# Peer Gynt

Aase and Solveig in Act Two, Scene Two, of a recent production at the Festival d'Arras, France. *Lipnitzki*

Aase's death-bed scene, Hamburg, 1951. *Rosemarie Clausen*

Fantasy and the Grotesque: Peer Gynt at the Hall of the Troll King in Tyrone Guthrie's production of Ibsen's play, London, 1944. *John Vickers*

# Ghosts

Alla Nazimova and Harry Ellerbe, New York, 1935. Oswald's expression of longing for the "joy of life." *Vandamm, from the Theatre Collection, New York Public Library*

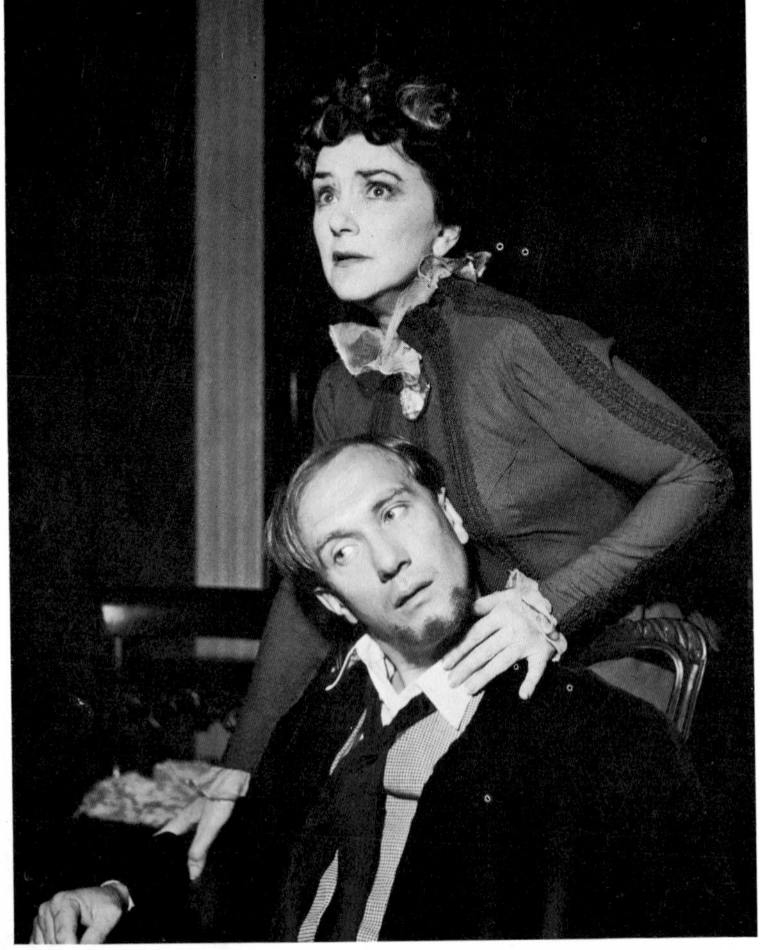

Lillebil Ibsen and Espen Skjoenberg: final scene of the production at the International Theatre Festival, Paris, 1954. *Lipnitzki*

# Miss Julie

Contrasting views of the relationship between Julie and Jean. Inga Tidblad and Ulf Palme at the Royal Dramatic Theatre in Stockholm. *American Swedish News Exchange*

Viveca Lindfors and James Daly in a recent New York production. *Friedman-Abeles*

Opening scene of Strindberg's play, at the Théâtre Gaité-Montparnasse, Paris. *Lipnitzki*

# The Ghost Sonata

Expressionist staging: The climax of Scene Two. *School of Drama, Yale University*

# The Weavers

A famous example of naturalistic staging: Act Two of Hauptmann's play, at the Grosses Schauspielhaus, Berlin, 1921. Old Ansorge is weaving on the floor with Moritz Jaeger seated nearby. *Ullstein*

# The Sea Gull

Komisarjevsky's production of Chekhov's play, London, 1936. A scene from Act One, with the curtain of the inner stage open. *Houston Rogers*

Nina and Trepleff in Act Four of a recent production. *Ohio State University*

Scene from Act Two, London, 1936, with Stephen Haggard as Trepleff and Peggy Ashcroft as Nina. *Houston Rogers*

A scene from Komisarjevsky's production in 1941 at Yale University. *School of Drama, Yale University*

# The Cherry Orchard

A scene from the Moscow Art Theatre production, 1904, with Olga Knipper-Chekhova as Lyuboff Andreevna. *By courtesy of Faubion Bowers*

A performance by the Theatre of the U.S.S.R. at the International Theatre Festival, Paris, 1958. *Lipnitzki*

Stanislavski as Satin, Moscow Art Theatre, 1923. *Theatre Collection, New York Public Library*

# The Lower Depths

A wistful moment from Act Two, Schauspielhaus, Düsseldorf, 1956. *Elfi Hess, from the Düsseldorf Schauspielhaus*

The violent climax of Act Three, Théâtre de l'Œuvre, Paris. *Lipnitzki*

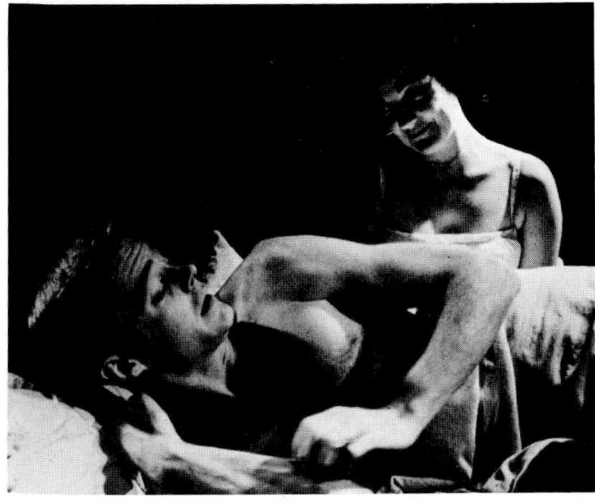

Young Gentleman and Young Wife

Actress and Count

# La Ronde

Patterns of character relationships in Schnitzler's play, as performed at the Theatre Marquee, New York, 1960, and directed by Patricia Newhall. *Photos by Claudio Campuzano*

Young Wife and Husband

Poet and Actress

Husband and Young Miss

Young Miss and Poet

Scene on a country road near the Whitefield house, from Act Two of a revival of *Man and Superman* at the New Theatre, London, 1951. *Houston Rogers*

# Man and Superman

The political debate in the Sierra Nevada, in the opening scene of Act Three, London, 1951. *Houston Rogers*

## Major Barbara

Charles Laughton as Undershaft and, from left, Nancy Malone, Eli Wallach, Burgess Meredith, and Glynis Johns in a New York production at the Morosco Theatre in 1956. *Friedman-Abeles.*

## No Exit

Scene from a revival of Sartre's *No Exit* at the Théâtre de la Potinière, Paris, with Tania Balachova as Inez, Michel Vitold as Garcin, and Gaby Sylvia as Estelle. *Lipnitzki*

## Riders to the Sea

Cathleen and Nora consoling Maurya: a scene from a Theatre East production, New York, 1956, with Elspeth March as Maurya. *Marga Kassimir*

## The Playboy of the Western World

Scene from Act One. The rural Irish pub was designed by Klaus Holm for a 1950 production at Yale. *School of Drama, Yale University*

# At the Hawk's Well

Stage, mask, and costume designs created by Edmund Dulac in 1916 for Yeats' play, as published in Harper's Bazaar.

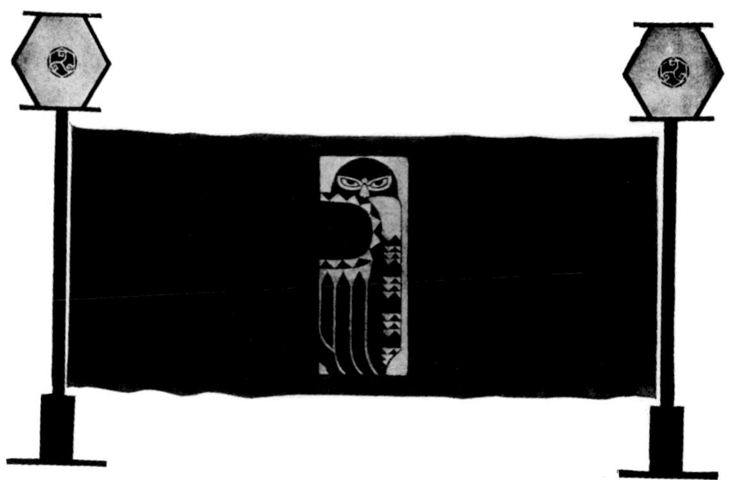

The setting: a patterned screen placed before a bare wall.

The Old Man at the well

The First Musician

The Young Man

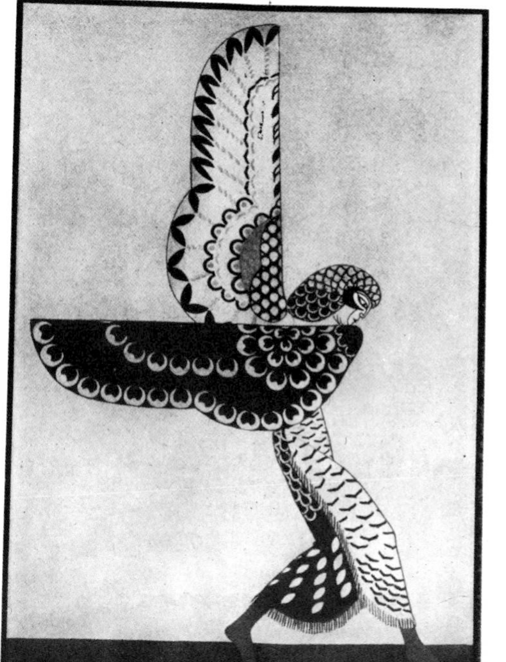

The Hawk

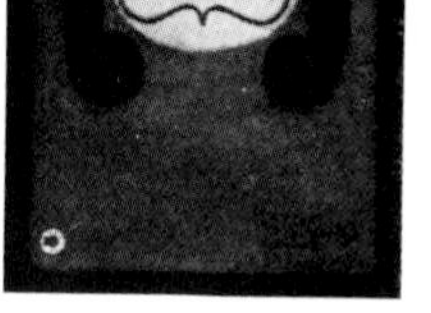

The Young Man's mask

The Old Man's mask

Contrasting views of Juno and Captain Boyle: (*right*) Mary Agnes Doyle and Whitford Kane, Chicago, 1926; (*below*) Sara Allgood and Barry Fitzgerald, New York, 1940. *The Art Institute of Chicago; Vandamm, from the Theatre Collection, New York Public Library*

Juno and the Paycock

Cock-a-Doodle Dandy

Magic Realism: Father Domineer defying the Cock in Scene Three at Yale University, 1955, directed by Frank McMullen with costumes by Carl Michell and setting by Henry Lowenstein. *School of Drama, Yale University*

Pirandello's Henry IV and his counselors, with (*right*) Jean Vilar and (*below*) François Chaumette in the lead role. *Lipnitzki; French Cultural Services*

## Henry IV

## Orphée

Surrealist staging: Jean Cocteau's play at Yale University, 1935. Setting designed by John Koenig. *School of Drama, Yale University*

Atmospheric evocation in poetic drama: Leonardo and the Bride in Act Three, Scene One at the Actors Playhouse, New York. *Avery Willard*

# Blood Wedding

Portrait of Tania Balachova as she appears in the last scene, in the 1951 production at the Studio des Champs-Elysées, Paris. *Thérèse Le Prat*

The final scene, with the Bride at the Mother's feet. *Emil Cadoo*

## The Emperor Jones

Scene Seven of O'Neill's *The Emperor Jones. Ohio State University*

Harry Hope's birthday party in the back room of the bar, in Act Two. *Vandamm, from the Theatre Collection, New York Public Library*

## The Iceman Cometh

Scene from Act Four with James Barton as Hickey. *George Karger—Pix*

# Awake and Sing!

Social Realism. Opening setting of Act Two of the Group Theatre production, New York, 1935. Actors are John Garfield, Morris Carnovsky, Stella and Luther Adler, and J. Edward Bromberg. *Vandamm, from the Theatre Collection, New York Public Library*

Close-up from Act Two with J. Edward Bromberg, Stella Adler, and Morris Carnovsky. *Alfredo Valente*

Setting for Act One as produced in New York in 1940. *Vandamm, from the Theatre Collection, New York Public Library*

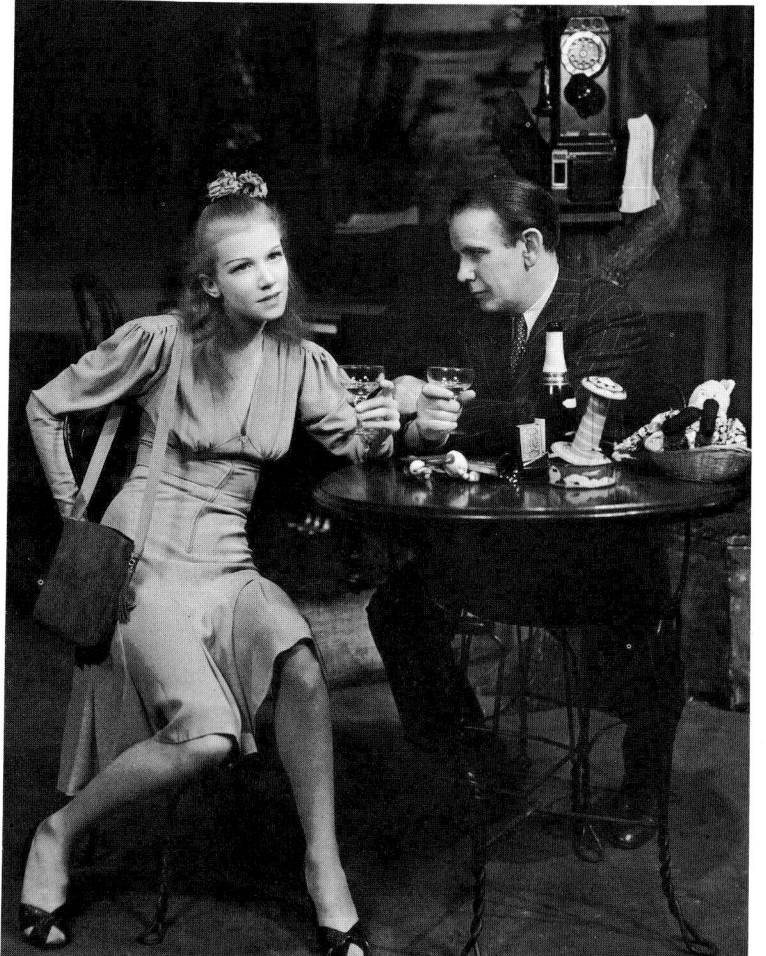

# The Time of Your Life

Julie Haydon as Kitty and Eddie Dowling as Joe, in a scene from Act Five. *Vandamm, from the Theatre Collection, New York Public Library*

Contrasting views of the opening scene: (*right*) Marguerite Moreno, in the lead role in the original French production, directed by Louis Jouvet; (*below*) Hermine Körner, in a Düsseldorf production of 1957, directed by Karl Heinz Stroux. *French Cultural Services; Elfi Hess, from the Düsseldorf Schauspielhaus*

# The Madwoman of Chaillot

The Ragpicker on trial in Act Two of the Düsseldorf production. *Elfi Hess, from the Düsseldorf Schauspielhaus*

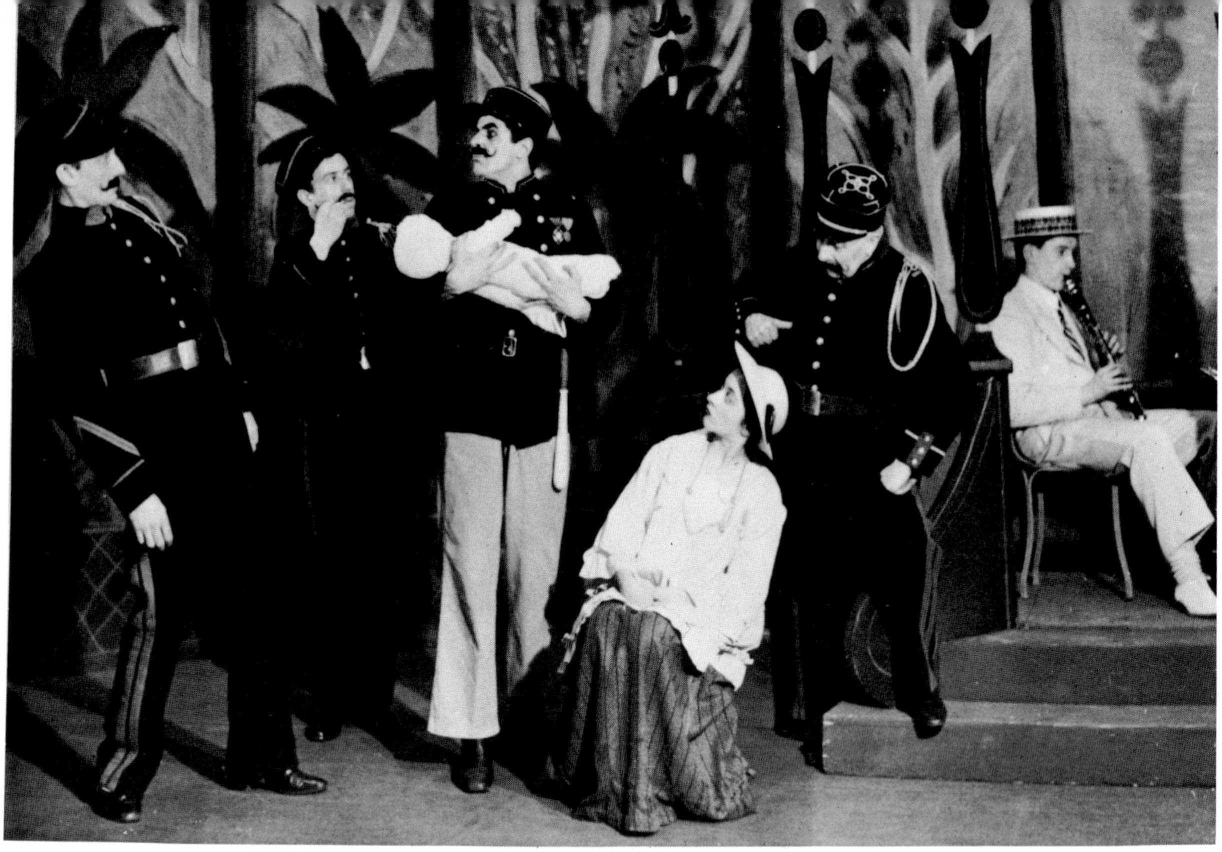

Policemen and thieves in Act One of a production at the Théâtre de l'Atelier, Paris, 1950. *French Cultural Services*

# Thieves' Carnival

Farcical extravaganza in Act Four. *French Cultural Services*

Classical Myth in Modern Dress: The opening scene as staged by Theatre Outlook, Liverpool. *Eric Salmon*

# Antigone

Creon and Antigone in Anouilh's play as performed in a revival at the Théâtre de l'Atelier, Paris. *Lipnitzki*

# Electra

Classical settings in the French theatre: (*above*) Giraudoux's *Electra* at the Théâtre de l'Athenée, Paris, 1937, with Louis Jouvet as the Beggar; (*left*) Camus' *Caligula* at the Théâtre Hébertot, Paris, 1945, with Gerard Philipe in the lead role. *Lipnitzki; French Cultural Services*

*Caligula* as staged by Albert Camus at the Nouveau Théâtre, Paris, 1958. *French Cultural Services*

# Caligula

# Mother Courage and Her Children

"Epic Theatre": Helene Weigel in the lead role in the Berliner Ensemble production.
*Ullstein–Croner*

Contrasting productions of Scene One. The block letters ("Schweden") in the production of the Berliner Ensemble (*below*) identify the setting, Sweden. The contrasting scene (*left*) is from the production of the Théâtre National Populaire, Paris, with Germaine Montero as Mother Courage.
*Ullstein–Croner; Lipnitzki*

Scene Three of Bertolt Brecht's play as produced by the Hacameri Theatre of Tel Aviv at the International Theatre Festival, Paris, 1956. *Pic, Paris*

# The Good Woman of Setzuan

Scenes Eight and Ten from the Zurich premiere, 1943. *Leonard Steckel*

# The Matchmaker

Theatrical Realism: Contrasting views of the restaurant scene, Act Three, as produced in (*above*) New York and (*below*) Helsinki. *Werner J. Kuhn; Lehtikuva Oy*

The final curtain scene with Ruth Gordon as Dolly Levi and Loring Smith as Horace Vandergelder in the New York production of 1955. *Werner J. Kuhn*

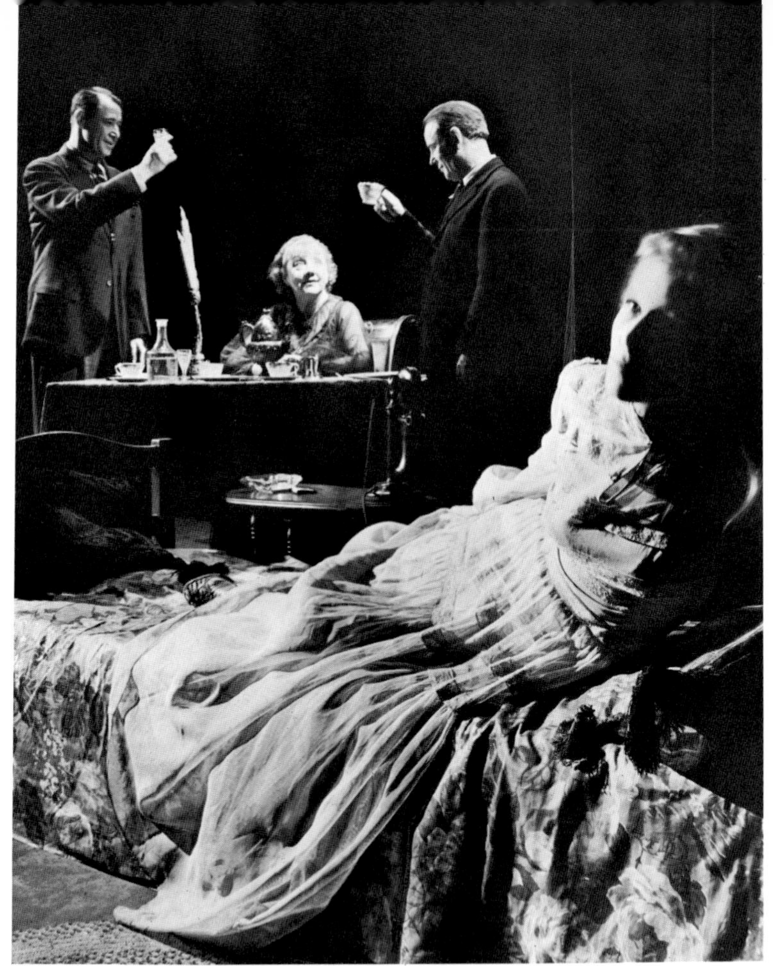

# The Glass Menagerie

Julie Haydon as Laura, New York, 1945, with Laurette Taylor as Amanda Wingfield, Eddie Dowling as Tom, and Anthony Ross as Jim O'Connor. *George Karger—Pix*

Williams' play as produced in modified "arena" style at the Alley Theatre, Houston, Texas, 1956. *Jack Richburg*

Jo Mielziner's transparent setting for the New York production, 1949, with Lee J. Cobb as Willy Loman, Mildred Dunnock as Linda, Arthur Kennedy as Biff, and Cameron Mitchell as Happy. *Graphic House*

# Death of a Salesman

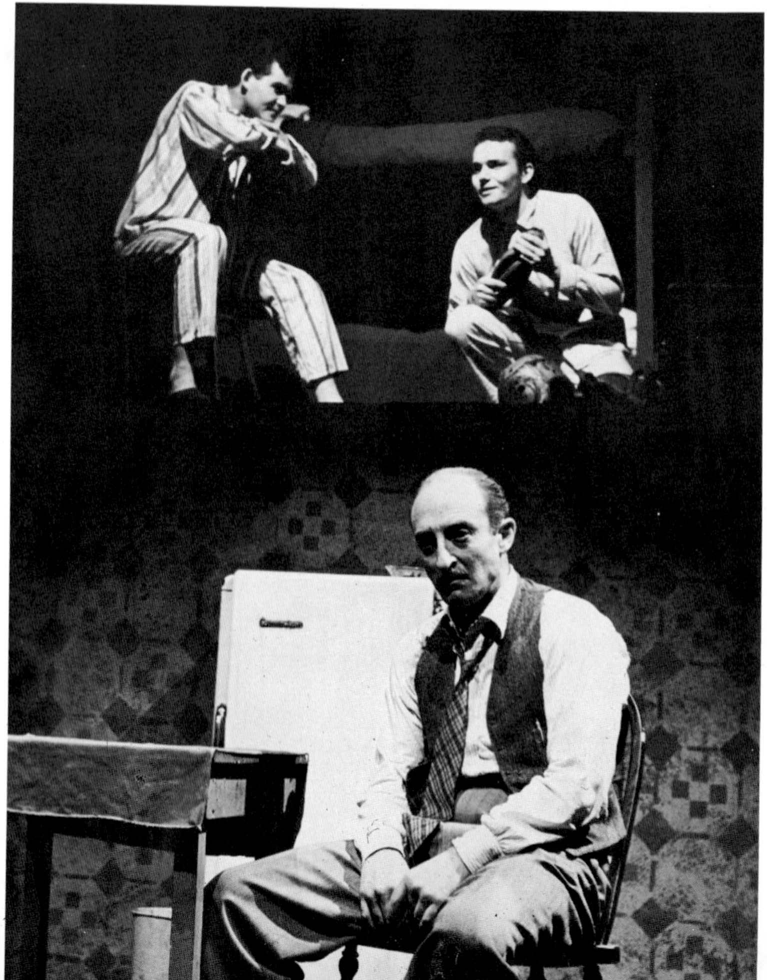

A contrasting scene from Act One of a recent production at the Actor's Workshop, San Francisco. *Ralph McCormic*

## Marty

Ernest Borgnine as Marty. *Culver*

Osborne's *Look Back in Anger* in two contrasting productions: (*above*) at the Royal Court Theatre in London in 1956; (*left*) at the Düsseldorf Schauspielhaus in 1958. *Houston Rogers; Elfi Hess, from the Düsseldorf Schauspielhaus*

## Look Back in Anger

## Endgame

Beckett's play as produced at the Encore Theatre of the Actor's Workshop, San Francisco, in 1959. Clov is feeling Nell's pulse. *Chic Lloyd*

## The Bald Soprano

Entrance of the Fire Chief, Théâtre des Noctambules, Paris. *Lipnitzki*

Alfred Lunt as Schill and Lynn Fontanne as Claire in a scene from Act One. *Vandamm, from the Theatre Collection, New York Public Library*

The departure from Güllen in the final scene as produced in Düsseldorf, 1956, with Hermine Körner as Claire. *Elfi Hess, from the Düsseldorf Schauspielhaus*

# The Visit

Setting for the Zurich premiere of Max Frisch's play in 1958, Scene Eight, with scenery by the playwright. *Bernhard Obrecht*

# Biedermann and the Firebugs

Biedermann between Schmitz and Eisenring after the last toast at the end of Scene Eight. *Bernhard Obrecht*

# MASTERS OF MODERN DRAMA

# MASTERS OF MODERN DRAMA

Edited, with Introductions and Notes, by

HASKELL M. BLOCK
*Brooklyn College of the City University of New York*

and

ROBERT G. SHEDD
*University of Maryland*

Random House New York

B98765



Library of Congress Catalog Card Number: 62-10776

Manufactured in the United States of America



## ACKNOWLEDGMENTS

PEER GYNT by Henrik Ibsen. Copyright, 1945, 1946 by Norman Ginsbury. Reprinted by permission of the William Morris Agency, Inc.

GHOSTS by Henrik Ibsen. From *Six Plays by Henrik Ibsen,* copyright 1951 by Eva Le Gallienne, in care of Brandt & Brandt, 101 Park Avenue, New York, New York. Reprinted by permission of Random House, Inc.

MISS JULIE by August Strindberg. Translated by Elizabeth Sprigge. Copyright 1955, by Elizabeth Sprigge. Reprinted by permission of Willis Kingsley Wing, 24 East 38th Street, New York 16, New York.

THE GHOST SONATA by August Strindberg. Translated by Elizabeth Sprigge. Copyright 1951, by Prentice-Hall, Inc. Reprinted by permission of Willis Kingsley Wing, 24 East 38th Street, New York 16, New York.

THE WEAVERS by Gerhart Hauptmann. From *Gerhart Hauptmann: The Weavers, Hannele, The Beaver Coat,* translated from the German by Horst Frenz and Miles Waggoner. Copyright, 1951, by Horst Frenz. Reprinted by permission of Holt, Rinehart and Winston, Inc.

THE INTRUDER by Maurice Maeterlinck. Translated by Haskell M. Block. © 1962, by Random House, Inc.

DEATH AND THE FOOL by Hugo von Hofmannsthal. Translated by Michael Hamburger. © 1961 by Bollingen Foundation, Inc.

THE SEA GULL by Anton Chekhov. Copyright, 1950, by Stark Young, in care of Leah Salisbury, 234 West 44th Street, New York, New York.

THE CHERRY ORCHARD by Anton Chekhov. Copyright, 1947, by Stark Young, in care of Leah Salisbury, 234 West 44th Street, New York, New York.

THE LOWER DEPTHS by Maxim Gorki. Translated by Alexander Bakshy. Reprinted by permission of Yale University Press.

LA RONDE by Arthur Schnitzler. Translated by Patricia Newhall and Hans Weigert. © Copyright, 1960, as an unpublished work, by Patricia Newhall and Hans Weigert. © Copyright, 1962, by Patricia Newhall and Hans Weigert.

THE MARQUIS OF KEITH by Frank Wedekind. Copyright, 1951, © 1962 by Beatrice Gottlieb. Printed by permission of Beatrice Gottlieb.

MAN AND SUPERMAN by Bernard Shaw. Used by permission of The Public Trustee, The Society of Authors and Dodd, Mead & Co., Inc.

MAJOR BARBARA by Bernard Shaw. Copyright, 1913, 1941 by George Bernard Shaw. Used by permission of The Public Trustee, The Society of Authors and Dodd, Mead & Co., Inc.

RIDERS TO THE SEA by John M. Synge. Copyright, 1935, by The Modern Library, Inc. Reprinted from *The Complete Works of John M. Synge* by permission of Random House, Inc.

THE PLAYBOY OF THE WESTERN WORLD by John M. Synge. Copyright, 1907 and Renewed, 1934 by the executors of the Estate of John M. Synge. Reprinted from *The Complete Works of John M. Synge* by permission of Random House, Inc.

AT THE HAWK'S WELL by W. B. Yeats. From *The Collected Plays of W. B. Yeats.* Copyright, 1934, 1952, by The Macmillan Company and used with their permission.

JUNO AND THE PAYCOCK by Sean O'Casey. Reprinted by permission of Macmillan & Company, Ltd. (London) and St. Martin's Press, Inc. (New York).

COCK-A-DOODLE DANDY by Sean O'Casey. Copyright, 1948, by Sean O'Casey. From *Collected Plays* by Sean O'Casey. Used by permission of The Macmillan Company.

FROM MORN TO MIDNIGHT by Georg Kaiser. Copyright, 1920, 1949, by Ashley Dukes. By permission of the executors of the estate of Ashley Dukes and of Curtis Brown, Ltd.

HENRY IV by Luigi Pirandello. From *Naked Masks: Five Plays* by Luigi Pirandello. Copyright, 1922, by E. P. Dutton & Co., Inc. Renewal, 1950, by Stefano, Fausto and Lietta Pirandello. Dutton Everyman Paperback. Reprinted by permission.

ORPHEE by Jean Cocteau. Translated by Carl Wildman. Copyright, 1933. Reprinted by permission of Dr. Jan van Loewen Ltd. of 81-83 Shaftesbury Avenue, London, W.1, England.

BLOOD WEDDING by Federico García Lorca. Copyright, 1945 by James Graham-Luján and Richard L. O'Connell. Copyright, 1947 by New Directions. Reprinted by permission of New Directions.

THE EMPEROR JONES by Eugene O'Neill. Copyright 1921 and Renewed 1948 by Eugene O'Neill, in care of Richard J. Madden, 522 Fifth Avenue, New York City, New York. Reprinted from *Nine Plays by Eugene O'Neill* by permission of Random House, Inc.

THE ICEMAN COMETH by Eugene O'Neill. Copyright 1940, 1946, by Eugene O'Neill, in care of Richard J. Madden, 522 Fifth Avenue, New York, New York. Reprinted from *The Plays of Eugene O'Neill* by permission of Random House, Inc.

AWAKE AND SING! by Clifford Odets. Copyright, 1933, 1935, by Clifford Odets, in care of Harold Freedman, Brandt & Brandt Dramatic Department, Inc., 101 Park Avenue, New York 17, New York.

THE TIME OF YOUR LIFE by William Saroyan. Copyright, 1939, by Harcourt, Brace and World, Inc., and reprinted with their permission.

ELECTRA by Jean Giraudoux. Copyright, 1955, by Winifred Smith. Published in French as *Electre,* Copyright, 1937, by B. Grasset, Paris. *Electra* was first published (in English) in Eric Bentley's *From the Modern Repertoire* (Indiana University Press) and then reprinted in the same editor's *The Modern Theatre* (Doubleday Anchor Books). Reprinted by permission of Mrs. Ninon Tallon Karlweis, 57 West 58th Street, New York 19, New York.

THE MADWOMAN OF CHAILLOT by Jean Giraudoux, adapted by Maurice Valency. Copyright, 1949, by Maurice Valency, in care of MCA Artists, Ltd., 598 Madison Avenue, New York, New York. Reprinted by permission of Random House, Inc.

THIEVES' CARNIVAL by Jean Anouilh. Copyright, 1952, by Jean Anouilh and Lucienne Hill. Reprinted by permission of Dr. Jan van Loewen Ltd., of 81-83 Shaftesbury Avenue, London, W.1, England.

ANTIGONE by Jean Anouilh (in care of Dr. Jan van Loewen Ltd. 81-83 Shaftesbury Avenue, London, W.1, England), adapted and translated by Lewis Galantière. Copyright, 1946, by Random House, Inc. Reprinted by permission.

NO EXIT by Jean-Paul Sartre. Translated by Stuart Gilbert. Copyright, 1946, by Stuart Gilbert. Reprinted from *No Exit and The Flies* by Jean-Paul Sartre, by permission of Alfred A. Knopf, Inc.

CALIGULA by Albert Camus. Copyright, 1958, by Alfred A. Knopf, Inc. Reprinted from *Caligula and Three Other Plays* by Albert Camus, translated by Stuart Gilbert, by permission of Alfred A. Knopf, Inc.

MOTHER COURAGE AND HER CHILDREN by Bertolt Brecht. English version by Eric Bentley. Copyright, 1955, 1959, © 1961, by Eric Bentley. Reprinted by permission.

THE GOOD WOMAN OF SETZUAN by Bertolt Brecht, translated by Eric Bentley. Copyright 1947 in manuscript form by Eric Russell Bentley. Copyright 1948, © 1962 by Eric Bentley. Originally published in the volume *Parables for the Theatre* by the University of Minnesota Press, Minneapolis.

THE DEVIL'S GENERAL by Carl Zuckmayer. © 1946 by Bermann-Fischer Verlag. Translated by Ingrid G. Gilbert and William F. Gilbert. © Copyright, 1962, by S. Fischer Verlag, in care of Marie Rodell and Joan Daves, Inc., 15 East 48th Street, New York 17, New York.

THE MATCHMAKER by Thornton Wilder. Copyright © 1955, 1957 by Thornton Wilder. Reprinted by permission of Harper & Brothers.

# Preface

MASTERS OF MODERN DRAMA attempts to bring together in a single volume the great plays of the contemporary theatre, so that the reader may experience and enjoy the variety and richness of the art of drama in our time. Each new generation of readers and theatre-goers must make a fresh appraisal of our literary and artistic inheritance. We have prepared this collection from the vantage point of the second half of the twentieth century, mindful of the role of current knowledge and opinion in shaping our view of the major achievements in contemporary drama. We have aimed at an anthology as up-to-date and as nearly definitive as we could make it, in the hope that our book will constitute the strongest and most exciting collection of modern drama yet published.

The plays included in this volume have been selected primarily for their artistic greatness. We have made no arbitrary distinction between historical importance and intrinsic excellence. The most vital and significant plays of the modern repertoire must necessarily have a special historical importance. Without the work of the playwrights represented in our book, the history of the modern drama would be totally different. These plays are landmarks in the contemporary theatre, not only because they broke new ground at the time they were performed, but because readers and theatre-goers of a later time can return to them again and again with new understanding and enjoyment.

Students of the drama have often disagreed over the relative greatness of individual playwrights. We claim no infallibility in matters of judgment and taste; our introductions are meant to be suggestive and not prescriptive. Nevertheless, we are fully convinced of the central role in the making of modern drama of the playwrights and plays presented in this book. These dramatists are in fact true masters of their art. There may be disagreement over their respective claims to our attention, but we do not believe that any of the writers or works here included are of second-rate or merely incidental importance.

While we have organized our book around individual playwrights, we have also aimed at a collection of plays of representative significance from the standpoint of themes, forms, and styles. In the General Introduction as well as in our individual introductions, we have sought to call attention to the interplay of theory and technique, of idea and accomplishment, and to the broad trends and movements of modern drama which link together in a common tradition writers often widely separated in time and space. Our approach has been comparative and international throughout, emphasizing the interrelatedness and the community of effort increasingly characteristic of the drama since the second half of the nineteenth century. We have not sought to represent the drama of every country or to distribute our plays in strict geographical proportion. Regardless of national origin, each selection has been considered in its own right as among the most significant achievements of a major contemporary playwright. In some instances we have selected two of an author's great plays, without presuming to choose between them; in other instances, we have had to take account of limitations of space and availability inherent in the preparation of any anthology. Even a collection of 45 plays must leave a good deal out. Nevertheless, we trust that experienced readers and lovers of the theatre will not find many favorite plays absent. It is our hope that the study of the plays in *Masters of Modern Drama* will whet the reader's appetite and lead him to enlarge his knowledge and appreciation of the riches of modern dramatic literature.

A large number of the plays in our book are translations. Throughout the collection, we have given special attention to the freshness, accuracy, and readability of English versions. With proper authorization, we have on occasion revised older translations, and have reexamined recent ones in close association with the translator. In several instances we have commissioned new translations specifically for this volume, and more than one play appears in English for the first time in this book. It is our hope that all of these translations, whether of long familiar or very recent plays, recapture the spirit as well as the letter of the original compositions.

In preparing the section of photographs and the bibliography, we have had in mind the needs of the student of modern drama who may wish to pursue the examination of particular playwrights and plays. The photographs are all presentations of significant moments in the plays that make up our collection; they should serve to remind the reader that notwithstanding its genuine literary appeal, a great play acquires flesh and blood through the act of performance. We hope that at many points, the analysis and interpretation of the plays in our book will be facilitated by the photographs. The bibliography is frankly selective but no major scholarly or critical works in the English language have been knowingly omitted.

We are grateful to all who have aided us in the completion of our work. No editor of a comprehensive anthology of modern drama can escape a deep feeling of obligation to John Gassner, who has done more than anyone to shape the study of contemporary drama in our colleges and universities. It would be impossible for us to thank all of the critics and scholars, European as well as American, whose studies of modern drama have entered into the formation of our attitudes and values. Scholarship and criticism, like art itself, is a vast collaborative enterprise, and our book could not have been conceived were it not for the collective efforts of dedicated lovers of the drama, past as well as present.

For generous and often frequent help during the preparation of our book, we wish to express our thanks to: Russell K. Alspach, Eric Bentley, Herbert Blau, Faubion Bowers, Sigurd Burckhardt, Jean Cocteau, Hugh Dickinson, A. C. Edwards, Robert C. Elliott, Richard Ellmann, John Enck, Edwin Engel, George Freedley, Lewis Galantière, Ingrid Gilbert, Vaun Gillmor, Norman Ginsbury, Mordecai Gorelik, Michael Hamburger, Kurt Hellmer, W. R. Jones, Betty Judkins, G. Johannes Klose, Jackson Mathews, Charles McGaw, Frank McMullan, Paul Myers, Patricia Newhall, Elizabeth Towne Norton, Sean O'Casey, Clifford Odets, Neal Oxenhandler, John Reich, Kenneth Rowe, Herman Salinger, Eric Salmon, William Saroyan, George Brandon Saul, Alfred Schwarz, Oskar Seidlin, Gleb Struve, Florence Vandamm, Richard Vowles, Gerald Weales, and Carl Zuckmayer. Finally, we wish to record our grateful appreciation for the kind and constant collaboration of the Random House staff, especially Jane P. Alles, Leonore C. Hauck, Charles Lieber, and Jess Stein.

H. M. B.
R. G. S.

Brooklyn, New York
Columbus, Ohio

# Contents

# MASTERS OF MODERN DRAMA

# General Introduction

THE MAKING of modern drama is the consequence of an immense collaborative activity. No single playwright, institution, or nation can lay claim to the creation of the drama of our day. It emerged as the complex and dynamic expression of cumulative artistic experience. Forms and attitudes, techniques and styles, do not come about by themselves. The drama as we now know it is the product of an accretion of resources, contributed by playwrights of the remote as well as the recent past. From the days of Thespis in Athens to our own times is a period of 2500 years. Although few epochs in world history can rival, let alone surpass, the achievement of the modern theatre, the contemporary playwright has returned again and again to the art of his predecessors.

All the same, modern drama has unique characteristics that have come about in response to the particular conditions of contemporary life. It is far from a mere imitation of the drama of ancient Greece or Rome, the Middle Ages or the Renaissance, or of other great epochs in the history of the theatre. The developments in the playwright's art in our time have their origins in the closing decades of the nineteenth century, in a period of intense intellectual probing into the tensions and cleavages of the modern world. This was an age of active and noble discontent, of searching and restless criticism. The pioneers of the modern theatre, Ibsen and Strindberg, Hauptmann and Gorki, Chekhov and Shaw, were men preoccupied with the vital ideological and social issues of their day. The conception of drama as both preachment and prophecy, expressing the theories and attitudes of the playwright in opposition to those of the great majority of men of his time, marks the early modern dramatist as an embattled revolutionary, seeking to change men's minds and hearts as well as their institutions and laws. The heritage of an era of protest and revolt is a permanent possession of contemporary drama.

Our debt to the early masters of the modern stage is enormous, yet it must be seen in proper perspective. We have come a long way from the realism and naturalism of the end of the last century. Variety and eclecticism are the dominant characteristics of twentieth century drama. Realism and naturalism, symbolist and poetic drama, expressionism and existentialism, these and many other styles may be found in active co-existence in the modern theatre. Not only in the work of the same playwright but in the same play, mixed and even contradictory styles jostle one another. Hard and fast distinctions between "comedy," "tragedy," and other genres have altogether broken down. Attempts to blend and reconcile seemingly disparate techniques and forms have been far more common than efforts to achieve formal or stylistic purity. Most major contemporary playwrights have been boldly experimental in their view of traditional forms; neither doctrinaire nor completely attached to a single, absolute style of playwriting, they have frequently sought to enlarge as well as to explore the boundaries of their art. Although such terms as naturalism and symbolism, realism and theatricalism, are often artificial, we must recognize the distinctive qualities of these and other movements if we are to understand modern drama.

Naturalism as a literary movement in the closing years of the nineteenth century is largely the creation of Émile Zola. Under the influence of the positivistic currents of his time, he sought to apply the clinical method of experimental biology to all of life. A work of art is thus a demonstration of a problem: given certain facts (a particular milieu and set of circumstances), certain consequences must follow. In his rigorous determinism, Zola insisted on a complete, objective, and impersonal representation of truth. Out of his analogy between art and science came a significant expansion of the subject-matter of literature and the development of techniques and styles that transformed both fiction and drama. In his essay, "Naturalism in the Theatre" (1879), Zola sought to transfer the gains made by the novel to the stage. His own dramatic efforts fell far short of his aims, but Zola insisted that his plea for a new theatre of contemporary actuality should not be judged by his own success or failure as a playwright. He saw the theatre of his day in urgent need of revitalization and, in retrospect, we recognize that he was right. The trivial melodrama and thesis plays of the heirs and followers of Scribe reduced drama to an art of facile moralizing and superficial entertainment. The corrosive social criticism of Henry Becque, expressed in such remarkable plays as *The Vultures* (*Les Corbeaux*, 1882) and *La Parisienne* (1885), was discouraged or ignored. Zola's battle cry proclaimed his acute awareness of a crisis in the theatre: "Our theatre," he declared, "will be naturalistic or it will not exist!"

The objectives of naturalness and truthfulness which Zola sought to bring to the French stage were shared by reformers of the theatre in Germany in the second half of the nineteenth century. In the 1860's, in protest against the acting style of rhetorical and bombastic declamation, Duke Georg II of Saxe-Meiningen began his program for revitalizing the German stage. "I was vexed," he laconically remarked, "that Shakespeare was played so badly in Germany." The Duke recruited talented actors whom he schooled through painstaking rehearsals in the art of ensemble acting. Roles were rotated; the star of one performance became an extra in the next. Under his influence, acting acquired a consistent style and production a new stress on scenic detail, with setting and costumes, reproduced with minute historical exactitude, made part of a unified theatrical conception. The walls of the closed room conveyed the illusion of real life, and the literalness of stage properties, with gardens that looked like real gardens, reinforced the air of authenticity. The Meiningen players were especially noted for crowd scenes and mass effects. Their virtuosity and discipline captivated theatre-goers everywhere and instructed directors and stage-managers all over Europe in the techniques of realism. It was appropriate that the Meiningen company should be the first troupe to perform Ibsen on the German stage, in 1875. In the 1880's it became an international road company, traveling to London, St. Petersburg, and New York, and influencing theatrical style throughout the Western world.

The most significant consequence in France of Zola's propaganda on behalf of naturalism was the founding of the *Théâtre Libre* (Free Theatre) by André Antoine in 1887. Antoine viewed his theatre as a "trial laboratory" for the production of new and unpublished plays by young writers. In practice, this meant plays that other producers had refused—mainly naturalistic plays. Antoine was not a theoretician or a propagandist in any strict sense, yet it is altogether understandable that Strindberg should refer to him in a letter of 1888 as "the director of the naturalists' stage in Paris." Many of the new French playwrights whose works were performed at the Théâtre Libre clung to a drama of shocking and horrific effects, such as a detailed account of a guillotine execution, or the murder of an illegitimate child whose body is then thrown to the pigs. Not all of the early naturalistic plays were so harsh, but most of them portrayed the experiences of poor and uneducated people, living perforce in a milieu of vice, filth, and squalor. As a result, naturalism came to be equated with a gray and dreary slice-of-life documentation of coarse and brutal reality. A typical definition is the following, from an English review of an adaptation of one of Zola's novels, performed in London in 1889: "What naturalism on the stage means, in theory, is the throwing overboard of the conventions—no 'points,' no 'curtains,' no 'crisis,' often no 'dénouement,' simply a page cut, without erasure or addition, from the book of life. . . . The point of the piece, as of all naturalistic pieces, is in its photographic truth of detail. At the most harrowing point of the interview between the wife and the returned husband, customers come to the door (the scene is laid in the butcher's 'back-shop') and have their little scraps of meat duly weighed out." The work of Strindberg and of Hauptmann was to demonstrate that, even at its inception, naturalism could transcend the limits of documentary realism to embrace symbolic as well as psychological techniques; nonetheless, to this day, many critics and historians have preferred to over-simplify dramatic naturalism and to see it merely as the counterpart of Zola's theories.

The foreign repertoire of the Théâtre Libre, which included French versions of Ibsen's *Ghosts*, Tolstoy's *Power of Darkness*, Verga's *Cavalleria Rusticana*, Strindberg's *Miss Julie*, and Hauptmann's *The Weavers*, reads like a compendium of European dramatic naturalism. The French playwrights in the naturalistic tradition—Brieux, Porto-Riche, Curel, and others, were far less significant. Despite the weakness of the French repertoire, the powerful example of Antoine's theatre led to the establishment of similar free and independent theatres all over Europe. What Antoine had done in Paris, Otto Brahm did in Berlin, J. T. Grein in London, and Stanislavsky and Nemirovich-Danchenko in Moscow.

The Berlin *Freie Bühne* (Free Stage), like the Théâtre Libre, was organized on a subscription basis as a private club in order to avoid censorship. Brahm shared the positivistic and deterministic assumptions of the French naturalists but aimed at a less rigid and more flexible theatre, capable of expressing truth in all its forms. Under Brahm's leadership, the Freie Bühne provided a tribune for the German naturalistic playwrights of the 1890's. Many of the younger German disciples of Zola, notably Arno Holz and Johannes Schlaf, were even more thorough-going than he had been in their analogy between the artist and scientist. Holz declared French naturalism unscientific, and set forth what he considered a "consistent naturalism": "Art has the tendency to return to nature. It does so according to its particular conditions of reproduction and their handling." Holz and Schlaf collaborated in writing the most completely naturalistic of all German plays, *Die Familie Selicke* (*The Selicke Family*), produced by the Freie Bühne in 1890. A gloomy and sordid presentation of suffering and death in a Berlin slum, it exemplifies the new passion for literal and detailed documentation. The language is Berlin dialect, colloquial or slang rather than literary. Trapped in their environment, the members of the family are but passive victims, crushed by material and spiritual poverty. Holz and Schlaf's play is significant for the new concern with a language mirroring the common speech of daily life, and the new control of space, limited to a single squalid room that confines and presses in on the Selicke household. The play is a dull and tedious composition, scarcely deserving of extended comment; nevertheless, the impulses that created it led directly to the powerful social naturalism of Hauptmann, who dedicated the first edition of his first play, *Before Dawn*, to Holz and Schlaf "in grateful acknowledgment of decisive stimulation."

In Victorian England, before the advent of Shaw, serious drama hardly existed. Melodrama, farce, comic opera, and other trivial fare dominated the scene.

Despite Shaw's campaign on behalf of Ibsen in the pages of *The Saturday Review*, virtually nothing written by his countrymen indicated that they were contemporaries of the Norwegian. In 1891, inspired by Antoine's venture, J. T. Grein founded the Independent Theatre in London; his first production was Ibsen's *Ghosts*, angrily denounced by the Victorian reviewers. Ibsen (derided in the press as "Henry Gibson") was at best the idol of a minority cult in the London of the 1890's, but the vigor and boldness of his art made an indelible impression on the young Shaw, and it was in response to Grein's appeal for a native drama of contemporary relevance that Shaw turned from criticism to the theatre. His first play, *Widower's Houses*, was produced by the Independent Theatre in 1892.

The same pioneering spirit animated Stanislavsky in the founding of the Moscow Art Theatre six years later: "We protested against the old manner of acting, against theatricalism, false pathos, declamation, artificiality in acting, bad staging and décor conventions, the emphasis on new productions that spoiled the ensemble work, the whole system of presentations, and the insignificant repertoires of the time." The impact of the Meiningen company and the wave of interest in Ibsen in Russia in the early 1890's are reflected in the Moscow enterprise. The old style of tortured rhetoric and bombast now gave way to a new and intense naturalness: the actor was to *live through* the experience of the character he recreates. What Hauptmann did for the Freie Bühne, Chekhov did for the Moscow Art Theatre; its distinct style emerged from the haunting inner dialogue of Chekhov's poetry of commonplace reality.

In the twentieth century the social and critical emphasis of realism and naturalism has come to be fused with studies of psychological aberration. The development of Ibsen from *Ghosts* to *Hedda Gabler* and the "great naturalism" of Strindberg are important anticipations of this tendency. Their latter-day successors have often combined psychological realism with the anatomy of the motives and values of a whole society. This is particularly true of recent American drama. No modern American playwright more fully shared Strindberg's awareness of the tensions of inner life, of love and hate as a life-and-death struggle, than Eugene O'Neill; yet O'Neill's late and greatest plays are at the same time squarely within the naturalist tradition. *Long Day's Journey into Night* offers further proof that naturalism need not be limited to the lower classes or to portrayals of slum and proletarian life. Whether O'Neill's technique in his last plays is best described as "intense realism" or "uncompromising naturalism," heredity and environment take their grim toll. Determinism does not rob O'Neill's characters of their individuality and responsibility any more than it does those of Strindberg. Similarly, in *Death of a Salesman*, Arthur Miller probes into Willy Loman's tangled and twisted motives even while revealing the contradictions of contemporary social processes and values. The playwright's art reaches out beyond the immediate crisis of isolated individuals to represent and often to criticize forces and institutions in contemporary society.

It is common today to speak of the excesses of realism or the dangers of naturalism, without recognizing that such playwrights as Ibsen and Strindberg, Chekhov and Gorki, Shaw and O'Casey, Odets and Miller, to name only a few, transcended the dogmas of restrictive theories to create a drama of imaginative power and deep human significance. The values of naturalism, when commanded by a powerful artistic vision, have never been merely photographic or documentary. The courage and dignity which the drama maintains, almost alone among the performing arts of our time, are due in large measure to the pioneering efforts of the creators of a drama of contemporary life.

Even at the end of the last century, when naturalism and social realism brought freshness and vigor into a theatre that had become little more than an elegant and comfortable place of fashionable amusement, radically different approaches to drama were also emerging. We no longer oppose naturalism and symbolism as sharply as did the avant-garde poets and playwrights of the 1890's; yet, in their time, the symbolists attempted a transformation of the theatre no less revolutionary than that of Zola and his followers. While naturalist playwrights demanded a drama reflecting the great social changes and ideological conflicts of the day, the symbolists sought for a drama evocative and suggestive rather than representational, reflecting the mystery and wonder of inner life. At the risk of over-simplification, we may distinguish two main traditions of symbolist drama: poetic and operatic. Not all of the symbolists wrote in verse, but many of them were preëminently poets attempting to transfer the rhythmic and introspective language of poetry to the stage. Writers in the poetic tradition saw the drama as an essentially literary art, free from any necessary dependence on artifice and theatricality. Décor was reduced to a few draperies or a curtain of blue gauze, to suggest the vague and remote. De-theatricalization went hand in hand with the new concern with language as the center of dramatic expression. The most significant formulation of the aims and premises of symbolist drama was the "Notes on the Theatre" written by the poet, Stéphane Mallarmé, for the *Revue Indépendante* in 1886 and 1887, and later collected in his prose essays entitled *Divagations*. Drama for Mallarmé is the expression of an inner condition, a "soul-state," rather than an external action. Hamlet, whose melancholy introspectiveness haunted the symbolist generation, was for Mallarmé "the unique character in an intimate and occult tragedy." Mallarmé's criticism of the vulgarity and mediocrity of the drama of his time was shared by his close friend, Villiers de l'Isle-Adam, author of *Axël* (1890). Their challenge was taken up by admirers and disciples in the 1890's: Van Lerberghe, Maeterlinck, Claudel, Régnier, Gide, Verhaeren, and many others. Some of the symbolists, notably Claudel, went on to forge dramatic styles of their own, but many remained essentially lyric poets.

While Mallarmé and his disciples viewed musicality as an inherent part of the character of poetic language, other symbolists, responding to the operatic currents of the time, considered music a principal element of dramatic structure. Wagner's ideal of a "total work of art" (*Gesamtkunstwerk*), fusing poetry, music, the dance, and the accessory arts of the theatre into a new spiritual harmony, inspired many ambitious and extravagant experiments. First and foremost a composer, Wagner nonetheless endowed the stage with the mysticism and fervor of religious ceremony. His view of drama as a grandiose celebration of mythic and ritualistic values, popularized by Nietzsche's account of the birth of tragedy, infused a new seriousness of purpose into the modern theatre. Talented and imaginative scene designers such as Adolphe Appia, Gordon Craig, and Vsevolod Meyerhold attempted to bring about the complex union of the arts which Wagner had envisaged, and drew upon the flexible properties of light and color to express the inner life or soul of the drama, as well as to sustain and enhance the emotional mood.

In the 1890's the symbolists, like the naturalists, enjoyed a theatre of their own. The *Théâtre d'Art* (Art Theatre) founded by Paul Fort in 1891 became, two years later, the *Théâtre de l'Œuvre* (Theatre of the Work of Art), directed by Lugné-Poe. Here, in a theatre where Lugné-Poe declared "poetry and silence would come together," the plays of Maeterlinck had their premiere. Until its dissolution in 1897, the Théâtre de l'Œuvre was the temple of symbolist drama; unfortunately, its history is that of a theatre in search of plays. Despite its all too numerous failures, in its intimate evocation of dream and reverie through half-tones and nuances, the symbolist theatre gave a new importance to the creation of atmosphere and mood. Bernard Shaw wrote plays far removed indeed from those of Maeterlinck, yet he could declare: "In the Théâtre de l'Œuvre there is not merely the ordinary theatrical intention, but a vigilant artistic conscience in the diction, the stage action, and the stage picture, producing a true poetic atmosphere, and triumphing easily over shabby appointments and ridiculous incidents." In the 1890's the symbolist drama was a source of vitality and freshness; it shaped the plays of Hofmannsthal and Yeats, and entered freely into combination with other styles in the work of Hauptmann, Strindberg, Claudel, García Lorca, Ghelderode, and many others. Hauptmann's "Dream Poem," *Hannele*, blends sordid naturalism with mysticism and spirituality. Strindberg wrote several plays in imitation of Maeterlinck; despite Strindberg's intense emotionalism and subjectivity, his preoccupation with dream and private vision in *A Dream Play* is not far removed from that of French playwrights of the 1890's. Paul Claudel, in his sprawling and turbulent early plays of crime and redemption as in his later experiments in total theatre, is markedly close to the symbolist tradition. García Lorca's surrealist fantasy and Ghelderode's grotesque farce both rely extensively on symbolist atmospheric evocation, as do the studied repetitions and silences of the "static drama" of Samuel Beckett. The failure of symbolist drama to dominate the theatre of its day should not blind us to its genuine contributions.

Modern poetic drama has been, in Jean Cocteau's words, a "poetry of the theatre," rather than simply drama written in lines that rhyme. Verse is a frequent but not an indispensable element in poetic drama. The literature of the past hundred years has demonstrated again and again that prose, through a sensitive exploitation of the figurative and musical properties of language, can be made to do the work of verse. Plays like Yeats' *At the Hawk's Well* and García Lorca's *Blood Wedding* are significant efforts in the creation of poetic drama. T. S. Eliot's *Murder in the Cathedral* (1935) revives the mystery and spirituality of the drama of the medieval church in the accents of the twentieth century. The play is an intensely moving expression of a profound religious experience. Eliot's later plays, like *The Cocktail Party* (1950), have moved toward drawing-room comedy but without abandoning the quest for "a rhythm close to contemporary speech" wherein poetry takes on the quality of actuality.

Poetry of the theatre in our time is part of a return to a drama of artifice and masquerade. Pirandello, in his assault on the notion of a unified personality and the theatre of literal representation, laid the groundwork for the revitalization of an art of elaborate pretense and make-believe. His successors, animated by the playful exuberance of Dada and surrealism, rediscovered the elasticity of dramatic form. Cocteau, Giraudoux and Anouilh; Saroyan, Wilder and Williams; Brecht, Duerrenmatt and Frisch—to name but a few, have repudiated the "four-wall" or "peep-hole" stage of the realistic tradition. Theatre is no longer a copy of something else; it is a show, a frankly artificial creation with unique claims and properties. Reinhardt, Meyerhold, Tairov, and other imaginative directors insisted that the theatre was superior to common reality, and demanded that plays be performed in such a way that the audience will not forget for a single moment that it is in the theatre. In the hands of jugglers and mere showmen, the theatre of magic and artifice has been little more than spectacular extravaganza or theatre for theatre's sake. Often, however, as the plays of Brecht or the experiments in epic style in the American Federal Theatre of the 1930's demonstrate, theatricalism has illuminated and enlarged the audience's perception of reality. Poetry of the theatre has sometimes served as mere escapism, but the most significant theatrical experimenters of our time have been motivated by a passionate dedication to humanity. Giraudoux' *Electra* and Wilder's *The Skin of Our Teeth* are unmistakably poetic dramas; their exploration of the interplay of fantasy and reality amid universal cataclysm enlarges our awareness of what it means to be alive in the middle years of the twentieth century.

The experimental techniques of poets of the theatre are in many instances a direct outgrowth of expressionism. No movement in the modern theatre was bolder in its claim to effect a reformulation of dramatic structure. Expressionism is sometimes mistakenly limited to German drama from about 1910 to 1924, but its processes may be found in many older as well as more recent playwrights throughout the Western world. Like naturalism and symbolism, expressionism embraced other arts and literary forms besides the drama. It sought to reveal a new "dynamics of the inner man" through the presentation of fantasies, hallucinations, nightmares, and other modes of intense subjective experience. We may see important anticipations in the strident and titanic emotionalism of the *Sturm und Drang* (Storm and Stress) movement of the later eighteenth century, the wild phantasmagoria of such scenes as the "Walpurgisnacht" in Goethe's *Faust,* or the episodic structure and stark violence of Büchner's *Woyzeck* (1837).

Strindberg, in his "dream plays," beginning with *The Road to Damascus,* virtually created the new dramatic style. The free transformation of external reality, redefined according to the irrational and frenzied behavior of the hidden self, resulted in a theatre of weird angularity and distortion. Linear narrative was replaced by fragmentary episodes. The unity of the single character gave way to multiple and depersonalized abstractions, transported into a paroxysm of exaltation and ecstasy. Dialogue became nervous and explosive, yielding to shrill soliloquy and grotesque pantomime.

Among the German playwrights, none was more responsible for the epigrammatic and ironic language of the new drama than Frank Wedekind, whose unmasking of instinctive animal forces revealed the anarchy and chaos beneath the surface of "civilization." All of the German expressionists—Sorge, Hasenclever, Kaiser, Toller, Kokoschka, Goll, and the others, shared Wedekind's rootlessness, alienation, and social discontent; it was from Wedekind far more than from Strindberg or other predecessors that Georg Kaiser derived the shrill and staccato idiom of *From Morn to Midnight* and his other expressionist plays. The impact of Kaiser, notably on American drama of the 1920's, was reinforced by that of Ernst Toller, even more extreme in his left-wing sympathies. Toller's best known plays, *Transfiguration* (*Die Wandlung,* 1919) and *Man and the Masses* (*Masse Mensch,* 1920) typify the depersonalization, abstraction, and revolutionary fervor of expressionism. The production of *Man and the Masses* by the Theatre Guild in New York in 1924, patterned directly after the Berlin production of Jürgen Fehling, introduced a new fluidity in the polarization of individuals and crowds, and breakneck shifts of planes of dramatic action.

Expressionism in the United States failed to achieve the distinctiveness of the German movement; it was rapidly diluted and trivialized in farcical or musical extravaganza, or reduced to stale imitation of purely visual effects. With the coming of the depression of the 1930's and a revival of social realism, the expressionist drama was perhaps too subjective in orientation to serve as a means of ideological or social preachment, even though its shrill assertion of alienation and inner torment was accompanied by a violent rejection of the existing social order. From Eugene O'Neill to Arthur Miller and Tennessee Williams, modern American playwrights have experimented with expressionist techniques, almost always in combination with other theatrical styles. In Europe as well, after the recent war the values of expressionism were again mirrored in the remarkable play of the young and short-lived Wolfgang Borchert, *Draussen vor der Tür* (*The Man Outside,* 1947), dominated by the same disillusionment and despair as the dramas of the preceding generation. As a play like Duerrenmatt's *The Visit* makes clear, by mid-century the techniques of expressionist drama have become so thoroughly assimilated as to constitute a permanent part of the resources available to the contemporary playwright.

The principal forces in European and American drama since World War II are primarily an extension of those of the inter-war period. The plays of Arthur Miller, Paddy Chayefsky, Carl Zuckmayer, and John Osborne, and the posthumous dramas of O'Neill offer convincing proof of the continuing vitality of social realism and naturalism, whether or not they are combined with other, less representational, techniques. The documentary, case study, or propaganda play can still make effective and moving theatre in the hands of a passionate and imaginatively gifted playwright. The honesty and stark simplicity of *A Streetcar Named Desire, The Diary of Anne Frank,* or *The Miracle Worker* made a deep impression in the theatres of a war-ravaged and politically divided Europe. A simultaneous revival of social satire—mordant, ironic, and at times rhetorical—can be traced to the belated discovery of Bertolt Brecht. Especially in the years immediately following his death, Brecht's plays pointed the way to transforming the patterns of social realism without abandoning social content. The improvisational style of "epic theatre" with its rapid alternations in mood and tempo and its wilful fragmentation of narrative marks a sharp departure from the naturalistic tradition, and it is understandable why a writer of *pièces à thèses* such as Sartre should accuse Brecht of indulging an excessive interest in form. Brecht was not merely a theatricalist experimenter, however. His social and humanistic passion was no less intense than that of the naturalists, and there can be no doubt that the devices and techniques of his "epic theatre" will be employed on behalf of causes remote indeed from Brecht's Marxism. Despite the relative decline of social drama in more recent years, the theatre may still serve as a pulpit or tribunal for an assault on false beliefs and values, and for an assertion of new truths.

Nevertheless, ideological preachment is hardly characteristic of the post-war stage. Out of the anarchy and nightmare of recent history has also come a distrust of ready-made ideologies and high-sounding phrases, in the theatre as well as in politics and public life. The corrosive pessimism of much of the theatre of fantasy and make-believe of the inter-war years is more than ever a part of the contemporary scene. The revival of the grotesque in modern drama, of paradoxical and irreconcilable contrasts that are not merely incongruous and bizarre, but mysterious and diabolical, indicates the dissolution of moral and spiritual absolutes in our time. Weird fantasy and gothic nightmare have moved so far beyond the plane of everyday reality as to call into question the existence of any norms. Yet, monstrous exaggeration and the complete abandonment of rational logic have also been ways of adventure and discovery. As Wedekind and Pirandello had discovered, the grotesque can illuminate recesses of experience that are inaccessible to the light of common day. The meditative theatricality of Wilder's *The Skin of Our Teeth* and the allegorical phantasmagoria of Frisch and Duerrenmatt are but perhaps the most striking examples of a radical reordering of literal events, no less distorted in the post-war theatre than in the hallucinatory vision of expressionism, but rendered more concrete and more objective. Viewed in the perspective of contemporary history, the grotesque acquires a rationale of its own.

Parallel impulses, such as surrealism and existentialism, have led to the "theatre of the absurd," projecting a reality beyond the limits of logic and literal observation, yet obliquely and indirectly enlarging our understanding of commonplace events. The "theatre of the absurd" owes much of its wild caprice and dark humor to surrealism and helps remind us that in the inter-war period, many of the stylistic tricks and dodges of the surrealist poets and painters were also practiced on the stage. Indeed, the term, *surrealism,* was first employed as the subtitle of a play by the cubist poet, Guillaume Apollinaire. Jean Cocteau, Gertrude Stein, and Federico García Lorca were but a few who astounded and at times infuriated theatre-goers with their utter disregard of representational reality. But surrealism, with its appeal to modes of unconscious experience, did not lend itself readily to theatrical appropriation. Its intense introspection and anguish flowed more readily into the private lyric, and it is only in mixed forms, in combination with other theatrical styles, that surrealism made an effective contribution to the stage. In some of García Lorca's most lyrical dramas, the distorted idiom of fantasy and dream blends hauntingly with the musicality and mystery of poetic utterance. In the post-war theatre, however, surrealism has moved away from lyricism and poetic drama toward a relentless probing into the meaning of metaphysical ultimates.

The alliance between philosophy and drama is not new. The vitality of antique myth and its interrogation into the meaning of life lent eloquence and passion to the theatre during the dark years of war and occupation. Existentialism, with its awareness of the absurdity of the universe and its preoccupation with a single ethical choice that determines the meaning of a whole existence, moved playwrights toward a drama of situations rather than a drama based upon psychological motivation or character. In such plays as Camus' *Caligula* and Sartre's *No Exit,* existential philosophy is no mere abstraction, but an organic part of a highly imaginative and effective theatrical framework. Thought and expression do not always blend so harmoniously in existential drama, and indeed, any drama of ideas runs the risk of unduly restricting the freedom and variety of dramatic experience for the sake of a theory. Philosophers in the theatre have sometimes forgotten their responsibilities as playwrights. Nevertheless, the heritage of existentialism remains a living part of the modern dramatist's almost obsessive concern with ambiguities and perplexities of cosmic dimension.

The interaction of surrealism and existentialism is a dominant force in the "theatre of the absurd." Adamov, Ionesco, Beckett, and their confreres have moved surrealism in the theatre from the realm of private incommunicability back to the context of ordinary life. Terrifying violence is no longer exceptional on the contemporary stage; it has become a casual and familiar part of everyday reality. In the influential manifesto of the surrealist poet, Antonin Artaud, *The Theatre and Its Double* (1938), a "theatre of cruelty" emerges from a new metaphysics of anarchy and horror: like the plague, Artaud insists, theatre must express a total crisis beyond which lies only death or purification. Artaud's theatre of frenzied exaltation relies not on words, but on images, gestures, and sensations. It constitutes an assault on the spectator's sensibility through a new dramatic language, liberated from the tyranny of speech. If Artaud's efforts to infuse a new vitality into the theatre were unduly neglected during his lifetime, his influence since his death has probably been somewhat exaggerated in recent studies of the "anti-theatre" of the absurd. Yet there can be no doubt of the deep spiritual kinship between the surrealist theorist and the playwrights of the new avant-garde.

In such plays as *The Bald Soprano* and *Endgame,* the absurd is made terrifyingly real. Both Ionesco and Beckett bear witness in their seemingly comic parables to the ambiguity and despair of any quest for spiritual meaning in an incoherent and irrational universe. In their early and most famous plays, neither narrative nor characterization has the slightest importance. What matters is the eternal situation of humanity, revealed through ironic commentary, elegiac lament, and pathetic or grotesque farce. Neither place nor time has any significance. Language is pulverized and reason shattered in the dramatization of the absurdity of the universe. The role of the theatre is to define and illustrate this absurdity, often through highly original stances and situations which constitute metaphors or parables of the human condition. Despite recent leanings in the direction of psychological exploration, the new avant-garde drama is essentially a theatre of artifice and gesture wherein lively and imaginative theatricality masks a serious attempt to fathom the mystery of human existence.

Whether the new avant-garde will have any durable effect on the forms and styles of modern drama remains to be seen. The popular triumphs of experimental dramatists are almost certain to come as the result of mutual adjustments between the playwright and the traditional representational theatre. The past half-century has shown that the distance between experimental and traditional theatres, or coteries and fashionable audiences, is often slight indeed. The multiplicity of styles and publics in the contemporary scene makes for refreshing variety, but also for confusion. Few of the playwrights of our time have enjoyed the sense of communal participation that characterized the relation of dramatist and audience in ancient Greece or the Middle Ages or Elizabethan England. Seldom indeed does the modern playwright create for a specific theatre and audience. Homogeneity of taste is perhaps not to be expected, much less sought for, in our pluralistic culture; nevertheless, the persistent quest for novelty and experiment, even while enriching artistic experience, is bound to aggravate the acute problem of communication in the theatre.

The patterns of dramatic form in our time are far from frozen in any permanent mold. The interaction of realism and naturalism, symbolism and expressionism, surrealism and existentialism, and other similarly powerful forces shaping modern drama, is far more significant than their opposition. The exaggeration of any particular style for the sake of novelty, or its reduction to a mere formula, are perhaps inevitable consequences of the way drama comes about, but have no larger importance. The achievements of the truly creative dramatic artists of our time are memorable not simply for the techniques they employ, but for the quality of vision that transforms the materials of their art into a unique, intrinsically rich and vital expression. The great dramas of the modern theatre, in their compelling illumination of human experience, are enduringly contemporary: their legacy is our inheritance.

# Henrik Ibsen

## (1828-1906)

Modern drama begins with Ibsen. Over a century has passed since he began his career as a playwright, yet he towers majestically over the contemporary stage. His great plays are a vital and enduring part of the modern repertory. Ibsen was a writer of prodigious range and depth, and it was his mission to endow the European theatre of the second half of the nineteenth century with profound human significance. The imaginative vigor of his drama has compelled readers and spectators everywhere to rediscover its immediacy and power. In its seemingly limitless capacity to respond to the changing needs and desires of successive generations of audiences, his work is truly classic, universal in implication and yet capable of endless transformation.

We do not see Ibsen today as our fathers and grandfathers saw him. Realism and the "problem play" are wholly inadequate definitions of his many-faceted art. Above all, Ibsen was a poet and not a photographer. It is true that part of his contribution to the drama of his day lies in his immense widening of the subject matter of theatrical expression, but this is an honor he shares with a number of other European playwrights of the last century. We have come to view the Norwegian as one of the great imaginative creators of dramatic art of all time. His innovations in construction, characterization, language, and other elements of drama express not only his mastery of the resources of dramatic form, but also a comprehensive quality of vision that both embraces and transcends technique and style. The complex allusiveness and dense symbolic implication familiar to readers of modern poetry and fiction are central to Ibsen's plays; no contemporary dramatist has probed with more subtlety or skill into man's nature and destiny. His art, like that of all great poets, is at once a revelation and a prophecy.

Ibsen belongs to European and world literature, yet his drama is closely bound up with the Norwegian cultural scene of his day. At the time of his birth Norway had only recently acquired its independence from Denmark. Ibsen matured in an age of fervent patriotism; the romantic nationalism of Western Europe was a powerful influence on his early career. Ibsen was poor and largely self-educated. At 15 he became a pharmacist's apprentice in Grimstad, a small port in the southeast corner of Norway. Here he lived in an attic on meager pay, and fed his imagination with romantic poetry, sagas and folk ballads, and histories of the struggles for Norse independence. He responded enthusiastically to the revolutions of 1848, and his vigorous participation in local politics often took the form of sharp attacks on the pettiness and hypocrisy of small town society. His first play, *Cataline* (1850), was inspired by his reading of Cicero while he was preparing for the entrance examination to the university, where he intended to study medicine. He passed only part of his examination and was not admitted, but in the process, he discovered his vocation. The alienated and despised revolutionary hero of Ibsen's first play undoubtedly reflects his own position in Grimstad. Later he declared: "*Cataline* was written in a little provincial town, where it was impossible for me to give expression to all that fermented in me except by mad, riotous pranks, which brought down upon me the ill will of all the respectable citizens who could not enter into that world which I was wrestling with alone."

For the next decade, Ibsen was an intimate part of the Norwegian theatrical scene. He worked hard to acquire a practical knowledge of the stage and travelled to Denmark and Germany to study foreign productions. At Bergen and later at Christiania, he produced dozens of plays, and gained a command of dramatic techniques and styles few playwrights have possessed. He was obliged to write a play a year and composed a number of romantic melodramas and history plays, but these were coldly received. His dramas of the 1850's are markedly indebted to the so-called "well-made play" of Scribe and his French successors, replete with artificial suspense created by secret confidences, muttered innuendoes, and sudden and improbable revelations. In later life, Ibsen was to adapt the formula of Scribe to a drama of profound human relevance, but the complicated plot and many of the older devices persisted as means of arousing and sustaining the interest of the audience.

Ibsen's early career as a playwright was accompanied by disappointment and failure. *Love's Comedy* (1862), a verse play on courtship and marriage, was refused performance. A significant improvement in Ibsen's fortune came with a historical play, *The Pretenders* (1863), a plea for Scandinavian unity with unmistakable reference to the need for common defense of Denmark and of Schleswig-Holstein against Prussia. The play was a great success and Ibsen was rewarded by the government with a travel grant that enabled him to move to Italy. For the greater part of his productive career he remained in self-imposed exile, never losing contact with the Norwegian scene, yet preferring to live and work abroad in undisturbed isolation. He did not return to live in Norway until 1891.

*Brand* (1866), the first fruit of exile, is the work of an angry man, deeply wounded by the failure of the Norwegians to go to the aid of the Danes. While working on the play, Ibsen was beset by mounting debts and by doubts about his powers, and was ill with malaria. *Brand* reflects the intensity and anguish of the playwright's inner life. A tyrant and martyr, Ibsen's clergyman hero makes impossible demands on his congregation, his family, and himself. All are sacrificed to the fanaticism of an impossible morality carried to its absolute limits. Brand's Kierkegaardian pursuit of "All or Nothing" dramatizes both the heroism and the inhumanity of blind and uncompromising idealism.

Buoyed up by the unprecedented success of *Brand,* Ibsen turned to his most exuberant and most poetic drama, *Peer Gynt* (1867). The last of his plays to be written in verse, it blends a capricious and free-wheeling fantasy with spirited satire and deep philosophical implications. Less solemn by far than Goethe's *Faust,* it embodies the same conception of drama as a vast cosmic quest, a revelation of the mystery and meaning of human existence. Ibsen found the wonderful adventures of Peer Gynt in traditional folklore, notably in Asbjörnsen's *Norwegian Fairy-Stories,* and combined them with recollections of his childhood in the mountains and valleys of central Norway. His mother, he declared, was the model for Aase, "with the necessary exaggerations."

Ibsen composed *Peer Gynt* with a shrewd awareness of the gap between the heroic boasting of his countrymen and their meager accomplishments. The first line of the play, "Peer, you're lying," sets the tone of the whole piece. An attractive but utterly unprincipled rogue, Peer never sees himself as he really is. Attracted to Solveig, he woos a troll, and follows the counsel of the Great Boyg, to "go round about." Peer's way becomes that of evasion and compromise. His complete dedication to the Gyntian Self transforms him into a troll without his knowing it. Whether in the north or south, in the ancient or modern world, Peer's code and conduct remain the same. At the final return home he gains a measure of insight into his condition, but it comes almost too late; the Button-Moulder will be waiting at the third crossroads. The closing lines suggest that Peer may be saved, either by Solveig's love or through an inner transformation; but Ibsen characteristically leaves the matter in doubt. *Peer Gynt* is a poetic drama, not a sermon or an allegory. The plight of the hero is that of Ibsen's countrymen and of all mankind, but Peer's imaginative vitality, his quick tongue and ready wit, his fanciful idealism and lively adaptability, make him a vigorous and wholly individual personality as well as a great symbolic creation. *Peer Gynt* achieved popularity somewhat later than Ibsen's mature dramas of contemporary life. The music of Edvard Grieg, composed in 1874, captures some but not all of the intoxication and frenzy of Ibsen's turbulent play. The wild phantasmagoria of *Peer Gynt* points directly to Strindberg's expressionism. In the twentieth century *Peer Gynt* has been seized upon repeatedly by daring and imaginative producers and directors. It may well emerge as Ibsen's greatest achievement.

Ibsen's first realistic social drama, *The League of Youth* (1869), a caustic satire of Norwegian class types and attitudes, introduced a new style of dialogue in modern drama. Written, as Ibsen declared, "without a single monologue, and even without a single aside," it offered an immediate representation of character in an idiom of contemporary speech. *Emperor and Galilean* (1873), his last historical play, is an expansive account of the vain struggle of Julian the Apostate to replace religious conformity with a new individual freedom. A brief visit to Norway in the following year made Ibsen acutely conscious of social injustice; he moved to Munich and wrote *Pillars of Society* (1877), a harsh indictment of moral corruption and crime for the sake of money and power. In the plays that followed, Ibsen moved beyond isolated abuses to an anatomy of complex character relationships surrounded by acute social tensions. *A Doll's House* (1879), *Ghosts* (1881), and *An Enemy of the People* (1882) mark the triumph of this phase of Ibsen's career.

The plays that followed are more enigmatic, more profoundly concerned with the contradictions and cleavages of inner experience, with the analysis of weakness and insufficiency that have their roots in character and in private life. *The Wild Duck* (1884) inverts the premises of the preceding social dramas in its justification of the necessity of make-believe for the sake of life itself. The meddling of the naïve idealist, Gregers Werle, leads to catastrophe. *Rosmersholm* (1886) similarly blends realistic and symbolic techniques in a portrayal of the fatal consequences of the effort to use another human being. In *Hedda Gabler* (1890) Ibsen created one of his most arresting characters in the heroine who refuses to face life and is entrapped by her own instability and the irony of circumstance. Hedda is a fascinating study in psychopathology and shows how far Ibsen had travelled in a single decade.

The late plays are dramas of remorse and suffering. In *The Master Builder* (1892), the elderly artist, Solness, has misused and compromised his art. His final act is a new consecration which brings his death. *Little Eyolf* (1894), close in idiom to the contemporary symbolist drama, portrays the painful fruits of self-deception in wrecked and empty lives. The hero of *John Gabriel Borkman* (1896), a miner's son turned banker and swindler, kills the love of those around him in a vain quest for greatness. Ibsen's last play, *When We Dead Awaken* (1899), "a dramatic epilogue," reveals the risks and perils of the artist's calling through the fate of the sculptor, Rubek, who has sacrificed life to art at the expense of the woman who loves him. In their final moment amid a mountain avalanche, they share a vision of their new life in death.

Through his powerful realization of the dramatic substance of human experience, Ibsen created the foundations of modern drama. New techniques have not outmoded his imaginative artistry and his profound understanding of humanity. He remains the giant of the modern theatre.

# PEER GYNT

Translated by Norman Ginsbury

## CHARACTERS

AASE, *a peasant's widow*
PEER GYNT, *her son*
TWO OLD WOMEN WITH CORN-SACKS
ASLAK, *a blacksmith*
WEDDING GUESTS, A STEWARD, A FIDDLER, *etc.*
A MAN
HIS WIFE
SOLVEIG } *their daughters*
HELGA }
THE FARMER AT HEGGSTAD
INGRID, *his daughter*
THE BRIDEGROOM AND HIS PARENTS
THREE COWHERD-GIRLS
A WOMAN IN GREEN
THE KING OF THE DOVRE
TROLL COURTIERS, TROLL YOUTHS AND MAIDENS; TWO WITCHES, GNOMES, HOBGOBLINS, NIXIES, *etc.*
AN UGLY BOY
VOICE IN THE DARK; BIRDS' CRIES
KARI, *a cotter's wife*
MR. COTTON, M. BALLON, HERR VON EBERKOPF, *and* HERR TRUMPETERSTRAALE, *tourists*
A THIEF, A RECEIVER
ANITRA, *daughter of an Arab chief*
ARABS, FEMALE SLAVES, DANCING GIRLS, *etc.*
THE STATUE OF MEMNON (*and song*); THE SPHINX AT GIZEH (*mute*)
PROFESSOR BEGRIFFENFELDT, PH.D., *Director of the lunatic asylum in Cairo*
HUHU, *a language-reformer from Malabar*
HUSSEIN, *an Eastern Vizier*
A FELLAH WITH A ROYAL MUMMY
SOME LUNATICS AND THEIR KEEPERS
A NORWEGIAN SKIPPER
HIS CREW
A STRANGE PASSENGER
A PARSON, A FUNERAL PARTY, A REPRESENTATIVE OF THE LAW
A BUTTON MOLDER
A THIN MAN

*The action begins in the early part of the nineteenth century and ends about 1867. It takes place partly in Gudbrandsdale and the surrounding mountains, partly on the Moroccan coast, in the Sahara desert, in the Lunatic Asylum in Cairo, at sea, etc.*

## Act One, Scene One

SCENE *Near* AASE'S *farm. A wooded hillside down which rushes a mountain stream. On the farther bank is an old mill. A hot summer's day.* PEER GYNT, *a well-built young man about twenty years old, is coming down the path. He is followed by a slight, frail, very angry woman. She is* AASE, PEER'S *mother.*

AASE Peer, you're lying.
PEER (*Without stopping*) What? Me? Lying?
AASE Well then, swear that it's the truth.
PEER Swear? Why should I?
AASE Pshaw, you're frightened!
Lies, lies, lies! That's all it is.
PEER Everything I've said is Gospel.
AASE (*Confronting him*)
Can you face me without blushing?
First, just when the busy season's
Starting, you go off for weeks,
Cutting capers in the mountains,
Stalking reindeer in the snow!
Back you come all torn and tattered—
Where's your game? And where's your gun?—
Thinking you can take me in
With idiotic hunting stories!
Tell me where you saw this buck?
PEER Just near Gendin.[1]
AASE (*With a mocking laugh*) That sounds likely!

[1] In the mountain country in central Norway.

PEER I was hidden in a thicket,
Sheltering from the icy blast.
He was pawing in the snow,
Foraging for lichen.
AASE (*As before*) No!
PEER I held my breath, I stood and listened,
Heard the crunching of his hoofs.
Then I saw his mighty antlers,
So I slowly slithered forward
On my belly. I was covered
By the boulders. I peeped out.
What a buck! So sleek, so fat!
I could scarcely believe my eyes.
AASE Scarcely!
PEER Bang! I took a shot.
The buck fell bump among the boulders.
In the twinkling of an eye
I was straddled on his shoulders,
Holding on to his left ear.
Just as I was going to plunge
My knife into his gullet--Hi!
The ugly brute reared up and screamed,
Tossed his head and knocked my knife
Clean from my hand, then braced his horns,
Pinned me to the loins and held me
By the legs in a steel vise.
Then he bounded off like lightning
Right along the Gendin Ridge.
AASE (*Involuntarily*)
Christ above!
PEER You know the ridge?
Half-a-mile from end to end
It stretches, sharp as any scythe.
Down beyond the glaciers,
Beyond the slopes and grey ravines,
You can see on either side,
Two thousand feet and more below,
The brooding waters of the lakes.
Along that edge, the buck and I
Clove a pathway through the sky.
What a ride and what a steed!
Far ahead of us, the sun
Was shining on the glaciers.
And in the terrifying void
That stretched from us to those dark lakes,
Golden eagles seemed to float
And fall away like motes in sunlight.
Avalanches hurtled down,
Yet no sound reached me; but all round,
Dancing, singing, circling, swinging,
Went the dizzy mountain sprites,
Blurring sight, confusing hearing.
AASE (*Faintly*)
Oh, God help me!
PEER Suddenly,
From his perilous retreat,
On the edge of the great chasm,
Right underneath the reindeer's hoof,
A ptarmigan rose in the air,
Cackling, flapping his great wings,
Terrified. The buck swung round,
Reared on his hind legs, made one bound
And out into sheer space we plunged.
(AASE *totters and holds on to a tree-trunk*)
Behind, the giant mountain wall!
Below, a bottomless abyss!
First, we tore through banks of cloud,
Then dispersed a flock of seagulls;
Screaming, circling all around us,
They scattered where the four winds bore them.
Down we went with gathering speed;
Far beneath us something gleamed
Whitish, like a reindeer's belly.
Mother, it was our reflection
Mirrored in the mountain lake.
Up, up, up it came to meet us
At the same mad pace as we
Hurtled downwards to the waters.
AASE (*Gasping for breath*)
Peer! God help me! Tell me quickly!
PEER Buck from air, buck from the depths
Clashed together violently,
Spraying foam for miles around.
There we were, half drowned. At last,
We scrambled to the northern shore.
The reindeer swam and I held tight
Till—here I am!
AASE But where's the buck?
PEER The buck? He's probably still there.
(*Snapping his fingers and turning on his heel*)
Findings keepings! Go and look!
AASE How is it that your neck's not broken?
Both your legs are right as rain.
You haven't even cracked your spine.
The Lord be praised! Cry out with joy
To God who shielded my dear boy!
Your breeches! They're not even torn! . . .
But that is quite a minor point
When you think what might have happened
From a fearful fall like that!
(*She stops suddenly, stares at him wide-eyed, open-mouthed and speechless, then suddenly breaks out*)
Oh, you liar! Oh, you devil!
Oh, my God! What lies, what lies!
It's all come back to me! I heard it
First when I was still a girl.
This fairy-tale you've just been telling,
It happened to that Gudbrand Glesne,[2]
Not to you——
PEER To me as well.
If he could do it so can I.
AASE (*Angrily*)
Yes, you can polish up your lies,
Adorn them and embellish them,
Dress them up in their Sunday-best
And hide the dried-up skin and ribs.
That's the way you spend your time,
Building castles in the air,

[2] A hunter who, according to ancient Norse legend, shot a reindeer and sat astride its back, only to see the animal come back to life and take him for a wild ride.

Inventing and imagining,
Riding on an eagle's wing,
Lying right and lying left,
Talking so much tommy-rot
That listeners are left bereft
And never know what's what—or not!

PEER If anybody else said that,
I'd waste no time; I'd knock him flat.

AASE (*Weeping*)
Oh, God, I wish that I were dead
And buried deep down in the earth!
Not even tears and prayers affect him.
You're damned—that's all there is to it!

PEER Dearest, pretty little mother,
Everything you say is true.
But why worry? Cheer up!

AASE Quiet!
Cheer up? How can I be happy?
I've reared a pig and not a son.
It's a lasting, crying scandal
That a poor defenseless widow
Should have to hang her head in shame.
(*She begins to cry again*)
What is left of all the wealth
Your rich grandfather used to own?
Where is all the solid cash
That Rasmus Gynt left? Flown, gone crash,
Squandered, dissolved! It ran like sand
Straight through your father's open hand.
He bought land here, there, everywhere,
Sported a gilded coach and pair.
And now where's all the cash he wasted
At that famous winter feast
When every guest there flung his glass
Crash against the wall behind?

PEER Where are the snows of yesteryear?

AASE Hold your tongue when mother's talking.
Take a look at our fine house.
Half the windows stopped with rags;
Fences, palings, hedges down;
The cattle out come wind come rain,
Fields and meadows never touched
And every month a new distraint.

PEER Stop your moaning and your groaning.
You know it never rains but pours.
Our luck is out—well, it will turn.

AASE The earth that used to be so rich
Is sour; but you—you walk around
As spry and smug and self-assured
And just as perky as that day
The parson came from Copenhagen
And asked you your baptismal name;
Then swore the town's most learned men
Would envy such a brilliant boy.
And so your father, pleased as Punch,
Gave him a horse and then a sledge,
All for his kindly condescension.
In those days nothing went amiss.
The Church, the Army, everyone
Who mattered hung around and ate
And drank until they nearly burst.
Adversity shows us our friends.
The very day John Money-bags
Set off with his peddler's pack,
This house became a silent tomb.
(*Drying her eyes with her apron*)
And you, you great big healthy lout,
You ought to be a rod and staff
To comfort me in my old age.
You should be wrapped up in the farm
And seeing to your heritage.
(*Beginning to cry again*)
God knows how much help I've had
From you, you scamp! When you're at home
You poke the fire—that's all you do.
You frighten all the girls you see
At dances in the neighborhood,
You make a laughing-stock of me,
You brawl and fight with everyone.

PEER (*Moving away from her*)
Shut up, Mother.

AASE (*Following him*) Is it true
That in that recent drinking bout
At Lunde,[3] where you scrapped like dogs,
You were the leader of the fight?
Can you deny that it was you
Who broke the blacksmith Aslak's arm?
Or, if that isn't quite the case,
You put his finger out of place.

PEER Who's been running to you with tales?

AASE (*Hotly*)
The cotter's wife. She heard the yells.

PEER (*Rubbing his elbow*)
Yes, but it was I who yelled.

AASE You?

PEER Yes, I. I got the licking.

AASE What's that?

PEER Have you felt his muscles?

AASE Whose?

PEER His, Aslak's. Well, I have!

AASE Good God! You make me want to spew.
An idle, tippling, leering sot,
A loafing, drunken idiot,
A silly lump like that has thrashed you.
(*Beginning to cry again*)
I've put up with shame and scorn
Because of you, but this, this is
The biggest blow of all to stomach.
Even if he has big muscles
Must you be a stupid weakling?

PEER It's of no account at all
If I thrash or if I'm thrashed,
As long as you can have your cry. (*Laughing*)
Cheer up, Mother!

AASE You've been lying!
Have you?

PEER Yes, this time I have.
Dry your eyes and stop your crying.
(*Clenches his left hand*)
Look! With this pair of pincers here

[3] A small town in north central Norway.

I held the smith and bent him double.
My sledge-hammer was my right hand.

AASE Ruffian! You'll bring me to the grave
With your madcap goings-on.

PEER Come, come! You're worth a better fate,
Better twenty thousand times!
Darling, simple little Mother,
Surely you can trust in me.
The countryside for miles around
Will bow and scrape to you. Just wait
Till I do something really great!

AASE (*Contemptuously*)
You?

PEER Who knows what the future holds?

AASE If you only had the sense
To darn your breeches I'd be thankful.

PEER (*Hotly*)
I'll be a King, an Emperor.

AASE God in Heaven, the poor boy's losing
The little bit of brain he's got!

PEER Give me time, that's all I ask.

AASE "Give me time, I'll reach the skies,"
That is how the saying goes.

PEER Mother, wait——

AASE Be quiet! You're mad!
Yet you might have got somewhere
If you had not spent your time
Building castles in the air.
The girl at Heggstad wanted you
And you could have won her, too,
If you'd gone about it properly.

PEER Do you think so?

AASE The old man
Can't resist his daughter's whims.
He's firm enough up to a point,
But in the end she gets her way.
Wherever Ingrid goes her father
Stamps behind and minds his step.
(*Begins to cry again*)
Ah, my Peer! She oozes gold!
An heiress! Think of it, if you
Had set your mind on it you could
Have been a handsome bridegroom now,
And not a filthy, smelly tramp.

PEER (*Briskly*)
Come with me, I'll start my courting.

AASE Where?

PEER At Heggstad.

AASE My poor boy,
That road is closed to lovers.

PEER Why?

AASE Oh, dear God, I'd like to cry!
You've lost your opportunity!

PEER Why?

AASE While you scoured the mountain tracks
And rode your reindeer through the sky,
Mads Moen went and got the girl!

PEER What? Him? That fool! That laughing-stock!

AASE Yes, that's the man she's marrying.

PEER Wait for me, I'll go and get
The mare and cart——
(*Begins to move off*)

AASE You needn't bother,
The wedding is to-morrow.

PEER Bah!
I can get there by to-night.

AASE You'll go and make things ten times worse.
They'll add insult to injury.

PEER Don't worry! It will be all right.
It takes too long to get the mare.
(*He shouts and laughs at the same time*)
Ready, Mother? We'll leave the cart.
(*He picks her up*)

AASE Let me go!

PEER No! I will carry
My mother to the wedding-feast.
(*Wades out into the stream*)

AASE Help! Oh, Lord, have mercy! Peer!
We're drowning!

PEER Not me! I was born
To die a glorious death.

AASE You will!
You'll swing for this in God's good time.
(*She pulls his hair*)
Oh, you beast, you!

PEER Stop your struggling.
The bottom's very slippery here!

AASE You donkey!

PEER Talk on! Words aren't dear.
Your sticks and stones will break no bones.
There now! It's getting shallower!

AASE Don't let me go!

PEER Gee-up, gee-up!
Shall we play at Peer and reindeer? (*Galloping*)
I'll be the reindeer, you be Peer.

AASE I'm fainting! Where am I? Oh dear!

PEER There now! We've reached the other side.
(*Climbing the bank*)
Now give the deer a nice big kiss
And thank him for the lovely ride.

AASE (*Boxing his ears*)
That's the thanks you'll get from me!

PEER Ow!
That's a handsome tip, I must say.

AASE Let me go!

PEER To the wedding first!
You are such a clever talker,
Reason with the silly fool,
Say Mads Moen is always drunk.

AASE Put me down!

PEER Let your smooth tongue run.
Tell him the virtues of your son.

AASE You can set your mind at rest,
You'll get a character—the best.
I'll tell him everything I can
About my good-for-nothing son.
Believe me, I won't be too brief.

PEER Indeed? Well, well!

AASE And I won't stop
Until the old man sets his dog
On you as though you were a thief.

PEER In that case I must go alone.
AASE In that case I will follow on.
PEER Mother dear, you haven't strength to——
AASE You shall see! I'm in the mood
When I could grind the rocks to flour!
Ha! I could make a meal of flints!
Let me down!
PEER Well, will you promise——
AASE No, I'm going there with you.
I'll tell them all just what you are!
PEER Then you shall stay just where I choose.
AASE Never! I'll follow on behind.
PEER Oh no, you won't!
AASE What will you do?
PEER I'll put you up here on the roof.
(*He puts her on the roof of the mill.* AASE *screams*)
AASE Lift me down!
PEER Will you listen then?
AASE No!
PEER Mother dear, take my advice.
AASE (*Throwing a lump of grass at him*)
Lift me down this instant, Peer.
PEER I can't, I dare not, else I would.
(*Goes nearer*)
Now remember, please, sit tight.
Don't move your legs, don't shift an inch,
Don't tear the thatch because you might
Fall off and then——
AASE You horrid beast!
PEER No kicking!
AASE I wish you'd been whisked,
Like a changeling, off the earth.
PEER Shame!
AASE Bah!
PEER You should give your blessing
On a trying trip like this.
Will you?
AASE I will wallop you,
Big and burly as you are.
PEER Well, good-bye then, dearest Mother.
Be patient! I won't be too long!
(*Goes off, but turns and shakes his finger at her*)
Remember now! Quiet as a mouse!
AASE Peer! God help me, he has gone!
Reindeer-rider! Liar! Hi!
Will you listen? No, he's off
Across the fields——
(*Shouting*) I'm fainting! Help!
(*Two* OLD WOMEN *with sacks on their backs are approaching the mill*)
FIRST OLD WOMAN Who can that be cackling?
AASE Me!
SECOND OLD WOMAN Aase! You've gone up in the world!
AASE The world? I'll rise to Heaven soon.
FIRST OLD WOMAN A pleasant trip!
AASE Fetch me a ladder!
Get me down! That King of Knaves——
SECOND OLD WOMAN That son of yours?
AASE Now you have seen
With your own eyes how he behaves.
FIRST OLD WOMAN We'll bear witness.
AASE Help me down!
I'm off to Heggstad instantly.
SECOND OLD WOMAN Has he gone there?
FIRST OLD WOMAN Then you're avenged.
The blacksmith's going to the feast.
AASE (*Wringing her hands*)
Oh, God help me! My poor boy!
They'll finish up by killing him.
FIRST OLD WOMAN I've often heard them give a hint.
Don't worry, you'll soon get the proof.
SECOND OLD WOMAN The old girl's dotty, that's quite clear. (*Shouting up the hill*)
Eyvind, Anders! Hi, come here!
A MAN'S VOICE Whatever's happened?
SECOND OLD WOMAN Look, Peer Gynt
Has stuck his mother on the roof.

# Act One, Scene Two

SCENE *A slope covered with bushes and heather. Behind it, and divided from it by a fence, runs the high road.* PEER GYNT *comes along the path, goes quickly to the fence and gazes out over the landscape.*

PEER Heggstad at last! I'll be there pretty soon.
(*Swings a leg over the fence, then hesitates*)
I wonder if Ingrid's alone in her room.
(*Shades his eyes and looks out into the distance*)
No! They'll be swarming around her like flies
With their gifts. I'm beginning to think I'll go home.
(*Withdraws his leg*)
They'll only start laughing behind my back,
And their whispers brand like a red-hot iron.
(*Moves a few steps from the fence and scratches his head thoughtfully*)
What I really need is a good stiff drink.
Perhaps I could slip in without being seen!
It's a pity they know me! Something damned strong
Would be best, then their sneers would pass over my head.
(*He looks round, startled, then hides in some bushes. People carrying wedding presents pass him on their way to the farm*)
A MAN (*In conversation with others*)
Drink finished his father, his mother's a slut——
A WOMAN Then it's not so surprising the son's what he is.
(*They pass on; a little later* PEER GYNT *emerges from his hiding-place. He is blushing with shame. He stares after them*)

PEER That was me they were praising!
(*Shrugs his shoulders*)
Oh, well! I won't fret!
I've never known gossip kill anyone yet.
(*Throws himself down on the heather and lies for some time on his back with his hands clasped behind his head, staring up into the sky*)
What a curious cloud! It looks like a charger.
There's a man on his back with bridle and saddle.
An old hag is following riding a broomstick.
(*Smiling to himself*)
It's Mother! She's scolding and screaming, "You beast!
Hi there, Peer!"
(*His eyes are closing gradually*)
Now she's shrinking. I think she's afraid.
At the head rides Peer Gynt; his vast host is behind him.
His harness is silver, his steed shod with gold.
He wears gauntlets and carries a sabre and scabbard.
His long flowing cloak is adorned with rich silk.
They are princely, the legion who ride in his train!
But not one sits his steed so nobly as Peer—
There's not one so resplendent as he in the sunlight.
In swarms by the sides of the streets are the people,
Flinging their hats in the air in their glee.
The women are curtsying; who does not know
The Emperor Peer Gynt and his myriad of men?
He scatters the roadway with pieces of silver;
Glistening shillings are spread there like pebbles.
In a trice, every man is as rich as a lord.
Then, over the seas, through the skies rides Peer Gynt,
And on the seashore awaits England's[1] own Prince.
The loveliest maidens in England are there.
The great men of England and England's great king
All rise from their seats as Peer Gynt comes in view,
And the king doffs his crown and respectfully speaks:
(ASLAK, *the smith, and some others pass on the other side of the fence*)

THE SMITH Look at that! It's Peer Gynt! The swine's dead drunk again!

PEER (*Starting violently*)
Your Majesty——

THE SMITH (*Leaning on the fence and grinning*)
Can't you stand up, my boy?

PEER What the devil! It's Aslak! And what do you want?

THE SMITH (*To the others*)
It's the after-effects of the Lunde affair.

PEER (*Jumping up*)
Clear off!

THE SMITH Don't you worry, we're not staying here.
But where have you been, man, where have you been hiding?
You've been gone six weeks! Were you caught by the trolls? [2]

PEER I'm astounded myself at the things I've been doing.

THE SMITH (*Winking to the others*)
Then tell us!

PEER No point! It would never sink in.

THE SMITH (*After a pause*)
Are you coming to Heggstad?

PEER No.

THE SMITH They used to say
That Ingrid had more than a passion for you.

PEER You grubby old crow——

THE SMITH (*Half turning away*) Now don't lose your temper.
If Ingrid has given you up there are others.
Don't forget you're the son of John Money-bags.
Come with us to the farm! You'll find girls there as playful
As lambs, and ripe widows ready to fall.

PEER Go to Hell!

THE SMITH You'll find someone or other who'll have you.
Good evening, I'll pay your respects to the bride.
(*They go off laughing and whispering.* PEER GYNT *stares after them for a moment, then tosses his head and turns half round*)

PEER As far as I'm concerned, Ingrid can marry
Whoever she pleases. I don't care a damn!
(*Takes stock of his clothes*)
My breeches in tatters, my clothes torn to shreds!
If only I sported a decent new suit!
(*Stamping*)
How I'd like to sharpen a butcher's knife
And carve the mockery out of their hearts!
(*Looks round suddenly*)
What's that? Who's that there? I heard somebody tittering!
I could swear I heard something! I must have been wrong!
I must get home to Mother.
(*Begins to go up the hill, stops again and listens, his ear cocked in the direction of the farm*)
The dancing is starting.
(*He strains his eyes and ears, then goes slowly down the road. His eyes are gleaming. He rubs his hands over his legs*)
Such girls, such girls! Seven or eight to each man!
Oh, Hell! I must join in, I can't miss a party!
But Mother will still be up there on the roof.
(*His eyes stray toward the farm again. He skips and laughs*)
Listen! The Halling! [3] They're putting some life in it!
And Guttorm's in form with that fiddle of his!
His notes flash and boom like a waterfall.

---

[1] Spelled "Engelland" in the original, either for metrical purposes or to indicate an imaginary country in Peer's mind (translator's note).

[2] In old Norse mythology, the trolls were evil spirits endowed with magical powers. Originally they were conceived as giants but later traditions depict them in all guises, capable of being invisible or of transforming themselves into any shape.

[3] A lively peasant dance, performed by men slapping their heels and backsides, with high jumps and kicks.

And then those girls, all these wonderful girls!
Oh, Hell! I must join in, I can't miss a party!

## Act One, Scene Three

SCENE *The courtyard at Heggstad. The farmhouse is at the back. It is full of guests and there is dancing on the grass. The* FIDDLER *is sitting on a table; the* STEWARD *is standing in the doorway. Maids are going backward and forward between the buildings. The older people are sitting around in groups having a good gossip. One of the* WOMEN *joins a group sitting on a pile of logs.*

WOMAN The bride? Well, of course, she's crying a bit.
But who ever took any notice of that?

STEWARD (*To another group*)
Come along, gents, drink up, there's lots more in the vat.

A MAN Thank you! I'm finding it hard to keep pace!

A YOUTH (*Flying past the* FIDDLER *and holding a girl by the hand*)
Keep at it, Guttorm, scrape away till you bust!

THE GIRL Scrape away! Let it echo over the hills.

GIRLS (*In a ring round a youth who is dancing*)
He can dance, can't he?

A GIRL He's got such long legs!

THE YOUTH (*Dancing*)
Well, the ceiling's quite high and the room's pretty big.
(*The* BRIDEGROOM, *half-crying, approaches his* FATHER *who is talking to a couple of guests. He pulls at his* FATHER'S *sleeve*)

BRIDEGROOM Father, I've tried but she won't! She's standoffish.

FATHER What won't she?

BRIDEGROOM She's gone and locked herself in——

FATHER Well, what about going and finding the key?

BRIDEGROOM I don't know where to look.

FATHER You're a blasted young fool.
(*He turns to the others. The* BRIDEGROOM *drifts away*)

A YOUTH (*Coming from behind the house*)
Peer Gynt's just arrived. Things are going to get lively.

THE SMITH (*Who has just arrived*)
Who asked him, anyway?

STEWARD That's what I'd like to know!
(*Goes to the house*)

THE SMITH (*To the* GIRLS)
Ignore the chap, girls, if he tries to get friendly.

A GIRL (*To the others*)
As far as we go, he doesn't exist!
(PEER GYNT *enters, brimming over with life. He stops in front of the group and rubs his hands together*)

PEER Who's the best dancer here? Which one is Twinkletoes?

A GIRL (*Whom he approaches*)
Not I.

ANOTHER GIRL Not I.

THIRD GIRL I'm certain I'm not.

PEER (*To a fourth*)
Well, then, you, before somebody better turns up!

GIRL (*Turning away*)
No time.

PEER (*To a fifth*) Well, then, you!

GIRL (*Walking off*) I'm afraid I'm just going.

PEER Going? So early! You can't be all there!

THE SMITH (*A moment later, in a low voice*)
Look, Peer! She's gone off with that scabby old ram!

PEER (*Turning quickly to an elderly man*)
Where are the girls sitting out?

THE MAN Go and look.
(*He walks away.* PEER GYNT *has suddenly lost his vitality. He glances shyly and furtively toward the group. They are all looking at him but not one of them speaks. He approaches other groups. He is met everywhere by stony silence. As he moves away, people smile and follow him with their eyes*)

PEER (*Low voice*)
Black looks, sharp answers, superior smiles!
Sneers! They grate like a file on the blade of a saw.
(*He shrinks away along the fence.* SOLVEIG, *leading little* HELGA, *comes into the courtyard with her parents*)

A MAN (*To another quite near* PEER GYNT)
Here are our new neighbors.

SECOND MAN The ones from the west?

FIRST MAN From Hedalen.[1]

SECOND MAN Oh, yes. I think you are right.
(PEER GYNT *approaches the newcomers, and, pointing to* SOLVEIG, *asks her father*)

PEER May I dance with your daughter?

THE MAN (*Quietly*) Yes, certainly, but first
We must go in and pay our respects to the host.
(*They go*)

STEWARD (*Offering* PEER GYNT *a drink*)
Since you're here you might as well try some of this.

PEER (*Staring fixedly after the newcomers*)
No, thanks, I'm not thirsty. I'm here for the dance.
(*The* STEWARD *walks away.* PEER *looks across to the house and smiles*)
How lovely she is! I know no one as lovely!
Her eyes cast down and her apron so white!
And the way she held on to her Mother's dress!
And carried her prayer-book wrapped in a kerchief!
I must see her again.
(*Turns to go into the house. Several* YOUTHS *come from the house*)

A YOUTH What, leaving so early?

PEER No.

YOUTH Then your sense of direction's gone wrong.

[1] A town in west central Norway.

(*Grasps him by the shoulders and turns him round*)

PEER Let me pass.

YOUTH Ah, I see! You're afraid of the smith!

PEER Me? Afraid?

YOUTH Yes, the Lunde affair's not blown over.

(*The group laugh and go toward the dancing-green*)

SOLVEIG (*In the doorway*)
I think it was you who asked me to dance.

PEER Of course! You can't have forgotten me, surely!
Come on!

SOLVEIG Mother says don't go too far away.

PEER Mother says, Mother says! Were you born yesterday?

SOLVIEG You're laughing at me!

PEER Why, you're still quite a baby!
You haven't grown up.

SOLVEIG I was confirmed last spring.

PEER Tell me your name, then we'll feel more at ease.

SOLVEIG My name is Solveig. And what is yours, please?

PEER I'm Peer Gynt.

SOLVEIG (*Pulling her hand away*)
Oh, my God!

PEER Well, what's wrong with that?

SOLVEIG My garter's worked loose. I must tie it up tighter.

(*She moves away from him*)

BRIDEGROOM (*Pulling at his* MOTHER)
Mother, I've tried but she won't——

MOTHER She won't what?

BRIDEGROOM She won't, Mother!

MOTHER What?

BRIDEGROOM She won't unlock the door.

FATHER (*In a low angry voice*)
The boy's only fit to be fed with a spoon!

MOTHER Don't scold the poor boy, he'll soon find his way.

(*They walk away. A* YOUTH, *surrounded by a crowd of people from the dance, approaches* PEER)

YOUTH Brandy, Peer?

PEER No, thanks!

YOUTH Come, come, just a tot!

PEER (*Looking darkly at him*)
Have you got any?

YOUTH Well, perhaps—and perhaps not!
(*Pulls a flask from his pocket and drinks*)
What a kick it's got! Well?

PEER Has it? Let's have a nip! (*Drinks*)

SECOND YOUTH Try some of this! Have a damned good swig!

PEER No!

SECOND YOUTH Oh, nonsense! What's wrong? You were never so slow
About having a drink.

PEER Well, a tot then, no more. (*Drinks again*)

A GIRL (*With lowered voice*)
We ought to be going.

PEER You're frightened of me.

THIRD YOUTH Who isn't?

FOURTH YOUTH You showed us a few things at Lunde.
You gave us a bit of an eye-opener then.

PEER Oh, I can do more than that once I start.

FIRST YOUTH (*Whispering*)
And he's starting, believe me!

SEVERAL (*Crowding round him*) Come on, let it rip!
Tell us what you can do.

PEER To-morrow.

SEVERAL No, now.

A GIRL Are you good at black magic?

PEER I've conjured Old Nick!

A MAN My grandmother did that before I was born.

PEER Liar! Nobody else can manage that trick.
I've conjured the Devil inside a nut!
The thing was worm-eaten.

SEVERAL (*Laughing*) Well, that's obvious!

PEER He swore and he cried and he tried hard to bribe me
With this and with that——

ONE OF THE CROWD Was he forced to get in?

PEER He was. Then I plugged up the hole with a pin.
Christ! You should have heard the buzz and the rumble!

A GIRL Should we?

PEER Oh, yes. It was like a great bee!

THE GIRL But where is he now? Is he still in the nut?

PEER Oh, no. He managed to get right away.
That's why the blacksmith hates me to this day.

A YOUTH Really?

PEER I went to the blacksmith and asked him
To hammer that nut for me. He said "Of course!"
He took hold of the nut to hammer it flat.
But being as clumsy as he always is
And swinging his hammer as he always does——

VOICE FROM CROWD Did he kill the Devil?

PEER He hit like a madman,
But the Devil went up in a fury of flame—
Hey presto! Straight through the roof and the walls.

SEVERAL And the smith?

PEER Just gaped, his hands roasted like beef!
And since that day we have never been friends.
(*Everybody laughs*)

SEVERAL That's a good story!

OTHERS Quite one of his best!

PEER Are you hinting that I made it up?

A MAN Not at all!
You couldn't have. It was one of my
Grandfather's stock stories.

PEER You liar! It happened
To me.

THE MAN We won't argue.

PEER (*Tossing his head*) Why, I can ride
Through the air on a horse. There are dozen of things
Beyond your comprehension that I can do.
(*More roars of laughter*)

ONE OF CROWD Come on, ride through the air!

CHORUS OF VOICES Get going, old chap!

PEER In my own good time, so stop begging and praying.

The day will come when I'll ride like a whirlwind
Over you all and you'll fall at my feet.

AN OLDER MAN Stark staring mad!

ANOTHER He's gone off his head!

A THIRD The boaster!

A FOURTH The liar!

PEER (*Threatening*) You wait! Mark my words!

A MAN (*Half drunk*)
You mark mine! We'll warm your breeches for you.

SEVERAL A bloody good hiding! A juicy black eye!
(*The crowd disperses, the older ones angrily, the younger ones laughing or mocking*)

BRIDEGROOM (*Near* PEER)
Listen, Peer! Is it true you can ride through the air?

PEER Of course it is, Mads. There's not much I can't do.

BRIDEGROOM I suppose you've got the invisible coat?

PEER The invisible hat,[2] you mean. Oh, I've got that!
(*He turns away from the* BRIDEGROOM. SOLVEIG *crosses the courtyard leading* HELGA *by the hand.* PEER GYNT *goes towards them. Life seems brighter*)
Solveig, you're back! I'm glad! Let's have a dance.
(*Grasps her wrists*)
I'll show you how light I can be on my feet.

SOLVEIG Please let me go.

PEER Let you go?

SOLVEIG You're so wild!

PEER Like the reindeer, when the summer comes on?
Come along, girl, don't be so obstinate.

SOLVEIG (*Dragging her arm away*)
I can't! No, I dare not!

PEER Why?

SOLVEIG You've been drinking.
(*Goes with* HELGA)

PEER Why didn't I get my knife and stick it
Right through the lot of them—yes, everyone?

BRIDEGROOM (*Nudging* PEER *with his elbow*)
I wish you'd help me get into her room.

PEER (*Absently*)
The bride's? Where is she?

BRIDEGROOM The loft.

PEER Ah, I see!

BRIDEGROOM It's the least you can do, Peer. You might have a try.

PEER To get at your bride? You must do that yourself.
(*Suddenly, a thought strikes him. He speaks softly but significantly*)
Ingrid in the loft!
(*Goes up to* SOLVEIG)
Have you changed your mind?
(SOLVEIG *tries to go. He bars her path*)
You're ashamed of me! I look like a tramp!

SOLVEIG But you don't! It's not true! I don't think it at all.

PEER Yes, I do, and what's more, I'm a little bit drunk.
I was piqued. You'd annoyed me. That's why I did it.
Now will you—?

[2] The invisible hat occurs frequently in Norse folklore. It is supposedly found in the mist around mountains.

SOLVEIG I'm frightened. Even if——

PEER Frightened? Of whom?

SOLVEIG Mostly of Father.

PEER Father! I see! He's so very correct!
Does he rule with an iron rod? Well, answer me.

SOLVEIG What can I say?

PEER Does he sing in the choir?
And you and your Mother? Are you just the same?
Why don't you answer me?

SOLVEIG Please, let me go!

PEER (*In a low threatening voice*)
I won't! I can turn myself into a troll!
At the stroke of twelve I'll be in your room,
And you'll hear a strange noise—a hissing and spitting,
Next to your bed, and it won't be your cat
But me! I'll drain your blood into a cup,
And I'll grab your sister and eat her up,
For every night I turn myself into a werewolf!
I'll bite your loins and I'll bite your back—
(*Suddenly turns round and entreats her*)
Dance with me, Solveig!

SOLVEIG (*Looking at him darkly*)
No, you've been horrible!
(*She returns to the house. The* BRIDEGROOM *comes drifting back to* PEER)

BRIDEGROOM I'll give you an ox if you'll help me.

PEER Come on!
(*They go behind the house. At the same time a crowd comes from the green where the dancing has been taking place. Most of them are drunk. There is noise and confusion.* SOLVEIG *and* HELGA *come out of the house with their parents and other people*)

STEWARD (*To the* SMITH *who is in front*)
Shut up!

SMITH (*Taking his coat off*)
No, we'll have this out once and for all.
It's Peer Gynt or I and it's now or never.

SOME OF CROWD Let them fight it out.

OTHERS No, let them fight with words.

SMITH Words! Words be damned! It's fists or it's nothing.

SOLVEIG'S FATHER Control yourself, man!

HELGA Are they going to hit him?

A YOUTH Why not pull his leg with his silly old lies?

SECOND YOUTH Kick him out of the place!

THIRD YOUTH I'll spit in his eye.

FOURTH YOUTH (*To* SMITH)
Are you backing out, you?

SMITH (*Throwing coat away*) No, I'll murder him.

SOLVEIG'S MOTHER (*To* SOLVEIG)
Now you can see what they think of the fellow!
(AASE *comes in with a stick in her hand*)

AASE Is he here? Where's my son? I'll give him what for!
My God! What a walloping he's going to get!

SMITH (*Rolling up his shirt-sleeves*)
For a scoundrel like him that cudgel's too soft.

VOICES The blacksmith will bash him!

OTHERS Will thrash him!

SMITH I'll smash him!
(*Spits on his hands and nods to* AASE)
AASE What? You smash my Peer? Just try if you dare!
His old mother Aase's got sharp teeth and claws!
Where is he? (*She calls*) Peer!
(BRIDEGROOM *comes running in*)
BRIDEGROOM Father! Mother!
FATHER What's happened?
BRIDEGROOM What do you think? Peer Gynt——
AASE (*Shrieking*) Have you killed him?
BRIDEGROOM No, Peer Gynt has—— Look! Up there! On the hills!
CROWD With the bride!
AASE (*Letting her stick fall*)
Oh, the beast!
SMITH (*Thunderstruck*) It's a sheer precipice!
He's clambering up! My God, like a goat!
BRIDEGROOM (*Crying*)
Look how he's carrying her! She might be a pig!
(AASE *shakes her fists threateningly at* PEER)
AASE I hope he falls! (*Shrieks in terror*)
Oh, take care! It's not safe!
(INGRID'S FATHER *comes out bareheaded and white with anger*)
INGRID'S FATHER He's raped my daughter! I'll strike him dead.
AASE God punish me if you touch a hair of his head!

## Act Two, Scene One

SCENE *A narrow path high up in the mountains. Early morning.* PEER GYNT *is walking along, very sullen.* INGRID, *still in the remnants of her bridal dress, is trying to hold him back.*

PEER Clear off!
INGRID (*Weeping*) But where can I go
After this?
PEER Go where you like.
INGRID (*Wringing her hands*)
You villain, you!
PEER Oh, hold your tongue!
This is where we part for good.
INGRID Memories bind us forever.
PEER The devil take all memories!
The devil take all women too,
Excepting one——!
INGRID Who *is* the one?
PEER Not you!
INGRID Well then, who is she?
PEER Go away! Go home, go back
To your father.
INGRID Dearest sweetheart——!
PEER Oh, for God's sake——!
INGRID You can't mean
What you're saying.
PEER Every word!
INGRID You get your way, then pack me off.
PEER Tell me what you have to offer.
INGRID Heggstad farm and more besides.
PEER Is your prayer-book in your kerchief?
Where's your plait of golden hair?
Do you gaze down at your apron?
Do you cling to your mother's dress?
Answer!
INGRID No——
PEER Were you confirmed
Last spring?
INGRID No, but listen, Peer——
PEER Have your eyes that dear, shy look?
Can you refuse me when I beg?
INGRID Christ! The man's gone raving mad!
PEER Does the grace of God descend
On those who see you? Answer me!
INGRID No, but——
PEER That is all that matters.
(*Turns to go*)
INGRID (*Stopping him*)
They'll hang you if you fail me now.
PEER It's a risk worth hanging for.
INGRID You'll be wealthy, you'll be honored
If you take me——
PEER Impossible.
INGRID (*Bursting into tears*)
Oh, you swindler!
PEER You were willing!
INGRID I was desperate——
PEER I was daft.
INGRID (*Threatening*)
You'll pay heavily for this!
PEER The heaviest price will be dirt-cheap.
INGRID You stand by that?
PEER Firm as a rock.
INGRID All right then! We'll see who'll win!
(INGRID *goes down the slope*)
PEER (*After a pause*)
The devil take all memories!
The devil take all women too!
INGRID (*Turning her head and calling back mockingly*)
Excepting one!
PEER Excepting one.
(*They go their different ways*)

## Act Two, Scene Two

SCENE *A mountain lake surrounded by moorland. A storm is brewing.* AASE *is shouting and peering all round her. She is in despair.* SOLVEIG *can barely keep up with her.* SOLVEIG'S *parents and* HELGA *are a little way behind.* AASE *clenches her fists and tears her hair.*

AASE Everything's against me with the powers of evil,
The mists, the waters and the cursed mountains!

Mists are rolling down to blind and confuse him.
Treacherous waters are waiting to drown him.
Mountains will open up chasms or crush him.
And the people! All of them out for his life!
Please, God, protect him! I can't live without him.
The rascal! To think that the Devil should tempt him!
(*Turns to* SOLVEIG)
I can't believe this has really happened.
He, who did nothing but lie and romance,
He, whose strength lay in his powers of boasting,
He, who has done not one stroke of real work,
He—! I could laugh and cry at the same time!
We were as one in our sorrow and need.
You are sure to have heard of my husband's bad name—
How he roamed round the district throwing away
His money like dirt, how he drank and he swore,
While I and my Peer sat alone at home.
What could we do but try to forget?
I hadn't the strength to take matters in hand.
It's ghastly to see Fate staring at you.
You are desperate to shake off your cares,
But thought brings nothing but grief and tears,
So you take to drink or you sham romance.
Well, we—we resorted to fairy-tales
About princes and trolls and strange animals too,
And also of brides who are stolen. But who
Could know that these tales would stick in his head?
(*Getting frightened again*)
Ugh, what a yell! It's a troll or a demon!
Peer, are you there? Up there on the hill——?
(*Runs to the top of the rise and gazes out over the lake.* SOLVEIG'S *parents join her*)
Not a thing in sight!

THE HUSBAND (*Quietly*) It is worse for him!

AASE (*Crying*)
Oh, my Peer! My poor lost lamb!

HUSBAND (*Nodding gently*) You are right,
He is lost.

AASE No, no! You mustn't say that!
He is so clever. There's no one like him!

HUSBAND You speak like a fool!

AASE Yes, yes, I know!
I may be foolish, but my boy's all right!

HUSBAND (*Still quietly and gently*)
He's hardened his heart, his soul is lost!

AASE (*Fearfully*)
No, no! Our Lord will have pity on him.

HUSBAND He's weighed down by his sins. Do you think he'll repent?

AASE No, but he'll ride through the air on a buck!

THE WIFE Great God! Are you mad?

HUSBAND What's that you're saying?

AASE Nothing's beyond him, I tell you! You wait!
If he lives long enough, he'll do something great.

HUSBAND It would be better to see him hang.

AASE (*Screaming*)
In Christ's name—!

HUSBAND With a rope round his neck,
His eyes might open; he might repent.

AASE (*Bewildered*)
You're driving me crazy with all your talk!
We must find him!

HUSBAND To save his soul!

AASE And body!
If he's in the marsh we must drag him out.
We must ring the bells if the trolls have caught him.

HUSBAND Look, here's a track!

AASE God will reward you
For aiding me.

HUSBAND It's my Christian duty.

AASE The rest of them are nothing but heathens.
Not one would lift a finger to help me!

HUSBAND They knew him too well.

AASE He was too good for them.
(*Wringing her hands*)
And to think—to think that his life's at stake!

HUSBAND There's a footprint! Look!

AASE Then we're on the right road.

HUSBAND We'll scatter and try the moors down there.
(*He and his* WIFE *go on ahead*)

SOLVEIG (*To* AASE)
Please tell me some more.

AASE (*Drying her eyes*) About my son?

SOLVEIG Yes, everything!

AASE (*Smiling and holding her head high*)
Tell you everything?
I'd tire you out!

SOLVEIG You'd tire of talking
Long before I'd tire of listening.

# Act Two, Scene Three

SCENE *Low bare hills below the mountain plateau. Snowclad peaks in the distance. It is early evening and the shadows are lengthening.* PEER GYNT *comes running in and stops on the slope.*

PEER The whole of the parish is on my track.
They've armed themselves with guns and clubs.
The old man from Heggstad is at the head.
I can hear him howling! The news has spread
That Peer Gynt's on the run. Not quite the same thing
As a scrap with the smith! This is life! I'm as strong
As a bear!
(*He flings his arms about and leaps in the air*)
I'll swim rapids, pull fir-trees up
By the roots! Smash! I'll overturn the whole world!
This is life! It makes your spirits rise,
Steels and toughens! To hell with paltry lies!
(*Three* COWHERD-GIRLS *from the mountains run across the hillside, singing wildly*)

COWHERD-GIRLS Trond of Valfjeld! Baard and Kaare! [1]
Sleep with us, trolls, and hear our story!

[1] Names of Trolls. Valfjeld refers to a region of mountains in central Norway.

PEER Who are you screeching for?
COWHERD-GIRLS Trolls, the whole crew!
FIRST COWHERD-GIRL Trond, be strong!
SECOND COWHERD-GIRL Baard, be gentle and true!
THIRD COWHERD-GIRL There's lots of room in our hut on the hay.
FIRST COWHERD-GIRL Strength is gentle!
SECOND COWHERD-GIRL And gentleness strong!
THIRD COWHERD-GIRL We sleep with trolls the whole night long!
PEER Where are your men then?
THE THREE (*Laughing coarsely*) They've gone away!
FIRST COWHERD-GIRL Mine called me darling and sweetheart, too. Now he's married a middle-age shrew!
SECOND COWHERD-GIRL Mine found a gypsy asleep in the heather. Now they are tramping the roads together!
THIRD COWHERD-GIRL Mine murdered our bastard, and now he grins on the end of a stake for his clumsy sins.
ALL THREE Trond of Valfjeld! Baard and Kaare!
Sleep with us, trolls, and hear our story!
PEER (*Leaping among them*)
I'm a three-headed troll and your man for today.
ALL THREE You're as sturdy as that?
PEER You'll very soon know!
FIRST COWHERD-GIRL To the hut! Let us go!
SECOND COWHERD-GIRL We have mead!
PEER Let it flow!
THIRD COWHERD-GIRL In the hut, to-night, we'll rumple the hay.
SECOND COWHERD-GIRL (*Kissing him*)
He glows and gleams like metal—feel!
THIRD COWHERD-GIRL (*Kissing him*)
A baby's eyes but limbs like steel!
PEER (*Dancing with them*)
Gloomy forebodings, dark thoughts waking,
Laughing eyes but a heart that's breaking!
(*The three* COWHERD-GIRLS *cock snooks at the mountains, singing wildly*)
ALL THREE Trond of Valfjeld! Baard and Kaare!
You've slept with us, trolls, you've heard our story.
(*They dance away over the hills,* PEER GYNT *between them*)

## Act Two, Scene Four

SCENE *Among the Ronde Mountains.*[1] *Sunset. Glistening snowclad peaks all around.*

PEER (*Entering wild and confused*)
Castle on castle is rising!
Look at that glistening gate!
Stop! Will you stop! It's drifting
Farther and farther away!
The cock on the weather-vane's lifting
His wings as though for a flight.
It's melted into the blue haze,
And the mountain is locked and barred.
What are those trees and bracken
That grow in the clefts of the rocks?
They are giants with feet of herons,
And now they are fading, too.
The air is flecked like the rainbow,
It's racking my eyes and mind.
Far off, there's a sound of bells ringing,
My eyes are weighted with lead.
Hell! It's a dreadful throbbing,
Like a glowing band clamped tight,
But I can't think who the devil
Has fastened it round my head!
(*Sinks down*)
A ride on the Gendin Ridge,
Romancing and silly lies!
A climb up the sharpest rock
With the bride—and drunk a whole day,
Chasing away hawks and kites,
Threatened by goblins and trolls,
An orgy with crazy women,
Romancing and silly lies!
(*Gazing upwards for a long time*)
There go two golden eagles!
The wild geese are flying south!
And here am I plodding and stumbling
Knee-deep in the mud and filth.
(*Jumps up*)
I'll join them! I'll wash off my sins
In a bath of the keenest winds!
I'll soar up and up, then plunge deep
In that shining christening font,
And emerge, at last, purged of vice!
I'll fly out over the meadows,
I'll fly till I'm pure of soul,
Over the salty ocean,
High above England's prince.
Yes, you may stare, you maidens,
But don't think I'm coming to you;
So you needn't trouble to wait!
Well, perhaps, I might swoop down on you.
Well, I'm damned! Those two golden eagles?
The Devil has taken them!
Look! There's the end of a gable,
And a house rising stone by stone
Out of those moldy ruins!
And now the door's wide open!
So that's what it is! I know it!
It's my old grandfather's farm!
The rags have gone from the windows,
The palings are spruce and new,
In every room lights are blazing,
There's a banquet in the hall.
I can hear the parson tapping
His knife against his glass.
The captain flings his bottle

[1] Part of the Dovre-fjeld, a range of mountains separating north from south Norway.

And smashes the mirror to bits.
Let them be lavish and squander!
Does it matter? Mother, be quiet!
Rich John Gynt is giving a party.
Hurrah for the house of Gynt!
What's all this bustle and hubbub?
Why all this hullabaloo?
The captain is calling for me,
The parson is drinking my health.
In you go then, Peer Gynt, to the toasting,
It rings out in clamor and song,
Peer Gynt, you were born into greatness,
And great you'll become before long.
(*Rushes forward but hits his nose against a rock and falls senseless*)

## Act Two, Scene Five

SCENE *A mountain slope with great trees through which the wind is sighing. Stars are twinkling through the leaves and birds singing in the branches. A* WOMAN, *dressed in green, is walking on the hillside. Behind her, comes* PEER GYNT, *making all sorts of amorous gestures. The* WOMAN *stops and turns round.*

WOMAN Is that true?
PEER (*Drawing his finger across his throat*)
As true as the fact that I'm Peer,
As true as the fact that you're gracious and fair,
Will you have me? You'll see how nice I'll be;
You won't have to weave or spin or mend,
You'll have lots to eat and lots more to spend,
And I'll never, never pull your hair——
WOMAN Nor beat me?
PEER No, it would be unheard-of!
We sons of kings do not beat our women.
WOMAN You're a king's son?
PEER Yes.
WOMAN Well, I happen to be
The daughter of the Dovre king.
PEER Do you now! Well, what a coincidence!
WOMAN My Father's palace is deep in the Ronde.
PEER I feel quite sure my Mother's is grander.
WOMAN Do you know my Father? His name is King Brose.
PEER Do you know my Mother? Her name is Queen Aase.
WOMAN When my Father's angry, the four winds awake.
PEER When my Mother starts scolding, the earth starts to quake.
WOMAN My Father can kick as high as a tower.
PEER My Mother can grind the rocks to flour.
WOMAN Have you nothing to wear except rags and tatters?
PEER It's the man inside the breeches that matters.
WOMAN Everyday I wear silk and a golden pelisse.
PEER It looks more like tow and verdigris.
WOMAN Ah, yes! There's one thing you must remember;
In the Ronde we see with another sense,
And everything seems to have a double
Form. When you enter my Father's hall,
You might think it a hideous pile of rubble.
PEER How peculiar! It's the same with us!
You might fancy that gold is worthless dross,
And a glittering window-pane will look
Like a bundle of stockings and dirt and moss.
WOMAN Evil seems good and black becomes white.
PEER Big becomes little and dull looks bright.
WOMAN (*Falling on his neck*)
I see we're made for each other, Peer!
PEER Like trousers for legs or a comb for hair.
WOMAN (*Shouting over the hill*)
My wedding-steed! Come! On your back we'll leap!
(*A gigantic pig comes trotting in. Its bridle is a piece of cord, its saddle an old sacking.* PEER GYNT *swings himself on its back and seats the* WOMAN *in front of him*)
PEER Heigh-ho! Through the Ronde gates we'll sweep!
Gee-up, hop-hop! My trusty sow!
WOMAN (*Lovingly*)
And I was feeling so sad just now!
It goes to show that it's Fate that counts!
PEER (*Whipping the pig, which trots away*)
You can tell great folk by the style of their mounts.

## Act Two, Scene Six

SCENE *The Royal Hall of the King of the Dovre Mountains.*[1] *A great assembly of* TROLL COURTIERS *of all ages, sizes and descriptions. The* KING *is seated on his throne, wearing his crown and carrying his sceptre. His children and nearest relatives are grouped round him.* PEER GYNT *is facing him. A good deal of commotion.*

COURTIERS Kill him! A Christian has dared to beguile
The Dovre king's most beautiful daughter!
YOUNG TROLL Let me slice his fingers!
ANOTHER YOUNG TROLL Let me pull his hair!
TROLL MAIDEN Let me bite a great big lump from his rump!
A WITCH (*Holding ladle*)
Shall we have him as porridge or in the stock-pot?
ANOTHER WITCH (*With chopper*)
Shall we eat him roasted or browned in a grill?

[1] Mountains of central Norway.

KING Keep cool! (*Beckons counselors*)
Now it's time we stopped preening ourselves.
Our affairs, of late, have been going down-hill;
No one knows whether we'll crash or recover,
So we can't refuse help, whatever the source.
Besides, the young man has hardly a blemish,
And he's virile, too, unless I'm mistaken.
It's true he has only a single head,
But my daughter herself hasn't more than one.
Three-headed trolls are quite out of fashion;
Even two-headed ones are rare enough now,
And I'm bound to say they're not much to look at.
(*To* PEER GYNT)
So you're after my daughter?

PEER Your daughter and
Your kingdom thrown in as her dowry, of course.

KING I'll give you half while I'm still alive,
You can have the rest the day I snuff out.

PEER That's fair enough.

KING Wait a moment, my lad!
You've got to make a few promises, too.
If you break one of them our pact becomes void
And you'll never get out of here alive.
First of all, you must swear to wipe from your mind
The world outside the Ronde. Avoid
The day, its affairs, never walk in the sun.

PEER If I'm king that ought to be easy enough.

KING Secondly—now we'll see what you don't know.
(*Stands up*)

OLDEST TROLL COURTIER (*To* PEER)
Now we'll see whether your wisdom tooth
Can crack the nut of an old man's riddles.

KING What's the difference between a troll and a man?

PEER None at all, as far as I can see.
Big trolls would roast you and little trolls skin you.
We'd do just the same if we only dared.

KING That's true! There are numerous points of resemblance,
But morning is morning and night is night,
And the difference is plain if you've got good sight.
Now, I'll tell you what that difference is.
Out there, among men living under the blue,
The saying goes, "Man, to thyself be true!"
In the hills, we've no time for such self-righteous stuff.
Our saying goes, "Troll, to thyself be enough."

TROLL COURTIER (*To* PEER)
Do you see it?

PEER It seems a bit indistinct.

KING That all-embracing "Enough," my son,
Must be emblazoned on your coat-of-arms.

PEER (*Scratching himself behind his ear*)
But——

KING It must if you're going to be king here!

PEER If it must, then it must. It isn't worse——

KING Next, you must learn to adjust yourself
To our homely, straightforward, plain way of living.
(*He beckons. Two* TROLLS *with pigs' heads and white nightcaps bring food and drink*)
Our cows give cakes and our bullocks mead;
Do not ask whether they taste sweet or sour;
The real point is, and you mustn't forget it,
The cakes are home-baked and the mead home-brewed.[2]

PEER (*Pushing the things away from him*)
To the Devil with your mysterious drinks!
I'll never get used to your country's ways.

KING The bowl is part of the drink and it's gold.
Who takes the bowl takes my daughter, as well.

PEER (*Thoughtfully*)
Well, they say we must overcome our dislikes;
I've no doubt I'll get used to the taste in time.
So here goes! (*Drinks*)

KING That was very wisely spoken!
You spit?

PEER That was merely force of habit.

KING Next, you must shed your Christian clothes.
In the Dovre, I'm proud to say, everything
Is mountain-made; nothing comes from the valley
Except the silk tassel on our tails.

PEER (*Angrily*)
I haven't a tail.

KING I can give you one.[3]
Chamberlain, fasten my Sunday tail on him.

PEER Don't you dare! You're making a fool of me!

KING You can't woo my child with a bare backside!

PEER You'd turn men into beasts!

KING My son, you're wrong!
I'm turning you into a gallant beau.
We'll give you a flame-yellow tip for your tail!
We could heap no higher honor on you.

PEER (*Thoughtfully*)
Well, they say we are feathers in the wind,
And custom and fashion must carry us with them.
All right, go ahead!

KING You're a wise young man.

COURTIER Now, see with what panache you wag it and whisk it.

PEER (*Annoyed*)
Is there anything else I'm supposed to do?
What about giving up my Christian faith?

KING You can stick to that if it eases your mind.
Belief is free; there's no tax on it.
You can tell a troll by the cut of his coat.
If we can agree about manners and dress,
You may hold beliefs that would give us the creeps.

PEER In spite of the terms that you impose,
You're much more moderate than I expected.

KING Alas, my son, we trolls are belied
By our reputations, and that's another
Distinction between you and us. However,
The serious part of our business is ended.
Now, we will feast our eyes and our ears.
Harpist! Pluck gently the Dovre harp-strings!
Dancer! Tread lightly the Dovre hall's floor!
(*Music and dancing*)

COURTIER How do you like it?

[2] Here Ibsen is satirizing a political faction demanding high tariffs and a policy of "Buy Norwegian."

[3] The tails indicate that the trolls are part of the devil's crew.

PEER Like it!

KING Speak your mind.
What do you see?

PEER Something incredible!
A bell-cow twanging a string with her hoof,
A sow in short socks out of step with the discord.

COURTIERS Eat him!

KING Remember his standards are human.

TROLL MAIDENS Let's lop off his ears, let's scratch out his eyes!

WOMAN IN GREEN (*Weeping*)
Boo-hoo! To think we must put up with that!
When my sister and I dance and play so well!

PEER Oh dear! Was it you? I was only teasing.
At a party everything's said in good fun.

WOMAN IN GREEN Will you swear you were teasing?

PEER The music and dance
Were quite entrancing, I swear they were.

KING It's a very strange thing, this human nature;
It sticks to a man like a layer of skin.
If it's hurt in a fight—well, it leaves a scar,
But it doesn't take long for the scar to heal.
Now, my son-in-law is very compliant.
He's taken his Christian breeches off,
He's willingly drunk our bowl of mead,
And willingly fastened a tail on his rump.
So willingly has he met our demands,
That I felt convinced *Homo sapiens*
Had been chased away forever. But no!
In double-quick time he's back again!
And so, my son, I must do what I can
To cure your peculiar human traits.

PEER How will you do that?

KING I'll scratch your left eye
So that you begin to see awry,
And everything that you gaze upon
Will bear the hall-mark of excellence.
Then I'll cut out your right window-pane——

PEER Are you drunk?

KING (*Putting some sharp instruments on the table*)
Here are the glazier's tools.
You'll be tamed as though you're a bull run amok;
And then you'll see that your bride is lovely;
Your eyes will never mislead you again
With sows out-of-step and bell-cows with hoofs.

PEER This is lunacy.

OLDEST COURTIER It's the Troll king's decision.
He is the wise one; it's you who are mad!

KING Think of all the annoyance and worry
You'll manage to dodge in the course of the years.
And try to remember that the eyes
Are the source of bitter, angry tears.

PEER That's true enough and the Bible says,
"If thy right eye offend thee pluck it out."
Now tell me, when will my sight be restored
To normal again?

KING Never, my friend!

PEER If that's the case, I must say, "No, thank you."

KING Then what are you going to do?

PEER Leave at once!

KING Indeed? Well, it's easy to get in here,
But the Dovre king's gate doesn't open outward.

PEER Are you going to keep me here by force?

KING Now listen, Prince Peer, and try to be prudent!
Your gifts mark you out to be a troll—
Hasn't he got the stamp and the carriage?—
And you would like to be a troll, wouldn't you?

PEER God knows I would! It's worth giving up
Something to win a beautiful bride
With a model kingdom thrown in besides.
But there's a limit to everything.
I've put on a tail, that's perfectly true;
But what's to stop me from casting it off?
I've cast off my breeches; they were old
And torn. But what's to stop me from putting
Them on again? And the Devil take me
If I can't cast off your troll's way of life.
If you like I'll swear that a cow's a maiden;
I can always release myself from my oath.
But to know I can never be free again;
That I can't even die like a decent man,
That I'll end my days like a mountain troll
And never go home again, as the book says—
A point which you stress so insistently—
To that, I'm afraid, I cannot agree.

KING Now, on my life, I'm losing my temper.
And I'm not here to be trifled with.
You long-legged ass! Do you know who I am?
In the first place you're much too free with my daughter——

PEER That's a lie!

KING You'll have to marry her!

PEER Do you dare to make out—?

KING Can you deny
That you had a hankering after her?

PEER (*Whistling*)
That's not such a serious crime, after all.

KING Human beings are all the same.
You talk, talk, talk about your souls,
But you're much more interested in flesh.
So you think desire is of no account?
Well, you'll very soon learn to think otherwise.

PEER You won't catch me with your bait of lies.

WOMAN IN GREEN
By the end of the year you'll be a proud father.

PEER Let me get out of here.

KING We'll send you your child
Wrapped up in a goatskin.

PEER (*Wiping the sweat from his forehead*)
If I could wake up!

KING Shall we send him to your palace?

PEER The parish!

KING Very good, Prince Peer, it's your own concern.
But one thing is certain, what's done is done.
You'll be surprised when you see your son;
Half-breeds grow at prodigious speed.

PEER Old man, you're as obstinate as a mule.
Dear lady, keep cool! We may yet strike a bargain.
I must make it plain that I'm neither a prince
Nor am I rich. Paint me how you like,
And I still won't be a credit to you.

KING (*Looks at him with disdain, then says*)

Dash him to bits on the rocks, my sons.

YOUNG TROLLS Mayn't we first play at Eagles and Owls?
Or the Wolf Game? Or Grey Mouse and Fierce-eyed Puss?

KING Well, be quick! I'm annoyed and I'm sleepy. Good night! (*Goes*)

PEER (*Chased by* YOUNG TROLLS)
Clear off, you devils!
(*Tries to get up chimney*)

YOUNG TROLLS Hobgoblins, imps!
Bite him all over!

PEER Ow!
(*Tries to get through trap-door to cellar*)

YOUNG TROLLS Shut all the exits.

COURTIER They're enjoying themselves, the little dears!

PEER (*Fighting with a little* TROLL *who is clinging to his ear*)
Let go, you maggot!

COURTIER (*Rapping* PEER *over knuckles*)
You're speaking to royalty.

PEER A rat-hole! (*Rushes towards it*)

YOUNG TROLLS Hobgoblins, bung up that hole!

PEER The old man was hellish; the young ones are worse.

YOUNG TROLLS Skin him!

PEER (*Running round and round*)
If I were as small as a mouse—

YOUNG TROLLS (*Swarming round him*)
Close in! We've got him!

PEER If I were a louse——(*Falls*)

YOUNG TROLLS Scratch his eyes out!

PEER (*Buried under a heap of* TROLLS)
Help, Mother, they're killing me!
(*Church bells far away*)

TROLL URCHINS Bells in the mountains! The Black-frock's cows! [4]
(*The* TROLLS *flee. Uproar and wild shrieks. The King's Hall collapses. Everything disappears*)

## Act Two, Scene Seven

SCENE *It is pitch-dark.* PEER GYNT *can be heard slashing out with the branch of a tree.*

PEER Tell me! Who are you?

VOICE IN THE DARKNESS Myself.

PEER Move aside.

VOICE Go round about, Peer. There's room on the mountain.
(PEER GYNT *tries to pass in another direction, but comes up against "the thing."*)

PEER Who are you?

VOICE Myself. Can you say the same?

[4] The black-frock refers to the priest. Trolls, as part of the devil's family, cannot abide the sound of church bells.

PEER I can say what I like and my sword can strike hard!
Take care or I'll bring it down on your head!
King Saul slew his hundreds; Peer Gynt slays his thousands. (*Slashes out*)
Who are you?

VOICE Myself!

PEER That's a stupid reply.
Keep it yourself. And try to be clearer.
What are you?

VOICE The Great Boyg.[1]

PEER That's a bit better.
Your riddle is clearing. The black's turned to gray.
Get out of the way, Boyg!

VOICE Go round about, Peer!

PEER I'll go through you. (*Slashes with his branch*)
He's fallen!
(*Tries to go forward but again comes up against "the thing."*)
Aha! There are more!

VOICE The Boyg, Peer Gynt! There is only one.
The Boyg that's unharmed, the Boyg that was wounded.
The Boyg that is dead, the Boyg that's alive.
(PEER GYNT *throws away the branch*)

PEER My sword is no good; but I have my fists.
(*He hits out*)

VOICE Rely on your fists; have faith in your strength.
Ha-ha! Peer Gynt, then you'll reach great heights.

PEER (*Returning*)
Backward or forward, it's just as far—
Within or without, the path is as narrow!
He's there! And he's there! He's all round. I seem
To be clear! No! A magic circle is round me!
Who are you? Show yourself! Say what you are!

VOICE I'm the Boyg.

PEER (*Feeling blindly*) Not dead nor alive, without shape,
Slimy and hazy; growling bears, half-asleep,
Seem to be swarming all over me. (*Shrieks*)
Hit out, can't you?

VOICE The Boyg is not mad.

PEER Hit out!

VOICE There's no need.

PEER Fight! You must fight!

VOICE The great Boyg wins but he doesn't fight.

PEER Give me only a goblin to pinch me or sting me!
Give me only as much as a year-old troll!
Something to fight with! Not emptiness!
Ah! He's snoring! Boyg?

VOICE Well?

PEER Why don't you fight?

VOICE The great Boyg gets his way by keeping the peace.
(PEER *bites his own arms and hands*)

PEER Give me claws and teeth to rend my flesh!
Let me feel my own blood, let me taste my own blood!

[1] In older legend, the Boyg is an invisible but enormous troll, related to giants: an incarnation of the spirit of evil. *Boyg* means "curve" or "bend."

(*A sound like the wings of great birds*[2] *is heard*)

BIRDS Is he coming, Boyg?

VOICE Yes, foot by foot!

BIRDS Our sisters are flying from far away!

PEER If you want to save me, girl, do it now.
Don't stand there gazing shyly downward.
Your prayer-book! Fling it straight in his face!

BIRDS He's weakening!

VOICE We've got him!

BIRDS Sisters, make haste!

PEER Such an hour of racking strife
Is too much to pay for life. (*Sinks down*)

BIRDS Boyg, he's fallen! Seize him! Seize him now!
(*Church bells and the singing of hymns is heard in the distance*)

BOYG (*With a gasp, as his voice gradually fades away*)
He was too strong! He was shielded by women.

# Act Two, Scene Eight

SCENE *Dawn. On the mountain-side outside* AASE'S *hut. The door is closed. The place is silent and deserted.* PEER GYNT *is asleep, lying by the side of the wall. He wakes, looks around him with dull, listless eyes, then spits.*

PEER What would I give for a pickled herring!
(*He spits again. At the same time he sees* HELGA *approaching and carrying a basket of food*)
Hi, little 'un, what are you doing here?

HELGA Solveig——

PEER (*Springing up*) Where is she?

HELGA Behind the hut.

SOLVEIG (*Hidden*) If you come over here, I'll run away!

PEER (*Stopping*) Are you still afraid I might cuddle you?

SOLVEIG You're shameless!

PEER Do you know where I was last night?
The Dovre king's daughter was chasing me!

SOLVEIG Then we did right to ring the church bells.

PEER Peer Gynt's not the sort who's so easily caught.
Well, say something!

HELGA (*Crying*) Oh, she's running away!
(*Runs after her*)
Wait!

PEER (*Catching her by the arm*)
Look what I've got in my pocket here!
A silver button! I'll give it to you
If you'll say a good word for me!

HELGA Please let me go!

PEER Here it is.

[2] Troll-birds who assist the dark powers.

HELGA Let me go. Here is the basket!

PEER If you don't, God help——

HELGA You're hurting! Please let me——.

PEER (*Quietly, letting her go*)
I meant no harm; beg her not to forget me!
(*Helga runs away*)

# Act Three, Scene One

SCENE *In the depths of the pine forest. A gray autumn day. Snow is falling.* PEER GYNT *is in his shirt-sleeves, felling the trees. He is hacking at a tall fir with crooked branches.*

PEER Oh yes, you're tough, my dear old friend!
But it won't avail you; your days are numbered.
(*Starts hacking again*)
I know you're wearing a coat of mail,
But I'll pierce it through, strong as it is.
Oh yes, you can shake your twisted arms;
You're resentful and angry. I understand.
But I'm going to make you fall to your knees—!
(*Breaks off suddenly*)
More lies! This is no hero in armor;
More lies! It's nothing but an old tree,
Only a fir with its bark all cracked.
It's heavy work, this timber-felling,
But it's worse when you muddle it up with day-dreams.
They must stop, these wonderful cloudy flights
To an airy world that never was.
You're an outlaw, my lad, a forest outlaw.
(*Hacks away for a time in a great hurry*)
Yes, a fugitive! You've no mother now
To lay your table and bring you your food.
If you want to eat you must help yourself,
Hunt in the forest and fish in the streams,
Chop your own wood and light your own fire,
Build your own house and set it in order.
You want warm clothes? You must kill a reindeer.
You want your own house? You must break the stones.
You want oak beams? You must saw the wood
And carry it home on your own broad back.
(*Lowers his axe and stares straight in front of him*)
I'll build myself a thing of beauty,
With a tower and a weather-vane;
And on the gable-end I will carve
A mermaid with a long swishing tail.
The weather-vane and the locks will be
Embossed with brass. I might get some glass
For the windows: and strangers far off will gape
And wonder at the glory of it.
(*Laughing uncomfortably*)

Romancing and lies! I'm at it again.
You're an outlaw!
(*Starts working again with a new relish*)
A hut with a decent roof
Will keep out the rain as well as the frost.
(*Looks up at the tree*)
He's beginning to totter. One more blow!
He's fallen! He's prostrate at my feet.
The young trees are trembling all around.
(*Begins to lop off the branches; suddenly, he stops and listens, his axe upraised*)
There's someone after me! Can it be
The old man from Heggstad trying his tricks?
(*Crouches behind a tree and peeps out cautiously*)
A boy! Just a lad! He seems afraid;
So furtive, too. What's that he's hidden
Under his jacket? A sickle? He's peering
All round him. He's putting his hand on a branch.
What's he doing now? He's so still, so tense. . . .
Oh, horrible! He's chopped his finger off!
Right off! And he's bleeding like an ox.
He's running off with a rag round his hand.
(*Goes nearer*)
This is the very Devil! A finger!
Right off! And he did it deliberately.
Aha! Now I see! It's a certain way
Of keeping out of the King's Service.
That must be it! They wanted him to fight
And he had his own ideas about war.
But to chop it off—! To maim himself—!
Think about it, yes; have the wish, the intention.
But do it! No! That is beyond me.
(*He shakes his head, then carries on with his work*)

# Act Three, Scene Two

SCENE *A room in* AASE'S *house. It is in a state of confusion. The chest is empty; clothes are scattered about all over the room; a cat is lying on the bed.* AASE *and the cotter's wife,* KARI, *are doing their best to tidy up.*

AASE (*Hurrying to one side of the room*)
Kari, listen!
KARI What's the matter?
AASE (*At far end of room*) Where is—
I wonder where— Tell me. Tell me where—
What am I looking for? I'm going mad!
Where is the key to the chest?
KARI In the keyhole.
AASE What is that rumbling?
KARI It's the last load
Going to Heggstad.
AASE (*Weeping*) If only they were
Carrying me out in my coffin!
What we poor creatures have to put up with!
Have mercy, God! The whole house cleaned out!
What Heggstad forgot, the bailiffs have taken.
They've left me barely a rag to my back.
It's disgusting that people can be so harsh!
(*Sits on edge of bed*)
The farm and the land have gone for good.
Old Heggstad was hard but the law was harder.
Not a soul would help me; not one showed pity;
My Peer away, no one to advise me.
KARI This house is yours till the day you die.
AASE Bread of Charity for me and my cat!
KARI God help you! You've got Peer to thank for all this!
AASE Peer? I'm afraid you're getting muddled!
Ingrid got home safe enough in the end.
They'd have shown more sense if they'd blamed the Devil;
He's the offender and no one else.
The Father of Lies tempted my poor boy!
KARI Wouldn't it be best to send for the parson?
You may be even worse than you think.
AASE Send for the parson? I suppose I should.
(*Gets up*)
But, O God! No, I can't! I'm the boy's own mother!
I must help him! It's my sacred duty.
They've all deserted me. Let me do
What I can. They've left him this coat. I'll patch
It up. Would to God I'd dared filch the rug!
Where are the stockings?
KARI With that pile of rubbish.
AASE (*Rummaging in pile of rubbish*)
What's this we've got here? Oh yes, it's an old
Casting ladle. It was one of his toys.
He used to smelt buttons and mold them with it.
One day, at a party, my Peer marched in
And asked his father for a piece of tin.
"Not tin," said my husband; "I'll give you silver;
King Christian's coin for the son of John Gynt!"
God pardon him, he was in such a state
That he couldn't distinguish between tin and gold.
Here are the stockings. They're full of holes.
I must darn them, Kari.
KARI It won't be too soon.
AASE When I've finished them I'm going to bed.
I'm tired out and I feel so sick and ill.
(*Gleefully*)
Look, Kari! Two shirts! They've forgotten to take them.
KARI So they have!
AASE Well, that's a bit of good luck!
I think I can safely keep one of them here.
No! I don't see why we shouldn't keep both.
The one he's wearing is quite threadbare.
KARI But, goodness! Aase, you know that's a sin.
AASE I do know. I also know that repentance
Absolves us from sin. Well, I'll repent!

# Act Three, Scene Three

SCENE *Outside a newly built hut in the forest. Reindeer antlers over the door. The snow is piled high. It is dusk.* PEER GYNT *is standing outside the door and fastening a large wooden bolt. Now and again he stops and laughs.*

PEER I must fix a bolt; a bolt to secure
The door against trolls, against men and women.
I must fix a bolt, a bolt to keep out
The venomous breed of hobgoblins.
They come when night falls; they knock and they rap,
Open, Peer Gynt, we're as nimble as thoughts!
We'll crawl under the bed, rake about in the ashes,
Blow down the chimney like flaming dragons.
Hee-hee! Peer Gynt, do you think nails or boards
Can shut out evil hobgoblin thoughts?

(SOLVEIG *enters on skis. She has come across the moor; she wears a shawl and is carrying a bundle in her hand*)

SOLVEIG God speed your work! Please don't send me away.
You sent and I came. And now I am yours.

PEER Solveig! No, it can't be—! Yes, it is—!
And you're not afraid to come so close!

SOLVEIG You sent a message with little Helga;
Others came, too, with the wind and the silence.
There were messages in your mother's words,
Messages in my crowded dreams.
The long, long nights and the empty days
Brought me the message that I must come.
Down there, the joy had gone out of life;
Laughter and tears were denied to me.
I did not know what was in your mind.
I only knew what I should and must do.

PEER But your father—?

SOLVEIG In the whole wide world
I've no one now to call Father or Mother.
I have left them for ever.

PEER Solveig, my precious!
All this for me?

SOLVEIG Yes, for you alone.
You must be all to me, my friend, my life.
(*Crying*)
It was worst to part from my little sister,
And even worse to leave my Father,
But worst of all to leave her who had
Carried me in her arms at her breast.
No, God forgive me, by far the worst
Was the sorrow of leaving them all—yes, all.

PEER Do you know the sentence they passed on me?
How they even took my inheritance?

SOLVEIG It was not for your goods nor your chattels
That I parted from those I loved so much.

PEER Do you know the rest? My life is at stake
If anyone captures me outside this forest.

SOLVEIG I came on snow-shoes. I asked my way here.
They said, "Where are you going?" I answered "Home."

PEER Then away with nails and bars and boards!
I need no bolts to protect me from
Hobgoblin thoughts. If you dare to dwell
With me here, my hut will be sanctified.
Let me look at you, Solveig! No, not too near!
Let me gaze on you, you're so pure and fair!
Let me carry you, you're so slender and light!
May I carry you, Solveig? I'll never tire!
I will not soil you. I'll hold you away
From me. You're so lovely, so warm! Who would
Have thought I could make you love me?
How I have longed for you, night and day!
Look! I built this! Hewed the timber, too.
It's coming down! It's too small and mean——

SOLVEIG Little or big, I love it; it's yours.
It's so easy to breathe in the wind up here.
The valley was stifling. I felt entombed.
That was one reason why I came away.
But here, I can hear the soughing pines—
Silence and song—here, I am at home.

PEER And are you quite sure? It will be forever.

SOLVEIG I have come to you. There is no way back.

PEER Then you're mine! Go in! Let me see you inside.
Go in! I will get some logs for a fire.
It will soon be snug and bright and warm.
It will always be cosy. You'll never be cold.

(*He opens the door.* SOLVEIG *enters. He stands still for a moment, then laughs and leaps with joy*)

My king's daughter! I've found her and won her at last!
Now, a king's palace shall rise from the ground.

(*He takes up his axe and begins to move away. An elderly* WOMAN, *dressed in a tattered green dress, approaches him from the pine-wood. An* UGLY BOY *with a flask in his hand limps after her, holding her by the dress*)

WOMAN Good evening, Peer Nimblefoot!

PEER What? Who's that?

WOMAN Old friends, Peer Gynt! My house is near by.
We're neighbors.

PEER Are we? That's news to me.

WOMAN As your hut was built, mine rose at its side

PEER (*Trying to go*)
I'm in a hurry——

WOMAN You always were.
But I'll plod along and still keep you in sight.

PEER You've made a mistake.

WOMAN Oh no! I did once. . . .
When you made me your marvelous promises.

PEER Promises? I? What the Hell do you mean?

WOMAN That evening you came and drank with my father—
Have you forgotten?

PEER What never happened!
What is all this? When did we meet last?

WOMAN The last time we met was the first time we met.
(*To the boy*)

Your father's thirsty. Give him a drink.
PEER Father? Are you drunk? Are you trying to say—
WOMAN You can always tell a pig by its skin!
Where are your eyes? Can't you see he's as crooked
In the shanks as you are in the mind?
PEER Are you trying——
WOMAN Are you trying to wriggle out?
PEER This long-legged brat——
WOMAN He has grown very quickly.
PEER You old witch, do you dare to tell me that I——
WOMAN Listen, Peer Gynt, you're as crude as an ox!
(*Crying*)
Is it my fault if I'm not as fair as I was
That day you enticed me out on the hills?
Last autumn, when my labor began,
The only doctor there was the Devil,
So it's not very strange that my looks all went.
If you want to see me as fair as before,
You need only show that girl there the door,
Put her out of your mind and out of your sight;
Do that, my dear, and my looks will return.
PEER Get away, you old hag!
WOMAN You'll see if I do!
PEER I'll split your skull open——
WOMAN You try if you dare!
Oh no, Peer Gynt, I can stand hard knocks.
I'll come back here every single day.
I'll open the door and spy on you both.
When you're sitting in the fireside glow,
And you want to love her and kiss and embrace,
I'll be at your side in my rightful place.
We'll share you. We'll take it in turns in your bed.
Farewell, my dear Peer, now go and get wed!
PEER You hell-fiend!
WOMAN Oh dear, I nearly forgot!
You'll have to bring up your son, you wretch!
Go along, little devil, go to your father.
CHILD (*Spitting*)
I'll brain you with my ax. You wait! Just you wait.
WOMAN (*Kissing the child*)
Oh dear! What a head he has on his shoulders!
You'll be daddy's double when you grow up!
PEER (*Stamping*)
I wish you as far——
WOMAN Away as we're near?
PEER (*Clenching fists*)
And all this——
WOMAN Arises from thoughts and desires.
It's hard on you, Peer!
PEER It's worse for her!
Solveig! My loveliest, purest gold!
WOMAN Oh yes! It's the innocent who suffer.
The Devil said that when his mother beat him
Because his father turned up dead drunk!
(*She goes off into the undergrowth with the* CHILD, *who throws the flask at* PEER'*s head*)
PEER (*After a pause*)
Go round about, said the Boyg; that's what
I must do. My king's palace has collapsed.
We were so near; and now she's walled in.
And beauty and joy have departed forever.
Go round about. There is no way
Straight through from me to her. Straight through?
Well . . . perhaps . . . there still might be a way.
I think the Bible has something to say
About repentance. But what does it say?
I have no Bible. I have forgotten.
There's no one to guide me here in the forest.
Repentance? It might take years and years
To win my way through! And life would be empty;
The pure and the beautiful would be destroyed.
Could I piece it together with scraps and shards?
You can patch up a fiddle but not a watch;
If you want your field green, you don't trample it down.
All the same, the old witch was telling lies!
She's out of my sight with her filthy ideas.
Yes, out of my sight, but not out of my mind.
Insidious thoughts will follow me.
Ingrid! And those three who sported and screamed
On the hills! Will they come and scoff and sneer,
And demand to be crushed to my breast like her?
Or carried so tenderly on outstretched arms?
Round about! No, no, if my arm were as long
As the pine-tree's branch, or the fir-tree's trunk,
I would still be holding her too close to me
To put her down again pure as before.
No, no, I must find my way round about,
Not for gain nor for loss but only to cleanse
Myself from things that are best forgotten.
(*Moves a few paces, then stops*)
Go in after this? So foul and smirched?
Go in with this retinue of trolls;
Speak but be silent, confess yet conceal?
(*Throws his ax away*)
It's a holy day; to go to her now
As I am would be nothing but sacrilege.
SOLVEIG (*In doorway*)
Are you coming?
PEER (*Half to himself*) Go round about.
SOLVEIG What?
PEER You must wait.
It's dark here and I've a heavy load.
SOLVEIG Wait! Let me help! I will come and share it.
PEER No, stay where you are. I must manage myself.
SOLVEIG Well, don't be too long!
PEER Be patient, dear.
No matter how long I may be——
SOLVEIG (*Nodding*) I will wait.
(*He goes into the forest.* SOLVEIG *remains standing in the half-open door*)

# Act Three, Scene Four

SCENE AASE'S *room. Evening. A log-fire lights the room. The cat is on the chair at the foot of the bed.* AASE *is in bed and is plucking restlessly at the sheets.*

AASE Lord God, will he never come back here?
The hours drag on endlessly.
I can't even send a message
And I have so much to say.
There's no time to be lost, not a moment.
So soon! It has come so soon!
I only wish I could feel that
I've not been too strict with him.

PEER (*Entering*)
Good evening!

AASE Is that Peer? Thank God!
Here at last, my own dear boy!
It's an awful risk you're running,
Your life is in danger here.

PEER My life? What does my life matter?
I felt I must see you at once.

AASE Well, you've given the lie to Kari.
I can leave you now in peace.

PEER Leave me? What's this you're saying?
Where are you going then?

AASE Ah, Peer! My time's nearly over.
I'm not very long for this world.

PEER (*Turning away and walking across the room*)
There! I thought I was flying from trouble;
Here, at least, I thought I'd be free.
Are you cold? Your feet? And your hands?

AASE Yes, Peer; it will soon be over.
When you notice my eyes grow dim,
You must close them very gently.
Then, you must see to my coffin;
It must be a good one, dear.
No; of course not——

PEER Please be quiet!
There's time to think of all that.

AASE Yes, yes. (*Looks restlessly round room*)
Do you see how much
They've left us? It's just like them.

PEER (*Turning sharply*)
Again!
(*Harshly*) I know it was my fault.
There's no point in reminding me.

AASE You! No, it was that damned liquor.
That's the cause of all the fuss.
You were drunk, my boy, my dear boy.
You didn't know what you were doing.
And that dreadful ride on the reindeer!
No wonder you were so strange!

PEER Yes, yes, let's forget all that nonsense.
Let's forget the whole damned thing.
Let's store up all our sorrows
Till later, some other day.
(*Sitting down on edge of bed*)
Now, let's have a nice long talk
About this, that and everything.
Let's forget what's sad or unpleasant.
Why, look! There's our dear old pussy!
Still alive! After all this time!

AASE At night she seems so restless.
You know what that means, don't you?

PEER (*Changing the subject*)
Is there any local gossip?

AASE (*Smiling*)
They say there's a girl in the district
Who's pining for the heights——

PEER (*Quickly*)
And Mads Moen, is he settling down?

AASE They say that she pays no heed
To the old folks' tears and prayers.
You ought to pay them a visit.
You might be helpful to them.

PEER And the smith? What's Aslak doing?

AASE Don't speak about that filthy smith.
I'd rather tell you her name. . . .
The girl is—you know—her name is——

PEER Now let's have our nice long talk,
About this, that and everything,
Except what's sad or unpleasant.
Are you thirsty? I'll bring some water.
Have you room to stretch yourself?
That bed seems so small. Why, it must
Be the bed I had when a boy.
Every evening you used to sit
On the edge and tuck me in,
And sing me your lullabies.
Sometimes, you would call the cattle
Home again. Do you remember?

AASE Yes, yes. And do you remember
How we used to play at sledges
When your father had gone away?
A blanket was our sledge-apron.
The floor was an ice-bound fjord.

PEER Yes, yes, but do you remember
What was the best thing of all?
Our fiery Arab horses . . . !

AASE As though I could ever forget it!
It was Kari's cat we borrowed.
We perched her up on the stool——

PEER And drove away up hill and down dale
To Soria-Moria Castle,[1]
The castle that's west of the moon,
The castle that's east of the sun.
A stick you found in a corner
Of the cupboard was your whip.

AASE I sat in front like the driver.

PEER Yes, you let the reins go loose
And turned round as we went along
And asked me if I were cold.
Bless you, you ugly old beauty,
You were always a loving soul—!
Why are you moaning?

AASE My back, dear,
It's aching on these hard boards.

PEER Sit up then, and let me hold you. . . .
There now! That's more comfortable.

AASE (*Uneasily*)
I want Him to take me, Peer.

[1] The name comes from Arabic and refers to a group of small islands beyond the Red Sea, which Arabs believed to be the isles of the blessed.

PEER Take you?

AASE I'm longing to get away.

PEER Wrap yourself up in the bedclothes.
I'll sit on the edge of the bed
And we'll while away the evening.
I'll sing as you once sang to me.
And I'll call the cattle home.

AASE Please, Peer, will you bring my prayer-book?
I'm uneasy in my mind.

PEER In Soria-Moria Castle,
King and Prince are giving a feast.
Now lie back upon your pillow,
I'm going to drive you there.

AASE But, Peer dear, am I invited?

PEER Yes, both of us will be there.
(*He throws a piece of string round the cat's chair, takes a stick in his hand and sits on the end of the bed*)
Gee-up! Look alive there, Blackie!
Mother, you're not cold, are you?
Ah! Now, we're making headway.
Grane's got into her stride.

AASE Peer dear, I can hear bells ringing.

PEER The glittering sledge-bells, dear!

AASE It's a ghostly hollow clanging.

PEER We're driving over a fjord.

AASE Peer, I'm frightened. What's that sighing?
And that eerie whispering?

PEER It's only the pine-trees, Mother,
Murmuring on the hills.

AASE Lights are gleaming in the distance.
Can you see where they're coming from?

PEER From the windows of the castle.
Can you hear them dancing?

AASE Yes.

PEER On guard, outside, stands Saint Peter.
He's inviting you straight inside.

AASE Is he greeting me?

PEER Yes, with honor,
And he's offering you sweet wine.

AASE Has he cakes to give me with it?

PEER He has! A plateful of them.
And our parson's wife is making
Your coffee and your dessert.

AASE Oh, God! Am I going to meet her?

PEER If you want to, dear, of course.

AASE You're driving your poor old mother
To a lovely party, Peer.

PEER (*Cracking his whip*)
Gee-up! Look alive there, Blackie!

AASE Are you sure you're on the right road?

PEER (*Cracking whip again*)
It's an easy road to follow.

AASE But the journey's long and tiring.

PEER The castle is there before us.
We'll be inside very soon.

AASE I'll lie back and close my eyes now
And trust to you, my own boy.

PEER Put your best foot forward, Grane.
There's a huge crowd in the grounds.
They are clamoring at the entrance.
Peer Gynt and his mother are here!
What was that, Mister Saint Peter?
My mother may not come in?
You'd search far and wide, let me tell you,
And not find so honest a soul.
I'll leave myself out of the counting;
I can go back the way I came.
If you ask me, well, I'd stay here.
If not, well, I'd still be content.
I have told as many whoppers
As the Father of Lies himself.
I've called my mother an old hen
Because she cackled and clucked,
But you must esteem and honor
And please her and make her happy.
You won't find anyone better
In our part of the world these days.
Ho-ho, there is God the Father!
Saint Peter, you're in for it now.
(*In a deep voice*)
"Stop being so high and mighty!
Mother Aase is welcome here."
(*Laughs aloud and turns to his mother*)
There you are! What did I tell you?
Saint Peter has piped down already.
(*Anxiously*)
Mother, what is it? Tell me,
Have you gone clean out of your mind?
(*Goes to head of bed*)
Don't stare at me like that, Mother!
Say something! It's Peer, your boy!
(*Tenderly feels her forehead and hands. Then he throws the string on to the chair and says in a low voice*)
Well, you can rest now, Grane.
The journey has come to an end.
(*Closes her eyes and bends over her*)
Thank you, dear, for all you gave me,
The thrashings and kisses, too.
But, now, you must thank me also.
(*Presses his cheek against her mouth*)
That was your fare for the drive.

KARI (*Entering*)
What? Peer! Well, you've put an end
To her sorrow and suffering.
Dear God, she is sleeping soundly—
Or is she—?

PEER Ssh! Ssh! She is dead.
(KARI *weeps beside the corpse.* PEER GYNT *walks up and down the room for a long time. He stops near the bed*)
See that she's buried with honor.
I must get away from here.

KARI Are you going far?

PEER Yes, to sea.

KARI So far?

PEER Yes, and farther still.

# Act Four, Scene One

SCENE *The southwest coast of Morocco. A table is set for dinner in a palm-grove, under an awning. Palm-matting on the ground. Farther back hammocks are hanging. A steam-yacht is lying offshore, flying the Norwegian and American flags. A jolly-boat is drawn up on the shore. Just before sunset.* PEER GYNT, *good-looking and middle-aged, is in an elegant traveling suit; gold-mounted eyeglasses are pinned to his coat. He is at the head of the table.* MR. COTTON,[1] MONSIEUR BALLON, HERR VON EBERKOPF *and* HERR TRUMPETERSTRAALE[2] *are dining with him.*

PEER Drink, gentlemen! If man was made
For pleasure let him have his fill.
They say that what is gone is gone.
The Past is past. What will you have?
TRUMPETERSTRAALE
You're a host of hosts, dear brother Gynt.
PEER Let my money share the honor
With my cook and steward.
COTTON Very well!
BALLON Monsieur, yours is a *goût,* a *ton*[3]
That nowadays is rarely found
In bachelors living *en garçon*—[4]
There's something which I can't define——
EBERKOPF It's in that fine wave of the hand!
A mirror of emancipation,
Spiritual meditation,
And citizenship of the world,
Vision that can pierce the clouds,
A mind devoid of prejudice
But tinged with higher criticism;
*Ur—natur,*[5] real knowledge of life;
These admirable traits all bound
Into an all-embracing whole.
Isn't that what you meant, monsieur?
BALLON Yes, very possibly; although
In French it sounds much less high-flown.
EBERKOPF *Ei was,* your tongue is limited.
But we are looking for the cause
Of this phenomenon——
PEER It's found.
Gentlemen, I am not married;
That will explain everything.
What is our duty? Well, in brief,
A man should always be himself,
Without reserve, devote himself
To himself and what concerns him.
What chance has he of doing this
If he's burdened like a camel
With someone else's joys and sorrows?
EBERKOPF This being everything to yourself—
Surely you've had to fight for it?
PEER I've had to fight unendingly,
But I have always managed to
Emerge with honor, although there
Was one occasion when I nearly
Tripped up. I was a gay young rip;
The lady whom I thought I loved
Boasted a royal lineage.
BALLON Royalty?
PEER (*Carelessly*) One of those families—
You must have met them——
TRUMPETERSTRAALE (*Thumping the table*) Blue blooded fools—
PEER (*Shrugging his shoulders*)
With outworn pedigrees, whose pride
Aimed at keeping their escutcheons
Free from any plebeian smudge.
COTTON What happened? Did it peter out?
BALLON The family opposed the match?
PEER The contrary.
BALLON Ah!
PEER (*Coolly*) Well, you'll smile!
Matters became so compromising
That it was deemed advisable
That we should marry there and then.
But, candidly, from first to last,
I found the matter most unwholesome.
In many ways I'm finicky.
I like to stand on my own feet.
So when her father started hinting
Demands that he thought right and proper,
Such as—that I should change my name
And my position and join his set,
Together with a good deal more
I could not and would not accept—
Well, I turned down his ultimatum,
Withdrew with proper dignity
And released my blossoming bride.
(*Drums on the table and adopts a pious air*)
Yes, yes; Fate is there to guide us.
Humanity can depend on it.
And it's a comfort, I can tell you.
BALLON And did the matter end with that?
PEER Oh no, it went a good deal further.
Others got mixed up in the business.
There was an outcry; younger members
Of the family demanded
Satisfaction. I fought duels
With no fewer than seven of them.
I'll remember that until I die.
But, once more, I emerged with honor;
Blood flowed, of course, but that same blood
Confirmed my lion's reputation
And stressed, what I have pointed out,
That Fate is always there to guide us.
EBERKOPF Your outlook upon life has raised you
To the ranks of the great thinkers.
While most people can only view

[1] An allusion to British commercialism abroad.
[2] "Trumpet-blast." The word is Swedish, as is presumably the character.
[3] "A taste, a tone."
[4] "By themselves."
[5] Elemental nature.

Each scene disjointed from the whole,
And do not see the panorama,
You have a comprehensive range.
Your norm embraces everything;
Your rules of life are like the rays
Proceeding from a central sun,
The core of deepest meditation.
And yet you tell us you're untutored.

PEER I am, as I've already mentioned,
A simple man, self-educated.
There was no method in my schooling,
But I have thought and speculated
And read a good deal on most subjects.
Unfortunately, I did not start
Until I was well past my youth;
And then, of course, it's heavy work
Plowing along, page after page,
Trying to take in everything.
I learned my history in fits
And starts. I had no time for more
Concentrated study; and then,
As we need something to fall back
Upon when our affairs don't prosper,
I took to religion bit by bit.
In that way it was easier
To swallow—like a sugared pill.
There's no point in too much reading;
Pick out what can be used—that's all.

COTTON That's practical, at least.

PEER (*Lighting a cigar*) My friends,
Consider my career. When first
I went out West I was a pauper;
My hands were empty and I had
To labor for my daily bread.
Believe me, it was difficult.
But life is sweet and death is bitter!
Well, Fortune was accommodating
And Destiny was very kind.
I learned for I was pliable.
Things went well and then went better.
Ten years later I had become
A Crœsus among Charleston traders;
My fame had spread from port to port;
My ships were harbingers of luck.

COTTON What was your trade?

PEER Black ivory!
Sending slaves to Carolina
And shipping images to China.

BALLON *Fi donc!* [6]

TRUMPETERSTRAALE You're joking, Uncle Gynt!

PEER No doubt you think the business hovered
On the verge of what was lawful.
I felt it too, felt it intensely.
In fact, it became odious.
But, once begun, I can assure you
It wasn't easy to wind up.
And anyhow, an undertaking
Of such enormous size, involving
Thousands, could hardly be wound up
Without calamitous results.

[6] "Come now!"

I always loathed winding things up.
On the other hand, I must confess
I've always had a keen respect
For what we call the consequences,
And when obliged to go beyond
The law I've always felt unhappy.
Moreover, I was growing older,
I was getting near the fifties
And my hair was going gray.
My health was excellent and yet
One thought was always uppermost:
"Who knows how soon my hour will come?
How soon will judgment be pronounced
And the sheep parted from the goats?"
What could I do? To stop the trade
With China was impossible.
I found a way! I soon arranged
Other interests in China.
I still sent idols every spring,
But every autumn I despatched
Missionaries well equipped
With all essentials for conversion—
Stockings and Bibles, rum and rice

COTTON At a good profit!

PEER Naturally!
What's more, it worked. My missionaries
Labored. For every idol bought
They had a coolie well baptized.
They worked like Hell and, more or less,
Offset my idols. They never ceased
To try to catch up on the hordes
Of idols we distributed.

COTTON And what about your trade in Negroes?

PEER Once more my moral feelings gained
The day. I knew it was no trade
For people of advancing years.
You never know when you might die.
Besides, there were the thousand snares
Laid by our dear philanthropists;
The ship might be seized any day.
There was the risk of wind and weather.
Thoughts of this sort made me decide.
"Peter," I said, "take in your sails.
See that your errors are made good."
And so, I bought land in the South,
Kept back my last cargo of meat,
Whose quality, by the way, was prime,
And settled them upon the land.
They flourished, soon grew fat and sleek
And were a veritable credit
To themselves and me. Without
Boasting, I may say that I
Was like a father to them all.
Profits were good. I built them schools
So that their morals might be kept
At a *niveau*[7] of excellence.
There was the strictest supervision
To prevent any back-sliding.
Eventually, I withdrew
From these activities. I sold

[7] "Standard."

The plantation, lock, stock and barrel,
And, as a parting gift, I gave
To everybody, big and little,
A measure of grog gratis till
Each man and woman had had his fill.
The widows got snuff, in addition.
And so, in all sincerity,
I trust the text which says that he
Who does no evil does some good
Is not all eyewash and that my sins
Are now redeemed. I think I can
State with much more truth than most
That my good deeds cancel my errors.

EBERKOPF (*Clinking glasses with him*)
It's really edifying to hear
A plan of life so practical,
Unhampered by dim theories,
Oblivious of unrest without.
(*During his last speech* PEER GYNT *has been diligently applying himself to the bottle*)

PEER We Northerners learned long ago
Never to trust to half-measures.
The key to living is simply this:
Keep your ear closed tight against
The venom of a dangerous viper.

COTTON What sort of viper, my dear friend?

PEER A little one who tempts you to
Make moves from which you can't draw back.
(*Drinks again*)
Everyone can act with courage
And keep his nerve as long as he
Fights to avoid life's many snares,
Fights with the knowledge that the day
Of battle is not the final one,
And keeps behind him an open bridge
Which he can cross to safer country.
That policy has kept me going
And has colored my behavior.
It's a family heritage
Picked up in my early childhood.

BALLON You're a Norwegian, aren't you?

PEER Yes,
By birth, but cosmopolitan
As anyone by inclination.
For the prosperity I've tasted
I have to thank America.
My well-stocked library derives
From Germany's most modern scholars.
From France I get my style in clothes,
My manners and my pretty wit;
From England a bent for industry
Together with a sharpened sense
Of what is for my own advantage.
The Jew has taught me to be patient.
In Italy I soon acquired
A love for *dolce far niente,*[8]
And once, when in a nasty corner,
I saved my bacon with the help
Of Swedish steel.

TRUMPETERSTRAALE (*Lifting his glass*) Yes, Swedish steel!

EBERKOPF Let us pay homage to the man
Who wields a sword with such success.
(*They clink glasses and drink.* PEER GYNT *is getting flushed with wine*)

COTTON What you have said is most absorbing.
But, sir, I am interested
In knowing what you hope to do
With all your money.

PEER Hm! Do with it?

ALL FOUR (*Drawing nearer*)
Yes, let's hear!

PEER Well, in the first place,
I'm going to travel. That is why
I took you on board at Gibraltar.
I need traveling companions,
Priests who will dance attendance at
My Altar of the Golden Calf.

EBERKOPF How very witty!

COTTON But no one
Sails just for a cruise alone.
You have a purpose, surely, and
That purpose is . . . ?

PEER To be Emperor!

ALL FOUR What?

PEER (*Nods*) Emperor.

ALL FOUR Where?

PEER Of the whole world.

BALLON But how, my friend?

PEER By the power of gold!
The idea is by no means new.
It has inspired me throughout life.
As a boy I used to dream and soar
Over the oceans on a cloud.
I'd fly adorned in silk and gold
And then I'd drop down on all fours.
But, my friends, the goal was always there.
Someone or other said somewhere,
I really can't remember where,
That if you gain the whole earth but
Lose your own self your gain would be
A crown upon a grinning skull.
That's what he said—or something like it—
And—well—they are not idle words.

EBERKOPF Tell me, what is the Gyntian "self"?

PEER The world that's here inside my head;
That makes me "me" and no one else,
No more than God could be the Devil.

TRUMPETERSTRAALE Now I see what you're aiming at.

BALLON Sublime thinker!

EBERKOPF A great poet!

PEER (*With increasing emotion*)
The Gyntian self—it is an army
Of wishes, hankerings, desires;
The Gyntian self—it is a sea
Of fancies, cravings and dictates.
It's all that swells within my breast,
It's all that makes me live the life
I live. It's all that makes me "me."
But, as our Lord needed the earth

[8] "Sweet idleness."

To make himself God of the Earth,
So I, Peer Gynt, have need of gold
To make myself an Emperor.

BALLON But you're rolling in it.

PEER Not
Enough except for a short reign
Of one or two days as a Duke
*À la* Lippe-Detmold;[9] that's all.
No, I must be myself, *en bloc.*
I want to be Gynt everywhere,
Sir Peter Gynt from top to toe.

BALLON (*Enraptured*)
And own the world's most beautiful
Treasures.

EBERKOPF Such as cellars of
Century-old Johannisburger.[10]

TRUMPETERSTRAALE Every weapon of Charles the Twelfth.[11]

COTTON But first, the opportunity
Of bigger profits.

PEER I think that chance
Has come while we've been anchored here.
This evening, we are steering north.
The papers that were brought aboard
Have given me important news.
(*Rises and lifts his glass*)
It shows that Fortune always helps
Those who always help themselves.

ALL FOUR What?
What's happened?

PEER Greece is in a ferment.

ALL FOUR (*Jumping to their feet*)
What? The Greeks?

PEER Yes, they have risen.

ALL FOUR Hurrah!

PEER The Turks are in a mess.
(*Empties his glass*)

BALLON To Greece! The path to glory's there!
I'll help them with the sword of France!

EBERKOPF I'll urge them on—but at a distance!

COTTON I'll urge them on—with a big contract!

TRUMPETERSTRAALE Forward! In Bender[12] I will find
The far-famed spurs of Charles the Twelfth.

BALLON (*Falling on* PEER's *neck*)
My friend, forgive me. For a time
I misunderstood your motives.

EBERKOPF (*Pressing his hand*)
I, the fool, thought you a rogue.

COTTON Too strong. I thought you were obtuse.

TRUMPETERSTRAALE (*Trying to kiss him*)
And I, my uncle, summed you up
As the lowest type of Yankee—!
Forgive me!

EBERKOPF We were all mistaken.

PEER I don't follow you.

[9] A petty principality of north central Germany.

[10] A famous Rhine wine.

[11] King of Sweden, 1697-1718, famous for his foreign military campaigns.

[12] A town in southeast Europe where Charles XII was captured by the Turks in 1713.

EBERKOPF Now we see
The splendor of the Gyntian army
Of wishes, hankerings, desires.

BALLON (*Admiringly*)
Monsieur Gynt! That's what you meant!

EBERKOPF (*Also admiringly*)
This is an honorable Gynt!

PEER But tell me—?

BALLON Don't you understand?

PEER Understand? I'm damned if I do.

BALLON You're going to assist the Greeks
With money and your fleet of ships!

PEER (*Whistling*)
No, thanks, I believe that might is right.
I'll lend my money to the Turks.

BALLON You can't!

EBERKOPF Amusing! A good joke!
(PEER GYNT *is silent for a while, then he leans against a chair and adopts an air of superiority*)

PEER Listen, gentlemen, the last shred
Of our friendship is dissolving;
It's best that we should part at once.
The man who has nothing to lose
Can gamble anything he likes.
If you only own a plot of earth
The length of your own shadow then
Your obvious fate is cannon-fodder.
But when a man's as comfortable
As I he runs far greater risks.
You're going to Greece! I'll take you there
For nothing. I'll put you ashore
Well armed. The more you fan the flames
Of war the better I shall like it.
Strike hard for freedom and for right!
Forward! On! On! Give the heathen Hell!
And end your days with glory, spiked
Upon a janissary's spear!
But make my apologies for me!
(*Slaps his pocket*)
Money! Myself! Sir Peter Gynt!
(*Opens his parasol and goes into the palm-grove, where the hammocks can be seen*)

TRUMPETERSTRAALE The swine!

BALLON Where is his sense of honor?

COTTON Honor be hanged! Think of the profits
We could make if Greece succeeded
In getting independence.

BALLON I
Saw myself crowned a conqueror,
Fêted by lovely Grecian women.

TRUMPETERSTRAALE I saw those celebrated spurs
Securely held in my Swedish hands.

EBERKOPF I saw my Fatherland's Kultur
Creeping out over land and sea.

COTTON The material loss is greatest.
Goddam! I could shed tears of rage!
I saw myself owning Olympus.
And if that mountain only lives
Up to its reputation there's
A mint of copper to be mined.

And then that river, the Kastale,[13]
People talk a lot about it,
But they don't know its waterfalls
Will generate a thousand horse-power.

TRUMPETERSTRAALE I'm going in spite of everything.
My Swedish sword is worth much more
Than Yankee gold. . . .

COTTON Perhaps, but when
We're in the ranks—and we *will* be—
We'll be drowned by a mob of others,
And what will happen to our profits?

BALLON So near success and now so far!

COTTON (*Shaking his fist at the yacht*)
That nigger-driving Nabob's gold
Is in that coffin of a ship!

EBERKOPF A marvelous idea! Quick, quick!
His empire's going to collapse!
Hurrah!

BALLON What is it?

EBERKOPF Seize the ship.
We'll bribe the crew. That won't be hard!
On board! Expropriate the yacht!

COTTON You can't!

EBERKOPF We'll pinch the whole damned thing!
(*He goes to the jolly-boat*)

COTTON In that case, my own interests
Advise me to do some pinching, too.
(*Follows* VON EBERKOPF)

TRUMPETERSTRAALE That man's a crook!

BALLON What villainy!
*Enfin!*
(*They follow the others*)

TRUMPETERSTRAALE All right, I'll go with them, but first
I register my protestations
Before the world court of the nations.
(*Follows them*)

# Act Four, Scene Two

SCENE *Another part of the coast. Moonlight and driving cloud. The yacht is far out to sea, steaming full speed ahead.* PEER GYNT *is running along the beach. First he pinches his arm, then he gazes out over the sea.*

PEER Nightmare! Delusions! I'll wake up soon!
She's putting to sea! And at top speed, too!
I'm dreaming! I'm sleeping! I'm dotty! I'm drunk!
(*Wrings his hands*)
I'm not going to die here! Impossible!
(*Tears his hair*)
It's a dream! I've made up my mind it's a dream.
It's frightening! But, oh dear, it's true!
Those verminous friends of mine! Hear me, O Lord!
You're wise. You're righteous! Then judge between us!
(*With outstretched arms*)
It is I! Peer Gynt! Pay attention please, Lord!
Help me, O Father, or I shall expire!
Make them turn it round! Make them lower the dinghy!
Stop thief! Make something or other go wrong!
Hear me! Forget other people *pro tem!*
The world will take care of itself for a while!
No, God isn't listening! He's deafer than ever!
What a state of affairs! A God who can't help!
(*Signals heavenward*)
Hi! I've given up the nigger plantation!
I've sent out missionaries to Asia!
Surely, one good turn deserves another!
Help me get on board—!
(*A column of fire shoots into the sky from the yacht and a thick cloud of smoke follows it.* PEER GYNT *utters a shriek and sinks down in the sand. By degrees the smoke clears away. The yacht has disappeared.* PEER GYNT *is pale and subdued*)
My God! What a judgment!
Plop to the bottom, all hands, man and mouse!
Thanks, eternal thanks, for this lucky escape!
(*Emotionally*)
Lucky escape! There's more to it than that!
That I should be saved and that they should be sunk!
All praise to the Lord who has sheltered me
And looked after me despite all my faults.
(*Takes a deep breath*)
What a wonderful feeling of safety and peace
You get when you know that you're specially shielded!
But I'm out in the desert! Where will I find
Food and drink? Oh, I'll come across something, no doubt.
It will be all right!
(*Loudly and ingratiatingly*)
He will never allow
A poor little sparrow like me to pop off.
I'll be humble—and then I'll give Him some time.
I must trust in the Lord. I am full of faith.
(*Jumps to his feet in terror*)
Did I hear a lion growl in the shrubs?
(*His teeth chattering*)
It couldn't have been. . . .
(*Pulling himself together*)
I believe it was!
They say that carnivora keep clear of men.
They've learned not to bite their superiors.
They've an instinct; they feel—what is perfectly true—
That it's dangerous to play with fire.
Nevertheless, I must find a tree;
There are palms and acacias over there.
If I were up there I'd be safe enough,

[13] Cotton is confused. The Kastale is not a river but a fountain on Mount Parnassus, sacred to Apollo and the Muses.

Especially if I knew a few psalms.
(*Climbs up*)
"Morning is morning and night is night."
That's a text that is often weighed up and discussed.
(*Settles down comfortably*)
How delightful to feel one's spirit exalted!
Noble thoughts are more precious than purple and gold.
Only trust in Him! He alone knows how much
Of the cup of misery I can drink.
He has quite a fatherly feeling for me.
(*Glances out across the sea and sighs*)
But no one could say He was frugal about it!

## Act Four, Scene Three

SCENE *Night. A Moroccan camp on the edge of the desert. Warriors resting by the camp-fire. A* SLAVE *runs in, tearing his hair.*

SLAVE The Emperor's white steed has disappeared.
(*Another* SLAVE *runs in rending his garments*)
SECOND SLAVE The Emperor's sacred attire has been stolen.
CHIEF EUNUCH (*Entering*)
A hundred strokes of the bastinado
For each man who fails to catch the thief!
(WARRIORS *mount their horses and gallop away in all directions*)

## Act Four, Scene Four

SCENE *Dawn. The same group of trees as before.* PEER GYNT *is still in his tree. He is hitting about him with a branch, keeping a tribe of Barbary apes at bay.*

PEER Awful! A most uncomfortable night!
(*He hits out*)
They're back again! Damn the lot of them!
Now they're throwing fruit. No, it's something else!
A loathsome animal, the ape!
There's a saying: "Keep your eyes open and fight."
But that's just it, I can't. I'm much too tired.
(*Is attacked again. He loses his patience*)
I must put an end to this, once and for all.
I'll get hold of one of them and then
I'll hang him and skin him and dress myself
As well as I can in his shaggy coat.
They'll think I'm the genuine article.
What are men? Only feathers blown by the wind.
We have to fit our environment.
More of them! They're everywhere. Cheeky, too!
You devils! Shoo! They're behaving like madmen!
I wish I could tie a tail on myself!
Something to make me look like an ape!
What's that? Something's rustling over my head!
(*Looks up*)
It's the old one; his fists are full of mire.
(*He crouches down anxiously, remaining quite still. The ape makes a threatening movement.* PEER GYNT *begins to coax him and talk to him as if he were a dog*)
Aha! There you are! There's a good fellow!
He's a clever boy, isn't he? He knows what's right!
He wouldn't throw dirt! No, I'm sure he wouldn't!
It is I! Cheerio! We're good friends, aren't we?
Bow-wow! Did you hear? I can speak your lingo!
Why, you and I are like cousins, old man.
Tomorrow, I'll give you some sugar. The beast!
The whole cartload over me! Horrible!
Perhaps it was food! The taste was unusual;
But taste, after all, is something acquired.
Who was the philosopher who once said,
"Spit and depend on the force of habit"?
Here come the little ones!
(*Gesticulates and hits all round him*)
It's too bad
That man, who is really the Lord of Creation,
Should find that he's got to——Help! Murder! Help!
The old man was hellish; the young ones are worse.

## Act Four, Scene Five

SCENE *Early morning. A rocky place with a view over the desert. On one side, a cleft in the rocks and a cave. A* THIEF *and a* RECEIVER *of stolen goods are hiding in the cleft with the Emperor's clothes and charger. The horse, very richly caparisoned, is tied to a stone. Riders can be seen in the distance.*

THIEF The blades of the lances
Are flashing and sparkling.
See, see!
RECEIVER My head will soon
Roll in the sand.
Woe! Woe!
THIEF (*Folding his arms*)
My father stole
So I must steal.
RECEIVER My father received
So I must receive.

THIEF You must bear your lot.
You must be yourself.
RECEIVER Footsteps approaching!
Run! Run! But where?
THIEF Deep is the grave
And the Prophet great.
(*They flee, leaving the booty. The riders disappear in the distance.* PEER GYNT *comes in cutting a reed pipe*)
PEER Well, what a perfectly lovely morning!
The dung-beetle is rolling himself in the sand;
The snail is creeping out of his shell.
Morning! Yes, it is far above gold!
Nature has done quite a wonderful thing
In endowing the daylight with such magic powers.
You feel so secure, your courage rises.
You would willingly drag a wild bull by the horns.
What peace there is! Oh, the countryside!
Looking back, I can't believe I abjured it
To shut myself up in a teeming city
And be stung by all sorts and conditions of men.
Just look at those lizards fussing around,
Or basking and thinking of nothing at all!
How innocent they are, these animals!
Each one carries out his Maker's intention,
Each one wears the permanent stamp of his tribe,
Each one is himself whether playing or quarreling,
Himself as he was on the day of creation.
(*Puts on his eyeglasses*)
A toad! Just there, in that clump of sandstone,
Half-hidden, only his head peeping out.
There he sits, gazing out on the world,
As though from a window. To himself
He is enough. Enough! Be yourself!
Where have I seen that? In the Bible, I think.
Or was it the Prayer-Book? Or was it Proverbs?
It's curious! As the years roll on
My memory for dates and for places gets worse.
(*Sits down in the shade*)
Here's a cool spot. I'll rest here and stretch my legs.
Look, there are plants here with edible roots.
(*Nibbles one*)
It's food for animals; but there's a saying:
"Overcome your dislikes." There's another one:
"Pride goeth before a fall." And again:
"He that shall humble himself shall be
Exalted." (*Troubled*) Exalted? Yes, that's what will happen
To me. I can see no alternative.
Fate will take me away from this place
And see that I get under way again.
This is my hour of trial. I will be saved,
If only our Lord will give me the strength.
(*He pushes thought away from him, lights a cigar, stretches himself and gazes over the desert*)
What an immense and limitless waste!
Away in the distance an ostrich is pacing.
I wonder what God's intention was
When He made this enormous desolate space?
This desert that lacks the essentials of life,
This perfectly useless dried-up land,
These arid areas of the earth,
This corpse, which since the world's beginning,
Hasn't given its Maker as much as a "Thank you"?
Why was it made? Nature's unbusinesslike.
Is that the sea over there in the East?
It can't be. It must be a mirage.
The sea's in the West; it's there behind me.
And that hill is the dyke which is keeping it out.
(*A thought strikes him*)
A dyke! Well, perhaps—! It's not much of a hill.
A dyke! A bit of blasting! Then a canal!
Like a river of life, it would lead the waters
Right through the channel, drowning the desert.
Soon, the whole of this smoking Hell
Would be as fresh as a rippling sea.
Island oases would soon appear,
Atlas would be green like our Northern shores,
Ships would speed southward like homing birds
On routes that were once the caravan tracks;
Gentle zephyrs would blow and would lower
The temperature; dew would fall from the skies;
Cities would spring up all over the place;
Grass would grow around each swaying palm;
South of the Sahara, a healthy country
With spacious harbors would come into being;
Steam would start Timbuctoo's factories working;
Bornu[1] would very soon be colonized;
The explorer would travel by express train
Via Habes[2] to the Upper Nile.
On a fertile oasis set in my seas,
I would propagate my Norwegian race.
The dalesman's blood is almost royal,
And an Arab cross would do the rest.
Around a lagoon, on rising land,
I will found my capital! Peeropolis!
The world's obsolete! Now it's the turn
Of Gyntiana, my nascent state!
(*Springs up*)
Give me the money! It can be done!
A key of gold to the door of the ocean!
A crusade against Death! That greedy old skinflint
Will have to open his sack of loot.
Just now, every country is crying for Freedom.
Like the ass in the Ark I will send my cry
Right round the world. Freedom's baptism's nigh!
To those lovely, harnessed, newborn shores
I must make my way. I'll raise capital
Everywhere, in the East and the West! On! On!
My kingdom—no, half my kingdom for a horse!
(*The horse whinnies in the ravine*)
A horse! And clothes! And jewels! And a sword!
(*Goes nearer*)
It can't be! It is! Yes, really! I've read
Somewhere or other that faith can move mountains,
But that doesn't mean it can move a horse, too!
But a fact's a fact! There is the horse!
*Ab esse ad posse*[3] and so on, and so on.

[1] Bornu is a city in the French Sudan, south of the Sahara Desert.
[2] Habes or Habesch is the Arabic name for Ethiopia.
[3] "From the reality to the power."

(*Puts on the robe and looks himself over*)
Sir Peter—and Turk from head to heels!
Look alive there, Grane, my trusty steed!
(*Mounts*)
Gold stirrups, too, to support my feet!
It goes to show that it's Fate that counts.
You can tell great folk by the style of their mounts!
(*Gallops off into the desert*)

# Act Four, Scene Six

SCENE *The tent of an Arab chief in the middle of an oasis.* PEER GYNT, *in Eastern dress, is reclining on some cushions. He is drinking coffee and smoking a long pipe.* ANITRA *and other girls are entertaining him with dancing and singing.*

CHORUS The prophet has come!
The prophet, the lord of all the land,
Unto us the lord has come
Riding across the sea of sand.
The prophet, the lord, the all-wise one,
Unto us the lord has come
Sailing across the sea of sand.
Blow the flute, beat the drum;
The prophet, the prophet has come.

ANITRA His steed is as white as the milk
That flows in the rivers of Paradise.
Bend the knee! Bow low! Bow down!
His loving eyes are stars that can frown.
No son of man can face
The heavenly radiance of those eyes.
Over the desert he came apace;
Gold and pearls adorned his breast.
He rode, and there was light!
Behind him it was night,
Behind him was drought and the simoom.
He, the Magnificent, came.
Across the desert he came,
Decked in his earthly guise.
Kaaba,[1] Kaaba is empty.
He has spoken, the All-Wise!

CHORUS Blow the flute, beat the drum;
The prophet, the prophet has come!
(*They dance to soft music*)

PEER I have seen it in print—so it must be true—
"No man's a prophet in his own country."
This is a much more pleasant existence
Than the life over there as a Charleston merchant.
There was something hollow about all that—
Something foreign; I might even say corrupt.
I never really felt quite at home,
And I never made quite a man of the world.
What was I doing in such company?
Rummaging in the cesspool of trade?
I think about it but light won't dawn.
It happened—and that's all there was to it!
To be yourself on the gold standard
Is exactly like building a house on sand.
If you flash a ring and a watch and fine clothes,
Your fellow-men crawl and lick your toes.
They raise their hats to a diamond-pin;
But the ring and the pin are not the man.
A prophet! That makes my position clear.
At least, I know what my profession is.
If men praise me now it's because I am I,
Not because of the size of my bank balance.
We are what we are! Don't philosophize,
Don't rely on luck or contingencies,
Don't depend on patents and permits and grants.
A prophet! Yes, that suits me down to the ground.
And I found myself numbered among them by chance,
Just by going and cantering over the sand
And running across these children of nature.
The prophet had come! They asked no more.
I didn't intend to deceive them. Oh no!
Prophetic replies are certainly not lies.
And, anyway, I can always resign.
I'm not tied. No, things might be much worse.
It's purely a personal private affair.
I can go as I came; my charger is ready.
In short, I am master of the situation.

ANITRA (*Approaching*)
Prophet and lord!

PEER What does my slave desire?

ANITRA The sons of the desert are waiting outside.
They beg permission to gaze on your face——

PEER Stop! Tell them to muster a long way away.
I'll give them audience from afar.
You may add that I'll tolerate no men in here.
Men, my dear child, are a rotten lot,
In fact, they're nothing but dirty swine.
Anitra, if you knew the brazen way
They've cheated, I mean sinned, against me, my child!
Never mind! Enough of them! Dance for me, daughter.
The prophet desires to forget these afflictions.

CHORUS (*Dancing*)
The prophet is good; the prophet is sad
At the evil deeds of the sons of man.
The prophet is kind; may his kindness be praised!
To sinners he opens up Paradise!

PEER (*His eyes following* ANITRA *during the dance*)
Her legs are working as fast as drumsticks.
She's a tasty piece of flesh, the hussy.
Here and there she bulges a bit too much.
Hardly a Northern conception of beauty!
But what is Beauty? Convention! No more!
A coinage that's minted and standardized
In certain places for certain occasions.
The man who's a lifelong teetotaler
Never knows the joys of drunkenness.
Yes, the extravagant makes its appeal

[1] A holy building at Mecca.

To a tongue overfed with normal fare.
And the normal's never exactly right.
If she's not too fat, she's a bag of bones,
If she's not too young, she's one leg in the grave,
If her age *is* right, she's an imbecile.
No! The normal is humdrum and tedious.
Her feet—well, they're not conspicuously clean,
Nor her arms—one of them, anyway;
But who cares a jot about things like that?
In fact, I would call them a qualification.
Anitra, listen.

ANITRA (*Approaching*) Thy slave has heard.

PEER You're alluring, my daughter! The prophet is moved.
If you don't believe me, here is the proof—
I'll make you a Houri in Paradise!

ANITRA Impossible, lord.

PEER You think I'm lying?
I'm dead serious, as I'm alive!

ANITRA But I have no soul.

PEER Then I'll get you one!

ANITRA But how, my lord?

PEER You leave that to me!
I'll make it my duty to educate you.
No soul! There's no doubt that you're rather silly;
That's an obvious fact and it's caused me some pain,
But you've ample room for a small-sized soul.
Come here! Let me measure your brain-box, my dear.
There's room! Lots of room! I knew there was!
It's true it will never get you far;
You must face the fact—it will be a small soul,
But dammit, you'll have to be satisfied!
You'll have quite enough to save you from feeling
Ashamed——

ANITRA The prophet is very kind——

PEER Why hesitate? Speak!

ANITRA I would rather have——

PEER Speak out, my daughter, don't dawdle and stutter.

ANITRA I'm not bothered so much about getting a soul;
I'd rather you gave me——

PEER What?

ANITRA (*Pointing to his turban*) That lovely opal!

PEER (*Giving her the jewel. He is overwhelmed with delight*)
Anitra! You're a true daughter of Eve!
You draw me like a magnet for I'm a man,
And as a well-known writer has said:
*"Das ewig Weibliche ziehet uns an!"* [1]

# Act Four, Scene Seven

SCENE *Outside* ANITRA'S *tent. Palm-trees near by. A full moon.* PEER GYNT, *with an Arabian lute in his hand, is sitting under a tree. His beard and hair have been trimmed; in consequence, he is looking much younger. He is singing and accompanying himself on the lute.*

PEER I locked the gates of Paradise
And took the key away.
I put to sea while north winds swept
The depths, and lovely women wept
In undisguised dismay.

Through salty seas my frigate sped
Southward to lands remote.
Where palm-trees proud and slender sway
Around a happy sunlit bay,
I stayed and burned my boat.

I boarded then the desert ship,
Four-leggèd, swift and free.
It skimmed along on wingèd feet.
A bird of passage, I! Tweet-tweet!
I twitter on a tree.

Anitra, thou art palm-tree milk
Which I will sample now.
Angora goats-milk cheese is nice
But has not half the bite or spice,
Anitra dear, as thou.

(*He hangs his lute over his shoulder and draws nearer*)

Silence! Is my fair one listening?
Did she hear me make sweet moan?
Is she peeping through the curtain,
Veils and suchlike thrown aside?
Hush! A sound as though a cork
Had been violently drawn
From a bottle! There! Again!
Sighs of love? A serenade?
No, it was an obvious snore!
Divine music! Anitra sleeps.
Nightingale, have done with singing!
All sorts of plagues will visit you
If you dare, with chirps and gurgles——
All right, continue! Destiny
Made the nightingale a songster
Even as I am myself.
He, as I, can win with music
Tender beating little hearts.
The cool night was made for song.
Music is our common sphere,
The fact of singing makes us us,
Peer Gynt and the nightingale,
As the fact that she is sleeping
Is the crest of my love's bliss. . . .
As though my lips had touched the beaker
And left the nectar there untasted. . . .
Why, there she is! Well, it is best
That she should appear in person.

ANITRA (*From the tent*) Is my lord calling in the night?

PEER Yes, your lord is. He's calling still.
I was wakened by the cats
Kicking up an awful row.

[1] A misquotation of the final lines of Goethe's *Faust*, Part 2: "The Eternal Feminine draws us on high."

ANITRA Don't think that they were quarreling.
It was something worse than that.
PEER What was it then?
ANITRA Oh, spare me!
PEER Speak.
ANITRA Oh, I'm blushing!
PEER (*Approaching her*) Perhaps it was
The feeling that suffused me when
I gave you that lovely opal.
ANITRA (*Horrified*)
My Treasure, how can you compare
A prophet with a mangy cat?
PEER Anitra, from a lover's viewpoint
There is nothing to distinguish
A prophet from an old tom-cat.
ANITRA Jokes, O Master, flow like honey
From your lips.
PEER Dear little friend—
You, like other maidens, judge
Great men by their exteriors.
At bottom, I am very frisky,
Especially when we're alone.
I am bound, by my position,
To wear a mask of gravity.
The world import of my routine,
The grave decisions, knotty points,
Crowding on me day by day,
Make my manner as a prophet
Rather terse. Yes, I admit it.
But that's the superficial "Me."
When we're alone I'm not like that.
I'm just plain Peer, my own straight self.
Hey presto! Now, the prophet's gone!
I, myself, am here before you!
(*He sits down under a tree and draws her to him*)
Come, Anitra, we will sport
Beneath this palm-tree's shady branches!
I will whisper, you will simper;
Later on, we'll change our roles;
Then your rosy lips will whisper
Words of love while I sit simpering.
ANITRA (*Lying at his feet*)
Every word is a sweet song,
Though they're past my understanding.
Tell me, prophet, can your daughter
Get a soul by listening?
PEER A soul, the light of life and knowledge!
Yes, you will acquire one soon.
When the East, with flaming pencil,
Writes in words of fire, "Day dawneth,"
Then, my child, I'll start your lessons.
We'll make a little lady of you.
But it would be silly if
I tried to act the pedagogue
And forced my threadbare wisdom on you
In the silent hours of night.
The soul should never really be
Our primary consideration.
It's the heart that matters most.
ANITRA Speak on, my lord, for when you speak
I see glimpses of more opals!
PEER Excess knowledge leads to folly
And the bud of cowardice
Flowers into cruelty.
Truth, when carried to excess,
Is wisdom's pillar upside down.
Yes, my child, people exist
Who are so steeped in their souls
That their vision's out of focus.
If that's not true, my name's not Peer!
I knew a fellow just like that.
He seemed a diamond among paste;
Fine verbiage fell from his lips,
But, in time, he lost himself
In his wood of eloquence.
Take a look at that vast desert
Round about this oasis.
If I cared to swing my turban
I could make the five great oceans
Swallow every nook and cranny.
But why should I start creating
Continents and oceans now?
It's a mug's game, nothing else.
Do you know what life is, child?
ANITRA No, but teach me, please.
PEER To float
Dry-shod down the stream of time
Being yourself—that, that is life.
In youth and in manhood alone
Can I be really what I am.
Age makes eagles shed their feathers,
Age gives old men rheumatism,
Age makes old women lose their teeth,
Age gives old misers skinny hands,
And, one and all, their souls dry up.
Youth! As Sultan I must rule,
Fiery with youth, and unimpaired,
Not in the fields of Gyntiana
Underneath palms and spreading vines,
But in the greener, fresher fields
Of a maiden's virgin thoughts.
So you see, my dear Anitra,
Why I've been so gracious with you,
Why I took your tender heart
And established there the Holy
Of Holies of my Caliphate.
I must know your every longing,
Be the despot of your love!
You must be mine alone; you must
Be my prisoner, bound to me
Like jewels to a golden chain.
If we part life will be ended,
*Your* life, *nota bene,* please.
Every fibre of your being,
Every cell and every pore,
Must acknowledge my dominion,
Must be conscript to my will.
Your locks, blacker than the midnight,
Your beauty, all that ravishes,
Shall draw me, your Sultan, to
A trysting-place more lovely than
The Hanging Gardens of Babel.

Therefore, it is fortunate
That you're such a little fool.
People who possess a soul
Become consumed by introspection.
Now, as we are on the subject,
You shall have this golden bracelet
To encircle your fine ankle.
That should satisfy us both;
No soul but I will now possess you.
If not—well, the *status quo.*
(ANITRA *snores*)
She's sleeping! The infectious beauty
Of my words has glided past her.
No, it shows my power established.
She has floated off in dreams
Upon the stream of my pure song.
(*Rises and puts some jewels in her lap*)
Here, then, are jewels! And more! And more!
Sleep on, Anitra! Dream of Peer!
Sleep! For in sleeping you have crowned
Your Emperor! Tonight, Peer Gynt
By personality alone,
Has won his greatest victory.

## Act Four, Scene Eight

SCENE *A caravan route. The oasis can be seen in the distance, far behind.* PEER GYNT, *on his white horse, is galloping over the desert with* ANITRA *in front of him on the saddle.*

ANITRA Let me go! I'll bite you!
PEER You little minx!
ANITRA What do you want?
PEER Want? I want to play
At dove and falcon! To carry you off
And do the maddest, most skittish things.
ANITRA Shame on you! An old prophet!
PEER Tommy-rot!
The prophet is not so old, you goose!
Does this bare-back ride point to old age?
ANITRA Let me go! I want to go home!
PEER Little rogue!
Home, home! My in-laws! That *is* an idea!
But birds who have once flown out of a cage
Take very good care not to fly back again.
Besides, my child, you should never remain
Too long in one place, for you lose in respect
What you gain in knowledge of other people,
Especially when you come as a prophet.
You should come and go, like a lovely poem.
It was quite time my visit came to an end.
They're capricious people, these sons of the desert!
Their incense and prayers have both fallen off lately.
ANITRA But *are* you a prophet?
PEER I'm your Emperor!
(*He tries to kiss her*)
See how perky the little woodpecker is!
ANITRA Give me that ring you have on your finger.
PEER Anitra darling, take everything.
ANITRA Your words are music. How noble they sound!
PEER What joy to know that you love me so dearly!
Let's away! I'll lead your horse like a slave.
(*Gives her the riding-whip and dismounts*)
There, there, my rose, my exquisite flower,,
I will trudge beside you in the sand
Till the sun strikes me down and I lie at your feet.
I am young, Anitra, remember that!
You mustn't judge my escapades harshly.
We recognize youth by the pranks he plays.
If only you weren't such a sillybilly,
You'd appreciate, my sweet oleander,
That your lover is full of pranks—*ergo,* he's young!
ANITRA Yes, you are young. Have you any more rings?
PEER Of course I'm young. Catch! I can leap like a buck!
If you had any vine-leaves I'd wear a wreath.
Oh yes! I'm young! Look, I'll dance for you.
(*Sings and dances*)
I am a cockadoodledoo;
Peck me, little pullet.
Oopsie, Twinkleshoe!
I am a cockadoodledoo.
ANITRA You're sweating, O prophet; I'm afraid you will melt.
Hand over that weighty thing there on your belt.
PEER Such tender anxiety! Of course you shall hold
My purse. Loving hearts can do without gold.
(*Sings and dances again*)
Young Peer Gynt is a very crazy chap!
He hardly knows himself from you!
"Pshaw," says Peer. "Pshaw, pshaw! Pooh, pooh."
Young Peer Gynt is a very crazy chap.
ANITRA What sight is finer than a prophet dancing?
PEER To Hell with this prophet business! Let's change our clothes!
Hurry up!
ANITRA Your burnoose would be too long,
Your girdle too ample, your stockings too short.
PEER *Eh bien!*
(*Kneels down*)
Then rack me with torment and pangs;
It is sweet for loving hearts to suffer!
When we get home to my castle, Anitra——
ANITRA Your Paradise! Have we far to go?
PEER A thousand miles or——
ANITRA Too far! Too far!
PEER You shall have the soul I promised you——
ANITRA No, thanks! I can manage without a soul.
But you were yearning for pangs——
PEER (*Getting up*) And torment!
Exquisite, ephemeral—a spasm of pain!
ANITRA Anitra obeys the prophet! Farewell!
(*She raps him over the knuckles with the whip and gallops off at top speed across the desert*)
PEER (*Thunderstruck*). Well, I'm b———! [1]

[1] The line is left incomplete in the original text.

# Act Four, Scene Nine

SCENE *The same. An hour later.* PEER GYNT, *chastened and thoughtful, is stripping himself of his Oriental robes. Finally, he pulls his little traveling-cap out of his pocket, puts it on his head and stands there attired in European dress once more. He throws his turban as far away as possible.*

PEER There lies the Turk and here stand I!
These heathen manners can do us no good.
It's lucky they're coming off with my clothes,
And were not tattooed right into my flesh.
What was I doing in such company?
I'm a Christian! What could be better than that?
Away with this peacock ostentation!
Be lawful, be moral; that's how to live!
I must be myself and assure myself
Of a graveside sermon and flowers on my coffin.
(*Takes a few steps forward*)
That little minx—I only escaped
From having my head turned by a hair's-breadth.
I'd have to be a troll to make out
What it was that captivated me.
Thank God it's over! Had that joke gone
A step further I'd have looked quite silly.
I have erred—that's so! But it's a relief
To know that I only erred by proxy.
It was not I who fell, not I, myself;
It was the prophet; my life as a prophet
Was denied the sperm of activity,
And consoled itself by making a show
Of these sorry, unfortunate acts of bad taste.
A prophet's life is a difficult one.
He must stand aloof, must live in the clouds.
If he shows a gleam of worldliness
He's put out of business in less than no time.
I thought I was going along pretty well
By paying court to that silly goose!
Still, in spite of everything——
(*Bursts out laughing*)
Just think of it!
I tried to bring time to a standstill by dancing,
By singing and sighing and sloppy canoodling!
And how did I finish? Like a plucked hen!
Even a holy man sows his wild oats!
Yes, plucked! Good God, how I've been plucked!
It's lucky I've kept a bit in reserve;
I've a bit in my pocket and a bit more
In America so I'm not on my beam-ends.
Middle-class! Yes, that's the thing to be!
I haven't got a coachman and pair
And I don't have to bother with trunks or carriage,
So I'm still master of the situation.
Many roads are open. Which one shall I choose?
The wise man can winnow the chaff from the wheat.
My business life is a finished chapter,
My love affairs are cast-off clothing,
And I don't want to double back on my tracks.
"Backward or forward, it's just as far,
Within or without the path is as narrow."
That comes from some holy book or other.
I must think something out, something new and ennobling,
Something that's worthy of labor and cash.
Should I write my autobiography,
Unexpurgated, to guide the guileless?
No, wait! Since I've plenty of time on my hands,
How would it be if I gave myself
*Carte blanche* to travel so that I might
Study Humanity throughout the ages?
Of course, that's it! It's the very thing.
In my younger days I used to pore
Over ancient manuscripts. History
And Humanity always appealed to me.
I'll study them. Like a feather I'll float
Down the unending stream of Time,
Live over the past, as in a dream,
See heroes do battle for worthy causes.
I'll be an onlooker, at a safe distance.
I'll see thinkers tortured and martyrs bleed,
See kingdoms crumble and empires fall,
See great things develop from small beginnings;
In short, skim the cream of history.
I must try to get a copy of Becker,[1]
Go from place to place chronologically.
I know that my groundwork is not very thorough
And history is a subtle subject,
But the crudest experiments have been known
To yield the most astounding results.
It's a great thing to set yourself a task,
Clench your teeth, steel your nerves and achieve your aim.
(*Moved but restrained*)
To break the bonds that hamper your Self,
Leave family, home and dearest friends,
Scatter your wealth and your earthly goods,
Turn a deaf ear to the wiles of love,
All in the cause of ultimate truth,
(*Wipes a tear from his eye*)
That is the way of the scientist!
Yes, I've solved the riddle of my life's work,
And now I'm happy beyond compare.
I will carry on through thick and thin;
If I hold my head high, it's forgivable.
I have found myself—the Man, Peer Gynt,
The Emperor of Humanity!
The Past will become my hunting-ground;
Let the modern, the living, pass me by;
I'll waste no shoe-leather on today;
There's no faith, no spine in modern man,
His soul has no light, his deeds have no weight.
(*Shrugs his shoulders*)
And women—well, frailty, thy name is woman!
(*He goes*)

[1] The reference is to K. F. Becker's *History of the World.* which had recently been translated from German into Danish.

## Act Four, Scene Ten

SCENE *A hut in a large forest in northern Norway. An open door with a large wooden bolt. Reindeer antlers over the door. A flock of goats near the hut. A bright summer's day.* SOLVEIG, *now a fair, good-looking, middle-aged woman, is sitting in the sunshine, spinning. She gazes down the pathway and sings.*

SOLVEIG The winter and spring may come and go,
The summer-time and the long year, too;
But some day, I know, you'll come back to me,
And I will wait, as I promised you.
(*She calls the goats, then starts spinning and singing again*)
God give you His love wherever you are,
If you are on earth or in His care.
I will wait here till you come back to me,
And if you're in Heaven I will meet you there.

## Act Four, Scene Eleven

SCENE *In Egypt. The statue of Memnon*[1] *in the middle of the desert. Dawn.* PEER GYNT *walks in and looks around him.*

PEER I could easily start my travels here.
For a change I'll become an Egyptian,
But on the basis of the Gyntian "self";
Then, I'll wend my way to Assyria;
But not as far back as the very Beginning;
That would only lead to embarrassment.
No, I'll go round about Bible history.
I'm sure to find some traces of it;
But I won't delve into it very deeply;
That's not in my power nor is it my plan.
(*Sits down on a rock*)
Now, I'll sit here and rest and wait patiently till
The Statue has sung its morning song.
After breakfast I'll climb the Pyramid;
If I've time I'll investigate the inside.
Then, by land round the north shore of the Red Sea;
Perhaps I will find King Potiphar's[2] grave.
Next, to Asia! In Babylon I will seek
The Hanging Gardens and concubines—
The earliest signs of civilization.

[1] Son of the dawn in ancient Egyptian religion. The statue is connected with an ancient Pharaoh.

[2] There was no king named Potiphar. He was a prominent Egyptian who figures in the Bible as chief of Pharaoh's bodyguard.

Then, on seven-league boots to the walls of Troy,
And from Troy by the direct sea-route across
To glorious, ancient Athens. There,
On the very spot, stone by stone, I'll explore
The pass that Leonidas[3] defended.
I will read the higher philosophers,
Find the prison where Socrates martyred himself.
But stop! I'm forgetting! There's a war on!
Hellenism must be laid aside.
(*Looks at his watch*)
It's quite absurd—the time the sun
Takes to rise! I've got no time to waste.
Oh yes, from Troy—it was there I stopped—
(*Gets up and listens*)
What is that peculiar murmuring sound?
(*Sunrise*)

MEMNON STATUE (*Singing*)
From the demi-god's ashes new-born there sprang
Birds that sang.
Zeus the All-knowing
Shaped birds of prey.
Owls of Wisdom deep,
Where do my birds sleep?
Then solve the riddle
Of the song—or die!

PEER I really think a sound came from the statue.
It was music of the Past. I heard
The rise and fall of a voice of stone.
I'll make a note; let the learned ponder.
(*Jots it down in his note-book*)
"The statue sang. I heard it distinctly.
But did not quite get the gist of the words.
It must have been a delusion, of course.
Nothing else of importance observed today."
(*Goes off*)

## Act Four, Scene Twelve

SCENE *Near the village of Gizeh. The Great* SPHINX, *and in the far distance the spires and minarets of Cairo.* PEER GYNT *enters. He looks carefully at the Sphinx, then puts on his glasses and continues to stare at it, sometimes through his glasses and sometimes through his hollowed hands.*

PEER Now where have I met this thing before?
This hideous image reminds me of something.
I've certainly met it up north or down south.
Now who was it? Was it a man? If so, who?
It occurs to me now that the Memnon statue
Was like the so-called King of the Dovre;
He sat just like that, just as stiff and straight,

[3] Leonidas defended the pass of Thermopylae against the Persians in 480 B.C. All the defenders were killed.

With his bottom firm on a pillar-seat.
But this strange half-breed monstrosity,
This freak, this cross between lion and woman,
Did I meet him on one of my flights of fancy
Or is he an actual memory?
Someone I know? Ha! I remember him now.
It's the Boyg, of course, whose skull I smashed.
At least, I dreamt I smashed it. I was
Delirious at the time with fever.
(*Goes nearer*)
Same eyes, same mouth, less sluggish, more crafty.
But otherwise very much the same.
Well, there you are, Boyg, you look like a lion
When viewed from behind in the light of day!
Do you still speak in riddles? Let's try you out.
Let's see if you still give the same answers!
(*Shouts to Sphinx*)
Hi, Boyg, who are you?

VOICE (*Behind Sphinx*) *Ach Sfinx, wer bist du?* [1]

PEER What's that? An echo in German! Unheard of!

VOICE *Wer bist du?*

PEER It talks just like a native!
A new observation and all my own.
(*Makes a note in his book*)
"Echo in German. Berlin accent."
(BEGRIFFENFELDT[2] *emerges from behind Sphinx*)

BEGRIFFENFELDT A man!

PEER I suppose it was he who was speaking.
(*Makes another note*)
"Later came to other conclusions."

BEGRIFFENFELDT (*Very excited*)
*Mein Herr,* excuse me—! *Eine Lebensfrage—!* [3]
Please tell me what brought you here to-day.

PEER I'm making a call on a boyhood friend.

BEGRIFFENFELDT The Sphinx?

PEER Yes, I knew him well in the past.

BEGRIFFENFELDT *Famos!* [4] After such a worried night, too!
My head is just on the point of splitting.
You know him, *mein Herr!* Then tell me, what is he?

PEER What is he? That's easy! He is himself!

BEGRIFFENFELDT (*Jumping*)
I see it! It's flashed before my eyes
Like lightning! The riddle of life is solved.
One thing is certain! He is himself!

PEER That's what he says, at any rate.

BEGRIFFENFELDT Himself! The Day of Knowledge has dawned.
(*Takes off his hat*)
Your name, *mein Herr?*

PEER I was christened Peer Gynt.

BEGRIFFENFELDT (*With restrained admiration*)
Peer Gynt! Allegorical! I guessed as much!
Peer Gynt! In other words, the Unknown One!
The Messiah whose coming was revealed to me.

PEER But—really! Did you come here to meet—?

BEGRIFFENFELDT Peer Gynt! Profound, mystifying, intense!
Each word is a mine of unplumbed ideas.
What are you?

PEER (*Modestly*) I've always tried to be
Myself. However, here is my passport.

BEGRIFFENFELDT Once again that baffling mysterious word!
(*Grasps his wrist*)
To Cairo! I've found the Emperor
Of Revelation.

PEER The Emperor?

BEGRIFFENFELDT Come!

PEER Do they know me here?

BEGRIFFENFELDT (*Dragging* PEER *with him*) The Emperor
Of Revelation based on Self!

# Act Four, Scene Thirteen

SCENE *Cairo. A lunatic asylum. A large courtyard surrounded by high walls and buildings. Barred windows and iron cages. Three* KEEPERS *in the courtyard; a fourth enters.*

FOURTH KEEPER Schaffmann, tell me, where's the Director?

A KEEPER He went out this morning before it was light.

FOURTH KEEPER Something must have annoyed him, I think. Last night——

ANOTHER Be quiet! There he is at the door!
(BEGRIFFENFELDT *comes in with* PEER GYNT. *He locks the door and puts the key in his pocket*)

PEER (*To himself*)
Undoubtedly a most talented man;
I can't understand a thing he says.
(*Stares round*)
So this is the Scholars' Club, is it?

BEGRIFFENFELDT Yes, you'll find them all here, every one of them.
Threescore and ten—the Interpreters' Circle.
One hundred and sixty have been added lately.
(*Calls to the* KEEPERS)
Mikkel, Schlingelberg, Schaffmann, Fuchs,
Into the cages with you at once!

KEEPERS Us?

BEGRIFFENFELDT Who else? Come along! Hurry up!
The world's upside down and so are we.
(*Pushes the* KEEPERS *into the cages*)
The great Peer has come to us to-day;
You can draw your own conclusion from that.
I'll say no more.
(*Locks the cages and throws the keys in a well*)

PEER *Herr Doktor, Herr Direktor——*

[1] "Sphinx, who are you?"
[2] The name means: "Field of concepts," a satire on German abstract science.
[3] "A philosophical question."
[4] "Wonderful!"

BEGRIFFENFELDT I'm neither; I used to be but now——
Herr Peer, can you keep a secret? I must
Pour out my heart to someone or other.

PEER (*Increasingly uncomfortable*)
What is it?

BEGRIFFENFELDT Promise me you won't faint.

PEER I will do my best.

BEGRIFFENFELDT (*Draws him into a corner and whispers*)
Absolute Reason
Died last night at eleven o'clock.

PEER Good God!

BEGRIFFENFELDT Yes, it's most lamentable,
And in my position, doubly so.
Up till now, this place has been looked upon
As a Lunatic Asylum.

PEER Asylum?

BEGRIFFENFELDT Not now.

PEER (*Growing pale and lowering his voice*)
I'm beginning to understand.
The man is mad and no one knows it!
(*Moves away*)

BEGRIFFENFELDT (*Following him*)
And now, I hope you see everything clearly.
When I say he's dead I'm talking nonsense.
He's beside himself; he's got out of his skin
Like my countryman Munchausen's fox.[1]

PEER Excuse me a moment——

BEGRIFFENFELDT (*Catching hold of him*) He was like an eel,
Not like a fox. A pin through his eye,
And he was wriggling away on the wall——

PEER What can I do to save myself?

BEGRIFFENFELDT A slit round his throat and then whip! He's out
Of his skin!

PEER Raving mad!

BEGRIFFENFELDT It's perfectly clear
That this "exit from self" can only result
In a revolution, world-wide in scope.
Those people who were thought to be mad
Became normal last night at eleven o'clock
In accordance with this new phase of Reason.
What's more, looked at from this new angle,
It becomes apparent that those we thought sane
All went off their heads at that very same hour.

PEER Talking of time, I'm in a great hurry——

BEGRIFFENFELDT Your time? There! You've jolted my memory.
(*Opens a door and shouts*)
Come out! The hour of re-birth has come!
Reason is dead! Long live Peer Gynt—!

PEER But, my dear man——
(*The* LUNATICS *follow each other into the courtyard*)

BEGRIFFENFELDT Hail to this festive morn!
Greet the dawn of our deliverance!
Your Emperor has come!

PEER Emperor?

BEGRIFFENFELDT Emperor!

PEER But the honor's too great; it goes beyond——

BEGRIFFENFELDT At a time like this, don't allow yourself
To be ruled by false modesty.

PEER Give me time!
I'm not fit; I'm completely stupefied.

BEGRIFFENFELDT Stupefied? You? A man who has solved
The Sphinx's riddle! A man who's himself!

PEER That's exactly the point! I am myself
In everything; but here, it appears,
It's a question of being beside yourself.

BEGRIFFENFELDT Beside? Oh no! You're sadly mistaken.
Here, we're ourselves from the very word "Go!"
We're ourselves and nothing but ourselves,
We speed full sail ahead as ourselves,
We shut ourselves up in a keg of self,
We stew in our own juice, we seal ourselves up
Hermetically with a bung of self
And get seasoned in a well of self.
We never consider anyone else;
There are no thoughts nor sorrows outside our own;
We are ourselves in thought and in word,
Ourselves to the farthest, the uttermost edge;
And so, since we must have an Emperor,
It's clear that you are the very man.

PEER If only the Devil——

BEGRIFFENFELDT Now, don't get discouraged.
Every new task must have a beginning.
"Oneself." Come here, we'll look for examples;
We'll take a chance and choose one at random.
(*To a gloomy person, near by*)
Good day, Hu-hu! Well, my man, are you still
Bowed down by your melancholia?

HUHU What else can I be when droves
Of people die misunderstood?
(*To* PEER)
You're a stranger. Shall I tell you?

PEER (*Bowing*) Certainly.

HUHU Well, listen then.
In the East, like crowns of garlands,
Lie the coasts of Malabar.
Portuguese and Hollanders
Sow the seeds of culture there;
But side by side with them there live
Tribes of native Malabaris
Who have muddled up the language
But who are the overlords.
In ages past, the orang-outang
Ruled the forest undisputed,
Was the lord and master there.
He was free to fight and gibber,
Free to grin and free to gape,
Just as Nature had intended.
He could snarl in perfect freedom;
He was king in his own house;

[1] An allusion to an adventure of Baron Munchausen wherein he put his hand into a fox's mouth and groped further and further until he caught the tail and, pulling it, turned the fox inside out.

But—the foreign conquest came,
And the language of the forest
Lost its primeval purity.
A long night of four hundred years
Glowered over the race of apes.
A night like that must kill all progress;
The old primeval forest noises
Are heard no longer. No one growls;
If we want to indicate
Our thoughts we have to do it by
Means of speech. What a restraint!
Portuguese and Hollanders,
Malabaris and Eurasians,
All have suffered equally.
I have tried to fight the fight
For our own true forest language,
Tried to resurrect its corpse,
Maintained the people's right to gibber,[2]
Gibbered myself and shown the need
For gibbering in our folk-songs,
But my struggles came to nothing.
Now you know why I am bitter.
Thanks for listening. If you have
Suggestions I would like to hear them.

PEER (*To himself*)
They say it's always safe to howl
With the wolves when they're abroad.
(*Aloud*) Dear friend, if my memory serves me,
There's a tribe of orang-outangs
In Morocco, which has neither
Interpreter nor national bard.
Their language sounds like Malabari.
Wouldn't it be a fine gesture
If you, great leader that you are,
Wandered forth to serve these people?

HUHU Thanks for listening to my story.
I will do as you advise. (*With a low bow*)
The Orient has spurned its bard;
The Occident has orang-outangs. (*Goes*)

BEGRIFFENFELDT Well, was he himself? I fancy he was!
He's full of himself and himself alone.
He's himself in every idea he expounds,
Himself because he's beside himself.
Come here! I'll show you another one
Whose sanity came back to him last night.
(*To a* FELLAH[3] *who is carrying a mummy on his back*)
King Apis,[4] Illustrious One, how are things going?

FELLAH (*Wildly to* PEER)
Am *I* King Apis?

PEER (*Getting behind doctor*) I must confess
That I'm not familiar with your case.
But if I can judge from your manner I'd say——

FELLAH You're lying, as well.

BEGRIFFENFELDT Will your Majesty
Report on the situation?

FELLAH I will.
(*Turning to* PEER
Do you see this thing on my back?
He was once a king called Apis;
To-day he is known as a mummy;
In addition, he is dead.
He built those pyramids yonder,
And carved the mighty Sphinx,
And fought, as the Doctor tells us,
With Turks on *rechts* and *links*.[5]
And so, the whole of Egypt
Exalted him into a God,
Placed his image in their temples
In the likeness of a bull.
But I am this same King Apis;
It's as clear as clear to me;
And if you cannot grasp it,
Understanding will soon dawn.
One day, when King Apis was hunting,
He suddenly got off his horse
And excused himself and went off
Into my grandfather's field.
The earth that King Apis manured
Has nourished me with its corn;
And if further proof is needed,
Well—I have an invisible horn.
So it's more than hellish, isn't it,
That no one admits my right?
By birth I am King Apis,
But a fellah in everyone's sight.
Now give me some sound advice, will you?
This is the question at stake:
How can I become like King Apis
And confound those who think I'm a fake?

PEER Your Majesty must build pyramids
And carve a more massive Sphinx,
And fight, as the Herr Doctor tells you,
With Turks on *rechts* and *links*.

FELLAH Well of course, that's marvelous counsel!
A fellah! A starving louse
Who has barely the means to keep
The rats and mice out of his house!
Quick, man! Think of something better,
That will give me what others lack,
That will give me royal features
Like King Apis here on my back.

PEER Your Majesty, may I suggest that
You hang yourself, and then
In your coffin, in the earth's bosom,
You behave as though you were dead?

FELLAH I'll do it! My life for a halter!
A rope around my neck!
At first I'll feel a bit different,
But time will soon smooth that out.
(*Goes away and begins making arrangements to hang himself*)

BEGRIFFENFELDT Herr Peer, I call that personality,
A man with method——

PEER Undoubtedly—

[2] The whole passage is an attack on ultra-nationalistic language reformers in Norway.

[3] A hungry and wretched servant.

[4] Apis, king of Argos, is confused here with the sacred bull of the Egyptians.

[5] "Right and left."

But he's really hanging himself! Oh, God!
Have mercy! I'm ill! My head's in a whirl!

BEGRIFFENFELDT A transitional stage; it won't last long.

PEER Transition? What to? Forgive me—I'm going——

BEGRIFFENFELDT (*Holding him*)
Are you mad?

PEER Not yet. Mad? Heaven forbid!
(*Uproar.* HUSSEIN, *a minister, pushes his way through the crowd*)

HUSSEIN I've been told that an Emperor arrived to-day.
(*To* PEER)
Is it you?

PEER (*In despair*) That seems to have been decided.

HUSSEIN Then you'll have some documents to sign.

PEER (*Tearing his hair*)
All right! Carry on! The madder the better!

HUSSEIN Will you honor me by taking a dip?
(*He bows low*)
I am a pen.

PEER (*Bowing even lower*) And I am only
A useless piece of imperial parchment.

HUSSEIN In short, *mein Herr,* my story is this:
They all say I'm a sand-box whereas I'm a pen.

PEER My history, Herr Pen, is just as brief—
I'm a sheet of paper that's been left blank.

HUSSEIN No one has an inkling of what I can do.
They only use me for sprinkling sand.

PEER I belonged to a woman, a silver-clasped book!
Sane or insane—it's a printer's error.

HUSSEIN Just think how nerve-racking it must be
To be a pen and not feel a knife's-edge.

PEER (*Jumping high*)
Just think what it's like to be a reindeer,
To spring from the rocks, to fall, fall, fall
Without feeling the ground beneath your hoofs!

HUSSEIN A knife! I am blunt! Quick, cut me! Slit me!
The world will end if I'm not sharpened.

PEER I fear for the world! Like so much else
It was thought by the Lord to be well-nigh perfect.

BEGRIFFENFELDT Here's a knife!

HUSSEIN (*Seizing it*) Ah! Now I can lick up the ink!
What joy, what ecstasy to slash oneself!
(*Cuts his throat*)

BEGRIFFENFELDT (*Turning away*)
There's no need to bleed all over me!

PEER (*In growing terror*)
Hold him!

HUSSEIN Yes, hold me! That's the word!
Hold! Hold the pen! Put pen to paper! (*Falls*)
I'm finished. The postscript—don't forget it:
He lived and he died, a pen guided by others.

PEER (*Wildly*)
What shall I—? What am I? Great God—hold fast!
I'm all that You wish—a Turk, a sinner,
A troll—but help me; something has burst!
(*Screaming*)
Your name—it's gone—I can't remember—
Help me, Thou! Oh, Protector of Madmen, help!
(*He sinks down exhausted.* BEGRIFFENFELDT, *with a crown of straw in his hand, makes a spring and seats himself astride* PEER)

BEGRIFFENFELDT Ha! Look at him sitting enthroned in the mire! He's beside himself! We'll crown him there!
(*Places the crown on* PEER'*s head and cries*)
Long live the Emperor, the Emperor of Self!

SCHAFFMANN (*In cage*)
*Es lebe hoch der grosse Peer!* [6]

# Act Five, Scene One

SCENE *On board a ship in the North Sea, off the Norwegian coast. Sunset. Stormy weather.* PEER GYNT, *a hale old man with grey hair and beard, is on the poop. He is dressed in semi-nautical fashion with a sailor's jacket and sea-boots. His clothes are rather threadbare. He is weather-beaten and his face seems harder. The* CAPTAIN *and* STEERSMAN *are at the wheel. The crew are for'ard.* PEER GYNT *is resting his arms on the rails, his eyes fixed on the coastline.*

PEER Look at the Hallingskarv[1] wearing his winter clothes;
The old man's showing off in the evening sun.
There's his brother, the Jøkel,[1] standing behind,
With his ice-green cape still slung on his back.
And there, like a virgin in pure white,
Is the Folgefaann,[2] unblemished still.
Stay there! Stay forever! No tricks with me,
My dear old friends! You are only stone.

CAPTAIN (*Shouting for'ard*)
Two men to the wheel—and the lantern set!

PEER There's a stiff breeze blowing.

CAPTAIN The storm's on its way.

PEER Can you see the Ronde hills from the sea?

CAPTAIN No, they're behind the glaciers.

PEER Or Blaahø? [3]

CAPTAIN No, but in the rigging,
From up aloft when the weather's fine,
Galdhøpiggen[3] can be clearly seen.

PEER Where is Haarteigen? [3]

CAPTAIN (*Pointing*) Over there.

PEER Yes, of course.

CAPTAIN You seem to know these parts.

PEER I sailed past here when I left my home.
Someone once said that our minds are like
Lumber-rooms, full of old memories.
(*He spits and gazes again at the coast*)

[6] "Long live great Peer!"

[1] Names of famous mountains on the Norwegian coast between Stavanger and Bergen.

[2] An immense glacier.

[3] Names of famous mountain tops to the east.

That's where they live, down in the blue dales
And the black mountain-valleys, like narrow ditches,
Right on the shores of the open fjords.
(*Looks at the* CAPTAIN)
The houses are very scattered here.

CAPTAIN You can walk for miles without seeing a dwelling.

PEER Will we land by the morning?

CAPTAIN Just about,
Unless we have a dirty night.

PEER It looks a bit threatening in the west.

CAPTAIN Aye!

PEER When I pay my bill remind me
To tip the crew. I'd like to give something
To all of them!

CAPTAIN Thank you.

PEER It won't be much.
I made my pile but most of it vanished.
Fate and I are at odds just now.
You know how much I've got here on board.
That's all that's left! The rest went west!

CAPTAIN It's more than enough to give you a standing
With the folk here at home.

PEER I've no family.
There's no one expecting this prodigal son.
I'll escape all the scenes at the pier when we land.

CAPTAIN Look! Here comes the storm!

PEER You won't forget?
If anyone here is really in need
I won't look too closely at my money.

CAPTAIN That's handsome of you. Nearly all are hard up.
And they all have wives and children at home.
They can't make ends meet on their wages alone.
If they can go back with a bit more to spend,
It would be the homecoming of their lives.

PEER What was that you said? They've got wives and children?
They're married then?

CAPTAIN Every man-jack of them!
The cook's the one who's most in need.
His family are all half-starved.

PEER Married? A home? Someone waiting for them?
Someone to welcome them when they return?

CAPTAIN Yes, a poor man's welcome.

PEER And if they get back
At night, what then?

CAPTAIN Then you can be sure
There'll be something special ready for supper.

PEER A light on the table?

CAPTAIN And something to drink.

PEER And there they'll sit snug with a flickering fire,
With their wives and children around them; such bustle
And noise—they'll all be talking together,
Too happy to listen to one another!

CAPTAIN Yes, that will all happen; that's why it was
So good of you to promise to give them
A little bit more to add to their wages.

PEER (*Banging the gunwale*)
No, I'm damned if I do! Do you think I'm mad?
Do you really expect me to empty my pockets
For the sake of other people's children?
I've had to slave for what I've got.
There's no one waiting for old Peer Gynt.

CAPTAIN Do as you like; the money's yours.

PEER It certainly is! And mine it will stay.
I'll pay my bill the moment we berth!
My fare from Panama; then I'll stand
A round of drinks for the crew—nothing else.
If I give any more, you can punch my nose!

CAPTAIN I'll put my fist to your bill, not your nose.
Excuse me now; the wind's getting up.
(*He crosses the deck. It has grown dark. A lamp is lit in the cabin. The pitching and tossing increases. Mist and heavy skies*)

PEER Support other people's swarming brats,
Make them laugh, bring joy into their homes,
Know that they're always in someone's thoughts!
There's no one at all to think of me.
A light to welcome them? I'll put it out!
I'll think of a way! I'll make them all drunk.
Those devils! I'll see that they don't stay sober.
They'll go back to their wives and children dead drunk.
Let them swear, bang the table until it rings,
Let them frighten their families out of their wits,
Let their wives start crying and run from the house
With the children. I'll give them happiness!
(*The ship rolls heavily. He staggers and keeps his feet with difficulty*)
Well, that was nasty! The sea is working
As though it were paid for every wave.
These northern waters are always themselves,
Always raging, wayward, tempestuous.
(*Listens*)
What was that? I heard——

THE WATCH (*For'ard*) A wreck to leeward.

CAPTAIN (*Amidships*)
Starboard the helm! Close to the wind!

FIRST MATE Any men on the wreck?

WATCH I can see three.

PEER Quick! Lower a boat.

CAPTAIN It would never get there.
(*Goes for'ard*)

PEER How can you talk like that? If you're men
You'll try. What does it matter if you
Get wet?

BO'SUN It's impossible in this sea.

PEER They're shouting again. The wind's dying down.
You, cook! Will you? I'll make it worth-while.

COOK Not for twenty pounds.

PEER You curs, you cowards!
They're men, with wives and children at home
Waiting——

BO'SUN Well, patience is a virtue.

CAPTAIN Bear away from the breakers.

FIRST MATE The wreck's gone under.

PEER This silence—? What?

BO'SUN If they were married,
As you seem to think, then three new widows

Have just been born into the world.
(*The storm increases in fury.* PEER GYNT *goes aft*)

PEER Faith among men is dying out.
Christianity's only seen in print.
Good deeds are rare. People never pray.
They've no respect for the Powers above.
It's in storms like this that our Lord shows His might.
These swine should take care and think of the proverb,
"It's dangerous to play with fire."
But no, they persist in flouting Him.
But *I* am innocent; on the Day,
I can prove I stood ready, my cash in my hand.
Will I get a reward? Of course, there's a saying,
"A good conscience makes a soft pillow."
That would hold good on shore but not on board ship
Where a decent man's such a rarity.
At sea, you can never be yourself,
You sink or swim with the rest of them.
If the hour of vengeance strikes for the cook
Or the bo'sun, it strikes for me as well.
Personal interests don't count at all.
You're only a sausage from a machine.
I've made the mistake of being too meek,
And it's never got me anywhere.
If I were younger I'd alter my tactics,
I'd be much more authoritative.
There's still time. Very soon it will get around
That Peer Gynt's back home from his travels abroad.
I'll get back my farm by fair means or foul.
I'll rebuild it; I'll make a palace of it;
But I won't allow anyone inside.
They'll stand at the door fumbling with their caps,
They'll beg and they'll pray. I wouldn't mind that.
But I won't give them anything—not a sou.
I've had to cower under the blows of Fate.
I'll make a few others start cowering now.
(A STRANGE PASSENGER *appears in the darkness beside* PEER GYNT *and greets him in a friendly voice*)

PASSENGER Good evening!

PEER Good evening! What? Who are you?

PASSENGER Your fellow-passenger.

PEER Well, that's funny!
I thought I was the only one here.

PASSENGER A small mistake. We've put it right.

PEER Why is it I've never seen you before?

PASSENGER I don't go on deck during the day.

PEER Have you been ill? You're as white as a sheet.

PASSENGER Not at all. I'm in the best of health.

PEER What a fearful storm!

PASSENGER Yes, a good thing, too.

PEER A good thing?

PASSENGER The waves are as high as a house.
I'm licking my lips. Just think of all
The ships that are going under! Just think
Of all the corpses that will be washed up!

PEER Good God!

PASSENGER Have you ever seen anyone hanged?
Or throttled—or drowned?

PEER Here! You're going too far!

PASSENGER The corpses all grin, a mocking grin,
And they've nearly all bitten off their tongues.

PEER Here! Keep away!

PASSENGER Let me ask you a question.
Just imagine that we run aground
And sink in the dark——

PEER You think we're in danger?

PASSENGER I couldn't say. I really don't know.
But suppose I'm saved and you go to the bottom——

PEER Nonsense!

PASSENGER It could easily happen.
When a person has one foot in the grave,
He starts to get generous, gives things away.

PEER (*Feeling in his pocket*)
Ah! Money?

PASSENGER No! But would you care
To give me your highly valuable corpse?

PEER This is really too much!

PASSENGER Your corpse, nothing else!
In the interests of science——

PEER Get away!

PASSENGER My dear sir, just think what you will gain!
I'll open you up and have you displayed.
I'm trying to find the seat of dreams.
I'd scrutinize every bit of you.

PEER Get away!

PASSENGER My dear sir, a useless drowned body!

PEER You blaspheming fool! You're helping the storm.
Are you mad? Here, in this wind, in this rain,
On this raging sea, with all the signs
That something disastrous may soon occur,
You go and start tempting Providence.

PASSENGER You're not in the humor for further talk,
But maybe you'll change your mind, in time.
(*Nods in a friendly way*)
We'll meet when the ship sinks, if not before!
By then you may be in a better mood.
(*Goes into the cabin*)

PEER They're sinister men, these scientists!
Free-thinkers, as well——
(*To the* BO'SUN, *who is passing*)
Just a word, my friend!
That passenger? What sort of madman is he?

BO'SUN You're the only one I know on board.

PEER Only me? This is getting worse and worse.
(*To a* SAILOR *who comes out of the cabin*)
Who was that who just went through the cabin door?

SAILOR The ship's dog, sir.
(*Passes on*)

WATCH (*Shouting*) Land just ahead!

PEER Get my trunk and my box! All my luggage on deck!

BO'SUN We've more important things to do.

PEER I was joking, Captain; it's only my fun!
I'll help the cook! Depend on it!

CAPTAIN The jib has gone!

FIRST MATE That was the foresail!

BO'SUN (*Shouting from for'ard*)
Breakers ahead!
CAPTAIN She's smashing up!
(*The ship founders. Noise and confusion*)

# Act Five, Scene Two

SCENE *Close to land, among the rocks and breakers. The ship is sinking. Through the mist glimpses can be seen of a boat with two men. A breaker engulfs it and it overturns. There is a scream. Then silence. A little later the boat's keel emerges.* PEER GYNT *comes to the surface close to the overturned boat.*

PEER Help! I'm drowning! Send a lifeboat!
Save me, Lord—that's in the Bible.
(*He is clinging to the keel. The* COOK *breaks surface on the other side of the boat*)
COOK Dear Lord, take pity on my children.
Be merciful! Help me reach shore.
(*He holds on to the upturned boat*)
PEER Let go!
COOK Get off!
PEER I'll hit——
COOK I'll smash——
PEER I'll kick you off! I'll do you in!
Let go, can't you? She won't take two.
COOK I know! Let go!
PEER Get off!
COOK Never!
(*They fight. The* COOK *hurts his hand. He hangs on with the other one*)
PEER Away with that hand!
COOK Spare me, please.
Think of my little ones at home.
PEER I need life even more than you.
Up till now I have no children.
COOK Let go! You've lived. I am still young!
PEER Get off! Quick! You'll drag us down!
COOK Have pity! In God's name, give way!
You have no one to grieve for you.
(*Screams as he slips off*)
I'm drowning!
PEER (*Catching hold of him*) No, I'm holding you
By your hair. Now say your prayers.
COOK I can't remember. Everything
Is black——
PEER Then say what's most important.
COOK "Give us this day——"
PEER Forget all that.
You'll soon get everything you want.
COOK "Give us this day——"
PEER The same old song!
It's obvious you were a cook.
(*His grip on the* COOK *loosens*)

COOK (*Sinking*)
"Give us this day our——" (*Goes under*)
PEER Amen, lad!
You were yourself right to the end.
(*Climbs into the boat*)
While there's life there's always hope.
(*The* STRANGE PASSENGER *is seen to be holding on to the boat*)
PASSENGER Good morning!
PEER You?
PASSENGER I heard you scream.
Amusing to run into you!
Well, was my prophecy correct?
PEER Let go! There's scarcely room for one.
PASSENGER Oh, I can swim with my left leg.
I'll float by holding on to this
Chink here with my finger-tip.
But apropos the corpse——
PEER Shut up!
PASSENGER The rest is finished off——
PEER Shut up!
PASSENGER Very well.
(*Silence*)
PEER Well?
PASSENGER I've shut up.
PEER You devil, you! What are you up to?
PASSENGER Waiting.
PEER (*Tearing his hair*) I'll go mad. What are you?
PASSENGER (*Nodding*)
A friend.
PEER What else?
PASSENGER What do you think?
Can't you think of anyone who
Looks like me?
PEER Only the Devil!
PASSENGER (*Softly*)
Does he show us a light when fear
Consumes us and when life is black?
PEER I see! Then in reality,
You're my guardian angel, are you?
PASSENGER Friend, have you, say once in six months,
Felt fear strike right into your heart?
PEER When danger threatens, I'm afraid.
But your talk will get us nowhere.
PASSENGER Friend, have you, say once in your life,
Won a victory from fear?
PEER (*Looking at him*)
If you are here to light my way,
You should have come much earlier.
There's not much sense in coming when
The sea's about to swallow me.
PASSENGER But would your victory be more sure
In a quiet corner by your fire?
PEER Who knows? Your talk has led nowhere.
Did you expect to give me faith?
PASSENGER Where I come from a smile is rated
Higher than affected pathos.
PEER There is a time for everything.
A proverb says that what is seemly
In a bartender would be
Quite outrageous in a bishop.

PASSENGER The Great Majority do not
Always strut about in buskins.
PEER You bugbear, you! Get off! Get off!
I won't die. I shall reach land yet.
PASSENGER Yes, ease your mind. One doesn't die
Half-way through the final act. (*Glides away*)
PEER He blurted it out in the end—
He was a tiresome moralist.

## Act Five, Scene Three

SCENE *A churchyard high up in the mountains. A funeral. A* PARSON *and congregation. The last verses of the psalm are being sung.* PEER GYNT *appears on the road outside the churchyard. He stops at the gate.*

PEER Here's another one gone the way of all flesh.
I can thank my stars it isn't me! (*Goes inside*)
PARSON (*At the graveside*)
Now, as his soul is summoned to his God,
And as his dust lies here, an empty shell,
Now, my dear friends, let us say a few words
About the dead man's pilgrimage on earth.
He was not rich nor was his mind profound;
He was not brave nor was his bearing manly.
In manner he was hesitant and shy.
He scarcely seemed master in his own house.
He crept into this church as though he begged
Our leave to be here and to pray with us.
He came from Gudbrandsdalen;[1] you all know
How he moved here while he was still a boy.
And I am sure that you must all remember
How his right hand was always in his pocket.
Indeed, it was that little mannerism,
Together with his awkwardness and shyness,
His silent, self-effacing reticence,
That stamped his image firmly on our minds.
But though he walked a lonely path among us,
Though he remained a stranger, we all knew—
Despite his vain attempts to hide the fact—
The hand he covered only had four fingers.
I can recall a morning, years ago;
The war was at its height and down at Lunde
Recruiting was in full swing. We knew too well
The dangers that confronted us. The captain
Sat at a table in between the Mayor
And sergeants. I was looking on. Recruits,
In turn, were being measured and examined,
Enrolled, sworn in and taken for the Army.
The room was full of men; outside we heard
A burst of laughter from the volunteers.
A name was called; another lad came in,
As white as snow around the glaciers.
His hand was wrapped in rags. They ordered him
To step up to the table where the captain
Interrogated him; and there the youth
Just stood and gasped, stuttered and swallowed, could
Not find his voice. And then, at last, he spoke.
His cheeks were burning and, from time to time,
His voice would fail him or his words would tumble
Over each other. In this way he mumbled
Something about a sickle that had slipped,
Gone through the bone and cut a finger off.
A silence fell. Quick glances shot across
The room. Lips curled; the silence stoned the boy.
He did not see their scorn and yet it stung him.
And then the captain, a grey-haired old man,
Got up and spat and pointed to the door
And said, "Get out!" The lad went. The crowd parted,
Making a path through which he had to run
The gauntlet to reach the door. Then he began
To race toward the hills. Up through the woods,
Over the rocks and boulders, stumbling, breathless.
His home was far away among the mountains.
It was six months before he joined us here;
His mother, baby, and betrothed were with him.
He leased some land upon the hillside where
The heath spreads out and reaches up to Lomb.[2]
The moment it was feasible he married,
Built his own house, broke up the stony ground
And worked and worked till patches of golden corn,
Billowing in his fields, told their own tale.
And yet, in church, that hand always remained
Deep in his pocket; but in his own home,
I am quite certain that he did as much
With nine fingers as others do with ten.
One spring, the floods came and his place was wrecked.
They managed to escape but they were left
Ruined and destitute; so, once again
Began the work of clearing and of building.
By autumn, smoke was rising from the chimneys
Of a more sheltered farm upon the mountains.
Did I say sheltered? Well, yes, from the floods,
But not from avalanches. Within two years,
His farm was lying underneath the snows.
And yet, not even avalanches could
Crush the man's courage. He dug, he cleared the snow,
Bore off the rubbish, stored his piles of logs,
And before winter came around again,
He built his humble home for the third time.
He had three sons, three splendid boys they were.
Their school was far away. Where the road stopped
They had to make their way across the narrow
Tracks and steep ice-fields. So, what did he do?
The eldest had to manage for himself;
But where the path grew difficult the man
Roped the boy to him. The other two he bore,
One in his arms, the second on his back.

[1] A deep valley in central Norway.

[2] A town in east central Norway.

And so he toiled, year in year out, till they
Were men. He had good reason now to hope
For some return from his three sons, from three
Rich gentlemen in the New World, but they
Forgot their father living here in Norway,
And the good schooling he had slaved to give them.
He was shortsighted. He could never see
Beyond the little circle of his home.
Words that should ring deep down in all men's hearts
Were distant bells to him; they struck no echo.
Fatherland, Race—ideals that shine so bright—
Were lost in mist before his swimming eyes.
But he was humble; yes, this man was humble.
And ever since that fateful day at Lunde,
The badge of shame was worn upon his heart
As surely as the blush upon his cheeks
And those four fingers hidden in his pocket.
A man who broke his country's laws? No doubt.
But just as clouds like soaring peaks climb over
The dazzling tent of Glittertind,[3] so there
Is something that stands higher than the law.
He was not a good patriot. To State
And Church he was a hollow pillar; but
Out on the barren moors, within his own
Family circle, where his life's work centered,
There he was great, because he was himself.
The substance of the inner man rang true.
His life was music played on muted strings.
So, rest in peace, you silent warrior,
Who fought the peasants' little fight and fell.
We will not search into his heart and veins;
That is no task for us but for his God.
But freely, and in all sincerity,
I hope that, as he takes his place before
His God, this man no longer is a cripple.

PEER Now that's what I call Christianity.
There was nothing to make you uncomfortable.
Yes, the subject of the parson's discourse,
The idea of always being yourself,
Is, in itself, most edifying.
(*Gazes into the grave*)
I wonder if this is the boy I saw
Slash off his finger that day I was chopping
Trees in the forest? Who knows? If I weren't
Standing here with my stick at the edge of the grave
Of this kindred spirit, I could imagine
That I, myself, was sleeping down there,
Hearing in dreams my own praises sung.
It's a most praiseworthy Christian custom
To review the life of the dear departed
With a charitable retrospective glance.
I, myself, would accept judgment willingly
From a parish priest as right-minded as this one.
Well, I daresay I've got a bit of time left
Before the gravedigger calls me home.
As the Bible says "The best is the best."
And further, "Sufficient for the day
Is the evil thereof." Still further on,
"Don't borrow for your funeral."
Yes, the Church is the only true Consoler;
And I've only just begun to see it.
And now I realize how good it is
To be assured by the well-informed
That "As ye sow so shall ye reap."
You must be yourself. In small things and great,
You must look to yourself. You must take great care
Of everything that belongs to yourself.
And then, if luck is dead against you,
At least the credit of having shaped
Your own divinity will be yours.
Now for home! Let the road be steep and narrow,
Let Fate be unkind to the very end,
Still old Peer Gynt will go his own way
And will be himself, poor but virtuous. (*Goes*)

[3] A tall mountain in east central Norway.

# Act Five, Scene Four

SCENE *A hill with a dry river-bed. A ruined mill on the bank of the river. The ground is broken up; there is desolation everywhere. Higher up is a big farm and outside it an auction is taking place. A large noisy crowd has gathered; a good deal of drinking is going on.* PEER GYNT *is sitting on a rubbish-heap near the mill.*

PEER Backward or forward it's just as far,
Within or without the path is as narrow.
Time and tide wait for no man. "Go round about,"
Said the Boyg, and it's what I must do here.

MAN IN MOURNING Now there's only the rubbish left.
(*Sees* PEER GYNT)
We have strangers, too! God bless you, my friend!

PEER Good day! This is quite a festive occasion.
Is it a christening or a wedding?

MAN IN MOURNING Call it rather a home-coming party.
The bride is asleep on a bed of worms.

PEER And worms are fighting for bits and pieces.

MAN IN MOURNING It is the end, the end of life's story.

PEER Every story is old, every story has
The same ending. I knew them when I was a boy.

YOUTH (*With a casting-ladle*)
Look at this! I've just bought it! Isn't it splendid?
Peer Gynt used to cast silver buttons in this.

SECOND YOUTH What about me? A purse for a ha'-penny!

THIRD YOUTH And me? A peddler's pack for twopence.

PEER Peer Gynt? Who was he?

MAN IN MOURNING I only know
That he was brother-in-law to Death
And to Aslak, the smith.

MAN IN GRAY You're forgetting me.
Are you drunk or mad?

MAN IN MOURNING You're forgetting the loft
At Heggstad.

MAN IN GRAY That's true! But when were you squeamish?

MAN IN MOURNING Supposing she plays fast and loose with Death!

MAN IN GREY Come along, have a drink with your brother-in-law.

MAN IN MOURNING Brother-in-law! Go to Hell! You're raving!

MAN IN GRAY Oh, nonsense! Blood isn't as watery as that!
We're both related somehow to Peer Gynt.
(*They go off together*)

PEER (*Softly*)
I *am* meeting old friends and no mistake.
(*A* BOY *calls after the* MAN IN MOURNING)

BOY Poor mother will haunt you, Aslak, if you
Start drinking again.

PEER (*Getting up*) The farmer's saying,
"The deeper you dig the better it smells,"
Doesn't hold.

YOUTH (*With bearskin*) Look here! It's the Dovre-cat! [1]
Or anyway, it's his skin. It's the one
Who went chasing the troll on Christmas Eve.

SECOND YOUTH (*With reindeer horns*)
Here's the reindeer's horns on which Peer Gynt
Went over the top of the Gendin Ridge.
(THIRD YOUTH, *holding a hammer, calls across to the* MAN IN MOURNING)

THIRD YOUTH Hi, you, Aslak, look at this hammer!
Was it the one you used when the Devil
Broke through the wall?

FOURTH YOUTH (*Empty-handed*) Mads Moen, here it is!
The invisible cloak in which Peer Gynt
And Ingrid flew off and disappeared!

PEER Some brandy here, boys! I'm feeling my age!
I'll put all my rubbish up to auction.

YOUTH What have you got?

PEER I've got a Palace
With big, thick walls. It's in the Ronde.

YOUTH I bid one button.

PEER Make it one tot.
It's a sin and a shame to bid less than that.

ANOTHER YOUTH He's a funny old fellow!
(*The people surge round him*)

PEER Grane, my horse!
Any bids?

ONE OF CROWD Where is he?

PEER Out in the west!
Near the setting sun, boys! Grane can run
As fast, yes as fast, as Peer Gynt could tell lies.

VOICES What else have you got?

PEER I've got gold and dross.
I bought them, soiled. I'll sell at a loss.

YOUTH Put them up!

PEER I've a dream about a prayer-book!
You can have it for a hook and eye.

YOUTH To the Devil with dreams!

[1] A legendary animal that frightened away the trolls in a haunted house.

PEER Then there's my Empire!
I'll toss it to you; you can scramble for it.

YOUTH Is the crown thrown in?

PEER A crown of straw!
It will fit the first man who tries it on.
Hi, there's still more! An addled egg!
A madman's gray hair! The prophet's beard!
I'll give the lot to the person who
Can show me the signpost out on the moor,
The signpost which says "This is the way."
(*A* REPRESENTATIVE OF THE LAW *arrives*)

REPRESENTATIVE OF LAW I don't like your behavior, my man.
Your signpost will take you straight to jail.

PEER (*Hat in hand*)
That may be, but tell me, who was Peer Gynt?

REPRESENTATIVE OF LAW What—!

PEER If you don't mind,
I'd like to find out.

REPRESENTATIVE OF LAW Well, they say he was a silly romancer.

PEER Romancer?

REPRESENTATIVE OF LAW Yes, he wove together
All the famous exploits he'd read about,
Then claimed them as his very own.
But excuse me, my friend, I've no time to waste.
(*Goes*)

PEER And where is he now, this remarkable fellow?

ELDERLY MAN He emigrated—some foreign land—
Went from bad to worse, as you might have guessed,
And got himself hanged. It was years ago.

PEER Hanged? Fancy that! I'm not really surprised.
The late Peer Gynt was himself to the end.
(*Bows*)
Good-by—and thank you all for your kindness.
(*Begins to go, then stops*)
All you happy men, all you pretty girls,
Would you like to hear one of my yarns?

VOICES What sort of yarns?

PEER Oh, quite simple ones.
(*He draws nearer. A strange look comes over his face*)
I used to dig gold in San Francisco.
The whole town was crammed with conjurers.
One played the fiddle with his toes,
Another could tango on his knees,
A third, I was told, kept on making rhymes
While his skull was being bored through and through.
One day, the Devil turned up at the Fair;
He wanted to try his luck as well.
He had the knack of being able
To grunt like a pig; it was true to life.
Although nobody recognized him,
His personality drew the crowds.
The house was full and expectations
Rose to fever-heat. Then he went on,
Wearing a long and flowing cape—
*"Man muss sich drapieren,"* [2] as the Germans say.
But under the cape—and no one knew it—
He'd managed to stow away a pig.

[2] "A person must be covered."

The show began. The Devil pinched
The pig, which squealed. The whole show was meant
To be a fantasy on the life
Of a pig from the suckling stage to the final
Squeal at the thrust of the slaughterer's knife.
At the finish, the artist bowed low and went off.
Critics discussed the actor's performance.
Opinions varied. Some praised, some condemned.
Some thought the tone of the squeals too thin;
Others considered the death-shriek too studied.
But on one thing everyone agreed—
That the act *qua* grunt was overdone
Ridiculously. That's what Satan got
For his crass stupidity in failing
To take the measure of his public.
(*He bows and goes. An uneasy silence falls on the crowd*)

## Act Five, Scene Five

SCENE *Whitsun eve. In the depths of the forest. Farther away, in a clearing, is a hut with reindeer antlers over the door.* PEER GYNT *is on his hands and knees in the undergrowth gathering wild onions.*

PEER This is one point of view. Where is the next one?
You must try everything, then choose the best.
Well, I've done that. I was Cæsar once.
And now I'm another Nebuchadnezzar.
I'm going right through Bible history.
This old boy's gone back to his mother again.
Of course, the Bible says, "Dust thou art!"
The main thing in life is to fill your belly.
Fill it with onions? No, that won't do.
I will be cunning. I'll set some snares.
There's a stream near by so I'll never be thirsty.
I'll still be a lord of creation here.
And when I die—as I dare say I will—
I'll creep under a tree blown down by the wind;
I'll cover myself with leaves, like a bear,
And on the bark I'll scratch in big letters,
"Here lies Peer Gynt, quite a decent fellow,
Emperor over all the beasts."
Emperor? (*Laughs to himself*)
You silly old buffoon!
You're no Emperor; you are just an onion.
And I'm going to peel you, my dear Peer!
Neither tears nor prayers will help you now.
(*Takes an onion and peels it layer by layer*)
There's the outer layer, all bruised and broken;
It's the drowning man hanging on to the wreck.
This is the wisp of a passenger;
He seems to taste a bit like Peer Gynt.
And inside here is the gold-digging "I."
The juice has gone—if it ever had any.
This layer here with the hard coarse skin
Is the fur-trapper of Hudson's Bay.
The next layer's like a crown. Thank you!
We'll throw it away without more ado.
Here's the archæologist, short but powerful,
And here is the prophet, juicy and fresh;
He stinks, as the proverb says, of lies,
Enough to bring tears to an honest man's eyes.
This layer, so soft and immaculate,
Is the man who lived for gaiety.
The next one looks poorly; it's shot through with black.
It brings Negroes and missionaries to mind.
(*Picks several at a time*)
There's quite a multitude of layers.
When am I going to get to the heart?
(*Pulls the whole onion to pieces*)
God, it hasn't got one! Right to the middle,
It's layers and layers, each getting smaller.
Nature is witty!
(*Throws the bits away*)
To Hell with thought!
Once you start thinking, you start stumbling, too.
As a matter of fact, I can smile at that danger;
I seem to be firmly set on all fours.
(*Scratches the back of his neck*)
Life itself is really a funny affair.
People say it pulls the wool over your eyes,
You make a grab for it—and it's gone,
And you get the wrong thing—or nothing at all.
(*He has approached close to the hut. He sees it and starts*)
That hut? In the forest! But—
(*Rubs his eyes*)
I could swear—!
I know I've seen this building before.
Those reindeer antlers over the door!
That mermaid with the long swishing tail—
Lies! It's no mermaid but nails and boards,
And a bolt to keep out hobgoblin thoughts!
(SOLVEIG'S *voice is heard in the hut*)

SOLVEIG Now all is ready for Pentecost,
Dear love of mine so far away,
When will you come back?
Your burden is heavy?
Then rest, rest awhile;
I will wait, I promised
You long, long ago. . . .
(PEER GYNT *rises, white as death*)

PEER One who remembered, and one who forgot,
One who had faith, and one who had none.
The game is over; my race is run!
What a trickster is Fate! My Empire was here.

## Act Five, Scene Six

SCENE *Night. A moor with pine trees. The place has been ravaged by a forest fire; charred tree trunks can be seen for miles around. Patches of mist here and there on the ground.* PEER GYNT *runs in across the moor.*

PEER Ashes, mists and driving dust-storms—
They're the stuff from which to build!
Stench and rottenness inside them;
All a whited sepulcher.
Dreams, romance, and still-born wisdom
For foundations, and above
The pyramid will rise complete
With its steps and stairs of lies.
"Flight from truth and from repentance."
Let it fly out like a banner,
Let the horn of doom ring out with
*"Petrus Gyntus Cæsar fecit."* [1]
(*Listens*)
I hear the sound of children weeping,
Weeping that is half a song.
Threadballs are rolling at my feet!
(*Kicking them*)
Get away! You block the path!

THREADBALLS (*On the ground*)
We are thoughts;
You should have thought us!
Legs to move on,
You should have brought us!

PEER Once, I gave life to a thought;
It was deformed, with crooked legs.

THREADBALLS
We should have soared skyward,
A tremulous choir.
Instead, as gray threadballs,
We roll in the mire.

PEER (*Stumbling*)
Threadballs, you confounded devils!
Are you tripping up your father?
(*Runs away*)

WITHERED LEAVES (*Flying before the wind*)
We are passwords;
You should have known us!
See where your indolence
Has torn and blown us.
The worm has gnawed us
In every vein;
We have never warmed
The fruit within.

PEER Despite that, you weren't born in vain;
Lie still; you'll make a good manure.

A SIGHING IN THE AIR
We are songs
You have left unsung!
In the depths of your heart
To hope we clung.
A thousand times over
We were stifled and killed;
We were never called;
May your voice be stilled!

PEER Be stilled yourself, with your rhyme and curse!
What time have I for nonsense verse?
(*Turns aside*)

DEWDROPS (*Dripping from the trees*)
We are tears
That would never fall!
We could have melted
The ice-spears of gall.
Now the barb remains
In the stubborn breast;
The wound is closed;
Our power has passed.

PEER Thanks—I wept in Rondesvalen,[2]
And got a kick in the behind!

BROKEN STRAWS
We are deeds
You have left undone!
Doubt, the Destroyer,
Assailed us and won.
On the Day of Judgment
We shall be there
To tell our story
And then, beware!

PEER You rascals! Would you dare to censure
Me for what I haven't done?
(*Runs away*)

AASE'S VOICE (*Far away*)
Pshaw! What a driver!
You've thrown me in
To an icy puddle;
I'm soaked to the skin!
You're on the wrong road, Peer;
Where is the Castle?
The Devil's misled you
With that whip you've got there.

PEER I think I'd better hurry off.
I'd sink into the hillside if
I had to bear the Devil's sins.
My own are hard enough to carry.
(*Runs away*)

[1] Made by the Emperor, Peer Gynt."

[2] The Ronde cloisters.

# Act Five, Scene Seven

SCENE *Part of the moor.*

PEER (*Singing*)
A sexton, a sexton! Where are you, you hounds?
Bleating notes from the preceptors' mouths.
Around your hats, black mourning-bands!
Let me follow the coffins of my dear friends!
(*The* BUTTON MOLDER, *with his box of tools and a large casting-ladle, enters from the side-path*)

BUTTON MOLDER
Good evening, old man!

PEER Good evening, my friend!
BUTTON MOLDER
You're in a great hurry. Where are you off to?
PEER A funeral.
BUTTON MOLDER Oh? My sight's not so good—
Excuse me—your name isn't Peer, I suppose?
PEER Yes, it is—Peer Gynt.
BUTTON MOLDER Well, I call that luck!
I've been searching for Peer Gynt everywhere.
PEER Oh? What do you want?
BUTTON MOLDER You can see what I am.
I'm a button molder. I want you for my spoon.
PEER What for?
BUTTON MOLDER You are to be melted down.
PEER Melted?
BUTTON MOLDER
Yes, look! It's been cleaned and it's empty.
Your grave is dug, your coffin is ready.
The worms will have a high time with your carcass.
I have orders from here from my Employer
To bring Him your soul without any delay.
PEER You can't do that! I've had no warning.
BUTTON MOLDER
It's the custom at funerals and births
To give the guest a tremendous surprise.
No one ever tells him the fateful day.
PEER Yes, I know. My brain is in a whirl.
You are—?
BUTTON MOLDER I told you! A button molder.
PEER I see! But a pet child has lots of nicknames.
So it's come to this, Peer, you end up in that spoon!
But, my good man, surely there's some mistake.
I'm worthy of better treatment than this;
I'm not as bad as you seem to think;
I've done my share of good deeds on earth;
At the worst, I'm no more than a bungling ass;
I'm certainly not a confirmed reprobate.
BUTTON MOLDER
You're getting away from the point, my dear man.
Because your sins were such puny ones
You're being let off perpetual torment
And are ending, like most, in the casting-ladle.
PEER Call it what you like—ladle or sulphur-pool,
Light ale or dark ale—they're both of them ale,
Get behind me, Satan.
BUTTON MOLDER You can't be so rude
As to think my foot is a horse's hoof?
PEER A horse's hoof or a fox's claw!
Off you go! And stick to your own affairs!
BUTTON MOLDER
My friend, you're making a great mistake.
As we're both in a hurry I'll put the case
As concisely as possible. It will save time.
You are not, as you yourself have confessed,
A sinner in a magnificent way.
You're about mediocre——
PEER Well, you're beginning
To talk sense at last.
BUTTON MOLDER Now wait a minute!
I'd be going too far if I called you righteous.
PEER That's something I would never expect.
BUTTON MOLDER You've steered the usual middle course.
A sinner in the really grand manner
Is hardly ever met nowadays.
There's more to it than wallowing in filth.
Strength and purpose are needed for epic sinning.
PEER What you've said just now is true enough;
You must rush at it like the berserkers.
BUTTON MOLDER
You didn't do that; you took sin lightly.
PEER Superficially, like a splash of mud.
BUTTON MOLDER
Now we're reaching agreement. The sulphur-pool
Is not for those who have splashed in the mud——
PEER And therefore, my friend, I can go as I came?
BUTTON MOLDER
And therefore, my friend, you'll be melted down.
PEER What sort of dodges have you been up to
Here at home while I've been abroad?
BUTTON MOLDER
The method's as old as the world's creation.
Its aim is the conservation of matter.
You know the trade, so you're well aware
That a casting may frequently have a flaw.
For example, a button may have no loop.
What would you have done with it?
PEER Thrown it away.
BUTTON MOLDER
Oh yes! John Gynt was a squanderer
As long as he had something left in his pocket.
But my Employer is very careful;
That's why he's become so prosperous.
He throws nothing away; he finds a use
For the useless as raw material.
You were going to be a shining button
On the world's waistcoat; but your loop gave way.
So you must be merged into the mass.
PEER You don't mean that you're going to melt me down
With any old Tom, Dick and Harry into
Something new?
BUTTON MOLDER That's exactly what I do mean.
We've done that with others, time and again.
They do the same thing at the Mint with coins
Which have worn thin with being handled too much.
PEER It's nothing but out-and-out stinginess!
My dear old friend, won't you let me off?
A button with no loop! A shilling worn smooth!
What are they to a man of your Master's standing?
BUTTON MOLDER
Oh, you have a soul and that's sufficient
To give you some value as metal-scrap.
PEER No, I say, no; I'll fight to the end.
I protest! I'd do anything rather than that.
BUTTON MOLDER
But what else is there? Come, be sensible.
You'd never feel at home in Heaven.
PEER I'm easy to please. I don't aim so high.
But I won't give up a jot of myself.
Judge me in the good old-fashioned way,
Send me to Him with the hoof for a time,

A hundred years if you think I deserve it;
I fancy I'd manage to last it out.
After all, it would only be moral torture,
So it wouldn't be really unbearable.
It's a transition stage, as the proverb has it;
Or as the fox said, "You wait and the hour
Of deliverance comes, and you double back
And hope that better days will come."
But this other thing—to have to be merged
Into some other body, a particle,
This ladle-business, this ending at Gynt—
My innermost soul rebels at it.

BUTTON MOLDER
But, my dear Peer, it's really unnecessary
To take on so much about such a small thing.
You have never really been yourself,
So why bother now if you go for good?

PEER I've not been myself! I could almost laugh!
Peer Gynt not himself! Well, well, we shall see!
No, Button Molder, your judgment is blind;
If you could see right into my mind,
Then and only then you would meet me, Peer,
And nothing but Peer and nothing else.

BUTTON MOLDER
That's quite impossible. Here are my orders.
They're in black and white: "You will bring Peer Gynt.
He has defied his life's destiny.
To the ladle with him as damaged goods!"

PEER What nonsense! They must mean somebody else.
Does it really say "Peer"? Not Rasmus nor John?

BUTTON MOLDER
I melted them down a long time ago.
Now come with a good grace and don't waste time.

PEER I'm damned if I will! A very nice thing
If you found out later you'd made a mistake!
You'd better take care, my man. Just think
Of the onus attached.

BUTTON MOLDER It's in writing here.

PEER Give me time.

BUTTON MOLDER Why should I?

PEER I'll go and get proof.
That I've been myself as long as I've lived.
That's the crux of our argument, isn't it?

BUTTON MOLDER Proof? How?

PEER Witnesses? Certificates!

BUTTON MOLDER
I'm afraid my Employer won't be impressed.

PEER I'm sure he would. However, "Sufficient
For the day is the evil thereof." My friend,
Only let me loan myself out on trust.
I'll soon be back. We're only born once,
So we do our best to cling to the self
That was born with us. Well? Do you agree?

BUTTON MOLDER Very well then, we'll let it go at that.
But remember, we'll meet at the next crossroads.
(PEER GYNT *runs away*)

# Act Five, Scene Eight

SCENE *Another part of the moors.* PEER GYNT *runs in.*

PEER Time is money; the good book says so.
If only I knew where the crossroads are!
They may be near and they may be far.
The earth is burning like red-hot iron.
A witness! A witness! Where's a witness?
I won't find one here in the depths of the forest.
A world where a man has to prove his rights
Which are clear as daylight, must be in a mess.
It's badly managed!
(*A bent old man with a staff in his hand and a bag on his back is trundling along in front of* PEER. *He is the* KING OF THE DOVRE MOUNTAINS)

KING (*Stopping*) Please, sir, a coin
For a homeless beggar.

PEER I've no small change.

KING Prince Peer! Just fancy us meeting again!

PEER Who are you?

KING You remember the Dovre King?

PEER You're never——

KING The King of the Ronde mountains!

PEER The Dovre King? Really? The Troll King? Tell me!

KING Yes, but I'm not what I used to be.

PEER Ruined?

KING And robbed; stripped of everything;
I'm a tramp now, as hungry as a wolf!

PEER Hurrah! You're the witness I'm looking for!

KING Prince Peer, you've aged a bit since our meeting.

PEER Dear Father-in-law, the years gobble us up.
Well, an armistice to our private affairs,
And above all to our family quarrels.
When we met before I was just a raw youth.

KING Prince Peer, you were young and youth will be served.
And you did the right thing when you threw your bride over.
You've saved yourself lots of shame and distress.
Later on, she went to the bad completely.

PEER Really?

KING She's just an abandoned woman.
Only think—she's living with that dirty Trond.

PEER Which Trond?

KING Of Valfjeld.

PEER That one? Aha!
I took his three cowherd-girls from him.

KING But my grandson has grown fat and prosperous;
He has bouncing babies all over the land.

PEER My dear man, please spare me these intimate details;
Something else is preying on my mind.
I happen to be in serious trouble—
I want a good-conduct certificate.
Now, you can help me, dear Father-in-law;

In return, I daresay I could stand you a drink.
KING Can I really help you in any way, Prince?
Will you give me a character in return?
PEER Certainly. At present I'm rather hard up.
I have to stint and save what I can.
Now listen, I'll tell you what it's about.
You remember the day I arrived in the Ronde
And asked you for your daughter's hand?
KING Of course I do, Prince!
PEER Drop this "Prince" business.
You wanted to lay rough hands on me,
Slit the lens of my eye, make me see awry
And transform Peer Gynt into a troll.
What did I do then? I rose up and fought you;
I swore that I'd stand on my own firm feet;
I rejected love and power and a kingdom,
Gave up everything just to be myself.
And that's what I'd like you to swear to when——
KING No, I can't.
PEER What are you talking about?
KING You wouldn't want me to tell lies, would you?
Don't you remember wearing a tail,
Drinking our mead?
PEER Yes, you coaxed me to do it;
But I lasted out and I won in the end.
A man is judged by such deeds as that.
The last verse is always the one that counts.
KING But, Peer, the result was just the reverse.
PEER What do you mean?
KING When you left my palace,
You'd written my motto on your coat-of-arms.
PEER What motto?
KING That all-embracing word——
PEER What word?
KING The word that distinguishes
Human beings from trolls, "Troll, to thyself
Be—enough."
PEER (*Stepping back*) Enough!
KING And that's how you've lived
With every fibre of your being.
PEER What? I? Peer Gynt?
KING (*Weeping*) You're very ungrateful.
You've lived like a troll but you've kept it dark.
The word I taught you established you
As a man of the world; it gave you fame.
And now you come here and start to sneer
At me and the word that gave you so much.
PEER Enough! A troll! Just an egoist!
It's a lot of rubbish! I'm certain it is!
(*The old man pulls out a bundle of newspapers*)
KING I expect you think we have no papers.
Look! In black and white! For all eyes to see!
How the *Bloksberg*[1] *Post* has been patting your back
And the *Heklefjeld*[1] *Express* as well,
Ever since that winter you went away.
Would you like to read them, Peer? Here, take a look!
Here's a leader signed by "Stallion's Hoof."
Here's another on "Troll Nationalism."

[1] Bloksberg and Heklefjeld were regarded as meeting places of witches.

The writer shows that you don't have to wear
A horn or a tail to be a troll.
The feeling! The outlook! That's what matters!
"Our 'Enough,'" he ends, "gives the character
Of Trolldom to Man"; and then he cites
The case of Peer Gynt as the best example.
PEER A troll? I!
KING Yes, that seems perfectly clear.
PEER I might just as well have stayed where I was,
And lived in the Ronde in comfort and peace,
And saved myself shoe-leather, toil and trouble!
Peer Gynt—a troll! It's nonsense! It's lies!
Good-bye! Here's a penny to buy tobacco!
KING Dear Prince Peer——
PEER Stop all that! You're mad or else
You're doting. Go off to a hospital.
KING That's the very thing I'm looking for.
But, as I've told you, my grandson's offspring
Are very powerful in the country;
They're spreading the news that I'm only a myth.
People say you should never trust relatives;
To my sorrow, I've learned how true it is.
It's hard to think I'm only a myth.
PEER My dear man, it's happened to others as well.
KING And we trolls can't depend on a Pension Fund,
Nor Post Office Books, nor alms-boxes.
They would be incongruous in the Ronde.
PEER No, the only things that mattered up there
Were those cursed words, "To thyself be—enough."
KING Prince Peer, you should be the last to complain.
And if, in some way or other, you could——
PEER My man, I'm afraid you're on the wrong scent.
The wolf's at my door; you know what that means.
KING You don't say so! You? A beggar, too?
PEER Stony-broke! My princely "self" is in pawn;
And who have I got to thank for that?
You trolls! Now, you see what low company does!
KING So my hope's gone west! Good-by! I must
Make my way into town somehow or other.
PEER What will you do there?
KING I'll go on the stage.
They're on the look out for native talent.
PEER The best of luck! Give them greetings from me.
If I can get free I'll do the same thing.
I'm going to write a comedy,
Profound and witty in turns. It will
Be called, *"Sic transit gloria mundi."*
(*Goes off along the path leaving the old man shouting after him*)

## Act Five, Scene Nine

SCENE *Crossroads.*

PEER You're in for a nasty time, friend Peer;
The trolls' "Enough" has let you down.

Your ship has sunk; you must cling to a spar,
To anything, rather than go to the scrap-heap.
BUTTON MOLDER (*At the crossroads*)
Well, Peer Gynt, where's your certificate?
PEER What? Crossroads again? That was pretty quick.
BUTTON MOLDER I can read your face like an open book.
I don't need the papers to tell me the news.
PEER I'm worn out with looking; you soon get lost.
BUTTON MOLDER
And besides, where is your road leading you?
PEER Yes, where? In the forest at nightfall, too——
BUTTON MOLDER
There's an old tramp there; shall we call him over?
PEER No, let him go! He's drunk, anyway!
BUTTON MOLDER But he might be able——
PEER No, let him go!
BUTTON MOLDER Well then, let's begin.
PEER A question first:
What do you mean by "being yourself"?
BUTTON MOLDER
That's an astounding question from you.
Why, a moment ago——
PEER Come, come, answer me.
BUTTON MOLDER To be yourself is to kill the worst
And so to bring out the best in yourself.
But I'm certain that would be lost on you,
So let's put it more simply: To carry out
The Master's intention in every detail.
PEER How about the man who has never learned
What the Master intended to do with him?
BUTTON MOLDER His intuition should tell him that.
PEER Intuitions are frequently wide of the mark.
They may send you *"ad undas"* [1] and kill your career.
BUTTON MOLDER
That's true, but when you lack intuition
You give the Devil his opening.
PEER This is a very knotty affair.
I'll waive my plea about being myself.
It wouldn't be easy to prove, anyhow.
I'll accept that part of the case as lost.
But as I was roaming the moors just before,
I felt the shoes of my conscience pinch,
And I said to myself, "Yes, you're a sinner——"
BUTTON MOLDER
Now, you're beginning all over again——
PEER No, I'm not; I mean sinning on the grand scale,
Not in deeds alone but in purpose and word.
When I was abroad I sank so low——
BUTTON MOLDER
So you say, but why don't you show me the proof?
PEER Give me time; I'll go and find a parson,
Confess at top speed and bring you his notes.
BUTTON MOLDER All right! If you can confirm your claim,
You may yet keep out of the casting-ladle.
But my orders, Peer——
PEER It was years ago;
It goes back to the days when I was a young fool,
When I believed in Fate, when I played at being

[1] "Into the waves."

A prophet. Well? May I . . . ?
BUTTON MOLDER But——
PEER My dear friend,
You haven't got much to do, after all;
And the air round here's so keen and crisp
That it adds years and years to the normal span.
The parson at Justedal always said,
"Hardly anyone ever dies down here." [2]
BUTTON MOLDER
To the next crossroads, then, but no further than that
PEER A parson! I must get hold of a parson
Even if I have to handcuff him.

# Act Five, Scene Ten

SCENE *A heather slope. A road winds away upward into the mountains.*

PEER "This may come in useful for many things,"
Said Esben,[1] when he found the magpie's wing.
Who would have thought that these sins of mine
Would have got me out of that last-minute scrape?
In any case, it's a rotten position.
I may jump from the frying-pan into the fire.
But there's also a saying that has stood
The test of time, "While there's life there's hope."
(*A thin person, wearing a cassock well hitched up, and carrying a fowler's net over his shoulder, comes running down the path*)
Who's there? A priest with a fowling-net?
Heigho! I seem to be in luck's way!
Good evening, sir! This road's hard going.
THIN MAN I agree, but I'd go through more than this
For a soul.
PEER So there's someone on his way
To Heaven.
THIN MAN I hope to the other place.
PEER Do you mind if I walk with you part of the way?
THIN MAN Not at all! I'm looking for company.
PEER I'm very worried——
THIN MAN *Heraus!* Out with it!
PEER You'll find that I'm quite a respectable fellow;
I've kept to the law most scrupulously;
I have never been handcuffed nor put behind bars;
Yet, the best of us sometimes loses his way
And stumbles——
THIN MAN That might happen to anyone.
PEER You see, these little things——
THIN MAN Are they so little?

[2] A humorous reference to a pastor named Matthias Foss, who wrote a description of the area in 1750, pointing out the long lives of the local inhabitants.

[1] A figure in a folk tale who finds things of apparently no value which make it possible for him to marry a princess.

PEER Yes, I've managed to steer clear of sins *en gros.*
THIN MAN In that case, old chap, you can leave me in peace;
I'm not what you seem to think I am.
You appear very interested in my hands?
PEER Your nails are very well manicured.
THIN MAN And my feet? You're having a jolly good look.
PEER (*Pointing*)
Is that hoof natural?
THIN MAN I flatter myself
That it is.
PEER (*Lifting his hat*) I'd have sworn you were a priest.
So I have the honor—the best is the best.
When the front door's open, you don't try the back;
When you meet a king, you don't bother with lackeys.
THIN MAN
Shake hands. You don't seem the least bit biased.
Well, well! And what can I do for you?
No, don't start asking for money or power.
I couldn't oblige you for anything.
There's been an awful slump in business;
Trade has gone completely to pot;
New souls are rare; now and then, an odd one——
PEER Has Mankind improved so noticeably?
THIN MAN On the contrary, he gets worse and worse;
Most people end up in the casting-ladle.
PEER I've heard more than enough about that ladle;
It's in that connection that I am here.
THIN MAN What's on your mind?
PEER Would it look very bad
If I asked you for——
THIN MAN A decent home, eh?
PEER You've guessed what I want before I ask.
Trade has, as you've said, gone to rack and ruin,
So you need not be overscrupulous——
THIN MAN My dear fellow——
PEER My needs are quite moderate.
I don't even ask for a living wage.
I just want to be a friendly tenant.
THIN MAN A warm room?
PEER Not too warm and, if possible,
Permission to come and go, as I like;
And the right—may I call it such?—to move out
Should the chance of better times come round.
THIN MAN
My dear friend, it hurts me; you'd hardly believe
What a glut of similar applications
Comes from other dear friends when they learn
That they're going to leave their earthly home.
PEER But when I consider my past behavior,
I feel I've more than a right to get in.
THIN MAN But your sins were such little ones.
PEER Yes, in a way—
If you exclude my traffic in niggers.
THIN MAN
There were some who trafficked in minds and souls,
But who messed it up badly and weren't allowed in.
PEER What about the idols I sent to China?
THIN MAN Fatuous stuff! It just makes us laugh.
There are people who've sent out far worse muck
In sermons and art and literature,
And they've had to stay outside. . . .
PEER Do you know
I once pretended to be a prophet?
THIN MAN
Overseas? Pure nonsense! Most people's *Sehen Ins blaue*[2] ends in the casting-ladle.
If that's all you've got to support your case
Then I can't let you in, however much
I might want to.
PEER Then listen. When I was shipwrecked
I scrambled onto an upturned boat.
There's a proverb, "A drowning man grasps at a straw."
There's another one, "Every man for himself."
Well, I, more or less, robbed the cook of his life.
THIN MAN I wouldn't care if you'd, more or less,
Robbed your kitchenmaid of something else.
What's all this talk about "more or less"?
With all due deference let me ask you,
Who's going to throw away precious fuel
In times like these on such feeble stuff?
Now don't lose your temper; it's your sins
I'm mocking—forgive me for being so frank.
Come, come, dearest friend, forget the idea;
Prepare yourself for the casting-ladle.
What would you gain if I gave you board
And lodging? Just think; you're a sensible man.
Well, you'd keep your memory; perfectly true!
And what would that do for you? Neither your heart
Nor your head would get any pleasure from it.
No! You'd get what the Swedes call, "Very poor sport."
You've little to laugh or to cry about,
Nothing to make you rejoice or despair,
Nothing to make you go hot or cold,
But only a constant anxiety.
PEER They say you can't find out where the shoe
Is pinching when you're not wearing it.
THIN MAN That's quite true. Thanks be to so-and-so,
I only wear one shoe. All the same,
It was fortunate that we talked about shoes;
It reminds me I must be going at once.
I'm collecting a steak; I hope he turns out
Nice and juicy. I'm off! No time for gossip.
PEER And may I ask what misdemeanors
Have fattened this friend of yours?
THIN MAN I believe
He has been himself by night and by day;
And that, at bottom, is the chief thing.
PEER Himself? Then does that sort belong to you?
THIN MAN They may or may not; the door's always ajar.
Remember that you can be yourself
In two sorts of ways—the right and the wrong.
Perhaps you know that someone in Paris
Has recently found out how to make
Portraits by using the sun. You can get

[2] "Gaze into the distance."

Direct pictures or else what are known
As negatives. Light and shade are reversed
In the latter, and to the unpracticed eye
They're not attractive, but the likeness is there,
And it only remains to bring it out.
Now if, in the course of its life, a soul
Has portrayed itself in the negative way,
The plate is sent on to me. It is not
Discarded. I start to work on it,
And the metamorphosis takes place.
I dip it and steam it, burn it and clean it
With sulphur and other chemicals
Until the picture that should have appeared
*Does* appear; we call it the positive.
But if anyone goes and does what you've done
And, more or less, blots himself out, then no
Amount of sulphur or potash will help.

PEER So they go to you as black as a raven
And leave you as white as a ptarmigan?
Dare I ask you whose the negative is
That you're turning into a positive now?

THIN MAN The name's Peter Gynt.

PEER Peter Gynt indeed?
And is he himself?

THIN MAN He swears he is.

PEER He's a trustworthy man—this Peter Gynt.

THIN MAN You know him?

PEER Oh yes, we're on nodding terms.
A sort of acquaintance, you know.

THIN MAN I'm late.
Where did you see him last?

PEER Down at the Cape.

THIN MAN *Di Buona Speranza?* [3]

PEER Yes, but I don't
Expect he'll be staying there much longer.

THIN MAN Then I must fly. I hope I don't miss him.
The Cape, the Cape! Not a very good spot;
Full of missionaries from Stavanger.[4]
(*Races off southward*)

PEER The dirty dog! Look at him bounding away
With his dribbling tongue; he'll be disappointed.
It was very nice to take in such an ass.
The airs he gives himself! Oh, the grand lord!
He's got a fat lot to swank about!
And he won't get rich on his present job;
He'll fall from his perch with his whole bag of tricks.
Not that I'm safe in the saddle myself!
The "self" nobility's thrown me out.
(*A shooting star is seen. He nods after it*)
Greetings from Peer Gynt, brother shooting star!
Shine forth, be extinguished, disappear for ever.
(*He seems to draw into himself as if in fear; he goes deeper into the mists. Quiet for a time, then he shouts*)
Is there no one, no one in this great world,
No one in the depths, no one in Heaven?
(*Returns, throws his hat on the ground and tears his hair. Gradually, a great stillness comes over him*)
So a soul can go back, so wretchedly poor,
Into the grey mists of nothingness.
Beautiful earth, do not be angry
That I have trod you and left no mark.
Beautiful sun, you have squandered your light,
Your glorious light, on an empty house.
There was no one within to be heartened and cheered:
The owner had gone. You beautiful sun,
You beautiful earth who wasted your warmth
And sustenance on my mother's womb!
How mean is the spirit, how lavish is nature!
How costly to pay with one's life for one's birth!
I will climb to the top of the highest peak,
I will see the sun rise once again,
I will gaze on the promised land till my eyes
Are tired out. Then let the snow pile over me,
And above my tomb write, "Here No One is buried."
And afterwards, well—let come what will.

CHURCHGOERS (*Singing on the path*)
Most blessed of mornings,
When the tongues of the Kingdom of God
Struck the earth like flaming swords!
Now His sons' hymns rise up
From the earth to His Heaven
In the tongue of the Kingdom of God.
(PEER GYNT *shrinks into himself in fright*)

PEER No, don't look there; it's a desert waste.
Alas! I was dead long before my death.
(*He tries to creep in among the bushes but comes out on the crossroads*)

BUTTON MOLDER
Good morning, Peer Gynt! Where's your list of sins?

PEER I've shouted and whistled all over the place.

BUTTON MOLDER And you've seen no one?

PEER A traveling
Photographer

BUTTON MOLDER Then your time is up.

PEER Everything is up. Can you hear that owl
Hooting? He must have smelled the dawn.

BUTTON MOLDER It's the matins ringing.

PEER (*Pointing*) What's that light over there?

BUTTON MOLDER Only a cottage.

PEER I can hear a sound
Like the wind in the trees.

BUTTON MOLDER It's a woman singing.

PEER There—there I shall find my list of sins.
(*The* BUTTON MOLDER *takes hold of him*)

BUTTON MOLDER It's time to set your house in order.
(*They have come out of the thicket and are standing near the hut. Dawn*)

PEER Set my house in order? It's there! Clear off!
If your ladle were as big as a coffin,
It would still be too small for me and my list.

BUTTON MOLDER
To the third crossroads, Peer Gynt, but then——!
(*Turns away and goes*)

PEER (*Approaching the hut*)
Backward or forward, it's just as far,
Within or without the path is as narrow. (*Stops*)
No! I can hear it—a wild endless cry

[3] "The Cape of Good Hope."
[4] Seat of the Norwegian Missionary Society.

Telling me go in, go back, go back home.
(*Advances a few steps but stops again*)
"Round about," said the Boyg.
(*Hears singing in the hut*)
No! No! This time,
It's straight through no matter how narrow the path!
(*He runs toward the hut. At that moment* SOLVEIG *comes out. She is dressed for church, and her prayer-book is wrapped in a handkerchief; she carries a stick in her hand. She stands there erect and gentle.* PEER GYNT *throws himself down on the threshold*)
Pass judgment on the sinner before you!

SOLVEIG It is he! It is he! Praise be to God!
(*She gropes for him*)

PEER Cry out how wickedly I have sinned!

SOLVEIG You have sinned in nothing, my only love.
(*Gropes for him again and finds him*)

BUTTON MOLDER (*Behind the hut*)
The list, Peer Gynt?

PEER Cry my sins aloud!

SOLVEIG (*Sitting down beside him*)
You have made my life a beautiful song.
Bless you for having come back at last!
And blessed, oh, blessed, be this Whitsun morn!

PEER I am lost!

SOLVEIG There is One who understands.

PEER (*Laughs*) Lost! Unless you can answer a riddle!

SOLVEIG Ask it!

PEER Ask it? Yes, you must answer it.
Can you tell me where Peer Gynt has been
Since you saw him last?

SOLVEIG Where he has been?

PEER With the mark of destiny on his brow,
Where has he been since he first sprang forth
As a thought newly born in the mind of God?
Can you tell me that? If not I must go
Home to the land of the valley of shadows.

SOLVEIG (*Smiling*)
Your riddle is easy.

PEER Then tell me, where
Was I, my real self, my whole self, my true self?
Where was I, with God's seal upon my brow?

SOLVEIG In my faith, my hope and in my love.

PEER (*Starting back*)
What are you saying? *You're* talking in riddles.
You speak as a mother speaks of her child.

SOLVEIG That is true; but who is his father? He
Who forgives in answer to a mother's prayers.
(*A gleam of light seems to break over* PEER GYNT. *He cries out*)

PEER My Mother! My wife! You holy woman!
Oh, hide me, hide me within your love!
(*He clings to her and hides his face in her lap. A long silence. The sun rises*)

SOLVEIG (*Singing softly*)
Sleep, my dear, my dearest love!
I will rock you and watch beside you.
The boy has sat on his mother's lap.
They've played together the whole day long.
The boy shall lie in his mother's arms
The whole day long. God bless you, my love!
The boy shall lie against his mother's heart
The whole day long. He is weary now.
Sleep, my dear, my precious one, sleep, sleep.
I will rock you, my boy, my darling. Sleep, sleep.

BUTTON MOLDER'S VOICE (*Behind hut*)
We shall meet at the last crossroads, Peer,
And then we'll see if—— I say no more.

SOLVEIG (*Singing louder as the sunshine bursts forth*)
I will rock you and watch beside you.
Sleep and dream, my own dear love!

*Curtain*

# GHOSTS

IBSEN completed *Ghosts* at Rome in the summer and fall of 1881, but he had thought about the play and had begun working on it several months earlier. Its origins lie in the same intellectual ferment which gave rise to *A Doll's House*; despite Ibsen's disclaimer, *Ghosts* can be viewed as a sequel to the immediately preceding drama. It is unmistakably the playwright's answer to the orthodox moralists who condemned Nora for walking out on her husband and children. Mrs. Alving is a Nora who stayed, and her misfortunes and those of Osvald are the consequence of her failure of nerve. Both plays examine in different ways the price a woman has to pay for the assertion of her individuality and freedom, but Ibsen was no militant feminist; his concern is not with the enunciation of a thesis or a slogan, but with the examination and judgment of individual and social motives and values.

The sources of *Ghosts* are literary and personal as well as ideological. A short novel by Mauritz Hansen, *The Daughter* (1837), tells of the secret of the Hedelbrandt family. The head of the family, a dissolute colonel, has a child by the maid, Else. Before the birth occurs she is married off to a wooden-legged janitor. Else later goes mad and her daughter is raised in the household, in daily association with the janitor, whom she views with fear and disdain. Ibsen also may have drawn Regine after one of his maids in Munich. A recent and controversial Danish drama on mercy-killing may have stimulated his thought in this direction. Contemporary Darwinian and naturalistic preoccupations are not far from the surface of the action. In particular, the current of biological and social determinism shaped the logic as well as the substance of Ibsen's drama.

None of his other plays is so rigorously constructed. The economy and concentration is almost breath-taking. The reduction of length from five acts to three helped Ibsen gain compression, but the unusual coherence of the play is due to the intricate organization of scenes and acts and the figurative and symbolic character of language. There is not a single line, not a single word, that fails to serve a vital organic purpose. Realism and naturalism are pale descriptions of the complexity of Ibsen's art. In his notes for *Ghosts* he remarked, "The play is to be like a picture of life." Nevertheless, the rearrangement of life in the relentless and inevitable movement of the play is not realistic in any strict sense. The rigorous enchainment of events makes for a drama of strict causality, but the contrivance of sequence is the work of an artist practicing an art of dramatic illusion, without any necessary dependence on our sense of the way things really happen.

*Ghosts* is unique among modern plays in its strict observance of the unities of time, place and action. Thirty years are compressed into twelve hours, and all events antecedent to the crucial action are set forth through exposition. It is characteristic of Ibsen's technique that revelation of the relevant past continues almost down to the final moment of the play. Nowhere do we find lumps of exposition, divorced from the tensions of the drama. Ibsen is a master of the art of informing the audience about the past while simultaneously sustaining and enhancing the interest of the immediate present. From the opening line, we are confronted with a situation in which one character wants something from another. This interaction at once defines character in the same instant that it arouses tension and expectation. The revelation of the past bears directly on relationships in the present. Each act is marked by antagonism, suspense, and climax. Ibsen does not scruple to force this pattern through rash coincidence, yet the behavior of all the characters is thoroughly and convincingly motivated, and the final catastrophe is both probable and necessary.

None of Ibsen's plays so infuriated his public. In Norway the *Morganbladet* declared, "This book has no place on the Christmas table of a Christian home." In England *Ghosts* was castigated as "An open drain; a loathsome sore unbandaged; a dirty act done publicly." It would be altogether wrong to view the play as a medical or sociological tract. The "Ghosts" are not merely figures out of the past; they represent all the dead lumber of institutional and ideological forces that blunt the free expression of individuality and stifle "the joy of life." In his notes for the play, Ibsen declared, "Marriage for external reasons, even when these are religious or moral, brings a Nemesis upon the offspring." The grim fatality and cruel irony of *Ghosts* recaptures the implacable tragedy of the ancient Greeks in an intricate pattern of theme and image, idea and symbol. The rising sun casts its luminous rays on the dark drama of guilt and retribution.

# GHOSTS

## *A Domestic Drama in Three Acts*

### Translated by Eva LeGallienne

CHARACTERS

MRS. HELENE ALVING, *the widow of Captain (Chamberlain) Alving*
OSVALD ALVING, *her son; a painter*
PASTOR MANDERS
JAKOB ENGSTRAND, *a carpenter*
REGINE ENGSTRAND,[1] *a member of the Alving household*

*The action takes place on* MRS. ALVING'S *country estate on one of the large fjords in the west of Norway.*

## Act One

*A spacious garden-room; in the left wall a door, and in the right wall two doors. In the center of the room a round table, with chairs about it. On the table lie books, periodicals, and newspapers. In the foreground to the left a window, and by it a small sofa, with a work-table in front of it. In the background, the room is continued into a somewhat narrower conservatory, the walls of which are formed by large panes of glass. In the right-hand wall of the conservatory is a door leading down into the garden. Through the glass wall a gloomy fjord landscape is faintly visible, veiled by steady rain.*

ENGSTRAND, *the carpenter, stands by the garden door. His left leg is somewhat bent; he has a clump of wood under the sole of his boot.* REGINE, *with an empty garden syringe in her hand, hinders him from advancing.*

REGINE (*In a low voice*) Well—what is it you want? No!—stay where you are—you're dripping wet!

ENGSTRAND It's only God's rain, my child.

REGINE It's the devil's rain, that's what it is!

ENGSTRAND Lord, how you talk, Regine! (*Limping a few steps into the room*) But, here's what I want to tell you—

REGINE Don't go clumping about with that foot of yours! The young master's upstairs asleep.

ENGSTRAND Asleep at this hour—in broad daylight?

REGINE It's none of your business.

ENGSTRAND Now—look at *me*—I was on a bit of a spree last night—

REGINE That's nothing new!

ENGSTRAND Well—we're all frail creatures, my child—

REGINE We are that!

ENGSTRAND And temptations are manifold in this world, you see—but that didn't prevent me from going to work at half past five as usual!

REGINE That's as it may be—and now, get out! I can't stand here having a rendezvous with you.

ENGSTRAND What's that?

REGINE I don't want anyone to see you here—so get out!

ENGSTRAND (*Comes a few steps nearer*) Damned if I go till I've had a talk with you. Listen—I'll be through with my work at the school-house this afternoon—then I'm going right back to town by the night boat—

REGINE (*Mutters*) A pleasant journey to you!

ENGSTRAND Thank you, my child! Tomorrow's the opening of the Orphanage, they'll all be celebrating—sure to be a lot of drinking too—I'll prove to them that Jakob Engstrand can keep out of the way of temptation—

REGINE Ha! . . .

ENGSTRAND Lots of grand people'll be here—Pastor Manders is expected from town—

REGINE He gets here today.

ENGSTRAND There—you see! Damned if I give *him* a chance to say anything against me!

REGINE So that's it, is it?

ENGSTRAND That's what?

REGINE (*Gives him a searching look*) What are you going to try and put over on him this time?

ENGSTRAND Are you crazy? As if I'd try and put anything over on *him!* No—Pastor Manders has been too good a friend to me—and that's just what I want to talk to you about. As I was saying, I'm going back home tonight—

[1] For stage purposes, often REGINA.

REGINE You can't go soon enough to please me!

ENGSTRAND But I want you to come with me, Regine.

REGINE (*Open-mouthed*) *I*, go with *you?*

ENGSTRAND Yes—I want you to come home with me.

REGINE (*Scornfully*) You'll never get me to do that!

ENGSTRAND Well—we'll see.

REGINE Yes! You'll see all right! After being brought up here by Mrs. Alving—treated almost like one of the family—do you suppose I'd go home with you—back to that kind of a house? You're crazy!

ENGSTRAND What kind of talk's that! You'd defy your own father, would you?

REGINE (*Mutters, without looking at him*) You've said often enough I'm no concern of yours—

ENGSTRAND Never mind about that—

REGINE Many's the time you've cursed at me and called me a—*Fi donc!*

ENGSTRAND When did I ever use a foul word like that?

REGINE I know well enough what word you used!

ENGSTRAND Well—maybe—when I wasn't feeling quite myself—hm. Temptations are manifold in this world, Regine!

REGINE Pah! . . .

ENGSTRAND And then your mother used to drive me crazy—I had to find some way to get back at her. She put on so many airs: (*Mimicking her*) "Let me go, Engstrand! Leave me alone! Don't forget I spent three years in Chamberlain Alving's house at Rosenvold!" (*Laughs*) God Almighty! She never got over the Captain being made Chamberlain while she was working here!

REGINE Poor mother! You certainly hounded her into her grave!

ENGSTRAND (*Shrugging his shoulders*) Oh, of course! I'm to blame for everything!

REGINE (*Under her breath as she turns away*) Ugh! And then that leg of yours!

ENGSTRAND What did you say, my child?

REGINE *Pied de mouton!* [1]

ENGSTRAND What's that? English?

REGINE Yes.

ENGSTRAND Yes—well; you've certainly got educated here—and that may come in handy too.

REGINE (*After a short silence*) Why do you want me to go back with you?

ENGSTRAND Why wouldn't a father want his only child with him? Aren't I a lonely, deserted widower?

REGINE Oh, don't talk rubbish to me! Why do you want me with you?

ENGSTRAND Well—I'll tell you—I'm thinking of setting up in a new line of business—

REGINE (*Whistles*) What, again! What is it this time?

ENGSTRAND You'll see—this time it'll be different. Christ Almighty—!

REGINE Stop your swearing! (*She stamps her foot*)

ENGSTRAND Sh! You're right, my child. Well—what I wanted to say was—I've managed to save quite a bit of money—from this work on the Orphanage—

REGINE You have, have you? So much the better for you.

[1] A pig's foot.

ENGSTRAND There's nothing to spend your money on in this God-forsaken hole—

REGINE Well?

ENGSTRAND So I thought I'd invest it in a paying concern. I thought of starting a sort of tavern—for seamen—

REGINE Ugh!

ENGSTRAND A really high-class tavern, you know—none of your cheap dives. No—by God! I'd cater to Captains and First-mates—really high-class people.

REGINE And I suppose I'd be expected to—

ENGSTRAND Oh, you could be a great help, Regine. You wouldn't have to do anything—it wouldn't be hard on you, my child—you'd have everything your own way!

REGINE Oh yes, of course!

ENGSTRAND After all there must be some women in the house—that goes without saying. We'd have to have a bit of fun in the evenings, singing and dancing—and that sort of thing. You've got to remember—these poor fellows are sailors—wanderers on the seas of the world. (*Comes nearer to her*) Don't be a fool and stand in your own way. What future is there for you out here? What good's all this education the Mrs. has paid for? You're to look after the kids in the new Orphanage I hear—is that a job for you? Do you want to wear yourself to the bone looking after a lot of dirty brats?

REGINE If things turn out as I hope—well—it could be—it could be—

ENGSTRAND What "could be"?

REGINE You keep your nose out of that! How much money did you save?

ENGSTRAND I'd say—in all—close to two hundred dollars.

REGINE Not so bad!

ENGSTRAND Enough to get me started, my child.

REGINE Do I get any of it?

ENGSTRAND You do not!

REGINE Not even enough to buy myself a new dress?

ENGSTRAND You come with me—you'll get plenty of new dresses then!

REGINE I can get them myself, if I set my mind to it.

ENGSTRAND But a father's guiding hand is a good thing, Regine. There's a nice little house right on Harbor Street—not much money down either—it'd be like a kind of Seamen's Home, you know.

REGINE But I don't want to live with you! I don't want to have anything to do with you! So now—get out!

ENGSTRAND You wouldn't be with me for long, my child—I know that well enough. All you've got to do is use your wits—you've turned into a handsome wench—do you know that?

REGINE Well—what of it?

ENGSTRAND Before you know it, some First-mate'll come along—maybe even a Captain.

REGINE I don't intend to marry any such trash. Sailors have no "savoir vivre." [2]

ENGSTRAND Well—I couldn't say about that—

[2] Refinement.

REGINE I tell you I know all about sailors. I wouldn't think of marrying one of them!

ENGSTRAND Who says you'd have to marry? You can make it pay just the same. (*More confidentially*) That Englishman—the one with the yacht—he gave three hundred dollars, he did—and she wasn't any better looking than you are.

REGINE (*Goes towards him*) Get out of here!

ENGSTRAND (*Retreating*) Now, now! You wouldn't hit me, would you?

REGINE You just say anything against Mother, and you'll see whether I'd hit you or not! Get out, I say! (*She pushes him toward the garden door*) And don't bang the door; young Mister Alving—

ENGSTRAND Is asleep—I know! Why should you be so worried about him? (*In a lower tone*) God—Almighty! You don't mean to tell me that *he*—?

REGINE You must be out of your head—you fool! Go on now—get out this minute. No—not that way—here comes Pastor Manders; the back stairs for you!

ENGSTRAND (*Goes toward door right*) All right—I'll go. But listen—you have a talk with him—he'll tell you what you owe your father—for I am your father after all, you know; I can prove that by the Church Register.

(*He goes out through the other door that* REGINE *has opened for him and closes after him. She glances at herself quickly in the mirror, fans herself with her handkerchief and straightens her collar; then she sets about tending the flowers.* PASTOR MANDERS *enters the conservatory by the garden door. He wears an overcoat, carries an umbrella and has a small traveling-bag slung over his shoulder*)

MANDERS Good-day, Miss Engstrand.

REGINE (*Turning in glad surprise*) Well! Good-day, Pastor Manders! Fancy! So the steamer's in, is it?

MANDERS (*He comes into the room*) Yes—just docked. Dreadful weather we've had these last few days.

REGINE (*Following him*) It's a blessing for the farmers, Pastor Manders.

MANDERS Quite right, Miss Engstrand! We city-folk never think of that. (*He begins taking off his overcoat*)

REGINE Do let me help you! My goodness! It's soaking wet! I'll just hang it in the hall—and, let me take your umbrella—I'll open it up—so it'll dry quicker.

(*She goes out with the things by the second door on the right.* MANDERS *puts his traveling-bag on a chair with his hat. Meanwhile,* REGINE *comes in again*)

MANDERS It's very pleasant to be indoors. And how are things going here? All well, I trust?

REGINE Yes—many thanks.

MANDERS I expect you've been very busy with tomorrow's preparations.

REGINE Yes—there's been so much to do!

MANDERS And Mrs. Alving is at home, I hope?

REGINE Oh yes, indeed. She just went upstairs to give the young master his hot chocolate.

MANDERS Tell me—I heard down at the pier that Osvald had come home—

REGINE He arrived the day before yesterday—we didn't expect him until today.

MANDERS In good health and spirits, I trust?

REGINE Yes, thank you, he seems to be—but dreadfully tired after his journey. He came straight through from Paris—without a stop; I mean, he came the whole way without a break. I think he's taking a little nap—so we must talk very quietly.

MANDERS Sh! We'll be still as mice!

REGINE (*She moves an armchair up to the table*) Do sit down, Pastor Manders, and make yourself comfortable. (*He sits; she places a footstool under his feet*) There! How does that feel?

MANDERS Most comfortable, thank you! (*He looks at her*) Do you know, Miss Engstrand, I really believe you've grown since I saw you last.

REGINE Do you think so, Pastor Manders? Mrs. Alving says I've filled out too.

MANDERS Filled out, eh? Yes, yes—perhaps a little—just suitably.

(*Short pause*)

REGINE Shall I tell Mrs. Alving you're here?

MANDERS Thank you—there's no hurry, my dear child— Well—tell me, my dear Regine, how is your father getting on out here?

REGINE Pretty well, thank you, Mr. Manders.

MANDERS He came in to see me last time he was in town.

REGINE Did he really? He's always so grateful for a talk with you, Mr. Manders.

MANDERS I suppose you see him regularly, every day?

REGINE I?— Oh, yes—of course.— Whenever I have time—that is—

MANDERS I'm afraid your father is not a very strong character, Miss Engstrand. He badly needs a guiding hand.

REGINE Yes, I dare say he does, Mr. Manders.

MANDERS He needs someone near him—someone he can lean on—whose judgment he respects. He admitted as much, quite candidly, last time he came to see me.

REGINE Yes—he said something of the sort to me. But I don't know if Mrs. Alving would want to let me go—especially now that we'll have the Orphanage to manage. And I really couldn't bear to leave Mrs. Alving—she's always been so good to me.

MANDERS But a daughter's duty, my dear child—of course, we would first have to gain Mrs. Alving's consent.

REGINE But would it be quite the thing, at my age, to keep house for a single man?

MANDERS What do you mean? My dear Miss Engstrand, it's a question of your own father!

REGINE Yes, I know—but all the same—of course if it were a *proper* kind of house—belonging to a real gentleman—

MANDERS Why—my dear Regine—!

REGINE Oh, I mean a man I could look up to—respect—become attached to—as though I were really his daughter—

MANDERS But, my dear child—

REGINE Then I'd gladly live in town again—for I'm often very lonely here—and you know yourself, Mr. Manders, what it is to be all alone in the world. And I'm capable and willing—though I say it myself as shouldn't. Mr. Manders—I suppose you couldn't find me a position of that sort?

MANDERS I? No—I'm really afraid I can't.

REGINE But, you will think of me, dear, dear Mr. Manders—you'll keep me in mind in case—

MANDERS (*Gets up*) Yes, yes—of course, Miss Engstrand—

REGINE Because, you see—if I could only—

MANDERS Would you be so kind as to tell Mrs. Alving I am here?

REGINE I'll go and call her at once, Mr. Manders.

(*She goes out left.* MANDERS *paces up and down the room a couple of times, then stands for a moment upstage with his hands behind his back looking out into the garden. Then he comes back to the table, picks up a book and glances at the title page. He gives a start and examines some of the others*)

MANDERS Hm!—Well—well! Really!

(MRS. ALVING *comes in by the door left followed by* REGINE *who immediately goes out by the first door on the right*)

MRS. ALVING (*With outstretched hand*) Welcome, dear Mr. Manders!

MANDERS Good-day, Mrs. Alving. Well—here I am—as I promised.

MRS. ALVING And punctual as usual!

MANDERS I had great trouble getting away. As you know—I'm chairman of so many organizations—and what with my committee meetings—

MRS. ALVING I'm all the more grateful to you for coming so promptly. Now we shall be able to get all our business settled before dinner. But, where is your luggage?

MANDERS (*Hastily*) I left my things down at the Inn—I'll put up there for the night.

MRS. ALVING (*Repressing a smile*) Can't I really persuade you to spend the night here this time?

MANDERS No, no, Mrs. Alving—thank you all the same—but I prefer to stay there as usual. It's so convenient—right by the pier, you know.

MRS. ALVING Well—just as you wish! I should have thought, that perhaps, at our age—!

MANDERS Ah—yes, of course—you will have your little joke! Well—I suppose you're radiantly happy today—what with tomorrow's ceremony—and having Osvald home again—

MRS. ALVING Yes—isn't it wonderful! He hasn't been home for over two years, you know. And he's promised to spend the whole winter with me!

MANDERS Has he really? That's a nice filial gesture—for I'm sure his life in Rome and Paris must offer many attractions.

MRS. ALVING Yes, no doubt—but after all, he has his mother here. God bless him—he still has a place in his heart for me.

MANDERS It would be regrettable indeed if separation and his interest in such a thing as Art were to interfere with his natural affections.

MRS. ALVING That's true. But fortunately, there's no danger of that with him. I'll be curious to see if you recognize him after all these years—he'll be down presently—he's just having a little rest upstairs. But—do sit down, dear Mr. Manders.

MANDERS Thank you. You're sure I'm not disturbing you?

MRS. ALVING (*Sits by table*) Of course not!

MANDERS Splendid—then suppose we get down to business. (*He goes to the chair and takes a bundle of papers out of his traveling-bag. Then sits down at the table opposite* MRS. ALVING. *He tries to arrange a space on which to lay out the papers*) Now first of all there's the question of—(*Breaks off*) Tell me, Mrs. Alving—what are those books doing here?

MRS. ALVING These? I happen to be reading them.

MANDERS You really read this sort of thing?

MRS. ALVING Of course I do.

MANDERS Do you feel that this type of reading makes you any better—any happier?

MRS. ALVING It gives me a certain confidence.

MANDERS Extraordinary! How do you mean?

MRS. ALVING It seems to clarify and confirm many things I've thought about myself. The strange thing is, Mr. Manders, there's really nothing new in any of these books; they deal with subjects that most of us think about and believe in; though I dare say most people don't take the trouble to look into them very deeply—or face them very honestly.

MANDERS But, good Heavens—you don't seriously believe that most people—?

MRS. ALVING I most emphatically do.

MANDERS But surely not here—surely not *our* kind of people—

MRS. ALVING Yes! "Our kind of people" too.

MANDERS Well—I really must say—!

MRS. ALVING But, what precisely do you object to in these books?

MANDERS Object to? You don't imagine I waste my time delving into such subjects!

MRS. ALVING Then you're condemning them without knowing them?

MANDERS I've read quite enough about these books to disapprove of them.

MRS. ALVING But, how can you form an opinion if you haven't—?

MANDERS My dear Mrs. Alving—in some things it is wiser to depend on the opinion of others. That is the way our world functions—and it is best that it should be so. Otherwise, what would become of Society?

MRS. ALVING Well—you may be right.

MANDERS I don't deny that such books may have a certain fascination. And I don't blame you for wishing to familiarize yourself with certain intellectual trends which, I understand, are current in the sophisticated world where your son has been allowed to roam so freely. But—

MRS. ALVING But—?

MANDERS (*Lowering his voice*) But one doesn't discuss such things openly, Mrs. Alving. There is no reason to give an account to all and sundry of what one reads, or thinks, in the privacy of one's own room.

MRS. ALVING Certainly not—I agree with you—

MANDERS Think of your new responsibilities toward the Orphanage. When you decided to found it, your feelings on certain subjects were decidedly at variance with those you now entertain—unless I am greatly mistaken.

MRS. ALVING I grant you that. But, let's get back to the Orphanage, Mr. Manders.

MANDERS By all means—only, remember: caution, my dear Mrs. Alving! And now—to work! (*Opens an envelope and takes out some papers*) You see these papers—?

MRS. ALVING The deeds?

MANDERS Yes—all in order at last! I had great trouble in getting them in time. I had to bring strong pressure to bear on the authorities; they are painfully conscientious when it comes to property settlements of any kind, but here they are at last. (*Turns over the papers*) This is the deed of conveyance for that part of the Rosenvold estate known as the Slovik property, together with all the newly erected buildings, the school, the teacher's house, and the chapel. And here is the Charter of the Institution: "Charter of the Orphanage in memory of Captain Alving."

MRS. ALVING (*After examining the papers at some length*) That all seems clear—

MANDERS I used the title "Captain" instead of "Court Chamberlain"—it seemed less ostentatious.

MRS. ALVING Whatever you think best.

MANDERS Here is the bank-book controlling the invested capital—the interest on which will be used to defray the running expenses of the institution.

MRS. ALVING Thank you—you'll take charge of that, won't you?

MANDERS Certainly, if you wish. For the time being, I think it would be wise to leave the entire sum in the bank—the interest is not very attractive it's true—but we could then take our time and later on find a good mortgage—it would of course have to be a first mortgage and on unexceptionable security—we can afford to take no risks—but we can discuss that matter at a later date.

MRS. ALVING Yes, dear Mr. Manders—I leave all that to you.

MANDERS I'll keep a sharp look-out. Now, there's something else—I've meant to take it up with you several times.

MRS. ALVING And what it that?

MANDERS The question of insurance. Do you wish me to take out insurance on the Orphanage or not?

MRS. ALVING Well of course it must be insured!

MANDERS Just a moment, Mrs. Alving—let us examine the matter more carefully.

MRS. ALVING But, everything I own is insured—my house and its contents—the livestock—everything.

MANDERS Your personal property, of course. All my things are insured too. But this is quite a different matter. The Orphanage is dedicated to a high spiritual purpose—

MRS. ALVING Yes, but—

MANDERS As far as I am personally concerned, I can't see the slightest objection to safe-guarding ourselves against all possible risks—

MRS. ALVING I quite agree—

MANDERS But what about public opinion?

MRS. ALVING Public opinion—?

MANDERS Are there any groups of people here—people who matter, I mean—who might take exception to it?

MRS. ALVING What do you mean by "people who matter"?

MANDERS I mean men of wealth and influence whose opinion it might be unwise to overlook.

MRS. ALVING I see what you mean—yes, there may be a few people here who might object—

MANDERS There, you see! In town I think there might be a strong feeling against it—among my colleagues for instance, and some of the more influential members of their congregations; it could be implied that we hadn't sufficient faith in Divine Providence.

MRS. ALVING But, surely, Mr. Manders, you have no such feeling—

MANDERS Oh, as far as I am personally concerned, I have no qualms in the matter; but we might not be able to prevent our action from being interpreted in an erroneous and unfortunate light—and this in turn might reflect on the work of the Orphanage.

MRS. ALVING Of course, if that were to be the case—

MANDERS And I admit, I can't quite overlook the embarrassing—I might even say difficult position—I should find myself in. In town this Orphanage has been much discussed by the leading citizens. They are well aware of the benefits that would accrue to the town from such an institution—its existence would undoubtedly reduce to an important degree the yearly sums they are expected to donate to charitable works. And, since I have been your adviser in this matter—your business representative from the beginning—most of the blame and criticism would inevitably fall on me—

MRS. ALVING I wouldn't want you to be exposed to that.

MANDERS Not to speak of the attacks that would unquestionably be made against me by certain newspapers—

MRS. ALVING That settles it, Mr. Manders—we'll say no more about it!

MANDERS Then, we decide against insurance?

MRS. ALVING Yes—we'll let that go.

MANDERS (*Leaning back in his chair*) But, on the other hand, Mrs. Alving, suppose there *should* be an accident—one never knows—would you be prepared to make good the damage?

MRS. ALVING No, I must tell you quite frankly, that would be out of the question.

MANDERS In that case we are assuming a very grave responsibility.

MRS. ALVING Well—do you see anything else to do?

MANDERS I'm afraid not—I don't really see that there's anything else we *can* do; we don't want to be placed in a false position—and we have no right to arouse the antagonism of the Community.

MRS. ALVING Especially you—as a clergyman.

MANDERS We must simply have faith that our institution will be under the special protection of Providence.

MRS. ALVING Let us hope so, Mr. Manders.

MANDERS Then—we'll let it go?

MRS. ALVING By all means.

MANDERS As you wish. (*Makes a note*) No insurance.

MRS. ALVING It's strange you should happen to bring this up today—

MANDERS I've often meant to discuss it with you—

MRS. ALVING Because only yesterday we nearly had a fire down there.

MANDERS What!

MRS. ALVING Nothing came of it, fortunately—some woodshavings caught fire—in the carpenter's shop—

MANDERS Where Engstrand works?

MRS. ALVING Yes. They say he's often very careless with matches—

MANDERS Poor man—he has so much on his mind—so many worries. I'm happy to say he's decided to turn over a new leaf.

MRS. ALVING Indeed? Who told you that?

MANDERS He assured me so himself. I'm very glad—he's such an excellent worker.

MRS. ALVING Yes—when he's sober.

MANDERS That unfortunate weakness! He tells me it relieves the pain in that poor leg of his. Last time he came to see me in town, he was really very touching. He was so grateful to me for getting him this work here—where he could be near Regine.

MRS. ALVING I don't think he sees much of her.

MANDERS Oh yes, he sees her every day—he told me so himself.

MRS. ALVING Well—it's possible.

MANDERS He realizes the need of someone near him, to help him when temptation gets too strong for him. That's what is so endearing about Jakob Engstrand—he admits how weak he is—and is so anxious to reform. Mrs. Alving—suppose it should become a real necessity for him to have Regine home with him again—?

MRS. ALVING (*Rises quickly*) Regine—?

MANDERS I urge you not to oppose it.

MRS. ALVING I most certainly would oppose it! And besides—Regine is to work at the Orphanage.

MANDERS But—he *is* her father after all—

MRS. ALVING I know only too well the kind of father he is! No! She shall never go back to him while I have anything to say in the matter!

MANDERS (*Gets up*) But, my dear Mrs. Alving, why be so violent about it! It's a great pity that you misjudge Engstrand so. One would think you were actually afraid—

MRS. ALVING (*More calmly*) That's not the point. I am looking after Regine now and she will stay here with me. (*Listen*) Sh! Dear Mr. Manders, let's not discuss this any further. (*Her face lights up with joy*) Here comes Osvald. We'll think about *him* now.

(OSVALD ALVING *enters left. He has on a light overcoat and is carrying his hat. He is smoking a large Meerschaum pipe*)

OSVALD (*Standing in the doorway*) Oh, I'm sorry—I thought you were in the library—I didn't mean to disturb you. (*Comes in*) How do you do, Mr. Manders!

MANDERS (*Stares at him*) Well, what an amazing—!

MRS. ALVING What do you think of him, Mr. Manders?

MANDERS Can it really be—?

OSVALD Yes—it's the Prodigal Son, Mr. Manders!

MANDERS My dear boy—!

OSVALD Or the wandering son returned to the fold—if you prefer.

MRS. ALVING He's only joking, Mr. Manders— He's referring to your disapproval of an artist's career.

MANDERS We are not infallible in our judgments; certain steps may seem to us dangerous that turn out in the end to be—(*Shakes hands with him*) So, welcome! Welcome home, my dear Osvald!—I may still call you Osvald, I trust?

OSVALD What else should you call me, Mr. Manders?

MANDERS Splendid!—I was just going to say—you must not imagine, my dear Osvald, that I unconditionally condemn the artist's life. I dare say there are many who succeed, in spite of everything, in preserving their integrity of character.

OSVALD Let us hope so!

MRS. ALVING (*Beaming with pleasure*) Well—this one's managed to do so, Mr. Manders—you've only to look at him to see that!

OSVALD (*Pacing the room*) There, there—Mother, dear—never mind—!

MANDERS Yes, fortunately, that's undeniable! And you've begun to make quite a name for yourself. I've often seen you mentioned in the papers, and always most favorably. Though recently I haven't seen so much about your work.

OSVALD (*Going up to the conservatory*) No—I haven't done much painting lately.

MRS. ALVING Even an artist needs to rest now and then.

MANDERS Most understandable— At such times you gather new strength, for even finer work.

OSVALD Quite so— Will dinner be ready soon, Mother?

MRS. ALVING In half an hour, dear. There's nothing wrong with his appetite, thank God!

MANDERS And I see he's partial to tobacco too.

OSVALD I found this old pipe of Father's up in his study—

MANDERS Oh—so that accounts for it!

MRS. ALVING How do you mean?

MANDERS When Osvald came in just now—with that pipe in his mouth—I thought for a moment it was his father come to life again.

OSVALD Really?

MRS. ALVING How can you say that! Osvald takes after me.

MANDERS Yes—perhaps; but, still, there's something about his mouth—something in the expression—that reminds me very strongly of Alving—especially when he smokes.

MRS. ALVING I don't see it at all—Osvald's mouth is much more sensitive. There's something almost ascetic about it.

MANDERS It's true—some of my colleagues have a similar expression.

MRS. ALVING But put down your pipe now, Osvald, dear. I don't allow smoking in this room.

OSVALD (*Puts down the pipe*) Very well, Mother. I only wanted to try it; I smoked it once before you see—when I was a child.

MRS. ALVING *You* did?

OSVALD Yes—I was very little at the time—I remember I went up to Father's study one evening; he was in a very gay, jolly mood.

MRS. ALVING How could you possibly remember? It's so long ago!

OSVALD Oh, but I do! I remember it very distinctly; he sat me on his knee and told me to smoke his pipe: Smoke, Son, he said—go on, Son—have a good smoke; so I smoked away with all my might, until I felt deathly ill and great beads of perspiration stood out on my forehead. He thought it was very funny. I remember he roared with laughter at me.

MANDERS What a very odd thing to do!

MRS. ALVING It's a lot of nonsense. Osvald must have dreamed it.

OSVALD No, Mother, I assure you I didn't! Don't you remember, you came in and rushed me off to the nursery. And then I was sick—and I noticed you'd been crying—I suppose it *was* rather odd—did Father often play tricks like that?

MANDERS He was a great joker in his young days.

OSVALD Yet think of all the good he did. The fine and useful things he was able to accomplish—though he died comparatively young.

MANDERS Yes—you have a fine heritage, Osvald Alving. It should be a great incentive to you!

OSVALD Yes, you're right! Indeed it should.

MANDERS And it was good of you to come home for the ceremony tomorrow.

OSVALD That's the least I could do for Father's memory.

MRS. ALVING And he plans to stay here for a while—that's the nicest thing of all!

MANDERS Yes, I understand you intend to spend the winter here.

OSVALD I plan to stay here indefinitely, Mr. Manders. It's so good to be home again!

MRS. ALVING (*Beaming*) Yes, it is, isn't it, dear?

MANDERS (*Looks at him sympathetically*) You were very young when you left home, my dear Osvald.

OSVALD A little too young, perhaps.

MRS. ALVING What nonsense! It's good for a strong healthy boy—especially an only child—to get away from home. Much better than being petted and spoiled by doting parents!

MANDERS I think that is open to debate, Mrs. Alving. A home and parents are still a child's best refuge.

OSVALD I'm inclined to agree with Mr. Manders there.

MANDERS Take your own son here as an example—there's no harm in discussing it before him—what has been the result in his case? Here he is, twenty-three or twenty-four years old, and he has never yet known what a normal, well-regulated home can be.

OSVALD I beg your pardon, Mr. Manders—you're quite wrong in that.

MANDERS Really? But, I thought you'd been living exclusively in artistic circles.

OSVALD So I have.

MANDERS And mostly among the younger artists, I believe.

OSVALD Quite right.

MANDERS But surely the majority of such people are in no position to found a home and family.

OSVALD Most of them are in no position to get married—that's true enough—

MANDERS That's just what I say—

OSVALD But that doesn't necessarily mean that they can't have homes of their *own*—and many of them have—very comfortable and well-run homes too.

(MRS. ALVING, *who has been listening attentively, nods in agreement but says nothing*)

MANDERS I'm not thinking of bachelor-establishments: when I use the word "home," I mean a family—a home where a man lives with his wife and children.

OSVALD Or with his children—and their mother.

MANDERS (*With a start, clasping his hands*) Good Heavens!

OSVALD Well?

MANDERS —lives with—with—his children's mother!

OSVALD Would you rather he abandoned her?

MANDERS Then you're speaking of illegal unions—dissolute relationships—!

OSVALD I've never noticed anything especially dissolute in the lives these people lead.

MANDERS How can any decent young man or woman possibly degrade themselves by living openly in such shameful circumstances!

OSVALD Well—what do you expect them to do? A poor young artist—a poor young girl—marriage is an expensive business—what do you expect them to do?

MANDERS I would expect them to resist temptation, Mr. Alving—to part before it is too late.

OSVALD That's a lot to expect of young people in love, Mr. Manders.

MRS. ALVING Indeed it is!

MANDERS (*Persistently*) And to think that the authorities put up with such behavior—that it should be openly tolerated. (*To* MRS. ALVING) You see how right I was to be concerned about your son. Living in circles where such rampant immorality prevails, where it's taken for granted, one might say—

OSVALD Let me tell you something, Mr. Manders—I've spent many a Sunday at some of these "illegal homes"—as you call them—

MANDERS On a Sunday too—!

OSVALD Sunday happens to be a holiday—I've never once heard a single vulgar or indecent word—nor have I ever witnessed any behavior that could possibly be called immoral. But do you know when and where I *have* met with such behavior?

MANDERS No! God forbid!

OSVALD Then permit me to tell you: When some of your highly-respected citizens—your model fathers and husbands from back home here—when they take a trip abroad to "see a bit of life"—when *they* condescend to honor us poor artists with their presence—then you would see "rampant immorality" if you like! These respectable gentlemen could tell us about things that we had never even dreamed of!

MANDERS You dare imply that honorable men here from home—?

OSVALD You must have heard these same "honorable men" when they get safely home again, hold forth on the outrageous immorality that prevails abroad?

MANDERS Of course I have.

MRS. ALVING I've heard them too—

OSVALD Well you may take their word for it! They speak with true authority! (*Clutches his head in his hands*) It's an outrage that that free and beautiful life should be distorted by their filth!

MRS. ALVING Don't get so excited, Osvald. It's bad for you.

OSVALD You're right, Mother. It's bad for me I know—it's just that I'm so tired. I think I'll take a little walk before dinner. Forgive me, Mr. Manders—I shouldn't have let go like that. I know you can't possibly understand my feelings. (*He goes out by the up-stage door right*)

MRS. ALVING Poor boy!

MANDERS You may well say so! —That he should have sunk to this! (MRS. ALVING *looks at him in silence.* MANDERS *paces up and down*) He called himself the Prodigal Son—Tragic!—Tragic! (MRS. ALVING *continues to look at him silently*) And what do you say to all this?

MRS. ALVING I say Osvald was right in every word he said.

MANDERS (*Stops pacing*) Right? —You mean you agree to such principles?

MRS. ALVING Living here alone all these years, I've come to the same conclusions—but I've never put my thoughts into words— Well—now my boy can speak for me.

MANDERS You are greatly to be pitied, Mrs. Alving! —I have always had your best interests at heart; for many years I have advised you in business matters; for many years I have been your friend and your late husband's friend; as your spiritual adviser I once saved you from a reckless and fool-hardy action; and it is as your spiritual adviser that I now feel it my duty to talk to you with the utmost solemnity.

MRS. ALVING And what have you to say to me, as my "spiritual adviser," Mr. Manders?

MANDERS Look back over the years—it's appropriate that you should do so today, for tomorrow is the tenth anniversary of your husband's death and his Memorial will be unveiled; tomorrow I shall speak to the crowd assembled in his honor—but today I must speak to you alone.

MRS. ALVING I'm listening.

MANDERS You had been married scarcely a year when you took the step that might have wrecked your life: You left house and home and ran away from your husband—yes, Mrs. Alving, ran away—and refused to go back to him in spite of all his entreaties.

MRS. ALVING I was miserably unhappy that first year—don't forget that.

MANDERS What right have we to expect happiness in this life? It is the sign of a rebellious spirit— No! Mrs. Alving we are here to do our duty, and it was your duty to stay with the man you had chosen and to whom you were bound in Holy Matrimony.

MRS. ALVING You know the kind of life Alving led in those days; his dissipation—his excesses—

MANDERS It's true, I heard many rumors about him—and had those rumors been true, I should have been the first to condemn his conduct at that time; but it is not a wife's place to judge her husband; your duty was to resign yourself and bear your cross with true humility. But you rebelled against it and instead of giving your husband the help and support he needed, you deserted him, and by so doing jeopardized your own good name and reputation—and that of others too.

MRS. ALVING Of "others"? Of *one*, you mean.

MANDERS It was highly imprudent to come to me, of all people, for help.

MRS. ALVING But why? Weren't you our "spiritual adviser" as well as our friend?

MANDERS All the more reason. You should go down on your knees and thank God that I found the necessary strength of mind to dissuade you from your reckless purpose, to guide you back to the path of duty, and home to your husband.

MRS. ALVING Yes, Mr. Manders—that was certainly your doing.

MANDERS I was merely an instrument in God's hand. And, as I had foreseen—once you had returned to your duties, and humbled your spirit in obedience—you were repaid an hundredfold. Alving reformed entirely, and remained a good and loving husband to the end of his days. He became a real benefactor to this whole community, and he allowed you to share, as his fellow-worker, in all his enterprises—and a very able fellow-worker too—I am aware of that, Mrs. Alving—I must pay you that tribute; but now I come to the second great error of your life.

MRS. ALVING What do you mean by that?

MANDERS You first betrayed your duty as a wife—you later betrayed your duty as a mother.

MRS. ALVING Ah—!

MANDERS All your life you have been possessed by a willful, rebellious spirit. Your natural inclinations always led you toward the undisciplined and lawless. You could never tolerate the slightest restraint; you have always disregarded any responsibility—carelessly and unscrupulously—as though it were a burden you had a right to cast aside. It no longer suited you to be a wife—so you left your husband. The cares of motherhood were too much for you—so you sent your child away to be brought up by strangers.

MRS. ALVING That's true—I did do that.

MANDERS And for that reason you are now a stranger to him.

MRS. ALVING No! No! I'm not!

MANDERS Of course you are! How could you be otherwise? And now you see the result of your conduct. You have much to atone for; you were guilty as a wife, Mrs. Alving, you failed your husband miserably—you are seeking to atone for that by raising this Memorial in his honor; how are you going to atone for your failure toward your son? It may not be too late to save him: by redeeming yourself—you may still help him to redemption! I warn you! (*With raised forefinger*) You are guilty as a mother, Mrs. Alving. I felt it my duty to tell you this.

(*Pause*)

MRS. ALVING (*Slowly, with great control*) I have listened to you talk, Mr. Manders. Tomorrow you will be making speeches in my husband's honor; I shall not make any speeches tomorrow; but now I intend to talk to you—just as frankly—just as brutally—as you have talked to me!

MANDERS Of course—it's natural that you should try and justify your conduct.

MRS. ALVING No—I only want to make a few things clear to you.

MANDERS Well?

MRS. ALVING You've just talked a great deal about my married life after you—as you put it—"led me back to the path of duty." What do you really know about it? From that day on you never set foot inside our house—you who had been our closest friend—

MANDERS But, you and your husband left town, immediately afterwards—

MRS. ALVING And you never once came out here to see us during my husband's lifetime. It wasn't until this Orphanage business, that you felt compelled to visit me.

MANDERS (*In a low uncertain tone*) If that is meant as a reproach, my dear Helene, I beg you to consider—

MRS. ALVING —that in your position you had to protect your reputation! After all—I was a wife who had tried to leave her husband! One can't be too careful with such disreputable women!

MANDERS My dear!—Mrs. Alving—what a gross exaggeration!

MRS. ALVING Well—never mind about that—the point is this: your opinions of my married life are based on nothing but hearsay.

MANDERS That may be so—what then?

MRS. ALVING Just this: that now, Manders, I am going to tell you the truth! I swore to myself that one day I would tell it to you—to you alone!

MANDERS Well? And what is the truth?

MRS. ALVING The truth is this: My husband continued to be a depraved profligate to the day of his death.

MANDERS (*Feeling for a chair*) What did you say?

MRS. ALVING After nineteen years of marriage—just as depraved, just as dissolute—as he was the day you married us.

MANDERS How can you use such words—!

MRS. ALVING They are the words our doctor used.

MANDERS I don't understand you.

MRS. ALVING It's not necessary that you should.

MANDERS I can't take it in. You mean—that this seemingly happy marriage—those long years of comradeship—all that was only a pretense—to cover up this hideous abyss?

MRS. ALVING That is just exactly what it was—nothing else.

MANDERS But—it's inconceivable—I can't grasp it! How was it possible to—? How could the truth remain concealed?

MRS. ALVING My life became one long fight to that end: After Osvald was born, Alving seemed to me a little better—but it didn't last long! And then I had to fight for my son as well: I was determined that no living soul should ever know the kind of father my boy had— As a matter of fact, you know how charming Alving could be—it was hard for people to think ill of him. He was one of those fortunate men whose private lives never seem to damage their public reputation. But then, Manders—I want you to know the whole story—then the most horrible thing of all happened.

MANDERS How could anything be worse than—?

MRS. ALVING I knew well enough all that was going on—and I put up with it as long as I didn't have to see it—but, when I was faced with it here—in my own home—!

MANDERS Here?

MRS. ALVING Yes—in this very house. The first time I became aware of it, I was in there—(*Points to the down-stage door right*) in the dining room—I was busy with something, and the door was ajar—then I heard the maid come up from the garden with water for the plants—

MANDERS Yes?

MRS. ALVING In a few moments, I heard Alving come in after her—he said something to her in a low voice—and then I heard—(*With a short laugh*) it still rings in my ears—it was so horrible, and yet somehow so ludicrous—I heard my own servant-girl whisper: "Let me go, Mr. Alving!—Leave me alone!"

MANDERS But he couldn't have meant anything by it, Mrs. Alving—believe me—I'm sure he didn't—!

MRS. ALVING I soon found out what to believe: My husband had his way with the girl, and there were—consequences, Mr. Manders.

MANDERS (*As though turned to stone*) To think—that in this house—!

MRS. ALVING I had been through a lot in this house! Night after night—in order to keep him home—I sat up in his study with him—pretending to join him in his private drinking-bouts. I sat there alone with him for hours on end listening to his obscene, senseless talk—I had to struggle with him—fight with sheer brute force—in order to drag him to his bed.

MANDERS (*Shaken*) How were you able to endure all this?

MRS. ALVING I had to endure it—I had my little boy to think of. But when I discovered this final outrage—with a servant—in our own house—! That was the end. From that day on I became master here. I took full control—over him and over everything. Alving didn't dare say a word—he knew he was in my power. It was then I decided to send Osvald away. He was nearly seven and was beginning to notice things and ask questions, as children do. This I could not endure, Manders. I felt the child would be poisoned in this sordid, degraded home. That's why I sent him away. Now perhaps you understand why I never let him set foot in this house as long as his father was alive. What you could never understand—is what agony it was to have to do it!

MANDERS To think of all you have been through—!

MRS. ALVING I could never have stood it if I hadn't had my work. For I can honestly say I have worked! Alving received all the praise—all the credit—but don't imagine he had anything to do with it! The increase in the value of our property—the improvements—all those fine enterprises you spoke of—all that was *my* work. All he did was to sprawl on the sofa in his study reading old newspapers. In his few lucid moments I did try to spur him to some effort—but it was no use. He sank back again into his old habits and then spent days in a maudlin state of penitence and self-pity.

MANDERS And you're building a Memorial to such a man—?

MRS. ALVING That's what comes of having a bad conscience.

MANDERS A bad—? What do you mean?

MRS. ALVING It seemed to me inevitable that the truth must come out, and that people would believe it; so I decided to dedicate this Orphanage to Alving—in order to dispel once and for all any possible rumors—any possible doubts.

MANDERS You've fully succeeded in that.

MRS. ALVING But I had another reason: I didn't want my son to inherit anything whatsoever from his father.

MANDERS I see—so you used Alving's money to—?

MRS. ALVING Precisely. The money that has gone into the Orphanage amounts to the exact sum—I've calculated it very carefully—to the exact sum of the fortune, that once made people consider Lt. Alving a good match.

MANDERS I understand you.

MRS. ALVING I sold myself for that sum. I don't want Osvald to touch a penny of it. Everything he has will come from me—everything!

(OSVALD *enters from the door up-stage right. He has left his hat and coat outside*)

MRS. ALVING (*Goes toward him*) Back already, dear?

OSVALD Yes—what can one do—out in this everlasting rain! But I hear dinner's nearly ready—splendid!

(REGINE *enters from the dining room carrying a small parcel*)

REGINE This parcel just came for you, Mrs. Alving. (*Hands her the parcel*)

MRS. ALVING (*With a glance at* MANDERS) Ah! The songs for tomorrow's ceremony, I expect.

MANDERS Hm—

REGINE And dinner is served, Mrs. Alving.

MRS. ALVING Good; we'll be there in a moment. I just want to see—

REGINE (*To* OSVALD) Would you like red or white wine, Mr. Alving?

OSVALD Both, by all means, Miss Engstrand.

REGINE *Bien*— Very good, Mr. Alving. (*Exits into dining room*)

OSVALD Let me help you uncork it—(*Follows her into the dining room, half closing the door*)

MRS. ALVING (*Who has opened the parcel*) Yes—just as I thought—the songs for tomorrow, Mr. Manders.

MANDERS (*Clasping his hands*) How I shall ever have the courage to make my speech tomorrow—!

MRS. ALVING You'll manage—somehow.

MANDERS (*Softly, so as not to be heard in the dining room*) It would never do to arouse suspicion—

MRS. ALVING (*Quietly but firmly*) No— And from tomorrow on, I shall be free at last—the long, hideous farce will be over—I shall forget that such a person as Alving ever lived in this house—there'll be no one here but my son and me. (*The noise of a chair being overturned is heard from the dining room—at the same time* REGINE'*s voice*)

REGINE'S *voice* (*In a sharp whisper*) Osvald!—Are you mad?—Let me go!

MRS. ALVING (*Stiffens with horror*) Ah—!

(*She gazes distractedly at the half-open door.* OSVALD *is heard coughing and humming a tune—then the sound of a bottle being uncorked*)

MANDERS (*In agitation*) But what *is* all this? What's the *matter,* Mrs. Alving?

MRS. ALVING (*Hoarsely*) Ghosts— Those two in the conservatory— Ghosts— They've come to life again!

MANDERS What do you mean? Regine—? Is *she*—?

MRS. ALVING Yes— Come— Not a word!

(*She takes* MANDERS' *arm and goes falteringly toward the dining room*)

*Curtain*

# Act Two

*The same room. The landscape is still shrouded in rain and mist.* MANDERS *and* MRS. ALVING *enter from the dining room.*

MRS. ALVING (*In the doorway, calls back into the dining room*) Aren't you coming too, Osvald?

OSVALD (*Off stage*) No, thanks; I think I'll go out for a bit.

MRS. ALVING Yes, do, dear; I think it's cleared up a little. (*She closes the dining room door, crosses to the hall door and calls*) Regine!

REGINE (*Off stage*) Yes, Mrs. Alving?

MRS. ALVING Go down to the laundry and help them with the wreaths.

REGINE Very well, Mrs. Alving.

(MRS. ALVING *makes sure that* REGINE *has gone and then closes the door*)

MANDERS You're sure he can't hear us in there?

MRS. ALVING Not with the door shut—besides, he's going out.

MANDERS I'm still so overcome. I don't know how I managed to eat a morsel of that delicious food.

MRS. ALVING (*In suppressed anguish, pacing up and down*) No— Well—what's to be done?

MANDERS What's to be done indeed? I wish I knew what to suggest— I don't feel competent to deal with a crisis of this sort.

MRS. ALVING One thing I'm convinced of—that, so far, nothing serious has happened.

MANDERS God forbid!— But it's a shameful business all the same.

MRS. ALVING It's just a foolish whim on Osvald's part; I'm sure of that.

MANDERS As I said before—I have no experience in such things—but I can't help thinking—

MRS. ALVING One thing's clear: she must leave this house at once—before it's too late.

MANDERS That goes without saying.

MRS. ALVING But where can she go? We certainly wouldn't be justified in—

MANDERS She must go home to her father, of course.

MRS. ALVING To whom—did you say?

MANDERS To her— But of course. Engstrand isn't her— Good Heavens, Mrs. Alving—all this is impossible—there must be some mistake!

MRS. ALVING I'm afraid there is no mistake, Manders. The girl confessed to me herself. And Alving didn't deny it; so the only thing we could do was to try and hush the matter up.

MANDERS Yes—I suppose so.

MRS. ALVING The girl left my service at once and was given a handsome sum to keep her mouth shut. She then took matters into her own hands—went back to town and renewed an old friendship with the carpenter, Engstrand. She hinted that she had money—told him some cock-and-bull story about a foreigner with a yacht—the outcome of all this was, that they were married in great haste. You married them yourself, I believe.

MANDERS But—I can't understand it! I remember distinctly Engstrand coming to arrange about the wedding: He was overcome with confusion—and kept reproaching himself bitterly for his and his fiancée's shameless behavior.

MRS. ALVING Well—I suppose he had to take the blame on himself.

MANDERS I certainly never would have believed Jakob Engstrand capable of such duplicity—and to me of all people! I shall have to teach him a good lesson, I can see that— The immorality of such a marriage—and for money too! How much did the girl receive?

MRS. ALVING Three hundred dollars.

MANDERS It's almost unbelievable—for a paltry three hundred dollars—consenting to marry a loose woman.

MRS. ALVING What about me? Didn't I marry a "loose" man.

MANDERS What on earth are you talking about!

MRS. ALVING Was Alving any better when he married me, than the girl Johanna was when she married Engstrand?

MANDERS But—good Heavens—the two cases are utterly different—

MRS. ALVING Perhaps not so very different, after all. There was a colossal difference in the price—that's true enough! A paltry three hundred dollars as against a large fortune.

MANDERS But there *can* be no comparison in this instance! Your decision was based on the advice of relatives and friends—as well as the promptings of your heart.

MRS. ALVING (*Without looking at him*) My heart, as you call it, was involved elsewhere at the time—as I thought you knew.

MANDERS (*In a reserved tone*) Had I known any such thing, I should not have been a constant visitor in your husband's house.

MRS. ALVING One thing is certain; I never really consulted my own feelings in the matter.

MANDERS Perhaps not—but you consulted your mother—your two aunts—all those nearest to you—as was only right.

MRS. ALVING Yes—those three! They were the ones that settled the whole business for me. As I look back on it, it seems incredible. They pointed out, in the most forceful terms, that it would be nothing short of folly to refuse an offer of such magnificence! Poor Mother. If she only knew what that "magnificence" has led to.

MANDERS No one can be held responsible for the outcome— The fact remains, that your marriage in every way conformed to the strictest rules of law and order.

MRS. ALVING (*At the window*): All this talk about law and order!—I often think all the suffering in the world is due to that.

MANDERS That is a very wicked thing to say, Mrs. Alving.

MRS. ALVING That may be; but I will not be bound by these responsibilities, these hypocritical conventions any longer—I simply cannot! I must work my way through to freedom.

MANDERS What do you mean by that?

MRS. ALVING (*Drumming on the windowpane*) I should never have lied about Alving—but I didn't dare do anything else at the time—and it wasn't only for Osvald's sake—it was for my own sake too. What a coward I've been!

MANDERS A coward?

MRS. ALVING A coward, yes— I could just hear what people would say if they found out the truth: Poor man! One can hardly blame him with a wife like that! She tried to leave him, you know!

MANDERS They would have been justified to some extent.

MRS. ALVING (*Looking at him steadily*) If I'd had the strength I should have taken Osvald into my confidence; I should have said: Listen, my son, your father was a corrupt, contaminated man—

MANDERS Good God—!

MRS. ALVING And then I should have told him the whole story—word for word—just as I told it to you.

MANDERS You horrify me, Mrs. Alving!

MRS. ALVING I know—God, yes!— I know!— I'm horrified myself at the thought of it!— That's how much of a coward I am.

MANDERS How can you call yourself a coward for doing what was merely your duty? Have you forgotten that a child should love and honor his father and mother?

MRS. ALVING Don't let us talk in generalities! Let us ask: Should Osvald love and honor Captain Alving?

MANDERS You're his mother—how could you find it in your heart to shatter his ideals?

MRS. ALVING Oh—ideals, ideals! What about the Truth?—If only I weren't such a coward!

MANDERS You shouldn't scoff at ideals, Mrs. Alving—they have a way of avenging themselves. God knows—Osvald doesn't seem to have many—unfortunately. But his father seems to be somewhat of an ideal to him.

MRS. ALVING Yes, that's quite true.

MANDERS Your letters must be responsible for that feeling in him—you must have fostered it.

MRS. ALVING Yes. I was treading the path of duty and obedience, Mr. Manders—I therefore lied to my son, religiously, year after year. What a coward—what a coward I was!

MANDERS You have fostered a happy illusion in your son's mind, Mrs. Alving—you shouldn't underestimate its value.

MRS. ALVING Its value may turn out to be dubious, who knows? But I won't tolerate any nonsense with Regine—he mustn't be allowed to get her into trouble.

MANDERS Good Heavens, no—that would be unthinkable!

MRS. ALVING If I thought she would really make him happy—if he were really serious about it—

MANDERS What do you mean?

MRS. ALVING Oh, but he couldn't be—Regine could never be enough for him—

MANDERS What are you talking about?

MRS. ALVING If I weren't such a miserable coward I'd say to him: marry her—come to any arrangement you like with her—only be honest about it!

MANDERS A marriage between them—? How could you condone anything so abominable—so unheard of!

MRS. ALVING Unheard of, you say? Why not face the truth, Manders? You know there are dozens of married couples out here in the country who are related in the same way.

MANDERS I refuse to understand you.

MRS. ALVING But you *do* understand me all the same!

MANDERS There may be a few instances—family life is not always as blameless as it should be, unfortunately. But in nine cases out of ten the relationship is unsuspected—or at worst, unconfirmed. Here—on the other hand— That you a mother, should be willing to allow your son—!

MRS. ALVING But I'm *not* willing to allow it—that's just what I'm saying— I wouldn't allow it for anything in the world.

MANDERS Only because you're a coward—as you express it. But if you weren't a coward—! Such a revolting marriage—God forgive you!

MRS. ALVING We're all of us descended from that kind of marriage—so they say. And who was responsible for that arrangement, Mr. Manders?

MANDERS I refuse to discuss these matters with you, Mrs. Alving—you are in no fit state to touch on such things— How you can have the effrontery to call yourself a coward for not—!

MRS. ALVING I'll tell you what I mean by that; I live in constant fear and terror, because I can't rid myself of all these ghosts that haunt me.

MANDERS Ghosts, you say?

MRS. ALVING Yes— Just now, when I heard Regine and Osvald in there—I felt hemmed in by ghosts— You know, Manders, the longer I live the more convinced I am that we're all haunted in this world—not only by the things we inherit from our parents—but by the ghosts of innumerable old prejudices and beliefs—half-forgotten cruelties and betrayals—we may not even be aware of them—but they're there just the same—and we can't get rid of them. The whole world is haunted by these ghosts of the dead past; you have only to pick up a newspaper to see them weaving in and out between the lines—Ah! if we only had the courage to sweep them all out and let in the light!

MANDERS So this is the result of all this reading of yours—this detestable, pernicious, free-thinking literature!

MRS. ALVING You're mistaken, my dear Manders. It

was you who first goaded me into thinking—I shall always be grateful to you for that.

MANDERS I?

MRS. ALVING Yes. When you forced me to obey what you called my conscience and my duty; when you hailed as right and noble what my whole soul rebelled against as false and ugly—that's when I started to analyze your teachings; that's when I first started to *think*. And one day I saw quite clearly that all you stand for—all that you preach—is artificial and dead—there's no life or truth in it.

MANDERS (*Softly, with emotion*) So that's all I achieved by the hardest struggle of my life.

MRS. ALVING I'd call it your most ignominious defeat.

MANDERS It was a victory over myself, Helene; my greatest victory.

MRS. ALVING It was a crime against us both.

MANDERS The fact that by my entreaties I persuaded you to return to your lawful husband, when you came to me distracted and overwrought crying: "Here I am. Take me!" You consider that a crime?

MRS. ALVING Yes; I think it was.

MANDERS There is no possible understanding between us.

MRS. ALVING Not any more, at any rate.

MANDERS You have always been to me—even in my most secret thoughts—another man's wife.

MRS. ALVING You really believe that, Manders?

MANDERS Helene—!

MRS. ALVING It's so easy to forget one's feelings!

MANDERS I don't forget. I am exactly the same as I always was.

MRS. ALVING (*With a change of tone*) Oh, don't let's talk any more about the old days! Now you're up to your eyes in committee meetings and advisory boards—and I sit out here and battle with ghosts—the ghosts within myself and those all around me.

MANDERS Those around you, I can at least help you to conquer. After the dreadful things you've said to me today, I couldn't dream of leaving a young, unprotected girl alone in your house.

MRS. ALVING I think the best thing would be to arrange a good match for her—don't you agree?

MANDERS Unquestionably. It would be best for her in every respect. Regine has reached the age when —of course, I know very little about these things—

MRS. ALVING Yes—she developed early.

MANDERS So it seemed to me. I remember thinking when I prepared her for Confirmation, that she was remarkably well-developed for a child of her age. For the present she had better go home, under her father's care—but, of course, Engstrand isn't—How could he—*he* of all people—conceal the truth from me!

(*There is a knock at the hall door*)

MRS. ALVING Who can *that* be? Come in!

(ENGSTRAND *appears in the doorway; he is in his Sunday clothes*)

ENGSTRAND I most humbly beg pardon—but—

MRS. ALVING Oh, it's you, Engstrand

ENGSTRAND None of the maids seemed to be about —so I took the liberty of knocking, Ma'am—

MRS. ALVING Oh, very well—come in. Do you wish to speak to me?

ENGSTRAND (*Coming in*) No—thank you all the same, Mrs. Alving. But—if I might have a word with the Reverend—

MANDERS (*Pacing up and down*) With me—eh? So you want to talk to me, do you?

ENGSTRAND I'd be most grateful—

MANDERS (*Stopping in front of him*) Well—what is it?

ENGSTRAND It's just this, Sir; we're being paid off down there—and many thanks to you, Ma'am—our work's all finished; and, I thought how nice and helpful it would be to all of us who've worked together so hard and faithfully—if we could have a few prayers this evening.

MANDERS Prayers?—Down at the Orphanage?

ENGSTRAND Yes, Sir; of course if it isn't convenient to you, Sir—

MANDERS Oh, it's convenient enough—but—hm—

ENGSTRAND I've taken to saying a few prayers myself down there of an evening—

MRS. ALVING *You* have?

ENGSTRAND Yes—now and then; we can all do with a little edification, I thought; but I'm just a simple, humble fellow—I'm not much good at it, God help me! But as long as the Reverend happened to be here—I thought—

MANDERS Look here, Engstrand; I must first ask you a question: Are you in a proper state of mind for prayer? Have you a clear untroubled conscience?

ENGSTRAND God help me! Perhaps we'd better not talk about my conscience, Mr. Manders.

MANDERS That is exactly what we must talk about. Well—answer me!

ENGSTRAND Well, Sir—of course, now and then, it does trouble me a bit—

MANDERS I'm glad you admit that at least. Now—will you be so kind as to tell me honestly—what is the truth about Regine?

MRS. ALVING (*Rapidly*) Mr. Manders!

MANDERS (*Calming her*) I'll handle this—

ENGSTRAND Regine! —Lord, how you frightened me! (*Gives* MRS. ALVING *a look*) There's nothing wrong with Regine, is there?

MANDERS It is to be hoped not. But what I mean is this: What is your true relationship to Regine? You pretend to be her father, do you not?

ENGSTRAND (*Uncertain*) Yes—hm—well, Sir—you know all about me and poor Johanna—

MANDERS No more prevarication, please! Your late wife confessed the whole truth to Mrs. Alving before she left her service.

ENGSTRAND Do you mean to say she—? Oh, she did, did she?

MANDERS Yes; so it's no use lying any longer, Engstrand.

ENGSTRAND Well! And after her swearing up and down—

MANDERS Swearing, you say—?

ENGSTRAND I mean, she gave me her solemn word, Sir.

MANDERS And all these years you've kept the truth from me—from *me,* who have always had the utmost faith in you!

ENGSTRAND Yes, Sir—I'm afraid I have.

MANDERS Have I deserved that, Engstrand? Haven't I always done everything in my power to help you? Answer me—haven't I?

ENGSTRAND Yes, Sir. Things would often have looked pretty black for me, if it hadn't been for Mr. Manders.

MANDERS And this is how you repay me! You cause me to enter erroneous statements in the Church Register, and withhold from me for years the truth which it was your duty to impart to me. Your conduct has been inexcusable, Engstrand; from now on, I shall have nothing more to do with you.

ENGSTRAND (*With a sigh*) Yes, Sir; I suppose that's how it has to be!

MANDERS I don't see how you can possibly justify your conduct.

ENGSTRAND We felt it better not to add to her shame by talking about it. Supposing you'd been in poor Johanna's place, Mr. Manders—

MANDERS I!

ENGSTRAND Lord bless me! I don't mean that the way it sounds! What I mean is: suppose you had done something you were ashamed of in the eyes of the world, as they say; we men oughtn't to judge a poor woman too hard, Mr. Manders.

MANDERS But I don't judge her—it's *you* I'm accusing.

ENGSTRAND Mr. Manders, would you allow me to ask you just one little question?

MANDERS Very well—what is it?

ENGSTRAND Shouldn't a decent honorable man help those who've gone astray?

MANDERS Well—naturally—

ENGSTRAND And isn't a man bound to keep his word of honor?

MANDERS Yes, of course, but—

ENGSTRAND Well—you see, after Johanna got into trouble with that Englishman—or maybe he was American—or one of those Russians even—anyway, she came back to town. Poor thing—she'd already refused me twice; she only had eyes for the handsome fellows—and, of course, I had this deformed leg of mine. You remember, Sir, I was once rash enough to enter one of those dance-halls—one of those dives where sailors spend their time drinking and carousing, as they say—I was just trying to persuade them to try another kind of life—

MRS. ALVING (*By the window*) Hm—

MANDERS Yes, I know, Engstrand; those dreadful men threw you downstairs; I remember your telling me of that tragic experience; you bear your deformity with honor.

ENGSTRAND I don't mean to brag about it, Sir. Well—anyway, she came to me, and confided her whole trouble to me, with tears and lamentations—it broke my heart to listen to her—

MANDERS Did it, indeed, Engstrand! Well—and then—?

ENGSTRAND Well, then I said to her, I said: that American is wandering on the seas of the world; and you, Johanna, are a sinful fallen creature, I said. But Jakob Engstrand, I said, stands here on two solid legs, I said; of course I only meant that in a manner of speaking, you know, Sir—

MANDERS Yes, yes—I understand—go on—

ENGSTRAND Well then, Sir, I married her—I made her an honest woman—so no one would know of her reckless behavior with that foreigner—

MANDERS All of that was very right and good of you, Engstrand; but I cannot condone your consenting to accept money—

ENGSTRAND Money? Me? Not a penny—

MANDERS (*In a questioning tone, to* MRS. ALVING) But—?

ENGSTRAND Oh yes—wait a bit—now I remember. Johanna did say something about some money she had—but I refused to hear anything about it! Get Thee behind me, Satan, I said; it's Mammon's gold (or bank-notes or whatever it was), we'll throw it back in the American's face, I said; but, of course, he had disappeared, Sir—disappeared over the vast ocean, you see—

MANDERS Yes—I see—my dear Engstrand—

ENGSTRAND Yes, Sir; and then Johanna and I agreed that every penny of that money should go to the child's upbringing; and that's where it went, Sir; and I can account for every cent of it.

MANDERS But this puts things in an entirely different light—

ENGSTRAND That's the way it was, Mr. Manders. And, though I say it myself, I've tried to be a good father to Regine—to the best of my ability, that is—you know what a weak man I am, Sir—unfortunately—

MANDERS Yes, yes—I know, dear Engstrand—

ENGSTRAND I can truly say I gave the child a decent upbringing and made poor Johanna a good and loving husband; but it never would have occurred to me to go to you, Mr. Manders, and brag about it and pat myself on the back for doing a good action; I'm not made like that. And most of the time, unfortunately, I've little enough to brag about. When I go and talk to you, Sir, it's mostly to confess my sins and weaknesses. For, as I said just now, my conscience troubles me quite a bit, Mr. Manders—

MANDERS Give me your hand, Jakob Engstrand.

ENGSTRAND Oh—Lord, Sir!—

MANDERS Come now—no nonsense! (*Grasps his hand*) There!

ENGSTRAND I most humbly ask you to forgive me, Sir—

MANDERS On the contrary—it's I who must ask your forgiveness—

ENGSTRAND Oh, no, Sir!

MANDERS Most certainly—and I do so with all my heart. Forgive me, dear Engstrand, for so misjudging you. I wish I might give you some proof of my sincere regret and of the esteem in which I hold you—

ENGSTRAND You'd really like to do that, Sir?

MANDERS It would give me the greatest of pleasure.

ENGSTRAND Well—it just happens—there is something you could do for me, Sir; I've managed to put by a bit of money from my earnings here, and I'm thinking of opening a kind of Seamen's Home when I get back to town, Sir—

MRS. ALVING You—*what?*

ENGSTRAND It'd be like a kind of refuge for them, you see, Ma'am. These poor sailors have so many temptations when they get to port—I thought in my house, they'd find a father's care—

MANDERS What do you say to that, Mrs. Alving?

ENGSTRAND Of course, I haven't much capital to go on—and I thought if I could just find a helping hand—

MANDERS I shall give it some thought. I find your scheme most interesting. But now, go and get everything ready—light the lights—and prepare for our little celebration. Now I feel sure you are in a fit state for prayer, my dear Engstrand—

ENGSTRAND Yes—I really believe I am. Well, goodbye, Mrs. Alving, and thank you for everything; be sure and take good care of Regine for me. (*Wipes away a tear*) Poor Johanna's child—it's strange how she's managed to creep into my heart—but, she has—there's no denying it! (*He bows and goes out by the hall door*)

MANDERS Well—what do you think of him now, Mrs. Alving? It certainly puts things in an entirely different light.

MRS. ALVING It does indeed!

MANDERS It just shows you how careful one must be in judging one's fellow-men. And what a satisfaction to find oneself mistaken! What do you say now?

MRS. ALVING I say you're a great big baby, Manders, and always will be!

MANDERS *I!*

MRS. ALVING (*Puts her hands on his shoulders*) Yes; and I say I should like very much to give you a big hug!

MANDERS (*Hastily drawing back*) Good Heavens—What ideas you have!

MRS. ALVING (*With a smile*) Oh, you needn't be afraid of me!

MANDERS (*By the table*) You have such an extravagant way of expressing yourself! I'll just gather up all these documents and put them in my bag. (*He does so*) There! Keep an eye on Osvald when he returns; I'll leave you for the present—but I'll come back and see you later. (*He takes his hat and goes out through the hall door*)

MRS. ALVING (*Gives a sigh, glances out of the window, straightens up one or two things in the room and is about to go into the dining room but stops in the doorway and gives a low exclamation*) Osvald—are you still there?

OSVALD (*From the dining room*) I'm just finishing my cigar.

MRS. ALVING I thought you'd gone out for a walk.

OSVALD In this kind of weather?

(*Noise of a glass clinking.* MRS. ALVING *leaves the door open, and sits down on the sofa with some knitting*)

OSVALD (*Off stage*) Was that Mr. Manders who went out just now?

MRS. ALVING Yes, he went down to the Orphanage.

OSVALD Hm—

(*The clinking of a bottle on a glass is heard again*)

MRS. ALVING (*With an uneasy glance*) Osvald dear—be careful with that liqueur—it's quite strong, you know.

OSVALD It'll do me good, Mother! I feel so chilly.

MRS. ALVING Wouldn't you rather come in here with me?

OSVALD You don't allow smoking in there, you said.

MRS. ALVING I don't mind a cigar, dear.

OSVALD Very well, then I'll come in—I'll just have another little drop—there! (*He comes in smoking a cigar. Closes the door after him. A short silence*) Where did Mr. Manders go?

MRS. ALVING I just told you; he went down to the Orphanage.

OSVALD Oh, yes—so you did.

MRS. ALVING It's not good for you to sit so long at table, Osvald, dear.

OSVALD (*Holding his cigar behind his back*) But it's so cozy, Mother. (*He pats her face and caresses her*) You don't know what it means: To be home! To sit at my mother's table—in my mother's own room—to eat my mother's delicious food—!

MRS. ALVING My dear, dear boy!

OSVALD (*Walks up and down impatiently*) And what on earth is there to do here? I can't seem to settle to anything—

MRS. ALVING Can't you?

OSVALD In this gloomy weather—never a ray of sunshine. (*Paces up and down*) God! Not to be able to work—!

MRS. ALVING Perhaps you shouldn't have come home, Osvald.

OSVALD I had to come, Mother.

MRS. ALVING But, if you're unhappy, Osvald. You know I'd ten times rather give up the joy of having you here, than—

OSVALD (*Stopping by the table*) Tell me honestly, Mother—is it really such a joy to you to have me home again?

MRS. ALVING How can you ask such a thing!

OSVALD (*Crumpling up a newspaper*) I should have thought you didn't much care one way or the other.

MRS. ALVING How have you the heart to say that to me, Osvald?

OSVALD After all—you managed to live without me all these years.

MRS. ALVING That's true—I've managed to live without you— (*A pause. Twilight is falling gradually.*

OSVALD *paces up and down. He has put out his cigar. He suddenly stops in front of* MRS. ALVING)

OSVALD May I sit beside you on the sofa, Mother?

MRS. ALVING (*Making room for him*) Of course, dear.

OSVALD (*Sits beside her*) There's something I must tell you.

MRS. ALVING (*Anxiously*) Well?

OSVALD (*Staring in front of him*) I don't think I can bear it any longer.

MRS. ALVING Bear what? What is it?

OSVALD (*As before*) I somehow couldn't bring myself to write to you about it—and, since I've been home—

MRS. ALVING (*Grips his arm*) Osvald—what is it?

OSVALD All day yesterday and again today, I've tried to get rid of the thought—free myself of it—but I can't—

MRS. ALVING (*Rising*) You must be honest with me, Osvald—

OSVALD (*Pulls her down on the sofa again*) No, don't get up! Sit still! I'll try and tell you. I've complained a lot about being tired after my journey—

MRS. ALVING Yes—well, what of that—?

OSVALD But that isn't really what's the matter with me; this is no ordinary fatigue—

MRS. ALVING (*Tries to get up*) You're not ill, are you, Osvald?

OSVALD (*Pulling her down again*) No, don't get up, Mother. Try and be calm. I'm not really ill either—not in the usual sort of way—(*Clasping his head in his hands*) It's a kind of mental breakdown, Mother—I'm destroyed—I'll never be able to work again. (*He hides his face in his hands, and lets his head fall into her lap—shaking with sobs*)

MRS. ALVING (*Pale and trembling*) Osvald! It's not true! Look at me!

OSVALD (*Looking up in despair*) I'll never be able to work again! Never—never! I'll be like a living corpse! Mother—can you imagine anything more frightful—?

MRS. ALVING But, my darling! How could such a dreadful thing happen to you?

OSVALD (*Sitting up again*) That's just it—I don't know! I can't possibly imagine! I've never lived a dissipated life—not in any kind of way—you must believe that, Mother—I haven't!

MRS. ALVING I believe that, Osvald.

OSVALD And yet, in spite of that—this ghastly thing has taken hold of me!

MRS. ALVING It'll come out all right, my darling. It's just overwork—believe me!

OSVALD (*Dully*) Yes—I thought that too at first—but it's not so.

MRS. ALVING Tell me all about it.

OSVALD Yes, I will.

MRS. ALVING When did you first notice anything?

OSVALD It was just after I went back to Paris—after my last visit here. I started to get terrible headaches—all up the back of my head—it was as if an iron band was screwed round my head—from the neck up—

MRS. ALVING And then—?

OSVALD At first I thought it was just the usual kind of headache I'd always had—since I was a child—

MRS. ALVING Yes—?

OSVALD But it wasn't that—I soon found that out, I was no longer able to work. I'd start on a new picture and all my strength would suddenly fail me—it was as though I were paralyzed; I couldn't concentrate—and I felt sick and dizzy; it was the most ghastly sensation; at last I went to see a doctor—and then I found out the truth.

MRS. ALVING What do you mean?

OSVALD He was one of the best doctors there. I described to him just how I felt—and then he started asking me all sorts of questions—questions about things that seemed to have no bearing on the case—I couldn't make out what he was driving at—

MRS. ALVING Well—?

OSVALD At last he said: your constitution has been undermined from birth; he used the word *vermoulu*.[1]

MRS. ALVING (*Anxiously*) What did he mean by that?

OSVALD I didn't know what he meant either; I asked him to explain. And do you know what he said—that cynical old man—? (*Clenching his fist*) Oh!—

MRS. ALVING No—what?

OSVALD He said: the sins of the fathers are visited upon the children.

MRS. ALVING (*Rises slowly*) The sins of the fathers—!

OSVALD I almost hit him in the face.

MRS. ALVING (*Pacing the floor*) The sins of the fathers—

OSVALD (*With a sad smile*) Can you believe it? Of course I assured him that such a thing was out of the question—but he paid no attention—he repeated what he'd said. I had some of your letters with me—and I had to translate to him the parts that referred to Father—

MRS. ALVING Yes—?

OSVALD Then he had to admit he must be on the wrong tack. And then I learned the truth—the incredible truth! The sort of life I'd been leading—gay and carefree but innocent enough I thought—had been too much for my strength; I should have been more careful. So, you see, I've brought it on myself—

MRS. ALVING No! You mustn't believe that, Osvald!

OSVALD He said that was the only possible explanation. My whole life ruined—thrown away—through my own carelessness. All that I dreamt of achieving, of accomplishing—I dare not think of it—I mustn't think of it! If I could only live my life over again—if I could wipe it all out and start afresh! (*He flings himself face downward on the sofa. After a pause looks up, leaning on his elbows*) It wouldn't be so bad if it was something I'd inherited—if it were something I couldn't help. But, deliberately—

[1] Worm-eaten.

out of carelessness—out of shameful stupidity to throw away happiness, health—everything that's worthwhile in this world—my future—my whole life—!

MRS. ALVING No—no! It's impossible, Osvald—my darling—my boy! (*Bending over him*) It's not true—it's not as desperate as that—!

OSVALD (*Jumping up*) Oh, Mother, you don't know! And to think I should bring you such unhappiness! I've often hoped and prayed that you didn't care much about me, after all—

MRS. ALVING Not care about you, Osvald? You're all I have in the world—you're the only thing on earth that matters to me—

OSVALD (*Takes both her hands and kisses them*) Yes, Mother, I know; when I'm home I realize that—and it makes it doubly hard for me. Well—now you know all about it; don't let's discuss it any more today; I can't bear to dwell on it too long. (*Paces about the room*) Give me something to drink, Mother.

MRS. ALVING To drink? What do you want, Osvald?

OSVALD Oh, it doesn't matter—anything! You must have something in the house—

MRS. ALVING Yes, but Osvald—don't you think—?

OSVALD Don't refuse me, Mother—be a dear! I must have something to help me drown these agonizing thoughts! (*He goes up to the conservatory and looks out*) Oh, it's so dark—so terribly dark! (MRS. ALVING *goes to the bell-pull and rings*) This incessant rain! It may go on for weeks—for months! Never a ray of sunshine! I never remember seeing any sunshine here!

MRS. ALVING You're not thinking of leaving me, Osvald?

OSVALD (*With a deep sigh*) I'm not thinking of anything, Mother; I'm not capable of thinking—(*In a low voice*) I've had to give that up!

(REGINE *comes in from the dining room*)

REGINE Did you ring, Mrs. Alving?

MRS. ALVING Yes; bring in the lamp.

REGINE At once, Mrs. Alving—I have it ready. (*She goes out*)

MRS. ALVING (*Goes to* OSVALD) Don't keep anything from me, Osvald.

OSVALD I won't, Mother. (*Goes to the table*) It seems to me I've been very frank with you.

(REGINE *brings in the lamp and puts it on the table*)

MRS. ALVING Oh, and Regine—you might bring us a half bottle of champagne.

REGINE Very good, Mrs. Alving. (*She goes out*)

OSVALD (*Takes her face in his hands*) That's right, Mother! I knew you wouldn't let me go thirsty!

MRS. ALVING My own poor boy! As if I could refuse you anything!

OSVALD (*Eagerly*) You really mean that, Mother?

MRS. ALVING What?

OSVALD That you couldn't refuse me anything?

MRS. ALVING But, my dear Osvald—

OSVALD Sh!

(REGINE *enters with a small tray on which are a bottle of champagne and two glasses; she sets it down on the table*)

REGINE Shall I open it, Mrs. Alving?

OSVALD No thanks—I'll do it myself.

(REGINE *goes out*)

MRS. ALVING (*Sits down at the table*) Osvald—be honest with me—what is it you don't want me to refuse you—?

OSVALD (*Busy opening the bottle*) First, let's have a glass of wine—(*He opens the bottle and pours out one glass and is about to pour another*)

MRS. ALVING (*Puts her hand over the glass*) Thanks—not for me.

OSVALD For me, then! (*He empties his glass, refills it and empties it again; he sits down at the table*)

MRS. ALVING (*Expectantly*) Well—

OSVALD Mother, tell me—what was the matter with you and Mr. Manders at dinner, just now? Why were you so quiet and solemn?

MRS. ALVING Oh—did you notice that?

OSVALD Yes. Hm—(*A pause*) Mother, what do you think of Regine?

MRS. ALVING What do I think of her?

OSVALD Don't you think she's wonderful?

MRS. ALVING You don't know her as well as I do, Osvald—

OSVALD Well—what of that?

MRS. ALVING I should have taken charge of her sooner— I'm afraid she spent too many years at home—

OSVALD But she's so wonderful to look at, Mother! (*Fills up his glass*)

MRS. ALVING She has many grave faults, Osvald—

OSVALD As if that mattered—! (*He drinks*)

MRS. ALVING But I'm fond of her all the same; I feel responsible for her. I wouldn't have anything happen to her for all the world.

OSVALD (*Jumps up*) Mother! The one thing that could save me, is Regine!

MRS. ALVING (*Rising*) What do you mean?

OSVALD I mean I can't endure this agony alone!

MRS. ALVING But I'm here to help you, Osvald—

OSVALD Yes, I know; I thought that would be enough—that's why I came home to you; but it's no use; I see that now. My life here would be intolerable.

MRS. ALVING Osvald—!

OSVALD I must live a different sort of life; that's why I must go away again. I don't want you to see it happening to me—

MRS. ALVING But you can't go away when you're so ill, Osvald.

OSVALD If it were just an ordinary illness, of course I'd stay home, Mother; I know you're the best friend I have in the world—

MRS. ALVING You do know that—don't you?

OSVALD (*Moves about the room restlessly*) But it's the anguish, the remorse, the deadly fear—oh—that terrible fear!

MRS. ALVING (*Follows after him*) Fear? Fear of what?

OSVALD Don't ask me any more about it! I don't know —I can't describe it to you—(MRS. ALVING *goes to the bell-pull and rings*) What do you want?

MRS. ALVING I want my boy to be happy, that's what I want—I won't let you suffer here! (*To* REGINE) More champagne, Regine! A whole bottle!

(REGINE *goes*)

OSVALD Mother!

MRS. ALVING We country-people know how to live too —you'll see.

OSVALD Isn't she wonderful to look at? So beautifully built! So radiant with health.

MRS. ALVING (*Sitting down at the table*) Sit down, Osvald; let's talk quietly for a moment—

OSVALD (*Sits down*) You don't know about it, Mother —but I haven't been quite fair to Regine—

MRS. ALVING Not fair—?

OSVALD No—it was just thoughtlessness on my part— nothing serious; but last time I was home—

MRS. ALVING Yes—?

OSVALD She kept on asking questions about Paris—I told her a bit about my life there—and one day I said to her, quite casually: "Perhaps you'd like to go there and see it all for yourself, Regine—"

MRS. ALVING Well—?

OSVALD Then she blushed and got quite excited and said she'd give anything to go; then I said, perhaps some day it might be arranged—or something of that sort—

MRS. ALVING I see.

OSVALD Of course I'd forgotten all about it; but the other day, when I arrived, I asked her if she was glad I intended to spend such a long time here—

MRS. ALVING Yes—?

OSVALD And then she looked at me so strangely and said: "Then what about my trip to Paris?"

MRS. ALVING Her trip—?

OSVALD Yes—it seems she'd taken me quite seriously; she'd been thinking about it all this time—thinking about *me*. She'd even tried to teach herself some French—

MRS. ALVING So that was why—

OSVALD I'd never noticed her much before, Mother— but suddenly I saw her there—so beautiful—so vital —she stood there as though waiting to come into my arms—

MRS. ALVING Osvald—!

OSVALD I suddenly realized that she could save me; she was so full of the joy of life!

MRS. ALVING (*Startled*) Joy of life—? Is there salvation in that?

(REGINE *comes in with the champagne*)

REGINE Excuse me for being so long, Mrs. Alving. I had to go down to the cellar—(*Puts the bottle on the table*)

OSVALD Fetch another glass.

REGINE (*Looks at him surprised*) Mrs. Alving has a glass, Sir.

OSVALD Yes—but fetch one for yourself, Regine. (REGINE *starts and gives a quick frightened glance at* MRS. ALVING) Well?

REGINE (*Softly, with hesitation*) Do you wish me to, Mrs. Alving?

MRS. ALVING Fetch the glass, Regine.

(REGINE *goes into the dining room*)

OSVALD (*Looking after her*) Have you noticed her walk, Mother—so strong—so sure.

MRS. ALVING This can't be allowed to happen, Osvald.

OSVALD But it's all settled—you must see that—there's no use forbidding it. (REGINE *comes in with an empty glass and keeps it in her hand*) Sit down, Regine. (REGINE *looks questioningly at* MRS. ALVING)

MRS. ALVING Sit down. (REGINE *sits on a chair by the dining room door, with the empty glass in her hand*) Osvald— What were you saying about the joy of life?

OSVALD Yes—the joy of life, Mother—you don't know much about that here at home. I could never find it here.

MRS. ALVING Not here with me?

OSVALD No. Never at home. But you don't understand that.

MRS. ALVING Yes—I believe I'm beginning to understand it—now.

OSVALD That—and the joy of work. They're really the same thing you know. But of course, you don't know anything about that here either.

MRS. ALVING No; you may be right. Tell me more about it.

OSVALD Well—I simply mean that here people look on work as a curse—as a kind of punishment. They look on *life* as a wretched, miserable business—to be got through as soon as possible—

MRS. ALVING I know—a "vale of tears"—we do our best to make it so—

OSVALD But, you see, abroad, people don't look at it like that. They don't believe in that old-fashioned preaching any longer. The mere fact of being alive in this world seems to them joyous and marvelous. You must have noticed, Mother, everything I paint is filled with this joy of life; always and forever the joy of life! My paintings are full of light, of sunshine, of glowing happy faces. That's why I'm afraid to stay here, Mother.

MRS. ALVING Afraid? What are you afraid of—here with me?

OSVALD I'm afraid that all the strongest traits in my nature would become warped here—would degenerate into ugliness.

MRS. ALVING (*Looks at him intently*) You really believe that is what would happen?

OSVALD Yes—I'm convinced of it! Even if I lived the same life here as I live abroad—it still wouldn't *be* the same life.

MRS. ALVING (*Who has listened intently, rises; a thoughtful look in her eyes*) Now I see it! It's all becoming clear to me—

OSVALD What do you see?

MRS. ALVING The whole pattern—for the first time, I see it—and now I can speak.

OSVALD (*Rising*) I don't understand you, Mother.

REGINE (*Who has risen too*) Perhaps I'd better go—

MRS. ALVING No, no—stay where you are. Now I

can speak. Now you must know everything, Osvald—and then you can choose. Osvald! Regine!

OSVALD Sh! Here comes Manders.

MANDERS (*Enters from hall door*) Well—I must say—we've had a most edifying time—

OSVALD So have we.

MANDERS There can be no doubt about it— We must make it possible for Engstrand to start that seamen's home of his. Regine must go back with him; she can be most helpful—

REGINE No thank you, Mr. Manders!

MANDERS (*Notices her for the first time*) What—? You in here? And with a glass in your hand?

REGINE (*Hastily puts down her glass*) *Pardon!*

OSVALD Regine is going with me, Mr. Manders.

MANDERS Going with you—?

OSVALD Yes; as my wife—if she insists on that.

MANDERS But—good Heavens—!

REGINE It's no fault of mine, Mr. Manders—

OSVALD Or if I decide to stay here—she'll stay too.

REGINE (*Involuntarily*) Stay here—!

MANDERS I am amazed at you, Mrs. Alving.

MRS. ALVING None of this will happen—for now I can tell the truth at last.

MANDERS But you won't—you can't!

MRS. ALVING I can and I will—and nobody's ideals will be the worse for it.

OSVALD Mother, what is all this—what are you hiding from me?

REGINE (*Listening*) Mrs. Alving—Listen!—I hear people shouting out there. (*She goes up to the conservatory*)

OSVALD (*Going to the window stage left*) What's happening? What's that glare in the sky?

REGINE (*Calls out*) It's the Orphanage—the Orphanage is on fire!

MRS. ALVING (*Going to the window*) On fire—?

MANDERS On fire—? Impossible! I've just come from there.

OSVALD Give me my hat!—Oh never mind— Father's Orphanage! (*He runs out into the garden*)

MRS. ALVING My shawl, Regine! The whole place is in flames!

MANDERS How horrible! It's a judgment, Mrs. Alving—a judgment on this house.

MRS. ALVING Yes—undoubtedly, Manders. Come, Regine.

(MRS. ALVING *and* REGINE *hurry out through the hall door*)

MANDERS (*Clasping his hands*) And to think it's not insured!

(*He follows them as the curtain falls*)

## Act Three

*The room as before. All the doors stand open. The lamp is still burning on the table. It is dark out of doors; there is only a faint glow from the fire in the background to the left.*

MRS. ALVING, *with a shawl over her head, stands in the conservatory looking out.* REGINE, *also with a shawl on, stands a little behind her.*

MRS. ALVING Nothing left—burned to the ground!

REGINE The cellar is still in flames.

MRS. ALVING Why doesn't Osvald come?—there's no hope of saving anything.

REGINE Shall I take his hat down to him?

MRS. ALVING Is he out there without it?

REGINE (*Pointing to the hall*) Yes—it's hanging in the hall—

MRS. ALVING No—leave it—he'll be back in a moment—I think I'll go and look for him. (*Exits to the garden*)

MANDERS (*Enters from hall*) Isn't Mrs. Alving here?

REGINE She just went down to the garden.

MANDERS What a night—I've never gone through anything as dreadful!

REGINE It's a terrible thing, Mr. Manders!

MANDERS Don't speak of it!— I can't bear the thought of it.

REGINE But how could it possibly have happened?

MANDERS Oh, don't ask me, Miss Engstrand—how should I know! You're not implying—? Isn't it enough that your father should—?

REGINE What's he been up to—?

MANDERS He's driven me half mad—

ENGSTRAND (*Enters through hall*) Oh there you are, Mr. Manders—

MANDERS (*Turning around with a start*) Must you follow me in here too!

ENGSTRAND Oh, Mr. Manders!— Such a terrible thing, Sir—!

MANDERS (*Pacing up and down*) Yes, yes! We know! We know!—

REGINE What's the meaning of this?

ENGSTRAND It was all due to the prayer meeting, you see! (*Aside to* REGINE) We've hooked the old fool now, my girl! (*Aloud*) That poor Mr. Manders should be the cause of such a calamity—and through my fault too!

MANDERS But I tell you, Engstrand—

ENGSTRAND No one touched the lights but you, Sir!

MANDERS (*Standing still*) That's what *you* claim—but I could swear I never went *near* the lights!

ENGSTRAND But I saw you with my own eyes, Sir!—I saw you snuff one of the candles and throw the bit of wick right into a pile of shavings!

MANDERS You say you *saw* this?

ENGSTRAND So help me God, Sir!

MANDERS Incredible!— I'm not in the habit of snuffing candles with my fingers.

ENGSTRAND No Sir—I thought at the time it didn't look quite like you. It'll be quite a serious thing, won't it, Sir?

MANDERS (*Walks restlessly back and forth*) Don't ask me about it!

ENGSTRAND (*Follows him about*) You hadn't insured the place, had you, Sir?

MANDERS (*Still pacing*) I told you I hadn't!

ENGSTRAND (*Following him*) Hadn't insured it!— And then to go and set the whole place on fire like that! Lord! What a bit of bad luck, Sir!

MANDERS (*Wipes the perspiration from his brow*) You may well say so, Engstrand.

ENGSTRAND A charitable institution too! A place dedicated, you might say, to the good of the Community! — It's likely the papers won't treat you any too kindly, Mr. Manders.

MANDERS That's just it! That's what I'm thinking about —all the spiteful attacks and accusations! That's the worst part of the whole business—I can't bear the thought of it!

MRS. ALVING (*Enters from the garden*) He won't come —he can't seem to tear himself away.

MANDERS Oh, it's you, Mrs. Alving.

MRS. ALVING Well, Manders! You got out of making your speech after all!

MANDERS I'd be only too glad to make it!

MRS. ALVING (*In a subdued tone*) It's all for the best; that poor Orphanage could never have brought good to anyone!

MANDERS You really feel that?

MRS. ALVING Well—don't you?

MANDERS All the same—it's a great tragedy.

MRS. ALVING Nonsense! Now—let's discuss it from a business point of view— Are you waiting for Mr. Manders, Engstrand?

ENSTRAND (*By the hall door*) Yes, Ma'am, I am.

MRS. ALVING Well then—sit down.

ENSTRAND I'd rather stand, thank you, Ma'am.

MRS. ALVING (*To* MANDERS) I suppose you'll be leaving by the next boat?

MANDERS Yes—there's one in an hour.

MRS. ALVING Please take all the documents with you —I don't want to hear another word about it! I've other things to think about now.

MANDERS Mrs. Alving—

MRS. ALVING I'll arrange to send you Power of Attorney and you can wind things up as you think best.

MANDERS I'll be glad to look after it for you. Of course now, the original terms of the bequest will have to be radically altered.

MRS. ALVING Naturally—

MANDERS I would suggest making the actual land over to the Parish under the circumstances; it's not without value, and could be used for many purposes. As to the interest on the capital—I feel sure I can find some worthy project in need of support—something that would prove beneficial to the life of the community.

MRS. ALVING Do anything you like with it—it makes no difference to me.

ENGSTRAND You might give a thought to my Seamen's Home, Mr. Manders.

MANDERS To be sure. A good suggestion. Well worth looking into.

ENGSTRAND (*Aside*) Looking into! That's a good one!

MANDERS (*With a sigh*) Of course I may not be long in charge of these affairs; public opinion may compel me to withdraw; there will naturally be an investigation to determine the cause of the fire; it all depends on the outcome of that.

MRS. ALVING What *are* you talking about, Manders?

MANDERS It's impossible to tell what the outcome will be.

ENGSTRAND (*Coming closer*) Oh no it's not, Mr. Manders! Don't forget *me*—don't forget Jakob Engstrand!

MANDERS But—I don't see—

ENGSTRAND (*In a low voice*) And Jakob Engstrand is not one to desert a benefactor in his hour of need— as they say!

MANDERS But, my dear man—how could you possibly—?

ENGSTRAND Jakob Engstrand won't desert you, Sir! He'll be like a guardian angel to you, Sir!

MANDERS But I could never consent—!

ENGSTRAND You'll have nothing to do with it, Sir. It wouldn't be the first time I'd taken the blame for others.

MANDER Jakob! (*Wringing his hands*) You're one in a million! I'll see that you get funds for your Seamen's Home— You can count on that. (ENGSTRAND *tries to thank him but is overcome with emotion;* MANDERS *slings his traveling-bag over his shoulder*) And now —let's be off. We'll travel together, of course.

ENGSTRAND (*At the hall door, aside to* REGINE) You'd better come with me, hussy! You'll live like a Queen!

REGINE (*Tosses her head*) *Merci!* (*She fetches* MANDERS' *things from the hall*)

MANDERS Goodbye, Mrs. Alving. May the Spirit of Truth and Righteousness soon enter into this house.

MRS. ALVING Goodbye, Manders. (*She goes to meet* OSVALD *who enters from the garden*)

ENGSTRAND (*As he and* REGINE *help* MANDERS *with his coat*) Goodbye, my dear child. And if anything should happen to you, remember Jakob Engstrand's always there—you know where to find him. Harbor Street—you know! (*To* MRS. ALVING *and* OSVALD) My home for poor Seamen shall be called "Captain Alving's Haven" and if it turns out the way I want it, Ma'am—I humbly hope it may prove worthy of Captain Alving's memory!

MANDERS (*In the doorway*) Hm—yes. Come along my dear Engstrand. Goodbye again—goodbye! (*They exit through the hall*)

OSVALD (*Goes toward the table*) What does he mean? What "home" is he talking about?

MRS. ALVING It's some sort of a hostel he and Manders are thinking of starting.

OSVALD It'll only burn down—just like this one.

MRS. ALVING Why do you say that?

OSVALD Everything will be burnt. Father's memory will be wiped out. I shall soon be burnt up too.

(REGINE *looks at him in amazement*)

MRS. ALVING Osvald!— You poor boy! You shouldn't have stayed down there so long.

OSVALD (*Sits down at the table*) I expect you're right about that.

MRS. ALVING Your face is wet, Osvald; let me dry it for you.

(*Wipes his face with her handkerchief*)

OSVALD (*Indifferently*) Thanks, Mother.

MRS. ALVING You must be tired, Osvald. You'd better get some sleep.

OSVALD (*Apprehensively*) No! No! I don't want to sleep! I never sleep—I only pretend to—(*Dully*) I'll sleep soon enough!

MRS. ALVING (*Looking at him anxiously*) I'm afraid you're really ill, my darling!

REGINE (*Intently*) Is Mr. Alving ill?

OSVALD (*Impatiently*) And close the doors!—I want all the doors closed!—this terrible fear—

MRS. ALVING Close the doors, Regine.

(REGINE *closes the doors and remains standing by the one to the hall.* MRS. ALVING *takes off her shawl, and* REGINE *does likewise*)

MRS. ALVING (*Draws up a chair and sits next to* OSVALD) There!—I'll sit here beside you.

OSVALD Yes—do, Mother. And Regine must stay here too—she must never leave me. You'll be there to help me, won't you, Regine?

REGINE I don't understand—

MRS. ALVING —There to help you?

OSVALD Yes—when the time comes.

MRS. ALVING Can't you trust your mother to do that?

OSVALD You? (*Smiles*) You'd never do it. (*With a melancholy laugh*) You! (*Looks at her gravely*) And yet you're the only one who has the right to do it. Why are you always so formal with me, Regine? Why don't you call me Osvald?

REGINE (*In a low voice*) Mrs. Alving might not like it.

MRS. ALVING You may soon have a right to—so sit down with us, Regine. (REGINE *hesitates, then sits down quietly at the far side of the table*) And now, my darling, I'm going to free you from this torment; you won't have to bear this dreadful burden any longer.

OSVALD You're going to free me, Mother?

MRS. ALVING Yes—from this remorse, this sense of guilt, this self-reproach—

OSVALD —Do you think you can do that?

MRS. ALVING Yes, I believe I can now. Earlier this evening you were talking about the joy of life—and suddenly everything became clear to me; I saw my whole life in a new light.

OSVALD (*Shaking his head*) I don't understand this.

MRS. ALVING You should have known your father when he was a young lieutenant. He was filled with that joy of life, I can tell you!

OSVALD Yes—so I've heard.

MRS. ALVING He seemed to radiate light and warmth—he was filled with a turbulent, joyous vitality.

OSVALD Well—?

MRS. ALVING And this boy, so full of the joy of life—he was like a boy then—was cooped up in this drab little provincial town—which could offer him no real joy—only dissipation. He had no real aim in life—no work that could stimulate his mind or feed his spirit—nothing but a dull, petty, routine job. He found no one here who understood that pure joy of life that was in him; what friends he had were bent on idling their time away or drinking themselves into a stupor—

OSVALD Mother—!

MRS. ALVING And so, the inevitable happened.

OSVALD The inevitable?

MRS. ALVING You told me a little while ago, what would happen to you if you stayed here.

OSVALD Do you mean by that—that Father—?

MRS. ALVING Your poor father could find no outlet for that overpowering joy of life that was in him—and I'm afraid I brought him no happiness either.

OSVALD Why, Mother?

MRS. ALVING All my life I'd been taught a great deal about duty—that seemed the all-important thing. Everything was reduced to a question of duty—*my* duty—*his* duty—your poor father—I'm afraid I must have made home intolerable for him, Osvald.

OSVALD Why did you never write me about all this?

MRS. ALVING You were his son—I felt it would be wrong to talk to you about it; you see, I didn't see things clearly then.

OSVALD How did you see them?

MRS. ALVING (*Slowly*) I was aware of one thing only; that your father was a broken, dissolute man, long before you were born.

OSVALD (*A smothered cry*) Ah! (*He rises and goes to the window*)

MRS. ALVING And day in and day out I was tormented by the thought that Regine actually had the same rights in this house that you have.

OSVALD (*Turns quickly*) Regine!

REGINE (*Jumps up and says in a choking voice*) I—!

MRS. ALVING Yes. Now you know everything—both of you.

OSVALD Regine!

REGINE (*To herself*) So mother was—*that* sort of woman.

MRS. ALVING Your mother had many fine qualities, Regine.

REGINE She was that sort all the same. There've been times when I guessed she might be—but—Mrs. Alving! Please allow me to leave at once.

MRS. ALVING You really want to go, Regine?

REGINE I certainly do, Mrs. Alving.

MRS. ALVING Of course you must do as you wish, but—

OSVALD (*Goes to* REGINE) Leave now? But you belong here.

REGINE *Merci,* Mr. Alving—I suppose I can call you Osvald now—though this wasn't the way I wanted it to happen.

MRS. ALVING Regine—I haven't been honest with you—

REGINE No! You certainly haven't, Mrs. Alving! If I'd known that Osvald was a sick man— And now that there can never be anything serious between us— No! I can't waste my time out here in the country looking after invalids.

OSVALD Not when it's your own brother, Regine?

REGINE I should say not! I'm poor—all I have is my youth—I can't afford to waste it. I don't want to be left stranded. I have some of that "joy of life" in me too, Mrs. Alving!

MRS. ALVING No doubt. But don't throw yourself away, Regine.

REGINE If I do—I *do*—that's all! If Osvald takes after his father, I take after my mother, I suppose. —May I ask, Mrs. Alving, if Mr. Manders knows about all this?

MRS. ALVING Mr. Manders knows everything.

REGINE (*Rapidly putting on her shawl*) Then I'd better try and catch that boat. Mr. Manders is such a kind man, he's sure to help me. It seems to me I have a right to some of that money too—a better right than that filthy old carpenter.

MRS. ALVING You're welcome to it, Regine.

REGINE (*With a hard look*) And I must say, Mrs. Alving—it seems to me I also had a right to a decent up-bringing—one suited to a gentleman's daughter. (*Tosses her head*) Well—what do I care! (*Casts a bitter glance at the unopened bottle*) Some day I may be drinking champagne with the best of them—who knows?

MRS. ALVING If you should ever need a home, Regine —come to me.

REGINE No thank you, Mrs. Alving! Mr. Manders'll look after me I'm sure. And if the worst comes to the worst, I know of a place where I'd be quite at home.

MRS. ALVING Where do you mean?

REGINE In Captain Alving's Hostel, of course!

MRS. ALVING Be careful, Regine! Don't destroy yourself!

REGINE What do I care!—Well—goodbye! (*She bows to them and goes out through the hall*)

OSVALD (*Stands at the window gazing out*) Has she gone?

MRS. ALVING Yes.

OSVALD (*Mutters to himself*) How stupid it all is!

MRS. ALVING (*Stands behind him and puts her hands on his shoulders*) Osvald—my dear; has it been a very great shock to you?

OSVALD (*Turns his face toward her*) All that about Father, you mean?

MRS. ALVING Yes, your poor father!—I'm afraid it's been too much for you.

OSVALD Why do you say that? It was a great surprise to me, I admit; but after all, it doesn't really matter.

MRS. ALVING (*Withdraws her hands*) Not matter? That your father was so unspeakably unhappy?

OSVALD I feel sorry for him of course—as I would for anyone who suffered.

MRS. ALVING No more than that?—But he was your *father*, Osvald.

OSVALD (*Impatiently*) Father! Father! I never *knew* my father. The only thing I remember about him is that he once made me sick!

MRS. ALVING What a dreadful thought! But surely a child must have some love for his father, in spite of everything.

OSVALD Even if he owes his father nothing? Even if he never knew him? Come now, Mother! You're too broadminded to believe in that superstitious nonsense!

MRS. ALVING Superstitious nonsense—you think that's all it is?

OSVALD Of course, Mother—you must see that. It's one of those old-fashioned illusions people go on clinging to—

MRS. ALVING (*Shaken*) Ghosts—

OSVALD (*Paces up and down*) Yes—call them ghosts if you like.

MRS. ALVING (*In a burst of emotion*) Osvald— Then you don't love me either!

OSVALD Well, at least I know *you*—

MRS. ALVING You know me—yes; but is that all?

OSVALD I know how much you care for me; I should be grateful to you for that. And now that I'm ill, you can be of great help to me.

MRS. ALVING I can—can't I, Osvald? I'm almost glad you're ill—since it's brought you home to me. I understand—you don't belong to me yet—I'll have to win you.

OSVALD (*Impatiently*) Oh, don't let's have a lot of phrases, Mother! You must remember I'm ill. I can't be bothered with other people; I've got to think about myself.

MRS. ALVING (*Gently*) I'll be very quiet and patient, Osvald.

OSVALD And, for God's sake, *happy*, Mother!

MRS. ALVING Yes, my darling—you're right. (*Goes to him*) And you've no more doubts, no more remorse? I've freed you of all that?

OSVALD Yes, Mother, you have. But who's to free me of the terror—?

MRS. ALVING Terror!

OSVALD (*Pacing up and down*) Regine would have done it, if I'd asked her.

MRS. ALVING I don't understand. What is this terror—and what has Regine to do with it?

OSWALD Mother—is it very late?

MRS. ALVING It's early morning. (*She goes to the conservatory and looks out*) The dawn is just breaking. It's going to be a lovely day, Osvald! In a little while you'll see the sun!

OSVALD I'll be glad of that. Perhaps after all there are lots of things I could be glad about, Mother—lots of things I'd like to live for—

MRS. ALVING Of course there are!

OSVALD And even if I'm not able to work—

MRS. ALVING You'll soon be able to work again, you'll see. Now that you're rid of all those depressing, gloomy thoughts.

OSVALD Yes—it's good that you were able to wipe out that obsession. Now, if I can just get over this other—(*Sits down on the sofa*) Come here, Mother. I want to talk to you—

MRS. ALVIN Yes, Osvald. (*She pushes an armchair over near the sofa and sits close to him*)

OSVALD Meanwhile the sun is rising. And now that you know—I don't feel—so afraid any more.

MRS. ALVING Now that I know—what?

OSVALD (*Without listening to her*) Mother—didn't you say a little while ago that there was nothing in this world you wouldn't do for me, if I asked you?

MRS. ALVING Yes—of course I did.

OSVALD And you stand by that, Mother?

MRS. ALVING You can depend on me, my darling. You're the only thing on earth I have to live for.

OSVALD Well then—listen, Mother; you have a strong, gallant spirit—I know that; I want you to sit quite still while I tell you something.

MRS. ALVING What dreadful thing are you going to—?

OSVALD Don't scream or get excited, do you hear? Promise me! We'll sit here and talk it over quietly. Promise!

MRS. ALVING Yes, yes—I promise! Tell me what it is!

OSVALD Well then—listen: this fatigue of mine—my inability to work—all of that is not the *essence* of my illness—

MRS. ALVING How do you mean?

OSVALD You see—my illness *is* hereditary—it—(*Touches his forehead and speaks very quietly*) It is centered—*here.*

MRS. ALVING (*Almost speechless*) Osvald! No—no!

OSVALD Don't scream, Mother—I can't stand it! It's lurking here—lying in wait—ready to spring at any moment.

MRS. ALVING How horrible—!

OSVALD Quiet, Mother!— Now you understand the state I'm in.

MRS. ALVING (*Springing up*) It's not true, Osvald—it's impossible!

OSVALD I had one attack while I was abroad—it didn't last long. But when I realized the condition I'd been in, I was filled with unspeakable terror—and I could think of nothing but getting home to you.

MRS. ALVING So that's what you mean by "the terror"!

OSVALD Yes—unspeakable, sickening terror! If it had only been an ordinary illness—even a fatal one—I wouldn't have minded so much—I'm not afraid of death—though I should like to live as long as possible—

MRS. ALVING You will, Osvald—you must!

OSVALD But there's something so utterly revolting about this! To become a child again—a helpless child—to have to be fed—to have to be—oh! It's too ghastly to think of!

MRS. ALVING I'll be here to look after you, Osvald.

OSVALD (*Jumping up*) No, never; I won't stand it! I can't endure the thought of lingering on like that—of growing old like that—old and gray-haired like that! And you might die and I should be left alone. (*Sits down in* MRS. ALVING'S *chair*) For the doctor said I might live for years, you see. He called it "Softening of the brain" or something of the sort. (*With a sad smile*) Charming expression! It makes one think of cherry-colored velvet curtains—soft and delicate to stroke—

MRS. ALVING (*Screams*) Osvald!

OSVALD (*Springs up and paces up and down*) And now you've taken Regine away from me—if only I had her. She'd have been willing to help me, I know.

MRS. ALVING (*Goes to him*) What do you mean by that, my darling?—You know I'd give my life to help you—

OSVALD I recovered from that attack abroad—but the doctor said that the next time—and there's bound to be a "next time"—it would be hopeless.

MRS. ALVING How could he be so brutal—!

OSVALD I insisted on the truth—I made him tell me. I explained that I had certain arrangements to make (*With a cunning smile*) and so I had. (*Takes a small box from his breast pocket*) Do you see this, Mother?

MRS. ALVING What is it?

OSVALD Morphine tablets—

MRS. ALVING (*Looks at him in terror*) Osvald—

OSVALD I managed to save up twelve of them—

MRS. ALVING (*Snatching at it*) Give me the box, Osvald!

OSVALD Not yet, Mother. (*Puts the box in his pocket*)

MRS. ALVING I can't endure this!

OSVALD You must endure it, Mother. If only Regine were here—I'd have explained to her how matters stood; I'd have asked her to help me put an end to it; she'd have done it, I know.

MRS. ALVING Never!

OSVALD Oh yes she would! If she'd seen that ghastly thing take hold of me—if she'd seen me lying there like an imbecile child—beyond help—hopelessly, irrevocably lost—

MRS. ALVING Regine would never have done it!

OSVALD Oh yes! She'd have done it! Regine has such a magnificently light and buoyant nature. She wouldn't have put up long with an invalid like me!

MRS. ALVING Then I can only thank God Regine is not here!

OSVALD Yes, but then you'll have to help me, Mother.

MRS. ALVING (*With a loud scream*) I!

OSVALD Who has a better right?

MRS. ALVING I—your mother.

OSVALD For that very reason.

MRS. ALVING I, who gave you life!

OSVALD I didn't ask you for life—and what kind of a life did you give me! I don't want it—take it back again!

MRS. ALVING Help—help! (*She runs out into the hall*)

OSVALD (*Following her*) Don't leave me! Where are you going?

MRS. ALVING (*In the hall*) I must fetch a doctor, Osvald—let me out!

OSVALD (*In the hall*) You shall not go out—and no one shall come in.

(*Sound of a key turning in the lock*)

MRS. ALVING (*Re-entering the room*) Osvald—Osvald! My little one!

OSVALD (*Follows her in*) Mother—if you love me—how can you bear to see me suffer this agony of fear!

MRS. ALVING (*After a moment's silence, in a firm voice*) I give you my word, Osvald.

OSVALD Then, you will—?

MRS. ALVING Yes— If it becomes necessary—but it won't become necessary! That's impossible!

OSVALD Let us hope so— Meanwhile we'll live together as long as we can. Thank you, Mother. (*He sits in the armchair that* MRS. ALVING *had moved to the sofa*)

(*Day breaks; the lamp is still burning on the table*)

MRS. ALVING (*Approaching him cautiously*) Do you feel calmer now?

OSVALD Yes.

MRS. ALVING (*Bends over him*) This has all been a nightmare, Osvald—just something you've imagined. It's been a dreadful strain, but now you're home with me and you'll be able to get some rest. I'll spoil you as I did when you were a tiny little boy—you shall have everything you want. There! The attack's over now— You see how easily it passed. It's not so serious—I was sure it couldn't be! And it's going to be such a lovely day, Osvald. Bright sunshine! Now you'll really be able to see your home.

(*She goes to the table and puts out the lamp. The sun rises. The glaciers and peaks in the background are bathed in the bright morning light*)

OSVALD (*Immovable in his armchair with his back to the view outside, suddenly speaks*) Mother—give me the sun.

MRS. ALVING (*By the table, looks at him in amazement*) What did you say?

OSVALD (*Repeats in a dull toneless voice*) The sun— The sun.

MRS. ALVING (*Goes to him*) Osvald—what's the matter with you?

(OSVALD *seems to crumple up in the chair; all his muscles relax; his face is expressionless—his eyes vacant and staring*)

MRS. ALVING (*Trembling with terror*) What is it? (*Screams*) Osvald! What's the matter with you? (*Throws herself on her knees beside him and shakes him*) Osvald! Osvald! Look at me! Don't you know me?

OSVALD (*Tonelessly as before*) The sun— The sun.

MRS. ALVING (*Springs up in despair, tears at her hair with both hands and screams*) I can't bear it! (*Whispers, paralyzed with fear*) I can't bear it! Never! (*Suddenly*) Where did he put them? (*Passes her hand rapidly over his breast*) Here! (*Draws back a couple of steps and cries*) No; no; no!— Yes! No; no! (*She stands a few steps away from him, her hands clutching her hair, and stares at him in speechless terror*)

OSVALD (*Immovable as before*) The sun— The sun.

*Curtain*

# August Strindberg

## (1849-1912)

Great writers invariably resist the easy generalizations that seek to reduce their art to a simple formula. No modern playwright was bolder, more original, more complex, than Strindberg. Alive to the intellectual and artistic currents of his time but not imprisoned by them, he transformed the mechanical and rigid dogmas of French naturalism into a pulsating revelation of the tension and anguish of inner life. His early plays mark the triumph of naturalism even while they break new ground in the exploration of instinctive and abnormal behavior. A masterful psychologist as well as a brilliant craftsman, in his later work Strindberg created the style and technique of dramatic expressionism. Now, half a century after his death, Strindberg is a classic of the contemporary theatre.

Born in Stockholm of poor parents, Strindberg was raised in an atmosphere of moral and physical squalor. His mother had been his father's mistress and had given birth to three illegitimate children before their marriage; at the time of Strindberg's birth his father, a shipping agent, was bankrupt. One of twelve children, Strindberg as a boy was treated with harshness or neglect. His mother died when the boy was thirteen; his father remarried soon after, and the step-mother added to the hardship of his daily life. After completing secondary school, the young Strindberg attended the University of Uppsala. He resisted the authority and discipline of school as he had that of his family; he despised formal studies and often quarreled with his professors. While a student, he tried to become an actor and failed, but this experience turned him to playwriting. His earliest extant play, *The Free Thinker* (1869), echoes the unyielding morality of Ibsen's *Brand* in its opposition of individual conscience and social convention. Strindberg's first production was a one-act play in verse, *In Rome* (1870), portraying the early struggles of the sculptor, Thorvaldsen, and reflecting the young Strindberg's questioning of his own vocation. The king gave the playwright a small sum to pursue his studies; encouraged, he composed a historical play, *Master Olof,* an ambitious drama of conspiracy and cowardice during the Swedish Reformation. In its vigorous characterization it is a remarkable achievement for a youth of 23. Strindberg frequently returned to Swedish history and achieved some of his most striking successes in a form closely akin to that of Shakespeare's chronicle plays.

Unconventional and reckless in his private life, Strindberg in 1875 had a passionate love affair with a married woman, Siri von Essen. She left her husband and, two years later, married Strindberg. Out of the tensions of their domestic life came some of Strindberg's most powerful fiction and drama. His frank and irreverent short stories, *Married* (1884), inflamed orthodox opinion. Strindberg was prosecuted for blasphemy and although he was found not guilty, the trial left psychological wounds that soon festered into delusions of persecution and fits of madness. On learning that his wife had privately sought medical advice concerning his condition, Strindberg was sure that she planned to have him locked up. Out of this imbalance and suffering came two plays of 1886, *Comrades* and *The Father*.

In Paris three years earlier, Strindberg had become familiar with the naturalism of Zola, whose doctrines he applied in modified form. *Comrades* began as a satire of feminism, one of many counterblasts at Ibsen's *A Doll's House,* but the tone harshened in the process of composition and the play in its final form is a bitter exposure of a wife's mediocrity and duplicity. *The Father* is more concentrated in structure and more soul-searching in its anatomy of the war between the sexes. Strindberg composed this masterpiece with remarkable facility, completing it in two months. In writing the play he aimed at a modern parallel to Agamemnon and Clytemnestra. The Captain and Laura have little of the grandeur of the ancient heroes, but the instinctive cunning and treachery of his heroine represented for Strindberg a permanent quality of the species. The dramatic effectiveness of *The Father* has virtually nothing to do with the biological determinism underlying the Captain's explanation of his defeat, or the pseudo-scientific doctrine of the privation of the will. His collapse presents the painful image of a man of talent and apparent strength unbalanced by suspicion and goaded into insanity. "All boilers explode," the Captain tells his doctor, "when the pressure gauge shows 100; but 100 is not the same for all boilers." The explosion of the Captain's mind in the third act, when he rushes out of his room with a pile of books bearing documentary proof of female betrayal and corruption, is one of the great moments of modern drama. Through this play Strindberg hoped to make his way on the Paris stage, but Antoine, producer of the Théâtre Libre, rejected it. *The Father* was first produced at the Casino Theatre in Copenhagen in

November 1887; it was not performed in Paris until late in 1894.

*Miss Julie* (1888) is much closer to our own day in its complex portrayal of personality. Strindberg's neurotic heroine yields to erotic compulsion and all but loses control over herself. In his "Foreword" Strindberg takes great pains to make her seduction probable; perhaps not all of the causes are made explicit in the play itself, but it is clear that Julie actively collaborates in her fall. It is important to keep in mind the social background of the lovers' relationship. Jean is a servant, Julie an aristocrat, and in the Sweden of Strindberg's day, class lines constituted an impassable barrier. The consciousness of the gulf between the very poor and the very rich underlies and intensifies the central conflict. For the playwright, as he indicates in his "Foreword," this antagonism, and its resolution in the drama, was symbolic of changing social processes in modern life: not merely the rise of the lower classes at the expense of their so-called betters, but the decline of "inferior" and degenerate types and the rise of "superior" beings to strength and power. It is characteristic of Strindberg's greatness as a playwright that despite his misogyny and his hatred for the social class to which his heroine belongs, he could portray her suffering with understanding and compassion.

The manuscript of *Miss Julie* bears the notation in Strindberg's hand, "A naturalistic tragedy." The Darwinian principle of the survival of the fittest enters forcefully into Strindberg's view of social processes and personal relationships. The "Foreword" and play in their original form were far more vigorous in their onslaught on traditional morality and religion. Strindberg's publisher made numerous alterations that the playwright was unable to prevent. All current editions of the play, whether in Swedish or in translation, reflect these changes; nevertheless, in its essential details *Miss Julie* is still as Strindberg wrote it. He was not mistaken in proclaiming to a prospective publisher, "this play will be a milestone in history." Although written for the Théâtre Libre in Paris, it received its premiere in Copenhagen in 1889; Antoine's production of *Miss Julie* in 1893 marks the first performance of a Strindberg play in Paris. *Miss Julie* was not performed in Sweden until 1906. Its recent film success has made it one of the best known of Strindberg's plays.

In 1888 Strindberg felt he had mastered the theory and technique of the new naturalistic drama, redefined so as to take full account of the gains of the psychology of his time: "The French today are looking for the formula but I have found it." The following year in his essay, "On Modern Drama and Modern Theatre," he gave programmatic utterance to "the great naturalism," which has nothing to do with photographic realism but "delights in the struggle between natural forces, whether these forces are called love and hate, rebellious or social instincts. . . ." For Strindberg, vital naturalistic theatre is concerned above all with the quest for significant motive and the polarization of essential conflicts of life, conceived as a life-and-death struggle. This same point of view is present in Strindberg's expressionist plays. After his divorce in 1891, he went to Germany, then the promised land for Scandinavian authors. He moved in the circles of Berlin naturalists and there met a young journalist, Frida Uhl, whom he married in 1893. They separated the next year and Strindberg went to Paris, where he gave himself over to studies in chemistry and alchemy, hoping to achieve the transmutation of elements and convinced that the periodic table was a fraud. He also took up theosophy and occult speculation. Moody and depressed, he became increasingly suspicious of all around him and subject to violent hallucinations; while in Paris, he was hospitalized for several months. The suffering Strindberg experienced during this "Inferno Crisis" from 1894 to 1896 was positive proof to him of his guilt and depravity. He emerged a broken man, yet out of this inner torment came an almost incredible release of creative energy: 29 more plays, to say nothing of novels, poems, critical essays, and other writings.

Of his later works, Strindberg's so-called dream plays, especially *The Road to Damascus, A Dream Play,* and *The Ghost Sonata,* have aroused the most interest. The new flexibility of dramatic form was encouraged by his return to the spacious panorama of the history play, and also by his experiments in symbolist drama. The best of the history plays are probably *Gustave Vasa* (1899) and *Erik XIV* (1899), psychological interpretations of the great rulers of sixteenth-century Sweden. The inner transformation of the ruthless king in the final scene of *Gustave Vasa* follows the pattern of guilt and expiation of Strindberg's dramas of contemporary life. The symbolist play, *Swanwhite* (1901), combines lyricism and romance in a fairy tale celebration of the triumph of love over evil. A similar evocation of fantasy and the supernatural is found in *The Crown Bride* (1901), and, in a more somber vein, in *Easter* (1901), written for his third wife, Harriet Bosse, whom he married in 1901 and from whom he separated two years later. Repeatedly in his later work, Strindberg drew directly upon his marital trials for the purposes of his art.

These departures from the literal representation of external reality were interrupted by occasional returns to the naturalism of Strindberg's earlier plays. *There Are Crimes and Crimes* (1899) is a drama of sin and retribution wherein a successful playwright abandons his mistress and daughter, and then must expiate his spiritual guilt for the child's death. The relentless struggle between husband and wife takes on grotesque horror and poignant sadness in *The Dance of Death* (1901); Alice's triumph over the captain after a life of venomous hatred is softened by her recollection of their long-lost love. Even at the height of his most daring experimentation, Strindberg could still create moving and effective drama in the naturalistic style. The imaginative brilliance of the "dream plays" should not obscure the achievement of his other work. Strindberg's naturalistic plays, early and late, rank among his very best. They are a living tribute to the authenticity and courage which naturalism brought to the modern stage.

# MISS JULIE

## *A Naturalistic Tragedy*

Translated by Elizabeth Sprigge

## Author's Foreword

Theatre has long seemed to me—in common with much other art—a *Biblia Pauperum,* a Bible in pictures for those who cannot read what is written or printed; and I see the playwright as a lay preacher peddling the ideas of his time in popular form, popular enough for the middle-classes, mainstay of theatre audiences, to grasp the gist of the matter without troubling their brains too much. For this reason theatre has always been an elementary school for the young, the semi-educated, and for women who still have a primitive capacity for deceiving themselves and letting themselves be deceived—who, that is to say, are susceptible to illusion and to suggestion from the author. I have therefore thought it not unlikely that in these days, when that rudimentary and immature thought-process operating through fantasy appears to be developing into reflection, research and analysis, that theatre, like religion, might be discarded as an outworn form for whose appreciation we lack the necessary conditions. This opinion is confirmed by the major crisis still prevailing in the theatres of Europe, and still more by the fact that in those countries of culture, producing the greatest thinkers of the age, namely England and Germany, drama—like other fine arts—is dead.

Some countries, it is true, have attempted to create a new drama by using the old forms with up-to-date contents, but not only has there been insufficient time for these new ideas to be popularized, so that the audience can grasp them, but also people have been so wrought up by the taking of sides that pure, disinterested appreciation has become impossible. One's deepest impressions are upset when an applauding or a hissing majority dominates as forcefully and openly as it can in the theatre. Moreover, as no new form has been devised for these new contents, the new wine has burst the old bottles.

In this play I have not tried to do anything new, for this cannot be done, but only to modernize the form to meet the demands which may, I think, be made on this art today. To this end I chose—or surrendered myself to—a theme which claims to be outside the controversial issues of today, since questions of social climbing or falling, of higher or lower, better or worse, of man and woman, are, have been, and will be of lasting interest. When I took this theme from a true story told me some years ago, which made a deep impression, I saw it as a subject for tragedy, for as yet it is tragic to see one favored by fortune go under, and still more to see a family heritage die out, although a time may come when we have grown so developed and enlightened that we shall view with indifference life's spectacle, now seeming so brutal, cynical, and heartless. Then we shall have dispensed with those inferior, unreliable instruments of thought called feelings, which become harmful and superfluous as reasoning develops.

The fact that my heroine rouses pity is solely due to weakness; we cannot resist fear of the same fate overtaking us. The hyper-sensitive spectator may, it is true, go beyond this kind of pity, while the man with belief in the future may actually demand some suggestion for remedying the evil—in other words some kind of policy. But, to begin with, there is no such thing as absolute evil; the downfall of one family is the good fortune of another, which thereby gets a chance to rise, and, fortune being only comparative, the alternation of rising and falling is one of life's principal charms. Also, to the man of policy, who wants to remedy the painful fact that the bird of prey devours the dove, and lice the bird of prey, I should like to put the question: why should it be remedied? Life is not so mathematically idiotic as only to permit the big to eat the small; it happens just as often that the bee kills the lion or at least drives it mad.

That my tragedy depresses many people is their own fault. When we have grown strong as the pioneers of the French revolution, we shall be happy and relieved to see the national parks cleared of ancient rotting trees which have stood too long in the way of others equally entitled to a period of growth—as relieved as we are when an incurable invalid dies.

My tragedy "The Father" was recently criticized for being too sad—as if one wants cheerful tragedies! Everybody is clamoring for this supposed "joy of life," and theatre managers demand farces, as if the joy of life consisted in being ridiculous and portraying all human beings as suffering from St. Vitus's dance or total idiocy. I myself find the joy of life in its strong and cruel struggles, and my pleasure in learning, in adding to my knowledge. For this reason I have chosen for this play an unusual situation, but an instructive one—an exception, that is to say, but a great exception, one proving the rule, which will no doubt annoy all lovers of the commonplace. What will offend simple minds is that my plot is not simple, nor its point of view single. In real life an action—this, by the way, is a somewhat new discovery—is generally caused by a whole series of motives, more or less fundamental, but as a rule the spectator chooses just one of these—the one which his mind can most easily grasp or that does most credit to his intelligence. A suicide is committed. Business troubles, says the man of affairs. Unrequited love, say the women. Sickness, says the invalid. Despair, says the down-and-out. But it is possible that the motive lay in all or none of these directions, or that the dead man concealed his actual motive by revealing quite another, likely to reflect more to his glory.

I see Miss Julie's tragic fate to be the result of many circumstances: the mother's character, the father's mistaken upbringing of the girl, her own nature, and the influence of her fiancé on a weak, degenerate mind. Also, more directly, the festive mood of Midsummer Eve, her father's absence, her monthly indisposition, her pre-occupation with animals, the excitement of dancing, the magic of dusk, the strongly aphrodisiac influence of flowers, and finally the chance that drives the couple into a room alone—to which must be added the urgency of the excited man.

My treatment of the theme, moreover, is neither exclusively physiological nor psychological. I have not put the blame wholly on the inheritance from her mother, nor on her physical condition at the time, nor on immorality. I have not even preached a moral sermon; in the absence of a priest I leave this to the cook.

I congratulate myself on this multiplicity of motives as being up-to-date, and if others have done the same thing before me, then I congratulate myself on not being alone in my "paradoxes," as all innovations are called.

In regard to the drawing of the characters, I have made my people somewhat "characterless" for the following reasons. In the course of time the word character has assumed manifold meanings. It must have originally signified the dominating trait of the soul-complex, and this was confused with temperament. Later it became the middle-class term for the automaton, one whose nature had become fixed or who had adapted himself to a particular rôle in life. In fact a person who had ceased to grow was called a character, while one continuing to develop—the skilful navigator of life's river, sailing not with sheets set fast, but veering before the wind to luff again—was called characterless, in a derogatory sense, of course, because he was so hard to catch, classify, and keep track of. This middle-class conception of the immobility of the soul was transferred to the stage where the middle-class has always ruled. A character came to signify a man fixed and finished: one who invariably appeared either drunk or jocular or melancholy, and characterization required nothing more than a physical defect such as a club-foot, a wooden leg, a red nose; or the fellow might be made to repeat some such phrase as: "That's capital!" or: "Barkis is willin'!" This simple way of regarding human beings still survives in the great Molière. Harpagon is nothing but a miser, although Harpagon might have been not only a miser, but also a first-rate financier, an excellent father, and a good citizen. Worse still, his "failing" is a distinct advantage to his son-in-law and his daughter, who are his heirs, and who therefore cannot criticize him, even if they have to wait a while to get to bed. I do not believe, therefore, in simple stage characters; and the summary judgments of authors—this man is stupid, that one brutal, this jealous, that stingy, and so forth—should be challenged by the Naturalists who know the richness of the soul-complex and realize that vice has a reverse side very much like virtue.

Because they are modern characters, living in a period of transition more feverishly hysterical than its predecessor at least, I have drawn my figures vacillating, disintegrated, a blend of old and new. Nor does it seem to me unlikely that, through newspapers and conversations, modern ideas may have filtered down to the level of the domestic servant.

My souls (characters) are conglomerations of past and present stages of civilization, bits from books and newspapers, scraps of humanity, rags and tatters of fine clothing, patched together as is the human soul. And I have added a little evolutionary history by making the weaker steal and repeat the words of the stronger, and by making the characters borrow ideas or "suggestions" from one another.

Miss Julie is a modern character, not that the half-woman, the man-hater, has not existed always, but because now that she has been discovered she has stepped to the front and begun to make a noise. The half-woman is a type who thrusts herself forward, selling herself nowadays for power, decorations, distinctions, diplomas, as formerly for money. The type implies degeneration; it is not a good type and it does not endure; but it can unfortunately transmit its misery, and degenerate men seem instinctively to choose their mates from among such women, and so they breed, producing offspring of indeterminate sex to whom life is torture. But fortunately they perish, either because they cannot come to terms with reality, or because their repressed instincts break out uncontrollably, or again because their hopes of catching up with men are shattered. The type is tragic, revealing a desperate fight against nature, tragic too in its Romantic inheritance now dissipated by Naturalism, which wants nothing but happiness—and for happiness strong and sound species are required.

But Miss Julie is also a relic of the old warrior nobility now giving way to the new nobility of nerve and brain. She is a victim of the discord which a mother's "crime" has produced in a family, a victim too of the day's complaisance, of circumstances, of her own defective constitution, all of which are equivalent to the Fate or Universal Law of former days. The Naturalist has abolished guilt with God, but the consequences of the action—

punishment, imprisonment or the fear of it—he cannot abolish, for the simple reason that they remain whether he is acquitted or not. An injured fellow-being is not so complacent as outsiders, who have not been injured, can afford to be. Even if the father had felt impelled to take no vengeance, the daughter would have taken vengeance on herself, as she does here, from that innate or acquired sense of honor which the upper-classes inherit—whether from Barbarism or Aryan forebears, or from the chivalry of the Middle Ages, who knows? It is a very beautiful thing, but it has become a danger nowadays to the preservation of the race. It is the nobleman's *hara-kiri,* the Japanese law of inner conscience which compels him to cut his own stomach open at the insult of another, and which survives in modified form in the duel, a privilege of the nobility. And so the valet Jean lives on, but Miss Julie cannot live without honor. This is the thrall's advantage over the nobleman, that he lacks this fatal preoccupation with honor. And in all of us Aryans there is something of the nobleman, or the Don Quixote, which makes us sympathize with the man who commits suicide because he has done something ignoble and lost his honor. And we are noblemen enough to suffer at the sight of fallen greatness littering the earth like a corpse —yes, even if the fallen rise again and make restitution by honorable deeds. Jean, the valet, is a race-builder, a man of marked characteristics. He was a laborer's son who has educated himself towards becoming a gentleman. He has learnt easily, through his well-developed senses (smell, taste, vision)—and he also has a sense of beauty. He has already bettered himself, and is thick-skinned enough to have no scruples about using other people's services. He is already foreign to his associates, despising them as part of the life he has turned his back on, yet also fearing and fleeing from them because they know his secrets, pry into his plans, watch his rise with envy, and look forward with pleasure to his fall. Hence his dual, indeterminate character, vacillating between love of the heights and hatred of those who have already achieved them. He is, he says himself, an aristocrat; he has learned the secrets of good society. He is polished, but vulgar within; he already wears his tails with taste, but there is no guarantee of his personal cleanliness.

He has some respect for his young lady, but he is frightened of Kristin, who knows his dangerous secrets, and he is sufficiently callous not to allow the night's events to wreck his plans for the future. Having both the slave's brutality and the master's lack of squeamishness, he can see blood without fainting and take disaster by the horns. Consequently he emerges from the battle unscathed, and probably ends his days as a hotel-keeper. And even if *he* does not become a Rumanian Count, his son will doubtless go to the university and perhaps become a county attorney.

The light which Jean sheds on a lower-class conception of life, life seen from below, is on the whole illuminating—when he speaks the truth, which is not often, for he says what is favorable to himself rather than what is true. When Miss Julie suggests that the lower-classes must be oppressed by the attitude of their superiors, Jean naturally agrees, as his object is to gain her sympathy; but when he perceives the advantage of separating himself from the common herd, he at once takes back his words.

It is not because Jean is now rising that he has the upper hand of Miss Julie, but because he is a man. Sexually he is the aristocrat because of his virility, his keener senses, and his capacity for taking the initiative. His inferiority is mainly due to the social environment in which he lives, and he can probably shed it with his valet's livery.

The slave mentality expresses itself in his worship of the Count (the boots), and his religious superstition; but he worships the Count chiefly because he holds that higher position for which Jean himself is striving. And this worship remains even when he has won the daughter of the house and seen how empty is that lovely shell.

I do not believe that a love relationship in the "higher" sense could exist between two individuals of such different quality, but I have made Miss Julie imagine that she is in love, so as to lessen her sense of guilt, and I let Jean suppose that if his social position were altered he would truly love her. I think love is like the hyacinth which has to strike roots in darkness *before* it can produce a vigorous flower. In this case it shoots up quickly, blossoms and goes to seed all at the same time, which is why the plant dies so soon.

As for Kristin, she is a female slave, full of servility and sluggishness acquired in front of the kitchen fire, and stuffed full of morality and religion, which are her cloak and scape-goat. She goes to church as a quick and easy way of unloading her household thefts on to Jesus and taking on a fresh cargo of guiltlessness. For the rest she is a minor character, and I have therefore sketched her in the same manner as the Pastor and the Doctor in "The Father," where I wanted ordinary human beings, as are most country pastors and provincial doctors. If these minor characters seem abstract to some people this is due to the fact that ordinary people are to a certain extent abstract in pursuit of their work; that is to say, they are without individuality, showing, while working, only one side of themselves. And as long as the spectator does not feel a need to see them from other sides, there is nothing wrong with my abstract presentation.

In regard to the dialogue, I have departed somewhat from tradition by not making my characters catechists who ask stupid questions in order to elicit a smart reply. I have avoided the symmetrical, mathematical construction of French dialogue, and let people's minds work irregularly, as they do in real life where, during a conversation, no topic is drained to the dregs, and one mind finds in another a chance cog to engage in. So too the dialogue wanders, gathering in the opening scenes material which is later picked up, worked over, repeated, expounded and developed like the theme in a musical composition.

The plot speaks for itself, and as it really only concerns two people, I have concentrated on these, introducing only one minor character, the cook, and keeping the unhappy spirit of the father above and behind the action. I have done this because it seems to me that the psychological process is what interests people most today. Our inquisitive souls are no longer satisfied with seeing a thing happen; we must also know how it happens. We want to see the wires themselves, to watch the machinery, to examine the box with the false bottom, to take hold of the magic ring in order to find the join, and look at the cards to see how they are marked.

In this connection I have had in view the documentary novels of the Goncourt brothers, which appeal to me more than any other modern literature.

As far as the technical side of the work is concerned I have made the experiment of abolishing the division into acts. This is because I have come to the conclusion that our capacity for illusion is disturbed by the intervals, during which the audience has time to reflect and escape from the suggestive influence of the author-hypnotist. My play will probably take an hour and a half, and as one can listen to a lecture, a sermon, or a parliamentary debate for as long as that or longer, I do not think a theatrical performance will be fatiguing in the same length of time. As early as 1872, in one of my first dramatic attempts, "The Outlaw," I tried this concentrated form, although with scant success. The play was written in five acts, and only when finished did I become aware of the restless, disjointed effect that it produced. The script was burnt and from the ashes rose a single well-knit act—fifty pages of print, playable in one hour. The form of the present play is, therefore, not new, but it appears to be my own, and changing tastes may make it timely. My hope is one day to have an audience educated enough to sit through a whole evening's entertainment in one act, but one would have to try this out to see. Meanwhile, in order to provide respite for the audience and the players, without allowing the audience to escape from the illusion, I have introduced three art forms: monologue, mime, and ballet. These are all part of drama, having their origins in classic tragedy, monody having become monologue and the chorus, ballet.

Monologue is now condemned by our realists as unnatural, but if one provides motives for it one makes it natural, and then can use it to advantage. It is, surely, natural for a public speaker to walk up and down the room practicing his speech, natural for an actor to read his part aloud, for a servant girl to talk to her cat, a mother to prattle to her child, an old maid to chatter to her parrot, and a sleeper to talk in his sleep. And in order that the actor may have a chance, for once, of working independently, free from the author's direction, it is better that the monologue should not be written, but only indicated. For since it is of small importance what is said in one's sleep or to the parrot or to the cat—none of it influences the action—a talented actor, identifying himself with the atmosphere and the situation, may improvise better than the author, who cannot calculate ahead how much may be said or how long taken without waking the audience from the illusion.

Some Italian theatres have, as we know, returned to improvisation, thereby producing actors who are creative, although within the bounds set by the author. This may well be a step forward, or even the beginning of a new art-form worthy to be called *productive*.

In places where monologue would be unnatural I have used mime, leaving here an even wider scope for the actor's imagination, and more chance for him to win independent laurels. But so as not to try the audience beyond endurance, I have introduced music—fully justified by the Midsummer Eve dance—to exercise its powers of persuasion during the dumb show. But I beg the musical director to consider carefully his choice of compositions, so that conflicting moods are not induced by selections from the current operetta or dance show, or by folk-tunes of too local a character.

The ballet I have introduced cannot be replaced by the usual kind of "crowd-scene," for such scenes are too badly played—a lot of grinning idiots seizing the opportunity to show off and thus destroying the illusion. And as peasants cannot improvise their taunts, but use ready-made phrases with a double meaning, I have not composed their lampoon, but taken a little-known song and dance which I myself noted down in the Stockholm district. The words are not quite to the point, but this too is intentional, for the cunning, i.e. weakness, of the slave prevents him from direct attack. Nor can there be clowning in a serious action, or coarse joking in a situation which nails the lid on a family coffin.

As regards the scenery, I have borrowed from impressionist painting its asymmetry and its economy; thus, I think, strengthening the illusion. For the fact that one does not see the whole room and all the furniture leaves scope for conjecture—that is to say imagination is roused and complements what is seen. I have succeeded too in getting rid of those tiresome exits through doors, since scenery doors are made of canvas, and rock at the slightest touch. They cannot even express the wrath of an irate head of the family who, after a bad dinner, goes out slamming the door behind him, "so that the whole house shakes." On the stage it rocks. I have also kept to a single set, both in order to let the characters develop in their métier and to break away from over-decoration. When one has only one set, one may expect it to be realistic; but as a matter of fact nothing is harder than to get a stage room that looks something like a room, however easily the scene painter can produce flaming volcanoes and water-falls. Presumably the walls must be of canvas; but it seems about time to dispense with painted shelves and cooking utensils. We are asked to accept so many stage conventions that we might at least be spared the pain of painted pots and pans.

I have set the back wall and the table diagonally so that the actors may play full-face and in half-profile when they are sitting opposite one another at the table. In the opera *Aïda* I saw a diagonal background, which led the eye to unfamiliar perspectives and did not look like mere reaction against boring straight lines.

Another much needed innovation is the abolition of foot-lights. This lighting from below is said to have the purpose of making the actors' faces fatter. But why, I ask, should all actors have fat faces? Does not this under-lighting flatten out all the subtlety of the lower part of the face, specially the jaw, falsify the shape of the nose and throw shadows up over the eyes? Even if this were not so, one thing is certain: that the lights hurt the performers' eyes, so that the full play of their expression is lost. The foot-lights strike part of the retina usually protected—except in sailors who have to watch sunlight on water—and therefore one seldom sees anything other than a crude rolling of the eyes, either sideways or up towards the gallery, showing their whites. Perhaps this too causes that tiresome blinking of the eyelashes, especially by actresses. And when anyone on the stage wants to speak with his eyes, the only thing he can do is to look straight at the audience, with whom he or she then gets into direct communication, outside the framework of the set—a habit called, rightly or wrongly, "greeting one's friends."

Would not sufficiently strong side-lighting, with some kind of reflectors, add to the actor's powers of expression by allowing him to use the face's greatest asset:—the play of the eyes?

I have few illusions about getting the actors to play *to* the audience instead of *with* it, although this is what I want. That I shall see an actor's back throughout a critical scene is beyond my dreams, but I do wish crucial scenes could be played, not in front of the prompter's box, like duets expecting applause, but in the place required by the action. So, no revolutions, but just some small modifications, for to make the stage into a real room with the fourth wall missing would be too upsetting altogether.

I dare not hope that the actresses will listen to what I have to say about make-up, for they would rather be beautiful than life-like, but the actor might consider whether it is to his advantage to create an abstract character with grease-paints, and cover his face with it like a mask. Take the case of a man who draws a choleric charcoal line between his eyes and then, in this fixed state of wrath, has to smile at some repartee. What a frightful grimace the result is! And equally, how is that false forehead, smooth as a billiard ball, to wrinkle when the old man loses his temper?

In a modern psychological drama, where the subtlest reactions of a character need to be mirrored in the face rather than expressed by sound and gesture, it would be worth while experimenting with powerful side-lighting on a small stage and a cast without make-up, or at least with the minimum.

If, in addition, we could abolish the visible orchestra, with its distracting lamps and its faces turned toward the audience; if we could have the stalls raised so that the spectators' eyes were higher than the players' knees; if we could get rid of the boxes (the center of my target), with their tittering diners and supper-parties, and have total darkness in the auditorium during the performance; and if, first and foremost, we could have a *small* stage and a *small* house, then perhaps a new dramatic art might arise, and theatre once more become a place of entertainment for educated people. While waiting for such a theatre we may as well go on writing so as to stock that repertory of the future.

I have made an attempt! If it has failed, there is time enough to try again!

## CHARACTERS

MISS JULIE, *aged 25*
JEAN, *the valet, aged 30*
KRISTIN, *the cook, aged 35*

SCENE *The large kitchen of a Swedish manor house in a country district in the 1880's.*

*Midsummer Eve.*

*The kitchen has three doors, two small ones into Jean's and Kristin's bedrooms, and a large, glass-fronted double one, opening on to a courtyard. This is the only way to the rest of the house.*

*Through these glass doors can be seen part of a fountain with a cupid, lilac bushes in flower and the tops of some Lombardy poplars. On one wall are shelves edged with scalloped paper on which are kitchen utensils of copper, iron and tin.*

*To the left is the corner of a large tiled range and part of its chimney-hood, to the right the end of the servants' dinner table with chairs beside it.*

*The stove is decorated with birch boughs, the floor strewn with twigs of juniper. On the end of the table is a large Japanese spice jar full of lilac.*

*There are also an ice-box, a scullery table and a sink.*

*Above the double door hangs a big old-fashioned bell; near it is a speaking-tube.*

*A fiddle can be heard from the dance in the barn near-by.*

*Kristin is standing at the stove, frying something in a pan. She wears a light-colored cotton dress and a big apron.*

*Jean enters, wearing livery and carrying a pair of large riding-boots with spurs, which he puts in a conspicuous place.*

JEAN Miss Julie's crazy again to-night, absolutely crazy.

KRISTIN Oh, so you're back, are you?

JEAN When I'd taken the Count to the station, I came back and dropped in at the Barn for a dance. And who did I see there but our young lady leading off with the gamekeeper. But the moment she sets eyes on me, up she rushes and invites me to waltz with her. And how she waltzed—I've never seen anything like it! She's crazy.

KRISTIN Always has been, but never so bad as this last fortnight since the engagement was broken off.

JEAN Yes, that was a pretty business, to be sure. He's a decent enough chap, too, even if he isn't rich. Oh, but they're choosy! (*Sits down at the end of the table*) In any case, it's a bit odd that our young—er—lady would rather stay at home with yokels than go with her father to visit her relations.

KRISTIN Perhaps she feels a bit awkward, after that bust-up with her fiancé.

JEAN Maybe. That chap had some guts, though. Do you know the sort of thing that was going on, Kristin? I saw it with my own eyes, though I didn't let on I had.

KRISTIN You saw them . . . ?

JEAN Didn't I just! Came across the pair of them one evening in the stable-yard. Miss Julie was doing what she called "training" him. Know what that was? Making him jump over her riding-whip—the way you teach a dog. He did it twice and got a cut each time for his pains, but when it came to the third go, he snatched the whip out of her hand and broke it into smithereens. And then he cleared off.

KRISTIN What goings on! I never did!

JEAN Well, that's how it was with that little affair . . . Now, what have you got for me, Kristin? Something tasty?

KRISTIN (*Serving from the pan to his plate*) Well, it's just a little bit of kidney I cut off their joint.

JEAN (*Smelling it*) Fine! That's my special delice. (*Feels the plate*) But you might have warmed the plate.

KRISTIN When you choose to be finicky you're worse than the Count himself. (*Pulls his hair affectionately*)

JEAN (*Crossly*) Stop pulling my hair. You know how sensitive I am.

KRISTIN There, there! It's only love, you know.

(JEAN *eats.* KRISTIN *brings a bottle of beer*)

JEAN Beer on Midsummer Eve? No thanks! I've got something better than that. (*From a drawer in the table brings out a bottle of red wine with a yellow seal*) Yellow seal, see! Now get me a glass. You use a glass with a stem of course when you're drinking it straight.

KRISTIN (*Giving him a wine-glass*) Lord help the woman who gets you for a husband, you old fusser! (*She puts the beer in the ice-box and sets a small saucepan on the stove*)

JEAN Nonsense! You'll be glad enough to get a fellow as smart as me. And I don't think it's done you any harm, people calling me your fiancé. (*Tastes the wine*) Good. Very good indeed. But not quite warmed enough. (*Warms the glass in his hand*) We bought this in Dijon. Four francs the liter without the bottle, and duty on top of that. What are you cooking now? It stinks.

KRISTIN Some bloody muck Miss Julie wants for Diana.

JEAN You should be more refined in your speech, Kristin. But why should you spend a holiday cooking for that bitch? Is she sick or what?

KRISTIN Yes, she's sick. She sneaked out with the pug at the lodge and got in the usual mess. And that, you know, Miss Julie won't have.

JEAN Miss Julie's too high-and-mighty in some respects, and not enough in others, just like her mother before her. The Countess was more at home in the kitchen and cowsheds than anywhere else, but would she ever go driving with only one horse? She went round with her cuffs filthy, but she had to have the coronet on the cuff-links. Our young lady—to come back to her—hasn't any proper respect for herself or her position. I mean she isn't refined. In the Barn just now she dragged the gamekeeper away from Anna and made him dance with her—no waiting to be asked. We wouldn't do a thing like that. But that's what happens when the gentry try to behave like the common people—they become common . . . Still she's a fine girl. Smashing! What shoulders! And what—er—etcetera!

KRISTIN Oh come off it! I know what Clara says, and she dresses her.

JEAN Clara? Pooh, you're all jealous! But I've been out riding with her . . . and as for her dancing!

KRISTIN Listen, Jean. You will dance with me, won't you, as soon as I'm through.

JEAN Of course I will.

KRISTIN Promise?

JEAN Promise? When I say I'll do a thing I do it. Well, thanks for the supper. It was a real treat. (*Corks the bottle*)

(JULIE *appears in the doorway, speaking to someone outside*)

JULIE I'll be back in a moment. Don't wait.

(JEAN *slips the bottle into the drawer and rises respectfully.* JULIE *enters and joins* KRISTIN *at the stove*)

Well, have you made it? (KRISTIN *signs that* JEAN *is near them*)

JEAN (*Gallantly*) Have you ladies got some secret?

JULIE (*Flipping his face with her handkerchief*) You're very inquisitive.

JEAN What a delicious smell! Violets.

JULIE (*Coquettishly*) Impertinence! Are you an expert of scent too? I must say you know how to dance. Now don't look. Go away. (*The music of a schottische begins*)

JEAN (*With impudent politeness*) Is it some witches' brew you're cooking on Midsummer Eve? Something to tell your stars by, so you can see your future?

JULIE (*Sharply*) If you could see that you'd have good eyes. (*To* KRISTIN) Put it in a bottle and cork it tight. Come and dance this schottische with me, Jean.

JEAN (*Hesitating*) I don't want to be rude, but I've promised to dance this one with Kristin.

JULIE Well, she can have another, can't you, Kristin? You'll lend me Jean, won't you?

KRISTIN (*Bottling*) It's nothing to do with me. When you're so condescending, Miss, it's not his place to say no. Go on, Jean, and thank Miss Julie for the honor.

JEAN Frankly speaking, Miss, and no offense meant, I wonder if it's wise for you to dance twice running with the same partner, specially as those people are so ready to jump to conclusions.

JULIE (*Flaring up*) What did you say? What sort of conclusions? What do you mean?

JEAN (*Meekly*) As you choose not to understand, Miss Julie, I'll have to speak more plainly. It looks bad to show a preference for one of your retainers when they're all hoping for the same unusual favor.

JULIE Show a preference! The very idea! I'm surprised at you. I'm doing the people an honor by attending their ball when I'm mistress of the house, but if I'm really going to dance, I mean to have a partner who can lead and doesn't make me look ridiculous.

JEAN If those are your orders, Miss, I'm at your service.

JULIE (*Gently*) Don't take it as an order. Tonight we're all just people enjoying a party. There's no question of class. So now give me your arm. Don't worry, Kristin. I shan't steal your sweetheart.

(JEAN *gives* JULIE *his arm and leads her out*)

(*Left alone,* KRISTIN *plays her scene in an unhurried, natural way, humming to the tune of the schottische, played on a distant violin. She clears* JEAN's *place, washes up and puts things away, then takes off her apron, brings out a small mirror from a drawer, props it against the jar of lilac, lights a candle, warms a small pair of tongs and curls her fringe. She goes to the door and listens, then turning back to the table finds* MISS JULIE's *handkerchief. She smells it, then meditatively smooths it out and folds it*)

(*Enter* JEAN)

JEAN She really *is* crazy. What a way to dance! With people standing grinning at her too from behind the doors. What's got into her, Kristin?

KRISTIN Oh, it's just her time coming on. She's always queer then. Are you going to dance with me now?

JEAN Then you're not wild with me for cutting that one.

KRISTIN You know I'm not—for a little thing like that. Besides, I know my place.

JEAN (*Putting his arm round her waist*) You're a sensible girl, Kristin, and you'll make a very good wife . . .

(*Enter* JULIE, *unpleasantly surprised*)

JULIE (*With forced gaiety*) You're a fine beau—running away from your partner.

JEAN Not away, Miss Julie, but as you see back to the one I deserted.

JULIE (*Changing her tone*) You really can dance, you know. But why are you wearing your livery on a holiday. Take it off at once.

JEAN Then I must ask you to go away for a moment, Miss. My black coat's here. (*Indicates it hanging on the door to his room*)

JULIE Are you so shy of me—just over changing a coat? Go into your room then—or stay here and I'll turn my back.

JEAN Excuse me then, Miss. (*He goes to his room and is partly visible as he changes his coat*)

JULIE Tell me, Kristin, is Jean your fiancé? You seem very intimate.

KRISTIN My fiancé? Yes, if you like. We call it that.

JULIE Call it?

KRISTIN Well, you've had a fiancé yourself, Miss, and . . .

JULIE But we really were engaged.

KRISTIN All the same it didn't come to anything.

(JEAN *returns in his black coat*)

JULIE *Très gentil, Monsieur Jean. Très gentil.*[1]

JEAN *Vous voulez plaisanter, Madame.*

JULIE *Et vous voulez parler français.* Where did you learn it?

JEAN In Switzerland, when I was steward at one of the biggest hotels in Lucerne.

JULIE You look quite the gentleman in that get-up. Charming. (*Sits at the table*)

JEAN Oh, you're just flattering me!

JULIE (*Annoyed*) Flattering you?

JEAN I'm too modest to believe you would pay real compliments to a man like me, so I must take it you are exaggerating—that this is what's known as flattery.

JULIE Where on earth did you learn to make speeches like that? Perhaps you've been to the theater a lot.

JEAN That's right. And traveled a lot too.

JULIE But you come from this neighborhood, don't you?

JEAN Yes, my father was a laborer on the next estate—the District Attorney's place. I often used to see you, Miss Julie, when you were little, though you never noticed me.

JULIE Did you really?

JEAN Yes. One time specially I remember . . . but I can't tell you about that.

JULIE Oh do! Why not? This is just the time.

JEAN No, I really can't now. Another time perhaps.

JULIE Another time means never. What harm in now?

JEAN No harm, but I'd rather not. (*Points to* KRISTIN, *now fast asleep*) Look at her.

JULIE She'll make a charming wife, won't she? I wonder if she snores.

JEAN No, she doesn't, but she talks in her sleep.

JULIE (*Cynically*) How do you know she talks in her sleep?

JEAN (*Brazenly*) I've heard her. (*Pause. They look at one another*)

JULIE Why don't you sit down?

JEAN I can't take such a liberty in your presence.

JULIE Supposing I order you to.

JEAN I'll obey.

JULIE Then sit down. No, wait a minute. Will you get me a drink first?

[1] JULIE Very nice, Monsieur Jean, very nice.
JEAN You like to joke, Madame.
JULIE And you want to speak French.

JEAN I don't know what's in the ice-box. Only beer, I expect.

JULIE There's no only about it. My taste is so simple I prefer it to wine.

(JEAN *takes a bottle from the ice-box, fetches a glass and plate and serves the beer*)

JEAN At your service.

JULIE Thank you. Won't you have some yourself?

JEAN I'm not really a beer-drinker, but if it's an order . . .

JULIE Order? I should have thought it was ordinary manners to keep your partner company.

JEAN That's a good way of putting it. (*He opens another bottle and fetches a glass*)

JULIE Now drink my health. (*He hesitates*) I believe the man really is shy.

(JEAN *kneels and raises his glass with mock ceremony*)

JEAN To the health of my lady!

JULIE Bravo! Now kiss my shoe and everything will be perfect. (*He hesitates, then boldly takes hold of her foot and lightly kisses it*) Splendid. You ought to have been an actor.

JEAN (*Rising*) We can't go on like this, Miss Julie. Someone might come in and see us.

JULIE Why would that matter?

JEAN For the simple reason that they'd talk. And if you knew the way their tongues were wagging out there just now, you . . .

JULIE What were they saying? Tell me. Sit down.

JEAN (*Sitting*) No offense meant, Miss, but . . . well, their language wasn't nice, and they were hinting . . . oh, you know quite well what. You're not a child, and if a lady's seen drinking alone at night with a man—and a servant at that—then . . .

JULIE Then what? Besides, we're not alone. Kristin's here.

JEAN Yes, asleep.

JULIE I'll wake her up. (*Rises*) Kristin, are you asleep? (KRISTIN *mumbles in her sleep*) Kristin! Goodness, how she sleeps!

KRISTIN (*In her sleep*) The Count's boots are cleaned —put the coffee on—yes, yes, at once . . . (*Mumbles incoherently*)

JULIE (*Tweaking her nose*) Wake up, can't you!

JEAN (*Sharply*) Let her sleep.

JULIE What?

JEAN When you've been standing at the stove all day you're likely to be tired at night. And sleep should be respected.

JULIE (*Changing her tone*) What a nice idea. It does you credit. Thank you for it. (*Holds out her hand to him*) Now come out and pick some lilac for me.

(*During the following* KRISTIN *goes sleepily in to her bedroom*)

JEAN Out with you, Miss Julie?

JULIE Yes.

JEAN It wouldn't do. It really wouldn't.

JULIE I don't know what you mean. You can't possibly imagine that . . .

JEAN I don't, but others do.

JULIE What? That I'm in love with the valet?

JEAN I'm not a conceited man, but such a thing's been known to happen, and to these rustics nothing's sacred.

JULIE You, I take it, are an aristocrat.

JEAN Yes, I am.

JULIE And I am coming down in the world.

JEAN Don't come down, Miss Julie. Take my advice. No one will believe you came down of your own accord. They'll all say you fell.

JULIE I have a higher opinion of our people than you. Come and put it to the test. Come on. (*Gazes into his eyes*)

JEAN You're very strange, you know.

JULIE Perhaps I am, but so are you. For that matter everything is strange. Life, human beings, everything, just scum drifting about on the water until it sinks—down and down. That reminds me of a dream I sometimes have, in which I'm on top of a pillar and can't see any way of getting down. When I look down I'm dizzy; I have to get down but I haven't the courage to jump. I can't stay there and I long to fall, but I don't fall. There's no respite. There can't be any peace at all for me until I'm down, right down on the ground. And if I did get to the ground I'd want to be under the ground . . . Have you ever felt like that?

JEAN No. In my dream I'm lying under a great tree in a dark wood. I want to get up, up to the top of it, and look out over the bright landscape where the sun is shining and rob that high nest of its golden eggs. And I climb and climb, but the trunk is so thick and smooth and it's so far to the first branch. But I know if I can once reach that first branch I'll go to the top just as if I'm on a ladder. I haven't reached it yet, but I shall get there, even if only in my dreams.

JULIE Here I am chattering about dreams with you. Come on. Only into the park. (*She takes his arm and they go toward the door*)

JEAN We must sleep on nine midsummer flowers tonight; then our dreams will come true, Miss Julie. (*They turn at the door. He has a hand to his eye*)

JULIE Have you got something in your eye? Let me see.

JEAN Oh, it's nothing. Just a speck of dust. It'll be gone in a minute.

JULIE My sleeve must have rubbed against you. Sit down and let me see to it. (*Takes him by the arm and makes him sit down, bends his head back and tries to get the speck out with the corner of her handkerchief*) Keep still now, quite still. (*Slaps his hand*) Do as I tell you. Why, I believe you're trembling, big, strong man though you are! (*Feels his biceps*) What muscles!

JEAN (*Warning*) Miss Julie!

JULIE Yes, Monsieur Jean?

JEAN *Attention. Je ne suis qu'un homme.*[2]

JULIE Will you stay still! There now. It's out. Kiss my hand and say thank you.

[2] Careful. I'm only a man.

JEAN (*Rising*) Miss Julie, listen. Kristin's gone to bed now. Will you listen?

JULIE Kiss my hand first.

JEAN Very well, but you'll have only yourself to blame.

JULIE For what?

JEAN For what! Are you still a child at twenty-five? Don't you know it's dangerous to play with fire?

JULIE Not for me. I'm insured.

JEAN (*Bluntly*) No, you're not. And even if you are, there's still stuff here to kindle a flame.

JULIE Meaning yourself?

JEAN Yes. Not because I'm me, but because I'm a man and young and . . .

JULIE And good-looking? What incredible conceit! A Don Juan perhaps? Or a Joseph? Good Lord, I do believe you are a Joseph!

JEAN Do you?

JULIE I'm rather afraid so.

(JEAN *goes boldly up and tries to put his arms round her and kiss her. She boxes his ears*)

How dare you!

JEAN Was that in earnest or a joke?

JULIE In earnest.

JEAN Then what went before was in earnest too. You take your games too seriously and that's dangerous. Anyhow I'm tired of playing now and beg leave to return to my work. The Count will want his boots first thing and it's past midnight now.

JULIE Put those boots down.

JEAN No. This is my work, which it's my duty to do. But I never undertook to be your playfellow and I never will be. I consider myself too good for that.

JULIE You're proud.

JEAN In some ways—not all.

JULIE Have you ever been in love?

JEAN We don't put it that way, but I've been gone on quite a few girls. And once I went sick because I couldn't have the one I wanted. Sick, I mean, like those princes in the Arabian Nights who couldn't eat or drink for love.

JULIE Who was she? (*No answer*) Who was she?

JEAN You can't force me to tell you that.

JULIE If I ask as an equal, ask as a—friend? Who was she?

JEAN You.

JULIE (*Sitting*) How absurd!

JEAN Yes, ludicrous if you like. That's the story I wouldn't tell you before, see, but now I will . . . Do you know what the world looks like from below? No, you don't. No more than the hawks and falcons do whose backs one hardly ever sees because they're always soaring up aloft. I lived in a laborer's hovel with seven other children and a pig, out in the gray fields where there isn't a single tree. But from the window I could see the wall round the Count's park with apple-trees above it. That was the Garden of Eden, guarded by many terrible angels with flaming swords. All the same I and the other boys managed to get to the tree of life. Does all this make you despise me?

JULIE Goodness, all boys steal apples!

JEAN You say that now, but all the same you do despise me. However, one time I went into the Garden of Eden with my mother to weed the onion beds. Close to the kitchen garden there was a Turkish pavilion hung all over with jasmine and honeysuckle. I hadn't any idea what it was used for, but I'd never seen such a beautiful building. People used to go in and then come out again, and one day the door was left open. I crept up and saw the walls covered with pictures of kings and emperors, and the windows had red curtains with fringes—you know now what the place was, don't you? I . . . (*Breaks off a piece of lilac and holds it for* JULIE *to smell. As he talks, she takes it from him*) I had never been inside the manor, never seen anything but the church, and this was more beautiful. No matter where my thoughts went, they always came back—to that place. The longing went on growing in me to enjoy it fully, just once. *Enfin,*[3] I sneaked in, gazed and admired. Then I heard someone coming. There was only one way out for the gentry, but for me there was another and I had no choice but to take it. (JULIE *drops the lilac on the table*) Then I took to my heels, plunged through the raspberry canes, dashed across the strawberry beds and found myself on the rose terrace. There I saw a pink dress and a pair of white stockings—it was you. I crawled into a weed pile and lay there right under it among prickly thistles and damp rank earth. I watched you walking among the roses and said to myself: "If it's true that a thief can get to heaven and be with the angels, it's pretty strange that a laborer's child here on God's earth mayn't come in the park and play with the Count's daughter."

JULIE (*Sentimentally*) Do you think all poor children feel the way you did?

JEAN (*Taken aback, then rallying*) *All* poor children? . . . Yes, of course they do. Of course.

JULIE It must be terrible to be poor.

JEAN (*With exaggerated distress*) Oh yes, Miss Julie, yes. A dog may lie on the Countess's sofa, a horse may have his nose stroked by a young lady, but a servant . . . (*Change of tone*) well, yes, now and then you meet one with guts enough to rise in the world, but how often? Anyhow, do you know what I did? Jumped in the millstream with my clothes on, was pulled out and got a hiding. But the next Sunday, when Father and all the rest went to Granny's, I managed to get left behind. Then I washed with soap and hot water, put my best clothes on and went to church so as to see you. I did see you and went home determined to die. But I wanted to die beautifully and peacefully, without any pain. Then I remembered it was dangerous to sleep under an elder bush. We had a big one in full bloom, so I stripped it and climbed into the oats-bin with the flowers. Have you ever noticed how smooth oats are? Soft to touch as human skin . . . Well, I closed the lid and shut my eyes, fell asleep, and when they woke me I was very

[3] Well,

ill. But I didn't die, as you see. What I meant by all that I don't know. There was no hope of winning you—you were simply a symbol of the hopelessness of ever getting out of the class I was born in.

JULIE You put things very well, you know. Did you go to school?

JEAN For a while. But I've read a lot of novels and been to the theater. Besides, I've heard educated folk talking—that's what's taught me most.

JULIE Do you stand round listening to what we're saying?

JEAN Yes, of course. And I've heard quite a bit too! On the carriage box or rowing the boat. Once I heard you, Miss Julie, and one of your young lady friends . . .

JULIE Oh! Whatever did you hear?

JEAN Well, it wouldn't be nice to repeat it. And I must say I was pretty startled. I couldn't think where you had learnt such words. Perhaps, at bottom, there isn't as much difference between people as one's led to believe.

JULIE How dare you! We don't behave as you do when we're engaged.

JEAN (*Looking hard at her*) Are you sure? It's no use making out so innocent to me.

JULIE The man I gave my love to was a scoundrel.

JEAN That's what you always say—afterward.

JULIE Always?

JEAN I think it must be always. I've heard the expression several times in similar circumstances.

JULIE What circumstances?

JEAN Like those in question. The last time . . .

JULIE (*Rising*) Stop. I don't want to hear any more.

JEAN Nor did *she*—curiously enough. May I go to bed now please?

JULIE (*Gently*) Go to bed on Midsummer Eve?

JEAN Yes. Dancing with that crowd doesn't really amuse me.

JULIE Get the key of the boathouse and row me out on the lake. I want to see the sun rise.

JEAN Would that be wise?

JULIE You sound as though you're frightened for your reputation.

JEAN Why not? I don't want to be made a fool of, nor to be sent packing without references when I'm trying to better myself. Besides, I have Kristin to consider.

JULIE So now it's Kristin.

JEAN Yes, but it's you I'm thinking about too. Take my advice and go to bed.

JULIE Am I to take orders from you?

JEAN Just this once, for your own sake. Please. It's very late and sleepiness goes to one's head and makes one rash. Go to bed. What's more, if my ears don't deceive me, I hear people coming this way. They'll be looking for me, and if they find us here, you're done for.

(*The* CHORUS *approaches, singing. During the following dialogue the song is heard in snatches, and in full when the peasants enter*)

Out of the wood two women came,
Tridiri-ralla, tridiri-ra.
The feet of one were bare and cold,
Tridiri-ralla-la.

The other talked of bags of gold,
Tridiri-ralla, tridiri-ra.
But neither had a sou to her name,
Tridiri-ralla-la.

The bridal wreath I give to you,
Tridiri-ralla, tridiri-ra.
But to another I'll be true,
Tridiri-ralla-la.

JULIE I know our people and I love them, just as they do me. Let them come. You'll see.

JEAN No, Miss Julie, they don't love you. They take your food, then spit at it. You must believe me. Listen to them, just listen to what they're singing . . . No, don't listen.

JULIE (*Listening*) What are they singing?

JEAN They're mocking—you and me.

JULIE Oh no! How horrible! What cowards!

JEAN A pack like that's always cowardly. But against such odds there's nothing we can do but run away.

JULIE Run away? Where to? We can't get out and we can't go into Kristin's room.

JEAN Into mine then. Necessity knows no rules. And you can trust me. I really am your true and devoted friend.

JULIE But supposing . . . supposing they were to look for you in there?

JEAN I'll bolt the door, and if they try to break in I'll shoot. Come on. (*Pleading*) Please come.

JULIE (*Tensely*) Do you promise . . . ?

JEAN I swear!

(JULIE *goes quickly into his room and he excitedly follows her.*

*Led by the fiddler, the peasants enter in festive attire with flowers in their hats. They put a barrel of beer and a keg of spirits, garlanded with leaves, on the table, fetch glasses and begin to carouse. The scene becomes a ballet. They form a ring and dance and sing and mime:* "Out of the wood two women came." *Finally they go out, still singing.*

JULIE *comes in alone. She looks at the havoc in the kitchen, wrings her hands, then takes out her powder puff and powders her face.*

JEAN *enters in high spirits*)

JEAN Now you see! And you heard, didn't you? Do you still think it's possible for us to stay here?

JULIE No, I don't. But what can we do?

JEAN Run away. Far away. Take a journey.

JULIE Journey? But where to?

JEAN Switzerland. The Italian lakes. Ever been there?

JULIE No. Is it nice?

JEAN Ah! Eternal summer, oranges, evergreens . . . ah!

JULIE But what would we do there?

JEAN I'll start a hotel. First-class accommodation and first-class customers.

JULIE Hotel?

JEAN There's life for you. New faces all the time, new languages—no time for nerves or worries, no need to look for something to do—work rolling up of its own accord. Bells ringing night and day, trains whistling, buses coming and going, and all the time gold pieces rolling on to the counter. There's life for you!

JULIE For *you*. And I?

JEAN Mistress of the house, ornament of the firm. With your looks, and your style . . . oh, it's bound to be a success! Terrific! You'll sit like a queen in the office and set your slaves in motion by pressing an electric button. The guests will file past your throne and nervously lay their treasure on your table. You've no idea the way people tremble when they get their bills. I'll salt the bills and you'll sugar them with your sweetest smiles. Ah, let's get away from here! (*Produces a time-table*) At once, by the next train. We shall be at Malmö at six-thirty, Hamburg eight-forty next morning, Frankfurt-Basle the following day, and Como by the St. Gotthard Pass in—let's see—three days. Three days!

JULIE That's all very well. But Jean, you must give me courage. Tell me you love me. Come and take me in your arms.

JEAN (*Reluctantly*) I'd like to, but I daren't. Not again in this house. I love you—that goes without saying. You can't doubt that, Miss Julie, can you?

JULIE (*Shyly, very feminine*) Miss? Call me Julie. There aren't any barriers between us now. Call me Julie.

JEAN (*Uneasily*) I can't. As long as we're in this house, there *are* barriers between us. There's the past and there's the Count. I've never been so servile to anyone as I am to him. I've only got to see his gloves on a chair to feel small. I've only to hear his bell and I shy like a horse. Even now, when I look at his boots, standing there so proud and stiff, I feel my back beginning to bend. (*Kicks the boots*) It's those old, narrow-minded notions drummed into us as children . . . but they can soon be forgotten. You've only got to get to another country, a republic, and people will bend themselves double before my porter's livery. Yes, double they'll bend themselves, but I shan't. I wasn't born to bend. I've got guts, I've got character, and once I reach that first branch, you'll watch me climb. Today I'm valet, next year I'll be proprietor, in ten years I'll have made a fortune, and then I'll go to Rumania, get myself decorated and I may, I only say *may,* mind you, end up as a Count.

JULIE (*Sadly*) That would be very nice.

JEAN You see in Rumania one can buy a title, and then you'll be a Countess after all. My Countess.

JULIE What do I care about all that? I'm putting those things behind me. Tell me you love me, because if you don't . . . if you don't, what am I?

JEAN I'll tell you a thousand times over—later. But not here. No sentimentality now or everything will be lost. We must consider this thing calmly like reasonable people. (*Takes a cigar, cuts and lights it*) You sit down there and I'll sit here and we'll talk as if nothing has happened.

JULIE My God, have you no feelings at all?

JEAN Nobody has more. But I know how to control them.

JULIE A short time ago you were kissing my shoe. And now . . .

JEAN (*Harshly*) Yes, that was then. Now we have something else to think about.

JULIE Don't speak to me so brutally.

JEAN I'm not. Just sensibly. One folly's been committed, don't let's have more. The Count will be back at any moment and we've got to settle our future before that. Now, what do you think of my plans? Do you approve?

JULIE It seems a very good idea—but just one thing. Such a big undertaking would need a lot of capital. Have you got any?

JEAN (*Chewing his cigar*) I certainly have. I've got my professional skill, my wide experience, and my knowledge of foreign languages. That's capital worth having, it seems to me.

JULIE But it won't buy even one railway ticket.

JEAN Quite true. That's why I need a backer to advance some ready cash.

JULIE How could you get that at a moment's notice?

JEAN You must get it, if you want to be my partner.

JULIE I can't. I haven't any money of my own. (*Pause*)

JEAN Then the whole thing's off.

JULIE And . . . ?

JEAN We go on as we are.

JULIE Do you think I'm going to stay under this roof as your mistress? With everyone pointing at me. Do you think I can face my father after this? No. Take me away from here, away from this shame, this humiliation. Oh my God, what have I done? My God, my God! (*Weeps*)

JEAN So that's the tune now, is it? What have you done? Same as many before you.

JULIE (*Hysterically*) And now you despise me. I'm falling, I'm falling.

JEAN Fall as far as me and I'll lift you up again.

JULIE Why was I so terribly attracted to you? The weak to the strong, the falling to the rising? Or was it love? Is that love? Do you know what love is?

JEAN Do I? You bet I do. Do you think I never had a girl before?

JULIE The things you say, the things you think!

JEAN That's what life's taught me, and that's what I am. It's no good getting hysterical or giving yourself airs. We're both in the same boat now. Here, my dear girl, let me give you a glass of something special. (*Opens the drawer, takes out the bottle of wine and fills two used glasses*)

JULIE Where did you get that wine?

JEAN From the cellar.

JULIE My father's burgundy.

JEAN Why not, for his son-in-law?

JULIE And I drink beer.

JEAN That only shows your taste's not so good as mine.

JULIE Thief!

JEAN Are you going to tell on me?

JULIE Oh God! The accomplice of a petty thief! Was I blind drunk? Have I dreamt this whole night? Midsummer Eve, the night for innocent merrymaking.

JEAN Innocent, eh?

JULIE Is anyone on earth as wretched as I am now?

JEAN Why should *you* be? After such a conquest. What about Kristin in there? Don't you think she has any feelings?

JULIE I did think so, but I don't any longer. No. A menial is a menial . . .

JEAN And a whore is a whore.

JULIE (*Falling to her knees, her hands clasped*) O God in heaven, put an end to my miserable life! Lift me out of this filth in which I'm sinking. Save me! Save me!

JEAN I must admit I'm sorry for you. When I was in the onion bed and saw you up there among the roses, I . . . yes, I'll tell you now . . . I had the same dirty thoughts as all boys.

JULIE You, who wanted to die because of me?

JEAN In the oats-bin? That was just talk.

JULIE Lies, you mean.

JEAN (*Getting sleepy*) More or less. I think I read a story in some paper about a chimney-sweep who shut himself up in a chest full of lilac because he'd been summonsed for not supporting some brat . . .

JULIE So this is what you're like.

JEAN I had to think up something. It's always the fancy stuff that catches the women.

JULIE Beast!

JEAN *Merde!*

JULIE Now you have seen the falcon's back.

JEAN Not exactly its *back*.

JULIE I was to be the first branch.

JEAN But the branch was rotten.

JULIE I was to be a hotel sign.

JEAN And I the hotel.

JULIE Sit at your counter, attract your clients and cook their accounts.

JEAN I'd have done that myself.

JULIE That any human being can be so steeped in filth!

JEAN Clean it up then.

JULIE Menial! Lackey! Stand up when I speak to you.

JEAN Menial's whore, lackey's harlot, shut your mouth and get out of here! Are you the one to lecture me for being coarse? Nobody of my kind would ever be as coarse as you were tonight. Do you think any servant girl would throw herself at a man that way? Have you ever seen a girl of my class asking for it like that? I haven't. Only animals and prostitutes.

JULIE (*Broken*) Go on. Hit me, trample on me—it's all I deserve. I'm rotten. But help me! If there's any way out at all, help me.

JEAN (*More gently*) I'm not denying myself a share in the honor of seducing you, but do you think anybody in my place would have dared look in your direction if you yourself hadn't asked for it? I'm still amazed . . .

JULIE And proud.

JEAN Why not? Though I must admit the victory was too easy to make me lose my head.

JULIE Go on hitting me.

JEAN (*Rising*) No. On the contrary I apologize for what I've said. I don't hit a person who's down—least of all a woman. I can't deny there's a certain satisfaction in finding that what dazzled one below was just moonshine, that that falcon's back is gray after all, that there's powder on the lovely cheek, that polished nails can have black tips, that the handkerchief is dirty although it smells of scent. On the other hand it hurts to find that what I was struggling to reach wasn't high and isn't real. It hurts to see you fallen so low you're far lower than your own cook. Hurts like when you see the last flowers of summer lashed to pieces by rain and turned to mud.

JULIE You're talking as if you're already my superior.

JEAN I am. I might make you a Countess, but you could never make me a Count, you know.

JULIE But I am the child of a Count, and you could never be that.

JEAN True, but I might be the father of Counts if . . .

JULIE You're a thief. I'm not.

JEAN There are worse things than being a thief—much lower. Besides, when I'm in a place I regard myself as a member of the family to some extent, as one of the children. You don't call it stealing when children pinch a berry from overladen bushes. (*His passion is roused again*) Miss Julie, you're a glorious woman, far too good for a man like me. You were carried away by some kind of madness, and now you're trying to cover up your mistake by persuading yourself you're in love with me. You're not, although you may find me physically attractive, which means your love's no better than mine. But I wouldn't be satisfied with being nothing but an animal for you, and I could never make you love me.

JULIE Are you sure?

JEAN You think there's a chance? Of my loving you, yes, of course. You're beautiful, refined, (*Takes her hand*) educated, and you can be nice when you want to be. The fire you kindle in a man isn't likely to go out. (*Puts his arm round her*) You're like mulled wine, full of spices, and your kisses . . . (*He tries to pull her to him, but she breaks away*)

JULIE Let go of me! You won't win me that way.

JEAN Not that way, how then? Not by kisses and fine speeches, not by planning the future and saving you from shame? How then?

JULIE How? How? I don't know. There isn't any way. I loathe you—loathe you as I loathe rats, but I can't escape from you.

JEAN Escape with me.

JULIE (*Pulling herself together*) Escape? Yes, we must escape. But I'm so tired. Give me a glass of wine.

(*He pours it out. She looks at her watch*) First we must talk. We still have a little time. (*Empties the glass and holds it out for more*)

JEAN Don't drink like that. You'll get tipsy.

JULIE What's that matter?

JEAN What's it matter? It's vulgar to get drunk. Well, what have you got to say?

JULIE We've got to run away, but we must talk first —or rather, I must, for so far you've done all the talking. You've told me about your life, now I want to tell you about mine, so that we really know each other before we begin this journey together.

EAN Wait. Excuse my saying so, but don't you think you may be sorry afterward if you give away your secrets to me?

JULIE Aren't you my friend?

JEAN On the whole. But don't rely on me.

JULIE You can't mean that. But anyway everyone knows my secrets. Listen. My mother wasn't wellborn; she came of quite humble people, and was brought up with all those new ideas of sex-equality and women's rights and so on. She thought marriage was quite wrong. So when my father proposed to her, she said she would never become his *wife* . . . but in the end she did. I came into the world, as far as I can make out, against my mother's will, and I was left to run wild, but I had to do all the things a boy does—to prove women are as good as men. I had to wear boys' clothes; I was taught to handle horses —and I wasn't allowed in the dairy. She made me groom and harness and go out hunting; I even had to try to plough. All the men on the estate were given the women's jobs, and the women the men's, until the whole place went to rack and ruin and we were the laughing-stock of the neighborhood. At last my father seemed to have come to his senses and rebelled. He changed everything and ran the place his own way. My mother got ill—I don't know what was the matter with her, but she used to have strange attacks and hide herself in the attic or the garden. Sometimes she stayed out all night. Then came the great fire which you have heard people talking about. The house and the stables and the barns—the whole place burnt to the ground. In very suspicious circumstances. Because the accident happened the very day the insurance had to be renewed, and my father had sent the new premium, but through some carelessness of the messenger it arrived too late. (*Refills her glass and drinks*)

JEAN Don't drink any more.

JULIE Oh, what does it matter? We were destitute and had to sleep in the carriages. My father didn't know how to get money to rebuild, and then my mother suggested he should borrow from an old friend of hers, a local brick manufacturer. My father got the loan and, to his surprise, without having to pay interest. So the place was rebuilt. (*Drinks*) Do you know who set fire to it?

JEAN Your lady mother.

JULIE Do you know who the brick manufacturer was?

JEAN Your mother's lover?

JULIE Do you know whose the money was?

JEAN Wait . . . no, I don't know that.

JULIE It was my mother's.

JEAN In other words the Count's, unless there was a settlement.

JULIE There wasn't any settlement. My mother had a little money of her own which she didn't want my father to control, so she invested it with her—friend.

JEAN Who grabbed it.

JULIE Exactly. He appropriated it. My father came to know all this. He couldn't bring an action, couldn't pay his wife's lover, nor prove it was his wife's money. That was my mother's revenge because he made himself master in his own house. He nearly shot himself then—at least there's a rumor he tried and didn't bring it off. So he went on living, and my mother had to pay dearly for what she'd done. Imagine what those five years were like for me. My natural sympathies were with my father, yet I took my mother's side, because I didn't know the facts. I'd learnt from her to hate and distrust men—you know how she loathed the whole male sex. And I swore to her I'd never become the slave of any man.

JEAN And so you got engaged to that attorney.

JULIE So that he should be my slave.

JEAN But he wouldn't be.

JULIE Oh yes, he wanted to be, but he didn't have the chance. I got bored with him.

JEAN Is that what I saw—in the stable-yard?

JULIE What did you see?

JEAN What I saw was him breaking off the engagement.

JULIE That's a lie. It was I who broke it off. Did he say it was him? The cad.

JEAN He's not a cad. Do you hate men, Miss Julie?

JULIE Yes . . . most of the time. But when that weakness comes, oh . . . the shame!

JEAN Then do you hate me?

JULIE Beyond words. I'd gladly have you killed like an animal.

JEAN Quick as you'd shoot a mad dog, eh?

JULIE Yes.

JEAN But there's nothing here to shoot with—and there isn't a dog. So what do we do now?

JULIE Go abroad.

JEAN To make each other miserable for the rest of our lives?

JULIE No, to enjoy ourselves for a day or two, for a week, for as long as enjoyment lasts, and then—to die . . .

JEAN Die? How silly! I think it would be far better to start a hotel.

JULIE (*Without listening*) . . . die on the shores of Lake Como, where the sun always shines and at Christmas time there are green trees and glowing oranges.

JEAN Lake Como's a rainy hole and I didn't see any oranges outside the shops. But it's a good place for tourists. Plenty of villas to be rented by—er—honeymoon couples. Profitable business that. Know why?

Because they all sign a lease for six months and all leave after three weeks.

JULIE (*Naïvely*) After three weeks? Why?

JEAN They quarrel, of course. But the rent has to be paid just the same. And then it's let again. So it goes on and on, for there's plenty of love although it doesn't last long.

JULIE You don't want to die with me?

JEAN I don't want to die at all. For one thing I like living and for another I consider suicide's a sin against the Creator who gave us life.

JULIE You believe in God—*you?*

JEAN Yes, of course. And I go to church every Sunday. Look here, I'm tired of all this. I'm going to bed.

JULIE Indeed! And do you think I'm going to leave things like this? Don't you know what you owe the woman you've ruined?

JEAN (*Taking out his purse and throwing a silver coin on the table*) There you are. I don't want to be in anybody's debt.

JULIE (*Pretending not to notice the insult*) Don't you know what the law is?

JEAN There's no law unfortunately that punishes a woman for seducing a man.

JULIE But can you see anything for it but to go abroad, get married and then divorce?

JEAN What if I refuse this misalliance?

JULIE Misalliance?

JEAN Yes, for me. I'm better bred than you, see! Nobody in my family committed arson.

JULIE How do you know?

JEAN Well, you can't prove otherwise, because we haven't any family records outside the Registrar's office. But I've seen your family tree in that book on the drawing-room table. Do you know who the founder of your family was? A miller who let his wife sleep with the King one night during the Danish war. I haven't any ancestors like that. I haven't any ancestors at all, but I might become one.

JULIE This is what I get for confiding in someone so low, for sacrificing my family honor . . .

JEAN Dishonor! Well, I told you so. One shouldn't drink, because then one talks. And one shouldn't talk.

JULIE Oh, how ashamed I am, how bitterly ashamed! If at least you loved me!

JEAN Look here—for the last time—what do you want? Am I to burst into tears? Am I to jump over your riding whip? Shall I kiss you and carry you off to Lake Como for three weeks, after which . . . What am I to do? What do you want? This is getting unbearable, but that's what comes of playing around with women. Miss Julie, I can see how miserable you are; I know you're going through hell, but I don't understand you. We don't have scenes like this; we don't go in for hating each other. We make love for fun in our spare time, but we haven't all day and all night for it like you. I think you must be ill. I'm sure you're ill.

JULIE Then you must be kind to me. You sound almost human now.

JEAN Well, be human yourself. You spit at me, then won't let me wipe it off—on you.

JULIE Help me, help me! Tell me what to do, where to go.

JEAN Jesus, as if I knew!

JULIE I've been mad, raving mad, but there must be a way out.

JEAN Stay here and keep quiet. Nobody knows anything.

JULIE I can't. People do know. Kristin knows.

JEAN They don't know and they wouldn't believe such a thing.

JULIE (*Hesitating*) But—it might happen again.

JEAN That's true.

JULIE And there might be—consequences.

JEAN (*In panic*) Consequences! Fool that I am I never thought of that. Yes, there's nothing for it but to go. At once. I can't come with you. That would be a complete give-away. You must go alone—abroad—anywhere.

JULIE Alone? Where to? I can't.

JEAN You must. And before the Count gets back. If you stay, we know what will happen. Once you've sinned you feel you might as well go on, as the harm's done. Then you get more and more reckless and in the end you're found out. No. You must go abroad. Then write to the Count and tell him everything, except that it was me. He'll never guess that—and I don't think he'll want to.

JULIE I'll go if you come with me.

JEAN Are you crazy, woman? "Miss Julie elopes with valet." Next day it would be in the headlines, and the Count would never live it down.

JULIE I can't go. I can't stay. I'm so tired, so completely worn out. Give me orders. Set me going. I can't think any more, can't act . . .

JEAN You see what weaklings you are. Why do you give yourselves airs and turn up your noses as if you're the lords of creation? Very well, I'll give you your orders. Go upstairs and dress. Get money for the journey and come down here again.

JULIE (*Softly*) Come up with me.

JEAN To your room? Now you've gone crazy again. (*Hesitates a moment*) No! Go along at once. (*Takes her hand and pulls her to the door*)

JULIE (*As she goes*) Speak kindly to me, Jean.

JEAN Orders always sound unkind. Now you know. Now you know.

(*Left alone,* JEAN *sighs with relief, sits down at the table, takes out a note-book and pencil and adds up figures, now and then aloud. Dawn begins to break.* KRISTIN *enters dressed for church, carrying his white dickey and tie*)

KRISTIN Lord Jesus, look at the state the place is in! What have you been up to? (*Turns out the lamp*)

JEAN Oh, Miss Julie invited the crowd in. Did you sleep through it? Didn't you hear anything?

KRISTIN I slept like a log.

JEAN And dressed for church already.

KRISTIN Yes, you promised to come to Communion with me today.

JEAN Why, so I did. And you've got my bib and tucker, I see. Come on then. (*Sits.* KRISTIN *begins to put his things on. Pause. Sleepily*) What's the lesson today?

KRISTIN It's about the beheading of John the Baptist, I think.

JEAN That's sure to be horribly long. Hi, you're choking me! Oh Lord, I'm so sleepy, so sleepy!

KRISTIN Yes, what have you been doing up all night? You look absolutely green.

JEAN Just sitting here talking with Miss Julie.

KRISTIN She doesn't know what's proper, that one. (*Pause*)

JEAN I say, Kristin.

KRISTIN What?

JEAN It's queer really, isn't it, when you come to think of it? Her.

KRISTIN What's queer?

JEAN The whole thing. (*Pause*)

KRISTIN (*Looking at the half-filled glasses on the table*) Have you been drinking together too?

JEAN Yes.

KRISTIN More shame you. Look me straight in the face.

JEAN Yes.

KRISTIN Is it possible? Is it possible?

JEAN (*After a moment*) Yes, it is.

KRISTIN Oh! This I would never have believed. How low!

JEAN You're not jealous of her, surely?

KRISTIN No, I'm not. If it had been Clara or Sophie I'd have scratched your eyes out. But not of her. I don't know why; that's how it is though. But it's disgusting.

JEAN You're angry with her then.

KRISTIN No. With you. It was wicked of you, very very wicked. Poor girl. And, mark my words, I won't stay here any longer now—in a place where one can't respect one's employers.

JEAN Why should one respect them?

KRISTIN You should know since you're so smart. But you don't want to stay in the service of people who aren't respectable, do you? I wouldn't demean myself.

JEAN But it's rather a comfort to find out they're no better than us.

KRISTIN I don't think so. If they're no better there's nothing for us to live up to. Oh and think of the Count! Think of him. He's been through so much already. No, I won't stay in the place any longer. A fellow like you too! If it had been that attorney now or somebody of her own class . . .

JEAN Why, what's wrong with . . .

KRISTIN Oh, you're all right in your own way, but when all's said and done there is a difference between one class and another. No, this is something I'll never be able to stomach. That our young lady who was so proud and so down on men you'd never believe she'd let one come near her should go and give herself to one like you. She who wanted to have poor Diana shot for running after the lodge-keeper's pug. No. I must say . . . ! Well, I won't stay here any longer. On the twenty-fourth of October I quit.

JEAN And then?

KRISTIN Well, since you mention it, it's about time you began to look around, if we're ever going to get married.

JEAN But what am I to look for? I shan't get a place like this when I'm married.

KRISTIN I know you won't. But you might get a job as porter or caretaker in some public institution. Government rations are small but sure, and there's a pension for the widow and children.

JEAN That's all very fine, but it's not in my line to start thinking at once about dying for my wife and children. I must say I had rather bigger ideas.

KRISTIN You and your ideas! You've got obligations too, and you'd better start thinking about them.

JEAN Don't *you* start pestering me about obligations. I've had enough of that. (*Listens to a sound upstairs*) Anyway we've plenty of time to work things out. Go and get ready now and we'll be off to church.

KRISTIN Who's that walking about upstairs?

JEAN Don't know—unless it's Clara.

KRISTIN (*Going*) You don't think the Count could have come back without our hearing him?

JEAN (*Scared*) The Count? No, he can't have. He'd have rung for me.

KRISTIN God help us! I've never known such goings on. (*Exit*)

(*The sun has now risen and is shining on the treetops. The light gradually changes until it slants in through the windows.* JEAN *goes to the door and beckons.* JULIE *enters in traveling clothes, carrying a small bird-cage covered with a cloth which she puts on a chair*)

JULIE I'm ready.

JEAN Hush! Kristin's up.

JULIE (*In a very nervous state*) Does she suspect anything?

JEAN Not a thing. But, my God, what a sight you are!

JULIE Sight? What do you mean?

JEAN You're white as a corpse and—pardon me—your face is dirty.

JULIE Let me wash then. (*Goes to the sink and washes her face and hands*) There. Give me a towel. Oh! The sun is rising!

JEAN And that breaks the spell.

JULIE Yes. The spell of Midsummer Eve . . . But listen, Jean. Come with me. I've got the money.

JEAN (*Skeptically*) Enough?

JULIE Enough to start with. Come with me. I can't travel alone today. It's Midsummer Day, remember. I'd be packed into a suffocating train among crowds of people who'd all stare at me. And it would stop at every station while I yearned for wings. No, I can't do that, I simply can't. There will be memories too; memories of Midsummer Days when I was little. The leafy church—birch and lilac—the gaily spread dinner table, relatives, friends—evening in the park—dancing and music and flowers and fun. Oh, however far you run away—there'll always be memories in the baggage car—and remorse and guilt.

JEAN I will come with you, but quickly now then, before it's too late. At once.

JULIE Put on your things. (*Picks up the cage*)

JEAN No luggage, mind. That would give us away.

JULIE No, only what we can take with us in the carriage.

JEAN (*Fetching his hat*) What on earth have you got there? What is it?

JULIE Only my greenfinch. I don't want to leave it behind.

JEAN Well, I'll be damned! We're to take a bird-cage along, are we? You're crazy. Put that cage down.

JULIE It's the only thing I'm taking from my home. The only living creature who cares for me since Diana went off like that. Don't be cruel. Let me take it.

JEAN Put that cage down, I tell you—and don't talk so loud. Kristin will hear.

JULIE No, I won't leave it in strange hands. I'd rather you killed it.

JEAN Give the little beast here then and I'll wring its neck.

JULIE But don't hurt it, don't . . . no, I can't.

JEAN Give it here. I *can*.

JULIE (*Taking the bird out of the cage and kissing it*) Dear little Serena, must you die and leave your mistress?

JEAN Please don't make a scene. It's *your* life and future we're worrying about. Come on, quick now!

(*He snatches the bird from her, puts it on a board and picks up a chopper.* JULIE *turns away*)

You should have learnt how to kill chickens instead of target-shooting. Then you wouldn't faint at a drop of blood.

JULIE (*Screaming*) Kill me too! Kill me! You who can butcher an innocent creature without a quiver. Oh, how I hate you, how I loathe you! There is blood between us now. I curse the hour I first saw you. I curse the hour I was conceived in my mother's womb.

JEAN What's the use of cursing. Let's go.

JULIE (*Going to the chopping-block as if drawn against her will*) No, I won't go yet. I can't . . . I must look. Listen! There's a carriage. (*Listens without taking her eyes off the board and chopper*) You don't think I can bear the sight of blood. You think I'm so weak. Oh, how I should like to see your blood and your brains on a chopping-block! I'd like to see the whole of your sex swimming like that in a sea of blood. I think I could drink out of your skull, bathe my feet in your broken breast and eat your heart roasted whole. You think I'm weak. You think I love you, that my womb yearned for your seed and I want to carry your offspring under my heart and nourish it with my blood. You think I want to bear your child and take your name. By the way, what is your name? I've never heard your surname. I don't suppose you've got one. I should be "Mrs. Hovel" or "Madam Dunghill." You dog wearing my collar, you lackey with my crest on your buttons! I share you with my cook; I'm my own servant's rival! Oh! Oh! Oh! . . . You think I'm a coward and will run away. No, now I'm going to stay—and let the storm break. My father will come back . . . find his desk broken open . . . his money gone. Then he'll ring that bell—twice for the valet—and then he'll send for the police . . . and I shall tell everything. Everything. Oh how wonderful to make an end of it all—a real end! He has a stroke and dies and that's the end of all of us. Just peace and quietness . . . eternal rest. The coat of arms broken on the coffin and the Count's line extinct . . . But the valet's line goes on in an orphanage, wins laurels in the gutter and ends in jail.

JEAN There speaks the noble blood! Bravo, Miss Julie. But now, don't let the cat out of the bag.

(KRISTIN *enters dressed for church, carrying a prayer-book.* JULIE *rushes to her and flings herself into her arms for protection*)

JULIE Help me, Kristin! Protect me from this man!

KRISTIN (*Unmoved and cold*) What goings-on for a feast day morning! (*Sees the board*) And what a filthy mess. What's it all about? Why are you screaming and carrying on so?

JULIE Kristin, you're a woman and my friend. Beware of that scoundrel!

JEAN (*Embarrassed*) While you ladies are talking things over, I'll go and shave. (*Slips into his room*)

JULIE You must understand. You must listen to me.

KRISTIN I certainly don't understand such loose ways. Where are you off to in those traveling clothes? And he had his hat on, didn't he, eh?

JULIE Listen, Kristin. Listen, I'll tell you everything.

KRISTIN I don't want to know anything.

JULIE You must listen.

KRISTIN What to? Your nonsense with Jean? I don't care a rap about that; it's nothing to do with me. But if you're thinking of getting him to run off with you, we'll soon put a stop to that.

JULIE (*Very nervously*) Please try to be calm, Kristin, and listen. I can't stay here, nor can Jean—so we must go abroad.

KRISTIN Hm, hm!

JULIE (*Brightening*) But you see, I've had an idea. Supposing we all three go—abroad—to Switzerland and start a hotel together . . . I've got some money, you see . . . and Jean and I could run the whole thing—and I thought you would take charge of the kitchen. Wouldn't that be splendid? Say yes, do. If you come with us everything will be fine. Oh do say yes! (*Puts her arms round* KRISTIN)

KRISTIN (*Coolly thinking*) Hm, hm.

JULIE (*Presto tempo*) You've never traveled, Kristin. You should go abroad and see the world. You've no idea how nice it is traveling by train—new faces all the time and new countries. On our way through Hamburg we'll go to the zoo—you'll love that—and we'll go to the theater and the opera too . . . and when we get to Munich there'll be the museums, dear, and pictures by Rubens and Raphael—the great painters, you know . . . You've heard of Munich, haven't you? Where King Ludwig lived—you know, the king who went mad. . . . We'll see his castles —some of his castles are still just like in fairy-tales . . . and from there it's not far to Switzerland—and the Alps. Think of the Alps, Kristin dear, covered with snow in the middle of summer . . . and there are oranges there and trees that are green the whole year round . . .

(JEAN *is seen in the door of his room, sharpening his razor on a strop which he holds with his teeth and his left hand. He listens to the talk with satisfaction and now and then nods approval.* JULIE *continues, tempo prestissimo*)

And then we'll get a hotel . . . and I'll sit at the desk, while Jean receives the guests and goes out marketing and writes letters . . . There's life for you! Trains whistling, buses driving up, bells ringing upstairs and downstairs . . . and I shall make out the bills—and I shall cook them too . . . you've no idea how nervous travelers are when it comes to paying their bills. And you—you'll sit like a queen in the kitchen . . . of course there won't be any standing at the stove for you. You'll always have to be nicely dressed and ready to be seen, and with your looks —no, I'm not flattering you—one fine day you'll catch yourself a husband . . . some rich Englishman, I shouldn't wonder—they're the ones who are easy (*Slowing down*) to catch . . . and then we'll get rich and build ourselves a villa on Lake Como . . . of course it rains there a little now and then —but (*Dully*) the sun must shine there too sometimes—even though it seems gloomy—and if not —then we can come home again—come back— (*Pause*)—here—or somewhere else . . .

KRISTIN Look here, Miss Julie, do you believe all that yourself?

JULIE (*Exhausted*) Do I believe it?

KRISTIN Yes.

JULIE (*Wearily*) I don't know. I don't believe anything any more. (*Sinks down on the bench; her head in her arms on the table*) Nothing. Nothing at all.

KRISTIN (*Turning to* JEAN) So you meant to beat it, did you?

JEAN (*Disconcerted, putting the razor on the table*) Beat it? What are you talking about? You've heard Miss Julie's plan, and though she's tired now with being up all night, it's a perfectly sound plan.

KRISTIN Oh, is it? If you thought I'd work for that . . .

JEAN (*Interrupting*) Kindly use decent language in front of your mistress. Do you hear?

KRISTIN Mistress?

JEAN Yes.

KRISTIN Well, well, just listen to that!

JEAN Yes, it would be a good thing if you did listen and talked less. Miss Julie is your mistress and what's made you lose your respect for her now ought to make you feel the same about yourself.

KRISTIN I've always had enough self-respect——

JEAN To despise other people.

KRISTIN —not to go below my own station. Has the Count's cook ever gone with the groom or the swineherd? Tell me that.

JEAN No, you were lucky enough to have a high-class chap for your beau.

KRISTIN High-class all right—selling the oats out of the Count's stable.

JEAN You're a fine one to talk—taking a commission on the groceries and bribes from the butcher.

KRISTIN What the devil . . . ?

JEAN And now you can't feel any respect for your employers. You, you!

KRISTIN Are you coming to church with me? I should think you need a good sermon after your fine deeds.

JEAN No, I'm not going to church today. You can go alone and confess your own sins.

KRISTIN Yes, I'll do that and bring back enough forgiveness to cover yours too. The Saviour suffered and died on the cross for all our sins, and if we go to Him with faith and a penitent heart, He takes all our sins upon Himself.

JEAN Even grocery thefts?

JULIE Do you believe that, Kristin?

KRISTIN That is my living faith, as sure as I stand here. The faith I learnt as a child and have kept ever since, Miss Julie. "But where sin abounded, grace did much more abound."

JULIE Oh, if I had your faith! Oh, if . . .

KRISTIN But you see you can't have it without God's special grace, and it's not given to all to have that.

JULIE Who is it given to then?

KRISTIN That's the great secret of the workings of grace, Miss Julie. God is no respecter of persons, and with Him the last shall be first . . .

JULIE Then I suppose He does respect the last.

KRISTIN (*Continuing*) . . . and it is easier for a camel to go through the eye of a needle than for a rich man to enter into the kingdom of God. That's how it is, Miss Julie. Now I'm going—alone, and on my way I shall tell the groom not to let any of the horses out, in case anyone should want to leave before the Count gets back. Good-by.

(*Exit*)

JEAN What a devil! And all on account of a greenfinch.

JULIE (*Wearily*) Never mind the greenfinch. Do you see any way out of this, any end to it?

JEAN (*Pondering*) No.

JULIE If you were in my place, what would you do?

JEAN In your place? Wait a bit. If I was a woman—a lady of rank who had—fallen. I don't know. Yes, I do know now.

JULIE (*Picking up the razor and making a gesture*) This?

JEAN Yes. But *I* wouldn't do it, you know. There's a difference between us.

JULIE Because you're a man and I'm a woman? What is the difference?

JEAN The usual difference—between man and woman.

JULIE (*Holding the razor*) I'd like to. But I can't. My father couldn't either, that time he wanted to.

JEAN No, he didn't want to. He had to be revenged first.

JULIE And now my mother is revenged again, through me.

JEAN Didn't you ever love your father, Miss Julie?

JULIE Deeply, but I must have hated him too—unconsciously. And he let me be brought up to despise my own sex, to be half woman, half man. Whose fault is what's happened? My father's, my mother's, or my own? My own? I haven't anything that's my own. I haven't one single thought that I didn't get from my father, one emotion that didn't come from my mother, and as for this last idea—about all people being equal—I got that from him, my fiancé—that's why I call him a cad. How can it be my fault? Push the responsibility on to Jesus, like Kristin does? No, I'm too proud and—thanks to my father's teaching—too intelligent. As for all that about a rich person not being able to get into heaven, it's just a lie, but Kristin, who has money in the savings-bank, will certainly not get in. Whose fault is it? What does it matter whose fault it is? In any case I must take the blame and bear the consequences.

JEAN Yes, but . . . (*There are two sharp rings on the bell.* JULIE *jumps to her feet.* JEAN *changes into his livery*) The Count is back. Supposing Kristin . . . (*Goes to the speaking-tube, presses it and listens*)

JULIE Has he been to his desk yet?

JEAN This is Jean, sir. (*Listens*) Yes, sir. (*Listens*) Yes, sir, very good, sir. (*Listens*) At once, sir? (*Listens*) Very good, sir. In half an hour.

JULIE (*In panic*) What did he say? My God, what did he say?

JEAN He ordered his boots and his coffee in half an hour.

JULIE Then there's half an hour . . . Oh, I'm so tired! I can't do anything. Can't be sorry, can't run away, can't stay, can't live—can't die. Help me. Order me, and I'll obey like a dog. Do me this last service—save my honor, save his name. You know what I ought to do, but haven't the strength to do. Use your strength and order me to do it.

JEAN I don't know why—I can't now—I don't understand . . . It's just as if this coat made me—I can't give you orders—and now that the Count has spoken to me—I can't quite explain, but . . . well, that devil of a lackey is bending my back again. I believe if the Count came down now and ordered me to cut my throat, I'd do it on the spot.

JULIE Then pretend you're him and I'm you. You did some fine acting before, when you knelt to me and played the aristocrat. Or . . . Have you ever seen a hypnotist at the theater? (*He nods*) He says to the person "Take the broom," and he takes it. He says "Sweep," and he sweeps . . .

JEAN But the person has to be asleep.

JULIE (*As if in a trance*) I am asleep already . . . the whole room has turned to smoke—and you look like a stove—a stove like a man in black with a tall hat—your eyes are glowing like coals when the fire is low—and your face is a white patch like ashes. (*The sunlight has now reached the floor and lights up* JEAN) How nice and warm it is! (*She holds out her hands as though warming them at a fire*) And so light—and so peaceful.

JEAN (*Putting the razor in her hand*) Here is the broom. Go now while it's light—out to the barn—and . . . (*Whispers in her ear*)

JULIE (*Waking*) Thank you. I am going now—to rest. But just tell me that even the first can receive the gift of grace.

JEAN The first? No, I can't tell you that. But wait . . . Miss Julie, I've got it! You aren't one of the first any longer. You're one of the last.

JULIE That's true. I'm one of the very last. I *am* the last. Oh! . . . But now I can't go. Tell me again to go.

JEAN No, I can't now either. I can't.

JULIE And the first shall be last.

JEAN Don't think, don't think. You're taking my strength away too and making me a coward. What's that? I thought I saw the bell move . . . To be so frightened of a bell! Yes, but it's not just a bell. There's somebody behind it—a hand moving it—and something else moving the hand—and if you stop your ears—if you stop your ears—yes, then it rings louder than ever. Rings and rings until you answer—and then it's too late. Then the police come and . . . and . . . (*The bell rings twice loudly.* JEAN *flinches, then straightens himself up*) It's horrible. But there's no other way to end it . . . Go!

(JULIE *walks firmly out through the door*)

*Curtain*

# THE GHOST SONATA

STRINDBERG'S expressionism begins with *The Road to Damascus* (Parts One and Two, 1898; Part Three, 1904), the first consequence of the "Inferno" period. The title alludes not only to the conversion of St. Paul, but to that of Strindberg's hero, the Stranger, *alter ego* of the playwright. In this play, unlike the earlier ones, there is virtually no concern with exposition or causal explanation. The Stranger's quest for sanity and redemption leads, in the final scene before the church, to the possibility of conversion. In Part Three the hero ends in monastic consecration; but there is no assurance that the newly-gained peace will endure.

Strindberg's capacity for self-renewal at the age of 50 is astounding. In a burst of productivity, he moved beyond historical chronicle and symbolist fantasy to a redefinition of dramatic form. In the Prologue to *A Dream Play,* written in 1906, four years after the play itself, Strindberg formulated the premises of expressionist drama. Here, he states, "the writer has tried to imitate the disjointed but apparently logical form of a dream. Anything may happen: everything is possible and probable. Time and space do not exist. . . . The characters are split, doubled, and multiplied: they evaporate and are condensed, are diffused and concentrated. But a single consciousness holds sway over them all—that of the dreamer." The new dramatic structure combines patterns of repetition and distortion with symbolic imagery and philosophical exploration. The dark theodicy of *A Dream Play* attacks not only social and institutional abuses, but the inner suffering which mortals inflict on one another. The endless pain of existence is set forth in the *leitmotif* of the play, "Mankind is pitiable." Life is a turbulent, agonizing dream and death is a deliverance.

Strindberg's last work consists of the Chamber Plays written between 1907 and 1909 for the Intimate Theatre, a little theatre in Stockholm founded specifically for the performance of Strindberg's dramas. The term "chamber theatre" was inspired by Max Reinhardt's Kammerspielhaus in Berlin where many of Strindberg's plays were performed, but the parallel to chamber music is also evident in the contrapuntal structure of the plays. Strindberg's writing even at the end of his life shows no falling off in quality. The best of the Chamber Plays are *The Pelican* and *The Ghost Sonata,* but all of them are arresting and moving.

In *The Ghost Sonata* (1907) the freedom of composition made possible by the Intimate Theatre takes the form of a bold and violent transposition of reality. The second sight of the "Sunday child" enables the Student to see the reappearance of the dead: the phantom of the drowned milkmaid stands before him in the opening scene, and soon afterwards, the body of the dead Consul, wrapped in a winding sheet, rolls out of the door of his home. The spirit world, mystifying and weird, is intertwined with that of everyday life. Through a process of unmasking, *The Ghost Sonata* reveals the anguish and brutality of existence. The vampire-like Hummel has led a life of monstrous depravity and crime. He exposes the sordidness and decay behind the façade of respectability in the house with the Round Room, and is in turn denounced and sentenced at the grotesque "ghost supper." The death which comes to the Girl in the final scene is in fact a liberation. The Student projects in his achieved wisdom the final message of the play: life is illusion, guilt and pain, but a time will come when God will redeem mankind and put an end to suffering and death. The mingling of dream and hallucination issues in a terrifying vision of reality, relieved only by lament and supplication.

In a fragmentary play, *Toten-Insel* (*The Isle of the Dead,* 1906), inspired by the painting by Böcklin which forms the background of the final scene in *The Ghost Sonata,* the Instructor remarks: "If life is a dream, then a drama is a dream of a dream, even though you have employed it as reality." In Strindberg's expressionist plays the boundaries of the imaginary and the real are submerged in the depths of an apocalyptic nightmare. Strindberg's frenzied and hallucinatory dramas achieved an enormous success on the German stage immediately after his death; over a thousand performances of his plays were given in 62 German cities in the period 1913-1915 alone. In France and southern Europe as well as England and the United States, the world-wide acclaim of Strindberg frequently mentioned by critics has been dubious indeed, but his influence has been far more significant than his public reception. Eugene O'Neill, his most gifted successor, unerringly fixed Strindberg's place in twentieth-century drama when he declared: "Strindberg was the precursor of all modernity in our present theatre. . . . Strindberg still remains among the most modern of moderns, the greatest interpreter in the theatre of the characteristic spiritual conflicts which constitute the drama—the blood—of our lives today."

# THE GHOST SONATA

Translated by Elizabeth Sprigge

CHARACTERS

THE OLD MAN (HUMMEL), *a Company Director*
THE STUDENT, (ARKENHOLTZ)
THE MILKMAID, *an apparition*
THE CARETAKER'S WIFE
THE CARETAKER
THE LADY IN BLACK, *the daughter of the Caretaker's Wife and the Dead Man. Also referred to as the Dark Lady*
THE COLONEL
THE MUMMY (AMELIA), *the Colonel's wife*
THE GIRL (ADÈLE), *the Colonel's daughter, actually the daughter of the Old Man*
THE ARISTOCRAT (BARON SKANSKORG), *Engaged to the Lady in Black*
JOHANSSON, *the Old Man's servant*
BENGTSSON, *the Colonel's servant*
THE FIANCÉE, (BEATRICE VON HOLSTEINKRONA), *a white-haired old woman, once betrothed to the Old Man*
THE COOK
A MAIDSERVANT
BEGGARS

## Scene One

*Outside the house. The corner of the façade of a modern house, showing the ground floor above, and the street in front. The ground floor terminates on the right in the Round Room, above which, on the first floor, is a balcony with a flagstaff. The windows of the Round Room face the street in front of the house, and at the corner look on to the suggestion of a side-street running toward the back. At the beginning of the scene the blinds of the Round Room are down. When, later, they are raised, the white marble statue of a young woman can be seen, surrounded with palms and brightly lighted by rays of sunshine.*

*To the left of the Round Room is the Hyacinth Room; its window filled with pots of hyacinths, blue, white, and pink. Further left, at the back, is an imposing double front door with laurels in tubs on either side of it. The doors are wide open, showing a staircase of white marble with a banister of mahogany and brass. To the left of the front door is another ground-floor window, with a window-mirror.*[1] *On the balcony rail in the corner above the Round Room are a blue silk quilt and two white pillows. The windows to the left of this are hung with white sheets.*[2]

*In the foreground, in front of the house, is a green bench; to the right a street drinking-fountain, to the left an advertisement column.*

*It is a bright Sunday morning, and as the curtain rises the bells of several churches, some near, some far away, are ringing.*

*On the staircase the* LADY IN BLACK *stands motionless.*

*The* CARETAKER'S WIFE *sweeps the doorstep, then polishes the brass on the door and waters the laurels.*

*In a wheel-chair by the advertisement column sits the* OLD MAN, *reading a newspaper. His hair and beard are white and he wears spectacles.*

*The* MILKMAID *comes round the corner on the right, carrying milk bottles in a wire basket. She is wearing a summer dress with brown shoes, black stockings and a white cap. She takes off her cap and hangs it on the fountain, wipes the perspiration from her forehead, washes her hands and arranges her hair, using the water as a mirror.*

[1] Set at an angle inside the window, so as to show what is going on in the street.—Tr.
[2] Sign of mourning.—Tr.

*A steamship bell is heard, and now and then the silence is broken by the deep notes of an organ in a nearby church.*

*After a few moments, when all is silent and the* MILKMAID *has finished her toilet, the* STUDENT *enters from the left. He has had a sleepless night and is unshaven. He goes straight up to the fountain. There is a pause before he speaks.*

STUDENT May I have the cup? (*The* MILKMAID *clutches the cup to her*) Haven't you finished yet?

(*The* MILKMAID *looks at him with horror*)

OLD MAN (*To himself*) Who's he talking to? I don't see anybody. Is he crazy?

(*He goes on watching them in great astonishment*)

STUDENT (*To the* MILKMAID) What are you staring at? Do I look so terrible? Well, I've had no sleep, and of course you think I've been making a night of it . . . (*The* MILKMAID *stays just as she is*) You think I've been drinking, eh? Do I smell of liquor? (*The* MILKMAID *does not change*) I haven't shaved, I know. Give me a drink of water, girl. I've earned it. (*Pause*) Oh well, I suppose I'll have to tell you. I spent the whole night dressing wounds and looking after the injured. You see, I was there when that house collapsed last night. Now you know. (*The* MILKMAID *rinses the cup and gives him a drink*) Thanks. (*The* MILKMAID *stands motionless. Slowly*) Will you do me a great favor? (*Pause*) The thing is, my eyes, as you can see, are inflamed, but my hands have been touching wounds and corpses, so it would be dangerous to put them near my eyes. Will you take my handkerchief—it's quite clean—and dip it in the fresh water and bathe my eyes? Will you do this? Will you play the good Samaritan? (*The* MILKMAID *hesitates, but does as he bids*) Thank you, my dear. (*He takes out his purse. She makes a gesture of refusal*) Forgive my stupidity, but I'm only half-awake. . . .

(*The* MILKMAID *disappears*)

OLD MAN (*To the* STUDENT) Excuse me speaking to you, but I heard you say you were at the scene of the accident last night. I was just reading about it in the paper.

STUDENT Is it in the paper already?

OLD MAN The whole thing, including your portrait. But they regret that they have been unable to find out the name of the splendid young student. . . .

STUDENT Really? (*Glances at the paper*) Yes, that's me. Well I never!

OLD MAN Who was it you were talking to just now?

STUDENT Didn't you see? (*Pause*)

OLD MAN Would it be impertinent to inquire—what in fact your name is?

STUDENT What would be the point? I don't care for publicity. If you get any praise, there's always disapproval too. The art of running people down has been developed to such a pitch. . . . Besides, I don't want any reward.

OLD MAN You're well off, perhaps.

STUDENT No, indeed. On the contrary, I'm very poor.

OLD MAN Do you know, it seems to me I've heard your voice before. When I was young I had a friend who pronounced certain words just as you do. I've never met anyone else with quite that pronunciation. Only him—and you. Are you by any chance related to Mr. Arkenholtz, the merchant?

STUDENT He was my father.

OLD MAN Strange are the paths of fate. I saw you when you were an infant, under very painful circumstances.

STUDENT Yes, I understand I came into the world in the middle of a bankruptcy.

OLD MAN Just that.

STUDENT Perhaps I might ask your name.

OLD MAN I am Mr. Hummel.

STUDENT Are you the? . . . I remember that . . .

OLD MAN Have you often heard my name mentioned in your family?

STUDENT Yes.

OLD MAN And mentioned perhaps with a certain aversion? (*The* STUDENT *is silent*) Yes, I can imagine it. You were told, I suppose, that I was the man who ruined your father? All who ruin themselves through foolish speculations consider they were ruined by those they couldn't fool. (*Pause*) Now these are the facts. Your father robbed me of seventeen thousand crowns—the whole of my savings at that time.

STUDENT It's queer that the same story can be told in two such different ways.

OLD MAN You surely don't believe I'm telling you what isn't true?

STUDENT What am I to believe? My father didn't lie.

OLD MAN That is so true. A father never lies. But I too am a father, and so it follows . . .

STUDENT What are you driving at?

OLD MAN I saved your father from disaster, and he repaid me with all the frightful hatred that is born of an obligation to be grateful. He taught his family to speak ill of me.

STUDENT Perhaps you made him ungrateful by poisoning your help with unnecessary humiliation.

OLD MAN All help is humiliating, sir.

STUDENT What do you want from me?

OLD MAN I'm not asking for the money, but if you will render me a few small services, I shall consider myself well paid. You see that I am a cripple. Some say it is my own fault; others lay the blame on my parents. I prefer to blame life itself, with its pitfalls. For if you escape one snare, you fall headlong into another. In any case, I am unable to climb stairs or ring doorbells, and that is why I am asking you to help me.

STUDENT What can I do?

OLD MAN To begin with, push my chair so that I can read those playbills. I want to see what is on tonight.

STUDENT (*Pushing the chair*) Haven't you got an attendant?

OLD MAN Yes, but he has gone on an errand. He'll be back soon. Are you a medical student?

STUDENT No, I am studying languages, but I don't

know at all what I'm going to do.

OLD MAN Aha! Are you good at mathematics?

STUDENT Yes, fairly.

OLD MAN Good. Perhaps you would like a job.

STUDENT Yes, why not?

OLD MAN Splendid. (*He studies the playbills*) They are doing *The Valkyrie* for the matinée. That means the Colonel will be there with his daughter, and as he always sits at the end of the sixth row, I'll put you next to him. Go to that telephone kiosk please and order a ticket for seat eighty-two in the sixth row.

STUDENT Am I to go to the Opera in the middle of the day?

OLD MAN Yes. Do as I tell you and things will go well with you. I want to see you happy, rich, and honored. Your début last night as the brave rescuer will make you famous by tomorrow and then your name will be worth something.

STUDENT (*Going to the telephone kiosk*) What an odd adventure!

OLD MAN Are you a gambler?

STUDENT Yes, unfortunately.

OLD MAN We'll make it fortunately. Go on now, telephone. (*The* STUDENT *goes. The* OLD MAN *reads his paper. The* LADY IN BLACK *comes out on to the pavement and talks to the* CARETAKER'S WIFE. *The* OLD MAN *listens, but the audience hears nothing. The* STUDENT *returns*) Did you fix it up?

STUDENT It's done.

OLD MAN You see that house?

STUDENT Yes, I've been looking at it a lot. I passed it yesterday when the sun was shining on the window-panes, and I imagined all the beauty and elegance there must be inside. I said to my companion: "Think of living up there in the top flat, with a beautiful young wife, two pretty little children and an income of twenty thousand crowns a year."

OLD MAN So that's what you said. That's what you said. Well, well! I too am very fond of this house.

STUDENT Do you speculate in houses?

OLD MAN Mm—yes. But not in the way you mean.

STUDENT Do you know the people who live here?

OLD MAN Every one of them. At my age one knows everybody, and their parents and grandparents too, and one's always related to them in some way or other. I am just eighty, but no one knows me—not really. I take an interest in human destiny. (*The blinds of the Round Room are drawn up. The* COLONEL *is seen, wearing mufti. He looks at the thermometer outside one of the windows, then turns back into the room and stands in front of the marble statue*) Look, that's the Colonel, whom you will sit next to this afternoon.

STUDENT Is he—the Colonel? I don't understand any of this, but it's like a fairy story.

OLD MAN My whole life's like a book of fairy stories, sir. And although the stories are different, they are held together by one thread, and the main theme constantly recurs.

STUDENT Who is that marble statue of?

OLD MAN That, naturally, is his wife.

STUDENT Was she such a wonderful person?

OLD MAN Er . . . yes.

STUDENT Tell me.

OLD MAN We can't judge people, young man. If I were to tell you that she left him, that he beat her, that she returned to him and married him a second time, and that now she is sitting inside there like a mummy, worshipping her own statue—then you would think me crazy.

STUDENT I don't understand.

OLD MAN I didn't think you would. Well, then we have the window with the hyacinths. His daughter lives there. She has gone out for a ride, but she will be home soon.

STUDENT And who is the dark lady talking to the caretaker?

OLD MAN Well, that's a bit complicated, but it is connected with the dead man, up there where you see the white sheets.

STUDENT Why, who was he?

OLD MAN A human being like you or me, but the most conspicuous thing about him was his vanity. If you were a Sunday child, you would see him presently come out of that door to look at the Consulate flag flying at half-mast. He was, you understand, a Consul, and he reveled in coronets and lions and plumed hats and colored ribbons.

STUDENT Sunday child, you say? I'm told I was born on a Sunday.

OLD MAN No, were you really? I might have known it. I saw it from the color of your eyes. Then you can see what others can't. Have you noticed that?

STUDENT I don't know what others do see, but at times. . . . Oh, but one doesn't talk of such things!

OLD MAN I was almost sure of it. But you can talk to me, because I understand such things.

STUDENT Yesterday, for instance . . . I was drawn to that obscure little street where later on the house collapsed. I went there and stopped in front of that building which I had never seen before. Then I noticed a crack in the wall. . . . I heard the floor boards snapping. . . . I dashed over and picked up a child that was passing under the wall. . . . The next moment the house collapsed. I was saved, but in my arms, which I thought held the child, was nothing at all.

OLD MAN Yes, yes, just as I thought. Tell me something. Why were you gesticulating that way just now by the fountain? And why were you talking to yourself?

STUDENT Didn't you see the milkmaid I was talking to?

OLD MAN (*In horror*) Milkmaid?

STUDENT Surely. The girl who handed me the cup.

OLD MAN Really? So that's what was going on. Ah well, I haven't second sight, but there are things I can do. (THE FIANCÉE *is now seen to sit down by the window which has the window-mirror*) Look at that old woman in the window. Do you see her? Well, she was my fiancée once, sixty years ago. I was twenty. Don't be alarmed. She doesn't recognize me. We see one another every day, and it makes no impression on me, although once we vowed to love one another eternally. Eternally!

STUDENT How foolish you were in those days! We never talk to our girls like that.

OLD MAN Forgive us, young man. We didn't know any better. But can you see that that old woman was once young and beautiful?

STUDENT It doesn't show. And yet there's some charm in her looks. I can't see her eyes.

(*The* CARETAKER'S WIFE *comes out with a basket of chopped fir branches*)[3]

OLD MAN Ah, the caretaker's wife! That dark lady is her daughter by the dead man. That's why her husband was given the job of caretaker. But the dark lady has a suitor, who is an aristocrat with great expectations. He is in the process of getting a divorce —from his present wife, you understand. She's presenting him with a stone mansion in order to be rid of him. This aristocratic suitor is the son-in-law of the dead man, and you can see his bedclothes being aired on the balcony upstairs. It is complicated, I must say.

STUDENT It's fearfully complicated.

OLD MAN Yes, that it is, internally and externally, although it looks quite simple.

STUDENT But then who was the dead man?

OLD MAN You asked me that just now, and I answered. If you were to look round the corner, where the tradesmen's entrance is, you would see a lot of poor people whom he used to help—when it suited him.

STUDENT He was a kind man then.

OLD MAN Yes—sometimes.

STUDENT Not always?

OLD MAN No-o. That's the way of people. Now, sir, will you push my chair a little, so that it gets into the sun. I'm horribly cold. When you're never able to move about, the blood congeals. I'm going to die soon, I know that, but I have a few things to do first. Take my hand and feel how cold I am.

STUDENT (*Taking it*) Yes, inconceivably. (*He shrinks back, trying in vain to free his hand*)

OLD MAN Don't leave me. I am tired now and lonely, but I haven't always been like this, you know. I have an enormously long life behind me, enormously long. I have made people unhappy and people have made me unhappy—the one cancels out the other—but before I die I want to see you happy. Our fates are entwined through your father—and other things.

STUDENT Let go of my hand. You are taking all my strength. You are freezing me. What do you want with me?

OLD MAN (*Letting go*) Be patient and you shall see and understand. Here comes the young lady.

(*They watch the* GIRL *approaching, though the audience cannot yet see her*)

STUDENT The Colonel's daughter?

OLD MAN His daughter—yes. Look at her. Have you ever seen such a masterpiece?

[3] It was customary in Sweden to strew the ground with these for a funeral.—Tr.

STUDENT She is like the marble statue in there.

OLD MAN That's her mother, you know.

STUDENT You are right. Never have I seen such a woman of woman born. Happy the man who may lead her to the altar and his home.

OLD MAN You can see it. Not everyone recognizes her beauty. So, then, it is written.

(*The* GIRL *enters, wearing an English riding habit. Without noticing anyone she walks slowly to the door, where she stops to say a few words to the* CARETAKER'S WIFE. *Then she goes into the house. The* STUDENT *covers his eyes with his hand*)

OLD MAN Are you weeping?

STUDENT In the face of what's hopeless there can be nothing but despair.

OLD MAN I can open doors and hearts, if only I find an arm to do my will. Serve me and you shall have power.

STUDENT Is it a bargain? Am I to sell my soul?

OLD MAN Sell nothing. Listen. All my life I have *taken.* Now I have a craving to give—give. But no one will accept. I am rich, very rich, but I have no heirs, except for a good-for-nothing who torments the life out of me. Become my son. Inherit me while I am still alive. Enjoy life so that I can watch, at least from a distance.

STUDENT What am I to do?

OLD MAN First go to *The Valkyrie.*

STUDENT That's settled. What else?

OLD MAN This evening you must be in there—in the Round Room.

STUDENT How am I to get there?

OLD MAN By way of *The Valkyrie.*

STUDENT Why have you chosen me as your medium? Did you know me before?

OLD MAN Yes, of course. I have had my eye on you for a long time. But now look up there at the balcony. The maid is hoisting the flag to half-mast for the Consul. And now she is turning the bedclothes. Do you see that blue quilt? It was made for two to sleep under, but now it covers only one. (*The* GIRL, *having changed her dress, appears in the window and waters the hyacinths*) There is my little girl. Look at her, look! She is talking to the flowers. Is she not like that blue hyacinth herself? She gives them drink —nothing but pure water, and they transform the water into color and fragrance. Now here comes the Colonel with the newspaper. He is showing her the bit about the house that collapsed. Now he's pointing to your portrait. She's not indifferent. She's reading of your brave deed. . . .

I believe it's clouding over. If it turns to rain I shall be in a pretty fix, unless Johansson comes back soon. (*It grows cloudy and dark. The* FIANCÉE *at the window-mirror closes her window*) Now my fiancée is closing the window. Seventy-nine years old. The window-mirror is the only mirror she uses, because in it she sees not herself, but the world outside—in two directions. But the world can see her; she hasn't thought of that. Anyhow she's a handsome old woman.

(*Now the* DEAD MAN, *wrapped in a winding sheet, comes out of the door*)

STUDENT Good God, what do I see?

OLD MAN What do you see?

STUDENT Don't *you* see? There, in the doorway, the dead man?

OLD MAN I see nothing, but I expected this. Tell me.

STUDENT He is coming out into the street. (*Pause*) Now he is turning his head and looking up at the flag.

OLD MAN What did I tell you? You may be sure he'll count the wreaths and read the visiting cards. Woe to him who's missing.

STUDENT Now he's turning the corner.

OLD MAN He's gone to count the poor at the back door. The poor are in the nature of a decoration, you see. "Followed by the blessings of many." Well, he's not going to have my blessing. Between ourselves he was a great scoundrel.

STUDENT But charitable.

OLD MAN A charitable scoundrel, always thinking of his grand funeral. When he knew his end was near, he cheated the State out of fifty thousand crowns. Now his daughter has relations with another woman's husband and is wondering about the will. Yes, the scoundrel can hear every word we're saying, and he's welcome to it. Ah, here comes Johansson! (JOHANSSON *enters*) Report! (JOHANSSON *speaks, but the audience does not hear*) Not at home, eh? You are an ass. And the telegram? Nothing? Go on. . . . At six this evening? That's good. Special edition, you say? With his name in full. Arkenholtz, a student, born . . . parents . . . That's splendid. . . . I think it's beginning to rain. . . . What did he say about it? So—so. He wouldn't? Well, he must. Here comes the aristocrat. Push me round the corner, Johansson, so I can hear what the poor are saying. And, Arkenholtz, you wait for me here. Understand? (*To* JOHANSSON) Hurry up now, hurry up.

(JOHANSSON *wheels the chair round the corner. The* STUDENT *remains watching the* GIRL, *who is now loosening the earth round the hyacinths. The* ARISTOCRAT, *wearing mourning, comes in and speaks to the* DARK LADY, *who has been walking to and fro on the pavement*)

ARISTOCRAT But what can we do about it? We shall have to wait.

LADY I can't wait.

ARISTOCRAT You can't? Well then, go into the country.

LADY I don't want to do that.

ARISTOCRAT Come over here or they will hear what we are saying.

(*They move toward the advertisement column and continue their conversation inaudibly.* JOHANSSON *returns*)

JOHANSSON (*To the* STUDENT) My master asks you not to forget that other thing, sir.

STUDENT (*Hesitating*) Look here . . . first of all tell me . . . who is your master?

JOHANSSON Well, he's so many things, and he has been everything.

STUDENT Is he a wise man?

JOHANSSON Depends what that is. He says all his life he's been looking for a Sunday child, but that may not be true.

STUDENT What does he want? He's grasping, isn't he?

JOHANSSON It's power he wants. The whole day long he rides round in his chariot like the god Thor himself. He looks at houses, pulls them down, opens up new streets, builds squares. . . . But he breaks into houses too, sneaks through windows, plays havoc with human destinies, kills his enemies—and never forgives. Can you imagine it, sir? This miserable cripple was once a Don Juan—although he always lost his women.

STUDENT How do you account for that?

JOHANSSON You see he's so cunning he makes the women leave him when he's tired of them. But what he's most like now is a horse-thief in the human market. He steals human beings in all sorts of different ways. He literally stole me out of the hands of the law. Well, as a matter of fact I'd made a slip —hm, yes—and only he knew about it. Instead of getting me put in jail, he turned me into a slave. I slave—for my food alone, and that's none of the best.

STUDENT Then what is it he means to do in this house?

JOHANSSON I'm not going to talk about that. It's too complicated.

STUDENT I think I'd better get away from it all.

(*The* GIRL *drops a bracelet out the window*)

JOHANSSON Look! The young lady has dropped her bracelet out of the window. (*The* STUDENT *goes slowly over, picks up the bracelet and returns it to the* GIRL, *who thanks him stiffly. The* STUDENT *goes back to* JOHANSSON) So you mean to get away. That's not so easy as you think, once he's got you in his net. And he's afraid of nothing between heaven and earth—yes, of one thing he is—of one person rather. . . .

STUDENT Don't tell me. I think perhaps I know.

JOHANSSON How can you know?

STUDENT I'm guessing. Is it a little milkmaid he's afraid of?

JOHANSSON He turns his head the other way whenever he meets a milk cart. Besides, he talks in his sleep. It seems he was once in Hamburg. . . .

STUDENT Can one trust this man?

JOHANSSON You can trust him—to do anything.

STUDENT What's he doing now round the corner?

JOHANSSON Listening to the poor. Sowing a little word, loosening one stone at a time, till the house falls down—metaphorically speaking. You see I'm an educated man. I was once a book-seller. . . . Do you still mean to go away?

STUDENT I don't like to be ungrateful. He saved my father once, and now he only asks a small service in return.

JOHANSSON What is that?

STUDENT I am to go to *The Valkyrie*.

JOHANSSON That's beyond me. But he's always up to new tricks. Look at him now, talking to that policeman. He is always thick with the police. He uses them, gets them involved in his interests, holds them with false promises and expectations, while all the time he's pumping them. You'll see that before the day is over he'll be received in the Round Room.

STUDENT What does he want there? What connection has he with the Colonel?

JOHANSSON I think I can guess, but I'm not sure. You'll see for yourself once you're in there.

STUDENT I shall never be in there.

JOHANSSON That depends on yourself. Go to *The Valkyrie.*

STUDENT Is that the way?

JOHANSSON Yes, if he said so. Look. Look at him in his war chariot, drawn in triumph by the beggars, who get nothing for their pains but the hint of a treat at his funeral.

(*The* OLD MAN *appears standing up in his wheelchair, drawn by one of the beggars and followed by the rest*)

OLD MAN Hail the noble youth who, at the risk of his own life, saved so many others in yesterday's accident. Three cheers for Arkenholtz! (*The* BEGGARS *bare their heads but do not cheer. The* GIRL *at the window waves her handkerchief. The* COLONEL *gazes from the window of the Round Room. The* OLD WOMAN *rises at her window. The* MAID *on the balcony hoists the flag to the top*) Clap your hands, citizens. True, it is Sunday, but the ass in the pit and the ear in the corn field will absolve us. And although I am not a Sunday child, I have the gift of prophecy and also that of healing. Once I brought a drowned person back to life. That was in Hamburg on a Sunday morning just like this. . . .

(*The* MILKMAID *enters, seen only by the* STUDENT *and the* OLD MAN. *She raises her arms like one who is drowning and gazes fixedly at the* OLD MAN. *He sits down, then crumples up, stricken with horror*) Johansson! Take me away! Quick! . . . Arkenholtz, don't forget *The Valkyrie.*

STUDENT What is all this?

JOHANSSON We shall see. We shall see.

## Scene Two

*Inside the Round Room. At the back is a white porcelain stove. On either side of it are a mirror, a pendulum clock, and candelabra. On the right of the stove is the entrance to the hall beyond which is a glimpse of a room furnished in green and mahogany. On the left of the stove is the door to a cupboard, papered like the wall. The statue, shaded by palms has a curtain which can be drawn to conceal it.*

*A door on the left leads into the Hyacinth Room, where the* GIRL *sits reading.*

*The back of the* COLONEL *can be seen, as he sits in the Green Room, writing.*

BENGTSSON, *the Colonel's servant, comes in from the hall. He is wearing livery, and is followed by* JOHANSSON, *dressed as a waiter.*

BENGTSSON Now you'll have to serve the tea, Johansson, while I take the coats. Have you ever done it before?

JOHANSSON It's true I push a war chariot in the daytime, as you know, but in the evenings I go as a waiter to receptions and so forth. It's always been my dream to get into this house. They're queer people here, aren't they?

BENGTSSON Ye-es. A bit out of the ordinary anyhow.

JOHANSSON Is it to be a musical party or what?

BENGTSSON The usual ghost supper, as we call it. They drink tea and don't say a word—or else the Colonel does all the talking. And they crunch their biscuits, all at the same time. It sounds like rats in an attic.

JOHANSSON Why do you call it the ghost supper?

BENGTSSON They look like ghosts. And they've kept this up for twenty years, always the same people saying the same things or saying nothing at all for fear of being found out.

JOHANSSON Isn't there a mistress of the house?

BENGTSSON Oh yes, but she's crazy. She sits in a cupboard because her eyes can't bear the light. (*He points to the papered door*) She sits in there.

JOHANSSON In there?

BENGTSSON Well, I told you they were a bit out of the ordinary.

JOHANSSON But then—what does she look like?

BENGTSSON Like a mummy. Do you want to have a look at her? (*He opens the door*) There she is.

(*The figure of the* COLONEL'S WIFE *is seen, white and shriveled into a* MUMMY)

JOHANSSON Oh my God!

MUMMY (*Babbling*) Why do you open the door? Haven't I told you to keep it closed?

BENGTSSON (*In a wheedling tone*) Ta, ta, ta, ta. Be a good girl now, then you'll get something nice. Pretty Polly.

MUMMY (*Parrot-like*) Pretty Polly. Are you there, Jacob? Currrrr!

BENGTSSON She thinks she's a parrot, and maybe she's right. (*To the* MUMMY) Whistle for us, Polly.

(*The* MUMMY *whistles*)

JOHANSSON Well, I've seen a few things in my day, but this beats everything.

BENGTSSON You see, when a house gets old, it grows moldy, and when people stay a long time together and torment each other they go mad. The mistress of the house—shut up, Polly!—that mummy there, has been living here for forty years—same husband, same furniture, same relatives, same friends. (*He closes the papered door*) And the goings-on in this house—well, they're beyond me. Look at that statue—that's her when she was young.

JOHANSSON Good Lord! Is that the mummy?

BENGTSSON Yes. It's enough to make you weep. And somehow, carried away by her own imagination or something, she's got to be a bit like a parrot—the way she talks and the way she can't stand cripples or sick people. She can't stand the sight of her own daughter, because she's sick.

JOHANSSON Is the young lady sick?

BENGTSSON Didn't you know that?

JOHANSSON No. And the Colonel, who is he?

BENGTSSON You'll see.

JOHANSSON (*Looking at the statue*) It's horrible to think that . . . How old is she now?

BENGTSSON Nobody knows. But it's said that when she was thirty-five she looked nineteen, and that's what she made the Colonel believe she was—here in this very house. Do you know what that black Japanese screen by the couch is for? They call it the death-screen, and when someone's going to die, they put it round—same as in a hospital.

JOHANSSON What a horrible house! And the student was longing to get in, as if it were paradise.

BENGTSSON What student? Oh, I know. The one who's coming here this evening. The Colonel and the young lady happened to meet him at the Opera, and both of them took a fancy to him. Hm. Now it's my turn to ask questions. Who is your master—the man in the wheelchair?

JOHANSSON Well, he er . . . Is he coming here too?

BENGTSSON He hasn't been invited.

JOHANSSON He'll come uninvited—if need be.

(*The* OLD MAN *appears in the hall on crutches, wearing a frock-coat and top-hat. He steals forward and listens*)

BENGTSSON He's a regular old devil, isn't he?

JOHANSSON Up to the ears.

BENGTSSON He looks like Old Nick himself.

JOHANSSON And he must be a wizard too, for he goes through locked doors.

(*The* OLD MAN *comes forward and takes hold of* JOHANSSON *by the ear*)

OLD MAN Rascal—take care! (*To* BENGTSSON) Tell the Colonel I am here.

BENGTSSON But we are expecting guests.

OLD MAN I know. But my visit is as good as expected, if not exactly looked forward to.

BENGTSSON I see. What name shall I say? Mr. Hummel?

OLD MAN Exactly. Yes. (BENGTSSON *crosses the hall to the Green Room, the door of which he closes behind him. To* JOHANSSON) Get out! (JOHANSSON *hesitates*) Get out! (JOHANSSON *disappears into the hall. The* OLD MAN *inspects the room and stops in front of the statue in much astonishment*) Amelia! It is she—she!

MUMMY (*From the cupboard*) Prrr-etty Polly. (*The* OLD MAN *starts*)

OLD MAN What was that? Is there a parrot in the room? I don't see it.

MUMMY Are you there, Jacob?

OLD MAN The house is haunted.

MUMMY Jacob!

OLD MAN I'm scared. So these are the kind of secrets they guard in this house. (*With his back turned to the cupboard he stands looking at a portrait*) There he is—he!

(*The* MUMMY *comes out behind the* OLD MAN *and gives a pull at his wig*)

MUMMY Currrrr! Is it . . . ? Currrrr!

OLD MAN (*Jumping out of his skin*) God in heaven! Who is it?

MUMMY (*In a natural voice*) Is it Jacob?

OLD MAN Yes, my name is Jacob.

MUMMY (*With emotion*) And my name is Amelia.

OLD MAN No, no, no . . . Oh my God!

MUMMY That's how I look. Yes. (*Pointing to the statue*) And that's how I *did* look. Life opens one's eyes, does it not? I live mostly in the cupboard to avoid seeing and being seen. . . . But, Jacob, what do you want here?

OLD MAN My child. Our child.

MUMMY There she is.

OLD MAN Where?

MUMMY There—in the Hyacinth Room.

OLD MAN (*Looking at the* GIRL) Yes, that is she. (*Pause*) And what about her father—the Colonel, I mean—your husband?

MUMMY Once, when I was angry with him, I told him everything.

OLD MAN Well . . . ?

MUMMY He didn't believe me. He just said: "That's what all wives say when they want to murder their husbands." It was a terrible crime none the less. It has falsified his whole life—his family tree too. Sometimes I take a look in the Peerage, and then I say to myself: Here she is, going about with a false birth certificate like some servant girl, and for such things people are sent to the reformatory.

OLD MAN Many do it. I seem to remember your own date of birth was given incorrectly.

MUMMY My mother made me do that. I was not to blame. And in our crime, *you* played the biggest part.

OLD MAN No. Your husband caused that crime, when he took my fiancée from me. I was born one who cannot forgive until he has punished. That was to me an imperative duty—and is so still.

MUMMY What are you expecting to find in this house? What do you want? How did you get in? Is it to do with my daughter? If you touch her, you shall die.

OLD MAN I mean well by her.

MUMMY Then you must spare her father.

OLD MAN No.

MUMMY Then you shall die. In this room, behind that screen.

OLD MAN That may be. But I can't let go once I've got my teeth into a thing.

MUMMY You want to marry her to that student. Why? He is nothing and has nothing.

OLD MAN He will be rich, through me.

MUMMY Have you been invited here tonight?

OLD MAN No, but I propose to get myself an invitation to this ghost supper.

MUMMY Do you know who is coming?

OLD MAN Not exactly.

MUMMY The Baron. The man who lives up above—whose father-in-law was buried this afternoon.

OLD MAN The man who is getting a divorce in order to marry the daughter of the Caretaker's wife . . . The man who used to be—your lover.

MUMMY Another guest will be your former fiancée, who was seduced by my husband.

OLD MAN A select gathering.

MUMMY Oh God, if only we might die, might die!

OLD MAN Then why have you stayed together?

MUMMY Crime and secrets and guilt bind us together. We have broken our bonds and gone our own ways, times without number, but we are always drawn together again.

OLD MAN I think the Colonel is coming.

MUMMY Then I will go in to Adèle. (*Pause*) Jacob, mind what you do. Spare him. (*Pause. She goes into the Hyacinth Room and disappears*)

(*The* COLONEL *enters, cold and reserved, with a letter in his hand*)

COLONEL Be seated, please. (*Slowly the* OLD MAN *sits down. Pause. The* COLONEL *stares at him*) You wrote this letter, sir?

OLD MAN I did.

COLONEL Your name is Hummel?

OLD MAN It is. (*Pause*)

COLONEL As I understand, you have bought in all my unpaid promissory notes. I can only conclude that I am in your hands. What do you want?

OLD MAN I want payment, in one way or another.

COLONEL In what way?

OLD MAN A very simple one. Let us not mention the money. Just bear with me in your house as a guest.

COLONEL If so little will satisfy you . . .

OLD MAN Thank you.

COLONEL What else?

OLD MAN Dismiss Bengtsson.

COLONEL Why should I do that? My devoted servant, who has been with me a lifetime, who has the national medal for long and faithful service—why should I do that?

OLD MAN That's how you see him—full of excellent qualities. He is not the man he appears to be.

COLONEL Who is?

OLD MAN (*Taken aback*) True. But Bengtsson must go.

COLONEL Are you going to run my house?

OLD MAN Yes. Since everything here belongs to me—furniture, curtains, dinner service, linen . . . and more too.

COLONEL How do you mean—more?

OLD MAN Everything. I own everything here. It is mine.

COLONEL Very well, it is yours. But my family escutcheon and my good name remain my own.

OLD MAN No, not even those. (*Pause*) You are not a nobleman.

COLONEL How dare you!

OLD MAN (*Producing a document*) If you read this extract from *The Armorial Gazette*, you will see that the family whose name you are using has been extinct for a hundred years.

COLONEL I have heard rumors to this effect, but I inherited the name from my father. (*Reads*) It is true. You are right. I am not a nobleman. Then I must take off my signet ring. It is true, it belongs to you. (*Gives it to him*) There you are.

OLD MAN (*Pocketing the ring*) Now we will continue. You are not a Colonel either.

COLONEL I am not . . . ?

OLD MAN No. You once held the temporary rank of Colonel in the American Volunteer Force, but after the war in Cuba and the reorganization of the Army, all such titles were abolished.

COLONEL Is this true?

OLD MAN (*Indicating his pocket*) Do you want to read it?

COLONEL No, that's not necessary. Who are you, and what right have you to sit there stripping me in this fashion?

OLD MAN You will see. But as far as stripping you goes . . . do you know who you are?

COLONEL How dare you?

OLD MAN Take off that wig and have a look at yourself in the mirror. But take your teeth out at the same time and shave off your moustache. Let Bengtsson unlace your metal stays and perhaps a certain X.Y.Z., a lackey, will recognize himself. The fellow who was a cupboard lover in a certain kitchen . . . (*The* COLONEL *reaches for the bell on the table, but* HUMMEL *checks him*) Don't touch that bell, and don't call Bengtsson. If you do, I'll have him arrested. (*Pause*) And now the guests are beginning to arrive. Keep your composure and we will continue to play our old parts for a while.

COLONEL Who are you? I recognize your voice and eyes.

OLD MAN Don't try to find out. Keep silent and obey.

(*The* STUDENT *enters and bows to the* COLONEL.)

STUDENT How do you do, sir.

COLONEL Welcome to my house, young man. Your splendid behavior at that great disaster has brought your name to everybody's lips, and I count it an honor to receive you in my home.

STUDENT My humble descent, sir . . . Your illustrious name and noble birth . . .

COLONEL May I introduce Mr. Arkenholtz—Mr. Hummel. If you will join the ladies in here, Mr. Arkenholtz—I must conclude my conversation with Mr. Hummel. (*He shows the* STUDENT *into the Hyacinth Room, where he remains visible, talking shyly to the* GIRL) A splendid young man, musical, sings, writes poetry. If he only had blue blood in him, if he were of the same station, I don't think I should object . . .

OLD MAN To what?

COLONEL To my daughter . . .

OLD MAN *Your* daughter! But apropos of that, why does she spend all her time in there?

COLONEL She insists on being in the Hyacinth Room except when she is out-of-doors. It's a peculiarity of hers. Ah, here comes Miss Beatrice von Holsteinkrona—a charming woman, a pillar of the Church, with just enough money of her own to suit her birth and position.

OLD MAN (*To himself*) My fiancée.

(*The* FIANCÉE *enters, looking a little crazy*)

COLONEL Miss Holsteinkrona—Mr. Hummel. (*The* FIANCÉE *curtseys and takes a seat. The* ARISTOCRAT *enters and seats himself. He wears mourning and looks mysterious*) Baron Skanskorg . . .

OLD MAN (*Aside, without rising*) That's the jewel-thief, I think. (*To the* COLONEL) If you bring in the Mummy, the party will be complete.

COLONEL (*At the door of the Hyacinth Room*) Polly!

MUMMY (*Entering*) Currrrr . . . !

COLONEL Are the young people to come in too?

OLD MAN No, not the young people. They shall be spared.

(*They all sit silent in a circle*)

COLONEL Shall we have the tea brought in?

OLD MAN What's the use? No one wants tea. Why should we pretend about it?

COLONEL Then shall we talk?

OLD MAN Talk of the weather, which we know? Inquire about each other's health, which we know just as well. I prefer silence—then one can hear thoughts and see the past. Silence cannot hide anything—but words can. I read the other day that differences of language originated among savages for the purpose of keeping one tribe's secrets hidden from another. Every language therefore is a code, and he who finds the key can understand every language in the world. But this does not prevent secrets from being exposed without a key, specially when there is a question of paternity to be proved. Proof in a Court of Law is another matter. Two false witnesses suffice to prove anything about which they are agreed, but one does not take witnesses along on the kind of explorations I have in mind. Nature herself has instilled in human beings a sense of modesty which tries to hide what should be hidden, but we slip into situations unintentionally, and by chance sometimes the deepest secret is divulged—the mask torn from the impostor, the villain exposed. . . . (*Pause. All look at each other in silence*) What a silence there is now! (*Long silence*) Here, for instance, in this honorable house, in this elegant home, where beauty, wealth and culture are united. . . . (*Long silence*) All of us now sitting here know who we are—do we not? There's no need for me to tell you. And you know me, although you pretend ignorance. (*He indicates the Hyacinth Room*) In there is my daughter. *Mine*—you know that too. She had lost the desire to live, without knowing why. The fact is she was withering away in this air charged with crime and deceit and falseness of every kind. That is why I looked for a friend for her in whose company she might enjoy the light and warmth of noble deeds. (*Long silence*) That was my mission in this house: to pull up the weeds, to expose the crimes, to settle all accounts, so that those young people might start afresh in this home, which is my gift to them. (*Long silence*) Now I am going to grant safe-conduct, to each of you in his and her proper time and turn. Whoever stays I shall have arrested. (*Long silence*) Do you hear the clock ticking like a death-watch beetle in the wall? Do you hear what it says? "It's time, it's time, it's time." When it strikes, in a few moments, your time will be up. Then you can go, but not before. It's raising its arm against you before it strikes. Listen! It is warning you. "The clock can strike." And I can strike too. (*He strikes the table with one of his crutches*) Do you hear?

(*Silence. The* MUMMY *goes up to the clock and stops it, then speaks in a normal and serious voice*)

MUMMY But I can stop time in its course. I can wipe out the past and undo what is done. But not with bribes, not with threats—only through suffering and repentance. (*She goes up to the* OLD MAN) We are miserable human beings, that we know. We have erred and we have sinned, we like all the rest. We are not what we seem, because at bottom we are better than ourselves, since we detest our sins. But when you, Jacob Hummel, with your false name, choose to sit in judgment over us, you prove yourself worse than us miserable sinners. For you are not the one you appear to be. You are a thief of human souls. You stole me once with false promises. You murdered the Consul who was buried today; you strangled him with debts. You have stolen the student, binding him by the pretence of a claim on his father, who never owed you a farthing. (*Having tried to rise and speak, the* OLD MAN *sinks back in his chair and crumples up more and more as she goes on*) But there is one dark spot in your life which I am not quite sure about, although I have my suspicions. I think Bengtsson knows. (*She rings the bell on the table*)

OLD MAN No, not Bengtsson, not him.

MUMMY So he does know. (*She rings again. The* MILKMAID *appears in the hallway door, unseen by all but the* OLD MAN, *who shrinks back in horror. The* MILKMAID *vanishes as* BENGTSSON *enters*) Do you know this man, Bengtsson?

BENGTSSON Yes, I know him and he knows me. Life, as you are aware, has its ups and downs. I have been in his service; another time he was in mine. For two whole years he was a sponger in my kitchen. As he had to be away by three, the dinner was got ready at two, and the family had to eat the warmed-up leavings of that brute. He drank the soup stock, which the cook then filled up with water. He sat out there like a vampire, sucking the marrow out of the house, so that we became like skeletons. And he nearly got us put in prison when we called the cook a thief. Later I met this man in Hamburg under another name. He was a usurer then, a blood-sucker. But while he was there he was charged with having lured a young girl out on to the ice so as to drown her, because she had seen him commit a crime he was afraid would be discovered. . . .

(*The* MUMMY *passes her hand over the* OLD MAN'S *face*)

MUMMY *This* is you. Now give up the notes and the will. (JOHANSSON *appears in the hallway door and watches the scene with great interest, knowing he is now to be freed from slavery. The* OLD MAN *produces a bundle of papers and throws it on the table. The* MUMMY *goes over and strokes his back*) Parrot. Are you there, Jacob?

OLD MAN (*Like a parrot*) Jacob is here. Pretty Polly. Currrrr!

MUMMY May the clock strike?

OLD MAN (*With a clucking sound*) The clock may strike. (*Imitating a cuckoo clock*) Cuckoo, cuckoo, cuckoo. . . .

(*The* MUMMY *opens the cupboard door*)

MUMMY Now the clock has struck. Rise, and enter the cupboard where I have spent twenty years repenting our crime. A rope is hanging there, which you can take as the one with which you strangled the Consul, and with which you meant to strangle your benefactor. . . . Go! (*The* OLD MAN *goes in to the cupboard. The* MUMMY *closes the door*) Bengtsson! Put up the screen—the death-screen. (BENGTSSON *places the screen in front of the door*) It is finished. God have mercy on his soul.

ALL Amen. (*Long silence*)

(*The* GIRL *and the* STUDENT *appear in the Hyacinth Room. She has a harp, on which she plays a prelude, and then accompanies the* STUDENT'S *recitation*)

STUDENT

I saw the sun. To me it seemed
that I beheld the Hidden.
Men must reap what they have sown;
blest is he whose deeds are good.
Deeds which you have wrought in fury,
cannot in evil find redress.
Comfort him you have distressed
with loving-kindness—this will heal.
No fear has he who does no ill.
Sweet is innocence.

# Scene Three

*Inside the Hyacinth Room. The general effect of the room is exotic and oriental. There are hyacinths everywhere, of every color, some in pots, some with the bulbs in glass vases and the roots going down into the water.*

*On top of the tiled stove is a large seated Buddha, in whose lap rests a bulb from which rises the stem of a shallot (Allium ascalonicum), bearing its globular cluster of white, starlike flowers.*

*On the right is an open door, leading into the Round Room, where the* COLONEL *and the* MUMMY *are seated, inactive and silent. A part of the death-screen is also visible.*

*On the left is a door to the pantry and kitchen.*

*The* STUDENT *and the* GIRL (Adèle) *are beside the table; he standing, she seated with her harp.*

GIRL Now sing to my flowers.

STUDENT Is this the flower of your soul?

GIRL The one and only. Do you too love the hyacinth?

STUDENT I love it above all other flowers—its virginal shape rising straight and slender out of the bulb, resting on the water and sending its pure white roots down into the colorless fluid. I love its colors: the snow-white, pure as innocence, the yellow honey-sweet, the youthful pink, the ripe red, but best of all the blue—the dewy blue, deep-eyed and full of faith. I love them all, more than gold or pearls. I have loved them ever since I was a child, have worshipped them because they have all the fine qualities I lack. . . . And yet . . .

GIRL Go on.

STUDENT My love is not returned, for these beautiful blossoms hate me.

GIRL How do you mean?

STUDENT Their fragrance, strong and pure as the early winds of spring which have passed over melting snows, confuses my senses, deafens me, blinds me, thrusts me out of the room, bombards me with poisoned arrows that wound my heart and set my head on fire. Do you know the legend of that flower?

GIRL Tell it to me.

STUDENT First its meaning. The bulb is the earth, resting on the water or buried in the soil. Then the stalk rises, straight as the axis of the world, and at the top are the six-pointed star-flowers.

GIRL Above the earth—the stars. Oh, that is wonderful! Where did you learn this? How did you find it out?

STUDENT Let me think . . . In your eyes. And so, you see, it is an image of the Cosmos. This is why Buddha sits holding the earth-bulb, his eyes brooding as he watches it grow, outward and upward, transforming itself into a heaven. This poor earth will become a heaven. It is for this that Buddha waits.

GIRL I see it now. Is not the snowflake six-pointed too like the hyacinth flower?

STUDENT You are right. The snowflakes must be falling stars.

GIRL And the snowdrop is a snow-star, grown out of snow.

STUDENT But the largest and most beautiful of all the stars in the firmament, the golden-red Sirius, is the narcissus with its gold and red chalice and its six white rays.

GIRL Have you seen the shallot in bloom?

STUDENT Indeed I have. It bears its blossoms within a

ball, a globe like the celestial one, strewn with white stars.

GIRL Oh how glorious! Whose thought was that?

STUDENT Yours.

GIRL Yours.

STUDENT Ours. We have given birth to it together. We are wedded.

GIRL Not yet.

STUDENT What's still to do?

GIRL Waiting, ordeals, patience.

STUDENT Very well. Put me to the test. (*Pause*) Tell me. Why do your parents sit in there so silently, not saying a single word?

GIRL Because they have nothing to say to each other, and because neither believes what the other says. This is how my father puts it: What's the point of talking, when neither of us can fool the other?

STUDENT What a horrible thing to hear!

GIRL Here comes the Cook. Look at her, how big and fat she is. (*They watch the* COOK, *although the audience cannot yet see her*)

STUDENT What does she want?

GIRL To ask me about the dinner. I have to do the housekeeping as my mother's ill.

STUDENT What have we to do with the kitchen?

GIRL We must eat. Look at the Cook. I can't bear the sight of her.

STUDENT Who is that ogress?

GIRL She belongs to the Hummel family of vampires. She is eating us.

STUDENT Why don't you dismiss her?

GIRL She won't go. We have no control over her. We've got her for our sins. Can't you see that we are pining and wasting away?

STUDENT Don't you get enough to eat?

GIRL Yes, we get many dishes, but all the strength has gone. She boils the nourishment out of the meat and gives us the fibre and water, while she drinks the stock herself. And when there's a roast, she first boils out the marrow, eats the gravy and drinks the juices herself. Everything she touches loses its savor. It's as if she sucked with her eyes. We get the grounds when she has drunk the coffee. She drinks the wine and fills the bottles up with water.

STUDENT Send her packing.

GIRL We can't.

STUDENT Why not?

GIRL We don't know. She won't go. No one has any control over her. She has taken all our strength from us.

STUDENT May I get rid of her?

GIRL No. It must be as it is. Here she is. She will ask me what is to be for dinner. I shall tell her. She will make objections and get her own way.

STUDENT Let her do the ordering herself then.

GIRL She won't do that.

STUDENT What an extraordinary house! It is bewitched.

GIRL Yes. But now she is turning back, because she has seen you.

THE COOK (*In the doorway*) No, that wasn't the reason. (*She grins, showing all her teeth*)

STUDENT Get out!

COOK When it suits me. (*Pause*) It does suit me now. (*She disappears*)

GIRL Don't lose your temper. Practice patience. She is one of the ordeals we have to go through in this house. You see, we have a housemaid too, whom we have to clean up after.

STUDENT I am done for. *Cor in æthere.*[1] Music!

GIRL Wait.

STUDENT Music!

GIRL Patience. This room is called the room of ordeals. It looks beautiful, but it is full of defects.

STUDENT Really? Well, such things must be seen to. It is very beautiful, but a little cold. Why don't you have a fire?

GIRL Because it smokes.

STUDENT Can't you have the chimney swept?

GIRL It doesn't help. You see that writing-desk there?

STUDENT An unusually fine piece.

GIRL But it wobbles. Every day I put a piece of cork under that leg, and every day the housemaid takes it away when she sweeps and I have to cut a new piece. The penholder is covered with ink every morning and so is the inkstand. I have to clean them up every morning after that woman, as sure as the sun rises. (*Pause*) What's the worst job you can think of?

STUDENT To count the washing. Ugh!

GIRL That I have to do. Ugh!

STUDENT What else?

GIRL To be waked in the middle of the night and have to get up and see to the window, which the housemaid has left banging.

STUDENT What else?

GIRL To get up on a ladder and tie the cord on the damper to the big stove, which the housemaid has torn off.

STUDENT What else?

GIRL To sweep after her, to dust after her, to light the fire in the stove when all she's done is throw in some wood. To see to the damper, to wipe the glasses, to lay the table over again, to open the bottles, to see that the rooms are aired, to remake my bed, to rinse the water-bottle when it's green with sediment, to buy matches and soap which are always lacking, to wipe the chimneys and trim the wicks to keep the lamps from smoking—and so that they don't go out when we have company, I have to fill them myself. . . .

STUDENT Music!

GIRL Wait. The labor comes first. The labor of keeping the dirt of life at a distance.

STUDENT But you are wealthy and have two servants.

GIRL It doesn't help. Even if we had three. Living is hard work, and sometimes I grow tired. (*Pause*) Think then if there were a nursery as well.

STUDENT The greatest of joys.

GIRL And the costliest. Is life worth so much hardship?

STUDENT That must depend on the reward you expect for your labors. I would not shrink from anything to win your hand.

[1] Lift up your heart.

GIRL Don't say that. You can never have me.

STUDENT Why not?

GIRL You mustn't ask. (*Pause*)

STUDENT You dropped your bracelet out of the window. . . .

GIRL Because my hand has grown so thin. (*Pause*)

(*The* COOK *appears with a Japanese bottle in her hand*)

There she is—the one who devours me and all of us.

STUDENT What has she in her hand?

GIRL It is the bottle of coloring matter that has letters like scorpions on it. It is the soy which turns water into soup and takes the place of gravy. She makes cabbage soup with it—and mock-turtle soup too.

STUDENT (*To* COOK) Get out!

COOK You drain us of sap, and we drain you. We take the blood and leave you the water, but colored . . . colored. I am going now, but all the same I shall stay, as long as I please.

(*She goes out*)

STUDENT Why did Bengtsson get a medal?

GIRL For his great merits.

STUDENT Has he no defects?

GIRL Yes, great ones. But you don't get a medal for them.

(*They smile*)

STUDENT You have many secrets in this house.

GIRL As in all others. Permit us to keep ours.

STUDENT Don't you approve of candor?

GIRL Yes—within reason.

STUDENT Sometimes I'm seized with a raging desire to say all I think. But I know the world would go to pieces if one were completely candid. (*Pause*) I went to a funeral the other day . . . in church. It was very solemn and beautiful.

GIRL Was it Mr. Hummel's?

STUDENT My false benefactor's—yes. At the head of the coffin stood an old friend of the deceased. He carried the mace. I was deeply impressed by the dignified manner and moving words of the clergyman. I cried. We all cried. Afterward we went to a tavern, and there I learned that the man with the mace had been in love with the dead man's son. . . . (*The* GIRL *stares at him, trying to understand*) And that the dead man had borrowed money from his son's admirer. (*Pause*) Next day the clergyman was arrested for embezzling the church funds. A pretty story.

GIRL Oh . . . ! (*Pause*)

STUDENT Do you know how I am thinking about you now?

GIRL Don't tell me, or I shall die.

STUDENT I must, or I shall die.

GIRL It is in asylums that people say everything they think.

STUDENT Exactly. My father finished up in an asylum.

GIRL Was he ill?

STUDENT No, he was well, but he was mad. You see, he broke out once—in these circumstances. Like all of us, he was surrounded with a circle of acquaintances; he called them friends for short. They were a lot of rotters, of course, as most people are, but he had to have some society—he couldn't get on all alone. Well, as you know, in everyday life no one tells people what he thinks of them, and he didn't either. He knew perfectly well what frauds they were—he'd sounded the depths of their deceit—but as he was a wise and well-bred man, he was always courteous to them. Then one day he gave a big party. It was in the evening and he was tired by the day's work and by the strain of holding his tongue and at the same time talking rubbish with his guests. . . . (*The* GIRL *is frightened*) Well, at the dinner table he rapped for silence, raised his glass, and began to speak. Then something loosed the trigger. He made an enormous speech in which he stripped the whole company naked, one after the other, and told them of all their treachery. Then, tired out, he sat down on the table and told them all to go to hell.

GIRL Oh!

STUDENT I was there, and I shall never forget what happened then. Father and Mother came to blows, the guests rushed for the door . . . and my father was taken to a madhouse, where he died. (*Pause*) Water that is still too long stagnates, and so it is in this house too. There is something stagnating here. And yet I thought it was paradise itself that first time I saw you coming in here. There I stood that Sunday morning, gazing in. I saw a Colonel who was no Colonel. I had a benefactor who was a thief and had to hang himself. I saw a mummy who was not a mummy and an old maid—what of the maidenhood, by the way? Where is beauty to be found? In nature, and in my own mind, when it is in its Sunday clothes. Where are honor and faith? In fairy-tales and children's fancies. Where is anything that fulfills its promise? In my imagination. Now your flowers have poisoned me and I have given the poison back to you. I asked you to become my wife in a home full of poetry and song and music. Then the Cook came. . . . *Sursum Corda!* [2] Try once more to strike fire and glory out of the golden harp. Try, I beg you, I implore you on my knees. (*Pause*) Then I will do it myself. (*He picks up the harp, but the strings give no sound*) It is dumb and deaf. To think that the most beautiful flowers are so poisonous, are the most poisonous. The curse lies over the whole of creation, over life itself. Why will you not be my bride? Because the very life-spring within you is sick . . . now I can feel that vampire in the kitchen beginning to suck me. I believe she is a Lamia, one of those that suck the blood of children. It is always in the kitchen quarters that the seed-leaves of the children are nipped, if it has not already happened in the bedroom. There are poisons that destroy the sight and poisons that open the eyes. I seem to have been born with the latter kind, for I cannot see what is ugly as beautiful, nor call evil good. I cannot. Jesus Christ descended into hell. That was His pilgrimage on earth—to this madhouse, this prison, this charnel-house, this earth. And the mad-

[2] Lift up your hearts.

men killed Him when He wanted to set them free; but the robber they let go. The robber always gets the sympathy. Woe! Woe to us all. Saviour of the world, save us! We perish.

(*And now the* GIRL *has drooped, and it is seen that she is dying. She rings*)

(BENGTSSON *enters*)

GIRL Bring the screen. Quick. I am dying.

(BENGTSSON *comes back with the screen, opens it and arranges it in front of the* GIRL)

STUDENT The Liberator is coming. Welcome, pale and gentle one. Sleep, you lovely, innocent, doomed creature, suffering for no fault of your own. Sleep without dreaming, and when you wake again . . . may you be greeted by a sun that does not burn, in a home without dust, by friends without stain, by a love without flaw. You wise and gentle Buddha, sitting there waiting for a Heaven to sprout from the earth, grant us patience in our ordeal and purity of will, so that this hope may not be confounded.

(*The strings of the harp hum softly and a white light fills the room*)

I saw the sun. To me it seemed
that I beheld the Hidden.
Men must reap what they have sown;
blest is he whose deeds are good.
Deeds which you have wrought in fury,
cannot in evil find redress.
Comfort him you have distressed
with loving-kindness—this will heal.
No fear has he who does no ill.
Sweet is innocence.

(*A faint moaning is heard behind the screen*) You poor little child, child of this world of illusion, guilt, suffering and death, this world of endless change, disappointment, and pain. May the Lord of Heaven be merciful to you upon your journey.

(*The room disappears. Böcklin's picture,* The Island of the Dead, *is seen in the distance,*[3] *and from the island comes music, soft, sweet, and melancholy*)

*Curtain*

[3] Arnold Böcklin (1827-1901) was a Swiss painter noted for landscape and mythological frescoes. "The Island of the Dead" (*Die Toteninsel*) is his most famous work.

# Gerhart Hauptmann

## (1862-1946)

GERHART HAUPTMANN is unquestionably one of the great playwrights of the modern theatre. His contribution to the character and direction of the drama in the late nineteenth and early twentieth centuries is immense, yet outside of Germany, where his best plays still command a lively interest, he is viewed today as a writer of far more historical than intrinsic importance. It is unusual today to see any of Hauptmann's plays in the United States; and even in European centers, the transformation or abandonment of naturalism has led to techniques and styles far removed from the solid traditionalism of Hauptmann's work. The sheer bulk of his output is at first glance intimidating: over 40 plays, as well as a number of short stories and novels, poems, essays, aphorisms, and other writings. Many of his plays have never been translated, and even his best-known dramas do not yield easily to translation. In part, Hauptmann's recurrent use of dialects is responsible, but virtually everything he wrote is so intensely German in its dependence on specific and often local historical, geographical, and cultural values as to make translation peculiarly difficult. Another reason for his decline in popularity may have been his failure to protest publicly against the Nazi regime. Other German playwrights—Kaiser, Brecht, Zuckmayer, to name but a few—left no doubt of their position. Perhaps Hauptmann was too old to risk exile or worse. Even his late plays seldom reflect a consciousness of the moral and spiritual anarchy of recent times. For all these reasons his work appears dated and remote to many; all the same, we should not confuse topicality or popularity with the true measure of a playwright's worth. The strength and power of Hauptmann's art marks him as one of the leading dramatists of our time.

Hauptmann is the outstanding naturalistic playwright of the German theatre, but he is much more than this. The styles of the ancient Greeks, Shakespeare, the historical and philosophical drama of Schiller and Goethe, the mythical drama of Wagner, the mystical and symbolic drama of the late Ibsen, all enter directly into his art. Naturalism is only one facet of Hauptmann's larger poetic achievement, but it is the best-known aspect of his work and probably the most enduring. In his comic as well as his serious plays, Hauptmann was at his best depicting characters and events drawn from his own observation of the working classes, especially from his Silesian environment.

His grandfather had been a weaver, his father a hotelkeeper in the town of Salzbrunn. The elder Hauptmann had traveled widely in his youth. In 1848 he had seen the storming of the barricades in Paris, and had returned home with deep and lasting feelings of social discontent. His neighbors referred to him as "the red Hauptmann." Even more important as part of the playwright's background was his mother's Moravian mystical piety, the source of a profound religious fervor in both the man and his work. He was a weak student, failing in his agricultural studies, but evincing a talent for sculpture. For a time, he attended the art academy in Breslau and then gave himself over to desultory scientific and philosophical studies under the guidance of his elder brother, Carl. His first contact with the theatre also came through his brother, who took him to see the performances of the traveling company of the Duke of Saxe-Meiningen in Breslau in 1876. At the time, the Meiningen players constituted the leading company of the European stage; from their performances Hauptmann acquired a vision of what the theatre could become.

His first attempts at drama were historical plays begun at Jena, where he studied art history, philosophy and science, and listened to the lectures of the celebrated materialist, Haeckel. The positivism of Auguste Comte, Darwin's evolutionary theories, and the biological and social determinism of Taine and Zola were widely diffused in Germany in the early 1880's. Even at this time, one of Hauptmann's professors referred to him as a "dramatic Zola." In 1885 he moved to Berlin, where he continued his scientific and social studies and saw performances of a number of Ibsen's plays. Hauptmann wavered at this time between fiction and drama. A number of his early jotted notes for short stories or novels were later expanded into some of his most famous plays. His naturalistic short story, "Flagman Thiel," is a classic of its kind. Of crucial importance was Hauptmann's visit to Zurich in 1888, where his brother was studying physiology and psychology. Rapidly drawn into the most advanced intellectual circles, Hauptmann entered into vigorous discussion of such burning questions as women's rights, sanitary conditions of miners and factory workers, socialist theories of economic organization, and the like. He later remarked, "My brother Carl's little house in the Freie Strasse was something like a Platonic Academy." The members of their circle included Karl Steinmetz, who later became chief assistant to Edison; the young Frank

Wedekind; the biologist, Alfred Ploetz; and a Polish girl who was among the few female students at the university, and whose daring notions of female emancipation mark her as the probable model for Anna Mahr of *Lonely Lives*. It was at this time that Hauptmann conceived of the plays, *Before Dawn* and *The Weavers*.

*Before Dawn* (*Vor Sonnenaufgang,* 1889) is a landmark in the emergence of European naturalism. Alcoholism, hereditary disease, and the sordid milieu of a rural mining community furnish the background to the drama of Alfred Loth. An idealistic reformer, he falls in love with Helene Krause, only to abandon her on learning that she is marked by the disease and degeneration of her family. There is no appeal beyond the harsh implacable law of heredity. Loth leaves, and Helene kills herself. The brutality of the surrounding characters and milieu suggests Tolstoy's *The Power of Darkness,* produced in Berlin by Otto Brahm's Freie Bühne (Free Stage), a society dedicated to the establishment of a German naturalistic theatre. *Before Dawn* also was produced by Brahm at a sensational premiere in October, 1889. Strindberg, who had little sympathy with the sociological bias of German naturalism, was genuinely moved by the love scene in the third act, and Hauptmann himself considered this scene the most realistic of the play.

With *Lonely Lives* (*Einsame Menschen,* 1891) and especially with *The Weavers* (*Die Weber,* 1892), Hauptmann gained international acclaim. *Lonely Lives* reveals an immense growth in depth and skill in a remarkably short time. Hauptmann was helped considerably by the study of Ibsen's fusion of exposition and action and concentration on inner development, revealed in a series of crises within as well as around the hero. The play is in some ways close to *Rosmersholm.* Johannes Vockerat, student of Darwin and Haeckel, is torn between the claims of duty and love, and is unable to resolve them. His suicide is no solution, but Hauptmann makes it not only convincing, but psychologically necessary.

*The Weavers* was originally written in Silesian dialect (entitled *De Waber*), then rewritten in High German. Hauptmann's interest was aroused by recent studies of the plight of the weaving industry in his native community, where, in 1891 as in the earlier years of the century, misery and suffering were widespread. Hauptmann traveled through the district, observing conditions with a keen and sensitive eye, and gathering details of the uprising of 1844 from surviving witnesses and participants. He was not a radical reformer, let alone a revolutionary; his weavers have no program, no ideology, no clear awareness of the economic and social causes of their plight. Nevertheless, the portrayal of their utter wretchedness and destitution is marked throughout by the playwright's compassion for their suffering and his indignation over their conditions. As the subtitle, "A Play of the Eighteen-Forties," suggests, *The Weavers* is a historical play, based on sources that reveal an even harsher reality. Hauptmann broke with traditional form in refusing to build his drama around a single hero; the masses are raised to the level of collective heroism in the succession of scenes that chart the course of the weavers' uprising. Despite its epic elements, the play is marked by detailed individualization of character and by a coherent structure, derived from rhythmic waves of mounting tension and from the interweaving of the *leitmotif* of the weavers' song. The final presence of the soldiers portends the defeat of the revolt, yet the protest is an act of heroism that commands our admiration and sympathy. Hauptmann's intimate awareness of the pathos of existence is perhaps best revealed in the final line of Act Three: "every man has his dream."

Among the later naturalistic plays, the best are *Drayman Henschel* (1898) and *Rose Bernd* (1903), the one culminating in suicide, the other in murder of a newly-born illegitimate child. Hauptmann's heroes and heroines are generally passive and suffering, driven by a dark fatality relieved only by the playwright's genuine compassion. Pain and hardship are bound up with life itself. The young James Joyce wrote of his *alter ego,* Stephen Dedalus: "The rain laden trees of the avenue evoked in him, as always, memories of the girls and women in the plays of Gerhart Hauptmann; and the memory of their pale sorrows. . . ." As the curtain falls in *Rose Bernd,* her betrothed, August, exclaims: "This girl . . . what she must have suffered!"

Not all of Hauptmann's work is dark and painful. In *The Beaver Coat* (1893) he proved that he could create lively folk comedy. The central figure, Frau Wolff, is a clever and crafty rogue whose brazen thefts assure her continued success. She has no illusions over the respectability of the wealthy: "If you're once rich, Julius," she tells her husband, "and can sit in a carriage, then nobody asks ya where ya got your money." A biting satire on petty self-important bureaucrats, the comedy ends with no one any the wiser and Frau Wolff launched in full career. Naturalism took yet a different form in the fantasy, *Hannele* (1893), wherein brutal suffering is assuaged by religious hope and wish-fulfillment. Hauptmann also applied naturalistic techniques to the history play in *Florian Geyer,* a tragedy of the Peasant War of 1525, marked by an effort at authenticity of speech in the idiom of the Reformation and by perhaps too heavy a reliance on historical and linguistic research. In the same year, 1896, Hauptmann also produced *The Sunken Bell,* a romantic blending of realism and fantasy that brought him his greatest theatrical success. Many of his subsequent plays are broadly symbolic dramatizations of Greek or Germanic myth, expressive of the aged writer's quest for cosmic unity.

Hauptmann's naturalism brought vigor and freshness to the theatre of his day. In his plays the stage took on an actuality and a social passion that are of continuing significance in the contemporary theatre. A poet as well as a humanitarian, Hauptmann gave enduring life to the pain and struggle of men and women crushed by forces beyond their control. His warm understanding of the pathos and tragedy of the lives of ordinary and seemingly insignificant people is a permanent possession of the modern drama.

# THE WEAVERS

## *A Play of the Eighteen-Forties*

Translated by Horst Frenz and Miles Waggoner

### CHARACTERS

DREISSIGER, *a cotton manufacturer*
MRS. DREISSIGER, *his wife*
PFEIFER, *a manager* — at DREISSIGER'S
NEUMANN, *a cashier* — at DREISSIGER'S
AN APPRENTICE — at DREISSIGER'S
JOHANN, *a coachman* — at DREISSIGER'S
A YOUNG GIRL — at DREISSIGER'S
WEINHOLD, *a tutor for* DREISSIGER'S *sons*
PASTOR KITTELHAUS
MRS. KITTELHAUS, *his wife*
HEIDE, *the Chief of Police*
KUTSCHE, *a policeman*
WELZEL, *an innkeeper*
MRS. WELZEL, *his wife*
ANNA WELZEL, *their daughter*
WIEGAND, *a carpenter*
A TRAVELING SALESMAN
A FARMER
A FORESTER
SCHMIDT, *a physician*
HORNIG, *a rag picker*
OLD WITTIG, *a smith*

WEAVERS *Baecker—Moritz Jaeger—Old Baumert—Mother Baumert—Bertha Baumert—Emma Baumert—Fritz, Emma's son, four years old—August Baumert—Ansorge—Mrs. Heinrich—Old Hilse—Gottlieb Hilse—Luise, Gottlieb's wife—Mielchen, his daughter, six years old—Reimann—Heiber—A weaver woman—A boy, eight years old—A large crowd of young and old weavers and weaver women.*

*The action of the play takes place in the 1840's in Kaschbach, Peterswaldau, and Langenbielau, cities at the foot of the mountains known as the Eulengebirge.*

## Act One

*A spacious whitewashed room in Dreissiger's house at Peterswaldau, where the weavers must deliver their finished webs. At the left are uncurtained windows; in the back wall, a glass door. At the right is a similar door through which weavers, men, women, and children continuously come and go. Along the right wall, which, like the others, is almost entirely hidden by wooden stands for cotton, there is a bench on which the weavers, as they come in, spread out their finished webs to be examined. They step forward in the order of their arrival and offer their finished products.* PFEIFER, *the manager, stands behind a large table on which the weavers lay their webs for inspection. He makes the inspection with the use of dividers and a magnifying glass. When he is finished, he lays the cotton on the scales, where an apprentice tests its weight. The same apprentice shoves the goods taken from the scales onto the stock shelves.* PFEIFER *calls out the amount to be paid to each weaver to* NEUMANN, *the cashier, who sits at a small table.*

*It is a sultry day toward the end of May. The clock points to twelve. Most of the waiting weavers stand like men before the bar of justice where, tortured and anxious, they must await a life-and-death decision. They all give the impression of being crushed, like beggars. Passing from humiliation to humiliation and convinced that they are only tolerated, they are used to making themselves as inconspicuous as possible. Also, they have a stark, irresolute look—gnawing, brooding faces. Most of the men resemble each other, half-dwarf, half-schoolmaster. They are flat-chested, coughing creatures with ashen gray faces: creatures of the looms, whose knees are bent with much sitting. At first glance, their women folk are less typical. They are broken, harried, worn out, while the men still have a certain look of pathetic gravity. The women's clothes are ragged, while those of the men are patched. Some of the young girls are not without charm—they have pale waxen complexions, delicate figures, large protruding melancholy eyes.*

CASHIER NEUMANN (*Counting out money*) That leaves 16 silver groschen and 2 pfennigs.

FIRST WEAVER WOMAN (*In her thirties, very emaciated, puts the money away with trembling fingers*) Thank ya, kindly, sir.

NEUMANN (*As the woman does not move on*) Well, is something wrong again?

FIRST WEAVER WOMAN (*Excitedly, in begging tone*) I'd like a few pfennigs in advance. I need it awful bad.

NEUMANN And I need a few hundred thalers. If it was just a matter of needing—! (*Already busy counting out money to another weaver, curtly*) Mr. Dreissiger himself has to decide about advances.

FIRST WEAVER WOMAN Then, maybe I could talk to Mr. Dreissiger hisself?

PFEIFER (*He was formerly a weaver. The type is unmistakable; only he is well-groomed, well-fed, well-clothed, clean-shaven; also, a heavy user of snuff. He calls across brusquely*) Mr. Dreissiger would have plenty to do, God knows, if he had to bother himself with every trifle. That's what we're here for. (*He measures and inspects a web with the magnifying glass*)

Damn it all! There's a draft! (*He wraps a heavy scarf around his neck*) Shut the door when ya come in.

THE APPRENTICE (*In a loud voice to* PFEIFER) It's just like talkin' to a block of wood.

PFEIFER That's settled then! Weigh it! (*The weaver lays his web on the scales*) If ya only understood your work better. It's got lumps in it again—I can tell without looking. A good weaver doesn't put off the winding who knows how long.

BAECKER (*Enters. A young, exceptionally strong weaver whose behavior is free and easy, almost impertinent.* PFEIFER, NEUMANN, *and* THE APPRENTICE *glance at each other understandingly when he enters*) Damn it, I'm sweatin' like a dog again.

FIRST WEAVER (*Softly*) Feels like rain.

OLD BAUMERT (*Pushes through the glass door at the right. Behind the door, waiting weavers are seen jammed together, shoulder to shoulder.* OLD BAUMERT *has hobbled forward and has laid his bundle on a bench near* BAECKER'S. *He sits down next to it and wipes the sweat from his face*) Ya sure earn a rest here.

BAECKER Rest is better than money.

OLD BAUMERT Ya need money too. Good day to ya, Baecker!

BAECKER And good day to you, Father Baumert! Who knows how long we'll have to be waitin' around here again.

FIRST WEAVER It don't matter whether a weaver has to wait an hour or a day. He just don't count.

PFEIFER Be quiet, back there. I can't hear myself think.

BAECKER (*Softly*) Today's one of his bad days again.

PFEIFER (*To the weavers standing in front of him*) How many times have I told you already. Ya ought to clean up the webs better. What sort of a mess is this? There are chunks of dirt in it, as long as my finger—and straw, and all kinds of rubbish.

WEAVER REIMANN I guess I need a new pair of pincers.

THE APPRENTICE (*Has weighed the web*) And it's short weight, too.

PFEIFER The kind of weavers ya have nowadays! You hate to hand out the yarn. Oh, Lord, in my time! My master would've made me pay for it. I tell you, weaving was a different thing in those days. Then, a man had to understand his business. Today it's not necessary any more. Reimann, 10 groschen.

WEAVER REIMANN Yes, but one pound is allowed for waste.

PFEIFER I haven't time. That's settled. (*To the next weaver*) What have you got?

WEAVER HEIBER (*Puts his web up on the counter. While* PFEIFER *is inspecting it,* HEIBER *steps up to him and speaks softly and eagerly*) Please, forgive me, Mr. Pfeifer, I would like to ask ya, sir, if perhaps ya would be so kind as to do me a favor and not deduct my advance this time.

PFEIFER (*Measuring with the dividers and inspecting, jeers*) Well, now! That's just fine. It looks as if about half the woof has been left on the spool again.

HEIBER (*Continuing, as before*) I'd be glad to make it up next week for sure. Last week I had to put in two days' work on the estate. And my wife's home, sick in bed. . . .

PFEIFER (*Putting the web on the scales*) Here's another piece of real sloppy work. (*Already taking a new web for inspection*) What a selvage—now it's broad, then it's narrow. In one place the woof's all gathered together, who knows how much, then the reed has been pulled apart. And scarcely seventy threads to the inch. Whatever happened to the rest? Is that honest work? I never saw such a thing!

(HEIBER, *suppressing tears, stands humiliated and helpless*)

BAECKER (*Low, to* BAUMERT) I guess this riffraff would like us to pay for the yarn, too.

FIRST WEAVER WOMAN (*Who has withdrawn only a few steps from the cashier's table, stares about from time to time, seeking help, without moving from the spot. Then she takes heart and once more turns imploringly to the cashier*) I can hardly . . . I don't know . . . if ya don't give me an advance this time . . . O, Lord, Lord. . . .

PFEIFER (*Calls across*) All this calling on the Lord! Just leave the Lord in peace. You haven't been bothering much about the Lord up to now. It'd be better if you'd look after your husband instead, so he isn't seen sitting in the tavern window all day long. We can't give advances. We have to account for every cent. It's not our own money. Later they'd be asking us for it. People who are industrious and understand their business and do their work in fear of God don't ever need advances. So, that's settled.

NEUMANN And if a Bielau weaver got four times as much pay, he'd squander four times as much and be in debt in the bargain.

FIRST WEAVER WOMAN (*In a loud voice, as if appealing to everyone's sense of justice*) I'm certainly not lazy, but I just can't go on this way much longer. I've had two miscarriages, and my husband, he can't do no more than half the work neither; he went up to the shepherd at Zerlau, but he couldn't do nothin' for his trouble either . . . there's just so much a body can do. . . . We sure do work as much as we can. I ain't had much sleep for weeks, and everything'll be all right again if I can only get a bit of this weakness out of my bones. But ya got to have a little consideration. (*Beseeching him and fawning*) Ya'll have to be good enough to let me have a few groschen, this time.

PFEIFER (*Unperturbed*) Fiedler, 11 groschen.

FIRST WEAVER WOMAN Just a few groschen, so we can get some bread. The farmer won't give us no more credit. We got a house full of children. . . .

NEUMANN (*Softly and with mock seriousness to* THE APPRENTICE) Once a year the linen weaver has a brat, fa, la, la, la, la.

THE APPRENTICE (*Chiming in*) The first six weeks it's blind as a bat, fa, la, la, la, la.

REIMANN (*Not touching the money that the cashier has counted out for him*) We've always been gettin' 13½ groschen for a web.

PFEIFER (*Calls across*) If it doesn't suit you, Reimann, all you have to do is say the word. There are plenty of weavers. Especially weavers like you. For full weight, you'll get full pay.

REIMANN That something should be wrong with the weight. . . .

PFEIFER If there's nothing wrong with the cotton you bring, there'll be nothing wrong with your pay.

REIMANN It really can't be that this web, here, should have too many flaws in it.

PFEIFER (*Inspecting*) He who weaves well, lives well.

HEIBER (*He has stayed close to* PFEIFER *waiting for a favorable opportunity. He smiled with the others at* PFEIFER'S *remark; now he steps forward and speaks to him as he did before*) I would like to ask ya, sir, if perhaps ya would be so kind and not deduct the 5 groschen advance this time. My wife's been sick in bed since before Ash Wednesday. She can't do a lick of work. And I have to pay a girl to tend the bobbin. And so—

PFEIFER (*Takes a pinch of snuff*) Heiber, you're not the only one I have to attend to. The others want their turn, too.

REIMANN The way the warp was given to me—that's the way I wound it and that's the way I took it off again. I can't bring back better yarn than I take home.

PFEIFER If ya don't like it, ya simply don't need to get any more warp here. There are plenty who'd run their feet off for it.

NEUMANN (*To* REIMANN) Aren't you going to take the money?

REIMANN I just can't take such pay.

NEUMANN (*Without troubling himself further about* REIMANN) Heiber, 10 groschen—take off the 5 groschen advance—leaves 5 groschen.

HEIBER (*Steps up, looks at the money, stands there, shakes his head as if there were something he could not believe, and then quietly and carefully pockets the money*) O my God—! (*Sighing*) Ah, well!

OLD BAUMERT (*Looking straight at* HEIBER) Yes, yes, Franz! You've got cause for sighing there.

HEIBER (*Speaking wearily*) Ya see, I've got a sick girl layin' home. She needs a bottle of medicine.

OLD BAUMERT What's wrong with her?

HEIBER Ya see, she's been a sickly little thing from the time she was born. I really don't know . . . well, I can tell you: she brought it into the world with her. Such trouble's in the blood, and it keeps breakin' out over and over again.

OLD BAUMERT There's something the matter everywhere. When you're poor, there's nothing but bad luck. There's no end to it and no salvation.

HEIBER What have ya got in that bundle?

OLD BAUMERT We haven't got a thing in the house. So I had our little dog killed. There ain't much to him, he was half-starved. He was a nice little dog. I couldn't kill him myself. I didn't have the heart.

PFEIFER (*Has inspected* BAECKER'S *web, calls out*) Baecker, 13½ groschen.

BAECKER That's a measly hand-out for a beggar, not pay.

PFEIFER Those who are done, have to get out. It's so crowded, we can't move around in here.

BAECKER (*To those standing about, without lowering his voice*) That's a measly hand-out, that's all it is. And for that a man's to work the treadle from early morning till late at night. And after a man's been workin' behind a loom for eighteen days, evenin' after evenin'—worn out, dizzy with the dust and terrible heat, then he's lucky if he gets 13½ groschen for his drudgery.

PFEIFER We'll have no back-talk here.

BAECKER You can't make me hold my tongue.

PFEIFER (*Jumps up, shouting*) We'll see about that. (*Walks toward the glass door and calls into the office*) Mr. Dreissiger! Mr. Dreissiger, if you'll be so kind!

DREISSIGER (*Enters. He is about forty, fat, asthmatic. With a severe look*) What's—the matter, Pfeifer?

PFEIFER (*Angrily*) Baecker won't hold his tongue.

DREISSIGER (*Draws himself up, throws his head back, and stares at* BAECKER *with quivering nostrils*) Oh, yes—Baecker—(*To* PFEIFER) Is that him—? (*The clerk nods*)

BAECKER (*Impudently*) Yes, indeed, Mr. Dreissiger! (*Pointing to himself*) That's him. (*Pointing to* DREISSIGER) And that's him.

DREISSIGER (*Indignantly*) How can he dare?

PFEIFER He's too well off, that's what he is. He'll skate on thin ice once too often.

BAECKER (*Roughly*) You shut up, you fool! Once, in

the new moon, your mother must have been ridin' a broomstick with Satan to beget such a devil as you for a son.

DREISSIGER (*In sudden anger, bellows*) Shut up! Shut up this minute, or else—(*He trembles, takes a few steps forward*)

BAECKER (*With determination, standing up to him*) I'm not deaf. I still hear good.

DREISSIGER (*Controls himself, asks with apparent businesslike calm*) Isn't he one of those—?

PFEIFER He's a Bielau weaver. They can always be found where trouble is brewing.

DREISSIGER (*Trembling*) Then I'm warning you: if it happens once more, and if such a gang of half-drunken young louts passes my house once again, as they did last night, singing that vile song. . . .

BAECKER I guess you mean "Bloody Justice"?

DREISSIGER You know exactly what I mean. Let me tell you, if I hear that song once more, I'll get hold of one of you, and—on my honor, joking aside, I promise you I'll turn him over to the state's attorney. And if I find out who wrote this wretched song. . . .

BAECKER That's a beautiful song—it is!

DREISSIGER Another word and I'll send for the police—immediately. I won't lose any time! We know how to deal with young fellows like you. I've taken care of your kind before.

BAECKER Well, now, that I can believe. A real manufacturer like you can gobble up two or three hundred weavers before a person has time to turn around . . . and not so much as a bone left over. Such a man's got four stomachs like a cow and teeth like a wolf. No, indeed—that's nothing at all to him!

DREISSIGER (*To the clerks*) See to it that that fellow doesn't get another stick of work from us.

BAECKER Oh, it's all the same to me whether I starve behind the loom or in a ditch by the side of the road.

DREISSIGER Get out, this minute! Get out of here!

BAECKER (*Firmly*) I'll take my pay first.

DREISSIGER How much has the man got coming, Neumann?

NEUMANN Twelve groschen and five pfennigs.

DREISSIGER (*Takes the money from the cashier in great haste and throws it down on the counter so that a few coins roll onto the floor*) There you are—and now hurry—get out of my sight!

BAECKER I'll take my pay first.

DREISSIGER There's your pay; and if you don't hurry and get out. . . . It's exactly twelve . . . my dyers are taking off for lunch. . . .

BAECKER My pay belongs in my hand. My pay belongs here. (*He points to the palm of his left hand*)

DREISSIGER (*To* THE APPRENTICE) Pick it up, Tilgner.

(THE APPRENTICE *picks up the money and lays it in* BAECKER'S *hand*)

BAECKER Everything's got to be done right. (*He puts the money slowly in an old purse*)

DREISSIGER Well? (*As* BAECKER *still does not leave, impatiently*) Shall I help you?

(*There is excited movement among the crowd of weavers. A long, deep sigh is heard, then a fall. Everyone's attention is turned to this new event*)

DREISSIGER What's happened there?

VARIOUS WEAVERS *and* WEAVER WOMEN Someone's fainted. It's a sickly little boy. What's wrong? Is it consumption, maybe?

DREISSIGER Why . . . what's that? Fainted? (*He goes up closer*)

AN OLD WEAVER He's layin' there. (*They make room. A little boy, about eight years old, is seen lying on the floor as if dead*)

DREISSIGER Does somebody know this boy?

OLD WEAVER He's not from our village.

OLD BAUMERT He looks like one of Heinrich's boys. (*He looks at him more closely*) Yes, indeed! That is Heinrich's little Gustav.

DREISSIGER Where do they live, these people?

OLD BAUMERT Why, near us in Kaschbach, Mr. Dreissiger. He goes around playin' music, and in the daytime he works at the loom. They have nine children and the tenth's on the way.

VARIOUS WEAVERS *and* WEAVER WOMEN They sure got a lot of trouble. Their roof leaks. The woman ain't got two shirts for the nine children.

OLD BAUMERT (*Taking hold of the boy*) Why, my child, what's wrong with ya? Wake up, there now!

DREISSIGER Take hold of him—here, help me—we'll pick him up. It's incomprehensible that anybody should let a weak child like that come such a long way. Bring some water, Pfeifer!

WEAVER WOMAN (*Helps him sit up*) Don't ya up and die on us, boy!

DREISSIGER Or brandy, Pfeifer, brandy is better.

BAECKER (*Forgotten by everybody, has been watching. Now, with one hand on the doorknob, he calls across in a loud voice, mockingly*) Give him something to eat, too, and he'll come to all right. (*Exit*)

DREISSIGER That fellow will come to no good. Take him under the arm, Neumann. Slowly—slowly . . . that's it . . . there, now . . . we'll take him into my room. Why, what is it?

NEUMANN He's said something, Mr. Dreissiger! He's moving his lips.

DREISSIGER What is it, little boy?

THE BOY (*Whispers*) I'm—hungry!

DREISSIGER (*Turns pale*) I can't understand him.

WEAVER WOMAN I think he said. . . .

DREISSIGER Well, we'll see. Let's not lose any time—he can lie on my sofa. We'll hear, then, what the doctor says.

(DREISSIGER, NEUMANN, *and the* WEAVER WOMAN *carry the boy into the office. There is a commotion among the weavers, as among school children when the teacher leaves the classroom. They stretch, they whisper, they shift from one foot to the other. Soon there is loud and general conversation among them*)

OLD BAUMERT I really do believe Baecker is right.

SEVERAL WEAVERS *and* WEAVER WOMEN He said something like that, too. That's nothing new around here—people faintin' from hunger. Yes, and who knows what'll happen this winter if this cuttin' of wages keeps on. . . . And the potatoes bein' so bad this year. . . . It won't be no different here till we're all of us flat on our backs.

OLD BAUMERT Ya might just as well put a rope 'round your neck and hang yourself on your loom like the Nentwich weaver did. Here, take a pinch of snuff—I was in Neurode, where my brother-in-law works in the snuff factory. He gave me a few grains. You carryin' anything nice in your kerchief?

AN OLD WEAVER It's only a little bit of barley. The wagon from the Ullbrich miller was drivin' ahead of me, and there was a little slit in one of the sacks. That comes in handy, believe me.

OLD BAUMERT There are twenty-two mills in Peterswaldau, and still there's nothin' left over for the likes of us.

AN OLD WEAVER Ah, we mustn't get discouraged. Something always turns up and helps a little bit.

HEIBER When we're hungry, we have to pray to the fourteen guardian angels, and if that don't fill ya up, then ya have to put a pebble in your mouth and suck on it. Right, Baumert?

(DREISSIGER *and* PFEIFER, *as well as the cashier, return*)

DREISSIGER It was nothing of any importance. The boy's quite all right again. (*Goes around excited and puffing*) And yet it is a disgrace. A bit of wind would blow that wisp of a child away. It's really unbelievable how people—how parents can be so irresponsible. To load him down with two bundles of cotton and send him a good seven and a half miles on the road. It's really quite unbelievable. I will simply have to take steps to see to it that goods brought by children will not be accepted. (*He walks silently back and forth*) In any case, I certainly hope that nothing of this sort happens again. On whose shoulders does the blame finally rest? The manufacturers, of course. We're blamed for everything. When a poor little fellow falls asleep in the snow in the wintertime, one of these reporter chaps comes running up, and in two days the gruesome story is in all the papers. The father, the parents, the ones who send the child out . . . oh, no . . . they aren't guilty, certainly not! It must be the manufacturer; the manufacturer is the goat. The weaver is always let off easy, the manufacturer is the one who catches it; he's a man without a heart, dangerous fellow who can be bitten in the leg by every mad dog of a reporter. He lives in splendor and in comfort and pays the poor weavers starvation wages. These scribblers are absolutely silent about the fact that such a man has troubles, too, and sleepless nights; that he runs great risks such as the weaver never dreams of; that often he does nothing but calculate—dividing, adding, and multiplying, calculating and recalculating until he's nearly out of his mind; that he has to consider and weigh a hundred different kinds of things, and always has to fight and compete, you might say, as a matter of life and death; that not a single day goes by without annoyances and losses. All the people who're dependent on the manufacturer, who suck him dry and want to live off of him . . . think of that! No, no! You ought to be in my shoes for a while, then you'd get fed up with it soon enough, I tell you. (*After a little reflection*) How that fellow, that scoundrel there, that Baecker, behaved! Now he'll go around and tell everybody how hard-hearted I am. That at the slightest opportunity I throw the weavers out. Is that true? Am I so hard-hearted?

MANY VOICES No, Mr. Dreissiger!

DREISSIGER Well, it doesn't look like that to me, either. And yet these rascals go around here and sing nasty songs about us manufacturers. They talk of hunger and yet they have so much money to spend that they can consume their liquor by the quart. They ought to look around in other places, and see how things are among the linen weavers. They can really talk of hard times. But you here, you cotton weavers, you can quietly thank God that things are as they are. And I ask the old, industrious, skilled weavers who are here: Tell me, can a worker, who does a good job, earn his living, working for me or can't he?

VERY MANY VOICES Yes, Mr. Dreissiger!

DREISSIGER There, you see! A fellow like Baecker can't, of course. But I advise you, keep those fellows in check; if this goes too far, I'll just quit. Then I'll give up the whole business, and you'll see where you are. You'll see who'll give you work. Certainly not your fine Mr. Baecker.

FIRST WEAVER WOMAN (*Has come up close to* DREISSIGER *and with fawning humility brushes some dust from his coat*) You've gone and rubbed against something, Mr. Dreissiger, sir, you have.

DREISSIGER Business is terrible, you know that yourselves. Instead of earning money, I'm actually losing it. If, in spite of this, I see to it that my weavers always have work, I expect them to appreciate it. The goods lie stocked up here in thousands of yards, and I don't know today if I'll ever sell them. Well, I've heard that a great number of weavers around here have no work at all, and so . . . well, Pfeifer can give you the details. The fact of the matter is this: so you'll see my good intentions . . . naturally, I can't just hand out charity. I'm not rich enough for that. But I can, up to a certain point, give the unemployed a chance to earn at least a little something. That I'm running a tremendous risk in doing that, well, that's my own affair. I think it's always better if a man can earn a piece of bread and cheese for himself every day rather than starve. Don't you think I'm right?

MANY VOICES Yes, yes, Mr. Dreissiger.

DREISSIGER I am therefore willing to put an additional two hundred weavers to work. Pfeifer will explain to you, under what conditions. (*He is about to leave*)

FIRST WEAVER WOMAN (*Steps in his path, speaks quickly, imploringly, urgently*) Mr. Dreissiger, sir, I wanted to ask ya real kindly, if perhaps you . . . I've been laid up twice. . . .

DREISSIGER (*In haste*) Speak to Pfeifer, my good woman, I'm late as it is. (*He turns away from her*)

REIMANN (*Stops him. In the tone of an injured and accusing man*) Mr. Dreissiger, I really have a complaint to make. Mr. Pfeifer has . . . I always get 12½ groschen for a web, and. . . .

DREISSIGER (*Interrupts him*) There's the manager. Talk to him: he's the person to see.

HEIBER (*Stops* DREISSIGER) Mr. Dreissiger, sir, (*Stuttering, in confusion and haste*) I wanted to ask ya if perhaps ya could . . . if maybe Mr. Pfeifer could . . . if he could. . . .

DREISSIGER What is it you want?

HEIBER The advance pay that I got last time. I mean that I. . . .

DREISSIGER I really do not understand you.

HEIBER I was pretty hard up, because. . . .

DREISSIGER Pfeifer's business, that's Pfeifer's business. I really can't . . . take it up with Pfeifer. (*He escapes into the office*)

(*The supplicants look helplessly at one another. One after the other, they step back, sighing*)

PFEIFER (*Starts the inspection again*) Well, Annie, and what are you bringing us?

OLD BAUMERT How much for a web, then, Mr. Pfeifer?

PFEIFER Ten groschen for each web.

OLD BAUMERT Ain't that something!

(*Excitement among the weavers, whispers and grumblings*)

*Curtain*

# Act Two

*A small room in the cottage of* WILHELM ANSORGE *in Kaschbach in the mountains called Eulengebirge.*

*The narrow room measures less than six feet from the dilapidated floor to the smoke-blackened rafters. Two young girls,* EMMA *and* BERTHA BAUMERT, *sit at looms.* MOTHER BAUMERT, *a crippled old woman, sits on a stool by the bed, at her spooling wheel. Her son,* AUGUST, *twenty years old, an idiot with small body and head and long spiderlike limbs, sits on a footstool, also reeling yarn.*

*The weak, rosy light of the setting sun shines through two small window openings in the left wall. These are partly pasted over with paper and partly filled up with straw. The light falls on the pale, blond, loose hair of the girls, on their bare, bony shoulders and thin waxen necks, on the folds of their coarse chemises, which, with a short skirt of the roughest linen, constitute their entire clothing. The warm glow lights up the entire face, neck, and chest of the old woman. Her face is emaciated to a skeleton, with folds and wrinkles in the anemic skin. The sunken eyes are reddened and watery from the lint and smoke and from working by lamplight. She has a long goiter neck with sinews standing out. Her narrow chest is covered with faded shawls and rags. Part of the right wall, with the stove, stove bench, bedstead, and several gaudily tinted pictures of saints, is also lighted up. There are rags hanging on the bar of the stove to dry, and behind the stove, old worthless rubbish is piled up. On the bench are a few old pots and kitchen utensils; a heap of potato peelings is laid out to dry on a piece of paper. Skeins of yarn and reels hang from the rafters. Small baskets with bobbins stand beside the looms. In the back there is a low door without a lock; next to it, a bundle of willow switches leans against the wall. Several broken peck baskets lie about. The room is filled with the noise of the looms: the rhythmic movement of the lathe which shakes the walls and the floor, the shuffle and clicking of the shuttle moving rapidly back and forth. This blends with the low constant humming of the spooling wheels that sounds like the buzzing of bumble bees.*

MOTHER BAUMERT (*In a pitiful, exhausted voice, as the girls stop their weaving and bend over their webs*) Do ya have to make knots again?

EMMA (*The elder of the girls, twenty-two years old, is tying up the torn threads*) This is the worst yarn!

BERTHA (*Fifteen years old*) The warp sure causes a lot of trouble.

EMMA Where's he been so long? He's been gone since nine o'clock.

MOTHER BAUMERT I should say so! Where can he be, girls?

BERTHA Don't ya worry, Mother!

MOTHER BAUMERT I can't help it!

(EMMA *continues weaving*)

BERTHA Wait a minute, Emma!

EMMA What is it?

BERTHA I thought I heard somebody comin'.

EMMA That'll be Ansorge comin' home.

FRITZ (*A small four-year-old boy, barefoot and dressed in rags, comes in crying*) Mother, I'm hungry.

EMMA Wait, Fritzi, just you wait a bit. Grandfather's comin' soon. He's bringin' bread and grain.

FRITZ But I'm so hungry, Mama.

EMMA I just told ya. Don't be so silly. He's comin' right away. He'll bring some nice bread and some coffee grain. When we stop workin', Mama'll take the potato peelin's to the farmer, and he'll give her a bit of buttermilk for her boy.

FRITZ But where's grandfather gone?

EMMA He's at the manufacturer's, deliverin' a web.

FRITZ At the manufacturer's?

EMMA Yes, Fritzi! Down at Dreissiger's, in Peterswaldau.

FRITZ Will he get some bread there?

EMMA Yes, yes, they'll give him some money, and then he can buy some bread.

FRITZ Will they give grandfather lots a money?

EMMA Oh, stop talkin', boy. (*She continues weaving, as does* BERTHA. *Then both stop again*)

BERTHA August, go and ask Ansorge if he won't give us a light.

(AUGUST *leaves together with* FRITZ)

MOTHER BAUMERT (*With ever-increasing childlike fear, almost whining*) Children, children! Where can the man be?

BERTHA Maybe he dropped in to see Hauffen.

MOTHER BAUMERT (*Crying*) If he just ain't gone to the tavern.

EMMA I hope not, Mother! But our father ain't that kind.

MOTHER BAUMERT (*Quite beside herself with a host of fears*) Well . . . well . . . well, tell me what'll happen if he . . . if he comes home . . . if he drinks it all up and don't bring nothin' home? There ain't a handful of salt in the house, not a piece of bread . . . we need a shovelful of fuel. . . .

BERTHA Don't ya worry, Mother! The moon's shining. We'll go to the woods. We'll take August along and bring back some firewood.

MOTHER BAUMERT Sure, so the forester can catch ya?

ANSORGE (*An old weaver, with a gigantic frame, who has to bend low in order to enter the room, sticks his head and the upper part of his body through the door. His hair and beard are unkempt*) Well, what do ya want?

BERTHA Ya could give us a light!

ANSORGE (*Muffled, as if speaking in the presence of a sick person*) It's still light enough.

MOTHER BAUMERT Now ya'll even make us sit in the dark.

ANSORGE I've got to do the best I can. (*He goes out*)

BERTHA Now ya see how stingy he is.

EMMA Yeah, we got to sit here till he gets good and ready.

MRS. HEINRICH (*Enters. She is thirty years old, pregnant. Her face is worn from sorrow and anxious waiting*) Good evenin' to ya all.

MOTHER BAUMERT Well, Mother Heinrich, what's the news?

MRS. HEINRICH (*Limping*) I've stepped on a piece of glass.

BERTHA Come over here and set down. I'll see if I can't get it out.

MRS. HEINRICH (*Sits down;* BERTHA *kneels in front of her and busies herself with* MRS. HEINRICH'*s foot*)

MOTHER BAUMERT How's things at home, Mother Heinrich?

MRS. HEINRICH (*Breaks out in despair*) Soon I won't be able to stand it no more. (*She fights in vain against a flood of tears. Then she weeps silently*)

MOTHER BAUMERT It'd be the best for the likes of us, Mother Heinrich, if the dear Lord would have pity on us and take us out of this world.

MRS. HEINRICH (*Losing her self-control, weeps and cries out*) My poor children are starvin'! (*She sobs and moans*) I just don't know what to do. Ya try as hard as ya can, ya wear yourself out till ya drop. I'm more dead than alive, and still it ain't no different. Nine hungry mouths to feed and not enough to feed them. Where am I to get the food, huh? Last night I had a little bit of bread—it wasn't enough for the two littlest ones. Who was I supposed to give it to, huh? They all cried: Mama, me, Mama, me. . . . No, no! And all this while I'm still up and about. What'll it be when I have to take to my bed? The few potatoes we had was washed away. We ain't got a bite to eat.

BERTHA (*Has removed the splinter and washed out the wound*) We'll put a piece of cloth around it. (*To* EMMA) Look and see if ya can find one.

MOTHER BAUMERT We ain't no better off, Mother Heinrich.

MRS. HEINRICH At least ya've still got your girls. Ya've got a husband who can work for ya, but mine—he fell down again this past week. He's had another spell, and I was that scared to death—I didn't know what to do. And after he's had one of them fits, he's laid up for at least a week.

MOTHER BAUMERT Mine ain't no better. He's ready to collapse, too. He's got trouble with his chest and his back. And there ain't a single pfennig in the house either. If he don't bring some money home today, I don't know what we're goin' to do either.

EMMA That's so, Mother Heinrich. We're so bad off, Father had to take little Ami with him . . . we had to have him butchered so we can get something real in our stomachs again.

MRS. HEINRICH Ain't ya even got a handful of flour left over?

MOTHER BAUMERT Not even that much, Mother Heinrich; there ain't a pinch of salt left in the house.

MRS. HEINRICH Well, then I don't know what to do! (*Gets up, stands brooding*) I really don't know what to do! (*Crying out in anger and panic*) I'd be satisfied if it was nothin' but pig swill!—but I just can't go home empty-handed again. That just won't do. God forgive me. I don't know nothin' else to do. (*She limps out quickly, stepping only on the heel of her left foot*)

MOTHER BAUMERT (*Calls after her, warning*) Mother Heinrich, don't ya go an' do nothin' foolish.

BERTHA She won't do no harm to herself. Don't ya worry.

EMMA She always acts like that. (*She sits at the loom again and weaves for a few seconds*)

(AUGUST *enters with a candle, lighting the way for his father,* OLD BAUMERT, *who drags in a bundle of yarn*)

MOTHER BAUMERT My God, man, where in the world have ya been so long?

OLD BAUMERT Ya don't have to snap at me like that, right away. Just let me catch my breath first. Better look an' see who's come in with me.

MORITZ JAEGER (*Enters, stooping, through the door. He is a well-built, average-sized, red-cheeked soldier. His Hussar's cap sits jauntily on the side of his head; he wears good clothes and shoes and a clean shirt without a collar. He stands erect and gives a military salute. In a hearty voice*) Good evening, Auntie Baumert.

MOTHER BAUMERT Well, well, now! So you've come home again? And ya didn't forget us? Why, set down. Come here, set down.

EMMA (*With her skirt cleans off a wooden stool and shoves it toward* JAEGER) Good evenin', Moritz! Did ya come back to have another look at how poor folks is living?

JAEGER Well, now, say, Emma! I never really could believe it! Why, you've got a boy who'll soon be big enough to be a soldier. Where did ya get him?

BERTHA (*Takes the small amount of food that her father brought in, puts the meat in a pan, and shoves it in the oven while* AUGUST *builds a fire*) Ya know the Weaver Finger, don't ya?

MOTHER BAUMERT He used to live here in the cottage with us. He would have married her, but his lungs was almost completely gone then. I warned the girl often enough. But would she listen to me? Now, he's dead and gone and forgotten a long time and she'll have to see how she can support the boy. But now, you tell me, Moritz, how's things been goin' with you?

OLD BAUMERT You be quiet, Mother, can't ya see he's had plenty to eat; he's laughin' at all of us; he's got clothes like a prince and a silver pocket watch, and on top of all that, ten silver thalers in cash.

JAEGER (*Stands with his legs apart, showing off, a boastful smile on his face*) I can't complain. I didn't have a bad time in the army.

OLD BAUMERT He was an orderly to a captain. Just listen to him—he talks like elegant folks.

JAEGER I've got so used to fine talk that I can't help it.

MOTHER BAUMERT No, no, well, I never! Such a good-for-nothin' as you was, and comin' into such money. You never was good for nothin' much; ya couldn't unwind two spools in a row. But you was always off and away, settin' wrenboxes and robin snares. You'd rather do that. Well, ain't that the truth?

JAEGER It's true, Auntie Baumert. And I didn't catch just robins, I caught swallows, too.

EMMA No matter how often we used to say swallows was poison.

JAEGER It was all the same to me. But how have all of you been getting along, Auntie Baumert?

MOTHER BAUMERT O dear Lord Jesus, it's been awful hard these last four years. I've been havin' bad pains. Just look at my fingers. I really don't know if it's the rheumatiz or what. I'm in such misery! I can hardly move a muscle. Nobody knows the kind of pain I have to put up with.

OLD BAUMERT She really has it bad now. She won't be with us long.

BERTHA In the mornin' we got to dress her, in the evenin' we got to undress her. We got to feed her like a little baby.

MOTHER BAUMERT (*Continuing in a complaining, tearful voice*) I got to be waited on, hand and foot. I ain't just sick. I'm also a burden. How often I've prayed to the good Lord if he'd only call me away. O Lord, O Lord, my life's too hard, it really is. I don't know . . . people might think . . . but I've been used to working hard from the time I was a child. I've always been able to do my share and now, all at once —(*She tries, in vain, to get up*)—I just can't do nothin', no more! I've got a good husband and good children, but if I've got to sit by and see. . . . See how those girls look! They ain't got hardly no blood in 'em. They got as much color as a sheet. They keep workin' away at the treadle if they get anything for it or not. What kind of a life is that? They ain't been away from the treadle all year long. They ain't even earned enough so they could buy just a few clothes so they could be seen in public, or could step into church and get some comfort. They look like skeletons, they do, young girls of fifteen and twenty.

BERTHA (*At the stove*) It's smokin' again.

OLD BAUMERT Yeah, just look at that smoke. Do ya think something can be done about it? It'll damn soon collapse, that stove. We'll have to let it collapse, and we'll just have to swallow the soot. All of us cough, one worse than the other. Anyone as coughs, coughs, and if it chokes us, and if our lungs are coughed up with it, nobody cares a bit.

JAEGER Why, that's Ansorge's business, he has to fix it, doesn't he?

BERTHA A lot he cares. He does enough complainin'.

MOTHER BAUMERT He thinks we're takin' up too much room, as it is.

OLD BAUMERT And if we make a fuss, out we go. He ain't seen a bit of rent from us for almost half a year.

MOTHER BAUMERT A man like that livin' alone could at least be civil.

OLD BAUMERT He ain't got nothin' neither, Mother. Things is hard enough with him, too, even if he don't make a fuss about his troubles.

MOTHER BAUMERT He's still got his house.

OLD BAUMERT Oh, no, Mother, what are ya talkin' about? There ain't hardly a stick of wood in this house he can call his own.

JAEGER (*Has sat down. He takes a short pipe with a decorative tassel out of one coat pocket and a flask of whiskey out of the other*) This can't go on much longer. I'm amazed at how things are with you people around here. Why, dogs in the city live better than you live.

OLD BAUMERT (*Eagerly*) That's the truth, ain't it? You know it, too? And if ya complain, they tell ya it's just hard times.

ANSORGE (*Enters with an earthen bowl full of soup in one hand, a half-finished basket in the other*) Welcome home, Moritz! So you're here again?

JAEGER Thank you, Father Ansorge.

ANSORGE (*Shoving his bowl into the oven*) Say, if you don't look like a count!

OLD BAUMERT Show him your fine watch. He's brought back a new suit, too, and ten silver thalers in cash.

ANSORGE (*Shaking his head*) Well, well! Well, well!

EMMA (*Putting the potato peelings into a little sack*) I'll take the peelin's over now. Maybe it'll be enough for a little skimmed milk. (*She goes out*)

JAEGER (*While all pay close and eager attention to him*) Well, now, just think how often you've made it hot as hell for me. They'll teach you manners, Moritz, you always said, just you wait, when they take you into the army. Well, now you see, it's gone pretty well with me. In half a year, I had my stripes. You have to be willing, that's the main thing. I polished the sergeant's boots; I curried his horse, I brought him his beer. I was as quick as a weasel. And I was always on my toes; damn it, my gear was always clean and sparkling. I was the first one in the stable, the first one at roll call, the first one in the saddle; and when it came to the attack—forward! Hell and damnation! I was as keen as a hunting dog. I always said to myself, nobody'll help you here, you can't get out of this job; and I'd pull myself together and do it; and then, finally, the captain said about me, in front of the whole squadron: That's the way a Hussar ought to be. (*Silence. He lights his pipe*)

ANSORGE (*Shaking his head*) My, and such luck you had! Well, well! Well, well! (*He sits down on the floor, with the willow switches beside him. Holding the basket between his legs, he continues mending it*)

OLD BAUMERT Let's just hope that ya brought us some of your good luck along with ya. Now maybe we could have a drink with ya, huh?

JAEGER Why, sure, Father Baumert, and when this is gone, there'll be more. (*He throws a coin down on the table*)

ANSORGE (*With foolish, grinning amazement*) O Lord, such goin's on . . . over there, there's a roast sizzlin' and here's a quart of whiskey—(*He drinks from the bottle*)—to your health, Moritz. Well, well! Well, well! (*From now on, the whiskey bottle is passed around*)

OLD BAUMERT If we could only have a little roast on holidays, instead of not seein' no meat at all, year in and year out. This way, ya've got to wait till a little dog crosses your path like this one did four weeks ago. And that don't happen often these days.

ANSORGE Did ya have Ami killed?

OLD BAUMERT He would've starved to death. . . .

ANSORGE Well, well! Well, well!

MOTHER BAUMERT And he was such a nice, friendly little dog.

JAEGER Are you still so eager 'round here for roast dog?

OLD BAUMERT O Lord, Lord, if we could only get our fill of it.

MOTHER BAUMERT Yes, a piece of meat like that is sure rare around here.

OLD BAUMERT Ain't ya got no appetite for such things no more? Well, just stay here with us, Moritz, and ya'll soon get it back.

ANSORGE (*Sniffing*) Well, well! Well, well! That's something that tastes good, and it sure gives off a nice smell.

OLD BAUMERT (*Sniffing*) The real thing, ya might say.

ANSORGE Now tell us what you think, Moritz. You know how things go, out there in the world. Will things ever be different here with us weavers, or what?

JAEGER I should hope so.

ANSORGE We can't live and we can't die up here. Things is really bad with us, believe me. We fight to the last, but in the end we have to give in. The wolf is always at the door. In the old days, when I could still work at the looms, I could half-way get along, in spite of hunger and hardship. It's been a long time since I've been able to get some real work. I can hardly make a livin' weavin' baskets. I work till late into the night and when I fall worn out into bed, I've slaved for just a few pfennigs. You got a' education, now you tell me—can anyone really make out in such hard times? I got to lay out three thalers for taxes on the house, one thaler for land taxes, three thalers for interest. I can figure on makin' fourteen thalers. That leaves me seven thalers to live on all year. Out of that, I have to buy food, firewood, clothes, shoes, and patches and thread for mendin', and ya have to have a place to live, and goodness knows what else. Is it any wonder a man can't pay the interest?

OLD BAUMERT Somebody sure ought to go to Berlin and explain to the King how things is with us.

JAEGER That won't do much good, either, Father Baumert. There's already been plenty said about it in the newspapers. But the rich, they turn and twist the whole thing so . . . they out-devil the very best Christians.

OLD BAUMERT (*Shaking his head*) To think that in Berlin they ain't got no more sense than that.

ANSORGE Tell me, Moritz, do you think that can really be? Ain't there a law against it? When I go and pinch and scrape and work my fingers to the bone weaving baskets and still can't pay the interest, can the farmer take my cottage away from me? There ain't a farmer who don't want his money. I just don't know what's to become of me if I've got to get out of my cottage. . . . (*Speaking with a choked voice, through tears*) Here I was born, here my father sat at his loom, for more than forty years. How often he said to Mother: Mother, he said, when my time comes, you hold on to the cottage. This cottage I've worked for, he told her. Here, every single nail stands for a night's work, every board, a year's dry bread. Ya'd really think. . . .

JAEGER They'll take your last pfennig, they're capable of it.

ANSORGE Well, well! Well, well! But if it comes to that, I'd rather they carried me out than have to walk out in my old age. Dyin' ain't nothin'! My father was glad enough to die—only at the end, the very end, he was a bit scared. But when I crawled into the bed with him, he quieted down again. When ya think about it, at the time I was a boy of thirteen. I was tired, and I fell asleep by the sick man. I didn't know no better —and when I woke up, he was stone cold.

MOTHER BAUMERT (*After a pause*) Reach into the stove, Bertha, and hand Ansorge his soup.

BERTHA Here it is, Father Ansorge.

ANSORGE (*Weeping, while he eats*) Well, well! Well, well!

(OLD BAUMERT *has begun to eat meat out of the pan*)

MOTHER BAUMERT Why, Father—Father, you wait. Let Bertha set it out on the table, proper.

OLD BAUMERT (*Chewing*) It was two years ago that I took the sacrament last. I sold my Sunday suit right afterward. We bought a little piece of pork with the money. I ain't had no meat to eat since then till this very evenin'.

JAEGER We don't need meat; the manufacturers eat it for us. They wade around in fat way up to here. If anybody doesn't believe that, he only needs to go down to Bielau or Peterswaldau. They'd be amazed—one manufacturer's mansion right after the other—one palace right after the other. With plate glass windows and little towers and fine iron fences. No, no, that doesn't look anything like hard times. There's plenty there for roasts and pastries, for carriages and coaches, for governesses, and who knows what all. They're so puffed up they don't really know what to do with all their high and mighty riches.

ANSORGE In the old days, it was all different. In those days the manufacturers gave the weavers enough to get along on. Today, they squander it all themselves. I say that's because them people in high places don't believe in God no more, or in the devil, neither. They don't know nothin' about commandments and punishment. So they steal our last bite of bread, and weaken and undermine us wherever they can. Them people are the ones that's causin' all the trouble. If our manufacturers was good men, there wouldn't be no hard times for us.

JAEGER You listen here, and I'll read you something nice. (*He takes a few sheets of paper from his pocket*) Come on, August, run to the tavern and get another bottle. Why, August, you're always laughing.

MOTHER BAUMERT I don't know what's the matter with the boy, he's always happy. No matter what happens, he laughs till his sides are ready to split. Now, quick! (AUGUST *goes out with the empty whiskey flask*) Huh, Father, you know what tastes good, don't ya?

OLD BAUMERT (*Chewing, his spirits rising from the food and the whiskey*) Moritz, you're our man. You can read and write. You know how things is with the weavers. You have a heart for us poor weaver folk. You ought to take up our cause around here.

JAEGER If that's all. That'd be fine with me. I'd be glad to give those devils of manufacturers something to think about. I wouldn't mind a bit. I'm an easy-going fellow, but when I once get my dander up and get mad, I'd take Dreissiger in one hand and Dittrich in the other and I'd knock their heads together so hard sparks would shoot out of their eyes. If we could manage to stick together, we could start such an uproar against the manufacturers. . . . We wouldn't need the King for that, or the government, either; we could simply say, we want this and that, and we do not want this or that, and they'd soon whistle a different tune. If they once see we've got spunk, they'd soon pull in their horns. I know their kind! They're cowardly bastards.

MOTHER BAUMERT And that's really the truth. I certainly ain't bad. I was always one to say, there has to be rich people, too. But when it comes to this. . . .

JAEGER For my part, the devil can take them all. That's what the whole bunch deserves.

BERTHA Where's father? (OLD BAUMERT *has quietly left*)

MOTHER BAUMERT I don't know where he could've gone.

BERTHA Could it be he ain't used to meat no more?

MOTHER BAUMERT (*Beside herself, crying*) Now, ya see, now ya see! He can't even keep it down. He's had to throw it up, all that nice little bit of good food.

OLD BAUMERT (*Re-enters, crying with rage*) No, no! It'll soon be all over with me. I'm too far gone. Ya finally got ahold of something good, and ya can't even keep it down. (*He sits down on the stove bench, weeping*)

JAEGER (*In a sudden fanatic outburst*) And, at the same time, there are people, judges, not far from here—pot-bellies—who haven't a thing to do all year long except idle away their time. And they'll say the weavers could get along fine, if only they weren't so lazy.

ANSORGE They ain't men, they're monsters.

JAEGER Never mind, he's got what's coming to him. Baecker and I, we've given him a piece of our mind, and before we left, we sang "Bloody Justice."

ANSORGE O Lord, O Lord, is that the song?

JAEGER Yes, yes, and I have it here.

ANSORGE I think it's called "Dreissiger's Song," ain't it?

JAEGER I'll read it to you.

MOTHER BAUMERT Who made up the song?

JAEGER That, nobody knows. Now listen.

(*He reads, spelling it out like a schoolboy, accenting it badly, but with unmistakably strong feeling. Despair, pain, courage, hate, thirst for revenge—are all expressed*)

JAEGER

Here a bloody justice thrives
More terrible than lynching.
Here sentence isn't even passed
To quickly end a poor man's life.

Men are slowly tortured here,
Here is the torture chamber,
Here every heavy sigh that's heard
Bears witness to man's misery.

OLD BAUMERT (*Is deeply moved by the words of the song. He frequently has difficulty in resisting the temptation to interrupt* JAEGER. *Now he can no longer contain himself; stammering amid laughter and tears, to his wife*) "Here is the torture chamber." Whoever wrote that, Mother, spoke the truth. You can bear witness to that . . . how does it go? "Here every sigh that's heard. . . ." What's the rest? . . . "bear witness . . ."

JAEGER "Bears witness to man's misery."

OLD BAUMERT Ya know, standin' or sittin', we sigh with misery day after day.

(ANSORGE *has stopped working, his body bent over in deep emotion.* MOTHER BAUMERT *and* BERTHA *are continuously wiping their eyes*)

JAEGER (*Continues reading*)

The Dreissigers are hangmen all,
Their servants are the henchmen
All of them oppressing us
And never showing mercy.

You scoundrels all, you devil's brood

OLD BAUMERT (*Trembling with rage, stamps the floor*) Yes, devil's brood!!!

JAEGER (*Reads*)

You demons from the pit of hell
Who steal the poor man's house and home
A curse will be your payment.

ANSORGE Well, well, and that deserves a curse.

OLD BAUMERT (*Doubling his fist, threatening*) "Who steal the poor man's house and home . . . !"

JAEGER (*Reads*)

Begging, pleading doesn't help,
In vain is all complaining,
"If you don't like it you can go,
And starve until you're dead."

OLD BAUMERT What does it say? "In vain is all complaining"? Every word, every single word. . . . It's all as true as the Bible. "Begging, pleading doesn't help."

ANSORGE Well, well! Well, well! Then nothin' will help.

JAEGER (*Reads*)

Now think about the misery
And pain of these poor wretches
Without a bite of bread at home
Are they not to be pitied?

Pitied! Ha! Such human feeling
Is unknown to you savages.
Your goal is known to everyone,
To bleed us poor men dry.

OLD BAUMERT (*Springs up, in mad frenzy*) "Bleed us poor men dry." That's right, bleed a poor man dry. Here I stand, Robert Baumert, master weaver from Kaschbach, who can step up and say . . . I've been a good man all my life, and now look at me. What good's it done me? How do I look? What have they made of me? "Men are slowly tortured here." (*He stretches out his arms*) Here, feel these, nothin' but skin and bones. "You scoundrels all, you devil's brood!!" (*He collapses onto a chair, weeping with anger and despair*)

ANSORGE (*Flings the basket into the corner, gets up, his entire body trembling with rage, stammers*) There must be a change, I tell ya, here and now. We won't stand for it no more! We won't stand for it no more, come what may.

*Curtain*

# Act Three

*The tap room in the principal tavern in Peterswaldau. It is a large room, the raftered ceiling of which is supported at the center by a wooden pillar, around which there is a table. To the right of the pillar—one of its jambs hidden by the pillar—is a door in the back wall leading to another large room in which barrels and brewing utensils can be seen. In the corner to the right of the door is the bar—a high wooden counter with shelves for mugs, glasses, and the like; behind the bar is a cupboard with rows of liquor bottles; between the counter and the liquor cabinet there is a narrow space for the bartender. In front of the bar there is a table covered with a brightly colored cloth. A decorative lamp hangs above the table, around which there are a number of cane-chairs. Not far off in the right wall, a door leads to a room used for special occasions. Nearer the front, to the right, an old grandfather's clock is ticking. To the left of the entrance, against the rear wall, stands a table with bottles and glasses, and beyond it, in the corner, a large tile stove. There are three small windows in the left wall, under them a bench. In front of each window there is a large wooden table with its narrow end toward the wall. On the broad side of the tables are benches with backs and at the other narrow end, a single wooden chair. The walls are painted blue and are hung with placards, posters, and oil prints, among them the portrait of the King of Prussia, William IV.*

*Innkeeper* WELZEL, *a good-natured giant of around fifty, is drawing beer into a glass from a barrel behind the counter.* MRS. WELZEL *is ironing at the stove. She is a dignified-looking woman, neatly dressed, not quite thirty-five years old.* ANNA WELZEL, *a well-dressed, pretty girl of seventeen with magnificent reddish-blonde hair, sits behind the table, embroidering. For a moment she looks up from her work and listens to the sounds of children's voices singing a funeral hymn, off in the distance.* WIEGAND, *the carpenter, in his work clothes, sits at the same table with a glass of Bavarian beer in front of him. He gives the appearance of being the sort of man who knows what is needed to get ahead in the world: cunning, speed, and ruthless determination.* A TRAVELING SALESMAN *sits at the pillar table, busily devouring a chopped steak. He is of medium height, well-fed, rather puffy, disposed to heartiness, lively and impudent. He is dressed in the latest fashion. His baggage, consisting of traveling bag, sample case, umbrella, overcoat, and steamer rug—lie on chairs beside him.*

WELZEL (*Carrying a glass of beer to the* SALESMAN, *aside to* WIEGAND) The devil's loose in Peterswaldau today.

WIEGAND (*In a sharp, trumpeting voice*) Well, of course, it's delivery day up at Dreissiger's.

MRS. WELZEL Yes, but they weren't always so noisy.

WIEGAND Well, it might be on account of the two hundred additional weavers that Dreissiger's gettin' ready to take on.

MRS. WELZEL (*At her ironing*) Yes, yes, that's it. If he wanted two hundred, probably six hundred will have showed up. We've got more'n enough of that sort.

WIEGAND Lord, yes, there's plenty of them. And no matter how hard it goes with them, they don't die out. They bring more children into the world than we can ever use. (*For a moment, the hymn can be more clearly heard*) And to add to it, there's a funeral today, too. Weaver Fabich died.

WELZEL It took him long enough. He's been goin' around for years lookin' like a ghost.

WIEGAND I tell ya, Welzel, never in all my life have I glued together such a tiny, shabby coffin. It was such a measly little corpse, it didn't even weigh ninety pounds.

SALESMAN (*Chewing*) I really don't understand . . . wherever you look, in all the newspapers, you read the most horrible stories about conditions among the weavers, and you get the impression that all the people here are half-starved. And then you see such a funeral! Just as I came into the village, there were brass bands, schoolteachers, children, the Pastor, and a whole string of people; my God, you'd think the Emperor of China was being buried. If these people can pay for that. . . ! (*He drinks his beer. Then he puts the glass down and suddenly speaks in a frivolous tone*) Isn't that so, Miss? Don't you agree with me?

(ANNA *smiles, embarrassed, and continues busily with her embroidery*)

SALESMAN Those must be slippers for Papa.

WELZEL Oh, I don't like to wear them things.

SALESMAN Just listen to that! I'd give half my fortune if those slippers were for me.

MRS. WELZEL He just don't appreciate such things.

WIEGAND (*After he has coughed several times and moved his chair about, as if he wanted to speak*) The gentleman has expressed himself mighty well about the funeral. Now tell us, young lady, isn't that just a small funeral?

SALESMAN Yes, I must say. . . . That must cost a tremendous amount of money. Where do these people get the money for it?

WIEGAND You'll forgive me for sayin' it, sir, there is so much folly among the poorer classes hereabouts. If you don't mind my sayin' so, they have such exaggerated ideas of the dutiful respect and the obligations that's due the deceased and the blessed dead. And when it's a matter of deceased parents, they are so superstitious that the descendants and the next of kin scrape together their last penny. And what the children can't raise, they borrow from the nearest money lender. And then they're in debts up to their necks; they'll be owing His Reverence the Pastor, the sexton, and everybody else in the neighborhood. And drinks and victuals and all the other necessary things. Oh yes, I approve of respectful duty on the part of children toward their parents, but not so that the mourners are burdened down the rest of their lives by such obligations.

SALESMAN I beg your pardon, but I should think the Pastor would talk them out of it.

WIEGAND Beggin' your pardon, sir, but here I would like to interpose that every little congregation has its ecclesiastical house of worship and must support its reverend pastor. The high clergy get a wonderful revenue and profit from such a big funeral. The more elaborate such a funeral can be arranged, the more profitable is the offertory that flows from it. Whoever knows the conditions of the workers hereabouts can, with unauthoritative certainty, affirm that the pastors only with reluctance tolerate small and quiet funerals.

HORNIG (*Enters. A small, bow-legged old man with a strap over his shoulders and chest. He is a rag picker*) Good mornin'. I'd like a drink. Well, young lady, any rags? Miss Anna, in my cart I've got beautiful hair ribbons, lingerie, ribbons, garters, pins and hairpins, hooks and eyes. I'll give them all to ya for a few rags. (*Changing his tone*) Then, out of rags, they'll make fine white paper, and your sweetheart'll write ya a lovely letter on it.

ANNA Oh no, thank you, I don't want a sweetheart.

MRS. WELZEL (*Puts a hot bolt in the iron*) That's the way the girl is. She don't want to think of gettin' married.

SALESMAN (*Jumps up, apparently surprised and pleased, steps up to the table, and holds out his hand to* ANNA) That's sensible, Miss. You're just like me. O.K., let's shake on it! We'll both stay single.

ANNA (*Blushing, gives him her hand*) But surely you are married?

SALESMAN God forbid, I just make believe I am. You think, perhaps, because I wear this ring? I just put it on my finger to prevent people from taking unfair advantage of my charming personality. Of you, I'm not afraid. (*He puts the ring in his pocket*) Seriously, Miss, tell me, don't you ever want to get just the least bit married?

ANNA (*Shaking her head*) And why should I?

MRS. WELZEL She'll stay single unless something very special turns up.

SALESMAN Well, why not? One wealthy Silesian businessman married his mother's maid, and that rich manufacturer, Dreissiger, took an innkeeper's daughter, too. She isn't half as pretty as you, Miss, and now she rides in a carriage with liveried servants. Why not, indeed? (*He walks around, stretching his legs*) I'll have a cup of coffee.

(ANSORGE *and* OLD BAUMERT *enter, each with a bundle, and quietly and humbly join* HORNIG *at the front table to the left*)

WELZEL Welcome, Father Ansorge. Is it you we're seein' again?

HORNIG Did ya finally crawl out of your smoky nest?

ANSORGE (*Awkwardly and visibly embarrassed*) I went and got myself another web.

OLD BAUMERT He's ready to work for 10 groschen.

ANSORGE I never would've done it, but there's been an end to my basket weavin'.

WIEGAND It's always better than nothin'. Ya know he's doin' it so ya'll have work. I'm very well acquainted with Dreissiger. A week ago I took out the storm windows for him. We were talkin' about it. He just does it out of pity.

ANSORGE Well, well—well, well.

WELZEL (*Setting a glass of whiskey in front of each of the weavers*) Your health! Now tell me, Ansorge, how long has it been since ya stopped shavin'? The gentleman would like to know.

SALESMAN (*Calls across*) Now, Mr. Welzel, you know I didn't say that. I just noticed the master weaver because of his venerable appearance. One doesn't often run across such a powerful figure.

ANSORGE (*Scratches his head, embarrassed*) Well, well —well, well.

SALESMAN Such extremely powerful, primitive men are seldom seen these days. We are so softened by civilization . . . but I find I still get pleasure out of such natural, unspoiled strength. What bushy eyebrows! Such a heavy beard. . . .

HORNIG Well, look here, now I'll tell ya, sir . . . the people hereabouts are too poor to go to the barber, and they haven't been able to afford a razor in many a day. What grows, grows. They haven't anything to spend on the outer man.

SALESMAN But I ask you, my good man, where would I. . . . (*Softly, to the tavern keeper*) Would it be proper to offer the hairy one a glass of beer?

WELZEL God forbid. He'll take nothin'. He's got queer notions.

SALESMAN Well, then I won't. With your permission, Miss? (*He takes a seat at the table with her*) I can assure you, from the time I came in, I've been so struck by your hair, such luster, such softness, such a mass of it! (*Delighted, he kisses his finger tips*) And what color . . . like ripe wheat. What a furor you would cause if you came to Berlin with hair like that. *Parole d'honneur,*[1] with such hair you could be presented at Court. (*Leaning back, looking at her hair*) Exquisite, really exquisite.

WIEGAND It's on account of her hair that she's got such a pretty nickname.

SALESMAN What do they call her?

ANNA (*Keeps on laughing to herself*) Oh, don't you listen to them.

HORNIG They call you Red Fox, don't they?

WELZEL Now stop that! Stop turnin' the girl's head altogether. They've already put enough high and mighty ideas in her head. Today she wants a count, tomorrow it'll have to be a prince.

MRS. WELZEL Don't ya run the girl down, man. It's no crime for a person to want to get ahead. Not everybody thinks the way you do. That wouldn't be good, either. Then nobody'd get ahead, then everybody'd always stay in the same old place. If Dreissiger's grandfather had thought the way you do, he'd still be a poor weaver. Now they're rich as can be. Old Tromtra, too, was no more than a poor weaver, now he owns twelve big estates and on top of that, he's got a title.

WIEGAND You must admit, Welzel, on that score, your wife's right. I can vouch for that. If I'd thought like you, would I have seven journeymen today?

HORNIG You sure know how to bide your time, we'll have to give ya credit for that. Even before the weaver's off his feet, you're already gettin' his coffin ready.

WIEGAND You've got to tend to business if you want to get ahead.

HORNIG Yes, you tend to yours, all right. You know better than the doctor does, when a weaver's child is goin' to die.

WIEGAND (*No longer smiling, suddenly furious*) And you know better than the police does where the thieves sit among the weavers, the ones who hold out a few bobbins every week. Ya come after rags and ya get a bobbin of yarn, too, if there's a chance.

HORNIG And your livin' lays in the graveyard. The more that go to rest on your wood shavings, the better it is for you. When ya look at all the children's graves, ya pat your belly and ya say, this year's been a good one again; the little rascals dropped like June bugs from the trees. So I can afford a bottle of whiskey again this week.

WIEGAND Anyhow, at least I don't trade in stolen goods.

HORNIG At the most, you bill some rich cotton manufacturer twice, or you take a few extra boards from Dreissiger's barn if the moon ain't shinin'.

WIEGAND (*Turning his back on* HORNIG) Oh, go on talkin' to anyone you please, but leave me alone. (*Suddenly*) Hornig, the liar!

HORNIG Coffin-maker!

WIEGAND (*To the others*) He knows how to bewitch cattle.

HORNIG Look out, let me tell ya, or I'll put the sign on you.

(WIEGAND *turns pale*)

MRS. WELZEL (*Had gone out, and now sets a cup of coffee down in front of the* SALESMAN) Would you perhaps rather have your coffee in the other room?

SALESMAN Whatever put that idea in your head? (*With a longing look at* ANNA) I'll stay here until I die.

(A YOUNG FORESTER *and a* FARMER *enter, the latter carrying a whip*)

FORESTER *and* FARMER Good morning! (*They stop at the bar*)

FARMER We'll have two ginger beers.

WELZEL Welcome to both of you! (*He pours the drinks; they both take their glasses, touch them to each other, take a sip, and place them back on the bar*)

SALESMAN Well, Forester, have you had a long trip?

FORESTER Pretty far. I've come from Steinseiffersdorf.

(FIRST *and* SECOND OLD WEAVERS *enter and sit down next to* ANSORGE, BAUMERT, *and* HORNIG)

SALESMAN Pardon me, sir, are you one of Count Hochheim's foresters?

[1] On my word of honor.

FORESTER No, I'm one of Count Kailsch's.

SALESMAN Oh, of course, of course—that's what I meant to say. It's most confusing here with all the counts and barons and other people of rank. You've got to have a good memory. What are you carrying the ax for?

FORESTER I took it away from some thieves I caught stealing wood.

OLD BAUMERT His Lordship is sure strict about a few sticks of firewood.

SALESMAN I beg your pardon, it would scarcely do if everybody were to take. . . .

OLD BAUMERT Beggin' your pardon, it's the same here as everywhere else with the big and the little thieves; there are those that carry on a wholesale lumber business and get rich from stolen wood, but if a poor weaver so much as. . . .

FIRST OLD WEAVER (*Interrupts* BAUMERT) We don't dare pick up a single twig, but the lords, they skin us alive. There's insurance money to pay, spinnin' money, payments in kind; then we have to run errands for nothin' and work on the estate, whether we want to or not.

ANSORGE And that's the truth: what the manufacturers leave us, the noblemen take away.

SECOND OLD WEAVER (*Has taken a seat at the next table*) I've said it to the gentleman hisself. Beggin' your pardon, sir, I says to him, I can't do so many days' work on the estate this year. I just can't do it! And why not? Forgive me, but the water has ruined everything. My little bit of ground's been all washed away. I've got to slave night and day if I'm to keep alive. Such a flood . . . I tell ya, I just stood there and wrung my hands. That good soil washed right down the hill and straight into my cottage; and that fine, expensive seed. . . ! Oh my Lord, I just howled into the wind. I cried for a week, till I couldn't see no more. . . . And after that I wore myself out pushin' eighty wheelbarrows of dirt up the hill.

FARMER (*Roughly*) You do set up an awful howl, I must say. We all have to put up with what Heaven sends us. And if it don't go good in other ways with ya, who's to blame but yourselves? When times was good, what did ya do then? Ya gambled and drank it all up, that's what ya did. If ya had put something aside at that time, ya'd have had something saved for now, and ya wouldn't have had to steal wood and yarn.

FIRST YOUNG WEAVER (*Standing with several friends in the other room, shouts through the door*) A farmer's always a farmer, even if he sleeps till nine every mornin'.

FIRST OLD WEAVER That's a fact; the farmer and the nobleman, they're two of a kind. If a weaver wants a place to live, the farmer says I'll give ya a little hole to live in. You pay me a nice rent, and help me bring in my hay and my grain, and if ya don't like it, ya'll see what happens. Every one of them's just like the next one.

OLD BAUMERT (*Fiercely*) We're just like an old apple that everybody takes a bite out of.

FARMER (*Irritated*) Oh, you starved wretches, what are you good for, anyway? Can ya handle a plow? Can ya even plow a straight furrow, or pitch fifteen shocks of oats onto a wagon? You're good for nothin' but loafin', and lyin' abed with your women. You're no good at all. You're no-account bums. No use at all.

(*He pays and leaves. The* FORESTER *follows him, laughing.* WELZEL, *the* CARPENTER, *and* MRS. WELZEL *laugh out loud, the* SALESMAN *chuckles. Then the laughter quiets down, and there is silence*)

HORNIG A farmer like that's just like a bull. As if I didn't know how bad things was around here. All the things ya get to see up here in the villages. Four and five people layin' naked on a single straw ticking.

SALESMAN (*In a gently, rebuking tone*) Permit me, my good man, to observe that there is a wide difference of opinion in regard to the distress in this region. If you can read. . . .

HORNIG Oh, I read everything in the papers as well as you do. No, no, I know these things from goin' around and mixin' with the people. When a man's lugged a pack around for forty years, he learns a thing or two. What happened at the Fullers? The children, they scratched around in the dung heap with the neighbors' geese. Those people died there—naked—on the cold stone floor. They had to eat stinkin' weaver's glue, they was so hungry. Hunger killed them off by the hundreds.

SALESMAN If you can read, you must be aware that the government has had a thorough investigation made and that. . . .

HORNIG We know all that. We know all that. The government sends a gentleman who before he sets out knows everything better than if he'd seen it himself. He walks around the village a little where the brook widens and where the best houses are. He won't dirty his good, shiny shoes goin' any farther. He thinks everything is probably just as beautiful everywhere else, and climbs into his carriage, and drives home again. And then he writes to Berlin that he saw no hardships at all. If he'd had a little bit of patience, though, and had climbed around in the village up to where the brook comes in and across it or, even better, off to the side where the little shacks are scattered, the old straw huts on the hills that are sometimes so black and broken-down they wouldn't be worth the match it'd take to set 'em afire, then he'd have made an altogether different report to Berlin. Those gentlemen from the government ought to have come to me, them that didn't want to believe that there was no hardships here. I would've showed them something, I would've opened their eyes to all the hunger-holes around here.

(*The singing of the "Weavers' Song" is heard outside*)

WELZEL They're singin' that devil's song again.

WIEGAND Yes, they're turnin' the whole village upside down.

MRS. WELZEL It's like there's something in the air.

(JAEGER *and* BAECKER, *arm in arm, at the head of a band of young weavers, noisily enter the other room, and then come into the bar*)

JAEGER Squadron halt! Dismount!

(*The new arrivals seat themselves at the various tables at which weavers are already sitting, and start conversations with them*)

HORNIG (*Calling to* BAECKER) Say, tell me, what's up that ya've got such a big crowd together?

BAECKER (*Significantly*) Maybe something's goin' to happen. Right, Moritz?

HORNIG You don't say! Don't do nothin' foolish.

BAECKER Blood's flowed already. Do ya want to see? (*He pushes back his sleeve, stretches out his arm and shows him bleeding tattoo marks on his upper arm. Many of the young weavers at the other tables do the same*)

BAECKER We were at Barber Schmidt's havin' ourselves tattooed.

HORNIG Well, now that's clear. No wonder there's so much noise in the streets, with such rascals tearin' around. . . !

JAEGER (*Showing off, in a loud voice*) Two quarts, right away, Welzel! I'll pay for it. Maybe you think I don't have the dough? Well, just you wait! If we wanted to, we could drink beer and lap up coffee till tomorrow morning as well as a traveling salesman. (*Laughter among the young weavers*)

SALESMAN (*With comic surprise*) Who or whom are you talking about—me?

(*The tavern keeper, his wife, their daughter,* WIEGAND, *and the* SALESMAN, *all laugh*)

JAEGER Always him who asks.

SALESMAN Allow me to say, young man, that things seem to be going right well with you.

JAEGER I can't complain, I'm a salesman for ready-made clothing. I go fifty-fifty with the manufacturers. The hungrier the weavers grow, the fatter I get. The greater their poverty, the fuller my cupboard.

BAECKER Well done. Your health, Moritz!

WELZEL (*Has brought the whiskey; on the way back to the bar, he stops and, in his usual phlegmatic and even manner, turns slowly to the weavers. Quietly and emphatically*) You let the gentleman alone. He ain't done nothin' to you.

YOUNG WEAVERS' VOICES We ain't done nothin' to him, either.

(MRS. WELZEL *has exchanged a few words with the* SALESMAN. *She takes the cup and the rest of the coffee into the next room. The* SALESMAN *follows her amidst the laughter of the weavers*)

YOUNG WEAVERS' VOICES (*Singing*) The Dreissigers are hangmen all, Their servants are the henchmen. . . .

WELZEL Sh, Sh! Sing that song wherever else ya want to, but I won't allow it here.

FIRST OLD WEAVER He's quite right. Stop that singin'.

BAECKER (*Shouts*) But we've got to march past Dreissiger's again. He's got to hear our song once more.

WIEGAND Don't go too far, or he might take it the wrong way.

(*Laughter and cries of "Ho-ho"*)

OLD WITTIG (*A gray-haired blacksmith, bareheaded, wearing a leather apron and wooden shoes, and covered with soot, as if he had just come from the smithy, enters and stands at the bar, waiting for a glass of brandy*) Let 'em make a little noise. Barkin' dogs don't bite.

OLD WEAVERS' VOICES Wittig, Wittig!

WITTIG Here he is. What do ya want?

OLD WEAVERS' VOICES Wittig is here—Wittig, Wittig!—Come here, Wittig, set with us!—Come over here, Wittig!

WITTIG I'm awful careful about settin' with such blockheads.

JAEGER Come on, have a drink on me.

WITTIG Oh, you keep your liquor. When I drink, I'll pay for my own.

(*He takes his glass of brandy and sits down at the table with* BAUMERT *and* ANSORGE. *He pats the latter on the belly*) What do the weavers eat nowadays? Sauerkraut and plenty of lice.

OLD BAUMERT (*Ecstatically*) But what if they wasn't to put up with it no more?

WITTIG (*With feigned surprise, staring stupidly at the weaver*) Well, well, well, Heinerle, tell me, is that really you? (*Laughs without restraint*) I laugh myself sick at you people. Old Baumert wants to start a rebellion. Now we're in for it: now the tailors'll start, too, then the baa-lambs'll be rising up, then the mice and the rats. Good Lord, what a time that'll be!

(*He holds his sides with laughter*)

OLD BAUMERT Look here, Wittig, I'm the same man I used to be. And I tell ya even now if things could be settled peaceable, it'd be better.

WITTIG Like hell it'll be settled peaceable. Where has anything like this ever been settled peaceable? Maybe things was settled peaceable in France? Maybe Robespierre patted the hands of the rich? There it was just "allay," go ahead! Always up to the guillotine! Let's go. It had to be "along songfong." Roast geese just don't fly into your mouth.

OLD BAUMERT If I could just halfway earn my livin'. . . .

FIRST OLD WEAVER We're fed up, up to here, Wittig.

SECOND OLD WEAVER We don't even want to go home, no more. . . . Whether we work or whether we lay down and sleep, we starve either way.

FIRST OLD WEAVER At home ya go completely crazy.

ANSORGE It's all the same to me now, no matter what happens.

OLD WEAVERS' VOICES (*With mounting excitement*) There's no peace left nowhere. . . . We ain't even got the spirit to work no more. . . . Up our way in Steinkunzendorf there's a man settin' by the brook all day long and washin' hisself, naked as God made him. . . . He's gone completely out of his head.

THIRD OLD WEAVER (*Rises, moved by the spirit, and begins to "speak with tongues," raising his finger threateningly*) Judgment Day is comin'! Don't join with the rich and the gentry. Judgment Day is comin'! Lord God of Sabaoth. . . .

(*Several laugh. He is pushed down into his chair*)

WELZEL All he has to do is drink just one glass of liquor and his head's in a whirl.

THIRD OLD WEAVER (*Continues*) Hearken, they don't believe in God nor hell nor heaven. They just mock at religion.

FIRST OLD WEAVER That's enough, now, that's enough.

BAECKER You let the man say his prayers. Many a man could take it to heart.

MANY VOICES (*In a tumult*) Let him talk—let him!

THIRD OLD WEAVER (*Raising his voice*) Hell has opened wide and its jaws are gaping open, wide open, crashing down all those who do harm to the poor and violence to the cause of the afflicted, saith the Lord.

(*Tumult. Suddenly reciting like a schoolboy*)

And then how strange it is.
If you will carefully observe
How they the linen weavers' work despise.

BAECKER But we're cotton weavers. (*Laughter*)

HORNIG The linen weavers are even worse off. They wander like ghosts around the mountains. Here you at least have the courage to rebel.

WITTIG Do ya think, maybe, that here the worst is over? That little bit of courage that they still have left in their bodies the manufacturers will knock right out of them.

BAECKER Why, he said that the weavers will get so they'll work for just a slice of bread and cheese. (*Tumult*)

VARIOUS OLD *and* YOUNG WEAVERS Who said that?

BAECKER That's what Dreissiger said about the weavers.

A YOUNG WEAVER That son of a bitch ought to be strung up.

JAEGER Listen to me, Wittig, you've always talked so much about the French Revolution. You always bragged so much. Now maybe the chance'll soon come for everybody to show how much of a man he is . . . whether he is a loud-mouth or a man of honor.

WITTIG (*Starting up in a rage*) Say one more word, boy! Did you ever hear the whistle of bullets? Did you ever stand at an outpost in enemy territory?

JAEGER Now don't get mad. You know we're all comrades. I didn't mean any harm.

WITTIG I don't give a rap for your comradeship. You puffed up fool!

(POLICEMAN KUTSCHE *enters*)

SEVERAL VOICES Sh! Sh! The Police!

(*There is a relatively long period of sh-ing before complete silence reigns*)

KUTSCHE (*Sits down by the center pillar amid the deep silence of all the others*) I'd like a shot of whiskey, please.

(*Again complete silence*)

WITTIG Well, Kutsche, you here to see that everything's all right with us?

KUTSCHE (*Not listening to* WITTIG) Good mornin', Mr. Wiegand.

WIEGAND (*Still in the corner of the bar*) Good mornin', Kutsche.

KUTSCHE How's business?

WIEGAND Fine, thanks for askin'.

BAECKER The Chief of Police is afraid we might spoil our stomachs on all the wages we get. (*Laughter*)

JAEGER Isn't that so, Welzel, we've all had pork roast and gravy and dumplings and sauerkraut, and now we're getting ready to drink our champagne. (*Laughter*)

WELZEL Everything's the other way 'round.

KUTSCHE And if ya did have champagne and roast, ya'd still not be satisfied. I don't have no champagne, neither, and I manage to get along.

BAECKER (*Referring to* KUTSCHE'S *nose*) He waters his red beet with brandy and beer. That's how it got so nice and ripe. (*Laughter*)

WITTIG A cop like him's got a hard life. Now, he's got to throw a starvin' little boy in jail for beggin', then he has to seduce a weaver's pretty daughter, then he has to get dead drunk and beat his wife so she goes runnin' to the neighbors for fear of her life. Ridin' about on his horse, lyin' in his featherbed . . . till nine, I tell ya, ain't that easy.

KUTSCHE Always a'talkin'! You'll talk yourself into a big mess one of these days. It's been known for a long time what sort of a fellow you are. Even as high as the judge they've known about your rebellious tongue for a long time. I know someone who'll bring his wife and children to the poorhouse with his drinkin' and hangin' around taverns, and hisself into jail. He'll agitate and agitate until he comes to a terrible end.

WITTIG (*Laughs bitterly*) Who know what's ahead? You might be right after all. (*Breaking out angrily*) But if it comes to that, then I'll know who I can thank, who has blabbed to the manufacturers and to the nobles, and reviled and slandered me so I don't get a lick of work no more. . . . Who set the farmers and the millers against me so that, for a whole week, I haven't had a single horse to shoe or a wheel to put a rim on. I know who that is. I once yanked the damned scoundrel off his horse because he was thrashing a poor little nitwit boy with a horsewhip for stealin' a few green pears. I tell ya, and ya know me, put me in jail, and ya'd better be makin' out your will at the same time. If I get the slightest warnin', I'll take whatever I can get my hands on, whether it's a horseshoe or a hammer, a wagon spoke or a bucket, and I'll go lookin' for ya, and if I have to pull ya out of bed, away from your woman, I'll do it and I'll cave your skull in, as sure as my name is Wittig.

(*He has jumped up and is about to attack* KUTSCHE)

OLD *and* YOUNG WEAVERS (*Holding him back*) Wittig, Wittig, don't lose your head.

KUTSCHE (*Has stood up involuntarily; his face is pale. During what follows he keeps moving backward. The nearer he gets to the door, the braver he becomes.*

*He speaks the last few words at the very threshold, and then immediately disappears)* What do ya want with me? I've got nothin' to do with you. I've got to talk to one of the weavers here. I've done nothin' to you and I've got no business with you. But I'm to tell you weavers this: the Chief of Police forbids ya to sing that song—"Dreissiger's Song," or whatever it's called. And if that singin' in the streets don't stop right away, he'll see to it that you get plenty of time and rest in jail. Then ya can sing on bread and water as long as ya like.

(*Leaves*)

WITTIG (*Shouts after him*) He ain't got no right to forbid us anything, and if we roar till the windows rattle and they can hear us way off in Reichenbach, and if we sing so the houses tumble down on all the manufacturers and all the policemen's helmets dance on their heads, it's nobody's business.

BAECKER (*In the meantime has stood up, and has given the signal for the singing to begin. He begins to sing, together with the others*)

Here a bloody justice thrives
More terrible than lynching
Here sentence isn't even passed
To quickly end a poor man's life.

(WELZEL *tries to quiet them, but no one listens to him.* WIEGAND *holds his hands over his ears and runs away. The weavers get up and, singing the following verses, march after* WITTIG *and* BAECKER, *who, by nods, gestures, have signaled for everyone to leave*)

Men are slowly tortured here,
Here is the torture chamber,
Here every heavy sigh that's heard
Bears witness to the misery.

(*Most of the weavers sing the following verse when they are in the street; only a few young fellows are still inside the taproom, paying for their drinks. At the end of the next verse the room is empty except for* WELZEL, *his wife, his daughter,* HORNIG, *and* OLD BAUMERT)

You scoundrels all, you devil's brood
You demons from the pit of hell
Who steal the poor man's house and home
A curse will be your payment.

WELZEL (*Calmly gathers up the glasses*) Why, they're completely out of their heads today.

(OLD BAUMERT *is about to leave*)

HORNIG Tell me, Baumert, what's goin' to happen?

OLD BAUMERT They'll be goin' to Dreissiger's to see if he'll add to their wages.

WELZEL Are you goin' to join up with such madness?

OLD BAUMERT Well, you see, Welzel, it ain't up to me. A young man sometimes may, and an old man must. (*A trifle embarrassed, leaves*)

HORNIG (*Rises*) It'll sure surprise me if things don't come to a bad end here.

WELZEL Who'd think the old fellows would completely lose their heads?

HORNIG Well, every man has his dream.

*Curtain*

# Act Four

*Peterswaldau—A living room in the house of the cotton manufacturer,* DREISSIGER. *It is luxuriously furnished in the cold style of the first half of the nineteenth century. The ceiling, stove, and doors are white; the wallpaper is a cold grayish blue, with straight lines and little flowers. The room is filled with red upholstered mahogany furniture, including chairs and cupboards, richly decorated and carved. The furniture is placed as follows: on the right, between two windows with cherry-red damask curtains, is a secretary with a drop leaf that folds down to form a desk; directly opposite it, the sofa, with an iron safe nearby; in front of the sofa a table, armchairs, and straight chairs; against the back wall, a gun case. Pictures reflecting poor taste hang in gilt frames on the walls. Above the sofa hangs a mirror with a heavily gilded rococo frame. A door on the left leads to the vestibule; an open double door in the back wall leads into the drawing room, also overloaded with uncomfortable, showy furnishings. In the drawing room,* MRS. DREISSIGER *and* MRS. KITTELHAUS, *the pastor's wife, can be seen looking at pictures while* PASTOR KITTELHAUS *converses with the tutor,* WEINHOLD, *a student of theology.*

KITTELHAUS (*A small, friendly man, enters the front room, smoking and chatting amiably with the tutor, who is also smoking.* KITTELHAUS *looks around and, when he sees no one is in the room, shakes his head in amazement*) Of course it is not at all surprising, Weinhold; you are young. At your age, we old fellows had—I won't say the same views—but yet, similar ones. Similar ones, at any rate. And there is, after all, something wonderful about youth—and all its beautiful ideals. Unfortunately, however, they are fleeting—fleeting as April sunshine. Just wait till you are my age. When once a man has said his say to the people from the pulpit for thirty years, fifty-two times a year, not counting holidays—then he, of necessity, becomes quieter. Think of me, Weinhold, when that time comes for you.

WEINHOLD (*Nineteen years old, pale, emaciated, tall and thin, with long, straight, blond hair. He is very restless and nervous in his movements*) With all respect, sir . . . I really don't know . . . there certainly is a great difference in temperaments.

KITTELHAUS My dear Weinhold, you may be ever so restless a soul—(*In a tone of reproof*) and that you are—you may be ever so violent—and rudely attack existing conditions, but that will subside. Yes, yes, I certainly do admit that we have colleagues who, though rather advanced in years, still play rather childish and foolish tricks. One preaches against drinking and founds temperance societies; another writes appeals which, undeniably, are most touching to read. But what does he accomplish with it? The distress among the weavers, where it exists, is not relieved thereby. And yet the peace of society is undermined by it. No, no, in such a case one might almost say, cobbler, stick to your last! A keeper of souls should not concern himself with bellies. Preach the pure word of God and, for the rest, let Him take care who provides shelter and food for the birds and sees that the lily in the field does not perish. . . . But now I would really like to know where our worthy host went so suddenly.

MRS. DREISSIGER (*Comes into the front room with the Pastor's wife. She is a pretty woman, thirty years old, a robust, healthy type. A certain discrepancy is noticeable between her manner of speaking or moving and her elegant attire*) You're quite right, Pastor. Wilhelm's always that way. When something strikes him, he runs off and leaves me alone. I've talked to him about it plenty, but you can say what you will, that's the way it is.

KITTELHAUS That's the way with businessmen, Madam.

WEINHOLD If I'm not mistaken, something's been happening downstairs.

DREISSIGER (*Enters, out of breath and excited*) Well, Rosa, has the coffee been served?

MRS. DREISSIGER (*Pouting*) Oh, why do you always have to run away?

DREISSIGER (*Lightly*) Oh, what do you know about it?

KITTELHAUS I beg your pardon! Have you had trouble, Mr. Dreissiger?

DREISSIGER God knows, that I have every single day, my dear Pastor. I'm used to that. Well, Rosa? I guess you're taking care of it?

(MRS. DREISSIGER *in a bad temper pulls violently several times at the broad, embroidered bell pull*)

DREISSIGER Just now—(*After walking up and down a few times*)—Mr. Weinhold, I would have liked you to have been there. You would have had an experience. At any rate . . . come, let's have a game of whist.

KITTELHAUS Yes, yes, by all means. Shake the dust and trouble of the day from your shoulders, and come and be one of us.

DREISSIGER (*Has stepped to the window, pushes the drapery aside, and looks out. Involuntarily*) Rabble! —come here, Rosa! (*She comes*) Tell me . . . that tall, red-headed fellow there. . . .

KITTELHAUS That is the one they call Red Baecker.

DREISSIGER Tell me, is he by any chance the one who insulted you, two days ago? You know, what you told me, when Johann helped you into the carriage.

MRS. DREISSIGER (*Makes a wry face, drawls*) I don't remember.

DREISSIGER Now don't be that way. I've got to know. I'm fed up with this impudence. If he's the one, I'll make him answer for it. (*The "Weavers' Song" is heard*) Just listen to it! Just listen to it!

KITTELHAUS (*Extremely indignant*) Won't this nonsense ever come to an end? Now, really, I too must say, it's time the police took a hand. Permit me. (*He steps to the window*) Look at that, Weinhold! Those aren't only young people; the old, steady weavers are running with the crowd. Men whom for years I have considered to be respectable and pious are in with them. They're taking part in this unheard-of nonsense. They are trampling God's law under their feet. Perhaps you would still like to defend these people, even now?

WEINHOLD Certainly not, sir. That is, sir, *cum grano salis*.[1] You must realize they are just hungry, ignorant men. They are expressing their dissatisfaction in the only way they know how. I don't expect such people. . . .

MRS. KITTELHAUS (*Small, thin, faded, more like an old maid than a married woman*) Mr. Weinhold, Mr. Weinhold! I must beg of you!

DREISSIGER Mr. Weinhold, I regret very much. . . . I did not take you into my house so that you should give me lectures on humanitarianism. I must request that you restrict yourself to the education of my sons, and for the rest, leave my affairs to me—completely—to me alone! Do you understand?

WEINHOLD (*Stands a moment, motionless and deathly pale, and then bows with a strange smile, softly*) Of course, of course, I understand. I have seen it coming: that is why I wish to leave. (*Exit*)

DREISSIGER (*Brutally*) Then, as soon as possible. We need the room.

MRS. DREISSIGER Please, Wilhelm, Wilhelm!

DREISSIGER Are you out of your mind? Are you defending a man that takes sides with such vulgarity and rowdyism as this insulting song?

MRS. DREISSIGER But hubby, hubby, he really didn't. . . .

DREISSIGER Reverend Kittelhaus, did he or did he not defend it?

KITTELHAUS Mr. Dreissiger, one must ascribe it to his youth.

MRS. KITTELHAUS I don't know—the young man comes from such a good and respectable family. His father was a civil servant for forty years and never allowed the slightest reproach to fall on himself. His mother was so overjoyed that he had found such an excellent position here. And now . . . now he shows so little appreciation of it.

PFEIFER (*Tears open the vestibule door, shouts in*) Mr. Dreissiger, Mr. Dreissiger! They've caught him. You ought to come. They've caught one of them.

DREISSIGER (*Hastily*) Has someone gone for the police?

PFEIFER The Chief of Police is comin' up the stairs right now.

DREISSIGER (*At the door*) Your humble servant, sir! I am very glad that you have come.

[1] With a grain of salt.

(KITTELHAUS *gestures to the ladies that it would be better if they withdrew. He, his wife, and Mrs. Dreissiger disappear into the drawing room*)

DREISSIGER (*Very excited, to the* CHIEF OF POLICE, *who has entered in the meantime*) I have finally had my dyers catch one of the ringleaders. I couldn't put up with it any longer. This impudence simply goes beyond all bounds. It's shocking. I have guests, and these rascals dare . . . they insult my wife when she shows herself; my children aren't sure of their lives. Chances are my guests will be beaten up. I assure you . . . if blameless people . . . such as me and my family . . . in a law-abiding community . . . can be openly and continuously insulted . . . without proper punishment, really . . . then I regret that I have different ideas of law and order.

POLICE CHIEF (*A man of perhaps fifty, of medium height, fat, red-faced. He is wearing a cavalry uniform, saber and spurs*) Certainly not . . . no . . . certainly not, Mr. Dreissiger! . . . I am at your service. Calm yourself, I am completely at your service. It is quite all right. . . . I am, in fact, very glad that you had one of the ringleaders caught. I am glad that this thing has finally come to a head. There are a few troublemakers around here that I've had it in for, for quite a long time.

DREISSIGER You are right, a few young fellows, thoroughly shiftless rabble, lazy rascals, who lead a dissolute life, day after day, sitting around in the taverns till the last penny has trickled down their throats. But now I am determined, I will put an end to these professional slanderers, once and for all. It's in the common interest, not merely in my own.

POLICE CHIEF By all means! Certainly—by all means, Mr. Dreissiger. Nobody could find fault with you there. And as far as it's within my power. . . .

DREISSIGER The whip should be used on these ruffians.

POLICE CHIEF Quite right, quite right. We must set an example.

KUTSCHE (*Enters and salutes. As the vestibule door opens, the noise of heavy feet stumbling up the steps is heard*) Chief, it's my duty to inform you that we have caught a man.

DREISSIGER Would you like to see him, Chief?

POLICE CHIEF Why, of course, of course. First of all, let's have a close look at him. Please do me the favor, Mr. Dreissiger, of not interfering. I'll see to it that you're given satisfaction, or my name isn't Heide.

DREISSIGER I won't be satisfied—not until that man is brought before the state's attorney.

JAEGER (*Is led in by five dyers. They have come directly from work. Their faces, hands, and clothes are stained with dye. The captured man has his cap cocked on the side of his head and displays a cheerful impudence. A few drinks of whiskey have put him in high spirits*) You miserable wretches, you! You want to be workers, huh? You want to be comrades, huh? Why, before I'd do a thing like this . . . before I'd lay hands on a fellow worker of mine, I think I'd let my hand rot off first.

(*At a signal from the* POLICE CHIEF, KUTSCHE *orders the dyers to take their hands off the victim and to guard the doors.* JAEGER, *now free, stands there impudently*)

POLICE CHIEF (*Shouts at* JAEGER) Take your cap off, you! (JAEGER *removes it, but very slowly. He continues to smile ironically*) What's your name? [2]

JAEGER (*Simply and quietly*) That's none of your business!

(*The impact of the words creates a stir among the others*)

DREISSIGER This is too much.

POLICE CHIEF (*Changes color, is about to burst out, but conquers his anger*) We'll see about this later. I'm asking you what your name is! (*When there is no reply, in rage*) Speak up, you scoundrel, or I'll have you whipped.

JAEGER (*Perfectly cheerful and without batting an eye at the furious outburst, calls over the heads of the spectators to a pretty servant girl about to serve coffee. She is perplexed at the unexpected sight and stands still, open-mouthed*) Why, tell me, Emily, are you in service in high society now? Well, then, see to it that you get out of here. The wind might start blowing around here one of these days, and it'll blow everything away . . . overnight.

(*The girl stares at* JAEGER. *When she realizes that the speech is meant for her, she blushes with shame, covers her eyes with her hands and runs out, leaving the dishes in confusion on the table. Again there is a commotion among the spectators*)

POLICE CHIEF (*Almost losing control of himself, to* DREISSIGER) As old as I am . . . I've never encountered such unheard-of impudence. . . .

(JAEGER *spits on the floor*)

DREISSIGER See here, you! You're not in a stable—understand?

POLICE CHIEF Now, I'm at the end of my patience. For the last time—what is your name?

KITTELHAUS (*During this past scene has been peeking out from behind the partly open door of the drawing room and listening. Now, carried away by the incident and trembling with excitement, he comes forward to intervene*) His name's Jaeger, Chief. Moritz . . . isn't it? Moritz Jaeger. (*To* JAEGER) Why, Jaeger, don't you remember me?

JAEGER (*Seriously*) You are Reverend Kittelhaus.

KITTELHAUS Yes, your pastor, Jaeger! If I'm the one who received you as an infant into the Communion of the Saints. This one . . . from whose hands you first received Holy Communion. Do you remember? There . . . I've worked and worked and brought the Word of God to your heart. Is this the thanks I get?

JAEGER (*Gloomily, like a schoolboy who has been scolded*) I've paid my thaler.

KITTELHAUS Money, money—do you really believe that that vile, miserable money will. . . . Keep your money. . . . I'd much rather you did. What nonsense

[2] In the original, the chief of police uses the familiar "Du," whereupon Jaeger makes the remark that the two had never gone "tending swine together," i.e., they had not been on familiar terms.—Tr.

that is! Behave yourself—be a good Christian! Think of what you've promised. Keep God's commandments —be good and pious. Money, money. . . .

JAEGER I'm a Quaker now, Reverend. I don't believe in anything any more.

KITTELHAUS What? A Quaker? Don't talk that way! Try to reform and leave words that you don't understand out of this! They're pious folk, not heathens like you. Quaker! What do you mean, Quaker?

POLICE CHIEF With your permission, Reverend. (*He steps between him and* JAEGER) Kutsche! Tie his hands!

(*Wild shouting outside:* "Jaeger! Let Jaeger come on out!")

DREISSIGER (*A little bit frightened, as are the others, has stepped instinctively to the window*) Now, what does this mean?

POLICE CHIEF I know. It means that they want this ruffian back. But that favor we won't do them this time. Understand, Kutsche? He goes to jail.

KUTSCHE (*The rope in his hand, hesitating*) With all respect, I'd like to say, Chief, we'll be havin' trouble. That's a damn big crowd. A regular gang of cutthroats, Chief. Baecker is among them, and the blacksmith. . . .

KITTELHAUS With your kind permission . . . in order not to create more ill-feeling, wouldn't it be more appropriate, Chief, if we tried to settle this peaceably? Perhaps Jaeger will promise that he'll go along quietly or. . . .

POLICE CHIEF What are you thinking? This is my responsibility. I can't possibly agree to a thing like that. Come on, Kutsche! Don't lose any time!

JAEGER (*Putting his hands together and holding them out, laughing*) Tie them tight—as tight as you can. It won't be for long.

(KUTSCHE, *with the help of the dyers, ties his hands*)

POLICE CHIEF Now, come on, march! (*To* DREISSIGER) If you're worried about this, have six of the dyers go along. They can put him in the middle. I'll ride ahead —Kutsche will follow. Whoever gets in our way . . . will be cut down.

(*Cries from outside: "Cock-a-doodle-doo!! Woof, woof, woof!"*)

POLICE CHIEF (*Threatening, toward the window*) Rabble! I'll cock-a-doodle-doo and woof-woof you. Get going! Forward! March!

(*He marches out ahead, with drawn saber; the others follow with* JAEGER)

JAEGER (*Shouts as he leaves*) And even if Milady Dreissiger acts so proud . . . she's no better than the likes of us. She's served my father his bit of whiskey a hundred times. Squadron, left wheel, ma-a-arch!

(*Leaves, laughing*)

DREISSIGER (*After a pause, apparently composed*) What do you think, Pastor? Shall we begin our game of whist now? I don't think anything else will interfere now. (*He lights a cigar, gives several short laughs. As soon as the cigar is lit, he laughs out loud*) Now I'm beginning to find this business funny. That fellow! (*In a nervous burst of laughter*) It really is indescribably funny. First the dispute at dinner with the tutor. Five minutes later, he leaves. Good riddance! Then this business. And now—let's get on with our whist.

KITTELHAUS Yes, but. . . . (*Roars from downstairs*) Yes, but . . . you know, those people are making a terrible row.

DREISSIGER We'll simply retire to the other room. We'll be quite undisturbed there.

KITTELHAUS (*Shaking his head*) If I only knew what has happened to these people. I must admit that the tutor was right in this respect. At least—until a short time ago—I, too, was of the opinion that the weavers were humble, patient, compliant people. Don't you think so too, Mr. Dreissiger?

DREISSIGER Certainly they used to be patient and easily managed—certainly they used to be a civilized and orderly people—as long as the so-called "humanitarians" kept their hands out of it. Then for the longest time the terrible misery of their lives was pointed out to them. Think of all the societies and committees for the relief of distress among the weavers. Finally the weaver himself believes it—and now he's all mixed up. Let some one come in and set him straight again. He won't be stopped now. Now he complains endlessly. This doesn't please him and that doesn't please him. Now, everything has to be just so.

(*Suddenly a swelling roar of "Hurrah!" is heard from the crowd*)

KITTELHAUS So—with all their humanitarianism, they have accomplished nothing more than literally making wolves out of lambs, overnight.

DREISSIGER No, Reverend, by the use of cool logic we might even be able to see the good side of this affair. Perhaps such happenings won't pass unnoticed in leading circles. Possibly at last they will come to the conclusion that such things can not go on any longer— that something must be done—if our home industries are not to collapse completely.

KITTELHAUS Yes, but what would you say was the cause of this enormous falling off of trade?

DREISSIGER Foreign countries have put up high tariff walls against our goods. Our best markets are thus cut off, and at home we've got to compete for our very lives. We have no protection—absolutely no protection.

PFEIFER (*Staggers in, breathless and pale*) Mr. Dreissiger! Oh, Mr. Dreissiger!

DREISSIGER (*Standing in the doorway, about to enter the drawing room, turns, angrily*) Well, Pfeifer, what is it this time?

PFEIFER No . . . no. . . . This is the limit.

DREISSIGER What's wrong now?

KITTELHAUS You're alarming us—speak up!

PFEIFER (*Hasn't recovered himself yet*) This is the limit! I never saw anything like it! The authorities . . . they'll make them pay for it.

DREISSIGER What the devil's got into you? Has anyone been—killed?

PFEIFER (*Almost weeping with fear, cries out*) They've

set Moritz Jaeger free, they've beaten up the Chief of Police, and chased him away, they've beaten up the policeman . . . and chased him away, too . . . without his helmet . . . his saber broken. . . . Oh, I never. . . .

DREISSIGER Pfeifer, you've lost your mind.

KITTELHAUS Why, that would be revolution.

PFEIFER (*Sitting down in a chair, his whole body trembling, moaning*) It's gettin' serious, Mr. Dreissiger! It's gettin' serious, Mr. Dreissiger.

DREISSIGER Well, then, the entire police force isn't. . . .

PFEIFER It's gettin' serious, Mr. Dreissiger!

DREISSIGER Damn it all, Pfeifer, shut up!

MRS. DREISSIGER (*Comes from the drawing room with* MRS. KITTELHAUS) Oh, but this is really shocking, Wilhelm. Our lovely evening is being ruined. There you are, now Mrs. Kittelhaus wants to go home.

KITTELHAUS My dear Mrs. Dreissiger, perhaps it would be best today. . . .

MRS. DREISSIGER Wilhelm, you should put a stop to this.

DREISSIGER You go and talk to them. You go! Go on! (*Stopping in front of the Pastor, bursts out*) Am I really a tyrant? Am I really a slave-driver?

JOHANN, THE COACHMAN (*Enters*) If you please, ma'am, I've harnessed the horses. The tutor has already put Georgie and Carl in the carriage. If things get worse we'll drive off.

MRS. DREISSIGER If what gets worse?

JOHANN Well, I don't know, either. I'm just thinkin'—the crowds are gettin' bigger all the time. After all, they have chased off the Chief of Police along with Kutsche.

PFEIFER I'm tellin' ya, it's gettin' serious, Mr. Dreissiger! It's gettin' serious!

MRS. DREISSIGER (*With mounting fear*) What's going to happen? What do these people want? They couldn't attack us, Johann, could they?

JOHANN There are some mangy dogs among them, ma'am.

PFEIFER It's gettin' serious—deadly serious.

DREISSIGER Shut up, you ass! Are the doors barred?

KITTELHAUS Do me a favor . . . do me a favor . . . I have decided to . . . please do me a favor. . . . (*To* JOHANN) What is it that the people really want?

JOHANN (*Embarrassed*) The stupid good-for-nothin's, they want more pay, that's what they want.

KITTELHAUS Good, fine! I will go out and do my duty. I will have a serious talk with them.

JOHANN Reverend, don't do that. Words won't do no good, here.

KITTELHAUS My dear Mr. Dreissiger, just one word more. I would like to ask you to post some men behind the door and lock it immediately after I've gone.

MRS. KITTELHAUS Oh, Joseph, are you really going to do this?

KITTELHAUS I'll do it, of course . . . I'll do it! I know what I'm doing. Have no fear, the Lord will protect me.

(MRS. KITTELHAUS *presses his hand, steps back, and wipes tears from her eyes*)

KITTELHAUS (*All the time the muffled noise of a large crowd is heard from below*) I'll act . . . I'll act as if I were just quietly going home. I want to see whether my holy office . . . whether I still command the respect of these people . . . I want to see . . . (*He takes his hat and stick*) Forward then, in God's name. (*Leaves, accompanied by* DREISSIGER, PFEIFER, *and* JOHANN)

MRS. KITTELHAUS Dear Mrs. Dreissiger—(*She bursts into tears and puts her arms around* MRS. DREISSIGER'S *neck*)—if only nothing happens to him!

MRS. DREISSIGER (*Absently*) I really don't know, Mrs. Kittelhaus—I am so . . . I really don't know how I feel. Such a thing can't hardly be humanly possible. If that's how it is . . . then it's like it was a sin to be rich. You know, if somebody had told me, I don't know but what, in the long run, I would rather have stayed in—in my humble circumstances.

MRS. KITTELHAUS Dear Mrs. Dreissiger, believe me, there are disappointments and troubles enough in all walks of life.

MRS. DREISSIGER Yes, of course—of course. I believe that, too. And if we've got more than other people . . . Lord knows, we certainly didn't steal it. Every single pfennig's been honestly earned. Surely it can't be that the people are going to attack us. Is it my husband's fault if business is bad?

(*From below comes tumultuous shouting. While the two women stare at each other, pale and terrified,* DREISSIGER *bursts in*)

DREISSIGER Rosa, throw on a coat and get into the carriage. I'll follow right after you!

(*He hurries to the safe, opens it, and takes out various valuables*)

JOHANN (*Enters*) Everything's ready! But hurry, before they get to the back gate!

MRS. DREISSIGER (*Panic-stricken, throws her arms around the coachman's neck*) Johann, dear—good Johann! Save us, dearest Johann! Save my children, oh, oh. . . .

DREISSIGER Be reasonable! Let go of Johann!

JOHANN Madam, madam! Aw, don't be scared. Our horses are in good shape. Nobody can catch up with them. If they don't get out of the way, they'll get run over. (*Exit*)

MRS. KITTELHAUS (*In helpless anxiety*) But my husband? What about my husband? What will become of him, Mr. Dreissiger?

DREISSIGER He is all right, Mrs. Kittelhaus. Just calm down, he is all right.

MRS. KITTELHAUS I know something terrible's happened to him. You just won't tell me. You just won't say.

DREISSIGER They'll be sorry for this, you mark my words. I know exactly who is responsible for it. Such unheard of, shameless impudence will not go unpunished. A community that does harm to its pastor—it's terrible! Mad dogs, that's what they are—beasts gone mad. And they should be treated accordingly. (*To* MRS. DREISSIGER, *who stands there, as if stunned*) Now go, and hurry up! (*Sounds of beating against the entrance door are heard*) Don't you hear me? The mob's gone mad. (*The smashing of the downstairs windows is heard*) They've gone absolutely insane. There's nothing left to do but to get out.

(*A chorus of shouts is heard, "We want Pfeifer!" "Pfeifer come out!"*)

MRS. DREISSIGER Pfeifer, Pfeifer! They want Pfeifer outside.

PFEIFER (*Rushes in*) They're at the back gate, too. The front door won't hold out another minute. Wittig is beating it in with a stable bucket—like—like a mad man.

(*From downstairs, the shouts become louder and clearer, "Pfeifer come out!" "Pfeifer come out!"* MRS. DREISSIGER *rushes off, as if pursued.* MRS. KITTELHAUS *follows*)

PFEIFER (*Listens. His face changes color. Once he makes out the cries, he is seized with an insane fear. He speaks the following words frantically, crying, whimpering, pleading, whining all at the same time. He overwhelms* DREISSIGER *with childish caresses, strokes his cheeks and arms, kisses his hands, and, finally, like a drowning man, put his arms around him, clutching him and not letting him go*) Oh, good, kind, merciful Mr. Dreissiger! Don't leave me behind. I have always served you loyally—I always treated the people well. Wages were fixed—I couldn't give them more. Don't leave me in the lurch. Don't! I beg you. They'll kill me. If they find me—they'll strike me dead. O, God in heaven, God in heaven, my wife, my children. . . .

DREISSIGER (*As he leaves, vainly trying to free himself from* PFEIFER) Let go of me, man! We'll see, we'll see!

(*Leaves with* PFEIFER)

(*The room remains empty for a few seconds. In the drawing room, window panes are being smashed. A loud crash resounds through the house, followed by a roar of "Hurray," then silence. A few seconds pass, then soft and cautious footsteps of people coming upstairs to the second floor are heard; then, timid and shy cries: "To the left!—Get upstairs!—Sh!—Slow!—Don't shove!—Help push!—Smash!—Here we are!—Move on! We're goin' to a weddin'—You go in first!—No, you go!"*

*Young weavers and weaver girls appear in the vestibule door. They don't dare to enter, and each one tries to push the other one in. After a few moments, they overcome their timidity, and the poor, thin figures, some of them sickly, some ragged or patched, disperse throughout* DREISSIGER'S *room and the drawing room. At first they look around curiously and shyly, then they touch everything. The girls try out the sofas; they form groups that admire their reflections in the mirror. A few climb up on chairs to look at pictures and to take them down, and in the meantime a steady stream of wretched-looking figures moves in from the vestibule*)

FIRST OLD WEAVER (*Enters*) No, no, this is goin' too far. Downstairs they're already startin' to break things up. It's crazy. There ain't no rhyme nor reason to it. In the end, that'll be a bad thing. Nobody with a clear head . . . would go along. I'll be careful and won't take part in such goin's on!

(JAEGER, BAECKER, WITTIG *with a wooden bucket,* BAUMERT *and a number of* YOUNG *and* OLD WEAVERS *come storming in as if they were chasing something, yelling back and forth in hoarse voices*)

JAEGER Where is he?

BAECKER Where is that dirty slave-driver?

OLD BAUMERT If we're to eat grass, let him eat sawdust.

WITTIG When we catch him, we'll string him up.

FIRST OLD WEAVER We'll take him by the legs and throw him out of the window so he'll never get up again.

SECOND YOUNG WEAVER (*Enters*) He's flown the coop.

ALL Who?

SECOND YOUNG WEAVER Dreissiger.

BAECKER Pfeifer, too?

VOICES Let's look for Pfeifer! Look for Pfeifer!

OLD BAUMERT Look for him, Little Pfeifer—there's a weaver for ya to starve! (*Laughter*)

JAEGER If we can't get this beast Dreissiger—we'll make him poor.

OLD BAUMERT He'll be as poor as a churchmouse—just as poor.

(*All rush to the door of the drawing room, ready to destroy everything*)

BAECKER (*Runs ahead, turns around, and stops the others*) Stop—listen to me! Once we're through here, we'll really get goin'. From here we'll go over to Bielau—to Dittrich's—he's the one who's got the steam power looms. . . . All the trouble comes from those factories.

ANSORGE (*Comes in from the vestibule. After he has taken a few steps, he stands still, looks unbelievingly about, shakes his head, strikes his forehead, and says*) Who am I? The Weaver Anton Ansorge? Has he gone crazy, Ansorge? It's true—things are buzzin' around in my head like a gadfly. What's he doin' here? He'll do whatever he wants to. Where is he, Ansorge? (*He strikes himself on the forehead*) I ain't myself! I don't understand, I ain't quite right. Go away—you go away! Go away, you rebels! Heads off—legs off—hands off! You take my cottage, I'll take yours. Go to it!

(*With a yell, he goes into the drawing room. The rest follow him amid yells and laughter*)

*Curtain*

# Act Five

*The tiny weaver's room at* OLD HILSE'S. *To the left is a small window, in front of it a loom; to the right, a bed with a table pushed up close to it. In the corner, to the right is the stove with a bench. Around the table, on the foot bench, on the edge of the bed, and on a wooden stool, the following persons are seated:* OLD HILSE; *his old, blind, and almost deaf wife; his son,* GOTTLIEB; *and* GOTTLIEB'S *wife,* LUISE. *They are at morning prayers. A winding wheel with bobbins stands between table and loom. On top of the smoky, brown rafters, all kinds of old spinning, winding, and weaving implements are stored. Long hanks of yarn hang down; all sorts of rubbish are strewn about the room. The very low, narrow room has a door leading to the hall in the back wall. Opposite it, another door in the entrance hall stands open and affords a view into a second weaver's room similar to the first. The hall is paved with stones, the plaster is crumbling, and a dilapidated wooden stair leads to the attic. A washtub on a wooden stool is partly visible; shabby bits of laundry and household goods of the poor are scattered about. The light falls from the left into all the rooms.*

OLD HILSE (*A bearded, heavy-boned man, now bent and worn with age, hard work, sickness, and exertion. An ex-soldier, he has lost one arm. He has a sharp nose, livid coloring. His hands tremble, and his body seems to be just skin, bones, and sinews. He has the deep-set, sore eyes characteristic of the weavers. He stands up, together with his son and daughter-in-law, and begins to pray*) O Lord, we cannot be grateful enough that Thou this night, in Thy grace and goodness . . . hast taken pity upon us. That we have come to no harm this night. "Lord, Thy mercy reaches so far," and we are but poor, evil, and sinful human beings not worthy to be trampled under Thy feet, so sinful and corrupted are we. But Thou, dear Father, willst look upon us and accept us for the sake of Thy beloved Son, our Lord and Savior, Jesus Christ. "Jesus' blood and righteousness, they are my jewels and my robe of glory. . . ." And if sometimes we despair under Thy scourge—when the fire of purification burns too raging hot, then do not count it too highly against us—forgive us our trespasses. Give us patience, O Heavenly Father, that after this suffering we may become part of Thy eternal blessedness. Amen.

MOTHER HILSE (*Who has been bending forward in a great effort to hear, weeping*) Father, you always say such a beautiful prayer.

(LUISE *goes to the washtub,* GOTTLIEB *into the room on the other side of the hall*)

OLD HILSE Wherever is the girl?

LUISE She went over to Peterswaldau—to Dreissiger's. She finished windin' a few hanks of yarn again last night.

OLD HILSE (*Speaking in a very loud voice*) Well, Mother, now I'll bring ya the wheel.

MOTHER HILSE Yes, bring it, bring it to me, Father.

OLD HILSE (*Placing the wheel in front of her*) I'd be glad to do it for ya. . . .

MOTHER HILSE No . . . no. . . . What would I be doin' then with all that time?

OLD HILSE I'll wipe your fingers off for ya a bit, so the yarn won't get greasy . . . do ya hear? (*He wipes her hands with a rag*)

LUISE (*At the washtub*) When did we have anything fat to eat?

OLD HILSE If we don't have fat, we'll eat dry bread—if we don't have bread, we'll eat potatoes—and if we don't have potatoes neither, then we'll eat dry bran.

LUISE (*Insolently*) And if we ain't got rye flour, we'll do like the Wenglers . . . we'll find out where the flayer has buried an old dead horse. We'll dig it up and live off the rotten beast . . . for a couple of weeks . . . that's what we'll do, won't we?

GOTTLIEB (*From the back room*) What kind of damn nonsense are ya spoutin'?

OLD HILSE Ya ought to be more careful with such godless talk! (*He goes to the loom, calls*) Won't ya help me, Gottlieb—there's a few threads to pull through.

LUISE (*From her work at the washtub*) Gottlieb, you're to lend a hand to your father.

(GOTTLIEB *enters. The old man and his son begin the tiresome job of reeding. They have hardly begun when* HORNIG *appears in the entrance hall*)

HORNIG (*In the doorway*) Good luck to your work!

OLD HILSE AND HIS SON Thank ya, Hornig!

OLD HILSE Tell me, when do ya sleep, anyhow? In the daytime ya go about tradin' . . . in the night ya stand watch.

HORNIG Why, I don't get no sleep at all no more!

LUISE Glad to see ya, Hornig!

OLD HILSE Any good news?

HORNIG A pretty piece of news. The people in Peterswaldau have risked their necks and have chased out Dreissiger and his whole family.

LUISE (*With signs of excitement*) Hornig's lyin' his head off again.

HORNIG Not this time, young woman! Not this time. . . . I have some pretty pinafores in the cart. . . . No, no, I'm tellin' the honest-to-God truth. They've up and chased him out. Yesterday evenin' he got to Reichenbach. By God! They didn't dare keep him there—for fear of the weavers—so he had to hurry off to Schweidnitz.

OLD HILSE (*Picks up the thread of the warp carefully and pulls it close to the reed. His son catches the thread with a hook and pulls it through*) Now, it's time for ya to stop, Hornig!

HORNIG If I'm lyin', I don't want to leave this place alive, I swear. There ain't a child that don't know the story.

OLD HILSE Now tell me, am I all mixed up, or are you?

HORNIG Well, now. What I'm tellin' ya is as true as Amen in the church. I wouldn't of said nothin' if I hadn't been standin' right there, but that's the way I saw it. With my own eyes, just like I see you here, Gottlieb. They've smashed up the manufacturer's house, from cellar to attic. They threw the fine china from the attic window and smashed it—right down over the roof. Hundreds of pieces of cotton are layin' in the bottom of the brook! Believe me, the water can't even flow on no more; it swelled up over the banks; it turned real blue from all the indigo they poured out of the windows. The air itself was filled with all them blue clouds. No, no, they did a terrible job there. Not just in the house, mind you, . . . in the dye plant . . . in the warehouse. . . ! Banisters smashed, the floors torn up—mirrors broken—sofas, arm chairs—everything—torn and slashed—cut to pieces and smashed—trampled and hacked to pieces—damn it! believe me, it was worse than war!

OLD HILSE And you say those were weavers from around here?

(*Slowly and incredulously, he shakes his head. A group of tenants of the house has gathered at the door, listening intently*)

HORNIG Well, who else? I could mention all of them by name. I led the Commissioner through the house. I talked with plenty of them. They were just as friendly as usual. They went about the whole business quietly—but they were thorough. The Commissioner talked with a lot of them. They were just as polite as usual. But they wouldn't stop. They hacked at the elegant furniture, just like they were workin' for wages.

OLD HILSE You led the Commissioner through the house?

HORNIG Well, I sure wasn't afraid. The people all know me, always turnin' up like a bad penny. I never had trouble with nobody. I'm in good with all of them. As sure as my name is Hornig, I went through the house. Yes—and ya can really believe it—I was sore at heart . . . and I can tell ya about the Commissioner . . . he took it to heart, too. And why? Ya couldn't hear a single word the whole time, it was that quiet. It gave ya a real solemn feelin'—the way them poor hungry devils was takin' their revenge.

LUISE (*Bursting out with excitement, trembling and wiping her eyes with her apron*) That's only right . . . that had to happen!

VOICES OF THE TENANTS There's enough slave-drivers 'round here. There's one livin' right over there. . . . He's got four horses and six coaches in his stable, and he lets his weavers starve!

OLD HILSE (*Still incredulous*) How could that have started over there?

HORNIG Who knows? Who knows? One says this—another that.

OLD HILSE What do they say?

HORNIG By God, Dreissiger is supposed to have said the weavers could eat grass if they got hungry. I don't know no more.

(*Commotion among the tenants, who repeat it to each other with signs of indignation*)

OLD HILSE Now just listen to me, Hornig. For all I care, ya might say to me, Father Hilse, tomorrow you've got to die. That's likely, I'd answer, why not? . . . You might say, Father Hilse, tomorrow the King of Prussia will come to visit ya . . . but that weavers, men like me and my son . . . should be up to such things, never in the world, never, never will I believe that.

MIELCHEN (*A pretty girl of seven, with long, loose, flaxen hair. She runs in with a basket on her arms. She holds out a silver spoon to her mother*) Mama, Mama, look what I've got! Ya can buy me a dress with it!

LUISE Why are ya in such a hurry, child? (*With mounting excitement and curiosity*) Tell me, what did ya come draggin' in this time? You're all out of breath. And the bobbins are still in the basket. What's the meanin' of all this, child?

OLD HILSE Where did ya get the spoon?

LUISE Could be she found it.

HORNIG It's worth at least two or three thalers.

OLD HILSE (*Beside himself*) Get out, girl! Hurry up and get out! Will ya do what I say, or do I have to get a stick to ya! And take the spoon back where ya got it. Out with you! Do ya want to make thieves out of all of us, huh? You—I'll knock the thievin' out of ya—(*He looks for something with which to hit her*)

MIELCHEN (*Clinging to her mother's skirt, cries*) Grandpapa, don't hit me . . . we, we . . . really found it. The bob-bobbin girls . . . they all . . . got . . . one, too.

LUISE (*Bursts out, torn between fear and anxiety*) There now—ya see. She found it. That's what she did. Where did ya find it?

MIELCHEN (*Sobbing*) In Peters—waldau . . . we . . . found 'em . . . in front of . . . Dreissiger's house.

OLD HILSE Well, now we're in a fine mess. Hurry up, now, or I'll help ya to get goin'.

MOTHER HILSE What's goin' on?

HORNIG I'll tell ya what, Father Hilse. Let Gottlieb put on his coat and take the spoon to the police.

OLD HILSE Gottlieb, put your coat on.

GOTTLIEB (*Already doing so, eagerly*) And then I'll go on up to the office and I'll say, they shouldn't blame us, a child like that just don't understand such things. And so I'm bringin' the spoon back. Stop that cryin', girl!

(*The mother takes the crying child into the back room and shuts the door on her.* LUISE *returns*)

HORNIG That might well be worth all of three thalers.

GOTTLIEB Come, give me a piece of cloth so it don't get hurt, Luise. My, my . . . what an expensive thing. (*He has tears in his eyes while he wraps up the spoon*)

LUISE If it was ours, we could live on it for weeks.

OLD HILSE Hurry up! Get a move on. Go as fast as ya can. That would be something! That would just about finish me. Hurry up, so we get rid of that devil's spoon. (GOTTLIEB *leaves with the spoon*)

HORNIG Well, I'd better be goin'. (*He talks to some of the tenants for a few seconds on his way out, then leaves*)

PHYSICIAN SCHMIDT (*A fidgety fat little man, with a cunning face, red from drinking, enters the house through the entrance hall*) Good morning, people!

Well, that's a fine business, that is. You can't fool me! (*Raising a warning finger*) I know what you're up to. (*In the doorway, without coming into the room*) Good morning, Father Hilse! (*To a woman in the hall*) Well, Mother, how's the rheumatism? Better, eh? There you are! Now, let me see how things are with you, Father Hilse. What the devil's wrong with Mama Hilse?

LUISE Doctor, the veins in her eyes are all dried up and she can't see at all no more.

SCHMIDT That comes from the dust and the weaving by candlelight. Now tell me, do you know what it all means? All of Peterswaldau is on its feet, heading this way. I started out this morning in my buggy, thinking nothing was wrong, nothing at all. Then, I keep hearing the most amazing things. What in the devil's gotten into these people, Hilse? Raging like a pack of wolves. Starting a revolution, a rebellion: starting to riot; plundering and marauding. . . . Mielchen! Why, where is Mielchen? (MIELCHEN, *her eyes still red from weeping, is pushed in by her mother*) There, Mielchen, you just reach into my coat pocket. (MIELCHEN *does so*) Those ginger snaps are for you. Well, well, not all at once, you rascal. First, a little song! "Fox, you stole the . . ." well? "Fox, you stole . . . the goose. . . ." Just you wait, what you did—you called the sparrows on the church fence dirty names. They reported you to the teacher. Now, what do you say to that! Close to fifteen hundred people are on the march. (*Ringing of bells in the distance*) Listen! . . . they're ringing the alarm bells in Reichenbach. Fifteen hundred people. It's really the end of the world. Uncanny!

OLD HILSE Are they really comin' over here to Bielau?

SCHMIDT Yes, of course, of course. . . . I drove right through. Right through the whole crowd. I wanted to get out and give each one of them a pill. They trudged along, one behind the other—like misery itself—and sang a song—it really turned your stomach—you actually began to gag. My driver, Friedrich, he trembled like an old woman. We had to have some strong bitters right afterward. I wouldn't want to be a manufacturer—not even if I could afford to have fine rubber tires on my carriage. (*Distant singing*) Just listen! As if you beat on an old cracked boiler with your knuckles. I tell you, they'll be here on top of us in less than five minutes. Good-bye, people. Don't do anything foolish. The soldiers'll be right behind them. Don't lose your heads. The people from Peterswaldau have lost theirs. (*Bells ring close by*) Heavens, now our bells are beginning to ring, too. It'll drive the people completely crazy. (*Goes upstairs*)

GOTTLIEB (*Enters again. Still in the entrance hall, panting*) I've seen them—I've seen them. (*To a woman in the hall*) They're here, Auntie, they're here! (*In the doorway*) They're here, Father, they're here! They've got beanpoles and spikes and axes. They're stoppin' at Dittrich's and kickin' up a terrible row. I think he's givin' them money. Oh, my God, whatever is goin' to happen here? I won't look. So many people! So many people! If once they get goin' and make an attack . . . oh, damn it, damn it! Then our manufacturers'll have a bad time of it.

OLD HILSE Why did you run so? You'll run like that till ya get your old trouble back, till you're flat on your back again, kickin' and hittin' all around ya.

GOTTLIEB (*With increasing excitement and joy*) I had to run, or else they would've caught me and kept me there. They were all yellin' I should hold out my hand, too. Godfather Baumert was one of them. He said to me, Come and get your two bits, you're a poor starvin' creature too. He even said, Tell your Father . . . he said I should tell ya, Father, you should come and help make the manufacturers pay back for all the terrible drudgery. (*Passionately*) Now times've changed, he said. Now it'd be different with us weavers. We should all of us come and help bring it about. Now we'd all have our half pound of meat on Sundays and blood sausage and cabbage on Holy Days. Now everything would be changed, he said to me.

OLD HILSE (*With repressed indignation*) And he calls himself your godfather! And asked ya to take part in such criminal doin's? Don't ya have nothin' to do with such things, Gottlieb. The devil's got his hand in such carryin's on. That's Satan's work, what they're doin'.

LUISE (*Overcome by passionate feeling, vehemently*) Yes, yes, Gottlieb, just you hide behind the stove—crawl into the chimney corner—take a ladle in your hand and put a dish of buttermilk on your knee, . . . put on a petticoat and say nice little prayers so you'll please Father! . . . And ya call that a man?

(*Laughter from the people in the entrance hall*)

OLD HILSE (*Trembling, with suppressed rage*) And ya call that a proper wife, huh? Let me tell ya straight out—you call yourself a mother and have a vile tongue like that? Ya think ya can tell your daughter what she should do, and stir up your husband to crime and wickedness?

LUISE (*Completely uncontrolled*) You with your bigoted talk! It never filled one of my babies' bellies. All four of 'em laid in filth and rags on account of it. That didn't so much as dry one single diaper. I do call myself a mother, now you know it! And ya know that's why I wish all the manufacturers was in hell and damnation! It's because I am a mother. . . . Can I keep a little worm like that alive? I've cried more than I've breathed, from the moment one of them tender, little creatures first came into the world, until death took pity on it, and took it away. You . . . you didn't give a damn. Ya prayed and ya sang, and I walked my feet bloody, for just a drop of skim milk. How many hundreds of nights I've racked my brains, just once to cheat the graveyard of a baby of mine. And tell me, what's the wrong that a little baby like that has done, huh? That he has to come to such a miserable end . . . and over there . . . at Dittrich's they're bathed in wine and washed in milk. No, no, I tell ya, if it starts here, ten horses won't hold me back. And this I'll say, too, if they was to attack Dittrich's, I'll be the first one—and God help them that tries to stop me. I'm fed up—and that's the truth.

OLD HILSE You're lost . . . you're past helpin'.

LUISE (*In a frenzy*) You're the ones that's past helpin'! You're dishrags—not men! Fools to be spit at. Milksops who'd run away in fright if they so much as heard a child's rattle. Ya'd say "Thank ya kindly" three times for every thrashin' ya get. They haven't left enough blood in your veins so ya can get red in the face. Somebody ought to take a whip to ya, and beat some courage into your rotten bones! (*Leaves hurriedly*)

(*A moment of embarrassment*)

MOTHER HILSE What's wrong with Luise, Father?

OLD HILSE Nothin', Mama. What would be wrong with her?

MOTHER HILSE Tell me, Father, am I just imaginin' it, or are the bells ringin'?

OLD HILSE I guess they're buryin' somebody, Mother.

MOTHER HILSE And for me the end never seems to come. Tell me, Father, why don't I ever die? (*Pause*)

OLD HILSE (*Leaves his work, draws himself up, solemnly*) Gottlieb! Your wife has said such things to us. Gottlieb, look here! (*He bares his breast*) Here laid a bullet as big as a thimble. And the King himself knows where I lost my arm. It wasn't the mice that ate it. (*He walks back and forth*) Your wife—before she was even thought of, I shed my blood by the quart for the Fatherland. So let her rave on as much as she wants to. . . . That's all right with me. I don't give a damn. . . . Afraid? Me, afraid? What would I be afraid of, I'd like to know. Of the few soldiers who'll be rushin' after the rioters, maybe? Oh, Lord, if that was it—that wouldn't be nothin'! If I'm a bit brittle in my bones, when it comes to action, they're like iron. I wouldn't be scared to stand up against a few miserable bayonets . . . and, if it comes to the worst? Oh, how glad I'd be to take a rest. I certainly ain't afraid to die. Better today than tomorrow. No. No. And it'd be a good thing. For what would we be leavin'? Nobody'd weep for our poor old tortured bodies. That little heap of fear and pain and drudgery that we call life—we'd be glad enough to leave behind. But afterward, Gottlieb, afterward there's something—and if ya throw that away, too—then everything's really gone.

GOTTLIEB Who knows what happens when you're dead? Ain't nobody seen it.

OLD HILSE I'm tellin' ya, Gottlieb! Don't go and doubt the only thing poor folks have got. Why would I have set here—and worked the treadle like a slave for forty years and more? And watched quietly how that fellow over there lives in pride and gluttony . . . and makes money out of my hunger and hardship. And for what? Because I've got hope. I've got something, in all this misery. (*Pointing out the window*) You've got your share here . . . me, in the world beyond. That's what I've been thinkin'. And I'd let myself be drawn and quartered—I'm that sure. It has been promised to us. Judgment Day is comin', but we are not the judges, no, on the contrary, "Vengeance is mine, saith the Lord."

A VOICE (*Through the window*) Weavers, come on out!

OLD HILSE I don't care . . . do what ya want. (*He sits down at the loom*) You'll have to leave me in here.

GOTTLIEB (*After a short struggle*) I'll go and work, come what will.

(*Leaves*)

(*Many hundreds of voices are heard near-by singing the "Weavers' Song"; it sounds like a dull, monotonous lament*)

VOICES OF THE TENANTS (*In the entrance hall*) My God! My God! Now they're comin' like ants. . . . Where'd so many weavers come from? . . . Don't push—I want to see, too. . . . Look at that lanky fellow who's walkin' out front. Oh! Oh! . . . They're comin' in swarms!

HORNIG (*Joins the people in the entrance hall*) It's quite a show, ain't it? Ya don't see the likes of that every day. Ya ought to come around to Dittrich's. What they've done up there is really something. He ain't got no house, no more . . . no factory, no wine cellar . . . no nothin' at all. The wine bottles, they're drinkin' them all up . . . they don't even take the time to pull out the corks. One, two, three—the necks come off; nobody cares if they cut their mouths on the broken glass or not. Lots of 'em are runnin' around bleedin' like stuck pigs. . . . Now they're lookin' for the other Dittrich, the one here.

(*The singing of the crowd has stopped*)

VOICES OF THE TENANTS They really don't look so mad.

HORNIG Don't ya worry. You just wait. Now they're takin' a good look at everything. See how they're lookin' over the place from all sides. Watch that little fat man—him with the stable bucket. That's the blacksmith from Peterswaldau, and a quick worker he is, too. He breaks down doors like they was pretzels—ya can believe me. If that man ever gets a manufacturer in his claws—he'll be done for!

VOICES OF THE TENANTS Smash! Something happened! That was a stone flyin' through the window! . . . Now old Dittrich's gettin' scared. . . . He's hangin' out a sign! . . . What's on it? . . . Can't ya read? Where'd I be if I couldn't read? . . . Well, read it! "Your demands will be met." "Your demands will be met."

HORNIG He could've spared hisself that. It won't help much. The weavers have their own ideas. Here it's the factory they're after. They want to put an end to the power looms. They're the things that are ruinin' the handweavers—even a blind man can see that. No, no! Those fellows won't stop now. They don't pay no attention to the judge, or to the chief of police—and certainly not to a sign. Anybody who's seen them kick up a riot, knows what it means.

VOICES OF THE TENANTS All them people! What do they want? (*Hastily*) They're comin' across the bridge! (*Anxiously*) Are they comin' over on this side? (*In great surprise and fear*) They're comin' this way, they're comin' this way. . . . They're pullin' the weavers out of their houses!

(*Everybody flees; the entrance hall is empty. A disorderly crowd of rioters, dirty, dusty, their faces red with liquor and exertion, wild-looking, ex-*

*hausted, as if they had been up all night, tattered, pushes its way in, with the cry, "Come on out, weavers!" The crowd disperses through the various rooms.* BAECKER *and a few* YOUNG WEAVERS, *armed with cudgels and poles, enter* OLD HILSE'S *room. When they recognize* OLD HILSE, *they are taken aback and calm down a little*)

BAECKER Father Hilse, stop that slavin'! Let whoever wants to work the treadle. Ya don't need to work till ya've harmed yourself. We'll see to that.

FIRST YOUNG WEAVER Ya won't have to go to bed hungry another day.

SECOND YOUNG WEAVER Weavers'll have a roof over their heads and a shirt on their backs once more.

OLD HILSE What's the devil makin' ya come in here for, with poles and axes?

BAECKER These we're goin' to break in pieces on Dittrich's back.

SECOND YOUNG WEAVER We'll get 'em red-hot and shove 'em down the manufacturers' throats, so they'll know how hunger burns.

THIRD YOUNG WEAVER Come along, Father Hilse. We don't give no quarter.

SECOND YOUNG WEAVER They took no pity on us. Neither God nor man. Now we're makin' our own justice.

OLD BAUMERT (*Comes in, somewhat unsteady on his feet, with a newly killed chicken under his arm. He stretches out his arm*) My dear . . . dear . . . br-brother . . . we are all brothers! Come to my heart, brother! (*Laughter*)

OLD HILSE Is that you, Willem?

OLD BAUMERT Gustav! . . . Gustav, poor, old wretch, come to my heart. (*Moved*)

OLD HILSE (*Growls*) Let me alone.

OLD BAUMERT Gustav, that's the way it is. A man's got to have luck! Gustav, just look at me. How do I look? A man's got to have luck. Don't I look like a count? (*Patting his belly*) Guess what's in my belly. Food fit for a prince is in my belly. A man's got to have luck. Then he gets champagne and roast hare. I'll tell ya something—we've been makin' a mistake—we've got to help ourselves.

ALL (*Speaking at once*) We've got to help ourselves. Hurray!

OLD BAUMERT And once ya've had your first good bite to eat, ya feel like a different man. Jesus! Then ya get to feelin' strong like a bull. Then the strength goes through your limbs so ya don't even see no more what ya're strikin' at. Damn it, that's fun!

JAEGER (*In the door, armed with an old cavalry saber*) We've made a few excellent attacks.

BAECKER Yes, we've got the hang of it, now. One, two, three, and we're inside the house. Then it goes like wild fire—cracklin' and shiverin'—like sparks flyin' in a forge.

FIRST YOUNG WEAVER We ought to make a little fire.

SECOND YOUNG WEAVER We're marchin' on to Reichenbach and burnin' the houses of the rich right over their heads.

JAEGER I bet they'd like that. Then they'd get a lot of insurance money. (*Laughter*)

BAECKER From here we'll march to Freiburg, to Tromtra's.[1]

JAEGER We ought to string up some of the officials. I've read all the trouble comes from the bureaucrats.

SECOND YOUNG WEAVER Soon we'll be marchin' to Breslau. The crowd keeps gettin' bigger.

OLD BAUMERT (*To* HILSE) Have a drink, Gustav! Come on!

OLD HILSE I never drink.

OLD BAUMERT That was in the old times—today things is different, Gustav.

FIRST YOUNG WEAVER Everyday ain't a holiday. (*Laughter*)

OLD HILSE (*Impatiently*) You infernal firebrands, what do ya want here in my house?

OLD BAUMERT (*Somewhat intimidated, overly friendly*) Now look, I wanted to bring ya a little chicken, so's you can cook some soup for Mother.

OLD HILSE (*Perplexed, half-friendly*) Oh, go and tell Mother.

MOTHER HILSE (*Her hand to her ear, has been listening with difficulty. Now she wards* BAUMERT *off*) You let me alone. I don't want no chicken soup.

OLD HILSE You're right, Mother. Me, neither. Not that kind, anyway. And you, Baumert! I'll tell ya one thing. When old men talk like little children, then the devil claps his hands with joy. And let me tell ya this: you and me, we have nothin' in common. You're not here because I want ya here. Accordin' to law and justice and righteousness, you ain't got no business here!

A VOICE Who ain't with us, is against us.

JAEGER (*Threatens brutally*) You've got the whole thing wrong. Listen here, old man, we aren't thieves.

A VOICE We're hungry, that's all.

FIRST YOUNG WEAVER We want to live, and that's all. And that's why we've cut the rope 'round our necks.

JAEGER And that was right! (*Holding his fist in front of* OLD HILSE'S *face*) Just say another word! Ya'll get a punch—right between the eyes.

BAECKER Be quiet, be quiet! Let the old man alone. . . . Father Hilse, this is the way we look at it. Better dead than start the old life again.

OLD HILSE Haven't I lived that kind of a life for sixty years or more?

BAECKER That don't matter. There's got to be a change, anyway.

OLD HILSE That day'll never come.

BAECKER What they don't give us willingly, we'll take by force.

OLD HILSE By force? (*Laughs*) Ya might as well go and dig your own graves. They'll show you where the force is. Just wait, young man!

JAEGER Maybe—because of the soldiers? I've been a soldier, too. We can handle a few companies of soldiers.

OLD HILSE With your loud mouths, that I'll believe.

[1] Freiburg in Silesia, the nearest big town. Tromtra was another rich manufacturer.

And if ya chase a couple of them out, a dozen more'll come back.

VOICES (*Through the window*) The soldiers are comin'! Look out! (*Suddenly everyone is silent. For a moment, the faint sound of fifes and drums can be heard. In the stillness a short, involuntary cry*) Damn it, I'm gettin' out! (*General laughter*)

BAECKER Who's talkin' of gettin' out? Who was it?

JAEGER Who's afraid of a few lousy soldiers? I'll give the commands. I've been in the army. I know the tricks.

OLD HILSE What'll ya shoot 'em with? With clubs, maybe, huh?

FIRST YOUNG WEAVER Never mind that old man—he ain't quite right in the head.

SECOND YOUNG WEAVER Yes, he is a bit crazy.

GOTTLIEB (*Has come into the room, unnoticed, and grabs hold of the speaker*) Ought ya to be so impudent to an old man?

FIRST YOUNG WEAVER Let me alone. I ain't said nothin' bad.

OLD HILSE (*Meditating*) Oh, let him talk. Don't meddle, Gottlieb. He'll see soon enough who's crazy—me or him.

BAECKER You goin' with us, Gottlieb?

OLD HILSE He'll have nothin' to do with it.

LUISE (*Comes into the entrance hall, calls in*) Don't keep hangin' around here. Don't lose no time with such prayer-book hypocrites. Come on out to the square! Ya ought to come on to the square. Uncle Baumert is comin' as fast as he can. The Major's speakin' to the people from horseback. He's tellin' 'em to go home. If ya don't come quick, we're through.

JAEGER (*As he leaves*) A fine, brave man you have for a husband!

LUISE A man for a husband? I ain't got no man for a husband.

(*Several in the entrance hall sing*)

Once there was a man so small,
Heigh-ho!
He would have a wife so tall,
Heigh diddle diddle, dum, dum, dum, hurrah!

WITTIG (*Has entered from upstairs, a stable bucket in his hand. As he is about to go out, he stops for a minute in the entrance hall*) Forward! Those that ain't cowards, hurray!

(*He rushes out. A crowd, among them* LUISE *and* JAEGER, *follow him amid shouts of "hurray"*)

BAECKER Good luck to ya, Father Hilse, we'll be seein' each other again. (*Is about to leave*)

OLD HILSE I doubt that. I won't last another five years. And you won't be out before that.

BAECKER (*Surprised, standing still*) Get out of where, Father Hilse?

OLD HILSE Out of jail—where else?

BAECKER (*Laughing wildly*) That wouldn't be so bad. At least I'd get enough to eat there, Father Hilse. (*Leaves*)

OLD BAUMERT (*Has been sitting slumped on a stool, moodily meditating; now he gets up*) It's true, Gustav—I am sorta drunk. But even so, my head's clear enough. You've got your opinion in this matter—I've got mine. I say Baecker's right—if it ends in chains and ropes—it's better in prison than at home. There, they at least take care of ya; there, ya don't have to starve. I didn't want to join 'em. But ya see, Gustav, there comes a time when a man has to have a breath of air. (*Going slowly toward the door*) Good luck to ya, Gustav. If something was to happen, say a prayer for me, will ya? (*Leaves*)

(*The mob of rioters has now left the stage. The entrance hall gradually fills up with curious tenants.* OLD HILSE *goes about tying knots in his web.* GOTTLIEB *has taken an ax from behind the stove and instinctively is testing its edge. Both* OLD HILSE *and* GOTTLIEB *are agitated, but remain silent. From outside come the buzz and roar of a large crowd*)

MOTHER HILSE Tell me, Father, the boards is shakin' so—what's goin' on here? What's goin' to happen? (*Pause*)

OLD HILSE Gottlieb!

GOTTLIEB What do ya want?

OLD HILSE Put down that ax.

GOTTLIEB And who'll chop the wood? (*He leans the ax against the stove. Pause*)

MOTHER HILSE Gottlieb, listen to what your father says.

A VOICE (*Singing outside the window*)

The little man at home will stay
Heigh-ho!
And wash the dishes all the day
Heigh diddle diddle, dum, dum, dum, hurrah!

(*It fades out*)

GOTTLIEB (*Leaps up, shakes his fist at the window*) You son of a bitch, don't make me mad!

(*A volley is fired*)

MOTHER HILSE (*Starts up in alarm*) Oh, dear Lord, is it thunderin' again?

OLD HILSE (*Instinctively folding his hands*) Dear God in heaven, protect the poor weavers, protect my poor brothers!

(*There is a short silence*)

OLD HILSE (*To himself, deeply moved*) Now the blood'll flow.

GOTTLIEB (*When the shots were heard, jumped up and held the ax tight in his hand. He is pale and scarcely able to control his great excitement*) Well, are we to take it layin' down, even now?

GIRL (*Calling into the room from the entrance hall*) Father Hilse, Father Hilse, get away from that window. A bullet came right through our window upstairs. (*Disappears*)

MIELCHEN (*Puts her head in through the window, laughing*) Grandpa, Grandpa, they're shootin' with guns. A couple of 'em fell down. One of 'em turned 'round in a circle—'round and 'round like a top. One's all floppin' like a sparrow with its head tore off. Oh, and so much blood spurtin' out—! (*She disappears*)

A WOMAN WEAVER They've killed some of 'em.

AN OLD WEAVER (*In the entrance hall*) Watch out! They're goin' at the soldiers.

A SECOND WEAVER (*Beside himself*) Look at the women! Just look at the women! If they aren't liftin' up their skirts, and spittin' at the soldiers!

A WOMAN WEAVER (*Calls in*) Gottlieb, look at your wife. She's got more courage than you. She's jumpin' around in front of the bayonets like she was dancin' to music.

(FOUR MEN *carry a wounded man through the entrance hall. Silence. A voice is clearly heard saying, "It's Weaver Ullbrich." After a few seconds, the voice says again, "He's done for, I guess—a bullet got him in the ear." The men are heard walking up the wooden stairs. Sudden shouts from outside, "Hurray, hurray!"*)

VOICES IN THE HOUSE Where'd they get the stones? Ya'd better run for it! From the road construction. . . . So long, soldiers! Now it's rainin' pavin' stones.

(*Shrieks of terror and yelling are heard outside and continuing in the entrance hall. There is a cry of fear, and the entrance door is banged shut*)

VOICES IN THE ENTRANCE HALL They're loadin' again. . . . They're goin' to shoot again. . . . Father Hilse, get away from that window.

GOTTLIEB (*Runs for the ax*) What! Are we mad dogs? Are we to eat powder and shot instead of bread? (*Hesitating a minute with the ax in his hand. To the old man*) Am I to stand by and let my wife get shot? No, that mustn't happen! (*As he rushes out*) Watch out—here I come!

(*Leaves*)

OLD HILSE Gottlieb, Gottlieb!

MOTHER HILSE Where's Gottlieb?

OLD HILSE He's gone to the devil.

VOICES (*From the entrance hall*) Get away from the window, Father Hilse!

OLD HILSE Not me! Not if ya all go crazy. (*To* MOTHER HILSE *with mounting excitement*) Here my Heavenly Father put me. Right, Mother? Here we'll stay sittin' and doin' what's our duty—even if the snow was to catch fire.

(*He begins to weave. A volley is fired. Fatally hit,* OLD HILSE *rises from his stool and then falls forward over the loom. At the same time loud cries of "Hurray" are heard. Shouting "Hurray" the people who have been standing in the entrance hall rush outside. The old woman asks several times:* "Father . . . Father . . . What's wrong with ya?" *The steady shouting grows more and more distant. Suddenly* MIELCHEN *comes running into the room*)

MIELCHEN Grandpa, Grandpa, they're drivin' the soldiers out of town. They've attacked Dittrich's house. They did like at Dreissiger's, Grandpa! (*Frightened, the child sees that something is wrong—sticks her finger in her mouth and cautiously steps close to the dead man*) Grandpa!

MOTHER HILSE Come now, Father . . . say something! You're scarin' me!

*Curtain*

# Maurice Maeterlinck

## (1862-1949)

MORE than any other writer of his time, Maeterlinck gave substance and expression to the ideal of a symbolist drama. The theories and techniques developed in French poetry by Baudelaire and Mallarmé led to attempts in the closing decades of the nineteenth century to bring poetry and drama into nearer accord. The aim of the symbolist poet was to reveal the mystery of inner life and the spiritual harmony between visible and invisible reality, expressed through analogies and *correspondances* which the poet alone can grasp. Applied to the drama by Mallarmé and his followers, the new aesthetic imposed the reduction or elimination of anecdote, the displacement of statement by suggestion, the evocation of mood or atmosphere rather than the presentation of concrete events. Dissatisfied by the monotony of a theatre of literal representation, the symbolists sought to redefine drama in accordance with the same tenets that revolutionized modern poetry. The success and the limits of this experiment are in large measure the result of Maeterlinck's efforts.

Maeterlinck's pursuit of a literary career reflects the Belgian literary renaissance of the 1880's, a development inspired by the French symbolists. Such elder contemporaries as Rodenbach, Verhaeren and Van Lerberghe warmly responded to the appeal of a poetry of musicality and mystery, and directed younger writers to French literature and the French language. Maeterlinck was raised in Ghent in a bilingual environment, with Flemish the language of everyday speech and French the language of polite society. His first publications are signed Mooris Maeterlinck. His parents belonged to the solid upper middle classes, well-to-do, but utterly uninterested in literature; their son was trained as a lawyer, and after receiving his diploma in 1885, he was permitted to go to Paris, ostensibly to pursue advanced legal studies. Here in the Latin Quarter he came under the spell of the symbolist playwright, Villiers de l'Isle-Adam, who persuaded him to devote himself to writing. The young Maeterlinck had already published a number of poems, marked by imagery of desolate landscapes, naked trees, and barren, empty fields, and by a mood of tender melancholy. His early plays are characterized by a similar awareness of cosmic mystery and the universal presence of death. *The Princess Maleine*, Maeterlinck's first drama, was printed in 1889 at his own expense; he sent a copy to Mallarmé who passed it on to the popular playwright and novelist, Octave Mirbeau. Maeterlinck's fame dates from Mirbeau's enthusiastic review; he hailed the play as the greatest masterpiece of the modern drama, "superior in beauty to the most beautiful things in Shakespeare." Literally overnight, the unknown Flemish writer, who had yet to see one of his plays performed, became a literary sensation.

*The Princess Maleine* is hardly a classic of the modern theatre, but it introduces the characteristic qualities of Maeterlinck's art. Its five acts are filled with an elaborate and highly melodramatic plot, but the pace of the action is retarded at every turn by repetitions of speech or intensifications of mood through such atmospheric effects as the incessant pounding at the door or the raging of a violent storm. The play depicts the helplessness of innocence confronted by evil: in the absence of her betrothed, Prince Hjalmar, Maleine is murdered by Queen Anne. The prince kills the queen and then takes his own life, leaving behind the old king, babbling like a madman. The lurid and macabre action blends uneasily with the dream-like haze surrounding the characters. Maeterlinck later explained that he wrote the play "in the style of Shakespeare for a theatre of marionettes." In his later dramas as well, the characters are at best vague abstractions.

Through the manipulation of atmospheric devices to create a mood of mystery and terror, Maeterlinck created a new dramatic style. Action gives way to intuition, and speech alternates with silence. *The Intruder* (*L'Intruse*, 1891) is his most striking dramatization of the presence of invisible and hostile powers in a world of apparent clarity and order. All of the grim and foreboding events of the play can be given a natural explanation, yet only the blind grandfather can see that death has secretly entered the room. The play is a studied creation of mood through carefully contrived repetitions and nuances. Tightly enclosed in their little world, the characters have no identity apart from their relation to the movement of events. Condemned to passive suffering, they wait in hushed and fearful expectation while death, as a moving presence, invades the scene. The one-act structure intensifies both the suspense and the climax, yet virtually nothing happens on the plane of physical action. The fear of the swans and fishes, the dimming of the lamp, the silence of the nightingales, the cold wind, all point to a secret and unknown reality outside the plane of earthly existence. Maeterlinck was inspired to write *The Intruder* by a now undeservedly forgotten one-act play by Van

Lerberghe, *Les Flaireurs* (*The Scenters*, 1889), an evocation of the terror aroused by the frenzied beating of death on the door amid futile attempts to protect a dying woman inside the house. In *The Intruder*, suggestion and silence take the place of physical violence. The production of the play at the Théâtre d'Art in Paris in May 1891, at a benefit for the poet Verlaine and the painter Gauguin, marked the first performance of any of Maeterlinck's plays.

Maeterlinck's evocation of invisible supernatural forces moved toward allegory in *The Blind* (*Les Aveugles*, 1891). Unlike the characters in *The Intruder*, all of the participants share the same perception of the mystery surrounding them. Abandoned to their fate by the sudden death of the priest, the blind sense the nearness of death through the cries of the child. The repetition of phrases points up the anxiety and fear of the victims; the deliberate monotony of their choral intonation emphasizes their helplessness and entrapment. The fate of the blind suggests the loss of faith in the modern world and the futility of man's groping for illumination and guidance. In its almost total absence of physical action, *The Blind* is Maeterlinck's nearest approximation to his ideal of "static drama." In a programmatic essay of 1890, the young Belgian called for a recovery of "the mystical density of the work of art." The new theatre, he insists, will turn away from anecdote and external reality, and will replace individual experience "by a shadow, a reflection, a projection of symbolic forms."

These values are far more evident in Maeterlinck's one-act plays than in his more ambitious dramas, yet it was only when he turned to violent and melodramatic action that he achieved a measure of popular success. *Pelléas and Mélisande* (1893) is a lurid drama of illicit love and bloody revenge, reminiscent of *Tristan* and of the tale of Paolo and Francesca related in the fifth canto of Dante's *Inferno*. The child-like heroine seems to possess an intuitive foreknowledge of death; her love for Pelléas is doomed from the start, and their tense, broken dialogue underscores this hopelessness. Mélisande is too fragile to endure in a world of savage violence and revenge; she dies "of a tiny little wound that would not kill a pigeon." The décor, with its castle, forest, grotto, pool, and tower, enhances the sense of mystery and legend. Maeterlinck gave convincing proof in *Pelléas and Mélisande* of his ability to compose sustained and rounded action without abandoning the techniques of static drama. Debussy's opera based on the play and the European tour of the Théâtre d'Art helped make *Pelléas* one of Maeterlinck's best-known works.

The playwright returned to the brief and concentrated "drama of silence" in three plays for marionettes composed in 1894. The best of these is *Interior*, wherein a small group bears the body of a drowned girl to the home of her unsuspecting family. The puppet-like characters have no names; they are essentially devices for the creation of mood. In keeping with the theory of drama expressed in Maeterlinck's essay, "The Tragic in Daily Life" (1896), *Interior* points to the hidden operation of the "silent, discreet, and slow-moving" laws of the universe. Tragedy, he declares, is "a sudden revelation of life in its stupendous grandeur, in its submissiveness to the unknown powers, in its endless affinities, in its awe-inspiring mystery." The sudden destruction of the calm and contentment of the victim's family in *Interior* points to the pathos and suffering latent in everyday existence.

Maeterlinck's contribution to modern drama is virtually limited to his plays of the 1890's. His later dramas attempted to treat moral and philosophical problems through the techniques of romantic melodrama or fairyland fantasy. *Aglavaine and Sélysette* (1896) is a dramatized essay on love wherein the victim of a triangular relationship liberates her husband through suicide. *Monna Vanna* (1902), based on one of Robert Browning's dramas of tangled love and bloodshed in the Italian Renaissance, was largely a vehicle for Maeterlinck's mistress, the actress Georgette Leblanc. With *The Blue Bird* (1905) Maeterlinck achieved his greatest box office triumph. A fairy play akin to Barrie's *Peter Pan*, it attempts to set forth deep philosophical truths concerning the survival of the dead, the meaning of happiness, the triumph of man over nature, and the like. By 1911 when Maeterlinck was awarded the Nobel Prize for literature, he had long ceased to create any vitally imaginative theatre. His last decades were years of increasing withdrawal. The romantic mysticism of his youth took the form in later life of strange experiments in the occult: telepathy, spiritualism, animal magnetism, theosophy, and other forms of psychic exoticism. During World War II he became a familiar figure among the men of letters who took refuge in the United States, but he had long ceased to have any living connection with the theatre and viewed his early symbolist dramas as puerile experiments.

At the time of his death, Maeterlinck was almost a forgotten man, yet his work is an inseparable part of the twentieth-century theatre. Such varied playwrights as Chekhov, Hofmannsthal, Yeats, Hauptmann, Strindberg, García Lorca and Ghelderode, to name but a few, hailed him as a genius and drew inspiration from his art. Great directors like Lugné-Poe and Reinhardt, Stanislavsky and Meyerhold, responded to the imaginative appeal of his plays. Maeterlinck did not succeed any more than other playwrights of the 1890's in creating a durable symbolist drama, but the characteristic techniques and devices of his best plays were soon assimilated by other dramatists, and have entered freely into the mixed styles of the contemporary theatre.

# THE INTRUDER

Translated by Haskell M. Block

## CHARACTERS

THE GRANDFATHER (*He is blind*)
THE FATHER (PAUL)
THE UNCLE (OLIVER)
THE THREE DAUGHTERS (URSULA, GENEVIEVE, *and* GERTRUDE)
THE SISTER OF MERCY
THE MAID

*A dimly lit room in an old country-house. A door on the right, a door on the left, and a small concealed door in a corner. At the back, stained-glass windows in which the color green predominates, and a glass door opening on to a terrace. A tall Dutch clock in one corner. A lighted lamp.*

THE THREE DAUGHTERS Come here, grandfather. Sit down under the lamp.

THE GRANDFATHER It does not seem to be very light here.

THE FATHER Shall we go on to the terrace, or stay in this room?

THE UNCLE Would it not be better to stay here? It has rained the whole week, and the nights are damp and cold.

THE ELDEST DAUGHTER Still, the stars are shining.

THE UNCLE Oh, the stars—that's nothing.

THE GRANDFATHER We had better stay here. You never know what may happen.

THE FATHER We don't have to worry any more. The danger is past, and she is saved. . . .

THE GRANDFATHER I believe she is not doing well. . . .

THE FATHER Why do you say that?

THE GRANDFATHER I have heard her voice.

THE FATHER But since the doctors assure us that we need not worry . . .

THE UNCLE You know quite well that your father-in-law likes to worry us needlessly.

THE GRANDFATHER I don't see these things as you do.

THE UNCLE Then you ought to rely on those who see. She looked very well this afternoon. She is sleeping quietly now, and we are not going to spoil the first pleasant evening that luck has given us. . . . It seems to me we have a right to relax and even to laugh a little this evening, without being afraid.

THE FATHER That's right; this is the first time I have felt at home with my family since this terrible childbirth.

THE UNCLE Once illness has come into a house, it is as though there were a stranger in the family.

THE FATHER And then, you see too, that apart from the family, you cannot count on anyone.

THE UNCLE You are absolutely right.

THE GRANDFATHER Why could I not see my poor daughter today?

THE UNCLE You know quite well that the doctor has forbidden it.

THE GRANDFATHER I do not know what to think. . . .

THE UNCLE There is no point in worrying.

THE GRANDFATHER (*Pointing to the door on the left*) She cannot hear us?

THE FATHER We won't talk too loud; besides, the door is very thick, and the Sister of Mercy is with her and would warn us if we made too much noise.

THE GRANDFATHER (*Pointing to the door on the right*) He cannot hear us?

THE FATHER No, no.

THE GRANDFATHER He is asleep?

THE FATHER I suppose so.

THE GRANDFATHER Someone should go and see.

THE UNCLE I would worry more about the little one than about your wife. It is now several weeks since he was born, and he has hardly moved. He has not cried once all the time. He is like a wax doll.

THE GRANDFATHER I think he will be deaf—dumb too, perhaps. The usual result of marriage between cousins. . . . (*A reproving silence*)

THE FATHER I am almost angry with him for the suffering he has caused his mother.

THE UNCLE We must be reasonable; it is not the poor little one's fault. He is all alone in the room?

THE FATHER Yes. The doctor does not want him to stay in his mother's room any longer.

THE UNCLE But the nurse is with him?

THE FATHER No. She has gone to rest a little; she has earned it these past few days. Ursula, just go and see if he is sleeping well.

THE ELDEST DAUGHTER Yes, father. (THE THREE

DAUGHTERS *get up, and go into the room on the right, hand in hand*)

THE FATHER When is our sister coming?

THE UNCLE I think she will come about nine.

THE FATHER It is after nine. I hope she will come this evening. My wife is anxious to see her.

THE UNCLE She is sure to come. This will be the first time she has been here?

THE FATHER She has never been in the house.

THE UNCLE It is very difficult for her to leave her convent.

THE FATHER She will be alone?

THE UNCLE I think one of the nuns will come with her. They cannot go out alone.

THE FATHER But she is the Superior.

THE UNCLE The rule is the same for all.

THE GRANDFATHER You are no longer anxious?

THE UNCLE Why should we feel anxious? What's the good of harping on that? There is nothing more to fear.

THE GRANDFATHER Your sister is older than you?

THE UNCLE She is the eldest of us all.

THE GRANDFATHER I do not know what is wrong with me; I feel uneasy. I wish your sister were here.

THE UNCLE She will come; she promised to.

THE GRANDFATHER I wish this evening were over!

(THE THREE DAUGHTERS *come in again*)

THE FATHER He is asleep?

THE ELDEST DAUGHTER Yes, father, very soundly.

THE UNCLE What shall we do while waiting?

THE GRANDFATHER Waiting for what?

THE UNCLE Waiting for our sister.

THE FATHER You see nothing coming, Ursula?

THE ELDEST DAUGHTER (*At the window*) No, father.

THE FATHER Not in the avenue? Can you see the avenue?

THE DAUGHTER Yes, father; there is moonlight, and I can see the avenue as far as the cypress woods.

THE GRANDFATHER And you do not see anyone?

THE DAUGHTER No one, grandfather.

THE UNCLE How is it outside?

THE DAUGHTER Beautiful. Do you hear the nightingales?

THE UNCLE Yes, yes.

THE DAUGHTER A little wind is rising in the avenue.

THE GRANDFATHER A little wind in the avenue?

THE DAUGHTER Yes; the trees are trembling a little.

THE UNCLE I am surprised that my sister is not here yet.

THE GRANDFATHER I do not hear the nightingales any more.

THE DAUGHTER I think someone has come into the garden, grandfather.

THE GRANDFATHER Who is it?

THE DAUGHTER I do not know; I can't see anyone.

THE UNCLE Because there is no one there.

THE DAUGHTER There must be someone in the garden; the nightingales have suddenly stopped singing.

THE GRANDFATHER But I do not hear anyone walking.

THE DAUGHTER Someone must be passing by the pond, because the swans are frightened.

ANOTHER DAUGHTER All the fishes in the pond are diving suddenly.

THE FATHER You cannot see anyone?

THE DAUGHTER No one, father.

THE FATHER But yet the pond is in the moonlight . . .

THE DAUGHTER Yes; I can see that the swans are frightened.

THE UNCLE I am sure it is my sister who frightens them. She must have come in by the little gate.

THE FATHER I cannot understand why the dogs do not bark.

THE DAUGHTER I can see the watch-dog at the very back of his kennel. The swans are crossing to the other bank! . . .

THE UNCLE They are afraid of my sister. I will go and see. (*He calls*) Sister! Sister! Is that you? . . . There is no one there.

THE DAUGHTER I am sure that someone has come into the garden. You will see.

THE UNCLE But she would answer me!

THE GRANDFATHER Are not the nightingales beginning to sing again, Ursula?

THE DAUGHTER I cannot hear a single one anywhere.

THE GRANDFATHER And yet there is no noise.

THE FATHER There is a stillness of death.

THE GRANDFATHER It must be some stranger who frightens them, for if it were someone from the house, they would not be silent.

THE UNCLE Are you going to talk about nightingales now?

THE GRANDFATHER Are all the windows open, Ursula?

THE DAUGHTER The glass door is open, grandfather.

THE GRANDFATHER It seems to me that the cold is coming into the room.

THE DAUGHTER There is a little wind in the garden, grandfather, and the rose leaves are falling.

THE FATHER Well then, shut the door. It is late.

THE DAUGHTER Yes, father— I cannot shut the door.

THE TWO OTHER DAUGHTERS We cannot shut it.

THE GRANDFATHER Why, what is the matter with the door, my children?

THE UNCLE You need not say that in such an extraordinary voice. I will go and help them.

THE ELDEST DAUGHTER We cannot quite shut it all the way.

THE UNCLE It is because of the damp. Let us all lean on it together. There must be something in the way.

THE FATHER The carpenter will fix it tomorrow.

THE GRANDFATHER Is the carpenter coming tomorrow?

THE DAUGHTER Yes, grandfather; he is coming to do some work in the cellar.

THE GRANDFATHER He will make a noise in the house!

THE DAUGHTER I will tell him to work quietly.

(*Suddenly the sound is heard of a scythe being sharpened outside*)

THE GRANDFATHER (*With a shudder*) Oh!

THE UNCLE What is that?

THE DAUGHTER I don't exactly know; I think it is the gardener. I cannot quite see; he is in the shadow of the house.

THE FATHER It is the gardener going to mow.

THE UNCLE He mows at night?

THE FATHER Is not tomorrow Sunday? Yes— I noticed that the grass was very long around the house.

THE GRANDFATHER It seems to me that his scythe makes a good deal of noise. . . .

THE DAUGHTER He is mowing around the house.

THE GRANDFATHER Can you see him, Ursula?

THE DAUGHTER No, grandfather. He is in the dark.

THE GRANDFATHER I am afraid he will wake up my daughter.

THE UNCLE We can hardly hear him.

THE GRANDFATHER It sounds to me as if he were mowing inside the house.

THE UNCLE The sick one will not hear it; there is no danger.

THE FATHER It seems to me that the lamp is not burning well tonight.

THE UNCLE It needs oil.

THE FATHER I saw it oiled this morning. It has been burning badly ever since the window was shut.

THE UNCLE I think the chimney is dirty.

THE FATHER It will burn better soon.

THE DAUGHTER Grandfather is sleeping. He has not slept for three nights.

THE FATHER He has been worried a lot.

THE UNCLE He always worries too much. At times he will not listen to reason.

THE FATHER It is quite excusable at his age.

THE UNCLE God knows what we shall be like at his age!

THE FATHER He is almost eighty.

THE UNCLE Then he has a right to be queer.

THE FATHER He is like all blind people.

THE UNCLE They meditate a little too much.

THE FATHER They have too much time to spare.

THE UNCLE They don't have anything else to do.

THE FATHER And besides, they have no fun.

THE UNCLE It must be terrible.

THE FATHER Apparently you get used to it.

THE UNCLE I cannot imagine it.

THE FATHER They are certainly to be pitied.

THE UNCLE Not to know where you are, not to know where you have come from, not to know where you are going, not to be able to tell noon from midnight, or summer from winter—and always the darkness, the darkness! I would rather not live. Is it absolutely incurable?

THE FATHER Apparently.

THE UNCLE But he is not completely blind?

THE FATHER He can make out strong lights.

THE UNCLE We must take care of our poor eyes.

THE FATHER He often has strange ideas.

THE UNCLE There are times when he is not a bit funny.

THE FATHER He says absolutely everything he thinks.

THE UNCLE But he was not always like this?

THE FATHER Certainly not. Once he was as normal as we are; he never said a thing out of the way. It is true that Ursula encourages him a little too much; she answers all his questions. . . .

THE UNCLE It would be better not to answer them. It's not a favor to him. (*Ten o'clock strikes*)

THE GRANDFATHER (*Waking up*) Am I facing the glass door?

THE DAUGHTER You have had a good sleep, grandfather?

THE GRANDFATHER Am I facing the glass door?

THE DAUGHTER Yes, grandfather.

THE GRANDFATHER There is no one at the glass door?

THE DAUGHTER No, grandfather, I do not see any one.

THE GRANDFATHER I thought someone was waiting. No one has come?

THE DAUGHTER No one, grandfather.

THE GRANDFATHER (*To the* UNCLE *and* FATHER) And your sister has not come?

THE UNCLE It is too late; she will not come now. It is not nice of her.

THE FATHER I'm beginning to worry about her. (*A noise, as of someone coming into the house*)

THE UNCLE She is here! Did you hear?

THE FATHER Yes; someone has come in through the basement.

THE UNCLE It must be our sister. I recognized her step.

THE GRANDFATHER I heard slow footsteps.

THE FATHER She came in very quietly.

THE UNCLE She knows there is a sick person here.

THE GRANDFATHER I don't hear anything now.

THE UNCLE She will come up at once; they will tell her we are here.

THE FATHER I am glad she has come.

THE UNCLE I was sure she would come tonight.

THE GRANDFATHER She is slow in coming up.

THE UNCLE However, it must be she.

THE FATHER We are not expecting any other visitors.

THE GRANDFATHER I cannot hear any noise in the basement.

THE FATHER I will call the maid. We shall see what's going on. (*He pulls a bell-rope*)

THE GRANDFATHER I can hear a noise on the stairs already.

THE FATHER It is the maid coming up.

THE GRANDFATHER It seems to me that she is not alone.

THE FATHER She is coming up slowly. . . . . .

THE GRANDFATHER I hear your sister's step!

THE FATHER I can only hear the maid.

THE GRANDFATHER It is your sister! It is your sister! (*There is a knock at the little door*)

THE UNCLE She is knocking at the door of the back stairs.

THE FATHER I will go and open it myself because that little door makes too much noise. We use it only when we want to come up without being seen. (*He partly opens the little door; the* MAID *remains outside in the opening*) Where are you?

THE MAID Here, sir.

THE GRANDFATHER Your sister is at the door?

THE UNCLE I can only see the maid.

THE FATHER It is only the maid. (*To the* MAID) Who came into the house?

THE MAID Came into the house?

THE FATHER Yes, some one came in just now?

THE MAID No one came in, sir.

THE GRANDFATHER Who is sighing like that?

THE UNCLE It is the maid; she is out of breath.

THE GRANDFATHER Is she crying?

THE UNCLE No. Why should she be crying?

THE FATHER (*To the* MAID) No one came in just now?

THE MAID No, sir.

THE FATHER But we heard the door open!

THE MAID It was I, shutting the door.

THE FATHER It was open?

THE MAID Yes, sir.

THE FATHER Why was it open at this time of night?

THE MAID I do not know, sir. I had shut it.

THE FATHER Then who opened it?

THE MAID I do not know, sir. Someone must have gone out after me, sir. . . .

THE FATHER You must be careful. But don't push the door; you know what a noise it makes!

THE MAID But sir, I am not touching the door.

THE FATHER You are too! You are pushing as if you were trying to get into the room!

THE MAID But sir, I am three steps away from the door!

THE FATHER Don't talk so loud.

THE GRANDFATHER Are they putting out the light?

THE ELDEST DAUGHTER No, grandfather.

THE GRANDFATHER It seems to me it has suddenly grown dark.

THE FATHER (*To the* MAID) You can go down again now; but do not make any more noise on the stairs.

THE MAID I did not make any noise.

THE FATHER I tell you that you did make a noise. Go down quietly; you might wake your mistress. And if anyone comes, say that we are not in.

THE UNCLE Yes; say that we are not in.

THE GRANDFATHER (*Trembling*) You must not say that!

THE FATHER . . . Except to my sister and the doctor.

THE UNCLE When will the doctor come?

THE FATHER He cannot come before midnight. (*He shuts the door. A clock is heard striking eleven*)

THE GRANDFATHER She has come in?

THE FATHER Who?

THE GRANDFATHER The maid.

THE FATHER No, she has gone downstairs.

THE GRANDFATHER I thought she was sitting at the table.

THE UNCLE The maid?

THE GRANDFATHER Yes.

THE UNCLE That is all we need!

THE GRANDFATHER No one has come into the room?

THE FATHER No, no one has come in.

THE GRANDFATHER And your sister is not here?

THE UNCLE Our sister has not come.

THE GRANDFATHER You are trying to deceive me!

THE UNCLE Deceive you?

THE GRANDFATHER Ursula, tell me the truth, for the love of God!

THE ELDEST DAUGHTER Grandfather! Grandfather! What is the matter with you?

THE GRANDFATHER Something has happened! I am sure my daughter is worse! . . .

THE UNCLE Are you dreaming?

THE GRANDFATHER You do not want to tell me! . . . I can see that there is something . . .

THE UNCLE In that case you can see better than we can.

THE GRANDFATHER Ursula, tell me the truth!

THE DAUGHTER But we have told you the truth, grandfather!

THE GRANDFATHER You are not speaking in your usual voice.

THE FATHER That is because you frighten her.

THE GRANDFATHER Your voice is changed too.

THE FATHER You are going crazy! (*He and the* UNCLE *make signs to each other to show that the* GRANDFATHER *has lost his reason*)

THE GRANDFATHER I can hear clearly that you are afraid.

THE FATHER But what should we be afraid of?

THE GRANDFATHER Why do you want to deceive me?

THE UNCLE Who is thinking of deceiving you?

THE GRANDFATHER Why have you put out the light?

THE UNCLE But the light is not out; it is as bright as it was before.

THE DAUGHTER It seems to me that the lamp has dimmed.

THE FATHER I see as well as ever.

THE GRANDFATHER I have millstones on my eyes! Tell me, girls, what is going on here! Tell me, for the love of God, you who can see! I am here, all alone, in darkness without end! I do not know who sits down alongside of me! I do not know what is happening two feet from me! . . . Why were you talking under your breath just now?

THE FATHER No one was talking under his breath.

THE GRANDFATHER You were talking softly, near the door.

THE FATHER You heard all I said.

THE GRANDFATHER You brought some one into the room?

THE FATHER But I tell you no one has come in!

THE GRANDFATHER Is it your sister or a priest? You should not try to deceive me— Ursula, who came in?

THE DAUGHTER No one, grandfather.

THE GRANDFATHER You should not try to deceive me. I know what I know! How many of us are there here?

THE DAUGHTER There are six of us around the table, grandfather.

THE GRANDFATHER You are all around the table?

THE DAUGHTER Yes, grandfather.

THE GRANDFATHER You are there, Paul?

THE FATHER Yes.

THE GRANDFATHER You are there, Oliver?

THE UNCLE Of course, of course I am here, in my usual place. That's not alarming, is it?

THE GRANDFATHER You are there, Genevieve?

ONE OF THE DAUGHTERS Yes, grandfather.

THE GRANDFATHER You are there, Gertrude?

ANOTHER DAUGHTER Yes, grandfather.

THE GRANDFATHER You are here, Ursula?

THE ELDEST DAUGHTER Yes, grandfather, next to you.

THE GRANDFATHER And who is sitting there?

THE DAUGHTER Where do you mean, grandfather? There is no one.

THE GRANDFATHER There, there—in the midst of us!

THE DAUGHTER But there is no one, grandfather!

THE FATHER We tell you there is no one!

THE GRANDFATHER But you don't see—any of you!

THE UNCLE Look, are you joking?

THE GRANDFATHER I do not want to joke, I assure you.

THE UNCLE Then trust those who can see.

THE GRANDFATHER (*Undecidedly*) I thought there was someone . . . I believe I shall not live much longer. . . .

THE UNCLE Why should we deceive you? What use would there be in that?

THE FATHER We should certainly tell you the truth.

THE UNCLE What would be the good of deceiving each other?

THE FATHER You would not be long in finding it out.

THE GRANDFATHER (*Trying to rise*) I should like to break through this darkness! . . .

THE FATHER Where do you want to go?

THE GRANDFATHER Over there. . . .

THE FATHER Don't worry so much. . . .

THE UNCLE You are strange tonight.

THE GRANDFATHER It is all of you who seem strange to me!

THE FATHER What are you looking for? . . .

THE GRANDFATHER I do not know what is the matter!

THE ELDEST DAUGHTER Grandfather! Grandfather! What do you want, grandfather!

THE GRANDFATHER Give me your little hands, my children.

THE THREE DAUGHTERS Yes, grandfather.

THE GRANDFATHER Why are you all three of you trembling, my children?

THE ELDEST DAUGHTER We are hardly trembling at all, grandfather.

THE GRANDFATHER I believe you are all three quite pale.

THE ELDEST DAUGHTER It is late, grandfather, and we are tired.

THE FATHER You must go to bed, and grandfather himself would do well to take a little rest.

THE GRANDFATHER I could not sleep tonight!

THE UNCLE We will wait for the doctor.

THE GRANDFATHER Prepare me for the truth.

THE UNCLE But there is no truth!

THE GRANDFATHER Then I do not know what there is!

THE UNCLE I tell you there is nothing at all!

THE GRANDFATHER I want to see my poor daughter!

THE FATHER But you know quite well that is impossible; she must not be wakened unnecessarily.

THE UNCLE You will see her tomorrow.

THE GRANDFATHER You can't hear a sound in her room.

THE UNCLE I would be worried if I heard any sound.

THE GRANDFATHER It is a long long time since I saw my daughter! . . . I took her hands yesterday evening, but I did not see her! . . . I do not know what has become of her. . . . I do not know how she is. . . . I do not know what her face is like anymore. . . . She must have changed these past weeks! . . . I felt her little cheek bones under my hands. . . . There is nothing but the darkness between her and me, and the rest of you! . . . I cannot go on living like this. . . . This is not living! . . . You sit there, all of you, looking with open eyes at my dead eyes, and not one of you has pity! . . . I do not know what is the matter with me. . . . No one says what ought to be said. . . . And everything is terrifying when you dream about it. . . . But why aren't you talking?

THE UNCLE What should we say, since you will not believe us?

THE GRANDFATHER You are afraid of betraying yourselves!

THE FATHER Come now, be reasonable!

THE GRANDFATHER You have been hiding something from me for a long time! . . . Something has happened in the house. . . . But I am beginning to understand now. . . . I have been deceived for too long! You think that I will never know anything? There are moments when I am less blind than you, do you understand? . . . Haven't I heard you whispering—for days and days—as if you were in the house of someone who had been hanged? I dare not say what I know tonight. . . . But I will know the truth! . . . I will wait for you to tell me the truth; but I have known it for a long time, in spite of you! And now, I know that you are all more pale than the dead!

THE THREE DAUGHTERS Grandfather! Grandfather! What is wrong with you, grandfather?

THE GRANDFATHER I am not talking about you, my girls. No, I am not talking about you. . . . I know quite well you would tell me the truth—if they were not around you! . . . And besides, I am sure that they are deceiving you as well. . . . You will see, children—you will see! . . . Don't I hear all three of you sobbing?

THE FATHER Is my wife really in danger?

THE GRANDFATHER It is no good trying to deceive me any more; it is too late now, and I know the truth better than you! . . .

THE UNCLE But really, now, we are not blind!

THE FATHER Would you like to go into your daughter's room? There is a misunderstanding here that must end. Would you like to?

THE GRANDFATHER (*Suddenly undecided*) No, no, not now . . . not yet . . .

THE UNCLE You see, you are not reasonable.

THE GRANDFATHER One never knows all that a man has been unable to say in his life! . . . Who made that noise?

THE ELDEST DAUGHTER It is the lamp flickering, grandfather.

THE GRANDFATHER It seems to be very unsteady . . . very unsteady . . .

THE DAUGHTER It is the cold wind troubling it. . . .

THE UNCLE There is no cold wind, the windows are closed.

THE DAUGHTER I think it is going out.

THE FATHER There is no more oil.

THE DAUGHTER It has gone completely out.

THE FATHER We cannot stay in the dark like this.

THE UNCLE Why not? I am used to it already.

THE FATHER There is a light in my wife's room.

THE UNCLE We will get it later, after the doctor has come.

THE FATHER We can really see enough here; there is light from outside.

THE GRANDFATHER Is it light outside?

THE FATHER Lighter than here.

THE UNCLE For my part, I would just as soon talk in the dark.

THE FATHER So would I. (*Silence*)

THE GRANDFATHER It seems to me the clock makes a great deal of noise! . . .

THE ELDEST DAUGHTER That is because we are not talking any more, grandfather.

THE GRANDFATHER But why are you all quiet?

THE UNCLE What do you want us to talk about? You are not acting right tonight.

THE GRANDFATHER Is it very dark in this room?

THE UNCLE It is not very light. (*Silence*)

THE GRANDFATHER I do not feel well, Ursula; open the window a little.

THE FATHER Yes, daughter; open the window a little. I need a little air myself. (THE DAUGHTER *opens the window*)

THE UNCLE I really believe we have stayed inside too long.

THE GRANDFATHER Is the window open?

THE DAUGHTER Yes, grandfather, it is wide open.

THE GRANDFATHER You would not think so; there is not a sound from outside.

THE DAUGHTER No, grandfather; there is not the slightest sound.

THE FATHER The silence is extraordinary.

THE DAUGHTER You could hear an angel walking.

THE UNCLE That is why I do not like the country.

THE GRANDFATHER I wish I could hear a little noise. What time is it, Ursula?

THE DAUGHTER Almost midnight, grandfather. (THE UNCLE *begins to pace up and down the room*)

THE GRANDFATHER Who is walking around us like that?

THE UNCLE It is I! It is I! Don't be afraid. I have to walk around a little. (*Silence*)— But I am going to sit down again. I cannot see where I am going. (*Silence*)

THE GRANDFATHER I wish I were some place else!

THE DAUGHTER Where would you like to go, grandfather?

THE GRANDFATHER I do not know—into another room, no matter where! no matter where!

THE FATHER Where could we go?

THE UNCLE It is too late to go anywhere else. (*Silence. They are sitting, motionless, around the table*)

THE GRANDFATHER What do I hear, Ursula?

THE DAUGHTER Nothing, grandfather; it is the leaves falling. Yes it is the leaves falling on the terrace.

THE GRANDFATHER Go and close the window, Ursula.

THE DAUGHTER Yes, grandfather. (*She closes the window, comes back, and sits down*)

THE GRANDFATHER I am cold. (*Silence.* THE THREE DAUGHTERS *kiss each other*) What do I hear now?

THE FATHER It is the three sisters kissing each other.

THE UNCLE It seems to me they are very pale tonight. (*Silence*)

THE GRANDFATHER What do I hear now?

THE DAUGHTER Nothing, grandfather; it is the clasping of my hands. (*Silence*)

THE GRANDFATHER And that? . . .

THE DAUGHTER I do not know, grandfather. . . . perhaps my sisters are trembling a little? . . .

THE GRANDFATHER I am afraid, too, my children. (*A ray of moonlight enters through a corner of the stained glass and throws strange gleams here and there in the room. Midnight sounds, and at the last stroke a vague sound is heard, as of some one getting up hurriedly*)

THE GRANDFATHER (*Trembling with unusual dread*) Who got up?

THE UNCLE No one got up!

THE FATHER I did not get up!

THE THREE DAUGHTERS Nor I! Nor I! Nor I!

THE GRANDFATHER Someone got up from the table!

THE UNCLE Light the lamp! . . . (*Suddenly a cry of fear is heard from the child's room, on the right; this cry continues with increasing terror until the end of the scene*)

THE FATHER Listen! The baby!

THE UNCLE He has never cried before!

THE FATHER Let us go and see!

THE UNCLE The light! The light! (*At this moment, rapid and heavy steps are heard in the room on the left. Then, a deathly silence. They listen in mute terror, until the door of the room opens slowly. Its light spurts into the room where they are sitting, and the* SISTER OF MERCY *in her black garments appears on the threshold, and bows as she makes the sign of the cross, to announce the wife's death. They understand, and after a moment of hesitation and fear, silently enter the room of the deceased. At the threshold the* UNCLE *courteously steps aside to let the three girls pass. The blind man, left alone, gets up and gropes his way excitedly around the table in the darkness*)

THE GRANDFATHER Where are you going? Where are you going? They have left me all alone!

# Hugo von Hofmannsthal

## (1874-1929)

THE rediscovery of Hugo von Hofmannsthal is one of the most striking events of the postwar literary scene. More than any other writer of Central Europe, he embodies a sense of tradition, of continuity with the past, that has become of special importance in a war-torn and chaotic world. Hofmannsthal thought of himself not simply as an Austrian, but as a European, seeking to establish through his plays and other writings a new cultural identity transcending the old nationalistic cleavages. Yet, he was an artist far more than a social or political thinker, and the purity and richness of his art is as compelling a reason as any for his renewed importance in our time.

The sophistication and authority of imperial Vienna are an essential part of the background of Hofmannsthal's art. Under the Hapsburgs, Austria was unmistakably the leading power of Central Europe, and even though the Empire was in process of steady decay and dissolution during Hofmannsthal's lifetime, its artistic and spiritual traditions had not lost their imaginative power. In the nineteenth century the Viennese theatre audience was the finest in all of Europe, sensitive and alive to varied forms of theatrical expression, from the high tragedies of Grillparzer to the romantic fantasies of Raimund or the satiric comedies of Nestroy. The old folk theatre with its passion plays, mysteries and moralities, and ribald comedies was also a living part of the Viennese scene. The geographical position of Austria, flanked by Italy on the south and by Slavic Europe on the east, contributed to the varied and cosmopolitan literary and theatrical tradition which Hofmannsthal inherited. His family origins reflected this wonderful variety, for he could point to Italian, Bohemian, and Jewish ancestry. All of these factors, along with Hofmannsthal's rare personal genius, help us understand his unusual precocity.

Hofmannsthal's first play was completed at the age of 16, before he had finished secondary school. By 18, he had published some of the finest poetry in the German language, poetry of solitude and mystical experience, revealing the intensity of adolescent inner life and marked by a seemingly instinctive command of the resources of poetic art. Hofmannsthal was to abandon lyric poetry a few years later, yet it was essentially as a poet that he first approached the drama, and his whole dramatic career must be seen as an effort to conciliate the private vision of the poet with the outward, public demands of theatrical performance.

The young playwright was learned as well as gifted. His range of literary knowledge was astonishing, extending into several literatures and widely separated epochs. Hofmannsthal was to compose a number of adaptations of older plays, ranging from the Greek tragedies to medieval drama, the Renaissance and seventeenth century, and including such varied playwrights as Calderón, Molière, and Otway. His critical essays, first published under the pen name "Loris," embrace the whole of imaginative literature. Some of his earliest efforts in literary prose deal with actors and actresses of the 1890's and with great theatrical performances at the Vienna *Burgtheater*. Hofmannsthal's early prose recreates the colorful theatrical scene of *fin de siècle* Vienna at the same time that it bears witness to the unusual sensitivity of the young poet and playwright.

The lyric dramas of the 1890's are essentially mood pieces, often in the form of the dramatic monologue inspired by Browning or of the dramatic proverb after Musset. The impact of Maeterlinck and the symbolist aesthetic is especially pronounced in these early plays. The preoccupation with the idyllic and dreamlike, with suggestion as opposed to statement, the evocation of a *"Seelenzustand"* or *"état d'âme,"* an inner spiritual condition rather than an outer action, follows directly from the symbolist tradition. From Novalis and Stefan George, as well as from Baudelaire and Mallarmé, Hofmannsthal acquired the conviction that poetry is an expression of the divine mystery of the cosmos, an intimation of its wonder. The art of the lyric drama is an art of nuances and half-tones, of an absorption with inner life within a slight and fragile narrative frame, set forth in a highly charged and rhythmic verse.

*Death and the Fool* (*Der Tor und der Tod*), the third of Hofmannsthal's lyric dramas, was completed in 1893. Its brevity is altogether in keeping with the form of the dramatic proverb, here combined with elements of the medieval morality play. In his prologue Hofmannsthal calls the work a "Totentanzkomödie," a "dance of death" akin to dramatic representations of the late Middle Ages. Nonetheless, the action is far more than macabre spectacle, for it resides essentially in Claudio's discovery of the meaning of his existence. Wealthy, independent, free of all care, luxuriating in the splendors of art, he is nevertheless a wretched and insensitive being whose artificial aestheticism is only an evasion of life. A younger brother to Huysmans' Des Esseintes or Wilde's Dorian Gray, he learns from Death of the emptiness of his past life. His conversion coincides with his dissolution. Far from justifying Claudio's aesthetic narcissism, the play is a sharp critique of the futility of a life directed solely to self-gratification. Despite the internalization of action, the impact of the play is outward: a moral exhortation to the spectator to reflect on his own existence.

Hofmannsthal was to return many times to the structure of the morality play, but nowhere is his fusion of poetry and drama more complete. His subsequent plays of the 1890's are even more restricted in movement, increasingly expressive of the poet's own spiritual crises. The sense of futility and loneliness and the pervasive pessimism clearly owe something to Maeterlinck, as does the décor of walls, corridors, pools, towers, fountains and grottoes reinforcing the shadowy atmosphere of events. This phase of Hofmannsthal's art was to end in the complex drama of spiritual transformation, *Das Bergwerk zu Falun* (*The Mines of Falun*), written in 1899. Hofmannsthal permitted only the first act to be published during his life. The play is of central importance for the study of the writer's inner conflict at this time, but its privacy of vision collides with the physical demands of dramatic representation. As Hofmannsthal was to suggest in his prose study, *The Letter of Lord Chandos* (1901), the inability of language to reveal the magic and wonder of the universe ultimately calls into question all human utterance and communication. Applied to the drama, the implication is clear: a symbolist drama founded on a thoroughgoing mysticism runs the risk of ending in a drama of silence.

At the turn of the century, Hofmannsthal experimented with mixed dramatic forms: ballet, pantomime, and dance-dramas. His short lyric dramas were rejected by the popular theatre, and he felt for a time that he had written himself out. For creative renewal he turned, like many other modern playwrights, to the myths and legends of Greek drama. As early as 1894 he had attempted a reworking of Euripides' *Alcestis*. His first popular success on the stage came with *Electra* (1903), written for Max Reinhardt's theatre in Berlin. It is interesting to note that despite his deep identification with Vienna, most of Hofmannsthal's plays opened in Berlin, Dresden, Munich, or Salzburg. The production of *Electra* was remarkable for its setting, more oriental than Greek, suggestive of the bloody violence surrounding the action, and marked by an imaginative modification of costume and color to fit the changing moods of the play. Hofmannsthal never had any sympathy for the drama of historical or realistic representation; his next play, a reworking of Otway's *Venice Preserved* (1905), was bound to fail in Otto Brahm's naturalistic theatre in Berlin. Hofmannsthal then returned to a happy and fruitful collaboration with Reinhardt, and also, from 1906 to the end of his life, collaborated with Richard Strauss as opera librettist. Their six operas are unusual for the close fitting together of words and music. The most famous of their efforts, *Der Rosenkavalier* (1911), recreates the gaiety and glitter of Viennese society under Maria Theresa in a spirited comedy wherein a pompous, fat and elderly suitor is bested by a dashing young lover. Hofmannsthal also achieved wide acclaim for his recreation in 1911 of the fifteenth-century English morality play, *Everyman* (*Jedermann*). Reminiscent of *Death and the Fool,* it expresses his growing awareness of the ethical and religious function of drama, not as moral preachment but as a festive ceremony. *Jedermann* is no mere translation, for Hofmannsthal has borrowed less than 100 lines from his English source. The play is thoroughly modern, not only in its pageantry, embracing music and dance along with lavish visual effects, but also in its direct concern with the dominance of monetary values in a materialistic society. The dinner scene which shows rather than describes the character of "Everyman" is Hofmannsthal's own invention, as is the comic figure of the devil, cheated of his prey at the end. In 1919 Max Reinhardt and Richard Strauss joined the playwright in founding the Salzburg Festival, and the play has since been staged many times in the Cathedral Square. It corresponds fully to Hofmannsthal's conception of drama as a vast collective ritual, embracing the deepest spiritual values of the audience.

The playwright's growing concern with theatrical values from the middle of his career also led him towards prose comedy. His most successful play in this vein is *Der Schwierige* (*The Difficult Man,* 1921). Here again, the hero calls into question the very possibility of communication with others, and carries his reticence and silence to such a point that they almost prevent him from winning the woman he loves. Hofmannsthal's later plays are far removed indeed from the ivory tower. His last major drama, *Der Turm* (*The Tower*), absorbed his interest over several years. Two years after its publication in 1925, the playwright brought out another version, aimed more directly at stage presentation. The play is based on Calderón's *La Vida es sueño* (*Life Is a Dream*), and explores the consequences of the unjust imprisonment of the young prince, Sigismund. The tower represents the corruption and injustice of the world as well as the seat of the prince's betrayal. The central problem of the drama is ethical: how to respond to brute force and violence. In the revised version, the saintlike hero succumbs to the chaotic impulses of mob hysteria, a portent of the spiritual anarchy soon to overwhelm Europe. The opposition of guilt and innocence, of the world and the self, along with the desperate quest for the meaning of inner freedom and for a center to personal existence, invest *The Tower* with representative significance as a mirror of the moral and philosophical perplexities of our time.

The steady growth of Hofmannsthal's literary reputation in recent years rests on the intrinsic excellence of his work: the intensity of his poetry, the sensitivity and brilliance of his prose, the scope and variety of imaginative endeavor in his theatre. His plays at their best are not merely period pieces. They illustrate the achievement as well as the trials of the poet in the theatre and the complexities inherent in creating a drama of mystery and wonder, of both high poetic and social significance.

# DEATH AND THE FOOL

Translated by Michael Hamburger

DEATH
CLAUDIO, *a nobleman*
HIS SERVANT
CLAUDIO'S MOTHER } *Dead*
A MISTRESS OF CLAUDIO } *Dead*
A FRIEND } *Dead*

*Claudio's house.*

*Costume of the eighteen-twenties.*

*Claudio's study, Empire style. In the background, left and right, large windows, in the center a glass door opening on to the balcony, from which a suspended wooden staircase leads to the garden. A white double door left, another right, leading to the bedroom, a green plush curtain in front of it. By the window, left, a writing-desk, an arm-chair in front of it. On the walls, glass cases containing bric-a-brac. Against the wall, right, a dark, carved Gothic chest, above it old-fashioned musical instruments. A picture by an Old Master, Italian, almost black with age. Wallpaper light in color, almost white, with stucco and gilt decorations.*

CLAUDIO (*Alone. He is sitting by the window. Evening sunlight*) Now the last mountains lie in gleaming shrouds,
Clothed in the moistened glow of sun-steeped air.
There hangs a wreath of alabaster clouds
Above, here rimmed with gold, gray shadows there:
So once did Masters of past centuries
Paint clouds which bear Our Lady through the skies.
Down on the slope some blue cloud-shadows lie,
The shadows of high mountains fill the valley,
Matting the meadows to a greenish gray;
The summit glistens in the last full ray.
How near to my deep longing have they grown
Who there on the wide pastures live alone,
Whose weariness of limb is well rewarded
By wealth which their own hands have plucked and hoarded.
The morning wind, the wonderful and wild,
That travels barefoot in the scent of heather,
Wakes them each day; around them wild bees build,
Fill with their humming God's pellucid air.
Nature has lent herself to be their ploy,
In all their wishes Nature wells each day,
Rest renews vigor, and in that interplay
All of this life's warm pleasures they enjoy.
Now moves the golden ball, now it inclines
Toward green crystals of the farthest seas;
Through distant trees the dying radiance shines.
Now red smoke breathes, a wall of glowing haze
Fills the sea-shore where all the cities are
Whose naiad arms, emerging from the tide,
In tall ships rock their children, cradled there,
A people reckless, cunning, full of pride.
Across the marvelous ocean, silent, far
As keel has never ventured yet, they glide;
Stirred by the fury of the savage main,
Their breasts are healed of folly and of pain.
Thus I see sense and blessings everywhere
And, full of yearning, stare across at them;
But when my gaze approaches what is near
All things grow bleak, offensive, dull, and dim.
Just as though all my missed and wasted days,
With their lost joys and tears unshed, were thronging
Around these streets, this house—my life a maze,
A search for ever vain, and aimless longing.
(*Going up to the window*)
But now they light the lamps and so confine
A shapeless world within their narrow walls,
Complete with all the liquors, tears, and wine
And other stuff that interests or enthralls.
They are so intimately near
And grieve for someone who is far away;
And if a man has suffered here
They comfort him . . . with words I cannot say.
In simple words they can convey
All that is wanted for laughter or tears,
Need not beat with bleeding fingers all day
At the seven nailed-up doors.

What do I know about human life?
True, I appeared to stand inside it,
But, at the most, I studied it,

Never was caught, but held aloof,
Never lost myself but, alien, eyed it.
Where others give and others take
I stood aside, my inmost center dumb.
From all those charming lips I did not suck
The true, essential potion, life by name,
Have never been pierced and shaken with true pain
And never, sobbing, walked the streets alone.
If ever I felt a feeble breath or stir
Of natural emotion or desire,
At once my conscious mind, which never yet
Has learnt to sleep or to forget,
Would leap awake to meddle in the game
And kill the urge by giving it a name.
When thousands of comparisons occurred,
Then faith was gone and bliss an empty word.
And suffering, too! All shredded, torn, devoured
With too much thinking, faded, wrung, and scoured!
Yet how I yearned to clasp it to my breast,
From pain and sorrow yearned to suck delight:
His wing soon grazed me, and I wanted rest,
Instead of pain, discomfort was my plight. . . .
(*Starting*)
Night falls. These are vain questions, vain retorts.
No doubt: the age has children of all sorts.
But I am tired and ought to go to bed.
(*The* SERVANT *brings a lamp, then goes out again*)
Now in the brightness that the lamp has shed
I see the lumber-room, full of bric-a-brac,
By which I still had hoped to creep or crawl
Into the life I long for, though I lack
The straight and open highway walked by all.
(*In front of the Crucifix*)
Down here beneath your wounded ivory feet,
O Lord upon the Cross, many have lain,
Praying that those high flames, so pure and sweet,
Descend to their own hearts and enter in again,
And if, instead of heat, gray coldness came
They were consumed with dread, remorse, and shame.
(*In front of an old picture*)
Gioconda, shining in the marvelous gloom,
With limbs that with the soul's suffusion gleam,
With sweet and bitter lips forever dumb,
Splendor of eyelids weighted with a dream:
Just so much life you have revealed to me
As, questioning, I lent your secrecy.
(*Turning away, in front of a chest*)
You cups to whose cool metal rim
How many mouths most blissfully have clung,
You ancient lutes whose music, when you rang,
Moved many hearts most deeply for a time,
If only I could live in servitude
To your old spell, how readily I would!
You ancient emblems, carved or cast,
Confusing, rich in images made to last,
You toads and angels, gargoyles, fauns,
Fantastic birds and gilded fruit in rings,
Intoxicating, terrifying things,
You, too, must have been felt before,
Conceived by twitching nerves, internal storms,
By the great ocean washed ashore
And, just as nets catch fish, so you were caught in forms!
In vain I have pursued you, all in vain,
Too much addicted to your curious charms:
By feeling through your masks, I could attain
Each of your obstinate souls at last; but then
My life, my heart, the world were overcast
And, an encircling swarm, you held me fast,
Inexorable harpies who devour
All that new sources water, the new flower. . . .
Too much attracted to mere artifice,
I saw the very sun with eyes long dead
And through dead ears drew sounds into my head:
Not wholly conscious, nor free from consciousness,
My sufferings petty and my joys gone stale,
Always I dragged along that awful curse
Which made my life a book, some twice-told tale
Partly not yet intelligible, partly no longer so,
And which, to grasp the living truth, we must reverse—
Whatever hurt or pleased me did not seem
To represent its proper meaning—no!
It was some future life's projected beam,
Void image of some richer life to come.
So in my cares and loves I did no more
Than brawl with shadows, dizzy on the verge,
Exhausting, not enjoying, every urge,
Dreaming of dawn, and the untrodden shore.
I turned about and contemplated life:
In which the runner does not gain by speed,
Nor courage help the fighter in his strife,
Misfortune need not sadden, nor luck lead
To happiness; vain question, vain reply;
From the dark threshold rises a tangled dream,
And all is chance: the hour, the wind, the stream.
Hiding such painful cleverness behind
My languid pride, a disenchanted mind
Spun deep into renunciation, I
Live uncomplaining in these rooms, this city.
People have ceased to trouble me with their pity,
Ask me no questions and think I'm of their kind.
(*Enter the* SERVANT, *who sets a plate of cherries on the table, then is about to close the door to the balcony*)
Leave the doors open. . . . Well, what's frightening you?

SERVANT I fear you won't believe me, your lordship.
(*Half to himself, afraid*)
Now they've hidden in the pavilion, sir.

CLAUDIO Who has?

SERVANT Excuse me, your lordship, I don't know.
A whole pack of uncanny fellows, sir.

CLAUDIO Beggars?

SERVANT I don't know.

CLAUDIO Then lock the door,
The one that leads from the garden to the street;
And go to bed, and leave me alone: good night.

SERVANT That's just what frightens me so, your lordship.
I *have* locked the garden door, but . . .

CLAUDIO Well, but what?

SERVANT Now they're sitting on the garden seat,
Just next to where the sandstone Apollo stands,
A few of them in the shade, on the fountain's edge,
And one of them has sat down on the sphinx.
He can't be seen, the yew-tree's just in front.

CLAUDIO Are they men?

SERVANT Well, some of them are. But women too.
Not like beggars, only old-fashioned in dress,
Wearing such clothes as you'd find on old engravings,
With such a gruesome way of sitting still
And staring at you with eyes that look dead,
Eyes that seem lost in space—they can't be human.
Please don't be angry, your lordship, but not
For anything in the world would I go
Too near to them. God willing, they may be gone
Early tomorrow morning, or sooner still.
Now—with your kind permission, sir—I'll go
And bolt the main door of the house, then sprinkle
The lock with holy water, to keep them out.
For never have I looked upon such humans,
And never has a human had such eyes.

CLAUDIO Do as you please; good night.
(*For a while he walks up and down, pensive. Behind the scenes the nostalgic and moving strains of a violin are heard, more distant at first, then gradually closer, finally warm and full, as if they came from the next room*)
Can this be music?
And music by which the soul is strangely stirred!
Has that man's raving then unhinged me, too?
Such tones I never yet have heard
Coming from human violins. . . .
(*He stands listening, facing right*)
In shuddering and long-awaited gusts
Most mightily this music thrusts
At me: unending hope it seems
And infinite regret, that streams
As if from all these ancient, silent walls
My life, transformed, were flowing back to me.
As when a mother or a loved one calls,
Like the return of anything long lost,
It stirs up thoughts, warm, pious ones, a host
Of thoughts that beckon like a youthful sea:
So once, a boy, I stood in gleaming spring
Feeling that I could float and melt in air,
Transcend the bounds of matter—anything,
Such fervent longing I experienced there!
Then came the roaming years; when without wine
I was so drunk, the whole world seemed to shine,
Bells pealed and roses glowed; all things were bright,
Radiant and jubilant with alien light:
How full of life created things were then,
How near to the beholder's loving mind,
How overjoyed I was, how rapt to find
Myself a link in life's encircling chain!
And, guided by the heart, I soon divined
The stream of love that nourishes all hearts,
Yet by a strange sufficiency retained
Such peace as hardly dreaming now imparts.
Music, play on, continue for a while
So to stir up my darkest memories:
My life grows warm and joyful by degrees
As now, I live it backwards, mile by mile:
For all the sweetest flames, blaze after blaze,
Melting my frozen past, rise and defile;
And that great load of twisted facts, conferred
Upon my shoulders, knowledge old and stale,
These tones remove, sound of the primal word,
Childishly deep, that heals when it is heard.
From far away, amidst the clang of bells,
Great news has been announced, news which foretells
No less than this: a different way of living,
Simple, yet strong in taking and in giving.
(*The music stops almost abruptly*)
But now the music that so moved me ends,
In which the human with the godlike blends.
He who, unknowing, sent it on this mission
Will now be holding out his hat for coins,
A beggarly, belated street musician.
(*At the right-hand window*)
How very strange! No sign of him down here.
Where, then? I'd better try the other window. . . .
(*As he walks to the door, right, the curtain is pulled aside gently, and in the doorway stands* DEATH, *the bow of his violin in one hand, the violin hanging from his belt. He looks at* CLAUDIO, *calmly, but* CLAUDIO *recoils in horror*)
What senseless, nameless horror can this be?
Why, when your violin's music was so sweet,
Now does your aspect freeze and shatter me,
Tighten my throat, make all my pulses beat?
Away! You're Death. What is your business here?
I am afraid. Away! I cannot scream.
(*Swooning*)
My foothold and the breath of life are gone.
Away! Who called you? Go! Who let you in?

DEATH Get up! Cast off hereditary fear!
I am not gruesome, am no skeleton.
As a great god of the soul I now appear,
To Dionysos, Venus most akin.
When in the stillness of a summer evening
Through warm and golden air a leaf came down,
My wafted breath was in your shuddering,
My breath which to ripe things adheres; and when
A brimming-over and uprush of feeling
In a warm torrent flooded your trembling soul;
Or when a sudden spasm was revealing
Your kinship with the vast and the unknown,
And you, abandoned to the cosmic dance,
Received the whole world's rhythm as your own:
In every hour pregnant with more than chance
Experienced fully in your earthly station,
'Twas I who touched your very soul's foundation
With power most holy, fraught with mystery.

CLAUDIO Enough. I greet you, though with a troubled heart.
(*Short pause*)
But tell me: for what purpose have you come?

DEATH My coming, friend, never has more than *one*.

CLAUDIO Oh, as for *that,* I'll wait. I've just begun.
Mark this: before the leaf glides to the ground,
Much heavy sap prepares it for its falling.

I'm far from that: I've scarcely felt the sun.
DEATH Like other men, you have pursued your calling.
CLAUDIO As meadow flowers, uprooted, flow
In dark flood water, driven on,
So my young days have passed and gone;
If that was really life, I never called it so.
Then . . . then I stood behind the gate of life,
Awed by its wonders, full of deep desire
That mighty storms should blast it with lightning's fire,
Cut every bar as with a marvelous knife.
It would not happen . . . but I stood inside,
Bereft of grace, and could not recollect
Even myself or my most fervent wishes,
Bound by a spell that froze and petrified.
Half-blind in twilight, buried beneath the rubble,
Half-hearted and my senses stupefied,
Shattered and dazed, it seemed, in my deep trouble,
Held back from every kind of wholeness, tied,
I never felt the authentic glow within;
Never could feel quite flooded by the tide,
Never on all my ways could meet the God
With whom one wrestles till He blesses one.
DEATH What all men have, you, too, were given:
An earthly life, to be lived in earthly fashion.
Inside you all a faithful spirit dwells
Who to this chaos of dead matter
Can lend significance and tells
Each one to make his garden so
That, in it, joys and cares and work may grow.
And woe to you, if *I* must tell you this!
A man binds others and is bound,
In wild, in tedious hours much gain is found;
Crying yourselves to sleep, worn out with toil,
Still hoping, full of longing, brave or timid,
Or breathing deeply, clinging to life's charms . . .
No matter—*ripe,* you fall into my arms.
CLAUDIO But ripe is what I'm not, so leave me here.
No longer foolishly I shall complain,
But gladly to my little plot adhere,
Avid for life, its pleasure and its pain.
The wildest fear rips up the ancient curse,
At last I feel that I can live—and *must!*
I know it by this boundless urge, this lust:
Oh, you shall see! No mere dumb animal
Or lifeless doll the others will remain,
I shall be moved by that which moves them all,
Plunge into every pleasure, every pain.
Faith I shall learn, and loyalty, the foundation
On which all being rests. . . . Soon I shall know
Both good and evil and their domination,
Be wild and cheerful—I will have it so!
Then soon these lifeless patterns will be living
And on my way men, women will be found,
I'll not be dumb in taking and in giving,
But strongly bind and—yes!—be strongly bound.
(*Seeing the unmoved expression on* DEATH'S *face, with mounting terror*)
For, look, believe me, it wasn't so before:
You think that I *did* love, that I *did* hate . . .
No, never did I dream of such a state.
It was all words and lies and metaphor!
Look here. I'll show you: letters, sent to me.
(*He tears open a drawer and takes out a bundle of old letters*)
Full of endearments, oaths, entreaties, sighs;
Do you think I ever felt as much as *they*—
Felt what I seemed to say in my replies?
(*He throws the bundle at* DEATH'S *feet, so that some letters fly out*)
There, now you have it all, my love-life's essence
In which myself and only I resided,
And leaving nothing sacred underided
I foamed with every passing effervescence.
There! There! And all the others are the same:
Void of all sense, and love, and hate, and shame!
DEATH You fool! Pernicious fool, I'll teach you yet
To honor life—before you part with it.
Stand over there, keep quiet, look this way
And learn that all the others from their birth
With soul and senses loved their native earth,
And you alone were different—hollow clay.
(DEATH *plays a few notes on his violin, as if calling. He stands near the bedroom door, in the foreground, right,* CLAUDIO *by the wall, left, in semi-darkness. From the door, right, enter the* MOTHER. *She is not very old. She wears a long black velvet dress, a bonnet to match, with a white ruche, in which her face is framed. A small lace handkerchief in her slender, white fingers. She steps from the door softly and walks about, silently*)
THE MOTHER How many dear, sweet sorrows I inhale
Together with this air. Like fine dead breath
Of dried, old lavender, one half of all
My life on earth wafts at me in this room:
A mother's life, a third of which is pain,
One trouble, grief the last. What does a man
Know of such things?
(*Near the chest*)
The corner there still sharp?
There once he struck his temple, made it bleed;
Of course, he was young then, impatient, wild
In his movements, headstrong. And the window, there!
Often I stood there, listening into the night
For his dear footfall, listening with such greed,
When fear and worry drove me from my bed;
When it struck two, then three, and when already
A pale dawn rose—and still he did not come . . .
How often . . . yet next day he never knew—
And in the daytime, too, I was much alone.
This hand: it waters flowers, beats the dust
From cushions, rubs brass handles bright and clean—
So the day passes; but the head has nothing
To do: all day a padded wheel revolves,
With premonitions, nightmare anxieties,
Mysterious feelings of unwarranted pain,
Connected, I suppose, with the obscure,
Unfathomable sacrament of motherhood
Which is akin to all the deepest workings
Of this world. But no longer I am allowed

To breathe the sweet, oppressive, painfully
Nourishing air of a life that's past and gone.
I must be leaving, leaving. . . .
(*Exit by the middle door*)

CLAUDIO Mother!

DEATH Quiet!
You'll never bring her back.

CLAUDIO O Mother, stay!
For once with trembling lips—the very same
Which, always tightly pressed, haughtily dumb,
Could not relax—here, on my knees with shame,
Oh, let me . . . Call her back! Don't let her go!
She did not want to go! Didn't you see?
Why do you force her to, Monstrosity?

DEATH Leave me what's mine. Once it *was* yours.

CLAUDIO Yet never
Felt to be so. But withered, all was withered.
When did I ever feel that all the roots
Of my life cried out for her? Or that her nearness
Filled me with awe like some great godhead's nearness,
As it was meant to do, miraculously
Filled me with human longing, joy, and grief?
(DEATH, *unmoved by this lamentation, plays the tune of an old popular song. Slowly a* YOUNG GIRL *enters wearing a flowered dress, very simple, cross-laced shoes, wisp of a veil about her neck, her head bare*)

THE YOUNG GIRL Yes, it was lovely. . . . Have you quite forgotten?
It's true, you hurt me, hurt me, oh, so much. . . .
But, after all, what doesn't end in pain?
I've known so very few untroubled days,
And these were lovely, lovely as a dream!
The flowers in front of my window, my own flowers,
The little rickety virginal, the cupboard
In which I put your letters and the things
You used to give to me at first . . . all this—
Don't laugh at me—all this grew beautiful
And spoke to me with dear and eloquent lips.
When after sultry evenings there was rain,
We stood at the open window together—
Oh, the fragrance of trees in the rain!—All that
Is gone, and what was living in it, dead.
All buried in the little grave of our love.
Yet it was beautiful, too, and you're to blame
That it *was* so beautiful; and that afterward
You threw me away, unthinkingly cruel,
Like a child who, tired of playing, drops his flowers. . . .
God knows I had nothing to hold you with.
(*Short pause*)
But when your letter, the last, the bad one, came
I wanted to die. Not to torment you now
Do I tell you this. I wanted to write
A farewell letter, gentle, uncomplaining,
Quite without bitterness or unbridled grief;
Only so that for my love and for myself
One day you might feel some longing and weep
A little, knowing it was too late for tears.
I did not write to you. Why should I write?
How can I know how much of your own heart
Was in it all—all that had filled my mind
And senses with such radiance, such a fever
That as though dreaming I walked in brightest day.
Good will can never cure unfaithfulness,
And tears can never waken what has died.
Nor does one die of it. Only much later,
After much long and lonely wretchedness,
I was allowed to die. Then I requested
That I might join you at your dying hour;
Not horribly, not to torment you now,
Only as when one drinks a glass of wine
And for a moment its taste or smell recalls
Some long-forgotten place or dim delight.
(*Exit;* CLAUDIO *covers his face with his hands. Immediately after her exit, enter a* MAN. *He is of about* CLAUDIO'S *age, wears an untidy, dusty traveling suit. The wooden grip of a knife sticks out from his chest, over his heart. He remains in the middle of the stage, facing* CLAUDIO)

THE MAN What, still alive, still always playing at life?
Still reading Horace and still taking pleasure
In mocking, clever, unimpassioned things?
With your fine words you came quite close to me,
Seemingly gripped by that which moved me, too. . . .
You said I had reminded you of things
That, latent in you, slept, as the night wind
Will speak of destinations out of mind. . . .
Oh yes, a fine Aeolian harp you were,
And always the love-sick wind that made it play
Was another's exploited breath, my own
Or someone else's. Friends we called ourselves
For quite some time. Yes, friends indeed! That means
We talked together daily and late at night,
Knew the same people, flirted and played about
With the same woman, shared our lives. We shared
As slave and master share a single house,
One litter, dinner table, dog, and whip:
To one the house means pleasure, jail to the other;
One rides aloft, the other's shoulder smarts,
Cut by the litter's carvings; one delights
To see the dog jump through a lifted hoop
Down in the park; the other serves the dog! . . .
Half-completed feelings, pearls of my soul
Painfully born, you took away from me
And juggled with them, toys you thought your own,
You, quick to make new friends and quick to drop them,
I, with a dumb devotion in my soul,
Teeth tightly clenched; you, touching everything,
Devoid of shame, while, diffident, unsure,
The word I groped for withered on the way.
A woman crossed our path. What pounced on me
And penetrated as an illness does
In which the senses, over-wakeful, swoon
With too much concentration on one aim. . . .
For such an aim, which tender gloom surrounds,
A lovely scent and luster that seem woven
Out of deep darkness and sheet-lightning. . . . This
You, too, observed, and it excited you! . . .

"Oh yes, because at times I feel the same,
The weary, languid manner of this girl,
Her hard and bitter haughtiness excited me—
So disillusioned, yet so young." These were
Your very words to me. Excited you!
More than this blood and brain she meant to me!
And, sick of the game, you threw the doll to me,
To me, when her whole image was defaced
By your own surfeit, horribly distorted,
Stripped of her spell by your satiety,
Her features meaningless, her living hair
Dead where it hung—threw me an empty mask,
Reducing sweet and enigmatic charm
To nothing with abominable art.
For this, at last, I hated you as much
As my forebodings always hated you,
And shunned you.
But my fate, which even then
Blessed me, the broken-down, with adamant will,
With resolution and a conscious end—
Even your poisonous proximity
Had not quite killed all passion, every urge—
My fate, I say, in a high cause impelled me
To meet this murderous blade and virile death;
But, cast into a ditch and lying there,
Rotting away, still I had time to think
Of things that you will never understand,
Still thrice as blessed, as fortunate as you,
The utterly unloving and unloved.
(*Exit*)

CLAUDIO Indeed unloving and indeed unloved.
(*Slowly drawing himself up*)
As on the stage a bad comedian passes—
He enters on his cue, recites his part
And, deaf to all that's not himself, walks off,
Not even moved by hearing his own voice,
Nor, ringing hollow, able to move others—
So, too, across this larger stage of life
I passed, without conviction, strength or worth.
Why was this done to me? Why, tell me, Death,
Did I need *you* to teach me to see life
Not only through a veil, but clear and whole,
And, rousing up so much, must you move on?
Why is the childish mind so richly blessed
With high presentiment of earthly things,
Why do those very things, once realized,
Grant only faint, remembered whisperings?
Why does your violin not sound its tune
And so stir up the hidden world of spirits
Which secretly the heart inherits,
But buries it so far from consciousness,
As flowers are buried under sliding stone?
If I could stay where you alone are heard,
Untroubled by the vain and trivial word!
I can! Now grant me that with which you threatened:
Since all my life was dead, Death, be my life!
Admitting neither, I can save my breath:
Need not call past things life, nor call you Death.
Into one hour you can compress more life
Than once the whole of life had space to hold.
All that is dim and vague I shall forget,
Into your powers and miracles enrolled.
(*He reflects for a moment*)
All this, it may be, is mere dying thought
Raised by the throbbing blood so nearly spent,
Yet never have my living senses caught
And grasped so much; therefore I am content.
If now, extinguished, I must pass away,
My brain replete with this last ecstasy,
This poor and faded life will not be missed:
Dying, at last I feel that I exist.
When a man sleeps, often his dream will break
With too much dreamed emotion, dream's excess;
So from the dream of life I now may wake,
Cloyed with emotion, to death's wakefulness.
(*He falls dead at* DEATH'S *feet*)

DEATH (*As he slowly leaves the stage, shaking his head*)
Strange are these creatures, strange indeed,
Who what's unfathomable, fathom,
What never yet was written, read,
Knit and command the tangled mystery
And in the eternal dark yet find a way.
(*Exit by the middle door; his words fade away*)
(*The room remains silent. Outside, through the window, we see* DEATH *pass by, playing his violin; behind him the* MOTHER, *also the* GIRL *and, close to them, a figure resembling* CLAUDIO)

*Curtain*

# Anton Chekhov

## (1860-1904)

Anton Chekhov's central importance in twentieth-century drama was prophesied long ago by one of his greatest contemporaries, Count Leo Tolstoi. Puzzled by the apparent shapelessness of Chekhovian drama and irritated by Chekhov's refusal to moralize or play the prophet, Tolstoi still sensed the younger playwright's unique gift for suffusing with compassion the characters he created in a spirit of objective and dispassionate analysis: "I have as yet no clear picture of Chekhov's plays. But it is possible that in the future, perhaps a hundred years hence, people will be amazed at what they find in Chekhov about the inner workings of the human soul." If Tolstoi would not be surprised at Chekhov's present reputation, Chekhov himself would certainly be. He would be astounded to discover how widely his plays, conceived only for Russian audiences, have been studied and produced throughout the world. He might recognize the same problems of interpretation over which he originally quarreled with his directors, but he would not be prepared to find even an early work such as *Platonov* (the long-lost play he himself discarded) delighting audiences in London and New York. Although he was aware that Stanislavski and Nemirovich-Danchenko had to devise special actor-training and production methods before they could present his last plays in their full power, Chekhov would be astonished to discover the revolutionizing force the "Method" developed by Stanislavski in the Moscow Art Theatre has had in our own theatre. Most of all, he would be dumfounded to discover how he has baffled biographers and critics who seek to explain how a writer so impervious to the revolutionary politics of his age could recreate so definitively and with such telling economy the social fabric of a Russia poised on the brink of devastating upheaval.

Born in 1860 in Taganrog, a dreary port in the Black Sea area, Chekhov was the son of a storekeeper whose father had bought himself and his family out of serfdom. Chekhov's father was an arrogant and despotic man less suited to shopkeeping than to the artistic life which, as choirmaster, violinist, and occasional painter, he allowed to take precedence over more practical affairs. Although in later years he spoke bitterly of his father, Chekhov enjoyed an easy companionship with his brothers and sister, and he received a sound education. His mother gave him the humane tolerance exemplified in his central belief, "People must never be humiliated—that is the important thing." Chekhov's interest in the theatre began early in trips to the Taganrog Theatre, and especially in reënacting at home such plays as Gogol's *The Inspector General* and other popular, if less effectively satirical, plays of the period.

When Chekhov was 16, his father, facing bankruptcy, fled to Moscow and an anonymity in which most of his family soon joined him. Chekhov was left in Taganrog until 1879, to complete his preparatory studies. Before he could join his family in the Moscow slums where he found them living, Chekhov sent the little money he could spare from his salary as tutor, but he was not prepared to find himself eagerly awaited in Moscow as the real head of the family. Before he left Taganrog, he had written three plays, none of which survive. While he studied medicine at the University of Moscow, he supplemented the family income by potboiling countless sketches and short stories. Except for the play now known as *Platonov*, written soon after he arrived in Moscow, fiction absorbed his energies during his years of study. In December, 1884, when he finally took up medical practice, Chekhov could measure the results of his five-year residence in Moscow: he had considerably improved family finances, he had acquired a wide circle of friends (especially among the ladies), he had gained a substantial reputation as a short-story writer, and he had contracted tuberculosis. Torn between medicine ("my lawful spouse") and writing ("my mistress"), Chekhov satisfied both sets of demands on his time: he treated thousands of patients while he wrote the more than 300 stories he published between 1885 and 1887. At 27, he directed his attention back to drama, his first love among the literary forms.

Chekhov's drama falls into two periods: the first (from about 1881 until 1895) is marked chiefly by adaptations of his stories into the farcical "vaudevilles" extremely popular in the Russian theatre; the second period (from 1896 until his untimely death in 1904) is notable for the full-length plays on which his world reputation rests. The earlier works are, for the most part, one-act farces lightly spiced with satiric commentary, clearly conceived with one eye on the public censor and the other on popular tastes. In writing these uproarious curtain-raisers, Chekhov followed a formula which included utter confusion, idiosyncratic behavior and language for each character, and the avoidance of long speeches or any action which might check a rapid flow of movement. Unabashedly, he tailored characters for particular actors. Among the most effective of these one-act plays were several Chekhov adapted from his own stories: *A Tragedian in Spite of Himself* concerned an officeworker commuting between his city job and a summer cottage; *The Wedding* is an hilarious romp involving wedding-guests who include a Greek pastry-cook, a flirtatious midwife, a quarrelsome telegraphist, and a retired naval officer; *The Anniversary* shows the chaos created in a bank by an old woman's simple request. *On the Harmfulness of Tobacco,* a monologue Chekhov constantly reworked, finally became, by 1903, a successful exercise in subtle internalized action. More nearly original were *The Bear* (or *The Boor*) and *The Proposal,* both dealing with marriage arrangements between canny landowners. Echoes of the imbroglios which propel the action of these short plays can be heard in Chekhov's last plays, especially among his secondary characters. In other works of this first period, Chekhov was less successful. *On the Highway,* a gloomy piece of naturalism, was rejected by the censor and Chekhov was content to forget it. Earlier, he had written a full-length study of a provincial Don Juan, a once-rich landowner reduced to being village schoolmaster. Its spineless hero is pursued by four women, all as bored with small town life as he. Long lost and recovered in an incomplete and untitled draft years after Chekhov's death, this play was a challenge for adaptors and translators: as *A Country Scandal* or *Platonov,* it has been successfully produced in the contemporary theatre.

Chekhov created in *Ivanov* a Hamlet figure, the provincial Everyman of the late 1880's. Seeking to shape a drama as close as possible to reality, Chekhov kept revising this play, but never quite succeeded in superseding the fashionable theatrical conventions of the time. Each act ends with an "effective curtain," there are rhetorical flights a Bernhardt would cherish, and every important action (including the hero's suicide) is depicted in full view. In its "direct action," *Ivanov* proved a great success. The central character was disturbingly familiar: stalemated in life, his youthful vigor and crusading zeal replaced by self-contempt, Ivanov kills himself, another victim of the *ennui* and inertia of provincial existence. Although *Ivanov* proved his mastery of popular stage conventions, Chekhov's impatience with formula playmaking led him to write *The Wood Demon,* a play ahead of its time. After this experiment was rejected for production, Chekhov abandoned drama for seven years.

From 1890 until 1896, Chekhov led an active life, partly out of a Tolstoyan humanitarianism, partly to forget a married woman with whom he had fallen in love. In 1890, he journeyed across Siberia to study penal conditions on Sakhalin Island, the Devil's Island of Russia. On his return to Moscow, he bought a country estate where, until poor health necessitated a move to Yalta's milder climate, he lived as a country gentleman, participating in local affairs, serving as country doctor, and directing experiments in scientific farming. At his Melikhovo estate in 1895, Chekhov wrote *The Sea Gull,* its origins buried deep in a complex set of personal experiences, several of which (like the shooting of the gull) became central elements in the play. He described it as "a comedy, three female parts, six male, four acts, landscape (view of a lake); lots of talk about literature, little action, five tons of love." Aware that he was "sinning terribly against the rules of the stage," he achieved his earlier ideal of a drama in which every character—or no character—is a protagonist and violent actions (such as Trepleff's suicide attempts) are kept offstage. Most important, he now knew how to employ fragments of speech and gesture, and the arrestingly intricate soliloquies in which private soul-searching and public utterance merge into dazzling patterns of unconscious self-revelation. Biographers disagree about the influence of Ibsen's *The Wild Duck* on Chekhov's conception of *The Sea Gull,* but there is no disagreement about both dramatists' skill in expanding a central image into a richly ambiguous set of symbolic values to unify their plays. Nor is there any doubt about the skill with which Chekhov made theatrical conventions work for instead of against the realism he sought to capture. The flamboyant histrionics and pseudo-realism of Arkadina's theatre is contrasted sharply with the evanescent symbolism and precious lyricism of Trepleff's theatre of "new forms," but Chekhov's own play is destined for a theatre which transcends both. As it was first produced in 1896, *The Sea Gull* only demonstrated to Chekhov that such a theatre did not yet exist. Two years later, however, *The Sea Gull* found its home at the newly created Moscow Art Theatre in the production which has become a landmark in the history of modern theatre.

Chekhov's "five tons of love" provides the key to one important unifying theme. In constantly shifting romantic triangles, Chekhov diagrams the changing changelessness of his characters' lives. The exhausted affair of Arkadina and Trigorin is counterpointed by the writer's passion for fishing, by the refreshing novelty of Nina's offerings, even by the complexly oedipal relationship of mother and son. Trepleff's schoolboyish love for Nina is enriched, if not reciprocated, with the passage of time. Weary of Trepleff's lack of interest in her, Masha weds a wearisome schoolmaster, and repeats the pattern of Pauline, married to one man but loving another. Each character, trapped in unrequited love, builds a bastion to protect his ego. When she sees Trepleff, Arkadina's professional youthfulness, physical attractiveness, poise, and artistry temporarily vanish. In the presence of Arkadina and Trigorin, Trepieff's literary aspirations crumble into nagging fears that he is mediocre, a mere Kiev burgher's brat. In the arrivals, departures, and occasional stayings-put which separate one year from another, the characters find their fortresses under attack. Chekhov's finest achievement was to reveal the comedy of their pathetic attempts to guard themselves against their greatest enemy, time.

# THE SEA GULL

*A Comedy in Four Acts*

Translated by Stark Young

CHARACTERS

IRINA NIKOLAEVNA ARKADINA, MADAME TREPLEFF, *an actress*
KONSTANTINE GAVRILOVICH TREPLEFF (KOSTYA), *her son*
PETER NIKOLAEVICH SORIN, *her brother*
NINA MIKHAILOVNA ZARYECHNY, *a young girl, the daughter of a wealthy landowner*
ILYA AFANASEVICH SHAMREYEFF, *a retired lieutenant,* SORIN'S *steward*
PAULINE ANDREEVNA, *his wife*
MASHA (MARIA ILYINISHNA), *his daughter*
BORIS ALEXEEVICH TRIGORIN, *a literary man*
EUGENE SERGEEVICH DORN, *a doctor*
SEMYON SEMYONOVICH MEDVEDENKO, *a schoolmaster*
YAKOV, *a laborer*
COOK
TWO HOUSEMAIDS

*The action takes place at* SORIN'S *country estate in the late 1890's.*

*Between Acts III and IV two years elapse.*

## Act One

*A section of the park on* SORIN'S *estate. The wide avenue leading away from the spectators into the depths of the park toward the lake is closed by a platform hurriedly put together for private theatricals, so that the lake is not seen at all. To left and right of the platform there are bushes. A few chairs, a small table.*

*The sun has just set. On the platform behind the curtain are* YAKOV *and other workmen; sounds of coughing and hammering are heard.* MASHA *and* MEDVEDENKO *enter on the left, returning from a walk.*

MEDVEDENKO Why do you always wear black?

MASHA I am in mourning for my life. I'm unhappy.

MEDVEDENKO You unhappy? I can't understand it. Your health is good, and your father is not rich but he's well enough off. My life is much harder to bear than yours. I get twenty-three rubles a month, and that's all, and then out of that the pension fund has to be deducted, but I don't wear mourning.

(*They sit down*)

MASHA It isn't a question of money. Even a beggar can be happy.

MEDVEDENKO Yes, theoretically he can, but not when you come right down to it. Look at me, with my mother, my two sisters and my little brother, and my salary twenty-three rubles in all. Well, people have to eat and drink, don't they? Have to have tea and sugar? Have tobacco? So it just goes round and round.

MASHA (*Glancing toward the stage*) The play will begin soon.

MEDVEDENKO Yes. The acting will be done by Nina Zaryechny and the play was written by Konstantine Gavrilovich. They are in love with each other, and today their souls are mingled in a longing to create some image both can share and true to both. But my soul and your soul can't find any ground to meet on. You see how it is. I love you; I can't stay at home because I keep wishing so for you; and so every day I walk four miles here and four miles back and meet with nothing but indifference on your part. That's only natural. I've got nothing, we're a big family. Who wants to marry a man who can't even feed himself?

MASHA Fiddlesticks! (*She takes snuff*) Your love touches me, but I can't return it, that's all. (*Offers him snuff*) Help yourself.

MEDVEDENKO I'd as soon not.

(*A pause*)

MASHA My, how close it is! It must be going to storm tonight. All you do is philosophize or talk about money. You think the worst misery we can have is poverty. But I think it's a thousand times easier to go ragged and beg for bread than. . . . But you'd never understand that. . . .

(*Enter* SORIN, *leaning on his walking stick, and* TREPLEFF)

SORIN For some reason, who knows, my dear boy, the country's not my style. Naturally. You can't teach an old horse new tricks. Last night I went to bed at ten o'clock, and at nine this morning I awoke feeling as if my brain stuck to my skull, and so on. (*Laughing*) And then on top of all that I fell asleep after dinner just the same. And so now I'm a wreck, I'm still lost in a nightmare, and all the rest of it. . . .

TREPLEFF That's true, Uncle, you really ought to live in town. (*Sees* MASHA *and* MEDVEDENKO) Look, my friends, we'll call you when the play starts, but don't stay here now. I'll have to ask you to go.

SORIN (*To* MASHA) Maria Ilyinishna, won't you kindly ask your father to leave that dog unchained, to stop that howling? All last night again my sister couldn't sleep.

MASHA You'll have to tell my father yourself. I shan't do it, so please don't ask me to. (*To* MEDVEDENKO) Let's go.

MEDVEDENKO Then you'll let us know before the play starts.

(MASHA *and* MEDVEDENKO *go out*)

SORIN That just means the dog will howl all night again. You see how 'tis; in the country I have never had what I wanted. It used to be I'd get leave for twenty-eight days, say, and come down here to recoup, and so on; but they plagued me so with one silly piece of nonsense after another that the very first day I wanted to be out of it. (*Laughs*) I've always left here with relish. . . . Well, now that I'm retired, I have nowhere to go and all the rest of it. Like it—like it not, I live. . . .

YAKOV We're going for a swim, Konstantine Gavrilovich.

TREPLEFF So long as you are back in ten minutes. (*Looks at his watch*) We're about to begin.

YAKOV Yes, sir.

TREPLEFF Here's your theater. The curtain, then the first wing, then the second wing, and still further open space. No scenery at all. You see what the background is—it stretches to the lake and on to the horizon. And the curtain will go up at 8:30, just when the moon's rising.

SORIN Magnificent!

TREPLEFF If Nina's late, then, of course, the whole effect will be spoilt. It's time she was here now. But her father and stepmother watch her so she can hardly get out of the house, it's like escaping from prison. (*Straightening his uncle's tie*) Uncle, your hair and beard are rumpled up—you ought to have them trimmed. . . .

SORIN (*Combing his beard*) It's the tragedy of my life. I always look as if I'd been drunk, even when I was young I did—and so on. Women never have loved me. (*Sits down*) Why is my sister in such bad humor?

TREPLEFF Why? Bored. (*Sits down by* SORIN) Jealous. She's set against me, against the performance and against my play, because Nina's going to act in it and she's not. She's never read my play but she hates it.

SORIN You (*Laughing*) imagine things, really . . .

TREPLEFF Yes, she's furious because even on this little stage it's Nina will have a success and not she. (*Looks at his watch*) A psychological case, my mother. She's undeniably talented, intelligent, capable of sobbing over a novel; she recites all of Nekrasov's poetry[1] by heart; she nurses the sick like an angel; but you just try praising Duse to her; oh, ho! You praise nobody but her, write about her, rave about her, go into ecstasies over her marvelous performance in *La Dame Aux Camélias* or in *The Whirl of Life*.[2] But all that is a drug she can't get in the country, so she's bored and cross. We are all her enemies—it's all our fault. And then she's superstitious, afraid of three candles or number thirteen. She's stingy. She's got seventy thousand rubles in an Odessa bank—I know that for a fact. But ask her for a loan, she'll burst into tears.

SORIN You've got it into your head your play annoys your mother, and that upsets you, and so on. Don't worry, your mother worships the ground you walk on.

TREPLEFF (*Picking petals from a flower*) Loves me—loves me not, loves me—loves me not, loves me—loves me not. (*Laughing*) You see, my mother doesn't love me, of course not. I should say not! What she wants is to live, and love, and wear pretty clothes; and here I am twenty-five-years old and a perpetual reminder that she's no longer young. You see, when I'm not there she's only thirty-two, and when I am she's forty-three . . . and for that she hates me. She knows too that I refuse to respect her idea of the theatre. She loves the theatre; it seems to her that she's working for humanity, for holy art. But to my thinking her theatre today is nothing but routine, convention. When the curtain goes up, and by artificial light in a room with three walls, these great geniuses, these priests of holy art, show how people eat, drink, make love, move about and wear their jackets; when they try to fish a moral out of these flat pictures and phrases, some sweet little bit anybody could understand and any fool take home; when in a thousand different dishes they serve me the same thing over and over, over and over, over and over—well, it's then I run and run like Maupassant from the Eiffel Tower and all that vulgarity about to bury him.

SORIN But we can't do without the theatre.

TREPLEFF We must have new forms. New forms we must have, and if we can't get them we'd better have

[1] Nikolai Nekrasov (1821-1877) wrote many poems portraying the life of both urban and rural lower classes.

[2] Both plays demand virtuoso performances. The first, better known as *Camille,* details the loves of a brilliant Parisian courtesan; Alexander Dumas *fils* (1824-1895) adapted the play from his own successful novel. The second play (sometimes called *The Fumes of Life*) was written by Boleslav Markevich, a contemporary writer Chekhov held in very low esteem.

nothing at all. (*He looks at his watch*) I love my mother, I love her very much; but she leads a senseless life, always making a fuss over this novelist, her name forever chucked about in the papers . . . it disgusts me. It's merely the simple egotism of an ordinary mortal, I suppose, stirring me up sometimes that makes me wish I had somebody besides a famous actress for a mother, and fancy if she had been an ordinary woman I'd have been happier. Uncle, can you imagine anything more hopeless than my position is in her house? It used to be she'd entertain, all famous people . . . actors and authors—and among them all I was the only one who was nothing, and they put up with me only because I was her son. Who am I? What am I? I left the university in my third year, owing to circumstances, as they say, for which the editors are not responsible; I've no talent at all, not a kopeck on me; and according to my passport I am—a burgher of Kiev. My father, as you know, was a burgher of Kiev, though he was also a famous actor. So when these actors and writers of hers bestowed on me their gracious attentions, it seemed to me their eyes were measuring my insignificance—I guessed their thoughts and felt humiliated.

SORIN By the by, listen, can you please tell me what sort of man this novelist is? You see, I can't make him out. He never opens his mouth.

TREPLEFF He's an intelligent man, he's simple, apt to be melancholy. Quite decent. He's well under forty yet but he's already celebrated, he's had more than enough of everything. As for his writings . . . well, we'll say charming, full of talent, but after Tolstoi or Zola, of course, a little of Trigorin goes a long way.

SORIN My boy, I'm fond of writers, you know. Once there were two things I wanted passionately. To marry and to be an author. I never succeeded in doing either. It must be pleasant being a minor writer even, and all the rest of it.

TREPLEFF I hear footsteps. (*Embraces his uncle*) I can't live without her. Just the sound of her footsteps is lovely. (*Going to meet* NINA ZARYECHNY *as she enters*) I'm insanely happy! My enchantress! My dream!

NINA I'm not late. . . . Surely I'm not late. . . .

TREPLEFF (*Kissing her hands*) No, no, no.

NINA All day I worried, was so frightened. . . . I was so afraid father wouldn't let me come. But at last he's gone out. He went out just now with my stepmother. The sky has turned red, the moon will soon be up, and I raced the horse, raced him. (*Laughs*) But I'm so happy. (*Warmly shaking* SORIN'S *hand*)

SORIN (*Laughing*) You've been crying, I see by your little eyes. That's not fair.

NINA That's so. You can see how out of breath I am. Do let's hurry. I've got to go in half an hour. I must. Don't ask me to stay, my father doesn't know I'm here.

TREPLEFF It's time to begin anyhow. . . . I'll go call them.

SORIN I'll go. I'll go this minute. (*Begins to sing "The Two Grenadiers," then stops*) Once I started singing like that and a deputy who was standing by said, "Your Excellency has a very strong voice" . . . then he thought awhile and said, "Strong but unpleasant." (*Exits, laughing*)

NINA My father and his wife won't let me come here; they say it's Bohemia. They are afraid I'll go on the stage. But I am drawn here to this lake like a sea gull. My heart is full of you.

TREPLEFF We're alone.

NINA Isn't that someone over there?

TREPLEFF No, nobody. (*Kisses her*)

NINA What kind of tree is that?

TREPLEFF It's an elm.

NINA Why does it look so dark?

TREPLEFF Because it's evening and everything looks darker. Don't go away early, please don't.

NINA I must.

TREPLEFF But if I should follow you, Nina? I'll stand all night in the garden, looking up at your window.

NINA Oh, no! You mustn't. The watchman would see you and Treasure doesn't know you yet, he'd bark.

TREPLEFF I love you.

NINA Ssh . . . !

TREPLEFF Who's that? . . . You, Yakov?

YAKOV (*From behind stage*) Yes, sir.

TREPLEFF You must get to your seats, it's time to begin. The moon's coming up.

YAKOV Yes, sir.

TREPLEFF Have you got that methylated spirits? Is the sulphur ready? (*To* NINA) You see when the red eyes appear there must be a smell of sulphur around. You'd better go now, everything's ready. Do you feel nervous?

NINA Yes, awfully. It's not that I'm afraid of your mother so much, it's Boris Trigorin terrifies me, acting before him, a famous author like him. Tell me, is he young?

TREPLEFF Yes.

NINA What marvelous stories he writes!

TREPLEFF (*Coldly*) I don't know. I don't read them.

NINA It's hard to act in your play. There are no living characters in it.

TREPLEFF Living characters! I must represent life not as it is and not as it should be, but as it appears in my dreams.

NINA In your play there's no action; it's all recitation. It seems to me a play must have some love in it.

(*They go out by way of the stage. Enter* PAULINE ANDREEVNA *and* DORN)

PAULINE It's getting damp, go back and put on your galoshes.

DORN I'm hot.

PAULINE You don't take any care of yourself and it's just contrariness. You're a doctor and know very well how bad damp air is for you, but you like to make me miserable. You sat out on that terrace all last evening on purpose.

DORN (*Sings low*) Oh, never say that I . . .

PAULINE You were so enchanted by Madame Arkadina's conversation you didn't even notice the cold. . . . You may as well own up—she charms you. . . .

DORN I'm fifty-five.

PAULINE Fiddlesticks! What's that for a man, it's not old. You're still young enough looking, women still like you.

DORN (*Gently*) Tell me, what is it you want?

PAULINE Before an actress you are all ready to kiss the ground. All of you!

DORN (*Sings low*) Once more I stand before thee . . . If society does make a fuss over actors, treats them differently from, say shopkeepers—it's only right and natural. That's the pursuit of the ideal.

PAULINE Women have always fallen in love with you and hung on your neck. Is that the pursuit of the ideal too?

DORN (*Shrugs his shoulders*) Why? In the relations women have had with me there has been a great deal that was fine. What they chiefly loved in me was the fact that I was a first-class doctor for childbirths. Ten or fifteen years ago, you remember, I was the only decent obstetrician they had in all this part of the country. Besides, I've always been an honorable man.

PAULINE (*Clasping his hand*) My dear!

DORN Ssh . . . here they come!

(*Enter* MADAME ARKADINA *on* SORIN'S *arm*, TRIGORIN, SHAMREYEFF, MEDVEDENKO, *and* MASHA)

SHAMREYEFF In '73 at the Poltava Fair . . . pure delight . . . I can assure you she was magnificent, ah, magnificent! Pure delight! But tell me if you know where Chadin, Paul Semyonovich, the comedian, is now? Take his Raspluyef . . . 'twas better than Sadovsky's,[3] I can assure you, most esteemed lady. But what's become of him?

ARKADINA You keep asking me about someone before the flood . . . how should I know? (*Sits down*)

SHAMREYEFF Ah. (*Sighs*) Paulie Chadin! Nobody like that now. The stage is not what it was, Irina Nikolaevna, ah, no! In those days there were mighty oaks, now we have nothing but stumps.

DORN There are not many brilliant talents nowadays, it's true, but the general average of the acting is much higher.

SHAMREYEFF I can't agree with you there. However, that's a matter of taste, *De gustibus aut bene, aut nihil.*[4]

(TREPLEFF *comes out from behind the stage*)

ARKADINA My dear son, when does it begin?

TREPLEFF Please be patient. It's only a moment.

ARKADINA (*Reciting from* Hamlet) My son!

"Thou turnst mine eyes into my very soul,
And there I see such black and grained spots
As will not leave their tinct."

TREPLEFF (*Paraphrasing from* Hamlet) Nay, but to live in wickedness, seek love in the depths of sin. . . . (*Behind the stage a horn blows*) Ladies and gentlemen, we begin! I beg your attention. (*A pause*) I begin. (*Tapping the floor with a stick. In a loud voice*) Harken ye mists, out of ancient time, that drift by night over the bosom of this lake, darken our eyes with sleep and in our dream show us what will be in 200,000 years.

SORIN In 200,000 years nothing will be.

TREPLEFF Then let them present to us that nothing.

ARKADINA Let them. We are asleep.

(*The curtain rises. Vista opens across the lake. Low on the horizon the moon hangs, reflected in the water.* NINA ZARYECHNY *all in white, seated on a rock*)

NINA Men and beasts, lions, eagles and partridges, antlered deer, mute fishes dwelling in the water, starfish and small creatures invisible to the eye . . . these and all life have run their sad course and are no more. Thousands of creatures have come and gone since there was life on the earth. Vainly now the pallid moon doth light her lamp. In the meadows the cranes wake and cry no longer; and the beetles' hum is silent in the linden groves. Cold, cold, cold. Empty, empty, empty! Terrible, terrible, terrible. (*A pause*) Living bodies have crumbled to dust, and Eternal Matter has changed them into stones and water and clouds and there is one soul of many souls. I am that soul of the world. . . . In me the soul of Alexander the Great, of Cæsar, of Shakespeare, of Napoleon and of the lowest worm. The mind of man and the brute's instinct mingle in me. I remember all, all, and in me lives each several life again.

(*The will-o'-the-wisps appear*)

ARKADINA (*In a stage whisper*) We're in for something Decadent.

TREPLEFF (*Imploring and reproaching*) Mother!

NINA I am alone. Once in a hundred years I open my lips to speak, and in this void my sad echo is unheard. And you, pale fires, you do not hear me. . . . Before daybreak the putrid marsh begets you, and you wander until sunrise, but without thought, without will, without the throb of life. For fear life should spring in you, the Father of Eternal Matter, the Devil, causes every instant in you, as in stones and in water, an interchange of the atoms, and you are changing endlessly. I, only, the World's Soul, remain unchanged and am eternal. (*A pause*) I am like a prisoner cast into a deep, empty well, and know not where I am nor what awaits me. One thing only is not hidden from me: in the stubborn, savage fight with the Devil, the Principle of Material Forces, I am destined to conquer; and when that has been, matter and spirit shall be made one in the shadow of my soul forever. And lo, the kingdom of universal will is at hand. But that cannot be before long centuries of the moon, the shining dog star, and the earth, have run to dust. And till that time horror shall be, horror, horror, horror! (*A pause; upon the background of the lake appear two red spots*) Behold, my mighty adversary, the Devil, approaches. I see his awful, blood-red eyes.

ARKADINA I smell sulphur, is that necessary?

TREPLEFF Yes, it is.

ARKADINA (*Laughing*) Yes, it's a stage effect!

TREPLEFF Mother!

NINA But without man he is lost. . . .

[3] Shamreyeff's tastes in drama are distinctly for low comedy, in which Chadin and Sadovsky made their reputations.

[4] It's good or bad, depending on one's tastes.

PAULINE (*To* DORN) You're taking your hat off. Put it on, you'll catch cold.

ARKADINA The doctor has taken off his hat to the Devil, the Father of Eternal Matter?

TREPLEFF (*Blazing up, in a loud voice*) The play's over! That's enough! Curtain!

ARKADINA Why are you angry?

TREPLEFF That's enough. Curtain! Drop the curtain! (*Stamping his foot*) Curtain! (*The curtain falls*) You must excuse me! I don't know how it was but I forgot somehow that only a chosen few can write plays and act them. I was infringing on a monopoly. . . . My . . . I . . . (*Instead of saying more he makes a gesture of having done with it and goes out to the left*)

ARKADINA What's the matter with him?

SORIN Irina, my dear, you mustn't treat a young man's pride like that.

ARKADINA Now what have I said?

SORIN You've hurt his feelings.

ARKADINA But he told us beforehand it was all in fun, that's the way I took it . . . of course.

SORIN All the same . . .

ARKADINA And now it appears he's produced a masterpiece. Well, I declare! Evidently he had no intention of amusing us, not at all; he got up this performance and fumigated us with sulphur to demonstrate to us how plays should be written and what's worth acting in. I'm sick of him. Nobody could stand his everlasting digs and outbursts. He's an unruly, conceited boy.

SORIN He was only hoping to give you some pleasure.

ARKADINA Yes? I notice he didn't choose some familiar sort of play, but forced his own decadent raving on us. I can listen to raving. I don't mind listening to it, so long as I'm not asked to take it seriously; but this of his is not like that. Not at all, it's introducing us to a new epoch in art, inaugurating a new era in art. But to my mind it's not new forms or epochs, it's simply bad temper.

TRIGORIN Everyone writes as he wants to and as he can.

ARKADINA Well, let him write as he wants to and as he can, so long as he leaves me out of it.

DORN Great Jove angry is no longer Jove.

ARKADINA I'm not Jove, I'm a woman. (*Lighting a cigarette*) I'm not angry. . . . I'm merely vexed to see a young man wasting his time so. I didn't mean to hurt him.

MEDVEDENKO Nobody has any grounds for separating matter from spirit, for it may be this very spirit itself is a union of material atoms. (*Excitedly, to* TRIGORIN) You know, somebody ought to put in a play, and then act on the stage, how we poor schoolmasters live. It's a hard, hard life.

ARKADINA That's so, but we shan't talk of plays or atoms. The evening is so lovely. Listen . . . they're singing! (*Pausing to listen*) How good it is!

PAULINE It's on the other side of the lake.

(*A pause*)

ARKADINA Sit down by me here. (*To* TRIGORIN) You know, ten or fifteen years ago we had music on this lake every night almost. There were six big country houses then around the shore; and it was all laughter, noise, shooting and lovemaking . . . making love without end. The *jeune premier*[5] and the idol of all six houses was our friend here, I must present (*Nods toward* DORN) Doctor Eugene Sergeevich. He's charming now, but then he was irresistible. Why did I hurt my poor boy's feelings? I'm worried about him. (*Calls*) Kostya! Son! Kostya!

MASHA I'll go look for him.

ARKADINA Would you, my dear?

MASHA (*Calling*) Ah-oo! Konstantine. Ah-oo! (*She goes out*)

NINA (*Coming from behind the stage*) Evidently we're not going on, so I may as well come out. Good evening! (*Kisses* MADAME ARKADINA *and* PAULINE ANDREEVNA)

SORIN Bravo! Bravo!

ARKADINA Bravo! Bravo! We were all enchanted. With such looks and such a lovely voice, it's a sin for you to stay here in the country. You have talent indeed. Do you hear? You owe it to yourself to go on the stage.

NINA Oh, that's my dream. (*Sighing*) But it will never come true.

ARKADINA Who can tell? Let me present Boris Alexeevich Trigorin.

NINA Oh, I'm so glad . . . (*Much embarrassed*) I'm always reading your . . .

ARKADINA (*Drawing* NINA *down beside her*) Don't be shy, dear. He may be a famous author, but his heart's quite simple. Look, he's embarrassed, too.

DORN I suppose we may raise the curtain now. This way it's frightening.

SHAMREYEFF (*Loudly*) Yakov, my man, raise the curtain!

(*The curtain is raised*)

NINA (*To* TRIGORIN) It's a strange play, isn't it?

TRIGORIN I didn't understand a word of it. However, I enjoyed watching it. You acted with so much sincerity, and the scenery was so lovely. (*A pause*) I dare say there are quantities of fish in this lake.

NINA Yes.

TRIGORIN I love fishing. I can think of no greater pleasure than to sit along toward evening by the water and watch a float.

NINA But, I'd have thought that for anyone who had tasted the joy of creation, no other pleasures could exist.

ARKADINA (*Laughing*) Don't talk like that. When people make him pretty speeches he simply crumples up.

SHAMREYEFF I remember one evening at the Opera in Moscow when the celebrated Silva was singing, how delighted we were when he took low C. Imagine our surprise . . . it so happened the bass from our church choir was there and all at once we heard "Bravo Silva" from the gallery a whole octave lower . . . like this . . . "Bravo Silva." The audience was thunderstruck.

[5] Literally, "first young man," the actor in a stock company who plays a dashing young lover.

(*A pause*)

DORN The angel of silence is flying over us.

NINA Oh, I must go. Good-by.

ARKADINA Where to? Where so early? We won't allow it.

NINA Papa is waiting for me.

ARKADINA What a man, really! (*Kissing her*) Well, there's no help for it. It's too sad losing you.

NINA If you only knew how I don't want to go.

ARKADINA Somebody must see you home, child.

NINA (*Frightened*) Oh, no, no.

SORIN (*Imploring her*) Don't go.

NINA I must, Peter Nikolaevich.

SORIN Stay an hour more, and so on. Come now, really . . .

NINA (*Hesitating with tears in her eyes*) I can't! (*She shakes hands and hurries out*)

ARKADINA Now there's a really poor, unfortunate girl. They say her mother when she died willed the husband all her immense fortune, everything to the very last kopeck, and now this little girl is left with nothing, since her father has already willed everything he has to the second wife. That's shocking.

DORN Yes, her papa is rather a beast, I must grant him that.

SORIN (*Rubbing his hands to warm them*) What do you say, we'd better go in too, it's getting damp. My legs ache.

ARKADINA It's like having wooden legs, you can hardly walk on them. Come on, you poor old patriarch. (*She takes his arm*)

SHAMREYEFF (*Offering his arm to his wife*) Madame?

SORIN There's that dog howling again. (*To* SHAMREYEFF) Be good enough, Ilya Afanasevich, to tell them to let that dog off the chain.

SHAMREYEFF It can't be done, Peter Nikolaevich, or we'll be having thieves in the barn, and the millet's there. (*To* MEDVEDENKO, *walking beside him*) Yes, a whole octave lower. "Bravo Silva!" And not your concert singer, mind you, just ordinary church choir.

MEDVEDENKO And what salary does a church singer get?

(*All except* DORN *go out*)

DORN (*Alone*) I don't know . . . maybe I'm no judge, I may be going off my head, but I liked that play. There's something in it. When the girl spoke of the vast solitude, and afterward when the Devil's eyes appeared, I could feel my hands trembling. It was all so fresh and naïve. But here he comes. I want to say all the nice things I can to him.

(*Enter* TREPLEFF)

TREPLEFF They've all gone.

DORN I'm here.

TREPLEFF Masha's been hunting for me all over the park. Unbearable creature!

DORN Konstantine Gavrilovich, I admired your play extremely. It's a curious kind of thing and I haven't heard the end, but still it made a deep impression on me. You've got great talent. You must keep on! (KONSTANTINE *presses his hand and embraces him impulsively*) Phew, what a nervous fellow! Tears in his eyes! What I wanted to say is you chose your subject from the realm of abstract ideas, and that's right . . . a work of art should express a great idea. There is no beauty without seriousness. My, you are pale!

TREPLEFF So you think I ought to go on?

DORN Yes. But write only of what is profound and eternal. You know how I have lived my life, I have lived it with variety and choiceness; and I have enjoyed it; and I am content. But if ever I had felt the elevation of spirit that comes to artists in their creative moments I believe I should have despised this body and all its usages, and tried to soar above all earthly things.

TREPLEFF Forgive me, where's Nina?

DORN And another thing. In a work of art there must be a clear, definite idea. You must know what your object is in writing, for if you follow that picturesque road without a definite aim, you will go astray and your talent will be your ruin.

TREPLEFF (*Impatiently*) Where is Nina?

DORN She's gone home.

TREPLEFF (*In despair*) What shall I do? I want to see her. I must see her. I'm going . . .

(MASHA *enters*)

DORN Calm yourself, my friend!

TREPLEFF But all the same I'm going. I must go.

MASHA Konstantine Gavrilovich, come indoors. Your mother wants you. She's anxious.

TREPLEFF Tell her I've gone . . . and please . . . all of you let me alone! Don't follow me around.

DORN Come, come, come, boy, you mustn't act like this . . . it won't do.

TREPLEFF (*In tears*) Good-by, Doctor . . . and thank you. . . . (*Exits*)

DORN (*Sighing*) Ah, youth, youth . . .

MASHA When there is nothing else left to say, people always say, "Ah, youth, youth." (*Takes a pinch of snuff*)

DORN (*Takes snuffbox out of her hand and flings it into the bushes*) It's disgusting. (*A pause*) There in the house they seem to be playing. We'd better go in.

MASHA No, no, wait a minute.

DORN What is it?

MASHA Let me talk to you. . . . I don't love my father, I can't talk to him, but I feel with all my heart that you are near me. . . . Help me . . . help me . . . (*Starts to sob*) or I shall do something silly, I'll make my life a mockery, ruin it . . . I can't keep on . . .

DORN How? Help you how?

MASHA I'm tortured. No one, no one knows what I'm suffering . . . (*Laying her head on his breast, softly*) I love Konstantine.

DORN How nervous they all are! How nervous they all are! And so much love! O magic lake! (*Tenderly*) What can I do for you, child? What, what?

*Curtain*

## Act Two

*A croquet lawn. In the background on the right is the house with a large terrace; on the left is seen the lake, in which the blazing sun is reflected. Flowerbeds. Noon. Hot. On one side of the croquet lawn, in the shade of an old linden tree,* MADAME ARKADINA, DORN *and* MASHA *are sitting on a garden bench.* DORN *has an open book on his knees.*

ARKADINA (*To* MASHA) Here, let's stand up. (*They both stand up*) Side by side. You are twenty-two and I am nearly twice that. Doctor Dorn, tell us, which one of us looks the younger?

DORN You, of course.

ARKADINA There you are . . . you see? . . . And why is it? Because I work, I feel, I'm always on the go, but you sit in the same spot all the time, you're not living. I make it a rule never to look ahead into the future. I let myself think neither of old age nor of death. What will be will be.

MASHA But I feel as if I were a thousand, I trail my life along after me like an endless train. . . . Often I have no wish to be living at all. (*Sits down*) Of course that's all nonsense. I ought to shake myself and throw it all off.

DORN (*Sings softly*) "Tell her, pretty flowers . . ."[1]

ARKADINA Then I'm correct as an Englishman. I'm always dressed and my hair always *comme il faut.* Would I permit myself to leave the house, even to come out here in the garden, in a dressing gown or with my hair blowzy? Never, I should say not! The reason I have kept my looks is because I've never been a frump, never let myself go, as some do. (*Arms akimbo, she walks up and down the croquet green*) Here I am, light as a bird. Ready to play a girl of fifteen any day.

DORN Well, at any rate, I'll go on with my reading. (*Takes up the book*) We stopped at the corn merchants and the rats.

ARKADINA And the rats. Go on. (*Sits*) Let me have it, I'll read. It's my turn anyhow. (*She takes the book and looks for the place*) And the rats . . . here we are . . . (*Reads*) "And certainly, for people of the world to pamper the romantics and make them at home in their houses is as dangerous as for corn merchants to raise rats in their granaries. And yet they are beloved. And so when a woman has picked out the author she wants to entrap, she besieges him with compliments, amenities, and favors." Well, among the French that may be, but certainly here with us there's nothing of the kind, we've no set program. Here with us a woman before she ever sets out to capture an author is usually head over heels in love with him herself. To go no further, take me and Trigorin . . .

[1] Here and elsewhere Dorn sings Siebel's Song, from Gounod's *Faust.*

(*Enter* SORIN, *leaning on a stick, with* NINA *at his side.* MEDVEDENKO *follows him, pushing a wheel chair*)

SORIN (*Caressingly, as if to a child*) Yes? We're all joy, eh? We're happy today after all. (*To his sister*) We're all joy. Father and Stepmother are gone to Tver, and we are free now for three whole days.

NINA (*Sits down beside* ARKADINA *and embraces her*) I am so happy! I belong now to you.

SORIN (*Sitting down in the wheel chair*) She looks lovely today.

ARKADINA Beautifully dressed, intriguing . . . that's a clever girl. (*She kisses* NINA) We mustn't praise her too much. It's bad luck. Where's Boris Alexeevich?

NINA He's at the bathhouse fishing.

ARKADINA You'd think he'd be sick of it. (*She begins reading again*)

NINA What is that you have?

ARKADINA Maupassant's "On the Water," darling. (*Reads a few lines to herself*) Well, the rest is uninteresting and untrue. (*Shutting the book*) I'm troubled in my soul. Tell me, what's the matter with my son? Why is he so sad and morose? He spends day after day on the lake and I hardly ever see him any more.

MASHA His heart's troubled. (*To* NINA, *timidly*) Please, Nina, read something out of his play, won't you?

NINA (*Shrugging her shoulders*) You really want me to? It's so uninteresting.

MASHA (*With restrained eagerness*) When he recites anything his eyes shine and his face grows pale. He has a beautiful sad voice, and a manner like a poet's.

(*Sound of* SORIN's *snoring*)

DORN Pleasant dreams.

ARKADINA (*To* SORIN) Petrusha!

SORIN Eh?

ARKADINA Are you asleep?

SORIN Not at all.

(*A pause*)

ARKADINA You are not following any treatment for yourself, that's not right, brother.

SORIN I'd be glad to follow a treatment, but the doctor won't give me any.

DORN Take care of yourself at sixty!

SORIN Even at sixty a man wants to live.

DORN (*Impatiently*) Bah! Take your valerian drops.

ARKADINA I'd think it would do him good to take a cure at some springs.

DORN Well . . . he might take it. He might not take it.

ARKADINA Try and understand that!

DORN Nothing to understand. It's all clear.

(*A pause*)

MEDVEDENKO Peter Nikolaevich ought to give up smoking.

SORIN Fiddlesticks!

DORN No, it's not fiddlesticks! Wine and tobacco rob us of our personality. After a cigar or a vodka, you're not Peter Nikolaevich, you're Peter Nikolaevich plus somebody else; your ego splits up, and you begin to see yourself as a third person.

SORIN Fine (*Laughs*) for you to argue! You've lived your life, but what about me? I've served the Department of Justice twenty-eight years, but I've never lived, never seen anything, and all the rest of it, so naturally I want to have my life. You've had your fill and that's why you turn to philosophy. I want to live, and that's why I turn to sherry and smoking cigars after dinner, and so on. And that's that.

DORN One must look seriously at life, but to go in for cures at sixty and regret the pleasures you missed in your youth, is, if you'll forgive me, frivolous.

MASHA (*Gets up*) It must be time for lunch. (*Walking slow and hobbling*) My foot's gone to sleep. (*Exits*)

DORN She'll down a couple of glasses before lunch.

SORIN The poor thing gets no happiness of her own.

DORN Fiddlesticks, your Excellency.

SORIN You argue like a man who's had his fill.

ARKADINA Oh, what can be duller than this darling country duliness! Hot, quiet, nobody ever does anything, everybody philosophizes. It's good to be here with you, my friends, delightful listening to you, but . . . sitting in my hotel room, all by myself, studying my part . . . how much better!

NINA (*Ecstatically*) Good! I understand you.

SORIN Of course, in town's better. You sit in your study, the footman lets nobody in without announcing them, there's the telephone . . . on the street, cabs and so on . . .

DORN (*Singing sotto voce*) "Tell her, my flowers . . ."

(*Enter* SHAMREYEFF, *behind him* PAULINE)

SHAMREYEFF Here they are. Good morning! (*Kisses* MADAME ARKADINA'S *hand, then* NINA'S) Very glad to see you looking so well. (*To* MADAME ARKADINA) My wife tells me you are thinking of driving into town with her today. Is that so?

ARKADINA Yes, we are thinking of it.

SHAMREYEFF Hm! That's magnificent, but what will you travel on, my most esteemed lady? Today around here we are hauling rye, all the hands are busy. And what horses would you take, may I ask?

ARKADINA What horses? How should I know . . . what horses!

SORIN There are carriage horses here!

SHAMREYEFF (*Flaring up*) Carriage horses? But where do I get the harness? Where do I get the harness? It's amazing. It's incomprehensible! Most esteemed lady! Excuse me, I am on my knees before your talent, I'd gladly give ten years of my life for you, but I cannot let you have the horses!

ARKADINA But what if I have to go? A fine business this is!

SHAMREYEFF Most esteemed lady! You don't know what a farm means.

ARKADINA (*Flaring up*) The same old story! In that case I'll start for Moscow today. Order me horses from the village, or I'll walk to the station.

SHAMREYEFF (*Flaring up*) In that case I resign my position! Find yourself another steward! (*Exits*)

ARKADINA Every summer it's like this, every summer here they insult me! I'll never put my foot here again!

(*Goes out in the direction of the bath-house. Presently she is seen going into the house.* TRIGORIN *follows, with fishing rods and a pail*)

SORIN (*Flaring up*) This is insolent! The devil knows what it is! I'm sick of it, and so on. Bring all the horses here this very minute!

NINA (*To* PAULINE) To refuse Irina Nikolaevna, the famous actress! Any little wish of hers, the least whim, is worth more than all your farm. It's simply unbelievable!

PAULINE (*In despair*) What can I do? Put yourself in my shoes, what can I do?

SORIN (*To* NINA) Let's go find my sister. We'll all beg her not to leave us. Isn't that so? (*Looking in the direction* SHAMREYEFF *went*) You insufferable man! Tyrant!

NINA (*Prevents his getting up*) Sit still, sit still. We'll wheel you. (*She and* MEDVEDENKO *push the wheel chair*) Oh, how awful it is!

SORIN Yes, yes, it's awful. But he won't leave, I'll speak to him right off.

(*They go out.* DORN *and* PAULINE *remain*)

DORN People are certainly tiresome. Really the thing to do, of course, is throw that husband of yours out by the neck; but it will all end by this old woman, Peter Nikolaevich, and his sister begging him to pardon them. See if they don't.

PAULINE He has put the carriage horses in the fields, too. And these misunderstandings happen every day. If you only knew how it all upsets me. It's making me sick; you see how I'm trembling. I can't bear his coarseness. (*Entreating*) Eugene, my darling, light of my eyes . . . take me with you. Our time is passing, we're not young any longer; if . . . if only we could . . . for the rest of our lives at least . . . stop concealing things, stop pretending.

(*A pause*)

DORN I am fifty-five, it's too late to change now.

PAULINE I know, you refuse me because there are other women close to you. It's impossible for you to take them all with you. I understand. I apologize! Forgive me, you are tired of me.

(NINA *appears before the house, picking a bunch of flowers*)

DORN No, not all that.

PAULINE I am miserable with jealousy. Of course you are a doctor. You can't escape women. I understand.

DORN (*To* NINA, *as she joins them*) What's happening?

NINA Irina Nikolaevna is crying and Peter Nikolaevich having his asthma.

DORN (*Rising*) I must go and give them both some valerian drops.

NINA (*Giving him the flowers*) Won't you?

DORN *Merci bien.* (*Goes toward the house*)

PAULINE What pretty flowers! (*Nearing the house, in a low voice*) Give me those flowers! Give me those flowers!

(*He hands her the flowers, she tears them to pieces and flings them away. They go into the house*)

NINA (*Alone*) How strange it is seeing a famous actress

cry, and about such a little nothing! And isn't it strange that a famous author should sit all day long fishing? The darling of the public, his name in the papers every day, his photograph for sale in shop windows, his book translated into foreign languages, and he's delighted because he's caught two chub. I imagined famous people were proud and distant, and that they despised the crowd, and used their fame and the glamor of their names to revenge themselves on the world for putting birth and money first. But here I see them crying or fishing, playing cards, laughing or losing their tempers, like everybody else.

(TREPLEFF *enters, without a hat, carrying a gun and a dead sea gull*)

TREPLEFF Are you here alone?

NINA Alone. (TREPLEFF *lays the sea gull at her feet*) What does that mean?

TREPLEFF I was low enough today to kill this sea gull. I lay it at your feet.

NINA What's the matter with you? (*Picks up sea gull and looks at it*)

TREPLEFF (*Pause*) It's the way I'll soon end my own life.

NINA I don't even recognize you.

TREPLEFF Yes, ever since I stopped recognizing you. You've changed toward me. Your eyes are cold. You hate to have me near you.

NINA You are so irritable lately, and you talk . . . it's as if you were talking in symbols. And this sea gull, I suppose that's a symbol, too. Forgive me, but I don't understand it. (*Lays the sea gull on the seat*) I'm too simple to understand you.

TREPLEFF This began that evening when my play failed so stupidly. Women will never forgive failure. I've burnt it all, every scrap of it. If you only knew what I'm going through! Your growing cold to me is terrible, unbelievable; it's as if I had suddenly waked and found this lake dried up and sunk in the ground. You say you are too simple to understand me. Oh, what is there to understand? My play didn't catch your fancy, you despise my kind of imagination, you already consider me commonplace, insignificant, like so many others. (*Stamping his foot*) How well I understand it all, how I understand it. It's like a spike in my brain, may it be damned along with my pride, which is sucking my blood, sucking it like a snake. (*He sees* TRIGORIN, *who enters reading a book*) Here comes the real genius, he walks like Hamlet, and with a book too. (*Mimicking*) "Words, words, words." [2] This sun has hardly reached you, and you are already smiling, your glance is melting in his rays. I won't stand in your way. (*He goes out*)

TRIGORIN (*Making notes in a book*) Takes snuff and drinks vodka, always wears black. The schoolmaster in love with her.

NINA Good morning, Boris Alexeevich!

TRIGORIN Good morning. It seems that things have taken a turn we hadn't expected, so we are leaving today. You and I aren't likely to meet again. I'm sorry. I don't often meet young women, young and charming. I've forgotten how one feels at eighteen or nineteen, I can't picture it very clearly, and so the girls I draw in my stories and novels are mostly wrong. I'd like to be in your shoes for just one hour, to see things through your eyes, and find out just what sort of a little person you are.

NINA And how I'd like to be in your shoes!

TRIGORIN Why?

NINA To know how it feels being a famous genius. What's it like being famous? How does it make you feel?

TRIGORIN How? Nohow, I should think. I'd never thought about it. (*Reflecting*) One of two things: either you exaggerate my fame, or else my fame hasn't made me feel it.

NINA But if you read about yourself in the papers?

TRIGORIN When they praise me I'm pleased; when they abuse me, I feel whipped for a day or so.

NINA It's a marvelous world! If you only knew how I envy you! Look how different different people's lots are! Some have all they can do to drag through their dull, obscure lives; they are all just alike, all miserable; others . . . well, you for instance . . . have a bright, interesting life that means something. You are happy.

TRIGORIN I? (*Shrugging his shoulders*) Hm . . . I hear you speak of fame and happiness, of a bright, interesting life, but for me that's all words, pretty words that . . . if you'll forgive my saying so . . . mean about the same to me as candied fruits, which I never eat. You are very young and very kind.

NINA Your life is beautiful.

TRIGORIN I don't see anything so very beautiful about it. (*Looks at his watch*) I must get to my writing. Excuse me, I'm busy. . . . (*Laughs*) You've stepped on my pet corn, as they say, and here I am, beginning to get excited and a little cross. At any rate let's talk. Let's talk about my beautiful, bright life. Well, where shall we begin? (*After reflecting a moment*) You know, sometimes violent obsessions take hold of a man, some fixed idea pursues him, the moon for example, day and night he thinks of nothing but the moon. Well, I have just such a moon. Day and night one thought obsesses me: I must be writing, I must be writing, I must be . . . I've scarcely finished one novel when somehow I'm driven on to write another, then a third, and after the third a fourth. I write incessantly, and always at a breakneck speed, and that's the only way I can write. What's beautiful and bright about that, I ask you? Oh, what a wild life! Why, now even, I'm here talking to you, I'm excited, but every minute I remember that the story I haven't finished is there waiting for me. I see that cloud up there, it's shaped like a grand piano . . . instantly a mental note . . . I must remember to put that in my story . . . a cloud sailing by . . . grand piano. A whiff of heliotrope. Quickly I make note of it: cloying smell, widow's color . . . put that in next time I describe a summer evening. Every sentence, every word I say and you say, I lie in wait for it, snap it up for my literary store-

[2] Chekhov uses Hamlet's response when Polonius asks the Prince what he is reading (Act II, Scene 2).

room . . . it might come in handy. . . . As soon as I put my work down, I race off to the theatre or go fishing, hoping to find a rest, but not at all . . . a new idea for a story comes rolling around in my head like a cannon ball, and I'm back at my desk, and writing and writing and writing. And it's always like that, everlastingly. I have no rest from myself, and I feel that I am consuming my own life, that for the honey I'm giving to someone in the void, I rob my best flowers of their pollen, I tear up those flowers and trample on their roots. Do I seem mad? Do my friends seem to talk with me as they would to a sane man? "What are you writing at now? What shall we have next?" Over and over it's like that, till I think all this attention and praise is said only out of kindness to a sick man . . . deceive him, and soothe him, and then any minute come stealing up behind and pack him off to the madhouse. And in those years, my young best years, when I was beginning, why then writing made my life a torment. A minor writer, especially when he's not successful, feels clumsy, he's all thumbs, the world has no need for him; his nerves are about to go; he can't resist hanging around people in the arts, where nobody knows him, or takes any notice of him, and he's afraid to look them straight in the eyes, like a man with a passion for gambling who hasn't any money to play with. I'd never seen my readers but for some reason or other I pictured them as hating me and mistrusting me, I had a deathly fear of the public, and when my first play was produced it seemed to me all the dark eyes in the audience were looking at it with hostility and all the light eyes with frigid indifference. Oh how awful that was! What torment it was!

NINA But surely the inspiration you feel and the creation itself of something must give you a moment of high, sweet happiness, don't they?

TRIGORIN Yes. When I'm writing I enjoy it and I enjoy reading my proofs, but the minute it comes out I detest it; I see it's not what I meant it to be; I was wrong to write it at all, and I'm vexed and sick at heart about it. (*Laughs*) Then the public reads it. "Yes, charming, clever. . . . Charming but nothing like Tolstoi: A very fine thing, but Turgenev's *Fathers and Sons* is finer." To my dying day that's what it will be, clever and charming, charming and clever . . . nothing more. And when I'm dead they'll be saying at my grave, "Here lies Trigorin, a delightful writer but not so good as Turgenev."

NINA Excuse me, but I refuse to understand you. You are simply spoiled by success.

TRIGORIN What success? I have never pleased myself. I don't like myself as a writer. The worst of it is that I am in a sort of daze and often don't understand what I write. . . . I love this water here, the trees, the sky, I feel nature, it stirs in me a passion, an irresistible desire to write. But I am not only a landscape painter, I am a citizen too, I love my country, the people, I feel that if I am a writer I ought to speak also of the people, of their sufferings, of their future, speak of science, of the rights of man, and so forth, and I speak of everything, I hurry up, on all sides they are after me, are annoyed at me, I dash from side to side like a fox the hounds are baiting, I see life and science getting always farther and farther ahead as I fall always more and more behind, like a peasant missing his train, and the upshot is I feel that I can write only landscape, and in all the rest I am false and false to the marrow of my bones.

NINA You work too hard, and have no time and no wish to feel your own importance. You may be dissatisfied with yourself, of course, but other people think you are great and excellent. If I were such a writer as you are I'd give my whole life to the people, but I should feel that the only happiness for them would be in rising to me; and they should draw my chariot.

TRIGORIN Well, in a chariot . . . Agamemnon am I, or what? (*They are smiling*)

NINA For the happiness of being an author or an actress I would bear any poverty, disillusionment, I'd have people hate me. I'd live in a garret and eat black bread, I'd endure my own dissatisfaction with myself and all my faults, but in return I should ask for fame . . . real resounding fame. (*Covers her face with her hands*) My head's swimming. . . . Ouf!

ARKADINA (*From within the house*) Boris Alexeevich!

TRIGORIN She's calling me. I dare say, to come and pack. But I don't feel like going away. (*He glances at the lake*) Look, how beautiful it is! Marvelous!

NINA Do you see over there, that house and garden?

TRIGORIN Yes.

NINA It used to belong to my dear mother, I was born there. I've spent all my life by this lake and I know every little island on it.

TRIGORIN It's all very charming. (*Seeing the sea gull*) What is that?

NINA A sea gull. Konstantine shot it.

TRIGORIN It's a lovely bird. Really, I don't want to leave here. Do try and persuade Irina Nikolaevna to stay. (*Makes a note in his book*)

NINA What is it you're writing?

TRIGORIN Only a note. An idea struck me. (*Putting the notebook away*) An idea for a short story: a young girl, one like you, has lived all her life beside a lake; she loves the lake like a sea gull and is happy and free like a sea gull. But by chance a man comes, sees her, and out of nothing better to do, destroys her, like this sea gull here.

(*A pause.* MADAME ARKADINA *appears at the window*)

ARKADINA Boris Alexeevich, where are you?

TRIGORIN Right away! (*Goes toward the house, looking back at* NINA. MADAME ARKADINA *remains at the window*) What is it?

ARKADINA We're staying.

(TRIGORIN *enters the house*)

NINA (*Coming forward, standing lost in thought*) It's a dream!

*Curtain*

# Act Three

*The dining room in* SORIN'S *house. On the right and left are doors. A sideboard. A medicine cupboard. In the middle of the room a table. A small trunk and hatboxes, signs of preparations for leaving.*

TRIGORIN *is at lunch,* MASHA *standing by the table.*

MASHA I tell you this because you're a writer. You might use it. I tell you the truth: if he had died when he shot himself I wouldn't live another minute. Just the same I'm getting braver; I've just made up my mind to tear this love out of my heart by the roots.

TRIGORIN How will you do it?

MASHA I'm going to get married. To Medvedenko.

TRIGORIN Is that the schoolmaster?

MASHA Yes.

TRIGORIN I don't see why you must do that.

MASHA Loving without hope, waiting the whole year long for something . . . but when I'm married I won't have any time for love, there'll be plenty of new things I'll have to do to make me forget the past. Anyhow it will be a change, you know. Shall we have another?

TRIGORIN Haven't you had about enough?

MASHA Ah! (*Pours two glasses*) Here! Don't look at me like that! Women drink oftener than you imagine. Not so many of them drink openly like me. Most of them hide it. Yes. And it's always vodka or cognac. (*Clinks glasses*) Your health. You're a decent sort, I'm sorry to be parting from you.

(*They drink*)

TRIGORIN I don't want to leave here myself.

MASHA You should beg her to stay.

TRIGORIN She'd never do that now. Her son is behaving himself very tactlessly. First he tries shooting himself and now, they say, he's going to challenge me to a duel. But what for? He sulks, he snorts, he preaches new art forms . . . but there's room for all, the new and the old . . . why elbow?

MASHA Well, and there's jealousy. However, that's not my business.

(*Pause.* YAKOV *crosses right to left with a piece of luggage.* NINA *enters, stops near window*)

MASHA That schoolmaster of mine is none too clever, but he's a good man and he's poor, and he loves me dearly. I'm sorry for him, and I'm sorry for his old mother. Well, let me wish you every happiness. Think kindly of me. (*Warmly shakes his hand*) Let me thank you for your friendly interest. Send me your books, be sure to write in them. Only don't put "esteemed lady," but simply this: "To Maria, who, not remembering her origin, does not know why she is living in this world." Good-by. (*Goes out*)

NINA (*Holding out her hand closed to* TRIGORIN) Even or odd?

TRIGORIN Even.

NINA (*Sighing*) No. I had only one pea in my hand. I was trying my fortune: To be an actress or not. I wish somebody would advise me.

TRIGORIN There's no advice in this sort of thing.

(*A pause*)

NINA We are going to part . . . I may never see you again. Won't you take this little medal to remember me? I've had it engraved with your initials and on the other side the title of your book: *Days and Nights.*

TRIGORIN What a graceful thing to do! (*Kisses the medal*) It's a charming present.

NINA Sometimes think of me.

TRIGORIN I'll think of you. I'll think of you as I saw you that sunny day . . . do you remember . . . a week ago when you had on your white dress . . . we were talking . . . a white sea gull was lying on the bench beside us.

NINA (*Pensive*) Yes, the sea gull. (*A pause*) Someone's coming . . . let me see you two minutes before you go, won't you? (*Goes out on the left as* MADAME ARKADINA *and* SORIN, *in full dress, with a decoration, enter, then* YAKOV, *busy with the packing*)

ARKADINA Stay at home, old man. How could you be running about with your rheumatism? (*To* TRIGORIN) Who was it just went out? Nina?

TRIGORIN Yes.

ARKADINA *Pardon!* We intruded. (*Sits down*) I believe everything's packed. I'm exhausted.

TRIGORIN *Days and Nights,* page 121, lines eleven and twelve.

YAKOV (*Clearing the table*) Shall I pack your fishing rods as well?

TRIGORIN Yes, I'll want them again. But the books you can give away.

YAKOV Yes, sir.

TRIGORIN (*To himself*) Page 121, lines eleven and twelve. What's in those lines? (*To* ARKADINA) Have you my works here in the house?

ARKADINA Yes, in my brother's study, the corner bookcase.

TRIGORIN Page 121. (*Exits*)

ARKADINA Really, Petrusha, you'd better stay at home.

SORIN You're going away. It's dreary for me here at home without you.

ARKADINA But what's there in town?

SORIN Nothing in particular, but all the same. (*Laughs*) There's the laying of the foundation stone for the town hall, and all that sort of thing. A man longs, if only for an hour or so, to get out of this gudgeon existence, and it's much too long I've been lying around like an old cigarette holder. I've ordered the horses at one o'clock, we'll set off at the same time.

ARKADINA (*After a pause*) Oh, stay here, don't be lonesome, don't take cold. Look after my son. Take care of him. Advise him. (*A pause*) Here I am leaving and so shall never know why Konstantine tried to kill himself. I have a notion the main reason was jealousy. and the sooner I take Trigorin away from here the better.

SORIN How should I explain it to you? There were

other reasons besides jealousy. Here we have a man who is young, intelligent, living in the country in solitude, without money, without position, without a future. He has nothing to do. He is ashamed and afraid of his idleness. I love him very much and he's attached to me, but he feels just the same that he's superfluous in this house, and a sort of dependent here, a poor relation. That's something we can understand, it's pride, of course.

ARKADINA I'm worried about him. (*Reflecting*) He might go into the service, perhaps.

SORIN (*Whistling, then hesitatingly*) It seems to me the best thing you could do would be to let him have a little money. In the first place he ought to be able to dress himself like other people, and so on. Look how he's worn that same old jacket these past three years; he runs around without an overcoat. (*Laughs*) Yes, and it wouldn't harm him to have a little fun . . . he might go abroad, perhaps . . . it wouldn't cost much.

ARKADINA Perhaps I could manage a suit, but as for going abroad . . . no. Just at this moment I can't even manage the suit. (*Firmly*) I haven't any money! (SORIN *laughs*) I haven't. No.

SORIN (*Whistling*) Very well. Forgive me, my dear, don't be angry. You're a generous, noble woman.

ARKADINA (*Weeping*) I haven't any money.

SORIN Of course, if I had any money, I'd give him some myself, but I haven't anything, not a kopeck. (*Laugh*) My manager takes all my pension and spends it on agriculture, cattle-raising, bee-keeping, and my money goes for nothing. The bees die, the cows die, horses they never let me have.

ARKADINA Yes, I have some money, but I'm an actress, my costumes alone are enough to ruin me.

SORIN You are very good, my dear. I respect you. Yes. . . . But there again something's coming over me. . . . (*Staggers*) My head's swimming. (*Leans on table*) I feel faint, and so on.

ARKADINA (*Alarmed*) Petrusha! (*Trying to support him*) Petrusha, my darling! (*Calls*) Help me! Help!

(*Enter* TREPLEFF, *his head bandaged, and* MEDVEDENKO)

ARKADINA He feels faint.

SORIN It's nothing, it's nothing. . . . (*Smiles and drinks water*) It's gone already . . . and so on.

TREPLEFF (*To his mother*) Don't be alarmed, Mother, it's not serious. It often happens now to my uncle. Uncle, you must lie down a little.

SORIN A little, yes. All the same I'm going to town. . . . I'm lying down a little and I'm going to town. . . . that's clear. (*He goes, leaning on his stick*)

MEDVEDENKO (*Gives him his arm*) There's a riddle: in the morning it's on four legs, at noon on two, in the evening on three.

SORIN (*Laughs*) That's it. And on the back at night. Thank you, I can manage alone.

MEDVEDENKO My, what ceremony! (*He and* SORIN *go out*)

ARKADINA How he frightened me!

TREPLEFF It's not good for him to live in the country. He's low in his mind. Now, Mother, if you'd only have a burst of sudden generosity and lend him a thousand or fifteen hundred, he could spend a whole year in town.

ARKADINA I haven't any money. I'm an actress, not a banker.

(*A pause*)

TREPLEFF Mother, change my bandage. You do it so well.

ARKADINA (*Takes bottle of iodoform and a box of bandages from cupboard*) And the doctor's late.

TREPLEFF He promised to be here at ten, but it's already noon.

ARKADINA Sit down. (*Takes off bandage*) You look as if you were in a turban. Some man who came by the kitchen yesterday asked what nationality you were. But it's almost entirely healed. What's left is nothing. (*Kisses him on the head*) While I'm away, you won't do any more click-click?

TREPLEFF No, Mother. That was a moment when I was out of my head with despair, and couldn't control myself. It won't happen again. (*Kisses her fingers*) You have clever fingers. I remember long, long ago when you were still playing at the Imperial Theatre . . . there was a fight one day in our court, and a washerwoman who was one of the tenants got beaten almost to death. Do you remember? She was picked up unconscious. . . . You nursed her, took medicines to her, bathed her children in the washtub. Don't you remember?

ARKADINA No. (*Puts on fresh bandage*)

TREPLEFF Two ballet dancers were living then in the same house we did, they used to come and drink coffee with you.

ARKADINA That I remember.

TREPLEFF They were very pious. (*A pause*) Lately, these last days, I have loved you as tenderly and fully as when I was a child. Except for you, there's nobody left me now. Only why, why do you subject yourself to the influence of that man?

ARKADINA You don't understand him, Konstantine. He's a very noble character.

TREPLEFF Nevertheless, when he was told I was going to challenge him to a duel, this nobility didn't keep him from playing the coward. He's leaving. Ignominious retreat!

ARKADINA Such nonsense! I myself begged him to leave here.

TREPLEFF Noble character! Here we both are nearly quarreling over him, and right now very likely he's in the drawing room or in the garden laughing at us . . . developing Nina, trying once and for all to convince her he's a genius.

ARKADINA For you it's a pleasure . . . saying disagreeable things to me. I respect that man and must ask you not to speak ill of him in my presence.

TREPLEFF And I don't respect him. You want me too to think he's a genius, but, forgive me, I can't tell lies . . . his creations make me sick.

ARKADINA That's envy. People who are not talented but pretend to be have nothing better to do than to disparage real talents. It must be a fine consolation!

TREPLEFF (*Sarcastically*) Real talents! (*Angrily*) I'm more talented than both of you put together, if it comes to that! (*Tears off the bandage*) You two, with your stale routine, have grabbed first place in art and think that only what you do is real or legitimate; the rest you'd like to stifle and keep down. I don't believe in you two. I don't believe in you or in him.

ARKADINA Decadent!

TREPLEFF Go back to your darling theatre and act there in trashy, stupid plays!

ARKADINA Never did I act in such plays. Leave me alone! You are not fit to write even wretched vaudeville. Kiev burgher! Sponge!

TREPLEFF Miser!

ARKADINA Beggar! (*He sits down, cries softly*) Nonentity! (*Walks up and down*) Don't cry! You mustn't cry! (*Weeps. Kisses him on his forehead, his cheeks, his head*) My dear child, forgive me! Forgive me, your wicked mother! Forgive miserable me!

TREPLEFF (*Embracing her*) If you only knew! I've lost everything. She doesn't love me, now I can't write. All my hopes are gone.

ARKADINA Don't despair. It will all pass. He's leaving right away. She'll love you again. (*Dries his tears*) That's enough. We've made it up now.

TREPLEFF (*Kissing her hands*) Yes, Mother.

ARKADINA (*Tenderly*) Make it up with him, too. You don't want a duel. You don't, do you?

TREPLEFF Very well. Only, Mother, don't let me see him. It's painful to me. It's beyond me. (TRIGORIN *comes in*) There he is. I'm going. (*Quickly puts dressings away in cupboard*) The doctor will do my bandage later.

TRIGORIN (*Looking through a book*) Page 121 . . . lines eleven and twelve. Here it is. (*Reads*) "If you ever, ever need my life, come and take it."

(TREPLEFF *picks up the bandage from the floor and goes out*)

ARKADINA (*Looking at her watch*) The horses will be here soon.

TRIGORIN (*To himself*) If you ever, ever need my life, come and take it.

ARKADINA I hope you are all packed.

TRIGORIN (*Impatiently*) Yes, yes. . . . (*In deep thought*) Why is it I seem to feel sadness in that call from a pure soul, and my heart aches so with pity? If you ever, ever need my life, come and take it. (*To* MADAME ARKADINA) Let's stay just one more day. (*She shakes her head*)

TRIGORIN Let's stay!

ARKADINA Darling, I know what keeps you here. But have some self control. You're a little drunk, be sober.

TRIGORIN You be sober, too, be understanding, reasonable, I beg you; look at all this like a true friend. . . . (*Presses her hand*) You are capable of sacrificing. Be my friend, let me be free.

ARKADINA (*Excited*) Are you so infatuated?

TRIGORIN I am drawn to her! Perhaps this is just what I need.

ARKADINA The love of some provincial girl? Oh, how little you know yourself!

TRIGORIN Sometimes people talk but are asleep. That's how it is now. . . . I'm talking to you but in my dream I see her. I'm possessed by sweet, marvelous dreams. Let me go. . . .

ARKADINA (*Trembling*) No, no, I'm an ordinary woman like any other woman, you shouldn't talk to me like this. Don't torture me, Boris. It frightens me.

TRIGORIN If you wanted to, you could be far from ordinary. There is a kind of love that's young, and beautiful, and is all poetry, and carries us away into a world of dreams; on earth it alone can ever give us happiness. Such a love I still have never known. In my youth there wasn't time, I was always around some editor's office, fighting off starvation. Now it's here, that love, it's come, it beckons me. What sense, then, is there in running away from it?

ARKADINA (*Angry*) You've gone mad.

TRIGORIN Well, let me!

ARKADINA You've all conspired today just to torment me. (*Weeps*)

TRIGORIN (*Clutching at his breast*) She doesn't understand. She doesn't want to understand.

ARKADINA Am I so old or ugly that you don't mind talking to me about other women? (*Embracing and kissing him*) Oh, you madman! My beautiful, my marvel . . . you are the last chapter of my life. (*Falls on knees*) My joy, my pride, my blessedness! (*Embracing his knees*) If you forsake me for one hour even, I'll never survive it, I'll go out of my mind, my wonderful, magnificent one, my master.

TRIGORIN Somebody might come in. (*Helps her to rise*)

ARKADINA Let them, I am not ashamed of my love for you. (*Kisses his hands*) My treasure! You reckless boy, you want to be mad, but I won't have it, I won't let you. (*Laughs*) You are mine . . . you are mine. This brow is mine, and the eyes mine, and this beautiful silky hair, too, is mine. You are all mine. You are so talented, so intelligent, the best of all modern writers; you are the one and only hope of Russia . . . you have such sincerity, simplicity, healthy humor. In one stroke you go to the very heart of a character or a scene; your people are like life itself. Oh, it's impossible to read you without rapture! Do you think this is just narcotic? that I'm only flattering you? Come, look me in the eyes. . . . Do I look like a liar? There you see, only I can appreciate you; only I tell you the truth, my lovely darling. . . . You are coming? Yes? You won't leave me?

TRIGORIN I have no will of my own. . . . I've never had a will of my own. Flabby, weak, always submitting! Is it possible that might please women? Take me, carry me away, only never let me be one step away from you.

ARKADINA (*To herself*) Now he's mine. (*Casually, as if nothing had happened*) However, if you like you may stay. I'll go by myself, and you come later, in a week. After all, where would you hurry to?

TRIGORIN No, let's go together.

ARKADINA As you like. Together, together, then. (*A

*pause.* TRIGORIN *writes in notebook*) What are you writing?

TRIGORIN This morning I heard a happy expression: "Virgin forest." It might be useful in a story. (*Yawns*) So, we're off. Once more the cars, stations, station buffets, stews, and conversations!

(SHAMREYEFF *enters*)

SHAMREYEFF I have the honor with deep regret to announce that the horses are ready. It's time, most esteemed lady, to be off to the station; the train arrives at five minutes after two. So will you do me the favor, Irina Nikolaevna, not to forget to inquire about this: Where's the actor Suzdaltsev now? Is he alive? Is he well? We used to drink together once upon a time. In *The Stolen Mail* he was inimitable. In the same company with him at Elisavetgrad, I remember, was the tragedian Izmailov, also a remarkable personality. Don't hurry, most esteemed lady, there are five minutes still. Once in some melodrama they were playing conspirators, and when they were suddenly discovered, he had to say, "We are caught in a trap," but Izmailov said, "We are traught in a clap." (*Laughs*) Clap!

(YAKOV *is busy with luggage.* MAID *brings* ARKADINA'S *hat, coat, parasol, gloves. All help her put them on. The* COOK *peers through door on left, as if hesitating, then he comes in. Enter* PAULINE, SORIN, *and* MEDVEDENKO)

PAULINE (*With basket*) Here are some plums for the journey. They are sweet ones. In case you'd like some little thing.

ARKADINA You are very kind, Pauline Andreevna.

PAULINE Good-by, my dear. If anything has been not quite so, forgive it. (*Cries*)

ARKADINA (*Embracing her*) Everything has been charming, everything's been charming. Only you mustn't cry.

PAULINE Time goes so.

ARKADINA There's nothing we can do about that.

SORIN (*In a greatcoat with a cape, his hat on and his stick in his hand, crossing the stage*) Sister, you'd better start if you don't want to be late. I'll go get in the carriage. (*Exits*)

MEDVEDENKO And I'll walk to the station . . . to see you off. I'll step lively.

ARKADINA Good-by, my friends. If we are alive and well next summer we'll meet again. (*The* MAID, COOK, *and* YAKOV *kiss her hand*) Don't forget me. (*Gives* COOK *a ruble*) Here's a ruble for the three of you.

COOK We humbly thank you, Madame. Pleasant journey to you. Many thanks to you.

YAKOV God bless you!

SHAMREYEFF Make us happy with a letter. Good-by, Boris Alexeevich.

ARKADINA Where's Konstantine? Tell him I'm off now. I must say good-by to him. Well, remember me kindly. (*To* YAKOV) I gave the cook a ruble. It's for the three of you.

(*All go out. The stage is empty. Offstage are heard the usual sounds when people are going away. The* MAID *comes back for the basket of plums from the table and goes out again*)

TRIGORIN (*Returning*) I forgot my stick. It's out there on the terrace, I think. (*As he starts to go out by the door on the left, he meets* NINA *coming in*) Is it you? We are just going. . . .

NINA I felt we should meet again. (*Excited*) Boris Alexeevich, I've come to a decision, the die is cast. I am going on the stage. Tomorrow I shall not be here. I am leaving my father, deserting everything, beginning a new life. I'm off like you . . . for Moscow . . . we shall meet there.

TRIGORIN (*Glancing around him*) Stay at Hotel Slavyansky Bazaar. Let me know at once. Molchanovka, Groholsky House. I must hurry.

(*A pause*)

NINA One minute yet.

TRIGORIN (*In a low voice*) You are so beautiful. . . . Oh, how happy to think we'll be meeting soon. (*She puts her head on his breast*) I shall see those lovely eyes again, that ineffably beautiful, tender smile . . . those gentle features, their pure, angelic expression . . . my darling . . .

(*A long kiss*)

*Curtain*

(*Two years pass between the Third and Fourth Acts*)

# Act Four

*One of the drawing rooms in* SORIN'S *house, turned by* KONSTANTINE TREPLEFF *into a study. On the right and left, doors leading into other parts of the house. Facing us, glass doors on to the terrace. Besides the usual furniture of a drawing room, there is a writing table in the corner to the right; near the door on the left, a sofa, a bookcase full of books, and books in the windows and on the chairs.*

*Evening. A single lamp with a shade is lighted. Semidarkness. The sound from outside of trees rustling and the wind howling in the chimney. The night watchman is knocking.* MEDVEDENKO *and* MASHA *come in.*

MASHA Konstantine Gavrilovich! Konstantine Gavrilovich! (*Looking around*) Nobody here. Every other minute all day long the old man keeps asking where's Kostya, where's Kostya? He can't live without him.

MEDVEDENKO He's afraid to be alone. (*Listening*) What terrible weather! It's two days now.

MASHA (*Turning up the lamp*) Out on the lake there are waves. Tremendous.

MEDVEDENKO The garden's black. We ought to have told them to pull down that stage. It stands all bare and hideous, like a skeleton, and the curtain flaps in the wind. When I passed there last night it seemed to me that in the wind I heard someone crying.

MASHA Well, here . . . (*Pause*)

MEDVEDENKO Masha, let's go home.

MASHA (*Shakes her head*) I'm going to stay here tonight.

MEDVEDENKO (*Imploring*) Masha, let's go. Our baby must be hungry.

MASHA Nonsense. Matriona will feed it.

(*A pause*)

MEDVEDENKO It's hard on him. He's been three nights now without his mother.

MASHA You're getting just too tiresome. In the old days you'd at least philosophize a little, but now it's all baby, home, baby, home . . . and that's all I can get out of you.

MEDVEDENKO Let's go, Masha.

MASHA Go yourself.

MEDVEDENKO Your father won't let me have a horse.

MASHA He will if you just ask him.

MEDVEDENKO Very well, I'll try. Then you'll come tomorrow.

MASHA (*Taking snuff*) Well, tomorrow. Stop bothering me.

(*Enter* TREPLEFF *and* PAULINE; TREPLEFF *carries pillows and a blanket,* PAULINE *sheets and pillowcases. They lay them on the sofa, then* TREPLEFF *goes and sits down at his desk*)

MASHA Why's that, Mama?

PAULINE Peter Nikolaevich asked to sleep in Kostya's room.

MASHA Let me. . . . (*She makes the bed*)

PAULINE (*Sighing*) Old people, what children. . . . (*Goes to the desk. Leaning on her elbows she gazes at the manuscript. A pause*)

MEDVEDENKO So I'm going. Good-by, Masha. (*Kisses her hand*) Good-by, Mother. (*Tries to kiss her hand*)

PAULINE (*With annoyance*) Well, go if you're going.

MEDVEDENKO Good-by, Konstantine Gavrilovich.

(TREPLEFF, *without speaking, gives him his hand.* MEDVEDENKO *goes out*)

PAULINE (*Gazing at the manuscript*) Nobody ever thought or dreamed that some day, Kostya, you'd turn out to be a real author. But now, thank God, the magazines send you money for your stories. (*Passing her hand over his hair*) And you've grown handsome . . . dear, good Kostya, be kind to my little Masha.

MASHA (*Making the bed*) Let him alone, Mama.

PAULINE She's a sweet little thing. (*A pause*) A woman, Kostya, doesn't ask much . . . only kind looks. As I well know.

(TREPLEFF *rises from the desk and without speaking goes out*)

MASHA You shouldn't have bothered him.

PAULINE I feel sorry for you, Masha.

MASHA Why should you?

PAULINE My heart aches and aches for you. I see it all.

MASHA It's all foolishness! Hopeless love . . . that's only in novels. No matter. Only you mustn't let yourself go, and be always waiting for something, waiting for fine weather by the sea. If love stirs in your heart, stamp it out. Now they've promised to transfer my husband to another district. As soon as we get there . . . I'll forget it all. . . . I'll tear it out of my heart by the roots.

(*Two rooms off is heard a melancholy waltz*)

PAULINE Kostya is playing. That means he's feeling sad.

MASHA (*Waltzes silently a few turns*) The great thing, Mama, is to be where I don't see him. If only my Semyon could get his transfer, I promise you I'd forget in a month. It's all nonsense.

(*Door on left opens.* DORN *and* MEDVEDENKO *come in, wheeling* SORIN *in his chair*)

MEDVEDENKO I have six souls at home now. And flour at seventy kopecks.

DORN So it just goes round and round.

MEDVEDENKO It's easy for you to smile. You've got more money than the chickens could pick up.

DORN Money! After practicing medicine thirty years, my friend, so driven day and night that I could never call my soul my own, I managed to save up at last two thousand rubles; and I've just spent all that on a trip abroad. I've got nothing at all.

MASHA (*To her husband*) Aren't you gone yet?

MEDVEDENKO (*Apologizing*) How can I, when they won't let me have a horse?

MASHA (*Under her breath angrily*) I wish I'd never lay eyes on you again.

(SORIN'*s wheel chair remains left center.* PAULINE, MASHA, *and* DORN *sit down beside him.* MEDVEDENKO *stands to one side gloomily*)

DORN Look how many changes they have made here! The drawing room is turned into a study.

MASHA Konstantine Gavrilovich likes to work in here. He can go into the garden whenever he likes and think.

(*A watchman's rattle sounds*)

SORIN Where's my sister?

DORN She went to the station to meet Trigorin. She'll be right back.

SORIN If you thought you had to send for my sister, that shows I'm very ill. (*Reflecting*) Now that's odd, isn't it? I'm very ill, but they won't let me have any medicine around here.

DORN And what would you like? Valerian drops? Soda? Quinine?

SORIN So it's more philosophy, I suppose. Oh, what an affliction! (*He motions with his head toward the sofa*) Is that for me?

PAULINE Yes, for you, Peter Nikolaevich.

SORIN Thank you.

DORN (*Singing sotto voce*) The moon drifts in the sky tonight.

SORIN Listen, I want to give Kostya a subject for a story. It should be called: "The Man Who Wanted To" . . . *L'homme qui a voulu.* In my youth long ago wanted to become an author . . . and never became one; wanted to speak eloquently . . . and spoke execrably (*Mimicking himself*) and so on and so forth, and all the rest of it, yes and no, and in the résumé would drag on, drag on, till the sweat broke out; wanted to marry . . . and never married; wanted always to live in town . . . and now am ending up my life in the country, and so on.

DORN Wanted to become a State Counselor . . . and became one.

SORIN (*Laughing*) For that I never longed. That came to me of itself.

DORN Come now, to be picking faults with life at sixty-two, you must confess, that's not magnanimous.

SORIN How bullheaded you are! Can't you take it in? I want to live.

DORN That's frivolous, it's the law of nature that every life must come to an end.

SORIN You argue like a man who's had his fill. You've had your fill and so you're indifferent to living, it's all one to you. But at that even you will be afraid to die.

DORN The fear of death . . . a brute fear. We must overcome it. The fear of death is reasonable only in those who believe in an eternal life, and shudder to think of the sins they have committed. But you in the first place don't believe, in the second place what sins have you? For twenty-five years you served as State Counselor . . . and that's all.

SORIN (*Laughing*) Twenty-eight.

(TREPLEFF *enters and sits on the stool beside* SORIN. MASHA *never takes her eyes off his face*)

DORN We are keeping Konstantine Gavrilovich from his work.

TREPLEFF No, it's nothing.

(*A pause*)

MEDVEDENKO Permit me to ask you, Doctor, what town in your travels did you most prefer?

DORN Genoa.

TREPLEFF Why Genoa?

DORN Because of the marvelous street crowd. When you go out of your hotel in the evening you find the whole street surging with people. You let yourself drift among the crowd, zigzagging back and forth, you live its life, its soul pours into you, until finally you begin to believe there might really be a world spirit after all, like that Nina Zaryechny acted in your play. By the way, where is Nina now? Where is she and how is she?

TREPLEFF Very well, I imagine.

DORN I've been told she was leading rather an odd sort of life. How's that?

TREPLEFF It's a long story, Doctor.

DORN You can shorten it.

(*A pause*)

TREPLEFF She ran away from home and joined Trigorin. That you knew?

DORN I know.

TREPLEFF She had a child. The child died. Trigorin got tired of her, and went back to his old ties, as might be expected. He'd never broken these old ties anyhow, but flitted in that backboneless style of his from one to the other. As far as I could say from what I know, Nina's private life didn't quite work out.

DORN And on the stage?

TREPLEFF I believe even worse. She made her debut in Moscow at a summer theatre, and afterward a tour in the provinces. At that time I never let her out of my sight, and wherever she was I was. She always attempted big parts, but her acting was crude, without any taste, her gestures were clumsy. There were moments when she did some talented screaming, talented dying, but those were only moments.

DORN It means, though, she has talent?

TREPLEFF I could never make out. I imagine she has. I saw her, but she didn't want to see me, and her maid wouldn't let me in her rooms. I understood how she felt, and never insisted on seeing her. (*A pause*) What more is there to tell you? Afterward, when I'd come back home here, she wrote me some letters. They were clever, tender, interesting; she didn't complain, but I could see she was profoundly unhappy; there was not a word that didn't show her exhausted nerves. And she'd taken a strange fancy. She always signed herself the sea gull. In *The Mermaid* [1] the miller says that he's a crow; the same way in all her letters she kept repeating she was a sea gull. Now she's here.

DORN How do you mean, here?

TREPLEFF In town, staying at the inn. She's already been here five days, living there in rooms. Masha drove in, but she never sees anybody. Semyon Semyonovich declares that last night after dinner he saw her in the fields, a mile and a half from here.

MEDVEDENKO Yes, I saw her. (*A pause*) Going in the opposite direction from here, toward town. I bowed to her, asked why she had not been out to see us. She said she'd come.

TREPLEFF Well, she won't. (*A pause*) Her father and stepmother don't want to know her. They've set watchmen to keep her off the grounds. (*Goes toward the desk with* DORN) How easy it is, Doctor, to be a philosopher on paper, and how hard it is in life!

SORIN She was a beautiful girl.

DORN How's that?

SORIN I say she was a beautiful girl. State Counselor Sorin was downright in love with her himself once for a while.

DORN You old Lovelace! [2]

(*They hear* SHAMREYEFF'S *laugh*)

PAULINE I imagine they're back from the station.

TREPLEFF Yes, I hear Mother.

(*Enter* MADAME ARKADINA *and* TRIGORIN, SHAMREYEFF *following*)

SHAMREYEFF We all get old and fade with the elements, esteemed lady, but you, most honored lady, are still young . . . white dress, vivacity . . . grace.

[1] Play by Aleksander Pushkin (1799-1837), Russia's great Romantic poet.

[2] The synonym for unscrupulous libertines, the term derives from Richardson's *Clarissa Harlowe*.

ARKADINA You still want to bring me bad luck, you tiresome creature!

TRIGORIN (*To* SORIN) How are you, Peter Nikolaevich? Are you still indisposed? That's not so good.

(*Pleased at seeing* MASHA) Masha Ilyinishna!

MASHA You know me? (*Grasps his hand*)

TRIGORIN Married?

MASHA Long ago.

TRIGORIN Are you happy? (*Bows to* DORN *and* MEDVEDENKO, *then hesitatingly goes to* TREPLEFF) Irina Nikolaevna tells me you have forgotten the past and given up being angry.

(TREPLEFF *holds out his hand*)

ARKADINA (*To her son*) Look, Boris Alexeevich has brought you the magazine with your last story.

TREPLEFF (*Taking the magazine. To* TRIGORIN) Thank you. You're very kind.

(*They sit down*)

TRIGORIN Your admirers send their respects to you. In Petersburg and in Moscow, everywhere, there's a great deal of interest in your work, and they all ask me about you. They ask: what is he like, what age is he, is he dark or fair? For some reason they all think you are no longer young. And nobody knows your real name, since you always publish under a pseudonym. You're a mystery, like the Man in the Iron Mask.[3]

TREPLEFF Will you be with us long?

TRIGORIN No, tomorrow I think I'll go to Moscow. I must. I'm in a hurry to finish a story, and besides I've promised to write something for an annual. In a word it's the same old thing.

(MADAME ARKADINA *and* PAULINE *have set up a card table.* SHAMREYEFF *lights candles, arranges chairs, gets box of lotto from a cupboard*)

TRIGORIN The weather's given me a poor welcome. The wind is ferocious. Tomorrow morning if it dies down I'm going out to the lake to fish. And I want to look around the garden and the place where . . . do you remember? . . . your play was done. The idea for a story is all worked out in my mind, I want only to refresh my memory of the place where it's laid.

MASHA Papa, let my husband have a horse! He must get home.

SHAMREYEFF (*Mimics*) A horse . . . home. (*Sternly*) See for yourself: they are just back from the station. They'll not go out again.

MASHA They're not the only horses. . . . (*Seeing that he says nothing, she makes an impatient gesture*) Nobody can do anything with you. . . .

MEDVEDENKO I can walk, Masha. Truly . . .

PAULINE (*Sighs*) Walk, in such weather! (*Sits down at card table*) Sit down, friends.

MEDVEDENKO It's only four miles. . . . Good-by. (*Kisses wife's hand*) Good-by, Mama. (*His mother-in-law puts out her hand reluctantly*) I should not have troubled anybody, but the little baby. . . . (*Bowing to them*) Good-by. (*He goes out as if apologizing*)

SHAMREYEFF He'll make it. He's not a general.

PAULINE (*Taps on table*) Sit down, friends. Let's not lose time, they'll be calling us to supper soon.

(SHAMREYEFF, MASHA, *and* DORN *sit at the card table*)

ARKADINA (*To* TRIGORIN) When these long autumn evenings draw on we pass the time out here with lotto. And look: the old lotto set we had when my mother used to play with us children. Don't you want to take a hand with us till suppertime? (*She and* TRIGORIN *sit down at the table*) It's a tiresome game, but it does well enough when you're used to it. (*She deals three cards to each one*)

TREPLEFF (*Turns magazine pages*) He's read his own story, but mine he hasn't even cut. (*He lays the magazine on the desk; on his way out, as he passes his mother, he kisses her on the head*)

ARKADINA But you, Kostya?

TREPLEFF Sorry, I don't care to. I'm going for a walk. (*Goes out*)

ARKADINA Stake . . . ten kopecks. Put it down for me, Doctor.

DORN Command me.

MASHA Has everybody bet? I'll begin. Twenty-two.

ARKADINA I have it.

MASHA Three.

DORN Here you are.

MASHA Did you put down three? Eight! Eighty-one! Ten!

SHAMREYEFF Not so fast.

ARKADINA What a reception they gave me at Kharkov! Can you believe it, my head's spinning yet.

MASHA Thirty-four.

(*A sad waltz is heard*)

ARKADINA The students gave me an ovation, three baskets of flowers, two wreaths and look . . . (*She takes off a brooch and puts it on the table*)

SHAMREYEFF Yes, that's the real . . .

MASHA Fifty!

DORN Fifty, you say?

ARKADINA I had a superb costume. Say what you like, but really when it comes to dressing myself I am no fool.

PAULINE Kostya is playing. The poor boy's sad.

SHAMREYEFF In the papers they often abuse him.

MASHA Seventy-seven.

ARKADINA Who cares what they say?

TRIGORIN He hasn't any luck. He still can't discover how to write a style of his own. There is something strange, vague, at times even like delirious raving. Not a single character that is alive.

MASHA Eleven!

ARKADINA (*Glancing at* SORIN) Petrusha, are you bored? (*A pause*) He's asleep.

DORN He's asleep, the State Counselor.

MASHA Seven! Ninety!

TRIGORIN Do you think if I lived in such a place as this and by this lake, I would write? I should overcome such a passion and devote my life to fishing.

[3] A political prisoner kept in the Bastille during the reign of Louis XIV, the Man's identity was concealed by a heavy black velvet mask. The case has invited many fictional treatments.

MASHA Twenty-eight!

TRIGORIN To catch a perch or a bass . . . that's something like happiness!

DORN Well, I believe in Konstantine Gavrilovich. He has something! He has something! He thinks in images, his stories are bright and full of color, I always feel them strongly. It's only a pity that he's got no definite purpose. He creates impressions, never more than that, but on mere impressions you don't go far. Irina Nikolaevna, are you glad your son is a writer?

ARKADINA Imagine, I have not read him yet. There's never time.

MASHA Twenty-six!

(TREPLEFF *enters without saying anything, sits at his desk*)

SHAMREYEFF And, Boris Alexeevich, we've still got something of yours here.

TRIGORIN What's that?

SHAMREYEFF Somehow or other Konstantine Gavrilovich shot a sea gull, and you asked me to have it stuffed for you.

TRIGORIN I don't remember. (*Reflecting*) I don't remember.

MASHA Sixty-six! One!

TREPLEFF (*Throwing open the window, stands listening*) How dark! I don't know why I feel so uneasy.

ARKADINA Kostya, shut the window, there's a draught.

(TREPLEFF *shuts window*)

MASHA Ninety-eight.

TRIGORIN I've made a game.

ARKADINA (*Gaily*) Bravo! Bravo!

SHAMREYEFF Bravo!

ARKADINA This man's lucky in everything, always. (*Rises*) And now let's go have a bite of something. Our celebrated author didn't have any dinner today. After supper we'll go on. Kostya, leave your manuscript, come have something to eat.

TREPLEFF I don't want to, Mother, I've had enough.

ARKADINA As you please. (*Wakes* SORIN) Petrusha, supper! (*Takes* SHAMREYEFF'S *arm*) I'll tell you how they received me in Kharkov.

(PAULINE *blows out candles on table. She and* DORN *wheel* SORIN'S *chair out of the room. All but* TREPLEFF *go out. He gets ready to write. Runs his eye over what's already written*)

TREPLEFF I've talked so much about new forms, but now I feel that little by little I am slipping into mere routine myself. (*Reads*) "The placards on the wall proclaimed" . . . "pale face in a frame of dark hair" . . . frame . . . that's flat. (*Scratches out what he's written*) I'll begin where the hero is awakened by the rain, and throw out all the rest. This description of a moonlight night is too long and too precious. Trigorin has worked out his own method, it's easy for him. With him a broken bottleneck lying on the dam glitters in the moonlight and the mill wheel casts a black shadow . . . and there before you is the moonlight night; but with me it's the shimmering light, and the silent twinkling of the stars, and the faroff sound of a piano dying away in the still, sweet-scented air. It's painful. (*A pause*) Yes, I'm coming more and more to the conclusion that it's a matter not of old forms and not of new forms, but that a man writes, not thinking at all of what form to choose, writes because it comes pouring out from his soul. (*A tap at the window nearest the desk*) What's that? (*Looks out*) I don't see anything. (*Opens the door and peers into the garden*) Someone ran down the steps. (*Calls*) Who's there? (*Goes out. The sound of his steps along the veranda. A moment later returns with* NINA) Nina! Nina! (*She lays her head on his breast, with restrained sobbing*)

TREPLEFF (*Moved*) Nina! Nina! It's you . . . you. I had a presentiment, all day my soul was tormented. (*Takes off her hat and cape*) Oh, my sweet, my darling, she has come! Let's not cry, let's not.

NINA There's someone here.

TREPLEFF No one.

NINA Lock the doors. Someone might come in.

TREPLEFF Nobody's coming in.

NINA I know Irina Nikolaevna is here. Lock the doors.

TREPLEFF (*Locks door on right. Goes to door on left*) This one doesn't lock. I'll put a chair against it. (*Puts chair against door*) Don't be afraid, nobody's coming in.

NINA (*As if studying his face*) Let me look at you. (*Glancing around her*) It's warm, cozy. . . . This used to be the drawing room. Am I very much changed?

TREPLEFF Yes . . . you are thinner and your eyes are bigger. Nina, how strange it is I'm seeing you. Why wouldn't you let me come to see you? Why didn't you come sooner? I know you've been here now for nearly a week. I have been every day there where you were, I stood under your window like a beggar.

NINA I was afraid you might hate me. I dream every night that you look at me and don't recognize me. If you only knew! Ever since I came I've been here walking about . . . by the lake. I've been near your house often, and couldn't make up my mind to come in. Let's sit down. (*They sit*) Let's sit down and let's talk, talk. It's pleasant here, warm, cozy. . . . You hear . . . the wind? There's a place in Turgenev: "Happy is he who on such a night is under his own roof, who has a warm corner." I . . . a sea gull . . . no, that's not it. (*Rubs her forehead*) What was I saying? Yes . . . Turgenev. "And may the Lord help all homeless wanderers." It's nothing. (*Sobs*)

TREPLEFF Nina, again . . . Nina!

NINA It's nothing. It will make me feel better. I've not cried for two years. Last night I came to the garden to see whether our theatre was still there, and it's there still. I cried for the first time in two years, and my heart grew lighter and my soul was clearer. Look, I'm not crying now. (*Takes his hand*) You are an author, I . . . an actress. We have both been drawn into the whirlpool. I used to be as happy as a child. I used to wake up in the morning singing. I loved you and dreamed of being famous, and now? Tomorrow early I must go to Yelets in the third class . . . with peasants, and at Yelets the cultured merchants will plague me with attentions. Life's brutal!

TREPLEFF Why Yelets?

NINA I've taken an engagement there for the winter. It's time I was going.

TREPLEFF Nina, I cursed you and hated you. I tore up all your letters, tore up your photograph, and yet I knew every minute that my heart was bound to yours forever. It's not in my power to stop loving you, Nina. Ever since I lost you and began to get my work published, my life has been unbearable. . . . I'm miserable. . . . All of a sudden my youth was snatched from me, and now I feel as if I'd been living in the world for ninety years. I call out to you, I kiss the ground you walk on, I see your face wherever I look, the tender smile that shone on me those best years of my life.

NINA (*In despair*) Why does he talk like that? Why does he talk like that?

TREPLEFF I'm alone, not warmed by anybody's affection. I'm all chilled . . . it's cold like living in a cave. And no matter what I write it's dry, gloomy, and harsh. Stay here, Nina, if you only would! And if you won't, then take me with you.

(NINA *quickly puts on her hat and cape*)

TREPLEFF Nina, why? For God's sake, Nina. (*He is looking at her as she puts her things on. A pause*)

NINA My horses are just out there. Don't see me off. I'll manage by myself. (*Sobbing*) Give me some water.

(*He gives her a glass of water*)

TREPLEFF Where are you going now?

NINA To town. (*A pause*) Is Irina Nikolaevna here?

TREPLEFF Yes, Thursday my uncle was not well, we telegraphed her to come.

NINA Why do you say you kiss the ground I walk on? I ought to be killed. (*Bends over desk*) I'm so tired. If I could rest . . . rest. I'm a sea gull. No, that's not it. I'm an actress. Well, no matter. . . . (*Hears* ARKADINA *and* TRIGORIN *laughing in the dining room. She listens, runs to the door on the left and peeps through the keyhole*) And he's here too. (*Goes to* TREPLEFF) Well, no matter. He didn't believe in the theatre, all my dreams he'd laugh at, and little by little I quit believing in it myself, and lost heart. And there was the strain of love, jealousy, constant anxiety about my little baby. I got to be small and trashy, and played without thinking. I didn't know what to do with my hands, couldn't stand properly on the stage, couldn't control my voice. You can't imagine the feeling when you are acting and know it's dull. I'm a sea gull. No, that's not it. Do you remember, you shot a sea gull? A man comes by chance, sees it, and out of nothing else to do, destroys it. That's not it. . . . (*Puts her hand to her forehead*) What was I . . . I was talking about the stage. Now I'm not like that. I'm a real actress, I act with delight, with rapture, I'm drunk when I'm on the stage, and feel that I am beautiful. And now, ever since I've been here, I've kept walking about, kept walking and thinking, thinking and believing my soul grows stronger every day. Now I know, I understand, Kostya, that in our work . . . acting or writing . . . what matters is not fame, not glory, not what I used to dream about, it's how to endure, to bear my cross, and have faith. I have faith and it all doesn't hurt me so much, and when I think of my calling I'm not afraid of life.

TREPLEFF (*Sadly*) You've found your way, you know where you are going, but I still move in a chaos of images and dreams, not knowing why or who it's for. I have no faith, and I don't know where my calling lies.

NINA (*Listening*) Ssh . . . I'm going. Good-by. When I'm a great actress, come and look at me. You promise? But now. . . . (*Takes his hand*) It's late. I can hardly stand on my feet, I feel faint. I'd like something to eat.

TREPLEFF Stay, I'll bring you some supper here.

NINA No, no . . . I can manage by myself. The horses are just out there. So, she brought him along with her? But that's all one. When you see Trigorin . . . don't ever tell him anything. I love him. I love him even more than before. "An idea for a short story"—I love, I love passionately, I love to desperation. How nice it used to be, Kostya! You remember? How gay and warm and pure our life was; what things we felt, tender, delicate like flowers. . . . Do you remember? . . . (*Recites*) "Men and beasts, lions, eagles and partridges, antlered deer, mute fishes dwelling in the water, starfish and small creatures invisible to the eye . . . these and all life have run their sad course and are no more. Thousands of creatures have come and gone since there was life on the earth. Vainly now the pallid moon doth light her lamp. In the meadows the cranes wake and cry no longer; and the beetles' hum is silent in the linden groves. . . ." (*Impulsively embraces* TREPLEFF, *and runs out by the terrace door. A pause*)

TREPLEFF Too bad if any one meets her in the garden and tells Mother. That might upset Mother. (*He stands for two minutes tearing up all his manuscripts and throwing them under the desk, then unlocks door on right, and goes out*)

DORN (*Trying to open the door on the left*) That's funny. This door seems to be locked. (*Enters and puts chair back in its place*) A regular hurdle race . . .

(*Enter* MADAME ARKADINA *and* PAULINE, *behind them* YAKOV *with a tray and bottles;* MASHA, *then* SHAMREYEFF *and* TRIGORIN)

ARKADINA Put the claret and the beer for Boris Alexeevich here on the table. We'll play and drink. Let's sit down, friends.

PAULINE (*To* YAKOV) Bring the tea now, too. (*Lights the candles and sits down*)

SHAMREYEFF (*Leading* TRIGORIN *to the cupboard*) Here's the thing I was telling you about just now. By your order.

TRIGORIN (*Looking at the sea gull*) I don't remember. (*Reflecting*) I don't remember.

(*Sound of a shot offstage right. Everybody jumps*)

ARKADINA (*Alarmed*) What's that?

DORN Nothing. It must be . . . in my medicine case . . . something blew up. Don't you worry. (*He goes out right, in a moment returns*) So it was. A bottle of ether blew up. (*Sings*) Again I stand before thee! Enchanted. . . .

ARKADINA (*Sitting down at the table*) Phew, I was frightened! It reminded me of how . . . (*Puts her hands over her face*) Everything's black before my eyes.

DORN (*Turning through the magazine, to* TRIGORIN) About two months ago in this magazine there was an article . . . a letter from America, and I wanted to ask you among other things . . . (*Puts his arm around* TRIGORIN's *waist and leads him toward the front of the stage*) since I'm very much interested in this question. . . . (*Dropping his voice*) Get Irina Nikolaevna somewhere away from here. The fact is Konstantine Gavrilovich has shot himself. . . .

*Curtain*

# THE CHERRY ORCHARD

If Chekhov's friend, Vladimir Nemirovich-Danchenko, had not admired *The Sea Gull* in spite of its unsatisfactory 1896 production, Chekhov might never again have written for the theatre. In 1898, however, the founding of The People's (later, Moscow) Art Theatre proved as important in Chekhov's career as the Abbey Theatre was in Synge's. Nemirovich-Danchenko and an actor-director Chekhov did not greatly admire, Stanislavski, started a theatre where declamatory acting and the star-system were to be replaced by "natural" ensemble-playing. With Nemirovich-Danchenko as mediator, Chekhov was persuaded to entrust *The Sea Gull* to the new theatre. On December 17, 1898, the play was reborn with a success immortalized in the adoption of a sea gull as the Moscow Art emblem.

By 1898 Chekhov's tuberculosis was advancing beyond cure. Even before *The Sea Gull*'s triumphant production, he had moved to Yalta, and until the Moscow Art Theatre's Crimean tour in 1900, he did not see his plays staged. At a rehearsal of *The Sea Gull,* however, he had met the actress, Olga Knipper, who was to play Arkadina. In May, 1901, they were married.

After *The Sea Gull,* the Moscow Art Theatre was eager to produce other Chekhov plays. In 1899, he gave them *Uncle Vanya,* a new version of *The Wood Demon,* a failure when it had been produced ten years earlier. The play centers around disturbances created when a retired professor, a pompous sponger, takes up residence at the country home where his daughter lives with his first wife's family. The professor's young second wife is a vapid Helen of Troy to a selfish, vain Menelaus; out of boredom she flirts with Astroff, the provincial doctor whose deepest dedication is to reforestation projects. Uncle Vanya, the professor's brother-in-law and one-time research assistant, has finally penetrated the scholarly pretentiousness to discover what an egotist the professor is. In the last act, the professor leaves, but it is clear that he will return to resume his retirement in the provinces.

*The Three Sisters* (1901), the most richly textured of Chekhov's plays, was the first written expressly for the Moscow Art Theatre. Here Chekhov worked on an almost panoramic scale, tracing the lives of General Prozoroff's son and three daughters over a period of several years. Increasingly isolated since their father's death, the younger Prozoroffs have become immobilized in the provinces amid fading recollections of their youth in Moscow. Andrei, the son, has married a stupid baggage, Natasha, who gradually drives the sisters out of the family home. The middle sister, Masha, married to a mild teacher, finds love briefly in an affair with an army officer. The oldest, Olga, throws herself into her work as a schoolmistress. The youngest, Irina, longs to lead a useful life in a "New" Russia, and at the end of the play she is on her way to becoming another Olga. The four acts follow a diurnal progression (midday, evening, early morning, noon) which actually covers the years of Andrei's progress from embarrassed swain to cuckold pushing the baby-carriage of the son who may not even be his.

Completed less than a year before Chekhov's death, *The Cherry Orchard* lacks the complexity of *The Three Sisters,* but its meaning has proved to be more universally accessible. Again building his action around arrivals and departures, Chekhov prided himself in this play on doing without offstage pistol-fire and triangulated love affairs. No play better illustrates the effectiveness of Chekhov's selection of details. Chekhov fused isolated bits of color into a brilliant design. Only rarely have his imitators approached his artistry, a situation which has given rise to endless conjecture about the nature of Chekhov's genius. Chekhov was able to accept life as process and change without succumbing to the sentimentality or special pleading which mars his imitators' works. *The Cherry Orchard* caused the widely reported dispute in which Chekhov denounced Stanislavski for turning his comic characters into cry-babies, merely pathetic and near-tragic victims of cultural changes beyond individual control or understanding. The quarrel exemplifies the slipperiness of such critical terms as *comedy* and *tragedy, optimism* and *pessimism.* Ironically enough, it was Stanislavski himself who belatedly found the key to Chekhov's elusive art. In 1907, three years after Chekhov's death, Stanislavski described Chekhov as a realistic optimist: "He painted a cheerful, always lively and confident, beautiful picture of future Russian life. It was only that he looked at the present without falsifying it. He was not afraid of the truth."

# THE CHERRY ORCHARD

## *A Comedy in Four Acts*

Translated by Stark Young

### CHARACTERS

RANEVSKAYA, LYUBOFF ANDREEVNA (LYUBA), *a landowner*
ANYA (ANITCHKA), *her daughter, 17 years old*
VARYA (VARVARA MIKHAILOVNA), *her adopted daughter, 24 years old*
GAYEFF, LEONID ANDREEVICH (LENYA *or* LYONYA), *her brother*
LOPAHIN, YERMOLAY ALEXEEVICH, *a merchant*
TROFIMOFF, PYOTR SERGEEVICH (PETYA), *a student, about 30 years old*
SEMYONOFF-PISHTCHIK, BORIS BORISOVICH, *a landowner*
CHARLOTTA IVANOVNA, *a governess*
EPIHODOFF, SEMYON PANTELEEVICH, *a clerk*
DUNYASHA (AVDOTYA FEODOROVNA), *a maid*
FIERS, *valet to Gayeff; 87 years old*
YASHA, *a young valet*
A STRANGER PASSING THROUGH THE ESTATE
STATION-MASTER
A POST-OFFICE CLERK
VISITORS, SERVANTS

*The action takes place on the estate of Ranevskaya.*

*The time is the beginning of the twentieth century, about forty years after the Emancipation of the Serfs (1861) and the end of the Russian feudal system.*

## Act One

*A room that is still called the nursery. One of the doors leads into* ANYA'S *room. Dawn, the sun will soon be rising. It is May, the cherry trees are in blossom but in the orchard it is cold, with a morning frost. The windows in the room are closed. Enter* DUNYASHA *with a candle and* LOPAHIN *with a book in his hand.*

LOPAHIN The train got in, thank God! What time is it?

DUNYASHA It's nearly two. (*Blows out her candle*) It's already daylight.

LOPAHIN But how late was the train? Two hours at least. (*Yawning and stretching*) I'm a fine one, I am, look what a fool thing I did! I drove here on purpose just to meet them at the station, and then all of a sudden I'd overslept myself! Fell asleep in my chair. How provoking!— You could have waked me up.

DUNYASHA I thought you had gone. (*Listening*) Listen, I think they are coming now.

LOPAHIN (*Listening*) No—No, there's the luggage and one thing and another. (*A pause*) Lyuboff Andreevna has been living abroad five years. I don't know what she is like now. She is a good woman. An easy-going, simple woman. I remember when I was a boy about fifteen, my father, who is at rest—in those days he ran a shop here in the village—hit me in the face with his fist, my nose was bleeding. We'd come to the yard together for something or other, and he was a little drunk. Lyuboff Andreevna, I can see her now, still so young, so slim, led me to the washbasin here in this very room, in the nursery. "Don't cry," she says, "little peasant, it will be well in time for your wedding"— (*A pause*) Yes, "little peasant"—my father was a peasant truly, and here I am in a white waistcoat and yellow shoes. Like a pig rooting in a pastry shop—I've got this rich, lots of money, but if you really stop and think of it, I'm just a peasant— (*Turning the pages of a book*) Here I was reading a book and didn't get a thing out of it. Reading and went to sleep. (*A pause*)

DUNYASHA And all night long the dogs were not asleep, they know their masters are coming.

LOPAHIN What is it, Dunyasha, you're so—

DUNYASHA My hands are shaking. I'm going to faint.

LOPAHIN You're just so delicate, Dunyasha. And all dressed up like a lady, and your hair all done up! Mustn't do that. Must know your place.

(*Enter* EPIHODOFF, *with a bouquet: he wears a*

*jacket and highly polished boots with a loud squeak. As he enters he drops the bouquet.)*

EPIHODOFF (*Picking up the bouquet*) Look, the gardener sent these, he says to put them in the dining room.

(*Giving the bouquet to* DUNYASHA)

LOPAHIN And bring me some *kvass.*

DUNYASHA Yes, sir. (*Goes out*)

EPIHODOFF There is a morning frost now, three degrees of frost (*Sighing*) and the cherries all in bloom. I cannot approve of our climate— I cannot. Our climate can never quite rise to the occasion. Listen, Yermolay Alexeevich, allow me to acquaint you with the fact that I bought myself, day before yesterday, some boots and they, I venture to assure you, squeak so that they are, well, impossible. What could I grease them with?

LOPAHIN Go on. You annoy me.

EPIHODOFF Every day some misfortune happens to me. But I don't complain, I am used to it, and I even smile.

(DUNYASHA *enters, serves* LOPAHIN *the kvass*)

EPIHODOFF I'm going. (*Stumbling over a chair and upsetting it*) There (*As if triumphant*) there, you see, pardon the expression, a circumstance like that, among others— It is simply quite remarkable. (*Goes out*)

DUNYASHA And I must tell you, Yermolay Alexeevich, that Epihodoff has proposed to me.

LOPAHIN Ah!

DUNYASHA I don't know really what to— He is a quiet man but sometimes when he starts talking, you can't understand a thing he means. It's all very nice, and full of feeling, but just doesn't make any sense. I sort of like him. He loves me madly. He's a man that's unfortunate, every day there's something or other. They tease him around here, call him "twenty-two misfortunes—"

LOPAHIN (*Cocking his ear*) Listen, I think they are coming—

DUNYASHA They are coming! But what's the matter with me— I'm cold all over.

LOPAHIN They're really coming. Let's go meet them. Will she recognize me? It's five years we haven't seen each other.

DUNYASHA (*Excitedly*) I'm going to faint this very minute. Ah, I'm going to faint!

(*Two carriages can be heard driving up to the house.* LOPAHIN *and* DUNYASHA *hurry out. The stage is empty. In the adjoining rooms a noise begins.* FIERS *hurries across the stage, leaning on a stick; he has been to meet* LYUBOFF ANDREEVNA, *and wears an old-fashioned livery and a high hat; he mutters something to himself, but one cannot understand a word of it. The noise offstage gets louder and louder. A voice: "Look! Let's go through here—"* LYUBOFF ANDREEVNA, ANYA *and* CHARLOTTA IVANOVNA, *with a little dog on a chain, all of them dressed for traveling,* VARYA, *in a coat and kerchief,* GAYEFF, SEMYONOFF-PISHTCHIK, LOPAHIN, DUNYASHA, *with a bundle and an umbrella, servants with pieces of luggage—all pass through the room.*)

ANYA Let's go through here. Mama, do you remember what room this is?

LYUBOFF (*Happily, through her tears*) The nursery!

VARYA How cold it is, my hands are stiff. (*To* LYUBOFF) Your rooms, the white one and the violet, are just the same as ever, Mama.

LYUBOFF The nursery, my dear beautiful room—I slept here when I was little— (*Crying*) And now I am like a child— (*Kisses her brother and* VARYA, *then her brother again*) And Varya is just the same as ever, looks like a nun. And I knew Dunyasha— (*Kisses* DUNYASHA)

GAYEFF The train was two hours late. How's that? How's that for good management?

CHARLOTTA (*To* PISHTCHIK) My dog—he eats nuts, too.

PISHTCHIK (*Astonished*) Think of that!

(*Everybody goes out except* ANYA *and* DUNYASHA.)

DUNYASHA We waited so long— (*Taking off* ANYA'S *coat and hat.*)

ANYA I didn't sleep all four nights on the way. And now I feel so chilly.

DUNYASHA It was Lent when you left, there was some snow then, there was frost, and now? My darling (*Laughing and kissing her*), I waited so long for you, my joy, my life— I'm telling you now, I can't keep from it another minute.

ANYA (*Wearily*) There we go again—

DUNYASHA The clerk, Epihodoff, proposed to me after Holy Week.

ANYA You're always talking about the same thing— (*Arranging her hair*) I've lost all my hairpins— (*She is tired to the point of staggering*)

DUNYASHA I just don't know what to think. He loves me, loves me so!

ANYA (*Looks in through her door, tenderly*) My room, my windows, it's just as if I had never been away. I'm home! Tomorrow morning I'll get up, I'll run into the orchard— Oh, if I only could go to sleep! I haven't slept all the way, I was tormented by anxiety.

DUNYASHA Day before yesterday, Pyotr Sergeevich arrived.

ANYA (*Joyfully*) Petya!

DUNYASHA He's asleep in the bathhouse, he lives there. I am afraid, he says, of being in the way. (*Taking her watch from her pocket and looking at it*) Somebody ought to wake him up. It's only that Varvara Mikhailovna told us not to. Don't you wake him up, she said.

(*Enter* VARYA *with a bunch of keys at her belt*)

VARYA Dunyasha, coffee, quick—Mama is asking for coffee.

DUNYASHA This minute. (*Goes out*)

VARYA Well, thank goodness, you've come back. You are home again. (*Caressingly*) My darling is back! My precious is back!

ANYA I've had such a time.

VARYA I can imagine!

ANYA I left during Holy Week, it was cold then. Charlotta talked all the way and did her tricks. Why did you fasten Charlotta on to me—?

VARYA But you couldn't have traveled alone, darling; not at seventeen!

ANYA We arrived in Paris, it was cold there and snowing. I speak terrible French. Mama lived on the fifth floor; I went to see her; there were some French people in her room, ladies, an old priest with his prayer book, and the place was full of tobacco smoke —very dreary. Suddenly I began to feel sorry for Mama, so sorry, I drew her to me, held her close and couldn't let her go. Then Mama kept hugging me, crying—yes—

VARYA (*Tearfully*) Don't—oh, don't—

ANYA Her villa near Mentone she had already sold, she had nothing left, nothing. And I didn't have a kopeck left. It was all we could do to get here. And Mama doesn't understand! We sit down to dinner at a station and she orders, insists on the most expensive things and gives the waiters rouble tips. Charlotta does the same. Yasha too demands his share; it's simply dreadful. Mama has her butler, Yasha, we've brought him here—

VARYA I saw the wretch.

ANYA Well, how are things? Has the interest on the mortgage been paid?

VARYA How could we?

ANYA Oh, my God, my God—!

VARYA In August the estate is to be sold—

ANYA My God—!

LOPAHIN (*Looking in through the door and mooing like a cow*) Moo-o-o— (*Goes away*)

VARYA (*Tearfully*) I'd land him one like that— (*Shaking her fist*)

ANYA (*Embracing* VARYA *gently*) Varya, has he proposed? (VARYA *shakes her head*) But he loves you— Why don't you have it out with him, what are you waiting for?

VARYA I don't think anything will come of it for us. He is very busy, he hasn't any time for me— And doesn't notice me. God knows, it's painful for me to see him— Everybody talks about our marriage, everybody congratulates us, and the truth is, there's nothing to it—it's all like a dream— (*In a different tone*) You have a brooch looks like a bee.

ANYA (*Sadly*) Mama bought it. (*Going toward her room, speaking gaily, like a child*) And in Paris I went up in a balloon!

VARYA My darling is back! My precious is back! (DUNYASHA *has returned with the coffee pot and is making coffee.* VARYA *is standing by the door*) Darling, I'm busy all day long with the house and I go around thinking things. If only you could be married to a rich man, I'd be more at peace, too. I would go all by myself to a hermitage—then to Kiev—to Moscow, and I'd keep going like that from one holy place to another—I would go on and on. Heavenly!

ANYA The birds are singing in the orchard. What time is it now?

VARYA It must be after two. It's time you were asleep, darling. (*Going into* ANYA's *room*) Heavenly!

YASHA (YASHA *enters with a lap robe and a traveling bag. Crossing the stage airily*) May I go through here?

DUNYASHA We'd hardly recognize you, Yasha; you've changed so abroad!

YASHA Hm— And who are you?

DUNYASHA When you left here, I was like that— (*Her hand so high from the floor*) I'm Dunyasha, Fyodor Kozoyedoff's daughter. You don't remember!

YASHA Hm— You little peach!

(*Looking around before he embraces her; she shrieks and drops a saucer;* YASHA *hurries out*)

VARYA (*At the door, in a vexed tone*) And what's going on here?

DUNYASHA (*Tearfully*) I broke a saucer—

VARYA That's good luck.

ANYA (*Emerging from her room*) We ought to tell Mama beforehand: Petya is here—

VARYA I told them not to wake him up.

ANYA (*Pensively*) Six years ago our father died, a month later our brother Grisha was drowned in the river. Such a pretty little boy, just seven. Mama couldn't bear it, she went away, went away without ever looking back— (*Shuddering*) How I understand her, if she only knew I did. (*A pause*) And Petya Trofimoff was Grisha's tutor. he might remind—

(*Enter* FIERS; *he is in a jacket and white waistcoat*)

FIERS (*Going to the coffee urn, busy with it*) The mistress will have her breakfast here— (*Putting on white gloves*) Is the coffee ready? (*To* DUNYASHA, *sternly*) You! What about the cream?

DUNYASHA Oh, my God— (*Hurrying out*)

FIERS (*Busy at the coffee urn*) Oh, you good-for-nothing—![1] (*Muttering to himself*) Come back from Paris—And the master used to go to Paris by coach— (*Laughing*)

VARYA Fiers, what are you—?

FIERS At your service. (*Joyfully*) My mistress is back! It's what I've been waiting for! Now I'm ready to die— (*Crying for joy*)

(LYUBOFF, GAYEFF *and* SEMYONOFF-PISHTCHIK *enter;* SEMYONOFF-PISHTCHIK *wears a full-length short-waisted peasant coat of fine cloth* [*podyovka*] *and wide, full trousers designed to be worn tucked inside high boots* [*sharovary*]. GAYEFF *enters, making gestures with his hands and body as if he were playing billiards.*)

LYUBOFF How is it? Let me remember— Yellow into the corner! Duplicate in the middle![2]

GAYEFF I cut into the corner. Sister, you and I slept here in this very room once, and now I am fifty-one years old, strange as that may seem—

LOPAHIN Yes, time passes.

[1] No translator of Chekhov has ever found an adequate English equivalent for Chekhov's phrase here, *nedotyopa*. It was originally a brilliant creation by Chekhov, a term given wide currency because of its effective use in this play. Literally, it means "half-chopped." In English, "daffy" and "wooly-headed" are close approximations, but these terms do not convey the overtone of "mediocre" or "unpromising" also found in the Russian word.

[2] The terms from billiards used throughout the play usually refer to difficult, if not impossible shots, classic problems in billiards the avid player might spend his life trying to master.

GAYEFF What?

LOPAHIN Time, I say, passes.

GAYEFF And it smells like patchouli here.[3]

ANYA I'm going to bed. Good night, Mama. (*Kissing her mother*)

LYUBOFF My sweet little child. (*Kissing her hands*) You're glad you are home? I still can't get myself together.

ANYA Good-by, Uncle.

GAYEFF (*Kissing her face and hands*) God be with you. How like your mother you are! (*To his sister*) Lyuba, at her age you were exactly like her.

(ANYA *shakes hands with* LOPAHIN *and* PISHTCHIK, *goes out and closes the door behind her*)

LYUBOFF She's very tired.

PISHTCHIK It is a long trip, I imagine.

VARYA (*To* LOPAHIN *and* PISHTCHIK) Well, then, sirs? It's going on three o'clock, time for gentlemen to be going.

LYUBOFF (*Laughing*) The same old Varya. (*Drawing her to her and kissing her*) There, I'll drink my coffee, then we'll all go. (FIERS *puts a small cushion under her feet*) Thank you, my dear. I am used to coffee. Drink it day and night. Thank you, my dear old soul. (*Kissing* FIERS)

VARYA I'll go see if all the things have come. (*Goes out*)

LYUBOFF Is it really me sitting here? (*Laughing*) I'd like to jump around and wave my arms. (*Covering her face with her hands*) But I may be dreaming! God knows I love my country, love it deeply, I couldn't look out of the car window, I just kept crying. (*Tearfully*) However, I must drink my coffee. Thank you, Fiers, thank you, my dear old friend. I'm so glad you're still alive.

FIERS Day before yesterday.

GAYEFF He doesn't hear well.

LOPAHIN And I must leave right now for Kharkov. It's nearly five o'clock in the morning. What a nuisance! I wanted to look at you—talk— You are as beautiful as ever.

PISHTCHIK (*Breathing heavily*) Even more beautiful— In your Paris clothes— It's a feast for the eyes—

LOPAHIN Your brother, Leonid Andreevich here, says I'm a boor, a peasant money grubber, but that's all the same to me, absolutely. Let him say it. All I wish is you'd trust me as you used to, and your wonderful, touching eyes would look at me as they did. Merciful God! My father was a serf; belonged to your grandfather and your father; but you, your own self, you did so much for me once that I've forgotten all that and love you like my own kin—more than my kin.

LYUBOFF I can't sit still—I can't. (*Jumping up and walking about in great excitement*) I'll never live through this happiness— Laugh at me, I'm silly— My own little bookcase—! (*Kissing the bookcase*) My little table!

GAYEFF And in your absence the nurse here died.

[3] A strong mentholated perfume frequently used by men as shaving lotion. Lopahin apparently applies it too copiously.

LYUBOFF (*Sitting down and drinking coffee*) Yes, may she rest in Heaven! They wrote me.

GAYEFF And Anastasy died. Cross-eyed Petrushka left me and lives in town now at the police officer's. (*Taking out of his pocket a box of hard candy and sucking a piece*)

PISHTCHIK My daughter, Dashenka—sends you her greetings—

LOPAHIN I want to tell you something very pleasant, cheerful. (*Glancing at his watch*) I'm going right away. There's no time for talking. Well, I'll make it two or three words. As you know, your cherry orchard is to be sold for your debts; the auction is set for August 22nd, but don't you worry, my dear, you just sleep in peace, there's a way out of it. Here's my plan. Please listen to me. Your estate is only thirteen miles from town. They've run the railroad by it. Now if the cherry orchard and the land along the river were cut up into building lots and leased for summer cottages, you'd have at the very lowest twenty-five thousand roubles per year income.

GAYEFF Excuse me, what rot!

LYUBOFF I don't quite understand you, Yermolay Alexeevich.

LOPAHIN At the very least you will get from the summer residents twenty-five roubles per year for a two-and-a-half acre lot and if you post a notice right off, I'll bet you anything that by autumn you won't have a single patch of land free, everything will be taken. In a word, my congratulations, you are saved. The location is wonderful, the river's so deep. Except, of course, it all needs to be tidied up, cleared— For instance, let's say, tear all the old buildings down and this house, which is no good any more, and cut down the old cherry orchard—

LYUBOFF Cut down? My dear, forgive me, you don't understand at all. If there's one thing in the whole province that's interesting—not to say remarkable—it's our cherry orchard.

LOPAHIN The only remarkable thing about this cherry orchard is that it's very big. There's a crop of cherries once every two years and even that's hard to get rid of. Nobody buys them.

GAYEFF This orchard is even mentioned in the encyclopedia.

LOPAHIN (*Glancing at his watch*) If we don't cook up something and don't get somewhere, the cherry orchard and the entire estate will be sold at auction on the twenty-second of August. Do get it settled then! I swear there is no other way out. Not a one!

FIERS There was a time, forty-fifty years ago when the cherries were dried, soaked, pickled, cooked into jam and it used to be—

GAYEFF Keep quiet, Fiers.

FIERS And it used to be that the dried cherries were shipped by the wagon-load to Moscow and to Kharkov. And the money there was! And the dried cherries were soft then, juicy, sweet, fragrant— They had a way of treating them then—

LYUBOFF And where is that way now?

FIERS They have forgotten it. Nobody remembers it.

PISHTCHIK (*To* LYUBOFF) What's happening in Paris? How is everything? Did you eat frogs?

LYUBOFF I ate crocodiles.

PISHTCHIK Think of it—!

LOPAHIN Up to now in the country there have been only the gentry and the peasants, but now in summer the villa people too are coming in. All the towns, even the least big ones, are surrounded with cottages. In about twenty years very likely the summer resident will multiply enormously. He merely drinks tea on the porch now, but it might well happen that on this two-and-a-half acre lot of his, he'll go in for farming, and then your cherry orchard would be happy, rich, splendid—

GAYEFF (*Getting hot*) What rot!

(*Enter* VARYA *and* YASHA)

VARYA Here, Mama. Two telegrams for you. (*Choosing a key and opening the old bookcase noisily*) Here they are.

LYUBOFF From Paris. (*Tearing up the telegrams without reading them*) Paris, that's all over—

GAYEFF Do you know how old this bookcase is, Lyuba? A week ago I pulled out the bottom drawer and looked, and there the figures were burned on it. The bookcase was made exactly a hundred years ago. How's that? Eh? You might celebrate its jubilee. It's an inanimate object, but all the same, be that as it may, it's a bookcase.

PISHTCHIK (*In astonishment*) A hundred years—! Think of it—!

GAYEFF Yes—quite something— (*Shaking the bookcase*) Dear, honored bookcase! I saluted your existence, which for more than a hundred years has been directed toward the clear ideals of goodness and justice; your silent appeal to fruitful endeavor has not flagged in all the course of a hundred years, sustaining (*Tearfully*) through the generations of our family, our courage and our faith in a better future and nurturing in us ideals of goodness and of a social consciousness.

(*A pause*)

LOPAHIN Yes.

LYUBOFF You're the same as ever, Lenya.

GAYEFF (*Slightly embarrassed*) Carom to the right into the corner pocket. I cut into the side pocket!

LOPAHIN (*Glancing at his watch*) Well, it's time for me to go.

YASHA (*Handing medicine to* LYUBOFF) Perhaps you'll take the pills now—

PISHTCHIK You should never take medicaments, dear madam— They do neither harm nor good— Hand them here, dearest lady. (*He takes the pillbox, shakes the pills out into his palm, blows on them, puts them in his mouth and washes them down with kvass*) There! Now!

LYUBOFF (*Startled*) Why, you've lost your mind!

PISHTCHIK I took all the pills.

LOPAHIN Such a glutton!

(*Everyone laughs*)

FIERS The gentleman stayed with us during Holy Week, he ate half a bucket of pickles— (*Muttering*)

LYUBOFF What is he muttering about?

VARYA He's been muttering like that for three years. We're used to it.

YASHA In his dotage.

(CHARLOTTA IVANOVNA *in a white dress—she is very thin, her corset laced very tight—with a lorgnette at her belt, crosses the stage*)

LOPAHIN Excuse me, Charlotta Ivanovna, I haven't had a chance yet to welcome you. (*Trying to kiss her hand*)

CHARLOTTA (*Drawing her hand away*) If I let you kiss my hand, 'twould be my elbow next, then my shoulder—

LOPAHIN No luck for me today. (*Everyone laughs*) Charlotta Ivanovna, show us a trick!

CHARLOTTA No. I want to go to bed. (*Exit*)

LOPAHIN In three weeks we shall see each other. (*Kissing* LYUBOFF'S *hand*) Till then, good-by. It's time. (*To* GAYEFF) See you soon. (*Kissing* PISHTCHIK) See you soon. (*Shaking* VARYA'S *hand, then* FIERS' *and* YASHA'S) I don't feel like going. (*To* LYUBOFF) If you think it over and make up your mind about the summer cottages, let me know and I'll arrange a loan of something like fifty thousand roubles. Think it over seriously.

VARYA (*Angrily*) Do go on, anyhow, will you!

LOPAHIN I'm going, I'm going— (*Exit*)

GAYEFF Boor. However, pardon—Varya is going to marry him, it's Varya's little fiancé.

VARYA Don't talk too much, Uncle.

LYUBOFF Well, Varya, I should be very glad. He's a good man.

PISHTCHIK A man, one must say truthfully— A most worthy— And my Dashenka—says also that—she says all sorts of things— (*Snoring but immediately waking up*) Nevertheless, dearest lady, oblige me—with a loan of two hundred and forty rubles— Tomorrow the interest on my mortgage has got to be paid—

VARYA (*Startled*) There's not any money, none at all.

LYUBOFF Really, I haven't got anything.

PISHTCHIK I'll find it, somehow. (*Laughing*) I never give up hope. There, I think to myself, all is lost, I am ruined and lo and behold—a railroad is put through my land and—they paid me. And then, just watch, something else will turn up—if not today, then tomorrow— Dashenka will win two hundred thousand— She has a ticket.

LYUBOFF We've finished the coffee, now we can go to bed.

FIERS (*Brushing* GAYEFF'S *clothes, reprovingly*) You put on the wrong trousers again. What am I going to do with you!

VARYA (*Softly*) Anya is asleep. (*Opening the window softly*) Already the sun's rising—it's not cold. Look, Mama! What beautiful trees! My Lord, what air! The starlings are singing!

GAYEFF (*Opening another window*) The orchard is all white. You haven't forgotten, Lyuba? That long lane there runs straight—as a strap stretched out. It glistens on moonlight nights. Do you remember? You haven't forgotten it?

LYUBOFF (*Looking out of the window on to the orchard*) Oh, my childhood, my innocence! I slept in this nursery and looked out on the orchard from here, every morning happiness awoke with me, it was just as it is now, then—nothing has changed. (*Laughing with joy*) All, all white! Oh, my orchard! After a dark, rainy autumn and cold winter, you are young again and full of happiness. The heavenly angels have not deserted you— If I only could lift the weight from my breast, from my shoulders, if I could only forget my past!

GAYEFF Yes, and the orchard will be sold for debt, strange as that may seem.

LYUBOFF Look, our dear mother is walking through the orchard—in a white dress! (*Laughing happily*) It's she.

GAYEFF Where?

VARYA God be with you, Mama!

LYUBOFF There's not anybody, it only seemed so. To the right, as you turn to the summerhouse, a little white tree is leaning there, looks like a woman— (*Enter* TROFIMOFF, *in a student's uniform, well worn, and glasses*) What a wonderful orchard! The white masses of blossoms, the sky all blue.

TROFIMOFF Lyuboff Andreevna! (*She looks around at him*) I will just greet you and go immediately. (*Kissing her hand warmly*) I was told to wait until morning, but I hadn't the patience—

(LYUBOFF *looks at him puzzled*)

VARYA (*Tearfully*) This is Petya Trofimoff—

TROFIMOFF Petya Trofimoff, the former tutor of your Grisha— Have I really changed so?

(LYUBOFF *embraces him; and crying quietly*)

GAYEFF (*Embarrassed*) There, there, Lyuba.

VARYA (*Crying*) I told you, Petya, to wait till tomorrow.

LYUBOFF My Grisha— My boy— Grisha— Son—

VARYA What can we do, Mama? It's God's will.

TROFIMOFF (*In a low voice tearfully*) There, there—

LYUBOFF (*Weeping softly*) My boy was lost, drowned — Why? Why, my friend? (*More quietly*) Anya is asleep there, and I am talking so loud— Making so much noise— But why, Petya? Why have you lost your looks? Why do you look so much older?

TROFIMOFF A peasant woman on the train called me a mangy-looking gentleman.

LYUBOFF You were a mere boy then, a charming young student, and now your hair's not very thick any more and you wear glasses. Are you really a student still? (*Going to the door*)

TROFIMOFF Very likely I'll be a perennial student.

LYUBOFF (*Kissing her brother, then* VARYA) Well, go to bed— You've grown older too, Leonid.

PISHTCHIK (*Following her*) So that's it, we are going to bed now. Oh, my gout! I'm staying here— I'd like, Lyuboff Andreevna, my soul, tomorrow morning— Two hundred and forty rubles—

GAYEFF He's still at it.

PISHTCHIK Two hundred and forty rubles— To pay interest on the mortgage.

LYUBOFF I haven't any money, my dove.

PISHTCHIK I'll pay it back, my dear— It's a trifling sum—

LYUBOFF Oh, very well, Leonid will give— You give it to him, Leonid.

GAYEFF Oh, certainly, I'll give it to him. Hold out your pockets.

LYUBOFF What can we do, give it, he needs it— He'll pay it back.

(LYUBOFF, TROFIMOFF, PISHTCHIK *and* FIERS *go out.* GAYEFF, VARYA *and* YASHA *remain*)

GAYEFF My sister hasn't yet lost her habit of throwing money away. (*To* YASHA) Get away, my good fellow, you smell like hens.

YASHA (*With a grin*) And you are just the same as you used to be, Leonid Andreevich.

GAYEFF What? (*To* VARYA) What did he say?

VARYA (*To* YASHA) Your mother has come from the village, she's been sitting in the servants' hall ever since yesterday, she wants to see you—

YASHA The devil take her!

VARYA Ach, shameless creature!

YASHA A lot I need her! She might have come tomorrow.

(*Goes out*)

VARYA Mama is just the same as she was, she hasn't changed at all. If she could, she'd give away everything she has.

GAYEFF Yes— If many remedies are prescribed for an illness, you may know the illness is incurable. I keep thinking, I wrack my brains, I have many remedies, a great many, and that means, really, I haven't any at all. It would be fine to inherit a fortune from somebody, it would be fine to marry off our Anya to a very rich man, it would be fine to go to Yaroslavl and try our luck with our old aunt, the Countess. Auntie is very, very rich.

VARYA (*Crying*) If God would only help us!

GAYEFF Don't bawl! Auntie is very rich but she doesn't like us. To begin with, Sister married a lawyer, not a nobleman— (ANYA *appears at the door*) Married not a nobleman and behaved herself, you could say, not very virtuously. She is good, kind, nice, I love her very much, but no matter how much you allow for the extenuating circumstances, you must admit she's a depraved woman. You feel it in her slightest movement.

VARYA (*Whispering*) Anya is standing in the door there.

GAYEFF What? (*A pause*) It's amazing, something got in my right eye. I am beginning to see poorly. And on Thursday, when I was in the District Court—

(ANYA *enters*)

VARYA But why aren't you asleep, Anya?

ANYA I don't feel like sleeping. I can't.

GAYEFF My little girl— (*Kissing* ANYA'*s face and hands*) My child— (*Tearfully*) You are not my niece, you are my angel, you are everything to me. Believe me, believe—

ANYA I believe you, Uncle. Everybody loves you, respects you— But dear Uncle, you must keep quiet, just keep quiet— What were you saying, just now, about my mother, about your own sister? What did you say that for?

GAYEFF Yes, yes— (*Putting her hand up over his face*) Really, it's terrible! My God! Oh, God, save me! And today I made a speech to the bookcase— So silly! And it was only when I finished it that I could see it was silly.

VARYA It's true, Uncle, you ought to keep quiet. Just keep quiet. That's all.

ANYA If you kept quiet, you'd have more peace.

GAYEFF I'll keep quiet. (*Kissing* ANYA's *and* VARYA's *hands*) I'll keep quiet. Only this, it's about business. On Thursday I was in the District Court; well, a few of us gathered around and a conversation began about this and that, about lots of things; apparently it will be possible to arrange a loan on a promissory note to pay the bank the interest due.

VARYA If the Lord would only help us!

GAYEFF Tuesday I shall go and talk it over again. (*To* VARYA) Don't bawl! (*To* ANYA) Your mother will talk to Lopahin; of course, he won't refuse her . . . And as soon as you rest up, you will go to Yaroslavl to your great-aunt, the Countess. There, that's how we will move from three directions, and the business is in the bag. We'll pay the interest. I am convinced of that— (*Putting a hard candy in his mouth*) On my honor I'll swear, by anything you like, that the estate shall not be sold! (*Excitedly*) By my happiness, I swear! Here's my hand, call me a worthless, dishonorable man, if I allow it to come up for auction! With all my soul I swear it!

ANYA (*A quieter mood returns to her; she is happy*) How good you are, Uncle, how clever! (*Embracing her uncle*) I feel easy now! I feel easy! I'm happy!

(FIERS *enters*)

FIERS (*Reproachfully*) Leonid Andreevich, have you no fear of God! When are you going to bed?

GAYEFF Right away, right away. You may go, Fiers. For this once I'll undress myself. Well, children, beddy bye— More details tomorrow, and now, go to bed. (*Kissing* ANYA *and* VARYA) I am a man of the eighties— It is a period that's not admired, but I can say, nevertheless, that I've suffered no little for my convictions in the course of my life. It is not for nothing that the peasant loves me. One must know the peasant! One must know from what—

ANYA Again, Uncle!

VARYA You, Uncle dear, keep quiet.

FIERS (*Angrily*) Leonid Andreevich!

GAYEFF I'm coming, I'm coming— Go to bed. A double bank into the side pocket! A clean shot—

(*Goes out,* FIERS *hobbling after him*)

ANYA I feel easy now. I don't feel like going to Yaroslavl; I don't like Great-aunt, but still I feel easy. Thanks to Uncle. (*Sits down*)

VARYA I must get to sleep. I'm going. And there was unpleasantness here during your absence. In the old servants' quarters, as you know, live only the old servants: Yephemushka, Polya, Yevstignay, well, and Karp. They began to let every sort of creature spend the night with them—I didn't say anything. But then I hear they've spread the rumor that I'd given orders to feed them nothing but beans. Out of stinginess, you see— And all that from Yevstignay— Very well, I think to myself. If that's the way it is, I think to myself, then you just wait. I call in Yevstignay— (*Yawning*) He comes— How is it, I say, that you, Yevstignay— You're such a fool— (*Glancing at* ANYA) Anitchka!— (*A pause*) Asleep! (*Takes* ANYA *by her arm*) Let's go to bed— Come on!— (*Leading her*) My little darling fell asleep! Come on— (*They go. Far away beyond the orchard a shepherd is playing on a pipe.* TROFIMOFF *walks across the stage and, seeing* VARYA *and* ANYA, *stops*) Shh— She is asleep—asleep— Let's go, dear.

ANYA (*Softly, half dreaming*) I'm so tired— All the bells!— Uncle—dear— And Mama and Uncle—

VARYA Come on, my dear, come on. (*They go into* ANYA's *room*)

TROFIMOFF (*Tenderly*) My little sun! My spring!

*Curtain*

# Act Two

*A field. An old chapel, long abandoned, with crooked walls, near it a well, big stones that apparently were once tombstones, and an old bench. A road to the estate of* GAYEFF *can be seen. On one side poplars rise, casting their shadows, the cherry orchard begins there. In the distance a row of telegraph poles; and far, far away, faintly traced on the horizon, is a large town, visible only in the clearest weather. The sun will soon be down.* CHARLOTTA, YASHA *and* DUNYASHA *are sitting on the bench;* EPIHODOFF *is standing near and playing the guitar; everyone sits lost in thought.* CHARLOTTA *wears a man's old peaked cap (fourrage); she has taken a rifle from off her shoulders and is adjusting the buckle on the strap.*

CHARLOTTA (*Pensively*) I have no proper passport, I don't know how old I am—it always seems to me I'm very young. When I was a little girl, my father and mother traveled from fair to fair and gave performances, very good ones. And I did *salto mortale*[1] and different tricks. And when Papa and Mama died, a German lady took me to live with her and began teaching me. Good. I grew up. And became a governess. But where I came from and who I am I don't know— Who my parents were, perhaps they weren't

[1] A "death-defying" jump or leap.

even married—I don't know. (*Taking a cucumber out of her pocket and beginning to eat it*) I don't know a thing. (*A pause*) I'd like so much to talk but there's not anybody. I haven't anybody.

EPIHODOFF (*Playing the guitar and singing*) "What care I for the noisy world, what care I for friends and foes."— How pleasant it is to play the mandolin!

DUNYASHA That's a guitar, not a mandolin. (*Looking into a little mirror and powdering her face*)

EPIHODOFF For a madman who is in love this is a mandolin— (*Singing*) "If only my heart were warm with the fire of requited love."

(YASHA *sings with him*)

CHARLOTTA How dreadfully these people sing— Phooey! Like jackals.

DUNYASHA (*To* YASHA) All the same what happiness to have been abroad.

YASHA Yes, of course. I cannot disagree with you.

(*Yawning and then lighting a cigar*)

EPIHODOFF That's easily understood. Abroad everything long since attained its complete development.

YASHA That's obvious.

EPIHODOFF I am a cultured man. I read all kinds of remarkable books, but the trouble is I cannot discover my own inclinations, whether to live or to shoot myself. But nevertheless, I always carry a revolver on me. Here it is— (*Showing a revolver*)

CHARLOTTA That's done. Now I am going. (*Slinging the rifle over her shoulder*) You are a very clever man, Epihodoff, and a very terrible one; the women must love you madly. Brrrr-r-r-r! (*Going*) These clever people are all so silly, I haven't anybody to talk with. I'm always alone, alone, I have nobody and— Who I am, why I am, is unknown— (*Goes out without hurrying*)

EPIHODOFF Strictly speaking, not touching on other subjects, I must state about myself, in passing, that fate treats me mercilessly, as a storm does a small ship. If, let us suppose, I am mistaken, then why, to mention one instance, do I wake up this morning, look and there on my chest is a spider of terrific size— There, like that. (*Showing the size with both hands*) And also I take some *kvass* to drink and in it I find something in the highest degree indecent, such as a cockroach. (*A pause*) Have you read Buckle? [2] (*A pause*) I desire to trouble you, Avdotya Feodorovna, with a couple of words.

DUNYASHA Speak.

EPIHODOFF I have a desire to speak with you alone— (*Sighing*)

DUNYASHA (*Embarrassed*) Very well— But bring me my cape first—by the cupboard— It's rather damp here—

EPIHODOFF Very well—I'll fetch it— Now I know what I should do with my revolver— (*Takes the guitar and goes out playing*)

YASHA "Twenty-two misfortunes!" Between us he's a stupid man, it must be said. (*Yawning*)

DUNYASHA God forbid he should shoot himself. (*A pause*) I've grown so uneasy, I'm always fretting. I was only a girl when I was taken into the master's house, and now I've lost the habit of simple living—and here are my hands white, white as a lady's. I've become so delicate, fragile, ladylike, afraid of everything— Frightfully so. And, Yasha, if you deceive me, I don't know what will happen to my nerves.

YASHA (*Kissing her*) You little cucumber! Of course every girl must behave properly. What I dislike above everything is for a girl to conduct herself badly.

DUNYASHA I have come to love you passionately, you are educated, you can discuss anything. (*A pause*)

YASHA (*Yawning*) Yes, sir— To my mind it is like this: If a girl loves someone, it means she is immoral. (*A pause*) It is pleasant to smoke a cigar in the clear air— (*Listening*) They are coming here— It is the ladies and gentlemen— (DUNYASHA *impulsively embraces him*) Go to the house, as though you had been to bathe in the river, go by this path, otherwise, they might meet you and suspect me of making a rendezvous with you. That I cannot tolerate.

DUNYASHA (*With a little cough*) Your cigar has given me the headache. (*Goes out*)

(YASHA *remains, sitting near the chapel.* LYUBOFF, GAYEFF *and* LOPAHIN *enter*)

LOPAHIN We must decide definitely, time doesn't wait. Why, the matter's quite simple. Are you willing to lease your land for summer cottages or are you not? Answer in one word, yes or no? Just one word!

LYUBOFF Who is it smokes those disgusting cigars out here—? (*Sitting down*)

GAYEFF The railroad running so near is a great convenience. (*Sitting down*) We made a trip to town and lunched there— Yellow in the side pocket! Perhaps I should go in the house first and play one game—

LYUBOFF You'll have time.

LOPAHIN Just one word! (*Imploringly*) Do give me your answer!

GAYEFF (*Yawning*) What?

LYUBOFF (*Looking in her purse*) Yesterday there was lots of money in it. Today there's very little. My poor Varya! For the sake of economy she feeds everybody milk soup, and in the kitchen the old people get nothing but beans, and here I spend money—senselessly— (*Dropping her purse and scattering gold coins*) There they go scattering! (*She is vexed*)

YASHA Allow me, I'll pick them up in a second. (*Picking up the coins*)

LYUBOFF If you will, Yasha. And why did I go in town for lunch—? Your restaurant with its music is trashy, the tablecloths smell of soap— Why drink so much, Lyonya? Why eat so much? Why talk so much? Today in the restaurant you were talking a lot again, and all of it beside the point. About the seventies, about the decadents. And to whom? Talking to waiters about the decadents!

LOPAHIN Yes.

GAYEFF (*Waving his hand*) I am incorrigible, that's evident— (*To* YASHA *irritably*) What is it?— You are forever swirling around in front of us?

[2] Henry Thomas Buckle (1821-1862), a nineteenth century historian.

YASHA (*Laughing*) I cannot hear your voice without laughing.

GAYEFF (*To his sister*) Either I or he—

LYUBOFF Go away, Yasha. Go on—

YASHA (*Giving* LYUBOFF *her purse*) I am going right away. (*Barely suppressing his laughter*) This minute. (*Goes out*)

LOPAHIN The rich Deriganoff intends to buy your estate. They say he is coming personally to the auction.

LYUBOFF And where did you hear that?

LOPAHIN In town they are saying it.

GAYEFF Our Yaroslavl aunt promised to send us something, but when and how much she will send, nobody knows—

LOPAHIN How much will she send? A hundred thousand? Two hundred?

LYUBOFF Well—maybe ten, fifteen thousand—we'd be thankful for that.

LOPAHIN Excuse me, but such light-minded people as you are, such odd, unbusinesslike people, I never saw. You are told in plain Russian that your estate is being sold up and you just don't seem to take it in.

LYUBOFF But what are we to do? Tell us what?

LOPAHIN I tell you every day. Every day I tell you the same thing. Both the cherry orchard and the land have got to be leased for summer cottages, it has to be done right now, quick— The auction is right under your noses. Do understand! Once you finally decide that there are to be summer cottages, you will get all the money you want, and then you'll be saved.

LYUBOFF Summer cottages and summer residents—it is so common, excuse me, but that's what it is.

GAYEFF I absolutely agreed with you.

LOPAHIN I'll either burst out crying, or scream, oı faint. I can't bear it! You are torturing me! (*To* GAYEFF) You're a perfect old woman!

GAYEFF What?

LOPAHIN A perfect old woman! (*About to go*)

LYUBOFF (*Alarmed*) No, don't go, stay, my lamb, I beg you. Perhaps we will think of something!

LOPAHIN What is there to think about?

LYUBOFF Don't go, I beg you. With you here it is more cheerful anyhow— (*A pause*) I keep waiting for something, as if the house were about to tumble down on our heads.

GAYEFF (*Deep in thought*) Double into the corner pocket— Bank into the wide pocket—

LYUBOFF We have sinned so much—

LOPAHIN What sins have you—?

GAYEFF (*Puts a hard candy into his mouth*) They say I've eaten my fortune up in hard candies— (*Laughing*)

LYUBOFF Oh, my sins—I've always thrown money around like mad, recklessly, and I married a man who accumulated nothing but debts. My husband died from champagne—he drank fearfully—and to my misfortune I fell in love with another man. I lived with him, and just at that time—it was my first punishment—a blow over the head: right here in the river my boy was drowned and I went abroad—went away for good, never to return, never to see this river again—I shut my eyes, ran away, beside myself, and he after me—mercilessly, brutally. I bought a villa near Mentone, because he fell ill there, and for three years I knew no rest day or night, the sick man exhausted me, my soul dried up. And last year when the villa was sold for debts, I went to Paris and there he robbed me of everything, threw me over, took up with another woman; I tried to poison myself—so stupid, so shameful— And suddenly I was seized with longing for Russia, for my own country, for my little girl— (*Wiping away her tears*) Lord, Lord, have mercy, forgive me my sins! Don't punish me any more! (*Getting a telegram out of her pocket*) I got this today from Paris, he asks forgiveness, begs me to return— (*Tears up the telegram*) That sounds like music somewhere.

(*Listening*)

GAYEFF It is our famous Jewish orchestra. You remember, four violins, a flute and double bass.

LYUBOFF Does it still exist? We ought to get hold of it sometime and give a party.

LOPAHIN (*Listening*) Can't hear it— (*Singing softly*) "And for money the Germans will frenchify a Russian." (*Laughing*) What a play I saw yesterday at the theatre, very funny!

LYUBOFF And most likely there was nothing funny about it. You shouldn't look at plays, but look oftener at yourselves. How gray all your lives are, what a lot of idle things you say!

LOPAHIN That's true. It must be said frankly this life of ours is idiotic— (*A pause*) My father was a peasant, an idiot, he understood nothing, he taught me nothing, he just beat me in his drunken fits and always with a stick. At bottom I am just as big a dolt and idiot as he was. I wasn't taught anything, my handwriting is vile, I write like a pig—I am ashamed for people to see it.

LYUBOFF You ought to get married, my friend.

LOPAHIN Yes— That's true.

LYUBOFF To our Varya, perhaps. She is a good girl.

LOPAHIN Yes.

LYUBOFF She comes from simple people, and she works all day long, but the main thing is she loves you. And you, too, have liked her a long time.

LOPAHIN Why not? I am not against it— She's a good girl. (*A pause*)

GAYEFF They are offering me a position in a bank. Six thousand a year— Have you heard that?

LYUBOFF Not you! You stay where you are—

(FIERS *enters, bringing an overcoat*)

FIERS (*To* GAYEFF) Pray, Sir, put this on, it's damp.

GAYEFF (*Putting on the overcoat*) You're a pest, old man.

FIERS That's all right— This morning you went off without letting me know. (*Looking him over*)

LYUBOFF How old you've grown, Fiers!

FIERS At your service.

LOPAHIN She says you've grown very old!

FIERS I've lived a long time. They were planning to marry me off before your papa was born. (*Laughing*) And at the time the serfs were freed I was already the head footman. I didn't want to be freed then, I stayed with the masters— (*A pause*) And I remember, everybody was happy, but what they were happy about they didn't know themselves.

LOPAHIN In the old days it was fine. At least they flogged.

FIERS (*Not hearing*) But, of course. The peasants stuck to the masters, the masters stuck to the peasants, and now everything is all smashed up, you can't tell about anything.

GAYEFF Keep still, Fiers. Tomorrow I must go to town. They have promised to introduce me to a certain general who might make us a loan.

LOPAHIN Nothing will come of it. And you can rest assured you won't pay the interest.

LYUBOFF He's just raving on. There aren't any such generals.

(TROFIMOFF, ANYA *and* VARYA *enter*)

GAYEFF Here they come.

ANYA There is Mama sitting there.

LYUBOFF (*Tenderly*) Come, come— My darlings— (*Embracing* ANYA *and* VARYA) If you only knew how I love you both! Come sit by me—there—like that.

(*Everybody sits down*)

LOPAHIN Our perennial student is always strolling with the young ladies.

TROFIMOFF It's none of your business.

LOPAHIN He will soon be fifty and he's still a student.

TROFIMOFF Stop your stupid jokes.

LOPAHIN But why are you so peevish, you queer duck?

TROFIMOFF Don't you pester me.

LOPAHIN (*Laughing*) Permit me to ask you, what do you make of me?

TROFIMOFF Yermolay Alexeevich, I make this of you: you are a rich man, you'll soon be a millionaire. Just as it is in the metabolism of nature, a wild beast is needed to eat up everything that comes his way; so you, too, are needed.

(*Everyone laughs*)

VARYA Petya, you'd better tell us about the planets.

LYUBOFF No, let's go on with yesterday's conversation.

TROFIMOFF What was it about?

GAYEFF About the proud man.

TROFIMOFF We talked a long time yesterday, but didn't get anywhere. In a proud man, in your sense of the word, there is something mystical. Maybe you are right, from your standpoint, but if we are to discuss it in simple terms, without whimsy, then what pride can there be, is there any sense in it, if man physiologically is poorly constructed, if in the great majority he is crude, unintelligent, profoundly miserable. One must stop admiring oneself. One must only work.

GAYEFF All the same, you will die.

TROFIMOFF Who knows? And what does it mean—you will die? Man may have a hundred senses, and when he dies only the five that are known to us may perish, and the remaining ninety-five go on living.

LYUBOFF How clever you are, Petya!

LOPAHIN (*Ironically*) Terribly!

TROFIMOFF Humanity goes forward, perfecting its powers. Everything that's unattainable now will some day become familiar, understandable; it is only that one must work and must help with all one's might those who seek the truth. With us in Russia so far only a very few work. The great majority of the intelligentsia that I know are looking for nothing, doing nothing, and as yet have no capacity for work. They call themselves intelligentsia, are free and easy with the servants, treat the peasants like animals, educate themselves poorly, read nothing seriously, do absolutely nothing; about science they just talk and about art they understand very little. Every one of them is serious, all have stern faces; they all talk of nothing but important things, philosophize, and all the time everybody can see that the workmen eat abominably, sleep without any pillows, thirty or forty to a room, and everywhere there are bedbugs, stench, dampness, moral uncleanness— And apparently with us, all the fine talk is only to divert the attention of ourselves and of others. Show me where we have the day nurseries they are always talking so much about, where are the reading rooms? They only write of these in novels, for the truth is there are not any at all. There is only filth, vulgarity, orientalism— I am afraid of very serious faces and dislike them. I'm afraid of serious conversations. Rather than that let's just keep still.

LOPAHIN You know I get up before five o'clock in the morning and work from morning till night. Well, I always have money, my own and other people's, on hand, and I see what the people around me are. One has only to start doing something to find out how few honest and decent people there are. At times when I can't go to sleep, I think: Lord, thou gavest us immense forests, unbounded fields and the widest horizons, and living in the midst of them we should indeed be giants—

LYUBOFF You feel the need for giants— They are good only in fairy tales; anywhere else they only frighten us.

(*At the back of the stage* EPIHODOFF *passes by, playing the guitar*)

LYUBOFF (*Lost in thought*) Epihodoff is coming—

ANYA (*Lost in thought*) Epihodoff is coming.

GAYEFF The sun has set, ladies and gentlemen.

TROFIMOFF Yes.

GAYEFF (*Not loud and as if he were declaiming*) Oh, Nature, wonderful, you gleam with eternal radiance, beautiful and indifferent, you, whom we call Mother, combine in yourself both life and death, you give life and you take it away.

VARYA (*Beseechingly*) Uncle!

ANYA Uncle, you're doing it again!

TROFIMOFF You'd better bank the yellow into the side pocket.

GAYEFF I'll be quiet, quiet.

(*All sit absorbed in their thoughts. There is only the silence.* FIERS *is heard muttering to himself softly. Suddenly a distant sound is heard, as if from the sky, like the sound of a snapped string, dying away, mournful*)

LYUBOFF What's that?

LOPAHIN I don't know. Somewhere far off in a mine shaft a lift cable must have broken. But somewhere very far off.

GAYEFF Or it may be some bird—like a heron.

TROFIMOFF Or an owl—

LYUBOFF (*Shivering*) It's unpleasant, somehow. (*A pause*)

FIERS Before the disaster it was like that. The owl hooted and the samovar hummed without stopping, both.

GAYEFF Before what disaster?

FIERS Before the emancipation.

(*A pause*)

LYUBOFF You know, my friends, let's go. Twilight is falling. (*To* ANYA) You have tears in your eyes— What is it, my dear little girl? (*Embracing her*)

ANYA It's just that, Mama. It's nothing.

TROFIMOFF Somebody is coming.

(*A* STRANGER *appears in a shabby white cap, and an overcoat; he is a little drunk*)

THE STRANGER Allow me to ask you, can I go straight through here to the station?

GAYEFF You can. Go by that road.

THE STRANGER I am heartily grateful to you. (*Coughing*) The weather is splendid— (*Declaiming*) "Brother of mine, suffering brother— Go out to the Volga, whose moans—" (*To* VARYA) Mademoiselle, grant a hungry Russian man some thirty kopecks—

(VARYA *is frightened and gives a shriek*)

LOPAHIN (*Angrily*) There's a limit to everything.

LYUBOFF (*Flustered*) Take this— Here's this for you— (*Searching in her purse*) No silver— It's all the same, here's a gold piece for you—

THE STRANGER I am heartily grateful to you. (*Goes out. Laughter*)

VARYA (*Frightened*) I'm going—I'm going— Oh, Mama, you poor little Mama! There's nothing in the house for people to eat, and you gave him a gold piece.

LYUBOFF What is to be done with me, so silly? I shall give you all I have in the house. Yermolay Alexeevich, you will lend me some this once more!—

LOPAHIN Agreed.

LYUBOFF Let's go, ladies and gentlemen, it's time. And here, Varya, we have definitely made a match for you, I congratulate you.

VARYA (*Through her tears*) Mama, that's not something to joke about.

LOPAHIN Achmelia, get thee to a nunnery.[3]

GAYEFF And my hands are trembling; it is a long time since I have played billiards.

LOPAHIN Achmelia, Oh nymph, in thine orisons be all my sins remember'd—

LYUBOFF Let's go, my dear friends, it will soon be suppertime.

VARYA He frightened me. My heart is thumping so!

LOPAHIN I remind you, ladies and gentlemen: August 22nd the cherry orchard will be auctioned off. Think about that!— Think!—

(*All go out except* TROFIMOFF *and* ANYA)

ANYA (*Laughing*) My thanks to the stranger, he frightened Varya. Now we are alone.

TROFIMOFF Varya is afraid we might begin to love each other and all day long she won't leave us to ourselves. With her narrow mind she cannot understand that we are above love. To sidestep the petty and illusory, which prevent our being free and happy, that is the aim and meaning of our life. Forward! We march on irresistibly toward the bright star that burns there in the distance. Forward! Do not fall behind, friends!

ANYA (*Extending her arms upward*) How well you talk! (*A pause*) It's wonderful here today!

TROFIMOFF Yes, the weather is marvelous.

ANYA What have you done to me, Petya? Why don't I love the cherry orchard any longer the way I used to? I loved it so tenderly, it seemed to me there was not a better place on earth than our orchard.

TROFIMOFF All Russia is our orchard. The earth is immense and beautiful, and on it are many wonderful places. (*A pause*) Just think, Anya: your grandfather, great-grandfather and all your ancestors were slave owners, in possession of living souls, and can you doubt that from every cherry in the orchard, from every leaf, from every trunk, human beings are looking at you. Can it be that you don't hear their voices? To possess living souls, well, that depraved all of you who lived before and who are living now, so that your mother and you, and your uncle no longer notice that you live by debt, at somebody else's expense, at the expense of those very people whom you wouldn't let past your front door— We are at least two hundred years behind the times, we have as yet absolutely nothing, we have no definite attitude toward the past, we only philosophize, complain of our sadness or drink vodka. Why, it is quite clear that to begin to live in the present we must first atone for our past, must be done with it; and we can atone for it only through suffering, only through uncommon, incessant labor. Understand that, Anya.

ANYA The house we live in ceased to be ours long ago, and I'll go away, I give you my word.

TROFIMOFF If you have the household keys, throw them in the well and go away. Be free as the wind.

ANYA (*Transported*) How well you said that!

TROFIMOFF Believe me, Anya, believe me! I am not thirty yet, I am young, I am still a student, but I have already borne so much! Every winter I am hungry, sick, anxious, poor as a beggar, and—where has destiny not chased me, where haven't I been! And yet, my soul has always, every minute, day and night, been full of inexplicable premonitions. I have a premonition of happiness, Anya, I see it already—

ANYA (*Pensively*) The moon is rising.

(EPIHODOFF *is heard playing on the guitar, always the same sad song. The moon rises. Somewhere near the poplars* VARYA *is looking for* ANYA *and calling: "Anya! Where are you?"*)

TROFIMOFF Yes, the moon is rising. (*A pause*) Here is

[3] Here and below Lopahin is quoting somewhat distortedly Hamlet's advice to Ophelia (Act III, Scene 1).

happiness, here it comes, comes always nearer and nearer, I hear its footsteps now. And if we shall not see it, shall not come to know it, what does that matter? Others will see it!

VARYA (*Off*) Anya! Where are you?

TROFIMOFF Again, that Varya! (*Angrily*) It's scandalous!

ANYA Well, let's go to the river. It's lovely there.

TROFIMOFF Let's go. (*They go out*)

VARYA (*Off*) Anya! Anya!

*Curtain*

# Act Three

*The drawing room, separated by an arch from the ballroom. A chandelier is lighted. A Jewish orchestra is playing—the same that was mentioned in Act Two. Evening. In the ballroom they are dancing grand rond. The* VOICE *of* SEMYONOFF-PISHTCHIK: *"Promenade à une paire!" They enter the drawing room; in the first couple are* PISHTCHIK *and* CHARLOTTA IVANOVNA; *in the second,* TROFIMOFF *and* LYUBOFF ANDREEVNA; *in the third,* ANYA *with the* POST-OFFICE CLERK; *in the fourth,* VARYA *with the* STATIONMASTER, *et cetera—*VARYA *is crying softly and wipes away her tears while she is dancing.* DUNYASHA *is in the last couple through the drawing room,* PISHTCHIK *shouts: "Grand rond, balancez!" and "Les Cavaliers à genoux et remerciez vos dames!"* [1]

FIERS *in a frock coat goes by with seltzer water on a tray.* PISHTCHIK *and* TROFIMOFF *come into the drawing room.*

PISHTCHIK I am full-blooded, I have had two strokes already, and dancing is hard for me, but as they say, if you are in a pack of dogs, you may bark and bark, but you must still wag your tail. At that, I have the health of a horse. My dear father—he was a great joker—may he dwell in Heaven—used to talk as if our ancient line, the Semyonoff-Pishtchiks, were descended from the very horse that Caligula made a Senator— (*Sitting down*) But here's my trouble: I haven't any money. A hungry dog believes in nothing but meat— (*Snoring but waking at once*) And the same way with me—I can't talk about anything but money.

TROFIMOFF Well, to tell you the truth, there *is* something horsy about your figure.

[1] The pattern of the *Grand Rond* is close to the familiar American square dances. The last of Pishtchik's calls signalizes the end of the full set: "Gentlemen, on your knees and thank your ladies."

PISHTCHIK Well—a horse is a fine animal— You can sell a horse—

(*The sound of playing billiards comes from the next room.* VARYA *appears under the arch to the ballroom*)

TROFIMOFF (*Teasing*) Madam Lopahin! Madam Lopahin!

VARYA (*Angrily*) A mangy-looking gentleman!

TROFIMOFF Yes, I am a mangy-looking gentleman, and proud of it!

VARYA (*In bitter thought*) Here we have gone and hired musicians and what are we going to pay them with? (*Goes out*)

TROFIMOFF (*To* PISHTCHIK) If the energy you have wasted in the course of your life trying to find money to pay the interest had gone into something else, you could very likely have turned the world upside down before you were done with it.

PISHTCHIK Nietzsche—the philosopher—the greatest—the most celebrated—a man of tremendous mind—says in his works that one may make counterfeit money.

TROFIMOFF And have you read Nietzsche?

PISHTCHIK Well—Dashenka told me. And I'm in such a state now that I could make counterfeit money myself— Day after tomorrow three hundred and ten roubles must be paid—one hundred and thirty I've on hand— (*Feeling in his pockets, alarmed*) The money is gone! I have lost the money! (*Tearfully*) Where is the money? (*Joyfully*) Here it is, inside the lining—I was in quite a sweat—

(LYUBOFF *and* CHARLOTTA IVANOVNA *come in*)

LYUBOFF (*Humming the "Lezginka," a Georgian dance*) Why does Leonid take so long? What's he doing in town? (*To* DUNYASHA) Dunyasha, offer the musicians some tea—

TROFIMOFF In all probability the auction did not take place.

LYUBOFF And the musicians came at an unfortunate moment and we planned the ball at an unfortunate moment— Well, it doesn't matter. (*Sitting down and singing softly*)

CHARLOTTA (*Gives* PISHTCHIK *a deck of cards*) Here is a deck of cards for you, think of some one card.

PISHTCHIK I have thought of one.

CHARLOTTA Now, shuffle the deck. Very good. Hand it here; oh, my dear Monsieur Pishtchik. *Ein, zwei, drei!* Now look for it, it's in your coat pocket—

PISHTCHIK (*Getting a card out of his coat pocket*) The eight of spades, that's absolutely right! (*Amazed*) Fancy that!

CHARLOTTA (*Holding a deck of cards in her palm; to* TROFIMOFF) Tell me quick now, which card is on top?

TROFIMOFF What is it? Well—the Queen of Spades.

CHARLOTTA Right! (*To* PISHTCHIK) Well? Which card's on top?

PISHTCHIK The Ace of Hearts.

CHARLOTTA Right! (*Strikes the deck against her palm; the deck of cards disappears*) And what beautiful weather we are having today!

(*A mysterious feminine voice answers her, as if from under the floor*)

VOICE Oh, yes. The weather is splendid, madam.

CHARLOTTA You are so nice, you're my ideal—

VOICE Madam, you too please me greatly.

THE STATIONMASTER (*Applauding*) Madam Ventriloquist, bravo!

PISHTCHIK (*Amazed*) Fancy that! Most charming Charlotta Ivanovna—I am simply in love with you.

CHARLOTTA In love? (*Shrugging her shoulders*) Is it possible that you can love? *Guter mensch aber schlechter musikant.*[2]

TROFIMOFF (*Slapping* PISHTCHIK *on the shoulder*) You horse, you—

CHARLOTTA I beg your attention, one more trick. (*Taking a lap robe from the chair*) Here is a very fine lap robe—I want to sell it— (*Shaking it out*) Wouldn't somebody like to buy it?

PISHTCHIK (*Amazed*) Fancy that!

CHARLOTTA *Ein, zwei, drei!*

(*She quickly raises the lowered robe, behind it stands* ANYA, *who curtseys, runs to her mother, embraces her and runs back into the ballroom amid the general delight*)

LYUBOFF (*Applauding*) Bravo, bravo—!

CHARLOTTA Now again! *Ein, zwei, drei!*

(*Lifting the robe: behind it stands* VARYA, *who bows*)

PISHTCHIK (*Amazed*) Fancy that!

CHARLOTTA That's all. (*Throwing the robe at* PISHTCHIK, *curtseying and running into the ballroom*)

PISHTCHIK (*Hurrying after her*) You little rascal—What a girl! What a girl! (*Goes out*)

LYUBOFF And Leonid is not here yet. What he's doing in town so long, I don't understand! Everything is finished there, either the estate is sold by now, or the auction didn't take place. Why keep it from us so long?

VARYA (*Trying to comfort her*) Uncle has bought it, I am sure of that.

TROFIMOFF (*Mockingly*) Yes.

VARYA Great-aunt sent him power of attorney to buy it in her name and transfer the debt. She did this for Anya. And I feel certain, God willing, that Uncle will buy it.

LYUBOFF Our great-aunt in Yaroslavl has sent fifteen thousand to buy the estate in her name— She doesn't trust us, but that wouldn't be enough to pay the interest even— (*Covering her face with her hands*) Today my fate will be decided, my fate—

TROFIMOFF (*Teasing* VARYA) Madam Lopahin!

VARYA (*Angrily*) Perennial student! You have already been expelled from the University twice.

LYUBOFF But why are you angry, Varya? He teases you about Lopahin, what of it? Marry Lopahin if you want to, he is a good man, interesting. If you don't want to, don't marry him; darling, nobody is making you do it.

[2] Literally, "a good man but a poor music-maker." Its modern equivalent would be "a nice guy but a lousy lover."

VARYA I look at this matter seriously, Mama, one must speak straight out. He's a good man, I like him.

LYUBOFF Then marry him. What there is to wait for I don't understand!

VARYA But I can't propose to him myself, Mama. It's two years now; everyone has been talking to me about him, everyone talks, and he either remains silent or jokes. I understand. He's getting rich, he's busy with his own affairs, and has no time for me. If there were money, ever so little, even a hundred roubles, I would drop everything, and go far away. I'd go to a nunnery.

TROFIMOFF How saintly!

VARYA (*To* TROFIMOFF) A student should be intelligent! (*In a low voice, tearfully*) How homely you have grown, Petya, how old you've got. (*To* LYUBOFF, *no longer crying*) It is just that I can't live without working, Mama. I must be doing something every minute.

(YASHA *enters*)

YASHA (*Barely restraining his laughter*) Epihodoff has broken a billiard cue!— (*Goes out*)

VARYA But why is Epihodoff here? Who allowed him to play billiards? I don't understand these people— (*Goes out*)

LYUBOFF Don't tease her, Petya; you can see she has troubles enough without that.

TROFIMOFF She is just too zealous. Sticking her nose into things that are none of her business. All summer she gave us no peace, neither me nor Anya; she was afraid a romance would spring up between us. What business is that of hers? And besides I haven't shown any signs of it. I am so remote from triviality. We are above love!

LYUBOFF Well, then, I must be beneath love. (*Very anxiously*) Why isn't Leonid here? Just to tell us whether the estate is sold or not? Calamity seems to me so incredible that I don't know what to think, I'm lost—I could scream this minute—I could do something insane. Save me, Petya. Say something, do say. . . .

TROFIMOFF Whether the estate is sold today or is not sold—is it not the same? There is no turning back, the path is all grown over. Calm yourself, my dear, all that was over long ago. One mustn't deceive oneself; one must for once at least in one's life look truth straight in the eye.

LYUBOFF What truth? You see where the truth is and where the untruth is, but as for me, it's as if I had lost my sight, I see nothing. You boldly decide all important questions, but tell me, my dear boy, isn't that because you are young and haven't had time yet to suffer through any one of your problems? You look boldly ahead, and isn't that because you don't see and don't expect anything terrible, since life is still hidden from your young eyes? You are braver, more honest, more profound than we are, but stop and think, be magnanimous, have a little mercy on me, just a little. Why, I was born here. My father and mother lived here and my grandfather. I love this house, I can't imagine my life without the cherry orchard and if it is very necessary to sell it, then sell me along with the orchard— (*Embracing* TROFIMOFF *and kissing him on the forehead*) Why, my son was drowned here— (*Crying*) Have mercy on me, good, kind man.

TROFIMOFF You know I sympathize with you from the bottom of my heart.

LYUBOFF But that should be said differently, differently— (*Taking out her handkerchief; a telegram falls on the floor*) My heart is heavy today, you can't imagine how heavy. It is too noisy for me here, my soul trembles at every sound, I tremble all over and yet I can't go off by myself. When I am alone the silence frightens me. Don't blame me, Petya—I love you as one of my own. I should gladly have given you Anya's hand, I assure you, only, my dear, you must study and finish your course. You do nothing. Fate simply flings you about from place to place, and that's so strange— Isn't that so? Yes? And you must do something about your beard, to make it grow somehow— (*Laughing*) You look funny!

TROFIMOFF (*Picking up the telegram*) I do not desire to be beautiful.

LYUBOFF This telegram is from Paris. I get one every day. Yesterday and today too. That wild man has fallen ill again, something is wrong again with him— He asks forgiveness, begs me to come, and really I ought to make a trip to Paris and stay awhile near him. Your face looks stern, Petya, but what is there to do, my dear, what am I to do, he is ill, he is alone, unhappy and who will look after him there, who will keep him from doing the wrong thing, who will give him his medicine on time? And what is there to hide or keep still about? I love him, that's plain. I love him, love him— It's a stone about my neck, I'm sinking to the bottom with it, but I love that stone and live without it I cannot. (*Pressing* TROFIMOFF'S *hand*) Don't think harshly of me, Petya, don't say anything to me, don't—

TROFIMOFF (*Tearfully*) Forgive my frankness, for God's sake! Why, he picked your bones.

LYUBOFF No, no, no, you must not talk like that. (*Stopping her ears*)

TROFIMOFF But he is a scoundrel. Only you, you are the only one that doesn't know it. He is a petty scoundrel, a nonentity—

LYUBOFF (*Angry but controlling herself*) You are twenty-six years old or twenty-seven, but you are still a schoolboy in the second grade!

TROFIMOFF Very well!

LYUBOFF You should be a man—at your age you should understand people who love. And you yourself should love someone—you should fall in love! (*Angrily*) Yes, yes! And there is no purity in you; you are simply smug, a ridiculous crank, a freak—

TROFIMOFF (*Horrified*) What is she saying!

LYUBOFF "I am above love!" You are not above love, Petya. You are, as our Fiers would say, just a good-for-nothing. Imagine, at your age, not having a mistress—!

TROFIMOFF (*Horrified*) This is terrible! What is she saying! (*Goes quickly into the ballroom, clutching his head*) This is horrible—I can't bear it, I am going— (*Goes out but immediately returns*) All is over between us. (*Goes out into the hall*)

LYUBOFF (*Shouting after him*) Petya, wait! You funny creature, I was joking! Petya! (*In the hall you hear someone running up the stairs and suddenly falling back down with a crash. You hear* ANYA *and* VARYA *scream but immediately you hear laughter*) What's that?

(ANYA *runs in*)

ANYA (*Laughing*) Petya fell down the stairs! (*Runs out*)

LYUBOFF What a funny boy that Petya is—! (*The* STATIONMASTER *stops in the center of the ballroom and begins to recite "The Sinner" by A. Tolstoi.*[3] *They listen to him but he has recited only a few lines when the strains of a waltz are heard from the hall and the recitation is broken off. They all dance.* TROFIMOFF, ANYA, VARYA *and* LYUBOFF *come in from the hall*) But, Petya—but, dear soul—I beg your forgiveness— Let's go dance.

(*She dances with* TROFIMOFF. ANYA *and* VARYA *dance.* FIERS *enters, leaving his stick by the side door.* YASHA *also comes into the drawing room and watches the dancers*)

YASHA What is it, Grandpa?

FIERS I don't feel very well. In the old days there were generals, barons, admirals dancing at our parties, and now we send for the post-office clerk and the stationmaster, and even they are none too anxious to come. Somehow I've grown feeble. The old master, the grandfather, treated everybody with sealing-wax for all sicknesses. I take sealing-wax every day, have done so for twenty-odd years or more; it may be due to that that I'm alive.

YASHA You are tiresome, Grandpa. (*Yawning*) Why don't you go off and die?

FIERS Aw, you—good-for-nothing!— (*Muttering*)

(TROFIMOFF *and* LYUBOFF *dance in the ballroom and then in the drawing room*)

LYUBOFF *Merci.* I'll sit down awhile— (*Sitting down*) I'm tired.

(ANYA *enters*)

ANYA (*Agitated*) And just now in the kitchen some man was saying that the cherry orchard had been sold today.

LYUBOFF Sold to whom?

ANYA He didn't say. He's gone.

(*Dancing with* TROFIMOFF, *they pass into the ballroom*)

YASHA It was some old man babbling there. A stranger.

FIERS And Leonid Andreevich is still not here, he has not arrived. The overcoat he has on is light, mid-season—let's hope he won't catch cold. Ach, these young things!

LYUBOFF I shall die this minute. Go, Yasha, find out who it was sold to.

YASHA But he's been gone a long time, the old fellow. (*Laughing*)

[3] Alexei Tolstoi (1817-1875), a popular poet.

LYUBOFF (*With some annoyance*) Well, what are you laughing at? What are you so amused at?

YASHA Epihodoff is just too funny. An empty-headed man. "Twenty-two misfortunes!"

LYUBOFF Fiers, if the estate is sold, where will you go?

FIERS Wherever you say, there I'll go.

LYUBOFF Why do you look like that? Aren't you well? You know you ought to go to bed—

FIERS Yes— (*With a sneer*) I go to bed and without me who's going to serve, who'll take care of things? I'm the only one in the whole house.

YASHA Lyuboff Andreevna, let me ask a favor of you, do be so kind! If you ever go back to Paris, take me with you, please do! It's impossible for me to stay here. (*Looking around him, and speaking in a low voice*) Why talk about it? You can see for yourself it's an uncivilized country, an immoral people and not only that, there's the boredom of it. The food they give us in that kitchen is abominable and there's that Fiers, too, walking about and muttering all kinds of words that are out of place. Take me with you, be so kind!

PISHTCHIK (*Entering*) Allow me to ask you—for a little waltz, most beautiful lady— (LYUBOFF *goes with him*) Charming lady, I must borrow a hundred and eighty roubles from you—will borrow— (*Dancing*) a hundred and eighty roubles— (*They pass into the ballroom*)

YASHA (*Singing low*) "Wilt thou know the unrest in my soul!"

(*In the ballroom a figure in a gray top hat and checked trousers waves both hands and jumps about; there are shouts of "Bravo, Charlotta Ivanovna!"*)

DUNYASHA (*Stopping to powder her face*) The young lady orders me to dance—there are a lot of gentlemen and very few ladies—but dancing makes my head swim and my heart thump. Fiers Nikolaevich, the post-office clerk said something to me just now that took my breath away.

(*The music plays more softly*)

FIERS What did he say to you?

DUNYASHA You are like a flower, he says.

YASHA (*Yawning*) What ignorance—! (*Goes out*)

DUNYASHA Like a flower—I am such a sensitive girl, I love tender words awfully.

FIERS You'll be getting your head turned.

(EPIHODOFF *enters*)

EPIHODOFF Avdotya Feodorovna, you don't want to see me— It's as if I were some sort of insect. (*Sighing*) Ach, life!

DUNYASHA What do you want?

EPIHODOFF Undoubtedly you may be right. (*Sighing*) But of course, if one considers it from a given point of view, then you—I will allow myself so to express it, forgive my frankness—absolutely led me into such a state of mind. I know my fate, every day some misfortune happens to me, but I have long since become accustomed to that, and so I look on my misfortunes with a smile. You gave me your word and, although I—

DUNYASHA I beg you, we'll talk later on, but leave me now in peace. I'm in a dream now. (*Playing with her fan*)

EPIHODOFF I have something wrong happen every day —I will allow myself so to express it—I just smile, I even laugh.

VARYA (*Entering from the ballroom*) You are not gone yet, Semyon? What a really disrespectful man you are! (*To* DUNYASHA) Get out of here, Dunyasha. (*To* EPIHODOFF) You either play billiards and break a cue or you walk about the drawing room like a guest.

EPIHODOFF Allow me to tell you, you cannot make any demands on me.

VARYA I'm not making any demands on you, I'm talking to you. All you know is to walk from place to place but not do any work. We keep a clerk, but what for, nobody knows.

EPIHODOFF (*Offended*) Whether I work, whether I walk, whether I eat, or whether I play billiards are matters to be discussed only by people of understanding and my seniors.

VARYA You dare to say that to me! (*Flying into a temper*) You dare? So I don't understand anything? Get out of here! This minute!

EPIHODOFF (*Alarmed*) I beg you to express yourself in a delicate manner.

VARYA (*Beside herself*) This very minute, get out of here! Get out! (*He goes to the door; she follows him*) "Twenty-two misfortunes!" Don't you dare breathe in here! Don't let me set eyes on you! (EPIHODOFF *has gone out, but his voice comes from outside the door: "I shall complain about you."*) Ah, you are coming back? (*Grabbing the stick that* FIERS *put by the door*) Come on, come—come on, I'll show you— Ah, you are coming? You are coming? Take that then—!

(*She swings the stick, at the very moment when* LOPAHIN *is coming in*)

LOPAHIN Most humbly, I thank you.

VARYA (*Angrily and ironically*) I beg your pardon!

LOPAHIN It's nothing at all. I humbly thank you for the pleasant treat.

VARYA It isn't worth your thanks. (*Moving away, then looking back and asking gently*) I haven't hurt you?

LOPAHIN No, it's nothing. (*Pause*) There's a great bump coming, though.

(*Voices in the ballroom: "Lopahin has come back." "Yermolay Alexeevich!"*)

PISHTCHIK (*Enters*) See what we see, hear what we hear—! (*He and* LOPAHIN *kiss one another*) You smell slightly of cognac, my dear, my good old chap. And we are amusing ourselves here too.

LYUBOFF (*Entering*) Is that you, Yermolay Alexeevich? Why were you so long? Where is Leonid?

LOPAHIN Leonid Andreevich got back when I did, he's coming.

LYUBOFF (*Agitated*) Well, what happened? Was there an auction? Do speak!

LOPAHIN (*Embarrassed, afraid of showing the joy he feels*) The auction was over by four o'clock— We were late for the train, had to wait till half-past nine. (*Sighing heavily*) Ugh, my head's swimming a bit!

(GAYEFF *enters; with his right hand he carries his purchases, with his left he wipes away his tears*)

LYUBOFF Lyona, what? Lyona, eh? (*Impatiently, with tears in her eyes*) Quick, for God's sake—

GAYEFF (*Not answering her, merely waving his hand; to* FIERS, *crying*) Here, take it— There are anchovies, some Kertch herrings— I haven't eaten anything all day— What I have suffered! (*The door into the billiard room is open; you hear the balls clicking and* YASHA'S *voice: "Seven and eighteen!"* GAYEFF'S *expression changes, he is no longer crying*) I'm terribly tired. You help me change, Fiers. (*Goes to his room through the ballroom,* FIERS *behind him*)

PISHTCHIK What happened at the auction? Go on, tell us!

LYUBOFF Is the cherry orchard sold?

LOPAHIN It's sold.

LYUBOFF Who bought it?

LOPAHIN I bought it. (*A pause.* LYUBOFF *is overcome. She would have fallen had she not been standing near the chair and table.* VARYA *takes the keys from her belt, throws them on the floor in the middle of the drawing room and goes out*) I bought it. Kindly wait a moment, ladies and gentlemen, everything is muddled up in my head, I can't speak— (*Laughing*) We arrived at the auction, Deriganoff was already there. Leonid Andreevich had only fifteen thousand and Deriganoff right off bids thirty over and above indebtedness. I see how things are, I match him with forty thousand. He forty-five. I fifty-five. That is to say he raises it by fives, I by tens— So it ended. Over and above the indebtedness, I bid up to ninety thousand, it was knocked down to me. The cherry orchard is mine now. Mine! (*Guffawing*) My God, Lord, the cherry orchard is mine! Tell me I'm drunk, out of my head, that I'm imagining all this— (*Stamps his feet*) Don't laugh at me! If only my father and grandfather could rise from their graves and see this whole business, see how their Yermolay, beaten, half-illiterate Yermolay, who used to run around barefoot in winter, how that very Yermolay has bought an estate that nothing in the world can beat. I bought the estate where grandfather and father were slaves, where you wouldn't even let me in the kitchen. I am asleep, it's only some dream of mine, it only seems so to me— That's nothing but the fruit of my imagination, covered with the darkness of the unknown— (*Picking up the keys, with a gentle smile*) She threw down the keys, wants to show she is not mistress any more— (*Jingling the keys*) Well, it's all the same. (*The orchestra is heard tuning up*) Hey, musicians, play, I want to hear you! Come on, everybody, and see how Yermolay Lopahin will swing the ax in the cherry orchard, how the trees will fall to the ground! We are going to build villas and our grandsons and great-grandsons will see a new life here— Music, play! (*The music is playing.* LYUBOFF *has sunk into a chair, crying bitterly.* LOPAHIN *reproachfully*) Why, then, didn't you listen to me? My poor dear, it can't be undone now. (*With tears*) Oh, if this could all be over soon, if somehow our awkward, unhappy life would be changed!

PISHTCHIK (*Taking him by the arm, in a low voice*) She is crying. Come on into the ballroom, let her be by herself— Come on— (*Taking him by the arm and leading him into the ballroom*)

LOPAHIN What's the matter? Music, there, play up! (*Ironically*) Everything is to be as I want it! Here comes the new squire, the owner of the cherry orchard. (*Quite accidentally, he bumps into the little table, and very nearly upsets the candelabra*) I can pay for everything! (*Goes out with* PISHTCHIK)

*There is nobody left either in the ballroom or the drawing room but* LYUBOFF, *who sits all huddled up and crying bitterly. The music plays softly.* ANYA *and* TROFIMOFF *enter hurriedly.* ANYA *comes up to her mother and kneels in front of her.* TROFIMOFF *remains at the ballroom door*)

ANYA Mama—! Mama, you are crying? My dear, kind, good Mama, my beautiful, I love you—I bless you. The cherry orchard is sold, it's not ours any more, that's true, true; but don't cry, Mama, you've your life ahead of you, you've your good, pure heart still left you— Come with me, come on, darling, away from here, come on— We will plant a new orchard, finer than this one, you'll see it, you'll understand; and joy, quiet, deep joy will sink into your heart, like the sun at evening, and you'll smile, Mama! Come, darling, come on!

*Curtain*

# Act Four

*The same setting as in Act One. There are no curtains on the windows or any pictures on the walls. Only a little furniture remains piled up in one corner as if for sale. A sense of emptiness is felt. Near the outer door, at the rear of the stage, is a pile of suitcases, traveling bags, and so on. The door on the left is open, and through it* VARYA'S *and* ANYA'S *voices are heard.* LOPAHIN *stands waiting.* YASHA *is holding a tray with glasses of champagne. In the hall* EPIHODOFF *is tying up a box, offstage at the rear there is a hum of voices. It is the peasants who have come to say good-by.* GAYEFF'S *voice: "Thanks, friends, thank you."*

YASHA The simple folk have come to say good-by. I am of the opinion, Yermolay Alexeevich, that the people are kind enough but don't understand anything.

(*The hum subsides.* LYUBOFF *enters through the hall with* GAYEFF; *she is not crying, but is pale, her face quivers, she is not able to speak*)

GAYEFF You gave them your purse, Lyuba. Mustn't do that! Mustn't do that!

LYUBOFF I couldn't help it! I couldn't help it!

(*Both go out*)

LOPAHIN (*Calling through the door after them*) Please, I humbly beg you! A little glass at parting. I didn't think to bring some from town, and at the station I found just one bottle. Please! (*A pause*) Well, then, ladies and gentlemen! You don't want it? (*Moving away from the door*) If I'd known that, I wouldn't have bought it. Well, then I won't drink any either. (YASHA *carefully sets the tray down on a chair*) At least, you have some, Yasha.

YASHA To those who are departing! Pleasant days to those who stay behind! (*Drinking*) This champagne is not the real stuff, I can assure you.

LOPAHIN Eight roubles a bottle. (*A pause*) It's devilish cold in here.

YASHA They didn't heat up today. We are leaving anyway. (*Laughing*)

LOPAHIN What are you laughing about?

YASHA For joy.

LOPAHIN Outside it's October, but it's sunny and still, like summer. Good for building. (*Looking at his watch, then through the door*) Ladies and gentlemen, bear in mind we have forty-six minutes in all till train time! Which means you have to go to the station in twenty minutes. Hurry up a little.

TROFIMOFF (*In an overcoat, entering from outside*) Seems to me it is time to go. The carriages are ready. The devil knows where my rubbers are. They've disappeared. (*In the door*) Anya, my rubbers are not here! I can't find them.

LOPAHIN And I have to go to Kharkov. I'm going on the same train with you. I'm going to live in Kharkov all winter. I've been dilly-dallying along with you, I'm tired of doing nothing. I can't be without work; look, I don't know what to do with my hands here. See, they are dangling somehow, as if they didn't belong to me.

TROFIMOFF We are leaving right away, and you'll set about your useful labors again.

LOPAHIN Here, drink a glass.

TROFIMOFF I shan't.

LOPAHIN It's to Moscow now?

TROFIMOFF Yes. I'll see them off to town, and tomorrow to Moscow.

LOPAHIN Yes— Maybe the professors are not giving their lectures. I imagine they are waiting till you arrive.

TROFIMOFF That's none of your business.

LOPAHIN How many years is it you've been studying at the University?

TROFIMOFF Think of something newer. This is old and flat. (*Looking for his rubbers*) You know, perhaps, we shall not see each other again; therefore, permit me to give you one piece of advice at parting! Don't wave your arms! Cure yourself of that habit—of arm waving. And also of building summer cottages, figuring that the summer residents will in time become individual landowners; figuring like that is arm-waving too— Just the same, however, I like you. You have delicate soft fingers like an artist, you have a delicate soft heart—

LOPAHIN (*Embracing him*) Good-by, my dear boy. Thanks for everything. If you need it, take some money from me for the trip.

TROFIMOFF Why should I? There's no need for it.

LOPAHIN But you haven't any!

TROFIMOFF I have. Thank you. I got some for a translation. Here it is my pocket. (*Anxiously*) But my rubbers are gone.

VARYA (*From another room*) Take your nasty things! (*Throws a pair of rubbers on to the stage*)

TROFIMOFF But what are you angry about, Varya? Hm— Why, these are not my rubbers.

LOPAHIN In the spring I planted twenty-seven hundred acres of poppies and now I've made forty thousand clear profit. And when my poppies were in bloom, what a picture it was! So look, as I say, I've made forty thousand, which means I'm offering you a loan because I can afford to. Why turn up your nose? I'm a peasant—I speak straight out.

TROFIMOFF Your father was a peasant, mine—an apothecary—and from that absolutely nothing follows. (LOPAHIN *takes out his wallet*) Leave it alone, leave it alone— If you gave me two hundred thousand even, I wouldn't take it. I am a free man. And everything that you—you rich men and beggars—all value so highly and dearly, has not the slightest power over me, it's like a mere feather floating in the air. I can get along without you, I can pass you by, I am strong and proud. Humanity is moving toward the loftiest truth, toward the loftiest happiness that is possible on earth and I am in the front ranks.

LOPAHIN Will you get there?

TROFIMOFF I'll get there. (*A pause*) I'll get there, or I'll show the others the way to get there.

(*In the distance is heard the sound of an ax on a tree*)

LOPAHIN Well, good-by, my dear boy. It's time to go. We turn up our noses at one another, but life keeps on passing. When I work a long time without stopping, my thoughts are clearer, and it seems as if I, too, know what I exist for. And, brother, how many people are there in Russia who exist, nobody knows for what! Well, all the same, it's not that that keeps things circulating. Leonid Andreevich, they say, has accepted a position—he'll be in a bank, six thousand a year—the only thing is, he won't stay there, he's very lazy—

ANYA (*In the doorway*) Mama begs you not to cut down the orchard until she's gone.

TROFIMOFF Honestly, haven't you enough tact to— (*Goes out through the hall*)

LOPAHIN Right away, right away— What people, really!

(*Goes out after him*)

ANYA Has Fiers been sent to the hospital?

YASHA I told them to this morning. They must have sent him.

ANYA (*To* EPIHODOFF, *who is passing through the room*) Semyon Panteleevich, please inquire whether or not they have taken Fiers to the hospital.

YASHA (*Huffily*) This morning, I told Igor. Why ask ten times over!

EPIHODOFF The venerable Fiers, in my opinion, is not worth mending, he ought to join his forefathers. And I can only envy him. (*Putting a suitcase on a hatbox and crushing it*) Well, there you are, of course. I knew it. (*Goes out*)

YASHA (*Mockingly*) "Twenty-two misfortunes—"

VARYA (*On the other side of the door*) Have they taken Fiers to the hospital?

ANYA They have.

VARYA Then why didn't they take the letter to the doctor?

ANYA We must send it on after them— (*Goes out*)

VARYA (*From the next room*) Where is Yasha? Tell him his mother has come, she wants to say good-by to him.

YASHA (*Waving his hand*) She merely tries my patience.

(DUNYASHA *has been busying herself with the luggage; now when* YASHA *is left alone, she goes up to him*)

DUNYASHA If you'd only look at me once, Yasha. You are going away—leaving me— (*Crying and throwing herself on his neck*)

YASHA Why are you crying? (*Drinking champagne*) In six days I'll be in Paris again. Tomorrow we will board the express train and dash off out of sight; somehow, I can't believe it. *Vive la France!* It doesn't suit me here—I can't live here— Can't help that. I've seen enough ignorance—enough for me. (*Drinking champagne*) Why do you cry? Behave yourself properly, then you won't be crying.

DUNYASHA (*Powdering her face, looking into a small mirror*) Send me a letter from Paris. I loved you, Yasha, you know, loved you so! I am a tender creature, Yasha!

YASHA They are coming here. (*Bustling about near the suitcases, humming low*)

(LYUBOFF, GAYEFF, ANYA *and* CHARLOTTA IVANOVNA *enter*)

GAYEFF We should be going. There is very little time left. (*Looking at* YASHA) Who is it smells like herring!

LYUBOFF In about ten minutes let's be in the carriage— (*Glancing around the room*) Good-by, dear house, old Grandfather. Winter will pass, spring will be here, but you won't be here any longer, they'll tear you down. How much these walls have seen! (*Kissing her daughter warmly*) My treasure, you are beaming, your eyes are dancing like two diamonds. Are you happy? Very?

ANYA Very! It's the beginning of a new life, Mama!

GAYEFF (*Gaily*) Yes, indeed, everything is fine now. Before the sale of the cherry orchard, we all were troubled, distressed, and then when the question was settled definitely, irrevocably, we all calmed down and were even cheerful— I'm a bank official. I am a financier now— Yellow ball into the side pocket. Anyway, Lyuba, you look better, no doubt about that.

LYUBOFF Yes. My nerves are better, that's true. (*They hand her her hat and coat*) I sleep well. Carry out my things, Yasha. It's time. (*To* ANYA) My little girl, we shall see each other again soon— I am going to Paris, I shall live there on the money your Yaroslavl great-aunt sent for the purchase of the estate—long live Great-aunt! But that money won't last long.

ANYA Mama, you'll come back soon, soon— Isn't that so? I'll prepare myself, pass the examination at high school, and then I'll work, I will help you. We'll read all sorts of books together. Mama, isn't that so? (*Kissing her mother's hands*) We'll read in the autumn evenings, read lots of books, and a new, wonderful world will open up before us— (*Daydreaming*) Mama, do come—

LYUBOFF I'll come, my precious. (*Embracing her daughter*)

(LOPAHIN *enters with* CHARLOTTA *who is softly humming a song*)

GAYEFF Lucky Charlotta: she's singing!

CHARLOTTA (*Taking a bundle that looks like a baby wrapped up*) My baby, bye, bye— (*A baby's cry is heard: Ooah, ooah—!*) Hush, my darling, my dear little boy. (*Ooah, ooah—!*) I am so sorry for you! (*Throwing the bundle back*) Will you please find me a position? I cannot go on like this.

LOPAHIN We will find something, Charlotta Ivanovna, don't worry.

GAYEFF Everybody is dropping us, Varya is going away— All of a sudden we are not needed.

CHARLOTTA I have no place in town to live. I must go away. (*Humming*) It's all the same—

(PISHTCHIK *enters*)

LOPAHIN The freak of nature—!

PISHTCHIK (*Out of breath*) Ugh, let me catch my breath—I'm exhausted— My honored friends— Give me some water—

GAYEFF After money, I suppose? This humble servant will flee from sin! (*Goes out*)

PISHTCHIK It's a long time since I was here— Most beautiful lady— (*To* LOPAHIN) You here—? Glad to see you—a man of the greatest intellect— Here— Take it— (*Giving* LOPAHIN *some money*) Four hundred rubles— That leaves eight hundred and forty I still owe you—

LOPAHIN (*With astonishment, shrugging his shoulders*) I must be dreaming. But where did you get it?

PISHTCHIK Wait—I'm hot— Most extraordinary event. Some Englishmen came and found on my land some kind of white clay— (*To* LYUBOFF) And four hundred for you— Beautiful lady— Wonderful lady— (*Handing over the money*) The rest later. (*Taking a drink of water*) Just now a young man was saying on the train that some great philosopher recommends jumping off roofs—"Jump!" he says, "and that settles the whole problem." (*With astonishment*) You don't say! Water!

LOPAHIN And what Englishmen were they?

PISHTCHIK I leased them the parcel of land with the clay for twenty-four years— And now, excuse me, I haven't time—I must run along—I'm going to Znoykoff's— To Kardamonoff's— I owe everybody— (*Drinking*) I wish you well— I'll drop in on Thursday—

LYUBOFF We are moving to town right away, and tomorrow I'm going abroad—

PISHTCHIK What? (*Alarmed*) Why to town? That's why I see furniture— Suitcases— Well, no matter— (*Tearfully*) No matter— Men of the greatest minds —those Englishmen— No matter— Good luck! God will help you— No matter— Everything in this world comes to an end— (*Kissing* LYUBOFF'S *hand*) And should the report reach you that my end has come, think of that well-known horse and say: "There was once on earth a so and so—Semyonoff Pishtchik— The kingdom of Heaven be his." Most remarkable weather—yes— (*Going out greatly disconcerted, but immediately returning and speaking from the door*) Dashenka sends her greetings!

(*Goes out*)

LYUBOFF And now we can go. I am leaving with two worries. First, that Fiers is sick. (*Glancing at her watch*) We still have five minutes—

ANYA Mama, Fiers has already been sent to the hospital. Yasha sent him off this morning.

LYUBOFF My second worry—is Varya. She is used to getting up early and working, and now without any work she is like a fish out of water. She has grown thin, pale and she cries all the time, poor thing— (*A pause*) You know this, Yermolay Alexeevich: I dreamed—of marrying her to you. And there was every sign of your getting married. (*Whispering to* ANYA, *who beckons to* CHARLOTTA; *both go out*) She loves you, you are fond of her, and I don't know, I just don't know why it is you seem to avoid each other—I don't understand it!

LOPAHIN I don't understand it either, I must confess. It's all strange somehow— If there's still time, I am ready right now even— Let's settle it now—and get it over and done with. (*Pause*) But without you, I doubt if I would ever propose to her.

LYUBOFF But that's excellent. Surely it takes only a minute. I'll call her at once.

LOPAHIN And to fit the occasion there's the champagne. (*Looking at the glasses*) Empty, somebody has already drunk them. (YASHA *coughs*) That's what's called lapping it up—

LYUBOFF (*Vivaciously*) Splendid! We'll go out— Yasha, *allez!* I'll call her— (*Through the door*) Varya, drop everything and come here. Come on! (*Goes out with* YASHA)

LOPAHIN (*Looking at his watch*) Yes—

(*A pause. Behind the door you hear smothered laughter, whispering, finally* VARYA *enters*)

VARYA (*Looking at the luggage a long time*) That's strange, I just can't find it—

LOPAHIN What are you looking for?

VARYA I packed it myself and don't remember where. (*A pause*)

LOPAHIN Where do you expect to go now, Varvara Mikhailovna?

VARYA I? To the Regulins. I agreed to go there to look after the house— As a sort of housekeeper.

LOPAHIN That's in Yashnevo? It's nigh on to seventy miles. (*A pause*) And here ends life in this house—

VARYA (*Examining the luggage*) But where is it? Either I put it in the trunk, perhaps— Yes, life in this house is ended—it won't be any more—

LOPAHIN And I am going to Kharkov now—by the next train. I've a lot to do. And I am leaving Epihodoff—on the ground here—I've hired him.

VARYA Well!

LOPAHIN Last year at this time it had already been snowing, if you remember, and now it's quiet, it's sunny. It's only that it's cold, about three degrees of frost.

VARYA I haven't noticed. (*A pause*) And besides— our thermometer is broken—

(*A pause. A voice is heard from the yard beyond the door:* Yermolay Alexeevich!)

LOPAHIN (*As if he had been expecting this call for a long time*) This minute! (*Goes out quickly*)

(VARYA, *sitting on the floor, puts her head on a bundle of clothes and sobs quietly. The door opens and* LYUBOFF *enters cautiously.*)

VARYA (*Stops crying and wipes her eyes*) Yes, it's time, Mama. (*Pause*) I can get to the Regulins today —if we are just not too late for the train!

LYUBOFF (*Calling through the door*) Anya, put your things on! (ANYA, *then* GAYEFF *and* CHARLOTTA IVANOVNA *enter.* GAYEFF *has on a warm overcoat, with a hood. The servants gather, also the drivers.* EPIHODOFF *busies himself with the luggage*) Now we can be on our way.

ANYA (*Joyfully*) On our way!

GAYEFF My friends, my dear, kind friends! Leaving this house forever, can I remain silent, can I restrain myself from expressing, as we say, farewell, those feelings that fill now my whole being—

ANYA (*Beseechingly*) Uncle!

VARYA Dear Uncle, don't!

GAYEFF (*Dejectedly*) Bank the yellow into the side pocket— I am silent—

(TROFIMOFF *and then* LOPAHIN *enter*)

TROFIMOFF Well, ladies and gentlemen, it's time to go!

LOPAHIN Epihodoff, my coat!

LYUBOFF I'll sit here just a minute more. It's as if I had never seen before what the walls in this house are like, what kind of ceilings, and now I look at them greedily, with such tender love—

GAYEFF I remember when I was six years old, on Trinity Day, I sat in this window and watched my father going to Church—

LYUBOFF Are all the things taken out?

LOPAHIN Everything, I think. (*Putting on his overcoat. To* EPIHODOFF) Epihodoff, you see that everything is in order.

EPIHODOFF (*Talking in a hoarse voice*) Don't worry, Yermolay Alexeevich!

LOPAHIN Why is your voice like that?

EPIHODOFF Just drank some water, swallowed something.

YASHA (*With contempt*) The ignorance—

LYUBOFF We are going and there won't be a soul left here—

LOPAHIN Till spring.

VARYA (*She pulls an umbrella out from a bundle; it looks as if she were going to hit someone;* LOPAHIN *pretends to be frightened*) What do you, what do you— I never thought of it.

TROFIMOFF Ladies and gentlemen, let's get in the carriage— It's time! The train is coming any minute.

VARYA Petya, here they are, your rubbers, by the suitcase. (*Tearfully*) And how dirty yours are, how old—!

TROFIMOFF (*Putting on the rubbers*) Let's go, ladies and gentlemen!

GAYEFF (*Greatly embarrassed, afraid he will cry*) The train— The station— Cross into the side, combination off the white into the corner—

LYUBOFF Let's go!

LOPAHIN Everybody here? Nobody there? (*Locking the side door on the left*) Things are stored here, it must be locked up. Let's go!

ANYA Good-by, house! Good-by, the old life!

TROFIMOFF Long live the new life!

(*Goes out with* ANYA. VARYA *casts a glance around the room and, without hurrying, goes out.* YASHA *and* CHARLOTTA, *with her dog, go out*)

LOPAHIN And so, till spring. Come along, ladies and gentlemen— Till we meet. (*Goes out*)

(LYUBOFF *and* GAYEFF *are left alone. As if they had been waiting for this, they throw themselves on one another's necks sobbing, but smothering their sobs as if afraid of being heard*)

GAYEFF (*In despair*) Oh, Sister, Sister—

LYUBOFF Oh, my dear, my lovely, beautiful orchard! My life, my youth, my happiness, good-by!

ANYA'S VOICE, *gaily, appealingly* Mama—!

TROFIMOFF'S VOICE (*Gaily, excitedly*) Aaooch!

LYUBOFF For the last time, just to look at the walls, at the window— My dear mother used to love to walk around in this room—

GAYEFF Oh, Sister, Sister—!

ANYA'S VOICE Mama—!

TROFIMOFF'S VOICE Aaooch—!

LYUBOFF We are coming! (*They go out.*)

(*The stage is empty. You hear the keys locking all the doors, then the carriages drive off. It grows quiet. In the silence you hear the dull thud of an ax on a tree, a lonely, mournful sound. Footsteps are heard. From the door on the right* FIERS *appears. He is dressed as usual, in a jacket and a white waistcoat, slippers on his feet. He is sick*)

FIERS (*Going to the door and trying the knob*) Locked. They've gone. (*Sitting down on the sofa*) They forgot about me— No matter— I'll sit here awhile— And Leonid Andreevich, for sure, didn't put on his fur coat, he went off in his topcoat— (*Sighing anxiously*) And I didn't see to it— The young saplings! (*He mutters something that cannot be understood*) Life has gone by, as if I hadn't lived at all— (*Lying down*) I'll lie down awhile— You haven't got any strength, nothing is left, nothing— Ach, you—good-for-nothing— (*He lies still*)

(*There is a far-off sound as if out of the sky, the sound of a snapped string, dying away, sad. A stillness falls, and there is only the thud of an ax on a tree, far away in the orchard*)

*Curtain*

# Maxim Gorki

## (1868-1936)

The only one of Maxim Gorki's plays which has been widely produced outside Russia is *The Lower Depths.* So powerful, however, is this one work that Gorki's right to be included among the masters of modern drama is never challenged. He brought to his depiction of the pre-1905 life of Russia's urban masses a fund of direct experience few Russian writers could match. He brought into drama the down-and-outers, the thieves, stevedores, prostitutes, pilgrims, and migratory day-laborers ("stormy petrels") who swarmed into Russia's slum tenements.

Gorki was born Alexei Maximovich Pyeshkov in 1868 in a port city on the upper reaches of the Volga, Nizhni Novgorod (in 1932, renamed Gorki in his honor). He was orphaned before he was ten, and his maternal grandparents grudgingly gave him a home. In their world of poverty, brutal beatings, and pietistic sermonizing, he became keenly aware of differences between highminded idealism and practical morality. He enjoyed the tales his grandmother told him whenever her rag-picking labors had not exhausted her energy or whenever his tyrannical grandfather was not present to interrupt her story-telling with one of his violent outbursts. Sent out to earn his own way at ten, Gorki held an incredible variety of jobs. He thought he was beyond being shocked at anything life could bring him, but he was appalled when, as apprentice in an icon shop, he was taught to lie about the age and worth of the religious images and to "hustle" prospective buyers away from other shops. As dishwasher on a Volga steamer, Gorki worked for a cook who encouraged him to read widely. He tried without success to enroll at the University of Kazan, but remained in Kazan to continue his round of odd jobs and feverish self-education. At 19, he reviewed his past life and, seeing no brighter future ahead, made a suicide attempt which almost succeeded. In Kazan he associated with the radical group of university students, learning much even though he was puzzled by the unrealistic tone of their visionary talk about the proletariat. Before he was 30, he had contracted tuberculosis, had been kept under surveillance by czarist police, and had made some friends who encouraged him to write.

In 1898, two volumes of sketches and stories, his first major publication, brought him immediate fame. His manner of dress (black blouse buttoned at the collar, workers' boots, and knobby walking stick) became the sartorial model for thousands of young Russians. Gorki's roustabout characters, audacious exponents of Nietzschean brigandage and romantic individualism, took Russia by storm. He sent his work to Chekhov, who was at first impressed by Gorki's exultant lyricism, and later, as they became close friends, by the man himself. Chekhov tried to smooth some of the rough edges of Gorki's personality, just as he advised him to tone down his highly ornate literary style. He sent him plays like Strindberg's *Miss Julie* in the hope Gorki might learn a greater economy of style. Most important, he introduced him to the Moscow Art Theatre group at a time when they were eager for new playwrights' works. In 1902, Chekhov took a strong stand on a political issue involving Gorki: when, at the Czar's request, Gorki's election to the Russian Academy was rescinded, Chekhov resigned in protest from the Academy. Nothing was changed by the resignation, but the act, surprising because of Chekhov's political neutrality, was widely admired as a sign of great courage.

In 1892, when his first story was accepted for publication, Gorki had adopted his pen-name (literally, "Maxim the Bitter"), obviously appropriate for an author who was to unveil so much misery and oppression in his works. When Stanislavski first solicited a play from Gorki, he hoped for the work Gorki had outlined to him at their first meeting in Yalta in 1900. The central character of that work, which later became *The Lower Depths,* was an ex-waiter who treasured above all else his dress collar and a shirt-front as mementos of his past service. In *My Life in Art,* Stanislavski recalled Gorki's outline of the play: "The second act finished with an unexpected police raid, at the news of which, the whole anthill came to life, trying to hide stolen goods. In the third act came the spring, the sun; nature bloomed again; the inhabitants of the foul-smelling lodging came out into the clean air to work on a farm; they sang songs under the sun, forgetting their former hatred of each other." The final version of *The Lower Depths* differed greatly from Gorki's original conception. He kept the rebirth theme, but the effects of Luka's departure and the Actor's suicide give it a grotesque ironic value.

When *The Lower Depths* was not finished on schedule, the Moscow Art Theatre accepted another play Gorki had completed. Variously translated as *Small People, The Smug Citizens, The Petty Bourgeois,* or *Philistines,* the play disappointed actors and audiences because it included none of the tramps Gorki had popularized in his stories. An angry attack on middle-class complacency fed by others' labor, it contained a mechanic who has since been recognized as perhaps the first of the proletarian heroes so familiar in later Marxist literature. Chekhov thought the play immature, but he predicted Gorki's achievement would transcend the merit of his plays: "Gorki's strength as a dramatist is not that audiences like him but that he is the first in Russia and in the world generally to speak out with contempt and disgust against the philistine—and that he did so just when society was ready to hear such criticism." Society may have been ready for Gorki's strictures, but czarist authorities were not. The dress rehearsal swarmed with so many policemen Stanislavski was reminded of battle preparations. Then and later there were censorship problems, which only added to Gorki's luster as a courageous upholder of the freedom which would be born in the "New Russia."

Before the end of the 1902 season, Gorki had finished *The Lower Depths* and the Moscow Art Theatre rushed it into production following Tolstoi's *The Power of Darkness.* The play was a challenge, for its characters were outside the actors' experience. To supplement the details Gorki provided concerning his "creatures who once were men," the acting company went into areas where the real lower depths could be studied. Stanislavski reported that these expeditions by the actors imparted "an aura of romanticism and a peculiar savage beauty" to the tramps: the play's "inner meaning" came through as "Freedom at any cost!" Although Stanislavski was not satisfied with his own portrayal of Satin, the opening of *The Lower Depths* (1902) was, if anything, an even greater success than *The Sea Gull* had been in 1898. Years later, when the Stalinist government was honoring Gorki, the Moscow Art Theatre was renamed in his honor.

*The Lower Depths* was immediately translated for productions in Berlin and London; New York also had a production in 1903, but of the German version. After *The Lower Depths,* however, Gorki's phenomenal success in the theatre was not to be repeated. Soon after the 1905 Revolution, he went into political exile, traveling to America, Finland, France, and later to Capri where he met Lenin. Only after 1917 was he able to remain safely in Russia for any extended period. When the masses were ready to exterminate the intellectuals, despised for their gradualism, Gorki used his popularity to save them, arguing that their services would be needed in building the new Russia. During the last fifteen years of his life, Gorki's failing health required that he stay for long periods in warmer climates outside Russia. He remains, however, even after his death 'under mysterious circumstances" in 1936, the most honored of Soviet writers.

After *The Lower Depths,* Gorki's writings, his stirring autobiographical volumes and novels as well as his plays, took on a polemical quality not always valued highly even by Russian critics. In plays like *Children of the Sun* (or *Summer Residents*) he resumed his attack on pink-lemonade intellectuals. Produced by the Moscow Art group in 1905, it was sharply criticized for shapelessness and stridency, flaws which marked the strongly didactic *Barbarians* and *Enemies* which followed. In America in 1906, Gorki wrote *Mother,* the prototype of the proletarian revolutionary novels which soon began to appear throughout the world. Some measure of *Mother*'s continuing popularity is found in Brecht's adaptation of it in the early 1930's. Gorki's last plays, *Egor Bulychev* and *Dostigaev and Others* (1932-1933) were studies of empire-builders whose capitalist values crumble on the eve of the Bolshevik revolution. Two plays, published posthumously, failed to stir interest outside Russia, although one of them, *Somov and Others,* is a revealing study of power struggles in Soviet Russia.

Few masterworks in modern drama have been translated so frequently or under so many titles as *The Lower Depths.* In English alone can be found translations with such titles as *A Night's Lodging* and *At the Bottom* (closest to the Russian title), to name only a few. Despite its great success, the play did not escape adverse criticism, some of which Gorki accepted. Chekhov criticized him for leaving "all the most interesting characters (except the Actor)" out of the last act, for insufficient characterization of the Baron, and for his failure to prepare the audience for the Actor's shocking suicide. Others have been puzzled by Gorki's conception of Luka: is the folk-philosopher with his easy consolation a fraud or a savior? By 1932, Gorki regarded his portrait of Luka as "false," but by then he was no longer influenced by Tolstoi's tenets of passive resistance and mysticism. Other critics have misunderstood the central importance of Satin, spokesman—despite his apparently unfeeling cynicism—for Gorki's faith in man. In the character sketches of the Baron, Satin, and Luka which Gorki later prepared for the opening scenes of a film version of the play, some details only implied in the play became clear: the Baron had indeed been an aristocrat and military officer flawed by laziness and sensuality, Satin was once a wastrel nobleman and a promising student, and, most important, Luka had been a leader whose perfidy had caused much anguish in the peasant community where he lived. The puzzles of interpretation somehow enhance the attractiveness of *The Lower Depths.* Certainly this was the case for Eugene O'Neill, whose *The Iceman Cometh* is a striking variation on Gorki's play. However it is interpreted, *The Lower Depths* remains a fine example of naturalism employed to delineate vestiges of decency in a morally anarchic world. The degenerate Peppel (literally, "ashes") trying too late to act on an honest impulse, the Actor who cannot remember the words by which actors live, the pander-prostitute pair who carp at one another's pipedreams, the illiterates who have only brute strength to offer in the labor market, the dying consumptive, the generous-hearted dumpling-peddler who becomes a lodgekeeper—all Gorki's characters preserve some glimmer of integrity to redeem them in their own eyes. Gorki sounded no notes of easy optimism anywhere in the play, but *The Lower Depths* leaves, unmistakably, the impression that it is a work of compassionate understanding.

# THE LOWER DEPTHS

Translated by Alexander Bakshy

GORKY's original title for this play was "At the Bottom of Life." On the advice of a friend he soon shortened it to "At the Bottom," under which name the play was given its first production on the stage of the Moscow Art Theater. The play has been translated into English under a variety of titles, but "The Lower Depths" is the one best known in English-speaking countries.

The action of the play is laid in a Volga town at the turn of the century. The characters inhabiting Kostylyov's lodging house are representatives of the type known in Russia as *bosyák,* the name, literally meaning "a barefoot," having come to be applied to the whole class of people who did occasional odd jobs but lived mostly by their wits. They formed a motley, shiftless, and often criminal fringe of the population of most Russian towns and used to be particularly numerous in port towns.

Three of the characters in "The Lower Depths" (the Baron, Satin, and Peppel), are former jailbirds, and Luka (judging by Gorky's film scenario based on the play) is one of them, too, though obviously reformed. Three other characters, the locksmith, Klestch, and the two longshoremen, the Tartar and the Goiter, typify the conscientious, upright working man. Even the cynical capmaker, Bubnov, is honest in his own way. The contrast is significant. But it is Satin, Luka, and Peppel through whom the moral message of the play is mostly conveyed. The translator must own to inconsistency in retaining the Russian nickname "Kvashnya" (which means "a tub for leavening dough") for one of the characters, while translating the nickname of another character, "Goiter" (which is "Krivoy Zob" in Russian, meaning "a lopsided Adam's apple"). His main excuse, aside from reasons of convenience, is that as used in the play "Kvashnya" takes on almost the quality of a proper name.

A. B.

## CHARACTERS

THE BARON, *age 33*
KVASHNYA, *peddles dumplings in the market, age close to 40*
BUBNOV, *a capmaker, age 45*
ANDREY DMITRICH KLESTCH, *a locksmith, age 40*
NASTYA, *a girl of the streets, age 24*
ANNA, KLESTCH'S *wife, age 30*
KONSTANTIN SATIN, *age close to 40*
THE ACTOR, *age close to 40*
MIKHAIL IVANOVICH KOSTYLYOV, *keeper of the lodgings, age 54*
VASSILY (VASSYA) PEPPEL, *age 28*
NATASHA, *sister of* VASSILISSA KOSTYLYOVA, *age 20*
LUKA, *a pilgrim, age 60*
ALYOSHKA, *a cobbler, age 20*
VASSILISSA KARPOVNA KOSTYLYOVA, *wife of* MIKHAIL KOSTYLYOV, *age 26*
ABRAM IVANYCH MEDVEDEV, *a policeman,* VASSILISSA'S *and* NATASHA'S *uncle, age 50*
ASSAN, THE TARTAR } *longshoremen*
KRIVOY ZOB, THE GOITER } *longshoremen*

## Act One

*A cavelike basement. A heavy vaulted ceiling, blackened with smoke, with patches where the plaster has fallen off. The light comes from the direction of the audience and from a square window high up the wall, right. The right corner is cut off by a thin partition behind which is* PEPPEL'S *room. Near the door leading into it is* BUBNOV'S *plank bed.*[1] *In the left corner is a big Russian stove. In the stone wall, left, is a door to the kitchen, where* KVASHNYA, *the* BARON, *and* NASTYA *live. By the wall between the stove and the door stands a wide bed screened off by a dirty cotton-print curtain. Everywhere along the walls are plank beds. Near the left wall, down-*

[1] A plank bed is a low wooden platform, which was used in Russian prisons and cheap lodging houses to provide sleeping accommodations, generally for several persons lying alongside one another. In the play Bubnov has a small plank bed to himself.—Tr.

*stage, stands a block of wood with a vise and a small anvil mounted upon it. Sitting before it, on a smaller block of wood, is* KLESTCH, *who is busy trying keys in old locks. On the floor lie two bunches of keys strung on wire rings, a battered tin samovar, a hammer, and some files. In the center of the basement stand a big table with a samovar, two benches, and a square stool—all unpainted and dirty. At the table* KVASHNYA *is serving tea, the* BARON *is munching black bread, and* NASTYA, *seated on the stool and leaning on the table, is reading a battered book.* ANNA, *lying on the bed behind the curtain, is heard coughing. On his plank bed the capmaker* BUBNOV, *holding a hat block between his legs, is fitting a ripped pair of pants over it, figuring out the best way to cut the cloth. Scattered about him are a torn hatbox containing cap visors, scraps of oilcloth, and cast-off clothing.* SATIN, *just awake, lies on a plank bed emitting loud guttural sounds. On top of the stove, unseen by the audience, the* ACTOR *is puttering around and coughing.*

*It is morning in early spring.*

BARON Go on.

KVASHNYA Oh, no, my friend, says I, keep away from me with that. I went through all that before, says I, and now you won't make me go to the altar even if you give me a hundred boiled crawfish.

BUBNOV (*To* SATIN) What are you snorting about? (SATIN *continues to grunt*)

KVASHNYA That I, a free woman and my own mistress, says I—that I should enter myself in somebody else's passport and make myself a man's slave—never! I wouldn't marry him even if he were an American prince.

KLESTCH Liar.

KVASHNYA What's that?

KLESTCH You're lying. You'll marry Abram all right.

BARON (*Snatches* NASTYA's *book and reads the title*) *Fatal Love.* (*He laughs*)

NASTYA (*Stretching out her hand*) Oh, give it back. Don't be childish. (*The* BARON *gazes at her, waving the book in the air.*

KVASHNYA (*To* KLESTCH) You red-haired goat! I'm lying, am I? How dare you speak to me like that?

BARON (*Hitting* NASTYA *on the head with the book*) You *are* a fool, Nastya—

NASTYA (*Wresting the book from him*) Let me have it.

KLESTCH Ha! A great lady. And you *will* marry Abram all the same—that's all you've been waiting for.

KVASHNYA Oh, of course! I haven't got anything better to do. You've driven your wife till she's nearly dead—

KLESTCH Shut up, you old sow! It's none of your business!

KVASHNYA Oh, you don't like to hear the truth!

BARON There it goes! What's doing, Nastya?

NASTYA (*Without lifting her head*) Go away!

ANNA (*Thrusting her head out from behind the curtain*) Another day starting! For heaven's sake, stop shouting and quarreling!

KLESTCH Now she's whining again.

ANNA Every day it's the same thing. Won't you let me die in peace?

BUBNOV Noise never stopped anybody from dying.

KVASHNYA (*Walking up to* ANNA) How could you live with such a brute?

ANNA Leave me alone—

KVASHNYA Well, you *are* a patient sufferer, poor soul. How does your chest feel? Any easier?

BARON Kvashnya! It's time to go to market!

KVASHNYA I'm coming. (*To* ANNA) Would you like some hot meat dumplings?

ANNA No, thank you. Why should I bother to eat?

KVASHNYA Never you mind. Heat softens your innards. I'll put some in a cup and leave it for you—eat them when you feel like it. Come on, nobleman— (*To* KLESTCH) You devil, you! (*Goes off to the kitchen*)

ANNA (*Coughing*) Oh, Lord—

BARON (*Giving* NASTYA *a nudge on the back of the neck*) Drop it, silly!

NASTYA (*In a loud voice*) Go away—I'm not keeping you.

(*The* BARON *follows* KVASHNYA *off, whistling*)

SATIN (*Half rising from his plank bed*) Who beat me up last night?

BUBNOV Does it make any difference?

SATIN You're right, I suppose. But why did they beat me?

BUBNOV Did you have a card game?

SATIN I did.

BUBNOV That's why they beat you up.

SATIN The dirty swine!

ACTOR (*Poking his head down from the stove*) They'll beat you to death one time—

SATIN You're a blockhead.

ACTOR Why?

SATIN Because you can't kill a man two times.

ACTOR (*After a pause*) I don't understand—why not.

KLESTCH You'd better come down off the stove and clean the place up— You've been loafing up there long enough.

ACTOR That's none of your business.

KLESTCH Wait till Vassilissa comes in—she'll show you whose business it is.

ACTOR To hell with Vassilissa! Today it's the Baron's turn to clean. Baron!

BARON (*Coming in from the kitchen*) I've no time for cleaning—I'm going to market with Kvashnya.

ACTOR That has nothing to do with me—you can go to jail for all I care, but it's your turn to sweep the floor —I'm not going to do other people's work.

BARON Oh, the devil with it! Nastya will sweep up. Hey, you, Fatal Love! Wake up! (*Snatches* NASTYA's *book from her*)

NASTYA (*Rising*) What do you want? Give it back, you boor. Call yourself a nobleman.

BARON (*Returning the book*) Nastya, sweep the floor for me, will you?

NASTYA (*Going off to the kitchen*) No, thank you!

(KVASHNYA *appears at the door*)

KVASHNYA (*To the* BARON) Come along with me. They

can clean up without you. You've been asked, Actor, and you should do it. It won't break your back.

ACTOR It's always me—I don't get it.

BARON (*Coming in with a yoke over his shoulders, two baskets containing large cloth-covered pots hanging from the ends*) It's rather heavy today.

SATIN Hardly worth your while to have been born a baron.

KVASHNYA (*To the* ACTOR) Now, mind you sweep the floor.

(*Preceded by the* BARON, KVASHNYA *goes off*)

ACTOR (*Coming down from the stove*) It's hard for me to breathe dust. (*Speaking with pride*) My organism is poisoned with alcohol. (*He sits on a plank bed, sunk in thought*)

SATIN Organism—organon—

ANNA Andrey Dmitrich—

KLESTCH What is it now?

ANNA Kvashnya has left me some dumplings in there—you eat them.

KLESTCH (*Walking up to her*) Aren't you going to?

ANNA No, I don't want any. Why should I eat? You work—you need it.

KLESTCH Are you afraid? Don't be. You may pull through—

ANNA Go eat the dumplings. I feel all in. Seems as though it's coming soon—

KLESTCH (*Moving away*) Never mind—you may get up yet—that happens sometimes. (*Goes off into the kitchen*)

ACTOR (*In a loud voice, as if waking up suddenly*) Yesterday, in the hospital, the doctor said to me: Your organism, he said, is completely poisoned with alcohol—

SATIN (*Smiling*) Organon—

ACTOR (*Insistently*) Not organon, but or-gan-ism—

SATIN Sycamore—

ACTOR (*Waving his hand at him*) You and your nonsense. I'm speaking seriously—I am. If my organism is poisoned, then it's bad for me to sweep the floor—to breathe dust—

SATIN Macrobiotics— Ha!

BUBNOV What are you mumbling about?

SATIN Words— Here's another—transit-dental—

BUBNOV What does that mean?

SATIN Don't know—I can't remember.

BUBNOV Why do you say them then?

SATIN Because. I'm tired, my friend, of all human words, our words. I'm fed up with them. I've heard every one of them a thousand times, if I've heard them once.

ACTOR There's a line in the play *Hamlet:* "Words—words—words!" A fine piece of work. I played the gravedigger.

KLESTCH (*Coming in from the kitchen*) How soon are you going to play with the broom?

ACTOR None of your business. (*Striking himself on the chest*) "The fair Ophelia! Nymph, in thy orisons be all my sins remembered!"

(*From off stage, somewhere in the distance, can be heard a muffled noise—followed by shouts and a policeman's whistle.* KLESTCH *resumes his work, rasping with a file*)

SATIN I love rare words I can't understand. When I was a boy I had a job in a telegraph office—used to read lots of books—

BUBNOV So you were a telegrapher too?

SATIN I was. There are some fine books—with lots of odd words. I was an educated man, you know.

BUBNOV I've heard that a hundred times. So you were. So what? I was a fur-dresser at one time—had my own shop. My hands and arms got so yellow from dyeing furs—oh, so yellow—up to the elbow, I tell you. I thought I'd never wash it off—even go to my grave with yellow arms. Well, look at them now—they're just dirty. Yes.

SATIN And so?

BUBNOV Nothing. That's all.

SATIN Well, what are you driving at?

BUBNOV Oh, just something to think over. It comes to this—no matter how you paint yourself up, it'll all rub off—yes, it'll all rub off.

SATIN Oh—my bones are sore.

ACTOR (*Sitting with his arms around his knees*) Education is rubbish. The main thing is talent. I knew an actor—he could scarcely read—but when he played his part the theater shook and rattled with the audience's raptures.

SATIN Bubnov, give me five kopecks.

BUBNOV All I've got is two kopecks.

ACTOR Talent, I say, is what an actor needs. And talent is faith in oneself, in one's own powers.

SATIN Give me five kopecks and I'll believe you're a talent, a hero, a crocodile, a bailiff— Klestch, give me five kopecks.

KLESTCH Go to hell! There are too many of your kind around here.

SATIN What are you cursing for? I know you haven't a kopeck.

ANNA Andrey Dmitrich—I'm suffocating, I feel awful—

KLESTCH What can I do?

BUBNOV Open the door to the front hall.

KLESTCH Thank you. You sit there on a plank bed, and I'm on the floor. Let me have your place, and you can open the door all you want. I have a cold as it is.

BUBNOV (*Calmly*) There's no reason for me to open the door. It's your own wife asking.

KLESTCH (*Sullenly*) People will ask for anything.

SATIN Wow, my head's ringing! Why, I'd like to know, do people punch each other in the head?

BUBNOV Not only heads—they do it to the rest of the body too. (*Rising*) Got to go buy myself some thread. Funny, our landlord and his lady haven't shown up today—maybe they've dropped in their tracks. (*Goes off*)

(ANNA *coughs.* SATIN *lies motionless, his arms under his head*)

ACTOR (*Looks around with sad eyes and walks up to* ANNA) Feeling bad?

ANNA It's too stuffy in here.

ACTOR If you like, I'll take you out into the hallway.

Here, get up. (*He helps* ANNA *to rise, throws some old garment over her shoulders, and, holding her under the arm, leads her out to the hallway*) Come, come—step out. I'm sick myself—poisoned with alcohol.

(KOSTYLYOV *appears in the doorway*)

KOSTYLYOV Going out for a walk? A fine couple—a ram and a lamb.

ACTOR Make way—you see invalids are going out, don't you?

KOSTYLYOV Pass on, if you please. (*Humming some hymn, he looks the place over suspiciously and inclines his head to the left as if trying to hear something in* PEPPEL'S *room.* KLESTCH *tinkles his keys and rasps his file with great firmness, meanwhile watching his landlord from under his brows*) Grating away, are you?

KLESTCH What?

KOSTYLYOV You're grating, I say. (*After a pause*) Oh—yes—what is it I wanted to ask you? (*Quickly, in a low voice*) Has my wife been here?

KLESTCH I haven't seen her.

KOSTYLYOV (*Moving cautiously toward* PEPPEL'S *room*) What a lot of space you get from me for two rubles a month! A bed—a place to sit—h'm—it's worth all of five rubles, I swear! I think I'll raise you half a ruble.

KLESTCH Raise me by the neck and strangle me while you're at it. You'll be dead soon, but all you think about is half rubles.

KOSTYLYOV Why should I strangle you? What good will it do anybody? God be with you, my good man, live to your heart's content. But I *will* raise your rent a half ruble. That'll buy me more oil for my icon lamp—and my sacrifice will burn before the holy icon. That sacrifice will be reckoned for me as amends for my sins, and for yours too. You never think of your sins, do you? So there it is. Oh, Andrey! You're such a spiteful man. Your wife has withered away because of your spitefulness. Nobody likes or respects you—and your work grates on people's ears, disturbs everybody—

KLESTCH (*Shouting*) Have you come to plague me?

(SATIN *emits a loud roar*)

KOSTYLYOV (*Startled*) My goodness!

(*Enter the* ACTOR)

ACTOR I've seated the lady in the hallway, wrapped her up—

KOSTYLYOV You have a kind heart, my friend. That's fine—that'll be credited to you.

ACTOR When?

KOSTYLYOV In the next world, my friend. Every deed, everything, is entered in a man's account there.

ACTOR That's there. You ought to reward me for my kindness here.

KOSTYLYOV Now, how could I do that?

ACTOR Slash my debt in half.

KOSTYLYOV Hee-hee! You will have your little joke, my dear fellow, you will keep play acting. Why, is kindness of heart comparable to money? Kindness stands above all benefits. And your debt to me is just what it is—a debt. Therefore you have to pay it back. To me who am an old man you must show kindness without looking for rewards—

ACTOR Old man, you're a rogue.

(*The* ACTOR *goes off to the kitchen.* KLESTCH *rises and exits to the hallway*)

KOSTYLYOV (*To* SATIN) He's run away, the grater—hee-hee! He doesn't like me.

SATIN Who does like you, outside the devil?

KOSTYLYOV (*Laughingly*) You *are* sharp. For myself, I like all of you—I understand you, my wretched, worthless, ruined brethren. (*Suddenly, quickly*) Is Vassily in?

SATIN Go look.

KOSTYLYOV (*Walks up to* PEPPEL'S *door and knocks*) Vassya!

(*The* ACTOR *appears at the kitchen door, munching*)

PEPPEL (*Off stage*) Who's there?

KOSTYLYOV It's me, Vassya.

PEPPEL (*From his room*) What do you want?

KOSTYLYOV (*Moving back from the door*) Open the door—

SATIN (*Without looking at* KOSTYLYOV) He'll open, and she's there.

(*The* ACTOR *laughs*)

KOSTYLYOV (*Alarmed, in a low voice*) What's that? Who's there? What do you mean?

SATIN Are you speaking to me?

KOSTYLYOV What was it you just said?

SATIN I was talking to myself.

KOSTYLYOV Look out, my friend. Know when to stop with your jokes—yes! (*Knocks loudly on* PEPPEL'S *door*) Vassily!

(PEPPEL *opens his door*)

PEPPEL Well? What's the idea of disturbing me?

KOSTYLYOV (*Peeking into the room*) You see, I have—

PEPPEL Have you brought the money?

KOSTYLYOV I have some business to talk over with you.

PEPPEL Have you brought the money?

KOSTYLYOV What money? Wait—

PEPPEL I say the money, the seven rubles for the watch. Come on.

KOSTYLYOV What watch? Oh, Vassya—

PEPPEL Now look! Yesterday, before witnesses, I sold you a watch for ten rubles. I received three rubles, now hand over the other seven. Why are you blinking at me like that? You wander around here, disturb other people's sleep, but don't know your business.

KOSTYLYOV Sh-sh! Don't lose your temper, Vassya. The watch—that's—

SATIN Stolen goods—

KOSTYLYOV (*Sternly*) I don't take stolen goods—how can you say—

PEPPEL (*Seizing* KOSTYLYOV *by the shoulder*) Why did you wake me up? What do you want?

KOSTYLYOV I don't want anything—I'll go—if you feel that way.

PEPPEL Go bring the money.

KOSTYLYOV Such rude people! I must say! (*Goes off*)

ACTOR A regular comedy!

SATIN Wonderful! I love it!

PEPPEL What brought him here?

SATIN Don't you understand? He's looking for his wife. Why don't you finish him off, Vassily?

PEPPEL It's not worth spoiling my life over trash like him.

SATIN You ought to make a neat job of it. Then you can marry Vassilissa—become our landlord—

PEPPEL I can hardly wait! With your kind hearts you'll drink up all my property in a barroom, and me too. (*He sits down on a plank bed*) The old pest—woke me up! And I had such a fine dream. I was fishing some place and caught a huge perch. It was such a size, it could only happen in a dream. Well, I pull it along on the hook and all the time I'm afraid the line will snap. I keep the bag ready hoping to get the perch in any minute—

SATIN It wasn't a perch—it was Vassilissa.

ACTOR He caught Vassilissa a long time ago.

PEPPEL Go to hell, all of you—you *and* Vassilissa!

(KLESTCH *enters from the front hall*)

KLESTCH Damn cold out!

ACTOR Why didn't you bring Anna in? She'll freeze to death.

KLESTCH Natasha took her into her kitchen.

ACTOR The old man will throw her out.

KLESTCH (*Sitting down to resume his work*) Well, then Natasha will bring her here.

SATIN Let me have five kopecks, Vassily.

ACTOR (*To* SATIN) Five kopecks! Look, Vassya! Give us a quarter of a ruble.

PEPPEL I'd better give it to you quick—before you ask for a ruble. Here!

SATIN Gibraltar! There are no better people in the world than thieves.

KLESTCH Money comes easy to them—they don't have to work.

SATIN Money comes easy to many people, but it doesn't come so easy to let it go. As for work, just you make it pleasant for me and I'll probably work—Yes, I probably will. When work is a pleasure, life is a joy! When work is a duty, life is slavery. (*To* ACTOR) Let's go, Sardanapalus.

ACTOR Let's go, Nebuchadnezzar. I'm going to get boiled—like forty thousand sots.

(SATIN *and the* ACTOR *go off*)

PEPPEL (*Yawning*) Well, how's your wife?

KLESTCH (*After a pause*) Looks like it'll be pretty soon now.

PEPPEL You know, looking at you—I can't see any sense to your grating.

KLESTCH What else can I do?

PEPPEL Do nothing.

KLESTCH How am I supposed to eat?

PEPPEL Other people manage to live.

KLESTCH You mean the ones here? They're not people. Scum, hoodlums—that's all they are. I'm a worker—I feel ashamed to set eyes on them—I've been working since I was a kid. You think I won't get out of here? I'll wriggle out of this hole even if it tears my skin off. Just wait till my wife dies—I've lived six months here, but it feels more like six years—

PEPPEL Nobody here is any worse than you are—you're wrong about that.

KLESTCH They're not! These men with no honor or conscience—

PEPPEL (*Indifferently*) What good are honor and conscience? You can't put them on your feet instead of boots. Honor and conscience are only important to those who have power—force—

(*Enter* BUBNOV)

BUBNOV Whew, I'm shivering!

PEPPEL Bubnov, have you got a conscience?

BUBNOV What? Conscience?

PEPPEL That's what I said.

BUBNOV What do I want a conscience for? I'm no moneybags.

PEPPEL That's just what I say. Only rich people need honor and conscience. And Klestch here criticizes us, says we have no conscience.

BUBNOV Why, does he want to borrow some?

PEPPEL He has plenty of his own.

BUBNOV (*To* KLESTCH) Then you're selling it? Well, you'll have a tough time finding customers here. There's one thing I would buy—marked cards—but even those would have to be on credit.

PEPPEL (*Lecturing him*) You're a fool, Andrey. You ought to listen to Satin—or the Baron about conscience.

KLESTCH I have nothing to talk to them about.

PEPPEL They've got more brains than you have—even if they are drunks.

BUBNOV Be both drunk and smart—you've got a good start.

PEPPEL Satin says—everybody wants his neighbor to have a conscience, but it turns out nobody can afford one. And it's the truth.

(*Enter* NATASHA. *She is followed by* LUKA *who has a stick in his hand, a peasant knapsack on his back, and a kettle and teapot hanging from his waist*)

LUKA Good health to you, honest people.

PEPPEL (*Smoothing down his mustache*) Ah, Natasha!

BUBNOV (*To* LUKA) We were honest, you bet—so far back we forget.

NATASHA This is a new lodger.

LUKA It's all the same to me. I have just as much respect for crooks. To my way of thinking, every flea is a good flea—they're all dark and all good jumpers. Where do I accommodate myself here, my dear?

NATASHA (*Pointing to the kitchen door*) Step in there, grandpa.

LUKA Thank you, girlie. Anywhere you say. To an old man any place that's warm is homeland. (LUKA *goes off*)

PEPPEL What an interesting old man you've brought, Natasha.

NATASHA More interesting than you are. Your wife's in our kitchen, Andrey. Come get her in a little while.

KLESTCH All right, I will.

NATASHA You ought to treat her more kindly, Andrey. It won't be long now—

KLESTCH I know.

NATASHA You know. It's not enough to know—you have to understand. It's a frightening thing to die.

PEPPEL I'm not afraid of death.

NATASHA You *are* a brave man.

BUBNOV (*Whistles*) This thread is rotten.

PEPPEL Really, I'm not afraid. I'll accept my death any time—right now. Take a knife and stab me to the heart, I'll die without a sigh of regret. Even with joy, because it comes from a pure hand.

NATASHA (*As she turns to go off*) Well—you'd better pull the wool over somebody else's eyes.

BUBNOV (*Drawling*) The thread is rotten, it's a fact.

NATASHA (*At the door*) Don't forget about your wife, Andrey.

(NATASHA *goes off*)

KLESTCH All right.

PEPPEL A fine girl.

BUBNOV Not bad.

PEPPEL Why is she so uppity with me—turning me down? She'll get ruined here anyway.

BUBNOV She will—through you.

PEPPEL Why through me? I feel sorry for her.

BUBNOV Like a wolf for a sheep.

PEPPEL That's a lie. I feel very sorry for her. She has a hard time of it here—I see it.

KLESTCH Wait till Vassilissa catches you talking to her.

BUBNOV Vassilissa? Y-yes, that one doesn't make anybody a present of what's hers.

PEPPEL (*Lying down on a plank bed*) Go to hell, both of you— Prophets, too!

KLESTCH You'll see—just wait.

LUKA (*In the kitchen, singing*) "In the darkness of the night you can't see the road aright—"

KLESTCH Listen to that howling. New lodger! Hmph! (*Goes off into the hall*)

PEPPEL God, I'm bored. What is it makes me feel bored? You go on living, everything is fine. Suddenly, as if you'd caught a chill—you feel bored.

BUBNOV Bored? H'm!

PEPPEL Up to here.

LUKA (*Singing in the kitchen*) "No, sir, you can't see your road aright—"

PEPPEL Hey, there, old man!

LUKA (*Peeping out of the kitchen*) You mean me?

PEPPEL Yes, you. Stop singing.

LUKA (*Coming in*) Don't you like it?

PEPPEL I do when the singing's good.

LUKA Then mine is bad?

PEPPEL It seems so.

LUKA Imagine! And I thought I sang well. It's always like that. A man thinks to himself: I'm doing a good job. Then bang—everybody is displeased.

PEPPEL (*Laughing*) That's true!

BUBNOV You say you're bored, and there you're laughing.

PEPPEL What's that to you? The croaking raven.

LUKA Who's bored around here?

PEPPEL I am.

(*Enter the* BARON)

LUKA Imagine that! In the kitchen there a girl is sitting. She's reading a book and crying—yes, crying! Tears roll down from her eyes. I say to her, What's the matter, my dear? And she answers, I feel so sorry for him. For who? I ask her. And she says, The man here, in this book. Some people find strange things to bother them, don't they? Must be from boredom too.

BARON That one is a fool.

PEPPEL Baron, have you had tea?

BARON Yes. Go on.

PEPPEL Would you like me to treat you to half a bottle?

BARON Of course I would. Go on.

PEPPEL Get down on all fours and bark like a dog.

BARON Idiot! Who are you—a wealthy merchant? Or are you drunk?

PEPPEL Oh, come on—do some barking. It'll amuse me. You're one of the high and mighty. Time was when you looked upon the common folk like me as if we weren't human beings and all that sort of thing—

BARON Go on.

PEPPEL Well, today I'll make you bark like a dog, and you will bark. You know you will.

BARON So I will. Fathead! What sort of pleasure can you derive from that, when I know myself I've grown perhaps even worse than you. You should have tried to make me walk on all fours when you weren't my equal.

BUBNOV That's true.

LUKA Very good, if you ask me.

BUBNOV What's gone is gone, and what's left isn't worth talking about. We have no high and mighty gentlemen here—everything has washed off—only the naked man remains.

LUKA Therefore all are equal. Were you a baron, dear fellow?

BARON What is this? Who are you, you old goblin?

LUKA I've met a count, and a prince too—but this is the first time I've ever seen a baron, and a damaged one at that.

PEPPEL (*Laughs*) You know, Baron, you've made me feel a bit ashamed of myself.

BARON It's time you showed more intelligence, Vassily.

LUKA Oh-ho-ho! Just look at you, my good friends, one can see what kind of a life—

BUBNOV Every morning's so foul we wake up with a howl.

BARON We knew better times too. I used to wake up in the morning and drink coffee in bed—yes, coffee with cream!

LUKA Yet all of you are just human beings. Yes, put on as much as you like, wriggle as much as you can, but just as you were born a man, so you'll die a man. And as I look on I see everybody getting cleverer and more interesting. They all live worse, it's true, but they all want something better—a stubborn lot.

BARON Who are you, old man? Where do you come from?

LUKA Who, me?

BARON Are you a pilgrim?

LUKA All of us are pilgrims on this earth. I've even heard people say that the earth itself is a pilgrim in the heavens.

BARON (*Sternly*) That may be, but how about a passport? Have you got one?

LUKA And who are you, a detective?

PEPPEL (*Delightedly*) That's the ticket, old man. Got it in the neck, eh, Baron?

BUBNOV Y-yes, our gentleman got it good and proper.

BARON (*Embarrassed*) What's the matter? I'm only joking, old man. Why, my friend, I have no papers myself.

BUBNOV Liar.

BARON That is, I have papers, but they're no good for anything.

LUKA All papers are like that—no good for anything.

PEPPEL Baron, let's go have a drink.

BARON I'm ready. Good-by, old man. You are a rogue, though.

LUKA All's possible, my friend.

PEPPEL (*At the hallway door*) Well, come on.

(PEPPEL *goes off, the* BARON *hurrying after him*)

LUKA The fellow actually was a baron?

BUBNOV God knows! But he's an aristocrat all right. Even now it breaks out all of a sudden. Seems it never got completely rubbed off.

LUKA Maybe aristocracy is just like smallpox. A man gets well, but the pock marks remain.

BUBNOV He's not bad, though. Only sometimes he's got to kick up a fuss—like about your passport today.

(*Enter* ALYOSHKA. *He is tipsy, carries an accordion, and is whistling as he comes in*)

ALYOSHKA Hey, inhabitants!

BUBNOV What are you yelling for?

ALYOSHKA Excuse me. Pardon me. I'm a polite man—

BUBNOV Off on a binge again?

ALYOSHKA All I can hold! Just a minute ago Sub-inspector Medyakin threw me out of the police station. Don't let me even get the smell of you in the streets, says he, ever! And I'm a man of character. My boss spits at me like a cat. And what's a boss? Pooh! He's a drunkard, my boss is. And I'm a man—who wants nothing. Nothing—and that's that! You can have me for a ruble twenty! But I want nothing! Give me a million—I don't want it. And to let my fellow worker who's a drunkard order me around—I won't have it. I won't, no, I won't!

(NASTYA *appears in the kitchen doorway and shakes her head as she watches* ALYOSHKA)

LUKA (*Good-humoredly*) You *have* got yourself in a tangle, young man—

BUBNOV Just human foolishness.

ALYOSHKA (*Stretching himself out on the floor*) There, you can eat me up for all I care. But I want nothing. I'm a reckless man. Explain to me—why am I worse than other people, and who are they? Medyakin says: Keep off the street or I'll knock your block off. But I will go out. I'll lie in the middle of the street—let them run over me! I want nothing!

NASTYA Poor thing! So young, and already—makes a fool of himself.

ALYOSHKA (*Noticing* NASTYA, *raises himself to his knees*) *Mamselle! Parlez français? Prix-fixe?* [2] I'm painting the town red—

NASTYA (*In a loud whisper*) Vassilissa!

(*Flinging open the hallway door,* VASSILISSA *enters*)

VASSILISSA (*To* ALYOSHKA) You here again?

ALYOSHKA Good morning—please step right in—

VASSILISSA I told you, dog, not to show your face around here, didn't I? And you're here again?

ALYOSHKA Vassilissa Karpovna— I'll play you a funeral march, shall I?

VASSILISSA (*Pushing him by the shoulder*) Get out!

ALYOSHKA (*Moving toward the door*) Now wait—you can't do that. A funeral march—I've just learned it—fresh music. No, wait—you can't do that.

VASSILISSA I'll show you what I can't do. I'll set the whole street on you, you dirty prattler. You're too young to go around yapping about me.

ALYOSHKA All right, I'm going. (*Runs out*)

VASSILISSA Don't let him set foot in here ever again. You hear me?

BUBNOV I'm not your watchman.

VASSILISSA I don't care who you are. You're living here on charity, remember that. How much do you owe me?

BUBNOV (*Calmly*) I haven't counted it.

VASSILISSA Look out, or I will!

(ALYOSHKA *opens the door*)

ALYOSHKA (*Shouting*) Vassilissa Karpovna! I'm not afraid of you—not that much!

(*He sneaks into the kitchen.* LUKA *laughs*)

VASSILISSA Who are you?

LUKA A wayfarer—a pilgrim.

VASSILISSA For a night or to stay?

LUKA That depends.

VASSILISSA Your passport.

LUKA You shall have it.

VASSILISSA Let me see.

LUKA I'll bring it to you—drag it up to your very own door.

VASSILISSA Wayfarer indeed! You should have called yourself a tramp—that would have been nearer the truth.

LUKA (*With a sigh*) Not much kindliness in you, woman.

(VASSILISSA *moves toward* PEPPEL'S *room.* ALYOSHKA *peeps out of the kitchen*)

ALYOSHKA (*In a whisper*) Has she gone?

VASSILISSA (*Turning toward him*) You still here?

(ALYOSHKA *disappears, whistling.* NASTYA *and* LUKA *laugh*)

[2] Alyoshka's drunken babblings are acknowledgment of Nastya's trade as prostitute: "Speak French, Miss? Do you have a fixed price?"

BUBNOV (*To* VASSILISSA) He's out.
VASSILISSA Who is?
BUBNOV Vassily.
VASSILISSA Have I asked you about him?
BUBNOV I see you're looking in everywhere.
VASSILISSA I'm looking to see that things are in order—understand? And why hasn't the floor been swept at this hour? How many times have I ordered you to keep the place clean?
BUBNOV It's the Actor's turn—
VASSILISSA I don't care whose it is. But if the sanitation inspectors come and I'm fined, I'll throw the whole damn lot of you out!
BUBNOV (*Calmly*) What will you live on then?
VASSILISSA Don't let me see a speck of dust here! (*Walks toward the kitchen and stops before* NASTYA) What are you sticking around for? And your face all swollen up too. Don't stand there like a stump. Sweep the floor. Have you seen—Natasha? Has she been here?
NASTYA I don't know— I haven't seen her.
VASSILISSA Bubnov! Has my sister been here?
BUBNOV (*Pointing at* LUKA) She brought him in.
VASSILISSA And that one—was he in?
BUBNOV Vassily? Yes, he was. She talked to Klestch here, your Natasha.
VASSILISSA I'm not asking you who she talked to. Dirt—filth everywhere! Oh, pigs! See that this place is clean, hear me? (*She goes off quickly*)
BUBNOV God, what a brute that woman is!
LUKA A peppery madam.
NASTYA Anybody would be a brute leading such a life. Tie any live human being to a husband like hers—
BUBNOV Well, she's not tied too fast—
LUKA Does she always act up like this?
BUBNOV Always. You see, she came to see her lover, and he's out.
LUKA So she felt hurt— I see. Oh-ho! So many different people order others around on this earth—and try to throw all sorts of scares into each other, but still there's no order in life—nor cleanliness.
BUBNOV Everybody wants order, but their brains are in disorder. Anyway—somebody's got to sweep the floor. Nastya, you take care of it.
NASTYA Oh, of course! I'm not your maid here. (*After a pause*) I'm going to get drunk today—gloriously drunk!
BUBNOV That's an idea.
LUKA Why do you want to get drunk, girlie? Just a while ago you were crying—now you say you want to get drunk.
NASTYA (*Challengingly*) And when I'm drunk I'll cry again—that's all.
BUBNOV All—that isn't much
LUKA But what's the reason, tell me? Even a pimple doesn't just spring up, without a reason. (NASTYA *makes no answer, only shakes her head*) I see— Oh-ho-ho! You human beings! What's going to happen to you? Well, let me sweep up here then. Where's your broom?
BUBNOV Behind the door, in the hallway. (LUKA *goes into the hallway*) Nastya!
NASTYA Yes?
BUBNOV Why did Vassilissa jump on Alyoshka?
NASTYA He's been telling everybody Vassily's sick of her and wants to drop her for Natasha. I'm going to get out of here and move to other lodgings.
BUBNOV What for? And where?
NASTYA I'm fed up— I'm not needed here.
BUBNOV (*Calmly*) You're not needed anywhere. For that matter all humans on this earth are not needed.
(NASTYA *shakes her head, rises, and goes out into the hallway. Enter* MEDVEDEV, *a policeman, followed by* LUKA *carrying a broom*)
MEDVEDEV I don't think I know you.
LUKA Do you know everybody else?
MEDVEDEV On my beat I have to know everybody. But I don't know you.
LUKA That's because the earth couldn't squeeze all of itself into your beat, Uncle—a bit of it has remained outside. (*He goes off to the kitchen*)
MEDVEDEV (*Walking up to* BUBNOV) He's right, mine is a small beat—though it's worse than any big one. Just a while ago, before going off duty, I took the cobbler Alyoshka to the station. He stretched himself out in the middle of the street, began playing his accordion, and yelled—I don't want anything—I don't want anything. There were horses in the street and all sorts of traffic—he could have been crushed to death and all that. A wild fellow. Well, I took him in—he's too fond of disorder.
BUBNOV Coming for a game of checkers tonight?
MEDVEDEV I am. Y-yes. And how is—Vassily?
BUBNOV He's all right. The same as always.
MEDVEDEV Then he's still carrying on?
BUBNOV Why shouldn't he? He can carry on—
MEDVEDEV (*Doubtfully*) Can he? (LUKA, *carrying a bucket, crosses the room to the hallway*) Y-yes—There's been some talk about Vassily around here—have you heard it?
BUBNOV I hear all sorts of talk—
MEDVEDEV About him and Vassilissa— Have you noticed anything?
BUBNOV Noticed what?
MEDVEDEV Just in general— Or maybe you know and are lying to me? Everybody knows it— (*Severely*) One mustn't lie, my friend.
BUBNOV Why should I lie?
MEDVEDEV Glad you see it my way. Oh, the swine! They say Peppel and Vassilissa—are like that—What's that got to do with me? I'm not her father—only her uncle. Why should they make fun of me?
(*Enter* KVASHNYA)
God knows what people are coming to—they laugh at everything. Ah! It's you!
KVASHNYA It's me, my precious uniform! Bubnov, he pestered me again at the market to marry him—
BUBNOV Why not? Go to it! He's got money, and still makes a presentable swain.
MEDVEDEV Me? Ho! Ho!
KVASHNYA Ah, so? Don't touch my sore spot, police-

man. I went through it once before, dear man. When a woman gets married it's like jumping into a hole in the ice in the middle of winter: you do it once, and you remember it the rest of your days.

MEDVEDEV Wait a minute. Husbands aren't all alike.

KVASHNYA But I'm always the same. When my darling husband—God blast his soul—gave up the ghost, I was so happy I stayed in alone the whole day— I sat and couldn't believe my good luck.

MEDVEDEV If your husband beat you—for no good reason, you should have complained to the police.

KVASHNYA I kept complaining to God for eight years—he never helped.

MEDVEDEV Today wife-beating is forbidden. Today there's law and order in everything. You can't beat anybody for nothing. If you do beat anyone, it's got to be for the sake of order.

(*Enter* LUKA, *leading* ANNA)

LUKA Here, we've made it. Don't you know you mustn't walk around alone with your weak constitution? Where's your place?

ANNA (*Pointing to her bed*) Thank you, Grandpa!

KVASHNYA There's a married one. Look at her.

LUKA The little woman has a very weak constitution. She was walking along the hallway, clinging to the walls, and moaning. Why do you let her walk by herself?

KVASHNYA It was careless of us, sir, please forgive us. And her chambermaid must have gone out for a stroll.

LUKA You're making a joke of it—but how can anybody cast off a human being? Whatever condition he's in, a human being is always worth something.

MEDVEDEV You have to keep your eye on a person. What if she dies? There'll be a lot of complications. Yes, you have to keep an eye open.

LUKA Very true, master sergeant.

MEDVEDEV Y-yes—though I'm not quite a master sergeant yet—

LUKA Ain't you? You look like a hero.

(*There is noise and a stamping of feet in the hallway. Muffled sounds of shouting are heard*)

MEDVEDEV Must be a brawl?

BUBNOV Sounds like it.

KVASHNYA I'm going to take a look.

MEDVEDEV I'll have to be going too. Duty is duty! I wish when people started a fight other people would leave them alone. They'd stop fighting themselves—when they got tired. They should be allowed to knock each other around without interference, for all they're worth. They wouldn't be so keen to get into scrapes again—they'd remember their bruises—

BUBNOV (*Getting up from his plank bed*) You ought to tell that to the Chief of Police—

(*The door bursts wide open, revealing* KOSTYLYOV *on the threshold*)

KOSTYLYOV (*Shouting*) Abram! Come quick! Vassilissa's—killing—Natasha! Quick!

(KVASHNYA, MEDVEDEV, *and* BUBNOV *rush out into the hallway.* LUKA *gazes after them, shaking his head*)

ANNA Oh, God! Poor little Natasha!

LUKA Who's fighting out there?

ANNA Our landladies—sisters—

LUKA (*Walking up to* ANNA) What are they dividing up?

ANNA They've nothing better to do—they're well fed and strong—

LUKA What's your name?

ANNA Anna. You know, as I look at you, you remind me of my father—just as kind—and soft.

LUKA I've been through the wringer—that's why I'm soft. (*He laughs with a cracked senile laugh*)

# Act Two

*The same basement. On the plank bed near the stove* SATIN, *the* BARON, *the* GOITER, *and the* TARTAR *are playing cards.* KLESTCH *and the* ACTOR *are watching the game. On his plank bed* BUBNOV *is playing checkers with* MEDVEDEV. LUKA *is sitting on a square stool by* ANNA'S *bed.*

*It is evening. The place is lighted by two lamps: one hanging from the wall near the cardplayers, the other on* BUBNOV'S *plank bed.*

TARTAR I play one more game—then I play no more—

BUBNOV Goiter, sing! (*Striking up*) "The sun comes up, the sun goes down again—"

GOITER (*Continuing*) "But in my cell it's never light—"

TARTAR (*To* SATIN) Mix cards—mix 'em good! I know good what you are.

BUBNOV *and* GOITER (*Singing together*) "The guards are watching my barred window—e-eh! Watching closely day and night—"

ANNA Beatings—harsh words, that's all I've ever known in my life. Nothing but that—

LUKA Forget it, my good woman. Don't upset yourself.

MEDVEDEV Where are you moving your man? Are you blind?

BUBNOV A-ah! I see—I see—

TARTAR (*Threatening* SATIN *with his fist*) Why you try hide a card? I see it— Oh!

GOITER Don't bother, Assan! They'll clean up on us anyway! Bubnov, sing.

ANNA I don't remember a time I didn't feel hungry. I counted every piece of bread. All my life I've trembled and worried that I might eat more than my share. All my life I've been wearing rags—all my miserable life. What have I done to deserve this?

LUKA Poor child! You are worn out. Never mind.

ACTOR (*To the* GOITER) Play the jack—the jack, you fool!

BARON And we have a king.

KLESTCH They'll always beat your card.

SATIN Such is our habit.

MEDVEDEV King!

BUBNOV Mine too. Well—

ANNA I'm dying now—

KLESTCH Oh, oh! Stop playing, Assan, take a tip from me and get out of the game.

ACTOR He can't do without your advice, can he?

BARON Watch out, Andrey, or I'll send you packing to hell!

TARTAR Deal again. The jug went for water—broke himself—and me too!

(*Shaking his head,* KLESTCH *moves over to* BUBNOV)

ANNA I keep thinking: O God! Am I to be punished with suffering in the next world too? Even there, O God?

LUKA You won't be. Don't worry. Nothing will happen to you. You'll have a good rest there. Just bear up a little more. Everybody bears his life, my dear, each in his own way. (*He rises and walks quickly to the kitchen*)

BUBNOV (*Singing*) "You guards can watch my window closely—"

GOITER (*Singing*) "I will not try my leave to take—"

BUBNOV *and* GOITER (*Together*) "I'd surely like to get my freedom—e-eh! But no—my chains I cannot break."

TARTAR (*Shouting*) Ah! You push a card up your sleeve.

BARON (*Embarrassed*) Well—where do you want me to push it—up your nose?

ACTOR You're wrong, Assan—nobody would do that —never.

TARTAR I saw it. Crook. I no play.

SATIN (*Gathering the cards*) Leave off, Assan. You knew we were crooks. If so, why did you play with us?

BARON You've lost two quarter rubles, but make three rubles' worth of noise. Ah!

TARTAR (*Heatedly*) You must play honest.

SATIN What for?

TARTAR What you mean, what for?

SATIN Just that—what for?

TARTAR You not know?

SATIN I don't. Do you?

(*The* TARTAR *spits in bitter disgust. The others laugh at him*)

GOITER (*Good-humoredly*) You're a funny man, Assan. Can't you understand? If they're going to start living honestly, they'll die of hunger in three days.

TARTAR That no my business. People must live honest.

GOITER There he goes—like a parrot. We'll do better to go have tea, Bubnov! (*Singing*) "O chains, you heavy chains that bind me—"

BUBNOV "You are my iron guards in truth—"

GOITER Come on, Assan. (*Goes off, singing*) "I know I cannot break you ever—e-eh!"

(*The* TARTAR *shakes his fist at the* BARON *and follows his friend*)

SATIN (*To the* BARON) Your Excellency, you made a magnificent fool of yourself once again. You're an educated man, and still you can't do a proper job of cheating at cards—

BARON (*Spreading his hands*) Devil knows how I muffed it.

ACTOR You lack talent—faith in yourself—and without that a man can do nothing—ever.

MEDVEDEV I have one king, and you have two. H'mm!

BUBNOV Even one is all right if he's clever and bright. Your move.

KLESTCH Your game is lost, Abram Ivanych.

MEDVEDEV Mind your own business, understand? Hold your tongue.

SATIN Winnings—fifty-three kopecks.

ACTOR Three kopecks go to me. Though what do I want three kopecks for?

(*Enter* LUKA *from the kitchen*)

LUKA Well, you've cleaned up the Tartar. Now you'll go drink some vodka, I take it?

BARON Come with us.

SATIN I'd like to see what sort of a man you are when drunk.

LUKA No better than when I'm sober.

ACTOR Come along, grandpa—I'll recite some verses to you.

LUKA What are those?

ACTOR You know—poems.

LUKA Oh, poems! And what do I want poems for?

ACTOR They make one laugh—or sometimes sad.

SATIN Are you coming, reciter? (SATIN *and the* BARON *go off*)

ACTOR In a minute. I'll catch up with you. Here, grandpa, is something from a poem—I forget how it begins— H'm, I forget— (*He rubs his forehead*)

BUBNOV There! It's good-by to your king. Your move.

MEDVEDEV Damn it—I made the wrong move.

ACTOR In the old days, old man, when my organism wasn't yet poisoned with alcohol, I had a good memory. Now it's all over with me—it's all over. I always read that poem with great success—it brought the house down. You don't know what applause is— It's like vodka, my friend. I would come on the stage, stand like this— (*Assumes a pose*) Yes, stand like this and— (*A long pause*) I can't remember a thing—not a single word! And it's the poem I loved best of all— That's bad, old man, isn't it?

LUKA It can't be good if you've forgotten something you loved best. All our soul is in what we love.

ACTOR I've drunk up my soul, old man. I'm lost. And why am I lost? Because I had no faith in myself. I'm finished.

LUKA Why finished? You get yourself treated. They treat for drunkenness today, so I hear. Free of charge, too. There's a special hospital for drunkards—so they can be treated for nothing. They've decided, you see, that a drunkard is a human being like everybody else, and they're even glad when he wants to be treated. There's a chance for you—go there right away.

ACTOR (*Reflectively*) Go where? Where is it?

LUKA It's—in a town—what's its name? It's called— Never mind, I'll give you the name! Only you know what—you prepare yourself in the meantime. Keep away from vodka. Pull yourself together and bear up! Then later you'll be cured—and you'll start your life all over again. Yes, all over again—wouldn't it be fine, my friend? Well, make up your mind—and be quick about it!

ACTOR (*Smiling*) All over again—from the start— That'll be fine— Yes, yes. Again. (*He laughs*) Of course. I can do that. Surely I can, don't you think?

LUKA Why, certainly. A man can do anything, if he only wants to.

ACTOR (*As if suddenly awakened*) You're a queer fellow. So long! (*Whistles*) So long, old man. (*Goes off*)

ANNA Grandpa!

LUKA What is it, my dear?

ANNA Talk to me.

LUKA (*Coming up to her*) All right, let's talk.

(KLESTCH *looks about, walks up to his wife, gazes at her, and gesticulates as if wishing to say something*)

What is it, my friend?

KLESTCH (*In a low voice*) Nothing. (*He walks slowly toward the hallway, stops for a few seconds at the threshold, and goes off*)

LUKA (*After following* KLESTCH *with his eyes*) Your husband finds it hard to bear.

ANNA I have other things than him to think of now.

LUKA Did he beat you?

ANNA Didn't he though! It's through him, I think, that I took sick—

BUBNOV My wife—had a lover. The rascal was awfully good at checkers—

MEDVEDEV H'm—

ANNA Talk to me, grandpa dear. I feel sick—

LUKA It's all right. It's before death, dear. It's all right. You keep hoping. You'll die, you see, and then you'll have peace. You'll have nothing to fear—nothing at all. There'll be peace and quiet—and you'll have nothing to do but lie. Death quiets everything. It's kind to us humans. When you die you'll have rest, folks say. It's true, my dear. For where can a human being find rest in this world?

(*Enter* PEPPEL. *He is slightly tipsy, and looks disheveled and sullen. He sits down on a plank bed near the door and remains silent and motionless*)

ANNA But has one to suffer there too?

LUKA There'll be nothing there, nothing. Believe me. Peace and nothing more. They'll call you before the Lord and say: Look, O Lord, here's your servant Anna—

MEDVEDEV (*Sharply*) How do you know what they'll say there?

(*At the sound of* MEDVEDEV'S *voice* PEPPEL *raises his head and listens*)

LUKA It must be I do, master sergeant—

MEDVEDEV (*In a conciliatory tone*) I—see. Well, it's your business. Though I'm not quite a master sergeant yet—

BUBNOV I take two.

MEDVEDEV Drat it.

LUKA And the Lord will look at you gently and caressingly and will say: I know this Anna. Well, he'll say, conduct Anna to heaven. Let her rest—I know she's had a very hard life and is very tired. Give Anna rest—

ANNA (*Gasping*) Oh, grandpa dear—if it were only like that! If I could only have rest—feel nothing—

LUKA You won't, I tell you. You have to believe. You have to die with joy, without fear. To us, I tell you, death is like a mother to little children.

ANNA But maybe—I'll get better?

LUKA (*Ironically*) What for? For more suffering?

ANNA Well—just to live a little longer—just a little. If there isn't going to be any suffering there, I can bear it here—yes, I can.

LUKA There'll be nothing there. Just—

PEPPEL (*Rising*) That's true— Or maybe it isn't.

ANNA (*In a frightened voice*) O God—

LUKA (*Calling* PEPPEL) Hey, handsome—

MEDVEDEV Who's hollering?

PEPPEL (*Walking up to him*) I am. Why?

MEDVEDEV There's no call for your hollering—that's why. Every man must behave himself quietly.

PEPPEL Blockhead! Call yourself an uncle— Ho! Ho!

LUKA (*To* PEPPEL, *in a low voice*) You there—don't shout. There's a woman dying here—her lips are already brushed with earth—don't interfere.

PEPPEL For you, grandfather, I'll be glad to do it. You're a smart fellow. You tell lies and pleasant tales mighty well. That's all right with me. Go on lying. There's damn little in this world that's pleasant.

BUBNOV Is the woman really dying?

LUKA She doesn't look like she's joking—

BUBNOV Well, then she'll stop coughing. Her coughing's been disturbing everybody. I take two.

MEDVEDEV Ah, blast your hide!

PEPPEL Abram.

MEDVEDEV I'm no Abram to you.

PEPPEL Abrashka, is Natasha ill?

MEDVEDEV What business is that of yours?

PEPPEL Come on, tell me: did Vassilissa beat her up badly?

MEDVEDEV That has nothing to do with you either. It's a family affair. And who are you, anyway?

PEPPEL Never mind who I am. But if I decide so, you'll never see Natasha again.

MEDVEDEV (*Interrupting his game*) What's that? Do you know who you're talking about? That my niece should ever become— You thief!

PEPPEL I may be a thief, but you never caught me—

MEDVEDEV You wait. I'll catch you yet—it won't be long!

PEPPEL If you catch me, it will be so much the worse for your whole brood. Do you think I'm going to keep mum before the court examiner? Expect good deeds from a wolf! Who kept after me to start thieving and who showed me the places? Mishka Kostylyov and his wife. Who took in what I stole? Mishka Kostylyov and his wife.

MEDVEDEV Liar. They won't believe you.

PEPPEL They will—because it's the truth. I'll drag you into it too—ha! I'll ruin all of you, you scoundrel, you'll see.

MEDVEDEV (*Taken aback*) You're lying. Just lying. And when have I done you any harm? A mad dog, that's what you are.

PEPPEL And when have you done me any good?

LUKA Aha—

MEDVEDEV (*To* LUKA) What are you croaking about? You have no business here. This is a family affair.

BUBNOV (*To* LUKA) Leave off. They're not tying nooses for you and me.

LUKA (*Meekly*) I know. I only say if a man hasn't done somebody good, he's done him ill.

MEDVEDEV (*Missing* LUKA's *point*) That's better. Around here we all know one another. And who are you? (*Spitting like an angry cat, he goes off quickly*)

LUKA The gentleman lost his temper. Oh-ho-ho! You *have* got yourselves into all sorts of mix-ups, my friends—

PEPPEL He's run to complain to Vassilissa.

BUBNOV You're playing the fool, Vassily. What's all this showing off how brave you are? Bravery is all right when you go picking mushrooms in the woods. It's not much use in these parts. They'll wring your neck in no time here.

PEPPEL Oh, no. We folks from Yaroslavl don't knuckle down without a fight. And if it's going to be a fight, I'm ready for it.

LUKA Really, young man, why don't you go away from here?

PEPPEL Where to? Can you tell me?

LUKA Go to—Siberia.

PEPPEL Oh, yes? No, I'll wait until I'm sent there at government expense.

LUKA You listen to me—go to Siberia. New paths will open up for you there. Men like you are needed there.

PEPPEL My life is cut out for me. My father spent all his life in prisons and taught me to do the same. I was only a tyke when everybody already called me a thief, a thief's son—

LUKA Well, Siberia's a fine place—a golden land. For a man who's strong and has a good head on his shoulders it's like a hothouse for a cucumber.

PEPPEL Why do you tell lies, old man?

LUKA What?

PEPPEL Gone deaf suddenly. Why do you lie, I say?

LUKA Where do you see me lying?

PEPPEL Everywhere. You keep saying it's fine here and it's fine there, but you know you're lying. What for?

LUKA Well, take my word for it and go look it over for yourself. You'll thank me for it. What's the good of sticking around here? Anyway, what do you want the truth for? The truth might come down on you like an ax.

PEPPEL I don't care. An ax is all right with me.

LUKA You're a queer fellow. Why be your own killer?

BUBNOV I don't understand what all this silly talk is about. What truth do you want, Vassily? And what for? You know the truth about yourself—everybody knows it.

PEPPEL Shut up, Bubnov, don't croak. I want him to tell me— Listen, old man: Does God exist?

(LUKA *smiles, making no answer*)

BUBNOV People live like chips floating down the river. The house is built, but the chips are thrown away to take care of themselves.

PEPPEL Well? Does he? Answer me.

LUKA (*In a low voice*) If you believe in him, he exists. If you don't, he doesn't. Whatever you believe in exists.

(PEPPEL, *puzzled, stares at* LUKA *in silence*)

BUBNOV I'm going to have some tea. Come along, you two!

LUKA Why are you looking at me?

PEPPEL Well—wait. So you say—

BUBNOV I'll go alone then— (*He walks toward the door as* VASSILISSA *enters*)

PEPPEL So you mean to say—

VASSILISSA (*To* BUBNOV) Is Nastya in?

BUBNOV No. (*He goes off*)

PEPPEL Oh, it's you.

VASSILISSA (*Going up to* ANNA) Still alive?

LUKA Don't disturb her.

VASSILISSA Why are you hanging around here?

LUKA I can leave, if necessary.

VASSILISSA (*Walking toward* PEPPEL's *room*) I want to talk over some business with you, Vassily. (*She enters* PEPPEL's *room, while* LUKA *moves to the hallway door, opens it, slams it loudly, and cautiously climbs over a plank bed onto the stove*) Come here, Vassya.

PEPPEL I don't want to.

VASSILISSA (*Coming out*) Why not? What makes you cross with me?

PEPPEL I'm bored—fed up with all this business.

VASSILISSA Fed up with me too?

PEPPEL Yes, with you too. (VASSILISSA *pulls her shoulder kerchief tight, pressing her hands to her breast, then walks to* ANNA's *bed, peeps silently behind the curtain, and returns to* PEPPEL) Well, if you have anything to say—

VASSILISSA What is there to say? You can't force one to like you—and it's not in my character to beg for alms. Thank you for speaking the truth.

PEPPEL What truth?

VASSILISSA That you're fed up with me. Or isn't it true? (PEPPEL *gazes at her in silence. She moves up to him*) Why are you staring at me? Don't you recognize me?

PEPPEL (*With a sigh*) You *are* beautiful to look at, Vassilissa— (VASSILISSA *puts an arm around his neck, but he shakes it off with a shrug of his shoulders*) But you never touched my heart. I lived with you and all that sort of thing—but I never really cared for you—

VASSILISSA (*In a low voice*) I see— Well?

PEPPEL Well—there's nothing we can talk about—nothing at all! Just leave me.

VASSILISSA You've taken a fancy to somebody else?

PEPPEL That's none of your business. If I have, I won't ask you to be my matchmaker.

VASSILISSA (*Significantly*) That's a pity. I could probably get you the right party.

PEPPEL (*Suspiciously*) Who do you mean?

VASSILISSA You know who—why pretend? Vassily, I'm a straightforward person— (*Lowering her voice*) I won't hide it—you've hurt me. For no reason whatever you struck me as if with a whip. You were telling me you loved me and then all of a sudden—

PEPPEL It wasn't sudden at all. I've felt like that for a long time. There's no soul in you, Vassilissa. A woman must have a soul. We men are brutes. We should be—we have to be tamed and trained. And what kind of training have you been giving me?

VASSILISSA What's gone is gone. I know we're not masters of our feelings. If you don't love me any more—all right—so be it.

PEPPEL Well, then, that's that. We'll each go our own way, quietly, without any fuss, and that's fine.

VASSILISSA No, wait. That's not all. When I lived with you I was always counting on you to help me get out of this mess—free me from my husband, my uncle—this whole life. Maybe it wasn't you I loved, Vassya, but this hope, this constant thought on my mind, that I loved in you. You understand? I was waiting for you to pull me out of here—

PEPPEL You're no nail, and I'm no pair of pliers. I thought myself that with your brains—you *are* clever—and smart too—aren't you?

VASSILISSA (*Bending closer to him*) Vassya, let's—help each other.

PEPPEL How?

VASSILISSA (*Quietly, but strongly*) I know you like—my sister.

PEPPEL That's why you're so brutal—always beating her. Look out, Vassilissa. Keep your hands off her.

VASSILISSA Wait. Don't excite yourself. It can all be done quietly—arranged in a friendly way. You want to marry Natasha? All right—marry her. I'll even give you some money—say three hundred rubles. When I've saved more, I'll give you more.

PEPPEL (*Moving away from* VASSILISSA) Now just a minute— What's that for? What's the idea?

VASSILISSA Free me from my husband— Take that noose off my neck.

PEPPEL (*Whistles quietly*) So that's it! I see. Very neat on your part—the husband packed off into the grave, the lover to Siberia, and you yourself—

VASSILISSA No, Vassya—why Siberia? You don't have to do it yourself—you can get others. And even if you do it, who'll know? Think of Natasha. And you'll have money—you'll go away somewhere—you'll free me for life—and as far as my sister's concerned, it'll be better for her, too, to be away from me. It's hard for me to see her— I get bitter because of you—and I can't restrain myself. I torment her, beat her—beat her so hard I cry myself for pity of her. But I keep beating her and will go right on doing it.

PEPPEL A demon—that's what you are. And you're boasting about it.

VASSILISSA I'm not boasting—I'm speaking the truth. Think, Vassya. Twice you did time on account of my husband—because of his greed. He's sucking my blood like a bedbug—been doing it for four years. What sort of a husband is that? And he's harsh with Natasha, taunts her, calls her a beggar. He's poison to everybody.

PEPPEL There's something too clever in all this.

VASSILISSA My meaning is clear—only a fool can fail to understand what I want.

(KOSTYLYOV *enters cautiously and moves stealthily forward*)

PEPPEL (*To* VASSILISSA) Well, you'd better go now.

VASSILISSA Think it over. (*Noticing her husband*) What brings you here? Looking for me?

(PEPPEL *jumps to his feet and stares wildly at* KOSTYLYOV)

KOSTYLYOV It's me—it's me. And you're alone here? Ah—you have been having a chat? (*Suddenly stamps his feet and squeals at* VASSILISSA) You slut! You dirty trash! (*He is frightened by his own voice, as the other two look at him silently without moving*) God forgive me—you've led me into sin again, Vassilissa. I've been looking for you everywhere. (*Squealing again*) Time to go to bed! You've forgotten to put oil in the icon lamps! You—miserable swine.

(*He shakes his trembling hands at* VASSILISSA. *She walks slowly to the hallway, looking back at* PEPPEL)

PEPPEL (*To* KOSTYLYOV) Get out of here!

KOSTYLYOV (*Shouting*) It's my house! You get out of here! Thief!

PEPPEL (*In a low voice*) Get out, Mishka!

KOSTYLYOV Don't you dare! I'll—I'll—

(PEPPEL *grabs him by the collar and shakes him. A loud shuffling and a long animal-like yawn are heard from the top of the stove.* PEPPEL *releases* KOSTYLYOV, *who runs into the hallway screaming*)

PEPPEL (*Jumping onto the plank bed*) Who's up there—on the stove?

LUKA (*Popping out*) What?

PEPPEL You?

LUKA (*Calmly*) Yes—it's me—none other— O Lord Jesus Christ!

PEPPEL (*Closes the hallway door and looks for the bolt, but cannot find it*) Ah, those devils! Come down, old man!

LUKA I'm coming—right away. (*He comes down*)

PEPPEL (*Roughly*) Why did you get up on top of the stove?

LUKA Was there somewhere else I should have gone?

PEPPEL But you went into the hall?

LUKA It's too cold out there for an old man like me.

PEPPEL Did you—hear?

LUKA I heard. How could I help hearing? I ain't deaf. Ah, what luck has come to you, my boy—what luck!

PEPPEL (*Suspiciously*) What sort of luck?

LUKA That I got up on the stove.

PEPPEL And why did you start shuffling around up there?

LUKA Because I felt hot—fortunately for you, my boy. Besides, I figured the fellow can make a mistake and squeeze the old man to death.

PEPPEL Yes—I could've done that— I hate him—

LUKA Nothing easier. Anybody could do it. People often make that mistake.

PEPPEL (*Smiling*) Say, maybe you made it yourself once?

LUKA Listen to what I'm going to tell you, my boy. You've got to cut yourself off from that woman. Don't let her come near you—ever. She'll drive her husband into the grave herself, and she'll do a neater job of it than you can—believe me! Don't listen to that witch. Look at my head. Bald, isn't it? And why? Because of these same women. I've known more of them maybe than I had hair on my head. And this Vassilissa woman is worse than a savage.

PEPPEL I don't understand. Am I supposed to say thank you, or are you just another—

LUKA Don't say anything. You can't improve on what I said. Better listen to me—whoever she is, the girl you like around here, take her by the arm and be off with you! Get away from here—as fast as you can!

PEPPEL (*Somberly*) I can't make people out—which are kind and which are out to get you—I can't understand anything.

LUKA What is there to understand? A man can live any which way—however his heart tells him—kind today, mean tomorrow. If that girl here has touched your heart real strong, go away with her and that's all there is to that. Or you can go away alone. You're still young—you have plenty of time to settle down with a woman.

PEPPEL (*Taking* LUKA *by the shoulder*) Now, tell me what are you getting out of all this?

LUKA Now wait—let go. I want to have a look at Anna —there's been too much rattle in her breathing. (*Walks up to* ANNA'*s bed, draws the curtain, looks, touches her with his hand.* PEPPEL *watches him attentively, with a puzzled air*) Jesus Christ, the all-merciful. Receive the soul of thy newly departed servant, Anna, with peace.

PEPPEL (*Quietly*) Is she dead? (*Staying where he is, he straightens up and gazes at the bed*)

LUKA (*Quietly*) Her suffering has ended. Where's her man?

PEPPEL Over at the inn, most likely.

LUKA I must go tell him.

PEPPEL (*With a shudder*) I don't like dead people.

LUKA (*Walking toward the hall door*) What's there to like them for? It's the living people we should like—yes, the living ones.

PEPPEL I'll go along with you.

LUKA Are you afraid?

PEPPEL I don't like—

(*They hurry out. The place is deserted and quiet. After a time a noise is heard beyond the hallway door—it is indistinct, uneven, and unintelligible. Then the* ACTOR *enters*)

ACTOR (*Stops just across the threshold without closing the door, and, holding onto the jamb with both hands, shouts*) Hey, old man! Where are you? It's come back to me—listen. (*Staggering, takes two steps forward and, assuming a stage pose, recites*)

"If the world, my friends, is unable to find
The road to justice and truth,
Honor be to the madman who weaves golden dreams
Giving mankind surcease."

(NATASHA *appears at the door behind the* ACTOR)

Old man, listen.

"If tomorrow the sun should forget to light up
Our planet's eternal path,
A thought of some madman will instantly flash
To illumine the darkened earth."

NATASHA (*Laughing*) You loon! Been out getting crocked?

ACTOR (*Turning to* NATASHA) Ah! It's you? And where's the old man, the darling little old man? There's nobody here, it seems. Well, farewell Natasha—yes, farewell!

NATASHA (*Stepping forward*) You never said good evening, and now you're saying farewell.

ACTOR (*Barring her way*) I'm leaving, going away. Spring will come, but I'll be here no more.

NATASHA Let me pass. Where are you off to?

ACTOR I'm going to look for a town—to get treatment. You should go too. "Ophelia—get thee to a nunnery." You see, there's a hospital for organisms—for drunkards. A splendid hospital—marble everywhere—marble floors—bright, clean rooms—food—everything free! And yes, marble floors! I'll find this hospital, get cured, and once again I'll—act. I'm on the road to rebirth, as King—Lear said.[1] My stage name is Sverchkov-Zavolzhsky—nobody knows that—nobody. I have no name here. Do you realize how it hurts to lose one's name? Even dogs have names.

(NATASHA *quietly moves around the* ACTOR, *stops at* ANNA'*s bed, and looks*)

Without a name there's no man.

NATASHA Look—but she's dead!

ACTOR (*Shaking his head*) That can't be.

NATASHA (*Stepping back*) Really—look.

(BUBNOV *appears at the door*)

BUBNOV Look at what?

NATASHA Anna's—dead.

BUBNOV That means the end of her coughing. (*Walks up to* ANNA'*s bed, looks at her, and proceeds to his own place*) Somebody should tell Klestch about it—it's his business.

ACTOR I'm going—I'll tell him— She's lost her name! (*He goes off*)

NATASHA (*Standing in the center of the room*) Some day I will end like that—in a basement—forgotten by everybody—

BUBNOV (*Spreading some tattered clothes on his plank*

[1] The Actor's memory is playing tricks again as he freely paraphrases ideas to be found in *King Lear.*

*bed*) What? What are you mumbling there?

NATASHA Nothing—I was talking to myself.

BUBNOV Waiting for Vassily? Look out! He'll break your neck for you.

NATASHA What's the difference who breaks it? I'd rather it's him.

BUBNOV (*Lying down*) Well, it's up to you.

NATASHA It's a good thing she died—but I can't help feeling sorry for her. God! What did she live for?

BUBNOV It's like that with everybody—a man is born, lives a while, and dies. I'll die too—and so will you. Nothing to be sorry about.

(*Enter* LUKA, *the* TARTAR, *the* GOITER, *and* KLESTCH. KLESTCH *walks slowly behind the others, stooped over*)

NATASHA Sh-sh! Anna—

GOITER We know— God rest her soul, if she's dead.

TARTAR (*To* KLESTCH) You must pull her out! Pull her out hallway! Here no dead people. Here live people will sleep.

KLESTCH (*In a low voice*) I'll pull her out.

(*They all walk up to the bed.* KLESTCH *gazes at his wife over the shoulders of the others*)

GOITER (*To the* TARTAR) You think there'll be a bad smell from her? No! She dried up while she was still alive.

NATASHA God! Not one to feel sorry for her—not a single kind word from anybody— Shame on you!

LUKA Don't take it that way, girlie— It's all right. How can we feel sorry for the dead? Why, girlie, we don't feel sorry for the living—even for ourselves. So what can you expect?

BUBNOV (*Yawning*) And another thing—death isn't afraid of words— Sickness is, but not death.

TARTAR (*Moving away*) Must call police.

GOITER The police? Positively. Did you report to the police, Klestch?

KLESTCH No. I have to bury her—and all I have is forty kopecks.

GOITER Well, in a case like that, borrow somewhere. Or we can take up a collection—five kopecks from this one, as much as he can spare from that. But you have to report to the police—and do it quick—or they'll think you've killed the woman—or something— (*Walks to his plank bed and prepares to lie down alongside the* TARTAR)

NATASHA (*Moving away toward* BUBNOV'*s plank bed*) Now I'll be seeing her in my dreams. I always see dead people in my dreams—I'm afraid to go back alone—it's dark in the hall.

LUKA (*Following her*) The people to fear are the living ones—take it from me—

NATASHA Come with me to the door, grandpa.

LUKA All right—let's go.

(*The two exit. There is a pause*)

GOITER Oh-ho-ho! Assan! Spring is coming, friend—life will be warm again! In the villages the peasants are already mending their plows, harrows—getting ready to turn the earth—y-yes! And we? Assan! The cursed Mohammed, he's dead to the world.

BUBNOV Tartars love to sleep.

KLESTCH (*Standing in the center of the room and gazing dully into space*) What am I to do now?

GOITER Lie down and sleep—that's all.

KLESTCH (*In a low voice*) And how—about her?

(*Nobody answers him. Enter* SATIN *and the* ACTOR)

ACTOR (*Shouts*) Old man! "Come here, my faithful Kent!" [2]

SATIN Behold the great explorer! Ho-ho!

ACTOR It's all settled and done with! Where's the town, old man? Where are you?

SATIN Fata-morgana! The old man lied to you. There's nothing! No town, no people—nothing!

ACTOR You're lying!

TARTAR (*Jumping up from his bed*) Where's landlord? I go see landlord. I not sleep, I not pay money. Dead people—drunken people— (*He rushes out.* SATIN *whistles after him*)

BUBNOV (*In a sleepy voice*) Come to bed, fellows, stop making so much noise. People are supposed to sleep at night.

ACTOR Oh, yes—there's a dead body here. "Daddy, Daddy, have you heard? Our nets have caught a corpse"—a poem by—Shakespeare or someone[3]. . . .

SATIN (*Shouts*) Corpses don't hear! Corpses don't feel! Shout—yell—corpses don't hear!

(LUKA *appears at the door*)

# Act Three

*A vacant plot of ground littered with junk and overgrown with weeds. At the rear a high red-brick wall cuts off the sky. Near the wall is a cluster of elder. To the right of it runs a dark log wall which is part of some kind of shed or stables. To the left is a gray wall with patches of plaster. This belongs to the Kostylyov lodging house and stands at an angle, its far corner jutting out almost to the center of the plot, and a narrow passage showing between it and the red-brick wall. In the gray wall are two windows, one at ground level, the other up about five feet and nearer the corner. Alongside this wall lie a country sleigh, turned upside down, and a log about ten feet long. Piled against the wall on the right are some beams and old wooden planks.*

*It is early spring, and the snow has already melted away. The black twigs of the elder bush have not*

[2] Kent is King Lear's faithful servant. The Actor is play-acting and Satin joins in the game with his improvised entrance-line.

[3] Most translators have chosen to imply the Actor's imprecise memory by using the name of Pierre Jean de Béranger, the popular French song writer.

*yet budded. The setting sun casts a red glow on the brick wall, rear.*

*Sitting on the log, side by side, are* NATASHA *and* NASTYA. LUKA *and the* BARON *are seated on the sledge.* KLESTCH *is lying on the heap of wood across from them.* BUBNOV'S *head is visible in the lower window.*

NASTYA (*Speaking in a singsong voice, her eyes closed and her head beating time to her words*) So one night he comes to the garden, to the arbor, as we arranged—and I'm already there waiting for him a long time, trembling with fear and grief. He too is trembling all over, his face white as chalk, and a revolver in his hand—

NATASHA (*Cracking sunflower seeds*) Imagine that! It seems to be true what people say about students being desperate—

NASTYA And he says to me in a ghastly voice: My dearest, my precious love—

BUBNOV Ho-ho! Precious?

BARON Just a minute. Don't like it, don't listen—but don't spoil a good lie. Go on.

NASTYA My adorable one, says he. My parents refuse to give their consent, says he, to my taking you for my spouse and threaten to put an eternal curse on me for my love of you. On account of this, says he, I'm obliged to take my life. And the revolver in his hand is ever so big and has ten bullets in it. Farewell, dear heart, says he, nothing can make me change my mind, for I could never live without you—never! And I answered him: My never-to-be-forgotten friend—Marcel—

BUBNOV (*With surprise*) Morsel? What's that? Something to eat?

BARON (*Laughing*) But listen, Nastya—last time it was Gaston!

NASTYA (*Jumping to her feet*) Keep quiet, you miserable things! You're nothing but stray dogs! How can you understand what love—real love is? And I did have real love! (*To the* BARON) You pitiful wretch! You're an educated man. You drank coffee in bed, you say—

LUKA Now wait, folks! You mustn't interrupt her. Oblige the girl, let her have her way. It doesn't matter what's said, but why it's said. Never mind them, girlie, go on with your story.

BUBNOV Paint your feathers, crow. Fire away!

BARON Well, go on.

NATASHA Take no notice of them. Who are they? They're just envious—they have nothing to say about themselves.

NASTYA (*Resuming her seat*) I don't want to laugh any more. No, I won't. If they don't believe me—if they laugh at me— (*She stops abruptly, pauses for a few seconds, then, closing her eyes again, continues in a fervent, loud voice, waving her hand to the beat of her speech as if listening to distant music*) And so I reply to him: Joy of my life! My bright star! For me too it's positively impossible to live in this world—because I love you madly and will go on loving you as long as my heart beats in my breast. But, says I, you mustn't destroy your young life—as it's needed by your dear parents for whom you are their only joy—Forget me! Better that I suffer—the heartache of missing you— For I have nobody—my kind never has! Better let me be destroyed—it won't matter now! I'm not fit for anything and I've nothing—nothing— (*She covers her face with her hands and weeps silently*)

NATASHA (*Turning away from* NASTYA, *in a low voice*) Don't cry—don't!

(*A smile on his face,* LUKA *strokes* NASTYA'S *head*)

BUBNOV (*Roars with laughter*) Damn fool!

BARON (*Laughing*) Do you think this true, grandpa? She took it all from the book *Fatal Love*— It's all bunk! Don't bother with her!

NATASHA What's that to you? Better hold your tongue—if you have no heart left in you.

NASTYA (*Fiercely*) You godforsaken, empty man! Where's your soul?

LUKA (*Taking* NASTYA *by the arm*) Come along, dear. Don't mind them—calm yourself. I know—I believe you. Yours is the truth, not theirs. If you believe you had a real love, then you did have it—you certainly did. And don't be angry with your Baron. Maybe he does laugh from plain envy—maybe he never knew anything true and real in his life. Come along.

NASTYA (*Pressing her hands to her breast*) Honest, grandpa, it's true, it did happen. He was a student, a Frenchman—Gaston was his name— He had a small black beard and wore patent leather boots—may lightning strike me dead! And he loved me so dearly—so dearly!

LUKA I know. I believe you. You say he wore patent leather boots? My goodness! And you loved him too?

(*The two go off around the corner*)

BARON That girl is so stupid—kind, but so unbearably stupid.

BUBNOV What is it that makes human beings so fond of lying? As if they were always facing a court examiner—

NATASHA Lies must be more pleasant than the truth, it seems. I too—

BARON Well—go on.

NATASHA I too like to imagine things. I imagine them and—wait.

BARON For what?

NATASHA (*Smiling embarrassedly*) Oh, I don't know. Maybe tomorrow, I think, somebody will come—somebody—quite different— Or maybe something will happen—something that's never happened before. I wait and wait—I'm always waiting. But really, come to think of it, what have I to wait for?

(*A pause*)

BARON (*Ironically*) There's nothing to wait for. I don't expect anything. Everything has already happened. It's over—and done with! Go on.

NATASHA Or sometimes I imagine that tomorrow—I'll suddenly die. It gives you such a creepy feeling. Summer is a fine time for imagining death— All those thunderstorms in summer—it's easy to get killed by lightning.

BARON You have a hard life. That sister of yours has a devilish character.

NATASHA And who has a good life? Nobody. I see it all around me.

KLESTCH (*Until this moment motionless and indifferent, suddenly springing to his feet*) Nobody? That's a lie! Some people have it! If everybody suffered, it'd be all right. You wouldn't feel then that life's been unfair to you.

BUBNOV What's got into you? The devil? Howling like that! Huh!

(KLESTCH *lies down on the heap, as before, mumbling to himself*)

BARON I suppose I have to go and make up with Nastya —or she won't give me anything for a drink.

BUBNOV H'mm— People do love telling lies. With Nastya, I can understand it. She's used to painting her face—so she wants to paint her soul too—put rouge on it. But why do others do it? Take Luka for instance—he lies an awful lot—gets nothing out of it. And he's already an old man. What does he do it for?

BARON (*Moving away, with a smile*) All human beings have gray little souls—and they all want to rouge them up.

LUKA (*Returning from around the corner*) Look, my dear man, why do you upset the girl? You should leave her alone. Let her amuse herself by crying. You know she cries for her own pleasure—what harm does it do you?

BARON The whole thing is stupid, old man. I'm tired of it. Today it's Marcel, tomorrow Gaston—and every day it's the same story! However, I'm off to make up with her. (*He goes*)

LUKA Go and be gentle with her. It never does any harm to be gentle to a human being.

NATASHA You're a kind man, grandpa. What makes you that way?

LUKA Kind, you say? That's all right, if it's true. (*Soft sounds of an accordion and a song drift on from behind the red wall*) Somebody has to be kind, my girl —we have to feel sorry for people. Christ felt sorry for everybody and bid us do the same. Believe me— feeling sorry for a man at the right moment can do a lot of good. One time, for instance, I was a watchman in a country house in Siberia, near Tomsk, working for an engineer, you know. Well, the house stood in the woods, all by itself—no other homes around. It was winter and I was all alone in the house. I felt fine. One day I hear noises at a window!

NATASHA Burglars?

LUKA That's right. Trying to break in. Well, I picked up my rifle and went out. I look around and there I see two men trying to open the window—and working so hard at it they didn't even notice me. I shout at them: Hey, you! Get out of here! And what do they do? They turn around and rush at me with an ax. I warn them, Keep away, I say, or I'll shoot, and at the same time I cover them with my rifle, now one, now the other. Down on their knees they went as if begging me to let them go. But by now I felt very cross with them—for the ax, you know. You devils wouldn't go away when I told you, says I, now, says I, break off some twigs from a tree, one of you. That was done. And now, I order, one of you lie down and let the other lash him with the twigs. So by my order they gave each other a fine lashing. And after they did it they say to me, grandpa, they say, for mercy's sake give us some bread. We've been tramping around on an empty belly. So there are your burglars, my dear— (*Laughing*) And with an ax too! Yes, fine fellows they were, both of them. I say to them: You devils should have asked for bread right away. And they answer me— We're tired of asking. You keep asking people—and nobody gives you anything—it makes you feel pretty sore. And so they stayed with me right through the winter. One of them, Stepan, would take a rifle sometimes and go into the woods for days. The other, Yakov, was sickly, coughed all the time. And so the three of us kept watch over that country house. When spring came they said, good-by, grandpa! and left—to tramp their way to Russia.

NATASHA Were they runaway convicts?

LUKA They were—they ran away from a convict camp. Fine fellows! If I hadn't felt sorry for them, they might have killed me—or something. And then they would have been tried, sent to jail, to Siberia—what sense in that? Jail doesn't teach anyone to do good, nor Siberia, but a man—yes! A man can teach another man to do good—believe me! (*A pause*)

BUBNOV Y-yes! Now *I* don't know how to tell lies. What good are they? What I say is—give 'em the whole truth just as it is. Why feel shy about it?

KLESTCH (*Again jumping suddenly to his feet, as if burned, and shouting*) What truth? Where's the truth? (*Running his hands through his tatters*) Here's the truth! No work, no strength, not even a place to live. The only thing left is to die like a dog! This is the truth! Good God! What do I want the truth for? I want to breathe more freely—that's all I ask. What have I done wrong? Why should I have been given the truth? No chance to live—Christ Almighty—not a chance—that's the truth!

BUBNOV Whew! It certainly got him!

LUKA Lord Jesus— Look, my friend, you should—

KLESTCH (*Shaking with emotion*) You keep saying, The truth—the truth! And you, old man, keep comforting everybody. So I tell you—I hate you all—and this truth too—to hell with it. Understand? To hell with it! (*Rushes off around the corner, glancing back as he goes*)

LUKA My, my! How upset he got! And where is he off to?

NATASHA He acted as if he suddenly went off his nut.

BUBNOV A fine show, I call it. Just like on the stage— That kind of thing happens, though, every once in a while. The man hasn't got used to life yet—

(PEPPEL *enters slowly from around the corner*)

PEPPEL Peace to you honest people! Well, Luka, you sly old man—still telling stories?

LUKA You should have been here—a man was screaming his lungs out.

PEPPEL Was it Klestch? What got into him? I saw him running as if he was on fire.

LUKA Who won't run when it gets you right in the heart?

PEPPEL I don't like him—he's too bitter and proud (*Imitating* KLESTCH) "I'm a working man"—and everybody's below him, he'll have you think. Well, work if you like it—what's there to be proud of? If we're supposed to judge people by their work, the horse is better than any man—you drive it—and it doesn't speak. Are your folks at home, Natasha?

NATASHA They've gone to the cemetery—said they'd go to the evening mass afterward.

PEPPEL And I've been wondering why you're free. It's a rare sight.

LUKA (*To* BUBNOV, *reflectively*) You've been saying we need the truth. But it isn't always that truth is good for what ails a man—you can't always cure the soul with truth. I remember this case, for instance. I knew a man who believed in the true and just land—

BUBNOV Believed in what?

LUKA In the true and just land. There must be such a land in the world, he'd say. The people in that land, says he, are of a special kind—a fine people. They respect one another, help one another, and everything they do is decent and fine. And so every day this man was thinking of going to look for that true and just land. He was a poor man, and had a hard life. But whenever things were so bad he was ready to lie down and die, he didn't let himself lose heart; he just smiled and said: It's all right—I can bear it. I'll wait a while, and then I'll give up this life and go to the true and just land. He had only one joy in life—that land—

PEPPEL Did he go?

BUBNOV Where? Ho! Ho!

LUKA Then there came to that place—all this happened in Siberia—a man exiled by the government, a learned man, with books, maps, and all sorts of things like that. So our man says to the scientist: Do me a favor, please, show me where the true and just land lies and how to get there. The scientist at once opens his books, spreads his maps—looks here, looks there—there's no true and just land anywhere. Everything is right, all the lands are shown—but the true and just land is just not there.

PEPPEL (*In a low voice*) Not there? Really?

(BUBNOV *laughs*)

NATASHA Don't interrupt. Go on, grandpa.

LUKA My man doesn't believe him. It must be there, says he, look harder for it. Otherwise your books and maps, says he—they're all worthless if they fail to show the true and just land. The scientist is sore at that. My maps, says he, are the truest of all, and the true and just land doesn't exist anywhere. Hearing that, my man too gets angry. What? says he. I've lived and suffered all these years believing it exists, and your maps make out it doesn't? It's robbery! And he says to the scientist: You dirty swine. You're a crook, not a scientist. And bang! he punches him in the nose, and bang! again! (*He pauses*) After that he went home—and hung himself.

(*All are silent.* LUKA *looks at* PEPPEL *and* NATASHA *with a smile*)

PEPPEL (*In a low voice*) What the devil! That's not what I'd call a gay story—

NATASHA He couldn't bear having been deceived.

BUBNOV (*Somberly*) It's all tales.

PEPPEL Y-yes. There is the true and just land for you. None such, it turns out.

NATASHA I feel sorry for the man.

BUBNOV It's all make-believe. Ho! Ho! The true and just land! How do you like that? Ho! Ho! Ho! (*He vanishes from his window*)

LUKA (*Nodding in the direction of* BUBNOV's *window*) He's laughing. Hee-hee! (*He pauses*) Well, friends, may you come to good ends. I'm leaving you soon.

PEPPEL Where are you off to now?

LUKA To the Ukrainians. I've heard they've discovered a new faith down there—I must have a look at it. Yes, people keep looking—keep wishing for something better. God give them patience!

PEPPEL What's your opinion? Will they find it?

LUKA Who, people? They'll find it. Look for something—want something with all your heart—you'll find it.

NATASHA If they would only find something—think up something good—

LUKA They'll think it up. Only we have to help them, girlie—make it easier for them.

NATASHA How can I help? I get no help myself.

PEPPEL (*Resolutely*) I'm going to—I will talk to you again, Natasha— Let him hear it too—he knows all about it. Come—with me!

NATASHA Where? From one jail to another?

PEPPEL I said I'd give up thieving. I swear I will. And I mean it. I'm not an illiterate—I'll work. Luka here says one ought to go to Siberia of his own free will. Let's go there. Don't you think I'm sick of my life? I know, Natasha, I see it all. I try to make myself feel better thinking others steal much more than I do and have honors heaped on them—but that doesn't help me—it's no answer. I'm not letting conscience prick me into saying this—I don't believe in conscience. But one thing I do know—this is not the way to live. I must live a better life. I must live—in such a way that I can respect myself—

LUKA You're right, my boy. May the Lord Jesus Christ help you. You're right—a man must respect himself.

PEPPEL I've been a thief from the time I was a kid. Everybody called me Vasska the thief! Vasska the thief's son! Ah, so? Then have it your way. Here I am—a thief! You must understand—I'm a thief maybe only out of spite—only because nobody ever thought of calling me by any other name. You'll call me something else, Natasha, won't you?

NATASHA (*In a melancholy tone*) I can't believe any words—somehow. And I feel uneasy today—my heart aches—as if I were expecting something to happen. I'm sorry you've started this conversation, Vassily—

PEPPEL How long should I have waited? This isn't the first time I've brought it up.

NATASHA Well, I don't know how I could go with you. Frankly, I can't say I love you very much. Sometimes

I seem to like you. Other times it makes me sick to look at you. It must be I don't really love you. When you love somebody you don't see anything wrong with them. I do.

PEPPEL You'll love me all right—don't worry. I'll see you get to like me—if you'll only say yes. I've been watching you for over a year—I can see you're a good girl—strict with yourself—dependable—and I've fallen in love with you—deeply.

(VASSILISSA, *in her best finery, appears at the higher window and listens, standing by the jamb*)

NATASHA I see. You say you love me—and what about my sister?

PEPPEL (*Embarrassed*) Oh, she's nothing to me. There are lots of her kind—

LUKA Don't mind that, girlie. When there's no bread, you eat grass—

PEPPEL (*Somberly*) I ask you to bear with me. Mine is a bitter life—a hungry wolf's life—there's no joy in it. I feel as if I'm sinking in a bog—whatever I lay hold of is rotten, nothing can keep me from going down. Your sister—I thought she was different. If she weren't so greedy for money—I'd have done anything for her. Only she had to be all mine. But she's after something else—she wants money—and freedom too—freedom to play around with men. She can't help me. But you—you're like a young fir tree—prickly to touch, but strong to hold on to—

LUKA My advice too, girlie—marry him. He's all right—he's a good fellow. Only you have to remind him as often as you can that he's a good fellow—so he doesn't forget it. He'll believe you. Just keep telling him—you're a good man, Vassya, remember that! And besides, my dear, where else can you go? Your sister is a wicked wild beast, and as for her husband—well, nothing you can say about him can be as bad as he is. Then, all this life around here—it can take you nowhere. And Vassily—he's substantial, there's something to him.

NATASHA I know I have nowhere else to go—I've thought of that myself. Only—I have no faith in anybody. But you're right, I've nowhere to go—

PEPPEL There's one road for you here—but I won't let you go that way—I'd rather kill you.

NATASHA There! I'm not your wife yet, and you already want to kill me.

PEPPEL (*Putting his arms around her*) Stop it, Natasha. Let's not say any more!

NATASHA (*Pressing close to him*) I'll say one thing, Vassily—and let God be my witness—the very first time you strike me—or wrong me in some other way—I won't spare my life—I'll either hang myself or—

PEPPEL May my hand wither away, if I ever touch you!

LUKA Have no doubts, dear. He needs you more than you need him.

VASSILISSA (*From the window*) Congratulations on the happy ending!

NATASHA They're back! God, they've seen us. Oh, Vassily!

PEPPEL What are you scared of? Nobodv will dare touch you now.

VASSILISSA Don't be afraid, Natasha. He won't beat you. He can neither beat nor love—I know.

LUKA (*In a low voice*) Oh, what a woman—a regular viper—

VASSILISSA He's brave mostly with words—

(*Enter* KOSTYLYOV)

KOSTYLYOV Natashka! What are you doing here, loafer? Scandal-mongering? Complaining about your family? And all this time the samovar hasn't been prepared, the table hasn't been cleared—ah?

NATASHA But you said you wanted to go to church.

KOSTYLYOV What we wanted to do is none of your business! You have to see to your own work—do what you're told!

PEPPEL You shut up! She's not your servant any more. Don't go, Natasha—don't do anything!

NATASHA Don't you give orders—it's too early for you. (*She goes off*)

PEPPEL (*To* KOSTYLYOV) Enough! You've bullied the girl all you're going to. Now she's mine.

KOSTYLYOV Yours? When did you buy her? How much did you pay?

(VASSILISSA *laughs loudly*)

LUKA Go away, Vassya.

PEPPEL Watch out, you—laughers! See you don't have to cry!

VASSILISSA Oh, how frightening! Oh, I'm so scared!

LUKA Go away, Vassily. Don't you see she's egging you on, trying to get you worked up?

PEPPEL Oh, so? Not me! I'll be damned if you have your own way!

VASSILISSA And I'll be damned if I don't, Vassya!

PEPPEL (*Shaking his fist at her*) We'll see about that! (*He goes off*)

VASSILISSA (*Disappearing from the window*) I'll fix you a nice wedding!

KOSTYLYOV (*Walking up to* LUKA) What's doing, old man?

LUKA Nothing doing, old man.

KOSTYLYOV Really. I hear you're leaving?

LUKA It's time to go.

KOSTYLYOV Where to?

LUKA Where my nose leads me.

KOSTYLYOV I see, tramping about. Seems you find it uncomfortable to stay in one place?

LUKA That's for stones. And they say even water won't flow under a stone.

KOSTYLYOV We're not talking about stones. A man must live in one place. You can't let people live like cockroaches—crawling every which way. A man ought to stick to his place—not wander about the earth for nothing.

LUKA What if a man's place is everywhere?

KOSTYLYOV Then he's a tramp, a useless man. A man must be useful, he must work—

LUKA You don't say.

KOSTYLYOV Yes—certainly. What's a pilgrim? A pilgrim, I've heard tell, means a foreigner, a stranger. He's a strange man, not like other people. If he's really strange—if he knows something—has learned something that's of no use to anybody—it may even be some truth—but not every truth is useful—not by a long shot— Well, let him keep what he knows to himself—and hold his tongue. If he's a real pilgrim he doesn't talk—or talks so nobody understands him. He doesn't want anything, minds his own business, and doesn't stir up trouble for nothing. It's none of his business how people live. Let him follow a righteous life—live in the woods—in the thickets—out of everybody's sight. It's not for him to interfere or criticize, but to pray for everybody—for all worldly sins—mine and yours—for everything. That's why he puts worldly vanity behind him—just so he can pray. Exactly! (*He pauses*) And what sort of pilgrim are you? You have no passport. A good man must have a passport. All good people have passports—yes.

LUKA There are people, and there are also just plain men.

KOSTYLYOV Don't try to be funny. And don't talk to me in riddles. I'm no more stupid than you are. What do you mean by people and men?

LUKA This is no riddle. I say there's soil unfit for sowing, and there's fertile soil—whatever you sow on it grows— That's all the difference.

KOSTYLYOV Well? What do you mean by that?

LUKA Take yourself, for instance. If the Lord God himself says to you: Mikhail, be a man!—he'll be wasting his breath—as you are, so you'll stay—

KOSTYLYOV And do you know my wife has an uncle who's a policeman? And if I—

(*Enter* VASSILISSA)

VASSILISSA Come have tea, Mikhail Ivanovich.

KOSTYLYOV (*To* LUKA) Listen, you—get out of here! Clear out of the house!

VASSILISSA Yes, old man, be off with you. Your tongue is much too sharp. And who knows—maybe you're a fugitive—

KOSTYLYOV If I see hide or hair of you after today—I'll take steps!

LUKA Call your uncle? Call him. Tell him you've caught a fugitive. He may get a reward—about three kopecks—

(BUBNOV *reappears in the lower window*)

BUBNOV What's up? What's being sold for three kopecks?

LUKA He's threatening to sell me.

VASSILISSA (*To* KOSTYLYOV) Come on.

BUBNOV For three kopecks? Watch out, old man, they'll sell you for one kopeck.

KOSTYLYOV (*To* BUBNOV) You would pop your head out like a devil in an oven!

VASSILISSA (*As she goes*) The world seems to be full of suspicious characters—and all sorts of crooks.

LUKA Hope you'll enjoy your tea.

VASSILISSA (*Glancing back*) Hold your tongue—you dirty toadstool!

(*She and* KOSTYLYOV *disappear around the corner*)

LUKA Tonight I'll be out of here.

BUBNOV The best thing you can do. It's always better to go away while there's still time.

LUKA You're right.

BUBNOV I know what I'm talking about. I probably saved myself from Siberia by going away in time.

LUKA Did you?

BUBNOV That's the truth. It was this way. My wife got mixed up with a furrier. He was a fine worker—I must say—very clever in dyeing dog skins to look like raccoon—also turning cat skins into kangaroo fur—muskrat—and all sorts of other furs. He *was* clever. Well, my wife got mixed up with him, and the two of them were so close I began to be afraid they'd poison me any minute or think up some other way to get rid of me. I started beating my wife, and the furrier beat me. He was a fierce fighter. Once he pulled half my beard out and broke a rib. I got angry too—one day I whacked my wife on the head with a poker—and all in all it was quite a war going on. Well, I realized I couldn't get any place that way—they were getting the best of me. So I made up my mind to kill my wife—I was in dead earnest about it. But I woke up in time and went away instead.

LUKA That was a better idea. Let them make dogs into raccoons.

BUBNOV Only, my workshop was in my wife's name—and I was left—as you see me now. Though, to tell the truth, I'd have drunk up my shop anyway. You see, I have spells of heavy drinking—

LUKA Have you? A-ah!

BUBNOV Terrific spells. When it comes over me I drink up every little thing I have—about all I end up with is my skin. And another thing—I'm lazy. You can't imagine how I hate work.

(SATIN *and the* ACTOR *enter, arguing*)

SATIN Bunk! You'll go nowhere. It's nothing but a damn pipe dream. Look here, old man. What sort of ideas have you been giving this broken-down old windbag?

ACTOR You lie. Grandpa, tell him he's lying. I'm going. I had work today, I swept the street—but I haven't touched vodka. How's that? Here are the thirty kopecks, but I'm sober.

SATIN It's crazy, that's all. Give them to me—I'll drink them up for you—or gamble them away—

ACTOR Go away! It's for the trip.

LUKA (*To* SATIN) Now why do you discourage the poor fellow?

SATIN Tell me, O wizard, belov'd by the gods, what fate do my stars hold in store? I lost every kopeck I had, brother. The world hasn't entirely gone to the dogs, grandpa—there are still cardsharpers cleverer than I am.

LUKA You're a jolly fellow, Konstantin, and a real pleasant one.

BUBNOV Come here, Actor.

(*The* ACTOR *walks over to the window and squats before* BUBNOV. *They talk in low voices*)

SATIN In my young days I was quite amusing, old man. It's pleasant to think back to those days. I was a happy-go-lucky sort of fellow—danced beautifully, performed on the stage, liked to make people laugh—it was a fine time.

LUKA What made you stray from the path then?

SATIN You're very curious, old man. You want to know everything— What for?

LUKA To understand the affairs of human beings, my man. Now I look at you and can't make you out. You're so manly, Konstantin, and you've got brains too. Why, then, suddenly—

SATIN It's jail, old man. I was four years and seven months in jail—and after jail a man can go nowhere.

LUKA So. And what did you do time for?

SATIN For a dirty swine—I killed him in a fit of temper. It was in jail that I learned to play cards too.

LUKA Did you kill because of a woman?

SATIN Because of my sister. But don't bother me. I don't like being questioned. Besides, it was all long ago—my sister's dead—nine years since. A fine little person my sister was.

LUKA I must say you take life lightly. Now the locksmith here let out such a scream a while ago, it was something frightful.

SATIN Who, Klestch?

LUKA That's the one. No work, he shouts, no nothing!

SATIN He'll get used to it. What shall I do with myself now, I wonder?

LUKA (*Quietly*) Look, here he comes.

(*His head bent low,* KLESTCH *enters slowly*)

SATIN Hey, widower! Why so down in the dumps? What's on your mind?

KLESTCH I'm trying to think what to do. I've no tools. The funeral swallowed up everything.

SATIN I'll give you a word of advice—don't do anything. Just let yourself be a burden on the world at large!

KLESTCH You with your talk. I have some shame before other people.

SATIN Forget it. People aren't ashamed at your living worse than a dog. Think this over—you stop working —I stop—hundreds and thousands of others—everybody—understand?—everybody stops working. Nobody wants to do any work—what'll happen then?

KLESTCH Everybody will drop dead from hunger.

LUKA (*To* SATIN) You ought to join the Wanderers with your ideas. There are such people, called Wanderers.[1]

SATIN I know—they're no fools, grandpa.

(*From the* KOSTYLYOVS' *window come* NATASHA'S *cries:* "What have I done wrong? Please, what have I done?")

LUKA (*With alarm*) Sounds like Natasha. Oh, God!

(*Noise, uproar, the sound of dishes being smashed in the* KOSTYLYOVS' *apartment*)

KOSTYLYOV (*Off stage*) You heathen—you slut—

VASSILISSA (*Off*) Wait, I'll fix her—

NATASHA (*Off*) They're beating me! They're killing me!

SATIN (*Shouting through the window*) Hey, you there!

LUKA (*Fidgeting*) We ought to call Vassily— Oh, God! Boys, friends—

ACTOR (*Running off*) I'll get him—

BUBNOV They do beat her an awful lot now.

SATIN Come on, old man—we'll be witnesses.

LUKA (*Following* SATIN) I'm no good as a witness—no! If only Vassily would come quick— (*The two go off*)

NATASHA (*Off stage*) Vassilissa! Sister! Vassi—

BUBNOV They've gagged her—I'll go look—

(*The disturbance in the* KOSTYLYOV *apartment dies down, apparently moving out of the room into the hall.* LUKA'S *shout,* "Stop!" *is heard. A door is slammed loudly, chopping off the noise as with a hatchet. All is quiet on the stage. Twilight*)

KLESTCH (*He is sitting indifferently on the upturned sleigh, rubbing his hands hard. Then he begins muttering something—at first indistinctly*) How now? I have to live— (*Raising his voice*) I have to have a place to live in—don't I? I haven't one. I have nothing. Only myself. Just one solitary being. No help from anybody.

(*Hunching over, he goes off slowly. There are a few seconds of sinister silence. Then a low, confused din rises somewhere in the passage. It swells and draws nearer. Individual voices can be distinguished off stage*)

VASSILISSA I'm her sister! Let go!

KOSTYLYOV What right have you?

VASSILISSA Jailbird!

SATIN Call Vassya, quick! Lay into him, Goiter!

(*A police whistle is heard. The* TARTAR, *his right arm in a sling, rushes on*)

TARTAR What such law is there—kill in daytime?

(*The* GOITER *enters, followed by* MEDVEDEV)

GOITER Ah, what a wallop I gave him!

MEDVEDEV How dare you strike people?

TARTAR And you? What's your duty?

MEDVEDEV (*Running after the* GOITER) Stop. Give me my whistle.

(KOSTYLYOV *runs on*)

KOSTYLYOV Abram! Catch him—arrest him!

(KVASHNYA *and* NASTYA *come on from around the corner, supporting a disheveled* NATASHA *under the arms. They are followed by* SATIN, *stepping backward as he fends off* VASSILISSA, *who, arms waving, tries to reach out and hit* NATASHA. ALYOSHKA *skips madly around* VASSILISSA, *blowing a whistle into her ears, shouting, and yelling. A few tattered figures, men and women, drift in to join the others*)

SATIN (*To* VASSILISSA) Where are you pushing? You damned hoot owl—

VASSILISSA Keep away, jailbird! I'll tear her to pieces if it kills me too!

KVASHNYA (*Moving* NATASHA *away*) Come, Vassilissa. You ought to be ashamed. Stop acting like a wild animal.

MEDVEDEV (*Catching hold of* SATIN) Now I've got you!

SATIN Goiter! Give it to them! Vasska! Vasska!

(NATASHA *is led to the pile of wood, right, where she can sit down. The rest are bunched together*

[1] A Russian religious sect dating from the time of Peter the Great and called Wanderers (or sometimes Runners) because they preached running away from places where the government-instituted religious reforms were being enforced. —Tr.

*near the passage, against the red wall.* PEPPEL, *rushing out of the passage, elbows his way through the crowd silently and vigorously*)

PEPPEL Where's Natasha? Ah, it's you—

(KOSTYLYOV *slips around the corner*)

KOSTYLYOV (*Off stage*) Abram! Get hold of Vasska! Boys, help him catch Vasska! He's a robber, a thief!

PEPPEL Ah, you old goat!

(*Swinging his fist, he belabors* KOSTYLYOV. *The latter falls to the ground, only the upper part of his body showing around the corner.* PEPPEL *dashes over to* NATASHA)

VASSILISSA Do something to Vasska! All you good people, beat him up—the dirty thief!

MEDVEDEV (*Shouting to* SATIN) Keep out of this! This is a family affair! They're relations—and who are you?

PEPPEL What did she do to you? Stab you?

KVASHNYA Just look what the brutes did—scalded the girl's feet with boiling water.

NASTYA Toppled the samovar on her.

TARTAR Maybe accident— You must know certain—you mustn't talk if you not know—

NATASHA (*Almost fainting*) Take me away, Vassily—hide me—

VASSILISSA My God! Look! He's dead. They've killed him—

(*Everybody crowds around* KOSTYLYOV *in the passage.* BUBNOV *comes out of the crowd and walks up to* PEPPEL)

BUBNOV (*In a low voice*) Look, Vasska. The old man is—you know what—finished.

PEPPEL (*Looking at* BUBNOV *without understanding a word*) Go call somebody—to take her to a hospital— Well, I'll get even with them!

BUBNOV I was saying—somebody has flattened the old man—

(*The noise on the stage dies down like a campfire doused with water. Random exclamations uttered in undertones can be heard:* "Is it really?" "What do you know!" "Well?" "Let's get away from here." "Oh, hell!" "Now look out!" *The crowd dwindles.* BUBNOV, *the* TARTAR, NASTYA, *and* KVASHNYA *rush over to* KOSTYLYOV'S *body*)

VASSILISSA (*Rises from the ground and shouts*) They've killed him! They've killed my husband! (*In a triumphant voice*) Here's the murderer. Vasska did it. I saw it. Good people, I saw it with my own eyes. Well, Vasska? What'll you say to the police now?

PEPPEL (*Leaving* NATASHA) Get out of the way! (*Gazes at the dead man. To* VASSILISSA) Well? You're glad? (*Touches the body with his foot*) The old pig has popped off! You've had your way. Well, I'd better finish you off too!

(*He makes a dash for her, but* SATIN *and the* GOITER *stop him quickly.* VASSILISSA *flees into the passage*)

SATIN Come to your senses!

GOITER Whoa! Where are you galloping?

(VASSILISSA *returns*)

VASSILISSA Now what, my dear friend Vasska? One can't escape his fate. Call the police inspector, Abram! Blow your whistle!

MEDVEDEV They've swiped my whistle, those bastards!

ALYOSHKA Here it is— (*He blows the whistle.* MEDVEDEV *runs after him*)

SATIN (*Leading* PEPPEL *to* NATASHA) Don't be afraid, Vasska! Killing a man in a fight is nothing serious. It doesn't cost much—

VASSILISSA Hold Vasska! He killed him—I saw him do it!

SATIN I punched the old man a few times myself. He didn't need much to keel over. Call me as a witness, Vasska.

PEPPEL I need no alibis. What I need is to get Vassilissa into it, and that I will do. It was she who wanted all this—egged me on to kill her husband!

NATASHA (*Suddenly, in a loud voice*) Oh, now I understand! So that's it, Vassily? Kind people! They're in this together! My sister and him—they're together! They've plotted all this. Isn't that so, Vassily? You talked to me today the way you did—so she'd hear everything? Kind people! She's his mistress—you know that—everybody knows it—they're both guilty! It was she who got him to kill her husband— He was in their way—and I was too. So they've maimed me—

PEPPEL Natasha—what are you saying?

SATIN What the hell!

VASSILISSA Liar! She lies—I—it was he, Vasska—he killed him!

NATASHA They're in it together! I curse you! I curse you both!

SATIN Such goings on! Watch out, Vassily! They'll be the death of you.

GOITER This is more than I can understand. Good God, what a business!

PEPPEL Do you really mean it, Natasha? Do you really believe that I and she—

SATIN Honest, Natasha, think—

VASSILISSA (*In the passage*) My husband has been killed, sir. Vasska Peppel, the thief—he killed him, Inspector. I saw it—everybody saw it—

NATASHA (*Tossing about, almost unconscious*) Kind people! My sister and Vasska killed him. Listen to me, police! That one, my sister, taught—got him—her lover—there he is, damn him—they killed the man! Arrest them—try them. Take me too—to jail! For Christ's sake, take me to jail!

# Act Four

*The same setting as the first act. The partitions forming* PEPPEL'S *room have been removed, and the room no longer exists. Lying in that corner now is the* TARTAR; *he is restless and groans occasionally. The wood block with anvil, at which* KLESTCH *used to work, is also gone.* KLESTCH *himself is sitting at the table tinkering with an accordion and trying the scales. At the other end of the table are* SATIN, *the* BARON, *and* NASTYA. *In front of them they have a bottle of vodka, three bottles of beer, and a big chunk of black bread. The* ACTOR *is on the stove, and can be heard moving about and coughing.*

*It is night. The place is lit by a lamp standing in the center of the table. Outside a wind is blowing.*

KLESTCH Y-yes—it was during all that mix-up that he disappeared.

BARON Vanished from the police—like unto smoke fleeing from the face of fire.

SATIN Thus do sinners vanish from the sight of the righteous.

NASTYA He was a good old man. And you—you're not men, you're just rust.

BARON (*Drinking*) Here's to you, your ladyship!

SATIN Yes, he was an interesting old gaffer. Nastya fell plumb in love with him.

NASTYA I did fall in love with him. I won't deny it. He saw—he understood everything—

SATIN (*Laughing*) And, all in all, to quite a few people he was like soft bread to the toothless.

BARON (*Laughing*) Like plaster to an abscess.

KLESTCH He had pity for other people. You haven't.

SATIN What good will it do you if I pity you?

KLESTCH You know—well, if not how to pity a man—you know how not to hurt him.

TARTAR (*Sitting up on his plank bed and rocking his wounded arm, as if it were a baby*) Old man was good. He had the law in his soul. Who has the law in his soul—he is good. Who lost the law, he is lost.

BARON What kind of law, Assan?

TARTAR Different kind. You know what kind.

BARON Go on.

TARTAR Not hurt a man—this is the law!

SATIN It's called "The code of criminal and reformatory penalties."

BARON Also "The code of penalties imposed by Justices of the Peace."

TARTAR Is called Koran. Your Koran called the law. In every soul must be Koran—yes.

KLESTCH (*Trying the accordion*) Damn it, listen to it hiss. Assan is right. We must live according to the law—according to the Gospels—

SATIN Do that.

BARON Yes, try it.

TARTAR Mohammed gave Koran, said: Here is law! Do as written here. Then time come—Koran is not enough—time will give new law. Every new time will give its law.

SATIN That's right. Time came, and it gave us the Penal Code. A strong law—not to be worn out in a hurry.

NASTYA (*Banging on the table with her glass*) Why do I go on living with you—here? I'm going away—anywhere—to the world's end!

BARON Without shoes, your ladyship?

NASTYA Stark naked! Even if I have to crawl on all fours!

BARON It'll make a delightful picture, your ladyship—particularly on all fours.

NASTYA Yes, I'm willing to crawl—just so long as I don't have to see your faces any more. Oh, I'm so disgusted with everything—with all life—all people!

SATIN When you leave, take the Actor with you. He's about ready to go there too. It's come to his knowledge that half a mile from the world's end there is a hospital for organons—

ACTOR (*Peeping out from the top of the stove*) For organisms, you fool!

SATIN For organons poisoned by alcohol—

ACTOR And he will go! Yes, he will. Just wait!

BARON Who's he, sir?

ACTOR I!

BARON Thank you, servant of the goddess—what's her name?—the goddess of drama, of tragedy—what was she called?

ACTOR A muse, fathead! A muse, not a goddess.

SATIN Lachesis—Hera—Aphrodite—Atropos—devil knows which. Do you see what the old man did, Baron? It was he who worked the Actor up to this state.

BARON The old man is a fool—

ACTOR Savages! Ignoramuses! Mel-po-me-ne! Clods! He'll go, you'll see. "Guzzle ye, O somber minds"—a poem by Béranger—yes! He'll find himself a place where there's no—no—

BARON Where there's nothing, sir?

ACTOR Yes, nothing! "This hole—my grave will be—I die of sickness and infirmity!" Why do you live? Why?

BARON You, Edmund Kean or Genius and Dissipation! Stop yelling!

ACTOR Not on your life! I will yell!

NASTYA (*Lifts her head from the table and flings her arms out*) Yell! Let 'em hear you!

BARON What's the sense, your ladyship?

SATIN Leave them alone, Baron! To hell with them! Let them holler! Let them split their heads wide open! There's sense enough in that! Keep out of people's way, as the old man used to say. Yes, he was like yeast, leavening our crowd here—

KLESTCH He beckoned them to go somewhere, but he didn't show them the road.

BARON The old man is a faker.

NASTYA Liar! You're a faker yourself.

BARON Shush, your ladyship.

KLESTCH The old man didn't like the truth—dead set against it, he was— And he was right. I say too—what can we do with the truth when even without it we can't breathe? There's Assan—had his arm crushed on the job—it'll have to be cut off, I suppose—that's truth for you.

SATIN (*Banging on the table with his fist*) Shut up, you brutes, numskulls! That's enough about the old man! (*In a calmer tone*) You're the worst of all,

Baron. You understand nothing—and lie. The old man is not a faker. What's truth? Man—that's the truth! He understood this—you don't. You're dull, like a brick. I understand the old man—I do. Certainly he lied—but it was out of pity for you, the devil take you! There are lots of people who lie out of pity for others—I know it—I've read about it. They lie beautifully, excitingly, with a kind of inspiration. There are lies that soothe, that reconcile one to his lot. There are lies that justify the load that crushed a worker's arm—and hold a man to blame for dying of starvation—I know lies! People weak in spirit—and those who live on the sweat of others—these need lies—the weak find support in them, the exploiters use them as a screen. But a man who is his own master, who is independent and doesn't batten on others—he can get along without lies. Lies are the religion of slaves and bosses. Truth is the god of the free man.

BARON Bravo! Splendid! I agree with you. You speak—like a decent man.

SATIN Why shouldn't a cheat speak well sometimes, when the decent people—speak like cheats? Yes, I've forgotten a lot, but I still know some things. The old man had a head on his shoulders. He had the same effect on me as acid on an old, dirty coin. Let's drink to his health! Fill the glasses—

(NASTYA *pours a glass of beer and hands it to* SATIN, *who continues with a smile*)

The old man lives from within—he looks at everything through his own eyes. I asked him once: Grandpa, what do people live for? (*Trying to imitate* LUKA's *voice and manner*) "They live for something better to come, my friend. Let's say, there are cabinetmakers. They live on, and all of them are just trash. But one day a cabinetmaker is born—such a cabinetmaker as has never been seen on this earth—there's no equal to him—he outshines everybody. The whole cabinetmaking trade is changed by him—and in one jump it moves twenty years ahead. Likewise, all the rest—locksmiths, say—cobblers and other working people—and peasants, too—and even the masters—they all live for something better to come. They live a hundred—and maybe more years for a better man."

(NASTYA *regards* SATIN *fixedly.* KLESTCH *stops work on the accordion and listens. The* BARON, *his head bowed low, drums quietly with his fingers on the table. The* ACTOR, *leaning over from the stove, cautiously tries to lower himself onto the plank bed*)

"Everybody, my friend, everybody lives for something better to come. That's why we have to be considerate of every man— Who knows what's in him, why he was born and what he can do? Maybe he was born for our good fortune—for our greater benefit. And most especially we have to be considerate of youngsters. Kids need plenty of elbowroom. Don't interfere with their life. Be kind to them."

BARON (*Reflectively*) H'm—for something better to come? That reminds me of our family. An old family—goes back to the time of Catherine the Great—noblemen—warriors! The founders came from France. They served the government, kept rising higher and higher. In the reign of Nicholas I, my grandfather, Gustave Debil, held a high post— There was wealth—hundreds of serfs—horses—cooks—

NASTYA Liar! There was not!

BARON (*Jumping to his feet*) What? Well, go on.

NASTYA There wasn't.

BARON (*Shouting*) A house in Moscow! A house in St. Petersburg! Carriages—with the coat of arms!

(KLESTCH *picks up the accordion and, moving to one side, watches the scene*)

NASTYA There wasn't!

BARON Shut up! I say dozens of flunkies!

NASTYA (*With relish*) There wasn't.

BARON I'll kill you.

NASTYA (*Ready to run off*) There weren't any carriages!

SATIN Chuck it, Nastya! Don't tease him.

BARON Just wait—you scum! My grandfather—

NASTYA There was no grandfather! There was nothing!

(SATIN *laughs*)

BARON (*Exhausted by his outburst, sits down on the bench*) Satin, tell this slut— You're laughing too? You don't believe me either? (*Shouts in despair, banging the table*) There was, the devil take you!

NASTYA (*Triumphantly*) A-ah, you scream? You understand now how it feels when somebody doesn't believe you?

KLESTCH (*Returning to the table*) I thought there was going to be a fight—

TARTAR A-ah, people are stupid. Very bad.

BARON I can't permit anybody to insult me! I have proofs—documents, damn it!

SATIN Chuck them! And forget about your grandfather's carriages. In the carriages of the past you can't go anywhere.

BARON But how dare she?

NASTYA Imagine! How dare I!

SATIN You see, she dares. Is she any worse than you? Although, in her past—she certainly didn't have not only carriages and a grandfather, but even a father and mother—

BARON (*Calming down*) Damn you—you can reason calmly. I don't seem to have any character—

SATIN Get yourself one. They're useful. (*A pause*) Have you been visiting the hospital, Nastya?

NASTYA What for?

SATIN To see Natasha.

NASTYA A little late, aren't you? She left the hospital a long time ago. She came out—and vanished. Nobody's seen her anywhere.

SATIN She must have evaporated—fizzed out.

KLESTCH It'll be interesting to see which one does the most to ruin the other one—whether Vasska drags Vassilissa down, or the other way around.

NASTYA Vassilissa will wriggle out of it—she's clever. And Vasska will go to Siberia.

SATIN The penalty for killing in a fight is only jail.

NASTYA That's a pity. Siberia's more his style. I wish

you'd all be packed off to Siberia—or swept off like dirt—into some pit.

SATIN (*Startled*) Have you gone raving mad?

BARON I'll bloody her nose—for her impertinence.

NASTYA You try—just touch me.

BARON I certainly will.

SATIN Drop it. Don't touch her. Don't hurt another human being. I can't get that old man out of my head. (*Laughs*) Don't hurt another human being! But I was hurt once—hurt for the rest of my life with a single blow. What am I supposed to do? Forgive it? Not on your life! Never!

BARON (*To* NASTYA) You have to understand once and for all, you're not my equal. You're—dirt under my feet!

NASTYA You good-for-nothing! Why, you're living off me like a worm off an apple.

(*The men all burst into laughter*)

KLESTCH A sweet little apple! Ah, what a crackbrain!

BARON You can't be cross with this idiot!

NASTYA You're laughing? You faker! You don't think it's funny.

ACTOR (*Somberly*) Give it to them good!

NASTYA If I had the power—I'd smash you all like this! (*She picks up a cup from the table and smashes it on the floor*)

TARTAR Why break cup? Such—pighead!

BARON (*Rising*) I'll teach her good manners!

NASTYA (*Running toward the hall door*) You go to hell!

SATIN (*After her*) Hey! Stop it! Who are you scaring? And what's it all about, anyway?

NASTYA Beasts! I hope you'll be struck dead! Beasts! (*She disappears into the hallway*)

ACTOR (*Somberly*) Amen.

TARTAR Oh! Russian woman, spiteful woman! Too free! Tartar woman—no! She know the law! Nothing stop her!

KLESTCH She needs a good beating.

BARON What a bitch!

KLESTCH (*Trying the accordion*) It's finished. But no sign of the owner. The boy is on a binge again.

SATIN Have a drink.

KLESTCH Thanks! It's time to turn in too.

SATIN Getting used to us?

KLESTCH (*Downs his drink and moves to his plank bed in the corner*) It's all right. It's the same human beings everywhere. At first, you don't see it. Then, you get a good look at them, and it turns out they're all human beings—they're all right.

(*The* TARTAR *spreads out some garment on his plank bed, kneels down, and begins to pray*)

BARON (*To* SATIN, *pointing at the* TARTAR) Look.

SATIN Leave him alone. He's a good fellow. (*Laughs*) I'm in a kind mood today—the devil knows why.

BARON You're always kind when you're oiled—kind and brainy.

SATIN When I'm drunk I like everything. Yes, sir. He's praying? Fine. A man can believe or not believe—it's his own affair. A man is free—he pays for everything himself—for belief and disbelief, for love, for intelligence, and that makes him free. Man—that's the truth. What is man? It's not you, nor I, nor they— No, it's you, I, they, the old man, Napoleon, Mohammed—all in one. (*Outlines the figure of a man in the air*) You understand? It's tremendous! In this are all the beginnings and all the ends. Everything in man, everything for man. Only man exists, the rest is the work of his hands and his brain. Man! It's magnificent! It has a proud ring! Man! We have to respect man, not pity him, not demean him— Respect him, that's what we have to do. Let's drink to man, Baron! (*Rises*) It's good to feel oneself a man! I'm a jailbird, a murderer, a cheat—granted! When I walk down the street, people look at me as at a crook—they side-step and glance back at me—and often say to me: Scoundrel! Charlatan! Work! Work? For what? So that I have what my body needs and feel satisfied? (*Laughs*) I've always despised people whose main thought in life is to feel satisfied. That's not important, Baron—no! Man is above that! Man is above satisfaction!

BARON (*Shaking his head*) You can reason. It's a fine thing—it must warm your heart. I haven't got that—I can't reason. (*Looks around and speaks in a low voice, cautiously*) I feel scared sometimes, old fellow. You know? I get panicky. Because, what's to become of me?

SATIN (*Walking up and down*) Nonsense! What can a man fear?

BARON You know, ever since I can remember myself I've always felt a sort of fog in my head. I could never understand anything. I have an awkward feeling as if all my life I've done nothing but change clothes— But to what end? I can't figure it out. I was given education, wore the uniform of a college for the nobility—but what did I study? I don't remember. I got married—to a woman who was no good, wore tails, then a dressing gown—why? I don't know. I went through my fortune—came to wear an old gray jacket and faded pants— But how did I go broke? I didn't notice. I got a job on a government board—wore a uniform, a cap with a badge—then embezzled government money, had prison clothes put on me, and later changed into this. And all that as if in a dream. It's funny.

SATIN Not very. Stupid, rather.

BARON Yes—I too think it's stupid. Yet there must have been some purpose that I was born for—don't you think?

SATIN (*Laughing*) Probably. A man is born for something better to come. (*Nods his head*)

BARON That Nastya! Where did she run off to? I'd better go look. After all, she's—(*He goes out. There is a pause*)

ACTOR Tartar! (*A pause*) Assan! (*The* TARTAR *turns his head*) Pray—for me.

TARTAR What?

ACTOR (*In a lower voice*) Pray—for me.

TARTAR (*After a pause*) Pray yourself.

ACTOR (*Coming down hurriedly from the stove, walks up to the table, pours himself some vodka with a trembling hand, downs it, and almost runs into the hallway)* I'm gone.

SATIN Hey, you, Sycamore! Where are you going? (*He whistles*)

(*Enter* MEDVEDEV, *wearing a woman's quilted jacket, and* BUBNOV. *They are both slightly drunk.* BUBNOV *carries a string of pretzels in one hand and a few small smoked fishes in the other, with a bottle of vodka under his arm and another sticking out of his pocket*)

MEDVEDEV The camel is a kind of—donkey, only without ears.

BUBNOV Forget it. You're kind of a donkey yourself.

MEDVEDEV The camel has no ears at all—he hears with his nostrils.

BUBNOV (*To* SATIN) Friend! I've been looking for you in all the barrooms. Take a bottle, my hands are full.

SATIN Put the pretzels on the table and that'll free your hand.

BUBNOV You're right, by God! Look, policeman—here's a clever fellow, isn't he?

MEDVEDEV Crooks are all clever—I know. They can't do without brains. A good man can be stupid and still be good. But a bad man must have brains—absolutely. As for the camel, you're wrong. He's a beast of burden, and has no horns—nor teeth—

BUBNOV Where is everybody? Why isn't there anybody here? Hey, you! Come out! I'm treating everybody! Who's over in the corner?

SATIN How soon are you going to drink up your money? Scarecrow!

BUBNOV It'll be soon. This time I've saved up only a little capital. Goiter! Where's Goiter?

KLESTCH (*Walking up to the table*) He's out.

BUBNOV B-rr! Fido! Brlyn—brlyn—brlyn! Turkey! Don't bark, don't cackle! Drink! Enjoy yourselves! Get out of the dumps! I'm treating everybody. I love treating people. If I was rich—I'd have a free barroom—you bet I would. With music—and a choir singing too. Everybody could come, drink, eat, listen to songs—ease their hearts! You're a poor man? Step right in—into my free barroom! Satin! I'd make you—I'd give you half of all my capital! There!

SATIN Give me all you have now.

BUBNOV My whole capital? Now? Take it. Here's a ruble—here's a quarter—here are the coppers—everything!

SATIN That's fine. They'll be safer in my hands—I'll have a game with them—

MEDVEDEV I'm witness—the money's been given for safekeeping—to what amount?

BUBNOV You? You're a camel. We don't need witnesses.

(*Enter* ALYOSHKA, *barefoot*)

ALYOSHKA Folks! I got my feet wet.

BUBNOV Come! Wet your whistle! That'll set you right. My dear fellow—you sing and play—that's fine. But you shouldn't drink. Drinking's bad for a person, my friend. It certainly is.

ALYOSHKA I can tell that by looking at you. The only time you look like a man is when you're drunk. Klestch, have you fixed my accordion? (*Sings, dancing*)

"If this here phiz
Weren't so fair to see,
My girl wouldn't be
So sweet on me."

I'm shivering, boys. It's cold.

MEDVEDEV H'mm!—And may I ask who the girl friend is?

BUBNOV Leave him alone. You're off the police force now, my friend. It's all over, finished. You're neither a policeman nor an uncle any more.

ALYOSHKA Just Aunt Kvashnya's husband.

BUBNOV One of your nieces is in jail, the other is dying.

MEDVEDEV (*Haughtily*) Liar! She's not dying—she's missing!

(SATIN *laughs*)

BUBNOV It's all the same, brother. A man without nieces is no uncle.

ALYOSHKA Your Excellency! (*Sings*)

"My girl friend has money,
I haven't a sou!
But I'm a gay lad,
And the girls think so too!"

Damn, it's cold.

(*Enter the* GOITER. *From time to time, up till the end of the act, other figures, men and women, come in. They undress for sleep and take their places on the plank beds, muttering to themselves*)

GOITER Bubnov! Why did you run away?

BUBNOV Come here! sit down. Now let's sing—you know, my favorite—eh?

TARTAR Night all must sleep. Sing song daytime.

SATIN It's all right, Assan! Come over here!

TARTAR How is all right? Will be noise. When you sing song, is noise.

BUBNOV (*Walking up to the* TARTAR) How's your hand, Assan? Have they cut it off?

TARTAR Why cut off? I wait. Maybe they no have cut it off. Hand is not iron, you cut it off quick.

GOITER You're in a rotten way, Assan. Without a hand you're no good for anything. The likes of us are valued for their hands and their backs. No hand, no man. Yes, yours is a bad case. Come have some vodka—and to hell with it all!

(*Enter* KVASHNYA)

KVASHNYA Ah, my dear lodgers! And isn't it terrible outdoors? Cold—wet! Is my policeman here? Policeman!

MEDVEDEV Here I am.

KVASHNYA Wearing my blouse again? And from the looks of it—a bit under the influence, ain't you? How does that happen?

MEDVEDEV It's on account of his birthday—Bubnov's—And it's cold and wet.

KVASHNYA Wet! Look out! Don't give me any of that! Go to bed.

MEDVEDEV (*Going off to the kitchen*) To bed—that I can—I want to go to bed—it's time.

SATIN You *are* strict with him. Why?

KVASHNYA You can't be otherwise, my friend. A man like him has to be kept in line. I took him on for a companion thinking I'd benefit by it—after all, he's a military man, and you're wild people, while I'm only a woman— And right off the bat he takes to drink! That's of no use to me.

SATIN You didn't choose your assistant very well.

KVASHNYA No, you're wrong. You wouldn't want to live with me—you wouldn't have me. And even if you did, within a week you'd gamble me away at cards—me and my tripe!

SATIN (*Laughing*) You're right there, landlady. I certainly would.

KVASHNYA There you are. Alyoshka!

ALYOSHKA Here he is—that's me.

KVASHNYA What sort of tales are you telling about me?

ALYOSHKA Me? I tell everything—just as it is, honestly. There's a woman, says I. A remarkable woman. In flesh, fat, and bones she's a heavyweight twice over. But she hasn't an ounce of brains!

KVASHNYA Now, that's a lie. I have plenty of brains. But why do you say I beat my policeman?

ALYOSHKA I thought you were beating him when you pulled his hair.

KVASHNYA (*Laughing*) You're a fool! As if you didn't see. Why carry dirt out of the house? Besides, it hurt his pride. He took to drink because of your tales.

ALYOSHKA Then it's true what they say—hens drink too.

(SATIN *and* KLESTCH *laugh*)

KVASHNYA You do have a wicked tongue! I can't make out what sort of man you are, Alyoshka.

ALYOSHKA The very finest sort of man! Can do anything. Something catches my eye, and off I fly.

BUBNOV (*Near the* TARTAR'S *plank bed*) Come along. We'll keep you awake anyway. We'll be singing—all night. Goiter!

GOITER Want a song? All right.

ALYOSHKA I'll play the accompaniment.

SATIN I'm all ears.

TARTAR (*Smiling*) Well, devil Bubnov—now we have some your vodka. Drink we will, play we will, death will come, die we will!

BUBNOV Fill his glass, Satin. Sit down, Goiter. Ah, friends! A man doesn't need much, does he? Here am I—I've had some drink—and I'm happy. Goiter, start my favorite one. I'll sing and weep!

GOITER (*Sings*) "The sun comes up, the sun goes down again—"

BUBNOV (*Picking it up*) "But in my cell it's never light—"

(*The hallway door is flung open. The* BARON, *standing on the threshold, shouts*)

BARON Hey, you! Come—come here! Out there—in the vacant lot the Actor—has hanged himself!

(*There is a general silence. Everybody gazes at the* BARON. NASTYA *appears from behind the* BARON'S *back and slowly, her eyes wide open, walks up to the table*)

SATIN (*In a low voice*) Ah, spoiled the song—the fool!

*Curtain*

# Arthur Schnitzler

## (1862-1931)

No writer gave more vivid and enduring expression to the gaiety and love of pleasure of Viennese society at the turn of the century than Arthur Schnitzler. The witty badinage of the salons and cafés, the reckless bohemianism of artists and men-about-town, the mad pursuit of adventure and love, are all recreated in his plays. Here old Vienna comes back to life: the *Korso* with its broad promenade, the *Ring* with its luxurious shops, the park and gardens of the *Prater,* the secluded walks along the Danube, the dazzling spectacle of the *Burgtheater,* the concert halls and the cafés. Schnitzler's Viennese were men and women of wealth and leisure, bent above all on savoring the pleasures of the moment. The sense of the flight of time, of the transiency of all experience, tinges Schnitzler's dramas with an autumnal sadness, a sign of the decaying world of *fin de siècle* Vienna. A mirror of his times, Schnitzler wrote of his fellow citizens with delicacy and grace, with charm and refinement, but also with a melancholy awareness of the emptiness of their daily lives.

Schnitzler spent his whole life in Vienna. His father was a famous Jewish throat specialist and the founder of one of the leading medical journals of the day. His son followed in his profession, receiving his medical degree at the University of Vienna in 1885 with a thesis on the hypnotic treatment of neurosis. Schnitzler was one of the first writers to embody the findings of modern psychiatric investigations in his works, and Sigmund Freud, who moved in the same Viennese circles, acknowledged his independent discoveries in depth psychology. Even while beginning his literary career, the young doctor reviewed medical publications on such subjects as hysteria, nervous disorders, hypnosis, sexual pathology, and psychotherapy. Illness of the mind and spirit, as well as of the body, is a persistent theme in Schnitzler's work, and is treated with the clinical scrutiny and compassionate understanding of a skilled physician. Many of the *raisonneurs* of his plays are in fact medical practitioners, seeking to diagnose human ailments and to prescribe a remedy. Yet like a man of science, the playwright is skeptical of automatic or universal solutions. This skepticism moves hand in hand with a genuine sympathy for human suffering and a pervasive melancholy inspired by an awareness of the dying and the dead. The absorption of the individual in the pleasures of the moment is an instinctive effort to escape from the certainty of death. The charm of imperial Vienna, which Schnitzler depicts with wonderful exuberance, is itself a mirage that cannot last.

Schnitzler's early writings prefigure the course of his entire career. His first publications were satiric poems, written at 18, pointing in a light-hearted and sardonic way to the close connection of sex and money. Illicit love is indeed the central theme of all of his work—short stories and novels as well as poems and plays. The relationship of the spurned lover to his former mistress, of the deceived husband to his unfaithful wife, and the like, provides the playwright with an unusual range of emotional experience, embracing rage and hysteria as well as compassionate and sympathetic understanding. Sexual adventure is wanton and anarchic in Schnitzler's plays, but this anarchy is often concealed by an illusion of "love" that makes life bearable.

His first play, *Anatol* (1892), is a triumph of wit and polished urbanity. The refined and sophisticated dialogue of the passionate but frivolous lover, Anatol, and his cynical and intellectual companion, Max, is itself a commentary on the emptiness of reckless hedonism. Anatol is close indeed to Hofmannsthal's Claudio of *Death and the Fool,* and it was fitting that Schnitzler's younger Viennese contemporary should write the prologue to the play. Schnitzler himself had used the pen name of Anatol in his earlier writings. In his morbidity and self-involvement, Anatol is typical of the young aristocrat of the *fin de siècle:* "There are so many diseases and only one health. . . . One must always be just as healthy as the others—but one can be ill quite differently from anyone else!" Each of the seven scenes of the play presents a new aspect of Anatol's private life and love affairs. The talk is always amusing and clever but the vignettes of sexual dalliance reveal the underlying vanity of Anatol's turbulent and confused existence. Life is nothing more to him than a series of easy flirtations and passing romances, where men and women are slaves of habit, whim, or desire, but where no one is deeply committed or badly hurt. Anatol moves from scene to scene changing partners as he might change his hat, never facing the reality of his situation. As Max remarks in a moment of apparent crisis: "You don't want the truth . . . you want to keep your illusions." Like Pirandello and other masters of the grotesque whom he anticipates, Schnitzler sees illusion as the necessary evasion of the pain and suffering of naked truth.

The irony of fate and the hollowness of convention are the principal implications of Schnitzler's next play,

*Liebelei* (*Light-o'-Love*). The protagonist, Fritz, is compelled to fight a duel over a woman in whom he has not the slightest interest. He is killed and his beloved Christine, feeling that he has died for another, commits suicide. For her, Fritz has meant everything; for him, she believes, she was only a passing flirtation. Christine is a larger figure than the "sweet young thing" who flits in and out of Schnitzler's comedies, light and free, caring only for the love of the moment. Fritz cannot defy the "call of honor" and dooms himself and the woman who might have made him capable of genuine love.

The world of dream, pretense, and illusion moves side by side in Schnitzler's art with the moral and social corruption of the times. His interest in the ebb and flow of inner life led him to write what is probably the first stream-of-consciousness narrative in German literature in the story, *Leutnant Gustl*. His immediate source of inspiration was the French symbolist, Edouard Dujardin, from whom James Joyce developed the interior monologue in his novel, *Ulysses*. Schnitzler's tale presented an Austrian army officer in an unfavorable light, and, as a result, he was tried by court-martial in 1901 and deprived of his commission as a medical officer in the army reserve. The nationalistic and anti-Semitic press acclaimed the decision while abusing Schnitzler in vile and filthy terms. Yet, this abuse was mild compared to the reaction to his next play.

*Reigen* (*Hands Around* or *La Ronde*) was written in the winter of 1896-97 and then, as was Schnitzler's habit with a new play, set aside for a time. The original title was *Liebesreigen* (*Hands Around in Love*) but he shortened it at the suggestion of the Berlin drama critic, Alfred Kerr. In 1900 Schnitzler had 200 copies of the play printed at his own expense, not for sale but for distribution to friends. The book was soon a sensation in literary circles, moving rapidly from hand to hand. In 1903 Schnitzler's publisher brought out a regular edition. At once it was condemned as a subversive and obscene work and many papers would not review it. A public reading in Vienna was forbidden by the police; in Germany, the play was confiscated and banned. For many years Schnitzler refused to authorize its performance. It was first produced in Budapest in 1912, for the play was not copyrighted in Hungary and the author could not prevent it. The performance was tactless and offensive, and the police banned the play two days later. It is almost incredible now to look back on the riots in Munich and Berlin, the sensational trial, and the stormy scenes in the Austrian parliament produced by the play in the years immediately after World War I. Max Reinhardt's company attempted to give the play a serious artistic performance, but the effort ended in the courts after hostile spectators hurled stinkbombs in the theatre. The Viennese premiere took place in February, 1921. Angry denunciations of *La Ronde* as "Jewish filth" followed in the press, and after a few performances 600 members of the proto-Nazi Deutsche Volkspartei (German People's Party) stormed the theatre and wrecked it. The event was hailed in the nationalistic press as "A Triumph of Viennese Christian Youth." Schnitzler's play may have offended the Viennese, but not because of any eroticism or pornography. Much must depend on the tact and sensitivity of the actors, for the play could readily become obscene in coarse hands. As Schnitzler wrote it, however, it is a somber and melancholy portrayal of the manners and morals of his countrymen. The sexual looseness of both men and women which reduces all human relationships to physical pleasure could be found in any metropolitan city of wealth and leisure. In mirroring the corruption of his society, Schnitzler refused to sentimentalize "love" or to idealize it with a false luster. His view of the sordid and commonplace character of sex is uncompromisingly frank, yet he depicts his characters with a verve and humor that makes for exhilarating if thoughtful comedy. It is fitting that in the final scene he should bring together the highest and lowest members of the community. The final "Good morning!" is in effect an invitation to the Viennese to see themselves as they really are.

*La Ronde* was followed by a number of "problem plays," of which the most important is *Professor Bernhardi* (1912), a study of official anti-Semitism. Schnitzler thought of himself as a German rather than a Jewish writer, but he suffered from anti-Semitism all his life, and once barely escaped injury in Prague at the hands of Jew-baiting thugs. His play therefore rests, at least in part, on personal experience. Professor Bernhardi, a director of a hospital, is concerned above all with the welfare of his patients. He refuses to admit a priest to a dying invalid's room because the mere sight of the cleric, come to administer last rites, would rob the patient of her blissful ignorance of her condition. The patient dies, a scandal ensues, and Bernhardi is forced to resign. He is tried and convicted of forcibly hindering a priest from the exercise of his sacred duty, and goes to jail for two months. Despite the help of politicians and a shift in public opinion in his favor, Bernhardi refuses to let himself become a political issue. He is released from jail, regains his license, and goes back to his work as a doctor. Schnitzler clearly sees an analogy between the artist's dedication to his calling and the scientist's pursuit of his convictions and his science, come what may.

Schnitzler's plays were banned by the Nazis, and in recent years his works have not recovered their former popularity. Yet our debt to him is considerable: few modern playwrights have surpassed him in courage and fortitude. The naturalistic subject matter of *La Ronde* was hardly usual in dramas of contemporary life sixty years ago, and Schnitzler must be placed alongside of Ibsen and Strindberg, Hauptmann and Wedekind, for his contribution to the expansion of the materials of the drama. A master of psychological realism, he possessed a limited but sure talent that enabled him to probe sensitively and deftly, like a skillful physician, into the innermost recesses and cleavages of modern life.

# LA RONDE

## *Ten Dialogues*

Translated by Hans Weigert and Patricia Newhall

CHARACTERS

THE GIRL OF THE STREETS
THE SOLDIER
THE MAID
THE YOUNG GENTLEMAN
THE YOUNG WIFE
THE HUSBAND
THE SWEET YOUNG MISS
THE POET
THE ACTRESS
THE COUNT

## Scene One

### *The Girl of the Streets and the Soldier*

*Late in the evening. At the Augarten Bridge.*[1] A SOLDIER *on his way home comes in whistling*

GIRL OF THE STREETS Hey there, my beautiful angel. (SOLDIER *turns back, then walks on again*)

GIRL OF THE STREETS Aren't you going to come along?

SOLDIER You mean me? Beautiful angel, ha!

GIRL OF THE STREETS Of course, who else? Do come with me. I live close by.

SOLDIER I've got no time. I'm due back at the barracks.

GIRL OF THE STREETS You'll be back there in plenty of time. It's nicer with me.

SOLDIER (*Near her*) Well, maybe.

GIRL OF THE STREETS Hey! A patrol may pass by any moment.

SOLDIER A patrol? I'm armed too.

GIRL OF THE STREETS Well let's go then.

SOLDIER Leave me alone. Anyway, I'm broke.

[1] A bridge over the Danube Canal in the center of Vienna.

GIRL OF THE STREETS You don't need money.

SOLDIER (*Stops. They are under a street light*) You don't want money? Then why are you here?

GIRL OF THE STREETS Civilians pay me. I'll always give it to someone like you for free.

SOLDIER Oh, you're the one Huber told me about. . . .

GIRL OF THE STREETS I don't know any Huber.

SOLDIER Yeh, you'd be the one. That's right. The café over there. He went home with you.

GIRL OF THE STREETS Lots have gone home with me from that café . . . oh, lots!

SOLDIER All right, then. Let's go.

GIRL OF THE STREETS What now? You're in a hurry now, huh?

SOLDIER Well, what's the point of waiting? I'm back on duty at ten.

GIRL OF THE STREETS How long have you been in the army?

SOLDIER That's none of your business. Live far from here?

GIRL OF THE STREETS Ten minutes' walk.

SOLDIER That's too far for me. Give me a kiss?

GIRL OF THE STREETS (*Kisses him*) I like it better that way when I like someone.

SOLDIER I don't. No. I'm not going with you. It's too far for me.

GIRL OF THE STREETS Tell you what. Come tomorrow afternoon.

SOLDIER Okay. Give me the address.

GIRL OF THE STREETS Only—maybe you won't come.

SOLDIER You have my word.

GIRL OF THE STREETS Say . . . know something—if it's too far to my place tonight . . . then . . . ah . . . (*She points toward the Danube*)

SOLDIER What's there?

GIRL OF THE STREETS It's nice and quiet there. No one around there this time of night.

SOLDIER Okay, then. But hurry.

GIRL OF THE STREETS Be careful. It's dark there. One slip, and you're in the Danube.

SOLDIER Might be the best thing.

GIRL OF THE STREETS Hey! Hold on a moment. We'll be coming to a bench.

SOLDIER You know your way around.

GIRL OF THE STREETS I'd like to have someone like you for a sweetheart.
SOLDIER I'd make you jealous.
GIRL OF THE STREETS I'd cure you soon enough.
SOLDIER Ha!
GIRL OF THE STREETS Not so loud. Sometimes a cop stumbles down here. You'd never think we were right in the middle of Vienna, would you?
SOLDIER Come here!
GIRL OF THE STREETS Hey, go easy there. One slip and we're in the river.
SOLDIER (*Has grabbed hold of her*) Oh, don't be silly.
GIRL OF THE STREETS Hold on tight then.
SOLDIER Don't be afraid. . . .

* * *

GIRL OF THE STREETS It'd have been nicer on the bench.
SOLDIER Well, what's the difference? Okay, up you come! (*Giving her a hand*)
GIRL OF THE STREETS What's the hurry?
SOLDIER Got to get back to the barracks. I'm late now.
GIRL OF THE STREETS Tell me, what's your name?
SOLDIER Why do you want to know my name?
GIRL OF THE STREETS Mine's—Leocadia.
SOLDIER Ha! I never heard of that name before.
GIRL OF THE STREETS Listen . . .
SOLDIER What is it now?
GIRL OF THE STREETS How about a dime for the janitor?
SOLDIER Ha! . . . Think I'm your meal ticket? So long Leocadia!
GIRL OF THE STREETS Tight wad . . . pimp!
(*He is gone*)

## Scene Two

### *The Soldier and the Maid*

*The Prater.*[1] *Sunday evening. A path leading from the Wurstelprater or amusement park out into dark avenues of trees. The conglomeration of music from the Wurstelprater is heard—also a dance band, composed mainly of wind instruments, playing a polka.*

MAID Please tell me, sir, why did you have to leave so urgently?
(SOLDIER *laughs embarrassedly*)
MAID It was so beautiful and I just love to dance.
(SOLDIER *puts his arm around her waist*)
MAID (*Letting him*) Why are you holding me so tight? We're not dancing now.

[1] A large and fashionable park along the Danube.

SOLDIER What's your name? Kathi?
MAID You've got a Kathi on your mind.
SOLDIER Oh yes. I remember. Marie.
MAID Goodness it's dark over here. I'm getting scared.
SOLDIER When I'm with you you've got nothing to fear. You're quite safe.
MAID But where are we going? There's no one around at all. Please let's go back.
SOLDIER (*Puffing at his cigar till it glows*) There! It's already getting lighter.
MAID Ooh! What are you doing? If I thought you were going to. . . .
SOLDIER Devil take me if any of the others at the dance were as soft as you Marie.
MAID Have you tried out all of them this way?
SOLDIER Oh, you notice. Dancing. You find out a lot of things. Ha!
MAID You danced more with the blond with the sour face than you did with me.
SOLDIER She's a friend of one of my pals.
MAID The corporal with the turned-up mustache?
SOLDIER No, no, of the civilian. You know—the one talking with me at the table before, with the hoarse voice?
MAID Oh, yes. I know. He's a fresh guy.
SOLDIER Did he try something with you? I'll show him. What did he do?
MAID Oh, nothing. I just saw him playing around with the others.
SOLDIER Tell me, Miss . . .
MAID Ooh! You'll burn me with your cigar.
SOLDIER Oh, pardon, Miss . . . or may I call you . . . Marie?
MAID We're not such good friends yet.
SOLDIER There's many people who act like good friends who can't even stand each other.
MAID Next time, when we . . . But Mr. Frank
SOLDIER You remember my name!
MAID But Mr. Frank . . .
SOLDIER Just say, "Frank," Miss Marie.
MAID Now don't get so fresh. Sh! What if somebody should come!
SOLDIER What if they did come? They couldn't see two steps in front of them.
MAID But, Mercy sake, where are we going to?
SOLDIER Look! There's a couple just like us!
MAID Where? I can't see a thing.
SOLDIER There. Just ahead of us.
MAID Why do you say like us?
SOLDIER Oh, I just mean—they like each other too.
MAID (*Stumbles*) Hey look out! What was that? I nearly fell.
SOLDIER It's the railings they put around the grass.
MAID Don't push me. I'll fall.
SOLDIER Sh! Not so loud!
MAID Sir! Now I'm really going to scream! What are you doing . . . hey . . .
SOLDIER There's no one around for miles.
MAID Let's go back with the rest of them.
SOLDIER But we don't need them, Marie, what we need is . . . uh, huh . . . (*Laughs*)

MAID Mr. Frank, please! For Heaven's sake!! Now listen, if I'd had . . . any idea . . . oh! . . . oh! . . . all right. . . .

* * *

SOLDIER (*Blissfully*) Come on again . . . Ah-h! . . .
MAID I can't see your face at all.
SOLDIER My face? so what . . . !

* * *

SOLDIER Well, Miss Marie. You can't remain here on the grass.
MAID Come, Frank, help me up!
SOLDIER (*He grabs her*) Okay. Upsa daisy.
MAID Mercy me, Frank.
SOLDIER What's the matter with Frank?
MAID You're a bad man, Frank.
SOLDIER Yes I am. Wait a moment.
MAID What did you let me go for?
SOLDIER I just want to light my cigar.
MAID It's pitch dark.
SOLDIER Well, tomorrow morning it'll be light again.
MAID Tell me at least—do you like me?
SOLDIER Well you must have felt that, Miss Marie. (*He laughs*)
MAID Where are we going?
SOLDIER Why back, of course!
MAID Oh, please, Frank, don't walk so fast.
SOLDIER Why not? I don't like walking around in the pitch dark.
MAID Tell me, Frank, do you—like me?
SOLDIER But I just now told you I liked you.
MAID Will you give me a kiss?
SOLDIER (*Condescending*) There . . . listen! There's the music again.
MAID I do declare. You want to go back dancing again?
SOLDIER Of course. What else?
MAID But, Frank, listen. I must be going home. I'll get a scolding anyhow, the lady of the house is such a . . . she'd like it best if I never went out at all.
SOLDIER All right, run along then.
MAID I just had an idea, Mr. Frank . . . that you might take me home.
SOLDIER Home? Huh?
MAID Oh, please, it's so sad—going home alone!
SOLDIER Where do you live?
MAID Not too far—Porzellanstrasse.
SOLDIER Oh! Then we go the same way. . . . But it's still too early for me! I want to have some fun. . . . I have a late pass tonight. Don't have to be back before twelve. I'm going to dance.
MAID I know. It's that blond's turn. The one with the sour face.
SOLDIER Ha! . . . Her face isn't that bad.
MAID Heavens, how wicked you men are! I bet you do this to every girl.
SOLDIER That'd be too many.
MAID Frank, please. Not tonight—stay just with me tonight . . . huh. . . .
SOLDIER Okay, okay. But I suppose I can dance.
MAID I'm not going to dance with anyone else tonight.
SOLDIER There it is already.
MAID What?
SOLDIER The hall. That was fast wasn't it? And they're still playing that piece. (*Humming with the band*) Ta-ta-ta-tum. All right if you want to wait for me to take you home. Otherwise, so long. . . .
MAID Yes, I'll be waiting.
SOLDIER Why don't you order a glass of beer, Miss Marie? (*Turning to a blond dancing*) Miss, may I have the next dance?

## Scene Three

### *The Maid and the Young Gentleman*

*A hot summer afternoon. The parents have already left for the country. It is the cook's afternoon off. The* MAID *is in the kitchen writing a letter to her lover, the soldier. A bell rings from the room of the* YOUNG GENTLEMAN. *She gets up and goes to answer.*

*The* YOUNG MAN *is lying on a chaise longue, smoking and reading a French novel.*

MAID What do you wish, Sir?
GENTLEMAN Oh, yes . . . Marie . . . yes, I did ring. . . . Now what was it I wanted? . . . Oh, that's right, you might let down the blinds, Marie. . . . It's cooler with the blinds down. . . . (MAID *goes to the window and lets the Venetian blinds down. The* YOUNG GENTLEMAN *goes on reading*) That's too much, Marie. Now I haven't any light at all.
MAID (*As she adjusts the blinds*) The young master is always so hard at work.
GENTLEMAN (*Passing over this loftily*) That's better. (*The* MAID *goes out. The* YOUNG GENTLEMAN *tries to go on reading; soon he lets the book fall; rings again. The* MAID *comes in again*)
GENTLEMAN Listen, Marie . . . now, um, what was I going to say? . . . Oh . . . yes, do we have any cognac in the house?
MAID Yes, Master Alfred, but it'll be locked away.
GENTLEMAN Well, who's got the key?
MAID Lini has the key.
GENTLEMAN Who's Lini?
MAID The cook, Master Alfred.
GENTLEMAN Well then, ask Lini for it.
MAID Yes, but it's Lini's afternoon off.
GENTLEMAN I see.
MAID Should I run over to the cafe and bring the young master . . . ?

GENTLEMAN No, no. . . . It's too hot today. I don't really need cognac. Listen, Marie, just bring me a glass of water. Wait, Marie—let it run. I want it cold.

(*The* MAID *leaves. The* YOUNG GENTLEMAN *watches her as she goes off. At the door she turns; he is now looking up into space. The* MAID *turns on the faucet and lets the water run. In the meantime, she goes into her little closet, washes her hands, arranges her braids, curled against her ears, in the mirror. She brings the* YOUNG GENTLEMAN *the water, stepping close to the chaise. The* YOUNG GENTLEMAN *half rises. The* MAID *takes the glass from the saucer and puts it into the* YOUNG GENTLEMAN'S *hand. Their fingers touch.*)

GENTLEMAN Thank you. . . . What's the matter? Be careful. Put the glass back on the saucer. (*He lies back and stretches himself*) What's the time?

MAID Five o'clock, Master Alfred.

GENTLEMAN I see. Five o'clock. That's all right. . . .

(*The* MAID *goes; at the door she turns; the* YOUNG GENTLEMAN *has been looking at her; she notices and smiles. The* YOUNG GENTLEMAN *lies where he is for awhile, then suddenly gets up. He walks to the door; then returns and lies down on the chaise. He tries to read again. In a couple of minutes he again rings. The* MAID *enters with a smile which she makes no attempt to hide*)

GENTLEMAN Listen, Marie, what was I going to ask you. . . . Oh, yes, did Dr. Schueller come by this morning?

MAID No. No one was here this morning.

GENTLEMAN That's strange. Then Dr. Schueller wasn't here? You know who Dr. Schueller is?

MAID Certainly. The big gentleman with the big black beard.

GENTLEMAN Yes, but perhaps he *did* call?

MAID No, sir. No one at all was here.

GENTLEMAN (*Taking the plunge*) Come here, Marie.

MAID (*Coming a little closer*) Yes, Sir.

GENTLEMAN Nearer . . . yes . . . um. . . . I just thought. . . .

MAID What did you do, Sir?

GENTLEMAN I just thought . . . I thought . . . about your blouse. What sort of material is it?

MAID (*Comes forward*) What's wrong with my blouse. Don't you like it, Sir?

GENTLEMAN (*Takes hold of the blouse and, in so doing, draws the* MAID *down on him*) Blue!! That's a very nice blue. (*Simply*) You're very prettily dressed, Marie.

MAID But Sir.

GENTLEMAN Oh, what's the matter? (*He has opened the blouse. Matter-of-fact*) You've got beautiful white skin, Marie.

MAID Sir, you flatter me.

GENTLEMAN (*Kissing her bosom*) That can't hurt you.

MAID Oh no!

GENTLEMAN Because you're sighing! Why do you sigh so deeply?

MAID But Master Alfred!!!

GENTLEMAN And what pretty slippers you have on. . . .

MAID . . . but . . . Sir . . . if the doorbell . . . should ring. . . .

GENTLEMAN Who's going to ring at this time of day?

MAID But, Master Alfred . . . Look, it's so light!

GENTLEMAN Don't make such a fuss, Marie. I've seen you with less than this on. A couple of nights ago when I came home late and went for a glass of water, the door to your room was open . . . well. . . .

MAID (*Hides her face*) Oh, my, I didn't know Master Alfred could be so wicked.

GENTLEMAN Well, that time I saw a whole lot . . . this . . . and this . . . and this . . . and . . .

MAID But Master Alfred!

GENTLEMAN Come here . . . closer . . . that's right, yes . . .

MAID But if someone should ring now . . .

GENTLEMAN Now stop it, for Heaven's sake. If worst comes to worst we just won't open the door. . . .

* * *

(*The doorbell rings*)

GENTLEMAN Damn it! (*Pause*) What a racket the fellow's making! Maybe he rang earlier and we just didn't notice.

MAID Oh, no, I was listening all the time.

GENTLEMAN Well, go and have a look—through the peephole.

MAID Master Alfred . . . You're . . . really so . . . wicked!

GENTLEMAN Run along now. Go take a look.

(*The* MAID *goes. The* YOUNG GENTLEMAN *quickly pulls up the Venetian blinds*)

MAID (*Comes back*) Well, anyway, he's gone now. There's no one there. Maybe it was Dr. Schueller.

GENTLEMAN (*Disagreeably affected*) Well, all right, thank you. (MAID *comes closer,* YOUNG GENTLEMAN *retreating*) Look Marie, I'm going to the café.

MAID (*Tenderly*) Already . . . Master Alfred?

GENTLEMAN (*Severely*) I'm going to the café now. If Dr. Schueller should come, I . . . I . . . I'm—in the Café.

(*He goes into the next room. The* MAID *takes a cigar from the smoking table, slips it into her blouse, and goes out*)

## Scene Four

### *The Young Gentleman and the Young Wife*

*A house in the Schwindgasse furnished with banal elegance. Evening. The* YOUNG GENTLEMAN *has just entered and lights the candles, still wearing his hat and overcoat. He opens the door to the next room and glances in. The candles in the living room throw enough light through the door to reveal a four-poster bed against the opposite wall. A fireplace in the corner of the bedroom illuminates the bed curtains with a red glow. He takes an atomizer from the dresser and sprays the pillows with violet perfume. Then he goes through both rooms, continually squeezing the bulb until the scent of violets is everywhere. Only then does he remove his hat and overcoat. Sitting down in the blue velvet easy chair, he lights a cigarette. After a few moments he jumps up to make sure that the shutters are closed. Suddenly he goes to the bedroom again and opens the drawer of the bedside table. He finds a tortoise shell hairpin. Looking for a place to hide it, he finally puts it in the pocket of his overcoat. Next he opens a cupboard in the living room, takes out a silver tray with a bottle of cognac and two liquor glasses and puts everything on the table. Going to the overcoat, he withdraws a small white package, opens it and puts it next to the cognac; from the cupboard he now takes two plates and cutlery which he also puts on the table (meanwhile taking a candied chestnut from the package and eating it). He then pours himself a glass of cognac, drinks it, looks at his watch and starts pacing up and down the room, pausing in front of a mirror to comb his hair and small mustache. Then he listens at the door to the lobby—there is not a sound—and finally he closes the blue curtains over the door leading to the bedroom. A bell rings, startling him slightly, and he sits down in the easy chair, to rise as the door opens and the* YOUNG WIFE *enters.*

*The* YOUNG WIFE, *heavily veiled, closes the door behind her and stands still with her left hand on her heart as though calming a tremendous emotion.*

GENTLEMAN (*Approaching the* YOUNG WIFE, *takes her left hand and imprints a kiss on the white, black trimmed glove; softly*) I thank you.

WIFE Alfred—Alfred!

GENTLEMAN Come in, dear lady . . . come in, Madame Emma.

WIFE Let me be for a moment, please—oh, please, Alfred! (*She stays close by the door. The* YOUNG GENTLEMAN *stands before her holding her hand*) But where am I actually?

GENTLEMAN With me.

WIFE This house is terrifying, Alfred.

GENTLEMAN But it's a very elegant house.

WIFE I met two gentlemen on the stairs.

GENTLEMAN Acquaintances?

WIFE I don't know. It's possible.

GENTLEMAN Pardon, dear lady—surely—you know your acquaintances.

WIFE But I couldn't see a thing.

GENTLEMAN Even if it had been your best friends, they couldn't possibly have recognized you. Even if I didn't know it were you . . . this veil . . .

WIFE There are two.

GENTLEMAN Wouldn't you like to come in? At least do take off your hat.

WIFE What are you thinking of, Alfred? I told you—five minutes. No, not a moment longer! I swear. . . .

GENTLEMAN And the veil?

WIFE There are two.

GENTLEMAN All right, both veils then . . . at least I might be able to see you.

WIFE Do you love me, Alfred?

GENTLEMAN (*Deeply hurt*) Emma, need you ask me . . . ?

WIFE It's so warm in here.

GENTLEMAN But you're wearing your fur cape—really you'll catch cold!

WIFE (*At last comes into the room, throwing herself into an armchair*) I'm exhausted.

GENTLEMAN Permit me. (*He takes her veils off, takes out the hatpin, puts hat, pin, and veil aside. The* YOUNG WIFE *allows him*)

(*The* GENTLEMAN *stands before her shaking his head*)

WIFE What is it?

GENTLEMAN I've never seen you looking so beautiful.

WIFE Why is that?

GENTLEMAN Alone . . . alone with you . . . Emma . . . I. (*He sinks on one knee beside the armchair, takes both her hands and covers them with kisses*)

WIFE And now, let me go. What you asked of me I have done. (*The* YOUNG GENTLEMAN *lets his head sink on to her lap*) You promised me to be good.

GENTLEMAN Yes.

WIFE It's stifling in this room.

GENTLEMAN (*Gets up*) You still have your cape on.

WIFE Lay it next to my hat. (*The* YOUNG GENTLEMAN *takes off her cape and puts it on the sofa along with the hat and the other things*) And now—adieu—

GENTLEMAN Emma!

WIFE The five minutes are long past.

GENTLEMAN No, not even one.

WIFE Alfred, please, tell me to the minute what the time is.

GENTLEMAN It is exactly quarter past six.

WIFE I should have been at my sister's long ago.

GENTLEMAN You can often see your sister. . . .

WIFE Oh dear, Alfred, why did you tempt me to come?

GENTLEMAN Because I . . . adore you, Emma.

WIFE How many have you told the same thing?

GENTLEMAN Since I met you, none.

WIFE What a frivolous woman I am! If anyone had predicted this a week ago . . . or even yesterday . . .

GENTLEMAN And the day before yesterday you had already promised me.

WIFE You urged me so. But I didn't want to, God is my witness—I didn't want to do it. Yesterday I had firmly decided . . . Do you know that as late as last night I wrote you a long letter?

GENTLEMAN I didn't receive any.

WIFE I tore it up. I should have sent it to you instead.

GENTLEMAN It's better like this.

WIFE Oh, no, it's terrible . . . of me. I don't understand myself. Alfred. Adieu, Alfred, please let me go. (*The* YOUNG GENTLEMAN *takes her in his arms and covers her face with passionate kisses*) Is this . . . the way you keep your promise?

GENTLEMAN One more kiss! Just one.

WIFE The last! (*He kisses her, she reciprocates, and their lips stay together a long time*)

GENTLEMAN Shall I tell you something, Emma? It is only now that I realize what happiness is. (*The* YOUNG WIFE *sinks back in the armchair. The* YOUNG GENTLEMAN *sits on the arm of the chair putting his arm gently around her neck*) Or rather, realize what happiness might be. (*The* YOUNG WIFE *gives a profound sigh. The* YOUNG GENTLEMAN *kisses her again*)

WIFE Alfred, Alfred, what are you doing to me?

GENTLEMAN It's not really so uncomfortable here, is it? And we are so safe. It's a thousand times more beautiful than a meeting in the open air. . . .

WIFE Oh, please don't remind me of those.

GENTLEMAN I shall remember even those with a thousand delights! For me every minute that I can spend at your side is a sweet memory.

WIFE Do you still remember the Industry Ball?

GENTLEMAN Do I remember? That's where I sat near you through the whole of the supper . . . quite near you. The champagne your husband—

(*The* YOUNG WIFE *gives him a hurt look*)

GENTLEMAN And speaking of champagne—Emma, wouldn't you like a glass of cognac?

WIFE Maybe just a drop. But first, give me a glass of water.

GENTLEMAN Oh, certainly . . . now, where is . . . oh, yes.

(*He draws the curtains back and goes into the bedroom. The* YOUNG WIFE *looks after him. The* YOUNG GENTLEMAN *returns with a decanter of water and two glasses*)

WIFE Where have you been?

GENTLEMAN In the—next room. (*He pours a glass of water for her*)

WIFE Now I'm going to ask you something, Alfred, and promise me you will tell me the truth.

GENTLEMAN I promise. . . .

WIFE Was there ever another woman in this apartment?

GENTLEMAN But, Emma, this house is twenty years old!

WIFE . . . Alfred . . . with you . . . together . . . You know what I mean.

GENTLEMAN With me, here? Emma! Oh, Emma, how could you think anything like that!

WIFE So you have . . . how shall I . . . ? But no, I mustn't ask. It's better not to ask questions which bring their own punishment.

GENTLEMAN But what's wrong? What's happened to you? What punishment?

WIFE No, no, no, I mustn't think about it—otherwise I'd sink into the ground for very shame.

GENTLEMAN (*Still with the decanter in his hand, sadly shakes his head*) Emma, if only you had any idea how much you hurt me! (*The* YOUNG WIFE *pours herself a glass of cognac*) I'll tell you something, Emma. If you're ashamed to be here—that is to say, if you're so indifferent to me—if you don't feel that for me you represent all the happiness in the world —then please go.

WIFE Yes, I think I'd better.

GENTLEMAN (*Seizing her hand*) But if you realize that I cannot live without you, that to kiss your hand means more to me than all the caresses of all the women in the world! Emma, I'm not like other young men who can turn a beautiful phrase . . . perhaps I am too naive.

WIFE But what if you *were* like the other young men?

GENTLEMAN Then you would not be here today because you are not like the other women.

WIFE How do you know that?

GENTLEMAN (*He draws her down to the sofa and sits close beside her*) I've thought a great deal about you. I know you are unhappy.

(*The* YOUNG WIFE *looks pleased*)

WIFE That's right.

GENTLEMAN Life is so empty—so meaningless. And so short . . . so terribly short. There is only one way to happiness; to find someone to love you. . . . Give me half.

(*The* YOUNG WIFE *has taken a candied pear from the table and put it into her mouth. She offers it to him with her lips*)

WIFE (*She catches the* YOUNG GENTLEMAN'S *hands, which threaten to go astray*) What are you doing, Alfred? Is this the way to keep your promise?

GENTLEMAN (*Swallows the candied fruit; then says, more boldly*) But life is so short!

WIFE (*Weakly*) But that's no reason . . .

GENTLEMAN (*Mechanically*) But it is.

WIFE (*More weakly*) Now look, Alfred, you promised to be good . . . and it's so light. . . .

GENTLEMAN Come, come, my only one, my only. . . . (*He lifts her off the sofa*)

WIFE What are you doing?

GENTLEMAN Inside it's not light at all.

WIFE Is there another room?

GENTLEMAN (*Carrying her*) A lovely one . . . and quite dark.

WIFE Let's stay here instead. (*The* YOUNG GENTLEMAN *has already got her through the curtains into the bedroom—he begins to unhook her dress at the waist*) You're so . . . oh, Heavens, what are you doing to me? . . . Alfred!

GENTLEMAN Emma, I worship you!

WIFE Wait, please, at least wait. . . . (*Weakly*) Go, I'll call you . . .

GENTLEMAN Let me . . . let you help me . . . let . . . me . . . help . . . you. . . .

WIFE No, no, you'll tear everything!

GENTLEMAN You don't wear a corset?

WIFE I never wear a corset. Neither does the Empress. But you may undo my boots. (*The* YOUNG GENTLE-

MAN *unbuttons her boots, kisses her feet, and goes into the other room. The* YOUNG WIFE *slips into bed*) Ooh, it's so chilly.

GENTLEMAN It'll be warm in a minute.

WIFE (*Laughing softly*) You think so?

GENTLEMAN (*Somewhat worried, to himself*) She shouldn't have said that!

(*He undresses in the dark*)

WIFE (*Tenderly*) Come, come, come.

GENTLEMAN (*In a better mood at once*) At once. . . .

WIFE There's such a scent of violets here.

GENTLEMAN That's yourself . . . yes . . . you. (*He comes to her*)

WIFE Alfred . . . Alfred!!!!!!

GENTLEMAN Emma . . .

* * *

Obviously I love you far too much . . . that's why . . . I'm nearly out of my mind!

WIFE. . . .

GENTLEMAN I've been delirious for days. I dreamed about this.

WIFE Don't make so much of it.

GENTLEMAN Oh, of course not, but it's only natural that . . .

WIFE Don't . . . don't . . . You're nervous. Calm down a little.

GENTLEMAN Do you know Stendhal?

WIFE Stendhal?

GENTLEMAN His book, *Psychology of Love.*

WIFE No, why do you ask?

GENTLEMAN There's a story in it which is very much to the point.

WIFE What is it about?

GENTLEMAN There is a party of cavalry officers . . .

WIFE Yes.

GENTLEMAN Who are telling of their adventures in love. Each tells that with the woman he loved most . . . you know, with the most passion . . . that he . . . that she . . . well in short that with each of those women the same thing happened, as . . with me just now.

WIFE I see.

GENTLEMAN That's quite characteristic.

WIFE Yes.

GENTLEMAN But that's not all. One of them claimed . . . it had never happened to him in all his life. But . . . Stendhal adds—this man was a notorious boaster.

WIFE Oh.

GENTLEMAN The stupid thing is that it made me feel unhappy, even though it's not the least important.

WIFE That's right . . . anyway . . . you did promise me to be good.

GENTLEMAN Please don't laugh! That doesn't make things any better.

WIFE I'm not laughing at all. This story of Stendhal is very interesting. I'd always thought that only with older . . . or with very . . . well, you know, with men who've lived a lot . . .

GENTLEMAN What do you mean! That has nothing to do with it. By the way, I quite forgot the nicest story in Stendhal. A cavalry officer said that he even spent three nights—or was it six? I can't remember—with a woman he'd been wanting for weeks—desired her, you know—and all those nights they did nothing but weep with happiness—both of them. . . .

WIFE Both of them?

GENTLEMAN *Both* of them. Are you surprised? I feel so much in sympathy with them. Especially since they were in love.

WIFE But surely there are many who don't cry.

GENTLEMAN (*Nervously*) Certainly . . . but this was an exceptional case.

WIFE Oh. . . . I thought Stendhal said all cavalry officers wept under these circumstances.

GENTLEMEN There! You're making fun of me. . . .

WIFE The idea of it. Don't be such a child, Alfred.

GENTLEMAN I can't help it, it makes me very sensitive . . . and also I have the feeling you're thinking about it all the time. That really makes me feel embarrassed.

WIFE I am not thinking about it at all.

GENTLEMAN All right. If I could only be sure you love me!

WIFE Do you want still more proof . . . ?

GENTLEMAN You see! You're making fun of me.

WIFE What? Come put your little head here.

GENTLEMAN Oh, that feels good.

WIFE Do you love me?

GENTLEMAN Oh, I'm so happy!

WIFE But you don't have to cry as well!

GENTLEMAN (*Moves away, highly irritated*) There you go again. And I did ask you so much.

WIFE I only said you shouldn't cry . . .

GENTLEMAN You said cry as well.

WIFE Oh, darling, you're so tense.

GENTLEMAN I know.

WIFE But you shouldn't be. I even prefer that . . . that—we—that we—we're—good friends.

GENTLEMAN Oh, there you go again.

WIFE But don't you remember? It was one of our very first talks: we just wanted to be . . . good friends, nothing more. . . . It was so pleasant. . . . That was at my sister's in January, at the great ball . . . during the quadrille. . . . Oh, my God, I should have left long ago! My sister is expecting me—what am I going to tell her? Adieu, Alfred. . . .

GENTLEMAN Emma. You're going to leave me like this?

WIFE Yes, like this!

GENTLEMAN Just five minutes more. . . .

WIFE All right, another five minutes. But you must promise me not to move . . . all right. . . . I'll just kiss you goodbye once. . . . Sh . . . be still, don't move . . . or I'll get up right away. My sweet . . . sweetheart.

GENTLEMAN Emma . . . my adorable . . .

* * *

WIFE My Alfred . . .
GENTLEMAN Oh, with you it is heavenly.
WIFE But now I really must go.
GENTLEMAN Oh, let your sister wait.
WIFE I must go home. It's much too late for my sister's. Just what time is it?
GENTLEMAN How can I judge that?
WIFE Well, you might look at your watch!
GENTLEMAN My watch is in my waistcoat.
WIFE All right, go get it.
GENTLEMAN (*With a start*) Eight o'clock.
WIFE For God's sake! Quickly, Alfred, give me my stockings—whatever am I going to tell them at home . . . eight o'clock.
GENTLEMAN When am I going to see you again?
WIFE Never.
GENTLEMAN Emma! Don't you love me any more?
WIFE Just because I do. Give me my boots.
GENTLEMAN Never again? . . . Here are your boots.
WIFE There's a buttonhook in my purse. Please, quickly. . . .
GENTLEMAN Here it is. . . .
WIFE Alfred, this might cost us both our lives.
GENTLEMAN (*Unnerved*) Why?
WIFE Well, what am I going to tell him when he asks me where I've been?
GENTLEMAN At your sister's.
WIFE Yes, if only I were a good liar.
GENTLEMAN You'll just have to be.
WIFE What I won't go through for a man like you. . . . Come here. Let me give you another kiss. (*She embraces him*) And now leave me by myself, go into the next room. I can't dress with you present.

(*The* YOUNG GENTLEMAN *goes to the drawing room and gets dressed. He eats a little of the pastry, drinks a glass of cognac*)

WIFE (*After a while, calling out*) Alfred!
GENTLEMAN Yes, my treasure?
WIFE I'm much happier that we didn't cry.
GENTLEMAN (*Smiles, not without pride*) How can you be so frivolous?
WIFE How will we behave, if by chance we should meet at a party someday in public?
GENTLEMAN One day? By chance? Surely you'll be at the Lobheimers' tomorrow?
WIFE Yes, you too!
GENTLEMAN Of course. May I ask you for the cotillion?
WIFE Oh, I'm not going to go. How can you think . . . ? Why . . . (*She enters the drawing room, fully dressed, and takes a chocolate pastry*) I'd sink into the ground!
GENTLEMAN Well, tomorrow at the Lobheimers! That's settled.
WIFE No, no, I'm going to send word I can't come. . . . I assure you. . . .
GENTLEMAN All right. The day after tomorrow, here. . . .
WIFE What impudence.
GENTLEMAN At six.
WIFE I can get a cab at the corner, can't I?
GENTLEMAN As many as you like. Then it's the day after tomorrow, six o'clock, here. Please say yes, my dearest treasure.
WIFE . . . we'll talk it over tomorrow . . . during the cotillion.
GENTLEMAN (*Embracing her*) My angel!
WIFE Don't muss up my hair again.
GENTLEMAN So, it's tomorrow at the Lobheimers' and the day after, here . . . in my arms.
WIFE Bye-bye.
GENTLEMAN (*Suddenly worried again*) And what are you going to tell him tonight?
WIFE Don't ask . . . don't ask me . . . it's too dreadful. . . . Why do I love you so much? Goodbye. If I meet people on the stairs again, I shall have a stroke.

(*The* YOUNG GENTLEMAN *kisses her hand yet again. The* YOUNG WIFE *goes*)

GENTLEMAN (*The* YOUNG GENTLEMAN *is left alone. He sits down on the sofa. Then he smiles to himself*) At last, a real woman.

## Scene Five

### *The Young Wife and the Husband*

(*A comfortable bedroom. It is 10:30 at night. The* YOUNG WIFE *is lying in bed, reading. The* HUSBAND *comes into the room in his dressing gown*)

WIFE (*Without looking up*) You've stopped working?
HUSBAND Yes. I'm too tired. And besides . . .
WIFE Yes?
HUSBAND I suddenly felt so lonely at my desk. I began to long for you.
WIFE (*Looks up*) Honestly?
HUSBAND (*Sits by her on her bed*) Don't read any more tonight. You'll ruin your eyes.
WIFE (*Closes the book*) What's come over you?
HUSBAND Nothing, my child. I'm in love with you. But you know that.
WIFE Sometimes I might almost forget it.
HUSBAND One should forget it sometimes.
WIFE Why?
HUSBAND Marriage would be incomplete otherwise. It would—how shall I put it? It would lose its sanctity.
WIFE Oh. . . .
HUSBAND Believe me—it is so. . . . If during the five years we've been married we hadn't sometimes forgotten we're in love with one another, we probably *wouldn't* be in love any more.
WIFE That's above me.
HUSBAND The fact is simply this: we've had ten or

twelve affairs with one another . . . doesn't it seem so with you too?

WIFE I haven't been counting.

HUSBAND If we'd experienced our first affair to the limit, if I'd blindly surrendered myself to my passion for you from the beginning, we'd have gone the way of millions of others. It would be over for us.

WIFE I see what you mean.

HUSBAND Believe me—Emma—in the first days of our marriage I was afraid that this would be the case.

WIFE I too.

HUSBAND You see? Wasn't I right? That's why it's always good to live together just as friends for a while.

WIFE I see.

HUSBAND And that is how it is that we can always have new honeymoons. That is why I never permit the honeymoon weeks . . .

WIFE . . . to extend into months.

HUSBAND Exactly.

WIFE And now it seems that we have come to the end of one of those friendship periods?

HUSBAND (*Tenderly pressing her to him*) It could be so!

WIFE But suppose it would be otherwise—with me?

HUSBAND It is no different with you. You see, you are the cleverest and most enchanting being alive. I am so happy that I have found you.

WIFE It's nice that you should court me—from time to time. I'm glad.

HUSBAND (*Has got into bed*) For a man who has been around the world a little—there, put your head on my shoulder—who has been around the world a little, marriage holds far more secrets than for you young girls from good families. You enter into it innocent, to a degree—ignorant, and that is where you have a much clearer view of the true nature of love than we.

WIFE (*Laughing*) Oh!

HUSBAND Certainly. Because we're confused, made insecure by the various experiences we are forced to have before marriage. You young women hear too much, and know too much, and probably read too much too, but you don't have a real understanding of what we men experience. What is commonly called love is made disgusting—because, after all, what are the sort of creatures to which we must resort?

WIFE Yes, what sort of creatures are they?

HUSBAND (*Kisses her on the forehead*) Be happy, my child, that you never understood these relationships. Anyhow, they are really rather pitiable beings. Let us not cast stones at them.

WIFE Oh, please. This sympathy. It doesn't seem quite appropriate. . . .

HUSBAND (*With a kindly indulgence*) They deserve it. You who are girls from good families, who can patiently wait under the care of your parents for the groom who wants you in marriage—you have no conception of the misery that drives those poor creatures into the arms of sin.

WIFE Do they all sell themselves, then?

HUSBAND I wouldn't quite say *that*. I don't mean only material misery. There is also—one might say—a moral misery; a faulty conception of that which is permitted and especially of that which is noble.

WIFE But why are they to be pitied? They seem to be quite happy.

HUSBAND You have peculiar views, my child. You must not forget that such people are meant by nature to sink forever lower and lower. There is no stopping it.

WIFE (*Snuggles up to him*) Obviously they seem to enjoy sinking!

HUSBAND (*Pained*) How can you talk like that, Emma? I think that especially for you decent women, it would be more frightening than to those others.

WIFE Of course, Karl, of course. I was only talking. Go on, tell me more. I so enjoy hearing you talk. Tell me something?

HUSBAND What?

WIFE Well, about these creatures.

HUSBAND But what an idea!

WIFE Look, a long time ago, right at the beginning, I always asked you to tell me something about your youth.

HUSBAND Why should *that* interest you?

WIFE Aren't you my husband? And isn't it an injustice that I should know absolutely nothing about your past?

HUSBAND Surely you don't think I would have . . . such bad taste . . . enough, Emma! It would be like sacrilege!

WIFE And yet you have . . . had I don't know how many other young women in your arms just like me.

HUSBAND Don't say "women." You are *the* woman!

WIFE But one question you *must* answer. Otherwise . . . no honeymoon.

HUSBAND What a way to talk . . . remember, that you're a mother—that our daughter is sleeping in there.

WIFE (*Cuddling against him*) But I want a boy too.

HUSBAND Emma!

WIFE Oh, don't be so. . . . Of course I'm your wife, but I'd like to be—your sweetheart a little.

HUSBAND Would you?

WIFE But first, my question!

HUSBAND (*Submissive*) Well, what is it?

WIFE Among them was there a—married woman?

HUSBAND Why? How do you mean that?

WIFE *You* know.

HUSBAND (*Somewhat disturbed*) What makes you ask this?

WIFE I'd like to know if it . . . well, I mean . . . there *are* such women, I know, . . . but if you . . .

HUSBAND (*Gravely*) Do you know any such woman?

WIFE Well, I don't really know. . . .

HUSBAND Among your friends, is there perhaps such a one?

WIFE Well, how can I give you a definite yes—or no —and be sure?

HUSBAND Perhaps some of your women friends . .

You discuss a lot . . . especially women among themselves . . . has one of them confessed?

WIFE (*Uncertainly*) No. . . .

HUSBAND Well, perhaps you *suspect* that one of your friends may be. . . .

WIFE Suspect . . . well . . . suspect . . .

HUSBAND Well it seems so!

WIFE Surely not, Karl. Certainly not. When I think it over, I wouldn't believe it of any of them.

HUSBAND None.

WIFE Of my friends, none.

HUSBAND Promise me something, Emma.

WIFE Well?

HUSBAND That you will never associate with a woman who is touched by the least suspicion. . . .

WIFE You need a promise for that?

HUSBAND I know, of course, that you would never choose such women for friends, but circumstances could be such. . . . In fact it is quite frequent that those women whose reputation is somewhat tarnished seek the company of decent women, partly for the association and partly out of a certain—how shall I put it?—out of a certain homesickness.

WIFE Well.

HUSBAND Yes, I believe that what I have just said is completely accurate. Homesickness for virtue! Because, believe me, in reality all these women are very unhappy.

WIFE But why?

HUSBAND Need you ask that, Emma? Just imagine what sort of an existence these women have. Full of lies, deceit, vulgarity—and full of danger.

WIFE Yes, of course, you are quite right.

HUSBAND Surely, they pay for that little bit of happiness . . . that little bit of . . .

WIFE . . . pleasure.

HUSBAND Why "pleasure"? How can you call it "pleasure"?

WIFE Well, there must be something to it. Otherwise they wouldn't do it.

HUSBAND It is nothing. An uncontrolled passion.

WIFE (*Thoughtfully*) An uncontrolled passion . . .

HUSBAND No, it is not even passion. However, she pays heavily, that is certain.

WIFE So . . . you have been through it once?

HUSBAND Yes, Emma. It is one of my saddest memories.

WIFE Who was it? Tell me. Do I know her?

HUSBAND Emma! How could you!

WIFE Was it long ago? Was it a long time before you married me?

HUSBAND Don't ask. I beg you don't ask.

WIFE But Karl!

HUSBAND She is dead.

WIFE Honestly?

HUSBAND Yes, . . . it may seem ridiculous, but I have the feeling that all these women die young.

WIFE Did you love her very much?

HUSBAND One does not love deceivers.

WIFE Then, why . . . ?

HUSBAND A passion. . . .

WIFE So that's it. . . .

HUSBAND Please, don't talk about it any more. All of this was over long ago. I have loved only once. That is you. One loves only where there is purity and truth.

WIFE Karl!

HUSBAND Oh how safe, how happy one feels in such arms! Why did I not know you even as a child? I believe I would never have looked at another woman.

WIFE Karl!

HUSBAND And you're so beautiful . . . beautiful. . . . Come.

(*He puts the light out*)

* * *

WIFE You know what I can't help thinking of tonight?

HUSBAND What, my treasure?

WIFE Of . . . of . . . of . . . Venice.

HUSBAND The first night . . .

WIFE Yes, that's right.

HUSBAND What was it? Tell me.

WIFE Tonight . . . you love me like that.

HUSBAND Yes, just as much.

WIFE Ah . . . if you could always . . .

HUSBAND (*In her arms*) Yes?

WIFE My Karl!

HUSBAND What do you mean? If I could always . . . ?

WIFE Well, yes.

HUSBAND Well, what then if I could always . . . ?

WIFE Then I'd always know that you loved me.

HUSBAND Yes. But you should know that anyway. One cannot always be the lover. He must go out into a hostile world and fight and struggle. Never forget that, my child. Everything has its time in marriage. That's the wonderful thing about it. There aren't many who can remember their Venice after five years.

WIFE That's true.

HUSBAND And now . . . good-night, my child.

WIFE Good-night!

## Scene Six

### *The Husband and the Sweet Young Miss*

*A private dining room at the Riedhof Restaurant. Comfortable, fairly elegant. The gas fireplace is lit. The remains of a meal are on the table, a dessert filled with whipped cream, fruit, cheese. A white Hungarian wine is in the wineglasses. The* HUSBAND, *sitting comfortably on the sofa, has lit a Havana cigar.*

*The* SWEET YOUNG MISS, *next to him on a chair, is intensely concentrated on scooping the whipped cream out of the pastry.*

HUSBAND Good?
MISS (*Without stopping*) Mm—mm—m.
HUSBAND Another one?
MISS No, I've eaten too much already.
HUSBAND You've no wine left. (*He fills up her glass*)
MISS No . . . I'll only leave it anyway.
HUSBAND Why are you so shy?
MISS Am I? Well, it takes time to change.
HUSBAND Don't be so formal. Come and sit by me.
MISS In one minute—I'm not finished yet.
(*The* HUSBAND *gets up, stands behind her chair and puts his arms around her, turning her head toward him*)
MISS What is it?
HUSBAND I'd like a kiss.
MISS (*Gives him a kiss*) You're awfully fresh.
HUSBAND You're just finding that out.
MISS Oh, no, I noticed earlier . . . in the street. You must have . . .
HUSBAND What?
MISS You must have a nice opinion of me.
HUSBAND Why?
MISS Going to a private room with you right away.
HUSBAND Well, I wouldn't say right away.
MISS You've a nice way of asking.
HUSBAND You think so?
MISS And, after all, what's wrong with it?
HUSBAND Precisely.
MISS Whether we go for a walk or . . .
HUSBAND And, besides, it's much too cold for a walk.
MISS Of course it was too cold.
HUSBAND But this is pleasantly warm, eh? (*He sits down again and puts his arm around the* SWEET YOUNG MISS, *drawing her near*)
MISS (*Weakly*) Well.
HUSBAND Now tell me . . . You noticed me previously, didn't you?
MISS Of course . . . in the Singerstrasse.
HUSBAND No, I don't mean today. You had noticed me the day before yesterday and the day before that when I followed you.
MISS Oh, many people follow me.
HUSBAND I can well imagine. But did you notice me?
MISS . . . You know what happened to me recently? My cousin's husband followed me in the dark, and didn't recognize me.
HUSBAND Did he accost you?
MISS Well! You think everybody's as fresh as you?
HUSBAND But it does happen, doesn't it?
MISS Sure it happens.
HUSBAND Well, what do you do?
MISS Me? Nothing. I just don't answer.
HUSBAND Hmm . . . but you answered me.
MISS Well, are you annoyed?
HUSBAND (*Kisses her violently*) Your lips taste of whipped cream.
MISS Oh, they're naturally sweet.
HUSBAND Many men have told you that, have they?
MISS Many! What an imagination you've got.
HUSBAND Now be honest with me. How many have kissed your lips before?
MISS Why do you ask me? You won't believe me if I told you.
HUSBAND Why not?
MISS Well, guess.
HUSBAND Let's say . . . um . . . but you mustn't be angry!
MISS Why should I be?
HUSBAND Well, I would guess . . . about twenty.
MISS (*Breaking away from him*) Well, why not a hundred while you're at it?
HUSBAND Well, I was just guessing.
MISS Well, you didn't guess well.
HUSBAND All right . . . ten.
MISS (*Offended*) Oh, of course! A girl who lets you talk to her in the street and goes to a private dining room right away!
HUSBAND Don't be foolish. Whether we walk in a street or sit together in a room . . . Remember we're in a restaurant, any moment the waiter might come in . . . it doesn't mean anything.
MISS That's just what *I* thought.
HUSBAND Have you ever been in a private dining room before?
MISS Well, to tell the truth; yes.
HUSBAND You see, I appreciate that. You're honest.
MISS But not . . . in the way that you're thinking of. I was with my girl friend and her husband during the Carnival.
HUSBAND Well, it wouldn't be a tragedy if you'd been . . . with your sweetheart . . .
MISS Of course, it wouldn't be a tragedy. But I haven't got a sweetheart.
HUSBAND Go on!
MISS Cross my heart. I haven't any.
HUSBAND You don't expect me to believe that. . . .
MISS Well, what? . . . There hasn't been anyone . . . for more than six months.
HUSBAND Oh . . . Well, previously? Who was it?
MISS Why are you so curious?
HUSBAND Because . . . I love you.
MISS Really?
HUSBAND Certainly, you should have noticed that. Tell me. (*He hugs her*)
MISS What should I tell you.
HUSBAND Don't make me ask so much. I would like to know who it was.
MISS (*Giggling*) Oh, a man.
HUSBAND Well, who was he?
MISS He looked a little like you.
HUSBAND Oh.
MISS If you didn't look so much like him . . .
HUSBAND Then what?
MISS Now, don't ask. You see that's why . . .
HUSBAND Oh, that's why you let me speak to you!
MISS Well, yes.
HUSBAND Now I really don't know whether I should be pleased or annoyed.
MISS Well, in your place, I'd be glad.
HUSBAND All right.
MISS Also, the way you talk reminds me of him . . . and the way you look at me.

HUSBAND What was he?

MISS No, those eyes . . .

HUSBAND What was his name?

MISS Don't look at me like that, no, please! (*The* HUSBAND *takes her in his arms: a long burning kiss. The* SWEET YOUNG MISS *shakes herself free and tries to get up*)

HUSBAND Why do you want to leave me?

MISS It's time to go.

HUSBAND Later.

MISS No, I must really be going home. What do you think my mother will say?

HUSBAND You live with your mother?

MISS Of course with my mother. What did you think?

HUSBAND So . . . with your mother. You live alone with her?

MISS Alone . . . ! There are five of us. Two boys and another two girls.

HUSBAND Don't sit so far away. Are you the oldest?

MISS No. I'm the second. First there's Kathi, she works in a flower shop. Then me.

HUSBAND What do you do?

MISS I'm at home.

HUSBAND All the time?

MISS Well, one of us has to be at home.

HUSBAND Of course, but what do you tell your mother when you . . . come home late?

MISS It doesn't happen often.

HUSBAND Tonight, for example, surely your mother will ask you?

MISS Of course she's going to ask me. I can be as careful as anything but when I come home she's awake.

HUSBAND What do you tell her?

MISS Oh, well, I'll tell her I've been to the theatre.

HUSBAND And will she believe it?

MISS Why shouldn't she? I often go to the theatre. Only last Sunday I was at the Opera with my girl friend and her fiancé . . . and my oldest brother.

HUSBAND Where do you get the tickets?

MISS My brother is a hairdresser.

HUSBAND Oh, yes, hairdresser . . . Oh, probably a *theatrical* barber?

MISS Why do you ask me so many questions?

HUSBAND I am just interested. And what does your other brother do?

MISS Oh, he's still going to school. He wants to become a teacher. Can you imagine that!

HUSBAND And, you have another little sister too?

MISS Yes, she's still a kid, but already you've got to keep an eye on her. You've no idea how these girls are spoiled at school. Would you believe it, the other day I caught her having a date!

HUSBAND Really?

MISS Yes, with a boy from the school across the street. She was walking with him in the park at half-past seven at night . . . and such a child!

HUSBAND What did you do?

MISS Well, I spanked her.

HUSBAND You are as strict as all that?

MISS Well, who else. My older sister is in the shop. Mother does nothing but grumble—and so everything depends on me.

HUSBAND My God, you are a darling! (*He kisses her and grows more tender*) You also remind me of someone.

MISS Oh, of whom?

HUSBAND No one in particular . . . of the time . . . well, of my youth! Come, have another drink, my child.

MISS Well, how old are you? Um . . . I don't even know what your name is.

HUSBAND Karl.

MISS Honestly? Your name is Karl?

HUSBAND Was his name also Karl?

MISS Really, it's a miracle . . . it's too . . . No, these eyes! that expression! (*She shakes her head*)

HUSBAND And you still haven't told me who he was.

MISS A bad man, that's for sure . . . otherwise he wouldn't have left me.

HUSBAND Did you like him very much?

MISS Of course I liked him.

HUSBAND I know what he was; a lieutenant.

MISS No, he wasn't in the Army. They wouldn't take him. His father has a house in the . . . but why should you need to know?

HUSBAND (*Kisses her*) You actually have gray eyes. At first I thought they were black.

MISS Aren't they pretty enough for you?

(*The* HUSBAND *kisses her eyes*)

MISS Oh, no . . . I can't bear it . . . please, please . . . Oh, God . . . No, let me get up . . . just for a minute, oh, please!

HUSBAND (*Increasingly tender*) Oh! no, no!

MISS But Karl, please!

HUSBAND How old are you? Eighteen perhaps?

MISS Past nineteen.

HUSBAND Nineteen . . . and I . . .

MISS You're thirty . . .

HUSBAND And . . . a little more . . . Don't let us talk about it.

MISS Karl was also thirty-two when I met him.

HUSBAND How long ago was that?

MISS I don't remember . . . you know something must have been in the wine!

HUSBAND How's that!

MISS I'm quite . . . you know . . . everything's turning around.

HUSBAND Hold tight to me. Like this . . . (*He pulls her to him and becomes more and more tender; she hardly resists*) I'll tell you something, treasure. We could really go now.

MISS Yes . . . home.

HUSBAND Not home, exactly.

MISS What do you mean? Oh, no . . . no! . . . I'm not going anywhere . . . what do you think I am?

HUSBAND Now, listen to me, my child, next time we meet, you know, we shall arrange things so that . . . (*He has slipped to the floor, his head in her lap*) That's good; oh, that is so good!

MISS What are you doing? (*She kisses his hair*) You know there must have been something in the wine

. . . so sleepy . . . Tell me what's going to happen if I can't get up again? But . . . look here, Karl! if somebody should come . . . Please . . . the waiter!

HUSBAND No waiter will ever . . . come in here . . . not in . . . your lifetime.

* * *

(*The* SWEET YOUNG MISS *is leaning back in a corner of the sofa, her eyes shut. The* HUSBAND *paces up and down the small room after lighting a cigar. A long silence*)

HUSBAND (*Looks at the girl for a long time, then says to himself*) Who knows what sort of person she really is . . . Dammit . . . So quickly . . . wasn't very careful of me . . .

MISS (*Without opening her eyes*) There must have been something in that wine.

HUSBAND But why?

MISS Otherwise . . .

HUSBAND Why do you blame everything on the wine?

MISS Where are you? Why are you so far away? Come here to me.

(*The* HUSBAND *goes to her, sits down*)

MISS Now tell me if you really like me. . . .

HUSBAND But you should know. . . . (*As if to his wife; then interrupting himself quickly*) Of course, I do.

MISS You know . . . it's so . . . Tell me the truth, what was in that wine?

HUSBAND Well, do you think that I drugged your wine?

MISS Well, you see, I just don't understand. I'm not what . . . we've known each other only . . . Listen, I'm not like that, cross my heart . . . if you think that of me . . .

HUSBAND There, you don't need to worry about that! I don't think anything the worse of you. I do believe that you love me.

MISS Yes . . .

HUSBAND After all, when two young people are alone in a room, and eat dinner and drink wine . . . there doesn't have to be anything in the wine.

MISS Oh, I was just talking.

HUSBAND But why?

MISS (*Somewhat defiantly*) Because I was ashamed.

HUSBAND That's ridiculous. There is absolutely no reason for it. Especially since I remind you of your first lover.

MISS Yes.

HUSBAND Of the first one.

MISS Well, yes. . . .

HUSBAND Now I would really like to know who the others were.

MISS There weren't any.

HUSBAND That isn't true. That can't be true.

MISS Oh, please don't tease me!

HUSBAND Cigarette?

MISS No, thank you!

HUSBAND Do you know what time it is?

MISS What?

HUSBAND Half-past eleven.

MISS Oh!

HUSBAND Well . . . and your mother . . . is she used to it?

MISS Do you want to send me home already?

HUSBAND But . . . you yourself said earlier . . .

MISS Oh, but you've changed completely. What have I done to you?

HUSBAND My dear child, what has happened to you? What are you thinking of?

MISS It was . . . only your face, believe me. Otherwise I would never . . . A lot of men have asked me to go to a private dining room with them!

HUSBAND Well, would you like to . . . to come here again with me soon? Or somewhere else?

MISS I don't know.

HUSBAND Now what does that mean, you don't know?

MISS Well, if you have to ask me . . .

HUSBAND All right . . . when? But first I must make it clear that I do not live in Vienna. I just come here from time to time. For a few days.

MISS Go on—you aren't Viennese?

HUSBAND Well, yes, I am Viennese, but I live . . . out of town.

MISS Where?

HUSBAND That doesn't matter . . .

MISS Don't be afraid. I won't come to see you.

HUSBAND Heavens, if it gives you pleasure, you can come. I live in Graz.

MISS Honestly?

HUSBAND Yes . . . yes . . . why should that surprise you?

MISS Then you're married, right?

HUSBAND (*Greatly surprised*) Whatever makes you think so?

MISS Well, I just got the impression.

HUSBAND And you wouldn't mind that?

MISS Well, I would prefer you were single. But you're married. I know.

HUSBAND But tell me, what makes you think so?

MISS Well, when you tell me you don't live in Vienna . . . that you don't have time.

HUSBAND That is not so improbable.

MISS I don't believe it.

HUSBAND And it doesn't bother your conscience that you should cause a married man to become unfaithful?

MISS Never mind. . . . I'm sure your wife is no different.

HUSBAND (*Very indignant*) That is enough! I forbid such remarks. . . .

MISS But I thought you didn't have a wife!

HUSBAND It doesn't matter whether I have one or not. You shouldn't make such remarks. (*He has risen*)

MISS Karl, oh, Karl, what is it? Are you angry? Look, I honestly didn't know you were married. I was just talking. Come on, be nice again.

HUSBAND (*Goes to her after a couple of seconds*) You women really are remarkable beings. (*He begins to caress her again*) Oh, the female of the species!

MISS . . . don't . . . and it's so late. . . .

HUSBAND All right. Now listen. Let's be serious for a moment. I would like to see you again, often.

MISS Truly?

HUSBAND But it is necessary . . . I must be able to rely on you. I cannot look after you.

MISS Oh, I can look after myself.

HUSBAND You are . . . well, I cannot say inexperienced exactly, but you are so young, and . . . men in general are so unscrupulous.

MISS Oh dear.

HUSBAND I don't mean that only in a moral sense . . . I am sure you know what I mean.

MISS Yes. Tell me what do you think I am?

HUSBAND Well, if you want me, me only, we can arrange it, even if I do live in Graz. But a place like this, where somebody might come in at any time, is not the right thing.

(*The* SWEET YOUNG MISS *snuggles up to him*)

HUSBAND Next time we will be together somewhere else, won't we?

MISS Yes.

HUSBAND Where we can't be disturbed?

MISS Yes.

HUSBAND (*He embraces her with fervor*) And the rest we can discuss on the way home. (*He gets up, opens the door*) Waiter . . . the check!

# Scene Seven

## *The Sweet Young Miss and the Poet*

*A small room, furnished with unobtrusive good taste. Curtains shut off most of the light coming in through the window. A large writing desk covered with books and paper dominates the room. A small upright piano is against one wall.*

*The* SWEET YOUNG MISS *and the* POET *are just entering the room; the* POET *locks the door.*

POET Here we are, my pet. (*Kisses her*)

MISS (*In hat and cloak*) Oh, that's nice! Only I can't see a thing.

POET Your eyes will have to get used to the darkness. Those sweet eyes! (*Kisses her eyelids*)

MISS But these sweet eyes won't have time for that.

POET Why not?

MISS Because I'm only going to stay a minute.

POET But take off your hat anyway.

MISS For only a minute?

POET (*Pulls her hatpin out, takes hat, puts it aside*) And the cloak.

MISS What are you doing? I must go in a few moments.

POET But you must rest a little. We've been walking three hours.

MISS We rode in the carriage.

POET Yes, coming home. But in Weidling-am-Bach we walked a full three hours. Now do sit down, child . . . wherever you like . . . here at the desk. . . . No, that isn't comfortable. Sit on the divan. So. (*He puts her down on the divan*) If you're very tired, you can even lie down. So. (*He makes her lie down*) With your little head on the cushion.

MISS (*Laughing*) But I'm not a bit tired!

POET You only think so, and if you feel sleepy you can even sleep. I'll be very quiet. Besides I can play you a lullaby . . . one of my own. (*He goes to the piano*)

MISS Your own?

POET Yes.

MISS But, Robert, I thought you were a doctor.

POET How come? I told you I was a writer.

MISS Well, all writers are doctors, aren't they?

POET No, not all of them—for example I'm not. But what made you think of that now?

MISS Well, because you said the piece you were going to play was one of your own.

POET Oh well . . . maybe it isn't. It doesn't matter. Right? Anyhow, it's not important who did compose it—just so long as it's beautiful—true?

MISS Of course . . . it must be beautiful. That's the main thing.

POET Do you know how I meant that?

MISS What?

POET Well, what I just said.

MISS (*Drowsily*) Of course.

POET (*Gets up, goes to her and strokes her hair*) You didn't understand a word.

MISS Now look, I'm not that stupid.

POET Certainly you are. That's why I love you. It's so wonderful when you're stupid. I mean, in your way.

MISS Come on, don't be mean.

POET Little angel! It's good just to lie there on the soft Persian carpet.

MISS Oh yes. Aren't you going to go on playing the piano?

POET No, I'd rather be with you. (*Caressing her*)

MISS Look, couldn't we have some light?

POET Oh no . . . this dusk is so restful. The whole day we were bathed in sunshine. Now we've come out of the bath, so to speak, and we're wrapping the dusk around us like a bathrobe. (*He laughs*) No, this should be said differently—don't you think?

MISS I don't know.

POET (*Withdrawing a little*) Divine! This stupidity! (*He takes out a notebook and writes a few words in it*)

MISS What are you doing? (*Turns round to look at him*) What are you writing down?

POET (*Mumbling to himself*) Sun—bath—dusk—bathrobe . . . (*He puts the notebook in his pocket, laughs*) Nothing. And now tell me, my pet, wouldn't you like something to eat or drink?

MISS I'm really not thirsty. But I *am* hungry.

POET Hm . . . now, I'd prefer you were thirsty.

Cognac I have here, but I'll have to go out to get food.

MISS Can't you send out for some?

POET That's difficult. My servant isn't here any more . . . never mind. I'll go. What would you like?

MISS Oh, it's not worthwhile. I've got to go home anyway.

POET Child, don't talk about it. But I'll tell you; if we go out, let's go out together to have dinner.

MISS Oh, no, I haven't got time for that. And—where could we go? Somebody might see us.

POET Do you know so many people?

MISS Only one needs to see me and the fat's in the fire.

POET How so? What fat in what fire?

MISS What do you think? If Mother heard anything. . . .

POET We could go somewhere where nobody *could* see us. There are restaurants with private rooms after all. . . .

MISS (*Sings*) "Just to share a private room with you" . . .

POET Have you ever been to a private dining room?

MISS To tell the truth, yes.

POET Who was the lucky man?

MISS Oh, it wasn't what you think . . . I was with my girl friend and her husband. They took me.

POET Well, and you expect me to believe that?

MISS You don't have to.

POET (*Close to her*) Are you blushing? I can't see a thing. I can't see your face any more. (*He touches her cheek with his hand*) Even so—I recognize you.

MISS Well, just be careful you don't mistake me for someone else.

POET It's strange. I don't recall any more just how you look.

MISS Thank you.

POET (*Seriously*) Do you know, it's almost uncanny —I can't visualize you any more—in a certain sense I've already *forgotten* you. Now, if I should fail to recall the sound of your voice also, what would you be? Near and far at the same time—uncanny.

MISS Go on. What are you talking about?

POET Nothing, my angel, nothing. Where are your lips? (*He kisses her*)

MISS Aren't you going to give us some light?

POET No. (*He grows very tender*) Tell me, do you love me?

MISS Yes, very much.

POET Have you ever loved anyone else as much?

MISS I told you I haven't.

POET But . . . (*He sighs*)

MISS Well, that was my fiancé.

POET I'd much rather you wouldn't think of him now.

MISS Say . . . what are you doing . . . now look . . . now we should . . .

POET Let's imagine we're in a palace in India.

MISS I'm sure people there couldn't be as fresh as you are.

POET How divinely stupid. Ah, if only you had an inkling of what you mean to me.

MISS Well?

POET Don't always push me away. I'm not doing anything to you . . . yet.

MISS But my corset is hurting me.

POET (*Simply*) Take it off.

MISS All right, but you mustn't start getting forward on that account.

POET Oh, no. (*The* SWEET YOUNG MISS *rises and takes off her corset in the dark;* POET *sitting on the sofa in the meanwhile*) Tell me, aren't you the least bit interested to know my last name?

MISS Oh yes, what is your name?

POET I'd rather not tell you what my name is. But what I call myself.

MISS Why? Is there a difference?

POET Well, the name I go by as a writer.

MISS You don't write under your real name? (*The* POET *gets closer to her*) Ah . . . don't . . . please!

POET Ah, what perfume greets me. How sweet! (*He kisses her bosom*)

MISS You're tearing my chemise.

POET Away with it! Away with all that is superfluous!

MISS Tell me first if you really love me.

POET But I adore you. (*He kisses her passionately*) My treasure, I adore you, my spring . . . my . . .

MISS Robert . . . Robert . . .

* * *

POET That was unearthly ecstasy . . . I call myself . . .

MISS Robert, my Robert.

POET I call myself Biebitz.

MISS Why do you call yourself Biebitz?

POET My name isn't Biebitz. I just call myself that. Well, don't you know the name?

MISS No.

POET You don't know the name of Biebitz? How divine! Really? You're just saying you don't know. Isn't that so?

MISS Truly, I've never heard it.

POET Don't you ever go to the theater?

MISS Oh, yes. Just recently I was there with—you know—with a friend of mine and her uncle—to the Opera—Cavalleria!

POET Hmmm, then you never go to see plays.

MISS I never get a pass for those.

POET I'll send you a ticket soon.

MISS Oh yes! Don't forget now. But make it something funny.

POET Yes . . . funny . . . don't you want to see something sad?

MISS Not as much.

POET Even when it's a play by me?

MISS Go on, one of your plays? You write for the theater?

POET Excuse me, I just want to light a candle. I haven't seen you since you became my beloved. Angel! (*He lights a candle*)

MISS Please. I'm shy— At least, give me a blanket.

POET In a little while. (*He comes toward her with the light and studies her for a long while*)

MISS (*Covers her face with her hands*) Please, Robert!

POET You're so beautiful. You're Beauty itself. Perhaps you are Nature itself. You are Sacred Simplicity!

MISS Ouch! You're dropping wax on me! Why don't you be more careful?

POET (*Puts the candlestick down*) You are that for which I have been seeking all this time. You love me —only me—you would love me even if I were a sales clerk. It makes me feel good. I must confess something. Up until this moment I had a faint suspicion. Tell me truly, had you no idea that I am Biebitz?

MISS Look, I don't know what you want with me. I don't know any Biebitz.

POET What is fame! No, forget what I said, forget even the name that I told you. Robert I am and Robert I shall remain for you. I was joking. (*Gaily*) I'm not a writer at all, I'm a sales clerk. In the evenings I play the piano for folk singers!

MISS Well, now I am completely mixed up . . . and the way you look at me! What is it? What's happened to you?

POET It's curious. Something that's almost never happened to me, my treasure—I'm almost in tears. You affect me deeply. We shall live together. We shall love each other very much.

MISS Tell me, is that true about the folk singers?

POET Yes, but don't ask any further. If you love me, ask no questions. Tell me, could you be completely free for a couple of weeks?

MISS What do you mean completely free?

POET Well, away from your house.

MISS What! But how can I? What would my Mother say? Anyway, everything would go wrong at home without me.

POET I'd imagined it so beautiful. Together for a few weeks, quite alone, somewhere, in distant solitude, in the depths of Nature's forests. Thou, Nature, art my Goddess! And then one day to say goodbye, to part. . . .

MISS And now you're already talking of saying goodbye. And I thought you loved me so much.

POET That's just why. (*He bends down and kisses her on the forehead*) Oh you sweet creature.

MISS Come, hold me close. I'm so cold.

POET It's almost time for you to dress. Wait, I'll light some more candles.

MISS (*Gets up*) But don't look!

POET All right. (*At the window*) Tell me, child, are you happy?

MISS How do you mean?

POET I mean in general, Are you happy?

MISS Things could be better.

POET You don't understand me. You've told me enough about your conditions at home. I know you aren't exactly a princess. I mean, apart from that— When you notice that you're alive, do you feel you are really alive? *Do* you ever notice that you are alive?

MISS Have you got a comb?

POET (*Goes to the dressing table, gives her a comb, contemplates her*) God how enchanting you look!

MISS No . . . don't!

POET Please stay here just awhile. I'll get something for our supper, and . . .

MISS But it's already too late.

POET It's not even nine.

MISS Oh, don't! I must hurry.

POET When shall we meet again?

MISS Well, when do you want to see me?

POET Tomorrow?

MISS What day is tomorrow?

POET Saturday.

MISS Oh, I can't—I must take my little sister to her guardian.

POET Sunday, then . . . hm . . . on Sunday . . . I must explain something to you. I'm not Biebitz. Biebitz is my friend. I'll introduce him to you someday. But Sunday they're giving the play by Biebitz. I'll send you a ticket, and then call for you at the theatre. You'll tell me how you like the play, won't you?

MISS This story about Biebitz . . . well I must be completely confused. . . .

POET I'll know you completely only when I know your feelings about this play.

MISS All right. I'm ready.

POET Let's go, then, my treasure.

## Scene Eight

### *The Poet and the Actress*

*A room in an inn in the country. It is evening in Spring. A full moon illuminates the hills and meadows. The windows are open. All is stillness. The* POET *and the* ACTRESS *enter, and as they do, the lamp which he is carrying is blown out.*

POET Oh!

ACTRESS What is it?

POET The light. But we don't need any. Look. It's quite light! Wonderful! (*The* ACTRESS *suddenly sinks to her knees at the window, folding her hands*)

POET What's the matter? (*The* ACTRESS *is silent*)

POET (*Goes to her*) What are you doing?

ACTRESS (*Indignant*) Can't you see I'm praying?

POET You believe in God?

ACTRESS Certainly. I'm no atheist.

POET I see.

ACTRESS Come over here. Kneel down next to me! You can pray too, for once. It won't make your hair fall out. (*The* POET *kneels down beside her, then puts his arms around her)* Libertine! *(She gets up)* And do you know to whom I was praying?

POET To God, I presume.

ACTRESS *(With great contempt)* Oh, yes! I was praying to you.

POET Then why were you looking out of the window?

ACTRESS Tell me rather where you've dragged me off? Seducer!

POET But darling, it was your idea. You wanted to go into the country—expressly here.

ACTRESS Well, wasn't I right?

POET Certainly, it's charming. When you imagine it's only two hours away from Vienna—and complete solitude! Beautiful scenery!

ACTRESS Isn't it? If you happened to have *talent,* you might be able to write poetry here.

POET Were you ever here before?

ACTRESS Was I ever here before? I lived here for years.

POET With whom?

ACTRESS Oh, with Fritz, of course.

POET I see.

ACTRESS I adored that man.

POET Yes, you told me.

ACTRESS All right, I can leave if I bore you.

POET You bore me? You have not even a faint idea what you mean to me. . . . You are a world in yourself . . . You are the epitome . . . the Genius . . . You are . . . The truth is you are actually Sacred Simplicity . . . yes, you. . . . But you shouldn't speak of Fritz—now.

ACTRESS Perhaps that was a mistake . . . yes . . .

POET It's decent of you to admit that.

ACTRESS Come here and kiss me. *(The* POET *kisses her)*

ACTRESS And now we shall say good-night. Bye, bye, my darling.

POET How do you mean that?

ACTRESS Now I'm going to lie down and sleep.

POET Yes, all right. But what's this about saying, good-night . . . where am I supposed to sleep?

ACTRESS I'm sure there are many more rooms in this inn.

POET The others don't hold any appeal for me. Anyhow, I think I should light the candle now.

ACTRESS Yes.

POET *(Lights the candle on the bedside table)* What a pretty room. . . . And such devout people, nothing but religious pictures. It would be interesting to spend some time among these people—a completely different world. We know so little about the way others live.

ACTRESS Stop talking nonsense and give me the bag that's on the table.

POET Here, my only one. *(The* ACTRESS *takes out a small framed picture and puts it on the table)*

POET What's that?

ACTRESS The Madonna.

POET You always take her along?

ACTRESS She's my mascot. Now be off with you, Robert.

POET Are you making jokes with me? Be off with me! Don't you need help?

ACTRESS No. Now you must leave.

POET And when shall I return?

ACTRESS In ten minutes.

POET *(Kisses her)* Good-bye.

ACTRESS Where are you going?

POET I shall pace up and down in front of the window. I love to walk outside at night. My best inspirations come then. Especially near you—enveloped in your longing, enmeshed in your art.

ACTRESS You talk like an idiot.

POET *(With pain)* Some women might have said—like a poet.

ACTRESS All right, get going. And don't start seducing the waitress. *(The* POET *exits, the* ACTRESS *undresses. She hears the* POET *going down the wooden staircase, then hears him pacing under the window. When she is ready, she goes to the window, looks down, calls in a whisper: "Come." The* POET *hurries upstairs, locks the door, and rushes toward her. She is in bed and has put out the light)* Now sit here and tell me something.

POET *(Sits by her on the bed)* Shouldn't I close the window? Aren't you cold?

ACTRESS Oh, no.

POET What should I tell you?

ACTRESS Well, tell me—to whom are you being unfaithful—at this moment?

POET Unfortunately to nobody . . . yet.

ACTRESS Never mind, I'm also deceiving someone.

POET That I can well believe.

ACTRESS Of whom would you believe it?

POET But darling, I haven't the faintest idea!

ACTRESS Well, guess.

POET Wait a moment. . . . Well, your manager.

ACTRESS My pet, I'm not a chorus girl.

POET Well, I was only guessing.

ACTRESS Guess again.

POET All right, you're deceiving your leading man—Benno.

ACTRESS Pooh, that man doesn't like women, didn't you know that? He's having an affair with his mail man.

POET No, really?

ACTRESS Give me a kiss instead . . . *(The* POET *embraces her)* But what are you doing?

POET Stop torturing me.

ACTRESS Listen, Robert. I'll make you a proposition. Lie down with me in the bed.

POET Accepted.

ACTRESS Hurry up! Hurry up!

POET Well . . . If I'd had my way, I'd have been there long ago. . . . Listen!

ACTRESS What?

POET The crickets are chirping outside.

ACTRESS You must be mad, my dear. There are no crickets here.

POET But you can hear them!

ACTRESS All right, come on then.

POET Here I am. (*He goes to her*)

ACTRESS And now lie still . . . shh . . . Don't move!

POET Say, what's the idea?

ACTRESS I suppose you'd like to have an affair with me?

POET That should be clear by now.

ACTRESS There are many who would like to.

POET There's no doubt about that, but at this moment I have the best chance.

ACTRESS Come, my cricket. From now on I'll call you only Cricket.

POET . . . Good.

ACTRESS Well, whom am I deceiving?

POET Whom? Perhaps me.

ACTRESS My child, you have a softening of the brain.

POET Or someone whom . . . you have never seen . . . one whom you don't know. . . . One who is meant for you but whom you will never find.

ACTRESS Please don't talk such fabulous rubbish.

POET . . . Isn't it curious . . . even you . . . and I would have thought—but no, it would mean . . . robbing you of your . . . if I should . . . come, come, come.

* * *

ACTRESS That's better than acting in idiotic silly plays. Don't you think?

POET Well, I think it's good that at times you get to act in an intelligent one.

ACTRESS Meaning yours, you conceited pup.

POET Of course.

ACTRESS (*Seriously*) It really is an excellent play.

POET Well, then.

ACTRESS You're really a great genius, Robert!

POET At this opportunity you might tell me why you canceled your performance two nights ago. There was nothing wrong with you.

ACTRESS I wanted to annoy you.

POET Why? What had I done to you?

ACTRESS You were arrogant.

POET In what way?

ACTRESS Everybody in the theatre thinks so.

POET Really.

ACTRESS But I told them, that man has a right to be conceited.

POET And what did the others say?

ACTRESS Well, what should they tell me? We're not on speaking terms.

POET I see.

ACTRESS They'd all love to poison me. (*Pause*) But they won't succeed.

POET Don't think of other people now. Be glad that we're here and tell me that you really love me.

ACTRESS You need still further proof?

POET Oh, that's something that can never be *proved.*

ACTRESS That's marvelous! What more do you want then?

POET And to how many have you tried to prove it in this manner; did you love them all?

ACTRESS Oh, no! I loved only one.

POET (*Embracing her*) My . . .

ACTRESS Fritz.

POET But I'm Robert! What am I to you, if it's Fritz you're thinking of?

ACTRESS You're a whim.

POET Nice to know it!

ACTRESS Tell me, aren't you proud?

POET Why should I be proud?

ACTRESS I think you should have a little reason for it.

POET Oh, for that?

ACTRESS Yes, for that, my pale cricket. Now what about the chirping? Are they still chirping?

POET Continuously. Can't you hear them?

ACTRESS Certainly, I can hear them. But those are frogs, my pet.

POET You're wrong there; frogs croak.

ACTRESS Certainly they croak.

POET But not here, my child. This is chirping.

ACTRESS You're the most obstinate thing that I have ever met. Kiss me, my frog.

POET Please don't call me that. It gets on my nerves.

ACTRESS Well, what should I call you?

POET I've got a name; Robert.

ACTRESS Oh, that's too silly.

POET But it would please me if you would call me simply by my own name.

ACTRESS All right, Robert, give me a kiss . . . Ah! (*She kisses him*) Are you satisfied now, Frog? (*She laughs*)

POET Will you permit me to light a cigarette?

ACTRESS Give me one too. (*The* POET *takes the cigarette case from the dresser, lights two cigarettes and hands her one*)

ACTRESS By the way, you never said a word about my performance yesterday.

POET Which performance?

ACTRESS Well . . . !

POET Oh, yes. I wasn't at the theatre.

ACTRESS I guess you like your little joke.

POET Not in the least. When you canceled your performance the day before yesterday, I assumed that yesterday you wouldn't be completely recovered. So I decided not to go.

ACTRESS You missed a great deal.

POET Indeed?

ACTRESS I was sensational. People turned pale.

POET You could see them?

ACTRESS Benno said to me, Darling, you played like a goddess.

POET Ha . . . and so ill the day before.

ACTRESS Indeed I was. And do you know why? Because of longing for you.

POET Just now you said you canceled to annoy me!

ACTRESS What do you know of my love for you? Everything leaves you untouched. All night long I lay with a fever of 104 degrees.

POET For a whim, that's pretty high.

ACTRESS A whim, you call it? I am dying for love of you and you call it a whim.

POET And what about Fritz?

ACTRESS Fritz! Don't talk to me about that galley slave!

## Scene Nine

### *The Actress and the Count*

*The* ACTRESS' *bedroom, furnished luxuriously. It is noon, the shades are still down. A candle is burning on the side table, the* ACTRESS *is in a sumptuous bed, the quilts covered by newspapers. The* COUNT *enters in the uniform of a* CAPTAIN OF THE DRAGOONS. *He remains at the door.*

ACTRESS Ah, the Count!

COUNT Your mother gave me permission, otherwise I should not . . .

ACTRESS Please do come in.

COUNT Your hand? I beg your pardon. I just came in from the street—you know, and I still cannot see a thing. Yes . . . here we are. (*At the bed*) Your hand. (*Kisses her hand*)

ACTRESS Please sit down, Count.

COUNT Your mother gave me to understand that you are not in good health? It is to be hoped that it is nothing serious?

ACTRESS Nothing serious! I was on the verge of death.

COUNT Oh, for Heavens sake!—How is it possible?

ACTRESS In any case it is very kind of you to . . . trouble yourself to visit me.

COUNT The verge of death! And only last night you acted like a goddess.

ACTRESS I suppose it was a great triumph.

COUNT Colossal! People were all carried away. . . . And I will not even talk about myself.

ACTRESS I thank you for those beautiful flowers.

COUNT Oh, it was nothing, Mademoiselle.

ACTRESS (*Turns her eyes to a large basket of flowers which is on a small table by the window*) There they are!

COUNT Last night you were really overwhelmed with flowers and garlands!

ACTRESS They're all still in my dressing room. Yours were the only ones I brought home.

COUNT (*Kisses her hand*) That is very sweet of you. (*The* ACTRESS *suddenly takes his hand and kisses it*) Mademoiselle!

ACTRESS Oh, Count, don't be frightened. It doesn't commit you to anything.

COUNT You are a strange creature . . . one might almost say a conundrum.

ACTRESS (*Pause*) I suppose Miss Birken is . . . easier to solve?

COUNT Yes, the little Birken is no puzzle, although . . . I know her only superficially.

ACTRESS Really?

COUNT Oh, please believe me. But you are a problem. And I have always had a yearning for one. Actually, last night I realized what a great pleasure I had been missing. You see, it was the first time I had ever seen you act.

ACTRESS Impossible!

COUNT Well, yes. You see, it is like this: I have difficulty in getting to the theatre. I am used to dining late. So when I arrive there the greater part of the play is always over.

ACTRESS From now on, you'll just have to dine earlier.

COUNT Yes, I had already thought of that. Dining is really not much of a pleasure, is it?

ACTRESS What can you still find pleasure in, you young fossil?

COUNT That is a question I ask myself sometimes. But I am not petrified yet. There must be another reason.

ACTRESS You think so?

COUNT Yes, Lulu, for example, always says I am a philosopher. You know, Mademoiselle, what he means is: that I think too much.

ACTRESS He's right. . . . Thinking is a bore.

COUNT I have too much free time: that's why I think such a lot. You see, Mademoiselle, when they transferred me to Vienna, I thought things would be better; here I could find discussions and stimulation. But basically, it is really much the same here as up there.

ACTRESS And where is "up there"?

COUNT Well, down there—you know—Mademoiselle, is Hungary. The village where I was in charge of the garrison.

ACTRESS Yes, but what were you doing in Hungary?

COUNT As I just said, Mademoiselle—Service.

ACTRESS And why did you stay there so long?

COUNT Well, it just happens, that's all.

ACTRESS It's enough to drive one mad!

COUNT Oh, no, actually there is quite a lot to do. You know, Mademoiselle, to train recruits, break in new horses. And the country itself is not as bad as its reputation. The lowlands are really quite beautiful; and those sunsets—it is a pity I am no painter. I have thought sometimes if I were a painter, I would paint it. One we had in the regiment—a boy named Splany—he could.[1] But I am afraid I am telling you a very dull story.

ACTRESS Oh, no, go on. I'm being entertained most elegantly.

COUNT You know, Mademoiselle, it is so easy to talk with you. Lulu told me it would be. That is what one finds so rarely.

ACTRESS Well, certainly, in Hungary.

COUNT Also in Vienna! People are the same everywhere. Where there are more people, there is a greater crowd, but that is the only difference. Tell me, Mademoiselle, do you like people?

[1] Probably a Hungarian named Splényi, serving in the Austrian army.

ACTRESS Like them? I detest them! I don't want to see anybody and I don't see anybody. I'm always alone. Nobody ever comes into this house.

COUNT You know, that is just as I imagined; you hate people, I suppose. It often happens to artists. Where you are in the high places . . . well, you are fortunate; at least you know your purpose in life.

ACTRESS Who told you that? I haven't the remotest idea what I am living for.

COUNT Not really, Mademoiselle . . . famous . . . celebrated. . . .

ACTRESS Is that . . . happiness?

COUNT Happiness? Now Mademoiselle, happiness doesn't exist. Nor do all those other things people discuss *most* . . . for example, love . . . that is one of them.

ACTRESS You may be right.

COUNT Pleasure . . . passion . . . All right, you cannot argue against them, they are real. If I enjoy something now, I am *aware* of the enjoyment—or I am even carried away! All right. That also is real. And when it is *over,* it is over, that is all.

ACTRESS (*Grandly*) It is over.

COUNT But as soon as one—how shall I say it—as soon as one does not live for the moment, or begins to think of the consequences or causes, then everything is destroyed—the pleasure is gone. For consequences are sad, causes are filled with uncertainty. In one word, one only becomes . . . confused. Isn't that so?

ACTRESS (*Nods, her eyes very wide*) You've got the very essence of it.

COUNT And you see Mademoiselle, once one has become clear on that point, it is all the same—whether one lives in Vienna or in the lowlands or in the tiny town of Steinamanger.[2] For instance . . . where can I put down my helmet, . . . yes, thank you. Now what were we discussing?

ACTRESS The village of Steinamanger.

COUNT That's right. Well as I was saying, the difference is not excessive. Whether I spend the evening at the Casino or at the Club is *much* the *same* thing.

ACTRESS How does that bear on love?

COUNT When one believes in it, there will always be *someone* to love.

ACTRESS Miss Birken, for example.

COUNT I really do not know why you are always mentioning the little Birken.

ACTRESS After all, she is your mistress.

COUNT Who says that?

ACTRESS Everyone knows it.

COUNT Strange to say, I am the only one who does not.

ACTRESS Well, you fought a duel on her account.

COUNT Maybe I was even shot dead and didn't notice it.

ACTRESS Well, my love, since you are a gentleman, sit a little closer.

COUNT With great pleasure.

[2] Steinamanger was another name for the Hungarian city of Szombathely, not far from the Austrian border.

ACTRESS Here. (*She draws him closer, and runs her fingers through his hair*) I knew that you would come to see me today.

COUNT How so?

ACTRESS I knew it last night at the theatre.

COUNT Oh, did you see me while you were on the stage?

ACTRESS Certainly, didn't you notice I was acting only for you?

COUNT How is it possible?

ACTRESS When I saw you sitting in the first row, I was on wings.

COUNT On my account? I had no idea you would even notice me.

ACTRESS Oh, you can drive a woman to despair with that dignity of yours!

COUNT Well, Mademoiselle!

ACTRESS "Well, Mademoiselle"? At least take your sword off!

COUNT If you permit? (*He unbuckles the belt and leans the sword against the bed*)

ACTRESS And *now* kiss me. (*The* COUNT *kisses her. She does not let him go*) I wish I had never set eyes on you.

COUNT I prefer it like this.

ACTRESS Count, you are a hypocrite.

COUNT I? But why?

ACTRESS Well, consider how many men would be happy to be in your place right now.

COUNT I am extremely happy.

ACTRESS Well, I thought there was no such thing as happiness. Why are you looking at me like that? Count, I believe you are afraid of me!

COUNT I told you Mademoiselle, you are a problem.

ACTRESS Oh, leave me alone with your philosophy. . . . Come here. And now ask me for something. You can have anything you want. You're so handsome.

COUNT Very well, I will ask permission . . . (*He kisses her hand*) to return here tonight.

ACTRESS Tonight? . . . But I'm playing tonight.

COUNT After the theatre.

ACTRESS You're not going to ask for anything else?

COUNT I'll ask for everything else . . . after the theater.

ACTRESS (*Hurt*) You can beg a long while then, you horrible hypocrite.

COUNT Look now, we have been perfectly open with one another. It would be so much more beautiful in the evening, after the theatre. More relaxed than now. I always have the feeling as though the door might open at any moment.

ACTRESS It can't be opened from the outside.

COUNT Well you see, I think one shouldn't spoil something in advance that could turn out to be very beautiful.

ACTRESS "That could"?

COUNT And to tell the truth, I detest love in the morning.

ACTRESS Well, you are the craziest thing that has ever happened to me.

COUNT I am not just talking about any woman. After all, in general, it is much the same thing. But women like you—you can call me a fool a hundred times, but women like you—I haven't the heart to take before breakfast. And so you see—

ACTRESS Oh, my, you're so sweet!

COUNT You realize the truth of what I have said . . . I imagined something like. . . .

ACTRESS Well, how did you imagine?

COUNT Well, like this. . . . After the theatre, I shall wait for you in my carriage, then we shall drive somewhere for supper and . . .

ACTRESS I am not Miss Birken!

COUNT I didn't say you were. I just think for everything there should be the right mood. . . . I find supper sets that mood. And the most beautiful part is driving home together . . . and then.

ACTRESS Well, what then?

COUNT And then? . . . Well, it depends on how circumstances develop.

ACTRESS Sit a little closer. Closer!

COUNT (*Sits down on the bed*) I do think there is a wonderful fragrance coming from the pillows—mignonette, isn't it?

ACTRESS Don't you think it's very warm in here? (*The* COUNT *bends down and kisses her neck*) My dear Count, that's not according to your schedule.

COUNT Who says that? I've got no schedule. (*The* ACTRESS *draws him close*) It really is warm.

ACTRESS Isn't it? And as dark as though it were evening . . . (*Pulling him to her, tearing at him*) It *is* evening. It's night . . . Close your eyes if it is too light for you. Come here.

(*The* COUNT *no longer defends himself*)

* * *

ACTRESS Well, what about mood, now, hypocrite?

COUNT You are a little devil.

ACTRESS Well, what a thing to say!

COUNT Very well, then, a little angel.

ACTRESS And you should have become an actor. Really! You know women. Do you know what I am going to do now?

COUNT Well?

ACTRESS I am going to tell you that I do not want to see you again.

COUNT But why?

ACTRESS No, never. You are too dangerous for me. You drive me out of my mind. And now you stand there as if nothing had happened.

COUNT But . . .

ACTRESS I beg you to remember, Count, that I have just been your mistress.

COUNT I shall never forget it!

ACTRESS And what about tonight?

COUNT What do you mean?

ACTRESS Well, you were going to wait for me after the theatre.

COUNT Oh, yes, all right; let's say the day after tomorrow.

ACTRESS What do you mean the day after tomorrow? I was talking about today.

COUNT There wouldn't be much sense to that.

ACTRESS Fossil!

COUNT You don't quite understand me. What I mean—how shall I say it—has more to do with the soul.

ACTRESS I'm not interested in your soul.

COUNT Believe me, it belongs there, too. I do not agree that you can separate the two.

ACTRESS Leave your philosophy out of it. If I want any, I'll read books.

COUNT Well, you don't learn from books anyway.

ACTRESS Quite true, and that is why you are going to wait for me tonight. Regarding your soul, we shall come to some sort of agreement, you scoundrel!

COUNT If you permit—I shall wait in my carriage.

ACTRESS You'll wait here. In my house.

COUNT . . . *After* the theatre.

ACTRESS Naturally. (*The* COUNT *puts on his sword*)

ACTRESS What are you doing?

COUNT I think it is time for me to go. Considering it is a formal call, I think I have stayed just a little over my time.

ACTRESS Tonight it won't be a formal call.

COUNT You think so?

ACTRESS Depend upon me. And now, give me another kiss, my little philosopher. Here, you seducer . . . you . . . sweet child, you devil, you tiger, you . . . (*After several ardent kisses, she thrusts him away*) Count, it was a great honor.

COUNT Your hand, Mademoiselle. (*At the door*) Au revoir!

ACTRESS Adieu, Steinamanger!

## Scene Ten

### *The Count and the Girl of the Streets*

*6 A.M. The room is shabby with one window. A dirty yellow roller blind is down and covered by faded green curtains. On the dresser, are a few photographs and a lady's hat in obvious bad taste. A few cheap Japanese fans are stuck behind the mirror. The table is covered with a cheap reddish cloth. On top of the table is a kerosene lamp; it is burning feebly and is covered by a cheap yellow lampshade. Beside it is a pitcher with some remaining beer, and a half-empty glass. On the floor, next to the bed, is an untidy pile of feminine clothing thrown there after having been taken off in a hurry. The* GIRL OF THE STREETS *is in bed asleep, breathing evenly. The* COUNT, *fully dressed, is on the divan, lying on his cape. His hat is on the floor at the head of the divan.*

COUNT Well, how did I . . . I see . . . so I actually did go home with this woman. . . . (*He rises rapidly, sees her in the bed*) Well, here she is. The adventures one can still have at my age. I haven't the faintest recollection . . . did they carry me up here. No . . . I saw it. I came into the room. Yes, I was still awake . . . or did I wake up . . . or maybe it is just that this room reminds me of something. Upon my soul. . . . No, I must have seen it yesterday. (*Looks at his watch*) What, yesterday? A few hours ago. But I knew that something would happen. I had a feeling . . . but what happened? Well, nothing—or maybe nothing—or maybe . . . ? Upon my soul—must be about ten years since I was in such a state that I just cannot remember. Well, in short, I was drunk. If I could just remember when I . . . Oh, yes, I recall exactly how I went into this street-walkers' café with Lulu and . . . no, no—we left the café . . . and then on the way it was . . . that's right. I drove in my carriage with Lulu—Oh, what am I breaking my head for? It makes no difference. Now then, let's get a move on. (*Sits up and the light shakes; he looks at the girl who is asleep*) Well, she is fast asleep. I don't remember anything but . . . I'll put some money on the table and adieu. (*Stands in front of her and looks at her awhile*) If only I didn't know what she is. (*Studies her again*) I have known many who didn't look as virtuous, even when they were asleep. Upon my soul—well, Lulu would say, I am philosophizing again. But it's true, sleep makes people alike—seems to me, like his brother death . . . but I would like to know it. . . . Well, it can't have slipped my mind . . . no, no, I just fell down on the divan . . . and nothing happened. . . . It is incredible how sometimes all women look alike— Well, let's go. (*Turns to go*) Oh, yes, that's right. (*He is about to get a bill from his wallet*)

GIRL (*Wakes up*) Well, who's that so early? (*Recognizing him*) Good morning, lover!

COUNT Good morning. Sleep well?

GIRL (*Stretches*) Oh, come over here. Give me a kiss.

COUNT (*Bends down, comes to his senses and pulls up short*) I was just going. . . .

GIRL Going?

COUNT It's high time.

GIRL You really want to go?

COUNT (*A little embarrassed*) Well . . .

GIRL All right, good-bye then. Come back some other time.

COUNT Yes, adieu then. Well, won't you give me your hand? (GIRL *pulls her hand from beneath the covers and extends it. He takes her hand mechanically, kisses it, catches himself, and laughs*) Like a princess! By the way, if I only . . .

GIRL Why are you looking at me that way?

COUNT If I saw only your head as now . . . on waking up. . . . One always looks so innocent. . . . Upon my soul . . . I could imagine all sorts of things if only it didn't smell so badly of kerosene. . . .

GIRL Yes, that lamp has always been a bother.

COUNT How old are you, anyway?

GIRL Well, guess?

COUNT Twenty-four.

GIRL Oh, yes—

COUNT You mean you are older?

GIRL I'm going on twenty.

COUNT And how long have you been . . .

GIRL I've been in the business a year.

COUNT Well, you started early.

GIRL Better too early than too late.

COUNT (*Sits down on the bed*) Tell me something, are you really happy?

GIRL What?

COUNT Well, I mean, are you . . . successful?

GIRL Oh, I do pretty well.

COUNT So . . . But has it never struck you that you might become something else?

GIRL What should I become?

COUNT Well, you're a very pretty girl. For instance, you could have a lover.

GIRL You think I don't have any?

COUNT Oh, yes, I know— But I mean one, you know —just one who would keep you so that you don't have to go with just anybody.

GIRL I don't go with just anybody. Thank God, that isn't necessary. I can take my pick. (*The* COUNT *looks around the room, the girl notices this*) Next month we're going to move into town. The Spiegelgasse.

COUNT We? Who is we?

GIRL Well, the madam and the few other girls who are living here.

COUNT There are more such—

GIRL Next door . . . listen? That's Milli, she was in the café too.

COUNT Somebody is snoring.

GIRL Yeh, that's Milli. She'll snore the whole day long till ten in the evening. Then she'll get up and go into the café.

COUNT But that is a horrible life!

GIRL Of course. And the madam gets disgusted with her. I'm always on the streets by twelve noon.

COUNT But what do you do on the streets at twelve noon!

GIRL What should I do? I'm looking for customers.

COUNT Oh . . . naturally . . . yes . . . (*He gets up again, takes out his wallet and puts a bill on the table*) Adieu.

GIRL Going already? . . . So long. . . . Come again soon. (*She turns over on her side*)

COUNT (*Stops again*) Tell me something. It doesn't mean a thing to you any more, right?

GIRL What?

COUNT I mean you don't get pleasure out of it any more?

GIRL (*Yawning*) I'm sleepy.

COUNT It is all the same to you, young or old, or whether . . .

GIRL Why are you asking?

COUNT Because . . . (*Suddenly remembering something*) Upon my soul, now I know who you remind me of . . . that is . . .

GIRL Do I look like somebody?

COUNT Incredible . . . incredible . . . now I would just like to ask something of you. Don't say a thing for at least a minute . . . (*He stares at her*) The same face, exactly the same face. (*He kisses her on the eyes*)

GIRL Well!

COUNT Upon my soul, it is a pity that you . . . are not something else . . . you could make a fortune.

GIRL You're just like Franz.

COUNT Who's Franz?

GIRL He's the waiter at our café.

COUNT Why am I just like Franz?

GIRL He also says I could make my fortune—and I should marry him!

COUNT Why don't you?

GIRL No thank you . . . I don't want to get married, not for any price. Later on, perhaps.

COUNT Those eyes . . . the same eyes. . . . Lulu would surely say I am a fool . . . but I would like to kiss your eyes once more . . . like this. And now adieu. Now I must go.

GIRL So long.

COUNT (*Turning at the door*) Say . . . doesn't it surprise you . . . ?

GIRL Well . . . what?

COUNT That I don't want anything from you.

GIRL There are many men who aren't in the mood in the morning.

COUNT . . . All right. (*To himself*) It's stupid of me that I would like her to wonder . . . Well, goodbye. (*At the door*) Actually, I am annoyed at myself. I *know* that these women are only after money . . . at least it is nice that she doesn't pretend, that should rather make me glad . . . (*To her*) you know, I will come again soon.

GIRL (*With her eyes closed*) Good.

COUNT When are you usually home?

GIRL I'm always at home. You just have to ask for Leocadia.

COUNT Leocadia . . . Good. Well, adieu. (*At the door*) I still have the wine in my head. This beats everything . . . in here with this one . . . and did nothing but kiss her eyes because she reminded me of someone. (*He turns to her*) Tell me, Leocadia, does it happen to you often that a man goes away like this?

GIRL Like how?

COUNT Like me.

GIRL In the morning?

COUNT . . . That men were with you and did not want anything of you?

GIRL No, it's never happened to me.

COUNT What do you think then? Do you think I don't like you?

GIRL Why shouldn't you like me? Last night you liked me.

COUNT I like you now too.

GIRL But last night you liked me better.

COUNT What makes you say that?

GIRL Well, what a thing to ask!

COUNT Last night . . . Tell me then, didn't I just fall down on the divan?

GIRL Sure . . . together with me.

COUNT With you?

GIRL Yes, don't you remember?

COUNT Did? . . . together with you . . . yes . . .

GIRL But you fell asleep right afterward.

COUNT Right afterward. . . . Oh . . . so that was it.

GIRL Yes, dear. You must have been good and drunk that you can't remember anything.

COUNT So . . . and yet . . . there is a remote resemblance . . . so long . . . (*He listens*) What's going on?

GIRL The maid is working. Give her something when you leave. The downstairs door is open, so you don't have to worry about the janitor.

COUNT Yes. . . . (*In the entrance hall, to himself*) It would have been beautiful if I had only kissed her eyes. It would have been almost an adventure . . . well, it wasn't meant to happen. (*The* MAID *opens the door for him*) Oh . . . here you are . . . Goodnight!

MAID Good morning!

COUNT Yes certainly . . . Good morning . . . Good morning!

# Frank Wedekind

## (1864-1918)

Despite the growing recognition of his genius by playwrights, producers, critics, and historians of the theatre, Frank Wedekind is perhaps the least popular major dramatist of our time. This is partly because he is not a "nice" playwright. His obsession with sexual perversion and aberration reflects a deep discontent with existing social and ethical values. Wedekind is a disturbing playwright. He wrote consciously in the face of conventional morality, attacking the prejudices of his public in a harsh and brutal way, and this is one reason for his failure to win acceptance on the stage. From a commercial standpoint, he is a bad risk. Critics and historians have found his work strange and bewildering, resisting easy labeling and classification. He refused to affiliate himself with any of the recognized literary groups, and this individualism is a further source of complexity in attempting to situate and evaluate his art. In particular, he had no use at all for naturalism, and constantly sought to go beyond the limits of naturalistic techniques. This is yet another source of difficulty: Wedekind's style makes special demands on the actor and director, and conventional realistic or naturalistic methods simply will not do. Finally, his work has appeared strange and mystifying because, in both attitudes and techniques, he was far in advance of his time. Even at mid-century, although many of his structural and stylistic devices have been widely adapted, he is, from a moral and psychological standpoint, in advance of our time as well. Increasingly, his works have imposed a claim on the attention of readers and spectators who are concerned with widening the boundaries of theatrical art.

Wedekind's background was international. He was born Benjamin Franklin Wedekind in Hanover, Germany, shortly after the return of his parents from America. His father, a physician who had spent ten years in the service of the sultan of Turkey, engaged in revolutionary activities in 1848, and the following year left for California in the gold rush. In San Francisco he married a German singer and actress half his age. The marriage was unhappy, and as a boy, Frank Wedekind suffered cruelly as a result of his parents' incompatibility. In 1872 the family moved to Switzerland, near Aarau, where the father bought an old castle and secluded himself on the top floor, seeing other members of the family only by accident. He destined Frank for a legal career, and the youth went to Munich to study law, but took up literary pursuits instead. In 1886 he told his father he wanted to be a writer. A terrible scene ensued and Wedekind struck his father with his fists. When later, in Zurich, he became friendly with the young Gerhart Hauptmann, he told Hauptmann about the event, and the latter used it as the basis of his second play, *Das Friedensfest* (*The Reconciliation*). The wounded Wedekind was to caricature Hauptmann in his early play of 1890, *Kinder und Narren* (*Children and Fools*), in the role of the poet Meier, who goes everywhere with his notebook seeking out material. Wedekind has Meier's girl-friend remark: "When he kissed me he always had his notebook in his hand, and with the other hand he noted down what kind of face I made." Even at the beginning of his career, Wedekind saw naturalism as a gray, dreary, and too-serious approach to the drama. In later life he disliked Hauptmann and his adherents partly from a sense of rivalry, but more because he felt that naturalism, with its conventional style and rejection of theatricality, gave the actor nothing to do. The sense of spectacle, of performance, is essential to all of Wedekind's work.

He began his career as a publicist and journalist in Zurich and Munich. In 1896 he collaborated in the founding of the famous satirical journal, *Simplizissimus,* to which Thomas Mann was an early contributor. Wedekind wrote political articles and satiric poetry for two years, then left Munich for Leipzig, where he served as play reader and director. He was also a gifted actor, and supported himself for long periods by performing in cabarets or in the theatre. As playwright and as satirist, he was frequently in collision with the authorities, and went to jail for a short time in 1900 for insulting the Emperor in print. The social attitudes of his central characters are often those of the convict or outlaw. Well before his jail sentence, Wedekind took a position in his plays which was boldly antagonistic to the moral conventions of his time.

His first major play, *Frühlings Erwachen* (*Spring's Awakening,* 1891) is revolutionary in both theme and technique. Subtitled "A Tragedy of Childhood," the drama unfolds in a series of short, fragmentary scenes, similar in manner to Goethe's *Faust* or the plays of Buechner and pointing directly to present-day epic style. Wedekind's adolescents run wild and end in disaster: one is a suicide, another is expelled from school and sent to a reformatory, a third dies after an abortion. The central characters, Moritz and Melchoir, are finally reunited in the graveyard where Moritz lies buried. His ghost appears, carrying its head in its hands.

Melchoir is torn between life and death, and must be rescued by the Man in the Mask (to whom the play is dedicated) who points the way to a life wherein man's physical needs and desires will be recognized rather than extirpated. *Spring's Awakening* is clearly among Wedekind's best plays and has enjoyed occasional waves of popularity, notably in Max Reinhardt's Berlin production of 1906 when it ran for 360 performances.

Wedekind's later dramas are harsher and even more violent. Lulu, the heroine of *Erdgeist* (*Earth Spirit,* 1894) and of *Büchse der Pandora* (*Pandora's Box,* 1901), is the incarnation of sexual compulsion and frenzy. Pandora-like in the false view of bliss she offers her admirers, Lulu is cursed by sexual abnormality and depravity that first attracts and then destroys her lovers. In *Earth Spirit* three husbands are driven to death by her. Wedekind originally planned to represent Lulu's career in a single play, but evidently could not get it all in and felt compelled to stretch it into two dramas. The second play presents a relatively passive Lulu, a fugitive from jail where she has served 18 months imprisonment. She barely escapes from the blackmailer and whoremaster, Casti-Piani, only to end as a streetwalker in London. In the final scene she suffers an excruciating death, butchered by the sex maniac, Jack the Ripper. Melodramatic and horrifying, the Lulu plays represent Wedekind's deepest probing into the psychopathology of sex.

In an essay of 1905, "Über Erotik," ("On Eroticism"), the playwright struck out vigorously at the traditional antithesis of body and soul, and the praise of spirit at the expense of flesh: "The body has a soul of its own." Modern life, he insists, is an evasion of emotion and of sexual experience. His plays are a deliberate attempt to overcome sexual taboos in the theatre as well as in society; they aim at clarification and enlightenment. Many of his short plays are in fact hymns to the joy of sensual pleasure; they demonstrate the triumph of male lucidity over female demoralization. Thus, *The Tenor* (1897) was described by the playwright as "the collision of a brutal intelligence with blind passions." Gerardo is unruffled by the desperation and ruin of the women who pursue him. Casti-Piani in *Death and Devil* (1905) is an even more outspoken moralist. He sees the persecution of vice as inverted sensuality, and prostitution as an altogether natural occupation. Sex is a trade like any other; life is essentially pain and suffering, redeemed only by the joys of the senses. Casti-Piani's suicide is sheer melodrama bordering on the farcical; his assault on moral hypocrisy is passionate and sincere.

Wedekind considered *The Marquis of Keith* (1900) his best play. The hero, a bold adventurer and master crook, was in fact modeled on one Willy Gretor whose company Wedekind frequented in Paris. Gretor was an art dealer and forger, a notorious swindler, a journalist and promoter, forever scheming and always surrounded by women. The self-styled Marquis of Keith is a master rogue who sees society as a contest between knaves and fools. Wedekind may have drawn for inspiration on Cagliostro or Casanova, or on Balzac's clever speculator, Mercadet. Keith is daring, inventive, reckless, inordinately fond of gambling for its own sake, one day on top and the next day on the bottom. His success is possible only by dint of unusual energy, concentration, and nerve. He overreaches himself and loses control of the enterprise he has created, yet even at the end he refuses to go under. The wonderful elasticity and adaptability of Keith is demonstrated repeatedly in the rapidity of his wit and his incredible composure in the most trying of circumstances. His principle that morality is simply good business and sin bad business is a logical extension of the code by which men actually live as opposed to that they profess. The object of satire is clearly not Keith but society.

Wedekind admired the play not only for the strength of character of his hero, who triumphs over physical infirmity and his lowly origins to become a genius of enterprise; he wrote the play, he told Thomas Mann, for the sake of the last scene between Keith and Scholz, in Act Five. Nowhere is his rapid, staccato dialogue more effective. The economy, lucidity, and concentration of language is breath-taking, and offers conclusive proof of the artistry Wedekind could command. The sharp, clear opposition of values juxtaposes the practical man and the ethical man, the sensualist and the moralist, life as affirmation and life as withdrawal. In the final interview Keith re-asserts his faith in his way of life in spite of everything, and vanquishes Scholz' temptations. We can well understand why Thomas Mann called this scene "the deepest, most terrifying and most moving of all that this deep, tormented playwright has written."

In all, Wedekind wrote over twenty plays. The best of his later works are probably *King Nicolo* (1905), a grotesque comedy wherein a deposed king becomes his successor's court fool, and *Franziska* (1911), in which illicit love and a pact with the devil lead to a rustic paradise that is perhaps an ironic version of the traditional happy ending. His attempts at historical drama (*Bismarck,* 1915) and at classical verse drama late in his career are distinctly inferior to his earlier work. Wedekind was at his best in the underworld of acrobats, clowns, gamblers, prostitutes, whoremasters, nymphomaniacs, and other raffish and sordid creatures who see respectable society at a tilted angle, but whose distortion is at the same time a source of profound insight into social values. Even more than a reformer, Wedekind was a keen psychologist, seeking to explore naked and bestial passion uncompromisingly. His love of parody, irony, burlesque, and artificiality is an actor's love of the theatre, an expression of an effort to recover the theatrical and spectacular at a time when naturalism had all but driven it underground. In his experimentation in epic structure and the grotesque, he looks forward to Brecht, Duerrenmatt, and the theatre of cruelty. A forceful and striking playwright, his work will continue to exert a strange fascination as a revelation of the inner self and as a prophecy of the violence of our times.

# THE MARQUIS OF KEITH

## (Scenes of Munich)

### *A Play in Five Acts*

Translated by Beatrice Gottlieb[1]

CHARACTERS

CONSUL CASIMIR, *a merchant*
HERMANN CASIMIR, *his son (15 years old)*
THE MARQUIS OF KEITH
ERNST SCHOLZ
MOLLY GRIESINGER
ANNA, *the widowed* COUNTESS WERDENFELS
SARANIEFF, *a painter*
ZAMRIAKI, *a composer*
SOMMERSBERG, *a man of letters*
RASPE, *a police inspector*
OSTERMEIER, *proprietor of a brewery*
KRENTZL, *a builder*
GRANDAUER, *a restaurateur*
FRAU OSTERMEIER
FRAU KRENTZL
BARONESS VON ROSENKRON } *divorcées*
BARONESS VON TOTLEBEN } *divorcées*
SASHA
SIMBA
A BUTCHER'S ASSISTANT
A BAKERY WOMAN
A PORTER
PATRONS OF THE HOFBRAUHÄUS

*The action takes place in Munich, late summer, 1899.*

## Act One

*A study, the walls of which are hung with pictures. In the rear wall, on the right, is the door to the hall; on the left is the door to a waiting room. Downstage right is a door which leads to the living room. Downstage left is a writing table on which are lying unrolled plans. On the wall near the writing table, a telephone. Downstage right, a sofa; in front of it a smallish table; in the center, partly upstage, is a large table. Bookcases, full of books. Musical instruments. Sheafs of documents, sheet music.*

THE MARQUIS OF KEITH *is sitting at the writing table, absorbed in one of the plans. He is about twenty-seven years old: medium height, slim, bony physique. He would be perfectly built if not for the limp in his left leg. His expressive features are nervous, at the same time have a certain hardness. He has piercing gray eyes, a small blond mustache; his unruly short straw-blond hair is carefully parted in the middle. He is carefully but not foppishly dressed in a finely tailored suit. He has the coarse red hands of a clown.*

MOLLY GRIESINGER *comes out of the living room and puts a tray with food on the small table in front of the sofa. She is a plain creature with brunette hair, somewhat shy and harassed looking, wearing a plain house dress; but she has large, black, soulful eyes.*

MOLLY Here, dear. Here's tea and caviar and cold meat. You were up at nine o'clock today.

KEITH (*Without moving*) Thank you, my dear child.

MOLLY You must be awfully hungry. Have you found out if the Fairyland Palace is going to be built?

KEITH Can't you see I'm working?

MOLLY You're always working when I come in. That's why I have to find out about you and your projects from your lady friends.

KEITH (*Turning around in his chair*) I once knew a woman who covered her ears when I spoke about plans. She'd say, "Come and tell me when you've *done* something!"

MOLLY That's what makes me miserable, that you've known all kinds of women. (*A bell rings*) God in Heaven, who can that be now! (*She goes into the hall to open the door*)

[1] From the text published by Albert Langen Verlag, Munich, 1901.

KEITH (*To himself*) Poor little wretch!

MOLLY (*Returns with a card*) A young gentleman wishes to see you. I told him you were working.

KEITH (*After reading the card*) Just the person I wanted to see!

(MOLLY *shows* HERMANN CASIMIR *in and exits into the living room*)

HERMANN CASIMIR (*A student of fifteen, in an exquisitely tailored cycling suit*) Good morning, Herr Baron.

KEITH What brings you here?

HERMANN The best thing is for me to come right out with it. Last night I was at the Café Luitpold with Saranieff and Zamriaki. I told them I was in desperate need of a hundred marks. Saranieff thought I could ask you.

KEITH Everyone in Munich thinks I'm an American railroad tycoon.

HERMANN Zamriaki said you always had money.

KEITH I am Zamriaki's patron because he is the greatest musical genius since Richard Wagner. But those bohemians aren't fit company for you!

HERMANN I think they are interesting. I made the acquaintance of the gentlemen at a meeting of the "Independents."

KEITH It must be a pleasant shock to your father to know that you're making your start in life by going to revolutionary meetings.

HERMANN Why doesn't my father let me leave Munich!

KEITH Because you're too young.

HERMANN But I think that at my age you learn so much more from real experience than by squirming on a school bench until you're grown up.

KEITH Real experience would strip you of your natural gifts. Particularly in your case, the son and sole heir of the greatest financial genius in Germany— What does your father say about me?

HERMANN My father never talks to me.

KEITH But he talks to other people.

HERMANN I'm not at home very much.

KEITH That's wrong of you. I've followed your father's financial operations since before I left America. Unfortunately, your father thinks no one else can be as clever as he is. That's why he stubbornly refuses to join my project.

HERMANN Try as I may, I can't imagine ever being happy with a life like my father's.

KEITH What if your father doesn't know how to make you interested in his work . . . ?

HERMANN But the important thing is not just to live. What's important is to learn everything about life and the world.

KEITH Your desire to learn everything about the world will be your ruin. The thing for you to do is to cultivate a favorable attitude toward the environment into which you were born. It will keep you from degrading yourself so cheerfully.

HERMANN There are things of higher value than money!

KEITH That's what they teach you in school. They are called "higher" because they're built on money; they're possible only because of money. You can devote yourself to an artistic or scientific career because your father's already made a fortune. But if, in doing so, you lose sight of the world's guiding principle your legacy will drop right into the clutches of swindlers.

HERMANN If Jesus Christ had acted according to that guiding principle . . .

KEITH Christianity liberated two-thirds of mankind from slavery. No ideas—social, scientific, or artistic —deal with anything but property. That's why the "Independents" are sworn enemies of property. And don't think the world will ever change. It's man who adjusts or perishes. (*Has sat down at the writing table*) I will give you the hundred marks. But come around some time when you don't need money. How long is it since your mother died?

HERMANN This spring will be three years.

KEITH (*Handing him a sealed note*) You're to take this to Countess Werdenfels, 25 Brienner Street. Tell her I send my very best regards. I happen to have nothing on me today.

HERMANN Thank you, Herr Baron.

KEITH (*Shows him out; as he closes the door after him*) To be sure, the pleasure was mine. (*He goes back to the writing table; rummaging among the plans*) His old man treats me like a dog catcher. I must arrange a concert as soon as possible. Then public opinion will force him to join my project. If worst comes to worst it will have to go ahead without him. (*There is a knock at the door*) Come in!

(ANNA, COUNTESS WERDENFELS *enters. She is a voluptuous beauty of thirty. White skin, turned-up nose, pale eyes, luxuriant chestnut-brown hair*)

KEITH (*Goes up to her*) Well, here you are, my queen! I just sent young Casimir to you with a little request.

ANNA So that was young Herr Casimir?

KEITH (*After kissing her lightly on her mouth, which she has offered him*) He'll come again if he doesn't find you.

ANNA He doesn't look at all like his father.

KEITH Let's forget his father. I have approached some people who are such parvenus I think they will be extremely enthusiastic about our project.

ANNA Everyone says that Casimir patronizes young artists.

KEITH When I look at you I become another person, as though you were the living pledge of my good luck. Won't you have breakfast with me? There's tea and caviar and cold meat.

ANNA (*Sits down on the sofa and eats*) I have a lesson at eleven. I've come for just a moment. Madame Bianchi tells me that in a year I could be the best Wagnerian soprano in Germany.

KEITH (*Lights a cigarette*) Perhaps in a year you will have done so well that the best Wagnerian sopranos will want your patronage.

ANNA That's fine! It's hard for me, with my limited woman's intelligence, to see how I can reach the heights so soon.

KEITH I don't take any responsibility for it. I just let myself be pulled along without resisting until I get to a spot where I feel at home and then I say to myself: this is where to build!

ANNA I can't feel that way. For some time now I've been so desperately in love with life I've sometimes thought of suicide.

KEITH Some men take what they want, others get it as a gift. When I went out into the world my highest hope was to end up as a village schoolmaster in Upper Silesia.

ANNA You never dreamt that one day Munich would lie at your feet.

KEITH Munich was something I'd only heard about in geography class. If my reputation isn't exactly spotless, don't forget the depths from which I have risen.

ANNA Every night I pray to God to transmit some of your energy to me.

KEITH I have no energy.

ANNA But you have a compulsion to keep running your head against stone walls.

KEITH Unfortunately, my talent is limited by the fact that I can't breathe in a middle-class atmosphere. If I get what I want in spite of this limitation I can't take any credit for it. Other men are planted in a certain spot and vegetate there without ever coming into conflict with the world.

ANNA But, after all, you didn't fall from the sky.

KEITH I am, however, a bastard. My father was a very distinguished intellectual, particularly in the field of mathematics and such scientific matters, and my mother was a Gypsy.

ANNA If I could read the secrets in people's faces, as you do, I'd grind their noses into the ground with my foot.

KEITH Gifts like that only arouse distrust. Middle-class society has been secretly afraid of me all my life because of it.

ANNA For three years I've gone about in society with lowered eyelids and raised eyebrows, and all that time I've longed to be able to open my eyes.

KEITH Because of its timidity, society is responsible for my success. The higher I go the more they trust me. In fact, I expect to reach the point some day where the mixture of philosopher and horse thief will be fully appreciated.

ANNA The whole town is talking about nothing but your Fairyland Palace.

KEITH The Fairyland Palace is merely a rallying point for my powers. I know myself too well to expect myself to audit account books all my life.

ANNA And I don't want to sing scales and exercises all my life. You said that the Fairyland Palace would be built for me. Why are you throwing away all this money on my training?

KEITH Certainly not so that you should spend the rest of your life prancing on your hind legs and being criticized by the idiots on newspapers. You could use a few more highlights in your past.

ANNA Well, I have no family tree, like Mesdames von Rosenkron and von Totleben.

KEITH You needn't envy anyone for that.

ANNA Are there any feminine charms I should envy any woman for?

KEITH You don't have the slightest reason.

ANNA I know it. And there isn't the slightest cause for you to have any doubts about it.

KEITH I had to take over both ladies with the concert agency as a legacy from my predecessor.

ANNA There are thousands of women like that, who need a man to make them aware of their worth.

KEITH Well, there are thousands of men who love women like that.

ANNA Are you one of them?

KEITH As soon as I get myself established, I don't care if they sell radishes or write novels for a living.

ANNA I care more about the shine on my shoes than I do for your feelings. Shall I tell you why? Because you are the most inconsiderate person in the world. You only care about your own gratification. On the other hand, I really don't think I could feel anything but pity for a man who left me.

KEITH Behind me is a life full of sudden changes, but now I'm thinking seriously of building a house—a house with high-ceilinged rooms, a park, and broad steps leading up to the entrance. Complete with beggars to give the driveway some tone. I've cut myself off from my past and have no wish to go back. It was too often a life-and-death struggle. I wouldn't advise a friend to take my career as a model.

ANNA You're indestructible.

KEITH Yes, I can thank that for everything I've accomplished till now. Anna, I think that if we had been born in two different worlds we would have had to find each other.

ANNA I'm rather indestructible too.

KEITH Even if Providence hadn't shown us we were meant for each other by giving us the same tastes, we have something else in common—

ANNA Excellent health.

KEITH As far as women are concerned, I believe that intelligence, health, sensitivity, and beauty are inseparable; any one leads automatically to the other three. If these traits are intensified . . .

(SASHA, *a thirteen-year-old errand boy in braid jacket and knee breeches, enters from the hall and places an armful of newspapers on the center table*)

KEITH What does Councillor Ostermeier say?

SASHA The Councillor gave me a letter. It's with the newspapers. (*He goes into the waiting room*)

KEITH (*Has opened the letter*) This is because you're with me! (*Reads*) ". . . I have been told something about your plans and am very interested in them. Meet me at noon today in the Café Maximilian. . . ." This puts the world right in the palm of my hand! Now I can turn my back on old Casimir if he decides to come along. With these worthy burghers, my authority is unchallenged.

ANNA (*Has risen*) Can you give me a thousand marks?

KEITH Are you in the red again?

ANNA The rent is due.

KEITH That can wait till tomorrow. Don't worry about it.

ANNA As you think best. Count Werdenfels prophesied on his deathbed that I would learn about life's bitter realities some day.

KEITH If he had appreciated you more he might still be alive.

ANNA So far his prophecy has not been fulfilled.

KEITH I'll send you the money tomorrow at noon.

ANNA (*As* KEITH *sees her out*) No, please don't; I'll come and get it.

(*The stage remains empty for a moment. Then* MOLLY GRIESINGER *comes out of the living room and clears away the dishes.* KEITH *returns from the hall*)

KEITH (*Calls*) Sasha! (*Takes one of the pictures off the wall*) This will have to see me through the next two weeks.

MOLLY You still hope we can keep going like this?

SASHA (*Comes out of the waiting room*) Herr Baron?

KEITH (*Gives him the picture*) Go to Tannhäuser. Tell him to put this Saranieff in his window. I'll give it to him for three thousand marks.

SASHA Very good, Herr Baron.

KEITH I'll be there myself in five minutes. Wait! (*He takes from the writing table a card which says "3,000 M." and slips it into the picture frame*) Three thousand marks! (*Goes to the writing table*) I just have to dash off a newspaper article about it.

(SASHA *exits with the picture*)

MOLLY If we could ever see the smallest result come out of all this big talk.

KEITH (*Writing*) "The Aesthetic Ideal in the Modern Landscape."

MOLLY If Saranieff could paint, you wouldn't have to write articles about him.

KEITH (*Turning around*) I beg your pardon?

MOLLY I know, you're working.

KEITH What did you want to say?

MOLLY I got a letter from Bückeburg.

KEITH From your mama?

MOLLY (*Takes the letter out of her pocket and reads*) "You are both welcome here at any time. You can have the two front rooms on the third floor. Then you can take it easy until your business in Munich is settled."

KEITH Don't you see, my dear child, that these little letters of yours undermine my credit?

MOLLY There's no bread for tomorrow.

KEITH Then we'll dine at the Hotel Continental.

MOLLY I wouldn't be able to swallow a bite for fear the bailiff would come and attach our beds in the meantime.

KEITH He's still in the process of thinking about it. Why is there nothing in your little head but food and drink? Your life could be so much happier if you looked at the brighter side of things. You have an incorrigible affection for misfortune.

MOLLY *You* do! Other people have such an easy time of it; they don't ever have to worry. They live for each other, in comfortable homes where their happiness is secure. But you, with all your gifts, behave like a madman, ruining your health, and we still never have a penny in the house.

KEITH But you've always had enough to eat! If you don't spend anything on clothes it's not my fault. As soon as I write this article I'll have three thousand marks. Take a cab and buy everything you can think of on the spur of the moment.

MOLLY He's as likely to pay three thousand marks for that picture as I am to wear silk stockings!

KEITH You're a jewel!

MOLLY (*Throws her arms around him*) Have I hurt you, darling? Forgive me! What I just told you—I'm convinced it's the solemn truth.

KEITH Even if the money lasts only until tomorrow, I won't regret the sacrifice.

MOLLY I know how awful it was of me. Beat me!

KEITH The Fairyland Palace is as good as certain.

MOLLY At least let me kiss your hand. Please, please, let me kiss your hand.

KEITH If I can only preserve my composure for the next few days.

MOLLY Won't you let me? How can you be so inhuman?

KEITH (*Takes his hand out of his pocket*) It's about time you looked to yourself. Otherwise you're in for a big surprise.

MOLLY (*Covering his hand with kisses*) Why won't you beat me? I deserve it.

KEITH You are deceiving yourself about your happiness with all the means a woman has at her disposal.

MOLLY Don't think that I'm frightened by your flirtations! We're held together by too strong a bond. If it ever breaks I won't keep you. But as long as your luck is bad you belong to me.

KEITH It will be your downfall that you fear my good fortune more than death. If my hands are free tomorrow you won't stay here another minute.

MOLLY That's fine. I'm glad you're so sure.

KEITH But my luck isn't bad now!

MOLLY At least let me keep on working for you until your hands are free.

KEITH Very well, do what you won't let me do. You know there's nothing I dislike more than a woman who works.

MOLLY I will not make myself a doll or a peacock for your sake. If I stand over a washtub instead of riding about half-naked to masquerades with you, it certainly can't ruin me.

KEITH Your obstinacy is superhuman.

MOLLY I'm sure it's beyond your comprehension.

KEITH Even if I understood, it wouldn't help you.

MOLLY I don't *have* to push it in your face, but I'll spell it out for you, if you want! I wouldn't be any happier if I acted differently and thought I was better than God made me, because you love me!

KEITH That's obvious.

MOLLY Because you can't live without me. Have your hands as free as you want! If I stay with you, it's up to me. Let women dress themselves in finery and idolize you as much as they please; it saves me the trouble of going to comedies. Oh, you're an idealist;

I know all about that. But if you ever did anything about your ideals—a fine chance there is of it!—I'd gladly let myself be buried alive.

KEITH If you would only take what you're offered!

MOLLY (*Tenderly*) What am I offered, my love? We had these endless fears in America, too. Everything always fell apart in the end. In Santiago you weren't elected president and were nearly sentenced to be shot because on the crucial evening we had no brandy to put on the table. Remember how you shouted, "A dollar, a dollar, a republic for a dollar!"

KEITH I came into the world a cripple. I do not feel I'm destined to be a slave because of it. And the fact that I was born a beggar does not prevent me from looking at the most extravagant luxury as my rightful heritage.

MOLLY As long as you live you'll only *look* at luxury.

KEITH Only death can change what I'm telling you. And death doesn't dare attack me, because it's afraid of making itself ridiculous. If I die without having lived, my ghost will come back.

MOLLY You have a swelled head.

KEITH I know I'm right! When you ran away to America with me you were an irresponsible child of fifteen, right out of school. If we part now and you're left to fend for yourself, you'll come to the worst end imaginable.

MOLLY (*Pleading*) Come to Bückeburg, then! My parents haven't seen their Molly in three years. They'll be so overjoyed they'll give you half their money. And how well we could live!

KEITH In Bückeburg? [1]

MOLLY All troubles come to an end sometime.

KEITH I'd rather pick up cigar butts in the cafés.

SASHA (*Returns with the picture*) Herr Tannhäuser says he can't put it in the window. Herr Tannhäuser says he has another picture by Herr Saranieff.

MOLLY I knew it all along!

KEITH That's why I keep you with me! Then I don't have to write the article!

(SASHA *puts the picture on the table and goes into the waiting room*)

MOLLY These Saranieffs and Zamriakis, you see, are people who belong to an entirely different race from us. They know how to empty people's pockets. We're both of us too simple for the great world.

KEITH Your kingdom is not yet come. Leave me alone. Bückeburg will have to wait.

MOLLY (*At a ring in the corridor*) The bailiff!

(*She runs to open the door*)

KEITH (*Looks at his watch*) What else can be sacrificed to fortune . . . ?

MOLLY (*Shows in* ERNST SCHOLZ) The gentleman won't give me his name.

(ERNST SCHOLZ *is a slim man of extremely aristocratic appearance, about twenty-seven years old; black, wavy hair; a Vandyke; under powerful elongated eyebrows big watery-blue eyes with a helpless expression*)

[1] Bückeburg is a small city in an agricultural section of northern Germany, not far from Hanover.

KEITH Gaston! Where have you come from?

SCHOLZ Your greeting is a good sign. I am so changed I thought you would have trouble recognizing me.

(MOLLY *is about to remove the breakfast dishes but, after a glance at* SCHOLZ, *is afraid that she will disturb them; she goes into the living room without the dishes*)

KEITH You look a little worn out; but the world is no puppet show.

SCHOLZ Certainly not for me; that's why I'm here. It's because of you that I've come to Munich.

KEITH Thank you; whatever I have left over from my business is yours.

SCHOLZ I know that life is a hard struggle for you. I want to be associated with you now on a personal basis. I would like to submit myself to your spiritual guidance for a time, but on one condition; you must allow me to help you financially as much as you need.

KEITH I'm about to become the director of a corporation. But what are you doing? If I'm not mistaken, the last time we saw each other was four years ago.

SCHOLZ At the legal convention in Brussels.

KEITH You had just passed your state examination.

SCHOLZ You were already writing for all the daily papers. Do you recall how I reproached you for your cynicism at the ball in the Palace of Justice?

KEITH You had fallen in love with the daughter of the Danish ambassador, and you were furious with me when I maintained that women are by nature more materialistic than men could ever be, even after experiencing the greatest luxury.

SCHOLZ I still think you are an unscrupulous monster, as I did all through our boyhood; but—you were absolutely right.

KEITH I've never been more flattered.

SCHOLZ I am worn out. Although I abhor your view of life from the bottom of my heart, I place in your hands today the riddle of my existence, which I find insoluble.

KEITH But why so solemn? I hope you are abandoning melancholy and turning toward the sun.

SCHOLZ My own inclinations would never have allowed me to do this; but certain things happened.

KEITH So much the better for you!

SCHOLZ This is not a cowardly surrender. I've tried in every way to solve the riddle myself, but in vain.

KEITH In Cuba I was to be shot with twelve conspirators. At the first shot I fell down, and stayed "dead" until they came to bury me. We incur no obligations at birth, and the most we can do is renounce everything. If that doesn't help, we can go outside the rules. In Brussels at that time you intended going into government work?

SCHOLZ I went into our Ministry of Railroads.

KEITH I wondered why, with your enormous wealth, you didn't prefer to be your own master.

SCHOLZ I intended to become, first, a useful member of human society. If I had been the son of a laborer it would have happened as a matter of course.

KEITH In this world you can help your fellow men most when you work for your own advantage. The broader my interest, the more people depend on me. Whoever thinks he's accomplishing something by merely doing his job and feeding his children is pulling the wool over his own eyes. The children would be thankful never to have been brought into the world, and a hundred poor devils are begging for the same job.

SCHOLZ But I didn't see why my wealth was any reason for me to be a useless idler. I have no artistic talent, and I did not consider myself insignificant enough to be satisfied merely with a happy marriage.

KEITH You've left the government?

SCHOLZ Because I was responsible for a terrible accident.

KEITH When I came back from America, someone who had seen you the year before in Constantinople told me you had spent two years traveling but that you were back home and going to be married.

SCHOLZ I broke my engagement yesterday. I was only half a man. Since I came of age I was guided by the idea that I would not be able to enjoy my existence until I had justified it through honest work. This point of view has now led me to seek pleasure, through sense of duty, nothing else, as though I were doing some kind of penance. But every time I want to open my arms to life I am paralyzed by the thought of those happy people who lost their lives and their happiness because I was overly conscientious.

KEITH What happened?

SCHOLZ I changed one of the railroad regulations. There had been some danger that it could not possibly be obeyed to the letter. My fears were exaggerated, but every day I seemed to see disaster come closer. I didn't have the mental equilibrium of people who come from homes where human values are respected. The first day after my new regulation went into effect there was a collision in which five people lost their lives. I visited the scene of the accident myself. It's not my fault I am still alive after seeing it.

KEITH And then you went traveling?

SCHOLZ I went to England, to Italy, but still felt cut off from all human life. In pleasant, gay surroundings, in the midst of deafeningly loud music, I suddenly hear a piercing cry, because I become aware of myself. In the Orient too I lived like an exiled wretch. To be frank, since that awful day I have become thoroughly convinced that I can buy back my life only through self-sacrifice. But I must have access to the world. I hoped I had found the way when I became engaged to a very wonderful girl of lower-class origins.

KEITH You really wanted to make her Countess Trautenau?

SCHOLZ I am no longer Count Trautenau. You can't understand that. The press quite effectively played up the contrast between my title and the accident I was responsible for. I felt it was my duty to my family to take another name. For two years my name has been Ernst Scholz. That is why my engagement could occasion no surprise; but disaster would have come from that, too. In her heart, not a spark of love; in mine, only the need to sacrifice myself; our relationship an endless chain of the most trivial misunderstandings. . . . I've given the girl an ample dowry so that she will be a good match for anyone in her class. She is overjoyed at having her freedom again. And now at last I must acquire the difficult art of forgetting myself. Men face death with complete awareness; but living is impossible unless one can forget oneself.

KEITH My father would turn over in his grave if he knew that you—were asking for my advice.

SCHOLZ That's how life contradicts bookish wisdom. Your father contributed his share to my one-sided development.

KEITH My father was as selfless and conscientious as the tutor and mentor of a Count Trautenau should be. You were his model student, and I was the whipping boy.

SCHOLZ Don't you remember how you used to be kissed by the maids, and all the more passionately when I happened to be around? I shall spend the next two or three years solely in training myself to be a sensualist.

KEITH Let's go tonight to the pleasure garden at Nymphenburg.[2] It's as unsuitable for people like us as you can imagine. But with all the rain and sleet falling on my head, I'm tempted to bathe in mud again.

SCHOLZ I don't have any great desire for the noises of the marketplace.

KEITH You won't hear a single loud word, just something like the hollow roar of the ocean uprooted from its bed. Munich is both Arcadia and Babylon. The silent Saturnalian frenzy that overpowers the soul here at every turn retains its charm even for the most blasé.

SCHOLZ How could I be blasé? I have never in my life had any pleasure.

KEITH We shall have to keep the crowd away. When I appear in such places they react like flies to carrion. But I can guarantee that you will forget yourself. If only you can laugh again with a full heart.

SCHOLZ I have actually asked myself if my tremendous wealth is not the only reason for my misfortune.

KEITH That's blasphemy!

SCHOLZ I really considered giving up my wealth as I did my title. As long as I am alive, however, that could benefit only my family. I can wait till I am on my deathbed to dispose of my property best, after it has ruined my life. If I had had to struggle from my youth, with my moral earnestness and my diligence I would probably be in the middle of a brilliant career today, instead of being an outcast.

KEITH Or else you would be wallowing with your lower-class girl in a thousand ecstasies and cleaning other men's dirty shoes.

SCHOLZ I would exchange that for my lot anytime.

KEITH Get rid of the idea that your memories are an obstacle to the enjoyment of life. You feed on

[2] A suburb of Munich noted for its castle, parks, and gardens.

them only because you're too inept to provide yourself with more delicate nourishment.

SCHOLZ You may be right. That is why I am here.

KEITH We'll find some kind of morsel. I'm sorry I can't ask you to have breakfast with me. I have a business appointment at twelve with a local big-wig. But I will write you a few words for you to take to my friend Raspe. Spend the afternoon with him; we will meet at six at the Hofgarten Café. (*He has gone to the writing table and is writing a note*)

SCHOLZ What kind of business are you in?

KEITH I am an art dealer. I write for the papers. I have a concert agency—none of it worth talking about. You have come just in time to see the founding of a concert hall which is being built for the exclusive use of my artists.

SCHOLZ (*Takes the picture from the table and examines it*) You have a nice picture collection.

KEITH I wouldn't take ten thousand marks for that. A Saranieff. You have to hold it this way.

SCHOLZ I don't know anything about art. In all my travels, I never visited a museum.

KEITH (*Gives him the note*) This man is an international police official; so don't be too open with him at first. A charming man, but people never know whether they should keep an eye on me or whether I am here to keep an eye on them.

SCHOLZ Thank you for your kind welcome. This evening, then, at six.

KEITH Then to Nymphenburg. Thank you for finally having some confidence in me.

(KEITH *shows* SCHOLZ *out. The stage is empty for a moment. Then* MOLLY GRIESINGER *comes out of the living room and removes the dishes from the table.* KEITH *returns immediately*)

KEITH (*Calling*) Sasha! (*Goes to the telephone and rings up*) Seventeen thirty-five—Inspector Raspe!

SASHA (*Comes out of the waiting room*) Herr Baron!

KEITH My hat! My overcoat!

(SASHA *hurries into the hall*)

MOLLY I beg you not to have anything to do with this patron! He wouldn't have come if he didn't want to take advantage of us.

KEITH (*Speaks into the telephone*) Thank God, you're there! Just wait ten minutes. You'll see for yourself. (*To* MOLLY, *as* SASHA *helps him on with his overcoat*) I'm rushing out to the newspaper offices.

MOLLY What should I write to Mama?

KEITH (*To* SASHA) A carriage!

SASHA Yes, Herr Baron. (*Exit*)

KEITH Tell her I pay her my deepest respects. (*Goes to the writing table*) The plans—Ostermeier's letter—tomorrow morning Munich must know that the Fairyland Palace is going to be built!

MOLLY Then you're not coming to Bückeburg?

KEITH (*The rolled-up plans under his arm, takes his hat from the center table and puts it on at an angle*) I can't help wondering how he's going to become a sensualist! (*Exit hastily*)

# Act Two

*In the* MARQUIS OF KEITH'S *study the center table is laid for breakfast: champagne and a large dish of oysters. The* MARQUIS OF KEITH *is sitting with his back to the writing table and his left foot on a stool, as* SASHA, *kneeling in front of him, buttons his shoes with a button hook.* ERNST SCHOLZ *is standing behind the sofa, trying out a guitar which he has taken from the wall.*

SCHOLZ After last night's conversations about art and modern literature I wonder if I shouldn't take lessons from that girl. I was amazed when she asked if she could wait on your guests at that garden party you spoke of, which is going to be such a sensation.

KEITH I know with whom I'm dealing! Anyway, there's time to talk about the garden party. Tomorrow I'm going to Paris for a few days.

SCHOLZ This comes at a very inconvenient time for me.

KEITH Come along. I want one of my artists to sing for Madam Marquesi before she makes her debut here.

SCHOLZ Must I relive the mental anguish I suffered in Paris?

KEITH I hoped that last night would have a more salutary effect. Very well, spend your time with Saranieff in my absence. He'll probably turn up somewhere today.

SCHOLZ She told me he was a Satanist, that his studio was a chamber of horrors, full of all the shocking atrocities known to man.

KEITH That is to make the pre-Raphaelite angels' heads he paints seem more valuable to his customers.

SCHOLZ She chattered in the most delightful way about her childhood, how she used to spend all summer sitting in the cherry trees in the Tyrol and how on winter afternoons she used to go sleigh-riding with the village children till nightfall. How can such a girl consider it an honor to be a maid at your party?

KEITH Till now the girl has had no more right to exist than the grass between the Munich cobblestones. She has not yet been crushed; so she is taking advantage of the opportunity to pay her humble respects to the present social order, which has the deepest contempt for her.

SCHOLZ How can the contempt be justified? How many hundreds of women in the best circles of society live desolate lives because the wellsprings of life are dried up in them! In her they overflow. The child's excesses of joy are no sin like the deadly discord in which my parents managed to endure each other for twenty years!

KEITH What is sin!

SCHOLZ Even yesterday I thought I was sure I knew. But today I can come right out and say what thousands and thousands of respectable people like me have felt. A man whose life is unfulfilled is bitterly envious of those who have strayed from the path of virtue.

KEITH The happiness of those creatures would not be so despised if it weren't the most unprofitable business in the world. Sin is simply a ridiculous term for bad business. Good business must fit into the existing social order! No one knows that better than I. As far as my European reputation is concerned, I am as much outside the pale of society as that girl. In fact, that's the reason I'm giving the garden party. I can't have her as one of my guests. It will be in much better taste if she is one of the servants.

SASHA (*Has risen*) Does the Herr Baron wish me to call a carriage?

KEITH Yes.

(SASHA *exit*)

KEITH (*Stamping his feet to get his shoes on securely*) Did you read that The Fairyland Palace Company was formed yesterday?

SCHOLZ I haven't looked at a newspaper since yesterday.

(*They both sit down at the breakfast table*)

KEITH The project rests on a brewer, a builder, and a restaurant owner. They are the caryatids who support the pediment of the temple.

SCHOLZ Your friend Raspe, the police official, is a charming person.

KEITH He's a scoundrel, but I like him anyway.

SCHOLZ He told me he was originally a theology student, but he lost his faith from studying too much, and tried to get it back the way the prodigal son did.

KEITH He sank lower and lower until finally the arm of the law embraced him and gave the precious thing back to him by keeping him under lock and key for two years. He is still so concerned about it, that he continues to spend all his time on the most worldly matters.

SCHOLZ That girl simply could not understand why I had never learned to ride a bicycle. She thought it was very clever of me not to ride a bicycle in Asia and Africa, because of the wild animals. But I could have begun in Italy!

KEITH I warn you again, my dear friend, don't be too open with people! Truth is our most precious possession and we must use it sparingly.

SCHOLZ Is that why you've taken the name Marquis of Keith?

KEITH I have as much right to be called the Marquis of Keith as you have to be called Ernst Scholz. I am the adopted son of Lord Keith, who in 1863 . . .

SASHA (*Enters from the hall, announcing*) Professor Saranieff!

(SARANIEFF *enters. Wears a black frock coat with sleeves a little too long, light-colored trousers that are a little too short, thick shoes, and bright red gloves; his somewhat long, bristling black hair is cut straight all around; in front of his eyes, which are full of anticipation, is a pince-nez on a black ribbon à la Murillo; his profile is very expressive; he has a small Spanish mustache. After his greeting he hands his top hat to* SASHA.)

SARANIEFF I wish you the best of luck from the bottom of my heart, my dear friend. At last the moorings are cut and the balloon can rise!

KEITH My high command is awaiting me; I'm sorry I can't invite you to breakfast now.

SARANIEFF (*Sitting down at the table*) I release you from the obligation of issuing an invitation.

KEITH Another place, Sasha!

(SASHA *has hung the hat up in the hall and goes into the living room*)

SARANIEFF The only thing that surprises me is that the great Casimir's name is not included on the board of directors.

KEITH That is because I don't want to lose the credit for having created my own work. (*Introducing them*) Saranieff, the painter—Count Trautenau.

SARANIEFF (*Takes a glass and plate and helps himself. To* SCHOLZ) Count, I know you already, inside and out. (*To* KEITH) Simba was just with me; she's sitting for a Boecklin.

KEITH (*To* SCHOLZ) Boecklin is a great painter too, you know. (*To* SARANIEFF) You don't have to boast about your tricks!

SARANIEFF Just make me famous! I'll pay you ten percent for life. Look at Zamriaki; his mind is tottering like a rickety fencepost because he wants so much to be immortal.

KEITH I am concerned only with his music. For the true composer a mind is a hindrance.

SCHOLZ To want immortality one must have an extraordinary love of life.

SARANIEFF (*To* SCHOLZ) By the way, our Simba described you to me as an extremely interesting person.

SCHOLZ Yes, I'm sure she doesn't come across many wet blankets like me.

SARANIEFF She put you with the Symbolists. (*To* KEITH) And then she raved about some forthcoming festivities to celebrate the founding with wonderful fireworks.

KEITH You can't impress a dog with fireworks, but the most rational man feels hurt if you don't give him any. At any rate, I'm going to Paris for a few days first.

SARANIEFF You've been asked for your opinion on a mutual-aid treaty between Germany and France?

KEITH But don't say anything about it!

SCHOLZ I had no idea you were active in politics, too!

SARANIEFF Do you know anything the Marquis of Keith is not active in?

KEITH I don't want it said of me that I had no concern for the times I lived in.

SCHOLZ Don't your own affairs keep you busy enough if you take life seriously?

SARANIEFF You certainly take it damned seriously! Tell me, did a laundress in the village of Gizeh, at the foot of the pyramids, once give you the wrong collar by mistake?

SCHOLZ You seem to have been thorougly informed about me. Will you permit me to visit you in your studio?

SARANIEFF If it suits you we can have coffee at my

place right now. You'll find your Simba still there.

SCHOLZ Simba—Simba—You keep talking about Simba. The girl told me her name was Kathi!

SARANIEFF Her real name is Kathi; but the Marquis christened her Simba.

SCHOLZ (*To* KEITH) I suppose because of her striking red hair?

KEITH With all the best intentions, I can give you no information on the subject.

SARANIEFF She's made herself comfortable on my Persian divan and is sleeping the sleep of the just.

(MOLLY GRIESINGER *comes out of the living room and sets a place for* SARANIEFF)

SARANIEFF Heartiest thanks, my dear madam; as you can see, I have already finished eating. Forgive me, I have not yet had the opportunity of kissing your hand.

MOLLY Save your flattery for better occasions. (*A bell rings in the corridor;* MOLLY *goes to open the door*)

KEITH (*Looks at his watch and gets up*) You will have to excuse me, gentlemen. (*Calls*) Sasha!

SARANIEFF (*Wipes his mouth*) We're going with you, of course. (*He and* SCHOLZ *get up*)

(SASHA *comes from the waiting room with the coats and helps* KEITH *and* SCHOLZ *put theirs on*)

SCHOLZ (*To* KEITH) Why didn't you tell me you were married?

KEITH Here, let me fix your tie. (*He does so*) You must be more careful about your appearance.

(MOLLY *comes back from the hall with* HERMANN CASIMIR)

MOLLY Herr Casimir wishes to see you.

KEITH (*To* HERMANN) Did you convey my respects yesterday?

HERMANN The countess was waiting for money herself!

KEITH Wait here a moment. I'll be back at once. (*To* SCHOLZ *and* SARANIEFF) Shall we, gentlemen?

SARANIEFF (*Taking his hat from* SASHA) With you through thick and thin!

SASHA The carriage is waiting, Herr Baron.

KEITH Sit with the driver!

(*Exeunt* SCHOLZ, SARANIEFF, KEITH, *and* SASHA)

MOLLY (*Putting the breakfast dishes together*) I wonder what you're after in this madhouse! You would be much better off at home with your mama!

HERMANN (*Wishes to leave at once*) My mother is not alive, madam; but I don't wish to disturb you.

MOLLY For heaven's sake, stay! You're not in anyone's way here. But what inhuman parents, not to protect their child from associating with such scoundrels! I had a happy home like yours and was no older or wiser than you when I jumped into the bottomless pit and never gave it a second thought.

HERMANN (*Greatly agitated*) Heaven have pity on me—I must find a way! I'll be ruined if I stay in Munich! But the Marquis will refuse to help me if he suspects what I have in mind. I beg you, madam, don't betray me!

MOLLY If you knew the state I was in you wouldn't have the slightest fear I'd be concerned with your problems! I only hope you get off no worse than I did! If my mother had let me work as I do now, instead of sending me off to skate every afternoon, I would still have some happiness to look forward to!

HERMANN But—if you're so unhappy and know—that you could still be happy, why—why don't you get a divorce?

MOLLY For heaven's sake, don't talk about things you don't understand! That's not the trouble. If you want to go about getting a divorce you have to be married first.

HERMANN I'm sorry, I—thought you were married.

MOLLY God knows, I don't want to complain about anybody! But to get married anywhere in the world you need to have some papers. And that's beneath his notice, having papers! (*As a bell rings in the corridor*) From morning to night it's just like a post office! (*Exit to the hall*)

HERMANN (*Collecting himself*) How could I have made such a blunder!

(MOLLY *shows in* COUNTESS WERDENFELS)

MOLLY You may wait for my husband here. He will probably be here any minute. May I introduce you?

ANNA We are acquainted.

MOLLY Hmm. Then I'm not needed. (*Exit into the living room*)

ANNA (*Sits down on the writing-table bench next to* HERMANN *and puts her hand on his*) Now tell me frankly, my dear young friend, why you need so much money at school.

HERMANN I won't tell you.

ANNA But I want to know so badly!

HERMANN I can believe that!

ANNA Stubborn mule!

HERMANN (*Pulls his hand away from hers*) I won't be bribed!

ANNA Who's bribing you? Don't flatter yourself! You see, I divide mankind into two general classes. Gay blades and old maids.

HERMANN Of course in your opinion I am an old maid.

ANNA If you can't even say why you need all that money . . .

HERMANN Of course I can't. I'm an old maid!

ANNA No, I could tell right away you're a gay blade!

HERMANN Of course I am; otherwise I'd be content to stay in Munich.

ANNA You want to go out into the world!

HERMANN And you'd like to know where. To Paris—to London.

ANNA Paris isn't at all fashionable any more!

HERMANN I don't really care about going to Paris.

ANNA Why don't you stay here in Munich? You have a father who's rolling in money. . . .

HERMANN Because you don't have experiences here! I'll go to pieces in Munich, especially if I have to waste any more time at school. A former classmate of mine writes me from London that when you're unhappy in London you're ten times happier than when you're happy in Munich.

ANNA I'll tell you something; your friend is an old

maid. Don't go to London. Better stay in Munich with us and have an experience.

HERMANN But that's impossible in Munich!

(MOLLY *shows in* POLICE INSPECTOR RASPE. RASPE *is in his early twenties, is wearing a light-colored summer suit and a straw hat, has the innocent childlike features of an angel by Guido Reni. Short blond hair, the beginnings of a mustache. When he thinks he is being observed he puts on blue spectacles.*)

MOLLY My husband will be here soon; if you wish to wait a moment. May I introduce . . .

RASPE I really don't know, my dear madam, if it would be doing the Baron a service.

MOLLY Oh, all right then!—for heaven's sake! (*Exit into the living room*)

ANNA Your precautions are quite unnecessary.

RASPE Hm—I shall have to recollect . . .

ANNA And then I'd like to ask you not to introduce me either.

RASPE How is it that I've never heard a word about you?

ANNA I heard about you—you spent two years in complete solitude.

RASPE And of course you let on to no one that you knew me at the height of my glory.

ANNA Who has not been known in his glory!

RASPE You're quite right. Pity is blasphemy. I was a victim of the insane confidence everyone had in me.

ANNA But now you're on top again?

RASPE Now I know what my talents are and use them for the good of my fellow men. By the way, can you tell me anything more about this sensualist?

ANNA I'm terribly sorry; he hasn't been introduced to me yet.

RASPE It's quite remarkable. A certain Herr Scholz, who wants to become a sensualist here in Munich.

ANNA What did he want with you?

RASPE That's what I asked myself. I took him to the Hofbräuhaus. It's right next door.

(MOLLY *opens the entrance door and shows in* CONSUL CASIMIR. *He is a man in his middle forties, somewhat thick-set, very well dressed; a full face with thick whiskers, a powerful mustache, bushy eyebrows, his hair carefully parted in the middle.*)

MOLLY My husband is not at home. (*Exit*)

CASIMIR (*Without speaking to anyone, goes up to* HERMANN) There's the door!— I have to hunt you up in this den of thieves!

HERMANN You wouldn't have come looking for me here if you weren't afraid it would be bad for your business!

CASIMIR (*Threatens him*) Will you be quiet!—Get a move on!

HERMANN (*Takes out a pocket revolver*) Don't touch me, Papa!—Don't touch me! I'll shoot myself if you touch me!

CASIMIR I'll make you pay for this at home!

RASPE Why should anyone let himself be pushed around like that!

CASIMIR Must I be insulted here too . . . !

ANNA (*Walks up to him*) Please, sir, or something terrible will happen. Calm yourself first. (*To* HERMANN) Be reasonable; go with your father.

HERMANN There's nothing for me at home. He wouldn't even notice if I drank myself into a stupor because I don't know what I'm living for!

ANNA Then tell him calmly what you intend to do; but don't threaten him with that revolver. Give me that thing.

HERMANN A fine idea.

ANNA You won't be sorry. I'll give it back when you've calmed down— Do you think I'm a liar?

(HERMANN *hesitatingly gives her the revolver*)

ANNA Now ask your father to forgive you. If you have a spark of honor in you, you can't expect your father to make the first move.

HERMANN But I will not let myself be destroyed!

ANNA First ask his forgiveness. You know your father can be reasoned with then.

HERMANN I—I—beg you to . . . (*He falls to his knees sobbing*)

ANNA (*Trying to raise him up*) Shame on you! Look your father in the eye!

CASIMIR His mother's nerves!

ANNA Prove to your father that he can have confidence in you— Now go home, and when you have calmed down, tell your father your plans and wishes.

(*She leads him out*)

CASIMIR (*To* RASPE) Who is this lady?

RASPE This is the first time I've seen her in two years. She used to be a clerk in a shop on Perusa Street, and her name was Müller, if I remember correctly. But if you want to know any more about her—

CASIMIR Thank you very much. At your service! (*Exit*)

(MOLLY *comes out of the living room to carry out the breakfast things*)

RASPE Excuse me, madam, did the Baron really intend to come back before dinner?

MOLLY For God's sake, please don't ask me such foolish things!

ANNA (*Comes back from the hall, to* MOLLY) Is there something I can take?

MOLLY You ask me if there's something. . . . (*Putting the serving tray back on the table*) Anyone who wants to can clear the table; I didn't eat there! (*Exit into the living room*)

RASPE You were absolutely perfect with the boy.

ANNA How I envy the handsome carriage his old man is taking him home in.

RASPE Tell me, what became of that Count Werdenfels who gave one champagne party after another two years ago?

ANNA I have his name.

RASPE I should have guessed it!—Will you convey to the Count my sincerest felicitations on his choice?

ANNA That's impossible.

RASPE Obviously, you're not living together.

ANNA Yes, obviously. (*As voices become audible in the corridor*) I'll tell you about it some other time.

(KEITH *enters with* HERR OSTERMEIER, HERR

KRENTZL, *and* HERR GRANDAUER, *all three of them more or less big-bellied, blear-eyed Munich Philistines. They are followed by* SASHA)

KEITH What a wonderful coincidence! I can introduce you right away to one of our leading artists— Sasha, remove this stuff!

(SASHA *exit into the living room with the breakfast things*)

KEITH (*Introducing them*) Herr Ostermeier, the brewery proprietor, Herr Krentzl, the builder, and Herr Grandauer, the restaurateur, the caryatids of the Fairyland Palace—Countess Werdenfels. But your time is limited, gentlemen; you want to see the plans. (*Takes the plans from the writing table and unrolls them on the center table*)

OSTERMEIER Take your time, my friend. Five minutes more or less won't matter.

KEITH (*To* GRANDAUER) Will you please hold this. —What you see here is the large concert hall with retracting ceiling and skylight, so that it may be used as an exhibition hall in the summer. Next to it is a smaller theatre, which I shall design for popular taste, using the most modern style of decoration—you know, half dancehall and half mortuary. The most modern is always cheapest and most effective.

OSTERMEIER Hm—you haven't forgotten the lavatories?

KEITH Here are the cloakroom and lavatory facilities in complete detail. Here, Herr Krentzl, is the front elevation: driveway, pediment, and caryatids.

KRENTZL Well, now, I sure wouldn't want to be one of those things!

KEITH That's just my little joke, honored sir!

KRENTZL What would my old lady say if I let myself be carved into a caryatid up there, especially on a Fairyland Palace!

GRANDAUER Remember, my main concern is to have enough room.

KEITH As for the location of the restaurant, my dear Herr Grandauer, the entire ground floor is set aside for it.

GRANDAUER You can't pack folks in for food and drink like you can for art.

KEITH For afternoon coffee, my dear Herr Grandauer, there is a terrace here on the second floor with a magnificent view of the grounds along the Isar.

OSTERMEIER I'd just like to ask you, my friend, if we could see your preliminary expense sheet.

KEITH (*Producing a piece of writing*) Two thousand shares at 500. I am going on the assumption that each of us, gentlemen, subscribes for twenty shares, preferred, and pays for them at once. As you can see, the estimated dividend is exceptionally low.

KRENTZL Then all we need is the city council's approval.

KEITH For that reason we are going to put out, in addition to shares, a number of interest-drawing bonds, and some of these we will allot to the city to use for worthy purposes— It is proposed that members of the board get ten percent of the net profit before deductions for depreciation and reserves.

OSTERMEIER All as it should be. Can't ask for more.

KEITH As for the stock market, we'll have to work at that a bit. I am going to Paris tomorrow for that purpose. Two weeks from now we will have our founders' party at my villa on Brienner Street.

OSTERMEIER If you could only convince Consul Casimir to come in with us before the party!

KRENTZL That would be really shrewd. If we had Casimir the city council would agree to everything.

KEITH I hope, gentlemen, that we will be able to call a general meeting before the party. Then we will see whether I've done anything about your suggestions.

OSTERMEIER (*Shakes his hand*) Then I wish you a pleasant journey, my friend. Write to us from Paris. (*Bowing to* ANNA) Allow me to wish you good day; my compliments.

GRANDAUER My respects; allow me to wish you good afternoon.

KRENTZL I'm honored.

(KEITH *shows the gentlemen out*)

ANNA (*When he returns*) What in the world do you mean by having your founders' party at my house?!

KEITH I'm going to have a concert gown made for you in Paris that will make it unnecessary for you to be able to sing. (*To* RASPE) I expect that at the founders' party you will use all your charms to bewitch the wives of the three caryatids.

RASPE They will have nothing to complain of.

KEITH (*Giving him money*) Here are three hundred marks. I'm going to bring back fireworks from Paris such as Munich has never seen.

RASPE This could be wonderful!

KEITH (*To* ANNA) I use all people according to their talents, and I must recommend caution in dealing with my dear friend, Herr Raspe.

RASPE When a man looks as though he has just been cut down from the gallows, getting through life honestly is no art. I'd like to see where you would be today if you had my face!

KEITH With your face I would have married a princess.

ANNA If I remember correctly, you were introduced to me under a French name.

RASPE I no longer use it, now that I've become a useful member of society— Permit me to pay my respects. (*Exit*)

ANNA But I don't have a staff of servants for big suppers!

KEITH (*Calls*) Sasha!

SASHA (*Comes out of the waiting room*) Herr Baron?

KEITH Will you help serve at my friend's garden party?

SASHA The pleasure's all mine, Herr Baron. (*Exit*)

KEITH Would you like to meet my oldest boyhood friend, Count Trautenau, today?

ANNA I have no luck with counts, but it doesn't matter.

KEITH I only ask you not to discuss my domestic arrangements with him. He is a real moralist, by nature and conviction. He has already questioned me about my household today.

ANNA Heavens, he's not the one who wants to become a sensualist?!

KEITH It's a complete self-contradiction. Ever since I've known him he has done nothing but sacrifice himself, without ever being aware that there are two souls in his breast.

ANNA He should have been satisfied. I find one is too many— But isn't his name Scholz?

KEITH One of his souls is named Ernst Scholz, the other is named Count Trautenau.

ANNA Then forget about the introduction. I won't have anything to do with people who can't come to an understanding with themselves.

KEITH He understands himself perfectly. He's at the highest point of human development. The world has nothing more to offer him, and life would mean nothing to him if he did not start again from the bottom.

ANNA He would do better to climb a step higher.

KEITH What's upsetting you?

ANNA That you want to bring me together with such a dangerous person.

KEITH He's as gentle as a lamb.

ANNA Thank you so much! If you have nothing to lose you can try anything. I will not allow disaster personified to come into my house. A man like that can bring a woman to life-long ruin, and neither he nor she nor anyone else gets anything out of it!

KEITH You don't understand me at all. I can't do without his confidence and so I don't want to expose myself to his censure in my present difficulties. If he doesn't meet you, so much the better; I will not have to fear any reproaches.

ANNA Who can ever guess where your schemes are leading?

KEITH What did you think?

ANNA I thought you wanted me as a lure for your friend.

KEITH You can believe that of me?

ANNA Why not? You said just a moment ago that you use every person according to his talents.

KEITH That's just what I'm doing. I should have liked my friend to get to know in you a woman of unimpeachable reputation.

ANNA How can you speak so ecstatically about another man in my presence!

KEITH Ann—I am going to Paris tomorrow, not because of art or politics, certainly not to see about the stock market or fireworks, but because I must breathe fresh air, because I must stretch out my arms, if I am not to lose the careful façade I've put on here in Munich. Would I ask you to come to Paris with me, Anna, if you weren't everything to me?— Do you know, Anna, not a night goes by that I do not dream of you with a diadem in your hair? If you asked me to get you a star out of the firmanent, I wouldn't hesitate, I'd find a way.

ANNA If your friend's confidence means so much, you can't make a greater sacrifice for him than the woman whom you know through and through.

KEITH And at this moment I have no thought in my head but for the gown I'm going to have St. Hilaire make for you. . . .

SASHA (*Enters from the hall*) A Herr Sommersberg asks if he may see you.

KEITH Have him come in. (*To* ANNA, *describing the gown*) A sea-blue gown, as light as possible, with a low square neckline, strewn with deep blue pearls, slits trimmed with wide gold lace; the coat of red velvet, bordered with ermine, with a simple sea-blue panel. . . .

(SOMMERSBERG *has entered. Late thirties, deeply lined face, hair and beard unkempt and streaked with gray. A thick winter overcoat covers his shabby clothes. He wears torn kid gloves*)

SOMMERSBERG I am the author of *Songs of a Happy Man*. I don't look it.

KEITH I once looked like that!

SOMMERSBERG I wouldn't have found the courage to come to you except that I've hardly eaten a thing in the last two days.

KEITH That's happened to me hundreds of times. How can I help you?

SOMMERSBERG A little something—for lunch . . .

KEITH You don't think I'm capable of doing any more for you?

SOMMERSBERG I'm an invalid.

KEITH But half your life is still ahead of you!

SOMMERSBERG I have thrown my life away in order to come up to the expectations people had of me.

KEITH You may still find a current to take you out to sea again. Or are you afraid?

SOMMERSBERG I can't swim; and here in Munich resignation isn't hard.

KEITH Come to our founders' party two weeks from today. You can make some very valuable contacts there. (*Gives him money*) Here are a hundred marks. Keep enough in reserve to rent yourself a dress suit for that evening.

SOMMERSBERG (*Hesitatingly taking the money*) I have a feeling I'm deceiving you. . . .

KEITH Don't deceive yourself! You are doing a good turn to the next poor devil who comes to me.

SOMMERSBERG Thank you, Herr Baron. (*Exit*)

KEITH My pleasure. (*After he shuts the door, taking* ANNA *in his arms*) And now, my queen, we're off to Paris!

## Act Three

*A garden room is seen, illuminated by electric lights; a wide glass door on the right leads into the garden. The center door in the rear wall leads into the dining room, where a meal is in progress. When the door is open the upper end of the table is visible. At the left, a door with a curtain leads into the game room, through which there is also access to the dining room. Near this door, an upright piano. Downstage right, a lady's writing table; downstage left, a settee, chairs, tables, etc. In the corner upstage right is a door leading to the entrance hall.*

*In the dining room a toast is being drunk. As the glasses clink,* SOMMERSBERG, *in shabby evening clothes, and* KEITH, *in a full-dress suit, enter the salon through the center door.*

KEITH (*Closing the door behind him*) You've composed the telegram?

SOMMERSBERG (*Paper in hand, reads*) "The founding of the Munich Fairyland Palace Company was the occasion yesterday evening of a gathering of prominent citizens of the gay city on the Isar at a lively garden party held at the Marquis of Keith's villa. A remarkable fireworks display entertained residents of the neighboring streets till after midnight. To this project, which has begun under such favorable auspices, we wish to extend . . ."

KEITH Excellent!— Who can go to the telegraph office . . . ?

SOMMERSBERG Let me take care of it. A little fresh air will do me good.

(*Exit* SOMMERSBERG *to the hall; at the same moment enter* ERNST SCHOLZ; *he is wearing a full-dess suit and an overcoat*)

KEITH You've kept us waiting a long time!

SCHOLZ And I've only come to tell you that I can't stay.

KEITH I'm being made a laughing stock! Old Casimir has stood me up; but at least he sent a congratulatory telegram.

SCHOLZ I don't belong among men! You complain that you are outside society; I am outside humanity!

KEITH Don't you now have every pleasure a man can dream of?!

SCHOLZ What pleasures! The riot of joys I'm wallowing in has made me no different from a barbarian. True, I have learned to appreciate Rubens and Wagner. The accident that used to arouse my pity is now almost unbearable because of its ugliness. I've become a connoisseur of the artistic creations of dancers and acrobats— If only I had made any real progress! Because of my money I am *treated* like a human being. As soon as I want to *be* one I run up against invisible walls!

KEITH If you envy human weeds who take root wherever they can and are uprooted as easily, don't come to me for sympathy! The world is a cursedly sly beast, not easily conquered. But once you succeed, you are proof against any misfortune.

SCHOLZ If such phrases give you satisfaction, I can hope to gain nothing from your company.

KEITH They are not phrases! Today no misfortune can touch me. We know each other too well, the world and I. For me, misfortune is an opportunity, like anything else. Any ass can suffer misfortune; it takes skill to exploit it to one's advantage.

SCHOLZ You cling to the world like a girl to her lover. You don't understand that a person can become as vile as carrion to himself if he exists only for himself

KEITH Then why don't you measure up to your convictions? Once this purgatory of earthly joys is behind you, you will be able to look down like a demi-god on this poor slave of passion.

SCHOLZ If only I had my human birthright! Better to crawl into the wilderness like a beast than to have to apologize for my existence every step of the way!— I can't stay— I met Countess Werdenfels yesterday— I can only guess at what I did to offend her. I suppose I unconsciously adopted the tone I've become accustomed to use with the little one.

KEITH I've received more rebuffs from women than I have hairs on my head! But not one of them has ever laughed at me behind my back!

SCHOLZ I am a man without breeding—and with a woman for whom I have the highest respect!

KEITH A man like you, whose every step from earliest youth has led to a spiritual conflict, can end up as the ruler of the world long after we others have gone to our rest.

SCHOLZ And then there's the little one, who is playing the serving maid here tonight!— The most skillful man of the world couldn't handle such a situation!

KEITH She doesn't know you!

SCHOLZ I'm not afraid that she will be too friendly with me; I am afraid of offending her by ignoring her for no good reason.

KEITH How could you offend her that way! The girl understands class distinctions better than you do.

SCHOLZ I've learned all about class distinctions! They are the chains which make man most aware of his complete weakness!

KEITH As far as this weakness goes, we're fellow sufferers. Even if my conduct is as correct as the course of the planets, even if I dress in the best clothes, it is as impossible to change this plebeian hand as it is for an imbecile to become a paragon of intellect! With my gifts, I would have a much better reputation in the world, if not for my hand— Come, you would do better to leave your coat in the game room!

SCHOLZ Let me alone! It's impossible for me to exchange a single calm word with the lady today.

KEITH Then stay with the two divorcées; they're going through conflicts similar to yours.

SCHOLZ Who are they?

KEITH Neither over twenty-five, perfect beauties, ancient Nordic stock, and so modern in their mode of life I feel like an old flintlock by comparison.

SCHOLZ It seems to me that I too am not very far from being a modern.

(SCHOLZ *goes into the game room;* KEITH *is about to follow him, but at that moment* SARANIEFF *enters from the hall*)

SARANIEFF Tell me, is there still something to eat?

KEITH Please don't wear that tweed coat in here!— I haven't eaten a thing all day.

SARANIEFF They're not so fussy here. I have to ask you something very important first.

(SARANIEFF *hangs his hat and coat in the hall; meanwhile* SASHA, *in frock coat and satin breeches, comes out of the game room with a cooler full of champagne and is about to go into the dining room*)

KEITH When you set off the fireworks, Sasha, be careful of the big mortar.

SASHA I'm not scared, Herr Baron! (*Exit into the dining room, closing the door behind him*)

SARANIEFF (*Comes back from the hall*) Do you have any money?

KEITH But you just sold a picture! Why do you think I sent my friend to you!

SARANIEFF What could I get from that squeezed lemon? You've already finished robbing him. He has to wait three days before he can pay me a penny.

KEITH (*Gives him a note*) Here are a thousand marks.

(SIMBA, *a typical Munich girl, with fresh coloring, a light step, luxuriant red hair, in a tasteful black dress with a white pinafore, comes out of the dining room with a tray of half-empty wineglasses*)

SIMBA The Councillor'd like to propose another toast to the Herr Baron.

(KEITH *takes one of the glasses from the tray and steps through the open door to the table. Exit* SIMBA *into the game room. A hurrah, then the clinking of glasses*)

KEITH Ladies and gentlemen! Tonight's festivities mark the beginning of an era for Munich which will eclipse everything that has gone before. We are creating an art center in which all the arts of the world will find a welcome home. If our project has occasioned general astonishment, you must remember that only what is truly astounding has ever been crowned with great success. I empty my glass to the vital principle that has preordained Munich a city of the arts, to Munich's citizenry and its beautiful women.

(*As the glasses are still clinking,* SASHA *comes out of the dining room, closes the door behind him, and goes into the game room.* SIMBA *comes out of the game room with a platter of cheese and is about to go into the dining room*)

SARANIEFF (*Stopping her*) Simba, what's the matter! How can you let the sensualist escape from your clutches!

SIMBA Why are you staying out here?— Go ahead, sit down at the table with the others!

SARANIEFF Me sit down with the caryatids!

SIMBA Oh, leave me be! I have work to do!

SARANIEFF (*Leads her downstage*) They don't need any more cheese! Let them wipe their mouths and be finished! (*Puts the cheese platter on the table*) Simba, you don't deserve the happiness that lies ready at your feet!

SIMBA Oh, please! Thanks a lot! Never has anyone in the world plagued me like this fellow with his compassion.

SARANIEFF And that's why you're abandoning me to the mercies of this worthless pirate again.

SIMBA I told him: Look here, I said, I'm no martyr to civilization! Tell that to your society ladies, I said. They like it when you think they're martyrs to civilization! When I drink champagne and have a wonderful time, I'm supposed to turn into a martyr!

SARANIEFF Why did the devil make me a man?

SIMBA Well, that's how he talks! He asks me why he's a man. As if there aren't enough ghosts in the world! Do you hear me asking people why I'm a girl?!

SARANIEFF You don't care that because of your self-indulgence you're throwing fifteen million out the window!

SIMBA Oh, my, those sad millions! You know, I've seen him laugh just once in all the time I've known him.

SARANIEFF You could have become an Imperial countess!

SIMBA A Social Democrat, that's what I could have become! Improving the world, humanitarianism, those are his specialties.

SARANIEFF If you were married to him for a couple of years, you would get used to his specialties.

SIMBA I'll tell you what, I'm not right for Social Democrats. They're so moralistic; if they ever get into power, that's the end of champagne suppers— Tell me, have you seen my sweetheart?

SARANIEFF Have I seen whom?

SIMBA My sweetheart!

SARANIEFF That's me, isn't it?

SIMBA Anybody might claim the honor!— You know, I have to watch that he doesn't get tipsy, or the Marquis won't hire him for the new Fairyland Palace.

SARANIEFF That at my age I should come to grief because of my faith in a woman's loyalty!

SIMBA Listen to me! I told him, the sensualist, that he had to learn to ride a bicycle. So he learned. So we cycled to Schleisheim, and while we were in the woods such a storm broke that I honestly thought the world was coming to an end. So then, for the first time since I met him, he started to laugh. The more it thundered and lightninged, the more he laughed, like an idiot.

SARANIEFF That gave you goose-pimples!

SIMBA I'm not afraid of any man or any storm; but I don't care for specialties. Hey, don't stand under the tree, says I, it'll be struck by lightning! No lightning will strike me, says he, and laughs. . . .

(SOMMERSBERG *enters from the hall*)

SIMBA Here he is! Where in the world have you been all this time?

SOMMERSBERG I sent a telegram.

SARANIEFF The graves are opening up! Sommersberg! Aren't you ashamed to rise from the dead to become the secretary of this Fairyland Palace?!

SOMMERSBERG This angel has restored me to the world.

SIMBA Oh, go on, lovey!— He comes to me and asks me where he can get money— Oh, says I, go straight to the Marquis of Keith; if he doesn't have any, you won't find a penny in the whole city of Munich.

RASPE (*In extremely elegant evening clothes, a small chain with an order on his chest, comes out of the game room*) Simba, it's downright scandalous of you to make the whole Fairyland Palace Company wait for its cheese!

SIMBA (*Seizes the cheese platter*) Saints alive—I'm coming right away!

SARANIEFF Why don't you stay with the old ladies you were hired to amuse?

SIMBA (*Taking* RASPE's *arm*) Leave the boy alone!—You'd be tickled pink, both of you, if you were as handsome as him!

SARANIEFF Simba—you're a born whore!

SIMBA What am I?

SARANIEFF You're a born whore!

SOMMERSBERG Let her go, for Heaven's sake!

SARANIEFF You're a born whore!

SIMBA Say that again?

SARANIEFF You're a born whore!!

SIMBA No, I'm not a born whore. I'm a born cloud lifter. (*Exit with* RASPE *into the game room*)

SOMMERSBERG I dictate all kinds of letters for her.

SARANIEFF Then I have you to thank for destroying my hopes.

(SASHA *comes out of the game room with a glowing lantern*)

SARANIEFF For God's sake, are you decked out! You want to make your fortune here too?

SASHA I'm going to set off the fireworks now. When I light that big mortar, you'll see something! The Marquis says it's loaded with all the fires of hell. (*Exit into the garden*)

SARANIEFF His master is afraid he might be blown into the air if he set it off himself!— Lady Luck is very wise not to let him get the upper hand!— Once he's in the saddle he rides anything so hard not a shred of flesh is left on its bones! (*As the center door opens and the guests leave the dining room*) Come, Sommersberg! Now we will have our Simba dish us up something!

(*The guests stream into the salon; first,* RASPE, *between* FRAU OSTERMEIER *and* FRAU KRENTZL; *then* KEITH, *with* OSTERMEIER, KRENTZL, *and* GRANDAUER; *then* ZAMRIAKI *with* BARONESS VON ROSENKRON *and* BARONESS VON TOTLEBEN; *finally,* SCHOLZ *and* ANNA. SARANIEFF *and* SOMMERSBERG *seat themselves at the table in the dining room*)

RASPE Will the esteemed ladies join me in a cup of fine coffee?

FRAU OSTERMEIER My word, a gracious cavalier like you isn't to be found in all of Munich!

FRAU KRENTZL Our young gentlemen could learn a few things from you!

RASPE This is the happiest moment of my life. (*Exit with the two ladies into the game room*)

OSTERMEIER (*To* KEITH) Well, it was really nice of him to send a telegram. But, as you see, my worthy friend, old Casimir is a very cautious man!

KEITH No matter! No matter! At the first general meeting we will have him among us— Would you gentlemen care for a cup of coffee?

(*Exeunt* OSTERMEIER, KRENTZL, *and* GRANDAUER *into the game room*)

BARONESS V. ROSENKRON (*To* KEITH, *who is about to follow the other men*) Promise me, Marquis, that you'll let me train as a dancer for the Fairyland Palace.

BARONESS V. TOTLEBEN And me as a trick rider!

KEITH You may rest assured, ladies, that we are counting fully on your participation— What's the matter with you, Zamriaki? You're as white as a corpse. . . .

ZAMRIAKI (*A slender, short, conservatory musician with long, black hair, carefully parted; speaks with a Polish accent*) Day and night I am working on my symphony. (*Taking* KEITH *to one side*) Permit, Marquis, I wish to ask, please, for advance of twenty marks on wages of conductor of orchestra.

KEITH With the greatest of pleasure. (*Gives him money*) Won't you give us a preview of your new symphony at a concert in the next few days?

ZAMRIAKI I will play scherzo. Scherzo will have great success.

BARONESS V. ROSENKRON (*At the glass door to the garden*) My word, a sea of lights! Look, Martha!— Come, Zamriaki, escort us into the garden!

ZAMRIAKI I come at once, ladies! (*Exit into the garden with* BARONESS VON ROSENKRON *and* BARONESS VON TOTLEBEN)

KEITH (*Following them*) Good heavens, children, stay away from the fireworks!

(*Exit into the garden.* SIMBA *shuts the center door from the dining room side*)

ANNA I haven't the slightest idea what I could have taken amiss; but you're terribly sensitive.

SCHOLZ I am as happy as a person who's been in a dungeon since earliest childhood and for the first time in his life breathes free air. I'm uncertain of every step I take; I'm so afraid of losing my happiness. Imagine, for ten whole years I groped about in broad daylight with my eyes shut, and tortured myself with the pangs of conscience because nothing in the world would make me happy.

ANNA I can't imagine why this dungeon was not unbearably tedious for you. I understand how someone could live with his eyes shut, but then he would know nothing of conscience.

SCHOLZ I wasn't lucky that way. Here in Munich it's becoming clearer and clearer to me that a life without higher meaning and purpose is not for me. And now that my eyes have been opened I no longer have any doubt that I shall reach my goal. If I succeed in putting my life in jeopardy for an idea, I shall not be able to thank my Creator enough.

ANNA Is there anything in the whole world without higher meaning and purpose? A pretty girl can get a man who is either cleverer, kinder, or richer. In any case, her children are better off than if their mother had been ugly.

SCHOLZ For me, the simple worker who does his duty has always been a shining example. But, God knows, the kind of work that takes care of everyday needs will not help me with the burden of existence!

ANNA Good Heavens! Is a man who supports his family and raises his children to be upright men and women only taking care of everyday needs?

SCHOLZ I've tried everything humanly possible to get my nature in tune with the outlook of the ordinary good man. I had no success. I was living proof that nobility of birth is an empty concept. Now I act on the premise that if there really is such a thing, it has to prove its existence by the mortal risks a man is willing to take for what he considers good and worth fighting for, as though he were taking possession of a promised land. This is the basis of my happiness about the future, and this knowledge makes me supremely confident.

ANNA But I think that even the most exalted endeavors have to do one's life some good.

SCHOLZ Don't think I'm raving! There's a lot left to fight for in the world! I will soon find a place for myself. There are still plenty of oppressed, mistreated people, whose suffering cries out for deliverance. As the blows fall down on me, my skin will become more precious to me, though I've found it such a burden up to now. And I am certain of one thing: if I ever succeed in placing myself at the service of my fellow men, I won't boast about it. Whether my path leads me up or leads me down, I will only obey the ruthless instinct of self-preservation!

ANNA Who knows, perhaps it's always been the case with famous people that they became famous because they couldn't stand being with us ordinary mortals!

SCHOLZ But you still do not understand, my dear lady. As soon as I have found my proper sphere, I shall be the most unassuming, pleasant, gracious company. I've already started, here in Munich, by learning how to ride a bicycle. I was as pleased as though I hadn't looked at the world since the earliest days of my childhood. Every tree, every bit of water, the hills, the sky—all were like a great revelation of which I once had a presentiment in another life.

ANNA That's the way everyone probably feels when he starts.

SCHOLZ My enthusiasm may seem childish to you.

ANNA Quite the contrary! It just surprises me because of the image I had formed of you.

SCHOLZ May I take you out with me?

ANNA I have very little time for bicycle riding now.

SCHOLZ You could give me no nicer proof that you are really not annoyed with me.

ANNA Is tomorrow morning at seven all right for you? Or aren't you fond of getting up early?

SCHOLZ It is really high time I helped you for a more correct judgment of me. Tomorrow morning at seven . . .

ANNA But don't keep me waiting!

SCHOLZ (*Kissing her hand*) How could you think that I would!

(ZAMRIAKI, BARONESS VON ROSENKRON, *and* BARONESS VON TOTLEBEN *come in from the garden.* SIMBA *comes out of the game room and serves coffee*)

BARONESS V. ROSENKRON Oh, it's cold! Martha, we'll have to take our shawls next time we go out. Play us a cancan, Zamriaki! (*To* SCHOLZ) Can you do the cancan?

SCHOLZ I regret that I cannot, Madam.

BARONESS V. ROSENKRON (*To* BARONESS V. TOTLEBEN) Then we'll dance with each other!

(ZAMRIAKI *has sat down at the piano and struck up a waltz*)

BARONESS V. ROSENKRON Do you call that a cancan, Maestro?

ANNA (*To* SIMBA) You can do the waltz, can't you?

SIMBA If Madam wishes. . . .

ANNA Come!

(BARONESS V. ROSENKRON, BARONESS V. TOTLEBEN, ANNA, *and* SIMBA *dance a waltz*)

BARONESS V. ROSENKRON Faster tempo, please!

(KEITH *comes in from the garden and turns out all but a few of the lights, so that the salon is dimly lit*)

ZAMRIAKI (*Breaking off his playing with annoyance*) With each beat I am coming closer to my symphony!

BARONESS V. TOTLEBEN Why is it dark all of a sudden?

KEITH So that my rockets will be more impressive! (*Opens the door to the game room*) I should like to ask you, ladies and gentlemen . . .

(RASPE, HERR *and* FRAU OSTERMEIER, *and* HERR *and* FRAU KRENTZL *enter the salon. Exit* SIMBA)

KEITH I am pleased to be able to inform you that in the course of the next week the first of our Fairyland Palace concerts will take place. They will be excellent advance publicity for us among the people of Munich. Countess Werdenfels will introduce several songs of recent composition, while our conductor, Herr Zamriaki, will personally direct the playing of several excerpts from his symphonic poem *The Wisdom of Brahma.*

(*General expressions of approval. In the garden a rocket rises hissing into the air and throws a reddish glow into the salon.* KEITH *turns off all the lights and opens the glass door*)

KEITH Into the garden, ladies and gentlemen! Into the garden, if you want to see anything!

(*A second rocket goes up as the guests leave the salon.* KEITH, *who is about to follow them, is held back by* ANNA. *The stage remains dark*)

ANNA Why did you say that I would take part in the concert?

KEITH If you wait until your teacher pronounces you ready to appear in public there won't be much time left for singing.

ANNA You might at least have said something to me about it first.

KEITH Don't worry! (*Throws himself into a chair*) At last, at last, the precarious tightrope performance is coming to an end! I had to use up all my energy for ten years in the effort to keep my balance— From now on the way is up!

ANNA Where am I supposed to get the nerve to appear before a Munich audience with my so-called singing?!

KEITH Weren't you going to be the best Wagnerian soprano in Germany in two years?

ANNA I said that as a joke.

KEITH How could I know?

ANNA Concerts are usually prepared months in advance!

KEITH I have not suffered self-denial thousands of times in my life in order to do what people usually do. Those who don't like your singing will be entranced by your brilliant Paris gown.

ANNA If only others looked at me with your eyes!

KEITH I'll furnish the audience with the right glasses!

ANNA You see and hear fantastic day-dreams whenever you look at me. You overrate my looks as much as you do my talent.

KEITH I have never been suspected of overrating women, but I knew you for what you were at first sight! Is it any wonder, when I searched for you for ten years on two continents! You had met me several times, but you were either in the clutches of another scoundrel like myself, or I was reduced to such a state that there was no practical advantage to appearing in your luminous circle.

ANNA If you are losing your mind out of love for me, is that any reason for me to heap the scorn of all Munich on myself?

KEITH Other women have heaped worse on themselves for my sake!

ANNA But I'm not infatuated with you!

KEITH They all say that! Submit to your inevitable good fortune. I will inspire you with the necessary confidence for your debut—even if I have to force you on with a loaded revolver!

ANNA If you treat me like your property everything will soon be over between us!

KEITH Take comfort from the fact that I am a man who takes life damned seriously! Although I like to drown in champagne, I can, unlike most people, deny myself all pleasure if necessary. No hour of my existence is bearable unless it brings me closer to my goal!

ANNA If I submit to your commands, tomorrow you'll find a woman you've been searching for on two continents for *twenty* years!

KEITH Anna, do you really think I would arrange the concert if I were not absolutely sure you would enjoy a brilliant triumph?!— Let me tell you something; I am a man of *faith*—

(*In the garden a rocket goes up with a hissing sound*)

KEITH —I have a firm faith that we are rewarded in *this* world for our efforts and sacrifices!

ANNA You need that faith to wear yourself out as you do!

KEITH If we aren't rewarded, our children will be!

ANNA You haven't any!

KEITH You will give them to me, Anna—children with my mind, with bodies that radiate health, and with aristocratic hands. And I will build you a home fit for a queen, one that a woman like you deserves! (*Tenderly*) And I will place at your side a husband who has the power to gratify every wish expressed by your great, dark eyes! (*He kisses her passionately. In the garden crackling fireworks are set off, bathing the pair in a lurid glow for a moment*)

KEITH —Go into the garden. The caryatids are dying to kneel before the Goddess!

ANNA Aren't you coming too?

KEITH (*Turns on two of the electric lights, so that the salon is dimly lit*) I'll just write a brief newspaper notice about our concert. It has to appear in tomorrow's paper. In it I shall congratulate you in advance on your triumph.

(*Exit* ANNA *into the garden.* KEITH *sits down at the table and jots down a few words.* MOLLY GRIESINGER, *a colorful shawl on her head, hurriedly enters from the hall, greatly agitated and disturbed*)

MOLLY I have to speak to you for just a minute.

KEITH As long as you want, my dear child; you're not disturbing me. I told you you wouldn't be able to stand it alone at home.

MOLLY I pray to heaven a dreadful misfortune will overtake us! It's the only thing that will save us!

KEITH But why don't you come with me when I ask you?!

MOLLY To your friends?

KEITH The people here are my *business.* You can't stand it if I'm here with my thoughts and not with you.

MOLLY Does that surprise you?!— You know, when you're with these people you're an entirely different person; you're someone I never knew, never loved, would never have followed so much as one step, let alone have given up my happiness and everything for— You're so good, so wonderful, so dear!— But with these people—as far as I'm concerned—you're worse than dead!

KEITH Go home and dress up a bit; Sasha will accompany you. You *must* not be alone tonight.

MOLLY I'm just in the mood for getting dolled up. Your behavior upsets me; I feel as though the world is going to end tomorrow. I have the feeling I must do *something,* no matter what, to protect us from something horrible.

KEITH Yesterday I started getting a yearly salary of twenty thousand marks. You need no longer fear that we're going to die of hunger.

MOLLY Don't joke! You're sinning against me! I can hardly bring myself to say what I'm afraid of!

KEITH Tell me what I can do to calm you. I'll do it at once.

MOLLY Come with me! Come out of this murderers' den, where they are all determined to destroy you. I know I've put the blame on you instead of on others, but I did it because I couldn't endure your childish delusions. You're so stupid, as stupid as you can be. Yes, you are! You let yourself be taken in by the lowest, most ordinary swindlers, and you willingly let them cut your throat.

KEITH It is better, my child, to suffer injustice than to be unjust.

MOLLY Yes, if you only knew it was happening! But they make sure that your eyes are not opened. They flatter you by telling you that you are Heaven knows what sort of miracle of cleverness and diplomacy! Because your vanity doesn't aim at anything higher! And all the time they are cold-bloodedly putting the rope around your neck!

KEITH What terrible thing are you afraid of?

MOLLY I can't say it! I can't put it into words!

KEITH Please say it; then you'll laugh about it.

MOLLY I'm afraid that . . . I'm afraid . . . (*A muffled report sounds from the garden;* MOLLY *cries out and falls to her knees*)

KEITH That was the big mortar— You must calm yourself! Come, have a couple of glasses of champagne; then we'll both go and watch the fireworks—

MOLLY There are enough fireworks in my head!— You were in Paris! Who was you with in Paris!— I swear to you by all that's holy, I will forget how I trembled for you, I will forget how I suffered, if you come with me now!

KEITH (*Kisses her*) Poor child.

MOLLY A crust to a beggar— Yes, yes, I'm going now. . . .

KEITH You're staying here; what are you thinking of! Dry your tears! Someone is coming up from the garden—

MOLLY (*Throws her arms around him passionately and kisses him several times*) You're so dear!—so wonderful!—so good! (*She frees herself, smiling*) It just happens that I wanted to see you once with your friends. You know I'm sometimes a little . . . (*She rotates her fist in front of her forehead*)

KEITH (*Wants to keep her*) You're staying here, girl—!

(*Exit* MOLLY *through the hall door.* SCHOLZ *enters from the garden through the glass door, limping and holding his knee*)

SCHOLZ Please don't be alarmed! Turn out the light, so that they can't see me from outside. No one of your company has noticed it. (*He drags himself to a chair, into which he lowers himself*)

KEITH What's the matter with you?

SCHOLZ Turn out the light first— It's really nothing. One of the rockets in the big mortar hit me in the kneecap!

KEITH (*Has turned out the lights; the stage is dark*) It would happen to you!

SCHOLZ The pains are already beginning to subside —Believe me, I am the happiest creature under the sun! Of course, I will hardly be able to keep my appointment to go cycling with Countess Werdenfels tomorrow morning. But what does that matter! I have vanquished the evil spirits; happiness lies before me; I belong to life! From this day forward I am another man. . . .

(*A rocket goes off in the garden and bathes* SCHOLZ'S *features in a lurid glow*)

KEITH For God's sake—I hardly recognized you just now!

SCHOLZ For ten years I considered myself disinherited, outlawed! To think that it was all my imagination! Nothing but imagination!

# Act Four

*In the* COUNTESS WERDENFELS'S *garden room a number of huge laurel wreaths are lying about on armchairs; there is an elaborate bouquet of flowers in a vase on the table.* ANNA, COUNTESS WERDENFELS, *wearing an attractive morning gown, is discovered in conversation with* POLICE INSPECTOR RASPE *and* HERMANN CASIMIR. *It is forenoon.*

ANNA (*A sheet of tinted notepaper in her hand, to* HERMANN) Thank you, my young friend, for the pretty verses you composed for me and for your splendid flowers. (*To* RASPE) But it's strange that you, sir, should come to me on this of all mornings with these rumors about your benefactor.

RASPE My benefactor? Two years ago I asked him to be a witness at my trial. He could have saved me six months. But instead he streaked off to America with some young thing.

(SIMBA, *wearing a tasteful maid's uniform, enters from the hall and hands* ANNA *a card*)

SIMBA The gentleman asks if he may see you.

ANNA (*To* HERMANN) Heavens, your father!

HERMANN (*Frightened*) How did my father know I was here!

ANNA (*Lifts the curtain to the game room*) Go in there. I'll send him away at once.

(*Exit* HERMANN *into the game room*)

RASPE Then it's best to pay my respects and leave at once. (*Exit*)

ANNA (*To* SIMBA) Ask the gentleman to come in.

(*Simba shows in Consul Casimir, behind whom is a* FOOTMAN *from whom he has taken a bouquet; exit* SIMBA)

CONSUL CASIMIR (*Handing her the flowers*) Allow me, madam, to offer you my sincerest congratulations on your triumph of last evening. Your debut has taken all Munich by storm; but you cannot have made a deeper impression on any of your audience than you did on me.

ANNA Nevertheless, I am overwhelmed by your coming to tell me so.

CASIMIR Do you have a moment? I wish to discuss a practical matter.

ANNA (*Offers him a seat*) I'm sure you must be on the wrong track.

CASIMIR (*After both have sat down*) We shall see in a moment. I wanted to ask you if you would like to become my wife.

ANNA I don't understand—

CASIMIR That is why I am here, for us to come to an understanding about it. Permit me to tell you from the outset that you would of course have to give up the attractive artistic career that you embarked on last evening.

ANNA You've surely not considered this step carefully.

CASIMIR At my age, madam, one takes no ill-considered step. Later, yes—or earlier. Will you let me know what other scruples present themselves to you.

ANNA You know, of course, that I can't give you an answer?

CASIMIR Of course I know. I say all this, however, in case you are ever completely free to make a decision about yourself and your future.

ANNA At the moment I can't imagine the possibility of such a thing.

CASIMIR Today, you see, I am the most respected man in Munich, but tomorrow I might be under lock and key. I would not blame my best friend if he had doubts about standing by me in such a case.

ANNA Wouldn't you find fault with your wife if she had doubts?

CASIMIR My wife, certainly; my mistress, never.

ANNA Wouldn't you think a person the most despicable creature alive if she gave you an answer qualified by such conditions?

CASIMIR Of course. Please don't. I don't want an answer now. I speak only in case you are left high and dry or circumstances arise which release you from your obligations; to be brief, in case you do not know where to turn next.

ANNA And then you would want me to be your wife?

CASIMIR I suppose it seems insane to you. But my reasons need to satisfy me, no one else. As you perhaps know, I have two small children at home, girls of three and six. And, as you can imagine, there are other considerations. . . . As for you, I take all responsibility upon myself that you will not disappoint my expectations—even in spite of yourself.

ANNA I admire your self-confidence.

CASIMIR You may depend on me completely.

ANNA But after a success like last night! It seemed as though an entirely new spirit had come over the people of Munich.

CASIMIR Believe me, I sincerely envy the perspicacity of the founder of the project. And, by the way, I must pay you a particular compliment on the choice of your gown last night. You seemed so confident that it showed you off to your best advantage that I was hardly able—I admit it—to follow your singing with the attention it deserved.

ANNA Please don't think the applause gave me an inflated opinion of my artistic performance.

CASIMIR Your teacher tells me that success like yours has brought misfortune to many. There is one thing you must not forget: Where would the most famous of singers be if rich men did not consider it their moral duty to regard them as sound financial investments? No matter how brilliant the fees some artists earn, such people actually always live on charity.

ANNA I was amazed at the favorable reception our program got.

CASIMIR (*Rising*) Till that man Zamriaki's wretched symphony.

ANNA But every other number got a thunderous ovation.

CASIMIR I haven't the slightest doubt that in time we will come to venerate the noise produced by Herr Zamriaki as the revelation of divine genius. Let us allow the world its ways, hope for the best, and be prepared for the worst— Allow me, madam, to wish you good day. (*Exit*)

(ANNA *clutches her temples with both hands, goes to the game room, lifts the curtain, and steps back*)

ANNA Didn't even shut the door!

(HERMANN CASIMIR *steps out of the game room*)

HERMANN I never would have dreamed a person could have such an experience!

ANNA Go now, so your father will find you at home.

HERMANN (*Notices the second bouquet*) The flowers are his?— I seem to have inherited that from him. But he doesn't feel the expense as much as I do.

ANNA How do you come to have money for such crazy purchases?

HERMANN From the Marquis of Keith.

ANNA Please go now! You look tired. Did the party go on till very late last night?

HERMANN I helped to save Zamriaki's life.

ANNA Do you consider that a worthy occupation for yourself?

HERMANN What do I have to do that's any better?

ANNA It's quite nice of you to have a heart for unfortunate people; but you don't have to sit at the same table with them. Misfortune is contagious.

HERMANN That's what the Marquis of Keith says.

ANNA Go now! I beg you.

(*Simba enters from the hall and hands* ANNA *a card*)

SIMBA The gentleman would like to see you.

ANNA (*Reading the card*) "Representative of the South German Concert Agency." Tell him to come back in two weeks.

(*Exit* SIMBA)

HERMANN What answer will you give my father?

ANNA Now it's really time for you to go! You're becoming insolent!

HERMANN I'm going to London even if I have to steal the money. My father won't have me to complain about any more.

ANNA You're the one who'll benefit most.

HERMANN (*Uneasily*) I owe it to my two little sisters. (*Exit*)

ANNA (*Ponders a moment, then calls*) Kathi!

(SIMBA *comes out of the dining room*)

SIMBA Madam?

ANNA I want to dress.

(*A bell rings in the corridor*)

SIMBA At once, madam. (*Goes to open the door*)

(*Exit* ANNA *into the game room. Immediately afterward* SIMBA *shows in* ERNST SCHOLZ; *he walks with the aid of an elegant walking stick, limping because of his stiff knee, and he carries a large bunch of flowers.*)

ERNST SCHOLZ I have not had an opportunity, my dear child, to thank you for your tactful, sensitive conduct the other evening at the garden party.

SIMBA Does the Baron wish to be announced to madam?

(*Enter* KEITH *from the hall, in a light-colored overcoat, a bundle of newspapers in his hand*)

KEITH (*Removing his overcoat*) It's the will of Heaven that I should find you here! (*To* SIMBA) What are you still doing here?

SIMBA Madam took me into her service as a housemaid.

KEITH You see, I've made your fortune— Announce us!

SIMBA Very good, Herr Baron. (*Exit into the game room*)

KEITH The morning papers have the most enthusiastic reviews of our concert!

SCHOLZ Have you finally heard where your wife is staying?

KEITH She's with her parents in Bückeburg. You suddenly disappeared during the banquet last night?

SCHOLZ I desperately needed to be alone. How is your wife?

KEITH Thanks; her father is about to go bankrupt.

SCHOLZ Surely you can spare enough to protect her family from that!

KEITH Do you know what the concert yesterday cost me?

SCHOLZ You take these things too lightly!

KEITH You really want me to help you hatch the eggs of eternity?

SCHOLZ I would consider myself fortunate if I could transmit some of the overflow of my sense of duty to you.

KEITH Lord protect me from that! I need all the elasticity imaginable now to make the most of this success.

SCHOLZ I have you to thank for the fact that today I face life calmly and confidently. I therefore consider it my duty to speak to you as frankly as you spoke to me two weeks ago.

KEITH The only difference is that I have not asked for your advice.

SCHOLZ As far as I am concerned, that is only another reason for complete candor. My exaggerated passion for duty caused the death of five people; but you behave as though one had absolutely no duties toward one's fellow men. What is more, you like to play with people's lives!

KEITH In my case they get away with just a few scratches.

SCHOLZ That is because you are incredibly lucky! You do not realize that others have exactly the same rights to the enjoyment of life as you. And as for the area of mankind's greatest achievements, that which is most properly called *morality*, you haven't the slightest understanding of it.

KEITH You remain true to your nature. You come to Munich with the express purpose of being trained as a sensualist, but through some oversight train as a moralist.

SCHOLZ By means of the variegated life of Munich I have arrived at a self-evaluation which is modest but quite accurate. In these two weeks I have experienced such tremendous inner transformations that if you wish to listen to me I really can speak as a moralist.

KEITH My good fortune galls you!

SCHOLZ I don't believe in your good fortune! I am so unspeakably happy that I could embrace the whole world, and I really and sincerely wish you the same happiness. But you will never have it as long as you continue to joke about the highest values of life in your puerile way. Till I came to Munich I appreciated only the spiritual side of the relationship between men and women, and thought sensual gratification something vulgar. It was really the other way around. But all your life you have never valued a woman for anything but what is purely material. You judge a woman by standards that are no higher than those I would use in horse-trading. As long as you make no concessions to the moral order, as I had to, all your good fortune stands on quicksand!

KEITH That's not how it is. I owe to the last two weeks my *material* freedom and, as a result, am at last able to enjoy my life. You owe to the last two weeks your *spiritual* freedom and are at last able to enjoy your life.

SCHOLZ Except that I am concerned with becoming a useful member of human society.

KEITH Why does one have to become a useful member of human society?

SCHOLZ Because otherwise there is no justification for one's existence!

KEITH I need no justification for my existence! I asked no one for my existence, and from that I deduce that I'm justified in existing as I please.

SCHOLZ And so with complete peace of mind you let your wife be ruined, though she has shared all your dangers and hardships for three years!

KEITH What can I do! My expenses are so steep I don't have a single penny left for my own use. I paid up my share of the founding capital with the first payment of my salary. For a moment I thought of appropriating the money that was given me for financing the preliminary work. But I can't do that— Or would you advise me to?

SCHOLZ I may be able to give you ten or twenty thousand marks if you can't help yourself any other way. It happens that I received a note from my steward today for ten thousand marks. (*Removes a note from his wallet and hands it to* KEITH)

KEITH (*Putting it in his pocket*) But please don't come to me tomorrow and tell me you want the money back!

SCHOLZ I don't need it now. The remaining ten thousand has to be sent through my banker in Breslau.

(ANNA, *in elegant street clothes, comes out of the game room*)

ANNA Forgive me for making you wait, gentlemen.

SCHOLZ (*Hands her his flowers*) I could not deny myself the pleasure, madam, of wishing you luck with all my heart on the first morning of your promising artistic career.

ANNA (*Puts the flowers in a vase*) Thank you. I've not had the pleasure of seeing you here since our founders' party. In my excitement last night I completely forgot to ask you how your injuries are coming along.

SCHOLZ Heaven knows, they're not worth talking about. My doctor says that in a week I can climb mountains if I like. What really pained me was the loud, scornful laughter that greeted Zamriaki's symphony.

KEITH I can do no more than give people a chance to show what they can do. Those who fail to make the grade are left by the wayside. I'll find plenty of conductors in Munich.

SCHOLZ Didn't you yourself say that he was the greatest musical genius since Richard Wagner?

KEITH I wouldn't say my own horse was a nag! I have to be responsible for the accuracy of my accounts at every moment. I've just been at the city council with the caryatids. The council was asked to consider whether the Fairyland Palace is something Munich needs. It answered unanimously in the affirmative. A city like Munich can hardly begin to dream of all it needs!

SCHOLZ (*To* ANNA) I suppose madam has world-embracing plans to discuss with her lucky impresario.

ANNA No, thank you, we have nothing to discuss. Are you leaving us already?

SCHOLZ You will allow me to come again some time in the next few days?

ANNA Please do; you're always welcome.

(SCHOLZ *has shaken* KEITH'S *hand. Exit*)

KEITH The morning papers have very enthusiastic notices of your performance. . . .

ANNA Have you heard where Molly is?

KEITH She's with her parents in Bückeburg. She's wallowing in an ocean of petit-bourgeois sentimentality.

ANNA Next time no one will get so frightened about her! But, you know, you really needed her to prove how completely unnecessary she is to you!

KEITH Thank God for the fact that to you overwhelming passion is a book with seven seals. If a person who is passionately in love with you can't make you happy, she wants at the very least to set fire to the roof over your head!

ANNA But you ought to give people more reason to trust in your business enterprises without fear and trembling.

KEITH Why must I hear lectures from all sides today!

ANNA Because you act as though you were a drug addict! You never rest. I've found that when one is uncertain about choosing between two things, it's best to do nothing at all. It's only doing things that lays one open to all kinds of unpleasantness. I do as little as I possibly can and have always been happy. You can blame nobody for distrusting you if you chase after luck day and night like a starving wolf.

KEITH I can't help being insatiable.

ANNA Sometimes there are people with loaded rifles sitting in the sleigh and they go bang-bang.

KEITH I am bulletproof. There are still two Spanish bullets in my body from the fighting in Cuba. And besides, I have a positive guaranty that I will have good luck.

ANNA This is too much!

KEITH Too much, perhaps, for the common herd to grasp— It must have been twenty years ago that young Trautenau and I, in short trousers, were standing at the altar of the whitewashed village church. My father was playing the organ. The village priest handed us each a picture with a Bible verse. Since then I've scarcely seen the inside of a church, but that verse has been fulfilled in ways that have amazed me. If an obstacle is placed in my path today I always smile scornfully as I remember it: "We know that all things work together for good to them that love God."

ANNA (*In amazement*) Do you care about religion?

KEITH As to whether I love God, I've examined all existing religions and in no religion have I found any distinction between love of God and love of one's self. Love of God is everywhere only a concentrated, symbolic way of expressing love of self.

(SIMBA *enters from the hall*)

SIMBA Will the Marquis please come out a moment? Sasha's here.

KEITH Why doesn't he come in?

(*Enter* SASHA *with a telegram*)

SASHA I didn't know if I should or shouldn't, because the Baron said never to deliver a telegram in company.

KEITH (*Opens the telegram, crumples it into a ball and throws it down*) Damn it again!— My coat!

ANNA From Molly?

KEITH No!— I only hope to Heaven not a soul finds out!

ANNA She isn't with her parents?

KEITH (*As* SASHA *helps him into his overcoat*) No!

ANNA But you just said—

KEITH Is it my fault if she isn't there?— As soon as I have a little success, something happens to gum up the works! (*Exeunt* KEITH *and* SASHA)

SIMBA (*Picks up the telegram and gives it to* ANNA) The Marquis has forgotten his telegram.

ANNA Where does Sasha come from?

SIMBA Sasha's from Swabia. His mother's a housekeeper.

ANNA Then his name couldn't be Sasha?

SIMBA Originally his name was Sepperl, but the Marquis christened him Sasha.

ANNA Bring me my hat.

(*A bell rings in the corridor*)

SIMBA At once, madam. (*Goes to open the door*)

ANNA (*Reads the telegram*) ". . . Molly not here. Please inform by return wire if you have had any word of her."

(SIMBA *returns*)

SIMBA The Baron has forgotten his gloves.

ANNA Which Baron?

SIMBA Oh, I meant the sensualist.

ANNA (*Searching hastily*) Lord, where are those gloves. . . .

(*Enter* ERNST SCHOLZ)

SCHOLZ Permit me two more words, madam.

ANNA I'm about to go out. (*To* SIMBA) My hat. (*Exit* SIMBA)

SCHOLZ My friends' presence prevented me from saying what is in my heart.

ANNA Say it, if it's not too much.

SCHOLZ You make it hard for me to find the proper tone.

ANNA Perhaps we'd better wait for a more suitable occasion.

SCHOLZ I hoped I could wait a few more days for your decision. My feelings overpower me. So that you will have no doubts that it is your happiness alone which I seek when I make my offer, let me confess that I am—unutterably—I love you.

ANNA Well?

SCHOLZ If I have been mistaken about your wishes, blame only my anxiety or my awkwardness.

ANNA What might your offer be?

SCHOLZ Until you reap the fruits of uncontested recognition as an artist, there will be many obstacles in your path. Permit me to use everything I possess to make it easier for you to achieve your goal.

ANNA Thank you, but I don't expect to sing any more.

SCHOLZ You aren't going to give up your career now!

ANNA Yes, I'm afraid I am.

SCHOLZ How many unhappy artists would give half their lives for your voice.

ANNA You have nothing else to say to me?

SCHOLZ You're offended. You expected that I would offer you my hand—

ANNA Isn't that what you wanted to do?

SCHOLZ While I was sick at home I asked myself a hundred times if you, with your independent nature, would ever be willing to submit to legal bondage

ANNA What did you think I would want?

SCHOLZ You have me on the rack! I have only one desire: to do what will make you happy.

ANNA But you didn't want to marry me?

SCHOLZ I wanted to ask you to be my *mistress*— I could honor you as my wife no more than I would esteem you as my mistress. Whether wife or mistress, I offer you my life, I offer you everything I possess. You know that it was only after the most complete self-conquest that I reconciled myself to the attitudes current here in Munich. You will forgive the insult if you think what ordeals I went through to free myself from social prejudice. If my happiness should be dashed to pieces because of a reconciliation I made just so that I could share my fellow men's happiness, what a revolting farce!

ANNA Didn't you have some career in mind that would offer you great satisfaction?

SCHOLZ I dreamed about improving the world as a prisoner behind iron bars dreams about snow on the mountains! When I experienced the rapture that makes all living things love life, joy and calm came over me. No longer do I torture myself, no longer do I struggle. Now I hope for only one thing, to make the woman I love so happy that she will never regret her choice.

ANNA I'm sorry to have to tell you that I don't care for you.

SCHOLZ You are ashamed to admit that you do.

ANNA I don't know what would make me do that.

SCHOLZ I've never had more proof of inclination from any woman than I've had from you!

ANNA That's not my fault. Your friend described you to me as a philosopher, with no concern for reality.

SCHOLZ It was reality that tore me away from my philosophy! I am not the kind of person who preaches against earthly vanity all his life and then when he is deaf and lame has to be bludgeoned into accepting death!

ANNA Can't religion offer you the peace you vainly seek in worldly pursuits?

SCHOLZ Without the belief in providence, I could not endure my existence for a single minute. That has nothing to do with the fact that I cannot live without you.

ANNA The Marquis is helped to overcome every stroke of bad luck by his confirmation verse, which he considers an inviolable guaranty of his success.

SCHOLZ A man's life is no game of chance. I do not stoop to believing in omens! If he is right, then at my confirmation I received just as unambiguous a guaranty of misfortune. Our pastor gave me the verse: "Many are called but few are chosen."—But that doesn't bother me! Even if I had definite proof that I did not belong to the chosen, it would only strengthen me in my fight against my destiny!

ANNA Please spare me your fight!

SCHOLZ I swear to you that I would sooner give up my reason than allow that reason to convince me that certain people are shut off from all happiness at the very outset through no fault of their own!

ANNA But what good does talk like this do?

SCHOLZ I'm not complaining! The more meager the favors of fortune, the more powerful becomes the strength of the soul; the longer the hard school of misfortune lasts, the more intrepid becomes the mind's power of resistance. People like me can be transformed. *My spirit is indestructible!*

ANNA I congratulate you!

SCHOLZ That is the source of my irresistible power! The less you care for me the greater and more powerful becomes my love for you, the surer I am of my victory, the sooner do I envision the moment when you will say: I fought against you with all the means in my power, but I love you!

ANNA Heaven protect me from that!!

SCHOLZ Heaven will not protect you! If a man with my strength of will, which cannot be broken by any reversal, concentrates all his thought and endeavor on *one* thing, there are only two possibilities: he reaches his goal or he loses his mind.

ANNA I think you're right.

SCHOLZ I will run the risk! The prize is worth it. Everything depends on which can persevere longer, which is better able to resist, your lack of feeling or my mind. I expect the worst to happen and will not look behind me until I reach my goal; for if I cannot fashion a happy life out of the bliss that fills me at this moment, there is no hope left for me. Never again will the opportunity offer itself!

ANNA I thank you with all my heart for reminding me of that! (*She sits down at the writing table*)

SCHOLZ For the last time the world lies before me in all its splendor!

ANNA (*Writing a note*) Thank you. (*Calls*) Kathi! (*To herself*) The opportunity won't offer itself again to me either.

SCHOLZ (*Suddenly coming to himself*) Why are you apprehensive, madam?! Why are you apprehensive? You're mistaken! You harbor a terrible suspicion—

ANNA Can't you see that you're keeping me? (*Calls*) Kathi!

SCHOLZ I can't possibly leave you like this! Give me your assurance that you have no doubts about my sanity!

(*Enter* SIMBA *with* ANNA'S *hat*)

ANNA Where have you been so long?

SIMBA I was scared to come in.

SCHOLZ Simba, you know that I'm in command of my senses—

SIMBA (*Pushing him away*) Go on, don't say stupid things!

ANNA Please leave my maid alone. (*To* SIMBA) Do you know Consul Casimir's address?

SCHOLZ —The mark of Cain is on my brow. . . .

# Act Five

*In the Marquis of Keith's study all the doors are wide open. As* HERMANN CASIMIR *leans on the center table,* KEITH *calls into the living room.*

KEITH Sasha! (*As he gets no answer, he goes to the waiting room; to* HERMANN) Excuse me. (*Calls into the waiting room*) Sasha! (*Comes downstage; to* HERMANN) So you're going to London with your father's consent. I can give you excellent recommendations to take to London. (*Throws himself into a chair*) First of all, I recommend that you leave your German sentimentality at home. Social Democracy and anarchism no longer create a stir in London. Let me tell you one more thing: The only way to use one's fellow men for one's own advantage is by appealing to the good in them. Therein lies the art of being well liked, the art of getting what one wants. The more you get out of your fellow men the more careful you have to be that the right is on your side. Never seek your advantage at the expense of a virtuous man, but always at the expense of scoundrels and blockheads. And now I bequeath you the philosopher's stone; the most splendid business in the world is *morality*. I haven't got to the point of going into that business myself but I would not be the Marquis of Keith if I passed it up altogether.

(*A bell rings in the corridor*)

KEITH (*Calls*) Sasha. (*Rising*) I'll box that rascal's ears. (*He goes to the hall and comes back with* COUNCILLOR OSTERMEIER) You couldn't have come at a better time, my dear Herr Ostermeier—

OSTERMEIER My colleagues on the board of directors have delegated me, my friend—

KEITH I have a plan to discuss with you which will triple our receipts.

OSTERMEIER Do you want me to state at our general meeting that it was again impossible for me to examine your account books?

KEITH You're raving! Won't you explain to me calmly and objectively what it is you want?

OSTERMEIER Your account books, my friend.

KEITH (*Irritably*) I work and slave for those numbskulls—

OSTERMEIER So he's right! (*Turning to go*) At your service!

KEITH (*Pulling open the drawer in the writing table*) Here, have yourself a time with account books! (*Turning to* OSTERMEIER) Who's right?

OSTERMEIER A certain Herr Raspe, who bet five bottles of Pommery at the American Bar last night that you don't keep any books.

KEITH It's true, I do not keep books.

OSTERMEIER Then let me see your notebook.

KEITH How could I have had the time to set up an office since the company was founded?

OSTERMEIER Let me see your notebook.

KEITH I have no notebook.

OSTERMEIER Then let me see the deposit receipts from the bank.

KEITH Did I take your money in order to collect interest on it?

OSTERMEIER Don't get excited, my friend. If you have no books you must surely make notes of your expenditures somewhere. Any errand boy does that.

KEITH (*Throws his memorandum book on the table*) Here is my memorandum book.

OSTERMEIER (*Opens it up and reads*) "A sea-blue gown—gold lace—velvet coat—" That's all there is!

KEITH If, after I have won success after success, you want to put stumbling blocks in my path, you can be absolutely certain that you will never see your money again, in this world or the next!

OSTERMEIER Fairyland Palace shares are not so worthless, my friend. We'll see our money again— At your service! (*Is about to go*)

KEITH (*Holding him back*) You're undermining the project with your snooping! Forgive me, sir; I'm upset because my feelings about the Fairyland Palace are those of a father toward his child.

OSTERMEIER Then you needn't have any more worries about your child. The Fairyland Palace is secured and will be built.

KEITH Without me?

OSTERMEIER If necessary, without you, my friend!

KEITH You can't do that!

OSTERMEIER Well, you are the last person to stop us!

KEITH That would be a low, rotten trick!

OSTERMEIER That's good! Because we won't let ourselves be cheated by you, you call us cheats!

KEITH If you think you're being cheated, you should sue me for your money!

OSTERMEIER Very nice idea, my friend, if we didn't belong to the board of directors!

KEITH What are you thinking of! You are on the board of directors in order to support me in my work.

OSTERMEIER And that's why I've come to you; but you don't seem to be working at anything.

KEITH My dear Herr Ostermeier, you cannot expect me as a man of honor to allow myself to be treated so abominably. Take over the business end; let me be the artistic manager of the project. I admit to certain irregularities in my running of the business, but I allowed them because I was convinced it was the last time it would happen; that after my position was secure, I would never be guilty of the slightest fault.

OSTERMEIER You could have said that yesterday when I was here with the others; but instead you talked our ears off. Even today I could say: Let's try again—if you had at least shown that you were sincere. But if we are always to hear lies. . . .

KEITH Tell the gentlemen: I will build the Fairyland Palace as surely as the idea for it sprang from my brain. If you build it, however—tell this to your gentlemen—I will see that the Fairyland Palace along with the board of directors *and* the stockholders is blown to bits!

OSTERMEIER I will give an accurate report, neighbor! You know, I don't like to insult a man to his face, let alone throw him out on his. . . . At your service! (*Exit*)

KEITH (*Staring after him*) . . . on his ass! I thought something was up. (*To* HERMANN) Don't leave me alone now or I'm afraid I'll go to pieces and nothing will be left of me— Is it possible? After all those fireworks!— Shall I be an outcast again, driven from country to country?!— I must not let myself be pushed to the wall!!— This is the last time in my life I will have an opportunity to get a firm footing. No!— I'm not tottering yet. On the contrary, I'll make a leap that will astound Munich. Then, while the town's still stunned with amazement, I'll land on its prostrate body to the sound of drums and trumpets and tear it limb from limb. Then we'll see who gets back on his feet first!

(COUNTESS WERDENFELS *enters*)

KEITH (*Hurrying to her*) My queen—

ANNA (*To* HERMANN) Please leave us alone for a moment.

(KEITH *shows* HERMANN *into the living room*)

KEITH (*Shutting the door behind him*) You look so sure of yourself?

ANNA That's possible. Since our Fairyland Palace concert I've had half a dozen proposals of marriage every day.

KEITH That means damned little to me!

ANNA But not to me.

KEITH Have you fallen in love with him?

ANNA Whom are you talking about?

KEITH The sensualist!

ANNA You're making fun of me!

KEITH Whom are you talking about?

ANNA (*Indicating the living room*) His father.

KEITH And you want to discuss it with me?

ANNA No, I only wanted to ask you if you've had any word of Molly.

KEITH No, but what about Casimir?

ANNA What about Molly?— You're keeping her disappearance a secret?

KEITH (*Uneasily*) Frankly, I'm not so afraid that she has had an accident as that her disappearance may knock the ground out from under me. If that seems inhuman, I've made up for it by spending the last three nights at the telegraph office— My offense to her consists in her never having heard an angry word from me since we've known each other. She is consumed by a longing for her petit-bourgeois world, where people live packed tightly together, in humiliation, drudgery—and love. No free outlook, no free air! Nothing but love! As much as possible and of the most vulgar sort!

ANNA If she can't be found, what then?

KEITH I am fully confident that when my house has crashed about my ears she will return with a contrite smile and say: "I won't ever do it again." Her goal has been reached; I can pack up.

ANNA And what will become of me?

KEITH So far you've gained most from our project, and I hope you will gain even more. You can lose nothing, because you've invested nothing.

ANNA Are you sure?

KEITH Why, what . . . ?

ANNA Yes, yes!

KEITH —What answer did you give him?

ANNA I wrote him that I couldn't give him an answer just yet.

KEITH You wrote him that!!

ANNA I wanted to discuss it with you first.

KEITH If it's only a matter of discussing it with me— marry him!!

ANNA A person who is as scornful of feelings as you are is surely capable of discussing practical matters!

KEITH Let's not discuss my feelings! I'm furious because you have so little pride, to be able to sell your birthright for a mess of pottage!

ANNA Anything that isn't you is a mess of pottage!

KEITH I know my weak points; but those men are domesticated animals! One of them has a weak head, another a weak spine! Do you want to bring monsters into the world, who can't see until the eighth day?!— If all is over with me, I will gladly bequeath you whatever glowing spirit I imbued in you for you to use in your career. But if you hide from the artist's hard lot behind a moneybag, you deserve nothing more valuable than the grass that will grow out of your grave!

ANNA If you only had the slightest inkling of what has become of Molly!

KEITH Don't abuse me!— (*Calls*) Sasha!

ANNA If you insist that we part—

KEITH Of course I insist.

ANNA Then give me back my letters!

KEITH Do you want to write your memoirs?

ANNA No, but they might fall into the wrong hands.

KEITH (*Jumping up*) Sasha!!

ANNA What do you want with him? I sent him on an errand.

KEITH How did you happen to do that?!

ANNA Because he came to me. I've done it several times. If worst comes to worst, the boy knows where he can earn something.

KEITH (*Sinks down into the chair at the writing table*) My Sasha! You haven't forgotten him either!— If you leave the room now, Anna, I'll collapse like an ox in the slaughterhouse— Give me a reprieve!

ANNA I have no time to lose.

KEITH Only until I've become accustomed to doing without you, Anna! No longer. I need mental balance now more than ever. . . .

ANNA Will you give me back my letters?

KEITH You're horrible!— But you're doing it out of pity! I should at least be able to curse you now that you're no longer mine.

ANNA As long as you live you'll never learn to understand women!

KEITH I will not renounce my faith, even on the rack! You're going toward good fortune; that's human. You are still what you were to me.

ANNA Then give me back my letters.

KEITH No, my child! Otherwise one day when I am on my deathbed I'll wonder whether you were only a phantom of my imagination. (*Kissing her hand*) Good luck!

ANNA Adieu! (*Exit*)

KEITH (*Alone, wrenched by heart spasms*) Ah! Ah! This is death! (*He staggers to the writing table, removes a handful of letters from a drawer and rushes toward the door*) Anna! Anna!

(*In the open door he is met by* ERNST SCHOLZ. SCHOLZ *is walking without difficulty, without a trace of his injury*)

KEITH I was just going to your hotel.

SCHOLZ There's no point to that. I am leaving.

KEITH Then give me the twenty thousand marks you promised me!

SCHOLZ I shall give you no more money.

KEITH The caryatids are crushing me! They want to take my directorship away!

SCHOLZ That confirms me in my resolution.

KEITH It's only a matter of weathering a temporary crisis!

SCHOLZ My wealth is more important than you! My wealth guarantees the members of my family a lofty and unhampered position of power for all time! But you will never reach the point where you will do anyone any good!

KEITH You parasite, how can you have the nerve to accuse me of being good for nothing?

SCHOLZ Let's not quarrel!— I am finally making the great renunciation many a man must make at one point in his life.

KEITH What's that?

SCHOLZ I have freed myself of my illusions.

KEITH Are you wallowing in the love of a lower-class girl again?

SCHOLZ I have freed myself of everything— I am going into a private sanatorium.

KEITH There's nothing more shameful than being a traitor to yourself!

SCHOLZ Your anger is very understandable— In the last three days I've fought the most horrible battle that can fall to the lot of an ordinary mortal.

KEITH And ended up by crawling away like a coward?! Can you consider yourself the victor, when you are renouncing your worth as a human being?

SCHOLZ (*Irritably*) I'm not renouncing my worth as a human being! You have no reason either to insult me or to make fun of me!— If a man allows himself *against* his will to be restricted by the restraints which I am imposing on myself, he may lose his worth as a human being. But in that case he is relatively happy; he is preserving his illusions— A man who settles his account with reality coldly and dispassionately as I do forfeits neither the esteem nor the sympathy of his fellow men.

KEITH I'd take a little more time to think it over.

SCHOLZ I have thought it over. It is the last duty my destiny requires me to fufill.

KEITH Once you're in it's not so easy to get out.

SCHOLZ If I had the slightest hope of ever coming out, I wouldn't go in. The burden of renunciation which I laid on myself, the self-conquest and joyful hope which I was able to wrest from my soul—I undertook all that in order to change my fate. I no longer have any doubt, for which I bewail God, that I am different from other men!

KEITH Thank God, I have never doubted that I'm different from other men!

SCHOLZ Bewail God or thank God—up to now I considered you the most cunning of scoundrels! I've given up that illusion, too. A scoundrel has luck on his side, as surely as an honest man keeps his good conscience even in irrevocable misfortune. You are no luckier than I am, and you don't know it. That's the frightful danger that hangs over you!

KEITH There's no danger hanging over me except that I will have no money tomorrow!

SCHOLZ As long as you live you will have no money tomorrow! I wish I could be sure you were safe from the disastrous consequences of your delusions. That's why I've come to you once more. I'm firmly convinced that the best thing for you is to accompany me.

KEITH Where?

SCHOLZ To the sanatorium.

KEITH Give me the thirty thousand marks and I'll come along!

SCHOLZ If you accompany me you will not need money any more. You'll find a more comfortable life than you've ever known. We'll keep a horse and carriage, play billiards—

KEITH Give me the thirty thousand marks!! Do you want me to grovel before you? I can be arrested on the spot!

SCHOLZ Have things gone so far? I don't give sums like that to madmen!

KEITH You're the madman!

SCHOLZ I have come to my senses.

KEITH If you want to go into a lunatic asylum because you've come to your senses—go right ahead!

SCHOLZ You're one of those who must be taken there by force!

KEITH I suppose you'll resume your title in the lunatic asylum?

SCHOLZ Haven't you gone into every possible variety of bankruptcy on two continents?

KEITH If you consider it your moral duty to free the world of your superfluous existence you can find more radical means than going for drives and playing billiards!

SCHOLZ I tried that a long time ago.

KEITH Then what are you still doing here?!

SCHOLZ I was unsuccessful in that as in everything else.

KEITH Through some oversight, I suppose, you killed someone else!

SCHOLZ They removed the bullet, near the spinal column— Today is the last time in your life that you will be offered a helping hand. What sort of experiences lie ahead of you, you know.

KEITH (*Embracing him beseechingly*) Give me the forty thousand marks and I am saved!

SCHOLZ They won't save you from the penitentiary!

KEITH Quiet!!

SCHOLZ Come with me and you will be safe. We grew up together; I don't see why we should not wait for the end together. Society judges you a criminal and subjects you to all kinds of medieval tortures—

KEITH (*Passionately*) If you don't want to help me, go, I beg you!

SCHOLZ Don't turn your back on your only refuge! I know that you are no more responsible for the choice of your deplorable fate than I am for mine.

KEITH Go! Go!

SCHOLZ Come. Come. In me you will have a companion as gentle as a lamb. It would be a dim ray of light in the nighttime of my life if I could rescue my boyhood friend from his terrible fate.

KEITH Go! I beg you!

SCHOLZ Entrust yourself to my guidance from now on, as I wanted to entrust myself to you. . . .

KEITH (*Calls in despair*) Sasha! Sasha!

SCHOLZ Then don't forget where you have a friend to whom you will always be welcome. (*Exit*)

KEITH (*Looks about, searching*) Molly! Molly!— It's the first time in my life I've ever cried on my knees in front of a woman! (*Suddenly hearing a sound in the living room*) There . . . ! (*After he has opened the living-room door*) Oh, it's you? (HERMANN CASIMIR *comes out of the living room*)

KEITH I can't ask you to stay here any longer. I am—not quite well. I have to—first—sleep on it, to become master of the situation again. Have a good . . . good . . .

(*Heavy footsteps and many voices are heard on the front stairs*)

KEITH Listen. . . . That noise! It means something bad. . . .

HERMANN Why don't you close the door?

KEITH I can't! I can't— It's her . . . !

(*A number of patrons from the Hofbräuhaus drag in* MOLLY'S *lifeless body. Water drips from her body, her clothing is in tatters. Her loosened hair covers her face*)

A BUTCHER'S ASSISTANT Well, here's the crook! (*To those behind him*) Is this him? Sure! (*To* KEITH) Look what we fished out! Look what we're bringing you! Look, if you have the guts!

A PORTER We pulled her out of the city pond! From under the iron grating! She was probably in the water there almost a week!

A BAKERY WOMAN And meanwhile the filthy tramp runs around with his shameless crowd! Six weeks he hasn't paid for his bread! Let's his poor wife go begging at all the shops for something to eat! It would have melted a stone to see how she looked toward the end!

KEITH (*Retreating to the writing table as the crowd presses around him with the body*) I beg you, please calm yourselves!

THE BUTCHER'S ASSISTANT Oh, shut your trap, you swindler! You fake, you! Or you'll get a wad on the nose from me that'll knock you off your feet!— Look over here!— Is it her or isn't it?!— Look here, I said!

KEITH (*Has grasped* HERMANN'S *revolver behind him on the desk, where* COUNTESS WERDENFELS *had left it lying earlier*) Don't touch me or I'll make use of this weapon!

THE BUTCHER'S ASSISTANT What's the lily-livered bastard saying?! What's he saying?!— Give me that revolver!— Haven't you done enough harm to *her*, you rat?!— Give it here, I said . . . !

(THE BUTCHER'S ASSISTANT *grapples with* KEITH, *who succeeds in reaching the outside door, through which* CONSUL CASIMIR *enters at that moment.* HERMANN CASIMIR *has meanwhile approached the body; he and the* BAKERY WOMAN *carry it to the sofa*)

KEITH (*Defending himself like a desperate man, calls*) Police! Police! (*Catches sight of* CASIMIR *and clings to him*) Save me, for God's sake!

CONSUL CASIMIR (*To the crowd*) Now look here, if this keeps up, you'll see another side of me!— Leave that woman on the couch there!— What do you want?— Now, get out!— That's where the door is, see! (*Dragging forward his son, who is about to leave with the crowd*) Wait a minute, sonny! We're both staying. You're going to have a nice lesson to take with you on your trip to London!

(*The people from the Hofbräuhaus have left the room*)

CASIMIR (*To* KEITH) I was about to ask you to leave Munich within twenty-four hours; but now I think it would be best if you left on the next train.

KEITH (*Still holding the revolver in his left hand*) I—I am not responsible—for this disaster. . . .

CASIMIR You can work that out with yourself! But you *are* responsible for forging my signature on a congratulatory telegram sent to your founders' party.

KEITH I can't leave. . . .

CASIMIR (*Gives him a paper*) Please sign this receipt. In it you vouch for the fact that the sum of ten thousand marks owed you by Countess Werdenfels has been received from me.

(KEITH *goes to the writing table and signs*)

CASIMIR (*Counting the money out of his wallet*) As your successor as director of the Fairyland Palace Company I am asking you in the interests of our project's success not to appear in Munich in the near future!

KEITH (*Standing at the writing table, gives* CASIMIR *the note and mechanically receives the money*)

CASIMIR (*Pocketing the note*) Pleasant journey! (*To* HERMANN) Get going! (HERMANN *slips out shyly.* CASIMIR *follows*)

KEITH (*The revolver in his left hand, the money in his right, takes several steps toward the couch but shrinks back in horror. Then he irresolutely looks at the revolver and the money in turn. As he lays the revolver behind him on the center table, with a grin*) Life is a slippery business. . . .

*Curtain*

# George Bernard Shaw

## (1856-1950)

At the center of any attempt to measure George Bernard Shaw's pre-eminence in the modern theatre lies a paradox of exactly the sort to delight the Anglo-Irish master of paradoxes: unquestionably the most influential twentieth-century playwright, Shaw is so absolutely inimitable that it is difficult to pinpoint evidence of his influence. The contemporary theatre would be richer in comic drama and more exciting generally if a Shavian school of playwrights had arisen; in truth, however, the vitality of his best plays is so unique that would-be imitators have been discouraged.

In his lifetime, he moved from the gaslit bleakness of the 1850's to the mushroom-clouded Atomic Age. To rapid and far-reaching changes which reduced others to despair and bewilderment, Shaw responded with deep concern, but with zestful good humor as well. With the optimism of "a confirmed Life Force worshipper" he ushered in the turbulent twentieth century without fear: he knew and accepted the fact that the modern experience is rooted in revolution and process. Two world wars and the emergence of freakish goosestepping mutants of his ideal "race of Supermen" made bold assault on his values, but he never fully retreated from the quintessential Shavian vitalist philosophy articulated in Act III of *Man and Superman.*

Shaw spent his youth in Dublin, where on July 26, 1856, he was born to "vaguely Protestant" parents. His father had been reared in the shabby-genteelism of British loyalists unable either to identify themselves with the Irish or to leave Ireland; he enjoyed drinking himself into the euphoric stupor which kept him ineligible for regular employment. Shaw's mother, on the other hand, was a self-sufficient "New Woman": leaving her husband to his alcoholic neurosis, she moved to London and a satisfying career as opera singer and voice-coach. Shaw remained with his father until, at 20, he decided he was wasting himself on a passion for neat bookkeeping. In 1876, he left the real estate agency where he had spent five dreary years, and joined his mother in London. The Dublin he left was still rocking along in the twilight of the eighteenth century, and Shaw was eager to embrace modern times as an energetic Victorian.

In London, doors slowly opened to Shaw as a journalist-critic who could review concerts, art exhibitions, books, and the theatre with a trenchancy Londoners had rarely encountered. Horrified by the bored Philistinism he observed in the arts, Shaw set himself the task of improving audiences' tastes and performers' standards: in music, he championed Wagnerianism and Mozartian opera (especially the *Don Giovanni* so important to the conception of *Man and Superman*); in the graphic arts, he attacked the wanly decorative Decadents and welcomed photography as a handmaiden of "realist" painting; in the theatre, he attacked the shoddy mechanics of melodrama and, by writing *The Quintessence of Ibsenism* (first published in 1891), participated in the revolution which gained the great Norwegian some acceptance by English audiences. The hedonistic "Art for Art's sake" doctrines held no appeal for Shaw, whose dedication to the arts was closely bound up with his development as a moral philosopher.

In his insistence on art's larger usefulness in the campaign to win men's souls for a better world, Shaw was guided by his study of political economy. In 1882, soon after hearing Henry George lecture on his mildly socialistic single-tax theory, he was absorbing the primary texts of modern socialism. Shaw's early brief association with the activist revolutionary, Henry Hyndman, was followed by a longer alignment with the gradualist Fabian Society, where his skepticism and conservative radicalism found more congenial fellowship. Shaw's exposure to the varieties of Victorian radicalism is apparent in *Man and Superman.* Jack Tanner was modeled in part on Hyndman, whose eloquence and high-minded revolutionary fervor impressed and amused Shaw long after they came to a parting of ideological ways. The lesser revolutionists holed up in the Sierra Nevada with the Byronic romantic brigand, Mendoza (later The Devil), show the internationalism of the Socialist movement as well as Shaw's impatience with the momentous hairsplitting he had so wearily endured on the debate platform. Shaw's double-vision of the socialism to which he remained permanently committed is most clearly shown in "The Revolutionist's Handbook and Pocket Companion," the work supposedly written by Jack Tanner, M.I.R.C. (Member of the Idle Rich Class), which Shaw appended to *Man and Superman.* The method employed and the ideas expressed in this pseudo-book are at once Shavian and not Shavian: it was written while Shaw was still taking Tanner's parlor Fabianism in the spirit of jesting irony with which he created his puritanical Don Juan protagonist.

For a playwright whose comic genius so clearly belongs in the theatre, Shaw found his calling almost by accident. During his early years in London (1879-1883), he had devoted himself to becoming a novelist: from the first novel, aptly titled *Immaturity*, to the fifth and last he wrote during this period, *An Unsocial Socialist*, it is possible to trace his intellectual development. The novels afford, however, only occasional glimpses of the brilliant Shavian stylistics of his maturity. In 1885, Shaw and William Archer, the influential drama critic who shared Shaw's enthusiasm for Ibsen, tried to collaborate on a play: Archer provided a Scribean well-made plot, and Shaw was to write the dialogue. When Archer heard enough of Shaw's embryonic play to recognize that his plot had been almost ignored, the partnership was quietly dissolved. Seven years later, Shaw offered to write a play for J. T. Grein's Independent Theatre, which had, since its opening in 1891, specialized in the works of continental playwrights popular in Antoine's *Théâtre Libre*. Grein was eager to make his "art theatre" available to promising young British playwrights; Shaw, neither promising nor young (at 36), became a playwright in what he felt was a worthy cause. His first play was rushed into production in 1892, ran for the usual nine days, lost money, but created a furor both in the press and in the theatre. Archer recognized in *Widowers' Houses* the end-product of the abortive 1885 collaboration; speaking as a critic, he urged Shaw to give up playwriting, advice which Shaw ignored as blithely as he had once ignored Archer's plot. Delighted by his success in outraging the moral sensibilities of his first audiences, Shaw began to think seriously of the theatre as the pulpit best suited to his talents.

*Widowers' Houses* contained the characteristically Shavian elements: his socialism, his utilitarian view of art, indebtedness to his own brand of "Ibsenism," and, above all, his superb sense of the theatre. Starting from the Biblical injunction against destroying widows' houses, he wrote a Shavian injunction against wealthy widowers who own slum properties. Once his prodigious energy was released by his tumultuous arrival in the theatre, Shaw wrote nine more plays before the 1890 decade ended. In 1898, his first seven plays were published in two volumes under the general title, *Plays Pleasant and Unpleasant*. The "unpleasant" plays were *Widowers' Houses, The Philanderer*, and *Mrs. Warren's Profession*, the play which provides the first stunning evidence of Shaw's dramatic mastery. In it, he traces prostitution back to the middle-class institutions which feed on its profits, but the play's greatest interest lies in the clash between the elegant and affluent brothel owner-operator, Kitty Warren, and her college-educated, "New Woman" offspring. In the "pleasant" plays (*Arms and the Man, Candida*, the long one-act play, *Man of Destiny*, and *You Never Can Tell*), Shaw demonstrated his extraordinary versatility: he ranged from a pacifist debunking of romanticized views of war and love, through an ironic inversion of Ibsen's *A Doll's House,* to the Shavian portrait of Napoleon as Organization Man, and, finally, to the farcical capriciousness of transferring a "sex-duelist" dentist to the potted-palms atmosphere of a seaside hotel.

In 1901 appeared *Plays for Puritans*, a collection of plays (*The Devil's Disciple, Caesar and Cleopatra*, and *Captain Brassbound's Conversion*) in which Shaw refined his technique for making the educator-pupil relationship wholly dramatic. In each of these works, an archetypal Shavian realist imparts a vitalist dedication to work and action to a reluctant student. Against a background of the American Revolution, Shaw's "devil's disciple" ridicules the stiff-necked, life-denying morality of false puritanism. Shaw's Caesar guides Cleopatra from childish fantasies to the threshold of political wisdom. Lady Cicely Waynflete converts a foolishly melodramatic pirate to an awareness of such modern realities as the U.S. Navy and common sense. In each play, education is as rewarding to the teacher as to the student. Shaw knew from his own experience that before the teacher can impart a philosophy, he must first articulate it for himself, and that to protect himself, the educator must avoid becoming merely doctrinaire: none of Shaw's characters is more Shavian than Lady Cicely when she exclaims, "As if anybody ever knew the whole truth about anything!"

During the 1890's Shaw established himself as a playwright but did not gain a real foothold in the theatre. Until 1904, when the Royal Court boldly launched a repertory of plays attractive to London's intellectuals, Shaw's plays were produced only in very limited runs at private theatres. After the brilliant 1904-1907 Royal Court productions, however, Shaw had a dedicated British audience. As world audiences scrambled to catch up with his early plays, Shaw tirelessly produced more plays, pamphlets, and pamphlet-prefaces to plays.

In *Man and Superman* (written between 1901 and 1903), the Shavian fun proceeds from the spectacle of a would-be teacher being caught—and taught—in a *terra incognita* uncharted on his Socialist maps. Basically a comedy of manners centered on the Battle of the Sexes, *Man and Superman* bursts excitingly out of its mold and defies classification as boldly as its Mozartian counterpart challenges traditional distinctions between comic and tragic opera. Shaw performed the remarkable feat of at once paralleling and extending *Don Giovanni.* In the controlling action (Ann Whitefield's shrewdly patient stalking of Tanner) Shaw followed Mozart to the edge of tragedy. In the extraordinary "Don Juan in Hell" dream-sequence, however, he brought Mozart's characters out on the other side of tragedy into the eternity which, for Shaw, is life. In scoring the interplay of his characters' voices, Shaw followed *Don Giovanni* as far as human imagination and spoken language can follow Mozart's orchestration. Finally, however, *Man and Superman* transcends all the sources in which its origins lie. It is more than a blend of Schopenhauer on will, Nietzsche on supermen beyond good and evil, and Bergson on creative evolution; it is more than literary and musical criticism of Molière, Mozart, and others who treated the Don Juan legend; it is more than a "Shavio-Socratic dialogue," "problem play," or "trumpery story of modern London life." As a play for the "pit of philosophers" Shaw always dreamed of entering, it is the most searching conversation on philosophy and religion in modern English.

# MAN AND SUPERMAN

## *A Comedy and a Philosophy*

### CHARACTERS

ROEBUCK RAMSDEN
PARLORMAID
MR OCTAVIUS ROBINSON
MR JOHN TANNER
MISS ANN WHITEFIELD
MRS WHITEFIELD
MISS SUSAN RAMSDEN
VIOLET ROBINSON
THE CHAUFFEUR—MR HENRY STRAKER
HECTOR MALONE
MENDOZA
THE ANARCHIST
THREE MEN IN SCARLET TIES:
{THE ROWDY SOCIAL-DEMOCRAT
{THE SULKY SOCIAL-DEMOCRAT
{THE FRENCH SOCIAL-DEMOCRAT (DUVAL)
GENUINELY ENGLISH BRIGANDS
GOATHERD
THE BULLFIGHTING INEBRIATE
{DON JUAN TENORIO
{OLD WOMAN—DOÑA ANA DE ULLOA
{THE STATUE—DON GONZALO
{THE DEVIL
THE OFFICER
THE IRISHMAN—HECTOR MALONE, SR

## Act One

ROEBUCK RAMSDEN *is in his study, opening the morning's letters. The study, handsomely and solidly furnished, proclaims the man of means. Not a speck of dust is visible: it is clear that there are at least two housemaids and a parlormaid downstairs, and a housekeeper upstairs who does not let them spare elbow-grease. Even the top of* ROEBUCK'S *head is polished: on a sunshiny day he could heliograph his orders to distant camps by merely nodding. In no other respect, however, does he suggest the military man. It is in active civil life that men get his broad air of importance, his dignified expectation of deference, his determinate mouth disarmed and refined since the hour of his success by the withdrawal of opposition and the concession of comfort and precedence and power. He is more than a highly respectable man: he is marked out as a president of highly respectable men, a chairman among directors, an alderman among councillors, a mayor among aldermen. Four tufts of iron-grey hair, which will soon be as white as isinglass, and are in other respects not at all unlike it, grow in two symmetrical pairs above his ears and at the angles of his spreading jaws. He wears a black frock coat, a white waistcoat (it is bright spring weather), and trousers, neither black nor perceptibly blue, of one of those indefinitely mixed hues which the modern clothier has produced to harmonize with the religions of respectable men. He has not been out of doors yet today; so he still wears his slippers, his boots being ready for him on the hearthrug. Surmising that he has no valet, and seeing that he has no secretary with a shorthand notebook and a typewriter, one meditates on how little our great burgess domesticity has been disturbed by new fashions and methods, or by the enterprise of the railway and hotel companies which sell you a Saturday to Monday of life at Folkestone as a real gentleman for two guineas, first class fares both ways included.*

*How old is* ROEBUCK? *The question is important on the threshold of a drama of ideas; for under such circumstances everything depends on whether his adolescence belonged to the sixties or to the eighties. He was born, as a matter of fact, in 1839, and was a Unitarian and Free Trader from his boyhood, and an Evolutionist from the publication of the* Origin of Species. *Consequently he has always classed himself as an advanced thinker and fearlessly outspoken reformer.*

*Sitting at his writing table, he has on his right the windows giving on Portland Place. Through these, as through a proscenium, the curious spectator may contemplate his profile as well as the blinds will permit. On his left is the inner wall, with a stately bookcase, and the door not quite in the middle, but somewhat further from him. Against the wall opposite him are two busts on pillars: one, to his left, of John Bright; the other, to his right, of Mr Herbert Spencer. Between them hang an engraved portrait of Richard Cobden; enlarged photographs of Martineau, Huxley, and George Eliot;*[1] *autotypes of allegories by Mr G. F. Watts*[2] *(for* ROEBUCK *believes in the fine arts with all the earnestness of a man who does not understand them), and an impression of Dupont's engraving of Delaroche's Beaux Arts hemicycle,*[3] *representing the great men of all ages. On the wall behind him, above the mantel-shelf, is a family portrait of impenetrable obscurity.*

*A chair stands near the writing table for the convenience of business visitors. Two other chairs are against the wall between the busts.*

*A* PARLORMAID *enters with a visitor's card.* ROEBUCK *takes it, and nods, pleased. Evidently a welcome caller.*

RAMSDEN Shew him in.

(*The* PARLORMAID *goes out and returns with the visitor*)

THE MAID Mr Robinson.

(MR ROBINSON *is really an uncommonly nice looking young fellow. He must, one thinks, be the* jeune premier;[4] *for it is not in reason to suppose that a second such attractive male figure should appear in one story. The slim, shapely frame, the elegant suit of new mourning, the small head and regular features, the pretty little moustache, the frank clear eyes, the wholesome bloom on the youthful complexion, the well brushed glossy hair, not curly, but of fine texture and good dark color, the arch of good nature in the eyebrows, the erect forehead and neatly pointed chin, all announce the man who will love and suffer later on. And that he will not do so without sympathy is guaranteed by an engaging sincerity and eager modest serviceableness which stamp him as a man of amiable nature. The moment he appears,* RAMSDEN'S *face expands into fatherly liking and welcome, an expression which drops into one of decorous grief as the young man approaches him with sorrow in his face as well as in his black clothes.* RAMSDEN *seems to know the nature of the bereavement. As the visitor advances silently to the writing table, the old man rises and shakes his hand across it without a word: a long, affectionate shake which tells the story of a recent sorrow common to both.*)

RAMSDEN (*Concluding the handshake and cheering up*) Well, well, Octavius, it's the common lot. We must all face it some day. Sit down.

(OCTAVIUS *takes the visitor's chair.* RAMSDEN *replaces himself in his own*)

OCTAVIUS Yes: we must face it, Mr Ramsden. But I owed him a great deal. He did everything for me that my father could have done if he had lived.

RAMSDEN He had no son of his own, you see.

OCTAVIUS But he had daughters; and yet he was as good to my sister as to me. And his death was so sudden! I always intended to thank him—to let him know that I had not taken all his care of me as a matter of course, as any boy takes his father's care. But I waited for an opportunity; and now he is dead—dropped without a moment's warning. He will never know what I felt. (*He takes out his handkerchief and cries unaffectedly*)

RAMSDEN How do we know that, Octavius? He may know it: we cannot tell. Come! don't grieve. (OCTAVIUS *masters himself and puts up his handkerchief*) That's right. Now let me tell you something to console you. The last time I saw him—it was in this very room—he said to me: "Tavy is a generous lad and the soul of honor; and when I see how little consideration other men get from their sons, I realize how much better than a son he's been to me." There! Doesn't that do you good?

OCTAVIUS Mr Ramsden: he used to say to me that he had met only one man in the world who was the soul of honor, and that was Roebuck Ramsden.

RAMSDEN Oh, that was his partiality: we were very old friends, you know. But there was something else he used to say about you. I wonder whether I ought to tell you or not!

OCTAVIUS You know best.

RAMSDEN It was something about his daughter.

OCTAVIUS (*Eagerly*) About Ann! Oh, do tell me that, Mr Ramsden.

RAMSDEN Well, he said he was glad, after all, you were not his son, because he thought that someday Annie and you—(OCTAVIUS *blushes vividly*) Well, perhaps I shouldn't have told you. But he was in earnest.

OCTAVIUS Oh, if only I thought I had a chance! You know, Mr Ramsden, I don't care about money or about what people call position; and I can't bring myself to take an interest in the business of struggling for them. Well, Ann has a most exquisite nature; but she is so accustomed to be in the thick of that sort of thing that she thinks a man's character incomplete if he is not ambitious. She knows that if she married me she would have to reason herself out of being ashamed of me for not being a big success of some kind.

RAMSDEN (*Getting up and planting himself with his back*

[1] Advanced "liberals" active in political, scientific, and social arenas, 1850-1875. Although they were the idols of a younger Roebuck, John Tanner would regard them as distinguished but outmoded conservatives.

[2] Watts' somber message-paintings (*e.g.*, "Life's Illusions," "Hope," "Love and Death") were widely reproduced.

[3] Hippolyte Delaroche, influential French historical painter, included 75 great artists from all periods and nations in this immense mural to be seen in the lecture theater of *École des Beaux-Arts,* Paris.

[4] The young actor in stock companies who plays the dashing heroes.

*to the fireplace*) Nonsense, my boy, nonsense! You're too modest. What does she know about the real value of men at her age? (*More seriously*) Besides, she's a wonderfully dutiful girl. Her father's wish would be sacred to her. Do you know that since she grew up to years of discretion, I don't believe she has ever once given her own wish as a reason for doing anything or not doing it. It's always "Father wishes me to," or "Mother wouldn't like it." It's really almost a fault in her. I have often told her she must learn to think for herself.

OCTAVIUS (*Shaking his head*) I couldn't ask her to marry me because her father wished it, Mr Ramsden.

RAMSDEN Well, perhaps not. No; of course not. I see that. No; you certainly couldn't. But when you win her on your own merits, it will be a great happiness to her to fulfill her father's desire as well as her own. Eh? Come! you'll ask her, won't you?

OCTAVIUS (*With sad gaiety*) At all events I promise you I shall never ask anyone else.

RAMSDEN Oh, you shan't need to. She'll accept you, my boy—although (*Here he suddenly becomes very serious indeed*) you have one great drawback.

OCTAVIUS (*Anxiously*) What drawback is that, Mr Ramsden? I should rather say which of my many drawbacks?

RAMSDEN I'll tell you, Octavius. (*He takes from the table a book bound in red cloth*) I have in my hand a copy of the most infamous, the most scandalous, the most mischievous, the most blackguardly book that ever escaped burning at the hands of the common hangman. I have not read it: I would not soil my mind with such filth; but I have read what the papers say of it. The title is quite enough for me. (*He reads it*) The Revolutionist's Handbook and Pocket Companion. By John Tanner, M.I.R.C., Member of the Idle Rich Class.

OCTAVIUS (*Smiling*) But Jack—

RAMSDEN (*Testily*) For goodness' sake, don't call him Jack under my roof. (*He throws the book violently down on the table. Then, somewhat relieved, he comes past the table to* OCTAVIUS, *and addresses him at close quarters with impressive gravity*) Now, Octavius, I know that my dead friend was right when he said you were a generous lad. I know that this man was your schoolfellow, and that you feel bound to stand by him because there was a boyish friendship between you. But I ask you to consider the altered circumstances. You were treated as a son in my friend's house. You lived there; and your friends could not be turned from the door. This man Tanner was in and out there on your account almost from his childhood. He addresses Annie by her Christian name as freely as you do. Well, while her father was alive, that was her father's business, not mine. This man Tanner was only a boy to him: his opinions were something to be laughed at, like a man's hat on a child's head. But now Tanner is a grown man and Annie a grown woman. And her father is gone. We don't as yet know the exact terms of his will; but he often talked it over with me; and I have no more doubt than I have that you're sitting there that the will appoints me Annie's trustee and guardian. (*Forcibly*) Now I tell you, once for all, I can't and I won't have Annie placed in such a position that she must, out of regard for you, suffer the intimacy of this fellow Tanner. It's not fair: it's not right: it's not kind. What are you going to do about it?

OCTAVIUS But Ann herself has told Jack that whatever his opinions are, he will always be welcome because he knew her dear father.

RAMSDEN (*Out of patience*) That girl's mad about her duty to her parents. (*He starts off like a goaded ox in the direction of John Bright, in whose expression there is no sympathy for him. As he speaks he fumes down to Herbert Spencer, who receives him still more coldly*) Excuse me, Octavius; but there are limits to social toleration. You know that I am not a bigoted or prejudiced man. You know that I am plain Roebuck Ramsden when other men who have done less have got handles to their names, because I have stood for equality and liberty of conscience while they were truckling to the Church and to the aristocracy. Whitefield and I lost chance after chance through our advanced opinions. But I draw the line at Anarchism and Free Love and that sort of thing. If I am to be Annie's guardian, she will have to learn that she has a duty to me. I won't have it: I will not have it. She must forbid John Tanner the house; and so must you.

(*The* PARLORMAID *returns*)

OCTAVIUS But—

RAMSDEN (*Calling his attention to the servant*) Ssh! Well?

THE MAID Mr Tanner wishes to see you, sir.

RAMSDEN Mr Tanner!

OCTAVIUS Jack!

RAMSDEN How dare Mr Tanner call on me! Say I cannot see him.

OCTAVIUS (*Hurt*) I am sorry you are turning my friend from your door like that.

THE MAID (*Calmly*) He's not at the door, sir. He's upstairs in the drawing room with Miss Ramsden. He came with Mrs Whitefield and Miss Ann and Miss Robinson, sir.

(RAMSDEN'S *feelings are beyond words*)

OCTAVIUS (*Grinning*) That's very like Jack, Mr Ramsden. You must see him, even if it's only to turn him out.

RAMSDEN (*Hammering out his words with suppressed fury*) Go upstairs and ask Mr Tanner to be good enough to step down here. (*The* PARLORMAID *goes out; and* RAMSDEN *returns to the fireplace, as to a fortified position*) I must say that of all the confounded pieces of impertinence—well, if these are Anarchist manners, I hope you like them. And Annie with him! Annie! A— (*He chokes*)

OCTAVIUS Yes: that's what surprises me. He's so desperately afraid of Ann. There must be something the matter.

*(*MR JOHN TANNER *suddenly opens the door and enters. He is too young to be described simply as a big man with a beard. But it is already plain that middle life will find him in that category. He has still some of the slimness of youth; but youthfulness is not the effect he aims at: his frock coat would befit a prime minister; and a certain high chested carriage of the shoulders, a lofty pose of the head, and the Olympian majesty with which a mane, or rather a huge wisp, of hazel colored hair is thrown back from an imposing brow, suggest Jupiter rather than Apollo. He is prodigiously fluent of speech, restless, excitable (mark the snorting nostril and the restless blue eye, just the thirty-secondth of an inch too wide open), possibly a little mad. He is carefully dressed, not from the vanity that cannot resist finery, but from a sense of the importance of everything he does which leads him to make as much of paying a call as other men do of getting married or laying a foundation stone. A sensitive, susceptible, exaggerative, earnest man: a megalomaniac, who would be lost without a sense of humor.*

*Just at present the sense of humor is in abeyance. To say that he is excited is nothing: all his moods are phases of excitement. He is now in the panic-stricken phase; and he walks straight up to* RAMSDEN *as if with the fixed intention of shooting him on his own hearthrug. But what he pulls from his breast pocket is not a pistol, but a foolscap document which he thrusts under the indignant nose of* RAMSDEN *as he exclaims*

TANNER Ramsden: do you know what that is?

RAMSDEN (*Loftily*) No, sir.

TANNER It's a copy of Whitefield's will. Ann got it this morning.

RAMSDEN When you say Ann, you mean, I presume, Miss Whitefield.

TANNER I mean our Ann, your Ann, Tavy's Ann, and now, Heaven help me, my Ann!

OCTAVIUS (*Rising, very pale*) What do you mean?

TANNER Mean! (*He holds up the will*) Do you know who is appointed Ann's guardian by this will?

RAMSDEN (*Coolly*) I believe I am.

TANNER You! You and I, man. I! I!! I!!! Both of us! (*He flings the will down on the writing table*)

RAMSDEN You! Impossible.

TANNER It's only too hideously true. (*He throws himself into* OCTAVIUS's *chair*) Ramsden: get me out of it somehow. You don't know Ann as well as I do. She'll commit every crime a respectable woman can; and she'll justify every one of them by saying that it was the wish of her guardians. She'll put everything on us; and we shall have no more control over her than a couple of mice over a cat.

OCTAVIUS Jack: I wish you wouldn't talk like that about Ann.

TANNER This chap's in love with her: that's another complication. Well, she'll either jilt him and say I didn't approve of him, or marry him and say you ordered her to. I tell you, this is the most staggering blow that has ever fallen on a man of my age and temperament.

RAMSDEN Let me see that will, sir. (*He goes to the writing table and picks it up*) I cannot believe that my old friend Whitefield would have shewn such a want of confidence in me as to associate me with— (*His countenance falls as he reads*)

TANNER It's all my own doing: that's the horrible irony of it. He told me one day that you were to be Ann's guardian; and like a fool I began arguing with him about the folly of leaving a young woman under the control of an old man with obsolete ideas.

RAMSDEN (*Stupended*) My ideas obsolete!!!!!!!

TANNER Totally. I had just finished an essay called Down with Government by the Greyhaired; and I was full of arguments and illustrations. I said the proper thing was to combine the experience of an old hand with the vitality of a young one. Hang me if he didn't take me at my word and alter his will—it's dated only a fortnight after that conversation—appointing me as joint guardian with you!

RAMSDEN (*Pale and determined*) I shall refuse to act.

TANNER What's the good of that? I've been refusing all the way from Richmond; but Ann keeps on saying that of course she's only an orphan; and that she can't expect the people who were glad to come to the house in her father's time to trouble much about her now. That's the latest game. An orphan! It's like hearing an ironclad talk about being at the mercy of the winds and waves.

OCTAVIUS This is not fair, Jack. She is an orphan. And you ought to stand by her.

TANNER Stand by her! What danger is she in? She has the law on her side; she has popular sentiment on her side; she has plenty of money and no conscience. All she wants with me is to load up all her moral responsibilities on me, and do as she likes at the expense of my character. I can't control her; and she can compromise me as much as she likes. I might as well be her husband.

RAMSDEN You can refuse to accept the guardianship. *I* shall certainly refuse to hold it jointly with you.

TANNER Yes; and what will she say to that? what does she say to it? Just that her father's wishes are sacred to her, and that she shall always look up to me as her guardian whether I care to face the responsibility or not. Refuse! You might as well refuse to accept the embraces of a boa constrictor when once it gets round your neck.

OCTAVIUS This sort of talk is not kind to me, Jack.

TANNER (*Rising and going to* OCTAVIUS *to consol him, but still lamenting*) If he wanted a young guardian, why didn't he appoint Tavy?

RAMSDEN Ah! why indeed?

OCTAVIUS I will tell you. He sounded me about it; but I refused the trust because I loved her. I had no right to let myself be forced on her as a guardian by her father. He spoke to her about it; and she said I was right. You know I love her, Mr Ramsden; and Jack knows it too. If Jack loved a woman, I would not compare her to a boa constrictor in his presence, however much I might dislike her. (*He sits down between the busts and turns his face to the wall*)

RAMSDEN I do not believe that Whitefield was in his right senses when he made that will. You have admitted that he made it under your influence.

TANNER You ought to be pretty well obliged to me for my influence. He leaves you two thousand five hundred for your trouble. He leaves Tavy a dowry for his sister and five thousand for himself.

OCTAVIUS (*His tears flowing afresh*) Oh, I can't take it. He was too good to us.

TANNER You won't get it, my boy, if Ramsden upsets the will.

RAMSDEN Ha! I see. You have got me in a cleft stick.

TANNER He leaves me nothing but the charge of Ann's morals, on the ground that I have already more money than is good for me. That shews that he had his wits about him, doesn't it?

RAMSDEN (*Grimly*) I admit that.

OCTAVIUS (*Rising and coming from his refuge by the wall*) Mr Ramsden: I think you are prejudiced against Jack. He is a man of honor, and incapable of abusing—

TANNER Don't, Tavy: you'll make me ill. I am not a man of honor: I am a man struck down by a dead hand. Tavy: you must marry her after all and take her off my hands. And I had set my heart on saving you from her!

OCTAVIUS Oh, Jack, you talk of saving me from my highest happiness.

TANNER Yes, a lifetime of happiness. If it were only the first half hour's happiness, Tavy, I would buy it for you with my last penny. But a lifetime of happiness! No man alive could bear it: it would be hell on earth.

RAMSDEN (*Violently*) Stuff, sir. Talk sense; or else go and waste someone else's time: I have something better to do than listen to your fooleries. (*He positively kicks his way to his table and resumes his seat*)

TANNER You hear him, Tavy! Not an idea in his head later than eighteen sixty. We can't leave Ann with no other guardian to turn to.

RAMSDEN I am proud of your contempt for my character and opinions, sir. Your own are set forth in that book, I believe.

TANNER (*Eagerly going to the table*) What! You've got my book! What do you think of it?

RAMSDEN Do you suppose I would read such a book, sir?

TANNER Then why did you buy it?

RAMSDEN I did not buy it, sir. It has been sent me by some foolish lady who seems to admire your views. I was about to dispose of it when Octavius interrupted me. I shall do so now, with your permission. (*He throws the book into the waste-paper basket with such vehemence that* TANNER *recoils under the impression that it is being thrown at his head*)

TANNER You have no more manners than I have myself. However, that saves ceremony between us. (*He sits down again*) What do you intend to do about this will?

OCTAVIUS May I make a suggestion?

RAMSDEN Certainly, Octavius.

OCTAVIUS Aren't we forgetting that Ann herself may have some wishes in this matter?

RAMSDEN I quite intend that Annie's wishes shall be consulted in every reasonable way. But she is only a woman, and a young and inexperienced woman at that.

TANNER Ramsden: I begin to pity you.

RAMSDEN (*Hotly*) I don't want to know how you feel towards me, Mr Tanner.

TANNER Ann will do just exactly as she likes. And what's more, she'll force us to advise her to do it; and she'll put the blame on us if it turns out badly. So, as Tavy is longing to see her—

OCTAVIUS (*Shyly*) I am not, Jack.

TANNER You lie, Tavy: you are. So let's have her down from the drawing room and ask her what she intends us to do. Off with you, Tavy, and fetch her. (TAVY *turns to go*) And don't be long; for the strained relations between myself and Ramsden will make the interval rather painful. (RAMSDEN *compresses his lips, but says nothing*)

OCTAVIUS Never mind him, Mr Ramsden. He's not serious. (*He goes out*)

RAMSDEN (*Very deliberately*) Mr Tanner: you are the most impudent person I have ever met.

TANNER (*Seriously*) I know it, Ramsden. Yet even I cannot wholly conquer shame. We live in an atmosphere of shame. We are ashamed of everything that is real about us; ashamed of ourselves, of our relatives, of our incomes, of our accents, of our opinions, of our experience, just as we are ashamed of our naked skins. Good Lord, my dear Ramsden, we are ashamed to walk, ashamed to ride in an omnibus, ashamed to hire a hansom instead of keeping a carriage, ashamed of keeping one horse instead of two and a groom-gardener instead of a coachman and footman. The more things a man is ashamed of, the more respectable he is. Why, you're ashamed to buy my book, ashamed to read it: the only thing you're not ashamed of is to judge me for it without having read it; and even that only means that you're ashamed to have heterodox opinions. Look at the effect I produce because my fairy godmother withheld from me this gift of shame. I have every possible virtue that a man can have except—

RAMSDEN I am glad you think so well of yourself.

TANNER All you mean by that is that you think I ought to be ashamed of talking about my virtues. You don't mean that I haven't got them: you know perfectly well that I am as sober and honest a citizen as yourself, as truthful personally, and much more truthful politically and morally.

RAMSDEN (*Touched on his most sensitive point*) I deny that. I will not allow you or any man to treat me as if I were a mere member of the British public.

I detest its prejudices; I scorn its narrowness; I demand the right to think for myself. You pose as an advanced man. Let me tell you that I was an advanced man before you were born.

TANNER I knew it was a long time ago.

RAMSDEN I am as advanced as ever I was. I defy you to prove that I have ever hauled down the flag. I am more advanced than ever I was. I grow more advanced every day.

TANNER More advanced in years, Polonius.

RAMSDEN Polonius! So you are Hamlet, I suppose.

TANNER No: I am only the most impudent person you've ever met. That's your notion of a thoroughly bad character. When you want to give me a piece of your mind, you ask yourself, as a just and upright man, what is the worst you can fairly say of me. Thief, liar, forger, adulterer, perjurer, glutton, drunkard? Not one of these names fit me. You have to fall back on my deficiency in shame. Well, I admit it. I even congratulate myself; for if I were ashamed of my real self, I should cut as stupid a figure as any of the rest of you. Cultivate a little impudence, Ramsden; and you will become quite a remarkable man.

RAMSDEN I have no—

TANNER You have no desire for that sort of notoriety. Bless you, I knew that answer would come as well as I know that a box of matches will come out of an automatic machine when I put a penny in the slot: you would be ashamed to say anything else.

*(The crushing retort for which Ramsden has been visibly collecting his forces is lost for ever; for at this point* OCTAVIUS *returns with* MISS ANN WHITEFIELD *and her mother; and* RAMSDEN *springs up and hurries to the door to receive them. Whether* ANN *is good-looking or not depends upon your taste; also and perhaps chiefly on your age and sex. To* OCTAVIUS *she is an enchantingly beautiful woman, in whose presence the world becomes transfigured, and the puny limits of individual consciousness are suddenly made infinite by a mystic memory of the whole life of the race to its beginnings in the east, or even back to the paradise from which it fell. She is to him the reality of romance, the inner good sense of nonsense, the unveiling of his eyes, the freeing of his soul, the abolition of time, place, and circumstance, the etherealization of his blood into rapturous rivers of the very water of life itself, the revelation of all the mysteries and the sanctification of all the dogmas. To her mother she is, to put it as moderately as possible, nothing whatever of the kind. Not that* OCTAVIUS'S *admiration is in any way ridiculous or discreditable.* ANN *is a well formed creature, as far as that goes; and she is perfectly ladylike, graceful, and comely, with ensnaring eyes and hair. Besides, instead of making herself an eyesore, like her mother, she has devised a mourning costume of black and violet silk which does honor to her late father and reveals the family tradition of brave unconventionality by which* RAMSDEN *sets such store.*

*But all this is beside the point as an explanation of* ANN'S *charm. Turn up her nose, give a cast to her eye, replace her black and violet confection by the apron and feathers of a flower girl, strike all the aitches out of her speech, and* ANN *would still make men dream. Vitality is as common as humanity; but, like humanity, it sometimes rises to genius; and* ANN *is one of the vital geniuses. Not at all, if you please, an oversexed person: that is a vital defect, not a true excess. She is a perfectly respectable, perfectly self-controlled woman, and looks it; though her pose is fashionably frank and impulsive. She inspires confidence as a person who will do nothing she does not mean to do; also some fear, perhaps, as a woman who will probably do everything she means to do without taking more account of other people than may be necessary and what she calls right. In short, what the weaker of her own sex sometimes call a cat.*

*Nothing can be more decorous than her entry and her reception by* RAMSDEN, *whom she kisses. The late Mr Whitefield would be gratified almost to impatience by the long faces of the men (except* TANNER, *who is fidgety), the silent handgrasps, the sympathetic placing of chairs, the sniffing of the widow, and the liquid eye of the daughter, whose heart, apparently will not let her control her tongue to speech.* RAMSDEN *and* OCTAVIUS *take the two chairs from the wall, and place them for the two ladies; but* ANN *comes to* TANNER *and takes his chair, which he offers with a brusque gesture, subsequently relieving his irritation by sitting down on the corner of the writing table with studied indecorum.* OCTAVIUS *gives* MRS WHITEFIELD *a chair next to* ANN, *and himself takes the vacant one which* RAMSDEN *has placed under the nose of the effigy of Mr Herbert Spencer.*

MRS WHITEFIELD, *by the way, is a little woman, whose faded flaxen hair looks like straw on an egg. She has an expression of muddled shrewdness, a squeak of protest in her voice, and an odd air of continually elbowing away some larger person who is crushing her into a corner. One guesses her as one of those women who are conscious of being treated as silly and negligible, and who, without having strength enough to assert themselves effectually, at any rate never submit to their fate. There is a touch of chivalry in* OCTAVIUS'S *scrupulous attention to her, even whilst his whole soul is absorbed by* ANN.

RAMSDEN *goes solemnly back to his magisterial seat at the writing table, ignoring* TANNER, *and opens the proceedings.)*

RAMSDEN I am sorry, Annie, to force business on you at a sad time like the present. But your poor dear father's will has raised a very serious question. You have read it, I believe?

(ANN *assents with a nod and a catch of her breath, too much affected to speak*)

I must say I am surprised to find Mr Tanner named as joint guardian and trustee with myself of you and Rhoda. (*A pause. They all look portentous; but they have nothing to say.* RAMSDEN, *a little ruffled by the lack of any response, continues*) I don't know that I can consent to act under such conditions. Mr Tanner has, I understand, some objection also; but I do not profess to understand its nature: he will no doubt speak for himself. But we are agreed that we can decide nothing until we know your views. I am afraid I shall have to ask you to choose between my sole guardianship and that of Mr Tanner; for I fear it is impossible for us to undertake a joint agreement.

ANN (*In a low musical voice*) Mamma—

MRS WHITEFIELD (*Hastily*) Now, Ann, I do beg you not to put it on me. I have no opinion on the subject; and if I had, it would probably not be attended to. I am quite content with whatever you three think best.

(TANNER *turns his head and looks fixedly at* RAMSDEN, *who angrily refuses to receive this mute communication*)

ANN (*Resuming in the same gentle voice, ignoring her mother's bad taste*) Mamma knows that she is not strong enough to bear the whole responsibility for me and Rhoda without some help and advice. Rhoda must have a guardian; and though I am older, I do not think any young unmarried woman should be left quite to her own guidance. I hope you agree with me, Granny?

TANNER (*Starting*) Granny! Do you intend to call your guardians Granny?

ANN Don't be foolish, Jack. Mr. Ramsden has always been Grandpapa Roebuck to me: I am Granny's Annie; and he is Annie's Granny. I christened him so when I first learned to speak.

RAMSDEN (*Sarcastically*) I hope you are satisfied, Mr. Tanner. Go on, Annie: I quite agree with you.

ANN Well, if I am to have a guardian, can I set aside anybody whom my dear father appointed for me?

RAMSDEN (*Biting his lip*) You approve of your father's choice, then?

ANN It is not for me to approve or disapprove. I accept it. My father loved me and knew best what was good for me.

RAMSDEN Of course I understand your feeling, Annie. It is what I should have expected of you; and it does you credit. But it does not settle the question so completely as you think. Let me put a case to you. Suppose you were to discover that I had been guilty of some disgraceful action—that I was not the man your poor dear father took me for! Would you still consider it right that I should be Rhoda's guardian?

ANN I can't imagine you doing anything disgraceful, Granny.

TANNER (*To* RAMSDEN) You havn't done anything of the sort, have you?

RAMSDEN (*Indignantly*) No, sir.

MRS WHITEFIELD (*Placidly*) Well, then, why suppose it?

ANN You see, Granny, Mamma would not like me to suppose it.

RAMSDEN (*Much perplexed*) You are both so full of natural and affectionate feeling in these family matters that it is very hard to put the situation fairly before you.

TANNER Besides, my friend, you are not putting the situation fairly before them.

RAMSDEN (*Sulkily*) Put it yourself, then.

TANNER I will. Ann: Ramsden thinks I am not fit to be your guardian; and I quite agree with him. He considers that if your father had read my book, he wouldn't have appointed me. That book is the disgraceful action he has been talking about. He thinks it's your duty for Rhoda's sake to ask him to act alone and to make me withdraw. Say the word; and I will.

ANN But I havn't read your book, Jack.

TANNER (*Diving at the waste-paper basket and fishing the book out for her*) Then read it at once and decide.

RAMSDEN (*Vehemently*) If I am to be your guardian, I positively forbid you to read that book, Annie. (*He smites the table with his fist and rises*)

ANN Of course not if you don't wish it. (*She puts the book on the table*)

TANNER If one guardian is to forbid you to read the other guardian's book, how are we to settle it? Suppose I order you to read it! What about your duty to me?

ANN (*Gently*) I am sure you would never purposely force me into a painful dilemma, Jack.

RAMSDEN (*Irritably*) Yes, yes, Annie: this is all very well, and, as I said, quite natural and becoming. But you must make a choice one way or the other. We are as much in a dilemma as you.

ANN I feel that I am too young, too inexperienced, to decide. My father's wishes are sacred to me.

MRS WHITEFIELD If you two men won't carry them out I must say it is rather hard that you should put the responsibility on Ann. It seems to me that people are always putting things on other people in this world.

RAMSDEN I am sorry you take it that way.

ANN (*Touchingly*) Do you refuse to accept me as your ward, Granny?

RAMSDEN No: I never said that. I greatly object to act with Mr Tanner: that's all.

MRS WHITEFIELD Why? What's the matter with poor Jack?

TANNER My views are too advanced for him.

RAMSDEN (*Indignantly*) They are not. I deny it.

ANN Of course not. What nonsense! Nobody is more advanced than Granny. I am sure it is Jack himself who has made all the difficulty. Come, Jack! be kind to me in my sorrow. You don't refuse to accept me as your ward, do you?

TANNER (*Gloomily*) No. I let myself in for it; so I suppose I must face it. (*He turns away to the bookcase, and stands there, moodily studying the titles of the volumes*)

ANN (*Rising and expanding with subdued but gushing delight*) Then we are all agreed; and my dear father's will is to be carried out. You don't know what a joy that is to me and to my mother! (*She goes to* RAMSDEN *and presses both his hands, saying*) And I shall have my dear Granny to help and advise me. (*She casts a glance at* TANNER *over her shoulder*) And Jack the Giant Killer. (*She goes past her mother to* OCTAVIUS) And Jack's inseparable friend Ricky-ticky-tavy.[5] (*He blushes and looks inexpressibly foolish*)

MRS WHITEFIELD (*Rising and shaking her widow's weeds straight*) Now that you are Ann's guardian, Mr Ramsden, I wish you would speak to her about her habit of giving people nicknames. They can't be expected to like it. (*She moves towards the door*)

ANN How can you say such a thing, Mamma! (*Glowing with affectionate remorse*) Oh, I wonder can you be right! Have I been inconsiderate? (*She turns to* OCTAVIUS, *who is sitting astride his chair with his elbows on the back of it. Putting her hand on his forehead she turns his face up suddenly*) Do you want to be treated like a grown-up man? Must I call you Mr Robinson in future?

OCTAVIUS (*Earnestly*) Oh please call me Ricky-ticky-tavy. "Mr Robinson" would hurt me cruelly. (*She laughs and pats his cheek with her finger; then comes back to* RAMSDEN) You know I'm beginning to think that Granny is rather a piece of impertinence. But I never dreamt of its hurting you.

RAMSDEN (*Breezily, as he pats her affectionately on the back*) My dear Annie, nonsense. I insist on Granny. I won't answer to any other name than Annie's Granny.

ANN (*Gratefully*) You all spoil me, except Jack.

TANNER (*Over his shoulder, from the bookcase*) I think you ought to call me Mr Tanner.

ANN (*Gently*) No you don't, Jack. That's like the things you say on purpose to shock people: those who know you pay no attention to them. But, if you like, I'll call you after your famous ancestor Don Juan.

RAMSDEN Don Juan!

ANN (*Innocently*) Oh, is there any harm in it? I didn't know. Then I certainly won't call you that. May I call you Jack until I can think of something else?

TANNER Oh, for Heaven's sake don't try to invent anything worse. I capitulate. I consent to Jack. I embrace Jack. Here endeth my first and last attempt to assert my authority.

ANN You see, Mamma, they all really like to have pet names.

MRS WHITEFIELD Well, I think you might at least drop them until we are out of mourning.

ANN (*Reproachfully, stricken to the soul*) Oh, how could you remind me, mother? (*She hastily leaves the room to conceal her emotion*)

MRS WHITEFIELD Of course. My fault as usual! (*She follows* ANN)

TANNER (*Coming from the bookcase*) Ramsden: we're beaten—smashed—nonentitized, like her mother.

[5] The name Kipling gave the mongoose in *The Jungle Book*.

RAMSDEN Stuff, sir. (*He follows* MRS WHITEFIELD *out of the room*)

TANNER (*Left alone with* OCTAVIUS, *stares whimsically at him*) Tavy: do you want to count for something in the world?

OCTAVIUS I want to count for something as a poet: I want to write a great play.

TANNER With Ann as the heroine?

OCTAVIUS Yes: I confess it.

TANNER Take care, Tavy. The play with Ann as the heroine is all right; but if you're not very careful, by Heaven she'll marry you.

OCTAVIUS (*Sighing*) No such luck, Jack!

TANNER Why, man, your head is in the lioness's mouth: you are half swallowed already—in three bites—Bite One, Ricky; Bite Two, Ticky; Bite Three, Tavy; and down you go.

OCTAVIUS She is the same to everybody, Jack: you know her ways.

TANNER Yes: she breaks everybody's back with the stroke of her paw; but the question is, which of us will she eat? My own opinion is that she means to eat you.

OCTAVIUS (*Rising, pettishly*) It's horrible to talk like that about her when she is upstairs crying for her father. But I do so want her to eat me that I can bear your brutalities because they give me hope.

TANNER Tavy: that's the devilish side of a woman's fascination: she makes you will your own destruction.

OCTAVIUS But it's not destruction: it's fulfilment.

TANNER Yes, of her purpose; and that purpose is neither her happiness nor yours, but Nature's. Vitality in a woman is a blind fury of creation. She sacrifices herself to it: do you think she will hesitate to sacrifice you?

OCTAVIUS Why, it is just because she is self-sacrificing that she will not sacrifice those she loves.

TANNER That is the profoundest of mistakes, Tavy. It is the self-sacrificing women that sacrifice others most recklessly. Because they are unselfish, they are kind in little things. Because they have a purpose which is not their own purpose, but that of the whole universe, a man is nothing to them but an instrument of that purpose.

OCTAVIUS Don't be ungenerous, Jack. They take the tenderest care of us.

TANNER Yes, as a soldier takes care of his rifle or a musician of his violin. But do they allow us any purpose or freedom of our own? Will they lend us to one another? Can the strongest man escape from them when once he is appropriated? They tremble when we are in danger, and weep when we die; but the tears are not for us, but for a father wasted, a son's breeding thrown away. They accuse us of treating them as a mere means to our pleasure; but how can so feeble and transient a folly as a man's selfish pleasure enslave a woman as the whole purpose of Nature embodied in a woman can enslave a man?

OCTAVIUS What matter, if the slavery makes us happy?

TANNER No matter at all if you have no purpose of your own, and are, like most men, a mere breadwinner. But you, Tavy, are an artist: that is, you have a purpose as absorbing and as unscrupulous as a woman's purpose.

OCTAVIUS Not unscrupulous.

TANNER Quite unscrupulous. The true artist will let his wife starve, his children go barefoot, his mother drudge for his living at seventy, sooner than work at anything but his art. To women he is half vivisector, half vampire. He gets into intimate relations with them to study them, to strip the mask of convention from them, to surprise their inmost secrets, knowing that they have the power to rouse his deepest creative energies, to rescue him from his cold reason, to make him see visions and dream dreams, to inspire him, as he calls it. He persuades women that they may do this for their own purpose whilst he really means them to do it for his. He steals the mother's milk and blackens it to make printer's ink to scoff at her and glorify ideal women with. He pretends to spare her the pangs of child-bearing so that he may have for himself the tenderness and fostering that belong of right to her children. Since marriage began, the great artist has been known as a bad husband. But he is worse: he is a child-robber, a blood-sucker, a hypocrite, and a cheat. Perish the race and wither a thousand women if only the sacrifice of them enable him to act Hamlet better, to paint a finer picture, to write a deeper poem, a greater play, a profounder philosophy! For mark you, Tavy, the artist's work is to shew us ourselves as we really are. Our minds are nothing but this knowledge of ourselves; and he who adds a jot to such knowledge creates new mind as surely as any woman creates new men. In the rage of that creation he is as ruthless as the woman, as dangerous to her as she to him, and as horribly fascinating. Of all human struggles there is none so treacherous and remorseless as the struggle between the artist man and the mother woman. Which shall use up the other? that is the issue between them. And it is all the deadlier because, in your romanticist cant, they love one another.

OCTAVIUS Even if it were so—and I don't admit it for a moment—it is out of the deadliest struggles that we get the noblest characters.

TANNER Remember that the next time you meet a grizzly bear or a Bengal tiger, Tavy.

OCTAVIUS I meant where there is love, Jack.

TANNER Oh, the tiger will love you. There is no love sincerer than the love of food. I think Ann loves you that way: she patted your cheek as if it were a nicely underdone chop.

OCTAVIUS You know, Jack, I should have to run away from you if I did not make it a fixed rule not to mind anything you say. You come out with perfectly revolting things sometimes.

(RAMSDEN *returns, followed by* ANN. *They come in quickly, with their former leisurely air of decorous grief changed to one of genuine concern, and, on* RAMSDEN'S *part, of worry. He comes between the two men, intending to address* OCTAVIUS, *but pulls himself up abruptly as he sees* TANNER)

RAMSDEN I hardly expected to find you still here, Mr Tanner.

TANNER Am I in the way? Good morning, fellow guardian. (*He goes towards the door*)

ANN Stop, Jack. Granny: he must know, sooner or later.

RAMSDEN Octavius: I have a very serious piece of news for you. It is of the most private and delicate nature—of the most painful nature too, I am sorry to say. Do you wish Mr Tanner to be present whilst I explain?

OCTAVIUS (*Turning pale*) I have no secrets from Jack.

RAMSDEN Before you decide that finally, let me say that the news concerns your sister, and that it is terrible news.

OCTAVIUS Violet! What has happened? Is she—dead?

RAMSDEN I am not sure that it is not even worse than that.

OCTAVIUS Is she badly hurt? Has there been an accident?

RAMSDEN No: nothing of that sort.

TANNER Ann: will you have the common humanity to tell us what the matter is?

ANN (*Half whispering*) I can't. Violet has done something dreadful. We shall have to get her away somewhere. (*She flutters to the writing table and sits in* RAMSDEN'S *chair, leaving the three men to fight it out between them*)

OCTAVIUS (*Enlightened*) Is that what you meant, Mr Ramsden?

RAMSDEN Yes. (OCTAVIUS *sinks upon a chair, crushed*) I am afraid there is no doubt that Violet did not really go to Eastbourne three weeks ago when we thought she was with the Parry Whitefields. And she called on a strange doctor yesterday with a wedding ring on her finger. Mrs Parry Whitefield met her there by chance; and so the whole thing came out.

OCTAVIUS (*Rising with his fists clenched*) Who is the scoundrel?

ANN She won't tell us.

OCTAVIUS (*Collapsing into the chair again*) What a frightful thing!

TANNER (*With angry sarcasm*) Dreadful. Appalling. Worse than death, as Ramsden says. (*He comes to* OCTAVIUS) What would you not give, Tavy, to turn it into a railway accident, with all her bones broken, or something equally respectable and deserving of sympathy?

OCTAVIUS Don't be brutal, Jack.

TANNER Brutal! Good Heavens, man, what are you crying for? Here is a woman whom we all supposed to be making bad water color sketches, practicing Grieg and Brahms, gadding about to concerts and parties, wasting her life and her money. We suddenly learn that she has turned from these sillinesses to the fulfilment of her highest purpose and greatest function—to increase, multiply, and replenish the earth. And instead of admiring her courage and rejoicing in her instinct; instead of crowning the completed womanhood and raising the triumphal strain of "Unto us a child is born: unto us a son is given," here you are—

you who have been as merry as grigs in your mourning for the dead—all pulling long faces and looking as ashamed and disgraced as if the girl had committed the vilest of crimes.

RAMSDEN (*Roaring with rage*) I will not have these abominations uttered in my house. (*He smites the writing-table with his fist*)

TANNER Look here: if you insult me again I'll take you at your word and leave your house. Ann: where is Violet now?

ANN Why? Are you going to her?

TANNER Of course I am going to her. She wants help; she wants money; she wants respect and congratulation; she wants every chance for her child. She does not seem likely to get it from you: she shall from me. Where is she?

ANN Don't be so headstrong, Jack. She's upstairs.

TANNER What! Under Ramsden's sacred roof! Go and do your miserable duty, Ramsden. Hunt her out into the street. Cleanse your threshold from her contamination. Vindicate the purity of your English home. I'll go for a cab.

ANN (*Alarmed*) Oh, Granny, you mustn't do that.

OCTAVIUS (*Broken-heartedly, rising*) I'll take her away, Mr Ramsden. She had no right to come to your house.

RAMSDEN (*Indignantly*) But I am only too anxious to help her. (*Turning on* TANNER) How dare you, sir, impute such monstrous intentions to me? I protest against it. I am ready to put down my last penny to save her from being driven to run to you for protection.

TANNER (*Subsiding*) It's all right, then. He's not going to act up to his principles. It's agreed that we all stand by Violet.

OCTAVIUS But who is the man? He can make reparation by marrying her; and he shall, or he shall answer for it to me.

RAMSDEN He shall, Octavius. There you speak like a man.

TANNER Then you don't think him a scoundrel, after all?

OCTAVIUS Not a scoundrel! He is a heartless scoundrel.

RAMSDEN A damned scoundrel. I beg your pardon, Annie; but I can say no less.

TANNER So we are to marry your sister to a damned scoundrel by way of reforming her character! On my soul, I think you are all mad.

ANN Don't be absurd, Jack. Of course you are quite right, Tavy; but we don't know who he is: Violet won't tell us.

TANNER What on earth does it matter who he is? He's done his part; and Violet must do the rest.

RAMSDEN (*Beside himself*) Stuff! lunacy! There is a rascal in our midst, a libertine, a villain worse than a murderer; and we are not to learn who he is! In our ignorance we are to shake him by the hand; to introduce him into our homes; to trust our daughters with him; to—to—

ANN (*Coaxingly*) There, Granny, don't talk so loud. It's most shocking: we must all admit that; but if Violet won't tell us, what can we do? Nothing. Simply *nothing*.

RAMSDEN Hmph! I'm not so sure of that. If any man has paid Violet any special attention, we can easily find that out. If there is any man of notoriously loose principles among us—

TANNER Ahem!

RAMSDEN (*Raising his voice*) Yes, sir, I repeat, if there is any man of notoriously loose principles among us—

TANNER Or any man notoriously lacking in self-control.

RAMSDEN (*Aghast*) Do you dare to suggest that *I* am capable of such an act?

TANNER My dear Ramsden, this is an act of which every man is capable. That is what comes of getting at cross purposes with Nature. The suspicion you have just flung at me clings to us all. It's a sort of mud that sticks to the judge's ermine or the cardinal's robe as fast as to the rags of the tramp. Come, Tavy! don't look so bewildered: it might have been me: it might have been Ramsden; just as it might have been anybody. If it had, what could we do but lie and protest—as Ramsden is going to protest.

RAMSDEN (*Choking*) I—I—I—

TANNER Guilt itself could not stammer more confusedly. And yet you know perfectly well he's innocent, Tavy.

RAMSDEN (*Exhausted*) I am glad you admit that, sir. I admit, myself, that there is an element of truth in what you say, grossly as you may distort it to gratify your malicious humor. I hope, Octavius, no suspicion of me is possible in your mind.

OCTAVIUS Of you! No, not for a moment.

TANNER (*Drily*) I think he suspects me just a little.

OCTAVIUS Jack: you couldn't—you wouldn't—

TANNER Why not?

OCTAVIUS (*Appalled*) Why not!

TANNER Oh, well, I'll tell you why not. First, you would feel bound to quarrel with me. Second, Violet doesn't like me. Third, if I had the honor of being the father of Violet's child, I should boast of it instead of denying it. So be easy: our friendship is not in danger.

OCTAVIUS I should have put away the suspicion with horror if only you would think and feel naturally about it. I beg your pardon.

TANNER My pardon! Nonsense! And now let's sit down and have a family council. (*He sits down. The rest follow his example, more or less under protest*) Violet is going to do the State a service; consequently she must be packed abroad like a criminal until it's over. What's happening upstairs?

ANN Violet is in the housekeeper's room—by herself, of course.

TANNER Why not in the drawing room?

ANN Don't be absurd, Jack. Miss Ramsden is in the drawing room with my mother, considering what to do.

TANNER Oh! the housekeeper's room is the penitentiary, I suppose; and the prisoner is waiting to be brought before her judges. The old cats!

ANN Oh, Jack!

RAMSDEN You are at present a guest beneath the roof of one of the old cats, sir. My sister is the mistress of this house.

TANNER She would put me in the housekeeper's room, too, if she dared, Ramsden. However, I withdraw cats. Cats would have more sense. Ann: as your guardian, I order you to go to Violet at once and be particularly kind to her.

ANN I have seen her, Jack. And I am sorry to say I am afraid she is going to be rather obstinate about going abroad. I think Tavy ought to speak to her about it.

OCTAVIUS How can I speak to her about such a thing? (*He breaks down*)

ANN Don't break down, Ricky. Try to bear it for all our sakes.

RAMSDEN Life is not all plays and poems, Octavius. Come! face it like a man.

TANNER (*Chafing again*) Poor dear brother! Poor dear friends of the family! Poor dear Tabbies and Grimalkins! Poor dear everybody except the woman who is going to risk her life to create another life! Tavy: don't you be a selfish ass. Away with you and talk to Violet; and bring her down here if she cares to come. (OCTAVIUS *rises*) Tell her we'll stand by her.

RAMSDEN (*Rising*) No, sir—

TANNER (*Rising also and interrupting him*) Oh, we understand: it's against your conscience; but still you'll do it.

OCTAVIUS I assure you all, on my word, I never meant to be selfish. It's so hard to know what to do when one wishes earnestly to do right.

TANNER My dear Tavy, your pious English habit of regarding the world as a moral gymnasium built expressly to strengthen your character in, occasionally leads you to think about your own confounded principles when you should be thinking about other people's necessities. The need of the present hour is a happy mother and a healthy baby. Bend your energies on that; and you will see your way clearly enough.

(OCTAVIUS, *much perplexed, goes out*)

RAMSDEN (*Facing* TANNER *impressively*) And Morality, sir? What is to become of that?

TANNER Meaning a weeping Magdalen and an innocent child branded with her shame. Not in our circle, thank you. Morality can go to its father the devil.

RAMSDEN I thought so, sir. Morality sent to the devil to please our libertines, male and female. That is to be the future of England, is it?

TANNER Oh, England will survive your disapproval. Meanwhile, I understand that you agree with me as to the practical course we are to take?

RAMSDEN Not in your spirit, sir. Not for your reasons.

TANNER You can explain that if anybody calls you to account, here or hereafter. (*He turns away, and plants himself in front of Mr Herbert Spencer, at whom he stares gloomily*)

ANN (*Rising and coming to* RAMSDEN) Granny: hadn't you better go up to the drawing room and tell them what we intend to do?

RAMSDEN (*Looking pointedly at* TANNER) I hardly like to leave you alone with this gentleman. Will you not come with me?

ANN Miss Ramsden would not like to speak about it before me, Granny. I ought not to be present.

RAMSDEN You are right: I should have thought of that. You are a good girl, Annie.

(*He pats her on the shoulder. She looks up at him with beaming eyes; and he goes out, much moved. Having disposed of him, she looks at* TANNER. *His back being turned to her, she gives a moment's attention to her personal appearance, then softly goes to him and speaks almost into his ear*)

ANN Jack (*He turns with a start*) are you glad that you are my guardian? You don't mind being made responsible for me, I hope.

TANNER The latest addition to your collection of scapegoats, eh?

ANN Oh, that stupid old joke of yours about me! Do please drop it. Why do you say things that you know must pain me? I do my best to please you, Jack: I suppose I may tell you so now that you are my guardian. You will make me so unhappy if you refuse to be friends with me.

TANNER (*Studying her as gloomily as he studied the bust*) You need not go begging for my regard. How unreal our moral judgments are! You seem to me to have absolutely no conscience—only hypocrisy; and you can't see the difference—yet there is a sort of fascination about you. I always attend to you, somehow. I should miss you if I lost you.

ANN (*Tranquilly slipping her arm into his and walking about with him*) But isn't that only natural, Jack? We have known each other since we were children. Do you remember—

TANNER (*Abruptly breaking loose*) Stop! I remember everything.

ANN Oh, I daresay we were often very silly; but—

TANNER I won't have it, Ann. I am no more that schoolboy now than I am the dotard of ninety I shall grow into if I live long enough. It is over: let me forget it.

ANN Wasn't it a happy time? (*She attempts to take his arm again*)

TANNER Sit down and behave yourself. (*He makes her sit down in the chair next to the writing table*) No doubt it was a happy time for you. You were a good girl and never compromised yourself. And yet the wickedest child that ever was slapped could hardly have had a better time. I can understand the success with which you bullied the other girls: your virtue imposed on them. But tell me this: did you ever know a good boy?

ANN Of course. All boys are foolish sometimes; but Tavy was always a really good boy.

TANNER (*Struck by this*) Yes: you're right. For some reason you never tempted Tavy.

ANN Tempted! Jack!

TANNER Yes, my dear Lady Mephistopheles, tempted. You were insatiably curious as to what a boy might be capable of, and diabolically clever at getting through his guard and surprising his inmost secrets.

ANN What nonsense! All because you used to tell me long stories of the wicked things you had done—silly boy's tricks! And you call such things inmost secrets! Boys' secrets are just like men's; and you know what they are!

TANNER (*Obstinately*) No I don't. What are they, pray?

ANN Why, the things they tell everybody, of course.

TANNER Now I swear I told you things I told no one else. You lured me into a compact by which we were to have no secrets from one another. We were to tell one another everything. I didn't notice that you never told me anything.

ANN You didn't want to talk about me, Jack. You wanted to talk about yourself.

TANNER Ah, true, horribly true. But what a devil of a child you must have been to know that weakness and to play on it for the satisfaction of your own curiosity! I wanted to brag to you, to make myself interesting. And I found myself doing all sorts of mischievous things simply to have something to tell you about. I fought with boys I didn't hate; I lied about things I might just as well have told the truth about; I stole things I didn't want; I kissed little girls I didn't care for. It was all bravado: passionless and therefore unreal.

ANN I never told of you, Jack.

TANNER No; but if you had wanted to stop me you would have told of me. You wanted me to go on.

ANN (*Flashing out*) Oh, that's not true: it's not true, Jack. I never wanted you to do those dull, disappointing, brutal, stupid, vulgar things. I always hoped that it would be something really heroic at last. (*Recovering herself*) Excuse me, Jack; but the things you did were never a bit like the things I wanted you to do. They often gave me great uneasiness; but I could not tell of you and get you into trouble. And you were only a boy. I knew you would grow out of them. Perhaps I was wrong.

TANNER (*Sardonically*) Do not give way to remorse, Ann. At least nineteen twentieths of the exploits I confessed to you were pure lies. I soon noticed that you didn't like the true stories.

ANN Of course I knew that some of the things couldn't have happened. But—

TANNER You are going to remind me that some of the most disgraceful ones did.

ANN (*Fondly, to his great terror*) I don't want to remind you of anything. But I knew the people they happened to, and heard about them.

TANNER Yes; but even the true stories were touched up for telling. A sensitive boy's humiliations may be very good fun for ordinary thickskinned grown-ups; but to the boy himself they are so acute, so ignominious, that he cannot confess them—cannot but deny them passionately. However, perhaps it was as well for me that I romanced a bit; for, on the one occasion when I told you the truth, you threatened to tell of me.

ANN Oh, never. Never once.

TANNER Yes, you did. Do you remember a dark-eyed girl named Rachel Rosetree? (ANN's *brows contract for an instant involuntarily*) I got up a love affair with her; and we met one night in the garden and walked about very uncomfortably with our arms round one another, and kissed at parting, and were most conscientiously romantic. If that love affair had gone on, it would have bored me to death; but it didn't go on; for the next thing that happened was that Rachel cut me because she found out that I had told you. How did she find it out? From you. You went to her and held the guilty secret over her head, leading her a life of abject terror and humiliation by threatening to tell of her.

ANN And a very good thing for her, too. It was my duty to stop her misconduct; and she is thankful to me for it now.

TANNER Is she?

ANN She ought to be, at all events.

TANNER It was not your duty to stop my misconduct, I suppose.

ANN I did stop it by stopping her.

TANNER Are you sure of that? You stopped my telling you about my adventures; but how do you know that you stopped the adventures?

ANN Do you mean to say that you went on in the same way with other girls?

TANNER No. I had enough of that sort of romantic tomfoolery with Rachel.

ANN (*Unconvinced*) Then why did you break off our confidences and become quite strange to me?

TANNER (*Enigmatically*) It happened just then that I got something that I wanted to keep all to myself instead of sharing it with you.

ANN I am sure I shouldn't have asked for any of it if you had grudged it.

TANNER It wasn't a box of sweets, Ann. It was something you'd never have let me call my own.

ANN (*Incredulously*) What?

TANNER My soul.

ANN Oh, do be sensible, Jack. You know you're talking nonsense.

TANNER The most solemn earnest, Ann. You didn't notice at that time that you were getting a soul too. But you were. It was not for nothing that you suddenly found you had a moral duty to chastise and reform Rachel. Up to that time you had traded pretty extensively in being a good child; but you had never set up a sense of duty to others. Well, I set one up too. Up to that time I had played the boy buccaneer with no more conscience than a fox in a poultry farm. But now I began to have scruples, to feel obligations, to find that veracity and honor were no longer goody-goody expressions in the mouths of grown-up people, but compelling principle in myself.

ANN (*Quietly*) Yes, I suppose you're right. You were beginning to be a man, and I to be a woman.

TANNER Are you sure it was not that we were beginning to be something more? What does the beginning of manhood and womanhood mean in most people's mouths? You know: it means the beginning of love. But love began long before that for me. Love played its part in the earliest dreams and follies and romances I can remember—may I say the earliest follies and romances we can remember?—though we did not understand it at the time. No: the change that came to me was the birth in me of moral passion; and I declare that according to my experience moral passion is the only real passion.

ANN All passions ought to be moral, Jack.

TANNER Ought! Do you think that anything is strong enough to impose oughts on a passion except a stronger passion still?

ANN Our moral sense controls passion, Jack. Don't be stupid.

TANNER Our moral sense! And is that not a passion? Is the devil to have all the passions as well as all the good tunes? If it were not a passion—if it were not the mightiest of the passions, all the other passions would sweep it away like a leaf before a hurricane. It is the birth of that passion that turns a child into a man.

ANN There are other passions, Jack. Very strong ones.

TANNER All the other passions were in me before; but they were idle and aimless—mere childish greedinesses and cruelties, curiosities and fancies, habits and superstitions, grotesque and ridiculous to the mature intelligence. When they suddenly began to shine like newly lit flames it was by no light of their own, but by the radiance of the dawning moral passion. That passion dignified them, gave them conscience and meaning, found them a mob of appetites and organized them into an army of purposes and principles. My soul was born of that passion.

ANN I noticed that you got more sense. You were a dreadfully destructive boy before that.

TANNER Destructive! Stuff! I was only mischievous.

ANN Oh, Jack, you were very destructive. You ruined all the young fir trees by chopping off their leaders with a wooden sword. You broke all the cucumber frames with your catapult. You set fire to the common: the police arrested Tavy for it because he ran away when he couldn't stop you. You—

TANNER Pooh! pooh! pooh! these were battles, bombardments, stratagems to save our scalps from the red Indians. You have no imagination, Ann. I am ten times more destructive now than I was then. The moral passion has taken my destructiveness in hand and directed it to moral ends. I have become a reformer, and, like all reformers, an iconoclast. I no longer break cucumber frames and burn gorse bushes: I shatter creeds and demolish idols.

ANN (*Bored*) I am afraid I am too feminine to see any sense in destruction. Destruction can only destroy.

TANNER Yes. That is why it is so useful. Construction cumbers the ground with institutions made by busybodies. Destruction clears it and gives us breathing space and liberty.

ANN It's no use, Jack. No woman will agree with you there.

TANNER That's because you confuse construction and destruction with creation and murder. They're quite different: I adore creation and abhor murder. Yes: I adore it in tree and flower, in bird and beast, even in you. (*A flush of interest and delight suddenly chases the growing perplexity and boredom from her face*) It was the creative instinct that led you to attach me to you by bonds that have left their mark on me to this day. Yes, Ann: the old childish compact between us was an unconscious love compact—

ANN Jack!

TANNER Oh, don't be alarmed—

ANN I am not alarmed.

TANNER (*Whimsically*) Then you ought to be: where are your principles?

ANN Jack: are you serious or are you not?

TANNER Do you mean about the moral passion?

ANN No, no: the other one. (*Confused*) Oh! you are so silly: one never knows how to take you.

TANNER You must take me quite seriously. I am your guardian; and it is my duty to improve your mind.

ANN The love compact is over, then, is it? I suppose you grew tired of me?

TANNER No; but the moral passion made our childish relations impossible. A jealous sense of my new individuality arose in me—

ANN You hated to be treated as a boy any longer. Poor Jack!

TANNER Yes, because to be treated as a boy was to be taken on the old footing. I had become a new person; and those who knew the old person laughed at me. The only man who behaved sensibly was my tailor: he took my measure anew every time he saw me, whilst all the rest went on with their old measurements and expected them to fit me.

ANN You became frightfully self-conscious.

TANNER When you go to heaven, Ann, you will be frightfully conscious of your wings for the first year or so. When you meet your relatives there, and they persist in treating you as if you were still a mortal, you will not be able to bear them. You will try to get into a circle which has never known you except as an angel.

ANN So it was only your vanity that made you run away from us after all?

TANNER Yes, only my vanity, as you call it.

ANN You need not have kept away from me on that account.

TANNER From you above all others. You fought harder than anybody against my emancipation.

ANN (*Earnestly*) Oh, how wrong you are! I would have done anything for you.

TANNER Anything except let me get loose from you. Even then you had acquired by instinct that damnable woman's trick of heaping obligations on a man, of placing yourself so entirely and helplessly at his mercy that at last he dare not take a step without running to you for leave. I know a poor wretch whose one desire in life is to run away from his wife. She prevents him by threatening to throw herself in front of the engine of the train he leaves her in. That is what all women do. If we try to go where you do not want us to go there is no law to prevent us; but when we take the first step your breasts are under our foot as it descends: your bodies are under our wheels as we start. No woman shall ever enslave me in that way.

ANN But, Jack, you cannot get through life without considering other people a little.

TANNER Ay; but what other people? It is this consideration of other people—or rather this cowardly fear of them which we call consideration—that makes us the sentimental slaves we are. To consider you, as you call it, is to substitute your will for my own. How if it be a baser will than mine? Are women taught better than men or worse? Are mobs of voters taught better than statesmen or worse? Worse, of course, in both cases. And then what sort of world are you going to get, with its public men considering its voting mobs, and its private men considering their wives? What does Church and State mean nowadays? The Woman and the Ratepayer.

ANN (*Placidly*) I am so glad you understand politics, Jack: it will be most useful to you if you go into parliament. (*He collapses like a pricked bladder*) But I am sorry you thought my influence a bad one.

TANNER I don't say it was a bad one. But bad or good, I didn't choose to be cut to your measure. And I won't be cut to it.

ANN Nobody wants you to, Jack. I assure you—really on my word—I don't mind your queer opinions one little bit. You know we have all been brought up to have advanced opinions. Why do you persist in thinking me so narrow minded?

TANNER That's the danger of it. I know you don't mind, because you've found out that it doesn't matter. The boa constrictor doesn't mind the opinions of a stag one little bit when once she has got her coils round it.

ANN (*Rising in sudden enlightenment*) O-o-o-o-oh! now I understand why you warned Tavy that I am a boa constrictor. Granny told me. (*She laughs and throws her boa round his neck*) Doesn't it feel nice and soft, Jack?

TANNER (*In the toils*) You scandalous woman, will you throw away even your hypocrisy?

ANN I am never hypocritical with you, Jack. Are you angry? (*She withdraws the boa and throws it on a chair*) Perhaps I shouldn't have done that.

TANNER (*Contemptuously*) Pooh, prudery! Why should you not, if it amuses you?

ANN (*Shyly*) Well, because—because I suppose what you really meant by the boa constrictor was this (*She puts her arms round his neck*)

TANNER (*Staring at her*) Magnificent audacity! (*She laughs and pats his cheeks*) Now just to think that if I mentioned this episode not a soul would believe me except the people who would cut me for telling, whilst if you accused me of it nobody would believe my denial!

ANN (*Taking her arms away with perfect dignity*) You are incorrigible, Jack. But you should not jest about our affection for one another. Nobody could possibly misunderstand it. You do not misunderstand it, I hope.

TANNER My blood interprets for me, Ann. Poor Ricky Ticky Tavy!

ANN (*Looking quickly at him as if this were a new light*) Surely you are not so absurd as to be jealous of Tavy.

TANNER Jealous! Why should I be? But I don't wonder at your grip of him. I feel the coils tightening round my very self, though you are only playing with me.

ANN Do you think I have designs on Tavy?

TANNER I know you have.

ANN (*Earnestly*) Take care, Jack. You may make Tavy very unhappy if you mislead him about me.

TANNER Never fear: he will not escape you.

ANN I wonder are you really a clever man!

TANNER Why this sudden misgiving on the subject?

ANN You seem to understand all the things I don't understand; but you are a perfect baby in the things I do understand.

TANNER I understand how Tavy feels for you, Ann; you may depend on that, at all events.

ANN And you think you understand how I feel for Tavy, don't you?

TANNER I know only too well what is going to happen to poor Tavy.

ANN I should laugh at you, Jack, if it were not for poor papa's death. Mind! Tavy will be very unhappy.

TANNER Yes; but he won't know it, poor devil. He is a thousand times too good for you. That's why he is going to make the mistake of his life about you.

ANN I think men make more mistakes by being too clever than by being too good. (*She sits down, with a trace of contempt for the whole male sex in the elegant carriage of her shoulders*)

TANNER Oh, I know you don't care very much about Tavy. But there is always one who kisses and one who only allows the kiss. Tavy will kiss; and you will only turn the cheek. And you will throw him over if anybody better turns up.

ANN (*Offended*) You have no right to say such things, Jack. They are not true, and not delicate. If you and Tavy choose to be stupid about me, that is not my fault.

TANNER (*Remorsefully*) Forgive my brutalities, Ann. They are leveled at this wicked world, not at you. (*She looks up at him, pleased and forgiving. He becomes cautious at once*) All the same, I wish Ramsden would come back. I never feel safe with you: there is a devilish charm—or no: not a charm, a subtle interest (*She laughs*)—Just so: you know it; and you triumph in it. Openly and shamelessly triumph in it!

ANN What a shocking flirt you are, Jack!

TANNER A flirt!! I!!!

ANN Yes, a flirt. You are always abusing and offending people; but you never really mean to let go your hold of them.

TANNER I will ring the bell. This conversation has already gone further than I intended.

(RAMSDEN *and* OCTAVIUS *come back with* MISS RAMSDEN, *a hardheaded old maiden lady in a plain brown silk gown, with enough rings, chains, and brooches to shew that her plainness of dress is a matter of principle, not of poverty. She comes into the room very determinedly: the two men, perplexed and downcast, following her.* ANN *rises and goes eagerly to meet her.* TANNER *retreats to the wall between the busts and pretends to study the pictures.* RAMSDEN *goes to his table as usual; and* OCTAVIUS *clings to the neighborhood of* TANNER)

MISS RAMSDEN (*Almost pushing* ANN *aside as she comes to* MRS WHITEFIELD'S *chair and plants herself there resolutely*) I wash my hands of the whole affair.

OCTAVIUS (*Very wretched*) I know you wish me to take Violet away, Miss Ramsden. I will. (*He turns irresolutely to the door*)

RAMSDEN No, no—

MISS RAMSDEN What is the use of saying no, Roebuck? Octavius knows that I would not turn any truly contrite and repentant woman from your doors. But when a woman is not only wicked, but intends to go on being wicked, she and I part company.

ANN Oh, Miss Ramsden, what do you mean? What has Violet said?

RAMSDEN Violet is certainly very obstinate. She won't leave London. I don't understand her.

MISS RAMSDEN I do. It's as plain as the nose on your face, Roebuck, that she won't go because she doesn't want to be separated from this man, whoever he is.

ANN Oh, surely, surely! Octavius: did you speak to her?

OCTAVIUS She won't tell us anything. She won't make any arrangement until she has consulted somebody. It can't be anybody else than the scoundrel who has betrayed her.

TANNER (*To* OCTAVIUS) Well, let her consult him. He will be glad enough to have her sent abroad. Where is the difficulty?

MISS RAMSDEN (*Taking the answer out of* OCTAVIUS'S *mouth*) The difficulty, Mr Jack, is that when I offered to help her I didn't offer to become her accomplice in her wickedness. She either pledges her word never to see that man again, or else she finds some new friends; and the sooner the better.

(*The* PARLORMAID *appears at the door.* ANN *hastily resumes her seat, and looks as unconcerned as possible.* OCTAVIUS *instinctively imitates her*)

THE MAID The cab is at the door, ma'am.

MISS RAMSDEN What cab?

THE MAID For Miss Robinson.

MISS RAMSDEN Oh! (*Recovering herself*) All right. (THE MAID *withdraws*) She has sent for a cab.

TANNER I wanted to send for that cab half an hour ago.

MISS RAMSDEN I am glad she understands the position she has placed herself in.

RAMSDEN I don't like her going away in this fashion, Susan. We had better not do anything harsh.

OCTAVIUS No: thank you again and again; but Miss Ramsden is quite right. Violet cannot expect to stay.

ANN Hadn't you better go with her, Tavy?

OCTAVIUS She won't have me.

MISS RAMSDEN Of course she won't. She's going straight to that man.

TANNER As a natural result of her virtuous reception here.

RAMSDEN (*Much troubled*) There, Susan! You hear! and there's some truth in it. I wish you could reconcile it with your principles to be a little patient with this poor girl. She's very young; and there's a time for everything.

MISS RAMSDEN Oh, she will get all the sympathy she wants from the men. I'm surprised at you, Roebuck.

TANNER So am I, Ramsden, most favorably.

(VIOLET *appears at the door. She is as impenitent and self-possessed a young lady as one would desire to see among the best behaved of her sex. Her small head and tiny resolute mouth and chin; her haughty crispness of speech and trimness of carriage; the ruthless elegance of her equipment, which includes a very smart hat with a dead bird in it, mark a personality which is as formidable as it is exquisitely pretty. She is not a siren, like* ANN: *admiration comes to her without any compulsion or even interest on her part; besides, there is some fun in* ANN, *but in this woman none, perhaps no mercy either: if anything restrains her, it is intelligence and pride, not compassion. Her voice might be the voice of a schoolmistress addressing a class of girls who had disgraced themselves, as she proceeds with complete composure and some disgust to say what she has come to say*)

VIOLET I have only looked in to tell Miss Ramsden that she will find her birthday present to me, the filagree bracelet, in the housekeeper's room.

TANNER Do come in, Violet; and talk to us sensibly.

VIOLET Thank you: I have had quite enough of the family conversation this morning. So has your mother, Ann: she has gone home crying. But at all events, I have found out what some of my pretended friends are worth. Goodbye.

TANNER No, no: one moment. I have something to say which I beg you to hear. (*She looks at him without the slightest curiosity, but waits, apparently as much to finish getting her glove on as to hear what he has to say*) I am altogether on your side in this matter. I congratulate you, with the sincerest respect, on having the courage to do what you have done. You are entirely in the right; and the family is entirely in the wrong.

(*Sensation.* ANN *and* MISS RAMSDEN *rise and turn towards the two.* VIOLET, *more surprised than any of the others, forgets her glove, and comes forward into the middle of the room, both puzzled and displeased.* OCTAVIUS *alone does not move nor raise his head: he is overwhelmed with shame*)

ANN (*Pleading to* TANNER *to be sensible*) Jack!

MISS RAMSDEN (*Outraged*) Well, I must say!

VIOLET (*Sharply to* TANNER) Who told you?

TANNER Why, Ramsden and Tavy of course. Why should they not?

VIOLET But they don't know.

TANNER Don't know what?

VIOLET They don't know that I am in the right, I mean.

TANNER Oh, they know it in their hearts, though they think themselves bound to blame you by their silly superstitions about morality and propriety and so forth. But I know, and the whole world really knows, though it dare not say so, that you were right to follow your instinct; that vitality and bravery are the greatest qualities a woman can have, and motherhood her solemn initiation into womanhood; and that the fact of your not being legally married matters not one scrap either to your own worth or to our real regard for you.

VIOLET (*Flushing with indignation*) Oh! You think me a wicked woman, like the rest. You think I have not only been vile, but that I share your abominable opinions. Miss Ramsden: I have borne your hard words because I knew you would be sorry for them when you found out the truth. But I won't bear such a horrible insult as to be complimented by Jack on being one of the wretches of whom he approves. I have kept my marriage a secret for my husband's sake. But now I claim my right as a married woman not to be insulted.

OCTAVIUS (*Raising his head with inexpressible relief*) You are married!

VIOLET Yes; and I think you might have guessed it. What business had you all to take it for granted that I had no right to wear my wedding ring? Not one of you even asked me: I cannot forget that.

TANNER (*In ruins*) I am utterly crushed. I meant well. I apologize—abjectly apologize.

VIOLET I hope you will be more careful in future about the things you say. Of course one does not take them seriously; but they are very disagreeable, and rather in bad taste, I think.

TANNER (*Bowing to the storm*) I have no defence: I shall know better in future than to take any woman's part. We have all disgraced ourselves in your eyes, I am afraid, except Ann. She befriended you. For Ann's sake, forgive us.

VIOLET Yes! Ann has been kind; but then Ann knew.

TANNER (*With a desperate gesture*) Oh!!! Unfathomable deceit! Double crossed!

MISS RAMSDEN (*Stiffly*) And who, pray, is the gentleman who does not acknowledge his wife?

VIOLET (*Promptly*) That is my business, Miss Ramsden, and not yours. I have my reasons for keeping my marriage a secret for the present.

RAMSDEN All I can say is that we are extremely sorry, Violet. I am shocked to think of how we have treated you.

OCTAVIUS (*Awkwardly*) I beg your pardon, Violet. I can say no more.

MISS RAMSDEN (*Still loth to surrender*) Of course what you say puts a very different complexion on the matter. All the same, I owe it to myself—

VIOLET (*Cutting her short*) You owe me an apology, Miss Ramsden: that's what you owe both to yourself and to me. If you were a married woman you would not like sitting in the housekeeper's room and being treated like a naughty child by young girls and old ladies without any serious duties and responsibilities.

TANNER Don't hit us when we're down, Violet. We seem to have made fools of ourselves; but really it was you who made fools of us.

VIOLET It was no business of yours, Jack, in any case.

TANNER No business of mine! Why, Ramsden as good as accused me of being the unknown gentleman.

(RAMSDEN *makes a frantic demonstration; but* VIOLET'S *cool keen anger extinguishes it*)

VIOLET You! Oh, how infamous! how abominable! how disgracefully you have all been talking about me! If my husband knew it he would never let me speak to any of you again. (*To* RAMSDEN) I think you might have spared me that, at least.

RAMSDEN But I assure you I never—at least it is a monstrous perversion of something I said that—

MISS RAMSDEN You needn't apologize, Roebuck. She brought it all on herself. It is for her to apologize for having deceived us.

VIOLET I can make allowances for you, Miss Ramsden: you cannot understand how I feel on this subject, though I should have expected rather better taste from people of greater experience. However, I quite feel that you have placed yourselves in a very painful position; and the most truly considerate thing for me to do is to go at once. Good morning.

(*She goes, leaving them staring*)

MISS RAMSDEN Well, I must say!

RAMSDEN (*Plaintively*) I don't think she is quite fair to us.

TANNER You must cower before the wedding ring like the rest of us, Ramsden. The cup of our ignominy is full.

# Act Two

*On the carriage drive in the park of a country house near Richmond an open touring car has broken down. It stands in front of a clump of trees round which the drive sweeps to the house, which is partly visible through them: indeed* TANNER, *standing in the drive with his back to us, could get an unobstructed view of the west corner of the house on his left were he not far too much interested in a pair of supine legs in dungaree overalls which protrude from beneath the machine. He is watching them intently with bent back and hands supported on his knees. His leathern overcoat and peaked cap proclaim him one of the dismounted passengers.*

THE LEGS Aha! I got him.

TANNER All right now?

THE LEGS Aw rawt nah.

(TANNER *stoops and takes the legs by the ankles, drawing their owner forth like a wheelbarrow, walking on his hands, with a hammer in his mouth. He is a young man in a neat suit of blue serge, clean shaven, dark eyed, square fingered, with short well brushed black hair and rather irregular sceptically turned eyebrows. When he is manipulating the car his movements are swift and sudden, yet attentive and deliberate. With* TANNER *and* TANNER'S *friends his manner is not in the least deferential, but cool and reticent, keeping them quite effectually at a distance whilst giving them no excuse for complaining of him. Nevertheless he has a vigilant eye on them always, and that, too, rather cynically, like a man who knows the world well from its seamy side. He speaks slowly and with a touch of sarcasm; and as he does not at all affect the gentleman in his speech, it may be inferred that his smart appearance is a mark of respect to himself and his own class, not to that which employs him.*

*He now gets into the car to stow away his tools and divest himself of his overalls.* TANNER *takes off his leathern overcoat and pitches it into the car with a sigh of relief, glad to be rid of it.* THE CHAUFFEUR, *noting this, tosses his head contemptuously, and surveys his employer sardonically*)

THE CHAUFFEUR Had enough of it, eh?

TANNER I may as well walk to the house and stretch my legs and calm my nerves a little. (*Looking at his watch*) I suppose you know that we have come from Hyde Park Corner to Richmond in twenty-one minutes.

THE CHAUFFEUR I'd ha' done it under fifteen if I'd had a clear road all the way.

TANNER Why do you do it? Is it for love of sport or for the fun of terrifying your unfortunate employer?

THE CHAUFFEUR What are you afraid of?

TANNER The police, and breaking my neck.

THE CHAUFFEUR Well, if you like easy going, you can take a bus, you know. It's cheaper. You pay me to save your time and give you the value of what you paid for the car. (*He sits down calmly*)

TANNER I am the slave of that car and of you too. I dream of the accursed thing at night.

THE CHAUFFEUR You'll get over that all right. If you're going up to the house, may I ask how long you're goin' to stay? Because if you mean to put in the whole morning in there, talkin' to the ladies, I'll put the car in the garage and make myself agreeable with a view to lunching here. If not, I'll keep the car on the go about here till you come.

TANNER Better wait here. We shan't be long. There's a young American gentleman, a Mr Malone, who is driving Mr Robinson down in his new American steam car.

THE CHAUFFEUR (*Springing up and coming hastily out of the car to* TANNER) American steam car! Wot! racin' us dahn from London!

TANNER Perhaps they're here already.

THE CHAUFFEUR If I'd known it! (*With deep reproach*) Why didn't you tell me, Mr Tanner?

TANNER Because I've been told that this car is capable of 84 miles an hour; and I already know what you are capable of when there is a rival car on the road. No, Henry: there are things it is not good for you to know; and this was one of them. However, cheer up: we are going to have a day after your own heart. The American is to take Mr Robinson and his sister and Miss Whitefield. We are to take Miss Rhoda.

THE CHAUFFEUR (*Consoled, and musing on another matter*) That's Miss Whitefield's sister, isn't it?

TANNER Yes.

THE CHAUFFEUR And Miss Whitefield herself is goin' in the other car? Not with you?

TANNER Why the devil should she come with me? Mr Robinson will be in the other car. (THE CHAUFFEUR *looks at* TANNER *with cool incredulity, and turns to the car, whistling a popular air softly to himself.* TANNER, *a little annoyed, is about to pursue the subject when he hears the footsteps of* OCTAVIUS *on the gravel.* OCTAVIUS *is coming from the house, dressed for motoring, but without his overcoat*) We've lost the race, thank Heaven: here's Mr Robinson. Well, Tavy, is the steam car a success?

OCTAVIUS I think so. We came from Hyde Park Corner here in seventeen minutes. (THE CHAUFFEUR, *furious, kicks the car with a groan of vexation*) How long were you?

TANNER Oh, about three quarters of an hour or so.

THE CHAUFFEUR (*Remonstrating*) Now, now, Mr Tanner, come now! We could ha' done it easy under fifteen.

TANNER By the way, let me introduce you. Mr Octavius Robinson: Mr Enry Straker.

STRAKER Pleased to meet you, sir. Mr. Tanner is gittin' at you with 'is Enry Straker, you know. You call it Henery. But I don't mind, bless you!

TANNER You think it's simply bad taste in me to chaff him, Tavy. But you're wrong. This man takes more trouble to drop his aitches than ever his father did to pick them up. It's a mark of caste to him. I have never met anybody more swollen with the pride of class than Enry is.

STRAKER Easy, easy! A little moderation, Mr Tanner.

TANNER A little moderation, Tavy, you observe. You would tell me to draw it mild. But this chap has been educated. What's more, he knows that we haven't. What was the Board School[1] of yours, Straker?

STRAKER Sherbrooke Road.

TANNER Sherbrooke Road! Would any of us say Rugby! Harrow! Eton! in that tone of intellectual snobbery? Sherbrooke Road is a place where boys learn something: Eton is a boy farm where we are

[1] Board schools, supervised by local school boards, are equivalent to American public schools.

sent because we are nuisances at home, and because in after life, whenever a Duke is mentioned, we can claim him as an old school-fellow.

STRAKER You don't know nothing about it, Mr Tanner. It's not the Board School that does it: it's the Polytechnic.

TANNER His university, Octavius. Not Oxford, Cambridge, Durham, Dublin, or Glasgow. Not even those Nonconformist holes in Wales. No, Tavy. Regent Street! Chelsea! the Borough!—I don't know half their confounded names: these are his universities, not mere shops for selling class limitations like ours. You despise Oxford, Enry, don't you?

STRAKER No, I don't. Very nice sort of place, Oxford, I should think, for people that like that sort of place. They teach you to be a gentleman there. In the Polytechnic they teach you to be an engineer or such like. See?

TANNER Sarcasm, Tavy, sarcasm! Oh, if you could only see into Enry's soul, the depth of his contempt for a gentleman, the arrogance of his pride in being an engineer, would appal you. He positively likes the car to break down because it brings out my gentlemanly helplessness and his workmanlike skill and resource.

STRAKER Never you mind him, Mr Robinson. He likes to talk. We know him, don't we?

OCTAVIUS (*Earnestly*) But there's a great truth at the bottom of what he says. I believe most intensely in the dignity of labor.

STRAKER (*Unimpressed*) That's because you never done any, Mr Robinson. My business is to do away with labor. You'll get more out of me and a machine than you will out of twenty laborers, and not so much to drink either.

TANNER For Heaven's sake, Tavy, don't start him on political economy. He knows all about it; and we don't. You're only a poetic Socialist, Tavy: he's a scientific one.

STRAKER (*Unperturbed*) Yes. Well, this conversation is very improvin'; but I've got to look after the car; and you two want to talk about your ladies. *I* know. (*He pretends to busy himself about the car, but presently saunters off to indulge in a cigaret*)

TANNER That's a very momentous social phenomenon.

OCTAVIUS What is?

TANNER Straker is. Here have we literary and cultured persons been for years setting up a cry of the New Woman whenever some unusually old fashioned female came along and never noticing the advent of the New Man. Straker's the New Man.

OCTAVIUS I see nothing new about him, except your way of chaffing him. But I don't want to talk about him just now. I want to speak to you about Ann.

TANNER Straker knew even that. He learnt it at the Polytechnic, probably. Well, what about Ann? Have you proposed to her?

OCTAVIUS (*Self-reproachfully*) I was brute enough to do so last night.

TANNER Brute enough! What do you mean?

OCTAVIUS (*Dithyrambically*) Jack: we men are all coarse: we never understand how exquisite a woman's sensibilities are. How could I have done such a thing!

TANNER Done what, you maudlin idiot?

OCTAVIUS Yes, I am an idiot. Jack: if you had heard her voice! If you had seen her tears! I have lain awake all night thinking of them. If she had reproached me, I could have borne it better.

TANNER Tears! that's dangerous. What did she say?

OCTAVIUS She asked me how she could think of anything now but her dear father. She stifled a sob— (*He breaks down*)

TANNER (*Patting him on the back*) Bear it like a man, Tavy, even if you feel it like an ass. It's the old game: she's not tired of playing with you yet.

OCTAVIUS (*Impatiently*) Oh, don't be a fool, Jack. Do you suppose this eternal shallow cynicism of yours has any real bearing on a nature like hers?

TANNER Hm! Did she say anything else?

OCTAVIUS Yes; and that is why I expose myself and her to your ridicule by telling you what passed.

TANNER (*Remorsefully*) No, dear Tavy, not ridicule, on my honor! However, no matter. Go on.

OCTAVIUS Her sense of duty is so devout, so perfect, so—

TANNER Yes: I know. Go on.

OCTAVIUS You see, under this new arrangement, you and Ramsden are her guardians; and she considers that all her duty to her father is now transferred to you. She said she thought I ought to have spoken to you both in the first instance. Of course she is right; but somehow it seems rather absurd that I am to come to you and formally ask to be received as a suitor for your ward's hand.

TANNER I am glad that love has not totally extinguished your sense of humor, Tavy.

OCTAVIUS That answer won't satisfy her.

TANNER My official answer is, obviously, Bless you, my children: may you be happy!

OCTAVIUS I wish you would stop playing the fool about this. If it is not serious to you, it is to me, and to her.

TANNER You know very well that she is as free to choose as you are.

OCTAVIUS She does not think so.

TANNER Oh, doesn't she! just! However, say what you want me to do?

OCTAVIUS I want you to tell her sincerely and earnestly what you think about me. I want you to tell her that you can trust her to me—that is, if you feel you can.

TANNER I have no doubt that I can trust her to you. What worries me is the idea of trusting you to her. Have you read Maeterlinck's book about the bee?[2]

OCTAVIUS (*Keeping his temper with difficulty*) I am not discussing literature at present.

TANNER Be just a little patient with me. *I* am not discussing literature: the book about the bee is natural history. It's an awful lesson to mankind. You think that you are Ann's suitor; that you are the

[2] Maeterlinck's *The Life of Bees,* first published in 1901, was a current bestseller when Shaw wrote this play.

pursuer and she the pursued; that it is your part to woo, to persuade, to prevail, to overcome. Fool: it is you who are the pursued, the marked down quarry, the destined prey. You need not sit looking longingly at the bait through the wires of the trap: the door is open, and will remain so until it shuts behind you for ever.

OCTAVIUS I wish I could believe that, vilely as you put it.

TANNER Why, man, what other work has she in life but to get a husband? It is a woman's business to get married as soon as possible, and a man's to keep unmarried as long as he can. You have your poems and your tragedies to work at: Ann has nothing.

OCTAVIUS I cannot write without inspiration. And nobody can give me that except Ann.

TANNER Well, hadn't you better get it from her at a safe distance? Petrarch didn't see half as much of Laura, nor Dante of Beatrice, as you see of Ann now; and yet they wrote first-rate poetry—at least so I'm told. They never exposed their idolatry to the test of domestic familiarity; and it lasted them to their graves. Marry Ann; and at the end of a week you'll find no more inspiration in her than in a plate of muffins.

OCTAVIUS You think I shall tire of her!

TANNER Not at all: you don't get tired of muffins. But you don't find inspiration in them; and you won't in her when she ceases to be a poet's dream and becomes a solid eleven stone wife. You'll be forced to dream about somebody else; and then there will be a row.

OCTAVIUS This sort of talk is no use, Jack. You don't understand. You have never been in love.

TANNER I! I have never been out of it. Why, I am in love even with Ann. But I am neither the slave of love nor its dupe. Go to the bee, thou poet: consider her ways and be wise. By Heaven, Tavy, if women could do without our work, and we ate their children's bread instead of making it, they would kill us as the spider kills her mate or as the bees kill the drone. And they would be right if we were good for nothing but love.

OCTAVIUS Ah, if we were only good enough for Love! There is nothing like Love: there is nothing else but Love: without it the world would be a dream of sordid horror.

TANNER And this—this is the man who asks me to give him the hand of my ward! Tavy: I believe we were changed in our cradles, and that you are the real descendant of Don Juan.

OCTAVIUS I beg you not to say anything like that to Ann.

TANNER Don't be afraid. She has marked you for her own; and nothing will stop her now. You are doomed. (STRAKER *comes back with a newspaper*) Here comes the New Man, demoralizing himself with a halfpenny paper as usual.

STRAKER Now would you believe it, Mr Robinson, when we're out motoring we take in two papers: the Times for him, the Leader or the Echo for me. And do you think I ever see my paper? Not much. He grabs the Leader and leaves me to stodge myself with his Times.

OCTAVIUS Are there no winners in the Times?

TANNER Enry don't 'old with bettin', Tavy. Motor records are his weakness. What's the latest?

STRAKER Paris to Biskra at forty mile an hour average, not countin' the Mediterranean.

TANNER How many killed?

STRAKER Two silly sheep. What does it matter? Sheep don't cost such a lot: they were glad to 'ave the price without the trouble o' sellin' 'em to the butcher. All the same, d'y'see, there'll be a clamor agin it presently; and then the French Government'll stop it; an' our chance'll be gone, see? That's what makes me fairly mad: Mr Tanner won't do a good run while he can.

TANNER Tavy: do you remember my uncle James?

OCTAVIUS Yes. Why?

TANNER Uncle James had a first rate cook: he couldn't digest anything except what she cooked. Well, the poor man was shy and hated society. But his cook was proud of her skill, and wanted to serve up dinners to princes and ambassadors. To prevent her from leaving him, that poor old man had to give a big dinner twice a month, and suffer agonies of awkwardness. Now here am I; and here is this chap Enry Straker, the New Man. I loathe traveling; but I rather like Enry. He cares for nothing but tearing along in a leather coat and goggles, with two inches of dust all over him, at sixty miles an hour and the risk of his life and mine. Except, of course, when he is lying on his back in the mud under the machine trying to find out where it has given way. Well, if I don't give him a thousand mile run at least once a fortnight I shall lose him. He will give me the sack and go to some American millionaire; and I shall have to put up with a nice respectful groom-gardener-amateur, who will touch his hat and know his place. I am Enry's slave, just as Uncle James was his cook's slave.

STRAKER (*Exasperated*) Garn! I wish I had a car that would go as fast as you can talk, Mr Tanner. What I say is that you lose money by a motor car unless you keep it workin'. Might as well 'ave a pram and a nussmaid to wheel you in it as that car and me if you don't git the last inch out of us both.

TANNER (*Soothingly*) All right, Henry, all right. We'll go out for half an hour presently.

STRAKER (*In disgust*) Arf an ahr! (*He returns to his machine; seats himself in it; and turns up a fresh page of his paper in search of more news*)

OCTAVIUS Oh, that reminds me. I have a note for you from Rhoda. (*He gives* TANNER *a note*)

TANNER (*Opening it*) I rather think Rhoda is heading for a row with Ann. As a rule there is only one person an English girl hates more than she hates her eldest sister; and that's her mother. But Rhoda positively prefers her mother to Ann. She—(*Indignantly*) Oh, I say!

OCTAVIUS What's the matter?

TANNER Rhoda was to have come with me for a ride

in the motor car She says Ann has forbidden her to go out with me.

(STRAKER *suddenly begins whistling his favorite air with remarkable deliberation. Surprised by this burst of larklike melody, and jarred by a sardonic note in its cheerfulness, they turn and look inquiringly at him. But he is busy with his paper; and nothing comes of their movement*)

OCTAVIUS (*Recovering himself*) Does she give any reason?

TANNER Reason! An insult is not a reason. Ann forbids her to be alone with me on any occasion. Says I am not a fit person for a young girl to be with. What do you think of your paragon now?

OCTAVIUS You must remember that she has a very heavy responsibility now that her father is dead. Mrs Whitefield is too weak to control Rhoda.

TANNER (*Staring at him*) In short, you agree with Ann.

OCTAVIUS No; but I think I understand her. You must admit that your views are hardly suited for the formation of a young girl's mind and character.

TANNER I admit nothing of the sort. I admit that the formation of a young lady's mind and character usually consists in telling her lies; but I object to the particular lie that I am in the habit of abusing the confidence of girls.

OCTAVIUS Ann doesn't say that, Jack.

TANNER What else does she mean?

STRAKER (*Catching sight of* ANN *coming from the house*) Miss Whitefield, gentlemen. (*He dismounts and strolls away down the avenue with the air of a man who knows he is no longer wanted*)

ANN (*Coming between* OCTAVIUS *and* TANNER) Good morning, Jack. I have come to tell you that poor Rhoda has got one of her headaches and cannot go out with you today in the car. It is a cruel disappointment to her, poor child!

TANNER What do you say now, Tavy?

OCTAVIUS Surely you cannot misunderstand, Jack. Ann is shewing you the kindest consideration, even at the cost of deceiving you.

ANN What do you mean?

TANNER Would you like to cure Rhoda's headache, Ann?

ANN Of course.

TANNER Then tell her what you said just now; and add that you arrived about two minutes after I had received her letter and read it.

ANN Rhoda has written to you!

TANNER With full particulars.

OCTAVIUS Never mind him, Ann. You were right—quite right. Ann was only doing her duty, Jack; and you know it. Doing it in the kindest way, too.

ANN (*Going to* OCTAVIUS) How kind you are, Tavy! How helpful! How well you understand!

(OCTAVIUS *beams*)

TANNER Ay: tighten the coils. You love her, Tavy, don't you?

OCTAVIUS She knows I do.

ANN Hush. For shame, Tavy!

TANNER Oh, I give you leave. I am your guardian; and I commit you to Tavy's care for the next hour. I am off for a turn in the car.

ANN No, Jack. I must speak to you about Rhoda. Ricky: will you go back to the house and entertain your American friend. He's rather on Mamma's hands so early in the morning. She wants to finish her housekeeping.

OCTAVIUS I fly, dearest Ann (*He kisses her hand*)

ANN (*Tenderly*) Ricky Ticky Tavy!

(*He looks at her with an eloquent blush, and runs off*)

TANNER (*Bluntly*) Now look here, Ann. This time you've landed yourself; and if Tavy were not in love with you past all salvation he'd have found out what an incorrigible liar you are.

ANN You misunderstand, Jack. I didn't dare tell Tavy the truth.

TANNER No: your daring is generally in the opposite direction. What the devil do you mean by telling Rhoda that I am too vicious to associate with her? How can I ever have any human or decent relations with her again, now that you have poisoned her mind in that abominable way?

ANN I know you are incapable of behaving badly—

TANNER Then why did you lie to her?

ANN I had to.

TANNER Had to!

ANN Mother made me.

TANNER (*His eye flashing*) Ha! I might have known it. The mother! Always the mother!

ANN It was that dreadful book of yours. You know how timid mother is. All timid women are conventional: we must be conventional, Jack, or we are so cruelly, so vilely misunderstood. Even you, who are a man, cannot say what you think without being misunderstood and vilified—yes: I admit it: I have had to vilify you. Do you want to have poor Rhoda misunderstood and vilified in the same way? Would it be right for mother to let her expose herself to such treatment before she is old enough to judge for herself?

TANNER In short, the way to avoid misunderstanding is for everybody to lie and slander and insinuate and pretend as hard as they can. That is what obeying your mother comes to.

ANN I love my mother, Jack.

TANNER (*Working himself up into a sociological rage*) Is that any reason why you are not to call your soul your own? Oh, I protest against this vile abjection of youth to age! Look at fashionable society as you know it. What does it pretend to be? An exquisite dance of nymphs. What is it? A horrible procession of wretched girls, each in the claws of a cynical, cunning, avaricious, disillusioned, ignorantly experienced, foulminded old woman whom she calls mother, and whose duty it is to corrupt her mind and sell her to the highest bidder. Why do these unhappy slaves marry anybody, however old and vile, sooner than not marry at all? Because marriage is their only means of escape from these decrepit fiends who hide their selfish ambitions, their jealous hatreds of the young rivals who have supplanted them, under the mask of maternal duty and family affection. Such things are abominable: the voice of nature proclaims for the daughter a father's care and for the son a mother's. The law for father and son and mother and daughter is not the law of love: it is the law of revolution, of emancipation, of final supersession of the old and worn-out by the young and capable. I tell you, the first duty of manhood and womanhood is a Declaration of Independence: the man who pleads his father's authority is no man: the woman who pleads her mother's authority is unfit to bear citizens to a free people.

ANN (*Watching him with quiet curiosity*) I suppose you will go in seriously for politics some day, Jack.

TANNER (*Heavily let down*) Eh? What? Wh—? (*Collecting his scattered wits*) What has that got to do with what I have been saying?

ANN You talk so well.

TANNER Talk! Talk! It means nothing to you but talk. Well, go back to your mother, and help her to poison Rhoda's imagination as she has poisoned yours. It is the tame elephants who enjoy capturing the wild ones.

ANN I am getting on. Yesterday I was a boa constrictor: today I am an elephant.

TANNER Yes. So pack your trunk and begone: I have no more to say to you.

ANN You are so utterly unreasonable and impracticable. What can I do?

TANNER Do! Break your chains. Go your way according to your own conscience and not according to your mother's. Get your mind clean and vigorous; and learn to enjoy a fast ride in a motor car instead of seeing nothing in it but an excuse for a detestable intrigue. Come with me to Marseilles and across to Algiers and to Biskra, at sixty miles an hour. Come right down to the Cape if you like. That will be a Declaration of Independence with a vengeance. You can write a book about it afterwards. That will finish your mother and make a woman of you.

ANN (*Thoughtfully*) I don't think there would be any harm in that, Jack. You are my guardian: you stand in my father's place, by his own wish. Nobody could say a word against our traveling together. It would be delightful: thank you a thousand times, Jack. I'll come.

TANNER (*Aghast*) You'll come!!!

ANN Of course.

TANNER But—(*He stops, utterly appalled; then resumes feebly*) No: look here, Ann: if there's no harm in it there's no point in doing it.

ANN How absurd you are! You don't want to compromise me, do you?

TANNER Yes: that's the whole sense of my proposal.

ANN You are talking the greatest nonsense; and you know it. You would never do anything to hurt me.

TANNER Well, if you don't want to be compromised, don't come.

ANN (*With simple earnestness*) Yes, I will come, Jack, since you wish it. You are my guardian; and I think we ought to see more of one another and come to know one another better. (*Gratefully*) It's very thoughtful and very kind of you, Jack, to offer me this lovely holiday, especially after what I said about Rhoda. You really are good—much better than you think. When do we start?

TANNER But—

(*The conversation is interrupted by the arrival of* MRS WHITEFIELD *from the house. She is accompanied by the American gentleman, and followed by* RAMSDEN *and* OCTAVIUS.

HECTOR MALONE *is an Eastern American; but he is not at all ashamed of his nationality. This makes English people of fashion think well of him, as of a young fellow who is manly enough to confess to an obvious disadvantage without any attempt to conceal or extenuate it. They feel that he ought not to be made to suffer for what is clearly not his fault, and make a point of being specially kind to him. His chivalrous manners to women, and his elevated moral sentiments, being both gratuitous and unusual, strike them as perhaps a little unfortunate; and though they find his vein of easy humor rather amusing when it has ceased to puzzle them (as it does at first), they have had to make him understand that he really must not tell anecdotes unless they are strictly personal and scandalous, and also that oratory is an accomplishment which belongs to a cruder stage of civilization than that in which his migration has landed him. On these points* HECTOR *is not quite convinced: he still thinks that the British are apt to make merits of their stupidities, and to represent their various incapacities as points of good breeding. English life seems to him to suffer from a lack of edifying rhetoric (which he calls moral tone); English behavior to shew a want of respect for womanhood; English pronunciation to fail very vulgarly in tackling such words as world, girl, bird, etc.; English society to be plain spoken to an extent which stretches occasionally to intolerable coarseness; and English intercourse to need enlivening by games and stories and other pastimes; so he does not feel called upon to acquire these defects after taking great pains to cultivate himself in a first rate manner before venturing across the Atlantic. To this culture he finds English people either totally indifferent, as they very commonly are to all culture, or else politely evasive, the truth being that* HECTOR'S *culture is nothing but a state of saturation with our literary exports of thirty years ago, reimported by him to be unpacked at a moment's notice and hurled at the head of English literature, science, and art, at every conversational opportunity. The dismay set up by these sallies encourages him in his belief that he is helping to educate England. When he finds people chattering harmlessly about Anatole France and Nietzsche, he devastates them with Matthew Arnold, the Autocrat of the Breakfast Table, and even Macaulay; and as he is devoutly religious at bottom, he first leads the unwary, by humorous irreverence, to leave popular theology out of account in discussing moral questions with him, and then scatters them in confusion by demanding whether the carrying out of his ideals of conduct was not the manifest object of God Almighty in creating honest men and pure women. The engaging freshness of his personality and the dumbfoundering staleness of his culture make it extremely difficult to decide whether he is worth knowing; for whilst his company is undeniably pleasant and enlivening, there is intellectually nothing new to be got out of him, especially as he despises politics, and is careful not to talk commercial shop, in which department he is probably much in advance of his English capitalist friends. He gets on best with romantic Christians of the amoristic sect: hence the friendship which has sprung up between him and* OCTAVIUS.

*In appearance* HECTOR *is a neatly built young man of twenty-four, with a short, smartly trimmed black beard, clear, well shaped eyes, and an ingratiating vivacity of expression. He is, from the fashionable point of view, faultlessly dressed. As he comes along the drive from the house with* MRS WHITEFIELD *he is sedulously making himself agreeable and entertaining, and thereby placing on her slender wit a burden it is unable to bear. An Englishman would let her alone, accepting boredom and indifference as their common lot; and the poor lady wants to be either let alone or let prattle about the things that interest her.*

RAMSDEN *strolls over to inspect the motor car.* OCTAVIUS *joins* HECTOR)

ANN (*Pouncing on her mother joyously*) Oh, mamma, what do you think! Jack is going to take me to Nice in his motor car. Isn't it lovely? I am the happiest person in London.

TANNER (*Desperately*) Mrs Whitefield objects. I am sure she objects. Doesn't she, Ramsden?

RAMSDEN I should think it very likely indeed.

ANN You don't object, do you, mother?

MRS WHITEFIELD *I* object! Why should I? I think it will do you good, Ann. (*Trotting over to* TANNER) I meant to ask you to take Rhoda out for a run occasionally: she is too much in the house; but it will do when you come back.

TANNER Abyss beneath abyss of perfidy!

ANN (*Hastily, to distract attention from this outburst*) Oh, I forgot: you have not met Mr Malone. Mr Tanner, my guardian: Mr Hector Malone.

HECTOR Pleased to meet you, Mr Tanner. I should like to suggest an extension of the traveling party to Nice, if I may.

ANN Oh, we're all coming. That's understood, isn't it?

HECTOR I also am the mawdest professor of a motor car. If Miss Rawbnsn will allow me the privilege of taking her, my car is at her service.

OCTAVIUS Violet!

(*General constraint*)

ANN (*Subduedly*) Come, mother: we must leave them to talk over the arrangements. I must see to my traveling kit.

(MRS WHITEFIELD *looks bewildered; but* ANN *draws her discreetly away; and they disappear round the corner towards the house*)

HECTOR I think I may go so far as to say that I can depend on Miss Rawbnsn's consent.

(*Continued embarrassment*)

OCTAVIUS I'm afraid we must leave Violet behind. There are circumstances which make it impossible for her to come on such an expedition.

HECTOR (*Amused and not at all convinced*) Too American, eh? Must the young lady have a chaperone?

OCTAVIUS It's not that, Malone—at least not altogether.

HECTOR Indeed! May I ask what other objection applies?

TANNER (*Impatiently*) Oh, tell him, tell him. We shall never be able to keep the secret unless everybody knows what it is. Mr Malone: if you go to Nice with Violet, you go with another man's wife. She is married.

HECTOR (*Thunderstruck*) You don't tell me so!

TANNER We do. In confidence.

RAMSDEN (*With an air of importance, lest* MALONE *should suspect a misalliance*) Her marriage has not yet been made known: she desires that it shall not be mentioned for the present.

HECTOR I shall respect the lady's wishes. Would it be indiscreet to ask who her husband is, in case I should have an opportunity of cawnsulting him about this trip?

TANNER We don't know who he is.

HECTOR (*Retiring into his shell in a very marked manner*) In that case, I have no more to say.

(*They become more embarrassed than ever*)

OCTAVIUS You must think this very strange.

HECTOR A little singular. Pardn mee for saying so.

RAMSDEN (*Half apologetic, half huffy*) The young lady was married secretly; and her husband has forbidden her, it seems, to declare his name. It is only right to tell you, since you are interested in Miss—er—in Violet.

OCTAVIUS (*Sympathetically*) I hope this is not a disappointment to you.

HECTOR (*Softened, coming out of his shell again*) Well: it is a blow. I can hardly understand how a man can leave his wife in such a position. Surely it's not customary. It's not manly. It's not considerate.

OCTAVIUS We feel that, as you may imagine, pretty deeply.

RAMSDEN (*Testily*) It is some young fool who has not enough experience to know what mystifications of this kind lead to.

HECTOR (*With strong symptoms of moral repugnance*) I hope so. A man need be very young and pretty foolish too to be excused for such conduct. You take a very lenient view, Mr Ramsden. Too lenient to my mind. Surely marriage should ennoble a man.

TANNER (*Sardonically*) Ha!

HECTOR Am I to gather from that cachinnation that you don't agree with me, Mr Tanner?

TANNER (*Drily*) Get married and try. You may find it delightful for a while: you certainly won't find it ennobling. The greatest common measure of a man and a woman is not necessarily greater than the man's single measure.

HECTOR Well, we think in America that a woman's morl number is higher than a man's, and that the purer nature of a woman lifts a man right out of himself, and makes him better than he was.

OCTAVIUS (*With conviction*) So it does.

TANNER No wonder American women prefer to live in Europe! It's more comfortable than standing all their lives on an altar to be worshipped. Anyhow, Violet's husband has not been ennobled. So what's to be done?

HECTOR (*Shaking his head*) I can't dismiss that man's cawnduct as lightly as you do, Mr Tanner. However, I'll say no more. Whoever he is, he's Miss Rawbnsn's husband; and I should be glad for her sake to think better of him.

OCTAVIUS (*Touched; for he divines a secret sorrow*) I'm very sorry, Malone. Very sorry.

HECTOR (*Gratefully*) You're a good fellow, Rawbnsn. Thank you.

TANNER Talk about something else. Violet's coming from the house.

HECTOR I should esteem it a very great favor, gentlemen, if you would take the opportunity to let me have a few words with the lady alone. I shall have to cry off this trip; and it's rather a dullicate—

RAMSDEN (*Glad to escape*) Say no more. Come, Tanner. Come, Tavy. (*He strolls away into the park with* OCTAVIUS *and* TANNER, *past the motor car*)

(VIOLET *comes down the avenue to* HECTOR)

VIOLET Are they looking?

HECTOR No.

(*She kisses him*)

VIOLET Have you been telling lies for my sake?

HECTOR Lying! Lying hardly describes it. I overdo it. I get carried away in an ecstasy of mendacity. Violet: I wish you'd let me own up.

VIOLET (*Instantly becoming serious and resolute*) No, no, Hector: you promised me not to.

HECTOR I'll keep my prawmis until you release me from it. But I feel mean, lying to those men, and denying my wife. Just dastardly.

VIOLET I wish your father were not so unreasonable.

HECTOR He's not unreasonable. He's right from his point of view. He has a prejudice against the English middle class.

VIOLET It's too ridiculous. You know how I dislike saying such things to you, Hector, but if I were to —oh, well, no matter.

HECTOR I know. If you were to marry the son of an English manufacturer of awffice furniture, your friends would consider it a misalliance. And here's my silly old dad, who is the biggest awffice furniture man in the world, would shew me the door for marrying the most perfect lady in England merely because she has no handle to her name. Of course it's just absurd. But I tell you, Violet, I don't like deceiving him. I feel as if I was stealing his money. Why won't you let me own up?

VIOLET We can't afford it. You can be as romantic as you please about love, Hector; but you mustn't be romantic about money.

HECTOR (*Divided between his uxoriousness and his habitual elevation of moral sentiment*) That's very English. (*Appealing to her impulsively*) Violet: dad's bound to find us out someday.

VIOLET Oh yes, later on of course. But don't let's go over this every time we meet, dear. You promised—

HECTOR All right, all right, I—

VIOLET (*Not to be silenced*) It is I and not you who suffer by this concealment; and as to facing a struggle and poverty and all that sort of thing I simply will not do it. It's too silly.

HECTOR You shall not. I'll sort of borrow the money from my dad until I get on my own feet; and then I can own up and pay up at the same time.

VIOLET (*Alarmed and indignant*) Do you mean to work? Do you want to spoil our marriage?

HECTOR Well, I don't mean to let marriage spoil my character. Your friend Mr Tanner has got the laugh on me a bit already about that; and—

VIOLET The beast! I hate Jack Tanner.

HECTOR (*Magnanimously*) Oh hee's all right: he only needs the love of a good woman to ennoble him. Besides, he's proposed a motoring trip to Nice; and I'm going to take you.

VIOLET How jolly!

HECTOR Yes; but how are we going to manage? You see, they've warned me off going with you, so to speak. They've told me in cawnfidnce that you're married. That's just the most overwhelming cawnfidence I've ever been honored with.

(TANNER *returns with* STRAKER, *who goes to his car*)

TANNER Your car is a great success, Mr Malone. Your engineer is showing it off to Mr Ramsden.

HECTOR (*Eagerly—forgetting himself*) Let's come, Vi.

VIOLET (*Coldly, warning him with her eyes*) I beg your pardon, Mr Malone: I did not quite catch—

HECTOR (*Recollecting himself*) I ask to be allowed the pleasure of shewing you my little American steam car, Miss Rawbnsn.

VIOLET I shall be very pleased. (*They go off together down the avenue*)

TANNER About this trip, Straker.

STRAKER (*Preoccupied with the car*) Yes?

TANNER Miss Whitefield is supposed to be coming with me.

STRAKER So I gather.

TANNER Mr Robinson is to be one of the party.

STRAKER Yes.

TANNER Well, if you can manage so as to be a good deal occupied with me, and leave Mr Robinson a good deal occupied with Miss Whitefield, he will be deeply grateful to you.

STRAKER (*Looking round at him*) Evidently.

TANNER "Evidently!" Your grandfather would have simply winked.

STRAKER My grandfather would have touched his 'at.

TANNER And I should have given your good nice respectful grandfather a sovereign.

STRAKER Five shillin's, more likely. (*He leaves the car and approaches* TANNER) What about the lady's views?

TANNER She is just as willing to be left to Mr Robinson as Mr Robinson is to be left to her. (STRAKER *looks at his principal with cool skepticism; then turns to the car whistling his favorite air*) Stop that aggravating noise. What do you mean by it? (STRAKER *calmly resumes the melody and finishes it.* TANNER *politely hears it out before he again addresses* STRAKER, *this time with elaborate seriousness*) Enry: I have ever been a warm advocate of the spread of music among the masses; but I object to your obliging the company whenever Miss Whitefield's name is mentioned. You did it this morning, too.

STRAKER (*Obstinately*) It's not a bit o' use. Mr Robinson may as well give it up first as last.

TANNER Why?

STRAKER Garn! You know why. Course it's not my business; but you needn't start kiddin' me about it.

TANNER I am not kidding. I don't know why.

STRAKER (*Cheerfully sulky*) Oh, very well. All right. It ain't my business.

TANNER (*Impressively*) I trust, Enry, that, as between employer and engineer, I shall always know how to keep my proper distance, and not intrude my private affairs on you. Even our business arrangements are subject to the approval of your Trade Union. But don't abuse your advantages. Let me remind you that Voltaire said that what was too silly to be said could be sung.

STRAKER It wasn't Voltaire: it was Bow Mar Shay.

TANNER I stand corrected: Beaumarchais of course. Now you seem to think that what is too delicate to be said can be whistled. Unfortunately your whistling, though melodious, is unintelligible. Come! there's nobody listening: neither my genteel relatives nor the secretary of your confounded Union. As man to man, Enry, why do you think that my friend has no chance with Miss Whitefield?

STRAKER Cause she's arter summun else.

TANNER Bosh! who else?

STRAKER You.

TANNER Me!!!

STRAKER Mean to tell me you don't know? Oh, come, Mr Tanner!

TANNER (*In fierce earnest*) Are you playing the fool, or do you mean it?

STRAKER (*With a flash of temper*) I'm not playin' no fool. (*More coolly*) Why, it's as plain as the nose on your face. If you ain't spotted that, you don't know much about these sort of things. (*Serene again*) Ex-cuse me, you know, Mr Tanner; but you asked me as man to man; and I told you as man to man.

TANNER (*Wildly appealing to the heavens*) Then I—*I* am the bee, the spider, the marked down victim, the destined prey.

STRAKER I dunno about the bee and the spider. But the marked down victim, that's what you are and no mistake; and a jolly good job for you, too, I should say.

TANNER (*Momentously*) Henry Straker: the golden moment of your life has arrived.

STRAKER What d'y mean?

TANNER That record to Biskra.

STRAKER (*Eagerly*) Yes?

TANNER Break it.

STRAKER (*Rising to the height of his destiny*) D'y' mean it?

TANNER I do.

STRAKER When?

TANNER Now. Is that machine ready to start?

STRAKER (*Quailing*) But you can't—

TANNER (*Cutting him short by getting into the car*) Off we go. First to the bank for money; then to my rooms for my kit; then to your rooms for your kit; then break the record from London to Dover or Folkestone; then across the channel and away like mad to Marseilles, Gibraltar, Genoa, any port from which we can sail to a Mahometan country where men are protected from women.

STRAKER Garn! you're kiddin'.

TANNER (*Resolutely*) Stay behind then. If you won't come I'll do it alone. (*He starts the motor*)

STRAKER (*Running after him*) Here! Mister! arf a mo! steady on! (*He scrambles in as the car plunges forward*)

# Act Three

*Evening in the Sierra Nevada. Rolling slopes of brown with olive trees instead of apple trees in the cultivated patches, and occasional prickly pears instead of gorse and bracken in the wilds. Higher up, tall stone peaks and precipices, all handsome and distinguished. No wild nature here: rather a most aristocratic mountain landscape made by a fastidious artist-creator. No vulgar profusion of vegetation: even a touch of aridity in the frequent patches of stones: Spanish magnificence and Spanish economy everywhere.*

*Not very far north of a spot at which the high road over one of the passes crosses a tunnel on the railway from Malaga to Granada, is one of the mountain amphitheatres of the Sierra. Looking at it from the wide end of the horse-shoe, one sees, a little to the right, in the face of the cliff, a romantic cave which is really an abandoned quarry, and towards the left a little hill, commanding a view of the road, which skirts the amphitheatre on the left, maintaining its higher level on embankments and an occasional stone arch. On the hill, watching the road, is a man who is either a Spaniard or a Scotchman. Probably a Spaniard, since he wears the dress of a Spanish goatherd and seems at home in the Sierra Nevada, but very like a Scotchman for all that. In the hollow, on the slope leading to the quarry-cave, are about a dozen men who, as they recline at their ease round a heap of smouldering white ashes of dead leaf and brushwood, have an air of being conscious of themselves as picturesque scoundrels honoring the Sierra by using it as an effective pictorial background. As a matter of artistic fact they are not picturesque; and the mountains tolerate them as lions tolerate lice. An English policeman or Poor Law Guardian would recognize them as a selected band of tramps and ablebodied paupers.*

*This description of them is not wholly contemptuous. Whoever has intelligently observed the tramp, or visited the ablebodied ward of a workhouse, will admit that our social failures are not all drunkards and weaklings. Some of them are men who do not fit the class they were born into. Precisely the same qualities that make the educated gentleman an artist may make an uneducated manual laborer an ablebodied pauper. There are men who fall helplessly into the workhouse because they are good for nothing; but there are also men who are there because they are strong-minded enough to disregard the social convention (obviously not a disinterested one on the part of the ratepayer) which bids a man live by heavy and badly paid drudgery when he has the alternative of walking into the workhouse, announcing himself as a destitute person, and legally compelling the Guardians to feed, clothe, and house him better than he could feed, clothe, and house himself without great exertion. When a man who is born a poet refuses a stool in a stockbroker's office, and starves in a garret, sponging on a poor landlady or on his friends and relatives sooner than work against his grain; or when a lady, because she is a lady, will face an extremity of parasitic dependence rather than take a situation as cook or parlormaid, we make large allowances for them. To such allowances the ablebodied pauper, and his nomadic variant, the tramp, are equally entitled.*

*Further, the imaginative man, if his life is to be tolerable to him, must have leisure to tell himself stories, and a position which lends itself to imaginative decoration. The ranks of unskilled labor offer no such positions. We misuse our laborers horribly; and when a man refuses to be misused, we have no right to say that he is refusing honest work. Let us be frank in this matter before we go on with our play; so that we may enjoy it without hypocrisy. If we were reasoning, far-sighted people, four fifths of us would go straight to the Guardians for relief, and knock the whole social system to pieces with most beneficial reconstructive results. The reason we do not do this is because we work like bees or ants, by instinct or habit, not reasoning about the matter at all. Therefore when a man comes along who can and does reason, and who, applying the Kantian test to his conduct, can truly say to us, If everybody did as I do, the world would be compelled to reform itself industrially, and abolish slavery and squalor, which exist only because everybody does as you do, let us honor that man and seriously consider the advisability of following his example. Such a man is the ablebodied, ableminded pauper. Were he a gentleman doing his best to get a pension or a sinecure instead of sweeping a crossing, nobody would blame him for deciding that so long as the alternative lies between living mainly at the expense of the community and allowing the community to live mainly at his, it would be folly to accept what is to him personally the greater of the two evils.*

*We may therefore contemplate the tramps of the Sierra without prejudice, admitting cheerfully that our objects—briefly, to be gentlemen of fortune—are much the same as theirs, and the difference in our position and methods merely accidental. One or two of them, perhaps, it would be wiser to kill without malice in a friendly and frank manner; for there are bipeds, just as there are quadrupeds, who are too dangerous to be left unchained and unmuzzled; and these cannot fairly expect to have other men's lives wasted in the work of watching them. But as society has not the courage to kill them, and, when it catches them, simply wreaks on them some superstitious expiatory rites of torture and degradation, and then lets them loose with heightened qualifications for mischief, it is just as well that they are at large in the Sierra, and in the hands of a* CHIEF *who looks as if he might possibly, on provocation, order them to be shot.*

*This* CHIEF*, seated in the centre of the group on a squared block of stone from the quarry, is a tall strong man, with a striking cockatoo nose, glossy black hair, pointed beard, upturned moustache, and a Mephistophelean affectation which is fairly imposing, perhaps because the scenery admits of a larger swagger than Piccadilly, perhaps because of a certain sentimentality in the man which gives him that touch of grace which alone can excuse deliberate picturesqueness. His eyes and mouth are by no means rascally; he has a fine voice and a ready wit; and whether he is really the strongest man in the party or not, he looks it. He is certainly the best fed, the best dressed, and the best trained. The fact that he speaks English is not unexpected, in spite of the Spanish landscape; for with the exception of one man who might be guessed as a bullfighter ruined by drink, and one unmistakable Frenchman, they are all cockney or American; therefore, in a land of cloaks and sombreros, they mostly wear seedy overcoats, woollen mufflers, hard hemispherical hats, and dirty brown gloves. Only a very few dress after their leader, whose* *broad sombrero with a cock's feather in the band, and voluminous cloak descending to his high boots, are as un-English as possible. None of them are armed; and the ungloved ones keep their hands in their pockets because it is their national belief that it must be dangerously cold in the open air with the night coming on. (It is as warm an evening as any reasonable man could desire.)*

*Except the bullfighting inebriate there is only one person in the company who looks more than, say, thirty-three. He is a small man with reddish whiskers, weak eyes, and the anxious look of a small tradesman in difficulties. He wears the only tall hat visible: it shines in the sunset with the sticky glow of some sixpenny patent hat reviver, often applied and constantly tending to produce a worse state of the original surface than the ruin it was applied to remedy. He has a collar and cuffs of celluloid: and his brown Chesterfield overcoat, with velvet collar, is still presentable. He is preeminently the respectable man of the party, and is certainly over forty, possibly over fifty. He is the corner man on the leader's right, opposite three men in scarlet ties on his left. One of these three is the Frenchman. Of the remaining two, who are both English, one is argumentative, solemn, and obstinate; the other rowdy and mischievous.*

*The* CHIEF, *with a magnificent fling of the end of his cloak across his left shoulder, rises to address them. The applause which greets him shews that he is a favorite orator.*

THE CHIEF Friends and fellow brigands. I have a proposal to make to this meeting. We have now spent three evenings in discussing the question Have Anarchists or Social-Democrats the most personal courage? We have gone into the principles of Anarchism and Social-Democracy at great length. The cause of Anarchy has been ably represented by our one Anarchist, who doesn't know what Anarchism means (*Laughter*)—

THE ANARCHIST (*Rising*) A point of order, Mendoza—

MENDOZA (*Forcibly*) No, by thunder: your last point of order took half an hour. Besides, Anarchists don't believe in order.

THE ANARCHIST (*Mild, polite but persistent: he is, in fact, the respectable looking elderly man in the celluloid collar and cuffs*) That is a vulgar error. I can prove—

MENDOZA Order, order.

THE OTHERS (*Shouting*) Order, order. Sit down. Chair! Shut up.

(THE ANARCHIST *is suppressed*)

MENDOZA On the other hand we have three Social-Democrats among us. They are not on speaking terms; and they have put before us three distinct and incompatible views of Social-Democracy.

THE THREE MEN IN SCARLET TIES 1. Mr Chairman, I protest. A personal explanation. 2. It's a lie. I never said so. Be fair, Mendoza. 3. *Je demande la parole. C'est absolument faux. C'est faux! faux! faux!!! Assas-s-s-s-sin!!!!!!* [1]

MENDOZA Order, order.

THE OTHERS Order, order, order Chair!

(*The Social-Democrats are suppressed*)

MENDOZA Now, we tolerate all opinions here. But after all, comrades, the vast majority of us are neither Anarchists nor Socialists, but gentlemen and Christians.

THE MAJORITY (*Shouting assent*) Hear, hear! So we are. Right.

THE ROWDY SOCIAL-DEMOCRAT (*Smarting under suppression*) You ain't no Christian. You're a Sheeny, you are.

MENDOZA (*With crushing magnanimity*) My friend: *I* am an exception to all rules. It is true that I have the honor to be a Jew; and when the Zionists need a leader to reassemble our race on its historic soil of Palestine, Mendoza will not be the last to volunteer. (*Sympathetic applause*—hear, hear, etc.) But I am not a slave to any superstition. I have swallowed all the formulas, even that of Socialism; though, in a sense, once a Socialist, always a Socialist.

THE SOCIAL-DEMOCRATS Hear, hear!

MENDOZA But I am well aware that the ordinary man—even the ordinary brigand, who can scarcely be called an ordinary man (Hear, hear!)—is not a philosopher. Common sense is good enough for him; and in our business affairs common sense is good enough for me. Well, what is our business here in the Sierra Nevada, chosen by the Moors as the fairest spot in Spain? Is it to discuss abstruse questions of political economy? No: it is to hold up motor cars and secure a more equitable distribution of wealth.

THE SULKY SOCIAL-DEMOCRAT All made by labor, mind you.

MENDOZA (*Urbanely*) Undoubtedly. All made by labor, and on its way to be squandered by wealthy vagabonds in the dens of vice that disfigure the sunny shores of the Mediterranean. We intercept that wealth. We restore it to circulation among the class that produced it and that chiefly needs it: the working class. We do this at the risk of our lives and liberties, by the exercise of the virtues of courage, endurance, foresight, and abstinence—especially abstinence. I myself have eaten nothing but prickly pears and broiled rabbit for three days.

THE SULKY SOCIAL-DEMOCRAT (*Stubbornly*) No more ain't we.

MENDOZA (*Indignantly*) Have I taken more than my share?

THE SULKY SOCIAL-DEMOCRAT (*Unmoved*) Why should you?

THE ANARCHIST Why should he not? To each according to his needs: from each according to his means.

THE FRENCHMAN (*Shaking his fist at* THE ANARCHIST) *Fumiste!* [2]

MENDOZA (*Diplomatically*) I agree with both of you.

[1] I demand the floor. It's completely wrong. It's false! false! false! you assassin!

[2] Humbug! drivel!

THE GENUINELY ENGLISH BRIGANDS Hear, hear! Bravo Mendoza!

MENDOZA What I say is, let us treat one another as gentlemen, and strive to excel in personal courage only when we take the field.

THE ROWDY SOCIAL-DEMOCRAT (*Derisively*) Shikespear.

(*A whistle comes from* THE GOATHERD *on the hill. He springs up and points excitedly forward along the road to the north*)

THE GOATHERD Automobile! Automobile! (*He rushes down the hill and joins the rest, who all scramble to their feet*)

MENDOZA (*In ringing tones*) To arms! Who has the gun?

THE SULKY SOCIAL-DEMOCRAT (*Handing a rifle to* MENDOZA) Here.

MENDOZA Have the nails been strewn in the road?

THE ROWDY SOCIAL-DEMOCRAT Two ahnces of 'em.

MENDOZA Good! (*To* THE FRENCHMAN) With me, Duval. If the nails fail, puncture their tires with a bullet. (*He gives the rifle to* DUVAL, *who follows him up the hill.* MENDOZA *produces an opera glass. The others hurry across to the road and disappear to the north*)

MENDOZA (*On the hill, using his glass*) Two only, a capitalist and his chauffeur. They look English.

DUVAL Angliche! Aoh yess. *Cochons!* (*Handling the rifle*) *Faut tirer, n'est-ce-pas?* [3]

MENDOZA No: the nails have gone home. Their tire is down: they stop.

DUVAL (*Shouting to the others*) *Fondez sur eux, nom de Dieu!* [4]

MENDOZA (*Rebuking his excitement*) *Du calme.*[5]

DUVAL Keep your hair on. They take it quietly. Let us descend and receive them.

(MENDOZA *descends, passing behind the fire and coming forward, whilst* TANNER *and* STRAKER, *in their motoring goggles, leather coats, and caps, are led in from the road by the brigands*)

TANNER Is this the gentleman you describe as your boss? Does he speak English?

THE ROWDY SOCIAL-DEMOCRAT Course 'e daz. Y' down't suppowz we Hinglishmen luts ahrselves be bossed by a bloomin' Spenniard, do you?

MENDOZA (*With dignity*) Allow me to introduce myself: Mendoza, President of the League of the Sierra! (*Posing loftily*) I am a brigand: I live by robbing the rich.

TANNER (*Promptly*) I am a gentleman: I live by robbing the poor. Shake hands.

THE ENGLISH SOCIAL-DEMOCRAT Hear, hear!

(*General laughter and good humor.* TANNER *and* MENDOZA *shake hands. The Brigands drop into their former places*)

STRAKER 'Ere! where do I come in?

TANNER (*Introducing*) My friend and chauffeur.

THE SULKY SOCIAL-DEMOCRAT (*Suspiciously*) Well, which is he? friend or show-foor? It makes all the difference, you know.

MENDOZA (*Explaining*) We should expect ransom for a friend. A professional chauffeur is free of the mountains. He even takes a trifling percentage of his principal's ransom if he will honor us by accepting it.

STRAKER I see. Just to encourage me to come this way again. Well, I'll think about it.

DUVAL (*Impulsively rushing across to* STRAKER) *Mon frère!* (*He embraces him rapturously and kisses him on both cheeks*)

STRAKER (*Disgusted*) 'Ere, git aht: don't be silly. Who are you, pray?

DUVAL Duval: Social-Democrat.

STRAKER Oh, you're a Social-Democrat, are you?

THE ANARCHIST He means that he has sold out to the parliamentary humbugs and the bourgeoisie. Compromise! that is his faith.

DUVAL (*Furiously*) I understand what he say. He say Bourgeois. He say Compromise. *Jamais de la vie! Misérable menteur*—[6]

STRAKER See here, Captain Mendoza, ah mach o' this sort o' thing do you put up with here? Are we avin' a pleasure trip in the mountains, or are we at a Socialist meetin'?

THE MAJORITY Here, hear! Shut up. Chuck it. Sit down, etc. etc. (THE SOCIAL-DEMOCRATS *and the* ANARCHIST *are hustled into the background.* STRAKER, *after superintending this proceeding with satisfaction, places himself on* MENDOZA'S *left,* TANNER *being on his right*)

MENDOZA Can we offer you anything? Broiled rabbit and prickly pears—

TANNER Thank you: we have dined.

MENDOZA (*To his followers*) Gentlemen: business is over for the day. Go as you please until morning.

(*The Brigands disperse into groups lazily. Some go into the cave. Others sit down or lie down to sleep in the open. A few produce a pack of cards and move off towards the road; for it is now starlight; and they know that motor cars have lamps which can be turned to account for lighting a card party*)

STRAKER (*Calling after him*) Don't none of you go fooling with that car, d'ye hear?

MENDOZA No fear, *Monsieur le Chauffeur*. The first one we captured cured us of that.

STRAKER (*Interested*) What did it do?

MENDOZA It carried three brave comrades of ours, who did not know how to stop it, into Granada, and capsized them opposite the police station. Since then we never touch one without sending for the chauffeur. Shall we chat at our ease?

TANNER By all means.

(TANNER, MENDOZA, *and* STRAKER *sit down on the turf by the fire.* MENDOZA *delicately waives his presidential dignity, of which the right to sit on the squared stone block is the appanage, by sitting on the ground like his guests, and using the stone only as a support for his back*)

MENDOZA It is the custom in Spain always to put off

[3] English! 'Aoh yess.' Pigs! We shoot, don't we?

[4] Rush on them, for God's sake!

[5] Keep calm.

[6] Never in my life! Wretched liar!

business until tomorrow. In fact, you have arrived out of office hours. However, if you would prefer to settle the question of ransom at once, I am at your service.

TANNER Tomorrow will do for me. I am rich enough to pay anything in reason.

MENDOZA (*Respectfully, much struck by this admission*) You are a remarkable man, sir. Our guests usually describe themselves as miserably poor.

TANNER Pooh! Miserably poor people don't own motor cars.

MENDOZA Precisely what we say to them.

TANNER Treat us well: we shall not prove ungrateful.

STRAKER No prickly pears and broiled rabbits, you know. Don't tell me you can't do us a bit better than that if you like.

MENDOZA Wine, kids, milk, cheese, and bread can be procured for ready money.

STRAKER (*Graciously*) Now you're talkin'.

TANNER Are you all Socialists here, may I ask?

MENDOZA (*Repudiating this humiliating misconception*) Oh, no, no, no: nothing of the kind, I assure you. We naturally have modern views as to the injustice of the existing distribution of wealth: otherwise we should lose our self-respect. But nothing that you could take exception to, except two or three faddists.

TANNER I had no intention of suggesting anything discreditable. In fact, I am a bit of a Socialist myself.

STRAKER (*Drily*) Most rich men are, I notice.

MENDOZA Quite so. It has reached us, I admit. It is in the air of the century.

STRAKER Socialism must be lookin' up a bit if your chaps are taking to it.

MENDOZA That is true, sir. A movement which is confined to philosophers and honest men can never exercise any real political influence: there are too few of them. Until a movement shews itself capable of spreading among brigands, it can never hope for a political majority.

TANNER But are your brigands any less honest than ordinary citizens?

MENDOZA Sir: I will be frank with you. Brigandage is abnormal. Abnormal professions attract two classes: those who are not good enough for ordinary bourgeois life and those who are too good for it. We are dregs and scum, sir: the dregs very filthy, the scum very superior.

STRAKER Take care! some o' the dregs'll hear you.

MENDOZA It does not matter: each brigand thinks himself scum, and likes to hear the others called dregs.

TANNER Come! you are a wit. (MENDOZA *inclines his head, flattered*) May one ask you a blunt question?

MENDOZA As blunt as you please.

TANNER How does it pay a man of your talent to shepherd such a flock as this on broiled rabbit and prickly pears? I have seen men less gifted, and I'll swear less honest, supping at the Savoy on foie gras and champagne.

MENDOZA Pooh! they have all had their turn at the broiled rabbit, just as I shall have my turn at the Savoy. Indeed, I have had a turn there already—as waiter.

TANNER A waiter! You astonish me!

MENDOZA (*Reflectively*) Yes: I, Mendoza of the Sierra, was a waiter. Hence, perhaps, my cosmopolitanism. (*With sudden intensity*) Shall I tell you the story of my life?

STRAKER (*Apprehensively*) If it ain't too long, old chap—

TANNER (*Interrupting him*) Tsh-sh: you are a Philistine, Henry: you have no romance in you. (*To* MENDOZA) You interest me extremely, President. Never mind Henry: he can go to sleep.

MENDOZA The woman I loved—

STRAKER Oh, this is a love story, is it? Right you are. Go on: I was only afraid you were going to talk about yourself.

MENDOZA Myself! I have thrown myself away for her sake: that is why I am here. No matter: I count the world well lost for her. She had, I pledge you my word, the most magnificent head of hair I ever saw. She had humor; she had intellect; she could cook to perfection; and her highly strung temperament made her uncertain, incalculable, variable, capricious, cruel, in a word, enchanting.

STRAKER A six shillin' novel sort o' woman, all but the cookin'. 'Er name was Lady Gladys Plantagenet, wasn't it?

MENDOZA No, sir: she was not an earl's daughter. Photography, reproduced by the half-tone process, has made me familiar with the appearance of the daughters of the English peerage; and I can honestly say that I would have sold the lot, faces, dowries, clothes, titles, and all, for a smile from this woman. Yet she was a woman of the people, a worker: otherwise—let me reciprocate your bluntness—I should have scorned her.

TANNER Very properly. And did she respond to your love?

MENDOZA Should I be here if she did? She objected to marry a Jew.

TANNER On religious grounds?

MENDOZA No: she was a freethinker. She said that every Jew considers in his heart that English people are dirty in their habits.

TANNER (*Surprised*) Dirty!

MENDOZA It shewed her extraordinary knowledge of the world; for it is undoubtedly true. Our elaborate sanitary code makes us unduly contemptuous of the Gentile.

TANNER Did you ever hear that, Henry?

STRAKER I've heard my sister say so. She was cook in a Jewish family once.

MENDOZA I could not deny it; neither could I eradicate the impression it made on her mind. I could have got round any other objection; but no woman can stand a suspicion of indelicacy as to her person. My entreaties were in vain: she always retorted that she wasn't good enough for me, and recommended me to marry an accursed barmaid named Rebecca Lazarus, whom I loathed. I talked of suicide: she offered me a packet of beetle poison to do it with. I hinted at murder: she went into hysterics; and as I am a living man I went to America so that she might sleep without dreaming that I was stealing upstairs to cut her throat. In America I went out west and fell in with a man who was wanted by the police for holding up trains. It was he who had the idea of holding up motor cars in the South of Europe: a welcome idea to a desperate and disappointed man. He gave me some valuable introductions to capitalists of the right sort. I formed a syndicate; and the present enterprise is the result. I became leader, as the Jew always becomes leader, by his brains and imagination. But with all my pride of race I would give everything I possess to be an Englishman. I am like a boy: I cut her name on the trees and her initials on the sod. When I am alone I lie down and tear my wretched hair and cry Louisa—

STRAKER (*Startled*) Louisa!

MENDOZA It is her name—Louisa—Louisa Straker—

TANNER Straker!

STRAKER (*Scrambling up on his knees most indignantly*) Look here: Louisa Straker is my sister, see? Wot do you mean by gassing about her like this? Wot's she got to do with you?

MENDOZA A dramatic coincidence! You are Enry, her favorite brother!

STRAKER 'Oo are you callin' Enry? What call have you to take a liberty with my name or with hers? For two pins I'd punch your fat 'edd, so I would.

MENDOZA (*With grandiose calm*) If I let you do it, will you promise to brag of it afterwards to her? She will be reminded of her Mendoza: that is all I desire.

TANNER This is genuine devotion, Henry. You should respect it.

STRAKER (*Fiercely*) Funk, more likely.

MENDOZA (*Springing to his feet*) Funk! Young man: I come of a famous family of fighters; and as your sister well knows, you would have as much chance against me as a perambulator against your motor car.

STRAKER (*Secretly daunted, but rising from his knees with an air of reckless pugnacity*) I ain't afraid of you. With your Louisa! Louisa! Miss Straker is good enough for you, I should think.

MENDOZA I wish you could persuade her to think so.

STRAKER (*Exasperated*) Here—

TANNER (*Rising quickly and interposing*) Oh come, Henry: even if you could fight the President you can't fight the whole League of the Sierra. Sit down again and be friendly. A cat may look at a king; and even a President of brigands may look at your sister. All this family pride is really very old fashioned.

STRAKER (*Subdued, but grumbling*) Let him look at her. But wot does he mean by makin' out that she ever looked at 'im? (*Reluctantly resuming his couch on the turf*) 'Ear him talk, one ud think she was keepin' company with him. (*He turns his back on them and composes himself to sleep*)

MENDOZA (*To* TANNER, *becoming more confidential as he finds himself virtually alone with a sympathetic listener in the still starlight of the mountains; for all the rest are asleep by this time*) It was just so with her, sir. Her intellect reached forward into the twentieth century: her social prejudices and family affections reached back into the dark ages. Ah, sir, how the words of Shakespear seem to fit every crisis in our emotions!

> I loved Louisa: 40,000 brothers
> Could not with all their quantity of love
> Make up my sum.

And so on. I forget the rest. Call it madness if you will—infatuation. I am an able man, a strong man: in ten years I should have owned a first-class hotel. I met her; and—you see!—I am a brigand, an outcast. Even Shakespear cannot do justice to what I feel for Louisa. Let me read you some lines that I have written about her myself. However slight their literary merit may be, they express what I feel better than any casual words can. (*He produces a packet of hotel bills scrawled with manuscript, and kneels at the fire to decipher them, poking it with a stick to make it glow*)

TANNER (*Slapping him rudely on the shoulder*) Put them in the fire, President.

MENDOZA (*Startled*) Eh?

TANNER You are sacrificing your career to a monomania.

MENDOZA I know it.

TANNER No, you don't. No man would commit such a crime against himself if he really knew what he was doing. How can you look round at these august hills, look up at this divine sky, taste this finely tempered air, and then talk like a literary hack on a second floor in Bloomsbury?

MENDOZA (*Shaking his head*) The Sierra is no better than Bloomsbury when once the novelty has worn off. Besides, these mountains make you dream of women—of women with magnificent hair.

TANNER Of Louisa, in short. They will not make me dream of women, my friend: I am heartwhole.

MENDOZA Do not boast until morning, sir. This is a strange country for dreams.

TANNER Well, we shall see. Goodnight. (*He lies down and composes himself to sleep*)

(MENDOZA, *with a sigh, follows his example; and for a few moments there is peace in the Sierra. Then* MENDOZA *sits up suddenly and says pleadingly to* TANNER—)

MENDOZA Just allow me to read a few lines before you go to sleep. I should really like your opinion of them.

TANNER (*Drowsily*) Go on. I am listening.

MENDOZA I saw thee first in Whitsun week
Louisa, Louisa—

TANNER (*Rousing himself*) My dear President, Louisa is a very pretty name; but it really doesn't rhyme well to Whitsun week.

MENDOZA Of course not. Louisa is not the rhyme, but the refrain.

TANNER (*Subsiding*) Ah, the refrain. I beg your pardon. Go on.

MENDOZA Perhaps you do not care for that one: I

think you will like this better. (*He recites, in rich soft tones, and in slow time*)

Louisa, I love thee.
I love thee, Louisa.
Louisa, Louisa, Louisa, I love thee.
One name and one phrase make my music, Louisa.
Louisa, Louisa, Louisa, I love thee.

Mendoza thy lover,
Thy lover, Mendoza,
Mendoza adoringly lives for Louisa.
There's nothing but that in the world for Mendoza.
Louisa, Louisa, Mendoza adores thee.

[*Affected*] There is no merit in producing beautiful lines upon such a name. Louisa is an exquisite name, it is not?

TANNER (*All but asleep, responds with a faint groan*)

MENDOZA

O wert thou, Louisa,
The wife of Mendoza,
Mendoza's Louisa, Louisa Mendoza,
How blest were the life of Louisa's Mendoza!
How painless his longing of love for Louisa!

That is real poetry—from the heart—from the heart of hearts. Don't you think it will move her?

(*No answer*)

(*Resignedly*) Asleep, as usual. Doggrel to all the world: heavenly music to me! Idiot that I am to wear my heart on my sleeve! (*He composes himself to sleep, murmuring*) Louisa, I love thee; I love thee, Louisa; Louisa, Louisa, Louisa, I—

(STRAKER *snores; rolls over on his side; and relapses into sleep. Stillness settles on the Sierra; and the darkness deepens. The fire has again buried itself in white ash and ceased to glow. The peaks shew unfathomably dark against the starry firmament; but now the stars dim and vanish; and the sky seems to steal away out of the universe. Instead of the Sierra there is nothing: omnipresent nothing. No sky, no peaks, no light, no sound, no time nor space, utter void. Then somewhere the beginning of a pallor, and with it a faint throbbing buzz as of a ghostly violincello palpitating on the same note endlessly. A couple of ghostly violins presently take advantage of this bass*[7]

*and therewith the pallor reveals a man in the void, an incorporeal but visible man, seated, absurdly enough, on nothing. For a moment he raises his head as the music passes him by. Then, with a heavy sigh, he droops in utter dejection; and the violins, discouraged, retrace their melody in despair and at last give it up, extinguished by wailings from uncanny wind instruments, thus:*

*It is all very odd. One recognizes the Mozartian strain; and on this hint, and by the aid of certain sparkles of violet light in the pallor, the man's costume explains itself as that of a Spanish nobleman of the XV-XVI century.* DON JUAN, *of course; but where? why? how? Besides, in the brief lifting of his face, now hidden by his hat brim, there was a curious suggestion of* TANNER. *A more critical, fastidious, handsome face, paler and colder, without* TANNER's *impetuous credulity and enthusiasm, and without a touch of his modern plutocratic vulgarity, but still a resemblance, even an identity. The name too:* DON JUAN TENORIO, JOHN TANNER. *Where on earth—or elsewhere—have we got to from the XX century and the Sierra?*

*Another pallor in the void, this time not violet, but a disagreeable smoky yellow. With it, the whisper of a ghostly clarionet turning this tune into infinite sadness:*[8]

*The yellowish pallor moves: there is an old crone wandering in the void, bent and toothless; draped as well as one can guess, in the coarse brown frock of some religious order. She wanders and wanders in her slow hopeless way, much as a wasp flies in its rapid busy way, until she blunders against the thing she seeks: companionship. With a sob of relief the poor old creature clutches at the presence of the man and addresses him in her dry unlovely voice, which can still express pride and resolution as well as suffering*)

THE OLD WOMAN Excuse me; but I am so lonely; and this place is so awful.

DON JUAN A new comer?

THE OLD WOMAN Yes: I suppose I died this morning. I confessed; I had extreme unction; I was in bed with my family about me and my eyes fixed on the cross. Then it grew dark; and when the light came

[7] This and the following musical quotation are derived from Mozart's overture to *Don Giovanni.*

[8] The beginning of Donna Anna's "Non mi dir" ["Say no more"] aria, *Don Giovanni,* Act II.

back it was this light by which I walk seeing nothing. I have wandered for hours in horrible loneliness.

DON JUAN (*Sighing*) Ah! you have not yet lost the sense of time. One soon does, in eternity.

THE OLD WOMAN Where are we?

DON JUAN In hell.

THE OLD WOMAN (*Proudly*) Hell! I in hell! How dare you?

DON JUAN (*Unimpressed*) Why not, Señora?

THE OLD WOMAN You do not know to whom you are speaking. I am a lady, and a faithful daughter of the Church.

DON JUAN I do not doubt it.

THE OLD WOMAN But how then can I be in hell? Purgatory, perhaps: I have not been perfect: who has? But hell! oh, you are lying.

DON JUAN Hell, Señora, I assure you; hell at its best: that is, its most solitary—though perhaps you would prefer company.

THE OLD WOMAN But I have sincerely repented; I have confessed—

DON JUAN How much?

THE OLD WOMAN More sins than I really committed. I loved confession.

DON JUAN Ah, that is perhaps as bad as confessing too little. At all events, Señora, whether by oversight or intention, you are certainly damned, like myself; and there is nothing for it now but to make the best of it.

THE OLD WOMAN (*Indignantly*) Oh! and I might have been so much wickeder! All my good deeds wasted! It is unjust.

DON JUAN No: you were fully and clearly warned. For your bad deeds, vicarious atonement, mercy without justice. For your good deeds, justice without mercy. We have many good people here.

THE OLD WOMAN Were you a good man?

DON JUAN I was a murderer.

THE OLD WOMAN A murderer! Oh, how dare they send me to herd with murderers! I was not as bad as that: I was a good woman. There is some mistake: where can I have it set right?

DON JUAN I do not know whether mistakes can be corrected here. Probably they will not admit a mistake even if they have made one.

THE OLD WOMAN But whom can I ask?

DON JUAN I should ask the Devil, Señora: he understands the ways of this place, which is more than I ever could.

THE OLD WOMAN The Devil! *I* speak to the Devil!

DON JUAN In hell, Señora, the Devil is the leader of the best society.

THE OLD WOMAN I tell you, wretch, I know I am not in hell.

DON JUAN How do you know?

THE OLD WOMAN Because I feel no pain.

DON JUAN Oh, then there is no mistake: you are intentionally damned.

THE OLD WOMAN Why do you say that?

DON JUAN Because hell, Señora, is a place for the wicked. The wicked are quite comfortable in it: it was made for them. You tell me you feel no pain. I conclude you are one of those for whom Hell exists.

THE OLD WOMAN Do you feel no pain?

DON JUAN I am not one of the wicked, Señora; therefore it bores me, bores me beyond description, beyond belief.

THE OLD WOMAN Not one of the wicked! You said you were a murderer.

DON JUAN Only a duel. I ran my sword through an old man who was trying to run his through me.

THE OLD WOMAN If you were a gentleman, that was not a murder.

DON JUAN The old man called it murder, because he was, he said, defending his daughter's honor. By this he meant that because I foolishly fell in love with her and told her so, she screamed; and he tried to assassinate me after calling me insulting names.

THE OLD WOMAN You were like all men. Libertines and murderers all, all, all!

DON JUAN And yet we meet here, dear lady.

THE OLD WOMAN Listen to me. My father was slain by just such a wretch as you, in just such a duel, for just such a cause. I screamed: it was my duty. My father drew on my assailant: his honor demanded it. He fell: that was the reward of honor. I am here: in hell, you tell me: that is the reward of duty. Is there justice in heaven?

DON JUAN No; but there is justice in hell: heaven is far above such idle human personalities. You will be welcome in hell, Señora. Hell is the home of honor, duty, justice, and the rest of the seven deadly virtues. All the wickedness on earth is done in their name: where else but in hell should they have their reward? Have I not told you that the truly damned are those who are happy in hell?

THE OLD WOMAN And are you happy here?

DON JUAN (*Springing to his feet*) No; and that is the enigma on which I ponder in darkness. Why am I here? I, who repudiated all duty, trampled honor underfoot, and laughed at justice!

THE OLD WOMAN Oh, what do I care why you are here? Why am *I* here? I, who sacrificed all my inclinations to womanly virtue and propriety!

DON JUAN Patience, lady: you will be perfectly happy and at home here. As saith the poet, "Hell is a city much like Seville." [9]

THE OLD WOMAN Happy! here! where I am nothing! where I am nobody!

DON JUAN Not at all: you are a lady; and wherever ladies are is hell. Do not be surprised or terrified: you will find everything here that a lady can desire, including devils who will serve you from sheer love of servitude, and magnify your importance for the sake of dignifying their service—the best of servants.

THE OLD WOMAN My servants will be devils!

DON JUAN Have you ever had servants who were not devils?

THE OLD WOMAN Never: they were devils, perfect devils, all of them. But that is only a manner of

[9] Shelley wrote, "Hell is a city much like London" in his "Peter Bell the Third."

speaking. I thought you meant that my servants here would be real devils.

DON JUAN No more real devils than you will be a real lady. Nothing is real here. That is the honor of damnation.

THE OLD WOMAN Oh, this is all madness. This is worse than fire and the worm.

DON JUAN For you, perhaps, there are consolations. For instance: how old were you when you changed from time to eternity?

THE OLD WOMAN Do not ask me how old I was—as if I were a thing of the past. I am 77.

DON JUAN A ripe age, Señora. But in hell old age is not tolerated. It is too real. Here we worship Love and Beauty. Our souls being entirely damned, we cultivate our hearts. As a lady of 77, you would not have a single acquaintance in hell.

THE OLD WOMAN How can I help my age, man?

DON JUAN You forget that you have left your age behind you in the realm of time. You are no more 77 than you are 7 or 17 or 27.

THE OLD WOMAN Nonsense!

DON JUAN Consider, Señora: was not this true even when you lived on earth? When you were 70, were you really older underneath your wrinkles and your grey hairs than when you were 30?

THE OLD WOMAN No, younger: at 30 I was a fool. But of what use is it to feel younger and look older?

DON JUAN You see, Señora, the look was only an illusion. Your wrinkles lied, just as the plump smooth skin of many a stupid girl of 17, with heavy spirits and decrepit ideas, lies about her age? Well, here we have no bodies: we see each other as bodies only because we learnt to think about one another under that aspect when we were alive; and we still think in that way, knowing no other. But we can appear to one another at what age we choose. You have but to will any of your old looks back, and back they will come.

THE OLD WOMAN It cannot be true

DON JUAN Try.

THE OLD WOMAN Seventeen!

DON JUAN Stop. Before you decide, I had better tell you that these things are a matter of fashion. Occasionally we have a rage for 17; but it does not last long. Just at present the fashionable age is 40—or say 37; but there are signs of a change. If you were at all good-looking at 27, I should suggest your trying that, and setting a new fashion.

THE OLD WOMAN I do not believe a word you are saying. However, 27 be it. (*Whisk! the old woman becomes a young one, magnificently attired, and so handsome that in the radiance into which her dull yellow halo has suddenly lightened one might almost mistake her for* ANN WHITEFIELD)

DON JUAN Doña Ana de Ulloa!

ANA What? You know me!

DON JUAN And you forget me!

ANA I cannot see your face. (*He raises his hat*) Don Juan Tenorio! Monster! You who slew my father! even here you pursue me.

DON JUAN I protest I do not pursue you. Allow me to withdraw (*Going*)

ANA (*Seizing his arm*) You shall not leave me alone in this dreadful place.

DON JUAN Provided my staying be not interpreted as pursuit.

ANA (*Releasing him*) You may well wonder how I can endure your presence. My dear, dear father!

DON JUAN Would you like to see him?

ANA My father here!!!

DON JUAN No: he is in heaven.

ANA I knew it. My noble father! He is looking down on us now. What must he feel to see his daughter in this place, and in conversation with his murderer!

DON JUAN By the way, if we should meet him—

ANA How can we meet him? He is in heaven.

DON JUAN He condescends to look in upon us here from time to time. Heaven bores him. So let me warn you that if you meet him he will be mortally offended if you speak of me as his murderer! He maintains that he was a much better swordsman than I, and that if his foot had not slipped he would have killed me. No doubt he is right: I was not a good fencer. I never dispute the point; so we are excellent friends.

ANA It is no dishonor to a soldier to be proud of his skill in arms.

DON JUAN You would rather not meet him, probably.

ANA How dare you say that?

DON JUAN Oh, that is the usual feeling here. You may remember that on earth—though of course we never confessed it—the death of anyone we knew, even those we liked best, was always mingled with a certain satisfaction at being finally done with them.

ANA Monster! Never, never.

DON JUAN (*Placidly*) I see you recognize the feeling. Yes: a funeral was always a festivity in black, especially the funeral of a relative. At all events, family ties are rarely kept up here. Your father is quite accustomed to this: he will not expect any devotion from you.

ANA Wretch: I wore mourning for him all my life.

DON JUAN Yes: it became you. But a life of mourning is one thing: an eternity of it quite another. Besides, here you are as dead as he. Can anything be more ridiculous than one dead person mourning for another? Do not look shocked, my dear Ana; and do not be alarmed: there is plenty of humbug in hell (indeed there is hardly anything else); but the humbug of death and age and change is dropped because here we are all dead and all eternal. You will pick up our ways soon.

ANA And will all the men call me their dear Ana?

DON JUAN No. That was a slip of the tongue. I beg your pardon.

ANA (*Almost tenderly*) Juan: did you really love me when you behaved so disgracefully to me?

DON JUAN (*Impatiently*) Oh, I beg you not to begin talking about love. Here they talk of nothing else but love: its beauty, its holiness, its spirituality, its devil knows what!—excuse me; but it does so bore me. They don't know what they're talking about: I do. They think they have achieved the perfection of love because they have no bodies. Sheer imaginative debauchery! Faugh!

ANA Has even death failed to refine your soul, Juan? Has the terrible judgment of which my father's statue was the minister taught you no reverence?

DON JUAN How is that very flattering statue, by the way? Does it still come to supper with naughty people and cast them into this bottomless pit? [10]

ANA It has been a great expense to me. The boys in the monastery school would not let it alone: the mischievous ones broke it; and the studious ones wrote their names on it. Three new noses in two years, and fingers without end. I had to leave it to its fate at last; and now I fear it is shockingly mutilated. My poor father!

DON JUAN Hush! Listen! (*Two great chords rolling on syncopated waves of sound break forth: D minor and its dominant:* [11] *a sound of dreadful joy to all musicians*) Ha! Mozart's statue music. It is your father. You had better disappear until I prepare him. (*She vanishes*)

(*From the void comes a living statue of white marble, designed to represent a majestic old man. But he waives his majesty with infinite grace; walks with a feather-like step; and makes every wrinkle in his war-worn visage brim over with holiday joyousness. To his sculptor he owes a perfectly trained figure, which he carries erect and trim; and the ends of his moustache curl up, elastic as watchsprings, giving him an air which, but for its Spanish dignity, would be called jaunty. He is on the pleasantest terms with* DON JUAN. *His voice, save for a much more distinguished intonation, is so like the voice of* ROEBUCK RAMSDEN *that it calls attention to the fact that they are not unlike one another in spite of their very different fashions of shaving*)

DON JUAN Ah, here you are, my friend. Why don't you learn to sing the splendid music Mozart has written for you?

THE STATUE Unluckily he has written it for a bass voice. Mine is a counter tenor. Well: have you repented yet?

DON JUAN I have too much consideration for you to repent, Don Gonzalo. If I did, you would have no excuse for coming from Heaven to argue with me.

THE STATUE True. Remain obdurate, my boy. I wish I had killed you, as I should have done but for an accident. Then I should have come here; and you would have had a statue and a reputation for piety to live up to. Any news?

DON JUAN Yes: your daughter is dead.

THE STATUE (*Puzzled*) My daughter? (*Recollecting*) Oh! the one you were taken with. Let me see: what was her name?

DON JUAN Ana.

THE STATUE To be sure: Ana. A goodlooking girl, if I recollect aright. Have you warned Whatshisname? her husband.

DON JUAN My friend Ottavio? No: I have not seen him since Ana arrived.

(ANA *comes indignantly to light*)

ANA What does this means? Ottavio here and your friend! And you, father, have forgotten my name. You are indeed turned to stone.

THE STATUE My dear: I am so much more admired in marble than I ever was in my own person that I have retained the shape the sculptor gave me. He was one of the first men of his day: you must acknowledge that.

ANA Father! Vanity! personal vanity! from you!

THE STATUE Ah, you outlived that weakness, my daughter: you must be nearly 80 by this time. I was cut off (by an accident) in my 64th year, and am considerably your junior in consequence. Besides, my child, in this place, what our libertine friend here would call the farce of parental wisdom is dropped. Regard me, I beg, as a fellow creature, not as a father.

ANA You speak as this villain speaks.

THE STATUE Juan is a sound thinker, Ana. A bad fencer, but a sound thinker.

ANA (*Horror creeping upon her*) I begin to understand. These are devils, mocking me. I had better pray.

THE STATUE (*Consoling her*) No, no, no, my child: do not pray. If you do, you will throw away the main advantage of this place. Written over the gate here are the words "Leave every hope behind, ye who enter." [12] Only think what a relief that is! For what is hope? A form of moral responsibility. Here there is no hope, and consequently no duty, no work, nothing to be gained by praying, nothing to be lost by doing what you like. Hell, in short, is a place where you have nothing to do but amuse yourself. [DON JUAN *sighs deeply*] You sigh, friend Juan; but if you dwelt in heaven, as I do, you would realize your advantages.

DON JUAN You are in good spirits today, Commander. You are positively brilliant. What is the matter?

THE STATUE I have come to a momentous decision, my boy. But first, where is our friend the Devil? I must consult him in the matter. And Ana would like to make his acquaintance, no doubt.

ANA You are preparing some torment for me.

DON JUAN All that is superstition, Ana. Reassure yourself. Remember: the devil is not so black as he is painted.

THE STATUE Let us give him a call.

(*At the wave of the statue's hand the great chords roll out again; but this time Mozart's music gets grotesquely adulterated with Gounod's.* [13] *A scarlet halo begins to glow; and into it* THE DEVIL *rises, very Mephistophelean, and not at all unlike* MENDOZA, *though not so interesting. He looks older; is*

[10] The action which brings *Don Giovanni* to its magnificent conclusion.

[11] The musical phrase, sounded chiefly by trombones, Mozart used to mark the appearance of the dead Commendatore to Don Giovanni (Act II).

[12] Part of the inscription on the Door of Hell, as recorded by Dante in his *Inferno*.

[13] Gounod's *Faust* has Mephistopheles as a character.

*getting prematurely bald; and, in spite of an effusion of goodnature and friendliness, is peevish and sensitive when his advances are not reciprocated. He does not inspire much confidence in his powers of hard work or endurance, and is, on the whole, a disagreeably self-indulgent looking person; but he is clever and plausible, though perceptibly less well bred than the two other men, and enormously less vital than the woman)*

THE DEVIL (*Heartily*) Have I the pleasure of again receiving a visit from the illustrious Commander of Calatrava? (*Coldly*) Don Juan, your servant. (*Politely*) And a strange lady? My respects, Señora.

ANA Are you—

THE DEVIL (*Bowing*) Lucifer, at your service.

ANA I shall go mad.

THE DEVIL (*Gallantly*) Ah, Señora, do not be anxious. You come to us from earth, full of the prejudices and terrors of that priest-ridden place. You have heard me ill spoken of; and yet, believe me, I have hosts of friends there.

ANA Yes: you reign in their hearts.

THE DEVIL (*Shaking his head*) You flatter me, Señora; but you are mistaken. It is true that the world cannot get on without me; but it never gives me credit for that: in its heart it mistrusts and hates me. Its sympathies are all with misery, with poverty, with starvation of the body and of the heart. I call on it to sympathize with joy, with love, with happiness, with beauty—

DON JUAN (*Nauseated*) Excuse me: I am going. You know I cannot stand this.

THE DEVIL (*Angrily*) Yes: I know that you are no friend of mine.

THE STATUE What harm is he doing you, Juan? It seems to me that he was talking excellent sense when you interrupted him.

THE DEVIL (*Warmly patting the statue's hand*) Thank you, my friend: thank you. You have always understood me: he has always disparaged and avoided me.

DON JUAN I have treated you with perfect courtesy.

THE DEVIL Courtesy! What is courtesy? I care nothing for mere courtesy. Give me warmth of heart, true sincerity, the bond of sympathy with love and joy—

DON JUAN You are making me ill.

THE DEVIL There! (*Appealing to* THE STATUE) You hear, sir! Oh, by what irony of fate was this cold selfish egotist sent to my kingdom, and you taken to the icy mansions of the sky!

THE STATUE I can't complain. I was a hypocrite; and it served me right to be sent to heaven.

THE DEVIL Why, sir, do you not join us, and leave a sphere for which your temperament is too sympathetic, your heart too warm, your capacity for enjoyment too generous?

THE STATUE I have this day resolved to do so. In future, excellent Son of the Morning, I am yours. I have left Heaven for ever.

THE DEVIL (*Again touching the marble hand*) Ah, what an honor! what a triumph for our cause! Thank you, thank you. And now, my friend—I may call you so at last—could you not persuade him to take the place you have left vacant above?

THE STATUE (*Shaking his head*) I cannot conscientiously recommend anybody with whom I am on friendly terms to deliberately make himself dull and uncomfortable.

THE DEVIL Of course not; but are you sure he would be uncomfortable? Of course you know best: you brought him here originally; and we had the greatest hopes of him. His sentiments were in the best taste of our best people. You remember how he sang? (*He begins to sing in a nasal operatic baritone, tremulous from an eternity of misuse in the French manner*)

*Vivan le femmine!*
*Viva il buon vino!*

THE STATUE (*Taking up the tune an octave higher in his counter tenor*)

*Sostegno e gloria*
*D'umanità.*[14]

THE DEVIL Precisely. Well, he never sings for us now.

DON JUAN Do you complain of that? Hell is full of musical amateurs: music is the brandy of the damned. May not one lost soul be permitted to abstain?

THE DEVIL You dare blaspheme against the sublimest of the arts!

DON JUAN (*With cold disgust*) You talk like a hysterical woman fawning on a fiddler.

THE DEVIL I am not angry. I merely pity you. You have no soul; and you are unconscious of all that you lose. Now you, Señor Commander, are a born musician. How well you sing! Mozart would be delighted if he were still here; but he moped and went to heaven. Curious how these clever men, whom you would have supposed born to be popular here, have turned out social failures, like Don Juan!

DON JUAN I am really very sorry to be a social failure.

THE DEVIL Not that we don't admire your intellect, you know. We do. But I look at the matter from your own point of view. You don't get on with us. The place doesn't suit you. The truth is, you have—I won't say no heart; for we know that beneath all your affected cynicism you have a warm one—

DON JUAN (*Shrinking*) Don't, please don't.

THE DEVIL (*Nettled*) Well, you've no capacity for enjoyment. Will that satisfy you?

DON JUAN It is a somewhat less insufferable form of cant than the other. But if you'll allow me, I'll take refuge, as usual, in solitude.

THE DEVIL Why not take refuge in Heaven? That's the proper place for you. (*To* ANA) Come, Señora! could you not persuade him for his own good to try change of air?

ANA But can he go to Heaven if he wants to?

THE DEVIL What's to prevent him?

ANA Can anybody—can *I* go to Heaven if I want to?

[14] "Here's to the ladies! Here's to good wine! They nourish and glorify all mankind," Don Giovanni's mocking toast, sung just before the arrival of the Statue (Act II).

THE DEVIL (*Rather contemptuously*) Certainly, if your taste lies that way.

ANA But why doesn't everybody go to Heaven, then?

THE STATUE (*Chuckling*) *I* can tell you that, my dear. It's because heaven is the most angelically dull place in all creation: that's why.

THE DEVIL His excellency the Commander puts it with military bluntness; but the strain of living in Heaven is intolerable. There is a notion that I was turned out of it; but as a matter of fact nothing could have induced me to stay there. I simply left it and organized this place.

THE STATUE I don't wonder at it. Nobody could stand an eternity of Heaven.

THE DEVIL Oh, it suits some people. Let us be just, Commander: it is a question of temperament. I don't admire the heavenly temperament: I don't understand it: I don't know that I particularly want to understand it; but it takes all sorts to make a universe. There is no accounting for tastes; there are people who like it. I think Don Juan would like it.

DON JUAN But—pardon my frankness—could you really go back there if you desired to; or are the grapes sour?

THE DEVIL Back there! I often go back there. Have you never read the book of Job? Have you any canonical authority for assuming that there is any barrier between our circle and the other one? [15]

ANA But surely there is a great gulf fixed.

THE DEVIL Dear lady: a parable must not be taken literally. The gulf is the difference between the angelic and the diabolic temperament. What more impassable gulf could you have? Think of what you have seen on earth. There is no physical gulf between the philosopher's class room and the bull ring; but the bull fighters do not come to the class room for all that. Have you ever been in the country where I have the largest following? England. There they have great racecourses, and also concert rooms where they play the classical compositions of his Excellency's friend Mozart. Those who go to the racecourses can stay away from them and go to the classical concerts instead if they like: there is no law against it; for Englishmen never will be slaves: they are free to do whatever the Government and public opinion allow them to do. And the classical concert is admitted to be a higher, more cultivated, poetic, intellectual, ennobling place than the racecourse. But do the lovers of racing desert their sport and flock to the concert room? Not they. They would suffer there all the weariness the Commander has suffered in heaven. There is the great gulf of the parable between the two places. A mere physical gulf they could bridge; or at least I could bridge it for them (the earth is full of Devil's Bridges); but the gulf of dislike is impassable and eternal. And that is the only gulf that separates my friends here from those who are invidiously called the blest.

ANA I shall go to heaven at once.

THE STATUE My child: one word of warning first. Let me complete my friend Lucifer's similitude of the classical concert. At every one of those concerts in England you will find rows of weary people who are there, not because they really like classical music, but because they think they ought to like it. Well, there is the same thing in heaven. A number of people sit there in glory, not because they are happy, but because they think they owe it to their position to be in heaven. They are almost all English.

THE DEVIL Yes: the Southerners give it up and join me just as you have done. But the English really do not seem to know when they are thoroughly miserable. An Englishman thinks he is moral when he is only uncomfortable.

THE STATUE In short, my daughter, if you go to Heaven without being naturally qualified for it, you will not enjoy yourself there.

ANA And who dares say that I am not naturally qualified for it? The most distinguished princes of the Church have never questioned it. I owe it to myself to leave this place at once.

THE DEVIL (*Offended*) As you please, Señora. I should have expected better taste from you.

ANA Father: I shall expect you to come with me. You cannot stay here. What will people say?

THE STATUE People! Why, the best people are here —princes of the church and all. So few go to Heaven, and so many come here, that the blest, once called a heavenly host, are a continually dwindling minority. The saints, the fathers, the elect of long ago are the cranks, the faddists, the outsiders of today.

THE DEVIL It is true. From the beginning of my career I knew that I should win in the long run by sheer weight of public opinion, in spite of the long campaign of misrepresentation and calumny against me. At bottom the universe is a constitutional one; and with such a majority as mine I cannot be kept permanently out of office.

DON JUAN I think, Ana, you had better stay here.

ANA (*Jealously*) You do not want me to go with you.

DON JUAN Surely you do not want to enter Heaven in the company of a reprobate like me.

ANA All souls are equally precious. You repent, do you not?

DON JUAN My dear Ana, you are silly. Do you suppose Heaven is like earth, where people persuade themselves that what is done can be undone by repentance; that what is spoken can be unspoken by withdrawing it; that what is true can be annihilated by a general agreement to give it the lie? No: Heaven is the home of the masters of reality: that is why I am going thither.

ANA Thank you: I am going to heaven for happiness. I have had quite enough of reality on earth.

DON JUAN Then you must stay here; for hell is the home of the unreal and of the seekers for happiness. It is the only refuge from heaven, which is, as I tell you, the home of the masters of reality, and from earth, which is the home of the slaves of reality. The earth is a nursery in which men and women play at being heroes and heroines, saints and sinners; but

[15] See *Job*, 1:6, where Satan presents himself before the Lord along with the other sons of God.

they are dragged down from their fool's paradise by their bodies: hunger and cold and thirst, age and decay and disease, death above all, make them slaves of reality: thrice a day meals must be eaten and digested: thrice a century a new generation must be engendered: ages of faith, of romance, and of science are all driven at last to have but one prayer "Make me a healthy animal." But here you escape this tyranny of the flesh; for here you are not an animal at all: you are a ghost, an appearance, an illusion, a convention, deathless, ageless: in a word, bodiless. There are no social questions here, no political questions, no religious questions, best of all, perhaps, no sanitary questions. Here you call your appearance beauty, your emotions love, your sentiments heroism, your aspirations virtue, just as you did on earth; but here there are no hard facts to contradict you, no ironic contrast of your needs with your pretensions, no human comedy, nothing but a perpetual romance, a universal melodrama. As our German friend put it in his poem, "the poetically nonsensical here is good sense; and the Eternal Feminine draws us ever upward and on" [16]—without getting us a step farther. And yet you want to leave this paradise!

ANA But if Hell be so beautiful as this, how glorious must Heaven be!

(THE DEVIL, THE STATUE, *and* DON JUAN *all begin to speak at once in violent protest; then stop abashed*)

DON JUAN I beg your pardon.

THE DEVIL Not at all. I interrupted you.

THE STATUE You were going to say something.

DON JUAN After you, gentlemen.

THE DEVIL (*To* DON JUAN) You have been so eloquent on the advantages of my dominions that I leave you to do equal justice to the drawbacks of the alternative establishment.

DON JUAN In Heaven, as I picture it, dear lady, you live and work instead of playing and pretending. You face things as they are; you escape nothing but glamor; and your steadfastness and your peril are your glory. If the play still goes on here and on earth, and all the world is a stage, Heaven is at least behind the scenes. But Heaven cannot be described by a metaphor. Thither I shall go presently, because there I hope to escape at last from lies and from the tedious, vulgar pursuit of happiness, to spend my eons in contemplation—

THE STATUE Ugh!

DON JUAN Señor Commander: I do not blame your disgust: a picture gallery is a dull place for a blind man. But even as you enjoy the contemplation of such romantic mirages as beauty and pleasure; so would I enjoy the contemplation of that which interests me above all things: namely, Life: the force that ever strives to attain greater power of contemplating itself. What made this brain of mine, do you think? Not the need to move my limbs; for a rat with half my brains moves as well as I. Not merely the need to do, but the need to know what I do, lest in my blind efforts to live I should be slaying myself.

THE STATUE You would have slain yourself in your blind efforts to fence but for my foot slipping, my friend.

DON JUAN Audacious ribald: your laughter will finish in hideous boredom before morning.

THE STATUE Ha ha! Do you remember how I frightened you when I said something like that[17] to you from my pedestal in Seville? It sounds rather flat without my trombones.

DON JUAN They tell me it generally sounds flat with them, Commander.

ANA Oh, do not interrupt with these frivolities, father. Is there nothing in Heaven but contemplation, Juan?

DON JUAN In the Heaven I seek, no other joy. But there is the work of helping Life in its struggle upward. Think of how it wastes and scatters itself, how it raises up obstacles to itself and destroys itself in its ignorance and blindness. It needs a brain, this irresistible force, lest in its ignorance it should resist itself. What a piece of work is man! says the poet. Yes; but what a blunderer! Here is the highest miracle of organization yet attained by life, the most intensely alive thing that exists, the most conscious of all the organisms; and yet, how wretched are his brains! Stupidity made sordid and cruel by the realities learnt from toil and poverty: Imagination resolved to starve sooner than face these realities, piling up illusions to hide them, and calling itself cleverness, genius! And each accusing the other of its own defect: Stupidity accusing Imagination of folly, and Imagination accusing Stupidity of ignorance: whereas, alas! Stupidity has all the knowledge, and Imagination all the intelligence.

THE DEVIL And a pretty kettle of fish they make of it between them. Did I not say, when I was arranging that affair of Faust's, that all Man's reason has done for him is to make him beastlier than any beast.[18] One splendid body is worth the brains of a hundred dyspeptic, flatulent philosophers.

DON JUAN You forget that brainless magnificence of body has been tried. Things immeasurably greater than man in every respect but brain have existed and perished. The megatherium, the icthyosaurus have paced the earth with seven-league steps and hidden the day with cloud vast wings. Where are they now? Fossils in museums, and so few and imperfect at that, that a knuckle bone or a tooth of one of them is prized beyond the lives of a thousand soldiers. These things lived and wanted to live; but for lack of brains they did not know how to carry out their purpose, and so destroyed themselves.

THE DEVIL And is Man any the less destroying himself for all this boasted brain of his? Have you walked up and down upon the earth lately? I have; and I have examined Man's wonderful inventions. And I tell you that in the arts of life man invents nothing; but in the arts of death he outdoes Nature herself,

[16] The last four lines of Goethe's *Faust,* Part II, are here rather freely translated.

[17] In *Don Giovanni,* the first phrase sung by the Statue is the prophetic "Your laughter will die before morning."

[18] See Mephistopheles' first speech in "The Prologue in Heaven," Goethe's *Faust, I.*

and produces by chemistry and machinery all the slaughter of plague, pestilence, and famine. The peasant I tempt today eats and drinks what was eaten and drunk by the peasants of ten thousand years ago; and the house he lives in has not altered as much in a thousand centuries as the fashion of a lady's bonnet in a score of weeks. But when he goes out to slay, he carries a marvel of mechanism that lets loose at the touch of his finger all the hidden molecular energies, and leaves the javelin, the arrow, the blowpipe of his fathers far behind. In the arts of peace Man is a bungler. I have seen his cotton factories and the like, with machinery that a greedy dog could have invented if it had wanted money instead of food. I know his clumsy typewriters and bungling locomotives and tedious bicycles: they are toys compared to the Maxim gun, the submarine torpedo boat. There is nothing in Man's industrial machinery but his greed and sloth: his heart is in his weapons. This marvelous force of Life of which you boast is a force of Death: Man measures his strength by his destructiveness. What is his religion? An excuse for hating me. What is his law? An excuse for hanging you. What is his morality? Gentility! an excuse for consuming without producing. What is his art? An excuse for gloating over pictures of slaughter. What are his politics? Either the worship of a despot because a despot can kill, or parliamentary cockfighting. I spent an evening lately in a certain celebrated legislature, and heard the pot lecturing the kettle for its blackness, and ministers answering questions. When I left I chalked upon the door the old nursery saying "Ask no questions and you will be told no lies." I bought a sixpenny family magazine, and found it full of pictures of young men shooting and stabbing one another. I saw a man die: he was a London bricklayer's laborer with seven children. He left seventeen pounds club money; and his wife spent it all on his funeral and went into the workhouse with the children next day. She would not have spent sevenpence on her children's schooling: the law had to force her to let them be taught gratuitously; but on death she spent all she had. Their imagination glows, their energies rise up at the idea of death, these people: they love it; and the more horrible it is the more they enjoy it. Hell is a place far above their comprehension: they derive their notion of it from two of the greatest fools that ever lived, an Italian and an Englishman.[19] The Italian described it as a place of mud, frost, filth, fire, and venomous serpents: all torture. This ass, when he was not lying about me, was maundering about some woman whom he saw once in the street. The Englishman described me as being expelled from Heaven by cannons and gunpowder; and to this day every Briton believes that the whole of his silly story is in the Bible. What else he says I do not know; for it is all in a long poem which neither I nor anyone else ever succeeded in wading through. It is the same in everything. The highest form of literature is the tragedy, a play in which everybody is murdered at the end. In the old chronicles you read of earthquakes and pestilences, and are told that these shewed the power and majesty of God and the littleness of Man. Nowadays the chronicles describe battles. In a battle two bodies of men shoot at one another with bullets and explosive shells until one body runs away, when the others chase the fugitives on horseback and cut them to pieces as they fly. And this, the chronicle concludes, shews the greatness and majesty of empires, and the littleness of the vanquished. Over such battles the people run about the streets yelling with delight, and egg their Governments on to spend hundreds of millions of money in the slaughter, whilst the strongest Ministers dare not spend an extra penny in the pound against the poverty and pestilence through which they themselves daily walk. I could give you a thousand instances; but they all come to the same thing: the power that governs the earth is not the power of Life but of Death; and the inner need that has nerved Life to the effort of organizing itself into the human being is not the need for higher life but for a more efficient engine of destruction. The plague, the famine, the earthquake, the tempest were too spasmodic in their action; the tiger and crocodile were too easily satiated and not cruel enough: something more constantly, more ruthlessly, more ingeniously destructive was needed; and that something was Man, the inventor of the rack, the stake, the gallows, the electric chair; of sword and gun and poison gas: above all, of justice, duty, patriotism, and all the other isms by which even those who are clever enough to be humanely disposed are persuaded to become the most destructive of all the destroyers.

DON JUAN Pshaw! all this is old. Your weak side, my diabolic friend, is that you have always been a gull: you take Man at his own valuation. Nothing would flatter him more than your opinion of him. He loves to think of himself as bold and bad. He is neither one nor the other: he is only a coward. Call him tyrant, murderer, pirate, bully; and he will adore you, and swagger about with the consciousness of having the blood of the old sea kings in his veins. Call him liar and thief; and he will only take an action against you for libel. But call him coward; and he will go mad with rage: he will face death to outface that stinging truth. Man gives every reason for his conduct save one, every excuse for his crimes save one, every plea for his safety save one; and that one is his cowardice. Yet all his civilization is founded on his cowardice, on his abject tameness, which he calls his respectability. There are limits to what a mule or an ass will stand; but Man will suffer himself to be degraded until his vileness becomes so loathsome to his oppressors that they themselves are forced to reform it.

THE DEVIL Precisely. And these are the creatures in whom you discover what you call a Life Force!

DON JUAN Yes; for now comes the most surprising part of the whole business.

THE STATUE What's that?

DON JUAN Why, that you can make any of these

[19] Dante and Milton; see especially *Paradise Lost,* Book VI.

cowards brave by simply putting an idea into his head.

THE STATUE Stuff! As an old soldier I admit the cowardice: it's as universal as sea sickness, and matters just as little. But that about putting an idea into a man's head is stuff and nonsense. In a battle all you need to make you fight is a little hot blood and the knowledge that it's more dangerous to lose than to win.

DON JUAN That is perhaps why battles are so useless. But men never really overcome fear until they imagine they are fighting to further a universal purpose—fighting for an idea, as they call it. Why was the Crusader braver than the pirate? Because he fought, not for himself, but for the Cross. What force was it that met him with a valor as reckless as his own? The force of men who fought, not for themselves, but for Islam. They took Spain from us, though we were fighting for our very hearths and homes; but when we, too, fought for that mighty idea, a Catholic Church, we swept them back to Africa.

THE DEVIL (*Ironically*) What! you a Catholic, Señor Don Juan! A devotee! My congratulations.

THE STATUE (*Seriously*) Come, come! as a soldier, I can listen to nothing against the Church.

DON JUAN Have no fear, Commander: this idea of a Catholic Church will survive Islam, will survive the Cross, will survive even that vulgar pageant of incompetent schoolboyish gladiators which you call the Army.

THE STATUE Juan: you will force me to call you to account for this.

DON JUAN Useless: I cannot fence. Every idea for which Man will die will be a Catholic idea. When the Spaniard learns at last that he is no better than the Saracen, and his prophet no better than Mahomet, he will arise, more Catholic than ever, and die on a barricade across the filthy slum he starves in, for universal liberty and equality.

THE STATUE Bosh!

DON JUAN What you call bosh is the only thing men dare die for. Later on, Liberty will not be Catholic enough: men will die for human perfection, to which they will sacrifice all their liberty gladly.

THE DEVIL Ay: they will never be at a loss for an excuse for killing one another.

DON JUAN What of that? It is not death that matters, but the fear of death. It is not killing and dying that degrades us, but base living, and accepting the wages and profits of degradation. Better ten dead men than one live slave or his master. Men shall yet rise up, father against son and brother against brother, and kill one another for the great Catholic idea of abolishing slavery.

THE DEVIL Yes, when the Liberty and Equality of which you prate shall have made free white Christians cheaper in the labor market than black heathen slaves sold by auction at the block.

DON JUAN Never fear! the white laborer shall have his turn too. But I am not now defending the illusory forms the great ideas take. I am giving you examples of the fact that this creature Man, who in his own selfish affairs is a coward to the backbone, will fight for an idea like a hero. He may be abject as a citizen; but he is dangerous as a fanatic. He can only be enslaved whilst he is spiritually weak enough to listen to reason. I tell you, gentlemen, if you can shew a man a piece of what he now calls God's work to do, and what he will later on call by many new names, you can make him entirely reckless of the consequences to himself personally.

ANA Yes: he shirks all his responsibilities, and leaves his wife to grapple with them.

THE STATUE Well said, daughter. Do not let him talk you out of your common sense.

THE DEVIL Alas! Señor Commander, now that we have got on to the subject of Woman, he will talk more than ever. However, I confess it is for me the one supremely interesting subject.

DON JUAN To a woman, Señora, man's duties and responsibilities begin and end with the task of getting bread for her children. To her, Man is only a means to the end of getting children and rearing them.

ANA Is that your idea of a woman's mind? I call it cynical and disgusting animalism.

DON JUAN Pardon me, Ana: I said nothing about a woman's whole mind. I spoke of her view of Man as a separate sex. It is no more cynical than her view of herself as above all things a Mother. Sexually, Woman is Nature's contrivance for perpetuating its highest achievement. Sexually, Man is Woman's contrivance for fulfilling Nature's behest in the most economical way. She knows by instinct that far back in the evolutional process she invented him, differentiated him, created him in order to produce something better than the single-sexed process can produce. Whilst he fulfils the purpose for which she made him, he is welcome to his dreams, his follies, his ideals, his heroisms, provided that the keystone of them all is the worship of woman, of motherhood, of the family, of the hearth. But how rash and dangerous it was to invent a separate creature whose sole function was her own impregnation! For mark what has happened. First, Man has multiplied on her hands until there are as many men as women; so that she has been unable to employ for her purposes more than a fraction of the immense energy she has left at his disposal by saving him the exhausting labor of gestation. This superfluous energy has gone to his brain and to his muscle. He has become too strong to be controlled by her bodily, and too imaginative and mentally vigorous to be content with mere self-reproduction. He has created civilization without consulting her, taking her domestic labor for granted as the foundation of it.

ANA That is true, at all events.

THE DEVIL Yes; and this civilization! what is it, after all?

DON JUAN After all, an excellent peg to hang your cynical commonplaces on; but before all, it is an attempt on Man's part to make himself something more than the mere instrument of Woman's purpose. So far, the result of Life's continual effort not only to maintain itself, but to achieve higher and higher organization and completer self-consciousness, is only, at best, a doubtful campaign between its forces and those of Death and Degeneration. The battles in this campaign are mere blunders, mostly won, like actual military battles, in spite of the commanders.

THE STATUE That is a dig at me. No matter: go on, go on.

DON JUAN It is a dig at a much higher power than you, Commander. Still, you must have noticed in your profession that even a stupid general can win battles when the enemy's general is a little stupider.

THE STATUE (*Very seriously*) Most true, Juan, most true. Some donkeys have amazing luck.

DON JUAN Well, the Life Force is stupid; but it is not so stupid as the forces of Death and Degeneration. Besides, these are in its pay all the time. And so Life wins, after a fashion. What mere copiousness of fecundity can supply and mere greed preserve, we possess. The survival of whatever form of civilization can produce the best rifle and the best fed riflemen is assured.

THE DEVIL Exactly! the survival, not of the most effective means of Life but of the most effective means of Death. You always come back to my point, in spite of your wrigglings and evasions and sophistries, not to mention the intolerable length of your speeches.

DON JUAN Oh, come! who began making long speeches? However, if I overtax your intellect, you can leave us and seek the society of love and beauty and the rest of your favorite boredoms.

THE DEVIL (*Much offended*) This is not fair, Don Juan, and not civil. I am also on the intellectual plane. Nobody can appreciate it more than I do. I am arguing fairly with you, and, I think, successfully refuting you. Let us go on for another hour if you like.

DON JUAN Good: let us.

THE STATUE Not that I see any prospect of your coming to any point in particular, Juan. Still, since in this place, instead of merely killing time we have to kill eternity, go ahead by all means.

DON JUAN (*Somewhat impatiently*) My point, you marbleheaded old masterpiece, is only a step ahead of you. Are we agreed that Life is a force which has made innumerable experiments in organizing itself; that the mammoth and the man, the mouse and the megatherium, the flies and the fleas and the Fathers of the Church, are more or less successful attempts to build up that raw force into higher and higher individuals, the ideal individual being omnipotent, omniscient, infallible, and withal completely, unilludedly self-conscious: in short, a god?

THE DEVIL I agree, for the sake of argument.

THE STATUE I agree, for the sake of avoiding argument.

ANA I most emphatically disagree as regards the Fathers of the Church; and I must beg you not to drag them into the argument.

DON JUAN I did so purely for the sake of alliteration, Ana; and I shall make no further allusion to them. And now, since we are, with that exception, agreed so far, will you not agree with me further that Life has not measured the success of its attempts at godhead by the beauty or bodily perfection of the result, since in both these respects the birds, as our friend Aristophanes long ago pointed out, are so extraordinarily superior, with their power of flight and their lovely plumage, and, may I add, the touching poetry of their loves and nestings, that it is inconceivable that Life, having once produced them, should, if love and beauty were her object, start off on another line and labor at the clumsy elephant and the hideous ape, whose grandchildren we are?

ANA Aristophanes was a heathen; and you, Juan, I am afraid, are very little better.

THE DEVIL You conclude, then, that Life was driving at clumsiness and ugliness?

DON JUAN No, perverse devil that you are, a thousand times no. Life was driving at brains—at its darling object: an organ by which it can attain not only self-consciousness but self-understanding.

THE STATUE This is metaphysics, Juan. Why the devil should—(*To* THE DEVIL) I beg your pardon.

THE DEVIL Pray don't mention it. I have always regarded the use of my name to secure additional emphasis as a high compliment to me. It is quite at your service, Commander.

THE STATUE Thank you: that's very good of you. Even in heaven, I never quite got out of my old military habits of speech. What I was going to ask Juan was why Life should bother itself about getting a brain. Why should it want to understand itself? Why not be content to enjoy itself?

DON JUAN Without a brain, Commander, you would enjoy yourself without knowing it, and so lose all the fun.

THE STATUE True, most true. But I am quite content with brain enough to know that I'm enjoying myself. I don't want to understand why. In fact, I'd rather not. My experience is that one's pleasures don't bear thinking about.

DON JUAN That is why intellect is so unpopular. But to Life, the force behind the Man, intellect is a necessity, because without it he blunders into death. Just as Life, after ages of struggle, evolved that wonderful bodily organ the eye, so that the living organism could see where it was going and what was coming to help or threaten it, and thus avoid a thousand dangers that formerly slew it, so it is evolving today a mind's eye that shall see, not the physical world, but the purpose of Life, and thereby enable the individual to work for that purpose instead of thwarting and baffling it by setting up shortsighted personal aims as at present. Even as it is, only one sort of man has ever been happy, has ever been universally respected among all the conflicts of interests and illusions.

THE STATUE You mean the military man.

DON JUAN Commander: I do not mean the military man. When the military man approaches, the world locks up its spoons and packs off its womankind. No: I sing, not arms and the hero, but the philosophic man: he who seeks in contemplation to discover the inner will of the world, in invention to discover the means of fulfilling that will, and in action to do that will by the so-discovered means. Of all other sorts of men I declare myself tired. They are tedious failures. When I was on earth, professors of all sorts prowled round me feeling for an unhealthy spot in me on which they could fasten. The doctors of medicine bade me consider what I must do to save my body, and offered me quack cures for imaginary diseases. I replied that I was not a hypochondriac; so they called me Ignoramus and went their way. The doctors of divinity bade me consider what I must do to save my soul; but I was not a spiritual hypochondriac any more than a bodily one, and would not trouble myself about that either; so they called me Atheist and went their way. After them came the politician, who said there was only one purpose in nature, and that was to get him into parliament. I told him I did not care whether he got into parliament or not; so he called me Mugwump and went his way. Then came the romantic man, the Artist, with his love songs and his paintings and his poems; and with him I had great delight for many years, and some profit; for I cultivated my senses for his sake; and his songs taught me to hear better, his paintings to see better, and his poems to feel more deeply. But he led me at last into the worship of Woman.

ANA Juan!

DON JUAN Yes: I came to believe that in her voice was all the music of the song, in her face all the beauty of the painting, and in her soul all the emotion of the poem.

ANA And you were disappointed, I suppose. Well, was it her fault that you attributed all these perfections to her?

DON JUAN Yes, partly. For with a wonderful instinctive cunning, she kept silent and allowed me to glorify her: to mistake my own visions, thoughts, and feelings for hers. Now my friend the romantic man was often too poor or too timid to approach those women who were beautiful or refined enough to seem to realize his ideal; and so he went to his grave believing in his dream. But I was more favored by nature and circumstance. I was of noble birth and rich; and when my person did not please, my conversation flattered, though I generally found myself fortunate in both.

THE STATUE Coxcomb!

DON JUAN Yes; but even my coxcombry pleased. Well, I found that when I had touched a woman's imagination, she would allow me to persuade myself that she loved me; but when my suit was granted she never said "I am happy: my love is satisfied": she always said, first, "At last, the barriers are down," and second, "When will you come again?"

ANA That is exactly what men say.

DON JUAN I protest I never said it. But all women say it. Well, these two speeches always alarmed me; for the first meant that the lady's impulse had been solely to throw down my fortifications and gain my citadel; and the second openly announced that henceforth she regarded me as her property, and counted my time as already wholly at her disposal.

THE DEVIL That is where your want of heart came in.

THE STATUE (*Shaking his head*) You shouldn't repeat what a woman says, Juan.

ANA (*Severely*) It should be sacred to you.

THE STATUE Still, they certainly do say it. I never minded the barriers; but there was always a slight shock about the other, unless one was very hard hit indeed.

DON JUAN Then the lady, who had been happy and idle enough before, became anxious, preoccupied with me, always intriguing, conspiring, pursuing, watching, waiting, bent wholly on making sure of her prey: I being the prey, you understand. Now this was not what I had bargained for. It may have been very proper and very natural; but it was not music, painting, poetry, and joy incarnated in a beautiful woman. I ran away from it. I ran away from it very often: in fact I became famous for running away from it.

ANA Infamous, you mean.

DON JUAN I did not run away from you. Do you blame me for running away from the others?

ANA Nonsense, man. You are talking to a woman of 77 now. If you had had the chance, you would have run away from me too—if I had let you. You would not have found it so easy with me as with some of the others. If men will not be faithful to their home and their duties, they must be made to be. I daresay you all want to marry lovely incarnations of music and painting and poetry. Well, you can't have them, because they don't exist. If flesh and blood is not good enough for you you must go without; that's all. Women have to put up with flesh-and-blood husbands—and little enough of that too, sometimes; and you will have to put up with flesh-and-blood wives. (THE DEVIL *looks dubious.* THE STATUE *makes a wry face*) I see you don't like that, any of you; but it's true, for all that; so if you don't like it you can lump it.

DON JUAN My dear lady, you have put my whole case against romance into a few sentences. That is just why I turned my back on the romantic man with the artist nature, as he called his infatuation. I thanked him for teaching me to use my eyes and ears; but I told him that his beauty worshipping and happiness hunting and woman idealizing was not worth a dump as a philosophy of life; so he called me Philistine and went his way.

ANA It seems that Woman taught you something, too, with all her defects.

DON JUAN She did more: she interpreted all the other teaching for me. Ah, my friends, when the barriers were down for the first time, what an astounding illumination! I had been prepared for infatuation, for intoxication, for all the illusions of love's young dream; and lo! never was my perception clearer, nor my criticism more ruthless. The most jealous rival of my mistress never saw every blemish in her more keenly than I. I was not duped: I took her without chloroform.

ANA But you did take her.

DON JUAN That was the revelation. Up to that moment I had never lost the sense of being my own master; never consciously taken a single step until my reason had examined and approved it. I had come to believe that I was a purely rational creature: a thinker! I said, with the foolish philosopher, "I think; therefore I am." [20] It was Woman who taught me to say "I am; therefore I think." And also "I would think more; therefore I must be more."

THE STATUE This is extremely abstract and metaphysical, Juan. If you would stick to the concrete, and put your discoveries in the form of entertaining anecdotes about your adventures with women, your conversation would be easier to follow.

DON JUAN Bah! what need I add? Do you not understand that when I stood face to face with Woman, every fibre in my clear critical brain warned me to spare her and save myself. My morals said No. My conscience said No. My chivalry and pity for her said No. My prudent regard for myself said No. My ear, practiced on a thousand songs and symphonies; my eye, exercised on a thousand paintings; tore her voice, her features, her color to shreds. I caught all those tell-tale resemblances to her father and mother by which I knew what she would be like in thirty years' time. I noted the gleam of gold from a dead tooth in the laughing mouth: I made curious observations of the strange odors of the chemistry of the nerves. The visions of my romantic reveries, in which I had trod the plains of heaven with a deathless, ageless creature of coral and ivory, deserted me in that supreme hour. I remembered them and desperately strove to recover their illusion; but they now seemed the emptiest of inventions: my judgment was not to be corrupted: my brain still said No on every issue. And whilst I was in the act of framing my excuse to the lady, Life seized me and threw me into her arms as a sailor throws a scrap of fish into the mouth of a seabird.

THE STATUE You might as well have gone without thinking such a lot about it, Juan. You are like all the clever men: you have more brains than is good for you.

THE DEVIL And were you not the happier for the experience, Señor Don Juan?

DON JUAN The happier, no: the wiser, yes. That moment introduced me for the first time to myself, and, through myself, to the world. I saw then how useless it is to attempt to impose conditions on the irresistible force of Life; to preach prudence, careful selection, virtue, honor, chastity—

ANA Don Juan: a word against chastity is an insult to me.

DON JUAN I say nothing against your chastity, Señora, since it took the form of a husband and twelve children. What more could you have done had you been the most abandoned of women?

ANA I could have had twelve husbands and no children: that's what I could have done, Juan. And let me tell you that that would have made all the difference to the earth which I replenished.

THE STATUE Bravo Ana! Juan: you are floored, quelled, annihilated.

DON JUAN No; for though that difference is the true essential difference—Doña Ana has, I admit, gone straight to the real point—yet it is not a difference of love or chastity, or even constancy; for twelve children by twelve different husbands would have replenished the earth perhaps more effectively. Suppose my friend Ottavio had died when you were thirty, you would never have remained a widow: you were too beautiful. Suppose the successor of Ottavio had died when you were forty, you would still have been irresistible; and a woman who marries twice marries three times if she becomes free to do so. Twelve lawful children borne by one highly respectable lady to three different fathers is not impossible nor condemned by public opinion. That such a lady may be more law abiding than the poor girl whom we used to spurn into the gutter for bearing one unlawful infant is no doubt true; but dare you say she is less self-indulgent?

ANA She is more virtuous: that is enough for me.

DON JUAN In that case, what is virtue but the Trade Unionism of the married? Let us face the facts, dear Ana. The Life Force respects marriage only because marriage is a contrivance of its own to secure the greatest number of children and the closest care of them. For honor, chastity, and all the rest of your moral figments it cares not a rap. Marriage is the most licentious of human institutions—

ANA Juan!

THE STATUE (*Protesting*) Really!—

DON JUAN (*Determinedly*) I say the most licentious of human institutions: that is the secret of its popularity. And a woman seeking a husband is the most unscrupulous of all the beasts of prey. The confusion of marriage with morality has done more to destroy the conscience of the human race than any other single error. Come, Ana! do not look shocked: you know better than any of us that marriage is a mantrap baited with simulated accomplishments and delusive idealizations. When your sainted mother, by dint of scoldings and punishments, forced you to learn how to play half a dozen pieces on the spinet—which she hated as much as you did—had she any other purpose than to delude your suitors into the belief that your husband would have in his home an angel who would fill it with melody, or at least play him to sleep after dinner? You married my friend Ottavio: well, did you ever open the spinet from the hour when the Church united him to you?

ANA You are a fool, Juan. A young married woman has something else to do than sit at the spinet without any support for her back; so she gets out of the habit of playing.

DON JUAN Not if she loves music. No: believe me, she only throws away the bait when the bird is in the net.

ANA (*Bitterly*) And men, I suppose, never throw off

[20] Descartes, "*Je pense, donc je suis.*"

the mask when their bird is in the net. The husband never becomes negligent, selfish, brutal—oh, never!

DON JUAN What do these recriminations prove, Ana? Only that the hero is as gross an imposture as the heroine.

ANA It is all nonsense: most marriages are perfectly comfortable.

DON JUAN "Perfectly" is a strong expression, Ana. What you mean is that sensible people make the best of one another. Send me to the galleys and chain me to the felon whose number happens to be next before mine; and I must accept the inevitable and make the best of the companionship. Many such companionships, they tell me, are touchingly affectionate; and most are at least tolerably friendly. But that does not make a chain a desirable ornament nor the galleys an abode of bliss. Those who talk most about the blessings of marriage and the constancy of its vows are the very people who declare that if the chain were broken and the prisoners left free to choose, the whole social fabric would fly asunder. You cannot have the argument both ways. If the prisoner is happy, why lock him in? If he is not, why pretend that he is?

ANA At all events, let me take an old woman's privilege again, and tell you flatly that marriage peoples the world and debauchery does not.

DON JUAN How if a time come when this shall cease to be true? Do you not know that where there is a will there is a way? that whatever Man really wishes to do he will finally discover a means of doing? Well, you have done your best, you virtuous ladies, and others of your way of thinking, to bend Man's mind wholly towards honorable love as the highest good, and to understand by honorable love, romance and beauty and happiness in the possession of beautiful, refined, delicate, affectionate women. You have taught women to value their own youth, health, shapeliness, and refinement above all things. Well, what place have squalling babies and household cares in this exquisite paradise of the sense and emotions? Is it not the inevitable end of it all that the human will shall say to the human brain: Invent me a means by which I can have love, beauty, romance, emotion, passion, without their wretched penalties, their expenses, their worries, their trials, their illnesses and agonies and risks of death, their retinue of servants and nurses and doctors and schoolmasters.

THE DEVIL All this, Señor Don Juan, is realized here in my realm.

DON JUAN Yes, at the cost of death. Man will not take it at that price: he demands the romantic delights of your hell whilst he is still on earth. Well, the means will be found: the brain will not fail when the will is in earnest. The day is coming when great nations will find their numbers dwindling from census to census; when the six roomed villa will rise in price above the family mansion; when the viciously reckless poor and the stupidly pious rich will delay the extinction of the race only by degrading it; whilst the boldly prudent, the thriftily selfish and ambitious, the imaginative and poetic, the lovers of money and solid comfort, the worshippers of success, of art, and of love, will all oppose to the Force of Life the device of sterility.

THE STATUE That is all very eloquent, my young friend; but if you had lived to Ana's age, or even to mine, you would have learned that the people who get rid of the fear of poverty and children and all the other family troubles, and devote themselves to having a good time of it, only leave their minds free for the fear of old age and ugliness and impotence and death. The childless laborer is more tormented by his wife's idleness and her constant demands for amusement and distraction than he could be by twenty children; and his wife is more wretched than he. I have had my share of vanity; for as a young man I was admired by women; and as a statue I am praised by art critics. But I confess that had I found nothing to do in the world but wallow in these delights I should have cut my throat. When I married Ana's mother—or perhaps, to be strictly correct, I should rather say when I at last gave in and allowed Ana's mother to marry me—I knew that I was planting thorns in my pillow, and that marriage for me, a swaggering young officer thitherto unvanquished, meant defeat and capture.

ANA (*Scandalized*) Father!

THE STATUE I am sorry to shock you, my love; but since Juan has stripped every rag of decency from the discussion I may as well tell the frozen truth.

ANA Hmf! I suppose I was one of the thorns.

THE STATUE By no means: you were often a rose. You see, your mother had most of the trouble you gave.

DON JUAN Then may I ask, Commander, why you have left Heaven to come here and wallow, as you express it, in sentimental beatitudes which you confess would once have driven you to cut your throat?

THE STATUE (*Struck by this*) Egad, that's true.

THE DEVIL (*Alarmed*) What! You are going back from your word! (*To* DON JUAN) And all your philosophizing has been nothing but a mask for proselytizing! (*To* THE STATUE) Have you forgotten already the hideous dulness from which I am offering you a refuge here? (*To* DON JUAN) And does your demonstration of the approaching sterilization and extinction of mankind lead to anything better than making the most of those pleasures of art and love which you yourself admit refined you, elevated you, developed you?

DON JUAN I never demonstrated the extinction of mankind. Life cannot will its own extinction either in its blind amorphous state or in any of the forms into which it has organized itself. I had not finished when His Excellency interrupted me.

THE STATUE I begin to doubt whether you ever will finish, my friend. You are extremely fond of hearing yourself talk.

DON JUAN True; but since you have endured so much, you may as well endure to the end. Long before this sterilization which I described becomes more than a clearly foreseen possibility, the reaction will begin. The great central purpose of breeding the race: ay, breeding it to heights now deemed superhuman: that purpose which is now hidden in a mephitic cloud of love and romance and prudery and fastidiousness, will break through into clear sunlight as a purpose no longer to be confused with the gratification of personal fancies, the impossible realization of boys' and girls' dreams of bliss, or the need of older people for companionship or money. The plain-spoken marriage services of the vernacular Churches will no longer be abbreviated and half suppressed as indelicate. The sober decency, earnestness, and authority of their declaration of the real purpose of marriage will be honored and accepted, whilst their romantic vowings and pledgings and until-death-do-us-partings and the like will be expunged as unbearable frivolities. Do my sex the justice to admit, Señora, that we have always recognized that the sex relation is not a personal or friendly relation at all.

ANA Not a personal or friendly relation! What relation is more personal? more sacred? more holy?

DON JUAN Sacred and holy, if you like, Ana, but not personally friendly. Your relation to God is sacred and holy: dare you call it personally friendly? In the sex relation the universal creative energy, of which the parties are both the helpless agents, over-rides and sweeps away all personal consideration, and dispenses with all personal relations. The pair may be utter strangers to one another, speaking different languages, differing in race and color, in age and disposition, with no bond between them but a possibility of that fecundity for the sake of which the Life Force throws them into one another's arms at the exchange of a glance. Do we not recognize this by allowing marriages to be made by parents without consulting the woman? Have you not often expressed your disgust at the immorality of the English nation, in which women and men of noble birth become acquainted and court each other like peasants? And how much does even the peasant know of his bride or she of him before he engages himself? Why, you would not make a man your lawyer or your family doctor on so slight an acquaintance as you would fall in love with and marry him!

ANA Yes, Juan: we know the libertine's philosophy. Always ignore the consequences to the woman.

DON JUAN The consequences, yes: they justify her fierce grip of the man. But surely you do not call that attachment a sentimental one. As well call the policeman's attachment to his prisoner a love relation.

ANA You see you have to confess that marriage is necessary, though, according to you, love is the slightest of all human relations.

DON JUAN How do you know that it is not the greatest of all human relations? far too great to be a personal matter. Could your father have served his country if he had refused to kill any enemy of Spain unless he personally hated him? Can a woman serve her country if she refuses to marry any man she does not personally love? You know it is not so: the woman of noble birth marries as the man of noble birth fights, on political and family grounds, not on personal ones.

THE STATUE (*Impressed*) A very clever point that, Juan: I must think it over. You are really full of ideas. How did you come to think of this one?

DON JUAN I learnt it by experience. When I was on earth, and made those proposals to ladies which, though universally condemned, have made me so interesting a hero of legend, I was not infrequently met in some such way as this. The lady would say that she would countenance my advances, provided they were honorable. On inquiring what that proviso meant, I found that it meant that I proposed to get possession of her property if she had any, or to undertake her support for life if she had not; that I desired her continual companionship, counsel, and conversation to the end of my days, and would take a most solemn oath to be always enraptured by them: above all, that I would turn my back on all other women for ever for her sake. I did not object to these conditions because they were exorbitant and inhuman: it was their extraordinary irrelevance that prostrated me. I invariably replied with perfect frankness that I had never dreamt of any of these things; that unless the lady's character and intellect were equal or superior to my own, her conversation must degrade and her counsel mislead me; that her constant companionship might, for all I knew, become intolerably tedious to me; that I could not answer for my feelings for a week in advance, much less to the end of my life; that to cut me off from all natural and unconstrained intercourse with half my fellow-creatures would narrow and warp me if I submitted to it, and, if not, would bring me under the curse of clandestinity; that, finally, my proposals to her were wholly unconnected with any of these matters, and were the outcome of a perfectly simple impulse of my manhood towards her womanhood.

ANA You mean that it was an immoral impulse.

DON JUAN Nature, my dear lady, is what you call immoral. I blush for it; but I cannot help it. Nature is a pandar, Time a wrecker, and Death a murderer. I have always preferred to stand up to those facts and build institutions on their recognition. You prefer to propitiate the three devils by proclaiming their chastity, their thrift, and their loving kindness; and to base your institutions on these flatteries. Is it any wonder that the institutions do not work smoothly?

THE STATUE What used the ladies to say, Juan?

DON JUAN Oh, come! Confidence for confidence. First tell me what you used to say to the ladies.

THE STATUE I! Oh, I swore that I would be faithful to the death; that I should die if they refused me; that no woman could ever be to me what she was—

ANA She! Who?

THE STATUE Whoever it happened to be at the time, my dear. I had certain things I always said. One of them was that even when I was eighty, one white hair of the woman I loved would make me tremble more than the thickest gold tress from the most beautiful young head. Another was that I could not bear the thought of anyone else being the mother of my children.

DON JUAN (*Revolted*) You old rascal!

THE STATUE (*Stoutly*) Not a bit; for I really believed it with all my soul at the moment, I had a heart: not like you. And it was this sincerity that made me successful.

DON JUAN Sincerity! To be fool enough to believe a ramping, stamping, thumping lie: that is what you call sincerity! To be so greedy for a woman that you deceive yourself in your eagerness to deceive her: sincerity, you call it!

THE STATUE Oh, damn your sophistries! I was a man in love, not a lawyer. And the women loved me for it, bless them!

DON JUAN They made you think so. What will you say when I tell you that though I played the lawyer so callously, they made me think so too? I also had my moments of infatuation in which I gushed nonsense and believed it. Sometimes the desire to give pleasure by saying beautiful things so rose in me on the flood of emotion that I said them recklessly. At other times I argued against myself with a devilish coldness that drew tears. But I found it just as hard to escape when I was cruel as when I was kind. When the lady's instinct was set on me, there was nothing for it but lifelong servitude or flight.

ANA You dare boast, before me and my father, that every woman found you irresistible.

DON JUAN Am I boasting? It seems to me that I cut the most pitiable of figures. Besides, I said "when the lady's instinct was set on me." It was not always so; and then, heavens! what transports of virtuous indignation! what overwhelming defiance to the dastardly seducer! what scenes of Imogen and Iachimo![21]

ANA I made no scenes. I simply called my father.

DON JUAN And he came, sword in hand, to vindicate outraged honor and morality by murdering me.

THE STATUE Murdering! What do you mean? Did I kill you or did you kill me?

DON JUAN Which of us was the better fencer?

THE STATUE I was.

DON JUAN Of course you were. And yet you, the hero of those scandalous adventures you have just been relating to us, you had the effrontery to pose as the avenger of outraged morality and condemn me to death! You would have slain me but for an accident.

THE STATUE I was expected to, Juan. That is how things were arranged on earth. I was not a social reformer; and I always did what it was customary for a gentleman to do.

DON JUAN That may account for your attacking me, but not for the revolting hypocrisy of your subsequent proceedings as a statue.

THE STATUE That all came of my going to Heaven.

THE DEVIL I still fail to see, Señor Don Juan, that these episodes in your earthly career and in that of the Señor Commander in any way discredit my view of life. Here, I repeat, you have all that you sought without anything that you shrank from.

DON JUAN On the contrary, here I have everything that disappointed me without anything that I have not already tried and found wanting. I tell you that as long as I can conceive something better than myself I cannot be easy unless I am striving to bring it into existence or clearing the way for it. That is the law of my life. That is the working within me of Life's incessant aspiration to higher organization, wider, deeper, intenser self-consciousness, and clearer self-understanding. It was the supremacy of this purpose that reduced love for me to the mere pleasure of a moment, art for me to the mere schooling of my faculties, religion for me to a mere excuse for laziness, since it had set up a God who looked at the world and saw that it was good, against the instinct in me that looked through my eyes at the world and saw that it could be improved. I tell you that in the pursuit of my own pleasure, my own health, my own fortune, I have never known happiness. It was not love for Woman that delivered me into her hands: it was fatigue, exhaustion. When I was a child, and bruised my head against a stone, I ran to the nearest woman and cried away my pain against her apron. When I grew up, and bruised my soul against the brutalities and stupidities with which I had to strive, I did again just what I had done as a child. I have enjoyed, too, my rests, my recuperations, my breathing times, my very prostrations after strife; but rather would I be dragged through all the circles of the foolish Italian's Inferno than through the pleasures of Europe. That is what has made this place of eternal pleasures so deadly to me. It is the absence of this instinct in you that makes you that strange monster called a Devil. It is the success with which you have diverted the attention of men from their real purpose, which in one degree or another is the same as mine, to yours, that has earned you the name of The Tempter. It is the fact that they are doing your will, or rather drifting with your want of will, instead of doing their own, that makes them the uncomfortable, false, restless, artificial, petulant, wretched creatures they are.

THE DEVIL (*Mortified*) Señor Don Juan: you are uncivil to my friends.

DON JUAN Pooh! why should I be civil to them or to you? In this Palace of Lies a truth or two will not hurt you. Your friends are all the dullest dogs I know. They are not beautiful: they are only decorated. They are not clean: they are only shaved and starched. They are not dignified: they are only fashionably dressed. They are not educated: they are only college passmen.[22] They are not religious: they are only pewrenters. They are not moral: they are only conventional. They are not virtuous: they are only cowardly. They are not even vicious: they are only "frail." They are not artistic: they are only lascivious. They are not prosperous: they are only rich. They are not loyal, they are only servile; not dutiful, only sheepish; not public spirited, only patriotic; not courageous, only quarrelsome; not

[21] In Shakespeare's *Cymbeline,* Iachimo wagers Posthumus that he can seduce the latter's virtuous wife, the princess Imogen.

[22] Students content to make the "gentleman's C" in courses.

determined, only obstinate; not masterful, only domineering; not self-controlled, only obtuse; not self-respecting, only vain; not kind, only sentimental; not social, only gregarious; not considerate, only polite; not intelligent, only opinionated; not progressive, only factious; not imaginative, only superstitious; not just, only vindictive; not generous, only propitiatory; not disciplined, only cowed; and not truthful at all: liars every one of them, to the very backbone of their souls.

THE STATUE Your flow of words is simply amazing, Juan. How I wish I could have talked like that to my soldiers.

THE DEVIL It is mere talk, though. It has all been said before; but what change has it ever made? What notice has the world ever taken of it?

DON JUAN Yes, it is mere talk. But why is it mere talk? Because, my friend, beauty, purity, respectability, religion, morality, art, patriotism, bravery, and the rest are nothing but words which I or anyone else can turn inside out like a glove. Were they realities, you would have to plead guilty to my indictment; but fortunately for your self-respect, my diabolical friend, they are not realities. As you say, they are mere words, useful for duping barbarians into adopting civilization, or the civilized poor into submitting to be robbed and enslaved. That is the family secret of the governing caste; and if we who are of that caste aimed at more Life for the world instead of at more power and luxury for our miserable selves, that secret would make us great. Now, since I, being a nobleman, am in the secret too, think how tedious to me must be your unending cant about all these moralistic figments, and how squalidly disastrous your sacrifice of your lives to them! If you even believed in your moral game enough to play it fairly, it would be interesting to watch; but you don't: you cheat at every trick; and if your opponent outcheats you, you upset the table and try to murder him.

THE DEVIL On earth there may be some truth in this, because the people are uneducated and cannot appreciate my religion of love and beauty; but here—

DON JUAN Oh yes: I know. Here there is nothing but love and beauty. Ugh! it is like sitting for all eternity at the first act of a fashionable play, before the complications begin. Never in my worst moments of superstitious terror on earth did I dream that Hell was so horrible. I live, like a hairdresser, in the continual contemplation of beauty, toying with silken tresses. I breathe an atmosphere of sweetness, like a confectioner's shopboy. Commander: are there any beautiful women in Heaven?

THE STATUE None. Absolutely none. All dowdies. Not two pennorth of jewellery among a dozen of them. They might be men of fifty.

DON JUAN I am impatient to get there. Is the word beauty ever mentioned; and are there any artistic people?

THE STATUE I give you my word they won't admire a fine statue even when it walks past them.

DON JUAN I go.

THE DEVIL Don Juan: shall I be frank with you?

DON JUAN Were you not so before?

THE DEVIL As far as I went, yes. But I will now go further, and confess to you that men get tired of everything, of heaven no less than of hell; and that all history is nothing but a record of the oscillations of the world between these two extremes. An epoch is but a swing of the pendulum; and each generation thinks the world is progressing because it is always moving. But when you are as old as I am; when you have a thousand times wearied of heaven, like myself and the Commander, and a thousand times wearied of hell, as you are wearied now, you will no longer imagine that every swing from heaven to hell is an emancipation, every swing from hell to heaven an evolution. Where you now see reform, progress, fulfillment of upward tendency, continual ascent by Man on the stepping stones of his dead selves to higher things, you will see nothing but an infinite comedy of illusion. You will discover the profound truth of the saying of my friend Koheleth,[23] that there is nothing new under the sun. Vanitas vanitatum—

DON JUAN (*Out of all patience*) By Heaven, this is worse than your cant about love and beauty. Clever dolt that you are, is a man no better than a worm, or a dog than a wolf, because he gets tired of everything? Shall he give up eating because he destroys his appetite in the act of gratifying it? Is a field idle when it is fallow? Can the Commander expend his hellish energy here without accumulating heavenly energy for his next term of blessedness? Granted that the great Life Force has hit on the device of the clockmaker's pendulum, and uses the earth for its bob; that the history of each oscillation, which seems so novel to us the actors, is but the history of the last oscillation repeated; nay more, that in the unthinkable infinitude of time the sun throws off the earth and catches it again a thousand times as a circus rider throws up a ball, and that our agelong epochs are but the moments between the toss and the catch, has the colossal mechanism no purpose?

THE DEVIL None, my friend. You think, because you have a purpose, Nature must have one. You might as well expect it to have fingers and toes because you have them.

DON JUAN But I should not have them if they served no purpose. And I, my friend, am as much a part of Nature as my own finger is a part of me. If my finger is the organ by which I grasp the sword and the mandoline, my brain is the organ by which Nature strives to understand itself. My dog's brain serves only my dog's purposes; but my own brain labors at a knowledge which does nothing for me personally but make my body bitter to me and my decay and death a calamity. Were I not possessed with a purpose beyond my own I had better be a ploughman than a philosopher; for the ploughman lives as long as the philosopher, eats more, sleeps better, and rejoices in

[23] The name [Hebrew, 'preacher'] given Solomon as author of *Ecclesiastes*. See *Eccles*. 1:9 and 1:2 for the quoted phrases.

the wife of his bosom with less misgiving. This is because the philosopher is in the grip of the Life Force. This Life Force says to him "I have done a thousand wonderful things unconsciously by merely willing to live and following the line of least resistance: now I want to know myself and my destination, and choose my path; so I have made a special brain—a philosopher's brain—to grasp this knowledge for me as the husbandman's hand grasps the plough for me. "And this" says the Life Force to the philosopher "must thou strive to do for me until thou diest, when I will make another brain and another philosopher to carry on the work."

THE DEVIL What is the use of knowing?

DON JUAN Why, to be able to choose the line of greatest advantage instead of yielding in the direction of the least resistance. Does a ship sail to its destination no better than a log drifts nowhither? The philosopher is Nature's pilot. And there you have our difference: to be in Hell is to drift: to be in Heaven is to steer.

THE DEVIL On the rocks, most likely.

DON JUAN Pooh! which ship goes oftenest on the rocks or to the bottom? the drifting ship or the ship with a pilot on board?

THE DEVIL Well, well, go your way, Señor Don Juan. I prefer to be my own master and not the tool of any blundering universal force. I know that beauty is good to look at; that music is good to hear; that love is good to feel; and that they are all good to think about and talk about. I know that to be well exercised in these sensations, emotions, and studies is to be a refined and cultivated being. Whatever they may say of me in churches on earth, I know that it is universally admitted in good society that the Prince of Darkness is a gentleman; and that is enough for me. As to your Life Force, which you think irresistible, it is the most resistible thing in the world for a person of any character. But if you are naturally vulgar and credulous, as all reformers are, it will thrust you first into religion, where you will sprinkle water on babies to save their souls from me; then it will drive you from religion into science, where you will snatch the babies from the water sprinkling and inoculate them with disease to save them from catching it accidentally; then you will take to politics, where you will become the catspaw of corrupt functionaries and the henchman of ambitious humbugs; and the end will be despair and decrepitude, broken nerve and shattered hopes, vain regrets for that worst and silliest of wastes and sacrifices, the waste and sacrifice of the power of enjoyment: in a word, the punishment of the fool who pursues the better before he has secured the good.

DON JUAN But at least I shall not be bored. The service of the Life Force has that advantage, at all events. So fare you well, Señor Satan.

THE DEVIL (*Amiably*) Fare you well, Don Juan. I shall often think of our interesting chats about things in general. I wish you every happiness: Heaven, as I said before, suits some people. But if you should change your mind, do not forget that the gates are always open here to the repentant prodigal. If you feel at any time that warmth of heart, sincere unforced affection, innocent enjoyment, and warm, breathing, palpitating reality—

DON JUAN Why not say flesh and blood at once, though we have left those two greasy commonplaces behind us?

THE DEVIL (*Angrily*) You throw my friendly farewell back in my teeth, then, Don Juan?

DON JUAN By no means. But though there is much to be learnt from a cynical devil, I really cannot stand a sentimental one. Señor Commander: you know the way to the frontier of hell and heaven. Be good enough to direct me.

THE STATUE Oh, the frontier is only the difference between two ways of looking at things. Any road will take you across it if you really want to get there.

DON JUAN Good. (*Saluting* DOÑA ANA) Señora: your servant.

ANA But I am going with you.

DON JUAN I can find my own way to heaven, Ana; not yours (*He vanishes*)

ANA How annoying!

THE STATUE (*Calling after him*) Bon voyage, Juan! (*He wafts a final blast of his great rolling chords after him as a parting salute. A faint echo of the first ghostly melody comes back in acknowledgment*) Ah! there he goes. (*Puffing a long breath out through his lips*) Whew! How he does talk! They'll never stand it in heaven.

THE DEVIL (*Gloomily*) His going is a political defeat. I cannot keep these Life Worshippers: they all go. This is the greatest loss I have had since that Dutch painter went: a fellow who would paint a hag of 70 with as much enjoyment as a Venus of 20.

THE STATUE I remember: he came to heaven. Rembrandt.

THE DEVIL Ay, Rembrandt. There is something unnatural about these fellows. Do not listen to their gospel, Señor Commander: it is dangerous. Beware of the pursuit of the Superhuman: it leads to an indiscriminate contempt for the Human. To a man, horses and dogs and cats are mere species, outside the moral world. Well, to the Superman, men and women are a mere species too, also outside the moral world. This Don Juan was kind to women and courteous to men as your daughter here was kind to her pet cats and dogs; but such kindness is a denial of the exclusively human character of the soul.

THE STATUE And who the deuce is the Superman?

THE DEVIL Oh, the latest fashion among the Life Force fanatics. Did you not meet in Heaven, among the new arrivals, that German Polish madman? what was his name? Nietzsche?

THE STATUE Never heard of him.

THE DEVIL Well, he came here first, before he recovered his wits. I had some hopes of him; but he was a confirmed Life Force worshipper. It was he who raked up the Superman, who is as old as Prometheus; and the 20th century will run after this newest of the old crazes when it gets tired of the world, the flesh, and your humble servant.

THE STATUE Superman is a good cry; and a good cry is half the battle. I should like to see this Nietzsche.

THE DEVIL Unfortunately he met Wagner here, and had a quarrel with him.

THE STATUE Quite right, too. Mozart for me!

THE DEVIL Oh, it was not about music. Wagner once drifted into Life Force worship, and invented a Superman called Siegfried. But he came to his senses afterwards. So when they met here, Nietzsche denounced him as a renegade; and Wagner wrote a pamphlet to prove that Nietzsche was a Jew; and it ended in Nietzsche's going to Heaven in a huff. And a good riddance too. And now, my friend, let us hasten to my palace and celebrate your arrival with a grand musical service.

THE STATUE With pleasure: you're most kind.

THE DEVIL This way, Commander. We go down the old trap (*He places himself on the grave trap*)

THE STATUE Good. (*Reflectively*) All the same, the Superman is a fine conception. There is something statuesque about it. (*He places himself on the grave trap beside The Devil. It begins to descend slowly. Red glow from the abyss*) Ah, this reminds me of old times.

THE DEVIL And me also.

ANA Stop! (*The trap stops*)

THE DEVIL You, Señora, cannot come this way. You will have an apotheosis. But you will be at the palace before us.

ANA That is not what I stopped you for. Tell me: where can I find the Superman?

THE DEVIL He is not yet created, Señora.

THE STATUE And never will be, probably. Let us proceed: the red fire will make me sneeze. (*They descend*)

ANA Not yet created! Then my work is not yet done. (*Crossing herself devoutly*) I believe in the Life to Come. (*Crying to the universe*) A father! a father for the Superman!

(*She vanishes into the void; and again there is nothing: all existence seems suspended infinitely. Then, vaguely, there is a live human voice crying somewhere. One sees, with a shock, a mountain peak shewing faintly against a lighter background. The sky has returned from afar; and we suddenly remember where we were. The cry becomes distinct and urgent: it says* Automobile, Automobile. *The complete reality comes back with a rush: in a moment it is full morning in the Sierra; and the brigands are scrambling to their feet and making for the road as the* GOATHERD *runs down from the hill, warning them of the approach of another motor.* TANNER *and* MENDOZA *rise amazedly and stare at one another with scattered wits.* STRAKER *sits up to yawn for a moment before he gets on his feet, making it a point of honor not to shew any undue interest in the excitement of the bandits.* MENDOZA *gives a quick look to see that his followers are attending to the alarm; then exchanges a private word with* TANNER.)

MENDOZA Did you dream?

TANNER Damnably. Did you?

MENDOZA Yes. I forget what. You were in it.

TANNER So were you. Amazing!

MENDOZA I warned you. (*A shot is heard from the road*) Dolts! they will play with that gun. (*The brigands come running back scared*) Who fired that shot? (*To* DUVAL) Was it you?

DUVAL (*Breathless*) I have not shoot. Dey shoot first.

ANARCHIST I told you to begin by abolishing the State. Now we are all lost.

THE ROWDY SOCIAL-DEMOCRAT (*Stampeding across the amphitheatre*) Run, everybody.

MENDOZA (*Collaring him; throwing him on his back; and drawing a knife*) I stab the man who stirs. (*He blocks the way. The stampede is checked*) What has happened?

THE SULKY SOCIAL-DEMOCRAT A motor—

THE ANARCHIST Three men—

DUVAL *Deux femmes*—

MENDOZA Three men and two women! Why have you not brought them here? Are you afraid of them?

THE ROWDY ONE (*Getting up*) Thy've a hescort. Ow, de-ooh luts ook it, Mendowza.

THE SULKY ONE Two armored cars full o' soldiers at the 'ed o' the valley.

ANARCHIST The shot was fired in the air. It was a signal.

(STRAKER *whistles his favorite air, which falls on the ears of the brigands like a funeral march*)

TANNER It is not an escort, but an expedition to capture you. We were advised to wait for it; but I was in a hurry.

THE ROWDY ONE (*In an agony of apprehension*) And 'Ow my good Lord, 'ere we are, wytin' for 'em! Lut's tike to the mahntns.

MENDOZA Idiot, what do you know about the mountains? Are you a Spaniard? You would be given up by the first shepherd you met. Besides, we are already within range of their rifles.

THE ROWDY ONE Bat—

MENDOZA Silence. Leave this to me. (*To* TANNER) Comrade: you will not betray us.

STRAKER 'Oo are you callin' comrade?

MENDOZA Last night the advantage was with me. The robber of the poor was at the mercy of the robber of the rich. You offered your hand: I took it.

TANNER I bring no charge against you, comrade. We have spent a pleasant evening with you: that is all.

STRAKER I gev my 'and to nobody, see?

MENDOZA (*Turning on him impressively*) Young man: if I am tried, I shall plead guilty, and explain what drove me from England, home, and duty. Do you wish to have the respectable name of Straker dragged through the mud of a Spanish criminal court? The police will search me. They will find Louisa's portrait. It will be published in the illustrated papers. You blench. It will be your doing, remember.

STRAKER (*With baffled rage*) I don't care about the

court. It's 'avin' our name mixed up with yours that I object to, you blackmailin' swine, you.

MENDOZA Language unworthy of Louisa's brother! But no matter: you are muzzled: that is enough for us. (*He turns to face his own men, who back uneasily across the amphitheatre towards the cave to take refuge behind him, as a fresh party, muffled for motoring, comes from the road in riotous spirits.* ANN *who makes straight for* TANNER, *comes first; then* VIOLET, *helped over the rough ground by* HECTOR *holding her right hand and* RAMSDEN *her left.* MENDOZA *goes to his presidential block and seats himself calmly with his rank and file grouped behind him, and his Staff, consisting of* DUVAL *and the* ANARCHIST *on his right and the two* SOCIAL-DEMOCRATS *on his left, supporting him in flank.*)

ANN It's Jack!

TANNER Caught!

HECTOR Why, certainly it is. I said it was you, Tanner. We've just been stopped by a puncture: the road is full of nails.

VIOLET What are you doing here with all these men?

ANN Why did you leave us without a word of warning?

HECTOR I wawnt that bunch of roses, Miss Whitefield. (*To* TANNER) When we found you were gone, Miss Whitefield bet me a bunch of roses my car would not overtake yours before you reached Monte Carlo.

TANNER But this is not the road to Monte Carlo.

HECTOR No matter. Miss Whitefield tracked you at every stopping place: she is a regular Sherlock Holmes.

TANNER The Life Force! I am lost.

OCTAVIUS (*Bounding gaily down from the road into the amphitheatre, and coming between* TANNER *and* STRAKER) I am so glad you are safe, old chap. We were afraid you had been captured by brigands.

RAMSDEN (*Who has been staring at* MENDOZA) I seem to remember the face of your friend here. (MENDOZA *rises politely and advances with a smile between* ANN *and* RAMSDEN)

HECTOR Why, so do I.

OCTAVIUS I know you perfectly well, sir; but I can't think where I have met you.

MENDOZA (*To* VIOLET) Do you remember me, madam?

VIOLET Oh, quite well; but I am so stupid about names.

MENDOZA It was at the Savoy Hotel. (*To* HECTOR) You, sir, used to come with this lady (VIOLET) to lunch. (*To* OCTAVIUS) You, sir, often brought this lady (ANN) and her mother to dinner on your way to the Lyceum Theatre. (*To* RAMSDEN) You, sir, used to come to supper, with (*Dropping his voice to a confidential but perfectly audible whisper*) several different ladies.

RAMSDEN (*Angrily*) Well, what is that to you, pray?

OCTAVIUS Why, Violet, I thought you hardly knew one another before this trip, you and Malone!

VIOLET (*Vexed*) I suppose this person was the manager.

MENDOZA The waiter, madam. I have a grateful recollection of you all. I gathered from the bountiful way in which you treated me that you all enjoyed your visits very much.

VIOLET What impertinence! (*She turns her back on him, and goes up the hill with* HECTOR)

RAMSDEN That will do, my friend. You do not expect these ladies to treat you as an acquaintance, I suppose, because you have waited on them at table.

MENDOZA Pardon me: it was you who claimed my acquaintance. The ladies followed your example. However, this display of the unfortunate manners of your class closes the incident. For the future, you will please address me with the respect due to a stranger and fellow traveler. (*He turns haughtily away and resumes his presidential seat*)

TANNER There! I have found one man on my journey capable of reasonable conversation; and you all instinctively insult him. Even the New Man is as bad as any of you. Enry: you have behaved just like a miserable gentleman.

STRAKER Gentleman! Not me.

RAMSDEN Really, Tanner, this tone—

ANN Don't mind him, Granny: you ought to know him by this time. (*She takes his arm and coaxes him away to the hill to join* VIOLET *and* HECTOR. OCTAVIUS *follows her, dog-like*)

VIOLET (*Calling from the hill*) Here are the soldiers. They are getting out of their motors.

DUVAL (*Panicstricken*) Oh, *nom de Dieu!*

THE ANARCHIST Fools: the State is about to crush you because you spared it at the prompting of the political hangers-on of the bourgeoisie.

THE SULKY SOCIAL-DEMOCRAT (*Argumentative to the last*) On the contrary, only by capturing the State machine—

THE ANARCHIST It is going to capture you.

THE ROWDY SOCIAL-DEMOCRAT (*His anguish culminating*) Ow, chack it. Wot are we 'ere for? Wot are we wytin' for?

MENDOZA (*Between his teeth*) Go on. Talk politics, you idiots: nothing sounds more respectable. Keep it up, I tell you.

(*The soldiers line the road, commanding the amphitheatre with their rifles. The brigands, struggling with an overwhelming impulse to hide behind one another, look as unconcerned as they can.* MENDOZA *rises superbly, with undaunted front.* THE OFFICER IN COMMAND *steps down from the road into the amphitheatre; looks hard at the brigands; and then inquiringly at* TANNER)

THE OFFICER Who are these men, Señor Ingles?

TANNER My escort.

(MENDOZA, *with a Mephistophelean smile, bows profoundly. An irrepressible grin runs from face to face among the brigands. They touch their hats, except the* ANARCHIST, *who defies the State with folded arms*)

# Act Four

*The garden of a villa in Granada. Whoever wishes to know what it is like must go to Granada to see. One may prosaically specify a group of hills dotted with villas, the Alhambra on the top of one of the hills, and a considerable town in the valley, approached by dusty white roads in which the children, no matter what they are doing or thinking about, automatically whine for halfpence and reach out little clutching brown palms for them; but there is nothing in this description except the Alhambra, the begging, and the color of the roads, that does not fit Surrey as well as Spain. The difference is that the Surrey hills are comparatively small and ugly, and should properly be called the Surrey Protuberances; but these Spanish hills are of mountain stock: the amenity which conceals their size does not compromise their dignity.*

*This particular garden is on a hill opposite the Alhambra; and the villa is as expensive and pretentious as a villa must be if it is to be let furnished by the week to opulent American and English visitors. If we stand on the lawn at the foot of the garden and look uphill, our horizon is the stone balustrade of a flagged platform on the edge of infinite space at the top of the hill. Between us and this platform is a flower garden with a circular basin and fountain in the centre, surrounded by geometrical flower beds, gravel paths, and clipped yew trees in the genteelest order. The garden is higher than our lawn; so we reach it by a few steps in the middle of its embankment. The platform is higher again than the garden, from which we mount a couple more steps to look over the balustrade at a fine view of the town up the valley and of the hills that stretch away beyond it to where, in the remotest distance, they become mountains. On our left is the villa, accessible by steps from the left hand corner of the garden. Returning from the platform through the garden and down again to the lawn (a movement which leaves the villa behind us on our right) we find evidence of literary interests on the part of the tenants in the fact that there is no tennis net nor set of croquet hoops, but, on our left, a little iron garden table with books on it, mostly yellow-backed, and a chair beside it. A chair on the right has also a couple of open books upon it. There are no newspapers, a circumstance which, with the absence of games, might lead an intelligent spectator to the most far reaching conclusions as to the sort of people who live in the villa. Such speculations are checked, however, on this delightfully fine afternoon, by the appearance at a little gate in a paling on our left, of* HENRY STRAKER *in his professional costume. He opens the gate for an elderly gentleman, and follows him on to the lawn.*

*This elderly gentleman defies the Spanish sun in a black frock coat, tall silk hat, trousers in which narrow stripes of dark grey and lilac blend into a highly respectable color, and a black necktie tied into a bow over spotless linen. Probably therefore a man whose social position needs constant and scrupulous affirmation without regard to climate: one who would dress thus for the middle of the Sahara or the top of Mont Blanc. And since he has not the stamp of the class which accepts as its life-mission the advertising and maintenance of first rate tailoring and millinery, he looks vulgar in his finery, though in a working dress of any kind he would look dignified enough. He is a bullet-cheeked man with a red complexion, stubbly hair, smallish eyes, a hard mouth that folds down at the corners, and a dogged chin. The looseness of skin that comes with age has attacked his throat and the laps of his cheeks; but he is still hard as an apple above the mouth; so that the upper half of his face looks younger than the lower. He has the self-confidence of one who has made money, and something of the truculence of one who has made it in a brutalizing struggle, his civility having under it a perceptible menace that he has other methods in reserve if necessary. Withal, a man to be rather pitied when he is not to be feared; for there is something pathetic about him at times, as if the huge commercial machine which has worked him into his frock coat had allowed him very little of his own way and left his affections hungry and baffled. At the first word that falls from him it is clear that he is an Irishman whose native intonation has clung to him through many changes of place and rank. One can only guess that the original material of his speech was perhaps the surly Kerry brogue; but the degradation of speech that occurs in London, Glasgow, Dublin, and big cities generally has been at work on it so long that nobody but an arrant cockney would dream of calling it a brogue now; for its music is almost gone, though its surliness is still perceptible.* STRAKER, *being a very obvious cockney, inspires him with implacable contempt, as a stupid Englishman who cannot even speak his own language properly.* STRAKER, *on the other hand, regards the old gentleman's accent as a joke thoughtfully provided by Providence expressly for the amusement of the British race, and treats him normally with the indulgence due to an inferior and unlucky species, but occasionally with indignant alarm when the old gentleman shews signs of intending his Irish nonsense to be taken seriously.*

STRAKER I'll go tell the young lady. She said you'd prefer to stay here. (*He turns to go up through the garden to the villa*)

THE IRISHMAN (*Who has been looking round him with lively curiosity*) The young lady? That's Miss Violet, eh?

STRAKER (*Stopping on the steps with sudden suspicion*) Well, you know, don't you?

THE IRISHMAN Do I?

STRAKER (*His temper rising*) Well, do you or don't you?

THE IRISHMAN What business is that of yours?

(STRAKER, *now highly indignant, comes back from the steps and confronts the visitor*)

STRAKER I'll tell you what business it is of mine. Miss Robinson—

THE IRISHMAN (*Interrupting*) Oh, her name is Robinson, is it? Thank you.

STRAKER Why, you don't know even her name?

THE IRISHMAN Yes I do, now that you've told me.

STRAKER (*After a moment of stupefaction at the old man's readiness in repartee*) Look here: what do you mean by gittin' into my car and lettin' me bring you here if you're not the person I took that note to?

THE IRISHMAN Who else did you take it to, pray?

STRAKER I took it to Mr Ector Malone, at Miss Robinson's request, see? Miss Robinson is not my principal: I took it to oblige her. I know Mr Malone; and he ain't you, not by a long chalk. At the hotel they told me that your name is Ector Malone—

MALONE Hector Malone.

STRAKER (*With calm superiority*) Hector in your own country: that's what comes o' livin' in provincial places like Ireland and America. Over here you're Ector: if you 'aven't noticed it before you soon will.

(*The growing strain of the conversation is here relieved by* VIOLET, *who has sallied from the villa and through the garden to the steps, which she now descends, coming very opportunely between* MALONE *and* STRAKER)

VIOLET (*To* STRAKER) Did you take my message?

STRAKER Yes, miss. I took it to the hotel and sent it up, expecting to see young Mr Malone. Then out walks this gent, and says it's all right and he'll come with me. So as the hotel people said he was Mr Ector Malone, I fetched him. And now he goes back on what he said. But if he isn't the gentleman you meant, say the word: it's easy enough to fetch him back again.

MALONE I should esteem it a great favor if I might have a short conversation with you, madam. I am Hector's father, as this bright Britisher would have guessed in the course of another hour or so.

STRAKER (*Coolly defiant*) No, not in another year or so. When we've 'ad you as long to polish up as we've 'ad 'im, perhaps you'll begin to look a little bit up to 'is mark. At present you fall a long way short. You've got too many aitches, for one thing. (*To* VIOLET, *amiably*) All right, Miss: you want to talk to him: I shan't intrude. (*He nods affably to* MALONE *and goes out through the little gate in the paling*)

VIOLET (*Very civilly*) I am so sorry, Mr Malone, if that man has been rude to you. But what can we do? He is our chauffeur.

MALONE Your what?

VIOLET The driver of our automobile. He can drive a motor car at seventy miles an hour, and mend it when it breaks down. We are dependent on our motor cars; and our motor cars are dependent on him; so of course we are dependent on him.

MALONE I've noticed, madam, that every thousand dollars an Englishman gets seems to add one to the number of people he's dependent on. However, you needn't apologize for your man: I made him talk on purpose. By doing so I learnt that you're stayin' here in Grannida with a party of English, including my son Hector.

VIOLET (*Conversationally*) Yes. We intended to go to Nice; but we had to follow a rather eccentric member of our party who started first and came here. Won't you sit down? (*She clears the nearest chair of the two books on it*)

MALONE (*Impressed by this attention*) Thank you. (*He sits down, examining her curiously as she goes to the iron table to put down the books. When she turns to him again, he says*) Miss Robinson, I believe?

VIOLET (*Sitting down*) Yes.

MALONE (*Taking a letter from his pocket*) Your note to Hector runs as follows (VIOLET *is unable to repress a start. He pauses quietly to take out and put on his spectacles, which have gold rims*) "Dearest: they have all gone to the Alhambra for the afternoon. I have shammed headache and have the garden all to myself. Jump into Jack's motor: Straker will rattle you here in a jiffy. Quick, quick, quick. Your loving Violet." (*He looks at her; but by this time she has recovered herself, and meets his spectacles with perfect composure. He continues slowly*) Now I don't know on hwat terms young people associate in English society; but in America that note would be considered to imply a very considerable degree of affectionate intimacy between the parties.

VIOLET Yes: I know your son very well, Mr Malone. Have you any objection?

MALONE (*Somewhat taken aback*) No, no objection exactly. Provided it is understood that my son is altogether dependent on me, and that I have to be consulted in any important step he may propose to take.

VIOLET I am sure you would not be unreasonable with him, Mr Malone.

MALONE I hope not, Miss Robinson; but at your age you might think many things unreasonable that don't seem so to me.

VIOLET (*With a little shrug*) Oh, well, I suppose there's no use our playing at cross purposes, Mr Malone. Hector wants to marry me.

MALONE I inferred from your note that he might. Well, Miss Robinson, he is his own master; but if he marries you he shall not have a rap from me. (*He takes off his spectacles and pockets them with the note*)

VIOLET (*With some severity*) That is not very complimentary to me, Mr Malone.

MALONE I say nothing against you, Miss Robinson: I daresay you are an amiable and excellent young lady. But I have other views for Hector.

VIOLET Hector may not have other views for himself, Mr Malone.

MALONE Possibly not. Then he does without me: that's

all. I daresay you are prepared for that. When a young lady writes to a young man to come to her quick, quick, quick, money seems nothing and love seems everything.

VIOLET (*Sharply*) I beg your pardon, Mr Malone: I do not think anything so foolish. Hector must have money.

MALONE (*Staggered*) Oh, very well, very well. No doubt he can work for it.

VIOLET What is the use of having money if you have to work for it? (*She rises impatiently*) It's all nonsense, Mr Malone: you must enable your son to keep up his position. It is his right.

MALONE (*Grimly*) I should not advise you to marry him on the strength of that right, Miss Robinson.

(VIOLET, *who has almost lost her temper, controls herself with an effort; unclenches her fingers; and resumes her seat with studied tranquillity and reasonableness*)

VIOLET What objection have you to me, pray? My social position is as good as Hector's, to say the least. He admits it.

MALONE (*Shrewdly*) You tell him so from time to time, eh? Hector's social position in England, Miss Robinson, is just what I choose to buy for him. I have made him a fair offer. Let him pick out the most historic house, castle, or abbey that England contains. The very day he tells me he wants it for a wife worthy of its traditions, I buy it for him, and give him the means of keeping it up.

VIOLET What do you mean by a wife worthy of its traditions? Cannot any well bred woman keep such a house for him?

MALONE No: she must be born to it.

VIOLET Hector was not born to it, was he?

MALONE His granmother was a barefooted Irish girl that nursed me by a turf fire. Let him marry another such, and I will not stint her marriage portion. Let him raise himself socially with my money or raise somebody else: so long as there is a social profit somewhere, I'll regard my expenditure as justified. But there must be a profit for someone. A marriage with you would leave things just where they are.

VIOLET Many of my relations would object very much to my marrying the grandson of a common woman, Mr Malone. That may be prejudice; but so is your desire to have him marry a title prejudice.

MALONE (*Rising, and approaching her with a scrutiny in which there is a good deal of reluctant respect*) You seem a pretty straightforward downright sort of a young woman.

VIOLET I do not see why I should be made miserably poor because I cannot make profits for you. Why do you want to make Hector unhappy?

MALONE He will get over it all right enough. Men thrive better on disappointments in love than on disappointments in money. I daresay you think that sordid; but I know what I'm talking about. Me father died of starvation in Ireland in the black 47. Maybe you've heard of it.

VIOLET The Famine?

MALONE (*With smouldering passion*) No, the starvation. When a country is full o' food, and exporting it, there can be no famine. Me father was starved dead; and I was starved out to America in me mother's arms. English rule drove me and mine out of Ireland. Well, you can keep Ireland. Me and me like are coming back to buy England; and we'll buy the best of it. I want no middle class properties and no middle class women for Hector. That's straightforward, isn't it, like yourself?

VIOLET (*Icily pitying his sentimentality*) Really, Mr Malone, I am astonished to hear a man of your age and good sense talking in that romantic way. Do you suppose English noblemen will sell their places to you for the asking?

MALONE I have the refusal of two of the oldest family mansions in England. One historic owner can't afford to keep all the rooms dusted: the other can't afford the death duties. What do you say now?

VIOLET Of course it is very scandalous; but surely you know that the Government will sooner or later put a stop to all these Socialistic attacks on property.

MALONE (*Grinning*) D'y'think they'll be able to get that done before I buy the house—or rather the abbey? They're both abbeys.

VIOLET (*Putting that aside rather impatiently*) Oh, well, let us talk sense, Mr Malone. You must feel that we haven't been talking sense so far.

MALONE I can't say I do. I mean all I say.

VIOLET Then you don't know Hector as I do. He is romantic and faddy—he gets it from you, I fancy—and he wants a certain sort of wife to take care of him. Not a faddy sort of person, you know.

MALONE Somebody like you, perhaps?

VIOLET (*Quietly*) Well, yes. But you cannot very well ask me to undertake this with absolutely no means of keeping up his position.

MALONE (*Alarmed*) Stop a bit, stop a bit. Where are we getting to? I'm not aware that I'm asking you to undertake anything.

VIOLET Of course, Mr Malone, you can make it very difficult for me to speak to you if you choose to misunderstand me.

MALONE (*Half bewildered*) I don't wish to take any unfair advantage; but we seem to have got off the straight track somehow.

(STRAKER, *with the air of a man who has been making haste, opens the little gate, and admits* HECTOR, *who, snorting with indignation, comes upon the lawn, and is making for his father when* VIOLET, *greatly dismayed, springs up and intercepts him.* STRAKER *does not wait; at least he does not remain visibly within earshot*)

VIOLET Oh, how unlucky! Now please, Hector, say nothing. Go away until I have finished speaking to your father.

HECTOR (*Inexorably*) No, Violet: I mean to have this thing out, right away. (*He puts her aside; passes her by; and faces his father, whose cheeks darken as his Irish blood begins to simmer*) Dad: you've not played this hand straight.

MALONE Hwat d'y' mean?

HECTOR You've opened a letter addressed to me. You've impersonated me and stolen a march on this lady. That's disawnerable.

MALONE (*Threateningly*) Now you take care what you're saying, Hector. Take care, I tell you.

HECTOR I have taken care. I am taking care. I'm taking care of my honor and my position in English society.

MALONE (*Hotly*) Your position has been got by my money: do you know that?

HECTOR Well, you've just spoiled it all by opening that letter. A letter from an English lady, not addressed to you—a cawnfidential letter! a dullicate letter! a private letter! opened by my father! That's a sort of thing a man can't struggle against in England. The sooner we go back together the better. (*He appeals mutely to the heavens to witness the shame and anguish of two outcasts*)

VIOLET (*Snubbing him with an instinctive dislike for scene-making*) Don't be unreasonable, Hector. It was quite natural for Mr Malone to open my letter: his name was on the envelope.

MALONE There! You've no common sense, Hector. I thank you, Miss Robinson.

HECTOR I thank you, too. It's very kind of you. My father knows no better.

MALONE (*Furiously clenching his fists*) Hector—

HECTOR (*With undaunted moral force*) Oh, it's no use hectoring me. A private letter's a private letter, dad: you can't get over that.

MALONE (*Raising his voice*) I won't be talked back to by you, d'y'hear?

VIOLET Ssh! please, please. Here they all come.

(*Father and son, checked, glare mutely at one another as* TANNER *comes in through the little gate with* RAMSDEN, *followed by* OCTAVIUS *and* ANN)

VIOLET Back already!

TANNER The Alhambra is not open this afternoon.

VIOLET What a sell!

(TANNER *passes on, and presently finds himself between* HECTOR *and a strange elder, both apparently on the verge of personal combat. He looks from one to the other for an explanation. They sulkily avoid his eye, and nurse their wrath in silence*)

RAMSDEN Is it wise for you to be out in the sunshine with such a headache, Violet?

TANNER Have you recovered too, Malone?

VIOLET Oh, I forgot. We have not all met before. Mr Malone: won't you introduce your father?

HECTOR (*With Roman firmness*) No, I will not. He is no father of mine.

MALONE (*Very angry*) You disown your dad before your English friends, do you?

VIOLET Oh, please don't make a scene.

(ANN *and* OCTAVIUS, *lingering near the gate, exchange an astonished glance, and discreetly withdraw up the steps to the garden, where they can enjoy the disturbance without intruding. On their way to the steps* ANN *sends a little grimace of mute sympathy to* VIOLET, *who is standing with her back to the little table, looking on in helpless annoyance as her husband soars to higher and higher moral eminence without the least regard to the old man's millions*)

HECTOR I'm very sorry, Miss Rawbnsn; but I'm contending for a principle. I am a son, and, I hope, a dutiful one; but before everything I'm a Mahn!!! And when dad treats my private letters as his own, and takes it on himself to say that I shan't marry you if I am happy and fortunate enough to gain your consent, then I just snap my fingers and go my own way.

TANNER Marry Violet!

RAMSDEN Are you in your senses?

TANNER Do you forget what we told you?

HECTOR (*Recklessly*) I don't care what you told me.

RAMSDEN (*Scandalized*) Tut tut, sir! Monstrous! (*He flings away towards the gate, his elbows quivering with indignation*)

TANNER Another madman! These men in love should be locked up. (*He gives* HECTOR *up as hopeless, and turns away towards the garden; but* MALONE, *taking offence in a new direction, follows him and compels him, by the aggressiveness of his tone, to stop*)

MALONE I don't understand this. Is Hector not good enough for this lady, pray?

TANNER My dear sir, the lady is married already. Hector knows it; and yet he persists in his infatuation. Take him home and lock him up.

MALONE (*Bitterly*) So this is the highborn social tone I've spoilt be me ignorant, uncultivated behavior! Makin' love to a married woman! (*He comes angrily between* HECTOR *and* VIOLET, *and almost bawls into* HECTOR'S *left ear*) You've picked up that habit of the British aristocracy, have you?

HECTOR That's all right. Don't you trouble yourself about that. I'll answer for the morality of what I'm doing.

TANNER (*Coming forward to* HECTOR'S *right hand with flashing eyes*) Well said, Malone! You also see that mere marriage laws are not morality! I agree with you; but unfortunately Violet does not.

MALONE I take leave to doubt that, sir. (*Turning on* VIOLET) Let me tell you, Mrs Robinson, or whatever your right name is, you had no right to send that letter to my son when you were the wife of another man.

HECTOR (*Outraged*) This is the last straw. Dad: you have insulted my wife.

MALONE Your wife!

TANNER You the missing husband! Another moral impostor! (*He smites his brow, and collapses into* MALONE'S *chair*)

MALONE You've married without my consent!

RAMSDEN You have deliberately humbugged us, sir!

HECTOR Here: I have had just about enough of being badgered. Violet and I are married: that's the long and the short of it. Now what have you got to say—any of you?

MALONE I know what I've got to say. She's married a beggar.

HECTOR No: she's married a Worker. (*His American pronunciation imparts an overwhelming intensity to this simple and unpopular word*) I start to earn my own living this very afternoon.

MALONE (*Sneering angrily*) Yes: you're very plucky now, because you got your remittance from me yesterday or this morning, I reckon. Wait'l it's spent. You won't be so full of cheek then.

HECTOR (*Producing a letter from his pocketbook*) Here it is. (*Thrusting it on his father*) Now you just take your remittance and yourself out of my life. I'm done with remittances; and I'm done with you. I don't sell the privilege of insulting my wife for a thousand dollars.

MALONE (*Deeply wounded and full of concern*) Hector: you don't know what poverty is.

HECTOR (*Fervidly*) Well, I wawnt to know what it is. I wawnt'be a Mahn. Violet: you come along with me, to your own home: I'll see you through.

OCTAVIUS (*Jumping down from the garden to the lawn and running to* HECTOR'S *left hand*) I hope you'll shake hands with me before you go, Hector. I admire and respect you more than I can say. (*He is affected almost to tears as they shake hands*)

VIOLET (*Also almost in tears, but of vexation*) Oh, don't be an idiot, Tavy. Hector's about as fit to become a workman as you are.

TANNER (*Rising from his chair on the other side of* HECTOR) Never fear: there's no question of his becoming a navvy, Mrs Malone. (*To* HECTOR) There's really no difficulty about capital to start with. Treat me as a friend: draw on me.

OCTAVIUS (*Impulsively*) Or on me.

MALONE (*With fierce jealousy*) Who wants your durty money? Who should he draw on but his own father? (TANNER *and* OCTAVIUS *recoil,* OCTAVIUS *rather hurt,* TANNER *consoled by the solution of the money difficulty.* VIOLET *looks up hopefully*) Hector: don't be rash, my boy. I'm sorry for what I said: I never meant to insult Violet: I take it all back. She's just the wife you want: there!

HECTOR (*Patting him on the shoulder*) Well, that's all right, dad. Say no more: we're friends again. Only, I take no money from anybody.

MALONE (*Pleading abjectly*) Don't be hard on me, Hector. I'd rather you quarreled and took the money than made friends and starved. You don't know what the world is: I do.

HECTOR No, no, NO. That's fixed: that's not going to change. (*He passes his father inexorably by, and goes to* VIOLET) Come, Mrs Malone: you've got to move to the hotel with me, and take your proper place before the world.

VIOLET But I must go in, dear, and tell Davis to pack. Won't you go on and make them give you a room overlooking the garden for me? I'll join you in half an hour.

HECTOR Very well. You'll dine with us, Dad, won't you?

MALONE (*Eager to conciliate him*) Yes, yes.

HECTOR See you all later. (*He waves his hand to* ANN, *who has now been joined by* TANNER, OCTAVIUS, *and* RAMSDEN *in the garden, and goes out through the little gate, leaving his father and* VIOLET *together on the lawn*)

MALONE You'll try to bring him to his senses, Violet: I know you will.

VIOLET I had no idea he could be so headstrong. If he goes on like that, what can I do?

MALONE Don't be discurridged: domestic pressure may be slow; but it's sure. You'll wear him down. Promise me you will.

VIOLET I will do my best. Of course I think it's the greatest nonsense deliberately making us poor like that.

MALONE Of course it is.

VIOLET (*After a moment's reflection*) You had better give me the remittance. He will want it for his hotel bill. I'll see whether I can induce him to accept it. Not now, of course, but presently.

MALONE (*Eagerly*) Yes, yes, yes: that's just the thing. (*He hands her the thousand dollar bill, and adds cunningly*) Y'understand that this is only a bachelor allowance.

VIOLET (*Coolly*) Oh, quite. (*She takes it*) Thank you. By the way, Mr Malone, those two houses you mentioned—the abbeys.

MALONE Yes?

VIOLET Don't take one of them until I've seen it. One never knows what may be wrong with these places.

MALONE I won't. I'll do nothing without consulting you, never fear.

VIOLET (*Politely, but without a ray of gratitude*) Thanks: that will be much the best way. (*She goes calmly back to the villa, escorted obsequiously by* MALONE *to the upper end of the garden*)

TANNER (*Drawing* RAMSDEN'S *attention to* MALONE'S *cringing attitude as he takes leave of* VIOLET) And that poor devil is a billionaire! one of the master spirits of the age! Led in a string like a pug dog by the first girl who takes the trouble to despise him! I wonder will it ever come to that with me. (*He comes down to the lawn*)

RAMSDEN (*Following him*) The sooner the better for you.

MALONE (*Slapping his hands as he returns through the garden*) That'll be a grand woman for Hector. I wouldn't exchange her for ten duchesses. (*He descends to the lawn and comes between* TANNER *and* RAMSDEN)

RAMSDEN (*Very civil to the billionaire*) It's an unexpected pleasure to find you in this corner of the world, Mr Malone. Have you come to buy up the Alhambra?

MALONE Well, I don't say I mightn't. I think I could do better with it than the Spanish government. But that's not what I came about. To tell you the truth, about a month ago I overheard a deal between two men over a bundle of shares. They differed about the price: they were young and greedy, and didn't know that if the shares were worth what was bid for them they must be worth what was asked, the margin being too small to be of any account, you see. To amuse meself, I cut in and bought the shares. Well, to this day I haven't found out what the business is. The office is in this town; and the name is Mendoza, Limited. Now whether Mendoza's a mine, or a steamboat line, or a bank, or a patent article—

TANNER He's a man. I know him: his principles are thoroughly commercial. Let us take you round the town in our motor, Mr Malone, and call on him on the way.

MALONE If you'll be so kind, yes. And may I ask who—

TANNER Mr Roebuck Ramsden, a very old friend of your daughter-in-law.

MALONE Happy to meet you, Mr Ramsden.

RAMSDEN Thank you. Mr Tanner is also one of our circle.

MALONE Glad to know you also, Mr Tanner.

TANNER Thanks. (MALONE *and* RAMSDEN *go out very amicably through the little gate.* TANNER *calls to* OCTAVIUS, *who is wandering in the garden with* ANN) Tavy! (TAVY *comes to the steps,* TANNER *whispers loudly to him*) Violet's father-in-law is a financier of brigands. (TANNER *hurries away to overtake* MALONE *and* RAMSDEN. ANN *strolls to the steps with an idle impulse to torment* OCTAVIUS)

ANN Won't you go with them, Tavy?

OCTAVIUS (*Tears suddenly flushing his eyes*) You cut me to the heart, Ann, by wanting me to go. (*He comes down on the lawn to hide his face from her. She follows him caressingly*)

ANN Poor Ricky Ticky Tavy! Poor heart!

OCTAVIUS It belongs to you, Ann. Forgive me: I must speak of it. I love you. You know I love you.

ANN What's the good, Tavy? You know that my mother is determined that I shall marry Jack.

OCTAVIUS (*Amazed*) Jack!

ANN It seems absurd, doesn't it?

OCTAVIUS (*With growing resentment*) Do you mean to say that Jack has been playing with me all this time? That he has been urging me not to marry you because he intends to marry you himself?

ANN (*Alarmed*) No, no: you mustn't lead him to believe that I said that. I don't for a moment think that Jack knows his own mind. But it's clear from my father's will that he wished me to marry Jack. And my mother is set on it.

OCTAVIUS But you are not bound to sacrifice yourself always to the wishes of your parents.

ANN My father loved me. My mother loves me. Surely their wishes are a better guide than my own selfishness.

OCTAVIUS Oh, I know how unselfish you are, Ann. But believe me—though I know I am speaking in my own interest—there is another side to this question. Is it fair to Jack to marry him if you do not love him? Is it fair to destroy my happiness as well as your own if you can bring yourself to love me?

ANN (*Looking at him with a faint impulse of pity*) Tavy, my dear, you are a nice creature—a good boy.

OCTAVIUS (*Humiliated*) Is that all?

ANN (*Mischievously in spite of her pity*) That's a great deal, I assure you. You would always worship the ground I trod on, wouldn't you?

OCTAVIUS I do. It sounds ridiculous; but it's no exaggeration. I do; and I always shall.

ANN Always is a long word, Tavy. You see, I shall have to live up always to your idea of my divinity; and I don't think I could do that if we were married. But if I marry Jack, you'll never be disillusioned—at least not until I grow too old.

OCTAVIUS I too shall grow old, Ann. And when I am eighty, one white hair of the woman I love will make me tremble more than the thickest gold tress from the most beautiful young head.[1]

ANN (*Quite touched*) Oh, that's poetry, Tavy, real poetry. It gives me that strange sudden sense of an echo from a former existence which always seems to me such a striking proof that we have immortal souls.

OCTAVIUS Do you believe that it is true?

ANN Tavy: if it is to come true, you must lose me as well as love me.

OCTAVIUS Oh! (*He hastily sits down at the little table and covers his face with his hands*)

ANN (*With conviction*) Tavy: I wouldn't for worlds destroy your illusions. I can neither take you nor let you go. I can see exactly what will suit you. You must be a sentimental old bachelor for my sake.

OCTAVIUS (*Desperately*) Ann: I'll kill myself.

ANN Oh no, you won't: that wouldn't be kind. You won't have a bad time. You will be very nice to women; and you will go a good deal to the opera. A broken heart is a very pleasant complaint for a man in London if he has a comfortable income.

OCTAVIUS (*Considerably cooled, but believing that he is only recovering his self-control*) I know you mean to be kind, Ann. Jack has persuaded you that cynicism is a good tonic for me. (*He rises with quiet dignity*)

ANN (*Studying him slyly*) You see, I'm disillusionizing you already. That's what I dread.

OCTAVIUS You do not dread disillusionizing Jack.

ANN (*Her face lighting up with mischievous ecstasy—whispering*) I can't: he has no illusions about me. I shall surprise Jack the other way. Getting over an unfavorable impression is ever so much easier than living up to an ideal. Oh, I shall enrapture Jack sometimes!

OCTAVIUS (*Resuming the calm phase of despair, and beginning to enjoy his broken heart and delicate attitude without knowing it*) I don't doubt that. You will enrapture him always. And he—the fool!—thinks you would make him wretched.

ANN Yes: that's the difficulty, so far.

OCTAVIUS (*Heroically*) Shall *I* tell him that you love him?

ANN (*Quickly*) Oh no: he'd run away again.

OCTAVIUS (*Shocked*) Ann: would you marry an unwilling man?

ANN What a queer creature you are, Tavy! There's

[1] See the Statue's account of what he "used to say to the ladies," in Act III.

no such thing as a willing man when you really go for him. (*She laughs naughtily*) I'm shocking you, I suppose. But you know you are really getting a sort of satisfaction already in being out of danger yourself.

OCTAVIUS (*Startled*) Satisfaction! (*Reproachfully*) You say that to me!

ANN Well, if it were really agony, would you ask for more of it?

OCTAVIUS Have I asked for more of it?

ANN You have offered to tell Jack that I love him. That's self-sacrifice, I suppose; but there must be some satisfaction in it. Perhaps it's because you're a poet. You are like the bird that presses its breast against the sharp thorn to make itself sing.

OCTAVIUS It's quite simple. I love you; and I want you to be happy. You don't love me; so I can't make you happy myself; but I can help another man to do it.

ANN Yes: it seems quite simple. But I doubt if we ever know why we do things. The only really simple thing is to go straight for what you want and grab it. I suppose I don't love you, Tavy; but sometimes I feel as if I should like to make a man of you somehow. You are very foolish about women.

OCTAVIUS (*Almost coldly*) I am content to be what I am in that respect.

ANN Then you must keep away from them, and only dream about them. I wouldn't marry you for worlds, Tavy.

OCTAVIUS I have no hope, Ann: I accept my ill luck. But I don't think you quite know how much it hurts.

ANN You are so softhearted! It's queer that you should be so different from Violet. Violet's as hard as nails.

OCTAVIUS Oh no. I am sure Violet is thoroughly womanly at heart.

ANN (*With some impatience*) Why do you say that? Is it unwomanly to be thoughtful and businesslike and sensible? Do you want Violet to be an idiot—or something worse, like me?

OCTAVIUS Something worse—like you! What do you mean, Ann?

ANN Oh well, I don't mean that, of course. But I have a great respect for Violet. She gets her own way always.

OCTAVIUS (*Sighing*) So do you.

ANN Yes; but somehow she gets it without coaxing—without having to make people sentimental about her.

OCTAVIUS (*With brotherly callousness*) Nobody could get very sentimental about Violet, I think, pretty as she is.

ANN Oh, yes, they could, if she made them.

OCTAVIUS But surely no really nice woman would deliberately practice on men's instincts in that way.

ANN (*Throwing up her hands*) Oh, Tavy, Tavy, Ricky Ticky Tavy, heaven help the woman who marries you!

OCTAVIUS (*His passion reviving at the name*) Oh why, why, why do you say that? Don't torment me. I don't understand.

ANN Suppose she were to tell fibs, and lay snares for men?

OCTAVIUS Do you think *I* could marry such a woman—I, who have known and loved you?

ANN Hm! Well, at all events, she wouldn't let you if she were wise. So that's settled. And now I can't talk any more. Say you forgive me, and that the subject is closed.

OCTAVIUS I have nothing to forgive; and the subject is closed. And if the wound is open, at least you shall never see it bleed.

ANN Poetic to the last, Tavy. Goodbye, dear. (*She pats his cheek; has an impulse to kiss him and then another impulse of distaste which prevents her; finally runs away through the garden and into the villa*)

(OCTAVIUS *again takes refuge at the table, bowing his head on his arms and sobbing softly.* MRS WHITEFIELD, *who has been pottering round the Granada shops, and has a net full of little parcels in her hand, comes in through the gate and sees him*)

MRS WHITEFIELD (*Running to him and lifting his head*) What's the matter, Tavy? Are you ill?

OCTAVIUS No, nothing, nothing.

MRS WHITEFIELD (*Still holding his head, anxiously*) But you're crying. Is it about Violet's marriage?

OCTAVIUS No, no. Who told you about Violet?

MRS WHITEFIELD (*Restoring the head to its owner*) I met Roebuck and that awful old Irishman. Are you sure you're not ill? What's the matter?

OCTAVIUS (*Affectionately*) It's nothing. Only a man's broken heart. Doesn't that sound ridiculous?

MRS WHITEFIELD But what is it all about? Has Ann been doing anything to you?

OCTAVIUS It's not Ann's fault. And don't think for a moment that I blame you.

MRS WHITEFIELD (*Startled*) For what?

OCTAVIUS (*Pressing her hand consolingly*) For nothing. I said I didn't blame you.

MRS WHITEFIELD But I havn't done anything. What's the matter?

OCTAVIUS (*Smiling sadly*) Can't you guess? I daresay you are right to prefer Jack to me as a husband for Ann; but I love Ann; and it hurts rather. (*He rises and moves away from her towards the middle of the lawn*)

MRS WHITEFIELD (*Following him hastily*) Does Ann say that I want her to marry Jack?

OCTAVIUS Yes: she has told me.

MRS WHITEFIELD (*Thoughtfully*) Then I'm very sorry for you, Tavy. It's only her way of saying she wants to marry Jack. Little she cares what *I* say or what *I* want!

OCTAVIUS But she would not say it unless she believed it. Surely you don't suspect Ann of—of deceit!!

MRS WHITEFIELD Well, never mind, Tavy. I don't know which is best for a young man: to know too little, like you, or too much, like Jack.

(TANNER *returns*)

TANNER Well, I've disposed of old Malone. I've introduced him to Mendoza, Limited; and left the two brigands together to talk it out. Hullo, Tavy! anything wrong?

OCTAVIUS I must go wash my face, I see. (*To* MRS WHITEFIELD) Tell him what you wish. (*To* TANNER) You may take it from me, Jack, that Ann approves of it.

TANNER (*Puzzled by his manner*) Approves of what?

OCTAVIUS Of what Mrs Whitefield wishes. (*He goes his way with sad dignity to the villa*)

TANNER (*To* MRS WHITEFIELD) This is very mysterious. What is it you wish? It shall be done, whatever it is.

MRS WHITEFIELD (*With snivelling gratitude*) Thank you, Jack. (*She sits down.* TANNER *brings the other chair from the table and sits close to her with his elbows on his knees, giving her his whole attention*) I don't know why it is that other people's children are so nice to me, and that my own have so little consideration for me. It's no wonder I don't seem able to care for Ann and Rhoda as I do for you and Tavy and Violet. It's a very queer world. It used to be so straight-forward and simple; and now nobody seems to think and feel as they ought. Nothing has been right since that speech that Professor Tyndall made at Belfast.[2]

TANNER Yes: life is more complicated than we used to think. But what am I to do for you?

MRS WHITEFIELD That's just what I want to tell you. Of course you'll marry Ann whether I like it or not—

TANNER (*Starting*) It seems to me that I shall presently be married to Ann whether I like it myself or not.

MRS WHITEFIELD (*Peacefully*) Oh, very likely you will: you know what she is when she has set her mind on anything. But don't put it on me: that's all I ask. Tavy has just let out that she's been saying that I am making her marry you; and the poor boy is breaking his heart about it; for he is in love with her himself, though what he sees in her so wonderful, goodness knows: *I* don't. It's no use telling Tavy that Ann puts things into people's heads by telling them that I want them when the thought of them never crossed my mind. It only sets Tavy against me. But you know better than that. So if you marry her, don't put the blame on me.

TANNER (*Emphatically*) I haven't the slightest intention of marrying her.

MRS WHITEFIELD (*Slyly*) She'd suit you better than Tavy. She'd meet her match in you, Jack. I'd like to see her meet her match.

TANNER No man is a match for a woman, except with a poker and a pair of hobnailed boots. Not always even then. Anyhow, *I* can't take the poker to her. I should be a mere slave.

MRS WHITEFIELD No: she's afraid of you. At all events, you would tell her the truth about herself. She wouldn't be able to slip out of it as she does with me.

TANNER Everybody would call me a brute if I told Ann the truth about herself in terms of her own moral code. To begin with, Ann says things that are not strictly true.

MRS WHITEFIELD I'm glad somebody sees she is not an angel.

TANNER In short—to put it as a husband would put it when exasperated to the point of speaking out—she is a liar. And since she has plunged Tavy head over ears in love with her without any intention of marrying him, she is a coquette, according to the standard definition of a coquette as a woman who rouses passions she has no intention of gratifying. And as she has now reduced you to the point of being willing to sacrifice me at the altar for the mere satisfaction of getting me to call her a liar to her face, I may conclude that she is a bully as well. She can't bully men as she bullies women; so she habitually and unscrupulously uses her personal fascination to make men give her whatever she wants. That makes her almost something for which I know no polite name.

MRS WHITEFIELD (*In mild expostulation*) Well, you can't expect perfection, Jack.

TANNER I don't. But what annoys me is that Ann does. I know perfectly well that all this about her being a liar and a bully and a coquette and so forth is a trumped-up moral indictment which might be brought against anybody. We all lie; we all bully as much as we dare; we all bid for admiration without the least intention of earning it; we all get as much rent as we can out of our powers of fascination. If Ann would admit this I shouldn't quarrel with her. But she won't. If she has children she'll take advantage of their telling lies to amuse herself by whacking them. If another woman makes eyes at me, she'll refuse to know a coquette. She will do just what she likes herself whilst insisting on everybody else doing what the conventional code prescribes. In short, I can stand everything except her confounded hypocrisy. That's what beats me.

MRS WHITEFIELD (*Carried away by the relief of hearing her own opinion so eloquently expressed*) Oh, she is a hypocrite. She is: she is. Isn't she?

TANNER Then why do you want to marry me to her?

MRS WHITEFIELD (*Querulously*) There now! put it on me, of course. I never thought of it until Tavy told me she said I did. But, you know, I'm very fond of Tavy: he's a sort of son to me; and I don't want him to be trampled on and made wretched.

TANNER Whereas I don't matter, I suppose.

MRS WHITEFIELD Oh, you are different, somehow: you are able to take care of yourself. You'd serve her out. And anyhow, she must marry somebody.

TANNER Aha! there speaks the life instinct. You detest her; but you feel that you must get her married.

MRS WHITEFIELD (*Rising, shocked*) Do you mean that I detest my own daughter! Surely you don't believe me to be so wicked and unnatural as that, merely because I see her faults.

TANNER (*Cynically*) You love her, then?

MRS WHITEFIELD Why, of course I do. What queer

[2] John Tyndall (1820-1893), British physicist: while president of the British Association, he defended materialism against religion (1874).

things you say, Jack! We can't help loving our own blood relations.

TANNER Well, perhaps it saves unpleasantness to say so. But for my part, I suspect that the tables of consanguinity have a natural basis in a natural repugnance. (*He rises*)

MRS WHITEFIELD You shouldn't say things like that, Jack. I hope you won't tell Ann that I have been speaking to you. I only wanted to set myself right with you and Tavy. I couldn't sit mumchance[3] and have everything put on me.

TANNER (*Politely*) Quite so.

MRS WHITEFIELD (*Dissatisfied*) And now I've only made matters worse. Tavy's angry with me because I don't worship Ann. And when it's been put into my head that Ann ought to marry you, what can I say except that it would serve her right?

TANNER Thank you.

MRS WHITEFIELD Now don't be silly and twist what I say into something I don't mean. I ought to have fair play—

(ANN *comes from the villa, followed presently by* VIOLET, *who is dressed for driving*)

ANN (*Coming to her mother's right hand with threatening suavity*) Well, mamma darling, you seem to be having a delightful chat with Jack. We can hear you all over the place.

MRS WHITEFIELD (*Appalled*) Have you overheard—

TANNER Never fear: Ann is only—well, we were discussing that habit of hers just now. She hasn't heard a word.

MRS WHITEFIELD (*Stoutly*) I don't care whether she has or not: I have a right to say what I please.

VIOLET (*Arriving on the lawn and coming between* MRS WHITEFIELD *and* TANNER) I've come to say goodbye. I'm off for my honeymoon.

MRS WHITEFIELD (*Crying*) Oh, don't say that, Violet. And no wedding, no breakfast, no clothes, nor anything.

VIOLET (*Petting her*) It won't be for long.

MRS WHITEFIELD Don't let him take you to America. Promise me that you won't.

VIOLET (*Very decidedly*) I should think not, indeed. Don't cry, dear: I'm only going to the hotel.

MRS WHITEFIELD But going in that dress, with your luggage, makes one realize— (*She chokes, and then breaks out again*) How I wish you were my daughter, Violet!

VIOLET (*Soothing her*) There, there: so I am. Ann will be jealous.

MRS WHITEFIELD Ann doesn't care a bit for me.

ANN Fie, mother! Come, now: you mustn't cry any more: you know Violet doesn't like it. (MRS WHITEFIELD *dries her eyes, and subsides*)

VIOLET Goodbye, Jack.

TANNER Goodbye, Violet.

VIOLET The sooner you get married too, the better. You will be much less misunderstood.

TANNER (*Restively*) I quite expect to get married in the course of the afternoon. You all seem to have set your minds on it.

VIOLET You might do worse. (*To* MRS WHITEFIELD: *putting her arm round her*) Let me take you to the hotel with me: the drive will do you good. Come in and get a wrap. (*She takes her towards the villa*)

MRS WHITEFIELD (*As they go up through the garden*) I don't know what I shall do when you are gone, with no one but Ann in the house; and she always occupied with the men! It's not to be expected that your husband will care to be bothered with an old woman like me. Oh, you needn't tell me: politeness is all very well; but I know what people think— (*She talks herself and* VIOLET *out of sight and hearing*)

(ANN, *alone with* TANNER, *watches him and waits. He makes an irresolute movement towards the gate; but some magnetism in her draws him to her, a broken man*)

ANN Violet is quite right. You ought to get married.

TANNER (*Explosively*) Ann: I will not marry you. Do you hear? I won't, won't, won't, won't, WON'T marry you.

ANN (*Placidly*) Well, nobody axd you, sir she said, sir she said, sir she said. So that's settled.

TANNER Yes, nobody has asked me; but everybody treats the thing as settled. It's in the air. When we meet, the others go away on absurd pretexts to leave us alone together. Ramsden no longer scowls at me: his eye beams, as if he were already giving you away to me in church. Tavy refers me to your mother and gives me his blessing. Straker openly treats you as his future employer: it was he who first told me of it.

ANN Was that why you ran away?

TANNER Yes, only to be stopped by a lovesick brigand and run down like a truant schoolboy.

ANN Well, if you don't want to be married, you needn't be. (*She turns away from him and sits down, much at her ease*)

TANNER (*Following her*) Does any man want to be hanged? Yet men let themselves be hanged without a struggle for life, though they could at least give the chaplain a black eye. We do the world's will, not our own. I have a frightful feeling that I shall let myself be married because it is the world's will that you should have a husband.

ANN I daresay I shall, someday.

TANNER But why me? me of all men! Marriage is to me apostasy, profanation of the sanctuary of my soul, violation of my manhood, sale of my birthright, shameful surrender, ignominious capitulation, acceptance of defeat. I shall decay like a thing that has served its purpose and is done with; I shall change from a man with a future to a man with a past; I shall see in the greasy eyes of all the other husbands their relief at the arrival of a new prisoner to share their ignominy. The young men will scorn me as one who has sold out: to the women I, who have always been an enigma and a possibility, shall be merely somebody else's property—and damaged goods at that: a secondhand man at best.

ANN Well, your wife can put on a cap and make her-

[3] Trying hard to keep from speaking.

self ugly to keep you in countenance, like my grandmother.

TANNER So that she may make her triumph more insolent by publicly throwing away the bait the moment the trap snaps on the victim!

ANN After all, though, what difference would it make? Beauty is all very well at first sight; but who ever looks at it when it has been in the house three days? I thought our pictures very lovely when papa bought them; but I haven't looked at them for years. You never bother about my looks: you are too well used to me. I might be the umbrella stand.

TANNER You lie, you vampire: you lie.

ANN Flatterer. Why are you trying to fascinate me, Jack, if you don't want to marry me?

TANNER The Life Force. I am in the grip of the Life Force.

ANN I don't understand in the least: it sounds like the Life Guards.

TANNER Why don't you marry Tavy? He is willing. Can you not be satisfied unless your prey struggles?

ANN (*Turning to him as if to let him into a secret*) Tavy will never marry. Haven't you noticed that that sort of man never marries?

TANNER What! a man who idolizes women! who sees nothing in nature but romantic scenery for love duets! Tavy, the chivalrous, the faithful, the tenderhearted and true! Tavy never marry! Why, he was born to be swept up by the first pair of blue eyes he meets in the street.

ANN Yes, I know. All the same, Jack, men like that always live in comfortable bachelor lodgings with broken hearts, and are adored by their landladies, and never get married. Men like you always get married.

TANNER (*Smiting his brow*) How frightfully, horribly true! It has been staring me in the face all my life; and I never saw it before.

ANN Oh, it's the same with women. The poetic temperament's a very nice temperament, very amiable, very harmless and poetic, I daresay; but it's an old maid's temperament.

TANNER Barren. The Life Force passes it by.

ANN If that's what you mean by the Life Force, yes.

TANNER You don't care for Tavy?

ANN (*Looking round carefully to make sure that Tavy is not within earshot*) No.

TANNER And you do care for me?

ANN (*Rising quietly and shaking her finger at him*) Now, Jack! Behave yourself.

TANNER Infamous, abandoned woman! Devil!

ANN Boa-constrictor! Elephant!

TANNER Hypocrite!

ANN (*Softly*) I must be, for my future husband's sake.

TANNER For mine. (*Correcting himself savagely*) I mean for his.

ANN (*Ignoring the correction*) Yes, for yours. You had better marry what you call a hypocrite, Jack. Women who are not hypocrites go about in rational dress and are insulted and get into all sorts of hot water. And then their husbands get dragged in too. and live in continual dread of fresh complications. Wouldn't you prefer a wife you could depend on?

TANNER No: a thousand times no: hot water is the revolutionist's element. You clean men as you clean milkpails, by scalding them.

ANN Cold water has its uses too. It's healthy.

TANNER (*Despairingly*) Oh, you are witty: at the supreme moment the Life Force endows you with every quality. Well, I too can be a hypocrite. Your father's will appointed me your guardian, not your suitor. I shall be faithful to my trust.

ANN (*In low siren tones*) He asked me who I would have as my guardian before he made that will. I chose you!

TANNER The will is yours then! The trap was laid from the beginning.

ANN (*Concentrating all her magic*) From the beginning—from our childhood—for both of us—by the Life Force.

TANNER I will not marry you. I will not marry you.

ANN Oh, you will, you will.

TANNER I tell you, no, no, no.

ANN I tell you, yes, yes, yes.

TANNER No.

ANN (*Coaxing—imploring—almost exhausted*) Yes. Before it is too late for repentance. Yes.

TANNER (*Struck by the echo from the past*) When did all this happen to me before? Are we two dreaming?

ANN (*Suddenly losing her courage, with an anguish that she does not conceal*) No. We are awake; and you have said no: that is all.

TANNER (*Brutally*) Well?

ANN Well, I made a mistake: you do not love me.

TANNER (*Seizing her in his arms*) It is false: I love you. The Life Force enchants me: I have the whole world in my arms when I clasp you. But I am fighting for my freedom, for my honor, for my self, one and indivisible.

ANN Your happiness will be worth them all.

TANNER You would sell freedom and honor and self for happiness?

ANN It will not be all happiness for me. Perhaps death.

TANNER (*Groaning*) Oh, that clutch holds and hurts. What have you grasped in me? Is there a father's heart as well as a mother's?

ANN Take care, Jack: if anyone comes while we are like this, you will have to marry me.

TANNER If we two stood now on the edge of a precipice, I would hold you tight and jump.

ANN (*Panting, failing more and more under the strain*) Jack; let me go. I have dared so frightfully—it is lasting longer than I thought. Let me go: I can't bear it.

TANNER Nor I. Let it kill us.

ANN Yes: I don't care. I am at the end of my forces. I don't care. I think I am going to faint.

(*At this moment* VIOLET *and* OCTAVIUS *come from the villa with* MRS WHITEFIELD, *who is wrapped up for driving. Simultaneously* MALONE *and* RAMSDEN, *followed by* MENDOZA *and* STRAKER, *come in through the little gate in the paling.* TANNER *shame-*

*facedly releases* ANN, *who raises her hand giddily to her forehead*)

MALONE Take care. Something's the matter with the lady.

RAMSDEN What does this mean?

VIOLET (*Running between* ANN *and* TANNER) Are you ill?

ANN (*Reeling, with a supreme effort*) I have promised to marry Jack. (*She swoons.* VIOLET *kneels by her and chafes her hand.* TANNER *runs round to her other hand, and tries to lift her head.* OCTAVIUS *goes to* VIOLET'S *assistance, but does not know what to do.* MRS WHITEFIELD *hurries back into the villa.* OCTAVIUS, MALONE, *and* RAMSDEN *run to* ANN *and crowd round her, stooping to assist.* STRAKER *coolly comes to* ANN'S *feet, and* MENDOZA *to her head, both upright and self-possessed*)

STRAKER Now then, ladies and gentlemen: she don't want a crowd round her: she wants air—all the air she can git. If you please, gents— (MALONE *and* RAMSDEN *allow him to drive them gently past* ANN *and up the lawn towards the garden, where* OCTAVIUS, *who has already become conscious of his uselessness, joins them.* STRAKER, *following them up, pauses for a moment to instruct* TANNER) Don't lift 'er 'ed, Mr Tanner: let it go flat so's the blood can run back into it.

MENDOZA He is right, Mr Tanner. Trust to the air of the Sierra. (*He withdraws delicately to the garden steps*)

TANNER (*Rising*) I yield to your superior knowledge of physiology, Henry. (*He withdraws to the corner of the lawn; and* OCTAVIUS *immediately hurries down to him*)

TAVY (*Aside to* TANNER, *grasping his hand*) Jack: be very happy.

TANNER (*Aside to* TAVY) I never asked her. It is a trap for me. (*He goes up the lawn towards the garden.* OCTAVIUS *remains petrified*)

MENDOZA (*Intercepting* MRS WHITEFIELD, *who comes from the villa with a glass of brandy*) What is this, madam (*He takes it from her*)?

MRS WHITEFIELD A little brandy.

MENDOZA The worst thing you could give her. Allow me. (*He swallows it*) Trust to the air of the Sierra, madam.

(*For a moment the men all forget* ANN *and stare at* MENDOZA)

ANN (*In* VIOLET'S *ear, clutching her round the neck*) Violet: did Jack say anything when I fainted?

VIOLET No.

ANN Ah! (*With a sigh of intense relief she relapses*)

MRS WHITEFIELD Oh, she's fainted again.

(*They are about to rush back to her; but* MENDOZA *stops them with a warning gesture*)

ANN (*Supine*) No, I haven't. I'm quite happy.

TANNER (*Suddenly walking determinedly to her, and snatching her hand from* VIOLET *to feel her pulse*) Why, her pulse is positively bounding. Come! get up. What nonsense! Up with you. (*He hauls her up summarily*)

ANN Yes: I feel strong enough now. But you very nearly killed me, Jack, for all that.

MALONE A rough wooer, eh? They're the best sort, Miss Whitefield. I congratulate Mr Tanner; and I hope to meet you and him as frequent guests at the abbey.

ANN Thank you. (*She goes past* MALONE *to* OCTAVIUS) Ricky Ticky Tavy: congratulate me. (*Aside to him*) I want to make you cry for the last time.

TAVY (*Steadfastly*) No more tears. I am happy in your happiness. And I believe in you in spite of everything.

RAMSDEN (*Coming between* MALONE *and* TANNER) You are a happy man, Jack Tanner. I envy you.

MENDOZA (*Advancing between* VIOLET *and* TANNER) Sir: there are two tragedies in life. One is to lose your heart's desire. The other is to gain it. Mine and yours, sir.

TANNER Mr Mendoza: I have no heart's desires. Ramsden: it is very easy for you to call me a happy man: you are only a spectator. I am one of the principals; and I know better. Ann: stop tempting Tavy, and come back to me.

ANN (*Complying*) You are absurd, Jack. (*She takes his proffered arm*)

TANNER (*Continuing*) I solemnly say that I am not a happy man. Ann looks happy; but she is only triumphant, successful, victorious. That is not happiness, but the price for which the strong sell their happiness. What we have both done this afternoon is to renounce happiness, renounce freedom, renounce tranquillity, above all, renounce the romantic possibilities of an unknown future, for the cares of a household and a family. I beg that no man may seize the occasion to get half drunk and utter imbecile speeches and coarse pleasantries at my expense. We propose to furnish our own house according to our own taste; and I hereby give notice that the seven or eight traveling clocks, the four or five dressing cases, the carvers and fish slices, the copies of Patmore's Angel In The House[4] in extra morocco, and the other articles you are preparing to heap upon us, will be instantly sold, and the proceeds devoted to circulating free copies of the Revolutionist's Handbook. The wedding will take place three days after our return to England, by special licence, at the office of the district superintendent registrar, in the presence of my solicitor and his clerk, who, like his clients, will be in ordinary walking dress—

VIOLET (*With intense conviction*) You are a brute, Jack.

ANN (*Looking at him with fond pride and caressing his arm*) Never mind her, dear. Go on talking.

TANNER Talking!

(*Universal laughter*)

*Curtain*

[4] A four-part narrative poem, by Coventry Patmore (1823-1896), on married life and love.

# MAJOR BARBARA

AFTER 1903, George Bernard Shaw continued the freewheeling experimentalism first apparent in the expressionist pyrotechnics of the dream-sequence in *Man and Superman*. In *John Bull's Other Island* (1904), he examined several varieties of Ireland. His characters included a Grasshopper along with a "professional" stage-Irishman, a Briton captivated by sentimental myths of Celtic twilight, a clearheaded Irishman happy and prosperous in England, and Father Keegan, one of Shaw's most appealing visionary characters.

In *Major Barbara* (1905), Shaw pitted a passionate Salvation Army visionary against Cusins, the sardonic classicist whose love she has won, and Andrew Undershaft, the poverty-hating capitalist father whose soul she hopes to win. Few Shavian plays have so challenged critics' ingenuity, for Shaw used his dialectics with such outrageous daring as to give his mystical munitions-maker arguments of a cogency his other characters cannot easily match. Here Shaw, who had long since dismissed the stage-villain as a moral anachronism, created an ostensible devil cloaked in the neutralism and amorality so repugnant to pacifist and militaristic chauvinist sensibilities alike. In the Preface to *Major Barbara*, Shaw called Undershaft "the hero" of the play; in the play, however, Shaw baited his dialectic trap with enticements for audiences to take sides against Undershaft. The questions he left unanswered at the final curtain are purposely irritant, designed with Socratic mastery to keep discussion going when audiences have left the theatre-classroom. The issues Shaw raised in this play over fifty years ago have lost none of their immediacy with the passage of time.

In *The Doctor's Dilemma* (1906), Shaw surveyed the medical profession's charlatanry as well as its progress. In *Getting Married* (1908) and *Misalliance* (1910), he experimented with near-plotlessness and wrote uninterrupted exchanges between shrewdly individualized spokesmen for popular and unpopular opinions about love, sex, marriage, and child-raising. In *Fanny's First Play* (1911), a set of plays-within-plays arranged like Chinese boxes, Shaw played some private jokes on London drama critics. The "fable play," *Androcles and the Lion* (1912), and the "romance in five acts," *Pygmalion* (1912), are marked by a joyful spirit which, in his later plays, Shaw never quite recaptured. In *Androcles*, Shaw combined farce with seriousness as he showed Christian martyrs preparing for a fate from which they are rescued by a lion fond of dancing with a little Greek tailor; equally memorable is the Preface (entitled "Why Not Give Christianity a Trial?"), an outwardly whimsical version of the New Testament which, in fact, records a deep understanding of Christianity. As *My Fair Lady*, Shaw's *Pygmalion* has lost all traces of the anti-romantic epilogue Shaw wrote to discourage actors from suggesting that Henry Higgins and his Galatea, Eliza Doolittle, will retire into quiet domesticity. Its appeal, however, remains undiminished.

World War I and Britain's participation in it dismayed Shaw (then in his early 60's). In *Heartbreak House* (1913-1916), subtitled "A Fantasia in the Russian manner on English themes," a self-destructive culture listlessly assists at its own wake. Although intended as a Shavian *Cherry Orchard*, it is most remarkable as anguished self-revelation of a Shaw whose values were being severely tested. *Back to Methuselah* (completed, 1921) is the Shavian version of Genesis and Revelation, a five-play work advancing his thesis that the world will be better only when man lives long enough to conquer his senses. The cycle begins in the Garden of Eden and ends in an eternity beyond 31,920 A.D. In *Saint Joan* (1923), Shaw looked backward and forward from the Maid's then-recent canonization and wrote one of modern drama's undoubted masterpieces. Critics have made *Saint Joan* a storm-center in the tragedy/comedy controversy Shaw himself dodged by labeling it "a chronicle play." Audiences, however, have grasped without difficulty Shaw's view that Joan's spiritual victory signifies mankind's failure. In 1925, Shaw refused and then accepted the Nobel Prize, but directed the prize money into a fund for translating Strindberg. From 1929 until his death, Shaw wrote as vigorously as ever, but few of his late plays have won wide popular or critical esteem. The best of these, *The Apple Cart* (1929), *Too True to Be Good* (1932), *The Simpleton of the Unexpected Isles* (1934), and *In Good King Charles's Golden Days* (1939), avoid the excessive topicality which marks some of the late works. All of them, however, deserve to find their way onto stages which, resourceful in the contemporary theatricalist tradition, can comfortably accommodate modern drama's greatest comic genius—the brilliant flow of words, the playful mischief only his highly civilized mind could invent and sustain, his communication of moral outrage without becoming strident or outrageous, and his way of attacking human follies without making humanity seem incurably foolish.

# MAJOR BARBARA

## CHARACTERS

SIR ANDREW UNDERSHAFT
LADY BRITOMART UNDERSHAFT, *his wife*
BARBARA, *his elder daughter, a Major in the Salvation Army*
SARAH, *his younger daughter*
STEPHEN, *his son*
ADOLPHUS CUSINS, *a professor of Greek in love with Barbara*
CHARLES LOMAX, *young-man-about-town engaged to Sarah*
MORRISON, *Lady Britomart's butler*
BRONTERRE O'BRIEN ("Snobby") PRICE, *a cobbler-carpenter down on his luck*
MRS ROMOLA ("Rummy") MITCHENS, *a worn-out lady who relies on the Salvation Army*
JENNY HILL, *a young Salvation Army worker*
PETER SHIRLEY, *an unemployed coal-broker*
BILL WALKER, *a bully*
MRS BAINES, *Commissioner in the Salvation Army*
BILTON, *a foreman at Perivale St. Andrews*

*The action of the play occurs within several days in January, 1906.*

ACT I *The library of Lady Britomart's house in Wilton Crescent, a fashionable London suburb.*

ACT II *The yard of the Salvation Army shelter in West Ham, an industrial suburb in London's East End.*

ACT III *The library in Lady Britomart's house; a parapet overlooking Perivale St Andrews, a region in Middlesex northwest of London.*

## Act One

*It is after dinner in January 1906, in the library in* LADY BRITOMART UNDERSHAFT'S *house in Wilton Crescent. A large and comfortable settee is in the middle of the room, upholstered in dark leather. A person sitting on it (it is vacant at present) would have, on his right,* LADY BRITOMART'S *writing-table, with the lady herself busy at it; a smaller writing-table behind him on his left; the door behind him on* LADY BRITOMART'S *side; and a window with a window-seat directly on his left. Near the window is an armchair.*

LADY BRITOMART *is a woman of fifty or thereabouts, well dressed and yet careless of her dress, well bred and quite reckless of her breeding, well mannered and yet appallingly outspoken and indifferent to the opinion of her interlocutors, amiable and yet peremptory, arbitrary, and hightempered to the last bearable degree, and withal a very typical managing matron of the upper class, treated as a naughty child until she grew into a scolding mother, and finally settling down with plenty of practical ability and worldly experience, limited in the oddest way with domestic and class limitations, conceiving the universe exactly as if it were a large house in Wilton Crescent, though handling her corner of it very effectively on that assumption, and being quite enlightened and liberal as to the books in the library, the pictures on the walls, the music in the portfolios, and the articles in the papers.*

*Her son,* STEPHEN, *comes in. He is a gravely correct young man under 25, taking himself very seriously, but still in some awe of his mother, from childish habit and bachelor shyness rather than from any weakness of character.*

STEPHEN What's the matter?

LADY BRITOMART Presently, Stephen.

(STEPHEN *submissively walks to the settee and sits down. He takes up a liberal weekly called* The Speaker)

LADY BRITOMART Don't begin to read, Stephen. I shall require all your attention.

STEPHEN It was only while I was waiting—

LADY BRITOMART Don't make excuses, Stephen. (*He puts down* The Speaker) Now! (*She finishes her writing; rises; and comes to the settee*) I have not kept you waiting very long, I think.

STEPHEN Not at all, mother.

LADY BRITOMART Bring me my cushion. (*He takes the cushion from the chair at the desk and arranges it for her as she sits down on the settee*) Sit down. (*He sits down and fingers his tie nervously*) Don't fiddle with your tie, Stephen: there is nothing the matter with it.

STEPHEN I beg your pardon. (*He fiddles with his watch chain instead*)

LADY BRITOMART Now are you attending to me, Stephen?

STEPHEN Of course, mother.

LADY BRITOMART No: it's not of course. I want something much more than your everyday matter-of-course attention. I am going to speak to you very seriously, Stephen. I wish you would let that chain alone.

STEPHEN (*Hastily relinquishing the chain*) Have I done anything to annoy you, mother? If so, it was quite unintentional.

LADY BRITOMART (*Astonished*) Nonsense! (*With some remorse*) My poor boy, did you think I was angry with you?

STEPHEN What is it, then, mother? You are making me very uneasy.

LADY BRITOMART (*Squaring herself at him rather aggressively*) Stephen: may I ask how soon you intend to realize that you are a grown-up man, and that I am only a woman?

STEPHEN (*Amazed*) Only a—

LADY BRITOMART Don't repeat my words, please: it is a most aggravating habit. You must learn to face life seriously, Stephen. I really cannot bear the whole burden of our family affairs any longer. You must advise me: you must assume the responsibility.

STEPHEN I!

LADY BRITOMART Yes, you, of course. You were twenty-four last June. You've been at Harrow and Cambridge. You've been to India and Japan. You must know a lot of things, now; unless you have wasted your time most scandalously. Well, advise me.

STEPHEN (*Much perplexed*) You know I have never interfered in the household—

LADY BRITOMART No: I should think not. I don't want you to order the dinner.

STEPHEN I mean in our family affairs.

LADY BRITOMART Well, you must interfere now; for they are getting quite beyond me.

STEPHEN (*Troubled*) I have thought sometimes that perhaps I ought; but really, mother, I know so little about them; and what I do know is so painful—it is so impossible to mention some things to you— (*He stops, ashamed*)

LADY BRITOMART I suppose you mean your father.

STEPHEN (*Almost inaudibly*) Yes.

LADY BRITOMART My dear: we can't go on all our lives not mentioning him. Of course you were quite right not to open the subject until I asked you to; but you are old enough now to be taken into my confidence, and to help me to deal with him about the girls.

STEPHEN But the girls are all right. They are engaged.

LADY BRITOMART (*Complacently*) Yes: I have made a very good match for Sarah. Charles Lomax will be a millionaire at thirty-five. But that is ten years ahead; and in the meantime his trustees cannot under the terms of his father's will allow him more than £800 a year.

STEPHEN But the will says also that if he increases his income by his own exertions, they may double the increase.

LADY BRITOMART Charles Lomax's exertions are much more likely to decrease his income than to increase it. Sarah will have to find at least another £800 a year for the next ten years; and even then they will be as poor as church mice. And what about Barbara? I thought Barbara was going to make the most brilliant career of all of you. And what does she do? Joins the Salvation Army; discharges her maid; lives on a pound a week; and walks in one evening with a professor of Greek whom she has picked up in the street, and who pretends to be a Salvationist, and actually plays the big drum for her in public because he has fallen head over ears in love with her.

STEPHEN I was certainly rather taken aback when I heard they were engaged. Cusins is a very nice fellow, certainly: nobody would ever guess that he was born in Australia; but—

LADY BRITOMART Oh, Adolphus Cusins will make a very good husband. After all, nobody can say a word against Greek: it stamps a man at once as an educated gentleman. And my family, thank Heaven, is not a pigheaded Tory one. We are Whigs, and believe in liberty. Let snobbish people say what they please: Barbara shall marry, not the man they like, but the man *I* like.

STEPHEN Of course I was thinking only of his income. However, he is not likely to be extravagant.

LADY BRITOMART Don't be too sure of that, Stephen. I know your quiet, simple, refined, poetic people like Adolphus—quite content with the best of everything! They cost more than your extravagant people, who are always as mean as they are second rate. No: Barbara will need at least £2000 a year. You see it means two additional households. Besides, my dear, you must marry soon. I don't approve of the present fashion of philandering bachelors and late marriages; and I am trying to arrange something for you.

STEPHEN It's very good of you, mother; but perhaps I had better arrange that for myself.

LADY BRITOMART Nonsense! you are much too young to begin matchmaking: you would be taken in by some pretty little nobody. Of course I don't mean that you are not to be consulted: you know that as well as I do. (STEPHEN *closes his lips and is silent*) Now don't sulk, Stephen.

STEPHEN I am not sulking, mother. What has all this got to do with—with—with my father?

LADY BRITOMART My dear Stephen: where is the money to come from? It is easy enough for you and the other children to live on my income as long as we are in the same house; but I can't keep four families in four separate houses. You know how poor my father is: he has barely seven thousand a year now; and really, if he were not the Earl of Stevenage, he would have to give up society. He can do nothing for us. He says, naturally enough, that it is absurd that he should be asked to provide for the children of a man who is rolling in money. You see, Stephen, your father must be fabulously wealthy, because there is always a war going on somewhere.

STEPHEN You need not remind me of that, mother. I have hardly ever opened a newspaper in my life without seeing our name in it. The Undershaft torpedo! The Undershaft quick firers! The Undershaft ten inch! The Undershaft disappearing rampart gun! The Undershaft submarine! and now the Undershaft aerial battleship! At Harrow they called me the Woolwich Infant.[1] At Cambridge it was the same. A little brute at King's who was always trying to get up revivals, spoilt my Bible—your first birthday present to me—by writing under my name, "Son and heir to Undershaft and Lazarus, Death and Destruction Dealers: address, Christendom and Judea." But that was not so bad as the way I was kowtowed to everywhere because my father was making millions by selling cannons.

LADY BRITOMART It is not only the cannons, but the war loans that Lazarus arranges under cover of giving credit for the cannons. You know, Stephen, it's perfectly scandalous. Those two men, Andrew Undershaft and Lazarus, positively have Europe under their thumbs. That is why your father is able to behave as he does. He is above the law. Do you think Bismarck or Gladstone or Disraeli could have openly defied every social and moral obligation all their lives as your father has? They simply wouldn't have dared. I asked Gladstone to take it up. I asked *The Times* to take it up. I asked the Lord Chamberlain to take it up. But it was just like asking them to declare war on the Sultan. They wouldn't. They said they couldn't touch him. I believe they were afraid.

STEPHEN What could they do? He does not actually break the law.

LADY BRITOMART Not break the law! He is always breaking the law. He broke the law when he was born: his parents were not married.

STEPHEN Mother! Is that true?

LADY BRITOMART Of course it's true: that was why we separated.

STEPHEN He married without letting you know this!

LADY BRITOMART (*Rather taken aback by this inference*) Oh no. To do Andrew justice, that was not the sort of thing he did. Besides, you know the Undershaft motto: Unashamed. Everybody knew.

STEPHEN But you said that was why you separated.

LADY BRITOMART Yes, because he was not content with being a foundling himself: he wanted to disinherit you for another foundling. That was what I couldn't stand.

STEPHEN (*Ashamed*) Do you mean for—for—for—

LADY BRITOMART Don't stammer, Stephen. Speak distinctly.

STEPHEN But this is so frightful to me, mother. To have to speak to you about such things!

LADY BRITOMART It's not pleasant for me, either, especially if you are still so childish that you must make it worse by a display of embarrassment. It is only in the middle classes, Stephen, that people get into a state of dumb helpless horror when they find that there are wicked people in the world. In our class, we have to decide what is to be done with wicked people; and nothing should disturb our self-possession. Now ask your question properly.

STEPHEN Mother: you have no consideration for me. For Heaven's sake either treat me as a child, as you always do, and tell me nothing at all; or tell me everything and let me take it as best I can.

LADY BRITOMART Treat you as a child! What do you mean? It is most unkind and ungrateful of you to say such a thing. You know I have never treated any of you as children. I have always made you my companions and friends, and allowed you perfect freedom to do and say whatever you liked, so long as you liked what I could approve of.

STEPHEN (*Desperately*) I daresay we have been the very imperfect children of a very perfect mother; but I do beg of you to let me alone for once, and tell me about this horrible business of my father wanting to set me aside for another son.

LADY BRITOMART (*Amazed*) Another son! I never said anything of the kind. I never dreamt of such a thing. This is what comes of interrupting me.

STEPHEN But you said—

LADY BRITOMART (*Cutting him short*) Now be a good boy, Stephen, and listen to me patiently. The Undershafts are descended from a foundling in the parish of St Andrew Undershaft in the city. That was long ago, in the reign of James the First. Well, this foundling was adopted by an armorer and gunmaker. In the course of time the foundling succeeded to the business; and from some notion of gratitude, or some vow or something, he adopted another foundling, and left the business to him. And that foundling did the

[1] The nickname puns on Stephen's connection with the Undershaft cannon business and the popular name for a widely used heavy gun.

same. Ever since that, the cannon business has always been left to an adopted foundling named Andrew Undershaft.

STEPHEN But did they never marry? Were there no legitimate sons?

LADY BRITOMART Oh yes: they married just as your father did; and they were rich enough to buy land for their own children and leave them well provided for. But they always adopted and trained some foundling to succeed them in the business; and of course they always quarreled with their wives furiously over it. Your father was adopted in that way; and he pretends to consider himself bound to keep up the tradition and adopt somebody to leave the business to. Of course I was not going to stand that. There may have been some reason for it when the Undershafts could only marry women in their own class, whose sons were not fit to govern great estates. But there could be no excuse for passing over my son.

STEPHEN (*Dubiously*) I am afraid I should make a poor hand of managing a cannon foundry.

LADY BRITOMART Nonsense! you could easily get a manager and pay him a salary.

STEPHEN My father evidently had no great opinion of my capacity.

LADY BRITOMART Stuff, child! you were only a baby: it had nothing to do with your capacity. Andrew did it on principle, just as he did every perverse and wicked thing on principle. When my father remonstrated, Andrew actually told him to his face that history tells us of only two successful institutions: one the Undershaft firm, and the other the Roman Empire under the Antonines. That was because the Antonine emperors all adopted their successors. Such rubbish! The Stevenages are as good as the Antonines, I hope; and you are a Stevenage. But that was Andrew all over. There you have the man! Always clever and unanswerable when he was defending nonsense and wickedness: always awkward and sullen when he had to behave sensibly and decently.

STEPHEN Then it was on my account that your home life was broken up, mother. I am sorry.

LADY BRITOMART Well, dear, there were other differences. I really cannot bear an immoral man. I am not a Pharisee, I hope; and I should not have minded his merely doing wrong things: we are none of us perfect. But your father didn't exactly do wrong things: he said them and thought them: that was what was so dreadful. He really had a sort of religion of wrongness. Just as one doesn't mind men practicing immorality so long as they own that they are in the wrong by preaching morality; so I couldn't forgive Andrew for preaching immorality while he practiced morality. You would all have grown up without principles, without any knowledge of right and wrong, if he had been in the house. You know, my dear, your father was a very attractive man in some ways. Children did not dislike him; and he took advantage of it to put the wickedest ideas into their heads, and make them quite unmanageable. I did not dislike him myself: very far from it; but nothing can bridge over moral disagreement.

STEPHEN All this simply bewilders me, mother. People may differ about matters of opinion, or even about religion; but how can they differ about right and wrong? Right is right; and wrong is wrong; and if a man cannot distinguish them properly, he is either a fool or a rascal: that's all.

LADY BRITOMART (*Touched*) That's my own boy! (*She pats his cheek*) Your father never could answer that: he used to laugh and get out of it under cover of some affectionate nonsense. And now that you understand the situation, what do you advise me to do?

STEPHEN Well, what can you do?

LADY BRITOMART I must get the money somehow.

STEPHEN We cannot take money from him. I had rather go and live in some cheap place like Bedford Square or even Hampstead than take a farthing of his money.

LADY BRITOMART But after all, Stephen, our present income comes from Andrew.

STEPHEN (*Shocked*) I never knew that.

LADY BRITOMART Well, you surely didn't suppose your grandfather had anything to give me. The Stevenages could not do everything for you. We gave you social position. Andrew had to contribute something. He had a very good bargain, I think.

STEPHEN (*Bitterly*) We are utterly dependent on him and his cannons, then?

LADY BRITOMART Certainly not: the money is settled. But he provided it. So you see it is not a question of taking money from him or not: it is simply a question of how much. I don't want any more for myself.

STEPHEN Nor do I.

LADY BRITOMART But Sarah does; and Barbara does. That is, Charles Lomax and Adolphus Cusins will cost them more. So I must put my pride in my pocket and ask for it, I suppose. That is your advice, Stephen, is it not?

STEPHEN No.

LADY BRITOMART (*Sharply*) Stephen!

STEPHEN Of course if you are determined—

LADY BRITOMART I am not determined: I ask your advice; and I am waiting for it. I will not have all the responsibility thrown on my shoulders.

STEPHEN (*Obstinately*) I would die sooner than ask him for another penny.

LADY BRITOMART (*Resignedly*) You mean that *I* must ask him. Very well, Stephen: it shall be as you wish. You will be glad to know that your grandfather concurs. But he thinks I ought to ask Andrew to come here and see the girls. After all he must have some natural affection for them.

STEPHEN Ask him here!!!

LADY BRITOMART Do not repeat my words, Stephen. Where else can I ask him?

STEPHEN I never expected you to ask him at all.

LADY BRITOMART Now don't tease, Stephen. Come! you see that it is necessary that he should pay us a visit, don't you?

STEPHEN (*Reluctantly*) I suppose so, if the girls cannot do without his money.

LADY BRITOMART Thank you, Stephen: I knew you would give me the right advice when it was properly explained to you. I have asked your father to come this evening. (STEPHEN *bounds from his seat*) Don't jump, Stephen: it fidgets me.

STEPHEN (*In utter consternation*) Do you mean to say that my father is coming here to-night—that he may be here at any moment?

LADY BRITOMART (*Looking at her watch*) I said nine. (*He gasps. She rises*) Ring the bell, please. (STEPHEN *goes to the smaller writing table; presses a button on it; and sits at it with his elbows on the table and his head in his hands, outwitted and overwhelmed*) It is ten minutes to nine yet; and I have to prepare the girls. I asked Charles Lomax and Adolphus to dinner on purpose that they might be here. Andrew had better see them in case he should cherish any delusions as to their being capable of supporting their wives. (*The butler enters:* LADY BRITOMART *goes behind the settee to speak to him*) Morrison: go up to the drawing-room and tell everybody to come down here at once. (MORRISON *withdraws.* LADY BRITOMART *turns to* STEPHEN) Now remember, Stephen: I shall need all your countenance and authority. (*He rises and tries to recover some vestige of these attributes*) Give me a chair, dear. (*He pushes a chair forward from the wall to where she stands, near the smaller writing table. She sits down; and he goes to the armchair, into which he throws himself*) I don't know how Barbara will take it. Ever since they made her a major in the Salvation Army she has developed a propensity to have her own way and order people about which quite cows me sometimes. It's not ladylike: I'm sure I don't know where she picked it up. Anyhow, Barbara shan't bully me; but still it's just as well that your father should be here before she has time to refuse to meet him or make a fuss. Don't look nervous, Stephen: it will only encourage Barbara to make difficulties. *I* am nervous enough, goodness knows; but I don't shew it.

(SARAH *and* BARBARA *come in with their respective young men,* CHARLES LOMAX *and* ADOLPHUS CUSINS. SARAH *is slender, bored, and mundane.* BARBARA *is robuster, jollier, much more energetic.* SARAH *is fashionably dressed:* BARBARA *is in Salvation Army uniform.* LOMAX, *a young man about town, is like many other young men about town. He is afflicted with a frivolous sense of humor which plunges him at the most inopportune moments into paroxysms of imperfectly suppressed laughter.* CUSINS *is a spectacled student, slight, thin haired, and sweet voiced, with a more complex form of* LOMAX*'s complaint. His sense of humor is intellectual and subtle, and is complicated by an appalling temper. The life-long struggle of a benevolent temperament and a high conscience against impulses of inhuman ridicule and fierce impatience has set up a chronic strain which has visibly wrecked his constitution. He is a most implacable, determined, tenacious, intolerant person who by mere force of character presents himself as—and indeed actually is—considerate, gentle, explanatory, even mild and apologetic, capable possibly of murder, but not of cruelty or coarseness. By the operation of some instinct which is not merciful enough to blind him with the illusions of love, he is obstinately bent on marrying* BARBARA. LOMAX *likes* SARAH *and thinks it will be rather a lark to marry her. Consequently he has not attempted to resist* LADY BRITOMART*'s arrangements to that end.*

*All four look as if they had been having a good deal of fun in the drawing room. The girls enter first, leaving the swains outside.* SARAH *comes to the settee.* BARBARA *comes in after her and stops at the door*)

BARBARA Are Cholly and Dolly to come in?

LADY BRITOMART (*Forcibly*) Barbara: I will not have Charles called Cholly: the vulgarity of it positively makes me ill.

BARBARA It's all right, mother: Cholly is quite correct nowadays. Are they to come in?

LADY BRITOMART Yes, if they will behave themselves.

BARBARA (*Through the door*) Come in, Dolly; and behave yourself.

(BARBARA *comes to her mother's writing table.* CUSINS *enters smiling, and wanders towards* LADY BRITOMART)

SARAH (*Calling*) Come in, Cholly. (LOMAX *enters, controlling his features very imperfectly, and places himself vaguely between* SARAH *and* BARBARA)

LADY BRITOMART (*Peremptorily*) Sit down, all of you. (*They sit.* CUSINS *crosses to the window and seats himself there.* LOMAX *takes a chair.* BARBARA *sits at the writing table and* SARAH *on the settee*) I don't in the least know what you are laughing at, Adolphus. I am surprised at you, though I expected nothing better from Charles Lomax.

CUSINS (*In a remarkably gentle voice*) Barbara has been trying to teach me the West Ham Salvation March.

LADY BRITOMART I see nothing to laugh at in that; nor should you if you are really converted.

CUSINS (*Sweetly*) You were not present. It was really funny, I believe.

LOMAX Ripping.

LADY BRITOMART Be quiet, Charles. Now listen to me, children. Your father is coming here this evening.

(*General stupefaction.* LOMAX, SARAH, *and* BARBARA *rise:* SARAH *scared, and* BARBARA *amused and expectant*)

LOMAX (*Remonstrating*) Oh I say!

LADY BRITOMART You are not called on to say anything, Charles.

SARAH Are you serious, mother?

LADY BRITOMART Of course I am serious. It is on your account, Sarah, and also on Charles's. (*Silence.* SARAH *sits, with a shrug.* CHARLES *looks painfully unworthy*) I hope you are not going to object, Barbara.

BARBARA I! why should I? My father has a soul to be saved like anybody else. He's quite welcome as far as

I am concerned. (*She sits on the table, and softly whistles "Onward, Christian Soldiers"*)

LOMAX (*Still remonstrant*) But really, don't you know! Oh I say!

LADY BRITOMART (*Frigidly*) What do you wish to convey, Charles?

LOMAX Well, you must admit that this is a bit thick.

LADY BRITOMART (*Turning with ominous suavity to* CUSINS) Adolphus: you are a professor of Greek. Can you translate Charles Lomax's remarks into reputable English for us?

CUSINS (*Cautiously*) If I may say so, Lady Brit, I think Charles has rather happily expressed what we all feel. Homer, speaking of Autolycus, uses the same phrase. πυκινὸν δόμον ἐλθεῖν means a bit thick.[2]

LOMAX (*Handsomely*) Not that I mind, you know, if Sarah don't. (*He sits*)

LADY BRITOMART (*Crushingly*) Thank you. Have I your permission, Adolphus, to invite my own husband to my own house?

CUSINS (*Gallantly*) You have my unhesitating support in everything you do.

LADY BRITOMART Tush! Sarah: have you nothing to say?

SARAH Do you mean that he is coming regularly to live here?

LADY BRITOMART Certainly not. The spare room is ready for him if he likes to stay for a day or two and see a little more of you; but there are limits.

SARAH Well, he can't eat us, I suppose. *I* don't mind.

LOMAX (*Chuckling*) I wonder how the old man will take it.

LADY BRITOMART Much as the old woman will, no doubt, Charles.

LOMAX (*Abashed*) I didn't mean—at least—

LADY BRITOMART You didn't think, Charles. You never do; and the result is, you never mean anything. And now please attend to me, children. Your father will be quite a stranger to us.

LOMAX I suppose he hasn't seen Sarah since she was a little kid.

LADY BRITOMART Not since she was a little kid, Charles, as you express it with that elegance of diction and refinement of thought that seem never to desert you. Accordingly—er— (*Impatiently*) Now I have forgotten what I was going to say. That comes of your provoking me to be sarcastic, Charles. Adolphus: will you kindly tell me where I was.

CUSINS (*Sweetly*) You were saying that as Mr. Undershaft has not seen his children since they were babies, he will form his opinion of the way you have brought them up from their behavior to-night, and that therefore you wish us all to be particularly careful to conduct ourselves well, especially Charles.

LADY BRITOMART (*With emphatic approval*) Precisely.

LOMAX Look here, Dolly: Lady Brit didn't say that.

LADY BRITOMART (*Vehemently*) I did, Charles. Adolphus's recollection is perfectly correct. It is most important that you should be good; and I do beg you for once not to pair off into opposite corners and giggle and whisper while I am speaking to your father.

BARBARA All right, mother. We'll do you credit. (*She comes off the table, and sits in her chair with ladylike elegance*)

LADY BRITOMART Remember, Charles, that Sarah will want to feel proud of you instead of ashamed of you.

LOMAX Oh I say! there's nothing to be exactly proud of, don't you know.

LADY BRITOMART Well, try and look as if there was.

(MORRISON, *pale and dismayed, breaks into the room in unconcealed disorder*)

MORRISON Might I speak a word to you, my lady?

LADY BRITOMART Nonsense! Shew him up.

MORRISON Yes, my lady. (*He goes*)

LOMAX Does Morrison know who it is?

LADY BRITOMART Of course. Morrison has always been with us.

LOMAX It must be a regular corker for him, don't you know.

LADY BRITOMART Is this a moment to get on my nerves, Charles, with your outrageous expressions?

LOMAX But this is something out of the ordinary, really—

MORRISON (*At the door*) The—er—Mr. Undershaft. (*He retreats in confusion*)

(ANDREW UNDERSHAFT *comes in. All rise.* LADY BRITOMART *meets him in the middle of the room behind the settee.*

ANDREW *is, on the surface, a stoutish, easygoing elderly man, with kindly patient manners, and an engaging simplicity of character. But he has a watchful, deliberate, waiting, listening face, and formidable reserves of power, both bodily and mental, in his capacious chest and long head. His gentleness is partly that of a strong man who has learnt by experience that his natural grip hurts ordinary people unless he handles them very carefully, and partly the mellowness of age and success. He is also a little shy in his present very delicate situation*)

LADY BRITOMART Good evening, Andrew.

UNDERSHAFT How d'ye do, my dear.

LADY BRITOMART You look a good deal older.

UNDERSHAFT (*Apologetically*) I am somewhat older. (*Taking her hand with a touch of courtship*) Time has stood still with you.

LADY BRITOMART (*Throwing away his hand*) Rubbish! This is your family.

UNDERSHAFT (*Surprised*) Is it so large? I am sorry to say my memory is failing very badly in some things. (*He offers his hand with paternal kindness to* LOMAX)

LOMAX (*Jerkily shaking his hand*) Ahdedoo.

[2] The Greek *pykinon domon elthein* (*Iliad,* Book X, line 267) translates literally as "to come to a thick [*i.e.,* well-built] house." Lomax's university-slang *thick* implies "It just isn't done." Cusins is punning on Undershaft's homecoming and a more literal sense of *thick.* Autolycus, famous in Greek legend as a thief with the power of making himself and his stolen goods invisible, captures the young Undershafts' impression of their father.

UNDERSHAFT I can see you are my eldest. I am very glad to meet you again, my boy.

LOMAX (*Remonstrating*) No, but look here don't you know—(*Overcome*) Oh I say!

LADY BRITOMART (*Recovering from momentary speechlessness*) Andrew: do you mean to say that you don't remember how many children you have?

UNDERSHAFT Well, I am afraid I— They have grown so much—er. Am I making any ridiculous mistake? I may as well confess: I recollect only one son. But so many things have happened since, of course—er—

LADY BRITOMART (*Decisively*) Andrew: you are talking nonsense. Of course you have only one son.

UNDERSHAFT Perhaps you will be good enough to introduce me, my dear.

LADY BRITOMART That is Charles Lomax, who is engaged to Sarah.

UNDERSHAFT My dear sir, I beg your pardon.

LOMAX Notatall. Delighted, I assure you.

LADY BRITOMART This is Stephen.

UNDERSHAFT (*Bowing*) Happy to make your acquaintance, Mr. Stephen. Then (*Going to* CUSINS) you must be my son. (*Taking* CUSINS' *hands in his*) How are you, my young friend? (*To* LADY BRITOMART) He is very like you, my love.

CUSINS You flatter me, Mr. Undershaft. My name is Cusins: engaged to Barbara. (*Very explicitly*) That is Major Barbara Undershaft, of the Salvation Army. That is Sarah, your second daughter. This is Stephen Undershaft, your son.

UNDERSHAFT My dear Stephen, I beg your pardon.

STEPHEN Not at all.

UNDERSHAFT Mr. Cusins: I am indebted to you for explaining so precisely. (*Turning to* SARAH) Barbara, my dear—

SARAH (*Prompting him*) Sarah.

UNDERSHAFT Sarah, of course. (*They shake hands. He goes over to* BARBARA) Barbara—I am right this time, I hope.

BARBARA Quite right. (*They shake hands*)

LADY BRITOMART (*Resuming command*) Sit down, all of you. Sit down, Andrew. (*She comes forward and sits on the settee.* CUSINS *also brings his chair forward on her left.* BARBARA *and* STEPHEN *resume their seats.* LOMAX *gives his chair to* SARAH *and goes for another*)

UNDERSHAFT Thank you, my love.

LOMAX (*Conversationally, as he brings a chair forward between the writing table and the settee, and offers it to* UNDERSHAFT) Takes you some time to find out exactly where you are, don't it?

UNDERSHAFT (*Accepting the chair, but remaining standing*) That is not what embarrasses me, Mr. Lomax. My difficulty is that if I play the part of a father, I shall produce the effect of an intrusive stranger; and if I play the part of a discreet stranger, I may appear a callous father.

LADY BRITOMART There is no need for you to play any part at all, Andrew. You had much better be sincere and natural.

UNDERSHAFT (*Submissively*) Yes, my dear: I daresay that will be best. (*He sits down comfortably*) Well, here I am. Now what can I do for you all?

LADY BRITOMART You need not do anything, Andrew. You are one of the family. You can sit with us and enjoy yourself. (*A painfully conscious pause.* BARBARA *makes a face at* LOMAX, *whose too long suppressed mirth immediately explodes in agonized neighings*)

LADY BRITOMART (*Outraged*) Charles Lomax: if you can behave yourself, behave yourself. If not, leave the room.

LOMAX I'm awfully sorry, Lady Brit; but really, you know, upon my soul! (*He sits on the settee between* LADY BRITOMART *and* UNDERSHAFT, *quite overcome*)

BARBARA Why don't you laugh if you want to, Cholly? It's good for your inside.

LADY BRITOMART Barbara: you have had the education of a lady. Please let your father see that; and don't talk like a street girl.

UNDERSHAFT Never mind me, my dear. As you know, I am not a gentleman; and I was never educated.

LOMAX (*Encouragingly*) Nobody'd know it, I assure you. You look all right, you know.

CUSINS Let me advise you to study Greek, Mr Undershaft. Greek scholars are privileged men. Few of them know Greek; and none of them know anything else; but their position is unchallengeable. Other languages are the qualifications of waiters and commercial travellers: Greek is to a man of position what the hallmark is to silver.

BARBARA Dolly: don't be insincere. Cholly: fetch your concertina and play something for us.

LOMAX (*Jumps up eagerly, but checks himself to remark doubtfully to* UNDERSHAFT) Perhaps that sort of thing isn't in your line, eh?

UNDERSHAFT I am particularly fond of music.

LOMAX (*Delighted*) Are you? Then I'll get it. (*He goes upstairs for the instrument*).

UNDERSHAFT Do you play, Barbara?

BARBARA Only the tambourine. But Cholly's teaching me the concertina.

UNDERSHAFT Is Cholly also a member of the Salvation Army?

BARBARA No: he says it's bad form to be a dissenter. But I don't despair of Cholly. I made him come yesterday to a meeting at the dock gates, and take the collection in his hat.

UNDERSHAFT (*Looks whimsically at his wife*)!!

LADY BRITOMART It is not my doing, Andrew. Barbara is old enough to take her own way. She has no father to advise her.

BARBARA Oh yes she has. There are no orphans in the Salvation Army.

UNDERSHAFT Your father there has a great many children and plenty of experience, eh?

BARBARA (*Looking at him with quick interest and nodding*) Just so. How did you come to understand that? (LOMAX *is heard at the door trying the concertina*)

LADY BRITOMART Come in, Charles. Play us something at once.

LOMAX Righto! (*He sits down in his former place, and preludes*)

UNDERSHAFT One moment, Mr Lomax, I am rather interested in the Salvation Army. Its motto might be my own: Blood and Fire.

LOMAX (*Shocked*) But not your sort of blood and fire, you know.

UNDERSHAFT My sort of blood cleanses: my sort of fire purifies.

BARBARA So do ours. Come down tomorrow to my shelter—the West Ham shelter—and see what we're doing. We're going to march to a great meeting in the Assembly Hall at Mile End.[3] Come and see the shelter and then march with us: it will do you a lot of good. Can you play anything?

UNDERSHAFT In my youth I earned pennies, and even shillings occasionally, in the streets and in public house parlors by my natural talent for stepdancing. Later on, I became a member of the Undershaft orchestral society, and performed passably on the tenor trombone.

LOMAX (*Scandalized—putting down the concertina*) Oh I say!

BARBARA Many a sinner has played himself into heaven on the trombone, thanks to the Army.

LOMAX (*To* BARBARA, *still rather shocked*) Yes; but what about the cannon business, don't you know? (*To* UNDERSHAFT) Getting into heaven is not exactly in your line, is it?

LADY BRITOMART Charles!!!

LOMAX Well; but it stands to reason, don't it? The cannon business may be necessary and all that: we can't get on without cannons; but it isn't right, you know. On the other hand, there may be a certain amount of tosh about the Salvation Army—I belong to the Established Church myself—but still you can't deny that it's religion; and you can't go against religion, can you? At least unless you're downright immoral, don't you know.

UNDERSHAFT You hardly appreciate my position, Mr. Lomax—

LOMAX (*Hastily*) I'm not saying anything against you personally—

UNDERSHAFT Quite so, quite so. But consider for a moment. Here I am, a profiteer in mutilation and murder. I find myself in a specially amiable humor just now because, this morning, down at the foundry, we blew twenty-seven dummy soldiers into fragments with a gun which formerly destroyed only thirteen.

LOMAX (*Leniently*) Well, the more destructive war becomes, the sooner it will be abolished, eh?

UNDERSHAFT Not at all. The more destructive war becomes, the more fascinating we find it. No, Mr. Lomax: I am obliged to you for making the usual excuse for my trade; but I am not ashamed of it. I am not one of those men who keep their morals and their business in watertight compartments. All the spare money my trade rivals spend on hospitals, cathedrals, and other receptacles for conscience money, I devote to experiments and researches in improved methods of destroying life and property. I have always done so; and I always shall. Therefore your Christmas card moralities of peace on earth and goodwill among men are of no use to me. Your Christianity, which enjoins you to resist not evil, and to turn the other cheek, would make me a bankrupt. My morality—my religion—must have a place for cannons and torpedoes in it.

STEPHEN (*Coldly—almost sullenly*) You speak as if there were half a dozen moralities and religions to choose from, instead of one true morality and one true religion.

UNDERSHAFT For me there is only one true morality; but it might not fit you, as you do not manufacture aerial battleships. There is only one true morality for every man; but every man has not the same true morality.

LOMAX (*Overtaxed*) Would you mind saying that again? I didn't quite follow it.

CUSINS It's quite simple. As Euripides says, one man's meat is another man's poison morally as well as physically.

UNDERSHAFT Precisely.

LOMAX Oh, that. Yes, yes, yes. True. True.

STEPHEN In other words, some men are honest and some are scoundrels.

BARBARA Bosh. There are no scoundrels.

UNDERSHAFT Indeed? Are there any good men?

BARBARA No. Not one. There are neither good men nor scoundrels: there are just children of one Father; and the sooner they stop calling one another names the better. You needn't talk to me: I know them. I've had scores of them through my hands: scoundrels, criminals, infidels, philanthropists, missionaries, county councillors, all sorts. They're all just the same sort of sinner; and there's the same salvation ready for them all.

UNDERSHAFT May I ask have you ever saved a maker of cannons?

BARBARA No. Will you let me try?

UNDERSHAFT Well, I will make a bargain with you. If I go to see you tomorrow in your Salvation Shelter, will you come the day after to see me in my cannon works?

BARBARA Take care. It may end in your giving up the cannons for the sake of the Salvation Army.

UNDERSHAFT Are you sure it will not end in your giving up the Salvation Army for the sake of cannons?

BARBARA I will take my chance of that.

UNDERSHAFT And I will take my chance of the other. (*They shake hands on it*) Where is your shelter?

BARBARA In West Ham. At the sign of the cross. Ask anybody in Canning Town. Where are your works?

UNDERSHAFT In Perivale St Andrews. At the sign of the sword. Ask anybody in Europe.

LOMAX Hadn't I better play something?

[3] The Salvation Army began when William Booth conducted a religious meeting at Mile End Waste, one of London's oldest sections.

BARBARA Yes. Give us "Onward, Christian Soldiers."

LOMAX Well, that's rather a strong order to begin with, don't you know. Suppose I sing "Thou're passing hence, my brother." It's much the same tune.

BARBARA It's too melancholy. You get saved, Cholly; and you'll pass hence, my brother, without making such a fuss about it.

LADY BRITOMART Really, Barbara, you go on as if religion were a pleasant subject. Do have some sense of propriety.

UNDERSHAFT I do not find it an unpleasant subject, my dear. It is the only one that capable people really care for.

LADY BRITOMART (*Looking at her watch*) Well, if you are determined to have it, I insist on having it in a proper and respectable way. Charles: ring for prayers. (*General amazement.* STEPHEN *rises in dismay*)

LOMAX (*Rising*) Oh I say!

UNDERSHAFT (*Rising*) I am afraid I must be going.

LADY BRITOMART You cannot go now, Andrew: it would be most improper. Sit down. What will the servants think?

UNDERSHAFT My dear: I have conscientious scruples. May I suggest a compromise? If Barbara will conduct a little service in the drawing room, with Mr. Lomax as organist, I will attend it willingly. I will even take part, if a trombone can be procured.

LADY BRITOMART Don't mock, Andrew.

UNDERSHAFT (*Shocked—to* BARBARA) You don't think I am mocking, my love, I hope.

BARBARA No, of course not; and it wouldn't matter if you were: half the Army came to their first meeting for a lark. (*Rising*) Come along. (*She throws her arm round her father and sweeps him out, calling to the others from the threshold*) Come, Dolly. Come, Cholly.

(CUSINS *rises*)

LADY BRITOMART I will not be disobeyed by everybody. Adolphus: sit down. (*He does not*) Charles: you may go. You are not fit for prayers: you cannot keep your countenance.

LOMAX Oh I say! (*He goes out*)

LADY BRITOMART (*Continuing*) But you, Adolphus, can behave yourself if you choose to. I insist on your staying.

CUSINS My dear Lady Brit: there are things in the family prayer book that I couldn't bear to hear you say.

LADY BRITOMART What things, pray?

CUSINS Well, you would have to say before all the servants that we have done things we ought not to have done, and left undone things we ought to have done, and that there is no health in us. I cannot bear to hear you doing yourself such an injustice, and Barbara such an injustice. As for myself, I flatly deny it: I have done my best. I shouldn't dare to marry Barbara—I couldn't look you in the face—if it were true. So I must go to the drawing room.

LADY BRITOMART (*Offended*) Well, go. (*He starts for the door*) And remember this, Adolphus (*He turns to listen*) I have a strong suspicion that you went to the Salvation Army to worship Barbara and nothing else. And I quite appreciate the clever way in which you systematically humbug me. I have found you out. Take care Barbara doesn't. That's all.

CUSINS (*With unruffled sweetness*) Don't tell on me. (*He steals out*)

LADY BRITOMART Sarah: if you want to go, go. Anything's better than to sit there as if you wished you were a thousand miles away.

SARAH (*Languidly*) Very well, mamma. (*She goes*).

(LADY BRITOMART, *with a sudden flounce, gives way to a little gust of tears*)

STEPHEN (*Going to her*) Mother: what's the matter?

LADY BRITOMART (*Swishing away her tears with her handkerchief*) Nothing. Foolishness. You can go with him, too, if you like, and leave me with the servants.

STEPHEN Oh, you mustn't think that, mother. I—I don't like him.

LADY BRITOMART The others do. That is the injustice of a woman's lot. A woman has to bring up her children; and that means to restrain them, to deny them things they want, to set them tasks, to punish them when they do wrong, to do all the unpleasant things. And then the father, who has nothing to do but pet them and spoil them, comes in when all her work is done and steals their affection from her.

STEPHEN He has not stolen our affection from you. It is only curiosity.

LADY BRITOMART (*Violently*) I won't be consoled, Stephen. There is nothing the matter with me. (*She rises and goes towards the door*)

STEPHEN Where are you going, mother?

LADY BRITOMART To the drawing room, of course. (*She goes out. "Onward, Christian Soldiers," on the concertina, with tambourine accompaniment, is heard when the door opens*) Are you coming, Stephen?

STEPHEN No. Certainly not. (*She goes. He sits down on the settee, with compressed lips and an expression of strong dislike*)

END OF ACT I

# Act Two

*The yard of the West Ham shelter of the Salvation Army is a cold place on a January morning. The building itself, an old warehouse, is newly whitewashed. Its gabled end projects into the yard in the middle, with a door on the ground floor, and another in the loft above it without any balcony or ladder, but with a pulley rigged over it for hoisting sacks. Those who come from this central gable end into the yard have the gateway leading to the street on their left, with a stone horse-trough just beyond it, and, on the right, a penthouse shielding a table from the weather. There are forms at the table; and on them are seated a man and a woman, both much down on their luck, finishing a meal of bread (one thick slice each, with margarine and golden syrup) and diluted milk.*

*The man, a workman out of employment, is young, agile, a talker, a poser, sharp enough to be capable of anything in reason except honesty or altruistic considerations of any kind. The woman is a commonplace old bundle of poverty and hard-worn humanity. She looks sixty and probably is forty-five. If they were rich people, gloved and muffed and well wrapped up in furs and overcoats, they would be numbed and miserable; for it is a grindingly cold, raw, January day; and a glance at the background of grimy warehouses and leaden sky visible over the whitewashed walls of the yard would drive any idle rich person straight to the Mediterranean. But these two, being no more troubled with visions of the Mediterranean than of the moon, and being compelled to keep more of their clothes in the pawnshop, and less on their persons, in winter than in summer, are not depressed by the cold: rather are they stung into vivacity, to which their meal has just now given an almost jolly turn. The man takes a pull at his mug, and then gets up and moves about the yard with his hands deep in his pockets, occasionally breaking into a stepdance.*

THE WOMAN Feel better arter your meal, sir?

THE MAN No. Call that a meal! Good enough for you, p'raps; but wot is it to me, an intelligent workin' man?

THE WOMAN Workin' man! Wot are you?

THE MAN Painter.

THE WOMAN (*Skeptically*) Yus, I dessay.

THE MAN Yus, you dessay! I know. Every loafer that can't do nothink calls 'isself a painter. Well, I'm a real painter: grainer, finisher, thirty-eight bob a week when I can get it.

THE WOMAN Then why don't you go and get it?

THE MAN I'll tell you why. Fust: I'm intelligent—fffff! it's rotten cold here (*He dances a step or two*)—yes; intelligent beyond the station o' life into which it has pleased the capitalists to call me; and they don't like a man that sees through 'em. Second, an intelligent bein' needs a doo share of 'appiness; so I drink somethink cruel when I get the chawnce. Third, I stand by my class and do as little as I can so's to leave 'arf the job for me fellow workers. Fourth, I'm fly[1] enough to know wot's inside the law and wot's outside it; and inside it I do as the capitalists do: pinch wot I can lay me 'ands on. In a proper state of society I am sober, industrious, and honest: in Rome, so to speak, I do as the Romans do. Wot's the consequence? When trade is bad—and it's rotten bad just now—and the employers 'az to sack 'arf their men, they generally start on me.

THE WOMAN What's your name?

THE MAN Price. Bronterre O'Brien Price. Usually called Snobby Price, for short.

THE WOMAN Snobby's a carpenter, ain't it? You said you was a painter.

PRICE Not that kind of snob, but the genteel sort. I'm too uppish, owing to my intelligence, and my father being a Chartist and a reading, thinking man: a stationer, too. I'm none of your common hewers of wood and drawers of water; and don't you forget it. (*He returns to his seat at the table, and takes up his mug*) Wot's your name?

THE WOMAN Rummy Mitchens, sir.

PRICE (*Quaffing the remains of his milk to her*) Your 'elth, Miss Mitchens.

RUMMY (*Correcting him*) Missis Mitchens.

PRICE Wot! Oh Rummy, Rummy! Respectable married woman, Rummy, gittin' rescued by the Salvation Army by pretendin' to be a bad un. Same old game!

RUMMY What am I to do? I can't starve. Them Salvation lasses is dear good girls; but the better you are, the worse they likes to think you were before they rescued you. Why shouldn't they 'av a bit o' credit, poor loves? they're worn to rags by their work. And where would they get the money to rescue us if we was to let on we're no worse than other people? You know what ladies and gentlemen are.

PRICE Thievin' swine! Wish I 'ad their job, Rummy, all the same. Wot does Rummy stand for? Pet name p'raps?

RUMMY Short for Romola.

PRICE For wot!?

RUMMY Romola. It was out of a new book.[2] Somebody me mother wanted me to grow up like.

PRICE We're companions in misfortune, Rummy. Both of us got names that nobody cawn't pronounce. Consequently I'm Snobby and you're Rummy because Bill and Sally wasn't good enough for our parents. Such is life!

RUMMY Who saved you, Mr Price? Was it Major Barbara?

PRICE No: I come here on my own. I'm goin' to be Bronterre O'Brien Price, the converted painter. I know wot they like. I'll tell 'em how I blasphemed and gambled and wopped my poor old mother—

RUMMY (*Shocked*) Used you to beat your mother?

PRICE Not likely. She used to beat me. No matter: you come and listen to the converted painter, and you'll hear how she was a pious woman that taught me me prayers at 'er knee, an' how I used to come home drunk and drag her out o' bed be 'er snow-white 'airs, an' lam into 'er with the poker.

RUMMY That's what's so unfair to us women. Your

[1] Sharp, shrewd.

[2] Probably George Eliot's impressive historical novel, *Romola*, first published in the early 1860's. Eliot's heroine finds peace of mind and spirit under the guidance of Savonarola; Shaw achieves an ironically distorted parallel in Rummy Mitchens' reliance on the Salvation Army.

confessions is just as big lies as ours: you don't tell what you really done no more than us; but you men can tell your lies right out at the meetin's and be made much of for it; while the sort o' confessions we 'az to make 'az to be whispered to one lady at a time. It ain't right, spite of all their piety.

PRICE Right! Do you s'pose the Army 'd be allowed if it went and did right? Not much. It combs our 'air and makes us good little blokes to be robbed and put upon. But I'll play the game as good as any of 'em. I'll see somebody struck by lightnin', or hear a voice sayin' "Snobby Price: where will you spend eternity?" I'll 'ave a time of it, I tell you.

RUMMY You won't be let drink, though.

PRICE I'll take it out in gorspellin', then. I don't want to drink if I can get fun enough any other way.

(JENNY HILL, *a pale, overwrought, pretty Salvation lass of eighteen, comes in through the yard gate, leading* PETER SHIRLEY, *a half hardened, half worn-out elderly man, weak with hunger*)

JENNY (*Supporting him*) Come! pluck up. I'll get you something to eat. You'll be all right then.

PRICE (*Rising and hurrying officiously to take the old man off* JENNY's *hands*) Poor old man! Cheer up, brother: you'll find rest and peace and 'appiness 'ere. Hurry up with the food, miss: 'e's fair done. (JENNY *hurries into the shelter*) 'Ere, buck up, daddy! she's fetchin y'a thick slice o' bread'n treacle, an' a mug o' skyblue.[3] (*He seats him at the corner of the table*)

RUMMY (*Gaily*) Keep up your old 'art! Never say die!

SHIRLEY I'm not an old man. I'm only forty-six. I'm as good as ever I was. The grey patch come in my hair before I was thirty. All it wants is three pennorth o' hair dye: am I to be turned on the streets to starve for it? Holy God! I've worked ten to twelve hours a day since I was thirteen, and paid my way all through; and now am I to be thrown into the gutter and my job given to a young man that can do it no better than me because I've black hair that goes white at the first change?

PRICE (*Cheerfully*) No good jawrin' about it. You're only a jumped-up, jerked-off, 'orspittle-turned-out incurable of an ole workin' man: who cares about you? Eh? Make the thievin' swine give you a meal: they've stole many a one from you. Get a bit o' your own back. (JENNY *returns with the usual meal*) There you are, brother. Awsk a blessin' an' tuck that into you.

SHIRLEY (*Looking at it ravenously but not touching it, and crying like a child*) I never took anything before.

JENNY (*Petting him*) Come, come! the Lord sends it to you: he wasn't above taking bread from his friends; and why should you be? Besides, when we find you a job you can pay us for it if you like.

SHIRLEY (*Eagerly*) Yes, yes: that's true. I can pay you back: it's only a loan. (*Shivering*) Oh Lord! oh Lord! (*He turns to the table and attacks the meal ravenously*)

[3] Diluted, watery milk.

JENNY Well, Rummy, are you more comfortable now?

RUMMY God bless you, lovey! you've fed my body and saved my soul, haven't you? (JENNY, *touched, kisses her*) Sit down and rest a bit: you must be ready to drop.

JENNY I've been going hard since morning. But there's more work than we can do. I mustn't stop.

RUMMY Try a prayer for just two minutes. You'll work all the better after.

JENNY (*Her eyes lighting up*) Oh isn't it wonderful how a few minutes prayer revives you! I was quite lightheaded at twelve o'clock, I was so tired; but Major Barbara just sent me to pray for five minutes; and I was able to go on as if I had only just begun. (*To* PRICE) Did you have a piece of bread?

PRICE (*With unction*) Yes, miss; but I've got the piece that I value more; and that's the peace that passeth hall hannerstennin.

RUMMY (*Fervently*) Glory Hallelujah!

(BILL WALKER, *a rough customer of about twenty-five, appears at the yard gate and looks malevolently at* JENNY)

JENNY That makes me so happy. When you say that, I feel wicked for loitering here. I must get to work again.

(*She is hurrying to the shelter, when the new-comer moves quickly up to the door and intercepts her. His manner is so threatening that she retreats as he comes at her truculently, driving her down the yard*)

BILL Aw knaow you. You're the one that took aw'y maw girl. You're the one that set 'er agen me. Well, I'm gowin' to 'ev 'er aht. Not that Aw care a carse for 'er or you: see? But Aw'll let 'er knaow; and Aw'll let you knaow. Aw'm gowin' to give her a doin' that'll teach 'er to cat aw'y from me. Nah in wiv you and tell 'er to cam aht afore Aw cam in and kick 'er aht. Tell 'er Bill Walker wants 'er. She'll knaow wot thet means; and if she keeps me witin' it'll be worse. You stop to jawr beck at me; and Aw'll stawt on you: d'ye 'eah? There's your w'y. In you gow. (*He takes her by the arm and slings her towards the door of the shelter. She falls on her hand and knee.* RUMMY *helps her up again*)

PRICE (*Rising, and venturing irresolutely towards* BILL) Easy there, mate. She ain't doin' you no 'arm.

BILL 'Oo are you callin' mite? (*Standing over him threateningly*) Youre gowin' to stend up for 'er, aw yer? Put ap your 'ends.

RUMMY (*Running indignantly to him to scold him*) Oh, you great brute— (*He instantly swings his left hand back against her face. She screams and reels back to the trough, where she sits down, covering her bruised face with her hands and rocking herself and moaning with pain*)

JENNY (*Going to her*) Oh, God forgive you! How could you strike an old woman like that?

BILL (*Seizing her by the hair so violently that she also screams, and tearing her away from the old woman*) You Gawd forgimme again and Aw'll Gawd forgive you one on the jawr thet'll stop you pryin' for a week.

(*Holding her and turning fiercely on* PRICE) 'Ev you ennything to s'y agen it?

PRICE (*Intimidated*) No, matey: she ain't anything to do with me.

BILL Good job for you! Aw'd pat two meals into you and fawt you with one finger arter, you stawved cur. (*To* JENNY) Nah are you gowin' to fetch aht Mog Ebbijem; or em Aw to knock your fice off you and fetch her meself?

JENNY (*Writhing in his grasp*) Oh, please, someone go in and tell Major Barbara— (*She screams again as he wrenches her head down; and* PRICE *and* RUMMY *flee into the shelter*)

BILL You want to gow in and tell your Mijor of me, do you?

JENNY Oh, please, don't drag my hair. Let me go.

BILL Do you or down't you? (*She stifles a scream*) Yus or nao?

JENNY God give me strength—

BILL (*Striking her with his fist in the face*) Gow an' shaow her thet, and tell her if she wants one lawk it to cam and interfere with me. (JENNY, *crying with pain, goes into the shed. He goes to the form and addresses the old man*) 'Eah: finish your mess; and git aht o' maw w'y.

SHIRLEY (*Springing up and facing him fiercely, with the mug in his hand*) You take a liberty with me, and I'll smash you over the face with the mug and cut your eye out. Ain't you satisfied—young whelps like you—with takin' the bread out o' the mouths of your elders that have brought you up and slaved for you, but you must come shovin and cheekin' and bullyin' in here, where the bread o' charity is sickenin' in our stummicks?

BILL (*Contemptuously, but backing a little*) Wot good are you, you aold palsy mag? Wot good are you?

SHIRLEY As good as you and better. I'll do a day's work agen you or any fat young soaker of your age. Go and take my job at Horrockses, where I worked for ten year. They want young men there: they can't afford to keep men over forty-five. They're very sorry—give you a character and happy to help you to get anything suited to your years—sure a steady man won't be long out of a job. Well, let 'em try you. They'll find the differ. What do you know? Not as much as how to beeyave yourself—layin' your dirty fist across the mouth of a respectable woman!

BILL Downt provowk me to l'y it acrost yours: d'ye 'eah?

SHIRLEY (*With blighting contempt*) Yes: you like an old man to hit, don't you, when you've finished with the women. I ain't seen you hit a young one yet.

BILL (*Stung*) You loy, you aold soupkitchener, you. There was a yang menn 'eah. Did Aw offer to 'itt him or did Aw not?

SHIRLEY Was he starvin' or was he not? Was he a man or only a crosseyed thief an' a loafer? Would you hit my son-in-law's brother?

BILL 'Oo's 'ee?

SHIRLEY Todger Fairmile o' Balls Pond. Him that won £20 off the Japanese wrastler at the music hall by standin' out 17 minutes 4 seconds agen him.

BILL (*Sullenly*) Aw'm nao music 'awl wrastler. Ken he box?

SHIRLEY Yes: an' you can't.

BILL Wot! Aw cawn't, cawn't Aw? Wot's they you s'y? (*Threatening him*)

SHIRLEY (*Not budging an inch*) Will you box Todger Fairmile if I put him on to you? Say the word.

BILL (*Subsiding with a slouch*) Aw'll stend ap to enny menn alawv, if he was ten Todger Fairmawls. But Aw down't set ap to be a perfeshnal.

SHIRLEY (*Looking down on him with unfathomable disdain*) You box! Slap an old woman with the back o' your hand! You hadn't even the sense to hit her where a magistrate couldn't see the mark of it, you silly young lump of conceit and ignorance. Hit a girl in the jaw and on'y make her cry! If Todger Fairmile'd done it, she wouldn't 'a got up inside o' ten minutes, no more than you would if he got on to you. Yah! I'd set about you myself if I had a week's feedin' in me instead o' two months' starvation. (*He turns his back on him and sits down moodily at the table*)

BILL (*Following him and stooping over him to drive the taunt in*) You loy! you've the bread and treacle in you that you cam 'eah to beg.

SHIRLEY (*Bursting into tears*) Oh God! it's true: I'm only an old pauper on the scrap heap. (*Furiously*) But you'll come to it yourself; and then you'll know. You'll come to it sooner than a teetotaller like me, fillin' yourself with gin at this hour o' the mornin!

BILL Aw'm nao gin drinker, you oald lawr; bat wen Aw want to give my girl a bloomin' good 'awdin' Aw lawk to 'ev a bit o' devil in me: see? An' 'eah Aw emm, talking to a rotten aold blawter like you stead o' given' 'er wot for. (*Working himself into a rage*) Aw'm gowin' in there to fetch her aht. (*He makes vengefully for the shelter door*)

SHIRLEY You're goin' to the station on a stretcher, more likely; and they'll take the gin and the devil out of you there when they get you inside. You mind what you're about: the major here is the Earl o' Stevenage's granddaughter.

BILL (*Checked*) Garn!

SHIRLEY You'll see.

BILL (*His resolution oozing*) Well, Aw ain't dan nathin' to 'er.

SHIRLEY S'pose she said you did! who'd believe you?

BILL (*Very uneasy, skulking back to the corner of the penthouse*) Gawd! there's no jastice in this cantry. To think wot them people can do! Aw'm as good as 'er.

SHIRLEY Tell her so. It's just what a fool like you would do.

(BARBARA, *brisk and businesslike, comes from the shelter with a note book, and addresses herself to* SHIRLEY. BILL, *cowed, sits down in the corner on a form, and turns his back on them*)

BARBARA Good morning.

SHIRLEY (*Standing up and taking off his hat*) Good morning, miss.

BARBARA Sit down: make yourself at home. (*He hesitates; but she puts a friendly hand on his shoulder and makes him obey*) Now then! since you've made friends with us, we want to know all about you. Names and addresses and trades.

SHIRLEY Peter Shirley. Fitter. Chucked out two months ago because I was too old.

BARBARA (*Not at all surprised*) You'd pass still. Why didn't you dye your hair?

SHIRLEY I did. Me age come out at a coroner's inquest on me daughter.

BARBARA Steady?

SHIRLEY Teetotaller. Never out of a job before. Good worker. And sent to the knackers like an old horse!

BARBARA No matter: if you did your part God will do his.

SHIRLEY (*Suddenly stubborn*) My religion's no concern of anybody but myself.

BARBARA (*Guessing*) *I* know. Secularist?

SHIRLEY (*Hotly*) Did I offer to deny it?

BARBARA Why should you? My own father's a Secularist, I think. Our Father—yours and mine—fulfils himself in many ways; and I daresay he knew what he was about when he made a Secularist of you. So buck up, Peter! we can always find a job for a steady man like you. (SHIRLEY, *disarmed and a little bewildered, touches his hat. She turns from him to* BILL) What's your name?

BILL (*Insolently*) Wot's thet to you?

BARBARA (*Calmly making a note*) Afraid to give his name. Any trade?

BILL 'Oo's afride to give 'is nime? (*Doggedly, with a sense of heroically defying the House of Lords in the person of Lord Stevenage*) If you want to bring a chawge agen me, bring it. (*She waits, unruffled*) Moy nime's Bill Walker.

BARBARA (*As if the name were familiar: trying to remember how*) Bill Walker? (*Recollecting*) Oh, I know: you're the man that Jenny Hill was praying for inside just now. (*She enters his name in her note book*)

BILL 'Oo's Jenny 'Ill? And wot call 'as she to pr'y for me?

BARBARA I don't know. Perhaps it was you that cut her lip.

BILL (*Defiantly*) Yus, it was me that cat her lip. Aw ain't afride o' you.

BARBARA How could you be, since you're not afraid of God? You're a brave man, Mr Walker. It takes some pluck to do our work here; but none of us dare lift our hand against a girl like that, for fear of her father in heaven.

BILL (*Sullenly*) I want nan o' your kentin' jawr.[4] I spowse you think Aw cam 'eah to beg from you, like this demmiged lot 'eah. Not me. Aw down't want your bread and scripe[5] and ketlep.[6] Aw don't b'lieve in your Gawd, no more than you do yourself.

BARBARA (*Sunnily apologetic and ladylike, as on a new footing with him*) Oh, I beg your pardon for putting your name down, Mr Walker. I didn't understand. I'll strike it out.

BILL (*Taking this as a slight, and deeply wounded by it*) 'Eah! you let maw nime alown. Ain't it good enaff to be in your book?

BARBARA (*Considering*) Well, you see, there's no use putting down your name unless I can do something for you, is there? What's your trade?

BILL (*Still smarting*) Thets nao concern o' yours.

BARBARA Just so. (*Very businesslike*) I'll put you down as (*Writing*) the man who—struck—poor little Jenny Hill—in the mouth.

BILL (*Rising threateningly*) See 'eah. Awve 'ed enaff o this.

BARBARA (*Quite sunny and fearless*) What did you come to us for?

BILL Aw cam for maw gel, see? Aw cam to tike her aht o' this and to brike 'er jawr for 'er.

BARBARA (*Complacently*) You see I was right about your trade. (BILL, *on the point of retorting furiously, finds himself, to his great shame and terror, in danger of crying instead. He sits down again suddenly*) What's her name?

BILL (*Dogged*) 'Er nime's Mog Ebbijem: thet's wot her nime is.

BARBARA Mog Habbijam! Oh, she's gone to Canning Town, to our barracks there.

BILL (*Fortified by his resentment of* MOG'S *perfidy*) Is she? (*Vindictively*) Then Aw'm gowin' to Kennintahn arter her. (*He crosses to the gate; hesitates; finally comes back at* BARBARA) Are you loyin' to me to git shat o' me?

BARBARA I don't want to get shut of you. I want to keep you here and save your soul. You'd better stay: you're going to have a bad time today, Bill.

BILL 'Oo's gowin' to give it to me? You, p'reps?

BARBARA Someone you don't believe in. But you'll be glad afterwards.

BILL (*Slinking off*) Aw'll gow to Kennintahn to be aht o' reach o' your tangue. (*Suddenly turning on her with intense malice*) And if Aw down't fawnd Mog there, Aw'll cam beck and do two years for you, s'elp me Gawd if Aw downt!

BARBARA (*A shade kindlier, if possible*) It's no use, Bill. She's got another bloke.

BILL Wot!

BARBARA One of her own converts. He fell in love with her when he saw her with her soul saved, and her face clean, and her hair washed.

BILL (*Surprised*) Wottud she wash it for, the carroty slat? It's red.

BARBARA It's quite lovely now, because she wears a new look in her eyes with it. It's a pity you're too late. The new bloke has put your nose out of joint, Bill.

BILL Aw'll put his nowse aht o' joint for him. Not that Aw care a carse for 'er, mawnd thet. But Aw'll teach her to drop me as if Aw was dirt. And Aw'll teach him to meddle with maw judy. Wots 'iz bleedin' nime?

BARBARA Sergeant Todger Fairmile.

SHIRLEY (*Rising with grim joy*) I'll go with him, miss.

[4] Special Salvation Army talk (canting jaw).
[5] Thinly spread butter (scrape).
[6] Thin drink, usually tea and milk (cat lap).

I want to see them two meet. I'll take him to the infirmary when it's over.

BILL (*To* SHIRLEY, *with undissembled misgiving*) Is thet 'im you was speakin' on?

SHIRLEY That's him.

BILL 'Im that wrastled in the music 'awl?

SHIRLEY The competitions at the National Sportin' Club was worth nigh a hundred a year to him. He's gev 'em up now for religion; so he's a bit fresh for want of the exercise he was accustomed to. He'll be glad to see you. Come along.

BILL Wot's 'is wight?

SHIRLEY Thirteen four. (BILL's *last hope expires*)

BARBARA Go and talk to him, Bill. He'll convert you.

SHIRLEY He'll convert your head into a mashed potato.

BILL (*Sullenly*) Aw ain't afride of 'im. Aw ain't afride of ennybody. Bat 'e can lick me. She's dan me. (*He sits down moodily on the edge of the horse trough*)

SHIRLEY You ain't goin'. I thought not. (*He resumes his seat*)

BARBARA (*Calling*) Jenny!

JENNY (*Appearing at the shelter door with a plaster on the corner of her mouth*) Yes, Major.

BARBARA Send Rummy Mitchens out to clear away here.

JENNY I think she's afraid.

BARBARA (*Her resemblance to her mother flashing out for a moment*) Nonsense! she must do as she's told.

JENNY (*Calling into the shelter*) Rummy: the Major says you must come.

(JENNY *comes to* BARBARA, *purposely keeping on the side next* BILL, *lest he should suppose that she shrank from him or bore malice*)

BARBARA Poor little Jenny! Are you tired? (*Looking at the wounded cheek*) Does it hurt?

JENNY No: it's all right now. It was nothing.

BARBARA (*Critically*) It was as hard as he could hit, I expect. Poor Bill! You don't feel angry with him, do you?

JENNY Oh no, no, no: indeed I don't, Major, bless his poor heart! (BARBARA *kisses her; and she runs away merrily into the shelter.* BILL *writhes with an agonizing return of his new and alarming symptoms, but says nothing.* RUMMY MITCHENS *comes from the shelter*)

BARBARA (*Going to meet* RUMMY) Now Rummy, bustle. Take in those mugs and plates to be washed; and throw the crumbs about for the birds.

(RUMMY *takes the three plates and mugs; but* SHIRLEY *takes back his mug from her, as there is still some milk left in it*)

RUMMY There ain't any crumbs. This ain't a time to waste good bread on birds.

PRICE (*Appearing at the shelter door*) Gentleman come to see the shelter, Major. Says he's your father.

BARBARA All right. Coming. (SNOBBY *goes back into the shelter, followed by* BARBARA)

RUMMY (*Stealing across to Bill and addressing him in a subdued voice, but with intense conviction*) I'd 'av the lor of you, you flat eared pignosed potwalloper, if she'd let me. You're no gentleman, to hit a lady in the face. (BILL, *with greater things moving in him, takes no notice*)

SHIRLEY (*Following her*) Here! in with you and don't get yourself into more trouble by talking.

RUMMY (*With hauteur*) I ain't 'ad the pleasure o' being hintroduced to you, as I can remember. (*She goes into the shelter with the plates*)

SHIRLEY That's the—

BILL (*Savagely*) Downt you talk to me, d'ye 'eah? You lea' me alown, or Aw'll do you a mischief. Aw'm not dirt under your feet, ennywy.

SHIRLEY (*Calmly*) Don't you be afeerd. You ain't such prime company that you need expect to be sought after. (*He is about to go into the shelter when* BARBARA *comes out, with* UNDERSHAFT *on her right*)

BARBARA Oh, there you are, Mr Shirley! (*Between them*) This is my father: I told you he was a Secularist, didn't I? Perhaps you'll be able to comfort one another.

UNDERSHAFT (*Startled*) A Secularist! Not the least in the world: on the contrary, a confirmed mystic.

BARBARA Sorry, I'm sure. By the way, papa, what is your religion? in case I have to introduce you again.

UNDERSHAFT My religion? Well, my dear, I am a Millionaire. That is my religion.

BARBARA Then I'm afraid you and Mr Shirley won't be able to comfort one another after all. You're not a Millionaire, are you, Peter?

SHIRLEY No; and proud of it.

UNDERSHAFT (*Gravely*) Poverty, my friend, is not a thing to be proud of.

SHIRLEY (*Angrily*) Who made your millions for you? Me and my like. What's kep' us poor? Keepin' you rich. I wouldn't have your conscience, not for all your income.

UNDERSHAFT I wouldn't have your income, not for all your conscience, Mr Shirley. (*He goes to the penthouse and sits down on a form*)

BARBARA (*Stopping* SHIRLEY *adroitly as he is about to retort*) You wouldn't think he was my father, would you, Peter? Will you go into the shelter and lend the lasses a hand for a while: we're worked off our feet.

SHIRLEY (*Bitterly*) Yes: I'm in their debt for a meal, ain't I?

BARBARA Oh, not because you're in their debt, but for love of them, Peter, for love of them. (*He cannot understand, and is rather scandalized*) There! don't stare at me. In with you; and give that conscience of yours a holiday. (*Bustling him into the shelter*)

SHIRLEY (*As he goes in*) Ah! it's a pity you never was trained to use your reason, miss. You'd have been a very taking lecturer on Secularism.

(BARBARA *turns to her father*)

UNDERSHAFT Never mind me, my dear. Go about your work; and let me watch it for a while.

BARBARA All right.

UNDERSHAFT For instance, what's the matter with that outpatient over there?

BARBARA (*Looking at* BILL, *whose attitude has never changed, and whose expression of brooding wrath has deepened*) Oh, we shall cure him in no time. Just watch. (*She goes over to* BILL *and waits. He glances up at her and casts his eyes down again, uneasy, but grimmer than ever*) It would be nice to just stamp on Mog Habbijam's face, wouldn't it, Bill?

BILL (*Starting up from the trough in consternation*) It's a loy: Aw never said so. (*She shakes her head*) 'Oo taold you wot was in moy mawnd?

BARBARA Only your new friend.

BILL Wot new friend?

BARBARA The devil, Bill. When he gets round people they get miserable, just like you.

BILL (*With a heartbreaking attempt at devil-may-care cheerfulness*) Aw ain't miserable. (*He sits down again, and stretches his legs in an attempt to seem indifferent*)

BARBARA Well, if you're happy, why don't you look happy, as we do?

BILL (*His legs curling back in spite of him*) Aw'm 'eppy enaff, Aw tell you. Woy cawn't you lea' me alown? Wot 'ev I dan to you? Aw ain't smashed your fice, 'ev Aw?

BARBARA (*Softly: wooing his soul*) It's not me that's getting at you, Bill.

BILL 'Oo else is it?

BARBARA Somebody that doesn't intend you to smash women's faces, I suppose. Somebody or something that wants to make a man of you.

BILL (*Blustering*) Mike a menn o' me! Ain't Aw a menn? eh? 'Oo sez Aw'n not a menn?

BARBARA There's a man in you somewhere, I suppose. But why did he let you hit poor little Jenny Hill? That wasn't very manly of him, was it?

BILL (*Tormented*) 'Ev dan wiv it, Aw tell you. Chack it. Aw'm sick o' your Jenny 'Ill and 'er silly little fice.

BARBARA Then why do you keep thinking about it? Why does it keep coming up against you in your mind? You're not getting converted, are you?

BILL (*With conviction*) Not ME. Not lawkly.

BARBARA That's right, Bill. Hold out against it. Put out your strength. Don't let's get you cheap. Todger Fairmile said he wrestled for three nights against his salvation harder than he ever wrestled with the Jap at the music hall. He gave in to the Jap when his arm was going to break. But he didn't give in to his salvation until his heart was going to break. Perhaps you'll escape that. You havn't any heart, have you?

BILL Wot d'ye mean? Woy ain't Aw got a 'awt the sime as ennybody else?

BARBARA A man with a heart wouldn't have bashed poor little Jenny's face, would he?

BILL (*Almost crying*) Ow, will you lea' me alown? 'Ev Aw ever offered to meddle with you, that you cam neggin' and provowkin' me lawk this? (*He writhes convulsively from his eyes to his toes*)

BARBARA (*With a steady soothing hand on his arm and a gentle voice that never lets go*) It's your soul that's hurting you, Bill, and not me. We've been through it all ourselves. Come with us, Bill. (*He looks wildly round*) To brave manhood on earth and eternal glory in heaven. (*He is on the point of breaking down*) Come. (*A drum is heard in the shelter; and* BILL, *with a gasp, escapes from the spell as* BARBARA *turns quickly.* ADOLPHUS *enters from the shelter with a big drum*) Oh! there you are, Dolly. Let me introduce a new friend of mine, Mr Bill Walker. This is my bloke, Bill: Mr Cusins. (CUSINS *salutes with his drumstick*)

BILL Gowin to merry 'im?

BARBARA Yes.

BILL (*Fervently*) Gawd 'elp 'im! Gaw-aw-aw-awd 'elp 'im!

BARBARA Why? Do you think he won't be happy with me?

BILL Awve aony 'ed to stend it for a mawnin': 'e'll 'ev to stend it for a lawftawm.

CUSINS That is a frightful reflection, Mr Walker. But I can't tear myself away from her.

BILL Well, Aw ken. (*To* BARBARA) 'Eah! do you knaow where Aw'm gowin' to, and wot Aw'm gowin' to do?

BARBARA Yes: you're going to heaven; and you're coming back here before the week's out to tell me so.

BILL You loy. Aw'm gowin to Kennintahn, to spit in Todger Fairmawl's eye. Aw beshed Jenny 'Ill's fice; an nar Aw'll git me aown fice beshed and cam beck and shaow it to 'er. 'Ee'll 'itt me 'ardern Aw 'itt 'er. That'll mike us square. (*To* ADOLPHUS) Is that fair or is it not? You're a genlm'n: you oughter knaow.

BARBARA Two black eyes won't make one white one, Bill.

BILL Aw didn't awst you. Cawnt you never keep your mahth shat? Oy awst the genlm'n.

CUSINS (*Reflectively*) Yes: I think you're right, Mr Walker. Yes: I should do it. It's curious: it's exactly what an ancient Greek would have done.

BARBARA But what good will it do?

CUSINS Well, it will give Mr Fairmile some exercise; and it will satisfy Mr Walker's soul.

BILL Rot! there ain't nao sach a thing as a saoul. Ah kin you tell wevver Aw've a saoul or not? You never seen it.

BARBARA I've seen it hurting you when you went against it.

BILL (*With compressed aggravation*) If you was maw gel and took the word aht o' me mahth lawk thet, Aw'd give you sathink you'd feel 'urtin, Aw would. (*To* ADOLPHUS) You tike maw tip, mite. Stop 'er jawr; or you'll doy afoah your tawm. (*With intense expression*) Wore aht: thet's you'll be: wore aht. (*He goes away through the gate*)

CUSINS (*Looking after him*) I wonder!

BARBARA Dolly! (*Indignant, in her mother's manner*)

CUSINS Yes, my dear, it's very wearing to be in love with you. If it lasts, I quite think I shall die young.

BARBARA Should you mind?

CUSINS Not at all. (*He is suddenly softened, and kisses her over the drum, evidently not for the first time, as people cannot kiss over a big drum without practice.* UNDERSHAFT *coughs*)

BARBARA It's all right, papa, we've not forgotten you. Dolly: explain the place to papa: I havn't time. (*She goes busily into the shelter*)

(UNDERSHAFT *and* ADOLPHUS *now have the yard to themselves.* UNDERSHAFT, *seated on a form, and still keenly attentive, looks hard at* ADOLPHUS. ADOLPHUS *looks hard at him*)

UNDERSHAFT I fancy you guess something of what is in my mind, Mr Cusins. (CUSINS *flourishes his drumsticks as if in the act of beating a lively rataplan, but makes no sound*) Exactly so. But suppose Barbara finds you out!

CUSINS You know, I do not admit that I am imposing on Barbara. I am quite genuinely interested in the views of the Salvation Army. The fact is, I am a sort of collector of religions; and the curious thing is that I find I can believe them all. By the way, have you any religion?

UNDERSHAFT Yes.

CUSINS Anything out of the common?

UNDERSHAFT Only that there are two things necessary to Salvation.

CUSINS (*Disappointed, but polite*) Ah, the Church Catechism. Charles Lomax also belongs to the Established Church.

UNDERSHAFT The two things are—

CUSINS Baptism and—

UNDERSHAFT No. Money and gunpowder.

CUSINS (*Surprised, but interested*) That is the general opinion of our governing classes. The novelty is in hearing any man confess it.

UNDERSHAFT Just so.

CUSINS Excuse me: is there any place in your religion for honor, justice, truth, love, mercy and so forth?

UNDERSHAFT Yes: they are the graces and luxuries of a rich, strong, and safe life.

CUSINS Suppose one is forced to choose between them and money or gunpowder?

UNDERSHAFT Choose money and gunpowder; for without enough of both you cannot afford the others.

CUSINS That is your religion?

UNDERSHAFT Yes.

(*The cadence of this reply makes a full close in the conversation.* CUSINS *twists his face dubiously and contemplates* UNDERSHAFT. UNDERSHAFT *contemplates him*)

CUSINS Barbara won't stand that. You will have to choose between your religion and Barbara.

UNDERSHAFT So will you, my friend. She will find out that that drum of yours is hollow.

CUSINS Father Undershaft: you are mistaken: I am a sincere Salvationist. You do not understand the Salvation Army. It is the army of joy, of love, of courage: it has banished the fear and remorse and despair of the old hell-ridden evangelical sects: it marches to fight the devil with trumpet and drum, with music and dancing, with banner and palm, as becomes a sally from heaven by its happy garrison. It picks the waster out of the public house and makes a man of him: it finds a worm wriggling in a back kitchen, and lo! a woman! Men and women of rank too, sons and daughters of the Highest. It takes the poor professor of Greek, the most artificial and self-suppressed of human creatures, from his meal of roots, and lets loose the rhapsodist in him; reveals the true worship of Dionysos to him; sends him down the public street drumming dithyrambs. (*He plays a thundering flourish on the drum*)

UNDERSHAFT You will alarm the shelter.

CUSINS Oh, they are accustomed to these sudden ecstasies of piety. However, if the drum worries you— (*He pockets the drumsticks; unhooks the drum; and stands it on the ground opposite the gateway*)

UNDERSHAFT Thank you.

CUSINS You remember what Euripides says about your money and gunpowder?

UNDERSHAFT No.

CUSINS (*Declaiming*)

One and another
In money and guns may outpass his brother;
And men in their millions float and flow
And seethe with a million hopes as leaven;
And they win their will; or they miss their will;
And their hopes are dead or are pined for still;
But whoe'er can know
As the long days go
That to live is happy, has found his heaven.

My translation: what do you think of it?

UNDERSHAFT I think, my friend, that if you wish to know, as the long days go, that to live is happy, you must first acquire money enough for a decent life, and power enough to be your own master.

CUSINS You are damnably discouraging. (*He resumes his declamation*)

Is it so hard a thing to see
That the spirit of God—whate'er it be—
The law that abides and changes not, ages long,
The Eternal and Nature-born: these things be strong?
What else is Wisdom? What of Man's endeavor,
Or God's high grace so lovely and so great?
To stand from fear set free? to breathe and wait?
To hold a hand uplifted over Fate?
And shall not Barbara be loved for ever?

UNDERSHAFT Euripides mentions Barbara, does he?

CUSINS It is a fair translation. The word means Loveliness.

UNDERSHAFT May I ask—as Barbara's father—how much a year she is to be loved for ever on?

CUSINS As Barbara's father, that is more your affair than mine. I can feed her by teaching Greek: that is about all.

UNDERSHAFT Do you consider it a good match for her?

CUSINS (*With polite obstinacy*) Mr Undershaft: I am in many ways a weak, timid, ineffectual person; and my health is far from satisfactory. But whenever I feel that I must have anything, I get it, sooner or later. I feel that way about Barbara. I don't like marriage: I feel intensely afraid of it; and I don't know what I shall do with Barbara or what she will do with me. But I feel that I and nobody else must marry her. Please regard that as settled— Not that I wish to be arbitrary; but why should I waste your time in discussing what is inevitable?

UNDERSHAFT You mean that you will stick at nothing: not even the conversion of the Salvation Army to the worship of Dionysos.

CUSINS The business of the Salvation Army is to save, not to wrangle about the name of the pathfinder. Dionysos or another: what does it matter?

UNDERSHAFT (*Rising and approaching him*) Professor Cusins: you are a young man after my own heart.

CUSINS Mr Undershaft: you are, as far as I am able to gather, a most infernal old rascal; but you appeal very strongly to my sense of ironic humor.

(UNDERSHAFT *mutely offers his hand. They shake*)

UNDERSHAFT (*Suddenly concentrating himself*) And now to business.

CUSINS Pardon me. We were discussing religion. Why go back to such an uninteresting and unimportant subject as business?

UNDERSHAFT Religion is our business at present, because it is through religion alone that we can win Barbara.

CUSINS Have you, too, fallen in love with Barbara?

UNDERSHAFT Yes, with a father's love.

CUSINS A father's love for a grown-up daughter is the most dangerous of all infatuations. I apologize for mentioning my own pale, coy, mistrustful fancy in the same breath with it.

UNDERSHAFT Keep to the point. We have to win her; and we are neither of us Methodists.

CUSINS That doesn't matter. The power Barbara wields here—the power that wields Barbara herself—is not Calvinism, not Presbyterianism, not Methodism—

UNDERSHAFT Not Greek Paganism either, eh?

CUSINS I admit that. Barbara is quite original in her religion.

UNDERSHAFT (*Triumphantly*) Aha! Barbara Undershaft would be. Her inspiration comes from within herself.

CUSINS How do you suppose it got there?

UNDERSHAFT (*In towering excitement*) It is the Undershaft inheritance. I shall hand on my torch to my daughter. She shall make my converts and preach my gospel—

CUSINS What! Money and gunpowder!

UNDERSHAFT Yes, money and gunpowder; freedom and power; command of life and command of death.

CUSINS (*Urbanely: trying to bring him down to earth*) This is extremely interesting, Mr Undershaft. Of course you know that you are mad.

UNDERSHAFT (*With redoubled force*) And you?

CUSINS Oh, mad as a hatter. You are welcome to my secret since I have discovered yours. But I am astonished. Can a madman make cannons?

UNDERSHAFT Would anyone else than a madman make them? And now (*With surging energy*) question for question. Can a sane man translate Euripides?

CUSINS No.

UNDERSHAFT (*Seizing him by the shoulder*) Can a sane woman make a man of a waster or a woman of a worm?

CUSINS (*Reeling before the storm*) Father Colossus—Mammoth Millionaire—

UNDERSHAFT (*Pressing him*) Are there two mad people or three in this Salvation shelter to-day?

CUSINS You mean Barbara is as mad as we are?

UNDERSHAFT (*Pushing him lightly off and resuming his equanimity suddenly and completely*) Pooh, Professor! let us call things by their proper names. I am a millionaire; you are a poet; Barbara is a savior of souls. What have we three to do with the common mob of slaves and idolaters? (*He sits down again with a shrug of contempt for the mob*)

CUSINS Take care! Barbara is in love with the common people. So am I. Have you never felt the romance of that love?

UNDERSHAFT (*Cold and sardonic*) Have you ever been in love with Poverty, like St. Francis? Have you ever been in love with Dirt, like St Simeon? Have you ever been in love with disease and suffering, like our nurses and philanthropists? Such passions are not virtues, but the most unnatural of all the vices. This love of the common people may please an earl's granddaughter and a university professor; but I have been a common man and a poor man; and it has no romance for me. Leave it to the poor to pretend that poverty is a blessing: leave it to the coward to make a religion of his cowardice by preaching humility: we know better than that. We three must stand together above the common people: how else can we help their children to climb up beside us? Barbara must belong to us, not to the Salvation Army.

CUSINS Well, I can only say that if you think you will get her away from the Salvation Army by talking to her as you have been talking to me, you don't know Barbara.

UNDERSHAFT My friend: I never ask for what I can buy.

CUSINS (*In a white fury*) Do I understand you to imply that you can buy Barbara?

UNDERSHAFT No; but I can buy the Salvation Army.

CUSINS Quite impossible.

UNDERSHAFT You shall see. All religious organizations exist by selling themselves to the rich.

CUSINS Not the Army. That is the Church of the poor.

UNDERSHAFT All the more reason for buying it.

CUSINS I don't think you quite know what the Army does for the poor.

UNDERSHAFT Oh, yes, I do. It draws their teeth: that is enough for me—as a man of business—

CUSINS Nonsense! It makes them sober—

UNDERSHAFT I prefer sober workmen. The profits are larger.

CUSINS —honest—

UNDERSHAFT Honest workmen are the most economical.

CUSINS —attached to their homes—

UNDERSHAFT So much the better: they will put up with anything sooner than change their shop.

CUSINS —happy—

UNDERSHAFT An invaluable safeguard against revolution.

CUSINS —unselfish—

UNDERSHAFT Indifferent to their own interests, which suits me exactly.

CUSINS —with their thoughts on heavenly things—

UNDERSHAFT (*Rising*) And not on Trade Unionism nor Socialism. Excellent.

CUSINS (*Revolted*) You really are an infernal old rascal.

UNDERSHAFT (*Indicating* PETER SHIRLEY, *who has just come from the shelter and strolled dejectedly down the yard between them*) And this is an honest man!

SHIRLEY Yes; and what 'av I got by it? (*He passes on bitterly and sits on the form, in the corner of the penthouse*)

(SNOBBY PRICE, *beaming sanctimoniously, and* JENNY HILL, *with a tambourine full of coppers, come from the shelter and go to the drum, on which* JENNY *begins to count the money*)

UNDERSHAFT (*Replying to* SHIRLEY) Oh, your employers must have got a good deal by it from first to last. (*He sits on the table, with one foot on the side form.* CUSINS, *overwhelmed, sits down on the same form nearer the shelter.* BARBARA *comes from the shelter to the middle of the yard. She is excited and a little overwrought*)

BARBARA We've just had a splendid experience meeting at the other gate in Cripp's Lane. I've hardly ever seen them so much moved as they were by your confession, Mr Price.

PRICE I could almost be glad of my past wickedness if I could believe that it would 'elp to keep hathers stright.

BARBARA So it will, Snobby. How much, Jenny?

JENNY Four and tenpence, Major.

BARBARA Oh, Snobby, if you had given your poor mother just one more kick, we should have got the whole five shillings!

PRICE If she heard you say that, miss, she'd be sorry I didn't. But I'm glad. Oh what a joy it will be to her when she hears I'm saved!

UNDERSHAFT Shall I contribute the odd twopence, Barbara? The millionaire's mite, eh? (*He takes a couple of pennies from his pocket*)

BARBARA How did you make that twopence?

UNDERSHAFT As usual. By selling cannons, torpedoes, submarines, and my new patent Grand Duke hand grenade.

BARBARA Put it back in your pocket. You can't buy your Salvation here for twopence: you must work it out.

UNDERSHAFT Is twopence not enough? I can afford a little more, if you press me.

BARBARA Two million millions would not be enough. There is bad blood on your hands; and nothing but good blood can cleanse them. Money is no use. Take it away. (*She turns to* CUSINS) Dolly: you must write another letter for me to the papers. (*He makes a wry face*) Yes: I know you don't like it; but it must be done. The starvation this winter is beating us: everybody is unemployed. The General says we must close this shelter if we can't get more money. I force the collections at the meetings until I am ashamed: don't I, Snobby?

PRICE It's a fair treat to see you work it, Miss. The way you got them up from three-and-six to four-and-ten with that hymn, penny by penny and verse by verse, was a caution. Not a Cheap Jack[7] on Mile End Waste could touch you at it.

BARBARA Yes; but I wish we could do without it. I am getting at last to think more of the collection than of the people's souls. And what are those hatfuls of pence and halfpence? We want thousands! tens of thousands! hundreds of thousands! I want to convert people, not to be always begging for the Army in a way I'd die sooner than beg for myself.

UNDERSHAFT (*In profound irony*) Genuine unselfishness is capable of anything, my dear.

BARBARA (*Unsuspectingly, as she turns away to take the money from the drum and put it in a cash bag she carries*) Yes, isn't it? (UNDERSHAFT *looks sardonically at* CUSINS)

CUSINS (*Aside to* UNDERSHAFT) Mephistopheles! Machiavelli!

BARBARA (*Tears coming into her eyes as she ties the bag and pockets it*) How are we to feed them? I can't talk religion to a man with bodily hunger in his eyes. (*Almost breaking down*) It's frightful.

JENNY (*Running to her*) Major, dear—

BARBARA (*Rebounding*) No: don't comfort me. It will be all right. We shall get the money.

UNDERSHAFT How?

JENNY By praying for it, of course. Mrs Baines says she prayed for it last night; and she has never prayed for it in vain: never once. (*She goes to the gate and looks out into the street*)

BARBARA (*Who has dried her eyes and regained her composure*) By the way, dad, Mrs Baines has come to march with us to our big meeting this afternoon; and she is very anxious to meet you, for some reason or other. Perhaps she'll convert you.

UNDERSHAFT I shall be delighted, my dear.

JENNY (*At the gate: excitedly*) Major! Major! here's that man back again.

BARBARA What man?

JENNY The man that hit me. Oh, I hope he's coming back to join us.

(BILL WALKER, *with frost on his jacket, comes through the gate, his hands deep in his pockets and his chin sunk between his shoulders, like a cleaned-out gambler. He halts between* BARBARA *and the drum*)

BARBARA Hullo, Bill! Back already!

BILL (*Nagging at her*) Bin talkin' ever sence, 'ev you?

BARBARA Pretty nearly. Well, has Todger paid you out for poor Jenny's jaw?

BILL Nao 'e ain't.

BARBARA I thought your jacket looked a bit snowy.

BILL Sao it is snaowy. You want to knaow where the snaow cam from, down't you?

BARBARA Yes.

[7] A salesman, usually hawking his ware on sidewalks.

BILL Well, it cam from orf the grahnd in Pawkinses Corner in Kennintahn. It got rabbed orf be maw shaoulders: see?

BARBARA Pity you didn't rub some off with your knees, Bill! That would have done you a lot of good.

BILL (*With sour mirthless humor*) Aw was sivin' anather menn's knees at the tawm. 'E was kneelin' on moy 'ed, 'e was.

JENNY Who was kneeling on your head?

BILL Todger was. 'E was pryin' for me: pryin' camfortable wiv me as a cawpet. Sow was Mog. Sao was the aol bloomin' meetin'. Mog she sez "Ow Lawd brike is stabborn sperrit; bat down't 'urt is dear 'art." Thet was wot she said. "Downt 'urt is dear 'art"! An 'er blowk—thirteen stun four!—kneelin' wiv all is wight on me. Fanny, aint it?

JENNY Oh no. We're so sorry, Mr Walker.

BARBARA (*Enjoying it frankly*) Nonsense! of course it's funny. Served you right, Bill! You must have done something to him first.

BILL (*Doggedly*) Aw did wot Aw said Aw'd do. Aw spit in 'is eye. 'E looks ap at the skoy and sez. "'Ow that Aw should be fahnd worthy to be spit upon for the gospel's sike!" 'e sez; an Mog sez "Glaory 'Allelloolier!"; an' then 'e called me Braddher, and dahned me as if Aw was a kid and 'e was me mather worshin' me a Setterda nawt. Aw 'ednt jast nao shaow wiv 'im at all. 'Arf the street pr'yed; and the tather 'arf larfed fit to split theirselves. (*To* BARBARA) There! are you settisfawd nah?

BARBARA (*Her eyes dancing*) Wish I'd been there, Bill.

BILL Yus: you'd 'a got in a hextra bit o' talk on me, wouldn't you?

JENNY I'm so sorry, Mr Walker.

BILL (*Fiercely*) Down't you gow bein' sorry for me: you've no call. Listen 'eah. Aw browk your jawr.

JENNY No, it didn't hurt me: indeed it didn't, except for a moment. It was only that I was frightened.

BILL Aw down't want to be forgive be you, or be ennybody. Wot Aw did Aw'll p'y for. Aw trawd to gat me aown jawr browk to settisfaw you—

JENNY (*Distressed*) Oh no—

BILL (*Impatiently*) Tell y' Aw did: cawnt you listen to wot's bein' taold you? All Aw got be it was being mide a sawt of in the pablic street for me pines. Well, if Aw cawnt settisfaw you one wy, Aw ken anather. Listen 'eah! Aw 'ed two quid sived agen the frost; an Aw've a pahnd of it left. A mite o' mawn last week 'ed words with the judy 'e's gowin to merry. 'E give 'er wotfor; an' 'e's bin fawnd fifteen bob. 'E 'ed a rawt to 'itt 'er cause they was gowin to be merrid; but Aw 'ednt nao rawt to 'itt you; sao put anather fawv bob on an cal it a pahnd's worth. (*He produces a sovereign*) 'Eahs the manney. Tike it; and lets 'ev no more o' your forgivin' an' pryin' and your Mijor jawrin' me. Let wot Aw dan be dan an' pide for; and let there be a end of it.

JENNY Oh, I couldn't take it, Mr Walker. But if you would give a shilling or two to poor Rummy Mitchens! you really did hurt her; and she's old.

BILL (*Contemptuously*) Not lawkly. Aw'd give her anather as soon as look at 'er. Let her 'ev the lawr o' me as she threatened! She ain't forgiven me: not mach. Wot Aw dan to 'er is not on me mawnd—wot she (*Indicating* BARBARA) mawt call on me conscience—no more than stickin' a pig. It's this Christian gime o' yours that Aw wown't 'ev pl'yed agen me: this bloomin' forgivin' an neggin' an jawrin' that mikes a menn thet sore that 'iz lawf's a burden to 'im. Aw wown't 'ev it, Aw tell you; sao tike your manney and stop thraowin' your silly beshed fice hap agen me.

JENNY Major: may I take a little of it for the Army?

BARBARA No: the Army is not to be bought. We want your soul, Bill; and we'll take nothing less.

BILL (*Bitterly*) Aw knaow. Me an' maw few shillin's is not good enaff for you. You're a earl's grendorter, you are. Nathink less than a 'anderd pahnd for you.

UNDERSHAFT Come, Barbara! you could do a great deal of good with a hundred pounds. If you will set this gentleman's mind at ease by taking his pound, I will give the other ninety-nine.

(BILL, *dazed by such opulence, instinctively touches his cap*)

BARBARA Oh, you're too extravagant, papa. Bill offers twenty pieces of silver. All you need offer is the other ten. That will make the standard price to buy anybody who's for sale. I'm not; and the Army's not. (*To* BILL) You'll never have another quiet moment, Bill, until you come round to us. You can't stand out against your salvation.

BILL (*Sullenly*) Aw cawnt stend aht agen music 'awl wrastlers and awtful tangued women. Aw've offered to p'y. Aw can do no more. Tike it or leave it. There it is. (*He throws the sovereign on the drum, and sits down on the horse trough. The coin fascinates* SNOBBY PRICE, *who takes an early opportunity of dropping his cap on it*)

(MRS BAINES *comes from the shelter. She is dressed as a Salvation Army Commissioner. She is an earnest looking woman of about forty, with a caressing, urgent voice, and an appealing manner*)

BARBARA This is my father, Mrs Baines. (UNDERSHAFT *comes from the table, taking his hat off with marked civility*) Try what you can do with him. He won't listen to me, because he remembers what a fool I was when I was a baby. (*She leaves them together and chats with* JENNY)

MRS BAINES Have you been shewn over the shelter, Mr Undershaft? You know the work we're doing, of course.

UNDERSHAFT (*Very civilly*) The whole nation knows it, Mrs Baines.

MRS BAINES No, sir: the whole nation does not know it, or we should not be crippled as we are for want of money to carry our work through the length and breadth of the land. Let me tell you that there would have been rioting this winter in London but for us.

UNDERSHAFT You really think so?

MRS BAINES I know it, I remember 1886, when you rich gentlemen hardened your hearts against the cry of the poor. They broke the windows of your clubs in Pall Mall.

UNDERSHAFT (*Gleaming with approval of their method*) And the Mansion House Fund went up next day from thirty thousand pounds to seventy-nine thousand! I remember quite well.

MRS BAINES Well, won't you help me to get at the people? They won't break windows then. Come here, Price. Let me shew you to this gentleman. (PRICE *comes to be inspected*) Do you remember the window breaking?

PRICE My ole father thought it was the revolution, ma'am.

MRS BAINES Would you break windows now?

PRICE Oh no ma'am. The windows of 'eaven 'av bin opened to me. I know now that the rich man is a sinner like myself.

RUMMY (*Appearing above at the loft door*) Snobby Price!

SNOBBY Wot is it?

RUMMY Your mother's askin' for you at the other gate in Crippses Lane. She's heard about your confession. (PRICE *turns pale*)

MRS BAINES Go, Mr Price; and pray with her.

JENNY You can go through the shelter, Snobby.

PRICE (*To* MRS BAINES) I couldn't face her now, ma'am, with all the weight of my sins fresh on me. Tell her she'll find her son at 'ome, waitin' for her in prayer. (*He skulks off through the gate, incidentally stealing the sovereign on his way out by picking up his cap from the drum*)

MRS BAINES (*With swimming eyes*) You see how we take the anger and the bitterness against you out of their hearts, Mr Undershaft.

UNDERSHAFT It is certainly most convenient and gratifying to all large employers of labor, Mrs Baines.

MRS BAINES Barbara: Jenny: I have good news: most wonderful news. (JENNY *runs to her*) My prayers have been answered. I told you they would, Jenny, didn't I?

JENNY Yes, yes.

BARBARA (*Moving nearer to the drum*) Have we got money enough to keep the shelter open?

MRS BAINES I hope we shall have enough to keep all the shelters open. Lord Saxmundham has promised us five thousand pounds—

BARBARA Hooray!

JENNY Glory!

MRS BAINES —if—

BARBARA "If!" If what?

MRS BAINES —if five other gentlemen will give a thousand each to make it up to ten thousand.

BARBARA Who is Lord Saxmundham? I never heard of him.

UNDERSHAFT (*Who has pricked up his ears at the peer's name, and is now watching* BARBARA *curiously*) A new creation, my dear. You have heard of Sir Horace Bodger?

BARBARA Bodger! Do you mean the distiller? Bodger's whisky!

UNDERSHAFT That is the man. He is one of the greatest of our public benefactors. He restored the cathedral at Hakington. They made him a baronet for that. He gave half a million to the funds of his party: they made him a baron for that.

SHIRLEY What will they give him for the five thousand?

UNDERSHAFT There is nothing left to give him. So the five thousand, I should think, is to save his soul.

MRS BAINES Heaven grant it may! Oh Mr Undershaft, you have some very rich friends. Can't you help us towards the other five thousand? We are going to hold a great meeting this afternoon at the Assembly Hall in the Mile End Road. If I could only announce that one gentleman had come forward to support Lord Saxmundham, others would follow. Don't you know somebody? couldn't you? wouldn't you? (*Her eyes fill with tears*) oh, think of those poor people, Mr Undershaft: think of how much it means to them, and how little to a great man like you.

UNDERSHAFT (*Sardonically gallant*) Mrs Baines: you are irresistible. I can't disappoint you; and I can't deny myself the satisfaction of making Bodger pay up. You shall have your five thousand pounds.

MRS BAINES Thank God!

UNDERSHAFT You don't thank me?

MRS BAINES Oh sir, don't try to be cynical: don't be ashamed of being a good man. The Lord will bless you abundantly; and our prayers will be like a strong fortification round you all the days of your life. (*With a touch of caution*) You will let me have the cheque to shew at the meeting, won't you? Jenny: go in and fetch a pen and ink. (JENNY *runs to the shelter door*)

UNDERSHAFT Do not disturb Miss Hill: I have a fountain pen. (JENNY *halts. He sits at the table and writes the cheque.* CUSINS *rises to make room for him. They all watch him silently*)

BILL (*Cynically, aside to* BARBARA, *his voice and accent horribly debased*) Wot prawce Selvytion nah?

BARBARA Stop. (UNDERSHAFT *stops writing: they all turn to her in surprise*) Mrs Baines: are you really going to take this money?

MRS BAINES (*Astonished*) Why not, dear?

BARBARA Why not! Do you know what my father is? Have you forgotten that Lord Saxmundham is Bodger the whisky man? Do you remember how we implored the County Council to stop him from writing Bodger's Whisky in letters of fire against the sky; so that the poor drink-ruined creatures on the Embankment could not wake up from their snatches of sleep without being reminded of their deadly thirst by that wicked sky sign? Do you know that the worst thing I have had to fight here is not the devil, but Bodger, Bodger, Bodger, with his whisky, his distilleries, and his tied houses?[7] Are you going to make our shelter another tied house for him, and ask me to keep it?

BILL Rotten dranken whisky it is too.

MRS BAINES Dear Barbara: Lord Saxmundham has a

[7] Taverns owned directly or indirectly by a brewer who expects the bars to serve only his own products.

soul to be saved like any of us. If heaven has found the way to make a good use of his money, are we to set ourselves up against the answer to our prayers?

BARBARA I know he has a soul to be saved. Let him come down here; and I'll do my best to help him to his salvation. But he wants to send his cheque down to buy us, and go on being as wicked as ever.

UNDERSHAFT (*With a reasonableness which* CUSINS *alone perceives to be ironical*) My dear Barbara: alcohol is a very necessary article. It heals the sick—

BARBARA It does nothing of the sort.

UNDERSHAFT Well, it assists the doctor: that is perhaps a less questionable way of putting it. It makes life bearable to millions of people who could not endure their existence if they were quite sober. It enables Parliament to do things at eleven at night that no sane person would do at eleven in the morning. Is it Bodger's fault that this inestimable gift is deplorably abused by less than one per cent of the poor? (*He turns again to the table; signs the cheque; and crosses it*)

MRS BAINES Barbara: will there be less drinking or more if all those poor souls we are saving come tomorrow and find the doors of our shelters shut in their faces? Lord Saxmundham gives us the money to stop drinking—to take his own business from him.

CUSINS (*Impishly*) Pure self-sacrifice on Bodger's part, clearly! Bless dear Bodger! (BARBARA *almost breaks down as Adolphus, too, fails her*)

UNDERSHAFT (*Tearing out the cheque and pocketing the book as he rises and goes past* CUSINS *to* MRS BAINES) I also, Mrs Baines, may claim a little disinterestedness. Think of my business! think of the widows and orphans! the men and lads torn to pieces with shrapnel and poisoned with lyddite! (MRS BAINES *shrinks; but he goes on remorselessly*) the oceans of blood, not one drop of which is shed in a really just cause! the ravaged crops! the peaceful peasants forced, women and men, to till their fields under the fire of opposing armies on pain of starvation! the bad blood of the fierce little cowards at home who egg on others to fight for the gratification of their national vanity! All this makes money for me: I am never richer, never busier than when the papers are full of it. Well, it is your work to preach peace on earth and goodwill to men. (MRS BAINES'S *face lights up again*) Every convert you make is a vote against war. (*Her lips move in prayer*) Yet I give you this money to help you to hasten my own commercial ruin. (*He gives her the cheque*)

CUSINS (*Mounting the form in an ecstasy of mischief*) The millennium will be inaugurated by the unselfishness of Undershaft and Bodger. Oh be joyful! (*He takes the drum-sticks from his pocket and flourishes them*)

MRS BAINES (*Taking the cheque*) The longer I live the more proof I see that there is an Infinite Goodness that turns everything to the work of salvation sooner or later. Who would have thought that any good could have come out of war and drink? And yet their profits are brought today to the feet of salvation to do its blessed work. (*She is affected to tears*)

JENNY (*Running to* MRS BAINES *and throwing her arms round her*) Oh dear! how blessed, how glorious it all is!

CUSINS (*In a convulsion of irony*) Let us seize this unspeakable moment. Let us march to the great meeting at once. Excuse me just an instant. (*He rushes into the shelter.* JENNY *takes her tambourine from the drum head*)

MRS BAINES Mr Undershaft: have you ever seen a thousand people fall on their knees with one impulse and pray? Come with us to the meeting. Barbara shall tell them that the Army is saved, and saved through you.

CUSINS (*Returning impetuously from the shelter with a flag and a trombone, and coming between* MRS BAINES *and* UNDERSHAFT) You will carry the flag down the first street, Mrs Baines. (*He gives her the flag*) Mr Undershaft is a gifted trombonist: he shall intone an Olympian diapason to the West Ham Salvation March. (*Aside to* UNDERSHAFT, *as he forces the trombone on him*) Blow, Machiavelli, blow.

UNDERSHAFT (*Aside to him, as he takes the trombone*) The trumpet in Zion! (CUSINS *rushes to the drum, which he takes up and puts on.* UNDERSHAFT *continues, aloud*) I will do my best. I could vamp a bass if I knew the tune.

CUSINS It is a wedding chorus from one of Donizetti's operas;[8] but we have converted it. We convert everything to good here, including Bodger. You remember the chorus. "For thee immense rejoicing—*immenso giubilo—immenso giubilo.*" (*With drum obbligato*) Rum tum ti tum tum, tum tum ti ta—

BARBARA Dolly: you are breaking my heart.

CUSINS What is a broken heart more or less here? Dionysos Undershaft has descended. I am possessed.

MRS BAINES Come, Barbara: I must have my dear Major to carry the flag with me.

JENNY Yes, yes, Major darling.

(CUSINS *snatches the tambourine out of* JENNY'S *hand and mutely offers it to* BARBARA)

BARBARA (*Coming forward a little as she puts the offer behind her with a shudder, whilst* CUSINS *recklessly tosses the tambourine back to* JENNY *and goes to the gate*) I can't come.

JENNY Not come!

MRS BAINES (*With tears in her eyes*) Barbara: do you think I am wrong to take the money?

BARBARA (*Impulsively going to her and kissing her*) No, no: God help you, dear, you must: you are saving the Army. Go; and may you have a great meeting!

JENNY But arn't you coming?

BARBARA No. (*She begins taking off the silver S brooch from her collar*)

MRS BAINES Barbara: what are you doing?

JENNY Why are you taking your badge off? You can't be going to leave us, Major.

BARBARA (*Quietly*) Father: come here.

[8] *Lucia di Lammermoor.*

UNDERSHAFT (*Coming to her*) My dear! (*Seeing that she is going to pin the badge on his collar, he retreats to the penthouse in some alarm*)

BARBARA (*Following him*) Don't be frightened. (*She pins the badge on and steps back towards the table, shewing him to the others*) There! It's not much for £5000, is it?

MRS BAINES Barbara: if you won't come and pray with us, promise me you will pray for us.

BARBARA I can't pray now. Perhaps I shall never pray again.

MRS BAINES Barbara!

JENNY Major!

BARBARA (*Almost delirious*) I can't bear any more. Quick march!

CUSINS (*Calling to the procession in the street outside*) Off we go. Play up, there! *Immenso giubilo.* (*He gives the time with his drum; and the band strikes up the march, which rapidly becomes more distant as the procession moves briskly away*)

MRS BAINES I must go, dear. You're overworked: you will be all right tomorrow. We'll never lose you. Now Jenny: step out with the old flag. Blood and Fire! (*She marches out through the gate with her flag*)

JENNY Glory Hallelujah! (*Flourishing her tambourine and marching*)

UNDERSHAFT (*To* CUSINS, *as he marches out past him easing the slide of his trombone*) "My ducats and my daughter"![9]

CUSINS (*Following him out*) Money and gunpowder!

BARBARA Drunkenness and Murder! My God: why hast thou forsaken me?

(*She sinks on the form with her face buried in her hands. The march passes away into silence.* BILL WALKER *steals across to her*)

BILL (*Taunting*) Wot prawce selvytion nah?

SHIRLEY Don't you hit her when she's down.

BILL She 'itt me wen aw wiz dahn. Waw shouldn't Aw git a bit o' me aown beck?

BARBARA (*Raising her head*) I didn't take your money, Bill. (*She crosses the yard to the gate and turns her back on the two men to hide her face from them*)

BILL (*Sneering after her*) Naow, it warn't enaff for you. (*Turning to the drum, he misses the money*) 'Ellow! If you ain't took it sammun else 'ez. Were's it gorn? Bly me if Jenny 'Ill didn't tike it arter all!

RUMMY (*Screaming at him from the loft*) You lie, you dirty blackguard! Snobby Price pinched it off the drum when he took up his cap. I was up here all the time an see 'im do it.

BILL Wot! Stowl maw manney! Waw didn't you call thief on him, you silly aold macker you?

RUMMY To serve you aht for 'ittin me acrost the face. It's cost y'pahnd, that 'az. (*Raising a pæan of squalid triumph*) I done you. I'm even with you. I've 'ad it aht o' y—(BILL *snatches up* SHIRLEY'S *mug and hurls it at her. She slams the loft door and vanishes. The mug smashes against the door and falls in fragments*)

BILL (*Beginning to chuckle*) Tell us, aol menn, wot o'clock this mawnin' was it wen 'im as they call Snobby Prawce was sived?

BARBARA (*Turning to him more composedly, and with unspoiled sweetness*) About half past twelve, Bill. And he pinched your pound at a quarter to two. *I* know. Well, you can't afford to lose it. I'll send it to you.

BILL (*His voice and accent suddenly improving*) Not if Aw wiz to stawve for it. Aw ain't to be bought.

SHIRLEY Ain't you? You'd sell yourself to the devil for a pint o' beer; only there ain't no devil to make the offer.

BILL (*Unshamed*) Sao Aw would, mite, and often 'ev, cheerful. But she cawn't baw me. (*Approaching* BARBARA) You wanted maw saoul, did you? Well, you ain't got it.

BARBARA I nearly got it, Bill. But we've sold it back to you for ten thousand pounds.

SHIRLEY And dear at the money!

BARBARA No, Peter: it was worth more than money.

BILL (*Salvationproof*) It's nao good: you cawn't get rahnd me nah. Aw down't b'lieve in it; and Aw've seen tod'y that Aw was rawt. (*Going*) Sao long, aol soupkitchener! Ta, ta, Mijor Earl's Grendorter! (*Turning at the gate*) Wot prawce selvytion nah? Snobby Prawce! Ha! ha!

BARBARA (*Offering her hand*) Goodbye, Bill.

BILL (*Taken aback, half plucks his cap off; then shoves it on again defiantly*) Git aht. (BARBARA *drops her hand, discouraged. He has a twinge of remorse*) But thet's aw rawt, you knaow. Nathink pasn'l. Naow mellice. Sao long, Judy. (*He goes*)

BARBARA No malice. So long, Bill.

SHIRLEY (*Shaking his head*) You make too much of him, Miss, in your innocence.

BARBARA (*Going to him*) Peter: I'm like you now. Cleaned out, and lost my job.

SHIRLEY You've youth and hope. That's two better than me.

BARBARA I'll get you a job, Peter. That's hope for you: the youth will have to be enough for me. (*She counts her money*) I have just enough left for two teas at Lockharts,[10] a Rowton doss[11] for you, and my tram and bus home. (*He frowns and rises with offended pride. She takes his arm*) Don't be proud, Peter: it's sharing between friends. And promise me you'll talk to me and not let me cry. (*She draws him towards the gate*)

SHIRLEY Well, I'm not accustomed to talk to the like of you—

BARBARA (*Urgently*) Yes, yes: you must talk to me. Tell me about Tom Paine's books and Bradlaugh's lectures.[12] Come along.

SHIRLEY Ah, if you would only read Tom Paine in the

[9] Undershaft recalls Salanio's report of Shylock's reaction to his daughter Jessica's elopement with Lorenzo (*The Merchant of Venice,* II, viii, 17).

[10] A fashionable tearoom in London.

[11] Mr. Rowton owned a string of inexpensive lodging-houses (doss); *cf.* our Skid Row flophouses.

[12] Charles Bradlaugh (1833-1891), like Paine, advocated free-thought in religion and republicanism in politics.

proper spirit, Miss! (*They go out through the gate together*)

END OF ACT II

# Act Three

*Next day after lunch* LADY BRITOMART *is writing in the library in Wilton Crescent.* SARAH *is reading in the armchair near the window.* BARBARA, *in ordinary fashionable dress, pale and brooding, is on the settee.* CHARLES LOMAX *enters. He starts on seeing* BARBARA *fashionably attired and in low spirits.*

LOMAX You've left off your uniform!

(BARBARA *says nothing; but an expression of pain passes over her face*)

LADY BRITOMART (*Warning him in low tones to be careful*) Charles!

LOMAX (*Much concerned, coming behind the settee and bending sympathetically over* BARBARA) I'm awfully sorry, Barbara. You know I helped you all I could with the concertina and so forth. (*Momentously*) Still, I have never shut my eyes to the fact that there is a certain amount of tosh about the Salvation Army. Now the claims of the Church of England—

LADY BRITOMART That's enough, Charles. Speak of something suited to your mental capacity.

LOMAX But surely the Church of England is suited to all our capacities.

BARBARA (*Pressing his hand*) Thank you for your sympathy, Cholly. Now go and spoon with Sarah.

LOMAX (*Dragging a chair from the writing table and seating himself affectionately by* SARAH's *side*) How is my ownest today?

SARAH I wish you wouldn't tell Cholly to do things, Barbara. He always comes straight and does them. Cholly: we're going to the works this afternoon.

LOMAX What works?

SARAH The cannon works.

LOMAX What? Your governor's shop!

SARAH Yes.

LOMAX Oh I say!

(CUSINS *enters in poor condition. He also starts visibly when he sees* BARBARA *without her uniform*)

BARBARA I expected you this morning, Dolly. Didn't you guess that?

CUSINS (*Sitting down beside her*) I'm sorry. I have only just breakfasted.

SARAH But we've just finished lunch.

BARBARA Have you had one of your bad nights?

CUSINS No: I had rather a good night: in fact, one of the most remarkable nights I have ever passed.

BARBARA The meeting?

CUSINS No: after the meeting.

LADY BRITOMART You should have gone to bed after the meeting. What were you doing?

CUSINS Drinking.

LADY BRITOMART Adolphus!<br>SARAH Dolly!<br>BARBARA Dolly!<br>LOMAX Oh I say!

LADY BRITOMART What were you drinking, may I ask?

CUSINS A most devilish kind of Spanish burgundy, warranted free from added alcohol: a Temperance burgundy in fact. Its richness in natural alcohol made any addition superfluous.

BARBARA Are you joking, Dolly?

CUSINS (*Patiently*) No. I have been making a night of it with the nominal head of this household: that is all.

LADY BRITOMART Andrew made you drunk!

CUSINS No: he only provided the wine. I think it was Dionysos who made me drunk. (*To* BARBARA) I told you I was possessed.

LADY BRITOMART You're not sober yet. Go home to bed at once.

CUSINS I have never before ventured to reproach you, Lady Brit; but how could you marry the Prince of Darkness?

LADY BRITOMART It was much more excusable to marry him than to get drunk with him. That is a new accomplishment of Andrew's, by the way. He usen't to drink.

CUSINS He doesn't now. He only sat there and completed the wreck of my moral basis, the rout of my convictions, the purchase of my soul. He cares for you, Barbara. That is what makes him so dangerous to me.

BARBARA That has nothing to do with it, Dolly. There are larger loves and diviner dreams than the fireside ones. You know that, don't you?

CUSINS Yes: that is our understanding. I know it. I hold to it. Unless he can win me on that holier ground he may amuse me for a while; but he can get no deeper hold, strong as he is.

BARBARA Keep to that; and the end will be right. Now tell me what happened at the meeting?

CUSINS It was an amazing meeting. Mrs Baines almost died of emotion. Jenny Hill simply gibbered with hysteria. The Prince of Darkness played his trombone like a madman: its brazen roarings were like the laughter of the damned. 117 conversions took place then and there. They prayed with the most touching sincerity and gratitude for Bodger, and for the anonymous donor of the £5000. Your father would not let his name be given.

LOMAX That was rather fine of the old man, you know. Most chaps would have wanted the advertisement.

CUSINS He said all the charitable institutions would be down on him like kites on a battle field if he gave his name.

LADY BRITOMART That's Andrew all over. He never does a proper thing without giving an improper reason for it.

CUSINS He convinced me that I have all my life been doing improper things for proper reasons.

LADY BRITOMART Adolphus: now that Barbara has left the Salvation Army, you had better leave it too. I will not have you playing that drum in the streets.

CUSINS Your orders are already obeyed, Lady Brit.

BARBARA Dolly: were you ever really in earnest about it? Would you have joined if you had never seen me?

CUSINS (*Disingenuously*) Well—er—well, possibly, as a collector of religions—

LOMAX (*Cunningly*) Not as a drummer, though, you know. You are a very clearheaded brainy chap, Dolly; and it must have been apparent to you that there is a certain amount of tosh about—

LADY BRITOMART Charles: if you must drivel, drivel like a grown-up man and not like a schoolboy.

LOMAX (*Out of countenance*) Well, drivel is drivel, don't you know, whatever a man's age.

LADY BRITOMART In good society in England, Charles, men drivel at all ages by repeating silly formulas with an air of wisdom. Schoolboys make their own formulas out of slang, like you. When they reach your age, and get political private secretaryships and things of that sort, they drop slang and get their formulas out of *The Spectator* or *The Times*. You had better confine yourself to *The Times*. You will find that there is a certain amount of tosh about *The Times*; but at least its language is reputable.

LOMAX (*Overwhelmed*) You are so awfully strongminded, Lady Brit—

LADY BRITOMART Rubbish! (MORRISON *comes in*) What is it?

MORRISON If you please, my lady, Mr Undershaft has just drove up to the door.

LADY BRITOMART Well, let him in. (MORRISON *hesitates*) What's the matter with you?

MORRISON Shall I announce him, my lady; or is he at home here, so to speak, my lady?

LADY BRITOMART Announce him.

MORRISON Thank you, my lady. You won't mind my asking, I hope. The occasion is in a manner of speaking new to me.

LADY BRITOMART Quite right. Go and let him in.

MORRISON Thank you, my lady. (*He withdraws*)

LADY BRITOMART Children: go and get ready. (SARAH *and* BARBARA *go upstairs for their out-of-door wraps*) Charles: go and tell Stephen to come down here in five minutes: you will find him in the drawing room. (CHARLES *goes*) Adolphus: tell them to send round the carriage in about fifteen minutes. (ADOLPHUS *goes*)

MORRISON (*At the door*) Mr Undershaft.

(UNDERSHAFT *comes in.* MORRISON *goes out*)

UNDERSHAFT Alone! How fortunate!

LADY BRITOMART (*Rising*) Don't be sentimental, Andrew. Sit down. (*She sits on the settee: he sits beside her, on her left. She comes to the point before he has time to breathe*) Sarah must have £800 a year until Charles Lomax comes into his property. Barbara will need more, and need it permanently, because Adolphus hasn't any property.

UNDERSHAFT (*Resignedly*) Yes, my dear: I will see to it. Anything else? for yourself, for instance?

LADY BRITOMART I want to talk to you about Stephen.

UNDERSHAFT (*Rather wearily*) Don't my dear. Stephen doesn't interest me.

LADY BRITOMART He does interest me. He is our son.

UNDERSHAFT Do you really think so? He has induced us to bring him into the world; but he chose his parents very incongruously, I think. I see nothing of myself in him, and less of you.

LADY BRITOMART Andrew: Stephen is an excellent son, and a most steady, capable, highminded young man. You are simply trying to find an excuse for disinheriting him.

UNDERSHAFT My dear Biddy: the Undershaft tradition disinherits him. It would be dishonest of me to leave the cannon foundry to my son.

LADY BRITOMART It would be most unnatural and improper of you to leave it to anyone else, Andrew. Do you suppose this wicked and immoral tradition can be kept up for ever? Do you pretend that Stephen could not carry on the foundry just as well as all the other sons of the big business houses?

UNDERSHAFT Yes: he could learn the office routine without understanding the business, like all the other sons; and the firm would go on by its own momentum until the real Undershaft—probably an Italian or a German—would invent a new method and cut him out.

LADY BRITOMART There is nothing that any Italian or German could do that Stephen could not do. And Stephen at least has breeding.

UNDERSHAFT The son of a foundling! Nonsense!

LADY BRITOMART My son, Andrew! And even you may have good blood in your veins for all you know.

UNDERSHAFT True. Probably I have. That is another argument in favor of a foundling.

LADY BRITOMART Andrew: don't be aggravating. And don't be wicked. At present you are both.

UNDERSHAFT This conversation is part of the Undershaft tradition, Biddy. Every Undershaft's wife has treated him to it ever since the house was founded. It is mere waste of breath. If the tradition be ever broken it will be for an abler man than Stephen.

LADY BRITOMART (*Pouting*) Then go away.

UNDERSHAFT (*Deprecatory*) Go away!

LADY BRITOMART Yes: go away. If you will do nothing for Stephen, you are not wanted here. Go to your foundling, whoever he is; and look after him.

UNDERSHAFT The fact is, Biddy—

LADY BRITOMART Don't call me Biddy. I don't call you Andy.

UNDERSHAFT I will not call my wife Britomart: it is not good sense. Seriously, my love, the Undershaft tradition has landed me in a difficulty. I am getting on in years; and my partner Lazarus has at last made a stand and insisted that the succession must be settled one way or the other; and of course he is quite right. You see, I haven't found a fit successor yet.

LADY BRITOMART (*Obstinately*) There is Stephen.

UNDERSHAFT That's just it: all the foundlings I can find are exactly like Stephen.

LADY BRITOMART Andrew!!

UNDERSHAFT I want a man with no relations and no schooling: that is, a man who would be out of the running altogether if he were not a strong man. And I can't find him. Every blessed foundling nowadays is snapped up in his infancy by Barnardo homes[1] or School Board officers, or Boards of Guardians; and if he shews the least ability, he is fastened on by schoolmasters; trained to win scholarships like a racehorse; crammed with secondhand ideas; drilled and disciplined in docility and what they call good taste; and lamed for life so that he is fit for nothing but teaching. If you want to keep the foundry in the family, you had better find an eligible foundling and marry him to Barbara.

LADY BRITOMART Ah! Barbara! Your pet! You would sacrifice Stephen to Barbara.

UNDERSHAFT Cheerfully. And you, my dear, would boil Barbara to make soup for Stephen.

LADY BRITOMART Andrew: this is not a question of our likings and dislikings: it is a question of duty. It is your duty to make Stephen your successor.

UNDERSHAFT Just as much as it is your duty to submit to your husband. Come, Biddy! these tricks of the governing class are of no use with me. I am one of the governing class myself; and it is waste of time giving tracts to a missionary. I have the power in this matter; and I am not to be humbugged into using it for your purposes.

LADY BRITOMART Andrew: you can talk my head off; but you can't change wrong into right. And your tie is all on one side. Put it straight.

UNDERSHAFT (*Disconcerted*) It won't stay unless it's pinned—(*He fumbles at it with childish grimaces*) (STEPHEN *comes in*)

STEPHEN (*At the door*) I beg your pardon. (*About to retire*)

LADY BRITOMART No: come in, Stephen. (STEPHEN *comes forward to his mother's writing table*)

UNDERSHAFT (*Not very cordially*) Good afternoon.

STEPHEN (*Coldly*) Good afternoon.

UNDERSHAFT (*To* LADY BRITOMART) He knows all about the tradition, I suppose?

LADY BRITOMART Yes. (*To* STEPHEN) It is what I told you last night, Stephen.

UNDERSHAFT (*Sulkily*) I understand you want to come into the cannon business.

STEPHEN *I* go into trade! Certainly not.

UNDERSHAFT (*Opening his eyes, greatly eased in mind and manner*) Oh! in that case—

LADY BRITOMART Cannons are not trade, Stephen. They are enterprise.

STEPHEN I have no intention of becoming a man of business in any sense. I have no capacity for business and no taste for it. I intend to devote myself to politics.

[1] Thomas J. Barnardo founded homes in which destitute children could be given industrial training.

UNDERSHAFT (*Rising*) My dear boy: this is an immense relief to me. And I trust it may prove an equally good thing for the country. I was afraid you would consider yourself disparaged and slighted. (*He moves towards* STEPHEN *as if to shake hands with him*)

LADY BRITOMART (*Rising and interposing*) Stephen: I cannot allow you to throw away an enormous property like this.

STEPHEN (*Stiffly*) Mother: there must be an end of treating me as a child, if you please. (LADY BRITOMART *recoils, deeply wounded by his tone*) Until last night I did not take your attitude seriously, because I did not think you meant it seriously. But I find now that you left me in the dark as to matters which you should have explained to me years ago. I am extremely hurt and offended. Any further discussion of my intentions had better take place with my father, as between one man and another.

LADY BRITOMART Stephen! (*She sits down again, her eyes filling with tears*)

UNDERSHAFT (*With grave compassion*) You see, my dear, it is only the big men who can be treated as children.

STEPHEN I am sorry, mother, that you have forced me—

UNDERSHAFT (*Stopping him*) Yes, yes, yes, yes: that's all right, Stephen. She won't interfere with you any more: your independence is achieved: you have won your latchkey. Don't rub it in; and above all, don't apologize. (*He resumes his seat*) Now what about your future, as between one man and another—I beg your pardon, Biddy: as between two men and a woman.

LADY BRITOMART (*Who has pulled herself together strongly*) I quite understand, Stephen. By all means go your own way if you feel strong enough. (STEPHEN *sits down magisterially in the chair at the writing table with an air of affirming his majority*)

UNDERSHAFT It is settled that you do not ask for the succession to the cannon business.

STEPHEN I hope it is settled that I repudiate the cannon business.

UNDERSHAFT Come, come! don't be so devilishly sulky: it's boyish. Freedom should be generous. Besides, I owe you a fair start in life in exchange for disinheriting you. You can't become prime minister all at once. Haven't you a turn for something? What about literature, art, and so forth?

STEPHEN I have nothing of the artist about me, either in faculty or character, thank Heaven!

UNDERSHAFT A philosopher, perhaps? Eh?

STEPHEN I make no such ridiculous pretension.

UNDERSHAFT Just so. Well, there is the army, the navy, the Church, the Bar. The Bar requires some ability. What about the Bar?

STEPHEN I have not studied law. And I am afraid I have not the necessary push—I believe that is the name barristers give to their vulgarity—for success in pleading.

UNDERSHAFT Rather a difficult case, Stephen. Hardly anything left but the stage, is there? (STEPHEN *makes an impatient movement*) Well, come! is there anything you know or care for?

STEPHEN (*Rising and looking at him steadily*) I know the difference between right and wrong.

UNDERSHAFT (*Hugely tickled*) You don't say so! What! no capacity for business, no knowledge of law, no sympathy with art, no pretension to philosophy; only a simple knowledge of the secret that has puzzled all the philosophers, baffled all the lawyers, muddled all the men of business, and ruined most of the artists: the secret of right and wrong. Why, man, you're a genius, a master of masters, a god! At twenty-four, too!

STEPHEN (*Keeping his temper with difficulty*) You are pleased to be facetious. I pretend to nothing more than any honorable English gentleman claims as his birthright. (*He sits down angrily*)

UNDERSHAFT Oh, that's everybody's birthright. Look at poor little Jenny Hill, the Salvation lassie! she would think you were laughing at her if you asked her to stand up in the street and teach grammar or geography or mathematics or even drawing room dancing; but it never occurs to her to doubt that she can teach morals and religion. You are all alike, you respectable people. You can't tell me the bursting strain of a ten-inch gun, which is a very simple matter; but you all think you can tell me the bursting strain of a man under temptation. You daren't handle high explosives; but you're all ready to handle honesty and truth and justice and the whole duty of man, and kill one another at that game. What a country! What a world!

LADY BRITOMART (*Uneasily*) What do you think he had better do, Andrew?

UNDERSHAFT Oh, just what he wants to do. He knows nothing and he thinks he knows everything. That points clearly to a political career. Get him a private secretaryship to someone who can get him an Under Secretaryship; and then leave him alone. He will find his natural and proper place in the end on the Treasury Bench.

STEPHEN (*Springing up again*) I am sorry, sir, that you force me to forget the respect due to you as my father. I am an Englishman and I will not hear the Government of my country insulted. (*He thrusts his hands in his pockets, and walks angrily across to the window*)

UNDERSHAFT (*With a touch of brutality*) The government of your country! *I* am the government of your country: I, and Lazarus. Do you suppose that you and half a dozen amateurs like you, sitting in a row in that foolish gabble shop, can govern Undershaft and Lazarus? No, my friend: you will do what pays us. You will make war when it suits us, and keep peace when it doesn't. You will find out that trade requires certain measures when we have decided on those measures. When I want anything to keep my dividends up, you will discover that my want is a national need. When other people want something to keep my dividends down, you will call out the police and military. And in return you shall have the support and applause of my newspapers, and the delight of imagining that you are a great statesman. Government of your country! Be off with you, my boy, and play with your caucuses and leading articles and historic parties and great leaders and burning questions and the rest of your toys. *I* am going back to my counting house to pay the piper and call the tune.

STEPHEN (*Actually smiling, and putting his hand on his father's shoulder with indulgent patronage*) Really, my dear father, it is impossible to be angry with you. You don't know how absurd all this sounds to me. You are very properly proud of having been industrious enough to make money; and it is greatly to your credit that you have made so much of it. But it has kept you in circles where you are valued for your money and deferred to for it, instead of in the doubtless very old-fashioned and behind-the-times public school and university where I formed my habits of mind. It is natural for you to think that money governs England; but you must allow me to think I know better.

UNDERSHAFT And what does govern England, pray?

STEPHEN Character, father, character.

UNDERSHAFT Whose character? Yours or mine?

STEPHEN Neither yours nor mine, father, but the best elements in the English national character.

UNDERSHAFT Stephen: I've found your profession for you. You're a born journalist. I'll start you with a hightoned weekly review. There!

(*Before* STEPHEN *can reply* SARAH, BARBARA, LOMAX, *and* CUSINS *come in ready for walking.* BARBARA *crosses the room to the window and looks out.* CUSINS *drifts amiably to the armchair.* LOMAX *remains near the door, whilst* SARAH *comes to her mother.*

STEPHEN *goes to the smaller writing table and busies himself with his letters*)

SARAH Go and get ready, mamma: the carriage is waiting. (LADY BRITOMART *leaves the room*)

UNDERSHAFT (*To* SARAH) Good day, my dear. Good afternoon, Mr Lomax.

LOMAX (*Vaguely*) Ahdedoo.

UNDERSHAFT (*To* CUSINS) Quite well after last night, Euripides, eh?

CUSINS As well as can be expected.

UNDERSHAFT That's right. (*To* BARBARA) So you are coming to see my death and devastation factory, Barbara?

BARBARA (*At the window*) You came yesterday to see my salvation factory. I promised you a return visit.

LOMAX (*Coming forward between* SARAH *and* UNDERSHAFT) You'll find it awfully interesting. I've been through the Woolwich Arsenal; and it gives you a ripping feeling of security, you know, to think of the lot of beggars we could kill if it came to fighting. (*To* UNDERSHAFT, *with sudden solemnity*) Still, it must be rather an awful reflection for you, from the religious point of view as it were. You're getting on, you know, and all that.

SARAH You don't mind Cholly's imbecility, papa, do you?

LOMAX (*Much taken aback*) Oh I say!

UNDERSHAFT Mr Lomax looks at the matter in a very proper spirit, my dear.

LOMAX Just so. That's all I meant, I assure you.

SARAH Are you coming, Stephen?

STEPHEN Well, I am rather busy—er— (*Magnanimously*) Oh well, yes: I'll come. That is, if there is room for me.

UNDERSHAFT I can take two with me in a little motor I am experimenting with for field use. You won't mind its being rather unfashionable. It's not painted yet; but it's bullet proof.

LOMAX (*Appalled at the prospect of confronting Wilton Crescent in an unpainted motor*) Oh I say!

SARAH The carriage for me, thank you. Barbara doesn't mind what she's seen in.

LOMAX I say, Dolly old chap: do you really mind the car being a guy? [2] Because of course if you do I'll go in it. Still—

CUSINS I prefer it.

LOMAX Thanks awfully, old man. Come, my ownest. (*He hurries out to secure his seat in the carriage.* SARAH *follows him*).

CUSINS (*Moodily walking across to* LADY BRITOMART'S *writing table*) Why are we two coming to this Works Department of Hell? that is what I ask myself.

BARBARA I have always thought of it as a sort of pit where lost creatures with blackened faces stirred up smoky fires and were driven and tormented by my father. Is it like that, dad?

UNDERSHAFT (*Scandalized*) My dear! It is a spotlessly clean and beautiful hillside town.

CUSINS With a Methodist chapel? Oh do say there's a Methodist chapel.

UNDERSHAFT There are two: a Primitive one and a sophisticated one. There is even an Ethical Society; but it is not much patronized, as my men are all strongly religious. In the High Explosives Sheds they object to the presence of Agnostics as unsafe.

CUSINS And yet they don't object to you!

BARBARA Do they obey all your orders?

UNDERSHAFT I never give them any orders. When I speak to one of them it is "Well, Jones, is the baby doing well? and has Mrs Jones made a good recovery?" "Nicely, thank you, sir." And that's all.

CUSINS But Jones has to be kept in order. How do you maintain discipline among your men?

UNDERSHAFT I don't. They do. You see, the one thing Jones won't stand is any rebellion from the man under him, or any assertion of social equality between the wife of the man with 4 shillings a week less than himself, and Mrs Jones! Of course they all rebel against me, theoretically. Practically, every man of them keeps the man just below him in his place. I never meddle with them. I never bully them. I don't even bully Lazarus. I say that certain things are to be done; but I don't order anybody to do them. I don't say, mind you, that there is no ordering about and snubbing and even bullying. The men snub the boys and order them about; the carmen snub the sweepers; the artisans snub the unskilled laborers; the foremen drive and bully both the laborers and artisans; the assistant engineers find fault with the foremen; the chief engineers drop on the assistants; the departmental managers worry the chiefs; and the clerks have tall hats and hymnbooks and keep up the social tone by refusing to associate on equal terms with anybody. The result is a colossal profit, which comes to me.

[2] A conspicuously grotesque object which invites ridicule.

CUSINS (*Revolted*) You really are a—well, what I was saying yesterday.

BARBARA What was he saying yesterday?

UNDERSHAFT Never mind, my dear. He thinks I have made you unhappy. Have I?

BARBARA Do you think I can be happy in this vulgar silly dress? I! who have worn the uniform. Do you understand what you have done to me? Yesterday I had a man's soul in my hand. I set him in the way of life with his face to salvation. But when we took your money he turned back to drunkenness and derision. (*With intense conviction*) I will never forgive you that. If I had a child, and you destroyed its body with your explosives—if you murdered Dolly with your horrible guns—I could forgive you if my forgiveness would open the gates of heaven to you. But to take a human soul from me, and turn it into the soul of a wolf! that is worse than any murder.

UNDERSHAFT Does my daughter despair so easily? Can you strike a man to the heart and leave no mark on him?

BARBARA (*Her face lighting up*) Oh, you are right: he can never be lost now: where was my faith?

CUSINS Oh, clever clever devil!

BARBARA You may be a devil; but God speaks through you sometimes. (*She takes her father's hands and kisses them*) You have given me back my happiness: I feel it deep down now, though my spirit is troubled.

UNDERSHAFT You have learnt something. That always feels at first as if you had lost something.

BARBARA Well, take me to the factory of death; and let me learn something more. There must be some truth or other behind all this frightful irony. Come, Dolly. (*She goes out*)

CUSINS My guardian angel! (*To* UNDERSHAFT) Avaunt! (*He follows* BARBARA)

STEPHEN (*Quietly, at the writing table*) You must not mind Cusins, father. He is a very amiable good fellow; but he is a Greek scholar and naturally a little eccentric.

UNDERSHAFT Ah, quite so. Thank you, Stephen. Thank you. (*He goes out*)

(STEPHEN *smiles patronizingly; buttons his coat responsibly; and crosses the room to the door.* LADY BRITOMART, *dressed for out-of-doors, opens it before he reaches it. She looks round for the others; looks at* STEPHEN; *and turns to go without a word*)

STEPHEN (*Embarrassed*) Mother—

LADY BRITOMART Don't be apologetic, Stephen. And don't forget that you have outgrown your mother. (*She goes out*)

(*Perivale St Andrews lies between two Middlesex*

*hills, half climbing the northern one. It is an almost smokeless town of white walls, roofs of narrow green slates or red tiles, tall trees, domes, campaniles, and slender chimney shafts, beautifully situated and beautiful in itself. The best view of it is obtained from the crest of a slope about half a mile to the east, where the high explosives are dealt with. The foundry lies hidden in the depths between, the tops of its chimneys sprouting like huge skittles into the middle distance. Across the crest runs an emplacement of concrete, with a firestep, and a parapet which suggests a fortification, because there is a huge cannon of the obsolete Woolwich Infant pattern peering across it at the town. The cannon is mounted on an experimental gun carriage: possibly the original model of the Undershaft disappearing rampart gun alluded to by Stephen. The firestep, being a convenient place to sit, is furnished here and there with straw disc cushions; and at one place there is the additional luxury of a fur rug.*

BARBARA *is standing on the firestep, looking over the parapet towards the town. On her right is the cannon; on her left the end of a shed raised on piles, with a ladder of three or four steps up to the door, which opens outwards and has a little wooden landing at the threshold, with a fire bucket in the corner of the landing. Several dummy soldiers more or less mutilated, with straw protruding from their gashes, have been shoved out of the way under the landing. A few others are nearly upright against the shed; and one has fallen forward and lies, like a grotesque corpse, on the emplacement. The parapet stops short of the shed, leaving a gap which is the beginning of the path down the hill through the foundry to the town. The rug is on the firestep near this gap. Down on the emplacement behind the cannon is a trolley carrying a huge conical bombshell with a red band painted on it. Further to the right is the door of an office, which, like the sheds, is of the lightest possible construction.*

CUSINS *arrives by the path from the town*)

BARBARA Well?

CUSINS Not a ray of hope. Everything perfect! wonderful! real! It only needs a cathedral to be a heavenly city instead of a hellish one.

BARBARA Have you found out whether they have done anything for old Peter Shirley?

CUSINS They have found him a job as gatekeeper and timekeeper. He's frightfully miserable. He calls the timekeeping brainwork, and says he isn't used to it; and his gate lodge is so splendid that he's ashamed to use the rooms, and skulks in the scullery.

BARBARA Poor Peter!

(STEPHEN *arrives from the town. He carries a field-glass*)

STEPHEN (*Enthusiastically*) Have you two seen the place? Why did you leave us?

CUSINS I wanted to see everything I was not intended to see; and Barbara wanted to make the men talk.

STEPHEN Have you found anything discreditable?

CUSINS No. They call him Dandy Andy and are proud of his being a cunning old rascal; but it's all horribly, frightfully, immorally, unanswerably perfect.

(SARAH *arrives*)

SARAH Heavens! what a place! (*She crosses to the trolley*) Did you see the nursing home!? (*She sits down on the shell*)

STEPHEN Did you see the libraries and schools!?

SARAH Did you see the ball room and the banqueting chamber in the Town Hall!?

STEPHEN Have you gone into the insurance fund, the pension fund, the building society, the various applications of cooperation!?

(UNDERSHAFT *comes from the office, with a sheaf of telegrams in his hand*)

UNDERSHAFT Well, have you seen everything? I'm sorry I was called away. (*Indicating the telegrams*) Good news from Manchuria.

STEPHEN Another Japanese victory?

UNDERSHAFT Oh, I don't know. Which side wins does not concern us here. No: the good news is that the aerial battleship is a tremendous success. At the first trial it has wiped out a fort with three hundred soldiers in it.

CUSINS (*From the platform*) Dummy soldiers?

UNDERSHAFT (*Striding across to* STEPHEN *and kicking the prostrate dummy brutally out of his way*) No: the real thing.

(CUSINS *and* BARBARA *exchange glances. Then* CUSINS *sits on the step and buries his face in his hands.* BARBARA *gravely lays her hand on his shoulder. He looks up at her in whimsical desperation*)

UNDERSHAFT Well, Stephen, what do you think of the place?

STEPHEN Oh, magnificent. A perfect triumph of modern industry. Frankly, my dear father, I have been a fool: I had no idea of what it all meant: of the wonderful forethought, the power of organization, the administrative capacity, the financial genius, the colossal capital it represents. I have been repeating to myself as I came through your streets "Peace hath her victories no less renowned than War." I have only one misgiving about it all.

UNDERSHAFT Out with it.

STEPHEN Well, I cannot help thinking that all this provision for every want of your workmen may sap their independence and weaken their sense of responsibility. And greatly as we enjoyed our tea at that splendid restaurant—how they gave us all that luxury and cake and jam and cream for threepence I really cannot imagine!—still you must remember that restaurants break up home life. Look at the continent, for instance! Are you sure so much pampering is really good for the men's characters?

UNDERSHAFT Well you see, my dear boy, when you are organizing civilization you have to make up your mind whether trouble and anxiety are good things or not. If you decide that they are, then, I take it, you simply don't organize civilization; and there you are, with trouble and anxiety enough to make us all angels! But if you decide the other way, you may as well go through with it. However, Stephen, our characters are safe here. A sufficient dose of anxiety is always provided by the fact that we may be blown to smithereens at any moment.

SARAH By the way, papa, where do you make the explosives?

UNDERSHAFT In separate little sheds, like that one. When one of them blows up, it costs very little; and only the people quite close to it are killed.

(STEPHEN, *who is quite close to it, looks at it rather scaredly, and moves away quickly to the cannon. At the same moment the door of the shed is thrown abruptly open; and a foreman in overalls and list slippers*[3] *comes out on the little landing and holds the door for* LOMAX, *who appears in the doorway*)

LOMAX (*With studied coolness*) My good fellow: you needn't get into a state of nerves. Nothing's going to happen to you; and I suppose it wouldn't be the end of the world if anything did. A little bit of British pluck is what you want, old chap. (*He descends and strolls across to* SARAH)

UNDERSHAFT (*To the foreman*) Anything wrong, Bilton?

BILTON (*With ironic calm*) Gentleman walked into the high explosives shed and lit a cigaret, sir: that's all.

UNDERSHAFT Ah, quite so. (*Going over to* LOMAX) Do you happen to remember what you did with the match?

LOMAX Oh come! I'm not a fool. I took jolly good care to blow it out before I chucked it away.

BILTON The top of it was red hot inside, sir.

LOMAX Well, suppose it was! I didn't chuck it into any of your messes.

UNDERSHAFT Think no more of it, Mr Lomax. By the way, would you mind lending me your matches?

LOMAX (*Offering his box*) Certainly.

UNDERSHAFT Thanks. (*He pockets the matches*)

LOMAX (*Lecturing to the company generally*) You know, these high explosives don't go off like gunpowder, except when they're in a gun. When they're spread loose, you can put a match to them without the least risk: they just burn quietly like a bit of paper. (*Warming to the scientific interest of the subject*) Did you know that, Undershaft? Have you ever tried?

UNDERSHAFT Not on a large scale, Mr Lomax. Bilton will give you a sample of gun cotton when you are leaving if you ask him. You can experiment with it at home. (BILTON *looks puzzled*)

SARAH Bilton will do nothing of the sort, papa. I suppose it's your business to blow up the Russians and Japs; but you might really stop short of blowing up poor Cholly. (BILTON *gives it up and retires into the shed*)

LOMAX My ownest, there is no danger. (*He sits beside her on the shell*)

(LADY BRITOMART *arrives from the town with a bouquet*)

[3] Soft cloth slippers used here to minimize friction.

LADY BRITOMART (*Impetuously*) Andrew: you shouldn't have let me see this place.

UNDERSHAFT Why, my dear?

LADY BRITOMART Never mind why: you shouldn't have: that's all. To think of all that (*Indicating the town*) being yours! and that you have kept it to yourself all these years!

UNDERSHAFT It does not belong to me. I belong to it. It is the Undershaft inheritance.

LADY BRITOMART It is not. Your ridiculous cannons and that noisy banging foundry may be the Undershaft inheritance; but all that plate and linen, all that furniture and those houses and orchards and gardens belong to us. They belong to me: they are not a man's business. I won't give them up. You must be out of your senses to throw them all away; and if you persist in such folly, I will call in a doctor.

UNDERSHAFT (*Stooping to smell the bouquet*) Where did you get the flowers, my dear?

LADY BRITOMART Your men presented them to me in your William Morris Labor Church.

CUSINS Oh! It needed only that. A Labor Church! (*He mounts the firestep distractedly, and leans with his elbows on the parapet, turning his back to them*)

LADY BRITOMART Yes, with Morris's words in mosaic letters ten feet high round the dome. NO MAN IS GOOD ENOUGH TO BE ANOTHER MAN'S MASTER. The cynicism of it!

UNDERSHAFT It shocked the men at first, I am afraid. But now they take no more notice of it than of the ten commandments in church.

LADY BRITOMART Andrew: you are trying to put me off the subject of the inheritance by profane jokes. Well, you shan't. I don't ask it any longer for Stephen: he has inherited far too much of your perversity to be fit for it. But Barbara has rights as well as Stephen. Why should not Adolphus succeed to the inheritance? I could manage the town for him; and he can look after the cannons, if they are really necessary.

UNDERSHAFT I should ask nothing better if Adolphus were a foundling. He is exactly the sort of new blood that is wanted in English business. But he's not a foundling; and there's an end of it. (*He makes for the office door*)

CUSINS (*Turning to them*) Not quite. (*They all turn and stare at him*) I think—Mind! I am not committing myself in any way as to my future course—but I think the foundling difficulty can be got over. (*He jumps down to the emplacement*)

UNDERSHAFT (*Coming back to him*) What do you mean?

CUSINS Well, I have something to say which is in the nature of a confession.

SARAH
LADY BRITOMART
BARBARA
STEPHEN } Confession!

LOMAX Oh I say!

CUSINS Yes, a confession. Listen, all. Until I met Barbara I thought myself in the main an honorable, truthful man, because I wanted the approval of my conscience more than I wanted anything else. But the moment I saw Barbara, I wanted her far more than the approval of my conscience.

LADY BRITOMART Adolphus!

CUSINS It is true. You accused me yourself, Lady Brit, of joining the Army to worship Barbara; and so I did. She bought my soul like a flower at a street corner; but she bought it for herself.

UNDERSHAFT What! Not for Dionysos or another?

CUSINS Dionysos and all the others are in herself. I adored what was divine in her, and was therefore a true worshipper. But I was romantic about her too. I thought she was a woman of the people, and that a marriage with a professor of Greek would be far beyond the wildest social ambitions of her rank.

LADY BRITOMART Adolphus!!

LOMAX Oh I say!!!

CUSINS When I learnt the horrible truth—

LADY BRITOMART What do you mean by the horrible truth, pray?

CUSINS That she was enormously rich; that her grandfather was an earl; that her father was the Prince of Darkness—

UNDERSHAFT Chut!

CUSINS —and that I was only an adventurer trying to catch a rich wife, then I stooped to deceive her about my birth.

BARBARA (*Rising*) Dolly!

LADY BRITOMART Your birth! Now Adolphus, don't dare to make up a wicked story for the sake of these wretched cannons. Remember: I have seen photographs of your parents; and the Agent General for South Western Australia knows them personally and has assured me that they are most respectable married people.

CUSINS So they are in Australia; but here they are outcasts. Their marriage is legal in Australia, but not in England. My mother is my father's deceased wife's sister; and in this island I am consequently a foundling. (*Sensation*)

BARBARA Silly! (*She climbs to the cannon, and leans, listening, in the angle it makes with the parapet*)

CUSINS Is the subterfuge good enough, Machiavelli?

UNDERSHAFT (*Thoughtfully*) Biddy: this may be a way out of the difficulty.

LADY BRITOMART Stuff! A man can't make cannons any the better for being his own cousin instead of his proper self. (*She sits down on the rug with a bounce that expresses her downright contempt for their casuistry*)

UNDERSHAFT (*To* CUSINS) You are an educated man. That is against the tradition.

CUSINS Once in ten thousand times it happens that the schoolboy is a born master of what they try to teach him. Greek has not destroyed my mind: it has nourished it. Besides, I did not learn it at an English public school.

UNDERSHAFT Hm! Well, I cannot afford to be too particular: you have cornered the foundling market. Let it pass. You are eligible, Euripides: you are eligible.

BARBARA Dolly: yesterday morning, when Stephen told us all about the tradition, you became very silent; and you have been strange and excited ever since. Were you thinking of your birth then?

CUSINS When the finger of Destiny suddenly points at a man in the middle of his breakfast, it makes him thoughtful.

UNDERSHAFT Aha! You have had your eye on the business, my young friend, have you?

CUSINS Take care! There is an abyss of moral horror between me and your accursed aerial battleships.

UNDERSHAFT Never mind the abyss for the present. Let us settle the practical details and leave your final decision open. You know that you will have to change your name. Do you object to that?

CUSINS Would any man named Adolphus—any man called Dolly!—object to be called something else?

UNDERSHAFT Good. Now, as to money! I propose to treat you handsomely from the beginning. You shall start at a thousand a year.

CUSINS (*With sudden heat, his spectacles twinkling with mischief*) A thousand! You dare offer a miserable thousand to the son-in-law of a millionaire! No, by Heavens, Machiavelli! you shall not cheat me. You cannot do without me; and I can do without you. I must have two thousand five hundred a year for two years. At the end of that time, if I am a failure, I go. But if I am a success, and stay on, you must give me the other five thousand.

UNDERSHAFT What other five thousand?

CUSINS To make the two years up to five thousand a year. The two thousand five hundred is only half pay in case I should turn out a failure. The third year I must have ten per cent on the profits.

UNDERSHAFT (*Taken aback*) Ten per cent! Why, man, do you know what my profits are?

CUSINS Enormous, I hope: otherwise I shall require twenty-five per cent.

UNDERSHAFT But, Mr Cusins, this is a serious matter of business. You are not bringing any capital into the concern.

CUSINS What! no capital! Is my mastery of Greek no capital? Is my access to the subtlest thought, the loftiest poetry yet attained by humanity, no capital? My character! my intellect! my life! my career! what Barbara calls my soul! are these no capital? Say another word; and I double my salary.

UNDERSHAFT Be reasonable—

CUSINS (*Peremptorily*) Mr Undershaft: you have my terms. Take them or leave them.

UNDERSHAFT (*Recovering himself*) Very well. I note your terms; and I offer you half.

CUSINS (*Disgusted*) Half!

UNDERSHAFT (*Firmly*) Half.

CUSINS You call yourself a gentleman; and you offer me half!!

UNDERSHAFT I do not call myself a gentleman; but I offer you half.

CUSINS This to your future partner! your successor! your son-in-law!

BARBARA You are selling your own soul, Dolly, not mine. Leave me out of the bargain, please.

UNDERSHAFT Come! I will go a step further for Barbara's sake. I will give you three fifths; but that is my last word.

CUSINS Done!

LOMAX Done in the eye! Why, *I* get only eight hundred, you know.

CUSINS By the way, Mac, I am a classical scholar, not an arithmetical one. Is three fifths more than half or less?

UNDERSHAFT More, of course.

CUSINS I would have taken two hundred and fifty. How you can succeed in business when you are willing to pay all that money to a University don who is obviously not worth a junior clerk's wages!—well! What will Lazarus say?

UNDERSHAFT Lazarus is a gentle romantic Jew who cares for nothing but string quartets and stalls at fashionable theatres. He will be blamed for your rapacity in money matters, poor fellow! as he has hitherto been blamed for mine. You are a shark of the first order, Euripides. So much the better for the firm!

BARBARA Is the bargain closed, Dolly? Does your soul belong to him now?

CUSINS No: the price is settled: that is all. The real tug of war is still to come. What about the moral question?

LADY BRITOMART There is no moral question in the matter at all, Adolphus. You must simply sell cannons and weapons to people whose cause is right and just, and refuse them to foreigners and criminals.

UNDERSHAFT (*Determinedly*) No: none of that. You must keep the true faith of an Armorer, or you don't come in here.

CUSINS What on earth is the true faith of an Armorer?

UNDERSHAFT To give arms to all men who offer an honest price for them, without respect of persons or principles: to aristocrat and republican, to Nihilist and Tsar, to Capitalist and Socialist, to Protestant and Catholic, to burglar and policeman, to black man, white man and yellow man, to all sorts and conditions, all nationalities, all faiths, all follies, all causes and all crimes. The first Undershaft wrote up in his shop IF GOD GAVE THE HAND, LET NOT MAN WITHHOLD THE SWORD. The second wrote up ALL HAVE THE RIGHT TO FIGHT: NONE HAVE THE RIGHT TO JUDGE. The third wrote up TO MAN THE WEAPON: TO HEAVEN THE VICTORY. The fourth had no literary turn; so he did not write up anything; but he sold cannons to Napoleon under the nose of George the Third. The fifth wrote up PEACE SHALL NOT PREVAIL SAVE WITH A SWORD IN HER HAND. The sixth, my master, was the best of all. He wrote up NOTHING IS EVER DONE IN THIS WORLD UNTIL MEN ARE PREPARED TO KILL ONE ANOTHER IF IT IS NOT DONE. After that, there was nothing left for the seventh to say. So he wrote up, simply, UNASHAMED.

CUSINS My good Machiavelli, I shall certainly write something up on the wall; only as I shall write it in Greek, you won't be able to read it. But as to your Armorer's faith, if I take my neck out of the noose of my own morality I am not going to put it into the noose of yours. I shall sell cannons to whom I please and refuse them to whom I please. So there!

UNDERSHAFT From the moment when you become Andrew Undershaft, you will never do as you please again. Don't come here lusting for power, young man.

CUSINS If power were my aim I should not come here for it. You have no power.

UNDERSHAFT None of my own, certainly.

CUSINS I have more power than you, more will. You do not drive this place: it drives you. And what drives the place?

UNDERSHAFT (*Enigmatically*) A will of which I am a part.

BARBARA (*Startled*) Father! Do you know what you are saying; or are you laying a snare for my soul?

CUSINS Don't listen to his metaphysics, Barbara. The place is driven by the most rascally part of society, the money hunters, the pleasure hunters, the military promotion hunters; and he is their slave.

UNDERSHAFT Not necessarily. Remember the Armorer's Faith. I will take an order from a good man as cheerfully as from a bad one. If you good people prefer preaching and shirking to buying my weapons and fighting the rascals, don't blame me. I cannot make courage and conviction. Bah! you tire me, Euripides, with your morality mongering. Ask Barbara: she understands. (*He suddenly reaches up and takes* BARBARA'S *hands, looking powerfully into her eyes*) Tell him, my love, what power really means.

BARBARA (*Hypnotized*) Before I joined the Salvation Army, I was in my own power; and the consequence was that I never knew what to do with myself. When I joined it, I had not time enough for all the things I had to do.

UNDERSHAFT (*Approvingly*) Just so. And why was that, do you suppose?

BARBARA Yesterday I should have said, because I was in the power of God. (*She resumes her self-possession, withdrawing her hands from his with a power equal to his own*) But you came and shewed me that I was in the power of Bodger and Undershaft. Today I feel—oh! how can I put it into words? Sarah: do you remember the earthquake at Cannes, when we were little children?—how little the surprise of the first shock mattered compared to the dread and horror of waiting for the second? That is how I feel in this place today. I stood on the rock I thought eternal; and without a word of warning it reeled and crumbled under me. I was safe with an infinite wisdom watching me, an army marching to Salvation with me; and in a moment, at a stroke of your pen in a cheque book, I stood alone; and the heavens were empty. That was the first shock of the earthquake: I am waiting for the second.

UNDERSHAFT Come, come, my daughter! don't make too much of your little tinpot tragedy. What do we do here when we spend years of work and thought and thousands of pounds of solid cash on a new gun or an aerial battleship that turns out just a hairsbreadth wrong after all? Scrap it. Scrap it without wasting another hour or another pound on it. Well, you have made for yourself something that you call a morality or a religion or what not. It doesn't fit the facts. Well, scrap it. Scrap it and get one that does fit. That is what is wrong with the world at present. It scraps its obsolete steam engines and dynamos; but it won't scrap its old prejudices and its old moralities and its old religions and its old political constitutions. What's the result? In machinery it does very well; but in morals and religion and politics it is working at a loss that brings it nearer bankruptcy every year. Don't persist in that folly. If your old religion broke down yesterday, get a newer and a better one for tomorrow.

BARBARA Oh how gladly I would take a better one to my soul! But you offer me a worse one. (*Turning on him with sudden vehemence*) Justify yourself: shew me some light through the darkness of this dreadful place, with its beautifully clean workshops, and respectable workmen, and model homes.

UNDERSHAFT Cleanliness and respectability do not need justification, Barbara: they justify themselves. I see no darkness here, no dreadfulness. In your Salvation shelter I saw poverty, misery, cold and hunger. You gave them bread and treacle and dreams of heaven. I give from thirty shillings a week to twelve thousand a year. They find their own dreams; but I look after the drainage.

BARBARA And their souls?

UNDERSHAFT I save their souls just as I saved yours.

BARBARA (*Revolted*) You saved my soul! What do you mean?

UNDERSHAFT I fed you and clothed you and housed you. I took care that you should have money enough to live handsomely—more than enough; so that you could be wasteful, careless, generous. That saved your soul from the seven deadly sins.

BARBARA (*Bewildered*) The seven deadly sins!

UNDERSHAFT Yes, the deadly seven. (*Counting on his fingers*) Food, clothing, firing, rent, taxes, respectability and children. Nothing can lift those seven millstones from Man's neck but money; and the spirit cannot soar until the millstones are lifted. I lifted them from your spirit. I enabled Barbara to become Major Barbara; and I saved her from the crime of poverty.

CUSINS Do you call poverty a crime?

UNDERSHAFT The worst of crimes. All the other crimes are virtues beside it: all the other dishonors are chivalry itself by comparison. Poverty blights whole cities; spreads horrible pestilences; strikes dead the very souls of all who come within sight, sound or smell of it. What you call crime is nothing: a murder here and a theft there, a blow now and a curse then: what do they matter? they are only the accidents and illnesses of life: there are not fifty genuine professional criminals in London. But there are millions of poor people, abject people, dirty people, ill fed, ill clothed people. They poison us morally and physically: they kill the happiness of society: they force us to do away with our own liberties and to organize unnatural cruelties for fear they should rise against us and drag us down into their abyss. Only fools fear crime: we all fear poverty. Pah! (*Turning on* BARBARA) you talk of your half-saved ruffian in West Ham: you accuse me of dragging his soul back to perdition. Well, bring him to me here; and I will drag his soul back again to salvation for you. Not by words and dreams; but by thirty-eight shillings a week, a sound house in a handsome street, and a permanent job. In three weeks he will have a fancy waistcoat; in three months a tall hat and a chapel sitting; before the end of the year he will shake hands with a duchess at a Primrose League[4] meeting, and join the Conservative Party.

BARBARA And will he be the better for that?

UNDERSHAFT You know he will. Don't be a hypocrite, Barbara. He will be better fed, better housed, better clothed, better behaved; and his children will be pounds heavier and bigger. That will be better than an American cloth[5] mattress in a shelter, chopping firewood, eating bread and treacle, and being forced to kneel down from time to time to thank heaven for it: knee drill, I think you call it. It is cheap work converting starving men with a Bible in one hand and a slice of bread in the other. I will undertake to convert West Ham to Mahometanism on the same terms. Try your hand on my men: their souls are hungry because their bodies are full.

BARBARA And leave the east end to starve?

UNDERSHAFT (*His energetic tone dropping into one of bitter and brooding remembrance*) *I* was an east ender. I moralized and starved until one day I swore that I would be a full-fed free man at all costs—that nothing should stop me except a bullet, neither reason nor morals nor the lives of other men. I said "Thou shalt starve ere I starve"; and with that word I became free and great. I was a dangerous man until I had my will: now I am a useful, beneficent, kindly person. That is the history of most self-made millionaires, I fancy. When it is the history of every Englishman we shall have an England worth living in.

LADY BRITOMART Stop making speeches, Andrew. This is not the place for them.

UNDERSHAFT (*Punctured*) My dear: I have no other means of conveying my ideas.

LADY BRITOMART Your ideas are nonsense. You got on because you were selfish and unscrupulous.

UNDERSHAFT Not at all. I had the strongest scruples about poverty and starvation. Your moralists are quite unscrupulous about both: they make virtues of them. I had rather be a thief than a pauper. I had rather be a murderer than a slave. I don't want to be

[4] Primrose League, named after Disraeli's favorite flower. Founded in 1883, the League followed Lord Beaconsfield's Conservative politics.

[5] "American cloth" was long used in England for oilcloth.

either; but if you force the alternative on me, then, by Heaven, I'll choose the braver and more moral one. I hate poverty and slavery worse than any other crimes whatsoever. And let me tell you this. Poverty and slavery have stood up for centuries to your sermons and leading articles: they will not stand up to my machine guns. Don't preach at them: don't reason with them. Kill them.

BARBARA Killing. Is that your remedy for everything?

UNDERSHAFT It is the final test of conviction, the only lever strong enough to overturn a social system, the only way of saying Must. Let six hundred and seventy fools loose in the street; and three policemen can scatter them. But huddle them together in a certain house in Westminster; and let them go through certain ceremonies and call themselves certain names until at last they get the courage to kill; and your six hundred and seventy fools become a government. Your pious mob fills up ballot papers and imagines it is governing its masters; but the ballot paper that really governs is the paper that has a bullet wrapped up in it.

CUSINS That is perhaps why, like most intelligent people, I never vote.

UNDERSHAFT Vote! Bah! When you vote, you only change the names of the cabinet. When you shoot, you pull down governments, inaugurate new epochs, abolish old orders and set up new. Is that historically true, Mr Learned Man, or is it not?

CUSINS It is historically true. I loathe having to admit it. I repudiate your sentiments. I abhor your nature. I defy you in every possible way. Still, it is true. But it ought not to be true.

UNDERSHAFT Ought! ought! ought! ought! ought! Are you going to spend your life saying ought, like the rest of our moralists? Turn your oughts into shalls, man. Come and make explosives with me. Whatever can blow men up can blow society up. The history of the world is the history of those who had courage enough to embrace this truth. Have you the courage to embrace it, Barbara?

LADY BRITOMART Barbara, I positively forbid you to listen to your father's abominable wickedness. And you, Adolphus, ought to know better than to go about saying that wrong things are true. What does it matter whether they are true if they are wrong?

UNDERSHAFT What does it matter whether they are wrong if they are true?

LADY BRITOMART (*Rising*) Children: come home instantly. Andrew: I am exceedingly sorry I allowed you to call on us. You are wickeder than ever. Come at once.

BARBARA (*Shaking her head*) It's no use running away from wicked people, mamma.

LADY BRITOMART It is every use. It shews your disapprobation of them.

BARBARA It does not save them.

LADY BRITOMART I can see that you are going to disobey me. Sarah: are you coming home or are you not?

SARAH I daresay it's very wicked of papa to make cannons; but I don't think I shall cut him on that account.

LOMAX (*Pouring oil on the troubled waters*) The fact is, you know, there is a certain amount of tosh about this notion of wickedness. It doesn't work. You must look at facts. Not that I would say a word in favor of anything wrong; but then, you see, all sorts of chaps are always doing all sorts of things; and we have to fit them in somehow, don't you know. What I mean is that you can't go cutting everybody; and that's about what it comes to. (*Their rapt attention to his eloquence makes him nervous*) Perhaps I don't make myself clear.

LADY BRITOMART You are lucidity itself, Charles. Because Andrew is successful and has plenty of money to give to Sarah, you will flatter him and encourage him in his wickedness.

LOMAX (*Unruffled*) Well, where the carcase is, there will the eagles be gathered, don't you know. (*To* UNDERSHAFT) Eh? What?

UNDERSHAFT Precisely. By the way, may I call you Charles?

LOMAX Delighted. Cholly is the usual ticket.

UNDERSHAFT (*To* LADY BRITOMART) Biddy—

LADY BRITOMART (*Violently*) Don't dare call me Biddy. Charles Lomax: you are a fool. Adolphus Cusins: you are a Jesuit. Stephen: you are a prig. Barbara: you are a lunatic. Andrew: you are a vulgar tradesman. Now you all know my opinion; and my conscience is clear, at all events. (*She sits down with a vehemence that the rug fortunately softens*)

UNDERSHAFT My dear: you are the incarnation of morality. (*She snorts*) Your conscience is clear and your duty done when you have called everybody names. Come, Euripides! it is getting late; and we all want to go home. Make up your mind.

CUSINS Understand this, you old demon—

LADY BRITOMART Adolphus!

UNDERSHAFT Let him alone, Biddy. Proceed, Euripides.

CUSINS You have me in a horrible dilemma. I want Barbara.

UNDERSHAFT Like all young men, you greatly exaggerate the difference between one young woman and another.

BARBARA Quite true, Dolly.

CUSINS I also want to avoid being a rascal.

UNDERSHAFT (*With biting contempt*) You lust for personal righteousness, for self-approval, for what you call a good conscience, for what Barbara calls salvation, for what I call patronizing people who are not so lucky as yourself.

CUSINS I do not: all the poet in me recoils from being a good man. But there are things in me that I must reckon with. Pity—

UNDERSHAFT Pity! The scavenger of misery.

CUSINS Well, love.

UNDERSHAFT I know. You love the needy and the outcast: you love the oppressed races, the negro, the Indian ryot, the underdog everywhere. Do you love the Japanese? Do you love the French? Do you love the English?

CUSINS No. Every true Englishman detests the English. We are the wickedest nation on earth; and our success is a moral horror.

UNDERSHAFT That is what comes of your gospel of love, is it?

CUSINS May I not love even my father-in-law?

UNDERSHAFT Who wants your love, man? By what right do you take the liberty of offering it to me? I will have your due heed and respect, or I will kill you. But your love! Damn your impertinence!

CUSINS (*Grinning*) I may not be able to control my affections, Mac.

UNDERSHAFT You are fencing, Euripides. You are weakening: your grip is slipping. Come! try your last weapon. Pity and love have broken in your hand: forgiveness is still left.

CUSINS No: forgiveness is a beggar's refuge. I am with you there: we must pay our debts.

UNDERSHAFT Well said. Come! you will suit me. Remember the words of Plato.

CUSINS (*Starting*) Plato! You dare quote Plato to me!

UNDERSHAFT Plato says, my friend, that society cannot be saved until either the Professors of Greek take to making gunpowder, or else the makers of gunpowder become Professors of Greek.

CUSINS Oh, tempter, cunning tempter!

UNDERSHAFT Come! choose, man, choose.

CUSINS But perhaps Barbara will not marry me if I make the wrong choice.

BARBARA Perhaps not.

CUSINS (*Desperately perplexed*) You hear!

BARBARA Father: do you love nobody?

UNDERSHAFT I love my best friend.

LADY BRITOMART And who is that, pray?

UNDERSHAFT My bravest enemy. That is the man who keeps me up to the mark.

CUSINS You know, the creature is really a sort of poet in his way. Suppose he is a great man, after all!

UNDERSHAFT Suppose you stop talking and make up your mind, my young friend.

CUSINS But you are driving me against my nature. I hate war.

UNDERSHAFT Hatred is the coward's revenge for being intimidated. Dare you make war on war? Here are the means: my friend Mr Lomax is sitting on them.

LOMAX (*Springing up*) Oh I say! You don't mean that this thing is loaded, do you? My ownest: come off it.

SARAH (*Sitting placidly on the shell*) If I am to be blown up, the more thoroughly it is done the better. Don't fuss, Cholly.

LOMAX (*To* UNDERSHAFT, *strongly remonstrant*) Your own daughter, you know.

UNDERSHAFT So I see. (*To* CUSINS) Well, my friend, may we expect you here at six tomorrow morning?

CUSINS (*Firmly*) Not on any account. I will see the whole establishment blown up with its own dynamite before I will get up at five. My hours are healthy, rational hours: eleven to five.

UNDERSHAFT Come when you please: before a week you will come at six and stay until I turn you out for the sake of your health. (*Calling*) Bilton! (*He turns to* LADY BRITOMART, *who rises*) My dear: let us leave these two young people to themselves for a moment. (BILTON *comes from the shed*) I am going to take you through the gun cotton shed.

BILTON (*Barring the way*) You can't take anything explosive in here, sir.

LADY BRITOMART What do you mean? Are you alluding to me?

BILTON (*Unmoved*) No, ma'am. Mr. Undershaft has the other gentleman's matches in his pocket.

LADY BRITOMART (*Abruptly*) Oh! I beg your pardon. (*She goes into the shed*)

UNDERSHAFT Quite right, Bilton, quite right: here you are. (*He gives* BILTON *the box of matches*) Come, Stephen. Come, Charles. Bring Sarah. (*He passes into the shed*)

(BILTON *opens the box and deliberately drops the matches into the fire-bucket*)

LOMAX Oh I say! (BILTON *stolidly hands him the empty box*) Infernal nonsense! Pure scientific ignorance! (*He goes in*)

SARAH Am I all right, Bilton?

BILTON You'll have to put on list slippers, miss: that's all. We've got 'em inside. (*She goes in*)

STEPHEN (*Very seriously to* CUSINS) Dolly, old fellow, think. Think before you decide. Do you feel that you are a sufficiently practical man? It is a huge undertaking, an enormous responsibility. All this mass of business will be Greek to you.

CUSINS Oh, I think it will be much less difficult than Greek.

STEPHEN Well, I just want to say this before I leave you to yourselves. Don't let anything I have said about right and wrong prejudice you against this great chance in life. I have satisfied myself that the business is one of the highest character and a credit to our country. (*Emotionally*) I am very proud of my father. I— (*Unable to proceed, he presses* CUSINS' *hand and goes hastily into the shed, followed by* BILTON)

(BARBARA *and* CUSINS, *left alone together, look at one another silently*)

CUSINS Barbara: I am going to accept this offer.

BARBARA I thought you would.

CUSINS You understand, don't you, that I had to decide without consulting you. If I had thrown the burden of the choice on you, you would sooner or later have despised me for it.

BARBARA Yes: I did not want you to sell your soul for me any more than for this inheritance.

CUSINS It is not the sale of my soul that troubles me: I have sold it too often to care about that. I have sold it for a professorship. I have sold it for an income. I have sold it to escape being imprisoned for refusing to pay taxes for hangmen's ropes and unjust wars and things that I abhor. What is all human conduct but the daily and hourly sale of our souls for trifles? What I am now selling it for is neither money nor position nor comfort, but for reality and for power.

BARBARA You know that you will have no power, and that he has none.

CUSINS I know. It is not for myself alone. I want to make power for the world.

BARBARA I want to make power for the world too; but it must be spiritual power.

CUSINS I think all power is spiritual: these cannons will not go off by themselves. I have tried to make spiritual power by teaching Greek. But the world can never be really touched by a dead language and a dead civilization. The people must have power; and the people cannot have Greek. Now the power that is made here can be wielded by all men.

BARBARA Power to burn women's houses down and kill their sons and tear their husbands to pieces.

CUSINS You cannot have power for good without having power for evil too. Even mother's milk nourishes murderers as well as heroes. This power which only tears men's bodies to pieces has never been so horribly abused as the intellectual power, the imaginative power, the poetic, religious power that can enslave men's souls. As a teacher of Greek I gave the intellectual man weapons against the common man. I now want to give the common man weapons against the intellectual man. I love the common people. I want to arm them against the lawyers, the doctors, the priests, the literary men, the professors, the artists, and the politicians, who, once in authority, are more disastrous and tyrannical than all the fools, rascals, and impostors. I want a power simple enough for common men to use, yet strong enough to force the intellectual oligarchy to use its genius for the general good.

BARBARA Is there no higher power than that? (*Pointing to the shell*)

CUSINS Yes; but that power can destroy the higher powers just as a tiger can destroy a man: therefore Man must master that power first. I admitted this when the Turks and Greeks were last at war. My best pupil went out to fight for Hellas. My parting gift to him was not a copy of Plato's *Republic*, but a revolver and a hundred Undershaft cartridges. The blood of every Turk he shot—if he shot any—is on my head as well as on Undershaft's. That act committed me to this place for ever. Your father's challenge has beaten me. Dare I make war on war? I dare. I must. I will. And now, is it all over between us?

BARBARA (*Touched by his evident dread of her answer*) Silly baby Dolly! How could it be!

CUSINS (*Overjoyed*) Then you—you—you— Oh for my drum! (*He flourishes imaginary drumsticks*)

BARBARA (*Angered by his levity*) Take care, Dolly, take care. Oh, if only I could get away from you and from father and from it all! if I could have the wings of a dove and fly away to heaven!

CUSINS And leave me!

BARBARA Yes, you, and all the other naughty mischievous children of men. But I can't. I was happy in the Salvation Army for a moment. I escaped from the world into a paradise of enthusiasm and prayer and soul saving; but the moment our money ran short, it all came back to Bodger: it was he who saved our people: he, and the Prince of Darkness, my papa. Undershaft and Bodger: their hands stretch everywhere: when we feed a starving fellow creature, it is with their bread, because there is no other bread; when we tend the sick, it is in the hospitals they endow; if we turn from the churches they build, we must kneel on the stones of the streets they pave. As long as that lasts, there is no getting away from them. Turning our backs on Bodger and Undershaft is turning our backs on life.

CUSINS I thought you were determined to turn your back on the wicked side of life.

BARBARA There is no wicked side: life is all one. And I never wanted to shirk my share in whatever evil must be endured, whether it be sin or suffering. I wish I could cure you of middle-class ideas, Dolly.

CUSINS (*Gasping*) Middle cl—! A snub! A social snub to me! from the daughter of a foundling!

BARBARA That is why I have no class, Dolly: I come straight out of the heart of the whole people. If I were middle-class I should turn my back on my father's business; and we should both live in an artistic drawing room, with you reading the reviews in one corner, and I in the other at the piano, playing Schumann: both very superior persons, and neither of us a bit of use. Sooner than that, I would sweep out the guncotton shed, or be one of Bodger's barmaids. Do you know what would have happened if you had refused papa's offer?

CUSINS I wonder!

BARBARA I should have given you up and married the man who accepted it. After all, my dear old mother has more sense than any of you. I felt like her when I saw this place—felt that I must have it—that never, never, never, could I let it go; only she thought it was the houses and the kitchen ranges and the linen and china, when it was really all the human souls to be saved: not weak souls in starved bodies, sobbing with gratitude for a scrap of bread and treacle, but fullfed, quarrelsome, snobbish, uppish creatures, all standing on their little rights and dignities, and thinking that my father ought to be greatly obliged to them for making so much money for him—and so he ought. That is where salvation is really wanted. My father shall never throw it in my teeth again that my converts were bribed with bread. (*She is transfigured*) I have got rid of the bribe of bread. I have got rid of the bribe of heaven. Let God's work be done for its own sake: the work he had to create us to do because it cannot be done except by living men and women. When I die, let him be in my debt, not I in his; and let me forgive him as becomes a woman of my rank.

CUSINS Then the way of life lies through the factory of death?

BARBARA Yes, through the raising of hell to heaven and of man to God, through the unveiling of an eternal light in the Valley of The Shadow. (*Seizing him with both hands*) Oh, did you think my courage would never come back? did you believe that I was a deserter? that I, who have stood in the streets, and taken my people to my heart, and talked of the holiest and greatest things with them, could ever turn back and chatter foolishly to fashionable people about nothing in a drawing room? Never, never, never, never: Major Barbara will die with the colors. Oh! and I have my dear little Dolly boy still; and he has found me my place and my work. Glory Hallelujah! (*She kisses him*)

CUSINS My dearest: consider my delicate health. I cannot stand as much happiness as you can.

BARBARA Yes: it is not easy work being in love with me, is it? But it's good for you. (*She runs to the shed, and calls, childlike*) Mamma! Mamma! (BILTON *comes out of the shed, followed by* UNDERSHAFT) I want mamma.

UNDERSHAFT She is taking off her list slippers, dear. (*He passes on to* CUSINS) Well? What does she say?

CUSINS She has gone right up into the skies.

LADY BRITOMART (*Coming from the shed and stopping on the steps, obstructing* SARAH, *who follows with* LOMAX. BARBARA *clutches like a baby at her mother's skirt*) Barbara: when will you learn to be independent and to act and think for yourself? I know as well as possible what that cry of "Mamma, Mamma," means. Always running to me!

SARAH (*Touching* LADY BRITOMART'S *ribs with her finger tips and imitating a bicycle horn*) Pip! pip!

LADY BRITOMART (*Highly indignant*) How dare you say Pip! pip! to me, Sarah? You are both very naughty children. What do you want, Barbara?

BARBARA I want a house in the village to live in with Dolly. (*Dragging at the skirt*) Come and tell me which one to take.

UNDERSHAFT (*To* CUSINS) Six o'clock tomorrow morning, Euripides.

*Curtain*

# John Millington Synge

## (1871-1909)

SUCH were the crosscurrents of art and politics in the Ireland of the 1890's that Synge's emergence as the first great modern Irish playwright still seems a small miracle of consummate artistry finding realization against patently insurmountable odds. Nothing in his education or in his generally withdrawn, reticent nature could respond to Yeats' ideal of a renascence of Irish life and literature through the glorification of the Celtic past; instead, Synge was to become, as Peter Kavanagh describes him in *The Story of the Abbey Theatre,* "the most hated of all the Abbey dramatists . . . detested by nationalists of every shade and degree of political thought." Fortunately for a world which can value his plays without becoming enmeshed in Irish political history, Synge remained largely unaffected by storms of controversy swirling about him. Even when his plays were received with shockingly unwarranted hostility, Synge guarded himself with what Yeats described as that "egotism of the man of genius which Nietzsche compares to the egotism of a woman with child."

The youngest of five children, Synge grew up in an atmosphere of strict, unimaginative Protestantism and unquestioning adherence to the values of a landed gentry proud of English lineage. His mother, widowed a year after his birth, expected him to prepare for a career suitable to his class, and when he replaced his early enthusiasm for such gentlemanly hobbies as naturalism with a determination to study music, she could only regard him as an enigma, disquieting and incomprehensible, a young man to be prayed for. Later, when he lost his religious faith and when he chose to pursue his studies on the Continent, he entered a world Mrs. Synge never understood. Illustrative of the gulf which, despite amicable relations, existed between mother and son was her failure ever to see one of his plays.

At Dublin's Trinity College, Synge took greatest satisfaction in his study at the Royal Irish Academy of Music. Although he took prizes in Hebrew and Irish, developed an informed interest in Irish antiquities, and made some attempts to write verse, his four years at Trinity are not notable for any discoveries he made either in himself or in the Ireland of his day.

From December 1892, when he received his college degree, until 1902, when he began to write his plays, Synge enjoyed what can best be called a prolonged *Wanderjahr* marked by quiet efforts to find himself. Never away from Ireland for any long period, he traveled—first to Germany for his musical studies, later to Paris, where he studied at the Sorbonne and in 1896 met Yeats, and to Italy, where he read Petrarch and recovered from a painfully unsuccessful love affair. Synge dabbled in many areas: he continued to write poems; he read widely in French letters from Villon to Baudelaire and the Symbolist poets, and tried his hand at translation; he worked on a play about a young Irish landlord who returns from Paris to defy his family by marrying the daughter of a cottager on his own estate; he participated, briefly, in the Irish League which Yeats and Maud Gonne founded in Paris, only to resign when he found his own gradualism at odds with his friends' "revolutionary and semi-military movement." Before 1898 (when, apparently at Yeats' urging, he made his first trip to the Aran Islands) Synge had dipped into the writings of Yeats and other young Irishmen seeking to recapture Celtic lyricism, interested himself in a scholarly way in Brittany and the Breton language as survivals of Celtic civilization on the continent, and studied with equal intensity both Renan's militantly agnostic *The Life of Jesus* and Thomas à Kempis' *The Imitation of Christ.* Unlike Yeats, whose interests and energies were strongly nationalistic, Synge seemed to be drifting everywhere—and nowhere.

Clearly, however, Synge's interests found sufficient focus during this period so that he could respond to Yeats' advice to go to the Aran Islands and "express a life which has never found expression." In *A Vision* (published in 1938, almost thirty years after Synge's death), Yeats was still marveling at Synge's sudden flowering into artistic maturity and comparing him with Rembrandt ("both delight in all that is willful, in all that flouts intellectual coherence, and conceive of the world as if it were an overflowing cauldron"). Yeats could apotheosize Synge by emphasizing that in his "early unpublished work, written before he found the dialects of Aran and of Wicklow, there is a brooding melancholy and self-pity. He had to undergo an aesthetic transformation, analogous to religious conversion, before he became the audacious, joyous, ironical man we know."

On the face of it, there would seem to be little in the harsh life on those islands in Galway Bay off Ireland's western coast to bring about the transformation Yeats described. The barren, primitive ways enforced upon the Islanders by the steady encroachment of sea on precious soil held for Synge, however, great fascination. So well did he document his visits in *The Aran Islands* (written before the plays, but not published until 1907) that many years later, while Robert Flaherty was making the documentary, *Man of Aran,* he credited Synge with teaching him what to photograph on those sea-swept islands. For Synge there was a way of life which, in its proud self-sufficiency and splendid isolation, mirrored his own nature. There was a copious larder of local legends and folklore, and although he set only *Riders to the Sea* against the Aran background, Synge found materials there for at least two other plays. Of equal importance and a source of continuing delight to Synge was the Islanders' rich idiom compounded of Elizabethan English and Gaelic, the language which gives his prose the vibrancy of verse.

For almost four years after his first Aran voyage, Synge's life continued largely unchanged. While Yeats was traveling the road of various theatrical ventures which led finally to the Abbey Theatre, Synge was back in Paris writing book reviews, trying again to write plays according to romantic formulas, polishing his Aran sketches, or studying long-familiar folkways in the mainland counties of Kerry and Wicklow with new interest. Finally, in the summer of 1902, spent in the small Wicklow cottage he describes in his Preface to *The Playboy of the Western World,* Synge hit his stride and wrote not only *In the Shadow of the Glen* and *Riders to the Sea* but a first (one-act) version of *The Tinker's Wedding* as well. In the relatively short period from 1902 until he died of cancer in 1909, Synge drove himself to complete the small but impressive group of six plays on which his fame rests so securely.

Sandwiched in a program of the Irish National Theatre Society between Yeats' *The King's Threshold* and the tried-and-true Nationalist flagwaver, *Cathleen ni Houlihan,* Synge's *In the Shadow of the Glen* was given its first production in October, 1903. Using a story he had heard in Aran but transferring the action to the "last cottage at the head of a long glen in County Wicklow," Synge offered a half-farcical, half-serious picture of a blasted May-December marriage. To test his young wife's fidelity, the old farmer, Dan Burke, feigns death. Into this remote setting wanders a Tramp who quickly becomes *confidant* of both husband and wife. At the play's end, Nora, discovered to be setting her cap for a dull but virile young sheep-farmer, is driven out by her husband. Her fate will be to wander the roads with the Tramp while Dan will live out his "black life" in even more lonely isolation. Although Synge could delight in the outrageous stratagem of the cuckoldry-obsessed old husband, he could also recognize the spiritual impoverishment such misalliances bring in their wake. The wit of this play has the sharp double edge of ironic tragicomedy Synge was to make his hallmark.

*In the Shadow of the Glen* was a harbinger of other things to come. Its first production set off, in the theatre, hissing barely drowned out by applause, and, in the press, a round of acrimonious exchanges between his supporters and detractors. Yeats' father, admiring the play as an attack on "our Irish institution, the loveless marriage," only exacerbated a situation in which Synge was being charged with insulting Irish womanhood and the Irish peasantry. In his "absorption in his own dream," Synge had cut himself off from such realities as the idealized Ireland existent in the tender sensibilities of ardent Nationalists. Except for the generally placid reception of *Riders to the Sea,* the history of his plays' initial performances is a catalogue of similarly stormy launchings, in light of which Synge's Preface (dated December, 1907) to *The Tinker's Wedding* is overcast with irony. Near the end of his life, Synge was again rejecting a drama of didacticism: "the drama, like the symphony, does not teach or prove anything." Citing Ibsen and "the Germans," he complained of the "analysts with their problems, and teachers with their systems" who were stocking modern playhouses with "the drugs of many seedy problems." The ring of deep conviction in these remarks may reflect Synge's discovery that, even when the dramatist disavows all intentions to "teach or prove anything," didactic purposes could still be imputed to him.

*Riders to the Sea* had appeared in Yeats' publication, *Samhain,* a month before *In the Shadow of the Glen* opened, but it was not produced until late February, 1904, on a bill with the *Deirdre* of AE (George Russell). Elaborate pains had been taken to costume the actors authentically (the women's red petticoats and the cowhide moccasins, or pampooties, designed as protection against the rocks), and the play interested its first audiences as much for its evocation of an exotic culture as for its large statements on life and death. The origins of Synge's conception can easily be traced in his Aran sketches: the apparitions of dead men; the discovery and identification of an Islander washed ashore (like Michael) in Donegal on the mainland; the Aran modes of keening and ritualized lamentation for the dead; the women's constant awareness of death as a living presence. To move from the sketches to the play is, however, to discover the superb orchestration of vividly recalled details into a unified prose-poem of extraordinary tragic beauty. With unparalleled economy of statement, in this play which can be performed in less than thirty minutes, Synge succeeded in mirroring the large world in the small: Maurya's complaint ("In the big world the old people do be leaving things after them for their sons and children, but in this place it is the young men do be leaving things behind for them that do be old") is placed against the Islanders' world of sea birds ("black hags") flying over churning surf, of the small boats (hookers and curaghs) at the mercy of tides and winds, of precious "fine white boards" brought from Connemara—and the nails Maurya forgot to order. Still without serious challenge as the perfect one-act play, *Riders to the Sea* shows Synge's mastery of the pattern of recurrences. As Maurya recalls the men and women bringing Patch home "in the half of a red sail" on a "dry day" long ago, the pattern begins to repeat itself as Bartley is brought home: "Is it Patch, or Michael, or what is it at all?" In showing Maurya's grief over the loss of all her men fusing into a single experience, Synge has dramatized the universal experience of grief.

# RIDERS TO THE SEA

## *A Play in One Act*

CHARACTERS

MAURYA, *an old woman*
BARTLEY, *her son*
CATHLEEN, *her daughter*
NORA, *a younger daughter*
MEN AND WOMEN

*An Island off the west of Ireland.*

*Cottage kitchen, with nets, oil-skins, spinning-wheel, some new boards standing by the wall, etc.* CATHLEEN, *a girl of about twenty, finishes kneading cake, and puts it down on the pot-oven by the fire; then wipes her hands, and begins to spin at the wheel.* NORA, *a young girl, puts her head in at the door.*

NORA (*In a low voice*) Where is she?

CATHLEEN She's lying down, God help her, and may be sleeping, if she's able.

(NORA *comes in softly, and takes a bundle from under her shawl*)

CATHLEEN (*Spinning the wheel rapidly*) What is it you have?

NORA The young priest is after bringing them. It's a shirt and a plain stocking were got off a drowned man in Donegal.

(CATHLEEN *stops her wheel with a sudden movement, and leans out to listen*)

NORA We're to find out if it's Michael's they are, some time herself will be down looking by the sea.

CATHLEEN How would they be Michael's, Nora? How would he go the length of that way to the Far North?

NORA The young priest says he's known the like of it. "If it's Michael's they are," says he, "you can tell herself he's got a clean burial by the grace of God, and if they're not his, let no one say a word about them, for she'll be getting her death," says he, "with crying and lamenting."

(*The door which* NORA *half closed is blown open by a gust of wind*)

CATHLEEN (*Looking out anxiously*) Did you ask him would he stop Bartley going this day with the horses to the Galway fair?

NORA "I won't stop him," says he, "but let you not be afraid. Herself does be saying prayers half through the night, and the Almighty God won't leave her destitute," says he, "with no son living."

CATHLEEN Is the sea bad by the white rocks, Nora?

NORA Middling bad, God help us. There's a great roaring in the west, and it's worse it'll be getting when the tide's turned to the wind. (*She goes over to the table with the bundle*) Shall I open it now?

CATHLEEN Maybe she'd wake up on us, and come in before we'd done. (*Coming to the table*) It's a long time we'll be, and the two of us crying.

NORA (*Goes to the inner door and listens*) She's moving about on the bed. She'll be coming in a minute.

CATHLEEN Give me the ladder, and I'll put them up in the turf-loft, the way she won't know of them at all, and maybe when the tide turns she'll be going down to see would he be floating from the east.

(*They put the ladder against the gable of the chimney;* CATHLEEN *goes up a few steps and hides the bundle in the turf-loft.* MAURYA *comes from the inner room*)

MAURYA (*Looking up at* CATHLEEN *and speaking querulously*) Isn't it turf enough you have for this day and evening?

CATHLEEN There's a cake baking at the fire for a short space (*Throwing down the turf*) and Bartley will want it when the tide turns if he goes to Connemara.

(NORA *picks up the turf and puts it round the pot-oven*)

MAURYA (*Sitting down on a stool at the fire*) He won't go this day with the wind rising from the south and west. He won't go this day, for the young priest will stop him surely.

NORA He'll not stop him, Mother, and I heard Eamon Simon and Stephen Pheety and Colum Shawn saying he would go.

MAURYA Where is he itself?

NORA He went down to see would there be another boat sailing in the week, and I'm thinking it won't be long till he's here now, for the tide's turning at the green head, and the hooker's[1] tacking from the east.

CATHLEEN I hear some one passing the big stones.

NORA (*Looking out*) He's coming now, and he in a hurry.

BARTLEY (*Comes in and looks round the room; speaking sadly and quietly*) Where is the bit of new rope, Cathleen, was bought in Connemara?

CATHLEEN (*Coming down*) Give it to him, Nora; it's on a nail by the white boards. I hung it up this morning, for the pig with the black feet was eating it.

NORA (*Giving him a rope*) Is that it, Bartley?

MAURYA You'd do right to leave that rope, Bartley, hanging by the boards. (BARTLEY *takes the rope*) It will be wanting in this place, I'm telling you, if Michael is washed up tomorrow morning, or the next morning, or any morning in the week, for it's a deep grave we'll make him by the grace of God.

BARTLEY (*Beginning to work with the rope*) I've no halter the way I can ride down on the mare, and I must go now quickly. This is the one boat going for two weeks or beyond it, and the fair will be a good fair for horses I heard them saying below.

MAURYA It's a hard thing they'll be saying below if the body is washed up and there's no man in it to make the coffin, and I after giving a big price for the finest white boards you'd find in Connemara. (*She looks round at the boards*)

BARTLEY How would it be washed up, and we after looking each day for nine days, and a strong wind blowing a while back from the west and south?

MAURYA If it wasn't found itself, that wind is raising the sea, and there was a star up against the moon, and it rising in the night. If it was a hundred horses, or a thousand horses you had itself, what is the price of a thousand horses against a son where there is one son only?

BARTLEY (*Working at the halter, to* CATHLEEN) Let you go down each day, and see the sheep aren't jumping in on the rye, and if the jobber comes you can sell the pig with the black feet if there is a good price going.

MAURYA How would the like of her get a good price for a pig?

BARTLEY (*To* CATHLEEN) If the west wind holds with the last bit of the moon let you and Nora get up weed enough for another cock[2] for the kelp. It's hard set we'll be from this day with no one in it but one man to work.

MAURYA It's hard set we'll be surely the day you're drownd'd with the rest. What way will I live and the girls with me, and I an old woman looking for the grave?

(BARTLEY *lays down the halter, takes off his old coat, and puts on a newer one of the same flannel*)

BARTLEY (*To* NORA) Is she coming to the pier?

NORA (*Looking out*) She's passing the green head and letting fall her sails.

[1] A single-masted fishing boat.

[2] A stack for burning seaweed into the ashes (kelp) useful as fertilizer.

BARTLEY (*Getting his purse and tobacco*) I'll have half an hour to go down, and you'll see me coming again in two days, or in three days, or maybe in four days if the wind is bad.

MAURYA (*Turning round to the fire, and putting her shawl over her head*) Isn't it a hard and cruel man won't hear a word from an old woman, and she holding him from the sea?

CATHLEEN It's the life of a young man to be going on the sea, and who would listen to an old woman with one thing and she saying it over?

BARTLEY (*Taking the halter*) I must go now quickly. I'll ride down on the red mare, and the gray pony'll run behind me. . . . The blessing of God on you. (*He goes out*)

MAURYA (*Crying out as he is in the door*) He's gone now, God spare us, and we'll not see him again. He's gone now, and when the black night is falling I'll have no son left me in the world.

CATHLEEN Why wouldn't you give him your blessing and he looking round in the door? Isn't it sorrow enough is on every one in this house without your sending him out with an unlucky word behind him, and a hard word in his ear?

(MAURYA *takes up the tongs and begins raking the fire aimlessly without looking round*)

NORA (*Turning toward her*) You're taking away the turf from the cake.

CATHLEEN (*Crying out*) The Son of God forgive us, Nora, we're after forgetting his bit of bread. (*She comes over to the fire*)

NORA And it's destroyed he'll be going till dark night, and he after eating nothing since the sun went up.

CATHLEEN (*Turning the cake out of the oven*) It's destroyed he'll be, surely. There's no sense left on any person in a house where an old woman will be talking forever.

(MAURYA *sways herself on her stool*)

CATHLEEN (*Cutting off some of the bread and rolling it in a cloth; to* MAURYA) Let you go down now to the spring well and give him this and he passing. You'll see him then and the dark word will be broken, and you can say "God speed you," the way he'll be easy in his mind.

MAURYA (*Taking the bread*) Will I be in it as soon as himself?

CATHLEEN If you go now quickly.

MAURYA (*Standing up unsteadily*) It's hard set I am to walk.

CATHLEEN (*Looking at her anxiously*) Give her the stick, Nora, or maybe she'll slip on the big stones.

NORA What stick?

CATHLEEN The stick Michael brought from Connemara.

MAURYA (*Taking a stick* NORA *gives her*) In the big world the old people do be leaving things after them for their sons and children, but in this place it is the young men do be leaving things behind for them that do be old.

(*She goes out slowly.* NORA *goes over to the ladder*)

CATHLEEN Wait, Nora, maybe she'd turn back quickly.

She's that sorry, God help her, you wouldn't know the thing she'd do.

NORA Is she gone round by the bush?

CATHLEEN (*Looking out*) She's gone now. Throw it down quickly, for the Lord knows when she'll be out of it again.

NORA (*Getting the bundle from the loft*) The young priest said he'd be passing tomorrow, and we might go down and speak to him below if it's Michael's they are surely.

CATHLEEN (*Taking the bundle*) Did he say what way they were found?

NORA (*Coming down*) "There were two men," says he, "and they rowing round with poteen[3] before the cocks crowed, and the oar of one of them caught the body, and they passing the black cliffs of the north."

CATHLEEN (*Trying to open the bundle*) Give me a knife, Nora, the string's perished with the salt water, and there's a black knot on it you wouldn't loosen in a week.

NORA (*Giving her a knife*) I've heard tell it was a long way to Donegal.

CATHLEEN (*Cutting the string*) It is surely. There was a man in here a while ago—the man sold us that knife—and he said if you set off walking from the rocks beyond, it would be seven days you'd be in Donegal.

NORA And what time would a man take, and he floating?

(CATHLEEN *opens the bundle and takes out a bit of a stocking. They look at them eagerly*)

CATHLEEN (*In a low voice*) The Lord spare us, Nora! isn't it a queer hard thing to say if it's his they are surely?

NORA I'll get his shirt off the hook the way we can put the one flannel on the other. (*She looks through some clothes hanging in the corner*) It's not with them, Cathleen, and where will it be?

CATHLEEN I'm thinking Bartley put it on him in the morning, for his own shirt was heavy with the salt in it. (*Pointing to the corner*) There's a bit of a sleeve was of the same stuff. Give me that and it will do.

(NORA *brings it to her and they compare the flannel*)

CATHLEEN It's the same stuff, Nora; but if it is itself aren't there great rolls of it in the shops of Galway, and isn't it many another man may have a shirt of it as well as Michael himself?

NORA (*Who has taken up the stocking and counted the stitches, crying out*) It's Michael, Cathleen, it's Michael; God spare his soul, and what will herself say when she hears this story, and Bartley on the sea?

CATHLEEN (*Taking the stocking*) It's a plain stocking.

NORA It's the second one of the third pair I knitted, and I put up threescore stitches, and I dropped four of them.

CATHLEEN (*Counts the stitches*) It's that number is in it. (*Crying out*) Ah, Nora, isn't it a bitter thing to think of him floating that way to the Far North, and no one to keen him but the black hags that do be flying on the sea?

NORA (*Swinging herself round, and throwing out her arms on the clothes*) And isn't it a pitiful thing when there is nothing left of a man who was a great rower and fisher, but a bit of an old shirt and a plain stocking?

CATHLEEN (*After an instant*) Tell me is herself coming, Nora? I hear a little sound on the path.

NORA (*Looking out*) She is, Cathleen. She's coming up to the door.

CATHLEEN Put these things away before she'll come in. Maybe it's easier she'll be after giving her blessing to Bartley, and we won't let on we've heard anything the time he's on the sea.

NORA (*Helping* CATHLEEN *to close the bundle*) We'll put them here in the corner.

(*They put them into a hole in the chimney corner.* CATHLEEN *goes back to the spinning-wheel*)

NORA Will she see it was crying I was?

CATHLEEN Keep your back to the door the way the light'll not be on you.

(NORA *sits down at the chimney corner, with her back to the door.* MAURYA *comes in very slowly, without looking at the girls, and goes over to her stool at the other side of the fire. The cloth with the bread is still in her hand. The girls look at each other, and* NORA *points to the bundle of bread*)

CATHLEEN (*After spinning for a moment*) You didn't give him his bit of bread? (MAURYA *begins to keen softly, without turning round*)

CATHLEEN Did you see him riding down?

(MAURYA *goes on keening*)

CATHLEEN (*A little impatiently*) God forgive you; isn't it a better thing to raise your voice and tell what you seen, than to be making lamentation for a thing that's done? Did you see Bartley, I'm saying to you.

MAURYA (*With a weak voice*) My heart's broken from this day.

CATHLEEN (*As before*) Did you see Bartley?

MAURYA I seen the fearfulest thing.

CATHLEEN (*Leaves her wheel and looks out*) God forgive you; he's riding the mare now over the green head, and the gray pony behind him.

MAURYA (*Starts, so that her shawl falls back from her head and shows her white tossed hair. With a frightened voice*) The gray pony behind him.

CATHLEEN (*Coming to the fire*) What is it ails you, at all?

MAURYA (*Speaking very slowly*) I've seen the fearfulest thing any person has seen, since the day Bride Dara seen the dead man with a child in his arms.

CATHLEEN AND NORA Uah.

(*They crouch down in front of the old woman at the fire*)

NORA Tell us what it is you seen.

MAURYA I went down to the spring well, and I stood there saying a prayer to myself. Then Bartley came along, and he riding on the red mare with the gray pony behind him. (*She puts up her hands, as if to*

[3] A strong whiskey illegally brewed and sold.

*hide something from her eyes)* The Son of God spare us, Nora!

CATHLEEN What is it you seen?

MAURYA I seen Michael himself.

CATHLEEN *(Speaking softly)* You did not, Mother; it wasn't Michael you seen, for his body is after being found in the Far North, and he's got a clean burial by the grace of God.

MAURYA *(A little defiantly)* I'm after seeing him this day, and he riding and galloping. Bartley came first on the red mare; and I tried to say, "God speed you," but something choked the words in my throat. He went by quickly; and "the blessing of God on you," says he, and I could say nothing. I looked up then, and I crying, at the gray pony, and there was Michael upon it—with fine clothes on him, and new shoes on his feet.

CATHLEEN *(Begins to keen)* It's destroyed we are from this day. It's destroyed, surely.

NORA Didn't the young priest say the Almighty God wouldn't leave her destitute with no son living?

MAURYA *(In a low voice, but clearly)* It's little the like of him knows of the sea. . . . Bartley will be lost now, and let you call in Eamon and make me a good coffin out of the white boards, for I won't live after them. I've had a husband, and a husband's father, and six sons in this house—six fine men, though it was a hard birth I had with every one of them and they coming to the world—and some of them were found and some of them were not found, but they're gone now the lot of them. . . . There were Stephen, and Shawn, were lost in the great wind, and found after in the Bay of Gregory of the Golden Mouth, and carried up the two of them on the one plank, and in by that door.

*(She pauses for a moment, the girls start as if they heard something through the door that is half open behind them)*

NORA *(In a whisper)* Did you hear that, Cathleen? Did you hear a noise in the northeast?

CATHLEEN *(In a whisper)* There's some one after crying out by the seashore.

MAURYA *(Continues without hearing anything)* There was Sheamus and his father, and his own father again, were lost in a dark night, and not a stick or sign was seen of them when the sun went up. There was Patch after was drowned out of a curagh that turned over. I was sitting here with Bartley, and he a baby, lying on my two knees, and I seen two women, and three women, and four women coming in, and they crossing themselves, and not saying a word. I looked out then, and there were men coming after them, and they holding a thing in the half of a red sail, and water dripping out of it—it was a dry day, Nora—and leaving a track to the door.

*(She pauses again with her hand stretched out toward the door. It opens softly and old women begin to come in, crossing themselves on the threshold, and kneeling down in front of the stage with red petticoats over their heads)*

MAURYA *(Half in a dream, to* CATHLEEN*)* Is it Patch, or Michael, or what is it at all?

CATHLEEN Michael is after being found in the Far North, and when he is found there how could he be here in this place?

MAURYA There does be a power of young men floating round in the sea, and what way would they know if it was Michael they had, or another man like him, for when a man is nine days in the sea, and the wind blowing, it's hard set his own mother would be to say what man was it.

CATHLEEN It's Michael, God spare him, for they're after sending us a bit of his clothes from the Far North.

*(She reaches out and hands* MAURYA *the clothes that belonged to Michael.* MAURYA *stands up slowly, and takes them in her hands.* NORA *looks out)*

NORA They're carrying a thing among them and there's water dripping out of it and leaving a track by the big stones.

CATHLEEN *(In a whisper to the women who have come in)* Is it Bartley it is?

ONE OF THE WOMEN It is surely, God rest his soul.

*(Two younger women come in and pull out the table. Then men carry in the body of* BARTLEY*, laid on a plank, with a bit of a sail over it, and lay it on the table)*

CATHLEEN *(To the women, as they are doing so)* What way was he drowned?

ONE OF THE WOMEN The gray pony knocked him into the sea, and he was washed out where there is a great surf on the white rocks.

*(*MAURYA *has gone over and knelt down at the head of the table. The women are keening softly and swaying themselves with a slow movement.* CATHLEEN *and* NORA *kneel at the other end of the table. The men kneel near the door)*

MAURYA *(Raising her head and speaking as if she did not see the people around her)* They're all gone now, and there isn't anything more the sea can do to me. . . . I'll have no call now to be up crying and praying when the wind breaks from the south, and you can hear the surf is in the east, and the surf is in the west, making a great stir with the two noises, and they hitting one on the other. I'll have no call now to be going down and getting Holy Water in the dark nights after Samhain,[4] and I won't care what way the sea is when the other women will be keening. *(To* NORA*)* Give me the Holy Water, Nora, there's a small sup still on the dresser.

*(*NORA *gives it to her)*

MAURYA *(Drops Michael's clothes across Bartley's feet, and sprinkles the Holy Water over him)* It isn't that I haven't prayed for you, Bartley, to the Almighty God. It isn't that I haven't said prayers in the dark night till you wouldn't know what I'd be saying; but it's a great rest I'll have now, and it's

[4] The equivalent of Allhallows. It falls on November 1 and marks the beginning of winter; it is celebrated with harvest rites and a Feast of the Dead.

time surely. It's a great rest I'll have now, and great sleeping in the long nights after Samhain, if it's only a bit of wet flour we do have to eat, and maybe a fish that would be stinking.

(*She kneels down again, crossing herself, and saying prayers under her breath*)

CATHLEEN (*To an old man*) Maybe yourself and Eamon would make a coffin when the sun rises. We have fine white boards herself bought, God help her, thinking Michael would be found, and I have a new cake you can eat while you'll be working.

THE OLD MAN (*Looking at the boards*) Are there nails with them?

CATHLEEN There are not, Colum; we didn't think of the nails.

ANOTHER MAN It's a great wonder she wouldn't think of the nails, and all the coffins she's seen made already.

CATHLEEN It's getting old she is, and broken.

(MAURYA *stands up again very slowly and spreads out the pieces of Michael's clothes beside the body, sprinkling them with the last of the Holy Water*)

NORA (*In a whisper to* CATHLEEN) She's quiet now and easy; but the day Michael was drowned you could hear her crying out from this to the spring well. It's fonder she was of Michael, and would any one have thought that?

CATHLEEN (*Slowly and clearly*) An old woman will be soon tired with anything she will do, and isn't it nine days herself is after crying and keening, and making great sorrow in the house?

MAURYA (*Puts the empty cup mouth downwards on the table, and lays her hands together on Bartley's feet*) They're all together this time, and the end is come. May the Almighty God have mercy on Bartley's soul, and on Michael's soul, and on the souls of Sheamus and Patch, and Stephen and Shawn; (*Bending her head*) and may He have mercy on my soul, Nora, and on the soul of every one is left living in the world.

(*She pauses, and the keen rises a little more loudly from the women, then sinks away*)

MAURYA (*Continuing*) Michael has a clean burial in the Far North, by the grace of the Almighty God. Bartley will have a fine coffin out of the white boards, and a deep grave surely. What more can we want than that? No man at all can be living forever, and we must be satisfied.

(*She kneels down again and the curtain falls slowly*)

# THE PLAYBOY OF THE WESTERN WORLD

During 1904 Synge participated from the sidelines in launching the theatre with which his name will always be linked. On Dublin's Abbey Street appeared a "people's theatre," the realization of a dream long held by Yeats and by the Fay brothers, men whose practical knowledge of the stage complemented Yeats' visionary idealism. Until it was destroyed by fire in 1951, the Abbey Theatre stood, embattled but indestructible in the face of forces only slightly less powerful than fire, as the headquarters of Ireland's vigorous drama.

The Abbey opened December 27, 1904, with a bill of four one-acts which included *In the Shadow of the Glen.* Even before the second bill, scheduled to introduce Synge's first full-length play to Dublin, opened on February 4, 1905, Synge was subjected to another round of attacks when the Nationalist zealot, Arthur Griffith, reopened his earlier campaign to unmask *In the Shadow of the Glen* as, among other things, "a foul echo from degenerate Greece." *The Well of the Saints,* Synge's third play to be produced, was derived from a fifteenth-century farce by Andrieu de la Vigne. It concerns a pair of blind beggars living "one or more centuries ago" in eastern Ireland. In their sightless world, Martin and Mary Doul have shaped illusions which make life bearable; with sight restored, however, they confront their grotesqueness in a world which does not extend to the seeing that same charity it offers to the blind. Like most of Synge's plays, this ends with a departure symbolic of the rejection of rootedness in favor of freedom and mobility. It greatly resembles another play which absorbed Synge's attention during this period: *The Tinker's Wedding,* deemed by the Abbey directors too inflammatory for production, could also be called, in Herbert Howarth's phrase, "a hymn to vagrancy." This short two-act play deals with a trio of footloose tinkers who trap a priest into agreeing to perform the marriage rites at reduced rates, and then joyously reject marriage. The characteristic tension in Synge's plays is illustrated again: opposed to the "rooted" Synge who could despair over the number of Irish emigrants is the "inner" Synge, himself "a migrant, relishing the liberty and apotheoses of eternal tinkerdom." Nowhere did Synge articulate more brilliantly these contrary impulses than in the Mahons, father and son, the heroes-in-spite-of-themselves of *The Playboy of the Western World.*

The genesis of Synge's exploration of hero-worship began in Aran where he heard of a Connaught man who fled to the Islands after he had, in a fit of anger, killed his father with a spade. Musing on the Islanders' willingness to hide the killer until he could sail for America, Synge conjectured that the impulse to protect the criminal is "universal in the west . . . partly due to the association between justice and the hated English jurisdiction, but more directly to the primitive feeling of these people—who are never criminals yet always capable of crime—that a man will not do wrong unless he is under the influence of a passion which is as irresponsible as a storm on the sea." Synge began outlining the play in 1903, using such early working titles as "The Fool of Farnham" and "Murder Will Out." By the time Synge found the richly suggestive title which changes in meaning as the play unfolds, he had poured into the play the wisdom, language, and details reflective of his lifetime, all tempered in the fire of his sardonic view that, at least in the Ireland he knew, heroes are not born but made, in the magic of words and in the deeply human need for excitement.

Before *The Playboy of the Western World* opened at the Abbey early in 1907, Synge had fallen in love with the young actress, Molly Allgood (or Maire O'Neill, as she was known professionally), for whom he began *Deirdre of the Sorrows,* his version of the tragic love story of Deirdre and Naisi. During this period of satisfying productiveness, Synge suddenly found himself involved again in controversy. On January 26, 1907, the opening-night audience, quietly receptive during two acts, suddenly erupted in a cacophony of hissing and applause which brought the first performance of *The Playboy of the Western World* to an end before it was finished. The line that set off the explosions which gave this play notoriety in America as well as in Ireland was Christy's reference (in Act Three) to "a drift of chosen females, standing in their shifts itself." For over a week thereafter, the Abbey was the scene of demonstrations beyond police control. Amid the clatter of riots and charges that he had plumbed new depths of vulgarity, Synge made a valiant effort, in a letter to *The Irish Times,* to explain his play: "not a play with 'a purpose' in the modern sense of the word, but although parts of it are, or are meant to be, extravagant comedy, still a great deal that is in it, and a great deal more that is behind it, is perfectly serious when looked at in a certain light. That is often the case, I think, with comedy, and no one is quite sure today whether Shylock and Alceste [Molière's Misanthrope] should be played seriously or not. There are, it may be hinted, several sides to *The Playboy.*" That there are, indeed, "several sides" to this play is a discovery later audiences and readers have rejoiced in making again and again.

# THE PLAYBOY OF THE WESTERN WORLD

## *A Play in Three Acts*

### Preface

In writing *The Playboy of the Western World,* as in my other plays, I have used one or two words only that I have not heard among the country people of Ireland, or spoken in my own nursery before I could read the newspapers. A certain number of the phrases I employ I have heard also from herds and fishermen along the coast from Kerry to Mayo, or from beggar-women and ballad-singers nearer Dublin; and I am glad to acknowledge how much I owe to the folk-imagination of these fine people. Anyone who has lived in real intimacy with the Irish peasantry will know that the wildest sayings and ideas in this play are tame indeed, compared with the fancies one may hear in any little hillside cabin in Geesala, or Carraroe, or Dingle Bay. All art is a collaboration; and there is little doubt that in the happy ages of literature, striking and beautiful phrases were as ready to the story-teller's or the playwright's hand, as the rich cloaks and dresses of his time. It is probable that when the Elizabethan dramatist took his ink-horn and sat down to his work he used many phrases that he had just heard, as he sat at dinner, from his mother or his children. In Ireland, those of us who know the people have the same privilege. When I was writing *The Shadow of the Glen,* some years ago, I got more aid than any learning could have given me from a chink in the floor of the old Wicklow house where I was staying, that let me hear what was being said by the servant girls in the kitchen. This matter, I think, is of importance, for in countries where the imagination of the people, and the language they use, is rich and living, it is possible for a writer to be rich and copious in his words, and at the same time to give the reality, which is the root of all poetry, in a comprehensive and natural form. In the modern literature of towns, however, richness is found only in sonnets, or prose poems, or in one or two elaborate books that are far away from the profound and common interests of life. One has, on one side, Mallarmé and Huysmans producing this literature; and on the other, Ibsen and Zola dealing with the reality of life in joyless and pallid words. On the stage one must have reality, and one must have joy; and that is why the intellectual modern drama has failed, and people have grown sick of the false joy of the musical comedy, that has been given them in place of the rich joy found only in what is superb and wild in reality. In a good play every speech should be as fully flavoured as a nut or apple, and such speeches cannot be written by anyone who works among people who have shut their lips on poetry. In Ireland, for a few years more, we have a popular imagination that is fiery and magnificent, and tender; so that those of us who wish to write start with a chance that is not given to writers in places where the springtime of the local life has been forgotten, and the harvest is a memory only, and the straw has been turned into bricks.

J. M. S.

*January* 21, 1907

### CHARACTERS

CHRISTOPHER MAHON
OLD MAHON (*his father, a squatter*)
MICHAEL JAMES FLAHERTY, called MICHAEL JAMES (*a publican*)
MARGARET FLAHERTY, called PEGEEN MIKE (*his daughter*)
SHAWN KEOGH (*her cousin, a young farmer*)
WIDOW QUIN (*a woman of about thirty*)
PHILLY CULLEN and JIMMY FARRELL (*small farmers*)
SARA TANSEY, SUSAN BRADY, HONOR BLAKE, and NELLY (*village girls*)
A BELLMAN (*or Town Crier*)
SOME PEASANTS

*The action takes place near a village, on a wild coast of Mayo.*[1] *The first Act passes on an evening of autumn, the other two Acts on the following day.*

[1] The county of Mayo is located in the northwest of Ireland, exposed to the Atlantic Ocean. Most of the communities and areas mentioned throughout the play can be located on a standard map of Ireland.

# Act One

SCENE *Country public-house or shebeen, very rough and untidy. There is a sort of counter on the right with shelves, holding many bottles and jugs, just seen above it. Empty barrels stand near the counter. At back, a little to left of counter, there is a door into the open air, then, more to the left, there is a settle with shelves above it, with more jugs, and a table beneath a window. At the left there is a large open fire place, with turf fire, and a small door into inner room.* PEGEEN, *a wild-looking but fine girl of about twenty, is writing at table. She is dressed in the usual peasant dress.*

PEGEEN (*Slowly as she writes*) Six yards of stuff for to make a yellow gown. A pair of lace boots with lengthy heels on them and brassy eyes. A hat is suited for a wedding-day. A fine tooth comb. To be sent with three barrels of porter in Jimmy Farrell's creel cart on the evening of the coming Fair to Mister Michael James Flaherty. With the best compliments of this season. Margaret Flaherty.

SHAWN KEOGH (*A fat and fair young man comes in as she signs, looks round awkwardly, when he sees she is alone*) Where's himself?

PEGEEN (*Without looking at him*) He's coming. (*She directs the letter*) To Master Sheamus Mulroy, Wine and Spirit Dealer, Castlebar.

SHAWN (*Uneasily*) I didn't see him on the road.

PEGEEN How would you see him (*Licks stamp and puts it on letter*) and it dark night this half hour gone by?

SHAWN (*Turning toward the door again*) I stood a while outside wondering would I have a right to pass on or to walk in and see you, Pegeen Mike, (*Comes to fire*) and I could hear the cows breathing, and sighing in the stillness of the air, and not a step moving any place from this gate to the bridge.

PEGEEN (*Putting letter in envelope*) It's above at the cross-roads he is, meeting Philly Cullen; and a couple more are going along with him to Kate Cassidy's wake.

SHAWN (*Looking at her blankly*) And he's going that length in the dark night?

PEGEEN (*Impatiently*) He is surely, and leaving me lonesome on the scruff of the hill. (*She gets up and puts envelope on dresser, then winds clock*) Isn't it long the nights are now, Shawn Keogh, to be leaving a poor girl with her own self counting the hours to the dawn of day?

SHAWN (*With awkward humour*) If it is, when we're wedded in a short while you'll have no call to complain, for I've little will to be walking off to wakes or weddings in the darkness of the night.

PEGEEN (*With rather scornful good humour*) You're making mighty certain, Shaneen, that I'll wed you now.

SHAWN Aren't we after making a good bargain, the way we're only waiting these days on Father Reilly's dispensation[2] from the bishops, or the Court of Rome?

PEGEEN (*Looking at him teasingly, washing up at dresser*) It's a wonder, Shaneen, the Holy Father'd be taking notice of the likes of you; for if I was him I wouldn't bother with this place where you'll meet none but Red Linahan, has a squint in his eye, and Patcheen is lame in his heel, or the mad Mulrannies were driven from California and they lost in their wits. We're a queer lot these times to go troubling the Holy Father on his sacred seat.

SHAWN (*Scandalized*) If we are, we're as good this place as another, maybe, and as good these times as we were for ever.

PEGEEN (*With scorn*) As good, is it? Where now will you meet the like of Daneen Sullivan knocked the eye from a peeler,[3] or Marcus Quin, God rest him, got six months for maiming ewes, and he a great warrant to tell stories of holy Ireland till he'd have the old women shedding down tears about their feet. Where will you find the like of them, I'm saying?

SHAWN (*Timidly*) If you don't, it's a good job, maybe; for (*With peculiar emphasis on the words*) Father Reilly has small conceit to have that kind walking around and talking to the girls.

PEGEEN (*Impatiently, throwing water from basin out of the door*) Stop tormenting me with Father Reilly (*Imitating his voice*) when I'm asking only what way I'll pass these twelve hours of dark, and not take my death with the fear. (*Looking out of door*)

SHAWN (*Timidly*) Would I fetch you the Widow Quin, maybe?

PEGEEN Is it the like of that murderer? You'll not, surely.

SHAWN (*Going to her, soothingly*) Then I'm thinking himself will stop along with you when he sees you taking on, for it'll be a long night-time with great darkness, and I'm after feeling a kind of fellow above in the furzy ditch, groaning wicked like a maddening dog, the way it's good cause you have, maybe, to be fearing now.

PEGEEN (*Turning on him sharply*) What's that? Is it a man you seen?

SHAWN (*Retreating*) I couldn't see him at all; but I heard him groaning out, and breaking his heart. It should have been a young man from his words speaking.

PEGEEN (*Going after him*) And you never went near to see was he hurted or what ailed him at all?

SHAWN I did not, Pegeen Mike. It was a dark, lonesome place to be hearing the like of him.

PEGEEN Well, you're a daring fellow, and if they find his corpse stretched above in the dews of dawn, what'll you say then to the peelers, or the Justice of the Peace?

SHAWN (*Thunderstruck*) I wasn't thinking of that. For

[2] A papal dispensation was required to permit marriage between cousins.

[3] A policeman.

the love of God, Pegeen Mike, don't let on I was speaking of him. Don't tell your father and the men is coming above; for if they heard that story, they'd have great blabbing this night at the wake.

PEGEEN I'll maybe tell them, and I'll maybe not.

SHAWN They are coming at the door. Will you whisht, I'm saying?

PEGEEN Whisht yourself. (*She goes behind counter.* MICHAEL JAMES, *fat jovial publican, comes in followed by* PHILLY CULLEN, *who is thin and mistrusting, and* JIMMY FARRELL, *who is fat and amorous, about forty-five*)

MEN (*Together*) God bless you. The blessing of God on this place.

PEGEEN God bless you kindly.

MICHAEL (*To men who go to the counter*) Sit down now, and take your rest. (*Crosses to* SHAWN *at the fire*) And how is it you are, Shawn Keogh? Are you coming over the sands to Kate Cassidy's wake?

SHAWN I am not, Michael James. I'm going home the short cut to my bed.

PEGEEN (*Speaking across the counter*) He's right too, and have you no shame, Michael James, to be quitting off for the whole night, and leaving myself lonesome in the shop?

MICHAEL (*Good-humouredly*) Isn't it the same whether I go for the whole night or a part only? and I'm thinking it's a queer daughter you are if you'd have me crossing backward through the Stooks[4] of the Dead Women, with a drop taken.

PEGEEN If I am a queer daughter, it's a queer father'd be leaving me lonesome these twelve hours of dark, and I piling the turf with the dogs barking, and the calves mooing, and my own teeth rattling with the fear.

JIMMY (*Flatteringly*) What is there to hurt you, and you a fine, hardy girl would knock the head of any two men in the place?

PEGEEN (*Working herself up*) Isn't there the harvest boys with their tongues red for drink, and the ten tinkers is camped in the east glen, and the thousand militia—bad cess to them!—walking idle through the land. There's lots surely to hurt me, and I won't stop alone in it, let himself do what he will.

MICHAEL If you're that afeard, let Shawn Keogh stop along with you. It's the will of God, I'm thinking, himself should be seeing to you now.

(*They all turn on* SHAWN)

SHAWN (*In horrified confusion*) I would and welcome, Michael James, but I'm afeard of Father Reilly; and what at all would the Holy Father and the Cardinals of Rome be saying if they heard I did the like of that?

MICHAEL (*With contempt*) God help you! Can't you sit in by the hearth with the light lit and herself beyond in the room? You'll do that surely, for I've heard tell there's a queer fellow above, going mad or getting his death, maybe, in the gripe of the ditch, so she'd be safer this night with a person here.

[4] Stacked sheaves of wheat; apparently superstition was attached to a field where grain was stacked.

SHAWN (*With plaintive despair*) I'm afeard of Father Reilly, I'm saying. Let you not be tempting me, and we near married itself.

PHILLY (*With cold contempt*) Lock him in the west room. He'll stay then and have no sin to be telling to the priest.

MICHAEL (*To* SHAWN, *getting between him and the door*) Go up now.

SHAWN (*At the top of his voice*) Don't stop me, Michael James. Let me out of the door, I'm saying, for the love of the Almighty God. Let me out. (*Trying to dodge past him*) Let me out of it, and may God grant you His indulgence in the hour of need.

MICHAEL (*Loudly*) Stop your noising, and sit down by the hearth. (*Gives him a push and goes to counter laughing*)

SHAWN (*Turning back, wringing his hands*) Oh, Father Reilly and the saints of God, where will I hide myself today? Oh, St. Joseph, and St. Patrick, and St. Brigid, and St. James, have mercy on me now! (SHAWN *turns round, sees door clear, and makes a rush for it*)

MICHAEL (*Catching him by the coat-tail*) You'd be going, is it?

SHAWN (*Screaming*) Leave me go, Michael James, leave me go, you old Pagan, leave me go, or I'll get the curse of the priests on you, and of the scarlet-coated bishops of the courts of Rome. (*With a sudden movement he pulls himself out of his coat, and disappears out of the door, leaving his coat in* MICHAEL'*s hands*)

MICHAEL (*Turning round, and holding up coat*) Well, there's the coat of a Christian man. Oh, there's sainted glory this day in the lonesome west; and by the will of God I've got you a decent man, Pegeen, you'll have no call to be spying after if you've a score of young girls, maybe, weeding in your fields.

PEGEEN (*Taking up the defence of her property*) What right have you to be making game of a poor fellow for minding the priest, when it's your own the fault is, not paying a penny pot-boy to stand along with me and give me courage in the doing of my work? (*She snaps the coat away from him, and goes behind counter with it*)

MICHAEL (*Taken aback*) Where would I get a pot-boy? Would you have me send the bellman screaming in the streets of Castlebar?

SHAWN (*Opening the door a chink and putting in his head, in a small voice*) Michael James!

MICHAEL (*Imitating him*) What ails you?

SHAWN The queer dying fellow's beyond looking over the ditch. He's come up, I'm thinking, stealing your hens. (*Looks over his shoulder*) God help me, he's following me now, (*He runs into room*) and if he's heard what I said, he'll be having my life, and I going home lonesome in the darkness of the night.

(*For a perceptible moment they watch the door with curiosity. Someone coughs outside. Then* CHRISTY MAHON, *a slight young man, comes in very tired and frightened and dirty*)

CHRISTY (*In a small voice*) God save all here!

MEN God save you kindly.

CHRISTY (*Going to the counter*) I'd trouble you for a glass of porter, woman of the house. (*He puts down coin*)

PEGEEN (*Serving him*) You're one of the tinkers, young fellow, is beyond camped in the glen?

CHRISTY I am not; but I'm destroyed walking.

MICHAEL (*Patronizingly*) Let you come up then to the fire. You're looking famished with the cold.

CHRISTY God reward you. (*He takes up his glass and goes a little way across to the left, then stops and looks about him*) Is it often the polis do be coming into this place, master of the house?

MICHAEL If you'd come in better hours, you'd have seen "Licensed for the sale of Beer and Spirits, to be consumed on the premises," written in white letters above the door, and what would the polis want spying on me, and not a decent house within four miles, the way every living Christian is a bona fide,[5] saving one widow alone?

CHRISTY (*With relief*) It's a safe house, so. (*He goes over to the fire, sighing and moaning. Then he sits down, putting his glass beside him and begins gnawing a turnip, too miserable to feel the others staring at him with curiosity*)

MICHAEL (*Going after him*) Is it yourself is fearing the polis? You're wanting, maybe?

CHRISTY There's many wanting.

MICHAEL Many surely, with the broken harvest and the ended wars. (*He picks up some stockings, etc., that are near the fire, and carries them away furtively*) It should be larceny, I'm thinking.

CHRISTY (*Dolefully*) I had it in my mind it was a different word and a bigger.

PEGEEN There's a queer lad. Were you never slapped in school, young fellow, that you don't know the name of your deed?

CHRISTY (*Bashfully*) I'm slow at learning, a middling scholar only.

MICHAEL If you're a dunce itself, you'd have a right to know that larceny's robbing and stealing. Is it for the like of that you're wanting?

CHRISTY (*With a flash of family pride*) And I the son of a strong farmer (*With a sudden qualm*), God rest his soul, could have bought up the whole of your old house awhile since, from the butt of his tail-pocket, and not have missed the weight of it gone.

MICHAEL (*Impressed*) If it's not stealing, it's maybe something big.

CHRISTY (*Flattered*) Aye; it's maybe something big.

JIMMY He's a wicked-looking young fellow. Maybe he followed after a young woman on a lonesome night.

CHRISTY (*Shocked*) Oh, the saints forbid, mister; I was all times a decent lad.

PHILLY (*Turning on* JIMMY) You're a silly man, Jimmy Farrell. He said his father was a farmer a while since, and there's himself now in a poor state. Maybe the land was grabbed from him, and he did what any decent man would do.

MICHAEL (*To* CHRISTY, *mysteriously*) Was it bailiffs?

CHRISTY The divil a one.[6]

MICHAEL Agents?

CHRISTY The divil a one.

MICHAEL Landlords?

CHRISTY (*Peevishly*) Ah, not at all, I'm saying. You'd see the like of them stories on any little paper of a Munster town. But I'm not calling to mind any person, gentle, simple, judge or jury, did the like of me.

(*They all draw nearer with delighted curiosity*)

PHILLY Well, that lad's a puzzle-the-world.

JIMMY He'd beat Dan Davies' circus, or the holy missioners making sermons on the villainy of man. Try him again, Philly.

PHILLY Did you strike golden guineas out of solder, young fellow, or shilling coins itself?

CHRISTY I did not, mister, not sixpence nor a farthing coin.

JIMMY Did you marry three wives maybe? I'm told there's a sprinkling have done that among the holy Luthers of the preaching north.

CHRISTY (*Shyly*) I never married with one, let alone with a couple or three.

PHILLY Maybe he went fighting for the Boers, the like of the man beyond, was judged to be hanged, quartered and drawn. Were you off east, young fellow, fighting bloody wars for Kruger and the freedom of the Boers?

CHRISTY I never left my own parish till Tuesday was a week.

PEGEEN (*Coming from counter*) He's done nothing, so. (*To* CHRISTY) If you didn't commit murder or a bad, nasty thing, or false coining, or robbery, or butchery, or the like of them, there isn't anything that would be worth your troubling for to run from now. You did nothing at all.

CHRISTY (*His feelings hurt*) That's an unkindly thing to be saying to a poor orphaned traveller, has a prison behind him, and hanging before, and hell's gap gaping below.

PEGEEN (*With a sign to the men to be quiet*) You're only saying it. You did nothing at all. A soft lad the like of you wouldn't slit the windpipe of a screeching sow.

CHRISTY (*Offended*) You're not speaking the truth.

PEGEEN (*In mock rage*) Not speaking the truth, is it? Would you have me knock the head off you with the butt of the broom?

CHRISTY (*Twisting round on her with a sharp cry of horror*) Don't strike me. I killed my poor father, Tuesday was a week, for doing the like of that.

PEGEEN (*With blank amazement*) Is it killed your father?

CHRISTY (*Subsiding*) With the help of God I did surely, and that the Holy Immaculate Mother may intercede for his soul.

[5] A person could be served drinks outside regular tavern hours if he had slept over three miles away on the previous night.

[6] Not a one.

PHILLY (*Retreating with* JIMMY) There's a daring fellow.

JIMMY Oh, glory be to God!

MICHAEL (*With great respect*) That was a hanging crime, mister honey. You should have had good reason for doing the like of that.

CHRISTY (*In a very reasonable tone*) He was a dirty man, God forgive him, and he getting old and crusty, the way I couldn't put up with him at all.

PEGEEN And you shot him dead?

CHRISTY (*Shaking his head*) I never used weapons. I've no license, and I'm a law-fearing man.

MICHAEL It was with a hilted knife maybe? I'm told, in the big world it's bloody knives they use.

CHRISTY (*Loudly, scandalized*) Do you take me for a slaughter-boy?

PEGEEN You never hanged him, the way Jimmy Farrell hanged his dog from the license,[7] and had it screeching and wriggling three hours at the butt of a string, and himself swearing it was a dead dog, and the peelers swearing it had life?

CHRISTY I did not then. I just riz the loy[8] and let fall the edge of it on the ridge of his skull, and he went down at my feet like an empty sack, and never let a grunt or groan from him at all.

MICHAEL (*Making a sign to* PEGEEN *to fill* CHRISTY'S *glass*) And what way weren't you hanged, mister? Did you bury him then?

CHRISTY (*Considering*) Aye. I buried him then. Wasn't I digging spuds in the field?

MICHAEL And the peelers never followed after you the eleven days that you're out?

CHRISTY (*Shaking his head*) Never a one of them, and I walking forward facing hog, dog, or divil on the highway of the road.

PHILLY (*Nodding wisely*) It's only with a common week-day kind of a murderer them lads would be trusting their carcase, and that man should be a great terror when his temper's roused.

MICHAEL He should then. (*To* CHRISTY) And where was it, mister honey, that you did the deed?

CHRISTY (*Looking at him with suspicion*) Oh, a distant place, master of the house, a windy corner of high, distant hills.

PHILLY (*Nodding with approval*) He's a close man, and he's right, surely.

PEGEEN That'd be a lad with the sense of Solomon to have for a pot-boy, Michael James, if it's the truth you're seeking one at all.

PHILLY The peelers is fearing him, and if you'd that lad in the house there isn't one of them would come smelling around if the dogs itself were lapping poteen[9] from the dung-pit of the yard.

JIMMY Bravery's a treasure in a lonesome place, and a lad would kill his father, I'm thinking, would face a foxy divil with a pitchpike on the flags of hell.

PEGEEN It's the truth they're saying, and if I'd that lad in the house, I wouldn't be fearing the loosèd kharki cut-throats,[10] or the walking dead.

CHRISTY (*Swelling with surprise and triumph*) Well, glory be to God!

MICHAEL (*With deference*) Would you think well to stop here and be pot-boy, mister honey, if we gave you good wages, and didn't destroy you with the weight of work?

SHAWN (*Coming forward uneasily*) That'd be a queer kind to bring into a decent quiet household with the like of Pegeen Mike.

PEGEEN (*Very sharply*) Will you whisht? Who's speaking to you?

SHAWN (*Retreating*) A bloody-handed murderer the like of . . .

PEGEEN (*Snapping at him*) Whisht I am saying; we'll take no fooling from your like at all. (*To* CHRISTY *with a honeyed voice*) And you, young fellow, you'd have a right to stop, I'm thinking, for we'd do our all and utmost to content your needs.

CHRISTY (*Overcome with wonder*) And I'd be safe in this place from the searching law?

MICHAEL You would, surely. If they're not fearing you, itself, the peelers in this place is decent droughty poor fellows, wouldn't touch a cur dog and not give warning in the dead of night.

PEGEEN (*Very kindly and persuasively*) Let you stop a short while anyhow. Aren't you destroyed walking with your feet in bleeding blisters, and your whole skin needing washing like a Wicklow sheep?

CHRISTY (*Looking round with satisfaction*) It's a nice room, and if it's not humbugging me you are, I'm thinking that I'll surely stay.

JIMMY (*Jumps up*) Now, by the grace of God, herself will be safe this night, with a man killed his father holding danger from the door, and let you come on, Michael James, or they'll have the best stuff drunk at the wake.

MICHAEL (*Going to the door with men*) And begging your pardon, mister, what name will we call you, for we'd like to know?

CHRISTY Christopher Mahon.

MICHAEL Well, God bless you, Christy, and a good rest till we meet again when the sun'll be rising to the noon of day.

CHRISTY God bless you all.

MEN God bless you.

(*They go out except* SHAWN, *who lingers at door*)

SHAWN (*To* PEGEEN) Are you wanting me to stop along with you and keep you from harm?

PEGEEN (*Gruffly*) Didn't you say you were fearing Father Reilly?

SHAWN There'd be no harm staying now, I'm thinking, and himself in it too.

PEGEEN You wouldn't stay when there was need for you, and let you step off nimble this time when there's none.

SHAWN Didn't I say it was Father Reilly . . .

PEGEEN Go on, then, to Father Reilly (*In a jeering*

[7] Because he had no license for the dog.

[8] A narrow spade widely used in Ireland for digging peat.

[9] It was illegal to distill or sell this strong whiskey.

[10] British soldiers

*tone*), and let him put you in the holy brotherhoods, and leave that lad to me.

SHAWN If I meet the Widow Quin . . .

PEGEEN Go on, I'm saying, and don't be waking this place with your noise. (*She hustles him out and bolts the door*) That lad would wear the spirits from the saints of peace. (*Bustles about, then takes off her apron and pins it up in the window as a blind.* CHRISTY *watching her timidly. Then she comes to him and speaks with bland good-humour*) Let you stretch out now by the fire, young fellow. You should be destroyed travelling.

CHRISTY (*Shyly again, drawing off his boots*) I'm tired, surely, walking wild eleven days, and waking fearful in the night. (*He holds up one of his feet, feeling his blisters, and looking at them with compassion*)

PEGEEN (*Standing beside him, watching him with delight*) You should have had great people in your family, I'm thinking, with the little, small feet you have, and you with a kind of a quality name, the like of what you'd find on the great powers and potentates of France and Spain.

CHRISTY (*With pride*) We were great surely, with wide and windy acres of rich Munster land.

PEGEEN Wasn't I telling you, and you a fine, handsome young fellow with a noble brow?

CHRISTY (*With a flash of delighted surprise*) Is it me?

PEGEEN Aye. Did you never hear that from the young girls where you come from in the west or south?

CHRISTY (*With venom*) I did not then. Oh, they're bloody liars in the naked parish where I grew a man.

PEGEEN If they are itself, you've heard it these days, I'm thinking, and you walking the world telling out your story to young girls or old.

CHRISTY I've told my story no place till this night, Pegeen Mike, and it's foolish I was here, maybe, to be talking free, but you're decent people, I'm thinking, and yourself a kindly woman, the way I wasn't fearing you at all.

PEGEEN (*Filling a sack with straw*) You've said the like of that, maybe, in every cot and cabin where you've met a young girl on your way.

CHRISTY (*Going over to her, gradually raising his voice*) I've said it nowhere till this night, I'm telling you, for I've seen none the like of you the eleven long days I am walking the world, looking over a low ditch or a high ditch on my north or my south, into stony scattered fields, or scribes[11] of bog, where you'd see young, limber girls, and fine prancing women making laughter with the men.

PEGEEN If you weren't destroyed travelling, you'd have as much talk and streeleen,[12] I'm thinking, as Owen Roe O'Sullivan[13] or the poets of the Dingle Bay, and I've heard all times it's the poets are your like, fine fiery fellows with great rages when their temper's roused.

CHRISTY (*Drawing a little nearer to her*) You've a power of rings, God bless you, and would there be any offence if I was asking are you single now?

PEGEEN What would I want wedding so young?

CHRISTY (*With relief*) We're alike, so.

PEGEEN (*She puts sack on settle and beats it up*) I never killed my father. I'd be afeard to do that, except I was the like of yourself with blind rages tearing me within, for I'm thinking you should have had great tussling when the end was come.

CHRISTY (*Expanding with delight at the first confidential talk he has ever had with a woman*) We had not then. It was a hard woman was come over the hill, and if he was always a crusty kind when he'd a hard woman setting him on, not the divil himself or his four fathers could put up with him at all.

PEGEEN (*With curiosity*) And isn't it a great wonder that one wasn't fearing you?

CHRISTY (*Very confidentially*) Up to the day I killed my father, there wasn't a person in Ireland knew the kind I was, and I there drinking, waking, eating, sleeping, a quiet, simple, poor fellow with no man giving me heed.

PEGEEN (*Getting a quilt out of the cupboard and putting it on the sack*) It was the girls were giving you heed maybe, and I'm thinking it's most conceit[14] you'd have to be gaming with their like.

CHRISTY (*Shaking his head, with simplicity*) Not the girls itself, and I won't tell you a lie. There wasn't anyone heeding me in that place saving only the dumb beasts of the field. (*He sits down at fire*)

PEGEEN (*With disappointment*) And I thinking you should have been living the like of a king of Norway or the Eastern world. (*She comes and sits beside him after placing bread and mug of milk on the table*)

CHRISTY (*Laughing piteously*) The like of a king, is it? And I after toiling, moiling, digging, dodging from the dawn till dusk with never a sight of joy or sport saving only when I'd be abroad in the dark night poaching rabbits on hills, for I was a divil to poach, God forgive me, (*Very naïvely*) and I near got six months for going with a dung fork and stabbing a fish.

PEGEEN And it's that you'd call sport, is it, to be abroad in the darkness with yourself alone?

CHRISTY I did, God help me, and there I'd be as happy as the sunshine of St. Martin's Day, watching the light passing the north or the patches of fog, till I'd hear a rabbit starting to screech and I'd go running in the furze. Then when I'd my full share I'd come walking down where you'd see the ducks and geese stretched sleeping on the highway of the road, and before I'd pass the dunghill, I'd hear himself snoring out, a loud lonesome snore he'd be making all times, the while he was sleeping, and he a man'd be raging all times, the while he was waking, like a gaudy officer you'd hear cursing and damning and swearing oaths.

[11] Wide expanses.

[12] Charmingly irresponsible, swaggering chatter; palaver.

[13] O'Sullivan (d. 1784) and other Jacobite poets from Munster in southern Ireland were strolling poets whose songs and deeds would excite Pegeen's imagination.

[14] Desire, inclination.

PEGEEN Providence and Mercy, spare us all!

CHRISTY It's that you'd say surely if you seen him and he after drinking for weeks, rising up in the red dawn, or before it maybe, and going out into the yard as naked as an ash tree in the moon of May, and shying clods against the visage of the stars till he'd put the fear of death into the banbhs[15] and the screeching sows.

PEGEEN I'd be well-nigh afeard of that lad myself, I'm thinking. And there was no one in it but the two of you alone?

CHRISTY The divil a one, though he'd sons and daughters walking all great states and territories of the world, and not a one of them, to this day, but would say their seven curses on him, and they rousing up to let a cough or sneeze, maybe, in the deadness of the night.

PEGEEN (*Nodding her head*) Well, you should have been a queer lot. I never cursed my father the like of that, though I'm twenty and more years of age.

CHRISTY Then you'd have cursed mine, I'm telling you, and he a man never gave peace to any, saving when he'd get two months or three, or be locked in the asylums for battering peelers or assaulting men (*With depression*) the way it was a bitter life he led me till I did up a Tuesday and halve his skull.

PEGEEN (*Putting her hand on his shoulder*) Well, you'll have peace in this place, Christy Mahon, and none to trouble you, and it's near time a fine lad like you should have your good share of the earth.

CHRISTY It's time surely, and I a seemly fellow with great strength in me and bravery of . . .

(*Someone knocks*)

CHRISTY (*Clinging to* PEGEEN) Oh, glory! it's late for knocking, and this last while I'm in terror of the peelers, and the walking dead.

(*Knocking again*)

PEGEEN Who's there?

VOICE (*Outside*) Me.

PEGEEN Who's me?

VOICE The Widow Quin.

PEGEEN (*Jumping up and giving him the bread and milk*) Go on now with your supper, and let on to be sleepy, for if she found you were such a warrant to talk, she'd be stringing gabble till the dawn of day. (*He takes bread and sits shyly with his back to the door*)

PEGEEN (*Opening door, with temper*) What ails you, or what is it you're wanting at this hour of the night?

WIDOW QUIN (*Coming in a step and peering at* CHRISTY) I'm after meeting Shawn Keogh and Father Reilly below, who told me of your curiosity man, and they fearing by this time he was maybe roaring, romping on your hands with drink.

PEGEEN (*Pointing to* CHRISTY) Look now is he roaring and he stretched away drowsy with his supper and his mug of milk. Walk down and tell that to Father Reilly and to Shaneen Keogh.

WIDOW QUIN (*Coming forward*) I'll not see them again, for I've their word to lead that lad forward for to lodge with me.

PEGEEN (*In blank amazement*) This night, is it?

WIDOW QUIN (*Going over*) This night. "It isn't fitting." says the priesteen, "to have his likeness lodging with an orphaned girl." (*To* CHRISTY) God save you, mister!

CHRISTY (*Shyly*) God save you kindly.

WIDOW QUIN (*Looking at him with half-amazed curiosity*) Well, aren't you a little smiling fellow? It should have been great and bitter torments did rouse your spirits to a deed of blood.

CHRISTY (*Doubtfully*) It should, maybe.

WIDOW QUIN It's more than "maybe" I'm saying, and it'd soften my heart to see you sitting so simple with your cup and cake, and you fitter to be saying your catechism than slaying your da.

PEGEEN (*At counter, washing glasses*) There's talking when any'd see he's fit to be holding his head high with the wonders of the world. Walk on from this, for I'll not have him tormented and he destroyed travelling since Tuesday was a week.

WIDOW QUIN (*Peaceably*) We'll be walking surely when his supper's done, and you'll find we're great company, young fellow, when it's of the like of you and me you'd hear the penny poets singing in an August Fair.

CHRISTY (*Innocently*) Did you kill your father?

PEGEEN (*Contemptuously*) She did not. She hit himself [16] with a worm pick, and the rusted poison did corrode his blood the way he never overed it, and died after. That was a sneaky kind of murder did win small glory with the boys itself. (*She crosses to* CHRISTY'S *left*)

WIDOW QUIN (*With good-humour*) If it didn't, maybe all knows a widow woman has buried her children and destroyed her man is a wiser comrade for a young lad than a girl, the like of you, who'd go helter-skeltering after any man would let you a wink upon the road.

PEGEEN (*Breaking out into wild rage*) And you'll say that, Widow Quin, and you gasping with the rage you had racing the hill beyond to look on his face.

WIDOW QUIN (*Laughing derisively*) Me, is it? Well, Father Reilly has cuteness to divide you now. (*She pulls* CHRISTY *up*) There's great temptation in a man did slay his da, and we'd best be going, young fellow; so rise up and come with me.

PEGEEN (*Seizing his arm*) He'll not stir. He's pot-boy in this place, and I'll not have him stolen off and kidnabbed while himself's abroad.

WIDOW QUIN It'd be a crazy pot-boy'd lodge him in the shebeen where he works by day, so you'd have a right to come on, young fellow, till you see my little houseen, a perch[17] off on the rising hill.

PEGEEN Wait till morning, Christy Mahon. Wait till you lay eyes on her leaky thatch is growing more pasture for her buck goat than her square of fields,

[15] Young pigs; sucklings.

[16] Her husband.

[17] Short distance.

and she without a tramp itself to keep in order her place at all.

WIDOW QUIN When you see me contriving in my little gardens, Christy Mahon, you'll swear the Lord God formed me to be living lone, and that there isn't my match in Mayo for thatching, or mowing, or shearing sheep.

PEGEEN (*With noisy scorn*) It's true the Lord God formed you to contrive indeed. Doesn't the world know you reared a black lamb at your own breast, so that the Lord Bishop of Connaught felt the elements of a Christian, and he eating it after in a kidney stew? Doesn't the world know you've been seen shaving the foxy skipper from France for a threepenny bit, and a sop of grass tobacco would wring the liver from a mountain goat you'd meet leaping the hills?

WIDOW QUIN (*With amusement*) Do you hear her now, young fellow? Do you hear the way she'll be rating at your own self when a week is by?

PEGEEN (*To* CHRISTY) Don't heed her. Tell her to go into her pigsty and not plague us here.

WIDOW QUIN I'm going; but he'll come with me.

PEGEEN (*Shaking him*) Are you dumb, young fellow?

CHRISTY (*Timidly, to* WIDOW QUIN) God increase you; but I'm pot-boy in this place, and it's here I'd liefer stay.

PEGEEN (*Triumphantly*) Now you have heard him, and go on from this.

WIDOW QUIN (*Looking round the room*) It's lonesome this hour crossing the hill, and if he won't come along with me, I'd have a right maybe to stop this night with yourselves. Let me stretch out on the settle, Pegeen Mike; and himself can lie by the hearth.

PEGEEN (*Short and fiercely*) Faith, I won't. Quit off or I will send you now.

WIDOW QUIN (*Gathering her shawl up*) Well, it's a terror to be aged a score.[18] (*To* CHRISTY) God bless you now, young fellow, and let you be wary, or there's right torment will await you here if you go romancing with her like, and she waiting only, as they bade me say, on a sheepskin parchment to be wed with Shawn Keogh of Killakeen.

CHRISTY (*Going to Pegeen as she bolts the door*) What's that she's after saying?

PEGEEN Lies and blather, you've no call to mind. Well, isn't Shawn Keogh an impudent fellow to send up spying on me? Wait till I lay hands on him. Let him wait, I'm saying.

CHRISTY And you're not wedding him at all?

PEGEEN I wouldn't wed him if a bishop came walking for to join us here.

CHRISTY That God in glory may be thanked for that.

PEGEEN There's your bed now. I've put a quilt upon you I'm after quilting a while since with my own two hands, and you'd best stretch out now for your sleep, and may God give you a good rest till I call you in the morning when the cocks will crow.

CHRISTY (*As she goes to inner room*) May God and Mary and St. Patrick bless you and reward you, for your kindly talk. (*She shuts the door behind her. He settles his bed slowly, feeling the quilt with immense satisfaction*) Well, it's a clean bed and soft with it, and it's great luck and company I've won me in the end of time—two fine women fighting for the likes of me—till I'm thinking this night wasn't I a foolish fellow not to kill my father in the years gone by.

*Curtain*

[18] She's a terror for a 20-year-old girl!

# Act Two

SCENE, *as before. Brilliant morning light.* CHRISTY, *looking bright and cheerful, is cleaning a girl's boots.*

CHRISTY (*To himself, counting jugs on dresser*) Half a hundred beyond. Ten there. A score that's above. Eighty jugs. Six cups and a broken one. Two plates. A power of glasses. Bottles, a school-master'd be hard set to count, and enough in them, I'm thinking, to drunken all the wealth and wisdom of the County Clare. (*He puts down the boot carefully*) There's her boots now, nice and decent for her evening use, and isn't it grand brushes she has? (*He puts them down and goes by degrees to the looking-glass*) Well, this'd be a fine place to be my whole life talking out with swearing Christians, in place of my old dogs and cat, and I stalking around, smoking my pipe and drinking my fill, and never a day's work but drawing a cork an odd time, or wiping a glass, or rinsing out a shiny tumbler for a decent man. (*He takes the looking-glass from the wall and puts it on the back of a chair; then sits down in front of it and begins washing his face*) Didn't I know rightly I was handsome, though it was the divil's own mirror we had beyond, would twist a squint across an angel's brow; and I'll be growing fine from this day, the way I'll have a soft lovely skin on me and won't be the like of the clumsy young fellows do be ploughing all times in the earth and dung. (*He starts*) Is she coming again? (*He looks out*) Stranger girls. God help me, where'll I hide myself away and my long neck naked to the world? (*He looks out*) I'd best go to the room maybe till I'm dressed again. (*He gathers up his coat and the looking-glass, and runs into the inner room. The door is pushed open, and* SUSAN BRADY *looks in, and knocks on door*)

SUSAN There's nobody in it. (*Knocks again*)

NELLY (*Pushing her in and following her, with* HONOR BLAKE *and* SARA TANSEY) It'd be early for them both to be out walking the hill.

SUSAN I'm thinking Shawn Keogh was making game of us and there's no such man in it at all.

HONOR (*Pointing to straw and quilt*) Look at that. He's been sleeping there in the night. Well, it'll be a hard case[1] if he's gone off now, the way we'll never set our eyes on a man killed his father, and we after rising early and destroying ourselves running fast on the hill.

NELLY Are you thinking them's his boots?

SARA (*Taking them up*) If they are, there should be his father's track on them. Did you never read in the papers the way murdered men do bleed and drip?

SUSAN Is that blood there, Sara Tansey?

SARA (*Smelling it*) That's bog water, I'm thinking, but it's his own they are surely, for I never seen the like of them for whity mud, and red mud, and turf on them, and the fine sands of the sea. That man's been walking, I'm telling you. (*She goes down right, putting on one of his boots*)

SUSAN (*Going to window*) Maybe he's stolen off to Belmullet with the boots of Michael James, and you'd have a right so to follow after him, Sara Tansey, and you the one yoked the ass cart and drove ten miles to set your eyes on the man bit the yellow lady's nostril on the northern shore. (*She looks out*)

SARA (*Running to window with one boot on*) Don't be talking, and we fooled today. (*Putting on other boot*) There's a pair do fit me well, and I'll be keeping them for walking to the priest, when you'd be ashamed this place, going up winter and summer with nothing worth while to confess at all.

HONOR (*Who has been listening at the door*) Whisht! there's someone inside the room. (*She pushes door a chink open*) It's a man.

(SARA *kicks off boots and puts them where they were. They all stand in a line looking through chink*)

SARA I'll call him. Mister! Mister! (*He puts in his head*) Is Pegeen within?

CHRISTY (*Coming in as meek as a mouse, with the looking-glass held behind his back*) She's above on the cnuceen,[2] seeking the nanny goats, the way she'd have a sup of goat's milk for to colour my tea.

SARA And asking your pardon, is it you's the man killed his father?

CHRISTY (*Sidling toward the nail where the glass was hanging*) I am, God help me!

SARA (*Taking eggs she has brought*) Then my thousand welcomes to you, and I've run up with a brace of duck's eggs for your food today. Pegeen's ducks is no use, but these are the real rich sort. Hold out your hand and you'll see it's no lie I'm telling you.

CHRISTY (*Coming forward shyly, and holding out his left hand*) They're a great and weighty size.

SUSAN And I run up with a pat of butter, for it'd be a poor thing to have you eating your spuds dry, and you after running a great way since you did destroy your da.

CHRISTY Thank you kindly.

HONOR And I brought you a little cut of cake, for you should have a thin stomach on you, and you that length walking the world.

NELLY And I brought you a little laying pullet—boiled and all she is—was crushed at the fall of night by the curate's car. Feel the fat of that breast, mister.

CHRISTY It's bursting, surely. (*He feels it with the back of his hand, in which he holds the presents*)

SARA Will you pinch it? Is your right hand too sacred for to use at all? (*She slips round behind him*) It's a glass he has. Well, I never seen to this day a man with a looking-glass held to his back. Them that kills their fathers is a vain lot surely.

(*Girls giggle*)

CHRISTY (*Smiling innocently and piling presents on glass*) I'm very thankful to you all today . . .

WIDOW QUIN (*Coming in quickly, at door*) Sara Tansey, Susan Brady, Honor Blake! What in glory has you here at this hour of day?

GIRLS (*Giggling*) That's the man killed his father.

WIDOW QUIN (*Coming to them*) I know well it's the man; and I'm after putting him down in the sports below for racing, leaping, pitching, and the Lord knows what.

SARA (*Exuberantly*) That's right, Widow Quin. I'll bet my dowry that he'll lick the world.

WIDOW QUIN If you will, you'd have a right to have him fresh and nourished in place of nursing a feast.[3] (*Taking presents*) Are you fasting or fed, young fellow?

CHRISTY Fasting, if you please.

WIDOW QUIN (*Loudly*) Well, you're the lot. Stir up now and give him his breakfast. (*To* CHRISTY) Come here to me (*She puts him on bench beside her while the girls make tea and get his breakfast*) and let you tell us your story before Pegeen will come, in place of grinning your ears off like the moon of May.

CHRISTY (*Beginning to be pleased*) It's a long story; you'd be destroyed listening.

WIDOW QUIN Don't be letting on to be shy, a fine, gamey, treacherous lad the like of you. Was it in your house beyond you cracked his skull?

CHRISTY (*Shy but flattered*) It was not. We were digging spuds in his cold, sloping, stony, divil's patch of a field.

WIDOW QUIN And you went asking money of him, or making talk of getting a wife would drive him from his farm?

CHRISTY I did not, then; but there I was, digging and digging, and "You squinting idiot," says he, "let you walk down now and tell the priest you'll wed the Widow Casey in a score of days."

WIDOW QUIN And what kind was she?

CHRISTY (*With horror*) A walking terror from beyond the hills, and she two score and five years, and two hundredweights and five pounds in the weighing scales, with a limping leg on her, and a blinded eye, and she a woman of noted misbehavior with the old and young.

GIRLS (*Clustering round him, serving him*) Glory be.

[1] Bad luck for us.

[2] Small hill.

[3] Needing to be fed.

WIDOW QUIN And what did he want driving you to wed with her? (*She takes a bit of the chicken*)

CHRISTY (*Eating with growing satisfaction*) He was letting on I was wanting a protector from the harshness of the world, and he without a thought the whole while but how he'd have her hut to live in and her gold to drink.

WIDOW QUIN There's maybe worse than a dry hearth and a widow woman and your glass at night. So you hit him then?

CHRISTY (*Getting almost excited*) I did not. "I won't wed her," says I, "when all know she did suckle me for six weeks when I came into the world, and she a hag this day with a tongue on her has the crows and seabirds scattered, the way they wouldn't cast a shadow on her garden with the dread of her curse."

WIDOW QUIN (*Teasingly*) That one should be right company.

SARA (*Eagerly*) Don't mind her. Did you kill him then?

CHRISTY "She's too good for the like of you," says he, "and go on now or I'll flatten you out like a crawling beast has passed under a dray." "You will not if I can help it," says I. "Go on," says he, "or I'll have the divil making garters of your limbs tonight." "You will not if I can help it," says I. (*He sits up, brandishing his mug*)

SARA You were right surely.

CHRISTY (*Impressively*) With that the sun came out between the cloud and the hill, and it shining green in my face. "God have mercy on your soul," says he, lifting a scythe; "or on your own," says I, raising the loy.

SUSAN That's a grand story.

HONOR He tells it lovely.

CHRISTY (*Flattered and confident, waving bone*) He gave a drive with the scythe, and I gave a lep to the east. Then I turned around with my back to the north, and I hit a blow on the ridge of his skull, laid him stretched out, and he split to the knob of his gullet. (*He raises the chicken bone to his Adam's apple*)

GIRLS (*Together*) Well, you're a marvel! Oh, God bless you! You're the lad surely!

SUSAN I'm thinking the Lord God sent him this road to make a second husband to the Widow Quin, and she with a great yearning to be wedded, though all dread her here. Lift him on her knee, Sara Tansey.

WIDOW QUIN Don't tease him.

SARA (*Going over to dresser and counter very quickly, and getting two glasses and porter*) You're heroes surely, and let you drink a supeen with your arms linked like the outlandish lovers in the sailor's song. (*She links their arms and gives them the glasses*) There now. Drink a health to the wonders of the western world, the pirates, preachers, poteen-makers, with the jobbing jockies;[4] parching peelers, and the juries fill their stomachs selling judgments of the English law. (*Brandishing the bottle*)

WIDOW QUIN That's a right toast, Sara Tansey. Now, Christy.

(*They drink with their arms linked, he drinking with his left hand, she with her right. As they are drinking,* PEGEEN MIKE *comes in with a milk can and stands aghast. They all spring away from* CHRISTY. *He goes down left.* WIDOW QUIN *remains seated*)

PEGEEN (*Angrily, to Sara*) What is it you're wanting?

SARA (*Twisting her apron*) An ounce of tobacco.

PEGEEN Have you tuppence?

SARA I've forgotten my purse.

PEGEEN Then you'd best be getting it and not fooling us here. (*To the* WIDOW QUIN, *with more elaborate scorn*) And what is it you're wanting, Widow Quin?

WIDOW QUIN (*Insolently*) A penn'orth of starch.

PEGEEN (*Breaking out*) And you without a white shift or a shirt in your whole family since the drying of the flood. I've no starch for the like of you, and let you walk on now to Killamuck.

WIDOW QUIN (*Turning to* CHRISTY, *as she goes out with the girls*) Well, you're mighty huffy this day, Pegeen Mike, and, you young fellow, let you not forget the sports and racing when the noon is by.

(*They go out*)

PEGEEN (*Imperiously*) Fling out that rubbish and put them cups away. (CHRISTY *tidies away in great haste*) Shove in the bench by the wall. (*He does so*) And hang that glass on the nail. What disturbed it at all?

CHRISTY (*Very meekly*) I was making myself decent only, and this a fine country for young lovely girls.

PEGEEN (*Sharply*) Whisht your talking of girls. (*Goes to counter, right*)

CHRISTY Wouldn't any wish to be decent in a place . . .

PEGEEN Whisht I'm saying.

CHRISTY (*Looks at her face for a moment with great misgivings, then as a last effort, takes up a loy, and goes toward her, with feigned assurance*) It was with a loy the like of that I killed my father.

PEGEEN (*Still sharply*) You've told me that story six times since the dawn of day.

CHRISTY (*Reproachfully*) It's a queer thing you wouldn't care to be hearing it and them girls after walking four miles to be listening to me now.

PEGEEN (*Turning around astonished*) Four miles!

CHRISTY (*Apologetically*) Didn't himself say there were only four bona fides living in the place?

PEGEEN It's bona fides by the road they are, but that lot came over the river lepping the stones. It's not three perches when you go like that, and I was down this morning looking on the papers the post-boy does have in his bag. (*With meaning and emphasis*) For there was great news this day, Christopher Mahon. (*She goes into room left*)

CHRISTY (*Suspiciously*) Is it news of my murder?

PEGEEN (*Inside*) Murder, indeed.

CHRISTY (*Loudly*) A murdered da?

PEGEEN (*Coming in again and crossing right*) There was not, but a story filled half a page of the hanging of a man. Ah, that should be a fearful end, young fellow, and it worst of all for a man who destroyed his da, for the like of him would get small mercies, and when it's dead he is, they'd put him in a narrow

[4] Petty crooks or poteen-peddlers.

grave, with cheap sacking wrapping him round, and pour down quicklime on his head, the way you'd see a woman pouring any frish-frash[5] from a cup.

CHRISTY (*Very miserably*) Oh, God help me. Are you thinking I'm safe? You were saying at the fall of night, I was shut of jeopardy and I here with yourselves.

PEGEEN (*Severely*) You'll be shut of jeopardy in no place if you go talking with a pack of wild girls the like of them do be walking abroad with the peelers, talking whispers at the fall of night.

CHRISTY (*With terror*) And you're thinking they'd tell?

PEGEEN (*With mock sympathy*) Who knows, God help you.

CHRISTY (*Loudly*) What joy would they have to bring hanging to the likes of me?

PEGEEN It's queer joys they have, and who knows the thing they'd do, if it'd make the green stones cry itself to think of you swaying and swiggling at the butt of a rope, and you with a fine, stout neck, God bless you! the way you'd be a half an hour, in great anguish, getting your death.

CHRISTY (*Getting his boots and putting them on*) If there's that terror of them, it'd be best, maybe, I went on wandering like Esau or Cain and Abel on the sides of Neifin or the Erris plain.

PEGEEN (*Beginning to play with him*) It would, maybe, for I've heard the Circuit Judges this place is a heartless crew.

CHRISTY (*Bitterly*) It's more than Judges this place is a heartless crew. (*Looking up at her*) And isn't it a poor thing to be starting again and I a lonesome fellow will be looking out on women and girls the way the needy fallen spirits do be looking on the Lord?

PEGEEN What call have you to be that lonesome when there's poor girls walking Mayo in their thousands now?

CHRISTY (*Grimly*) It's well you know what call I have. It's well you know it's a lonesome thing to be passing small towns with the lights shining sideways when the night is down, or going in strange places with a dog noising before you and a dog noising behind, or drawn to the cities where you'd hear a voice kissing and talking deep love in every shadow of the ditch, and you passing on with an empty, hungry stomach failing from your heart.

PEGEEN I'm thinking you're an odd man, Christy Mahon. The oddest walking fellow I ever set my eyes on to this hour today.

CHRISTY What would any be but odd men and they living lonesome in the world?

PEGEEN I'm not odd, and I'm my whole life with my father only.

CHRISTY (*With infinite admiration*) How would a lovely handsome woman the like of you be lonesome when all men should be thronging around to hear the sweetness of your voice, and the little infant children should be pestering your steps I'm thinking, and you walking the roads.

[5] Slops, dregs.

PEGEEN I'm hard set to know what way a coaxing fellow the like of yourself should be lonesome either.

CHRISTY Coaxing?

PEGEEN Would you have me think a man never talked with the girls would have the words you've spoken today? It's only letting on you are to be lonesome, the way you'd get around me now.

CHRISTY I wish to God I was letting on; but I was lonesome all times, and born lonesome, I'm thinking, as the moon of dawn. (*Going to door*)

PEGEEN (*Puzzled by his talk*) Well, it's a story I'm not understanding at all why you'd be worse than another, Christy Mahon, and you a fine lad with the great savagery to destroy your da.

CHRISTY It's little I'm understanding myself, saving only that my heart's scalded this day, and I am going off stretching out the earth between us, the way I'll not be waking near you another dawn of the year till the two of us do arise to hope or judgment with the saints of God, and now I'd best be going with my wattle in my hand, for hanging is a poor thing (*Turning to go*), and it's little welcome only is left me in this house today.

PEGEEN (*Sharply*) Christy! (*He turns round*) Come here to me. (*He goes toward her*) Lay down that switch and throw some sods on the fire. You're potboy in this place, and I'll not have you mitch[6] off from us now.

CHRISTY You were saying I'd be hanged if I stay.

PEGEEN (*Quite kindly at last*) I'm after going down and reading the fearful crimes of Ireland for two weeks or three, and there wasn't a word of your murder. (*Getting up and going over to the counter*) They've likely not found the body. You're safe so with ourselves.

CHRISTY (*Astonished, slowly*) It's making game of me you were, (*Following her with fearful joy*) and I can stay so, working at your side, and I not lonesome from this mortal day.

PEGEEN What's to hinder you from staying, except the widow woman or the young girls would inveigle you off?

CHRISTY (*With rapture*) And I'll have your words from this day filling my ears, and that look is come upon you meeting my two eyes, and I watching you loafing around in the warm sun, or rinsing your ankles when the night is come.

PEGEEN (*Kindly, but a little embarrassed*) I'm thinking you'll be a loyal young lad to have working around, and if you vexed me a while since with your leaguing with the girls, I wouldn't give a thraneen[7] for a lad hadn't a mighty spirit in him and a gamey heart.

(SHAWN KEOGH *runs in carrying a cleeve*[8] *on his back, followed by the* WIDOW QUIN)

SHAWN (*To* PEGEEN) I was passing below, and I seen your mountainy sheep eating cabbages in Jimmy's field. Run up or they'll be bursting surely.

[6] Sneak.
[7] Worthless token.
[8] Basket.

PEGEEN Oh, God mend them! (*She puts a shawl over her head and runs out*)

CHRISTY (*Looking from one to the other. Still in high spirits*) I'd best go to her aid maybe. I'm handy with ewes.

WIDOW QUIN (*Closing the door*) She can do that much, and there is Shaneen has long speeches for to tell you now. (*She sits down with an amused smile*)

SHAWN (*Taking something from his pocket and offering it to* CHRISTY) Do you see that, mister?

CHRISTY (*Looking at it*) The half of a ticket to the Western States! [9]

SHAWN (*Trembling with anxiety*) I'll give it to you and my new hat (*Pulling it out of hamper*); and my breeches with the double seat (*Pulling it off*); and my new coat is woven from the blackest shearings for three miles around (*Giving him the coat*); I'll give you the whole of them, and my blessing, and the blessing of Father Reilly itself, maybe, if you'll quit from this and leave us in the peace we had till last night at the fall of dark.

CHRISTY (*With a new arrogance*) And for what is it you're wanting to get shut of me?

SHAWN (*Looking to the* WIDOW *for help*) I'm a poor scholar with middling faculties to coin a lie, so I'll tell you the truth, Christy Mahon. I'm wedding with Pegeen beyond, and I don't think well of having a clever fearless man the like of you dwelling in her house.

CHRISTY (*Almost pugnaciously*) And you'd be using bribery for to banish me?

SHAWN (*In an imploring voice*) Let you not take it badly, mister honey, isn't beyond the best place for you where you'll have golden chains and shiny coats and you riding upon hunters with the ladies of the land. (*He makes an eager sign to the* WIDOW QUIN *to come to help him*)

WIDOW QUIN (*Coming over*) It's true for him, and you'd best quit off and not have that poor girl setting her mind on you, for there's Shaneen thinks she wouldn't suit you though all is saying that she'll wed you now.

(CHRISTY *beams with delight*)

SHAWN (*In terrified earnest*) She wouldn't suit you, and she with the divil's own temper the way you'd be strangling one another in a score of days. (*He makes the movement of strangling with his hands*) It's the like of me only that she's fit for, a quiet simple fellow wouldn't raise a hand upon her if she scratched itself.

WIDOW QUIN (*Putting* SHAWN'S *hat on* CHRISTY) Fit them clothes on you anyhow, young fellow, and he'd maybe loan them to you for the sports. (*Pushing him toward inner door*) Fit them on and you can give your answer when you have them tried.

CHRISTY (*Beaming, delighted with the clothes*) I will then. I'd like herself to see me in them tweeds and hat. (*He goes into room and shuts the door*)

SHAWN (*In great anxiety*) He'd like herself to see them. He'll not leave us, Widow Quin. He's a score of divils in him the way it's well nigh certain he will wed Pegeen.

WIDOW QUIN (*Jeeringly*) It's true all girls are fond of courage and do hate the like of you.

SHAWN (*Walking about in desperation*) Oh, Widow Quin, what'll I be doing now? I'd inform again him, but he'd burst from Kilmainham[10] and he'd be sure and certain to destroy me. If I wasn't so God-fearing, I'd near have courage to come behind him and run a pike into his side. Oh, it's a hard case to be an orphan and not to have your father that you're used to, and you'd easy kill and make yourself a hero in the sight of all. (*Coming up to her*) Oh, Widow Quin, will you find me some contrivance when I've promised you a ewe?

WIDOW QUIN A ewe's a small thing, but what would you give me if I did wed him and did save you so?

SHAWN (*With astonishment*) You?

WIDOW QUIN Aye. Would you give me the red cow you have and the mountainy ram, and the right of way across your rye path, and a load of dung at Michaelmas, and turbary[11] upon the western hill?

SHAWN (*Radiant with hope*) I would surely, and I'd give you the wedding-ring I have, and the loan of a new suit, the way you'd have him decent on the wedding-day. I'd give you two kids for your dinner, and a gallon of poteen, and I'd call the piper on the long car to your wedding from Crossmolina or from Ballina. I'd give you . . .

WIDOW QUIN That'll do so, and let you whisht, for he's coming now again.

(CHRISTY *comes in very natty in the new clothes.* WIDOW QUIN *goes to him admiringly*)

WIDOW QUIN If you seen yourself now, I'm thinking you'd be too proud to speak to us at all, and it'd be a pity surely to have your like sailing from Mayo to the Western World.

CHRISTY (*As proud as a peacock*) I'm not going. If this is a poor place itself, I'll make myself contented to be lodging here.

(WIDOW QUIN *makes a sign to* SHAWN *to leave them*)

SHAWN Well, I'm going measuring the race-course while the tide is low, so I'll leave you the garments and my blessing for the sports today. God bless you! (*He wriggles out*)

WIDOW QUIN (*Admiring* CHRISTY) Well, you're mighty spruce, young fellow. Sit down now while you're quiet till you talk with me.

CHRISTY (*Swaggering*) I'm going abroad on the hillside for to seek Pegeen.

WIDOW QUIN You'll have time and plenty for to seek Pegeen, and you heard me saying at the fall of night the two of us should be great company.

CHRISTY From this out I'll have no want of company when all sorts is bringing me their food and clothing, (*He swaggers to the door, tightening his belt*) the

9 The United States.

10 Penitentiary in Dublin.

11 The right to dig turf or peat on another's land, or the piece of land itself. Widow Quin seems most interested in the right.

way they'd set their eyes upon a gallant orphan cleft his father with one blow to the breeches belt. (*He opens door, then staggers back*) Saints of glory! Holy angels from the throne of light!

WIDOW QUIN (*Going over*) What ails you?

CHRISTY It's the walking spirit of my murdered da!

WIDOW QUIN (*Looking out*) Is it that tramper?

CHRISTY (*Wildly*) Where'll I hide my poor body from that ghost of hell?

(*The door is pushed open, and old* MAHON *appears on threshold.* CHRISTY *darts in behind door*)

WIDOW QUIN (*In great amusement*) God save you, my poor man.

MAHON (*Gruffly*) Did you see a young lad passing this way in the early morning or the fall of night?

WIDOW QUIN You're a queer kind to walk in not saluting at all.

MAHON Did you see the young lad?

WIDOW QUIN (*Stiffly*) What kind was he?

MAHON An ugly young streeler[12] with a murderous gob[13] on him, and a little switch in his hand. I met a tramper seen him coming this way at the fall of night.

WIDOW QUIN There's harvest hundreds do be passing these days for the Sligo boat. For what is it you're wanting him, my poor man?

MAHON I want to destroy him for breaking the head on me with the clout of a loy. (*He takes off a big hat, and shows his head in a mass of bandages and plaster, with some pride*) It was he did that, and amn't I a great wonder to think I've traced him ten days with that rent in my crown?

WIDOW QUIN (*Taking his head in both hands and examing it with extreme delight*) That was a great blow. And who hit you? A robber maybe?

MAHON It was my own son hit me, and he the divil a robber, or anything else, but a dirty, stuttering lout.

WIDOW QUIN (*Letting go his skull and wiping her hands in her apron*) You'd best be wary of a mortified[14] scalp, I think they call it, lepping around with that wound in the splendour of the sun. It was a bad blow surely, and you should have vexed him fearful to make him strike that gash in his da.

MAHON Is it me?

WIDOW QUIN (*Amusing herself*) Aye. And isn't it a great shame when the old and hardened do torment the young?

MAHON (*Raging*) Torment him, is it? And I after holding out with the patience of a martyred saint till there's nothing but destruction on, and I'm driven out in my old age with none to aid me.

WIDOW QUIN (*Greatly amused*) It's a sacred wonder the way that wickedness will spoil a man.

MAHON My wickedness, is it? Amn't I after saying it is himself has me destroyed, and he a lier on walls, a talker of folly, a man you'd see stretched the half of the day in the brown ferns with his belly to the sun.

[12] Stroller, vagrant.
[13] Face.
[14] Poisoned, perhaps gangrenous; dying.

WIDOW QUIN Not working at all?

MAHON The divil a work, or if he did itself, you'd see him raising up a haystack like the stalk of a rush, or driving our last cow till he broke her leg at the hip, and when he wasn't at that he'd be fooling over little birds he had—finches and felts[15]—or making mugs at his own self in the bit of a glass we had hung on the wall.

WIDOW QUIN (*Looking at* CHRISTY) What way was he so foolish? It was running wild after the girls maybe?

MAHON (*With a shout of derision*) Running wild, is it? If he seen a red petticoat coming swinging over the hill, he'd be off to hide in the sticks, and you'd see him shooting out his sheep's eyes between the little twigs and the leaves, and his two ears rising like a hare looking out through a gap. Girls, indeed!

WIDOW QUIN It was drink maybe?

MAHON And he a poor fellow would get drunk on the smell of a pint. He'd a queer rotten stomach, I'm telling you, and when I gave him three pulls from my pipe a while since, he was taken with contortions till I had to send him in the ass cart to the females' nurse.

WIDOW QUIN (*Clasping her hands*) Well, I never till this day heard tell of a man the like of that!

MAHON I'd take a mighty oath you didn't surely, and wasn't he the laughing joke of every female woman where four baronies meet, the way the girls would stop their weeding if they seen him coming the road to let a roar at him, and call him the looney of Mahon's.

WIDOW QUIN I'd give the world and all to see the like of him. What kind was he?

MAHON A small low fellow.

WIDOW QUIN And dark?

MAHON Dark and dirty.

WIDOW QUIN (*Considering*) I'm thinking I seen him.

MAHON (*Eagerly*) An ugly young blackguard.

WIDOW QUIN A hideous, fearful villain, and the spit of you.

MAHON What way is he fled?

WIDOW QUIN Gone over the hills to catch a coasting steamer to the north or south.

MAHON Could I pull up on him now?

WIDOW QUIN If you'll cross the sands below where the tide is out, you'll be in it as soon as himself, for he had to go round ten miles by the top of the bay. (*She points to the door*) Strike down by the head beyond and then follow on the roadway to the north and east.

(MAHON *goes abruptly*)

WIDOW QUIN (*Shouting after him*) Let you give him a good vengeance when you come up with him, but don't put yourself in the power of the law, for it'd be a poor thing to see a judge in his black cap reading out his sentence on a civil warrior the like of you. (*She swings the door to and looks at* CHRISTY, *who is cowering in terror, for a moment, then she bursts into a laugh*) Well, you're the walking Playboy[16] of

[15] Thrushes.
[16] Here used in the sense of *hoaxer* or *big talker.*

the Western World, and that's the poor man you had divided to his breeches belt.

CHRISTY (*Looking out: then, to her*) What'll Pegeen say when she hears that story? What'll she be saying to me now?

WIDOW QUIN She'll knock the head of you, I'm thinking, and drive you from the door. God help her to be taking you for a wonder, and you a little schemer making up the story you destroyed your da.

CHRISTY (*Turning to the door, nearly speechless with rage, half to himself*) To be letting on he was dead, and coming back to his life, and following after me like an old weasel tracing a rat, and coming in here laying desolation between my own self and the fine women of Ireland, and he a kind of carcase that you'd fling upon the sea . . .

WIDOW QUIN (*More soberly*) There's talking for a man's one only son.

CHRISTY (*Breaking out*) His one son, is it? May I meet him with one tooth and it aching, and one eye to be seeing seven and seventy divils in the twists of the road, and one old timber leg on him to limp into the scalding grave. (*Looking out*) There he is now crossing the strands, and that the Lord God would send a high wave to wash him from the world.

WIDOW QUIN (*Scandalized*) Have you no shame? (*Putting her hand on his shoulder and turning him round*) What ails you? Near crying, is it?

CHRISTY (*In despair and grief*) Amn't I after seeing the lovelight of the star of knowledge shining from her brow, and hearing words would put you thinking on the holy Brigid speaking to the infant saints, and now she'll be turning again, and speaking hard words to me, like an old woman with a spavindy[17] ass she'd have, urging on a hill.

WIDOW QUIN There's poetry talk for a girl you'd see itching and scratching, and she with a stale stink of poteen on her from selling in the shop.

CHRISTY (*Impatiently*) It's her like is fitted to be handling merchandise in the heavens above, and what'll I be doing now, I ask you, and I a kind of wonder was jilted by the heavens when a day was by.

(*There is a distant noise of girls' voices.* WIDOW QUIN *looks from window and comes to him, hurriedly*)

WIDOW QUIN You'll be doing like myself, I'm thinking, when I did destroy my man, for I'm above many's the day, odd times in great spirits, abroad in the sunshine, darning a stocking or stitching a shift; and odd times again looking out on the schooners, hookers, trawlers is sailing the sea, and I thinking on the gallant hairy fellows are drifting beyond, and myself long years living alone.

CHRISTY (*Interested*) You're like me, so.

WIDOW QUIN I am your like, and it's for that I'm taking a fancy to you, and I with my little houseen above where there'd be myself to tend you, and none to ask were you a murderer or what at all.

[17] Lame.

CHRISTY And what would I be doing if I left Pegeen?

WIDOW QUIN I've nice jobs you could be doing, gathering shells to make a whitewash for our hut within, building up a little goose-house, or stretching a new skin on an old curragh I have, and if my hut is far from all sides, it's there you'll meet the wisest old men, I tell you, at the corner of my wheel, and it's there yourself and me will have great times whispering and hugging. . . .

VOICES (*Outside, calling far away*) Christy! Christy Mahon! Christy!

CHRISTY Is it Pegeen Mike?

WIDOW QUIN It's the young girls, I'm thinking, coming to bring you to the sports below, and what is it you'll have me to tell them now?

CHRISTY Aid me for to win Pegeen. It's herself only that I'm seeking now. (WIDOW QUIN *gets up and goes to window*) Aid me for to win her, and I'll be asking God to stretch a hand to you in the hour of death, and lead you short cuts through the Meadows of Ease, and up the floor of Heaven to the Footstool of the Virgin's Son.

WIDOW QUIN There's praying.

VOICES (*Nearer*) Christy! Christy Mahon!

CHRISTY (*With agitation*) They're coming. Will you swear to aid and save me for the love of Christ?

WIDOW QUIN (*Looks at him for a moment*) If I aid you, will you swear to give me a right of way I want, and a mountainy ram, and a load of dung at Michaelmas, the time that you'll be master here?

CHRISTY I will, by the elements and stars of night.

WIDOW QUIN Then we'll not say a word of the old fellow, the way Pegeen won't know your story till the end of time.

CHRISTY And if he chances to return again?

WIDOW QUIN We'll swear he's a maniac and not your da. I could take an oath I seen him raving on the sands today.

(*Girls run in*)

SUSAN Come on to the sports below. Pegeen says you're to come.

SARA TANSEY The lepping's beginning, and we've a jockey's suit to fit upon you for the mule race on the sands below.

HONOR Come on, will you?

CHRISTY I will then if Pegeen's beyond.

SARA TANSEY She's in the boreen[18] making game of Shaneen Keogh.

CHRISTY Then I'll be going to her now. (*He runs out followed by the girls*)

WIDOW QUIN Well, if the worst comes in the end of all, it'll be great game to see there's none to pity him but a widow woman, the like of me, has buried her children and destroyed her man. (*She goes out*)

*Curtain*

[18] Lane, country road.

# Act Three

SCENE *As before. Later in the day.* JIMMY *comes in, slightly drunk.*

JIMMY (*Calls*) Pegeen! (*Crosses to inner door*) Pegeen Mike! (*Comes back again into the room*) Pegeen! (PHILLY *comes in in the same state*) (*To* PHILLY) Did you see herself?

PHILLY I did not; but I sent Shawn Keogh with the ass cart for to bear him home. (*Trying cupboards which are locked*) Well, isn't he a nasty man to get into such staggers at a morning wake? and isn't herself the divil's daughter for locking,[1] and she so fussy after that young gaffer, you might take your death with drought and none to heed you?

JIMMY It's little wonder she'd be fussy, and he after bringing bankrupt ruin on the roulette man, and the trick-o'-the-loop man, and breaking the nose of the cockshot-man, and winning all in the sports below, racing, lepping, dancing, and the Lord knows what! He's right luck, I'm telling you.

PHILLY If he has, he'll be rightly hobbled yet, and he not able to say ten words without making a brag of the way he killed his father, and the great blow he hit with the loy.

JIMMY A man can't hang by his own informing, and his father should be rotten by now.

(*Old* MAHON *passes window slowly*)

PHILLY Supposing a man's digging spuds in that field with a long spade, and supposing he flings up the two halves of that skull, what'll be said then in the papers and the courts of law?

JIMMY They'd say it was an old Dane, maybe, was drowned in the flood. (*Old* MAHON *comes in and sits down near door listening*) Did you never hear tell of the skulls they have in the city of Dublin, ranged out like blue jugs in a cabin of Connaught?

PHILLY And you believe that?

JIMMY (*Pugnaciously*) Didn't a lad see them and he after coming from harvesting in the Liverpool boat? "They have them there," says he, "making a show of the great people there was one time walking the world. White skulls and black skulls and yellow skulls, and some with full teeth, and some haven't only but one."

PHILLY It was no lie, maybe, for when I was a young lad there was a graveyard beyond the house with the remnants of a man who had thighs as long as your arm. He was a horrid man, I'm telling you, and there was many a fine Sunday I'd put him together for fun, and he with shiny bones, you wouldn't meet the like of these days in the cities of the world.

MAHON (*Getting up*) You wouldn't, is it? Lay your eyes on that skull, and tell me where and when there was another the like of it, is splintered only from the blow of a loy.

PHILLY Glory be to God! And who hit you at all?

[1] The Devil can't even keep track of her.

MAHON (*Triumphantly*) It was my own son hit me. Would you believe that?

JIMMY Well, there's wonders hidden in the heart of man!

PHILLY (*Suspiciously*) And what way was it done?

MAHON (*Wandering about the room*) I'm after walking hundreds and long scores of miles, winning clean beds and the fill of my belly four times in the day, and I doing nothing but telling stories of that naked truth. (*He comes to them a little aggressively*) Give me a supeen and I'll tell you now.

(WIDOW QUIN *comes in and stands aghast behind him. He is facing* JIMMY *and* PHILLY, *who are on the left*)

JIMMY Ask herself beyond. She's the stuff hidden in her shawl.

WIDOW QUIN (*Coming to* MAHON *quickly*) You here, is it? You didn't go far at all?

MAHON I seen the coasting steamer passing, and I got a drought upon me and a cramping leg, so I said, "The divil go along with him," and turned again. (*Looking under her shawl*) And let you give me a supeen, for I'm destroyed travelling since Tuesday was a week.

WIDOW QUIN (*Getting a glass, in a cajoling tone*) Sit down then by the fire and take your ease for a space. You've a right to be destroyed indeed, with your walking, and fighting, and facing the sun. (*Giving him poteen from a stone jar she has brought in*) There now is a drink for you, and may it be to your happiness and length of life.

MAHON (*Taking glass greedily and sitting down by fire*) God increase you!

WIDOW QUIN (*Taking men to the right stealthily*) Do you know what? That man's raving from his wound today, for I met him a while since telling a rambling tale of a tinker had him destroyed. Then he heard of Christy's deed, and he up and says it was his son had cracked his skull. O, isn't madness a fright, for he'll go killing someone yet, and he thinking it's the man has struck him so?

JIMMY (*Entirely convinced*) It's a fright, surely. I knew a party was kicked in the head by a red mare, and he went killing horses a great while, till he eat the insides of a clock and died after.

PHILLY (*With suspicion*) Did he see Christy?

WIDOW QUIN He didn't. (*With a warning gesture*) Let you not be putting him in mind of him, or you'll be likely summoned if there's murder done. (*Looking round at* MAHON) Whisht! He's listening. Wait now till you hear me taking him easy and unravelling all. (*She goes to* MAHON) And what way are you feeling, mister? Are you in contentment now?

MAHON (*Slightly emotional from his drink*) I'm poorly only, for it's a hard story the way I'm left today, when it was I did tend him from his hour of birth, and he a dunce never reached his second book, the way he'd come from school, many's the day, with his legs lamed under him, and he blackened with his beatings like a tinker's ass. It's a hard story, I'm saying, the way some do have their next and nighest raising up a hand of murder on them, and some is lonesome getting their death with lamentation in the dead of night.

WIDOW QUIN (*Not knowing what to say*) To hear you talking so quiet, who'd know you were the same fellow we seen pass today?

MAHON I'm the same surely. The wrack and ruin of three score years; and it's a terror to live that length, I tell you, and to have your sons going to the dogs against you, and you wore out scolding them, and skelping them, and God knows what.

PHILLY (*To* JIMMY) He's not raving. (*To* WIDOW QUIN) Will you ask him what kind was his son?

WIDOW QUIN (*To* MAHON, *with a peculiar look*) Was your son that hit you a lad of one year and a score maybe, a great hand at racing and lepping and licking the world?

MAHON (*Turning on her with a roar of rage*) Didn't you hear me say he was the fool of men, the way from this out he'll know the orphan's lot with old and young making game of him and they swearing, raging, kicking at him like a mangy cur.

(*A great burst of cheering outside, some way off*)

MAHON (*Putting his hands to his ears*) What in the name of God do they want roaring below?

WIDOW QUIN (*With the shade of a smile*) They're cheering a young lad, the champion Playboy of the Western World.

(*More cheering*)

MAHON (*Going to window*) It'd split my heart to hear them, and I with pulses in my brain-pan for a week gone by. Is it racing they are?

JIMMY (*Looking from door*) It is then. They are mounting him for the mule race will be run upon the sands. That's the playboy on the winkered mule.

MAHON (*Puzzled*) That lad, is it? If you said it was a fool he was, I'd have laid a mighty oath he was the likeness of my wandering son (*Uneasily, putting his hand to his head*) Faith, I'm thinking I'll go walking for to view the race.

WIDOW QUIN (*Stopping him, sharply*) You will not. You'd best take the road to Belmullet, and not be dilly-dallying in this place where there isn't a spot you could sleep.

PHILLY (*Coming forward*) Don't mind her. Mount there on the bench and you'll have a view of the whole. They're hurrying before the tide will rise, and it'd be near over if you went down the pathway through the crags below.

MAHON (*Mounts on bench,* WIDOW QUIN *beside him*) That's a right view again the edge of the sea. They're coming now from the point. He's leading. Who is he at all?

WIDOW QUIN He's the champion of the world, I tell you, and there isn't a hop'orth isn't falling lucky to his hands today.

PHILLY (*Looking out, interested in the race*) Look at that. They're pressing him now.

JIMMY He'll win it yet.

PHILLY Take your time, Jimmy Farrell. It's too soon to say.

WIDOW QUIN (*Shouting*) Watch him taking the gate. There's riding.

JIMMY (*Cheering*) More power to the young lad!

MAHON He's passing the third.

JIMMY He'll lick them yet!

WIDOW QUIN He'd lick them if he was running races with a score itself.

MAHON Look at the mule he has, kicking the stars.

WIDOW QUIN There was a lep! (*Catching hold of* MAHON *in her excitement*) He's fallen! He's mounted again! Faith, he's passing them all!

JIMMY Look at him skelping her!

PHILLY And the mountain girls hooshing him on!

JIMMY It's the last turn! The post's cleared for them now!

MAHON Look at the narrow place. He'll be into the bogs! (*With a yell*) Good rider! He's through it again!

JIMMY He's neck and neck!

MAHON Good boy to him! Flames, but he's in!

(*Great cheering, in which all join*)

MAHON (*With hesitation*) What's that? They're raising him up. They're coming this way. (*With a roar of rage and astonishment*) It's Christy! by the stars of God! I'd know his way of spitting and he astride the moon.

(*He jumps down and makes for the door, but* WIDOW QUIN *catches him and pulls him back*)

WIDOW QUIN Stay quiet, will you. That's not your son. (*To* JIMMY) Stop him, or you'll get a month for the abetting of manslaughter and be fined as well.

JIMMY I'll hold him.

MAHON (*Struggling*) Let me out! Let me out, the lot of you! till I have my vengeance on his head today.

WIDOW QUIN (*Shaking him, vehemently*) That's not your son. That's a man is going to make a marriage with the daughter of this house, a place with fine trade, with a license, and with poteen too.

MAHON (*Amazed*) That man marrying a decent and a moneyed girl! Is it mad yous are? Is it in a crazy-house for females that I'm landed now?

WIDOW QUIN It's mad yourself is with the blow upon your head. That lad is the wonder of the Western World.

MAHON I seen it's my son.

WIDOW QUIN You seen that you're mad. (*Cheering outside*) Do you hear them cheering him in the zig-zags of the road? Aren't you after saying that your son's a fool, and how would they be cheering a true idiot born?

MAHON (*Getting distressed*) It's maybe out of reason that that man's himself. (*Cheering again*) There's none surely will go cheering him. Oh, I'm raving with a madness that would fright the world! (*He sits down with his hand to his head*) There was one time I seen ten scarlet divils letting on they'd cork my spirit in a gallon can; and one time I seen rats as big as badgers sucking the life blood from the butt of my lug;[2] but I never till this day confused that dribbling idiot with a likely man. I'm destroyed surely.

[2] Lobe of my ear.

WIDOW QUIN And who'd wonder when it's your brain-pan that is gaping now?

MAHON Then the blight of the sacred drought upon myself and him, for I never went mad to this day, and I not three weeks with the Limerick girls drinking myself silly, and parlatic[3] from the dusk to dawn. (*To* WIDOW QUIN, *suddenly*) Is my visage astray?

WIDOW QUIN It is then. You're a sniggering maniac, a child could see.

MAHON (*Getting up more cheerfully*) Then I'd best be going to the union[4] beyond, and there'll be a welcome before me, I tell you (*With great pride*), and I a terrible and fearful case, the way that there I was one time, screeching in a straitened waistcoat, with seven doctors writing out my sayings in a printed book. Would you believe that?

WIDOW QUIN If you're a wonder itself, you'd best be hasty, for them lads caught a maniac one time and pelted the poor creature till he ran out, raving and foaming, and was drowned in the sea.

MAHON (*With philosophy*) It's true mankind is the divil when your head's astray. Let me out now and I'll slip down the boreen, and not see them so.

WIDOW QUIN (*Showing him out*) That's it. Run to the right, and not a one will see.

(*He runs off*)

PHILLY (*Wisely*) You're at some gaming, Widow Quin; but I'll walk after him and give him his dinner and a time to rest, and I'll see then if he's raving or as sane as you.

WIDOW QUIN (*Annoyed*) If you go near that lad, let you be wary of your head, I'm saying. Didn't you hear him telling he was crazed at times?

PHILLY I heard him telling a power; and I'm thinking we'll have right sport, before night will fall. (*He goes out*)

JIMMY Well, Philly's a conceited and foolish man. How could that madman have his senses and his brain-pan slit? I'll go after them and see him turn on Philly now.

(*He goes;* WIDOW QUIN *hides poteen behind counter. Then hubbub outside*)

VOICES There you are! Good jumper! Grand lepper! Darlint boy! He's the racer! Bear him on, will you!

(CHRISTY *comes in, in jockey's dress, with* PEGEEN MIKE, SARA, *and other girls, and men*)

PEGEEN (*To crowd*) Go on now and don't destroy him and he drenching with sweat. Go along, I'm saying, and have your tug-of-warring till he's dried his skin.

CROWD Here's his prizes! A bagpipes! A fiddle was played by a poet in the years gone by! A flat and three-thorned blackthorn would lick the scholars out of Dublin town!

CHRISTY (*Taking prizes from the men*) Thank you kindly, the lot of you. But you'd say it was little only I did this day if you'd seen me a while since striking my one single blow.

TOWN CRIER (*Outside, ringing a bell*) Take notice, last event of this day! Tug-of-warring on the green below! Come on, the lot of you! Great achievements for all Mayo men!

PEGEEN Go on, and leave him for to rest and dry. Go on, I tell you, for he'll do no more. (*She hustles crowd out;* WIDOW QUIN *following them*)

MEN (*Going*) Come on, then. Good luck for the while!

PEGEEN (*Radiantly, wiping his face with her shawl*) Well, you're the lad, and you'll have great times from this out when you could win that wealth of prizes, and you sweating in the heat of noon!

CHRISTY (*Looking at her with delight*) I'll have great times if I win the crowning prize I'm seeking now, and that's your promise that you'll wed me in a fortnight, when our banns is called.

PEGEEN (*Backing away from him*) You've right daring to go ask me that, when all knows you'll be starting to some girl in your own townland, when your father's rotten in four months, or five.

CHRISTY (*Indignantly*) Starting from you, is it? (*He follows her*) I will not, then, and when the airs is warming in four months, or five, it's then yourself and me should be pacing Neifin in the dews of night, the times sweet smells do be rising, and you'd see a little shiny new moon, maybe, sinking on the hills.

PEGEEN (*Looking at him playfully*) And it's that kind of a poacher's love you'd make, Christy Mahon, on the sides of Neifin, when the night is down?

CHRISTY It's little you'll think if my love's a poacher's, or an earl's itself, when you'll feel my two hands stretched around you, and I squeezing kisses on your puckered lips, till I'd feel a kind of pity for the Lord God in all ages sitting lonesome in his golden chair.

PEGEEN That'll be right fun, Christy Mahon, and any girl would walk her heart out before she'd meet a young man was your like for eloquence, or talk, at all.

CHRISTY (*Encouraged*) Let you wait, to hear me talking, till we're astray in Erris, when Good Friday's by, drinking a sup from a well, and making mighty kisses with our wetted mouths, or gaming in a gap of sunshine, with yourself stretched back unto your necklace, in the flowers of the earth.

PEGEEN (*In a lower voice, moved by his tone*) I'd be nice so, is it?

CHRISTY (*With rapture*) If the mitred bishops seen you that time, they'd be the like of the holy prophets, I'm thinking, do be straining the bars of Paradise to lay eyes on the Lady Helen of Troy, and she abroad, pacing back and forward, with a nosegay in her golden shawl.

PEGEEN (*With real tenderness*) And what is it I have, Christy Mahon, to make me fitting entertainment for the like of you, that has such poet's talking, and such bravery of heart?

CHRISTY (*In a low voice*) Isn't there the light of seven heavens in your heart alone, the way you'll be an angel's lamp to me from this out, and I abroad in the darkness, spearing salmons in the Owen, or the Carrowmore?

PEGEEN If I was your wife, I'd be along with you those nights, Christy Mahon, the way you'd see I was a

[3] Paralyzed; Mahon's version of *paralytic*.

[4] A workhouse and hospital for the unemployed.

great hand at coaxing bailiffs, or coining funny nicknames for the stars of night.

CHRISTY You, is it? Taking your death in the hailstones, or in the fogs of dawn.

PEGEEN Yourself and me would shelter easy in a narrow bush, (*With a qualm of dread*) but we're only talking, maybe, for this would be a poor, thatched place to hold a fine lad is the like of you.

CHRISTY (*Putting his arm around her*) If I wasn't a good Christian, it's on my naked knees I'd be saying my prayers and paters to every jackstraw you have roofing your head, and every stony pebble is paving the laneway to your door.

PEGEEN (*Radiantly*) If that's the truth, I'll be burning candles from this out to the miracles of God that have brought you from the south today, and I, with my gowns bought ready, the way that I can wed you, and not wait at all.

CHRISTY It's miracles, and that's the truth. Me there toiling a long while, and walking a long while, not knowing at all I was drawing all times nearer to this holy day.

PEGEEN And myself, a girl, was tempted often to go sailing the seas till I'd marry a Jew-man, with ten kegs of gold, and I not knowing at all there was the like of you drawing nearer, like the stars of God.

CHRISTY And to think I'm long years hearing women talking that talk, to all bloody fools, and this the first time I've heard the like of your voice talking sweetly for my own delight.

PEGEEN And to think it's me is talking sweetly, Christy Mahon, and I the fright of seven townlands for my biting tongue. Well, the heart's a wonder; and, I'm thinking, there won't be our like in Mayo, for gallant lovers, from this hour, today. (*Drunken singing is heard outside*) There's my father coming from the wake, and when he's had his sleep we'll tell him, for he's peaceful then. (*They separate*)

MICHAEL (*Singing outside*)

The jailor and the turnkey
They quickly ran us down,
And brought us back as prisoners
Once more to Cavan town.

(*He comes in supported by* SHAWN)

There we lay bewailing
All in a prison bound. . . .

(*He sees* CHRISTY. *Goes and shakes him drunkenly by the hand, while* PEGEEN *and* SHAWN *talk on the left*)

MICHAEL (*To* CHRISTY) The blessing of God and the holy angels on your head, young fellow. I hear tell you're after winning all in the sports below; and wasn't it a shame I didn't bear you along with me to Kate Cassidy's wake, a fine, stout lad, the like of you, for you'd never see the match of it for flows of drink, the way when we sunk her bones at noonday in her narrow grave, there were five men, aye, and six men, stretched out retching speechless on the holy stones.

CHRISTY (*Uneasily, watching* PEGEEN) Is that the truth?

MICHAEL It is then, and aren't you a louty schemer to go burying your poor father unbeknownst when you'd a right to throw him on the crupper of a Kerry mule and drive him westwards, like holy Joseph in the days gone by, the way we could have given him a decent burial, and not have him rotting beyond, and not a Christian drinking a smart drop to the glory of his soul?

CHRISTY (*Gruffly*) It's well enough he's lying, for the likes of him.

MICHAEL (*Slapping him on the back*) Well, aren't you a hardened slayer? It'll be a poor thing for the household man where you go sniffing for a female wife; and (*Pointing to* SHAWN) look beyond at that shy and decent Christian I have chosen for my daughter's hand, and I after getting the gilded dispensation this day for to wed them now.

CHRISTY And you'll be wedding them this day, is it?

MICHAEL (*Drawing himself up*) Aye. Are you thinking, if I'm drunk itself, I'd leave my daughter living single with a little frisky rascal is the like of you?

PEGEEN (*Breaking away from* SHAWN) Is it the truth the dispensation's come?

MICHAEL (*Triumphantly*) Father Reilly's after reading it in gallous[5] Latin, and "It's come in the nick of time," says he; "so I'll wed them in a hurry, dreading that young gaffer who'd capsize the stars."

PEGEEN (*Fiercely*) He's missed his nick of time, for it's that lad, Christy Mahon, that I'm wedding now.

MICHAEL (*Loudly with horror*) You'd be making him a son to me, and he wet and crusted with his father's blood?

PEGEEN Aye. Wouldn't it be a bitter thing for a girl to go marrying the like of Shaneen, and he a middling kind of a scarecrow, with no savagery or fine words in him at all?

MICHAEL (*Gasping and sinking on a chair*) Oh, aren't you a heathen daughter to go shaking the fat of my heart, and I swamped and drownded with the weight of drink? Would you have them turning on me the way that I'd be roaring to the dawn of day with the wind upon my heart? Have you not a word to aid me, Shaneen? Are you not jealous at all?

SHAWN (*In great misery*) I'd be afeard to be jealous of a man did slay his da.

PEGEEN Well, it'd be a poor thing to go marrying your like. I'm seeing there's a world of peril for an orphan girl, and isn't it a great blessing I didn't wed you, before himself came walking from the west or south?

SHAWN It's a queer story you'd go picking a dirty tramp up from the highways of the world.

PEGEEN (*Playfully*) And you think you're a likely beau to go straying along with, the shiny Sundays of the opening year, when it's sooner on a bullock's liver you'd put a poor girl thinking than on the lily or the rose?

SHAWN And have you no mind of my weight of

[5] Fine-sounding, over-acted.

passion, and the holy dispensation, and the drift of heifers I am giving, and the golden ring?

PEGEEN I'm thinking you're too fine for the like of me, Shawn Keogh of Killakeen, and let you go off till you'd find a radiant lady with droves of bullocks on the plains of Meath, and herself bedizened in the diamond jewelries of Pharaoh's ma. That'd be your match, Shaneen. So God save you now! (*She retreats behind* CHRISTY)

SHAWN Won't you hear me telling you . . . ?

CHRISTY (*With ferocity*) Take yourself from this, young fellow, or I'll maybe add a murder to my deeds today.

MICHAEL (*Springing up with a shriek*) Murder is it? Is it mad yous are? Would you go making murder in this place, and it piled with poteen for our drink tonight? Go on to the foreshore if it's fighting you want, where the rising tide will wash all traces from the memory of man. (*Pushing* SHAWN *toward* CHRISTY)

SHAWN (*Shaking himself free, and getting behind* MICHAEL) I'll not fight him, Michael James. I'd liefer live a bachelor, simmering in passions to the end of time, than face a lepping savage the like of him has descended from the Lord knows where. Strike him yourself, Michael James, or you'll lose my drift of heifers and my blue bull from Sneem.

MICHAEL Is it me fight him, when it's father-slaying he's bred to now? (*Pushing* SHAWN) Go on, you fool, and fight him now.

SHAWN (*Coming forward a little*) Will I strike him with my hand?

MICHAEL Take the loy is on your western side.

SHAWN I'd be afeard of the gallows if I struck him with that.

CHRISTY (*Taking up the loy*) Then I'll make you face the gallows or quit off from this.

(SHAWN *flies out of the door*)

CHRISTY Well, fine weather be after him (*Going to* MICHAEL, *coaxingly*) and I'm thinking you wouldn't wish to have that quaking blackguard in your house at all. Let you give us your blessing and hear her swear her faith to me, for I'm mounted on the springtide of the stars of luck, the way it'll be good for any to have me in the house.

PEGEEN (*At the other side of* MICHAEL) Bless us now, for I swear to God I'll wed him, and I'll not renege.

MICHAEL (*Standing up in the centre, holding on to both of them*) It's the will of God, I'm thinking, that all should win an easy or a cruel end, and it's the will of God that all should rear up lengthy families for the nurture of the earth. What's a single man, I ask you, eating a bit in one house and drinking a sup in another, and he with no place of his own, like an old braying jackass strayed upon the rocks? (*To* CHRISTY) It's many would be in dread to bring your like into their house for to end them, maybe, with a sudden end; but I'm a decent man of Ireland, and I liefer face the grave untimely and I seeing a score of grandsons growing up little gallant swearers by the name of God, than go peopling my bedside with puny weeds the like of what you'd breed, I'm thinking, out of Shaneen Keogh. (*He joins their hands*) A daring fellow is the jewel of the world, and a man did split his father's middle with a single clout, should have the bravery of ten, so may God and Mary and St. Patrick bless you, and increase you from this mortal day.

CHRISTY AND PEGEEN Amen, O Lord!

(*Hubbub outside*)

(*Old* MAHON *rushes in, followed by all the crowd, and* WIDOW QUIN. *He makes a rush at* CHRISTY, *knocks him down, and begins to beat him*)

PEGEEN (*Dragging back his arm*) Stop that, will you? Who are you at all?

MAHON His father, God forgive me!

PEGEEN (*Drawing back*) Is it rose from the dead?

MAHON Do you think I look so easy quenched with the tap of a loy? (*Beats* CHRISTY *again*)

PEGEEN (*Glaring at* CHRISTY) And it's lies you told, letting on you had him slitted, and you nothing at all.

CHRISTY (*Catching* MAHON'S *stick*) He's not my father. He's a raving maniac would scare the world. (*Pointing to* WIDOW QUIN) Herself knows it is true.

CROWD You're fooling Pegeen! The Widow Quin seen him this day, and you likely knew! You're a liar!

CHRISTY (*Dumbfounded*) It's himself was a liar, lying stretched out with an open head on him, letting on he was dead.

MAHON Weren't you off racing the hills before I got my breath with the start I had seeing you turn on me at all?

PEGEEN And to think of the coaxing glory we had given him, and he after doing nothing but hitting a soft blow and chasing northward in a sweat of fear. Quit off from this.

CHRISTY (*Piteously*) You've seen my doings this day, and let you save me from the old man; for why would you be in such a scorch of haste to spur me to destruction now?

PEGEEN It's there your treachery is spurring me, till I'm hard set to think you're the one I'm after lacing in my heart-strings half-an-hour gone by. (*To* MAHON) Take him on from this, for I think bad the world should see me raging for a Munster liar, and the fool of men.

MAHON Rise up now to retribution, and come on with me.

CROWD (*Jeeringly*) There's the playboy! There's the lad thought he'd rule the roost in Mayo. Slate[6] him now, mister.

CHRISTY (*Getting up in shy terror*) What is it drives you to torment me here, when I'd asked the thunders of the might of God to blast me if I ever did hurt to any saving only that one single blow.

MAHON (*Loudly*) If you didn't, you're a poor good-for-nothing, and isn't it by the like of you the sins of the whole world are committed?

CHRISTY (*Raising his hands*) In the name of the Almighty God. . . .

[6] Let him have it; give him a good scolding.

MAHON Leave troubling the Lord God. Would you have him sending down droughts, and fevers, and the old hen and the cholera morbus?

CHRISTY (*To* WIDOW QUIN) Will you come between us and protect me now?

WIDOW QUIN I've tried a lot, God help me, and my share is done.

CHRISTY (*Looking round in desperation*) And I must go back into my torment is it, or run off like a vagabond straying through the unions[7] with the dusts of August making mudstains in the gullet of my throat, or the winds of March blowing on me till I'd take an oath I felt them making whistles of my ribs within?

SARA Ask Pegeen to aid you. Her like does often change.

CHRISTY I will not then, for there's torment in the splendour of her like, and she a girl any moon of midnight would take pride to meet, facing southwards on the heaths of Keel. But what did I want crawling forward to scorch my understanding at her flaming brow?

PEGEEN (*To* MAHON, *vehemently, fearing she will break into tears*) Take him on from this or I'll set the young lads to destroy him here.

MAHON (*Going to him, shaking his stick*) Come on now if you wouldn't have the company to see you skelped.

PEGEEN (*Half laughing, through her tears*) That's it, now the world will see him pandied,[8] and he an ugly liar was playing off the hero, and the fright of men.

CHRISTY (*To* MAHON, *very sharply*) Leave me go!

CROWD That's it. Now, Christy. If them two set fighting, it will lick the world.

MAHON (*Making a grab at* CHRISTY) Come here to me.

CHRISTY (*More threateningly*) Leave me go, I'm saying.

MAHON I will maybe, when your legs is limping, and your back is blue.

CROWD Keep it up, the two of you. I'll back the old one. Now the playboy.

CHRISTY (*In low and intense voice*) Shut your yelling, for if you're after making a mighty man of me this day by the power of a lie, you're setting me now to think if it's a poor thing to be lonesome, it's worse maybe to go mixing with the fools of earth.

(MAHON *makes a movement toward him*)

CHRISTY (*Almost shouting*) Keep off . . . lest I do show a blow unto the lot of you would set the guardian angels winking in the clouds above. (*He swings round with a sudden rapid movement and picks up a loy*)

CROWD (*Half frightened, half amused*) He's going mad! Mind yourselves! Run from the idiot!

CHRISTY If I am an idiot, I'm after hearing my voice this day saying words would raise the topknot on a poet in a merchant's town. I've won your racing, your lepping, and . . .

MAHON Shut your gullet and come on with me.

CHRISTY I'm going, but I'll stretch you first.

(*He runs at old* MAHON *with the loy, chases him out of the door, followed by crowd and* WIDOW QUIN. *There is a great noise outside, then a yell, and dead silence for a moment.* CHRISTY *comes in, half dazed, and goes to fire*)

WIDOW QUIN (*Coming in, hurriedly, and going to him*) They're turning again you. Come on, or you'll be hanged, indeed.

CHRISTY I'm thinking, from this out, Pegeen'll be giving me praises the same as in the hours gone by.

WIDOW QUIN (*Impatiently*) Come by the back-door. I'd think bad to have you stifled on the gallows tree.

CHRISTY (*Indignantly*) I will not, then. What good'd be my life-time, if I left Pegeen?

WIDOW QUIN Come on, and you'll be no worse than you were last night; and you with a double murder this time to be telling to the girls.

CHRISTY I'll not leave Pegeen Mike.

WIDOW QUIN (*Impatiently*) Isn't there the match of her in every parish public, from Binghamstown unto the plain of Meath? Come on, I tell you, and I'll find you finer sweethearts at each waning moon.

CHRISTY It's Pegeen I'm seeking only, and what'd I care if you brought me a drift of chosen females, standing in their shifts itself, maybe, from this place to the Eastern World?

SARA (*Runs in, pulling off one of her petticoats*) They're going to hang him. (*Holding out petticoat and shawl*) Fit these upon him, and let him run off to the east.

WIDOW QUIN He's raving now; but we'll fit them on him, and I'll take him, in the ferry, to the Achill boat.

CHRISTY (*Struggling feebly*) Leave me go, will you? When I'm thinking of my luck today, for she will wed me surely, and I a proven hero in the end of all.

(*They try to fasten petticoat round him*)

WIDOW QUIN Take his left hand, and we'll pull him now. Come on, young fellow.

CHRISTY (*Suddenly starting up*) You'll be taking me from her? You're jealous, is it, of her wedding me? Go on from this. (*He snatches up a stool, and threatens them with it*)

WIDOW QUIN (*Going*) It's in the mad-house they should put him, not in jail, at all. We'll go by the back-door, to call the doctor, and we'll save him so.

(*She goes out, with* SARA, *through inner room. Men crowd in the doorway.* CHRISTY *sits down again by the fire*)

MICHAEL (*In a terrified whisper*) Is the old lad killed surely?

PHILLY I'm after feeling the last gasps quitting his heart.

(*They peer in at* CHRISTY)

MICHAEL (*With a rope*) Look at the way he is. Twist a hangman's knot on it, and slip it over his head, while he's not minding at all.

PHILLY Let you take it, Shaneen. You're the soberest of all that's here.

[7] Wandering from one parish workhouse to another.

[8] Beaten and exposed.

SHAWN Is it me to go near him, and he the wickedest and worst with me? Let you take it, Pegeen Mike.

PEGEEN Come on, so.

(*She goes forward with the others, and they drop the double hitch over his head*)

CHRISTY What ails you?

SHAWN (*Triumphantly, as they pull the rope tight on his arms*) Come on to the peelers, till they stretch you now.

CHRISTY Me!

MICHAEL If we took pity on you, the Lord God would, maybe, bring us ruin from the law today, so you'd best come easy, for hanging is an easy and a speedy end.

CHRISTY I'll not stir. (*To* PEGEEN) And what is it you'll say to me, and I after doing it this time in the face of all?

PEGEEN I'll say, a strange man is a marvel, with his mighty talk; but what's a squabble in your back-yard, and the blow of a loy, have taught me that there's a great gap between a gallous story and a dirty deed. (*To* MEN) Take him on from this, or the lot of us will be likely put on trial for his deed to-day.

CHRISTY (*With horror in his voice*) And it's yourself will send me off, to have a horny-fingered hangman hitching his bloody slip-knots at the butt of my ear.

MEN (*Pulling rope*) Come on, will you?

(*He is pulled down on the floor*)

CHRISTY (*Twisting his legs round the table*) Cut the rope, Pegeen, and I'll quit the lot of you, and live from this out, like the madmen of Keel, eating muck and green weeds, on the faces of the cliffs.

PEGEEN And leave us to hang, is it, for a saucy liar, the like of you? (*To* MEN) Take him on, out from this.

SHAWN Pull a twist on his neck, and squeeze him so.

PHILLY Twist yourself. Sure he cannot hurt you, if you keep your distance from his teeth alone.

SHAWN I'm afeard of him. (*To* PEGEEN) Lift a lighted sod, will you, and scorch his leg.

PEGEEN (*Blowing the fire, with a bellows*) Leave go now, young fellow, or I'll scorch your shins.

CHRISTY You're blowing for to torture me. (*His voice rising and growing stronger*) That's your kind, is it? Then let the lot of you be wary, for, if I've to face the gallows, I'll have a gay march down, I tell you, and shed the blood of some of you before I die.

SHAWN (*In terror*) Keep a good hold, Philly. Be wary, for the love of God. For I'm thinking he would liefest wreak his pains on me.

CHRISTY (*Almost gaily*) If I do lay my hands on you, it's the way you'll be at the fall of night, hanging as a scarecrow for the fowls of hell. Ah, you'll have a gallous jaunt I'm saying, coaching out through Limbo with my father's ghost.

SHAWN (*To* PEGEEN) Make haste, will you? Oh, isn't he a holy terror, and isn't it true for Father Reilly, that all drink's a curse that has the lot of you so shaky and uncertain now?

CHRISTY If I can wring a neck among you, I'll have a royal judgment looking on the trembling jury in the courts of law. And won't there be crying out in Mayo the day I'm stretched upon the rope with ladies in their silks and satins snivelling in their lacy kerchiefs, and they rhyming songs and ballads on the terror of my fate? (*He squirms round on the floor and bites* SHAWN'*s leg*)

SHAWN (*Shrieking*) My leg's bit on me. He's the like of a mad dog, I'm thinking, the way that I will surely die.

CHRISTY (*Delighted with himself*) You will then, the way you can shake out hell's flags of welcome for my coming in two weeks or three, for I'm thinking Satan hasn't many have killed their da in Kerry, and in Mayo too.

(*Old* MAHON *comes in behind on all fours and looks on unnoticed*)

MEN (*To* PEGEEN) Bring the sod, will you?

PEGEEN (*Coming over*) God help him so. (*Burns his leg*)

CHRISTY (*Kicking and screaming*) O, glory be to God!

(*He kicks loose from the table, and they all drag him toward the door*)

JIMMY (*Seeing old* MAHON) Will you look what's come in?

(*They all drop* CHRISTY *and run left*)

CHRISTY (*Scrambling on his knees face to face with old* MAHON) Are you coming to be killed a third time, or what ails you now?

MAHON For what is it they have you tied?

CHRISTY They're taking me to the peelers to have me hanged for slaying you.

MICHAEL (*Apologetically*) It is the will of God that all should guard their little cabins from the treachery of law, and what would my daughter be doing if I was ruined or was hanged itself?

MAHON (*Grimly, loosening* CHRISTY) It's little I care if you put a bag on her back, and went picking cockles till the hour of death; but my son and myself will be going our own way, and we'll have great times from this out telling stories of the villainy of Mayo, and the fools is here. (*To* CHRISTY, *who is freed*) Come on now.

CHRISTY Go with you, is it? I will then, like a gallant captain with his heathen slave. Go on now and I'll see you from this day stewing my oatmeal and washing my spuds, for I'm master of all fights from now. (*Pushing* MAHON) Go on, I'm saying.

MAHON Is it me?

CHRISTY Not a word out of you. Go on from this.

MAHON (*Walking out and looking back at* CHRISTY *over his shoulder*) Glory be to God! (*With a broad smile*) I am crazy again! (*Goes*)

CHRISTY Ten thousand blessings upon all that's here, for you've turned me a likely gaffer in the end of all, the way I'll go romancing through a romping lifetime from this hour to the dawning of the judgment day. (*He goes out*)

MICHAEL By the will of God, we'll have peace now for our drinks. Will you draw the porter, Pegeen?

SHAWN (*Going up to her*) It's a miracle Father Reilly can wed us in the end of all, and we'll have none to trouble us when his vicious bite is healed.

PEGEEN (*Hitting him a box on the ear*) Quit my sight. (*Putting her shawl over her head and breaking out into wild lamentations*) Oh, my grief, I've lost him surely. I've lost the only Playboy of the Western World.

*Curtain*

# William Butler Yeats

## (1865-1939)

INCREASINGLY regarded as the greatest poet of the English language in the twentieth century, Yeats deserves far more attention as a playwright than he has generally received. His great contribution to the modern theatre lies in his fusion of poetry and the drama. In the course of his long and productive career, Yeats wrote over 30 plays. His drama makes unusual and at times even impossible demands on actors and spectators, and it is no wonder that few of his plays are performed. Nevertheless, they represent a fresh and vital effort to reshape the contemporary theatre, and the best of them are in perpetual readiness for rediscovery.

Born near Dublin of a Protestant and Anglo-Irish family, Yeats spent much of his youth in London and always remained close to the English literary scene. His mother came from Sligo in western Ireland, where he came to know the rhythmic speech of the peasant and the folklore of popular superstition. A genuine belief in magic and the occult pervades all of Yeats' writing, early and late. He shares with the continental symbolist poets and playwrights an intimate concern with dream-life, reverie, and private vision as reflections of an underlying spiritual reality. Yeats saw the myths and legends of pagan Ireland as a means of recovering the supernatural in both poetry and the theatre. Under the impact of a surge of nationalism in Ireland at the end of the nineteenth century, and with the aid of a number of important new histories and collections of Celtic myth and legend, Yeats sought to recapture the bardic tradition of ancient saga and song. In 1899, with Lady Gregory, he launched the Irish Literary Theatre, aiming at a repertory of plays on native subjects written by native playwrights and performed by native actors. In 1904, aided by an English patron, Miss Horniman, he founded the Abbey Theatre in Dublin. It opened with a performance of his play, *On Baile's Strand*, and throughout most of its history the Abbey was closely connected with Yeats' efforts in the theatre. The creation of the Irish dramatic movement and its vital role in the theatre of our time are in large measure due to Yeats' integrity and dedication.

From the beginning, he aimed at an unpopular theatre. Lady Gregory later remarked, "We went on giving what we thought good until it became popular." Yeats refused to cater to the box office or to compromise with the demands of political or religious fanaticism. He tried for many years to turn the Dublin public away from Philistinism and crude prejudice, and to create conditions that would make possible a living poetic drama. "Our plays," he declared, "must be literature or written in the spirit of literature." The triumph of his aims may be seen in the plays of Synge, yet nothing so embittered Yeats' relation to his public as the riots of 1907 over *The Playboy of the Western World*. This event marks a turning point in Yeats' career in the theatre.

His early compositions of the 1890's and the following decade are pale reflections of what he called "the Celtic twilight," misty and romantic evocations of ancient legend and popular superstition. Many of the early plays were first written as dramatic poems and then revised, often more than once, for performance. Down to the end of his life Yeats continued to rework his early dramas, and it is revealing to compare the versions included in different editions of his works. *The Countess Cathleen* (1892), portraying the self-sacrifice and redemption of a great soul, freely combines the supernatural and the everyday. *The Land of Heart's Desire* (1894) reveals the presence of strange and magical powers free from human control: the pagan fairy-child summons the heroine to a new life through death. The quest for spiritual fulfillment through liberation from earth-bound experience is also present in *The Shadowy Waters* (1900), a verse play reminiscent of Villiers de l'Isle-Adam's *Axël* which Yeats saw in Paris in 1894 and which moved him toward symbolist drama. Dectora and Forgael become one through a death that transports them to the realm of transcendental love. As in many symbolist dramas, the lyricism moves inward toward the expression of mood and feeling rather than outward toward the concreteness of physical action.

Yet even in his early plays, Yeats attempted to go beyond "static drama" to the creation of a sustained pattern of action. As early as 1892 he had begun writing poetry based on the exploits of Cuchulain, the chief hero of the Ulster Cycle of Irish heroic myth. Reputed to be of divine origin, he acquired his name, meaning "Caulann's hound," at the age of six when he killed a bloodhound that had the strength of nine men. A druid predicted he would have great fame and a short life. According to the saga, Cuchulain died at 27, either in a war of revenge, or fighting the waves in a fit of madness after slaying an unknown challenger discovered to be his son. This last event is the subject of *On Baile's Strand* (1903), probably the best of Yeats' early plays. The dialogue of the Fool and the Blind Man provides a frame to the action as well as the requisite exposition, and mediates effectively between the heroic characters and the audience. In *Deirdre* (1907) Yeats fused a language of rich poetic evocation with a melodramatic portrayal of the lovers' doom. His efforts at comedy or realistic prose drama were written in collaboration with Lady Gregory, and are markedly inferior to the verse plays.

After 1907 Yeats turned his back on the theatre of public performance and the demands of a mass audience. Inspired by Wagner's and Mallarmé's vision of drama as a collective rite embodying a sacred mystery and prophecy, Yeats developed a drama of complex allusiveness and formal intricacy. From Gordon Craig he acquired a deep interest in the role of masks as an aid in maintaining "an appropriate distance from life." The decisive stimulus was provided by Ezra Pound, who served as Yeats' secretary from 1913 to 1916 and directed him to the Japanese Noh drama. Yeats admired its concentrated action and its complex interrelation of the arts, combining language, mask, mime, song and dance into a mystical and ceremonial revelation of spiritual truth. In his Noh plays Yeats claimed to have invented a new dramatic form, "distinguished, indirect and symbolic, and having no need of mob or press to pay its way—an aristocratic form." In its evocation of mood and feeling, the Noh play as Yeats conceived it is clearly in the symbolist tradition, but the language is stark, bare, and direct, markedly superior to the languorous poetic idiom of the previous decade.

*At the Hawk's Well* (1916) is the first of *Four Plays for Dancers.* Yeats wrote the play for performance in a drawing room before a select audience, with a bare stage and only a patterned screen for a set, and with the curtain replaced by the folding or unfolding of the cloth. The drama portrays events in the early history of Cuchulain which foreshadow his later career. Originally entitled *The Well of Immortality*, it depicts the futility of the hero's quest. Paralyzed by the dance of the hawk-like Guardian of the Well, he succumbs to the lure of eroticism and loses sight of his mission. Cuchulain is responsible for his own failure; the pursuit of his dream leads only to subsequent pain and destruction. The play is dominated throughout by a sense of defeat and disillusion. The old man exhausted by the quest for immortality points to the vanity of life, while the young and bold-hearted Cuchulain represents man's striving for spiritual transformation. The climax of the action lies not in words but in the dance, with the commentary provided by the final words of the musicians. In the first version of the play, they concluded with a brief statement: "Accursed the life of man—between passion/ and emptiness./ What he longs for never comes." In the final version, the claims of quiet contentment are more indirectly opposed to the vain pursuit of adventure.

Despite the severe demands made on director, actors, and audience, *At the Hawk's Well* is sufficiently distinct and coherent in its dramatic movement to communicate its complex symbolic experience. The subsequent Noh plays are even denser and more subjective. All of them are distinguished by magnificent lyric poetry that is often, but not always, made part of an absorbing dramatic situation. In *The Only Jealousy of Emer* (1918), Cuchulain's wife sacrifices herself that he may live. *The Dreaming of the Bones* (1918) welds together myth and recent history, with the ancient dead reliving the tragic experiences of their lives. *Calvary* (1920) contrasts Christ with those He cannot save—Lazarus, Judas, and the Roman soldiers: "God has not died for the white heron." Yeats was to treat this theme again in *Resurrection* (1925), a debate on the nature of Christ between three followers of Jesus. The ideological conflict is resolved by the sudden appearance of the figure of Jesus before the disputants—a momentous shock that brings the drama to a vivid climax. All of these plays are marked by the esoteric symbolism of the private mythology that Yeats invented late in life. Literal clarity is not to be sought for, yet the very density of Yeats' art is a source of compelling fascination and wonder.

Not all of Yeats' late dramas are Noh plays, but all are marked by the same passion for formal experiment and philosophical depth. *The Cat and the Moon* (1924) is at once personal satire and a reflection of the cyclical pattern of history. *The Words upon the Window Pane* (1932) invokes the spirits of Jonathan Swift and Vanessa through the seance of a Dublin medium. *A Full Moon in March* (1935), like its earlier version, *The King of the Great Clock Tower*, portrays the compulsion and pain of love in the history of a Swineherd, a mythic analogue of Orpheus and Dionysus, who comes to court a Queen and is slain for his presumption; his severed head triumphs in song over her "virgin cruelty." Perhaps the best known of the last plays is *Purgatory* (1938), a stark and dramatically effective re-enacting of an ancient crime during a futile attempt at expiation. The ritual murder reflects the aged Yeats' dark philosophy of history. *The Herne's Egg* (1938) reveals the sexual power of a mysterious deity and the disaster that comes to those who challenge him. Yeats' last play, *The Death of Cuchulain* (1939), explicitly re-echoes the themes and motifs of a number of the earlier dramas. The play is shocking not only in its brutal violence, but in its speech of blunt sexuality. The harlot's song at the end is a passionate questioning of the value of a life of poetic endeavor.

Yeats remarked of his *Four Plays for Dancers*, "In writing these little plays I knew that I was creating something which could only fully succeed in a civilization very unlike ours." His impact on the contemporary stage has been slight indeed, yet his exploration of the possibilities of dramatic expression is of enduring significance. As T. S. Eliot declared, in Yeats' work "the idea of the poetic drama was kept alive when everywhere else it had been driven underground." Eliot's personal indebtedness to Yeats' fusion of poetry and drama is incalculable. Yeats' later plays contain some of the most intense and arresting poetry in the English language, yet he was a playwright as well as a poet, keenly aware of the resources of the drama and the demands of the art form. His plays remain a powerful assertion of the claims of poetry in the theatre.

# AT THE HAWK'S WELL

PERSONS IN THE PLAY

THREE MUSICIANS (*their faces made up to resemble masks*)
THE GUARDIAN OF THE WELL (*with face made up to resemble a mask*)
AN OLD MAN (*wearing a mask*)
A YOUNG MAN (*wearing a mask*)

TIME *the Irish Heroic Age*

*The stage is any bare space before a wall against which stands a patterned screen. A drum and a gong and a zither have been laid close to the screen before the play begins. If necessary, they can be carried in, after the audience is seated, by the* FIRST MUSICIAN, *who also can attend to the lights if there is any special lighting. We had two lanterns upon posts—designed by Mr. Dulac—at the outer corners of the stage, but they did not give enough light, and we found it better to play by the light of a large chandelier. Indeed, I think, so far as my present experience goes, that the most effective lighting is the lighting we are most accustomed to in our rooms. These masked players seem stranger when there is no mechanical means of separating them from us. The* FIRST MUSICIAN *carries with him a folded black cloth and goes to the centre of the stage towards the front and stands motionless, the folded cloth hanging from between his hands. The two other* MUSICIANS *enter and, after standing a moment at either side of the stage, go towards him and slowly unfold the cloth, singing as they do so:*

I call to the eye of the mind
A well long choked up and dry
And boughs long stripped by the wind,
And I call to the mind's eye
Pallor of an ivory face,
Its lofty dissolute air,
A man climbing up to a place
The salt sea wind has swept bare.

*As they unfold the cloth, they go backward a little so that the stretched cloth and the wall make a triangle with the* FIRST MUSICIAN *at the apex supporting the centre of the cloth. On the black cloth is a gold pattern suggesting a hawk. The* SECOND *and* THIRD MUSICIANS *now slowly fold up the cloth again, pacing with a rhythmic movement of the arms towards the* FIRST MUSICIAN *and singing:*

What were his life soon done!
Would he lose by that or win?
A mother that saw her son
Doubled over a speckled shin,
Cross-grained with ninety years,
Would cry, "How little worth
Were all my hopes and fears
And the hard pain of his birth!"

*The words "a speckled shin" are familiar to readers of Irish legendary stories in descriptions of old men bent double over the fire. While the cloth has been spread out, the* GUARDIAN OF THE WELL *has entered and is now crouching upon the ground. She is entirely covered by a black cloak; beside her lies a square blue cloth to represent a well. The three* MUSICIANS *have taken their places against the wall beside their instruments of music; they will accompany the movements of the players with gong or drum or zither.*

FIRST MUSICIAN (*Singing*)
The boughs of the hazel shake,
The sun goes down in the west.

SECOND MUSICIAN (*Singing*)
The heart would be always awake,
The heart would turn to its rest.

(*They now go to one side of the stage rolling up the cloth*)

FIRST MUSICIAN (*Speaking*) Night falls;
The mountain-side grows dark;
The withered leaves of the hazel
Half choke the dry bed of the well;
The guardian of the well is sitting
Upon the old grey stone at its side,

Worn out from raking its dry bed,
Worn out from gathering up the leaves.
Her heavy eyes
Know nothing, or but look upon stone.
The wind that blows out of the sea
Turns over the heaped-up leaves at her side;
They rustle and diminish.

SECOND MUSICIAN I am afraid of this place.

BOTH MUSICIANS (*Singing*)
"Why should I sleep?" the heart cries,
"For the wind, the salt wind, the sea wind,
Is beating a cloud through the skies;
I would wander always like the wind."

(*An* OLD MAN *enters through the audience*)

FIRST MUSICIAN (*Speaking*) That old man climbs up hither,
Who has been watching by his well
These fifty years.
He is all doubled up with age;
The old thorn-trees are doubled so
Among the rocks where he is climbing.

(*The* OLD MAN *stands for a moment motionless by the side of the stage with bowed head. He lifts his head at the sound of a drumtap. He goes toward the front of the stage moving to the taps of the drum. He crouches and moves his hands as if making a fire. His movements, like those of the other persons of the play, suggest a marionette*)

FIRST MUSICIAN (*Speaking*) He has made a little heap of leaves;
He lays the dry sticks on the leaves
And, shivering with cold, he has taken up
The fire-stick and socket from its hole.
He whirls it round to get a flame;
And now the dry sticks take the fire,
And now the fire leaps up and shines
Upon the hazels and the empty well.

MUSICIANS (*Singing*)
"O wind, O salt wind, O sea wind!"
Cries the heart, "it is time to sleep;
Why wander and nothing to find?
Better grow old and sleep."

OLD MAN (*Speaking*) Why don't you speak to me? Why don't you say:
"Are you not weary gathering those sticks?
Are not your fingers cold?" You have not one word,
While yesterday you spoke three times. You said:
"The well is full of hazel leaves." You said:
"The wind is from the west." And after that:
"If there is rain it's likely there'll be mud."
To-day you are as stupid as a fish,
No, worse, worse, being less lively and as dumb.
(*He goes nearer*)
Your eyes are dazed and heavy. If the Sidhe[1]
Must have a guardian to clean out the well
And drive the cattle off, they might choose somebody
That can be pleasant and companionable
Once in the day. Why do you stare like that?
You had that glassy look about the eyes
Last time it happened. Do you know anything?
It is enough to drive an old man crazy
To look all day upon these broken rocks,
And ragged thorns, and that one stupid face,
And speak and get no answer.

YOUNG MAN (*Who has entered through the audience during the last speech*) Then speak to me,
For youth is not more patient than old age;
And though I have trod the rocks for half a day
I cannot find what I am looking for.

OLD MAN Who speaks?
Who comes so suddenly into this place
Where nothing thrives? If I may judge by the gold
On head and feet and glittering in your coat,
You are not of those who hate the living world.

YOUNG MAN I am named Cuchulain, I am Sualtim's son.[2]

OLD MAN I have never heard that name.

YOUNG MAN It is not unknown.
I have an ancient house beyond the sea.

OLD MAN What mischief brings you hither?—you are like those
Who are crazy for the shedding of men's blood,
And for the love of women.

YOUNG MAN A rumour has led me,
A story told over the wine towards dawn.
I rose from table, found a boat, spread sail,
And with a lucky wind under the sail
Crossed waves that have seemed charmed, and found this shore.

OLD MAN There is no house to sack among these hills
Nor beautiful woman to be carried off.

YOUNG MAN You should be native here, for that rough tongue
Matches the barbarous spot. You can, it may be,
Lead me to what I seek, a well wherein
Three hazels drop their nuts and withered leaves,
And where a solitary girl keeps watch
Among grey boulders. He who drinks, they say,
Of that miraculous water lives for ever.

OLD MAN And are there not before your eyes at the instant
Grey boulders and a solitary girl
And three stripped hazels?

YOUNG MAN But there is no well.

OLD MAN Can you see nothing yonder?

YOUNG MAN I but see
A hollow among stones half-full of leaves.

OLD MAN And do you think so great a gift is found
By no more toil than spreading out a sail,
And climbing a steep hill? O, folly of youth,
Why should that hollow place fill up for you,
That will not fill for me? I have lain in wait
For more than fifty years, to find it empty,
Or but to find the stupid wind of the sea

[1] An ancient divine race (pronounced "Shee") that had once possessed Ireland. Conquered by other gods, they became invisible and made their home in the hills and countryside.

[2] The warrior Sualtim, a vague and shadowy figure of Irish myth, was held to be Cuchulain's mortal father. Cuchulain claimed supernatural descent as the son of Lugh, the Sun-God.

Drive round the perishable leaves.
YOUNG MAN So it seems
There is some moment when the water fills it.
OLD MAN A secret moment that the holy shades
That dance upon the desolate mountain know,
And not a living man, and when it comes
The water has scarce plashed before it is gone.
YOUNG MAN I will stand here and wait. Why should the luck
Of Sualtim's son desert him now? For never
Have I had long to wait for anything.
OLD MAN No! Go from this accursed place! This place
Belongs to me, that girl there, and those others,
Deceivers of men.
YOUNG MAN And who are you who rail
Upon those dancers that all others bless?
OLD MAN One whom the dancers cheat. I came like you
When young in body and in mind, and blown
By what had seemed to me a lucky sail.
The well was dry, I sat upon its edge,
I waited the miraculous flood, I waited
While the years passed and withered me away.
I have snared the birds for food and eaten grass
And drunk the rain, and neither in dark nor shine
Wandered too far away to have heard the plash,
And yet the dancers have deceived me. Thrice
I have awakened from a sudden sleep
To find the stones were wet.
YOUNG MAN My luck is strong,
It will not leave me waiting, nor will they
That dance among the stones put me asleep;
If I grow drowsy I can pierce my foot.
OLD MAN No, do not pierce it, for the foot is tender,
It feels pain much. But find your sail again
And leave the well to me, for it belongs
To all that's old and withered.
YOUNG MAN No, I stay.
(*The* GUARDIAN OF THE WELL *gives the cry of the hawk*)
There is that bird again.
OLD MAN There is no bird.
YOUNG MAN It sounded like the sudden cry of a hawk,
But there's no wing in sight. As I came hither
A great grey hawk swept down out of the sky,
And though I have good hawks, the best in the world
I had fancied, I have not seen its like. It flew
As though it would have torn me with its beak,
Or blinded me, smiting with that great wing.
I had to draw my sword to drive it off,
And after that it flew from rock to rock.
I pelted it with stones, a good half-hour,
And just before I had turned the big rock there
And seen this place, it seemed to vanish away.
Could I but find a means to bring it down
I'd hood it.
OLD MAN The Woman of the Sidhe herself,
The mountain witch, the unappeasable shadow.
She is always flitting upon this mountain-side,
To allure or to destroy. When she has shown
Herself to the fierce women of the hills
Under that shape they offer sacrifice
And arm for battle. There falls a curse
On all who have gazed in her unmoistened eyes;
So get you gone while you have that proud step
And confident voice, for not a man alive
Has so much luck that he can play with it.
Those that have long to live should fear her most,
The old are cursed already. That curse may be
Never to win a woman's love and keep it;
Or always to mix hatred in the love;
Or it may be that she will kill your children,
That you will find them, their throats torn and bloody,
Or you will be so maddened that you kill them
With your own hand.
YOUNG MAN Have you been set down there
To threaten all who come, and scare them off?
You seem as dried up as the leaves and sticks,
As though you had no part in life.
(*The* GUARDIAN OF THE WELL *gives hawk cry again*)
That cry!
There is that cry again. That woman made it,
But why does she cry out as the hawk cries?
OLD MAN It was her mouth, and yet not she, that cried.
It was that shadow cried behind her mouth;
And now I know why she has been so stupid
All the day through, and had such heavy eyes.
Look at her shivering now, the terrible life
Is slipping through her veins. She is possessed.
Who knows whom she will murder or betray
Before she awakes in ignorance of it all,
And gathers up the leaves? But they'll be wet;
The water will have come and gone again;
That shivering is the sign. O, get you gone,
At any moment now I shall hear it bubble.
If you are good you will leave it. I am old,
And if I do not drink it now, will never;
I have been watching all my life and maybe
Only a little cupful will bubble up.
YOUNG MAN I'll take it in my hands. We shall both drink,
And even if there are but a few drops,
Share them.
OLD MAN But swear that I may drink the first;
The young are greedy, and if you drink the first
You'll drink it all. Ah, you have looked at her;
She has felt your gaze and turned her eyes on us;
I cannot bear her eyes, they are not of this world,
Nor moist, nor faltering; they are no girl's eyes.
(*He covers his head. The* GUARDIAN OF THE WELL *throws off her cloak and rises. Her dress under the cloak suggests a hawk*)
YOUNG MAN Why do you fix those eyes of a hawk upon me?
I am not afraid of you, bird, woman, or witch.
(*He goes to the side of the well, which the* GUARDIAN OF THE WELL *has left*)
Do what you will, I shall not leave this place
Till I have grown immortal like yourself.
(*He has sat down; the* GUARDIAN OF THE WELL *has*

*begun to dance, moving like a hawk. The* OLD MAN *sleeps. The dance goes on for some time*)

FIRST MUSICIAN (*Singing or half-singing*)

O God, protect me
From a horrible deathless body
Sliding through the veins of a sudden.

(*The dance goes on for some time. The* YOUNG MAN *rises slowly*)

FIRST MUSICIAN (*Speaking*) The madness has laid hold upon him now,
For he grows pale and staggers to his feet.

(*The dance goes on*)

YOUNG MAN Run where you will,
Grey bird, you shall be perched upon my wrist.
Some were called queens and yet have been perched there.

(*The dance goes on*)

FIRST MUSICIAN (*Speaking*) I have heard water plash; it comes, it comes;
Look where it glitters. He has heard the plash;
Look, he has turned his head.

(*The* GUARDIAN OF THE WELL *has gone out. The* YOUNG MAN *drops his spear as if in a dream and goes out*)

MUSICIANS (*Singing*)

He has lost what may not be found
Till men heap his burial-mound
And all the history ends.
He might have lived at his ease,
An old dog's head on his knees,
Among his children and friends.

(*The* OLD MAN *creeps up to the well*)

OLD MAN The accursed shadows have deluded me,
The stones are dark and yet the well is empty;
The water flowed and emptied while I slept.
You have deluded me my whole life through,
Accursed dancers, you have stolen my life.
That there should be such evil in a shadow!

YOUNG MAN (*Entering*) She has fled from me and hidden in the rocks.

OLD MAN She has but led you from the fountain. Look!
Though stones and leaves are dark where it has flowed,
There's not a drop to drink.

(*The* MUSICIANS *cry* "Aoife!" "Aoife!" *and strike gong*)

YOUNG MAN What are those cries?
What is that sound that runs along the hill?
Who are they that beat a sword upon a shield?

OLD MAN She has roused up the fierce women of the hills,
Aoife,[3] and all her troop, to take your life,
And never till you are lying in the earth
Can you know rest.

YOUNG MAN The clash of arms again!

OLD MAN O, do not go! The mountain is accursed;
Stay with me, I have nothing more to lose,
I do not now deceive you.

YOUNG MAN I will face them.

(*He goes out, no longer as if in a dream, but shouldering his spear and calling*)

He comes! Cuchulain, son of Sualtim, comes!

(*The* MUSICIANS *stand up; one goes to centre with folded cloth. The others unfold it. While they do so they sing. During the singing, and while hidden by the cloth, the* OLD MAN *goes out. When the play is performed with Mr. Dulac's music, the* MUSICIANS *do not rise or unfold the cloth till after they have sung the words* "a bitter life")

(*Songs for the unfolding and folding of the cloth*)

Come to me, human faces,
Familiar memories;
I have found hateful eyes
Among the desolate places,
Unfaltering, unmoistened eyes.

Folly alone I cherish,
I choose it for my share;
Being but a mouthful of air,
I am content to perish;
I am but a mouthful of sweet air.

O lamentable shadows,
Obscurity of strife!
I choose a pleasant life
Among indolent meadows;
Wisdom must live a bitter life.

(*They then fold up the cloth, singing*)

"The man that I praise,"
Cries out the empty well,
"Lives all his days
Where a hand on the bell
Can call the milch cows
To the comfortable door of his house.
Who but an idiot would praise
Dry stones in a well?"

"The man that I praise,"
Cries out the leafless tree,
"Has married and stays
By an old hearth, and he
On naught has set store
But children and dogs on the floor.
Who but an idiot would praise
A withered tree?"

(*They go out*)

*Curtain*

[3] Aoife was a warrior-queen whom Cuchulain defeated in battle. The two subsequently became lovers. After his departure, Aoife bore Cuchulain a son, Conlaoch, who was later killed by his father unwittingly, in combat.

# Sean O'Casey

## (1880-1964)

SEAN O'CASEY was 43 when, in 1923, he first saw the Abbey Theatre curtains go up on one of his plays. At 47, after three of his finest plays had been performed at the Abbey, he determined to leave Ireland forever. In light of his move in 1927 to England, it is possible to recognize two major periods in his development: the "Irish" and the "International." In the first period, culminating in his brief association with the Abbey directors and actors, O'Casey was deeply involved in modern Ireland's tumultuous history, several chapters of which he recorded in the early plays which brought him fame. During this time O'Casey upheld, but with diminishing enthusiasm, the ideals of Irish nationalism, and in his plays he mastered the realistic mode and the rich Dublin idiom and dialects which give his dialogue its exceptional vitality. The second period is marked by the greatly increased literary and dramatic productivity of an author seeking to support himself through his writings, and by O'Casey's commitment to such essentially international ideals as pacifism and communism. In his later plays, O'Casey abandoned naturalism in favor of allegory in the expressionist manner. Ironically, it is the "Irish" O'Casey whose plays are still most frequently performed. The "International" O'Casey is best known for his autobiographical volumes, several of which have been effectively adapted for concert readings. In both periods, however, O'Casey always dedicated himself to being the self-styled "green crow" whose commonness, despite its Irish greenness, in the Bird Kingdom mirrored O'Casey's sense of himself as a very common man very much a part of the brotherhood of man. O'Casey's early life was marred by strife, poverty, bitter controversy and lonely alienation, but he could still celebrate life in winged words: "Isn't everybody hurrahing for life? What are we going to do without it?"

The "green crow" began life on March 30, 1880, as John Casey, the thirteenth and last child born to Michael and Susan Casey. The predominantly Catholic Dublin of the 1880's was filthy and poverty-stricken, a dismally over-populated world of tenement squalor. O'Casey's parents were dedicated Protestants not, however, like Synge's parents, of the comfortable suburban Anglo-Irish variety. Synge could grow up largely untouched by Ireland's economic and political turmoil, but O'Casey knew the struggle for survival from early childhood. His father, a clerk who devoted much of his energy to the Protestant Irish Church Mission, died when O'Casey was six. His mother, left with the five children who had miraculously not become statistics in Dublin's infant-mortality lists, battled poverty and somehow managed to keep her family together. When O'Casey came to write *Juno and the Paycock* and, much later, *Red Roses for Me,* he paid tribute to her courage and gentle compassion by creating two of his most appealing characters in her image.

Afflicted with a painful eye disease, the young O'Casey was forced into a life of shadowy half-lights. At a very early age, he received slave-wages doing jobs for which, in his physical frailty and waspish temperament, he was ill-suited. In these various and never very permanent jobs, he worked alongside the willing and not-so-willing laborers whose speech and mannerisms later emerged in Jack Boyle and Joxer Daly (in *Juno and the Paycock*) or in The Covey, Fluther Good, and Peter Flynn (in *The Plough and the Stars*). Later, as he assisted Jim Larkin, the energetic union-organizer whose Irish Transport and General Workers Union was responsible for the 1913 Strike and Lock-Out, O'Casey found a cause to which he could subscribe. His unionist loyalties are reflected—not always without an ironic edge—in Mary Boyle and Jerry Devine in *Juno and the Paycock* as well as in the clashing employers, Father Domineer, and the truck-drivers in *Cock-a-Doodle Dandy*. During his early maturity, O'Casey saw the destiny of a free Ireland linked to Labor and Socialism, and he bitterly opposed Capitalism and Irish Clericalism.

In his conviction that Gaelic should be the official language of an Irish Republic, John Casey gaelicized his name as Sean O'Cathasaigh and, under the auspices of the Gaelic League, taught the language in Dublin's slums. In the cause of republicanism, he served as Secretary of the Union-sponsored Irish Citizen Army, created to protect striking workers against harassment by Dublin police. During his twenties, however, he began to realize that Ireland was not always kind to its men of principle, a discovery that became part of the stream of disillusioning events which ultimately led O'Casey into self-exile. He learned that he could support causes but not all the leaders working in those causes. In the Gaelic League, in the Irish Republican Brotherhood, finally even in the Irish Citizen Army, he found it easier to submit his resignation than to compromise his own beliefs. This disenchantment is everywhere apparent in his early plays: having heard highminded idealism and having seen self-serving tactics among nationalists of all persuasions, he brought a rare combination of sympathy and objectivity to his portrayal of Dubliners. As both Insider and Outsider, O'Casey greatly resembled Synge, and like Synge, O'Casey learned to his horror how easy it was to underestimate the emotional flammability of his contemporaries.

Before he began writing plays, O'Casey had achieved modest success with two collections of satirical songs (*Songs of the Wren* and *More Songs of the Wren*), several editorializing articles for labor publications, and two books dealing with the Citizen Army. An early attempt to combine satire and drama, the one-act play, *The Robe of Rosheen,* found its way into a Republican paper. In *Inishfallen Fare Thee Well,* the autobiographical volume dealing with 1916-1926, his last years in Dublin, O'Casey gives a third-person account of how, as he neared 40, he determined to devote more time to writing: "He had shifted away from the active Ireland, and was growing contentedly active in himself. Instead of trying to form Ireland's life, he would shape his own. He would splash his thoughts over what he had seen and heard; keep eyes and ears open to see and hear what life did, what life had to say, and how life said it; life drunk or sober; life sickly or sturdy; life sensible or half demented; life well-off or poor; life on its knees in prayer, or shouting up a wild curse to heaven's centre." All of these faces of life can be found in his plays.

O'Casey submitted three plays (*The Frost in the Flower, The Harvest Festival,* and *The Crimson and the Tri-Color*) before he provided one acceptable to all of the three Abbey Directors, Yeats, Lady Gregory, and Lennox Robinson. His stubborn determination to have an Abbey production of one of his works was surprising because, in the early 1920's, the theatre was, financially and artistically, in dire straits. In April, 1923, when the Abbey opened O'Casey's *The Shadow of a Gunman* for a limited run, it regained, if only for a few years, its lost luster. Submitted as *On the Run,* the play was, except for a title-change, accepted without revision. Set against the 1920 fighting in Dublin between the Irish Republican Army and the British forces, this short tragedy perfectly illustrates the essentially anti-heroic stance the pacifist O'Casey has always taken. Through her senseless, tragic death, a pretty and very impressionable working girl, Minnie Powell, demonstrates the meaning of courage to two self-deluding, ineffectual men: the peddler, Seumas Shields, and the poet-gunman who is neither poet nor brave Republican soldier, Donal Davoren. Although flawed with languor, Seumas also has the coward's wisdom usually found in O'Casey's male characters: "It's the civilians who suffer; when there's an ambush they don't know where to run. Shot in the back to save the British Empire, an' shot in the breast to save the soul of Ireland." When the play was first produced, the 1920 War of Independence had been safely won. Assuming the play was fashionably anti-British, O'Casey's audiences missed much of his double-edged commentary on the folly of one segment of the human community trying to destroy another.

Next, in *Juno and the Paycock* O'Casey explored the chaotic aftermath of the Free State Settlement. Produced just two years after the 1922 civil warfare, the play awakened painful memories of divisive partisanships, many of which were still unforgiven. From O'Casey's perspective, however, the sight of Irishmen interrupting domestic battles only long enough to resist the British was heartbreaking when it was not insanely comic: his compound of comic and tragic elements inevitably irritated some Irishmen. In 1922 the issue had been joined between Free Staters, willing to buy peace by accepting half-a-loaf of independence within the British Empire, and Die-hards, adamant for complete independence. Although O'Casey rose above nationalist politics, there were too many tender sensibilities, Diehard and Free Stater, anti-clericalist and pro-labor, ready to be affronted at any insult, real or imagined. The first rumbles of protest were faint but real. Ironically, however, controversy over O'Casey's political loyalties did not erupt in full violence until March, 1926, when *The Plough and the Stars* opened at the Abbey. In this play, O'Casey had moved back to what seemed a more safely distant period in recent Irish history: the complex 1916 Easter Uprising, when battle lines had been most clearly drawn between Irish and British. Taking his title from the unionist Citizen Army insignia, O'Casey had created a gallery of tenement dwellers who embody major political and religious loyalties of the time. The riots which marked the first performances of *The Plough and the Stars* stirred memories of 1907 and the violent christening of Synge's *Playboy.* Once again Yeats found himself proclaiming the "arrival of Irish genius" and trying to shame a clamorous audience into silence. To O'Casey, however, watching police pulling rioters out of the theatre, it was a sickening spectacle which strengthened his resolve to try his fortunes in another land where he could live and write on his own terms.

Of the three plays produced at the Abbey between 1923 and 1926, *Juno and the Paycock* is the most universal in its appeal. Its deceptively simple structure of a comic reversal-in-expectations is underlined throughout with the spiritual agonies of Johnny Boyle, the menacing presence of the Mobilizers who take justice into their own hands, and the death of Mrs. Tancred's son. By neoclassical standards, O'Casey's bold interweaving of comic and tragic incidents should result in an unsatisfactory play, but in the theatre *Juno and the Paycock* is a perfect fusion of theme and technique. In the final moments of the play, the tragic and the comic are combined in an overwhelming image. With Juno's magnificent final prayer still ringing in the nearly empty flat, O'Casey brings in for our final contemplation his grotesque travesty of the shining peacocks attendant on the classical Juno. Lost in alcoholic reveries of flying columns and dying comrades, Juno's "Paycock" drunkenly blabbers out his slogan, "Th' whole worl's . . . in a terr . . . ible state o' . . . chassis!" It is at once the whole truth and something less than the whole truth, the key to O'Casey's tragicomic view of the twentieth century.

# JUNO AND THE PAYCOCK

## *A Tragedy in Three Acts*

### CHARACTERS

"CAPTAIN" JACK BOYLE
JUNO BOYLE, *his wife*
JOHNNY BOYLE } *their children*
MARY BOYLE
"JOXER" DALY
MRS. MAISIE MADIGAN
"NEEDLE" NUGENT, *a tailor*
MRS. TANCRED
} *Residents in the Tenement*

JERRY DEVINE
CHARLIE BENTHAM, *a school teacher*
AN IRREGULAR MOBILIZER
TWO IRREGULARS
A COAL-BLOCK VENDOR
A SEWING MACHINE MAN
TWO FURNITURE REMOVAL MEN
TWO NEIGHBOURS

SCENE *the living apartment of a two-roomed tenancy of the Boyle family, in a tenement house in Dublin.*

PERIOD OF THE PLAY *1922. A few days elapse between Acts I and II, and two months elapse between Acts II and III. During Act III the curtain is lowered for a few minutes to denote the lapse of one hour.*

## Act One

*The living room of a two-room tenancy occupied by the* BOYLE *family in a tenement house in Dublin. Left, a door leading to another part of the house; left of door a window looking into the street; at back a dresser; farther to right at back, a window looking into the back of the house. Between the window and the dresser is a picture of the Virgin; below the picture, on a bracket, is a crimson bowl in which a floating votive light is burning. Farther to the right is a small bed partly concealed by cretonne hangings strung on a twine. To the right is the fireplace; near the fireplace is a door leading to the other room. Beside the fireplace is a box containing coal. On the mantelshelf is an alarm clock lying on its face. In a corner near the window looking into the back is a galvanized bath. A table and some chairs. On the table are breakfast things for one. A teapot is on the hob and a frying-pan stands inside the fender. There are a few books on the dresser and one on the table. Leaning against the dresser is a long-handled shovel—the kind invariably used by labourers when turning concrete or mixing mortar.* JOHNNY BOYLE *is sitting crouched beside the fire.* MARY *with her jumper off—it is lying on the back of a chair—is arranging her hair before a tiny mirror perched on the table. Beside the mirror is stretched out the morning paper, which she looks at when she isn't gazing into the mirror. She is a well-made and good-looking girl of twenty-two. Two forces are working in her mind—one, through the circumstances of her life, pulling her back; the other, through the influence of books she has read, pushing her forward. The opposing forces are apparent in her speech and her manners, both of which are degraded by her environment, and improved by her acquaintance—slight though it be—with literature. The time is early forenoon.*

MARY (*Looking at the paper*) On a little bye-road, out beyant Finglas, he was found.

(MRS. BOYLE *enters by door on right; she has been shopping and carries a small parcel in her hand. She is forty-five years of age, and twenty years ago she must have been a pretty woman; but her face has now assumed that look which ultimately settles down upon the faces of the women of the working-class; a look of listless monotony and harassed anxiety, blending with an expression of mechanical resistance. Were circumstances favourable, she would probably be a handsome, active and clever woman*)

MRS. BOYLE Isn't he come in yet?

MARY No, Mother.

MRS. BOYLE Oh, he'll come in when he likes; struttin' about the town like a paycock with Joxer, I suppose. I hear all about Mrs. Tancred's son is in this mornin's paper.

MARY The full details are in it this mornin'; seven wounds he had—one entherin' the neck, with an exit wound beneath the left shoulder-blade; another in the left breast penethratin' the heart, an' . . .

JOHNNY (*Springing up from the fire*) Oh, quit that readin', for God's sake! Are yous losin' all your feelin's? It'll soon be that none of yous'll read anythin' that's not about butcherin'! (*He goes quickly into the room on left*)

MARY He's gettin' very sensitive, all of a sudden!

MRS. BOYLE I'll read it myself, Mary, by an' by, when I come home. Everybody's sayin' that he was a Diehard[1]—thanks be to God that Johnny had nothin' to do with him this long time. . . . (*Opening the parcel and taking out some sausages, which she places on a plate*) Ah, then, if that father o' yours doesn't come in soon for his breakfast, he may go without any; I'll not wait much longer for him.

MARY Can't you let him get it himself when he comes in?

MRS. BOYLE Yes, an' let him bring in Joxer Daly along with him? Ay, that's what he'd like, an' that's what he's waitin' for—till he thinks I'm gone to work, an' then sail in with the boul' Joxer, to burn all the coal an' dhrink all the tea in the place, to show them what a good Samaritan he is! But I'll stop here till he comes in, if I have to wait till to-morrow mornin'.

VOICE OF JOHNNY (*Inside*) Mother!

MRS. BOYLE Yis?

VOICE OF JOHNNY Bring us in a dhrink o' wather.

MRS. BOYLE Bring in that fella a dhrink o' wather, for God's sake, Mary.

MARY Isn't he big an' able enough to come out an' get it himself?

MRS. BOYLE If you weren't well yourself you'd like somebody to bring you in a dhrink o' wather. (*She brings in drink and returns*)

MRS. BOYLE Isn't it terrible to have to be waitin' this way! You'd think he was bringin' twenty poun's a week into the house the way he's goin' on. He wore out the Health Insurance long ago, he's afther wearin' out the unemployment dole, an', now, he's thryin' to wear out me! An' constantly singin', no less, when he ought always to be on his knees offerin' up a Novena for a job!

MARY (*Tying a ribbon, fillet-wise around her head*) I don't like this ribbon, Ma; I think I'll wear the green —it looks betther than the blue.

MRS. BOYLE Ah, wear whatever ribbon you like, girl, only don't be botherin' me. I don't know what a girl on strike wants to be wearin' a ribbon round her head for or silk stockin's on her legs either; it's wearin' them things that make the employers think they're givin' yous too much money.

MARY The hour is past now when we'll ask the employers' permission to wear what we like.

MRS. BOYLE I don't know why you wanted to walk out for Jennie Claffey; up to this you never had a good word for her.

MARY What's the use of belongin' to a Trades Union if you won't stand up for your principles? Why did they sack her? It was a clear case of victimization. We couldn't let her walk the streets, could we?

MRS. BOYLE No, of course yous couldn't—yous wanted to keep her company. Wan victim wasn't enough. When the employers sacrifice wan victim, the Trades Unions go wan betther be sacrificin' a hundred.

MARY It doesn't matther what you say, Ma—a principle's a principle.

MRS. BOYLE Yis; an' when I go into oul' Murphy's tomorrow, an' he gets to know that, instead o' payin' all, I'm goin' to borry more, what'll he say when I tell him a principle's a principle? What'll we do if he refuses to give us any more on tick?

MARY He daren't refuse—if he does, can't you tell him he's paid?

MRS. BOYLE It's lookin' as if he was paid, whether he refuses or no.

(JOHNNY *appears at the door on left. He can be plainly seen now; he is a thin, delicate fellow, something younger than* MARY. *He has evidently gone through a rough time. His face is pale and drawn; there is a tremulous look of indefinite fear in his eyes. The left sleeve of his coat is empty, and he walks with a slight halt*)

JOHNNY I was lyin' down; I thought yous were gone. Oul' Simon Mackay is thrampin' about like a horse over me head, an' I can't sleep with him—they're like thunder-claps in me brain! The curse o'—God forgive me for goin' to curse!

MRS. BOYLE There, now; go back an' lie down agen, an' I'll bring you in a nice cup o' tay.

JOHNNY Tay, tay, tay! You're always thinkin' o' tay. If a man was dyin', you'd thry to make him swally a cup o' tay! (*He goes back*)

MRS. BOYLE I don't know what's goin' to be done with him. The bullet he got in the hip in Easter Week[2] was bad enough, but the bomb that shatthered his arm in the fight in O'Connell Street put the finishin' touch on him. I knew he was makin' a fool of himself. God knows I went down on me bended knees to him not to go agen the Free State.

MARY He stuck to his principles, an', no matther how you may argue, Ma, a principle's a principle.

VOICE OF JOHNNY Is Mary goin' to stay here?

MARY No, I'm not goin' to stay here; you can't expect me to be always at your beck an' call, can you?

VOICE OF JOHNNY I won't stop here be meself!

[1] A fervent Irish nationalist who resists the authority of the Irish Free State.

[2] Easter Week, 1916, when the Citizen Army fought British troops in the streets of Dublin.

MRS. BOYLE Amn't I nicely handicapped with the whole o' yous! I don't know what any o' yous ud do without your ma. (*To* JOHNNY) Your father'll be here in a minute, an' if you want anythin', he'll get it for you.

JOHNNY I hate assin' him for anythin'. . . . He hates to be assed to stir. . . . Is the light lightin' before the picture o' the Virgin?

MRS. BOYLE Yis, yis! The wan inside to St. Anthony isn't enough, but he must have another wan to the Virgin here!

(JERRY DEVINE *enters hastily. He is about twenty-five, well set, active and earnest. He is a type, becoming very common now in the Labour Movement, of a mind knowing enough to make the mass of his associates, who know less, a power, and too little to broaden that power for the benefit of all.* MARY *seizes her jumper and runs hastily into room left*)

JERRY (*Breathless*) Where's the Captain, Mrs. Boyle; where's the Captain?

MRS. BOYLE You may well ass a body that: he's wherever Joxer Daly is—dhrinkin' in some snug or another.

JERRY Father Farrell is just afther stoppin' to tell me to run up an' get him to go to the new job that's goin' on in Rathmines; his cousin is foreman o' the job, an' Father Farrell was speakin' to him about poor Johnny an' his father bein' idle so long, an' the foreman told Father Farrell to send the Captain up an' he'd give him a start—I wondher where I'd find him?

MRS. BOYLE You'll find he's ayther in Ryan's or Foley's.

JERRY I'll run round to Ryan's—I know it's a great house o' Joxer's. (*He rushes out*)

MRS. BOYLE (*Piteously*) There now, he'll miss that job, or I know for what! If he gets win' o' the word, he'll not come back till evenin', so that it'll be too late. There'll never be any good got out o' him so long as he goes with that shouldher-shruggin' Joxer. I killin' meself workin', an' he sthruttin' about from mornin' till night like a paycock!

(*The steps of two persons are heard coming up a flight of stairs. They are the footsteps of* CAPTAIN BOYLE *and* JOXER. CAPTAIN BOYLE *is singing in a deep, sonorous, self-honouring voice*)

THE CAPTAIN Sweet Spirit, hear me prayer! Hear . . . oh . . . hear . . . me prayer . . . hear, oh, hear . . . Oh, he . . . ar . . . oh, he . . . ar . . . me . . . pray . . . er!

JOXER (*Outside*) Ah, that's a darlin' song, a daaarlin' song!

MRS. BOYLE (*Viciously*) Sweet spirit hear his prayer! Ah, then, I'll take me solemn affeydavey, it's not for a job he's prayin'!

(*She sits down on the bed so that the cretonne hangings hide her from the view of those entering.*

THE CAPTAIN *comes slowly in. He is a man of about sixty; stout, grey-haired and stocky. His neck is short, and his head looks like a stone ball that one sometimes sees on top of a gatepost. His cheeks, reddish-purple, are puffed out, as if he were always repressing an almost irrepressible ejaculation. On his upper lip is a crisp, tightly cropped moustache; he carries himself with the upper part of his body slightly thrown back, and his stomach slightly thrust forward. His walk is a slow, consequential strut. His clothes are dingy, and he wears a faded seaman's cap with a glazed peak*)

BOYLE (*To* JOXER, *who is still outside*) Come on, come on in, Joxer; she's gone out long ago, man. If there's nothing else to be got, we'll furrage out a cup o' tay, anyway. It's the only bit I get in comfort when she's away. 'Tisn't Juno should be her pet name at all, but Deirdre of the Sorras, for she's always grousin'.

(JOXER *steps cautiously into the room. He may be younger than* THE CAPTAIN *but he looks a lot older. His face is like a bundle of crinkled paper; his eyes have a cunning twinkle; he is spare and loosely built; he has a habit of constantly shrugging his shoulders with a peculiar twitching movement, meant to be ingratiating. His face is invariably ornamented with a grin*)

JOXER It's a terrible thing to be tied to a woman that's always grousin'. I don't know how you stick it—it ud put years on me. It's a good job she has to be so ofen away, for (*With a shrug*) when the cat's away, the mice can play!

BOYLE (*With a commanding and complacent gesture*) Pull over to the fire, Joxer, an' we'll have a cup o' tay in a minute.

JOXER Ah, a cup o' tay's a darlin' thing, a daaarlin' thing—the cup that cheers but doesn't . . .

(JOXER'S *rhapsody is cut short by the sight of* JUNO *coming forward and confronting the two cronies. Both are stupefied*)

MRS. BOYLE (*With sweet irony—poking the fire, and turning her head to glare at* JOXER) Pull over to the fire, Joxer Daly, an' we'll have a cup o' tay in a minute! Are you sure, now, you wouldn't like an egg?

JOXER I can't stop, Mrs. Boyle; I'm in a desperate hurry, a desperate hurry.

MRS. BOYLE Pull over to the fire, Joxer Daly; people is always far more comfortabler here than they are in their own place.

(JOXER *makes hastily for the door.* BOYLE *stirs to follow him; thinks of something to relieve the situation—stops, and says suddenly:* Joxer!)

JOXER (*At door ready to bolt*) Yis?

BOYLE You know the foreman o' that job that's goin' on down in Killesther, don't you, Joxer?

JOXER (*Puzzled*) Foreman—Killesther?

BOYLE (*With a meaning look*) He's a butty o' yours, isn't he?

JOXER (*The truth dawning on him*) The foreman at Killesther—oh, yis, yis. He's an oul' butty o' mine—oh, he's a darlin' man, a daarlin' man.

BOYLE Oh, then, it's a sure thing. It's a pity we didn't go down at breakfast first thing this mornin'—we might ha' been working now; but you didn't know it then.

JOXER (*With a shrug*) It's betther late than never.

BOYLE It's nearly time we got a start, anyhow; I'm fed up knockin' round, doin' nothin'. He promised you—gave you the straight tip?

JOXER Yis. "Come down on the blow o' dinner," says he, "an' I'll start you, an' any friend you like to brin' with you." "Ah," says I, "you're a darlin' man, a daaarlin' man."

BOYLE Well, it couldn't come at a betther time—we're a long time waitin' for it.

JOXER Indeed we were; but it's a long lane that has no turnin'.

BOYLE The blow up for dinner is at one—wait till I see what time it 'tis. (*He goes over to the mantelpiece, and gingerly lifts the clock*)

MRS. BOYLE Min' now, how you go on fiddlin' with that clock—you know the least little thing sets it asthray.

BOYLE The job couldn't come at a betther time; I'm feelin' in great fettle, Joxer. I'd hardly believe I ever had a pain in me legs, an' last week I was nearly crippled with them.

JOXER That's betther and betther; ah, God never shut wan door but He opened another!

BOYLE It's only eleven o'clock; we've lashins o' time. I'll slip on me oul' moleskins afther breakfast, an' we can saunther down at our ayse. (*Putting his hand on the shovel*) I think, Joxer, we'd betther bring our shovels?

JOXER Yis, Captain, yis; it's betther to go fully prepared an' ready for all eventualities. You bring your long-tailed shovel, an' I'll bring me navvy. We mighten' want them, an', then agen, we might: for want of a nail the shoe was lost, for want of a shoe the horse was lost, an' for want of a horse the man was lost—aw, that's a darlin' proverb, a daarlin' . . .

(*As* JOXER *is finishing his sentence,* MRS. BOYLE *approaches the door and* JOXER *retreats hurriedly. She shuts the door with a bang*)

BOYLE (*Suggestively*) We won't be long pullin' ourselves together agen when I'm working for a few weeks.

(MRS. BOYLE *takes no notice*)

BOYLE The foreman on the job is an oul' butty o' Joxer's; I have an idea that I know him meself. (*Silence*) . . . There's a button off the back o' me moleskin trousers. . . . If you leave out a needle an' thread I'll sew it on meself. . . . Thanks be to God, the pains in me legs is gone, anyhow!

MRS. BOYLE (*With a burst*) Look here, Mr. Jacky Boyle, them yarns won't go down with Juno. I know you an' Joxer Daly of an oul' date, an', if you think you're able to come it over me with them fairy tales, you're in the wrong shop.

BOYLE (*Coughing subduedly to relieve the tenseness of the situation*) U-u-u-ugh.

MRS. BOYLE Butty o' Joxer's! Oh, you'll do a lot o' good as long as you continue to be a butty o' Joxer's!

BOYLE U-u-u-ugh.

MRS. BOYLE Shovel! Ah, then, me boyo, you'd do far more work with a knife an' fork than ever you'll do with a shovel! If there was e'er a genuine job goin' you'd be dh'other way about—not able to lift your arms with the pains in your legs! Your poor wife slavin' to keep the bit in your mouth, an' you gallivantin' about all the day like a paycock!

BOYLE It ud be betther for a man to be dead, betther for a man to be dead.

MRS. BOYLE (*Ignoring the interruption*) Everybody callin' you "Captain," an' you only wanst on the wather, in an oul' collier from here to Liverpool, when anybody, to listen or look at you, ud take you for a second Christo For Columbus!

BOYLE Are you never goin' to give us a rest?

MRS. BOYLE Oh, you're never tired o' lookin' for a rest.

BOYLE D'ye want to dhrive me out o' the house?

MRS. BOYLE It ud be easier to dhrive you out o' the house than to dhrive you into a job. Here, sit down an' take your breakfast—it may be the last you'll get, for I don't know where the next is goin' to come from.

BOYLE If I get this job we'll be all right.

MRS. BOYLE Did ye see Jerry Devine?

BOYLE (*Testily*) No, I didn't see him.

MRS. BOYLE No, but you seen Joxer. Well, he was here lookin' for you.

BOYLE Well, let him look!

MRS. BOYLE Oh, indeed, he may well look, for it ud be hard for him to see you, an' you stuck in Ryan's snug.

BOYLE I wasn't in Ryan's snug—I don't go into Ryan's.

MRS. BOYLE Oh, is there a mad dog there? Well, if you weren't in Ryan's you were in Foley's.

BOYLE I'm telling you for the last three weeks I haven't tasted a dhrop of intoxicatin' liquor. I wasn't in ayther wan snug or dh'other—I could swear that on a prayer-book—I'm as innocent as the child unborn!

MRS. BOYLE Well, if you'd been in for your breakfast you'd ha' seen him.

BOYLE (*Suspiciously*) What does he want me for?

MRS. BOYLE He'll be back any minute an' then you'll soon know.

BOYLE I'll dhrop out an' see if I can meet him.

MRS. BOYLE You'll sit down an' take your breakfast, an' let me go to me work, for I'm an hour late already waitin' for you.

BOYLE You needn't ha' waited, for I'll take no breakfast—I've a little spirit left in me still!

MRS. BOYLE Are you goin' to have your breakfast—yes or no?

BOYLE (*Too proud to yield*) I'll have no breakfast—yous can keep your breakfast. (*Plaintively*) I'll knock out a bit somewhere, never fear.

MRS. BOYLE Nobody's goin' to coax you—don't think that. (*She vigorously replaces the pan and the sausages in the press*)

BOYLE I've a little spirit left in me still.

(JERRY DEVINE *enters hastily*)

JERRY Oh, here you are at last! I've been searchin' for you everywhere. The foreman in Foley's told me you hadn't left the snug with Joxer ten minutes before I went in.

MRS. BOYLE An' he swearin' on the holy prayer-book that he wasn't in no snug!

BOYLE (*To* JERRY) What business is it o' yours whether I was in a snug or no? What do you want to be gallopin' about afther me for? Is a man not to be allowed to leave his house for a minute without havin' a pack o' spies, pimps an' informers cantherin' at his heels?

JERRY Oh, you're takin' a wrong view of it, Mr. Boyle; I simply was anxious to do you a good turn. I have a message for you from Father Farrell: he says that if you go to the job that's on in Rathmines, an' ask for Foreman Mangan, you'll get a start.

BOYLE That's all right, but I don't want the motions of me body to be watched the way an asthronomer ud watch a star. If you're folleyin' Mary aself, you've no pereeogative to be folleyin' me. (*Suddenly catching his thigh*) U-ugh, I'm afther gettin' a terrible twinge in me right leg!

MRS. BOYLE Oh, it won't be very long now till it travels into your left wan. It's miraculous that whenever he scents a job in front of him, his legs begin to fail him! Then, me bucko, if you lose this chance, you may go an' furrage for yourself!

JERRY This job'll last for some time, too, Captain, an' as soon as the foundations are in, it'll be cushy enough.

BOYLE Won't it be a climbin' job? How d'ye expect me to be able to go up a ladder with these legs? An', if I get up aself, how am I goin' to get down agen?

MRS. BOYLE (*Viciously*) Get wan o' the labourers to carry you down in a hod! You can't climb a laddher, but you can skip like a goat into a snug!

JERRY I wouldn't let meself be let down that easy, Mr. Boyle; a little exercise, now, might do you all the good in the world.

BOYLE It's a docthor you should have been, Devine—maybe you know more about the pains in me legs than meself that has them?

JERRY (*Irritated*) Oh, I know nothin' about the pains in your legs; I've brought the message that Father Farrell gave me, an' that's all I can do.

MRS. BOYLE Here, sit down an' take your breakfast, an' go an' get ready; an' don't be actin' as if you couldn't pull a wing out of a dead bee.

BOYLE I want no breakfast, I tell you; it ud choke me afther all that's been said. I've a little spirit left in me still.

MRS. BOYLE Well, let's see your spirit, then, an' go in at wanst an' put on your moleskin trousers!

BOYLE (*Moving towards the door on left*) It ud be betther for a man to be dead! U-ugh! There's another twinge in me other leg! Nobody but meself knows the sufferin' I'm goin' through with the pains in these legs o' mine! (*He goes into the room on left as* MARY *comes out with her hat in her hand*)

MRS. BOYLE I'll have to push off now, for I'm terrible late already, but I was determined to stay an' hunt that Joxer this time. (*She goes off*)

JERRY Are you going out, Mary?

MARY It looks like it when I'm putting on my hat, doesn't it?

JERRY The bitther word agen, Mary.

MARY You won't allow me to be friendly with you; if I thry, you deliberately misundherstand it.

JERRY I didn't always misundherstand it; you were ofen delighted to have the arms of Jerry around you.

MARY If you go on talkin' like this, Jerry Devine, you'll make me hate you!

JERRY Well, let it be either a weddin' or a wake! Listen, Mary, I'm standin' for the Secretaryship of our Union. There's only one opposin' me; I'm popular with all the men, an' a good speaker—all are sayin' that I'll get elected.

MARY Well?

JERRY The job's worth three hundred an' fifty pounds a year, Mary. You an' I could live nice an' cosily on that; it would lift you out o' this place an' . . .

MARY I haven't time to listen to you now—I have to go. (*She is going out when* JERRY *bars the way*)

JERRY (*Appealingly*). Mary, what's come over you with me for the last few weeks? You hardly speak to me, an' then only a word with a face o' bittherness on it. Have you forgotten, Mary, all the happy evenin's that were as sweet as the scented hawthorn that sheltered the sides o' the road as we saunthered through the country?

MARY That's all over now. When you get your new job, Jerry, you won't be long findin' a girl far betther than I am for your sweetheart.

JERRY Never, never, Mary! No matther what happens you'll always be the same to me.

MARY I must be off; please let me go, Jerry.

JERRY I'll go a bit o' the way with you.

MARY You needn't, thanks; I want to be by myself.

JERRY (*Catching her arm*) You're goin' to meet another fella; you've clicked with some one else, me lady!

MARY That's no concern o' yours, Jerry Devine; let me go!

JERRY I saw yous comin' out o' the Cornflower Dance Class, an' you hangin' on his arm—a thin, lanky strip of a Micky Dazzler,[3] with a walkin'-stick an' gloves!

VOICE OF JOHNNY (*Loudly*) What are you doin' there —pullin' about everything!

VOICE OF BOYLE (*Loudly and viciously*) I'm puttin' on me moleskin trousers!

MARY You're hurtin' me arm! Let me go, or I'll scream, an' then you'll have the oul' fella out on top of us!

JERRY Don't be so hard on a fella, Mary, don't be so hard.

BOYLE (*Appearing at the door*) What's the meanin' of all this hillabaloo?

MARY Let me go, let me go!

[3] A man-about-town, playboy, dude.

BOYLE D'ye hear me—what's all this hillabaloo about?

JERRY (*Plaintively*) Will you not give us one kind word, one kind word, Mary?

BOYLE D'ye hear me talkin' to yous? What's all this hillabaloo for?

JERRY Let me kiss your hand, your little, tiny, white hand!

BOYLE Your little, tiny, white hand—are you takin' leave o' your senses, man?

(MARY *breaks away and rushes out*)

BOYLE This is nice goin's on in front of her father!

JERRY Ah, dhry up, for God's sake! (*He follows* MARY)

BOYLE Chiselurs[4] don't care a damn now about their parents, they're bringin' their fathers' gray hairs down with sorra to the grave, an' laughin' at it, laughin' at it. Ah, I suppose it's just the same everywhere—the whole worl's in a state o' chassis! (*He sits by the fire*) Breakfast! Well, they can keep their breakfast for me. Not if they went down on their bended knees would I take it—I'll show them I've a little spirit left in me still! (*He goes over to the press, takes out a plate and looks at it*) Sassige! Well, let her keep her sassige. (*He returns to the fire, takes up the teapot and gives it a gentle shake*) The tay's wet right enough. (*A pause; he rises, goes to the press, takes out the sausage, puts it on the pan, and puts both on the fire. He attends the sausage with a fork*)

BOYLE (*Singing*)

When the robins nest agen,
And the flowers are in bloom,
When the Springtime's sunny smile seems to banish all sorrow an' gloom;
Then me bonny blue-ey'd lad, if me heart be true till then—
He's promised he'll come back to me,
When the robins nest agen!

(*He lifts his head at the high note, and then drops his eyes to the pan*)

BOYLE (*Singing*)

When the . . .

(*Steps are heard approaching; he whips the pan off the fire and puts it under the bed, then sits down at the fire. The door opens and a bearded man looking in says*)

You don't happen to want a sewin' machine?

BOYLE (*Furiously*) No, I don't want e'er a sewin' machine! (*He returns the pan to the fire, and commences to sing again*)

BOYLE (*Singing*)

When the robins nest agen,
And the flowers they are in bloom,
He's . . .

(*A thundering knock is heard at the street door*)

BOYLE There's a terrible tatheraraa—that's a stranger—that's nobody belongin' to the house. (*Another loud knock*)

JOXER (*Sticking his head in at the door*) Did ye hear them tatherarahs?

BOYLE Well, Joxer, I'm not deaf.

[4] Children, offspring (*cf.* brats).

JOHNNY (*Appearing in his shirt and trousers at the door on left; his face is anxious and his voice is tremulous*) Who's that at the door; who's that at the door? Who gave that knock—d'yous hear me—are yous deaf or dhrunk or what?

BOYLE (*to* JOHNNY) How the hell do I know who 'tis? Joxer, stick your head out o' the window an' see.

JOXER An' mebbe get a bullet in the kisser? Ah, none o' them thricks for Joxer! It's betther to be a coward than a corpse!

BOYLE (*Looking cautiously out of the window*) It's a fella in a thrench coat.

JOHNNY Holy Mary, Mother o' God, I . . .

BOYLE He's goin' away—he must ha' got tired knockin'.

(JOHNNY *returns to the room on left*)

BOYLE Sit down an' have a cup o' tay, Joxer.

JOXER I'm afraid the missus ud pop in on us agen before we'd know where we are. Somethin's tellin' me to go at wanst.

BOYLE Don't be superstitious, man; we're Dublin men, an' not boyos that's only afther comin' up from the bog o' Allen[5]—though if she did come in, right enough, we'd be caught like rats in a thrap.

JOXER An' you know the sort she is—she wouldn't listen to reason—an' wanse bitten twice shy.

BOYLE (*Going over to the window at back*) If the worst came to the worst, you could dart out here, Joxer; it's only a dhrop of a few feet to the roof of the return room, an' the first minute she goes into dh'other room, I'll give you the bend, an' you can slip in an' away.

JOXER (*Yielding to the temptation*) Ah, I won't stop very long anyhow. (*Picking up a book from the table*) Whose is the buk?

BOYLE Aw, one o' Mary's; she's always readin' lately—nothin' but thrash, too. There's one I was lookin' at dh'other day: three stories, The Doll's House, Ghosts, an' The Wild Duck—buks only fit for chiselurs!

JOXER Didja ever rade *Elizabeth, or Th' Exile o' Sibayria?* . . . Ah, it's a darlin' story, a daarlin' story!

BOYLE You eat your sassige, an' never min' *Th' Exile o' Sibayria.*

(*Both sit down;* BOYLE *fills out tea, pours gravy on* JOXER'*s plate, and keeps the sausage for himself*)

JOXER What are you wearin' your moleskin trousers for?

BOYLE I have to go to a job, Joxer. Just afther you'd gone, Devine kem runnin' in to tell us that Father Farrell said if I went down to the job that's goin' on in Rathmines I'd get a start.

JOXER Be the holy, that's good news!

BOYLE How is it good news? I wondher if you were in my condition, would you call it good news?

JOXER I thought . . .

BOYLE You thought! You think too sudden sometimes, Joxer. D'ye know, I'm hardly able to crawl with the pains in me legs!

[5] Irishmen who live in this peat bog of central Ireland are regarded as brutish, ignorant, vicious.

JOXER Yis, yis; I forgot the pains in your legs. I know you can do nothin' while they're at you.

BOYLE You forgot; I don't think any of yous realize the state I'm in with the pains in me legs. What ud happen if I had to carry a bag o' cement?

JOXER Ah, any man havin' the like of them pains id be down an' out, down an' out.

BOYLE I wouldn't mind if he had said it to meself; but, no, oh no, he rushes in an' shouts it out in front o' Juno, an' you know what Juno is, Joxer. We all know Devine knows a little more than the rest of us, but he doesn't act as if he did; he's a good boy, sober, able to talk an' all that, but still . . .

JOXER Oh ay; able to argufy, but still . . .

BOYLE If he's runnin' afther Mary, aself, he's not goin' to be runnin' afther me. Captain Boyle's able to take care of himself. Afther all, I'm not gettin' brought up on Virol.[6] I never heard him usin' a curse; I don't believe he was ever dhrunk in his life—sure he's not like a Christian at all!

JOXER You're afther takin' the word out o' me mouth—afther all, a Christian's natural, but he's unnatural.

BOYLE His oul' fella was just the same—a Wicklow man.

JOXER A Wicklow man! That explains the whole thing. I've met many a Wicklow man in me time, but I never met wan that was any good.

BOYLE "Father Farrell," says he, "sent me down to tell you." Father Farrell! . . . D'ye know, Joxer, I never like to be beholden to any o' the clergy.

JOXER It's dangerous, right enough.

BOYLE If they do anything for you, they'd want you to be livin' in the Chapel. . . . I'm goin' to tell you somethin', Joxer, that I wouldn't tell to anybody else—the clergy always had too much power over the people in this unfortunate country.

JOXER You could sing that if you had an air to it!

BOYLE (*Becoming enthusiastic*) Didn't they prevent the people in '47[7] from seizin' the corn, an' they starvin'; didn't they down Parnell;[8] didn't they say that hell wasn't hot enough nor eternity long enough to punish the Fenians?[9] We don't forget, we don't forget them things, Joxer. If they've taken everything else from us, Joxer, they've left us our memory.

JOXER (*Emotionally*) For mem'ry's the only friend that grief can call its own, that grief . . . can . . . call . . . its own!

BOYLE Father Farrell's beginnin' to take a great intherest in Captain Boyle; because of what Johnny did for his country, says he to me wan day. It's a curious way to reward Johnny be makin' his poor oul' father work. But, that's what the clergy want, Joxer—work, work, work for me an' you; havin' us mulin' from mornin' till night, so that they may be in betther fettle when they come hoppin' round for their dues! Job! Well, let him give his job to wan of his hymn-singin', prayer-spoutin', craw-thumpin' Confraternity men!

(*The voice of a coal-block vendor is heard chanting in the street*)

VOICE OF COAL VENDOR Blocks . . . coal-blocks! Blocks . . . coal-blocks!

JOXER God be with the young days when you were steppin' the deck of a manly ship, with the win' blowin' a hurricane through the masts, an' the only sound you'd hear was, "Port your helm!" an' the only answer, "Port it is, sir!"

BOYLE Them was days, Joxer, them was days. Nothin' was too hot or too heavy for me then. Sailin' from the Gulf o' Mexico to the Antanartic Ocean. I seen things, I seen things, Joxer, that no mortal man should speak about that knows his Catechism. Ofen, an' ofen, when I was fixed to the wheel with a marlin-spike, an' the win's blowin' fierce an' the waves lashin' an' lashin', till you'd think every minute was goin' to be your last, an' it blowed, an' blowed—blew is the right word, Joxer, but blowed is what the sailors use. . . .

JOXER Aw, it's a darlin' word, a daarlin' word.

BOYLE An', as it blowed an' blowed, I ofen looked up at the sky an' assed meself the question—what is the stars, what is the stars?

VOICE OF COAL VENDOR Any blocks, coal-blocks; blocks, coal-blocks!

JOXER Ah, that's the question, that's the question—what is the stars?

BOYLE An' then, I'd have another look, an' I'd ass meself—what is the moon?

JOXER Ah, that's the question—what is the moon, what is the moon?

(*Rapid steps are heard coming towards the door.* BOYLE *makes desperate efforts to hide everything;* JOXER *rushes to the window in a frantic effort to get out;* BOYLE *begins to innocently lilt— "Oh, me darlin' Jennie, I will be thrue to thee," when the door is opened, and the black face of the* COAL VENDOR *appears*)

THE COAL VENDOR D'yes want any blocks?

BOYLE (*With a roar*) No, we don't want any blocks!

JOXER (*Coming back with a sigh of relief*) That's afther puttin' the heart across me—I could ha' sworn it was Juno. I'd betther be goin', Captain; you couldn't tell the minute Juno'd hop in on us.

BOYLE Let her hop in; we may as well have it out first as at last. I've made up me mind—I'm not goin' to do only what she damn well likes.

JOXER Them sentiments does you credit, Captain; I don't like to say anything as between man an' wife, but I say as a butty, as a butty, Captain, that you've stuck it too long, an' that it's about time you showed a little spunk.

[6] A tonic comparable to vitaminized fortifiers sold in America.

[7] The worst year of the potato famine. Boyle can only have heard of events in 1847.

[8] Charles Stewart Parnell (1846-1891), whose success in leading the Irish toward home-rule was blocked when, in 1889, his adulterous affair with Mrs. Kitty O'Shea became public.

[9] A secret brotherhood, especially active in the 1860's, dedicated to Irish independence.

How can a man die betther than facin' fearful odds,
For th' ashes of his fathers an' the temples of his
gods.[10]

BOYLE She has her rights—there's no one denyin' it, but haven't I me rights too?

JOXER Of course you have—the sacred rights o' man!

BOYLE To-day, Joxer, there's goin' to be issued a proclamation be me, establishin' an independent Republic, an' Juno'll have to take an oath of allegiance.

JOXER Be firm, be firm, Captain; the first few minutes'll be the worst:—if you gently touch a nettle it'll sting you for your pains; grasp it like a lad of mettle, an' as soft as silk remains!

VOICE OF JUNO (*Outside*) Can't stop, Mrs. Madigan—I haven't a minute!

JOXER (*Flying out of the window*) Holy God, here she is!

BOYLE (*Packing the things away with a rush in the press*) I knew that fella ud stop till she was in on top of us! (*He sits down by the fire.* JUNO *enters hastily; she is flurried and excited*)

JUNO Oh, you're in—you must have been only afther comin' in?

BOYLE No, I never went out.

JUNO It's curious, then, you never heard the knockin'. (*She puts her coat and hat on bed*)

BOYLE Knockin'? Of course I heard the knockin'.

JUNO An' why didn't you open the door, then? I suppose you were so busy with Joxer that you hadn't time.

BOYLE I haven't seen Joxer since I seen him before. Joxer! What ud bring Joxer here?

JUNO D'ye mean to tell me that the pair of yous wasn't collogin' together here when me back was turned?

BOYLE What ud we be collogin' together about? I have somethin' else to think of besides collogin' with Joxer. I can swear on all the holy prayer-books . . .

MRS. BOYLE That you weren't in no snug! Go on in at wanst now, an' take off that moleskin trousers o' yours, an' put on a collar an' tie to smarten yourself up a bit. There's a visitor comin' with Mary in a minute, an' he has great news for you.

BOYLE A job, I suppose; let us get wan first before we start lookin' for another.

MRS. BOYLE That's the thing that's able to put the win' up you. Well, it's no job, but news that'll give you the chance o' your life.

BOYLE What's all the mysthery about?

MRS. BOYLE G'win an' take off the moleskin trousers when you're told!

(BOYLE *goes into room on left.* MRS. BOYLE *tidies up the room, puts the shovel under the bed, and goes to the press*)

MRS. BOYLE Oh, God bless us, looka the way everythin's thrun about! Oh, Joxer was here, Joxer was here!

(MARY *enters with* CHARLIE BENTHAM; *he is a young man of twenty-five, tall, good-looking, with a very high opinion of himself generally. He is dressed in a brown coat, brown knee-breeches, grey stockings, a brown sweater, with a deep blue tie; he carries gloves and a walking-stick*)

MRS. BOYLE (*Fussing round*) Come in, Mr. Bentham; sit down, Mr. Bentham, in this chair; it's more comfortabler than that, Mr. Bentham. Himself'll be here in a minute; he's just takin' off his trousers.

MARY Mother!

BENTHAM Please don't put yourself to any trouble, Mrs. Boyle—I'm quite all right here, thank you.

MRS. BOYLE An' to think of you knowin' Mary, an' she knowin' the news you had for us, an' wouldn't let on; but it's all the more welcomer now, for we were on our last lap!

VOICE OF JOHNNY (*Inside*) What are you kickin' up all the racket for?

BOYLE (*Roughly*) I'm takin' off me moleskin trousers!

JOHNNY Can't you do it, then, without lettin' th' whole house know you're takin' off your trousers? What d'ye want puttin' them on an' takin' them off again?

BOYLE Will you let me alone, will you let me alone? Am I never goin' to be done thryin' to please th' whole o' yous?

MRS. BOYLE (*To* BENTHAM) You must excuse th' state o' th' place, Mr. Bentham; th' minute I turn me back that man o' mine always makes a litther o' th' place, a litther o' th' place.

BENTHAM Don't worry, Mrs. Boyle; it's all right, I assure . . .

BOYLE (*Inside*) Where's me braces; where in th' name o' God did I leave me braces? . . . Ay, did you see where I put me braces?

JOHNNY (*Inside, calling out*) Ma, will you come in here an' take da away ou' o' this or he'll dhrive me mad.

MRS. BOYLE (*Going towards door*) Dear, dear, dear, that man'll be lookin' for somethin' on th' day o' Judgement. (*Looking into room and calling to* BOYLE) Look at your braces, man, hangin' round your neck!

BOYLE (*Inside*) Aw, Holy God!

MRS. BOYLE (*Calling*) Johnny, Johnny, come out here for a minute.

JOHNNY Oh, leave Johnny alone, an' don't be annoyin' him!

MRS. BOYLE Come on, Johnny, till I inthroduce you to Mr. Bentham. (*To* BENTHAM) Me son, Mr. Bentham; he's afther goin' through the mill. He was only a chiselur of a Boy Scout in Easter Week, when he got hit in the hip; and his arm was blew off in the fight in O'Connell Street. (JOHNNY *comes in*) Here he is, Mr. Bentham; Mr. Bentham, Johnny. None can deny he done his bit for Irelan', if that's going to do him any good.

JOHNNY (*Boastfully*) I'd do it agen, Ma, I'd do it agen; for a principle's a principle.

MRS. BOYLE Ah, you lost your best principle, me boy, when you lost your arm; them's the only sort o' principles that's any good to a workin' man.

JOHNNY Ireland only half free'll never be at peace while she has a son left to pull a trigger.

[10] Stanza 27 of Macaulay's "Horatius" in *The Lays of Ancient Rome.*

MRS. BOYLE To be sure, to be sure—no bread's a lot betther than half a loaf. (*Calling loudly in to* BOYLE) Will you hurry up there?

(BOYLE *enters in his best trousers, which aren't too good, and looks very uncomfortable in his collar and tie*)

MRS. BOYLE This is me husband; Mr. Boyle, Mr. Bentham.

BENTHAM Ah, very glad to know you, Mr. Boyle. How are you?

BOYLE Ah, I'm not too well at all; I suffer terrible with pains in me legs. Juno can tell you there what . . .

MRS. BOYLE You won't have many pains in your legs when you hear what Mr. Bentham has to tell you.

BENTHAM Juno! What an interesting name! It reminds one of Homer's glorious story of ancient gods and heroes.

BOYLE Yis, doesn't it? You see, Juno was born an' christened in June; I met her in June; we were married in June, an' Johnny was born in June, so wan day I says to her, "You should ha' been called Juno," an' the name stuck to her ever since.

MRS. BOYLE Here, we can talk o' them things agen; let Mr. Bentham say what he has to say now.

BENTHAM Well, Mr. Boyle, I suppose you'll remember a Mr. Ellison of Santry—he's a relative of yours, I think.

BOYLE (*Viciously*) Is it that prognosticator an' procrastinator! Of course I remember him.

BENTHAM Well, he's dead, Mr. Boyle . . .

BOYLE Sorra many'll[11] go into mournin' for him.

MRS. BOYLE Wait till you hear what Mr. Bentham has to say, an' then, maybe, you'll change your opinion.

BENTHAM A week before he died he sent for me to write his will for him. He told me that there were two only that he wished to leave his property to: his second cousin Michael Finnegan of Santry, and John Boyle, his first cousin of Dublin.

BOYLE (*Excitedly*) Me, is it me, me?

BENTHAM You, Mr. Boyle; I'll read a copy of the will that I have here with me, which has been duly filed in the Court of Probate. (*He takes a paper from his pocket and reads*)

*6th February* 1922.

This is the last Will and Testament of William Ellison, of Santry, in the County of Dublin. I hereby order and wish my property to be sold and divided as follows:—

£20 to the St. Vincent De Paul Society.

£60 for Masses for the repose of my soul (5s. for each Mass).

The rest of my property to be divided between my first and second cousins.

I hereby appoint Timothy Buckly, of Santry, and Hugh Brierly, of Coolock, to be my Executors.

(*Signed*) WILLIAM ELLISON.
HUGH BRIERLY.
TIMOTHY BUCKLY.
CHARLES BENTHAM, N.T.[12]

[11] Not many, very few.
[12] National Teacher.

BOYLE (*Eagerly*) An' how much'll be comin' out of it, Mr. Bentham?

BENTHAM The Executors told me that half of the property would be anything between £1500 and £2000.

MARY A fortune, father, a fortune!

JOHNNY We'll be able to get out o' this place now, an' go somewhere we're not known.

MRS. BOYLE You won't have to trouble about a job for a while, Jack.

BOYLE (*Fervently*) I'll never doubt the goodness o' God agen.

BENTHAM I congratulate you, Mr. Boyle. (*They shake hands*)

BOYLE An' now, Mr. Bentham, you'll have to have a wet.

BENTHAM A wet?

BOYLE A wet—a jar—a boul!

MRS. BOYLE Jack, you're speakin' to Mr. Bentham, an' not to Joxer.

BOYLE (*Solemnly*) Juno . . . Mary . . . Johnny . . . we'll have to go into mournin' at wanst. . . . I never expected that poor Bill ud die so sudden. . . . Well, we all have to die some day . . . you, Juno, today . . . an' me, maybe, tomorrow. . . . It's sad, but it can't be helped. . . . Requiescat in pace . . . or, usin' our oul' tongue like St. Patrick or St. Bridget, Guh sayeree jeea ayera!

MARY Oh, father, that's not Rest in Peace; that's God save Ireland.

BOYLE U-u-ugh, it's all the same—isn't it a prayer? . . . Juno, I'm done with Joxer; he's nothin' but a prognosticator an' a . . .

JOXER (*Climbing angrily through the window and bounding into the room*) You're done with Joxer, are you? Maybe you thought I'd stop on the roof all the night for you! Joxer out on the roof with the win' blowin' through him was nothin' to you an' your friend with the collar an' tie!

MRS. BOYLE What in the name o' God brought you out on the roof; what were you doin' there?

JOXER (*Ironically*) I was dhreamin' I was standin' on the bridge of a ship, an' she sailin' the Antartic Ocean, an' it blowed, an' blowed, an' I lookin' up at the sky an' sayin', what is the stars, what is the stars?

MRS. BOYLE (*Opening the door and standing at it*) Here, get ou' o' this, Joxer Daly; I was always thinkin' you had a slate off.[13]

JOXER (*Moving to the door*) I have to laugh every time I look at the deep-sea sailor; an' a row on a river ud make him sea-sick!

BOYLE Get ou' o' this before I take the law into me own hands!

JOXER (*Going out*) Say aw rewaeawr, but not good-bye. Lookin' for work, an' prayin' to God he won't get it! (*He goes*)

MRS. BOYLE I'm tired tellin' you what Joxer was; maybe now you see yourself the kind he is.

BOYLE He'll never blow the froth off a pint o' mine agen, that's a sure thing. Johnny . . . Mary . . .

[13] You were crazy.

you're to keep yourselves to yourselves for the future. Juno, I'm done with Joxer. . . . I'm a new man from this out. . . . (*Clasping* JUNO'S *hand, and singing emotionally*)

Oh, me darlin' Juno, I will be thrue to thee;
Me own, me darlin' Juno, you're all the world to me.

*Curtain*

# Act Two

SCENE *The same, but the furniture is more plentiful, and of a vulgar nature. A glaringly upholstered arm-chair and lounge; cheap pictures and photos everywhere. Every available spot is ornamented with huge vases filled with artificial flowers. Crossed festoons of coloured paper chains stretch from end to end of ceiling. On the table is an old attaché case. It is about six in the evening, and two days after the First Act.* BOYLE, *in his shirt sleeves, is voluptuously stretched on the sofa; he is smoking a clay pipe. He is half asleep. A lamp is lighting on the table. After a few moments' pause the voice of* JOXER *is heard singing softly outside at the door—"Me pipe I'll smoke, as I dhrive me moke*[1]*—are you there, Mor . . . ee . . . ar . . . i . . teee!"*

BOYLE (*Leaping up, takes a pen in his hand and busies himself with papers*) Come along, Joxer, me son, come along.

JOXER (*Putting his head in*) Are you be yourself?

BOYLE Come on, come on; that doesn't matther; I'm masther now, an' I'm goin' to remain masther.

(JOXER *comes in*)

JOXER How d'ye feel now, as a man o' money?

BOYLE (*Solemnly*) It's a responsibility, Joxer, a great responsibility.

JOXER I suppose 'tis now, though you wouldn't think it.

BOYLE Joxer, han' me over that attackey case on the table there. (JOXER *hands the case*) Ever since the Will was passed I've run hundhreds o' dockyments through me han's—I tell you, you have to keep your wits about you. (*He busies himself with papers*)

JOXER Well, I won't disturb you; I'll dhrop in when . . .

BOYLE (*Hastily*) It's all right, Joxer, this is the last one to be signed to-day. (*He signs a paper, puts it into the case, which he shuts with a snap, and sits back pompously in the chair*) Now, Joxer, you want to see me; I'm at your service—what can I do for you, me man?

[1] Donkey or mule.

JOXER I've just dhropped in with the £3:5s. that Mrs. Madigan riz on the blankets an' table for you, and she says you're to be in no hurry payin' it back.

BOYLE She won't be long without it; I expect the first cheque for a couple o' hundhred any day. There's the five bob for yourself—go on, take it, man; it'll not be the last you'll get from the Captain. Now an' agen we have our differ, but we're there together all the time.

JOXER Me for you, an' you for me, like the two Musketeers.

BOYLE Father Farrell stopped me to-day an' tole me how glad he was I fell in for the money.

JOXER He'll be stoppin' you ofen enough now; I suppose it was "Mr." Boyle with him?

BOYLE He shuk me be the han'. . . .

JOXER (*Ironically*) I met with Napper Tandy, an' he shuk me be the han'! [2]

BOYLE You're seldom asthray, Joxer, but you're wrong shipped this time. What you're sayin' of Father Farrell is very near to blasfeemey. I don't like any one to talk disrespectful of Father Farrell.

JOXER You're takin' me up wrong, Captain; I wouldn't let a word be said agen Father Farrell—the heart o' the rowl,[3] that's what he is; I always said he was a darlin' man, a daarlin' man.

BOYLE Comin' up the stairs who did I meet but that bummer, Nugent. "I seen you talkin' to Father Farrell," says he, with a grin on him. "He'll be folleyin' you," says he, "like a Guardian Angel from this out"—all the time the oul' grin on him, Joxer.

JOXER I never seen him yet but he had that oul' grin on him!

BOYLE "Mr. Nugent," says I, "Father Farrell is a man o' the people, an', as far as I know the History o' me country, the priests was always in the van of the fight for Irelan's freedom."

JOXER (*Fervently*)

Who was it led the van, Soggart Aroon?
Since the fight first began, Soggart Aroon? [4]

BOYLE "Who are you tellin'?" says he. "Didn't they let down the Fenians, an' didn't they do in Parnell? An' now . . ." "You ought to be ashamed o' yourself," says I, interruptin' him, "not to know the History o' your country." An' I left him gawkin' where he was.

JOXER Where ignorance 's bliss 'tis folly to be wise; I wondher did he ever read the Story o' Irelan'.

BOYLE Be J. L. Sullivan? [5] Don't you know he didn't?

JOXER Ah, it's a darlin' buk, a daarlin' buk!

BOYLE You'd betther be goin', now, Joxer; his Majesty, Bentham, 'll be here any minute, now.

[2] Opening line of "The Wearing of the Green," the patriotic song. Napper Tandy (1740-1803) was one of Ireland's great eighteenth-century nationalists.

[3] The "heart of the roll" (where the meat is) is used to describe a jolly good fellow, especially in drinking circles.

[4] Lines from a ballad honoring one Father Murphy, who took a major role in the 1798 rebellion of Irish against English. *Soggart[h]* = priest, and *Aroon* is an affectionate diminutive; Father Murphy is Ireland's "lovely little priest."

[5] A. M. Sullivan wrote a pro-nationalist book. *The Story of Ireland,* which Joxer has in mind. Boyle unconsciously attributes the book to the great Boston Irish prizefighter.

JOXER Be the way things is lookin', it'll be a match between him an' Mary. She's thrun over Jerry altogether. Well, I hope it will, for he's a darlin' man.

BOYLE I'm glad you think so—I don't. (*Irritably*) What's darlin' about him?

JOXER (*Nonplussed*) I only seen him twiced; if you want to know me, come an' live with me.

BOYLE He's too dignified for me—to hear him talk you'd think he knew as much as a Boney's Oraculum.[6] He's given up his job as teacher, an' is going to become a solicitor in Dublin—he's been studyin' law. I suppose he thinks I'll set him up, but he's wrong shipped. An' th' other fella—Jerry's as bad. The two o' them ud give you a pain in your face, listenin' to them; Jerry believin' in nothin', an' Bentham believin' in everythin'. One that says all is God an' no man; an' th' other that says all is man an' no God!

JOXER Well, I'll be off now.

BOYLE Don't forget to dhrop down afther a while; we'll have a quiet jar, an' a song or two.

JOXER Never fear.

BOYLE An' tell Mrs. Madigan that I hope we'll have the pleasure of her organization at our little enthertainment.

JOXER Righto; we'll come down together. (*He goes out*)

(JOHNNY *comes from room on left, and sits down moodily at the fire.* BOYLE *looks at him for a few moments, and shakes his head. He fills his pipe*)

VOICE OF JUNO AT THE DOOR Open the door, Jack; this thing has me nearly kilt with the weight.

(BOYLE *opens the door.* JUNO *enters carrying the box of a gramophone, followed by* MARY *carrying the horn, and some parcels.* JUNO *leaves the box on the table and flops into a chair*)

JUNO Carryin' that from Henry Street was no joke.

BOYLE U-u-ugh, that's a grand lookin' insthrument—how much was it?

JUNO Pound down, an' five to be paid at two shillin's a week.

BOYLE That's reasonable enough.

JUNO I'm afraid we're runnin' into too much debt; first the furniture, an' now this.

BOYLE The whole lot won't be much out of £2000.

MARY I don't know what you wanted a gramophone for—I know Charlie hates them; he says they're destructive of real music.

BOYLE Desthructive of music—that fella ud give you a pain in your face. All a gramophone wants is to be properly played; its thrue wondher is only felt when everythin's quiet—what a gramophone wants is dead silence!

MARY But, father, Jerry says the same; afther all, you can only appreciate music when your ear is properly trained.

BOYLE That's another fella ud give you a pain in your face. Properly thrained! I suppose you couldn't appreciate football unless your fut was properly thrained.

MRS. BOYLE (*To* MARY) Go on in ower that an' dress, or Charlie 'll be in on you, an' tay nor nothin' 'll be ready.

(MARY *goes into room left*)

MRS. BOYLE (*Arranging table for tea*) You didn't look at our new gramophone, Johnny?

JOHNNY 'Tisn't gramophones I'm thinking of.

MRS. BOYLE An' what is it you're thinkin' of, allanna?[7]

JOHNNY Nothin', nothin', nothin'.

MRS. BOYLE Sure, you must be thinkin' of somethin'; it's yourself that has yourself the way y'are; sleepin' wan night in me sisther's, an' the nex' in your father's brother's—you'll get no rest goin' on that way.

JOHNNY I can rest nowhere, nowhere, nowhere.

MRS. BOYLE Sure, you're not thryin' to rest anywhere.

JOHNNY Let me alone, let me alone, let me alone, for God's sake.

(*A knock at street door*)

MRS. BOYLE (*In a flutter*) Here he is; here's Mr. Bentham!

BOYLE Well, there's room for him; it's a pity there's not a brass band to play him in.

MRS. BOYLE We'll han' the tay round, an' not be clusthered round the table, as if we never seen nothin'.

(*Steps are heard approaching, and* JUNO, *opening the door, allows* BENTHAM *to enter*)

JUNO Give your hat an' stick to Jack, there . . . sit down, Mr. Bentham . . . no, not there . . . in th' easy chair be the fire . . . there, that's betther. Mary'll be out to you in a minute.

BOYLE (*Solemnly*) I seen be the paper this mornin' that Consols was down half per cent. That's serious, min' you, an' shows the whole counthry's in a state o' chassis.

MRS. BOYLE What's Consols, Jack?

BOYLE Consols? Oh, Consols is—oh, there's no use tellin' women what Consols is—th' wouldn't undherstand.

BENTHAM It's just as you were saying, Mr. Boyle . . .

(MARY *enters, charmingly dressed*)

BENTHAM Oh, good evening, Mary; how pretty you're looking!

MARY (*Archly*) Am I?

BOYLE We were just talkin' when you kem in, Mary; I was tellin' Mr. Bentham that the whole counthry's in a state o' chassis.

MARY (*To* BENTHAM) Would you prefer the green or the blue ribbon round me hair, Charlie?

MRS. BOYLE Mary, your father's speakin'.

BOYLE (*Rapidly*) I was jus' tellin' Mr. Bentham that the whole counthry's in a state o' chassis.

MARY I'm sure you're frettin', Da, whether it is or no.

MRS. BOYLE With all our churches an' religions, the worl's not a bit the betther.

BOYLE (*With a commanding gesture*) Tay!

(MARY *and* MRS. BOYLE *dispense the tea*)

MRS. BOYLE An' Irelan's takin' a leaf out o' the worl's buk; when we got the makin' of our own laws I

[6] O'Casey has explained that *Boneparte's Oraculum* was a popular penny-pamphlet containing interpretations of dreams, fortune-telling cards, and various signs and wonders.

[7] Dear, darling; an Irish word of deep affection.

thought we'd never stop to look behind us, but instead of that we never stopped to look before us! If the people ud folley up their religion betther there'd be a betther chance for us—what do you think, Mr. Bentham?

BENTHAM I'm afraid I can't venture to express an opinion on that point, Mrs. Boyle; dogma has no attraction for me.

MRS. BOYLE I forgot you didn't hold with us: what's this you said you were?

BENTHAM A Theosophist, Mrs. Boyle.

MRS. BOYLE An' what in the name o' God's a Theosophist?

BOYLE A Theosophist, Juno, 's a—tell her, Mr. Bentham, tell her.

BENTHAM It's hard to explain in a few words: Theosophy's founded on The Vedas, the religious books of the East. Its central theme is the existence of an all-pervading Spirit—the Life-Breath. Nothing really exists but this one Universal Life-Breath. And whatever even seems to exist separately from this Life-Breath, doesn't really exist at all. It is all vital force in man, in all animals, and in all vegetation. This Life-Breath is called the Prawna.

MRS. BOYLE The Prawna! What a comical name!

BOYLE Prawna; yis, the Prawna. (*Blowing gently through his lips*) That's the Prawna!

MRS. BOYLE Whist, whist, Jack.

BENTHAM The happiness of man depends upon his sympathy with this Spirit. Men who have reached a high state of excellence are called Yogi. Some men become Yogi in a short time, it may take others millions of years.

BOYLE Yogi! I seen hundhreds of them in the streets o' San Francisco.

BENTHAM It is said by these Yogi that if we practise certain mental exercises that we would have powers denied to others—for instance, the faculty of seeing things that happen miles and miles away.

MRS. BOYLE I wouldn't care to meddle with that sort o' belief; it's a very curious religion, altogether.

BOYLE What's curious about it? Isn't all religions curious? If they weren't, you wouldn't get any one to believe them. But religions is passin' away—they've had their day like everything else. Take the real Dublin people, f'rinstance: they know more about Charlie Chaplin an' Tommy Mix than they do about SS. Peter an' Paul!

MRS. BOYLE You don't believe in ghosts, Mr. Bentham?

MARY Don't you know he doesn't, Mother?

BENTHAM I don't know that, Mary. Scientists are beginning to think that what we call ghosts are sometimes seen by persons of a certain nature. They say that sensational actions, such as the killing of a person, demand great energy, and that that energy lingers in the place where the action occurred. People may live in the place and see nothing, when some one may come along whose personality has some peculiar connection with the energy of the place, and, in a flash, the person sees the whole affair.

JOHNNY (*Rising swiftly, pale and affected*) What sort o' talk is this to be goin' on with? Is there nothin' betther to be talkin' about but the killin' o' people? My God, isn't it bad enough for these things to happen without talkin' about them! (*He hurriedly goes into the room on left*)

BENTHAM Oh, I'm very sorry, Mrs. Boyle; I never thought . . .

MRS. BOYLE (*Apologetically*) Never mind, Mr. Bentham, he's very touchy. (*A frightened scream is heard from* JOHNNY *inside*)

MRS. BOYLE Mother of God? What's that?

(*He rushes out again, his face pale, his lips twitching, his limbs trembling*)

JOHNNY Shut the door, shut the door, quick, for God's sake! Great God, have mercy on me! Blessed Mother o' God, shelther me, shelther your son!

MRS. BOYLE (*Catching him in her arms*) What's wrong with you? What ails you? Sit down, sit down, here, on the bed . . . there now . . . there now.

MARY Johnny, Johnny, what ails you?

JOHNNY I seen him, I seen him . . . kneelin' in front o' the statue . . . merciful Jesus, have pity on me!

MRS. BOYLE (*To* BOYLE) Get him a glass o' whisky . . . quick, man, an' don't stand gawkin'.

(BOYLE *gets the whisky*)

JOHNNY Sit here, sit here, Mother . . . between me an' the door.

MRS. BOYLE I'll sit beside you as long as you like, only tell me what was it came across you at all?

JOHNNY (*After taking some drink*) I seen him. . . . I seen Robbie Tancred kneelin' down before the statue . . . an' the red light shinin' on him . . . an' when I went in . . . he turned an' looked at me . . . an' I seen the woun's bleedin' in his breast. . . . Oh, why did he look at me like that . . . it wasn't my fault that he was done in. . . . Mother o' God, keep him away from me!

MRS. BOYLE There, there, child, you've imagined it all. There was nothin' there at all—it was the red light you seen, an' the talk we had put all the rest into your head. Here, dhrink more o' this—it'll do you good. . . . An', now, stretch yourself down on the bed for a little. (*To* BOYLE) Go in, Jack, an' show him it was only in his own head it was.

BOYLE (*Making no move*) E-e-e-e-eh; it's all nonsense; it was only a shadda he saw.

MARY Mother o' God, he made me heart lep!

BENTHAM It was simply due to an overwrought imagination—we all get that way at times.

MRS. BOYLE There, dear, lie down in the bed, an I'll put the quilt across you . . . e-e-e-eh, that's it . . . you'll be as right as the mail in a few minutes.

JOHNNY Mother, go into the room an' see if the light's lightin' before the statue.

MRS. BOYLE (*To* BOYLE) Jack, run in an' see if the light's lightin' before the statue.

BOYLE (*To* MARY) Mary, slip in an' see if the light's lightin' before the statue.

(MARY *hesitates to go in*)

BENTHAM It's all right; Mary, I'll go. (*He goes into the room; remains for a few moments, and returns*)

BENTHAM Everything's just as it was—the light burning bravely before the statue.

BOYLE Of course; I knew it was all nonsense.

(*A knock at the door*)

BOYLE (*Going to open the door*) E-e-e-e-eh. (*He opens it, and* JOXER, *followed by* MRS. MADIGAN, *enters.* MRS. MADIGAN *is a strong, dapper little woman of about forty-five; her face is almost always a wide-spread smile of complacency. She is a woman who, in manner at least, can mourn with them that mourn, and rejoice with them that do rejoice. When she is feeling comfortable, she is inclined to be reminiscent; when others say anything, or following a statement made by herself, she has a habit of putting her head a little to one side, and nodding it rapidly several times in succession, like a bird pecking at a hard berry. Indeed, she has a good deal of the bird in her, but the bird instinct is by no means a melodious one. She is ignorant, vulgar and forward, but her heart is generous withal. For instance, she would help a neighbour's sick child; she would probably kill the child, but her intentions would be to cure it; she would be more at home helping a drayman to lift a fallen horse. She is dressed in a rather soiled grey dress and a vivid purple blouse; in her hair is a huge comb, ornamented with huge coloured beads. She enters with a gliding step, beaming smile and nodding head.* BOYLE *receives them effusively*)

BOYLE Come on in, Mrs. Madigan; come on in; I was afraid you weren't comin'. . . . (*Slyly*) There's some people able to dhress, ay, Joxer?

JOXER Fair as the blossoms that bloom in the May, an' sweet as the scent of the new mown hay. . . . Ah, well she may wear them.

MRS. MADIGAN (*Looking at* MARY) I know some as are as sweet as the blossoms that bloom in the May—oh, no names, no pack dhrill! [8]

BOYLE An' now, I'll inthroduce the pair o' yous to Mary's intended: Mr. Bentham, this is Mrs. Madigan, an oul' back-parlour neighbour, that, if she could help it at all, ud never see a body shuk! [9]

BENTHAM (*Rising, and tentatively shaking the hand of* MRS. MADIGAN) I'm sure, it's a great pleasure to know you, Mrs. Madigan.

MRS. MADIGAN An' I'm goin' to tell you, Mr. Bentham, you're goin' to get as nice a bit o' skirt in Mary, there, as ever you seen in your puff. Not like some of the dhressed up dolls that's knockin' about lookin' for men when it's a skelpin' they want. I remember as well as I remember yestherday, the day she was born—of a Tuesday, the 25th o' June, in the year 1901, at thirty-three minutes past wan in the day be Foley's clock, the pub at the corner o' the street. A cowld day it was too, for the season o' the year, an' I remember sayin' to Joxer, there, who I met comin' up th' stairs, that the new arrival in Boyle's ud grow up a hardy chiselur if it lived, an' that she'd be somethin' one o' these days that nobody suspected, an' so signs on it, here she is to-day, goin' to be married to a young man lookin' as if he'd be fit to commensurate in any position in life it ud please God to call him!

BOYLE (*Effusively*) Sit down, Mrs. Madigan, sit down, me oul' sport. (*To* BENTHAM) This is Joxer Daly, Past Chief Ranger of the Dear Little Shamrock Branch of the Irish National Foresters, an oul' front-top neighbour, that never despaired, even in the darkest days of Ireland's sorra.

JOXER Nil desperandum, Captain, nil desperandum.[10]

BOYLE Sit down, Joxer, sit down. The two of us was ofen in a tight corner.

MRS. BOYLE Ay, in Foley's snug!

JOXER An' we kem out of it flyin', we kem out of it flyin', Captain.

BOYLE An', now, for a dhrink—I know yous won't refuse an oul' friend.

MRS. MADIGAN (*To* JUNO) Is Johnny not well, Mrs. . . .

MRS. BOYLE (*Warningly*) S-s-s-sh.

MRS. MADIGAN Oh, the poor darlin'.

BOYLE Well, Mrs. Madigan, is it tay or what?

MRS. MADIGAN Well, speakin' for meself, I jus' had me tay a minute ago, an' I'm afraid to dhrink any more—I'm never the same when I dhrink too much tay. Thanks, all the same, Mr. Boyle.

BOYLE Well, what about a bottle o' stout or a dhrop o' whisky?

MRS. MADIGAN A bottle o' stout ud be a little too heavy for me stummock afther me tay. . . . A-a-ah, I'll thry the ball o' malt. (BOYLE *prepares the whisky*) There's nothin' like a ball o' malt occasional like—too much of it isn't good. (*To* BOYLE, *who is adding water*) Ah, God, Johnny, don't put too much wather on it! (*She drinks*) I suppose yous'll be lavin' this place.

BOYLE I'm looking for a place near the sea; I'd like the place that you might say was me cradle, to be me grave as well. The sea is always callin' me.

JOXER She is callin', callin', callin', in the win' an' on the sea.

BOYLE Another dhrop o' whisky, Mrs. Madigan?

MRS. MADIGAN Well, now, it ud be hard to refuse seein' the suspicious times that's in it.

BOYLE (*With a commanding gesture*) Song! . . . Juno . . . Mary . . . "Home to Our Mount'ins"!

MRS. MADIGAN (*Enthusiastically*) Hear, hear!

JOXER Oh, tha's a darlin' song, a daarlin' song!

MARY (*Bashfully*) Ah, no, Da; I'm not in a singin' humour.

MRS. MADIGAN Gawn with you, child, an' you only goin' to be marrid; I remember as well as I remember yestherday—it was on a lovely August evenin', exactly, accordin' to date, fifteen years ago, come the Tuesday folleyin' the nex' that's comin' on, when me own man (the Lord be good to him) an' me was sittin' shy together in a doty little nook on a counthry road, adjacent to The Stiles. "That'll scratch your lovely, little white neck," says he, ketchin' hould of a danglin' bramble branch, holdin' clusters of the love-

[8] A military punishment involving marching with full equipment.

[9] Would never see anyone taken advantage of.

[10] "There is nothing to cause despair."

liest flowers you ever seen, an' breakin' it off, so that his arm fell, accidental like, roun' me waist, an' as I felt it tightenin', an' tightenin', an' tightenin', I thought me buzzum was every minute goin' to burst out into a roystherin' song about

The little green leaves that were shakin' on the threes,
The gallivantin' buttherflies, an' buzzin' o' the bees!

BOYLE Ordher for the song!

JUNO Come on, Mary—we'll do our best. (JUNO *and* MARY *stand up, and choosing a suitable position, sing simply "Home to Our Mountains."*)

(*They bow to company, and return to their places*)

BOYLE (*Emotionally, at the end of the song*) Lull . . . me . . . to . . . rest!

JOXER (*Clapping his hands*) Bravo, bravo! Darlin' girulls, darlin' girulls!

MRS. MADIGAN Juno, I never seen you in betther form.

BENTHAM Very nicely rendered indeed.

MRS. MADIGAN A noble call, a noble call!

MRS. BOYLE What about yourself, Mrs. Madigan? (*After some coaxing,* MRS. MADIGAN *rises, and in a quavering voice sings the following verse*)

If I were a blackbird I'd whistle and sing;
I'd follow the ship that my thrue love was in;
An' on the top riggin', I'd there build me nest,
An' at night I would sleep on me Willie's white breast!

(*Becoming husky, amid applause, she sits down*)

MRS. MADIGAN Ah, me voice is too husky now, Juno; though I remember the time when Maisie Madigan could sing like a nightingale at matin' time. I remember as well as I remember yesthe rday, at a party given to celebrate the comin' of the first chiselur to Annie an' Benny Jimeson—who was the barber, yous may remember, in Henrietta Street, that, afther Easter Week, hung out a green, white an' orange pole, an', then, when the Tans started their Jazz dancin', whipped it in agen, an' stuck out a red, white an' blue wan instead,[11] givin' as an excuse that a barber's pole was strictly non-political—singin' "An' You'll Remember Me," with the top notes quiverin' in a dead hush of pethrified attention, folleyed by a clappin' o' han's that shuk the tumblers on the table, an' capped be Jimeson, the barber, sayin' that it was the best rendherin' of "You'll Remember Me" he ever heard in his natural!

BOYLE (*Peremptorily*) Ordher for Joxer's song!

JOXER Ah, no, I couldn't; don't ass me, Captain.

BOYLE Joxer's song, Joxer's song—give us wan of your shut-eyed wans. (JOXER *settles himself in his chair; takes a drink; clears his throat; solemnly closes his eyes, and begins to sing in a very querulous voice*)

JOXER She is far from the lan' where her young hero sleeps,
An' lovers around her are sighing (*He hesitates*)
An' lovers around her are sighin' . . . sighin' . . . sighin' . . . (*A pause*)

BOYLE (*imitating* JOXER)

And lovers around her are sighing!

What's the use of you thryin' to sing the song if you don't know it?

MARY Thry another one, Mr. Daly—maybe you'd be more fortunate.

MRS. MADIGAN Gawn, Joxer, thry another wan.

JOXER (*Starting again*)
I have heard the mavis singin' his love song to the morn;
I have seen the dew-dhrop clingin' to the rose jus' newly born; but . . . but . . . (*frantically*) to the rose jus' newly born . . . newly born . . . born.

JOHNNY Mother, put on the gramophone, for God's sake, an' stop Joxer's bawlin'.

BOYLE (*Commandingly*) Gramophone! . . . I hate to see fellas thryin' to do what they're not able to do. (BOYLE *arranges the gramophone, and is about to start it, when voices are heard of persons descending the stairs*)

MRS. BOYLE (*Warningly*) Whisht, Jack, don't put it on, don't put it on yet; this must be poor Mrs. Tancred comin' down to go to the hospital—I forgot all about them bringin' the body to the church tonight. Open the door, Mary, an' give them a bit o' light.

(MARY *opens the door, and* MRS. TANCRED*—a very old woman, obviously shaken by the death of her son—appears, accompanied by several neighbours. The first few phrases are spoken before they appear*)

FIRST NEIGHBOUR It's a sad journey we're goin' on, but God's good, an' the Republicans won't be always down.

MRS. TANCRED Ah, what good is that to me now? Whether they're up or down—it won't bring me darlin' boy from the grave.

MRS. BOYLE Come in an' have a hot cup o' tay, Mrs. Tancred, before you go.

MRS. TANCRED Ah, I can take nothin' now, Mrs. Boyle —I won't be long afther him.

FIRST NEIGHBOUR Still an' all, he died a noble death, an' we'll bury him like a king.

MRS. TANCRED An' I'll go on livin' like a pauper. Ah, what's the pains I suffered bringin' him into the world to carry him to his cradle, to the pains I'm sufferin' now, carryin' him out o' the world to bring him to his grave!

MARY It would be better for you not to go at all, Mrs. Tancred, but to stay at home beside the fire with some o' the neighbours.

MRS. TANCRED I seen the first of him, an' I'll see the last of him.

MRS. BOYLE You'd want a shawl, Mrs. Tancred; it's a cowld night, an' the win's blowin' sharp.

MRS. MADIGAN (*Rushing out*) I've a shawl above.

MRS. TANCRED Me home is gone, now; he was me only

[11] The Irish Free State colors were green, white and orange; the British flag is red, white and blue. The Tans (or Black-and-Tans) were British soldiers.

child, an' to think that he was lyin' for a whole night stretched out on the side of a lonely counthry lane, with his head, his darlin' head, that I ofen kissed an' fondled, half hidden in the wather of a runnin' brook. An' I'm told he was the leadher of the ambush where me nex' door neighbour, Mrs. Mannin', lost her Free State soldier son. An' now here's the two of us oul' women, standin' one on each side of a scales o' sorra, balanced be the bodies of our two dead darlin' sons. (MRS. MADIGAN *returns, and wraps a shawl around her*) God bless you, Mrs. Madigan. . . . (*She moves slowly towards the door*) Mother o' God, Mother o' God, have pity on the pair of us! . . . O Blessed Virgin, where were you when me darlin' son was riddled with bullets, when me darlin' son was riddled with bullets! . . . Sacred Heart of the Crucified Jesus, take away our hearts o' stone . . . an' give us hearts o' flesh! . . . Take away this murdherin' hate . . . an' give us Thine own eternal love! (*They pass out of the room*)

MRS. BOYLE (*Explanatorily to* BENTHAM) That was Mrs. Tancred of the two-pair[12] back; her son was found, e'er yestherday, lyin' out beyant Finglas riddled with bullets. A Die-hard he was, be all accounts. He was a nice quiet boy, but lattherly he went to hell, with his Republic first, an' Republic last an' Republic over all. He often took tea with us here, in the oul' days; an' Johnny, there, an' him used to be always together.

JOHNNY Am I always to be havin' to tell you that he was no friend o' mine? I never cared for him, an' he could never stick me. It's not because he was Commandant of the Battalion that I was Quarther-Masther of, that we were friends.

MRS. BOYLE He's gone, now—the Lord be good to him! God help his poor oul' creature of a mother, for no matther whose friend or enemy he was, he was her poor son.

BENTHAM The whole thing is terrible, Mrs. Boyle; but the only way to deal with a mad dog is to destroy him.

MRS. BOYLE An' to think of me forgettin' about him bein' brought to the church tonight, an' we singin' an' all, but it was well we hadn't the gramophone goin', anyhow.

BOYLE Even if we had aself. We've nothin' to do with these things, one way or t'other. That's the Government's business, an' let them do what we're payin' them for doin'.

MRS. BOYLE I'd like to know how a body's not to mind these things; look at the way they're afther leavin' the people in this very house. Hasn't the whole house, nearly, been massacreed? There's young Mrs. Dougherty's husband with his leg off; Mrs. Travers that had her son blew up be a mine in Inchegeela, in County Cork; Mrs. Mannin' that lost wan of her sons in an ambush a few weeks ago, an' now, poor Mrs. Tancred's only child gone West with his body made a collandher of. Sure, if it's not our business, I don't know whose business it is.

[12] Two-room apartment.

BOYLE Here, there, that's enough about them things; they don't affect us, an' we needn't give a damn. If they want a wake, well, let them have a wake. When I was a sailor, I was always resigned to meet with a wathery grave; an', if they want to be soldiers, well, there's no use o' them squealin' when they meet a soldier's fate.

JOXER Let me like a soldier fall—me breast expandin' to th' ball!

MRS. BOYLE In wan way, she deserves all she got; for lately, she let th' Die-hards make an open house of th' place; an' for th' last couple of months, either when th' sun was risin', or when th' sun was settin', you had C.I.D. men[13] burstin' into your room, assin' you where were you born, where were you christened, where were you married, an' where would you be buried!

JOHNNY For God's sake, let us have no more o' this talk.

MRS. MADIGAN What about Mr. Boyle's song before we start th' gramophone?

MARY (*Getting her hat, and putting it on*) Mother, Charlie and I are goin' out for a little shtroll.

MRS. BOYLE All right, darlin'.

BENTHAM (*Going out with* MARY) We won't be long away, Mrs. Boyle.

MRS. MADIGAN Gwan, Captain, gwan.

BOYLE E-e-e-e-eh, I'd want to have a few more jars in me, before I'd be in fettle for singin'.

JOXER Give us that poem you writ t'other day. (*To the rest*) Aw, it's a darlin' poem, a daarlin' poem.

MRS. BOYLE God bless us, is he startin' to write poetry!

BOYLE (*Rising to his feet*) E-e-e-e-eh. (*He recites in an emotional, consequential manner the following verses*)

Shawn an' I were friends, sir, to me he was all in all.
His work was very heavy and his wages were very small.
None betther on th' beach as Docker, I'll go bail,
'Tis now I'm feelin' lonely, for to-day he lies in jail.
He was not what some call pious—seldom at church or prayer;
For the greatest scoundrels I know, sir, goes every Sunday there.
Fond of his pint—well, rather, but hated the Boss by creed
But never refused a copper to comfort a pal in need.
E-e-e-e-eh. (*He sits down*)

MRS. MADIGAN Grand, grand; you should folley that up, you should folley that up.

JOXER It's a daarlin' poem!

BOYLE (*Delightedly*) E-e-e-e-eh.

JOHNNY Are yous goin' to put on th' gramophone tonight, or are yous not?

[13] Free State supporters recruited for the Irish counterpart of Britain's Criminal Investigation Department. Scotland Yard men had been active in Ireland during the 1916-1921 fighting.

MRS. BOYLE Gwan, Jack, put on a record.

MRS. MADIGAN Gwan, Captain, gwan.

BOYLE Well, yous'll want to keep a dead silence. (*He sets a record, starts the machine, and it begins to play "If you're Irish, come into the Parlour." As the tune is in full blare, the door is suddenly opened by a brisk, little, bald-headed man, dressed circumspectly in a black suit; he glares fiercely at all in the room; he is* "NEEDLE" NUGENT, *a tailor. He carries his hat in his hands*)

NUGENT (*Loudly, above the noise of the gramophone*) Are yous goin' to have that thing bawlin' an' the funeral of Mrs. Tancred's son passin' the house? Have none of yous any respect for the Irish people's National regard for the dead?

(BOYLE *stops the gramophone*)

MRS. BOYLE Maybe, Needle Nugent, it's nearly time we had a little less respect for the dead, an' a little more regard for the livin'.

MRS. MADIGAN We don't want you, Mr. Nugent, to teach us what we learned at our mother's knee. You don't look yourself as if you were dyin' of grief; if y'ass Maisie Madigan anything, I'd call you a real thrue Die-hard an' live-soft Republican, attendin' Republican funerals in the day, an' stoppin' up half the night makin' suits for the Civic Guards! [14] (*Persons are heard running down to the street, some saying, "Here it is, here it is."* NUGENT *withdraws, and the rest, except* JOHNNY, *go to the window looking into the street, and look out. Sounds of a crowd coming nearer are heard; portion are singing*)

To Jesus' Heart all burning
With fervent love for men,
My heart with fondest yearning
Shall raise its joyful strain.
While ages course along,
Blest be with loudest song,
The Sacred Heart of Jesus
By every heart and tongue.

MRS. BOYLE Here's the hearse, here's the hearse!

BOYLE There's t'oul' mother walkin' behin' the coffin.

MRS. MADIGAN You can hardly see the coffin with the wreaths.

JOXER Oh, it's a darlin' funeral, a daarlin' funeral!

MRS. MADIGAN We'd have a betther view from the street.

BOYLE Yes—this place ud give you a crick in your neck. (*They leave the room, and go down.* JOHNNY *sits moodily by the fire*)

(*A young man enters; he looks at* JOHNNY *for a moment*)

THE YOUNG MAN Quarther-Masther Boyle.

JOHNNY (*With a start*) The Mobilizer!

THE YOUNG MAN You're not at the funeral?

JOHNNY I'm not well.

THE YOUNG MAN I'm glad I've found you; you were stoppin' at your aunt's; I called there but you'd gone. I've to give you an ordher to attend a Battalion Staff meetin' the night afther tomorrow.

[14] Soldiers of the Irish Free State.

JOHNNY Where?

THE YOUNG MAN I don't know; you're to meet me at the Pillar at eight o'clock; then we're to go to a place I'll be told of tonight; there we'll meet a mothor that'll bring us to the meeting. They think you might be able to know somethin' about them that gave the bend where Commandant Tancred was shelterin'.

JOHNNY I'm not goin', then. I know nothing about Tancred.

THE YOUNG MAN (*At the door*) You'd betther come for your own sake—remember your oath.

JOHNNY (*Passionately*) I won't go! Haven't I done enough for Ireland! I've lost me arm, an' me hip's desthroyed so that I'll never be able to walk right agen! Good God, haven't I done enough for Ireland?

THE YOUNG MAN Boyle, no man can do enough for Ireland! (*He goes*)

(*Faintly in the distance the crowd is heard saying*)

Hail, Mary, full of grace, the Lord is with Thee;
Blessed art Thou amongst women, and blessed, etc.

*Curtain*

# Act Three

SCENE *The same as Act II. It is about half-past six on a November evening; a bright fire is burning in the grate;* MARY, *dressed to go out, is sitting on a chair by the fire, leaning forward, her hands under her chin, her elbows on her knees. A look of dejection, mingled with uncertain anxiety, is on her face. A lamp, turned low, is lighting on the table. The votive light under the picture of the Virgin gleams more redly than ever.* MRS. BOYLE *is putting on her hat and coat. It is two months later.*

MRS. BOYLE An' has Bentham never even written to you since—not one line for the past month?

MARY (*Tonelessly*) Not even a line, Mother.

MRS. BOYLE That's very curious. . . . What came between the two of yous at all? To leave you so sudden, an' yous so great together. . . . To go away t' England, an' not to even leave you his address. . . . The way he was always bringin' you to dances, I thought he was mad afther you. Are you sure you said nothin' to him?

MARY No, Mother—at least nothing could possibly explain his givin' me up.

MRS. BOYLE You know you're a bit hasty at times, Mary, an' say things you shouldn't say.

MARY I never said to him what I shouldn't say, I'm sure of that.

MRS. BOYLE How are you sure of it?

MARY Because I love him with all my heart and soul, Mother. Why, I don't know; I often thought to myself that he wasn't the man poor Jerry was, but I couldn't help loving him, all the same.

MRS. BOYLE But you shouldn't be frettin' the way you are; when a woman loses a man, she never knows what she's afther losin', to be sure, but, then, she never knows what she's afther gainin', either. You're not the one girl of a month ago—you look like one pinin' away. It's long ago I had a right to bring you to the doctor, instead of waitin' till tonight.

MARY There's no necessity, really, Mother, to go to the doctor; nothing serious is wrong with me—I'm run down and disappointed, that's all.

MRS. BOYLE I'll not wait another minute; I don't like the look of you at all. I'm afraid we made a mistake in throwin' over poor Jerry. . . . He'd have been betther for you than that Bentham.

MARY Mother, the best man for a woman is the one for whom she has the most love, and Charlie had it all.

MRS. BOYLE Well, there's one thing to be said for him—he couldn't have been thinkin' of the money, or he wouldn't ha' left you . . . it must ha' been somethin' else.

MARY (*Wearily*) I don't know . . . I don't know, Mother . . . only I think . . .

MRS. BOYLE What d'ye think?

MARY I imagine . . . he thought . . . we weren't . . . good enough for him.

MRS. BOYLE An' what was he himself, only a school teacher? Though I don't blame him for fightin' shy of people like that Joxer fella an' that oul' Madigan wan—nice sort o' people for your father to inthroduce to a man like Mr. Bentham. You might have told me all about this before now, Mary; I don't know why you like to hide everything from your mother; you knew Bentham, an' I'd ha' known nothin' about it if it hadn't bin for the Will; an' it was only today, afther long coaxin', that you let out that he's left you.

MARY It would have been useless to tell you—you wouldn't understand.

MRS. BOYLE (*Hurt*) Maybe not. . . . Maybe I wouldn't understand. . . . Well, we'll be off now. (*She goes over to the door left, and speaks to* BOYLE *inside*) We're goin' now to the doctor's. Are you goin' to get up this evenin'?

BOYLE (*From inside*) The pains in me legs is terrible! It's me should be poppin' off to the doctor instead o' Mary, the way I feel.

MRS. BOYLE Sorra mend you! A nice way you were in last night—carried in in a frog's march,[1] dead to the world. If that's the way you'll go on when you get the money it'll be the grave for you, an asylum for me and the Poorhouse for Johnny.

BOYLE I thought you were goin'?

MRS. BOYLE That's what has you as you are—you can't bear to be spoken to. Knowin' the way we are, up to our ears in debt, it's a wondher you wouldn't ha' got up to go to th' solicitor's an' see if we could ha' gotten a little o' the money even.

BOYLE (*Shouting*) I can't be goin' up there night, noon an' mornin', can I? He can't give the money till he gets it, can he? I can't get blood out of a turnip, can I?

MRS. BOYLE It's nearly two months since we heard of the Will, an' the money seems as far off as ever. . . . I suppose you know we owe twenty poun's to oul' Murphy?

BOYLE I've a faint recollection of you tellin' me that before.

MRS. BOYLE Well, you'll go over to the shop yourself for the things in future—I'll face him no more.

BOYLE I thought you said you were goin'?

MRS. BOYLE I'm goin' now; come on, Mary.

BOYLE Ey, Juno, ey!

MRS. BOYLE Well, what d'ye want now?

BOYLE Is there e'er a bottle o' stout left?

MRS. BOYLE There's two o' them here still.

BOYLE Show us in one o' them an' leave t'other there till I get up. An' throw us in the paper that's on the table, an' the bottle o' Sloan's Liniment that's in th' drawer.

MRS. BOYLE (*Getting the liniment and the stout*) What paper is it you want—the *Messenger?* [2]

BOYLE *Messenger! The News o' the World!* [3]

(MRS. BOYLE *brings in the things asked for and comes out again*)

MRS. BOYLE (*At door*) Mind the candle, now, an' don't burn the house over our heads. I left t'other bottle o' stout on the table. (*She puts bottle of stout on table. She goes out with* MARY. *A cork is heard popping inside*)

(*A pause; then outside the door is heard the voice of* JOXER *lilting softly: "Me pipe I'll smoke, as I dhrive me moke . . . are you . . . there . . . Mor . . . ee . . . ar . . . i . . . tee!" A gentle knock is heard and, after a pause, the door opens, and* JOXER, *followed by* NUGENT, *enters*)

JOXER Be God, they must all be out; I was thinkin' there was somethin' up when he didn't answer the signal. We seen Juno an' Mary goin', but I didn't see him, an' it's very seldom he escapes me.

NUGENT He's not goin' to escape me—he's not goin' to be let go to the fair altogether.

JOXER Sure, the house couldn't hould them lately; an' he goin' about like a masterpiece of the Free State counthry; forgettin' their friends; forgettin' God—wouldn't even lift his hat passin' a chapel! Sure they were bound to get a dhrop! An' you really think there's no money comin' to him afther all?

NUGENT Not as much as a red rex, man; I've been a bit anxious this long time over me money, an' I went up to the solicitor's to find out all I could—ah, man, they were goin' to throw me down the stairs. They toul' me that the oul' cock himself had the stairs worn away comin' up afther it, an' they black in the face tellin' him he'd get nothin'. Some way or another

[1] Juno means that the Captain was carried home, face downward, by his arms and legs.

[2] A conservative newspaper.

[3] The Sunday scandal-sheet.

that the Will is writ he won't be entitled to get as much as a make! [4]

JOXER Ah, I thought there was somethin' curious about the whole thing; I've bin havin' sthrange dreams for the last couple o' weeks. An' I notice that that Bentham fella doesn't be comin' here now—there must be somethin' on the mat there too. Anyhow, who, in the name o' God, ud leave anythin' to that oul' bummer? Sure it ud be unnatural. An' the way Juno an' him's been throwin' their weight about for the last few months! Ah, him that goes a borrowin' goes a sorrowin'!

NUGENT Well, he's not goin' to throw his weight about in the suit I made for him much longer. I'm tellin' you seven poun's aren't to be found growin' on the bushes these days.

JOXER An' there isn't hardly a neighbour in the whole street that hasn't lent him money on the strength of what he was goin' to get, but they're after backing the wrong horse. Wasn't it a mercy o' God that I'd nothin' to give him! The softy I am, you know, I'd ha' lent him me last juice! I must have had somebody's good prayers. Ah, afther all, an honest man's the noblest work o' God!

(BOYLE *coughs inside*)

JOXER Whisht, damn it, he must be inside in bed.

NUGENT Inside o' bed or outside of it he's goin' to pay me for that suit, or give it back—he'll not climb up my back as easily as he thinks.

JOXER Gwan in at wanst, man, an' get it off him, an' don't be a fool.

NUGENT (*Going to the door left, opening it and looking in*) Ah, don't disturb yourself, Mr. Boyle; I hope you're not sick?

BOYLE The' oul' legs, Mr. Nugent, the oul' legs.

NUGENT I just called over to see if you could let me have anything off the suit?

BOYLE E-e-e-eh, how much is this it is?

NUGENT It's the same as it was at the start—seven poun's.

BOYLE I'm glad you kem, Mr. Nugent; I want a good heavy top-coat—Irish frieze, if you have it. How much would a top-coat like that be, now?

NUGENT About six poun's.

BOYLE Six poun's—six an' seven, six an' seven is thirteen—that'll be thirteen poun's I'll owe you.

(JOXER *slips the bottle of stout that is on the table into his pocket.* NUGENT *rushes into the room, and returns with the suit on his arm; he pauses at the door*)

NUGENT You'll owe me no thirteen poun's. Maybe you think you're betther able to owe it than pay it!

BOYLE (*Frantically*) Here, come back to hell ower that—where're you goin' with them clothes o' mine?

NUGENT Where am I goin' with them clothes o' yours? Well, I like your damn cheek!

BOYLE Here, what am I going to dhress meself in when I'm goin' out?

NUGENT What do I care what you dhress yourself in? You can put yourself in a bolsther cover, if you like.

[4] A halfpenny.

(*He goes towards the other door, followed by* JOXER)

JOXER What'll he dhress himself in! Gentleman Jack an' his frieze coat!

(*They go out*)

BOYLE (*Inside*) Ey, Nugent, ey, Mr. Nugent, Mr. Nugent!

(*After a pause* BOYLE *enters hastily, buttoning the braces of his moleskin trousers; his coat and vest are on his arm; he throws these on a chair and hurries to the door on right*)

BOYLE Ey, Mr. Nugent, Mr. Nugent!

JOXER (*Meeting him at the door*) What's up, what's wrong, Captain?

BOYLE Nugent's been here an' took away me suit—the only things I had to go out in!

JOXER Tuk your suit—for God's sake! An' what were you doin' while he was takin' them?

BOYLE I was in bed when he stole in like a thief in the night, an' before I knew even what he was thinkin' of, he whipped them from the chair, an' was off like a redshank! [5]

JOXER An' what, in the name o' God, did he do that for?

BOYLE What he do it for? How the hell do I know what he done it for? Jealousy an' spite, I suppose.

JOXER Did he not say what he done it for?

BOYLE Amn't I afther tellin' you that he had them whipped up an' was gone before I could open me mouth?

JOXER That was a very sudden thing to do; there mus' be somethin' behin' it. Did he hear anythin', I wondher?

BOYLE Did he hear anythin'?—you talk very queer, Joxer—what could he hear?

JOXER About you not gettin' the money, in some way or t'other?

BOYLE An' what ud prevent me from gettin' th' money?

JOXER That's jus' what I was thinkin'—what ud prevent you from gettin' the money—nothin', as far as I can see.

BOYLE (*Looking round for bottle of stout with an exclamation*) Aw, holy God!

JOXER What's up, Jack?

BOYLE He must have afther lifted the bottle o' stout that Juno left on the table!

JOXER (*Horrified*) Ah, no, ah, no! He wouldn't be afther doin' that, now.

BOYLE An' who done it then? Juno left a bottle o' stout here, an' it's gone—it didn't walk, did it?

JOXER Oh, that's shockin'; ah, man's inhumanity to man makes countless thousands mourn! [6]

MRS. MADIGAN (*Appearing at the door*) I hope I'm not disturbin' you in any discussion on your forthcomin' legacy—if I may use the word—an' that

[5] O'Casey has explained that this is a red-legged seagull, notable because it is uncommon and because it never stays anywhere for long.

[6] Joxer is quoting from Robert Burns' "Man Was Made to Mourn."

you'll let me have a barny[7] for a minute or two with you, Mr. Boyle.

BOYLE (*Uneasily*) To be sure, Mrs. Madigan—an oul' friend's always welcome.

JOXER Come in the evenin', come in th' mornin'; come when you're assed, or come without warnin', Mrs. Madigan.

BOYLE Sit down, Mrs. Madigan.

MRS. MADIGAN (*Ominously*) Th' few words I have to say can be said standin'. Puttin' aside all formularies, I suppose you remember me lendin' you some time ago three poun's that I raised on blankets an' furniture in me uncle's?

BOYLE I remember it well. I have it recorded in me book—three poun's five shillin's from Maisie Madigan, raised on articles pawned; an', item: fourpence, given to make up the price of a pint, on th' principle that no bird ever flew on wan wing; all to be repaid at par, when the ship comes home.

MRS. MADIGAN Well, ever since I shoved in the blankets I've been perishing with th' cowld, an' I've decided, if I'll be too hot in th' nex' world aself, I'm not goin' to be too cowld in this wan; an' consequently, I want me three poun's, if you please.

BOYLE This is a very sudden demand, Mrs. Madigan, an' can't be met; but I'm willin' to give you a receipt in full, in full.

MRS. MADIGAN Come on, out with th' money, an' don't be jack-actin'.

BOYLE You can't get blood out of a turnip, can you?

MRS. MADIGAN (*Rushing over and shaking him*) Gimme me money, y'oul' reprobate, or I'll shake the worth of it out of you!

BOYLE Ey, houl' on, there; houl' on, there! You'll wait for your money now, me lassie!

MRS. MADIGAN (*Looking around the room and seeing the gramophone*) I'll wait for it, will I? Well, I'll not wait long; if I can't get th' cash, I'll get th' worth of it. (*She catches up the gramophone*)

BOYLE Ey, ey, there, wher'r' you goin' with that?

MRS. MADIGAN I'm goin' to th' pawn to get me three quid five shillin's; I'll brin' you th' ticket, an' then you can do what you like, me bucko.

BOYLE You can't touch that, you can't touch that! It's not my property, an' it's not ped for yet!

MRS. MADIGAN So much th' betther. It'll be an ayse to me conscience, for I'm takin' what doesn't belong to you. You're not goin' to be swankin' it like a paycock with Maisie Madigan's money—I'll pull some o' th' gorgeous feathers out o' your tail! (*She goes off with the gramophone*)

BOYLE What's th' world comin' to at all? I ass you, Joxer Daly, is there any morality left anywhere?

JOXER I wouldn't ha' believed it, only I seen it with me own two eyes. I didn't think Maisie Madigan was that sort of a woman; she has either a sup taken, or she's heard somethin'.

BOYLE Heard somethin'—about what, if it's not any harm to ass you?

[7] Conversation, talk.

JOXER She must ha' heard some rumour or other that you weren't goin' to get th' money.

BOYLE Who says I'm not goin' to get th' money?

JOXER Sure, I don't know—I was only sayin'.

BOYLE Only sayin' what?

JOXER Nothin'.

BOYLE You were goin' to say somethin'—don't be a twisther.

JOXER (*Angrily*) Who's a twisther?

BOYLE Why don't you speak your mind, then?

JOXER You never twisted yourself—no, you wouldn't know how!

BOYLE Did you ever know me to twist; did you ever know me to twist?

JOXER (*Fiercely*) Did you ever do anythin' else! Sure, you can't believe a word that comes out o' your mouth.

BOYLE Here, get out, ower o' this;[8] I always knew you were a prognosticator an' a procrastinator!

JOXER (*Going out as* JOHNNY *comes in*) The anchor's weighed, farewell, ree . . . mem . . . ber . . . me. Jacky Boyle, Esquire, infernal rogue an' damned liar!

JOHNNY Joxer an' you at it agen?—when are you goin' to have a little respect for yourself, an' not be always makin' a show of us all?

BOYLE Are you goin' to lecture me now?

JOHNNY Is mother back from the doctor yet, with Mary?

(MRS. BOYLE *enters; it is apparent from the serious look on her face that something has happened. She takes off her hat and coat without a word and puts them by. She then sits down near the fire, and there is a few moments' pause*)

BOYLE Well, what did the doctor say about Mary?

MRS. BOYLE (*In an earnest manner and with suppressed agitation*) Sit down here, Jack; I've something to say to you . . . about Mary.

BOYLE (*Awed by her manner*) About . . . Mary?

MRS. BOYLE Close that door there and sit down here.

BOYLE (*Closing the door*) More throuble in our native land, is it? (*He sits down*) Well, what is it?

MRS. BOYLE It's about Mary.

BOYLE Well, what about Mary—there's nothin' wrong with her, is there?

MRS. BOYLE I'm sorry to say there's a gradle wrong with her.

BOYLE A gradle wrong with her! (*Peevishly*) First Johnny an' now Mary; is the whole house goin' to become an hospital! It's not consumption, is it?

MRS. BOYLE No . . . it's not consumption . . . it's worse.

JOHNNY Worse! Well, we'll have to get her into some place ower this, there's no one here to mind her.

MRS. BOYLE We'll all have to mind her now. You might as well know now, Johnny, as another time. (*To* BOYLE) D'ye know what the doctor said to me about her, Jack?

BOYLE How ud I know—I wasn't there, was I?

MRS. BOYLE He told me to get her married at wanst.

[8] Enough of this.

BOYLE Married at wanst! An' why did he say the like o' that?

MRS. BOYLE Because Mary's goin' to have a baby in a short time.

BOYLE Goin' to have a baby!—my God, what'll Bentham say when he hears that?

MRS. BOYLE Are you blind, man, that you can't see that it was Bentham that has done this wrong to her?

BOYLE (*Passionately*) Then he'll marry her, he'll have to marry her!

MRS. BOYLE You know he's gone to England, an' God knows where he is now.

BOYLE I'll folley him, I'll folley him, an' bring him back, an' make him do her justice. The scoundrel, I might ha' known what he was, with his yogees an' his prawna!

MRS. BOYLE We'll have to keep it quiet till we see what we can do.

BOYLE Oh, isn't this a nice thing to come on top o' me, an' the state I'm in! A pretty show I'll be to Joxer an' to that oul' wan, Madigan! Amn't I afther goin' through enough without havin' to go through this!

MRS. BOYLE What you an' I'll have to go through'll be nothing to what poor Mary'll have to go through; for you an' me is middlin' old, an' most of our years is spent; but Mary'll have maybe forty years to face an' handle, an' every wan of them'll be tainted with a bitther memory.

BOYLE Where is she? Where is she till I tell her off? I'm tellin' you when I'm done with her she'll be a sorry girl!

MRS. BOYLE I left her in me sisther's till I came to speak to you. You'll say nothin' to her, Jack; ever since she left school she's earned her livin', an' your fatherly care never throubled the poor girl.

BOYLE Gwan, take her part agen her father! But I'll let you see whether I'll say nothin' to her or no! Her an' her readin'! That's more o' th' blasted nonsense that has the house fallin' down on top of us! What did th' likes of her, born in a tenement house, want with readin'? Her readin's afther bringin' her to a nice pass —oh, it's madnin', madnin', madnin'!

MRS. BOYLE When she comes back say nothin' to her, Jack, or she'll leave this place.

BOYLE Leave this place! Ay, she'll leave this place, an' quick too!

MRS. BOYLE If Mary goes, I'll go with her.

BOYLE Well, go with her! Well, go, th' pair o' yous! I lived before I seen yous, an' I can live when yous are gone. Isn't this a nice thing to come rollin' in on top o' me afther all your prayin' to St. Anthony an' The Little Flower. An' she's a Child o' Mary, too—I wonder what'll the nuns think of her now? An' it'll be bellows'd all over th' disthrict before you could say Jack Robinson; an' whenever I'm seen they'll whisper, "That's th' father of Mary Boyle that had th' kid be th' swank she used to go with; d'ye know, d'ye know?" To be sure they'll know—more about it than I will meself!

JOHNNY She should be dhriven out o' th' house she's brought disgrace on!

MRS. BOYLE Hush, you, Johnny. We needn't let it be bellows'd all over the place; all we've got to do is to leave this place quietly an' go somewhere where we're not known, an' nobody'll be the wiser.

BOYLE You're talkin' like a two-year-oul', woman. Where'll we get a place ou' o' this?—places aren't that easily got.

MRS. BOYLE But, Jack, when we get the money . . .

BOYLE Money—what money?

MRS. BOYLE Why, oul' Ellison's money, of course.

BOYLE There's no money comin' from oul' Ellison, or any one else. Since you heard of wan throuble, you might as well hear of another. There's no money comin' to us at all—the Will's a wash-out!

MRS. BOYLE What are you sayin', man—no money?

JOHNNY How could it be a wash-out?

BOYLE The boyo that's afther doin' it to Mary done it to me as well. The thick[9] made out the Will wrong; he said in th' Will, only first cousin an' second cousin, instead of mentionin' our names, an' now any one that thinks he's a first cousin or second cousin t'oul' Ellison can claim the money as well as me, an' they're springin' up in hundreds, an' comin' from America an' Australia, thinkin' to get their whack out of it, while all the time the lawyers is gobblin' it up, till there's not as much as ud buy a stockin' for your lovely daughter's baby!

MRS. BOYLE I don't believe it, I don't believe it, I don't believe it!

JOHNNY Why did you say nothin' about this before?

MRS. BOYLE You're not serious, Jack; you're not serious!

BOYLE I'm tellin' you the scholar, Bentham, made a banjax[10] o' th' Will; instead o' sayin', "th' rest o' me property to be divided between me first cousin, Jack Boyle, an' me second cousin, Mick Finnegan, o' Santhry," he writ down only, "me first an' second cousins," an' the world an' his wife are afther th' property now.

MRS. BOYLE Now, I know why Bentham left poor Mary in th' lurch; I can see it all now—oh, is there not even a middlin' honest man left in th' world?

JOHNNY (*To* BOYLE) An' you let us run into debt, an' you borreyed money from everybody to fill yourself with beer! An' now, you tell us the whole thing's a wash-out! Oh, if it's thrue, I'm done with you, for you're worse than me sisther Mary!

BOYLE You hole your tongue, d'ye hear? I'll not take any lip from you. Go an' get Bentham if you want satisfaction for all that's afther happenin' us.

JOHNNY I won't hole me tongue, I won't hole me tongue! I'll tell you what I think of you, father an' all as you are . . . you . . .

MRS. BOYLE Johnny, Johnny, Johnny, for God's sake, be quiet!

JOHNNY I'll not be quiet, I'll not be quiet; he's a nice father, isn't he? Is it any wondher Mary went asthray, when . . .

[9] Thickhead.

[10] Mess.

MRS. BOYLE Johnny, Johnny, for my sake be quiet—for your mother's sake!

BOYLE I'm goin' out now to have a few dhrinks with th' last few makes I have, an' tell that lassie o' yours not to be here when I come back; for if I lay me eyes on her, I'll lay me han's on her, an' if I lay me han's on her, I won't be accountable for me actions!

JOHNNY Take care somebody doesn't lay his han's on you—y'oul' . . .

MRS. BOYLE Johnny, Johnny!

BOYLE (*At door, about to go out*) Oh, a nice son, an' a nicer daughter, I have. (*Calling loudly upstairs*) Joxer, Joxer, are you there?

JOXER (*From a distance*) I'm here, More . . . ee . . . aar . . . i . . . tee!

BOYLE I'm goin' down to Foley's—are you comin'?

JOXER Come with you? With that sweet call me heart is stirred; I'm only waiting for the word, an' I'll be with you, like a bird!

(BOYLE *and* JOXER *pass the door going out*)

JOHNNY (*Throwing himself on the bed*) I've a nice sisther, an' a nice father, there's no bettin' on it. I wish to God a bullet or a bomb had whipped me ou' o' this long ago! Not one o' yous, not one o' yous, have any thought for me!

MRS. BOYLE (*With passionate remonstrance*) If you don't whisht, Johnny, you'll drive me mad. Who has kep' th' home together for the past few years—only me. An' who'll have to bear th' biggest part o' this throuble but me—but whinin' an' whingin' isn't going to do any good.

JOHNNY You're to blame yourself for a gradle of it—givin' him his own way in everything, an' never assin' to check him, no matther what he done. Why didn't you look afther th' money? why . . .

(*There is a knock at the door;* MRS. BOYLE *opens it;* JOHNNY *rises on his elbow to look and listen; two men enter*)

FIRST MAN We've been sent up be th' Manager of the Hibernian Furnishing Co., Mrs. Boyle, to take back the furniture that was got a while ago.

MRS. BOYLE Yous'll touch nothin' here—how do I know who yous are?

FIRST MAN (*Showing a paper*) There's the ordher, ma'am. (*Reading*) A chest o' drawers, a table, wan easy an' two ordinary chairs; wan mirror; wan chesterfield divan, an' a wardrobe an' two vases. (*To his comrade*) Come on, Bill, it's afther knockin' off time already.

JOHNNY For God's sake, Mother, run down to Foley's an' bring Father back, or we'll be left without a stick.

(*The men carry out the table*)

MRS. BOYLE What good would it be? You heard what he said before he went out.

JOHNNY Can't you thry? He ought to be here, an' the like of this goin' on.

(MRS. BOYLE *puts a shawl around her, as* MARY *enters*)

MARY What's up, Mother? I met men carryin' away the table, an' everybody's talking about us not gettin' the money after all.

MRS. BOYLE Everythin's gone wrong, Mary, everythin'. We're not gettin' a penny out o' the Will, not a penny—I'll tell you all when I come back; I'm goin' for your father. (*She runs out*)

JOHNNY (*To* MARY, *who has sat down by the fire*) It's a wondher you're not ashamed to show your face here, afther what has happened.

(JERRY *enters slowly; there is a look of earnest hope on his face. He looks at* MARY *for a few moments*)

JERRY (*Softly*) Mary!

(MARY *does not answer*)

JERRY Mary, I want to speak to you for a few moments, may I?

(MARY *remains silent;* JOHNNY *goes slowly into room on left*)

JERRY Your mother has told me everything, Mary, and I have come to you. . . . I have come to tell you, Mary, that my love for you is greater and deeper than ever. . . .

MARY (*With a sob*) Oh, Jerry, Jerry, say no more; all that is over now; anything like that is impossible now!

JERRY Impossible? Why do you talk like that, Mary?

MARY After all that has happened.

JERRY What does it matter what has happened? We are young enough to be able to forget all those things. (*He catches her hand*) Mary, Mary, I am pleading for your love. With Labor, Mary, humanity is above everything; we are the Leaders in the fight for a new life. I want to forget Bentham, I want to forget that you left me—even for a while.

MARY Oh, Jerry, Jerry, you haven't the bitter word of scorn for me after all.

JERRY (*Passionately*) Scorn! I love you, love you, Mary!

MARY (*Rising, and looking him in the eyes*) Even though . . .

JERRY Even though you threw me over for another man; even though you gave me many a bitter word!

MARY Yes, yes, I know; but you love me, even though . . . even though . . . I'm . . . goin' . . . goin' . . . (*He looks at her questioningly, and fear gathers in his eyes*) Ah, I was thinkin' so. . . . You don't know everything!

JERRY (*Poignantly*) Surely to God, Mary, you don't mean that . . . that . . . that . . .

MARY Now you know all, Jerry; now you know all!

JERRY My God, Mary, have you fallen as low as that?

MARY Yes, Jerry, as you say, I have fallen as low as that.

JERRY I didn't mean it that way, Mary . . . it came on me so sudden, that I didn't mind what I was sayin'. . . . I never expected this—your mother never told me. . . . I'm sorry . . . God knows, I'm sorry for you, Mary.

MARY Let us say no more, Jerry; I don't blame you for thinkin' it's terrible. . . . I suppose it is. . . . Everybody'll think the same. . . . It's only as I expected—your humanity is just as narrow as the humanity of the others.

JERRY I'm sorry, all the same. . . . I shouldn't have

troubled you. . . . I wouldn't if I'd known . . . if I can do anything for you . . . Mary . . . I will. (*He turns to go, and halts at the door*)

MARY Do you remember, Jerry, the verses you read when you gave the lecture in the Socialist Rooms some time ago, on Humanity's Strife with Nature?

JERRY The verses—no; I don't remember them.

MARY I do. They're runnin' in me head now—

An' we felt the power that fashion'd
All the lovely things we saw,
That created all the murmur
Of an everlasting law,
Was a hand of force an' beauty,
With an eagle's tearin' claw.

Then we saw our globe of beauty
Was an ugly thing as well,
A hymn divine whose chorus
Was an agonizin' yell;
Like the story of a demon,
That an angel had to tell;

Like a glowin' picture by a
Hand unsteady, brought to ruin;
Like her craters, if their deadness
Could give life unto the moon;
Like the agonizing horror
Of a violin out of tune.[11]

(*There is a pause, and* DEVINE *goes slowly out*)

JOHNNY (*Returning*) Is he gone?

MARY Yes.

(*The two men re-enter*)

FIRST MAN We can't wait any longer for t'oul' fella—sorry, Miss, but we have to live as well as th' nex' man.

(*They carry out some things*)

JOHNNY Oh, isn't this terrible! . . . I suppose you told him everything . . . couldn't you have waited for a few days . . . he'd have stopped th' takin' of the things, if you'd kep' your mouth shut. Are you burnin' to tell every one of the shame you've brought on us?

MARY (*Snatching up her hat and coat*) Oh, this is unbearable! (*She rushes out*)

FIRST MAN (*Re-entering*) We'll take the chest o' drawers next—it's the heaviest.

(*The votive light flickers for a moment, and goes out*)

JOHNNY (*In a cry of fear*) Mother o' God, the light's afther goin' out!

FIRST MAN You put the win' up me the way you bawled that time. The oil's all gone, that's all.

JOHNNY (*With an agonizing cry*) Mother o' God, there's a shot I'm afther gettin'!

FIRST MAN What's wrong with you, man? Is it a fit you're takin'?

JOHNNY I'm afther feelin' a pain in me breast, like the tearin' by of a bullet!

FIRST MAN He's goin' mad—it's a wondher they'd leave a chap like that here be himself.

[11] O'Casey has identified these lines as his own, written when he was a very young man.

(*Two* IRREGULARS *enter swiftly; they carry revolvers; one goes over to* JOHNNY; *the other covers the two furniture men*)

FIRST IRREGULAR (*To the men, quietly and incisively*) Who are you—what are yous doin' here—quick!

FIRST MAN Removin' furniture that's not paid for.

IRREGULAR Get over to the other end of the room an' turn your faces to the wall—quick.

(*The two men turn their faces to the wall, with their hands up*)

SECOND IRREGULAR (*To* JOHNNY) Come on, Sean Boyle, you're wanted; some of us have a word to say to you.

JOHNNY I'm sick, I can't—what do you want with me?

SECOND IRREGULAR Come on, come on; we've a distance to go, an' haven't much time—come on.

JOHNNY I'm an oul' comrade—yous wouldn't shoot an oul' comrade.

SECOND IRREGULAR Poor Tancred was an oul' comrade o' yours, but you didn't think o' that when you gave him away to the gang that sent him to his grave. But we've no time to waste; come on—here, Dermot, ketch his arm. (*To* JOHNNY) Have you your beads?

JOHNNY Me beads! Why do you ass me that, why do you ass me that?

SECOND IRREGULAR Go on, go on, march!

JOHNNY Are yous goin' to do in a comrade—look at me arm, I lost it for Ireland.

SECOND IRREGULAR Commandant Tancred lost his life for Ireland.

JOHNNY Sacred Heart of Jesus, have mercy on me! Mother o' God, pray for me—be with me now in the agonies o' death! . . . Hail, Mary, full o' grace . . . the Lord is . . . with Thee.

(*They drag out* JOHNNY BOYLE, *and the curtain falls. When it rises again the most of the furniture is gone.* MARY *and* MRS. BOYLE, *one on each side, are sitting in a darkened room, by the fire; it is an hour later*)

MRS. BOYLE I'll not wait much longer . . . what did they bring him away in the mothor for? Nugent says he thinks they had guns . . . is me throubles never goin' to be over? . . . If anything ud happen to poor Johnny, I think I'd lose me mind . . . I'll go to the Police Station, surely they ought to be able to do somethin'.

(*Below is heard the sound of voices*)

MRS. BOYLE Whisht, is that something? Maybe, it's your father, though when I left him in Foley's he was hardly able to lift his head. Whisht!

(*A knock at the door, and the voice of* MRS. MADIGAN, *speaking very softly*)

Mrs. Boyle, Mrs. Boyle. (MRS. BOYLE *opens the door*)

MRS. MADIGAN Oh, Mrs. Boyle, God an' His Blessed Mother be with you this night!

MRS. BOYLE (*Calmly*) What is it, Mrs. Madigan? It's Johnny—something about Johnny.

MRS. MADIGAN God send it's not. God send it's not Johnny!

MRS. BOYLE Don't keep me waitin', Mrs. Madigan; I've

gone through so much lately that I feel able for anything.

MRS. MADIGAN Two polismen below wantin' you.

MRS. BOYLE Wantin' me; an' why do they want me?

MRS. MADIGAN Some poor fella's been found, an' they think it's, it's . . .

MRS. BOYLE Johnny, Johnny!

MARY (*With her arms round her mother*) Oh, Mother, Mother, me poor, darlin' Mother.

MRS. BOYLE Hush, hush, darlin'; you'll shortly have your own throuble to bear. (*To* MRS. MADIGAN) An' why do the polis think it's Johnny, Mrs. Madigan?

MRS. MADIGAN Because one o' the doctors knew him when he was attendin' with his poor arm.

MRS. BOYLE Oh, it's thrue, then; it's Johnny, it's me son, me own son!

MARY Oh, it's thrue, it's thrue what Jerry Devine says —there isn't a God, there isn't a God; if there was He wouldn't let these things happen!

MRS. BOYLE Mary, Mary, you mustn't say them things. We'll want all the help we can get from God an' His Blessed Mother now! These things have nothin' to do with the Will o' God. Ah, what can God do agen the stupidity o' men!

MRS. MADIGAN The polis want you to go with them to the hospital to see the poor body—they're waitin' below.

MRS. BOYLE We'll go. Come, Mary, an' we'll never come back here agen. Let your father furrage for himself now; I've done all I could an' it was all no use—he'll be hopeless till the end of his days. I've got a little room in me sisther's where we'll stop till your throuble is over, an' then we'll work together for the sake of the baby.

MARY My poor little child that'll have no father!

MRS. BOYLE It'll have what's far bether—it'll have two mothers.

(*A rough voice shouting from below*) Are yous goin' to keep us waitin' for yous all night?

MRS. MADIGAN (*Going to the door, and shouting down*) Take your hour, there, take your hour! If yous are in such a hurry, skip off, then, for nobody wants you here—if they did yous wouldn't be found. For you're the same as yous were undher the British Government —never where yous are wanted! As far as I can see, the Polis as Polis, in this city, is Null an' Void!

MRS. BOYLE We'll go, Mary, we'll go; you to see your poor dead brother, an' me to see me poor dead son!

MARY I dhread it, Mother, I dhread it!

MRS. BOYLE I forgot, Mary, I forgot; your poor oul' selfish mother was only thinkin' of herself. No, no, you mustn't come—it wouldn't be good for you. You go on to me sisther's an' I'll face th' ordeal meself. Maybe I didn't feel sorry enough for Mrs. Tancred when her poor son was found as Johnny's been found now—because he was a Die-hard! Ah, why didn't I remember that then he wasn't a Die-hard or a Stater, but only a poor dead son! It's well I remember all that she said—an' it's my turn to say it now: What was the pain I suffered, Johnny, bringin' you into the world to carry you to your cradle, to the pains I'll suffer carryin' you out o' the world to bring you to your grave! Mother o' God, Mother o' God, have pity on us all! Blessed Virgin, where were you when me darlin' son was riddled with bullets, when me darlin' son was riddled with bullets? Sacred Heart o' Jesus, take away our hearts o' stone, and give us hearts o' flesh! Take away this murdherin' hate, an' give us Thine own eternal love!

(*They all go slowly out*)

(*There is a pause; then a sound of shuffling steps on the stairs outside. The door opens and* BOYLE *and* JOXER, *both of them very drunk, enter*)

BOYLE I'm able to go no farther. . . . Two polis, ey . . . what were they doin' here, I wondher? . . . Up to no good, anyhow . . . an' Juno an' that lovely daughter o' mine with them. (*Taking a sixpence from his pocket and looking at it*) Wan single, solithary tanner left out of all I borreyed. . . . (*He lets it fall*) The last o' the Mohicans. . . . The blinds is down, Joxer, the blinds is down!

JOXER (*Walking unsteadily across the room, and anchoring at the bed*) Put all . . . your throubles . . . in your oul' kit bag . . . an' smile . . . smile . . . smile! [12]

BOYLE The counthry'll have to steady itself . . . it's goin' . . . to hell. . . . Where'r all . . . the chairs . . . gone to . . . steady itself, Joxer. . . . Chairs'll . . . have to . . . steady themselves. . . . No matther . . . what any one may . . . say . . . Irelan' sober . . . is Irelan' . . . free.

JOXER (*Stretching himself on the bed*) Chains . . . an' . . . slaveree[13] . . . that's a darlin' motto . . . a daaarlin' . . . motto!

BOYLE If th' worst comes . . . to th' worse . . . I can join a . . . flyin' . . . column. . . . I done . . . me bit . . . in Easther Week . . . had no business . . . to . . . be . . . there . . . but Captain Boyle's Captain Boyle!

JOXER Breathes there a man with soul . . . so . . . de . . . ad . . . this . . . me . . . o . . . wn, me nat . . . ive l . . . an'! [14]

BOYLE (*Subsiding into a sitting posture on the floor*) Commandant Kelly died . . . in them . . . arms . . . Joxer. . . . Tell me Volunteer Butties . . . says he . . . that . . . I died for . . . Irelan'!

JOXER D'jever rade Willie . . . Reilly . . . an' his own . . . Colleen . . . Bawn? [15] It's a darlin' story, a daarlin' story!

BOYLE I'm telling you . . . Joxer . . . th' whole worl's . . . in a terr . . . ible state o' . . . chassis!

*Curtain*

[12] A popular song of the Allies during World War I.

[13] Derived from Patrick Henry's "Give me liberty" speech (1775) or Thomas Moore's ballad, "The Minstrel Boy."

[14] Joxer now quotes from Sir Walter Scott's *The Lay of the Last Minstrel.*

[15] The adventures of Willie Reilly and his Colleen Bawn (beautiful fairhaired sweetheart) are recounted in a folk ballad: a young man accepts his sweetheart's invitation to steal her away from her father's land.

# COCK-A-DOODLE DANDY

In 1927, O'Casey joined the ranks of such Irish expatriates as Shaw, Wilde, Joyce, and Beckett, men escaping Ireland's confining parochialism by becoming citizens of the world. Of these writers O'Casey was oldest when he wrenched himself free of a land which had brought him more anguish than joy. At 47, he celebrated a new life by again changing his name: once hopeful that Ireland could achieve the brotherhood of man, John Casey had gaelicized his name; now, despairing because Ireland Free seemed inhospitable to freedom, Sean O'Cathasaigh anglicized his name—and Sean O'Casey was officially born.

The fifth and sixth volumes of his autobiography (*Rose and Crown,* 1952, and *Sunset and Evening Star,* 1954) deal with his first 27 years in England, a period marked by satisfying new associations and brave but not always successful experiments in drama. He married a charming young actress, and parenthood became significant in his experience. He made such new friends as Shaw, O'Neill, George Jean Nathan and Brooks Atkinson, as well as such new enemies as James Agate, London's most influential drama critic.

In London on the eve of the Great Depression, O'Casey found himself out of step with the work of such fashionable young playwrights as Noel Coward (whose *Cavalcade,* an ultra-patriotic panorama of Establishment and Empire, O'Casey despised); later, as the bubble of postwar prosperity burst and the sound of tanks was again heard in the land, O'Casey found himself exalted to equivocal status as the world's most admired and least produced playwright. Warring against the "Green Goddess of Realism," O'Casey opposed the tradition in which he had initially established himself.

When O'Casey left Ireland, his feelings toward the Irish were bitter, but his relations with the Abbey directors were cordial. In 1928, however, Yeats alienated O'Casey by rejecting *The Silver Tassie.* O'Casey had little difficulty in meeting Yeats' criticisms—that he could not write about a war in which he had not participated, that he had injected too many of his own opinions, that he had failed to create "psychological unity" or "unity of action," but he did not succeed in changing Yeats' mind. *The Silver Tassie* embodies O'Casey's pacifist commentary on World War I: he widened his range, shifting the action from Dublin to the battlefields of France, from an army hospital to a football clubhouse, and proved, at least to his own satisfaction, that he could successfully use expressionist techniques in an essentially realistic play.

In his next play, *Within the Gates* (1933), O'Casey attempted a modern morality play in which a setting remindful of London's Hyde Park reinforces his symbolic characters in their quest for salvation. O'Casey's park is his Wasteland-symbol, and the play is his *Everyman,* an extension of Shaw's explorations—in *Major Barbara*—of the interaction of Capitalism and Organized Religion in the modern world. His indebtedness to German Expressionists such as Kaiser and Toller, and to O'Neill is everywhere apparent, but it is Strindberg's *Dream Play* which emerges most clearly as O'Casey's model. In subsequent plays, he continued to vary the ratio of expressionism to realism according to his needs. Only in two plays, however, did he hit upon the formula which led him toward his own "favorite play," *Cock-a-Doodle Dandy.* In *Purple Dust* (1940), O'Casey took a rollicking (but ill-timed) jab in the manner of Shaw's *John Bull's Other Island* at British attitudes toward Ireland, and in *Red Roses for Me* (1943) he effectively recreated the Dublin of the 1913 General Strike.

O'Casey continued to write until his death on September 18, 1964. It is doubtful, however, that any work ever supplanted *Cock-a-Doodle Dandy* in his esteem: "I think that's the most cockeyed, and it's a ball from start to finish. It's by far the best of all I've written." Written in 1949 when he was writing *Inishfallen Fare Thee Well,* this paean to the joy of living also reflects matters which came swimming back into his mind as he recalled his painful last years in Dublin.

In O'Casey's Nyadnanave (which he has explained as a pun on Gaelic words which coalesce "Nest of the Saints" with "Nest of Rogues—or Knaves"), anything can and does happen. Its "menacing fools" are Irishmen, but, as O'Casey has said, "the spirit is to be found in action everywhere: the fight made by many to drive the joy of life from the hearts of men. . . . It isn't the clergy alone who boo and bluster against this joy of life in living, in dance, song, and story . . . who interfere in the free flow of thought from man to man. Playwrights and poets have had, are having, a share in squeezing the mind of man into visions of woe and lamentations. . . . They labor hard to get us all down." The gorgeous Cock who struts through this play is the author's own zest for life, but O'Casey remained realist enough to see that, while the Cock endures, the Nyadnanaveans can still defeat its celebrants.

# COCK-A-DOODLE DANDY

## CHARACTERS

THE COCK
MICHAEL MARTHRAUN, *a small farmer, now the owner of a lucrative bog*
SAILOR MAHAN, *once a sailor, now the owner of a fleet of lorries* [*trucks*] *carrying turf from bog to town*
LORNA, *second young wife of* MARTHRAUN
LORELEEN, MARTHRAUN'S *daughter by his first young wife*
MARION, *helper in* LORNA'S *house*
SHANAAR, *a "very wise old crawthumper,"*[1] *really a dangerous old cod*[2]
FIRST ROUGH FELLOW } *peasants working on*
SECOND ROUGH FELLOW } *the bog*
FATHER DOMINEER, *the parish priest of Nyadnanave*
THE SERGEANT *of the Civic Guard*
JACK, MAHAN'S *foreman lorry driver*
JULIA, LORNA'S *sister, a paralytic on a visit to Lourdes*
HER FATHER
ONE-EYED LARRY, *a peasant lad and potential sacristan*
A MAYOR
A MACE-BEARER
THE MESSENGER [ROBIN ADAIR], *in love with* MARION
THE BELLMAN, *a kind of town crier*
A PORTER *of a general store in the near-by town*

### SCENES

SCENE 1 *The front garden outside Michael Marthraun's house, in Nyadnanave. Morning.*
SCENE 2 *The same. Midday.*
SCENE 3 *The same. Dusk.*

## Scene One

*Part of the garden outside the house of* MICHAEL MARTHRAUN. *It is rough and uncared for, with tough grass everywhere, sprinkled with buttercups and daisies. It is surrounded by a stone wall, three to four feet high, which is pierced by a wooden gate to the right of any visitor entering the garden. To the left, a little way from the gate, a clump of sunflowers, in full bloom, stand stiff and stately, their blossoms big as shields, the petals raying out widely and sharply, like rays from an angry sun. Glancing farther to the left, a visitor would see the gable end of the house, with a porch jutting from it, and a window above the porch. The porch is supported by twisted pillars of wood, looking like snakes, which are connected with latticework shaped like noughts and crosses. These are painted a dazzling white. The framework of the window above is a little on the skew, and the sashwork holding the glass is twisted into irregular lines. A little way from the porch, toward the wall, is a dignified-looking bronze urn holding a standoffish, cynical-looking evergreen. Farther up, near the wall, the Irish Tricolour flutters from a flagpole. The house itself is black in colour, the sash and frame of the window in it is a brilliant red.*

*It is a brilliantly fine day in summer, and as there is nothing in the garden to provide a shade, the place is a deep pool of heat, which, seemingly, has lasted for some time, for the grass has turned to a deep yellow hue, save where the house and porch throw a rich black shadow. Stretching away in the distance, beyond the wall, is a bog of a rich purple colour, dabbed here and there with black patches. The sky above it is a silvery grey, glittering like an Oriental canopy.*

*Some little distance away, an accordian is heard playing a dance tune, and, a few moments after, the* COCK *comes dancing in around the gable of the house, circles the dignified urn, and disappears round the farther end of the gable end as the music ceases.*

*He is of a deep black plumage, fitted to his agile and slender body like a glove on a lady's hand; yellow feet and ankles, bright green flaps like wings, and a stiff cloak falling like a tail behind him. A big crimson crest flowers over his head, and crimson flaps hang from his jaws. His face has the look of a cynical jester.*

MICHAEL MARTHRAUN, *followed by* SAILOR MAHAN, *comes into the garden by the porch. Each carries a kitchen chair, which he sets down some way from the house.* MICHAEL *is a man who is well*

[1] ostentatiously devout person ('breastbeater')
[2] fool

*over sixty years of age, clean-shaven, lean, and grim-looking. His lips twitch nervously whenever he forgets to keep his mouth tightly closed. He is dressed in a blackish tweed suit, and his legs are encased in black leggings. A heavy gold chain stretches across his waistcoat, and he wears a wide-leafed collar, under which a prim black bow is tied.*

SAILOR MAHAN *is a little over fifty, stouter than his companion, and of a more serene countenance. He has a short, pointed beard, just beginning to show signs of grayness. His face is of a ruddier hue, and shows that the wind and the stress of many storms have made it rugged, but in no way unpleasant. There is, maybe, a touch of the sea breeze in his way of talking and his way of walking. He is wearing light gray flannel trousers, a double-breasted royal blue coat, and has a white scarf round his neck, over a light blue shirt. They come to the two chairs, and stand there facing each other.*

MICHAEL Come out here, come on out here, where a body can talk free. There's whispers an' whispers in that house, upsettin' a man's mind.

MAHAN (*Puzzled*) Whispers? What kinda whispers?

MICHAEL Sthrange kinds; whispers good for neither soul nor body.

MAHAN But there's no one in the house but your wife, Lorna, Marion the maid, and your own girl Loreleen?

MICHAEL Ay, so you think; but I know different.

MAHAN (*Breezily*) Nonsense, Mick; you're haulin' on a rope that isn't there!

MICHAEL (*Raising his voice*) You don't live in th' house, do you?

(MAHAN *is silent*)

You don't live in th' house, do you?

MAHAN (*Raising his voice too*) I know I don't live in it, an' if it's like what you say, I don't want to live in it!

MICHAEL Well, then, keep quiet when a man speaks of what he knows.

MAHAN I know as much about a whisper as you do.

MICHAEL You know about th' whispers of wind an' wave, harmless an' innocent things; but I'm talkin' about whispers ebbin' an' flowin' about th' house, with an edge of evil on them, since that painted one, that godless an' laughin' little bitch left London to come here for a long an' leering holiday.

MAHAN Loreleen? Why, man, she's your own daughter by your first young wife!

MICHAEL So it was said at th' time, an' so it's believed still; but I had me doubts then, and I've more doubts now. I dhread meetin' her, dhread it, dhread it.

(*With a frightened laugh*)

Michael Marthraun's daughter!

(*Gripping* MAHAN'*s arm*)

Is she anyone's daughter, man?

MAHAN (*Impatiently*) She must be somebody's daughter, man!

MICHAEL (*Impatiently*) Why must she be, man? Remember what th' Missioner said last night: Sthrange things are foisted by the powers of evil into th' life o' man. Since that one come back from England, where evil things abound, there's sinisther signs appearin' everywhere, evil evocations floatin' through every room.

MAHAN (*Puzzled*) What kinda evocation an' significality is there?

MICHAEL (*Looking suspiciously at the porch, then at the window above it, and drawing* MAHAN *farther away from the house*) Looka, Sailor Mahan, (*He speaks furtively*) there's always a stern commotion among th' holy objects of th' house, when that one, Loreleen, goes sailin' by; an invisible wind blows th' pictures out, an' turns their frenzied faces to th' wall; once I seen the statue of St. Crankarius[3] standin' on his head to circumvent th' lurin' quality of her presence; an' another time, I seen th' image of our own St. Pathrick makin' a skelp at her with his crozier; fallin' flat on his face, stunned, when he missed!

MAHAN (*Doubtful, but a little impressed*) Good God, them's serious things, Michael Marthraun! (*A pause*) Are you sure, now, Mick, you're not deludin' yourself?

MICHAEL Have sense, man! An' me own wife, Lorna Marthraun, is mixin' herself with th' disordher, fondlin' herself with all sorts o' dismayin' decorations. Th' other day, I caught her gapin' into a lookin'-glass, an' when I looked meself, I seen gay-coloured horns branchin' from her head!

MAHAN No! Oh, Mick, you're fancyin' things. Lorna's a fine, upstandin' woman, an' should be respected.

MICHAEL Are you gone on her, too? I tell you, I seen the way th' eyes of young men stare at her face, an' follow th' movements of her lurin' legs—there's evil in that woman!

MAHAN But there's nothin' evil in a pretty face, or in a pair of lurin' legs.

MICHAEL Oh, man, your religion should tell you th' biggest fight th' holy saints ever had was with temptations from good-lookin' women.

MAHAN (*Getting nervous, and eager to change the subject*) Looka, let's sit down, an' thry to settle about what you're willin' to pay for th' cartage of th' turf.

MICHAEL (*Ignoring* MAHAN'*s attempt to change the tide of talk*) Up there in that room (*He points to the window above the porch*) she often dances be herself, but dancin' in her mind with hefty lads, plum'd with youth, an' spurred with looser thoughts of love.

(*As he speaks, the sounds of a gentle waltz are heard, played by harp, lute, or violin, or by all three, the sounds coming, apparently, from the room whose window is above the porch. Bitterly*)

There, d'ye hear that, man! Mockin' me. She'll hurt her soul, if she isn't careful.

MAHAN She's young enough yet to nourish th' need o' dancin'. An' anyway, why did you insist on marryin' her, an' she so young; an' she so gay? She was all again' it herself.

MICHAEL She consented to it, at last, didn't she?

MAHAN Ay, when you, her father, an' th' priest had

[3] O'Casey invented this saint as one "standing crankily in the way of life's enjoyments."

badgered th' girl's mind into disordered attention over th' catch she was gettin'.

MICHAEL Oh, well you know, Sailor Mahan, that she had her blue eye on th' fat little farm undher me feet; th' taut roof over me head; an' th' kind cushion I had in th' bank, against a hard day.

MAHAN I seen you meself throtting afther her from starboard to port, from poop to quarther-deck, hoistin' before her th' fancy of ribbon an' lace, silver-buckled shoes, an' a silk dhress for Sunday.

MICHAEL An' what had she but a patched petticoat, a worn look, an' broken brogues to wear to Mass on Sundays? An' didn't I give her oul' fella fifty solid pounds so that her ailin' sisther could thravel to Lourdes to get undher th' aegis of th' Blessed Virgin? An' what did I get for them but a scraggy oul' bog of two hundhred acres?

MAHAN An' you're makin' a good thing out of it since turf came into its own. It's made you a Councillor, a Justice of the Peace, an' th' fair-haired boy of th' clergy.

MICHAEL As you mentioned turf, we'd betther settle this question of you demandin', for carting it, an exthra amount I couldn't possibly pay.

MAHAN (*Stiffness coming into his voice*) You'll have to, Michael Marthraun, for it can't be done now for a cent less.

MICHAEL We'll have a drink while we're discussin'. I have a bottle of th' best, ten years maturin', inside. Sit down there till I get it.

(*He goes into the porch and, after a few moments, comes quickly out again, his mouth twitching, his voice toned to fear and hate*)

That one, Loreleen's comin' down th' stairs, an' I don't want to come too near her. We'll wait till she goes. Let's talk of our affairs, quietly, while she passes by. Th' thing to do, as Shanaar would tell you, when you hear a sound or see a shape of anything evil, is to take no notice of it.

(*Whispering impatiently*)

Sit down, man!

MAHAN (*Sitting down—dubiously*) Are you sure, Mick, you have a close-hauled comprehension of th' way you're thinkin'?

MICHAEL Ay, am I sure; as sure as I am that a cock crows!

(*A cock suddenly crows lustily as* LORELEEN *appears in the doorway of the porch. She is a very attractive young woman with an air of her own. A jaunty air it is, indicating that it is the sign of a handsome, gay, and intelligent woman. She is dressed in a darkish green dress, with dark red flashes on bodice and side of skirt. A saucy hat of a brighter green than the dress sports a scarlet ornament, its shape suggestive of a cock's crimson crest. Her legs—very charming ones—are clad in brown silk stockings; brown that flashes a golden sheen.* MICHAEL, *who has sat down, jumps startled to his feet at the sudden sound of the cock's crow and, stretching over the table, grips* MAHAN *by the shoulder*)

MICHAEL What's that, what's that?

MAHAN (*Startled by* MICHAEL's *frightened movement*) What's what, man?

MICHAEL (*Trying to recover himself*) Nothin', I heard nothin'. What was it you were sayin'?

(*In a whisper*)

Get goin' on th' turf, man.

MAHAN (*Mystified, but doing his best*) You'll have to grant th' two shillin's additional on each load, Mick. I'd work me lorries at a loss if I took less. (*Placing an affectionate hand on* MICHAEL's *shoulder*) An' you know well, you're such an oul' an' valued friend, I'd do it for affection's sake, if I only could.

MICHAEL (*Forgetting about* LORELEEN) Don't I know that well, Sailor Mahan; an' I'd do th' same, an' more, be you; but if I surrendhered two shillin's, I might as well give you th' bog as well. I have to live, Sailor Mahan.

MAHAN Damn it, man, haven't I to live too? How th' hell am I to give th' men a shillin' more without th' exthra two shillin's from you? Pray to th' saints to let them fall like rain from heaven, eh?

MICHAEL (*Putting his face closer to* MAHAN'S, *hotly*) Looka here, Sailor Mahan, you're not goin' to magicfy me into th' dhream of believin' you're not addin', every hurryin' week, a fine bundle o' notes to th' jubilant store you've there already, forcin' overtime on th' poor men o' th' bank, flickin' th' notes into imperial ordher.

MAHAN (*As fiercely—standing up to say it, his face close to the face of* MICHAEL) An' you yourself, Michael Marthraun, aren't worn away with th' punishment of poverty! Puttin' on a poor mouth, an' if you set out to count graciously all you have in hidlins,[4] you'd be workin' many a long, glad day, without supper or sleep, be daylight an' candlelight, till your mind centhred on th' sum dominated be th' last note flutherin' from your fingers!

LORELEEN (*Who has strolled slowly over to the gate, listening to the talk the while, turning at the gate to watch as well as listen*) Lay not up for yourselves treasures upon earth, where moth and rust doth corrupt, and where thieves break through and steal!

MICHAEL (*In a frightened whisper*) Don't turn your head; take no notice. Don't pretend to hear her lyin' hallucinations!

(*A young, rough-looking fellow, well set and strong, comes running along the pathway to the gate. He is wearing dark brown corduroy trousers, belted at waist, grey shirt, and scarf of bright green, with yellow dots. He pushes* LORELEEN *aside*)

FIRST ROUGH FELLOW (*Pushing* LORELEEN *out of his way*) Outa me way, woman! (*He sees how charming she is as he swings her aside*) Be God, but you're th' good-lookin' lass! What are you doin' in this hole?

LORELEEN Seeking happiness, an' failing to find it.

FIRST ROUGH FELLOW It isn't here you should be, lost among th' rough stones, th' twisty grass, an' th' moody misery of th' brown bog; but it's lyin' laughin'

[4] In secret; hidden away.

you should be where th' palms are tall, an' wherever a foot is planted, a scarlet flower is crushed; where there's levity living its life, an' not loneliness dyin' as it is here.

LORELEEN (*Dropping him a deep curtsy*) Thank you, sir knight, for th' silken compliments to your handmaiden.

(*She turns to go out, and the* ROUGH FELLOW *hurries in through the gate, down to the two men*)

FIRST ROUGH FELLOW (*Going through the gate down to where the two men are, and turning to speak up to* LORELEEN, *still standing at the gate*) If you wait till I'm done with these fellas (*Indicating* MICHAEL *and* MAHAN) I could go to th' bend o' th' road with you, for it's meself would surrendher a long spell of heaven's ease to go a long day's journey with a lass like you!

(*Another* ROUGH FELLOW *hurries in along the pathway outside to the gate, pulling* LORELEEN *aside when he finds her in his way. He wears light brown corduroy trousers, check shirt, and has a scarf of light yellow, with green stripes, round his neck*)

SECOND ROUGH FELLOW (*Pulling* LORELEEN *out of his way*) Eh, there, woman—outa me way! (*He sees, as she swings around, how charming she is*) Arra, what winsome wind blew such a flower into this dread, dhried-up desert? Deirdre come to life again, not to sorrow, but to dance! If Eve was as you are, no wondher Adam fell, for a lass like you could shutther th' world away with a kiss! (*He goes through the gate, and down to the other men, pausing to look up at* LORELEEN *again*)

SECOND ROUGH FELLOW (*To* LORELEEN) Wait, lass, till I'm done with these fellas, an' I'll go with you till youth's a shadow a long way left behind!

LORELEEN (*Down to the two* ROUGH FELLOWS) I'm not for you, friends, for I'm not good for decent men. The two old cronies will tell you a kiss from me must be taken undher a canopy of dangerous darkness. (*She kisses a hand to them*) Good-bye! (*She goes out*)

MICHAEL }
MAHAN } (*Together*) What d'ye th' two of yous want here? Why aren't yous at work?

FIRST ROUGH FELLOW (*Laying a hand sternly on the shoulder of* MAHAN) Looka, you; you give us th' exthra shillin', or we leave your lorries standin', helpless an' naked on th' roads!

SECOND ROUGH FELLOW (*Laying a hand sternly on* MICHAEL'S *shoulder*) Looka, you; looka that! (*He throws a cheque contemptuously on to the table*) D'ye think a good week's wages is in a cheque for tuppence?

MICHAEL You didn't work a week, because of th' rain, an' canteen contribution an' insurance brought your wage for the week to tuppence.

SECOND ROUGH FELLOW Tell me how I'm goin' to live a week on tuppence?

FIRST ROUGH FELLOW Seein' th' both of them's Knights o' Columbanus,[5] they should be able to say.

[5] St. Columbanus (543-615), an Irish missionary who founded several major abbeys in Europe, wrote a very strict rule which stresses the importance of manual labor.

MICHAEL That's a social question to be solved by th' Rerum Novarum.[6]

SECOND ROUGH FELLOW Fifty years old; not worth much when it was born, an' not worth a damn now. You give a guaranteed week, or th' men come off your bog! (*He goes off towards the gate*)

FIRST ROUGH FELLOW (*Going to the gate—to* MAHAN) Take our demand serious, or your lorries stand still on th' highways!

SECOND ROUGH FELLOW (*Impatiently*) Looka, there she is! (*He points a finger in front*) Let's hurry, an' we'll ketch up on th' fine, fair lady.

(*They hurry along the path, but suddenly stop to stare ahead*)

FIRST ROUGH FELLOW (*With awe in his voice*) What's happenin' to her? A cloud closin' in on her, flashes like lightning whirlin' round her head, an' her whole figure ripplin'!

SECOND ROUGH FELLOW (*Frightened*) Jasus, she's changin' into th' look of a fancy-bred fowl! It's turnin' to face us; it's openin' its bake as big as a bayonet!

(*The crow of a cock is heard in the distance*)

FIRST ROUGH FELLOW (*Frightened*) Here, man, th' other way for us! It's an omen, a warnin', a reminder of what th' Missioner said last night that young men should think of good-lookin' things in skirts only in th' presence of, an' undher the guidance of, old and pious people.

(*The two of them hurry away in the opposite direction*)

MICHAEL (*To* MAHAN) Did you hear that? I'm askin' you, Sailor Mahan, did you hear what them two graspin' rascals said?

MAHAN I heard, but I can see no significality in it, unless th' two of them had dhrink taken.

MICHAEL (*Warningly*) Looka, Sailor Mahan, if you aren't careful, your wilful disbelief in things'll lead you asthray! Loreleen isn't me daughter; she isn't even a woman: she's either undher a spell, or she's a possessed person.

MAHAN (*With contempt*) Aw, for God's sake, Mick, have sense, an' get that bottle o' whiskey out to put a spell on us.

MICHAEL (*Almost shouting*) Have you forgotten already th' case of th' Widow Malone who could turn, twinklin', into a dog or a hare, when she wanted to hide herself? An' how, one day, th' dogs followed what they thought was a hare that made for th' widow's cottage, an' dived through an open window, one o' th' dogs snappin' a leg off before it could get through? An' when th' door was burst open, there was th' oul' witch-widow screamin' on her oul' bed, one leg gone, with blood spoutin' from th' stump, so that all th' people heard her last screechin' as she went sliddherin' down to hell!

[6] The shortened and familiar name of Pope Leo XIII's encyclical of 1891. This document was designed to meet changes in the modern social and economic order, particularly the relations between employers and employees, trade-unionism, and the 'reconstruction and perfection of the social order.'

MAHAN I heard tell of it months after, when I come back from Valparaiso.

MICHAEL Well, if you heard of it, you know it must have happened. An' here you are, thinkin' only of whiskey, and showin' how ready you are to ruin me to be askin' more than I'm able to give. You, a good Christian, a Knight of Columbanus, a student in th' Circle studyin' th' Rerum Novarum, you should show a sign of charity an' justice, recognisin' th' needs of th' people rather than your own. (*Suddenly*) Here, I'll add thruppence, an' make th' offer ninepence. Hold out th' hand, an' clinch th' bargain.

MAHAN I'll be scuppered if I will! You'll not use me like th' oul' father of th' good woman within, who sold you th' bog when he thought it was derelict, though you're makin' thousands out of it now.

MICHAEL You forget I gave th' oul' cod enough to bring his other daughter to Lourdes for a cure!

MAHAN You know th' way th' men are actin' now—goin' slow, an' doin' two journeys where they used to do three.

MICHAEL An' aren't my men threatenin' to come off th' bog altogether? It's this materialism's doin' it—edgin' into revolt against Christian conduct. If they'd only judge o' things in th' proper Christian way, as we do, there'd be no disputes. Now let's be good sons of Columbanus—you thinkin' of my difficulties, an' me thinkin' of yours.

MAHAN Make your offer one an' sixpence, an' I'll hoist th' pennant of agreement?

MICHAEL I couldn't. Looka, Sailor Mahan, it would ruin me.

MAHAN (*Viciously*) You'd rather throw th' money after a tall-hat so that you could controvert yourself into a dapper disturbance th' time the President comes to view th' workin' of th' turf. Talk about Loreleen castin' a spell! Th' whole disthrict'll be paralysed in a spell when your top-hat comes out to meet the President's top-hat, th' two poor things tryin' to keep people from noticin' what's undher them! Two shillin's, now, or nothin'.

(*He sits down in disgust. Behind the wall,* SHANAAR *is seen coming along the road; he opens the gate, and comes slowly down to where the two men are. He is a very, very old man, wrinkled like a walnut, bent at the shoulders, with longish white hair, and a white beard—a bit dirty—reaching to his belly. He is dressed peasant-wise, thin, threadbare frieze coat, patched blackish corduroy trousers, thick boots, good and strong, a vivid blue muffler round his neck, and a sackcloth waistcoat, on which hangs a brass cross, suspended round his neck by twine. A round, wide-brimmed, black hat is on his head*)

SHANAAR (*Lifting his hat as he comes in by the gate*) God save all here! God save all that may be in th' house, barrin' th' cat an' th' dog!

MICHAEL (*With great respect*) An' you, too, Shanaar, old, old man, full of wisdom an' th' knowledge of deeper things.

SHANAAR Old, is it? Ever so old, thousands of years, thousands of years if all were told.

MICHAEL Me an' Sailor Mahan here were talkin' some time ago about th' sthrange dodges of unseen powers, an' of what the Missioner said about them last night, but th' easiness of his mind hasn't been hindhered.

SHANAAR (*Bending lower, and shoving his bearded face between the two men*) If it doesn't hindher th' easiness of his mind now, it will one day! Maybe this very day in this very place.

MICHAEL (*To* MAHAN) What d'ye say to that, now?

MAHAN (*Trying to be firm, but a little uneasy*) Nothin', nothin'.

SHANAAR (*Shoving his face closer to* MAHAN'*s*) Ah, me friend, for years an' years I've thravelled over hollow lands an' hilly lands, an' I know. Big powers of evil, with their little powers, an' them with their littler ones, an' them with their littlest ones, are everywhere. You might meet a bee that wasn't a bee; a bird that wasn't a bird; or a beautiful woman who wasn't a woman at all.

MICHAEL (*Excitedly*) I'm tellin' him that, I'm tellin' him that all along.

MAHAN (*A little doubtfully—to* SHANAAR) An' how's a poor body to know them?

SHANAAR (*Looking round cautiously, then speaking in a tense whisper*) A sure sign, if only you can get an all-round glimpse of them. (*He looks round him again*) *Daemones posteriora non habent*—they have no behinds!

MICHAEL (*Frightened a lot*) My God, what an awe-inspiring, expiring experience!

MAHAN (*Frightened too, but trying to appear brave*) That may be, but I wouldn't put innocent birds or bees in that category.

SHANAAR (*Full of pitying scorn for ignorance*) You wouldn't! Innocent birds! Listen all: There was a cuckoo once that led a holy brother to damnation. Th' cuckoo's call enticed th' brother to a silent glade where th' poor man saw a lovely woman, near naked, bathin' her legs in a pool, an' in an instant th' holy man was taken with desire. Lost! She told him he was handsome, but he must have money if he wanted to get her. Th' brother entered a noble's house, an' demanded a hundhred crowns for his convent; but the noble was a wise old bird, an' said he'd have to see the prior first. Thereupon, th' brother up with an axe, hidden undher his gown, an' cleft th' noble from skull to chin; robbed th' noble, dhressed himself in rare velvets, an' searched out all th' rosy rottenness of sin with th' damsel till th' money was gone. Then they caught him. Then they hanged him, an', mind you, (*The three heads come closer together*) while this poor brother sobbed on the scaffold, everyone heard th' mocking laughter of a girl and th' calling of a cuckoo!

(*As* SHANAAR *is speaking the three last things, the mocking laughter of a girl is heard, the call of a cuckoo, and a young man's sobbing, one after the other, at first, then they blend together for a few moments, and cease.* SHANAAR *stands as stiff as his bent back will allow, and the other two rise slowly from their chairs, stiff, too, and frightened*)

SHANAAR (*In a tense whisper*) Say nothing; take no notice. Sit down. Thry to continue as if yous hadn't heard!

MAHAN (*After a pause*) Ay, a cuckoo, maybe; but that's a foreign bird: no set harbour or home. No genuine decent Irish bird would do a thing like that on a man.

MICHAEL Looka here, Sailor Mahan, when th' powers of evil get goin', I wouldn't put anything past an ordinary hen!

SHANAAR An' you'd be right, Mr. Marthraun, though, as a rule, hens is always undher th' eye an' comprehension of a Christian. Innocent-looking things are often th' most dangerous. Looka th' lad whose mother had set her heart on him bein' a priest, an' one day, at home, he suddenly saw a corn crake flyin' into a house be an open window. Climbin' in afther it, he spied a glittherin' brooch on a table, an' couldn't resist th' temptation o' thievin' it. That lad spent th' next ten years in a reformatory; his mother died of a broken heart, and his father took to dhrink.

(*During the recital of* SHANAAR'S *story, the "crek crek, crek crek" of a corn crake is heard*)

MICHAEL (*In a tense whisper—to* MAHAN) D'ye hear that, Sailor Mahan?

SHANAAR (*Warningly*) Hush! Take no vocal notice. When yous hear anything or see anything suspicious, give it no notice, unless you know how to deal with it.

MICHAEL (*Solemnly*) A warnin' we'll remember. But supposin' a hen goes wrong, what are we to do?

SHANAAR (*Thoughtfully*) It isn't aysey to say, an' you have to go cautious. The one thing to do, if yous have the knowledge, is to parley with th' hens in a Latin dissertation. If among the fowl there's an illusion of a hen from Gehenna,[7] it won't endure th' Latin. She can't face th' Latin. The Latin downs her. She tangles herself in a helluva disordher. She busts asundher, an' disappears in a quick column of black an' blue smoke, a thrue ear ketchin' a screech of agony from its centre!

MICHAEL (*Tremendously impressed*) Looka that now. See what it is to know!

(*A commotion is heard within the house: a loud cackling, mingled with a short, sharpened crow of a cock; the breaking of delf; the half-angry, half-frightened cries of women. A cup, followed by a saucer, flies out through the open window, over the porch, past the heads of the three men, who duck violently, and then crouch, amazed, and a little frightened*)

What th' hell's happenin' now?

(MARION *rushes to the door of the porch, frightened and alarmed. She is a young girl of twenty or so, and very good-looking. Her skirts come just to her knees, for they are nice legs, and she likes to show them—and why shouldn't she? And when she does so, she can add the spice of a saucy look to her bright blue eyes. Instead of the usual maid's cap, she wears a scarf-bandeau round her head, ornamented with silver strips, joined in the centre above her forehead with an enamelled stone, each strip extending along the bandeau as far as either ear. She wears a dark green uniform, flashed with a brighter green on the sleeves and neck, and the buttons of the bodice are of the same colour. Her stockings and shoes are black. A small, neat, white apron, piped with green, protects her uniform*)

MARION (*Excitedly—to the men*) It's flyin' about th' house, an' behavin' outrageous! I guessed that that Loreleen's cluck, cluck, cluckin' would upset th' bird's respectable way of livin'!

MICHAEL (*Frightened*) What's wrong with you girl; what's up?

MARION Will one of yous come in, an' ketch it, for God's sake, before it ruins th' house?

MAHAN (*Shouting*) Ketch what, ketch what, woman?

MARION A wild goose! It's sent th' althar light flyin'; it's clawed the holy pictures; an' now it's peckin' at th' tall-hat!

MICHAEL A wild goose? Are you sure it was a wild one?

MARION (*In great distress*) I dunno, I dunno—maybe it's a wild duck. It's some flyin' thing tearin' th' house asundher.

MICHAEL (*Trembling—to* SHANAAR) D'ye think it might be what you know?

SHANAAR (*His knees shaking a little*) It might be, Mr. Marthraun! It might be, God help us!

MAHAN (*Nervous himself*) Keep your heads, keep your heads! It's nothin'.

MICHAEL (*Beside himself with anxiety and dread—shaking* MARION *roughly by the shoulders*) Conthrol yourself, girl, an' speak sensibly. Is it a goose or a duck or a hen, or what is it?

MARION (*Wildly*) It's a goose—no, it's a hen, it must be a hen! We thried to dhrive it out with flyin' cups and flyin' saucers, but it didn't notice them. Oh, someone should go in, or it'll peck th' place to pieces!

SHANAAR (*Prayerfully*) So long as it's not transmuted, so long as it's not been transmuted!

MICHAEL (*Shaking* MARION *again*) Where's Lorna, where's Lorna?

MARION (*Responding to the shaking listlessly*) Last I seen of her, she was barricadin' herself undher th' banisters!

MICHAEL (*Pleadingly—to* MAHAN) You've been free with whales an' dolphins an' octopususas, Sailor Mahan—you run in, like a good man, an' enthrone yourself on top of th' thing!

MAHAN (*Indignant*) Is it me? I'm not goin' to squandher meself conthrollin' live land fowl!

MICHAEL (*To* SHANAAR—*half-commandingly*) In case it's what we're afraid of, you pop in, Shanaar, an' liquidate whatever it is with your Latin.

SHANAAR (*Backing towards the wall*) No good in th' house: it's effective only in th' open air.

MICHAEL (*In a fury—to* MARION—*pushing her violently towards the gate*) You go, you gapin', frightened fool, an' bring Father Domineer quick!

[7] Originally, the Valley of Hinnom near Jerusalem where some Israelites sacrificed their children to Moloch; now, synonymous with Hell, a place of pestilence.

(*All this time, intermittent cackling has been heard, cackling with a note of satisfaction, or even victory in it, interspersed with the whirring sound of wings. As* MARION *rushes out through the gate, she runs into the arms of the* MESSENGER, *who carries a telegram in his hand. He clasps* MARION *tight in his arms, and kisses her. He wears a silver grey coat, buttoned over his breast, and trousers. On the right side of the coat is a flash of a pair of scarlet wings. A bright green beret is set jauntily on his head and he is wearing green-coloured sandals.*

MICHAEL *and* MAHAN *have moved farther from the house, and* SHANAAR *has edged to the gateway, where he stares at the house, ready to run if anything happens. His hands are piously folded in front of him, and his lips move as if he prayed*)

MESSENGER (*To* MARION) Ah, lovely one of grace an' gladness, whose kiss is like a honied flame, where are you rushin' to in such a hurry?

MICHAEL (*Angrily—up to the* MESSENGER) Let her go, you—she's runnin' for th' priest!

MESSENGER Th' priest—why?

(*The cackling breaks into intensity, the whirring of wings becomes louder, and a plate flies out through the window, followed by a squeal from* LORNA)

MESSENGER (*Astonished, but not startled*) What's goin' on in th' house?

MICHAEL There's a wild goose, or somethin', asthray in th' house, an' it's sent th' althar bowl flyin'!

MARION An' it's peckin' th' holy pictures hangin' on th' walls.

MAHAN Some think it's a wild duck.

SHANAAR It may be a hen, only a hen.

MESSENGER (*Releasing* MARION, *and handing the telegram to* MICHAEL) Here's a telegram for you. (MICHAEL *takes it mechanically, and stuffs it in a pocket*) Is it losin' your senses yous are to be afraid of a hen? (*He goes towards the porch*) I'll soon settle it!

SHANAAR (*Who is now outside, behind the wall*) If you value your mortal life, lad, don't go in, for th' hen in there isn't a hen at all!

MESSENGER If th' hen, that isn't a hen, in there, isn't a hen, then it must be a cock. I'll settle it!

(*He rushes into the house*)

MICHAEL (*In agony*) If it's a cock, we're done!

SHANAAR (*Fervently*) *Oh, rowelum randee, horrida aidus, sed spero spiro specialii spam!* [8]

(*The head of the* COCK, *with its huge, handsome crimson comb, is suddenly thrust through the window above the porch, and lets out a violent and triumphant crow.* SHANAAR *disappears behind the wall, and* MAHAN *and* MICHAEL *fall flat in the garden, as if in a dead faint*)

MICHAEL (*As he is falling*) Holy saints preserve us—it's th' Cock!

SHANAAR (*From behind the wall*) *Oh, dana eirebus, heniba et galli scatterum in multus parvum avic asthorum!*

[8] Here and elsewhere, Shanaar's Latin is gallimaufry, a hodgepodge which defies literal translation.

(*The* COCK*'s head is as suddenly withdrawn, and a louder commotion is heard to be going on in the house; the* MESSENGER *shouting, a woman's squeal. Then silence for a few moments as puffs of blue-black smoke jet out through the window. When the smoke has gone, the* MESSENGER *comes from the house into the garden. His cap is awry on his head, his face is a little flushed, and his mouth is smiling. He carries in his right hand what might have been a broomstick, but is now a silver staff, topped with a rosette of green and red ribbons. He is followed out by the* COCK, *whom he is leading by a green ribbon, the other end circling the* COCK*'s neck. The* COCK *follows the* MESSENGER *meekly, stopping when he stops, and moving when the* MESSENGER *moves*)

SHANAAR (*Peeping over the wall*) Boys an' girls, take no notice of it, or you're done! Talk only of th' first thing entherin' your minds.

MESSENGER (*Looking with astonishment at the two men sitting up now on the ground, as far as possible from the house, and moving away when the* COCK *comes nearer*) What's the matter with yous? Why are yous dodgin' about on your bums? Get up, get up, an' be sensible.

(MICHAEL *and* MAHAN *scramble to their feet, hurry out through the gate, and stand, warily, beside* SHANAAR. LORNA*'s head appears at the window above the porch, and it is at once evident that she is much younger than her husband, very good-looking still, but the bright and graceful contours of her face are somewhat troubled by a vague aspect of worry and inward timidity. Her face shows signs of excitement, and she speaks rather loudly down to the* MESSENGER)

LORNA (*To the* MESSENGER) Robin Adair, take that bird away at once. Hand him over to th' Civic Guard, or someone fit to take charge of him.

MESSENGER (*Up to* LORNA) Looka, lovely lady, there's no danger, an' there never was. He was lonely, an' was only goin' about in quest o' company. Instead of shyin' cups an' saucers at him, if only you'd given him your lily-white hand, he'd have led you through a wistful an' wondherful dance. But you frightened th' poor thing!

LORNA Frightened him, is it? It was me was frightened when I seen him tossin' down delf, clawin' holy pictures, and peckin' to pieces th' brand new tall-hat that Mr. Marthraun bought to wear, goin' with the Mayor to greet His Brightness, th' President of Eire, comin' to inaugerate th' new canteen for th' turf workers.

MICHAEL (*Enraged*) Is it me new hat he's desthroyed?

SHANAAR (*Pulling* MICHAEL*'s arm in warning*) Damnit, man, take no notice!

MICHAEL (*Turning indignantly on* SHANAAR) How'd you like your sumptous, silken hat to be mangled into a monstrosity!

SHANAAR (*With concentrated venom*) Hush, man, hush!

MARION (*Who has been looking at the* COCK *with admiration*) Sure, he's harmless when you know him.

MESSENGER (*Stroking its back*) 'Course he is! Just a gay bird, that's all. A bit unruly at times, but controllable be th' right persons.

(*To the* COCK)

Go on, comrade, lift up th' head an' clap th' wings, black cock, an' crow!

(*The* COCK *lifts up his head, claps his wings, and lets out a mighty crow, which is immediately followed by a rumbling roll of thunder*)

MICHAEL (*Almost in a state of collapse*) Aw, we're done for!

SHANAAR (*Violently*) No notice, no notice!

LORNA (*From the window*) God bless us, what's that?

(*Down to the* MESSENGER)

Robin, will you take that damned animal away before things happen that God won't know about!

MESSENGER (*Reassuringly—up to* LORNA) Lovely lady, you can let your little hands lie with idle quietness in your lap, for there's no harm in him beyond gaiety an' fine feelin'.

(*To the* COCK)

You know th' goose step done be the Irish Militia in th' city of Cork more'n a hundhred years ago? Well, we'll go home doin' it, to show there's nothing undher th' sun Ireland didn't know, before th' world sensed it. Ready?

One, two—quick march!

(*The* MESSENGER *and the* COCK *march off doing the goose step.* MARION *follows them, imitating the step, as far as the end of the garden; then she stands looking after them, waving them farewell.* MICHAEL *and* MAHAN *come slowly and stealthily into the garden as the* COCK *goes out. They go to the chairs, on which they sit, exhausted, wiping their foreheads with their handkerchiefs.* SHANAAR *comes towards them more slowly, keeping an eye in the direction taken by the* COCK *and the* MESSENGER. *When the place is clear, he anchors himself behind the table*)

LORNA (*Down to* MARION) Marion, dear, come on in, an' help me to straighten things up a little. (*She goes away from the window*)

MARION (*Going slowly towards the house, after having given a last farewell—gleefully*) Wasn't it a saucy bird! An' th' stately way he done th' goose step! (*She playfully shakes* MICHAEL's *shoulder*) Did you see it, sir?

(MICHAEL *takes no notice*)

God forgive me, but it gave us all an hilarious time—didn't it, sir?

MICHAEL (*Coldly*) Your misthress called you.

MARION I heard her, sir. What a clatther it all made! An' yous all quakin', an' even Sailor Mahan there, shakin' in his shoes, sure it was somethin' sinisther!

MAHAN (*Angrily*) You go in to your misthress, girl!

MARION (*Giggling*) Th' bould sailor lad! An' he gettin' rocked in th' cradle of th' deep! Me faltherin' tongue can't impart th' fun I felt at seein' yous all thinkin' th' anchor was bein' weighed for th' next world.

MICHAEL (*Loudly*) Go to your misthress when you're told.

MARION (*Giggling more than ever*) An' oul' dodderin' Shanaar, there, concoctin' his Latin, an' puttin' th' wall between himself an' th' blast! Well, while yous sit all alone there in th' gloamin', yous won't be in heart for singin'. (*She chants*) "Only to see his face again, only to hear him crow!" (*She runs merrily in*)

SHANAAR (*Warily—in a warning whisper*) Watch that one!

MICHAEL Th' ignorant, mockin', saucy face of her afther us bein' in danger of thransportation to where we couldn't know ourselves with agony an' consternation!

SHANAAR (*Fervently*) Sweet airs of heaven be round us all! Watch that one, Mr. Marthraun. Women is more flexible towards th' ungodly than us men, an' well th' old saints knew it. I'd recommend you to compel her, for a start, to lift her bodice higher up, an' pull her skirt lower down; for th' circumnambulatory nature of a woman's form often has a detonatin' effect on a man's idle thoughts.

MICHAEL (*Pensively*) How thrue, how thrue that is!

SHANAAR What we have to do now is to keep thought from dwellin' on th' things seen an' heard this day; for dwellin' on it may bring th' evil back again. So don't let any thought of it, *ab initio extensio,* remain in your minds, though, as a precaution, when I'm passin' th' barracks, I'll acquaint the Civic Guard. Now I must be off, for I've a long way to thravel.

(*He goes as far as the gate, and returns*)

Mr. Marthraun, don't forget to have th' room where th' commotion was manifested, *turbulenta concursio cockolorum,* purified an' surified be an understandin' clergyman. Good-bye.

(*Again he goes as far as the gate, and returns*)

Be on your guard against any unfamiliar motion or peculiar conspicuosity or quasimodical addendum, perceivable in any familiar thing or creature common to your general recognisances. A cat barkin' at a dog, or a dog miaouin' be a fire would atthract your attention, give you a shock, but don't, for th' love of God, notice it! It's this scourge of materialism sweepin' th' world that's incantatin' these evils to our senses and our doorsteps.

MAHAN (*Pensively*) That's th' way th' compass is pointin', Shanaar—everyone only thinkin', thinkin' of himself.

SHANAAR An' women's wily exhilarations are abettin' it, so that a man's measure of virtue is now made with money, used to buy ornaments, bestowed on girls to give a gaudy outside to the ugliness of hell.

MICHAEL (*Fervently*) Oh, how thrue, how thrue that is!

SHANAAR An' th' coruscatin' conduct in th' dance halls is completin' th' ruin.

MAHAN (*Solemnly*) Wise words from a wiser man! Afther a night in one of them, there isn't an ounce of energy left in a worker!

SHANAAR (*Whispering*) A last warnin'—don't forget that six thousand six hundhred an' sixty-six evil spirits can find ready lodgin's under th' skin of a single man!

MICHAEL (*Horrified*) What an appallin' thought!

SHANAAR So be on your guard. Well, good-bye.

MICHAEL (*Offering him a note*) Here's a pound to help you on your way.

SHANAAR (*Setting the note aside*) No, thanks. If I took it, I couldn't fuse th' inner with th' outher vision; I'd lose th' power of spiritual scansion. If you've a shillin' for a meal in th' town till I get to the counthry, where I'm always welcome, I'll take it, an' thank you.

(MICHAEL *gives him a shilling*)

SHANAAR Thank you kindly.

(*He goes out through the gate, and along the pathway outside. Just as he is about to disappear, he faces toward the two men, and stretches out a hand in a gesture of blessing. Fervently*)

*Ab tormentum sed absolvo, non revolvo, cockalorum credulum hibernica!*

MICHAEL (*With emotion*) You too, Shanaar, oul' son; you too! (SHANAAR *goes off.*)

MAHAN (*After a pause—viciously*) That Latin-lustrous oul' cod of a prayer-blower is a positive danger goin' about th' counthry!

MICHAEL (*Startled and offended*) Eh! I wouldn't go callin' him a cod, Sailor Mahan. A little asthray in a way, now an' again, but no cod. You should be th' last to call th' man a cod, for if it wasn't for his holy Latin aspirations, you mightn't be here now.

MAHAN (*With exasperation*) Aw, th' oul' fool, pipin' a gale into every breeze that blows! I don't believe there was ever anything engenderogically evil in that cock as a cock, or denounceable either! Lardin' a man's mind with his killakee Latin! An' looka th' way he slights th' women. I seen him lookin' at Lorna an' Marion as if they'd horns on their heads!

MICHAEL (*Doubtfully*) Maybe he's too down on th' women, though you have to allow women is temptin'.

MAHAN They wouldn't tempt man if they didn't damn well know he wanted to be tempted!

MICHAEL Yes, yes; but we must suffer th' temptation accordin' to the cognisances of th' canon law. But let's have a dhrink, for I'm near dead with th' drouth, an' we can sensify our discussion about th' increased price you're demandin' for carryin' th' turf; though, honest to God, Sailor Mahan, I can't add a ha'penny more to what I'm givin'.

MAHAN A dhrink would be welcome, an' we can talk over th' matter, though, honest to God, Michael Marthraun, blast th' penny less I'll take than what I'm askin'.

MICHAEL (*Going to the porch, and shouting into the house*) Marion, bring th' bottle of ten years' maturin', an' two glasses! (*He returns*) It's th' principle I'm thinkin' of.

MAHAN That's what's throublin' me, too.

(MARION *comes in with the bottle of whiskey and the two glasses. She places them on the table, getting between the two men to do so. Reading the label*)

Flanagan's First! Nyav na Nyale—th' heaven of th' clouds! An' brought be a lass who's a Flanagan's first too!

MARION (*In jovial mood*) G'long with you—you an' your blarney!

MICHAEL (*Enthusiastically*) Had you lived long ago, Emer[9] would have been jealous of you!

(*He playfully pinches her bottom*)

MARION (*Squealing*) Ouch! (*She breaks away, and makes for the porch*) A pair o' naughty men! (*She goes into the house*)

MICHAEL (*Calling after her*) I forgot th' soda, Marion; bring th' siphon, lass.

MAHAN (*Complacently*) I could hold that one in me arms for a long time, Mick.

MICHAEL Th' man would want to be dead who couldn't.

MAHAN (*Enthusiastically*) I'd welcome her, even if I seen her through th' vision of oul' Shanaar—with horns growin' out of her head!

(MARION *returns with the siphon, which she places on the table. The two men, looking in front of them, have silly, sly grins on their faces. The ornament which* MARION *wears round her head has separated into two parts, each of which has risen over her head, forming two branching horns, apparently sprouting from her forehead. The two men, shyly gazing in front, or at the table, do not see the change.* MARION'S *face has changed too, and now seems to wear a mocking, cynical look fitting the aspect of her face to the horns*)

MARION (*Jokingly*) Two wild men—it's afraid I am to come near yous.

MAHAN (*Slyly*) What about a kiss on your rosy mouth, darlin', to give a honied tang to th' whiskey?

MICHAEL An' one for me, too?

MARION (*With pretended demureness*) A thrue gentleman'll rise up an' never expect a thrue lady to bend down for a kiss. (*With vigour*) Up an' take it, before yous grow cold!

(*They rise from their chairs, foolish grins on their faces, settle themselves for a kiss, and then perceive the change that has taken place. They flop back on to the chairs, fright and dismay sweeping over their faces*)

MAHAN }<br>MICHAEL } (*Together*) Good God!

(*They slump in the chairs, overcome, their hands folded in front of their chests, palm to palm, as if in prayer.* MARION *looks at them in some astonishment*)

MARION What ails yous? Was th' excitement too much for yous, or what?

MICHAEL (*Plaintively*) Saints in heaven help us now!

MARION What's come over yous? Th' way yous slumped so sudden down, you'd think I'd horns on me, or somethin'!

MICHAEL (*Hoarsely*) G'way, g'way! Shanaar, Shanaar, where are you now!

MARION (*Going over to* MAHAN, *and putting an arm round his neck*) What about you, gay one?

[9] The wife of the great Irish legendary hero, Cuchulain. The story of her rivalry with other women for her husband's love has attracted many Irish authors.

MAHAN (*Gurgling with fright*) You're sthranglin' me! G'way, g'way, girl!

MARION Looka, a kiss would do yous good. Yous think too much of th' world!

MAHAN (*Chokingly*) St. Christopher, mainstay of mariners, be with me now!

(LORNA *thrusts her head out from the window over the porch*)

LORNA (*Down to* MARION) Let them two oul' life-frighteners fend for themselves, an' come in. From th' back window, I can see th' crowd gathered to give Julia a send-off to Lourdes, so come in to tidy if you want to join them with me.

MARION (*Half to herself—as she runs into the house*) God forgive me—I near forgot! Here we are followin' laughter, instead of seekin' succour from prayer!

(*She runs in, and* LORNA *takes her head back into the room again*)

MICHAEL (*Frightened and very angry*) Now, maybe, you'll quit your jeerin' at oul' Shanaar! Now, maybe, you'll let your mind concentrate on higher things! Now, maybe, you won't be runnin' loose afther girls!

MAHAN (*Indignantly*) Damnit, man, you were as eager for a cuddle as I was!

MICHAEL (*Lifting his eyes skywards*) Oh, d'ye hear that! I was only toleratin' your queer declivity, like a fool. An' afther all th' warnin's given be wise oul' Shanaar! Looka, Sailor Mahan, you'll have to be more on your guard!

MAHAN (*Trying to defend himself*) How could any man suspect such a thing? We'll have to think this thing out.

MICHAEL (*With exasperation*) Think it out! Oh, man, Sailor Mahan, have you nothin' more sensible to say than that we'll have to think it out?

MAHAN Let's have a drink, for God's sake, to steady us down!

MICHAEL (*Hurriedly putting bottle and glasses under the table*) What're you thinkin' of, Sailor Mahan? We can't dispense ourselves through a scene of jollification an' poor Julia passin' on her way to Lourdes!

(*Along the path, on a stretcher, carried by the two* ROUGH FELLOWS, *comes* JULIA, *followed by her father. The stretcher is borne to the gate, and there laid down, so that the head of it is flush with the gateposts and the rest of it within the garden. The framework of the gate makes a frame for* JULIA, *who is half sitting up, her head supported by a high pillow. Her face is a sad yellowish mask, pierced by wide eyes, surrounded by dark circles. Her father is a sturdy fellow of fifty, a scraggly greyish beard struggling from his chin. He is roughly dressed, as a poorer peasant might be, and his clothes are patched in places. He wears a brown muffler, and a faded black trilby-hat*[10] *is on his head. All the time, he looks straight in front with a passive and stony stare.*

*Before the stretcher walks the* MAYOR, *rather stout, clean-shaven, wearing a red robe over rough clothing; he has a very wide three-cornered hat, laced with gold, on his head. Behind him walks the* MACEBEARER, *a big silver and black mace on his shoulder. He is tall, and wears a bright blue robe, trimmed with silver; on his head is a huge cocked hat, laced, too, with silver. These two do not enter the garden, but walk on, and stand waiting near the house, beside the flagpole, but without the wall.*

LORNA, *followed by* MARION, *comes out of the house. Instead of the bright headgear worn before, they have black kerchiefs, worn peasant-wise on their heads—that is, they have been folded triangularly, draped over their heads, with the ends tied beneath their chins.*

LORNA *runs over to the stretcher, kneels down beside it, and kisses* JULIA)

LORNA (*Affectionately*) My sister, my little Julia, oh, how sorry I am that you have to go on this long, sad journey!

JULIA (*Her voice is low, but there is a hectic note of hope in it*) A long journey, Lorna darlin', but not a sad one; oh, no, not a sad one. Hope, Lorna, will have me be the hand all the long way. I go to kneel at the feet of the ever Blessed Virgin.

LORNA Oh, she will comfort you, me darlin'.

JULIA Yes, she will comfort me, Lorna; (*After a pause*) an' cure me too. Lorna, say she will cure me too.

LORNA (*Stifling a sob*) An' cure you too.

JULIA (*To* MICHAEL) Give me your good wishes, Mr. Marthraun.

MICHAEL (*With genuine emotion*) Julia, me best wishes go with you, an' me best prayers'll follow all th' long way!

JULIA (*To* MAHAN) An' you, Sailor Mahan—have you no good wish for the poor voyager?

MAHAN (*Fervently*) Young lass, may you go through healin' wathers, an' come back a clipper, with ne'er a spar, a sail, or a rope asthray!

(FATHER DOMINEER *comes quickly in on the path outside. He is a tall, rather heavily built man of forty. He has a breezy manner now, heading the forlorn hope. He is trying to smile now, but crack his mouth as he will, the tight, surly lines of his face refuse to furnish one. He is dressed in the usual clerical, outdoor garb, and his hard head is covered with a soft, rather widely brimmed black hat*)

FATHER DOMINEER (*As happily as he can*) Now, now, no halts on th' road, little daughter! The train won't wait, an' we must have a few minutes to spare to make you comfortable. Bring her along, Brancardiers![11] Forward, in th' name o' God and of Mary, ever Virgin, ever blessed, always bending to help poor, banished children of Eve!

(*The two* ROUGH MEN *take up the stretcher and carry it along the pathway outside, the* MAYOR, *followed by his* MACE-BEARER, *leading it on.* FATHER DOMINEER *follows immediately behind; then come*

[10] A soft felt hat, usually large-brimmed, named after the Latin Quarter laundress-model heroine of George du Maurier's popular novel.

[11] Stretcher- or litter-bearers.

LORNA *and* MARION, *followed by* MICHAEL *and* MAHAN.

*As the stretcher moves along the pathway outside, a band in the distance is heard playing "Star of the Sea," to which is added the voice of a crowd, singing the words:*

*Hail, Queen of Heav'n, the ocean Star!*
*Guide of the wand'rer here below!*
*Thrown on life's surge, we claim thy care—*
*Save us from peril and from woe.*
*Mother of Christ, Star of the Sea,*
*Pray for the wanderer, pray for me.*)

FATHER DOMINEER (*Enthusiastically*) Julia will bring us back a miracle, a glorious miracle! To Lourdes!

## Scene Two

*The scene is the same as before, though the sunshine isn't quite so bright and determined. The Irish Tricolour flies breezily from its flagpole; the table and chairs stand where they were, and the bottle and glasses are still under it.*

*No one is in the garden, all, apparently, having gone to see* JULIA *away on her long, long journey. Away in the distance the band is playing "Star of the Sea," and the tune can be softly heard from the garden.*

*After a few moments,* LORNA *and* MARION *come along the path outside, enter by the gate, and cross over into the house.*

MARION (*Anxiously*) What d'ye think of th' chance of a cure?

LORNA I'm afraid th' chance is a poor one; but we won't talk about it.

MARION (*Piously*) Well, it was a grand send-off, an' God is good.

LORNA (*Coldly*) An' th' devil's not a bad fella either.

(*They both go into the house, and, a few moments later,* MICHAEL *and* MAHAN *stroll along the path, come into the garden, and go to where the table and chairs are*)

MAHAN Well, th' anchor's weighed.

MICHAEL It was an edifyin' spectacle, Sailor Mahan, thrustin' us outa this world for th' time bein'. Julia's asked for a sign, Sailor Mahan, an', believe me, she'll get it.

MAHAN She will, she will, though I wouldn't like to bet on it.

MICHAEL She'll get what she's afther—a complete cure. Me own generous gift of fifty pounds for th' oul' bog'll be rewarded; an' th' spate o' prayin' goin' on, from the Mayor to the Bellman, is bound to get th' higher saints goin', persuadin' them to furnish a suitable answer to all we're askin'.

MAHAN (*Impatiently*) Arra, man alive, d'ye think th' skipper aloft an' his glitterin' crew is goin' to bother their heads about a call from a tiny town an' disthrict thryin' hard to thrive on turf?

MICHAEL (*Indignantly*) Looka, if you were only versed in th' endurin' promulgacity of th' gospels, you'd know th' man above's concerned as much about Nyadnanave as he is about a place where a swarm of cardinals saunther secure, decoratin' th' air with all their purple an' gold!

MAHAN (*As indignantly*) Are you goin' to tell me that th' skipper aloft an' his hierarchilogical crew are concerned about th' Mayor, the Messenger, Marion, me, an' you as much as they are about them who've been promoted to th' quarter-deck o' th' world's fame? Are you goin' to pit our palthry penances an' haltin' hummin' o' hymns against th' piercin' pipin' of th' rosary be Bing Bang Crosby an' other great film stars, who side-stepped from published greatness for a holy minute or two to send a blessed blast over th' wireless, callin' all Catholics to perpetuatin' prayer!

MICHAEL (*Sitting down on a chair*) Sailor Mahan, I ask you to thry to get your thoughts shipshaped in your mind.

(*While they have been talking, the* MESSENGER *has come running along the path outside, and is now leaning on the gate, listening to the two men, unnoticed by them*)

MAHAN (*Plumping down on the other chair—indignantly*) D'ye remember who you're talkin' to, man? Shipshape in me mind! Isn't a man bound to have his mind fitted together in a shipshape way, who, forced out of his thrue course be a nautical cathastrope, to wit, videliket, an act o' God, ploughed a way through th' Sargasso Sea, reachin' open wathers, long afther hope had troubled him no longer?

MICHAEL (*Wearily*) Aw, Sailor Mahan, what's them things got to do with th' things tantamount to heaven?

MESSENGER (*Over to them*) Mick's right—them things can't be tantamount to anything bar themselves.

MAHAN (*Turning fiercely on the* MESSENGER) What do you want? What're you doin' here? Your coalition of ignorant knowledge can't comprehend th' things we talk about!

MESSENGER (*With some excitement*) Listen, boys—I've a question to ask yous.

MICHAEL (*With a gesture signifying this isn't the time to ask it*) Ask it some time more convenient. An' don't refer to us as "boys"—we're gentlemen to you!

MAHAN (*To* MICHAEL) Looka, Mick, if you only listened to Bing Crosby, th' mighty film star, croonin' his Irish lullaby, (*He chants*) "Tooral ooral ooral, tooral ooral ay," you'd have th' visuality to see th' amazin' response he'd have from millions of admirers, if he crooned a hymn!

MESSENGER I was never sthruck be Bing Crosby's croonin'.[1]

[1] Teamed with the distinguished Abbey Theatre actor, Barry Fitzgerald, Crosby made a popular film, *Going My Way* (1944). In it Crosby sang the lullaby under discussion here.

MICHAEL (*Wrathfully—to* MESSENGER) You were never sthruck! An' who th' hell are you to be consulted? Please don't stand there interferin' with the earnest colloquy of betther men. (*To* MAHAN) Looka, Sailor Mahan, any priest'll tell you that in th' eyes of heaven all men are equal an' must be held in respect an' reverence.

MAHAN (*Mockingly*) Ay, they'll say that to me an' you, but will they say it to Bing Crosby, or any other famous film star?

MESSENGER Will they hell! Honour be th' clergy's regulated by how much a man can give!

MICHAEL (*Furiously—to the* MESSENGER) Get to hell outa here! With that kinda talk, we won't be able soon to sit steady on our chairs. Oh!

(*The chair he is sitting on collapses, and he comes down to the ground on his arse*)

MAHAN (*Astonished*) Holy saints, what's happened?

MICHAEL (*In a fierce whisper—to* MAHAN) Take no notice of it, fool. Go on talkin'!

MAHAN (*A little confused*) I'll say you're right, Mick; th' way things are goin' we won't be able much longer to sit serene on our chairs. Oh!

(*The chair collapses under* MAHAN, *and he, too, comes down to the ground*)

MICHAEL (*In a fierce whisper*) Don't notice it; go on's if nothin' happened!

MESSENGER (*Amused*) Well, yous have settled down now, anyhow! Will I get yous chairs sturdy enough to uphold th' wisdom of your talkin'?

MICHAEL (*Angrily—to* MESSENGER) There's nothin' wrong with th' chairs we have! You get outa here! Nothin's wrong with th' chairs at all. Get outa here—I don't trust you either!

MESSENGER I've somethin' important to ask yous.

MICHAEL Well, ask it at some more convenient time. (*To* MAHAN) It's a blessin' that so many lively-livin' oul' holy spots are still in th' land to help us an' keep us wary.

MESSENGER (*Scornfully*) An' where are th' lively holy spots still to be found? Sure, man, they're all gone west long ago, an' the whole face o' th' land is pock-marked with their ruins!

MICHAEL (*Shouting at the* MESSENGER) Where are th' lost an' ruined holy places? We've always cared for, an' honoured, our holy spots! Mention one of them, either lost or ruined!

MESSENGER (*Shouting back*) There are thousands of them, man; places founded by Finian, Finbarr, an' th' rest; places that are now only an oul' ruined wall, blighted be nettle an' dock, their only glory th' crimson berries of th' bright arbutus! Where's th' Seven Churches of Glendalough? Where's Durrow of Offally, founded be Columkille[2] himself? Known now only be the name of the Book of Durrow!

MICHAEL (*Ferociously*) Book o' Durrow! It's books that have us half th' woeful way we are, fillin' broody minds with loose scholasticality, infringin' th' holy beliefs an' thried impositions that our fathers' fathers' fathers gave our fathers' fathers, who gave our fathers what our fathers gave to us!

MESSENGER Faith, your fathers' faith is fear, an' now fear is your only fun.

MAHAN (*Impatiently*) Let him go, Mick, an' let's have that dhrink you mentioned a year ago.

(MARION'S *head appears at the window, looking down at the* MESSENGER. *The decorations on her head have now declined to their first place*)

MARION (*Down to the* MESSENGER) Hallo, Robin Adair!

(*He looks up*)

Where are th' two oul' woeful wondhers?

(*He points to where they are*)

Oh, they've brought the unsteady chairs out, and now they've broken them up! (*To* MICHAEL—*angrily*) You knew well th' chairs in the hall were there only to present an appearance.

MESSENGER (*Up to her*) Oh, Marion, Marion, sweet Marion, come down till I give you a kiss havin' in it all the life an' longin' of th' greater lovers of th' past!

MARION (*Leaving the window*) Now, now, naughty boy!

MICHAEL (*Sourly*) You'd do well to remember, lad, the month in jail you got for kissin' Marion, an' the forty-shillin' fine on Marion, for kissing you in a public place at th' crossroads.

(MARION *comes from the house, goes toward the* MESSENGER, *who seizes her in his arms and kisses her*)

MESSENGER I'd do a year an' a day in a cold cell of pressed-in loneliness, an' come out singin' a song, for a kiss from a lass like Marion!

MARION Don't think too much of me, Robin Adair, for I've some of th' devil in me, an' th' two fostherers of fear, there, think I wear horns on holy days.

MICHAEL (*Impressively*) See—she's warnin' you, herself, young man!

MARION (*To the* MESSENGER) An' what has you here arguin' with them two oul' fools?

MESSENGER I came to ask a question of them, but they were buried in their prayers. Did you see him? Did he come this way?

MICHAEL (*Suddenly alarmed*) Come where?

MAHAN (*Alarmed*) See who?

MESSENGER Th' Cock.

MAHAN, MICHAEL (*Together*) Th' Cock!

(*They carefully creep away from the broken chairs, and stand up when they are some distance from them*)

MESSENGER Ay. I thought he'd make for here first.

MICHAEL (*Echoing the* MESSENGER) Make for here first!

(*In the distance, the loud, exultant crow of the* COCK *is heard*)

MESSENGER (*Excitedly*) There he is! Away in the direction east of th' bog! I'll go get him, an' fetch him home.

[2] The ruins and relics are reminders of Ireland's past. Columkille (or St. Columba) is, with Saints Patrick and Bridget, one of Ireland's patron saints.

MARION (*Kissing the* MESSENGER) Bring him here first, Robin, an' I'll have a wreath of roses ready to hang round his neck.

MESSENGER (*Rushing away*) I will, I will, fair one!

(*He goes off. She takes the broken chairs into the house*)

MARION (*Carrying in the chairs*) Next time, you boyos, take out two steady ones.

MICHAEL (*Horrified*) Did you hear what she said, Sailor Mahan? Hang a wreath of roses round his neck! Well, I'll have th' gun ready! Ay, now!

(*He goes over to the porch, but* MAHAN *lays a restraining hand on his arm*)

MAHAN What good would th' gun be? Have you forgot what Shanaar told us? Your bullet would go clean through him, an' leave him untouched. Now that we're in peace here, let's have th' dhrink we were to have, an' which we both need.

MICHAEL (*Halting*) You're right, Sailor Mahan. If he comes here, what we have to do is to take no notice. Look through him, past him, over him, but never at him. (*He prepares the bottle of whiskey and the glasses*) There's sinisther enchantments all around us. God between us an' all harm! We'll have to be for ever on our guard.

MAHAN (*Impatiently*) Yis, yis; fill out th' dhrink, for God's sake!

MICHAEL May it give us courage. (*He tilts the bottle over the glass, but none of it spills out*) Good God, th' bottle's bewitched too!

MAHAN Bottle bewitched? How could a bottle be bewitched? Steady your nerves, man. Thry givin' it a shake.

MICHAEL (*Who has left the bottle on the table—retreating away from it*) Thry givin' it a shake yourself, since you're so darin'.

(MAHAN *goes over to the table with a forced swagger, and reaches out a cautious hand for the bottle. As he touches it, its colour changes to a glowing red*)

MAHAN (*Fervent and frightened*) St. Christopher, pathron of all mariners, defend us—th' bottle's changed its colour!

MICHAEL There's evil things cantherin' an' crawlin' about this place! You saw th' seal on th' bottle showin' it was untouched since it left th' store. Flanagan's finest, Jamieson's best, ten years maturin' —an' look at it now.

MAHAN How are we goin' to prevent ourselves from bein' the victims of sorcery an' ruin? You'd think good whiskey would be exempt from injury even be th' lowest of th' low.

MICHAEL It's th' women who're always intherceptin' our good intentions. Evil things is threatenin' us everywhere. Th' one safe method of turnin' our back to a power like this is to go forward an' meet it halfway. (*He comes close to* MAHAN, *and whispers hoarsely*) Selah! [3]

[3] The obscure Hebrew word which appears very frequently in *Psalms,* now widely presumed to be a musical notation for a pause.

MAHAN (*Mystified and frightened at what he thinks may be something sinister*) Selah?

MICHAEL (*Emphatically*) Selah!

MAHAN (*Agonisingly*) Good God!

MICHAEL Now, maybe, you'll believe what th' missioner said last night.

MAHAN (*A little dubiously*) He might have been exaggeratin' a bit, Mick.

MICHAEL Look at th' bottle, man! Demons can hide in th' froth of th' beer a man's dhrinkin'. An' all th' time, my turf-workers an' your lorry drivers are screwin' all they can out of us so that they'll have more to spend on pictures an' in th' dance halls, leavin' us to face th' foe alone.

MAHAN (*Abjectly*) What's a poor, good-livin', virtuous man to do then?

MICHAEL He must always be thinkin' of th' four last things—hell, heaven, death, an' th' judgment.

MAHAN (*Pitifully*) But that would sthrain a man's nerves, an' make life hardly worth livin'.

MICHAEL It's plain, Sailor Mahan, you're still hankerin' afther th' things o' th' world, an' the soft, stimulatin' touch of th' flesh. You're puttin' th' two of us in peril, Sailor Mahan.

MAHAN (*Protesting*) You're exaggeratin' now.

MICHAEL I am not. I seen your eyes followin' that Loreleen when she's about, hurtin' th' tendher muscles of your eye squintin' down at her legs. You'll have to curb your conthradictions, for you're puttin' us both in dire peril, Sailor Mahan. Looka what I've lost already! Me fine silk hat torn to shreds, so that Lorna's had to telephone th' firm for another, that I may suitably show meself when I meet His Brightness, the President; an' looka th' whiskey there—forced into a misundherstandin' of itself be some minor demon devisin' a spell on it! Guess how much good money I surrendhered to get that bottle, Sailor Mahan?

MAHAN I've no idea of what whiskey is a gallon now.

MICHAEL (*Impatiently*) What whiskey is a gallon now? Is there some kinda spell on you, too, Sailor Mahan? You can't think of whiskey in gallons now; you have to think of it in terms of sips; an' sips spaced out from each other like th' holy days of obligation.

MAHAN An' how are we goin' to get rid of it? We're in some danger while it's standin' there.

MICHAEL How th' hell do I know how we'll get rid of it? We'll have to get Shanaar to deal with it, an', mind you, don't go too near it.

(*The* PORTER *appears on the sidewalk outside the wall. He is a middle-aged man with an obstinate face, the chin hidden by a grizzled beard. He is wearing a pair of old brown trousers, an older grey coat, and an old blue shirt. On his head is a big cap, with a long, wide peak jutting out in front of it. The crown of the cap is a high one, and around the crown is a wide band of dazzling scarlet. He is carrying a parcel wrapped in brown paper, either side of which is a little torn. He looks north, south, west, and then, turning east, he sees the two men in the garden)*

PORTER (*To the two men*) Isn't it handy now that I've clapped eyes on two human bein's in this godforsaken hole! I've been trudhgin' about for hours thryin' to find th' one that'll claim what's in this parcel I'm bearin', an', maybe, th' two of yous, or maybe, one of yous, can tell me where I'll find him. I'm on th' thrack of an oul' fella callin' himself a Councillor an' a Jay Pee.[4]

MICHAEL What's his name?

PORTER That's more than I can say, for th' chit of th' girl in th' shop who took th' ordher forgot to write down th' name, an' then forgot th' name itself when she started to write it down. All I know is that in this disthrict I'm seekin' a Mr. Councillor So-an'-so; one havin' Councillor at his head an' Jay Pee at his tail.

MICHAEL (*With importance*) I'm a Councillor and a Jay Pee.

PORTER (*With some scorn*) D'ye tell me that now? (*He bends over the wall to come closer to* MICHAEL) Listen, me good man, me journey's been too long an' too dangerous for me to glorify any cod-actin'! It would be a quare place if you were a councillor. You'll have to grow a few more grey hairs before you can take a rise outa me!

MICHAEL (*Indignantly*) Tell us what you've got there, fella, an', if it's not for us, be off about your business!

PORTER (*Angrily*) Fella yourself! An' mend your manners, please! It's hardly th' like of you would be standin' in need of a silky, shinin' tall-hat.

MICHAEL If it's a tall-hat, it's for me! I'm Mr. Councillor Marthraun, Jay Pee—ordhered to be sent express by th' firm of Buckley's.

PORTER (*With a quick conciliatory change*) That's th' firm. I guessed you was th' man at once, at once. That man's a leadher in th' locality, I said, as soon as I clapped me eye on you. A fine, clever, upstandin' individual, I says to meself.

MICHAEL (*Shortly*) Hand over th' hat, and you can go.

PORTER Hould on a minute, sir; wait till I tell you: I'm sorry, but th' hat's been slightly damaged in thransit. (*He begins to take the hat from the paper*)

MICHAEL Damaged? How th' hell did you damage it?

PORTER Me, is it? No, not me, sir. (*He stretches over the wall towards them*) When I was bringin' it here, someone shot a bullet through it, east be west!

MICHAEL Nonsense, man, who'd be shootin' bullets round here?

PORTER Who indeed? That's th' mystery. Bullet it was. People told me the Civic Guards were out thryin' to shoot down an evil spirit flyin' th' air in th' shape of a bird.

MICHAEL (*Alarmed*) Th' Cock!

PORTER (*Placing the tall-hat on the wall carefully*) An', seein' how things are, an' th' fright I got, it's welcome a dhrink would be from th' handsome bottle I see paradin' on th' table.

[4] J.P., Justice of the Peace.

MICHAEL (*In a loud whisper*) To touch it is to go in danger of your life—th' bottle's bewitched!

PORTER Th' bottle bewitched? What sort of a place have me poor, wandherin' feet sthrayed into at all? Before I ventured to come here at all, I should have stayed at home. I'm already as uneasy as th' place itself!

(*A shot is heard, and the tall-hat is knocked from the wall on to the road*)

Saints in glory, there's another one!

MAHAN (*Excitedly*) It's your hat, man, th' red band on your hat!

PORTER (*To* MICHAEL*—speaking rapidly, picking the tall-hat from the road and offering it to* MICHAEL) Here, take your hat, sir, an' keep it safe, an' I'll be goin'.

MICHAEL (*Frightened and angry*) Take it back; it's damaged; take it back, fella!

PORTER (*Loudly and with anger*) Fella yourself! Is it takin' th' risk I'd be of a bullet rushin' through me instead of th' oul' hat? (*He flings it towards the two men*) Here, take your oul' hat an' th' risk along with it! Do what you want with it; do what you like with it; do what you can with it—I'm off! (*He runs off in the direction he came from, while the two men gaze doubtfully at the hat lying in the garden*)

MICHAEL (*Tremulously*) The cowards that are in this counthry leavin' a poor man alone in his dilemma! I'd be afraid to wear it now.

MAHAN Aw, give yourself a shake, Mick. You're not afraid of a poor tall-hat. An' throw away ten good pounds. (*He goes towards where the hat is, but* MICHAEL *holds him by the arm*)

MICHAEL (*With warning and appeal*) No, don't touch it till we see further.

(*The* SERGEANT *appears on the pathway outside. He has a rifle in his hands; he leans against the wall looking towards the two. He is obviously anxious, and in a state of fear*)

SERGEANT Yous didn't see it? It didn't come here, did it?

MICHAEL (*Breathless with the tension of fear*) No, no; not yet. (*With doleful appeal*) Oh, don't be prowlin' round here—you'll only be attractin' it to th' place!

SERGEANT (*Ignoring appeal*) Three times I shot at it; three times th' bullets went right through it; and twice th' thing flew away crowing.

MICHAEL (*Excitedly*) Did you get it th' third time, did you get it then?

SERGEANT Wait till I tell yous: sthrange things an' unruly are happenin' in this holy land of ours this day! Will I ever forget what happened th' third time I hot[5] it! Never, never. Isn't it a wondher an' a mercy of God that I'm left alive afther th' reverberatin' fright I got!

MICHAEL (*Eagerly*) Well, what happened when you hot it then?

MAHAN (*Eagerly*) When you hot it for th' third time?

SERGEANT Yous could never guess?

[5] Dialect past tense of *hit*.

MICHAEL (*Impatiently*) Oh, we know we'd never guess; no one can go guessin' about demonological disturbances.

MAHAN Tell us, will you, without any more of your sthructural suggestions!

SERGEANT As sure as I'm standin' here; as sure as this gun is in me left hand; (*He is holding it in his right one*) as sure as we're all poor, identified sinners; when I hot him for th' third time, I seen him changin' into a—

MICHAEL }
MAHAN } (*Together*) What?

SERGEANT (*Whisperingly*) What d'ye think?

MAHAN (*Explosively*) Oh, we're not thinkin'; we can't think; we're beyond thinkin'! We're waitin' for you to tell us!

SERGEANT Th' soul well-nigh left me body when I seen th' unholy novelty happenin': th' thing that couldn't be, yet th' thing that was. If I never prayed before, I prayed then—for hope; for holy considheration in th' quandary; for power to be usual an' spry again when th' thing was gone.

MICHAEL What thing, what thing, man?

MAHAN (*Despairingly*) Thry to tell us, Sergeant, what you said you said you seen.

SERGEANT I'm comin' to it; since what I seen was seen by no man never before, it's not easy for a man to describe with evidential accuracy th' consequential thoughts fluttherin' through me amazed mind at what was, an' what couldn't be, demonstrated there, or there, or anywhere else, where mortals congregate in ones or twos or crowds astoundin'.

MICHAEL (*Imploringly*) Looka, Sergeant, we're languishin' for th' information that may keep us from spendin' th' rest of our lives in constant consternation.

SERGEANT As I was tellin' you, there was th' crimson crest of th' Cock, enhancin' th' head lifted up to give a crow, an' when I riz th' gun to me shouldher, an' let bang, th' whole place went dead-dark; a flash of red lightning near blinded me; an' when it got light again, a second afther, there was the demonised Cock changin' himself into a silken glossified tall-hat!

MICHAEL (*Horrified*) A silken tall-hat!

MAHAN A glossified tall-hat!

MICHAEL (*To* MAHAN—*viciously*) Now you'll quit undherestimatin' what th' holy missioner said last night about th' desperate an' deranging thrickeries of evil things loose an' loungin' among us! Now can you see the significality of things?

MAHAN (*Going away as far as he can from the tall-hat lying in the garden*) Steer clear of it; get as far away from it as we can! Keep well abaft of it!

SERGEANT (*Puzzled*) Keep clear from what?

MAHAN (*Pointing to the hat*) Th' hat, man, th' hat!

SERGEANT (*Seeing the hat beside him, and jumping away from it*) I was near touchin' th' brim of it! Jasus! yous should have warned me!

MICHAEL (*Close to the* SERGEANT—*in a whisper*) Does it look anything like th' thing you shot?

SERGEANT (*Laying a shaking hand on* MICHAEL'*s arm*) It's th' dead spit of what I seen him changin' into durin' th' flash of lightining! I just riz th' gun to me shouldher—like this (*He raises the gun to his shoulder*) to let bang.

(*The garden is suddenly enveloped in darkness for a few moments. A fierce flash of lightning shoots through the darkness; the hat has disappeared, and where it stood now stands the* COCK. *While the lightning flashes, the* COCK *crows lustily. Then the light as suddenly comes back to the garden, and shows that the* COCK *and the hat have gone.* MICHAEL *and* MAHAN *are seen to be lying on the ground, and the* SERGEANT *is on his knees, as if in prayer*)

SERGEANT Holy St. Custodius, pathron of th' police, protect me!

MICHAEL (*In a whisper*) Are you there, Sailor Mahan?

MAHAN (*In a whisper*) Are you there, Michael Marthraun?

MICHAEL I'm done for.

MAHAN We're both done for.

SERGEANT We're all done for.

MAHAN Th' smell of th' sulphur an' brimstone's burnin' me.

MICHAEL Now you'll give up mockin' Shanaar, if it's not too late. You seen how Marion's head was ornamented, an' it'll not be long till Lorna has them too.

SERGEANT (*Now sitting down, so that he is to the left of* MICHAEL, *while* MAHAN *sits to the right of him, so frightened that he must blame someone*) We'll have to curtail th' gallivantin' of th' women afther th' men. Th' house is their province, as th' clergy's tired tellin' them. They'll have to realize that th' home's their only proper place.

MICHAEL An' demolish th' minds that babble about books.

SERGEANT (*Raising his voice*) Th' biggest curse of all! Books no decent mortal should touch, should never even see th' cover of one!

MICHAEL (*Warningly*) Hush! Don't speak so loud, or th' lesser boyo'll hear you!

SERGEANT (*Startled*) Lesser boyo? What lesser boyo?

MAHAN (*Whispering and pointing*) Th' boyo in th' bottle there.

SERGEANT (*Noticing it for the first time*) Why, what's in it?

MICHAEL Th' best of whiskey was in it till some evil spirit put a spell on it, desthroyin' its legitimate use.

SERGEANT (*Unbelievingly*) I don't believe it. Nothin' could translate good dhrink into anything but what it was made to be. We could do with a dhrink now. (*He advances cautiously towards the table*)

MICHAEL (*Excitedly*) Don't meddle with it, man; don't stimulate him!

(*The* SERGEANT *tiptoes over to the table, stretches his hand out, and touches the bottle. He immediately lets out a yelp, and jumps back*)

SERGEANT Oh! Be God, it's red-hot!

MAHAN (*Angrily*) You were told not to touch it! You're addin' to our dangers.

MICHAEL (*Shouting*) Good God, man, couldn't you

do what you're told! Now you've added anger to its impositional qualities!

SERGEANT (*Nursing his hand*) Aren't we in a nice quandary when an evil thing can insconce itself in a bottle!

MICHAEL Th' whole place's seethin' with them. You, Sergeant, watch th' road north; you, Sailor Mahan, watch it south; an' I'll keep an eye on th' house.

(MAHAN *goes to one end of the wall, the* SERGEANT *to the other, and both stretch over it to look different ways along the road. During the next discussion, whenever they leave where they are, they move cautiously, crouching a little, as if they were afraid to be seen; keeping as low as possible for security*)

One of us'll have to take th' risk, an' go for Father Domineer at once. (*He waits for a few moments, but no one answers*) Did yous hear me, or are yous lettin' on to be deaf? I said one of us'll have to go for Father Domineer. (*There is no reply*) Are you listenin' to me be any chance, Sailor Mahan?

MAHAN I heard you, I heard you.

MICHAEL An' why don't you go, then?

MAHAN (*Coming down towards* MICHAEL*—crouching low*) Nice thing if I met th' Cock barrin' me way? Why don't you go yourself?

MICHAEL What about th' possibility of me meetin' him? I'm more conspicuous in this disthrict than you, an' th' thing would take immediate recognisance of me.

SERGEANT (*Coming down towards them—crouching too*) Me an' Sailor Mahan'll go together.

MICHAEL (*Indignantly*) An' leave me to grapple with *mysteriosa Daemones* alone? (*He turns his face skywards*) Oh, in this disthrict there's not a sign of one willin' to do unto another what another would do to him!

MAHAN (*Fiercely*) That's a lie: there isn't a one who isn't eager to do to others what others would do to him!

(*The* BELLMAN, *dressed as a fireman, comes in, and walks along on the path outside. He has a huge brass fireman's helmet on his head, and is wearing a red shirt and blue trousers. He has a bell in his hand which he rings loudly before he shouts his orders. The three men cease their discussion, and give him their full attention*)

BELLMAN (*Shouting*) Into your houses all! Bar th' doors, shut th' windows! Th' Cock's comin'! In the shape of a woman! Gallus, Le Coq, an' Kyleloch,[6] th' Cock's comin' in th' shape of a woman! Into your houses, shut to th' windows, bar th' doors!

(*He goes out in the opposite direction, shouting his orders and ringing his bell, leaving the three men agitated and more frightened than ever*)

SERGEANT (*Frantically*) Into the house with us all—quick!

MICHAEL (*Hindering him—ferociously*) Not in there, you fool! Th' house is full o' them. You seen what happened to the whiskey? If he or she comes, th' thing to do is to take no notice; if he or she talks, not to answer; and take no notice of whatever questionable shape it takes. Sit down, quiet, th' three of us.

(*The three men sit down on the ground—*MICHAEL *to the right, the* SERGEANT *to the left, and* MAHAN *in the centre.*

MICHAEL (*Trembling*) Now, let th' two of yous pull yourselves together. An' you, Mahan, sing that favourite of yours, quietly, as if we were passing th' time pleasantly. (*As* MAHAN *hesitates*) Go on, man, for God's sake!

MAHAN (*Agitated*) I can't see how I'll do it justice undher these conditions. I'll thry. (*He sings, but his voice quavers occasionally*)

Long time ago when men was men
An' ships not ships that sail'd just to an' fro-o-o,
We hoisted sail an' sail'd, an' then sail'd on an' on to Jericho-o-o;
With silks an' spice came back again because we'd nowhere else to go!

MICHAEL, SERGEANT (*Together*) Go, go!

MAHAN (*Singing*)

Th' captain says, says he, we'll make
Th' pirates where th' palm trees wave an' grow-o-o,
Haul down their sable flag, an' pray, before we hang them all, heave yo-ho-ho;
Then fling their bodies in th' sea to feed th' fishes down below!

MICHAEL, SERGEANT (*Together*) Low, low!

(*A golden shaft of light streams in from the left of the road, and, a moment afterwards,* LORELEEN *appears in the midst of it. She stands in the gateway staring at the three men squatted on the ground*)

LORELEEN (*Puzzled*) What th' hell's wrong here?

MICHAEL (*In a whisper—motioning* MAHAN *to continue*) Go on, man.

MAHAN (*Singing—with more quavers in his voice*)

An' when we've swabb'd th' blood away,
We'll take their hundhred-ton gunn'd ship in tow-o-o;
Their precious jewels'll go to deck th' breasts of women, white as snow-o-o;
So hoist all sail an' make for home through waves that lash an' winds that blow!

MICHAEL, SERGEANT (*Together*) Blow, blow!

(LORELEEN *comes into the garden, and approaches the men. The golden light follows her, and partly shines on the three singers*)

LORELEEN (*Brightly*) Singin' is it the three of you are? Practisin' for the fancy-dress ball tonight, eh? Ye do well to bring a spray of light, now and again, into a dark place. The Sergeant's eyes, too, whenever Lorna or me passes by, are lit with a light that never was on sea or land. An' th' bould Sailor Mahan is smiling too; only Dad is dour. (*She glances at the*

[6] The Bellman shouts the Latin, the French, and the Gaelic for "cock."

*bottle on the table*) The song is heard, th' wine is seen, only th' women wanting. (*She runs over to the porchway, and shouts into the house*) Lorna, Marion, come on down, come out here, an' join th' enthertainment!

(LORNA *and* MARION *come trotting out of the house into the garden. They are both clad in what would be called fancy dress.* LORNA *is supposed to be a gypsy, and is wearing a short black skirt, low-cut green bodice, with a gay sash round her waist, sparkling with sequins. Her fair arms are bare. Her head is bound with a silver and black ornament, similar in shape to that already worn by* MARION. *Her legs are encased in black stockings, and dark red shoes cover her feet.* MARION *is dressed as a Nippy,*[7] *a gay one. She has on a short, bright green skirt, below which a black petticoat peeps; a low-cut bodice of a darker green, and sports a tiny black apron to protect her costume. She wears light brown silk stockings and brown shoes. Outside the white bandeau round her head she wears the ornament worn before. The two women stare at the three men*)

LORNA (*Vexatiously*) Dhrunk is it? To get in that state just when we were practisin' a few steps for tonight's fancy-dress dance! (*She notices the bottle*) Looka th' dhrink left out in th' sun an' air to dhry! (*She whips up the bottle, and places it inside on the floor of the porch*) An' even th' Sailor Mahan is moody too! (*She goes over to the* SERGEANT, *stands behind him, and lays a hand on his head. She is now in the golden light which shines down on the* SERGEANT *too*)

I saw a ship a-sailing, a-sailing on th' sea;
An' among its spicy cargo was a bonny lad for me!

(*The* SERGEANT *rises slowly, as if enchanted, with a foolish look of devotion on his face, till he stands upright beside* LORNA, *glancing at her face, now and again, very shy and uncertain. While this has been happening,* LORELEEN *has gone to* SAILOR MAHAN, *and now stands behind him with a hand on his head*)

LORELEEN (*Down to* SAILOR MAHAN)

I saw a man come running, come running o'er th' lea, sir,
And, lo, he carried silken gowns
That couldn't hide a knee,
That he had bought in saucy towns;
An' jewels he'd bought beyond th' bounds
Of Asia's furthest sea.
And all were lovely, all were fine,
An' all were meant for me!

(SAILOR MAHAN *rises, as if enchanted, till he stands upright beside* LORELEEN, *slyly looking at her now and again*)

MARION Aw, let's be sensible. (*She sees the gun*) What's th' gun doin'? Who owns th' gun?

SERGEANT It's mine. I'm on pathrol lookin' to shoot down th' demon bird loose among innocent people.

[7] A waitress, originally as employed by the British restaurant-chain of Lyons.

MARION Demon bird loose among innocent people! Yous must be mad.

SERGEANT (*Indignantly*) We're not mad! It's only that we were startled when th' darkness came, th' lightning flashed, an' we saw Mr. Marthraun's tall-hat turnin' itself into th' demon bird!

LORNA (*Mystified*) Th' darkness came, th' lightning flashed? A tall-hat changin' into a demon bird!

MICHAEL (*Springing to his feet*) Ay, an' this isn't th' time for gay disturbance! So go in, an' sthrip off them gaudy things, an' bend your mind to silent prayer an' long fastin'! Fall prostrate before God, admittin' your dire disthress, an' you may be admitted to a new dispensation!

LORNA (*To* MICHAEL) Nonsense! Your new tall-hat was delivered an hour ago, an' is upstairs now, waitin' for you to put it on. (*To* MARION) Take that gun in, dear, outa th' way, an' bring down th' tall-hat to show him he's dreamin'.

(MARION *takes up the gun, and goes into the house with it, as* MICHAEL, *in a great rage, shoves* MAHAN *aside to face* LORNA *fiercely*)

MICHAEL (*Loudly*) Who are you, you jade, to set yourself up against th' inner sight an' outer sight of genuine Christian men? (*He shouts*) We seen this thing, I tell you! If you knew what you ought to know, you'd acknowledge th' thrained tenacity of evil things. Betther had I left you soakin' in poverty, with your rags coverin' your thin legs, an' your cheeks hollow from mean feedin'. Through our bulgin' eyes, didn't we see th' horrification of me tall-hat turnin' into th' demonised cock? Me tall-hat, you bitch, me own tall-hat is roamin' round th' counthry, temptin' souls to desthroy themselves with dancin' an' desultory pleasures!

MAHAN (*Gripping* MICHAEL'S *arm*) Aw, draw it mild, Mick!

MICHAEL (*Flinging off* MAHAN'S *hold*) Go in, an' take them things, showy with sin, off you, an' dhress decent! (*He points to* LORELEEN) It's you who's brought this blast from th' undherworld, England, with you! It's easy seen what you learned while you worked there—a place where no God is; where pride and lust an' money are the brightest liveries of life! (*He advances as if to strike her, but* MAHAN *bars his way*) You painted slug!

(MARION *comes from the house, carrying a fresh, dignified tall-hat, noble in its silken glossiness. She offers it to* MICHAEL, *who jumps away from it*)

No, no, take it away; don't let it touch me.

(MARION *puts the hat on the table, and the three men stare at it as if expecting something to happen*)

LORNA (*Darting into the porch, and returning with the bottle. It has gone back to its former colour*) Let's have a dhrink to give us courage to fight our dangers. Fetch another glass, Marion.

(MARION *goes in, and returns with a glass.* LORNA *uncorks the bottle, and takes up a glass to fill it*)

MICHAEL (*Warningly*) Don't meddle with that dhrink, or harm may come to us all!

LORNA (*Recklessly*) If I can't wrap myself in th' arms

of a man, I'll wrap myself in a cordial. (*She fills the glass then she fills another one, and gives it to* LORELEEN; *then she fills a third, and gives it to* MARION) Here, Loreleen.

(LORELEEN *takes the glass*)

Here, Marion.

(MARION *takes the glass from her*)

MAHAN (*Doubtfully, and with some fear*) I wouldn't, Lorna, I wouldn't dhrink it—there's some kind of a spell on it.

LORNA Is there, now? I hope to God it's a strong one! (*Raising her glass*) Th' Cock-a-doodle Dandy!

MARION, LORELEEN (*Raising their glasses—together*) Th' Cock-a-doodle Dandy!

(*The three women empty their glasses together.* LORNA *fills her glass again, and goes over to the* SERGEANT)

LORNA (*Offering the glass to the* SERGEANT) Dhrink, hearty man, an' praise th' good things life can give.

(*As he hesitates*)

Dhrink from th' glass touched by th' lips of a very fair lady!

SERGEANT (*Impulsively*) Death an' bedamnit, ma'am, it's a fair lady you are. (*He takes the glass from her*) I'm not th' one to be short in salutin' loveliness! (*He drinks, and a look of delightful animation gradually comes on to his face*)

LORELEEN (*Who has filled her glass again—going over to* SAILOR MAHAN, *and offering him the drink*) Here, Sailor Mahan, man of th' wider waters, an' th' seven seas, dhrink!

(*As he hesitates*)

Dhrink from th' glass touched by th' lips of a very fair lady!

MAHAN (*Taking the glass—impulsively*) Here's a one who always yelled ahoy to a lovely face an' charmin' figure whenever they went sailin' by—*salud!* (*He drinks, and the look of animation gradually comes on to his face too*)

MARION (*Who has filled her glass the second time—going over to* MICHAEL *and offering him the drink*) Dark man, let th' light come to you be dhrinkin' from a glass touched be th' red lips of a fair young maiden!

MICHAEL (*Who has been watching the others enviously—taking the glass from her*) Gimme it! I won't be one odd. Yous can't best me! (*He drinks it down greedily. A reckless look steals over his face*)

(*During the last few moments,* LORNA *has been humming a tune, which has been taken up by an accordion, very softly. Then the* MESSENGER *appears on the pathway outside, and it can be seen that he is the player. He sits sideways on the wall, still playing softly a kind of a dance tune*)

MICHAEL (*To* MARION) In our heart of hearts, maid Marion, we care nothin' about th' world of men. Do we now, Sailor Mahan?

MAHAN (*Cautiously—though a reckless gleam is appearing in his eyes too*) We all have to think about th' world o' men at times.

MICHAEL Not with our hearts, Sailor Mahan; oh, not with our hearts. You're thinkin' now of th' exthra money you want off me, Sailor Mahan. Take it, man, an' welcome! (*Enthusiastically*) An' more! You can have double what you're askin', without a whimper, without a grudge!

MAHAN (*Enthusiastically*) No, damnit, Michael, not a penny from you! We're as good as bein' brothers! Looka th' lilies of th' field, an' ask yourself what th' hell's money!

MICHAEL (*Excitedly*) Dhross, be God! Dhross, an' nothin' else! (*To* MARION) Gimme that hat there!

(*She gives it to him. He puts it on, puts an arm round her waist, and they begin to move with the beat of the music. As* MICHAEL *puts his arm around her waist, the ornament on her head rises into a graceful, curving horn, but he does not notice it. At the same time, the* SERGEANT, *having put an arm round* LORNA, *moves in the dance, too. As he does so, the ornament on her head, too, becomes a curving horn, but he does not notice it. Then* MAHAN *goes over stealthily to* LORELEEN, *who is watching the others, and stabs her shyly in the ribs with a finger. She turns, smiles, takes hold of his arm, and puts it round her waist. Then the two of them join the others in moving round to the beat of the music, the cock-like crest in* LORELEEN'S *hat rising higher as she begins to move in the dance.*

*After a few moments, the dance quickens, the excitement grows, and the men stamp out the measure of the music fiercely, while the three women begin to whirl round them with ardour and abandon. While the excitement is at its height, a loud, long peal of thunder is heard, and in the midst of it, with a sliding, rushing pace,* FATHER DOMINEER *appears in the gateway, a green glow enveloping him as he glares down at the swinging dancers, and as a loud, lusty crow from the* COCK *rings out through the garden.*

*The dancers, excepting* LORELEEN, *suddenly stand stockstill, then fall on one knee, facing the priest, their heads bent in shame and some dismay.* LORELEEN *dances on for some few moments longer, the music becoming softer, then she slowly ends her dance to face forward towards the priest, the* MESSENGER *continuing to play the tune very softly, very faintly now*)

FATHER DOMINEER (*Down to those in the garden—with vicious intensity*) Stop that devil's dance! How often have yous been warned that th' avowed enemies of Christianity are on th' march everywhere! An' I find yous dancin'! How often have yous been told that pagan poison is floodin' th' world, an' that Ireland is dhrinkin' in generous doses through films, plays, an' books! An' yet I come here to find yous dancin'! Dancin', an' with th' Kyleloch, Le Coq, Gallus, th' Cock rampant in th' disthrict, destroyin' desire for prayer, desire for work, an' weakenin' th' authority of th' pastors an' masters of your souls! Th' empire of Satan's pushin' out its foundations everywhere, an' I find yous dancin', *ubique ululanti cockalorum ochone, ululo!*

MESSENGER (*Through his soft playing of the accordion*)

Th' devil was as often in th' street, an' as intimate in th' home when there was nor film nor play nor book.

FATHER DOMINEER There was singin' then, an' there's singin' now; there was dancin' then, an' there's dancin' now, leadin' innocent souls to perjure their perfection. (*To* LORELEEN) Kneel down, as th' others do, you proud an' dartin' cheat, an' beg a pardon!

LORELEEN (*Obstinately*) I seek no pardon for th' dance that's done.

FATHER DOMINEER (*Turning away from her*) Seek for it then when pardon hides away.

MICHAEL Oh, what have I done! I've bethrayed meself into a sudden misdoin'!

MAHAN *Mea culpa*, me, too, Father!

FATHER DOMINEER Oh, Michael Marthraun, an' you, Sailor Mahan, Knights of Columbanus, I come to help yous, an' I catch yous in th' act of prancin' about with shameless women, dhressed to stun th' virtue out of all beholdhers!

MICHAEL It was them, right enough, Father, helped be th' wine, that done poor me an' poor Sailor Mahan in! I should have remembered that a Columbanian knight told me a brother Columbanian knight told him another brother has said that St. Jerome told a brother once that woman was th' gate of hell! An' it's thrue—they stab a man with a knife wreathed with roses!

FATHER DOMINEER Get up, get up, an' stand away from me; an' let ye never be loungers again in th' fight for good against evil.

(*They all rise up humbly, the women to one side, the men to the other, and go back some way, as the priest comes into the garden.* LORELEEN *strolls defiantly over to the table, and sits sideways upon it. To* MAHAN)

An' now, Sailor Mahan, a special word for you. On my way here, I passed that man of yours who's livin' in sin with a lost an' wretched woman. He dodged down a lane to give me th' slip. I warned you, if he didn't leave her, to dismiss him—did you do so?

(MAHAN *is silent*)

I have asked you, Mahan, if you've dismissed him?

MAHAN (*Obstinately*) I see no reason why I should dismiss me best lorry driver.

FATHER DOMINEER (*Coldly*) You don't see a reason? An' who are you to have any need of a reason in a question of this kind? (*Loudly*) I have a reason, an' that's enough for you!

MAHAN (*Defensively*) He's a fine worker, Father, an' th' nation needs such as him.

FATHER DOMINEER (*Loudly*) We're above all nations. Nationality is mystical, maundering nonsense! It's a heresy! I'm the custodian of higher interests. (*Shouting*) Do as you're told—get rid of him!

MICHAEL (*Wheedling*) It's all right, Father—he'll do what your reverence tells him. Sailor Mahan's a thrue Columbanian.

MAHAN (*Angrily—to* MICHAEL) He won't do what his reverence tells him!

(*Down the path outside comes the* LORRY DRIVER, *a man of thirty years of age. He doesn't look a giant, but there is an air of independence and sturdiness about him. He is wearing a leather jacket, a pair of soldier's khaki trousers, and an oily-looking peaked cap. His face is tanned by the weather, and his upper lip is hidden by a well-trimmed moustache. He hesitates for a moment when he sees* FATHER DOMINEER; *but, stiffening a little, he continues his walk to the gateway, into the garden. He stands a little away from* MAHAN, *looking at him, evidently having something to say to him*)

FATHER DOMINEER (*Sneeringly*) Ah, the gentleman himself has arrived. (*To the man*) We were just talking of you, my man. I have told Mr. Mahan to dismiss you. You know why. You're a scandal to th' whole place; you're a shame to us all. Either leave this woman you're living with, or go to where that sort of thing's permitted. (*Loudly*) You heard me?

LORRY DRIVER (*Surlily*) I heard you.

FATHER DOMINEER (*Impatiently*) Well?

LORRY DRIVER I come to speak with Mr. Mahan, Father.

MAHAN (*Quickly*) Me, Jack! Oh, yes; what's the throuble now?

LORRY DRIVER Plenty, sir. The turf-workers have left th' bog, an' we've no turf to load. Th' delegate says he sent a telegram to Mr. Marthraun, sayin' th' men would leave th' bog, if no answer came within an hour.

MESSENGER He did, an' I delivered it.

MICHAEL Damnit, but I forgot about it! The tension here put it out of me mind!

FATHER DOMINEER (*Catching the* LORRY DRIVER *by an arm*) Never mind turf or tension now. Are you going to go from here?

LORRY DRIVER (*Obstinately*) I'll go, if Mr. Mahan tells me to go.

FATHER DOMINEER (*In a fury*) Isn't it a wondher God doesn't strike you dead! I tell you to give the wretched woman up, or go, an' that's enough for either Sailor Mahan or you. (*He shakes the* LORRY DRIVER'*s arm*) Will you give that wretched woman up; will you send that woman of yours away?

LORRY DRIVER (*Resentfully*) Eh, don't be pullin' th' arm outa me!

FATHER DOMINEER (*His fury growing*) Did you send that woman away; are you going to do it?

LORRY DRIVER (*Shaking his arm free, and stepping back*) Aw, let go! I didn't an' I won't!

FATHER DOMINEER (*In an ungovernable burst of fury*) You wretch, would you dare to outface your priest? Get out of me sight!

(*He lunges forward, and strikes the* LORRY DRIVER *swiftly and savagely on the side of the head. The man falls heavily; lies still for a moment; tries feebly to rise; falls down again, and lies quite still*)

MAHAN (*Frightened*) He's hurted, Father; you hot him far too hard.

FATHER DOMINEER (*Frightened too—with a forced laugh*) Nonsense! I just touched him. (*He touches the fallen man with his foot*) Get up, get up—you're not that much hurt.

MAHAN (*Bending over the* LORRY DRIVER, *and placing a hand on his breast*) I'm afraid he's either dyin' or dead, Father!

(FATHER DOMINEER *runs over agitatedly to the fallen man, kneels down beside him, and murmurs in his ear. Then he raises his head to face the others*)

FATHER DOMINEER (*To the others*) Yous all saw what happened. I just touched him, an' he fell. I'd no intention of hurting him—only to administer a rebuke.

SERGEANT (*Consolingly*) Sure, we know that, Father—it was a pure accident.

FATHER DOMINEER I murmured an act of contrition into th' poor man's ear.

MESSENGER (*Playing very softly*) It would have been far fitther, Father, if you'd murmured one into your own.

## Scene Three

*It is towards dusk in the garden now. The sun is setting, and the sky shows it. The rich blue of the sky has given place to a rich yellow, slashed with green and purple. The flagpole stands black against the green and yellow of the sky, and the flag, now, has the same sombre hue.*

*The big sunflowers against the wall have turned into a solemn black, too; the house has a dark look, save where a falling shaft from the sun turns the window above the porch into a golden eye of light. Far away, in the depths of the sky, the evening star can be faintly seen.*

*In the distance, for some time, the sounds of drumming, occasionally pierced by the shrill notes of a fife, can be heard.*

MAHAN *is sitting at the table, busy totting up figures on papers spread out before him, his face knotted into creases of anxiety and doubt.*

LORNA *and* MARION *are leaning against the wall, away from the gateway, and near the house. Their gay garments are covered with dark hooded cloaks to temper the coolness of the evening air.*

LORNA They all seem to be out on th' hunt—police an' soldiers, with th' bands to give them courage. Th' fools!

MARION D'ye think they'll get him? Th' place'll lose its brightness if th' Cock's killed.

LORNA How can they desthroy a thing they say themselves is not of this world? (*She goes over to* MAHAN, *and stares at him for a moment*) It's cooler. The sun's settin'.

MAHAN (*Hardly noticing*) Is it? I didn't notice. I'm busy. Everything thrust through everything else, since that damned Cock got loose. Th' drouth now dhryin' everything to dust; the turf-workers refusin' to work, th' women thinkin' only of dancin' an' dhress. But we'll lay him low, an' bury him deep enough to forget he ever came here!

LORNA Th' men on th' bog work hard; they should get all you've got to give them.

MAHAN (*Resentfully*) An' why th' hell shouldn't they work hard? Who'd keep th' fires of th' nation burning, if they didn't?

LORNA They work for you, too; an' for Michael. He's got a pile in th' bank, an' rumour says you've got one too.

MAHAN (*Whining*) Michael may; I never had, an' I'm losin' th' little I had since I lost me best lorry dhriver—blast th' hand that hot him!

(*The* COCK *suddenly glides in, weaving a way between* MAHAN *at the table and* LORNA, *circling the garden, and finally disappearing round the gable end of the house; the dance tune softly keeps time with his movements. Jumping to his feet*)

What was that? I thought I saw him prancin' by me!

LORNA (*Startled too*) What was what?

MAHAN Th' Cock in his black plumage, yellow legs, an' crimson crest!

MARION (*Who has gone tense*) You put th' heart across me! I thought you meant th' poor dead man. (*She turns to look along the road again*)

LORNA (*To* MAHAN) There's little use worryin' over figures till you settle with th' men.

MAHAN (*Irritably*) That's Mick's business, that's Mick's business!

MARION (*Running over to whisper excitedly to* LORNA) Here they are—Father Domineer an' Mr. Marthraun comin' along th' road!

MAHAN (*Irascibly*) Aw, what does that Father Domineer want comin' here when we've so much to think about! Delayin' things! I want to get away from here before it gets dark.

LORNA Didn't you know they're goin' to purge th' poor house of its evil influences?

MAHAN (*Irritably*) Oh, can't they do first things first?

(*Along the pathway outside come* FATHER DOMINEER *and* MICHAEL, *followed by a lad. The lad is* ONE-EYED LARRY. *His face is one alternately showing stupidity or cunning, according to whosoever may be speaking to him. Where his left eye was is a black cavity, giving him a somewhat sinister look. He is lanky and rather awkward looking. He is wearing a black cassock or soutane, piped with red braid, and is bareheaded. He is carrying a small bell, a book, and an unlighted candle. He shuffles along after the two men, and follows them into the garden*)

FATHER DOMINEER We'll banish them, never fear, Michael, before I have to leave th' parish because of that unhappy accident. I've faced worse. Be staunch. Th' bell is powerful, so is th' book, an' th' blessed candle, too. (*He glances at the women*) Let yous women keep to th' farther end of th' garden. (*He glances at* MAHAN) We won't be long, Sailor Mahan. (*Suddenly, as he,* MICHAEL, *and* ONE-EYED LARRY *reach the porch*) Where's that other one?

MICHAEL Is it Loreleen, me daughter, Father?

FATHER DOMINEER She's no daughter of yours, Michael. (*Bending down to whisper warningly*) Get rid of her, get rid of her—she's dangerous!

MICHAEL How get rid of her, Father?

FATHER DOMINEER Pack her off to America!

MICHAEL (*Respectfully—as they are about to go into the house*) I'll go first, Father.

FATHER DOMINEER (*Setting him gently aside*) No, no; mine th' gap of danger.

(*The three of them go in, the priest first, then* MICHAEL, *and, lastly,* ONE-EYED LARRY. MARION *and* LORNA *move over to the farther side of the garden*)

LORNA It's all damn nonsense, though Michael has me nerves in such a way that I'm near ready to believe in anything.

MAHAN Waste of time, too. It'll take a betther man than Father Domineer to dhrive evil things outa Eire.

MARION Messenger says he's only addin' to their number, an' soon a noddin' daffodil, when it dies, 'll know its own way to hell.

(*The roll of a drum is heard and a great booing.* MARION *runs to the wall to look over it, and up the road. Excitedly*)

A girl runnin' this way, hell for leather. My God, it's Loreleen!

(*After a few moments,* LORELEEN *runs along the pathway outside, and dashes in through the gateway to* LORNA, *who catches her in her arms. Clumps of grass and sods of turf, and a few stones follow* LORELEEN *in her rush along the road*)

LORELEEN (*Out of breath*) God damn th' dastards of this vile disthrict! They pelted me with whatever they could lay hands on—th' women because they couldn't stand beside me; th' men because there was ne'er a hope of usin' me as they'd like to! Is it any wondher that th' girls are fleein' in their tens of thousands from this bewildhered land? Blast them! I'll still be gay an' good-lookin'. Let them draw me as I am not, an' sketch in a devil where a maiden stands!

LORNA (*Soothingly*) Be calm, child! We can't go in, for Father Domineer's inside puttin' things in ordher. (*Releasing* LORELEEN) I'll run along th' road to them disturbers, an' give them a bit o' me mind! (*She catches hold of* MARION'S *arm*) Come on, Marion! (*She and* MARION *rush out along the road, and pass out of sight*)

LORELEEN (*Staring at the house*) He's inside, is he? That's not where th' evil is, th' gaum,[1] if he wants to know.

MAHAN (*Seriously*) Come here, Loreleen; nearer, for I've something to say to you. (*As she does not stir, he grips her arm, and draws her farther from the house*) We might be heard.

LORELEEN (*Suspiciously*) What do you want, Sailor Mahan? You're not of one mind with them who chased me?

MAHAN (*A little embarrassed*) Aw, God, no! Me sails of love are reefed at last, an' I lie quiet, restin' in a lonely harbour now, I'm too old to be flustered with that kinda folly. I just want to warn you to get outa this disthrict.

LORELEEN (*Bitterly*) Why must I go? Is it because I'm good-lookin' an' gay?

(*But the bold* MAHAN *isn't indifferent to the charms of* LORELEEN. *So he goes on to show* LORELEEN *the youthfulness of his old age; that his muscles are still strong, his fibres flexible. He becomes restless, and walks about, occasionally glancing at the house, nervous at what may be happening inside. When he comes to a chair, he nonchalantly swings a leg over the back of it, turning on the foot of the same leg to swing the other one back again. These actions, like the conversation, though not done in a hurry, are done quickly, as if he wanted to say all he had to say before any interruption*)

MAHAN (*Swinging a leg over a chair*) Partly because you're good-lookin' an' partly because of th' reckless way you talk. Remember what happened to poor Jack. I'd clear out if I were you. (*He vaults on to the table, swings round it on his backside, and vaults from it on the opposite side, a little stiffly*)

LORELEEN How'm I to clear out? I've no money left. Th' forty pounds I had, Dad put into his bank for me, an' now won't give me a penny of it, because he says if I got it, I'd go to England; an' if I went to England, I'd lose me soul, th' shaky, venomous lout! An' I keep quiet because of Lorna. (*Hurriedly, as* MAHAN *is stiffly climbing a few feet up the flagpole*) Oh, don't be doin' th' monkey on a stick! Maybe you could help me? Could you, would you?

MAHAN (*Sliddering from the pole, swinging a leg over a chair, and coming closer to her*) Now that's what I'd hoped you'd say. This is th' first time I've caught you alone. I'll give you what you need, an' you can weigh anchor, an' be off outa this damned place. Listen, darlin': you steal out tonight to th' Red Barn, west of th' Holy Cross, an' I'll dhrive there with what'll get you as far as you want to go. (*He suddenly puts an arm round her in a kind of clutch*) Jasus, you have lovely eyes!

LORELEEN (*Trying to pull his arm away*) Oh, Sailor Mahan, don't do that! Let me go—someone may see us!

MAHAN (*Recklessly*) You deserve to be ruffled a bit! Well, will you come to th' Red Barn, while th' rest are goin' to th' dance, an' save yourself? Yes or no!

LORELEEN Maybe, maybe; yes, yes, I'll go. Let go your clutch!

(*The house shakes; a sound of things moving and crockery breaking comes from it; several flashes of lightning spear out through the window over the porch; and the flagpole wags drunkenly from side to side.*

MARION *and* LORNA *appear on the pathway outside the wall, and hurry along into the garden just as* ONE-EYED LARRY *comes running out of the house, his face beset with fear. His one eye takes in the*

[1] O'Casey has indicated that this term is used to describe a soft and foolish person.

*picture of* LORELEEN *breaking away from* MAHAN. LORELEEN *turns aside from* ONE-EYED LARRY, *while* MAHAN, *embarrassed, turns to face him*)

ONE-EYED LARRY (*Excitedly*) It's startin' in earnest! There's a death sthruggle goin' on in there! Poor Father Domineer's got a bad black eye, an' Micky Marthraun's coat is torn to tatthers!

LORNA (*Hurrying into the garden*) What's happened, what's happenin'?

MAHAN (*With dignity—to* ONE-EYED LARRY) Misther Marthraun in your mouth, me lad.

LORELEEN (*Mischievously*) Let th' lad tell his funny story.

ONE-EYED LARRY (*Turning on* LORELEEN) It's funny to you because you're in league with th' evil ones! (*To the others*) One o' Father Domineer's feet is all burned be a touch from one o' them, an' one o' Micky's is frozen stiff be a touch from another. (*To* MAHAN) Maybe you'd ha' liked me to have lost me other eye while you were warmin' yourself in that one's arms!

(*He points to* LORELEEN)

MAHAN (*Furiously*) You one-eyed gett,[2] if you had two, I'd cyclonise you with a box!

LORELEEN (*Unmoved—a little mockingly*) An' how did th' poor lamb lose his eye?

MAHAN (*Indifferently*) Oh, when he was a kid, he was hammerin' a bottle, an' a flyin' piece cut it out of his head.

ONE-EYED LARRY (*Venomously*) You're a liar, that wasn't th' way! It was th' Demon Cock who done it to me. Only certain eyes can see him, an' I had one that could. He caught me once when I was spyin' on him, put a claw over me left eye, askin' if I could see him then; an' on me sayin' no, put th' claw over th' other one, an' when I said I could see him clear now, says he, that eye sees too well, an' on that, he pushed an' pushed till it was crushed into me head.

LORELEEN (*Mockingly*) What a sad thing to happen!

(*The house shakes worse than before, and seems to lurch over to one side. The flagpole wags from side to side merrily; there is a rumble of thunder, and blue lightning flashes from the window. All, except* LORELEEN, *cower together at the far end of the garden. She stands over by the wall, partly framed by the sable sunflowers*)

MARION (*Full of fright*) Sacred Heart! Th' house'll fall asundher!

LORELEEN (*Gleefully*) Let it! It's th' finest thing that could happen to it!

ONE-EYED LARRY (*Trembling violently*) It's now or never for them an' for us. They're terrible powerful spirits. Knocked th' bell outa me hand, blew out th' candle, an' tore th' book to threads! Thousands of them there are, led be th' bigger ones—Kissalass, Velvethighs, Reedabuck, Dancesolong, an' Sameagain. Keep close. Don't run. They might want help.

(*Screeches like those of barn owls are heard from the house, with the "too-whit too-whoo" of other kinds, the cackling of hens, and the loud cawing of crows. Frantically pushing his way to the back of the others*)

Oooh! Let me get back, get back!

(*The house shakes again; the flagpole totters and falls flat; blue and red lightning flashes from the window, and a great peal of thunder drums through the garden. Then all becomes suddenly silent. They all hang on to each other, shivering with fear, except* LORELEEN, *who lights a cigarette, puts a foot on a chair, leans on its back, looks at the house, and smokes away serenely*)

LORNA (*Tremulously*) Why has th' house gone so silent suddenly?

ONE-EYED LARRY (*From the rear*) They've either killed th' demons, or th' demons has killed them.

MARION God save us, they must be dead!

LORELEEN (*With quiet mockery*) Welcome be th' will o' God.

LORNA (*Suddenly—with great agitation*) Get back, get back! Run! There's something comin' out!

(*She,* MARION, *and* ONE-EYED LARRY *race for the gateway, rush on to the sidewalk, and bend down, so that only their heads can be seen peeping over the wall.* MAHAN *shrinks back to the far end of the garden, and* LORELEEN *remains where she is.*

*From the house, sideways, through the now lurching porch, come* FATHER DOMINEER *and* MICHAEL. *Both are limping,* FATHER DOMINEER *on his left foot,* MICHAEL *on his right one.* DOMINEER *has a big black eye, his coat is awry on his back, and his hair is widely tossed.* MICHAEL'*s coat hangs in tatters on him.* FATHER DOMINEER'S *face is begrimed with the smudges of smoke, and both look tired, but elated.*

ONE-EYED LARRY *at once runs out, and takes his place reverently behind them, standing with his hands folded piously in front of his breast, his eyes bent towards the ground.* MAHAN *straightens up, and* LORNA *and* MARION *return to the garden.* LORELEEN *remains as she was*)

FATHER DOMINEER (*As he enters with* MICHAEL) Be assured, good people, all's well, now. The house is safe for all. The evil things have been banished from the dwelling. Most of the myrmidons of Anticlericus, Secularius, an' Odeonius[3] have been destroyed. The Civic Guard and the soldiers of Feehanna Fawl[4] will see to the few who escaped. We can think quietly again of our Irish Sweep.[5] Now I must get to my car to go home, and have a wash an' brush up. (*To* MARION *and* LORNA) Off you go into the house, good women. Th' place, th' proper place, th' only place for th' woman. Straighten it out, and take pride in doing it. (*He shoves* MARION *toward the porch*) Go on, woman, when you're told! (*To* MICHAEL) You'll have to exert your authority more as head of the house.

MICHAEL (*Asserting it at once—to* LORNA) You heard

[2] Brat

[3] To the Anti-Clericals and the Secularists, Father Domineer adds the followers of the music-hall (*odeum*).

[4] Fianna Fail, the political party headed by De Valera; thus, the party in power.

[5] The Irish Sweepstakes race and lottery.

what Father Domineer said. Go on; in you go, an' show yourself a decent, God-fearin' woman.

FATHER DOMINEER (*Trying to be gracious—to* LORNA) Th' queen of th' household as th' husband is th' king.

(MARION *has gone into the house with a sour-looking face, and* LORNA *now follows her example, looking anything but charmed*)

FATHER DOMINEER (*Turning to* LORELEEN) And you—aren't you going in to help?

LORELEEN (*Quietly*) No, thanks; I prefer to stay on in the garden.

FATHER DOMINEER (*Thunderously*) Then learn to stand on the earth in a more modest and suitable way, woman! (*Pointing to ornaments on crest of hat and breast of bodice*) An' do you mind that th' ornaments ye have on of brooch an' bangle were invented be th' fallen angels, now condemned to everlastin' death for worshippin' beauty that faded before it could be clearly seen? (*Angrily*) Oh, woman, *de cultus feminarum malifico eradicum.*[6]

MICHAEL That one's mind is always mustherin' dangerous thoughts plundered outa evil books!

FATHER DOMINEER (*Startled*) Books? What kinda books? Where are they?

MICHAEL She has some o' them in th' house this minute.

FATHER DOMINEER (*Roaring*) Bring them out, bring them out! How often have I to warn you against books! Hell's bells tolling people away from th' thruth! Bring them out, *in annem fiat ecclesiam nonsensio,*[7] before th' demoneens we've banished flood back into th' house again!

(MICHAEL *and* ONE-EYED LARRY *jostle together into the porch and into the house to do* FATHER DOMINEER'S *bidding*)

LORELEEN (*Taking her leg down from the chair, and striding over to* FATHER DOMINEER) You fool, d'ye know what you're thryin' to do? You're thryin' to keep God from talkin'!

FATHER DOMINEER You're speakin' blasphemy, woman!

MAHAN What do people want with books? I don't remember readin' a book in me life.

(MICHAEL *comes back carrying a book, followed by* ONE-EYED LARRY *carrying another.* FATHER DOMINEER *takes the book from* MICHAEL, *and glances at the title page*)

FATHER DOMINEER (*Explosively*) A book about Voltaire! (*To* LORELEEN) This book has been banned, woman.

LORELEEN (*Innocently*) Has it now? If so, I must read it over again.

FATHER DOMINEER (*To* ONE-EYED LARRY) What's th' name of that one?

ONE-EYED LARRY (*Squinting at the title*) Ullisississies,[8] or something.

FATHER DOMINEER Worse than th' other one. (*He hands his to* ONE-EYED LARRY) Bring th' two o' them down to th' Presbytery, an' we'll desthroy them.

[6] "Eradicate evil from the tribe of women."
[7] Roughly, "let the church be purged of nonsense."
[8] James Joyce's *Ulysses,* long banned as 'obscene.'

(LORELEEN *snatches the two books from* ONE-EYED LARRY. ONE-EYED LARRY *tries to prevent her, but a sharp push from her sends him toppling over.* LORELEEN, *with great speed, darts out of the gateway, runs along the pathway, and disappears. Standing as if stuck to the ground*)

After her, afther her!

MICHAEL (*Astonished*) Me legs won't move!

MAHAN / ONE-EYED LARRY (*Together*) Nor mine, neither.

(*As* LORELEEN *disappears, the* COCK *suddenly springs over the wall, and pirouettes in and out between them as they stand stuck to the ground.*

*Cute*[9] *ears may hear the quick tune, played softly, of an accordion, as the* COCK *weaves his way about. The* SERGEANT *appears running outside, stops when he sees the* COCK, *leans over the wall, and presents a gun at* MICHAEL)

MICHAEL (*Frantically—to* SERGEANT) Not me, man, not me!

(*Terribly excited, the* SERGEANT *swings the gun till it is pointing at* MAHAN)

MAHAN (*Frantically*) Eh, not me, man!

(*After the* COCK *has pirouetted round for some moments, while they all remain transfixed, the scene suddenly goes dark, though the music continues to sound through it. Then two squib-like shots are heard, followed by a clash of thunder, and, when the garden enjoys the light of early dusk again, which comes immediately after the clap of thunder, the music as suddenly ceases.*

*The returning light shows that* FATHER DOMINEER *is not there; that* MICHAEL *and* MAHAN *are stretched out on the ground; and that* ONE-EYED LARRY *is half over the wall, his belly on it, his legs trailing in the garden, his head and shoulders protruding into the road*)

MICHAEL (*Moaning*) Shot through the soft flesh an' th' hard bone!

MAHAN (*Groaning*) Shot through th' hard bone an' th' soft flesh!

ONE-EYED LARRY (*Shouting*) Mrs. Marthraun, Marion, we're all killed be th' Cock an' th' Sergeant!

(LORNA *and* MARION *come running out of the house over to the two prostrate men*)

LORNA What's happened? Where's th' Sergeant?

ONE-EYED LARRY (*Sliddering over the wall, frantic with fear*) I seen him runnin' off when he'd shot us all! I'm goin' home, I'm goin' home! Father Domineer's been carried off be th' Demon Cock—I'm off! (*He runs swiftly down the road, and disappears*)

LORNA (*Bending over* MICHAEL) Where were you hit? D'ye think there's a chance of you dyin'?

MICHAEL (*Despairingly*) I'm riddled!

LORNA (*Feeling his body over*) I can't see a speck of damage on you anywhere, you fool.

MARION (*Who has been examining* MAHAN) No, nor on this fella either.

MICHAEL I tell you th' bullet careered through me breast an' come out be me back!

[9] Acute, sharp

MAHAN An' then tore through me back an' came out be me breast!

LORNA What darkness was One-eyed Larry talkin' about? An' Father Domineer carried off be the Cock! Me nerves are all gettin' shatthered. It's all very thryin'. (*She pokes* MICHAEL *roughly with her foot*) Here, get up, th' both of yous. There isn't a thing wrong with either of you.

MAHAN (*Sitting up cautiously, and feeling in his breast pocket*) What th' hell's this? (*He pulls out a bullet bigger than a cigar*) Looka, Michael Marthraun, th' size of th' bullet that went tearin' through you an' then through me! (*Very devoutly*) Good angels musta gone along with it, healin' all at th' same time that it tore our vitals.

MICHAEL (*As devoutly*) Some higher an' special power musta been watchin' over us, Sailor Mahan. Sharin' a miracle, now, Sailor Mahan, we're more than brothers.

MAHAN (*Fervently*) We are that, now; we are indeed. I'll keep this bullet till th' day I die as a momento of a mementous occasion!

LORNA (*Impatiently*) Get up, get up. An' don't disturb us again while we're practicin' for the fancy-dhress dance tonight in th' hope of winning a spot prize.[10]

MICHAEL (*Furiously to her*) You'll win no spot prize, an' there'll be no dance till that Demon Cock's laid low! (*To* MAHAN—*piously*) Thrue men we are, workin' in a thruly brotherly way for the good of th' entire community—aren't we, Sailor Mahan? That's what saved us!

MAHAN (*As piously*) We are that, Michael; we are indeed; especially now that we've settled th' question finally so long disputed between us.

MICHAEL (*Suspiciously, a note of sharpness in his voice*) How settled it?

MAHAN Be you arrangin' to give me, not only what I was askin', but twice as much.

MICHAEL (*Sarcastically*) Oh, did I now? That was damned good of me! (*Angrily*) No, nor what you were askin' either. D'ye want me to ruin meself to glorify you? An' didn't I hear a certain man promisin', nearly on his oath, he'd give his lorries for next to nothin' to serve th' community?

MAHAN (*Shouting*) When I was undher a spell, fosthered on me here! I'm goin', I'm goin'. I'll argue no more! (*He goes out by the gate and along the road, pausing as he is about to disappear*) For th' last time, Michael Marthraun, are you goin' to do th' decent for th' sake of th' nation, an' give me what I'm askin'?

MICHAEL (*With decision—quietly*) No, Sailor Mahan, I'm not. (*He shouts*) I'd see you in hell first!

MAHAN (*As he goes*) A sweet good-bye to you, an' take a dhrug to keep from stayin' awake o' nights thinkin' of the nation's needs!

LORNA (*Persuasively*) Be reasonable, Michael. You're makin' enough now to be well able to give him all he asks.

MICHAEL (*Savagely seizing her arm*) Listen, you: even though you keep th' accounts for me, it's a law of nature an' a law of God that a wife must be silent about her husband's secrets! D'ye hear me, you costumed slut?

[10] Prize given a dancing couple caught in a spotlight.

LORNA (*Freeing herself with an effort*) Don't tear th' arm out of me! If you want to embalm yourself in money, you won't get me to do it!

(*The sound of the wind rising is heard now—a long, sudden gust-like sound, causing* MICHAEL *to do a sudden rush towards the gate, pressing himself back all the time, and gripping the wall when he gets to it. The two women do not notice the wind*)

MICHAEL Jasus! that was a sudden blast!

LORNA (*Wonderingly*) Blast? I felt no blast.

MARION (*Shaking her head*) He's undher a spell again.

(ONE-EYED LARRY *comes running along the road outside, excited and shouting. He is holding on tensely to the waistband of his trousers*)

ONE-EYED LARRY (*Without the wall*) A miracle, a miracle! Father Domineer, outa th' darkness, was snatched from th' claws of the Demon Cock, an' carried home safe on th' back of a white duck!

LORNA (*Amazed*) On th' back of a white duck? When will wondhers cease! They're all goin' mad!

MICHAEL (*Clapping his hands*) Grand news! Was it a wild duck, now, or merely a domestic one?

ONE-EYED LARRY Wild or tame, what does it matther? It carried him cheerily through th' sky, an' deposited him dacently down on his own doorstep!

MICHAEL (*With deep thought*) It might well have been one of me own sensible ducks that done it.

ONE-EYED LARRY (*Coming to the gate*) Wait till I tell yous. Th' Demon Cock's furious at his escape, an' he's causin' consthernation. He's raised a fierce wind be th' beat of his wings, an' it's tossin' cattle on to their backs; whippin' th' guns from th' hands of Civic Guard an' soldier, so that th' guns go sailin' through th' sky like cranes; an' th' wind's tearin' at the clothes of th' people. It's only be hard holdin' that I can keep me own trousers on!

MICHAEL (*Eagerly*) Th' wind near whipped me on to th' road a minute ago.

(*The* BELLMAN *enters on the pathway outside, and meets* ONE-EYED LARRY *at the gateway, so that the two of them stand there, the one on the left, the other to the right of it. The collar and one arm are all that are left of the* BELLMAN'S *coat, and his shirt has been blown outside of his trousers. He is still wearing the brass hat. His right hand is gripping his waistband, and his left carries the bell that he is ringing*)

BELLMAN (*Shouting*) Get out, get in! Th' Demon Cock's scourin' the skies again, mettlesome, menacin', molestifyin' monsther! Fly to your houses, fall upon your knees, shut th' doors, close th' windows! In a tearin' rage, he's rippin' th' clouds outa th' sky, because Father Domineer was snatched away from him, an' carried home, fit an' well, on th' back of a speckled duck!

ONE-EYED LARRY (*Startled into anger*) You're a liar, it wasn't a speckled duck! What are you sayin', fella? It was a pure white duck that carried th' Father home!

BELLMAN (*Angrily—to* ONE-EYED LARRY) Liar yourself, an' you're wrong! It was a speckled duck that done it; speckled in black, brown, an' green spots. I seen it with me own two eyes doin' th' thrick.

ONE-EYED LARRY (*Vehemently*) I seen it with me one eye in concentration, an' it was a duck white as th' dhriven snow that brought him to his domiceel.

LORNA I'd say white's a sensible colour, an' more apter for th' job.

MICHAEL I'd say a speckled duck would look more handsome landin' on a doorstep than a white fowl.

MARION (*Thoughtfully*) I wondher, now, could it have been Mr. McGilligan's tame barnacle goose?

MICHAEL (*Explosively*) No, it couldn't have been Mr. McGilligan's tame barnacle goose! Don't be thryin' to scatther confusion over a miracle happenin' before our very eyes!

(*The* SERGEANT *comes rushing in along the pathway outside the wall, and runs into the garden through the gateway, roughly shoving the* BELLMAN *and* ONE-EYED LARRY *out of his way. His cap is gone, a piece of rope is tied round his chest to keep his coat on; and, when he reaches the gate, all can see that he wears no trousers, leaving him in a long shirt over short pants. He is excited, and his face is almost convulsed with fear and shame*)

SERGEANT (*Shoving* ONE-EYED LARRY *and* BELLMAN *aside*) Outa me way, you fools! (*Rushing into the garden—to* MICHAEL) Give me one of your oul' trousers, Mick, for th' love o' God! Whipped off me be a blast of th' wind me own were. When I seen them goin', me entire nature was galvanised into alarmin' anxiety as to what might happen next.

MICHAEL A terrible experience! What's to come of us, at all!

SERGEANT (*Tearfully*) Why isn't Father Domineer here to help? He doesn't care a damn now, since he was carried home, safe an' sound on th' back of a barnacle goose!

ONE-EYED LARRY (*Dumbfounded and angry*) A barnacle goose? What are you sayin', man? It was a dazzlin' white duck that brought him home.

BELLMAN (*To* ONE-EYED LARRY) I'm tellin' you it was a specially speckled duck that done it.

SERGEANT (*Emphatically*) It was a goose, I'm sayin'. Th' Inspector seen it through a field glass, an' identified it as a goose, a goose!

LORNA (*Amused—laying a hand on* MARION'S *shoulder*) Look at him, Marion. All dollied up for th' fancy-dhress dance!

MARION (*Hilariously*) It's lookin' like th' blue bonnets are over th' bordher!

MICHAEL (*Angrily—to the* SERGEANT) Get into th' house, man, an' don't be standin' there in that style of half-naked finality! You'll find some oul' trousers upstairs. (*Turning on* LORNA *and* MARION *as the* SERGEANT *trots timidly into the house*) You two hussies, have yous no semblance of sense of things past an' things to come? Here's a sweet miracle only afther happenin', an' there yous are, gigglin' an' gloatin' at an aspect in a man that should send th' two of yous screamin' away! Yous are as bad as that one possessed th' people call me daughter.

(*The sound of the wind now rises, swifter, shriller, and stronger, carrying in it an occasional moan, as in a gale, and with this stronger wind comes the* MESSENGER, *sauntering along outside the wall, sitting down on it when he reaches the end farthest from the house. Nothing in the garden is moved by the wind's whistling violence, except* MICHAEL, *the* BELLMAN, *and* ONE-EYED LARRY (*who have been suddenly hustled into the garden by the wind*). *These three now grip their waistbands, and begin to make sudden movements to and fro, as if dragged by an invisible force; each of them trying to hold back as the wind pushes them forward. The* MESSENGER *is coaxing a soft tune from his accordion; while* MARION *and* LORNA *are unaffected by the wind, and stand staring at the men, amused by their antics*)

MICHAEL (*A little frantic*) Listen to th' risin' evil of th' wind! Oh, th' beat of it, oh, th' beat of it! We know where it comes from—red wind on our backs, black wind on our breasts, thryin' to blow us to hell!

BELLMAN (*Gliding about, pushed by the wind; holding on to his trousers with one hand, while he rings his bell with the other one*) Fly into th' houses, close th' windows, shut th' doors!

ONE-EYED LARRY (*Gliding in opposite direction*) We can't, we can't—we go where th' wind blows us!

MESSENGER What ails yous? I feel only th' brisk breeze carryin' the smell of pinewoods, or th' softer one carryin' the scent of th' ripenin' apples.

MICHAEL (*To the women, while he holds fast to his waistband*) Get in, an' sthrip off them coloured deceits, smellin' of th' sly violet an' th' richer rose, sequestherin' a lure in every petal! Off with them, I say, an' put on a cautious grey, or th' stated humbleness of a coal-black gown!

(*The* SERGEANT *comes from the house wearing* MICHAEL'S *best black Sunday trousers. He comes from the porch shyly, but the moment he steps into the garden, his face flashes into a grim look, and he grabs hold of the waistband, and glides about as the others do.* MICHAEL, *seeing the trousers—with a squeal of indignation*)

Me best Sunday black ones! Couldn't your damned plundherin' paws pounce on something a little lowlier to wear?

BELLMAN Get into th' houses, shut to th' doors, close th' windows!

(FATHER DOMINEER *suddenly appears on the pathway outside, and stands at the gateway looking into the garden. A gust of wind, fierce and shrill, that preceded him, declines in a sad wail, and ceases altogether, leaving a sombre silence behind it.* FATHER DOMINEER'S *hair is tossed about; he has a wild look in his eyes, and he carries a walking stick to help him surmount the limp from the hurt he got when warring with the evil spirits*)

FATHER DOMINEER (*Stormily*) Stop where yous are! No hidin' from the enemy! Back to hell with all bad books, bad plays, bad pictures, and bad thoughts! Cock o' th' north, or cock o' th' south, we'll down derry-doh down him yet. Shoulder to shoulder, an' step together against th' onward rush of paganism! Boldly tread, firm each foot, erect each head!

ONE-EYED LARRY, MICHAEL, BELLMAN, SERGEANT (*Together—very feebly*) Hurrah!

FATHER DOMINEER Fixed in front be every glance, forward at th' word advance!

ONE-EYED LARRY, MICHAEL, BELLMAN, SERGEANT (*Together—very feebly*) Advance!

FATHER DOMINEER We know where we're goin', an' we know who's goin' with us.[11]

MICHAEL The minsthrel boy with th' dear harp of his country, an' Brian O'Lynn.

BELLMAN Danny Boy an' th' man who sthruck O'Hara.

ONE-EYED LARRY Not forgettin' Mick McGilligan's daughter, Maryann!

(*Sounds of fifing and drumming are heard, mingled with the sound of booing, a little distance away*)

FATHER DOMINEER (*Jubilantly*) Listen to th' band! We're closin' in; we're winnin'! (*He puts a hand up to shade his eyes, and peers forward*) They've collared one of them! Aha, a woman again! (*A pause*) A fine, familiar one too. (*He shouts*) Lead th' slut here, Shanaar, right here in front of me!

(*He goes through the gateway, and waits in the garden for things to come.*

SHANAAR *appears on the pathway, followed by the two* ROUGH FELLOWS *dragging* LORELEEN *along. She is in a sad way. Her hair is tumbled about; her clothes are disarranged; her bodice unbuttoned, and her skirt reefed halfway up, showing a slim leg, with the nylon stocking torn. One of the* ROUGH FELLOWS *is carrying her hat with its cock-like crest in his hand. A bloodstained streak stretches from a corner of an eye halfway down a cheek. Her face is very pale, and intense fright is vividly mirrored in it. She is dragged by the arms along the ground by the men, led by* SHANAAR, *to where the priest is standing. When she is nicely placed before him, she hangs her head, ashamed of her dishevelled state, and of the way she has been pulled before him. Other men and women follow them in, but are checked from crowding the pathway by an order from the priest. The* MESSENGER *rises from his seat on the wall, and comes near to where the men are holding* LORELEEN. *He has placed the carrying straps of his accordion over his shoulders, and now bears the instrument on his back.* MICHAEL, *the* BELLMAN, *and* ONE-EYED LARRY *stand some way behind the priest.* MARION *and* LORNA *have started to come to* LORELEEN'S *assistance, but have been imperiously waved back by* FATHER DOMINEER, *and have retreated back towards the house, where they stand to stare at what happens.* SHANAAR *stands at the gateway, gloating over the woeful condition of* LORELEEN)

FATHER DOMINEER (*To those following the men dragging in* LORELEEN) Go back; keep back there! Give th' honied harlot plenty of space to show herself off in.

SHANAAR (*Down to* FATHER DOMINEER) Tell her off, Father; speak to her in th' name of holy Ireland!

FATHER DOMINEER (*To* SERGEANT) You go, Sergeant, an' keep them from coming too close; (*To* SHANAAR) an' you, Shanaar, stand at the opposite end to keep any others from pressing in on us. (*To the men holding* LORELEEN) Bring her a little closer. (*The men drag her closer*)

FATHER DOMINEER Now, jerk her to her feet.

(*The men jerk her upright*)

Well, me painted paramour, you're not looking quite so gay now; your impudent confidence has left you to your self. Your jest with heaven is over, me lass! (*To the men*) How did you ketch her?

FIRST ROUGH FELLOW (*With pride*) We've been on her tail, Father, for some time. We ketched her in a grand car with a married man; with a married man, Father, an' he thryin' to put an arm round her.

SECOND ROUGH FELLOW (*Butting in to share the pride of capture*) So we hauled her outa th' car, and hustled her here to you.

LORNA (*Running over to the man nearest to her, and catching his arm*) Let th' poor lass go, you cowardly lout! I know you: your whole nature's a tuft of villainies! Lust inflames your flimsy eyes whenever a skirt passes you by. If God had given you a tusk, you'd rend asundher every woman of th' district!

FATHER DOMINEER (*Angrily—to* LORNA) Get back to your place, woman! (*Shouting, as she hesitates*) Get back when I tell you!

(LORNA *moves slowly away from* LORELEEN'S *side and goes into the house*)

MARION (*As she follows* LORNA *into the house*) Dastard Knights of Columbanus, do noble work an' do it well!

LORELEEN (*To* FATHER DOMINEER*—appealingly*) Make them let me go, Father, an' let me get into th' house! It was Sailor Mahan promised me enough to take me away from here that made me go to him. I shouldn't have gone, but I wanted to get away; (*Brokenly*) get away, away! Five pounds he gave me, an' they took them off me, with th' last two pounds of me own I had left.

FATHER DOMINEER (*Savagely*) Sailor Mahan's a decent, honest soul, woman! A man fresh for th' faith, full of good works for clergy an' his neighbours. (*He bends down to hiss in her ears*) An' this is th' man, you sinful slut, this is th' man you would pet an' probe into a scarlet sin!

LORELEEN I only wanted to get away. I wanted to get away from Sailor Mahan as much as I wanted to get away from all here.

FATHER DOMINEER (*To the two* ROUGH FELLOWS) Where's Sailor Mahan?

FIRST ROUGH FELLOW Th' people pelted him back to

[11] This and the next three 'exorcisms' are derived from popular songs.

his home an' proper wife, Father, an' he's there now, in bed, an' sorry for what he thried to do.

LORELEEN (*Plaintively*) Make them give me back th' last few pounds I had.

FATHER DOMINEER (*To the* ROUGH FELLOWS) You shouldn't have handled Sailor Mahan so roughly. Where's the money?

SECOND ROUGH FELLOW We tore it up, Father, thinkin' it wasn't fit to be handled be anyone of decent discernment.

LORELEEN (*Emphatically*) They didn't; they kept it. (*Stifling a scream*) Oh, they're twisting me arms!

FATHER DOMINEER (*Cynically*) Don't be timid of a little twinge of pain, woman, for, afther th' life you've lived, you'll welther in it later. (*To the two* ROUGH FELLOWS) Yous should have kept th' money to be given to th' poor.

MESSENGER (*Coming over to the* ROUGH FELLOW *on* LORELEEN's *right—calmly*) Let that fair arm go, me man, for, if you don't, there's a live arm here'll twist your neck instead. (*With a shout*) Let it go!

(*After a nod from the priest, the* FIRST ROUGH FELLOW *lets* LORELEEN's *arm go. The* MESSENGER *goes quietly round to the* SECOND ROUGH FELLOW)

Let that fair arm go, me man, or another arm may twist your own neck! Let it go!

(*The* SECOND ROUGH FELLOW *sullenly does so*)

Now stand a little away, an' give th' girl room to breathe.

(*The two* ROUGH FELLOWS *move a little away from* LORELEEN) Thank you.

(*To the priest*)

Now, Father, so full of pity an' loving-kindness, jet out your bitther blessin', an' let th' girl go. An' thry to mingle undherstandin' with your pride, so as to ease th' tangle God has suffered to be flung around us all.

FATHER DOMINEER (*Fiercely—to the* MESSENGER) Keep farther away, you, for th' crowd is angry and their arms are sthrong! We know you—enemy to th' glow of tradition's thruth, enemy to righteous reprobation, whose rowdy livery is but dyed in rust from th' gates of hell! (*To* LORELEEN) An' you, you'd hook your unholy reputation to a decent man's life. A man, like Sailor Mahan, diligent in his duty, th' echo of whose last prayer can ever be heard when another worshipper enters th' church. You'd sentence him to stand beside you, you shuttlecock of sin!

LORELEEN (*Roused to indignation*) Oh, end it, will you! You fail in honesty when you won't make them give me back what they robbed from me. When you condemn a fair face, you sneer at God's good handiwork. You are layin' your curse, sir, not upon a sin, but on a joy. Take care a divil doesn't climb up your own cassock into your own belfry!

FATHER DOMINEER (*Furiously*) You'll dhribble th' blackness of sin no longer over our virtuous bordhers! (*He hisses the words out*) *Stipendium peccati mors est!*[12] Get away from here quicker than you came, or it's in your coffin you'll be—in your coffin, your coffin!

[12] The wages of sin is death. (*Romans* 6:23)

SHANAAR (*From the gateway*) A merciful sentence, an aysey one, for a one like her!

LORELEEN (*Half defiantly*) How am I to go where I'd like to go, when they took all I had off me? How am I to go for miles with me clothes near rent from me back, an' frail shoes on me feet?

FATHER DOMINEER (*Putting his face closer to hers*) Thrudge it; thrudge on your two feet; an' when these burn an' blister, go on your knees; an' when your knees are broken an' bruised, go on your belly; crawl in th' dust, as did th' snake in th' Garden of Eden, for dust is th' right cushion for th' like of you! (*He raises himself erect, and commands in a loud voice*) Go now! ( LORELEEN *turns away, goes slowly through the gateway, and along the road outside. As* LORELEEN *reaches the gate,* LORNA *runs out of the house. She is wearing a dark red cloak, and carries a green one over her arm. She has a fairly large rucksack strapped on her back*)

LORNA (*Calling as she runs out of the house*) Loreleen! (LORELEEN *halts but does not turn her head*) Loreleen, I go with you!

(LORNA *shoves* FATHER DOMINEER *aside at the gateway, nearly knocks* SHANAAR *over, and hurries to* LORELEEN. *Draping the green cloak over* LORELEEN'S *shoulders*)

I go with you, love. I've got a sthrong pair of shoes in the sack you can put on when we're free from th' priest an' his rabble. Lift up your heart, lass: we go not towards an evil, but leave an evil behind us!

(*They go out slowly together*)

FATHER DOMINEER (*Taking the* SERGEANT *by the arm*) Let her go quietly to her own. We'll follow some of the way to prevent anyone from harming her. (*Down to* MICHAEL) Be of good cheer, Michael; th' demon is conquered—you can live peaceful an' happy in your own home now.

(*He goes out with the* SERGEANT, *followed by all who may be there, except* MICHAEL, *the* MESSENGER, *and* SHANAAR. *The* MESSENGER *goes back to the wall, sits on it sideways, takes the accordion from his back, and begins to play, very softly, the air of "Oh, Woman Gracious."* SHANAAR *leans on the wall from the outside, looking down at* MICHAEL, *who is now seated gloomily on a chair beside the table, an elbow resting on it, his head resting on his hand*)

SHANAAR (*Down to* MICHAEL) His reverence never spoke a thruer word, Mick, than that of you'd have happiness an' peace now. You were a long time without them, but you have them now.

MICHAEL (*Doubtfully*) Maybe I have, Shanaar, an', God knows, I need them. (*He pauses for a moment, thinking*) I wonder will Lorna come back?

SHANAAR (*Emphatically*) Oh, devil a come back! You need have no fear o' that, man. An' fortunate you are, for a woman's always a menace to a man's soul. Woman is th' passionate path to hell!

MESSENGER (*Playing softly on his accordion and singing*)

Oh, woman gracious, in golden garments,
Through life's dark places, all glintin' go;

Bring man, in search of th' thruth tremendous,
Th' joy that ev'ry young lad should know.

Then come out, darlin', in reckless raiment,
We'll dance along through Ireland gay,
An' clip from life life's rich enjoyments,
An' never want for a word to say.

(MARION *has come into the porch, and now stands at the door, watching the* MESSENGER. *She is covered to her knees by a bright blue cloak*)

Cling close to youth with your arms enthrancin',
For youth is restless, an' loth to stay;
So take your share of th' kisses goin',
Ere sly youth, tirin', can slink away!

(MARION *crosses the garden towards the gate, and is about to go through it when the* MESSENGER *catches her by the arm*)

Would you leave me here, alone, without a lass to love me?

MARION (*Gently removing the hold of his hand on her arm*) Your voice is dear to me; your arm around me near seals me to you; an' I'd love to have—

MESSENGER (*Quickly*) Your lips on mine!

MARION But not here, Robin Adair, oh, not here; for a whisper of love in this place bites away some of th' soul! (*She goes out by the gateway, and along the road taken by* LORNA *and* LORELEEN. *The* MESSENGER *stays where he is, wistful and still. Just before she goes*) Come, if you want to, Robin Adair; stay, if you will.

SHANAAR (*To the* MESSENGER) Stay, Messenger. Take a warnin' from a wise oul' man, a very wise oul' one, too. (*He turns his head to look peeringly to the left along the road*) What's this I see comin'? If it isn't Julia, back from Lourdes, an' she on her stretcher still! I'd best be off, for I've no inclination to thry a chatter with a one who's come back as bad as she was when she went.

(*He bends down nearly double, so as not to be seen, and slyly and quietly steals away.*

*After a pause,* JULIA *comes in on her stretcher, carried by the two* ROUGH FELLOWS *as before, her* FATHER, *silent and stony-faced, walking beside her. The stretcher is laid down in the garden just inside the gate.* JULIA *is covered with a rug, black as a winter's sky, and its sombre hue is enlivened only by the chalk-white face of the dying girl. The* MESSENGER *has gone from the gateway, and now stands in a half-to-attention, military way, a little distance from the stretcher, looking down at* JULIA. JULIA'S FATHER *stands, as before, behind her head.* MICHAEL *sits, unnoticing, elbow on table, his head resting on his hand*)

JULIA (*In a toneless voice—to no one in particular*) Lorna, I want Lorna.

MESSENGER (*Gently*) She's gone, Julia.

JULIA Gone? Gone where?

MESSENGER To a place where life resembles life more than it does here.

JULIA She's a long way to go, then. It's th' same everywhere. In Lourdes as here, with all its crowds an' all its candles. I want Loreleen.

MESSENGER She's gone with Lorna, an' Marion's followed them both.

JULIA Then there's no voice left to offer even th' taunting comfort of asking if I feel better.

MESSENGER There's Michael Marthraun there.

JULIA (*After a long look at* MICHAEL) He, poor man, is dyin' too. No one left, an' th' stir there was when I was goin'—th' Mayor there, with all his accouthered helperds; th' band playin'; Father Domineer spoutin' his blessin'; an' oul' Shanaar busy sayin' somersaultin' prayers; because they all thought I would bring a sweet miracle back. (*She pauses*) There was no miracle, Robin; she didn't cure me, she didn't cure me, Robin. I've come back, without even a gloamin' thought of hope. (*She pauses again; with a wan smile*) I can see your whole soul wishin' you could cure me. Touch me with your questionable blessin' before I go.

MESSENGER (*Very softly*) Be brave.

JULIA Nothin' else, Robin Adair?

MESSENGER Evermore be brave.

JULIA (*After a pause*) Dad, take me home.

(*The* ROUGH FELLOWS *take up the stretcher and carry it out, the stony-faced* FATHER *following in the rear without a word*)

MICHAEL (*Raising his head from his hand to look at the* MESSENGER) Maybe Lorna might come back. Maybe I mightn't have been so down on her fancy dhressin'.

MESSENGER (*Tonelessly*) Maybe she will; maybe you mightn't.

MICHAEL (*Tonelessly too*) It'll be very lonely for me now. All have left me. (*He takes a set of rosary beads from his pocket, and fingers them*) I've no one left to me but th' Son o' God. (*He notices the* MESSENGER *settling the accordion comfortably on his back, and watches him going to the gate*) Are you goin' too?

MESSENGER (*Shortly*) Ay.

MICHAEL Where?

MESSENGER To a place where life resembles life more than it does here.

MICHAEL (*After a pause*) What, Messenger, would you advise me to do?

MESSENGER (*Turning at the gate to reply*) Die. There is little else left useful for the likes of you to do. (*He swings his accordion comfortably before him, and plays a few preliminary notes. Then he starts to sing softly as he goes away along the pathway outside; while* MICHAEL *leans forward on to the table, and buries his head in his arms*)

MESSENGER (*Singing and accompanying himself on the accordion—as he is going off*)

She's just like a young star out taking the air—
Let others be good or be clever—

With Marion gay, a gay flow'r in her hair,
Life becomes but a pleasant endeavour.

When building a city or making the hay,
I'll follow her close as night follows day,

Or lads follow lasses out nutting in May,
For ever and ever and ever!

*Curtain*

# Georg Kaiser

## (1878-1945)

THE MOST significant playwright of German expressionism, Georg Kaiser pioneered in the development of the radically subjective and stridently emotional dramatic style. A writer of incredible facility, he wrote over 60 plays, as well as novels, poems, essays, and other works. In the 1917-18 season alone, 13 of his plays were produced on the German stage. No writer except Gerhart Hauptmann so completely dominated the attention of the German theatrical world in the years immediately following World War I. Despite the uneven quality of much of his work, his best plays continue to hold the stage. They have exerted a lasting influence on the technique of modern drama.

Kaiser began as a playwright relatively late. His first published work appeared when he was 33. His father, a moderately prosperous business man, had destined him for a business career, and he left his native Magdeburg at the age of 20 to emigrate to Buenos Aires, where he worked as a commercial representative for a German power corporation. He contracted malaria during a trip through the interior of Argentina and returned to Germany in precarious health, remaining so for several years. His first play, *Rektor Kleist* (1905), resembles Wedekind's *Spring's Awakening* in its assault on the stupidity of the German educational system and the callous treatment of adolescents by their elders. In 1911 he gained a degree of recognition in Berlin theatrical circles with the publication of *Die jüdische Witwe* (*The Jewish Widow*), an imaginative portrayal of Judith before and after her slaying of Holofernes. The spectacular and colorful use of mass scenes, along with the reduction of exposition to brief fragments of dialogue, prefigure the later, expressionist manner of Kaiser's major plays.

In 1913 Kaiser completed *The Citizens of Calais* (*Die Bürger von Calais*), one of his best-known plays. The action takes place in fourteenth-century France, and is based on an incident reported in Froissart's *Chronicles*. The King of England besieging Calais offers to spare the city and port from destruction if six citizens will give themselves up for execution. The initial conflict between hopeless resistance and acceptance of the terms of surrender is resolved by the arguments of the hero of the play, Eustache de Saint-Pierre, who places the work accomplished by the citizens in the construction of the port above all personal considerations. He volunteers to give himself up and under his influence, others do likewise. Six men are required but after five have volunteered, two brothers pledge themselves simultaneously. The action then turns on the determination of the seventh man, whose life will be spared. Eustache controls the drawing of lots so that all are elected to go. None of them, he tell his comrades, is ripe for the deed, but in the short time that follows, they all come to a realization of the necessity of self-sacrifice. Like the Cashier, the Billionaire, and other heroes of later plays, he finds the full meaning of life in a death of expiation and self-surrender. *The Citizens of Calais* is not primarily a historical play, but it is clearly a landmark. The premiere of the play in Frankfurt in 1917 was one of the great events of the modern German theatre.

Kaiser's mastery of dramatic form and his command of his devices and techniques are at their best in his most thoroughgoing expressionist plays: *From Morn to Midnight* (*Von Morgens bis Mitternachts*) and the *Gas* trilogy, comprising *The Coral, Gas I,* and *Gas II. From Morn to Midnight,* written in 1912 and first produced in 1916, is probably Kaiser's most famous work. It is the tragedy of a little man whose staid and placid way of life is demoralized by the sudden eruption of sexual desire. The Cashier, like the other characters of the play, has no name; he is a representative of his class and status. Tormented by the monotony of his robot-like existence, he protests through his crime against a meaningless, dehumanized way of life. The shrill soliloquy of the disoriented fugitive rises to an apocalyptic frenzy: "A catastrophe in the wash tubs! A world in chaos!" The drama unfolds not in the traditional sequence of acts, but in short scenes or *Stationen*, each of which presents a new phase in the hero's career. The patterned contrast of the individual and the crowd characteristic of expressionist staging is exemplified in Scene V, at the bicycle race, where the puppet-like gentlemen are all dressed alike. The reduction of the crowd from the human to the animal in a surge of mass delirium excites the frenzy of the Cashier's quest for meaning to its highest pitch. Naked passion is the essence of brute reality. The Cashier ends a martyr to the futility of life, yet his protest lends dignity and purpose to his crude assertion of individuality. His final words, echoing Pilate's description of Christ, call our attention to his abstract, symbolic function. Whether the Cashier is large enough to carry this symbolic weight is another matter; but there can be no doubt of the dramatic effectiveness of Kaiser's shrill and violent play.

The same fierce denunciation of the anarchy and

valuelessness of commonplace existence in a society dominated by the love of wealth and power runs through the *Gas* trilogy, composed from 1917 to 1919. The note of social protest is even harsher than in the earlier works. The images of violent destruction, inspired by the nightmare of chaos of World War I, are even more frenetic. The Billionaire in *The Coral* evades the grim realities of life through the substitution of a second self, and then experiences the demoralization of his dream-world through the refusal of his son to accept his standard of values. The murder he commits is a form of suicide, impelled by the realization that human progress will come not through class war and industrial violence, but only through the recovery of man's primal innocence, the regaining of a lost paradise. In *Gas I* the Billionaire's Son is head of a gas plant wherein the workers share in the profits; he has dedicated his life to social betterment, yet the plant and many of the workers are destroyed by the scientific monster they cannot control. Kaiser's apocalyptic view of cosmic destruction takes on new meaning in the wake of the atom bomb and the grim possibility of thermonuclear war. We see in *Gas II* the real prospect of total human annihilation through scientific invention and automation. The redemption of suffering humanity, as preached by the Billionaire Worker, lies not simply in a change in the social and economic order, but in a spiritual conversion that will make possible a renewal of man. Our deliverance, Kaiser affirms, lies within. The final holocaust is at the same time a proclamation of the need for human brotherhood and love, for the realization of a new vision of mankind.

The alternatives to chaos in Kaiser's major plays rest not so much on intellectual argument as on his shrill emotionalism, wherein dialogue gives way to monologue or to an almost breathless alternation of plea and exultation. There is little room in his expressionistic dramas for calm reflection or for psychological analyses of character or of character relationships. Yet, not all of Kaiser's plays are as markedly expressionistic as *From Morn to Midnight* or the *Gas* trilogy; indeed, much of his writing is not expressionistic at all. His eclecticism led him to exploit varied and often contradictory experiences and attitudes. Schopenhauerean resignation and Nietzschean affirmation move side by side. Often, in successive plays, he would offer completely opposite solutions to the same problem. Sometimes the solutions were too simple: to end unemployment by suppressing procreation; or to end materialism by destroying machinery. Much of his later work explores the conflicts and contradictions of intelligence and passion. He drew the sharp opposition of ideas, or of conflicting elements of his dramatic idea, from the structure of the Platonic dialogue, and also, perhaps, from his study of the plays of Shaw, whose work he admired immensely. Kaiser's preoccupation with abstract thought led critics to label him "Denkspieler," "writer of thought-plays." Yet, intellectual argumentation is but one aspect of the playwright's many-sided art, too rich and too varied to be reduced to an easy formula.

In 1921 Kaiser acquired considerable notoriety as the result of an act of embezzlement. Impractical in money matters, he sold the furnishings of an expensive house he had rented; as a result, he was sentenced to six months in jail. In his statement to the Munich court, Kaiser claimed that as an artist he was not subject to ordinary human standards; that the artist is outside the law. His defense caused a sensation, but he was found guilty and went to jail. Increasingly, his later plays are marked by pacifism, socialism, sympathy for the underdog, hatred of oppression of any kind. The Nazis attacked his work violently and in 1933 banned the production of his plays. Kaiser was dependent on royalties for his income and the ban forced him into dire poverty. In 1938 he left for Holland and then sought asylum in Switzerland, where he lived for the rest of his life. In exile, he continued his attack on uniformity, militarism, and the glorification of machines over men. Representative of this phase of his late work is *Soldier Tanaka* (*Der Soldat Tanaka*, 1940), about the revolt of a young Japanese soldier against the injustice of the social system. Court-martialed and sentenced to death, Tanaka is advised that he may request clemency from the Emperor. It is the Emperor, he exclaims, who should beg pardon for the degradation he imposes on his people. The court orders the sentence carried out at once and the volley of the firing squad ends the play. Kaiser saw certain analogies between Tanaka and Buechner's Woyzeck, but the inner tension is far more acute in the earlier play, while in Kaiser's play, the education of the hero is the dominant theme.

His last plays, published posthumously, consist of a "Hellenic Trilogy," a retelling in verse of the legends of Pygmalion, Amphitryon, and Bellerophon. Reflective in tone, they offer little resemblance to the expressionistic style. *Pygmalion* is a portrait of the artist, protected by Athene but doomed to isolation and suffering, and finding the meaning of his life in his dedication to the redemption of mankind. His Amphitryon play, in sharp contrast to the usual comic versions, offers a bitter condemnation of cold and selfish ambition, while in *Bellerophon*, the idealistic hero demonstrates the trials of pure goodness and innocence on earth. He ends transported to the heavens with the aid of the gods.

Kaiser was perhaps more convinced of his greatness as a playwright than are most of his present-day readers or spectators, yet there can be no question of the importance of his contribution to the modern theatre. However one-sided the view, he must be considered the representative playwright of German expressionism. The production of *From Morn to Midnight* by the Theatre Guild in New York in May, 1922, was, moreover, a major event in the course of modern American drama. Quite apart from the question of direct influence on Eugene O'Neill, Elmer Rice, and other American playwrights who responded to the challenge of expressionism, Kaiser's play was instrumental in establishing the new shrill, abrupt, and depersonalized style on the American stage. In his best work the humanistic passion of expressionism finds its most artistic embodiment.

# FROM MORN TO MIDNIGHT

Translated from the German by Ashley Dukes

## CHARACTERS

CASHIER
STOUT GENTLEMAN
CLERK
MESSENGER BOY
LADY
BANK MANAGER
MUFFLED GENTLEMAN
SERVING MAID
PORTER
THE LADY'S SON
THE CASHIER'S MOTHER
HIS DAUGHTERS
HIS WIFE
FIRST GENTLEMAN
SECOND GENTLEMAN
THIRD GENTLEMAN
FOURTH GENTLEMAN
FIFTH GENTLEMAN
SALVATION LASS
WAITER
FIRST MASK
SECOND MASK
THIRD MASK
FOURTH MASK
FIRST GUEST
SECOND GUEST
THIRD GUEST
OFFICER OF SALVATION ARMY
FIRST SOLDIER OF SALVATION ARMY
FIRST PENITENT
SECOND SOLDIER OF SALVATION ARMY
SECOND PENITENT
THIRD SOLDIER OF SALVATION ARMY
THIRD PENITENT
FOURTH SOLDIER OF SALVATION ARMY
POLICEMAN
AND THE CROWD AT VELODROME AND SALVATION ARMY HALL

## SCENES

I—*The Interior of a Provincial Bank*
II—*The Writing Room of a Hotel*
III—*A Field Deep in Snow*
IV—*The Parlor in the Cashier's Home*
V—*The Steward's Box at a Velodrome during Bicycle Races*
VI—*A Private Supper Room in a Cabaret*
VII—*A Salvation Army Hall*

*In a Small Town and a City in Germany at the Present Time*

## Scene One

SCENE *Interior of a provincial Bank.*

*On the right, pigeon-holes and a door inscribed Manager. Another door in the middle: Strong Room. Entrance from the lower left. In front of the* CASHIER'S *cage on the left hand side is a cane sofa, and in front of it a small table with a water-bottle and glass.*

*The* CASHIER *at the counter and the* CLERK *at a desk, both writing. On the cane sofa sits a* STOUT GENTLEMAN, *wheezing. In front of the counter stands a* MESSENGER BOY, *staring at the door through which some one has just gone out.*

(CASHIER *raps on the counter.* MESSENGER BOY *turns, hands in a check.* CASHIER *examines it, writes, takes a handful of silver from a drawer, counts it, pushes a small pile across the counter.* MESSENGER BOY *sweeps the money into a linen bag.*)

STOUT GENTLEMAN (*Rising*) Now the fat fellows take their turn. (*He pulls out a bag. Enter* LADY, *expensive furs; rustle of silk.* STOUT GENTLEMAN *stops short*)

LADY (*Smiles involuntarily in his direction*) At last! (STOUT GENTLEMAN *makes a wry face.* CASHIER *taps the counter impatiently.* LADY *looks at* STOUT GENTLEMAN)

STOUT GENTLEMAN (*Giving place to her*) The fat fellows can wait.

(LADY *bows distantly, comes to counter.* CASHIER *taps as before*)

LADY (*Opens her handbag, takes out a letter and hands it to* CASHIER) A letter of credit. Three thousand, please. (CASHIER *takes the envelope, turns it over, hands it back*) I beg your pardon. (*She pulls out the folded letter and offers it again.* CASHIER *turns it over, hands it back*)

LADY (*Unfolds the letter, hands it to him*) Three thousand, please.

(CASHIER *glances at it, puts it in front of the* CLERK. CLERK *takes the letter, rises, goes out by the door inscribed Manager*)

STOUT GENTLEMAN (*Retiring to sofa*) I can wait. The fat fellows can always wait.

(CASHIER *begins counting silver*)

LADY In notes, if you don't mind.

(CASHIER *ignores her*)

MANAGER (*Youthful, plump, comes in with the letter in his hand*) Who is—

(*He stops short on seeing the* LADY. CLERK *resumes work at his desk*)

STOUT GENTLEMAN Ahem! Good morning.

MANAGER (*Glancing at him*) How goes it?

STOUT GENTLEMAN (*Tapping his belly*) Oh, rounding out—rounding out!

MANAGER (*Laughs shortly. Turning to* LADY) I understand you want to draw on us?

LADY Three thousand marks.

MANAGER I would pay you three—(*Glancing at letter*) —three thousand with pleasure, but—

LADY Is anything wrong with the letter?

MANAGER (*Suave, important*) It's in the proper form. (*Reading the headlines*) "Not exceeding twelve thousand"—quite correct. (*Spelling out the address*) "B-A-N-C-O"—

LADY My bank in Florence assured me—

MANAGER Your bank in Florence is quite all right.

LADY Then I don't see why—

MANAGER I suppose you applied for this letter?

LADY Of course.

MANAGER Twelve thousand—payable at such cities—

LADY As I should touch on my trip.

MANAGER And you must have given your bank in Florence duplicate signatures.

LADY Certainly. To be sent to the banks mentioned in the list to identify me.

MANAGER (*Consults letter*) Ah! (*Looks up*) We have received no letter of advice. (STOUT GENTLEMAN *coughs; winks at the* MANAGER)

LADY That means I must wait until . . .

MANAGER Well, we must have something to go upon!

(MUFFLED GENTLEMAN, *in fur cap and shawl, comes in and takes his place at the counter. He darts angry glances at the* LADY)

LADY I was quite unprepared for this . . .

MANAGER (*With a clumsy laugh*) As you see, Madame, we are even less prepared; in fact—not at all.

LADY I need the money so badly . . . (STOUT GENTLEMAN *laughs aloud*)

MANAGER Who doesn't? (STOUT GENTLEMAN *neighs with delight. Looking round for an audience*) Myself, for instance—(*To the impatient* MUFFLED CUSTOMER) You have more time than I—don't you see I'm busy with this Lady? Now, Madame, what do you expect me to do—pay you money on your—ah—

(STOUT GENTLEMAN *titters*)

LADY (*Quickly*) I'm staying at the Elephant.

(STOUT GENTLEMAN *wheezes with laughter*)

MANAGER I am very glad to know your address. I always lunch there.

LADY Can't the proprietor vouch for me?

MANAGER Has he already had the pleasure?

(STOUT GENTLEMAN *rocks with delight*)

LADY Well, I have my luggage with me . . .

MANAGER Am I to examine it?

LADY A most embarrassing position. I can't . . .

MANAGER Then we're in the same boat. You can't—I can't—that's the situation.

(*He returns the letter*)

LADY What do you advise me to do?

MANAGER This is a snug little town of ours—it has surroundings— The Elephant is a well-known house . . . you'll make pleasant acquaintances of one sort or another . . . and time will pass—days—nights—well you know?

LADY I don't in the least mind passing a few days here.

MANAGER Your fellow-guests will be delighted to contribute something for your entertainment.

LADY But I must have three thousand today!

MANAGER (*To* STOUT GENTLEMAN) Will anybody here underwrite a lady from abroad for three thousand marks?

LADY I couldn't think of accepting that. I shall be in my room at the hotel. When the letter of advice arrives, will you please notify me at once by telephone?

MANAGER Personally, Madame, if you wish.

LADY In whatever way is quickest. (*She folds up the letter, replaces it in the envelope, and puts both into the handbag*) I shall call again in any case this afternoon.

MANAGER At your service. (LADY *bows coldly, goes out.* MUFFLED GENTLEMAN *moves up to counter, on which he leans, crackling his check impatiently.* MANAGER *ignoring him, looks merrily at the* STOUT GENTLEMAN. STOUT GENTLEMAN *sniffs the air. Laughs*) All the fragrance of Italy, eh? Straight from the perfume bottle. (STOUT GENTLEMAN *fans himself with his hand*) Warm, eh?

STOUT GENTLEMAN (*Pours out water*) Three thousand is not bad. (*Drinks*) I guess three hundred wouldn't sound bad to her either.

MANAGER Perhaps you would like to make a lower offer at the Elephant?—in her room?

STOUT GENTLEMAN No use for fat fellows.

MANAGER Our bellies protect our morals. (MUFFLED

GENTLEMAN *raps impatiently on the counter. Indifferently*) Well?

(*He takes the check, smoothes it out, and hands it to the* CASHIER)

(MESSENGER BOY *stares after the departing* LADY, *then at the last speakers, finally stumbles over the* STOUT GENTLEMAN *on the sofa*)

STOUT GENTLEMAN (*Robbing him of his wallet*) There, my boy, that's what comes of making eyes at pretty ladies. Now you've lost your money. (MESSENGER BOY *looks shyly at him*) How are you going to explain to your boss? (MESSENGER BOY *laughs*) Remember this for the rest of your life! (*Returning the wallet*) Your eyes run away and you bolt after them. You wouldn't be the first. (MESSENGER BOY *goes out*)

(CASHIER *has counted out some small silver*)

MANAGER And they trust money to a young fool like that.

STOUT GENTLEMAN Stupid!

MANAGER People should be more careful. That boy will abscond the first chance he gets—a born embezzler. (*To* MUFFLED GENTLEMAN) Is anything wrong? (MUFFLED GENTLEMAN *examines every coin*) That's a twenty-five pfennig piece. Forty-five pfennigs altogether; that's all that's coming to you.

(MUFFLED GENTLEMAN *pockets his money with great ceremony; buttons his coat over the pocket*)

STOUT GENTLEMAN (*Ironically*) You ought to deposit your capital in the vault. (*Rising*) Now it's time for fat fellows to unload.

(MUFFLED GENTLEMAN *turns away from counter, and goes out*)

MANAGER (*To* STOUT GENTLEMAN, *breezily*) What are you bringing us this morning?

STOUT GENTLEMAN (*Sets his attaché case on the counter and takes out a pocket-book*) With all the confidence that your elegant clientele inspires. (*He offers his hand*)

MANAGER (*Taking it*) In any case we are immune to a pretty face when it comes to business.

STOUT GENTLEMAN (*Counting out his money*) How old was she, at a guess?

MANAGER I haven't seen her without rouge—yet.

STOUT GENTLEMAN What's she doing here?

MANAGER We'll hear that tonight at the Elephant.

STOUT GENTLEMAN But who's she after?

MANAGER All of us, perhaps, before she gets through.

STOUT GENTLEMAN What can she do with three thousand in this town?

MANAGER Evidently she needs them.

STOUT GENTLEMAN I wish her luck.

MANAGER With what!

STOUT GENTLEMAN Getting her three thousand if she can.

MANAGER From me?

STOUT GENTLEMAN It doesn't matter from whom! (*They laugh*)

MANAGER I'm curious to see when that letter of advice from Florence will arrive.

STOUT GENTLEMAN If it arrives!

MANAGER Ah! If it arrives!

STOUT GENTLEMAN We might make a collection for her benefit.

MANAGER I dare say that's what she has in mind.

STOUT GENTLEMAN You don't need to tell me.

MANAGER Did you draw a winning number in the last lottery? (*They laugh*)

STOUT GENTLEMAN (*To* CASHIER) Take this. What's the difference if our money draws interest here or outside. Here—open an account for the Realty Construction Company.

MANAGER (*Sharply, to* CLERK) Account: "Realty Construction Company."

STOUT GENTLEMAN There's more to come.

MANAGER The more the merrier. We can use it just now.

STOUT GENTLEMAN Sixty thousand marks, fifty thousand in paper, ten thousand in gold.

(CASHIER *begins counting*)

MANAGER (*After a pause*) And how are you, otherwise?

STOUT GENTLEMAN (*To* CASHIER, *who pauses to examine a note*) Yes, that one's patched.

MANAGER We'll accept it, of course. We shall soon be rid of it. I'll reserve it for our fair client from Florence. She wore patches too.

STOUT GENTLEMAN But behind these you find—a thousand marks.

MANAGER Face value.

STOUT GENTLEMAN (*Laughing immoderately*) Face value—that's good!

MANAGER The face value! Here's your receipt. (*Choking with laughter*) Sixty—thousand—

STOUT GENTLEMAN (*Takes it, reads*) Sixty—thou—

MANAGER Face.

STOUT GENTLEMAN Value. (*They shake hands*)

MANAGER (*In tears*) I'll see you tonight.

STOUT GENTLEMAN (*Nods*) The face—the face—value! (*He buttons his overcoat, and goes out laughing*)

(MANAGER *wipes the tears from his pince-nez;* CASHIER *fastens the notes together in bundles*)

MANAGER This lady from Florence—who claims to come from Florence—has a vision like that ever visited you in your cage before? Furs—perfume! The fragrance lingers—you breathe adventure. Superbly staged. Italy . . . Enchantment—fairy-tale—Riviera—Mentone—Bordighera[1]—Nice—Monte Carlo,—where oranges blossom, fraud blooms, too. Swindlers—down there every square foot of earth breeds them. They organize crusades. The gang disperses to the four winds—preferably small towns—off the beaten track. Then—apparitions—billowing silks—furs—women—modern sirens. Refrains from the sunny south—o bella Napoli! One glance and you're stripped to your undershirt—to the bare skin—to the naked, naked skin. (*He drums with a pencil on the* CASHIER*'s hand*) Depend upon it, this bank in Florence knows as much about the lady as the man in the

[1] Mentone and Bordighera are famous resorts on the Riviera in France and Italy.

moon. The whole affair is a swindle, carefully arranged. And the web was woven not in Florence, but in Monte Carlo. That's the place to keep in mind. Take my word for it, you've just seen one of the gadflies that thrive in the swamp of the Casino. We shall never see her again. The first attempt missed fire; she'll scarcely risk a second! I joke about it but I have a keen eye—when you're a banker—I really should have tipped off the police! Well, it doesn't concern me—besides, banks must be discreet. Keep your eye on the out-of-town papers—the police news. When you find something there about an adventuress, safe under lock and key—then we'll talk about it again. You'll see I was right—then we'll hear more of our Florentine lady than we'll ever see of her and her furs again. (*Exit*)

(CASHIER *seals up rolls of bank notes*)

PORTER (*Enters with letters, hands them to* CLERK) One registered letter, I want the receipt.

(CLERK *stamps receipt form, hands it to* PORTER. PORTER *re-arranges glass and water-bottle on the table, and goes out.* CLERK *takes the letters into* MANAGER'S *room, and returns*)

LADY (*Re-enters; comes quickly to the counter*) I beg your pardon.

(CASHIER *stretches out his hand, without looking at her. Raps*)

LADY (*Louder*) If you please! (CASHIER *raps on the counter*) I don't want to trouble the Manager a second time. (CASHIER *raps on the counter*) Please tell me—would it be possible for me to leave you the letter of credit for the whole sum, and to receive an advance of three thousand in part payment? (CASHIER *raps impatiently*) I should be willing to deposit my diamonds as security, if required. Any jeweler in the town will appraise them for you. (*She takes off a glove and pulls at her bracelet.* SERVING MAID *comes in quickly, plumps down on sofa, and begins rummaging in her market-basket.* LADY *startled by the commotion, looks round. As she leans on the counter her hand sinks into the* CASHIER'S. CASHIER *bends over the hand which lies in his own. His spectacles glitter, his glance travels slowly upward from her wrist.* SERVING MAID *with a sigh of relief, discovers the check she is looking for.* LADY *nods kindly in her direction.* SERVING MAID *replaces vegetables, etc., in her basket.* LADY *turning again to the counter, meets the eyes of the* CASHIER. CASHIER *smiles at her*)

LADY (*Drawing back her hand*) Of course I shall not ask the bank to do anything irregular. (*She puts the bracelet on her wrist; the clasp refuses to catch. Stretching out her arm to the* CASHIER) Would you be so kind? I'm clumsy with the left hand. (CASHIER *stares at her as if mesmerized. His spectacles, bright points of light, seem almost to be swallowed up in the cavity of his wide-open eyes. To* SERVING MAID) You can help me, mademoiselle. (SERVING MAID *does so*) Now the safety catch. (*With a little cry*) You're pinching my flesh. Ah, that's better. Thank you so much. (*She bows to the* CASHIER *and goes out.* SERVING MAID *coming to the counter, planks down her check.* CASHIER *takes it in trembling hands, the slip of paper flutters and crackles; he fumbles under the counter, then counts out money*)

SERVING MAID (*Looking at the pile of coins*) That isn't all mine. (CASHIER *writes.* CLERK *becomes observant*)

SERVING MAID (*To* CLERK) But it's too much! (CLERK *looks at* CASHIER. CASHIER *rakes in part of the money*) Still too much! (CASHIER *ignores her and continues writing.* SERVING MAID *shaking her head, puts the money in her basket and goes out*)

CASHIER (*Hoarsely*) Get me a glass of water! (CLERK *hurries from behind the counter; comes to table*) That's been standing. Fresh water—cold water—from the faucet. (CLERK *hurries out with glass.* CASHIER *goes quickly to electric bell, and rings.* PORTER *enters from the hall*) Get me fresh water.

PORTER I'm not allowed to go so far from the door.

CASHIER (*Hoarsely*) For me. Not that slime. I want water from the faucet. (PORTER *seizes water bottle and hurries out.* CASHIER *quickly crams his pockets with bank notes. Then he takes his coat from a peg, throws it over his arm, and puts on his hat. He lifts a flap in the counter, passes through, and goes out*)

MANAGER (*Absorbed in reading a letter, enters from his room*) Here's the letter of advice from Florence, after all! (CLERK *enters with a glass of water.* PORTER *enters with a full water bottle*)

MANAGER (*Looking up*) What the devil . . . ?

*Curtain*

## Scene Two

SCENE *Writing-room of a hotel. Glass door in background. On right, desk with telephone. On the left, sofa and armchair with table and newspapers.*

LADY (*Writes.* SON, *in hat and coat, enters, carrying under his arm a large flat object wrapped in green baize. With surprise*) Have you brought it with you?

SON Hush! The wine dealer is downstairs. The old fool is afraid I'll run away with it.

LADY But I thought this morning he was glad to get rid of it.

SON Now he's suspicious.

LADY You must have given yourself away.

SON I did let him see I was pleased.

LADY (*Smiling*) That would open a blind man's eyes.

SON Let it. But don't be afraid, Mother, the price is the same as it was this morning.

LADY Is the man waiting for his money?

SON Let him wait.

LADY But, my dear boy, I must tell you—

SON (*Kissing her*) Hush, Mother. This is a great moment. You mustn't look until I say so. (*He takes off his hat and cloak, puts the picture on a chair and lifts the green baize covering*)

LADY Ready?

SON (*In a low tone*) Mother! (LADY *turns in her chair. Comes to her, puts his arm round her neck*) Well?

LADY That was never meant to hang in a restaurant.

SON It was turned to the wall. The old fellow had pasted his own photograph on the back of it.

LADY Was that included in the price?

SON (*Laughs*) Tell me, what do you think of it?

LADY I find it—very naïve.

SON Marvelous, isn't it? Extraordinary considering it's a Cranach.[1]

LADY Do you really prize it as a picture?

SON Of course! But just look at the peculiar conception—unique for Cranach. And a new treatment of this subject in the entire history of art. Where can you find anything like it—in the Pitti—the Uffizi—the Vatican? Even the Louvre has nothing to compare with it. Here we have without doubt the first and only erotic conception of Adam and Eve. The apple is still in the grass—the serpent leers from behind the indescribable green foliage—and that means that the drama is played in Paradise itself and not in the banishment. That's the original sin—the real fall! Cranach painted dozens of Adams and Eves—standing stiffly—always separated—with the apple bough between them. In those pictures Cranach says simply: they knew each other. But in this picture for the first time, he cries exultantly they loved each other. Here a German proves himself a master of an eroticism intensely southern in its feeling. (*In front of the picture*) And yet what restraint in this ecstasy! This line of the man's arm as it slants across the woman's hip. The horizontal line of her thighs and the opposing line of his—never weary the eyes. These flesh tones make their love a living thing—doesn't it affect you that way?

LADY I find it as naïve as your picture.

SON What does that mean?

LADY Please hide it in your room.

SON I won't get its full effect until we get home. This Cranach in Florence. Of course, I'll have to postpone finishing my book. I must digest this first. A man must live with a thing like this before he dares write about it. Just now I am overwhelmed. Think of finding this picture here—on the first stage of our trip!

LADY But you were almost certain that it must be in this neighborhood.

SON I am dazed nevertheless. Isn't it amazing! I am lucky.

LADY This is simply the result of your own careful research.

SON But not without your generosity? Your help?

LADY It makes me as happy as it does you.

SON Your patience is endless. I tear you from your beautiful quiet life in Fiesole.[2] You are an Italian, but I drag you through Germany in mid-winter. You live in sleeping cars or third-rate hotels; rub elbows with Tom, Dick, Harry!

LADY (*Smiling—patting his cheek*) Yes, I have had my fill of that.

SON But now I promise you to hurry. I'm madly impatient to get this treasure safely home. Let's take the three o'clock train. Will you give me the three thousand marks?

LADY I haven't them.

SON But the owner is here, in the hotel.

LADY The bank couldn't pay me. The letter of advice has somehow been delayed.

SON I've promised him the money.

LADY Then you must return the picture until the letter arrives.

SON Can't we hurry it in any way?

LADY (*Smiles*) I've written a telegram; I'll have it sent now. You see, we traveled so quickly that—(WAITER *knocks at the door. Phone rings*) Yes?

WAITER Someone from the bank.

LADY Send him up. (*To* SON) They must be sending the money.

SON Call me as soon as you've got it. I'd rather keep an eye on the old man.

LADY I'll send for you.

SON Then I'll wait downstairs. (*Pauses in front of picture.* LADY *closes her portfolio.* CASHIER *is seen behind the glass door, enters.* LADY *points to a chair, and starts to seat herself.* CASHIER *stands*)

LADY I hope the bank— (CASHIER *sees the picture, and starts violently*) My visit to the bank was closely connected with this picture.

CASHIER (*Staring*) You!

LADY Do you find any point of resemblance?

CASHIER (*Smiling*) In the wrist!

LADY Are you interested?

CASHIER I should like to discover more.

LADY Do such subjects interest you?

CASHIER (*Looking straight at her*) Yes—I understand them.

LADY Are there any more to be found here? You would do me a great favor—that's more important than the money.

CASHIER I have the money.

LADY I fear at this rate my letter of credit will soon be exhausted.

CASHIER (*Produces a roll of bank notes*) This will be enough.

LADY I can only draw twelve thousand in all.

CASHIER Sixty thousand!

LADY But—how did you—?

CASHIER That's my business.

LADY How am I to—?

CASHIER We shall bolt.

LADY Bolt? Where?

CASHIER Abroad. Anywhere. Pack your trunk, if you've got one. You can start from the station; I'll walk to the next stop and board the train. We'll spend the first night in—a timetable! (*He finds it*)

[1] Lucas Cranach (1472-1553), a noted German painter.
[2] A suburb of Florence.

LADY Have you brought more than three thousand from the Bank?

CASHIER (*Preoccupied with the timetable*) I have sixty thousand in my pocket—fifty thousand in notes and ten thousand in gold.

LADY And my part of that is—

CASHIER (*Opens a roll of notes, and counts them with professional skill, then lays a bundle of them on the table*) Your part. Take this. Put it away. We may be seen. The door has a glass panel. That's five hundred.

LADY Five hundred?

CASHIER More to come. All in good time. When we're in a safe place. Here we must be careful . . . hurry up—take it. No time for love-making. The wheel spins. An arm outstretched will be caught in the spokes. (*He springs to his feet*)

LADY But I need three thousand.

CASHIER If the police find them on you, you'll find yourself in jail!

LADY What have the police to do with it?

CASHIER You were in the Bank. Your presence filled the air. They'll suspect you; the link between us is clear as daylight.

LADY I went to—your Bank.

CASHIER As cool as a cucumber—

LADY I demanded—

CASHIER You tried to.

LADY I tried—

CASHIER You did. With your forged letter.

LADY (*Taking a paper from her handbag*) Isn't my letter genuine?

CASHIER As false as your diamonds.

LADY I offered them as a security. Why should my precious stones be paste?

CASHIER Ladies of your kind only dazzle.

LADY What do you think I am? I'm dark, it's true; a Southerner, a Tuscan.

CASHIER From Monte Carlo.

LADY (*Smiles*) No, from Florence!

CASHIER (*His glance lighting upon the* SON's *hat and cloak*) Ha! Have I come too late?

LADY Too late?

CASHIER Where is he? I'll bargain with him. He'll be willing. I have the means. How much shall I offer? How high do you put the indemnity? How much shall I cram into his pockets? I'll bid up to fifteen thousand. Is he asleep? Still rolling in bed? Where's your room? Twenty thousand—five thousand extra for instant withdrawal! (*Picking up hat and cloak*)

LADY (*In astonishment*) The gentleman is sitting in the lounge.

CASHIER Downstairs? Too risky! Too many people down there. Call him up; I'll settle with him here. Ring for him; let the Waiter hustle. Twenty thousand, cash down! (*He begins counting the money*)

LADY Can my son speak for me?

CASHIER (*Bounding back*) Your—son! ! !

LADY I'm traveling with him. He's collecting material for a book on the history of art. That's what brought us from Florence to Germany.

CASHIER (*Staring at her*) Son?

LADY Is that so appalling?

CASHIER But—but—this picture—

LADY A lucky find of his. My son is buying for three thousand marks; this was the amount needed so urgently. The owner is a wine dealer whom you will probably know by name . . .

CASHIER Furs . . . silk . . . rustle—glitter. The air was heavy with perfume!

LADY This is mid-winter. As far as I know, my way of dressing is not exceptional.

CASHIER The forged letter—

LADY I was about to wire to my bank.

CASHIER Your bare wrist—on which you wanted me to put the bracelet—

LADY We're all clumsy with the left hand.

CASHIER (*Dully, to himself*) And I—have stolen the money—

LADY (*Diverted*) Will that satisfy you and your police? My son is not utterly unknown in the art world.

CASHIER Now—at this very moment—they've discovered everything! I asked for water to get the clerk out of the way—and again for water to get the porter away from the door. The notes are gone; I'm an embezzler. I mustn't be seen in the streets; I can't go to the railway station; the police are warned, sixty thousand! I must slip away across the fields—through the snow—before the whole town is on my track!

LADY (*Shocked*) Be quiet!

CASHIER I took all the money. Your presence filled the Bank. Your scent hung on the air. You glistened and rustled—you put your naked hand in mine—your breath came warm across the counter—warm—

LADY (*Silencing him*) Please—I am a lady.

CASHIER But now you must—

LADY (*Controlling herself*) Tell me, are you married? Yes? (*Violent gesture from* CASHIER) Ah, that makes a difference. Unless I am to consider the whole thing a joke, you gave way to a foolish impulse. Listen. You can make good the loss. You can go back to your Bank and plead a passing illness—a lapse of memory. I suppose you still have the full amount.

CASHIER I've embezzled the money—

LADY (*Abruptly*) Then I can take no further interest in the matter.

CASHIER I've robbed the bank.

LADY You grow tedious, my dear sir.

CASHIER And now you must—

LADY The one thing I must do, is to—

CASHIER After this you must—

LADY Preposterous.

CASHIER I've robbed for you. I've delivered myself into your hands, destroyed my livelihood. I've burned my bridges behind me. I'm a thief and a criminal. (*Burying his face in his hands*) Now you must! . . . After all that you must!

LADY (*Turns*) I shall call my son. Perhaps he—

CASHIER (*With a change of tone, springs nimbly to his feet. Grabbing her arm*) Aha! Call him, would you? Rouse the hotel, give the alarm? A fine plan! Clumsy.

I'm not so easily caught as that. Not in that trap. I have my wits about me, ladies and gentlemen. Yours are asleep. I'm always five miles ahead of you. Don't move. Stay where you are until I . . . (*He puts the money in his pocket*) . . . until I . . . (*He presses his hat over his eyes*) . . . until I . . . (*He wraps his coat closely about him*) . . . until I . . . (*Softly he opens the glass door and slips out.* LADY *rises, stands motionless*)

SON (*Entering*) The man from the Bank has just gone out. You're looking worried, Mother. Is the money—?

LADY I found this interview trying. You know, my dear boy, how money matters get on my nerves.

SON Is there still trouble about the payment?

LADY Perhaps I ought to tell you—

SON Must I give back the picture?

LADY I'm not thinking of that—

SON But that's the chief question!

LADY I think I ought to notify the police.

SON Police?

LADY Send this telegram to my Bank. In future I must have proper documents that will satisfy everyone.

SON Isn't your letter of credit enough?

LADY Not quite. Go to the telegraph office for me. I don't want to send the porter.

SON And when shall we have the three thousand marks? (*Telephone bell rings*)

LADY (*Recoils*) They're ringing me up already. (*At the instrument*) Oh! Has it arrived? And I'm to call for it myself? Gladly. (*Change of tone*) I'm not in the least annoyed. Yes, of course. (*Change of tone*) Florence is a long way off. And then the Italian post-office—I beg your pardon? Oh, via Berlin—a roundabout way. That explains it. Not in the least. Thank you. In ten minutes. Good-by. (*To* SON) All settled, my dear boy. Never mind the telegram. (*She tears up the form*) You shall have the picture. Your wine dealer can come along. He'll get his money at the Bank. Pack up your treasure. We go straight from the Bank to the station. (*Telephoning while the* SON *wraps up the picture*) The bill, please. Rooms 14 and 16. Yes, immediately. Please.

*Curtain*

## Scene Three

SCENE *Aslant a field deep in snow. Through a tangle of low-hanging branches, blue shadows are cast by the midday sun.*

CASHIER (*Comes in backward, furtively*) What a marvelous contraption a man is. The mechanism runs in his joints—silently. Suddenly faculties are stimulated, action results. My hands, for instance, when did they ever shovel snow? And now they dig through snowdrifts without the slightest trouble. My footprints are all blotted out. I have achieved a complete incognito. (*Pause*) Frost and damp breed chills. Before you know it you've got a fever and that weakens the will—a man loses control over his actions if he's in bed sick. He's easily tracked. (*Throws cuffs to ground*) Lie there! You'll be missed in the wash! Lamentations fill the kitchen! A pair of cuffs is missing! A catastrophe in the wash tubs! The world in chaos! (*Pause*) Strange! How keen my wits are! Here I work like mad to efface my tracks and then betray myself by two bits of dirty linen. It is always a trifle, an oversight—carelessness that betrays the criminal. (*Pause*) I wonder what's going to happen. I am keyed up to the highest pitch! I have every reason to expect momentous discoveries. The last few hours prove it. This morning a trusted employee—fortunes passing through my hands. The Construction Company makes a huge deposit. At noon an out-and-out scoundrel. Up to all the tricks. The details of flight carefully worked out. Turn the trick and run. Marvelous accomplishment—and only half the day gone. I am prepared for anything. I know I can play the game. I am on the march! There is no turning back. I march—so out with your trumps without any fuss. I have put sixty thousand on a single card—it must be trumps. I play too high to lose. No nonsense—cards on the table—do you understand? Now you'll have to, my beautiful lady. Your cue—my silken lady, give it to me, my resplendent lady—or the scene will fall flat. (*Pause*) Idiot—and you think you can act! Perform your natural duties—breed children and don't bother the prompter. Ah, I beg your pardon—you have a son—you are completely absolved. I withdraw my aspersions. Good-by, give my compliments to the manager of the bank. His very glances cover you with slime, but don't let that worry you. He's been robbed of sixty thousand. His roof rattles and leaks—never mind, never mind—the Construction Company will mend it for him. I release you from all obligations—you are dismissed—you can go! Stop! Permit me to thank you! What's that you say? Nothing to thank you for? Yes! There is. Not worth mentioning? You are joking. You are my sole creditor. How so? I owe you my life! Good God—I exaggerate? You have electrified me—set me free. One step toward you and I enter a land of miracles. And with this load in my breast pocket I pay cash for all favors. And now fade away. You are outbid. Your means are too limited. Remember you have a son. Nothing will be knocked down to you. I'm paying cash down. (*Pause*) I have ready money. Come on—what's for sale? (*Pause*) Snow? Sunlight—stillness—. Blue snow at such a price. Outrageous, profiteering. I decline the offer. Your proposition is not *bona fide*. (*Pause*) But I must pay. I must spend, I've got the cash. Where are the goods that are worth the whole sum? Sixty thousand and the buyer to boot—flesh and bones—body and soul. Deal with me! Sell to me—I have the money, you have the goods—let us trade. (*The wind is blow-*

*ing, the sun is overcast, distant thunder is heard*) The earth is in labor—spring gales at last! That's better! I knew my cry could not be in vain. My demand was urgent. Chaos is insulted and will not be put to shame by my colossal deed of this morning. I knew it. In a case like mine never let up. Go at them hard—pull down their cloaks and you'll see something. (*The tree has changed to the form of a skeleton, the wind and thunder die down*) Have you been sitting behind me all this time eavesdropping? Are you an agent of the police? Not in the ordinary narrow sense—but (*pause*) comprising all. Police of Fate? Are you the all-embracing answer to my emphatic question? Does your rather well ventilated appearance suggest the final truth—emptiness? That's somewhat scanty—very threadbare—in fact nothing! I reject the information as being too full of gaps. Your services are not required. You can shut your rag and bone shop. I am not taken in as easily as that. (*Pause*) This procedure would be exceedingly simple—it's true—you would spare me further entanglements. But I prefer complications. So farewell—if that is possible, to you in your condition! I still have things to do. When one is traveling one can't enter every house on the road—not even at the friendliest invitations. I still have many obligations to fulfill before evening. You can't possibly be the first—perhaps the last—but even then only as a last resort. I won't want to do it. But, as I said, as a last resort—that's debatable. Ring me up at midnight—ask Central for my number. It will change from hour to hour. And excuse the coldness of my tone. We should be on friendlier terms, I know. We are closely bound. I really believe I carry you about with me now.

So, you see, we have come to a sort of understanding. That is a beginning which gives one confidence and backbone to face the future, whatever it is. I appreciate that fully. My most profound respects. (*After a peal of thunder and a last gust of wind the skeleton reverts to the tree. The sun comes out again*) There—I knew it wouldn't last.

*Curtain*

# Scene Four

SCENE *Parlor in* CASHIER'S *house. In the window-boxes, blown geraniums. Table and chairs. Piano right.* MOTHER (*hard of hearing*) *sits near the window.* FIRST DAUGHTER *is embroidering at the table.* SECOND DAUGHTER *is practicing the overture to* Tannhäuser. WIFE *comes and goes on the Left. The clock ticks interminably.*

MOTHER What's that you're playing?

FIRST DAUGHTER The Overture to *Tannhäuser.*

MOTHER "O Tannenbaum" is another pretty piece.

WIFE (*Entering*) It's time I began to fry the chops.

FIRST DAUGHTER Oh, not yet, Mama.

WIFE No, it's not time yet to fry the chops.

MOTHER What are you embroidering now?

FIRST DAUGHTER Father's slippers.

WIFE (*Coming to* MOTHER) Today we have chops for dinner.

MOTHER Are you frying them now?

WIFE Plenty of time. It's not twelve o'clock yet.

FIRST DAUGHTER Not nearly twelve, Mama.

WIFE No, not nearly twelve.

MOTHER When he comes, it will be twelve.

WIFE He hasn't come yet.

FIRST DAUGHTER When Father comes, it will be twelve o'clock.

WIFE Yes. (*Exit*)

SECOND DAUGHTER (*Stops playing, listens*) Is that Father?

FIRST DAUGHTER (*Listens*) Father?

WIFE (*Enters*) Is that my husband?

MOTHER Is that my son?

SECOND DAUGHTER Father!

FIRST DAUGHTER Father!

WIFE Husband!

MOTHER Son!

(CASHIER *enters Right, hangs up hat and cloak. Pause*)

WIFE Where do you come from?

CASHIER From the cemetery.

MOTHER Has somebody died suddenly?

CASHIER (*Patting her on the back*) You can have a sudden death, but not a sudden burial.

WIFE Where have you come from?

CASHIER From the grave. I burrowed through the clods with my forehead. See, here's a lump of ice. It was a great effort to get through—an extraordinary effort. I've dirtied my hands a little. You need a good grip to pull yourself up. You're buried deep. Life keeps on dumping dirt on you. Mountains of it—dust—ashes—the place is a rubbish heap. The dead lie at the usual depth—three yards. The living keep on sinking deeper and deeper.

WIFE You're frozen from head to foot.

CASHIER Thawed. Shaken by storms, like the spring. The wind whistled and roared; I tell you it stripped off my flesh until my bones were bare—a skeleton—bleached in a minute. A boneyard! At last the sun welded me together again. And here I am. Thus I've been renewed from the sole of my feet up.

MOTHER Have you been out in the open?

CASHIER In hideous dungeons, Mother. In bottomless pits beneath monstrous towers; deafened by clanking chains, blinded by darkness!

WIFE The Bank must be closed. You've been celebrating with the manager. Has there been a happy event in his family?

CASHIER He has his eye on a new mistress. Italian beauty—silks and furs—where oranges bloom. Wrists like polished ivory. Black tresses—olive complexion. Diamonds. Real . . . all real. Tus . . . tus . . .

the rest sounds like Canaan. Fetch me an atlas. Tus-Canaan. Is that right? Is there an island of that name? A mountain? A swamp? Geography can tell us everything. But he'll burn his fingers. She'll turn him down —brush him off like a bit of dirt. There he lies . . . sprawling on the carpet . . . legs in the air . . . our snug little manager!

WIFE The Bank is not closed?

CASHIER Never, Wife. Prisons are never closed. The procession is endless. An eternal pilgrimage. Like sheep rushing into the slaughter house. A seething mass. No escape—none—unless you jump over their backs.

MOTHER Your coat's torn in the back.

CASHIER And look at my hat! Fit for a tramp.

SECOND DAUGHTER The lining's torn.

CASHIER Look in my pockets. Left . . . right! (FIRST DAUGHTER *and* SECOND DAUGHTER *pull out cuffs*)

CASHIER Inventory.

DAUGHTERS Your cuffs.

CASHIER But not the buttons. Hat—coat—torn—what can you expect—jumping over backs. They kick—they scratch—hurdles and fences—silence in the pen —order in the fold—equal rights for all. But one jump—don't hesitate—and you are out of the pen. One mighty deed and here I am! Behind me nothing and before me— What? (*Sits. Pause*)

(WIFE *stares at him*)

MOTHER (*Half whispering*) He's sick.

CASHIER (*To one of the* DAUGHTERS) Get my jacket. (*To the other*) My slippers. (*To the first*) My cap. (*To the other*) My pipe. (*All are brought*)

MOTHER You oughtn't to smoke, when you've already been—

WIFE (*Motioning her to be silent*) Shall I give you a light?

CASHIER (*In jacket, slippers, and embroidered skull-cap, with pipe in hand, seats himself comfortably at the table*) Light up!

WIFE (*Anxiously*) Does it draw?

CASHIER (*Looking into pipe*) I shall have to send it for a thorough cleaning. There must be some bits of stale tobacco in the stem. Sometimes way in . . . there are obstructions. It means I have to draw harder than is strictly necessary.

WIFE Do you want me to take it now?

CASHIER No, stay here. (*Blowing great smoke-clouds*) It will do. (*To* SECOND DAUGHTER) Play something.

(SECOND DAUGHTER *at a sign from her mother, sits at piano and plays*)

CASHIER What piece is that?

SECOND DAUGHTER The Overture to *Tannhäuser.*

CASHIER (*Nods approval. To* FIRST DAUGHTER) Sewing? Mending? Darning?

FIRST DAUGHTER Embroidering your slippers.

CASHIER Very practical. And you, Grandma?

MOTHER (*Feeling the universal dread*) I was just having forty winks.

CASHIER In peace and quiet.

MOTHER Yes, my life is quiet now.

CASHIER (*To* WIFE) And you, Wife?

WIFE I was going to fry the chops.

CASHIER (*Nodding*) Mmm—kitchen.

WIFE I'll fry yours now.

CASHIER (*Nodding as before*) Kitchen! (*Exit* WIFE)

CASHIER (*To* DAUGHTERS) Open the doors.

(DAUGHTERS *exit Right and Left, returning immediately*)

WIFE (*Enters, Pause*) Are you too warm in here? (*She returns to her task*)

CASHIER (*Looking around him*) Grandmother at the window. Daughters—at the table embroidering . . . playing Wagner. Wife busy in the kitchen. Four walls . . . family life. Cozy . . . all of us together. Mother —son . . . child under one roof. The magic of familiar things. It spins a web. Room with a table. Piano. Kitchen . . . daily bread. Coffee in the morning . . . chops at noon. Bedroom . . . beds . . . in . . . out. More magic. In the end flat on your back . . . white and stiff. Table pushed against the wall . . . in the center a pine coffin . . . screw lid . . . silver mountings . . . but detachable . . . a bit of crepe on the lamp . . . piano unopened for a year.

(SECOND DAUGHTER *stops playing, and runs sobbing into the kitchen*)

WIFE (*Enters*) She is practicing the new piece.

MOTHER Why doesn't she try something simpler?

(CASHIER *knocks out his pipe, begins putting on his hat and overcoat*)

WIFE Are you going to the Bank? Are you going out on business?

CASHIER Bank—business? No.

WIFE Then where are you going?

CASHIER That's the question, Wife. I've climbed down from windswept trees to find an answer. I came here first. Warm and cozy, this nest; I won't deny its good points; but it doesn't stand the final test. No! The answer is clear. This is not the end of my journey, just a signpost; the road leads further on. (*He is now fully dressed*)

WIFE (*Distraught*) Husband, how wild you look!

CASHIER Like a tramp, as I told you. Never mind. Better a ragged wayfarer than an empty road!

WIFE But, it's dinner-time.

MOTHER (*Half rising*) And you're going out, just before a meal?

CASHIER I smell the pork chops. Full stomach, drowsy wits.

(MOTHER *beats the air suddenly with her arms, and falls senseless*)

FIRST DAUGHTER Grandma.

SECOND DAUGHTER Grandma! Mother. (*Both fall on their knees, beside her.* WIFE *stands motionless*)

CASHIER (*Going to* MOTHER'S *chair*) For once in his life a man goes out before his meal—and that kills her. (*He brushes the daughters aside and regards the body*) Grief? Mourning? Overflowing tears? Can they make me forget. Are these bonds so closely woven that when they break there's nothing left to me in life but grief?—Mother—son! (*He pulls the roll of banknotes out of his pocket and weighs it in his hand, then shakes his head and puts the money away*) Grief does not paralyze . . . the eyes are dry and the mind goes on. There's no time to lose, if my day is to be well spent. (*He lays his well-worn purse on the table*) Use it. There's money honestly earned. That may be worth remembering. Use it. (*He goes out on the left*)

(WIFE *stands motionless.* DAUGHTERS *bend over the dead* MOTHER)

BANK MANAGER (*Coming from the Right*) Is your husband at home? Has your husband been there? I have to bring you the painful news that he has absconded. We missed him some hours ago; since then we have been through his books. The sum involved is sixty thousand marks, deposited by the Realty Construction Company. So far, I've refrained from making the matter public, in the hope that he would come to his senses and return. This is my last attempt. You see I've made a personal call. Has your husband been here? (*He looks around him, and observes jacket, pipe, etc.*) It looks as though . . . (*His glance lights upon the group at the window. He nods*) I see! In that case . . . (*He shrugs his shoulders, puts on his hat*) I can only express my personal sympathy; be assured of that. The rest must take its course. (*Exit* MANAGER)

DAUGHTERS (*Coming to* WIFE) Mother—

WIFE (*Savagely*) Don't screech into my ears! Who are you? What do you want? Brats—monkeys. What have you to do with me? (*Breaking down*) My husband has left me.

(DAUGHTERS *stand shyly, holding hands*)

*Curtain*

## Scene Five

SCENE *The steward's box at a stadium during a bicycle race. Jewish* GENTLEMEN, *stewards, come and go. They are all alike; little animated figures in dinner jackets, with silk hats tilted back and binoculars slung in leather cases. Whistling, catcalls and a restless hum from the crowded tiers of spectators unseen, off right. Music. All the action takes place on the platform.*

FIRST GENTLEMAN (*Entering*) Is everything ready?

SECOND GENTLEMAN See for yourself.

FIRST GENTLEMAN (*Looking through glasses*) The palms—

SECOND GENTLEMAN What's the matter with the palms?

FIRST GENTLEMAN I thought as much.

SECOND GENTLEMAN But what's wrong with them?

FIRST GENTLEMAN Who arranged them like that?

THIRD GENTLEMAN Crazy.

SECOND GENTLEMAN Upon my soul, you're right!

FIRST GENTLEMAN Was nobody responsible for arranging them?

THIRD GENTLEMAN Ridiculous. Simply ridiculous.

FIRST GENTLEMAN Whoever it was, he's as blind as a bat!

THIRD GENTLEMAN Or fast asleep.

SECOND GENTLEMAN Asleep. But this is only the fourth night of the races.

FIRST GENTLEMAN The palm-tubs must be pushed on one side.

SECOND GENTLEMAN Will you see to it?

FIRST GENTLEMAN Right against the wall. There must be a clear view of the whole track. (*Exit*)

THIRD GENTLEMAN And of the royal box.

SECOND GENTLEMAN I'll go with you. (*Exit*)

(FOURTH GENTLEMAN *enters, fires a pistol-shot and withdraws.* FIFTH GENTLEMAN *enters with a red-lacquered megaphone*)

THIRD GENTLEMAN How much is the prize?

FIFTH GENTLEMAN Eighty marks. Fifty to the winner, thirty to the second.

FIRST GENTLEMAN (*Re-entering*) Three times round, no more. We're tiring them out.

FOURTH GENTLEMAN (*Through megaphone*) A prize is offered of eighty marks. The winner to receive fifty marks, the second thirty marks. (*Applause*)

(SECOND *and* THIRD GENTLEMEN *return, one carrying a flag*)

FIRST GENTLEMAN We can start them now.

SECOND GENTLEMAN Not yet. No. 7 is shifting.

FIRST GENTLEMAN Off!

(SECOND GENTLEMAN *lowers his flag. The race begins. Rising and falling volumes of applause, with silent intervals*)

THIRD GENTLEMAN The little fellows must win once in a while.

FOURTH GENTLEMAN It's a good thing the favorites are holding back.

FIFTH GENTLEMAN They'll have to work hard enough before the night's over.

THIRD GENTLEMAN The riders are terribly excited.

FOURTH GENTLEMAN And no wonder.

FIFTH GENTLEMAN Depend upon it, the championship will be settled tonight.

THIRD GENTLEMAN The Americans are still fresh.

FIFTH GENTLEMAN Our lads will make them hustle.

FOURTH GENTLEMAN Let's hope his Royal Highness will be pleased with the victory.

FIRST GENTLEMAN (*Looking through glasses*) The box is still empty. (*Outburst of applause*)

THIRD GENTLEMAN The result!

FOURTH GENTLEMAN Prizes in cash—fifty marks for No. 11, thirty marks for No. 4.

(SECOND GENTLEMAN *enters with* CASHIER. *The latter is in evening clothes, with silk hat, patent shoes, gloves, cloak, his beard trimmed, his hair carefully brushed*)

CASHIER Tell me what is this all about?

SECOND GENTLEMAN I'll introduce you to the stewards.

CASHIER My name doesn't matter.

SECOND GENTLEMAN But you ought to meet the management.

CASHIER I prefer to remain incognito.

SECOND GENTLEMAN But you seem interested in these races.

CASHIER I haven't the slightest idea what it's all about. What are they doing down there? I can see a round track with a bright moving line, like a snake. Now one comes in, another falls out. Why is that?

SECOND GENTLEMAN They ride in pairs. While one partner is pedaling—

CASHIER The other blockhead sleeps?

SECOND GENTLEMAN He's being massaged.

CASHIER And you call that a relay race?

SECOND GENTLEMAN Certainly.

CASHIER You might as well call it a relay rest.

FIRST GENTLEMAN (*Approaching*) Ahem! The enclosure is reserved for the management.

SECOND GENTLEMAN This gentleman offers a prize of a thousand marks.

FIRST GENTLEMAN (*Change of tone*) Allow me to introduce myself.

CASHIER On no account.

SECOND GENTLEMAN The gentleman wishes to preserve his incognito.

CASHIER Impenetrably.

SECOND GENTLEMAN I was just explaining the sport to him.

CASHIER Yes, don't you find it funny?

FIRST GENTLEMAN How do you mean?

CASHIER Why, this relay rest.

FOURTH GENTLEMAN A prize of a thousand marks! For how many laps?

CASHIER As many as you please.

FOURTH GENTLEMAN How much shall we allot to the winner?

CASHIER That's your affair.

FOURTH GENTLEMAN Eight hundred and two hundred. (*Through megaphone*) An anonymous gentleman offers the following prizes for an open race of ten laps: eight hundred marks to the winner; two hundred marks to the second; one thousand marks in all. (*Loud applause*)

SECONG GENTLEMAN But tell me, if you're not really interested in this sort of thing, why do you offer such a big prize?

CASHIER Because it works like magic.

SECOND GENTLEMAN On the pace of the riders, you mean?

CASHIER Rubbish.

THIRD GENTLEMAN (*Entering*) Are you the gentleman who is offering a thousand marks?

CASHIER In gold.

SECOND GENTLEMAN That would take too long to count . . .

CASHIER Watch me. (*He pulls out the money, moistens his finger and counts rapidly*) That makes less to carry.

SECOND GENTLEMAN I see you're an expert.

CASHIER A mere detail, sir. (*Handing him the money*) Accept payment.

SECOND GENTLEMAN Received with thanks.

FIFTH GENTLEMAN (*Approaching*) Where is the gentleman? Allow me to introduce—

CASHIER Certainly not!

THIRD GENTLEMAN (*With flag*) I shall give the start. (*General movement from the stand*)

FIFTH GENTLEMAN Now we shall see a tussle for the championship.

THIRD GENTLEMAN (*Joining group*) All the cracks are in the race.

FOURTH GENTLEMAN Off! (*Outburst of applause*)

CASHIER (*Taking* FIRST *and* SECOND GENTLEMEN *by the collar and turning them around*) Now I'll answer your question for you. Look up!

SECOND GENTLEMAN But you must keep your eye on the track, and watch how the race goes.

CASHIER Childish, this sport. One rider must win because the other loses. Look up, I say! It's there, among the crowd, that the magic works. Look at them—three tiers—one above the other—packed like sardines—excitement rages. Down there in the boxes the better classes are still controlling themselves. They're only looking on but, oh, what looks—wide-eyed—staring. One row higher, their bodies sway and vibrate. You hear exclamations. Way up—no restraint! Fanatic—yells—bellowing nakedness—a gallery of passion. Just look at that group! Five times entwined; five heads dancing on one shoulder, five pairs of arms beating time across one howling breast! At the head of this monster is a single man. He's being crushed . . . mangled . . . thrust over the railing. His hat, crumpled, falls through the murky atmosphere . . . flutters into the middle balcony, lights upon a lady's bosom. There it rests daintily . . . so daintily! She'll never notice the hat; she'll go to bed with it; year in, year in, year out, she'll carry this hat upon her breast!

(*The applause swells*)

FIRST GENTLEMAN The Dutchman is putting on speed.

CASHIER The second balcony joins in. An alliance has been made; the hat has done the trick. The lady crushes it against the railing. Pretty lady, your bosom will show the marks of this! There's no help for it. It's foolish to struggle. You are pushed to the wall and you've got to give yourself, just as you are, without a murmur.

SECOND GENTLEMAN Do you know the lady?

CASHIER Look! Someone is being pushed out over the railing. He swings free. He loses his hold, he drops—he sails down into the boxes. What has become of him? Vanished! Swallowed, stifled, absorbed! A raindrop in a maelstrom!

FIRST GENTLEMAN The fellow from Hamburg is making up ground.

CASHIER The boxes are frantic. The falling man has set up contact. Restraint can go to the devil! Dinner jackets quiver. Shirt fronts begin to split. Studs fly in all directions. Lips are parted, jaws are rattling. Above and below—all distinctions are lost. One universal yell from every tier. Pandemonium. Climax.

SECOND GENTLEMAN (*Turning*) He wins! He wins! The German wins! What do you say to that?

CASHIER Stuff and nonsense.

SECOND GENTLEMAN A marvelous spurt!

CASHIER Marvelous trash!

FIRST GENTLEMAN (*About to leave*) We'll just make certain—

CASHIER (*Holding him back*) Have you any doubts about it?

SECOND GENTLEMAN The German was leading, but—

CASHIER Never mind that, if you please. (*Pointing to the audience*) Up there you have the staggering fact. Watch the supreme effort, the lazy dizzy height of accomplishment. From boxes to gallery one seething flux, dissolving the individual, recreating-passion! Differences melt away, veils are torn away; passion rules! The trumpets blare and the walls come tumbling down. No restraint, no modesty, no motherhood, no childhood—nothing but passion! There's the real thing. That's worth the search. That justifies the price!

THIRD GENTLEMAN (*Entering*) The ambulance column is working splendidly.

CASHIER Is the man hurt who fell?

THIRD GENTLEMAN Crushed flat.

CASHIER When life is at fever heat some must die.

FOURTH GENTLEMAN (*With megaphone*) Result; eight hundred marks won by No. 2; two hundred marks won by No. 1 (*Loud applause*)

FIFTH GENTLEMAN The men are tired out.

SECOND GENTLEMAN You could see the pace dropping.

THIRD GENTLEMAN They need a rest.

CASHIER I've another prize to offer.

FIRST GENTLEMAN Presently, sir.

CASHIER No interruptions, no delays.

SECOND GENTLEMAN We must give them a chance to breathe.

CASHIER Bah! Don't talk to me of those fools! Look at the public, bursting with excitement. This power mustn't be wasted. We'll feed the flames; you shall see them leap into the sky. I offer fifty thousand marks.

SECOND GENTLEMAN Do you mean it?

THIRD GENTLEMAN How much did you say?

CASHIER Fifty thousand. Everything.

THIRD GENTLEMAN It's an unheard of sum—

CASHIER The effects will be unheard of. Warn your ambulance men on every floor.

FIRST GENTLEMAN We accept your offer. The contest shall begin when the box is occupied.

SECOND GENTLEMAN Capital idea!

THIRD GENTLEMAN Excellent!

FOURTH GENTLEMAN This is a profitable visitor.

FIFTH GENTLEMAN (*Digging him in the rib*) A paying guest.

CASHIER (*To* FIRST GENTLEMAN) What do you mean —when the box is occupied?

FIRST GENTLEMAN We'll talk over the conditions in the committee room. I suggest thirty thousand to the winner; fifteen thousand to the second; five thousand to the third.

SECOND GENTLEMAN Exactly.

THIRD GENTLEMAN (*Gloomily*) Downright waste, I call it.

FIFTH GENTLEMAN The sport's ruined for good and all.

FIRST GENTLEMAN (*Turning*) As soon as the box is occupied.

(*All go out, leaving* CASHIER *alone. Enter* SALVATION LASS)

SALVATION LASS The War Cry! Ten pfennigs, sir.

CASHIER Presently, presently.

SALVATION LASS The War Cry, sir.

CASHIER What trash are you trying to sell?

SALVATION LASS The War Cry, sir.

CASHIER You're too late. The battle's in full swing.

SALVATION LASS (*Shaking tin box*) Ten pfennigs, sir.

CASHIER So you expect to start a war for ten pfennigs?

SALVATION LASS Ten pfennigs, sir.

CASHIER I'm paying an indemnity of fifty thousand marks.

SALVATION LASS Ten pfennigs.

CASHIER Yours is a wretched scuffle. I only subscribe to pitched battles.

SALVATION LASS Ten pfennigs.

CASHIER I carry only gold.

SALVATION LASS Ten pfennigs.

CASHIER Gold—

SALVATION LASS Ten—

CASHIER (*Seizing megaphone, bellows at her through it*) Gold! Gold! Gold!

(SALVATION LASS *goes out. Many* GENTLEMEN *enter*)

FOURTH GENTLEMAN Would you care to announce your offer yourself?

CASHIER No, I'm a spectator. You stun them with the fifty thousand. (*Handing him the megaphone*)

FOURTH GENTLEMAN (*Through the megaphone*) A new prize is offered by the same anonymous gentleman. (*Cries of "Bravo!"*) The total sum is fifty thousand marks. Five thousand marks to the third, fifteen thousand to the second. The winner to receive thirty thousand marks. (*Ecstasy*)

CASHIER (*Stands apart, nodding his head*) There we have it, the pinnacle. The summit. The climbing hope fulfilled. The roar of a spring gale. The breaking wave of a human tide. All bonds are burst. Up with the veils—down with the shams! Humanity—free humanity, high and low, untroubled by class, unfettered by manners. Unclean, but free. That's a reward for my impudence. (*Pulling out a bundle of notes*) I can pay with a good heart! (*Sudden silence. The* GENTLEMEN *have taken off their silk hats and stand with bowed heads*)

FOURTH GENTLEMAN (*Coming to* CASHIER) If you'll hand me the money, we can have the race for your prize immediately.

CASHIER What's the meaning of this?

FOURTH GENTLEMAN Of what, my dear sir?

CASHIER Oh this sudden, unnatural silence.

FOURTH GENTLEMAN Unnatural? Not at all. His Royal Highness has just entered his box.

CASHIER Highness . . . the royal box . . . the house full.

FOURTH GENTLEMAN Your generous patronage comes at the most opportune moment.

CASHIER Thank you! I don't intend to waste my money.

FOURTH GENTLEMAN What do you mean?

CASHIER I find the sum too large . . . as a subscription to the society of backbenders!

FOURTH GENTLEMAN But pray explain . . .

CASHIER This fire that was raging a moment ago has been put out by the boot of his Highness. You take me for crazy, if you think I will throw one single penny under the snouts of these groveling dogs, these crooked lackeys! A kick where the bend is greatest, that's the prize they'll get from me.

FOURTH GENTLEMAN But the prize has been announced. His Royal Highness is in his box. The audience is showing a proper respect. What do you mean?

CASHIER If you don't understand my words, let deeds speak for me. (*With violent blow he crushes the other's silk hat down upon his shoulders. Exit.* FOURTH GENTLEMAN *rushes after him, but is restrained by the others*)

*Curtain*

## Scene Six

SCENE *Private supper room in a cabaret. Subdued dance music. A* WAITER *opens the door. The* CASHIER *enters; evening clothes, coat, silk muffler, gold-headed bamboo cane.*

WAITER Will this room suit you, sir?

CASHIER It'll do.

(WAITER *takes coat, etc.* CASHIER *turns his back and looks into a mirror*)

WAITER How many places shall I lay, sir?

CASHIER Twenty-four. I'm expecting my grandma, my mother, my wife, and several aunts. The supper is to celebrate my daughter's confirmation. (*The* WAITER *stares at him. To the other's reflection in the mirror*) Ass! Two! What are these private rooms for?

WAITER What brand would you prefer?

CASHIER Leave that to me, my oily friend. I shall know which flower to pluck in the ballroom . . . round or slender, a bud or a full-blown rose. I shall not require your invaluable services. No doubt they are invaluable . . . or have you a fixed tariff for that too?

WAITER What brand of champagne, if you please?

CASHIER Ahem! Grand Marnier.

WAITER That's a liqueur, sir.

CASHIER Then I leave it to you.

WAITER Two bottles of Pommery—extra dry. (*Producing menu card*) And for supper?

CASHIER Pinnacles!

WAITER *Oeufs pochés Bergère? Poulet grillé? Steak de veau truffé? Parfait de foie gras en croûte? Salade coeur de laitue?* [1]

CASHIER Pinnacles, pinnacles from soup to dessert.

WAITER Pardon?

CASHIER (*Tapping him on the nose*) A pinnacle is the point of perfection . . . the summit of a work of art. So it must be with your pots and pans. The last word in delicacy. The menu of menus. Fit to garnish great events. It's your affair, my friend. I'm not the cook.

WAITER (*Sets a large menu-card on the table*) It will be served in twenty minutes. (*He rearranges glasses, etc. Heads with silken masks peep through the doorway*)

CASHIER (*Sees them in the mirror. Shaking a warning finger at them*) Wait, my moths! Presently I shall have you in the lamplight!

(*The* MASKS *vanish, giggling.* WAITER *hangs a notice—"Reserved"—on the outside of the door, then withdraws and closes it behind him*)

CASHIER (*Pushes back his silk hat, takes out a gold cigarette case, strikes a match, sings*) "Tor . . . ea . . . dor, Tor . . . ea . . . dor . . ." Queer, how this stuff comes to your lips. A man's mind must be cram full of it . . . cram full. Everything. Toreador —Carmen—Caruso. I read all this somewhere . . . it stuck in my head. There it lies, piled up like a snowdrift. At this very moment I could give a history of the Bagdad railway. And how the Crown Prince of Roumania married the Czar's second daughter, Tatjana. Well, well, let them marry. The people need princes. (*Sings*) "Tat . . . tat . . . ja . . . na, Tat . . . ja . . . na . . ." (*Twirling his cane, exit*)

(WAITER *enters with bottles on ice. Uncorks, pours out wine. Exit*)

CASHIER (*Re-enters, driving before him a female* MASK *in a harlequin's red-and-yellow-quartered costume*) Fly, moth! Fly, moth!

FIRST MASK (*Running round the table*) Fizz! (*She drinks both of the filled glasses*) Fizz!

CASHIER (*Pouring out more wine*) Liquid powder. Load your painted body.

FIRST MASK (*Drinking*) Fizz!

CASHIER Battery mounted, action front.

FIRST MASK Fizz!

CASHIER (*Putting aside the bottles*) Loaded (*Coming to her*) Ready to fire. (*The* FIRST MASK *leans drunkenly towards him. Shaking her limp arm*) Look brighter, moth. (FIRST MASK *does not respond*) You're dizzy, my bright butterfly. You've been licking the prickly yellow honey. Open your wings, enfold me, cover me up. I'm an outlaw; give me a hiding-place; open your wings.

[1] Poached eggs, fried chicken, veal steak, liver pasty, hearts of lettuce.

FIRST MASK (*With a hiccough*) Fizz!

CASHIER No, my bird of paradise. You have your full load.

FIRST MASK Fizz! (*Sinking onto sofa*)

CASHIER Not another drop, or you'll be tipsy. Then what would you be worth?

FIRST MASK Fizz!

CASHIER How much are you worth? What have you to offer? (*Bending over her*)

FIRST MASK Fizz!

CASHIER I gave you that, but what can you give me? (FIRST MASK *falls asleep*) Ha! You'd sleep here, would you? Little imp! But I've no time for the joke; I find it too tedious. (*He rises, fills a glass of wine and throws it in her face*) Good morning to you! The cocks are crowing!

FIRST MASK (*Leaping to her feet*) Swine!

CASHIER A quaint name. Unfortunately I'm traveling incognito, and can't respond to the introduction. And so, my mask of the well-known snoutish family . . . get off my sofa!

FIRST MASK I'll make you pay for this!

CASHIER I've paid already. It was cheap at the price. (*Exit* FIRST MASK. CASHIER *drinks champagne; exits, singing.* WAITER *enters with caviar; collects empty glasses; exits.* CASHIER *enters with two black* MASKS)

SECOND MASK (*Slamming the door*) Reserved!

THIRD MASK (*At the table*) Caviar!

SECOND MASK (*Running to her*) Caviar?

CASHIER Black as your masks. Black as yourselves. Eat it up; gobble it, cram it down your throats. (*Seating himself between them*) Speak caviar. Sing wine. I've no use for your brains. (*He pours out champagne and fills their plates*) Not one word shall you utter. Not a syllable, not an exclamation. You shall be dumb as the fish that strewed this black spawn upon the Black Sea. You can giggle, you can bleat, but don't talk to me. You've nothing to say. You've nothing to shed but your finery . . . Be careful! I've settled one already! (MASKS *look at one another, sniggering. Taking* SECOND MASK *by the arm*) What color are your eyes? Green . . . yellow? (*Turning to* THIRD MASK) And yours? Blue . . . red? A play of glances through the eyeholes. That promises well. Come, I'll offer a beauty prize! (MASKS *laugh. To* SECOND MASK) You're the pretty one. You struggle hard, but wait! In a moment I'll tear down your curtain and look at the show (SECOND MASK *breaks away from him. To* THIRD MASK) You have something to hide. Modesty's your lure. You dropped in here by chance. You were looking for adventure. Well, here's your adventurer. Off with your mask. (THIRD MASK *slips away from him*) This is the goal? I sit here trembling. You've stirred my blood. Now let me pay. (*He pulls out a bundle of notes and divides it between them*) Pretty mask, this for your beauty. Pretty mask, this for your beauty. (*Holding his hand before his eyes*) One—two—three! (MASKS *lift their dominoes. Looking at them, he laughs hoarsely*) Cover them—cover them up! (*He runs round the table*) Monsters—horrors! Out with you this minute—this very second,—or I'll . . . (*He lifts his cane*)

SECOND MASK But you told us—

THIRD MASK You wanted us—

CASHIER I wanted to get at you! (*The* MASKS *run out. Shaking himself, he drinks champagne*) Sluts! (*Exits, humming*)

(WAITER *enters with fresh bottles, and exit*)

CASHIER (*Kicking the door open, entering with* FOURTH MASK, *a Pierrette in a domino cloak reaching to her shoes. He leaves her standing in the middle of the room, and throws himself in chair*) Dance! (*The* FOURTH MASK *stands still*) Dance! Spin your bag of bones. Dance, dance! Brains are nothing. Beauty doesn't count. Dancing's the thing—twisting, whirling! Dance, dance, dance! (FOURTH MASK *comes halting to the mirror. Waving her away*) No interruption, no delay. Dance! (FOURTH MASK *stands motionless*) Why don't you leap in the air? Have you never heard of Dervishes? Dancing-men. Men while they dance, corpses when they cease. Death and dancing—sign posts on the road of life. And between them— (*The* SALVATION LASS *enters*) Oh, Halleluja!

SALVATION LASS The War Cry!

CASHIER I know. Ten pfennigs. (SALVATION LASS *holds out her box*) When do you expect me to jump into your box?

SALVATION LASS The War Cry!

CASHIER I suppose you do expect it?

SALVATION LASS Ten pfennigs.

CASHIER When will it be?

SALVATION LASS Ten pfennigs.

CASHIER So you mean to hang on to my coattails, do you? (SALVATION LASS *shakes her box*) I'll shake you off! (SALVATION LASS *shakes box. To* MASK) Dance!

SALVATION LASS Oh! (*Exit*)

(FOURTH MASK *comes to table*)

CASHIER Why were you sitting in a corner of the ballroom, instead of dancing in the middle of the floor? That made me look at you. All the others went whirling by, and you were motionless. Why do you wear a long cloak, when they are dressed like slender boys?

FOURTH MASK I don't dance.

CASHIER You don't dance like the others.

FOURTH MASK I can't dance.

CASHIER Not to music, perhaps; not keeping time. You're right; that's too slow. But you can do other dances. You hide something under your cloak—your own particular spring, not to be cramped by step and measure! You have a quicker movement—a nimbler leap. (*Pushing everything off the table*) Here's your stage. Jump onto it. A boundless riot in this narrow circle. Jump now. One bound from the carpet. One effortless leap—on the springs that are rooted in your joints. Jump. Put spurs to your heels. Arch your knees. Let your dress float free over the dancing limbs!

FOURTH MASK (*Sits on the edge of the table*) I can't dance.

CASHIER You arouse my curiosity. Do you know what

price I can pay? (*Showing her a roll of bank notes*) All that!

FOURTH MASK (*Takes his hand and passes it down her leg*) You see—I can't.

CASHIER (*Leaping to his feet*) A wooden leg! (*He seizes a champagne cooler and upsets it over her*) I'll water it for you! We'll make the buds sprout!

FOURTH MASK I'll teach you a lesson.

CASHIER I'm out to learn!

FOURTH MASK Just wait! (*Exit*)

(CASHIER *puts a bank note on the table, takes cloak and stick. Exit.* GUESTS *in evening dress enter*)

FIRST GUEST Where is the fellow?

SECOND GUEST Let's have a closer look at him.

FIRST GUEST A blackguard who entices away our girls—

SECOND GUEST Stuffs them with caviar—

THIRD GUEST Drenches them in champagne—

SECOND GUEST And then insults them!

FIRST GUEST We'll find out his price—

SECOND GUEST Where is he?

THIRD GUEST Given us the slip!

FIRST GUEST He smelt trouble!

SECOND GUEST The place was too hot for him.

THIRD GUEST (*Finding the bank note*) A thousand!

SECOND GUEST Good God!

FIRST GUEST He must stink of money.

SECOND GUEST That's to pay the bill.

THIRD GUEST He's bolted. We'll do a vanishing trick too. (*He pockets the money*)

FIRST GUEST That's the indemnity for our girls.

SECOND GUEST Now let's give them the slip.

THIRD GUEST They're all drunk.

FIRST GUEST They'll only dirty our shirt-fronts for us.

SECOND GUEST Let's go to a brothel for a week.

THIRD GUEST Bravo! While the money lasts! Look out, here comes the waiter! (WAITER *entering with full tray, halts dismayed*)

FIRST GUEST Are you looking for anyone?

SECOND GUEST You might find him under the table. (*Laughter*)

WAITER (*In an outburst*) The champagne—the supper—the private room—nothing paid for. Five bottles of Pommery, two portions of caviar, two special suppers—I have to stand for everything. I've a wife and children. I've been four months out of a job, on account of a weak chest. You won't see me ruined, gentlemen?

THIRD GUEST What has your chest to do with us? We all have wives and children.

SECOND GUEST Have we done you out of anything? What are you talking about?

FIRST GUEST What sort of a place is this? Where are we? It's a common den of swindlers. And you lure people into a place like this? We're respectable people who pay for their drinks. Eh! What! Eh!

THIRD GUEST (*After changing the doorkey to the outer side*) Look under the table, there. Now we've paid too! (*He gives the* WAITER, *who turns round, a push which sends him sprawling.* WAITER *staggers, falls.* GENTLEMEN *exeunt*)

WAITER (*Rises, runs to the door, finds it locked. Beating his fists on the panels*) Let me out! Let me out! You needn't pay me! I'm going—into the river!

*Curtain*

## Scene Seven

SCENE *Salvation Army hall, seen in depth. The background is formed by a black curtain. In front of this stands the low platform on which is the penitent form.*

*In the body of the hall, the benches are crowded. A great hanging lamp, with a tangle of wires for electric lighting, is above the audience. In the foreground on the left, is the entrance. Music: "Jesus Lover of My Soul," played on an organ, and sung by the audience. From a corner, applause and laughter centering in one man.* SALVATION LASS *goes to this corner and sits near the disturber. She takes his hand in hers and whispers to him.*

VOICE (*From the other side*) Move up closer. Be careful, Bill! Ha, ha! Move there!

(SALVATION LASS, *goes to the speaker, a young workman*)

WORKMAN What are you after?

SALVATION LASS (*Looks at him, shaking her head gravely*) Merriment.

OFFICER (*Woman of thirty, coming to the front of the platform*) I've a question to ask you all.

SOME (*Cry*) Hush! (*Or whistle for silence*)

OTHERS Speech. None of your lip! . . . Music! . . .

VOICES Begin! Stop!

OFFICER Tell me . . . why are you sitting crowded there?

VOICE Why not?

OFFICER You're packed like herrings in a barrel. You're fighting for places . . . shoving one another off the forms. Yet one bench stands empty.

VOICE Nothing doing!

OFFICER Why do you sit squeezing and crowding there? Can't you see it's a nasty habit? Who knows his next-door neighbor? You rub shoulders with him, you press your knees against his, and for all you know he may be rotting. You look into his face—and perhaps his mind is full of murderous thoughts. I know there are sick men and criminals in this hall. So I give you warning! Mind your next-door neighbor! Beware of him! Those benches groan under sick men and criminals!

WOMAN'S VOICE Next to me?

SECOND VOICE Or me?

OFFICER I give you this word of advice; steer clear of your neighbor! In this asphalt city, disease and crime are everywhere. Which of you is without a scab? Your skin may be smooth and white, but your looks give you away. You have no eyes to see, but your eyes are wide open to betray you. You haven't escaped the great plague; the germs are too powerful. You've been sitting too long near bad neighbors. Come up here, come away from those benches, if you would not be as your neighbors are in this city of asphalt. This is the last warning. Repent. Repent. Come up here, come to the penitent form. Come to the penitent form, come to the penitent form.

(*Music "Jesus Lover of My Soul."* SALVATION LASS *leads in* CASHIER, *in evening dress, who arouses some notice.* SALVATION LASS *finds* CASHIER *a place among the crowd, stands next to him and explains the procedure.* CASHIER *looks around him amused. Music ceases, ironical applause*)

OFFICER (*Coming forward again*) One of our comrades will tell you how he found his way to the penitent bench.

(FIRST SOLDIER *of Salvation Army, a young man, steps onto the platform*)

VOICE So that's the mug! (*Some laughter*)

FIRST SOLDIER I want to tell you of my sin. I led a life without giving a thought to my soul. I cared only for my body. I built up my body like a strong wall; the soul was quite hidden behind it. I sought for glory with my body, and made broader the shadow in which my soul withered away. My sin was sport. I practiced it without a moment's pause; vain of the quickness of my feet on the pedals; and the ring of the applause among the spectators. I sent out many a challenge; I won many a prize. My name was printed on every billboard; my picture was in all the papers. I was in the running for the world championship . . . At last my soul spoke to me. Its patience was ended. I met with an accident. The injury was not fatal. My soul wanted to leave me time for repentance. My soul left me strength enough to rise from those benches where you sit, and to climb up here to the penitent form. There my soul could speak to me in peace. What it told me I can't tell you now. It's all too wonderful, and my words are too weak to describe it. You must come yourselves, and hear the voice speak within you! (*He steps in*)

(*A Man laughs obscenely*)

SEVERAL (*Cry*) Hush!

SALVATION LASS (*To* CASHIER, *in a low voice*) Do you hear him?

CASHIER Let me alone. (*Music plays and ceases*)

OFFICER (*Coming forward*) You've heard our comrade's testimony. Can you win anything nobler than your own? And it's quite easy, for the soul is there within you. You've only to give it peace . . . once, just once. The soul wants to sit with you for one quiet hour. Its favorite seat is on this bench. There must be one among you who sinned like our comrade here. Our comrade will help him. The way has been opened up. So come. Come to the penitent bench. Come to the penitent bench. Come to the penitent bench. (*Silence*)

(*The* FIRST PENITENT, *a young man of powerful build, with one arm in a sling, rises in a corner of the hall and makes his way through the crowd, smiling nervously. He mounts the platform. A Man laughs obscenely*)

ANOTHER (*Indignantly*) Where is that dirty lout!

(*The Man rises abashed, and makes his way toward the door*)

OTHERS That's the fellow!

(SALVATION LASS, *hurries to him and leads him back to the place*)

VOICE (*Facetiously*) Oh, let me go, Angelina!

SEVERAL OTHERS Bravo!

FIRST PENITENT (*On the platform*) In this city of asphalt there's a hall. Inside the hall is a cycle-track. This was my sin. I was a rider too. I was a rider in the relay races this week. On the second night I met with a collision. I was thrown; my arm was broken. The races are hurrying on, but I am at rest. All my life I have been riding without a thought. Now! I want to think of everything. (*Loudly*) I want to think of my sins at the penitent bench. (*Led by a* SOLDIER, *he sinks onto the bench;* SOLDIER *remains at his side*)

OFFICER A soul has been won! (*Music plays and ceases*)

SALVATION LASS (*To* CASHIER) Do you see him?

CASHIER My affair. My affair.

SALVATION LASS What are you muttering?

CASHIER The relay races.

SALVATION LASS Are you ready?

CASHIER Hold your tongue.

OFFICER (*Stepping forward*) Another comrade will testify.

(*A Man hisses*)

OTHERS Be quiet there!

SECOND SOLDIER (*Girl mounts the platform*) Whose sin is my sin? I'll tell you of my sin without shame. I had a wretched home, if you could call it a home. The man, a drunkard, was not my father. The woman—who was my mother—went with smart gentlemen. She gave me all the money I wanted; her bully gave me all the blows—I didn't want. (*Laughter*) No one thought of me; least of all did I think of myself. So I became a lost woman. I was blind in those days. I couldn't see that the miserable life at home was only meant to make me think of my soul and dedicate myself to its salvation. One night I learned the truth. I had a gentleman with me, and he asked me to darken the room. I turned out the gas, though I wasn't used to such ways. Presently I understood why he had asked me; for, I realized that I had with me only the trunk of a man whose legs had been cut off. He didn't want me to know that he had wooden legs, and that he had taken them off in the dark. Then horror took hold of me, and wouldn't let me go. I began to hate my body; it was only my soul that I could love. And now this soul of mine is my delight. It's so perfect, so beautiful; it's the bonniest thing I know. I know too much of it to tell you here. If you ask your souls, they'll tell you all—all! (*She steps down. Silence*)

OFFICER (*Coming forward*) You've heard our sister testify. Her soul offered itself to her, and she did not refuse. Now she tells you her story with joyful lips. Isn't a soul offering itself now, at this moment, to one of you? Let it come closer. Let it speak; here on this bench it will be undisturbed. Come to the penitent bench. Come to the penitent bench. (*Movement in the hall. Some turn round*)

SECOND PENITENT (*Elderly prostitute, begins to speak as she comes forward*) What do you think of me, ladies and gentlemen? I was just tired to death of streetwalking, and dropped in by chance for a rest. I'm not shy—oh, dear no! I don't know this hall; it's my first time here. Just dropped in by chance, as you might say. (*Speaking from the platform*) But you make a great mistake, ladies and gentlemen, if you think I should wait to be asked a second time! Not this child, thank you—oh, dear no! Take a good look at me, from tip to toe; it's your last chance; enjoy the treat while you can! It's quite all right; never mind me; I'm not a bit shy; look me up and down. Thank you, my soul's not for disposal. I've never sold that. You could offer me as much as you pleased, but my soul was always my own. I'm obliged to you for your compliments, ladies and gentlemen. You won't run up against me in the streets again. I've got no time to spare for you. My soul leaves me no peace. (*A* SOLDIER *leads her to the penitent form*)

OFFICER A soul has been won! (*Music. Jubilation of the* SOLDIERS. *Music ceases*)

SALVATION LASS (*To* CASHIER) Do you hear all?

CASHIER That's my affair. My affair.

SALVATION LASS What are you muttering about?

CASHIER The wooden leg. The wooden leg.

SALVATION LASS Are you ready?

CASHIER Not yet. Not yet.

A MAN (*Standing upright in the middle of the hall*) Tell me my sin. I want to hear my sin!

OFFICER (*Coming forward*) Our comrade here will tell you.

VOICES (*Excitedly*) Sit down! Keep quiet; give him a chance.

THIRD SOLDIER (*Elderly man*) Let me tell you my story. It's an everyday story.

VOICE Then why tell it?

THIRD SOLDIER That's how it came to be my sin. I had a snug home, a contented family, a comfortable job. Everything was just—everyday. In the evening, when I sat smoking my pipe at the table, under the lamp, with my wife and children round about me, I felt satisfied enough. I never felt the need of a change. Yet the change came, I forget what started it; perhaps I never knew. The soul knocks quietly at your door. It knows the right hour and uses it.

SECOND PENITENT Halleluja.

THIRD SOLDIER However that might be, I couldn't pass the warning by. I stood out at first in a sluggish sort of way, but the soul was stronger. More and more I felt its power. All my born days I'd been set upon comfort; now I knew that nothing could satisfy me fully but the soul.

SOLDIERS Halleluja.

THIRD SOLDIER I don't look for comfort any longer at the table under the lamp, with a pipe in my mouth; I find it here alone at the penitent bench. That's my everyday story. (*He stands back. Music plays and is interrupted by* THIRD PENITENT)

THIRD PENITENT (*Elbowing his way up*) My sin! My sin! (*From the platform*) I'm the father of a family!

VOICE Congratulations!

THIRD PENITENT I have two daughters. I have a wife. My mother is still with us. We live in four rooms. It's quite snug and cozy in our house. One of my daughters plays the piano, the other does embroideries. My wife cooks. My old mother waters the geraniums in the window-boxes. It's cozy in our house. Coziness itself. It's fine in our house. It's grand . . . first-rate . . . It's a model—a pattern of a home. (*With a change of voice*) Our house is loathsome . . . horrible . . . horrible . . . mean . . . paltry through and through. It stinks of paltriness in every room; with the piano-playing, the cooking, the embroidery, the watering-pots. (*Breaking out*) I have a soul! I have a soul! I have a soul! (*He stumbles to the penitent bench*)

SOLDIERS Halleluja.

OFFICER A soul has been won!

SALVATION LASS (*To* CASHIER) Do you see him?

CASHIER My daughters. My wife. My mother.

SALVATION LASS What do you keep mumbling?

CASHIER My affair. My affair.

SALVATION LASS Are you ready?

CASHIER Not yet. Not yet.

(*Jubilant music. Loud uproar in the hall*)

MAN (*Standing upright, and stretching out hands*) What's my sin? I want to know my sin? Tell me my sin.

OFFICER (*Coming forward*) Our comrade will tell you. (*Deep silence*)

FOURTH SOLDIER (*Middle-aged, comes forward*) My soul had a hard struggle to win the victory. It had to take me by the throat and shake me like a rat. It was rougher still with me. It sent me to jail. I'd stolen the money that was entrusted to me; I'd absconded with a big sum. They caught me; I was tried and sentenced. In my prison cell I found the rest my soul had been looking for. At the last it could speak to me in peace. At last I could hear its voice. Those days in the lonely cell became the happiest in my life. When my time was finished I could not part from my soul.

SOLDIERS Halleluja.

FOURTH SOLDIER I looked for a quiet place where we two could meet. I found it here on the penitent form; I find it here still, each evening that I feel the need of a happy hour! (*Standing aside*)

OFFICER (*Coming forward*) Our comrade has told you of his happy hours at the penitent form. Who is there among you who wants to escape from this sin? Here he will find peace! Come to the penitent bench!

MAN (*Standing up, shouting and gesticulating*) Nobody's sin! That's nobody's sin! I want to hear mine! My sin! My sin! (*Many join in*) My sin! My sin! My sin!

CASHIER My sin!

SALVATION LASS (*Above the uproar*) What are you shouting?

CASHIER The bank. The money.

SALVATION LASS (*Shaking him*) Are you ready?

CASHIER Yes, now I'm ready!

SALVATION LASS (*Taking his arm*) I'll lead you up there. I'll stand by you—always at your side. (*Turning to the crowd, ecstatically*) A soul is going to speak. I looked for this soul. I found this soul! (*The tumult ebbs into a quiet hum*)

CASHIER (*On the platform,* SALVATION LASS *by his side*) I've been on the road since this morning. I was driven out on this search. There was no chance of turning back. The earth gave way behind me, all bridges were broken. I had to march forward on a road that led me here. I won't weary you with the halting-places that wearied me. None of them were worth my break with the old life; none of them repaid me. I marched on with a searching eye, a sure touch, a clear head. I passed them all by, stage after stage; they dwindled and vanished in the distance. It wasn't this, it wasn't that, or the next—or the fourth or the fifth! What is the goal, what is the prize, that's worth the whole stake? This hall, humming with crowded benches, ringing with melody! This hall! Here, from bench to bench, the spirit thunders fulfillment! Here glow the twin crucibles; confession and repentance! Molten and free from dross, the soul stands like a glittering tower, strong and bright. You cry fulfillment for these benches. (*Pause*) I'll tell you my story.

SALVATION LASS Speak, I'm with you. I'll stand by you.

CASHIER I've been all day on the road. I confess; I'm a bank cashier. I embezzled the money that was entrusted me. A good round sum; sixty thousand marks! I fled with it into your city of asphalt. By this time, they're on my track; perhaps they've offered a big reward. I'm not in hiding any more. I confess! You can buy nothing worth having, even with all the money of all the banks in the world. You get less than you pay, every time. The more you spend, the less the goods are worth. The money corrupts them: the money veils the truth. Money's the meanest of the paltry swindles in this world! (*Pulling rolls of bank notes out of his breast pocket*) This hall is a burning oven; it glows with your contempt for all mean things. I throw the money to you; it shall be torn and stamped under foot. So much less deceit in the world! So much trash consumed. I'll go through your benches and give myself up to the first policeman; after confession, comes atonement. So the cup is filled!

(*With gloved hand he scatters bank notes broadcast into the hall. The money flutters down; all hands are stretched upward; a battle ensues. The crowd is tangled into a fighting coil. The* SOLDIERS *leap from the platform; benches are overturned, blows of fisticuffs resound above the shouting. At last, the cramped mass rolls to the door and out into the street. The* SALVATION LASS, *who has taken no part in the struggle, stands alone on the steps*)

CASHIER (*Smiling at her*) You are standing by me. You are with me still! (*Picking up an abandoned drum and a stick*) On we go. (*Roll of drum*) The crowd is left behind. (*Rolls of drum*) The yelping pack outrun. Vast emptiness. Elbow room! Room! Room! Room! (*Drum*) A maid remains . . . upright, steadfast! Maiden and man. The old garden is reopened. The sky is clear. A voice cries from the silent tree tops. It is well. (*Drum*) Maiden and man . . . eternal constancy. Maiden and man . . . fullness in the void. Maiden and man . . . the beginning and the end. Maiden and man . . . the seed and the flower. Maiden and man . . . sense and aim and goal! (*Rapid drumtaps, then a long roll.* SALVATION LASS *draws back to the door, and slips out.* CASHIER *beats a tattoo*)

SALVATION LASS (*Throws the door open. To* POLICEMAN) There he is! I've shown him to you! I've earned the reward.

CASHIER (*Letting fall the drumstick in the middle of a beat*) Here above you, I stand. Two are too many. Space holds but one. Space is loneliness. Loneliness is space. Coldness is sunshine. Sunshine is coldness. Fever heat burns you. Fever heat freezes you. Fields are deserted. Ice overgrows them. Who can escape? Where is the door?

POLICEMAN Is this the only entrance? (SALVATION LASS *nods.* CASHIER *feels in his pocket*)

POLICEMAN He's got his hand in his pocket. Switch off that light. We're a target for him!

(SALVATION LASS *obeys. All the lights of the hanging lamp are put out. Lights from the left illuminate the tangle of wires, forming a skeleton in outline*)

CASHIER (*Feeling with his left hand in his breast pocket, grasps with his right a trumpet, and blows a fanfare toward the lamp*) Ah!—Discovered. Scorned in the snow this morning—welcomed now in the tangled wires. I salute you. (*Trumpet*) The road is behind me. Panting, I climb the steep curves that lead upward. My forces are spent. I've spared myself nothing. I've made the path hard, where it might have been easy. This morning in the snow when we met, you and I, you should have been more pressing in your invitation. One spark of enlightenment would have helped me and spared me all trouble. It doesn't take much of a brain to see that— Why did I hesitate? Why take the road? Whither am I bound? From first to last you sit there, naked bone. From morn to midnight, I rage in a circle . . . and now your beckoning finger points the way . . . whither? (*He shoots the answer into his breast*)

POLICEMAN Switch on the light.

(SALVATION LASS *does so. The* CASHIER *has fallen back, with arms outstretched, tumbling headlong down the steps. His husky gasp is like an "Ecce," his heavy sigh is like a "Homo."* [1] *One second later all the lamps explode with a loud report*)

POLICEMAN There must be a short circuit in the main. (*Darkness*)

*Curtain*

[1] "Behold the Man," words uttered by Pilate immediately before Jesus' crucifixion. See *John*, 19:5.

# Luigi Pirandello

## (1867-1936)

There can be no question of the central importance of Luigi Pirandello in the shaping of the modern theatre. Easily the greatest Italian playwright of the twentieth century, Pirandello transformed the naturalists' concern with brute and instinctive passion into a broad philosophical commentary on the weaknesses and contradictions of human existence. It was his genius as a playwright to embody abstract thought in the concrete immediacy of living characters, whose problems and tensions are made alive on the stage. To speak of Pirandello as a writer of intellectual drama, of problem plays, or of plays of ideas is to emphasize only one aspect of his art, for in Pirandello's best work the plane of ideas cannot be separated from the vividness and immediacy of his dramatic representation.

Pirandello was born in Girgenti, Sicily, in 1867, the son of a prosperous owner of sulphur mines. All about him, however, was bleak poverty, an almost primitive environment in which violence substituted for the rule of law and where sudden outbursts of passion and crime lent savage and intense drama to everyday existence. The stark and smouldering Sicilian landscape is ever-present in Pirandello's work, and many of his early writings are in Sicilian dialect. Despite his father's wishes, young Pirandello was not cut out to be a businessman, and after an abortive attempt, was sent to the University of Rome. He continued his studies in Germany, receiving a doctorate at Bonn in 1891. Reminiscences of his residence in the Rhineland abound in his later work. On completing his studies, he returned to Rome to make his way in literature, through the writing of poetry, fiction, and literary criticism. Soon afterwards, in accordance with the wishes of his parents, he married a girl from his native village. To support his family of three children, Pirandello accepted a professorship of Italian literature at a teachers' college for girls in Rome. Severe family financial reverses along with the mental collapse of his wife brought new and continuing pressures. Friends urged him to commit his wife to an institution, especially as her derangement increased, but he refused, and kept her at home with him, both leading a life of torment and agony. The alternation between sanity and madness that plays so large a role in Pirandello's plays is undoubtedly based on personal experience. Yet, despite the difficulties of his private life, Pirandello was able, well before he became famous as a playwright, to compose a large number of successful novels and short stories. Indeed, many of his best plays had their inception in his earlier fiction. Pirandello was a master of the short story, and his command of the art of sharp compression, deft characterization, and sudden climax enter directly into his dramatic technique.

Pirandello's great success in the European theatre came in the 1920's, at a time when his pessimism and scepticism responded to the war-weariness and the radical questioning of traditional values that came in the wake of world chaos. Yet many of his most significant plays date from the years before and during World War I. Characteristic is *Così è (se vi pare)* (*It Is So! If You Think So*), produced in 1917, and dramatizing the contradiction between appearance and reality that makes the pursuit of absolute knowledge chimerical. Personal identity, Pirandello implies, is not intrinsic and individual, but extrinsic and multiple, produced by the roles and situations which circumstances force upon us. "Truth" cannot be described objectively or explored scientifically. Applied to the Ponza family, Pirandello's assault on the possibility of objective knowledge of human beings is, at the same time, a plea for individual privacy and for tolerance of ambiguities and eccentricities that are sometimes necessary for life to maintain a degree of balance. Illusion for Pirandello is a positive and indeed indispensable element amid circumstances that render existence wretched and all but unbearable.

Pirandello's plays are rescued from cold intellectual abstraction by a pervasive sympathy with those who suffer, whom chance or fate, passion or circumstance have twisted out of the quiet, ordinary pursuit of daily routine, and whose dislocation makes life itself impossible except through creating a mask, imposing a fictitious reality, reshaping the image of the self. Pirandello calls this process *"costruirsi,"* to build one's self up. Yet, despite this elaboration of illusion, at bottom there remains the elemental passion and seething torment revealed in a moment of crisis. Pirandello gave the title *Maschere Nude* (*Naked Masks*) to his collected plays by way of emphasizing the interplay between the make-believe and the real. Ultimately, however, it is not the alternation and contrast of mask and face which is of essential importance, but rather the understanding and compassion with which Pirandello dramatizes human suffering and pain. The intellectual analyses and contortions of his heroes and heroines are not games or empty abstractions, but expressions of a driving introspection born of the intensity of anguish. As The Father in *Six Characters in Search of an Author* protests, "I'm not philosophizing: I'm crying aloud the reason of my sufferings." Far more than a mere intellectual or philosophical riddle, the tormented self-analysis of Pirandello's victims is a haunting lament, a cry, a shriek, a supplication.

Pirandello's preoccupation with the gap between being and seeming, his spontaneity and love of artifice, coalesce in his plays to produce an effect of improvisation. Life itself, he insists, is performance; hence, the theatrical is implicit in our every action. Indeed, art, in its consistent and self-contained wholeness, is a fuller and more perfect mode of being than life with its indeterminate flux. The contrast between the fixity and permanence of art and the fluidity and evanescence of life underlies his most famous drama of improvisation, *Six Characters in Search of an Author* (1921). The setting is a theatre where a rehearsal of a Pirandello play is taking place. Suddenly the rehearsal is interrupted by the appearance of the six characters who claim to bear their own drama and who ask to be allowed to perform it. The action, then, is a play within a play, in which Pirandello contrasts appearance and reality, life and art, theatrical performance and the experience which it purports to represent. Imbedded in the play is a scathing criticism of the contemporary stage, its slovenliness, artificiality, and moral flabbiness; but the drama of the unrealized or partially realized characters is of central interest. The characters are creatures of fantasy but they embody values and feelings which are the natural expression of human desires and tensions, given a reality on the stage that, in Pirandello's terms, is more real than life itself.

In all, Pirandello wrote over forty plays. Many of them are repetitious and uneven in quality, but at his best, he is among the great dramatic artists of our time. In addition to *It Is So! (If You Think So)* and *Six Characters in Search of an Author,* his best plays include *Naked* (1922), *The Life I Gave You* (1923), and *Each in His Own Way* (1924). Illicit love, the anguish of bereavement, the necessity and cost of a life of illusion, again recur as central themes. The underlying ideas are relatively simple and familiar; what matters is the intensity and vividness with which they are made part of compelling dramatic situations. Pirandello's art is grounded on deep reflection and often issues in all-pervasive philosophical generalization, yet at the same time it is essentially human, close to the substance of concrete existence.

By common consent, the best of Pirandello's plays is *Enrico IV* (*Henry IV*), completed in 1922. Theme and technique fit perfectly together. On the surface, *Henry IV* resembles a historical play set in eleventh-century Germany, but the events of the drama take place in our own day. The contrast between past and present, between history and reality, functions precisely the same way as the contrast between art and life, form and flux, in *Six Characters in Search of an Author. Henry IV* is also theatrical in its reliance on masquerade, but for the hero, the realm of make-believe has become the world of essential reality. However, we know—or rather we learn in the second act—that Henry IV is not unconscious of his transformation, as is reported in the first act, but has chosen to maintain his role out of lucid reflection. Pirandello thus blurs the boundaries of pretence and reality, sanity and madness, and the distinction is further confounded by the frenzied savagery, akin to madness, with which Henry IV asserts his sanity. The long exposition of the first act may seem labored and clumsy, but it acquires its true meaning in the light of following events. The play must be viewed in retrospect as well as in a mounting sequence of climactic moments.

In calling his play a tragedy, Pirandello may have had in mind a conformity to traditional canons of tragic art, but the explanation is more likely to reside within the play itself. Up to the moment of his violent revenge, Henry IV enjoys the freedom of his masquerade. It is his by choice, not by necessity. At the end of the play, the mask of insanity remains his last and only defence. Henry IV ends bound in his role, a prisoner of his madness, no longer at liberty to assert his will, to militate against his condition. The absurdity of the masquerade becomes the final reality.

Domenico Vittorini reports of an interview with Pirandello in 1935: "In reply to my question as to which of his plays he considered the best, he showed his preference for *Enrico IV* (*Henry IV*)." The author's judgment has been amply confirmed by the unusual success of the play since the end of World War II, not only in Italy, but throughout the Western world. It is no surprise that at a time when the theatre has turned more intensively than ever to probing the depths of the irrational and the meaning of the absurd, Pirandello should emerge as an authentic precursor of existential drama. It is not merely his concepts and attitudes that keep his work alive, but the powerful artistry with which they are transmuted into drama. In the vividness of his dramatic dialogue, the trenchancy of his character analysis, the depth and poignancy of his rendering of passion, Pirandello is unsurpassed in the theatre of our time.

# HENRY IV

## *A Tragedy in Three Acts*

English version by Edward Storer

CHARACTERS

HENRY IV
THE MARCHIONESS MATILDA SPINA
FRIDA, *her daughter*
CHARLES DI NOLLI, *the young Marquis*
BARON TITO BELCREDI
DOCTOR DIONYSIUS GENONI
HAROLD (FRANK)
LANDOLPH (LOLO)
ORDULPH (MOMO)
BERTHOLD (FINO)
*The four private counsellors (The names in parentheses are nicknames)*
JOHN, *the old waiter*
THE TWO VALETS IN COSTUME

*A Solitary Villa in Italy in Our Own Time*

## Act One

*Salon in the villa, furnished and decorated so as to look exactly like the throne room of Henry IV in the royal residence at Goslar. Among the antique decorations there are two modern life-size portraits in oil painting. They are placed against the back wall, and mounted in a wooden stand that runs the whole length of the wall. (It is wide and protrudes, so that it is like a large bench.) One of the paintings is on the right; the other on the left of the throne, which is in the middle of the wall and divides the stand.*

*The Imperial chair and Baldachin.*

*The two portraits represent a lady and a gentleman, both young, dressed up in carnival costumes: one as "Henry IV," the other as the "Marchioness Matilda of Tuscany." Exits to right and left.*

*When the curtain goes up, the two valets jump down, as if surprised, from the stand on which they have been lying, and go and take their positions, as rigid as statues, on either side below the throne with their halberds in their hands. Soon after, from the second exit, right, enter* HAROLD, LANDOLPH, ORDULPH *and* BERTHOLD, *young men employed by the* MARQUIS CHARLES DI NOLLI *to play the part of "Secret Counsellors" at the court of "Henry IV." They are, therefore, dressed like German knights of the eleventh century.* BERTHOLD, *nicknamed Fino, is just entering on his duties for the first time. His companions are telling him what he has to do and amusing themselves at his expense. The scene is to be played rapidly and vivaciously.*

LANDOLPH (*To* BERTHOLD *as if explaining*) And this is the throne room.

HAROLD At Goslar.

ORDULPH Or at the castle in the Hartz, if you prefer.

HAROLD Or at Worms.

LANDOLPH According as to what's doing, it jumps about with us, now here, now there.

ORDULPH In Saxony.

HAROLD In Lombardy.

LANDOLPH On the Rhine.

ONE OF THE VALETS (*Without moving, just opening his lips*) I say . . .

HAROLD (*Turning round*) What is it?

FIRST VALET (*Like a statue*) Is he coming in or not? (*He alludes to* HENRY IV)

ORDULPH No, no, he's asleep. You needn't worry.

SECOND VALET (*Releasing his pose, taking a long breath and going to lie down again on the stand*) You might have told us at once.

FIRST VALET (*Going over to* HAROLD) Have you got a match, please?

LANDOLPH What? You can't smoke a pipe here, you know.

FIRST VALET (*While* HAROLD *offers him a light*) No; a cigarette. (*Lights his cigarette and lies down again on the stand*)

BERTHOLD (*Who has been looking on in amazement, walking round the room, regarding the costumes of the others*) I say . . . this room . . . these costumes . . . Which Henry IV is it? I don't quite get it. Is he Henry IV of France or not? (*At this* LANDOLPH, HAROLD, *and* ORDULPH, *burst out laughing*)

LANDOLPH (*Still laughing; and pointing to* BERTHOLD *as if inviting the others to make fun of him*) Henry of France he says: ha! ha!

ORDULPH He thought it was the king of France!

HAROLD Henry IV of Germany, my boy: the Salian dynasty!

ORDULPH The great and tragic Emperor!

LANDOLPH He of Canossa. Every day we carry on here the terrible war between Church and State, by Jove.

ORDULPH The Empire against the Papacy!

HAROLD Antipopes against the Pope!

LANDOLPH Kings against anti-kings!

ORDULPH War on the Saxons!

HAROLD And all the rebels Princes!

LANDOLPH Against the Emperor's own sons!

BERTHOLD (*Covering his head with his hands to protect himself against this avalanche of information*) I understand! I understand! Naturally, I didn't get the idea at first. I'm right then: these aren't costumes of the sixteenth century?

HAROLD Sixteenth century be hanged!

ORDULPH We're somewhere between a thousand and eleven hundred.

LANDOLPH Work it out for yourself: if we are before Canossa on the 25th of January, 1077 . . .

BERTHOLD (*More confused than ever*) Oh my God! What a mess I've made of it!

ORDULPH Well, just slightly, if you supposed you were at the French court.

BERTHOLD All that historical stuff I've worked up!

LANDOLPH My dear boy, it's four hundred years earlier.

BERTHOLD (*Getting angry*) Good Heavens! You ought to have told me it was Germany and not France. I can't tell you how many books I've read in the last fifteen days.

HAROLD But I say, surely you knew that poor Tito was Adalbert of Bremen, here?

BERTHOLD Not a damned bit!

LANDOLPH Well, don't you see how it is? When Tito died, the Marquis Di Nolli . . .

BERTHOLD Oh, it was he, was it? He might have told me.

HAROLD Perhaps he thought you knew.

LANDOLPH He didn't want to engage anyone else in substitution. He thought the remaining three of us would do. But *he* began to cry out: "With Adalbert driven away . . ." because, you see, he didn't imagine poor Tito was dead; but that, as Bishop Adalbert, the rival bishops of Cologne and Mayence had driven him off . . .

BERTHOLD (*Taking his head in his hand*) But I don't know a word of what you're talking about.

ORDULPH So much the worse for you, my boy!

HAROLD But the trouble is that not even we know who you are.

BERTHOLD What? Not even you? You don't know who I'm supposed to be?

ORDULPH Hum! "Berthold."

BERTHOLD But which Berthold? And why Berthold?

LANDOLPH (*Solemnly imitating* HENRY IV) "They've driven Adalbert away from me. Well then, I want Berthold! I want Berthold!" That's what he said.

HAROLD We three looked one another in the eyes: who's got to be Berthold?

ORDULPH And so here you are, "Berthold," my dear fellow!

LANDOLPH I'm afraid you will make a bit of a mess of it.

BERTHOLD (*Indignant, getting ready to go*) Ah, no! Thanks very much, but I'm off! I'm out of this!

HAROLD (*Restraining him with the other two, amid laughter*) Steady now! Don't get excited!

LANDOLPH Cheer up, my dear fellow! We don't any of us know who we are really. He's Harold; he's Ordulph; I'm Landolph! That's the way he calls us. We've got used to it. But who are we? Names of the period! Yours, too, is a name of the period: Berthold! Only one of us, poor Tito, had got a really decent part, as you can read in history: that of the Bishop of Bremen. He was just like a real bishop. Tito did it awfully well, poor chap!

HAROLD Look at the study he put into it!

LANDOLPH Why, he even ordered his Majesty about, opposed his views, guided and counselled him. We're "secret counsellors"—in a manner of speaking only; because it is written in history that Henry IV was hated by the upper aristocracy for surrounding himself at court with young men of the lower classes.

ORDULPH Us, that is.

LANDOLPH Yes, small devoted vassals, a bit dissolute and very gay . . .

BERTHOLD So I've got to be gay as well?

HAROLD I should say so! Same as we are!

ORDULPH And it isn't too easy, you know.

LANDOLPH It's a pity; because the way we're got up, we could do a fine historical reconstruction. There's any amount of material in the story of Henry IV. But, as a matter of fact, we do nothing. We have the form without the content. We're worse than the real secret counsellors of Henry IV; because certainly no one had given them a part to play—at any rate, they didn't feel they had a part to play. It was their life. They looked after their own interests at the expense of others, sold investitures and—what not! We stop here in this magnificent court—for what?— Just doing nothing. We're like so many puppets hung on the wall, waiting for someone to come and move us or make us talk.

HAROLD Ah, no, old sport, not quite that! We've got to give the proper answer, you know. There's trouble if he asks you something and you don't chip in with the cue.

LANDOLPH Yes, that's true.

BERTHOLD Don't rub it in too hard! How the devil am I to give him the proper answer, if I've worked up

Henry IV of France, and now he turns out to be Henry IV of Germany? (*The other three laugh*)

HAROLD You'd better start and prepare yourself at once.

ORDULPH We'll help you out.

HAROLD We've got any amount of books on the subject. A brief run through the main points will do to begin with.

ORDULPH At any rate, you must have got some sort of general idea.

HAROLD Look here! (*Turns him around and shows him the portrait of the Marchioness Matilda on the wall*) Who's that?

BERTHOLD (*Looking at it*) That? Well, the thing seems to me somewhat out of place, anyway: two modern paintings in the midst of all this respectable antiquity!

HAROLD You're right! They weren't there in the beginning. There are two niches there behind the pictures. They were going to put up two statues in the style of the period. Then the places were covered with those canvases there.

LANDOLPH (*Interrupting and continuing*) They would certainly be out of place if they really were paintings!

BERTHOLD What are they, if they aren't paintings?

LANDOLPH Go and touch them! Pictures all right . . . but for him! (*Makes a mysterious gesture to the right, alluding to* HENRY IV) . . . who never touches them! . . .

BERTHOLD No? What are they for him?

LANDOLPH Well, I'm only supposing, you know; but I imagine I'm about right. They're images such as . . . well—such as a mirror might throw back. Do you understand? That one there represents himself, as he is in this throne room, which is all in the style of the period. What's there to marvel at? If we put you before a mirror, won't you see yourself, alive, but dressed up in ancient costume? Well, it's as if there were two mirrors there, which cast back living images in the midst of a world which, as you will see, when you have lived with us, comes to life too.

BERTHOLD I say, look here . . . I've no particular desire to go mad here.

HAROLD Go mad, be hanged! You'll have a fine time!

BERTHOLD Tell me this: how have you all managed to become so learned?

LANDOLPH My dear fellow, you can't go back over eight hundred years of history without picking up a bit of experience.

HAROLD Come on! Come on! You'll see how quickly you get into it!

ORDULPH You'll learn wisdom, too, at this school.

BERTHOLD Well, for Heaven's sake, help me a bit! Give me the main lines, anyway.

HAROLD Leave it to us. We'll do it all between us.

LANDOLPH We'll put your wires on you and fix you up like a first-class marionette. Come along! (*They take him by the arm to lead him away*)

BERTHOLD (*Stopping and looking at the portrait on the wall*) Wait a minute! You haven't told me who that is. The Emperor's wife?

HAROLD No! The Emperor's wife is Bertha of Susa, the sister of Amadeus II of Savoy.

ORDULPH And the Emperor, who wants to be young with us, can't stand her, and wants to put her away.

LANDOLPH That is his most ferocious enemy: Matilda, Marchioness of Tuscany.

BERTHOLD Ah, I've got it: the one who gave hospitality to the Pope!

LANDOLPH Exactly: at Canossa!

ORDULPH Pope Gregory VII!

HAROLD Our *bête noire!*[1] Come on! come on! (*All four move toward the right to go out, when, from the left, the old servant* JOHN *enters in evening dress*)

JOHN (*Quickly, anxiously*) Hss! Hss! Frank! Lolo!

HAROLD (*Turning round*) What is it?

BERTHOLD (*Marveling at seeing a man in modern clothes enter the throne room*) Oh! I say, this is a bit too much, this chap here!

LANDOLPH A man of the twentieth century, here! Oh, go away! (*They run over to him, pretending to menace him and throw him out*)

ORDULPH (*Heroically*) Messenger of Gregory VII, away!

HAROLD Away! Away!

JOHN (*Annoyed, defending himself*) Oh, stop it! Stop it, I tell you!

ORDULPH No, you can't set foot here!

HAROLD Out with him!

LANDOLPH (*To* BERTHOLD) Magic, you know! He's a demon conjured up by the Wizard of Rome! Out with your swords! (*Makes as if to draw a sword*)

JOHN (*Shouting*) Stop it, will you? Don't play the fool with me! The Marquis has arrived with some friends . . .

LANDOLPH Good! Good! Are there ladies too?

ORDULPH Old or young?

JOHN There are two gentlemen.

HAROLD But the ladies, the ladies, who are they?

JOHN The Marchioness and her daughter.

LANDOLPH (*Surprised*) What do you say?

ORDULPH The Marchioness?

JOHN The Marchioness! The Marchioness!

HAROLD Who are the gentlemen?

JOHN I don't know.

HAROLD (*To* BERTHOLD) They're coming to bring us a message from the Pope, do you see?

ORDULPH All messengers of Gregory VII! What fun!

JOHN Will you let me speak, or not?

HAROLD Go on, then!

JOHN One of the two gentlemen is a doctor, I fancy.

LANDOLPH Oh, I see, one of the usual doctors.

HAROLD Bravo Berthold, you'll bring us luck!

LANDOLPH You wait and see how we'll manage this doctor!

BERTHOLD It looks as if I were going to get into a nice mess right away.

JOHN If the gentlemen would allow me to speak . . . they want to come here into the throne room.

[1] Hated enemy.

LANDOLPH (*Surprised*) What? She? The Marchioness here?

HAROLD Then this is something quite different! No play-acting this time!

LANDOLPH We'll have a real tragedy: that's what!

BERTHOLD (*Curious*) Why? Why?

ORDULPH (*Pointing to the portrait*) She is that person there, don't you understand?

LANDOLPH The daughter is the fiancée of the Marquis. But what have they come for, I should like to know?

ORDULPH If he sees her, there'll be trouble.

LANDOLPH Perhaps he won't recognize her any more.

JOHN You must keep him there, if he should wake up . . .

ORDULPH Easier said than done, by Jove!

HAROLD You know what he's like!

JOHN —even by force, if necessary! Those are my orders. Go on! Go on!

HAROLD Yes, because who knows if he hasn't already wakened up?

ORDULPH Come on then!

LANDOLPH (*Going toward* JOHN *with the others*) You'll tell us later what it all means.

JOHN (*Shouting after them*) Close the door there, and hide the key! That other door too. (*Pointing to the other door on right*)

JOHN (*To the* TWO VALETS) Be off, you two! There! (*Pointing to exit right*) Close the door after you, and hide the key!

(*The* TWO VALETS *go out by the first door on right.* JOHN *moves over to the left to show in:* DONNA MATILDA SPINA, *the young* MARCHIONESS FRIDA, DR. DIONYSIUS GENONI, *the* BARON TITO BELCREDI *and the young* MARQUIS CHARLES DI NOLLI, *who, as master of the house, enters last.*

DONNA MATILDA SPINA *is about forty-five, still handsome, although there are too patent signs of her attempts to remedy the ravages of time with make-up. Her head is thus rather like a Valkyrie. This facial make-up contrasts with her beautiful sad mouth. A widow for many years, she now has as her friend the* BARON TITO BELCREDI, *whom neither she nor anyone else takes seriously—at least so it would appear.*

*What* TITO BELCREDI *really is for her at bottom, he alone knows; and he is, therefore, entitled to laugh, if his friend feels the need of pretending not to know. He can always laugh at the jests which the beautiful Marchioness makes with the others at his expense. He is slim, prematurely gray, and younger than she is. His head is bird-like in shape. He would be a very vivacious person, if his ductile agility (which among other things makes him a redoubtable swordsman) were not enclosed in a sheath of Arab-like laziness, which is revealed in his strange, nasal drawn-out voice.*

FRIDA, *the daughter of the Marchioness is nineteen. She is sad; because her imperious and too beautiful mother puts her in the shade, and provokes facile gossip against her daughter as well as against herself. Fortunately for her, she is engaged to the* MARQUIS CHARLES DI NOLLI.

CHARLES DI NOLLI *is a stiff young man, very indulgent toward others, but sure of himself for what he amounts to in the world. He is worried about all the responsibilities which he believes weigh on him. He is dressed in deep mourning for the recent death of his mother.*

DR. DIONYSIUS GENONI *has a bold rubicund Satyr-like face, prominent eyes, a pointed beard (which is silvery and shiny) and elegant manners. He is nearly bald. All enter in a state of perturbation, almost as if afraid, and all (except* DI NOLLI*) looking curiously about the room. At first, they speak sotto voce*)

DI NOLLI (*To* JOHN) Have you given the orders properly?

JOHN Yes, my Lord; don't be anxious about that.

BELCREDI Ah, magnificent! magnificent!

DOCTOR How extremely interesting! Even in the surroundings his raving madness—is perfectly taken into account!

DONNA MATILDA (*Glancing round for her portrait, discovers it, and goes up close to it*) Ah! Here it is! (*Going back to admire it, while mixed emotions stir within her*) Yes . . . Yes . . . (*Calls her daughter* FRIDA)

FRIDA Ah, your portrait!

DONNA MATILDA No, no . . . look again; it's you, not I, there!

DI NOLLI Yes, it's quite true. I told you so, I . . .

DONNA MATILDA But I would never have believed it! (*Shaking as if with a chill*) What a strange feeling it gives one! (*Then looking at her daughter*) Frida, what's the matter? (*She pulls her to her side, and slips an arm round her waist*) Come: don't you see yourself in me there?

FRIDA Well, I really . . .

DONNA MATILDA Don't you think so? Don't you, really? (*Turning to* BELCREDI) Look at it, Tito! Speak up, man!

BELCREDI (*Without looking*) Ah, no! I shan't look at it. For me, *a priori*, certainly not!

DONNA MATILDA Stupid! You think you are paying me a compliment! (*Turning to* DOCTOR GENONI) What do you say, Doctor? Do say something, please!

(DOCTOR *makes a movement to go near to the picture*)

BELCREDI (*With his back turned, pretending to attract his attention secretly*) —Hss! No, Doctor! For the love of Heaven, have nothing to do with it!

DOCTOR (*Getting bewildered and smiling*) And why shouldn't I?

DONNA MATILDA Don't listen to him! Come here! He's insufferable!

FRIDA He acts the fool by profession, didn't you know that?

BELCREDI (*To the* DOCTOR, *seeing him go over*) Look at your feet, Doctor! Mind where you're going!

DOCTOR Why?

BELCREDI Be careful you don't put your foot in it!

DOCTOR (*Laughing feebly*) No, no. After all, it seems to me there's no reason to be astonished at the fact that a daughter should resemble her mother!

BELCREDI Oh oh! He's done it now; he's said it.

DONNA MATILDA (*With exaggerated anger, advancing toward* BELCREDI) What's the matter? What has he said? What has he done?

DOCTOR (*Candidly*) Well, isn't it so?

BELCREDI (*Answering the* MARCHIONESS) I said there was nothing to be astounded at—and you are astounded! And why so, then, if the thing is so simple and natural for you now?

DONNA MATILDA (*Still more angry*) Fool! fool! It's just because it is so natural! Just because it isn't my daughter who is there. (*Pointing to the canvas*) That is my portrait; and to find my daughter there instead of me fills me with astonishment, an astonishment which, I beg you to believe, is sincere. I forbid you to cast doubts on it.

FRIDA (*Slowly and wearily*) My God! It's always like this . . . quarrels over nothing . . .

BELCREDI (*Also slowly, looking dejected, in accents of apology*) I cast no doubt on anything! I noticed from the beginning that you haven't shared your mother's astonishment; or, if something did astonish you, it was because the likeness between you and the portrait seemed so strong.

DONNA MATILDA Naturally! She cannot recognize herself in me as I was at her age; while I, there, can very well recognize myself in her as she is now!

DOCTOR Quite right! Because a portrait is always there, fixed in the twinkling of an eye: for the young lady something far away and without memories, while, for the Marchioness, it can bring back everything: movements, gestures, looks, smiles, so many things . . .

DONNA MATILDA Exactly!

DOCTOR (*Continuing, turning toward her*) Naturally enough, you can live all these old sensations again in your daughter.

DONNA MATILDA He always spoils every innocent pleasure for me, every touch I have of spontaneous sentiment! He does it merely to annoy me.

DOCTOR (*Frightened at the disturbance he has caused, adopts a professorial tone*) Likeness, dear Baron, is often the result of imponderable things. So one explains that . . .

BELCREDI (*Interrupting the discourse*) Somebody will soon be finding a likeness between you and me, my dear Professor!

DI NOLLI Oh! let's finish with this, please! (*Points to the two doors on the right, as a warning that there is someone there who may be listening*) We've wasted too much time as it is!

FRIDA As one might expect when *he's* present. (*Alludes to* BELCREDI)

DI NOLLI Enough! The Doctor is here; and we have come for a very serious purpose which you all know is important for me.

DOCTOR Yes, that is so! But now, first of all, let's try to get some points down exactly. Excuse me, Marchioness, will you tell me why your portrait is here? Did you present it to him then?

DONNA MATILDA No, not at all. How could I have given it to him? I was just like Frida then—and not even engaged. I gave it to him three or four years after the accident. I gave it to him because his mother wished it so much . . . (*Points to* DI NOLLI)

DOCTOR She was his sister? (*Alludes to* HENRY IV)

DI NOLLI Yes, Doctor; and our coming here is a debt we pay to my mother who has been dead for more than a month. Instead of being here, she and I (*Indicating* FRIDA) ought to be traveling together . . .

DOCTOR . . . taking a cure of quite a different kind!

DI NOLLI —Hum! Mother died in the firm conviction that her adored brother was just about to be cured.

DOCTOR And can't you tell me, if you please, how she inferred this?

DI NOLLI The conviction would appear to have derived from certain strange remarks which he made, a little before mother died.

DOCTOR Oh, remarks! . . . Ah! . . . It would be extremely useful for me to have those remarks, word for word, if possible.

DI NOLLI I can't remember them. I know that mother returned awfully upset from her last visit with him. On her death-bed, she made me promise that I would never neglect him, that I would have doctors see him, and examine him.

DOCTOR Um! Um! Let me see! let me see! Sometimes very small reasons determine . . . and this portrait here then? . . .

DONNA MATILDA For Heaven's sake, Doctor, don't attach excessive importance to this. It made an impression on me because I had not seen it for so many years!

DOCTOR If you please, quietly, quietly . . .

DI NOLLI —Well, yes, it must be about fifteen years ago.

DONNA MATILDA More, more: eighteen!

DOCTOR Forgive me, but you don't quite know what I'm trying to get at. I attach a very great importance to these two portraits. . . . They were painted, naturally, prior to the famous—and most regrettable pageant, weren't they?

DONNA MATILDA Of course!

DOCTOR That is . . . when he was quite in his right mind—that's what I've been trying to say. Was it his suggestion that they should be painted?

DONNA MATILDA Lots of the people who took part in the pageant had theirs done as a souvenir. . . .

BELCREDI I had mine done—as "Charles of Anjou!"

DONNA MATILDA . . . as soon as the costumes were ready.

BELCREDI As a matter of fact, it was proposed that the whole lot of us should be hung together in a gallery of the villa where the pageant took place. But in the end, everybody wanted to keep his own portrait.

DONNA MATILDA And I gave him this portrait of me without very much regret . . . since his mother . . . (*Indicates* DI NOLLI)

DOCTOR You don't remember if it was he who asked for it?

DONNA MATILDA Ah, that I don't remember. . . . Maybe it was his sister, wanting to help out. . . .

DOCTOR One other thing: was it his idea, this pageant?

BELCREDI (*At once*) No, no, it was mine!

DOCTOR If you please . . .

DONNA MATILDA Don't listen to him! It was poor Belassi's idea.

BELCREDI Belassi! What had he got to do with it?

DONNA MATILDA Count Belassi, who died, poor fellow, two or three months after . . .

BELCREDI But if Belassi wasn't there when . . .

DI NOLLI Excuse me, Doctor; but is it really necessary to establish whose the original idea was?

DOCTOR It would help me, certainly!

BELCREDI I tell you the idea was mine! There's nothing to be proud of in it, seeing what the result's been. Look here, Doctor, it was like this. One evening, in the first days of November, I was looking at an illustrated German review in the club. I was merely glancing at the pictures, because I can't read German. There was a picture of the Kaiser, at some University town where he had been a student . . . I don't remember which.

DOCTOR Bonn, Bonn!

BELCREDI —You are right: Bonn! He was on horseback, dressed up in one of those ancient German student guild-costumes, followed by a procession of noble students, also in costume. The picture gave me the idea. Already someone at the club had spoken of a pageant for the forthcoming carnival. So I had the notion that each of us should choose for this Tower of Babel pageant to represent some character: a king, an emperor, a prince, with his queen, empress, or lady, alongside of him—and all on horseback. The suggestion was at once accepted.

DONNA MATILDA I had my invitation from Belassi.

BELCREDI Well, he wasn't speaking the truth! That's all I can say, if he told you the idea was his. He wasn't even at the club the evening I made the suggestion, just as he (*Meaning* HENRY IV) wasn't there either.

DOCTOR So he chose the character of Henry IV?

DONNA MATILDA Because I . . . thinking of my name, and not giving the choice any importance, said I would be the Marchioness Matilda of Tuscany.

DOCTOR I . . . don't understand the relation between the two.

DONNA MATILDA —Neither did I, to begin with, when he said that in that case he would be at my feet like Henry IV at Canossa. I had heard of Canossa of course; but to tell the truth, I'd forgotten most of the story; and I remember I received a curious impression when I had to get up my part, and found that I was the faithful and zealous friend of Pope Gregory VII in deadly enmity with the Emperor of Germany. Then I understood why, since I had chosen to represent his implacable enemy, he wanted to be near me in the pageant as Henry IV.

DOCTOR Ah, perhaps because . . .

BELCREDI —Good Heavens, Doctor, because he was then paying furious court to her! (*Indicates the* MARCHIONESS) And she, naturally . . .

DONNA MATILDA Naturally? Not naturally at all. . . .

BELCREDI (*Pointing to her*) She couldn't stand him . . .

DONNA MATILDA —No, that isn't true! I didn't dislike him. Not at all! But for me, when a man begins to want to be taken seriously, well . . .

BELCREDI (*Continuing for her*) He gives you the clearest proof of his stupidity.

DONNA MATILDA No, dear; not in this case; because he was never a fool like you.

BELCREDI Anyway, I've never asked you to take me seriously.

DONNA MATILDA Yes, I know. But with him one couldn't joke. (*Changing her tone and speaking to the* DOCTOR) One of the many misfortunes which happen to us women, Doctor, is to see before us every now and again a pair of eyes glaring at us with a contained intense promise of eternal devotion. (*Bursts out laughing*) There is nothing quite so funny. If men could only see themselves with that eternal look of fidelity in their faces! I've always thought it comic; then more even than now. But I want to make a confession—I can do so after twenty years or more. When I laughed at him then, it was partly out of fear. One might have almost believed a promise from those eyes of his. But it would have been very dangerous.

DOCTOR (*With lively interest*) Ah! ah! This is most interesting! Very dangerous, you say?

DONNA MATILDA Yes, because he was very different from the others. And then, I am . . . well . . . what shall I say? . . . a little impatient of all that is pondered, or tedious. But I was too young then, and a woman. I had the bit between my teeth. It would have required more courage than I felt I possessed. So I laughed at him too—with remorse, to spite myself, indeed; since I saw that my own laugh mingled with those of all the others—the other fools—who made fun of him.

BELCREDI My own case, more or less!

DONNA MATILDA You make people laugh at you, my dear, with your trick of always humiliating yourself. It was quite a different affair with him. There's a vast difference. And you—you know—people laugh in your face!

BELCREDI Well, that's better than behind one's back!

DOCTOR Let's get to the facts. He was then already somewhat exalted, if I understand rightly.

BELCREDI Yes, but in a curious fashion, Doctor.

DOCTOR How?

BELCREDI Well, cold-bloodedly so to speak.

DONNA MATILDA Not at all! It was like this, Doctor! He was a bit strange, certainly; but only because he was fond of life: eccentric, there!

BELCREDI I don't say he simulated exaltation. On the contrary, he was often genuinely exalted. But I could swear, Doctor, that he saw himself at once in his own exaltation. Moreover, I'm certain it made him suffer. Sometimes he had the most comical fits of rage against himself.

DOCTOR Yes?

DONNA MATILDA That is true.

BELCREDI (*To* DONNA MATILDA) And why? (*To the* DOCTOR) Evidently, because that immediate lucidity that comes from acting, assuming a part, at once put him out of key with his own feelings, which seemed to him not exactly false, but like something he was obliged to give the value there and then of—what shall I say—of an act of intelligence, to make up for that sincere cordial warmth he felt lacking. So he improvised, exaggerated, let himself go, so as to distract and forget himself. He appeared inconstant, fatuous, and —yes—even ridiculous, sometimes.

DOCTOR And may we say unsociable?

BELCREDI No, not at all. He was famous for getting up things: *tableaux vivants,*[1] dances, theatrical performances for charity: all for the fun of the thing, of course. He was a jolly good actor, you know!

DI NOLLI Madness has made a superb actor of him.

BELCREDI —Why, so he was even in the old days. When the accident happened, after the horse fell . . .

DOCTOR Hit the back of his head, didn't he?

DONNA MATILDA Oh, it was horrible! He was beside me! I saw him between the horse's hoofs! It was rearing!

BELCREDI None of us thought it was anything serious at first. There was a stop in the pageant, a bit of disorder. People wanted to know what had happened. But they'd already taken him off to the villa.

DONNA MATILDA There wasn't the least sign of a wound, not a drop of blood.

BELCREDI We thought he had merely fainted.

DONNA MATILDA But two hours afterward . . .

BELCREDI He reappeared in the drawing-room of the villa . . . that is what I wanted to say . . .

DONNA MATILDA My God! What a face he had. I saw the whole thing at once!

BELCREDI No, no! that isn't true. Nobody saw it, Doctor, believe me!

DONNA MATILDA Doubtless, because you were all like mad men.

BELCREDI Everybody was pretending to act his part for a joke. It was a regular Babel.

DONNA MATILDA And you can imagine, Doctor, what terror struck into us when we understood that he, on the contrary, was playing his part in deadly earnest . . .

DOCTOR Oh, he was there too, was he?

BELCREDI Of course! He came straight into the midst of us. We thought he'd quite recovered, and was pretending, fooling, like all the rest of us . . . only doing it rather better; because, as I say, he knew how to act.

DONNA MATILDA Some of them began to hit him with their whips and fans and sticks.

[1] Scenes in pantomime.

BELCREDI And then—as a king, he was armed, of course—he drew out his sword and menaced two or three of us. . . . It was a terrible moment, I can assure you!

DONNA MATILDA I shall never forget that scene—all our masked faces hideous and terrified gazing at him, at that terrible mask of his face, which was no longer a mask, but madness, madness personified.

BELCREDI He was Henry IV, Henry IV in person, in a moment of fury.

DONNA MATILDA He'd got into it all the detail and minute preparation of a month's careful study. And it all burned and blazed there in the terrible obsession which lit his face.

DOCTOR Yes, that is quite natural, of course. The momentary obsession of a dilettante became fixed, owing to the fall and the damage to the brain.

BELCREDI (*To* FRIDA *and* DI NOLLI) You see the kind of jokes life can play on us. (*To* DI NOLLI) You were four or five years old. (*To* FRIDA) Your mother imagines you've taken her place there in that portrait; when, at the time, she had not the remotest idea that she would bring you into the world. My hair is already gray; and he—look at him—(*Points to portrait*)—ha! A smack on the head, and he never moves again: Henry IV forever!

DOCTOR (*Seeking to draw the attention of the others, looking learned and imposing*) —Well, well, then it comes, we may say, to this. . . .

(*Suddenly the first exit to right, the one nearest footlights, opens, and* BERTHOLD *enters all excited*)

BERTHOLD (*Rushing in*) I say! I say! (*Stops for a moment, arrested by the astonishment which his appearance has caused in the others*)

FRIDA (*Running away terrified*) Oh dear! oh dear! it's he, it's . . .

DONNA MATILDA (*Covering her face with her hands so as not to see*) Is it, is it he?

DI NOLLI No, no, what are you talking about? Be calm!

DOCTOR Who is it then?

BELCREDI One of our masqueraders.

DI NOLLI He is one of the four youths we keep here to help him out in his madness. . . .

BERTHOLD I beg your pardon, Marquis. . . .

DI NOLLI Pardon be damned! I gave orders that the doors were to be closed, and that nobody should be allowed to enter.

BERTHOLD Yes, sir, but I can't stand it any longer, and I ask you to let me go away this very minute.

DI NOLLI Oh, you're the new valet, are you? You were supposed to begin this morning, weren't you?

BERTHOLD Yes, sir, and I can't stand it, I can't bear it.

DONNA MATILDA (*To* DI NOLLI *excitedly*) What? Then he's not so calm as you said?

BERTHOLD (*Quickly*) —No, no, my lady, it isn't he; it's my companions. You say "help him out with his madness," Marquis; but they don't do anything of the kind. They're the real madmen. I come here for the first time, and instead of helping me . . .

(LANDOLPH *and* HAROLD *come in from the same door, but hesitate on the threshold*)

LANDOLPH Excuse me?

HAROLD May I come in, my Lord?

DI NOLLI Come in! What's the matter? What are you all doing?

FRIDA Oh God! I'm frightened! I'm going to run away. (*Makes toward exit at left*)

DI NOLLI (*Restraining her at once*) No, no, Frida!

LANDOLPH My Lord, this fool here . . . (*Indicates* BERTHOLD)

BERTHOLD (*Protesting*) Ah, no thanks, my friends, no thanks! I'm not stopping here! I'm off!

LANDOLPH What do you mean—you're not stopping here?

HAROLD He's ruined everything, my Lord, running away in here!

LANDOLPH He's made him quite mad. We can't keep him in there any longer. He's given orders that he's to be arrested; and he wants to "judge" him at once from the throne: What is to be done?

DI NOLLI Shut the door, man! Shut the door! Go and close that door! (LANDOLPH *goes over to close it*)

HAROLD Ordulph, alone, won't be able to keep him there.

LANDOLPH —My Lord, perhaps if we could announce the visitors at once, it would turn his thoughts. Have the gentlemen thought under what pretext they will present themselves to him?

DI NOLLI —It's all been arranged! (*To the* DOCTOR) If you, Doctor, think it well to see him at once. . . .

FRIDA I'm not coming! I'm not coming! I'll keep out of this. You too, Mother, for Heaven's sake, come away with me!

DOCTOR —I say . . . I suppose he's not armed, is he?

DI NOLLI —Nonsense! Of course not. (*To* FRIDA) Frida, you know this is childish of you. You wanted to come!

FRIDA I didn't at all. It was mother's idea.

DONNA MATILDA And I'm quite ready to see him. What are we going to do?

BELCREDI Must we absolutely dress up in some fashion or other?

LANDOLPH —Absolutely essential, indispensable, sir. Alas! as you see . . . (*Shows his costume*), there'd be awful trouble if he saw you gentlemen in modern dress.

HAROLD He would think it was some diabolical masquerade.

DI NOLLI As these men seem to be in costume to you, so we appear to be in costume to him, in these modern clothes of ours.

LANDOLPH It wouldn't matter so much if he wouldn't suppose it to be the work of his mortal enemy.

BELCREDI Pope Gregory VII?

LANDOLPH Precisely. He calls him "a pagan."

BELCREDI The Pope a pagan? That's not bad!

LANDOLPH —Yes, sir . . . and a man who calls up the dead! He accuses him of all the diabolical arts. He's terribly afraid of him.

DOCTOR Persecution mania!

HAROLD He'd be simply furious.

DI NOLLI (*To* BELCREDI) But there's no need for you to be there, you know. It's sufficient for the Doctor to see him.

DOCTOR —What do you mean? . . . I? Alone?

DI NOLLI —But they are there. (*Indicates the three young men*)

DOCTOR I don't mean that. . . . I mean if the Marchioness . . .

DONNA MATILDA Of course. I mean to see him too, naturally. I want to see him again.

FRIDA Oh, why, Mother, why? Do come away with me, I implore you!

DONNA MATILDA (*Imperiously*) Let me do as I wish! I came here for this purpose! (*To* LANDOLPH) I shall be "Adelaide," the mother.

LANDOLPH Excellent! The mother of the Empress Bertha. Good! It will be enough if her Ladyship wears the ducal crown and puts on a mantle that will hide her other clothes entirely. (*To* HAROLD) Off you go, Harold!

HAROLD Wait a moment! And this gentleman here? . . . (*Alludes to the* DOCTOR)

DOCTOR —Ah yes . . . we decided I was to be . . . the Bishop of Cluny, Hugh of Cluny!

HAROLD The gentleman means the Abbot. Very good! Hugh of Cluny.

LANDOLPH —He's often been here before!

DOCTOR (*Amazed*) —What? Been here before?

LANDOLPH —Don't be alarmed! I mean that it's an easily prepared disguise. . . .

HAROLD We've made use of it on other occasions, you see!

DOCTOR But . . .

LANDOLPH Oh, no, there's no risk of his remembering. He pays more attention to the dress than to the person.

DONNA MATILDA That's fortunate for me too then.

DI NOLLI Frida, you and I'll get along. Come on, Tito!

BELCREDI Ah no. If she (*Indicates the* MARCHIONESS) stops here, so do I!

DONNA MATILDA But I don't need you at all.

BELCREDI You may not need me, but I should like to see him again myself. Mayn't I?

LANDOLPH Well, perhaps it would be better if there were three.

HAROLD How is the gentleman to be dressed then?

BELCREDI Oh, try and find some easy costume for me.

LANDOLPH (*To* HAROLD) Hum! Yes . . . he'd better be from Cluny too.

BELCREDI What do you mean—from Cluny?

LANDOLPH A Benedictine's habit of the Abbey of Cluny. He can be in attendance on Monsignor. (*To* HAROLD) Off you go! (*To* BERTHOLD) And you too get away and keep out of sight all today. No, wait a moment. (*To* BERTHOLD) You bring here the costumes he will give you. (*To* HAROLD) You go at once and announce the visit of the "Duchess Adelaide" and "Monsignor Hugh of Cluny." Do you understand? (HAROLD *and* BERTHOLD *go off by the first door on the right*)

DI NOLLI We'll retire now. (*Goes off with* FRIDA, *left*)

DOCTOR Shall I be a *persona grata*[2] to him, as Hugh of Cluny?

LANDOLPH Oh, rather! Don't worry about that! Monsignor has always been received here with great respect. You too, my Lady, he will be glad to see. He never forgets that it was owing to the intercession of you two that he was admitted to the Castle of Canossa and the presence of Gregory VII, who didn't want to receive him.

BELCREDI And what do I do?

LANDOLPH You stand a little apart, respectfully: that's all.

DONNA MATILDA (*Irritated, nervous*) You would do well to go away, you know.

BELCREDI (*Slowly, spitefully*) How upset you seem! . . .

DONNA MATILDA (*Proudly*) I am as I am. Leave me alone!

(BERTHOLD *comes in with the costumes*)

LANDOLPH (*Seeing him enter*) Ah, the costumes: here they are. This mantle is for the Marchioness . . .

DONNA MATILDA Wait a minute! I'll take off my hat. (*Does so and gives it to* BERTHOLD)

LANDOLPH Put it down there! (*Then to the* MARCHIONESS, *while he offers to put the ducal crown on her head*) Allow me!

DONNA MATILDA Dear, dear! Isn't there a mirror here?

LANDOLPH Yes, there's one there. (*Points to the door on the left*) If the Marchioness would rather put it on herself . . .

DONNA MATILDA Yes, yes, that will be better. Give it to me! (*Takes up her hat and goes off with* BERTHOLD, *who carries the cloak and the crown*)

BELCREDI Well, I must say, I never thought I should be a Benedictine monk! By the way, this business must cost an awful lot of money.

DOCTOR Like any other fantasy, naturally!

BELCREDI Well, there's a fortune to go upon.

LANDOLPH We have got there a whole wardrobe of costumes of the period, copied to perfection from old models. This is my special job. I get them from the best theatrical costumers. They cost lots of money. (DONNA MATILDA *re-enters, wearing mantle and crown*)

BELCREDI (*At once, in admiration*) Oh magnificent! Truly regal!

DONNA MATILDA (*Looking at* BELCREDI *and bursting out into laughter*) Oh no, no! Take it off! You're impossible. You look like an ostrich dressed up as a monk.

BELCREDI Well, how about the Doctor?

DOCTOR I don't think I look so bad, do I?

DONNA MATILDA No; the Doctor's all right, . . . but you are too funny for words.

DOCTOR Do you have many receptions here then?

LANDOLPH It depends. He often gives orders that such and such a person appear before him. Then we have to find someone who will take the part. Women too. . . .

[2] Acceptable.

DONNA MATILDA (*Hurt, but trying to hide the fact*) Ah, women too?

LANDOLPH Oh, yes; many at first.

BELCREDI (*Laughing*) Oh, that's great! In costume, like the Marchioness?

LANDOLPH Oh well, you know, women of the kind that lend themselves to . . . .

BELCREDI Ah, I see! (*Perfidiously to the* MARCHIONESS) Look out, you know he's becoming dangerous for you.

(*The second door on the right opens, and* HAROLD *appears making first of all a discreet sign that all conversation should cease*)

HAROLD His Majesty, the Emperor!

(*The* TWO VALETS *enter first, and go and stand on either side of the throne. Then* HENRY IV *comes in between* ORDULPH *and* HAROLD, *who keep a little in the rear respectfully.*

HENRY IV *is about fifty and very pale. The hair on the back of his head is already gray; over the temples and forehead it appears blond, owing to its having been tinted in an evident and puerile fashion. On his cheekbones he has two small, doll-like dabs of color, that stand out prominently against the rest of his tragic pallor. He is wearing a penitent's sack over his regal habit, as at Canossa. His eyes have a fixed look which is dreadful to see, and this expression is in strained contrast with the sackcloth.* ORDULPH *carries the Imperial crown;* HAROLD, *the sceptre with eagle, and the globe with the cross*)

HENRY IV (*Bowing first to* DONNA MATILDA *and afterward to the* DOCTOR) My lady . . . Monsignor . . . (*Then he looks at* BELCREDI *and seems about to greet him too; when, suddenly, he turns to* LANDOLPH, *who has approached him, and asks him sotto voce*[3] *and with diffidence*) Is that Peter Damiani?

LANDOLPH No, Sire. He is a monk from Cluny who is accompanying the Abbot.

HENRY IV (*Looks again at* BELCREDI *with increasing mistrust, and then noticing that he appears embarrassed and keeps glancing at* DONNA MATILDA *and the* DOCTOR, *stands upright and cries out*) No, it's Peter Damiani! It's no use, father, your looking at the Duchess. (*Then turning quickly to* DONNA MATILDA *and the* DOCTOR *as though to ward off a danger*) I swear it! I swear that my heart is changed toward your daughter. I confess that if he (*Indicates* BELCREDI) hadn't come to forbid it in the name of Pope Alexander, I'd have repudiated her. Yes, yes, there were people ready to favor the repudiation: the Bishop of Mayence would have done it for a matter of one hundred and twenty farms. (*Looks at* LANDOLPH *a little perplexed and adds*) But I mustn't speak ill of the bishops at this moment! (*More humbly to* BELCREDI) I am grateful to you, believe me, I am grateful to you for the hindrance you put in my way!—God knows, my life's been all made of humiliations: my mother, Adalbert, Tribur, Goslar! And now this sackcloth you see me

[3] In an undertone.

wearing! (*Changes tone suddenly and speaks like one who goes over his part in a parenthesis of astuteness*) It doesn't matter: clarity of ideas, perspicacity, firmness, and patience under adversity, that's the thing. (*Then turning to all and speaking solemnly*) I know how to make amends for the mistakes I have made; and I can humiliate myself even before you, Peter Damiani. (*Bows profoundly to him and remains curved. Then a suspicion is born in him which he is obliged to utter in menacing tones, almost against his will*) Was it not perhaps you who started that obscene rumor that my holy mother had illicit relations with the Bishop of Augusta?

BELCREDI (*Since* HENRY IV *has his finger pointed at him*) No, no, it wasn't I. . . .

HENRY IV (*Straightening up*) Not true, not true? Infamy! (*Looks at him and then adds*) I didn't think you capable of it! (*Goes to the* DOCTOR *and plucks his sleeve, while winking at him knowingly*) Always the same, Monsignor, those bishops, always the same!

HAROLD (*Softly, whispering as if to help out the doctor*) Yes, yes, the rapacious bishops!

DOCTOR (*To* HAROLD, *trying to keep it up*) Ah, yes, those fellows . . . ah yes . . .

HENRY IV Nothing satisfies them! I was a little boy, Monsignor . . . One passes the time, playing even, when, without knowing it, one is a king. I was six years old; and they tore me away from my mother, and made use of me against her without my knowing anything about it . . . always profaning, always stealing, stealing! . . . One greedier than the other. . . . Hanno worse than Stephen! Stephen worse than Hanno!

LANDOLPH (*Sotto voce, persuasively, to call his attention*) Majesty!

HENRY IV (*Turning round quickly*) Ah yes . . . this isn't the moment to speak ill of the bishops. But this infamy against my mother, Monsignor, is too much. (*Looks at the* MARCHIONESS *and grows tender*) And I can't even weep for her, Lady. . . . I appeal to you who have a mother's heart! She came here to see me from her convent a month ago. . . . They had told me she was dead! (*Sustained pause full of feeling. Then smiling sadly*) I can't weep for her; because if you are here now, and I am like this (*Shows the sackcloth he is wearing*) it means I am twenty-six years old!

HAROLD And that she is therefore alive, Majesty! . . .

ORDULPH Still in her convent!

HENRY IV (*Looking at them*) Ah yes! And I can postpone my grief to another time. (*Shows the* MARCHIONESS *almost with coquetry the tint he has given to his hair*) Look! I am still fair. . . . (*Then slowly as if in confidence*) For you . . . there's no need! But little exterior details do help! A matter of time, Monsignor, do you understand me? (*Turns to the* MARCHIONESS *and notices her hair*) Ah, but I see that you too, Duchess . . . Italian, eh? (*As much as to say "false"; but without any indignation, indeed rather with malicious admiration*) Heaven forbid that I should show disgust or surprise! Nobody cares to recognize that obscure and fatal power which sets limits to our will. But I say, if one is born and one dies . . . Did you want to be born, Monsignor? I didn't! And in both cases, independently of our wills, so many things happen we would wish didn't happen, and to which we resign ourselves as best we can! . . .

DOCTOR (*Merely to make a remark, while studying* HENRY IV *carefully*) Alas! Yes, alas!

HENRY IV It's like this: When we are not resigned, out come our desires. A woman wants to be a man . . . an old man would be young again. Desires, ridiculous fixed ideas of course— But reflect! Monsignor, those other desires are not less ridiculous: I mean, those desires where the will is kept within the limits of the possible. Not one of us can lie or pretend. We're all fixed in good faith in a certain concept of ourselves. However, Monsignor, while you keep yourself in order, holding on with both your hands to your holy habit, there slips down from your sleeves, there peels off from you like . . . like a serpent . . . something you don't notice: life, Monsignor! (*Turns to the* MARCHIONESS) Has it never happened to you, my Lady, to find a different self in yourself? Have you always been the same? My God! One day . . . how was it, how was it you were able to commit this or that action? (*Fixes her so intently in the eyes as almost to make her blanch*) Yes, that particular action, that very one: we understand each other! But don't be afraid: I shall reveal it to none. And you, Peter Damiani, how could you be a friend of that man? . . .

LANDOLPH Majesty!

HENRY IV (*At once*) No, I won't name him! (*Turning to* BELCREDI) What did you think of him? But we all of us cling tight to our conceptions of ourselves, just as he who is growing old dyes his hair. What does it matter that this dyed hair of mine isn't a reality for you, if it *is*, to some extent, for me?—you, you, my Lady, certainly don't dye your hair to deceive the others, nor even yourself; but only to cheat your own image a little before the looking-glass. I do it for a joke! You do it seriously! But I assure you that you too, Madam, are in masquerade, though it be in all seriousness; and I am not speaking of the venerable crown on your brows or the ducal mantle. I am speaking only of the memory you wish to fix in yourself of your fair complexion one day when it pleased you—or of your dark complexion, if you were dark: the fading image of your youth! For you, Peter Damiani, on the contrary, the memory of what you have been, of what you have done, seems to you a recognition of past realities that remain within you like a dream. I'm in the same case too: with so many inexplicable memories—like dreams! Ah! . . . There's nothing to marvel at in it, Peter Damiani! Tomorrow it will be the same thing with our life of today! (*Suddenly getting excited and taking hold of his sackcloth*) This sackcloth here . . . (*Beginning to take it off with a gesture of almost ferocious joy while the* THREE VALETS *run over to him, frightened, as if to prevent his doing so*) Ah, my God! (*Draws back and throws off sackcloth*) Tomorrow, at Bressanone, twenty-seven German and Lombard bishops will sign with me the act of deposition of Gregory VII! No Pope at all! Just a false monk!

ORDULPH (*With the other three*) Majesty! Majesty! In God's name! . . .

HAROLD (*Inviting him to put on the sackcloth again*) Listen to what he says, Majesty!

LANDOLPH Monsignor is here with the Duchess to intercede in your favor. (*Makes secret signs to the* DOCTOR *to say something at once*)

DOCTOR (*Foolishly*) Ah yes . . . yes . . . we are here to intercede . . .

HENRY IV (*Repenting at once, almost terrified, allowing the three to put on the sackcloth again, and pulling it down over him with his own hands*) Pardon . . . yes . . . yes . . . pardon, Monsignor: forgive me, my Lady. . . . I swear to you I feel the whole weight of the anathema. (*Bends himself, takes his face between his hands, as though waiting for something to crush him. Then changing tone, but without moving, says softly to* LANDOLPH, HAROLD, *and* ORDULPH) But I don't know why I cannot be humble before that man there! (*Indicates* BELCREDI)

LANDOLPH (*Sotto voce*) But why, Majesty, do you insist on believing he is Peter Damiani, when he isn't, at all?

HENRY IV (*Looking at him timorously*) He isn't Peter Damiani?

HAROLD No, no, he is a poor monk, Majesty.

HENRY IV (*Sadly with a touch of exasperation*) Ah! None of us can estimate what we do when we do it from instinct. . . . You perhaps, Madam, can understand me better than the others, since you are a woman and a Duchess. This is a solemn and decisive moment. I could, you know, accept the assistance of the Lombard bishops, arrest the Pope, lock him up here in the castle, run to Rome and elect an anti-Pope; offer alliance to Robert Guiscard—and Gregory VII would be lost! I resist the temptation; and, believe me, I am wise in doing so. I feel the atmosphere of our times and the majesty of one who knows how to be what he ought to be! a Pope! Do you feel inclined to laugh at me, seeing me like this? You would be foolish to do so; for you don't understand the political wisdom which makes this penitent's sack advisable. The parts may be changed tomorrow. What would you do then? Would you laugh to see the Pope a prisoner? No! It would come to the same thing: I dressed as a penitent, today; he, as prisoner tomorrow! But woe to him who doesn't know how to wear his mask, be he king or Pope!—Perhaps he is a bit too cruel! No! Yes, yes, maybe!—You remember, my Lady, how your daughter Bertha, for whom, I repeat, my feelings have changed (*Turns to* BELCREDI *and shouts to his face as if he were being contradicted by him*)—yes, changed on account of the affection and devotion she showed me in that terrible moment . . . (*Then once again to the* MARCHIONESS) . . . you remember how she came with me, my Lady, followed me like a beggar and passed two nights out in the open, in the snow? You are her mother! Doesn't this touch your mother's heart? Doesn't this urge you to pity, so that you will beg His Holiness for pardon, beg him to receive us?

DONNA MATILDA (*Trembling, with feeble voice*) Yes, yes, at once. . . .

DOCTOR It shall be done!

HENRY IV And one thing more! (*Draws them in to listen to him*) It isn't enough that he should receive me! You know he can do *everything—everything* I tell you! He can even call up the dead. (*Touches his chest*) Behold me! Do you see me? There is no magic art unknown to him. Well, Monsignor, my Lady, my torment is really this: that whether here or there (*Pointing to his portrait almost in fear*) I can't free myself from this magic. I am a penitent now, you see; and I swear to you I shall remain so until he receives me. But you two, when the excommunication is taken off, must ask the Pope to do this thing he can so easily do: to take me away from that; (*Indicating the portrait again*) and let me live wholly and freely my miserable life. A man can't always be twenty-six, my Lady. I ask this of you for your daughter's sake too; that I may love her as she deserves to be loved, well disposed as I am now, all tender toward her for her pity. There: it's all there! I am in your hands! (*Bows*) My Lady! Monsignor!

(*He goes off, bowing grandly, through the door by which he entered, leaving everyone stupefied, and the* MARCHIONESS *so profoundly touched, that no sooner has he gone than she breaks out into sobs and sits down almost fainting*)

# Act Two

*Another room of the villa, adjoining the throne room. Its furniture is antique and severe. Principal exit at rear in the background. To the left, two windows looking on the garden. To the right, a door opening into the throne room.*

*Late afternoon of the same day.*

DONNA MATILDA, *the* DOCTOR *and* BELCREDI *are on the stage engaged in conversation; but* DONNA MATILDA *stands to one side, evidently annoyed at what the other two are saying; although she cannot help listening, because, in her agitated state, everything interests her in spite of herself. The talk of the other two attracts her attention, because she instinctively feels the need for calm at the moment.*

BELCREDI It may be as you say, Doctor, but that was my impression.

DOCTOR I won't contradict you; but, believe me, it is only . . . an impression.

BELCREDI Pardon me, but he even said so, and quite clearly. (*Turning to the* MARCHIONESS) Didn't he, Marchioness?

DONNA MATILDA (*Turning round*) What did he say? . . . (*Then not agreeing*) Oh yes . . . but not for the reason you think!

DOCTOR He was alluding to the costumes we had slipped on. . . . Your cloak (*Indicating the* MARCHIONESS) our Benedictine habits. . . . But all this is childish!

DONNA MATILDA (*Turning quickly, indignant*) Childish? What do you mean, Doctor?

DOCTOR From one point of view, it is—I beg you to let me say so, Marchioness! Yet, on the other hand, it is much more complicated than you can imagine.

DONNA MATILDA To me, on the contrary, it is perfectly clear!

DOCTOR (*With a smile of pity of the competent person toward those who do not understand*) We must take into account the peculiar psychology of madmen; which, you must know, enables us to be certain that they observe things and can, for instance, easily detect people who are disguised; can in fact recognize the disguise and yet believe in it; just as children do, for whom disguise is both play and reality. That is why I used the word childish. But the thing is extremely complicated, inasmuch as he must be perfectly aware of being an image to himself and for himself—that image there, in fact! (*Alluding to the portrait in the throne room, and pointing to the left*)

BELCREDI That's what he said!

DOCTOR Very well then— An image before which other images, ours, have appeared: understand? Now he, in his acute and perfectly lucid delirium, was able to detect at once a difference between his image and ours: that is, he saw that ours were make-believes. So he suspected us; because all madmen are armed with a special diffidence. But that's all there is to it! Our make-believe, built up all round his, did not seem pitiful to him. While his seemed all the more tragic to us, in that he, as if in defiance—understand?—and induced by his suspicion, wanted to show us up merely as a joke. That was also partly the case with him, in coming before us with painted cheeks and hair, and saying he had done it on purpose for a jest.

DONNA MATILDA (*Impatiently*) No, it's not that, Doctor. It's not like that! It's not like that!

DOCTOR Why isn't it, may I ask?

DONNA MATILDA (*With decision but trembling*) I am perfectly certain he recognized me!

DOCTOR It's not possible . . . it's not possible!

BELCREDI (*At the same time*) Of course not!

DONNA MATILDA (*More than ever determined, almost convulsively*) I tell you, he recognized me! When he came close up to speak to me—looking in my eyes, right into my eyes—he recognized me!

BELCREDI But he was talking of your daughter!

DONNA MATILDA That's not true! He was talking of me! Of me!

BELCREDI Yes, perhaps, when he said . . .

DONNA MATILDA (*Letting herself go*) About my dyed hair! But didn't you notice that he added at once: "or the memory of your dark hair, if you were dark"? He remembered perfectly well that I was dark—then!

BELCREDI Nonsense! nonsense!

DONNA MATILDA (*Not listening to him, turning to the* DOCTOR) My hair, Doctor, is really dark—like my daughter's! That's why he spoke of her.

BELCREDI But he doesn't even know your daughter! He's never seen her!

DONNA MATILDA Exactly! Oh, you never understand anything! By my daughter, stupid, he meant me—as I was then!

BELCREDI Oh, this is catching! This is catching, this madness!

DONNA MATILDA (*Softly, with contempt*) Fool!

BELCREDI Excuse me, were you ever his wife? Your daughter is his wife—in his delirium: Bertha of Susa.

DONNA MATILDA Exactly! Because I, no longer dark—as he remembered me—but *fair,* introduced myself as "Adelaide," the mother. My daughter doesn't exist for him: he's never seen her—you said so yourself! So how can he know whether she's fair or dark?

BELCREDI But he said dark, speaking generally, just as anyone who wants to recall, whether fair or dark, a memory of youth in the color of the hair! And you, as usual, begin to imagine things! Doctor, you said I ought not to have come! It's she who ought not to have come!

DONNA MATILDA (*Upset for a moment by* BELCREDI'S *remark, recovers herself. Then with a touch of anger, because doubtful*) No, no . . . he spoke of me. . . . He spoke all the time to me, with me, of me. . . .

BELCREDI That's not bad! He didn't leave me a moment's breathing space; and you say he was talking all the time to you? Unless you think he was alluding to you too, when he was talking to Peter Damiani!

DONNA MATILDA (*Defiantly, almost exceeding the limits of courteous discussion*) Who knows? Can you tell me why, from the outset, he showed a strong dislike for you, for you alone? (*From the tone of the question, the expected answer must almost explicitly be: "because he understands you are my lover."* BELCREDI *feels this so well that he remains silent and can say nothing*)

DOCTOR The reason may also be found in the fact that only the visit of the Duchess Adelaide and the Abbot of Cluny was announced to him. Finding a third person present, who had not been announced, at once his suspicions . . .

BELCREDI Yes, exactly! His suspicion made him see an enemy in me: Peter Damiani! But she's got it into her head, that he recognized her . . .

DONNA MATILDA There's no doubt about it! I could see it from his eyes, doctor. You know, there's a way of looking that leaves no doubt whatever. . . . Perhaps it was only for an instant, but I am sure!

DOCTOR It is not impossible: a lucid moment . . .

DONNA MATILDA Yes, perhaps. . . . And then his speech seemed to me full of regret for his and my youth—for the horrible thing that happened to him, that has held him in that disguise from which he has never been able to free himself, and from which he longs to be free—he said so himself!

BELCREDI Yes, so as to be able to make love to your daughter, or you, as you believe—having been touched by your pity.

DONNA MATILDA Which is very great, I would ask you to believe.

BELCREDI As one can see, Marchioness; so much so that a miracle-worker might expect a miracle from it!

DOCTOR Will you let me speak? I don't work miracles, because I am a doctor and not a miracle-worker. I listened very intently to all he said; and I repeat that a certain analogical elasticity, common in all systematized delirium, is evidently with him much—what shall I say?—much relaxed! The elements, that is, of his delirium no longer hold together. It seems to me he has lost the equilibrium of his second personality and sudden recollections drag him—and this is very comforting—not from a state of incipient apathy, but rather from a morbid inclination to reflective melancholy, which shows a . . . a very considerable cerebral activity. Very comforting, I repeat! Now if, by this violent trick we've planned . . .

DONNA MATILDA (*Turning to the window, in the tone of a sick person complaining*) But how is it that the car has not returned? It's three hours and a half since . . .

DOCTOR What do you say?

DONNA MATILDA The car, Doctor! It's more than three hours and a half . . .

DOCTOR (*Taking out his watch and looking at it*) Yes, more than four hours, by this!

DONNA MATILDA It could have reached here an hour ago at least! But, as usual . . .

BELCREDI Perhaps they can't find the dress . . .

DONNA MATILDA But I explained exactly where it was! (*Impatiently*) And Frida . . . where is Frida?

BELCREDI (*Looking out of the window*) Perhaps she is in the garden with Charles. . . .

DOCTOR He'll talk her out of her fright.

BELCREDI She's not afraid, Doctor; don't you believe it: the thing bores her rather . . .

DONNA MATILDA Just don't ask anything of her! I know what she's like.

DOCTOR Let's wait patiently. Anyhow, it will soon be over, and it has to be in the evening . . . It will only be the matter of a moment! If we can succeed in rousing him, as I was saying, and in breaking at one go the threads—already slack—which still bind him to this fiction of his, giving him back what he himself asks for—you remember, he said: "one cannot always be twenty-six years old, madam!"—if we can give him freedom from this torment, which even *he* feels is a torment, then if he is able to recover at one bound the sensation of the distance of time . . .

BELCREDI (*Quickly*) He'll be cured! (*Then emphatically with irony*) We'll pull him out of it all!

DOCTOR Yes, we may hope to set him going again, like a watch which has stopped at a certain hour . . . just as if we had our watches in our hands and were waiting for that other watch to go again. A shake—so—and let's hope it'll tell the time again after its long stop. (*At this point the* MARQUIS CHARLES DI NOLLI *enters from the principal entrance*)

DONNA MATILDA Oh, Charles! . . . And Frida? Where is she?

DI NOLLI She'll be here in a moment.

DOCTOR Has the car arrived?

DI NOLLI Yes.

DONNA MATILDA Yes? Has the dress come?

DI NOLLI It's been here some time.

DOCTOR Good! Good!

DONNA MATILDA (*Trembling*) Where is she? Where's Frida?

DI NOLLI (*Shrugging his shoulders and smiling sadly, like one lending himself unwillingly to an untimely joke*) You'll see, you'll see! . . . (*Pointing toward the hall*) Here she is! . . . (BERTHOLD *appears at the threshold of the hall, and announces with solemnity*)

BERTHOLD Her Highness the Countess Matilda of Canossa! (FRIDA *enters, magnificent and beautiful, arrayed in the robes of her mother as "Countess Matilda of Tuscany," so that she is a living copy of the portrait in the throne room*)

FRIDA (*Passing* BERTHOLD, *who is bowing, says to him with disdain*) Of Tuscany, of Tuscany! Canossa is just one of my castles!

BELCREDI (*In admiration*) Look! Look! She seems another person. . . .

DONNA MATILDA One would say it were I! Look! Why, Frida, look! She's exactly my portrait, alive!

DOCTOR Yes, yes . . . Perfect! Perfect! The portrait, to the life.

BELCREDI Yes, there's no question about it. She *is* the portrait! Magnificent!

FRIDA Don't make me laugh, or I shall burst! I say, Mother, what a tiny waist you had! I had to squeeze so to get into this!

DONNA MATILDA (*Arranging her dress a little*) Wait! . . . Keep still! . . . These pleats . . . is it really so tight?

FRIDA I'm suffocating! I implore you, be quick! . . .

DOCTOR But we must wait till it's evening!

FRIDA No, no, I can't hold out till evening!

DONNA MATILDA Why did you put it on so soon?

FRIDA The moment I saw it, the temptation was irresistible. . . .

DONNA MATILDA At least you could have called me, or have had someone help you! It's still all crumpled.

FRIDA So I saw, Mother; but they are old creases; they won't come out.

DOCTOR It doesn't matter, Marchioness! The illusion is perfect. (*Then coming nearer and asking her to come in front of her daughter, without hiding her*)

If you please, stay there, there . . . at a certain distance . . . now a little more forward. . . .

BELCREDI For the feeling of the distance of time. . . .

DONNA MATILDA (*Slightly turning to him*) Twenty years after! A disaster! A tragedy!

BELCREDI Now don't let's exaggerate!

DOCTOR (*Embarrassed, trying to save the situation*) No, no! I meant the dress . . . so as to see . . . You know . . .

(*Pointing first to* FRIDA *and then to the* MARCHIONESS)

BELCREDI (*Laughing*) Oh, as for the dress, Doctor, it isn't a matter of twenty years! It's eight hundred! An abyss! Do you really want to shove him across it from there to here? But you'll have to pick him up in pieces with a basket! Just think now: for us it is a matter of twenty years, a couple of dresses, and a masquerade. But, if, as you say, Doctor, time has stopped for and around him: if he lives there (*Pointing to* FRIDA) with her, eight hundred years ago . . . I repeat: the giddiness of the jump will be such, that finding himself suddenly among us . . . (*The* DOCTOR *shakes his head in dissent*) You don't think so?

DOCTOR No, because life, my dear baron, can take up its rhythms. This—our life—will at once become real also to him; and will pull him up directly, wresting from him suddenly the illusion, and showing him that the eight hundred years, as you say, are only twenty! It will be like one of those tricks, such as the leap into space, for instance, of the Masonic rite, which appears to be heaven knows how far, and is only a step down the stairs.

BELCREDI Ah! An idea! Yes! Look at Frida and the Marchioness, doctor! Which is more advanced in time? We old people, Doctor! The young ones think they are more ahead; but it isn't true: we are more ahead, because time belongs to us more than to them.

DOCTOR If the past didn't alienate us. . . .

BELCREDI It doesn't matter at all! How does it alienate us? They (*Pointing to* FRIDA *and* DI NOLLI) have still to do what we have accomplished, Doctor: to grow old, doing the same foolish things, more or less, as we did. . . . This is the illusion: that one comes forward through a door to life. It isn't so! As soon as one is born, one starts dying; therefore, he who started first is the most advanced of all. The youngest of us is father Adam! Look there: (*Pointing to* FRIDA) eight hundred years younger than all of us—the Countess Matilda of Tuscany. (*He makes her a deep bow*)

DI NOLLI I say, Tito, don't start joking.

BELCREDI Oh, you think I am joking? . . .

DI NOLLI Of course, of course . . . all the time.

BELCREDI Impossible! I've even dressed up as a Benedictine. . . .

DI NOLLI Yes, but for a serious purpose.

BELCREDI Well, exactly. If it has been serious for the others . . . for Frida, now, for instance. (*Then turning to the* DOCTOR) I swear, Doctor, I don't yet understand what you want to do.

DOCTOR (*Annoyed*) You'll see! Let me do as I wish. . . . At present you see the Marchioness still dressed as . . .

BELCREDI Oh, she also . . . has to masquerade?

DOCTOR Of course! of course! In another dress that's in there ready to be used when it comes into his head he sees the Countess Matilda of Canossa before him.

FRIDA (*While talking quietly to* DI NOLLI *notices the doctor's mistake*) Of Tuscany, of Tuscany!

DOCTOR It's all the same!

BELCREDI Oh, I see; He'll be faced by two of them. . . .

DOCTOR Two, precisely! And then . . .

FRIDA (*Calling him aside*) Come here, doctor! Listen!

DOCTOR Here I am! (*Goes near the two young people and pretends to give some explanations to them*)

BELCREDI (*Softly to* DONNA MATILDA) I say, this is getting rather strong, you know!

DONNA MATILDA (*Looking him firmly in the face*) What?

BELCREDI Does it really interest you as much as all that—to make you willing to take part in . . . ? For a woman this is simply enormous! . . .

DONNA MATILDA Yes, for an ordinary woman.

BELCREDI Oh, no, my dear, for all women—in a question like this! It's an abnegation.

DONNA MATILDA I owe it to him.

BELCREDI Don't lie! You know well enough it's not hurting you!

DONNA MATILDA Well, then, where does the abnegation come in?

BELCREDI Just enough to prevent you losing caste in other people's eyes—and just enough to offend me! . . .

DONNA MATILDA But who is worrying about you now?

DI NOLLI (*Coming forward*) It's all right. It's all right. That's what we'll do! (*Turning toward* BERTHOLD) Here you, go and call one of those fellows!

BERTHOLD At once! (*Exit*)

DONNA MATILDA But first of all we've got to pretend that we are going away.

DI NOLLI Exactly! I'll see to that. . . . (*To* BELCREDI) You don't mind staying here?

BELCREDI (*Ironically*) Oh, no, I don't mind, I don't mind! . . .

DI NOLLI We must look out not to make him suspicious again, you know.

BELCREDI Oh, Lord! *He* doesn't amount to anything!

DOCTOR He must believe absolutely that we've gone away. (LANDOLPH *followed by* BERTHOLD *enters from the right*)

LANDOLPH May I come in?

DI NOLLI Come in! Come in! I say—your name's Lolo, isn't it?

LANDOLPH Lolo, or Landolph, just as you like!

DI NOLLI Well, look here: the Doctor and the Marchioness are leaving, at once.

LANDOLPH Very well. All we've got to say is that they have been able to obtain the permission for the reception from His Holiness. He's in there in his own apartments repenting of all he said—and in an awful state to have the pardon! Would you mind coming a minute? . . . If you would, just for a minute . . . put on the dress again. . . .

DOCTOR Why, of course, with pleasure. . . .

LANDOLPH Might I be allowed to make a suggestion? Why not add that the Marchioness of Tuscany has interceded with the Pope that he should be received?

DONNA MATILDA You see, he has recognized me!

LANDOLPH Forgive me . . . I don't know my history very well. I am sure you gentlemen know it much better! But I thought it was believed that Henry IV had a secret passion for the Marchioness of Tuscany.

DONNA MATILDA (*At once*) Nothing of the kind! Nothing of the kind!

LANDOLPH That's what I thought! But he says he's loved her . . . he's always saying it. . . . And now he fears that her indignation for this secret love of his will work him harm with the Pope.

BELCREDI We must let him understand that this aversion no longer exists.

LANDOLPH Exactly! Of course!

DONNA MATILDA (*To* BELCREDI) History says—I don't know whether you know it or not—that the Pope gave way to the supplications of the Marchioness Matilda and the Abbot of Cluny. And I may say, my dear Belcredi, that I intended to take advantage of this fact—at the time of the pageant—to show him my feelings were not so hostile to him as he supposed.

BELCREDI You are most faithful to history, Marchioness. . . .

LANDOLPH Well then, the Marchioness could spare herself a double disguise and present herself with Monsignor (*Indicating the* DOCTOR) as the Marchioness of Tuscany.

DOCTOR (*Quickly, energetically*) No, no! That won't do at all. It would ruin everything. The impression from the confrontation must be a sudden one, give a shock! No, no, Marchioness, you will appear again as the Duchess Adelaide, the mother of the Empress. And then we'll go away. This is most necessary: that he should know we've gone away. Come on! Don't let's waste any more time! There's a lot to prepare.

(*Exeunt the* DOCTOR, DONNA MATILDA, *and* LANDOLPH, *right*)

FRIDA I am beginning to feel afraid again.

DI NOLLI Again, Frida?

FRIDA It would have been better if I had seen him before.

DI NOLLI There's nothing to be frightened of, really.

FRIDA He isn't furious, is he?

DI NOLLI Of course not! he's quite calm.

BELCREDI (*With ironic sentimental affectation*) Melancholy! Didn't you hear that he loves you?

FRIDA Thanks! That's just why I am afraid.

BELCREDI He won't do you any harm.

DI NOLLI It'll only last a minute.

FRIDA Yes, but there in the dark with him. . . .

DI NOLLI Only for a moment; and I will be near you, and all the others behind the door ready to run in. As soon as you see your mother, your part will be finished.

BELCREDI I'm afraid of a different thing: that we're wasting our time. . . .

DI NOLLI Don't begin again! The remedy seems a sound one to me.

FRIDA I think so too! I feel it! I'm all trembling!

BELCREDI But, mad people, my dear friends—though they don't know it, alas—have this felicity which we don't take into account. . . .

DI NOLLI (*Interrupting, annoyed*) What felicity? Nonsense!

BELCREDI (*Forcefully*) They don't reason!

DI NOLLI What's reasoning got to do with it, anyway?

BELCREDI Don't you call it reasoning that he will have to do—according to us—when he sees her (*Indicates* FRIDA) and her mother? We've reasoned it all out, surely!

DI NOLLI Nothing of the kind: no reasoning at all! We put before him a double image of his own fantasy, or fiction, as the doctor says.

BELCREDI (*Suddenly*) I say, I've never understood why they take degrees in medicine.

DI NOLLI (*Amazed*) Who?

BELCREDI The psychiatrists.

DI NOLLI What ought they to take degrees in, then?

FRIDA If they are psychiatrists, in what else should they take degrees?

BELCREDI In law, of course! All a matter of talk! The more they talk, the more highly they are considered. "Analogous elasticity," "the sensation of distance in time!" And the first thing they tell you is that they don't work miracles—when a miracle's just what is wanted! But they know that the more they say they are not miracle-workers, the more people believe in their seriousness!

BERTHOLD (*Who has been looking through the keyhole of the door on right*) There they are! There they are! They're coming in here.

DI NOLLI Are they?

BERTHOLD He wants to come with them. . . . Yes! . . . He's coming too!

DI NOLLI Let's get away, then! Let's get away, at once! (*To* BERTHOLD) You stop here!

BERTHOLD Must I?

(*Without answering him,* DI NOLLI, FRIDA, *and* BELCREDI *go out by the main exit, leaving* BERTHOLD *surprised. The door on the right opens, and* LANDOLPH *enters first, bowing. Then* DONNA MATILDA *comes in, with mantle and ducal crown as in the first act; also the* DOCTOR *as the* ABBOT OF CLUNY. HENRY IV *is among them in royal dress.* ORDULPH *and* HAROLD *enter last of all*)

HENRY IV (*Following up what he has been saying in the other room*) And now I will ask you a question: how can I be astute, if you think me obstinate?

DOCTOR No, no, not obstinate!

HENRY IV (*Smiling, pleased*) Then you think me really astute?

DOCTOR No, no, neither obstinate, nor astute.

HENRY IV (*With benevolent irony*) Monsignor, if

obstinacy is not a vice which can go with astuteness, I hoped that in denying me the former, you would at least allow me a little of the latter. I can assure you I have great need of it. But if you want to keep it all for yourself . . .

DOCTOR I? I? Do I seem astute to you?

HENRY IV No. Monsignor! What do you say? Not in the least! Perhaps in this case, I may seem a little obstinate to you. . . . (*Cutting short to speak to* DONNA MATILDA) With your permission: a word in confidence to the Duchess. (*Leads her aside and asks her very earnestly*) Is your daughter really dear to you?

DONNA MATILDA (*Dismayed*) Why, yes, certainly. . . .

HENRY IV Do you wish me to compensate her with all my love, with all my devotion, for the grave wrongs I have done her—though you must not believe all the stories my enemies tell about my dissoluteness!

DONNA MATILDA No, no, I don't believe them. I never have believed such stories.

HENRY IV Well, then are you willing?

DONNA MATILDA (*Confused*) What?

HENRY IV That I return to love your daughter again? (*Looks at her and adds, in a mysterious tone of warning*) You mustn't be a friend of the Marchioness of Tuscany!

DONNA MATILDA I tell you again that she has begged and tried not less than ourselves to obtain your pardon. . . .

HENRY IV (*Softly, but excitedly*) Don't tell me that! Don't say that to me! Don't you see the effect it has on me, my Lady?

DONNA MATILDA (*Looks at him; then very softly as if in confidence*) You love her still?

HENRY IV (*Puzzled*) Still? Still, you say? You know, then? But nobody knows! Nobody must know!

DONNA MATILDA But perhaps she knows, if she has begged so hard for you!

HENRY IV (*Looks at her and says*) And you love your daughter? (*Brief pause. He turns to the* DOCTOR *with laughing accents*) Ah, Monsignor, it's strange how little I think of my wife! It may be a sin, but I swear to you that I hardly feel her at all in my heart. What is stranger is that her own mother scarcely feels her in her heart. Confess, my Lady, that she amounts to very little for you. (*Turning to* DOCTOR) She talks to me of that other woman, insistently, insistently, I don't know why! . . .

LANDOLPH (*Humbly*) Maybe, Majesty, it is to disabuse you of some ideas you have had about the Marchioness of Tuscany. (*Then, dismayed at having allowed himself this observation, adds*) I mean just now, of course. . . .

HENRY IV You too maintain that she has been friendly to me?

LANDOLPH Yes, at the moment, Majesty.

DONNA MATILDA Exactly! Exactly! . . .

HENRY IV I understand. That is to say, you don't believe I love her. I see! I see! Nobody's ever believed it, nobody's ever thought it. Better so, then! But enough, enough! (*Turns to the* DOCTOR *with changed expression*) Monsignor, you see? The reasons the Pope has had for revoking the excommunication have nothing at all to do with the reasons for which he excommunicated me originally. Tell Pope Gregory we shall meet again at Bressanone. And you, Madame, should you chance to meet your daughter in the courtyard of the castle of your friend the Marchioness, ask her to visit me. We shall see if I succeed in keeping her close beside me as wife and Empress. Many women have presented themselves here already assuring me that they were she. And I thought to have her—yes, I tried sometimes—there's no shame in it, with one's wife!—But when they said they were Bertha, and they were from Susa, all of them—I can't think why—started laughing! (*Confidentially*) Understand?—In bed—I undressed—so did she—yes, by God, undressed—a man and a woman—it's natural after all! Like that, we don't bother much about who we are. And one's dress is like a phantom that hovers always near one. Oh, Monsignor, phantoms in general are nothing more than trifling disorders of the spirit: images we cannot contain within the bounds of sleep. They reveal themselves even when we are awake, and they frighten us. I . . . ah . . . I am always afraid when, at nighttime, I see disordered images before me. Sometimes I am even afraid of my own blood pulsing loudly in my arteries in the silence of night, like the sound of a distant step in a lonely corridor! . . . But, forgive me! I have kept you standing too long already. I thank you, my Lady, I thank you, Monsignor. (DONNA MATILDA *and the* DOCTOR *go off bowing. As soon as they have gone,* HENRY IV *suddenly changes his tone*) Buffoons, buffoons! One can play any tune on them! And that other fellow . . . Pietro Damiani! . . . Caught him out perfectly! He's afraid to appear before me again. (*Moves up and down excitedly while saying this; then sees* BERTHOLD, *and points him out to the other three valets*) Oh, look at this imbecile watching me with his mouth wide open! (*Shakes him*) Don't you understand? Don't you see, idiot, how I treat them, how I play the fool with them, make them appear before me just as I wish? Miserable, frightened clowns that they are! And you (*Addressing the* VALETS) are amazed that I tear off their ridiculous masks now, just as if it wasn't I who had made them mask themselves to satisfy this taste of mine for playing the madman!

LANDOLPH—HAROLD—ORDULPH (*Bewildered, looking at one another*) What? What does he say? What?

HENRY IV (*Answers them imperiously*) Enough! enough! Let's stop it. I'm tired of it. (*Then as if the thought left him no peace*) By God! The impudence! To come here along with her lover! . . . And pretending to do it out of pity! So as not to infuriate a poor devil already out of the world, out of time, out of life! If it weren't supposed to be done out of pity, one can well imagine that fellow wouldn't have allowed it. Those people expect others to behave as they wish all the time. And, of course, there's nothing arrogant in that! Oh, no! Oh, no!

It's merely their way of thinking, of feeling, of seeing. Everybody has his own way of thinking; you fellows, too. Yours is that of a flock of sheep—miserable, feeble, uncertain. . . . But those others take advantage of this and make you accept their way of thinking; or, at least, they suppose they do; because, after all, what do they succeed in imposing on you? Words, words which anyone can interpret in his own manner! That's the way public opinion is formed! And it's a bad outlook for a man who finds himself labeled one day with one of these words which everyone repeats; for example "madman," or "imbecile." Don't you think it is rather hard for a man to keep quiet, when he knows that there is a fellow going about trying to persuade everybody that he is as he sees him, trying to fix him in other people's opinion as a "madman"—according to him? Now I am talking seriously! Before I hurt my head, falling from my horse . . . (*Stops suddenly, noticing the dismay of the four young men*) What's the matter with you? (*Imitates their amazed looks*) What? Am I, or am I not, mad? Oh, yes! I'm mad all right! (*He becomes terrible*) Well, then, by God, down on your knees, down on your knees! (*Makes them go down on their knees one by one*) I order you to go down on your knees before me! And touch the ground three times with your foreheads! Down, down! That's the way you've got to be before madmen! (*Then annoyed with their facile humiliation*) Get up, sheep! You obeyed me, didn't you? You might have put the strait jacket on me! . . . Crush a man with the weight of a word—it's nothing—a fly! All our life is crushed by the weight of words: the weight of the dead. Look at me here: can you really suppose that Henry IV is still alive? All the same, I speak, and order you live men about! Do you think it's a joke that the dead continue to live?—Yes, *here* it's a joke! But get out into the live world!—Ah, you say: what a beautiful sunrise—for us! All time is before us!—Dawn! We will do what we like with this day. . . . Ah, yes! To Hell with tradition, the old conventions! Well, go on! You will do nothing but repeat the old, old words, while you imagine you are living! (*Goes up to* BERTHOLD *who has now become quite stupid*) You don't understand a word of this, do you? What's your name?

BERTHOLD I? . . . What? . . . Berthold . . .

HENRY IV Poor Berthold! What's your name here?

BERTHOLD I . . . I . . . my name is Fino.

HENRY IV (*Feeling the warning and critical glances of the others, turns to them to reduce them to silence*) Fino?

BERTHOLD Fino Pagliuca, sire.

HENRY IV (*Turning to* LANDOLPH) I've heard you call each other by your nicknames often enough! Your name is Lolo, isn't it?

LANDOLPH Yes, sire . . . (*Then with a sense of immense joy*) Oh Lord! Oh Lord! Then he is not mad. . . .

HENRY IV (*Brusquely*) What?

LANDOLPH (*Hesitating*) No . . . I said . . .

HENRY IV Not mad, any more. No. Don't you see? We're having a joke on those that think I am mad! (*To* HAROLD) I say, boy, your name's Franco. . . . (*To* ORDULPH) And yours . . .

ORDULPH Momo.

HENRY IV Momo, Momo . . . A nice name that!

LANDOLPH So he isn't . . .

HENRY IV What are you talking about? Of course not! Let's have a jolly, good laugh! . . . (*Laughs*) Ah! . . . Ah! . . . Ah! . . .

LANDOLPH—HAROLD—ORDULPH (*Looking at each other half happy and half dismayed*) Then he's cured! . . . he's all right! . . .

HENRY IV Silence! Silence! . . . (*To* BERTHOLD) Why don't you laugh? Are you offended? I didn't mean it especially for you. It's convenient for everybody to insist that certain people are mad, so they can be shut up. Do you know why? Because it's impossible to hear them speak! What shall I say of these people who've just gone away? That one is a whore, another a libertine, another a swindler. . . . Don't you think so? You can't believe a word he says. . . . Don't you think so? By the way, they all listen to me terrified. And why are they terrified, if what I say isn't true? Of course, you can't believe what madmen say—yet, at the same time, they stand there with their eyes wide open with terror!—Why? Tell me, tell me, why?—You see I'm quite calm now!

BERTHOLD But, perhaps, they think that . . .

HENRY IV No, no, my dear fellow! Look me well in the eyes! . . . I don't say that it's true—nothing is true, Berthold! But . . . look me in the eyes!

BERTHOLD Well . . .

HENRY IV You see? You see? . . . You have terror in your own eyes now because I seem mad to you! There's the proof of it! (*Laughs*)

LANDOLPH (*Coming forward in the name of the others, exasperated*) What proof?

HENRY IV Your being so dismayed because now I seem again mad to you. You have thought me mad up to now, haven't you? You feel that this dismay of yours can become terror too—something to dash away the ground from under your feet and deprive you of the air you breathe! Do you know what it means to find yourselves face to face with a madman—with one who shakes the foundations of all you have built up in yourselves, your logic, the logic of all your constructions? Madmen, lucky folk, construct without logic, or rather with a logic that flies like a feather. Voluble! Voluble! Today like this and tomorrow—who knows? You say: "This cannot be"; but for them everything can be. You say: "This isn't true!" And why? Because it doesn't seem true to you, or you, or you. . . . (*Indicates the three of them in succession*) . . . and to a hundred thousand others! One must see what seems true to these hundred thousand others who are not supposed to be mad! What a magnificent spectacle they afford, when they reason! What flowers of logic they scatter! I know that when I was a child, I thought the moon in the pond was real. How many things I thought real! I believed everything I was told—and I was happy! Because it's a terrible thing if you don't hold on to that which seems true to you today—to that which will seem true to you tomorrow, even if it is the opposite of that which seemed true to you yesterday. I would never wish you to think, as I have done, on this horrible thing which really drives one mad: that if you were beside another and looking into his eyes—as I one day looked into somebody's eyes—you might as well be a beggar before a door never to be opened to you; for he who does enter there will never be you, but someone unknown to you with his own different and impenetrable world. . . . (*Long pause. Darkness gathers in the room, increasing the sense of strangeness and consternation in which the four young men are involved.* HENRY IV *remains aloof, pondering on the misery which is not only his, but everybody's. Then he pulls himself up, and says in an ordinary tone*) It's getting dark here. . . .

ORDULPH Shall I go for a lamp?

HENRY IV (*Ironically*) The lamp, yes the lamp! . . . Do you suppose I don't know that as soon as I turn my back with my oil lamp to go to bed, you turn on the electric light for yourselves, here, and even there, in the throne room? I pretend not to see it!

ORDULPH Well, then, shall I turn it on now?

HENRY IV No, it would blind me! I want my lamp!

ORDULPH It's ready here behind the door. (*Goes to the main exit, opens the door, goes out for a moment, and returns with an ancient lamp which is held by a ring at the top*)

HENRY IV Ah, a little light! Sit there around the table, no, not like that; in an elegant, easy, manner! . . . (*To* HAROLD) Yes, you, like that! (*Poses him*) (*Then to* BERTHOLD) You, so! . . . and I, here! (*Sits opposite them*) We could do with a little decorative moonlight. It's very useful for us, the moonlight. I feel a real necessity for it, and pass a lot of time looking up at the moon from my window. Who would think, to look at her that she knows that eight hundred years have passed, and that I, seated at the window, cannot really be Henry IV gazing at the moon like any poor devil? But, look, look! See what a magnificent night scene we have here: the emperor surrounded by his faithful counselors! . . . How do you like it?

LANDOLPH (*Softly to* HAROLD, *so as not to break the enchantment*) And to think it wasn't true! . . .

HENRY IV True? What wasn't true?

LANDOLPH (*Timidly as if to excuse himself*) No . . . I mean . . . I was saying this morning to him (*Indicates* BERTHOLD)—he has just started working here—I was saying: what a pity that dressed like this and with so many beautiful costumes in the wardrobe . . . and with a room like that . . . (*Indicates the throne room*)

HENRY IV Well? what's the pity?

LANDOLPH Well . . . that we didn't know . . .

HENRY IV That it was all done in jest, this comedy?

LANDOLPH Because we thought that . . .

HAROLD (*Coming to his assistance*) Yes . . . that it was done seriously!

HENRY IV What do you say? Doesn't it seem serious to you?

LANDOLPH But if you say that . . .

HENRY IV I say that—you are fools! You ought to have known how to create a fantasy for yourselves, not to act it for me, or anyone coming to see me; but naturally, simply, day by day, before nobody, feeling yourselves alive in the history of the eleventh century, here at the court of your emperor, Henry IV! You, Ordulph (*Taking him by the arm*), alive in the castle of Goslar, waking up in the morning, getting out of bed, and entering straight into the dream, clothing yourself in the dream that would be no more a dream, because you would have lived it, felt it all alive in you. You would have drunk it in with the air you breathed; yet knowing all the time that it was a dream, so you could better enjoy the privilege afforded you of having to do nothing else but live this dream, this far off and yet actual dream! And to think that at a distance of eight centuries from this remote age of ours, so colored and so sepulchral, the men of the twentieth century are torturing themselves in ceaseless anxiety to know how their fates and fortunes will work out! Whereas you are already in history with me. . . .

LANDOLPH Yes, yes, very good!

HENRY IV . . . Everything determined, everything settled!

ORDULPH Yes, yes!

HENRY IV And sad as is my lot, hideous as some of the events are, bitter the struggles, and troubled the time—still all history! All history that cannot change, understand? All fixed for ever! And you could have admired at your ease how every effect followed obediently its cause with perfect logic, how every event took place precisely and coherently in each minute particular! The pleasure, the pleasure of history, in fact, which is so great, was yours.

LANDOLPH Beautiful, beautiful!

HENRY IV Beautiful, but it's finished! Now that you know, I could not do it any more! (*Takes his lamp to go to bed*) Neither could you, if up to now you haven't understood the reason of it! I am sick of it now. (*Almost to himself with violent contained rage*) By God, I'll make her sorry she came here! Dressed herself up as a mother-in-law for me! . . . And he as an abbot! . . . And they bring a doctor with them to study me! . . . Who knows if they don't hope to cure me? . . . Clowns! . . . I'd like to smack one of them at least in the face: yes, that one—a famous swordsman, they say! . . . He'll kill me . . . Well, we'll see, we'll see! . . . (*A knock at the door*) Who is it?

THE VOICE OF JOHN Deo Gratias!

HAROLD (*Very pleased at the chance for another joke*) Oh, it's John, it's old John, who comes every night to play the monk.

ORDULPH (*Rubbing his hands*) Yes, yes! Let's make him do it!

HENRY IV (*At once, severely*) Fool, why? Just to play a joke on a poor old man who does it for love of me?

LANDOLPH (*To* ORDULPH) It has to be as if it were true.

HENRY IV Exactly, as if true! Because, only so, truth is not a jest. (*Opens the door and admits* JOHN *dressed as a humble friar with a roll of parchment under his arm*) Come in, come in, Father! (*Then assuming a tone of tragic gravity and deep resentment*) All the documents of my life and reign favorable to me were destroyed deliberately by my enemies. One only has escaped destruction, this, my life, written by a humble monk who is devoted to me. And you would laugh at him! (*Turns affectionately to* JOHN, *and invites him to sit down at the table*) Sit down, Father, sit down! Have the lamp near you! (*Puts the lamp near him*) Write! Write!

JOHN (*Opens the parchment and prepares to write from dictation*) I am ready, your Majesty!

HENRY IV (*Dictating*) "The decree of peace proclaimed at Mayence helped the poor and the good, while it damaged the powerful and the bad. (*Curtain begins to fall*) It brought wealth to the former, hunger and misery to the latter. . . ."

*Curtain*

# Act Three

*The throne room is so dark that the wall at the bottom is hardly seen. The canvases of the two portraits have been taken away; and, within their frames,* FRIDA, *dressed as the "Marchioness of Tuscany," and* CHARLES DI NOLLI, *as "Henry IV," have taken the exact positions of the portraits.*

*For a moment, after the raising of the curtain, the stage is empty. Then the door on the left opens; and* HENRY IV, *holding the lamp by the ring on top of it, enters. He looks back to speak to the four young men, who, with* JOHN, *are presumedly in the adjoining hall, as at the end of the second act.*

HENRY IV No, stay where you are, stay where you are. I shall manage all right by myself. Good night! (*Closes the door and walks, very sad and tired, across the hall toward the second door on the right, which leads into his apartments*)

FRIDA (*As soon as she sees that he has just passed the throne, whispers from the niche like one who is on the point of fainting away with fright*) Henry . . .

HENRY IV (*Stopping at the voice, as if someone had stabbed him traitorously in the back, turns a terror-stricken face toward the wall at the bottom of the room; raising an arm instinctively, as if to defend himself and ward off a blow*) Who is calling me? (*It is not a question, but an exclamation vibrating with terror, which does not expect a reply from the darkness and the terrible silence of the hall, which suddenly fills him with the suspicion that he is really mad*)

FRIDA (*At his shudder of terror, is herself not less frightened at the part she is playing, and repeats a little more loudly*) Henry! . . . (*But, although she wishes to act the part as they have given it to her, she stretches her head a little out of the frame toward the other frame*)

HENRY IV (*Gives a dreadful cry; lets the lamp fall from his hands to cover his head with his arms, and makes a movement as if to run away*)

FRIDA (*Jumping from the frame on to the stand and shouting like a mad woman*) Henry! . . . Henry! . . . I'm afraid! . . . I'm terrified! . . .

(*And while* DI NOLLI *jumps in turn on to the stand and thence to the floor and runs to* FRIDA *who, on the verge of fainting, continues to cry out, the* DOCTOR, DONNA MATILDA, *also dressed as "Matilda of Tuscany,"* TITO BELCREDI, LANDOLPH, BERTHOLD *and* JOHN *enter the hall from the doors on the right and on the left. One of them turns on the light: a strange light coming from lamps hidden in the ceiling so that only the upper part of the stage is well lighted. The others without taking notice of* HENRY IV, *who looks on astonished by the unexpected inrush, after the moment of terror which still causes him to tremble, run anxiously to support and comfort the still shaking* FRIDA, *who is moaning in the arms of her fiancé. All are speaking at the same time*)

DI NOLLI No, no, Frida . . . Here I am . . . I am beside you!

DOCTOR (*Coming with the others*) Enough! Enough! There's nothing more to be done! . . .

DONNA MATILDA He is cured, Frida. Look! He is cured! Don't you see?

DI NOLLI (*Astonished*) Cured?

BELCREDI It was only for fun! Be calm!

FRIDA No! I am afraid! I am afraid!

DONNA MATILDA Afraid of what? Look at him! He was never mad at all! . . .

DI NOLLI That isn't true! What are you saying? Cured?

DOCTOR It appears so. I should say so . . .

BELCREDI Yes, yes! They have told us so. (*Pointing to the four young men*)

DONNA MATILDA Yes, for a long time! He has confided in them, told them the truth!

DI NOLLI (*Now more indignant than astonished*) But what does it mean? If, up to a short time ago . . . ?

BELCREDI Hum! He was acting, to take you in and also us, who in good faith . . .

DI NOLLI Is it possible? To deceive his sister too, right up to the time of her death?

HENRY IV (*Remains apart, peering at one and now at the other under the accusation and the mockery of what all believe to be a cruel joke of his, which is now revealed. He has shown by the flashing of his eyes *that he is meditating a revenge, which his violent contempt prevents him from defining clearly, as yet. Stung to the quick and with a clear idea of accepting the fiction they have insidiously worked up as true, he bursts forth at this point*) Go on, I say! Go on!

DI NOLLI (*Astonished at the cry*) Go on! What do you mean?

HENRY IV It isn't *your* sister only that is dead!

DI NOLLI My sister? Yours, I say, whom you compelled up to the last moment, to present herself here as your mother, Agnes!

HENRY IV And was she not *your* mother?

DI NOLLI My mother? Certainly my mother!

HENRY IV But your mother is dead for me, *old and far away!* You have just got down now from there. (*Pointing to the frame from which he jumped down*) And how do you know whether I have not wept her long in secret, dressed even as I am?

DONNA MATILDA (*Dismayed, looking at the others*) What does he say?

DOCTOR (*Much impressed, observing him*) Quietly! quietly, for Heaven's sake!

HENRY IV What do I say? I ask all of you if Agnes was not the mother of Henry IV? (*Turns to* FRIDA *as if she were really the "Marchioness of Tuscany"*) You, Marchioness, it seems to me, ought to know.

FRIDA (*Still frightened, draws closer to* DI NOLLI) No, no, I don't know. Not I!

DOCTOR It's the madness returning. . . . Quiet now, everybody!

BELCREDI (*Indignant*) Madness indeed, Doctor! He's acting again! . . .

HENRY IV (*Suddenly*) I? You have emptied those two frames over there, and he stands before my eyes as Henry IV. . . .

BELCREDI We've had enough of this joke now.

HENRY IV Who said joke?

DOCTOR (*Loudly to* BELCREDI) Don't excite him, for the love of God!

BELCREDI (*Without lending an ear to him, but speaking louder*) But they have said so (*Pointing again to the four young men*), they, they!

HENRY IV (*Turning round and looking at them*) You? Did you say it was all a joke?

LANDOLPH (*Timid and embarrassed*) No . . . really we said that you were cured.

BELCREDI Look here! Enough of this! (*To* DONNA MATILDA) Doesn't it seem to you that the sight of him (*Pointing to* DI NOLLI), Marchioness, and that of your daughter dressed so, is becoming intolerably childish?

DONNA MATILDA Oh, be quiet! What does the dress matter, if he is cured?

HENRY IV Cured, yes! I am cured! (*To* BELCREDI) Ah, but not to let it end this way all at once, as you suppose! (*Attacks him*) Do you know that for twenty years nobody has ever dared to appear before me here like you and that gentleman? (*Pointing to the* DOCTOR)

BELCREDI Of course I know it. As a matter of fact, I too appeared before you this morning dressed . . .

HENRY IV As a monk, yes!

BELCREDI And you took me for Peter Damiani! And I didn't even laugh, believing, in fact, that . . .

HENRY IV That I was mad! Does it make you laugh seeing her like that, now that I am cured? And yet you might have remembered that in my eyes her appearance now . . . (*Interrupts himself with a gesture of contempt*) Ah! (*Suddenly turns to the* DOCTOR) You are a doctor, aren't you?

DOCTOR Yes.

HENRY IV And you also took part in dressing her up as the Marchioness of Tuscany? To prepare a counter-joke for me here, eh?

DONNA MATILDA (*Impetuously*) No, no! What do you say? It was done for you! I did it for your sake.

DOCTOR (*Quickly*) To attempt, to try, not knowing . . .

HENRY IV (*Cutting him short*) I understand. I say counter-joke, in his case (*Indicates* BELCREDI) because he believes that I have been carrying on a jest. . . .

BELCREDI But excuse me, what do you mean? You say yourself you are cured.

HENRY IV Let me speak! (*To the* DOCTOR) Do you know, Doctor, that for a moment you ran the risk of making me mad again? By God, to make the portraits speak; to make them jump alive out of their frames . . .

DOCTOR But you saw that all of us ran in at once, as soon as they told us . . .

HENRY IV Certainly! (*Contemplates* FRIDA *and* DI NOLLI, *and then looks at the* MARCHIONESS, *and finally at his own costume*) The combination is very beautiful. . . . Two couples. . . . Very good, very good, Doctor! For a madman, not bad! . . . (*With a slight wave of his hand to* BELCREDI) It seems to him now to be a carnival out of season, eh? (*Turns to look at him*) We'll get rid now of this masquerade costume of mine, so that I may come away with you. What do you say?

BELCREDI With me? With us!

HENRY IV Where shall we go? To the Club? In dress coats and with white ties? Or shall both of us go to the Marchioness' house?

BELCREDI Wherever you like! Do you want to remain here still, to continue—alone—what was nothing but the unfortunate joke of a day of carnival? It is really incredible, incredible how you have been able to do all this, freed from the disaster that befell you!

HENRY IV Yes, you see how it was! The fact is that falling from my horse and striking my head as I did, I was really mad for I know not how long. . . .

DOCTOR Ah! Did it last long?

HENRY IV (*Very quickly to the* DOCTOR) Yes, Doctor, a long time! I think it must have been about twelve years. (*Then suddenly turning to speak to* BELCREDI) Thus I saw nothing, my dear fellow, of all that, after that day of carnival, happened for you but not for me: how things changed, how my friends deceived me, how my place was taken by another, and all the rest of it! And suppose my place had been taken in the heart of the woman I loved? . . . And how should I know who was dead or who had disappeared? . . .

All this, you know, wasn't exactly a joke for me, as it seems to you. . . .

BELCREDI No, no! I don't mean that! I mean after . . .

HENRY IV Ah, yes? After? One day—(*Stops and addresses the* DOCTOR) A most interesting case, Doctor! Study me well! Study me carefully! (*Trembles while speaking*)—All by itself, who knows how, one day the trouble here (*Touches his forehead*) mended. Little by little, I open my eyes, and at first I don't know whether I am asleep or awake. Then I know I am awake. I touch this thing and that; I see clearly again. . . . Ah!—then, as *he* says (*Alludes to* BELCREDI) away, away with this masquerade, this incubus! Let's open the windows, breathe life once again! Away! Away! Let's run out! (*Suddenly pulling himself up*) But where? And to do what? To show myself to all, secretly, as Henry IV, not like this, but arm in arm with you, among my dear friends?

BELCREDI What are you saying?

DONNA MATILDA Who could think it? It's not to be imagined. It was an accident.

HENRY IV They all said I was mad before. (*To* BELCREDI) And you know it! You were more ferocious than anyone against those who tried to defend me.

BELCREDI Oh, that was only a joke!

HENRY IV Look at my hair! (*Shows him the hair on the nape of his neck*)

BELCREDI But mine is gray too!

HENRY IV Yes, with this difference: that mine went gray here, as Henry IV, do you understand? And I never knew it! I perceived it all of a sudden, one day, when I opened my eyes; and I was terrified because I understood at once that not only had my hair gone gray, but that I was all gray, inside; that everything had fallen to pieces, that everything was finished; and I was going to arrive, hungry as a wolf, at a banquet which had already been cleared away. . . .

BELCREDI Yes, but, what about the others? . . .

HENRY IV (*Quickly*) Ah, yes, I know! They couldn't wait until I was cured, not even those, who, behind my back, pricked my saddled horse till it bled. . . .

DI NOLLI (*Agitated*) What, what?

HENRY IV Yes, treacherously, to make it rear and cause me to fall.

DONNA MATILDA (*Quickly, in horror*) This is the first time I knew that.

HENRY IV That was also a joke, probably!

DONNA MATILDA But who did it? Who was behind us, then?

HENRY IV It doesn't matter who it was. All those that went on feasting and were ready to leave me their scrapings, Marchioness, of miserable pity, or some dirty remnant of remorse in the filthy plate! Thanks! (*Turning quickly to the* DOCTOR) Now, Doctor, the case must be absolutely new in the history of madness; I preferred to remain mad—since I found everything ready and at my disposal for this new exquisite fantasy. I would live it—this madness of mine—with the most lucid consciousness; and thus revenge myself on the brutality of a stone which had dented my head. The solitude—this solitude—squalid and empty as it appeared to me when I opened my eyes again—I determined to deck it out with all the colors and splendors of that far off day of carnival, when you (*Looks at* DONNA MATILDA *and points* FRIDA *out to her*)—when you, Marchioness, triumphed. So I would oblige all those who were around me to follow, by God, at my orders that famous pageant which had been—for you and not for me—the jest of a day. I would make it become—forever—no more a joke but a reality, the reality of a real madness: here, all in masquerade, with throne room, and these my four secret counselors: secret and, of course, traitors. (*He turns quickly toward them*) I should like to know what you have gained by revealing the fact that I was cured! If I am cured, there's no longer any need of you, and you will be discharged! To give anyone one's confidence . . . that is really the act of a madman. But now I accuse you in my turn. (*Turning to the others*) Do you know? They thought (*Alludes to the* VALETS) they could make fun of me too with you. (*Bursts out laughing. The others laugh, but shamefacedly, except* DONNA MATILDA)

BELCREDI (*To* DI NOLLI) Well, imagine that. . . . That's not bad. . . .

DI NOLLI (*To the four young men*) You?

HENRY IV We must pardon them. This dress (*Plucking his dress*) which is for me the evident, voluntary caricature of that other continuous, everlasting masquerade, of which we are the involuntary puppets (*Indicates* BELCREDI), when, without knowing it, we mask ourselves with that which we appear to be . . . ah, that dress of theirs, this masquerade of theirs, of course, we must forgive it them, since they do not yet see it is identical with themselves. . . . (*Turning again to* BELCREDI) You know, it is quite easy to get accustomed to it. One walks about as a tragic character, just as if it were nothing . . . (*Imitates the tragic manner*) in a room like this. . . . Look here, Doctor! I remember a priest, certainly Irish, a nice-looking priest, who was sleeping in the sun one November day, with his arm on the corner of the bench of a public garden. He was lost in the golden delight of the mild sunny air which must have seemed for him almost summery. One may be sure that in that moment he did not know any more that he was a priest, or even where he was. He was dreaming. . . . A little boy passed with a flower in his hand. He touched the priest with it here on the neck. I saw him open his laughing eyes, while all his mouth smiled with the beauty of his dream. He was forgetful of everything. . . . But all at once, he pulled himself together, and stretched out his priest's cassock; and there came back to his eyes the same seriousness which you have seen in mine; because the Irish priests defend the seriousness of their Catholic faith with the same zeal with which I defend the sacred rights of hereditary monarchy! I am cured, gentlemen: because I can act the madman to perfection, here; and I do it very quietly. I'm only sorry for you that have to live your madness so agitatedly, without knowing it or seeing it.

BELCREDI It comes to this, then, that it is we who are mad. That's what it is!

HENRY IV (*Containing his irritation*) But if you weren't mad, both you and she (*Indicating the* MARCHIONESS), would you have come here to see me?

BELCREDI To tell the truth, I came here believing that you were the madman.

HENRY IV (*Suddenly indicating the* MARCHIONESS) And she?

BELCREDI Ah, as for her . . . I can't say. I see she is fascinated by your words, by this *conscious* madness of yours. (*Turns to her*) Dressed as you are (*Speaking to her*), you could even remain here to live it out, Marchioness.

DONNA MATILDA You are insolent!

HENRY IV (*Conciliatingly*) No, Marchioness, what he means to say is that the miracle would be complete, according to him, with you here, who—as the Marchioness of Tuscany, you well know—could not be my friend, save, as at Canossa, to give me a little pity. . . .

BELCREDI Or even more than a little! She said so herself!

HENRY IV (*To the* MARCHIONESS, *continuing*) And even, shall we say, a little remorse! . . .

BELCREDI Yes, that too she has admitted.

DONNA MATILDA (*Angry*) Now look here . . .

HENRY IV (*Quickly, to placate her*) Don't bother about him! Don't mind him! Let him go on infuriating me—though the Doctor's told him not to. (*Turns to* BELCREDI) But do you suppose I am going to trouble myself any more about what happened between us—the share you had in my misfortune with her (*Indicates the* MARCHIONESS *to him and pointing* BELCREDI *out to her*), the part he has now in your life? This is my life! Quite a different thing from your life! Your life, the life in which you have grown old—I have not lived that life. (*To* DONNA MATILDA) Was this what you wanted to show me with this sacrifice of yours, dressing yourself up like this, according to the Doctor's idea? Excellently done, Doctor! Oh, an excellent idea: "As we were then, eh? and as we are now?" But I am not a madman according to your way of thinking, Doctor. I know very well that that man there (*Indicates* DI NOLLI) cannot be me; because I am Henry IV, and have been, these twenty years, cast in this eternal masquerade. She has lived these years! (*Indicates the* MARCHIONESS) She has enjoyed them and has become—look at her!—a woman I can no longer recognize. It is so that I knew her! (*Points to* FRIDA *and draws near her*) This is the Marchioness I know, always this one! . . . You seem a lot of children to be so easily frightened by me. . . . (*To* FRIDA) And you're frightened too, little girl, aren't you, by the jest that they made you take part in—though they didn't understand it wouldn't be the jest they meant it to be, for me? Oh miracle of miracles! Prodigy of prodigies! The dream alive in you! More than ever, alive in you! It was an image that wavered there and they've made you come to life! Oh, mine! You're mine, mine, mine, in my own right! (*He holds her in his arms, laughing like a madman, while all stand still terrified. Then as they advance to tear* FRIDA *from his arms, he becomes furious, terrible, and cries imperiously to his* VALETS) Hold them! Hold them! I order you to hold them!

(*The four young men amazed, yet fascinated, move to execute his orders, automatically, and seize* DI NOLLI, *the* DOCTOR, *and* BELCREDI)

BELCREDI (*Freeing himself*) Leave her alone! Leave her alone! You're no madman!

HENRY IV (*In a flash, draws the sword from the side of* LANDOLPH, *who is close to him*) I'm not mad, eh! Take that, you! . . . (*Drives sword into him. A cry of horror follows. All rush over to assist* BELCREDI, *crying out together*)

DI NOLLI Has he wounded you?

BERTHOLD He's wounded him seriously!

DOCTOR I told you so!

FRIDA Oh God, oh God!

DI NOLLI Frida, come here!

DONNA MATILDA He's mad, mad!

DI NOLLI Hold him!

BELCREDI (*While they take him away by the left exit, he protests as he is borne out*) No, no, you're not mad! You're not mad. He's not mad!

(*They go out by the left amid cries and excitement. After a moment, one hears a still sharper, more piercing cry from* DONNA MATILDA, *and then, silence*)

HENRY IV (*Who has remained on the stage between* LANDOLPH, HAROLD, *and* ORDULPH, *with his eyes almost starting out of his head, terrified by the life of his own masquerade which has driven him to crime*) Now, yes . . . we'll have to . . . (*Calls his* VALETS *around him as if to protect him*) Here we are . . . together . . . forever!

*Curtain*

# Jean Cocteau

# (1889-1963)

BAFFLING his critics and delighting the gossipmongers, Jean Cocteau spent his life responding to the imperative of the famous ballet impresario, Sergei Diaghilev, "Astound me!" Cocteau was in his early 20's when he heard Diaghilev's half-serious injunction, but one of his biographers has expressed astonishment that Cocteau was so *old* before the idea of "surprise" became central in his artistic values. In 1955, when he was elected to the French Academy of 40 "immortals," Cocteau seemed still to be leading critics and audiences in a merry game of hide-and-seek.

Cocteau was born in 1889 in Maisons-Laffitte where his well-to-do Parisian parents maintained a summer home. Cocteau's amazing catholicity of tastes in the arts was encouraged from his early youth. He moved easily, a madcap prince, through the world his friends, Proust and Colette, recorded in their novels. In his early 20's Cocteau joined the Parisian *haut monde* in adulation of Diaghilev's *Ballets Russes,* and associated easily with the great dancers and choreographers of that group—Nijinsky, Massine, and Fokine. The artistic revolution effected in all the arts by the *Ballets Russes* was epitomized in Cocteau's ballet-scenario, *Parade,* first performed in Paris in May, 1917. With music by Satie, costumes and décor by Picasso, choreography by Cocteau and Massine, this *ballet réaliste* created a sensation. The action concerned the tug-of-war between showmanship and bourgeois indifference, with audiences willing to accept the "come-on" performed outside a street theatre rather than paying to see the real "show" inside. Although *Parade* was an artistic failure, it is one of the most important events in modern theatre, particularly in foreshadowing the complex collaborations and experimentalism which flourished in Paris after World War I.

Not the least important aspect of Cocteau's stature is his success in linking the anti-bourgeois theatre of Alfred Jarry, whose *King Ubu* was first produced in 1896, and Guillaume Apollinaire, whose *Breasts of Tiresias* was produced soon after *Parade* in 1917, with the avant-garde theatre of France between the wars. In his "poetry of the theatre," he prepared the ground for Giraudoux, Anouilh, Sartre, and Camus. From Jarry's outrageous and hilarious *King Ubu,* Cocteau may have drawn, if not the inspiration, at least the precedent for the Rabelaisian shorthand Orphée's Horse taps out. Jarry had made explicit use of the French obscenity, *Merde,* which Cocteau more decorously buried in the first letters of the Horse's cryptic message: *"Madame Eurydice reviendra des enfers"* (literally, "Madame Eurydice will return from hell," but rendered innocuous in translation.)

Cocteau's influence on French theatre continued long after World War II. His illusionist theatricalism may be seen in the work of Jean Genet, whose plays in the tradition of the "theatre of cruelty" (*The Maids, Deathwatch, The Balcony, The Blacks*) have enlivened French —and American—theatre in recent years. In Genet's case, Cocteau's influence has been even more immediate since he, along with Sartre and other well-known French writers, joined in the successful effort to save the brilliant Baudelairean poet of perversion and satanism from life-imprisonment.

In the other arts, Cocteau was equally successful in expanding popular interest in works once regarded as eccentric or obscure. He carried his theory of aesthetics to music, especially during his association with *"Les Six"* (of whom Auric, Milhaud, Honegger, and Poulenc are best known) in the preparation of the farce, *The Wedding Party on the Eiffel Tower* (1921). In the graphic arts, especially as Picasso, Dufy, Bérard and others provided décor and costumes for his works, Cocteau made his theories viable. In addition to ballet-scenarios in which his cascades of shocking, fresh images broke the formality of classical ballet patterns, Cocteau prepared pantomimes like *Le Boeuf sur le Toit, or "The Do Nothing Bar"* (1920) for the popular Fratellini clowns, and material for popular cabaret entertainers of the 30's. He chose to adapt works as various as Sophocles' *Antigone* (1922) and *Oedipus Rex* (1937), Shakespeare's *Romeo and Juliet* (1924), and Williams' *A Streetcar Named Desire* (1949). When inevitably he addressed himself to the film medium, Cocteau found almost limitless the possibilities for conveying his highly subjective poetic vision and produced some of his finest work. His 1950 film adaptations of *Orphée* and of his major novel, *Les Enfants Terribles,* are among the most effective films produced since World War II. Apart from his work in the theatre and cinema, Cocteau also wrote extensively as poet, novelist, art and music critic. He has recorded not only his 1936 world trip *à la* Jules Verne's Phileas Fogg, but also such private agonies as his strange love affairs and the period of opium-addiction which account for so much of his restless productivity.

Cocteau's opium-taking may have been triggered by a well-meaning friend's efforts to keep Cocteau from the suicide he contemplated after the death, in 1923, of his *protégé*, the extraordinary young novelist, Raymond Radiguet. There is little doubt that in this difficult period Cocteau acquired the keen awareness of the hairline between life and death which is so important in *Orphée*. The strange name, *Heurtebise* (literally, "break-wind"), which Cocteau used first for an angel in a poem and later for the peculiarly un-Grecian Guardian Angel in *Orphée,* was revealed to him while he was under the effect of opium. Cocteau has recorded that, on a visit to Picasso, he saw *Heurtebise* on the manufacturer's plate in an elevator. The name obsessed him, filling him with a sense that another being was living inside him. Cocteau exorcised this phantom creature by objectifying it in his art. Years later, when he stepped into the elevator where he first met *Heurtebise,* he found the usual manufacturer's label, *Otis-Pifre*.

Cocteau has recorded that *Orphée* was originally conceived as a play about Mary and Joseph confronting their fellow Nazarenes' vicious gossip about the Virgin's pregnancy. He found this idea unworkable, however, and substituted the mysteries of artistic creation for the miracle of Christ's birth. Cocteau found the Orpheus-Eurydice myths mirrored his own vision of the poet in society and his preoccupation with Death and Eternity. In a very real sense, he saw himself as Orpheus, as suggested by his frequent returns to *Orphée,* first in the film version (1950) which considerably expanded Orpheus' love-affair with Death and reduced Heurtebise to a kind but prosaic chauffeur, and more recently in another film, *The Testament of Orpheus* (completed in 1959), in which Cocteau as Poet bequeaths his art to the future. In these works, Cocteau played very important roles on, as well as off, the screen. He is the Poet, directing in the manner of the Poet-Dreamer of Strindberg's *Dream Play* the flow of reality veiled behind familiar objects and practical affairs.

The mythological Orpheus captured Cocteau's sense of the poet as divine oracle holding the key to the mysteries of life. He can charm the beasts of the field, but he is victimized by their only partial apprehension of the universe. The classical Orpheus aroused jealousy among his human rivals and was persecuted for his superhuman powers, a treacherous relationship Cocteau has portrayed ironically in Aglaonice and her Bacchantes striking at Orphée through Eurydice. These outrageous bluestockings may symbolize the outraged ladies who threatened to blind Cocteau and Picasso with hatpins after the premiere of *Parade,* but the ladies are never far from their classical essence as The World. Written in 1925, *Orphée* was first performed in 1926. Although it was originally no more successful than *Parade* had been, *Orphée* has won many admirers and, along with Cocteau's equally theatricalist treatment of the Oedipus myth, *The Infernal Machine* (1934), it now ranks as one of his undoubted masterpieces.

Pursuing his policy of changing direction after each new work, Cocteau followed *Orphée* with a one-act monologue, *The Human Voice* (1930), accepted for production at the venerable Comédie-Française, and his first film, *The Blood of a Poet* (1932), in which Orphic themes were startlingly fragmentized in a "realistic documentary of unreal events." Next, with *The Infernal Machine,* Cocteau was at his most resourceful in shocking the atrophied imagination he has always despised. His version of the Oedipus myth eliminates suspense, builds the encounter between Oedipus and the Sphinx into an ironic courtship, and carries the archetypal seeker-after-truth through his incestuous wedding night to his bloody fate of self-inflicted blindness. The vision of a hellish machine symbolic of an essentially hostile universe is a victory for Cocteau's theatre: Oedipus, locked in timeless mythic truth, still accepts his destiny proudly as his own—and no other man's. In later works, Cocteau employed Arthurian legends (*Knights of the Round Table,* 1937), familiar domestic drama deployed in the naturalistic well-made-play tradition (*Intimate Relations,* or *Les Parents Terrible,* 1938; in film, 1948), formulas of classical verse tragedy (*Renaud et Armide,* 1943) and of romantic melodrama (*L'Aigle à deux Têtes,* 1946, but translated as *The Eagle Has Two Heads*), and, a historical drama enclosing a debate between symbolic exponents of religious freedom and church authority (*Bacchus,* 1951).

Until his death on October 11, 1963, Cocteau never ceased to live vigorously in his world of art and free spirits. One of his last works was *Patmos* (1962), an oratorio for which Paul Hindemith wrote the musical score. In this work, the secular replaced the traditional religious spirit of the classical oratorio form. Flying saucers rather than flying angels filled the outer space of this sensational success.

Both the iconoclast and dedicated aesthete in his pursuit of *magic, scandal,* and *spectacle,* Cocteau expanded the range of the modern theatre enormously, although in questing after the absolute limits of artistic freedom, he had courted disaster as much as success. In the process, however, he again demonstrated that the maximum freedom is open only to the experimentalist who respects simplicity and directness of style, explores the full resources of the modern theatre, and loves its masqueraders on both sides of the footlights.

# ORPHÉE

## *A Tragedy in One Act and an Interval*

Translated by Carl Wildman

### DRAMATIS PERSONAE

ORPHÉE (ORPHEUS), *a poet*
EURYDICE, *his wife*
HEURTEBISE, *a glazier*
THE HORSE
DEATH
AZRAEL, *experienced assistant to* DEATH
RAPHAEL, *novice assistant to* DEATH
COMMISSIONER OF POLICE
THE SCRIVENER
VOICE OF THE POSTMAN

## Notes on Costume (by Cocteau):

The costumes in fashion at the time of the performance should be adopted.

ORPHÉE and EURYDICE are in very inconspicuous country clothes.

HEURTEBISE wears pale blue workman's overalls with a dark muffler round his neck and white bathing-shoes. He is bronzed and hatless. He never leaves off his glazier's apparatus (window-panes).

The COMMISSIONER OF POLICE and the SCRIVENER wear black frock-coats, panamas, goatees, and buttoned boots.

DEATH is a very beautiful young woman in a bright pink evening dress and fur cloak. Her hair, frock, cloak, shoes, gestures, and gait are in the latest fashion. She has large blue eyes painted on a domino. Her nurse's tunic should also be of great elegance.[1]

Her assistants wear the uniform, linen masks, and rubber gloves of operating surgeons.

## Notes on Scenery (by Cocteau):

THRACE. A ROOM IN ORPHÉE'S VILLA. It is a strange room rather like the room of a conjuror. In spite of the April-blue sky and the clear light, one suspects that it is surrounded by mysterious forces. Even familiar objects have a suspicious air.

First of all, in a box in the form of a niche, well in the center, there lives a white horse, whose legs are very much like those of a man. On the right of the horse is another little niche in which an empty pedestal stands framed by laurel. On the extreme right a door which opens on to the garden; when the door is open, the leaf hides the pedestal. On the left of the horse an earthenware wash-basin. On the extreme left a French window, pushed half outwards—it looks on to the terrace which surrounds the villa.

In the foreground in the right wall is a very large mirror; in the background a bookcase. In the middle of the left wall a door opening into EURYDICE's room. A sloping ceiling closes in the room like a box.

The room is furnished with two tables and three white chairs. On the right a writing-table and one of the chairs.

On the left of the stage, the second table which is covered with a cloth reaching to the floor, and thereon fruits, plates, a decanter, and glasses, like the cardboard objects of jugglers. One chair stands squarely behind this table, and one near by on the right.

A chair cannot be added or taken away, nor the openings distributed otherwise, for this is a *practical* set, in which the smallest detail plays its part like the apparatus in an acrobatic number.

Apart from the sky-blue and the pad of dark red velvet that borders the top of the little door of the box dissimulating the middle of the horse's body—there is no color.

The scenery should recall the sham aeroplanes and ships of certain photographers.

After all, there is that same harmony, made of harsh simplicity, between the setting, characters, and events as between model and painted canvas in the plain *camaïeu* style of card portraits.

## Notes on Producing (by Cocteau):

THE MIRROR allows people to enter and leave the stage by an opening into the wings at the height of the frame. The opening is hidden by a glistening panel.

THE BOOKCASE should have one real pigeon-hole

[1] According to Cocteau's latest opinion both the non-human characters, DEATH and the guardian angel, should wear half-masks or masks in white. —Tr. *February 1933.*

in which a real book is slipped. At the top of the bookcase should be a slot from which a piece of paper can be taken.

THE PEDESTAL holds an actor kneeling on a cushion so that his head appears in the niche.

THE HORSE is the front of a horse; a horse's head with very curved neck, on a man in tights. The door of the box hides the upper part of the legs and the breast.

A BLACK CURTAIN on a rod can close the niche.

THE WASH-BASIN is a sham.

WHEN HEURTEBISE PRETENDS HE IS WORKING, he first frees the view of the window by carrying up to the wall on the left the table which is laid. Then, at the order ("Get up on this chair") he takes the chair which was behind the table and puts it in the frame of the French window. He puts his left foot on it and his right foot on a stool hidden behind the door. He lifts his hands up to the panes. A stage-hand holds him by an unseen belt from which a ring projects under his glazier's apparatus. When ORPHÉE removes the chair, he flies. This very simple arrangement, discovered by Pitoëff, is extraordinarily effective.

THE GLAZIER'S APPARATUS OF HEURTEBISE supports panes of various kinds. His head stands out against some mica. The panes behind him are of a glistening material which sends out gleams at all angles.

IN THE WINGS, near the audience, an electric machine with a deep roar. (A vacuum cleaner can be used.)

WHEN DEATH GOES INTO EURYDICE'S ROOM, she removes her bandage. A stage-hand gives her the dove which she takes by the legs so that its wings beat. She reappears. RAPHAEL cuts the thread. She disappears behind the scenery to the right of the window, where the dove is taken from her hands; she recoils on the terrace with a gesture as if having freed the dove into the air. (Note: "It is not necessary to say that there is no symbol in the play. Nothing but simple language, *acted poetry*. This dove is a commonplace.")

AFTER THE REMARK OF HEURTEBISE: "I will bring him back, I promise you," the light lowers and becomes milky. Once this new aquarium light is fixed, DEATH enters. Her arm appears through the mirror first and the left arms of the assistants before the assistants themselves.

ON LEAVING, DEATH hurries, freezes a moment, her hand extended in front of the mirror. Her assistants do the same.

WHEN THE CURTAIN FOR THE INTERVAL FALLS, wait a while to see if the spectators applaud before ringing up again, so that this card-trick in the abstract does not have the appearance of a false maneuver.

THE DISAPPEARANCE OF EURYDICE. In a theater without a trap, the light is lowered on a dimmer. EURYDICE rises with a gesture of horror and slips slowly behind the table. When darkness is complete, the end of some black material is passed to ORPHÉE who stands by the door of the bedroom. He stretches the material to the table and EURYDICE escapes behind it. The material is pulled sharply into the wings and the lights are thrown on full. The whole maneuver takes place in the winking of an eye. Even in a theater furnished with a trap, EURYDICE should disappear slowly and the light be lowered with her.

THREE MUSICIANS suffice for the arrival of the Bacchantes. One man: drums and cymbals. Another: jazz-set. A third: kettle-drums. The rhythms should torture like the tom-tom of savages.

AFTER THE THIRD "Ladies!" of ORPHÉE, the drums make a terrible noise. Windows are heard breaking, something heavy falls, and a chair goes over. A small lamp, hidden on the left in the footlights, comes on. It is the lighting given to the crimes in the Musée Grévin. On the ground near the cloth the head is seen against the white background of the overturned chair. The chair is knocked over and the head put into place during the blackout which blinds the spectators. The actor lies in the wings and speaks from the bedroom.

WHILE THE POLICE ARE KNOCKING ON THE DOOR AND THE ANGEL IS PICKING UP THE HEAD, putting it on the pedestal, and opening the door, full light is given and the actor substitutes his head for the mask. While the COMMISSIONER and the SCRIVENER are going out, the actor withdraws and replaces the mask.

## Prologue

*The actor who plays the part of* ORPHÉE *appears before the curtain.*

Ladies and gentlemen, this prologue is not by the author and I expect he would be surprised to hear it. The tragedy in which we are going to act develops on very delicate lines. I will ask you, therefore, if you are not satisfied with our work, to wait till the end before you express your feelings. Here is the reason for my request: we are playing at a great height, and without a safety-net. The slightest untimely noise and the lives of my comrades and my own may be imperiled. (*Exit*)

## Scene One

ORPHÉE *behind the table on the right, consulting a spiritualist alphabet.* EURYDICE *seated left, near the table which is laid.*

EURYDICE Can I move?

ORPHÉE One moment.

EURYDICE He's stopped tapping.

ORPHÉE Sometimes he leaves a long interval between the first letter and the others.

EURYDICE They can be guessed!

ORPHÉE Please, please!

EURYDICE You must admit, it's always the same word.

ORPHÉE H, H. . . . Carry on, horse. Go on, quick, after the letter H . . . I'm listening to you.

EURYDICE What patience! You have no mind, but your horse has—you think.

ORPHÉE I'm listening. Now, horse! H, H, after H. (*The* HORSE *moves*) You're moving, you're going to speak. Speak, horse! Dictate the letter after H. (*The* HORSE *strikes with its hoof,* ORPHÉE *counts*) A, B, C, D, E, is it E? (*The* HORSE *nods its head*)

EURYDICE Of course.

ORPHÉE (*Furious*) Sh! (*The* HORSE *taps*) A, B, C, D, E, F, G, H, I, J, K, L—L. A, B, C, D, E, F, G, H, I, J, K, L—L. (*To* EURYDICE) You're not to laugh. L, L, can it be L? H, E, L, L, hell? I can't have counted right. Horse! Is it really the letter L? If it is, tap once, and twice if it isn't. (*The* HORSE *taps once*)

EURYDICE You needn't insist.

ORPHÉE Look here, I ask you as a favor to keep quiet. Nothing disturbs this horse so much as incredulous people. Go to your room, or keep quiet.

EURYDICE I won't open my mouth again.

ORPHÉE So much the better. (*To the* HORSE) Hell, hell . . . and after hell? H, E, L, L, hell. I'm listening. Speak. Speak to me, horse. Horse! Come along, don't be afraid. After the letter L? (*The* HORSE *taps,* ORPHÉE *counts*) A, B, C, D, E, F, G, H, I, J, K, L, M, N, O—O. The letter O, my dear! H, E, L, L, O, hello. It was hello! Is that all? Is it just hello? (*The* HORSE *nods its head*) Just think of that. You see, Eurydice! I might have believed you with your wrong mind, I might have been weak enough to yield and be convinced. . . . Just "Hello," that's amazing!

EURYDICE Why?

ORPHÉE What do you mean, why?

EURYDICE Why amazing? This hello doesn't mean anything.

ORPHÉE What! This horse dictated to me last week one of the most moving sentences in the world . . .

EURYDICE Oh!

ORPHÉE . . . dictated one of the most moving sentences in the world. I'll work it out and I shall transfigure poetry. I am immortalizing my horse, and you're surprised to hear him greet me. That "hello" is a masterpiece of tact. And I who thought . . . (*He puts his arms round the* HORSE'S *neck*)

EURYDICE Listen, Orphée, my love; don't scold me. Be just! Since that famous sentence you've obtained one word and one word only, and this word isn't really poetic.

ORPHÉE Do we know what is poetic and what is not poetic?

EURYDICE Aglaonice used to do table-turning and her table always answered with that word.

ORPHÉE That's it! Drag that person into our business, as a last straw. I've told you already, I don't want to hear any more of her—a woman who nearly led you astray, a woman who drinks, takes tigers out for exercise, turns the heads of our wives, and prevents girls from marrying.

EURYDICE But that is the cult of the moon.

ORPHÉE Good! I can leave it to you to defend her. Return to the Bacchantes since their customs give you pleasure.

EURYDICE I'm just teasing. You know very well that it's only you I love, and you had but to give a sign to make me leave that circle.

ORPHÉE What a circle too! I shall never forget the tone in which Aglaonice said to me: "Take her, since she accepts. Stupid women adore artists, but—he who laughs last, laughs longest."

EURYDICE Ugh! That made my blood run cold.

ORPHÉE If ever I see her again! (*He strikes the inkwell on the table*)

EURYDICE Orphée, my poet. . . . Look how irritable you are ever since this horse business of yours. Before, you would laugh, kiss, and fondle me, you had a splendid situation, fame and fortune were yours. You would write poems which were snatched from hand to hand, and which all Thrace knew by heart. You would sing the praises of the sun, you were its high priest. But the horse has put an end to all that. Now we live in the country, you have given up your position and you refuse to write. Your life is passed in petting the horse, in questioning the horse, in hoping that the horse will answer you. That's not being serious.

ORPHÉE Not serious? My life, like game, was beginning to get high, and, on the turn, was beginning to stink of success and death. The sun and the moon are all the same to me. There remains night. But not the night of others! My night. This horse plunges into my night and reappears like a diver. He brings back sentences. Don't you feel that the least of these sentences is more remarkable than all the poems? I would give my complete works for one of those little sentences in which I listen to myself as you listen to the sea in a shell. Not serious? But what can you want, my dear? I am discovering a new world, I am living again, I am stalking the unknown.

EURYDICE You are going to quote me again the famous sentence?

ORPHÉE (*Gravely*) Yes. (*He goes toward the* HORSE *and recites*) "Orphée hunts Eurydice's lost life."

EURYDICE That sentence doesn't mean anything.

ORPHÉE It is indeed a question of meaning. Listen carefully to this sentence, listen to the mystery of it. Eurydice alone might be anybody and so might Orphée, but it is a Eurydice whose lost life Orphée would hunt! "Orphée hunts—" that exciting "hunts"—"Orphée hunts Eurydice's—" mark the possessive? and the close: "Eurydice's lost life." You ought to be pleased I am speaking about you.

EURYDICE It's not you who are speaking of me. It's the horse. (*Pointing*)

ORPHÉE Neither he, nor I, nor anyone else. What do we know? Who is speaking? We are knocking against each other in the dark; we are up to our necks in the supernatural. We are playing hide-and-seek with the gods. We know nothing, absolutely nothing. "Orphée hunts Eurydice's lost life"—that's not a sentence—it is a poem, a poem of vision, a flower deep-rooted in death.

EURYDICE And do you hope to convince the world? to make everyone admit that poetry consists in writing a sentence? to make a success with your horse's sentence?

ORPHÉE It's not a question of success, nor of the horse, nor of convincing the world. Besides, I no longer stand alone.

EURYDICE Don't talk to me about your public. Four or five heartless young hooligans, who think you're an anarchist, and a dozen fools who are trying to attract attention.

ORPHÉE I shall have a better following. I hope one day to charm even the beasts of the field.

EURYDICE If you despise success, why send this sentence to the Thracian competition? Why attach such importance to winning the prize?

ORPHÉE We must throw a bombshell and make a sensation. We must have a storm to clear the air. We are suffocating, we can no longer breathe.

EURYDICE We were so peaceful.

ORPHÉE Too peaceful.

EURYDICE You used to love me.

ORPHÉE I do love you.

EURYDICE You love the horse. I take second place.

ORPHÉE Don't be stupid. There's no connection. (*He kisses* EURYDICE *absent-mindedly and goes to the* HORSE) That's so, isn't it, old boy? Isn't it, my dear old brother, eh? Does he love his friend? Piece of sugar? Then kiss me. No, better than that. There . . . there . . . isn't he just fine! There! (*He takes some sugar out of his pocket and gives it to the* HORSE) That's right.

EURYDICE I don't count any more. If I were dead you wouldn't notice it.

ORPHÉE Without noticing it, we *were* dead.

EURYDICE Come near me.

ORPHÉE Sorry, I must be going out. I'm going into the town so as to have everything in order for the competition. Tomorrow's the last day. I haven't a minute to lose.

EURYDICE (*Bursting out*) Orphée! my Orphée! . . .

ORPHÉE You see this empty pedestal. Only a bust worthy of me shall be put there.

EURYDICE They will throw stones at you.

ORPHÉE I shall make my bust with them.

EURYDICE Beware of the Bacchantes.

ORPHÉE I'm not aware of their existence.

EURYDICE They do exist, and they are liked. I know their ways. Aglaonice hates you. She is going to take part in the competition.

ORPHÉE Oh! that woman! that woman!

EURYDICE Be just . . . she has ability.

ORPHÉE What?

EURYDICE Of a fearful kind, of course. But, from a certain angle and on a certain plane, she has ability. She creates fine images.

ORPHÉE Listen to that. *From a certain angle . . . on a certain plane. . . .* Did you learn that way of speaking from the Bacchantes? Then, on a certain plane her images please you. From a certain angle you approve of my mortal enemies. . . . And yet you insist that you love me. Very well then, by that angle and by that plane I declare that I have had enough of it; that I am persecuted, and this horse is the only being who understands me. (*He strikes his fist on the table*)

EURYDICE You needn't break everything.

ORPHÉE Break everything! That's the limit! Madam breaks a window-pane a day, and now it's I who break everything.

EURYDICE To begin with . . . .

ORPHÉE (*Walking up and down*) I know what you're going to say. You're going to say that you haven't broken a pane today.

EURYDICE But . . . .

ORPHÉE Very well, go on and break, break it, break the window-pane.

EURYDICE How can you get into such a state!

ORPHÉE See how sly. . . . You're not breaking a window-pane because I am going out.

EURYDICE (*Sharply*) What do you mean to insinuate?

ORPHÉE Do you think I am blind? You break a window-pane every day so that the glazier will come up.

EURYDICE Very well then, I do. I break a window-pane so that the glazier will come up. He's a good fellow, and he listens to me. He admires you.

ORPHÉE Too nice.

EURYDICE And when you are questioning the horse and leave me all alone, I break a pane. You're not jealous, I suppose?

ORPHÉE Jealous, I? Jealous of a boy-glazier? Why not of Aglaonice too! Upon my word! Look here, since you refuse to break a pane, I will break one. That'll soothe me. (*He breaks a pane*) Glazier! Glazier! Glazier! (*Is heard*) Hi! glazier! He's coming up. Jealous?

## Scene Two

*HEURTEBISE appears on the balcony. The sun beats on his window-panes. He enters, bends a knee, and crosses his hands over his heart.*

HEURTEBISE Good day, Ladies and Gentlemen.

ORPHÉE Good day, my friend. It was I, *I* who broke this pane. Put it in. I'm going. (*To* EURYDICE) My dear, you will superintend the work. (*To the* HORSE) Does he love his poet? (*He embraces him*) Till this evening. (*He goes out*)

## Scene Three

EURYDICE You see. I'm not inventing anything.
HEURTEBISE It's unheard of.
EURYDICE You understand me.
HEURTEBISE Poor lady.
EURYDICE Since that horse followed him in the street, and he brought it home with him, since it has lived here, and they talk together . . . .
HEURTEBISE The horse has spoken to him again?
EURYDICE It said "hello" to him.
HEURTEBISE It knows how to take him.
EURYDICE In short, for a month now, our life has been a torture.
HEURTEBISE Surely you can't be jealous of a horse!
EURYDICE I would rather know he had a mistress.
HEURTEBISE Do you mean that . . . ?
EURYDICE Without you and your friendship, I should have gone mad by now.
HEURTEBISE Poor Eurydice.
EURYDICE (*Looking at herself in the mirror and smiling*) Just think, I have a faint ray of hope. He has realized I break a window-pane every day, and, instead of saying I break a piece of glass to bring me luck, I told him I break it so that you come up to see me.
HEURTEBISE I should have thought . . . .
EURYDICE But listen. He made a scene, and he broke the pane. I believe he's still jealous.
HEURTEBISE How you love him . . . .
EURYDICE The more he ill-treats me the more I love him. I already had an idea that he might be jealous of Aglaonice.
HEURTEBISE Of Aglaonice?
EURYDICE He detests everything to do with my old circle. That is why I fear we may be committing a terrible indiscretion. Speak softly. I'm always afraid the horse may be listening to me. (*They tiptoe up to the niche*)
HEURTEBISE He's asleep. (*They return downstage*)
EURYDICE Have you seen Aglaonice?
HEURTEBISE Yes.
EURYDICE Orphée would kill you if that came to his ears.
HEURTEBISE It won't.
EURYDICE (*Pulling him still farther from the* HORSE, *towards her room*) Have you . . . got it?
HEURTEBISE I have.
EURYDICE In what form?
HEURTEBISE A piece of sugar.
EURYDICE What attitude did she take?
HEURTEBISE A very simple one. She said: "A bargain! Here is the poison, bring me back the letter."
EURYDICE That letter seems to cause her a lot of trouble.
HEURTEBISE She even added: "So that the poor dear doesn't compromise herself, here is an envelope with my address in my own handwriting. She will just have to put the letter in, stick the envelope down, and there'll be no trace of our communication."
EURYDICE Orphée is unjust. She can be very nice. Was she alone?
HEURTEBISE With a lady friend. It wasn't the sort of place for you.
EURYDICE Of course not, but I don't think Aglaonice is such a bad girl.
HEURTEBISE Beware of good girls and fine fellows. Here's your piece of sugar.
EURYDICE Thank you . . . . (*She takes the sugar with fear and approaches the* HORSE) I'm afraid.
HEURTEBISE Do you draw back?
EURYDICE No, I don't, but I'm afraid. I confess that when it comes to the point, in cold blood, my courage fails me. (*She returns in front of the writing-table*) Heurtebise?
HEURTEBISE What?
EURYDICE My dear Heurtebise, I suppose you wouldn't like to . . . ?
HEURTEBISE Oh! Ho! You are asking me to do something very serious.
EURYDICE You told me you would do anything to render me a service.
HEURTEBISE I repeat that, but . . . .
EURYDICE Oh! my dear, if it troubles you in the slightest . . . let us speak no more of it.
HEURTEBISE Pass me the sugar.
EURYDICE Thank you. You're a good fellow.
HEURTEBISE Only, will he take it from my hand?
EURYDICE Still, try.
HEURTEBISE (*Near the* HORSE) I confess I don't feel very firm on my feet.
EURYDICE Be a man! (*She crosses left and stops near the door of her room*)
HEURTEBISE Well, here goes. (*In a weak voice*) Horse . . . horse . . . .
EURYDICE (*Looking out of the window*) Heavens! Orphée! He's coming back. He's crossing the garden. Quick, quick, look as though you're working. (HEURTEBISE *throws the lump of sugar on to the set table and pushes it up against the wall between the window and the door of the bedroom*) Get up on this chair. (HEURTEBISE *gets up on the chair in the framework of the French window and pretends he is taking measurements.* EURYDICE *drops into the chair at the writing-table*)

## Scene Four

ORPHÉE (*Coming in*) I've forgotten my birth-certificate. Where did I put it?
EURYDICE On top of the bookcase, on the left. Shall I look for it?

ORPHÉE Sit still. I can find it myself. (*He passes in front of the* HORSE *and caresses it, takes the chair on which* HEURTEBISE *is standing, and carries it away.* HEURTEBISE *remains in the same pose, suspended in the air.* EURYDICE *stifles a cry.* ORPHÉE, *without noticing anything, gets up on the chair in front of the bookcase and says*) Here it is. (*Takes the birth-certificate, gets down from the chair, carries it back to its place beneath the feet of* HEURTEBISE, *and goes out*)

## Scene Five

EURYDICE Heurtebise! Will you explain this miracle?

HEURTEBISE What miracle?

EURYDICE You're not going to tell me you haven't noticed anything, and that it is natural to remain suspended in mid-air, instead of falling, when a chair is taken from under you?

HEURTEBISE Suspended in mid-air?

EURYDICE You needn't make out you are surprised, because I saw you. You stayed in mid-air. You stayed there two feet above the floor, with only emptiness round you.

HEURTEBISE You really do surprise me.

EURYDICE You remained a good minute between heaven and earth.

HEURTEBISE Impossible.

EURYDICE Exactly. That's why you owe me an explanation.

HEURTEBISE You mean to say that I stayed without a support between the ceiling and the floor?

EURYDICE Don't tell a lie, Heurtebise! I saw you, I saw you with my own eyes. I had the greatest difficulty in stifling a cry. In this mad-house, you were my last refuge, you were the only person who didn't frighten me, in your presence I regained my balance. It's all very well living with a horse that talks, but a friend who floats in the air becomes of necessity an object of suspicion. Don't come near me. At the moment even your glistening back gives me gooseflesh. Explain yourself, Heurtebise! I am listening.

HEURTEBISE I have no need to defend myself. Either I am dreaming or you have dreamt.

EURYDICE Yes, such things do happen in dreams, but neither of us was asleep.

HEURTEBISE You must have been the dupe of the mirage between my window-panes and yours. Things do lie at times. At the fair I saw a naked woman walking along the ceiling.

EURYDICE This was nothing to do with a machine. It was beautiful and outrageous. For the space of a second I saw you as outrageous as an accident and as beautiful as a rainbow. You were the cry of a man who falls from a window, and you were the silence of the stars. You frighten me. I'm too frank not to tell you. If you do not wish to answer me, you needn't, but our relationship can never be the same. I thought you were simple, but you are complex. I thought you were of my race, but you are of the race of the horse.

HEURTEBISE Eurydice, don't torture me. . . . Your voice is that of a sleep-talker. It's you who are frightening me.

EURYDICE Don't you use Orphée's method. Don't turn the tables on me. Don't try to make me believe I'm mad.

HEURTEBISE Eurydice, I swear that . . .

EURYDICE You needn't, Heurtebise. I have lost my confidence in you.

HEURTEBISE What's to be done?

EURYDICE One moment. (*She goes to the bookcase, gets up on the chair, pulls out a book, opens it, takes a letter from it, and returns the book to its place*) Give me Aglaonice's envelope. (*He gives it*) Thank you. (*She puts the letter in the envelope and licks the edge*) Oh!

HEURTEBISE Cut your tongue?

EURYDICE No—curious taste. Take the envelope to Aglaonice. Goodbye.

HEURTEBISE The window-pane hasn't been put in.

EURYDICE I'll do without it. Go along.

HEURTEBISE You want me to leave you?

EURYDICE I want to be alone.

HEURTEBISE You are unkind.

EURYDICE I don't like tradesmen who get suspended.

HEURTEBISE That cruel play on words isn't worthy of you.

EURYDICE It isn't a play on words.

HEURTEBISE (*Picking up his bag*) You'll be sorry you have hurt me. (*Silence*) Am I discharged?

EURYDICE All mystery is my enemy. I have decided to fight it.

HEURTEBISE I am going. I want to please you by my obedience. Goodbye, Madam.

EURYDICE Goodbye. (*They cross.* EURYDICE *goes toward her room.* HEURTEBISE *opens the door and goes out. The door remains open. His back is seen gleaming immobile in the sun. Suddenly* EURYDICE *stops and her expression changes. She staggers, puts her hand to her heart, and begins to cry*) Heurtebise! Heurtebise! quick, quick . . . .

HEURTEBISE (*Entering*) What is it?

EURYDICE Help! . . .

HEURTEBISE How pale you are! You're like ice.

EURYDICE I'm going paralyzed. My inside's burning and my heart's thumping.

HEURTEBISE The envelope!

EURYDICE The envelope?

HEURTEBISE (*Shouting*) Aglaonice's envelope. You licked it. You said it had a curious taste.

EURYDICE Ah! that wretched woman! Run quickly. Bring back Orphée. I am dying. I want to see Orphée again. Orphée! Orphée!

HEURTEBISE I can't leave you alone. There must be something that can be done—take an antidote.

EURYDICE I know the poison of the Bacchantes. It paralyzes. Nothing will save me. Run quickly. Fetch Orphée. I want to see him again. I want him to forgive me. I love him, Heurtebise. I am in pain. If you delay it'll be too late. I implore you, Heurtebise, Heurtebise, you are good to me, you pity me. Ah! They are sticking knives between my ribs. Quick, quick, run, fly! Take the short cut. If he's on the way back, you'll meet him. I am going to lie down in my room and wait for you. Help me. (HEURTEBISE *helps her to her room*) Quick, quick, quick. (*She disappears. At the moment* HEURTEBISE *is going to open the door she comes out of her room*) Heurtebise, listen, if you do know things . . . well . . . things like a moment ago . . . which allow lightning movement from one place to another. . . . You mustn't bear me ill will, I was irritable and silly . . . I really like you, Heurtebise . . . try everything. Ah! (*She goes back to her room*)

HEURTEBISE I will bring him back, I promise you. (*Exit*)

(*The stage remains empty a moment. The light changes. Rolling and syncopation of drums which accompanies the whole of the following scene—damped*)

## Scene Six

DEATH *comes on the stage through the mirror, followed by her two assistants,* AZRAEL *and* RAPHAEL. *She is wearing an evening dress and cloak. Her assistants wear surgeon's uniforms. Their eyes are just visible. The rest of the face is covered by a linen mask. Rubber gloves. They are carrying two very elegant large black bags.* DEATH *walks quickly and stops in the middle of the stage.*

DEATH Quickly!

RAPHAEL Where does Madam want us to put the bags?

DEATH On the ground, anywhere. Azrael will explain. Azrael, my cloak. (*He takes off the cloak*)

RAPHAEL It's because I'm afraid of making mistakes that I do silly things.

DEATH You can't pick up Azrael's job in two days. Azrael has been in my service for several centuries now. He was like you at first. My tunic. (AZRAEL *takes the white tunic out of one of the bags and helps* DEATH *to put it over her dress*)

AZRAEL (*To* RAPHAEL) Take the metal boxes and put them on the table. No, first of all, the cloths. Cover the table with them.

DEATH (*Going to the wash-basin*) Azrael will tell you that I insist on having everything clean and shipshape.

RAPHAEL Yes, Madam. I hope Madam will forgive me . . . but my attention was distracted by this horse.

DEATH (*Washing her hands*) Do you like him?

RAPHAEL Oh! yes, Madam. Very much.

DEATH What a child! I believe you'd like to have him for yourself. That's very easy. Azrael, the spirit. (*To* RAPHAEL) You'll find a piece of sugar on the other table.

RAPHAEL Yes, Madam, it is there.

DEATH Give it to him. If he refuses, I'll give it to him myself. Azrael, my rubber gloves. Thank you. (*She puts on the right-hand glove*)

RAPHAEL Madam, the horse won't take the sugar.

DEATH (*Taking the sugar*) Eat, horse; I wish it. (*The* HORSE *eats it, withdraws, and disappears. A black curtain closes the niche*) There you are. (*To* RAPHAEL) He's yours.

RAPHAEL Madam is too kind.

DEATH (*Putting on the left-hand glove*) Only a week ago you thought I was a skeleton with a winding-sheet and a scythe. You imagined me as a bug-bear and a scarecrow.

RAPHAEL Oh! Madam. . . . (*During these remarks* AZRAEL *is hiding the mirror with a cloth*)

DEATH (*Going to take a chair left by* HEURTEBISE *in the French window*) Oh! yes, you did. Everybody believes that. But, my dear child, if I were as people wish me to be, they would see me, whereas I must enter their homes unseen. (*She puts the chair near the footlights in the middle*) Azrael, try the contact.

AZRAEL It's working, Madam. (*Deep noise of an electric machine*)

DEATH (*Taking a handkerchief from out of her tunic*) Good! Raphael, would you be so kind as to bind my eyes with this handkerchief? (*While* RAPHAEL *is binding her eyes. . . .* ) We have a wave-length of seven and a range of seven to twelve. Set everything at four. If I amplify, go up to five. Don't exceed five on any account. Pull tight. Tie a double knot. Thank you. Are you at your posts? (AZRAEL *and* RAPHAEL *stand behind the table, side by side, their hands inside the metal boxes*) I'm beginning. (*She comes near the chair. Slow movement of the hands as of a masseuse and hypnotist round the invisible head*)

RAPHAEL (*Very softly*) Azrael . . . .

AZRAEL (*Very softly*) Sh!

DEATH You may talk. It doesn't disturb me.

RAPHAEL Azrael, where is Eurydice?

DEATH I was expecting that. You see, Azrael, they all ask the same question. Explain it to him.

AZRAEL Death, to reach living things, has to pass through an element which deforms and displaces them. Our apparatus allows her to reach them where she sees them, thus saving calculations and a considerable loss of time.

RAPHAEL It's like fishing with a gun.

DEATH (*Laughing*) Yes. (*Gravely*) Azrael, prepare the bobbin for me.

AZRAEL Yes, Madam. Does Madam know where Heurtebise is?

DEATH He's bringing Orphée back from town.

RAPHAEL If they are hurrying shall we have time to finish?

DEATH That is a question for Azrael. He changes our speeds. An hour for me is only a minute for them.

AZRAEL The hand is passing five. Does Madam want the bobbin?

DEATH Disconnect it and give it to me. (AZRAEL *disappears into* EURYDICE'S *room and comes on the stage again with the bobbin.* DEATH *counts the steps between her chair and the room. Than she stops, facing the door.* AZRAEL *gives her the bobbin which is a sort of automatic measure on which a white thread from the room will coil*)

AZRAEL Raphael, the chronometer.

RAPHAEL I've forgotten it!

AZRAEL Now we are in a fix.

DEATH Don't get alarmed. It's quite easy. (*She speaks softly to* AZRAEL)

AZRAEL Ladies and Gentlemen, I am instructed by Death to ask the audience if there's a spectator who would be so kind as to lend her a watch? (*To a gentleman in the first row, who raises his hand*) Thank you, Sir. Raphael, will you take the gentleman's watch? (*Business*)

DEATH All right?

AZRAEL Go! (*Rolling of drums. The wire comes from the room and enters the box held by* DEATH. AZRAEL *and* RAPHAEL, *backstage, turn their backs.* AZRAEL *counts with one hand in the air like a referee.* RAPHAEL *goes through movements like naval signals*) Whoa! (*Rolling of drums stops.* RAPHAEL *freezes. The wire tightens.* DEATH *rushes into the bedroom. She comes out without the bandage over her eyes, with a dove which flaps its wings attached to the thread. The machine is no longer heard*)

DEATH Phew! Quick, quick, Raphael, the scissors. (*She runs to the balcony*) Come here; cut this. (*He cuts the thread and the dove flies away*) Now clear the things up. Azrael, show him how. It's very simple. Let him do it, he's got to learn. (AZRAEL *and* RAPHAEL *pack up the metal boxes, tunic,* etc. DEATH *leans against the table on the right. She looks into space as if worn out. She slowly passes her right arm and hand across her brow, like a sleepwalker who is reawakening, as if recalling herself from the hypnotic state*)

AZRAEL Everything is in order, Madam.

DEATH And now, close the bags and lock them. I'm ready. My cloak. (AZRAEL *puts her cloak over her shoulders, while* RAPHAEL *is closing the bags*) Have we forgotten anything?

AZRAEL No, Madam.

DEATH Then, let's be going.

GENTLEMAN IN THE AUDIENCE Ssss!

AZRAEL Ah! Of course.

DEATH What is it?

AZRAEL The watch. Raphael, take the watch back to the gentleman and thank him. (*Business*)

DEATH Raphael, hurry up, hurry up.

RAPHAEL I'm coming, Madam. (DEATH *walks quickly and comes to a standstill with outstretched arms in front of the mirror. Then, she penetrates it. Her assistants follow her. They go through the same movements. She has forgotten her rubber gloves, which are well in evidence on the left-hand table*)

## Scene Seven

*Directly after* DEATH'S *last remark,* ORPHÉE'S *voice is heard in the garden.*

VOICE OF ORPHÉE You don't know her. You don't know what she's capable of. This is one of her theatricals to get me back home. (*The door opens and they enter.* HEURTEBISE *rushes to the room, looks in, recoils and kneels on the threshold*)

ORPHÉE Where is she? Eurydice! . . . She's sulking. Here, I shall go off my head! The horse! Where's the horse? (*He opens the niche*) Gone!—I'm lost. Some one has opened the door for him. Some one must have scared him; Eurydice must have done this. She shall pay for it! (*He makes a dash. . . .*)

HEURTEBISE Stop!

ORPHÉE Would you dare prevent me from going to my wife?

HEURTEBISE Look.

ORPHÉE Where?

HEURTEBISE Look through my panes.

ORPHÉE (*Looking*) She is sitting. She's asleep.

HEURTEBISE She is dead.

ORPHÉE What?

HEURTEBISE Dead. We've got here too late.

ORPHÉE It can't be. (*He knocks on the panes*) Eurydice! My darling! Answer me!

HEURTEBISE It's no good.

ORPHÉE You! Let me go in. (*He pushes* HEURTEBISE *aside*) Where is she? (*In the wings*) I saw her a moment ago, sitting near the bed. The room's empty. (*He re-enters*) Eurydice!

HEURTEBISE You only thought you saw her. Eurydice is living in the abode of Death.

ORPHÉE Ah! The horse is of little consequence! I want to see Eurydice again. I want her to forgive me for having neglected and misunderstood her. Help me. Save me. What can we do? We're losing precious time.

HEURTEBISE Those kind words save you, Orphée. . . .

ORPHÉE (*Weeping, collapsed on the table*) Dead. Eurydice is dead. (*He gets up*) Well, then . . . I'll snatch her away from death! To seek her, I'll brave the Underworld, if necessary.

HEURTEBISE Orphée . . . listen to me. Calm yourself. Are you going to listen to me? . . .

ORPHÉE Yes . . . I'll be calm. Let's consider things.

Let's find a plan. . . .

HEURTEBISE I know a way.

ORPHÉE You!

HEURTEBISE But you must obey me and not lose a minute.

ORPHÉE Yes. (*All* ORPHÉE'*s remarks are made in a feverish docility. The scene moves with extreme rapidity*)

HEURTEBISE Death came into your house to carry off Eurydice.

ORPHÉE Yes. . . .

HEURTEBISE She's forgotten her rubber gloves. (*Silence. He goes to the table, hesitates, and picks up the gloves at arm's length, as one touches a sacred object*)

ORPHÉE (*In terror*) Ah!

HEURTEBISE You'll put them on.

ORPHÉE Yes.

HEURTEBISE Put them on. (*He passes them to him.* ORPHÉE *puts them on*) You must go and see Death under the pretense of returning them, and thanks to them you'll be able to get to her.

ORPHÉE Right. . . .

HEURTEBISE Death is going to look for her gloves. If you take them to her, she'll give you a reward. She's miserly, she prefers receiving to giving, and as she never returns what anyone lets her take, your procedure will astonish her not a little. I don't suppose you'll get much, but still you'll get something.

ORPHÉE Good.

HEURTEBISE (*Leading him in front of the mirror*) That's your way.

ORPHÉE That mirror?

HEURTEBISE I'm entrusting you with the secret of secrets. Mirrors are the doors through which Death comes and goes. Don't tell any one. You only have to watch yourself all your life in a mirror, and you'll see Death at work like bees in a glass hive. Goodbye. Good luck!

ORPHÉE But a mirror—that's hard.

HEURTEBISE (*With hand raised*) With those gloves you'll pass through mirrors as through water.

ORPHÉE Where did you learn all these dreadful things?

HEURTEBISE (*His hand drops*) You know, mirrors are connected in a way with glazing. That's our trade.

ORPHÉE And once I'm past this . . . door. . . .

HEURTEBISE Breathe slowly and regularly. Don't be afraid; just walk straight ahead. Turn to the right, then to the left, then to the right, then go straight along. There, how can I explain it? . . . There's no more direction . . . you go round; it's a little difficult at first.

ORPHÉE And then?

HEURTEBISE Then? No one in the world can tell you. Death begins.

ORPHÉE I'm not afraid of her.

HEURTEBISE Farewell. I'll wait for you to come back.

ORPHÉE But I might be a long time.

HEURTEBISE A long time . . . for you. For us you'll scarcely do more than go in and come out.

ORPHÉE I can't see how this mirror can be soft. Anyhow, I'll try.

HEURTEBISE Yes, try. (ORPHÉE *begins to move*) First your hands! (ORPHÉE, *with arms outstretched and the red gloves on his hands, sinks into the mirror*)

ORPHÉE Eurydice! . . . (*He disappears*)

## Scene Eight (a)

HEURTEBISE, *alone, kneels in front of the* HORSE'*s niche. A knock.*

HEURTEBISE What is it?

POSTMAN'S VOICE Postman. I've a letter for you.

HEURTEBISE Master's not here.

POSTMAN'S VOICE And madam?

HEURTEBISE Not here either. Slip the letter under the door. (*A letter comes under the door*)

POSTMAN'S VOICE Have they gone out?

HEURTEBISE No . . . they're asleep.

(*The curtain for the Interval falls slowly and rises immediately*)

## Scene Eight (b)

HEURTEBISE *is discovered kneeling in front of the* HORSE'*s niche. A knock.*

HEURTEBISE What is it?

POSTMAN'S VOICE Postman. I've a letter for you.

HEURTEBISE Master's not here.

POSTMAN'S VOICE And madam?

HEURTEBISE Not here either. Slip the letter under the door. (*A letter comes under the door*)

POSTMAN'S VOICE Have they gone out?

HEURTEBISE No . . . they're asleep.

## Scene Nine

ORPHÉE (*Comes out of the mirror*) What, still here?

HEURTEBISE Now tell me quickly . . . .

ORPHÉE My dear fellow, you're an angel.

HEURTEBISE Not at all.

ORPHÉE Oh! yes, an angel, a real angel. You have saved me.

HEURTEBISE And Eurydice?

ORPHÉE A surprise. Just look.

HEURTEBISE Where?

ORPHÉE At the mirror. One, two, three. (EURYDICE *comes out of the mirror*)

HEURTEBISE It is she!

EURYDICE Yes, it is I. I, the happiest of wives; I, the first woman with a husband bold enough to recover her from the dead.

ORPHÉE "Orphée hunts Eurydice's lost life." And to think we refused to believe this sentence had a meaning.

EURYDICE Sh! my darling. Remember your promise. We weren't going to speak of the horse any more.

ORPHÉE Where was my head?

EURYDICE And you know, Heurtebise, he found the way all by himself. He didn't hesitate one second. He had the ingenious idea of putting on Death's gloves.

HEURTEBISE Hm! I think I shall have to take up the gloves for myself.

ORPHÉE (*Very quickly*) Anyway, the chief thing was to succeed. (*He makes as if to turn to* EURYDICE)

EURYDICE Careful!

ORPHÉE Oh! (*He freezes*)

HEURTEBISE What's the matter?

ORPHÉE A detail, a mere detail. At first it appears terrifying, but with a little care it'll be all right.

EURYDICE It'll become a matter of habit.

HEURTEBISE But what's it all about?

ORPHÉE A pact. I'm allowed to have Eurydice again, but I may not look at her. If I look at her, she'll disappear.

HEURTEBISE How dreadful!

EURYDICE How clever to discourage my husband!

ORPHÉE (*Making* HEURTEBISE *pass in front of him*) That's all right, I'm not discouraged. What is happening to him, happened to us. Think, after we'd accepted that clause—and we had to, whatever the cost—we went through all your apprehensions. Well, I repeat, it can be done. It isn't easy by any means, but it can be done. I maintain it isn't so hard as to become blind.

EURYDICE Or as to lose a leg.

ORPHÉE Besides . . . we had no choice.

EURYDICE There are even advantages. Orphée won't see my wrinkles.

HEURTEBISE Bravo! I have nothing more to do but to wish you good luck.

ORPHÉE Are you going to leave us?

HEURTEBISE I fear my presence may be embarrassing. You must have so many things to say to each other.

ORPHÉE We'll say them after lunch. The table is laid. I'm very hungry. You are too much a part of our adventure not to stay to lunch with us.

HEURTEBISE I'm afraid the presence of a third may vex your wife.

EURYDICE No, Heurtebise. (*Weighing the words*) The journey I've made transforms the face of the world. I have learned a lot. I'm ashamed of myself. From now on I shall be a new wife to Orphée, a honeymoon wife.

ORPHÉE Eurydice! Your promise. We weren't going to speak any more of the moon.

EURYDICE It's my turn to have no memory. Let's have lunch! Heurtebise on my right. Come and sit down. Orphée opposite me.

HEURTEBISE Not opposite!

ORPHÉE Heavens! I did right in keeping Heurtebise. I shall sit on your left with my back turned to you. I shall eat from my lap. (EURYDICE *serves them*)

HEURTEBISE I'm anxious to hear the story of your journey.

ORPHÉE Lord, I shall find it difficult to relate. It seems as if I'm recovering from an operation. I have a vague memory of it, like that of one of my poems which I recite to keep me awake, and of foul beasts falling asleep. Then a black hole. Then speaking with an invisible lady. She thanked me for the gloves. A sort of surgeon came to take them, and he told me to go, that Eurydice would follow me, and that I wasn't to look at her on any account. I am thirsty. (*He takes his glass and turns round*)

EURYDICE *and* HEURTEBISE (*Together*) Careful!

EURYDICE I had a rare fright! Without turning round, my dear, feel how my heart is beating.

ORPHÉE How silly it is. Supposing I bound my eyes!

HEURTEBISE I don't advise you to do that. You don't know the exact rules. If you cheat, all is lost.

ORPHÉE You would hardly credit how difficult it is to do such an idiotic thing, and the mental strain it involves.

EURYDICE What do you expect, my poor dear, when you are always mooning . . . .

ORPHÉE The moon again! You might as well call me a lunatic.

EURYDICE Orphée!

ORPHÉE I leave the moon to your late companions. (*Silence*)

HEURTEBISE Mr. Orphée!

ORPHÉE I am a sun-worshipper.

EURYDICE No longer, my love.

ORPHÉE Perhaps not. But I forbid mention of the moon in my house. (*Silence*)

EURYDICE If only you knew how little importance attaches to this talk of sun and moon.

ORPHÉE Madam is above these things.

EURYDICE If only I could speak. . . .

ORPHÉE It seems to me that for a person who can't speak, you speak quite a lot! A lot too much! (EURYDICE *weeps. Silence*)

HEURTEBISE You're making your wife cry.

ORPHÉE (*Threatening*) You! (*He turns round*)

EURYDICE Ah!

HEURTEBISE Take care!

ORPHÉE It's her fault. She would make the dead turn.

EURYDICE It would have been better to remain dead. (*Silence*)

ORPHÉE The moon! If I were to let her talk, where

would we get to? I ask you. We'd go back to the reign of the horse.

HEURTEBISE You're exaggerating. . . .

ORPHÉE I am exaggerating?

HEURTEBISE Yes.

ORPHÉE And even if I admit that I'm exaggerating . . . . (*He turns round*)

EURYDICE Look out!

HEURTEBISE (*To* EURYDICE) Calm yourself. Don't cry. The difficulty is making you nervous. Orphée, try and make an effort yourself. You'll bring about trouble in the end.

ORPHÉE And even if I admit that I'm exaggerating, who began it?

EURYDICE Not me.

ORPHÉE Not you! Not you! (*He turns round*)

EURYDICE *and* HEURTEBISE Heigh!

HEURTEBISE You're dangerous, my dear fellow.

ORPHÉE You're right. The best thing I can do is to leave the table, and rid you of my presence, since I'm dangerous. (*He rises.* EURYDICE *and* HEURTEBISE *hold him back by his coat*)

EURYDICE My dear . . . .

HEURTEBISE Orphée . . . .

ORPHÉE No, no. Let me go.

HEURTEBISE Be reasonable.

ORPHÉE I shall be what it pleases me to be.

EURYDICE Don't go. (*She pulls him, he loses his balance, and looks at her. He utters a cry.* EURYDICE, *petrified, rises. Her face expresses terror. The light lowers.* EURYDICE *sinks slowly into the mirror and disappears. The light rises again*)

HEURTEBISE It was to be.

ORPHÉE (*Pale and limp, with an expression of false grace*) Phew! That's better.

HEURTEBISE What!

ORPHÉE (*Same expression*) We can breathe now.

HEURTEBISE He's mad.

ORPHÉE (*Hiding his embarrassment more and more in anger*) You have to be firm with women, and show them you don't depend on them. You mustn't let them lead you by the nose.

HEURTEBISE That's going a bit strong, isn't it? Would you have me believe you looked at Eurydice on purpose?

ORPHÉE Am I an absent-minded man?

HEURTEBISE You don't lack boldness! You looked inadvertently. You lost your balance, and you turned your head inadvertently; I saw you.

ORPHÉE I lost my balance on purpose. I turned my head deliberately, and I forbid anyone to contradict me. (*Silence*)

HEURTEBISE Very well then, if you did turn your head deliberately, I don't congratulate you.

ORPHÉE I can do without your congratulations. *I* congratulate myself for having turned my head deliberately toward my wife. That's better than trying to turn the heads of other people's wives.

HEURTEBISE Is that meant for me?

ORPHÉE If the cap fits . . . .

HEURTEBISE That's very unkind. I've never allowed myself to make love to your wife. She would soon have sent me about my business. Your wife was a model wife. You had to lose her the first time to realize that, and you have just lost her a second time, lost her shamefully and tragically, and lost yourself. You have just killed a dead woman, and committed out of sheer wantonness an irreparable act. For she has died, died, died again. Never more will she come back.

ORPHÉE Oh! come on!

HEURTEBISE What do you mean, "Oh! come on!"?

ORPHÉE When have you seen a woman get up from table scolding and not come back?

HEURTEBISE I leave you five minutes to realize your misfortune.

(ORPHÉE *throws his napkin on the floor, rises, adjusts the table, goes to look at the mirror, touches it, goes to the door, and picks up the letter. Opens the letter*)

ORPHÉE What's this?

HEURTEBISE Some bad news?

ORPHÉE I can't read it; the letter is written backward.

HEURTEBISE That's a way of disguising the handwriting. Read it in the mirror.

ORPHÉE (*In front of the mirror, reads*) "Sir, excuse my preserving my incognito. Aglaonice has discovered that the initial letters of your sentence: 'Orphée Hunts Eurydice's Lost Life,' together form a word which is offensive to the jury of the competition." (ORPHÉE *says to himself*) O, H, E, L, L. O Hell! (ORPHÉE *continues to read*) "She has convinced the jury that you are a hoaxer. She has stirred up against you half of the women of the town. In short, an enormous troop of mad women under her orders is coming toward your house. The Bacchantes lead the way and demand your death. Escape and hide yourself. Do not lose a minute. From one who wishes you well."

HEURTEBISE There can't be a word of truth in it.

(*Drums are heard approaching from a distance, beating a furious rhythm*)

ORPHÉE Listen . . . .

HEURTEBISE Drums.

ORPHÉE *Their* drums. Eurydice saw aright. Heurtebise, the horse has befooled me.

HEURTEBISE A man isn't hacked to pieces for a couple of words.

ORPHÉE The words are a pretext which hides a deep and religious hatred. Aglaonice was biding her time. I am lost.

HEURTEBISE The drums are coming nearer.

ORPHÉE How was it I didn't see this letter? How long ago was it slipped under the door?

HEURTEBISE Orphée, I'm to blame. The letter was slipped in during your visit to the dead. Your wife's return engrossed me, and I forgot to tell you. Fly!

ORPHÉE Too late. (*The* HORSE'S *spell is ended.* ORPHÉE *is transfigured*)

HEURTEBISE Hide in the grove. I'll say you're traveling. . . .

ORPHÉE It's useless, Heurtebise. Things happen as they must.

HEURTEBISE I shall save you by force!

ORPHÉE I refuse.

HEURTEBISE This is madness!

ORPHÉE The mirror is hard. It read the letter for me. I know what I can still do.

HEURTEBISE What are you going to do?

ORPHÉE Rejoin Eurydice.

HEURTEBISE Not this time.

ORPHÉE Why not?

HEURTEBISE Even if you did manage it, there'd be more scenes between you.

ORPHÉE (*In ecstasy*) Not there, where she beckons me to join her.

HEURTEBISE Your face is drawn. You're suffering. I won't let you take your life.

ORPHÉE Oh! those drums, those drums! They are coming nearer, Heurtebise, they are rumbling and thundering, they'll soon be here.

HEURTEBISE You have already done the impossible.

ORPHÉE I have held by the impossible.

HEURTEBISE You have withstood other plots.

ORPHÉE Not at the cost of bloodshed, yet.

HEURTEBISE You frighten me. . . . (HEURTEBISE's *face expresses a supernatural joy*)

ORPHÉE What are the thoughts of the marble from which a sculptor shapes a masterpiece? It thinks: I am being struck, ruined, insulted, and broken, I am lost. This marble is stupid. Life is shaping me, Heurtebise. It is making a masterpiece. I must bear its blows without understanding them. I must stand firm. I must be still and accept the inevitable. I must help and bear my part, till the work is ended.

HEURTEBISE Stones! (*Some stones break the window and fall into the room*)

ORPHÉE Glass. That's good luck! Luck! I shall have the bust I wished for. (*A stone breaks the mirror*)

HEURTEBISE The mirror!

ORPHÉE Not the mirror! (*He rushes on to the balcony*)

HEURTEBISE They'll hack you to pieces. (*Clamoring and drums*)

ORPHÉE (*Back to audience, leans over the balcony*) Ladies! (*Roar of drums*) Ladies! (*Roar of drums*) Ladies! (*Roar of drums*)

(*He rushes to the right—invisible part of the balcony. The drums drown his voice. Darkness.* HEURTEBISE *falls on his knees and hides his face. Suddenly something flies through the window and falls into the room. It is* ORPHÉE's *head. It rolls to the right, and stops on the forestage.* HEURTEBISE *utters a weak cry. The drums are getting farther away*)

## Scene Ten

ORPHÉE'S HEAD (*Speaking in the voice of someone greatly hurt*) Where am I? How dark it is . . . how heavy my head is. And my body, my body hurts me so much. I must have fallen from the balcony. I must have fallen from a great height, a great height, from a great height on to my head. And my head . . . ? as a matter of fact . . . yes, I'm speaking about my head . . . where is my head? Eurydice! Heurtebise! Help me! Where are you? Light the lamp. Eurydice! I can't see my body. I can't find my head. I've lost my head, and my body; and I can't understand how. There's an emptiness, all about me there is an emptiness. Explain it to me. Wake me. Help! Help! Eurydice! (*Like a lament*) Eurydice . . . Eurydice . . . Eurydice . . . Eurydice . . . Eurydice . . . .

(EURYDICE *comes through the mirror. She remains on the spot*)

EURYDICE My darling?

ORPHÉE'S HEAD Eurydice . . . is it you?

EURYDICE It is.

ORPHÉE'S HEAD Where is my body? Where did I put my body?

EURYDICE Quiet. Don't upset yourself. Give me your hand.

ORPHÉE'S HEAD Where is my head?

EURYDICE (*Taking the invisible body by the hand*) I have your hand in mine. Walk. Don't be afraid. Let yourself go. . . .

ORPHÉE'S HEAD Where is my body?

EURYDICE Near me. Against me. You can't see me now, and I may take you away.

ORPHÉE'S HEAD And my head, Eurydice . . . my head . . . where did I put my head?

EURYDICE No more of that, my love, let your head be. . . .

(EURYDICE *and the invisible body of* ORPHÉE *sink into the mirror*)

## Scene Eleven

(*A knock on the door. Silence. Knock. Silence*)

VOICE OF THE COMMISSIONER OF POLICE Open, in the name of the law.

HEURTEBISE Who is it?

VOICE OF THE COMMISSIONER OF POLICE The police. Open or I'll break in the door.

HEURTEBISE I'll open it. (HEURTEBISE *rushes to* ORPHÉE's *head, picks it up, hesitates, puts it on the pedestal, and opens the door. The leaf of the door hides the pedestal. It is now that the actor who plays* ORPHÉE *substitutes his own head for that of the mask*)

C. OF POLICE Why didn't you reply to my first summons?

HEURTEBISE Your Worship . . . .

C. OF POLICE Commissioner of Police.

HEURTEBISE Sir, I'm a friend of the family . . . I was still suffering from the shock, as you may well imagine. . . .

C. OF POLICE Shock? What shock?

HEURTEBISE I must tell you. I was alone with Orphée at the moment of the drama.

C. OF POLICE What drama?

HEURTEBISE The murder of Orphée by the Bacchantes.

C. OF POLICE (*Turning to the* SCRIVENER) I was expecting this version. And . . . the wife of the victim . . . where is she? I should like to confront her with you.

HEURTEBISE She's not here.

C. OF POLICE Better and better.

HEURTEBISE She had even abandoned the conjugal domicile.

C. OF POLICE Do you hear that! (*To the* SCRIVENER) Sit down at that table, please (*He points to the right-hand table*) and take notes.

(*The* SCRIVENER *installs himself. Papers and pens. He turns his back to the mirror.* HEURTEBISE *is standing near the mirror. To be more at ease the* SCRIVENER *pulls the table back so that this table renders access to the door impossible*)

HEURTEBISE I have. . . .

SCRIVENER Silence.

C. OF POLICE Let's proceed in order. Don't speak unless I question you. Where's the body?

HEURTEBISE What body?

C. OF POLICE When there's a murder, there's a body. I am asking you—where is the body?

HEURTEBISE But, Sir, there isn't a body. It has been torn, decapitated, and carried away by those mad women!

C. OF POLICE Primo, I am not asking you to make a detrimental judgment on women who perform priestly rites. Secundo, your version is contradicted by five-hundred eye-witnesses.

HEURTEBISE Do you mean that I . . . .

C. OF POLICE Silence!

HEURTEBISE I . . . .

C. OF POLICE Silence! (*Pompous delivery*) You just listen to me, my lad. Today is the day of the eclipse. This eclipse of the sun has brought about a tremendous change of popular feeling in Orphée's favor. Mourning's being worn. Triumphal celebrations are being prepared, and the authorities claim his mortal remains. Now, the Bacchantes saw Orphée appear on his balcony, covered with blood and calling for help. They were astonished, as they had come there under his window with the sole purpose of fêting him. They would have flown to his aid, if he hadn't, as they say—and five-hundred mouths testify to it—if he hadn't, as I was saying, fallen dead before their eyes. To sum up. These ladies made a long procession. They arrive with cries of "Out with Orphée!" Suddenly Orphée covered with blood rushes out and calls for help. These ladies make ready to mount the steps. Too late! Orphée falls, and the whole troop—don't forget they are women . . . women who make a brave noise, but who are frightened at the sight of blood—the whole troop, I say, turns tail. Eclipse! The town saw in this eclipse the anger of the sun, because one of its late priests had been derided. The authorities came to meet the women, and the women, through the medium of Aglaonice, retailed the strange crime of which they had just been witnesses. The whole town wanted to rush to the scene of the tragedy. Severe measures were taken to suppress the disorder and I was given charge, I, *I,* the head of the Police force, I, who am conducting your examination—and I won't allow anyone to treat me like a country policeman, keep that well in mind.

HEURTEBISE But, I'm not . . . .

SCRIVENER Silence. You're not being questioned.

C. OF POLICE Let's proceed in order. (*To the* SCRIVENER) Where did I get to?

SCRIVENER The bust. I beg to remind you of the bust . . . .

C. OF POLICE Ah! yes. (*To* HEURTEBISE) Are you a relative?

HEURTEBISE A friend of the family.

C. OF POLICE A bust of Orphée is required for the celebrations. Do you know of one?

(HEURTEBISE *goes to the door and closes it. The head on the pedestal is discovered. The* C. OF POLICE *and* SCRIVENER *turn round*)

C. OF POLICE It isn't a likeness.

HEURTEBISE It's a very fine work.

C. OF POLICE Who by?

HEURTEBISE I don't know.

C. OF POLICE Is the bust not signed?

HEURTEBISE No.

C. OF POLICE (*To the* SCRIVENER) Write down: "Alleged bust of Orphée."

HEURTEBISE No, no. It is Orphée, of that we're sure. There's doubt only about the authorship.

C. OF POLICE Then put: "Head of Orphée by X." (*To* HEURTEBISE) Your name?

HEURTEBISE Pardon?

SCRIVENER You were asked for your full name.

C. OF POLICE For, as regards your profession, I'm not to be deceived. I have eyes. (*He goes to* HEURTEBISE *and fingers the panes*) You are a glazier, my fine fellow!

HEURTEBISE (*Smiling*) Yes, I am a glazier, I confess.

C. OF POLICE Confess, confess, it's the only defense which carries any weight.

SCRIVENER Excuse me, Sir, supposing we ask him for his papers. . . .

C. OF POLICE Quite right. (*He sits down*) Your papers.

HEURTEBISE I . . . I haven't any.

C. OF POLICE What?

SCRIVENER Ho! ho!

C. OF POLICE Going about without your papers? Where are they? Where do you live?

HEURTEBISE I live . . . that is to say—er—I used to live . . . .

C. OF POLICE I'm not asking you where you used to live. I'm asking where you're living now.

HEURTEBISE Now? . . . at the moment I am . . . without an address.

C. OF POLICE No papers, no fixed abode. Exactly. Vagrancy! a vagrant! Your case is clear, my friend. Your age?

HEURTEBISE I am . . . . (*He hesitates*)

C. OF POLICE (*He questions with his back turned, looking up to the ceiling, moving his feet, like an examiner*) I suppose, at least, you have some age . . . .

ORPHÉE'S HEAD I'm eighteen.

SCRIVENER (*Writing*) Seventeen.

ORPHÉE'S HEAD Eighteen.

C. OF POLICE Born at . . . .

SCRIVENER Half a minute, Sir. I'm erasing the figure.

(EURYDICE *comes half-way through the mirror*)

EURYDICE Heurtebise . . . Heurtebise. I know who you are. Come in, we were waiting for you. You alone were missing. (HEURTEBISE *hesitates*)

ORPHÉE'S HEAD Hurry up, Heurtebise. Follow my wife. I'll answer for you. I'll invent something, anything.

(HEURTEBISE *plunges into the mirror*)

## Scene Twelve

SCRIVENER Sir, at your service.

C. OF POLICE Born at . . . .

ORPHÉE'S HEAD Maisons-Laffitte.

C. OF POLICE Maisons what?

ORHPÉE'S HEAD Maisons-Laffitte, two F's, two T's.

C. OF POLICE As you can tell me your place of birth, perhaps you'll no longer refuse to tell me your name. You're called . . . .

ORPHÉE'S HEAD Jean.

C. OF POLICE Jean what?

ORPHÉE'S HEAD Jean Cocteau.

C. OF POLICE Coc . . . .

ORPHÉE'S HEAD C, O, C, T, E, A, U. Cocteau.

C. OF POLICE There's a name to go to bed with. Is it true you sleep out of doors? If you don't consent now to tell us where you live . . . .

ORPHÉE'S HEAD Rue d'Anjou. Number 10.

C. OF POLICE You're becoming reasonable.

SCRIVENER Your signature . . . .

C. OF POLICE Get a pen ready. (*To* HEURTEBISE) Come here. Come here, I won't eat you. (*Turns round*) Great . . . !

SCRIVENER What is it?

C. OF POLICE Great Heavens! The accused has disappeared.

SCRIVENER Miraculous!

C. OF POLICE Miraculous . . . miraculous . . . it's not miraculous at all. (*He strides up and down the stage*) I don't believe in miracles. An eclipse is an eclipse. A table's a table. An accused man's an accused man. Let's proceed in order. This door . . . .

SCRIVENER Impossible, Sir. To go out by this door, he would have to knock over my chair.

C. OF POLICE The window, then.

SCRIVENER For the window, he would have to pass in front of us. Besides, the accused was answering. He answered right up to the last minute.

C. OF POLICE Well?

SCRIVENER Well, I don't understand at all.

C. OF POLICE There must be a secret exit of which the assassin—for this flight gives us proof of the crime—of which the assassin, as I was saying, knew the existence. Sound the wall. (SCRIVENER *taps. Investigations*)

SCRIVENER The wall sounds solid. . . .

C. OF POLICE Right. This young dog may leave us and hide in this unmannerly fashion, but we won't give him the satisfaction of seeking him under his very nose. (*At the top of his voice*) I have men about the house. He can't take two steps outside without being caught, and if he persists, we'll surround him till hunger drives him out. Come on.

SCRIVENER What an extraordinary affair!

C. OF POLICE There's nothing extraordinary at all. You're always seeing something extraordinary somewhere.

(*They go out. While they are going out and the door hides the bust, the actor substitutes the mask for his own head. The stage remains empty*)

C. OF POLICE (*Returning*) We're forgetting the bust.

SCRIVENER We mustn't return empty-handed.

C. OF POLICE Take it. (*The* SCRIVENER *takes the head. Exeunt*)

## Scene Thirteen

*The scene changes to Heaven. Through the mirror come* EURYDICE *and* ORPHÉE, *led by* HEURTEBISE. *They look at their home as if they were seeing it for the first time. They sit down at table;* EURYDICE *beckons* HEURTEBISE *to her right. They smile and breathe calmness.*

EURYDICE You were wanting some wine, I think, my dear.

ORPHÉE One moment. First of all, the prayer.

(*He rises, also* EURYDICE *and* HEURTEBISE. *He recites*)

ORPHÉE O God, we thank thee for assigning us our house and home as the only paradise, and for having opened to us thy paradise. We thank thee for having sent Heurtebise to us, and we are guilty of not recognizing him as our Guardian Angel. We thank thee for having saved Eurydice, because, through love, she killed the devil in the shape of a horse, and in so doing she died. We thank thee for having saved me because I adored poetry, and thou art poetry. Amen.

(*They sit again*)

HEURTEBISE May I serve you?

ORPHÉE (*Respectfully*) Let Eurydice . . .

(EURYDICE *pours out for him to drink*)

HEURTEBISE Perhaps we can have lunch at last.

*Curtain*

# Federico García Lorca

# (1898-1936)

FEDERICO GARCÍA LORCA was one of the liveliest and most original talents of the modern theatre. His freely experimental plays combine elements of the romantic history play, the puppet show, farce, vaudeville, folk tragedy, and surrealist extravaganza. Above all else a poet, Lorca brought about a fusion of poetry and drama that remains among the unique theatrical achievements of our time.

Born in 1898 in Granada, a city of rich classical, Arabian, and gypsy traditions, Lorca found his principal sources of inspiration in the vibrancy and magic of the Spanish scene around him. He responded warmly to the demands of the "Generation of 1898" that Spain enter dynamically into the broad stream of European culture, and at the Residencia de Estudiantes in Madrid, where he went to study in 1919, Lorca came into direct contact with the new avant-garde painting and music as well as the French-influenced experimental poetry of his Spanish contemporaries. Lorca was a talented pianist as well as a gifted painter, and the interrelation of the arts is an important element of his dramatic work. In Madrid he studied music under Manuel de Falla, with whom he later collaborated in the composition of a comic ballet. Lorca himself provided the music for many of his folk ballads and poems of gypsy life, a poetry rich in dramatic episodes and techniques.

Lorca's first play, *The Witchery of the Butterfly* (*El Maleficio de la Mariposa*), was staged by the Spanish playwright, Martínez Sierra, at the Teatro Eslava, an art theatre dedicated to classic repertory as well as to new foreign and native experimental and serious drama. The poet's slight fantasy is set in the form of an insect parable: a lone cockroach is disoriented by the intrusion into its life of a light and colorful butterfly, suggestive of a world of magic and adventure that earthbound insects can never know. Lorca's play, closer perhaps to dramatic poetry than to poetic drama, had only one performance. It is a fragile and adolescent attempt, but it served to give the young poet direct contact with the theatre and to stimulate his dramatic ambitions.

Lorca's first full-length play, *Mariana Pineda,* was produced in 1927, with sets designed by Salvador Dalí. It demonstrates Lorca's keen affinity for traditional Spanish subjects and for the romantic history play. Set in the 1830's, the play portrays the heroism of a woman who embroiders a flag in preparation for a revolution. The plot is discovered and the conspirators flee, leaving Mariana Pineda to die on the scaffold. The play was viewed, mistakenly, as republican political propaganda, and it enjoyed considerable success on its initial production. Emboldened by his good fortune, Lorca turned to a livelier, more farcical setting in *The Love of Don Perlimplin for Belisa in His Garden* (*Amor de Don Perlimplín con Belisa en su Jardín*). The play is a series of tableaux in which Perlimplin, a well-to-do bachelor of 50, woos and wins the voluptuous Belisa, only to be made a cuckold on his wedding night, when his bedroom is entered by representatives of the five races of the earth: European, Indian, Negro, Yellow Man, and American. Perlimplin accepts Belisa's desire for the young lover from whom she receives passionate notes, but in the final scene he goes to intercept the meeting of the lovers and stabs himself, revealing to Belisa that he was her young lover in disguise. His suicide brings Belisa to a realization of the depth of his love for her, which she will now cherish as a permanent possession. The atmosphere of violent, primitive passion is reinforced by Belisa's large red cape and by the incidental music taken from Scarlatti. In *Don Perlimplin* Lorca combined elements of traditional Italian farce with a complex multiplicity of personality derived at least in part from the drama of Pirandello. More traditional in its farcical qualities is *The Shoemaker's Prodigious Wife* (*La Zapatera Prodigiosa*), written about the same time and first performed late in 1930. Lorca's flirtatious and hot-tempered heroine supports herself after her husband's desertion by turning his shop into a tavern. Lechers come to make advances but she holds them off in lively and spirited sallies reminiscent of Goldoni's *La Locandiera.* At the end, reunited with her husband, she turns her back on the mean and prying society. The accompanying music and dance as well as the conflict of barrenness and fecundity were to find fuller expression in Lorca's later, more ambitious plays. *The Shoemaker's Prodigious Wife* reveals his deep interest in feminine sexual and psychological frustrations.

In 1932, under the sponsorship of an enlightened ministry of education, Lorca organized a travelling troupe called *La Barraca* which travelled across rural Spain, performing all kinds of plays, classic and modern, largely for peasant audiences. Lorca worked at direction and production, acted, designed scenery, worked as a stage hand, played the piano, lectured to the audience on the play, performed magic tricks and stunts, and thereby achieved not only an intimate knowledge of the physical theatre, but a rare sense of community with the villages of Spain and their inhabitants.

The rural landscape dominates Lorca's late and major dramas: *Blood Wedding* (*Bodas de Sangre*), 1933; *Yerma*, 1934; and *The House of Bernarda Alba* (*La Casa de Bernarda Alba*), 1936. These works of the playwright's maturity reveal his concern with elemental psychological and social forces in the Spain of his day. All of them demonstrate the overwhelming power of erotic impulse in conflict with the restraints of civilization and social control. This conflict is particularly evident in *Yerma*, unique among Lorca's late plays in its concentration on a single character. Here Lorca probes sensitively into the frustrations of a passionate woman longing for a child and for emotional completeness. The title itself means "barren," but it is Yerma's husband, Juan, who is responsible for her condition. Yerma refuses to violate the sexual code of her community; as she murders Juan, she exclaims: "I've killed my son!" There is no confusion of identities. Her act of murder places her forever outside of the possibility of personal fulfillment. The pagan ritual in which she participates in Act III points toward an altogether different way of life from the stern social morality which coerces and dooms her to an empty existence.

Lorca moved to an increasingly broad conception of the social function of drama, the barometer, as he declared in 1935, of the greatness or decline of a whole people: "A theatre that is sensitive and well oriented in all of its branches, from tragedy to vaudeville, can in a few years change the sensibility of a people; and a shattered theatre, in which hoofs substitute for wings, can debase and benumb an entire nation." In his last plays and especially in *The House of Bernarda Alba*, Lorca subjected to rigorous scrutiny the outworn moral code of family honor subsisting at the expense of genuine passionate self-fulfillment. His late work constitutes a corrosive indictment of cold and bloodless institutional brutalization of the individual in present-day Spain. At the close of his life, the poet was moving in an ever more markedly realistic direction; in his last complete play, poetry had all but receded from the stage.

Federico García Lorca was executed in July, 1936, in the early days of the Spanish civil war, by a Fascist firing squad. To this date, no one has been able to explain this wanton murder satisfactorily. For although Lorca soon afterwards became a political martyr, his poetry and drama are essentially unpolitical. Curiously, he enjoyed the benefit of undeserved notoriety in 1928, when the role of Don Perlimplin was played by a well-known army commander. On learning that Perlimplin was a cuckold, the government censure office considered the play an affront to the army and banned further performances. As a result, Lorca was hailed as a satirist of the regime, although there is not the slightest support for this view within the play. His late works are devoid of any involvement in the bitter partisan political struggles of the time. His death was stupid and inexplicable; it came at the height of his artistic maturity.

*Blood Wedding* reveals Lorca's most characteristic attitudes and techniques. His rare gifts of fantasy and lyricism find full expression in a drama of violent passion. According to the poet's brother, the plot was taken from a newspaper account on which the poet meditated for a long time: the actual composition of the play required but a single week. The language of the drama is closely akin to Lorca's most famous collection of poetry, *Gypsy Ballads* (*Romancero Gitano*)—warm, sensuous, and stark. Yet the poetry serves to enlarge the plane of emotion even while it retards the dramatic action. The Lullaby in the second scene of Act I provides a wonderful example of the integration of lyricism and drama. In Act III, the vivid supernatural personifications combine the planes of fantasy and realism in an eery, surrealistic atmosphere wherein the human and the symbolic move side by side. The finale, with its painful lamentation, reconciles the conflicting personalities and principles in their common submission to human destiny. The fate of Lorca's tortured heroines merges with that of mankind.

# BLOOD WEDDING[1]

## *Tragedy in Three Acts and Seven Scenes*

Translated by James Graham-Luján and Richard L. O'Connell

### CHARACTERS

THE MOTHER
THE BRIDE
THE MOTHER-IN-LAW
LEONARDO'S WIFE
THE SERVANT WOMAN
THE NEIGHBOR WOMAN
YOUNG GIRLS
LEONARDO
THE BRIDEGROOM
THE BRIDE'S FATHER
THE MOON
WOODCUTTERS
YOUNG MEN

## Act One, Scene One

*A room painted yellow.*

BRIDEGROOM (*Entering*) Mother.
MOTHER What?
BRIDEGROOM I'm going.
MOTHER Where?
BRIDEGROOM To the vineyard.
(*He starts to go*)
MOTHER Wait.
BRIDEGROOM You want something?
MOTHER Your breakfast, son.
BRIDEGROOM Forget it. I'll eat grapes. Give me the knife.
MOTHER What for?

[1] NOTICE: This edition of *Blood Wedding* has been printed with the proper authorization. It was scrupulously revised in accordance with the original manuscript of Federico García Lorca which I have in my possession, and it contains his very latest revisions.

MARGARITA XIRGU

*Buenos Aires, July 1938*

BRIDEGROOM (*Laughing*) To cut the grapes with.
MOTHER (*Muttering as she looks for the knife*) Knives, knives. Cursed be all knives, and the scoundrel who invented them.
BRIDEGROOM Let's talk about something else.
MOTHER And guns and pistols and the smallest little knife—and even hoes and pitchforks.
BRIDEGROOM All right.
MOTHER Everything that can slice a man's body. A handsome man, full of young life, who goes out to the vineyards or to his own olive groves—his own because he's inherited them . . .
BRIDEGROOM (*Lowering his head*) Be quiet.
MOTHER . . . and then that man doesn't come back. Or if he does come back it's only for someone to cover him over with a palm leaf or a plate of rock salt so he won't bloat. I don't know how you dare carry a knife on your body—or how I let this serpent (*She takes a knife from a kitchen chest*) stay in the chest.
BRIDEGROOM Have you had your say?
MOTHER If I lived to be a hundred I'd talk of nothing else. First your father; to me he smelled like a carnation and I had him for barely three years. Then your brother. Oh, is it right—how can it be—that a small thing like a knife or a pistol can finish off a man—a bull of a man? No, I'll never be quiet. The months pass and the hopelessness of it stings in my eyes and even to the roots of my hair.
BRIDEGROOM (*Forcefully*) Let's quit this talk!
MOTHER No. No. Let's not quit this talk. Can anyone bring me your father back? Or your brother? Then there's the jail. What do they mean, jail? They eat there, smoke there, play music there! My dead men choking with weeds, silent, turning to dust. Two men like two beautiful flowers. The killers in jail, carefree, looking at the mountains.
BRIDEGROOM Do you want me to go kill them?
MOTHER No . . . If I talk about it it's because . . . Oh, how can I help talking about it, seeing you go out that door? It's . . . I don't like you to carry a knife. It's just that . . . that I wish you wouldn't go out to the fields.
BRIDEGROOM (*Laughing*) Oh, come now!
MOTHER I'd like it if you were a woman. Then you wouldn't be going out to the arroyo now and we'd

both of us embroider flounces and little woolly dogs.

BRIDEGROOM (*He puts his arm around his mother and laughs*) Mother, what if I should take you with me to the vineyards?

MOTHER What would an old lady do in the vineyards? Were you going to put me down under the young vines?

BRIDEGROOM (*Lifting her in his arms*) Old lady, old lady—you little old, little old lady!

MOTHER Your father, he used to take me. That's the way with men of good stock; good blood. Your grandfather left a son on every corner. That's what I like. Men, men; wheat, wheat.

BRIDEGROOM And I, Mother?

MOTHER You, what?

BRIDEGROOM Do I need to tell you again?

MOTHER (*Seriously*) Oh!

BRIDEGROOM Do you think it's bad?

MOTHER No.

BRIDEGROOM Well, then?

MOTHER I don't really know. Like this, suddenly, it always surprises me. I know the girl is good. Isn't she? Well behaved. Hard working. Kneads her bread, sews her skirts, but even so when I say her name I feel as though someone had hit me on the forehead with a rock.

BRIDEGROOM Foolishness.

MOTHER More than foolishness. I'll be left alone. Now only you are left me—I hate to see you go.

BRIDEGROOM But you'll come with us.

MOTHER No. I can't leave your father and brother here alone. I have to go to them every morning and if I go away it's possible one of the Félix family, one of the killers, might die—and they'd bury him next to ours. And that'll never happen! Oh, no! That'll never happen! Because I'd dig them out with my nails and, all by myself, crush them against the wall.

BRIDEGROOM (*Sternly*) There you go again.

MOTHER Forgive me.

(*Pause*)

How long have you known her?

BRIDEGROOM Three years. I've been able to buy the vineyard.

MOTHER Three years. She used to have another sweetheart, didn't she?

BRIDEGROOM I don't know. I don't think so. Girls have to look at what they'll marry.

MOTHER Yes. I looked at nobody. I looked at your father, and when they killed him I looked at the wall in front of me. One woman with one man, and that's all.

BRIDEGROOM You know my girl's good.

MOTHER I don't doubt it. All the same, I'm sorry not to have known what her mother was like.

BRIDEGROOM What difference does it make now?

MOTHER (*Looking at him*) Son.

BRIDEGROOM What is it?

MOTHER That's true! You're right! When do you want me to ask for her?

BRIDEGROOM (*Happily*) Does Sunday seem all right to you?

MOTHER (*Seriously*) I'll take her the bronze earrings, they're very old—and you buy her . . .

BRIDEGROOM You know more about that . . .

MOTHER . . . you buy her some open-work stockings —and for you, two suits—three! I have no one but you now!

BRIDEGROOM I'm going. Tomorrow I'll go see her.

MOTHER Yes, yes—and see if you can make me happy with six grandchildren—or as many as you want, since your father didn't live to give them to me.

BRIDEGROOM The first-born for you!

MOTHER Yes, but have some girls. I want to embroider and make lace, and be at peace.

BRIDEGROOM I'm sure you'll love my wife.

MOTHER I'll love her.

(*She starts to kiss him but changes her mind*)

Go on. You're too big now for kisses. Give them to your wife.

(*Pause. To herself*)

When she is your wife.

BRIDEGROOM I'm going.

MOTHER And that land around the little mill—work it over. You've not taken good care of it.

BRIDEGROOM You're right. I will.

MOTHER God keep you.

(*The Son goes out. The* MOTHER *remains seated—her back to the door. A* NEIGHBOR WOMAN *with a kerchief on her head appears in the door*)

Come in.

NEIGHBOR How are you?

MOTHER Just as you see me.

NEIGHBOR I came down to the store and stopped in to see you. We live so far away!

MOTHER It's twenty years since I've been up to the top of the street.

NEIGHBOR You're looking well.

MOTHER You think so?

NEIGHBOR Things happen. Two days ago they brought in my neighbor's son with both arms sliced off by the machine.

(*She sits down*)

MOTHER Rafael?

NEIGHBOR Yes. And there you have him. Many times I've thought your son and mine are better off where they are—sleeping, resting—not running the risk of being left helpless.

MOTHER Hush. That's all just something thought up—but no consolation.

NEIGHBOR (*Sighing*) Ay!

MOTHER (*Sighing*) Ay!

(*Pause*)

NEIGHBOR (*Sadly*) Where's your son?

MOTHER He went out.

NEIGHBOR He finally bought the vineyard!

MOTHER He was lucky.

NEIGHBOR Now he'll get married.

MOTHER (*As though reminded of something, she draws her chair near the* NEIGHBOR) Listen.

NEIGHBOR (*In a confidential manner*) Yes. What is it?

MOTHER You know my son's sweetheart?

NEIGHBOR A good girl!

MOTHER Yes, but . . .

NEIGHBOR But who knows her really well? There's nobody. She lives out there alone with her father—so far away—fifteen miles from the nearest house. But she's a good girl. Used to being alone.

MOTHER And her mother?

NEIGHBOR Her mother I *did* know. Beautiful. Her face glowed like a saint's—but *I* never liked her. She didn't love her husband.

MOTHER (*Sternly*) Well, what a lot of things certain people know!

NEIGHBOR I'm sorry. I didn't mean to offend—but it's true. Now, whether she was decent or not nobody said. That wasn't discussed. She was haughty.

MOTHER There you go again!

NEIGHBOR You asked me.

MOTHER I wish no one knew anything about them—either the live one or the dead one—that they were like two thistles no one even names but cuts off at the right moment.

NEIGHBOR You're right. Your son is worth a lot.

MOTHER Yes—a lot. That's why I look after him. They told me the girl had a sweetheart some time ago.

NEIGHBOR She was about fifteen. He's been married two years now—to a cousin of hers, as a matter of fact. But nobody remembers about their engagement.

MOTHER How do you remember it?

NEIGHBOR Oh, what questions you ask!

MOTHER We like to know all about the things that hurt us. Who was the boy?

NEIGHBOR Leonardo.

MOTHER What Leonardo?

NEIGHBOR Leonardo Félix.

MOTHER Félix!

NEIGHBOR Yes, but—how is Leonardo to blame for anything? He was eight years old when those things happened.

MOTHER That's true. But I hear that name—Félix—and it's all the same.
(*Muttering*)
Félix, a slimy mouthful.
(*She spits*)
It makes me spit—spit so I won't kill!

NEIGHBOR Control yourself. What good will it do?

MOTHER No good. But you see how it is.

NEIGHBOR Don't get in the way of your son's happiness. Don't say anything to him. You're old. So am I. It's time for you and me to keep quiet.

MOTHER I'll say nothing to him.

NEIGHBOR (*Kissing her*) Nothing.

MOTHER (*Calmly*) Such things . . . !

NEIGHBOR I'm going. My men will soon be coming in from the fields.

MOTHER Have you ever known such a hot sun?

NEIGHBOR The children carrying water out to the reapers are black with it. Goodbye, woman.

MOTHER Goodbye.

(*The* MOTHER *starts toward the door at the left. Halfway there she stops and slowly crosses herself*)

*Curtain*

# Act One, Scene Two

*A room painted rose with copperware and wreaths of common flowers. In the center of the room is a table with a tablecloth. It is morning.*

*Leonardo's* MOTHER-IN-LAW *sits in one corner holding a child in her arms and rocking it. His* WIFE *is in the other corner mending stockings.*

MOTHER-IN-LAW

Lullaby, my baby
once there was a big horse
who didn't like water.
The water was black there
under the branches.
When it reached the bridge
it stopped and it sang.
Who can say, my baby,
what the stream holds
with its long tail
in its green parlor?

WIFE (*Softly*)

Carnation, sleep and dream,
the horse won't drink from the stream.

MOTHER-IN-LAW

My rose, asleep now lie,
the horse is starting to cry.
His poor hooves were bleeding,
his long mane was frozen,
and deep in his eyes
stuck a silvery dagger.
Down he went to the river,
Oh, down he went down!
And his blood was running,
Oh, more than the water.

WIFE

Carnation, sleep and dream,
the horse won't drink from the stream.

MOTHER-IN-LAW

My rose, asleep now lie,
the horse is starting to cry.

WIFE

He never did touch
the dank river shore
though his muzzle was warm
and with silvery flies.
So, to the hard mountains
he could only whinny
just when the dead stream
covered his throat.

Ay-y-y, for the big horse
who didn't like water!
Ay-y-y, for the snow-wound,
big horse of the dawn!

MOTHER-IN-LAW

Don't come in! Stop him
and close up the window
with branches of dreams
and a dream of branches.

WIFE

My baby is sleeping.

MOTHER-IN-LAW

My baby is quiet.

WIFE

Look, horse, my baby
has him a pillow.

MOTHER-IN-LAW

His cradle is metal.

WIFE

His quilt a fine fabric.

MOTHER-IN-LAW

Lullaby, my baby.

WIFE

Ay-y-y, for the big horse
who didn't like water!

MOTHER-IN-LAW

Don't come near, don't come in!
Go away to the mountains
and through the gray valleys,
that's where your mare is.

WIFE (*Looking at the baby*)

My baby is sleeping.

MOTHER-IN-LAW

My baby is resting.

WIFE (*Softly*)

Carnation, sleep and dream,
The horse won't drink from the stream.

MOTHER-IN-LAW (*Getting up, very softly*)

My rose, asleep now lie
for the horse is starting to cry.

(*She carries the child out.* LEONARDO *enters*)

LEONARDO Where's the baby?

WIFE He's sleeping.

LEONARDO Yesterday he wasn't well. He cried during the night.

WIFE Today he's like a dahlia. And you? Were you at the blacksmith's?

LEONARDO I've just come from there. Would you believe it? For more than two months he's been putting new shoes on the horse and they're always coming off. As far as I can see he pulls them off on the stones.

WIFE Couldn't it just be that you use him so much?

LEONARDO No. I almost never use him.

WIFE Yesterday the neighbors told me they'd seen you on the far side of the plains.

LEONARDO Who said that?

WIFE The women who gather capers. It certainly surprised me. Was it you?

LEONARDO No. What would I be doing there, in that wasteland?

WIFE That's what I said. But the horse was streaming sweat.

LEONARDO Did you see him?

WIFE No. Mother did.

LEONARDO Is she with the baby?

WIFE Yes. Do you want some lemonade?

LEONARDO With good cold water.

WIFE And then you didn't come to eat!

LEONARDO I was with the wheat weighers. They always hold me up.

WIFE (*Very tenderly, while she makes the lemonade*) Did they pay you a good price?

LEONARDO Fair.

WIFE I need a new dress and the baby a bonnet with ribbons.

LEONARDO (*Getting up*) I'm going to take a look at him.

WIFE Be careful. He's asleep.

MOTHER-IN-LAW (*Coming in*) Well! Who's been racing the horse that way? He's down there, worn out, his eyes popping from their sockets as though he'd come from the ends of the earth.

LEONARDO (*Acidly*) I have.

MOTHER-IN-LAW Oh, excuse me! He's your horse.

WIFE (*Timidly*) He was at the wheat buyers.

MOTHER-IN-LAW He can burst for all of me!

(*She sits down. Pause*)

WIFE Your drink. Is it cold?

LEONARDO Yes.

WIFE Did you hear they're going to ask for my cousin?

LEONARDO When?

WIFE Tomorrow. The wedding will be within a month. I hope they're going to invite us.

LEONARDO (*Gravely*) I don't know.

MOTHER-IN-LAW His mother, I think, wasn't very happy about the match.

LEONARDO Well, she may be right. She's a girl to be careful with.

WIFE I don't like to have you thinking bad things about a good girl.

MOTHER-IN-LAW (*Meaningfully*) If he does, it's because he knows her. Didn't you know he courted her for three years?

LEONARDO But I left her.

(*To his* WIFE)

Are you going to cry now? Quit that!
*(He brusquely pulls her hands away from her face)*
Let's go see the baby.
*(They go in with their arms around each other. A* GIRL *appears. She is happy. She enters running)*

GIRL Señora.

MOTHER-IN-LAW What is it?

GIRL The groom came to the store and he's bought the best of everything they had.

MOTHER-IN-LAW Was he alone?

GIRL No. With his mother. Stern, tall.
*(She imitates her)*
And such extravagance!

MOTHER-IN-LAW They have money.

GIRL And they bought some open-work stockings! Oh, such stockings! A woman's dream of stockings! Look: a swallow here,
*(She points to her ankle)*
a ship here,
*(She points to her calf)*
and here,
*(She points to her thigh)*
a rose!

MOTHER-IN-LAW Child!

GIRL A rose with the seeds and the stem! Oh! All in silk.

MOTHER-IN-LAW Two rich families are being brought together.
*(*LEONARDO *and his* WIFE *appear)*

GIRL I came to tell you what they're buying.

LEONARDO *(Loudly)* We don't care.

WIFE Leave her alone.

MOTHER-IN-LAW Leonardo, it's not that important.

GIRL Please excuse me.
*(She leaves, weeping)*

MOTHER-IN-LAW Why do you always have to make trouble with people?

LEONARDO I didn't ask for your opinion.
*(He sits down)*

MOTHER-IN-LAW Very well.
*(Pause)*

WIFE *(To* LEONARDO*)* What's the matter with you? What idea've you got boiling there inside your head? Don't leave me like this, not knowing anything.

LEONARDO Stop that.

WIFE No. I want you to look at me and tell me.

LEONARDO Let me alone.
*(He rises)*

WIFE Where are you going, love?

LEONARDO *(Sharply)* Can't you shut up?

MOTHER-IN-LAW *(Energetically, to her daughter)* Be quiet!
*(*LEONARDO *goes out)*
The baby!
*(She goes into the bedroom and comes out again with the baby in her arms. The* WIFE *has remained standing, unmoving)*

MOTHER-IN-LAW

His poor hooves were bleeding,
his long mane was frozen,
and deep in his eyes
stuck a silvery dagger.
Down he went to the river,
Oh, down he went down!
And his blood was running,
Oh, more than the water.

WIFE *(Turning slowly, as though dreaming)*

Carnation, sleep and dream,
the horse is drinking from the stream.

MOTHER-IN-LAW

My rose, asleep now lie
the horse is starting to cry.

WIFE

Lullaby, my baby.

MOTHER-IN-LAW

Ay-y-y, for the big horse
who didn't like water!

WIFE *(Dramatically)*

Don't come near, don't come in!
Go away to the mountains!
Ay-y-y, for the snow-wound,
big horse of the dawn!

MOTHER-IN-LAW *(Weeping)*

My baby is sleeping . . .

WIFE *(Weeping, as she slowly moves closer)*

My baby is resting . . .

MOTHER-IN-LAW

Carnation, sleep and dream,
the horse won't drink from the stream.

WIFE *(Weeping, and leaning on the table)*

My rose, asleep now lie,
the horse is starting to cry.

*Curtain*

## Act One, Scene Three

*Interior of the cave where the* BRIDE *lives. At the back is a cross of large rose colored flowers. The round doors have lace curtains with rose colored ties. Around the walls, which are of a white and hard material, are round fans, blue jars, and little mirrors.*

SERVANT Come right in . . .

*(She is very affable, full of humble hypocrisy. The* BRIDEGROOM *and his* MOTHER *enter. The* MOTHER *is dressed in black satin and wears a lace mantilla; the* BRIDEGROOM *in black corduroy with a great golden chain)*

Won't you sit down? They'll be right here.

*(She leaves. The* MOTHER *and* SON *are left sitting motionless as statues. Long pause)*

MOTHER Did you wear the watch?

BRIDEGROOM Yes.

*(He takes it out and looks at it)*

MOTHER We have to be back on time. How far away these people live!

BRIDEGROOM But this is good land.

MOTHER Good; but much too lonesome. A four hour trip and not one house, not one tree.

BRIDEGROOM This is the wasteland.

MOTHER Your father would have covered it with trees.

BRIDEGROOM Without water?

MOTHER He would have found some. In the three years we were married he planted ten cherry trees, *(Remembering)* those three walnut trees by the mill, a whole vineyard and a plant called Jupiter which had scarlet flowers—but it dried up.

*(Pause)*

BRIDEGROOM *(Referring to the* BRIDE*)* She must be dressing.

*(The* BRIDE'S FATHER *enters. He is very old, with shining white hair. His head is bowed. The* MOTHER *and the* BRIDEGROOM *rise. They shake hands in silence)*

FATHER Was it a long trip?

MOTHER Four hours.

*(They sit down)*

FATHER You must have come the longest way.

MOTHER I'm too old to come along the cliffs by the river.

BRIDEGROOM She gets dizzy.

*(Pause)*

FATHER A good hemp harvest.

BRIDEGROOM A really good one.

FATHER When I was young this land didn't even grow hemp. We've had to punish it, even weep over it, to make it give us anything useful.

MOTHER But now it does. Don't complain. I'm not here to ask you for anything.

FATHER *(Smiling)* You're richer than I. Your vineyards are worth a fortune. Each young vine a silver coin. But—do you know?—what bothers me is that our lands are separated. I like to have everything together. One thorn I have in my heart, and that's the little orchard there, stuck in between my fields—and they won't sell it to me for all the gold in the world.

BRIDEGROOM That's the way it always is.

FATHER If we could just take twenty teams of oxen and move your vineyards over here, and put them down on that hillside, how happy I'd be!

MOTHER But why?

FATHER What's mine is hers and what's yours is his. That's why. Just to see it all together. How beautiful it is to bring things together!

BRIDEGROOM And it would be less work.

MOTHER When I die, you could sell ours and buy here, right alongside.

FATHER Sell, sell? Bah! Buy, my friend, buy everything. If I had had sons I would have bought all this mountainside right up to the part with the stream. It's not good land, but strong arms can make it good, and since no people pass by, they don't steal your fruit and you can sleep in peace.

*(Pause)*

MOTHER You know what I'm here for.

FATHER Yes.

MOTHER And?

FATHER It seems all right to me. They have talked it over.

MOTHER My son has money and knows how to manage it.

FATHER My daughter too.

MOTHER My son is handsome. He's never known a woman. His good name is cleaner than a sheet spread out in the sun.

FATHER No need to tell you about my daughter. At three, when the morning star shines, she prepares the bread. She never talks: soft as wool, she embroiders all kinds of fancy work and she can cut a strong cord with her teeth.

MOTHER God bless her house.

FATHER May God bless it.

*(The* SERVANT *appears with two trays. One with drinks and the other with sweets)*

MOTHER *(To the* SON*)* When would you like the wedding?

BRIDEGROOM Next Thursday.

FATHER The day on which she'll be exactly twenty-two years old.

MOTHER Twenty-two! My oldest son would be that age if he were alive. Warm and manly as he was, he'd be living now if men hadn't invented knives.

FATHER One mustn't think about that.

MOTHER Every minute. Always a hand on your breast.

FATHER Thursday, then? Is that right?

BRIDEGROOM That's right.

FATHER You and I and the bridal couple will go in a carriage to the church which is very far from here; the wedding party on the carts and horses they'll bring with them.

MOTHER Agreed.

*(The* SERVANT *passes through)*

FATHER Tell her she may come in now.

*(To the* MOTHER*)*

I shall be much pleased if you like her.

*(The* BRIDE *appears. Her hands fall in a modest pose and her head is bowed)*

MOTHER Come here. Are you happy?

BRIDE Yes, señora.

FATHER You shouldn't be so solemn. After all, she's going to be your mother.

BRIDE I'm happy. I've said "yes" because I wanted to.

MOTHER Naturally.

(*She takes her by the chin*)

Look at me.

FATHER She resembles my wife in every way.

MOTHER Yes? What a beautiful glance! Do you know what it is to be married, child?

BRIDE (*Seriously*) I do.

MOTHER A man, some children and a wall two yards thick for everything else.

BRIDEGROOM Is anything else needed?

MOTHER No. Just that you all live—that's it! Live long!

BRIDE I'll know how to keep my word.

MOTHER Here are some gifts for you.

BRIDE Thank you.

FATHER Shall we have something?

MOTHER Nothing for me.

(*To the* SON)

But you?

BRIDEGROOM Yes, thank you.

(*He takes one sweet, the* BRIDE *another*)

FATHER (*To the* BRIDEGROOM) Wine?

MOTHER He doesn't touch it.

FATHER All the better.

(*Pause. All are standing*)

BRIDEGROOM (*To the* BRIDE) I'll come tomorrow.

BRIDE What time?

BRIDEGROOM Five.

BRIDE I'll be waiting for you.

BRIDEGROOM When I leave your side I feel a great emptiness, and something like a knot in my throat.

BRIDE When you are my husband you won't have it any more.

BRIDEGROOM That's what I tell myself.

MOTHER Come. The sun doesn't wait.

(*To the* FATHER)

Are we agreed on everything?

FATHER Agreed.

MOTHER (*To the* SERVANT) Goodbye, woman.

SERVANT God go with you!

(*The* MOTHER *kisses the* BRIDE *and they begin to leave in silence*)

MOTHER (*At the door*) Goodbye, daughter.

(*The* BRIDE *answers with her hand*)

FATHER I'll go out with you.

(*They leave*)

SERVANT I'm bursting to see the presents.

BRIDE (*Sharply*) Stop that!

SERVANT Oh, child, show them to me.

BRIDE I don't want to.

SERVANT At least the stockings. They say they're all open work. Please!

BRIDE I said no.

SERVANT Well, my Lord. All right then. It looks as if you didn't want to get married.

BRIDE (*Biting her hand in anger*) Ay-y-y!

SERVANT Child, child! What's the matter with you? Are you sorry to give up your queen's life? Don't think of bitter things. Have you any reason to? None. Let's look at the presents.

(*She takes the box*)

BRIDE (*Holding her by the wrists*) Let go.

SERVANT Ay-y-y, girl!

BRIDE Let go, I said.

SERVANT You're stronger than a man.

BRIDE Haven't I done a man's work? I wish I were.

SERVANT Don't talk like that.

BRIDE Quiet, I said. Let's talk about something else.

(*The light is fading from the stage. Long pause*)

SERVANT Did you hear a horse last night?

BRIDE What time?

SERVANT Three.

BRIDE It might have been a stray horse—from the herd.

SERVANT No. It carried a rider.

BRIDE How do you know?

SERVANT Because I saw him. He was standing by your window. It shocked me greatly.

BRIDE Maybe it was my fiancé. Sometimes he comes by at that time.

SERVANT No.

BRIDE You saw him?

SERVANT Yes.

BRIDE Who was it?

SERVANT It was Leonardo.

BRIDE (*Strongly*) Liar! You liar! Why should he come here?

SERVANT He came.

BRIDE Shut up! Shut your cursed mouth.

(*The sound of a horse is heard*)

SERVANT (*At the window*) Look. Lean out. Was it Leonardo?

BRIDE It was!

*Quick Curtain*

# Act Two, Scene One

*The entrance hall of the* BRIDE*'s house. A large door in the back. It is night. The* BRIDE *enters wearing ruffled white petticoats full of laces and embroidered bands, and a sleeveless white bodice. The* SERVANT *is dressed the same way.*

SERVANT I'll finish combing your hair out here.

BRIDE It's too warm to stay in there.

SERVANT In this country it doesn't even cool off at dawn.

(*The* BRIDE *sits on a low chair and looks into a little hand mirror. The* SERVANT *combs her hair*)

BRIDE My mother came from a place with lots of trees—from a fertile country.

SERVANT And she was so happy!

BRIDE But she wasted away here.

SERVANT Fate.

BRIDE As we're all wasting away here. The very walls give off heat. Ay-y-y! Don't pull so hard.

SERVANT I'm only trying to fix this wave better. I want it to fall over your forehead.

(*The* BRIDE *looks at herself in the mirror*)

How beautiful you are! Ay-y-y!

(*She kisses her passionately*)

BRIDE (*Seriously*) Keep right on combing.

SERVANT (*Combing*) Oh, lucky you—going to put your arms around a man; and kiss him; and feel his weight.

BRIDE Hush.

SERVANT And the best part will be when you'll wake up and you'll feel him at your side and when he caresses your shoulders with his breath, like a little nightingale's feather.

BRIDE (*Sternly*) Will you be quiet.

SERVANT But, child! What *is* a wedding? A wedding is just that and nothing more. Is it the sweets—or the bouquets of flowers? No. It's a shining bed and a man and a woman.

BRIDE But you shouldn't talk about it.

SERVANT Oh, *that's* something else again. But fun enough too.

BRIDE Or bitter enough.

SERVANT I'm going to put the orange blossoms on from here to here, so the wreath will shine out on top of your hair.

(*She tries on the sprigs of orange blossom*)

BRIDE (*Looking at herself in the mirror*) Give it to me.

(*She takes the wreath, looks at it and lets her head fall in discouragement*)

SERVANT Now what's the matter?

BRIDE Leave me alone.

SERVANT This is no time for you to start feeling sad.

(*Encouragingly*)

Give me the wreath.

(*The* BRIDE *takes the wreath and hurls it away*)

Child! You're just asking God to punish you, throwing the wreath on the floor like that. Raise your head! Don't you want to get married? Say it. You can still withdraw.

(*The* BRIDE *rises*)

BRIDE Storm clouds. A chill wind that cuts through my heart. Who hasn't felt it?

SERVANT You love your sweetheart, don't you?

BRIDE I love him.

SERVANT Yes, yes. I'm sure you do.

BRIDE But this is a very serious step.

SERVANT You've got to take it.

BRIDE I've already given my word.

SERVANT I'll put on the wreath.

BRIDE (*She sits down*) Hurry. They should be arriving by now.

SERVANT They've already been at least two hours on the way.

BRIDE How far is it from here to the church?

SERVANT Five leagues by the stream, but twice that by the road.

(*The* BRIDE *rises and the* SERVANT *grows excited as she looks at her*)

SERVANT

Awake, O Bride, awaken,
On your wedding morning waken!
The world's rivers may all
Bear along your bridal Crown!

BRIDE (*Smiling*) Come now.

SERVANT (*Enthusiastically kissing her and dancing around her*)

Awake,
with the fresh bouquet
of flowering laurel.
Awake,
by the trunk and branch
of the laurels!

(*The banging of the front door latch is heard*)

BRIDE Open the door! That must be the first guests.

(*She leaves. The* SERVANT *opens the door*)

SERVANT (*In astonishment*) You!

LEONARDO Yes, me. Good morning.

SERVANT The first one!

LEONARDO Wasn't I invited?

SERVANT Yes.

LEONARDO That's why I'm here.

SERVANT Where's your wife?

LEONARDO I came on my horse. She's coming by the road.

SERVANT Didn't you meet anyone?

LEONARDO I *passed* them on my horse.

SERVANT You're going to kill that horse with so much racing.

LEONARDO When he dies, he's dead!

(*Pause*)

SERVANT Sit down. Nobody's up yet.

LEONARDO Where's the bride?

SERVANT I'm just on my way to dress her.

LEONARDO The bride! She ought to be happy!

SERVANT (*Changing the subject*) How's the baby?

LEONARDO What baby?

SERVANT Your son.

LEONARDO (*Remembering, as though in a dream*) Ah!

SERVANT Are they bringing him?

LEONARDO No.

(*Pause. Voices sing distantly*)

VOICES

Awake, O Bride, awaken,
On your wedding morning waken!

LEONARDO

Awake, O Bride, awaken,
On your wedding morning waken!

SERVANT It's the guests. They're still quite a way off.

LEONARDO The bride's going to wear a big wreath, isn't she? But it ought not to be so large. One a little smaller would look better on her. Has the groom already brought her the orange blossom that must be worn on the breast?

BRIDE (*Appearing, still in petticoats and wearing the wreath*) He brought it.

SERVANT (*Sternly*) Don't come out like that.

BRIDE What does it matter?

(*Seriously*)

Why do you ask if they brought the orange blossom? Do you have something in mind?

LEONARDO Nothing. What would I have in mind?

(*Drawing near her*)

You, you know me; you know I don't. Tell me so. What have I ever meant to you? Open your memory, refresh it. But two oxen and an ugly little hut are almost nothing. That's the thorn.

BRIDE What have you come here to do?

LEONARDO To see your wedding.

BRIDE Just as I saw yours!

LEONARDO Tied up by you, done with your two hands. Oh, they can kill me but they can't spit on me. But even money, which shines so much, spits sometimes.

BRIDE Liar!

LEONARDO I don't want to talk. I'm hot-blooded and I don't want to shout so all these hills will hear me.

BRIDE My shouts would be louder.

SERVANT You'll have to stop talking like this.

(*To the* BRIDE)

You don't have to talk about what's past.

(*The* SERVANT *looks around uneasily at the doors*)

BRIDE She's right. I shouldn't even talk to you. But it offends me to the soul that you come here to watch me, and spy on my wedding, and ask about the orange blossom with something on your mind. Go and wait for your wife at the door.

LEONARDO But, can't you and I even talk?

SERVANT (*With rage*) No! No, you can't talk.

LEONARDO Ever since I got married I've been thinking night and day about whose fault it was, and every time I think about it, out comes a new fault to eat up the old one; but always there's a fault left!

BRIDE A man with a horse knows a lot of things and can do a lot to ride roughshod over a girl stuck out in the desert. But I have my pride. And that's why I'm getting married. I'll lock myself in with my husband and then I'll have to love him above everyone else.

LEONARDO Pride won't help you a bit.

(*He draws near to her*)

BRIDE Don't come near me!

LEONARDO To burn with desire and keep quiet about it is the greatest punishment we can bring on ourselves. What good was pride to me—and not seeing you, and letting you lie awake night after night? No good! It only served to bring the fire down on me! You think that time heals and walls hide things, but it isn't true, it isn't true! When things get that deep inside you there isn't anybody can change them.

BRIDE (*Trembling*) I can't listen to you. I can't listen to your voice. It's as though I'd drunk a bottle of anise and fallen asleep wrapped in a quilt of roses. It pulls me along, and I know I'm drowning—but I go on down.

SERVANT (*Seizing* LEONARDO *by the lapels*) You've got to go right now!

LEONARDO This is the last time I'll ever talk to her. Don't you be afraid of anything.

BRIDE And I know I'm crazy and I know my breast rots with longing; but here I am—calmed by hearing him, by just seeing him move his arms.

LEONARDO I'd never be at peace if I didn't tell you these things. I got married. Now you get married.

SERVANT But she *is* getting married!

(*Voices are heard singing, nearer*)

VOICES

Awake, O Bride, awaken,
On your wedding morning waken!

BRIDE

Awake, O Bride, awaken,

(*She goes out, running toward her room*)

SERVANT The people are here now.

(*To* LEONARDO)

Don't you come near her again.

LEONARDO Don't worry.

(*He goes out to the left. Day begins to break*)

FIRST GIRL (*Entering*)

Awake, O Bride, awaken,
the morning you're to marry;
sing round and dance round;
balconies a wreath must carry.

VOICES

Bride, awaken!

SERVANT (*Creating enthusiasm*)

Awake,
with the green bouquet
of love in flower.
Awake,
by the trunk and the branch
of the laurels!

SECOND GIRL (*Entering*)

Awake,
with her long hair,
snowy sleeping gown,
patent leather boots with silver—
her forehead jasmines crown.

SERVANT

Oh, shepherdess,
the moon begins to shine!

FIRST GIRL

Oh, gallant,
leave your hat beneath the vine!

FIRST YOUNG MAN (*Entering, holding his hat on high*)

Bride, awaken,
for over the fields

the wedding draws nigh
with trays heaped with dahlias
and cakes piled high.

VOICES

Bride, awaken!

SECOND GIRL

The bride
has set her white wreath in place
and the groom
ties it on with a golden lace.

SERVANT

By the orange tree,
sleepless the bride will be.

THIRD GIRL (*Entering*)

By the citron vine,
gifts from the groom will shine.

(*Three* GUESTS *come in*)

FIRST YOUTH

Dove, awaken!
In the dawn
shadowy bells are shaken.

GUEST

The bride, the white bride
today a maiden,
tomorrow a wife.

FIRST GIRL

Dark one, come down
trailing the train of your silken gown.

GUEST

Little dark one, come down,
cold morning wears a dewy crown.

FIRST GUEST

Awaken, wife, awake,
orange blossoms the breezes shake.

SERVANT

A tree I would embroider her
with garnet sashes wound,
And on each sash a cupid,
with "Long Live" all around.

VOICES

Bride, awaken.

FIRST YOUTH

The morning you're to marry!

GUEST

The morning you're to marry
how elegant you'll seem;
worthy, mountain flower,
of a captain's dream.

FATHER (*Entering*)

A captain's wife
the groom will marry.
He comes with his oxen the treasure to carry!

THIRD GIRL

The groom
is like a flower of gold.
When he walks,
blossoms at his feet unfold.

SERVANT

Oh, my lucky girl!

SECOND YOUTH

Bride, awaken.

SERVANT

Oh, my elegant girl!

FIRST GIRL

Through the windows
hear the wedding shout.

SECOND GIRL

Let the bride come out.

FIRST GIRL

Come out, come out!

SERVANT

Let the bells
ring and ring out clear!

FIRST YOUTH

For here she comes!
For now she's near!

SERVANT

Like a bull, the wedding
is arising here!

(*The* BRIDE *appears. She wears a black dress in the style of 1900, with a bustle and large train covered with pleated gauzes and heavy laces. Upon her hair, brushed in a wave over her forehead, she wears an orange blossom wreath. Guitars sound. The* GIRLS *kiss the* BRIDE)

THIRD GIRL What scent did you put on your hair?

BRIDE (*Laughing*) None at all.

SECOND GIRL (*Looking at her dress*) This cloth is what you can't get.

FIRST YOUTH Here's the groom!

BRIDEGROOM *Salud!*

FIRST GIRL (*Putting a flower behind his ear*)

The groom
is like a flower of gold.

SECOND GIRL

Quiet breezes
from his eyes unfold.

(*The* GROOM *goes to the* BRIDE)

BRIDE Why did you put on those shoes?

BRIDEGROOM They're gayer than the black ones.

LEONARDO'S WIFE (*Entering and kissing the* BRIDE) *Salud!*

(*They all speak excitedly*)

LEONARDO (*Entering as one who performs a duty*)

The morning you're to marry
We give you a wreath to wear.

LEONARDO'S WIFE

So the fields may be made happy
with the dew dropped from your hair!

MOTHER (*To the* FATHER) Are those people here, too?

FATHER They're part of the family. Today is a day of forgiveness!

MOTHER I'll put up with it, but I don't forgive.

BRIDEGROOM With your wreath, it's a joy to look at you!

BRIDE Let's go to the church quickly.

BRIDEGROOM Are you in a hurry?

BRIDE Yes. I want to be your wife right now so that I can be with you alone, not hearing any voice but yours.

BRIDEGROOM That's what I want!

BRIDE And not seeing any eyes but yours. And for you to hug me so hard, that even though my dead mother should call me, I wouldn't be able to draw away from you.

BRIDEGROOM My arms are strong. I'll hug you for forty years without stopping.

BRIDE (*Taking his arm, dramatically*) Forever!

FATHER Quick now! Round up the teams and carts! The sun's already out.

MOTHER And go along carefully! Let's hope nothing goes wrong.

(*The great door in the background opens*)

SERVANT (*Weeping*)

As you set out from your house,
Oh, maiden white,
remember you leave shining
with a star's light.

FIRST GIRL

Clean of body, clean of clothes
from her home to church she goes.

(*They start leaving*)

SECOND GIRL

Now you leave your home
for the church!

SERVANT

The wind sets flowers
on the sands.

THIRD GIRL

Ah, the white maid!

SERVANT

Dark winds are the lace
of her mantilla.

(*They leave. Guitars, castanets and tambourines are heard.* LEONARDO *and his* WIFE *are left alone*)

WIFE Let's go.

LEONARDO Where?

WIFE To the church. But not on your horse. You're coming with me.

LEONARDO In the cart?

WIFE Is there anything else?

LEONARDO I'm not the kind of man to ride in a cart.

WIFE Nor I the wife to go to a wedding without her husband. I can't stand any more of this!

LEONARDO Neither can I!

WIFE And why do you look at me that way? With a thorn in each eye.

LEONARDO Let's go!

WIFE I don't know what's happening. But I think, and I don't want to think. One thing I do know. I'm already cast off by you. But I have a son. And another coming. And so it goes. My mother's fate was the same. Well, I'm not moving from here.

(VOICES *outside*)

VOICES

As you set out from your home
and to the church go
remember you leave shining
with a star's glow.

WIFE (*Weeping*)

Remember you leave shining
with a star's glow!

I left my house like that too. They could have stuffed the whole countryside in my mouth. I was that trusting.

LEONARDO (*Rising*) Let's go!

WIFE But you with me!

LEONARDO Yes.

(*Pause*)

Start moving!

(*They leave*)

VOICES

As you set out from your home
and to the church go,
remember you leave shining
with a star's glow.

*Slow Curtain*

# Act Two, Scene Two

*The exterior of the* BRIDE'S *Cave Home, in white gray and cold blue tones. Large cactus trees. Shadowy and silver tones. Panoramas of light tan tablelands, everything hard like a landscape in popular ceramics.*

SERVANT (*Arranging glasses and trays on a table*)

A-turning,
the wheel was a-turning
and the water was flowing,
for the wedding night comes.
May the branches part
and the moon be arrayed
at her white balcony rail.

(*In a loud voice*)
Set out the tablecloths!
(*In a pathetic voice*)

A-singing,
bride and groom were singing
and the water was flowing
for their wedding night comes.
Oh, rime-frost, flash!—
and almonds bitter
fill with honey!

(*In a loud voice*)
Get the wine ready!
(*In a poetic tone*)

Elegant girl,
most elegant in the world,
see the way the water is flowing,
for your wedding night comes.
Hold your skirts close in
under the bridegroom's wing
and never leave your house,
for the Bridegroom is a dove
with his breast a firebrand
and the fields wait for the whisper
of spurting blood.
A-turning
the wheel was a-turning
and the water was flowing
and your wedding night comes.
Oh, water, sparkle!

MOTHER (*Entering*) At last!

FATHER Are we the first ones?

SERVANT No. Leonardo and his wife arrived a while ago. They drove like demons. His wife got here dead with fright. They made the trip as though they'd come on horseback.

FATHER That one's looking for trouble. He's not of good blood.

MOTHER What blood would you expect him to have? His whole family's blood. It comes down from his great grandfather, who started in killing, and it goes on down through the whole evil breed of knife wielding and false smiling men.

FATHER Let's leave it at that!

SERVANT But how can she leave it at that?

MOTHER It hurts me to the tips of my veins. On the forehead of all of them I see only the hand with which they killed what was mine. Can you really see me? Don't I seem mad to you? Well, it's the madness of not having shrieked out all my breast needs to. Always in my breast there's a shriek standing tiptoe that I have to beat down and hold in under my shawls. But the dead are carried off and one has to keep still. And then, people find fault.

(*She removes her shawl*)

FATHER Today's not the day for you to be remembering these things.

MOTHER When the talk turns on it, I have to speak. And more so today. Because today I'm left alone in my house.

FATHER But with the expectation of having someone with you.

MOTHER That's my hope: grandchildren.

(*They sit down*)

FATHER I want them to have a lot of them. This land needs hands that aren't hired. There's a battle to be waged against weeds, the thistles, the big rocks that come from one doesn't know where. And those hands have to be the owner's, who chastises and dominates, who makes the seeds grow. Lots of sons are needed.

MOTHER And some daughters! Men are like the wind! They're forced to handle weapons. Girls never go out into the street.

FATHER (*Happily*) I think they'll have both.

MOTHER My son will cover her well. He's of good seed. His father could have had many sons with me.

FATHER What I'd like is to have all this happen in a day. So that right away they'd have two or three boys.

MOTHER But it's not like that. It takes a long time. That's why it's so terrible to see one's own blood spilled out on the ground. A fountain that spurts for a minute, but costs us years. When I got to my son, he lay fallen in the middle of the street. I wet my hands with his blood and licked them with my tongue —because it was my blood. You don't know what that's like. In a glass and topaz shrine I'd put the earth moistened by his blood.

FATHER Now you must hope. My daughter is wide-hipped and your son is strong.

MOTHER That's why I'm hoping.

(*They rise*)

FATHER Get the wheat trays ready!

SERVANT They're all ready.

LEONARDO'S WIFE (*Entering*) May it be for the best!

MOTHER Thank you.

LEONARDO Is there going to be a celebration?

FATHER A small one. People can't stay long.

SERVANT Here they are!

(*Guests begin entering in gay groups. The* BRIDE *and* GROOM *come in arm-in-arm.* LEONARDO *leaves*)

BRIDEGROOM There's never been a wedding with so many people!

BRIDE (*Sullen*) Never.

FATHER It was brilliant.

MOTHER Whole branches of families came.

BRIDEGROOM People who never went out of the house.

MOTHER Your father sowed well, and now you're reaping it.

BRIDEGROOM There were cousins of mine whom I no longer knew.

MOTHER All the people from the seacoast.

BRIDEGROOM (*Happily*) They were frightened of the horses.

(*They talk*)

MOTHER (*To the* BRIDE) What are you thinking about?

BRIDE I'm not thinking about anything.

MOTHER Your blessings weigh heavily.

(*Guitars are heard*)

BRIDE Like lead.

MOTHER (*Stern*) But they shouldn't weigh so. Happy as a dove you ought to be.

BRIDE Are you staying here tonight?

MOTHER No. My house is empty.

BRIDE You ought to stay!

FATHER (*To the* MOTHER) Look at the dance they're forming. Dances of the far away seashore.

(LEONARDO *enters and sits down. His* WIFE *stands rigidly behind him*)

MOTHER They're my husband's cousins. Stiff as stones at dancing.

FATHER It makes me happy to watch them. What a change for this house!

(*He leaves*)

BRIDEGROOM (*To the* BRIDE) Did you like the orange blossom?

BRIDE (*Looking at him fixedly*) Yes.

BRIDEGROOM It's all of wax. It will last forever. I'd like you to have had them all over your dress.

BRIDE No need of that.

(LEONARDO *goes off to the right*)

FIRST GIRL Let's go and take out your pins.

BRIDE (*To the* GROOM) I'll be right back.

LEONARDO'S WIFE I hope you'll be happy with my cousin!

BRIDEGROOM I'm sure I will.

LEONARDO'S WIFE The two of you here; never going out; building a home. I wish I could live far away like this, too!

BRIDEGROOM Why don't you buy land? The mountainside is cheap and children grow up better.

LEONARDO'S WIFE We don't have any money. And at the rate we're going . . . !

BRIDEGROOM Your husband is a good worker.

LEONARDO'S WIFE Yes, but he likes to fly around too much; from one thing to another. He's not a patient man.

SERVANT Aren't you having anything? I'm going to wrap up some wine cakes for your mother. She likes them so much.

BRIDEGROOM Put up three dozen for her.

LEONARDO'S WIFE No, no. A half-dozen's enough for her!

BRIDEGROOM But today's a day!

LEONARDO'S WIFE (*To the* SERVANT) Where's Leonardo?

BRIDEGROOM He must be with the guests.

LEONARDO'S WIFE I'm going to go see.

(*She leaves*)

SERVANT (*Looking off at the dance*) That's beautiful there.

BRIDEGROOM Aren't you dancing?

SERVANT No one will ask me.

(TWO GIRLS *pass across the back of the stage; during this whole scene the background should be an animated crossing of figures*)

BRIDEGROOM (*Happily*) They just don't know anything. Lively old girls like you dance better than the young ones.

SERVANT Well! Are you tossing me a compliment, boy? What a family yours is! Men among men! As a little girl I saw your grandfather's wedding. What a figure! It seemed as if a mountain were getting married.

BRIDEGROOM I'm not as tall.

SERVANT But there's the same twinkle in your eye Where's the girl?

BRIDEGROOM Taking off her wreath.

SERVANT Ah! Look. For midnight, since you won't be sleeping, I have prepared ham for you, and some large glasses of old wine. On the lower shelf of the cupboard. In case you need it.

BRIDEGROOM (*Smiling*) I won't be eating at midnight.

SERVANT (*Slyly*) If not you, maybe the bride.

(*She leaves*)

FIRST YOUTH (*Entering*) You've got to come have a drink with us!

BRIDEGROOM I'm waiting for the bride.

SECOND YOUTH You'll have her at dawn!

FIRST YOUTH That's when it's best!

SECOND YOUTH Just for a minute.

BRIDEGROOM Let's go.

(*They leave. Great excitement is heard. The* BRIDE *enters. From the opposite side* TWO GIRLS *come running to meet her*)

FIRST GIRL To whom did you give the first pin; me or this one?

BRIDE I don't remember.

FIRST GIRL To me, you gave it to me here.

SECOND GIRL To me, in front of the altar.

BRIDE (*Uneasily, with a great inner struggle*) I don't know anything about it.

FIRST GIRL It's just that I wish you'd . . .

BRIDE (*Interrupting*) Nor do I care. I have a lot to think about.

SECOND GIRL Your pardon.

(LEONARDO *crosses at the rear of the stage*)

BRIDE (*She sees* LEONARDO) And this is an upsetting time.

FIRST GIRL We wouldn't know anything about that!

BRIDE You'll know about it when your time comes. This step is a very hard one to take.

FIRST GIRL Has she offended you?
BRIDE No. You must pardon me.
SECOND GIRL What for? But *both* the pins are good for getting married, aren't they?
BRIDE Both of them.
FIRST GIRL Maybe now one will get married before the other.
BRIDE Are you so eager?
SECOND GIRL (*Shyly*) Yes.
BRIDE Why?
FIRST GIRL Well . . .

(*She embraces the* SECOND GIRL. *Both go running off. The* GROOM *comes in very slowly and embraces the* BRIDE *from behind*)

BRIDE (*In sudden fright*) Let go of me!
BRIDEGROOM Are you frightened of me?
BRIDE Ay-y-y! It's you?
BRIDEGROOM Who else would it be?

(*Pause*)

Your father or me.
BRIDE That's true!
BRIDEGROOM Of course, your father would have hugged you more gently.
BRIDE (*Darkly*) Of course!
BRIDEGROOM (*Embracing her strongly and a little bit brusquely*) Because he's old.
BRIDE (*Curtly*) Let me go!
BRIDEGROOM Why?

(*He lets her go*)

BRIDE Well . . . the people. They can see us.

(*The* SERVANT *crosses at the back of the stage again without looking at the* BRIDE *and* BRIDEGROOM)

BRIDEGROOM What of it? It's consecrated now.
BRIDE Yes, but let me be . . . Later.
BRIDEGROOM What's the matter with you? You look frightened!
BRIDE I'm all right. Don't go.

(LEONARDO'S WIFE *enters*)

LEONARDO'S WIFE I don't mean to intrude . . .
BRIDEGROOM What is it?
LEONARDO'S WIFE Did my husband come through here?
BRIDEGROOM No.
LEONARDO'S WIFE Because I can't find him, and his horse isn't in the stable either.
BRIDEGROOM (*Happily*) He must be out racing it.

(*The* WIFE *leaves, troubled. The* SERVANT *enters*)

SERVANT Aren't you two proud and happy with so many good wishes?
BRIDEGROOM I wish it were over with. The bride is a little tired.
SERVANT That's no way to act, child.
BRIDE It's as though I'd been struck on the head.
SERVANT A bride from these mountains must be strong.

(*To the* GROOM)

You're the only one who can cure her, because she's yours.

(*She goes running off*)

BRIDEGROOM (*Embracing the* BRIDE) Let's go dance a little.

(*He kisses her*)

BRIDE (*Worried*) No. I'd like to stretch out on my bed a little.
BRIDEGROOM I'll keep you company.
BRIDE Never! With all these people here? What would they say? Let me be quiet for a moment.
BRIDEGROOM Whatever you say! But don't be like that tonight!
BRIDE (*At the door*) I'll be better tonight.
BRIDEGROOM That's what I want.

(*The* MOTHER *appears*)

MOTHER Son.
BRIDEGROOM Where've you been?
MOTHER Out there—in all that noise. Are you happy?
BRIDEGROOM Yes.
MOTHER Where's your wife?
BRIDEGROOM Resting a little. It's a bad day for brides!
MOTHER A bad day? The only good one. To me it was like coming into my own.

(*The* SERVANT *enters and goes toward the* BRIDE'S *room*)

Like the breaking of new ground; the planting of new trees.
BRIDEGROOM Are you going to leave?
MOTHER Yes. I ought to be at home.
BRIDEGROOM Alone.
MOTHER Not alone. For my head is full of things: of men, and fights.
BRIDEGROOM But now the fights are no longer fights.

(*The* SERVANT *enters quickly; she disappears at the rear of the stage, running*)

MOTHER While you live, you have to fight.
BRIDEGROOM I'll always obey you!
MOTHER Try to be loving with your wife, and if you see she's acting foolish or touchy, caress her in a way that will hurt her a little: a strong hug, a bite and then a soft kiss. Not so she'll be angry, but just so she'll feel you're the man, the boss, the one who gives orders. I learned that from your father. And since you don't have him, I have to be the one to tell you about these strong defenses.
BRIDEGROOM I'll always do as you say.
FATHER (*Entering*) Where's my daughter?
BRIDEGROOM She's inside.

(*The* FATHER *goes to look for her*)

FIRST GIRL Get the bride and groom! We're going to dance a round!
FIRST YOUTH (*To the* BRIDEGROOM) You're going to lead it.
FATHER (*Entering*) She's not there.
BRIDEGROOM No?
FATHER She must have gone up to the railing.
BRIDEGROOM I'll go see!

(*He leaves. A hubbub of excitement and guitars is heard*)

FIRST GIRL They've started it already!

(*She leaves*)

BRIDEGROOM (*Entering*) She isn't there.

MOTHER (*Uneasily*) Isn't she?

FATHER But where could she have gone?

SERVANT (*Entering*) But where's the girl, where is she?

MOTHER (*Seriously*) That we don't know.

(*The* BRIDEGROOM *leaves. Three guests enter*)

FATHER (*Dramatically*) But, isn't she in the dance?

SERVANT She's not in the dance.

FATHER (*With a start*) There are a lot of people. Go look!

SERVANT I've already looked.

FATHER (*Tragically*) Then where is she?

BRIDEGROOM (*Entering*) Nowhere. Not anywhere.

MOTHER (*To the* FATHER) What does this mean? Where is your daughter?

(LEONARDO'S WIFE *enters*)

LEONARDO'S WIFE They've run away! They've run away! She and Leonardo. On the horse. With their arms around each other, they rode off like a shooting star!

FATHER That's not true! Not my daughter!

MOTHER Yes, your daughter! Spawn of a wicked mother, and he, he too. But now she's my son's wife!

BRIDEGROOM (*Entering*) Let's go after them! Who has a horse?

MOTHER Who has a horse? Right away! Who has a horse? I'll give him all I have—my eyes, my tongue even. . . .

VOICE Here's one.

MOTHER (*To the* SON) Go! After them!

(*He leaves with two young men*)

No. Don't go. Those people kill quickly and well . . . but yes, run, and I'll follow!

FATHER It couldn't be my daughter. Perhaps she's thrown herself in the well.

MOTHER Decent women throw themselves in water; not that one! But now she's my son's wife. Two groups. There are two groups here.

(*They all enter*)

My family and yours. Everyone set out from here. Shake the dust from your heels! We'll go help my son.

(*The people separate into two groups*)

For he has his family: his cousins from the sea, and all who came from inland. Out of here! On all roads. The hour of blood has come again. Two groups! You with yours and I with mine. After them! After them!

*Curtain*

# Act Three, Scene One

*A forest. It is nighttime. Great moist tree trunks. A dark atmosphere. Two violins are heard. Three* WOODCUTTERS *enter.*

FIRST WOODCUTTER And have they found them?

SECOND WOODCUTTER No. But they're looking for them everywhere.

THIRD WOODCUTTER They'll find them.

SECOND WOODCUTTER Sh-h-h!

THIRD WOODCUTTER What?

SECOND WOODCUTTER They seem to be coming closer on all the roads at once.

FIRST WOODCUTTER When the moon comes out they'll see them.

SECOND WOODCUTTER They ought to let them go.

FIRST WOODCUTTER The world is wide. Everybody can live in it.

THIRD WOODCUTTER But they'll kill them.

SECOND WOODCUTTER You have to follow your passion. They did right to run away.

FIRST WOODCUTTER They were deceiving themselves but at the last blood was stronger.

THIRD WOODCUTTER Blood!

FIRST WOODCUTTER You have to follow the path of your blood.

SECOND WOODCUTTER But blood that sees the light of day is drunk up by the earth.

FIRST WOODCUTTER What of it? Better dead with the blood drained away than alive with it rotting.

THIRD WOODCUTTER Hush!

FIRST WOODCUTTER What? Do you hear something?

THIRD WOODCUTTER I hear the crickets, the frogs, the night's ambush.

FIRST WOODCUTTER But not the horse.

THIRD WOODCUTTER No.

FIRST WOODCUTTER By now he must be loving her.

SECOND WOODCUTTER Her body for him; his body for her.

THIRD WOODCUTTER They'll find them and they'll kill them.

FIRST WOODCUTTER But by then they'll have mingled their bloods. They'll be like two empty jars, like two dry arroyos.

SECOND WOODCUTTER There are many clouds and it would be easy for the moon not to come out.

THIRD WOODCUTTER The bridegroom will find them with or without the moon. I saw him set out. Like a raging star. His face the color of ashes. He looked the fate of all his clan.

FIRST WOODCUTTER His clan of dead men lying in the middle of the street.

SECOND WOODCUTTER There you have it!

THIRD WOODCUTTER You think they'll be able to break through the circle?

SECOND WOODCUTTER It's hard to. There are knives and guns for ten leagues 'round.

THIRD WOODCUTTER He's riding a good horse.

SECOND WOODCUTTER But he's carrying a woman.

FIRST WOODCUTTER We're close by now.

SECOND WOODCUTTER A tree with forty branches. We'll soon cut it down.

THIRD WOODCUTTER The moon's coming out now. Let's hurry.

(*From the left shines a brightness*)

FIRST WOODCUTTER

O rising moon!
Moon among the great leaves.

SECOND WOODCUTTER

Cover the blood with jasmines!

FIRST WOODCUTTER

O lonely moon!
Moon among the great leaves.

SECOND WOODCUTTER

Silver on the bride's face.

THIRD WOODCUTTER

O evil moon!
Leave for their love a branch in shadow.

FIRST WOODCUTTER

O sorrowing moon!
Leave for their love a branch in shadow.

(*They go out. The* MOON *appears through the shining brightness at the left. The* MOON *is a young woodcutter with a white face. The stage takes on an intense blue radiance*)

MOON

Round swan in the river
and a cathedral's eye,
false dawn on the leaves,
they'll not escape; these things am I!
Who is hiding? And who sobs
in the thornbrakes of the valley?
The moon sets a knife
abandoned in the air
which being a leaden threat
yearns to be blood's pain.
Let me in! I come freezing
down to walls and windows!
Open roofs, open breasts
where I may warm myself!
I'm cold! My ashes
of somnolent metals
seek the fire's crest
on mountains and streets.
But the snow carries me
upon its mottled back
and pools soak me
in their water, hard and cold.
But this night there will be
red blood for my cheeks,
and for the reeds that cluster
at the wide feet of the wind.
Let there be neither shadow nor bower,
and then they can't get away!
O let me enter a breast
where I may get warm!
A heart for me!
Warm! That will spurt
over the mountains of my chest;
let me come in, oh let me!
(*To the branches*)
I want no shadows. My rays
must get in everywhere,
even among the dark trunks I want
the whisper of gleaming lights,
so that this night there will be
sweet blood for my cheeks,
and for the reeds that cluster
at the wide feet of the wind.
Who is hiding? Out, I say!
No! They will not get away!
I will light up the horse
with a fever bright as diamonds.

(*He disappears among the trunks, and the stage goes back to its dark lighting. An Old Woman comes out completely covered by thin green cloth. She is barefooted. Her face can barely be seen among the folds. This character does not appear in the cast*)

BEGGAR WOMAN

That moon's going away, just when they's near.
They won't get past here. The river's whisper
and the whispering tree trunks will muffle
the torn flight of their shrieks.
It has to be here, and soon. I'm worn out.
The coffins are ready, and white sheets
wait on the floor of the bedroom
for heavy bodies with torn throats.
Let not one bird awake, let the breeze,
gathering their moans in her skirt,
fly with them over black tree tops
or bury them in soft mud.
(*Impatiently*)
Oh, that moon! That moon!

(*The* MOON *appears. The intense blue light returns*)

MOON They're coming. One band through the ravine and the other along the river. I'm going to light up the boulders. What do you need?

BEGGAR WOMAN Nothing.

MOON The wind blows hard now, with a double edge.

BEGGAR WOMAN Light up the waistcoat and open the buttons; the knives will know the path after that.

MOON

But let them be a long time a-dying. So the blood
will slide its delicate hissing between my fingers.
Look how my ashen valleys already are waking
in longing for this fountain of shuddering gushes!

BEGGAR WOMAN Let's not let them get past the arroyo. Silence!

MOON There they come!
(*He goes. The stage is left dark*)

BEGGAR WOMAN Quick! Lots of light! Do you hear me? They can't get away!
(*The* BRIDEGROOM *and the* FIRST YOUTH *enter. The* BEGGAR WOMAN *sits down and covers herself with her cloak*)

BRIDEGROOM This way.
FIRST YOUTH You won't find them.
BRIDEGROOM (*Angrily*) Yes, I'll find them.
FIRST YOUTH I think they've taken another path.
BRIDEGROOM No. Just a moment ago I felt the galloping.
FIRST YOUTH It could have been another horse.
BRIDEGROOM (*Intensely*) Listen to me. There's only one horse in the whole world, and this one's it. Can't you understand that? If you're going to follow me, follow me without talking.
FIRST YOUTH It's only that I want to . . .
BRIDEGROOM Be quiet. I'm sure of meeting them there. Do you see this arm? Well, it's not my arm. It's my brother's arm, and my father's, and that of all the dead ones in my family. And it has so much strength that it can pull this tree up by the roots, if it wants to. And let's move on, because here I feel the clenched teeth of all my people in me so that I can't breathe easily.
BEGGAR WOMAN (*Whining*) Ay-y-y!
FIRST YOUTH Did you hear that?
BRIDEGROOM You go that way and then circle back.
FIRST YOUTH This is a hunt.
BRIDEGROOM A hunt. The greatest hunt there is.

(*The* YOUTH *goes off. The* BRIDEGROOM *goes rapidly to the left and stumbles over the* BEGGAR WOMAN, *Death*)

BEGGAR WOMAN Ay-y-y!
BRIDEGROOM What do you want?
BEGGAR WOMAN I'm cold.
BRIDEGROOM Which way are you going?
BEGGAR WOMAN (*Always whining like a beggar*) Over there, far away . . .
BRIDEGROOM Where are you from?
BEGGAR WOMAN Over there . . . very far away.
BRIDEGROOM Have you seen a man and a woman running away on a horse?
BEGGAR WOMAN (*Awakening*) Wait a minute . . .
(*She looks at him*)
Handsome young man.
(*She rises*)
But you'd be much handsomer sleeping.
BRIDEGROOM Tell me; answer me. Did you see them?
BEGGAR WOMAN Wait a minute . . . What broad shoulders! How would you like to be laid out on them and not have to walk on the soles of your feet which are so small?
BRIDEGROOM (*Shaking her*) I asked you if you saw them! Have they passed through here?
BEGGAR WOMAN (*Energetically*) No. They haven't passed; but they're coming from the hill. Don't you hear them?
BRIDEGROOM No.
BEGGAR WOMAN Do you know the road?
BRIDEGROOM I'll go, whatever it's like!
BEGGAR WOMAN I'll go along with you. I know this country.
BRIDEGROOM (*Impatiently*) Well, let's go! Which way?
BEGGAR WOMAN (*Dramatically*) This way!

(*They go rapidly out. Two violins, which represent the forest, are heard distantly. The* WOODCUTTERS *return. They have their axes on their shoulders. They move slowly among the tree trunks*)

FIRST WOODCUTTER

O rising death!
Death among the great leaves.

SECOND WOODCUTTER

Don't open the gush of blood!

FIRST WOODCUTTER

O lonely death!
Death among the dried leaves.

THIRD WOODCUTTER

Don't lay flowers over the wedding!

SECOND WOODCUTTER

O sad death!
Leave for their love a green branch.

FIRST WOODCUTTER

O evil death!
Leave for their love a branch of green!

(*They go out while they are talking.* LEONARDO *and the* BRIDE *appear*)

LEONARDO

Hush!

BRIDE

From here I'll go on alone.
You go now! I want you to turn back.

LEONARDO

Hush, I said!

BRIDE

With your teeth, with your hands, anyway you can,
take from my clean throat
the metal of this chain,
and let me live forgotten
back there in my house in the ground.
And if you don't want to kill me
as you would kill a tiny snake,
set in my hands, a bride's hands,
the barrel of your shotgun.
Oh, what lamenting, what fire,
sweeps upward through my head!
What glass splinters are stuck in my tongue!

LEONARDO

We've taken the step now; hush!
because they're close behind us,
and I must take you with me.

BRIDE

Then it must be by force!

LEONARDO

By force? Who was it first
went down the stairway?

BRIDE

I went down it.

LEONARDO

And who was it put
a new bridle on the horse?

BRIDE

I myself did it. It's true.

LEONARDO

And whose were the hands
strapped spurs to my boots?

BRIDE

The same hands, these that are yours,
but which when they see you would like
to break the blue branches
and sunder the purl of your veins.
I love you! I love you! But leave me!
For if I were able to kill you
I'd wrap you 'round in a shroud
with the edges bordered in violets.
Oh, what lamenting, what fire,
sweeps upward through my head!

LEONARDO

What glass splinters are stuck in my tongue!
Because I tried to forget you
and put a wall of stone
between your house and mine.
It's true. You remember?
And when I saw you in the distance
I threw sand in my eyes.
But I was riding a horse
and the horse went straight to your door.
And the silver pins of your wedding
turned my red blood black.
And in me our dream was choking
my flesh with its poisoned weeds.
Oh, it isn't my fault—
the fault is the earth's—
and this fragrance that you exhale
from your breasts and your braids.

BRIDE

Oh, how untrue! I want
from you neither bed nor food,
yet there's not a minute each day
that I don't want to be with you,
because you drag me, and I come,
then you tell me to go back
and I follow you,
like chaff blown on the breeze.
I have left a good, honest man,
and all his people,
with the wedding feast half over
and wearing my bridal wreath.
But you are the one will be punished
and that I don't want to happen.
Leave me alone now! You run away!
There is no one who will defend you.

LEONARDO

The birds of early morning
are calling among the trees.
The night is dying
on the stone's ridge.
Let's go to a hidden corner
where I may love you forever,
for to me the people don't matter,
nor the venom they throw on us.
(*He embraces her strongly*)

BRIDE

And I'll sleep at your feet,
to watch over your dreams.
Naked, looking over the fields,
as though I were a bitch.
Because that's what I am! Oh, I look at you
and your beauty sears me.

LEONARDO

Fire is stirred by fire.
The same tiny flame
will kill two wheat heads together.
Let's go!

BRIDE

Where are you taking me?

LEONARDO

Where they cannot come,
these men who surround us.
Where I can look at you!

BRIDE (*Sarcastically*)

Carry me with you from fair to fair,
a shame to clean women,
so that people will see me
with my wedding sheets
on the breeze like banners.

LEONARDO

I, too, would want to leave you
if I thought as men should.
But wherever you go, I go.
You're the same. Take a step. Try.
Nails of moonlight have fused
my waist and your thighs.

(*This whole scene is violent, full of great sensuality*)

BRIDE

Listen!

LEONARDO

They're coming.

BRIDE

Run!
It's fitting that I should die here,
with water over my feet,
with thorns upon my head.
And fitting the leaves should mourn me,
a woman lost and virgin.

LEONARDO

Be quiet. Now they're appearing.

BRIDE

Go now!

LEONARDO

Quiet. Don't let them hear us.
(*The* BRIDE *hesitates*)

BRIDE

Both of us!

LEONARDO (*Embracing her*)

Any way you want!
If they separate us, it will be
because I am dead.

BRIDE

And I dead too.
(*They go out in each other's arms.*
*The* MOON *appears very slowly. The stage takes on a strong blue light. The two violins are heard. Suddenly two long, ear-splitting shrieks are heard, and the music of the two violins is cut short. At the second shriek The* BEGGAR WOMAN *appears and stands with her back to the audience. She opens her cape and stands in the center of the stage like a great bird with immense wings. The* MOON *halts. The curtain comes down in absolute silence*)

***Curtain***

# Act Three, Scene Two

(*The Final Scene*)

*A white dwelling with arches and thick walls. To the right and left, are white stairs. At the back, a great arch and a wall of the same color. The floor also should be shining white. This simple dwelling should have the monumental feeling of a church. There should not be a single gray nor any shadow, not even what is necessary for perspective.*

*Two* GIRLS *dressed in dark blue are winding a red skein.*

FIRST GIRL

Wool, red wool,
what would you make?

SECOND GIRL

Oh, jasmine for dresses,
fine wool like glass.
At four o'clock born,
at ten o'clock dead.
A thread from this wool yarn,
a chain 'round your feet
a knot that will tighten
the bitter white wreath.

LITTLE GIRL (*Singing*)

Were you at the wedding?

FIRST GIRL

No.

LITTLE GIRL

Well, neither was I!
What could have happened
'midst the shoots of the vineyards?
What could have happened
'neath the branch of the olive?
What really happened
that no one came back?
Were you at the wedding?

SECOND GIRL

We told you once, no.

LITTLE GIRL (*Leaving*)

Well, neither was I!

SECOND GIRL

Wool, red wool,
what would you sing?

FIRST GIRL

Their wounds turning waxen
balm-myrtle for pain.
Asleep in the morning,
and watching at night.

LITTLE GIRL (*In the doorway*)

And then, the thread stumbled
on the flinty stones,
but mountains, blue mountains,
are letting it pass.
Running, running, running,
and finally to come

to stick in a knife blade,
to take back the bread.
(*She goes out*)

SECOND GIRL

Wool, red wool,
what would you tell?

FIRST GIRL

The lover is silent,
crimson the groom,
at the still shoreline
I saw them laid out.
(*She stops and looks at the skein*)

LITTLE GIRL (*Appearing in the doorway*)

Running, running, running,
the thread runs to here.
All covered with clay
I feel them draw near.
Bodies stretched stiffly
in ivory sheets!

(*The* WIFE *and* MOTHER-IN-LAW *of* LEONARDO *appear. They are anguished*)

FIRST GIRL Are they coming yet?

MOTHER-IN-LAW (*Harshly*) We don't know.

SECOND GIRL What can you tell us about the wedding?

FIRST GIRL Yes, tell me.

MOTHER-IN-LAW (*Curtly*) Nothing.

LEONARDO'S WIFE I want to go back and find out all about it.

MOTHER-IN-LAW (*Sternly*)

You, back to your house.
Brave and alone in your house.
To grow old and to weep.
But behind closed doors.
Never again. Neither dead nor alive.
We'll nail up our windows
and let rains and nights
fall on the bitter weeds.

LEONARDO'S WIFE What could have happened?

MOTHER-IN-LAW

It doesn't matter what.
Put a veil over your face.
Your children are yours,
that's all. On the bed
put a cross of ashes
where his pillow was.

(*They go out*)

BEGGAR WOMAN (*At the door*) A crust of bread, little girls.

LITTLE GIRL Go away!
(*The* GIRLS *huddle close together*)

BEGGAR WOMAN Why?

LITTLE GIRL Because you whine; go away!

FIRST GIRL Child!

BEGGAR WOMAN

I might have asked for your eyes! A cloud
of birds is following me. Will you have one?

LITTLE GIRL I want to get away from here!

SECOND GIRL (*To the* BEGGAR WOMAN) Don't mind her!

FIRST GIRL Did you come by the road through the arroyo?

BEGGAR WOMAN I came that way!

FIRST GIRL (*Timidly*) Can I ask you something?

BEGGAR WOMAN

I saw them: they'll be here soon; two torrents
still at last, among the great boulders,
two men at the horse's feet.
Two dead men in the night's splendor.

(*With pleasure*)
Dead, yes, dead.

FIRST GIRL Hush, old woman, hush!

BEGGAR WOMAN

Crushed flowers for eyes, and their teeth
two fistfuls of hard-frozen snow.
Both of them fell, and the Bride returns
with bloodstains on her skirt and hair.
And they come covered with two sheets
carried on the shoulders of two tall boys.
That's how it was; nothing more. What was fitting.
Over the golden flower, dirty sand.

(*She goes. The* GIRLS *bow their heads and start going out rhythmically*)

FIRST GIRL

Dirty sand.

SECOND GIRL

Over the golden flower.

LITTLE GIRL

Over the golden flower
they're bringing the dead from the arroyo.
Dark the one,
dark the other.
What shadowy nightingale flies and weeps
over the golden flower!

(*She goes. The stage is left empty. The* MOTHER *and a* NEIGHBOR WOMAN *appear. The* NEIGHBOR *is weeping*)

MOTHER Hush.

NEIGHBOR I can't.

MOTHER Hush, I said.
(*At the door*)
Is there nobody here?
(*She puts her hands to her forehead*)
My son ought to answer me. But now my son is an armful of shriveled flowers. My son is a fading voice beyond the mountains now.
(*With rage, to the* NEIGHBOR)
Will you shut up? I want no wailing in this house.

Your tears are only tears from your eyes, but when I'm alone mine will come—from the soles of my feet, from my roots—burning more than blood.

NEIGHBOR You come to my house; don't you stay here.

MOTHER I want to be here. Here. In peace. They're all dead now: and at midnight I'll sleep, sleep without terror of guns or knives. Other mothers will go to their windows, lashed by rain, to watch for their sons' faces. But not I. And of my dreams I'll make a cold ivory dove that will carry camellias of white frost to the graveyard. But no; not graveyard, not graveyard: the couch of earth, the bed that shelters them and rocks them in the sky.

(*A woman dressed in black enters, goes toward the right, and there kneels. To the* NEIGHBOR)

Take your hands from your face. We have terrible days ahead. I want to see no one. The earth and I. My grief and I. And these four walls. Ay-y-y! Ay-y-y!

(*She sits down, overcome*)

NEIGHBOR Take pity on yourself!

MOTHER (*Pushing back her hair*) I must be calm.

(*She sits down*)

Because the neighbor women will come and I don't want them to see me so poor. So poor! A woman without even one son to hold to her lips.

(*The* BRIDE *appears. She is without her wreath and wears a black shawl*)

NEIGHBOR (*With rage, seeing the* BRIDE) Where are you going?

BRIDE I'm coming here.

MOTHER (*To the* NEIGHBOR) Who is it?

NEIGHBOR Don't you recognize her?

MOTHER That's why I asked who it was. Because I don't want to recognize her, so I won't sink my teeth in her throat. You snake!

(*She moves wrathfully on the* BRIDE, *then stops. To the* NEIGHBOR)

Look at her! There she is, and she's crying, while I stand here calmly and don't tear her eyes out. I don't understand myself. Can it be I didn't love my son? But, where's his good name? Where is it now? Where is it?

(*She beats the* BRIDE *who drops to the floor*)

NEIGHBOR For God's sake!

(*She tries to separate them*)

BRIDE (*To the* NEIGHBOR) Let her; I came here so she'd kill me and they'd take me away with them.

(*To the* MOTHER)

But not with her hands; with grappling hooks, with a sickle—and with force—until they break on my bones. Let her! I want her to know I'm clean, that I may be crazy, but that they can bury me without a single man ever having seen himself in the whiteness of my breasts.

MOTHER Shut up, shut up; what do I care about that?

BRIDE Because I ran away with the other one; I ran away!

(*With anguish*)

You would have gone, too. I was a woman burning with desire, full of sores inside and out, and your son was a little bit of water from which I hoped for children, land, health; but the other one was a dark river, choked with brush, that brought near me the undertone of its rushes and its whispered song. And I went along with your son who was like a little boy of cold water—and the other sent against me hundreds of birds who got in my way and left white frost on my wounds, my wounds of a poor withered woman, of a girl caressed by fire. I didn't want to; remember that! I didn't want to. Your son was my destiny and I have not betrayed him, but the other one's arm dragged me along like the pull of the sea, like the head toss of a mule, and he would have dragged me always, always, always—even if I were an old woman and all your son's sons held me by the hair!

(*A* NEIGHBOR *enters*)

MOTHER She is not to blame; nor am I!

(*Sarcastically*)

Who is, then? It's a delicate, lazy, sleepless woman who throws away an orange blossom wreath and goes looking for a piece of bed warmed by another woman!

BRIDE Be still! Be still! Take your revenge on me; here I am! See how soft my throat is; it would be less work for you than cutting a dahlia in your garden. But never that! Clean, clean as a new-born little girl. And strong enough to prove it to you. Light the fire. Let's stick our hands in; you, for your son, I, for my body. *You'll* draw yours out first.

(*Another* NEIGHBOR *enters*)

MOTHER But what does your good name matter to me? What does your death matter to me? What does anything about anything matter to me? Blessed be the wheat stalks, because my sons are under them; blessed be the rain, because it wets the face of the dead. Blessed be God, who stretches us out together to rest.

(*Another* NEIGHBOR *enters*)

BRIDE Let me weep with you.

MOTHER Weep. But at the door.

(*The* GIRL *enters. The* BRIDE *stays at the door. The* MOTHER *is at the center of the stage*)

LEONARDO'S WIFE (*Entering and going to the left*)

He was a beautiful horseman,
now he's a heap of snow.
He rode to fairs and mountains
and women's arms.
Now, the night's dark moss
crowns his forehead.

MOTHER

A sunflower to your mother,
a mirror of the earth.
Let them put on your breast
the cross of bitter rosebay;
and over you a sheet
of shining silk;
between your quiet hands
let water form its lament.

WIFE

Ay-y-y, four gallant boys
come with tired shoulders!

BRIDE

Ay-y-y, four gallant boys
carry death on high!

MOTHER

Neighbors.

LITTLE GIRL (*At the door*)

They're bringing them now.

MOTHER

It's the same thing.
Always the cross, the cross.

WOMEN

Sweet nails,
cross adored,
sweet name
of Christ our Lord.

BRIDE May the cross protect both the quick and the dead.

MOTHER

Neighbors: with a knife,
with a little knife,
on their appointed day, between two and three,
these two men killed each other for love.
With a knife,
with a tiny knife
that barely fits the hand,
but that slides in clean
through the astonished flesh
and stops at the place
where trembles, enmeshed,
the dark root of a scream.

BRIDE

And this is a knife,
a tiny knife
that barely fits the hand;
fish without scales, without river,
so that on their appointed day, between two and three,
with this knife,
two men are left stiff,
with their lips turning yellow.

MOTHER

And it barely fits the hand
but it slides in clean
through the astonished flesh
and stops there, at the place
where trembles enmeshed
the dark root of a scream.

(*The* NEIGHBORS, *kneeling on the floor, sob*)

*Curtain*

# Eugene O'Neill

## (1888-1953)

WITH a single-mindedness rare in contemporary letters, Eugene Gladstone O'Neill reduced America's usual cultural lag behind Europe and brought the main currents of modern drama into the American theatre. He dedicated himself uncompromisingly to writing plays, not for the existing popular stage, but for the theatre he felt America needed. Although his posthumous *Long Day's Journey into Night* is not completely factual as autobiography, it shows with unquestionable accuracy the young O'Neill's contempt for the commercial theatre in which his actor-father squandered his talents. In addition to showing private family disagreements, the clashes between the elder O'Neill (James Tyrone in the play) and his playboy-radical sons symbolize the unbridgeable chasm between the American stage before World War I and the American theatre which came suddenly and gloriously of age in the postwar period. To the father, the stage was a risky venture which might, if the public was given what it wanted, make a fortune for an actor; to the son, it was a stronghold of anti-intellectualism waiting to be blasted out of existence.

Like the other arts in America, the theatre remained Tory long after the American Revolution. The earliest touring actors were English, with repertories of current London plays and the monstrous adaptations of Shakespeare popular until the early twentieth century. By the 1850's, a few dramatists were writing about American life with a vigor that almost made up for their derivativeness and over-reliance on popular formulas. The forte of Dublin-born Dion Boucicault was thrilling melodrama, but in *The Octoroon* (1859) and *Rip Van Winkle* (1865) he called younger writers' attention to the wealth of uniquely American materials waiting to be tapped for native drama. By the 1890's, several Americans were writing impressively about contemporary life: Bronson Howard dealt with Wall Street in *The Henrietta* and with the Civil War in *Shenandoah;* James A. Herne manifested his responsiveness to Ibsenism and to literary realism in such works as *Margaret Fleming* and *Shore Acres.* At the turn of the century, however, American theatre was dominated by Belasco's compulsive detailing of surface realism, by Daly's mass-produced showcases for individual performers, and by a powerful puritanism among local censors. The younger generation (which included O'Neill) had to read Ibsen, Strindberg, Shaw, and Chekhov instead of seeing their works on American stages. In 1905 Harvard University cautiously permitted Professor George Pierce Baker to offer a non-credit course in playwriting, a precedent-shattering experiment which spurred interest in drama as a serious art. With the belated emergence of an Art Theatre movement during the 1910-1920 decade, the ground was prepared for the appearance of a Eugene O'Neill.

The theatrical world into which O'Neill was born, however, existed blissfully oblivious to such faint stirrings of modernism as could be heard in William Dean Howells' campaign for "true realism" in American drama as well as fiction. O'Neill's father had once been a distinguished Shakespearean actor, but before Eugene was born, he had settled for the handsome guaranteed profits from touring in the popular *Count of Monte Cristo.* In an age when the acting profession was rated just this side of perdition, James O'Neill maintained a dignity which caused his non-theatrical associates to overlook two other matters not likely to inspire high esteem in the late nineteenth century: he was born in Ireland and he was a devout Catholic. O'Neill's mother had forsaken her dream of becoming a nun when she fell in love with James O'Neill. As a matinee idol's wife accompanying her husband on long tours, her life was taxing, at times unbearable. The first of the O'Neills' three sons, named for the father, was born in 1878—and grew up to waste himself in the easy profligacy in which he early initiated his youngest brother. "Jamie" O'Neill was recreated memorably in *A Moon for the Misbegotten* and *Long Day's Journey.* The second son, named Edmund Dantes after his father's Monte Cristo, was born in 1884 and died a year later; his name was borrowed for the Eugene-character in *Long Day's Journey.* Eugene, the third son, was born October 16, 1888, in a family hotel overlooking New York's Times Square.

His youth was crowded with experiences incredible in variety: touring the country with his father or attending different boarding schools; sampling, under his brother's tutelage, New York's high life of chorus girls and saloons; surviving a single year at Princeton (1906-1907); trying his hand at office jobs he detested; arranging a secret marriage, fathering Eugene O'Neill II, a child he never knew well, and playing adulterous mate long enough to provide grounds for divorce. The only home he knew was in New London, Connecticut, where his family usually spent the summer in the "Monte Cristo" cottage he later recreated in *Long Day's Journey.* Before 1912, when he discovered he had incipient tuberculosis, he had descended into the lower depths: gold-prospecting in Central America, where he contracted malaria and learned something about deep jungles he later used in *The Emperor Jones;* shipping out as seaman; trying office jobs in Argentina before sinking into dereliction as a heavy-drinking bum drifting from South American dives to such New York saloons as Jimmy-the-Priest's (recreated first as the setting of *Anna Christie,* later as the partial basis of Harry Hope's in *The Iceman Cometh*); serving briefly as "manager" and actor in his father's touring company, and later as a reporter for a New London newspaper. Although his tuberculosis was easily arrested, he was sobered by the illness; during his enforced convalescence (1912-1913) he read more deeply in world drama and brought into focus his plan to become a dramatist. In 1914 he enrolled in Harvard's 47 Workshop, where Professor Baker made him feel "it was worthwhile going ahead" as a playwright.

Living in Greenwich Village in 1915, O'Neill learned of a group of young writers trying out their plays on Cape Cod. In the summer of 1916, in the tiny Wharf Theatre in Provincetown, he first saw one of his plays (*Bound East for Cardiff*) produced; the following November, the Provincetown Players opened a theatre in Greenwich Village and produced the early one-acts O'Neill based chiefly on his seafaring and beach-bumming adventures. With the enthusiastic support of such Provincetown friends as Susan Glaspell, George Cram Cook, and stage-designer Robert Edmond Jones, and later with George Jean Nathan and H. L. Mencken printing his work in their *Smart Set* magazine, O'Neill felt he had finally found himself. The year 1920 brought the brilliantly successful production of *The Emperor Jones,* with its haunting evocation of jungle terrors and its exploration of Brutus' racial memory, and commercial success with *Beyond the Horizon,* the full-length play for which he received his first Pulitzer Prize. At 32, O'Neill had embarked on what seemed a successful second marriage, he had stabilized his life, he had won national acclaim as America's most exciting playwright, and he was bursting with ideas for other plays. From 1920 until 1934, when a disease like Parkinson's syndrome made writing increasingly difficult for him, O'Neill dominated the American theatre.

O'Neill's biographers have not determined exactly when he started writing plays. Before he enrolled at Harvard, however, he had written *Bound East for Cardiff* as well as the one-acts included in the *Thirst* collection (1914) financed by his father. His first impressive plays, the one-acts known as the "S.S. Glencairn" group, were essentially realistic in form. They show O'Neill's deep understanding of sailors' feelings toward the sea, and exhibit a dramatic economy not always within his grasp. The sea was a central symbol in *Anna Christie* (1921) as the "ol' davil" from which an old barge-captain tries to protect his ex-prostitute daughter. *Beyond the Horizon* used the lure of the sea as counter-symbol to land-bound existence, but the basic conflict between two brothers was so internalized that, in the play's too-obvious ironic conclusion, both rival fates, land and sea, are dismissed. In *The Hairy Ape* (1922), O'Neill's expressionist allegory, Yank begins as a happy stoker in the bowels of an oceanliner, loses his sense of "belonging" when a vapid passenger calls him a "filthy beast," and regains it only in the gorilla cage where he dies. The sea became merely incidental as O'Neill pursued his protagonists' dry-land quests for identity through Jungian and Freudian psychosexual jungles. In *Desire Under the Elms* (1924) O'Neill probed the struggle between Ephraim and Eben Cabot, father and son, for a spot of soil and the mastery of a passionate young woman, herself torn between desires for security (the farm) and love (her stepson, Eben). This work outraged the sanctimonious, but it remains America's first important tragic drama.

Relations between parents and children were also central in two of O'Neill's most ambitious undertakings. In *Strange Interlude* (1928), he traced Everywoman Nina Leeds' progress from romantic love, promiscuity, wifehood, and adultery, to maternal love and twilight calm. In his "trilogy of the damned," *Mourning Becomes Electra* (1931), he transferred the doomed progeny of Atreus—Agamemnon, Aegisthus, Electra, and Orestes—from mythic Greece to post-Civil War New England. In these works, O'Neill's experimental bent, which had first been clear in the accelerative tom-tom rhythms of *The Emperor Jones,* came close to overwhelming playgoers kept in the theatre from the late afternoon until late evening. Such, however, was his reputation that audiences bravely endured his demands. In his determination to recapture the communal experience of ancient tragedy, O'Neill experimented with masks (most notably, in *The Great God Brown* and the nearly unproducible *Lazarus Laughed*); with the aside as a means of contrasting masked private thoughts contrary to the masks of public utterance (in *Strange Interlude*); with a machine—a gigantic hydroelectric generator symbolizing the new "God of Electricity"—as a character (in *Dynamo*); and with translation of the grandeur of classical Greek tragedy into the substance of American experience (in *Mourning Becomes Electra*).

In *The Emperor Jones,* O'Neill first found the key to unlock the full resources of the modern theatre in the service of his psychological naturalism. Of all his plays, it is the least dependent on dialogue, but it remains typical for its reliance on scenic and sound effects to supplement language. Real masks are employed only incidentally here as costume details, but metaphorically, O'Neill stripped away the masks of Brutus Jones' civilized being as he pushed his protagonist through the jungle of memory back to his racial and human origins. Ironically, Brutus Jones is the inheritor of all the values of the white traders who brought his ancestors out of Africa onto slave auction-blocks. Such materialistic values as shrewd foresightedness ultimately contribute to Jones' destruction, for they have blinded him to the haunted primitive man who is susceptible to fear. After *The Emperor Jones,* audiences were ready to follow O'Neill in his lifelong exploration of the inner man, where O'Neill believed he had located the wellsprings of human destiny.

# THE EMPEROR JONES

## CHARACTERS

BRUTUS JONES, *Emperor*
HENRY SMITHERS, *a Cockney trader*
AN OLD NATIVE WOMAN
LEM, *a native chief*
SOLDIERS, *adherents of* LEM
THE LITTLE FORMLESS FEARS; JEFF; THE NEGRO CONVICTS; THE PRISON GUARD; THE PLANTERS; THE AUCTIONEER; THE SLAVES; THE CONGO WITCH DOCTOR; THE CROCODILE GOD

SCENE *An island in the West Indies as yet not self-determined by white Marines. The form of native government is, for the time being, an empire.*

## Scene One

*The audience chamber in the palace of the Emperor—a spacious, high-ceilinged room with bare, whitewashed walls. The floor is of white tiles. In the rear, to the left of the center, a wide archway giving out on a portico with white pillars. The palace is evidently situated on high ground, for beyond the portico nothing can be seen but a vista of distant hills, their summits crowned with thick groves of palm trees. In the right wall, center, a smaller arched doorway leading to the living quarters of the palace. The room is bare of furniture with the exception of one huge chair made of uncut wood which stands at the center, its back to the rear. This is very apparently the Emperor's throne. It is painted a dazzling, eye-smiting scarlet. There is a brilliant orange cushion on the seat and another smaller one is placed on the floor to serve as a footstool. Strips of matting, dyed scarlet, lead from the foot of the throne to the two entrances.*

*It is late afternoon, but the sunlight still blazes yellowly beyond the portico and there is an oppressive burden of exhausting heat in the air.*

*As the curtain rises, a native Negro* WOMAN *sneaks in cautiously from the entrance on the right. She is very old, dressed in cheap calico, barefooted, a red bandanna handkerchief covering all but a few stray wisps of white hair. A bundle bound in colored cloth is carried over her shoulder on the end of a stick. She hesitates beside the doorway, peering back as if in extreme dread of being discovered. Then she begins to glide noiselessly, a step at a time, toward the doorway in the rear. At this moment,* SMITHERS *appears beneath the portico.*

SMITHERS *is a tall, stoop-shouldered man about forty. His bald head, perched on a long neck with an enormous Adam's apple, looks like an egg. The tropics have tanned his naturally pasty face with its small, sharp features to a sickly yellow, and native rum has painted his pointed nose to a startling red. His little, washy-blue eyes are red-rimmed and dart about him like a ferret's. His expression is one of unscrupulous meanness, cowardly and dangerous. He is dressed in a worn riding suit of dirty white drill, puttees, spurs, and wears a white cork helmet. A cartridge belt with an automatic revolver is around his waist. He carries a riding whip in his hand. He sees the* WOMAN *and stops to watch her suspiciously. Then, making up his mind, he steps quickly on tiptoe into the room. The* WOMAN, *looking back over her shoulder continually, does not see him until it is too late. When she does* SMITHERS *springs forward and grabs her firmly by the shoulder. She struggles to get away, fiercely but silently.*

SMITHERS (*Tightening his grasp—roughly*) Easy! None o' that, me birdie. You can't wriggle out, now I got me 'ooks on yer.

WOMAN (*Seeing the uselessness of struggling, gives way to frantic terror, and sinks to the ground, embracing his knees supplicatingly*) No tell him! No tell him, mister!

SMITHERS (*With great curiosity*) Tell 'im? (*Then scornfully*) Oh, you mean 'is bloomin' Majesty. What's the gaime, any'ow? What are you sneakin' away for? Been stealin' a bit, I s'pose. (*He taps her bundle with his riding whip significantly*)

WOMAN (*Shaking her head vehemently*) No, me no steal.

SMITHERS Bloody liar! But tell me what's up. There's somethin' funny goin' on. I smelled it in the air first thing I got up this mornin'. You blacks are up to some devilment. This palace of 'is is like a bleedin' tomb. Where's all the 'ands? (*The woman keeps sullenly silent.* SMITHERS *raises his whip threateningly*) Ow, yer won't, won't yer? I'll show yer what's what.

WOMAN (*Coweringly*) I tell, mister. You no hit. They go—all go. (*She makes a sweeping gesture toward the hills in the distance*)

SMITHERS Run away—to the 'ills?

WOMAN Yes, mister. Him Emperor—Great Father. (*She touches her forehead to the floor with a quick mechanical jerk*) Him sleep after eat. Then they go—all go. Me old woman. Me left only. Now me go too.

SMITHERS (*His astonishment giving way to an immense, mean satisfaction*) Ow! So that's the ticket! Well, I know bloody well wot's in the air—when they runs orf to the 'ills. The tom-tom'll be thumpin' out there bloomin' soon. (*With extreme vindictiveness*) And I'm bloody glad of it, for one! Serve 'im right! Puttin' on airs, the stinkin' nigger! 'Is Majesty! Gawd blimey! I only 'opes I'm there when they takes 'im out to shoot 'im. (*Suddenly*) 'E's still 'ere all right, ain't 'e?

WOMAN Him sleep.

SMITHERS 'E's bound to find out soon as 'e wakes up. 'E's cunnin' enough to know when 'is time's come. (*He goes to the doorway on the right and whistles shrilly with his fingers in his mouth. The old woman springs to her feet and runs out of the doorway at the rear.* SMITHERS *goes after her, reaching for his revolver*) Stop or I'll shoot! (*Then, stopping—indifferently*) Pop orf, then, if yer like, yer black cow. (*He stands in the doorway, looking after her*)

(JONES *enters from the right. He is a tall, powerfully built, full-blooded Negro of middle age. His features are typically negroid, yet there is something decidedly distinctive about his face—an underlying strength of will, a hardy, self-reliant confidence in himself that inspires respect. His eyes are alive with a keen, cunning intelligence. In manner he is shrewd, suspicious, evasive. He wears a light-blue uniform coat sprayed with brass buttons, heavy gold chevrons on his shoulders, gold braid on the collar, cuffs, etc. His pants are bright-red with a light-blue stripe down the side. Patent-leather laced boots with brass spurs, and a belt with a long-barreled, pearl-handled revolver in a holster complete his make-up. Yet there is something not altogether ridiculous about his grandeur. He has a way of carrying it off*)

JONES (*Not seeing anyone—greatly irritated and blinking sleepily—shouts*) Who dare whistle dat way in my palace? Who dare wake up de Emperor? I'll git de hide frayled off some o' you niggers sho'!

SMITHERS (*Showing himself—in a manner half afraid and half defiant*) It was me whistled to yer. (*As* JONES *frowns angrily*) I got news for yer.

JONES (*Putting on his suavest manner, which fails to cover up his contempt for the white man*) Oh, it's you, Mr. Smithers. (*He sits down on his throne with easy dignity*) What news you got to tell me?

SMITHERS (*Coming close to enjoy his discomfiture*) Don't yer notice nothin' funny today?

JONES (*Coldly*) Funny? No. I ain't perceived nothin' of de kind!

SMITHERS Then yer ain't so foxy as I thought yer was. Where's all your court?—(*Sarcastically*)—the Generals and the Cabinet Ministers and all?

JONES (*Imperturbably*) Where dey mostly runs to minute I closes my eyes—drinkin' rum and talkin' big down in de town. (*Sarcastically*) How come you don't know dat? Ain't you sousin' with 'em most every day?

SMITHERS (*Stung, but pretending indifference—with a wink*) That's part of the day's work. I got ter—ain't I—in my business?

JONES (*Contemptuously*) Yo' business!

SMITHERS (*Imprudently enraged*) Gawd blimey, you was glad enough for me ter take yer in on it when you landed here first. You didn' 'ave no 'igh and mighty airs in them days!

JONES (*His hand going to his revolver like a flash—menacingly*) Talk polite, white man! Talk polite, you heah me! I'm boss heah now, is you fergettin'?

(*The Cockney seems about to challenge this last statement with the facts, but something in the other's eyes holds and cows him*)

SMITHERS (*In a cowardly whine*) No 'arm meant, old top.

JONES (*Condescendingly*) I accepts yo' apology. (*Lets his hand fall from his revolver*) No use'n you rakin' up ole times. What I was den is one thing. What I is now's another. You didn't let me in on yo' crooked work out o' no kind feelin's dat time. I done de dirty work fo' you—and most o' de brainwork, too, fo' dat matter—and I was wu'th money to you, dat's de reason.

SMITHERS Well, blimey, I give yer a start, didn't I?—when no one else would. I wasn't afraid to 'ire you like the rest was—'count of the story about your breakin' jail back in the States.

JONES No, you didn't have no 'scuse to look down on me fo' dat. You been in jail you'self more'n once.

SMITHERS (*Furiously*) It's a lie! (*Then trying to pass it off by an attempt at scorn*) Garn! Who told yer that fairy tale?

JONES Dey's some tings I ain't got to be tole. I kin see 'em in folks' eyes. (*Then after a pause—meditatively*) Yes, you sho' give me a start. And it didn't take long from dat time to git dese fool woods' niggers right where I wanted dem. (*With pride*) From stowaway to Emperor in two years! Dat's goin' some!

SMITHERS (*With curiosity*) And I bet you got yer pile o' money 'id safe some place.

JONES (*With satisfaction*) I sho' has! And it's in a foreign bank where no pusson don't ever git it out but me no matter what come. You didn't s'pose I was holdin' down dis Emperor job for de glory in it, did you? Sho'! De fuss and glory part of it, dat's only to turn de heads o' de low-flung bush niggers dat's here. Dey wants de big circus show for deir money. I gives it to 'em an' I gits de money. (*With a grin*) De long green, dat's me every time! (*Then rebukingly*) But you ain't got no kick agin me, Smithers. I'se paid you back all you done for me many times. Ain't I pertected you and winked at all de crooked tradin' you been doin' right out in de broad day? Sho' I has—and me makin' laws to stop it at de same time! (*He chuckles*)

SMITHERS (*Grinning*) But, meanin' no 'arm, you been grabbin' right and left yourself, ain't yer? Look at the taxes you've put on 'em! Blimey! You've squeezed 'em dry!

JONES (*Chuckling*) No, dey ain't *all* dry yet. I'se still heah, ain't I?

SMITHERS (*Smiling at his secret thought*) They re dry right now, you'll find out. (*Changing the subject abruptly*) And as for me breakin' laws, you've broke 'em all yerself just as fast as yer made 'em.

JONES Ain't I de Emperor? De laws don't go for him. (*Judicially*) You heah what I tells you, Smithers. Dere's little stealin' like you does, and dere's big stealin' like I does. For de little stealin' dey gits you in jail soon or late. For de big stealin' dey makes you Emperor and puts you in de Hall o' Fame when you croaks. (*Reminiscently*) If dey's one thing I learns in ten years on de Pullman ca's listenin' to de white quality talk, it's dat same fact. And when I gits a chance to use it I winds up Emperor in two years.

SMITHERS (*Unable to repress the genuine admiration of the small fry for the large*) Yes, yer turned the bleedin' trick, all right. Blimey, I never seen a bloke 'as 'ad the bloomin' luck you 'as.

JONES (*Severely*) Luck? What you mean—luck?

SMITHERS I suppose you'll say as that swank about the silver bullet ain't luck—and that was what first got the fool blacks on yer side the time of the revolution, wasn't it?

JONES (*With a laugh*) Oh, dat silver bullet! Sho' was luck! But I makes dat luck, you heah? I loads de dice! Yessuh! When dat murderin' nigger ole Lem hired to kill me takes aim ten feet away and his gun misses fire and I shoots him dead, what you heah me say?

SMITHERS You said yer'd got a charm so's no lead bullet'd kill yer. You was so strong only a silver bullet could kill yer, you told 'em. Blimey, wasn't that swank for yer—and plain, fat-'eaded luck?

JONES (*Proudly*) I got brains and I uses 'em quick. Dat ain't luck.

SMITHERS Yer know they wasn't 'ardly liable to get no silver bullets. And it was luck 'e didn't 'it you that time.

JONES (*Laughing*) And dere all dem fool bush niggers was kneelin' down and bumpin' deir heads on de ground like I was a miracle out o' de Bible. Oh Lawd, from dat time on I has dem all eatin' out of my hand. I cracks de whip and dey jumps through.

SMITHERS (*With a sniff*) Yankee bluff done it.

JONES Ain't a man's talkin' big what makes him big—long as he makes folks believe it? Sho', I talks large when I ain't got nothin' to back it up, but I ain't talkin' wild just de same. I knows I kin fool 'em—I *knows* it—and dat's backin' enough fo' my game. And ain't I got to learn deir lingo and teach some of dem English befo' I kin talk to 'em? Ain't dat wuk? You ain't never learned ary word er it, Smithers, in de ten years you been heah, dough you knows it's money in yo' pocket tradin' wid 'em if you does. But you'se too shiftless to take de trouble.

SMITHERS (*Flushing*) Never mind about me. What's this I've 'eard about yer really 'avin' a silver bullet molded for yourself.

JONES It's playin' out my bluff. I has de silver bullet molded and I tells 'em when de times comes I kills myself wid it. I tells 'em dat's 'cause I'm de on'y man in de world big enuff to git me. No use'n deir tryin'. And dey falls down and bumps deir heads. (*He laughs*) I does dat so's I kin take a walk in peace widout no jealous nigger gunnin' at me from behind de trees.

SMITHERS (*Astonished*) Then you 'ad it made—'onest?

JONES Sho' did. Heah she be. (*He takes out his revolver, breaks it, and takes the silver bullet out of one chamber*) Five lead an' dis silver baby at de last. Don't she shine pretty? (*He holds it in his hand, looking at it admiringly, as if strangely fascinated*)

SMITHERS Let me see. (*Reaches out his hand for it*)

JONES (*Harshly*) Keep yo' hands whar dey b'long, white man. (*He replaces it in the chamber and puts the revolver back on his hip*)

SMITHERS (*Snarling*) Gawd blimey! Think I'm a bleedin' thief, you would.

JONES No, 'tain't dat. I knows you'se scared to steal from me. On'y I ain't 'lowin' nary body to touch dis baby. She's my rabbit's foot.

SMITHERS (*Sneering*) A bloomin' charm, wot? (*Venomously*) Well, you'll need all the bloody charms you 'as before long, s' 'elp me!

JONES (*Judicially*) Oh, I'se good for six months yit 'fore dey gits sick o' my game. Den, when I sees trouble comin', I makes my getaway.

SMITHERS Ho! You got it all planned, ain't yer?

JONES I ain't no fool. I knows dis Emperor's time is sho't. Dat why I make hay when de sun shine. Was you thinkin' I'se aimin' to hold down dis job for life? No, suh! What good is gittin' money if you stays back in dis raggedy country? I wants action when I spends. And when I sees dese niggers gittin' up deir nerve to tu'n me out, and I'se got all de money in sight, I resigns on de spot and beats it quick.

SMITHERS Where to?

JONES None o' yo' business.

SMITHERS Not back to the bloody States, I'll lay my oath.

JONES (*Suspiciously*) Why don't I? (*Then with an easy laugh*) You mean 'count of dat story 'bout me breakin' from jail back dere? Dat's all talk.

SMITHERS (*Skeptically*) Ho, yes!

JONES (*Sharply*) You ain't 'sinuatin' I'se a liar, is you?

SMITHERS (*Hastily*) No, Gawd strike me! I was only thinkin' o' the bloody lies you told the blacks 'ere about killin' white men in the States.

JONES (*Angered*) How come dey're lies?

SMITHERS You'd 'ave been in jail if you 'ad, wouldn't yer then? (*With venom*) And from what I've 'eard, it ain't 'ealthy for a black to kill a white man in the States. They burns 'em in oil, don't they?

JONES (*With cool deadliness*) You mean lynchin' 'd scare me? Well, I tells you, Smithers, maybe I does kill one white man back dere. Maybe I does. And maybe I kills another right heah 'fore long if he don't look out.

SMITHERS (*Trying to force a laugh*) I was on'y spoofin' yer. Can't yer take a joke? And you was just sayin' you'd never been in jail.

JONES (*In the same tone—slightly boastful*) Maybe I goes to jail dere for gettin' in an argument wid razors ovah a crap game. Maybe I gits twenty years when dat colored man die. Maybe I gits in 'nother argument wid de prison guard was overseer ovah us when we're wukin' de road. Maybe he hits me wid a whip and I splits his head wid a shovel and runs away and files de chain off my leg and gits away safe. Maybe I does all dat an' maybe I don't. It's a story I tells you so's you knows I'se de kind of man dat if you evah repeats one word of it, I ends yo' stealin' on dis yearth mighty damn quick!

SMITHERS (*Terrified*) Think I'd peach on yer? Not me! Ain't I always been yer friend?

JONES (*Suddenly relaxing*) Sho' you has—and you better be.

SMITHERS (*Recovering his composure—and with it his malice*) And just to show yer I'm yer friend, I'll tell yer that bit o' news I was goin' to.

JONES Go ahead! Shoot de piece. Must be bad news from de happy way you look.

SMITHERS (*Warningly*) Maybe it's gettin' time for you to resign—with that bloomin' silver bullet, wot? (*He finishes with a mocking grin*)

JONES (*Puzzled*) What's dat you say? Talk plain.

SMITHERS Ain't noticed any of the guards or servants about the place today, I 'aven't.

JONES (*Carelessly*) Dey're all out in de garden sleepin' under de trees. When I sleeps, dey sneaks a sleep too, and I pretends I never suspicions it. All I got to do is to ring de bell and dey come flyin', makin' a bluff dey was wukin' all de time.

SMITHERS (*In the same mocking tone*) Ring the bell now an' you'll bloody well see what I means.

JONES (*Startled to alertness, but preserving the same careless tone*) Sho' I rings. (*He reaches below the throne and pulls out a big, common dinner bell which is painted the same vivid scarlet as the throne. He rings this vigorously—then stops to listen. Then he goes to both doors, rings again, and looks out*)

SMITHERS (*Watching him with malicious satisfaction, after a pause—mockingly*) The bloody ship is sinkin' an' the bleedin' rats 'as slung their 'ooks.

JONES (*In a sudden fit of anger flings the bell clattering into a corner*) Low-flung woods' niggers! (*Then catching* SMITHERS' *eye on him, he controls himself and suddenly bursts into a low chuckling laugh*) Reckon I overplays my hand dis once! A man can't take de pot on a bobtailed flush all de time. Was I sayin' I'd sit in six months mo'? Well, I'se changed my mind den. I cashes in and resigns de job of Emperor right dis minute.

SMITHERS (*With real admiration*) Blimey, but you're a cool bird, and no mistake.

JONES No use'n fussin'. When I knows de game's up I kisses it good-by widout no long waits. Dey've all run off to de hills, ain't dey?

SMITHERS Yes—every bleedin' man jack of 'em.

JONES Den de revolution is at de post. And de Emperor better git his feet smokin' up de trail. (*He starts for the door in the rear*)

SMITHERS Goin' out to look for your 'orse? Yer won't find any. They steals the 'orses first thing. Mine was gone when I went for 'im this mornin'. That's wot first give me a suspicion of wot was up.

JONES (*Alarmed for a second, scratches his head, then, philosophically*) Well, den I hoofs it. Feet, do yo' duty! (*He pulls out a gold watch and looks at it*) Three-thuty. Sundown's at six-thuty or dereabouts. (*Puts his watch back—with cool confidence*) I got plenty o' time to make it easy.

SMITHERS Don't be so bloomin' sure of it. They'll be after you 'ot and 'eavy. Ole Lem is at the bottom o' this business an' 'e 'ates you like 'ell. 'E'd rather do for you than eat 'is dinner, 'e would!

JONES (*Scornfully*) Dat fool no-count nigger! Does you think I'se scared o' him? I stands him on his thick head more'n once befo' dis, and I does it again if he comes in my way— (*Fiercely*) And dis time I leave him a dead nigger fo' sho'!

SMITHERS You'll 'ave to cut through the big forest—an' these blacks 'ere can sniff and follow a trail in the dark like 'ounds. You'd 'ave to 'ustle to get through that forest in twelve hours even if you knew all the bloomin' trails like a native.

JONES (*With indignant scorn*) Look-a-heah, white man! Does you think I'se a natural bo'n fool? Give me credit fo' havin' some sense, fo' Lawd's sake! Don't you s'pose I'se looked ahead and made sho' of all de chances? I'se gone out in dat big forest, pretendin' to hunt, so many times dat I knows it high an' low like a book. I could go through on dem trails wid my eyes shut. (*With great contempt*) Think dese ign'rent bush niggers dat ain't got brains enuff to know deir own names even can catch Brutus Jones? Huh, I s'pects not! Not on yo' life! Why, man, de white men went after me wid bloodhounds where I come from an' I jes' laughs at 'em. It's a shame to fool dese black trash around heah, dey're so easy. You watch me, man. I'll make dem look sick, I will. I'll be 'cross de plain to de edge of de forest by time dark comes. Once in de woods in de night, dey got a swell chance o' findin' dis baby! Dawn tomorrow I'll be out at de oder side and on de coast whar dat French gunboat is stayin'. She picks me up, takes me to Martinique when she go dar, and dere I is safe wid a mighty big bank roll in my jeans. It's easy as rollin' off a log.

SMITHERS (*Maliciously*) But s'posin' somethin' 'appens wrong an' they do nab yer?

JONES (*Decisively*) Dey don't—dat's de answer.

SMITHERS But, just for argyment's sake—what'd you do?

JONES (*Frowning*) I'se got five lead bullets in dis gun good enuff fo' common bush niggers—and after dat I got de silver bullet left to cheat 'em out o' gittin' me.

SMITHERS (*Jeeringly*) Ho, I was fergettin' that silver bullet. You'll bump yourself orf in style, won't yer? Blimey!

JONES (*Gloomily*) You kin bet yo' whole roll on one thing, white man. Dis baby plays out his string to de end and when he quits, he quits wid a bang de way he ought. Silver bullet ain't none too good for him when he go, dat's a fac'! (*Then, shaking off his nervousness—with a confident laugh*) Sho'! What is I talkin' about? Ain't come to dat yit and I never will —not wid trash niggers like dese yere. (*Boastfully*) Silver bullet bring me luck anyway. I kin outguess, outrun, outfight, an' outplay de whole lot o' dem all ovah de board any time o' de day er night! You watch me!

(*From the distant hills comes the faint, steady thump of a tom-tom, low and vibrating. It starts at a rate exactly corresponding to normal pulse beat—72 to the minute—and continues at a gradually accelerating rate from this point uninterruptedly to the very end of the play*)

JONES (*Starts at the sound; a strange look of apprehension creeps into his face for a moment as he listens; then he asks, with an attempt to regain his most casual manner*) What's dat drum beatin' fo'?

SMITHERS (*With a mean grin*) For you. That means the bleedin' ceremony 'as started. I've 'eard it before and I knows.

JONES Cer'mony? What cer'mony?

SMITHERS The blacks is 'oldin' a bloody meetin', 'avin' a war dance, gettin' their courage worked up b'fore they starts after you.

JONES Let dem! Dey'll sho' need it!

SMITHERS And they're there 'oldin' their 'eathen religious service—makin' no end of devil spells and charms to 'elp 'em against your silver bullet. (*He guffaws loudly*) Blimey, but they're balmy as 'ell!

JONES (*A tiny bit awed and shaken in spite of himself*) Huh! Takes more'n dat to scare dis chicken!

SMITHERS (*Scenting the other's feeling—maliciously*) Ternight when it's pitch-black in the forest, they'll 'ave their pet devils and ghosts 'oundin' after you. You'll find yer bloody 'air'll be standin' on end before termorrow mornin'. (*Seriously*) It's a bleedin' queer place, that stinkin' forest, even in daylight. Yer don't know what might 'appen in there, it's that rotten still. Always sends the cold shivers down my back minute I gets in it.

JONES (*With a contemptuous sniff*) I ain't no chicken-liver like you is. Trees an' me, we'se friends, and dar's a full moon comin' bring me light. And let dem po' niggers make all de fool spells dey'se a min' to. Does yo' s'pect I'se silly enuff to b'lieve in ghosts an' ha'nts an' all dat ole woman's talk? G'long, white man! You ain't talkin' to me. (*With a chuckle*) Doesn't you know dey's got to do wid a man was member in good standin' o' de Baptist Church? Sho' I was dat when I was porter on de Pullmans, befo' I gits into my little trouble. Let dem try deir heathen tricks. De Baptist Church done pertect me and land dem all in hell. (*Then with more confident satisfaction*) And I'se got little silver bullet o' my own, don't forgit!

SMITHERS Ho! You 'aven't give much 'eed to your Baptist Church since you been down 'ere. I've 'eard myself you 'ad turned yer coat an' was takin' up with their blarsted witch doctors, or whatever the 'ell yer calls the swine.

JONES (*Vehemently*) I pretends to! Sho' I pretends! Dat's part o' my game from de fust. If I finds out dem niggers believes dat black is white, den I yells it out louder'n deir loudest. It don't git me nothin' to do missionary work for de Baptist Church. I'se after de coin, an' I lays my Jesus on de shelf for de time bein'. (*Stops abruptly to look at his watch—alertly*) But I ain't got de time to waste on no more fool talk wid you. I'se gwine away from heah dis secon'. (*He reaches in under the throne and pulls out an expensive panama hat with a bright multicolored band and sets it jauntily on his head*) So long, white man! (*With a grin*) See you in jail sometime, maybe!

SMITHERS Not me, you won't. Well, I wouldn't be in yer bloody boots for no bloomin' money, but 'ere's wishin' yer luck just the same.

JONES (*Contemptuously*) You're de frightenedest man evah I see! I tells you I'se safe's 'f I was in New York City. It takes dem niggers from now to dark to git up de nerve to start somethin'. By dat time, I'se got a head start dey never kotch up wid.

SMITHERS (*Maliciously*) Give my regards to any ghosts yer meets up with.

JONES (*Grinning*) If dat ghost got money, I'll tell him never ha'nt you less'n he wants to lose it.

SMITHERS (*Flattered*) Garn! (*Then curiously*) Ain't yer takin' no luggage with yer?

JONES I travels light when I wants to move fast. And I got tinned grub buried on de edge o' de forest. (*Boastfully*) Now say dat I don't look ahead an' use my brains! (*With a wide, liberal gesture*) I will all dat's left in de palace to you—and you better grab all you kin sneak away wid befo' dey gits here.

SMITHERS (*Gratefully*) Righto—and thanks ter yer. (*As* JONES *walks toward the door in the rear—cautioningly*) Say! Look 'ere, you ain't goin' out that way, are yer?

JONES Does you think I'd slink out de back door like a common nigger? I'se Emperor yit, ain't I? And de Emperor Jones leaves de way he comes, and dat black trash don't dare stop him—not yit, leastways. (*He stops for a moment in the doorway, listening to the far-off but insistent beat of the tom-tom*) Listen to dat roll call, will you? Must be mighty big drum carry dat far. (*Then with a laugh*) Well, if dey ain't no whole brass band to see me off, I sho' got de drum part of it. So long, white man. (*He puts his hands in his pockets and with studied carelessness, whistling a tune, he saunters out of the doorway and off to the left*)

SMITHERS (*Looks after him with a puzzled admiration*) 'E's got 'is bloomin' nerve with 'im, s'elp me! (*Then angrily*) Ho—the bleedin' nigger—puttin' on 'is bloody airs! I 'opes they nabs 'im an' gives 'im what's what!

## Scene Two

*The end of the plain where the Great Forest begins. The foreground is sandy, level ground dotted by a few stones and clumps of stunted bushes cowering close against the earth to escape the buffeting of the trade wind. In the rear the forest is a wall of darkness dividing the world. Only when the eye becomes accustomed to the gloom can the outlines of separate trunks of the nearest trees be made out, enormous pillars of deeper blackness. A somber monotone of wind lost in the leaves moans in the air. Yet this sound serves but to intensify the impression of the forest's relentless immobility, to form a background throwing into relief its brooding, implacable silence.*

JONES *enters from the left, walking rapidly. He stops as he nears the edge of the forest, looks around him quickly, peering into the dark as if searching for some familiar landmark. Then, apparently satisfied that he is where he ought to be, he throws himself on the ground, dog-tired.*

JONES Well, heah I is. In de nick o' time, too! Little mo' an' it'd be blacker'n de ace of spades heahabouts. (*He pulls a bandanna handkerchief from his hip pocket and mops off his perspiring face*) Sho'! Gimme air! I'se tuckered out sho' 'nuff. Dat soft Emperor job ain't no trainin' fo' a long hike ovah dat plain in de brilin' sun. (*Then with a chuckle*) Cheer up, nigger, de worst is yet to come. (*He lifts his head and stares at the forest. His chuckle peters out abruptly. In a tone of awe*) My goodness, look at dem woods, will you? Dat no-count Smithers said dey'd be black an' he sho' called de turn. (*Turning away from them quickly and looking down at his feet, he snatches at a chance to change the subject—solicitously*) Feet, you is holdin' up yo' end fine an' I sutinly hopes you ain't blisterin' none. It's time you git a rest. (*He takes off his shoes, his eyes studiously avoiding the forest. He feels the soles of his feet gingerly*) You is still in de pink—on'y a little mite feverish. Cool yo'selfs. Remember you done got a long journey yit befo' you. (*He sits in a weary attitude, listening to the rhythmic beating of the tom-tom. He grumbles in a loud tone to cover up a growing uneasiness*) Bush niggers! Wonder dey wouldn't git sick o' beatin' dat drum. Sound louder, seem like. I wonder if dey's startin' after me? (*He scrambles to his feet, looking back across the plain*) Couldn't see dem now, nohow, if dey was hundred feet away. (*Then, shaking himself like a wet dog to get rid of these depressing thoughts*) Sho', dey's miles an' miles behind. What you gittin' fidgety about? (*But he sits down and begins to lace up his shoes in great haste, all the time muttering reassuringly*)

You know what? Yo' belly is empty, dat's what's de matter wid you. Come time to eat! Wid nothin' but wind on yo' stumach, o' course you feels jiggedy. Well, we eats right heah an' now soon's I gits dese pesky shoes laced up. (*He finishes lacing up his shoes*) Dere! Now le's see! (*Gets on his hands and knees and searches the ground around him with his eyes*) White stone, white stone, where is you? (*He sees the first white stone and crawls to it—with satisfaction*) Heah you is! I knowed dis was de right place. Box of grub, come to me. (*He turns over the stone and feels in under it—in a tone of dismay*) Ain't heah! Gorry, is I in de right place or isn't I? Dere's 'nother stone. Guess dat's it. (*He scrambles to the next stone and turns it over*) Ain't heah, neither! Grub, whar is you? Ain't heah. Gorry, has I got to go hungry into dem woods—all de night? (*While he is talking he scrambles from one stone to another, turning them over in frantic haste. Finally, he jumps to his feet excitedly*) Is I lost de place? Must have! But how dat happen when I was followin' de trail across de plain in broad daylight? (*Almost plaintively*) I'se hungry, I is! I gotta git my feed. Whar's my strength gonna come from if I doesn't? Gorry, I gotta find dat grub high an' low somehow! Why it come dark so quick like dat? Can't see nothin'. (*He scratches a match on his trousers and peers about him. The rate of the beat of the far-off tom-tom increases perceptibly as he does so. He mutters in a bewildered voice*) How come all dese white stones come heah when I only remembers one? (*Suddenly, with a frightened gasp, he flings the match on the ground and stamps on it*) Nigger, is you gone crazy mad? Is you lightin' matches to show dem whar you is? Fo' Lawd's sake, use yo' haid. Gorry, I'se got to be careful! (*He stares at the plain behind him apprehensively, his hand on his revolver*) But how come all dese white stones? And whar's dat tin box o' grub I hid all wrapped up in oilcloth?

*(While his back is turned, the* LITTLE FORMLESS FEARS *creep out from the deeper blackness of the forest. They are black, shapeless, only their glittering little eyes can be seen. If they have any describable form at all it is that of a grubworm about the size of a creeping child. They move noiselessly, but with deliberate, painful effort, striving to raise themselves on end, failing and sinking prone again.* JONES *turns about to face the forest. He stares up at the trees, seeking vainly to discover his whereabouts by their conformation)*

Can't tell nothin' from dem trees! Gorry, nothin' 'round heah looks like I evah seed it befo'. I'se done lost de place sho' 'nuff! *(With mournful foreboding)* It's mighty queer! It's mighty queer! *(With sudden forced defiance—in an angry tone)* Woods, is you tryin' to put somethin' ovah on me?

*(From the* FORMLESS CREATURES *on the ground in front of him comes a tiny gale of low mocking laughter like a rustling of leaves. They squirm upward toward him in twisted attitudes.* JONES *looks down, leaps backward with a yell of terror, yanking out his revolver as he does so—in a quavering voice)*

What's dat? Who's dar? What is you? Git away from me befo' I shoots you up! You don't?—

*(He fires. There is a flash, a loud report, then silence broken only by the far-off, quickened throb of the tom-tom. The* FORMLESS CREATURES *have scurried back into the forest.* JONES *remains fixed in his position, listening intently. The sound of the shot, the reassuring feel of the revolver in his hand, have somewhat restored his shaken nerve. He addresses himself with renewed confidence)*

Dey're gone. Dat shot fix 'em. Dey was only little animals—little wild pigs, I reckon. Dey've maybe rooted out yo' grub an' eat it. Sho', you fool nigger, what you think dey is—ha'nts? *(Excitedly)* Gorry, you give de game away when you fire dat shot. Dem niggers heah dat fo' sutin! Time you beat it in de woods widout no long waits. *(He starts for the forest —hesitates before the plunge—then urging himself in with manful resolution)* Git in, nigger! What you skeered at? Ain't nothin' dere but de trees! Git in! *(He plunges boldly into the forest)*

## Scene Three

*In the forest. The moon has just risen. Its beams, drifting through the canopy of leaves, make a barely perceptible, suffused, eerie glow. A dense low wall of underbrush and creepers is in the nearer foreground, fencing in a small triangular clearing. Beyond this is the massed blackness of the forest like an encompassing barrier. A path is dimly discerned leading down to the clearing from the left rear, and winding away from it again toward the right. As the scene opens nothing can be distinctly made out. Except for the beating of the tom-tom, which is a trifle louder and quicker than at the close of the previous scene, there is silence, broken every few seconds by a queer, clicking sound. Then gradually the figure of the Negro* JEFF *can be discerned crouching on his haunches at the rear of the triangle. He is middle-aged, thin, brown in color, is dressed in a Pullman porter's uniform and cap. He is throwing a pair of dice on the ground before him, picking them up, shaking them, casting them out, with the regular, rigid, mechanical movements of an automaton. The heavy, plodding footsteps of someone approaching along the trail from the left are heard and* JONES' *voice, pitched on a slightly higher key and strained in a cheery effort to overcome its own tremors.*

JONES De moon's rizen. Does you heah dat, nigger? You gits more light from dis out. No mo' buttin' yo' fool head agin de trunks an' scratchin' de hide off yo' legs in de bushes. Now you sees whar yo'se gwine. So cheer up! From now on you has a snap. *(He steps just to the rear of the triangular clearing and mops off his face on his sleeve. He has lost his panama hat. His face is scratched, his brilliant uniform shows several large rents)* What time's it gittin' to be, I wonder? I dassent light no match to find out. Phoo'. It's wa'm an' dat's a fac'! *(Wearily)* How long I been makin' tracks in dese woods? Must be hours an' hours. Seems like fo'evah! Yit can't be, when de moon's jes' riz. Dis am a long night fo' yo', yo' Majesty! *(With a mournful chuckle)* Majesty! Der ain't much majesty 'bout dis baby now. *(With attempted cheerfulness)* Never min'. It's all part o' de game. Dis night come to an end like everything else. And when you gits dar safe and has dat bankroll in yo' hands you laughs at all dis. *(He starts to whistle, but checks himself abruptly)* What yo' whistlin' for, you po' dope! Want all de worl' to heah you? *(He stops talking to listen)* Heah dat ole drum! Sho' gits nearer from de sound. Dey's packin' it along wid 'em. Time fo' me to move. *(He takes a step forward, then stops—worriedly)* What's dat odder queer clickety sound I heah? Dere it is! Sound close! Sound like— Sound like— Fo' God sake, sound like some nigger was shootin' crap! *(Frightenedly)* I better beat it quick when I gits dem notions. *(He walks quickly into the clear space—then stands transfixed as he sees* JEFF*—in a terrified gasp)* Who dar? Who dat? Is dat you, Jeff? *(Starting toward the other, forgetful for a moment of his surroundings and really believing it is a living man that he sees—in a tone of happy relief)* Jeff! I'se sho' mighty glad to see you! Dey tol' me you done died from dat razor cut I gives you. *(Stopping suddenly, bewilderedly)* But how you come to be heah, nigger? *(He stares fascinatedly at the other, who continues his mechanical play with the* *dice.* JONES' *eyes begin to roll wildly. He stutters*) Ain't you gwine—look up—can't you speak to me? Is you—is you—a ha'nt? (*He jerks out his revolver in a frenzy of terrified rage.*) Nigger, I kills you dead once. Has I got to kill you agin? You take it den. (*He fires. When the smoke clears away,* JEFF *has disappeared.* JONES *stands trembling—then with a certain reassurance*) He's gone, anyway. Ha'nt or no ha'nt, dat shot fix him. (*The beat of the far-off tom-tom is perceptibly louder and more rapid.* JONES *becomes conscious of it—with a start, looking back over his shoulder*) Dey's gittin' near! Dey's comin' fast! And heah I is shootin' shots to let 'em know jes' whar I is! Oh, Gorry, I'se got to run. (*Forgetting the path, he plunges wildly into the underbrush in the rear and disappears in the shadow*)

## Scene Four

*In the forest. A wide dirt road runs diagonally from the right front to the left rear. Rising sheer on both sides, the forest walls it in. The moon is now up. Under its light the road glimmers ghastly and unreal. It is as if the forest had stood aside momentarily to let the road pass through and accomplish its veiled purpose. This done, the forest will fold in upon itself again and the road will be no more.* JONES *stumbles in from the forest on the right. His uniform is ragged and torn. He looks about him with numbed surprise when he sees the road, his eyes blinking in the bright moonlight. He flops down exhaustedly and pants heavily for a while. Then with sudden anger*)

JONES I'm meltin' wid heat! Runnin' an' runnin' an' runnin'! Damn dis heah coat! Like a strait jacket! (*He tears off his coat and flings it away from him, revealing himself stripped to the waist*) Dere! Dat's better! Now I kin breathe! (*Looking down at his feet, the spurs catch his eye*) And to hell wid dese high-fangled spurs. Dey're what's been a-trippin' me up an' breakin' my neck. (*He unstraps them and flings them away disgustedly*) Dere! I gits rid o' dem frippety Emperor trappin's an' I travels lighter. Lawd! I'se tired! (*After a pause, listening to the insistent beat of the tom-tom in the distance*) I must 'a' put some distance between myself an' dem—runnin' like dat—and yit—dat damn drum sounds jes' de same—nearer, even. Well, I guess I a'most holds my lead anyhow. Dey won't never catch up. (*With a sigh*) If on'y my fool legs stands up. Oh, I'se sorry I evah went in for dis. Dat Emperor job is sho' hard to shake. (*He looks around him suspiciously*) How'd dis road evah git heah? Good level road, too. I never remembers seein' it befo'. (*Shaking his head apprehensively*) Dese woods is sho' full o' de queerest things at night. (*With a sudden terror*) Lawd God, don't let me see no more o' dem ha'nts! Dey gits my goat! (*Then, trying to talk himself into confidence*) Ha'nts! You fool nigger, dey ain't no such things. Don't de Baptist parson tell you dat many time? Is you civilized, or is you like dese ign'rent black niggers heah? Sho'! Dat was all in yo' own head. Wasn't nothin' dere. Wasn't no Jeff! Know what? You jes' get seein' dem things 'cause yo' belly's empty and you's sick wid hunger inside. Hunger 'fects yo' head and yo' eyes. Any fool know dat. (*Then, pleading fervently*) But bless God, I don't come across no more o' dem, whatever dey is! (*Then cautiously*) Rest! Don't talk! Rest! You needs it. Den you gits on yo' way again. (*Looking at the moon*) Night's half gone a'most. You hits de coast in de mawning! Den yo's all safe.

(*From the right forward a small gang of Negroes enter. They are dressed in striped convict suits, their heads are shaven, one leg drags limpingly, shackled to a heavy ball and chain. Some carry picks, the others shovels. They are followed by a white man dressed in the uniform of a* PRISON GUARD. *A Winchester rifle is slung across his shoulder and he carries a heavy whip. At a signal from the* GUARD *they stop on the road opposite where* JONES *is sitting.* JONES, *who has been staring up at the sky, unmindful of their noiseless approach, suddenly looks down and sees them. His eyes pop out, he tries to get to his feet and fly, but sinks back, too numbed by fright to move. His voice catches in a choking prayer*)

Lawd Jesus!

(*The* PRISON GUARD *cracks his whip—noiselessly—and at that signal all the convicts start to work on the road. They swing their picks, they shovel, but not a sound comes from their labor. Their movements, like those of* JEFF *in the preceding scene, are those of automatons—rigid, slow, and mechanical. The* PRISON GUARD *points sternly at* JONES *with his whip, motions him to take his place among the other shovelers.* JONES *gets to his feet in a hypnotized stupor. He mumbles subserviently*)

Yes, suh! Yes, suh! I'se comin'. (*As he shuffles, dragging one foot, over to his place, he curses under his breath with rage and hatred*) God damn yo' soul, I gits even wid you yit, some time.

(*As if there were a shovel in his hands he goes through weary, mechanical gestures of digging up dirt, and throwing it to the roadside. Suddenly the* GUARD *approaches him angrily, threateningly. He raises his whip and lashes* JONES *viciously across the shoulders with it.* JONES *winces with pain and cowers abjectly. The* GUARD *turns his back on him and walks away contemptuously. Instantly* JONES *straightens up. With arms upraised as if his shovel were a club in his hands, he springs murderously at the unsuspecting* GUARD. *In the act of crashing down his shovel on the white man's skull,* JONES *suddenly becomes aware that his hands are empty. He cries despairingly*)

What's my shovel? Gimme my shovel 'til I splits his damn head! (*Appealing to his fellow convicts*) Gimme a shovel, one o' you, fo' God sake!

(*They stand fixed in motionless attitudes, their eyes on the ground. The* GUARD *seems to wait expectantly, his back turned to the attacker.* JONES *bellows with baffled, terrified rage, tugging frantically at his revolver*)

I kills you, you white debil, if it's de last thing I evah does! Ghost or debil, I kill you agin!

(*He frees the revolver and fires point-blank at the* GUARD'S *back. Instantly the walls of the forest close in from both sides, the road and the figures of the convict gang are blotted out in an enshrouding darkness. The only sounds are a crashing in the underbrush as* JONES *leaps away in mad flight and the throbbing of the tom-tom, still far distant, but increased in volume of sound and rapidity of beat*)

## Scene Five

*A large circular clearing, enclosed by the serried ranks of gigantic trunks of tall trees whose tops are lost to view. In the center is a big dead stump worn by time into a curious resemblance to an auction block. The moon floods the clearing with a clear light.* JONES *forces his way through the forest on the left. He looks wildly about the clearing with hunted, fearful glances. His pants are in tatters, his shoes cut and misshapen, flapping about his feet. He slinks cautiously to the stump in the center and sits down in a tense position, ready for instant flight. Then he holds his head in his hands and rocks back and forth, moaning to himself miserably.*

JONES Oh, Lawd, Lawd! Oh, Lawd, Lawd! (*Suddenly he throws himself on his knees and raises his clasped hands to the sky—in a voice of agonized pleading*) Lawd Jesus, heah my prayer! I'se a po' sinner, a po' sinner! I knows I done wrong, I knows it! When I cotches Jeff cheatin' wid loaded dice my anger overcomes me and I kills him dead! Lawd, I done wrong! When dat guard hits me wid de whip, my anger overcomes me, and I kills him dead. Lawd, I done wrong! And down heah whar dese fool bush niggers raises me up to de seat o' de mighty, I steals all I could grab. Lawd, I done wrong! I knows it! I'se sorry! Forgive me, Lawd! Forgive dis po' sinner! (*Then, beseeching terrifiedly*) And keep dem away, Lawd! Keep dem away from me! And stop dat drum soundin' in my ears! Dat begin to sound ha'nted, too. (*He gets to his feet, evidently slightly reassured by his prayer—with attempted confidence*) De Lawd'll preserve me from dem ha'nts after dis. (*Sits down on the stump again*) I ain't skeered o' real men. Let dem come. But dem odders— (*He shudders—then looks down at his feet, working his toes inside the shoes—with a groan*) Oh, my po' feet! Dem shoes ain't no use no more 'ceptin' to hurt. I'se better off widout dem. (*He unlaces them and pulls them off—holds the wrecks of the shoes in his hands and regards them mournfully*) You was real, A-one patin' leather, too. Look at you now. Emperor, you'se gittin' mighty low!

(*He sighs dejectedly and remains with bowed shoulders, staring down at the shoes in his hands as if reluctant to throw them away. While his attention is thus occupied, a crowd of figures silently enter the clearing from all sides. All are dressed in Southern costumes of the period of the 1850's. There are middle-aged men who are evidently well-to-do* PLANTERS. *There is one spruce, authoritative individual—the* AUCTIONEER. *There is a crowd of curious spectators, chiefly young belles and dandies who have come to the slave market for diversion. All exchange courtly greetings in dumb show and chat silently together. There is something stiff, rigid, unreal, marionettish about their movements. They group themselves about the stump. Finally a batch of slaves is led in from the left by an attendant—three men of different ages, two women, one with a baby in her arms, nursing. They are placed to the left of the stump, beside* JONES. *The white planters look them over appraisingly as if they were cattle, and exchange judgments on each. The dandies point with their fingers and make witty remarks. The belles titter bewitchingly. All this in silence save for the ominous throb of the tom-tom. The* AUCTIONEER *holds up his hand, taking his place at the stump. The group strain forward attentively. He touches* JONES *on the shoulder peremptorily, motioning for him to stand on the stump—the auction block.* JONES *looks up, sees the figures on all sides, looks wildly for some opening to escape, sees none, screams, and leaps madly to the top of the stump to get as far away from them as possible. He stands there, cowering, paralyzed with horror. The* AUCTIONEER *begins his silent spiel. He points to* JONES, *appeals to the planters to see for themselves. Here is a good field hand, sound in wind and limb as they can see. Very strong still in spite of his being middle-aged. Look at that back. Look at those shoulders. Look at the muscles in his arms and his sturdy legs. Capable of any amount of hard labor. Moreover, of a good disposition, intelligent, and tractable. Will any gentleman start the bidding? The* PLANTERS *raise their fingers, make their bids. They are apparently all eager to possess* JONES. *The bidding is lively, the crowd interested. While this has been going on,* JONES *has been seized by the courage of desperation. He dares to look down and around him. Over his face abject terror gives way to mystification, to gradual realization—stutteringly)*

What you all doin', white folks? What's all dis? What you all lookin' at me fo'? What you doin' wid me, anyhow? (*Suddenly convulsed with raging hatred and fear*) Is dis a auction? Is you sellin' me like dey uster befo' de war? (*Jerking out his revolver just as the* AUCTIONEER *knocks him down to one of the* PLANTERS*—glaring from him to the purchaser*) And *you* sells me? And *you* buys me? I shows you I'se a free nigger, damn yo' souls!

(*He fires at the* AUCTIONEER *and at the* PLANTER *with such rapidity that the two shots are almost simultaneous. As if this were a signal the walls of the forest fold in. Only blackness remains and silence broken by* JONES *as he rushes off, crying with fear—and by the quickened, ever louder beat of the tom-tom*)

## Scene Six

*A cleared space in the forest. The limbs of the trees meet over it, forming a low ceiling about five feet from the ground. The interlocked ropes of creepers reaching upward to entwine the tree trunks give an arched appearance to the sides. The space thus enclosed is like the dark, noisome hold of some ancient vessel. The moonlight is almost completely shut out and only a vague wan light filters through. There is the noise of someone approaching from the left, stumbling and crawling through the undergrowth.* JONES' *voice is heard between chattering moans.*

JONES Oh Lawd! What I gwine do now? Ain't got no bullet left on'y de silver one. If mo' o' dem ha'nts come after me, how I gwine skeer dem away? Oh Lawd, on'y de silver one left—an' I gotta save dat fo' luck. If I shoots dat one I'm a goner sho'! Lawd, it's black heah! Whar's de moon? Oh Lawd, don't dis night evah come to an end? (*By the sounds, he is feeling his way cautiously forward*) Dere! Dis feels like a clear space. I gotta lie down an' rest. I don't care if dem niggers does cotch me. I gotta rest.

(*He is well forward now where his figure can be dimly made out. His pants have been so torn away that what is left of them is no better than a breechcloth. He flings himself full length, face downward on the ground, panting with exhaustion. Gradually it seems to grow lighter in the enclosed space and two rows of seated figures can be seen behind* JONES. *They are sitting in crumpled, despairing attitudes, hunched, facing one another with their backs touching the forest walls as if they were shackled to them. All are Negroes, naked save for loincloths. At first they are silent and motionless. Then they begin to sway slowly forward toward each and back again in unison, as if they were laxly letting themselves follow the long roll of a ship at sea. At the same time a low, melancholy murmur rises among them, increasing gradually by rhythmic degrees which seem to be directed and controlled by the throb of the tom-tom in the distance, to a long, tremulous wail of despair that reaches a certain pitch, unbearably acute, then falls by slow gradations of tone into silence and is taken up again.* JONES *starts, looks up, sees the figures, and throws himself down again to shut out the sight. A shudder of terror shakes his whole body as the wail rises up about him again. But the next time, his voice, as if under some uncanny compulsion, starts with the others. As their chorus lifts he rises to a sitting posture similar to the others, swaying back and forth. His voice reaches the highest pitch of sorrow, of desolation. The light fades out, the other voices cease, and only darkness is left.* JONES *can be heard scrambling to his feet and running off, his voice sinking down the scale and receding as he moves farther and farther away in the forest. The tom-tom beats louder, quicker, with a more insistent, triumphant pulsation*)

## Scene Seven

*The foot of a gigantic tree by the edge of a great river. A rough structure of boulders, like an altar, is by the tree. The raised riverbank is in the nearer background. Beyond this the surface of the river spreads out, brilliant and unruffled in the moonlight, blotted out and merged into a veil of bluish mist in the distance.* JONES' *voice is heard from the left rising and falling in the long, despairing wail of the chained slaves, to the rhythmic beat of the tom-tom. As his voice sinks into silence, he enters the open space. The expression of his face is fixed and stony, his eyes have an obsessed glare, he moves with a strange deliberation like a sleepwalker or one in a trance. He looks around at the tree, the rough stone altar, the moonlit surface of the river beyond, and passes his hand over his head with a vague gesture of puzzled bewilderment. Then, as if in obedience to some obscure impulse, he sinks into a kneeling, devotional posture before the altar. Then he seems to come to himself partly, to have an uncertain realization of what he is doing, for he straightens up and stares about him horrifiedly—in an incoherent mumble:*

JONES What—what is I doin'? What is—dis place? Seems like I know dat tree—an' dem stones—an' de river. I remember—seems like I been heah befo'. (*Tremblingly*) Oh, Gorry, I'se skeered in dis place! I'se skeered. Oh Lawd, pertect dis sinner!

(*Crawling away from the altar, he cowers close to the ground, his face hidden, his shoulders heaving with sobs of hysterical fright. From behind the trunk of the tree, as if he had sprung out of it, the figure of the* CONGO WITCH DOCTOR *appears. He is wizened and old, naked except for the fur of some small animal tied about his waist, its bushy tail hanging down in front. His body is stained all over a bright red. Antelope horns are on each side of his head, branching upward. In one hand he carries a bone rattle, in the other a charm stick with a bunch of white cockatoo feathers tied to the end. A great number of glass beads and bone ornaments are about his neck, ears, wrists, and ankles. He struts noiselessly with a queer prancing step to a position in the clear ground between* JONES *and the altar. Then with a preliminary, summoning stamp of his foot on the earth, he begins to dance and to chant. As if in response to his summons, the beating of the tom-tom grows to a fierce, exultant boom whose throbs seem to fill the air with vibrating rhythm.* JONES *looks up, starts to spring to his feet, reaches a half-kneeling, half-squatting position and remains rigidly fixed there, paralyzed with awed fascination by this new apparition. The* WITCH DOCTOR *sways, stamping with his foot, his bone rattle clicking the time. His voice rises and falls in a weird, monotonous croon, without articulate word divisions. Gradually his dance becomes clearly one of a narrative in pantomime, his croon is an incantation, a charm to allay the fierceness of some implacable deity demanding sacrifice. He flees, he is pursued by devils, he hides, he flees again. Ever wilder and wilder becomes his flight, nearer and nearer draws the pursuing evil, more and more the spirit of terror gains possession of him. His croon, rising to intensity, is punctuated by shrill cries.* JONES *has become completely hypnotized. His voice joins in the incantation, in the cries, he beats time with his hands and sways his body to and fro from the waist. The whole spirit and meaning of the dance has entered into him, has become his spirit. Finally the theme of the pantomime halts on a howl of despair, and is taken up again in a note of savage hope. There is a salvation. The forces of evil demand sacrifice. They must be appeased. The* WITCH DOCTOR *points with his wand to the sacred tree, to the river beyond, to the altar, and finally to* JONES, *with a ferocious command.* JONES *seems to sense the meaning of this. It is he who must offer himself for sacrifice. He beats his forehead abjectly on the ground, moaning hysterically*)

Mercy, O Lawd! Mercy! Mercy on dis po' sinner.

(*The* WITCH DOCTOR *springs to the riverbank. He stretches out his arms and calls to some god within its depths. Then he starts backward slowly, his arms remaining out. A huge head of a crocodile appears over the bank and its eyes, glittering greenly, fasten upon* JONES. *He stares into them fascinatedly. The* WITCH DOCTOR *prances up to him, touches him with his wand, motions with hideous command toward the waiting monster.* JONES *squirms on his belly nearer and nearer, moaning continually*)

Mercy, Lawd! Mercy!

(*The crocodile heaves more of his enormous hulk onto the land.* JONES *squirms toward him. The* WITCH DOCTOR'S *voice shrills out in furious exaltation, the tom-tom beats madly.* JONES *cries out in a fierce, exhausted spasm of anguished pleading*)

Lawd, save me! Lawd Jesus, heah my prayer!

(*Immediately, in answer to his prayer, comes the thought of the one bullet left him. He snatches at his hip, shouting defiantly*)

De silver bullet! You don't git me yit!

(*He fires at the green eyes in front of him. The head of the crocodile sinks back behind the riverbank, the* WITCH DOCTOR *springs behind the sacred tree and disappears.* JONES *lies with his face to the ground, his arms outstretched, whimpering with fear as the throb of the tom-tom fills the silence about him with a somber pulsation, a baffled but revengeful power*)

## Scene Eight

*Dawn. Same as Scene Two, the dividing line of forest and plain. The nearest tree trunks are dimly revealed, but the forest behind them is still a mass of glooming shadow. The tom-tom seems on the very spot, so loud and continuously vibrating are its beats.* LEM *enters from the left, followed by a small squad of his soldiers, and by the Cockney trader,* SMITHERS. LEM *is a heavy-set, ape-faced old savage of the extreme African type, dressed only in a loincloth. A revolver and a cartridge belt are about his waist. His soldiers are in different degrees of rag-concealed nakedness. All wear broad palm-leaf hats. Each one carries a rifle.* SMITHERS *is the same as in Scene One. One of the soldiers, evidently a tracker, is peering about keenly on the ground. He points to the spot where* JONES *entered the forest.* LEM *and* SMITHERS *come to look.*

SMITHERS (*After a glance, turns away in disgust*) That's where 'e went in right enough. Much good it'll do yer. 'E's miles orf by this an' safe to the Coast, damn 's 'ide! I tole yer yer'd lose 'im, didn't I?—wastin' the 'ole bloomin' night beatin' yer bloody drum and castin' yer silly spells! Gawd blimey, wot a pack!

LEM (*Gutturally*) We cotch him. (*He makes a motion to his soldiers, who squat down on their haunches in a semicircle*)

SMITHERS (*Exasperatedly*) Well, ain't yer goin' in an' 'unt 'im in the woods? What the 'ell's the good of waitin'?

LEM (*Imperturbably—squatting down himself*) We cotch him.

SMITHERS (*Turning away from him contemptuously*) Aw! Garn! 'E's a better man than the lot o' you together. I 'ates the sight o' 'im but I'll say that for 'im.

(*A sound comes from the forest. The soldiers jump to their feet, cocking their rifles alertly.* LEM *remains sitting with an imperturbable expression, but listening intently. He makes a quick signal with his hand. His followers creep quickly into the forest, scattering so that each enters at a different spot*)

SMITHERS You ain't thinkin' that would be 'im, I 'ope?

LEM (*Calmly*) We cotch him.

SMITHERS Blarsted fat'eads! (*Then after a second's thought—wonderingly*) Still an' all, it might 'appen. If 'e lost 'is bloody way in these stinkin' woods 'e'd likely turn in a circle without 'is knowin' it.

LEM (*Peremptorily*) Sssh! (*The reports of several rifles sound from the forest, followed a second later by savage, exultant yells. The beating of the tom-tom abruptly ceases.* LEM *looks up at the white man with a grin of satisfaction*) We cotch him. Him dead.

SMITHERS (*With a snarl*) 'Ow d'yer know it's 'im an' 'ow d'yer know 'e's dead?

LEM My mens dey got um silver bullets. Lead bullet no kill him. He got um strong charm. I cook um money, make um silver bullet, make um strong charm, too.

SMITHERS (*Astonished*) So that's wot you was up to all night, wot? You was scared to put after 'im till you'd molded silver bullets, eh?

LEM (*Simply stating a fact*) Yes. Him got strong charm. Lead no good.

SMITHERS (*Slapping his thigh and guffawing*) Haw-haw! If yer don't beat all 'ell. (*Then recovering himself—scornfully*) I'll bet yer it ain't 'im they shot at all, yer bleedin' looney!

LEM (*Calmly*) Dey come bring him now.

(*The soldiers come out of the forest, carrying* JONES' *limp body. He is dead. They carry him to* LEM, *who examines his body with great satisfaction*)

SMITHERS (*Leans over his shoulder—in a tone of frightened awe*) Well, they did for yer right enough, Jonesy me lad! Dead as a 'erring! (*Mockingly*) Where's yer 'igh an' mighty airs now, yer bloomin' Majesty? (*Then with a grin*) Silver bullets! Gawd blimey, but yer died in the 'eighth o' style, any'ow!

*Curtain*

# THE ICEMAN COMETH

"I HAVE always felt a sympathy for that tortured self-torturing man who offered himself to his own soul as Buddha offered himself to the famished tiger," wrote William Butler Yeats in *Dramatis Personae*. Yeats was speaking of Strindberg, but the description also fits the "bedeviled" Eugene O'Neill whose total indebtedness to the great Swedish playwright cannot be over-estimated. Unavoidably involved in a cursed and misbegotten human race they loved and despised, both lived with their private *daemons* of despairing nihilism. Both pursued the logic of their constant self-questioning to what was, for them, the ultimate conclusion: in the blind indifference of a senseless, godless universe, there is only the haunted man with his ego-sustaining mechanism for spawning and nurturing the illusions which separate the Living Dead from the Dead.

From 1934 until his death in 1953, O'Neill was represented in New York with only one new work: *The Iceman Cometh,* produced by the Theatre Guild in 1946. In *Ah, Wilderness!* and *Days Without End* (1933-1934), produced just before his "retirement" began, O'Neill displayed an uncharacteristic sunniness and affirmativeness. In *Ah, Wilderness!* he used his happiest memories of New London in a work which, now musicalized by both Hollywood and Broadway, has become his "most popular" play. In *Days Without End* O'Neill again explored the conflict between negation and religious faith. Because he had announced that the earlier *Dynamo* (1929) was to be part of a trilogy called *God Is Dead! Long Live—What?,* playgoers were astounded to find him following a Goethean instead of a Marlovian pattern in his Faust-play: the bifurcated protagonist of *Days Without End,* John Loving, is finally re-integrated in the forgiveness he receives from a priest. The play closes with Loving's exalted "Life laughs with God's love again. Life laughs with love!" *Ah, Wilderness!* ran long after *Days Without End,* a critical failure, had opened and closed, but the speculation the latter play evoked concerning O'Neill's alleged return to Catholicism went on until *The Iceman Cometh* opened twelve years later.

O'Neill's last years were filled with honors, with periods of tranquility, with deep personal sorrows, with poor health. In 1936 he received the Nobel Prize for *Mourning Becomes Electra;* he knew his works were being translated and produced throughout the world. Despite the satisfying life he knew with his third wife, he blamed himself for neglecting the three children of his previous marriages. The horrors of World War II deepened his despair, much of which was to be poured into *The Last Conquest,* a projected "fantasy of the future" in which Armageddon was to be shown. He planned extensive play-cycles and made elaborate notes on characters and action. *A Tale of Possessors Self-Dispossessed* was to be a cycle of nine or eleven plays chronicling a family's history in America; the posthumous *A Touch of the Poet* (produced, 1958) and, if it can ever be produced, *More Stately Mansions,* the other play surviving from this cycle, shed some light on O'Neill's larger design. In another cycle, *By Way of Obit,* only the one-act, *Hughie* (produced in Stockholm, 1958), is known. O'Neill's last plays are notable for his return to episodes recalled from his early life and to the naturalism in which he first established his reputation. *The Iceman Cometh* (completed in 1939) recreates two New York dives and many familiar Greenwich Village figures O'Neill knew in his twenties. Major Cornelius Melody, the colorful protagonist of *A Touch of the Poet,* was partly inspired by O'Neill's father. *A Moon for the Misbegotten* (produced on the road 1947, but not seen in New York until 1957) recreates his brother's search for peace. *Long Day's Journey into Night* (completed, 1941) covers a day in August, 1912, when O'Neill learned he was tubercular. It commemorates the complex of love and hate among "the four haunted Tyrones."

Although flawed by redundancy, *The Iceman Cometh* is one of O'Neill's greatest works. In this nihilistic version of the Last Supper, the salesman Hickey startles Harry Hope's "regulars" out of their torpor and into the bright glare of the world outside the saloon. In time they return to this graveyard of the living. O'Neill shows each character's unique response to Hickey's strange preachment, but firmly at the play's center he placed Larry Slade, the ex-Anarchist. Like Gorki's Satin, Slade begins without any of the "harmless pipe dreams" by which the other sterile denizens of Harry Hope's "keep up the appearances of life." At the end of the play, he knows he is "the only real convert to death Hickey made here." Ignoring Parritt, the young mother-betraying Judas who escapes his guilt by jumping off a fire escape, Harry Hope's regulars set up a cacophony and launch another *danse-macabre* birthday celebration. At the final curtain, Larry Slade—with a resolve O'Neill undoubtedly understood all too well—"stares in front of him, oblivious to their racket."

# THE ICEMAN COMETH

## CHARACTERS

HARRY HOPE, *proprietor of a saloon and rooming house*
ED MOSHER, *Hope's brother-in-law, one-time circus man**
PAT MCGLOIN, *one-time Police Lieutenant**
WILLIE OBAN, *a Harvard Law School alumnus**
JOE MOTT, *one-time proprietor of a Negro gambling house*
PIET WETJOEN ("THE GENERAL"), *one-time leader of a Boer commando**
CECIL LEWIS ("THE CAPTAIN"), *one-time Captain of British infantry**
JAMES CAMERON ("JIMMY TOMORROW"), *one-time Boer War correspondent**
HUGO KALMAR, *one-time editor of Anarchist periodicals**
LARRY SLADE, *one-time Syndicalist-Anarchist**
ROCKY PIOGGI, *night bartender**
DON PARRITT*
PEARL* }
MARGIE* } *street walkers*
CORA* }
CHUCK MORELLO, *day bartender**
THEODORE HICKMAN (HICKEY), *a hardware salesman*
MORAN
LIEB

## SCENES

### Act One

SCENE *Back room and a section of the bar at Harry Hope's—early morning in summer, 1912.*

### Act Two

SCENE *Back room, around midnight of the same day.*

### Act Three

SCENE *Bar and a section of the back room—morning of the following day.*

* Roomers at Harry Hope's.

### Act Four

SCENE *Same as Act One. Back room and a section of the bar—around 1:30 A.M. of the next day.*

HARRY HOPE'S *is a Raines-Law hotel*[1] *of the period, a cheap ginmill of the five-cent whiskey, last-resort variety situated on the downtown West Side of New York. The building, owned by* HOPE, *is a narrow five-story structure of the tenement type, the second floor a flat occupied by the proprietor. The renting of rooms on the upper floors, under the Raines-Law loopholes, makes the establishment legally a hotel and gives it the privilege of serving liquor in the back room of the bar after closing hours and on Sundays, provided a meal is served with the booze, thus making a back room legally a hotel restaurant. This food provision was generally circumvented by putting a property sandwich in the middle of each table, an old desiccated ruin of dust-laden bread and mummified ham or cheese which only the drunkest yokel from the sticks ever regarded as anything but a noisome table decoration. But at* HARRY HOPE'S, HOPE *being a former minor Tammanyite and still possessing friends, this food technicality is ignored as irrelevant, except during the fleeting alarms of reform agitation. Even* HOPE'S *back room is not a separate room, but simply the rear of the barroom divided from the bar by drawing a dirty black curtain across the room.*

## Act One

SCENE *The back room and a section of the bar of* HARRY HOPE'S *saloon on an early morning in sum-*

[1] The New York Raines Law restricted Sunday liquor sales to hotels; a Raines-Law hotel was usually a saloon provided with sleeping rooms, often a house of assignation.

*mer, 1912. The right wall of the back room is a dirty black curtain which separates it from the bar. At rear, this curtain is drawn back from the wall so the bartender can get in and out. The back room is crammed with round tables and chairs placed so close together that it is a difficult squeeze to pass between them. In the middle of the rear wall is a door opening on a hallway. In the left corner, built out into the room, is the toilet with a sign "This is it" on the door. Against the middle of the left wall is a nickel-in-the-slot phonograph. Two windows, so glazed with grime one cannot see through them, are in the left wall, looking out on a backyard. The walls and ceiling once were white, but it was a long time ago, and they are now so splotched, peeled, stained and dusty that their color can best be described as dirty. The floor, with iron spittoons placed here and there, is covered with sawdust. Lighting comes from single wall brackets, two at left and two at rear.*

*There are three rows of tables, from front to back. Three are in the front line. The one at left-front has four chairs; the one at center-front, four; the one at right-front, five. At rear of, and half between, front tables one and two is a table of the second row with five chairs. A table, similarly placed at rear of front tables two and three, also has five chairs. The third row of tables, four chairs to one and six to the other, is against the rear wall on either side of the door.*

*At right of this dividing curtain is a section of the barroom, with the end of the bar seen at rear, a door to the hall at left of it. At front is a table with four chairs. Light comes from the street windows off right, the gray subdued light of early morning in a narrow street. In the back room,* LARRY SLADE *and* HUGO KALMAR *are at the table at left-front,* HUGO *in a chair facing right,* LARRY at *rear of table facing front, with an empty chair between them. A fourth chair is at right of table, facing left.* HUGO *is a small man in his late fifties. He has a head much too big for his body, a high forehead, crinkly long black hair streaked with gray, a square face with a pug nose, a walrus mustache, black eyes which peer near-sightedly from behind thick-lensed spectacles, tiny hands and feet. He is dressed in threadbare black clothes and his white shirt is frayed at collar and cuffs, but everything about him is fastidiously clean. Even his flowing Windsor tie is neatly tied. There is a foreign atmosphere about him, the stamp of an alien radical, a strong resemblance to the type Anarchist as portrayed, bomb in hand, in newspaper cartoons. He is asleep now, bent forward in his chair, his arms folded on the table, his head resting sideways on his arms.*

LARRY SLADE *is sixty. He is tall, raw-boned, with coarse straight white hair, worn long and raggedly cut. He has a gaunt Irish face with a big nose, high cheekbones, a lantern jaw with a week's stubble of beard, a mystic's meditative pale-blue eyes with a gleam of sharp sardonic humor in them. As slovenly as* HUGO *is neat, his clothes are dirty and much slept in. His gray flannel shirt, open at the neck, has the appearance of having never been washed. From the way he methodically scratches himself with his long-fingered, hairy hands, he is lousy and reconciled to being so. He is the only occupant of the room who is not asleep. He stares in front of him, an expression of tired tolerance giving his face the quality of a pitying but weary old priest's.*

*All four chairs at the middle table, front, are occupied.* JOE MOTT *sits at left-front of the table, facing front. Behind him, facing right-front, is* PIET WETJOEN *("The General"). At center of the table, rear,* JAMES CAMERON *("Jimmy Tomorrow") sits facing front. At right of table, opposite* JOE, *is* CECIL LEWIS *("The Captain").*

JOE MOTT *is a Negro, about fifty years old, brown-skinned, stocky, wearing a light suit that had once been flashily sporty but is now about to fall apart. His pointed tan buttoned shoes, faded pink shirt and bright tie belong to the same vintage. Still, he manages to preserve an atmosphere of nattiness and there is nothing dirty about his appearance. His face is only mildly negroid in type. The nose is thin and his lips are not noticeably thick. His hair is crinkly and he is beginning to get bald. A scar from a knife slash runs from his left cheekbone to jaw. His face would be hard and tough if it were not for its good nature and lazy humor. He is asleep, his nodding head supported by his left hand.*

PIET WETJOEN, *the Boer, is in his fifties, a huge man with a bald head and a long grizzled beard. He is slovenly dressed in a dirty shapeless patched suit, spotted by food. A Dutch farmer type, his once great muscular strength has been debauched into flaccid tallow. But despite his blubbery mouth and sodden bloodshot blue eyes, there is still a suggestion of old authority lurking in him like a memory of the drowned. He is hunched forward, both elbows on the table, his hand on each side of his head for support.*

JAMES CAMERON *("Jimmy Tomorrow") is about the same size and age as* HUGO, *a small man. Like* HUGO, *he wears threadbare black, and everything about him is clean. But the resemblance ceases there.* JIMMY *has a face like an old well-bred, gentle bloodhound's, with folds of flesh hanging from each side of his mouth, and big brown friendly guileless eyes, more bloodshot than any bloodhound's ever were. He has mouse-colored thinning hair, a little bulbous nose, buck teeth in a small rabbit mouth. But his forehead is fine, his eyes are intelligent and there once was a competent ability in him. His speech is educated, with the ghost of a Scotch rhythm in it. His manners are those of a gentleman. There is a quality about him of a prim, Victorian old maid, and at the same time of a likeable, affectionate boy who has never grown up. He sleeps, chin on chest, hands folded in his lap.*

CECIL LEWIS *("The Captain") is as obviously English as Yorkshire pudding and just as obviously the former army officer. He is going on sixty. His hair and military mustache are white, his eyes bright blue, his complexion that of a turkey. His lean figure is still erect and square-shouldered. He is stripped to the waist, his coat, shirt, undershirt, collar and tie crushed up into a pillow on the table in front of him, his head sideways on this pillow, facing front, his arms dangling toward the floor. On his lower left shoulder is the big ragged scar of an old wound.*

*At the table at right, front,* HARRY HOPE, *the proprietor, sits in the middle, facing front, with* PAT MCGLOIN *on his right and* ED MOSHER *on his left, the other two chairs being unoccupied.*

*Both* MCGLOIN *and* MOSHER *are big paunchy men.* MCGLOIN *has his old occupation of policeman stamped all over him. He is in his fifties, sandy-haired, bullet-headed, jowly, with protruding ears and little round eyes. His face must once have been brutal and greedy, but time and whiskey have melted it down into a good-humored, parasite's characterlessness. He wears old clothes and is slovenly. He is slumped sideways on his chair, his head drooping jerkily toward one shoulder.*

ED MOSHER *is going on sixty. He has a round kewpie's face—a kewpie who is an unshaven habitual drunkard. He looks like an enlarged, elderly, bald edition of the village fat boy—a sly fat boy, congenitally indolent, a practical joker, a born grafter and con merchant. But amusing and essentially harmless, even in his most enterprising days, because always too lazy to carry crookedness beyond petty swindling. The influence of his old circus career is apparent in his get-up. His worn clothes are flashy; he wears phony rings and a heavy brass watch-chain (not connected to a watch). Like* MCGLOIN, *he is slovenly. His head is thrown back, his big mouth open.*

HARRY HOPE *is sixty, white-haired, so thin the description "bag of bones" was made for him. He has the face of an old family horse, prone to tantrums, with balkiness always smoldering in its wall eyes, waiting for any excuse to shy and pretend to take the bit in its teeth.* HOPE *is one of those men whom everyone likes on sight, a softhearted slob, without malice, feeling superior to no one, a sinner among sinners, a born easy mark for every appeal. He attempts to hide his defenselessness behind a testy truculent manner, but this has never fooled anyone. He is a little deaf, but not half as deaf as he sometimes pretends. His sight is failing but is not as bad as he complains it is. He wears five-and-ten-cent-store spectacles which are so out of alignment that one eye at times peers half over one glass while the other eye looks half under the other. He has badly fitting store teeth, which click like castanets when he begins to fume. He is dressed in an old coat from one suit and pants from another.*

*In a chair facing right at the table in the second line, between the first two tables, front, sits* WILLIE OBAN, *his head on his left arm outstretched along the table edge. He is in his late thirties, of average height, thin. His haggard, dissipated face has a small nose, a pointed chin, blue eyes with colorless lashes and brows. His blond hair, badly in need of a cut, clings in a limp part to his skull. His eyelids flutter continually as if any light were too strong for his eyes. The clothes he wears belong on a scarecrow. They seem constructed of an inferior grade of dirty blotting paper. His shoes are even more disreputable, wrecks of imitation leather, one laced with twine, the other with a bit of wire. He has no socks, and his bare feet show through holes in the soles, with his big toes sticking out of the uppers. He keeps muttering and twitching in his sleep.*

*As the curtain rises,* ROCKY, *the night bartender, comes from the bar through the curtain and stands looking over the back room. He is a Neapolitan-American in his late twenties, squat and muscular, with a flat, swarthy face and beady eyes. The sleeves of his collarless shirt are rolled up on his thick, powerful arms and he wears a soiled apron. A tough guy but sentimental, in his way, and good-natured. He signals to* LARRY *with a cautious "Sstt" and motions him to see if* HOPE *is asleep.* LARRY *rises from his chair to look at* HOPE *and nods to* ROCKY. ROCKY *goes back in the bar but immediately returns with a bottle of bar whiskey and a glass. He squeezes between the tables to* LARRY.

ROCKY (*In a low voice out of the side of his mouth*) Make it fast. (LARRY *pours a drink and gulps it down.* ROCKY *takes the bottle and puts it on the table where* WILLIE OBAN *is*) Don't want de Boss to get wise when he's got one of his tightwad buns on. (*He chuckles with an amused glance at* HOPE) Jees, ain't de old bastard a riot when he starts dat bull about turnin' over a new leaf? "Not a damned drink on de house," he tells me, "and all dese bums got to pay up deir room rent. Beginnin' tomorrow," he says. Jees, yuh'd tink he meant it! (*He sits down in the chair at* LARRY'S *left*)

LARRY (*Grinning*) I'll be glad to pay up—tomorrow.

And I know my fellow inmates will promise the same. They've all a touching credulity concerning tomorrows. (*A half-drunken mockery in his eyes*) It'll be a great day for them, tomorrow—the Feast of All Fools, with brass bands playing! Their ships will come in, loaded to the gunwales with canceled regrets and promises fulfilled and clean slates and new leases!

ROCKY (*Cynically*) Yeah, and a ton of hop!

LARRY (*Leans toward him, a comical intensity in his low voice*) Don't mock the faith! Have you no respect for religion, you unregenerate Wop? What's it matter if the truth is that their favoring breeze has the stink of nickel whiskey on its breath, and their sea is a growler of lager and ale, and their ships are long since looted and scuttled and sunk on the bottom? To hell with the truth! As the history of the world proves, the truth has no bearing on anything. It's irrelevant and immaterial, as the lawyers say. The lie of a pipe dream is what gives life to the whole misbegotten mad lot of us, drunk or sober. And that's enough philosophic wisdom to give you for one drink of rot-gut.

ROCKY (*Grins kiddingly*) De old Foolosopher, like Hickey calls yuh, ain't yuh? I s'pose you don't fall for no pipe dream?

LARRY (*A bit stiffly*) I don't, no. Mine are all dead and buried behind me. What's before me is the comforting fact that death is a fine long sleep, and I'm damned tired, and it can't come too soon for me.

ROCKY Yeah, just hangin' around hopin' you'll croak, ain't yuh? Well, I'm bettin' you'll have a good long wait. Jees, somebody'll have to take an axe to croak you!

LARRY (*Grins*) Yes, it's my bad luck to be cursed with an iron constitution that even Harry's booze can't corrode.

ROCKY De old anarchist wise guy dat knows all de answers! Dat's you, huh?

LARRY (*Frowns*) Forget the anarchist part of it. I'm through with the Movement long since. I saw men didn't want to be saved from themselves, for that would mean they'd have to give up greed, and they'll never pay that price for liberty. So I said to the world, God bless all here, and may the best man win and die of gluttony! And I took a seat in the grandstand of philosophical detachment to fall asleep observing the cannibals do their death dance. (*He chuckles at his own fancy—reaches over and shakes* HUGO's *shoulder*) Ain't I telling him the truth, Comrade Hugo?

ROCKY Aw, fer Chris' sake, don't get dat bughouse bum started!

HUGO (*Raises his head and peers at* ROCKY *blearily through his thick spectacles—in a guttural declamatory tone*) Capitalist swine! Bourgeois stool pigeons! Have the slaves no right to sleep even? (*Then he grins at* ROCKY *and his manner changes to a giggling, wheedling playfulness, as though he were talking to a child*) Hello, leedle Rocky! Leedle monkey-face! Vere is your leedle slave girls? (*With an abrupt change to a bullying tone*) Don't be a fool! Loan me a dollar! Damned bourgeois Wop! The great Malatesta[2] is my good friend! Buy me a trink! (*He seems to run down, and is overcome by drowsiness. His head sinks to the table again and he is at once fast asleep*)

ROCKY He's out again. (*More exasperated than angry*) He's lucky no one don't take his cracks serious or he'd wake up every mornin' in a hospital.

LARRY (*Regarding* HUGO *with pity*) No. No one takes him seriously. That's his epitaph. Not even the comrades any more. If I've been through with the Movement long since, it's been through with him, and, thanks to whiskey, he's the only one doesn't know it.

ROCKY I've let him get by wid too much. He's goin' to pull dat slave-girl stuff on me once too often. (*His manner changes to defensive argument*) Hell, yuh'd tink I wuz a pimp or somethin'. Everybody knows me knows I ain't. A pimp don't hold no job. I'm a bartender. Dem tarts, Margie and Poil, dey're just a side line to pick up some extra dough. Strictly business, like dey was fighters and I was deir manager, see? I fix the cops fer dem so's dey can hustle widout gettin' pinched. Hell, dey'd be on de Island most of de time if it wasn't fer me. And I don't beat dem up like a pimp would. I treat dem fine. Dey like me. We're pals, see? What if I do take deir dough? Dey'd on'y trow it away. Tarts can't hang on to dough. But I'm a bartender and I work hard for my livin' in dis dump. You know dat, Larry.

LARRY (*With inner sardonic amusement—flatteringly*) A shrewd business man, who doesn't miss any opportunity to get on in the world. That's what I'd call you.

ROCKY (*Pleased*) Sure ting. Dat's me. Grab another ball, Larry. (LARRY *pours a drink from the bottle on* WILLIE's *table and gulps it down.* ROCKY *glances around the room*) Yuh'd never tink all dese bums had a good bed upstairs to go to. Scared if dey hit the hay dey wouldn't be here when Hickey showed up, and dey'd miss a coupla drinks. Dat's what kept you up too, ain't it?

LARRY It is. But not so much the hope of booze, if you can believe that. I've got the blues and Hickey's a great one to make a joke of everything and cheer you up.

ROCKY Yeah, some kidder! Remember how he woiks up dat gag about his wife, when he's cockeyed, cryin' over her picture and den springin' it on yuh all of a sudden dat he left her in de hay wid de iceman? (*He laughs*) I wonder what's happened to him. Yuh could set your watch by his periodicals before dis. Always got here a coupla days before Harry's birthday party, and now he's on'y got till tonight to make it. I hope he shows soon. Dis dump is like de morgue wid all dese bums passed out. (WILLIE OBAN *jerks and twitches in his sleep and begins to mumble. They watch him*)

[2] Errico Malatesta (1853-1932) was a prominent Italian anarchist and agitator who, as a disciple of Bakunin, gained international repute for his revolutionary activism.

WILLIE (*Blurts from his dream*) It's a lie! (*Miserably*) Papa! Papa!

LARRY Poor devil. (*Then angry with himself*) But to hell with pity! It does no good. I'm through with it!

ROCKY Dreamin' about his old man. From what de old-timers say, de old gent sure made a pile of dough in de bucket-shop game before de cops got him. (*He considers* WILLIE *frowningly*) Jees, I've seen him bad but never dis bad. Look at dat get-up. Been playin' de old reliever game. Sold his suit and shoes at Solly's two days ago. Solly give him two bucks and a bum outfit. Yesterday he sells de bum one back to Solly for four bits and gets dese rags to put on. Now he's through. Dat's Solly's final edition he wouldn't take back for nuttin'. Willie sure is on de bottom. I ain't never seen no one so bad, except Hickey on de end of a coupla his bats.

LARRY (*Sardonically*) It's a great game, the pursuit of happiness.

ROCKY Harry don't know what to do about him. He called up his old lady's lawyer like he always does when Willie gets licked. Yuh remember dey used to send down a private dick to give him the rush to a cure, but de lawyer tells Harry nix, de old lady's off of Willie for keeps dis time and he can go to hell.

LARRY (*Watches* WILLIE, *who is shaking in his sleep like an old dog*) There's the consolation that he hasn't far to go! (*As if replying to this,* WILLIE *comes to a crisis of jerks and moans.* LARRY *adds in a comically intense, crazy whisper*) Be God, he's knocking on the door right now!

WILLIE (*Suddenly yells in his nightmare*) It's a God-damned lie! (*He begins to sob*) Oh, Papa! Jesus! (*All the occupants of the room stir on their chairs but none of them wakes up except* HOPE)

ROCKY (*Grabs his shoulder and shakes him*) Hey, you! Nix! Cut out de noise! (WILLIE *opens his eyes to stare around him with a bewildered horror*)

HOPE (*Opens one eye to peer over his spectacles—drowsily*) Who's that yelling?

ROCKY Willie, Boss. De Brooklyn boys is after him.

HOPE (*Querulously*) Well, why don't you give the poor feller a drink and keep him quiet? Bejees, can't I get a wink of sleep in my own back room?

ROCKY (*Indignantly to* LARRY) Listen to that blind-eyed, deef old bastard, will yuh? He give me strict orders not to let Willie hang up no more drinks, no matter—

HOPE (*Mechanically puts a hand to his ear in the gesture of deafness*) What's that? I can't hear you. (*Then drowsily irascible*) You're a cockeyed liar. Never refused a drink to anyone needed it bad in my life! Told you to use your judgment. Ought to know better. You're too busy thinking up ways to cheat me. Oh, I ain't as blind as you think. I can still see a cash register, bejees!

ROCKY (*Grins at him affectionately now—flatteringly*) Sure, Boss. Swell chance of foolin' you!

HOPE I'm wise to you and your sidekick, Chuck. Bejees, you're burglars, not barkeeps! Blind-eyed, deef old bastard, am I? Oh, I heard you! Heard you often when you didn't think. You and Chuck laughing behind my back, telling people you throw the money up in the air and whatever sticks to the ceiling is my share! A fine couple of crooks! You'd steal the pennies off your dead mother's eyes!

ROCKY (*Winks at* LARRY) Aw, Harry, me and Chuck was on'y kiddin'.

HOPE (*More drowsily*) I'll fire both of you. Bejees, if you think you can play me for an easy mark, you've come to the wrong house. No one ever played Harry Hope for a sucker!

ROCKY (*To* LARRY) No one but everybody.

HOPE (*His eyes shut again—mutters*) Least you could do—keep things quiet— (*He falls asleep*)

WILLIE (*Pleadingly*) Give me a drink, Rocky. Harry said it was all right. God, I need a drink.

ROCKY Den grab it. It's right under your nose.

WILLIE (*Avidly*) Thanks. (*He takes the bottle with both twitching hands and tilts it to his lips and gulps down the whiskey in big swallows*)

ROCKY (*Sharply*) When! When! (*He grabs the bottle*) I didn't say, take a bath! (*Showing the bottle to* LARRY—*indignantly*) Jees, look! He's killed a half pint or more! (*He turns on* WILLIE *angrily, but* WILLIE *has closed his eyes and is sitting quietly, shuddering, waiting for the effect*)

LARRY (*With a pitying glance*) Leave him be, the poor devil. A half pint of that dynamite in one swig will fix him for a while—if it doesn't kill him.

ROCKY (*Shrugs his shoulders and sits down again*) Aw right by me. It ain't my booze. (*Behind him, in the chair at left of the middle table,* JOE MOTT, *the Negro, has been waking up*)

JOE (*His eye blinking sleepily*) Whose booze? Gimme some. I don't care whose. Where's Hickey? Ain't he come yet? What time's it, Rocky?

ROCKY Gettin' near time to open up. Time you begun to sweep up in de bar.

JOE (*Lazily*) Never mind de time. If Hickey ain't come, it's time Joe goes to sleep again. I was dreamin' Hickey come in de door, crackin' one of dem drummer's jokes, wavin' a big bankroll and we was all goin' be drunk for two weeks. Wake up and no luck. (*Suddenly his eyes open wide*) Wait a minute, dough. I got idea. Say, Larry, how 'bout dat young guy, Parritt, came to look you up last night and rented a room? Where's he at?

LARRY Up in his room, asleep. No hope in him, anyway, Joe. He's broke.

JOE Dat what he told you? Me and Rocky knows different. Had a roll when he paid you his room rent, didn't he, Rocky? I seen it.

ROCKY Yeah. He flashed it like he forgot and den tried to hide it quick.

LARRY (*Surprised and resentful*) He did, did he?

ROCKY Yeah, I figgered he don't belong, but he said he was a friend of yours.

LARRY He's a liar. I wouldn't know him if he hadn't told me who he was. His mother and I were friends years ago on the Coast. (*He hesitates—then lowering his voice*) You've read in the papers about that bombing on the Coast when several people got killed? Well, the one woman they pinched, Rosa Parritt, is his mother. They'll be coming up for trial soon, and there's no chance for them. She'll get life, I think. I'm telling you this so you'll know why if Don acts a bit queer, and not jump on him. He must be hard hit. He's her only kid.

ROCKY (*Nods—then thoughtfully*) Why ain't he out dere stickin' by her?

LARRY (*Frowns*) Don't ask questions. Maybe there's a good reason.

ROCKY (*Stares at him—understandingly*) Sure. I get it. (*Then wonderingly*) But den what kind of a sap is he to hang on to his right name?

LARRY (*Irritably*) I'm telling you I don't know anything and I don't want to know. To hell with the Movement and all connected with it! I'm out of it, and everything else, and damned glad to be.

ROCKY (*Shrugs his shoulders—indifferently*) Well, don't tink I'm interested in dis Parritt guy. He's nuttin' to me.

JOE Me neider. If dere's one ting more'n anudder I cares nuttin' about, it's de sucker game you and Hugo call de Movement. (*He chuckles—reminiscently*) Reminds me of damn fool argument me and Mose Porter has de udder night. He's drunk and I'm drunker. He says, "Socialist and Anarchist, we ought to shoot dem dead. Dey's all no-good sons of bitches." I says, "Hold on, you talk 's if Anarchists and Socialists was de same." "Dey is," he says. "Dey's both no-good bastards." "No, dey ain't," I says. "I'll explain the difference. De Anarchist he never works. He drinks but he never buys, and if he do ever git a nickel, he blows it in on bombs, and he wouldn't give you nothin'. So go ahead and shoot him. But de Socialist, sometimes, he's got a job, and if he gets ten bucks, he's bound by his religion to split fifty-fifty wid you. You say—how about my cut, Comrade? And you gets de five. So you don't shoot no Socialists while I'm around. Dat is, not if dey got anything. Of course, if dey's broke, den dey's no-good bastards, too." (*He laughs, immensely tickled*)

LARRY (*Grins with sardonic appreciation*) Be God, Joe, you've got all the beauty of human nature and the practical wisdom of the world in that little parable.

ROCKY (*Winks at* JOE) Sure, Larry ain't de on'y wise guy in dis dump, hey, Joe? (*At a sound from the hall he turns as* DON PARRITT *appears in the doorway.* ROCKY *speaks to* LARRY *out of the side of his mouth*) Here's your guy. (PARRITT *comes forward. He is eighteen, tall and broad-shouldered but thin, gangling and awkward. His face is good-looking, with blond curly hair and large regular features, but his personality is unpleasant. There is a shifting defiance and ingratiation in his light-blue eyes and an irritating aggressiveness in his manner. His clothes and shoes are new, comparatively expensive, sporty in style. He looks as though he belonged in a pool room patronized by would-be sports. He glances around defensively, sees* LARRY *and comes forward*)

PARRITT Hello, Larry. (*He nods to* ROCKY *and* JOE) Hello. (*They nod and size him up with expressionless eyes*)

LARRY (*Without cordiality*) What's up? I thought you'd be asleep.

PARRITT Couldn't make it. I got sick of lying awake. Thought I might as well see if you were around.

LARRY (*Indicates the chair on the right of table*) Sit down and join the bums then. (PARRITT *sits down.* LARRY *adds meaningfully*) The rules of the house are that drinks may be served at all hours.

PARRITT (*Forcing a smile*) I get you. But, hell, I'm just about broke. (*He catches* ROCKY'*s and* JOE'*s contemptuous glances—quickly*) Oh, I know you guys saw— You think I've got a roll. Well, you're all wrong. I'll show you. (*He takes a small wad of dollar bills from his pocket*) It's all ones. And I've got to live on it till I get a job. (*Then with defensive truculence*) You think I fixed up a phony, don't you? Why the hell would I? Where would I get a real roll? You don't get rich doing what I've been doing. Ask Larry. You're lucky in the Movement if you have enough to eat. (LARRY *regards him puzzledly*)

ROCKY (*Coldly*) What's de song and dance about? We ain't said nuttin'.

PARRITT (*Lamely—placating them now*) Why, I was just putting you right. But I don't want you to think I'm a tightwad. I'll buy a drink if you want one.

JOE (*Cheering up*) If? Man, when I don't want a drink, you call de morgue, tell dem come take Joe's body away, 'cause he's sure enuf dead. Gimme de bottle quick, Rocky, before he changes his mind! (ROCKY *passes him the bottle and glass. He pours a brimful drink and tosses it down his throat, and hands the bottle and glass to* LARRY)

ROCKY I'll take a cigar when I go in de bar. What're you havin'?

PARRITT Nothing. I'm on the wagon. What's the damage? (*He holds out a dollar bill*)

ROCKY Fifteen cents. (*He makes change from his pocket*)

PARRITT Must be some booze!

LARRY It's cyanide cut with carbolic acid to give it a mellow flavor. Here's luck! (*He drinks*)

ROCKY Guess I'll get back in de bar and catch a coupla winks before opening-up time. (*He squeezes through the tables and disappears, right-rear, behind the curtain. In the section of bar at right, he comes forward and sits at the table and slumps back, closing his eyes and yawning*)

JOE (*Stares calculatingly at* PARRITT *and then looks away—aloud to himself, philosophically*) One-drink guy. Dat well done run dry. No hope till Harry's birthday party. 'Less Hickey shows up. (*He turns to* LARRY) If Hickey comes, Larry, you wake me up if you has to bat me wid a chair. (*He settles himself and immediately falls asleep*)

PARRITT Who's Hickey?

LARRY A hardware drummer. An old friend of Harry Hope's and all the gang. He's a grand guy. He comes here twice a year regularly on a periodical drunk and blows in all his money.

PARRITT (*With a disparaging glance around*) Must be hard up for a place to hang out.

LARRY It has its points for him. He never runs into anyone he knows in his business here.

PARRITT (*Lowering his voice*) Yes, that's what I want, too. I've got to stay under cover, Larry, like I told you last night.

LARRY You did a lot of hinting. You didn't tell me anything.

PARRITT You can guess, can't you? (*He changes the subject abruptly*) I've been in some dumps on the Coast, but this is the limit. What kind of joint is it, anyway?

LARRY (*With a sardonic grin*) What is it? It's the No Chance Saloon. It's Bedrock Bar, The End of the Line Café, The Bottom of the Sea Rathskeller! Don't you notice the beautiful calm in the atmosphere? That's because it's the last harbor. No one here has to worry about where they're going next, because there is no farther they can go. It's a great comfort to them. Although even here they keep up the appearances of life with a few harmless pipe dreams about their yesterdays and tomorrows, as you'll see for yourself if you're here long.

PARRITT (*Stares at him curiously*) What's your pipe dream, Larry?

LARRY (*Hiding resentment*) Oh, I'm the exception. I haven't any left, thank God. (*Shortly*) Don't complain about this place. You couldn't find a better for lying low.

PARRITT I'm glad of that, Larry. I don't feel any too damned good. I was knocked off my base by that business on the Coast, and since then it's been no fun dodging around the country, thinking every guy you see might be a dick.

LARRY (*Sympathetically now*) No, it wouldn't be. But you're safe here. The cops ignore this dump. They think it's as harmless as a graveyard. (*He grins sardonically*) And, be God, they're right.

PARRITT It's been lonely as hell. (*Impulsively*) Christ, Larry, I was glad to find you. I kept saying to myself, "If I can only find Larry. He's the one guy in the world who can understand—" (*He hesitates, staring at* LARRY *with a strange appeal*)

LARRY (*Watching him puzzledly*) Understand what?

PARRITT (*Hastily*) Why, all I've been through. (*Looking away*) Oh, I know you're thinking, This guy has a hell of a nerve. I haven't seen him since he was a kid. I'd forgotten he was alive. But I've never forgotten you, Larry. You were the only friend of Mother's who ever paid attention to me, or knew I was alive. All the others were too busy with the Movement. Even Mother. And I had no Old Man. You used to take me on your knee and tell me stories and crack jokes and make me laugh. You'd ask me questions and take what I said seriously. I guess I got to feel in the years you lived with us that you'd taken the place of my Old Man. (*Embarrassedly*) But, hell, that sounds like a lot of mush. I suppose you don't remember a damned thing about it.

LARRY (*Moved in spite of himself*) I remember well. You were a serious lonely little shaver. (*Then resenting being moved, changes the subject*) How is it they didn't pick you up when they got your mother and the rest?

PARRITT (*In a lowered voice but eagerly, as if he wanted this chance to tell about it*) I wasn't around, and as soon as I heard the news I went under cover. You've noticed my glad rags. I was staked to them—as a disguise, sort of. I hung around pool rooms and gambling joints and hooker shops, where they'd never look for a Wobblie,[3] pretending I was a sport. Anyway, they'd grabbed everyone important, so I suppose they didn't think of me until afterward.

LARRY The papers say the cops got them all dead to rights, that the Burns dicks knew every move before it was made, and someone inside the Movement must have sold out and tipped them off.

PARRITT (*Turns to look* LARRY *in the eyes—slowly*) Yes, I guess that must be true, Larry. It hasn't come out who it was. It may never come out. I suppose whoever it was made a bargain with the Burns men to keep him out of it. They won't need his evidence.

LARRY (*Tensely*) By God, I hate to believe it of any of the crowd, even if I am through long since with any connection with them. I know they're damned fools, most of them, as stupidly greedy for power as the worst capitalist they attack, but I'd swear there couldn't be a yellow stool pigeon among them.

PARRITT Sure. I'd have sworn that, too, Larry.

LARRY I hope his soul rots in hell, whoever it is!

PARRITT Yes, so do I.

LARRY (*After a pause—shortly*) How did you locate me? I hoped I'd found a place of retirement here where no one in the Movement would ever come to disturb my peace.

PARRITT I found out through Mother.

LARRY I asked her not to tell anyone.

PARRITT She didn't tell me, but she'd kept all your letters and I found where she'd hidden them in the flat. I sneaked up there one night after she was arrested.

LARRY I'd never have thought she was a woman who'd keep letters.

PARRITT No, I wouldn't, either. There's nothing soft or sentimental about Mother.

LARRY I never answered her last letters. I haven't written her in a couple of years—or anyone else. I've gotten beyond the desire to communicate with the world—or, what's more to the point, let it bother me any more with its greedy madness.

PARRITT It's funny Mother kept in touch with you so long. When she's finished with anyone, she's finished. She's always been proud of that. And you know how she feels about the Movement. Like a revivalist preacher about religion. Anyone who loses faith in it

[3] Familiar slang term for a member of the I.W.W. (Industrial Workers of the World).

is more than dead to her; he's a Judas who ought to be boiled in oil. Yet she seemed to forgive you.

LARRY (*Sardonically*) She didn't, don't worry. She wrote to denounce me and try to bring the sinner to repentance and a belief in the One True Faith again.

PARRITT What made you leave the Movement, Larry? Was it on account of Mother?

LARRY (*Starts*) Don't be a damned fool! What the hell put that in your head?

PARRITT Why, nothing—except I remember what a fight you had with her before you left.

LARRY (*Resentfully*) Well, if you do, I don't. That was eleven years ago. You were only seven. If we did quarrel, it was because I told her I'd become convinced the Movement was only a beautiful pipe dream.

PARRITT (*With a strange smile*) I don't remember it that way.

LARRY Then you can blame your imagination—and forget it. (*He changes the subject abruptly*) You asked me why I quit the Movement. I had a lot of good reasons. One was myself, and another was my comrades, and the last was the breed of swine called men in general. For myself, I was forced to admit, at the end of thirty years' devotion to the Cause, that I was never made for it. I was born condemned to be one of those who has to see all sides of a question. When you're damned like that, the questions multiply for you until in the end it's all question and no answer. As history proves, to be a worldly success at anything, especially revolution, you have to wear blinders like a horse and see only straight in front of you. You have to see, too, that this is all black, and that is all white. As for my comrades in the Great Cause, I felt as Horace Walpole did about England, that he could love it if it weren't for the people in it. The material the ideal free society must be constructed from is men themselves and you can't build a marble temple out of a mixture of mud and manure. When man's soul isn't a sow's ear, it will be time enough to dream of silk purses. (*He chuckles sardonically—then irritably as if suddenly provoked at himself for talking so much*) Well, that's why I quit the Movement, if it leaves you any wiser. At any rate, you see it had nothing to do with your mother.

PARRITT (*Smiles almost mockingly*) Oh, sure, I see. But I'll bet Mother has always thought it was on her account. You know her, Larry. To hear her go on sometimes, you'd think she was the Movement.

LARRY (*Stares at him, puzzled and repelled—sharply*) That's a hell of a way for you to talk, after what happened to her!

PARRITT (*At once confused and guilty*) Don't get me wrong. I wasn't sneering, Larry. Only kidding. I've said the same thing to her lots of times to kid her. But you're right. I know I shouldn't now. I keep forgetting she's in jail. It doesn't seem real. I can't believe it about her. She's always been so free. I— But I don't want to think of it. (LARRY *is moved to a puzzled pity in spite of himself.* PARRITT *changes the subject*) What have you been doing all the years since you left—the Coast, Larry?

LARRY (*Sardonically*) Nothing I could help doing. If I don't believe in the Movement, I don't believe in anything else either, especially not the State. I've refused to become a useful member of its society. I've been a philosophical drunken bum, and proud of it. (*Abruptly his tone sharpens with resentful warning*) Listen to me. I hope you've deduced that I've my own reason for answering the impertinent questions of a stranger, for that's all you are to me. I have a strong hunch you've come here expecting something of me. I'm warning you, at the start, so there'll be no misunderstanding, that I've nothing left to give, and I want to be left alone, and I'll thank you to keep your life to yourself. I feel you're looking for some answer to something. I have no answer to give anyone, not even myself. Unless you can call what Heine wrote in his poem to morphine an answer. (*He quotes a translation of the closing couplet sardonically*)

"Lo, sleep is good; better is death; in sooth,
The best of all were never to be born."

PARRITT (*Shrinks a bit frightenedly*) That's the hell of an answer. (*Then with a forced grin of bravado*) Still, you never know when it might come in handy. (*He looks away.* LARRY *stares at him puzzledly, interested in spite of himself and at the same time vaguely uneasy*)

LARRY (*Forcing a casual tone*) I don't suppose you've had much chance to hear news of your mother since she's been in jail?

PARRITT No. No chance. (*He hesitates—then blurts out*) Anyway, I don't think she wants to hear from me. We had a fight just before that business happened. She bawled me out because I was going around with tarts. That got my goat, coming from her. I told her, "You've always acted the free woman, you've never let anything stop you from—" (*He checks himself—goes on hurriedly*) That made her sore. She said she wouldn't give a damn what I did except she'd begun to suspect I was too interested in outside things and losing interest in the Movement.

LARRY (*Stares at him*) And were you?

PARRITT (*Hesitates—then with intensity*) Sure I was! I'm no damned fool! I couldn't go on believing forever that gang was going to change the world by shooting off their loud traps on soapboxes and sneaking around blowing up a lousy building or a bridge! I got wise it was all a crazy pipe dream! (*Appealingly*) The same as you did, Larry. That's why I came to you. I knew you'd understand. What finished me was this last business of someone selling out. How can you believe anything after a thing like that happens? It knocks you cold! You don't know what the hell is what! You're through! (*Appealingly*) You know how I feel, don't you, Larry? (LARRY *stares at him, moved by sympathy and pity in spite of himself, disturbed, and resentful at being disturbed, and puzzled by something he feels about* PARRITT *that isn't right. But before he can reply,* HUGO *suddenly raises his head from his arms in a half-awake alcoholic daze and speaks*)

HUGO (*Quotes aloud to himself in a guttural declamatory style*) "The days grow hot, O Babylon! 'Tis cool beneath thy villow trees!" (PARRITT *turns startledly as* HUGO *peers muzzily without recognition at him.* HUGO *exclaims automatically in his tone of denunciation*) Gottammed stool pigeon!

PARRITT (*Shrinks away—stammers*) What? Who do you mean? (*Then furiously*) You lousy bum, you can't call me that! (*He draws back his fist*)

HUGO (*Ignores this—recognizing him now, bursts into his childish teasing giggle*) Hello, leedle Don! Leedle monkey-face. I did not recognize you. You have grown big boy. How is your mother? Where you come from? (*He breaks into his wheedling, bullying tone*) Don't be a fool! Loan me a dollar! Buy me a trink! (*As if this exhausted him, he abruptly forgets it and plumps his head down on his arms again and is asleep*)

PARRITT (*With eager relief*) Sure, I'll buy you a drink, Hugo. I'm broke, but I can afford one for you. I'm sorry I got sore. I ought to have remembered when you're soused you call everyone a stool pigeon. But it's no damned joke right at this time. (*He turns to* LARRY, *who is regarding him now fixedly with an uneasy expression as if he suddenly were afraid of his own thoughts—forcing a smile*) Gee, he's passed out again. (*He stiffens defensively*) What are you giving me the hard look for? Oh, I know. You thought I was going to hit him? What do you think I am? I've always had a lot of respect for Hugo. I've always stood up for him when people in the Movement panned him for an old drunken has-been. He had the guts to serve ten years in the can in his own country and get his eyes ruined in solitary. I'd like to see some of them here stick that. Well, they'll get a chance now to show— (*Hastily*) I don't mean— But let's forget that. Tell me some more about this dump. Who are all these tanks? Who's that guy trying to catch pneumonia? (*He indicates* LEWIS)

LARRY (*Stares at him almost frightenedly—then looks away and grasps eagerly this chance to change the subject. He begins to describe the sleepers with sardonic relish but at the same time showing his affection for them*) That's Captain Lewis, a one-time hero of the British Army. He strips to display that scar on his back he got from a native spear whenever he's completely plastered. The bewhiskered bloke opposite him is General Wetjoen, who led a commando in the War. The two of them met when they came here to work in the Boer War spectacle at the St. Louis Fair and they've been bosom pals ever since. They dream the hours away in happy dispute over the brave days in South Africa when they tried to murder each other. The little guy between them was in it, too, as correspondent for some English paper. His nickname here is Jimmy Tomorrow. He's the leader of our Tomorrow Movement.

PARRITT What do they do for a living?

LARRY As little as possible. Once in a while one of them makes a successful touch somewhere, and some of them get a few dollars a month from connections at home who pay it on condition they never come back. For the rest, they live on free lunch and their old friend, Harry Hope, who doesn't give a damn what anyone does or doesn't do, as long as he likes you.

PARRITT It must be a tough life.

LARRY It's not. Don't waste your pity. They wouldn't thank you for it. They manage to get drunk, by hook or crook, and keep their pipe dreams, and that's all they ask of life. I've never known more contented men. It isn't often that men attain the true goal of their heart's desire. The same applies to Harry himself and his two cronies at the far table. He's so satisfied with life he's never set foot out of this place since his wife died twenty years ago. He has no need of the outside world at all. This place has a fine trade from the Market people across the street and the waterfront workers, so in spite of Harry's thirst and his generous heart, he comes out even. He never worries in hard times because there's always old friends from the days when he was a jitney Tammany politician, and a friendly brewery to tide him over. Don't ask me what his two pals work at because they don't. Except at being his lifetime guests. The one facing this way is his brother-in-law, Ed Mosher, who once worked for a circus in the ticket wagon. Pat McGloin, the other one, was a police lieutenant back in the flush times of graft when everything went. But he got too greedy and when the usual reform investigation came he was caught red-handed and thrown off the Force. (*He nods at* JOE) Joe here has a yesterday in the same flush period. He ran a colored gambling house then and was a hell of a sport, so they say. Well, that's our whole family circle of inmates, except the two barkeeps and their girls, three ladies of the pavement that room on the third floor.

PARRITT (*Bitterly*) To hell with them! I never want to see a whore again! (*As* LARRY *flashes him a puzzled glance, he adds confusedly*) I mean, they always get you in dutch. (*While he is speaking* WILLIE OBAN *has opened his eyes. He leans toward them, drunk now from the effect of the huge drink he took, and speaks with a mocking suavity*)

WILLIE Why omit me from your Who's Who in Dypsomania, Larry? An unpardonable slight, especially as I am the only inmate of royal blood. (*To* PARRITT *—ramblingly*) Educated at Harvard, too. You must have noticed the atmosphere of culture here. My humble contribution. Yes, Generous Stranger—I trust you're generous—I was born in the purple, the son, but unfortunately not the heir, of the late world-famous Bill Oban, King of the Bucket Shops. A revolution deposed him, conducted by the District Attorney. He was sent into exile. In fact, not to mince matters, they locked him in the can and threw away the key. Alas, his was an adventurous spirit that pined in confinement. And so he died. Forgive these reminiscences. Undoubtedly all this is well known to you. Everyone in the world knows.

PARRITT (*Uncomfortably*) Tough luck. No, I never heard of him.

WILLIE (*Blinks at him incredulously*) Never heard? I thought everyone in the world— Why, even at Harvard I discovered my father was well known by reputation, although that was some time before the District Attorney gave him so much unwelcome publicity. Yes, even as a freshman I was notorious. I was accepted socially with all the warm cordiality that Henry Wadsworth Longfellow would have shown a drunken Negress dancing the can can at high noon on Brattle Street. Harvard was my father's idea. He was an ambitious man. Dictatorial, too. Always knowing what was best for me. But I did make myself a brilliant student. A dirty trick on my classmates, inspired by revenge, I fear. (*He quotes*) "Dear college days, with pleasure rife! The grandest gladdest days of life!" But, of course, that is a Yale hymn, and they're given to rah-rah exaggeration at New Haven. I was a brilliant student at Law School, too. My father wanted a lawyer in the family. He was a calculating man. A thorough knowledge of the law close at hand in the house to help him find fresh ways to evade it. But I discovered the loophole of whiskey and escaped his jurisdiction. (*Abruptly to* PARRITT) Speaking of whiskey, sir, reminds me—and, I hope, reminds you—that when meeting a Prince the customary salutation is "What'll you have?"

PARRITT (*With defensive resentment*) Nix! All you guys seem to think I'm made of dough. Where would I get the coin to blow everyone?

WILLIE (*Skeptically*) Broke? You haven't the thirsty look of the impecunious. I'd judge you to be a plutocrat, your pockets stuffed with ill-gotten gains. Two or three dollars, at least. And don't think we will question how you got it. As Vespasian remarked, the smell of all whiskey is sweet.

PARRITT What do you mean, how I got it? (*To* LARRY, *forcing a laugh*) It's a laugh, calling me a plutocrat, isn't it, Larry, when I've been in the Movement all my life. (LARRY *gives him an uneasy suspicious glance, then looks away, as if avoiding something he does not wish to see*)

WILLIE (*Disgustedly*) Ah, one of those, eh? I believe you now, all right! Go away and blow yourself up, that's a good lad. Hugo is the only licensed preacher of that gospel here. A dangerous terrorist, Hugo! He would as soon blow the collar off a schooner of beer as look at you! (*To* LARRY) Let us ignore this useless youth, Larry. Let us join in prayer that Hickey, the Great Salesman, will soon arrive bringing the blessed bourgeois long green! Would that Hickey or Death would come! Meanwhile, I will sing a song. A beautiful old New England folk ballad which I picked up at Harvard amid the debris of education. (*He sings in a boisterous baritone, rapping on the table with his knuckles at the indicated spots in the song*)

"Jack, oh, Jack, was a sailor lad
And he came to a tavern for gin.
He rapped and he rapped with a (*Rap, rap, rap*)
But never a soul seemed in."

(*The drunks at the tables stir.* ROCKY *gets up from his chair in the bar and starts back for the entrance to the back room.* HOPE *cocks one irritable eye over his specs.* JOE MOTT *opens both of his and grins.* WILLIE *interposes some drunken whimsical exposition to* LARRY) The origin of this beautiful ditty is veiled in mystery, Larry. There was a legend bruited about in Cambridge lavatories that Waldo Emerson composed it during his uninformative period as a minister, while he was trying to write a sermon. But my own opinion is, it goes back much further, and Jonathan Edwards was the author of both words and music. (*He sings*)

"He rapped and rapped, and tapped and tapped
Enough to wake the dead
Till he heard a damsel (*Rap, rap, rap*)
On a window right over his head."

(*The drunks are blinking their eyes now, grumbling and cursing.* ROCKY *appears from the bar at rear, right, yawning*)

HOPE (*With fuming irritation*) Rocky! Bejees, can't you keep that crazy bastard quiet? (ROCKY *starts for* WILLIE)

WILLIE And now the influence of a good woman enters our mariner's life. Well, perhaps "good" isn't the word. But very, very kind. (*He sings*)

"Oh, come up," she cried, "my sailor lad,
And you and I'll agree,
And I'll show you the prettiest (*Rap, rap, rap*)
That ever you did see."

(*He speaks*) You see, Larry? The lewd Puritan touch, obviously, and it grows more marked as we go on. (*He sings*)

"Oh, he put his arm around her waist,
He gazed in her bright blue eyes
And then he—"

(*But here* ROCKY *shakes him roughly by the shoulder*)

ROCKY *Piano!*[4] What d'yuh tink dis dump is, a dump?

HOPE Give him the bum's rush upstairs! Lock him in his room!

ROCKY (*Yanks* WILLIE *by the arm*) Come on, Bum.

WILLIE (*Dissolves into pitiable terror*) No! Please, Rocky! I'll go crazy up in that room alone! It's haunted! I— (*He calls to* HOPE) Please, Harry! Let me stay here! I'll be quiet!

HOPE (*Immediately relents—indignantly*) What the hell you doing to him, Rocky? I didn't tell you to beat up the poor guy. Leave him alone, long as he's quiet. (ROCKY *lets go of* WILLIE *disgustedly and goes back to his chair in the bar*)

WILLIE (*Huskily*) Thanks, Harry. You're a good scout. (*He closes his eyes and sinks back in his chair exhaustedly, twitching and quivering again*)

[4] Quiet! (Italian)

HOPE (*Addressing* MCGLOIN *and* MOSHER, *who are sleepily awake—accusingly*) Always the way. Can't trust nobody. Leave it to that Dago to keep order and it's like bedlam in a cathouse, singing and everything. And you two big barflies are a hell of a help to me, ain't you? Eat and sleep and get drunk! All you're good for, bejees! Well, you can take that "I'll-have-the-same" look off your maps! There ain't going to be no more drinks on the house till hell freezes over! (*Neither of the two is impressed either by his insults or his threats. They grin hangover grins of tolerant affection at him and wink at each other.* HARRY *fumes*) Yeah, grin! Wink, bejees! Fine pair of sons of bitches to have glued on me for life! (*But he can't get a rise out of them and he subsides into a fuming mumble. Meanwhile, at the middle table,* CAPTAIN LEWIS *and* GENERAL WETJOEN *are as wide awake as heavy hangovers permit.* JIMMY TOMORROW *nods, his eyes blinking.* LEWIS *is gazing across the table at* JOE MOTT, *who is still chuckling to himself over* WILLIE'S *song. The expression on* LEWIS'S *face is that of one who can't believe his eyes*)

LEWIS (*Aloud to himself, with a muzzy wonder*) Good God! Have I been drinking at the same table with a bloody Kaffir?

JOE (*Grinning*) Hello, Captain. You comin' up for air? Kaffir? Who's he?

WETJOEN (*Blurrily*) Kaffir, dot's a nigger, Joe. (JOE *stiffens and his eyes narrow.* WETJOEN *goes on with heavy jocosity*) Dot's joke on him, Joe. He don't know you. He's still plind drunk, the ploody Limey chentleman! A great mistake I missed him at the pattle of Modder River.[5] Vit mine rifle I shoot damn fool Limey officers py the dozen, but him I miss. De pity of it! (*He chuckles and slaps* LEWIS *on his bare shoulder*) Hey, wake up, Cecil, you ploody fool! Don't you know your old friend, Joe? He's no damned Kaffir! He's white, Joe is!

LEWIS (*Light dawning—contritely*) My profound apologies, Joseph, old chum. Eyesight a trifle blurry, I'm afraid. Whitest colored man I ever knew. Proud to call you my friend. No hard feelings, what? (*He holds out his hand*)

JOE (*At once grins good-naturedly and shakes his hand*) No, Captain, I know it's mistake. Youse regular, if you is a Limey. (*Then his face hardening*) But I don't stand for "nigger" from nobody. Never did. In de old days, people calls me "nigger" wakes up in de hospital. I was de leader ob de Dirty Half-Dozen Gang. All six of us colored boys, we was tough and I was de toughest.

WETJOEN (*Inspired to boastful reminiscence*) Me, in old days in Transvaal, I vas so tough and strong I grab axle of ox wagon mit full load and lift like feather.

LEWIS (*Smiling amiably*) As for you, my balmy Boer that walks like a man, I say again it was a grave error in our foreign policy ever to set you free, once we nabbed you and your commando with Cronje.[6] We should have taken you to the London zoo and incarcerated you in the baboons' cage. With a sign: "Spectators may distinguish the true baboon by his blue behind."

WETJOEN (*Grins*) Gott! To dink, ten better Limey officers, at least, I shoot clean in the mittle of forehead at Spion Kopje,[7] and you I miss! I neffer forgive myself! (JIMMY TOMORROW *blinks benignantly from one to the other with a gentle drunken smile*)

JIMMY (*Sentimentally*) Now, come, Cecil, Piet! We must forget the War. Boer and Briton, each fought fairly and played the game till the better man won and then we shook hands. We are all brothers within the Empire united beneath the flag on which the sun never sets. (*Tears come to his eyes. He quotes with great sentiment, if with slight application*) "Ship me somewhere east of Suez—"

LARRY (*Breaks in sardonically*) Be God, you're there already, Jimmy. Worst is best here, and East is West, and tomorrow is yesterday. What more do you want?

JIMMY (*With bleary benevolence, shaking his head in mild rebuke*) No, Larry, old friend, you can't deceive me. You pretend a bitter, cynic philosophy, but in your heart you are the kindest man among us.

LARRY (*Disconcerted—irritably*) The hell you say!

PARRITT (*Leans toward him—confidentially*) What a bunch of cuckoos!

JIMMY (*As if reminded of something—with a pathetic attempt at a brisk, no-more-nonsense air*) Tomorrow, yes. It's high time I straightened out and got down to business again. (*He brushes his sleeve fastidiously*) I must have this suit cleaned and pressed. I can't look like a tramp when I—

JOE (*Who has been brooding—interrupts*) Yes, suh, white folks always said I was white. In de days when I was flush, Joe Mott's de only colored man dey allows in de white gamblin' houses. "You're all right, Joe, you're white," dey says. (*He chuckles*) Wouldn't let me play craps, dough. Dey know I could make dem dice behave. "Any odder game and any limit you like, Joe," dey says. Man, de money I lost! (*He chuckles—then with an underlying defensiveness*) Look at de Big Chief in dem days. He knew I was white. I'd saved my dough so I could start my own gamblin' house. Folks in de know tells me, see de man at de top, den you never has trouble. You git Harry Hope give you a letter to de Chief. And Harry does. Don't you, Harry?

HOPE (*Preoccupied with his own thoughts*) Eh? Sure. Big Bill was a good friend of mine. I had plenty of friends high up in those days. Still could have if I wanted to go out and see them. Sure, I gave you a letter. I said you was white. What the hell of it?

JOE (*To* CAPTAIN LEWIS *who has relapsed into a sleepy*

[5] An early and decisive engagement in the Boer War (November, 1899); it was a controversial and expensive British victory.

[6] P. A. Cronje, leader of the Transvaal forces; his surrender to Lord Roberts at Paardeberg (February, 1900) marked the beginning of the end of the war.

[7] A small mountain in Natal, seized but later abandoned by the British under severe attack by the Boers (January, 1900).

*daze and is listening to him with an absurd strained attention without comprehending a word*) Dere. You see, Captain. I went to see de Chief, shakin' in my boots, and dere he is sittin' behind a big desk, lookin' as big as a freight train. He don't look up. He keeps me waitin' and waitin', and after 'bout an hour, seems like to me, he says slow and quiet like dere wasn't no harm in him, "You want to open a gamblin' joint, does you, Joe?" But he don't give me no time to answer. He jumps up, lookin' as big as two freight trains, and he pounds his fist like a ham on de desk, and he shouts, "You black son of a bitch, Harry says you're white and you better be white or dere's a little iron room up de river waitin' for you!" Den he sits down and says quiet again, "All right. You can open. Git de hell outa here!" So I opens, and he finds out I'se white, sure 'nuff, 'cause I run wide open for years and pays my sugar on de dot, and de cops and I is friends. (*He chuckles with pride*) Dem old days! Many's de night I come in here. Dis was a first-class hangout for sports in dem days. Good whiskey, fifteen cents, two for two bits. I t'rows down a fifty-dollar bill like it was trash paper and says, "Drink it up, boys, I don't want no change." Ain't dat right, Harry?

HOPE (*Caustically*) Yes, and bejees, if I ever seen you throw fifty cents on the bar now, I'd know I had delirium tremens! You've told that story ten million times and if I have to hear it again, that'll give me D.T.s anyway!

JOE (*Chuckling*) Gittin' drunk every day for twenty years ain't give you de Brooklyn boys. You needn't be scared of me!

LEWIS (*Suddenly turns and beams on* HOPE) Thank you, Harry, old chum. I will have a drink, now you mention it, seeing it's so near your birthday. (*The others laugh*)

HOPE (*Puts his hand to his ear—angrily*) What's that? I can't hear you.

LEWIS (*Sadly*) No, I fancied you wouldn't.

HOPE I don't have to hear, bejees! Booze is the only thing you ever talk about!

LEWIS (*Sadly*) True. Yet there was a time when my conversation was more comprehensive. But as I became burdened with years, it seemed rather pointless to discuss my other subject.

HOPE You can't joke with me! How much room rent do you owe me, tell me that?

LEWIS Sorry. Adding has always baffled me. Subtraction is my forte.

HOPE (*Snarling*) Arrh! Think you're funny! Captain, bejees! Showing off your wounds! Put on your clothes, for Christ's sake! This ain't no Turkish bath! Lousy Limey army! Took 'em years to lick a gang of Dutch hayseeds!

WETJOEN Dot's right, Harry. Gif him hell!

HOPE No lip out of you, neither, you Dutch spinach! General, hell! Salvation Army, that's what you'd ought t'been General in! Bragging what a shot you were, and, bejees, you missed him! And he missed you, that's just as bad! And now the two of you bum on me! (*Threateningly*) But you've broke the camel's back this time, bejees! You pay up tomorrow or out you go!

LEWIS (*Earnestly*) My dear fellow, I give you my word of honor as an officer and a gentleman, you shall be paid tomorrow.

WETJOEN Ve swear it, Harry! Tomorrow vidout fail!

MCGLOIN (*A twinkle in his eye*) There you are, Harry. Sure, what could be fairer?

MOSHER (*With a wink at* MCGLOIN) Yes, you can't ask more than that, Harry. A promise is a promise—as I've often discovered.

HOPE (*Turns on them*) I mean the both of you, too! An old grafting flatfoot and a circus bunco steerer![8] Fine company for me, bejees! Couple of con men living in my flat since Christ knows when! Getting fat as hogs, too! And you ain't even got the decency to get me upstairs where I got a good bed! Let me sleep on a chair like a bum! Kept me down here waitin' for Hickey to show up, hoping I'd blow you to more drinks!

MCGLOIN Ed and I did our damnedest to get you up, didn't we, Ed?

MOSHER We did. But you said you couldn't bear the flat because it was one of those nights when memory brought poor old Bessie back to you.

HOPE (*His face instantly becoming long and sad and sentimental—mournfully*) Yes, that's right, boys. I remember now. I could almost see her in every room just as she used to be—and it's twenty years since she— (*His throat and eyes fill up. A suitable sentimental hush falls on the room*)

LARRY (*In a sardonic whisper to* PARRITT) Isn't a pipe dream of yesterday a touching thing? By all accounts, Bessie nagged the hell out of him.

JIMMY (*Who has been dreaming, a look of prim resolution on his face, speaks aloud to himself*) No more of this sitting around and loafing. Time I took hold of myself. I must have my shoes soled and heeled and shined first thing tomorrow morning. A general spruce-up. I want to have a well-groomed appearance when I— (*His voice fades out as he stares in front of him. No one pays any attention to him except* LARRY *and* PARRITT)

LARRY (*As before, in a sardonic aside to* PARRITT) The tomorrow movement is a sad and beautiful thing, too!

MCGLOIN (*With a huge sentimental sigh—and a calculating look at* HOPE) Poor old Bessie! You don't find her like in these days. A sweeter woman never drew breath.

MOSHER (*In a similar calculating mood*) Good old Bess. A man couldn't want a better sister than she was to me.

HOPE (*Mournfully*) Twenty years, and I've never set foot out of this house since the day I buried her. Didn't have the heart. Once she'd gone, I didn't give a damn for anything. I lost all my ambition. Without her, nothing seemed worth the trouble. You remember, Ed, you, too, Mac—the boys was going to nomi-

[8] A decoy in a swindling operation, useful for "convincing" the unsure victim.

nate me for Alderman. It was all fixed. Bessie wanted it and she was so proud. But when she was taken, I told them, "No, boys, I can't do it. I simply haven't the heart. I'm through." I would have won the election easy, too. (*He says this a bit defiantly*) Oh, I know there was jealous wise guys said the boys was giving me the nomination because they knew they couldn't win that year in this ward. But that's a damned lie! I knew every man, woman and child in the ward, almost. Bessie made me make friends with everyone, helped me remember all their names. I'd have been elected easy.

MCGLOIN You would, Harry. It was a sure thing.

MOSHER A dead cinch, Harry. Everyone knows that.

HOPE Sure they do. But after Bessie died, I didn't have the heart. Still, I know while she'd appreciate my grief, she wouldn't want it to keep me cooped up in here all my life. So I've made up my mind I'll go out soon. Take a walk around the ward, see all the friends I used to know, get together with the boys and maybe tell 'em I'll let 'em deal me a hand in their game again. Yes, bejees, I'll do it. My birthday, tomorrow, that'd be the right time to turn over a new leaf. Sixty. That ain't too old.

MCGLOIN (*Flatteringly*) It's the prime of life, Harry.

MOSHER Wonderful thing about you, Harry, you keep young as you ever was.

JIMMY (*Dreaming aloud again*) Get my things from the laundry. They must still have them. Clean collar and shirt. If I wash the ones I've got on any more, they'll fall apart. Socks, too. I want to make a good appearance. I met Dick Trumbull on the street a year or two ago. He said, "Jimmy, the publicity department's never been the same since you got—resigned. It's dead as hell." I said, "I know. I've heard rumors the management were at their wits' end and would be only too glad to have me run it for them again. I think all I'd have to do would be go and see them and they'd offer me the position. Don't you think so, Dick?" He said, "Sure, they would, Jimmy. Only take my advice and wait a while until business conditions are better. Then you can strike them for a bigger salary than you got before, do you see?" I said, "Yes, I do see, Dick, and many thanks for the tip." Well, conditions must be better by this time. All I have to do is get fixed up with a decent front tomorrow, and it's as good as done.

HOPE (*Glances at* JIMMY *with a condescending affectionate pity—in a hushed voice*) Poor Jimmy's off on his pipe dream again. Bejees, he takes the cake! (*This is too much for* LARRY. *He cannot restrain a sardonic guffaw. But no one pays any attention to him*)

LEWIS (*Opens his eyes, which are drowsing again—dreamily to* WETJOEN) I'm sorry we had to postpone our trip again this April, Piet. I hoped the blasted old estate would be settled up by then. The damned lawyers can't hold up the settlement much longer. We'll make it next year, even if we have to work and earn our passage money, eh? You'll stay with me at the old place as long as you like, then you can take the *Union Castle* from Southampton to Cape Town. (*Sentimentally, with real yearning*) England in April. I want you to see that, Piet. The old veldt has its points, I'll admit, but it isn't home—especially home in April.

WETJOEN (*Blinks drowsily at him—dreamily*) Ja, Cecil, I know how beautiful it must be, from all you tell me many times. I vill enjoy it. But I shall enjoy more ven I am home, too. The veldt, ja! You could put England on it, and it would look like a farmer's small garden. Py Gott, there is space to be free, the air like vine is, you don't need booze to be drunk! My relations vill so surprised be. They vill not know me, it is so many years. Dey vill be so glad I haf come home at last.

JOE (*Dreamily*) I'll make my stake and get my new gamblin' house open before you boys leave. You got to come to de openin'. I'll treat you white. If you're broke, I'll stake you to buck any game you chooses. If you wins, dat's velvet for you. If you loses, it don't count. Can't treat you no whiter dan dat, can I?

HOPE (*Again with condescending pity*) Bejees, Jimmy's started them off smoking the same hop. (*But the three are finished, their eyes closed again in sleep or a drowse*)

LARRY (*Aloud to himself—in his comically tense, crazy whisper*) Be God, this bughouse will drive me stark, raving loony yet!

HOPE (*Turns on him with fuming suspicion*) What? What d'you say?

LARRY (*Placatingly*) Nothing, Harry. I had a crazy thought in my head.

HOPE (*Irascibly*) Crazy is right! Yah! The old wise guy! Wise, hell! A damned old fool Anarchist I-Won't-Worker! [9] I'm sick of you and Hugo, too. Bejees, you'll pay up tomorrow, or I'll start a Harry Hope Revolution! I'll tie a dispossess bomb to your tails that'll blow you out in the street! Bejees, I'll make your Movement move! (*The witticism delights him and he bursts into a shrill cackle. At once* MCGLOIN *and* MOSHER *guffaw enthusiastically*)

MOSHER (*Flatteringly*) Harry, you sure say the funniest things! (*He reaches on the table as if he expected a glass to be there—then starts with well-acted surprise*) Hell, where's my drink? That Rocky is too damned fast cleaning tables. Why, I'd only take one sip of it.

HOPE (*His smiling face congealing*) No, you don't! (*Acidly*) Any time you only take one sip of a drink, you'll have lockjaw and paralysis! Think you can kid me with those old circus con games?—me, that's known you since you was knee-high, and, bejees, you was a crook even then!

MCGLOIN (*Grinning*) It's not like you to be so hard-hearted, Harry. Sure, it's hot, parching work laughing at your jokes so early in the morning on an empty stomach!

HOPE Yah! You, Mac! Another crook! Who asked you to laugh? We was talking about poor old Bessie, and you and her no-good brother start to laugh! A hell of

[9] A member of the I.W.W.

a thing! Talking mush about her, too! "Good old Bess." Bejees, she'd never forgive me if she knew I had you two bums living in her flat, throwing ashes and cigar butts on her carpet. You know her opinion of you, Mac. "That Pat McGloin is the biggest drunken grafter that ever disgraced the police force," she used to say to me. "I hope they send him to Sing Sing for life."

MCGLOIN (*Unperturbed*) She didn't mean it. She was angry at me because you used to get me drunk. But Bess had a heart of gold underneath her sharpness. She knew I was innocent of all the charges.

WILLIE (*Jumps to his feet drunkenly and points a finger at* MCGLOIN*—imitating the manner of a cross-examiner—coldly*) One moment, please. Lieutenant McGloin! Are you aware you are under oath? Do you realize what the penalty for perjury is? (*Purringly*) Come now, Lieutenant, isn't it a fact that you're as guilty as hell? No, don't say, "How about your old man?" I am asking the questions. The fact that he was a crooked old bucket-shop bastard has no bearing on your case. (*With a change to maudlin joviality*) Gentlemen of the Jury, court will now recess while the D.A. sings out a little ditty he learned at Harvard. It was composed in a wanton moment by the Dean of the Divinity School on a moonlight night in July, 1776, while sobering up in a Turkish bath. (*He sings*)

"Oh, come up," she cried, "my sailor lad,
And you and I'll agree.
And I'll show you the prettiest (*Rap, rap, rap on table*)
That ever you did see."

(*Suddenly he catches* HOPE'S *eyes fixed on him condemningly, and sees* ROCKY *appearing from the bar. He collapses back on his chair, pleading miserably*) Please, Harry! I'll be quiet! Don't make Rocky bounce me upstairs! I'll go crazy alone! (*To* MCGLOIN) I apologize, Mac. Don't get sore. I was only kidding you. (ROCKY, *at a relenting glance from* HOPE, *returns to the bar*)

MCGLOIN (*Good-naturedly*) Sure, kid all you like, Willie. I'm hardened to it. (*He pauses—seriously*) But I'm telling you some day before long I'm going to make them reopen my case. Everyone knows there was no real evidence against me, and I took the fall for the ones higher up. I'll be found innocent this time and reinstated. (*Wistfully*) I'd like to have my old job on the Force back. The boys tell me there's fine pickings these days, and I'm not getting rich here, sitting with a parched throat waiting for Harry Hope to buy a drink. (*He glances reproachfully at* HOPE)

WILLIE Of course, you'll be reinstated, Mac. All you need is a brilliant young attorney to handle your case. I'll be straightened out and on the wagon in a day or two. I've never practiced but I was one of the most brilliant students in Law School, and your case is just the opportunity I need to start. (*Darkly*) Don't worry about my not forcing the D.A. to reopen your case. I went through my father's papers befoie the cops destroyed them, and I remember a lot of people, even if I can't prove— (*Coaxingly*) You will let me take your case, won't you, Mac?

MCGLOIN (*Soothingly*) Sure I will and it'll make your reputation, Willie. (MOSHER *winks at* HOPE, *shaking his head, and* HOPE *answers with identical pantomime, as though to say, "Poor dopes, they're off again!"*)

LARRY (*Aloud to himself more than to* PARRITT*—with irritable wonder*) Ah, be damned! Haven't I heard their visions a thousand times? Why should they get under my skin now? I've got the blues, I guess. I wish to hell Hickey'd turn up.

MOSHER (*Calculatingly solicitous—whispering to* HOPE) Poor Willie needs a drink bad, Harry—and I think if we all joined him it'd make him feel he was among friends and cheer him up.

HOPE More circus con tricks! (*Scathingly*) You talking of your dear sister! Bessie had you sized up. She used to tell me, "I don't know what you can see in that worthless, drunken, petty-larceny brother of mine. If I had my way," she'd say, "he'd get booted out in the gutter on his fat behind." Sometimes she didn't say behind, either.

MOSHER (*Grins genially*) Yes, dear old Bess had a quick temper, but there was no real harm in her. (*He chuckles reminiscently*) Remember the time she sent me down to the bar to change a ten-dollar bill for her?

HOPE (*Has to grin himself*) Bejees, do I! She coulda bit a piece out of a stove lid, after she found it out. (*He cackles appreciatively*)

MOSHER I was sure surprised when she gave me the ten spot. Bess usually had better sense, but she was in a hurry to go to church. I didn't really mean to do it, but you know how habit gets you. Besides, I still worked then, and the circus season was going to begin soon, and I needed a little practice to keep my hand in. Or, you never can tell, the first rube that came to my wagon for a ticket might have left with the right change and I'd be disgraced. (*He chuckles*) I said, "I'm sorry, Bess, but I had to take it all in dimes. Here, hold out your hands and I'll count it out for you, so you won't kick afterwards I short-changed you." (*He begins a count which grows more rapid as he goes on*) Ten, twenty, thirty, forty, fifty, sixty, seventy, eighty, ninety, a dollar. Ten, twenty, thirty, forty, fifty, sixty— You're counting with me, Bess, aren't you?—eighty, ninety, two dollars. Ten, twenty— Those are pretty shoes you got on, Bess—forty, fifty, seventy, eighty, ninety, three dollars. Ten, twenty, thirty— What's on at the church tonight, Bess?—fifty, sixty, seventy, ninety, four dollars. Ten, twenty, thirty, fifty, seventy, eighty, ninety— That's a swell new hat, Bess, looks very becoming—six dollars. (*He chuckles*) And so on. I'm bum at it now for lack of practice, but in those days I could have short-changed the Keeper of the Mint.

HOPE (*Grinning*) Stung her for two dollars and a half, wasn't it, Ed?

MOSHER Yes. A fine percentage, if I do say so, when you're dealing to someone who's sober and can count.

I'm sorry to say she discovered my mistakes in arithmetic just after I beat it around the corner. She counted it over herself. Bess somehow never had the confidence in me a sister should. (*He sighs tenderly*) Dear old Bess.

HOPE (*Indignant now*) You're a fine guy bragging how you short-changed your own sister! Bejees, if there was a war and you was in it, they'd have to padlock the pockets of the dead!

MOSHER (*A bit hurt at this*) That's going pretty strong, Harry. I always gave a sucker some chance. There wouldn't be no fun robbing the dead. (*He becomes reminiscently melancholy*) Gosh, thinking of the old ticket wagon brings those days back. The greatest life on earth with the greatest show on earth! The grandest crowd of regular guys ever gathered under one tent! I'd sure like to shake their hands again!

HOPE (*Acidly*) They'd have guns in theirs. They'd shoot you on sight. You've touched every damned one of them. Bejees, you've even borrowed fish from the trained seals and peanuts from every elephant that remembered you! (*This fancy tickles him and he gives a cackling laugh*)

MOSHER (*Overlooking this—dreamily*) You know, Harry, I've made up my mind I'll see the boss in a couple of days and ask for my old job. I can get back my magic touch with change easy, and I can throw him a line of bull that'll kid him I won't be so unreasonable about sharing the profits next time. (*With insinuating complaint*) There's no percentage in hanging around this dive, taking care of you and shooing away your snakes, when I don't even get an eye-opener for my trouble.

HOPE (*Implacably*) No! (MOSHER *sighs and gives up and closes his eyes. The others, except* LARRY *and* PARRITT, *are all dozing again now.* HOPE *goes on grumbling*) Go to hell or the circus, for all I care. Good riddance, bejees! I'm sick of you! (*Then worriedly*) Say, Ed, what the hell you think's happened to Hickey? I hope he'll turn up. Always got a million funny stories. You and the other bums have begun to give me the graveyard fantods. I'd like a good laugh with old Hickey. (*He chuckles at a memory*) Remember that gag he always pulls about his wife and the iceman? He'd make a cat laugh! (ROCKY *appears from the bar. He comes front, behind* MOSHER'*s chair, and begins pushing the black curtain along the rod to the rear wall*)

ROCKY Openin' time, Boss. (*He presses a button at rear which switches off the lights. The back room becomes drabber and dingier than ever in the gray daylight that comes from the street windows, off right, and what light can penetrate the grime of the two backyard windows at left.* ROCKY *turns back to* HOPE *—grumpily*) Why don't you go up to bed, Boss? Hickey'd never turn up dis time of de mornin'!

HOPE (*Starts and listens*) Someone's coming now.

ROCKY (*Listens*) Aw, dat's on'y my two pigs. It's about time dey showed. (*He goes back toward the door at left of the bar*)

HOPE (*Sourly disappointed*) You keep them dumb broads quiet. I don't want to go to bed. I'm going to catch a couple more winks here and I don't want no damn-fool laughing and screeching. (*He settles himself in his chair, grumbling*) Never thought I'd see the day when Harry Hope's would have tarts rooming in it. What'd Bessie think? But I don't let 'em use my rooms for business. And they're good kids. Good as anyone else. They got to make a living. Pay their rent, too, which is more than I can say for— (*He cocks an eye over his specs at* MOSHER *and grins with satisfaction*) Bejees, Ed, I'll bet Bessie is doing somersaults in her grave! (*He chuckles. But* MOSHER'*s eyes are closed, his head nodding, and he doesn't reply, so* HOPE *closes his eyes.* ROCKY *has opened the barroom door at rear and is standing in the hall beyond it, facing right. A girl's laugh is heard*)

ROCKY (*Warningly*) Nix! *Piano!* (*He comes in, beckoning them to follow. He goes behind the bar and gets a whiskey bottle and glasses and chairs.* MARGIE *and* PEARL *follow him, casting a glance around. Everyone except* LARRY *and* PARRITT *is asleep or dozing. Even* PARRITT *has his eyes closed. The two girls, neither much over twenty, are typical dollar street walkers, dressed in the usual tawdry get-up.* PEARL *is obviously Italian with black hair and eyes.* MARGIE *has brown hair and hazel eyes, a slum New Yorker of mixed blood. Both are plump and have a certain prettiness that shows even through their blobby make-up. Each retains a vestige of youthful freshness, although the game is beginning to get them and give them hard, worn expressions. Both are sentimental, feather-brained, giggly, lazy, good-natured and reasonably contented with life. Their attitude toward* ROCKY *is much that of two maternal, affectionate sisters toward a bullying brother whom they like to tease and spoil. His attitude toward them is that of the owner of two performing pets he has trained to do a profitable act under his management. He feels a proud proprietor's affection for them, and is tolerantly lax in his discipline*)

MARGIE (*Glancing around*) Jees, Poil, it's de Morgue wid all de stiffs on deck. (*She catches* LARRY'*s eye and smiles affectionately*) Hello, Old Wise Guy, ain't you died yet?

LARRY (*Grinning*) Not yet, Margie. But I'm waiting impatiently for the end. (PARRITT *opens his eyes to look at the two girls, but as soon as they glance at him he closes them again and turns his head away*)

MARGIE (*As she and* PEARL *come to the table at right, front, followed by* ROCKY) Who's de new guy? Friend of yours, Larry? (*Automatically she smiles seductively at* PARRITT *and addresses him in a professional chant*) Wanta have a good time, kid?

PEARL Aw, he's passed out. Hell wid him!

HOPE (*Cocks an eye over his specs at them—with drowsy irritation*) You dumb broads cut the loud talk. (*He shuts his eye again*)

ROCKY (*Admonishing them good-naturedly*) Sit down before I knock yuh down. (MARGIE *and* PEARL *sit at left, and rear, of table,* ROCKY *at right of it. The girls pour drinks.* ROCKY *begins in a brisk, business-like manner but in a lowered voice with an eye on* HOPE) Well, how'd you tramps do?

MARGIE Pretty good. Didn't we, Poil?

PEARL Sure. We nailed a coupla all-night guys.

MARGIE On Sixth Avenoo. Boobs from de sticks.

PEARL Stinko, de bot' of 'em.

MARGIE We thought we was in luck. We steered dem to a real hotel. We figgered dey was too stinko to bother us much and we could cop a good sleep in beds that ain't got cobble stones in de mattress like de ones in dis dump.

PEARL But we was outa luck. Dey didn't bother us much dat way, but dey wouldn't go to sleep either, see? Jees, I never hoid such gabby guys.

MARGIE Dey got onta politics, drinkin' outa de bottle. Dey forgot we was around. "De Bull Moosers is de on'y reg'lar guys," one guy says. And de other guy says, "You're a God-damned liar! And I'm a Republican!" Den dey'd laugh.

PEARL Den dey'd get mad and make a bluff dey was goin' to scrap, and den dey'd make up and cry and sing "School Days." Jees, imagine tryin' to sleep wid dat on de phonograph!

MARGIE Maybe you tink we wasn't glad when de house dick come up and told us all to git dressed and take de air!

PEARL We told de guys we'd wait for dem 'round de corner.

MARGIE So here we are.

ROCKY (*Sententiously*) Yeah. I see you. But I don't see no dough yet.

PEARL (*With a wink at* MARGIE—*teasingly*) Right on de job, ain't he, Margie?

MARGIE Yeah, our little business man! Dat's him!

ROCKY Come on! Dig! (*They both pull up their skirts to get the money from their stockings.* ROCKY *watches this move carefully*)

PEARL (*Amused*) Pipe him keepin' cases, Margie.

MARGIE (*Amused*) Scared we're holdin' out on him.

PEARL Way he grabs, yuh'd tink it was him done de woik. (*She holds out a little roll of bills to* ROCKY) Here y'are, Grafter!

MARGIE (*Holding hers out*) We hope it chokes yuh. (ROCKY *counts the money quickly and shoves it in his pocket*)

ROCKY (*Genially*) You dumb baby dolls gimme a pain. What would you do wid money if I wasn't around? Give it all to some pimp.

PEARL (*Teasingly*) Jees, what's the difference—? (*Hastily*) Aw, I don't mean dat, Rocky.

ROCKY (*His eyes growing hard—slowly*) A lotta difference, get me?

PEARL Don't get sore. Jees, can't yuh take a little kiddin'?

MARGIE Sure, Rocky, Poil was on'y kiddin'. (*Soothingly*) We know yuh got a reg'lar job. Dat's why we like yuh, see? Yuh don't live offa us. Yuh're a bartender.

ROCKY (*Genially again*) Sure, I'm a bartender. Everyone knows me knows dat. And I treat you goils right, don't I? Jees, I'm wise yuh hold out on me, but I know it ain't much, so what the hell, I let yuh get away wid it. I tink yuh're a coupla good kids. Yuh're aces wid me, see?

PEARL You're aces wid us, too. Ain't he, Margie?

MARGIE Sure, he's aces. (ROCKY *beams complacently and takes the glasses back to the bar.* MARGIE *whispers*) Yuh sap, don't yuh know enough not to kid him on dat? Serve yuh right if he beat yuh up!

PEARL (*Admiringly*) Jees, I'll bet he'd give yuh an awful beatin', too, once he started. Ginnies[10] got awful tempers.

MARGIE Anyway, we wouldn't keep no pimp, like we was reg'lar old whores. We ain't dat bad.

PEARL No. We're tarts, but dat's all.

ROCKY (*Rinsing glasses behind the bar*) Cora got back around three o'clock. She woke up Chuck and dragged him outa de hay to go to a chop suey joint. (*Disgustedly*) Imagine him standin' for dat stuff!

MARGIE (*Disgustedly*) I'll bet dey been sittin' around kiddin' demselves wid dat old pipe dream about gettin' married and settlin' down on a farm. Jees, when Chuck's on de wagon, dey never lay off dat dope! Dey give yuh an earful every time yuh talk to 'em!

PEARL Yeah. Chuck wid a silly grin on his ugly map, de big boob, and Cora gigglin' like she was in grammar school and some tough guy'd just told her babies wasn't brung down de chimney by a boid!

MARGIE And her on de turf long before me and you was! And bot' of 'em arguin' all de time, Cora sayin' she's scared to marry him because he'll go on drunks again. Just as dough any drunk could scare Cora!

PEARL And him swearin', de big liar, he'll never go on no more periodicals! An' den her pretendin'— But it gives me a pain to talk about it. We ought to phone de booby hatch to send round de wagon for 'em.

ROCKY (*Comes back to the table—disgustedly*) Yeah, of all de pipe dreams in dis dump, dey got de nuttiest! And nuttin' stops dem. Dey been dreamin' it for years, every time Chuck goes on de wagon. I never could figger it. What would gettin' married get dem? But de farm stuff is de sappiest part. When bot' of 'em was dragged up in dis ward and ain't never been nearer a farm dan Coney Island! Jees, dey'd tink dey'd gone deef if dey didn't hear de El rattle! Dey'd get D.T.s if dey ever hoid a cricket choip! I hoid crickets once on my cousin's place in Joisey. I couldn't sleep a wink. Dey give me de heebie-jeebies. (*With deeper disgust*) Jees, can yuh picture a good barkeep like Chuck diggin' spuds? And imagine a whore hustlin' de cows home! For Christ sake! Ain't dat a sweet picture!

MARGIE (*Rebukingly*) Yuh oughtn't to call Cora dat, Rocky. She's a good kid. She may be a tart, but—

ROCKY (*Considerately*) Sure, dat's all I meant, a tart.

PEARL (*Giggling*) But he's right about de damned cows, Margie. Jees, I bet Cora don't know which end of de cow has de horns! I'm goin' to ask her. (*There is the noise of a door opening in the hall and the sound of a man's and woman's arguing voices*)

[10] Another of the many slang terms for Italians or Americans of Italian extraction.

ROCKY Here's your chance. Dat's dem two nuts now. (*CORA and CHUCK look in from the hallway and then come in. CORA is a thin peroxide blonde, a few years older than PEARL and MARGIE, dressed in similar style, her round face showing more of the wear and tear of her trade than theirs, but still with traces of a doll-like prettiness. CHUCK is a tough, thick-necked, barrel-chested Italian-American, with a fat, amiable, swarthy face. He has on a straw hat with a vivid band, a loud suit, tie and shirt, and yellow shoes. His eyes are clear and he looks healthy and strong as an ox*)

CORA (*Gaily*) Hello, bums. (*She looks around*) Jees, de Morgue on a rainy Sunday night! (*She waves to LARRY—affectionately*) Hello, Old Wise Guy! Ain't you croaked yet?

LARRY (*Grins*) Not yet, Cora. It's damned tiring, this waiting for the end.

CORA Aw, gwan, you'll never die! Yuh'll have to hire someone to croak yuh wid an axe.

HOPE (*Cocks one sleepy eye at her—irritably*) You dumb hookers, cut the loud noise! This ain't a cat-house!

CORA (*Teasingly*) My, Harry! Such language!

HOPE (*Closes his eyes—to himself with a gratified chuckle*) Bejees, I'll bet Bessie's turning over in her grave! (*CORA sits down between MARGIE and PEARL. CHUCK takes an empty chair from HOPE's table and puts it by hers and sits down. At LARRY's table, PARRITT is glaring resentfully toward the girls*)

PARRITT If I'd known this dump was a hooker hang-out, I'd never have come here.

LARRY (*Watching him*) You seem down on the ladies.

PARRITT (*Vindictively*) I hate every bitch that ever lived! They're all alike! (*Catching himself guiltily*) You can understand how I feel, can't you, when it was getting mixed up with a tart that made me have that fight with Mother? (*Then with a resentful sneer*) But what the hell does it matter to you? You're in the grandstand. You're through with life.

LARRY (*Sharply*) I'm glad you remember it. I don't want to know a damned thing about your business. (*He closes his eyes and settles on his chair as if preparing for sleep. PARRITT stares at him sneeringly. Then he looks away and his expression becomes furtive and frightened*)

CORA Who's de guy wid Larry?

ROCKY A tightwad. To hell wid him.

PEARL Say, Cora, wise me up. Which end of a cow is de horns on?

CORA (*Embarrassed*) Aw, don't bring dat up. I'm sick of hearin' about dat farm.

ROCKY You got nuttin' on us!

CORA (*Ignoring this*) Me and dis overgrown tramp has been scrappin' about it. He says Joisey's de best place, and I says Long Island because we'll be near Coney. And I tells him, How do I know yuh're off of periodicals for life? I don't give a damn how drunk yuh get, the way we are, but I don't wanta be married to no soak.

CHUCK And I tells her I'm off de stuff for life. Den she beefs we won't be married a month before I'll trow it in her face she was a tart. "Jees, Baby," I tells her. "Why should I? What de hell yuh tink I tink I'm marryin', a voigin? Why should I kick as long as yuh lay off it and don't do no cheatin' wid de ice-man or nobody? (*He gives her a rough hug*) Dat's on de level, Baby. (*He kisses her*)

CORA (*Kissing him*) Aw, yuh big tramp!

ROCKY (*Shakes his head with profound disgust*) Can yuh tie it? I'll buy a drink. I'll do anything. (*He gets up*)

CORA No, dis round's on me. I run into luck. Dat's why I dragged Chuck outa bed to celebrate. It was a sailor. I rolled him. (*She giggles*) Listen, it was a scream. I've run into some nutty souses, but dis guy was de nuttiest. De booze dey dish out around de Brooklyn Navy Yard must be as turrible bug-juice as Harry's. My dogs was givin' out when I seen dis guy holdin' up a lamppost, so I hurried to get him before a cop did. I says, "Hello, Handsome, wanta have a good time?" Jees, he was paralyzed! One of dem polite jags. He tries to bow to me, imagine, and I had to prop him up or he'd fell on his nose. And what d'yuh tink he said? "Lady," he says, "can yuh kindly tell me de nearest way to de Museum of Natural History?" (*They all laugh*) Can yuh imagine! At two A.M. As if I'd know where de dump was anyway. But I says, "Sure ting, Honey Boy, I'll be only too glad." So I steered him into a side street where it was dark and propped him against a wall and give him a frisk. (*She giggles*) And what d'yuh tink he does? Jees, I ain't lyin', he begins to laugh, de big sap! He says, "Quit ticklin' me." While I was friskin' him for his roll! I near died! Den I toined him 'round and give him a push to start him. "Just keep goin'," I told him. "It's a big white building on your right. You can't miss it." He must be swimmin' in de North River yet! (*They all laugh*)

CHUCK Ain't Uncle Sam de sap to trust guys like dat wid dough!

CORA (*With a business-like air*) I picked twelve bucks offa him. Come on, Rocky. Set 'em up. (*ROCKY goes back to the bar. CORA looks around the room*) Say, Chuck's kiddin' about de iceman a minute ago reminds me. Where de hell's Hickey?

ROCKY Dat's what we're all wonderin'.

CORA He oughta be here. Me and Chuck seen him.

ROCKY (*Excited, comes back from the bar, forgetting the drinks*) You seen Hickey? (*He nudges HOPE*) Hey, Boss, come to! Cora's seen Hickey. (*HOPE is instantly wide awake and everyone in the place, except HUGO and PARRITT, begins to rouse up hopefully, as if a mysterious wireless message had gone round*)

HOPE Where'd you see him, Cora?

CORA Right on de next corner. He was standin' dere. We said, "Welcome to our city. De gang is expectin' yuh wid deir tongues hangin' out a yard long." And I kidded him, "How's de iceman, Hickey? How's he doin' at your house?" He laughs and says, "Fine." And he says, "Tell de gang I'll be along in a minute.

I'm just finishin' figurin' out de best way to save dem and bring dem peace."

HOPE (*Chuckles*) Bejees, he's thought up a new gag! It's a wonder he didn't borry a Salvation Army uniform and show up in that! Go out and get him, Rocky. Tell him we're waitin' to be saved! (ROCKY *goes out, grinning*)

CORA Yeah, Harry, he was only kiddin'. But he was funny, too, somehow. He was different, or somethin'.

CHUCK Sure, he was sober, Baby. Dat's what made him different. We ain't never seen him when he wasn't on a drunk, or had de willies gettin' over it.

CORA Sure! Gee, ain't I dumb?

HOPE (*With conviction*) The dumbest broad I ever seen! (*Then puzzledly*) Sober? That's funny. He's always lapped up a good starter on his way here. Well, bejees, he won't be sober long! He'll be good and ripe for my birthday party tonight at twelve. (*He chuckles with excited anticipation—addressing all of them*) Listen! He's fixed some new gag to pull on us. We'll pretend to let him kid us, see? And we'll kid the pants off him. (*They all say laughingly, "Sure, Harry," "Righto," "That's the stuff," "We'll fix him," etc., etc., their faces excited with the same eager anticipation.* ROCKY *appears in the doorway at the end of the bar with* HICKEY, *his arm around* HICKEY'S *shoulders*)

ROCKY (*With an affectionate grin*) Here's the old son of a bitch! (*They all stand up and greet him with affectionate acclaim, "Hello, Hickey!" etc. Even* HUGO *comes out of his coma to raise his head and blink through his thick spectacles with a welcoming giggle*)

HICKEY (*Jovially*) Hello, Gang! (*He stands a moment, beaming around at all of them affectionately. He is about fifty, a little under medium height, with a stout, roly-poly figure. His face is round and smooth and big-boyish with bright blue eyes, a button nose, a small, pursed mouth. His head is bald except for a fringe of hair around his temples and the back of his head. His expression is fixed in a salesman's winning smile of self-confident affability and hearty good fellowship. His eyes have the twinkle of a humor which delights in kidding others but can also enjoy equally a joke on himself. He exudes a friendly, generous personality that makes everyone like him on sight. You get the impression, too, that he must have real ability in his line. There is an efficient, business-like approach in his manner, and his eyes can take you in shrewdly at a glance. He has the salesman's mannerisms of speech, an easy flow of glib, persuasive convincingness. His clothes are those of a successful drummer whose territory consists of minor cities and small towns—not flashy but conspicuously spic and span. He immediately puts on an entrance act, places a hand affectedly on his chest, throws back his head, and sings in a falsetto tenor*) "It's always fair weather, when good fellows get together!" (*Changing to a comic bass and another tune*) "And another little drink won't do us any harm!" (*They all roar with laughter at this burlesque which his personality makes really funny. He waves his hand in a lordly manner to* ROCKY) Do your duty, Brother Rocky. Bring on the rat poison! (ROCKY *grins and goes behind the bar to get drinks amid an approving cheer from the crowd.* HICKEY *comes forward to shake hands with* HOPE*—with affectionate heartiness*) How goes it, Governor?

HOPE (*Enthusiastically*) Bejees, Hickey, you old bastard, it's good to see you! (HICKEY *shakes hands with* MOSHER *and* MCGLOIN; *leans right to shake hands with* MARGIE *and* PEARL; *moves to the middle table to shake hands with* LEWIS, JOE MOTT, WETJOEN *and* JIMMY; *waves to* WILLIE, LARRY *and* HUGO. *He greets each by name with the same affectionate heartiness and there is an interchange of "How's the kid?" "How's the old scout?" "How's the boy?" "How's everything?" etc., etc.* ROCKY *begins setting out drinks, whiskey glasses with chasers, and a bottle for each table, starting with* LARRY'S *table.* HOPE *says:*) Sit down, Hickey. Sit down. (HICKEY *takes the chair, facing front, at the front of the table in the second row which is half between* HOPE'S *table and the one where* JIMMY TOMORROW *is.* HOPE *goes on with excited pleasure*) Bejees, Hickey, it seems natural to see your ugly, grinning map. (*With a scornful nod to* CORA) This dumb broad was tryin' to tell us you'd changed, but you ain't a damned bit. Tell us about yourself. How've you been doin'? Bejees, you look like a million dollars.

ROCKY (*Coming to* HICKEY'S *table, puts a bottle of whiskey, a glass and a chaser on it—then hands* HICKEY *a key*) Here's your key, Hickey. Same old room.

HICKEY (*Shoves the key in his pocket*) Thanks, Rocky. I'm going up in a little while and grab a snooze. Haven't been able to sleep lately and I'm tired as hell. A couple of hours good kip will fix me.

HOPE (*As* ROCKY *puts drinks on his table*) First time I ever heard you worry about sleep. Bejees, you never would go to bed. (*He raises his glass, and all the others except* PARRITT *do likewise*) Get a few slugs under your belt and you'll forget sleeping. Here's mud in your eye, Hickey. (*They all join in with the usual humorous toasts*)

HICKEY (*Heartily*) Drink hearty, boys and girls! (*They all drink, but* HICKEY *drinks only his chaser*)

HOPE Bejees, is that a new stunt, drinking your chaser first?

HICKEY No, I forgot to tell Rocky— You'll have to excuse me, boys and girls, but I'm off the stuff. For keeps. (*They stare at him in amazed incredulity*)

HOPE What the hell— (*Then with a wink at the others, kiddingly*) Sure! Joined the Salvation Army, ain't you? Been elected President of the W.C.T.U.? Take that bottle away from him, Rocky. We don't want to tempt him into sin. (*He chuckles and the others laugh*)

HICKEY (*Earnestly*) No, honest, Harry. I know it's hard to believe but— (*He pauses—then adds simply*) Cora was right, Harry. I have changed. I mean, about booze. I don't need it any more. (*They all stare, hop-*

*ing it's a gag, but impressed and disappointed and made vaguely uneasy by the change they now sense in him)*

HOPE (*His kidding a bit forced*) Yeah, go ahead, kid the pants off us! Bejees, Cora said you was coming to save us! Well, go on. Get this joke off your chest! Start the service! Sing a God-damned hymn if you like. We'll all join in the chorus. "No drunkard can enter this beautiful home." That's a good one. (*He forces a cackle*)

HICKEY (*Grinning*) Oh, hell, Governor! You don't think I'd come around here peddling some brand of temperance bunk, do you? You know me better than that! Just because I'm through with the stuff don't mean I'm going Prohibition. Hell, I'm not that ungrateful! It's given me too many good times. I feel exactly the same as I always did. If anyone wants to get drunk, if that's the only way they can be happy, and feel at peace with themselves, why the hell shouldn't they? They have my full and entire sympathy. I know all about that game from soup to nuts. I'm the guy that wrote the book. The only reason I've quit is— Well, I finally had the guts to face myself and throw overboard the damned lying pipe dream that'd been making me miserable, and do what I had to do for the happiness of all concerned—and then all at once I found I was at peace with myself and I didn't need booze any more. That's all there was to it. (*He pauses. They are staring at him, uneasy and beginning to feel defensive.* HICKEY *looks round and grins affectionately—apologetically*) But what the hell! Don't let me be a wet blanket, making fool speeches about myself. Set 'em up again, Rocky. Here. (*He pulls a big roll from his pocket and peels off a ten-dollar bill. The faces of all brighten*) Keep the balls coming until this is killed. Then ask for more.

ROCKY Jees, a roll dat'd choke a hippopotamus! Fill up, youse guys. (*They all pour out drinks*)

HOPE That sounds more like you, Hickey. That water-wagon bull— Cut out the act and have a drink, for Christ's sake.

HICKEY It's no act, Governor. But don't get me wrong. That don't mean I'm a teetotal grouch and can't be in the party. Hell, why d'you suppose I'm here except to have a party, same as I've always done, and help celebrate your birthday tonight? You've all been good pals to me, the best friends I've ever had. I've been thinking about you ever since I left the house —all the time I was walking over here—

HOPE Walking? Bejees, do you mean to say you walked?

HICKEY I sure did. All the way from the wilds of darkest Astoria. Didn't mind it a bit, either. I seemed to get here before I knew it. I'm a bit tired and sleepy but otherwise I feel great. (*Kiddingly*) That ought to encourage you, Governor—show you a little walk around the ward is nothing to be so scared about. (*He winks at the others.* HOPE *stiffens resentfully for a second.* HICKEY *goes on*) I didn't make such bad time either for a fat guy, considering it's a hell of a ways, and I sat in the park a while thinking. It was going on twelve when I went in the bedroom to tell Evelyn I was leaving. Six hours, say. No, less than that. I'd been standing on the corner some time before Cora and Chuck came along, thinking about all of you. Of course, I was only kidding Cora with that stuff about saving you. (*Then seriously*) No, I wasn't either. But I didn't mean booze. I meant save you from pipe dreams. I know now, from my experience, they're the things that really poison and ruin a guy's life and keep him from finding any peace. If you knew how free and contented I feel now. I'm like a new man. And the cure for them is so damned simple, once you have the nerve. Just the old dope of honesty is the best policy—honesty with yourself, I mean. Just stop lying about yourself and kidding yourself about tomorrows. (*He is staring ahead of him now as if he were talking aloud to himself as much as to them. Their eyes are fixed on him with uneasy resentment. His manner becomes apologetic again*) Hell, this begins to sound like a damned sermon on the way to lead the good life. Forget that part of it. It's in my blood, I guess. My old man used to whale salvation into my heinie with a birch rod. He was a preacher in the sticks of Indiana, like I've told you. I got my knack of sales gab from him, too. He was the boy who could sell those Hoosier hayseeds building lots along the Golden Street! (*Taking on a salesman's persuasiveness*) Now listen, boys and girls, don't look at me as if I was trying to sell you a goldbrick. Nothing up my sleeve, honest. Let's take an example. Any one of you. Take you, Governor. That walk around the ward you never take—

HOPE (*Defensively sharp*) What about it?

HICKEY (*Grinning affectionately*) Why, you know as well as I do, Harry. Everything about it.

HOPE (*Defiantly*) Bejees, I'm going to take it!

HICKEY Sure, you're going to—this time. Because I'm going to help you. I know it's the thing you've got to do before you'll ever know what real peace means. (*He looks at* JIMMY TOMORROW) Same thing with you, Jimmy. You've got to try and get your old job back. And no tomorrow about it! (*As* JIMMY *stiffens with a pathetic attempt at dignity—placatingly*) No, don't tell me, Jimmy. I know all about tomorrow. I'm the guy that wrote the book.

JIMMY I don't understand you. I admit I've foolishly delayed, but as it happens, I'd just made up my mind that as soon as I could get straightened out—

HICKEY Fine! That's the spirit! And I'm going to help you. You've been damned kind to me, Jimmy, and I want to prove how grateful I am. When it's all over and you don't have to nag at yourself any more, you'll be grateful to me, too! (*He looks around at the others*) And all the rest of you, ladies included, are in the same boat, one way or another.

LARRY (*Who has been listening with sardonic appreciation—in his comically intense, crazy whisper*) Be God, you've hit the nail on the head, Hickey! This dump is the Palace of Pipe Dreams!

HICKEY (*Grins at him with affectionate kidding*) Well,

well! The Old Grandstand Foolosopher speaks! You think you're the big exception, eh? Life doesn't mean a damn to you any more, does it? You're retired from the circus. You're just waiting impatiently for the end—the good old Long Sleep! (*He chuckles*) Well, I think a lot of you, Larry, you old bastard. I'll try and make an honest man of you, too!

LARRY (*Stung*) What the devil are you hinting at, anyway?

HICKEY You don't have to ask me, do you, a wise old guy like you? Just ask yourself. I'll bet you know.

PARRITT (*Is watching* LARRY's *face with a curious sneering satisfaction*) He's got your number all right, Larry! (*He turns to* HICKEY) That's the stuff, Hickey. Show the old faker up! He's got no right to sneak out of everything.

HICKEY (*Regards him with surprise at first, then with a puzzled interest*) Hello. A stranger in our midst. I didn't notice you before, Brother.

PARRITT (*Embarrassed, his eyes shifting away*) My name's Parritt. I'm an old friend of Larry's. (*His eyes come back to* HICKEY *to find him still sizing him up—defensively*) Well? What are you staring at?

HICKEY (*Continuing to stare—puzzledly*) No offense, Brother. I was trying to figure— Haven't we met before some place?

PARRITT (*Reassured*) No. First time I've ever been East.

HICKEY No, you're right. I know that's not it. In my game, to be a shark at it, you teach yourself never to forget a name or a face. But still I know damned well I recognized something about you. We're members of the same lodge—in some way.

PARRITT (*Uneasy again*) What are you talking about? You're nuts.

HICKEY (*Dryly*) Don't try to kid me, Little Boy. I'm a good salesman—so damned good the firm was glad to take me back after every drunk—and what made me good was I could size up anyone. (*Frowningly puzzled again*) But I don't see— (*Suddenly breezily good-natured*) Never mind. I can tell you're having trouble with yourself and I'll be glad to do anything I can to help a friend of Larry's.

LARRY Mind your own business, Hickey. He's nothing to you—or to me, either. (HICKEY *gives him a keen inquisitive glance.* LARRY *looks away and goes on sarcastically*) You're keeping us all in suspense. Tell us more about how you're going to save us.

HICKEY (*Good-naturedly but seeming a little hurt*) Hell, don't get sore, Larry. Not at me. We've always been good pals, haven't we? I know I've always liked you a lot.

LARRY (*A bit shamefaced*) Well, so have I liked you. Forget it, Hickey.

HICKEY (*Beaming*) Fine! That's the spirit! (*Looking around at the others, who have forgotten their drinks*) What's the matter, everybody? What is this, a funeral? Come on and drink up! A little action! (*They all drink*) Have another. Hell, this is a celebration! Forget it, if anything I've said sounds too serious. I don't want to be a pain in the neck. Any time you think I'm talking out of turn, just tell me to go chase myself! (*He yawns with growing drowsiness and his voice grows a bit muffled*) No, boys and girls, I'm not trying to put anything over on you. It's just that I know now from experience what a lying pipe dream can do to you—and how damned relieved and contented with yourself you feel when you're rid of it. (*He yawns again*) God, I'm sleepy all of a sudden. That long walk is beginning to get me. I better go upstairs. Hell of a trick to go dead on you like this. (*He starts to get up but relaxes again. His eyes blink as he tries to keep them open*) No, boys and girls, I've never known what real peace was until now. It's a grand feeling, like when you're sick and suffering like hell and the Doc gives you a shot in the arm, and the pain goes, and you drift off. (*His eyes close*) You can let go of yourself at last. Let yourself sink down to the bottom of the sea. Rest in peace. There's no farther you have to go. Not a single damned hope or dream left to nag you. You'll all know what I mean after you— (*He pauses—mumbles*) Excuse—all in —got to grab forty winks— Drink up, everybody—on me— (*The sleep of complete exhaustion overpowers him. His chin sags to his chest. They stare at him with puzzled uneasy fascination*)

HOPE (*Forcing a tone of irritation*) Bejees, that's a fine stunt, to go to sleep on us! (*Then fumingly to the crowd*) Well, what the hell's the matter with you bums? Why don't you drink up? You're always crying for booze, and now you've got it under your nose, you sit like dummies! (*They start and gulp down their whiskies and pour another.* HOPE *stares at* HICKEY) Bejees, I can't figure Hickey. I still say he's kidding us. Kid his own grandmother, Hickey would. What d'you think, Jimmy?

JIMMY (*Unconvincingly*) It must be another of his jokes, Harry, although— Well, he does appear changed. But he'll probably be his natural self again tomorrow— (*Hastily*) I mean, when he wakes up.

LARRY (*Staring at* HICKEY *frowningly—more aloud to himself than to them*) You'll make a mistake if you think he's only kidding.

PARRITT (*In a low confidential voice*) I don't like that guy, Larry. He's too damned nosy. I'm going to steer clear of him. (LARRY *gives him a suspicious glance, then looks hastily away*)

JIMMY (*With an attempt at open-minded reasonableness*) Still, Harry, I have to admit there was some sense in his nonsense. It is time I got my job back—although I hardly need him to remind me.

HOPE (*With an air of frankness*) Yes, and I ought to take a walk around the ward. But I don't need no Hickey to tell me, seeing I got it all set for my birthday tomorrow.

LARRY (*Sardonically*) Ha! (*Then in his comically intense, crazy whisper*) Be God, it looks like he's going to make two sales of his peace at least! But you'd better make sure first it's the real McCoy and not poison.

HOPE (*Disturbed—angrily*) You bughouse I-Won't-Work harp, who asked you to shove in an oar? What the hell d'you mean, poison? Just because he has your number— (*He immediately feels ashamed of this taunt and adds apologetically*) Bejees, Larry, you're always croaking about something to do with death. It gets my nanny. Come on, fellers, let's drink up. (*They drink.* HOPE'S *eyes are fixed on* HICKEY *again*) Stone cold sober and dead to the world! Spilling that business about pipe dreams! Bejees, I don't get it. (*He bursts out again in angry complaint*) He ain't like the old Hickey! He'll be a fine wet blanket to have around at my birthday party! I wish to hell he'd never turned up!

MOSHER (*Who has been the least impressed by* HICKEY'S *talk and is the first to recover and feel the effect of the drinks on top of his hangover—genially*) Give him time, Harry, and he'll come out of it. I've watched many cases of almost fatal teetotalism, but they all came out of it completely cured and as drunk as ever. My opinion is the poor sap is temporarily bughouse from overwork. (*Musingly*) You can't be too careful about work. It's the deadliest habit known to science, a great physician once told me. He practiced on street corners under a torchlight. He was positively the only doctor in the world who claimed that rattlesnake oil, rubbed on the prat, would cure heart failure in three days. I remember well his saying to me, "You are naturally delicate, Ed, but if you drink a pint of bad whiskey before breakfast every evening, and never work if you can help it, you may live to a ripe old age. It's staying sober and working that cuts men off in their prime." (*While he is talking, they turn to him with eager grins. They are longing to laugh, and as he finishes they roar. Even* PARRITT *laughs.* HICKEY *sleeps on like a dead man, but* HUGO, *who had passed into his customary coma again, head on table, looks up through his thick spectacles and giggles foolishly*)

HUGO (*Blinking around at them. As the laughter dies he speaks in his giggling, wheedling manner, as if he were playfully teasing children*) Laugh, leedle bourgeois monkey-faces! Laugh like fools, leedle stupid peoples! (*His tone suddenly changes to one of guttural soapbox denunciation and he pounds on the table with a small fist*) I vill laugh, too! But I vill laugh last! I vill laugh at you! (*He declaims his favorite quotation*) "The days grow hot, O Babylon! 'Tis cool beneath thy villow trees!" (*They all hoot him down in a chorus of amused jeering.* HUGO *is not offended. This is evidently their customary reaction. He giggles good-naturedly.* HICKEY *sleeps on. They have all forgotten their uneasiness about him now and ignore him*)

LEWIS (*Tipsily*) Well, now that our little Robespierre has got the daily bit of guillotining off his chest, tell me more about your doctor friend, Ed. He strikes me as the only bloody sensible medico I ever heard of. I think we should appoint him house physician here without a moment's delay. (*They all laughingly assent*)

MOSHER (*Warming to his subject, shakes his head sadly*) Too late! The old Doc has passed on to his Maker. A victim of overwork, too. He didn't follow his own advice. Kept his nose to the grindstone and sold one bottle of snake oil too many. Only eighty years old when he was taken. The saddest part was that he knew he was doomed. The last time we got paralyzed together he told me: "This game will get me yet, Ed. You see before you a broken man, a martyr to medical science. If I had any nerves I'd have a nervous breakdown. You won't believe me, but this last year there was actually one night I had so many patients, I didn't even have time to get drunk. The shock to my system brought on a stroke which, as a doctor, I recognized was the beginning of the end." Poor old Doc! When he said this he started crying. "I hate to go before my task is completed, Ed," he sobbed. "I'd hoped I'd live to see the day when, thanks to my miraculous cure, there wouldn't be a single vacant cemetery lot left in this glorious country." (*There is a roar of laughter. He waits for it to die and then goes on sadly*) I miss Doc. He was a gentleman of the old school. I'll bet he's standing on a street corner in hell right now, making suckers of the damned, telling them there's nothing like snake oil for a bad burn. (*There is another roar of laughter. This time it penetrates* HICKEY'S *exhausted slumber. He stirs on his chair, trying to wake up, managing to raise his head a little and force his eyes half open. He speaks with a drowsy, affectionately encouraging smile. At once the laughter stops abruptly and they turn to him startledly*)

HICKEY That's the spirit—don't let me be a wet blanket—all I want is to see you happy— (*He slips back into heavy sleep again. They all stare at him, their faces again puzzled, resentful and uneasy*)

*Curtain*

# Act Two

SCENE *The back room only. The black curtain dividing it from the bar is the right wall of the scene. It is getting on toward midnight of the same day.*

*The back room has been prepared for a festivity. At center, front, four of the circular tables are pushed together to form one long table with an uneven line of chairs behind it, and chairs at each end. This improvised banquet table is covered with old table cloths, borrowed from a neighboring beanery, and is laid with glasses, plates and cutlery before each of the seventeen chairs. Bottles of bar whiskey are placed at intervals within reach of any sitter. An old upright piano and stool have been moved in and stand against the wall at left, front.*

*At right, front, is a table without chairs. The other tables and chairs that had been in the room have been moved out, leaving a clear floor space at rear for dancing. The floor has been swept clean of sawdust and scrubbed. Even the walls show evidence of having been washed, although the result is only to heighten their splotchy leprous look. The electric light brackets are adorned with festoons of red ribbon. In the middle of the separate table at right, front, is a birthday cake with six candles. Several packages, tied with ribbon, are also on the table. There are two necktie boxes, two cigar boxes, a fifth containing a half dozen handkerchiefs, the sixth is a square jeweler's watch box.*

*As the curtain rises,* CORA, CHUCK, HUGO, LARRY, MARGIE, PEARL *and* ROCKY *are discovered.* CHUCK, ROCKY *and the three girls have dressed up for the occasion.* CORA *is arranging a bouquet of flowers in a vase, the vase being a big schooner glass from the bar, on top of the piano.* CHUCK *sits in a chair at the foot (left) of the banquet table. He has turned it so he can watch her. Near the middle of the row of chairs behind the table,* LARRY *sits, facing front, a drink of whiskey before him. He is staring before him in frowning, disturbed meditation. Next to him, on his left,* HUGO *is in his habitual position, passed out, arms on table, head on arms, a full whiskey glass by his head. By the separate table at right, front,* MARGIE *and* PEARL *are arranging the cake and presents, and* ROCKY *stands by them. All of them, with the exception of* CHUCK *and* ROCKY, *have had plenty to drink and show it, but no one, except* HUGO, *seems to be drunk. They are trying to act up in the spirit of the occasion but there is something forced about their manner, an undercurrent of nervous irritation and preoccupation.*

CORA (*Standing back from the piano to regard the flower effect*) How's dat, Kid?

CHUCK (*Grumpily*) What de hell do I know about flowers?

CORA Yuh can see dey're pretty, can't yuh, yuh big dummy?

CHUCK (*Mollifyingly*) Yeah, Baby, sure. If yuh like 'em, dey're aw right wid me. (CORA *goes back to give the schooner of flowers a few more touches*)

MARGIE (*Admiring the cake*) Some cake, huh, Poil? Lookit! Six candles. Each for ten years.

PEARL When do we light de candles, Rocky?

ROCKY (*Grumpily*) Ask dat bughouse Hickey. He's elected himself boss of dis boithday racket. Just before Harry comes down, he says. Den Harry blows dem out wid one breath, for luck. Hickey was goin' to have sixty candles, but I says, Jees, if de old guy took dat big a breath, he'd croak himself.

MARGIE (*Challengingly*) Well, anyways, it's some cake, ain't it?

ROCKY (*Without enthusiasm*) Sure, it's aw right by me. But what de hell is Harry goin' to do wid a cake? If he ever et a hunk, it'd croak him.

PEARL Jees, yuh're a dope! Ain't he, Margie?

MARGIE A dope is right!

ROCKY (*Stung*) You broads better watch your step or—

PEARL (*Defiantly*) Or what?

MARGIE Yeah! Or what? (*They glare at him truculently*)

ROCKY Say, what de hell's got into youse? It'll be twelve o'clock and Harry's boithday before long. I ain't lookin' for no trouble.

PEARL (*Ashamed*) Aw, we ain't neider, Rocky. (*For the moment this argument subsides*)

CORA (*Over her shoulder to* CHUCK—*acidly*) A guy what can't see flowers is pretty must be some dumbbell.

CHUCK Yeah? Well, if I was as dumb as you— (*Then mollifyingly*) Jees, yuh got your scrappin' pants on, ain't yuh? (*Grins good-naturedly*) Hell, Baby, what's eatin' yuh? All I'm tinkin' is, flowers is dat louse Hickey's stunt. We never had no flowers for Harry's boithday before. What de hell can Harry do wid flowers? He don't know a cauliflower from a geranium.

ROCKY Yeah, Chuck, it's like I'm tellin' dese broads about de cake. Dat's Hickey's wrinkle, too. (*Bitterly*) Jees, ever since he woke up, yuh can't hold him. He's taken on de party like it was his boithday.

MARGIE Well, he's payin' for everything, ain't he?

ROCKY Aw, I don't mind de boithday stuff so much. What gets my goat is de way he's tryin' to run de whole dump and everyone in it. He's buttin' in all over de place, tellin' everybody where dey get off. On'y he don't really tell yuh. He just keeps hintin' around.

PEARL Yeah. He was hintin' to me and Margie.

MARGIE Yeah, de lousy drummer.

ROCKY He just gives yuh an earful of dat line of bull about yuh got to be honest wid yourself and not kid yourself, and have de guts to be what yuh are. I got sore. I told him dat's aw right for de bums in dis dump. I hope he makes dem wake up. I'm sick of listenin' to dem hop demselves up. But it don't go wid me, see? I don't kid myself wid no pipe dream. (PEARL *and* MARGIE *exchange a derisive look. He catches it and his eyes narrow*) What are yuh grinnin' at?

PEARL (*Her face hard—scornfully*) Nuttin'.

MARGIE Nuttin'.

ROCKY It better be nuttin'! Don't let Hickey put no ideas in your nuts if you wanta stay healthy! (*Then angrily*) I wish de louse never showed up! I hope he don't come back from de delicatessen. He's gettin' everyone nuts. He's ridin' someone every minute. He's got Harry and Jimmy Tomorrow run ragged, and de rest is hidin' in deir rooms so dey won't have to listen to him. Dey're all actin' cagey wid de booze, too, like dey was scared if dey get too drunk, dey might spill deir guts, or somethin'. And everybody's gettin' a prize grouch on.

CORA Yeah, he's been hintin' around to me and Chuck,

too. Yuh'd tink he suspected me and Chuck hadn't no real intention of gettin' married. Yuh'd tink he suspected Chuck wasn't goin' to lay off periodicals—or maybe even didn't want to.

CHUCK He didn't say it right out or I'da socked him one. I told him, "I'm on de wagon for keeps and Cora knows it."

CORA I told him, "Sure, I know it. And Chuck ain't never goin' to trow it in my face dat I was a tart, neider. And if yuh tink we're just kiddin' ourselves, we'll show yuh!"

CHUCK We're goin' to show him!

CORA We got it all fixed. We've decided Joisey is where we want de farm, and we'll get married dere, too, because yuh don't need no license. We're goin' to get married tomorrow. Ain't we, Honey?

CHUCK You bet, Baby.

ROCKY (*Disgusted*) Christ, Chuck, are yuh lettin' dat bughouse louse Hickey kid yuh into—

CORA (*Turns on him angrily*) Nobody's kiddin' him into it, nor me neider! And Hickey's right. If dis big tramp's goin' to marry me, he ought to do it, and not just shoot off his old bazoo about it.

ROCKY (*Ignoring her*) Yuh can't be dat dumb, Chuck.

CORA You keep outa dis! And don't start beefin' about crickets on de farm drivin' us nuts. You and your crickets! Yuh'd tink dey was elephants!

MARGIE (*Coming to* ROCKY's *defense—sneeringly*) Don't notice dat broad, Rocky. Yuh heard her say "tomorrow," didn't yuh? It's de same old crap.

CORA (*Glares at her*) Is dat so?

PEARL (*Lines up with* MARGIE*—sneeringly*) Imagine Cora a bride! Dat's a hot one! Jees, Cora, if all de guys you've stayed wid was side by side, yuh could walk on 'em from here to Texas!

CORA (*Starts moving toward her threateningly*) Yuh can't talk like dat to me, yuh fat Dago hooker! I may be a tart, but I ain't a cheap old whore like you!

PEARL (*Furiously*) I'll show yuh who's a whore! (*They start to fly at each other, but* CHUCK *and* ROCKY *grab them from behind*)

CHUCK (*Forcing* CORA *onto a chair*) Sit down and cool off, Baby.

ROCKY (*Doing the same to* PEARL) Nix on de rough stuff, Poil.

MARGIE (*Glaring at* CORA) Why don't you leave Poil alone, Rocky? She'll fix dat blonde's clock! Or if she don't, I will!

ROCKY Shut up, you! (*Disgustedly*) Jees, what dames! D'yuh wanta gum Harry's party?

PEARL (*A bit shamefaced—sulkily*) Who wants to? But nobody can't call me a —.

ROCKY (*Exasperatedly*) Aw, bury it! What are you, a voigin? (PEARL *stares at him, her face growing hard and bitter. So does* MARGIE)

PEARL Yuh mean you tink I'm a whore, too, huh?

MARGIE Yeah, and me?

ROCKY Now don't start nuttin'!

PEARL I suppose it'd tickle you if me and Margie did what dat louse, Hickey, was hintin' and come right out and admitted we was whores.

ROCKY Aw right! What of it? It's de truth, ain't it?

CORA (*Lining up with* PEARL *and* MARGIE*—indignantly*) Jees, Rocky, dat's a fine hell of a ting to say to two goils dat's been as good to yuh as Poil and Margie! (*To* PEARL) I didn't mean to call yuh dat, Poil. I was on'y mad.

PEARL (*Accepts the apology gratefully*) Sure, I was mad, too, Cora. No hard feelin's.

ROCKY (*Relieved*) Dere. Dat fixes everyting, don't it?

PEARL (*Turns on him—hard and bitter*) Aw right, Rocky. We're whores. You know what dat makes you, don't you?

ROCKY (*Angrily*) Look out, now!

MARGIE A lousy little pimp, dat's what!

ROCKY I'll loin yuh! (*He gives her a slap on the side of the face*)

PEARL A dirty little Ginny pimp, dat's what!

ROCKY (*Gives her a slap, too*) And dat'll loin you! (*But they only stare at him with hard sneering eyes*)

MARGIE He's provin' it to us, Poil.

PEARL Yeah! Hickey's convoited him. He's give up his pipe dream!

ROCKY (*Furious and at the same time bewildered by their defiance*) Lay off me or I'll beat de hell—

CHUCK (*Growls*) Aw, lay off dem. Harry's party ain't no time to beat up your stable.

ROCKY (*Turns to him*) Whose stable? Who d'yuh tink yuh're talkin' to? I ain't never beat dem up! What d'yuh tink I am? I just give dem a slap, like any guy would his wife, if she got too gabby. Why don't yuh tell dem to lay off me? I don't want no trouble on Harry's boithday party.

MARGIE (*A victorious gleam in her eye—tauntingly*) Aw right, den, yuh poor little Ginny. I'll lay off yuh till de party's over if Poil will.

PEARL (*Tauntingly*) Sure, I will. For Harry's sake, not yours, yuh little Wop!

ROCKY (*Stung*) Say, listen, youse! Don't get no wrong idea— (*But an interruption comes from* LARRY *who bursts into a sardonic laugh. They all jump startledly and look at him with unanimous hostility.* ROCKY *transfers his anger to him*) Who de hell yuh laughin' at, yuh half-dead old stew bum?

CORA (*Sneeringly*) At himself, he ought to be! Jees, Hickey's sure got his number!

LARRY (*Ignoring them, turns to* HUGO *and shakes him by the shoulder—in his comically intense, crazy whisper*) Wake up, Comrade! Here's the Revolution starting on all sides of you and you're sleeping through it! Be God, it's not to Bakunin's ghost you ought to pray in your dreams, but to the great Nihilist, Hickey! He's started a movement that'll blow up the world!

HUGO (*Blinks at him through his thick spectacles—with guttural denunciation*) You, Larry! Renegade! Traitor! I vill have you shot! (*He giggles*) Don't be a fool! Buy me a trink! (*He sees the drink in front of him, and gulps it down. He begins to sing the Carmagnole*[1] *in a guttural basso, pounding on the table*

[1] A song popularized during the French Revolution.

*with his glass*) "Dansons la Carmagnole! Vive le son! Vive le son! Dansons la Carmagnole! Vive le son des canons!"

ROCKY Can dat noise!

HUGO (*Ignores this—to* LARRY, *in a low tone of hatred*) That bourgeois svine, Hickey! He laughs like good fellow, he makes jokes, he dares make hints to me so I see what he dares to think. He thinks I am finish, it is too late, and so I do not vish the Day come because it vill not be my Day. Oh, I see what he thinks! He thinks lies even vorse, dat I— (*He stops abruptly with a guilty look, as if afraid he was letting something slip—then revengefully*) I vill have him hanged the first one of all on de first lamppost! (*He changes his mood abruptly and peers around at* ROCKY *and the others—giggling again*) Vhy you so serious, leedle monkey-faces? It's all great joke, no? So ve get drunk, and ve laugh like hell, and den ve die, and de pipe dream vanish! (*A bitter mocking contempt creeps into his tone*) But be of good cheer, leedle stupid peoples! "The days grow hot, O Babylon!" Soon, leedle proletarians, ve vill have free picnic in the cool shade, ve vill eat hot dogs and trink free beer beneath the villow trees! Like hogs, yes! Like beautiful leedle hogs! (*He stops startledly, as if confused and amazed at what he has heard himself say. He mutters with hatred*) Dot Gottamned liar, Hickey. It is he who makes me sneer. I want to sleep. (*He lets his head fall forward on his folded arms again and closes his eyes.* LARRY *gives him a pitying look, then quickly drinks his drink*)

CORA (*Uneasily*) Hickey ain't overlookin' no bets, is he? He's even give Hugo de woiks.

LARRY I warned you this morning he wasn't kidding.

MARGIE (*Sneering*) De old wise guy!

PEARL Yeah, still pretendin' he's de one exception, like Hickey told him. He don't do no pipe dreamin'! Oh, no!

LARRY (*Sharply resentful*) I—! (*Then abruptly he is drunkenly good-natured, and you feel this drunken manner is an evasive exaggeration*) All right, take it out on me, if it makes you more content. Sure, I love every hair of your heads, my great big beautiful baby dolls, and there's nothing I wouldn't do for you!

PEARL (*Stiffly*) De old Irish bunk, huh? We ain't big. And we ain't your baby dolls! (*Suddenly she is mollified and smiles*) But we admit we're beautiful. Huh, Margie?

MARGIE (*Smiling*) Sure ting! But what would he do wid beautiful dolls, even if he had de price, de old goat? (*She laughs teasingly—then pats* LARRY *on the shoulder affectionately*) Aw, yuh're aw right at dat, Larry, if yuh are full of bull!

EARL Sure. Yuh're aces wid us. We're noivous, dat's all. Dat lousy drummer—why can't he be like he's always been? I never seen a guy change so. You pretend to be such a fox, Larry. What d'yuh tink's happened to him?

.RRY I don't know. With all his gab I notice he's kept that to himself so far. Maybe he's saving the great revelation for Harry's party. (*Then irritably*) To hell with him! I don't want to know. Let him mind his own business and I'll mind mine.

CHUCK Yeah, dat's what I say.

CORA Say, Larry, where's dat young friend of yours disappeared to?

LARRY I don't care where he is, except I wish it was a thousand miles away! (*Then, as he sees they are surprised at his vehemence, he adds hastily*) He's a pest.

ROCKY (*Breaks in with his own preoccupation*) I don't give a damn what happened to Hickey, but I know what's gonna happen if he don't watch his step. I told him, "I'll take a lot from you, Hickey, like everyone else in dis dump, because yuh've always been a grand guy. But dere's tings I don't take from you nor nobody, see? Remember dat, or you'll wake up in a hospital—or maybe worse, wid your wife and de iceman walkin' slow behind yuh."

CORA Aw, yuh shouldn't make dat iceman crack, Rocky. It's aw right for him to kid about it but—I notice Hickey ain't pulled dat old iceman gag dis time. (*Excitedly*) D'yuh suppose dat he did catch his wife cheatin'? I don't mean wid no iceman, but wid some guy.

ROCKY Aw, dat's de bunk. He ain't pulled dat gag or showed her photo around because he ain't drunk. And if he'd caught her cheatin' he'd be drunk, wouldn't he? He'd have beat her up and den gone on de woist drunk he'd ever staged. Like any other guy'd do. (*The girls nod, convinced by this reasoning*)

CHUCK Sure! Rocky's got de right dope, Baby. He'd be paralyzed. (*While he is speaking, the Negro,* JOE, *comes in from the hallway. There is a noticeable change in him. He walks with a tough, truculent swagger and his good-natured face is set in sullen suspicion*)

JOE (*To* ROCKY*—defiantly*) I's stood tellin' people dis dump is closed for de night all I's goin' to. Let Harry hire a doorman, pay him wages, if he wants one.

ROCKY (*Scowling*) Yeah? Harry's pretty damned good to you.

JOE (*Shamefaced*) Sure he is. I don't mean dat. Anyways, it's all right. I told Schwartz, de cop, we's closed for de party. He'll keep folks away. (*Aggressively again*) I want a big drink, dat's what!

CHUCK Who's stoppin' yuh? Yuh can have all yuh want on Hickey.

JOE (*Has taken a glass from the table and has his hand on a bottle when* HICKEY'S *name is mentioned. He draws his hand back as if he were going to refuse—then grabs it defiantly and pours a big drink*) All right, I's earned all de drinks on him I could drink in a year for listenin' to his crazy bull. And here's hopin' he gets de lockjaw! (*He drinks and pours out another*) I drinks on him but I don't drink wid him. No, suh, never no more!

ROCKY Aw, bull! Hickey's aw right. What's he done to you?

JOE (*Sullenly*) Dat's my business. I ain't buttin' in yours, is I? (*Bitterly*) Sure, you think he's all right.

He's a white man, ain't he? (*His tone becomes aggressive*) Listen to me, you white boys! Don't you get it in your heads I's pretendin' to be what I ain't, or dat I ain't proud to be what I is, get me? Or you and me's goin' to have trouble! (*He picks up his drink and walks left as far away from them as he can get and slumps down on the piano stool*)

MARGIE (*In a low angry tone*) What a noive! Just because we act nice to him, he gets a swelled nut! If dat ain't a coon all over!

CHUCK Talkin' fight talk, huh? I'll moider de nigger! (*He takes a threatening step toward* JOE, *who is staring before him guiltily now*)

JOE (*Speaks up shamefacedly*) Listen, boys, I's sorry. I didn't mean dat. You been good friends to me. I's nuts, I guess. Dat Hickey, he gets my head all mixed up wit' craziness. (*Their faces at once clear of resentment against him*)

CORA Aw, dat's aw right, Joe. De boys wasn't takin' yuh serious. (*Then to the others, forcing a laugh*) Jees, what'd I say, Hickey ain't overlookin' no bets. Even Joe. (*She pauses—then adds puzzledly*) De funny ting is, yuh can't stay sore at de bum when he's around. When he forgets de bughouse preachin', and quits tellin' yuh where yuh get off, he's de same old Hickey. Yuh can't help likin' de louse. And yuh got to admit he's got de right dope— (*She adds hastily*) I mean, on some of de bums here.

MARGIE (*With a sneering look at* ROCKY) Yeah, he's coitinly got one guy I know sized up right! Huh, Poil?

PEARL He coitinly has!

ROCKY Cut it out, I told yuh!

LARRY (*Is staring before him broodingly. He speaks more aloud to himself than to them*) It's nothing to me what happened to him. But I have a feeling he's dying to tell us, inside him, and yet he's afraid. He's like that damned kid. It's strange the queer way he seemed to recognize him. If he's afraid, it explains why he's off booze. Like that damned kid again. Afraid if he got drunk, he'd tell— (*While he is speaking,* HICKEY *comes in the doorway at rear. He looks the same as in the previous act, except that now his face beams with the excited expectation of a boy going to a party. His arms are piled with packages*)

HICKEY (*Booms in imitation of a familiar Polo Grounds bleacherite cry—with rising volume*) Well! Well!! Well!!! (*They all jump startledly. He comes forward, grinning*) Here I am in the nick of time. Give me a hand with these bundles, somebody. (MARGIE *and* PEARL *start taking them from his arms and putting them on the table. Now that he is present, all their attitudes show the reaction* CORA *has expressed. They can't help liking him and forgiving him*)

MARGIE Jees, Hickey, yuh scared me outa a year's growth, sneakin' in like dat.

HICKEY Sneaking? Why, me and the taxi man made enough noise getting my big surprise in the hall to wake the dead. You were all so busy drinking in words of wisdom from the Old Wise Guy here, you couldn't hear anything else. (*He grins at* LARRY) From what I heard, Larry, you're not so good when you start playing Sherlock Holmes. You've got me all wrong. I'm not afraid of anything now—not even myself. You better stick to the part of Old Cemetery, the Barker for the Big Sleep—that is, if you can still let yourself get away with it! (*He chuckles and gives* LARRY *a friendly slap on the back.* LARRY *gives him a bitter angry look*)

CORA (*Giggles*) Old Cemetery! That's him, Hickey. We'll have to call him dat.

HICKEY (*Watching* LARRY *quizzically*) Beginning to do a lot of puzzling about me, aren't you, Larry? But that won't help you. You've got to think of yourself. I couldn't give you my peace. You've got to find your own. All I can do is help you, and the rest of the gang, by showing you the way to find it. (*He has said this with a simple persuasive earnestness. He pauses, and for a second they stare at him with fascinated resentful uneasiness*)

ROCKY (*Breaks the spell*) Aw, hire a church!

HICKEY (*Placatingly*) All right! All right! Don't get sore, boys and girls. I guess that did sound too much like a lousy preacher. Let's forget it and get busy on the party. (*They look relieved*)

CHUCK Is dose bundles grub, Hickey? You bought enough already to feed an army.

HICKEY (*With boyish excitement again*) Can't be too much! I want this to be the biggest birthday Harry's ever had. You and Rocky go in the hall and get the big surprise. My arms are busted lugging it. (*They catch his excitement.* CHUCK *and* ROCKY *go out, grinning expectantly. The three girls gather around* HICKEY, *full of thrilled curiosity*)

PEARL Jees, yuh got us all het up! What is it, Hickey?

HICKEY Wait and see. I got it as a treat for the three of you more than anyone. I thought to myself, I'll bet this is what will please those whores more than anything. (*They wince as if he had slapped them, but before they have a chance to be angry, he goes on affectionately*) I said to myself, I don't care how much it costs, they're worth it. They're the best little scouts in the world, and they've been damned kind to me when I was down and out! Nothing is too good for them. (*Earnestly*) I mean every word of that, too —and then some! (*Then, as if he noticed the expression on their faces for the first time*) What's the matter? You look sore. What—? (*Then he chuckles*) Oh, I see. But you know how I feel about that. You know I didn't say it to offend you. So don't be silly now.

MARGIE (*Lets out a tense breath*) Aw right, Hickey. Let it slide.

HICKEY (*Jubilantly, as* CHUCK *and* ROCKY *enter carrying a big wicker basket*) Look! There it comes! Unveil it, boys. (*They pull off a covering burlap bag. The basket is piled with quarts of champagne*)

PEARL (*With childish excitement*) It's champagne! Jees, Hickey, if you ain't a sport! (*She gives him a hug, forgetting all animosity, as do the other girls*)

MARGIE I never been soused on champagne. Let's get stinko, Poil.

PEARL You betcha my life! De bot' of us! (*A holiday*

*spirit of gay festivity has seized them all. Even* JOE MOTT *is standing up to look at the wine with an admiring grin, and* HUGO *raises his head to blink at it)*

JOE You sure is hittin' de high spots, Hickey. (*Boastfully*) Man, when I runs my gamblin' house, I drinks dat old bubbly water in steins! (*He stops guiltily and gives* HICKEY *a look of defiance*) I's goin' to drink it dat way again, too, soon's I make my stake! And dat ain't no pipe dream, neider! (*He sits down where he was, his back turned to them*)

ROCKY What'll we drink it outa, Hickey? Dere ain't no wine glasses.

HICKEY (*Enthusiastically*) Joe has the right idea! Schooners! That's the spirit for Harry's birthday! (ROCKY *and* CHUCK *carry the basket of wine into the bar. The three girls go back and stand around the entrance to the bar, chatting excitedly among themselves and to* CHUCK *and* ROCKY *in the bar*)

HUGO (*With his silly giggle*) Ve vill trink vine beneath the villow trees!

HICKEY (*Grins at him*) That's the spirit, Brother—and let the lousy slaves drink vinegar! (HUGO *blinks at him startledly, then looks away*)

HUGO (*Mutters*) Gottamned liar! (*He puts his head back on his arms and closes his eyes, but this time his habitual pass-out has a quality of hiding*)

LARRY (*Gives* HUGO *a pitying glance—in a low tone of anger*) Leave Hugo be! He rotted ten years in prison for his faith! He's earned his dream! Have you no decency or pity?

HICKEY (*Quizzically*) Hello, what's this? I thought you were in the grandstand. (*Then with a simple earnestness, taking a chair by* LARRY, *and putting a hand on his shoulder*) Listen, Larry, you're getting me all wrong. Hell, you ought to know me better. I've always been the best-natured slob in the world. Of course, I have pity. But now I've seen the light, it isn't my old kind of pity—the kind yours is. It isn't the kind that lets itself off easy by encouraging some poor guy to go on kidding himself with a lie—the kind that leaves the poor slob worse off because it makes him feel guiltier than ever—the kind that makes his lying hopes nag at him and reproach him until he's a rotten skunk in his own eyes. I know all about that kind of pity. I've had a bellyful of it in my time, and it's all wrong! (*With a salesman's persuasiveness*) No, sir. The kind of pity I feel now is after final results that will really save the poor guy, and make him contented with what he is, and quit battling himself, and find peace for the rest of his life. Oh, I know how you resent the way I have to show you up to yourself. I don't blame you. I know from my own experience it's bitter medicine, facing yourself in the mirror with the old false whiskers off. But you forget that, once you're cured. You'll be grateful to me when all at once you find you're able to admit, without feeling ashamed, that all the grandstand foolosopher bunk and the waiting for the Big Sleep stuff is a pipe dream. You'll say to yourself, I'm just an old man who is scared of life, but even more scared of dying. So I'm keeping drunk and hanging on to life at any price, and what of it? Then you'll know what real peace means, Larry, because you won't be scared of either life or death any more. You simply won't give a damn! Any more than I do!

LARRY (*Has been staring into his eyes with a fascinated wondering dread*) Be God, if I'm not beginning to think you've gone mad! (*With a rush of anger*) You're a liar!

HICKEY (*Injuredly*) Now, listen, that's no way to talk to an old pal who's trying to help you. Hell, if you really wanted to die, you'd just take a hop off your fire escape, wouldn't you? And if you really were in the grandstand, you wouldn't be pitying everyone. Oh, I know the truth is tough at first. It was for me. All I ask is for you to suspend judgment and give it a chance. I'll absolutely guarantee— Hell, Larry, I'm no fool. Do you suppose I'd deliberately set out to get under everyone's skin and put myself in dutch with all my old pals, if I wasn't certain, from my own experience, that it means contentment in the end for all of you? (LARRY *again is staring at him fascinatedly.* HICKEY *grins*) As for my being bughouse, you can't crawl out of it that way. Hell, I'm too damned sane. I can size up guys, and turn 'em inside out, better than I ever could. Even where they're strangers like that Parritt kid. He's licked, Larry. I think there is only one possible way out you can help him to take. That is, if you have the right kind of pity for him.

LARRY (*Uneasily*) What do you mean? (*Attempting indifference*) I'm not advising him, except to leave me out of his troubles. He's nothing to me.

HICKEY (*Shakes his head*) You'll find he won't agree to that. He'll keep after you until he makes you help him. Because he has to be punished, so he can forgive himself. He's lost all his guts. He can't manage it alone, and you're the only one he can turn to.

LARRY For the love of God, mind your own business! (*With forced scorn*) A lot you know about him! He's hardly spoken to you!

HICKEY No, that's right. But I do know a lot about him just the same. I've had hell inside me. I can spot it in others. (*Frowning*) Maybe that's what gives me the feeling there's something familiar about him, something between us. (*He shakes his head*) No, it's more than that. I can't figure it. Tell me about him. For instance, I don't imagine he's married, is he?

LARRY No.

HICKEY Hasn't he been mixed up with some woman? I don't mean trollops. I mean the old real love stuff that crucifies you.

LARRY (*With a calculating relieved look at him—encouraging him along this line*) Maybe you're right. I wouldn't be surprised.

HICKEY (*Grins at him quizzically*) I see. You think I'm on the wrong track and you're glad I am. Because then I won't suspect whatever he did about the Great Cause. That's another lie you tell yourself, Larry, that the good old Cause means nothing to you any more. (LARRY *is about to burst out in denial but* HICKEY *goes on*) But you're all wrong about Parritt. That isn't what's got him stopped. It's what's behind that. And it's a woman. I recognize the symptoms.

LARRY (*Sneeringly*) And you're the boy who's never wrong! Don't be a damned fool. His trouble is he was brought up a devout believer in the Movement and now he's lost his faith. It's a shock, but he's young and he'll soon find another dream just as good. (*He adds sardonically*) Or as bad.

HICKEY All right. I'll let it go at that, Larry. He's nothing to me except I'm glad he's here because he'll help me make you wake up to yourself. I don't even like the guy, or the feeling there's anything between us. But you'll find I'm right just the same, when you get to the final showdown with him.

LARRY There'll be no showdown! I don't give a tinker's damn—

HICKEY Sticking to the old grandstand, eh? Well, I knew you'd be the toughest to convince of all the gang, Larry. And, along with Harry and Jimmy Tomorrow, you're the one I want most to help. (*He puts an arm around* LARRY'S *shoulder and gives him an affectionate hug*) I've always liked you a lot, you old bastard! (*He gets up and his manner changes to his bustling party excitement—glancing at his watch*) Well, well, not much time before twelve. Let's get busy, boys and girls. (*He looks over the table where the cake is*) Cake all set. Good. And my presents, and yours, girls, and Chuck's, and Rocky's. Fine. Harry'll certainly be touched by your thought of him. (*He goes back to the girls*) You go in the bar, Pearl and Margie, and get the grub ready so it can be brought right in. There'll be some drinking and toasts first, of course. My idea is to use the wine for that, so get it all set. I'll go upstairs now and root everyone out. Harry the last. I'll come back with him. Somebody light the candles on the cake when you hear us coming, and you start playing Harry's favorite tune, Cora. Hustle now, everybody. We want this to come off in style. (*He bustles into the hall.* MARGIE *and* PEARL *disappear in the bar.* CORA *goes to the piano.* JOE *gets off the stool sullenly to let her sit down*)

CORA I got to practice. I ain't laid my mits on a box in Gawd knows when. (*With the soft pedal down, she begins gropingly to pick out "The Sunshine of Paradise Alley"*) Is dat right, Joe? I've forgotten dat has-been tune. (*She picks out a few more notes*) Come on, Joe, hum de tune so I can follow. (JOE *begins to hum and sing in a low voice and correct her. He forgets his sullenness and becomes his old self again*)

LARRY (*Suddenly gives a laugh—in his comically intense, crazy tone*) Be God, it's a second feast of Belshazzar, with Hickey to do the writing on the wall!

CORA Aw, shut up, Old Cemetery! Always beefin'! (WILLIE *comes in from the hall. He is in a pitiable state, his face pasty, haggard with sleeplessness and nerves, his eyes sick and haunted. He is sober.* CORA *greets him over her shoulder kiddingly*) If it ain't Prince Willie! (*Then kindly*) Gee, kid, yuh look sick. Git a coupla shots in yuh.

WILLIE (*Tensely*) No, thanks. Not now. I'm tapering off. (*He sits down weakly on* LARRY'S *right*)

CORA (*Astonished*) What d'yuh know? He means it!

WILLIE (*Leaning toward* LARRY *confidentially—in a low shaken voice*) It's been hell up in that damned room, Larry! The things I've imagined! (*He shudders*) I thought I'd go crazy. (*With pathetic boastful pride*) But I've got it beat now. By tomorrow morning I'll be on the wagon. I'll get back my clothes the first thing. Hickey's loaning me the money. I'm going to do what I've always said—go to the D.A.'s office. He was a good friend of my Old Man's. He was only assistant, then. He was in on the graft, but my Old Man never squealed on him. So he certainly owes it to me to give me a chance. And he knows that I really was a brilliant law student. (*Self-reassuringly*) Oh, I know I can make good, now I'm getting off the booze forever. (*Moved*) I owe a lot to Hickey. He's made me wake up to myself—see what a fool— It wasn't nice to face but— (*With bitter resentment*) It isn't what he says. It's what you feel behind—what he hints— Christ, you'd think all I really wanted to do with my life was sit here and stay drunk. (*With hatred*) I'll show him!

LARRY (*Masking pity behind a sardonic tone*) If you want my advice, you'll put the nearest bottle to your mouth until you don't give a damn for Hickey!

WILLIE (*Stares at a bottle greedily, tempted for a moment—then bitterly*) That's fine advice! I thought you were my friend! (*He gets up with a hurt glance at* LARRY, *and moves away to take a chair in back of the left end of the table, where he sits in dejected, shaking misery, his chin on his chest*)

JOE (*To* CORA) No, like dis. (*He beats time with his finger and sings in a low voice*) "She is the sunshine of Paradise Alley." (*She plays*) Dat's more like it. Try it again. (*She begins to play through the chorus again.* DON PARRITT *enters from the hall. There is a frightened look on his face. He slinks in furtively, as if he were escaping from someone. He looks relieved when he sees* LARRY *and comes and slips into the chair on his right.* LARRY *pretends not to notice his coming, but he instinctively shrinks with repulsion.* PARRITT *leans toward him and speaks ingratiatingly in a low secretive tone*)

PARRITT Gee, I'm glad you're here, Larry. That damned fool, Hickey, knocked on my door. I opened up because I thought it must be you, and he came busting in and made me come downstairs. I don't know what for. I don't belong in this birthday celebration. I don't know this gang and I don't want to be mixed up with them. All I came here for was to find you.

LARRY (*Tensely*) I've warned you—

PARRITT (*Goes on as if he hadn't heard*) Can't you make Hickey mind his own business? I don't like that guy, Larry. The way he acts, you'd think he had something on me. Why, just now he pats me on the shoulder, like he was sympathizing with me, and says, "I know how it is, Son, but you can't hide from yourself, not even here on the bottom of the sea. You've got to face the truth and then do what must be done for your own peace and the happiness of all concerned." What did he mean by that, Larry?

LARRY How the hell would I know?

PARRITT Then he grins and says, "Never mind, Larry's getting wise to himself. I think you can rely on his help in the end. He'll have to choose between living and dying, and he'll never choose to die while there is a breath left in the old bastard!" And then he laughs like it was a joke on you. (*He pauses.* LARRY *is rigid on his chair, staring before him.* PARRITT *asks him with a sudden taunt in his voice*) Well, what do you say to that, Larry?

LARRY I've nothing to say. Except you're a bigger fool than he is to listen to him.

PARRITT (*With a sneer*) Is that so? He's no fool where you're concerned. He's got your number, all right! (LARRY'S *face tightens but he keeps silent.* PARRITT *changes to a contrite, appealing air*) I don't mean that. But you keep acting as if you were sore at me, and that gets my goat. You know what I want most is to be friends with you, Larry. I haven't a single friend left in the world. I hoped you— (*Bitterly*) And you could be, too, without it hurting you. You ought to, for Mother's sake. She really loved you. You loved her, too, didn't you?

LARRY (*Tensely*) Leave what's dead in its grave.

PARRITT I suppose, because I was only a kid, you didn't think I was wise about you and her. Well, I was. I've been wise, ever since I can remember, to all the guys she's had, although she'd tried to kid me along it wasn't so. That was a silly stunt for a free Anarchist woman, wasn't it, being ashamed of being free?

LARRY Shut your damned trap!

PARRITT (*Guiltily but with a strange undertone of satisfaction*) Yes, I know I shouldn't say that now. I keep forgetting she isn't free any more. (*He pauses*) Do you know, Larry, you're the one of them all she cared most about? Anyone else who left the Movement would have been dead to her, but she couldn't forget you. She'd always make excuses for you. I used to try and get her goat about you. I'd say, "Larry's got brains and yet he thinks the Movement is just a crazy pipe dream." She'd blame it on booze getting you. She'd kid herself that you'd give up booze and come back to the Movement—tomorrow! She'd say, "Larry can't kill in himself a faith he's given his life to, not without killing himself." (*He grins sneeringly*) How about it, Larry? Was she right? (LARRY *remains silent. He goes on insistently*) I suppose what she really meant was, come back to her. She was always getting the Movement mixed up with herself. But I'm sure she really must have loved you, Larry. As much as she could love anyone besides herself. But she wasn't faithful to you, even at that, was she? That's why you finally walked out on her, isn't it? I remember that last fight you had with her. I was listening. I was on your side, even if she was my mother, because I liked you so much; you'd been so good to me—like a father. I remember her putting on her high-and-mighty free-woman stuff, saying you were still a slave to bourgeois morality and jealousy and you thought a woman you loved was a piece of private property you owned. I remember that you got mad and you told her, "I don't like living with a whore, if that's what you mean!"

LARRY (*Bursts out*) You lie! I never called her that!

PARRITT (*Goes on as if* LARRY *hadn't spoken*) I think that's why she still respects you, because it was you who left her. You were the only one to beat her to it. She got sick of the others before they did of her. I don't think she ever cared much about them, anyway. She just had to keep on having lovers to prove to herself how free she was. (*He pauses—then with a bitter repulsion*) It made home a lousy place. I felt like you did about it. I'd get feeling it was like living in a whorehouse—only worse, because she didn't have to make her living—

LARRY You bastard! She's your mother! Have you no shame?

PARRITT (*Bitterly*) No! She brought me up to believe that family-respect stuff is all bourgeois, property-owning crap. Why should I be ashamed?

LARRY (*Making a move to get up*) I've had enough!

PARRITT (*Catches his arm—pleadingly*) No! Don't leave me! Please! I promise I won't mention her again! (LARRY *sinks back in his chair*) I only did it to make you understand better. I know this isn't the place to— Why didn't you come up to my room, like I asked you? I kept waiting. We could talk everything over there.

LARRY There's nothing to talk over!

PARRITT But I've got to talk to you. Or I'll talk to Hickey. He won't let me alone! I feel he knows, anyway! And I know he'd understand, all right—in his way. But I hate his guts! I don't want anything to do with him! I'm scared of him, honest. There's something not human behind his damned grinning and kidding.

LARRY (*Starts*) Ah! You feel that, too?

PARRITT (*Pleadingly*) But I can't go on like this. I've got to decide what I've got to do. I've got to tell you, Larry!

LARRY (*Again starts up*) I won't listen!

PARRITT (*Again holds him by the arm*) All right! I won't. Don't go! (LARRY *lets himself be pulled down on his chair.* PARRITT *examines his face and becomes insultingly scornful*) Who do you think you're kidding? I know damned well you've guessed—

LARRY I've guessed nothing!

PARRITT But I want you to guess now! I'm glad you have! I know now, since Hickey's been after me, that I meant you to guess right from the start. That's why I came to you. (*Hurrying on with an attempt at a plausible frank air that makes what he says seem doubly false*) I want you to understand the reason. You see, I began studying American history. I got admiring Washington and Jefferson and Jackson and Lincoln. I began to feel patriotic and love this country. I saw it was the best government in the world, where everybody was equal and had a chance. I saw that all the ideas behind the Movement came from a lot of Russians like Bakunin and Kropotkin and were meant for Europe, but we didn't need them here in a democracy where we were free already. I didn't want this country to be destroyed for a damned foreign pipe dream. After all, I'm from old American pioneer stock. I began to feel I was a traitor for helping a lot of cranks and bums and free women plot to overthrow our government. And then I saw it was my duty to my country—

LARRY (*Nauseated—turns on him*) You stinking rotten liar! Do you think you can fool me with such hypocrite's cant! (*Then turning away*) I don't give a damn what you did! It's on your head—whatever it was! I don't want to know—and I won't know!

PARRITT (*As if* LARRY *had never spoken—falteringly*) But I never thought Mother would be caught. Please believe that, Larry. You know I never would have—

LARRY (*His face haggard, drawing a deep breath and closing his eyes—as if he were trying to hammer something into his own brain*) All I know is I'm sick of life! I'm through! I've forgotten myself! I'm drowned and contented on the bottom of a bottle. Honor or dishonor, faith or treachery are nothing to me but the opposites of the same stupidity which is ruler and king of life, and in the end they rot into dust in the same grave. All things are the same meaningless joke to me, for they grin at me from the one skull of death. So go away. You're wasting breath. I've forgotten your mother.

PARRITT (*Jeers angrily*) The old foolosopher, eh? (*He spits out contemptuously*) You lousy old faker!

LARRY (*So distracted he pleads weakly*) For the love of God, leave me in peace the little time that's left to me!

PARRITT Aw, don't pull that pitiful old-man junk on me! You old bastard, you'll never die as long as there's a free drink of whiskey left!

LARRY (*Stung—furiously*) Look out how you try to taunt me back into life, I warn you! I might remember the thing they call justice there, and the punishment for—(*He checks himself with an effort—then with a real indifference that comes from exhaustion*) I'm old and tired. To hell with you! You're as mad as Hickey, and as big a liar. I'd never let myself believe a word you told me.

PARRITT (*Threateningly*) The hell you won't! Wait till Hickey gets through with you! (PEARL *and* MARGIE *come in from the bar. At the sight of them,* PARRITT *instantly subsides and becomes self-conscious and defensive, scowling at them and then quickly looking away*)

MARGIE (*Eyes him jeeringly*) Why, hello, Tightwad Kid. Come to join de party? Gee, don't he act bashful, Poil?

PEARL Yeah. Especially wid his dough. (PARRITT *slinks to a chair at the left end of the table, pretending he hasn't heard them. Suddenly there is a noise of angry, cursing voices and a scuffle from the hall.* PEARL *yells*) Hey, Rocky! Fight in de hall! (ROCKY *and* CHUCK *run from behind the bar curtain and rush into the hall.* ROCKY'S *voice is heard in irritated astonishment, "What de hell?" and then the scuffle stops and* ROCKY *appears holding* CAPTAIN LEWIS *by the arm, followed by* CHUCK *with a similar hold on* GENERAL WETJOEN. *Although these two have been drinking they are both sober, for them. Their faces are sullenly angry, their clothes disarranged from the tussle*)

ROCKY (*Leading* LEWIS *forward—astonished, amused and irritated*) Can yuh beat it? I've heard youse two call each other every name yuh could think of but I never seen you— (*Indignantly*) A swell time to stage your first bout, on Harry's boithday party! What started de scrap?

LEWIS (*Forcing a casual tone*) Nothing, old chap. Our business, you know. That bloody ass, Hickey, made some insinuation about me, and the boorish Boer had the impertinence to agree with him.

WETJOEN Dot's a lie! Hickey made joke about me, and this Limey said yes, it was true!

ROCKY Well, sit down, de bot' of yuh, and cut out de rough stuff. (*He and* CHUCK *dump them down in adjoining chairs toward the left end of the table, where, like two sulky boys, they turn their backs on each other as far as possible in chairs which both face front*)

MARGIE (*Laughs*) Jees, lookit de two bums! Like a coupla kids! Kiss and make up, for Gawd's sakes!

ROCKY Yeah. Harry's party begins in a minute and we don't want no soreheads around.

LEWIS (*Stiffly*) Very well. In deference to the occasion, I apologize, General Wetjoen—provided that you do also.

WETJOEN (*Sulkily*) I apologize, Captain Lewis—because Harry is my goot friend.

ROCKY Aw, hell! If yuh can't do better'n dat—! (MOSHER *and* MCGLOIN *enter together from the hall. Both have been drinking but are not drunk*)

PEARL Here's de star boarders. (*They advance, their heads together, so interested in a discussion they are oblivious to everyone*)

MCGLOIN I'm telling you, Ed, it's serious this time. That bastard, Hickey, has got Harry on the hip. (*As he talks,* MARGIE, PEARL, ROCKY *and* CHUCK *prick up their ears and gather round.* CORA, *at the piano, keeps running through the tune, with soft pedal, and singing the chorus half under her breath, with* JOE *still correcting her mistakes. At the table,* LARRY, PARRITT, WILLIE, WETJOEN *and* LEWIS *sit motionless, staring in front of them.* HUGO *seems asleep in his habitual position*) And you know it isn't going to do us no good if he gets him to take that walk tomorrow.

MOSHER You're damned right. Harry'll mosey around the ward, dropping in on everyone who knew him when. (*Indignantly*) And they'll all give him a phony glad hand and a ton of good advice about what a sucker he is to stand for us.

MCGLOIN He's sure to call on Bessie's relations to do a little cryin' over dear Bessie. And you know what that bitch and all her family thought of me.

MOSHER (*With a flash of his usual humor—rebukingly*)

Remember, Lieutenant, you are speaking of my sister! Dear Bessie wasn't a bitch. She was a God-damned bitch! But if you think my loving relatives will have time to discuss you, you don't know them. They'll be too busy telling Harry what a drunken crook I am and saying he ought to have me put in Sing Sing!

MCGLOIN (*Dejectedly*) Yes, once Bessie's relations get their hooks in him, it'll be as tough for us as if she wasn't gone.

MOSHER (*Dejectedly*) Yes, Harry has always been weak and easily influenced, and now he's getting old he'll be an easy mark for those grafters. (*Then with forced reassurance*) Oh, hell, Mac, we're saps to worry. We've heard Harry pull that bluff about taking a walk every birthday he's had for twenty years.

MCGLOIN (*Doubtfully*) But Hickey wasn't sicking him on those times. Just the opposite. He was asking Harry what he wanted to go out for when there was plenty of whiskey here.

MOSHER (*With a change to forced carelessness*) Well, after all, I don't care whether he goes out or not. I'm clearing out tomorrow morning anyway. I'm just sorry for you, Mac.

MCGLOIN (*Resentfully*) You needn't be, then. Ain't I going myself? I was only feeling sorry for you.

MOSHER Yes, my mind is made up. Hickey may be a lousy, interfering pest, now he's gone teetotal on us, but there's a lot of truth in some of his bull. Hanging around here getting plastered with you, Mac, is pleasant, I won't deny, but the old booze gets you in the end, if you keep lapping it up. It's time I quit for a while. (*With forced enthusiasm*) Besides, I feel the call of the old carefree circus life in my blood again. I'll see the boss tomorrow. It's late in the season but he'll be glad to take me on. And won't all the old gang be tickled to death when I show up on the lot!

MCGLOIN Maybe—if they've got a rope handy!

MOSHER (*Turns on him—angrily*) Listen! I'm damned sick of that kidding!

MCGLOIN You are, are you? Well, I'm sicker of your kidding me about getting reinstated on the Force. And whatever you'd like, I can't spend my life sitting here with you, ruining my stomach with rotgut. I'm tapering off, and in the morning I'll be fresh as a daisy. I'll go and have a private chin with the Commissioner. (*With forced enthusiasm*) Man alive, from what the boys tell me, there's sugar galore these days, and I'll soon be ridin' around in a big red automobile—

MOSHER (*Derisively—beckoning an imaginary Chinese*) Here, One Lung Hop! Put fresh peanut oil in the lamp and cook the Lieutenant another dozen pills! It's his gowed-up night!

MCGLOIN (*Stung—pulls back a fist threateningly*) One more crack like that and I'll—!

MOSHER (*Putting up his fists*) Yes? Just start—! (CHUCK *and* ROCKY *jump between them*)

ROCKY Hey! Are you guys nuts? Jees, it's Harry's boithday party! (*They both look guilty*) Sit down and behave.

MOSHER (*Grumpily*) All right. Only tell him to lay off me. (*He lets* ROCKY *push him in a chair, at the right end of the table, rear*)

MCGLOIN (*Grumpily*) Tell him to lay off me. (*He lets* CHUCK *push him into the chair on* MOSHER'S *left. At this moment* HICKEY *bursts in from the hall, bustling and excited*)

HICKEY Everything all set? Fine! (*He glances at his watch*) Half a minute to go. Harry's starting down with Jimmy. I had a hard time getting them to move! They'd rather stay hiding up there, kidding each other along. (*He chuckles*) Harry don't even want to remember it's his birthday now! (*He hears a noise from the stairs*) Here they come! (*Urgently*) Light the candles! Get ready to play, Cora! Stand up, everybody! Get that wine ready, Chuck and Rocky! (MARGIE *and* PEARL *light the candles on the cake.* CORA *gets her hands set over the piano keys, watching over her shoulder.* ROCKY *and* CHUCK *go in the bar. Everybody at the table stands up mechanically.* HUGO *is the last, suddenly coming to and scrambling to his feet.* HARRY HOPE *and* JIMMY TOMORROW *appear in the hall outside the door.* HICKEY *looks up from his watch*) On the dot! It's twelve! (*Like a cheer leader*) Come on now, everybody, with a Happy Birthday, Harry! (*With his voice leading they all shout "Happy Birthday, Harry!" in a spiritless chorus.* HICKEY *signals to* CORA, *who starts playing and singing in a whiskey soprano "She's the Sunshine of Paradise Alley."* HOPE *and* JIMMY *stand in the doorway. Both have been drinking heavily. In* HOPE *the effect is apparent only in a bristling, touchy, pugnacious attitude. It is entirely different from the usual irascible beefing he delights in and which no one takes seriously. Now he really has a chip on his shoulder.* JIMMY, *on the other hand, is plainly drunk, but it has not had the desired effect, for beneath a pathetic assumption of gentlemanly poise, he is obviously frightened and shrinking back within himself.* HICKEY *grabs* HOPE'S *hand and pumps it up and down. For a moment* HOPE *appears unconscious of this handshake. Then he jerks his hand away angrily*)

HOPE Cut out the glad hand, Hickey. D'you think I'm a sucker? I know you, bejees, you sneaking, lying drummer! (*With rising anger, to the others*) And all you bums! What the hell you trying to do, yelling and raising the roof? Want the cops to close the joint and get my license taken away? (*He yells at* CORA *who has stopped singing but continues to play mechanically with many mistakes*) Hey, you dumb tart, quit banging that box! Bejees, the least you could do is learn the tune!

CORA (*Stops—deeply hurt*) Aw, Harry! Jees, ain't I— (*Her eyes begin to fill*)

HOPE (*Glaring at the other girls*) And you two hookers, screaming at the top of your lungs! What d'you think this is, a dollar cathouse? Bejees, that's where you belong!

PEARL (*Miserably*) Aw, Harry— (*She begins to cry*)

MARGIE Jees, Harry, I never thought you'd say that—like yuh meant it. (*She puts her arm around* PEARL—

*on the verge of tears herself*) Aw, don't bawl, Poil. He don't mean it.

HICKEY (*Reproachfully*) Now, Harry! Don't take it out on the gang because you're upset about yourself. Anyway, I've promised you you'll come through all right, haven't I? So quit worrying. (*He slaps* HOPE *on the back encouragingly.* HOPE *flashes him a glance of hate*) Be yourself, Governor. You don't want to bawl out the old gang just when they're congratulating you on your birthday, do you? Hell, that's no way!

HOPE (*Looking guilty and shamefaced now—forcing an unconvincing attempt at his natural tone*) Bejees, they ain't as dumb as you. They know I was only kidding them. They know I appreciate their congratulations. Don't you, fellers? (*There is a listless chorus of "Sure, Harry," "Yes," "Of course we do," etc. He comes forward to the two girls, with* JIMMY *and* HICKEY *following him, and pats them clumsily*) Bejees, I like you broads. You know I was only kidding. (*Instantly they forgive him and smile affectionately*)

MARGIE Sure we know, Harry.

PEARL Sure.

HICKEY (*Grinning*) Sure. Harry's the greatest kidder in this dump and that's saying something! Look how he's kidded himself for twenty years! (*As* HOPE *gives him a bitter, angry glance, he digs him in the ribs with his elbow playfully*) Unless I'm wrong, Governor, and I'm betting I'm not. We'll soon know, eh? Tomorrow morning. No, by God, it's *this* morning now!

JIMMY (*With a dazed dread*) *This* morning?

HICKEY Yes, it's today at last, Jimmy. (*He pats him on the back*) Don't be so scared! I've promised I'll help you.

JIMMY (*Trying to hide his dread behind an offended, drunken dignity*) I don't understand you. Kindly remember I'm fully capable of settling my own affairs!

HICKEY (*Earnestly*) Well, isn't that exactly what I want you to do, settle with yourself once and for all? (*He speaks in his ear in confidential warning*) Only watch out on the booze, Jimmy. You know, not too much from now on. You've had a lot already, and you don't want to let yourself duck out of it by being too drunk to move—not this time! (JIMMY *gives him a guilty, stricken look and turns away and slumps into the chair on* MOSHER's *right*)

HOPE (*To* MARGIE*—still guiltily*) Bejees, Margie, you know I didn't mean it. It's that lousy drummer riding me that's got my goat.

MARGIE I know. (*She puts a protecting arm around* HOPE *and turns him to face the table with the cake and presents*) Come on. You ain't noticed your cake yet. Ain't it grand?

HOPE (*Trying to brighten up*) Say, that's pretty. Ain't ever had a cake since Bessie— Six candles. Each for ten years, eh? Bejees, that's thoughtful of you.

PEARL It was Hickey got it.

HOPE (*His tone forced*) Well, it was thoughtful of him. He means well, I guess. (*His eyes, fixed on the cake, harden angrily*) To hell with his cake. (*He starts to turn away.* PEARL *grabs his arm*)

PEARL Wait, Harry. Yuh ain't seen de presents from Margie and me and Cora and Chuck and Rocky. And dere's a watch all engraved wid your name and de date from Hickey.

HOPE To hell with it! Bejees, he can keep it! (*This time he does turn away*)

PEARL Jees, he ain't even goin' to look at our presents.

MARGIE (*Bitterly*) Dis is all wrong. We gotta put some life in dis party or I'll go nuts! Hey, Cora, what's de matter wid dat box? Can't yuh play for Harry? Yuh don't have to stop just because he kidded yuh!

HOPE (*Rouses himself—with forced heartiness*) Yes, come on, Cora. You was playing it fine. (CORA *begins to play half-heartedly.* HOPE *suddenly becomes almost tearfully sentimental*) It was Bessie's favorite tune. She was always singing it. It brings her back. I wish— (*He chokes up*)

HICKEY (*Grins at him—amusedly*) Yes, we've all heard you tell us you thought the world of her, Governor.

HOPE (*Looks at him with frightened suspicion*) Well, so I did, bejees! Everyone knows I did! (*Threateningly*) Bejees, if you say I didn't—

HICKEY (*Soothingly*) Now, Governor. I didn't say anything. You're the only one knows the truth about that. (HOPE *stares at him confusedly.* CORA *continues to play. For a moment there is a pause, broken by* JIMMY TOMORROW *who speaks with muzzy, self-pitying melancholy out of a sentimental dream*)

JIMMY Marjorie's favorite song was "Loch Lomond." She was beautiful and she played the piano beautifully and she had a beautiful voice. (*With gentle sorrow*) You were lucky, Harry. Bessie died. But there are more bitter sorrows than losing the woman one loves by the hand of death—

HICKEY (*With an amused wink at* HOPE) Now, listen, Jimmy, you needn't go on. We've all heard that story about how you came back to Cape Town and found her in the hay with a staff officer. We know you like to believe that was what started you on the booze and ruined your life.

JIMMY (*Stammers*) I—I'm talking to Harry. Will you kindly keep out of— (*With a pitiful defiance*) My life is not ruined!

HICKEY (*Ignoring this—with a kidding grin*) But I'll bet when you admit the truth to yourself, you'll confess you were pretty sick of her hating you for getting drunk. I'll bet you were really damned relieved when she gave you such a good excuse. (JIMMY *stares at him strickenly.* HICKEY *pats him on the back again—with sincere sympathy*) I know how it is, Jimmy. I— (*He stops abruptly and for a second he seems to lose his self-assurance and become confused*)

LARRY (*Seizing on this with vindictive relish*) Ha! So that's what happened to you, is it? Your iceman joke finally came home to roost, did it? (*He grins tauntingly*) You should have remembered there's truth in the old superstition that you'd better look out what you call because in the end it comes to you!

HICKEY (*Himself again—grins to* LARRY *kiddingly*) Is that a fact, Larry? Well, well! Then you'd better watch out how you keep calling for that old Big Sleep! (LARRY *starts and for a second looks superstitiously frightened. Abruptly* HICKEY *changes to his jovial, bustling, master-of-ceremonies manner*) But what are we waiting for, boys and girls? Let's start the party rolling! (*He shouts to the bar*) Hey, Chuck and Rocky! Bring on the big surprise! Governor, you sit at the head of the table here. (*He makes* HARRY *sit down on the chair at the end of the table, right. To* MARGIE *and* PEARL) Come on, girls, sit down. (*They sit side by side on* JIMMY'S *right.* HICKEY *bustles down to the left end of table*) I'll sit here at the foot. (*He sits, with* CORA *on his left and* JOE *on her left.* ROCKY *and* CHUCK *appear from the bar, each bearing a big tray laden with schooners of champagne which they start shoving in front of each member of the party*)

ROCKY (*With forced cheeriness*) Real champagne, bums! Cheer up! What is dis, a funeral? Jees, mixin' champagne wid Harry's redeye will knock yuh paralyzed! Ain't yuh never satisfied? (*He and* CHUCK *finish serving out the schooners, grab the last two themselves and sit down in the two vacant chairs remaining near the middle of the table. As they do so,* HICKEY *rises, a schooner in his hand*)

HICKEY (*Rapping on the table for order when there is nothing but a dead silence*) Order! Order, Ladies and Gents! (*He catches* LARRY'S *eyes on the glass in his hand*) Yes, Larry, I'm going to drink with you this time. To prove I'm not teetotal because I'm afraid booze would make me spill my secrets, as you think. (LARRY *looks sheepish.* HICKEY *chuckles and goes on*) No, I gave you the simple truth about that. I don't need booze or anything else any more. But I want to be sociable and propose a toast in honor of our old friend, Harry, and drink it with you. (*His eyes fix on* HUGO, *who is out again, his head on his plate— To* CHUCK, *who is on* HUGO'S *left*) Wake up our demon bomb-tosser, Chuck. We don't want corpses at this feast.

CHUCK (*Gives* HUGO *a shake*) Hey, Hugo, come up for air! Don't yuh see de champagne? (HUGO *blinks around and giggles foolishly*)

HUGO Ve vill eat birthday cake and trink champagne beneath the villow tree! (*He grabs his schooner and takes a greedy gulp—then sets it back on the table with a grimace of distaste—in a strange, arrogantly disdainful tone, as if he were rebuking a butler*) Dis vine is unfit to trink. It has not properly been iced.

HICKEY (*Amusedly*) Always a high-toned swell at heart, eh, Hugo? God help us poor bums if you'd ever get to telling us where to get off! You'd have been drinking our blood beneath those willow trees! (*He chuckles.* HUGO *shrinks back in his chair, blinking at him, but* HICKEY *is now looking up the table at* HOPE. *He starts his toast, and as he goes on he becomes more moved and obviously sincere*) Here's the toast, Ladies and Gents! Here's to Harry Hope, who's been a friend in need to every one of us! Here's to the old Governor, the best sport and the kindest, biggest-hearted guy in the world! Here's wishing you all the luck there is, Harry, and long life and happiness! Come on, everybody! To Harry! Bottoms up! (*They have all caught his sincerity with eager relief. They raise their schooners with an enthusiastic chorus of "Here's how, Harry!" "Here's luck, Harry!" etc., and gulp half the wine down,* HICKEY *leading them in this*)

HOPE (*Deeply moved—his voice husky*) Bejees, thanks, all of you. Bejees, Hickey, you old son of a bitch, that's white of you! Bejees, I know you meant it, too.

HICKEY (*Moved*) Of course I meant it, Harry, old friend! And I mean it when I say I hope today will be the biggest day in your life, and in the lives of everyone here, the beginning of a new life of peace and contentment where no pipe dreams can ever nag at you again. Here's to that, Harry! (*He drains the remainder of his drink, but this time he drinks alone. In an instant the attitude of everyone has reverted to uneasy, suspicious defensiveness*)

ROCKY (*Growls*) Aw, forget dat bughouse line of bull for a minute, can't yuh?

HICKEY (*Sitting down—good-naturedly*) You're right, Rocky, I'm talking too much. It's Harry we want to hear from. Come on, Harry! (*He pounds his schooner on the table*) Speech! Speech! (*They try to recapture their momentary enthusiasm, rap their schooners on the table, call "Speech," but there is a hollow ring in it.* HOPE *gets to his feet reluctantly, with a forced smile, a smoldering resentment beginning to show in his manner*)

HOPE (*Lamely*) Bejees, I'm no good at speeches. All I can say is thanks to everybody again for remembering me on my birthday. (*Bitterness coming out*) Only don't think because I'm sixty I'll be a bigger damned fool easy mark than ever! No, bejees! Like Hickey says, it's going to be a new day! This dump has got to be run like other dumps, so I can make some money and not just split even. People has got to pay what they owe me! I'm not running a damned orphan asylum for bums and crooks! Nor a God-damned hooker shanty, either! Nor an Old Men's Home for lousy Anarchist tramps that ought to be in jail! I'm sick of being played for a sucker! (*They stare at him with stunned, bewildered hurt. He goes on in a sort of furious desperation, as if he hated himself for every word he said, and yet couldn't stop*) And don't think you're kidding me right now, either! I know damned well you're giving me the laugh behind my back, thinking to yourselves, The old, lying, pipe-dreaming faker, we've heard his bull about taking a walk around the wards for years, he'll never make it! He's yellow, he ain't got the guts, he's scared he'll find out— (*He glares around at them almost with hatred*) But I'll show you, bejees! (*He glares at* HICKEY) I'll show you, too, you son of a bitch of a frying-pan-peddling bastard!

HICKEY (*Heartily encouraging*) That's the stuff, Harry! Of course you'll try to show me! That's what I want you to do! (HARRY *glances at him with helpless dread*

*—then drops his eyes and looks furtively around the table. All at once he becomes miserably contrite)*

HOPE (*His voice catching*) Listen, all of you! Bejees, forgive me. I lost my temper! I ain't feeling well! I got a hell of a grouch on! Bejees, you know you're all as welcome here as the flowers in May! (*They look at him with eager forgiveness.* ROCKY *is the first one who can voice it*)

ROCKY Aw, sure, Boss, you're always aces wid us, see?

HICKEY (*Rises to his feet again. He addresses them now with the simple, convincing sincerity of one making a confession of which he is genuinely ashamed*) Listen, everybody! I know you are sick of my gabbing, but I think this is the spot where I owe it to you to do a little explaining and apologize for some of the rough stuff I've had to pull on you. I know how it must look to you. As if I was a damned busybody who was not only interfering in your private business, but even sicking some of you on to nag at each other. Well, I have to admit that's true, and I'm damned sorry about it. But it simply had to be done! You must believe that! You know old Hickey. I was never one to start trouble. But this time I had to—for your own good! I had to make you help me with each other. I saw I couldn't do what I was after alone. Not in the time at my disposal. I knew when I came here I wouldn't be able to stay with you long. I'm slated to leave on a trip. I saw I'd have to hustle and use every means I could. (*With a joking boastfulness*) Why, if I had enough time, I'd get a lot of sport out of selling my line of salvation to each of you all by my lonesome. Like it was fun in the old days, when I traveled house to house, to convince some dame, who was sicking the dog on me, her house wouldn't be properly furnished unless she bought another wash boiler. And I could do it with you, all right. I know every one of you, inside and out, by heart. I may have been drunk when I've been here before, but old Hickey could never be so drunk he didn't have to see through people. I mean, everyone except himself. And, finally, he had to see through himself, too. (*He pauses. They stare at him, bitter, uneasy and fascinated. His manner changes to deep earnestness*) But here's the point to get. I swear I'd never act like I have if I wasn't absolutely sure it will be worth it to you in the end, after you're rid of the damned guilt that makes you lie to yourselves you're something you're not, and the remorse that nags at you and makes you hide behind lousy pipe dreams about tomorrow. You'll be in a today where there is no yesterday or tomorrow to worry you. You won't give a damn what you are any more. I wouldn't say this unless I knew, Brothers and Sisters. This peace is real! It's a fact! I know! Because I've got it! Here! Now! Right in front of you! You see the difference in me! You remember how I used to be! Even when I had two quarts of rotgut under my belt and joked and sang "Sweet Adeline," I still felt like a guilty skunk. But you can all see that I don't give a damn about anything now. And I promise you, by the time this day is over, I'll have every one of you feeling the same way! (*He pauses. They stare at him fascinatedly. He adds with a grin*) I guess that'll be about all from me, boys and girls—for the present. So let's get on with the party. (*He starts to sit down*)

LARRY (*Sharply*) Wait! (*Insistently—with a sneer*) I think it would help us poor pipe-dreaming sinners along the sawdust trail to salvation if you told us now what it was happened to you that converted you to this great peace you've found. (*More and more with a deliberate, provocative taunting*) I notice you didn't deny it when I asked you about the iceman. Did this great revelation of the evil habit of dreaming about tomorrow come to you after you found your wife was sick of you? (*While he is speaking the faces of the gang have lighted up vindictively, as if all at once they saw a chance to revenge themselves. As he finishes, a chorus of sneering taunts begins, punctuated by nasty, jeering laughter*)

HOPE Bejees, you've hit it, Larry! I've noticed he hasn't shown her picture around this time!

MOSHER He hasn't got it! The iceman took it away from him!

MARGIE Jees, look at him! Who could blame her?

PEARL She must be hard up to fall for an iceman!

CORA Imagine a sap like him advisin' me and Chuck to git married!

CHUCK Yeah! He done so good wid it!

JIMMY At least I can say Marjorie chose an officer and a gentleman.

LEWIS Come to look at you, Hickey, old chap, you've sprouted horns like a bloody antelope!

WETJOEN Pigger, py Gott! Like a water buffalo's!

WILLIE (*Sings to his Sailor Lad tune*)

"Come up," she cried, "my iceman lad,
And you and I'll agree—"

(*They all join in a jeering chorus, rapping with knuckles or glasses on the table at the indicated spot in the lyric*)

"And I'll show you the prettiest (*Rap, rap, rap*)
That ever you did see!"

(*A roar of derisive, dirty laughter. But* HICKEY *has remained unmoved by all this taunting. He grins good-naturedly, as if he enjoyed the poke at his expense, and joins in the laughter*)

HICKEY Well, boys and girls, I'm glad to see you getting in good spirits for Harry's party, even if the joke is on me. I admit I asked for it by always pulling that iceman gag in the old days. So laugh all you like. (*He pauses. They do not laugh now. They are again staring at him with baffled uneasiness. He goes on thoughtfully*) Well, this forces my hand, I guess, your bringing up the subject of Evelyn. I didn't want to tell you yet. It's hardly an appropriate time. I meant to wait until the party was over. But you're getting the wrong idea about poor Evelyn, and I've got to stop that. (*He pauses again. There is a tense stillness in the room. He bows his head a little and says quietly*) I'm sorry to tell you my dearly beloved wife is dead. (*A gasp comes from the stunned company. They look away from him, shocked and miserably ashamed of themselves, except* LARRY *who continues to stare at him)*

LARRY (*Aloud to himself with a superstitious shrinking*) Be God, I felt he'd brought the touch of death on him! (*Then suddenly he is even more ashamed of himself than the others and stammers*) Forgive me, Hickey! I'd like to cut my dirty tongue out! (*This releases a chorus of shamefaced mumbles from the crowd. "Sorry, Hickey." "I'm sorry, Hickey." "We're sorry, Hickey"*)

HICKEY (*Looking around at them—in a kindly, reassuring tone*) Now look here, everybody. You mustn't let this be a wet blanket on Harry's party. You're still getting me all wrong. There's no reason— You see, I don't feel any grief. (*They gaze at him startledly. He goes on with convincing sincerity*) I've got to feel glad, for her sake. Because she's at peace. She's rid of me at last. Hell, I don't have to tell you—you all know what I was like. You can imagine what she went through, married to a no-good cheater and drunk like I was. And there was no way out of it for her. Because she loved me. But now she is at peace like she always longed to be. So why should I feel sad? She wouldn't want me to feel sad. Why, all that Evelyn ever wanted out of life was to make me happy. (*He stops, looking around at them with a simple, gentle frankness. They stare at him in bewildered, incredulous confusion*)

*Curtain*

# Act Three

SCENE *Barroom of* HARRY HOPE'S, *including a part of what had been the back room in Acts One and Two. In the right wall are two big windows, with the swinging doors to the street between them. The bar itself is at rear. Behind it is a mirror, covered with white mosquito netting to keep off the flies, and a shelf on which are barrels of cheap whiskey with spiggots and a small show case of bottled goods. At left of the bar is the doorway to the hall. There is a table at left, front, of barroom proper, with four chairs. At right, front, is a small free-lunch counter, facing left, with a space between it and the window for the dealer to stand when he dishes out soup at the noon hour. Over the mirror behind the bar are framed photographs of Richard Croker and Big Tim Sullivan,*[1] *flanked by framed lithographs of John L. Sullivan and Gentleman Jim Corbett in ring costume.*

[1] Influential Tammanyites until around 1903.

*At left, in what had been the back room, with the dividing curtain drawn, the banquet table of Act Two has been broken up, and the tables are again in the crowded arrangement of Act One. Of these, we see one in the front row with five chairs at left of the barroom table, another with five chairs at left-rear of it, a third back by the rear wall with five chairs, and finally, at extreme left-front, one with four chairs, partly on and partly off stage, left.*

*It is around the middle of the morning of* HOPE'S *birthday, a hot summer day. There is sunlight in the street outside, but it does not hit the windows and the light in the back-room section is dim.*

JOE MOTT *is moving around, a box of sawdust under his arm, strewing it over the floor. His manner is sullen, his face set in gloom. He ignores everyone. As the scene progresses, he finishes his sawdusting job, goes behind the lunch counter and cuts loaves of bread.* ROCKY *is behind the bar, wiping it, washing glasses, etc. He wears his working clothes, sleeves rolled up. He looks sleepy, irritable and worried. At the barroom table, front,* LARRY *sits in a chair, facing right-front. He has no drink in front of him. He stares ahead, deep in harried thought. On his right, in a chair facing right,* HUGO *sits sprawled forward, arms and head on the table as usual, a whiskey glass beside his limp hand. At rear of the front table at left of them, in a chair facing left,* PARRITT *is sitting. He is staring in front of him in a tense, strained immobility.*

*As the curtain rises,* ROCKY *finishes his work behind the bar. He comes forward and drops wearily in the chair at right of* LARRY'S *table, facing left.*

ROCKY Nuttin' now till de noon rush from de Market. I'm goin' to rest my fanny. (*Irritably*) If I ain't a sap to let Chuck kid me into workin' his time so's he can take de mornin' off. But I got sick of arguin' wid 'im. I says, "Aw right, git married! What's it to me?" Hickey's got de bot' of dem bugs. (*Bitterly*) Some party last night, huh? Jees, what a funeral! It was jinxed from de start, but his tellin' about his wife croakin' put de K.O. on it.

LARRY Yes, it turned out it wasn't a birthday feast but a wake!

ROCKY Him promisin' he'd cut out de bughouse bull about peace—and den he went on talkin' and talkin' like he couldn't stop! And all de gang sneakin' upstairs, leavin' free booze and eats like dey was poison! It didn't do dem no good if dey thought dey'd shake him. He's been hoppin' from room to room all night. Yuh can't stop him. He's got his Reform Wave goin' strong dis mornin'! Did yuh notice him drag Jimmy out de foist ting to get his laundry and his clothes pressed so he wouldn't have no excuse? And he give Willie de dough to buy his stuff back from Solly's. And all de rest been brushin' and shavin' demselves wid de shakes—

LARRY (*Defiantly*) He didn't come to my room! He's afraid I might ask him a few questions.

ROCKY (*Scornfully*) Yeah? It don't look to me he's scared of yuh. I'd say you was scared of him.

LARRY (*Stung*) You'd lie, then!

PARRITT (*Jerks round to look at* LARRY—*sneeringly*) Don't let him kid you, Rocky. He had his door locked. I couldn't get in, either.

ROCKY Yeah, who d'yuh tink yuh're kiddin', Larry? He's showed you up, aw right. Like he says, if yuh was so anxious to croak, why wouldn't yuh hop off your fire escape long ago?

LARRY (*Defiantly*) Because it'd be a coward's quitting, that's why!

PARRITT He's all quitter, Rocky. He's a yellow old faker!

LARRY (*Turns on him*) You lying punk! Remember what I warned you—!

ROCKY (*Scowls at* PARRITT) Yeah, keep outta dis, you! Where d'yuh get a license to butt in? Shall I give him de bum's rush, Larry? If you don't want him around, nobody else don't.

LARRY (*Forcing an indifferent tone*) No. Let him stay. I don't mind him. He's nothing to me. (ROCKY *shrugs his shoulders and yawns sleepily*)

PARRITT You're right, I have nowhere to go now. You're the only one in the world I can turn to.

ROCKY (*Drowsily*) Yuh're a soft old sap, Larry. He's a no-good louse like Hickey. He don't belong. (*He yawns*) I'm all in. Not a wink of sleep. Can't keep my peepers open. (*His eyes close and his head nods.* PARRITT *gives him a glance and then gets up and slinks over to slide into the chair on* LARRY'S *left, between him and* ROCKY. LARRY *shrinks away, but determinedly ignores him*)

PARRITT (*Bending toward him—in a low, ingratiating, apologetic voice*) I'm sorry for riding you, Larry. But you get my goat when you act as if you didn't care a damn what happened to me, and keep your door locked so I can't talk to you. (*Then hopefully*) But that was to keep Hickey out, wasn't it? I don't blame you. I'm getting to hate him. I'm getting more and more scared of him. Especially since he told us his wife was dead. It's that queer feeling he gives me that I'm mixed up with him some way. I don't know why, but it started me thinking about Mother—as if she was dead. (*With a strange undercurrent of something like satisfaction in his pitying tone*) I suppose she might as well be. Inside herself, I mean. It must kill her when she thinks of me—I know she doesn't want to, but she can't help it. After all, I'm her only kid. She used to spoil me and made a pet of me. Once in a great while, I mean. When she remembered me. As if she wanted to make up for something. As if she felt guilty. So she must have loved me a little, even if she never let it interfere with her freedom. (*With a strange pathetic wistfulness*) Do you know, Larry, I once had a sneaking suspicion that maybe, if the truth was known, you were my father.

LARRY (*Violently*) You damned fool! Who put that insane idea in your head? You know it's a lie! Any-one in the Coast crowd could tell you I never laid eyes on your mother till after you were born.

PARRITT Well, I'd hardly ask them, would I? I know you're right, though, because I asked her. She brought me up to be frank and ask her anything, and she'd always tell me the truth. (*Abruptly*) But I was talking about how she must feel now about me. My getting through with the Movement. She'll never forgive that. The Movement is her life. And it must be the final knockout for her if she knows I was the one who sold—

LARRY Shut up, damn you!

PARRITT It'll kill her. And I'm sure she knows it must have been me. (*Suddenly with desperate urgency*) But I never thought the cops would get her! You've got to believe that! You've got to see what my only reason was! I'll admit what I told you last night was a lie—that bunk about getting patriotic and my duty to my country. But here's the true reason, Larry—the only reason! It was just for money! I got stuck on a whore and wanted dough to blow in on her and have a good time! That's all I did it for! Just money! Honest! (*He has the terrible grotesque air, in confessing his sordid baseness, of one who gives an excuse which exonerates him from any real guilt*)

LARRY (*Grabs him by the shoulder and shakes him*) God damn you, shut up! What the hell is it to me? (ROCKY *starts awake*)

ROCKY What's comin' off here?

LARRY (*Controlling himself*) Nothing. This gabby young punk was talking my ear off, that's all. He's a worse pest than Hickey.

ROCKY (*Drowsily*) Yeah, Hickey— Say, listen, what d'yuh mean about him bein' scared you'd ask him questions? What questions?

LARRY Well, I feel he's hiding something. You notice he didn't say what his wife died of.

ROCKY (*Rebukingly*) Aw, lay off dat. De poor guy— What are yuh gettin' at, anyway? Yuh don't tink it's just a gag of his?

LARRY I don't. I'm damned sure he's brought death here with him. I feel the cold touch of it on him.

ROCKY Aw, bunk! You got croakin' on de brain, Old Cemetery. (*Suddenly* ROCKY'S *eyes widen*) Say! D'yuh mean yuh tink she committed suicide, 'count of his cheatin' or someting?

LARRY (*Grimly*) It wouldn't surprise me. I'd be the last to blame her.

ROCKY (*Scornfully*) But dat's crazy! Jees, if she'd done dat, he wouldn't tell us he was glad about it, would he? He ain't dat big a bastard.

PARRITT (*Speaks up from his own preoccupation—strangely*) You know better than that, Larry. You know she'd never commit suicide. She's like you. She'll hang on to life even when there's nothing left but—

LARRY (*Stung—turns on him viciously*) And how about you? Be God, if you had any guts or decency—! (*He stops guiltily*)

PARRITT (*Sneeringly*) I'd take that hop off your fire escape you're too yellow to take, I suppose?

LARRY (*As if to himself*) No! Who am I to judge? I'm done with judging.

PARRITT (*Tauntingly*) Yes, I suppose you'd like that, wouldn't you?

ROCKY (*Irritably mystified*) What de hell's all dis about? (*To* PARRITT) What d'you know about Hickey's wife? How d'yuh know she didn't—?

LARRY (*With forced belittling casualness*) He doesn't. Hickey's addled the little brains he's got. Shove him back to his own table, Rocky. I'm sick of him.

ROCKY (*To* PARRITT, *threateningly*) Yuh heard Larry? I'd like an excuse to give yuh a good punch in de snoot. So move quick!

PARRITT (*Gets up—to* LARRY) If you think moving to another table will get rid of me! (*He moves away—then adds with bitter reproach*) Gee, Larry, that's a hell of a way to treat me, when I've trusted you, and I need your help. (*He sits down in his old place and sinks into a wounded, self-pitying brooding*)

ROCKY (*Going back to his train of thought*) Jees, if she committed suicide, yuh got to feel sorry for Hickey, huh? Yuh can understand how he'd go bughouse and not be responsible for all de crazy stunts he's stagin' here. (*Then puzzledly*) But how can yuh be sorry for him when he says he's glad she croaked, and yuh can tell he means it? (*With weary exasperation*) Aw, nuts! I don't get nowhere tryin' to figger his game. (*His face hardening*) But I know dis. He better lay off me and my stable! (*He pauses—then sighs*) Jees, Larry, what a night dem two pigs give me! When de party went dead, dey pinched a coupla bottles and brung dem up deir room and got stinko. I don't get a wink of sleep, see? Just as I'd drop off on a chair here, dey'd come down lookin' for trouble. Or else dey'd raise hell upstairs, laughin' and singin', so I'd get scared dey'd get de joint pinched and go up to tell dem to can de noise. And every time dey'd crawl my frame wid de same old argument. Dey'd say, "So yuh agreed wid Hickey, do yuh, yuh dirty little Ginny? We're whores, are we? Well, we agree wid Hickey about you, see! Yuh're nuttin' but a lousy pimp!" Den I'd slap dem. Not beat 'em up, like a pimp would. Just slap dem. But it don't do no good. Dey'd keep at it over and over. Jees, I get de earache just thinkin' of it! "Listen," dey'd say, "if we're whores we gotta right to have a reg'lar pimp and not stand for no punk imitation! We're sick of wearin' out our dogs poundin' sidewalks for a double-crossin' bartender, when all de thanks we get is he looks down on us. We'll find a guy who really needs us to take care of him and ain't ashamed of it. Don't expect us to work tonight, 'cause we won't, see? Not if de streets was blocked wid sailors! We're goin' on strike and yuh can like it or lump it!" (*He shakes his head*) Whores goin' on strike! Can yuh tie dat? (*Going on with his story*) Dey says, "We're takin' a holiday. We're goin' to beat it down to Coney Island and shoot the chutes and maybe we'll come back and maybe we won't. And you can go to hell!" So dey put on deir lids and beat it, de bot' of dem stinko. (*He sighs dejectedly. He seems grotesquely like a harried family man, henpecked and browbeaten by a nagging wife.* LARRY *is deep in his own bitter preoccupation and hasn't listened to him.* CHUCK *enters from the hall at rear. He has his straw hat with the gaudy band in his hand and wears a Sunday-best blue suit with a high stiff collar. He looks sleepy, hot, uncomfortable and grouchy*)

CHUCK (*Glumly*) Hey, Rocky. Cora wants a sherry flip. For her noives.

ROCKY (*Turns indignantly*) Sherry flip! Christ, she don't need nuttin' for her noive! What's she tink dis is, de Waldorf?

CHUCK Yeah, I told her, what would we use for sherry, and dere wasn't no egg unless she laid one. She says, "Is dere a law yuh can't go out and buy de makings, yuh big tramp?" (*Resentfully puts his straw hat on his head at a defiant tilt*) To hell wid her! She'll drink booze or nuttin'! (*He goes behind the bar to draw a glass of whiskey from a barrel*)

ROCKY (*Sarcastically*) Jees, a guy oughta give his bride anything she wants on de weddin' day, I should tink! (*As* CHUCK *comes from behind the bar,* ROCKY *surveys him derisively*) Pipe de bridegroom, Larry! All dolled up for de killin'! (LARRY *pays no attention*)

CHUCK Aw, shut up!

ROCKY One week on dat farm in Joisey, dat's what I give yuh! Yuh'll come runnin' in here some night yellin' for a shot of booze 'cause de crickets is after yuh! (*Disgustedly*) Jees, Chuck, dat louse Hickey's coitinly made a prize coupla suckers outa youse.

CHUCK (*Unguardedly*) Yeah. I'd like to give him one sock in de puss—just one! (*Then angrily*) Aw, can dat! What's he got to do wid it? Ain't we always said we was goin' to? So we're goin' to, see? And don't give me no argument! (*He stares at* ROCKY *truculently. But* ROCKY *only shrugs his shoulders with weary disgust and* CHUCK *subsides into complaining gloom*) If on'y Cora'd cut out de beefin'. She don't gimme a minute's rest all night. De same old stuff over and over! Do I really want to marry her? I says, "Sure, Baby, why not?" She says, "Yeah, but after a week yuh'll be tinkin' what a sap you was. Yuh'll make dat an excuse to go off on a periodical, and den I'll be tied for life to a no-good soak, and de foist ting I know yuh'll have me out hustlin' again, your own wife!" Den she'd bust out cryin', and I'd get sore. "Yuh're a liar," I'd say. "I ain't never taken your dough 'cept when I was drunk and not workin'!" "Yeah," she'd say, "and how long will yuh stay sober now? Don't tink yuh can kid me wid dat water-wagon bull! I've heard it too often." Dat'd make me sore and I'd say, "Don't call me a liar. But I wish I was drunk right now, because if I was, yuh wouldn't be keepin' me awake all night beefin'. If yuh opened your yap, I'd knock de stuffin' outa yuh!" Den she'd yell, "Dat's a sweet way to talk to de goil yuh're goin' to marry." (*He sighs explosively*) Jees, she's got me hangin' on de ropes! (*He glances with vengeful yearning at the drink of whiskey in his hand*) Jees, would I like to get a quart of dis redeye under my belt!

ROCKY Well, why de hell don't yuh?

CHUCK (*Instantly suspicious and angry*) Sure! You'd

like dat, wouldn't yuh? I'm wise to you! Yuh don't wanta see me get married and settle down like a reg'lar guy! Yuh'd like me to stay paralyzed all de time, so's I'd be like you, a lousy pimp!

ROCKY (*Springs to his feet, his face hardened viciously*) Listen! I don't take dat even from you, see!

CHUCK (*Puts his drink on the bar and clenches his fists*) Yeah? Wanta make sometin' of it? (*Jeeringly*) Don't make me laugh! I can lick ten of youse wid one mit!

ROCKY (*Reaching for his hip pocket*) Not wid lead in your belly, yuh won't!

JOE (*Has stopped cutting when the quarrel started—expostulating*) Hey, you, Rocky and Chuck! Cut it out! You's ole friends! Don't let dat Hickey make you crazy!

CHUCK (*Turns on him*) Keep outa our business, yuh black bastard!

ROCKY (*Like* CHUCK, *turns on* JOE, *as if their own quarrel was forgotten and they became natural allies against an alien*) Stay where yuh belong, yuh doity nigger!

JOE (*Snarling with rage, springs from behind the lunch counter with the bread knife in his hand*) You white sons of bitches! I'll rip your guts out! (CHUCK *snatches a whiskey bottle from the bar and raises it above his head to hurl at* JOE. ROCKY *jerks a short-barreled, nickel-plated revolver from his hip pocket. At this moment* LARRY *pounds on the table with his fist and bursts into a sardonic laugh*)

LARRY That's it! Murder each other, you damned loons, with Hickey's blessing! Didn't I tell you he'd brought death with him? (*His interruption startles them. They pause to stare at him, their fighting fury suddenly dies out and they appear deflated and sheepish*)

ROCKY (*To* JOE) Aw right, you. Leggo dat shiv and I'll put dis gat away. (JOE *sullenly goes back behind the counter and slaps the knife on top of it.* ROCKY *slips the revolver back in his pocket.* CHUCK *lowers the bottle to the bar.* HUGO, *who has awakened and raised his head when* LARRY *pounded on the table, now giggles foolishly*)

HUGO Hello, leedle peoples! Neffer mind! Soon you vill eat hot dogs beneath the villow trees and trink free vine— (*Abruptly in a haughty fastidious tone*) The champagne vas not properly iced. (*With guttural anger*) Gottamned liar, Hickey! Does that prove I vant to be aristocrat? I love only the proletariat! I vill lead them! I vill be like a Gott to them! They vill be my slaves! (*He stops in bewildered self-amazement—to* LARRY *appealingly*) I am very trunk, no, Larry? I talk foolishness. I am so trunk, Larry, old friend, am I not, I don't know vhat I say?

LARRY (*Pityingly*) You're raving drunk, Hugo. I've never seen you so paralyzed. Lay your head down now and sleep it off.

HUGO (*Gratefully*) Yes. I should sleep. I am too crazy trunk. (*He puts his head on his arms and closes his eyes*)

JOE (*Behind the lunch counter—brooding superstitiously*) You's right, Larry. Bad luck come in de door when Hickey come. I's an ole gamblin' man and I knows bad luck when I feels it! (*Then defiantly*) But it's white man's bad luck. He can't jinx me! (*He comes from behind the counter and goes to the bar—addressing* ROCKY *stiffly*) De bread's cut and I's finished my job. Do I get de drink I's earned? (ROCKY *gives him a hostile look but shoves a bottle and glass at him.* JOE *pours a brimful drink—sullenly*) I's finished wid dis dump for keeps. (*He takes a key from his pocket and slaps it on the bar*) Here's de key to my room. I ain't comin' back. I's goin' to my own folks where I belong. I don't stay where I's not wanted. I's sick and tired of messin' round wid white men. (*He gulps down his drink—then looking around defiantly he deliberately throws his whiskey glass on the floor and smashes it*)

ROCKY Hey! What de hell—!

JOE (*With a sneering dignity*) I's on'y savin' you de trouble, White Boy. Now you don't have to break it, soon's my back's turned, so's no white man kick about drinkin' from de same glass. (*He walks stiffly to the street door—then turns for a parting shot—boastfully*) I's tired of loafin' 'round wid a lot of bums. I's a gamblin' man. I's gonna get in a big crap game and win me a big bankroll. Den I'll get de okay to open up my old gamblin' house for colored men. Den maybe I comes back here sometime to see de bums. Maybe I throw a twenty-dollar bill on de bar and say, "Drink it up," and listen when dey all pat me on de back and say, "Joe, you sure is white." But I'll say, "No, I'm black and my dough is black man's dough, and you's proud to drink wid me or you don't get no drink!" Or maybe I just says, "You can all go to hell. I don't lower myself drinkin' wid no white trash!" (*He opens the door to go out—then turns again*) And dat ain't no pipe dream! I'll git de money for my stake today, somehow, somewheres! If I has to borrow a gun and stick up some white man, I gets it! You wait and see! (*He swaggers out through the swinging doors*)

CHUCK (*Angrily*) Can yuh beat de noive of dat dinge! Jees, if I wasn't dressed up, I'd go out and mop up de street wid him!

ROCKY Aw, let him go, de poor old dope! Him and his gamblin' house! He'll be back tonight askin' Harry for his room and bummin' me for a ball. (*Vengefully*) Den I'll be de one to smash de glass. I'll loin him his place! (*The swinging doors are pushed open and* WILLIE OBAN *enters from the street. He is shaved and wears an expensive, well-cut suit, good shoes and clean linen. He is absolutely sober, but his face is sick, and his nerves in a shocking state of shakes*)

CHUCK Another guy all dolled up! Got your clothes from Solly's, huh, Willie? (*Derisively*) Now yuh can sell dem back to him again tomorrow.

WILLIE (*Stiffly*) No, I—I'm through with that stuff. Never again. (*He comes to the bar*)

ROCKY (*Sympathetically*) Yuh look sick, Willie. Take a ball to pick yuh up. (*He pushes a bottle toward him*)

WILLIE (*Eyes the bottle yearningly but shakes his head—determinedly*) No, thanks. The only way to stop is to stop. I'd have no chance if I went to the D.A.'s office smelling of booze.

CHUCK Yuh're really goin' dere?

WILLIE (*Stiffly*) I said I was, didn't I? I just came back here to rest a few minutes, not because I needed any booze. I'll show that cheap drummer I don't have to have any Dutch courage— (*Guiltily*) But he's been very kind and generous staking me. He can't help his insulting manner, I suppose. (*He turns away from the bar*) My legs are a bit shaky yet. I better sit down a while. (*He goes back and sits at the left of the second table, facing* PARRITT, *who gives him a scowling, suspicious glance and then ignores him.* ROCKY *looks at* CHUCK *and taps his head disgustedly.* CAPTAIN LEWIS *appears in the doorway from the hall*)

CHUCK (*Mutters*) Here's anudder one. (LEWIS *looks spruce and clean-shaven. His ancient tweed suit has been brushed and his frayed linen is clean. His manner is full of a forced, jaunty self-assurance. But he is sick and beset by katzenjammer*[2])

LEWIS Good morning, gentlemen all. (*He passes along the front of bar to look out in the street*) A jolly fine morning, too. (*He turns back to the bar*) An eye-opener? I think not. Not required, Rocky, old chum. Feel extremely fit, as a matter of fact. Though can't say I slept much, thanks to that interfering ass, Hickey, and that stupid bounder of a Boer. (*His face hardens*) I've had about all I can take from that fellow. It's my own fault, of course, for allowing a brute of a Dutch farmer to become familiar. Well, it's come to a parting of the ways now, and good riddance. Which reminds me, here's my key. (*He puts it on the bar*) I shan't be coming back. Sorry to be leaving good old Harry and the rest of you, of course, but I can't continue to live under the same roof with that fellow. (*He stops, stiffening into hostility as* WETJOEN *enters from the hall, and pointedly turns his back on him.* WETJOEN *glares at him sneeringly. He, too, has made an effort to spruce up his appearance, and his bearing has a forced swagger of conscious physical strength. Behind this, he is sick and feebly holding his booze-sodden body together*)

ROCKY (*To* LEWIS*—disgustedly putting the key on the shelf in back of the bar*) So Hickey's kidded the pants offa you, too? Yuh tink yuh're leavin' here, huh?

WETJOEN (*Jeeringly*) Ja! Dot's vhat he kids himself.

LEWIS (*Ignores him—airily*) Yes, I'm leaving, Rocky. But that ass, Hickey, has nothing to do with it. Been thinking things over. Time I turned over a new leaf, and all that.

WETJOEN He's going to get a job! Dot's what he says!

ROCKY What at, for Chris' sake?

LEWIS (*Keeping his airy manner*) Oh, anything. I mean, not manual labor, naturally, but anything that calls for a bit of brains and education. However humble. Beggars can't be choosers. I'll see a pal of mine at the Consulate. He promised any time I felt an energetic fit he'd get me a post with the Cunard—clark in the office or something of the kind.

[2] A bad hangover, complete with headaches, nausea, and the jitters.

WETJOEN Ja! At Limey Consulate they promise anything to get rid of him vhen he comes there tronk! They're scared to call the police and have him pinched because it vould scandal in the papers make about a Limey officer and chentleman!

LEWIS As a matter of fact, Rocky, I only wish a post temporarily. Means to an end, you know. Save up enough for a first-class passage home, that's the bright idea.

WETJOEN He's sailing back to home, sveet home! Dot's biggest pipe dream of all. What leetle brain the poor Limey has left, dot isn't in whiskey pickled, Hickey has made crazy! (LEWIS' *fists clench, but he manages to ignore this*)

CHUCK (*Feels sorry for* LEWIS *and turns on* WETJOEN*—sarcastically*) Hickey ain't made no sucker outa you, huh? You're too foxy, huh? But I'll bet you tink yuh're goin' out and land a job, too.

WETJOEN (*Bristles*) I am, ja. For me, it is easy. Because I put on no airs of chentleman. I am not ashamed to vork vith my hands. I vas a farmer before the war ven ploody Limey thieves steal my country. (*Boastfully*) Anyone I ask for job can see vith one look I have the great strength to do work of ten ordinary mens.

LEWIS (*Sneeringly*) Yes, Chuck, you remember he gave a demonstration of his extraordinary muscles last night when he helped to move the piano.

CHUCK Yuh couldn't even hold up your corner. It was your fault de damned box almost fell down de stairs.

WETJOEN My hands vas sweaty! Could I help dot my hands slip? I could de whole veight of it lift! In old days in Transvaal, I lift loaded oxcart by the axle! So vhy shouldn't I get job? Dot longshoreman boss, Dan, he tell me any time I like, he take me on. And Benny from de Market he promise me same.

LEWIS You remember, Rocky, it was one of those rare occasions when the Boer that walks like a man—spelled with a double o, by the way—was buying drinks and Dan and Benny were stony. They'd bloody well have promised him the moon.

ROCKY Yeah, yuh big boob, dem boids was on'y kiddin' yuh.

WETJOEN (*Angrily*) Dot's lie! You vill see dis morning I get job! I'll show dot bloody Limey chentleman, and dot liar, Hickey! And I need vork only leetle vhile to save money for my passage home. I need not much money because I am not ashamed to travel steerage. I don't put on first-cabin airs! (*Tauntingly*) Und *I can* go home to my country! Vhen I get there, they vill let *me* come in!

LEWIS (*Grows rigid—his voice trembling with repressed anger*) There was a rumor in South Africa, Rocky, that a certain Boer officer—if you call the leaders of a rabble of farmers officers—kept advising Cronje to retreat and not stand and fight—

WETJOEN And I vas right! I vas right! He got surrounded at Paardeberg![3] He had to surrender!

[3] Cronje's surrender to the British forces under Lord Roberts at Paardeberg (February 28, 1900) was perhaps the tide-turning moment in the Boer War.

LEWIS (*Ignoring him*) Good strategy, no doubt, but a suspicion grew afterwards into a conviction among the Boers that the officer's caution was prompted by a desire to make his personal escape. His countrymen felt extremely savage about it, and his family disowned him. So I imagine there would be no welcoming committee waiting on the dock, nor delighted relatives making the veldt ring with their happy cries—

WETJOEN (*With guilty rage*) All lies! You Gottamned Limey— (*Trying to control himself and copy* LEWIS' *manner*) I also haf heard rumors of a Limey officer who, after the war, lost all his money gambling vhen he vas tronk. But they found out it vas regiment money, too, he lost—

LEWIS (*Loses his control and starts for him*) You bloody Dutch scum!

ROCKY (*Leans over the bar and stops* LEWIS *with a straight-arm swipe on the chest*) Cut it out! (*At the same moment* CHUCK *grabs* WETJOEN *and yanks him back*)

WETJOEN (*Struggling*) Let him come! I saw them come before—at Modder River, Magersfontein,[4] Spion Kopje—waving their silly swords, so afraid they couldn't show off how brave they vas!—and I kill them vith my rifle so easy! (*Vindictively*) Listen to me, you Cecil! Often vhen I am tronk and kidding you I say I am sorry I missed you, but now, py Gott, I am sober, and I don't joke, and I say it!

LARRY (*Gives a sardonic guffaw—with his comically crazy, intense whisper*) Be God, you can't say Hickey hasn't the miraculous touch to raise the dead, when he can start the Boer War raging again! (*This interruption acts like a cold douche on* LEWIS *and* WETJOEN. *They subside, and* ROCKY *and* CHUCK *let go of them.* LEWIS *turns his back on the Boer*)

LEWIS (*Attempting a return of his jaunty manner, as if nothing had happened*) Well, time I was on my merry way to see my chap at the Consulate. The early bird catches the job, what? Good-bye and good luck, Rocky, and everyone. (*He starts for the street door*)

WETJOEN Py Gott, if dot Limey can go, I can go! (*He hurries after* LEWIS. *But* LEWIS, *his hand about to push the swinging doors open, hesitates, as though struck by a sudden paralysis of the will, and* WETJOEN *has to jerk back to avoid bumping into him. For a second they stand there, one behind the other, staring over the swinging doors into the street*)

ROCKY Well, why don't yuh beat it?

LEWIS (*Guiltily casual*) Eh? Oh, just happened to think. Hardly the decent thing to pop off without saying good-bye to old Harry. One of the best, Harry. And good old Jimmy, too. They ought to be down any moment. (*He pretends to notice* WETJOEN *for the first time and steps away from the door—apologizing as to a stranger*) Sorry. I seem to be blocking your way out.

WETJOEN (*Stiffly*) No. I vait to say good-bye to Harry and Jimmy, too. (*He goes to right of door behind the lunch counter and looks through the window, his back to the room.* LEWIS *takes up a similar stand at the window on the left of door*)

CHUCK Jees, can yuh beat dem simps! (*He picks up* CORA'S *drink at the end of the bar*) Hell, I'd forgot Cora. She'll be trowin' a fit. (*He goes into the hall with the drink*)

ROCKY (*Looks after him disgustedly*) Dat's right, wait on her and spoil her, yuh poor sap! (*He shakes his head and begins to wipe the bar mechanically*)

WILLIE (*Is regarding* PARRITT *across the table from him with an eager, calculating eye. He leans over and speaks in a low confidential tone*) Look here, Parritt. I'd like to have a talk with you.

PARRITT (*Starts—scowling defensively*) What about?

WILLIE (*His manner becoming his idea of a crafty criminal lawyer's*) About the trouble you're in. Oh, I know. You don't admit it. You're quite right. That's my advice. Deny everything. Keep your mouth shut. Make no statements whatever without first consulting your attorney.

PARRITT Say! What the hell—?

WILLIE But you can trust me. I'm a lawyer, and it's just occurred to me you and I ought to co-operate. Of course I'm going to see the D.A. this morning about a job on his staff. But that may take time. There may not be an immediate opening. Meanwhile it would be a good idea for me to take a case or two, on my own, and prove my brilliant record in law school was no flash in the pan. So why not retain me as your attorney?

PARRITT You're crazy! What do I want with a lawyer?

WILLIE That's right. Don't admit anything. But you can trust me, so let's not beat about the bush. You got in trouble out on the Coast, eh? And now you're hiding out. Any fool can spot that. (*Lowering his voice still more*) You feel safe here, and maybe you are, for a while. But remember, they get you in the end. I know from my father's experience. No one could have felt safer than he did. When anyone mentioned the law to him, he nearly died laughing. But—

PARRITT You crazy mutt! (*Turning to* LARRY *with a strained laugh*) Did you get that, Larry? This damned fool thinks the cops are after me!

LARRY (*Bursts out with his true reaction before he thinks to ignore him*) I wish to God they were! And so should you, if you had the honor of a louse! (PARRITT *stares into his eyes guiltily for a second. Then he smiles sneeringly*)

PARRITT And you're the guy who kids himself he's through with the Movement! You old lying faker, you're still in love with it! (LARRY *ignores him again now*)

WILLIE (*Disappointedly*) Then you're not in trouble, Parritt? I was hoping— But never mind. No offense meant. Forget it.

PARRITT (*Condescendingly—his eyes on* LARRY) Sure. That's all right, Willie. I'm not sore at you. It's that damned old faker that gets my goat. (*He slips out of his chair and goes quietly over to sit in the chair*

[4] An early engagement in the Boer War in which the Highland Brigade under Wauchope suffered great losses.

*beside* LARRY *he had occupied before—in a low, insinuating, intimate tone*) I think I understand, Larry. It's really Mother you still love—isn't it?—in spite of the dirty deal she gave you. But hell, what did you expect? She was never true to anyone but herself and the Movement. But I understand how you can't help still feeling—because I still love her, too. (*Pleading in a strained, desperate tone*) You know I do, don't you? You must! So you see I couldn't have expected they'd catch her! You've got to believe me that I sold them out just to get a few lousy dollars to blow in on a whore. No other reason, honest! There couldn't possibly be any other reason! (*Again he has a strange air of exonerating himself from guilt by this shameless confession*)

LARRY (*Trying not to listen, has listened with increasing tension*) For the love of Christ will you leave me in peace! I've told you you can't make me judge you! But if you don't keep still, you'll be saying something soon that will make you vomit your own soul like a drink of nickel rotgut that won't stay down! (*He pushes back his chair and springs to his feet*) To hell with you! (*He goes to the bar*)

PARRITT (*Jumps up and starts to follow him—desperately*) Don't go, Larry! You've got to help me! (*But* LARRY *is at the bar, back turned, and* ROCKY *is scowling at him. He stops, shrinking back into himself helplessly, and turns away. He goes to the table where he had been before, and this time he takes the chair at rear facing directly front. He puts his elbows on the table, holding his head in his hands as if he had a splitting headache*)

LARRY Set 'em up, Rocky. I swore I'd have no more drinks on Hickey, if I died of drought, but I've changed my mind! Be God, he owes it to me, and I'd get blind to the world now if it was the Iceman of Death himself treating! (*He stops, startledly, a superstitious awe coming into his face*) What made me say that, I wonder. (*With a sardonic laugh*) Well, be God, it fits, for Death was the Iceman Hickey called to his home!

ROCKY Aw, forget dat iceman gag! De poor dame is dead. (*Pushing a bottle and glass at* LARRY) Gwan and get paralyzed! I'll be glad to see one bum in dis dump act natural. (LARRY *downs a drink and pours another*)

(ED MOSHER *appears in the doorway from the hall. The same change which is apparent in the manner and appearance of the others shows in him. He is sick, his nerves are shattered, his eyes are apprehensive, but he, too, puts on an exaggeratedly self-confident bearing. He saunters to the bar between* LARRY *and the street entrance*)

MOSHER Morning, Rocky. Hello, Larry. Glad to see Brother Hickey hasn't corrupted you to temperance. I wouldn't mind a shot myself. (*As* ROCKY *shoves a bottle toward him he shakes his head*) But I remember the only breath-killer in this dump is coffee beans. The boss would never fall for that. No man can run a circus successfully who believes guys chew coffee beans because they like them. (*He pushes the bottle away*) No, much as I need one after the hell of a night I've had— (*He scowls*) That drummer son of a drummer! I had to lock him out. But I could hear him through the wall doing his spiel to someone all night long. Still at it with Jimmy and Harry when I came down just now. But the hardest to take was that flannel-mouth, flatfoot Mick trying to tell me where I got off! I had to lock him out, too. (*As he says this,* MCGLOIN *comes in the doorway from the hall. The change in his appearance and manner is identical with that of* MOSHER *and the others*)

MCGLOIN He's a liar, Rocky! It was me locked him out! (MOSHER *starts to flare up—then ignores him. They turn their backs on each other.* MCGLOIN *starts into the back-room section*)

WILLIE Come and sit here, Mac. You're just the man I want to see. If I'm to take your case, we ought to have a talk before we leave.

MCGLOIN (*Contemptuously*) We'll have no talk. You damned fool, do you think I'd have your father's son for my lawyer? They'd take one look at you and bounce us both out on our necks! (WILLIE *winces and shrinks down in his chair.* MCGLOIN *goes to the first table beyond him and sits with his back to the bar*) I don't need a lawyer, anyway. To hell with the law! All I've got to do is see the right ones and get them to pass the word. They will, too. They know I was framed. And once they've passed the word, it's as good as done, law or no law.

MOSHER God, I'm glad I'm leaving this madhouse! (*He pulls his key from his pocket and slaps it on the bar*) Here's my key, Rocky.

MCGLOIN (*Pulls his from his pocket*) And here's mine. (*He tosses it to* ROCKY) I'd rather sleep in the gutter than pass another night under the same roof with that loon, Hickey, and a lying circus grifter! (*He adds darkly*) And if that hat fits anyone here, let him put it on! (MOSHER *turns toward him furiously but* ROCKY *leans over the bar and grabs his arm*)

ROCKY Nix! Take it easy! (MOSHER *subsides.* ROCKY *tosses the keys on the shelf—disgustedly*) You boids gimme a pain. It'd soive you right if I wouldn't give de keys back to yuh tonight. (*They both turn on him resentfully, but there is an interruption as* CORA *appears in the doorway from the hall with* CHUCK *behind her. She is drunk, dressed in her gaudy best, her face plastered with rouge and mascara, her hair a bit disheveled, her hat on anyhow*)

CORA (*Comes a few steps inside the bar—with a strained bright giggle*) Hello, everybody! Here we go! Hickey just told us, ain't it time we beat it, if we're really goin'. So we're showin' de bastard, ain't we, Honey? He's comin' right down wid Harry and Jimmy. Jees, dem two look like dey was goin' to de electric chair! (*With frightened anger*) If I had to listen to any more of Hickey's bunk, I'd brain him. (*She puts her hand on* CHUCK'S *arm*) Come on, Honey. Let's get started before he comes down.

CHUCK (*Sullenly*) Sure, anyting yuh say, Baby.

CORA (*Turns on him truculently*) Yeah? Well, I say we stop at de foist reg'lar dump and yuh gotta blow me to a sherry flip—or four or five, if I want 'em! —or all bets is off!

CHUCK Aw, yuh got a fine bun on now!

CORA Cheap skate! I know what's eatin' you, Tightwad! Well, use my dough, den, if yuh're so stingy. Yuh'll grab it all, anyway, right after de ceremony. I know you! (*She hikes her skirt up and reaches inside the top of her stocking*) Here, yuh big tramp!

CHUCK (*Knocks her hand away—angrily*) Keep your lousy dough! And don't show off your legs to dese bums when yuh're goin' to be married, if yuh don't want a sock in de puss!

CORA (*Pleased—meekly*) Aw right, Honey. (*Looking around with a foolish laugh*) Say, why don't all you barflies come to de weddin'? (*But they are all sunk in their own apprehensions and ignore her. She hesitates, miserably uncertain*) Well, we're goin', guys. (*There is no comment. Her eyes fasten on* ROCKY—*desperately*) Say, Rocky, yuh gone deef? I said me and Chuck was goin' now.

ROCKY (*Wiping the bar—with elaborate indifference*) Well, good-bye. Give my love to Joisey.

CORA (*Tearfully indignant*) Ain't yuh goin' to wish us happiness, yuh doity little Ginny?

ROCKY Sure. Here's hopin' yuh don't moider each odder before next week.

CHUCK (*Angrily*) Aw, Baby, what d'we care for dat pimp? (ROCKY *turns on him threateningly, but* CHUCK *hears someone upstairs in the hall and grabs* CORA's *arm*) Here's Hickey comin'! Let's get outa here! (*They hurry into the hall. The street door is heard slamming behind them*)

ROCKY (*Gloomily pronounces an obituary*) One regular guy and one all-right tart gone to hell! (*Fiercely*) Dat louse Hickey oughta be croaked! (*There is a muttered growl of assent from most of the gathering. Then* HARRY HOPE *enters from the hall, followed by* JIMMY TOMORROW, *with* HICKEY *on his heels.* HOPE *and* JIMMY *are both putting up a front of self-assurance, but* CORA's *description of them was apt. There is a desperate bluff in their manner as they walk in, which suggests the last march of the condemned.* HOPE *is dressed in an old black Sunday suit, black tie, shoes, socks, which give him the appearance of being in mourning.* JIMMY's *clothes are pressed, his shoes shined, his white linen immaculate. He has a hangover and his gently appealing dog's eyes have a boiled look.* HICKEY's *face is a bit drawn from lack of sleep and his voice is hoarse from continual talking, but his bustling energy appears nervously intensified, and his beaming expression is one of triumphant accomplishment*)

HICKEY Well, here we are! We've got this far, at least! (*He pats* JIMMY *on the back*) Good work, Jimmy. I told you you weren't half as sick as you pretended. No excuse whatever for postponing—

JIMMY I'll thank you to keep your hands off me! I merely mentioned I would feel more fit tomorrow. But it might as well be today, I suppose.

HICKEY Finish it now, so it'll be dead forever, and you can be free! (*He passes him to clap* HOPE *encouragingly on the shoulder*) Cheer up, Harry. You found your rheumatism didn't bother you coming downstairs, didn't you? I told you it wouldn't. (*He winks around at the others. With the exception of* HUGO *and* PARRITT, *all their eyes are fixed on him with bitter animosity. He gives* HOPE *a playful nudge in the ribs*) You're the damnedest one for alibis, Governor! As bad as Jimmy!

HOPE (*Putting on his deaf manner*) Eh? I can't hear— (*Defiantly*) You're a liar! I've had rheumatism on and off for twenty years. Ever since Bessie died. Everybody knows that.

HICKEY Yes, we know it's the kind of rheumatism you turn on and off! We're on to you, you old faker! (*He claps him on the shoulder again, chuckling*)

HOPE (*Looks humiliated and guilty—by way of escape he glares around at the others*) Bejees, what are all you bums hanging round staring at me for? Think you was watching a circus! Why don't you get the hell out of here and 'tend to your own business, like Hickey's told you? (*They look at him reproachfully, their eyes hurt. They fidget as if trying to move*)

HICKEY Yes, Harry, I certainly thought they'd have had the guts to be gone by this time. (*He grins*) Or maybe I did have my doubts. (*Abruptly he becomes sincerely sympathetic and earnest*) Because I know exactly what you're up against, boys. I know how damned yellow a man can be when it comes to making himself face the truth. I've been through the mill, and I had to face a worse bastard in myself than any of you will have to in yourselves. I know you become such a coward you'll grab at any lousy excuse to get out of killing your pipe dreams. And yet, as I've told you over and over, it's exactly those damned tomorrow dreams which keep you from making peace with yourself. So you've got to kill them like I did mine. (*He pauses. They glare at him with fear and hatred. They seem about to curse him, to spring at him. But they remain silent and motionless. His manner changes and he becomes kindly bullying*) Come on, boys! Get moving! Who'll start the ball rolling? You, Captain, and you, General. You're nearest the door. And besides, you're old war heroes! You ought to lead the forlorn hope! Come on, now, show us a little of that good old battle of Modder River spirit we've heard so much about! You can't hang around all day looking as if you were scared the street outside would bite you!

LEWIS (*Turns with humiliated rage—with an attempt at jaunty casualness*) Right you are, Mister Bloody Nosey Parker! Time I pushed off. Was only waiting to say good-bye to you, Harry, old chum.

HOPE (*Dejectedly*) Good-bye, Captain. Hope you have luck.

LEWIS Oh, I'm bound to, Old Chap, and the same to you. (*He pushes the swinging doors open and makes a brave exit, turning to his right and marching off outside the window at right of door*)

WETJOEN Py Gott, if dot Limey can, I can! (*He pushes the door open and lumbers through it like a *bull charging an obstacle. He turns left and disappears off rear, outside the farthest window*)

HICKEY (*Exhortingly*) Next? Come on, Ed. It's a fine summer's day and the call of the old circus lot must be in your blood! (MOSHER *glares at him, then goes to the door.* MCGLOIN *jumps up from his chair and starts moving toward the door.* HICKEY *claps him on the back as he passes*) That's the stuff, Mac.

MOSHER Good-bye, Harry. (*He goes out, turning right outside*)

MCGLOIN (*Glowering after him*) If that crooked grifter has the guts— (*He goes out, turning left outside.* HICKEY *glances at* WILLIE *who, before he can speak, jumps from his chair*)

WILLIE Good-bye, Harry, and thanks for all the kindness.

HICKEY (*Claps him on the back*) That's the way, Willie! The D.A.'s a busy man. He can't wait all day for you, you know. (WILLIE *hurries to the door*)

HOPE (*Dully*) Good luck, Willie. (WILLIE *goes out and turns right outside. While he is doing so,* JIMMY, *in a sick panic, sneaks to the bar and furtively reaches for* LARRY'S *glass of whiskey*)

HICKEY And now it's your turn, Jimmy, old pal. (*He sees what* JIMMY *is at and grabs his arm just as he is about to down the drink*) Now, now, Jimmy! You can't do that to yourself. One drink on top of your hangover and an empty stomach and you'll be oreyeyed.[5] Then you'll tell yourself you wouldn't stand a chance if you went up soused to get your old job back.

JIMMY (*Pleads abjectly*) Tomorrow! I will tomorrow! I'll be in good shape tomorrow! (*Abruptly getting control of himself—with shaken firmness*) All right. I'm going. Take your hands off me.

HICKEY That's the ticket! You'll thank me when it's all over.

JIMMY (*In a burst of futile fury*) You dirty swine! (*He tries to throw the drink in* HICKEY'S *face, but his aim is poor and it lands on* HICKEY'S *coat.* JIMMY *turns and dashes through the door, disappearing outside the window at right of door*)

HICKEY (*Brushing the whiskey off his coat—humorously*) All set for an alcohol rub! But no hard feelings. I know how he feels. I wrote the book. I've seen the day when if anyone forced me to face the truth about my pipe dreams, I'd have shot them dead. (*He turns to* HOPE*—encouragingly*) Well, Governor, Jimmy made the grade. It's up to you. If he's got the guts to go through with the test, then certainly you—

LARRY (*Burst out*) Leave Harry alone, damn you!

HICKEY (*Grins at him*) I'd make up my mind about myself if I was you, Larry, and not bother over Harry. He'll come through all right. I've promised him that. He doesn't need anyone's bum pity. Do you, Governor?

HOPE (*With a pathetic attempt at his old fuming assertiveness*) No, bejees! Keep your nose out of this, Larry. What's Hickey got to do with it? I've always been going to take this walk, ain't I? Bejees, you bums want to keep me locked up in here 's if I was in jail! I've stood it long enough! I'm free, white and twenty-one, and I'll do as I damned please, bejees! You keep your nose out, too, Hickey! You'd think you was boss of this dump, not me. Sure, I'm all right! Why shouldn't I be? What the hell's to be scared of, just taking a stroll around my own ward? (*As he talks he has been moving toward the door. Now he reaches it*) What's the weather like outside, Rocky?

ROCKY Fine day, Boss.

HOPE What's that? Can't hear you. Don't look fine to me. Looks 's if it'd pour down cats and dogs any minute. My rheumatism— (*He catches himself*) No, must be my eyes. Half blind, bejees. Makes things look black. I see now it's a fine day. Too damned hot for a walk, though, if you ask me. Well, do me good to sweat the booze out of me. But I'll have to watch out for the damned automobiles. Wasn't none of them around the last time, twenty years ago. From what I've seen of 'em through the window, they'd run over you as soon as look at you. Not that I'm scared of 'em. I can take care of myself. (*He puts a reluctant hand on the swinging door*) Well, so long— (*He stops and looks back—with frightened irascibility*) Bejees, where are you, Hickey? It's time we got started.

HICKEY (*Grins and shakes his head*) No, Harry. Can't be done. You've got to keep a date with yourself alone.

HOPE (*With forced fuming*) Hell of a guy, you are! Thought you'd be willing to help me across the street, knowing I'm half blind. Half deaf, too. Can't bear those damned automobiles. Hell with you! Bejees, I've never needed no one's help and I don't now! (*Egging himself on*) I'll take a good long walk now I've started. See all my old friends. Bejees, they must have given me up for dead. Twenty years is a long time. But they know it was grief over Bessie's death that made me— (*He puts his hand on the door*) Well, the sooner I get started— (*Then he drops his hand—with sentimental melancholy*) You know, Hickey, that's what gets me. Can't help thinking the last time I went out was to Bessie's funeral. After she'd gone, I didn't feel life was worth living. Swore I'd never go out again. (*Pathetically*) Somehow, I can't feel it's right for me to go, Hickey, even now. It's like I was doing wrong to her memory.

HICKEY Now, Governor, you can't let yourself get away with that one any more!

HOPE (*Cupping his hand to his ear*) What's that? Can't hear you. (*Sentimentally again but with desperation*) I remember now clear as day the last time before she— It was a fine Sunday morning. We went out to church together. (*His voice breaks on a sob*)

HICKEY (*Amused*) It's a great act, Governor. But I know better, and so do you. You never did want to go to church or any place else with her. She was always on your neck, making you have ambition and go out and do things, when all you wanted was to get drunk in peace.

HOPE (*Falteringly*) Can't hear a word you're saying. You're a God-damned liar, anyway! (*Then in a sud-*

[5] Cockeyed drunk.

*den fury, his voice trembling with hatred)* Bejees, you son of a bitch, if there was a mad dog outside I'd go and shake hands with it rather than stay here with you! *(The momentum of his fit of rage does it. He pushes the door open and strides blindly out into the street and as blindly past the window behind the free-lunch counter)*

ROCKY *(In amazement)* Jees, he made it! I'd a give yuh fifty to one he'd never— *(He goes to the end of the bar to look through the window—disgustedly)* Aw, he's stopped. I'll bet yuh he's comin' back.

HICKEY Of course, he's coming back. So are all the others. By tonight they'll all be here again. You dumbbell, that's the whole point.

ROCKY *(Excitedly)* No, he ain't neider! He's gone to de coib. He's lookin' up and down. Scared stiff of automobiles. Jees, dey ain't more'n two an hour comes down dis street, de old boob! *(He watches excitedly, as if it were a race he had a bet on, oblivious to what happens in the bar)*

LARRY *(Turns on* HICKEY *with bitter defiance)* And now it's my turn, I suppose? What is it I'm to do to achieve this blessed peace of yours?

HICKEY *(Grins at him)* Why, we've discussed all that, Larry. Just stop lying to yourself—

LARRY You think when I say I'm finished with life, and tired of watching the stupid greed of the human circus, and I'll welcome closing my eyes in the long sleep of death—you think that's a coward's lie?

HICKEY *(Chuckling)* Well, what do you think, Larry?

LARRY *(With increasing bitter intensity, more as if he were fighting with himself than with* HICKEY*)* I'm afraid to live, am I?—and even more afraid to die! So I sit here, with my pride drowned on the bottom of a bottle, keeping drunk so I won't see myself shaking in my britches with fright, or hear myself whining and praying: Beloved Christ, let me live a little longer at any price! If it's only for a few days more, or a few hours even, have mercy, Almighty God, and let me still clutch greedily to my yellow heart this sweet treasure, this jewel beyond price, the dirty, stinking bit of withered old flesh which is my beautiful little life! *(He laughs with a sneering, vindictive self-loathing, staring inward at himself with contempt and hatred. Then abruptly he makes* HICKEY *again the antagonist)* You think you'll make me admit that to myself?

HICKEY *(Chuckling)* But you just did admit it, didn't you?

PARRITT *(Lifts his head from his hands to glare at* LARRY*—jeeringly)* That's the stuff, Hickey! Show the old yellow faker up! He can't play dead on me like this! He's got to help me!

HICKEY Yes, Larry, you've got to settle with him. I'm leaving you entirely in his hands. He'll do as good a job as I could at making you give up that old grandstand bluff.

LARRY *(Angrily)* I'll see the two of you in hell first!

ROCKY *(Calls excitedly from the end of the bar)* Jees, Harry's startin' across de street! He's goin' to fool yuh, Hickey, yuh bastard! *(He pauses, watching—then worriedly)* What de hell's he stoppin' for? Right in de middle of de street! Yuh'd tink he was paralyzed or somethin'! *(Disgustedly)* Aw, he's quittin'! He's turned back! Jees, look at de old bastard travel! Here he comes! *(*HOPE *passes the window outside the free-lunch counter in a shambling, panic-stricken run. He comes lurching blindly through the swinging doors and stumbles to the bar at* LARRY's *right)*

HOPE Bejees, give me a drink quick! Scared me out of a year's growth! Bejees, that guy ought to be pinched! Bejees, it ain't safe to walk in the streets! Bejees, that ends me! Never again! Give me that bottle! *(He slops a glass full and drains it and pours another— To* ROCKY, *who is regarding him with scorn—appealingly)* You seen it, didn't you, Rocky?

ROCKY Seen what?

HOPE That automobile, you dumb Wop! Feller driving it must be drunk or crazy. He'd run right over me if I hadn't jumped. *(Ingratiatingly)* Come on, Larry, have a drink. Everybody have a drink. Have a cigar, Rocky. I know you hardly ever touch it.

ROCKY *(Resentfully)* Well, dis is de time I do touch it! *(Pouring a drink)* I'm goin' to get stinko, see! And if yuh don't like it, yuh know what yuh can do! I gotta good mind to chuck my job, anyways. *(Disgustedly)* Jees, Harry, I thought yuh had some guts! I was bettin' yuh'd make it and show dat four-flusher up. *(He nods at* HICKEY*—then snorts)* Automobile, hell! Who d'yuh tink yuh're kiddin'? Dey wasn' no automobile! Yuh just quit cold!

HOPE *(Feebly)* Guess I ought to know! Bejees, it almost killed me!

HICKEY *(Comes to the bar between him and* LARRY, *and puts a hand on his shoulder—kindly)* Now, now, Governor. Don't be foolish. You've faced the test and come through. You're rid of all that nagging dream stuff now. You know you can't believe it any more.

HOPE *(Appeals pleadingly to* LARRY*)* Larry, you saw it, didn't you? Drink up! Have another! Have all you want! Bejees, we'll go on a grand old souse together! You saw that automobile, didn't you?

LARRY *(Compassionately, avoiding his eyes)* Sure, I saw it, Harry. You had a narrow escape. Be God, I thought you were a goner!

HICKEY *(Turns on him with a flash of sincere indignation)* What the hell's the matter with you, Larry? You know what I told you about the wrong kind of pity. Leave Harry alone! You'd think I was trying to harm him, the fool way you act! My oldest friend! What kind of a louse do you think I am? There isn't anything I wouldn't do for Harry, and he knows it! All I've wanted to do is fix it so he'll be finally at peace with himself for the rest of his days! And if you'll only wait until the final returns are in, you'll find that's exactly what I've accomplished! *(He turns to* HOPE *and pats his shoulder—coaxingly)* Come now, Governor. What's the use of being stubborn, now when it's all over and dead? Give up that ghost automobile.

HOPE *(Beginning to collapse within himself—dully)*

Yes, what's the use—now? All a lie! No automobile. But, bejees, something ran over me! Must have been myself, I guess. (*He forces a feeble smile—then wearily*) Guess I'll sit down. Feel all in. Like a corpse, bejees. (*He picks a bottle and glass from the bar and walks to the first table and slumps down in the chair, facing left-front. His shaking hand misjudges the distance and he sets the bottle on the table with a jar that rouses* HUGO, *who lifts his head from his arms and blinks at him through his thick spectacles.* HOPE *speaks to him in a flat, dead voice*) Hello, Hugo. Coming up for air? Stay passed out, that's the right dope. There ain't any cool willow trees—except you grow your own in a bottle. (*He pours a drink and gulps it down*)

HUGO (*With his silly giggle*) Hello, Harry, stupid proletarian monkey-face! I will trink champagne beneath the villow— (*With a change to aristocratic fastidiousness*) But the slaves must ice it properly! (*With guttural rage*) Gottamned Hickey! Peddler pimp for nouveau-riche capitalism! Vhen I lead the jackass mob to the sack of Babylon, I vill make them hang him to a lamppost the first one!

HOPE (*Spiritlessly*) Good work. I'll help pull on the rope. Have a drink, Hugo.

HUGO (*Frightenedly*) No, thank you. I am too trunk now. I hear myself say crazy things. Do not listen, please. Larry vill tell you I haf never been so crazy trunk. I must sleep it off. (*He starts to put his head on his arms but stops and stares at* HOPE *with growing uneasiness*) Vhat's matter, Harry? You look funny. You look dead. Vhat's happened? I don't know you. Listen, I feel I am dying, too. Because I am so crazy trunk! It is very necessary I sleep. But I can't sleep here with you. You look dead. (*He scrambles to his feet in a confused panic, turns his back on* HOPE *and settles into the chair at the next table which faces left. He thrusts his head down on his arms like an ostrich hiding its head in the sand. He does not notice* PARRITT, *nor* PARRITT *him*)

LARRY (*To* HICKEY *with bitter condemnation*) Another one who's begun to enjoy your peace!

HICKEY Oh, I know it's tough on him right now, the same as it is on Harry. But that's only the first shock. I promise you they'll both come through all right.

LARRY And you believe that! I see you do! You mad fool!

HICKEY Of course, I believe it! I tell you I know from my own experience!

HOPE (*Spiritlessly*) Close that big clam of yours, Hickey. Bejees, you're a worse gabber than that nagging bitch, Bessie, was. (*He drinks his drink mechanically and pours another*)

ROCKY (*In amazement*) Jees, did yuh hear dat?

HOPE (*Dully*) What's wrong with this booze? There's no kick in it.

ROCKY (*Worriedly*) Jees, Larry, Hugo had it right. He does look like he'd croaked.

HICKEY (*Annoyed*) Don't be a damned fool! Give him time. He's coming along all right. (*He calls to* HOPE *with a first trace of underlying uneasiness*) You're all right, aren't you, Harry?

HOPE (*Dully*) I want to pass out like Hugo.

LARRY (*Turns to* HICKEY*—with bitter anger*) It's the peace of death you've brought him.

HICKEY (*For the first time loses his temper*) That's a lie! (*But he controls this instantly and grins*) Well, well, you did manage to get a rise out of me that time. I think such a hell of a lot of Harry— (*Impatiently*) You know that's damned foolishness. Look at me. I've been through it. Do I look dead? Just leave Harry alone and wait until the shock wears off and you'll see. He'll be a new man. Like I am. (*He calls to* HOPE *coaxingly*) How's it coming, Governor? Beginning to feel free, aren't you? Relieved and not guilty any more?

HOPE (*Grumbles spiritlessly*) Bejees, you must have been monkeying with the booze, too, you interfering bastard! There's no life in it now. I want to get drunk and pass out. Let's all pass out. Who the hell cares?

HICKEY (*Lowering his voice—worriedly to* LARRY) I admit I didn't think he'd be hit so hard. He's always been a happy-go-lucky slob. Like I was. Of course, it hit me hard, too. But only for a minute. Then I felt as if a ton of guilt had been lifted off my mind. I saw what had happened was the only possible way for the peace of all concerned.

LARRY (*Sharply*) What was it happened? Tell us that! And don't try to get out of it! I want a straight answer! (*Vindictively*) I think it was something you drove someone else to do!

HICKEY (*Puzzled*) Someone else?

LARRY (*Accusingly*) What did your wife die of? You've kept that a deep secret, I notice—for some reason!

HICKEY (*Reproachfully*) You're not very considerate, Larry. But, if you insist on knowing now, there's no reason you shouldn't. It was a bullet through the head that killed Evelyn. (*There is a second's tense silence*)

HOPE (*Dully*) Who the hell cares? To hell with her and that nagging old hag, Bessie.

ROCKY Christ. You had de right dope, Larry.

LARRY (*Revengefully*) You drove your poor wife to suicide? I knew it! Be God, I don't blame her! I'd almost do as much myself to be rid of you! It's what you'd like to drive us all to— (*Abruptly he is ashamed of himself and pitying*) I'm sorry, Hickey. I'm a rotten louse to throw that in your face.

HICKEY (*Quietly*) Oh, that's all right, Larry. But don't jump at conclusions. I didn't say poor Evelyn committed suicide. It's the last thing she'd ever have done, as long as I was alive for her to take care of and forgive. If you'd known her at all, you'd never get such a crazy suspicion. (*He pauses—then slowly*) No, I'm sorry to have to tell you my poor wife was killed. (LARRY *stares at him with growing horror and shrinks back along the bar away from him.* PARRITT *jerks his head up from his hands and looks around frightenedly, not at* HICKEY, *but at* LARRY. ROCKY'S *round eyes are popping.* HOPE *stares dully at the table top.*

HUGO, *his head hidden in his arms, gives no sign of life)*

LARRY (*Shakenly*) Then she—was murdered.

PARRITT (*Springs to his feet—stammers defensively*) You're a liar, Larry! You must be crazy to say that to me! You know she's still alive! (*But no one pays any attention to him*)

ROCKY (*Blurts out*) Moidered? Who done it?

LARRY (*His eyes fixed with fascinated horror on* HICKEY *—frightenedly*) Don't ask questions, you dumb Wop! It's none of our damned business! Leave Hickey alone!

HICKEY (*Smiles at him with affectionate amusement*) Still the old grandstand bluff, Larry? Or is it some more bum pity? (*He turns to* ROCKY*—matter-of-factly*) The police don't know who killed her yet, Rocky. But I expect they will before very long. (*As if that finished the subject, he comes forward to* HOPE *and sits beside him, with an arm around his shoulder —affectionately coaxing*) Coming along fine now, aren't you, Governor? Getting over the first shock? Beginning to feel free from guilt and lying hopes and at peace with yourself?

HOPE (*With a dull callousness*) Somebody croaked your Evelyn, eh? Bejees, my bets are on the iceman! But who the hell cares? Let's get drunk and pass out. (*He tosses down his drink with a lifeless, automatic movement—complainingly*) Bejees, what did you do to the booze, Hickey? There's no damned life left in it.

PARRITT (*Stammers, his eyes on* LARRY, *whose eyes in turn remain fixed on* HICKEY) Don't look like that, Larry! You've got to believe what I told you! It had nothing to do with her! It was just to get a few lousy dollars!

HUGO (*Suddenly raises his head from his arms and, looking straight in front of him, pounds on the table frightenedly with his small fists*) Don't be a fool! Buy me a trink! But no more vine! It is not properly iced! (*With guttural rage*) Gottamned stupid proletarian slaves! Buy me a trink or I vill have you shot! (*He collapses into abject begging*) Please, for Gott's sake! I am not trunk enough! I cannot sleep! Life is a crazy monkey-face! Always there is blood beneath the villow trees! I hate it and I am afraid! (*He hides his face on his arms, sobbing muffledly*) Please, I am crazy trunk! I say crazy things! For Gott's sake, do not listen to me! (*But no one pays any attention to him.* LARRY *stands shrunk back against the bar.* ROCKY *is leaning over it. They stare at* HICKEY. PARRITT *stands looking pleadingly at* LARRY)

HICKEY (*Gazes with worried kindliness at* HOPE) You're beginning to worry me, Governor. Something's holding you up somewhere. I don't see why— You've faced the truth about yourself. You've done what you had to do to kill your nagging pipe dreams. Oh, I know it knocks you cold. But only for a minute. Then you see it was the only possible way to peace. And you feel happy. Like I did. That's what worries me about you, Governor. It's time you began to feel happy—

*Curtain*

# Act Four

SCENE *Same as Act One—the back room with the curtain separating it from the section of the barroom with its single table at right of curtain, front. It is around half past one in the morning of the following day.*

*The tables in the back room have a new arrangement. The one at left, front, before the window to the yard, is in the same position. So is the one at the right, rear, of it in the second row. But this table now has only one chair. This chair is at right of it, facing directly front. The two tables on either side of the door at rear are unchanged. But the table which was at center, front, has been pushed toward right so that it and the table at right, rear, of it in the second row, and the last table at right in the front row, are now jammed so closely together that they form one group.*

LARRY, HUGO *and* PARRITT *are at the table at left, front.* LARRY *is at left of it, beside the window, facing front.* HUGO *sits at rear, facing front, his head on his arms in his habitual position, but he is not asleep. On* HUGO'S *left is* PARRITT, *his chair facing left, front. At right of table, an empty chair, facing left.* LARRY'S *chin is on his chest, his eyes fixed on the floor. He will not look at* PARRITT, *who keeps staring at him with a sneering, pleading challenge.*

*Two bottles of whiskey are on each table, whiskey and chaser glasses, a pitcher of water.*

*The one chair by the table at right, rear, of them is vacant. At the first table at right of center,* CORA *sits at left, front, of it, facing front. Around the rear of this table are four empty chairs. Opposite* CORA, *in a sixth chair, is* CAPTAIN LEWIS, *also facing front. On his left,* MCGLOIN *is facing front in a chair before the middle table of his group. At right, rear, of him, also at this table,* GENERAL WETJOEN *sits facing front. In back of this table are three empty chairs.*

*At right, rear, of* WETJOEN, *but beside the last table of the group, sits* WILLIE. *On* WILLIE'S *left, at rear of table, is* HOPE. *On* HOPE'S *left, at right, rear, of table, is* MOSHER. *Finally, at right of table is* JIMMY TOMORROW. *All of the four sit facing front.*

*There is an atmosphere of oppressive stagnation in the room, and a quality of insensibility about all the people in this group at right. They are like wax figures, set stiffly on their chairs, carrying out mechanically the motions of getting drunk but sunk in a numb stupor which is impervious to stimulation.*

*In the bar section,* JOE *is sprawled in the chair at right of table, facing left. His head rolls forward in a sodden slumber.* ROCKY *is standing behind his chair, regarding him with dull hostility.* ROCKY'S *face is set in an expression of tired, callous toughness. He looks now like a minor Wop gangster.*

ROCKY (*Shakes* JOE *by the shoulder*) Come on, yuh damned nigger! Beat it in de back room! It's after hours. (*But* JOE *remains inert.* ROCKY *gives up*) Aw, to hell wid it. Let de dump get pinched. I'm through wid dis lousy job, anyway! (*He hears someone at rear and calls*) Who's dat? (CHUCK *appears from rear. He has been drinking heavily, but there is no lift to his jag; his manner is grouchy and sullen. He has evidently been brawling. His knuckles are raw and there is a mouse under one eye. He has lost his straw hat, his tie is awry, and his blue suit is dirty.* ROCKY *eyes him indifferently*) Been scrappin', huh? Started off on your periodical, ain't yuh? (*For a second there is a gleam of satisfaction in his eyes*)

CHUCK Yeah, ain't yuh glad? (*Truculently*) What's it to yuh?

ROCKY Not a damn ting. But dis is someting to me. I'm cut on my feet holdin' down your job. Yuh said if I'd take your day, yuh'd relieve me at six, and here it's half past one A.M. Well, yuh're takin' over now, get me, no matter how plastered yuh are!

CHUCK Plastered, hell! I wisht I was. I've lapped up a gallon, but it don't hit me right. And to hell wid de job. I'm goin' to tell Harry I'm quittin'.

ROCKY Yeah? Well, I'm quittin', too.

CHUCK I've played sucker for dat crummy blonde long enough, lettin' her kid me into woikin'. From now on I take it easy.

ROCKY I'm glad yuh're gettin' some sense.

CHUCK And I hope yuh're gettin' some. What a prize sap you been, tendin' bar when yuh got two good hustlers in your stable!

ROCKY Yeah, but I ain't no sap now. I'll loin dem, when dey get back from Coney. (*Sneeringly*) Jees, dat Cora sure played you for a dope, feedin' yuh dat marriage-on-de-farm hop!

CHUCK (*Dully*) Yeah. Hickey got it right. A lousy pipe dream. It was her pulling sherry flips on me woke me up. All de way walkin' to de ferry, every ginmill we come to she'd drag me in to blow her. I got tinkin', Christ, what won't she want when she gets de ring on her finger and I'm hooked? So I tells her at de ferry, "Kiddo, yuh can go to Joisey, or to hell, but count me out."

ROCKY She says it was her told you to go to hell, because yuh'd started hittin' de booze.

CHUCK (*Ignoring this*) I got tinkin', too, Jees, won't I look sweet wid a wife dat if yuh put all de guys she's stayed wid side by side, dey'd reach to Chicago. (*He sighs gloomily*) Dat kind of dame, yuh can't trust 'em. De minute your back is toined, dey're cheatin' wid de iceman or someone. Hickey done me a favor, makin' me wake up. (*He pauses—then adds pathetically*) On'y it was fun, kinda, me and Cora kiddin' ourselves— (*Suddenly his face hardens with hatred*) Where is dat son of a bitch, Hickey? I want one good sock at dat guy—just one!—and de next buttin' in he'll do will be in de morgue! I'll take a chance on goin' to de Chair—!

ROCKY (*Starts—in a low warning voice*) *Piano!* Keep away from him, Chuck! He ain't here now, anyway. He went out to phone, he said. He wouldn't call from here. I got a hunch he's beat it. But if he does come back, yuh don't know him, if anyone asks yuh, get me? (*As* CHUCK *looks at him with dull surprise he lowers his voice to a whisper*) De Chair, maybe dat's where he's goin'. I don't know nuttin', see, but it looks like he croaked his wife.

CHUCK (*With a flash of interest*) Yuh mean she really was cheatin' on him? Den I don't blame de guy—

ROCKY Who's blamin' him? When a dame asks for it— But I don't know nuttin' about it, see?

CHUCK Is any of de gang wise?

ROCKY Larry is. And de boss ought to be. I tried to wise de rest of dem up to stay clear of him, but dey're all so licked, I don't know if dey got it. (*He pauses—vindictively*) I don't give a damn what he done to his wife, but if he gets de Hot Seat I won't go into no mournin'!

CHUCK Me, neider!

ROCKY Not after his trowin' it in my face I'm a pimp. What if I am? Why de hell not? And what he's done to Harry. Jees, de poor old slob is so licked he can't even get drunk. And all de gang. Dey're all licked. I couldn't help feelin' sorry for de poor bums when dey showed up tonight, one by one, lookin' like pooches wid deir tails between deir legs, dat everyone'd been kickin' till dey was too punch-drunk to feel it no more. Jimmy Tomorrow was de last. Schwartz, de copper, brung him in. Seen him sittin' on de dock on West Street, lookin' at de water and cryin'! Schwartz thought he was drunk and I let him tink it. But he was cold sober. He was tryin' to jump in and didn't have de noive, I figured it. Noive! Jees, dere ain't enough guts left in de whole gang to battle a mosquito!

CHUCK Aw, to hell wid 'em! Who cares? Gimme a drink. (ROCKY *pushes the bottle toward him apathetically*) I see you been hittin' de redeye, too.

ROCKY Yeah. But it don't do no good. I can't get drunk right. (CHUCK *drinks.* JOE *mumbles in his sleep.* CHUCK *regards him resentfully*) Dis doity dinge was able to get his snootful and pass out. Jees, even Hickey can't faze a nigger! Yuh'd tink he was fazed if yuh'd seen him come in. Stinko, and he pulled a gat and said he'd plug Hickey for insultin' him. Den he dropped it and begun to cry and said he wasn't a gamblin' man or a tough guy no more; he was yellow. He'd borrowed de gat to stick up someone, and den didn't have de guts. He got drunk panhandlin' drinks in nigger joints, I s'pose. I guess dey felt sorry for him.

CHUCK He ain't got no business in de bar after hours. Why don't yuh chuck him out?

ROCKY (*Apathetically*) Aw, to hell wid it. Who cares?

CHUCK (*Lapsing into the same mood*) Yeah. I don't.

JOE (*Suddenly lunges to his feet dazedly—mumbles in humbled apology*) Scuse me, White Boys. Scuse me for livin'. I don't want to be where I's not wanted

*(He makes his way swayingly to the opening in the curtain at rear and tacks down to the middle table of the three at right, front. He feels his way around it to the table at its left and gets to the chair in back of* CAPTAIN LEWIS*)*

CHUCK *(Gets up—in a callous, brutal tone)* My pig's in de back room, ain't she? I wanna collect de dough I wouldn't take dis mornin', like a sucker, before she blows it. *(He goes rear)*

ROCKY *(Getting up)* I'm comin', too. I'm trough woikin'. I ain't no lousy bartender. *(*CHUCK *comes through the curtain and looks for* CORA *as* JOE *flops down in the chair in back of* CAPTAIN LEWIS*)*

JOE *(Taps* LEWIS *on the shoulder—servilely apologetic)* If you objects to my sittin' here, Captain, just tell me and I pulls my freight.

LEWIS No apology required, old chap. Anybody could tell you I should feel honored a bloody Kaffir would lower himself to sit beside me. *(*JOE *stares at him with sodden perplexity—then closes his eyes.* CHUCK *comes forward to take the chair behind* CORA'S, *as* ROCKY *enters the back room and starts over toward* LARRY'S *table)*

CHUCK *(His voice hard)* I'm waitin', Baby. Dig!

CORA *(With apathetic obedience)* Sure. I been expectin' yuh. I got it all ready. Here. *(She passes a small roll of bills she has in her hand over her shoulder, without looking at him. He takes it, glances at it suspiciously, then shoves it in his pocket without a word of acknowledgment.* CORA *speaks with a tired wonder at herself rather than resentment toward him)* Jees, imagine me kiddin' myself I wanted to marry a drunken pimp.

CHUCK Dat's nuttin', Baby. Imagine de sap I'da been, when I can get your dough just as easy widout it!

ROCKY *(Takes the chair on* PARRITT'S *left, facing* LARRY *—dully)* Hello, Old Cemetery. *(*LARRY *doesn't seem to hear. To* PARRITT*)* Hello, Tightwad. You still around?

PARRITT *(Keeps his eyes on* LARRY*—in a jeeringly challenging tone)* Ask Larry! He knows I'm here, all right, although he's pretending not to! He'd like to forget I'm alive! He's trying to kid himself with that grandstand philosopher stuff! But he knows he can't get away with it now! He kept himself locked in his room until a while ago, alone with a bottle of booze, but he couldn't make it work! He couldn't even get drunk! He had to come out! There must have been something there he was even more scared to face than he is Hickey and me! I guess he got looking at the fire escape and thinking how handy it was, if he was really sick of life and only had the nerve to die! *(He pauses sneeringly.* LARRY'S *face has tautened, but he pretends he doesn't hear.* ROCKY *pays no attention. His head has sunk forward, and he stares at the table top, sunk in the same stupor as the other occupants of the room.* PARRITT *goes on, his tone becoming more insistent)* He's been thinking of me, too, Rocky. Trying to figure a way to get out of helping me! He doesn't want to be bothered understanding. But he does understand all right! He used to love her, too. So he thinks I ought to take a hop off the fire escape! *(He pauses.* LARRY'S *hands on the table have clinched into fists, as his nails dig into his palms, but he remains silent.* PARRITT *breaks and starts pleading)* For God's sake, Larry, can't you say something? Hickey's got me all balled up. Thinking of what he must have done has got me so I don't know any more what I did or why. I can't go on like this! I've got to know what I ought to do—

LARRY *(In a stifled tone)* God damn you! Are you trying to make me your executioner?

PARRITT *(Starts frightenedly)* Execution? Then you do think—?

LARRY I don't think anything!

PARRITT *(With forced jeering)* I suppose you think I ought to die because I sold out a lot of loud-mouthed fakers, who were cheating suckers with a phony pipe dream, and put them where they ought to be, in jail? *(He forces a laugh)* Don't make me laugh! I ought to get a medal! What a damned old sap you are! You must still believe in the Movement! *(He nudges* ROCKY *with his elbow)* Hickey's right about him, isn't he, Rocky? An old no-good drunken tramp, as dumb as he is, ought to take a hop off the fire escape!

ROCKY *(Dully)* Sure. Why don't he? Or you? Or me? What de hell's de difference? Who cares? *(There is a faint stir from all the crowd, as if this sentiment struck a responsive chord in their numbed minds. They mumble almost in chorus as one voice, like sleepers talking out of a dully irritating dream, "The hell with it!" "Who cares?" Then the sodden silence descends again on the room.* ROCKY *looks from* PARRITT *to* LARRY *puzzledly. He mutters)* What am I doin' here wid youse two? I remember I had someting on my mind to tell yuh. What—? Oh, I got it now. *(He looks from one to the other of their oblivious faces with a strange, sly, calculating look—ingratiatingly)* I was tinking how you was bot' reg'lar guys. I tinks, ain't two guys like dem saps to be hangin' round like a coupla stew bums and wastin' demselves. Not dat I blame yuh for not woikin'. On'y suckers woik. But dere's no percentage in bein' broke when yuh can grab good jack for yourself and make someone else woik for yuh, is dere? I mean, like I do. So I tinks, Dey're my pals and I ought to wise up two good guys like dem to play my system, and not be lousy barflies, no good to demselves or nobody else. *(He addresses* PARRITT *now—persuasively)* What yuh tink, Parritt? Ain't I right? Sure, I am. So don't be a sucker, see? Yuh ain't a bad-lookin' guy. Yuh could easy make some gal who's a good hustler, an' start a stable. I'd help yuh and wise yuh up to de inside dope on de game. *(He pauses inquiringly.* PARRITT *gives no sign of having heard him.* ROCKY *asks impatiently)* Well, what about it? What if dey do call yuh a pimp? What de hell do you care—any more'n I do.

PARRITT *(Without looking at him—vindictively)* I'm through with whores. I wish they were all in jail—or dead!

ROCKY *(Ignores this—disappointedly)* So yuh won't touch it, huh? Aw right, stay a bum! *(He turns to*

LARRY) Jees, Larry, he's sure one dumb boob, ain't he? Dead from de neck up! He don't know a good ting when he sees it. (*Oily, even persuasive again*) But how about you, Larry? You ain't dumb. So why not, huh? Sure, yuh're old, but dat don't matter. All de hustlers tink yuh're aces. Dey fall for yuh like yuh was deir uncle or old man or someting. Dey'd like takin' care of yuh. And de cops 'round here, dey like yuh, too. It'd be a pipe for yuh, 'specially wid me to help yuh and wise yuh up. Yuh wouldn't have to worry where de next drink's comin' from, or wear doity clothes. (*Hopefully*) Well, don't it look good to yuh?

LARRY (*Glances at him—for a moment he is stirred to sardonic pity*) No, it doesn't look good, Rocky. I mean, the peace Hickey's brought you. It isn't contented enough, if you have to make everyone else a pimp, too.

ROCKY (*Stares at him stupidly—then pushes his chair back and gets up, grumbling*) I'm a sap to waste time on yuh. A stew bum is a stew bum and yuh can't change him. (*He turns away—then turns back for an afterthought*) Like I was sayin' to Chuck, yuh better keep away from Hickey. If anyone asks yuh, yuh don't know nuttin', get me? Yuh never even hoid he had a wife. (*His face hardens*) Jees, we all ought to git drunk and stage a celebration when dat bastard goes to de Chair.

LARRY (*Vindictively*) Be God, I'll celebrate with you and drink long life to him in hell! (*Then guiltily and pityingly*) No! The poor mad devil— (*Then with angry self-contempt*) Ah, pity again! The wrong kind! He'll welcome the Chair!

PARRITT (*Contemptuously*) Yes, what are you so damned scared of death for? I don't want your lousy pity.

ROCKY Christ, I hope he don't come back, Larry. We don't know nuttin' now. We're on'y guessin', see? But if de bastard keeps on talkin'—

LARRY (*Grimly*) He'll come back. He'll keep on talking. He's got to. He's lost his confidence that the peace he's sold us is the real McCoy, and it's made him uneasy about his own. He'll have to prove to us— (*As he is speaking* HICKEY *appears silently in the doorway at rear. He has lost his beaming salesman's grin. His manner is no longer self-assured. His expression is uneasy, baffled and resentful. It has the stubborn set of an obsessed determination. His eyes are on* LARRY *as he comes in. As he speaks, there is a start from all the crowd, a shrinking away from him*)

HICKEY (*Angrily*) That's a damned lie, Larry! I haven't lost confidence a damned bit! Why should I? (*Boastfully*) By God, whenever I made up my mind to sell someone something I knew they ought to want, I've sold 'em! (*He suddenly looks confused—haltingly*) I mean— It isn't kind of you, Larry, to make that kind of crack when I've been doing my best to help—

ROCKY (*Moving away from him toward right—sharply*) Keep away from me! I don't know nuttin' about yuh, see? (*His tone is threatening but his manner as he turns his back and ducks quickly across to the bar entrance is that of one in flight. In the bar he comes forward and slumps in a chair at the table, facing front*)

HICKEY (*Comes to the table at right, rear, of* LARRY'S *table and sits in the one chair there, facing front. He looks over the crowd at right, hopefully and then disappointedly. He speaks with a strained attempt at his old affectionate jollying manner*) Well, well! How are you coming along, everybody? Sorry I had to leave you for a while, but there was something I had to get finally settled. It's all fixed now.

HOPE (*In the voice of one reiterating mechanically a hopeless complaint*) When are you going to do something about this booze, Hickey? Bejees, we all know you did something to take the life out of it. It's like drinking dishwater! We can't pass out! And you promised us peace. (*His group all join in in a dull, complaining chorus, "We can't pass out! You promised us peace!"*)

HICKEY (*Bursts into resentful exasperation*) For God's sake, Harry, are you still harping on that damned nonsense! You've kept it up all afternoon and night! And you've got everybody else singing the same crazy tune! I've had about all I can stand— That's why I phoned— (*He controls himself*) Excuse me, boys and girls. I don't mean that. I'm just worried about you, when you play dead on me like this. I was hoping by the time I got back you'd be like you ought to be! I thought you were deliberately holding back, while I was around, because you didn't want to give me the satisfaction of showing me I'd had the right dope. And I did have! I know from my own experience. (*Exasperatedly*) But I've explained that a million times! And you've all done what you needed to do! By rights you should be contented now, without a single damned hope or lying dream left to torment you! But here you are, acting like a lot of stiffs cheating the undertaker! (*He looks around accusingly*) I can't figure it—unless it's just your damned pigheaded stubbornness! (*He breaks—miserably*) Hell, you oughtn't to act this way with me! You're my old pals, the only friends I've got. You know the one thing I want is to see you all happy before I go— (*Rousing himself to his old brisk, master-of-ceremonies manner*) And there's damned little time left now. I've made a date for two o'clock. We've got to get busy right away and find out what's wrong. (*There is a sodden silence. He goes on exasperatedly*) Can't you appreciate what you've got, for God's sake? Don't you know you're free now to be yourselves, without having to feel remorse or guilt, or lie to yourselves about reforming tomorrow? Can't you see there is no tomorrow now? You're rid of it forever! You've killed it! You don't have to care a damn about anything any more! You've finally got the game of life licked, don't you see that? (*Angrily exhorting*) Then why the hell don't you get pie-eyed and celebrate? Why don't you laugh and sing "Sweet Adeline"? (*With bitterly hurt accusation*) The only reason I can think of is, you're putting on this rotten half-dead act just to get back at me! Because you hate my guts!

(*He breaks again*) God, don't do that, gang! It makes me feel like hell to think you hate me. It makes me feel you suspect I must have hated you. But that's a lie! Oh, I know I used to hate everyone in the world who wasn't as rotten a bastard as I was! But that was when I was still living in hell—before I faced the truth and saw the one possible way to free poor Evelyn and give her the peace she'd always dreamed about. (*He pauses. Everyone in the group stirs with awakening dread and they all begin to grow tense on their chairs*)

CHUCK (*Without looking at* HICKEY—*with dull, resentful viciousness*) Aw, put a bag over it! To hell wid Evelyn! What if she was cheatin'? And who cares what yuh did to her? Dat's your funeral. We don't give a damn, see? (*There is a dull, resentful chorus of assent, "We don't give a damn."* CHUCK *adds dully*) All we want outa you is keep de hell away from us and give us a rest. (*A muttered chorus of assent*)

HICKEY (*As if he hadn't heard this—an obsessed look on his face*) The one possible way to make up to her for all I'd made her go through, and get her rid of me so I couldn't make her suffer any more, and she wouldn't have to forgive me again! I saw I couldn't do it by killing myself, like I wanted to for a long time. That would have been the last straw for her. She'd have died of a broken heart to think I could do that to her. She'd have blamed herself for it, too. Or I couldn't just run away from her. She'd have died of grief and humiliation if I'd done that to her. She'd have thought I'd stopped loving her. (*He adds with a strange impressive simplicity*) You see, Evelyn loved me. And I loved her. That was the trouble. It would have been easy to find a way out if she hadn't loved me so much. Or if I hadn't loved her. But as it was, there was only one possible way. (*He pauses—then adds simply*) I had to kill her. (*There is a second's dead silence as he finishes—then a tense in-drawn breath like a gasp from the crowd, and a general shrinking movement*)

LARRY (*Bursts out*) You mad fool, can't you keep your mouth shut! We may hate you for what you've done here this time, but we remember the old times, too, when you brought kindness and laughter with you instead of death! We don't want to know things that will make us help send you to the Chair!

PARRITT (*With angry scorn*) Ah, shut up, you yellow faker! Can't you face anything? Wouldn't I deserve the Chair, too, if I'd— It's worse if you kill someone and they have to go on living. I'd be glad of the Chair! It'd wipe it out! It'd square me with myself!

HICKEY (*Disturbed—with a movement of repulsion*) I wish you'd get rid of that bastard, Larry. I can't have him pretending there's something in common between him and me. It's what's in your heart that counts. There was love in my heart, not hate.

PARRITT (*Glares at him in angry terror*) You're a liar! I don't hate her! I couldn't! And it had nothing to do with her, anyway! You ask Larry!

LARRY (*Grabs his shoulder and shakes him furiously*) God damn you, stop shoving your rotten soul in my lap! (PARRITT *subsides, hiding his face in his hands and shuddering*)

HICKEY (*Goes on quietly now*) Don't worry about the Chair, Larry. I know it's still hard for you not to be terrified by death, but when you've made peace with yourself, like I have, you won't give a damn. (*He addresses the group at right again—earnestly*) Listen, everybody. I've made up my mind the only way I can clear things up for you, so you'll realize how contented and carefree you ought to feel, now I've made you get rid of your pipe dreams, is to show you what a pipe dream did to me and Evelyn. I'm certain if I tell you about it from the beginning, you'll appreciate what I've done for you and why I did it, and how damned grateful you ought to be—instead of hating me. (*He begins eagerly in a strange running narrative manner*) You see, even when we were kids, Evelyn and me—

HOPE (*Bursts out, pounding with his glass on the table*) No! Who the hell cares? We don't want to hear it. All we want is to pass out and get drunk and a little peace! (*They are all, except* LARRY *and* PARRITT, *seized by the same fit and pound with their glasses, even* HUGO, *and* ROCKY *in the bar, and shout in chorus, "Who the hell cares? We want to pass out!"*)

HICKEY (*With an expression of wounded hurt*) All right, if that's the way you feel. I don't want to cram it down your throats. I don't need to tell anyone. I don't feel guilty. I'm only worried about you.

HOPE What did you do to this booze? That's what we'd like to hear. Bejees, you done something. There's no life or kick in it now. (*He appeals mechanically to* JIMMY TOMORROW) Ain't that right, Jimmy?

JIMMY (*More than any of them, his face has a wax-figure blankness that makes it look embalmed. He answers in a precise, completely lifeless voice, but his reply is not to* HARRY'S *question, and he does not look at him or anyone else*) Yes. Quite right. It was all a stupid lie—my nonsense about tomorrow. Naturally, they would never give me my position back. I would never dream of asking them. It would be hopeless. I didn't resign. I was fired for drunkenness. And that was years ago. I'm much worse now. And it was absurd of me to excuse my drunkenness by pretending it was my wife's adultery that ruined my life. As Hickey guessed, I was a drunkard before that. Long before. I discovered early in life that living frightened me when I was sober. I have forgotten why I married Marjorie. I can't even remember now if she was pretty. She was a blonde, I think, but I couldn't swear to it. I had some idea of wanting a home, perhaps. But, of course, I much preferred the nearest pub. Why Marjorie married me, God knows. It's impossible to believe she loved me. She soon found I much preferred drinking all night with my pals to being in bed with her. So, naturally, she was unfaithful. I didn't blame her. I really didn't care. I was glad to be free—even grateful to her, I think, for giving me such a good tragic excuse to drink as much as I damned well pleased. (*He stops like a mechanical doll that has run down. No one gives any sign of having heard him.*

*There is a heavy silence. Then* ROCKY, *at the table in the bar, turns grouchily as he hears a noise behind him. Two men come quietly forward. One,* MORAN, *is middle-aged. The other,* LIEB, *is in his twenties. They look ordinary in every way, without anything distinctive to indicate what they do for a living)*

ROCKY (*Grumpily*) In de back room if yuh wanta drink. (MORAN *makes a peremptory sign to be quiet. All of a sudden* ROCKY *senses they are detectives and springs up to face them, his expression freezing into a wary blankness.* MORAN *pulls back his coat to show his badge*)

MORAN (*In a low voice*) Guy named Hickman in the back room?

ROCKY Tink I know de names of all de guys—?

MORAN Listen, you! This is murder. And don't be a sap. It was Hickman himself phoned in and said we'd find him here around two.

ROCKY (*Dully*) So dat's who he phoned to. (*He shrugs his shoulders*) Aw right, if he asked for it. He's de fat guy sittin' alone. (*He slumps down in his chair again*) And if yuh want a confession all yuh got to do is listen. He'll be tellin' all about it soon. Yuh can't stop de bastard talkin'. (MORAN *gives him a curious look, then whispers to* LIEB, *who disappears rear and a moment later appears in the hall doorway of the back room. He spots* HICKEY *and slides into a chair at the left of the doorway, cutting off escape by the hall.* MORAN *goes back and stands in the opening in the curtain leading to the back room. He sees* HICKEY *and stands watching him and listening*)

HICKEY (*Suddenly bursts out*) I've got to tell you! Your being the way you are now gets my goat! It's all wrong! It puts things in my mind—about myself. It makes me think, if I got balled up about you, how do I know I wasn't balled up about myself? And that's plain damned foolishness. When you know the story of me and Evelyn, you'll see there wasn't any other possible way out of it, for her sake. Only I've got to start way back at the beginning or you won't understand. (*He starts his story, his tone again becoming musingly reminiscent*) You see, even as a kid I was always restless. I had to keep on the go. You've heard the old saying, "Ministers' sons are sons of guns." Well, that was me, and then some. Home was like a jail. I didn't fall for the religious bunk. Listening to my old man whooping up hell fire and scaring those Hoosier suckers into shelling out their dough only handed me a laugh, although I had to hand it to him, the way he sold them nothing for something. I guess I take after him, and that's what made me a good salesman. Well, anyway, as I said, home was like jail, and so was school, and so was that damned hick town. The only place I liked was the pool rooms, where I could smoke Sweet Caporals, and mop up a couple of beers, thinking I was a hell-on-wheels sport. We had one hooker shop in town, and, of course, I liked that, too. Not that I hardly ever had entrance money. My old man was a tight old bastard. But I liked to sit around in the parlor and joke with the girls, and they liked me because I could kid 'em along and make 'em laugh. Well, you know what a small town is. Everyone got wise to me. They all said I was a no-good tramp. I didn't give a damn what they said. I hated everybody in the place. That is, except Evelyn. I loved Evelyn. Even as a kid. And Evelyn loved me. (*He pauses. No one moves or gives any sign except by the dread in their eyes that they have heard him. Except* PARRITT, *who takes his hands from his face to look at* LARRY *pleadingly*)

PARRITT I loved Mother, Larry! No matter what she did! I still do! Even though I know she wishes now I was dead! You believe that, don't you? Christ, why can't you say something?

HICKEY (*Too absorbed in his story now to notice this—goes on in a tone of fond, sentimental reminiscence*) Yes, sir, as far back as I can remember, Evelyn and I loved each other. She always stuck up for me. She wouldn't believe the gossip—or she'd pretend she didn't. No one could convince her I was no good. Evelyn was stubborn as all hell once she'd made up her mind. Even when I'd admit things and ask her forgiveness, she'd make excuses for me and defend me against myself. She'd kiss me and say she knew I didn't mean it and I wouldn't do it again. So I'd promise I wouldn't. I'd have to promise, she was so sweet and good, though I knew darned well— (*A touch of strange bitterness comes into his voice for a moment*) No, sir, you couldn't stop Evelyn. Nothing on earth could shake her faith in me. Even I couldn't. She was a sucker for a pipe dream. (*Then quickly*) Well, naturally, her family forbid her seeing me. They were one of the town's best, rich for that hick burg, owned the trolley line and lumber company. Strict Methodists, too. They hated my guts. But they couldn't stop Evelyn. She'd sneak notes to me and meet me on the sly. I was getting more restless. The town was getting more like a jail. I made up my mind to beat it. I knew exactly what I wanted to be by that time. I'd met a lot of drummers around the hotel and liked 'em. They were always telling jokes. They were sports. They kept moving. I liked their life. And I knew I could kid people and sell things. The hitch was how to get the railroad fare to the Big Town. I told Mollie Arlington my trouble. She was the madame of the cathouse. She liked me. She laughed and said, "Hell, I'll stake you, Kid! I'll bet on you. With that grin of yours and that line of bull, you ought to be able to sell skunks for good ratters!" (*He chuckles*) Mollie was all right. She gave me confidence in myself. I paid her back, the first money I earned. Wrote her a kidding letter, I remember, saying I was peddling baby carriages and she and the girls had better take advantage of our bargain offer. (*He chuckles*) But that's ahead of my story. The night before I left town, I had a date with Evelyn. I got all worked up, she was so pretty and sweet and good. I told her straight, "You better forget me, Evelyn, for your own sake. I'm no good and never will be. I'm not worthy to wipe your shoes." I broke down and cried. She just said, looking white and scared, "Why, Teddy? Don't you still love me?" I said, "Love you? God, Evelyn, I love you more than anything in the world. And I always will!" She said, "Then nothing else matters, Teddy, because nothing but death could stop my loving you. So I'll wait, and when you're ready you send for me and we'll be married. I know I can make you happy, Teddy, and once you're happy you won't want to do any of the bad things you've done any more." And I said, "Of course, I won't, Evelyn!" I meant it, too. I believed it. I loved her so much she could make me believe anything. (*He sighs. There is a suspended, waiting silence. Even the two detectives are drawn into it. Then* HOPE *breaks into dully exasperated, brutally callous protest*)

HOPE Get it over, you long-winded bastard! You married her, and you caught her cheating with the iceman, and you croaked her, and who the hell cares? What's she to us? All we want is to pass out in peace, bejees! (*A chorus of dull, resentful protest from all the group. They mumble, like sleepers who curse a person who keeps awakening them, "What's it to us? We want to pass out in peace!"* HOPE *drinks and they mechanically follow his example. He pours another and they do the same. He complains with a stupid, nagging insistence*) No life in the booze! No kick! Dishwater. Bejees, I'll never pass out!

HICKEY (*Goes on as if there had been no interruption*) So I beat it to the Big Town. I got a job easy, and it was a cinch for me to make good. I had the knack. It was like a game, sizing people up quick, spotting what their pet pipe dreams were, and then kidding 'em along that line, pretending you believed what they wanted to believe about themselves. Then they liked you, they trusted you, they wanted to buy something to show their gratitude. It was fun. But still, all the while I felt guilty, as if I had no right to be having such a good time away from Evelyn. In each letter I'd tell her how I missed her, but I'd keep warning her, too. I'd tell her all my faults, how I liked my booze every once in a while, and so on. But there was no shaking Evelyn's belief in me, or her dreams about the future. After each letter of hers, I'd be as full of faith as she was. So as soon as I got enough saved to start us off, I sent for her and we got married. Christ, wasn't I happy for a while! And wasn't she happy! I don't care what anyone says, I'll bet there never was two people who loved each other more than me and Evelyn. Not only then but always after, in spite of everything I did— (*He pauses—then sadly*) Well, it's all there, at the start, everything that happened afterwards. I never could learn to handle temptation. I'd want to reform and mean it. I'd promise Evelyn, and I'd promise myself, and I'd believe it. I'd tell her, it's the last time. And she'd say, "I know it's the last time, Teddy. You'll never do it again." That's what made it so hard. That's what made me feel such a rotten skunk—her always forgiving me. My playing around with women, for instance. It was only a harmless good time to me. Didn't mean anything. But I'd know what it meant to Evelyn. So I'd say to myself, never again. But you know how it is, traveling around. The damned hotel rooms. I'd get seeing things in the wall paper. I'd get bored as hell. Lonely and homesick. But at the same time sick of home. I'd feel free and I'd want to celebrate a little. I never drank on the job, so it had to be dames. Any tart. What I'd want was some tramp I could be myself with without being ashamed—someone I could tell a dirty joke to and she'd laugh.

CORA (*With a dull, weary bitterness*) Jees, all de lousy jokes I've had to listen to and pretend was funny!

HICKEY (*Goes on obliviously*) Sometimes I'd try some joke I thought was a corker on Evelyn. She'd always make herself laugh. But I could tell she thought it was dirty, not funny. And Evelyn always knew about the tarts I'd been with when I came home from a trip. She'd kiss me and look in my eyes, and she'd know. I'd see in her eyes how she was trying not to know, and then telling herself even if it was true, he couldn't help it, they tempt him, and he's lonely, he hasn't got me, it's only his body, anyway, he doesn't love them, I'm the only one he loves. She was right, too. I never loved anyone else. Couldn't if I wanted to. (*He pauses*) She forgave me even when it all had to come out in the open. You know how it is when you keep taking chances. You may be lucky for a long time, but you get nicked in the end. I picked up a nail from some tart in Altoona.

CORA (*Dully, without resentment*) Yeah. And she picked it up from some guy. It's all in de game. What de hell of it?

HICKEY I had to do a lot of lying and stalling when I got home. It didn't do any good. The quack I went to got all my dough and then told me I was cured and I took his word. But I wasn't, and poor Evelyn— But she did her best to make me believe she fell for my lie about how traveling men get things from drinking cups on trains. Anyway, she forgave me. The same way she forgave me every time I'd turn up after a periodical drunk. You all know what I'd be like at the end of one. You've seen me. Like something lying in the gutter that no alley cat would lower itself to drag in—something they threw out of the D.T. ward in Bellevue along with the garbage, something that ought to be dead and isn't! (*His face is convulsed with self-loathing*) Evelyn wouldn't have heard from me in a month or more. She'd have been waiting there alone, with the neighbors shaking their heads and feeling sorry for her out loud. That was before she got me to move to the outskirts, where there weren't any next-door neighbors. And then the door would open and in I'd stumble—looking like what I've said—into her home, where she kept everything so spotless and clean. And I'd sworn it would never happen again, and now I'd have to start swearing again this was the last time. I could see disgust having a battle in her eyes with love. Love always won. She'd make herself kiss me, as if nothing had happened, as if I'd just come home from a business trip. She'd never complain or bawl me out. (*He bursts out in a tone of anguish that has anger and hatred beneath it*) Christ, can you imagine what a guilty skunk she made me feel! If she'd only admitted once she didn't believe any more in her pipe dream that some day I'd behave! But she never would. Evelyn was stubborn as hell. Once she'd set her heart on anything, you couldn't shake her faith that it had to come true—tomorrow! It was the same old story, over and over, for years and years. It kept piling up, inside her and inside me. God, can you picture all I made her suffer, and all the guilt she made me feel, and how I hated myself! If she only hadn't been so damned good—if she'd been the same kind of wife I was a husband. God, I used to pray sometimes she'd—I'd even say to her, "Go on, why don't you, Evelyn? It'd serve me right. I wouldn't mind. I'd forgive you." Of course, I'd pretend I was kidding—the same way I used to joke here about her being in the hay with the iceman. She'd have been so hurt if I'd said it seriously. She'd have thought I'd stopped loving her. (*He pauses—then looking around at them*) I suppose you think I'm a liar, that no woman could have stood all she stood and still loved me so much—that it isn't human for any woman to be so pitying and forgiving. Well, I'm not lying, and if you'd ever seen her, you'd realize I wasn't. It was written all over her face, sweetness and love and pity and forgiveness. (*He reaches mechanically for the inside pocket of his coat*) Wait! I'll show you. I always carry her picture. (*Suddenly he looks startled. He stares before him, his hand falling back —quietly*) No, I'm forgetting I tore it up—afterwards. I didn't need it any more. (*He pauses. The silence is like that in the room of a dying man where people hold their breath, waiting for him to die*)

CORA (*With a muffled sob*) Jees, Hickey! Jees! (*She shivers and puts her hands over her face*)

PARRITT (*To* LARRY *in a low insistent tone*) I burnt up Mother's picture, Larry. Her eyes followed me all the time. They seemed to be wishing I was dead!

HICKEY It kept piling up, like I've said. I got so I thought of it all the time. I hated myself more and more, thinking of all the wrong I'd done to the sweetest woman in the world who loved me so much. I got so I'd curse myself for a lousy bastard every time I saw myself in the mirror. I felt such pity for her it drove me crazy. You wouldn't believe a guy like me, that's knocked around so much, could feel such pity. It got so every night I'd wind up hiding my face in her lap, bawling and begging her forgiveness. And, of course, she'd always comfort me and say, "Never mind, Teddy, I know you won't ever again." Christ, I loved her so, but I began to hate that pipe dream! I began to be afraid I was going bughouse, because sometimes I couldn't forgive her for forgiving me. I even caught myself hating her for making me hate myself so much. There's a limit to the guilt you can feel and the forgiveness and the pity you can take! You have to begin blaming someone else, too. I got so sometimes when she'd kiss me it was like she did it on purpose to humiliate me, as if she'd spit in my face! But all the time I saw how crazy and rotten of me that was, and it made me hate myself all the more. You'd never believe I could hate so much, a good-natured, happy-go-lucky slob like me. And as the time got nearer to when I was due to come here for my drunk around Harry's birthday, I got nearly crazy. I kept swearing to her every night that this time I really wouldn't, until I'd made it a real final test to myself—and to her. And she kept encouraging me and saying, "I can see you really mean it now, Teddy. I know you'll conquer it this time, and we'll be so happy, dear." When she'd say that and kiss me, I'd believe it, too. Then she'd go to bed, and I'd stay up alone because I couldn't sleep and I didn't want to disturb her, tossing and rolling around. I'd get so damned lonely. I'd get thinking how peaceful it was here, sitting around with the old gang, getting drunk and forgetting love, joking and laughing and singing and swapping lies. And finally I knew I'd have to come. And I knew if I came this time, it was the finish. I'd never have the guts to go back and be forgiven again, and that would break Evelyn's heart because to her it would mean I didn't love her any more. (*He pauses*) That last night I'd driven myself crazy trying to figure some way out for her. I went in the bedroom. I was going to tell her it was the end. But I couldn't do that to her. She was sound asleep. I thought, God, if she'd only never wake up, she'd never know! And then it came to me—the only possible way out, for her sake. I remembered I'd given her a gun for protection while I was away and it was in the bureau drawer. She'd never feel any pain, never wake up from her dream. So I—

HOPE (*Tries to ward this off by pounding with his glass on the table—with brutal, callous exasperation*) Give us a rest, for the love of Christ! Who the hell cares? We want to pass out in peace! (*They all, except* PARRITT *and* LARRY, *pound with their glasses and grumble in chorus: "Who the hell cares? We want to pass out in peace!"* MORAN, *the detective, moves quietly from the entrance in the curtain across the back of the room to the table where his companion,* LIEB, *is sitting.* ROCKY *notices his leaving and gets up from the table in the rear and goes back to stand and watch in the entrance.* MORAN *exchanges a glance with* LIEB, *motioning him to get up. The latter does so. No one notices them. The clamor of banging glasses dies out as abruptly as it started.* HICKEY *hasn't appeared to hear it*)

HICKEY (*Simply*) So I killed her. (*There is a moment of dead silence. Even the detectives are caught in it and stand motionless*)

PARRITT (*Suddenly gives up and relaxes limply in his chair—in a low voice in which there is a strange exhausted relief*) I may as well confess, Larry. There's no use lying any more. You know, anyway. I didn't give a damn about the money. It was because I hated her.

HICKEY (*Obliviously*) And then I saw I'd always known that was the only possible way to give her peace and free her from the misery of loving me. I saw it meant peace for me, too, knowing she was at peace. I felt as though a ton of guilt was lifted off my mind. I remember I stood by the bed and suddenly I had to laugh. I couldn't help it, and I knew Evelyn would forgive me. I remember I heard myself speaking to her, as if it was something I'd always wanted to say: "Well, you know what you can do with your pipe dream now, you damned bitch!" (*He stops with a horrified start, as if shocked out of a nightmare, as if he couldn't believe he heard what he had just said. He stammers*) No! I never—!

PARRITT (*To* LARRY—*sneeringly*) Yes, that's it! Her and the damned old Movement pipe dream! Eh, Larry?

HICKEY (*Bursts into frantic denial*) No! That's a lie! I never said—! Good God, I couldn't have said that! If I did, I'd gone insane! Why, I loved Evelyn better than anything in life! (*He appeals brokenly to the crowd*) Boys, you're all my old pals! You've known old Hickey for years! You know I'd never— (*His eyes fix on* HOPE) You've known me longer than anyone, Harry. You know I must have been insane, don't you, Governor?

HOPE (*At first with the same defensive callousness—without looking at him*) Who the hell cares? (*Then suddenly he looks at* HICKEY *and there is an extraordinary change in his expression. His face lights up, as if he were grasping at some dawning hope in his mind. He speaks with a groping eagerness*) Insane? You mean—you went really insane? (*At the tone of his voice, all the group at the tables by him start and stare at him as if they caught his thought. Then they all look at* HICKEY *eagerly, too*)

HICKEY Yes! Or I couldn't have laughed! I couldn't have said that to her! (MORAN *walks up behind him on one side, while the second detective,* LIEB, *closes in on him from the other*)

MORAN (*Taps* HICKEY *on the shoulder*) That's enough, Hickman. You know who we are. You're under arrest. (*He nods to* LIEB, *who slips a pair of handcuffs on* HICKEY's *wrists.* HICKEY *stares at them with stupid incomprehension.* MORAN *takes his arm*) Come along and spill your guts where we can get it on paper.

HICKEY No, wait, Officer! You owe me a break! I phoned and made it easy for you, didn't I? Just a few minutes! (*To* HOPE—*pleadingly*) You know I couldn't say that to Evelyn, don't you, Harry—unless—

HOPE (*Eagerly*) And you've been crazy ever since? Everything you've said and done here—

HICKEY (*For a moment forgets his own obsession and his face takes on its familiar expression of affectionate amusement and he chuckles*) Now, Governor! Up to your old tricks, eh? I see what you're driving at, but I can't let you get away with— (*Then, as* HOPE's *expression turns to resentful callousness again and he looks away, he adds hastily with pleading desperation*) Yes, Harry, of course, I've been out of my mind ever since! All the time I've been here! You saw I was insane, didn't you?

MORAN (*With cynical disgust*) Can it! I've had enough of your act. Save it for the jury. (*Addressing the crowd, sharply*) Listen, you guys. Don't fall for his lies. He's starting to get foxy now and thinks he'll plead insanity. But he can't get away with it. (*The crowd at the grouped tables are grasping at hope now. They glare at him resentfully*)

HOPE (*Begins to bristle in his old-time manner*) Bejees, you dumb dick, you've got a crust trying to tell us about Hickey! We've known him for years, and every one of us noticed he was nutty the minute he showed up here! Bejees, if you'd heard all the crazy bull he was pulling about bringing us peace—like a bughouse preacher escaped from an asylum! If you'd seen all the damned-fool things he made us do! We only did them because— (*He hesitates—then defiantly*) Because we hoped he'd come out of it if we kidded him along and humored him. (*He looks around at the others*) Ain't that right, fellers? (*They burst into a chorus of eager assent: "Yes, Harry!" "That's it, Harry!" "That's why!" "We knew he was crazy!" "Just to humor him!"*)

MORAN A fine bunch of rats! Covering up for a dirty, cold-blooded murderer.

HOPE (*Stung into recovering all his old fuming truculence*) Is that so? Bejees, you know the old story, when Saint Patrick drove the snakes out of Ireland they swam to New York and joined the police force! Ha! (*He cackles insultingly*) Bejees, we can believe it now when we look at you, can't we, fellers? (*They all growl assent, glowering defiantly at* MORAN. MORAN *glares at them, looking as if he'd like to forget his prisoner and start cleaning out the place.* HOPE *goes on pugnaciously*) You stand up for your rights, bejees, Hickey! Don't let this smart-aleck dick get funny with you. If he pulls any rubber-hose tricks, you let me know! I've still got friends at the Hall! Bejees, I'll have him back in uniform pounding a beat where the only graft he'll get will be stealing tin cans from the goats!

MORAN (*Furiously*) Listen, you cockeyed old bum, for a plugged nickel I'd— (*Controlling himself, turns to* HICKEY, *who is oblivious to all this, and yanks his arm*) Come on, you!

HICKEY (*With a strange mad earnestness*) Oh, I want to go, Officer. I can hardly wait now. I should have phoned you from the house right afterwards. It was a waste of time coming here. I've got to explain to Evelyn. But I know she's forgiven me. She knows I was insane. You've got me all wrong, Officer. I want to go to the Chair.

MORAN Crap!

HICKEY (*Exasperatedly*) God, you're a dumb dick! Do you suppose I give a damn about life now? Why, you bonehead, I haven't got a single damned lying hope or pipe dream left!

MORAN (*Jerks him around to face the door to the hall*) Get a move on!

HICKEY (*As they start walking toward rear—insistently*) All I want you to see is I was out of my mind afterwards, when I laughed at her! I was a raving rotten lunatic or I couldn't have said— Why, Evelyn was the only thing on God's earth I ever loved! I'd have killed myself before I'd ever have hurt her! (*They disappear in the hall.* HICKEY's *voice keeps on protesting*)

HOPE (*Calls after him*) Don't worry, Hickey! They can't give you the Chair! We'll testify you was crazy! Won't we, fellers? (*They all assent. Two or three echo* HOPE's *"Don't worry, Hickey." Then from the hall comes the slam of the street door.* HOPE's *face falls—with genuine sorrow*) He's gone. Poor crazy son of a bitch! (*All the group around him are sad and sympathetic, too.* HOPE *reaches for his drink*) Bejees, I need a drink. (*They grab their glasses.* HOPE *says hopefully*) Bejees, maybe it'll have the old kick, now he's gone. (*He drinks and they follow suit*)

ROCKY (*Comes forward from where he has stood in the bar entrance—hopefully*) Yeah, Boss, maybe we can get drunk now. (*He sits in the chair by* CHUCK *and pours a drink and tosses it down. Then they all sit still, waiting for the effect, as if this drink were a crucial test, so absorbed in hopeful expectancy that they remain oblivious to what happens at* LARRY's *table*)

LARRY (*His eyes full of pain and pity—in a whisper, aloud to himself*) May the Chair bring him peace at last, the poor tortured bastard!

PARRITT (*Leans toward him—in a strange low insistent voice*) Yes, but he isn't the only one who needs peace, Larry. I can't feel sorry for him. He's lucky. He's through, now. It's all decided for him. I wish it was decided for me. I've never been any good at deciding things. Even about selling out, it was the tart the detective agency got after me who put it in my mind. You remember what Mother's like, Larry. She makes all the decisions. She's always decided what I must do. She doesn't like anyone to be free but herself. (*He pauses, as if waiting for comment, but* LARRY *ignores him*) I suppose you think I ought to have made those dicks take me away with Hickey. But how could I prove it, Larry? They'd think I was nutty. Because she's still alive. You're the only one who can understand how guilty I am. Because you know her and what I've done to her. You know I'm really much guiltier than he is. You know what I did is a much worse murder. Because she is dead and yet she has to live. For a while. But she can't live long in jail. She loves freedom too much. And I can't kid myself like Hickey, that she's at peace. As long as she lives, she'll never be able to forget what I've done to her even in her sleep. She'll never have a second's peace. (*He pauses—then bursts out*) Jesus, Larry, can't you say something? (LARRY *is at the breaking point.* PARRITT *goes on*) And I'm not putting up any bluff, either, that I was crazy afterwards when I laughed to myself and thought, "You know what you can do with your freedom pipe dream now, don't you, you damned old bitch!"

LARRY (*Snaps and turns on him, his face convulsed with detestation. His quivering voice has a condemning command in it*) Go! Get the hell out of life, God damn you, before I choke it out of you! Go up—!

PARRITT (*His manner is at once transformed. He seems suddenly at peace with himself. He speaks simply and gratefully*) Thanks, Larry. I just wanted to be sure. I can see now it's the only possible way I can ever get free from her. I guess I've really known that all my life. (*He pauses—then with a derisive smile*) It ought to comfort Mother a little, too. It'll give her the chance to play the great incorruptible Mother of the Revolution, whose only child is the Proletariat. She'll be able to say: "Justice is done! So may all traitors die!" She'll be able to say: "I am glad he's dead! Long live the Revolution!" (*He adds with a final implacable jeer*) You know her, Larry! Always a ham!

LARRY (*Pleads distractedly*) Go, for the love of Christ, you mad tortured bastard, for your own sake! (HUGO *is roused by this. He lifts his head and peers uncomprehendingly at* LARRY. *Neither* LARRY *nor* PARRITT *notices him*)

PARRITT (*Stares at* LARRY. *His face begins to crumble as if he were going to break down and sob. He turns his head away, but reaches out fumblingly and pats* LARRY's *arm and stammers*) Jesus, Larry, thanks. That's kind. I knew you were the only one who could understand my side of it. (*He gets to his feet and turns toward the door*)

HUGO (*Looks at* PARRITT *and bursts into his silly giggle*) Hello, leedle Don, leedle monkey-face! Don't be a fool! Buy me a trink!

PARRITT (*Puts on an act of dramatic bravado—forcing a grin*) Sure, I will, Hugo! Tomorrow! Beneath the willow trees! (*He walks to the door with a careless swagger and disappears in the hall. From now on,* LARRY *waits, listening for the sound he knows is coming from the backyard outside the window, but trying not to listen, in an agony of horror and cracking nerve*)

HUGO (*Stares after* PARRITT *stupidly*) Stupid fool! Hickey make you crazy, too. (*He turns to the oblivious* LARRY*—with a timid eagerness*) I'm glad, Larry, they take the crazy Hickey avay to asylum. He makes me have bad dreams. He makes me tell lies about myself. He makes me want to spit on all I have ever dreamed. Yes, I am glad they take him to asylum. I don't feel I am dying now. He vas selling death to me, that crazy salesman. I think I have a trink now, Larry. (*He pours a drink and gulps it down*)

HOPE (*Jubilantly*) Bejees, fellers, I'm feeling the old kick, or I'm a liar! It's putting life back in me! Bejees, if all I've lapped up begins to hit me, I'll be paralyzed before I know it! It was Hickey kept it from— Bejees, I know that sounds crazy, but he was crazy, and he'd got all of us as bughouse as he was. Bejees, it does queer things to you, having to listen day and night to a lunatic's pipe dreams—pretending you believe them, to kid him along and doing any crazy thing he wants to humor him. It's dangerous, too. Look at me pretending to start for a walk just to keep him quiet. I knew damned well it wasn't the right day for it. The sun was broiling and the streets full of automobiles. Bejees, I could feel myself getting sunstroke, and an automobile damn near ran over me. (*He appeals to* ROCKY, *afraid of the result, but daring it*) Ask Rocky. He was watching. Didn't it, Rocky?

ROCKY (*A bit tipsily*) What's dat, Boss? Jees, all de

booze I've mopped up is beginning to get to me. (*Earnestly*) De automobile, Boss? Sure, I seen it! Just missed yuh! I thought yuh was a goner. (*He pauses—then looks around at the others, and assumes the old kidding tone of the inmates, but hesitantly, as if still a little afraid*) On de woid of a honest bartender! (*He tries a wink at the others. They all respond with smiles that are still a little forced and uneasy*)

HOPE (*Flashes him a suspicious glance. Then he understands—with his natural testy manner*) You're a bartender, all right. No one can say different. (ROCKY *looks grateful*) But, bejees, don't pull that honest junk! You and Chuck ought to have cards in the Burglars' Union! (*This time there is an eager laugh from the group.* HOPE *is delighted*) Bejees, it's good to hear someone laugh again! All the time that bas—poor old Hickey was here, I didn't have the heart—Bejees, I'm getting drunk and glad of it! (*He cackles and reaches for the bottle*) Come on, fellers. It's on the house. (*They pour drinks. They begin rapidly to get drunk now.* HOPE *becomes sentimental*) Poor old Hickey! We mustn't hold him responsible for anything he's done. We'll forget that and only remember him the way we've always known him before—the kindest, biggest-hearted guy ever wore shoe leather. (*They all chorus hearty sentimental assent: "That's right, Harry!" "That's all!" "Finest fellow!" "Best scout!" etc.* HOPE *goes on*) Good luck to him in Matteawan! [1] Come on, bottoms up! (*They all drink. At the table by the window* LARRY'*s hands grip the edge of the table. Unconsciously his head is inclined toward the window as he listens*)

LARRY (*Cannot hold back an anguished exclamation*) Christ! Why don't he—!

HUGO (*Beginning to be drunk again—peers at him*) Vhy don't he what? Don't be a fool! Hickey's gone. He vas crazy. Have a trink. (*Then as he receives no reply—with vague uneasiness*) What's matter vith you, Larry? You look funny. What you listen to out in backyard, Larry? (CORA *begins to talk in the group at right*)

CORA (*Tipsily*) Well, I thank Gawd now me and Chuck did all we could to humor de poor nut. Jees, imagine us goin' off like we really meant to git married, when we ain't even picked out a farm yet!

CHUCK (*Eagerly*) Sure ting, Baby. We kidded him we was serious.

JIMMY (*Confidently—with a gentle, drunken unction*) I may as well say I detected his condition almost at once. All that talk of his about tomorrow, for example. He had the fixed idea of the insane. It only makes them worse to cross them.

WILLIE (*Eagerly*) Same with me, Jimmy. Only I spent the day in the park. I wasn't such a damned fool as to—

LEWIS (*Getting jauntily drunk*) Picture my predicament if I *had* gone to the Consulate. The pal of mine there is a humorous blighter. He would have got me a job out of pure spite. So I strolled about and finally came to roost in the park. (*He grins with affectionate kidding at* WETJOEN) And lo and behold, who was on the neighboring bench but my old battlefield companion, the Boer that walks like a man—who, if the British Government had taken my advice, would have been removed from his fetid kraal on the veldt straight to the baboon's cage at the London Zoo, and little children would now be asking their nurses: "Tell me, Nana, is that the Boer General, the one with the blue behind?" (*They all laugh uproariously.* LEWIS *leans over and slaps* WETJOEN *affectionately on the knee*) No offense meant, Piet, old chap.

WETJOEN (*Beaming at him*) No offense taken, you tamned Limey! (WETJOEN *goes on—grinningly*) About a job, I felt the same as you, Cecil.

(*At the table by the window* HUGO *speaks to* LARRY *again*)

HUGO (*With uneasy insistence*) What's matter, Larry? You look scared. What you listen for out there? (*But* LARRY *doesn't hear, and* JOE *begins talking in the group at right*)

JOE (*With drunken self-assurance*) No, suh, I wasn't fool enough to git in no crap game. Not while Hickey's around. Crazy people puts a jinx on you.

(MCGLOIN *is now heard. He is leaning across in front of* WETJOEN *to talk to* ED MOSHER *on* HOPE'S *left*)

MCGLOIN (*With drunken earnestness*) I know you saw how it was, Ed. There was no good trying to explain to a crazy guy, but it ain't the right time. You know how getting reinstated is.

MOSHER (*Decidedly*) Sure, Mac. The same way with the circus. The boys tell me the rubes are wasting all their money buying food and times never was so hard. And I never was one to cheat for chicken feed.

HOPE (*Looks around him in an ecstasy of bleary sentimental content*) Bejees, I'm cockeyed! Bejees, you're all cockeyed! Bejees, we're all all right! Let's have another! (*They pour out drinks. At the table by the window* LARRY *has unconsciously shut his eyes as he listens.* HUGO *is peering at him frightenedly now*)

HUGO (*Reiterates stupidly*) What's matter, Larry? Why you keep eyes shut? You look dead. What you listen for in backyard? (*Then, as* LARRY *doesn't open his eyes or answer, he gets up hastily and moves away from the table, mumbling with frightened anger*) Crazy fool! You vas crazy like Hickey! You give me bad dreams, too. (*He shrinks quickly past the table where* HICKEY *had sat to the rear of the group at right*)

ROCKY (*Greets him with boisterous affection*) Hello, dere, Hugo! Welcome to de party!

HOPE Yes, bejees, Hugo! Sit down! Have a drink! Have ten drinks, bejees!

HUGO (*Forgetting* LARRY *and bad dreams, gives his familiar giggle*) Hello, leedle Harry! Hello, nice, leedle, funny monkey-faces! (*Warming up, changes abruptly to his usual declamatory denunciation*) Gottamned stupid bourgeois! Soon comes the Day of Judgment! (*They make derisive noises and tell him to*

[1] A New York State Hospital for the Criminally Insane.

*sit down. He changes again, giggling good-naturedly, and sits at rear of the middle table)* Give me ten trinks, Harry. Don't be a fool. (*They laugh.* ROCKY *shoves a glass and bottle at him. The sound of* MARGIE's *and* PEARL's *voices is heard from the hall, drunkenly shrill. All of the group turn toward the door as the two appear. They are drunk and look blowsy and disheveled. Their manner as they enter hardens into a brazen defensive truculence*)

MARGIE (*Stridently*) Gangway for two good whores!

PEARL Yeah! and we want a drink quick!

MARGIE (*Glaring at* ROCKY) Shake de lead outa your pants, Pimp! A little soivice!

ROCKY (*His black bullet eyes sentimental, his round Wop face grinning welcome*) Well, look who's here! (*He goes to them unsteadily, opening his arms*) Hello, dere, Sweethearts! Jees, I was beginnin' to worry about yuh, honest! (*He tries to embrace them. They push his arms away, regarding him with amazed suspicion*)

PEARL What kind of a gag is dis?

HOPE (*Calls to them effusively*) Come on and join the party, you broads! Bejees, I'm glad to see you! (*The girls exchange a bewildered glance, taking in the party and the changed atmosphere*)

MARGIE Jees, what's come off here?

PEARL Where's dat louse, Hickey?

ROCKY De cops got him. He'd gone crazy and croaked his wife. (*The girls exclaim, "Jees!" But there is more relief than horror in it.* ROCKY *goes on*) He'll get Matteawan. He ain't responsible. What he's pulled don't mean nuttin'. So forget dat whore stuff. I'll knock de block off anyone calls you whores! I'll fill de bastard full of lead! Yuh're tarts, and what de hell of it? Yuh're as good as anyone! So forget it, see? (*They let him get his arms around them now. He gives them a hug. All the truculence leaves their faces. They smile and exchange maternally amused glances*)

MARGIE (*With a wink*) Our little bartender, ain't he, Poil?

PEARL Yeah, and a cute little Ginny at dat! (*They laugh*)

MARGIE And is he stinko!

PEARL Stinko is right. But he ain't got nuttin' on us. Jees, Rocky, did we have a big time at Coney!

HOPE Bejees, sit down, you dumb broads! Welcome home! Have a drink! Have ten drinks, bejees! (*They take the empty chairs on* CHUCK's *left, warmly welcomed by all.* ROCKY *stands in back of them, a hand on each of their shoulders, grinning with proud proprietorship.* HOPE *beams over and under his crooked spectacles with the air of a host whose party is a huge success, and rambles on happily*) Bejees, this is all right! We'll make this my birthday party, and forget the other. We'll get paralyzed! But who's missing? Where's the Old Wise Guy? Where's Larry?

ROCKY Over by de window, Boss. Jees, he's got his eyes shut. De old bastard's asleep. (*They turn to look.* ROCKY *dismisses him*) Aw, to hell wid him. Let's have a drink. (*They turn away and forget him*)

LARRY (*Torturedly arguing to himself in a shaken whisper*) It's the only way out for him! For the peace of all concerned, as Hickey said! (*Snapping*) God damn his yellow soul, if he doesn't soon, I'll go up and throw him off!—like a dog with its guts ripped out you'd put out of misery! (*He half rises from his chair just as from outside the window comes the sound of something hurtling down, followed by a muffled, crunching thud.* LARRY *gasps and drops back on his chair, shuddering, hiding his face in his hands. The group at right hear it but are too preoccupied with drinks to pay much attention*)

HOPE (*Wonderingly*) What the hell was that?

ROCKY Aw, nuttin'. Someting fell off de fire escape. A mattress, I'll bet. Some of dese bums been sleepin' on de fire escapes.

HOPE (*His interest diverted by this excuse to beef—testily*) They've got to cut it out! Bejees, this ain't a fresh-air cure. Mattresses cost money.

MOSHER Now don't start crabbing at the party, Harry. Let's drink up. (HOPE *forgets it and grabs his glass, and they all drink*)

LARRY (*In a whisper of horrified pity*) Poor devil! (*A long-forgotten faith returns to him for a moment and he mumbles*) God rest his soul in peace. (*He opens his eyes—with a bitter self-derision*) Ah, the damned pity—the wrong kind, as Hickey said! Be God, there's no hope! I'll never be a success in the grandstand—or anywhere else! Life is too much for me! I'll be a weak fool looking with pity at the two sides of everything till the day I die! (*With an intense bitter sincerity*) May that day come soon! (*He pauses startledly, surprised at himself—then with a sardonic grin*) Be God, I'm the only real convert to death Hickey made here. From the bottom of my coward's heart I mean that now!

HOPE (*Calls effusively*) Hey there, Larry! Come over and get paralyzed! What the hell you doing, sitting there? (*Then as* LARRY *doesn't reply he immediately forgets him and turns to the party. They are all very drunk now, just a few drinks ahead of the passing-out stage, and hilariously happy about it*) Bejees, let's sing! Let's celebrate! It's my birthday party! Bejees, I'm oreyeyed! I want to sing! (*He starts the chorus of "She's the Sunshine of Paradise Alley," and instantly they all burst into song. But not the same song. Each starts the chorus of his or her choice.* JIMMY TOMORROW's *is "A Wee Dock and Doris";* ED MOSHER's, *"Break the News to Mother";* WILLIE OBAN's, *the Sailor Lad ditty he sang in Act One;* GENERAL WETJOEN's, *"Waiting at the Church";* MCGLOIN's, *"Tammany";* CAPTAIN LEWIS's, *"The Old Kent Road";* JOE's, *"All I Got Was Sympathy";* PEARL's *and* MARGIE's, *"Everybody's Doing It";* ROCKY's, *"You Great Big Beautiful Doll";* CHUCK's, *"The Curse of an Aching Heart";* CORA's, *"The Oceana Roll"; while* HUGO *jumps to his feet and, pounding on the table with his fist, bellows in his guttural basso the French Revolutionary "Carmagnole." A weird cacophony results from this mixture and they stop singing to roar with laughter. All but* HUGO, *who keeps on with drunken fervor*)

HUGO *Dansons la Carmagnole!*
*Vive le son! Vive le son!*
*Dansons la Carmagnole!*
*Vive le son des canons!*

(*They all turn on him and howl him down with amused derision. He stops singing to denounce them in his most fiery style*) Capitalist svine! Stupid bourgeois monkeys! (*He declaims*) "The days grow hot, O Babylon!" (*They all take it up and shout in enthusiastic jeering chorus*) "'Tis cool beneath thy willow trees!" (*They pound their glasses on the table, roaring with laughter, and* HUGO *giggles with them. In his chair by the window,* LARRY *stares in front of him, oblivious to their racket*)

*Curtain*

# Clifford Odets

## (1906-1963)

In American history, 1935 was at once the bleakest of the Depression years and a turning point when New Deal emergency measures began to inch a sick economy toward recovery; it was a year in which the first pro-Nazi Bundist groups began to mushroom in American cities even while "Leftism" was still insurgent. In the annals of American drama, 1935 was the Year of Odets: a relatively unknown young actor challenged O'Neill's eminence when, in rapid succession, four of his plays were produced on Broadway. The Group Theatre, an energetic "collective" in which Odets had been a founding member, opened *Awake and Sing!* on February 19; a bill of long one-acts, *Waiting for Lefty* and *Till the Day I Die,* on March 26; and *Paradise Lost* on December 9. To these may be added the powerful monologue, "I Can't Sleep," in which Odets, writing for a union benefit, traced an ex-radical's insomnia back to his alienation from his working-class origins. By the end of 1935, Odets was hailed as a "revolutionary oracle," the "darling of the proletariat," the "prophet of the Left." He had participated in an unsuccessful fact-finding mission dispatched to Cuba by the League of American Writers, had ended a brief period of Communist Party membership, and was receiving Hollywood offers in astronomical figures. By January, 1938, after he had proved—with *Golden Boy,* his next major work—that he had not surrendered his mastery of dialogue by toiling in the Hollywood vineyards for a reported $2500 a week, Odets was profiled in *The New Yorker* as "Revolution's Number One Boy" even though he reminded his old friends of "a well-groomed capitalist playboy." Later in 1938 *Awake and Sing!*, revived by the Group as a modern classic, was given a warmer reception than it had been accorded on its maiden voyage three years earlier. By 1938, *Waiting for Lefty,* his most transparent use of theatre as a weapon in the class struggle, was being produced all over the world as, in Odets' report, "a kind of light-machine-gun that you wheeled in to use whenever there was any kind of strike trouble." By 1938, his anti-Nazi *Till the Day I Die,* dismissed as unwarrantedly alarmist in 1935, seemed prophetic for its depiction of Master Race sadism in persecution techniques.

Within four years Odets had established himself as a dominant force in American drama, a personality framed in controversy, perhaps, but exciting as much for what his future promised as for what he had already achieved. His path had started in Philadelphia, where he was born into a family of Jewish Lithuanian immigrants; it had carried him to the Bronx where, in sharp contrast to his parents' middle-class security, thousands of families lived on the fringe of poverty. Quitting high school before graduation, he sought jobs in radio and theatre. In the late 1920's, he was playing minor roles in Theatre Guild productions; in the Guild's acting studio he met Harold Clurman, Lee Strasberg, and Cheryl Crawford, prime movers in establishing the Group Theatre.

Odets continued to write for the theatre (at least up until 1954, when he staged *The Flowering Peach,* his moving tragicomic treatment of the Noah legend), but he was best known for his productive association with the Group. From 1931 when the Group broke away from the Theatre Guild, until 1941 when it ceased to function, Odets' activities were inextricably bound up with its history. Even after he departed in 1936 for Hollywood, the Group remained his home base in New York. This period has been well documented, especially in Harold Clurman's *The Fervent Years* (first published, 1945), the unofficial history of the Group and the troubled era in which it struggled to survive. The Group produced works by Sidney Kingsley, Maxwell Anderson, Robert Ardrey, Paul Green, Irwin Shaw, William Saroyan and, through its playwriting contest, encouraged a young Tennessee Williams, but it was best known for sponsoring Odets. Dedicated to studying Stanislavsky's methods and to establishing Moscow Art Theatre standards of ensemble-acting in America, the Group gave Odets an artistic challenge. In his turn, he wrote plays in which the Group could fully realize its artistic ideals.

More to the point, however, was the extent to which Depression psychology, marked, as Clurman has said, by "the appetite for meetings, collections, demonstrations, petitions, and parades," imparted special urgency to concerns which gave Odets and his Group colleagues a unity beyond their artistic goals. Odets was in no sense the first or even the angriest American dramatist to speak out against a life "printed on dollar bills." Criticism of bourgeois materialism had long been commonplace in American letters, and the playwrights emergent in the 1920's—O'Neill, Elmer Rice, Sidney Howard, S. N. Behrman, Maxwell Anderson—had all brought social commentary into the American theatre. Nor was the Group the first producing organization to accommodate itself to a Depression-heightened interest in the Marxist thesis. In comparison to the New Theatre League (for which Odets originally wrote *Waiting for*

*Lefty*), the Theatre of Action, Labor Stage, and other radical workers' theatre groups, the Group seemed almost moderate in its responsiveness to the period's widespread discontent. What made Odets' plays, especially as performed by Group actors, arrest the attention of audiences was his rare combination of sympathetic insight into characters trapped in the "struggle for life amidst petty conditions" and the unerring ability to create the voices through which his characters assert themselves. Had Odets been less than a master of dialogue, had he been less intimately involved in the lives of his characters, his plays, along with most of the period's drama of political commitment, would long since have lost their appeal.

It was his command of living language which led critics of widely divergent political beliefs to hail Odets as the most promising American dramatist since O'Neill. In *The Changing World in Plays and Theatre* (1939), Anita Block suggested why, for an audience which "comes in from passing a picket line and goes out to get news of a war," Odets' plays were superior to those of Shaw and O'Neill: "In the half-articulate idiom of the street, spoken by the ordinary folk who constitute the throbbing characters of a Clifford Odets, their counterparts in the audience hear their own inarticulate cries; in the taut monosyllables of frustration and longing, they hear their own eager and bursting hearts." A more conservative critic, John Mason Brown, balanced out Odets' strengths and weaknesses in his 1935 review of *Waiting for Lefty* and *Till the Day I Die*: "You may regret the simplicity of his Communist panaceas and look askance at his willful stacking of the cards. . . . You may point to scenes which he leaves as raw and as undeveloped as if he were dashing off a hurried first draft at midnight. . . . But . . . Mr. Odets is doing more than holding your attention. He is commanding it. As an emotionalist he has a sweeping, vigorous power which is as welcome as it is thundersome when encountered in our theatre." Although the eminent British critic, James Agate, felt that what Odets tried to convey in *Paradise Lost* was "complete nonsense," he also proclaimed him "a born dramatist whom no amount of pretentious thinking can make into anything else."

Odets' customary dramatic mode was allegory strongly rooted in realism. Especially in the early plays, his Pilgrims are Potential or Putative Proletarian Victims of the Capitalist System; his Slough of Despond is the Mausoleum of the Middle Class; his Celestial City is, variously, the Workers' Paradise, the State of Being Wanted, or the Land of Self-Respect. His morality plays are set against locales where Odets saw the mettle of modern man being tested: middle-class dwellings, the prizefight world juxtaposed with the world of violin lessons and simple humanity, a dentist's waiting room, a Hollywood star's pleasure-palace, and drafty Broadway dressing rooms. In *Night Music* (1940) Odets wrote of the Homeless and Unneeded, much in the manner of *Peer Gynt* or O'Casey's *Within the Gates*: his protagonists follow a Via Dolorosa marked out by police stations, stage doors, hotels, Central Park, the World's Fair, and an airport. In his maturest work, *The Flowering Peach,* he recreated the voices of *Awake and Sing!* with Everyman fragmentized into Noah and his family ("assorted clowns and acrobats") moving in a "Then, not now" between Noah's home and the new land on which the Ark finally comes aground.

The weight of his allegory varies from play to play, but there was a very discernible development away from the Marxist abstractions in *Waiting for Lefty,* with its heroes and villains conceived in comic-strip terms. In this agitprop (agitation-propaganda) minstrel show, Odets epitomized the evils of capitalism in Harry Fatt, the anti-strike union boss, and his gunmen. Among his Everyman-Taxidrivers were a victim of anti-Semitism in a hospital, a lab assistant who refused to spy on an associate for his poison-gas manufacturer boss, a young actor unable to find work in the face of Broadway's commercialist emphasis. Hovering throughout is Lefty, the pro-strike committee chairman who never appears. When his murder ("behind the car barns . . . a bullet in his head") is reported, the cry goes up—"WE'RE STORMBIRDS OF THE WORKING CLASS"—and the strike is called.

After *Waiting for Lefty,* Odets' other plays seem less boldly inventive in conception. When he chose to show characters oscillating between strongly contrasted worlds, he employed a freewheeling, loosely episodic form: this cinematic-picaresque structure is effective in *Golden Boy* and *Night Music,* both of which have twelve scenes, and in *Flowering Peach,* which has nine. More often he concentrated on a single environment within conventional three-act form. *Awake and Sing!* gains much of its power from its concentrated focus on the appalling reality of the Bergers' "typically furnished" Bronx apartment, the arena in which children and parents battle for survival. This setting is the "dust" out of which the younger Bergers must break before they can "awake and sing."

The Marxist emphasis, so apparent in Ralph's final speeches when *Awake and Sing!* was first produced, now seems merely a lyrically Romantic celebration of basic human rights. Unlike the 1935 audiences who were told that *Awake and Sing!* began as a despairingly pessimistic play entitled *I Got the Blues,* later audiences can accept its ending as appropriate in its desperate affirmation. It is now apparent that Depression-period audiences may have brought more Marxist dogma to the play than the play itself encourages anyone to carry away.

Until his death in August, 1963, Odets had spent his later years in Hollywood as writer-director, but occasionally he sought to reestablish his roots in the theatre. Large audiences have seen *The Big Knife* and *The Country Girl,* both on the stage and in the films. In 1961, Odets was honored by the American Academy of Arts and Letters for his dramatic achievements. Among his most significant contributions must be counted his influence on younger dramatists who have mastered the art of dialogue by studying his plays. As one of the great prose-poets of contemporary drama, Odets belongs among those dramatists who have touched universal concerns by mirroring, without succumbing to, the special circumstances of their moment in history.

# AWAKE AND SING!

## THE CHARACTERS OF THE PLAY

*All of the characters in* Awake and Sing! *share a fundamental activity: a struggle for life amidst petty conditions.*

BESSIE BERGER, *as she herself states, is not only the mother in this home but also the father. She is constantly arranging and taking care of her family. She loves life, likes to laugh, has great resourcefulness and enjoys living from day to day. A high degree of energy accounts for her quick exasperation at ineptitude. She is a shrewd judge of realistic qualities in people in the sense of being able to gauge quickly their effectiveness. In her eyes all of the people in the house are equal. She is naïve and quick in emotional response. She is afraid of utter poverty. She is proper according to her own standards, which are fairly close to those of most middle-class families. She knows that when one lives in the jungle one must look out for the wild life.*

MYRON, *her husband, is a born follower. He would like to be a leader. He would like to make a million dollars. He is not sad or ever depressed. Life is an even sweet event to him, but the "old days" were sweeter yet. He has a dignified sense of himself. He likes people. He likes everything. But he is heartbroken without being aware of it.*

HENNIE *is a girl who has had few friends, male or female. She is proud of her body. She won't ask favors. She travels alone. She is fatalistic about being trapped, but will escape if possible. She is self-reliant in the best sense. Till the day she dies she will be faithful to a loved man. She inherits her mother's sense of humor and energy.*

RALPH *is a boy with a clean spirit. He wants to know, wants to learn. He is ardent, he is romantic, he is sensitive. He is naïve too. He is trying to find why so much dirt must be cleared away before it is possible to "get to first base."*

JACOB, *too, is trying to find a right path for himself and the others. He is aware of justice, of dignity. He is an observer of the others, compares their activities with his real and ideal sense of life. This produces a reflective nature. In this home he is a constant boarder. He is a sentimental idealist with no power to turn ideal to action.*
*With physical facts—such as housework—he putters. But as a barber he demonstrates the flair of an artist. He is an old Jew with living eyes in his tired face.*

UNCLE MORTY *is a successful American business man with five good senses. Something sinister comes out of the fact that the lives of others seldom touch him deeply. He holds to his own line of life. When he is generous he wants others to be aware of it. He is pleased by attention—a rich relative to the* BERGER *family. He is a shrewd judge of material values. He will die unmarried. Two and two make four, never five with him. He can blink in the sun for hours, a fat tomcat. Tickle him, he laughs. He lives in a penthouse with a real Japanese butler to serve him. He sleeps with dress models, but not from his own showrooms. He plays cards for hours on end. He smokes expensive cigars. He sees every Mickey Mouse cartoon that appears. He is a 32-degree Mason. He is really deeply intolerant finally.*

MOE AXELROD *lost a leg in the war. He seldom forgets that fact. He has killed two men in extramartial activity. He is mordant, bitter. Life has taught him a disbelief in everything, but he will fight his way through. He seldom shows his feelings: fights against his own sensitivity. He has been everywhere and seen everything. All he wants is* HENNIE. *He is very proud. He scorns the inability of others to make their way in life, but he likes people for whatever good qualities they possess. His passionate outbursts come from a strong but contained emotional mechanism.*

SAM FEINSCHREIBER *wants to find a home. He is a lonely man, a foreigner in a strange land, hyper-*

*sensitive about this fact, conditioned by the humiliation of not making his way alone. He has a sense of others laughing at him. At night he gets up and sits alone in the dark. He hears acutely all the small sounds of life. He might have been a poet in another time and place. He approaches his wife as if he were always offering her a delicate flower. Life is a high chill wind weaving itself around his head.*

SCHLOSSER, *the janitor, is an overworked German whose wife ran away with another man and left him with a young daughter who in turn ran away and joined a burlesque show as chorus girl. The man suffers rheumatic pains. He has lost his identity twenty years before.*

THE SCENE *Exposed on the stage are the dining room and adjoining front room of the* BERGER *apartment. These two rooms are typically furnished. There is a curtain between them. A small door off the front room leads to* JACOB'S *room. When his door is open one sees a picture of Sacco and Vanzetti on the wall and several shelves of books. Stage left of this door presents the entrance to the foyer hall of the apartment. The two other bedrooms of the apartment are off this hall, but not necessarily shown.*
*Stage left of the dining room presents a swinging door which opens on the kitchen.*

*The entire action takes place in an apartment in the Bronx, New York City.*

*Awake and sing,* ye that dwell in dust:
ISAIAH—26:19

# Act One

TIME *The present (the middle 1930's); the family finishing supper.*

RALPH Where's advancement down the place? Work like crazy! Think they see it? You'd drop dead first.

MYRON Never mind, son, merit never goes unrewarded. Teddy Roosevelt used to say——

HENNIE It rewarded you—thirty years a haberdashery clerk! (JACOB *laughs*)

RALPH All I want's a chance to get to first base!

HENNIE That's all?

RALPH Stuck down in that joint on Fourth Avenue—a stock clerk in a silk house! Just look at Eddie. I'm as good as he is—pulling in two-fifty a week for forty-eight minutes a day. A headliner, his name in all the papers.

JACOB That's what you want, Ralphie? Your name in the paper?

RALPH I wanna make up my own mind about things . . . be something! Didn't I want to take up tap dancing, too?

BESSIE So take lessons. Who stopped you?

RALPH On what?

BESSIE On what? Save money.

RALPH Sure, five dollars a week for expenses and the rest in the house. I can't save even for shoe laces.

BESSIE You mean we shouldn't have food in the house, but you'll make a jig on the street corner?

RALPH I mean something.

BESSIE You also mean something when you studied on the drum, Mr. Smartie!

RALPH I don't know. . . . Every other day to sit around with the blues and mud in your mouth.

MYRON That's how it is—life is like that—a cake-walk.

RALPH What's it get you?

HENNIE A four-car funeral.

RALPH What's it for?

JACOB What's it for? If this life leads to a revolution it's a good life. Otherwise it's for nothing.

BESSIE Never mind, Pop! Pass me the salt.

RALPH It's crazy—all my life I want a pair of black and white shoes and can't get them. It's crazy!

BESSIE In a minute I'll get up from the table. I can't take a bite in my mouth no more.

MYRON (*Restraining her*) Now, Momma, just don't excite yourself——

BESSIE I'm so nervous I can't hold a knife in my hand.

MYRON Is that a way to talk, Ralphie? Don't Momma work hard enough all day? (BESSIE *allows herself to be reseated*)

BESSIE On my feet twenty-four hours?

MYRON On her feet——

RALPH (*Jumps up*) What do I do—go to night-clubs with Greta Garbo? Then when I come home can't even have my own room? Sleep on a day-bed in the front room! (*Choked, he exits to front room*)

BESSIE He's starting up that stuff again. (*Shouts to him*) When Hennie here marries you'll have her room—I should only live to see the day.

HENNIE Me, too. (*They settle down to serious eating*)

MYRON This morning the sink was full of ants. Where they come from I just don't know. I thought it was coffee grounds . . . and then they began moving.

BESSIE You gave the dog eat?

JACOB I gave the dog eat. (HENNIE *drops a knife and picks it up again*)

BESSIE You got dropsy tonight.

HENNIE Company's coming.

MYRON You can buy a ticket for fifty cents and win fortunes. A man came in the store—it's the Irish Sweepstakes.

BESSIE What?

MYRON Like a raffle, only different. A man came in——

BESSIE Who spends fifty-cent pieces for Irish raffles?

They threw out a family on Dawson Street today. All the furniture on the sidewalk. A fine old woman with gray hair.

JACOB Come eat, Ralph.

MYRON A butcher on Beck Street won eighty thousand dollars.

BESSIE Eighty thousand dollars! You'll excuse my expression, you're bughouse!

MYRON I seen it in the paper—on one ticket—765 Beck Street.

BESSIE Impossible!

MYRON He did . . . yes he did. He says he'll take his old mother to Europe . . . an Austrian——

HENNIE Europe . . .

MYRON Six per cent on eighty thousand—forty-eight hundred a year.

BESSIE I'll give you money. Buy a ticket in Hennie's name. Say, you can't tell—lightning never struck us yet. If they win on Beck Street we could win on Longwood Avenue.

JACOB (*Ironically*) If it rained pearls—who would work?

BESSIE Another county heard from. (RALPH *enters and silently seats himself*)

MYRON I forgot, Beauty—Sam Feinschreiber sent you a present. Since I brought him for supper he just can't stop talking about you.

HENNIE What's that "mockie" [1] bothering about? Who needs him?

MYRON He's a very lonely boy.

HENNIE So I'll sit down and bust out crying " 'cause he's lonely."

BESSIE (*Opening candy*) He'd marry you one two three.

HENNIE Too bad about him.

BESSIE (*Naïvely delighted*) Chocolate peanuts.

HENNIE Loft's week-end special, two for thirty-nine.

BESSIE You could think about it. It wouldn't hurt.

HENNIE (*Laughing*) To quote Moe Axelrod, "Don't make me laugh."

BESSIE Never mind laughing. It's time you already had in your head a serious thought. A girl twenty-six don't grow younger. When I was your age it was already a big family with responsibilities.

HENNIE (*Laughing*) Maybe that's what ails you, Mom.

BESSIE Don't you feel well?

HENNIE 'Cause I'm laughing? I feel fine. It's just funny—that poor guy sending me presents 'cause he loves me.

BESSIE I think it's very, very nice.

HENNIE Sure . . . swell!

BESSIE Mrs. Marcus' Rose is engaged to a Brooklyn boy, a dentist. He came in his car today. A little dope should get such a boy. (*Finished with the meal,* BESSIE, MYRON *and* JACOB *rise. Both* HENNIE *and* RALPH *sit silently at the table, he eating. Suddenly she rises*)

HENNIE Tell you what, Mom. I saved for a new dress, but I'll take you and Pop to the Franklin. Don't need a dress. From now on I'm planning to stay in nights. Hold everything!

BESSIE What's the matter—a bedbug bit you suddenly?

HENNIE It's a good bill—Belle Baker. Maybe she'll sing "Eli, Eli."

BESSIE We was going to a movie.

HENNIE Forget it. Let's go.

MYRON I see in the papers (*As he picks his teeth*) Sophie Tucker took off twenty-six pounds. Fearful business with Japan.

HENNIE Write a book, Pop! Come on, we'll go early for good seats.

MYRON Moe said you had a date with him for tonight.

BESSIE Axelrod?

HENNIE I told him no, but he don't believe it. I'll tell him no for the next hundred years, too.

MYRON Don't break appointments, Beauty, and hurt people's feelings. (BESSIE *exits*)

HENNIE His hands got free wheeling. (*She exits*)

MYRON I don't know . . . people ain't the same. N-O. The whole world's changing right under our eyes. Presto! No manners. Like the great Italian lover in the movies. What was his name? The Sheik. . . . No one remembers? (*Exits, shaking his head*)

RALPH (*Unmoving at the table*) Jake . . .

JACOB Noo?

RALPH I can't stand it.

JACOB There's an expression—"strong as iron you must be."

RALPH It's a cock-eyed world.

JACOB Boys like you could fix it some day. Look on the world, not on yourself so much. Every country with starving millions, no? In Germany and Poland a Jew couldn't walk in the street. Everybody hates, nobody loves.

RALPH I don't get all that.

JACOB For years, I watched you grow up. Wait! You'll graduate from my university. (*The others enter, dressed*)

MYRON (*Lighting*) Good cigars now for a nickel.

BESSIE (*To* JACOB) After take Tootsie on the roof. (*To* RALPH) What'll you do?

RALPH Don't know.

BESSIE You'll see the boys around the block?

RALPH I'll stay home every night!

MYRON Momma don't mean for you——

RALPH I'm flying to Hollywood by plane, that's what I'm doing.

(*Doorbell rings.* MYRON *answers it*)

BESSIE I don't like my boy to be seen with those tramps on the corner.

MYRON (*Without*) Schlosser's here, Momma, with the garbage can.

BESSIE Come in here, Schlosser. (*Sotto voce*) Wait, I'll give him a piece of my mind. (MYRON *ushers in* SCHLOSSER *who carries a garbage can in each hand*) What's the matter, the dumbwaiter's broken again?

SCHLOSSER Mr. Wimmer sends new ropes next week. I got a sore arm.

BESSIE He should live so long, your Mr. Wimmer. For

[1] A Jew not yet Americanized or successful.

seven years already he's sending new ropes. No dumbwaiter, no hot water, no steam—— In a respectable house, they don't allow such conditions.

SCHLOSSER In a decent house dogs are not running to make dirty the hallway.

BESSIE Tootsie's making dirty? Our Tootsie's making dirty in the hall?

SCHLOSSER (*To* JACOB) I tell you yesterday again. You must not leave her——

BESSIE (*Indignantly*) Excuse me! Please don't yell on an old man. He's got more brains in his finger than you got—I don't know where. Did you ever see—he should talk to you an old man?

MYRON Awful.

BESSIE From now on we don't walk up the stairs no more. You keep it so clean we'll fly in the windows.

SCHLOSSER I speak to Mr. Wimmer.

BESSIE Speak! Speak! Tootsie walks behind me like a lady any time, any place. So good-bye . . . good-bye, Mr. Schlosser.

SCHLOSSER I tell you dot—I verk verry hard here. My arms is. . . . (*Exits in confusion*)

BESSIE Tootsie should lay all day in the kitchen maybe. Give him back if he yells on you. What's funny?

JACOB (*Laughing*) Nothing.

BESSIE Come. (*Exits*)

JACOB Hennie, take care. . . .

HENNIE Sure.

JACOB Bye-bye. (HENNIE *exits.* MYRON *pops head back in door*)

MYRON Valentino! That's the one! (*He exits*)

RALPH I never in my life even had a birthday party. Every time I went and cried in the toilet when my birthday came.

JACOB (*Seeing* RALPH *remove his tie*) You're going to bed?

RALPH No, I'm putting on a clean shirt.

JACOB Why?

RALPH I got a girl. . . . Don't laugh!

JACOB Who laughs? Since when?

RALPH Three weeks. She lives in Yorkville with an aunt and uncle. A bunch of relatives, but no parents.

JACOB An orphan girl—tch, tch.

RALPH But she's got me! Boy, I'm telling you I could sing! Jake, she's like stars. She's so beautiful you look at her and cry! She's like French words! We went to the park the other night. Heard the last band concert.

JACOB Music. . . .

RALPH (*Stuffing shirt in trousers*) It got cold and I gave her my coat to wear. We just walked along like that, see, without a word, see. I never was so happy in all my life. It got late . . . we just sat there. She looked at me—you know what I mean, how a girl looks at you—right in the eyes? "I love you," she says, "Ralph." I took her home. . . . I wanted to cry. That's how I felt!

JACOB It's a beautiful feeling.

RALPH You said a mouthful!

JACOB Her name is——

RALPH Blanche.

JACOB A fine name. Bring her sometimes here.

RALPH She's scared to meet Mom.

JACOB Why?

RALPH You know Mom's not letting my sixteen bucks out of the house if she can help it. She'd take one look at Blanche and insult her in a minute—a kid who's got nothing.

JACOB Boychick!

RALPH What's the diff?

JACOB It's no difference—a plain bourgeois prejudice—but when they find out a poor girl—it ain't so kosher.

RALPH They don't have to know I've got a girl.

JACOB What's in the end?

RALPH Out I go! I don't mean maybe!

JACOB And then what?

RALPH Life begins.

JACOB What life?

RALPH Life with my girl. Boy, I could sing when I think about it! Her and me together—that's a new life!

JACOB Don't make a mistake! A new death!

RALPH What's the idea?

JACOB Me, I'm the idea! Once I had in *my* heart a dream, a vision, but came marriage and then you forget. Children come and you forget because——

RALPH Don't worry, Jake.

JACOB Remember, a woman insults a man's soul like no other thing in the whole world!

RALPH Why get so excited? No one——

JACOB Boychick, wake up! Be something! Make your life something good. For the love of an old man who sees in your young days his new life, for such love take the world in your two hands and make it like new. Go out and fight so life shouldn't be printed on dollar bills. A woman waits.

RALPH Say, I'm no fool!

JACOB From my heart I hope not. In the meantime—— (*Bell rings*)

RALPH See who it is, will you? (*Stands off*) Don't want Mom to catch me with a clean shirt.

JACOB (*Calls*) Come in. (*Sotto voce*) Moe Axelrod. (MOE *enters*)

MOE Hello, girls, how's your whiskers? (*To* RALPH) All dolled up. What's it, the weekly visit to the cat house?

RALPH Please mind your business.

MOE Okay, sweetheart.

RALPH (*Taking a hidden dollar from a book*) If Mom asks where I went——

JACOB I know. Enjoy yourself.

RALPH Bye-bye. (*He exits*)

JACOB Bye-bye.

MOE Who's home?

JACOB Me.

MOE Good. I'll stick around a few minutes. Where's Hennie?

JACOB She went with Bessie and Myron to a show.

MOE She what?!

JACOB You had a date?

MOE (*Hiding his feelings*) Here—I brought you some halavah.

JACOB Halavah? Thanks. I'll eat a piece after.

MOE So Ralph's got a dame? Hot stuff—a kid can't even play a card game.

JACOB Moe, you're a no-good, a bum of the first water. To your dying day you won't change.

MOE Where'd you get that stuff, a no-good?

JACOB But I like you.

MOE Didn't I go fight in France for democracy? Didn't I get my goddam leg shot off in that war the day before the armistice? Uncle Sam give me the Order of the Purple Heart, didn't he? What'd you mean, a no-good?

JACOB Excuse me.

MOE If you got an orange I'll eat an orange.

JACOB No orange. An apple.

MOE No oranges, huh?—what a dump!

JACOB Bessie hears you once talking like this she'll knock your head off.

MOE Hennie went with, huh? She wantsa see me squirm, only I don't squirm for dames.

JACOB You came to see her?

MOE What for? I got a present for our boy friend, Myron. He'll drop dead when I tell him his gentle horse galloped in fifteen to one. He'll die.

JACOB It really won? The first time I remember.

MOE Where'd they go?

JACOB A vaudeville by the Franklin.

MOE What's special tonight?

JACOB Someone tells a few jokes . . . and they forget the street is filled with starving beggars.

MOE What'll they do—start a war?

JACOB I don't know.

MOE You oughta know. What the hell you got all the books for?

JACOB It needs a new world.

MOE That's why they had the big war—to make a new world, they said—safe for democracy. Sure every big general laying up in a Paris hotel with a half dozen broads pinned on his mustache. Democracy! I learned a lesson.

JACOB An imperial war. You know what this means?

MOE Sure, I know everything!

JACOB By money men the interests must be protected. Who gave you such a rotten haircut? Please (*Fishing in his vest pocket*) give me for a cent a cigarette. I didn't have since yesterday——

MOE (*Giving one*) Don't make me laugh. (*A cent passes back and forth between them,* MOE *finally throwing it over his shoulder*) Don't look so tired all the time. You're a wow—always sore about something.

JACOB And you?

MOE You got one thing—you can play pinochle. I'll take you over in a game. Then you'll have something to be sore on.

JACOB Who'll wash dishes? (MOE *takes deck from buffet drawer*)

MOE Do 'em after. Ten cents a deal.

JACOB Who's got ten cents?

MOE I got ten cents. I'll lend it to you.

JACOB Commence.

MOE (*Shaking cards*) The first time I had my hands on a pack in two days. Lemme shake up these cards. I'll make 'em talk. (JACOB *goes to his room where he puts on a Caruso record*)

JACOB You should live so long.

MOE Ever see oranges grow? I know a certain place—— One summer I laid under a tree and let them fall right in my mouth.

JACOB (*Off, the music is playing; the card game begins*) From "L'Africana" . . . a big explorer comes on a new land—"O Paradiso." From act four this piece. Caruso stands on the ship and looks on a Utopia. You hear? "Oh paradise! Oh paradise on earth! Oh blue sky, oh fragrant air——"

MOE Ask him does he see any oranges? (BESSIE, MYRON *and* HENNIE *enter*)

JACOB You came back so soon?

BESSIE Hennie got sick on the way.

MYRON Hello, Moe. . . . (MOE *puts cards back in pocket*)

BESSIE Take off the phonograph, Pop. (*To* HENNIE) Lay down . . . I'll call the doctor. You should see how she got sick on Prospect Avenue. Two weeks already she don't feel right.

MYRON Moe . . . ?

BESSIE Go to bed, Hennie.

HENNIE I'll sit here.

BESSIE Such a girl I never saw! Now you'll be stubborn?

MYRON It's for your own good, Beauty. Influenza——

HENNIE I'll sit here.

BESSIE You ever seen a girl should say no to everything. She can't stand on her feet, so——

HENNIE Don't yell in my ears. I hear. Nothing's wrong. I ate tuna fish for lunch.

MYRON Canned goods. . . .

BESSIE Last week you also ate tuna fish?

HENNIE Yeah, I'm funny for tuna fish. Go to the show —have a good time.

BESSIE I don't understand what I did to God He blessed me with such children. From the whole world——

MOE (*Coming to aid of* HENNIE) For Chris' sake, don't kibitz so much!

BESSIE You don't like it?

MOE (*Aping*) No, I don't like it.

BESSIE That's too bad, Axelrod. Maybe it's better by your cigar-store friends. Here we're different people.

MOE Don't gimme that cigar store line, Bessie. I walked up five flights——

BESSIE To take out Hennie. But my daughter ain't in your class, Axelrod.

MOE To see Myron.

MYRON Did he, did he, Moe?

MOE Did he what?

MYRON "Sky Rocket"?

BESSIE You bet on a horse!

MOE Paid twelve and a half to one.

MYRON There! You hear that, Momma? Our horse

came in. You see, it happens, and twelve and a half to one. Just look at that!

MOE What the hell, a sure thing. I told you.

BESSIE If Moe said a sure thing, you couldn't bet a few dollars instead of fifty cents?

JACOB (*Laughs*) Aie, aie, aie.

MOE (*At his wallet*) I'm carrying six hundred "plunks" in big denominations.

BESSIE A banker!

MOE Uncle Sam sends me ninety a month.

BESSIE So you save it?

MOE Run it up. Run-it-up-Axelrod, that's me.

BESSIE The police should know how.

MOE (*Shutting her up*) All right, all right—— Change twenty, sweetheart.

MYRON Can you make change?

BESSIE Don't be crazy.

MOE I'll meet a guy in Goldman's restaurant. I'll meet 'im and come back with change.

MYRON (*Figuring on paper*) You can give it to me tomorrow in the store.

BESSIE (*Acquisitive*) He'll come back, he'll come back!

MOE Lucky I bet some bucks myself. (*In derision to* HENNIE) Let's step out tomorrow night, Par-a-dise. (*Thumbs his nose at her, laughs mordantly and exits*)

MYRON Oh, that's big percentage. If I picked a winner every day. . . .

BESSIE Poppa, did you take Tootsie on the roof?

JACOB All right.

MYRON Just look at that—a cake walk. We can make——

BESSIE It's enough talk. I got a splitting headache. Hennie, go in bed. I'll call Dr. Cantor.

HENNIE I'll sit here . . . and don't call that old Ignatz 'cause I won't see him.

MYRON If you get sick Momma can't nurse you. You don't want to go to a hospital.

JACOB She don't look sick, Bessie, it's a fact.

BESSIE She's got fever. I see in her eyes, so he tells me no. Myron, call Dr. Cantor. (MYRON *picks up phone, but* HENNIE *grabs it from him*)

HENNIE I don't want any doctor. I ain't sick. Leave me alone.

MYRON Beauty, it's for your own sake.

HENNIE Day in and day out pestering. Why are you always right and no one else can say a word?

BESSIE When you have your own children——

HENNIE I'm not sick! Hear what I say? I'm not sick! Nothing's the matter with me! I don't want a doctor. (BESSIE *is watching her with slow progressive understanding*)

BESSIE What's the matter?

HENNIE Nothing, I told you!

BESSIE You told me, but—— (*A long pause of examination follows*)

HENNIE See much?

BESSIE Myron, put down the . . . the . . . (*He slowly puts the phone down*) Tell me what happened. . . .

HENNIE Brooklyn Bridge fell down.

BESSIE (*Approaching*) I'm asking a question. . . .

MYRON What's happened, Momma?

BESSIE Listen to me!

HENNIE What the hell are you talking?

BESSIE Poppa—take Tootsie on the roof.

HENNIE (*Holding* JACOB *back*) If he wants he can stay here.

MYRON What's wrong, Momma?

BESSIE (*Her voice quivering slightly*) Myron, your fine Beauty's in trouble. Our society lady. . . .

MYRON Trouble? I don't under—is it——?

BESSIE Look in her face. (*He looks, understands and slowly sits in a chair, utterly crushed*) Who's the man?

HENNIE The Prince of Wales.

BESSIE My gall is busting in me. In two seconds——

HENNIE (*In a violent outburst*) Shut up! Shut up! I'll jump out the window in a minute! Shut up! (*Finally she gains control of herself, says in a low, hard voice*) You don't know him.

JACOB Bessie. . . .

BESSIE He's a Bronx boy?

HENNIE From out of town.

BESSIE What do you mean?

HENNIE From out of town!!

BESSIE A long time you know him? You were sleeping by a girl from the office Saturday nights? You slept good, my lovely lady. You'll go to him . . . he'll marry you.

HENNIE That's what you say.

BESSIE That's what I say! He'll do it, take *my* word he'll do it!

HENNIE Where? (*To* JACOB) Give her the letter. (JACOB *does so*)

BESSIE What? (*Reads*) "Dear sir: In reply to your request of the 14th inst., we can state that no Mr. Ben Grossman has ever been connected with our organization . . ." You don't know where he is?

HENNIE No.

BESSIE (*Walks back and forth*) Stop crying like a baby, Myron.

MYRON It's like a play on the stage. . . .

BESSIE To a mother you couldn't say something before. I'm old-fashioned—like your friends I'm not smart—I don't eat chop suey and run around Coney Island with tramps. (*She walks reflectively to buffet, picks up a box of candy, puts it down, says to* MYRON) Tomorrow night bring Sam Feinschreiber for supper.

HENNIE I won't do it.

BESSIE You'll do it, my fine beauty, you'll do it!

HENNIE I'm not marrying a poor foreigner like him. Can't even speak an English word. Not me! I'll go to my grave without a husband.

BESSIE You don't say! We'll find for you somewhere a millionaire with a pleasure boat. He's going to night school, Sam. For a boy only three years in the country he speaks very nice. In three years he put enough in the bank, a good living.

JACOB This is serious?

BESSIE What then? I'm talking for my health? He'll come tomorrow night for supper. By Saturday they're engaged.

JACOB Such a thing you can't do.

BESSIE Who asked your advice?

JACOB Such a thing——

BESSIE Never mind!

JACOB The lowest from the low!

BESSIE Don't talk! I'm warning you! A man who don't believe in God—with crazy ideas——

JACOB So bad I never imagined you could be.

BESSIE Maybe if you didn't talk so much it wouldn't happen like this. You with your ideas—I'm a mother. I raise a family they should have respect.

JACOB Respect? (*Spits*) Respect! For the neighbors' opinion! You insult me, Bessie!

BESSIE Go in your room, Poppa. Every job he ever had he lost because he's got a big mouth. He opens his mouth and the whole Bronx could fall in. Everybody said it——

MYRON Momma, they'll hear you down the dumbwaiter.

BESSIE A good barber not to hold a job a week. Maybe you never heard charity starts at home. You never heard it, Pop?

JACOB All you know, I heard, and more yet. But Ralph you don't make like you. Before you do it, I'll die first. He'll find a girl. He'll go in a fresh world with her. This is a house? Marx said it—abolish such families.

BESSIE Go in your room, Poppa.

JACOB Ralph you don't make like you!

BESSIE Go lay in your room with Caruso and the books together.

JACOB All right!

BESSIE Go in the room!

JACOB Some day I'll come out, I'll—— (*Unable to continue, he turns, looks at* HENNIE, *goes to his door and there says with an attempt at humor*) Bessie, some day you'll talk to me so fresh . . . I'll leave the house for good! (*He exits*)

BESSIE (*Crying*) You ever in your life seen it? He should dare! He should just dare say in the house another word. Your gall could bust from such a man. (*Bell rings,* MYRON *goes*) Go to sleep now. It won't hurt.

HENNIE Yeah? (MOE *enters, a box in his hand.* MYRON *follows and sits down*)

MOE (*Looks around first—putting box on table*) Cake. (*About to give* MYRON *the money, he turns instead to* BESSIE) Six fifty, four bits change . . . come on, hand over half a buck. (*She does so. Of* MYRON) Who bit him?

BESSIE We're soon losing our Hennie, Moe.

MOE Why? What's the matter?

BESSIE She made her engagement.

MOE Zat so?

BESSIE Today it happened . . . he asked her.

MOE Did he? Who? Who's the corpse?

BESSIE It's a secret.

MOE In the bag, huh?

HENNIE Yeah. . . .

BESSIE When a mother gives away an only daughter it's no joke. Wait, when you'll get married you'll know. . . .

MOE (*Bitterly*) Don't make me laugh—when I get married! What I think a women? Take 'em all, cut 'em in little pieces like a herring in Greek salad. A guy in France had the right idea—dropped his wife in a bathtub fulla acid. (*Whistles*) Sss, down the pipe! Pfft—not even a corset button left!

MYRON Corsets don't have buttons.

MOE (*To* HENNIE) What's the great idea? Gone big time, Paradise? Christ, it's suicide! Sure, kids you'll have, gold teeth, get fat, big in the tangerines——

HENNIE Shut your face!

MOE Who's it—some dope pullin' down twenty bucks a week? Cut your throat, sweetheart. Save time.

BESSIE Never mind your two cents, Axelrod.

MOE I say what I think—that's me!

HENNIE That's you—a lousy fourflusher who'd steal the glasses off a blind man.

MOE Get hot!

HENNIE My God, do I need it—to listen to this mutt shoot his mouth off?

MYRON Please. . . .

MOE Now wait a minute, sweetheart, wait a minute. I don't have to take that from you.

BESSIE Don't yell at her!

HENNIE For two cents I'd spit in your eye.

MOE (*Throwing coin to table*) Here's two bits. (HENNIE *looks at him and then starts across the room*)

BESSIE Where are you going?

HENNIE (*Crying*) For my beauty nap, Mussolini. Wake me up when it's apple blossom time in Normandy. (*Exits*)

MOE Pretty, pretty—a sweet gal, your Hennie. See the look in her eyes?

BESSIE She don't feel well. . . .

MYRON Canned goods. . . .

BESSIE So don't start with her.

MOE Like a battleship she's got it. Not like other dames—shove 'em and they lay. Not her. I got a yen for her and I don't mean a Chinee coin.

BESSIE Listen, Axelrod, in my house you don't talk this way. Either have respect or get out.

MOE When I think about it . . . maybe I'd marry her myself.

BESSIE (*Suddenly aware of* MOE) You could—— What do you mean, Moe?

MOE You ain't sunburnt—you heard me.

BESSIE Why don't you, Moe? An old friend of the family like you. It would be a blessing on all of us.

MOE You said she's engaged.

BESSIE But maybe she don't know her own mind. Say, it's——

MOE I need a wife like a hole in the head. . . . What's to know about women, I know. Even if I asked her. She won't do it! A guy with one leg—it gives her the heebie-jeebies. I know what she's looking for. An arrow-collar guy, a hero, but with a wad of jack. Only the two don't go together. But I got what it takes . . . plenty, and more where it comes from. (*Breaks off, snorts and rubs his knee. A pause. In his room* JACOB *puts on Caruso singing the lament from "The Pearl Fishers."*)

BESSIE It's right—she wants a millionaire with a mansion on Riverside Drive. So go fight City Hall. Cake?

MOE Cake.

BESSIE I'll make tea. But one thing—she's got a fine boy with a business brain. Caruso! (*Exits into the front room and stands in the dark, at the window*)

MOE No wet smack . . . a fine girl. . . . She'll burn that guy out in a month. (MOE *retrieves the quarter and spins it on the table*)

MYRON I remember that song . . . beautiful. Nora Bayes sang it at the old Proctor's Twenty-third Street —"When It's Apple Blossom Time in Normandy."

MOE She wantsa see me crawl—my head on a plate she wants! A snowball in hell's got a better chance. (*Out of sheer fury he spins the quarter in his fingers*)

MYRON (*As his eyes slowly fill with tears*) Beautiful . . .

MOE Match you for a quarter. Match you for any goddam thing you got. (*Spins the coin viciously*) What the hell kind of house is this it ain't got an orange!!

*Slow Curtain*

# Act Two, Scene One

*One year later, a Sunday afternoon. The front room.* JACOB *is giving his son* MORDECAI (UNCLE MORTY) *a haircut, newspapers spread around the base of the chair.* MOE *is reading a newspaper, leg propped on a chair.* RALPH, *in another chair, is spasmodically reading a paper.* UNCLE MORTY *reads colored jokes. Silence, then* BESSIE *enters.*

BESSIE Dinner's in half an hour, Morty.

MORTY (*Still reading jokes*) I got time.

BESSIE A duck. Don't get hair on the rug, Pop. (*Goes to window and pulls down shade*) What's the matter the shade's up to the ceiling?

JACOB (*Pulling it up again*) Since when do I give a haircut in the dark? (*He mimics her tone*)

BESSIE When you're finished, pull it down. I like my house to look respectable. Ralphie, bring up two bottles seltzer from Weiss.

RALPH I'm reading the paper.

BESSIE Uncle Morty likes a little seltzer.

RALPH I'm expecting a phone call.

BESSIE Noo, if it comes you'll be back. What's the matter? (*Gives him money from apron pocket*) Take down the old bottles.

RALPH (*To* JACOB) Get that call if it comes. Say I'll be right back. (JACOB *nods assent*)

MORTY (*Giving change from vest*) Get grandpa some cigarettes.

RALPH Okay. (*Exits*)

JACOB What's new in the paper, Moe?

MOE Still jumping off the high buildings like flies—the big shots who lost all their coconuts. Pfft!

JACOB Suicides?

MOE Plenty can't take it—good in the break, but can't take the whip in the stretch.

MORTY (*Without looking up*) I saw it happen Monday in my building. My hair stood up how they shoveled him together—like a pancake—a bankrupt manufacturer.

MOE No brains.

MORTY Enough . . . all over the sidewalk.

JACOB If someone said five-ten years ago I couldn't make for myself a living, I wouldn't believe——

MORTY Duck for dinner?

BESSIE The best Long Island duck.

MORTY I like goose.

BESSIE A duck is just like a goose, only better.

MORTY I like a goose.

BESSIE The next time you'll be for Sunday dinner I'll make a goose.

MORTY (*Sniffs deeply*) Smells good. I'm a great boy for smells.

BESSIE Ain't you ashamed? Once in a blue moon he should come to an only sister's house.

MORTY Bessie, leave me live.

BESSIE You should be ashamed!

MORTY Quack quack!

BESSIE No, better to lay around Mecca Temple playing cards with the Masons.

MORTY (*With good nature*) Bessie, don't you see Pop's giving me a haircut?

BESSIE You don't need no haircut. Look, two hairs he took off.

MORTY Pop likes to give me a haircut. If I said no he don't forget for a year, do you, Pop? An old man's like that.

JACOB I still do an A-1 job.

MORTY (*Winking*) Pop cuts hair to fit the face, don't you, Pop?

JACOB For sure, Morty. To each face a different haircut. Custom built, no ready made. A round face needs special——

BESSIE (*Cutting him short*) A graduate from the B.M.T. (*Going*) Don't forget the shade. (*The phone rings. She beats* JACOB *to it*) Hello? Who is it, please? . . . Who is it, please? . . . Miss Hirsch? No, he ain't here. . . . No, I couldn't say when. (*Hangs up sharply*)

JACOB For Ralph?

BESSIE A wrong number. (JACOB *looks at her and goes back to his job*)

JACOB Excuse me!

BESSIE (*To* MORTY) Ralphie took another cut down the place yesterday.

MORTY Business is bad. I saw his boss Harry Glicksman Thursday. I bought some velvets . . . they're coming in again.

BESSIE Do something for Ralphie down there.

MORTY What can I do? I mentioned it to Glicksman. He told me they squeezed out half the people. . . . (MYRON *enters dressed in apron*)

BESSIE What's gonna be the end? Myron's working only three days a week now.

MYRON It's conditions.

BESSIE Hennie's married with a baby . . . money just don't come in. I never saw conditions should be so bad.

MORTY Times'll change.

MOE The only thing'll change is my underwear.

MORTY These last few years I got my share of gray hairs. (*Still reading jokes without having looked up once*) Ha, ha, ha—Popeye the sailor ate spinach and knocked out four bums.

MYRON I'll tell you the way I see it. The country needs a great man now—a regular Teddy Roosevelt.

MOE What this country needs is a good five-cent earthquake.

JACOB So long labor lives it should increase private gain——

BESSIE (*To* JACOB) Listen, Poppa, go talk on the street corner. The government'll give you free board the rest of your life.

MORTY I'm surprised. Don't I send a five-dollar check for Pop every week?

BESSIE You could afford a couple more and not miss it.

MORTY Tell me jokes. Business is so rotten I could just as soon lay all day in the Turkish bath.

MYRON Why'd I come in here? (*Puzzled, he exits*)

MORTY (*To* MOE) I hear the bootleggers still do business, Moe.

MOE Wake up! I kissed bootlegging bye-bye two years back.

MORTY For a fact? What kind of racket is it now?

MOE If I told you, you'd know something. (HENNIE *comes from bedroom*)

HENNIE Where's Sam?

BESSIE Sam? In the kitchen.

HENNIE (*Calls*) Sam. Come take the diaper.

MORTY How's the Mickey Louse? Ha, ha, ha. . . .

HENNIE Sleeping.

MORTY Ah, that's life to a baby. He sleeps—gets it in the mouth—sleeps some more. To raise a family nowadays you must be a damn fool.

BESSIE Never mind, never mind, a woman who don't raise a family—a girl—should jump overboard. What's she good for? (*To* MOE*—to change the subject*) Your leg bothers you bad?

MOE It's okay, sweetheart.

BESSIE (*To* MORTY) It hurts him every time it's cold out. He's got four legs in the closet.

MORTY Four wooden legs?

MOE Three.

MORTY What's the big idea?

MOE Why not? Uncle Sam gives them out free.

MORTY Say, maybe if Uncle Sam gave out less legs we could balance the budget.

JACOB Or not have a war so they wouldn't have to give out legs.

MORTY Shame on you, Pop. Everybody knows war is necessary.

MOE Don't make me laugh. Ask me—the first time you pick up a dead one in the trench—then you learn war ain't so damn necessary.

MORTY Say, you should kick. The rest of your life Uncle Sam pays you ninety a month. Look, not a worry in the world.

MOE Don't make me laugh. Uncle Sam can take his *seventy* bucks and—— (*Finishes with a gesture*) Nothing good hurts. (*He rubs his stump*)

HENNIE Use a crutch, Axelrod. Give the stump a rest.

MOE Mind your business, Feinschreiber.

BESSIE It's a sensible idea.

MOE Who asked you?

BESSIE Look, he's ashamed.

MOE So's your Aunt Fanny.

BESSIE (*Naïvely*) Who's got an Aunt Fanny? (*She cleans a rubber plant's leaves with her apron*)

MORTY It's a joke!

MOE I don't want my paper creased before I read it. I want it fresh. Fifty times I said that.

BESSIE Don't get so excited for a five-cent paper—our star boarder.

MOE And I don't want no one using my razor either. Get it straight. I'm not buying ten blades a week for the Berger family. (*Furious, he limps out*)

BESSIE Maybe I'm using his razor too.

HENNIE Proud!

BESSIE You need luck with plants. I didn't clean off the leaves in a month.

MORTY You keep the house like a pin and I like your cooking. Any time Myron fires you, come to me, Bessie. I'll let the butler go and you'll be my housekeeper. I don't like Japs so much—sneaky.

BESSIE Say, you can't tell. Maybe any day I'm coming to stay. (HENNIE *exits*)

JACOB Finished.

MORTY How much, Ed. Pinaud? (*Disengages self from chair*)

JACOB Five cents.

MORTY Still five cents for a haircut to fit the face?

JACOB Prices don't change by me. (*Takes a dollar*) I can't change——

MORTY Keep it. Buy yourself a Packard. Ha, ha, ha.

JACOB (*Taking large envelope from pocket*) Please, you'll keep this for me. Put it away.

MORTY What is it?

JACOB My insurance policy. I don't like it should lay around where something could happen.

MORTY What could happen?

JACOB Who knows, robbers, fire . . . they took next door. Fifty dollars from O'Reilly.

MORTY Say, lucky a Berger didn't lose it.

JACOB Put it downtown in the safe. Bessie don't have to know.

MORTY It's made out to Bessie?

JACOB No, to Ralph.

MORTY To Ralph?

JACOB He don't know. Some day he'll get three thousand.

MORTY You got good years ahead.

JACOB Behind. (RALPH *enters*)

RALPH Cigarettes. Did a call come?

JACOB A few minutes. She don't let me answer it.

RALPH Did Mom say I was coming back?

JACOB No. (MORTY *is back at new jokes*)

RALPH She starting that stuff again? (BESSIE *enters*) A call come for me?

BESSIE (*Waters pot from milk bottle*) A wrong number.

JACOB Don't say a lie, Bessie.

RALPH Blanche said she'd call me at two—was it her?

BESSIE I said a wrong number.

RALPH Please, Mom, if it was her tell me.

BESSIE You call me a liar next. You got no shame—to start a scene in front of Uncle Morty. Once in a blue moon he comes——

RALPH What's the shame? If my girl calls I wanna know it.

BESSIE You made enough mish mosh with her until now.

MORTY I'm surprised, Bessie. For the love of Mike tell him yes or no.

BESSIE I didn't tell him? No!

MORTY (*To* RALPH) No! (RALPH *goes to a window and looks out*)

BESSIE Morty, I didn't say before—he runs around steady with a girl.

MORTY Terrible. Should he run around with a foxie-woxie?

BESSIE A girl with no parents.

MORTY An orphan?

BESSIE I could die from shame. A year already he runs around with her. He brought her once for supper. Believe me, she didn't come again, no!

RALPH Don't think I didn't ask her.

BESSIE You hear? You raise them and what's in the end for all your trouble?

JACOB When you'll lay in a grave, no more trouble. (*Exits*)

MORTY Quack quack!

BESSIE A girl like that he wants to marry. A skinny consumptive-looking . . . six months already she's not working—taking charity from an aunt. You should see her. In a year she's dead on his hands.

RALPH You'd cut her throat if you could.

BESSIE That's right! Before she'd ruin a nice boy's life I would first go to prison. Miss Nobody should step in the picture and I'll stand by with my mouth shut.

RALPH Miss Nobody! Who am I? Al Jolson?

BESSIE Fix your tie!

RALPH I'll take care of my own life.

BESSIE You'll take care? Excuse my expression, you can't even wipe your nose yet! He'll take care!

MORTY (*To* BESSIE) I'm surprised. Don't worry so much, Bessie. When it's time to settle down he won't marry a poor girl, will you? In the long run common sense is thicker than love. I'm a great boy for live and let live.

BESSIE Sure, it's easy to say. In the meantime he eats out my heart. You know I'm not strong.

MORTY I know . . . a pussy cat . . . ha, ha, ha.

BESSIE You got money and money talks. But without the dollar who sleeps at night?

RALPH I been working for years, bringing in money here—putting it in your hand like a kid. All right, I can't get my teeth fixed. All right, that a new suit's like trying to buy the Chrysler Building. You never in your life bought me a pair of skates even—things I died for when I was a kid. I don't care about that stuff, see. Only just remember I pay some of the bills around here, just a few . . . and if my girl calls me on the phone I'll talk to her any time I please. (*He exits.* HENNIE *applauds*)

BESSIE Don't be so smart, Miss America! (*To* MORTY) He didn't have skates! But when he got sick, a twelve-year-old boy, who called a big specialist for the last $25 in the house? Skates!

JACOB (*Just in. Adjusts window shade*) It looks like snow today.

MORTY It's about time—winter.

BESSIE Poppa here could talk like Samuel Webster, too, but it's just talk. He should try to buy a two-cent pickle in the Burland Market without money.

MORTY I'm getting an appetite.

BESSIE Right away we'll eat. I made chopped liver for you.

MORTY My specialty!

BESSIE Ralph should only be a success like you, Morty. I should only live to see the day when he rides up to the door in a big car with a chauffeur and a radio. I could die happy, believe me.

MORTY Success she says. She should see how we spend thousands of dollars making up a winter line and winter don't come—summer in January. Can you beat it?

JACOB Don't live, just make success.

MORTY Chopped liver—ha!

JACOB Ha! (*Exits*)

MORTY When they start arguing, I don't hear. Suddenly I'm deaf. I'm a great boy for the practical side. (*He looks over to* HENNIE *who sits rubbing her hands with lotion*)

HENNIE Hands like a raw potato.

MORTY What's the matter? You don't look so well . . . no pep.

HENNIE I'm swell.

MORTY You used to be such a pretty girl.

HENNIE Maybe I got the blues. You can't tell.

MORTY You could stand a new dress.

HENNIE That's not all I could stand.

MORTY Come down to the place tomorrow and pick out a couple from the "eleven-eighty" line. Only don't sing me the blues.

HENNIE Thanks. I need some new clothes.

MORTY I got two thousand pieces of merchandise waiting in the stock room for winter.

HENNIE I never had anything from life. Sam don't help.

MORTY He's crazy about the kid.

HENNIE Crazy is right. Twenty-one a week he brings in—a nigger don't have it so hard. I wore my fingers off on an Underwood for six years. For what? Now I wash baby diapers. Sure, I'm crazy about the kid too. But half the night the kid's up. Try to sleep. You don't know how it is, Uncle Morty.

MORTY No, I don't know. I was born yesterday. Ha, ha, ha. Some day I'll leave you a little nest egg. You like eggs? Ha?

HENNIE When? When I'm dead and buried?

MORTY No, when *I'm* dead and buried. Ha, ha, ha.

HENNIE You should know what I'm thinking.

MORTY Ha, ha, ha, I know. (MYRON *enters*)

MYRON I never take a drink. I'm just surprised at myself, I——

MORTY I got a pain. Maybe I'm hungry.

MYRON Come inside, Morty. Bessie's got some schnapps.

MORTY I'll take a drink. Yesterday I missed the Turkish bath.

MYRON I get so bitter when I take a drink, it just surprises me.

MORTY Look how fat. Say, you live once. . . . Quack, quack. (*Both exit.* MOE *stands silently in the doorway*)

SAM (*Entering*) I'll make Leon's bottle now!

HENNIE No, let him sleep, Sam. Take away the diaper. (*He does. Exits*)

MOE (*Advancing into the room*) That your husband?

HENNIE Don't you know?

MOE Maybe he's a nurse you hired for the kid—it looks it—how he tends it. A guy comes howling to your old lady every time you look cock-eyed. Does he sleep with you?

HENNIE Don't be so wise!

MOE (*Indicating newspaper*) Here's a dame strangled her hubby with wire. Claimed she didn't like him. Why don't you brain Sam with an ax some night?

HENNIE Why don't you lay an egg, Axelrod?

MOE I laid a few in my day, Feinschreiber. Hardboiled ones too.

HENNIE Yeah?

MOE Yeah. You wanna know what I see when I look in your eyes?

HENNIE No.

MOE Ted Lewis playing the clarinet—some of those high crazy notes! Christ, you coulda had a guy with some guts instead of a cluck stands around boilin' baby nipples.

HENNIE Meaning you?

MOE Meaning me, sweetheart.

HENNIE Think you're pretty good.

MOE You'd know if I slept with you again.

HENNIE I'll smack your face in a minute.

MOE You do and I'll break your arm. (*Holds up paper*) Take a look. (*Reads*) "Ten-day luxury cruise to Havana." That's the stuff you coulda had. Put up at ritzy hotels, frenchie soap, champagne. Now you're tied down to "Snake-Eye" here. What for? What's it get you? . . . a 2 x 4 flat on 108th Street . . . a pain in the bustle it gets you.

HENNIE What's it to you?

MOE I know you from the old days. How you like to spend it! What I mean! Lizard-skin shoes, perfume behind the ears. . . . You're in a mess, Paradise! Paradise—that's a hot one—yah, crazy to eat a knish at your own wedding.

HENNIE I get it—you're jealous. You can't get me.

MOE Don't make me laugh.

HENNIE Kid Jailbird's been trying to make me for years. You'd give your other leg. I'm hooked? Maybe, but you're in the same boat. Only it's worse for you. I don't give a damn no more, but you gotta yen makes you——

MOE Don't make me laugh.

HENNIE Compared to you I'm sittin' on top of the world.

MOE You're losing your looks. A dame don't stay young forever.

HENNIE You're a liar. I'm only twenty-four.

MOE When you comin' home to stay?

HENNIE Wouldn't you like to know?

MOE I'll get you again.

HENNIE Think so?

MOE Sure, whatever goes up comes down. You're easy —you remember—two for a nickel—a pushover! (*Suddenly she slaps him. They both seem stunned*) What's the idea?

HENNIE Go on . . . break my arm.

MOE (*As if saying "I love you"*) Listen, lousy.

HENNIE Go on, do something!

MOE Listen——

HENNIE You're so damn tough!

MOE You like me. (*He takes her*)

HENNIE Take your hand off! (*Pushes him away*) Come around when it's a flood again and they put you in the ark with the animals. Not even then—if you was the last man!

MOE Baby, if you had a dog I'd love the dog.

HENNIE Gorilla! (*Exits.* RALPH *enters*)

RALPH Were you here before?

MOE (*Sits*) What?

RALPH When the call came for me?

MOE What?

RALPH The call came. (JACOB *enters*)

MOE (*Rubbing his leg*) No.

JACOB Don't worry, Ralphie, she'll call back.

RALPH Maybe not. I think somethin's the matter.

JACOB What?

RALPH I don't know. I took her home from the movie last night. She asked me what I'd think if she went away.

JACOB Don't worry, she'll call again.

RALPH Maybe not, if Mom insulted her. She gets it on both ends, the poor kid. Lived in an orphan asylum most of her life. They shove her around like an empty freight train.

JACOB After dinner go see her.

RALPH Twice they kicked me down the stairs.

JACOB Life should have some dignity.

RALPH Every time I go near the place I get heart failure. The uncle drives a bus. You oughta see him —like Babe Ruth.

MOE Use your brains. Stop acting like a kid who still wets the bed. Hire a room somewhere—a club room for two members.

RALPH Not that kind of proposition, Moe.

MOE Don't be a bush leaguer all your life.

RALPH Cut it out!

MOE (*On a sudden upsurge of emotion*) Ever sleep with one? Look at 'im blush.

RALPH You don't know her.

MOE I seen her—the kind no one sees undressed till the undertaker works on her.

RALPH Why give me the needles all the time? What'd I ever do to you?

MOE Not a thing. You're a nice kid. But grow up! In life there's two kinds—the men that's sure of themselves and the ones who ain't! It's time you quit being a selling-plater[1] and got in the first class.

JACOB And you, Axelrod?

MOE (*To* JACOB) Scratch your whiskers! (*To* RALPH) Get independent. Get what-it-takes and be yourself. Do what you like.

RALPH Got a suggestion? (MORTY *enters, eating*)

MOE Sure, pick out a racket. Shake down the coconuts. See what that does.

MORTY We know what it does—puts a pudding on your nose! Sing Sing! Easy money's against the law. Against the law don't win. A racket is illegitimate, no?

MOE It's all a racket—from horse racing down. Marriage, politics, big business—everybody plays cops and robbers. You, you're a racketeer yourself.

MORTY Who? Me? Personally I manufacture dresses.

MOE Horse feathers!

MORTY (*Seriously*) Don't make such remarks to me without proof. I'm a great one for proof. That's why I made a success in business. Proof—put up or shut up, like a game of cards. I heard this remark before —a rich man's a crook who steals from the poor. Personally, I don't like it. It's a big lie!

MOE If you don't like it, buy yourself a fife and drum —and go fight your own war.

MORTY Sweatshop talk. Every Jew and Wop in the shop eats my bread and behind my back says, "a sonofabitch." I started from a poor boy who worked on an ice wagon for two dollars a week. Pop's right here—he'll tell you. I made it honest. In the whole industry nobody's got a better name.

JACOB It's an exception, such success.

MORTY Ralph can't do the same thing?

JACOB No, Morty, I don't think. In a house like this he don't realize even the possibilities of life. Economics comes down like a ton of coal on the head.

MOE Red rover, red rover, let Jacob come over!

JACOB In my day the propaganda was for God. Now it's for success. A boy don't turn around without having shoved in him he should make success

MORTY Pop, you're a comedian, a regular Charlie Chaplin.

JACOB He dreams all night of fortunes. Why not? Don't it say in the movies he should have a personal steamship, pajamas for fifty dollars a pair and a toilet like a monument? But in the morning he wakes up and for ten dollars he can't fix the teeth. And millions more worse off in the mills of the South—starvation wages. The blood from the worker's heart. (MORTY *laughs loud and long*) Laugh, laugh . . . tomorrow not.

MORTY A real, a real Boob McNutt[2] you're getting to be.

JACOB Laugh, my son. . . .

MORTY Here is the North, Pop.

JACOB North, south, it's one country.

MORTY The country's all right. A duck quacks in every pot!

JACOB You never heard how they shoot down men and women which ask a better wage? Kentucky 1932?

MORTY That's a pile of chopped liver, Pop. (BESSIE *and others enter*)

JACOB Pittsburgh, Passaic, Illinois—slavery—it begins where success begins in a competitive system. (MORTY *howls with delight*)

MORTY Oh, Pop, what are you bothering? Why? Tell me why? Ha, ha, ha. I bought you a phonograph . . . stick to Caruso.

BESSIE He's starting up again.

MORTY Don't bother with Kentucky. It's full of moonshiners.

JACOB Sure, sure——

MORTY You don't know practical affairs. Stay home and cut hair to fit the face.

JACOB It says in the Bible how the Red Sea opened and the Egyptians went in and the sea rolled over them. (*Quotes two lines of Hebrew*) In this boy's life a Red Sea will happen again. I see it!

MORTY I'm getting sore, Pop, with all this sweatshop talk.

BESSIE He don't stop a minute. The whole day, like a phonograph.

MORTY I'm surprised. Without a rich man you don't have a roof over your head. You don't know it?

MYRON Now you can't bite the hand that feeds you.

RALPH Let him alone—he's right!

BESSIE Another county heard from.

RALPH It's the truth. It's——

MORTY Keep quiet, snotnose!

JACOB For sure, charity, a bone for an old dog. But in Russia an old man don't take charity so his eyes turn black in his head. In Russia they got Marx.

MORTY (*Scoffingly*) Who's Marx?

MOE An outfielder for the Yanks. (MORTY *howls with delight*)

MORTY Ha, Ha, ha, it's better than the jokes. I'm telling you. This is Uncle Sam's country. Put it in your pipe and smoke it.

[1] An inferior horse. The term is appropriate coming from Moe, deriving as it does from the world of betting and *The Racing Form.*

[2] An early comic-strip character.

BESSIE Russia, he says! Read the papers.

SAM Here is opportunity.

MYRON People can't believe in God in Russia. The papers tell the truth, they do.

JACOB So you believe in God . . . you got something for it? You! You worked for all the capitalists. You harvested the fruit from your labor? You got God! But the past comforts you? The present smiles on you, yes? It promises you the future something? Did you found a piece of earth where you could live like a human being and die with the sun on your face? Tell me, yes, tell me. I would like to know myself. But on these questions, on this theme—the struggle for existence—you can't make an answer. The answer I see in your face . . . the answer is your mouth can't talk. In this dark corner you sit and you die. But abolish private property!

BESSIE (*Settling the issue*) Noo, go fight City Hall!

MORTY He's drunk!

JACOB I'm studying from books a whole lifetime.

MORTY That's what it is—he's drunk. What the hell does all that mean?

JACOB If you don't know, why should I tell you?

MORTY (*Triumphant at last*) You see? Hear him? Like all those nuts, don't know what they're saying.

JACOB I know, I know.

MORTY Like Boob McNutt you know! Don't go in the park, Pop—the squirrels'll get you. Ha, ha, ha. . . .

BESSIE Save your appetite, Morty. (*To* MYRON) Don't drop the duck.

MYRON We're ready to eat, Momma.

MORTY (*To* JACOB) Shame on you. It's your second childhood.

(*Now they file out.* MYRON *first with the duck, the others behind him*)

BESSIE Come eat. We had enough for one day. (*Exits*)

MORTY Ha, ha, ha. Quack, quack. (*Exits*)

(JACOB *sits there trembling and deeply humiliated.* MOE *approaches him and thumbs the old man's nose in the direction of the dining room*)

MOE Give 'em five. (*Takes his hand away*) They got you pasted on the wall like a picture, Jake. (*He limps out to seat himself at the table in the next room*)

JACOB Go eat, boychick. (RALPH *comes to him*) He gives me eat, so I'll climb in a needle. One time I saw an old horse in summer . . . he wore a straw hat . . . the ears stuck out on top. An old horse for hire. Give me back my young days . . . give me fresh blood . . . arms . . . give me—— (*The telephone rings. Quickly* RALPH *goes to it.* JACOB *pulls the curtains and stands there, a sentry on guard*)

RALPH Hello? . . . Yeah, I went to the store and came right back, right after you called. (*Looks at* JACOB)

JACOB Speak, speak. Don't be afraid they'll hear.

RALPH I'm sorry if Mom said something. You know how excitable Mom is . . . Sure! What? . . . Sure, I'm listening. . . . Put on the radio, Jake. (JACOB *does so. Music comes in and up, a tango, grating with an insistent nostalgic pulse. Under the cover of the music* RALPH *speaks more freely*) Yes . . . yes . . . What's the matter? Why're you crying? What happened? (*To* JACOB) She's putting her uncle on. Yes? . . . Listen, Mr. Hirsch, what're you trying to do? What's the big idea? Honest to God. I'm in no mood for joking! Lemme talk to her! Gimme Blanche! (*Waits*) Blanche? What's this? Is this a joke? Is that true? I'm coming right down! I know, but—— You wanna do that? . . . I know, but—— I'm coming down . . . tonight! Nine o'clock . . . sure . . . sure . . . sure. . . . (*Hangs up*)

JACOB What happened?

MORTY (*Enters*) Listen, Pop. I'm surprised you didn't —— (*He howls, shakes his head in mock despair, exits*)

JACOB Boychick, what?

RALPH I don't get it straight. (*To* JACOB) She's leaving. . . .

JACOB Where?

RALPH Out West—— To Cleveland.

JACOB Cleveland?

RALPH . . . In a week or two. Can you picture it? It's a put-up job. But they can't get away with that.

JACOB We'll find something.

RALPH Sure, the angels of heaven'll come down on her uncle's cab and whisper in his ear.

JACOB Come eat. . . . We'll find something.

RALPH I'm meeting her tonight, but I know—— (BESSIE *throws open the curtain between the two rooms and enters*)

BESSIE Maybe we'll serve for you a special blue plate supper in the garden?

JACOB All right, all right. (BESSIE *goes over to the window, levels the shade and on her way out, clicks off the radio*)

MORTY (*Within*) Leave the music, Bessie. (*She clicks it on again, looks at them, exits*)

RALPH I know . . .

JACOB Don't cry, boychick. (*Goes over to* RALPH) Why should you make like this? Tell me why you should cry, just tell me. . . . (JACOB *takes* RALPH *in his arms and both, trying to keep back the tears, trying fearfully not to be heard by the others in the dining room, begin crying*) You mustn't cry. . . .

(*The tango twists on. Inside the clatter of dishes and the clash of cutlery sound.* MORTY *begins to howl with laughter*)

*Curtain*

# Act Two, Scene Two

*That night. The dark dining room.*

*At rise:* JACOB *is heard in his lighted room, reading from a sheet, declaiming aloud as if to an audience.*

JACOB They are there to remind us of the horrors—under those crosses lie hundreds of thousands of workers and farmers who murdered each other in uniform for the greater glory of capitalism. (*Comes out of his room.*) The new imperialist war will send millions to their death, will bring prosperity to the pocket of the capitalist—aie, Morty—and will bring only greater hunger and misery to the masses of workers and farmers. The memories of the last world slaughter are still vivid in our minds. (*Hearing a noise he quickly retreats to his room.* RALPH *comes in from the street. He sits with hat and coat on.* JACOB *tentatively opens door and asks*) Ralphie?

RALPH It's getting pretty cold out.

JACOB (*Enters room fully, cleaning hair clippers*) We should have steam till twelve instead of ten. Go complain to the Board of Health.

RALPH It might snow.

JACOB It don't hurt . . . extra work for men.

RALPH When I was a kid I laid awake at nights and heard the sounds of trains . . . far-away lonesome sounds . . . boats going up and down the river. I used to think of all kinds of things I wanted to do. What was it, Jake? Just a bunch of noise in my head?

JACOB (*Waiting for news of the girl*) You wanted to make for yourself a certain kind of world.

RALPH I guess I didn't. I'm feeling pretty, pretty low.

JACOB You're a young boy and for you life is all in front like a big mountain. You got feet to climb.

RALPH I don't know how.

JACOB So you'll find out. Never a young man had such opportunity like today. He could make history.

RALPH Ten P.M. and all is well. Where's everybody?

JACOB They went.

RALPH Uncle Morty too?

JACOB Hennie and Sam he drove down.

RALPH I saw her.

JACOB (*Alert and eager*) Yes, yes, tell me.

RALPH I waited in Mount Morris Park till she came out. So cold I did a buck'n wing to keep warm. She's scared to death.

JACOB They made her?

RALPH Sure. She wants to go. They keep yelling at her—they want her to marry a millionaire, too.

JACOB You told her you love her?

RALPH Sure. "Marry me," I said. "Marry me tomorrow." On sixteen bucks a week. On top of that I had to admit Mom'd have Uncle Morty get me fired in a second. . . . Two can starve as cheap as one!

JACOB So what happened?

RALPH I made her promise to meet me tomorrow.

JACOB Now she'll go in the West?

RALPH I'd fight the whole goddam world with her, but not her. No guts. The hell with her. If she wantsa go—all right—I'll get along.

JACOB For sure, there's more important things than girls. . . .

RALPH You said a mouthful . . . and maybe I don't see it. She'll see what I can do. No one stops me when I get going. . . . (*Near to tears, he has to stop.* JACOB *examines his clippers very closely*)

JACOB Electric clippers never do a job like by hand.

RALPH Why won't Mom let us live here?

JACOB Why? Why? Because in a society like this today people don't love. Hate!

RALPH Gee, I'm no bum who hangs around pool parlors. I got the stuff to go ahead. I don't know what to do.

JACOB Look on me and learn what to do, boychick. Here sits an old man polishing tools. You think maybe I'll use them again! Look on this failure and see for seventy years he talked, with good ideas, but only in the head. It's enough for me now I should see your happiness. This is why I tell you—DO! Do what is in your heart and you carry in yourself a revolution. But you should act. Not like me. A man who had golden opportunities but drank instead a glass tea. No. . . . (*A pause of silence*)

RALPH (*Listening*) Hear it? The Boston air mail plane. Ten minutes late. I get a kick the way it cuts across the Bronx every night. (*The bell rings:* SAM, *excited, disheveled, enters*)

JACOB You came back so soon?

SAM Where's Mom?

JACOB Mom? Look on the chandelier.

SAM Nobody's home?

JACOB Sit down. Right away they're coming. You went in the street without a tie?

SAM Maybe it's a crime.

JACOB Excuse me.

RALPH You had a fight with Hennie again?

SAM She'll fight once . . . some day. . . . (*Lapses into silence*)

JACOB In my day the daughter came home. Now comes the son-in-law.

SAM Once too often she'll fight with me, Hennie. I mean it. I mean it like anything. I'm a person with a bad heart. I sit quiet, but inside I got a——

RALPH What happened?

SAM I'll talk to Mom. I'll see Mom.

JACOB Take an apple.

SAM Please . . . he tells me apples.

RALPH Why hop around like a billiard ball?

SAM Even in a joke she should dare say it.

JACOB My grandchild said something?

SAM To my father in the old country they did a joke . . . I'll tell you: One day in Odessa he talked to another Jew on the street. They didn't like it, they jumped on him like a wild wolf.

RALPH Who?

SAM Cossacks. They cut off his beard. A Jew without a beard! He came home—I remember like yesterday how he came home and went in bed for two days. He put like this the cover on his face. No one should see. The third morning he died.

RALPH From what?

SAM From a broken heart. . . . Some people are like this. Me too. I could die like this from shame.

JACOB Hennie told you something?

SAM Straight out she said it—like a lightning from the sky. The baby ain't mine. She said it.

RALPH Don't be a dope.

JACOB For sure, a joke.

RALPH She's kidding you.

SAM She should kid a policeman, not Sam Feinschreiber. Please . . . you don't know her like me. I wake up in the nighttime and she sits watching me like I don't know what. I make a nice living from the store. But it's no use—she looks for a star in the sky. I'm afraid like anything. You could go crazy from less even. What I shall do I'll ask Mom.

JACOB "Go home and sleep," she'll say. "It's a bad dream."

SAM It don't satisfy me more, such remarks, when Hennie could kill in the bed. (JACOB *laughs*) Don't laugh. I'm so nervous—look, two times I weighed myself on the subway station. (*Throws small cards to table*)

JACOB (*Examining one*) One hundred and thirty-eight —also a fortune. (*Turns it and reads*) "You are inclined to deep thinking, and have a high admiration for intellectual excellence and inclined to be very exclusive in the selection of friends." Correct! I think maybe you got mixed up in the wrong family, Sam. (MYRON *and* BESSIE *now enter*)

BESSIE Look, a guest! What's the matter? Something wrong with the baby? (*Waits*)

SAM No.

BESSIE Noo?

SAM (*In a burst*) I wash my hands from everything.

BESSIE Take off your coat and hat. Have a seat. Excitement don't help. Myron, make tea. You'll have a glass tea. We'll talk like civilized people. (MYRON *goes*) What is it, Ralph, you're all dressed up for a party? (*He looks at her silently and exits. To* SAM) We saw a very good movie, with Wallace Beery. He acts like life, very good.

MYRON (*Within*) Polly Moran too.

BESSIE Polly Moran too—a woman with a nose from here to Hunts Point, but a fine player. Poppa, take away the tools and the books.

JACOB All right. (*Exits to his room*)

BESSIE Noo, Sam, why do you look like a funeral?

SAM I can't stand it. . . .

BESSIE Wait. (*Yells*) You took up Tootsie on the roof.

JACOB (*Within*) In a minute.

BESSIE What can't you stand?

SAM She said I'm a second fiddle in my own house.

BESSIE Who?

SAM Hennie. In the second place, it ain't my baby, she said.

BESSIE What? What are you talking? (MYRON *enters with dishes*)

SAM From her own mouth. It went like a knife in my heart.

BESSIE Sam, what're you saying?

SAM Please, I'm making a story? I fell in the chair like a dead.

BESSIE Such a story you believe?

SAM I don't know.

BESSIE How you don't know?

SAM She told me even the man.

BESSIE Impossible!

SAM I can't believe myself. But she said it. I'm a second fiddle, she said. She made such a yell everybody heard for ten miles.

BESSIE Such a thing Hennie should say—impossible!

SAM What should I do? With my bad heart such a remark kills.

MYRON Hennie don't feel well, Sam. You see, she——

BESSIE What then?—a sick girl. Believe me, a mother knows. Nerves. Our Hennie's got a bad temper. You'll let her she says anything. She takes after me—nervous. (*To* MYRON) You ever heard such a remark in all your life? She should make such a statement! Bughouse.

MYRON The little one's been sick all these months. Hennie needs a rest. No doubt.

BESSIE Sam don't think she means it——

MYRON Oh, I know he don't, of course——

BESSIE I'll say the truth, Sam. We didn't half the time understand her ourselves. A girl with her own mind. When she makes it up, wild horses wouldn't change her.

SAM She don't love me.

BESSIE This is sensible, Sam?

SAM Not for a nickel.

BESSIE What do you think? She married you for your money? For your looks? You ain't no John Barrymore, Sam. No, she liked you.

SAM Please, not for a nickel. (JACOB *stands in the doorway*)

BESSIE We stood right here the first time she said it. "Sam Feinschreiber's a nice boy," she said it, "a boy he's got good common sense, with a business head." Right here she said it, in this room. You sent her two boxes of candy together, you remember?

MYRON Loft's candy.

BESSIE This is when she said it. What do you think?

MYRON You were just the only boy she cared for.

BESSIE So she married you. Such a world . . . plenty of boy friends she had, believe me!

JACOB A popular girl. . . .

MYRON Y-e-s.

BESSIE I'll say it plain out—Moe Axelrod offered her plenty—a servant, a house . . . she don't have to pick up a hand.

MYRON Oh, Moe? Just wild about her. . . .

SAM Moe Axelrod? He wanted to——

BESSIE But she didn't care. A girl like Hennie you don't buy. I should never live to see another day if I'm telling a lie.

SAM She was kidding me.

BESSIE What then? You shouldn't be foolish.

SAM The baby looks like my family. He's got Feinschreiber eyes.

BESSIE A blind man could see it.

JACOB Sure . . . sure. . . .

SAM The baby looks like me. Yes. . . .

BESSIE You could believe me.

JACOB Any day. . . .

SAM But she tells me the man. She made up his name too?

BESSIE Sam, Sam, look in the phone book—a million names.

MYRON Tom, Dick and Harry. (JACOB *laughs quietly, soberly*)

BESSIE Don't stand around, Poppa. Take Tootsie on the roof. And you don't let her go under the water tank.

JACOB *Schmah Yisroeal.*[1] Behold! (*Quietly laughing he goes back into his room, closing the door behind him*)

SAM I won't stand he should make insults. A man eats out his——

BESSIE No, no, he's an old man—a second childhood. Myron, bring in the tea. Open a jar of raspberry jelly. (MYRON *exits*)

SAM Mom, you think——?

BESSIE I'll talk to Hennie. It's all right.

SAM Tomorrow, I'll take her by the doctor. (RALPH *enters*)

BESSIE Stay for a little tea.

SAM No, I'll go home. I'm tired. Already I caught a cold in such weather. (*Blows his nose*)

MYRON (*Entering with stuffs*) Going home?

SAM I'll go in bed. I caught a cold.

MYRON Teddy Roosevelt used to say, "When you have a problem, sleep on it."

BESSIE My Sam is no problem.

MYRON I don't mean . . . I mean he said——

BESSIE Call me tomorrow, Sam.

SAM I'll phone supper time. Sometime I think there's something funny about me. (MYRON *sees him out. In the following pause Caruso is heard singing within*)

BESSIE A bargain! Second fiddle. By me he don't even play in the orchestra—a man like a mouse. Maybe she'll lay down and die 'cause he makes a living?

RALPH Can I talk to you about something?

BESSIE What's the matter—I'm biting you?

RALPH It's something about Blanche.

BESSIE Don't tell me.

RALPH Listen now——

BESSIE I don't wanna know.

RALPH She's got no place to go.

BESSIE I don't want to know.

RALPH Mom, I love this girl. . . .

BESSIE So go knock your head against the wall.

RALPH I want her to come here. Listen, Mom, I want you to let her live here for a while.

BESSIE You got funny ideas, my son.

RALPH I'm as good as anyone else. Don't I have some rights in the world? Listen, Mom, if I don't do something, she's going away. Why don't you do it? Why don't you let her stay here for a few weeks? Things'll pick up. Then we can——

BESSIE Sure, sure. I'll keep her fresh on ice for a wedding day. That's what you want?

RALPH No, I mean you should——

BESSIE Or maybe you'll sleep here in the same bed without marriage. (JACOB *stands in his doorway, dressed*)

[1] "Hear, O Israel," the beginning of a Jewish prayer.

RALPH Don't say that, Mom. I only mean. . . .

BESSIE What you mean, I know . . . and what I mean I also know. Make up your mind. For your own good, Ralphie. If she dropped in the ocean I don't lift a finger.

RALPH That's all, I suppose.

BESSIE With me it's one thing—a boy should have respect for his own future. Go to sleep, you look tired. In the morning you'll forget.

JACOB "Awake and sing, ye that dwell in dust, and the earth shall cast out the dead." It's cold out?

MYRON Oh, yes.

JACOB I'll take up Tootsie now.

MYRON (*Eating bread and jam*) He come on us like the wild man of Borneo, Sam. I don't think Hennie was fool enough to tell him the truth like that.

BESSIE Myron! (*A deep pause*)

RALPH What did he say?

BESSIE Never mind.

RALPH I heard him. I heard him. You don't needa tell me.

BESSIE Never mind.

RALPH You trapped that guy.

BESSIE Don't say another word.

RALPH Just have respect? That's the idea?

BESSIE Don't say another word. I'm boiling over ten times inside.

RALPH You won't let Blanche here, huh. I'm not sure I want her. You put one over on that little shrimp. The cat's whiskers, Mom?

BESSIE I'm telling you something!

RALPH I got the whole idea. I get it so quick my head's swimming. Boy, what a laugh! I suppose you know about this, Jake?

JACOB Yes.

RALPH Why didn't you do something?

JACOB I'm an old man.

RALPH What's that got to do with the price of bonds? Sits around and lets a thing like that happen! You make me sick too.

MYRON (*After a pause*) Let me say something, son.

RALPH Take your hand away! Sit in a corner and wag your tail. Keep on boasting you went to law school for two years.

MYRON I want to tell you——

RALPH You never in your life had a thing to tell me.

BESSIE (*Bitterly*) Don't say a word. Let him, let him run and tell Sam. Publish in the papers, give a broadcast on the radio. To him it don't matter nothing his family sits with tears pouring from the eyes. (*To* JACOB) What are you waiting for? I didn't tell you twice already about the dog? You'll stand around with Caruso and make a bughouse. It ain't enough all day long. Fifty times I told you I'll break every record in the house. (*She brushes past him, breaks the records, comes out*) The next time I say something you'll maybe believe it. Now maybe you learned a lesson. (*Pause*)

JACOB (*Quietly*) Bessie, new lessons . . . not for an old dog. (MOE *enters*)

MYRON You didn't have to do it, Momma.

BESSIE Talk better to your son, Mr. Berger! Me, I don't lay down and die for him and Poppa no more. I'll work like a nigger? For what? Wait, the day comes when you'll be punished. When it's too late you'll remember how you sucked away a mother's life. Talk to him, tell him how I don't sleep at night. (*Bursts into tears and exits*)

MOE (*Sings*) "Good-by to all your sorrows. You never hear them talk about the war, in the land of Yama Yama. . . ."

MYRON Yes, Momma's a sick woman, Ralphie.

RALPH Yeah?

MOE We'll be out of the trenches by Christmas. Putt, putt, putt . . . here, stinker. . . . (*Picks up Tootsie, a small, white poodle that just then enters from the hall*) If there's reincarnation in the next life I wanna be a dog and lay in a fat lady's lap. Barrage over? How 'bout a little pinochle, Pop?

JACOB Nnno.

RALPH (*Taking dog*) I'll take her up. (*Conciliatory*)

JACOB No, I'll do it. (*Takes dog*)

RALPH (*Ashamed*) It's cold out.

JACOB I was cold before in my life. A man sixty-seven. . . . (*Strokes the dog*) Tootsie is my favorite lady in the house. (*He slowly passes across the room and exits. A settling pause*)

MYRON She cried all last night—Tootsie—I heard her in the kitchen like a young girl.

MOE Tonight I could do something. I got a yen . . . I don't know.

MYRON (*Rubbing his head*) My scalp is impoverished.

RALPH Mom bust all his records.

MYRON She didn't have to do it.

MOE Tough tit! Now I can sleep in the morning. Who the hell wantsa hear a wop air his tonsils all day long!

RALPH (*Handling the fragment of a record*) "O Paradiso!"

MOE (*Gets cards*) It's snowing out, girls.

MYRON There's no more big snows like in the old days. I think the whole world's changing. I see it, right under our very eyes. No one hardly remembers any more when we used to have gaslight and all the dishes had little fishes on them.

MOE It's the system, girls.

MYRON I was a little boy when it happened—the Great Blizzard. It snowed three days without a stop that time. Yes, and the horse cars stopped. A silence of death was on the city and little babies got no milk . . . they say a lot of people died that year.

MOE (*Singing as he deals himself cards*)

"Lights are blinking while you're drinking,
That's the place where the good fellows go.
Good-by to all your sorrows,
You never hear them talk about the war,
In the land of Yama Yama
Funicalee, funicala, funicalo. . . ."

MYRON What can I say to you, Big Boy?

RALPH Not a damn word.

MOE (*Goes "ta ra ta ra" throughout*)

MYRON I know how you feel about all those things, I know.

RALPH Forget it.

MYRON And your girl. . . .

RALPH Don't soft soap me all of a sudden.

MYRON I'm not foreign born. I'm an American, and yet I never got close to you. It's an American father's duty to be his son's friend.

RALPH Who said that—Teddy R.?

MOE (*Dealing cards*) You're breaking his heart, *Litvak.*[2]

MYRON It just happened the other day. The moment I began losing my hair I just knew I was destined to be a failure in life . . . and when I grew bald I was. Now isn't that funny, Big Boy?

MOE It's a pisscutter!

MYRON I believe in Destiny.

MOE You get what-it-takes. Then they don't catch you with your pants down. (*Sings out*) Eight of clubs. . . .

MYRON I really don't know. I sold jewelry on the road before I married. It's one thing to—— Now here's a thing the druggist gave me. (*Reads*) "The Marvel Cosmetic Girl of Hollywood is going on the air. Give this charming little radio singer a name and win five thousand dollars. If you will send——"

MOE Your old man still believes in Santy Claus.

MYRON Someone's got to win. The government isn't gonna allow everything to be a fake.

MOE It's a fake. There ain't no prizes. It's a fake.

MYRON It says——

RALPH (*Snatching it*) For Christ's sake, Pop, forget it. Grow up. Jake's right—everybody's crazy. It's like a zoo in this house. I'm going to bed.

MOE In the land of Yama Yama. . . . (*Goes on with "ta ra"*)

MYRON Don't think life's easy with Momma. No, but she means for your good all the time. I tell you she does, she——

RALPH Maybe, but I'm going to bed. (*Downstairs doorbell rings violently*)

MOE (*Ring*) Enemy barrage begins on sector eight seventy-five.

RALPH That's downstairs.

MYRON We ain't expecting anyone this hour of the night.

MOE "Lights are blinking while you're drinking, that's the place where the good fellows go. Good-by to ta ra tara ra," etc.

RALPH I better see who it is.

MYRON I'll tick the button. (*As he starts, the apartment doorbell begins ringing, followed by large knocking.* MYRON *goes out*)

RALPH Who's ever ringing means it. (*A loud excited voice outside*)

MOE "In the land of Yama Yama, Funicalee, funicalo, funic——"

(MYRON *enters followed by* SCHLOSSER *the janitor.* BESSIE *cuts in from the other side*)

[2] Literally "Lithuanian," used by Moe to specify Myron's Jewish background.

BESSIE Who's ringing like a lunatic?

RALPH What's the matter?

MYRON Momma. . . .

BESSIE Noo, what's the matter? (*Downstairs bell continues*)

RALPH What's the matter?

BESSIE Well, well . . . ?

MYRON Poppa. . . .

BESSIE What happened?

SCHLOSSER He shlipped maybe in de snow.

RALPH Who?

SCHLOSSER (*To* BESSIE) Your fadder fall off de roof. . . . Ja. (*A dead pause.* RALPH *then runs out*)

BESSIE (*Dazed*) Myron. . . . Call Morty on the phone . . . call him. (MYRON *starts for phone*) No. I'll do it myself. I'll . . . do it. (MYRON *exits*)

SCHLOSSER (*Standing stupidly*) Since I was in dis country . . . I was pudding out de ash can . . . The snow is vet. . . .

MOE (*To* SCHLOSSER) Scram. (SCHLOSSER *exits*) (BESSIE *goes blindly to the phone, fumbles and gets it.* MOE *sits quietly, slowly turning cards over, but watching her*)

BESSIE He slipped. . . .

MOE (*Deeply moved*) Slipped?

BESSIE I can't see the numbers. Make it, Moe, make it. . . .

MOE Make it yourself. (*He looks at her and slowly goes back to his game of cards with shaking hands*)

BESSIE Riverside 7— . . . (*Unable to talk she dials slowly. The dial whizzes on*)

MOE Don't . . . make me laugh. . . . (*He turns over cards*)

*Curtain*

# Act Three

*A week later in the dining room.* MORTY, BESSIE *and* MYRON *eating. Sitting in the front room is* MOE *marking a "dope sheet," but really listening to the others.*

BESSIE You're sure he'll come tonight—the insurance man?

MORTY Why not? I shtupped him a ten-dollar bill. Everything's hot delicatessen.

BESSIE Why must he come so soon?

MORTY Because you had a big expense. You'll settle once and for all. I'm a great boy for making hay while the sun shines.

BESSIE Stay till he'll come, Morty. . . .

MORTY No, I got a strike downtown. Business don't stop for personal life. Two times already in the past week those bastards threw stink bombs in the showroom. Wait! We'll give them strikes—in the *kishkas*[1] we'll give them. . . .

BESSIE I'm a woman. I don't know about policies. Stay till he comes.

MORTY Bessie—sweetheart, leave me live.

BESSIE I'm afraid, Morty.

MORTY Be practical. They made an investigation. Everybody knows Pop had an accident. Now we'll collect.

MYRON Ralphie don't know Papa left the insurance in his name.

MORTY It's not his business. And I'll tell him.

BESSIE The way he feels. (*Enter* RALPH *into front room*) He'll do something crazy. He thinks Poppa jumped off the roof.

MORTY Be practical, Bessie. Ralphie will sign when I tell him. Everything is peaches and cream.

BESSIE Wait for a few minutes. . . .

MORTY Look, I'll show you in black on white what the policy says. *For God's sake, leave me live!* (*Angrily exits to kitchen. In parlor,* MOE *speaks to* RALPH *who is reading a letter*)

MOE What's the letter say?

RALPH Blanche won't see me no more, she says. I couldn't care very much, she says. If I didn't come like I said. . . . She'll phone before she leaves.

MOE She don't know about Pop?

RALPH She won't ever forget me she says. Look what she sends me . . . a little locket on a chain . . . if she calls I'm out.

MOE You mean it?

RALPH For a week I'm trying to go in his room. I guess he'd like me to have it, but I can't. . . .

MOE Wait a minute! (*Crosses over*) They're trying to rook you—a freeze-out.

RALPH Who?

MOE That bunch stuffin' their gut with hot pastrami. Morty in particular. Jake left the insurance—three thousand dollars—for you.

RALPH For me?

MOE Now you got wings, kid. Pop figured you could use it. That's why. . . .

RALPH That's why what?

MOE It ain't the only reason he done it.

RALPH He done it?

MOE You think a breeze blew him off? (HENNIE *enters and sits*)

RALPH I'm not sure what I think.

MOE The insurance guy's coming tonight. Morty "shtupped" him.

RALPH Yeah?

MOE I'll back you up. You're dead on your feet. Grab a sleep for yourself.

RALPH No!

MOE Go on! (*Pushes boy into room*)

SAM (*Whom* MORTY *has sent in for the paper*) Morty wants the paper.

HENNIE So?

SAM You're sitting on it. (*Gets paper*) We could go home now, Hennie! Leon is alone by Mrs. Strasberg a whole day.

[1] Intestines, i.e., guts.

HENNIE Go on home if you're so anxious. A full tub of diapers is waiting.

SAM Why should you act this way?

HENNIE 'Cause there's no bones in ice cream. Don't touch me.

SAM Please, what's the matter. . . .

MOE She don't like you. Plain as the face on your nose. . . .

SAM To me, my friend, you talk a foreign language.

MOE A quarter you're lousy. (SAM *exits*) Gimme a buck, I'll run it up to ten.

HENNIE Don't do me no favors.

MOE Take a chance. (*Stopping her as she crosses to doorway*)

HENNIE I'm a pushover.

MOE I say lotsa things. You don't know me.

HENNIE I know you—when you knock 'em down you're through.

MOE (*Sadly*) You still don't know me.

HENNIE I know what goes in your wise-guy head.

MOE Don't run away. . . . I ain't got hydrophobia. Wait. I want to tell you. . . . I'm leaving.

HENNIE Leaving?

MOE Tonight. Already packed.

HENNIE Where?

MORTY (*As he enters followed by the others*) My car goes through snow like a dose of salts.

BESSIE Hennie, go eat. . . .

MORTY Where's Ralphie?

MOE In his new room. (*Moves into dining room*)

MORTY I didn't have a piece of hot pastrami in my mouth for years.

BESSIE Take a sandwich, Hennie. You didn't eat all day. . . . (*At window*) A whole week it rained cats and dogs.

MYRON Rain, rain, go away. Come again some other day. (*Puts shawl on her*)

MORTY Where's my gloves?

SAM (*Sits on stool*) I'm sorry the old man lays in the rain.

MORTY Personally, Pop was a fine man. But I'm a great boy for an honest opinion. He had enough crazy ideas for a regiment.

MYRON Poppa never had a doctor in his whole life. . . . (*Enter* RALPH)

MORTY He had Caruso. Who's got more from life?

BESSIE Who's got more? . . .

MYRON And Marx he had.

(MYRON *and* BESSIE *sit on sofa*)

MORTY Marx! Some say Marx is the new God today. Maybe I'm wrong. Ha, ha, ha. . . . Personally I counted my ten million last night. . . . I'm sixteen cents short. So tomorrow I'll go to Union Square and yell no equality in the country! Ah, it's a new generation.

RALPH You said it!

MORTY What's the matter, Ralphie? What are you looking funny?

RALPH I hear I'm left insurance and the man's coming tonight.

MORTY Poppa didn't leave no insurance for you.

RALPH What?

MORTY In your name he left it—but not for you.

RALPH It's my name on the paper.

MORTY Who said so?

RALPH (*To his mother*) The insurance man's coming tonight?

MORTY What's the matter?

RALPH I'm not talking to you. (*To his mother*) Why?

BESSIE I don't know why.

RALPH He don't come in this house tonight.

MORTY That's what *you* say.

RALPH I'm not talking to you, Uncle Morty, but I'll tell you, too, he don't come here tonight when there's still mud on a grave. (*To his mother*) Couldn't you give the house a chance to cool off?

MORTY Is this a way to talk to your mother?

RALPH Was that a way to talk to your father?

MORTY Don't be so smart with me, Mr. Ralph Berger!

RALPH Don't be so smart with *me*.

MORTY What'll you do? I say he's coming tonight. Who says no?

MOE (*Suddenly, from the background*) Me.

MORTY Take a back seat, Axelrod. When you're in the family——

MOE I got a little document here. (*Produces paper*) I found it under his pillow that night. A guy who slips off a roof don't leave a note before he does it.

MORTY (*Starting for* MOE *after a horrified silence*) Let me see this note.

BESSIE Morty, don't touch it!

MOE Not if you crawled.

MORTY It's a fake. Poppa wouldn't——

MOE Get the insurance guy here and we'll see how—— (*The bell rings*) Speak of the devil. . . . Answer it, see what happens. (MORTY *starts for the ticker*)

BESSIE Morty, don't!

MORTY (*Stopping*) Be practical, Bessie.

MOE Sometimes you don't collect on suicides if they know about it.

MORTY You should let. . . . You should let him. . . . (*A pause in which* ALL *seem dazed. Bell rings insistently*)

MOE Well, we're waiting.

MORTY Give me the note.

MOE I'll give you the head off your shoulders.

MORTY Bessie, you'll stand for this? (*Points to* RALPH) Pull down his pants and give him with a strap.

RALPH (*As bell rings again*) How about it?

BESSIE Don't be crazy. It's not my fault. Morty said he should come tonight. It's not nice so soon. I didn't——

MORTY I said it? Me?

BESSIE Who then?

MORTY You didn't sing a song in my ear a whole week to settle quick?

BESSIE I'm surprised. Morty, you're a big liar.

MYRON Momma's telling the truth, she is!

MORTY Lissen. In two shakes of a lamb's tail, we'll start a real fight and then nobody won't like nobody.

Where's my fur gloves? I'm going downtown. (*To* SAM) You coming? I'll drive you down.

HENNIE (*To* SAM, *who looks questioningly at her*) Don't look at me. Go home if you want.

SAM If you're coming soon, I'll wait.

HENNIE Don't do me any favors. Night and day he pesters me.

MORTY You made a cushion——sleep!

SAM I'll go home. I know . . . to my worst enemy I don't wish such a life——

HENNIE Sam, keep quiet.

SAM (*Quietly; sadly*) No more free speech in America? (*Gets his hat and coat*) I'm a lonely person. Nobody likes me.

MYRON I like you, Sam.

HENNIE (*Going to him gently; sensing the end*) Please go home, Sam. I'll sleep here. . . . I'm tired and nervous. Tomorrow I'll come home. I love you . . . I mean it. (*She kisses him with real feeling*)

SAM I would die for you. . . . (SAM *looks at her. Tries to say something, but his voice chokes up with a mingled feeling. He turns and leaves the room*)

MORTY A bird in the hand is worth two in the bush. Remember I said it. Good night. (*Exits after* SAM) (HENNIE *sits depressed.* BESSIE *goes up and looks at the picture calendar again.* MYRON *finally breaks the silence*)

MYRON Yesterday a man wanted to sell me a saxophone with pearl buttons. But I——

BESSIE It's a beautiful picture. In this land, nobody works. . . . Nobody worries. . . . Come to bed, Myron. (*Stops at the door, and says to* RALPH) Please don't have foolish ideas about the money.

RALPH Let's call it a day.

BESSIE It belongs for the whole family. You'll get your teeth fixed——

RALPH And a pair of black and white shoes?

BESSIE Hennie needs a vacation. She'll take two weeks in the mountains and I'll mind the baby.

RALPH I'll take care of my own affairs.

BESSIE A family needs for a rainy day. Times is getting worse. Prospect Avenue, Dawson, Beck Street—every day furniture's on the sidewalk.

RALPH Forget it, Mom.

BESSIE Ralphie, I worked too hard all my years to be treated like dirt. It's no law we should be stuck together like Siamese twins. Summer shoes you didn't have, skates you never had, but I bought a new dress every week. A lover I kept—Mr. Gigolo! Did I ever play a game of cards like Mrs. Marcus? Or was Bessie Berger's children always the cleanest on the block?! Here I'm not only the mother, but also the father. The first two years I worked in a stocking factory for six dollars while Myron Berger went to law school. If I didn't worry about the family who would? On the calendar it's a different place, but here without a dollar you don't look the world in the eye. Talk from now to next year—this is life in America.

RALPH Then it's wrong. It don't make sense. If life made you this way, then it's wrong!

BESSIE Maybe you wanted me to give up twenty years ago. Where would you be now? You'll excuse my expression—a bum in the park!

RALPH I'm not blaming you, Mom. Sink or swim—I see it. But it can't stay like this.

BESSIE My foolish boy. . . .

RALPH No, I see every house lousy with lies and hate. He said it, Grandpa— Brooklyn hates the Bronx. Smacked on the nose twice a day. But boys and girls can get ahead like that, Mom. We don't want life printed on dollar bills, Mom!

BESSIE So go out and change the world if you don't like it.

RALPH I will! And why? 'Cause life's different in my head. Gimme the earth in two hands. I'm strong. There . . . hear him? The air mail off to Boston. Day or night, he flies away, a job to do. That's us and it's no time to die. (*The airplane sound fades off as* MYRON *gives alarm clock to* BESSIE *which she begins to wind*)

BESSIE "Mom, what does she know? She's old-fashioned!" But I'll tell you a big secret: My whole life I wanted to go away too, but with children a woman stays home. A fire burned in *my* heart too, but now it's too late. I'm no spring chicken. The clock goes and Bessie goes. Only my machinery can't be fixed. (*She lifts a button: the alarm rings on the clock; she stops it, says "Good night" and exits*)

MYRON I guess I'm no prize bag. . . .

BESSIE (*From within*) Come to bed, Myron.

MYRON (*Tears page off calendar*) Hmmm. . . . (*Exits to her*)

RALPH Look at him, draggin' after her like an old shoe.

MOE Punch drunk. (*Phone rings*) That's for me. (*At phone*) Yeah? . . . Just a minute. (*To* RALPH) Your girl . . .

RALPH Jeez, I don't know what to say to her.

MOE Hang up? (RALPH *slowly takes phone*)

RALPH Hello. . . . Blanche, I wish. . . . I don't know what to say. . . . Yes . . . Hello? . . . (*Puts phone down*) She hung up on me . . .

MOE Sorry?

RALPH No girl means anything to me until . . .

MOE Till when?

RALPH Till I can take care of her. Till we don't look out on an airshaft. Till we can take the world in two hands and polish off the dirt.

MOE That's a big order.

RALPH Once upon a time I thought I'd drown to death in bolts of silk and velour. But I grew up these last few weeks. Jake said a lot.

MOE Your memory's okay?

RALPH But take a look at this. (*Brings armful of books from* JACOB'*s room—dumps them on table*) His books, I got them too—the pages ain't cut in half of them.

MOE Perfect.

RALPH Does it prove something? Damn tootin'! A ten-cent nail-file cuts them. Uptown, downtown, I'll read them on the way. Get a big lamp over the bed. (*Picks up one*) My eyes are good. (*Puts book in pocket*)

Sure, inventory tomorrow. Coletti to Driscoll to Berger—that's how we work. It's a team down the warehouse. Driscoll's a show-off, a wiseguy, and Joe talks pigeons day and night. But they're like me, looking for a chance to get to first base too. Joe razzed me about my girl. But he don't know why. I'll tell him. Hell, he might tell me something I don't know. Get teams together all over. Spit on your hands and get to work. And with enough teams together maybe we'll get steam in the warehouse so our fingers don't freeze off. Maybe we'll fix it so life won't be printed on dollar bills.

MOE Graduation Day.

RALPH (*Starts for door of his room, stops*) Can I have . . . Grandpa's note?

MOE Sure you want it?

RALPH Please— (MOE *gives it*) It's blank!

MOE (*Taking note back and tearing it up*) That's right.

RALPH Thanks! (*Exits*)

MOE The kid's a fighter! (*To* HENNIE) Why are you crying?

HENNIE I never cried in my life. (*She is now*)

MOE (*Starts for door. Stops*) You told Sam you love him. . . .

HENNIE If I'm sore on life, why take it out on him?

MOE You won't forget me to your dyin' day—I was the first guy. Part of your insides. You won't forget. I wrote my name on you—indelible ink!

HENNIE One thing I won't forget—how you left me crying on the bed like I was two for a cent!

MOE Listen, do you think——

HENNIE Sure. Waits till the family goes to the open air movie. He brings me perfume. . . . He grabs my arms——

MOE You won't forget me!

HENNIE How you left the next week?

MOE So I made a mistake. For Chris' sake, don't act like the Queen of Roumania!

HENNIE Don't make me laugh!

MOE What the hell do you want, my head on a plate?! Was my life so happy? Chris', my old man was a bum. I supported the whole damn family—five kids and Mom. When they grew up they beat it the hell away like rabbits. Mom died. I went to the war; got clapped down like a bedbug; woke up in a room without a leg. What the hell do you think, anyone's got it better than you? I never had a home either. I'm lookin' too!

HENNIE So what?!

MOE So you're it—you're home for me, a place to live! That's the whole parade, sickness, eating out your heart! Sometimes you meet a girl—she stops it—that's love. . . . So take a chance! Be with me, Paradise. What's to lose?

HENNIE My pride!

MOE (*Grabbing her*) What do you want? Say the word—I'll tango on a dime. Don't gimme ice when your heart's on fire!

HENNIE Let me go! (*He stops her*)

MOE WHERE?!!

HENNIE What do you want, Moe, what do you want?

MOE You!

HENNIE You'll be sorry you ever started——

MOE You!

HENNIE Moe, lemme go—— (*Trying to leave*) I'm getting up early—lemme go.

MOE No! . . . I got enough fever to blow the whole damn town to hell. (*He suddenly releases her and half stumbles backwards. Forces himself to quiet down*) You wanna go back to him? Say the word. I'll know what to do. . . .

HENNIE (*Helplessly*) Moe, I don't know what to say.

MOE Listen to me.

HENNIE What?

MOE Come away. A certain place where it's moonlight and roses. We'll lay down, count stars. Hear the big ocean making noise. You lay under the trees. Champagne flows like—— (*Phone rings.* MOE *finally answers the telephone*) Hello? . . . Just a minute. (*Looks at* HENNIE)

HENNIE Who is it?

MOE Sam.

HENNIE (*Starts for phone, but changes her mind*) I'm sleeping. . . .

MOE (*In phone*) She's sleeping. . . . (*Hangs up. Watches* HENNIE *who slowly sits*) He wants you to know he got home O.K. . . . What's on your mind?

HENNIE Nothing.

MOE Sam?

HENNIE They say it's a palace on those Havana boats.

MOE What's on your mind?

HENNIE (*Trying to escape*) Moe, I don't care for Sam—I never loved him——

MOE But your kid—?

HENNIE All my life I waited for this minute.

MOE (*Holding her*) Me too. Made believe I was talkin' just bedroom golf, but you and me forever was what I meant! Christ, baby, there's one life to live! Live it!

HENNIE Leave the baby?

MOE Yeah!

HENNIE I can't. . . .

MOE You can!

HENNIE No. . . .

MOE But you're not sure!

HENNIE I don't know.

MOE Make a break or spend the rest of your life in a coffin.

HENNIE Oh God, I don't know where I stand.

MOE Don't look up there. Paradise, you're on a big boat headed south. No more pins and needles in your heart, no snake juice squirted in your arm. The whole world's green grass and when you cry it's because you're happy.

HENNIE Moe, I don't know. . . .

MOE Nobody knows, but you do it and find out. When you're scared the answer's zero.

HENNIE You're hurting my arm.

MOE The doctor said it—cut off your leg to save your life! And they done it—one thing to get another. (*Enter* RALPH)

RALPH I didn't hear a word, but do it, Hennie, do it!

MOE Mom can mind the kid. She'll go on forever, Mom. We'll send money back, and Easter eggs.

RALPH I'll be here.

MOE Get your coat . . . get it.

HENNIE Moe!

MOE I know . . . but get your coat and hat and kiss the house good-bye.

HENNIE The man I love. . . . (MYRON *entering*) I left my coat in Mom's room. (*Exits*)

MYRON Don't wake her up, Beauty. Momma fell asleep as soon as her head hit the pillow. I can't sleep. It was a long day. Hmmm. (*Examines his tongue in buffet mirror*) I was reading the other day a person with a thick tongue is feeble-minded. I can do anything with my tongue. Make it thick, flat. No fruit in the house lately. Just a lone apple. (*He gets apple and paring knife and starts paring*) Must be something wrong with me—I say I won't eat but I eat. (HENNIE *enters dressed to go out*) Where you going, little Red Riding Hood?

HENNIE Nobody knows, Peter Rabbit.

MYRON You're looking very pretty tonight. You were a beautiful baby too. 1910, that was the year you was born. The same year Teddy Roosevelt come back from Africa.

HENNIE Gee, Pop; you're such a funny guy.

MYRON He was a boisterous man, Teddy. Good night. (*He exits, paring apple*)

RALPH When I look at him, I'm sad. Let me die like a dog, if I can't get more from life.

HENNIE Where?

RALPH Right here in the house! My days won't be for nothing. Let Mom have the dough. I'm twenty-two and kickin'! I'll get along. Did Jake die for us to fight about nickels? No! "Awake and sing," he said. Right here he stood and said it. The night he died, I saw it like a thunderbolt! I saw he was dead and I was born! I swear to God, I'm one week old! I want the whole city to hear it—fresh blood, arms. We got 'em. We're glad we're living.

MOE I wouldn't trade you for two pitchers and an outfielder. Hold the fort!

RALPH So long.

MOE So long.

(*They go and* RALPH *stands full and strong in the doorway seeing them off as the curtain slowly falls*)

*Curtain*

# William Saroyan

# (1908-     )

When he began to spin out his uninhibitedly free-flowing fantasias which gave terms like *surrealist* and *dadaist* a measure of respectability in American drama, William Saroyan was just being William Saroyan—and not a writer associated with Dada, Dalí, André Breton's Surrealist Manifestoes, or the fetish of Automatic Writing. Using the same free-associational techniques which had made him prolific as a short-story writer, Saroyan took pride in the speed with which he wrote his plays: when, for example, *The Time of Your Life* took closer to five than to the six days he had allotted for its composition, it became a five-act instead of the six-act play he had set out to write. An incorrigible original, Saroyan filled his works with images welling up from his well-stocked unconscious: scraps of poetry, anecdotes, memories of sweet and bizarre people, strains of melody, flashes of color, childhood wishes, and occasionally phantoms (like Blick, the sadistic Vice Squad chief in *The Time of Your Life*) from the nightmarish world of everyday reality. With innocence and bravado, he cast aside "the rules other people make" and balanced his plays precariously on the fine line where private and public symbols coalesce and an essentially extra-logical communication between artist and audience occurs.

In the American theatre, 1939-1942 was the "Saroyan period," and he left his imprint as much by dint of his exuberant personality as through his plays. In the early 1940's, as Americans stopped worrying about the Depression only to start taking fascism seriously, Saroyan's flamboyant vitality in his love affair with America and its "beautiful people" was refreshing. His nonconformity was valued for his guarded optimism and his impatience with The Way Things Are Done in publishers' offices, in Hollywood studios, and New York theatres. He moved into the highly publicized entertainment world like a younger Bernard Shaw, the answer to a publicist's prayers: if he had not just returned from a remote part of the world, he was leaving for one; if he had not just finished one "classic," he was starting another; if he was not at war with New York critics or producers, he was warring with the U.S. Army; if he was not refusing Pulitzer money for *The Time of Your Life,* he was accepting the Critics Circle Award for the same play. In 1942, just three years after the successful production of his first play, *My Heart's in the Highlands,* Saroyan's irrepressible hoboism was so well known that in Samson Raphaelson's pungent comedy, *Jason,* the central characters are obviously based on Saroyan and George Jean Nathan, one of his earliest champions.

To some, Saroyan's plays were charming overflowings of boyish high spirits; to others, his works were signs that Peter Pan had come again, infantile pastoralist fantasies depressingly inappropriate in a war-wracked world. To his admirers, Saroyan was reasserting the Good, the True, and the Beautiful in the American Experience; to his detractors, his free-form vaudevilles were naive escapist exercises, puerile and unmanly in a time of crisis. To Saroyan in this period, however, the Light was Dark Enough, as the allegorical alignments in his best plays clearly indicate. He hoped that in the theatre, if not in the real world, the gathering forces of evil could be stayed long enough for his audiences to recall their essential humanity. *The Time of Your Life* contains both Blick and Nick, both the Arab ("No foundation") and Willie, the pinball addict ("Oh, boy, what a beautiful country"), and Saroyan never fails to underline the differences between the world inside Nick's Saloon and the world outside. His characters are all sharers in Harry's comic monologue, at once funny and inutterably sad, in its details as in its punch-line (*"Everybody's behind the eight-ball!"*).

Because of the compellingly subjective quality of his writing, Saroyan is only rarely recognized as one of this century's best regionalist authors. His world, centered around San Francisco and Fresno, California, is, however, supremely real to millions who have discovered that world only through his plays and stories. Born in 1908 in Fresno to parents recently arrived from Turkish Armenia, Saroyan early developed a profound awareness of himself as an American with a rich Armenian heritage. He knows the deep family-loyalties and the national-consciousness which bind Armenians together throughout the world, but pride in his Americanism has kept him from the chauvinism and clannishness of the "professional Armenian." His autobiographical *My Name Is Aram* (1940) shows his basic loyalties: it is dedicated both to Fresno ("the ugly little city containing the large comic world") and his family ("the proud and angry Saroyans containing all humanity").

Saroyan's father, a Presbyterian minister turned grape-grower, died in 1911, and his mother had to place her children in an orphanage until she could support them. In 1915, when the family was reunited in Fresno, Saroyan began a reluctant flirtation with public schools. After he had endured a few years of high school, he decided to educate himself. Drifting from job to job, he regarded the Fresno Public Library as a second home; he read widely and indiscriminately, absorbing personalities and ideas instead of formal techniques. Saroyan has said, "I am the kind of writer to live a life," and it is clear that he was drawn to writers who built similar bridges between life and literature: Jack London, Mencken, Twain, Whitman, Gorki, Chekhov, Sandburg, Hemingway. Inspired by Guy de Maupassant, Saroyan in his early teens tried the short story. The styles of Ibsen ("too cagey, crafty, and calculating") and Wilde "didn't seem right" for him. In Shaw, however, he found his idol, "the man who seemed to remind me of myself—of what I really was and would surely become." In his Preface to *Hello Out There,* perhaps his best and certainly his most carefully barbered one-act, Saroyan recalls telling, at 18, a fellow telegraph worker that Shaw "is health, wisdom, and comedy, and that's what I am, too." If the Shavian influence is not readily identifiable in his plays, it is inescapably present in Saroyan's iconoclasm.

Saroyan's feeling for theatre has been as instinctual as his approach to literature. Impatient with the drama of ideas, he prefers the excitement of movies, vaudeville or musical comedy, circuses and county fairs with their horse or automobile races. In 1938 when he adapted a short story into dramatic form, he resolved to put "play" back into plays. Never scorning entertainment, he has peopled his plays with characters who are either entertainers or simple people starved for entertainment, and he has recaptured the rhythms of the popular arts. In the Preface to *Love's Old Sweet Song,* Saroyan says that the "line of the play is melodic, the same as the line of a song," a description easily duplicated elsewhere in his many commentaries on his plays. Like Maeterlinck, Saroyan "saw drama in everything because," as he says, "there *was* drama in everything —because there was drama in myself." Like Cocteau and Lorca, Saroyan came to the theatre with the expectation that everything could and would be presented in its full poetic value. The first few minutes of *My Heart's in the Highlands* typify Saroyan's orchestration of familiar sights and sounds as, almost entirely in pantomime, Fresno's San Benito Avenue comes to life on a late afternoon in August, 1914: Johnny ("aged nine, but essentially ageless") is stirred out of a reverie by a train whistle so mournful he tries "to figure out everything"; eating an ice-cream cone, an older boy bicycles past but ignores Johnny's friendly wave; sitting again, Johnny listens to "a small overjoyed but angry bird"; the bird flies away; inside the house, Johnny's father is heard composing a poem; "a table or chair is pushed over in anger," this followed by a groan, then silence; Johnny finally succeeds in standing on his head; in this position, he hears "My Heart's in the Highlands" played on a bugle by an old man. After this overture of symbols, the play "begins." Saroyan's consciousness of approaching war is heard in the Father's cry ("Fire your feeble guns. You won't kill anything. There will always be poets in the world."), but Saroyan's interest is concentrated on the townspeople who long for music, poetry, and the magic of theatre. *The Time of Your Life* was also conceived in dance and musical patterns, as its earlier titles, "The Light Fantastic" and "Sunset Sonata," indicate. The play requires actors who can dance, play the piano or harmonica, sing, as well as act; it specifies the subtlest modulations of lighting; the properties-list includes toys, guns, newspapers with war-mongering headlines, maps, jellybeans in quantity, and the most vivacious pinball machine ever devised.

After his extraordinary success with *The Time of Your Life,* Saroyan was eager to try writing anything; irritated by the uncertainty he had detected in professional directors, Saroyan also determined to direct his own plays. His versatility is reflected in *Razzle Dazzle* (1942), a collection of 17 short works ranging in form from relatively conventional one-act plays and radio scripts to a "ballet-play," a "ballet-poem," a "ballet-scenario," an "Italian opera in English," and a "vaudeville." From 1941, when he failed with a theatre created so that he could direct his own works, until 1957, when *The Cave Dwellers* received critical acclaim, Saroyan's new plays were rarely produced in New York. In Hollywood he proved intractable when confronted with the success-formulas he later satirized in *Get Away Old Man* (1943); during the middle 1950's he found in the "Omnibus" television series a respectful sponsor for some of his best one-act plays. The London theatre was enlivened in 1960 with *Sam—The Highest Jumper of Them All,* designed to demonstrate that drama is a collaborative and improvisatory art; Saroyan and his actors made up the play as they went along, reportedly with disastrous results.

Like O'Casey, Saroyan has continued to write for a theatre reluctant to produce his later works. However, through frequent revivals of *The Time of Your Life* on film and television as well as in the theatre, he has maintained his popularity. Saroyan has always addressed himself to the Child in Man ("fresh, eager, interested, innocent, imaginative, healthy, and full of faith"). Most notably perhaps in *The Time of Your Life,* audiences have been glad to join in his make-believe.

Saroyan has been a liberating force whose experiments were far ahead of their time. In 1939, he described *Sweeney in the Trees,* written soon after *The Time of Your Life,* in terms taken as exhibitionist horseplay: "A play, a dream, a poem, a travesty, a fable, a symphony, a parable, a comedy, a tragedy, a farce, a vaudeville, a song and dance, a statement on money, a report on life, an essay on art and religion, a theatrical entertainment, a circus, anything you like, whatever you please." This now seems a banner under which Ionesco, Brendan Behan, Beckett, and lesser experimentalists might sell their wares. Both prodigious and prodigal in his talents, Saroyan has many plays awaiting the test of production, and there are encouraging signs that off-Broadway producers will bring these works to new audiences. In the 1960's, measured against the darker "Saroyanesque" works of the Theatre of the Absurd, Saroyan may once again become a formidable force in American drama.

# THE TIME OF YOUR LIFE

## CHARACTERS

| | |
|---|---|
| SAILOR | MARY L. |
| SAM | KRUPP |
| THE NEWSBOY | MC CARTHY |
| THE DRUNKARD | KIT CARSON |
| WILLIE | NICK'S MA |
| JOE | YOUNG SAILOR |
| NICK | ELSIE |
| TOM | ANNA, NICK'S DAUGHTER |
| KITTY DUVAL | |
| DUDLEY | KILLER |
| HARRY | HER SIDE KICK |
| WESLEY | A SOCIETY LADY |
| LORENE | A SOCIETY GENTLEMAN |
| BLICK | FIRST COP |
| ARAB | SECOND COP |

THE PLACE *Nick's Pacific Street Saloon, Restaurant, and Entertainment Palace at the foot of Embarcadero, in San Francisco. A suggestion of room 21 at The New York Hotel, upstairs, around the corner.*

THE TIME *Afternoon and night of a day in October, 1939.*

## Act One

*NICK'S is an American place: a San Francisco waterfront honky-tonk.*

*At a table, JOE: always calm, always quiet, always thinking, always eager, always bored, always superior. His expensive clothes are casually and youthfully worn and give him an almost boyish appearance. He is thinking.*

*Behind the bar, NICK: a big red-headed young Italian-American with an enormous naked woman tattooed in red on the inside of his right arm. He is studying* The Racing Form.

*The ARAB, at his place at the end of the bar. He is a lean old man with a rather ferocious old-country mustache, with the ends twisted up. Between the thumb and forefinger of his left hand is the Mohammedan tattoo indicating that he has been to Mecca. He is sipping a glass of beer.*

*It is about eleven-thirty in the morning. SAM is sweeping out. We see only his back. He disappears into the kitchen. The SAILOR at the bar finishes his drink and leaves, moving thoughtfully, as though he were trying very hard to discover how to live.*

*The NEWSBOY comes in.*

NEWSBOY (*Cheerfully*) Good-morning, everybody. (*No answer. To* NICK) Paper, Mister? (NICK *shakes his head, no. The* NEWSBOY *goes to* JOE) Paper, Mister? (JOE *shakes his head, no. The* NEWSBOY *walks away, counting papers*)

JOE (*Noticing him*) How many you got?

NEWSBOY Five. (JOE *gives him a quarter, takes all the papers, glances at the headlines with irritation, throws them away. The* NEWSBOY *watches carefully, then goes*)

ARAB (*Picks up paper, looks at headlines, shakes head as if rejecting everything else a man might say about the world*) No foundation. All the way down the line. (*The* DRUNK *comes in. Walks to the telephone, looks for a nickel in the chute, sits down at* JOE'S *table.* NICK *takes the* DRUNK *out. The* DRUNK *returns*)

DRUNK (*Champion of the Bill of Rights*) This is a free country, ain't it? (WILLIE, *the marble-game maniac, explodes through the swinging doors and lifts the forefinger of his right hand comically, indicating one beer. He is a very young man, not more than twenty. He is wearing heavy shoes, a pair of old and dirty corduroys, a light green turtle-neck jersey with a large letter "F" on the chest, an over-*

*size two-button tweed coat, and a green hat, with the brim up.* NICK *sets out a glass of beer for him, he drinks it, straightens up vigorously, saying "Aaah," makes a solemn face, gives* NICK *a one-finger salute of adieu, and begins to leave, refreshed and restored in spirit. He walks by the marble game, halts suddenly, turns, studies the contraption, gestures as if to say, Oh, no. Turns to go, stops, returns to the machine, studies it, takes a handful of small coins out of his pants pocket, lifts a nickel, indicates with a gesture, One game, no more. Puts the nickel in the slot, pushes in the slide, making an interesting noise*)

NICK You can't beat that machine.

WILLIE Oh, yeah? (*The marbles fall, roll, and take their place. He pushes down the lever, placing one marble in position. Takes a very deep breath, walks in a small circle, excited at the beginning of great drama. Stands straight and pious before the contest. Himself vs. the machine.* WILLIE *vs. Destiny. His skill and daring vs. the cunning and trickery of the novelty industry of America, and the whole challenging world. He is the last of the American pioneers, with nothing more to fight but the machine, with no other reward than lights going on and off, and six nickels for one. Before him is the last champion, the machine. He is the last challenger, the young man with nothing to do in the world.* WILLIE *grips the knob delicately, studies the situation carefully, draws the knob back, holds it a moment, and then releases it. The first marble rolls out among the hazards, and the contest is on. At the very beginning of the play "The Missouri Waltz" is coming from the phonograph. The music ends here. This is the signal for the beginning of the play.* JOE *suddenly comes out of his reverie. He whistles the way people do who are calling a cab that's about a block away, only he does it quietly.* WILLIE *turns around, but* JOE *gestures for him to return to his work.* NICK *looks up from* The Racing Form)

JOE (*Calling*) Tom. (*To himself*) Where the hell is he, every time I need him? (*He looks around calmly: the nickle-in-the-slot phonograph in the corner; the open public telephone; the stage; the marble-game; the bar; and so on. He calls again, this time very loud*) Hey, Tom.

NICK (*With morning irritation*) What do you want?

JOE (*Without thinking*) I want the boy to get me a watermelon, that's what *I* want. What do *you* want? Money, or love, or fame, or what? You won't get them studying *The Racing Form.*

NICK I like to keep abreast of the times. (TOM *comes hurrying in. He is a great big man of about thirty or so who appears to be much younger because of the childlike expression of his face: handsome, dumb, innocent, troubled, and a little bewildered by everything. He is obviously adult in years, but it seems as if by all rights he should still be a boy. He is defensive as clumsy, self-conscious, overgrown boys are. He is wearing a flashy cheap suit.* JOE *leans back and studies him with casual disapproval.* TOM *slackens his pace and becomes clumsy and embarrassed, waiting for the bawling-out he's pretty sure he's going to get*)

JOE (*Objectively, severely, but a little amused*) Who saved your life?

TOM (*Sincerely*) You did, Joe. Thanks.

JOE (*Interested*) How'd I do it?

TOM (*Confused*) What?

JOE (*Even more interested*) How'd I do it?

TOM Joe, you know how you did it.

JOE (*Softly*) I want you to answer me. How'd I save your life? I've forgotten.

TOM (*Remembering, with a big sorrowful smile*) You made me eat all that chicken soup three years ago when I was sick and hungry.

JOE (*Fascinated*) Chicken soup?

TOM (*Eagerly*) Yeah.

JOE Three years? Is it that long?

TOM (*Delighted to have the information*) Yeah, sure. 1937. 1938. 1939. This is 1939, Joe.

JOE (*Amused*) Never mind what year it is. Tell me the whole story.

TOM You took me to the doctor. You gave me money for food and clothes, and paid my room rent. Aw, Joe, you know all the different things you did. (JOE *nods, turning away from* TOM *after each question*)

JOE You in good health now?

TOM Yeah, Joe.

JOE You got clothes?

TOM Yeah, Joe.

JOE You eat three times a day. Sometimes four?

TOM Yeah, Joe. Sometimes five.

JOE You got a place to sleep?

TOM Yeah, Joe. (JOE *nods. Pauses. Studies* TOM *carefully*)

JOE Then, where the hell have you been?

TOM (*Humbly*) Joe, I was out in the street listening to the boys. They're talking about the trouble down here on the waterfront.

JOE (*Sharply*) I want you to be around when I need you.

TOM (*Pleased that the bawling-out is over*) I won't do it again. Joe, one guy out there says there's got to be a revolution before anything will ever be all right.

JOE (*Impatiently*) I know all about it. Now, here. Take this money. Go up to the Emporium. You know where the Emporium is?

TOM Yeah, sure, Joe.

JOE All right. Take the elevator and go up to the fourth floor. Walk around to the back, to the toy department. Buy me a couple of dollars' worth of toys and bring them here.

TOM (*Amazed*) Toys? What kind of toys, Joe?

JOE Any kind of toys. Little ones that I can put on this table.

TOM What do you want toys for, Joe?

JOE (*Mildly angry*) What?

TOM All right, all right. You don't have to get sore at *everything.* What'll people think, a big guy like me buying toys?

JOE *What people?*

TOM Aw, Joe, you're always making me do crazy

things for you, and *I'm* the guy that gets embarrassed. You just sit in this place and make me do all the dirty work.

JOE (*Looking away*) Do what I tell you.

TOM O.K., but I wish I knew why. (*He makes to go.*)

JOE Wait a minute. Here's a nickel. Put it in the phonograph. Number seven. I want to hear that waltz again.

TOM Boy, I'm glad *I* don't have to stay and listen to it. Joe, what do you hear in that song anyway? We listen to that song ten times a day. Why can't we hear number six, or two, or nine? There are a lot of other numbers.

JOE (*Emphatically*) Put the nickel in the phonograph. (*Pause*) Sit down and wait till the music's over. Then go get me some toys.

TOM O.K. O.K.

JOE (*Loudly*) Never mind being a martyr about it either. The cause isn't worth it. (TOM *puts the nickel into the machine, with a ritual of impatient and efficient movement which plainly shows his lack of sympathy or enthusiasm. His manner also reveals, however, that his lack of sympathy is spurious and exaggerated. Actually, he is fascinated by the music, but is so confused by it that he pretends he dislikes it. The music begins. It is another variation of "The Missouri Waltz," played dreamily and softly, with perfect orchestral form, and with a theme of weeping in the horns repeated a number of times. At first* TOM *listens with something close to irritation, since he can't understand what is so attractive in the music to* JOE, *and what is so painful and confusing in it to himself. Very soon, however, he is carried away by the melancholy story of grief and nostalgia of the song. He stands, troubled by the poetry and confusion in himself.* JOE, *on the other hand, listens as if he were not listening, indifferent and unmoved. What he's interested in is* TOM. *He turns and glances at* TOM. KITTY DUVAL, *who lives in a room in The New York Hotel, around the corner, comes beyond the swinging doors quietly, and walks slowly to the bar, her reality and rhythm a perfect accompaniment to the sorrowful American music, which is her music, as it is* TOM'*s, which the world drove out of her, putting in its place brokenness and all manner of spiritually crippled forms. She seems to understand this, and is angry. Angry with herself, full of hate for the poor world, and full of pity and contempt for its tragic, unbelievable, confounded people. She is a small powerful girl, with that kind of delicate and rugged beauty which no circumstance of evil or ugly reality can destroy. This beauty is that element of the immortal which is in the seed of good and common people, and which is kept alive in some of the female of our kind, no matter how accidentally or pointlessly they may have entered the world.* KITTY DUVAL *is somebody. There is an angry purity, and a fierce pride, in her. In her stance, and way of walking, there is grace and arrogance.* JOE *recognizes her as a great person immediately. She goes to the bar*)

KITTY Beer. (NICK *places a glass of beer before her mechanically. She swallows half the drink, and listens to the music again.* TOM *turns and sees her. He becomes dead to everything in the world but her. He stands like a lump, fascinated and undone by his almost religious adoration for her.* JOE *notices* TOM)

JOE (*Gently*) Tom. (TOM *begins to move toward the bar, where* KITTY *is standing. Loudly*) Tom. (TOM *halts, then turns, and* JOE *motions to him to come over to the table.* TOM *goes over. Quietly*) Have you got everything straight?

TOM (*Out of the world*) What?

JOE What do you mean, what? I just gave you some instructions.

TOM (*Pathetically*) What do you want, Joe?

JOE I want you to come to your senses. (*He stands up quietly and knocks* TOM'*s hat off.* TOM *picks up his hat quickly*)

TOM I got it, Joe. I got it. The Emporium. Fourth floor. In the back. The toy department. Two dollars' worth of toys. That you can put on a table.

KITTY (*To herself*) Who the hell is he to push a big man like that around?

JOE I'll expect you back in a half hour. Don't get side-tracked anywhere. Just do what I tell you.

TOM (*Pleading*) Joe? Can't I bet four bits on a horse race? There's a long shot—Precious Time—that's going to win by ten lengths. I got to have money. (JOE *points to the street.* TOM *goes out.* NICK *is combing his hair, looking in the mirror*)

NICK I thought you wanted him to get you a watermelon.

JOE I forgot. (*He watches* KITTY *a moment. To* KITTY, *clearly, slowly, with great compassion*) What's the dream?

KITTY (*Moving to* JOE, *coming to*) What?

JOE (*Holding the dream for her*) What's the dream, *now?*

KITTY (*Coming still closer*) What dream?

JOE What dream! The dream you're dreaming.

NICK Suppose he did bring you a watermelon? What the hell would you do with it?

JOE (*Irritated*) I'd put it on this table. I'd look at it. Then I'd eat it. What do you *think* I'd do with it, sell it for a profit?

NICK How should I know what *you'd* do with *anything?* What I'd like to know is, where do you get your money from? What work do you do?

JOE (*Looking at* KITTY) Bring us a bottle of champagne.

KITTY Champagne?

JOE (*Simply*) Would you rather have something else?

KITTY What's the big idea?

JOE I thought you might like some champagne. I myself am very fond of it.

KITTY Yeah, but what's the big idea? You can't push *me* around.

JOE (*Gently but severely*) It's not in my nature to be unkind to another human being. I have only contempt for wit. Otherwise I might say something obvious, therefore cruel, and perhaps untrue.

KITTY You be careful what you think about me.

JOE (*Slowly, not looking at her*) I have only the noblest thoughts for both your person and your spirit.

NICK (*Having listened carefully and not being able to make it out*) What are you talking about?

KITTY You shut up. You—

JOE He owns this place. He's an important man. All kinds of people come to him looking for work. Comedians. Singers. Dancers.

KITTY I don't care. He can't call me names.

NICK All right, sister. I know how it is with a two-dollar whore in the morning.

KITTY (*Furiously*) Don't you dare call me names. I used to be in burlesque.

NICK If you were ever in burlesque, I used to be Charlie Chaplin.

KITTY (*Angry and a little pathetic*) I *was* in burlesque. I played the burlesque circuit from coast to coast. I've had flowers sent to me by European royalty. I've had dinner with young men of wealth and social position.

NICK You're dreaming.

KITTY (*To* JOE) *I was in burlesque.* Kitty Duval. That was my name. Life-size photographs of me in costume in front of burlesque theaters all over the country.

JOE (*Gently, coaxingly*) I believe you. Have some champagne.

NICK (*Going to table, with champagne bottle and glasses*) There he goes again.

JOE Miss Duval?

KITTY (*Sincerely, going over*) That's not my *real* name. That's my *stage* name.

JOE I'll call you by your stage name.

NICK (*Pouring*) All right, sister, make up your mind. Are you going to have champagne with him, or not?

JOE Pour the lady some wine.

NICK O.K., Professor. Why you come to this joint instead of one of the high-class dumps uptown is more than I can understand. Why don't you have champagne at the St. Francis? Why don't you drink with a lady?

KITTY (*Furiously*) Don't you call me names—you dentist.

JOE Dentist?

NICK (*Amazed, loudly*) What kind of cussing is that? (*Pause. Looking at* KITTY, *then at* JOE, *bewildered*) This guy doesn't belong here. The only reason I've got champagne is because *he* keeps ordering it all the time. (*To* KITTY) Don't think you're the only one he drinks champagne with. He drinks with *all* of them. (*Pause*) He's crazy. Or something.

JOE (*Confidentially*) Nick, I think you're going to be all right in a couple of centuries.

NICK I'm sorry, I don't understand your English. (JOE *lifts his glass.* KITTY *slowly lifts hers, not quite sure of what's going on*)

JOE (*Sincerely*) To the spirit, Kitty Duval.

KITTY (*Beginning to understand, and very grateful, looking at him*) Thank you.

JOE (*Calling*) Nick.

NICK Yeah?

JOE Would you mind putting a nickel in the machine again? Number—

NICK Seven. I know. I know. I don't mind at all, Your Highness, although, personally, I'm not a lover of music. (*Going to the machine*) As a matter of fact I think Tchaikowsky was a dope.

JOE Tchaikowsky? Where'd you ever hear of Tchaikowsky?

NICK He was a dope.

JOE Yeah. Why?

NICK They talked about him on the radio one Sunday morning. He was a sucker. He let a woman drive him crazy.

JOE I see.

NICK I stood behind that bar listening to the God-damn stuff and cried like a baby. *None but the lonely heart!* He was a dope.

JOE What made you cry?

NICK What?

JOE (*Sternly*) What made you cry, Nick?

NICK (*Angry with himself*) I don't know.

JOE I've been underestimating you, Nick. Play number seven.

NICK They get everybody worked up. They give everybody stuff they shouldn't have. (NICK *puts the nickel into the machine and the Waltz begins again. He listens to the music. Then studies* The Racing Form)

KITTY (*To herself, dreaming*) I like champagne, and everything that goes with it. Big houses with big porches, and big rooms with big windows, and big lawns, and big trees, and flowers growing everywhere, and big shepherd dogs sleeping in the shade.

NICK I'm going next door to Frankie's to make a bet. I'll be right back.

JOE Make one for me.

NICK (*Going to* JOE) Who do you like?

JOE (*Giving him money*) Precious Time.

NICK Ten dollars? Across the board?

JOE No. On the nose.

NICK O.K. (*He goes.* DUDLEY R. BOSTWICK, *as he calls himself, breaks through the swinging doors, and practically flings himself upon the open telephone beside the phonograph.* DUDLEY *is a young man of about twenty-four or twenty-five, ordinary and yet extraordinary. He is smallish, as the saying is, neatly dressed in bargain clothes, overworked and irritated by the routine and dullness and monotony of his life, apparently nobody and nothing, but in reality a great personality. The swindled young man. Educated, but without the least real understanding. A brave, dumb, salmon-spirit struggling for life in weary, stupefied flesh, dueling ferociously with a banal mind which has been only irritated by what it has been taught. He is a great personality because, against all these handicaps, what he wants is simple and basic: a woman. This urgent and violent need, common yet miraculous enough in itself, considering the unhappy environment of the animal, is the force which elevates him from nothingness to greatness. A ridiculous greatness, but in the nature of things beautiful to behold. All that he has been taught, and everything he believes, is phony, and yet he himself is real, almost super-real, because of this indestructible force in himself. His face is ridiculous. His personal rhythm is tense and jittery. His speech is shrill and violent. His gestures are wild. His ego is disjointed and epileptic. And yet deeply he possesses the same wholeness of spirit, and directness of energy, that is in all species of animals. There is little innate or cultivated spirit in him, but there is no absence of innocent animal force. He is a young man who has been taught that he has a chance, as a person, and believes it. As a matter of fact, he hasn't a chance in the world, and should have been told by somebody, or should not have had his natural and valuable ignorance spoiled by education, ruining an otherwise perfectly good and charming member of the human race. At the telephone he immediately begins to dial furiously, hesitates, changes his mind, stops dialing, hangs up furiously, and suddenly begins again. Not more than half a minute after the firecracker arrival of* DUDLEY R. BOSTWICK, *occurs the polka-and-waltz arrival of* HARRY. HARRY *is another story. He comes in timidly, turning about uncertainly, awkward, out of place everywhere, embarrassed and encumbered by the contemporary costume, sick at heart, but determined to fit in somewhere. His arrival constitutes a dance. His clothes don't fit. The pants are a little too large. The coat, which doesn't match, is also a little too large, and loose. He is a dumb young fellow, but he has ideas. A philosophy, in fact. His philosophy is simple and beautiful. The world is sorrowful. The world needs laughter.* HARRY *is funny. The world needs* HARRY. HARRY *will make the world laugh. He has probably had a year or two of high school. He has also listened to the boys at the pool room. He's looking for* NICK. *He goes to the* ARAB, *and says, "Are you Nick?" The* ARAB *shakes his head. He stands at the bar, waiting. He waits very busily)*

HARRY (*As* NICK *returns*) You Nick?

NICK (*Very loudly*) *I am Nick.*

HARRY (*Acting*) Can you use a great comedian?

NICK (*Behind the bar*) Who, for instance?

HARRY (*Almost angry*) Me.

NICK You? What's funny about you? (DUDLEY *at the telephone, is dialing. Because of some defect in the apparatus the dialing is very loud*)

DUDLEY Hello. Sunset 7349? May I speak to Miss Elsie Mandelspiegel? (*Pause*)

HARRY (*With spirit and noise, dancing*) I dance and do gags and stuff.

NICK In costume? Or are you wearing your costume?

DUDLEY All I need is a cigar.

KITTY (*Continuing the dream of grace*) I'd walk out of the house, and stand on the porch, and look at the trees, and smell the flowers, and run across the lawn, and lie down under a tree, and read a book. (*Pause*) A book of poems, maybe.

DUDLEY (*Very, very clearly*) Elsie Mandelspiegel. (*Impatiently*) She has a room on the fourth floor. She's a nurse at the Southern Pacific Hospital. Elsie Mandelspiegel. She works at night. Elsie. Yes. (*He begins waiting again.* WESLEY, *a colored boy, comes to the bar and stands near* HARRY, *waiting*)

NICK Beer?

WESLEY No, sir. I'd like to talk to you.

NICK (*To* HARRY) All right. Get funny.

HARRY (*Getting funny, an altogether different person, an actor, with great energy, both in power of voice, and in force and speed of physical gesture*) Now, I'm standing on the corner of Third and Market. I'm looking around. I'm figuring it out. There it is. Right in front of me. The whole city. The whole world. People going by. They're going somewhere. I don't know where, but they're going. I ain't going *anywhere.* Where the hell can you go? I'm figuring it out. All right, I'm a citizen. A fat guy bumps his stomach into the face of an old lady. They were in a hurry. Fat and old. *They bumped.* Boom. I don't know. It may mean war. *War.* Germany. England. Russia. I don't know for sure. (*Loudly, dramatically, he salutes, about faces, presents arms, aims, and fires*) WAAAAAR. (*He blows a call to arms.* NICK *gets sick of this, indicates with a gesture that* HARRY *should hold it, and goes to* WESLEY)

NICK What's on your mind?

WESLEY (*Confused*) Well—

NICK Come on. Speak up. Are you hungry, or what?

WESLEY Honest to God, I ain't hungry. All I want is a job. I don't want no charity.

NICK Well, what can you do, and how good are you?

WESLEY I can run errands, clean up, wash dishes, anything.

DUDLEY (*On the telephone, very eagerly*) Elsie? Elsie, this is Dudley. Elsie, I'll jump in the bay if you don't marry me. Life isn't worth living without you. I can't sleep. I can't think of anything but you. All the time. Day and night and night and day. Elsie, I love you. I love you. What? (*Burning up*) Is this Sunset 7-3-4-9? (*Pause*) 7943? (*Calmly, while* WILLIE *begins making a small racket*) Well, what's *your* name? *Lorene?* Lorene Smith? I thought you were Elsie Mandelspiegel. What? Dudley. Yeah. Dudley R. Bostwick. Yeah. R. It stands for Raoul, but I never spell it out. I'm pleased to meet *you,* too. What? There's a lot of noise around here. (WILLIE *stops hitting the marble-game*) Where am I? At Nick's, on Pacific Street. I work at the S. P.[1] I told them I was sick and they gave me the afternoon off. Wait a minute. I'll ask them. I'd like to meet *you,* too. Sure. I'll ask them. (*Turns around to* NICK) What's this address?

NICK Number 3 Pacific Street, you cad.

DUDLEY Cad? You don't know how I've been suffering on account of Elsie. I take things too ceremoniously. I've got to be more lackadaisical. (*Into telephone*) Hello, Elenore? I mean, Lorene. It's number 3 Pacific Street. Yeah. Sure. I'll wait for you. How'll you know me? You'll *know* me. I'll recognize *you.* Good-by, now. (*He hangs up*)

HARRY (*Continuing his monologue, with gestures, movements, and so on*) I'm standing there. I didn't do

[1] Southern Pacific Railroad.

anything to anybody. Why should *I* be a soldier? (*Sincerely, insanely*) BOOOOOOOOOM. *WAR!* O.K. War. *I* retreat. *I* hate war. I move to Sacramento.

NICK (*Shouting*) All right, Comedian. Lay off a minute.

HARRY (*Broken-hearted, going to* WILLIE) Nobody's got a sense of humor any more. The world's dying for comedy like never before, but nobody knows how to *laugh*.

NICK (*To* WESLEY) Do you belong to the union?

WESLEY What union?

NICK For the love of Mike, where've you been? Don't you know you can't come into a place and ask for a job and get one and go to work, just like that. You've got to belong to one of the unions.

WESLEY I didn't know. I got to have a job. Real soon.

NICK Well, you've got to belong to a union.

WESLEY I don't want any favors. All I want is a chance to earn a living.

NICK Go on into the kitchen and tell Sam to give you some lunch.

WESLEY Honest, I ain't hungry.

DUDLEY (*Shouting*) What I've gone through for Elsie.

HARRY I've got all kinds of funny ideas in my head to help make the world happy again.

NICK (*Holding* WESLEY) No, he isn't hungry. (WESLEY *almost faints from hunger.* NICK *catches him just in time. The* ARAB *and* NICK *go off with* WESLEY *into the kitchen*)

HARRY (*To* WILLIE) See if you think this is funny. It's my own idea. I created this dance myself. It comes after the monologue. (HARRY *begins to dance.* WILLIE *watches a moment, and then goes back to the game. It's a goofy dance, which* HARRY *does with great sorrow, but much energy*)

DUDLEY Elsie. Aw, gee, Elsie. What the hell do I want to see Lorene Smith for? Some girl I don't know. (JOE *and* KITTY *have been drinking in silence. There is no sound now except the softshoe shuffling of* HARRY, *the Comedian*)

JOE What's the dream now, Kitty Duval?

KITTY (*Dreaming the words and pictures*) I dream of home. Christ, I always dream of home. I've no *home*. I've no place. But I always dream of all of us together again. We had a farm in Ohio. There was nothing good about it. It was always sad. There was always trouble. But I always dream about it as if I could go back and Papa would be there and Mamma and Louie and my little brother Stephen and my sister Mary. I'm Polish. Duval! My name isn't Duval, it's Koranovsky. Katerina Koranovsky. We lost everything. The house, the farm, the trees, the horses, the cows, the chickens. Papa died. He was old. He was thirteen years older than Mamma. We moved to Chicago. We tried to work. We tried to stay together. Louie got in trouble. The fellows he was with killed him for something. I don't know what. Stephen ran away from home. Seventeen years old. I don't know where he is. Then Mamma died. (*Pause*) What's the dream? I dream of home. (NICK *comes out of the kitchen with* WESLEY)

NICK Here. Sit down here and rest. That'll hold you for a *while*. Why didn't you tell me you were hungry? You all right now?

WESLEY (*Sitting down in the chair at the piano*) Yes, I am. Thank you. I didn't know I was *that* hungry.

NICK Fine. (*To* HARRY *who is dancing.*) Hey. What the hell do you think you're doing?

HARRY (*Stopping*) That's my own idea. I'm a natural-born dancer and comedian. (WESLEY *begins slowly, one note, one chord at a time, to play the piano*)

NICK You're no good. Why don't you try some other kind of work? Why don't you get a job in a store, selling something? What do you want to be a comedian for?

HARRY I've got something for the world and they haven't got sense enough to let me give it to them. Nobody knows me.

DUDLEY *Elsie*. Now I'm waiting for some dame I've never seen before. Lorene Smith. Never saw her in my life. Just happened to get the wrong number. She turns on the personality, and I'm a cooked Indian. Give me a beer, please.

HARRY Nick, you've got to see my act. It's the greatest thing of its kind in America. All I want is a chance. No salary to begin. Let me try it out tonight. If I don't wow 'em, O.K., I'll go home. If vaudeville wasn't dead, a guy like me would have a chance.

NICK You're not funny. You're a sad young punk. What the hell do you want to try to be funny for? You'll break everybody's heart. What's there for you to be funny about? You've been poor all your life, haven't you?

HARRY I've been poor all right, but don't forget that some things count more than some other things.

NICK What counts more, for instance, than what else, for instance?

HARRY Talent, for instance, counts more than money, for instance, that's what, and I've got talent. I get new ideas night and day. Everything comes natural to me. I've got style, but it'll take me a little time to round it out. That's all. (*By now* WESLEY *is playing something of his own which is very good and out of the world. He plays about half a minute, after which* HARRY *begins to dance*)

NICK (*Watching*) I run the lousiest dive in Frisco, and a guy arrives and makes me stock up with champagne. The whores come in and holler at me that they're ladies. Talent comes in and begs me for a chance to show itself. Even society people come here once in a while. I don't know what for. Maybe it's liquor. Maybe it's the location. Maybe it's my personality. Maybe it's the crazy personality of the joint. The old honky-tonk. (*Pause*) Maybe they can't feel at home anywhere else. (*By now* WESLEY *is really playing, and* HARRY *is going through a new routine.* DUDLEY *grows sadder and sadder*)

KITTY Please dance with me.

JOE (*Loudly*) I never learned to dance.

KITTY Anybody can dance. Just hold me in your arms.

JOE I'm very fond of you. I'm *sorry*. I *can't* dance. I wish to God I could.

KITTY Oh, please.

JOE Forgive me. I'd like to very much. (KITTY *dances alone.* TOM *comes in with a package. He sees* KITTY *and goes ga-ga again. He comes out of the trance and puts the bundle on the table in front of* JOE)

JOE (*Taking the package*) What'd you get?

TOM Two dollars' worth of toys. That's what you sent me for. The girl asked me what I wanted with toys. I didn't know what to tell her. (*He stares at* KITTY, *then back at* JOE) Joe? I've got to have some money. After all you've done for me, I'll do anything in the world for you, but, Joe, you got to give me some money once in a while.

JOE What do you want it for? (TOM *turns and stares at* KITTY *dancing*)

JOE (*Noticing*) Sure. Here. Here's five. (*Shouting*) Can you dance?

TOM (*Proudly*) I got second prize at the Palomar in Sacramento five years ago.

JOE (*Loudly, opening package*) O.K., dance with her.

TOM You mean *her?*

JOE (*Loudly*) I mean Kitty Duval, the burlesque queen. I mean the queen of the world burlesque. Dance with her. She wants to dance.

TOM (*Worshiping the name Kitty Duval, helplessly*) Joe, can I tell you something?

JOE (*He brings out a toy and winds it*) You don't have to. I know. You love her. You *really* love her. I'm not blind. I know. But take care of yourself. Don't get sick that way again.

NICK (*Looking at and listening to* WESLEY *with amazement*) Comes in here and wants to be a dishwasher. Faints from hunger. And then sits down and plays better than Heifetz.

JOE Heifetz plays the violin.

NICK All right, don't get careful. He's good, ain't he?

TOM (*To* KITTY) Kitty.

JOE (*He lets the toy go, loudly*) Don't *talk*. Just *dance.* (TOM *and* KITTY *dance.* NICK *is at the bar, watching everything.* HARRY *is dancing.* DUDLEY *is grieving into his beer.* LORENE SMITH, *about thirty-seven, very overbearing and funny-looking, comes to the bar*)

NICK What'll it be, lady?

LORENE (*Looking about and scaring all the young men*) I'm looking for the young man I talked to on the telephone. Dudley R. Bostwick.

DUDLEY (*Jumping, running to her, stopping, shocked*) Dudley R. (*Slowly*) Bostwick? Oh, yeah. He left here ten minutes ago. You mean Dudley Bostwick, that poor man on crutches?

LORENE Crutches?

DUDLEY Yeah. Dudley Bostwick. That's what he *said* his name was. He said to tell you not to wait.

LORENE Well. (*She begins to go, turns around*) Are you sure *you're* not Dudley Bostwick?

DUDLEY Who—me? (*Grandly*) My name is Roger Tenefrancia. I'm a French-Canadian. I never saw the poor fellow before.

LORENE It seems to me your voice is like the voice I heard over the telephone.

DUDLEY A coincidence. An accident. A quirk of fate. One of those things. Dismiss the thought. That poor cripple hobbled out of here ten minutes ago.

LORENE He said he was going to commit suicide. I only wanted to be of help. (*She goes*)

DUDLEY Be of help? What kind of help could she be of? (DUDLEY *runs to the telephone in the corner*) Gee whiz, Elsie. Gee whiz. I'll never leave you again. (*He turns the pages of a little address book*) Why do I always forget the number? I've tried to get her on the phone a hundred times this week and I still forget the number. She won't come to the phone, but I keep trying anyway. She's out. She's not in. She's working. I get the wrong number. Everything goes haywire. I can't sleep. (*Defiantly*) She'll come to the phone one of these days. If there's anything to true love at all, she'll come to the phone. Sunset 7349. (*He dials the number, as* JOE *goes on studying the toys. They are one big mechanical toy, whistles, and a music box.* JOE *blows into the whistle, quickly, by way of getting casually acquainted with them.* TOM *and* KITTY *stop dancing.* TOM *stares at her*)

DUDLEY Hello. Is this Sunset 7349? May I speak to Elsie? Yes. (*Emphatically, and bitterly*) No, this is *not* Dudley Bostwick. This is Roger Tenefrancia of Montreal, Canada. I'm a childhood friend of Miss Mandelspiegel. We went to kindergarten together. (*Hand over phone*) God damn it. (*Into phone*) Yes. I'll wait, thank you.

TOM I love you.

KITTY You want to go to my room? (TOM *can't answer*) Have you got two dollars?

TOM (*Shaking his head with confusion*) I've got *five* dollars, but I *love* you.

KITTY (*Looking at him*) You want to spend *all* that money? (TOM *embraces her. They go.* JOE *watches. Goes back to the toy*)

JOE Where's the longshoreman, McCarthy?

NICK He'll be around.

JOE What do you think he'll have to say today?

NICK Plenty, as usual. I'm going next door to see who won that third race at Laurel.

JOE Precious Time won it.

NICK That's what you think. (*He goes*)

JOE (*To himself*) A horse named McCarthy is running the sixth race today.

DUDLEY (*On the phone*) Hello. Hello, Elsie? Elsie? (*His voice weakens; also his limbs*) My God. She's come to the phone. Elsie, I'm at Nick's on Pacific Street. You've got to come here and talk to me. Hello. Hello, Elsie? (*Amazed*) Did she hang up? Or was I disconnected? (*He hangs up and goes to bar.* WESLEY *is still playing the piano.* HARRY *is still dancing.* JOE *has wound up the big mechanical toy and is watching it work.* NICK *returns*)

NICK (*Watching the toy*) Say. That's some gadget.

JOE How much did I win?

NICK How do you know you *won?*

JOE Don't be silly. He said Precious Time was going to win by ten lengths, didn't he? He's in love, isn't he?

NICK O.K. I don't know why, but Precious Time won. You got eighty for ten. How do you do it?

JOE (*Roaring*) Faith. Faith. How'd he win?

NICK By a nose. Look him up in *The Racing Form*. The slowest, the cheapest, the worst horse in the race, and the worst jockey. What's the matter with my luck?

JOE How much did you lose?

NICK Fifty cents.

JOE You should never gamble.

NICK Why not?

JOE You always bet fifty cents. You've got no more faith than a flea, that's why.

HARRY (*Shouting*) How do you like this, Nick? (*He is really busy now, all legs and arms*)

NICK (*Turning and watching*) Not bad. Hang around. You can wait table. (*To* WESLEY) Hey. Wesley. Can you play that again tonight?

WESLEY (*Turning, but still playing the piano*) I don't know for sure, Mr. Nick. I can play *something*.

NICK Good. *You* hang around, too. (*He goes behind the bar. The atmosphere is now one of warm, natural, American ease; every man innocent and good; each doing what he believes he should do, or what he must do. There is deep American naïveté and faith in the behavior of each person. No one is competing with anyone else. No one hates anyone else. Every man is living, and letting live. Each man is following his destiny as he feels it should be followed; or is abandoning it as he feels it must, by now, be abandoned; or is forgetting it for the moment as he feels he should forget it. Although everyone is dead serious, there is unmistakable smiling and humor in the scene; a sense of the human body and spirit emerging from the world-imposed state of stress and fretfulness, fear and awkwardness, to the more natural state of casualness and grace. Each person belongs to the environment, in his own person, as himself:* WESLEY *is playing better than ever.* HARRY *is hoofing better than ever.* NICK *is behind the bar shining glasses.* JOE *is smiling at the toy and studying it.* DUDLEY, *although still troubled is at least calm now and full of melancholy poise.* WILLIE, *at the marble game is happy. The* ARAB *is deep in his memories, where he wants to be. Into this scene and atmosphere comes* BLICK. BLICK *is the sort of human being you dislike at sight. He is no different from anybody else physically. His face is an ordinary face. There is nothing obviously wrong with him, and yet you know that it is impossible, even by the most generous expansion of understanding, to accept him as a human being. He is the strong man without strength—strong only among the weak—the weakling who uses force on the weaker.* BLICK *enters casually, as if he were a customer, and immediately* HARRY *begins slowing down*)

BLICK (*Oily, and with mock-friendliness*) Hello, Nick.

NICK (*Stopping his work and leaning across the bar*) What do you want to come here for? You're too big a man for a little honky-tonk.

BLICK (*Flattered*) Now, Nick.

NICK Important people never come here. *Here*. Have a drink. (*Whiskey bottle*)

BLICK Thanks, I don't drink.

NICK (*Drinking the drink himself*) Well, why don't you?

BLICK I have responsibilities.

NICK You're head of the lousy Vice Squad. There's no vice here.

BLICK (*Sharply*) Street-walkers are working out of this place.

NICK (*Angry*) What do you want?

BLICK (*Loudly*) I just want you to know that it's got to *stop*. (*The music stops. The mechanical toy runs down. There is absolute silence, and a strange fearfulness and disharmony in the atmosphere now.* HARRY *doesn't know what to do with his hands or feet.* WESLEY*'s arms hang at his sides.* JOE *quietly pushes the toy to one side of the table, eager to study what is happening.* WILLIE *stops playing the marble-game, turns around and begins to wait.* DUDLEY *straightens up very, very vigorously, as if to say: "Nothing can scare me. I know love is the only thing." The* ARAB *is the same as ever, but watchful.* NICK *is arrogantly aloof. There is a moment of this silence and tensions, as though* BLICK *were waiting for everybody to acknowledge his presence. He is obviously flattered by the acknowledgment of* HARRY, DUDLEY, WESLEY, *and* WILLIE, *but a little irritated by* NICK*'s aloofness and unfriendliness*)

NICK Don't look at me. I can't tell a street-walker from a lady. You married?

BLICK You're not asking *me* questions. *I'm* telling *you*.

NICK (*Interrupting*) You're a man of about forty-five or so. You *ought* to know better.

BLICK (*Angry*) Street-walkers are working out of this place.

NICK (*Beginning to shout*) Now, don't start any trouble with me. People come here to drink and loaf around. I don't care who they are.

BLICK Well, I do.

NICK The only way to find out if a lady is a street-walker is to walk the streets with her, go to bed, and make sure. You wouldn't want to do that. *You'd* like to, of course.

BLICK Any more of it, and I'll have your joint closed.

NICK (*Very casually, without ill-will*) Listen. I've got no use for you, or anybody like you. You're out to change the world from something bad to something worse. Something like yourself.

BLICK (*Furious pause, and contempt*) I'll be back tonight. (*He begins to go*)

NICK (*Very angry but very calm*) Do yourself a big favor and don't come back tonight. Send somebody else. I don't like your personality.

BLICK (*Casually, but with contempt*) Don't break any laws. I don't like yours, either. (*He looks the place *over, and goes. There is a moment of silence. Then* WILLIE *turns and puts a new nickel in the slot and starts a new game.* WESLEY *turns to the piano and rather falteringly begins to play. His heart really isn't in it.* HARRY *walks about, unable to dance.* DUDLEY *lapses into his customary melancholy, at a table.* NICK *whistles a little: suddenly stops.* JOE *winds the toy)*

JOE (*Comically*) Nick. You going to kill that man?

NICK I'm disgusted.

JOE Yeah? Why?

NICK Why should I get worked up over a guy like that? Why should I hate *him?* He's nothing. He's nobody. He's a mouse. But every time he comes into this place I get burned up. He doesn't want to drink. He doesn't want to sit down. He doesn't want to take things easy. Tell me one thing?

JOE Do my best.

NICK What's a punk like *that* want to go out and try to change the world for?

JOE (*Amazed*) Does *he* want to change the world, too?

NICK (*Irritated*) You know what I mean. What's he want to bother people for? He's *sick.*

JOE (*Almost to himself, reflecting on the fact that* BLICK *too wants to change the world*) I guess he wants to change the world at that.

NICK So I go to work and hate him.

JOE It's not him, Nick. It's everything.

NICK Yeah, *I know.* But I've still got no use for him. He's no good. You know what I mean? He hurts little people. (*Confused*) One of the girls tried to commit suicide on account of him. (*Furiously*) I'll break his head if he hurts anybody around here. This is *my* joint. (*Afterthought*) Or anybody's *feelings,* either.

JOE He may not be so bad, deep down underneath.

NICK I know all about him. He's no good. (*During this talk* WESLEY *has really begun to play the piano, the toy is rattling again, and little by little* HARRY *has begun to dance.* NICK *has come around the bar, and now, very much like a child—forgetting all his anger—is watching the toy work. He begins to smile at everything: turns and listens to* WESLEY: *watches* HARRY: *nods at the* ARAB: *shakes his head at* DUDLEY: *and gestures amiably about* WILLIE. *It's his joint all right. It's a good, low-down, honky-tonk American place that lets people alone*)

NICK I've got a good joint. There's nothing wrong here. Hey. Comedian. Stick to the dancing tonight. I think you're O.K. Wesley? Do some more of that tonight. That's fine.

HARRY Thanks, Nick. Gosh, I'm on my way at last. (*On telephone*) Hello, Ma? Is that you, Ma? Harry. I got the job. (*He hangs up and walks around, smiling*)

NICK (*Watching the toy all this time*) Say, that really is something. What is that, anyway? (MARY L. *comes in*)

JOE (*Holding it toward* NICK, *and* MARY L.) Nick, this is a toy. A contraption devised by the cunning of man to drive boredom, or grief, or anger out of children. A noble gadget. A gadget, I might say, infinitely nobler than any other I can think of at the moment. (*Everybody gathers around* JOE'S *table to look at the toy. The toy stops working.* JOE *winds the music box. Lifts a whistle: blows it, making a very strange, funny, and sorrowful sound*) Delightful. Tragic, but delightful. (WESLEY *plays the music-box theme on the piano.* MARY L. *takes a table*)

NICK Joe. That girl, Kitty. What's she mean, calling me a dentist? I wouldn't hurt anybody, let alone a tooth. (NICK *goes to* MARY L.'s *table.* HARRY *imitates the toy. Dances. The piano music comes up, the light dims slowly, while the piano solo continues*)

# Act Two

*An hour later. All the people who were at* NICK'S *when the curtain came down are still there.* JOE *at his table, quietly shuffling and turning a deck of cards, and at the same time watching the face of the* WOMAN, *and looking at the initials on her handbag, as though they were the symbols of the lost glory of the world. The woman, in turn, very casually regards* JOE *occasionally. Or rather senses him; has sensed him in fact the whole hour. She is mildly tight on beer, and* JOE *himself is tight, but is always completely under control; simply sharper. The others are about, at tables, and so on.*

JOE Is it Madge—Laubowitz?

MARY Is what *what?*

JOE Is the name Mabel Lepescu?

MARY What name?

JOE The name the initials M. L. stand for. The initials on your bag.

MARY No.

JOE (*After a long pause, thinking deeply what the name might be, turning a card, looking into the beautiful face of the woman*) Margie Longworthy?

MARY (*All this is very natural and sincere, no comedy on the part of the people involved: they are both solemn, being drunk*) No.

JOE (*His voice higher-pitched, as though he were growing a little alarmed*) Midge Laurie? (MARY *shakes her head*) My initials are J. T.

MARY (*Pause*) John?

JOE No. (*Pause*) Martha Lancaster?

MARY No. (*Slight pause*) Joseph?

JOE Well, not exactly. That's my first name, but everybody calls me Joe. The last name is the tough one. I'll help you a little. I'm Irish. (*Pause*) Is it just plain Mary?

MARY Yes, it is. I'm Irish, too. At least on my father's side. English on my mother's side.

JOE I'm Irish on both sides. Mary's one of my favorite names. I guess that's why I didn't think of it. I met a girl in Mexico City named Mary once. She was an American from Philadelphia. She got married there. In Mexico City, I mean. While I was *there*. We were in love, too. At least *I* was. You never know about anyone else. They were engaged, you see, and her mother was with her, so they went through with it. Must have been six or seven years ago. She's probably got three or four children by this time.

MARY Are you still in love with her?

JOE Well—no. To tell you the truth, I'm not sure. I guess I am. I didn't even know she was engaged until a couple of days before they got married. I thought *I* was going to marry her. I kept thinking all the time about the kind of kids we would be likely to have. My favorite was the third one. The first two were fine. Handsome and fine and intelligent, but that third one was different. Dumb and goofy-looking. I liked *him* a lot. When she told me she was going to be married, I didn't feel so bad about the first two, it was that dumb one.

MARY (*After a pause of some few seconds*) What do you do?

JOE Do? To tell you the truth, nothing.

MARY Do you always drink a great deal?

JOE (*Scientifically*) Not *always*. Only when I'm awake. I sleep seven or eight hours every night, you know.

MARY How nice. I mean to drink when you're awake.

JOE (*Thoughtfully*) It's a privilege.

MARY Do you really *like* to drink?

JOE (*Positively*) As much as I like to *breathe*.

MARY (*Beautifully*) Why?

JOE (*Dramatically*) Why do I like to drink? (*Pause*) Because I don't like to be gypped. Because I don't like to be dead most of the time and just a little alive every once in a long while. (*Pause*) If I don't drink, I become fascinated by unimportant things—like everybody else. I get busy. Do things. All kinds of little stupid things, for all kinds of little stupid reasons. Proud, selfish, *ordinary* things. I've done them. Now I don't do anything. *I live all the time.* Then I go to sleep. (*Pause*)

MARY Do you sleep well?

JOE (*Taking it for granted*) Of course.

MARY (*Quietly, almost with tenderness*) What are your plans?

JOE (*Loudly, but also tenderly*) Plans? I haven't *got* any. *I just get up.*

MARY (*Beginning to understand everything*) Oh, yes. Yes, of course. (DUDLEY *puts a nickel in the phonograph*)

JOE (*Thoughtfully*) Why do I drink? (*Pause, while he thinks about it. The thinking appears to be profound and complex, and has the effect of giving his face a very comical and naïve expression*) That question calls for a pretty complicated answer. (*He smiles abstractly*)

MARY Oh, I didn't mean—

JOE (*Swiftly, gallantly*) No. No. *I insist*. I *know* why. It's just a matter of finding words. Little ones.

MARY It really doesn't matter.

JOE (*Seriously*) Oh, yes, it does. (*Clinically*) Now, why do I drink? (*Scientifically*) No. Why does *anybody* drink? (*Working it out*) Every day has twenty-four hours.

MARY (*Sadly, but brightly*) Yes, that's true.

JOE Twenty-four hours. Out of the twenty-four hours at *least* twenty-three and a half are—my God, I don't know why—dull, dead, boring, empty, and murderous. Minutes on the clock, *not time of living*. It doesn't make any difference who you are or what you do, twenty-three and a half hours of the twenty-four are spent *waiting*.

MARY Waiting?

JOE (*Gesturing, loudly*) And the more you wait, the less there is to wait *for*.

MARY (*Attentively, beautifully his student*) Oh?

JOE (*Continuing*) That goes on for days and days, and weeks and months and years, and years, and the first thing you know *all* the years are dead. All the minutes are dead. You yourself are dead. There's nothing to wait for any more. Nothing except *minutes* on the *clock*. No time of life. Nothing but minutes, and idiocy. Beautiful, bright, intelligent idiocy. (*Pause*) Does that answer your question?

MARY (*Earnestly*) I'm afraid it does. Thank you. You shouldn't have gone to all the trouble.

JOE No trouble at all. (*Pause*) You have children?

MARY Yes. Two. A son and a daughter.

JOE (*Delighted*) How swell. Do they look like you?

MARY Yes.

JOE Then why are you sad?

MARY I was always sad. It's just that after I was married I was allowed to drink.

JOE (*Eagerly*) Who are you waiting for?

MARY No one.

JOE (*Smiling*) I'm not waiting for anybody, either.

MARY My husband, of course.

JOE Oh, sure.

MARY He's a lawyer.

JOE (*Standing, leaning on the table*) He's a great guy. I like him. I'm very fond of him.

MARY (*Listening*) You have responsibilities?

JOE (*Loudly*) *One*, and *thousands*. As a matter of fact, I feel responsible to everybody. At least to everybody I meet. I've been trying for three years to find out if it's possible to live what I think is a civilized life. I mean a life that can't hurt any other life.

MARY You're famous?

JOE Very. Utterly unknown, but very famous. Would you like to dance?

MARY All right.

JOE (*Loudly*) I'm *sorry*. I don't dance. I didn't think you'd like to.

MARY To tell you the truth, I don't like to dance at all.

JOE (*Proudly—commentator*) I can hardly walk.

MARY You mean you're tight?

JOE (*Smiling*) No. I mean *all* the time.

MARY (*Looking at him closely*) Were you ever in Paris?

JOE In 1929, and again in 1934.

MARY What month of 1934?

JOE Most of April, all of May, and a little of June.

MARY I was there in November and December that year.

JOE We were there almost at the same time. You were married?

MARY Engaged. (*They are silent a moment, looking at one another. Quietly and with great charm*) Are you *really* in love with me?

JOE Yes.

MARY Is it the champagne?

JOE Yes. Partly, at least. (*He sits down*)

MARY If you don't see me again, will you be very unhappy?

JOE Very.

MARY (*Getting up*) I'm so pleased. (JOE *is deeply grieved that she is going. In fact, he is almost panic-stricken about it, getting up in a way that is full of furious sorrow and regret*) I must go now. Please don't get up. (JOE *is up, staring at her with amazement*) Good-by.

JOE (*Simply*) Good-by. (*The woman stands looking at him a moment, then turns and goes.* JOE *stands staring after her for a long time. Just as he is slowly sitting down again, the* NEWSBOY *enters, and goes to* JOE'S *table*)

NEWSBOY Paper, Mister?

JOE How many you got this time?

NEWSBOY Eleven. (JOE *buys them all, looks at the lousy headlines, throws them away. The* NEWSBOY *looks at* JOE, *amazed. He walks over to* NICK *at the bar*)

NEWSBOY (*Troubled*) Hey, Mister, do you own this place?

NICK (*Casually but emphatically*) I own this place.

NEWSBOY Can you use a great lyric tenor?

NICK (*Almost to himself*) Great lyric tenor? (*Loudly*) Who?

NEWSBOY (*Loud and the least bit angry*) Me. I'm getting too big to sell papers. I don't want to holler headlines all the time. I want to *sing*. You can use a great lyric tenor, can't you?

NICK What's lyric about you?

NEWSBOY (*Voice high-pitched, confused*) My voice.

NICK Oh. (*Slight pause, giving in*) All right, then—sing! (*The* NEWSBOY *breaks into swift and beautiful song: "When Irish Eyes Are Smiling."* NICK *and* JOE *listen carefully:* NICK *with wonder,* JOE *with amazement and delight*)

NEWSBOY (*Singing*)

When Irish eyes are smiling,
Sure 'tis like a morn in Spring.
In the lilt of Irish laughter,
You can hear the angels sing.
When Irish hearts are happy,
All the world seems bright and gay.
But when Irish eyes are smiling—

NICK (*Loudly, swiftly*) Are you Irish?

NEWSBOY (*Speaking swiftly, loudly, a little impatient with the irrelevant question*) No. I'm Greek. (*He finishes the song, singing louder than ever*) Sure they steal your heart away. (*He turns to* NICK *dramatically, like a vaudeville singer begging his audience for applause.* NICK *studies the* BOY *eagerly.* JOE *gets to his feet and leans toward the* BOY *and* NICK)

NICK Not bad. Let me hear you again about a year from now.

NEWSBOY (*Thrilled*) Honest?

NICK Yeah. Along about November 7th, 1940.

NEWSBOY (*Happier than ever before in his life, running over to* JOE) Did you hear it too, Mister?

JOE Yes, and it's great. What part of Greece?

NEWSBOY Salonica. Gosh, Mister. Thanks.

JOE Don't wait a year. Come back with some papers a little later. You're a great singer.

NEWSBOY (*Thrilled and excited*) Aw, thanks, Mister. So long. (*Running, to* NICK) Thanks, Mister. (*He runs out.* JOE *and* NICK *look at the swinging doors.* JOE *sits down.* NICK *laughs*)

NICK Joe, people are so wonderful. Look at that kid.

JOE Of course they're wonderful. Every one of them is wonderful. (MC CARTHY *and* KRUPP *come in, talking.* MC CARTHY *is a big man in work clothes, which make him seem very young. He is wearing black jeans, and a blue workman's shirt. No tie. No hat. He has broad shoulders, a lean intelligent face, thick black hair. In his right back pocket is the longshoreman's book. His arms are long and hairy. His sleeves are rolled up to just below his elbows. He is a casual man, easy-going in movement, sharp in perception, swift in appreciation of charm or innocence or comedy, and gentle in spirit. His speech is clear and full of warmth. His voice is powerful, but modulated. He enjoys the world, in spite of the mess it is, and he is fond of people, in spite of the mess they are.* KRUPP *is not quite as tall or broad-shouldered as* MC CARTHY. *He is physically encumbered by his uniform, club, pistol, belt, and cap. And he is plainly not at home in the role of policeman. His movement is stiff and unintentionally pompous. He is a naïve man, essentially good. His understanding is less than* MC CARTHY'S, *but he is honest and he doesn't try to bluff*)

KRUPP You don't understand what I mean. Hi-ya, Joe.

JOE Hello, Krupp.

MC CARTHY Hi-ya, Joe.

JOE Hello, McCarthy.

KRUPP Two beers, Nick. (*To* MC CARTHY) All I do is carry out orders, carry out orders. I don't know what the idea is behind the order. Who it's for, or who it's against, or why. All I do is carry it out. (NICK *gives them beer*)

MC CARTHY You don't read enough.

KRUPP I do read. I read *The Examiner* every morning. *The Call-Bulletin* every night.

MC CARTHY And carry out orders. What are the orders now?

KRUPP To keep the peace down here on the waterfront.

MC CARTHY Keep it for who? (*To* JOE) Right?

JOE (*Sorrowfully*) Right.

KRUPP How do I know for who? The peace. Just keep it.

MC CARTHY It's got to be kept for somebody. Who would you suspect it's kept for?

KRUPP For citizens!

MC CARTHY I'm a citizen!

KRUPP All right, I'm keeping it for you.

MC CARTHY By hitting me over the head with a club? (*To* JOE) Right?

JOE (*Melancholy, with remembrance*) I don't know.

KRUPP Mac, you know I never hit you over the head with a club.

MC CARTHY But you will if you're on duty at the time and happen to stand on the opposite side of myself, on duty.

KRUPP We went to Mission High together. We were always good friends. The only time we ever fought was that time over Alma Haggerty. Did *you* marry Alma Haggerty? (*To* JOE) Right?

JOE Everything's right.

MC CARTHY No. Did you? (*To* JOE) Joe, are you with me or against me?

JOE I'm with everybody. One at a time.

KRUPP No. And that's just what I mean.

MC CARTHY You mean neither one of us is going to marry the thing we're fighting for?

KRUPP *I don't even know what it is.*

MC CARTHY You don't read enough, I tell you.

KRUPP Mac, you don't know what you're fighting for, either.

MC CARTHY It's so simple, it's fantastic.

KRUPP All right, what are you fighting for?

MC CARTHY For the rights of the inferior. Right?

JOE Something like that.

KRUPP The who?

MC CARTHY The inferior. The world is full of Mahoneys who haven't got what it takes to make monkeys out of everybody else, near by. The men who were created equal. Remember?

KRUPP Mac, you're not inferior.

MC CARTHY I'm a longshoreman. And an idealist. I'm a man with too much brawn to be an intellectual, exclusively. I married a small, sensitive, cultured woman so that my kids would be sissies instead of suckers. A strong man with any sensibility has no choice in this world but to be a heel, or a *worker*. I haven't the heart to be a heel, so I'm a worker. I've got a son in high school who's already thinking of being a writer.

KRUPP I wanted to be a writer once.

JOE Wonderful. (*He puts down the paper, looks at* KRUPP *and* MC CARTHY)

MC CARTHY They *all* wanted to be writers. Every maniac in the world that ever brought about the murder of people through war started out in an attic or a basement writing poetry. It stank. So they got even by becoming important heels. And it's still going on.

KRUPP Is it really, Joe?

JOE Look at today's paper.

MC CARTHY Right now on Telegraph Hill is some punk who is trying to be Shakespeare. Ten years from now he'll be a senator. Or a communist.

KRUPP Somebody ought to do something about it.

MC CARTHY (*Mischievously, with laughter in his voice*) The thing to do is to have more magazines. Hundreds of them. *Thousands.* Print everything they write, so they'll believe they're immortal. That way keep them from going haywire.

KRUPP Mac, you ought to be a writer yourself.

MC CARTHY I hate the tribe. They're mischief-makers. Right?

JOE (*Swiftly*) Everything's right. Right and wrong.

KRUPP Then why do you read?

MC CARTHY (*Laughing*) It's relaxing. It's soothing. (*Pause*) The lousiest people born into the world are writers. Language is all right. It's the people who use language that are lousy. (*The* ARAB *has moved a little closer, and is listening carefully. To the* ARAB) What do you think, Brother?

ARAB (*After making many faces, thinking very deeply*) No foundation. All the way down the line. What. What-not. Nothing. I go walk and look at sky. (*He goes*)

KRUPP What? What-not? (*To* JOE) What's that mean?

JOE (*Slowly, thinking, remembering*) What? What-not? That means this side, that side. Inhale, exhale. What: birth. What-not: death. The inevitable, the astounding, the magnificent seed of growth and decay in all things. Beginning, and end. That man, in his own way, is a prophet. He is one who, with the help of *beer,* is able to reach that state of deep understanding in which what and what-not, the reasonable and the unreasonable, are *one.*

MC CARTHY Right.

KRUPP If you can understand that kind of talk, how can you be a longshoreman?

MC CARTHY I come from a long line of McCarthys who never married or slept with anything but the most powerful and quarrelsome flesh. (*He drinks beer*)

KRUPP I could listen to you two guys for hours, but I'll be damned if I know what the hell you're talking about.

MC CARTHY The consequence is that all the McCarthys are too great and too strong to be heroes. Only the weak and unsure perform the heroic. They've *got* to. The more heroes you have, the worse the history of the world becomes. Right?

JOE Go outside and look at it.

KRUPP You sure can philos-philosoph—Boy, you can talk.

MC CARTHY I wouldn't talk this way to anyone but a man in uniform, and a man who couldn't understand a word of what I was saying. The party I'm speaking of, my friend, is *YOU.* (*The phone rings.* HARRY *gets up from his table suddenly and begins a new dance*)

KRUPP (*Noticing him, with great authority*) Here. Here. What do you think you're doing?

HARRY (*Stopping*) I just got an idea for a new dance. I'm trying it out. Nick. Nick, the phone's ringing.

KRUPP (*To* MC CARTHY) Has he got a right to do that?

MC CARTHY The living have danced from the beginning of time. I might even say, the dance and the life have moved along together, until now we have—(*To* HARRY) Go into your dance, son, and show us what we have.

HARRY I haven't got it worked out *completely* yet, but it starts out like this. (*He dances*)

NICK (*On phone*) Nick's Pacific Street Restaurant, Saloon, and Entertainment Palace. Good afternoon. Nick speaking. (*Listens*) Who? (*Turns around*) Is there a Dudley Bostwick in the joint? (DUDLEY *jumps to his feet and goes to phone*)

DUDLEY (*On phone*) Hello. Elsie? (*Listens*) You're coming down? (*Elated. To the saloon*) She's coming down. (*Pause*) No. I won't drink. Aw, gosh, Elsie. (*He hangs up, looks about him strangely, as if he were just born, walks around touching things, putting chairs in place, and so on*)

MC CARTHY (*To* HARRY) Splendid. Splendid.

HARRY Then I go into this little routine. (*He demonstrates*)

KRUPP Is that good, Mac?

MC CARTHY It's awful, but it's honest and ambitious, like everything else in this great country.

HARRY Then I work along into this. (*He demonstrates*) And *this* is where I *really* get going. (*He finishes the dance*)

MC CARTHY Excellent. A most satisfying demonstration of the present state of the American body and soul. Son, you're a genius.

HARRY (*Delighted, shaking hands with* MC CARTHY) I go on in front of an audience for the first time in my life tonight.

MC CARTHY They'll be delighted. Where'd you learn to dance?

HARRY Never took a lesson in my life. I'm a natural-born dancer. And *comedian*, too.

MC CARTHY (*Astounded*) You can make people *laugh?*

HARRY (*Dumbly*) I can be funny, but they won't laugh.

MC CARTHY That's odd. Why not?

HARRY I don't know. They just won't laugh.

MC CARTHY Would you care to be funny now?

HARRY I'd like to try out a new monologue I've been thinking about.

MC CARTHY Please do. I promise you if it's funny I shall *roar* with laughter.

HARRY This is it. (*Goes into the act, with much energy*) I'm up at Sharkey's on Turk Street. It's a quarter to nine, daylight saving. Wednesday, the eleventh. What I've got is a headache and a 1918 nickel. What I *want* is a cup of coffee. If I buy a cup of coffee with the nickel, I've got to walk home. I've got an eight-ball problem. George the Greek is shooting a game of snooker with Pedro the Filipino. *I'm in rags*. They're wearing thirty-five dollar suits, made to order. I haven't got a cigarette. They're smoking Bobby Burns panatelas. I'm thinking it over, like I always do. George the Greek is in a tough spot. If I buy a cup of coffee, I'll want another cup. What happens? My *ear* aches! My ear. George the Greek takes the cue. Chalks it. Studies the table. Touches the cueball delicately. Tick. What happens? He makes the three-ball! What do I do? I get confused. *I go out and buy a morning paper*. What the hell do I want with a morning paper? What I *want* is a cup of coffee, and a good used car. I go out and buy a morning paper. Thursday, the twelfth. Maybe the headline's about *me*. I take a quick look. *No. The headline is not about me*. It's about Hitler. Seven thousand miles away. I'm here. Who the hell is Hitler? Who's behind the eight-ball? I turn around. *Everybody's behind the eight-ball!* (*Pause.* KRUPP *moves toward* HARRY *as if to make an important arrest.* HARRY *moves to the swinging doors.* MC CARTHY *stops* KRUPP)

MC CARTHY (*To* HARRY) It's the funniest thing I've ever heard. Or seen, for that matter.

HARRY (*Coming back to* MC CARTHY) Then, why don't you laugh?

MC CARTHY I don't know, *yet*.

HARRY I'm always getting funny ideas that nobody will laugh at.

MC CARTHY (*Thoughtfully*) It may be that you've stumbled headlong into a new kind of comedy.

HARRY Well, what good is it if it doesn't make anybody laugh?

MC CARTHY There are *kinds* of laughter, son. I must say, in all truth, that I *am* laughing, although not *out loud*.

HARRY I want to *hear* people laugh. *Out loud*. That's why I keep thinking of funny things to say.

MC CARTHY Well. They may catch on in time. Let's go, Krupp. So long, Joe. (MC CARTHY *and* KRUPP *go*)

JOE So long. (*After a moment's pause*) Hey, Nick.

NICK Yeah.

JOE Bet McCarthy in the last race.

NICK You're crazy. That horse is a double-crossing, no-good—

JOE Bet everything you've got on McCarthy.

NICK I'm not betting a nickel on him. *You* bet everything you've got on McCarthy.

JOE I don't need money.

NICK What makes you think McCarthy's going to win?

JOE McCarthy's name's McCarthy, isn't it?

NICK Yeah. So what?

JOE The *horse* named McCarthy is going to win, *that's all*. Today.

NICK Why?

JOE You do what I tell you, and everything will be all right.

NICK McCarthy likes to talk, that's all. (*Pause*) Where's Tom?

JOE He'll be around. He'll be miserable, but he'll be around. Five or ten minutes more.

NICK You don't believe that Kitty, do you? About being in burlesque?

JOE (*Very clearly*) I believe dreams sooner than statistics.

NICK (*Remembering*) She sure is somebody. Called me a dentist. (TOM, *turning about, confused, troubled, comes in, and hurries to* JOE'S *table*)

JOE What's the matter?

TOM Here's your five, Joe. I'm in trouble again.

JOE If it's not organic, it'll cure itself. If it is organic, science will cure it. What is it, organic or non-organic?

TOM Joe, I don't know— (*He seems to be completely broken down*)

JOE What's eating you? I want you to go on an errand for me.

TOM It's Kitty.

JOE What about her?

TOM She's up in her room, crying.

JOE Crying?

TOM Yeah, she's been crying for over an hour. I been talking to her all this time, but she won't stop.

JOE What's she crying about?

TOM I don't know. I couldn't understand anything. She kept crying and telling me about a big house and collie dogs all around and flowers and one of her brothers dead and the other one lost somewhere. Joe, I can't stand Kitty crying.

JOE You want to marry the girl?

TOM (*Nodding*) Yeah.

JOE (*Curious and sincere*) Why?

TOM I don't know why, exactly, Joe. (*Pause*) Joe, I don't like to think of Kitty out in the streets. I guess I love her, that's all.

JOE She's a nice girl.

TOM She's like an angel. She's not like those other street-walkers.

JOE (*Swiftly*) Here. Take all this money and run next door to Frankie's and bet it on the nose of McCarthy.

TOM (*Swiftly*) All this money, Joe? McCarthy?

JOE Yeah. Hurry.

TOM (*Going*) Ah, Joe. If McCarthy wins we'll be rich.

JOE Get going, will you? (TOM *runs out and nearly knocks over the* ARAB *coming back in.* NICK *fills him a beer without a word*)

ARAB No foundation, anywhere. Whole world. No foundation. All the way down the line.

NICK (*Angry*) McCarthy! Just because you got a little lucky this morning, you have to go to work and throw away eighty bucks.

JOE He wants to marry her.

NICK Suppose she doesn't want to marry *him?*

JOE (*Amazed*) Oh, yeah. (*Thinking*) Now, why wouldn't she want to marry a nice guy like Tom?

NICK She's been in burlesque. She's had flowers sent to her by European royalty. She's dined with young men of quality and social position. She's above Tom. (TOM *comes running in*)

TOM (*Disgusted*) They were running when I got there. Frankie wouldn't take the bet. McCarthy didn't get a call till the stretch. I thought we were going to save all this money. Then McCarthy won by *two* lengths.

JOE What'd he pay, fifteen to one?

TOM Better, but Frankie wouldn't take the bet.

NICK (*Throwing a dish towel across the room*) Well, for the love of Mike.

JOE Give me the money.

TOM (*Giving back the money*) We would have had about a thousand five hundred dollars.

JOE (*Bored, casually, inventing*) Go up to Schwabacher-Frey and get me the biggest Rand-McNally map of the nations of Europe they've got. On your way back stop at one of the pawn shops on Third Street, and buy me a good revolver and some cartridges.

TOM She's up in her room crying, Joe.

JOE Go get me those things.

NICK What are you going to do, study the map, and then go out and shoot somebody?

JOE I want to read the names of some European towns and rivers and valleys and mountains.

NICK What do you want with the revolver?

JOE I want to study it. I'm interested in things. Here's twenty dollars, Tom. Now go get them things.

TOM A big map of Europe. And a revolver.

JOE Get a good one. Tell the man you don't know anything about firearms and you're trusting him not to fool you. Don't pay more than ten dollars.

TOM Joe, you got something on your mind. Don't go fool with a revolver.

JOE Be sure it's a good one.

TOM Joe.

JOE (*Irritated*) What, Tom?

TOM Joe, what do you send me out for crazy things for all the time?

JOE (*Angry*) They're not crazy, Tom. Now, get going.

TOM What about Kitty, Joe?

JOE Let her cry. It'll do her good.

TOM If she comes in here while I'm gone, talk to her, will you, Joe? Tell her about me.

JOE O.K. Get going. Don't load that gun. Just buy it and bring it here.

TOM (*Going*) You won't catch me loading any gun.

JOE Wait a minute. Take these toys away.

TOM Where'll I take them?

JOE Give them to some kid. (*Pause*) No. Take them up to Kitty. Toys stopped me from crying once. That's the reason I had you buy them. I wanted to see if I could find out *why* they stopped me from crying. I remember they seemed awfully stupid at the time.

TOM Shall I, Joe? Take them up to Kitty? Do you think they'd stop *her* from crying?

JOE They might. You get curious about the way they work and you forget whatever it is you're remembering that's making you cry. That's what they're for.

TOM Yeah. Sure. The girl at the store asked me what I wanted with toys. I'll take them up to Kitty. (*Tragically*) She's like a little girl. (*He goes*)

WESLEY Mr. Nick, can I play the piano again?

NICK Sure. Practice all you like—until I tell you to stop.

WESLEY You going to pay me for playing the piano?

NICK Sure. I'll give you enough to get by on.

WESLEY (*Amazed and delighted*) Get money for playing the piano? (*He goes to the piano and begins to play quietly.* HARRY *goes up on the little stage and listens to the music. After a while he begins a soft-shoe dance*)

NICK What were you crying about?

JOE My mother.

NICK What about her?

JOE She was dead. I stopped crying when they gave me the toys. (NICK'S MOTHER, *a little old woman of sixty or so, dressed plainly in black, her face shining, comes in briskly, chattering loudly in Italian, gesturing.* NICK *is delighted to see her*)

NICK'S MOTHER (*In Italian*) Everything all right, Nickie?

NICK (*In Italian*) Sure, Mamma. (NICK'S MOTHER *leaves as gaily and as noisily as she came, after half a minute of loud Italian family talk*)

JOE Who was that?

NICK (*To* JOE, *proudly and a little sadly*) My mother. (*Still looking at the swinging doors*)

JOE What'd she say?

NICK Nothing. Just wanted to see me. (*Pause*) What do you want with that gun?

JOE I study things, Nick. (*An old man who looks as if he might have been Kit Carson at one time walks in importantly, moves about, and finally stands at* JOE'S *table*)

KIT CARSON Murphy's the name. Just an old trapper. Mind if I sit down?

JOE Be delighted. What'll you drink?

KIT CARSON (*Sitting down*) Beer. Same as I've been drinking. And thanks.

JOE (*To* NICK) Glass of beer, Nick. (NICK *brings the beer to the table,* KIT CARSON *swallows it in one swig, wipes his big white mustache with the back of his right hand*)

KIT CARSON (*Moving in*) I don't suppose you ever fell in love with a midget weighing thirty-nine pounds?

JOE (*Studying the man*) Can't say I have, but have another beer.

KIT CARSON (*Intimately*) Thanks, thanks. Down in Gallup, twenty years ago. Fellow by the name of Rufus Jenkins came in town with six white horses and two black ones. Said he wanted a man to break the horses for him because his left leg was wood and he couldn't do it. Had a meeting at Parker's Mercantile Store and finally came to blows, me and Henry Walpal. Bashed his head with a brass cuspidor and ran away to Mexico, but he didn't die. Couldn't speak a word. Took up with a cattle-breeder named Diego, educated in California. Spoke the language better than you and me. Said, Your job, Murph, is to feed them prize bulls. I said, Fine, what'll I feed them? He said, Hay, lettuce, salt, beer, and aspirin. Came to blows two days later over an accordion he claimed I stole. I had *borrowed* it. During the fight I busted it over his head; ruined one of the finest accordions I ever saw. Grabbed a horse and rode back across the border. Texas. Got to talking with a fellow who looked honest. Turned out to be a Ranger who was looking for me.

JOE Yeah. You were saying, a thirty-nine-pound midget.

KIT CARSON Will I ever forget that lady? Will I ever get over that amazon of small proportions?

JOE Will you?

KIT CARSON If I live to be sixty.

JOE *Sixty?* You look more than sixty now.

KIT CARSON That's trouble showing in my face. Trouble and complications. I was fifty-eight three months ago.

JOE That accounts for it, then. Go ahead, tell me more.

KIT CARSON Told the Texas Ranger my name was Rothstein, mining engineer from Pennsylvania, looking for something worth while. Mentioned two places in Houston. Nearly lost an eye early one morning, going down the stairs. Ran into a six-footer with an iron claw where his right hand was supposed to be. Said, You broke up my home. Told him I was a stranger in Houston. The girls gathered at the top of the stairs to see a fight. Seven of them. Six feet and an iron claw. That's bad on the nerves. Kicked him in the mouth when he swung for my head with the claw. Would have lost an eye except for quick thinking. He rolled into the gutter and pulled a gun. Fired seven times. I was back upstairs. Left the place an hour later, dressed in silk and feathers, with a hat swung around over my face. Saw him standing on the corner, waiting. Said, Care for a wiggle? Said he didn't. I went on down the street and left town. I don't suppose you ever had to put a dress on to save your skin, did you?

JOE No, and I never fell in love with a midget weighing thirty-nine pounds. Have another beer?

KIT CARSON Thanks. (*Swallows glass of beer*) Ever try to herd cattle on a bicycle?

JOE No. I never got around to that.

KIT CARSON Left Houston with sixty cents in my pocket, gift of a girl named Lucinda. Walked fourteen miles in fourteen hours. Big house with barbwire all around, and big dogs. One thing I never could get around. Walked past the gate, anyway, from hunger and thirst. Dogs jumped up and came for me. Walked right into them, growing older every second. Went up to the door and knocked. Big negress opened the door, closed it quick. Said, On your way, white trash. Knocked again. Said, On your way. Again. On your way. Again. This time the old man himself opened the door, ninety, if he was a day. Sawed-off shotgun, too. Said, I ain't looking for trouble, Father. I'm hungry and thirsty, name's Cavanaugh. Took me in and made mint juleps for the two of us. Said, Living here alone, Father? Said, Drink and ask no questions. Maybe I am and maybe I ain't. You saw the lady. Draw your own conclusions. I'd heard of that, but didn't wink out of tact. If I told you that old Southern gentleman was my grandfather, you wouldn't believe me, would you?

JOE I might.

KIT CARSON Well, it so happens he wasn't. Would have been romantic if he had been, though.

JOE Where did you herd cattle on a bicycle?

KIT CARSON Toledo, Ohio, 1918.

JOE Toledo, Ohio? They don't herd cattle in Toledo.

KIT CARSON They don't anymore. They did in 1918. One fellow did, leastways. Bookkeeper named Sam Gold. Straight from the East Side, New York. Sombrero, lariats, Bull Durham, two head of cattle and two bicycles. Called his place The Gold Bar Ranch, two acres, just outside the city limits. That was the year of the War, you'll remember.

JOE Yeah, I remember, but how about herding them two cows on a bicycle? How'd you do it?

KIT CARSON Easiest thing in the world. Rode no hands. Had to, otherwise couldn't lasso the cows. Worked for Sam Gold till the cows ran away. Bicycles scared them. They went into Toledo. Never saw hide nor hair of them again. Advertised in every paper, but never got them back. Broke his heart. Sold both bikes and returned to New York. Took four aces from a deck of red cards and walked to town. Poker. Fellow in the game named Chuck Collins, liked to gamble. Told him with a smile I didn't suppose he'd care to bet a hundred dollars I wouldn't hold four aces the next hand. Called it. My cards were red on the blank side. The other cards were blue. Plumb forget all about it. Showed him four aces. Ace of spades, ace of clubs, ace of diamonds, ace of hearts. I'll remember them four cards if I live to be sixty. Would have been killed on the spot except for the hurricane that year.

JOE Hurricane?

KIT CARSON You haven't forgotten the Toledo hurricane of 1918, have you?

JOE No. There was no hurricane in Toledo in 1918, or any other year.

KIT CARSON For the love of God, then what do you suppose that commotion was? And how come I came to in Chicago, dream-walking down State Street?

JOE I guess they scared you.

KIT CARSON No, that wasn't it. You go back to the papers of November 1918, and I think you'll find there was a hurricane in Toledo. I remember sitting on the roof of a two-story house, floating northwest.

JOE (*Seriously*) Northwest?

KIT CARSON Now, son, don't tell me *you* don't believe me, either?

JOE (*Pause. Very seriously, energetically, and sharply*) Of course I believe you. Living is an art. It's not bookkeeping. It takes a lot of rehearsing for a man to get to be himself.

KIT CARSON (*Thoughtfully, smiling, and amazed*) You're the first man I've ever met who believes me.

JOE (*Seriously*) Have another beer. (TOM *comes in with the Rand-McNally book, the revolver, and the box of cartridges.* KIT *goes to bar*)

JOE (*To* TOM) Did you give her the toys?

TOM Yeah, I gave them to her.

JOE Did she stop crying?

TOM No. She started crying harder than ever.

JOE That's funny. I wonder why.

TOM Joe, if I was a minute earlier, Frankie would have taken the bet and now we'd have about a thousand five hundred dollars. How much of it would you have given me, Joe?

JOE If she'd marry you—*all* of it.

TOM Would you, Joe?

JOE (*Opening packages, examining book first, and revolver next*) Sure. In this realm there's only one subject, and you're it. It's my duty to see that my subject is happy.

TOM Joe, do you think we'll ever have eighty dollars for a race sometime again when there's a fifteen-to-one shot that we like, weather good, track fast, they get off to a good start, our horse doesn't get a call till the stretch, we think we're going to lose all that money, and then it wins, by a nose?

JOE I didn't quite get that.

TOM You know what I mean.

JOE You mean the impossible. No, Tom, we won't. We were just a little late, that's all.

TOM We might, Joe.

JOE It's not likely.

TOM Then how am I ever going to make enough money to marry her?

JOE I don't know, Tom. Maybe you aren't.

TOM Joe, I got to marry Kitty. (*Shaking his head*) You ought to see the crazy room she lives in.

JOE What kind of a room is it?

TOM It's little. It crowds you in. It's bad, Joe. Kitty don't belong in a place like that.

JOE You want to take her away from there?

TOM Yeah. I want her to live in a house where there's room enough to live. Kitty ought to have a garden, or something.

JOE You want to take care of her?

TOM Yeah, sure, Joe. I ought to take care of somebody good that makes me feel like *I'm* somebody.

JOE That means you'll have to get a job. What can you do?

TOM I finished high school, but I don't know what I can do.

JOE Sometimes when you think about it, what do you think you'd like to do?

TOM Just sit around like you, Joe, and have somebody run errands for me and drink champagne and take things easy and never be broke and never worry about money.

JOE That's a noble ambition.

NICK (*To* JOE) How do you do it?

JOE I really don't know, but I think you've got to have the full cooperation of the Good Lord.

NICK I can't understand the way you talk.

TOM Joe, shall I go back and see if I can get her to stop crying?

JOE Give me a hand and I'll go with you.

TOM (*Amazed*) What! You're going to get up already?

JOE She's crying, isn't she?

TOM She's crying. Worse than ever now.

JOE I thought the toys would stop her.

TOM I've seen you sit in one place from four in the morning till two the next morning.

JOE At my best, Tom, I don't travel by foot. That's all. Come on. Give me a hand. I'll find some way to stop her from crying.

TOM (*Helping* JOE) Joe, I never did tell you. You're a different kind of a guy.

JOE (*Swiftly, a little angry*) Don't be silly. I don't understand things. I'm trying to understand them. (JOE *is a little drunk. They go out together. The lights go down slowly, while* WESLEY *plays the piano, and come up slowly on . . .*)

# Act Three

*A cheap bed in* NICK'S *to indicate room 21 of The New York Hotel, upstairs, around the corner from* NICK'S. *The bed can be at the center of* NICK'S, *or up on the little stage. Everything in* NICK'S *is the same, except that all the people are silent, immobile, and in darkness, except* WESLEY *who is playing the piano softly and sadly.* KITTY DUVAL, *in a dress she has carried around with her from the early days in Ohio, is seated on the bed, tying a ribbon in her hair. She looks at herself in a hand mirror. She is deeply grieved at the change she sees in herself. She takes off the ribbon, angry and hurt. She lifts a book from the bed and tries to read. She begins to sob again. She picks up an old picture of herself and looks at it. Sobs harder than ever, falling on the bed and burying her face. There is a knock, as if at the door.*

KITTY (*Sobbing*) Who is it?

TOM'S VOICE Kitty, it's me. Tom. Me and Joe. (JOE, *followed by* TOM, *comes to the bed quietly.* JOE *is holding a rather large toy carousel.* JOE *studies* KITTY *a moment. He sets the toy carousel on the floor, at the foot of* KITTY'S *bed*)

TOM (*standing over* KITTY *and bending down close to her*) Don't cry any more, Kitty.

KITTY (*Not looking, sobbing*) I don't like this life. (JOE *starts the carousel which makes a strange, sorrowful, tinkling music. The music begins slowly, becomes swift, gradually slows down, and ends.* JOE *himself is interested in the toy, watches and listens to it carefully*)

TOM (*Eagerly*) Kitty. Joe got up from his chair at Nick's just to get you a toy and come here. This one makes music. We rode all over town in a cab to get it. Listen. (KITTY *sits up slowly, listening, while* TOM *watches her. Everything happens slowly and somberly.* KITTY *notices the photograph of herself when she was a little girl. Lifts it, and looks at it again*)

TOM (*Looking*) Who's that little girl, Kitty?

KITTY That's me. When I was seven.

TOM (*Looking, smiling*) Gee, you're pretty, Kitty. (JOE *reaches up for the photograph, which* TOM *hands to him.* TOM *returns to* KITTY *whom he finds as pretty now as she was at seven.* JOE *studies the photograph.* KITTY *looks up at* TOM. *There is no doubt that they really love one another.* JOE *looks up at them*)

KITTY Tom?

TOM (*Eagerly*) Yeah, Kitty.

KITTY Tom, when you were a little boy what did you want to be?

TOM (*A little bewildered, but eager to please her*) What, Kitty?

KITTY Do you remember when you were a little boy?

TOM (*Thoughtfully*) Yeah, I remember sometimes, Kitty.

KITTY What did you want to be?

TOM (*Looks at* JOE. JOE *holds* TOM'S *eyes a moment. Then* TOM *is able to speak*) Sometimes I wanted to be a locomotive engineer. Sometimes I wanted to be a policeman.

KITTY I wanted to be a great actress. (*She looks up into* TOM'S *face*) Tom, didn't you ever want to be a doctor?

TOM (*Looks at* JOE. JOE *holds* TOM'S *eyes again, encouraging* TOM *by his serious expression to go on talking*) Yeah, now I remember. Sure, Kitty. I wanted to be a doctor—once.

KITTY (*Smiling sadly*) I'm so glad. Because I wanted to be an actress and have a young doctor come to the theater and see me and fall in love with me and send me flowers. (JOE *pantomimes to* TOM, *demanding that he go on talking*)

TOM I would do that, Kitty.

KITTY I wouldn't know who it was and then one day I'd see him in the street and fall in love with him. I wouldn't know *he* was the one who was in love with me. I'd think about him all the time. I'd dream about him. I'd dream of being near him the rest of my life. I'd dream of having children that looked like him. I wouldn't be an actress all the time. Only until I found him and fell in love with him. After that we'd take a train and go to beautiful cities and see the wonderful people everywhere and give money to the poor and whenever people were sick he'd go to them and make them well again. (TOM *looks at* JOE, *bewildered, confused, and full of sorrow.* KITTY *is deep in memory, almost in a trance*)

JOE (*Gently*) Talk to her, Tom. Be the wonderful young doctor she dreamed about and never found. Go ahead. Correct the errors of the world.

TOM Joe. (*Pathetically*) I don't know what to say. (*There is rowdy singing in the hall. A loud young* VOICE *sings: "Sailing, sailing, over the bounding main"*)

VOICE Kitty. Oh, Kitty! (KITTY *stirs, shocked, coming out of the trance*) Where the hell are you? Oh, Kitty. (TOM *jumps up, furiously*)

WOMAN'S VOICE (*In the hall*) Who are you looking for, Sailor Boy?

VOICE The most beautiful lay in the world.

WOMAN'S VOICE Don't go any further.

VOICE (*With impersonal contempt*) You? No. Not you. Kitty. You stink.

WOMAN'S VOICE (*Rasping, angry*) Don't you dare talk to me that way. You pickpocket.

VOICE (*Still impersonal, but louder*) Oh, I see. Want to get tough, hey? Close the door. Go hide.

WOMAN'S VOICE You pickpocket. All of you. (*The door slams.*)

VOICE (*Roaring with laughter which is very sad*) Oh—Kitty. Room 21. Where the hell is that room?

TOM (*To* JOE) Joe, I'll kill him.

KITTY (*Fully herself again, terribly frightened*) Who is it? (*She looks long and steadily at* TOM *and* JOE. TOM *is standing, excited and angry.* JOE *is completely at ease, his expression full of pity.* KITTY *buries her face in the bed*)

JOE (*Gently*) Tom. Just take him away.

VOICE Here it is. Number 21. Three naturals. Heaven. My blue heaven. The west, a nest, and you. Just Molly and me. (*Tragically*) Ah, to hell with everything. (*A young* SAILOR, *a good-looking boy of no more than twenty or so, who is only drunk and lonely, comes to the bed, singing sadly*)

SAILOR Hi-ya, Kitty. (*Pause*) Oh. Visitors. Sorry. A thousand apologies. (*To* KITTY) I'll come back later.

TOM (*Taking him by the shoulders, furiously*) If you do, I'll kill you. (JOE *holds* TOM. TOM *pushes the frightened boy away*)

JOE (*Somberly*) Tom. You stay here with Kitty. I'm going down to Union Square to hire an automobile. I'll be back in a few minutes. We'll ride out to the ocean and watch the sun go down. Then we'll ride down the Great Highway to Half Moon Bay. We'll have supper down there, and you and Kitty can dance.

TOM (*Stupefied, unable to express his amazement and gratitude*) Joe, you mean you're going to go on an errand for *me?* You mean you're not going to send me?

JOE That's right. (*He gestures toward* KITTY, *indicating that* TOM *shall talk to her, protect the innocence in her which is in so much danger when* TOM *isn't near, which* TOM *loves so deeply.* JOE *leaves.* TOM *studies* KITTY, *his face becoming childlike and somber. He sets the carousel into motion, listens, watching* KITTY, *who lifts herself slowly, looking only at* TOM. TOM *lifts the turning carousel and moves it slowly toward* KITTY, *as though the toy were his heart. The piano music comes up loudly and the lights go down, while* HARRY *is heard dancing swiftly*)

# Act Four

*A little later.* WESLEY, *the colored boy, is at the piano.* HARRY *is on the little stage, dancing.* NICK *is behind the bar. The* ARAB *is in his place.* KIT CARSON *is asleep on his folded arms. The* DRUNKARD *comes in. Goes to the telephone for the nickel that might be in the return-chute.* NICK *comes to take him out. He gestures for* NICK *to hold on a minute. Then produces a half dollar.* NICK *goes behind the bar to serve the* DRUNKARD *whiskey.*

THE DRUNKARD To the old, God bless them. (*Another*) To the new, God love them. (*Another*) To—children and small animals, like little dogs that don't bite. (*Another. Loudly*) To reforestation. (*Searches for money. Finds some*) To—President Taft. (*He goes out. The telephone rings*)

KIT CARSON (*Jumping up, fighting*) Come on, *all* of you, if you're looking for trouble. I never asked for quarter and I always gave it.

NICK (*Reproachfully*) Hey, Kit Carson.

DUDLEY (*On the phone*) Hello. Who? Nick? Yes. He's here. (*To* NICK) It's for you. I think it's important.

NICK (*Going to the phone*) Important! *What's* important?

DUDLEY He sounded like big-shot.

NICK Big *what?* (*To* WESLEY *and* HARRY) Hey, you. Quiet. I want to hear this important stuff. (WESLEY *stops playing the piano.* HARRY *stops dancing.* KIT CARSON *comes close to* NICK)

KIT CARSON If there's anything I can do, name it. I'll do it for you. I'm fifty-eight years old; been through three wars; married four times; the father of countless children whose *names* I don't even know. I've got no money. I live from hand to mouth. But if there's anything I can do, name it. I'll do it.

NICK (*Patiently*) Listen, Pop. For a moment, please sit down and go back to sleep—for *me.*

KIT CARSON I can do that, too. (*He sits down, folds his arms, and puts his head into them. But not for long. As* NICK *begins to talk, he listens carefully, gets to his feet, and then begins to express in pantomime the moods of each of* NICK'S *remarks*)

NICK (*On phone*) Yeah? (*Pause*) Who? Oh, I see. (*Listens*) Why don't you leave them alone? (*Listens*) The church-people? Well, to hell with the church-people. I'm a Catholic myself. (*Listens*) All right. I'll send them away. I'll tell them to lay low for a couple of days. Yeah, I know how it is. (NICK'S *daughter* ANNA *comes in shyly, looking at her father, and stands unnoticed by the piano*) What? (*Very angry*) Listen. I don't like that Blick. He was here this morning, and I told him not to come back. I'll keep the girls out of here. You keep Blick out of here. (*Listens*) I know his brother-in-law is important, but I don't want him to come down here. He looks for trouble everywhere, and he always find it. I don't break any laws. I've got a dive in the lousiest part of town. Five years nobody's been robbed, murdered, or gypped. I leave people alone. Your swanky joints uptown make trouble for you every night. (NICK *gestures to* WESLEY*—keeps listening on the phone—puts his hand over the mouthpiece. To* WESLEY *and* HARRY) Start playing again. My ears have got a headache. Go into your dance, son. (WESLEY *begins to play again.* HARRY *begins to dance.* NICK, *into mouthpiece*) Yeah. I'll keep them out. Just see that Blick doesn't come around and start something. (*Pause*) O.K. (*He hangs up*)

KIT CARSON Trouble coming?

NICK That lousy Vice Squad again. It's that gorilla Blick.

KIT CARSON Anybody at all. You can count on me. What kind of a gorilla is this gorilla Blick?

NICK Very dignified. Toenails on his fingers.

ANNA (*To* KIT CARSON, *with great, warm, beautiful pride, pointing at* NICK) That's my father.

KIT CARSON (*Leaping with amazement at the beautiful voice, the wondrous face, the magnificent event*) Well, bless your heart, child. Bless your lovely heart. I had a little daughter point me out in a crowd once.

NICK (*Surprised*) Anna. What the hell are you doing here? Get back home where you belong and help Grandma cook me some supper. (ANNA *smiles at her father, understanding him, knowing that his words are words of love. She turns and goes, looking at him all the way out, as much as to say that she would cook for him the rest of her life.* NICK *stares at the swinging doors.* KIT CARSON *moves toward them, two or three steps.* ANNA *pushes open one of the doors and peeks in, to look at her father again. She waves to him. Turns and runs.* NICK *is very sad. He doesn't know what to do. He gets a glass and a bottle. Pours himself a drink. Swallows some. It isn't enough, so he pours more and swallows the whole drink. To himself*) My beautiful, beautiful baby. Anna, she is you again. (*He brings out a handkerchief, touches his eyes, and blows his nose.* KIT CARSON *moves close to* NICK, *watching* NICK'S *face.* NICK *looks at him. Loudly, almost making* KIT *jump*) You're broke, aren't you?

KIT CARSON Always. Always.

NICK All right. Go into the kitchen and give Sam a hand. Eat some food and when you come back you can have a couple of beers.

KIT CARSON (*Studying* NICK) Anything at all. I know a good man when I see one. (*He goes.* ELSIE MANDELSPIEGEL *comes into* NICK'S. *She is a beautiful, dark girl, with a sorrowful, wise, dreaming face, almost on the verge of tears, and full of pity. There is an aura of dream about her. She moves softly and gently, as if everything around her were unreal and pathetic.* DUDLEY *doesn't notice her for a moment or two. When he does finally see her, he is so amazed, he can barely move or speak. Her presence has the effect of changing him completely. He gets up from his chair, as if in a trance, and walks toward her, smiling sadly*)

ELSIE (*Looking at him*) Hello, Dudley.

DUDLEY (*Broken-hearted*) Elsie.

ELSIE I'm sorry. (*Explaining*) So many people are sick. Last night a little boy died. I love you, but— (*She gestures, trying to indicate how hopeless love is. They sit down*)

DUDLEY (*Staring at her, stunned and quieted*) Elsie. You'll never know how glad I am to see you. Just to see you. (*Pathetically*) I was afraid I'd never see you again. It was driving me crazy. I didn't want to live. Honest. (*He shakes his head mournfully, with dumb and beautiful affection.* TWO STREETWALKERS *come in, and pause near* DUDLEY, *at the bar*) I know. You told me before, but I can't help it, Elsie. I love you.

ELSIE (*Quietly, somberly, gently, with great compassion*) I know you love me, and I love you, but don't you see love is impossible in this world?

DUDLEY Maybe it isn't, Elsie.

ELSIE Love is for birds. They have wings to fly away on when it's time for flying. For tigers in the jungle because they don't know their end. We know *our* end. Every night I watch over poor, dying men. I hear them breathing, crying, talking in their sleep. Crying for air and water and love, for mother and field and sunlight. We can never know love or greatness. We *should* know both.

DUDLEY (*Deeply moved by her words*) Elsie, I love you.

ELSIE You want to live. *I* want to live, too, but where? Where can we escape our poor world?

DUDLEY Elsie, we'll find a place.

ELSIE (*Smiling at him*) All right. We'll try again. We'll go together to a room in a cheap hotel, and dream that the world is beautiful, and that living is full of love and greatness. But in the morning, can we forget debts, and duties, and the cost of ridiculous things?

DUDLEY (*With blind faith*) Sure, we can, Elsie.

ELSIE All right, Dudley. Of course. Come on. The time for the new pathetic war has come. Let's hurry, before they dress you, stand you in line, hand you a gun, and have you kill and be killed. (ELSIE *looks at him gently, and takes his hand.* DUDLEY *embraces her shyly, as if he might hurt her. They go, as if they were a couple of young animals. There is a moment of silence. One of the* STREETWALKERS *bursts out laughing*)

KILLER Nick, what the hell kind of a joint are you running?

NICK Well, it's not out of the world. It's on a street in a city, and people come and go. They bring whatever they've got with them and they say what they must say.

THE OTHER STREETWALKER It's floozies like her that raise hell with our racket.

NICK (*Remembering*) Oh, yeah. Finnegan telephoned.

KILLER That mouse in elephant's body?

THE OTHER STREETWALKER What the hell does *he* want?

NICK Spend your time at the movies for the next couple of days.

KILLER They're all lousy. (*Mocking*) All about love.

NICK Lousy or not lousy, for a couple of days the flatfoots are going to be romancing you, so stay out of here, and lay low.

KILLER I always was a pushover for a man in uniform, with a badge, a club, and a gun. (KRUPP *comes into the place. The girls put down their drinks*)

NICK O.K., get going. (*The* GIRLS *begin to leave and meet* KRUPP)

THE OTHER STREETWALKER We was just going.

KILLER We was formerly models at Magnin's. (*They go*)

KRUPP (*At the bar*) The strike isn't enough, so they've got to put us on the tails of the girls, too. I don't know. I wish to God I was back in the Sunset holding the hands of kids going home from school, where I belong. I don't like trouble. Give me a beer. (NICK *gives him a beer. He drinks some*) Right now, McCarthy, my best friend, is with sixty strikers who want to stop the finks who are going to try to unload the *Mary Luckenbach* tonight. Why the hell McCarthy ever became a longshoreman instead of a professor of some kind is something I'll never know.

NICK Cowboys and Indians, cops and robbers, longshoremen and finks.

KRUPP They're all guys who are trying to be happy; trying to make a living; support a family; bring up children; enjoy sleep. Go to a movie; take a drive on Sunday. They're all good guys, so out of nowhere comes trouble. All they want is a chance to get out of debt and relax in front of a radio while Amos and Andy go through their act. What the hell do they always want to make trouble for? I been thinking everything over, Nick, and you know what I think?

NICK No. What?

KRUPP I think we're all crazy. It came to me while I was on my way to Pier 27. All of a sudden it hit me like a ton of bricks. A thing like that never happened to me before. Here we are in this wonderful world, full of all the wonderful things—here we are—all of us, and look at us. Just look at us. We're crazy. We're nuts. We've got everything, but we always feel lousy and dissatisfied just the same.

NICK Of course we're crazy. Even so, we've got to go on living together. (*He waves at the people in his joint*)

KRUPP There's no hope. I don't suppose it's right for an officer of the law to feel the way I feel, but, by God, right or not right, that's how I feel. Why are we all so lousy? This is a good world. It's wonderful to get up in the morning and go out for a little walk and smell the trees and see the streets and the kids going to school and the clouds in the sky. It's wonderful just to be able to move around and whistle a song if you feel like it, or maybe try to sing one. This is a nice world. So why do they make all the trouble?

NICK I don't know. Why?

KRUPP We're crazy, that's why. We're no good any more. All the corruption everywhere. The poor kids selling themselves. A couple of years ago they were in grammar school. Everybody trying to get a lot of money in a hurry. Everybody betting the horses. Nobody going quietly for a little walk to the ocean. Nobody taking things easy and not wanting to make some kind of a killing. Nick, I'm going to quit being a cop. Let somebody else keep law and order. The stuff I hear about at headquarters. I'm thirty-seven years old, and I still can't get used to it. The only trouble is, the wife'll raise hell.

NICK Ah, the wife.

KRUPP She's a wonderful woman, Nick. We've got two of the swellest boys in the world. Twelve and seven years old. (*The* ARAB *gets up and moves closer to listen*)

NICK I didn't know that.

KRUPP Sure. But what'll I do? I've wanted to quit for seven years. I wanted to quit the day they began putting me through the school. I didn't quit. What'll I do if I quit? Where's money going to be coming in from?

NICK That's one of the reasons we're all crazy. We don't know where it's going to be coming in from, except from wherever it happens to be coming in from at the time, which we don't usually like.

KRUPP Every once in a while I catch myself being mean, hating people just because they're down and out, broke and hungry, sick or drunk. And then when I'm with the stuffed shirts at headquarters, all of a sudden I'm nice to them, trying to make an impression. On who? People I don't like. And I feel disgusted. (*With finality*) I'm going to quit. That's all. Quit. Out. I'm going to give them back the uniform and the gadgets that go with it. I don't want any part of it. This is a good world. What do they want to make all the trouble for all the time?

ARAB (*Quietly, gently, with great understanding*) No foundation. All the way down the line.

KRUPP What?

ARAB No foundation. No foundation.

KRUPP I'll say there's no foundation.

ARAB All the way down the line.

KRUPP (*To* NICK) Is that all he ever says?

NICK That's all he's been saying *this* week.

KRUPP What is he, anyway?

NICK He's an Arab, or something like that.

KRUPP No, I mean what's he do for a living?

NICK (*To* ARAB) What do you do for a living, brother?

ARAB Work. Work all my life. All my life, work. From small boy to old man, work. In old country, work. In new country, work. In New York. Pittsburgh. Detroit. Chicago. Imperial Valley. San Francisco. Work. No beg. Work. For what? Nothing. Three boys in old country. Twenty years, not see. Lost. Dead. Who knows? What. What-not. No foundation. All the way down the line.

KRUPP What'd he say last week?

NICK Didn't say anything. Played the harmonica.

ARAB Old country song, I play. (*He brings a harmonica from his back pocket*)

KRUPP Seems like a nice guy.

NICK Nicest guy in the world.

KRUPP (*Bitterly*) But crazy. Just like all the rest of us. Stark raving mad. (WESLEY *and* HARRY *long ago stopped playing and dancing. They sat at a table together and talked for a while; then began playing casino or rummy. When the* ARAB *begins his solo on the harmonica, they stop their game to listen*)

WESLEY You hear that?

HARRY That's *something.*

WESLEY That's crying. That's crying.

HARRY I want to make people laugh.

WESLEY That's deep, deep crying. That's crying a long time ago. That's crying a thousand years ago. Some place five thousand miles away.

HARRY Do you think you can play to that?

WESLEY I want to *sing* to that, but I can't *sing.*

HARRY You try and play to that. I'll try to dance. (WESLEY *goes to the piano, and after closer listening, he begins to accompany the harmonica solo.* HARRY *goes to the little stage and after a few efforts begins to dance to the song. This keeps up quietly for some time.* KRUPP *and* NICK *have been silent, and deeply moved*)

KRUPP (*Softly*) Well, anyhow, Nick.

NICK Hmmmmmmm?

KRUPP What I said. Forget it.

NICK Sure.

KRUPP It gets me down once in a while.

NICK No harm in talking.

KRUPP (*The* POLICEMAN *again, loudly*) Keep the girls out of here.

NICK (*Loud and friendly*) Take it easy. (*The music and dancing are now at their height*)

# Act Five

*That evening. Fog-horns are heard throughout the scene. A man in evening clothes and a top hat, and his woman, also in evening clothes, are entering.*

WILLIE *is still at the marble game.* NICK *is behind the bar.* JOE *is at his table, looking at the book of maps of the countries of Europe. The box containing the revolver and the box containing the cartridges are on the table, beside his glass. He is at peace, his hat tilted back on his head, a calm expression on his face.* TOM *is leaning against the bar, dreaming of love and* KITTY. *The* ARAB *is gone.* WESLEY *and* HARRY *are gone.* KIT CARSON *is watching the boy at the marble game.*

LADY Oh, come on, please. (*The gentleman follows miserably. The* SOCIETY MAN *and* WIFE *take a table.* NICK *gives them a menu. Outside, in the street, the Salvation Army people are playing a song. Big drum, tambourines, cornet, and singing. They are singing "The Blood of the Lamb." The music and words come into the place faintly and comically. This is followed by an old sinner testifying. It is the* DRUNKARD. *His words are not intelligible, but his message is unmistakable. He is saved. He wants to sin no more. And so on*)

DRUNKARD (*Testifying, unmistakably drunk*) Brothers and sisters. I was a sinner. I chewed tobacco and chased women. Oh, I sinned, brothers and sisters. And then I was saved. Saved by the Salvation Army, God forgive me.

JOE Let's see now. Here's a city. Pribor. Czechoslovakia. Little, lovely, lonely Czechoslovakia. I wonder what kind of a place Pribor was? (*Calling*) Pribor! *Pribor!* (TOM *leaps*)

LADY What's the matter with him?

MAN (*Crossing his legs, as if he ought to go to the men's room*) Drunk.

TOM Who you calling, Joe?

JOE Pribor.

TOM Who's Pribor?

JOE He's a Czech. And a Slav. A Czechoslovakian.

LADY How interesting.

MAN (*Uncrosses legs*) He's drunk.

JOE Tom, Pribor's a city in Czechoslovakia.

TOM Oh. (*Pause*) You sure were nice to her, Joe.

JOE Kitty Duval? She's one of the finest people in the world.

TOM It sure was nice of you to hire an automobile and take us for a drive along the ocean front and down to Half Moon Bay.

JOE Those three hours were the most delightful, the most somber, and the most beautiful I have ever known.

TOM Why, Joe?

JOE Why? I'm a student. (*Lifting his voice*) Tom. (*Quietly*) I'm a student. I study all things. All. All. And when my study reveals something of beauty in a place or in a person where by all rights only ugliness or death should be revealed, then I know how full of goodness this life is. And that's a good thing to know. That's a truth I shall always seek to verify.

LADY Are you *sure* he's drunk?

MAN (*Crossing his legs*) He's either drunk, or just naturally crazy.

TOM Joe?

JOE Yeah.

TOM You won't get sore or anything?

JOE (*Impatiently*) What is it, Tom?

TOM Joe, where do you get all that money? You paid for the automobile. You paid for supper and the two bottles of champagne at the Half Moon Bay Restaurant. You moved Kitty out of the New York Hotel around the corner to the St. Francis Hotel on Powell Street. I saw you pay her rent. I saw you give her money for new clothes. Where do you get all that money, Joe? Three years now and I've never asked.

JOE (*Looking at* TOM *sorrowfully, a little irritated, not so much with* TOM *as with the world and himself, his own superiority. He speaks clearly, slowly, and solemnly*) Now don't be a fool, Tom. Listen carefully. If anybody's got any money—to hoard or to throw away—you can be sure he stole it from other people. Not from rich people who can spare it, but from poor people who can't. From their lives and from their dreams. I'm no exception. I *earned* the money I throw away. I stole it like everybody else does. I hurt people to get it. Loafing around this way, I *still* earn money. The money itself earns *more*. I *still* hurt people. I don't know who they are, or where they are. If I did, I'd feel worse than I do. I've got a Christian conscience in a world that's got no conscience at all. The world's trying to get some sort of a *social* conscience, but it's having a devil of a time trying to do *that*. I've got money. I'll always have money, as long as this world stays the way it is. I don't work. I don't make anything. (*He sips*) I drink. I worked when I was a kid. I worked *hard*. I mean hard, Tom. People are supposed to enjoy living. I got tired. (*He lifts the gun and looks at it while he talks*) I decided to get even on the world. Well, you can't enjoy living unless you work. Unless you do something. I don't do anything. I don't *want* to do anything any more. There isn't anything I can do that won't make me feel embarrassed. Because I can't do simple, good things. I haven't the patience. And I'm too smart. Money is the guiltiest thing in the world. It stinks. Now, don't ever bother me about it again.

TOM I didn't mean to make you feel bad, Joe.

JOE (*Slowly*) Here. Take this gun out in the street and give it to some worthy hold-up man.

LADY What's he saying?

MAN (*Uncrosses legs*) You wanted to visit a honky-tonk. Well, *this* is a honky-tonk. (*To the world*) Married twenty-eight years and she's still looking for adventure.

TOM How should I know who's a hold-up man?

JOE Take it away. Give it to somebody.

TOM (*Bewildered*) Do I *have* to *give* it to somebody?

JOE Of course.

TOM Can't I take it back and get some of our money?

JOE Don't talk like a business man. Look around and find somebody who appears to be in need of a gun and give it to him. It's a good gun, isn't it?

TOM The man said it was, but how can I tell who needs a gun?

JOE Tom, you've seen good people who needed guns, haven't you?

TOM I don't remember. Joe, I might give it to the wrong kind of guy. He might do something crazy.

JOE All right. I'll find somebody myself. (TOM *rises*) Here's some money. Go get me this week's *Life, Liberty, Time,* and six or seven packages of chewing gum.

TOM (*Swiftly, in order to remember each item*) *Life, Liberty, Time,* and six or seven packages of chewing gum?

JOE That's right.

TOM All that chewing gum? What kind?

JOE Any kind. Mix 'em up. All kinds.

TOM Licorice, too?

JOE Licorice, by all means.

TOM Juicy Fruit?

JOE Juicy Fruit.

TOM Tutti-frutti?

JOE Is there such a gum?

TOM I think so.

JOE All right. Tutti-frutti, too. Get *all* the kinds. Get as many kinds as they're selling.

TOM *Life, Liberty, Time,* and all the different kinds of gum. (*He begins to go*)

JOE (*Calling after him loudly*) Get some jelly beans too. All the different colors.

TOM All right, Joe.

JOE And the longest panatela cigar you can find. Six of them.

TOM Panatela. I got it.

JOE Give a news-kid a dollar.

TOM O.K., Joe.

JOE Give some old man a dollar.

TOM O.K., Joe.

JOE Give them Salvation Army people in the street a couple of dollars and ask them to sing that song that goes— (*He sings loudly*)

Let the lower lights be burning, send a gleam across the wave.

TOM (*Swiftly*)

Let the lower lights be burning, send a gleam across the wave.

JOE That's it. (*He goes on with the song, very loudly and religiously*)

Some poor, dying, struggling seaman, you may rescue, you may save.

(*Halts*)

TOM O.K., Joe. I got it. *Life, Liberty, Time,* all the kinds of gum they're selling, jelly beans, six panatela cigars, a dollar for a news-kid, a dollar for an old man, two dollars for the Salvation Army. (*Going*)

Let the lower lights be burning, send a gleam across the wave.

JOE That's it.

LADY He's absolutely insane.

MAN (*Wearily crossing legs*) You asked me to take you to a honky-tonk, instead of to the Mark Hopkins. You're *here* in a honky-tonk. I can't help it if he's crazy. Do you want to go back to where people *aren't* crazy?

LADY No, not just yet.

MAN Well, all right then. Don't be telling me every minute that he's crazy.

LADY You needn't be huffy about it. (MAN *refuses to answer, uncrosses legs. When* JOE *began to sing,* KIT CARSON *turned away from the marble game and listened. While the man and woman are arguing he comes over to* JOE*'s table*)

KIT CARSON Presbyterian?

JOE I attended a Presbyterian Sunday School.

KIT CARSON Fond of singing?

JOE On occasion. Have a drink?

KIT CARSON Thanks.

JOE Get a glass and sit down. (KIT CARSON *gets a glass from* NICK*, returns to the table, sits down,* JOE *pours him a drink, they touch glasses just as the Salvation Army people begin to fulfill the request. They sip some champagne, and at the proper moment begin to sing the song together, sipping champagne, raising* *hell with the tune, swinging it, and so on. The* SOCIETY LADY *joins them, and is stopped by her husband*) Always was fond of that song. Used to sing it at the top of my voice. Never saved a seaman in my life.

KIT CARSON (*Flirting with the* SOCIETY LADY *who loves it*) I saved a seaman once. Well, he wasn't exactly a seaman. He was a darky named Wellington. Heavy-set sort of a fellow. Nice personality, but no friends to speak of. Not until I came along, at any rate. In New Orleans. In the summer of the year 1899. No. Ninety-eight. I was a lot younger of course, and had no mustache, but was regarded by many people as a man of means.

JOE Know anything about guns?

KIT CARSON (*Flirting*) All there is to know. Didn't fight the Ojibways for nothing. Up there in the Lake Takalooca country, in Michigan. (*Remembering*) Along about in 1881 or two. Fought 'em right up to the shore of the Lake. Made 'em swim for Canada. One fellow in particular, an Indian named Harry Daisy.

JOE (*Opening the box containing the revolver*) What sort of a gun would you say this is? Any good?

KIT CARSON (*At sight of gun, leaping*) Yep. That looks like a pretty nice hunk of shooting iron. That's a six-shooter. Shot a man with a six-shooter once. Got him through the palm of his right hand. Lifted his arm to wave to a friend. Thought it was a bird. Fellow named, I believe, Carroway. Larrimore Carroway.

JOE Know how to work one of these things? (*He offers* KIT CARSON *the revolver, which is old and enormous*)

KIT CARSON (*Laughing at the absurd question*) Know how to work it? Hand me that little gun, son, and I'll show you all about it. (JOE *hands* KIT *the revolver. Importantly*) Let's see now. This is probably a new kind of six-shooter. After my time. Haven't nicked an Indian in years. I believe this here place is supposed to move out. (*He fools around and gets the barrel out for loading*) That's it. There it is.

JOE Look all right?

KIT CARSON It's a good gun. You've got a good gun there, son. I'll explain it to you. You see these holes? Well, that's where you put the cartridges.

JOE (*Taking some cartridges out of the box*) Here. Show me how it's done.

KIT CARSON (*A little impatiently*) Well, son, you take 'em one by one and put 'em in the holes, like this. There's one. Two. Three. Four. Five. Six. Then you get the barrel back in place. Then cock it. Then all you got to do is aim and fire. (*He points the gun at the* LADY *and* GENTLEMAN *who scream and stand up, scaring* KIT CARSON *into paralysis. The gun is loaded, but uncocked*)

JOE It's all set?

KIT CARSON Ready to kill.

JOE Let me hold it. (KIT *hands* JOE *the gun. The* LADY *and* GENTLEMAN *watch, in terror*)

KIT CARSON Careful, now, son. Don't cock it. Many a man's lost an eye fooling with a loaded gun. Fellow I used to know named Danny Donovan lost a nose. Ruined his whole life. Hold it firm. Squeeze the trigger. Don't snap it. Spoils your aim.

JOE Thanks. Let's see if I can unload it. (*He begins to unload it*)

KIT CARSON Of course you can. (JOE *unloads the revolver, looks at it very closely, puts the cartridges back into the box*)

JOE (*Looking at gun*) I'm mighty grateful to you. Always wanted to see one of those things close up. Is it really a good one?

KIT CARSON It's a beaut, son.

JOE (*Aims the empty gun at a bottle on the bar*) Bang!

WILLIE (*At the marble game, as the machine groans*) Oh, Boy! (*Loudly, triumphantly*) There you are, Nick. Thought I couldn't do it, hey? *Now,* watch. (*The machine begins to make a special kind of noise. Lights go on and off. Some red, some green. A bell rings loudly six times*) One. Two. Three. Four. Five. Six. (*An American flag jumps up.* WILLIE *comes to attention. Salutes*) Oh, boy, what a beautiful country. (*A loud music-box version of the song "America."* JOE, KIT, *and the* LADY *get to their feet. Singing.* "My country, 'tis of thee, sweet land of liberty, of thee I sing." *Everything quiets down. The flag goes back into the machine.* WILLIE *is thrilled, amazed, delighted. Everybody has watched the performance of the defeated machine from wherever he happened to be when the performance began.* WILLIE, *looking around at everybody, as if they had all been on the side of the machine*) O.K. How's that? I knew I could do it. (*To* NICK) Six nickels. (NICK *hands him six nickels.* WILLIE *goes over to* JOE *and* KIT) Took me a little while, but I finally did it. It's scientific, really. With a little skill a man can make a modest living beating the marble games. Not that that's what I want to do. I just don't like the idea of anything getting the best of me. A machine or anything else. Myself, I'm the kind of a guy who makes up his mind to do something, and then goes to work and does it. There's no other way a man can be a success at anything. (*Indicating the letter "F" on his sweater*) See that letter? That don't stand for some little-bitty high school somewhere. That stands for *me.* Faroughli. Willie Faroughli. I'm an Assyrian. We've got a civilization six or seven centuries old, I think. Somewhere along in there. Ever hear of Osman? Harold Osman? He's an Assyrian, too. He's got an orchestra down in Fresno. (*He goes to the* LADY *and* GENTLEMAN) I've never seen you before in my life, but I can tell from the clothes you wear and the company you keep (*Graciously indicating the* LADY) that you're a man who looks every problem straight in the eye, and then goes to work and *solves* it. I'm that way myself. Well. (*He smiles beautifully, takes the* GENTLEMAN's *hand furiously*) It's been wonderful talking to a nicer type of people for a change. Well. I'll be seeing you. So long. (*He turns, takes two steps, returns to the table. Very politely and seriously*) Good-by, lady. You've got a good man there. Take good care of him. (WILLIE *goes, saluting* JOE *and the world*)

KIT CARSON (*To* JOE) By God, for a while there I didn't think that young Assyrian was going to do it. That fellow's got something. (TOM *comes back with the magazines and other stuff*)

JOE Get it all?

TOM Yeah. I had a little trouble finding the jelly beans.

JOE Let's take a look at them.

TOM These are the jelly beans. (JOE *puts his hand into the cellophane bag and takes out a handful of the jelly beans, looks at them, smiles, and tosses a couple into his mouth*)

JOE Same as ever. Have some. (*He offers the bag to* KIT)

KIT CARSON (*Flirting*) Thanks! I remember the first time I ever ate jelly beans. I was six, or at the most seven. Must have been in (*Slowly*) eighteen—seventy-seven. Seven or eight. Baltimore.

JOE Have some, Tom. (TOM *takes some*)

TOM Thanks, Joe.

JOE Let's have some of that chewing gum. (*He dumps all the packages of gum out of the bag onto the table*)

KIT CARSON (*Flirting*) Me and a boy named Clark. Quinton Clark. Became a Senator.

JOE Yeah. Tutti-frutti, all right. (*He opens a package and folds all five pieces into his mouth*) Always wanted to see how many I could chew at one time. Tell you what, Tom. I'll bet I can chew more at one time than you can.

TOM (*Delighted*) All right. (*They both begin to fold gum into their mouths*)

KIT CARSON I'll referee. Now, one at a time. How many you got?

JOE Six.

KIT CARSON All right. Let Tom catch up with you.

JOE (*While* TOM'*s catching up*) Did you give a dollar to a news-kid?

TOM Yeah, sure.

JOE What'd he say?

TOM Thanks.

JOE What sort of a kid was he?

TOM Little, dark kid. I guess he's Italian.

JOE Did he seem pleased?

TOM Yeah.

JOE That's good. Did you give a dollar to an old man?

TOM Yeah.

JOE Was he pleased?

TOM Yeah.

JOE Good. How many you got in your mouth?

TOM Six.

JOE All right. I got six, too. (*Folds one more in his mouth.* TOM *folds one too*)

KIT CARSON Seven. Seven each. (*They each fold one more into their mouths, very solemnly, chewing them into the main hunk of gum*) Eight. Nine. Ten.

JOE (*Delighted*) Always wanted to do this. (*He picks up one of the magazines*) Let's see what's going on in the world. (*He turns the pages and keeps folding gum into his mouth and chewing*)

KIT CARSON Eleven. Twelve. (KIT *continues to count while* JOE *and* TOM *continue the contest. In spite of what they are doing, each is very serious*)

TOM Joe, what'd you want to move Kitty into the St. Francis Hotel for?

JOE She's a better woman than any of them tramp society dames that hang around that lobby.

TOM Yeah, but do you think she'll feel at home up there?

JOE Maybe not at first, but after a couple of days she'll be all right. A nice big room. A bed for sleeping in. Good clothes. Good food. She'll be all right, Tom.

TOM I hope so. Don't you think she'll get lonely up there with nobody to talk to?

JOE (*Looking at* TOM *sharply, almost with admiration, pleased but severe*) There's nobody *anywhere* for *her* to talk to—except *you.*

TOM (*Amazed and delighted*) *Me,* Joe?

JOE (*While* TOM *and* KIT CARSON *listen carefully,* KIT *with great appreciation*) Yes, you. By the grace of God, you're the other half of that girl. Not the angry woman that swaggers into this waterfront dive and shouts because the world has kicked her around. *Anybody* can have *her*. You belong to the little kid in Ohio who once dreamed of living. Not with her carcass, for *money,* so she can have food and clothes, and pay rent. With *all* of her. I put her in that hotel, so she can have a chance to gather herself together again. She can't do that in the New York Hotel. You saw what happens there. There's nobody anywhere for her to talk to, except you. They all make her talk like a whore. After a while, she'll *believe* them. Then she won't be able to remember. She'll get lonely. Sure. People can get lonely for *misery,* even. I want her to go on being lonely for *you,* so she can come together again the way she was meant to be from the beginning. Loneliness is good for people. Right now it's the only thing for Kitty. Any more licorice?

TOM (*Dazed*) What? Licorice? (*Looking around busily*) I guess we've chewed all the licorice in. We still got Clove, Peppermint, Doublemint, Beechnut, Teaberry, and Juicy Fruit.

JOE Licorice used to be my favorite. Don't worry about her, Tom, she'll be all right. You really want to marry her, don't you?

TOM (*Nodding*) Honest to God, Joe. (*Pathetically*) Only, I haven't got any money.

JOE Couldn't you be a prize-fighter or something like that?

TOM Naaaah. I couldn't hit a man if I wasn't sore at him. He'd have to do something that made me hate him.

JOE You've got to figure out something to do that you won't mind doing very much.

TOM I wish I could, Joe.

JOE (*Thinking deeply, suddenly*) Tom, would you be embarrassed driving a truck?

TOM (*Hit by a thunderbolt*) Joe, I never thought of that. I'd like that. Travel. Highways. Little towns. Coffee and hot cakes. Beautiful valleys and mountains and streams and trees and daybreak and sunset.

JOE There *is* poetry in it, at that.

TOM Joe, that's just the kind of work I *should* do. Just sit there and travel, and look, and smile, and bust out laughing. Could Kitty go with me, sometimes?

JOE I don't know. Get me the phone book. Can you drive a truck?

TOM Joe, you know I can drive a truck, or any kind of thing with a motor and wheels. (TOM *takes* JOE *the phone book.* JOE *turns the pages*)

JOE (*Looking*) Here! Here it is. Tuxedo 7900. Here's a nickel. Get me that number. (TOM *goes to telephone, dials the number*)

TOM Hello.

JOE Ask for Mr. Keith.

TOM (*Mouth and language full of gum*) I'd like to talk to Mr. Keith. (*Pause*) Mr. Keith.

JOE Take that gum out of your mouth for a minute. (TOM *removes the gum*)

TOM Mr. Keith. Yeah. That's right. Hello, Mr. Keith?

JOE Tell him to hold the line.

TOM Hold the line, please.

JOE Give me a hand, Tom. (TOM *helps* JOE *to the telephone. At phone, wad of gum in fingers delicately*) Keith? Joe. Yeah. Fine. Forget it. (*Pause*) Have you got a place for a good driver? (*Pause*) I don't think so. (*To* TOM) You haven't got a driver's license, have you?

TOM (*Worried*) No. But I can get one, Joe.

JOE (*At phone*) No, but he can get one easy enough. To hell with the union. He'll join later. All right, call him a Vice-President and say he drives for relaxation. Sure. What do you mean? Tonight? I don't know why not. San Diego? All right, let him start driving without a license. What the hell's the difference? Yeah. Sure. Look him over. Yeah. I'll send him right over. Right. (*He hangs up*) Thanks. (*To telephone*)

TOM Am I going to get the job?

JOE He wants to take a look at you.

TOM Do I look all right, Joe?

JOE (*Looking at him carefully*) Hold up your head. Stick out your chest. How do you feel? (TOM *does these things*)

TOM Fine.

JOE You *look* fine, too. (JOE *takes his wad of gum out of his mouth and wraps* Liberty *magazine around it*)

JOE You win, Tom. Now, look. (*He bites off the tip of a very long panatela cigar, lights it, and hands one to* TOM, *and another to* KIT) Have yourselves a pleasant smoke. Here. (*He hands two more to* TOM) Give those slummers one each. (*He indicates the* SOCIETY LADY *and* GENTLEMAN. TOM *goes over and without a word gives a cigar each to the* MAN *and the* LADY. *The* MAN *is offended; he smells and tosses aside his cigar. The* WOMAN *looks at her cigar a moment, then puts the cigar in her mouth*)

MAN What do you think you're doing?

LADY Really, dear. I'd like to.

MAN Oh, this is too much.

LADY I'd *really*, really like to, dear. (*She laughs, puts the cigar in her mouth. Turns to* KIT. *He spits out tip. She does the same*)

MAN (*Loudly*) The mother of five grown men, and she's still looking for *romance*. (*Shouts as* KIT *lights her cigar*) No. I forbid it.

JOE (*Shouting*) What's the matter with you? Why don't you leave her alone? What are you always pushing your women around for? (*Almost without a pause*) Now, look, Tom. (*The* LADY *puts the lighted cigar in her mouth, and begins to smoke, feeling wonderful*) Here's ten bucks.

TOM Ten bucks?

JOE He may want you to get into a truck and begin driving to San Diego tonight.

TOM Joe, I got to tell Kitty.

JOE I'll tell her.

TOM Joe, take care of her.

JOE She'll be all right. Stop worrying about her. She's at the St. Francis Hotel. Now, look. Take a cab to Townsend and Fourth. You'll see the big sign. Keith Motor Transport Company. He'll be waiting for you.

TOM O.K., Joe. (*Trying hard*) Thanks, Joe.

JOE Don't be silly. Get going. (TOM *goes.* LADY *starts puffing on cigar. As* TOM *goes,* WESLEY *and* HARRY *come in together*)

NICK Where the hell have you been? We've got to have some entertainment around here. Can't you see them fine people from uptown? (*He points at the* SOCIETY LADY *and* GENTLEMAN)

WESLEY You said to come back at ten for the second show.

NICK Did I say that?

WESLEY Yes, sir, Mr. Nick, that's exactly what you said.

HARRY Was the first show all right?

NICK That wasn't a show. There was no one here to see it. How can it be a show when no one sees it? People are afraid to come down to the waterfront.

HARRY Yeah. We were just down to Pier 27. One of the longshoremen and a cop had a fight and the cop hit him over the head with a blackjack. We saw it happen, didn't we?

WESLEY Yes, sir, we was standing there looking when it happened.

NICK (*A little worried*) Anything else happen?

WESLEY They was all talking.

HARRY A man in a big car came up and said there was going to be a meeting right away and they hoped to satisfy everybody and stop the strike.

WESLEY Right away. *Tonight.*

NICK Well, it's about time. Them poor cops are liable to get nervous and—shoot somebody. (*To* HARRY, *suddenly*) Come back here. I want you to tend bar for a while. I'm going to take a walk over to the pier.

HARRY Yes, sir.

NICK (*To the* SOCIETY LADY *and* GENTLEMAN) You society people made up your minds yet?

LADY Have you champagne?

NICK (*Indicating* JOE) What do you think he's pouring out of that bottle, water or something?

LADY Have you a chilled bottle?

NICK I've got a dozen of them chilled. He's been drinking champagne here all day and all night for a month now.

LADY May we have a bottle?

NICK It's six dollars.

LADY I think we can manage.

MAN I don't know. I *know* I don't know. (NICK *takes off his coat and helps* HARRY *into it.* HARRY *takes a bottle of champagne and two glasses to the* LADY *and* GENTLEMAN, *dancing, collects six dollars, and goes back behind the bar, dancing.* NICK *gets his coat and hat*)

NICK (*To* WESLEY) Rattle the keys a little son. Rattle the keys.

WESLEY Yes, sir, Mr. Nick. (NICK *is on his way out. The* ARAB *enters*)

NICK Hi-ya, *Mahmed.*

ARAB No foundation.

NICK All the way down the line. (*He goes.* WESLEY *is at the piano, playing quietly. The* ARAB *swallows a glass of beer, takes out his harmonica, and begins to play.* WESLEY *fits his playing to the* ARAB'S. KITTY DUVAL, *strangely beautiful, in new clothes, comes in. She walks shyly, as if she were embarrassed by the fine clothes, as if she had no right to wear them. The* LADY *and* GENTLEMAN *are very impressed.* HARRY *looks at her with amazement.* JOE *is reading* Time *magazine.* KITTY *goes to his table.* JOE *looks up from the magazine, without the least amazement*)

JOE Hello, Kitty.

KITTY Hello, Joe.

JOE It's nice seeing you again.

KITTY I came in a cab.

JOE You been crying again? (KITTY *can't answer. To* HARRY) Bring a glass. (HARRY *comes over with a glass.* JOE *pours* KITTY *a drink*)

KITTY I've got to talk to you.

JOE Have a drink.

KITTY I've never been in burlesque. We were just poor.

JOE Sit down, Kitty.

KITTY (*Sits down*) I tried other things.

JOE Here's to you, Katerina Koranovsky. Here's to you. And Tom.

KITTY (*Sorrowfully*) Where *is* Tom?

JOE He's getting a job tonight driving a truck. He'll be back in a couple of days.

KITTY (*Sadly*) I told him I'd marry him.

JOE He wanted to see you and say good-by.

KITTY He's too good for me. He's like a little boy. (*Wearily*) I'm— Too many things have happened to me.

JOE Kitty Duval, you're one of the few truly innocent people I have ever known. He'll be back in a couple of days. Go back to the hotel and wait for him.

KITTY That's what I mean. I can't stand being alone. I'm no good. I tried very hard. I don't know what it is. I miss— (*She gestures*)

JOE (*Gently*) Do you really want to come back here, Kitty?

KITTY I don't know. I'm not sure. Everything *smells* different. I don't know how to feel, or what to think. (*Gesturing pathetically*) I know I don't belong there. It's what I've wanted all my life, but it's too *late.* I try to be happy about it, but all I can do is remember everything and cry.

JOE I don't know what to tell you, Kitty. I didn't mean to hurt you.

KITTY You haven't hurt me. You're the only person who's ever been good to me. I've never known anybody like you. I'm not sure about love any more, but I know I love you, and I know I love Tom.

JOE I love you too, Kitty Duval.

KITTY He'll want babies. I know he will. I know *I* will, too. Of course I will. I can't— (*She shakes her head*)

JOE Tom's a baby himself. You'll be very happy together. He wants you to ride with him in the truck. Tom's good for you. You're good for Tom.

KITTY (*Like a child*) Do you want me to go back and wait for him?

JOE I can't *tell* you what to do. I think it would be a good idea, though.

KITTY I wish I could tell you how it makes me feel to be alone. It's almost worse.

JOE It might take a whole week, Kitty. (*He looks at her sharply, at the arrival of an idea*) Didn't you speak of reading a book? A book of poems?

KITTY I didn't know what I was saying.

JOE (*Trying to get up*) Of course you knew. I think you'll like poetry. Wait here a minute, Kitty. I'll go see if I can find some books.

KITTY All right, Joe. (*He walks out of the place, trying very hard not to wobble. Fog-horn. Music. The* NEWSBOY *comes in. Looks for* JOE. *Is broken-hearted because* JOE *is gone*)

NEWSBOY (*To* SOCIETY GENTLEMAN) Paper?

MAN (*Angry*) No. (*The* NEWSBOY *goes to the* ARAB)

NEWSBOY Paper, Mister?

ARAB (*Irritated*) No foundation.

NEWSBOY What?

ARAB (*Very angry*) No foundation. (*The* NEWSBOY *starts out, turns, looks at the* ARAB, *shakes head*)

NEWSBOY No foundation? How do you figure? (BLICK *and* TWO COPS *enter*)

NEWSBOY (*To* BLICK) Paper, Mister? (BLICK *pushes him aside. The* NEWSBOY *goes*)

BLICK (*Walking authoritatively, about the place, to* HARRY) Where's Nick?

HARRY He went for a walk.

BLICK Who are you?

HARRY Harry.

BLICK (*To the* ARAB *and* WESLEY) Hey, you. Shut up. (*The* ARAB *stops playing the harmonica,* WESLEY *the piano*)

BLICK (*Studies* KITTY) What's your name, sister?

KITTY (*Looking at him*) Kitty Duval. What's it to you? (KITTY'S *voice is now like it was at the begin-*

*ning of the play: tough, independent, bitter, and hard*)

BLICK (*Angry*) Don't give me any of your gutter lip. Just answer my questions.

KITTY You go to hell, you.

BLICK (*Coming over, enraged*) Where do you live?

KITTY The New York Hotel. Room 21.

BLICK Where do you work?

KITTY I'm not working just now. I'm looking for work.

BLICK What kind of work? (KITTY *can't answer*) What kind of work? (KITTY *can't answer. Furiously*) WHAT KIND OF WORK? (KIT CARSON *comes over*)

KIT CARSON You can't talk to a lady that way in *my* presence. (BLICK *turns and stares at* KIT. *The* COPS *begin to move from the bar*)

BLICK (*To the* COPS) It's all right, boys. I'll take care of this. (*To* KIT) *What'd you say?*

KIT CARSON You got no right to hurt people. Who are you? (BLICK, *without a word, takes* KIT *to the street. Sounds of a blow and a groan.* BLICK *returns, breathing hard*)

BLICK (*To the* COPS) O.K., boys. You can go now. Take care of him. Put him on his feet and tell him to behave himself from now on. (*To* KITTY *again*) Now answer my question. What kind of work?

KITTY (*Quietly*) I'm a whore, you son of a bitch. You know what kind of work I do. And I know what kind you do.

MAN (*Shocked and really hurt*) Excuse me, officer, but it seems to me that your attitude—

BLICK Shut up.

MAN (*Quietly*) —is making the poor child say things that are not true.

BLICK Shut up, I said.

LADY Well. (*To the* MAN) Are you going to stand for such insolence?

BLICK (*To* MAN, *who is standing*) Are you?

MAN (*Taking the* WOMAN'*s arm*) I'll get a divorce. I'll start life all over again. (*Pushing the* WOMAN) Come on. Get the hell out of here! (*The* MAN *hurries his* WOMAN *out of the place,* BLICK *watching them go*)

BLICK (*To* KITTY) Now. Let's begin again, and see that you tell the truth. What's your name?

KITTY Kitty Duval.

BLICK Where do you live?

KITTY Until this evening I lived at the New York Hotel. Room 21. This evening I moved to the St. Francis Hotel.

BLICK Oh. To the St. Francis Hotel. Nice place. Where do you work?

KITTY I'm looking for work.

BLICK What kind of work do you do?

KITTY I'm an actress.

BLICK I see. What movies have I seen you in?

KITTY I've worked in burlesque.

BLICK You're a liar. (WESLEY *stands, worried and full of dumb resentment*)

KITTY (*Pathetically, as at the beginning of the play*) It's the truth.

BLICK What are you doing here?

KITTY I came to see if I could get a job here.

BLICK Doing what?

KITTY Singing—and—dancing.

BLICK You can't sing or dance. What are you lying for?

KITTY I can. I sang and danced in burlesque all over the country.

BLICK You're a liar.

KITTY I said lines, too.

BLICK So you danced in burlesque?

KITTY Yes.

BLICK All right. Let's see what you did.

KITTY I can't. There's no music, and I haven't got the right clothes.

BLICK There's music. (*To* WESLEY) Put a nickel in that phonograph. (WESLEY *can't move*) Come on. Put a nickel in that phonograph. (WESLEY *does so. To* KITTY) All right. Get up on that stage and do a hot little burlesque number. (KITTY *stands. Walks slowly to the stage, but is unable to move.* JOE *comes in, holding three books*) Get going, now. Let's see you dance the way you did in burlesque, all over the country. (KITTY *tries to do a burlesque dance. It is beautiful in a tragic way*)

BLICK All right, start taking them off! (KITTY *removes her hat and starts to remove her jacket.* JOE *moves closer to the stage, amazed*)

JOE (*Hurrying to* KITTY) Get down from there. (*He takes* KITTY *into his arms. She is crying. To* BLICK) What the hell do you think you're doing?

WESLEY (*Like a little boy, very angry*) It's that man, Blick. *He* made her take off her clothes. He beat up the old man, too. (BLICK *pushes* WESLEY *off, as* TOM *enters.* BLICK *begins beating up* WESLEY)

TOM What's the matter, Joe? What's happened?

JOE Is the truck out there?

TOM Yeah, but what's happened? Kitty's crying again!

JOE You driving to San Diego?

TOM Yeah, Joe. But what's he doing to that poor colored boy?

JOE Get going. Here's some money. Everything's O.K. (*To* KITTY) Dress in the truck. Take these books.

WESLEY'S VOICE You can't hurt me. You'll get yours. You wait and see.

TOM Joe, he's hurting that boy. I'll kill him!

JOE (*Pushing* TOM) Get out of here! Get married in San Diego. I'll see you when you get back. (TOM *and* KITTY *go.* NICK *enters and stands at the lower end of bar.* JOE *takes the revolver out of his pocket. Looks at it*) I've always wanted to kill somebody, but I never knew who it should be. (*He cocks the revolver, stands real straight, holds it in front of him firmly and walks to the door. He stands a moment watching* BLICK, *aims very carefully, and pulls trigger. There is no shot.* NICK *runs over and grabs the gun, and takes* JOE *aside*)

NICK What the hell do you think you're doing?

JOE (*Casually, but angry*) That dumb Tom. Buys a six-shooter that won't even shoot once. (JOE *sits down, dead to the world.* BLICK *comes out, panting for breath.* NICK *looks at him. He speaks slowly*)

NICK Blick! I told you to stay out of here! Now get

out of here. (*He takes* BLICK *by the collar, tightening his grip as he speaks, and pushing him out*) If you come back again, I'm going to take you in that room where you've been beating up that colored boy, and I'm going to murder you—slowly—with my hands. Beat it! (*He pushes* BLICK *out. To* HARRY) Go take care of the colored boy. (HARRY *runs out.* WILLIE *returns and doesn't sense that anything is changed.* WILLIE *puts another nickel into the machine, but he does so very violently. The consequence of this violence is that the flag comes up again.* WILLIE, *amazed, stands at attention and salutes. The flag goes down. He shakes his head*)

WILLIE (*Thoughtfully*) As far as I'm concerned, this is the *only* country in the world. If you ask me, *nuts* to Europe! (*He is about to push the slide in again when the flag comes up again. Furiously, to* NICK, *while he salutes and stands at attention, pleadingly*) Hey, Nick. This machine is out of order.

NICK (*Somberly*) Give it a whack on the side. (WILLIE *does so. A hell of a whack. The result is the flag comes up and down, and* WILLIE *keeps saluting*)

WILLIE (*Saluting*) Hey, Nick. Something's wrong. (*The machine quiets down abruptly.* WILLIE *very stealthily slides a new nickel in, and starts a new game. From a distance two pistol shots are heard, each carefully timed.* NICK *runs out. The* NEWSBOY *enters, crosses to* JOE'*s table, senses something is wrong*)

NEWSBOY (*Softly*) Paper, Mister? (JOE *can't hear him. The* NEWSBOY *backs away, studies* JOE, *wishes he could cheer* JOE *up. Notices the phonograph, goes to it, and puts a coin in it, hoping music will make* JOE *happier. The* NEWSBOY *sits down. Watches* JOE. *The music begins. "The Missouri Waltz." The* DRUNKARD *comes in and walks around. Then sits down.* NICK *comes back*)

NICK (*Delighted*) Joe, Blick's dead! Somebody just shot him, and none of the cops are trying to find out who. (JOE *doesn't hear.* NICK *steps back, studying* JOE. *Shouting*) Joe.

JOE (*Looking up*) What?

NICK Blick's dead.

JOE Blick? Dead? Good! That God-damn gun wouldn't go off. I *told* Tom to get a good one.

NICK (*Picking up gun and looking at it*) Joe, you wanted to kill that guy! (HARRY *returns.* JOE *puts the gun in his coat pocket*) I'm going to buy you a bottle of champagne. (NICK *goes to bar.* JOE *rises, takes hat from rack, puts coat on. The* NEWSBOY *jumps up, helps* JOE *with coat*)

NICK What's the matter, Joe?

JOE Nothing. Nothing.

NICK How about the champagne?

JOE Thanks. (*Going*)

NICK It's not eleven yet. Where you going, Joe?

JOE I don't know. Nowhere.

NICK Will I see you tomorrow?

JOE I don't know. I don't think so. (KIT CARSON *enters, walks to* JOE. JOE *and* KIT *look at one another knowingly*)

JOE Somebody just shot a man. How are you feeling?

KIT Never felt better in my life. (*Loudly, bragging, but somber*) I shot a man once. In San Francisco. Shot him two times. In 1939, I think it was. In October. Fellow named Blick or Glick or something like that. Couldn't stand the way he talked to ladies. Went up to my room and got my old pearl-handled revolver and waited for him on Pacific Street. Saw him walking, and let him have it, two times. Had to throw the beautiful revolver into the Bay. (HARRY, NICK, *the* ARAB, *and the* DRUNKARD *close in around him.* JOE *searches his pockets, brings out the revolver, puts it in* KIT'*s hand, looks at him with great admiration and affection.* JOE *walks slowly to the stairs leading to the street, turns and waves.* KIT, *and then one by one everybody else, waves, and the marble game goes into its beautiful American routine again: flag, lights, and music. The play ends*)

## Note Appended to THE TIME OF YOUR LIFE

In the time of your life, live—so that in that good time there shall be no ugliness or death for yourself or for any life your life touches. Seek goodness everywhere, and when it is found, bring it out of its hiding-place and let it be free and unashamed. Place in matter and in flesh the least of the values, for these are the things that hold death and must pass away. Discover in all things that which shines and is beyond corruption. Encourage virtue in whatever heart it may have been driven into secrecy and sorrow by the shame and terror of the world. Ignore the obvious, for it is unworthy of the clear eye and the kindly heart. Be the inferior of no man, nor of any man be the superior. Remember that every man is a variation of yourself. No man's guilt is not yours, nor is any man's innocence a thing apart. Despise evil and ungodliness, but not men of ungodliness or evil. These, understand. Have no shame in being kindly and gentle, but if the time comes in the time of your life to kill, kill and have no regret. In the time of your life, live—so that in that wondrous time you shall not add to the misery and sorrow of the world, but shall smile to the infinite delight and mystery of it.

# Jean Giraudoux

## (1882-1944)

In 1928 when Jean Giraudoux turned from fiction to drama, the French theatre was at a low point. Society dramas, love triangles, bedroom farces, and slice-of-life melodramas were turned out with monotonous regularity by such writers as Bataille, Bernstein, and Porto-Riche. The virtuosity and brilliance of the Paris stage in the 1920's contrasts sharply indeed with the poverty of the native repertory. It was an age of great directors and producers—Jacques Copeau, Georges Pitoëff, Charles Dullin, Gaston Baty, and Louis Jouvet—and of magnificent performances of French classic plays and of contemporary foreign plays by such masters as Chekhov, Shaw, and Pirandello. Jean Giraudoux had been writing clever but unpretentious fiction since 1909. He came to the stage at a time when imagination and style had all but vanished from the contemporary French theatrical scene, and although he began relatively late in life, within a few years he succeeded in transforming the character of modern French drama.

Giraudoux was by profession a diplomat; his writing was an avocation, but it was frequently marked by the qualities of delicacy, finesse, and tact that were natural to his occupation. He was born in the small town of Bellac in south central France, and after completing his secondary education, went to Paris for further study. At the Sorbonne he majored in German studies under the distinguished French Germanist, Charles Andler, and received a fellowship to study in Munich during the year 1905-06. German literature and thought made a profound impression on the young Giraudoux. He attempted fictional sketches in German and took particular delight in the study of German romanticism and nineteenth-century drama. La Motte Fouqué, Kleist, Wagner, and Hebbel were to provide materials for some of his most famous plays. During the interwar period Giraudoux served at the German desk of the Ministry of Foreign Affairs, and the complexities and mounting tensions of Franco-German political relationships, before and after Hitler's rise to power, are frequently reflected in his dramas.

Giraudoux's first play, *Siegfried* (1928), is clearly the work of a cultivated Frenchman, keenly aware of diplomatic tensions, but also sympathetic toward German culture. There are perhaps overtones of Pirandello in his hero's confusion over his identity: Siegfried, the savior of postwar Germany, is in fact a Frenchman named Jacques Forestier. He ends dedicated to the welfare of both countries. Some readers have seen this conclusion as a reflection of the *rapprochement* policies of the French Foreign Ministry under Briand. More striking is Giraudoux's style, which freely mixes the lofty and the mundane, the majesty of history and the wry humor of everyday life. He senses the dangers of a Germany in an endless process of becoming, animated by a demented and "almost physical love of the universe," but boldly transforms politics and ideology into a highly personal and poetic fantasy. The success of the Paris production of *Siegfried* marked the beginning of the warm collaboration of Giraudoux and the great actor-director, Louis Jouvet. Jouvet produced all but two of Giraudoux's fifteen plays, and stamped them with his personality.

The transformation of history in *Siegfried* was followed the next year by the recreation of classical myth in *Amphitryon 38*, so whimsically named because it was apparently preceded by 37 other plays on the same subject. In a light-hearted and delicate vein, Giraudoux probes tenderly into the nuances of married love. Jupiter would win Alkmena as a lover but is forced into the role of a husband. In *Judith* (1931), the playwright experimented even more freely with the restatement of history and legend. Far more serious in tone and implication than most of his dramas, it is the only play which Giraudoux subtitled "Tragedy." The Jewish virgin, forced by her people to give herself to the conquering giant, Holofernes, rebels against her entrapment by God and against her role in history. Passionately and sensuously, she enjoys Holofernes, then kills him so as not to lose him. The murder is an act of love, not hatred, yet Judith finally submits to the fraud of a divine miracle, and thereby becomes the image of herself as the popular imagination would have her be. The contrast between the mask and the face is absolute.

In his critical essays of the early 1930's Giraudoux vigorously defended his poetic conception of the theatre. "Our epoch," he declared in his "Discourse on the Theatre," "no longer demands works from the man of letters—the street and courtyards are filled with such useless furniture—it demands from him above all else a language." Giraudoux's language is that of an urbane and cultivated man—gay, light, witty, sophisticated, yet marked by an underlying seriousness that lends depth to his seemingly-frivolous neat turns of phrase. Much ink has been spilled by Giraudoux's admirers in the defense of his style from the charge of preciosity and over-refinement. Language in Giraudoux's plays is rarely an end in itself. The color and magic of the word is part of a larger poetic conception of the theatre, free from dependence on the literal or the verifiable. Giraudoux's style with its verve, glitter, and polish moves hand in hand with his love of artifice, elegant theatricality, and bold categorization. The world of myth, fantasy, and the supernatural is never far from the natural plane of events. In *The Impromptu of Paris* (1937), a critical essay in the form of a one-act play, Giraudoux again insists that "the theatre is a world of light, poetry, and imagination," the expression of dream and vision, of fantasy and wonder. As one of the actresses declares, "It's merely being real in the unreal." The playwright's language is part of a theatre that constitutes its own reality.

This does not mean that theatre for Giraudoux is trivial or inconsequential. In his "Discourse" of 1931 he asserted, "The stage is the only form of a nation's spiritual and artistic education." It is the measure of its cultural achievement, the index of the quality of experience of a whole people. Giraudoux sought in his theatre of magic to capture the free-wheeling irrationality which he so prized in his countrymen and which made him declare that "the mission of France is to infuriate the world." Drama, he insists, communicates through feeling rather than through understanding; without knowing it, the spectators, through their participation in an act of communal ritual, absorb the prophecy and vision of dramatic art at its highest reach.

The same grandeur of conception underlies Giraudoux's evocations of antique myth that pointed to the outbreak of a new world war, *The Trojan War Will Not Take Place* of 1935 (*La Guerre de Troie n'aura pas lieu*, translated by Christopher Fry as *Tiger at the Gates*) and *Electra* (1937). In the first play, Hector battles vainly against destiny and the gods. Despite his rational persuasion of Paris to yield Helen to the Greek ambassadors, and of Helen to return with them, accident and the irrational triumph over human calculation. Ulysses' famous speech on the inevitable war between two nations, each brought up to a future of similar invention and authority but with opposite scales of value, points unmistakably to the coming clash between France and Germany. Giraudoux's play was produced as Hitler's armies reoccupied the left bank of the Rhine. The political background provides a grim commentary on the efforts of the peacemakers.

In similar fashion, *Electra* is as close to contemporary history as to the ancient dramatizations of the story of the House of Atreus. The choice between a compromise peace and a destructive war confronted Giraudoux's countrymen squarely in 1937. Electra is the spokesman of the playwright in her declaration, "When the crime is an assault on human dignity, infects a nation, corrupts its loyalty, then—no pardon is possible." Aegisthus becomes a somewhat more sympathetic tyrant than we find in Greek drama, but we should not see him as a tragic hero; his fate is fully merited by his ruthlessness. In lively theatrical style, Giraudoux has modernized the legend by casting the furies as little girls and contriving the gardener, the beggar, and other supporting characters to heighten the fantasy. The exposition is long and complex, with dialogue carrying the weight of the action. In such scenes as the Interlude, Giraudoux indulges his fondness for long set speeches and monologues. The aside, the direct address to the audience, the interweaving of narration and action, are all part of his assertion of the histrionic qualities of performance. We move from the tale of the death of Agamemnon to the final catastrophe: the slaying of Aegisthus amid the violent destruction of the city. Electra's victory is expensive but the price is not too high; the *raisonneur* speaks for the playwright when he gives it all a beautiful name: "It is called the dawn." There is bitter irony in Electra's claim, "I have everything"; but Giraudoux is once more pointing to the mixed and painful character of human accomplishment in a world in which nothing pure can remain unalloyed.

In the United States, Giraudoux is better known for the charm, gaiety, and humor of his more romantic adventures into the realm of the fairy-like and supernatural, as in *Intermezzo*, known in America as *The Enchanted* (1933), and *Ondine* (1939). Isabel, the heroine of *Intermezzo*, is an early version of the naïve and beautiful water nymph, but she is called back to a world of human love and everyday events, whereas Ondine is separated from them forever. In keeping with the romantic legend, her knight, Hans, must die should he ever give up his love. Ondine's desertion of her fairyland home beneath the sea only demonstrates the fragility of human love and the pain and pathos of mortal existence. An even darker melancholy hovers over the anatomy of marriage in *Sodom and Gomorrah* (1943), a somewhat moralistic account of husband-wife relations much closer to the modern than to the biblical world, and ending in universal death and destruction echoing the holocaust of World War II. Giraudoux's final play, *Pour Lucrèce* (*Duel of Angels*, 1944) was only partially finished at the time of his death. Reminiscent of his early studies of love and desire and the interplay of the real and the imaginary, it explores virtuous love and the painful consequences of loss of faith in feminine purity. Giraudoux was poignantly aware of the suffering love brought to its victims, but in his earlier plays it is the triumph of love and the praise of lovers that dominates the action.

The somber hue that colored Giraudoux's late years is no doubt a reflection of the dark realities of life in France under Nazi control. Despite the melancholy pathos of his last plays, Giraudoux saw life as intrinsically good, to be seized and enjoyed to the limit of human capacity. Entertaining and thought-provoking, he moved away from the restrictions of literal representation and the *pièce à thèse* toward a vividly poetic expression of illusion, mystery, and the kingdom of the imagination. In Act II of *Ondine*, Giraudoux's Illusionist, when asked if the figures that prestidigitators produce out of thin air are real or contrived, replies with oblique allusion to the playwright's art, "It depends on the magician."

# ELECTRA

## English Version by Winifred Smith

### CHARACTERS

ORESTES
THE EUMENIDES, *first as three little girls, later as fifteen-year-olds*
GARDENER
PRESIDENT OF THE COUNCIL
AGATHA, *his young wife*
AEGISTHUS
BEGGAR
CLYTEMNESTRA
ELECTRA
YOUNG MAN
CAPTAIN
NARSES' WIFE
GUESTS, SERVANTS, MAIDS, SOLDIERS

## Act One

SCENE 1 *A stranger,* ORESTES, *enters, escorted by* THREE LITTLE GIRLS, *just as, from the opposite side, the* GARDENER *comes in dressed for a festival, and accompanied by guests from the village.*

FIRST LITTLE GIRL How fine the gardener looks!

SECOND LITTLE GIRL Of course! It's his wedding day.

THIRD LITTLE GIRL Here it is, sir, your Agamemnon's palace!

STRANGER What a strange façade! Is it straight?

FIRST LITTLE GIRL No. There's no right side to it. You think you see it, but that's a mirage. Like the gardener you see coming, who wants to speak to you. He's not coming. He won't be able to say a word.

SECOND LITTLE GIRL Or he'll bray—or meow—

GARDENER The façade is perfectly straight, stranger. Don't listen to these liars. You are confused because the right side is built of stones from Gaul and sweats at certain seasons; then the people say the palace is weeping. The left side is built of marble from Argos, which—no one knows why—will suddenly be flooded with sunshine, even at night. Then they say the palace laughs. Right now the palace is laughing and crying at the same time.

FIRST LITTLE GIRL So it's sure not to be mistaken.

SECOND LITTLE GIRL It's really a widow's palace.

FIRST LITTLE GIRL Or of childhood memories.

STRANGER I can't remember seeing such a sensitive building anywhere.

GARDENER Have you already visited the palace?

FIRST LITTLE GIRL As a baby.

SECOND LITTLE GIRL Twenty years ago.

THIRD LITTLE GIRL He couldn't walk yet.

GARDENER But he must remember if he saw it.

STRANGER All I can remember of Agamemnon's palace is a mosaic. They set me down on a square of tigers when I was naughty and on a hexagon of flowers when I was good—and I remember creeping from one to the other across some birds.

FIRST LITTLE GIRL And over a beetle.

STRANGER How do you know that, child?

GARDENER And did your family live in Argos?

STRANGER And I remember many, many bare feet. Not a face, faces were way up in the sky, but lots of bare feet. I tried to touch the gold rings under the edges of the skirts; some ankles were joined by chains, slaves' ankles. I remember two little feet, very white ones, the barest, the whitest. Their steps were always even, timid, measured by an invisible chain. I imagine they were Electra's. I must have kissed them, mustn't I? A baby kisses everything it touches.

SECOND LITTLE GIRL Anyway that would have been the only kiss Electra ever had.

GARDENER It surely would!

FIRST LITTLE GIRL Jealous, gardener?

STRANGER Electra still lives in the palace?

SECOND LITTLE GIRL Still. But not much longer.

STRANGER Is that her window, the one with jasmine?

GARDENER No. That's the room where Atreus, the first king of Argos, killed his brother's sons.

FIRST LITTLE GIRL The dinner when he served up their hearts took place in the room next to it. I'd love to know how they tasted.

THIRD LITTLE GIRL Did he cut them up or cook them whole?

SECOND LITTLE GIRL And Cassandra was strangled in the sentry box.

THIRD LITTLE GIRL They caught her in a net and stabbed her. She yelled like a crazy woman, through her veil. I'd love to have seen it.

FIRST LITTLE GIRL That all happened in the laughing wing, as you see.

STRANGER The one with roses?

GARDENER Stranger, don't try to connect the windows with flowers. I'm the palace gardener. I plant them at random. They're just flowers.

SECOND LITTLE GIRL Not at all. There are flowers and flowers. Phlox doesn't suit Thyestes.

THIRD LITTLE GIRL Nor mignonette Cassandra.

GARDENER Oh, be quiet! The window with the roses, stranger, is the one of the rooms where our king, Agamemnon, coming back from the war, slipped into the pool, fell on his sword and killed himself.

FIRST LITTLE GIRL He took his bath after his death. About two minutes after. That's the difference.

GARDENER That's Electra's window.

STRANGER Why is it so high up, almost on the roof?

GARDENER So she can see her father's tomb.

STRANGER Why is she there?

GARDENER Because it's Orestes' old room, her brother's. Her mother sent him out of the country when he was two and he's not been heard of since.

SECOND LITTLE GIRL Listen, sisters, listen! They're talking about Orestes!

GARDENER Will you clear out! Leave us! You're just like flies.

FIRST LITTLE GIRL We certainly won't leave. We're with this stranger.

GARDENER Do you know these girls?

STRANGER I met them at the door. They followed me in.

SECOND LITTLE GIRL We followed him because we like him.

THIRD LITTLE GIRL Because he's a lot better looking than you are, gardener.

FIRST LITTLE GIRL No caterpillars in his beard.

SECOND LITTLE GIRL Nor June bugs in his nose.

THIRD LITTLE GIRL If flowers are to smell sweet, the gardener has to smell bad.

STRANGER Be polite, children, and tell us what you do all the time.

FIRST LITTLE GIRL What we do is, we're not polite.

SECOND LITTLE GIRL We lie, we slander, we insult.

FIRST LITTLE GIRL But specially, we recite.

STRANGER And what do you recite?

FIRST LITTLE GIRL We never know ahead of time—we invent as we go along. But we're very, very good.

SECOND LITTLE GIRL The king of Mycenae, whose sister-in-law we insulted, said we were very, very good.

THIRD LITTLE GIRL We say all the bad things we can think up.

GARDENER Don't listen to them, stranger. No one knows who they are. They've been wandering about the town for two days without friends or family. If we ask who they are, they pretend they're the little Eumenides. And the horrible thing is that they grow and get fat as you look at them. Yesterday they were years younger than today. Come here, you!

SECOND LITTLE GIRL Is he rude, for a bridegroom!

GARDENER Look at her! See how her eyelashes grow. Look at her bosom. I understand such things, I've seen mushrooms grow. They grow fast, like an orange.

SECOND LITTLE GIRL Poisonous things always win out.

THIRD LITTLE GIRL (*To the* FIRST LITTLE GIRL) Really? You're growing a bosom?

FIRST LITTLE GIRL Are we going to recite or not?

STRANGER Let them recite, gardener.

FIRST LITTLE GIRL Let's recite Clytemnestra, Electra's mother— You agree? Clytemnestra?

SECOND LITTLE GIRL We agree.

FIRST LITTLE GIRL Queen Clytemnestra has a bad color. She uses rouge.

SECOND LITTLE GIRL Her color is bad because she sleeps badly.

THIRD LITTLE GIRL She sleeps badly because she's afraid.

FIRST LITTLE GIRL What is Queen Clytemnestra afraid of?

SECOND LITTLE GIRL Of everything.

FIRST LITTLE GIRL What's everything?

SECOND LITTLE GIRL Silence. Silences.

THIRD LITTLE GIRL Noise. Noises.

FIRST LITTLE GIRL The idea that midnight is near. That the spider on its thread is about to pass from the time of day when it brings good luck to the time when it brings bad luck.

SECOND LITTLE GIRL Of everything red, because blood is red.

FIRST LITTLE GIRL Queen Clytemnestra has a bad color. She puts on blood.

GARDENER What a silly story!

SECOND LITTLE GIRL Good, isn't it?

FIRST LITTLE GIRL See how the end goes back to the beginning—couldn't be more poetic!

STRANGER Very interesting.

FIRST LITTLE GIRL As you're interested in Electra we can recite about her. You agree, sisters? We can recite what she was like at our age.

SECOND LITTLE GIRL We certainly do agree!

THIRD LITTLE GIRL Even before we were born, before yesterday, we agreed.

FIRST LITTLE GIRL Electra amuses herself by making Orestes fall out of his mother's arms.

SECOND LITTLE GIRL Electra waxes the steps of the throne so her uncle, Aegisthus, will measure his length on the marble.

THIRD LITTLE GIRL Electra is preparing to spit in the face of her little brother, Orestes, if he ever returns.

FIRST LITTLE GIRL Of course, *that* isn't true, but it'd be a good story.

SECOND LITTLE GIRL For nineteen years she's prepared poisonous spittle in her mouth.

THIRD LITTLE GIRL She's thinking of your slugs, gardener, to make her mouth water more.

GARDENER Now stop, you dirty little vipers!

SECOND LITTLE GIRL Oh, ha, ha, the bridegroom gets mad!

STRANGER He's right. Get out!

GARDENER And don't come back!

FIRST LITTLE GIRL We'll come back tomorrow.

GARDENER Just try to! The palace is forbidden to girls of your age.

FIRST LITTLE GIRL Tomorrow we'll be grown up.

SECOND LITTLE GIRL Tomorrow will be the day after Electra's marriage to the gardener. We'll be grown up.

STRANGER What are they saying?

FIRST LITTLE GIRL You've not defended us, stranger. You'll be sorry for that.

GARDENER Horrible little beasts! You'd think they were three little Fates. Dreadful to be a child Fate!

SECOND LITTLE GIRL Fate shows you her tail, gardener. Watch out if it grows.

FIRST LITTLE GIRL Come, sisters. Let's leave them both in front of their tainted wall.

(*The little* EUMENIDES *go out, the* GUESTS *shrinking away from them in terror*)

SCENE 2 *The* STRANGER. *The* GARDENER. *The* PRESIDENT OF THE COUNCIL *and his young wife,* AGATHA THEOCATHOCLES. *Villagers*

STRANGER What did these girls say? That you are marrying Electra, gardener?

GARDENER She'll be my wife an hour from now.

AGATHA He'll *not* marry her. We've come to prevent that.

PRESIDENT I'm your distant cousin, gardener, and the Vice President of the Council; so I've a double right to advise you. Run away to your radishes and squashes. Don't marry Electra.

GARDENER Aegisthus orders me to.

STRANGER Am I crazy? If Agamemnon were alive, Electra's wedding would be a festival for all Greece—and Aegisthus gives her to a gardener, whose family, even, objects! Don't tell me Electra is ugly or hunch-backed!

GARDENER Electra is the most beautiful girl in Argos.

AGATHA Oh, she's not too bad looking.

PRESIDENT And she's perfectly straight. Like all flowers that grow in the shade.

STRANGER Is she backward? Feeble-minded?

PRESIDENT She's intelligence personified.

AGATHA An especially good memory. Not always for the same thing, though. I don't have a good memory. Except for your birthday, darling, *that* I never forget.

STRANGER What can she have done, or said, to be treated this way?

PRESIDENT She does nothing, says nothing. But she's always *here*.

AGATHA She's here now.

STRANGER She has a right to be. It's her father's palace. It's not her fault he's dead.

GARDENER I'd never have dreamed of marrying Electra, but as Aegisthus orders me to, I don't see why I'd be afraid.

PRESIDENT You have every reason to be afraid. She's the kind of woman that makes trouble.

AGATHA And you're not the only one! Our family has everything to fear.

GARDENER I don't understand you.

PRESIDENT You will understand. Life can be pleasant, can't it!

AGATHA Very pleasant! Immensely so!

PRESIDENT Don't interrupt me, darling, especially just to repeat what I say. It *can* be very pleasant. Everything has a way of settling itself in life—spiritual suffering can be cured more quickly than cancer, and mourning than a sty. Take any group of human beings at random, each will have the same percentage of crime, lies, vice and adultery.

AGATHA That's a horrid word, adultery, darling.

PRESIDENT Don't interrupt me, especially to contradict! How does it happen that in one group life slips by softly, conventionally, the dead are forgotten, the living get on well together, while in another there's hell to pay? It's simply that in the latter there's a woman who makes trouble.

STRANGER That means there's a conscience in the second group.

AGATHA I can't help thinking of your word, adultery—such a horrid word!

PRESIDENT Be quiet, Agatha. A conscience, you say! If criminals don't forget their sins, if the conquered don't forget their defeats, if there are curses, quarrels, hatreds, the fault is not with humanity's conscience, which always tends toward compromise and forgetfulness, it lies with ten or fifteen women who make trouble.

STRANGER I agree with you. Those ten or fifteen women save the world from egoism.

PRESIDENT They save it from happiness! I know Electra. Let's agree that she is what you say—justice, generosity, duty. But it's by justice, generosity, duty, and not by egoism and easygoing ways, that the state, individuals, and the best families are ruined.

AGATHA Absolutely! But why, darling? You've told me, but I forget.

PRESIDENT Because those three virtues have in common the one element fatal to humanity—implacability. Happiness is never the lot of implacable people. A happy family makes a surrender. A happy epoch demands unanimous capitulation.

STRANGER You surrendered at the first call?

PRESIDENT Alas, no! Some one else got in first. So I'm only the vice-president.

GARDENER Against what is Electra implacable? She goes every night to her father's tomb, is that all?

PRESIDENT I know. I've followed her. Along the same road which my duty made me take one night, pursuing our most dangerous murderer, along the same river I followed and saw the greatest innocent in Greece. A horrible walk, behind the two of them. They stopped at the same places, at the yew, at the corner of the bridge, at the thousand year old milestone, all made the same signs to innocence and to crime. But because the murderer was there, the night was bright, peaceful, clear. He was the kernel taken out of the fruit, which, in a tart, might have broken your tooth. Electra's presence, on the contrary, confused light and darkness, even spoiled the full moon. Have you seen a fisherman, who before going out to fish, arranges his bait? All the way along the river, that was she. Every evening she spreads her net for everything that without her would have abandoned this pleasant, agreeable earth—remorse, confessions, old blood stains, rust, bones of murdered men, a mass of accusations. In a short time everything will be ready for the fisherman to pass by.

STRANGER He always comes, sooner or later.

PRESIDENT That's not so.

AGATHA (*Much taken by the* STRANGER) A mistake!

PRESIDENT This child herself sees the leak in your argument. A triple layer of earth daily piles up over our sins, our failures, our crimes, and stifles their worst effects! Forgetfulness, death, human justice. It is madness to remember those things. A horrible country, one where because of an avenger of wrongs, ghosts walk, dead men, half asleep,—where no allowance is ever made for human weakness, or perjury, where a ghost and an avenger constantly threaten. When guilty men's sleep continues to be more troubled after legal prosecution than the sleep of an innocent, society is terribly disturbed. When I look at Electra, I'm troubled by the sins I committed in my cradle.

AGATHA And I by my future sins. I'll never commit them, darling. You know that. Especially that adultery, which you will talk about. But those other sins already bother me.

GARDENER I'm rather of Electra's opinion. I don't much care for wicked people. I love truth.

PRESIDENT Do you know what truth is for our family that you proclaim it so openly? A quiet, well-thought-of family, rising fast. You'll not deny my assertion that you are the least important member of it. But I know by experience that it's not safe to venture on thin ice. It won't be ten days, if you marry Electra, before the discovery—I'm just inventing this—that our old aunt, when a young girl, strangled her baby so her husband wouldn't find out about it, and in order to quiet suspicion, stopped hushing up the various aspersions on her grandfather's virtue. My little Agatha, in spite of being gaiety itself, can't sleep because of all this. You are the only one who doesn't see Aegisthus' trick. He wants to pass on to the Theocathocles family everything that might some day throw a sinister light on the Atrides.[1]

STRANGER And what have the Atrides to fear?

PRESIDENT Nothing. Nothing that I know of, it's like every happy family or couple, every satisfied person. Yet it does have to fear the most dangerous enemy in the world, who would eat it through to the bone, Electra's ally, uncompromising justice.

[1] Descendants of Atreus.

GARDENER Electra loves my garden. If she's a little nervous, the flowers will do her good.

AGATHA But she'll not do the flowers good.

PRESIDENT Certainly. You'll get to know your fuchias and geraniums. You'll see that they're not just pretty symbols. They'll show their knavery and their ingratitude. Electra in the garden is justice and memory among the flowers—that means hatred.

GARDENER Electra is devout. All the dead are for her.

PRESIDENT The dead! The murdered, half melted into the murderers, the shades of the robbed mingled with those of the thieves, rival families scattered among each other, and saying, "Oh, Heavens! here's Electra! And we were so peaceful."

AGATHA Here comes Electra!

GARDENER No, not yet. It's Aegisthus. Leave us, stranger, Aegisthus doesn't like strange faces.

PRESIDENT You, too. Agatha. He's rather too fond of well-known women's faces.

AGATHA (*With marked interest in the stranger's good looks*) Shall I show you the way, handsome stranger?

(AEGISTHUS *enters, to the hurrahs of the* GUESTS, *as* SERVANTS *set up his throne, and place a stool beside a pillar*)

SCENE 3 AEGISTHUS. *The* PRESIDENT. *The* BEGGAR. *The* GARDENER. SERVANT.

AEGISTHUS Why the stool? What's the stool for?

SERVANT For the beggar, my lord.

AEGISTHUS What beggar?

SERVANT The god, if you prefer. This beggar has been wandering through the city for several days. We've never seen a beggar who's so much a beggar, so it's thought he must be a god. We let him go wherever he likes. He's prowling around the palace now.

AEGISTHUS Changing wheat to gold? Seducing the maids?

SERVANT He does no harm.

AEGISTHUS A queer god! The priests haven't found out yet whether he's a rascal or Jupiter?

SERVANT The priests don't want to be asked.

AEGISTHUS Friends, shall we leave the stool here?

PRESIDENT I think it will be better to honor a beggar than to insult a god.

AEGISTHUS Leave the stool there. But if he comes, warn us. We'd like to be just a group of human beings for a few minutes. And don't be rude to him. Perhaps he is delegated by the gods to attend Electra's marriage. The gods invite themselves to this marriage, which the President considers an insult to his family.

PRESIDENT My lord . . .

AEGISTHUS Don't protest. I heard everything. The acoustics in this palace are extraordinary. The architect apparently wanted to listen to the council's discussions of his salary and bonus, he built it full of echoing passages.

PRESIDENT My lord . . .

AEGISTHUS Be quiet. I know everything you're about

to say on the subject of your fine honest family, your worthy sister-in-law, the baby-killer, your uncle, the satirist and your nephew, the slanderer.

PRESIDENT My lord . . .

AEGISTHUS An officer, in a battle, to whom the King's standard is given to turn the enemy's fire on him, carries it with more enthusiasm. You're losing your time. The gardener will marry Electra.

SERVANT Here is the beggar, my lord.

AEGISTHUS Detain him a moment. Offer him a drink. Wine is appropriate for a beggar or a god.

SERVANT God or beggar, he's drunk already.

AEGISTHUS Then let him come in. He'll not understand us, though we must speak of the gods. It might even be amusing to talk about them before him. Your notion of Electra, President, is true enough, but it's peculiar, definitely middle-class. As I'm the Regent, allow me to give you more elevated philosophical ideas. You believe in the gods, President?

PRESIDENT Do you, my lord?

AEGISTHUS My dear President, I've often asked myself if I believe in the gods. Asked myself because it's the only problem a statesman must decide for himself. I do believe in the gods. Or rather, I believe I believe in the gods. But I believe in them, not as great caretakers and great watchmen, but as great abstractions. Between space and time, always oscillating between gravitation and emptiness, there are the great indifferences. Those are the gods. I imagine them, not constantly concerned with that moving mould on the earth which is humanity, but as having reached the stage of serenity and universality. That is blessedness, the same thing as unconsciousness. They are unconscious at the top of the ladder of being, as the atom is at the bottom. The difference is that theirs is the unconsciousness of lightning, omniscient, thousand-faceted, so that in their normal state, like diamonds, powerless and deaf, they only *react* to light, to omens, without understanding them.

BEGGAR (*At last seated, feels he must applaud*) Well said! Bravo!

AEGISTHUS Thanks. On the other hand, President, it's undeniable that sometimes there seem to be interruptions in human life so opportune and extensive that it's possible to believe in an extraordinary superhuman interest or justice. Such events have something superhuman or divine about them, in that they are like coarse work, not at all well designed. The plague breaks out in a town which has sinned by impiety or folly, but it also ravages the neighboring city, a particularly holy one. War breaks out when a nation becomes degenerate and vile, but it destroys all the just, the brave, and preserves the cowards. Or, whose ever the fault, or by whom committed, it's the same family that pays, innocent or guilty. I know a mother of seven children, who always spanked the same child —she was a divine mother. This fits our idea of the gods, that they are blind boxers, always satisfied by finding the same cheeks to slap, the same bottoms to spank. We might even be surprised if we understood the confusion that comes from a sudden waking to beatitude, that their blows weren't given more at random; that the wife of a good man, and not a perjurer's, is brained by a shutter in a wind storm; that accidents strike down pilgrims and not troops. Always humanity suffers . . . I'm speaking generally. We see crows or deer struck down by an inexplicable epidemic—perhaps the blow intended for mankind went astray, either up or down. However it be, it's certain that the chief duty of a statesman is to watch fiercely that the gods are not shaken out of their lethargy, and to limit the harm they do to such reactions as sleepers snoring, or to thunder.

BEGGAR Bravo! That's very clear! I understand it very well!

AEGISTHUS Charmed, I'm sure!

BEGGAR It's truth itself. For example, look at the people walking along the roads. Sometimes every hundred feet you'll see a dead hedgehog. They go over the roads at night by tens, male and female, and get crushed. You'll say they're fools, that they could find their mates on their side of the road. I can't explain it, but love, for hedgehogs, begins by crossing a road. What the devil was I trying to say? I've lost the thread . . . Go on, it'll come back to me.

AEGISTHUS Indeed! What is he trying to say!

PRESIDENT Shall we talk about Electra, my lord?

AEGISTHUS What do you think we've been talking about? Our charming little Agatha? We were talking only about Electra, President, and about the need I feel to get her out of the royal family. Why, since I've been Regent, while other cities are devoured by dissension, other citizens by moral crises, are we alone satisfied with other people and with ourselves? Why are we so rich? Why in Argos alone are raw materials so dear and retail prices so low? Why, when we're exporting more cows, does butter go down in price? Why do storms pass by our vineyards, heresies our temples, animal diseases our barns? Because, in this city, I wage merciless war against all who signal to the gods.

PRESIDENT What do you mean, signal to the gods?

BEGGAR There! I've found it!

AEGISTHUS Found what?

BEGGAR My story, the thread of my story. I was speaking of the death of hedgehogs.

AEGISTHUS One moment, please. We're speaking of the gods.

BEGGAR To be sure! Gods come first, hedgehogs second. But I wonder if I'll remember.

AEGISTHUS There are no two ways of signaling, President: it's done by separating one's self from the crowd, climbing a hill and waving a lantern or a flag. The earth is betrayed, as is a besieged city, by signals. The philosopher signals from his roof, the poet or a desperate man signals from his balcony or his swimming pool. If for ten years the gods have not meddled with our lives, it's because I've kept the heights empty and the fairgrounds full. I've ordered dreamers, painters, and chemists to marry; and because, in order to avoid racial trouble between our citizens— something that can't help marking human beings as different in the eyes of the gods—I've always given great importance to misdemeanors and paid slight attention to crimes. Nothing keeps the gods so quiet as an equal value set on murder and on stealing bread. I must say the courts have supported me splendidly. Whenever I've been forced to be severe, they've overlooked it. None of my decisions has been so obvious as to allow the gods to avenge it. No exile. I kill. An exile tends to climb up a steep road, just like a ladybird. I never execute in public. Our poor neighboring cities betray themselves by erecting their gallows on the top of a hill; I crucify at the bottom of a valley. Now I've said everything about Electra.

GARDENER What have you said?

AEGISTHUS That there's just one person in Argos now to give a signal to the gods, and that's Electra. What's the matter?

(BEGGAR *moves about among the* GUESTS)

BEGGAR Nothing's the matter. But I'd better tell you my story now. In five minutes, at the rate you're talking, it won't make sense. It's just to support what you say. Among those crushed hedgehogs you'll see dozens who seem to have died a hedgehog's death. Their muzzles flattened by horse's hoofs, their spines broken under wheels, they're just smashed hedgehogs, nothing more. Smashed because of the original sin of hedgehogs—which is crossing the main or side road on the pretext that the snail or partridge egg on the far side tastes better but actually to make hedgehog love. That's their affair. No one stops them. Suddenly you see a little young one, not flattened like the others, not so dirty, his little paw stretched out, his lips closed, very dignified, and you feel that he's not died a hedgehog's death, but was struck down for someone else, for you. His cold little eye is your eye. His spikes, your beard. His blood, your blood. I always pick up those little ones, they're the youngest, the tenderest to eat. A year goes by, a hedgehog no longer sacrifices himself for mankind. You see I understand. The gods were mistaken, they wanted to strike a perjurer, a thief, and they kill a hedgehog. A young one.

AEGISTHUS Very well understood.

BEGGAR And what's true of hedgehogs holds for other species.

PRESIDENT Of course! Of course!

BEGGAR Why, of course? That's all wrong. Take the martin. Even though you're a President of the Council, you'll never pretend to have seen birds dying for you?

AEGISTHUS Will you let us go on talking about Electra?

BEGGAR Talk! Talk! But I must add, when you see dead men, many seem to have died for bulls or pigs or turtles, not many for mankind. A man who seems to have died for man, he's hard to find, or even for himself. Are we going to see her?

AEGISTHUS See whom?

BEGGAR Electra. I'd like to see her before she's killed.

AEGISTHUS Electra killed? Who says Electra's to be killed?

BEGGAR You.

PRESIDENT There's been no thought of killing Electra.

BEGGAR I have one gift. I don't understand words—I've had no education—but I do understand people. You want to kill Electra.

PRESIDENT You don't understand at all, stranger. This man is Aegisthus, Agamemnon's cousin, and Electra's his darling niece.

BEGGAR Are there two Electras? The one he was talking about who ruins everything, and the other one, his darling niece?

PRESIDENT No! There's only one.

BEGGAR Then he wants to kill her. No doubt of it. He wants to kill his darling niece.

PRESIDENT I repeat, you don't understand in the least.

BEGGAR Oh, I move about a lot. I knew a couple, he was called Narses. She was better than he. She was sick, her breathing bad. But a great deal better than he. No comparison.

GARDENER He's drunk, a beggar, you know.

PRESIDENT He's raving. He's a god.

BEGGAR No. I started to tell you they had a wolf cub. It was their darling little pet. But one day around noon, wolf cubs, you know, grow up. They couldn't foretell the day. Two minutes before noon they were petting her, one minute after twelve she jumped at their throats. I didn't mind about him!

AEGISTHUS Well?

BEGGAR Well, I was just passing by. And I killed the wolf. She was beginning to eat Narses' cheeks, she liked them. Narses' wife got away, not too badly hurt. Thanks! You'll see her. She's coming for me pretty soon.

AEGISTHUS What's the connection . . . ?

BEGGAR Oh, don't expect to see an Amazon queen. Varicose veins age a person.

PRESIDENT He asked, what's the connection?

BEGGAR The connection? It's because I think this man, as he's head of the state, must be more intelligent than Narses. No one could imagine such stupidity as Narses'. I never could teach him to smoke a cigar except by the lighted end. And what about knots? It's terribly important to know how to make knots. If you make a curlycue where you ought to have a knot, and vice versa, you're lost. You lose your money, you catch cold, you choke, your boat veers away or collides, you can't pull off your shoes. I mean if you want to pull them off. And the laces? You know Narses was a poacher.

PRESIDENT We've asked you, what is the connection?

BEGGAR Here's the connection. If this man distrusts his niece, if he knows that one of these days she'll give a signal, as he said, she'll begin to bite, to turn the city upside down, push up the price of butter, start a war, et cetera, he can't hesitate. He ought to kill her dead before she reveals herself. When will she reveal herself?

PRESIDENT What do you mean?

BEGGAR What day, at what time will she reveal herself? When will she turn into a wolf? When will she become Electra?

PRESIDENT But nothing tells us she'll turn into a wolf.

BEGGAR (*Pointing to* AEGISTHUS) Yes. He thinks so. He says so.

GARDENER Electra is the gentlest of women.

BEGGAR Narses' wolf cub was the gentlest of wolves.

PRESIDENT Your expression "reveal herself" doesn't make sense.

BEGGAR My expression doesn't make sense? You know nothing about life. The 29th of May, when you see the hills astir with thousands of little red, yellow, and green balls flying, squawling, quarreling over every little bit of thistle fluff, never making a mistake nor going after dandelion down, aren't the butterflies revealing themselves? And June 14th when you see on the river bank two reeds move without wind or wave till June 15th, and, too, without bubbles made by carp, isn't the pike revealing himself? And judges like you, the first time they condemn to death, when the condemned man appears, distraught, don't they reveal themselves by the taste of blood on their lips? Everything in nature reveals itself. Even the king. And the question today, if you'll believe me, is whether the king will reveal himself as Aegisthus before Electra reveals herself as Electra. So he has to know the day when it will happen to the girl, so he can kill her on the eve, down in a valley, as he said, down in a little valley, the handiest and least visible, in her bath.

PRESIDENT Isn't he awful?

AEGISTHUS You're forgetting the wedding, beggar.

BEGGAR True. I am forgetting the wedding. But a wedding, if you want to kill someone, isn't as sure as death. Especially as a girl like her, sensitive, rather retarded, et cetera, will reveal herself the moment a man takes her in his arms for the first time. You're marrying her?

AEGISTHUS At once. Right here.

BEGGAR Not to the king of a neighboring city, I hope?

AEGISTHUS Not on your life! To this gardener.

PRESIDENT To this gardener.

BEGGAR She'll take him? I'd not reveal myself in the arms of a gardener. But everyone to his taste. I revealed myself in Corfu, at the fountain near the bakery, under the plane trees. You should have seen me that day! In each tray of the scales I weighed a hand of the baker's wife. They never weighed the same. I evened them up in the right tray with flour, in the left with oatmeal . . . Where does the gardener live?

GARDENER Outside the walls.

BEGGAR In a village?

GARDENER No. My house stands alone.

BEGGAR (*To* AEGISTHUS) Bravo! I catch your idea. Not bad! It's quite easy to kill a gardener's wife. Much easier than a princess in a palace.

GARDENER Whoever you are, I beg you . . .

BEGGAR You'll not deny that it's easier to bury someone in compost than in marble?

GARDENER What are you imagining? For one thing she'll not be a minute out of my sight.

BEGGAR You'll bend down to plant a pear tree. Transplant it again because you hit a hard clod. Death has passed by.

PRESIDENT Stranger, I fear you don't know where you are. You're in Agamemnon's palace, in his family.

BEGGAR I see what I see, I see this man is afraid, he lives with fear, fear of Electra.

AEGISTHUS My dear guest, let's not misunderstand each other. I'll not deny I'm anxious about Electra. I know misfortunes and troubles will come to the family of the Atrides the day she reveals herself, as you say. And to us all, for every citizen is affected by what happens to the royal family. That's why I'm handing her over to a lowly family, unseen by the gods, where her eyes and gestures will not inflame, where the harm will be only local and in the middle class, the Theocathocles family.

BEGGAR A good idea, a good idea! But the family ought to be especially lowly.

AEGISTHUS It is, and I'll see that it stays so. I'll see that no Theocathocles distinguishes himself by talent or courage. As for boldness and genius, I'm not afraid they'll make their mark.

BEGGAR Take care! This little Agatha is not exactly ugly. Beauty too can give a signal.

PRESIDENT I beg you to leave Agatha out of our argument.

BEGGAR Of course it's possible to rub her face with vitriol.

PRESIDENT My lord!

AEGISTHUS The case has been argued.

PRESIDENT But I'm thinking of fate, Aegisthus! It's not a disease. You think it's infectious?

BEGGAR Yes. Like hunger among the poor.

PRESIDENT I can hardly believe that fate will be content with one obscure little clan instead of the royal family, or that it will become the fate of the Theocathocles instead of the Atrides.

BEGGAR Don't worry. A royal cancer spreads to the middle classes.

AEGISTHUS President, if you don't want Electra's entrance into your family to mark the disgrace of its members, don't add a word. In a third-class zone the most implacable fate will do only third-class harm. I personally am distressed, because of my great esteem for the Theocathocles family, but the dynasty, the state, and the city can no longer take risks.

BEGGAR And perhaps she can be killed a little anyway, if an occasion arises.

AEGISTHUS I have spoken. You may fetch Clytemnestra and Electra. They're waiting.

BEGGAR It's not too soon. Without blaming you, I must say our talk lacks women.

AEGISTHUS You'll have two, and talkers!

BEGGAR And they'll argue with you a little, I hope?

AEGISTHUS You like arguing women?

BEGGAR Adore them. This afternoon I was in a house where a dispute was going on. Not a very high-toned discussion. Not compared to here. Not a plot of royal assassins as here. They were arguing whether they ought to serve guests chickens with or without livers. And the neck, of course. The women were furious. Had to be separated. Now I think of it, it was a fierce dispute. Blood flowed.

SCENE 4 *The Same.* CLYTEMNESTRA. ELECTRA. MAIDS.

PRESIDENT Here they both are.

CLYTEMNESTRA Both! That's a manner of speaking. Electra is never more absent than when she's present.

ELECTRA No. Today I'm here.

AEGISTHUS Then let's make the most of it. You know why your mother has brought you here?

ELECTRA It's her habit. She's already led a daughter to sacrifice.

CLYTEMNESTRA There's Electra to the life! Never a word that's not treason or insinuation.

ELECTRA Excuse me, mother. The allusion is quite apropos in the family of the Atrides.

BEGGAR What does she mean? Is she angry with her mother?

GARDENER It would be the first time anyone has seen Electra angry.

BEGGAR All the more interesting!

AEGISTHUS Electra, your mother has told you of our decision. We've been anxious about you for a long time. I hardly think you realize that you're like a sleepwalker in broad daylight. In the palace and the city people speak of you only in whispers, they're so afraid you'd wake and fall if they raised their voices.

BEGGAR (*Shouting*) Electra!

AEGISTHUS What's the matter with him?

BEGGAR Oh, I'm sorry, it's just a joke. Excuse it. But you were scared, not she. Electra's no sleepwalker.

AEGISTHUS Please—

BEGGAR At least the experiment has been made. You were the one who flinched. What would you have done if I'd shouted, "Aegisthus"?

PRESIDENT Let our Regent speak.

BEGGAR I'll shout "Aegisthus" pretty soon, when nobody expects it.

AEGISTHUS You must get well, Electra, no matter what it costs.

ELECTRA To cure me, that's easy. Give life to a dead man.

AEGISTHUS You're not the only one who grieves for your father. But he'd not ask you to make your mourning an offense to the living. We wrong the dead to attach them to our lives, for that deprives them of the freedom of death, if they know it.

ELECTRA He's free. That's why he comes.

AEGISTHUS Do you really think he's pleased to see you weep for him, not like a daughter but like a wife?

ELECTRA I am my father's widow, for lack of another.

CLYTEMNESTRA Electra!

AEGISTHUS Widow or not, today we'll celebrate your marriage.

ELECTRA Yes, I know your plot.

CLYTEMNESTRA What plot? Is it a plot to marry a twenty-one year old daughter? At your age I had the two of you in my arms, you and Orestes.

ELECTRA You carried us badly. You let Orestes fall on the marble floor.

CLYTEMNESTRA What could I do? You pushed him.

ELECTRA That's a lie. I never pushed him.

CLYTEMNESTRA What do you know about it? You were only fifteen months old.

ELECTRA I did *not* push Orestes! I remember it, far back in my memory. Oh, Orestes, wherever you are, hear me! I did not push you.

AEGISTHUS That's enough, Electra.

BEGGAR This time they're really at it! It'd be funny if the little girl revealed herself right in front of us.

ELECTRA She lies. Orestes, she lies!

AEGISTHUS Please, Electra!

CLYTEMNESTRA She did push him. Obviously at her age she didn't know what she was doing. But she did push him.

ELECTRA With all my strength I tried to hold him: by his little blue tunic, by his arm, by the end of his fingers, by his shadow. I sobbed when I saw him on the floor, with the red mark on his forehead.

CLYTEMNESTRA You shouted with laughter. The tunic, by the way, was mauve.

ELECTRA It was blue. I know Orestes' tunic. When it was drying you couldn't see it against the sky.

AEGISTHUS Can *I* get a word in? Haven't you had time these twenty years to settle this debate?

ELECTRA For twenty years I've waited for this chance. Now I have it.

CLYTEMNESTRA Why can't she understand that she might be wrong, even honestly?

BEGGAR They're both honest. That's the truth.

PRESIDENT Princess, I beg of you! Of what interest is this question today?

CLYTEMNESTRA Of none, I grant you.

ELECTRA What interest? If I had pushed Orestes I'd rather die, I'd kill myself. My life would have no meaning.

AEGISTHUS Must I force you to keep quiet? Are you as mad as she, queen?

CLYTEMNESTRA Electra, listen. Let's not quarrel. This is exactly what happened: he was on my right arm.

ELECTRA On your left!

AEGISTHUS Have you finished, Clytemnestra, or haven't you?

CLYTEMNESTRA We've finished. But a right arm is a right arm, a mauve tunic is mauve, not blue.

ELECTRA It was blue. As blue as Orestes' forehead was red.

CLYTEMNESTRA That is true. Very red. You touched the wound with your finger and danced around the little prone body. You laughed as you tasted the blood.

ELECTRA I? I wanted to bruise my head on the step that hurt him. I trembled for a week.

AEGISTHUS Silence!

ELECTRA I'm still trembling.

BEGGAR Narses' wife tied hers with an elastic rope that had some play. Often it was askew, but he didn't fall.

AEGISTHUS Enough. We'll soon see how Electra will carry hers. For you agree, don't you? You accept this marriage?

ELECTRA I agree.

AEGISTHUS I must admit not many suitors throng around you.

BEGGAR They say . . .

AEGISTHUS What do they say?

BEGGAR They say you've threatened to kill the princes who might marry Electra. That's what they say in the city.

ELECTRA Good! I don't want any prince.

CLYTEMNESTRA You'd rather have a gardener?

ELECTRA I know you two have decided to marry me to my father's gardener. I accept.

CLYTEMNESTRA You shall not marry a gardener.

AEGISTHUS Queen, we settled that. Our word is given.

CLYTEMNESTRA I take mine back. It was a wicked word. If Electra is ill we'll care for her. I'll not give my daughter to a gardener.

ELECTRA Too late, mother. You have given me.

CLYTEMNESTRA Gardener, you dare to aspire to Electra?

GARDENER I'm unworthy, queen, but Aegisthus commands me.

AEGISTHUS I do command you. Here are the rings. Take your wife.

CLYTEMNESTRA If you persist, gardener, it's at the risk of your life.

BEGGAR Then don't persist. I'd rather see soldiers die than gardeners.

CLYTEMNESTRA What's that man saying? Marry Electra, gardener, and you die.

BEGGAR It's your business. But go into the garden a year after the death of the gardener. You'll see something. You'll see what's happened to the endive, widowed by its gardener. It's not like kings' widows.

CLYTEMNESTRA That garden won't suffer. Come, Electra.

GARDENER Queen, you can deny me Electra, but it's not nice to say bad things about a garden you don't know.

CLYTEMNESTRA I know it—empty land, with scattered plantings.

GARDENER Empty? The best tended garden in Argos.

PRESIDENT If he begins to talk about his garden we'll never finish.

AEGISTHUS Spare us your descriptions!

GARDENER The queen provoked me, and I answer. My garden is my dowry and my honor.

AEGISTHUS Never mind! Enough of quarrels.

GARDENER Empty, indeed! It covers ten acres of hilly land, and six of valley. No, no, you'll not silence me! Not a sterile inch, is there, Electra? On the terraces I have garlic and tomatoes, on the slopes grape vines and peach trees. On the level land vegetables, strawberries, and raspberries. A fig tree at the bottom of each slope against the wall, which warms the figs.

AEGISTHUS Fine! Let your figs get warm and take your wife.

CLYTEMNESTRA You dare talk of your garden! I've seen it from the road. It's all dry, a bald skull. You shall not have Electra.

GARDENER All dry! A brook flows between the box and the plane trees, never dry in hottest weather; I've dug two little trenches from it—one turned on the meadow, the other cut in the rock. Try to find skulls like that! And scattered plantings! In spring it's full of narcissus and jonquils. I've never seen Electra really smile, but in my garden, I saw something on her face almost like a smile.

CLYTEMNESTRA See if she's smiling now!

GARDENER I call that Electra's smile.

CLYTEMNESTRA Smiling at your dirty hands, your black nails . . .

ELECTRA Dear gardener . . .

GARDENER My black nails? Look, see if my nails are black! Don't believe it, Electra. You're unlucky today, queen, I spent this morning whitewashing my house, so there's not a sign of mice there, and my nails came out, not black, as you say, but mooned with white.

AEGISTHSUS That's enough, gardener.

GARDENER I know, I know it's enough. And my dirty hands! Look! Look at these dirty hands! Hands that I washed after taking down the dried mushrooms and onions, so nothing would trouble Electra's nights. I'll sleep in the outhouse, Electra; there I'll keep guard so that nothing disturbs your sleep, whether an owl, or the open floodgate, or a fox, hunting in the hedge, with a chicken in his mouth. I've said my say.

ELECTRA Thanks, gardener.

CLYTEMNESTRA And that's how Electra will live, Clytemnestra's daughter, watching her husband going around his border, two pails in his hands. . . .

AEGISTHUS There she can weep for her dead to her heart's content. Get ready your wreaths of everlasting tomorrow.

GARDENER And there she'll escape from anxiety, torture, and perhaps tragedy. I don't understand people, queen, but I do know the seasons. It's time, full time, to transplant misfortune from our city. The Atrides won't be grafted on our poor family, but on the seasons, the fields, the winds. I think they'll lose nothing by that.

BEGGAR Be persuaded, queen. Don't you see that Aegisthus hates Electra so much he'll be driven to kill her, giving her to the earth by a kind of play on words: he gives her to a garden. She gains by that, she gains life.

(AEGISTHUS *rises*)

What? Was I wrong to say that?

AEGISTHUS (*To* ELECTRA *and the* GARDENER) Come here, both of you.

CLYTEMNESTRA Electra, I beg you!

ELECTRA You're the one who wanted it, mother.

CLYTEMNESTRA I no longer want it. You see I don't want it now.

ELECTRA Why don't you want it? Are you afraid? Too late!

CLYTEMNESTRA How can I make you remember who I am and who you are?

ELECTRA You'll have to tell me I didn't push Orestes

CLYTEMNESTRA Stupid girl!

AEGISTHUS Are they beginning again?

BEGGAR Yes, yes, let them begin again.

CLYTEMNESTRA And unjust! And stubborn! I let Orestes fall! I who never break anything! Never let fall a glass or a ring! I'm so steady that birds light on my arms. It's possible to fly away from me but not to fall. That's just what I said when he lost his balance, "Why, why did an ill fate bring his sister so near him?"

AEGISTHUS They're crazy!

ELECTRA And I said to myself, as soon as I saw him slipping, "If she's a true mother she'll stoop to soften his fall, or she'll bend to make a slope and catch him on her thigh or her knees. We'll see if they'll catch him, the noble knees and thighs of my mother. I'm not sure. I'll see."

CLYTEMNESTRA Be quiet!

ELECTRA "Or she'll bend backward, so little Orestes will slip off her like a child from a tree where he's picked off a nest, or she'll fall so *he* won't, or so he'll fall on her. She knows all the ways a mother uses to catch her son, she still knows them. She can still be a curve, a shell, a motherly slope, a cradle." But she stood fixed, straight, and he fell right down from the full height of his mother.

AEGISTHUS The case is heard. Clytemnestra, we'll leave.

CLYTEMNESTRA Just let her remember what she saw when she was fifteen months old and what she didn't see. That's the point.

AEGISTHUS Who but you believes her or listens to her?

ELECTRA There are a thousand ways of preventing a fall, and she did nothing.

CLYTEMNESTRA The slightest movement, and *you* would have fallen.

ELECTRA Just as I said. You calculated. You figured it all out. You were a nurse, not a mother.

CLYTEMNESTRA My little Electra . . .

ELECTRA I'm not your little Electra. Your motherly feeling is tickled awake by your rubbing your two children against you. But it's too late.

CLYTEMNESTRA Please—!

ELECTRA There you are! Open your arms, see what you've done. Look, everybody. That's just what you did.

CLYTEMNESTRA Let's go, Aegisthus.

(*She leaves*)

BEGGAR I believe the mother is frightened.

AEGISTHUS (*To the* BEGGAR) What's that you say?

BEGGAR I? I say nothing. I never say anything. When I'm hungry I talk, everyone hears me. Today I've drunk a little something.

SCENE 5 ELECTRA. BEGGAR. GARDENER. STRANGER. AGATHA.

AGATHA This is the right time, Aegisthus isn't here. Get out, gardener.

GARDENER What do you mean?

AGATHA Get out, fast. This man will take your place.

GARDENER My place with Electra?

STRANGER Yes, I'll marry her.

ELECTRA Let go my hand.

STRANGER Never.

AGATHA Just look at him, Electra. Before you turn your back on a man, at least look at him. I'm sure you'll lose nothing by that.

ELECTRA Gardener, help!

STRANGER I owe you nothing, gardener. But look me in the eye. You understand species and kinds. Look at me and see the kind I am. So! Look, with your poor peasant eyes, with the gaze of humble folk, a bleareyed mixture of devotion and fear, the sterile look of the poor, unchanged by sunshine or misfortune, see if I can give way to you. Fine! Now give me your ring. Thanks!

ELECTRA Agatha, cousin! Help me! I swear I'll not tell about your rendezvous, your quarrels, I'll tell nothing.

AGATHA (*Leading off the* GARDENER) Come, the Theocathocles are saved. Let the Atrides work it out.

BEGGAR She runs away—like a wood-louse, hiding under a stone to escape from the sun.

SCENE 6 ELECTRA. STRANGER. BEGGAR.

STRANGER Struggle no more.

ELECTRA I'll struggle till I die.

STRANGER You think so? In a minute you'll take me in your arms.

ELECTRA No insults!

STRANGER In a minute you'll embrace me.

ELECTRA Shame on you for profiting from two infamies!

STRANGER See how I trust you. I let you go.

ELECTRA Farewell forever!

STRANGER No! I'll say one word to you and you'll come back to me, tenderly.

ELECTRA What lie is this?

STRANGER One word, and you'll be sobbing in my arms. One word, my name.

ELECTRA There's only one name in the world that could draw me to anyone.

STRANGER That's the one.

ELECTRA Are you Orestes?

ORESTES Ungrateful sister, only recognizing me by my name!

(CLYTEMNESTRA *appears*)

SCENE 7 CLYTEMNESTRA. ELECTRA. ORESTES. BEGGAR.

CLYTEMNESTRA Electra!

ELECTRA Mother?

CLYTEMNESTRA Come back to your place in the palace. Leave the gardener. Come!

ELECTRA The gardener has left, mother.

CLYTEMNESTRA Where is he?

ELECTRA He's given me to this man.

CLYTEMNESTRA What man?

ELECTRA This man. He's my husband now.

CLYTEMNESTRA This is no time for jokes. Come!

ELECTRA How can I come? He's holding my hand.

CLYTEMNESTRA Hurry!

ELECTRA You know, mother, those clogs they put on

the legs of foals to prevent their running away? This man has put them on my ankles.

CLYTEMNESTRA This time I command you. You must be in your room by tonight. Come!

ELECTRA What? Leave my husband the night of my wedding?

CLYTEMNESTRA What are you doing? Who are you?

ELECTRA He'll not answer you. This evening my husband's mouth belongs to me, and all the words he speaks.

CLYTEMNESTRA Where do you come from? Who is your father?

ELECTRA A misalliance maybe. But not such a bad one.

CLYTEMNESTRA Why do you look at me like that? Why the challenge in your eyes? Who was your mother?

ELECTRA He never saw her.

CLYTEMNESTRA She's dead?

ELECTRA Perhaps what you see in his eyes is that he never saw his mother. Handsome, isn't he?

CLYTEMNESTRA Yes. He looks like you.

ELECTRA If our first married hours make us look alike, that's a good omen, isn't it, mother?

CLYTEMNESTRA Who are you?

ELECTRA What does it matter to you? Never was a man less yours.

CLYTEMNESTRA Whatever or whoever you are, stranger, don't give in to her caprice. We'll see tomorrow if you're worthy of Electra. I'll win over Aegisthus. But I've never known a less propitious night. Leave this man, Electra.

ELECTRA Too late! His arms hold me.

CLYTEMNESTRA You can break iron if you want to.

ELECTRA Iron, yes, *this* iron, no!

CLYTEMNESTRA What has he said against your mother that you accept him this way?

ELECTRA We've had no time yet to speak of my mother or his. Go, we'll begin!

ORESTES Electra!

ELECTRA That's all he can say. If I take my hand from his mouth, he just says my name without stopping. You can't get anything else out of him. Oh, husband, now that your mouth is free, kiss me!

CLYTEMNESTRA Shame! So this madness is Electra's secret!

ELECTRA Kiss me, before my mother.

CLYTEMNESTRA Farewell! But I didn't think you were a girl to give yourself to the first passer-by.

ELECTRA Nor I. But I didn't know what the first kiss was like.

SCENE 8 ELECTRA. ORESTES. BEGGAR.

ORESTES Why do you hate our mother so, Electra?

ELECTRA Don't speak of her, above all not of her! Let's imagine for a minute that we were born without a mother. Don't talk.

ORESTES I have everything to tell you.

ELECTRA You tell me everything just by being here. Be quiet. Close your eyes. Your words and your look touch me too poignantly, they wound me. I often wished that I'd find you in your sleep, if I ever found you. Now I can't bear to have all at once the look, the voice, the life of Orestes. I ought to have stumbled on your image, dead at first, then coming alive little by little. But my brother was born like the sun, a golden animal at his rising. Either I'm blind or I find my brother by groping—oh, the joy of being blind for a sister who finds her brother! For twenty years my hands have fumbled over mean or indifferent things, and now they touch—a brother—a brother in whom everything is true. Some dubious or some false bits might have been in this head, this body, but by a wonderful chance, everything in Orestes is brotherly, everything is Orestes.

ORESTES You smother me.

ELECTRA I don't smother you. I don't kill you. I caress you. I'm calling you to life. From this brotherly shape which my dazzled eyes have scarcely seen I'm making my brother in all his features. See, how I've made my brother's hand, with its straight thumb. See how I've made my brother's chest, which I'm animating so it swells and breathes, giving life to my brother. See how I make this ear, little, curled, transparent like a bat's wing. One last touch and the ear is finished. I make the two alike. Quite a success, these ears! And now I'll make my brother's mouth, gentle and dry, and fasten it on his face. Take your life from me, Orestes, not from our mother.

ORESTES Why do you hate her? Listen . . .

ELECTRA What's the matter with you? Are you pushing me away? That's the ingratitude of sons. They're hardly finished before they get away and escape.

ORESTES Someone is watching us from the staircase.

ELECTRA It's she, certainly she. From jealousy or fear. It's our mother.

BEGGAR Yes, yes, it's she.

ELECTRA She suspects we're here, creating ourselves, freeing ourselves from her. She thinks that my caresses will cover you, wash you clear of her, make you an orphan. Oh, brother, who else could do me such a service!

ORESTES How can you speak so of her who bore you? Though she was harsh to me, I'm less hard on her.

ELECTRA That's just what I can't stand about her, that she bore me. That's my shame. I feel that I came into life in a dubious way, that her motherhood is only a plot to bind us together. I love everything that comes from my father. I love the way he put off his fine wedding garment and lay down to beget me, from his thought and from his body. I love his eyes, and his surprise the day I was born; I came from him far more than from my mother's pains. I was born from his nights of deep sleep, his nine months' emaciation, the comfort he found with other women while my mother was carrying me, his fatherly smile when I was born. I hate everything about my birth that comes from my mother.

ORESTES Why do you detest women so?

ELECTRA I don't detest women, I detest my mother. And I don't detest men, I detest Aegisthus.

ORESTES Why do you hate him?

ELECTRA I don't know yet. I only know it's the same hatred. That's why it's so hard to bear, that's why I'm suffocating. Many times I've tried to find out why I hate both of them with a special hatred. Two little hatreds could be borne—like sorrows—one balances the other. I tried to think I hated my mother because she let you fall when you were a baby, and Aegisthus because he stole your throne. But it's not true. I really pitied this great queen, who ruled the world, yet suddenly, frightened and humble, let her child fall, like a feeble grandmother. I pitied Aegisthus, that cruel tyrant, whose fate is to die miserably from your blows. All the reasons I had for hating them made me think them human, pitiable, but no sooner had my hatred washed them clean and re-clothed them and I found myself gentle, obedient before them, than a yet heavier wave, charged with a yet more virulent hatred, flowed over them. I hate them with a hatred that is not really me.

ORESTES I'm here. It will vanish.

ELECTRA You believe that? I used to think your return would free me of this hatred. I thought my illness was because you were far away. I prepared for your return by becoming all tenderness, tenderness for everyone, for them too. I was wrong. My pain tonight is caused by your being here and all the hatred in me laughs and welcomes you, it is my love for you. It caresses you as a dog does the hand that frees him. I know that you have given me the sight, the smell of hatred. The first scent, and now I follow the trail. Who's there? Is it she?

BEGGAR No, me. You're forgetting the time. She's gone up. She's undressing.

ELECTRA She's undressing. Before her mirror, looking long at herself, our mother, Clytemnestra, undresses. Our mother, whom I love for her beauty and pity because she's aging, whose voice and looks I admire, our mother, whom I hate.

ORESTES Electra, sister darling, please calm yourself.

ELECTRA Then I'm to follow the trail?

ORESTES Calm yourself.

ELECTRA I? I'm perfectly calm. I'm all sweetness. Sweet to my mother, very sweet. It's this hatred for her that swells up and kills me.

ORESTES Now it's your turn not to talk. We'll think about that hatred tomorrow. This evening let me taste, for an hour at least, the sweetness of the life I've never known and now return to.

ELECTRA An hour. All right, one hour.

ORESTES The palace is so beautiful beneath the moon. My palace. All the power of our family is emanating from it. My power. In your arms let me imagine all the happiness these walls might have held for calmer, more reasonable people. Oh, Electra, how many of our family's names were originally sweet and tender, and should have been happy names!

ELECTRA Yes, I know. Medea, Phaedra.[1]

ORESTES Even those, why not?

ELECTRA Electra. Orestes.

ORESTES Isn't there still time? I've come to save them.

ELECTRA Silence! She's there.

ORESTES Who?

ELECTRA She with the happy name: Clytemnestra.

SCENE 9 ELECTRA. ORESTES. BEGGAR. CLYTEMNESTRA, *then* AEGISTHUS.

CLYTEMNESTRA Electra?

ELECTRA Mother?

CLYTEMNESTRA Who is this man?

ELECTRA Guess.

CLYTEMNESTRA Let me see his face.

ELECTRA If you can't see it at a distance you'd see him less well near to.

CLYTEMNESTRA Electra, let's stop fighting. If you really want to marry this man, I'll agree. Why do you smile? Wasn't it I who wanted you to marry?

ELECTRA Not at all. You wanted me to be a woman.

CLYTEMNESTRA What's the difference?

ELECTRA You wanted me in your camp. You didn't want the face of your worst enemy constantly before you.

CLYTEMNESTRA You mean my daughter's?

ELECTRA Chastity, rather!

ORESTES Electra . . . !

ELECTRA Let me alone, let me alone. I've found the trail.

CLYTEMNESTRA Chastity! This girl who's devoured by desire talks about chastity! This girl at two years old couldn't see a boy without blushing. It was because you wanted to embrace Orestes, if you want to know, that you pulled him out of my arms.

ELECTRA Then I was right. I am proud of it. It was worth while.

(*Trumpets. Shouts. Faces in the windows.* AEGISTHUS *leans down from a balcony*)

AEGISTHUS Are you there, queen?

BEGGAR Yes, she's here.

AEGISTHUS Great news, queen. Orestes is not dead. He's escaped. He's coming toward Argos.

CLYTEMNESTRA Orestes!

AEGISTHUS I'm sending my bodyguard to meet him. I've posted my most faithful men around the walls. You say nothing?

CLYTEMNESTRA Orestes is coming back?

AEGISTHUS Coming back to seize his father's throne, to prevent my being regent, and you being queen. His emissaries are preparing a revolt. But don't worry. I'll keep order. Who's down there with you?

CLYTEMNESTRA Electra.

AEGISTHUS And her gardener?

BEGGAR And her gardener.

AEGISTHUS I hope you're not still trying to separate them? You see how well founded my fears were! You agree now?

CLYTEMNESTRA No. I'm not trying any more.

AEGISTHUS Don't let them leave the palace. Them especially. I've ordered the gates closed till the soldiers return. You hear me, gardener?

[1] Medea, a barbarian princess, was abandoned by Jason, and killed their children and Jason's bride by way of revenge. Phaedra, wife of Theseus, fell in love with her husband's illegitimate son, Hippolytus, and killed herself out of resentment of his scorn. Neither Medea nor Phaedra belonged to the house of Atreus.

ELECTRA We'll not leave.

AEGISTHUS Queen, come upstairs. Go back to your room. It's late and the Council is to meet at dawn. I wish you a goodnight.

ELECTRA Thanks, Aegisthus.

AEGISTHUS I was speaking to the queen, Electra. This is no time for irony. Come, queen.

CLYTEMNESTRA Good-by, Electra.

ELECTRA Good-bye, mother.

(CLYTEMNESTRA *goes, then turns back*)

CLYTEMNESTRA Good-by, my daughter's husband.

BEGGAR What you see in families! You see everything!

ELECTRA Who spoke?

BEGGAR No one! No one spoke. You think someone would speak at a time like this?

SCENE 10 ELECTRA. ORESTES. BEGGAR.

ORESTES Tell me, Electra! Tell me!

ELECTRA Tell you what?

ORESTES Your hatred. The reason for your hatred. You know it now, when you were talking to Clytemnestra a moment ago you almost fainted in my arms. It might have been from joy—or horror.

ELECTRA It was both joy *and* horror. Are you strong or weak, Orestes?

ORESTES Tell me your secret and I'll find out.

ELECTRA I don't know my secret yet. I hold only one end of the thread. Don't worry. Everything will follow. Take care! Here she is.

(CLYTEMNESTRA *appears at the back of the stage*)

SCENE 11 ELECTRA. CLYTEMNESTRA. ORESTES. BEGGAR. EUMENIDES.

CLYTEMNESTRA So it's you, Orestes?

ORESTES Yes, mother, it's I.

CLYTEMNESTRA Is it sweet to see a mother when you're twenty?

ORESTES A mother who sent you away? Sad and sweet.

CLYTEMNESTRA You look at her from far away.

ORESTES She's just as I imagined her.

CLYTEMNESTRA My son. Handsome. Regal. And yet I draw near.

ORESTES Not I. At a distance she's a magnificent mother.

CLYTEMNESTRA Who tells you that near to her magnificence remains?

ORESTES Or her motherliness? That's why I don't move.

CLYTEMNESTRA The mirage of a mother is enough for you?

ORESTES I've had so much less until today. At least I can tell the mirage what I'd never tell my real mother.

CLYTEMNESTRA If the mirage deserves it, that's all right. What will you tell her?

ORESTES Everything I never tell you. Everything that would be a lie if said to you.

CLYTEMNESTRA That you love her?

ORESTES Yes.

CLYTEMNESTRA That you respect her?

ORESTES Yes.

CLYTEMNESTRA That you admire her?

ORESTES That the mother and the mirage can share.

CLYTEMNESTRA It's the opposite for me. I don't love the mirage of my son. But when my son is actually before me, speaking, breathing, I lose my strength.

ORESTES Think of hurting him, you'll recover it.

CLYTEMNESTRA Why are you so hard? You don't look cruel. Your voice is gentle.

ORESTES Yes, I'm exactly like the son I might have been. You too, of course. You look so like a wonderful mother. If I weren't your son, I'd be deceived.

ELECTRA Why are you both talking? Where does this horrible maternal coquetry get you, mother? At midnight the little window which allows a mother and son to see each other as they are not opens for a minute. Shut it, the minute has passed.

CLYTEMNESTRA Why so quickly? How do you know one minute of maternal love is enough for Orestes?

ELECTRA Everything tells me you have no right to more than a minute of your son's love in your whole life. You've had it. And that's the end. What a comedy you're playing! Go!

CLYTEMNESTRA Very well. Good-by.

FIRST LITTLE GIRL (*Appearing from behind the columns*) Good-by, truth of my son!

ORESTES Good-by.

SECOND LITTLE GIRL Good-by, mirage of my mother!

ELECTRA You might say *au revoir*. You'll meet again.

SCENE 12 ELECTRA *and* ORESTES *asleep. The little* EUMENIDES. BEGGAR. *The* EUMENIDES *now seem to be about twelve or thirteen years old.*

FIRST GIRL They're asleep. It's our turn to play Clytemnestra and Orestes. But not the way they played. Let's play it truly.

BEGGAR (*To himself, though out loud*) The story of push or not push—I'd like to know . . .

SECOND GIRL You there, let us play. We're playing.

(*The three little* EUMENIDES *take the positions of the actors in the preceding scene and play it as a parody. Masks could be used*)

FIRST GIRL So it's you, Orestes?

SECOND GIRL Yes, it's me, mother.

FIRST GIRL You've come to kill me and Aegisthus?

SECOND GIRL News to me!

FIRST GIRL Not to your sister. You've done some killing, little Orestes?

SECOND GIRL The things one kills when one is good! A doe. And to be a little kind, I killed her fawn too, so it wouldn't be an orphan. But to kill my mother, never! That would be—parricide.

FIRST GIRL Was that the sword you did your killing with?

SECOND GIRL Yes. It will cut iron. See, it went through the fawn so fast he felt nothing.

FIRST GIRL I'm not suggesting anything. I don't want to influence you. But if a sword like that were to kill your sister, we'd all be at peace!

SECOND GIRL You want me to kill my sister?

FIRST GIRL Never! That would be—fratricide. If the sword were to kill her by itself, that would be ideal.

Let it come out of its scabbard, like this, and kill her by itself. I'd just quietly marry Aegisthus. We'd call you home, Aegisthus is getting old. You'd succeed him very soon. You'd be King Orestes.

SECOND GIRL A sword doesn't kill by itself. It needs an assassin.

FIRST GIRL Certainly! I should know! But I'm talking about the times when swords will kill by themselves. People who avenge wrongs are the curse of the world. And they get no better as they get older, I beg you to believe that. As criminals improve with age, good people always become criminals. Surely this is a fine moment for a sword to think for itself, move of itself, and kill by itself. They'd marry you to Alcmena's second daughter, the laughing one, with the fine teeth —you'd be Orestes, the married man.

SECOND GIRL I don't want to kill my sister, I love her, nor my mother, I detest her.

FIRST GIRL I know, I know. In a word you're weak and you have principles.

THIRD GIRL Why are you two talking? Because the moon is rising, the nightingale singing here in the middle of this night of hatred and threats; take your hand off the hilt of your sword, Orestes, and see if it will have the intelligence to act by itself.

FIRST GIRL That's right. Take it off . . . it's moving, friends, it's moving!

SECOND GIRL It really is! It's a thinking sword. It thinks so hard it's half out!

ORESTES (*Asleep*) Electra!

BEGGAR Off with you, screech owls! You're waking them.

ELECTRA (*Asleep*) Orestes!

SCENE 13 ELECTRA. ORESTES. BEGGAR.

BEGGAR I'd love to get straight that story of pushed or not pushed. For whether it's true or false, it would show whether Electra is truthful or lying and whether she lies knowingly or whether her memory plays her false. I don't believe she pushed him. Look at her: two inches above ground she's holding her sleeping brother as tight as if they were over an abyss. He's dreaming that he's falling, evidently, but that's not her fault. Now the queen looks like those bakers' wives who never stoop, even to pick up their money, or like those bitches who smother their prettiest pup while they sleep. Afterward they lick it as the queen licked Orestes, but no one ever made a child with saliva. I can see the story as if I'd been there. It's understandable, if you imagine the queen had put on a diamond pin and a white cat had passed by. She's holding Electra on her right arm, for the girl was getting heavy, and the baby on the left, a bit away from her so he'll not scratch himself on the brooch or drive it into him. It's a queen's pin, not a nurse's. And the child sees the white cat, a magnificent creature—a white life, white hair—his eyes follow it, he rocks himself, and she's an egotistical woman. Anyway, seeing the child capsizing, in order to hold him she need only free her arm of little Electra, throw little Electra off on the marble floor, get rid of little Electra. Let little Electra break her neck, so the son of the king of kings be unhurt! But she's an egotist. For her a woman is as good as a man, she's a woman; the womb as good as the phallus, and she's a womb; she wouldn't dream for a second of destroying her daughter to save her son, so she keeps Electra. Now look at Electra. She's revealed herself in her brother's arms, and she's right. She couldn't wish for a better moment. Fraternity is the mark of human beings. Beasts know only love . . . cats, parrots, et cetera, they only recognize fraternity by the hair. To find brothers they have to love men, to turn to men. . . . What does the duckling do when he gets away from the other ducks and, with his tender little eye shining on his slanting duck's cheek, he looks at us humans, eating and playing games, because he knows men and women are his brothers? I've taken little ducks in my hands, and could have wrung their necks, because they came to me so fraternally, trying to understand what I was doing, I, their brother, cutting my bread and cheese and adding an onion. Brother of ducks, that's our real title, for when they raise the little heads they've plunged into the water and look at a man, they're all neatness, intelligence and tenderness—not eatable except for their brains. I could teach those little duck heads to weep! . . . So Electra didn't push Orestes! That makes everything she says legitimate, everything she undertakes irrefutable. She's unadulterated truth, a lamp without a wick. So if she kills, as looks likely, all happiness and peace around her, it's because she's right. It's as if the soul of a girl, in bright sunlight, felt a moment of anguish, as if she sniffed escaping gas in the midst of splendid festivals, and had to go after it, for the young girl is the guardian of truth; she has to go after it whether or not the world bursts and cracks down to its foundations, whether innocents die the death of innocents to let the guilty live their guilty lives. Look at those two innocents! What will be the fruit of their marriage? To bring to life, for the world and for ages to come, a crime already forgotten, the punishment of which will be a worse crime? How right they are to sleep away this hour that is still theirs! Leave them. I'm going for a walk. If I stayed, I'd wake them. I always sneeze three times when the moon is full, and, right now, to sneeze would be taking a frightful risk. But all you who remain here, be quiet, now. This is Electra's first rest, and the last rest of Orestes.

*Curtain*

## Interlude: The Gardener's Lament

I'm not in the play any more. That's why I'm free to come and tell you what the play can't tell you. In stories like this the people won't stop killing and biting each other in order to tell you that the one aim of life is to love. It would be awkward to see the parricide stop, with upraised dagger, and make a speech praising love. That would seem artificial. A lot of people wouldn't believe him. But I really don't see what else I can do here in this loneliness and desolation. And I speak impartially. I'll never marry anyone but Electra, and I'll never have her. I was made to live with a woman day and night, but I'll always live alone. I was meant to give myself fully, and yet I have to keep myself to myself. This is my wedding night that I'm living through, all alone—but thank you for being here—and the orangeade I'd prepared for Electra I had to drink up myself; there's not a drop left, and this was a long wedding night. Now who will doubt my word? The trouble is that I always say the opposite of what I mean, and that would be miserable today when my heart is so heavy and my mouth so bitter—oranges are really bitter—and if I forgot for an instant that I must speak to you of joy. Yes, love and joy. I come to tell you they're preferable to bitterness and hate. That's a motto to carve on a porch, or to put on a handkerchief, or better, in dwarf begonias in a clump. Of course, life is a failure, yet it's very, very good. Of course, nothing ever goes right, never is well planned, yet you must confess, sometimes everything comes out splendidly, is splendidly planned. . . . Not for me . . . or perhaps just for me. . . . If I can judge from my wish to love everything and everyone, which is the result of the greatest misfortune in my life! What will happen to people who've had less bad luck? How much love must men feel who marry wives they don't love, what joy must those feel who leave a wife they adore, after having had her in their home one hour? And people whose children are ugly? Of course, tonight in my garden, I wasn't very happy. As a little festival it didn't come off. I pretended sometimes that Electra was near me, I talked to her and said: "Come in, Electra! Are you cold, Electra?" But no one was deceived, not even the dog, not to say myself. The dog thought: "He promised us a bride, and he only gives us a word. My master has married a word; he put on his white garment, the one my paws soil, which keeps me from caressing him, just to marry a word! He gives his orangeade to a word. He scolds me for barking at shadows, real shadows which aren't alive, yet he tries to embrace a word."

And I didn't lie down: to sleep with a word was impossible. I can speak with a word, that's all! But if you were sitting like me in this garden, where everything is confused at night, where the moon is shining on the sundial, and the blind owl tries to drink the cement walk instead of the brook, you'd understand what I've understood: the truth! You'd understand that the day your parents died, that day your parents were born; the day you were ruined, that day you were rich; when your child was ungrateful, he was gratitude itself; when you were abandoned, the whole world was coming to you in rapture and tenderness. That was what happened to me in this empty, silent suburb. All these stony trees, these immovable hills, rushed toward me. This all applies to our play. To be sure, we can't say Electra is all love for Clytemnestra. But note the difference: she tries to find a mother and would see one in the first comer. She was marrying me because I was the only man who could be a kind of mother to her, though I'm not *really* the only one. There are men who'd be glad to carry a child nine months, if they had to, just to have daughters. All men, actually. Nine months are rather long, but . . . a week, or a day . . . any man would be proud. Perhaps to find a mother in *her* mother she'd have to cut her breast open, though with royalty that's rather theoretical. Among kings there are experiences never found among humble folk, pure hatred, for instance, and pure wrath. Always purity. That's tragedy, with its incests and parricides: purity, meaning—innocence. I don't know if you're like me, but to me, in tragedy, Pharaoh's daughter killing herself means hope, the treasonous Marshall means faith, the Duke-Assassin speaks of tenderness. Cruelty is a deed of love—excuse me, I mean: tragedy is a deed of love. That's why I'm sure this morning, that if I asked, Heaven would approve me, would give a sign that a miracle is near, which would show you that joy and love are written in heaven, and that they echo my motto, though I'm abandoned and alone. If you wish, I'll ask. I'm as sure as I'm here that a voice from on high would answer me, that loud speakers and amplifiers and God's thunder are all prepared by God himself to shout, if I ask: "love and joy." But I'd rather you didn't ask. First it would be indecent. It's not the gardener's role to demand of God a storm, even a storm of tenderness. Moreover it would be useless. We know so well that at this moment, and yesterday and tomorrow and always, they're all up there, as many as there are, or perhaps only one, or even if that one is absent, they're all ready to shout: love and joy. It's much better for a man to take the gods at their word—this is euphemism—without forcing them to underline it, or to be held by it, or to create among themselves obligations of creditor and debtor. I'm always convinced by silences. Yes, I've begged them, haven't I? not to shout love and joy. But let them shout it if they really want to. Yet I'd rather conjure them, I conjure you, God, as a proof of your affections, of your voice and all your shouting, to keep silent, silent for one second. . . . That's much more convincing. . . . Listen! . . . Thanks!

# Act Two

SCENE 1 *The same setting, shortly before dawn.* ELECTRA, *seated, holding* ORESTES, *asleep.* BEGGAR *A cock. Sound of a trumpet in the distance.*

BEGGAR It won't be long now, eh, Electra?

ELECTRA No. It's not far away.

BEGGAR I said "it," I meant the day.

ELECTRA I meant the light.

BEGGAR It's not enough for you that liars' faces are shining in the sun? That adulterers and murderers move about freely? That's what the day brings—not too bad.

ELECTRA No. But I want their faces to look blank at noon, and their hands red. That's what light brings out. I want their eyes to be rotten, their mouths diseased.

BEGGAR As you say, one can't ask too much!

ELECTRA There's the cock . . . shall I wake him?

BEGGAR Wake him if you wish, but if I were you, I'd give him another five minutes.

ELECTRA Five minutes of nothingness! A poor gift!

BEGGAR You never know. I believe there's an insect that lives only five minutes. In five minutes he's young, adult, senile; he runs through childhood and adolescence, to the time of lame knees and cataract, and legitimate and morganatic unions. While I'm speaking he must be having measles and growing to puberty.

ELECTRA Let's wait till he dies. That's all I'll agree to.

BEGGAR Our brother sleeps well.

ELECTRA He went to sleep right away. He escaped from me. He slipped into sleep as though that were his real life.

BEGGAR He's smiling. It *is* his real life.

ELECTRA Tell me anything you like, beggar, except that Orestes' real life is a smile.

BEGGAR Loud laughter, love, fine clothes, happiness. I guessed that as soon as I saw him. Orestes would be gay as a lark, if life were good to him.

ELECTRA He has bad luck.

BEGGAR Yes, he's not very lucky. All the more reason for not hurrying him.

ELECTRA Good! As he was made to laugh, to dress well, as he's a lark, I'll give Orestes five minutes, for he'll wake to a lifetime of horror.

BEGGAR In your place, since you can choose, I'd see to it that this morning light and truth depart at the same time. That doesn't mean much, but it would be a young girl's role and would please me. Man's truth is part of his habits, it leaves him somehow, whether at nine o'clock in the morning when workers strike, or at six in the evening, when women confess, et cetera; these are always bad things, always unclear. Now I'm used to animals. They know when to leave. A rabbit's first jump in the heather, the very second the sun rises, the plover's first flight, the young bear's first run from his rock, these, I can tell you, go toward the truth. If they don't get there, that's because they don't have to. A mere nothing distracts them, a gudgeon, a bee. Do as they do, Electra, go toward the dawn.

ELECTRA A fine kingdom where gudgeons and bees are liars! But your animals are moving already!

BEGGAR No. Those are the night creatures turning in. Owls. Rats. The night's truth turning in. Hush! Listen to the last two, the nightingales, of course the nightingales' truth.

SCENE 2 *The same.* AGATHA. *A* YOUNG MAN.

AGATHA Darling, you do understand, don't you?

YOUNG MAN Yes, I have an answer for everything.

AGATHA If he sees you on the stairs?

YOUNG MAN I have come to see the doctor on the top floor.

AGATHA You forget already! He's a veterinary. Buy a dog. . . . If he finds me in your arms?

YOUNG MAN I've picked you up in the street, you've sprained your ankle.

AGATHA If it's in our kitchen?

YOUNG MAN I'll pretend to be drunk—I don't know where I am. I'll break the glasses.

AGATHA One will be enough, darling, a small one, the large ones are crystal. If it's in our room and we're dressed?

YOUNG MAN I'm looking for him, to talk politics. I had to go there to find him.

AGATHA If it's in our room and we're undressed?

YOUNG MAN I entered unexpectedly, you're resisting me, you are perfidy itself, you treat as a thief a man who's pursued you six months. . . . You're a tart!

AGATHA Darling!

YOUNG MAN A real tart!

AGATHA I understand. It's almost day, my love, and I've hardly had you for an hour, and how many more times do you think he'll believe I walk in my sleep, and that it's less dangerous to let me stroll in the grove than on the roof? Oh, my love, can you think of any pretext for letting me have you in *our* bed at night, me between you two, so it would seem quite natural to him?

YOUNG MAN Think! You'll invent something.

AGATHA A pretext for letting you two talk about your elections and the races over the body of your Agatha, so he'd not suspect anything. That's what we need —that's all.

YOUNG MAN All!

AGATHA Oh dear! Why is he so vain? Why is his sleep so light? Why does he adore me?

YOUNG MAN The eternal litany! Why did you marry him? Why did you love him?

AGATHA I? Liar! I never loved anyone but you!

YOUNG MAN I? Remember in whose arms I found you day before yesterday!

AGATHA That was only because I'd sprained my ankle. The man you mention was picking me up.

YOUNG MAN First I've heard of any sprain.

AGATHA You! You understand nothing. You don't realize that accident gave me an idea for us to use.

YOUNG MAN When I meet him on the stairs he has no dogs, I can tell you, and no cats.

AGATHA He rides horseback. You can't take a horse to the doctor upstairs.

YOUNG MAN And he's always leaving your room.

AGATHA Why do you force me to betray a state secret? He comes to consult my husband. They're afraid of a plot in the city. Please don't tell anyone, that would mean his dismissal. You'd bring me to the stake.

YOUNG MAN One evening he was hurrying, his scarf not fastened, his tunic half unbuttoned. . . .

AGATHA Of course, that was the day he tried to kiss me. I fixed him!

YOUNG MAN You didn't let him kiss you, and he so powerful? I was waiting downstairs. He stayed two hours. . . .

AGATHA He did stay two hours, but I didn't let him kiss me.

YOUNG MAN Then he kissed you without your leave. Confess, Agatha, or I'll go away.

AGATHA Force me to confess! That's a fine reward for my frankness. Yes, he did kiss me . . . once . . . on my forehead.

YOUNG MAN And that seems dreadful to you?

AGATHA Dreadful? Frightful!

YOUNG MAN And you don't suffer for it?

AGATHA Not at all! . . . Ah, do I suffer? It's killing me, killing me! Kiss me, darling. Now you know everything, and I'm glad of it. Aren't you happy everything is cleared up between us?

YOUNG MAN Yes. Anything is better than a lie.

AGATHA What a nice way you have of saying you prefer me to everything else, darling!

SCENE 3 ELECTRA. ORESTES. BEGGAR, *then the* EUMENIDES. *They are taller than before, and seem fifteen years old.*

BEGGAR A dawn song, at the dawn of such a day! It's always like this.

ELECTRA The insect is dead, beggar?

BEGGAR Dispersed in the universe. His great-grandchildren are now fighting gout.

ELECTRA Orestes!

BEGGAR You see he's no longer asleep. His eyes are open.

ELECTRA Where are you, Orestes? What are you thinking about?

FIRST FURY Orestes, there's just time. Don't listen to your sister.

SECOND FURY Don't listen to her. We have learned what life holds for you, it's wonderful!

THIRD FURY Just by chance. As we grew up during the night.

SECOND FURY We're not saying anything about love to you, does that seem strange?

FIRST FURY She's going to spoil everything with her poison.

THIRD FURY Her poison of *truth,* the only one that has no antidote.

FIRST FURY You're right. We know what you're thinking. Royalty is magnificent, Orestes: young girls in the royal parks, feeding bread to the swans, King Orestes' miniature hanging on their blouses—they kiss it secretly; soldiers going to war, the women on the roofs, the sky like a veil over them, a white horse prancing to music; the return from war, the king's face looking like the face of a god, just because he's chilly or hungry or a little frightened, or pitying his people. If the truth is going to spoil all that, let it perish!

SECOND FURY You're right. And love is magnificent. Orestes! Lovers, it seems, will never part. They're never separated but they rush back to each other, to clasp hands. Or if they go away, they find each other face to face again immediately. The earth is round for the sake of lovers. Everywhere I run into him I love, though he's not yet alive. All this Electra wants to take from you, and from us too, with her Truth. We want to love. Flee Electra!

ELECTRA Orestes!

ORESTES I'm awake, sister.

ELECTRA Wake from your awakening. Don't listen to these girls.

ORESTES Are you sure they aren't right? Are you sure that it's not the worst kind of arrogance for a human being to try to retrace his steps? Why not take the first road and go forward, at random? Trust yourself to me. At this moment I can see so clearly the track of the game called happiness.

ELECTRA Alas! That's not what we're hunting today.

ORESTES The only thing that's important is not to leave each other. Let's go to Thessaly. You'll see my house, covered with roses and jasmin.

ELECTRA Darling Orestes, you've saved me from the gardener not just to give me to flowers!

ORESTES Be persuaded! Let's slip out of the trap which will soon catch us! Let's rejoice that we woke up before it did! Come!

FIRST FURY It's awake! Look at its eyes!

THIRD FURY You're right. The spring is wonderful, Orestes. When you can see over the hedges only the moving backs of the beasts grazing in the new grass, and the donkey's head looking at you over them. That donkey's head would look funny if you murdered your uncle. Pretty funny, a donkey looking at you when your hands are red with your uncle's blood—

ORESTES What's she saying?

THIRD FURY Talk on about the spring! The buttery mould that floats on the watercress in the brooks—you'll see what a comfort that will be for a man who kills his mother. Spread your butter that day with a knife, even if it's not the knife that killed your mother, and you'll see!

ORESTES Help! Electra!

ELECTRA So! You're like all men, Orestes! The least little flattery relaxes them, the slightest breath captivates them. Help you? I know what you'd like me to say.

ORESTES Then tell me.

ELECTRA That on the whole human beings are good, that life, too, after all, is good.

ORESTES Isn't that true?

ELECTRA That it's not a bad fate to be young, handsome, and a prince, to have a young sister who's a princess. That it's enough to leave men alone in their mean, vain business—not lancing human ulcers, but living for the beauty of the earth.

ORESTES Isn't that what you're telling me?

ELECTRA No! I'm telling you our mother has a lover.

ORESTES You lie! That's impossible.

FIRST FURY She's a widow. She has the right.

ELECTRA I'm telling you our father was murdered.

ORESTES Agamemnon! Murdered!

ELECTRA Stabbed, by assassins.

SECOND FURY Seven years ago. It's ancient history.

ORESTES You knew that and let me sleep all night!

ELECTRA I didn't know it. It's the night's gift to me. These truths were tossed to me by the night. Now I know how prophetesses work. They hold their brother close to their heart through one night.

ORESTES Our father killed! Who told you?

ELECTRA He himself.

ORESTES He spoke to you before he died?

ELECTRA Dead, he spoke to me. The very day of his death, but it's taken seven years for his word to reach me.

ORESTES He appeared to you?

ELECTRA No. His corpse appeared to me last night, looking like him the day he was murdered, but illuminated; I just had to read. There was a fold of his garment which said, I'm not a fold of death but of murder. And on his shoe there was a buckle which repeated, I'm not an accidental buckle but a criminal buckle. And on his eyelid there was a wrinkle which said, I didn't see death, I saw regicides.

ORESTES And about our mother, who told you that?

ELECTRA She herself, herself again.

ORESTES She confessed?

ELECTRA No. I saw her dead. Her body betrayed her. There's no possible doubt. Her eyebrow was the eyebrow of a dead woman who'd had a lover.

ORESTES Who is this lover? Who is this murderer?

ELECTRA I've waked you so you can find out. Let's hope they're both the same, then you'll have to strike just one blow.

ORESTES Girls, I think you'll have to clear out. My sister presents me as I wake with a harlot queen and a murdered king . . . my parents.

FIRST FURY That's not too bad. Add nothing more.

ELECTRA Forgive me, Orestes.

SECOND FURY Now she's excusing herself.

THIRD FURY I'm killing you, but excuse it, please.

BEGGAR She's wrong to excuse herself. This is the kind of awakening we generally reserve for our wives and sisters. They seem to be made for that.

ELECTRA They are made just for that. Wives, sisters-in-law, mothers-in-law, they're the ones to shake up the men who, barely awake, see nothing but purple and gold, till the women give them, with their coffee and hot water, a hatred of injustice and a scorn for small joys.

ORESTES Forgive me, Electra!

SECOND FURY It's his turn to beg pardon. Aren't they polite in this family!

FIRST FURY They take off their heads and bow to each other.

ELECTRA And they watch for their waking. For men put on the armor of happiness if they sleep no more than five minutes: and with it satisfaction, indifference, generosity, appetite. And a spot of sunlight reconciles them to all blood spots. And a bird song to all lies. But the women are there, all of them, worn by insomnia, with jealousy, envy, love, memory and truth. Are you awake, Orestes?

FIRST FURY And we'll be as old as he in an hour! Let's hope heaven makes us different!

ORESTES I believe I'm waking up.

BEGGAR Here comes our mother, children.

ORESTES Where's my sword?

ELECTRA Bravo! That's what I call a good awakening. Take up your sword. Take up your hatred. Take up your strength.

SCENE 4 *The same.* CLYTEMNESTRA.

CLYTEMNESTRA Their mother appears. And they turn into statues.

ELECTRA Orphans, rather.

CLYTEMNESTRA I'm not going to listen to an insolent daughter any longer.

ELECTRA Listen to your son.

ORESTES Who is it, mother? Confess.

CLYTEMNESTRA What kind of children are you, turning our meeting into a melodrama? Leave me, or I'll call.

ELECTRA Whom will you call? Him?

ORESTES You struggle too much, mother.

BEGGAR Be careful, Orestes. An innocent creature struggles as much as a guilty.

CLYTEMNESTRA Creature? What kind of creature am I for my children? Speak, Orestes, speak!

ORESTES I don't dare.

CLYTEMNESTRA Electra, then. She'll dare.

ELECTRA Who is it, mother?

CLYTEMNESTRA Of whom, of what are you speaking?

ORESTES Mother, is it true you have . . . ?

ELECTRA Don't specify, Orestes. Just ask who it is. There's a name somewhere in her. However you ask your question, the name will come out.

ORESTES Mother, is it true you have a lover?

CLYTEMNESTRA That's your question too, Electra?

ELECTRA It might be put that way.

CLYTEMNESTRA My son and daughter ask if I have a lover?

ELECTRA Your husband can't ask it now.

CLYTEMNESTRA The gods would blush to hear you.

ELECTRA That would surprise me. They've not been doing much blushing lately.

CLYTEMNESTRA I have no lover. But watch your step. All the evil in the world is caused by the so-called pure people trying to dig up secrets and bring them to light.

ELECTRA Rottenness is born of sunshine, I grant that.

CLYTEMNESTRA I have no lover, I couldn't have a lover if I wanted one. But take care. Curious people have had no luck in our family: they tracked down a theft and found a sacrilege; they carried on a love affair and ran into an incest. You'll not find out I have a lover, because I haven't, but you'll stumble on a stone which will be fatal to your sisters and yourselves.

ELECTRA Who is your lover?

ORESTES Electra, at least listen to her.

CLYTEMNESTRA I have no lover. But who would call it a crime if I had?

ORESTES Oh, mother, you're a queen.

CLYTEMNESTRA The world is not old and day is just dawning. But it would take us at least till twilight to recite the list of queens who've had lovers.

ORESTES Mother, please! Fight on this way. Convince us. If this struggle restores a queen to us, it's blessed, everything is restored.

ELECTRA Don't you see you're giving her weapons, Orestes?

CLYTEMNESTRA That's enough. Orestes, leave me alone with Electra, will you?

ORESTES Must I, sister?

ELECTRA Yes. Yes. Wait there, under the arch. And run back to me as soon as I call, Orestes. Run as fast as you can. It will mean I know all.

SCENE 5 CLYTEMNESTRA. ELECTRA. *The* BEGGAR.

CLYTEMNESTRA Help me, Electra!

ELECTRA Help you to what? To tell the truth or to lie?

CLYTEMNESTRA Protect me.

ELECTRA It's the first time you stoop to your daughter, mother. You must be afraid.

CLYTEMNESTRA I'm afraid of Orestes.

ELECTRA You lie. You're not the least afraid of Orestes. You see what he is: passionate, changeable, weak—still dreaming of an idyl in the Atrides' family. It's I you're afraid of, it's for me you're playing this game, the meaning of which still escapes me. You have a lover, haven't you? Who is he?

CLYTEMNESTRA He knows nothing. And he's not in question.

ELECTRA He doesn't know he's your lover?

CLYTEMNESTRA Stop acting like a judge, Electra. Stop this pursuit. After all, you're my daughter.

ELECTRA After all! Exactly after all! That's why I'm questioning you.

CLYTEMNESTRA Then stop being my daughter. Stop hating me. Just be what I look for in you—a woman. Take up my cause, it's yours. Defend yourself by defending me.

ELECTRA I'm not a member of the Women's Association, and someone other than you would have to recruit me.

CLYTEMNESTRA You're wrong. If you betray your equal in body, in misfortune, you're the first one Orestes will loathe. Scandal always strikes back at the people who start it. What good does it do you to bespatter all women by bespattering me? In Orestes' eyes you'll sully all the qualities you get from me.

ELECTRA I'm not like you in anything. I never look in my mirror except to be certain of that piece of luck. All the shiny marble, all the fountains of the palace have cried out to me, your own face cries it: Electra's nose is not the least like Clytemnestra's nose. My forehead is my own. My mouth's my own. And I have no lover.

CLYTEMNESTRA Listen! I have no lover. I'm in love.

ELECTRA Don't try that trick. You throw love at me the way drivers pursued by wolves throw them a dog. Dog meat is not my food.

CLYTEMNESTRA We're women, Electra. We have a right to love.

ELECTRA There are many rights in the sisterhood of women. I know. If you pay the entrance fee, which is steep, which means admission only for weak, lying, base women, you have a right to be weak, lying, and base. Unfortunately women are strong, loyal, and noble, so you're wrong. You had the right to love my father only. Did you? On your wedding night, did you love him?

CLYTEMNESTRA What are you driving at? Do you want me to say that your birth owes nothing to love, that you were conceived in indifference? Be satisfied. Not everyone can be like your Aunt Leda, and lay eggs.[1] You never spoke in me. We were indifferent to each other from the first. You didn't even cause me pain at your birth. You were small and withdrawn, your lips tight. When you were a year old, your lips were sealed, so "mother" wouldn't be your first word. Neither of us cried that day. We've never wept together.

ELECTRA Weeping parties don't interest me.

CLYTEMNESTRA You'll weep soon, perhaps over me.

ELECTRA Eyes can weep by themselves. That's what they're there for.

CLYTEMNESTRA Yes, even yours, which look like two stones. Some day tears will drown them.

ELECTRA I hope that day comes! But why are you trying to hold me by cold words instead of by love?

CLYTEMNESTRA So you'll understand I have a right to love. So you'll know that my whole life has been as hard as my daughter from her very first day. Since my marriage I've never been alone, never at peace. I never went to the forest except for festivals. No rest, even for my body which was covered every day by golden robes and at night by a king. Always mistrust, even of things, animals, plants. I often said to myself, as I looked at cross, silent lindens, smelling like a wet nurse: "They're like Electra's head, the day she was born." No queen has ever suffered so deeply the fate of queens, a husband's absence, a son's suspicions, a daughter's hatred. What had I left?

ELECTRA What the others had left: waiting.

CLYTEMNESTRA Waiting, for what? Waiting is horrible.

ELECTRA For her who has caught you today, perhaps.

CLYTEMNESTRA Can you tell me what you're waiting for?

ELECTRA I no longer wait. For ten years I've waited—for my father. Waiting is the only happiness in the world.

CLYTEMNESTRA A virgin's happiness, a solitary happiness.

ELECTRA You think so? Except for you and the men, everything in the palace awaited my father with me, everything was party to my waiting. It began in the morning with my early walk under the lindens which

[1] Leda was loved by Zeus who disguised himself as a swan. Helen, sister of Clytemnestra, was among their offspring.

hate you, which waited for my father with an eagerness they tried in vain to repress; they were sorry to live by the year and not by the decade, ashamed every spring that they couldn't hold back their flowers and perfume, that they grew weak with me over his absence. It went on till noon when I went to the brook that was the luckiest of us all, for it awaited my father as it ran to the river that ran to the sea. And in the evening, when I wasn't strong enough to wait near his dogs and his horses, poor short-lived beasts, that couldn't wait for centuries, I took refuge with the columns and the statues. I modeled myself on them. I waited in the moonlight for hours, motionless like them, without thought, lifeless. I awaited him with a stony heart—marble, alabaster, onyx—though it was beating, shattering my breast. Where would I be if there weren't still hours to wait, to wait for the past, wait for him still?

CLYTEMNESTRA I'm not waiting. I love.

ELECTRA Everything goes well with you now?

CLYTEMNESTRA Very well.

ELECTRA Flowers obey you? Birds talk to you?

CLYTEMNESTRA Yes, your lindens signal to me.

ELECTRA Quite likely. You've robbed me of everything in life.

CLYTEMNESTRA Fall in love. We'll share.

ELECTRA Share love with you?! Are you offering to share your lover with me? Who is he?

CLYTEMNESTRA Electra, have pity! I'll tell you his name, though it will make you blush. But wait a few days. What good will a scandal do you? Think of your brother. Can you imagine the Argives letting Orestes succeed an unworthy mother?

ELECTRA An unworthy mother? What are you getting at with this confession? What time do you want to gain? What trap are you setting for me? What brood are you hoping to save, limping off like a partridge, toward love and unworthiness?

CLYTEMNESTRA Spare me public disgrace! Why do you force me to confess I love someone below me in rank?

ELECTRA Some little nameless lieutenant?

CLYTEMNESTRA Yes.

ELECTRA You're lying. If your lover were some little nameless inglorious officer, or a bathhouse attendant, or a groom, you'd love him. But you're not in love, you've never loved. Who is it? Why do you refuse to name him, as you'd refuse a key? What piece of furniture are you afraid of opening with that name?

CLYTEMNESTRA Something of my own, my love.

ELECTRA Tell me the name of your lover, and I'll tell you if you love. And we'll keep it to ourselves forever.

CLYTEMNESTRA Never!

ELECTRA You see! It's not your lover but your secret that you're hiding from me. You're afraid his name would give me the one proof I'm lacking in my pursuit.

CLYTEMNESTRA What proof? You're mad.

ELECTRA The proof of the crime. Everything tells me, mother, that you committed it. But what I don't yet see, what you must tell me, is why you committed it. I've tried all the keys, as you say. Not one opens it—yet. Not love. You love nothing. Not ambition. You scoff at queenship. Not anger. You're deliberate, calculating. But our lover's name would clear up everything, tell us everything, wouldn't it? Who do you love? Who is he?

SCENE 6 *The same.* AGATHA, *pursued by the* PRESIDENT.

PRESIDENT Who is he? Who do you love?

AGATHA I hate you.

PRESIDENT Who is it?

AGATHA I tell you that's enough. Enough lies. Electra's right. I'm on her side. Thanks, Electra, you give me life.

PRESIDENT What is this song?

AGATHA Wives' song. You'll soon know it.

PRESIDENT So, she's going to sing!

AGATHA Yes, we're all here, with our unsatisfactory husbands or our widowhood. And we all kill ourselves, trying to make life and death pleasant. And if they eat cooked lettuce they have to have salt and a smile with it. And if they smoke we have to light their horrid cigars with the flame of our hearts.

PRESIDENT Who are you talking about? I never ate cooked lettuce.

AGATHA Sorrel leaves, if you prefer.

PRESIDENT Your lover doesn't eat sorrel or smoke cigars?

AGATHA The sorrel my lover eats turns into ambrosia, and I lick up what's left. And everything soiled by my husband's touch is purified by his hands or lips. I myself! God knows!

ELECTRA I've found out, mother, I've found out!

PRESIDENT Collect yourself, Agatha.

AGATHA Precisely. I've done just that. Twenty-four hours a day we kill ourselves to please someone whose displeasure is our only joy, for a husband whose absence is our only delight, for the vanity of the only man who humiliates us daily by showing us his toes and his shirt tails. And he has the gall to reproach us for stealing from him one hour a week of this hell! But, sure enough, he's right. When this wonderful hour comes, we don't greet it with a dead hand!

PRESIDENT Electra, this is your work. This very morning she kissed me!

AGATHA I'm pretty and he's ugly. I'm young and he's old. I'm bright and he's stupid. I have a soul and he hasn't. Yet he has everything. At least he has me. And I have nothing, though I have him! Until this morning, I gave everything and had to seem grateful. Why? I black his shoes. Why? I brush off his dandruff. Why? I make his coffee. Why? The truth might be that I'm poisoning him, rubbing his collar with pitch and ashes. Of course you can understand about the shoes. I spit on them. I spit on you. But it's all over, finished. Welcome, truth! Electra has given me her courage. I'm through. I'd as soon die.

BEGGAR Don't these wives sing well!

PRESIDENT Who is it?

ELECTRA Listen, mother! Listen to yourself. It's you talking.

AGATHA Who is it? All husbands think it's just one person.

PRESIDENT Lovers? You have lovers?

AGATHA They think we deceive them only with lovers. Of course we have lovers, too. But we deceive you with everything. When I wake and my hand slips along the wooden bedstead, that's my first adultery. Let's use your word for once, adultery. How often, when I'm wakeful, I've caressed that wood—olive wood, so soft! What a pretty name! I start when I hear an olive tree mentioned in the street—I hear my lover's name! And my second adultery is when I open my eyes and see daylight through the blinds. And my third, when my foot touches the bathwater and when I jump in. I betray you with my fingers, with my eyes, with the soles of my feet. When I look at you, I deceive you. When I listen to you and pretend to admire you in court, I'm deceiving you. Kill the olive trees, the pigeons, the five year old children, boys and girls, and water and earth and fire! Kill this beggar. You're betrayed by all of them.

BEGGAR Thanks!

PRESIDENT And yesterday this woman was still pouring my tea! And finding it too cool, having the water boiled again! You're all pleased, aren't you? This little scandal within a great one can't displease you!

BEGGAR No. It's like the squirrel in a big wheel. It gives the right rhythm.

PRESIDENT And this scene before the queen herself. You'll pardon it?

ELECTRA The queen envies Agatha. The queen would give her life to have the chance Agatha has today. Who is it, mother?

BEGGAR Sure! Don't let anything distract you, president. It's almost a minute since you asked her who it is.

PRESIDENT Who is it?

AGATHA I've told you, Everybody. Everything.

PRESIDENT It's enough to drive me to suicide, to make me bash my head against the wall.

AGATHA Don't stop on my account. The Mycenean wall is solid.

PRESIDENT Is he young? Or old?

AGATHA A lover's age—between 16 and 80.

PRESIDENT And she thinks she's disgracing me by insulting me! Your insults only hurt yourself, abandoned woman!

AGATHA I know, I know. Outrage is called majesty. In the streets the most respectable people slip on dung.

PRESIDENT At last you'll find out who I am! Whoever your lovers are, I'll kill the first one I find here.

AGATHA The first one you find here? You choose the place badly.

PRESIDENT I'll make him kneel down and kiss the marble.

AGATHA You'll see how he'll kiss the marble when he comes into this court in a minute and sits on the throne.

PRESIDENT Wretch, what are you saying?

AGATHA I'm saying that at present I have two lovers, and one is Aegisthus.

CLYTEMNESTRA Liar!

AGATHA What! She too!

ELECTRA You too, mother?

BEGGAR That's funny. I'd have thought, if Aegisthus had a liking, it was for Electra.

PAGE (*Announcing*) Aegisthus!

ELECTRA At last!

THE FURIES Aegisthus!

(AEGISTHUS *comes in. Much more majestic and calm than in the first act. Far above him, a bird hovers in the air*)

SCENE 7 *The same.* AEGISTHUS. *A* CAPTAIN. SOLDIERS.

AEGISTHUS Electra is here. . . . Thanks, Electra! I'll stop here, Captain. Headquarters are here.

CLYTEMNESTRA I, too, am here.

AEGISTHUS I'm glad. Welcome, queen!

PRESIDENT I too, Aegisthus!

AEGISTHUS Good, president. I need your help.

PRESIDENT And now he insults us!

AEGISTHUS What's the matter with you all, that you stare at me so?

BEGGAR What's the matter is that the queen is waiting for a perjurer, Electra for an infidel, Agatha for a faithless lover. He's more humble, he's waiting for the man who seduced his wife. They're all waiting for you, but it's not you that's come!

AEGISTHUS They have no luck, have they, beggar?

BEGGAR No, they have no luck. Waiting for a rascal, they see a king enter! I don't care about the others, but for our little Electra, the situation is complicated.

AEGISTHUS You think so? I think not.

BEGGAR I knew it would happen. I told you so yesterday. I knew the king would reveal himself in you. He has your strength and your years. He finds the right moment. Electra is near. That might have involved a bloody act. But you've revealed yourself. Fine for Greece! But not so gay for the family.

CLYTEMNESTRA What do these riddles mean? What are you talking about?

BEGGAR Lucky for us, too! Since there has to be *some* kind of meeting, better let Electra meet nobility than wickedness. How did you get this way, Aegisthus?

AEGISTHUS (*Looking at* ELECTRA) Electra is here! I knew I'd find her looking toward me, her statuesque head, her eyes which see only when the lids are closed, deaf to human speech.

CLYTEMNESTRA Listen to me, Aegisthus!

PRESIDENT How well you choose your lovers, Agatha! What impudence!

CAPTAIN Aegisthus, there's no time!

AEGISTHUS Your ears are ornaments, aren't they, Electra? Mere ornaments. . . . The gods said, we gave her hands so she'd not touch, eyes so she'd be seen, we can't let her head be without ears! People would soon discover that she hears only us. . . . Tell me, what would we hear if we placed our ears near hers? What roaring! And where from?

CLYTEMNESTRA Are you mad? Take care! Electra's ears do hear you.

PRESIDENT They blush for it.

AEGISTHUS They hear me. I'm sure of that. Since what happened to me just now in the outskirts of Argos, my words come from beyond myself. And I know she sees me too, she's the only one who does see me. The only one to guess what I've become since that moment.

CLYTEMNESTRA You're talking to your worst enemy, Aegisthus!

AEGISTHUS She knows why I galloped toward the city from the mountains. Electra, you'd have thought my horse understood. He was beautiful, that light chestnut, charging toward Electra, followed by the thunder of the squadron, in which the knowledge of rushing toward Electra grew less, from the white stallions of the trumpeters to the piebald mares of the rear guard. Don't be surprised if my horse sticks his head between the pillars, neighing to you. He knew that I was strangling, with your name in my mouth like a golden stopper. I had to shout your name, and to you—shall I shout it, Electra?

CLYTEMNESTRA Stop this outrageous behavior, Aegisthus.

CAPTAIN Aegisthus! The city is in danger!

AEGISTHUS True! Pardon me! Where are they now, Captain?

CAPTAIN You can see their lances coming over the hills. I've never seen a harvest grow so fast. Nor so thick. There are thousands of them.

AEGISTHUS The cavalry's no use against them?

CAPTAIN Repulsed, prisoners taken.

CLYTEMNESTRA What's happening, Aegisthus?

CAPTAIN The Corinthians are surrounding us, no declaration of war, no reason for it. Their regiments entered our territory last night. The suburbs are on fire already.

AEGISTHUS What do the prisoners say?

CAPTAIN Their orders are to leave no stone standing in Argos.

CLYTEMNESTRA Show yourself, Aegisthus, and they'll flee!

AEGISTHUS I fear, queen, that wouldn't be enough.

CAPTAIN They have friends in the city. The reserves of pitch have been stolen, so the middle-class quarters can be burned. Gangs of beggars are gathering around the markets ready to start pillaging.

CLYTEMNESTRA If the guard is loyal, what is there to fear?

CAPTAIN The guard is ready to fight. But they're muttering. You know, they've never willingly obeyed a woman. The city's the same way. They both demand a king, a man.

AEGISTHUS They're right. They shall have one.

PRESIDENT Whoever wants to be king of Argos, Aegisthus, must first kill Clytemnestra.

BEGGAR Or simply marry her.

PRESIDENT Never!

AEGISTHUS Why, never? The queen can't deny that's the only way to save Argos. I don't doubt she'll consent. Captain, tell the guard the wedding has this moment taken place. Keep me informed of events. I'll wait here for your bulletins. And do you, president, go meet the rioters and tell them this news most enthusiastically.

PRESIDENT Never! I must first speak to you, man to man, no matter what happens.

AEGISTHUS No matter if Argos falls, if war comes? You're outrageous.

PRESIDENT My honor, the honor of all Greek judges, is at stake.

BEGGAR If Greek justice lies in Agatha's lap, that's just what it deserves. Don't hinder us at such a time. Look at Agatha, see if she cares for the honor of Greek judges, with her nose in the air.

PRESIDENT Her nose in the air! Agatha is your nose in the air?

AGATHA My nose *is* in the air. I'm looking at that bird hovering over Aegisthus.

PRESIDENT Lower it!

AEGISTHUS Queen, I'm waiting for your reply.

CLYTEMNESTRA A bird? What is that bird? Get away from under that bird, Aegisthus.

AEGISTHUS Why? He's not left me since sunrise. He must have his reasons. My horse noticed him first. He kicked without any provocation. I looked all around and then up there. He was kicking at that bird, and plunging and rearing. It's exactly above me, isn't it, beggar?

BEGGAR Exactly above. If you were a thousand feet tall, your head would be there.

AEGISTHUS Like a mark on a page, isn't it? A black mark.

BEGGAR Yes, at the moment you're the most marked man in Greece. We'll have to find out whether the mark is over the word "human" or the word "mortal."

CLYTEMNESTRA I don't like this hovering bird. What is it? A kite or an eagle?

BEGGAR He's too high up. I might recognize him by his shadow, but so high up we can't see it, it's lost.

CAPTAIN (*Returning*) The guards are delighted, Aegisthus. They're joyfully getting ready to fight. They're waiting for you to appear on the balcony with the queen, so they can cheer you.

AEGISTHUS My oath, and I'll go.

PRESIDENT Electra, help me! Why should this rake teach us courage?

BEGGAR Why? Listen! . . .

AEGISTHUS Oh, Heavenly Powers, since I must pray to you on the eve of battle, I thank you for the gift of this hill which overlooks Argos the moment the fog evaporates. I dismounted, weary from the night patrol, I leant against the battlement, and suddenly I saw Argos as I had never before seen it—new, rebuilt by me; you have given it to me. You've given it all to me, its towers, its bridges, the smoke from its farm machines, the flying pigeons, its first movements, the grinding of its locks, its first cry. Everything in your gift has equal value, Electra, the sunrise over Argos, the last lantern in the city, the temple, the ruins, the lake, the tanneries. And the gift is forever! This morning I was given my city for eternity, as a mother her child, and in agony I asked myself if the gift were not even greater, if you hadn't given me far more than Argos. In the morning God never counts his gifts: he might even have given me the whole world. That would have been dreadful. I should have felt a despair like that of a man who expects a diamond on his birthday and is given the sun. Electra, you see my anxiety! I anxiously stretched my foot and my thoughts beyond Argos. What joy! I had not been given the Orient, its plagues, earthquakes, famines: I realized that with a smile. My thirst was not like that of men who quench it in the great, warm rivers flowing through the desert, but, I discovered, I could quench it at an icy spring. And nothing in Africa is mine! Negresses can pound millet at the doors of their huts, the jaguar drive his claws into the crocodile's flank, not a drop of their soup or their blood is mine. I'm as happy over the gifts not given me as over the gift of Argos. In a fit of generosity the Gods have not given me Athens or Olympia or Mycenae. What joy! They have given me the Argive cattle markets, not the treasures of Corinth; the short noses of the Argive girls, not the nose of Athena; the wrinkled prune of Argos, not the golden fig of Thebes! That's what they gave me this morning; me, the wastrel, the parasite, the knave, a country where I feel myself pure, strong, perfect; a fatherland; a country where, instead of being a slave, I am king, where I swear to live and die—you hear me, judge—a country I swear to save.

PRESIDENT I rely on you only, Electra!

ELECTRA Rely on me. No one should save his fatherland with impure hands.

BEGGAR A coronation purifies everything.

ELECTRA Who crowned you? Who witnessed your coronation?

BEGGAR Can't you guess? Just what he begged of you. For the first time he sees you in your truth and power. The thought has suddenly dawned on him that Electra is included in this gift of Argos.

AEGISTHUS Everything on my way consecrated me, Electra. As I galloped I heard the trees, the children, the streams shout to me: I was king. But the holy oil was lacking. I was a coward yesterday. A rabbit, whose trembling ears showed over a furrow, gave me courage. I was a hypocrite. A fox crossed the road, his eyes crafty, and I became frank. And a couple of magpies gave me independence, an ant hill, generosity. And if I hurried back to you, Electra, it was because you are the only creature who can give me her very being.

ELECTRA And that is—?

AEGISTHUS I think it is rather like duty.

ELECTRA My duty is certainly the mortal enemy of yours. You shall not marry Clytemnestra.

PRESIDENT You shall not marry her.

CLYTEMNESTRA And why shan't we marry? Why should we sacrifice our lives to ungrateful children? Yes, I love Aegisthus. For ten years I've loved Aegisthus. For ten years I've postponed this marriage for your sake, Electra, and in memory of your father. Now you force us to it. Thanks! But not under that bird. That bird annoys me. As soon as the bird flies away, I consent.

AEGISTHUS Don't worry, queen. I'm not marrying you in order to create new lies. I don't know if I still love you, and the whole city doubts that you ever loved me. For ten years our liaison has dragged along between indifference and neglect. But marriage is the only way to cast a little truth over our past lies, and it will safeguard Argos. It must take place, this very hour.

ELECTRA I don't believe it will take place.

PRESIDENT Bravo!

AEGISTHUS Will you be quiet? Who are you in Argos? A deceived husband or the chief justice?

PRESIDENT Both, of course.

AEGISTHUS Then choose. I have no choice. Choose between duty and prison. Time is short.

PRESIDENT You took Agatha from me.

AEGISTHUS I'm not the one who took Agatha.

PRESIDENT Weren't you given all the deceived husbands in Argos this morning?

BEGGAR Yes. But he's not the man who deceived them.

PRESIDENT I understand. The new king forgets the outrages he committed as regent.

BEGGAR Agatha looks like a rose. Outrages make her rosy!

AEGISTHUS A king begs you to pardon today the insult a rake inflicted on you yesterday. That must satisfy you. Listen to my orders. Go quickly to your courtroom, try the rebels, and be severe with them.

AGATHA Be severe. I have a little lover among them.

PRESIDENT Will you stop looking at that bird? You irritate me.

AGATHA I'm sorry. It's the only thing in the world that interests me.

PRESIDENT Idiot! What will you do when it goes away?

AGATHA That's what I'm wondering.

AEGISTHUS Are you disobeying me, president? Don't you hear those shouts?

PRESIDENT I'll not go. I'll help Electra prevent your marriage.

ELECTRA I don't need your help, president. Your role ended when Agatha gave me the key to everything. Thanks, Agatha!

CLYTEMNESTRA What key?

AEGISTHUS Come, queen.

CLYTEMNESTRA What key did she give you? What new quarrel are you trying to start?

ELECTRA You hated my father! Oh, everything is clear in the light of Agatha's lamp.

CLYTEMNESTRA There she goes again! Protect me, Aegisthus!

ELECTRA How you envied Agatha just now! What joy to shout out your hatred to the husband you hate! That joy was not allowed you, mother. Never in your life will you have it. Till the day of his death he believed you admired and adored him. At banquets and festivals I've often seen your face harden, your lips move soundlessly, because you wanted to cry out you hated him. You wanted passers-by, guests, the servant pouring wine, the detective guarding the silver, to hear you, didn't you? Poor mother, you could never go to the country alone to cry out to the bushes! All the bushes say you adored him!

CLYTEMNESTRA Listen, Electra!

ELECTRA That's right, mother, cry it out to me! Though he's not here, I'm his substitute. Cry to me! That will do you as much good as to say it to him. You're not going to die without letting him know you hated him.

CLYTEMNESTRA Come, Aegisthus! Never mind the bird!

ELECTRA If you take one step, mother, I'll call.

AEGISTHUS Whom will you call, Electra? Is there anyone in the world who can take from us the right to save our city?

ELECTRA Save our city from hypocrisy, from corruption? There are thousands. The purest, the handsomest, the youngest is here, in this courtyard. If Clytemnestra takes a step, I'll call.

CLYTEMNESTRA Come, Aegisthus!

ELECTRA Orestes! Orestes!

(*The* EUMENIDES *appear and bar the way*)

FIRST FURY Poor girl! You're too naive! Do you think we'll let Orestes run around sword in hand? Accidents happen too quickly in this palace. We've gagged him and chained him up.

ELECTRA That's not true! Orestes! Orestes!

SECOND FURY You, too, it will happen to you.

AEGISTHUS Electra, dear Electra, listen to me. I want to persuade you.

CLYTEMNESTRA You're losing precious time, Aegisthus.

AEGISTHUS I'm coming! Electra, I know you're the only one who understands what I am today. Help me! Let me tell you why you must help me!

CLYTEMNESTRA What is this craze to explain, to argue? Are we roosters in this courtyard or human beings? Do we have to go on explaining till our eyes are gouged out? Must the three of us be carried off by force, to separate us?

PRESIDENT I think that's the only way, queen.

CAPTAIN I beseech you, Aegisthus! Hurry!

BEGGAR Don't you understand? Aegisthus must settle once and for all the business about Agamemnon—Clytemnestra—Electra. Then he'll come.

CAPTAIN In five minutes it will be too late.

BEGGAR We'll all do our bit. It will be settled in five minutes.

AEGISTHUS Take this man away.

(*Guards take out the* PRESIDENT. *All the spectators leave. Silence*)

AEGISTHUS Now, Electra, what do you want?

SCENE 8 ELECTRA. CLYTEMNESTRA. AEGISTHUS. BEGGAR.

ELECTRA She's not late, Aegisthus. She just won't come.

AEGISTHUS Of whom are you speaking?

ELECTRA Of her you're waiting for. The messenger of the gods. If divine justice absolves Aegisthus because he loves his city, and is marrying Clytemnestra because he despises lies and wants to save the middle class and the rich, this is the moment for her to appear before the two of you, bearing her diplomas and her laurels. But she'll not come.

AEGISTHUS You know she has come. This morning's sunbeam on my head was she.

ELECTRA That was a morning beam. Every scurvy child thinks he's a king when a morning sunbeam touches him.

AEGISTHUS Do you doubt my sincerity?

ELECTRA I don't doubt it. I recognize in it the hypocrisy and malice of the gods. They change a parasite into a just man, an adulterer into a husband, a usurper into a king. They thought my task not painful enough, so they made a figure of honor out of you, whom I despise! But there's one change they can't carry through! They can't transform a criminal into an innocent man. They bow to me there.

AEGISTHUS I don't know what you mean.

ELECTRA You have an inkling. Listen to the small voice beneath your heroic soul. You'll understand.

AEGISTHUS Who can explain what you're talking about?

CLYTEMNESTRA Of whom *can* she talk? What has she always talked about her whole life long? Of a father she never knew.

ELECTRA I? I never knew my father?

CLYTEMNESTRA You touched a corpse, ice that had been your father. But not your father.

AEGISTHUS Please, Clytemnestra! How can you quarrel at such a moment!

CLYTEMNESTRA Everyone must have a turn in this debate. It's my turn now.

ELECTRA For once you're right. We've come to the heart of the matter. If I'd not touched my living father, from whom would I have drawn my strength, my truth?

CLYTEMNESTRA Precisely. But now you're talking wildly. I wonder if you ever kissed him. I took care he didn't lick my children.

ELECTRA I never kissed my father?

CLYTEMNESTRA Your father's dead body, perhaps, not your father.

AEGISTHUS I beg you . . . !

ELECTRA Ah, now I see why you're so firm as you face me. You thought me unarmed, you thought I'd never touched my father. What a mistake!

CLYTEMNESTRA You're lying.

ELECTRA The day my father came home you two waited for him a minute too long on the palace stairs, didn't you?

CLYTEMNESTRA How do you know? You weren't there!

ELECTRA I was holding him back. I was in his arms.

AEGISTHUS Now listen, Electra . . .

ELECTRA I'd waited in the crowd, mother. I rushed toward him. His escorts were frightened, they feared an attempt on his life. But he recognized me, smiled at me. He understood Electra's attempt, and, brave father, went to meet it. And I touched him.

CLYTEMNESTRA You may have touched his leg armor, his horse, leather and hair!

ELECTRA He got down, mother. I touched his hands with these fingers, his lips with these lips. I touched a skin you'd never touched, purified from you by ten years of absence.

AEGISTHUS That's enough. She believes you!

ELECTRA My cheek on his, I felt my father's warmth. Sometimes in summer the whole world is just as warm as my father. I faint from it. And I did hug him in these arms. I thought I was taking the measure of my love—it was also that of my vengeance. He freed himself, mounted his horse, more agile, more resplendent than before. Electra's attempt on his life was over. He was more alive, more golden, because of it. And I ran to the palace to see him again, but I was really running not toward him, but toward you, his murderers.

AEGISTHUS Pull yourself together, Electra!

ELECTRA Perhaps I am out of breath. I've reached my goal.

CLYTEMNESTRA Rid us of this girl, Aegisthus. Give her back to the gardener. Or turn her over to her brother.

AEGISTHUS Stop, Electra! Why, at the very moment that I see you, that I love you, when I'm at the point of understanding you—your scorn for abuses, your courage, your disinterestedness—why do you persist in fighting?

ELECTRA I have only this moment.

AEGISTHUS Don't you know Argos is in danger?

ELECTRA We don't see the same dangers.

AEGISTHUS Don't you know that if I marry Clytemnestra, the city will quiet down, the Atrides will be saved? If not, riots, conflagrations?

ELECTRA Perhaps.

AEGISTHUS Don't you know that I alone can defend the city against the Corinthians who are already at the gates? If not, pillage, massacre?

ELECTRA Yes. You'd be victor.

AEGISTHUS Yet you are obstinate! You ruin my work. And you sacrifice your family and your country to a dream!

ELECTRA You're mocking me, Aegisthus! You pretend to know me yet you think I'm the kind to whom you can say, "If you lie and let other people lie, you'll have a prosperous country. If you hide your crimes, your country will be victorious." What is this poor country that you're all of a sudden placing between us and truth?

AEGISTHUS Your country—Argos.

ELECTRA You're wrong, Aegisthus. This morning, at the very hour you were given Argos, I also received a gift. I expected it, it had been promised me, but I still didn't know just what it would be. I had already been given a thousand gifts, which seemed incomplete, I couldn't see their appropriateness, but last night, near Orestes as he slept, I saw they were all one and the same gift. I'd been given the back of a truck driver, the smile of a laundress suddenly stopped in her work, watching the river. I'd been given a fat, naked little child, running across the street as his mother and the neighbors shouted to him. I'd been given the cry of a caged bird set free, and that of a mason I one day saw fall from a scaffold, his legs sprawling. I was given the water plant, resisting the current, fighting and dying; the sick young man, coughing, smiling and coughing; and my maid's red cheeks, puffed up each winter morning as she blows on the ashes of the fire. I too thought I was given Argos, everything in Argos that is modest, tender, beautiful and wretched, but just now I found out that it's not so. I knew I'd been given all the servants' cheeks as they blow on wood or coal, all the laundresses' eyes, whether round or almond-shaped, all the falling masons, all the water plants which seem lost and grow again in streams or the sea. But Argos is only a speck in this universe, my country only a village in that country. All the light and the cries in sad faces, all the wrinkles and shadows on joyful faces, all the desires and despair on indifferent faces—these are my new country. And this morning, at dawn, when you were given Argos and its narrow borders, I also saw it as tremendous, and I heard its name, which is not to be spoken, but which is both tenderness and justice.

CLYTEMNESTRA So that's Electra's motto! Tenderness! That's enough. Let's go.

AEGISTHUS And you dare call this justice, that makes you burn your city, damn your family, you dare call this the justice of the gods?

ELECTRA Far from it! In this country of mine, concern for justice is not the gods' business. The gods are only artists. A beautiful light from a conflagration, beautiful grass on a battle field, such is their justice. A magnificent repentance for a crime is the gods' verdict on your case. I don't accept it.

AEGISTHUS Electra's justice consists in re-examining every sin, making every act irreparable?

ELECTRA Oh, no! Some years, frost is justice for the trees, other times it's injustice. There are criminals we love, murderers we embrace. But when the crime is an assault on human dignity, infects a nation, corrupts its loyalty, then—no pardon is possible.

AEGISTHUS Have you any idea what a nation is, Electra?

ELECTRA When you see a huge face fill the horizon and you look straight at it with pure, brave eyes, that's a nation.

AEGISTHUS You talk like a young girl, not like a king. There's also a huge body to rule and to nourish.

ELECTRA I speak like a woman. There's a bright look to sift, to gild. And the only gold is truth. Those great eyes of truth, they're so beautiful, when you think of the real nations of the world.

AEGISTHUS There are truths that can kill nations, Electra.

ELECTRA Sometimes, the eyes of a dead nation shine forever. Pray Heaven, that will be the fate of Argos! But since my father's death, since our people's happiness came to be founded on injustice and crime, since everyone has become a cowardly accomplice in murder and lies, the city can prosper, sing, dance, conquer, heaven may shine on it, but it will be only a cellar where eyes are useless. Infants suck the breast without seeing it.

AEGISTHUS A scandal can only destroy it.

ELECTRA Possibly. But I can no longer endure the dim, lustreless look in its eyes.

AEGISTHUS That will cost thousands of glazed, dead eyes.

ELECTRA That's the price. It's not too high.

AEGISTHUS I must have this day. Give it to me. Your truth, if there is such a thing, will find a way to be revealed at a time more suitable for it.

ELECTRA The revolt shows this day is made for it.

AEGISTHUS I beseech you! Wait till tomorrow.

ELECTRA No. This is the day for it. I've seen too many truths fade away because they were a day too late. I know young girls who waited one second before saying no to an ugly, vile thing, and could then say nothing but yes, yes. The beautiful and cruel thing about truth is that she is eternal, but is also like a flash of lightning.

AEGISTHUS I must save the city and Greece.

ELECTRA That's a small duty. I'm saving their soul.—You did kill him, didn't you?

CLYTEMNESTRA How dare you say that, daughter? Everyone knows your father slipped on the tiles.

ELECTRA Everyone knows it because you said so.

CLYTEMNESTRA Crazy girl, he slipped and fell.

ELECTRA He did not slip. For one obvious reason. Because my father never slipped.

CLYTEMNESTRA How do you know?

ELECTRA For eight years I've been asking the grooms, the maids, his escort in rain and hail. He *never* slipped.

CLYTEMNESTRA The war came after.

ELECTRA I've asked his fellow soldiers. He crossed Scamander[1] without slipping. He took the battlements by assault without slipping. He never slipped, in water or in blood.

CLYTEMNESTRA He was in haste that day. You had made him late.

ELECTRA I'm the guilty one, am I? That's Clytemnestra's kind of truth. Your opinion, too, Aegisthus? Electra murdered Agamemnon?

CLYTEMNESTRA The maids had soaped the tiles too well. I know. I almost slipped myself.

ELECTRA Ah, you were in the bathroom, too, mother? Who held you up?

CLYTEMNESTRA What's wrong in my being there?

ELECTRA With Aegisthus, of course?

CLYTEMNESTRA With Aegisthus. And we weren't alone. Leo, my counsellor, was there, wasn't he, Aegisthus?

ELECTRA Leo, who died the next day?

CLYTEMNESTRA Did he die the next day?

ELECTRA Yes, Leo slipped, too. He lay down on his bed and in the morning was found dead. He found a way to slip into death—sleeping, not slipping! You had him killed, didn't you?

[1] A river in north-west Turkey before the ancient city of Troy.

CLYTEMNESTRA Aegisthus, defend me. I call on you for help.

ELECTRA He can do nothing for you. You've come to the place where you must defend yourself.

CLYTEMNESTRA Oh, God! Have I come to this? A mother! A queen!

ELECTRA Where is "this"? Tell us where you've come.

CLYTEMNESTRA Brought there by this heartless, joyless daughter! Happily, my little Chrysothemis loves flowers.

ELECTRA Don't I love flowers?

CLYTEMNESTRA To come to this! Through this idiotic journey called life, to come to this! I, who as a girl loved quiet, tending my pets, laughing at meal time, sewing! . . . I was so gentle, Aegisthus, I swear I was the gentlest. . . . There are still old men in my birthplace who call gentleness Clytemnestra.

ELECTRA If they die today, they needn't change their symbol. If they die this morning!

CLYTEMNESTRA To come to this! What injustice! Aegisthus, I spent my days in the meadows behind the palace. There were so many flowers I didn't have to stoop to pick them, I sat down. My dogs lay at my feet, the one who barked when Agamemnon came to take me away. I teased him with flowers and he ate them to please me. If I only had him! Anywhere else, if my husband had been a Persian, or an Egyptian, by now I'd be good, careless, gay! When I was young I had a voice, I trained birds! I might have been an Egyptian queen, singing gaily; I'd have had an Egyptian aviary! And we've come to this! What has this family, what have these walls done to us?

ELECTRA Murderers! . . . These are wicked walls.

MESSENGER My lord, they've forced an entrance. The postern gate gave way.

ELECTRA All right. Let the walls crumble.

AEGISTHUS Electra, heed my final word. I forgive everything—your foolish fancies, your insults. But can't you see your country is dying?

ELECTRA And I don't love flowers! Do you imagine flowers for a father's grave are picked sitting down?

CLYTEMNESTRA Well, let this father return! Let him stop being dead! What nonsense, this absence, this silence! Let him come back, in his pomp, his vanity, his beard! That beard must have grown in the grave—a good thing, too!

ELECTRA What are you saying?

AEGISTHUS Electra, I promise that tomorrow, as soon as Argos is saved, the guilty, if there are any, shall disappear, for good and all. But don't be stubborn. You're gentle, Electra, in your heart you're gentle. Listen! The city will perish.

ELECTRA Let it! I can already feel my love for a burnt and conquered Argos! No! My mother has begun to insult my father, let her finish!

CLYTEMNESTRA Why are you talking about the guilty? What do you mean, Aegisthus?

ELECTRA He's just told me in a word all that you deny!

CLYTEMNESTRA And what do I deny?

ELECTRA He's told me that you let Orestes fall, that I love flowers, and that my father didn't slip.

CLYTEMNESTRA He did slip. I swear he slipped. If there's a truth in the world, let lightning from heaven show it to us. You'll see it revealed in all its brilliance.

AEGISTHUS Electra, you're in my power. Your brother too. I can kill you. Yesterday I should have killed you. Instead of that I promise, as soon as the enemy is repulsed, to step down from the throne and place Orestes on it.

ELECTRA That's no longer the question, Aegisthus. If the gods for once change their methods, if they make you wise and just in order to ruin you, that's their affair. The question now is, will she dare tell us why she hated my father!

CLYTEMNESTRA Oh, you want to know that?

ELECTRA But you'll not dare tell.

AEGISTHUS Electra, tomorrow, before the altar where we celebrate our victory the guilty man shall stand, for there is only one guilty man, in a parricide's coat. He'll confess his crime publicly and determine his punishment himself. First let me save the city.

ELECTRA You've "saved" yourselves today, Aegisthus, and in my presence. That's enough. Now I want her to finish!

CLYTEMNESTRA So, you want me to finish!

ELECTRA I dare you to!

MESSENGER They're entering the court yards, Aegisthus!

AEGISTHUS Come, queen!

CLYTEMNESTRA Yes, I hated him. Yes, you shall know what this fine father was like. Yes, after twenty years I'll have the joy that Agatha had today. A woman might belong to anyone, but there was just one man in the world to whom I couldn't belong. That man was the king of kings, father of fathers! I hated him from the first day he came to wrench me from my home, with his curly beard and the hand with the little finger always sticking up. He raised it when he drank, when he drove, when he held his sceptre . . . and when he held me close I felt on my back only four fingers. It drove me wild, and the morning he sacrificed your sister, Iphigenia,[2]—horrible—I saw the little fingers of both his hands sticking out, dark against the sun—king of kings! What nonsense! He was pompous, indecisive, stupid. He was the fop of fops, the most credulous creature. The king of kings was never anything more than that little finger and the beard that nothing could soften. The bathwater I soaked his head in didn't soften it, nor did the nights of false love when I pulled and tangled it, nor the storm at Delphi which turned the dancers' hair into manes; it came out in gold ringlets from water, bed, and rain. He would beckon me with his little finger and I would go smiling. . . . Why? He would tell me to kiss his mouth in that fleece and I would run to kiss it. . . . Why? And when I woke and was unfaithful to him, like Agatha, with the wooden bedstead—a royal bed—and he bade me talk to him, though I knew he was vain, empty, tiresome, I told him he was modest, strange, even splendid. . . . Why? And if he persisted, stammering, pathetic, I swore to him he was a god. King of kings! The only excuse for that title is that it justifies a hatred of hatreds. Do you know what I did, Electra, the day of his departure, when his ship was still in sight? I sacrificed the curliest ram I could find and toward midnight I stole into the throne room quite alone, and took the sceptre in my hands! Now you know everything. You wanted a hymn to truth, and here's a beautiful one.

[2] She was sacrificed in order to enable the Greek fleet to sail to Troy.

ELECTRA Oh, father, forgive!

AEGISTHUS Come, queen.

CLYTEMNESTRA Take this girl first and chain her up.

ELECTRA Father, will you ever forgive me for listening to her? Aegisthus, should she not die?

AEGISTHUS Farewell, Electra.

ELECTRA Kill her, Aegisthus. And I'll forgive you.

CLYTEMNESTRA Don't let her go free, Aegisthus. They'll stab you in the back.

AEGISTHUS We'll see about that. Leave Electra alone. . . . Unbind Orestes.

(AEGISTHUS *and* CLYTEMNESTRA *go out*)

ELECTRA The bird is coming down, beggar, the bird is coming down.

BEGGAR Look, it's a vulture!

SCENE 9 ELECTRA. NARSES' WIFE. BEGGAR. *Then* ORESTES.

BEGGAR You here, Narses' wife?

NARSES' WIFE All of us beggars, the lame, the halt and the blind, have come to save Electra and her brother.

BEGGAR Justice, eh?

NARSES' WIFE There they are, untying Orestes.

(*A crowd of* BEGGARS *enter, a few at a time*)

BEGGAR This is how they did the killing, listen, woman. This is the way it all happened, I never invent anything. It was the queen who had the steps soaped that go down to the bath; the two of them did it. While all the housewives in Argos scrubbed their thresholds, the queen and her lover soaped the doorsill to his death. Think how clean their hands were when they greeted Agamemnon at his entrance! And your father slipped, Electra, as he reached out his arms to her. You were right except on this one point. He slipped on the steps, and the noise of his fall, because of his golden cuirass and helmet, was that of a king falling. And she threw herself on him, he thought, to raise him up, but she held him down. He didn't understand why his darling wife was holding him down, he wondered if it was a love transport, but then why did Aegisthus stay? Young Aegisthus was awkward and indiscreet. (We'll consider his promotion.) The ruler of the world, the conqueror of Troy, who had just reviewed the army and navy parade, must have been humiliated to fall like that.

on his back and in his noisy armor, even if his beard was untouched, in the presence of his loving wife and the young ensign. All the more annoyed because this might be a bad omen. The fall might mean he'd die in a year, or in five years. And he was surprised that his beloved wife caught his wrists and threw herself on him to hold him down, as fisherwomen do with big stranded turtles on the shore. She was wrong, and not so beautiful, her face flushed, her neck wrinkled. Not like young Aegisthus, who was trying to extricate his sword for fear he'd hurt himself, apparently, he looked handsomer every minute. What was strange, though, was that the two of them were silent. He said "Dear wife, how strong you are!" "Young man," he said, "pull out the sword—by its handle!" But they said nothing, the queen and the squire had become mutes in the last ten years, and no one had told him. They were as mute as travelers hurrying to pack a trunk when time is short. They had to do something quickly, before anyone else came in. What was it? Suddenly Aegisthus kicked his helmet as a dying man kicks his dog, and the truth was plain. And he cried, "Wife, let me go. Wife, what are you doing?" She took care not to answer, she couldn't say aloud, "I'm killing you, murdering you!" But she said to herself, "I'm killing you because there's not one gray hair on your beard, because it's the only way to murder that little finger."

She undid the laces of his cuirass with her teeth, and the gold turned scarlet, and Aegisthus—beautiful with the beauty of Achilles killing Hector, of Ulysses killing Dolon[3]—approached, with drawn sword. Then the king of kings kicked Clytemnestra's back, and she shook all over, her silent hand shook, and he shouted so loud Aegisthus had to roar with laughter to cover the noise. Then he drove in the sword. And the king of kings was no longer the mass of bronze and iron he'd thought himself, he was just soft flesh, as easy to pierce as a lamb, and the sword cut so deep it split the marble. The murderers were wrong to hurt the marble, for it revenged itself. I found out about the crime from that split tile.

So he stopped struggling, let himself go, between the woman, who became uglier every moment, and the man, who was handsomer and handsomer. One good thing about death is that you can trust yourself to her, death is your only friend in an ambush, she has a familiar look, he saw that and called on his children, first the boy, Orestes, then the girl, Electra, to thank them for avenging him in future, lending their hands of death. Clytemnestra, foam on her lips, did not let go of him, and Agamemnon as willing to die but not to have this woman spit in his face, on his beard. She didn't spit because she was walking around the corpse, trying not to get blood on her sandals; her red dress looked to the dying man like the sun. Then the shadow fell, because each of them took an arm and turned him over on the floor. On his right hand four fingers were already stiff. Then, as Aegisthus had pulled out the sword without thinking, they turned him over again and put it gently, deliberately, back in the wound. Aegisthus was grateful to the dead man for having let himself be killed so very easily. Dozens of kings of kings could be killed like that, if murder was so easy.

But Clytemnestra's hatred of the man who'd struggled so fiercely, so stupidly, grew as she foresaw how every night she would dream of this murder. That's just what happened. It's seven years since she killed, she's killed him three thousand times.

(ORESTES *has come in during this speech*)

NARSES' WIFE Here's the young man! Isn't he handsome?

BEGGAR As beautiful as Aegisthus when young.

ORESTES Where are they, Electra?

ELECTRA Dear Orestes!

NARSES' WIFE In the southern courtyard.

ORESTES I'll see you soon, Electra, and we'll never part.

ELECTRA Go, my lover.

ORESTES Don't stop, beggar. Go on, tell them about the death of Clytemnestra and Aegisthus.

(*He goes out, sword in hand*)

NARSES' WIFE Tell us, beggar.

BEGGAR In two minutes. Give him time to get there.

ELECTRA He has his sword?

NARSES' WIFE Yes, daughter.

BEGGAR Are you crazy? Calling the princess your daughter!

NARSES' WIFE I call her daughter, I don't say she's my daughter. I've often seen her father, though. Heavens, what a fine man!

ELECTRA He had a beard, hadn't he?

NARSES' WIFE Not a beard, a sun. A wavy, curly sun, a sun just rising from the sea. He stroked it with his hand. The most beautiful hand in the world.

ELECTRA Call me your daughter, Narses' wife! I am your daughter. . . . I heard a cry!

NARSES' WIFE No, my daughter.

ELECTRA You're sure he had his sword? He didn't go to them without a sword?

NARSES' WIFE You saw him going. He had a thousand swords. Be calm, be calm!

ELECTRA What a long minute, mother, you waited at the edge of the bath!

NARSES' WIFE Why don't you tell us? Everything will be over before we know it.

BEGGAR One minute! He's looking for them. Now! He's found them.

NARSES' WIFE Oh, I can wait. Little Electra is soft to touch. I had only boys, gangsters. Mothers who only have girls are happy.

ELECTRA Yes . . . happy. . . . This time I do hear a cry!

NARSES' WIFE Yes, my daughter.

BEGGAR So, here's the end. Narses' wife and the beggars untied Orestes. He rushed across the courtyard. He didn't touch or embrace Electra. He was wrong, for he'll never touch her again. He found the murderers on the marble balcony, calming the rioters.

[3] As related in *The Iliad.* For Dolon, see Book Ten.

As Aegisthus leaned down to tell the leaders that everything was going well, he heard behind him the cry of a wounded beast. But it wasn't a beast crying, it was Clytemnestra. She was bleeding. Her son had stabbed her. He struck at the couple blindly, his eyes closed. A mother, though, even when unworthy, is sensitive and human. She didn't call on Electra or Orestes but on her youngest daughter, Chrysothemis, so Orestes thought he had killed another, and an innocent, mother. She clung to Aegisthus' arm; she was right, that gave her a last chance to stand up. But she prevented Aegisthus from drawing his sword. He shook her, to free his arm. She was too heavy to serve as a shield. And that bird was beating his head with its wings and attacking him with its beak, so he struggled. Just with his unarmed left arm, the dead queen, loaded with necklace and pendants, on his right arm. He was in despair over dying like a criminal, when he had become pure and holy; to be fighting because of a crime which was no longer his; to find himself, though loyal and innocent, infamous before this parricide. He struggled with one hand, which the sword was cutting little by little, but the lacing of his cuirass caught on a brooch of Clytemnestra's, and it opened. Then he resisted no longer; he only shook his right arm to rid himself of the queen, not only to fight but to die alone, to lie far from Clytemnestra in death. He didn't succeed. Forever Clytemnestra and Aegisthus will be coupled. He died, calling a name I'll not repeat.

(AEGISTHUS' *voice off stage.* Electra!)

BEGGAR I talked too fast. He caught up with me.

SCENE 10 ELECTRA. BEGGAR. NARSES' WIFE. *The* EUMENIDES, *who are of exactly the same height and figure as Electra.*

SERVANT Flee, everybody, the palace is on fire!

FIRST FURY That's what Electra wanted. Three things: daylight, truth—and this fire!

SECOND FURY Satisfied, Electra? The city's dying.

ELECTRA I'm satisfied. I know now that it will be born again.

THIRD FURY And the people killing each other in the streets, will they be born again? The Corinthians have started the attack, and it's a massacre.

FIRST FURY Your pride has brought you to this, Electra. You have nothing left, nothing.

ELECTRA I have my conscience, I have Orestes, I have justice, I have everything.

SECOND FURY Your conscience! Will you listen to your conscience in the early mornings to come? For seven years you've not slept because of a crime that others committed. Now you're the guilty one.

ELECTRA I have Orestes, I have justice, I have everything.

THIRD FURY Orestes! You'll never see Orestes again. We're leaving *you*—to pursue *him.* We've taken on your age and your shape—to pursue him. Good-by! We'll not leave him until he's been driven to madness or suicide, cursing his sister.

ELECTRA I have justice. I have everything.

NARSES' WIFE What are they saying? They're back. What have we come to, my poor Electra, what have we come to?

ELECTRA What have we come to?

NARSES' WIFE Yes, tell me. I'm not very quick to understand. I know something's happened but I don't know just what. How can you explain it, when a day begins like today, and everything's ruined and pillaged—though we're still breathing, we've lost everything, the city's burning, innocent people are killing each other, the guilty are dying, too—and the sun still rises?

ELECTRA Ask the beggar. He knows.

BEGGAR It all has a beautiful name, Narses' wife, it is called the dawn.

*Curtain*

# THE MADWOMAN OF CHAILLOT

THE MADWOMAN OF CHAILLOT is Giraudoux's best-known play. It may not be as rich in psychological complexity or as deep in its probing of social morality as some of his earlier works, but it is a wonderful expression of the lightness and gaiety of Giraudoux's art. None of his other late plays so completely captivated his audience. Under Louis Jouvet's direction, with brilliantly imaginative sets and costumes by Christian Bérard, the play ran for 297 performances at the Théâtre de l'Athénée in 1945-46. Marguerite Moréno's performance as the Madwoman was one of the great events of the Paris stage in the early days of the Liberation. In 1949, with Martita Hunt in the leading role, *The Madwoman of Chaillot* enjoyed an impressive Broadway success and was awarded the prize of the New York Critics Circle for the best play of the year by a foreign author. For some theatregoers, nevertheless, the play seemed too remote from the harsh facts of contemporary history, and many wondered how Giraudoux could write so spirited a comedy during a period of national suffering and despair. Plainly, none of the anguish of the existential drama of the French Occupation is present in Giraudoux's extravaganza. *The Madwoman of Chaillot* is a poetic fantasy, not a realistic chronicle, and the remoteness of the mood and characters from the dark reality of the day is itself part of the play's charm.

At the time of his death, Giraudoux left the manuscript in a virtually finished state. *The Madwoman of Chaillot* is a posthumous play but it is clearly not a draft. The style is smooth and melodious, the movement is sure and swiftly paced; in every respect it is a finished play. Jouvet's assistance was never more valuable to the playwright. In keeping with his arduous but cleverly concealed habits of revision, Giraudoux left several versions for a number of the scenes; the form in which we see and read the play owes everything to Jouvet's instinctive awareness of the poetry of Giraudoux's theatre, based on years of intimate collaboration.

In its clear-cut opposition of good and evil, Giraudoux's fanciful comedy is a parody of modern finance capitalism. The fantastic stock manipulations might have reminded some Frenchmen of the Stavisky scandal of 1934, the consequence of a flotation of some 25 million dollars of bonds for a small rural pawnshop. Giraudoux himself, before taking his examination for the foreign service, may have seriously thought of a career as a financier and big business man. He knew many who had amassed huge fortunes through bold speculation, and tycoons of the business world recur in the pages of his novels. Yet, plainly, the satire of capitalism in *The Madwoman of Chaillot* is poetic rather than polemic. Giraudoux's imaginative sympathy with the dispossessed, with riffraff like the peddler, the ragpicker, the juggler, and the street singer, has nothing to do with ideology. Furthermore, Giraudoux's poor are not really wretched; like his lovable eccentrics, they live in a world of gay and carefree individualism. Evil, on the other hand, is incarnated in the presence of those who worship the Golden Calf and who are seemingly bent on the universal destruction of mankind.

The successful counterplot hatched by the madwoman is as fantastic as the heroine herself. In her Giraudoux has created one of his most wonderful characters. Is she really crazy after all? The inversion of sanity and madness moves hand in hand with the interplay of pretense and reality. The purification of the world only caps the wonderful fantasy of the play. One may sense an underlying tone of bitterness and pathos in the countess' poignant awareness of the flight of time and the fragility of existence, yet love and the world of the imagination offer what salvation man can achieve. In an age of increasing conformity and practicality, Giraudoux in *The Madwoman of Chaillot* takes his stand with the individualists and the irresponsibles. Nowhere in his drama is the humor more alive, the action more spontaneous, the characterization more engaging. In his exuberant comedy Giraudoux has recaptured the magic and wonder of the stage.

# THE MADWOMAN OF CHAILLOT

Adapted by Maurice Valency

## CHARACTERS

THE WAITER
THE LITTLE MAN
THE PROSPECTOR
THE PRESIDENT
THE BARON
THERESE
THE STREET SINGER
THE PROFESSOR
THE FLOWER GIRL
THE RAGPICKER
PAULETTE
THE DEAF-MUTE
IRMA
THE SHOE-LACE PEDDLER
THE BROKER
THE STREET JUGGLER
DR. JADIN
COUNTESS AURELIA, *The Madwoman of Chaillot*
THE DOORMAN
THE POLICEMAN
PIERRE
THE SERGEANT
THE SEWER-MAN
CONSTANCE, *The Madwoman of Passy*
GABRIELLE, *The Madwoman of St. Sulpice*
JOSEPHINE, *The Madwoman of La Concorde*
THE PRESIDENTS
THE PROSPECTORS
THE PRESS AGENTS
THE LADIES
THE ADOLPHE BERTAUTS

### SCENES

ACT ONE

*The Café Terrace of* Chez Francis.

ACT TWO

*The Countess' Cellar—21 Rue de Chaillot.*

## Act One

SCENE *The café terrace at* Chez Francis, *on the Place de l'Alma in Paris. The Alma is in the stately quarter of Paris known as Chaillot, between the Champs Élysées and the Seine, across the river from the Eiffel Tower.*

Chez Francis *has several rows of tables set out under its awning, and, as it is lunch time, a good many of them are occupied. At a table, downstage, a somewhat obvious* BLONDE *with ravishing legs is sipping a vermouth-cassis and trying hard to engage the attention of the* PROSPECTOR, *who sits at an adjacent table taking little sips of water and rolling them over his tongue with the air of a connoisseur. Downstage right, in front of the tables on the sidewalk, is the usual Paris bench, a stout and uncomfortable affair provided by the municipality for the benefit of those who prefer to sit without drinking. A* POLICEMAN *lounges about, keeping the peace without unnecessary exertion.*

TIME *It is a little before noon in the Spring of next year.*

AT RISE *The* PRESIDENT *and the* BARON *enter with importance, and are ushered to a front table by the* WAITER.

THE PRESIDENT Baron, sit down. This is a historic occasion. It must be properly celebrated. The waiter is going to bring out my special port.

THE BARON Splendid.

THE PRESIDENT (*Offers his cigar case*) Cigar? My private brand.

THE BARON Thank you. You know, this all gives me the feeling of one of those enchanted mornings in the *Arabian Nights* when thieves foregather in the market place. Thieves—pashas . . .

(*He sniffs the cigar judiciously, and begins lighting it*)

THE PRESIDENT (*Chuckles*) Tell me about yourself.

THE BARON Well, where shall I begin?

(*The* STREET SINGER *enters. He takes off a battered black felt with a flourish and begins singing an ancient mazurka*)

STREET SINGER (*Sings*)

Do you hear, Mademoiselle,
Those musicians of hell?

THE PRESIDENT Waiter! Get rid of that man.

WAITER He is singing *La Belle Polonaise.*

THE PRESIDENT I didn't ask for the program. I asked you to get rid of him. (*The* WAITER *doesn't budge. The* SINGER *goes by himself*) As you were saying, Baron . . . ?

THE BARON Well, until I was fifty . . . (*The* FLOWER GIRL *enters through the café door, center*) my life was relatively uncomplicated. It consisted of selling off one by one the various estates left me by my father. Three years ago, I parted with my last farm. Two years ago, I lost my last mistress. And now—all that is left me is . . .

THE FLOWER GIRL (*To the* BARON) Violets, sir?

THE PRESIDENT Run along. (*The* FLOWER GIRL *moves on*)

THE BARON (*Staring after her*) So that, in short, all I have left now is my name.

THE PRESIDENT Your name is precisely the name we need on our board of directors.

THE BARON (*With an inclination of his head*) Very flattering.

THE PRESIDENT You will understand when I tell you that mine has been a very different experience. I came up from the bottom. My mother spent most of her life bent over a washtub in order to send me to school. I'm eternally grateful to her, of course, but I must confess that I no longer remember her face. It was no doubt beautiful—but when I try to recall it, I see only the part she invariably showed me—her rear.

THE BARON Very touching.

THE PRESIDENT When I was thrown out of school for the fifth and last time, I decided to find out for myself what makes the world go round. I ran errands for an editor, a movie star, a financier. . . . I began to understand a little what life is. Then, one day, in the subway, I saw a face. . . . My rise in life dates from that day.

THE BARON Really?

THE PRESIDENT One look at that face, and I knew. One look at mine, and he knew. And so I made my first thousand—passing a boxful of counterfeit notes. A year later, I saw another such face. It got me a nice berth in the narcotics business. Since then, all I do is to look out for such faces. And now here I am—president of eleven corporations, director of fifty-two companies, and, beginning today, chairman of the board of the international combine in which you have been so good as to accept a post.

(*The* RAGPICKER *passes, sees something under the* PRESIDENT'S *table, and stoops to pick it up*)

Looking for something?

THE RAGPICKER Did you drop this?

THE PRESIDENT I never drop anything.

THE RAGPICKER Then this hundred-franc note isn't yours?

THE PRESIDENT Give it here.

(*The* RAGPICKER *gives him the note, and goes out*)

THE BARON Are you sure it's yours?

THE PRESIDENT All hundred-franc notes, Baron, are mine.

THE BARON Mr. President, there's something I've been wanting to ask you. What exactly is the purpose of our new company? Or is that an indiscreet question . . . ?

THE PRESIDENT Indiscreet? Not a bit. Merely unusual. As far as I know, you're the first member of a board of directors ever to ask such a question.

THE BARON Do we plan to exploit a commodity? A utility?

THE PRESIDENT My dear sir, I haven't the faintest idea.

THE BARON But if you don't know—who does?

THE PRESIDENT Nobody. And at the moment, it's becoming just a trifle embarrassing. Yes, my dear Baron, since we are now close business associates, I must confess that for the time being we're in a little trouble.

THE BARON I was afraid of that. The stock issue isn't going well?

THE PRESIDENT No, no—on the contrary. The stock issue is going beautifully. Yesterday morning at ten o'clock we offered 500,000 shares to the general public. By 10:05 they were all snapped up at par. By 10:20, when the police finally arrived, our offices were a shambles. . . . Windows smashed—doors torn off their hinges—you never saw anything so beautiful in your life! And this morning our stock is being quoted over the counter at 124 with no sellers, and the orders are still pouring in.

THE BARON But in that case—what is the trouble?

THE PRESIDENT The trouble is we have a tremendous capital, and not the slightest idea of what to do with it.

THE BARON You mean all those people are fighting to buy stock in a company that has no object?

THE PRESIDENT My dear Baron, do you imagine that when a subscriber buys a share of stock, he has any idea of getting behind a counter or digging a ditch? A stock certificate is not a tool, like a shovel or a commodity, like a pound of cheese. What we sell a customer is not a share in a business, but a view of the Elysian Fields. A financier is a creative artist. Our function is to stimulate the imagination. We are poets!

THE BARON But in order to stimulate the imagination, don't you need some field of activity?

THE PRESIDENT Not at all. What you need for that is a name. A name that will stir the pulse like a trumpet call, set the brain awhirl like a movie star, inspire reverence like a cathedral. *United General International Consolidated!* Of course that's been used. That's what a corporation needs.

THE BARON And do we have such a name?

THE PRESIDENT So far we have only a blank space. In that blank space a name must be printed. This name must be a masterpiece. And if I seem a little nervous today, it's because—somehow—I've racked my brains, but it hasn't come to me. Oho! Look at that! Just like the answer to a prayer . . . ! (*The* BARON *turns and stares in the direction of the* PROSPECTOR) You see? There's one. And what a beauty!

BARON You mean that girl?

THE PRESIDENT No, no, not the girl. That face. You see . . . ? The one that's drinking water.

THE BARON You call that a face? That's a tombstone.

THE PRESIDENT It's a milestone. It's a signpost. But is it pointing the way to steel, or wheat, or phosphates? That's what we have to find out. Ah! He sees me. He understands. He will be over.

THE BARON And when he comes . . . ?

THE PRESIDENT He will tell me what to do.

THE BARON You mean business is done this way? You mean, you would trust a stranger with a matter of this importance?

THE PRESIDENT Baron, I trust neither my wife, nor my daughter, nor my closest friend. My confidential secretary has no idea where I live. But a face like that I would trust with my inmost secrets. Though we have never laid eyes on each other before, that man and I know each other to the depths of our souls. He's no stranger—he's my brother, he's myself. You'll see. He'll be over in a minute. (*The* DEAF MUTE *enters and passes slowly among the tables, placing a small envelope before each customer. He comes to the* PRESIDENT'S *table*) What is this anyway? A conspiracy? We don't want your envelopes. Take them away. (*The* DEAF MUTE *makes a short but pointed speech in sign language*) Waiter, what the devil's he saying?

WAITER Only Irma understands him.

THE PRESIDENT Irma? Who's Irma?

WAITER (*Calls*) Irma! It's the waitress inside, sir. Irma!

(IRMA *comes out. She is twenty. She has the face and figure of an angel*)

IRMA Yes?

WAITER These gentlemen would . . .

THE PRESIDENT Tell this fellow to get out of here, for God's sake! (*The* DEAF MUTE *makes another manual oration*) What's he trying to say, anyway?

IRMA He says it's an exceptionally beautiful morning, sir. . . .

THE PRESIDENT Who asked him?

IRMA But, he says, it was nicer before the gentleman stuck his face in it.

THE PRESIDENT Call the manager!

(IRMA *shrugs. She goes back into the restaurant. The* DEAF MUTE *walks off, Left. Meanwhile a* SHOELACE PEDDLER *has arrived*)

PEDDLER Shoelaces? Postcards?

THE BARON I think I could use a shoelace.

THE PRESIDENT No, no . . .

PEDDLER Black? Tan?

THE BARON (*Showing his shoes*) What would you recommend?

PEDDLER Anybody's guess.

THE BARON Well, give me one of each.

THE PRESIDENT (*Putting a hand on the* BARON'S *arm*) Baron, although I am your chairman, I have no authority over your personal life—none, that is, except to fix the amount of your director's fees, and eventually to assign a motor car for your use. Therefore, I am asking you, as a personal favor to me, not to purchase anything from this fellow.

THE BARON How can I resist so gracious a request? (*The* PEDDLER *shrugs, and passes on*) But I really don't understand . . . What difference would it make?

THE PRESIDENT Look here, Baron. Now that you're with us, you must understand that between this irresponsible riff-raff and us there is an impenetrable barrier. *We* have no dealings whatever with *them.*

THE BARON But without us, the poor devil will starve.

THE PRESIDENT No, he won't. He expects nothing from us. He has a clientele of his own. He sells shoelaces exclusively to those who have no shoes. Just as the necktie peddler sells only to those who wear no shirts. And that's why these street hawkers can afford to be insolent, disrespectful, and independent. They don't need us. They have a world of their own. Ah! My broker. Splendid. He's beaming.

(*The* BROKER *walks up and grasps the* PRESIDENT'S *hand with enthusiasm*)

BROKER Mr. President! My heartiest congratulations! What a day! What a day!

(*The* STREET JUGGLER *appears, Right. He removes his coat, folds it carefully, and puts it on the bench. Then he opens a suitcase, from which he extracts a number of colored clubs*)

THE PRESIDENT (*Presenting the* BROKER) Baron Tommard, of our Board of Directors. My broker. (*The* BROKER *bows. So does the* JUGGLER. *The* BROKER *sits down and signals for a drink. The* JUGGLER *prepares to juggle*) What's happened?

BROKER Listen to this. Ten o'clock this morning. The market opens. (*As he speaks, the* JUGGLER *provides a visual counterpart to the* BROKER'S *lines, his clubs rising and falling in rhythm to the* BROKER'S *words*) Half million shares issued at par, par value a hundred, quoted on the curb at 124 and we start buying at 126, 127, 129—and it's going up—up—up—(*The* JUGGLER'S *clubs rise higher and higher*)—132—133—138—141—141—141—141 . . .

THE BARON May I ask . . . ?

THE PRESIDENT No, no—any explanation would only confuse you.

BROKER Ten forty-five we start selling short on rumors of a Communist plot, market bearish. . . . 141—138—133—132—and it's down—down—down—102—and we start buying back at 93. Eleven o'clock, rumors denied—95—98—101—106—124—141—

and by 11:30 we've got it all back—net profit three and a half million francs.

THE PRESIDENT Classical. Pure. (*The* JUGGLER *bows again. A* LITTLE MAN *leans over from a near-by table, listening intently, and trembling with excitement*) And how many shares do we reserve to each member of the board?

BROKER Fifty, as agreed.

THE PRESIDENT Bit stingy, don't you think?

BROKER All right—three thousand.

THE PRESIDENT That's a little better. (*To the* BARON) You get the idea?

THE BARON I'm beginning to get it.

BROKER And now we come to the exciting part . . . (*The* JUGGLER *prepares to juggle with balls of fire*) Listen carefully: With 35 percent of our funded capital under Section 32 I buy 50,000 United at 36 which I immediately reconvert into 32,000 National Amalgamated two's preferred which I set up as collateral on 150,000 General Consols which I deposit against a credit of fifteen billion to buy Eastern Hennequin which I immediately turn into Argentine wheat realizing 136 percent of the original investment which naturally accrues as capital gain and not as corporate income thus saving twelve millions in taxes, and at once convert the 25 percent cotton reserve into lignite, and as our people swing into action in London and New York, I beat up the price on greige goods from 26 to 92—114—203—306—(*The* JUGGLER *by now is juggling his fire-balls in the sky. The balls no longer return to his hands*) 404 . . . (*The* LITTLE MAN *can stand no more. He rushes over and dumps a sackful of money on the table*)

LITTLE MAN Here—take it—please, take it!

BROKER (*Frigidly*) Who is this man? What is this money?

LITTLE MAN It's my life's savings. Every cent. I put it all in your hands.

BROKER Can't you see we're busy?

LITTLE MAN But I beg you . . . It's my only chance . . . Please don't turn me away.

BROKER Oh, all right. (*He sweeps the money into his pocket*) Well?

LITTLE MAN I thought—perhaps you'd give me a little receipt. . . .

THE PRESIDENT My dear man, people like us don't give receipts for money. We take them.

LITTLE MAN Oh, pardon. Of course. I was confused. Here it is. (*Scribbles a receipt*) Thank you—thank you—thank you. (*He rushes off joyfully. The* STREET SINGER *reappears*)

STREET SINGER (*Sings*)

Do you hear, Mademoiselle,
Those musicians of hell?

THE PRESIDENT What, again? Why does he keep repeating those two lines like a parrot?

WAITER What else can he do? He doesn't know any more and the song's been out of print for years.

THE BARON Couldn't he sing a song he knows?

WAITER He likes this one. He hopes if he keeps singing the beginning someone will turn up to teach him the end.

THE PRESIDENT Tell him to move on. We don't know the song.

(*The* PROFESSOR *strolls by, swinging his cane. He overhears*)

PROFESSOR (*Stops and addresses the* PRESIDENT *politely*) Nor do I, my dear sir. Nor do I. And yet, I'm in exactly the same predicament. I remember just two lines of my favorite song, as a child. A mazurka also, in case you're interested. . . .

THE PRESIDENT I'm not.

PROFESSOR Why is it, I wonder, that one always forgets the words of a mazurka? I suppose they just get lost in that damnable rhythm. All I remember is: (*He sings*)

From England to Spain
I have drunk, it was bliss . . . .

STREET SINGER (*Walks over, and picks up the tune*)

Red wine and champagne
And many a kiss.

PROFESSOR Oh, God! It all comes back to me . . . ! (*He sings*)

Red lips and white hands I have known
Where the nightingales dwell. . . .

THE PRESIDENT (*Holding his hands to his ears*) Please —please . . .

STREET SINGER

And to each one I've whispered, "My own,"
And to each one, I've murmured: "Farewell."

THE PRESIDENT Farewell. Farewell.

STREET SINGER, PROFESSOR (*Duo*)

But there's one I shall never forget. . . .

THE PRESIDENT This isn't a café. It's a circus!

(*The two go off, still singing: "There is one that's engraved in my heart." The* PROSPECTOR *gets up slowly and walks toward the* PRESIDENT'S *table. He looks down without a word. There is a tense silence*)

PROSPECTOR Well?

THE PRESIDENT I need a name.

PROSPECTOR (*Nods, with complete comprehension*) I need fifty thousand.

THE PRESIDENT For a corporation.

PROSPECTOR For a woman.

THE PRESIDENT Immediately.

PROSPECTOR Before evening.

THE PRESIDENT Something . . .

PROSPECTOR Unusual?

THE PRESIDENT Something . . .

PROSPECTOR Provocative?

THE PRESIDENT Something . . .

PROSPECTOR Practical.

THE PRESIDENT Yes.

PROSPECTOR Fifty thousand. Cash.

THE PRESIDENT I'm listening.

PROSPECTOR *International Substrate of Paris, Inc.*

THE PRESIDENT (*Snaps his fingers*) That's it! (*To the* BROKER) Pay him off. (*The* BROKER *pays with the* LITTLE MAN'S *money*) Now—what does it mean?

PROSPECTOR It means what it says. I'm a prospector.

THE PRESIDENT (*Rises*) A prospector! Allow me to shake your hand. Baron. You are in the presence of one of nature's noblemen. Shake his hand. This is Baron Tommard. (*They shake hands*) It is this man, my dear Baron, who smells out in the bowels of the earth those deposits of metal or liquid on which can be founded the only social unit of which our age is capable—the corporation. Sit down, please. (*They all sit*) And now that we have a name . . .

PROSPECTOR You need a property.

THE PRESIDENT Precisely.

PROSPECTOR I have one.

THE PRESIDENT A claim?

PROSPECTOR Terrific.

THE PRESIDENT Foreign?

PROSPECTOR French.

THE BARON In Indo-China?

BROKER Morocco?

THE PRESIDENT In France?

PROSPECTOR (*Matter of fact*) In Paris.

THE PRESIDENT In Paris? You've been prospecting in Paris?

THE BARON For women, no doubt.

THE PRESIDENT For art?

BROKER For gold?

PROSPECTOR Oil.

BROKER He's crazy.

THE PRESIDENT Sh! He's inspired.

PROSPECTOR You think I'm crazy. Well, they thought Columbus was crazy.

THE BARON Oil in Paris?

BROKER But how is it possible?

PROSPECTOR It's not only possible. It's certain.

THE PRESIDENT Tell us.

PROSPECTOR You don't know, my dear sir, what treasures Paris conceals. Paris is the least prospected place in the world. We've gone over the rest of the planet with a fine-tooth comb. But has anyone ever thought of looking for oil in Paris? Nobody. Before me, that is.

THE PRESIDENT Genius!

PROSPECTOR No. Just a practical man. I use my head.

THE BARON But why has nobody ever thought of this before?

PROSPECTOR The treasures of the earth, my dear sir, are not easy to find nor to get at. They are invariably guarded by dragons. Doubtless there is some reason for this. For once we've dug out and consumed the internal ballast of the planet, the chances are it will shoot off on some irresponsible tangent and smash itself up in the sky. Well, that's the risk we take. Anyway, that's not my business. A prospector has enough to worry about.

THE BARON I know—snakes—tarantulas—fleas . . .

PROSPECTOR Worse than that, sir. Civilization.

THE PRESIDENT Does that annoy you?

PROSPECTOR Civilization gets in our way all the time. In the first place, it covers the earth with cities and towns which are damned awkward to dig up when you want to see what's underneath. It's not only the real-estate people—you can always do business with them—it's human sentimentality. How do you do business with that?

THE PRESIDENT I see what you mean.

PROSPECTOR They say that where we pass, nothing ever grows again. What of it? Is a park any better than a coal mine? What's a mountain got that a slag pile hasn't? What would you rather have in your garden—an almond tree or an oil well?

THE PRESIDENT Well . . .

PROSPECTOR Exactly. But what's the use of arguing with these fools? Imagine the choicest place you ever saw for an excavation, and what do they put there? A playground for children! Civilization!

THE PRESIDENT Just show us the point where you want to start digging. We'll do the rest. Even if it's in the middle of the Louvre. Where's the oil?

PROSPECTOR Perhaps you think it's easy to make an accurate fix in an area like Paris where everything conspires to put you off the scent? Women—perfume—flowers—history. You can talk all you like about geology, but an oil deposit, gentlemen, has to be smelled out. I have a good nose. I go further. I have a phenomenal nose. But the minute I get the right whiff—the minute I'm on the scent—a fragrance rises from what I take to be the spiritual deposits of the past—and I'm completely at sea. Now take this very point, for example, this very spot.

THE BARON You mean—right here in Chaillot?

PROSPECTOR Right under here.

THE PRESIDENT Good heavens! (*He looks under his chair*)

PROSPECTOR It's taken me months to locate this spot.

THE BARON But what in the world makes you think . . . ?

PROSPECTOR Do you know this place, Baron?

THE BARON Well, I've been sitting here for thirty years.

PROSPECTOR Did you ever taste the water?

THE BARON The water? Good God, no!

PROSPECTOR It's plain to see that you are no prospector! A prospector, Baron, is addicted to water as a drunkard to wine. Water, gentlemen, is the one substance from which the earth can conceal nothing. It sucks out its innermost secrets and brings them to our very lips. Well—beginning at Notre Dame, where I first caught the scent of oil three months ago, I worked my way across Paris, glassful by glassful, sampling the water, until at last I came to this café. And here—just two days ago—I took a sip. My heart began to thump. Was it possible that I was deceived? I took another, a third, a fourth, a fifth. I was trembling like a leaf. But there was no mistake. Each time that I drank, my taste-buds thrilled to the most exquisite flavor known to a prospector—the flavor of— (*With utmost lyricism*) Petroleum!

THE PRESIDENT Waiter! Some water and four glasses. Hurry. This round, gentlemen, is on me. And as a toast—I shall propose International Substrate of Paris, Incorporated. (*The* WAITER *brings a decanter and the glasses. The* PRESIDENT *pours out the water amid profound silence. They taste it with the air of connoisseurs savoring something that has never before passed human lips. Then they look at each other doubtfully. The* PROSPECTOR *pours himself a second glass and drinks it off*) Well . . .

BROKER Ye-es . . .

THE BARON Mm . . .

PROSPECTOR Get it?

THE BARON Tastes queer.

PROSPECTOR That's it. To the unpracticed palate it tastes queer. But to the taste-buds of the expert—ah!

THE BARON Still, there's one thing I don't quite understand . . .

PROSPECTOR Yes?

THE BARON This café doesn't have its own well, does it?

PROSPECTOR Of course not. This is Paris water.

BROKER Then why should it taste different here than anywhere else?

PROSPECTOR Because, my dear sir, the pipes that carry this water pass deep through the earth, and the earth just here is soaked with oil, and this oil permeates the pores of the iron and flavors the water it carries. Ever so little, yes—but quite enough to betray its presence to the sensitive tongue of the specialist.

THE BARON I see.

PROSPECTOR I don't say everyone is capable of tasting it. No. But I—I can detect the presence of oil in water that has passed within fifteen miles of a deposit. Under special circumstances, twenty.

THE PRESIDENT Phenomenal!

PROSPECTOR And so here I am with the greatest discovery of the age on my hands—but the blasted authorities won't let me drill a single well unless I show them the oil! Now how can I show them the oil unless they let me dig? Completely stymied! Eh?

THE PRESIDENT What? A man like you?

PROSPECTOR That's what they think. That's what they want. Have you noticed the strange glamor of the women this morning? And the quality of the sunshine? And this extraordinary convocation of vagabonds buzzing about protectively like bees around a hive? Do you know why it is? Because they know. It's a plot to distract us, to turn us from our purpose. Well, let them try. I know there's oil here. And I'm going to dig it up, even if I . . . (*He smiles*) Shall I tell you my little plan?

THE PRESIDENT By all means.

PROSPECTOR Well . . . For heaven's sake, what's that?

(*At this point, the* MADWOMAN *enters. She is dressed in the grand fashion of 1885, a taffeta skirt with an immense train—which she has gathered up by means of a clothespin—ancient button shoes, and a hat in the style of Marie Antoinette. She wears a lorgnette on a chain, and an enormous cameo pin at her throat. In her hand she carries a small basket. She walks in with great dignity, extracts a dinner bell from the bosom of her dress, and rings it sharply.* IRMA *appears*)

COUNTESS Are my bones ready, Irma?

IRMA There won't be much today, Countess. We had broilers. Can you wait? While the gentleman inside finishes eating?

COUNTESS And my gizzard?

IRMA I'll try to get it away from him.

COUNTESS If he eats my gizzard, save me the giblets. They will do for the tomcat that lives under the bridge. He likes a few giblets now and again.

IRMA Yes, Countess.

(IRMA *goes back into the café. The* COUNTESS *takes a few steps and stops in front of the* PRESIDENT*'s table. She examines him with undisguised disapproval*)

THE PRESIDENT Waiter. Ask that woman to move on.

WAITER Sorry, sir. This is her café.

THE PRESIDENT Is she the manager of the café?

WAITER She's the Madwoman of Chaillot.

THE PRESIDENT A Madwoman? She's mad?

WAITER Who says she's mad?

THE PRESIDENT You just said so yourself.

WAITER Look, sir. You asked me who she was. And I told you. What's mad about her? She's the Madwoman of Chaillot.

THE PRESIDENT Call a policeman.

(*The* COUNTESS *whistles through her fingers. At once, the* DOORMAN *runs out of the café. He has three scarves in his hands*)

COUNTESS Have you found it? My feather boa?

DOORMAN Not yet, Countess. Three scarves. But no boa.

COUNTESS It's five years since I lost it. Surely you've had time to find it.

DOORMAN Take one of these, Countess. Nobody's claimed them.

COUNTESS A boa like that doesn't vanish, you know. A feather boa nine feet long!

DOORMAN How about this blue one?

COUNTESS With my pink ruffle and my green veil? You're joking! Let me see the yellow. (*She tries it on*) How does it look?

DOORMAN Terrific.

(*With a magnificent gesture, she flings the scarf about her, upsetting the* PRESIDENT*'s glass and drenching his trousers with water. She stalks off without a glance at him*)

THE PRESIDENT Waiter! I'm making a complaint.

WAITER Against whom?

THE PRESIDENT Against her! Against you! The whole gang of you! That singer! That shoelace peddler! That female lunatic! Or whatever you call her!

THE BARON Calm yourself, Mr. President. . . .

THE PRESIDENT I'll do nothing of the sort! Baron, the first thing we have to do is get rid of these people! Good heavens, look at them! Every size, shape, color and period of history imaginable. It's utter anarchy! I tell you, sir, the only safeguard of order and discipline in the modern world is a standardized worker with interchangeable parts. That would solve the entire problem of management. Here, the manager . . . And there—one composite drudge grunting and sweating all over the world. Just we two. Ah, how beautiful! How easy on the eyes! How restful for the conscience!

THE BARON Yes, yes—of course.

THE PRESIDENT Order. Symmetry. Balance. But instead of that, what? Here in Chaillot, the very citadel of management, these insolent phantoms of the past come to beard us with their raffish individualism—with the right of the voiceless to sing, of the dumb to make speeches, of trousers to have no seats and bosoms to have dinner bells!

THE BARON But, after all, do these people matter?

THE PRESIDENT My dear sir, wherever the poor are happy, and the servants are proud, and the mad are respected, our power is at an end. Look at that! That waiter! That madwoman! That flower girl! Do I get that sort of service? And suppose that I—president of twelve corporations and ten times a millionaire—were to stick a gladiolus in my buttonhole and start yelling— (*He tinkles his spoon in a glass violently, yelling*) Are my bones ready, Irma?

THE BARON (*Reprovingly*) Mr. President . . .

(*People at the adjoining tables turn and stare with raised eyebrows. The* WAITER *starts to come over*)

THE PRESIDENT You see? Now.

PROSPECTOR We were discussing my plan.

THE PRESIDENT Ah, yes, your plan. (*He glances in the direction of the* MADWOMAN'S *table*) Careful—she's looking at us.

PROSPECTOR Do you know what a bomb is?

THE PRESIDENT I'm told they explode.

PROSPECTOR Exactly. You see that white building across the river. Do you happen to know what that is?

THE PRESIDENT I do not.

PROSPECTOR That's the office of the City Architect. That man has stubbornly refused to give me a permit to drill for oil anywhere within the limits of the city of Paris. I've tried everything with him—influence, bribes, threats. He says I'm crazy. And now . . .

THE PRESIDENT Oh, my God! What is this one trying to sell us?

(*A little* OLD MAN *enters left, and doffs his hat politely. He is somewhat ostentatiously respectable —gloved, pomaded, and carefully dressed, with a white handkerchief peeping out of his breast pocket*)

DR. JADIN Nothing but health, sir. Or rather the health of the feet. But remember—as the foot goes, so goes the man. May I present myself . . . ? Dr. Gaspard Jadin, French Navy, retired. Former specialist in the extraction of ticks and chiggers. At present specializing in the extraction of bunions and corns. In case of sudden emergency, Martial the waiter will furnish my home address. My office is here, second row, third table, week days, twelve to five. Thank you very much.

(*He sits at his table*)

WAITER Your vermouth, Doctor?

DR. JADIN My vermouth. My vermouths. How are your gallstones today, Martial?

WAITER Fine. Fine. They rattle like anything.

DR. JADIN Splendid. (*He spies the* COUNTESS) Good morning, Countess. How's the floating kidney? Still afloat? (*She nods graciously*) Splendid. Splendid. So long as it floats, it can't sink.

THE PRESIDENT This is impossible! Let's go somewhere else.

PROSPECTOR No. It's nearly noon.

THE PRESIDENT Yes. It is. Five to twelve.

PROSPECTOR In five minutes' time you're going to see that City Architect blown up, building and all—boom!

BROKER Are you serious?

PROSPECTOR That imbecile has no one to blame but himself. Yesterday noon, he got my ultimatum—he's had twenty-four hours to think it over. No permit? All right. Within two minutes my agent is going to drop a little package in his coal bin. And three minutes after that, precisely at noon . . .

THE BARON You prospectors certainly use modern methods.

PROSPECTOR The method may be modern. But the idea is old. To get at the treasure, it has always been necessary to slay the dragon. I guarantee that after this, the City Architect will be more reasonable. The new one, I mean.

THE PRESIDENT Don't you think we're sitting a little close for comfort?

PROSPECTOR Oh no, no. Don't worry. And, above all, don't stare. We may be watched. (*A clock strikes*) Why, that's noon. Something's wrong! Good God! What's this? (*A* POLICEMAN *staggers in bearing a lifeless body on his shoulders in the manner prescribed as "The Fireman's Lift"*) It's Pierre! My agent! (*He walks over with affected nonchalance*) I say, Officer, what's that you've got?

POLICEMAN Drowned man. (*He puts him down on the bench*)

WAITER He's not drowned. His clothes are dry. He's been slugged.

POLICEMAN Slugged is also correct. He was just jumping off the bridge when I came along and pulled him back. I slugged him, naturally, so he wouldn't drag me under. Life Saving Manual, Rule 5: "In cases where there is danger of being dragged under, it is necessary to render the subject unconscious by means of a sharp blow." He's had that. (*He loosens the clothes and begins applying artificial respiration*)

PROSPECTOR The stupid idiot! What the devil did he do with the bomb? That's what comes of employing amateurs!

THE PRESIDENT You don't think he'll give you away?

PROSPECTOR Don't worry. (*He walks over to the policeman*) Say, what do you think you're doing?

POLICEMAN Lifesaving. Artificial respiration. First aid to the drowning.

PROSPECTOR But he's not drowning.

POLICEMAN But he thinks he is.

PROSPECTOR You'll never bring him round that way

my friend. That's meant for people who drown in water. It's no good at all for those who drown without water.

POLICEMAN What am I supposed to do? I've just been sworn in. It's my first day on the beat. I can't afford to get in trouble. I've got to go by the book.

PROSPECTOR Perfectly simple. Take him back to the bridge where you found him and throw him in. Then you can save his life and you'll get a medal. This way, you'll only get fined for slugging an innocent man.

POLICEMAN What do you mean, innocent? He was just going to jump when I grabbed him.

PROSPECTOR Have you any proof of that?

POLICEMAN Well, I saw him.

PROSPECTOR Written proof? Witnesses?

POLICEMAN No, but . . .

PROSPECTOR Then don't waste time arguing. You're in trouble. Quick—before anybody notices—throw him in and dive after him. It's the only way out.

POLICEMAN But I don't swim.

THE PRESIDENT You'll learn how on the way down. Before you were born, did you know how to breathe?

POLICEMAN (*Convinced*) All right. Here we go. (*He starts lifting the body*)

DR. JADIN One moment, please. I don't like to interfere, but it's my professional duty to point out that medical science has definitely established the fact of intra-uterine respiration. Consequently, this policeman, even before he was born, knew not only how to breathe but also how to cough, hiccup, and belch.

THE PRESIDENT Suppose he did—how does it concern you?

DR. JADIN On the other hand, medical science has never established the fact of intra-uterine swimming or diving. Under the circumstances, we are forced to the opinion, Officer, that if you dive in you will probably drown.

POLICEMAN You think so?

PROSPECTOR Who asked you for an opinion?

THE PRESIDENT Pay no attention to that quack, Officer.

DR. JADIN Quack, sir?

PROSPECTOR This is not a medical matter. It's a legal problem. The officer has made a grave error. He's new. We're trying to help him.

BROKER He's probably afraid of the water.

POLICEMAN Nothing of the sort. Officially, I'm afraid of nothing. But I always follow doctor's orders.

DR. JADIN You see, Officer, when a child is born . . .

PROSPECTOR Now, what does he care about when a child is born? He's got a dying man on his hands. . . . Officer, if you want my advice . . .

POLICEMAN It so happens, I care a lot about when a child is born. It's part of my duty to aid and assist any woman in childbirth or labor.

THE PRESIDENT Can you imagine!

POLICEMAN Is it true, Doctor, what they say, that when you have twins, the first born is considered to be the youngest?

DR. JADIN Quite correct. And what's more, if the twins happen to be born at midnight on December 31st, the older is a whole year younger. He does his military service a year later. That's why you have to keep your eyes open. And that's the reason why a queen always gives birth before witnesses. . . .

POLICEMAN God! The things a policeman is supposed to know! Doctor, what does it mean if, when I get up in the morning sometimes . . .

PROSPECTOR (*Nudging the* PRESIDENT *meaningfully*) The old woman . . .

BROKER Come on, Baron.

THE PRESIDENT I think we'd better all run along.

PROSPECTOR Leave him to me.

THE PRESIDENT I'll see you later. (*The* PRESIDENT *steals off with the* BROKER *and the* BARON)

POLICEMAN (*Still in conference with* DR. JADIN) But what's really worrying me, Doctor, is this—don't you think it's a bit risky for a man to marry after forty-five?

(*The* BROKER *runs in breathlessly*)

BROKER Officer! Officer!

POLICEMAN What's the trouble?

BROKER Quick! Two women are calling for help—on the sidewalk—Avenue Wilson!

POLICEMAN Two women at once? Standing up or lying down?

BROKER You'd better go and see. Quick!

PROSPECTOR You'd better take the Doctor with you.

POLICEMAN Come along, Doctor, come along. . . . (*Pointing to* PIERRE) Tell him to wait till I get back. Come along, Doctor.

(*He runs out, the* DOCTOR *following. The* PROSPECTOR *moves over toward* PIERRE, *but* IRMA *crosses in front of him and takes the boy's hand*)

IRMA How beautiful he is! Is he dead, Martial?

WAITER (*Handing her a pocket mirror*) Hold this mirror to his mouth. If it clouds over . . .

IRMA It clouds over.

WAITER He's alive. (*He holds out his hand for the mirror*)

IRMA Just a sec— (*She rubs it clean and looks at herself intently. Before handing it back, she fixes her hair and applies her lipstick. Meanwhile the* PROSPECTOR *tries to get around the other side, but the* COUNTESS' *eagle eye drives him off. He shrugs his shoulders and exits with the* BARON) Oh, look—he's opened his eyes!

(PIERRE *opens his eyes, stares intently at* IRMA *and closes them again with the expression of a man who is among the angels*)

PIERRE (*Murmurs*) Oh! How beautiful!

VOICE (*From within the café*) Irma!

IRMA Coming. Coming.

(*She goes in, not without a certain reluctance. The* COUNTESS *at once takes her place on the bench, and also the young man's hand.* PIERRE *sits up suddenly, and finds himself staring, not at* IRMA, *but into the very peculiar face of the* COUNTESS. *His expression changes*)

COUNTESS You're looking at my iris? Isn't it beautiful?

PIERRE Very. (*He drops back, exhausted*)

COUNTESS The Sergeant was good enough to say it

becomes me. But I no longer trust his taste. Yesterday, the flower girl gave me a lily, and he said it didn't suit me.

PIERRE (*Weakly*) It's beautiful.

COUNTESS He'll be very happy to know that you agree with him. He's really quite sensitive. (*She calls*) Sergeant!

PIERRE No, please—don't call the police.

COUNTESS But I must. I think I hurt his feelings.

PIERRE Let me go, Madame.

COUNTESS No, no. Stay where you are. Sergeant! (PIERRE *struggles weakly to get up*)

PIERRE Please let me go.

COUNTESS I'll do nothing of the sort. When you let someone go, you never see him again. I let Charlotte Mazumet go. I never saw her again.

PIERRE Oh, my head.

COUNTESS I let Adolphe Bertaut go. And I was holding him. And I never saw him again.

PIERRE Oh, God!

COUNTESS Except once. Thirty years later. In the market. He had changed a great deal—he didn't know me. He sneaked a melon from right under my nose, the only good one of the year. Ah, here we are. Sergeant! (*The* POLICE SERGEANT *comes in with importance*)

SERGEANT I'm in a hurry, Countess.

COUNTESS With regard to the iris. This young man agrees with you. He says it suits me.

SERGEANT (*Going*) There's a man drowning in the Seine.

COUNTESS He's not drowning in the Seine. He's drowning here. Because I'm holding him tight—as I should have held Adolphe Bertaut. But if I let him go, I'm sure he will go and drown in the Seine. He's a lot better looking than Adolphe Bertaut, wouldn't you say?

(PIERRE *sighs deeply*)

SERGEANT How would I know?

COUNTESS I've shown you his photograph. The one with the bicycle.

SERGEANT Oh, yes. The one with the harelip.

COUNTESS I've told you a hundred times! Adolphe Bertaut had no harelip. That was a scratch in the negative. (*The* SERGEANT *takes out his notebook and pencil*) What are you doing?

SERGEANT I am taking down the drowned man's name, given name, and date of birth.

COUNTESS You think that's going to stop him from jumping in the river? Don't be silly, Sergeant. Put that book away and try to console him.

SERGEANT I should try and console him?

COUNTESS When people want to die, it is your job as a guardian of the state to speak out in praise of life. Not mine.

SERGEANT I should speak out in praise of life?

COUNTESS I assume you have some motive for interfering with people's attempts to kill each other, and rob each other, and run each other over? If you believe that life has some value, tell him what it is. Go on.

SERGEANT Well, all right. Now look, young man . . .

COUNTESS His name is Roderick.

PIERRE My name is not Roderick.

COUNTESS Yes, it is. It's noon. At noon all men become Roderick.

SERGEANT Except Adolphe Bertaut.

COUNTESS In the days of Adolphe Bertaut, we were forced to change the men when we got tired of their names. Nowadays, we're more practical—each hour on the hour all names are automatically changed. The men remain the same. But you're not here to discuss Adolphe Bertaut, Sergeant. You're here to convince the young man that life is worth living.

PIERRE It isn't.

SERGEANT Quiet. Now then—what was the idea of jumping off the bridge, anyway?

COUNTESS The idea was to land in the river. Roderick doesn't seem to be at all confused about that.

SERGEANT Now how can I convince anybody that life is worth living if you keep interrupting all the time?

COUNTESS I'll be quiet.

SERGEANT First of all, Mr. Roderick, you have to realize that suicide is a crime against the state. And why is it a crime against the state? Because every time anybody commits suicide, that means one soldier less for the army, one taxpayer less for the . . .

COUNTESS Sergeant, isn't there something about life that you really enjoy?

SERGEANT That I enjoy?

COUNTESS Well, surely, in all these years, you must have found something worth living for. Some secret pleasure, or passion. Don't blush. Tell him about it.

SERGEANT Who's blushing? Well, naturally, yes—I have my passions—like everybody else. The fact is, since you ask me—I love—to play—casino. And if the gentleman would like to join me, by and by when I go off duty, we can sit down to a nice little game in the back room with a nice cold glass of beer. If he wants to kill an hour, that is.

COUNTESS He doesn't want to kill an hour. He wants to kill himself. Well? Is that all the police force has to offer by way of earthly bliss?

SERGEANT Huh? You mean— (*He jerks a thumb in the direction of the pretty* BLONDE, *who has just been joined by a* BRUNETTE *of the same stamp*) Paulette? (*The young man groans*)

COUNTESS You're not earning your salary, Sergeant. I defy anybody to stop dying on your account.

SERGEANT Go ahead, if you can do any better. But you won't find it easy.

COUNTESS Oh, this is not a desperate case at all. A young man who has just fallen in love with someone who has fallen in love with him!

PIERRE She hasn't. How could she?

COUNTESS Oh, yes, she has. She was holding your hand, just as I'm holding it, when all of a sudden . . . Did you ever know Marshal Canrobert's[1] niece?

SERGEANT How could he know Marshal Canrobert's niece?

[1] Commander of French forces in the Crimean war, 1854-55

COUNTESS Lots of people knew her—when she was alive. (PIERRE *begins to struggle energetically*) No, no, Roderick—stop—stop!

SERGEANT You see? You won't do any better than I did.

COUNTESS No? Let's bet. I'll bet my iris against one of your gold buttons. Right?—Roderick, I know very well why you tried to drown yourself in the river.

PIERRE You don't at all.

COUNTESS It's because that Prospector wanted you to commit a horrible crime.

PIERRE How did you know that?

COUNTESS He stole my boa, and now he wants you to kill me.

PIERRE Not exactly.

COUNTESS It wouldn't be the first time they've tried it. But I'm not so easy to get rid of, my boy, oh, no . . . Because . . .

(*The* DOORMAN *rides in on his bicycle. He winks at the* SERGEANT, *who has now seated himself while the* WAITER *serves him a beer*)

DOORMAN Take it easy, Sergeant.

SERGEANT I'm busy saving a drowning man.

COUNTESS They can't kill me because—I have no desire to die.

PIERRE You're fortunate.

COUNTESS To be alive is to be fortunate, Roderick. Of course, in the morning, when you first awake, it does not always seem so very gay. When you take your hair out of the drawer, and your teeth out of the glass, you are apt to feel a little out of place in this world. Especially if you've just been dreaming that you're a little girl on a pony looking for strawberries in the woods. But all you need to feel the call of life once more is a letter in your mail giving you your schedule for the day—your mending, your shopping, that letter to your grandmother that you never seem to get around to. And so, when you've washed your face in rosewater, and powdered it—not with this awful rice-powder they sell nowadays, which does nothing for the skin, but with a cake of pure white starch—and put on your pins, your rings, your brooches, bracelets, earrings, and pearls—in short, when you are dressed for your morning coffee—and have had a good look at yourself—not in the glass, naturally—it lies—but in the side of the brass gong that once belonged to Admiral Courbet[2]—then, Roderick, then you're armed, you're strong, you're ready—you can begin again.

(PIERRE *is listening now intently. There are tears in his eyes*)

PIERRE Oh, Madame . . . ! Oh, Madame . . . !

COUNTESS After that, everything is pure delight. First the morning paper. Not, of course, these current sheets full of lies and vulgarity. I always read the *Gaulois,* the issue of March 22, 1903. It's by far the best. It has some delightful scandal, some excellent fashion notes, and, of course, the last-minute bulletin on the death of Leonide Leblanc. She used to live next door, poor woman, and when I learn of her death every morning, it gives me quite a shock. I'd gladly lend you my copy, but it's in tatters.

SERGEANT Couldn't we find him a copy in some library?

COUNTESS I doubt it. And so, when you've taken your fruit salts—not in water, naturally—no matter what they say, it's water that gives you gas—but with a bit of spiced cake—then in sunlight or rain, Chaillot calls. It is time to dress for your morning walk. This takes much longer, of course—without a maid, impossible to do it under an hour, what with your corset, corset-cover, and drawers all of which lace or button in the back. I asked Madame Lanvin, a while ago, to fit the drawers with zippers. She was quite charming, but she declined. She thought it would spoil the style.

(*The* DEAF MUTE *comes in*)

WAITER I know a place where they put zippers on anything.

(*The* RAGPICKER *enters*)

COUNTESS I think Lanvin knows best. But I really manage very well, Martial. What I do now is, I lace them up in front, then twist them around to the back. It's quite simple, really. Then you choose a lorgnette, and then the usual fruitless search for the feather boa that the prospector stole—I know it was he: he didn't dare look me in the eye—and then all you need is a rubber band to slip around your parasol—I lost the catch the day I struck the cat that was stalking the pigeon—it was worth it—ah, that day I earned my wages!

THE RAGPICKER Countess, if you can use it, I found a nice umbrella catch the other day with a cat's eye in it.

COUNTESS Thank you, Ragpicker. They say these eyes sometimes come to life and fill with tears. I'd be afraid . . .

PIERRE Go on, Madame, go on . . .

COUNTESS Ah! So life is beginning to interest you, is it? You see how beautiful it is?

PIERRE What a fool I've been!

COUNTESS Then, Roderick, I begin my rounds. I have my cats to feed, my dogs to pet, my plants to water. I have to see what the evil ones are up to in the district—those who hate people, those who hate plants, those who hate animals. I watch them sneaking off in the morning to put on their disguises—to the baths, to the beauty parlors, to the barbers. But they can't deceive me. And when they come out again with blonde hair and false whiskers, to pull up my flowers and poison my dogs, I'm there, and I'm ready. All you have to do to break their power is to cut across their path from the left. That isn't always easy. Vice moves swiftly. But I have a good long stride and I generally manage. . . . Right, my friends? (*The* WAITER *and the* RAGPICKER *nod their heads with evident approval*) Yes, the flowers have been marvelous this year. And the butcher's dog on the Rue Bizet, in spite of that wretch that tried to poison him, is friskier than ever. . . .

[2] Admiral Courbet commanded the French fleet in the Far East, 1883-84.

SERGEANT That dog had better look out. He has no license.

COUNTESS He doesn't seem to feel the need for one.

THE RAGPICKER The Duchess de la Rochefoucauld's whippet is getting awfully thin. . . .

COUNTESS What can I do? She bought that dog full grown from a kennel where they didn't know his right name. A dog without his right name is bound to get thin.

THE RAGPICKER I've got a friend who knows a lot about dogs—an Arab . . .

COUNTESS Ask him to call on the Duchess. She receives Thursdays, five to seven. You see, then, Roderick. That's life. Does it appeal to you now?

PIERRE It seems marvelous.

COUNTESS Ah! Sergeant. My button. (*The* SERGEANT *gives her his button and goes off. At this point the* PROSPECTOR *enters*) That's only the morning. Wait till I tell you about the afternoon!

PROSPECTOR All right, Pierre. Come along now.

PIERRE I'm perfectly all right here.

PROSPECTOR I said, come along now.

PIERRE (*To the* COUNTESS) I'd better go, Madame.

COUNTESS No.

PIERRE It's no use. Please let go my hand.

PROSPECTOR Madame, will you oblige me by letting my friend go?

COUNTESS I will not oblige you in any way.

PROSPECTOR All right. Then I'll oblige you . . . !

(*He tries to push her away. She catches up a soda water siphon and squirts it in his face*)

PIERRE Countess . . .

COUNTESS Stay where you are. This man isn't going to take you away. In the first place, I shall need you in a few minutes to take me home. I'm all alone here and I'm very easily frightened.

(*The* PROSPECTOR *makes a second attempt to drag* PIERRE *away. The* COUNTESS *cracks him over the skull with the siphon. They join battle. The* COUNTESS *whistles. The* DOORMAN *comes, then the other* VAGABONDS, *and lastly the* POLICE SERGEANT)

PROSPECTOR Officer! Arrest this woman!

SERGEANT What's the trouble here?

PROSPECTOR She refuses to let this man go.

SERGEANT Why should she?

PROSPECTOR It's against the law for a woman to detain a man on the street.

IRMA Suppose it's her son whom she's found again after twenty years?

THE RAGPICKER (*Gallantly*) Or her long-lost brother? The Countess is not so old.

PROSPECTOR Officer, this is a clear case of disorderly conduct.

(*The* DEAF-MUTE *interrupts with frantic signals*)

COUNTESS Irma, what is the Deaf-Mute saying?

IRMA (*Interpreting*) The young man is in danger of his life. He mustn't go with him.

PROSPECTOR What does he know?

IRMA He knows everything.

PROSPECTOR Officer, I'll have to take your number.

COUNTESS Take his number. It's 2133. It adds up to nine. It will bring you luck.

SERGEANT Countess, between ourselves, what are you holding him for, anyway?

COUNTESS I'm holding him because it's very pleasant to hold him. I've never really held anybody before, and I'm making the most of it. And because so long as *I* hold him, he's free.

PROSPECTOR Pierre, I'm giving you fair warning. . . .

COUNTESS And I'm holding him because Irma wants me to hold him. Because if I let him go, it will break her heart.

IRMA Oh, Countess!

SERGEANT (*To the* PROSPECTOR) All right, you—move on. Nobody's holding you. You're blocking traffic. Move on.

PROSPECTOR (*Menacingly*) I have your number. (*And murderously, to* PIERRE) You'll regret this, Pierre.

(*Exit* PROSPECTOR)

PIERRE Thank you, Countess.

COUNTESS They're blackmailing you, are they? (PIERRE *nods*) What have you done? Murdered somebody?

PIERRE No.

COUNTESS Stolen something?

PIERRE No.

COUNTESS What then?

PIERRE I forged a signature.

COUNTESS Whose signature?

PIERRE My father's. To a note.

COUNTESS And this man has the paper, I suppose?

PIERRE He promised to tear it up, if I did what he wanted. But I couldn't do it.

COUNTESS But the man is mad! Does he really want to destroy the whole neighborhood?

PIERRE He wants to destroy the whole city.

COUNTESS (*Laughs*) Fantastic.

PIERRE It's not funny, Countess. He can do it. He's mad, but he's powerful, and he has friends. Their machines are already drawn up and waiting. In three months' time you may see the city covered by a forest of derricks and drills.

COUNTESS But what are they looking for? Have they lost something?

PIERRE They're looking for oil. They're convinced that Paris is sitting on a lake of oil.

COUNTESS Suppose it is. What harm does it do?

PIERRE They want to bring the oil to the surface, Countess.

COUNTESS (*Laughs*) How silly! Is that a reason to destroy a city? What do they want with this oil?

PIERRE They want to make war, Countess.

COUNTESS Oh, dear, let's forget about these horrible men. The world is beautiful. It's happy. That's how God made it. No man can change it.

WAITER Ah, Countess, if you only knew . . .

COUNTESS If I only knew what?

WAITER Shall we tell her now? Shall we tell her?

COUNTESS What is it you are hiding from me?

THE RAGPICKER Nothing, Countess. It's you who are hiding.

WAITER You tell her. You've been a pitchman. You can talk.

ALL Tell her. Tell her. Tell her.

COUNTESS You're frightening me, my friends. Go on. I'm listening.

THE RAGPICKER Countess, there was a time when old clothes were as good as new—in fact, they were better. Because when people wore clothes, they gave something to them. You may not believe it, but right this minute, the highest-priced shops in Paris are selling clothes that were thrown away thirty years ago. They're selling them for new. That's how good they were.

COUNTESS Well?

THE RAGPICKER Countess, there was a time when garbage was a pleasure. A garbage can was not what it is now. If it smelled a little strange, it was because it was a little confused—there was everything there—sardines, cologne, iodine, roses. An amateur might jump to a wrong conclusion. But to a professional—it was the smell of God's plenty.

COUNTESS Well?

THE RAGPICKER Countess, the world has changed.

COUNTESS Nonsense. How could it change? People are the same, I hope.

THE RAGPICKER No, Countess. The people are not the same. The people are different. There's been an invasion. An infiltration. From another planet. The world is not beautiful any more. It's not happy.

COUNTESS Not happy? Is that true? Why didn't you tell me this before?

THE RAGPICKER Because you live in a dream, Countess. And we don't like to disturb you.

COUNTESS But how could it have happened?

THE RAGPICKER Countess, there was a time when you could walk around Paris, and all the people you met were just like yourself. A little cleaner, maybe, or dirtier, perhaps, or angry, or smiling—but you knew them. They were you. Well, Countess, twenty years ago, one day, on the street, I saw a face in the crowd. A face, you might say, without a face. The eyes—empty. The expression—not human. Not a human face. It saw me staring, and when it looked back at me with its gelatine eyes, I shuddered. Because I knew that to make room for this one, one of us must have left the earth. A while after, I saw another. And another. And since then, I've seen hundreds come in—yes—thousands.

COUNTESS Describe them to me.

THE RAGPICKER You've seen them yourself, Countess. Their clothes don't wrinkle. Their hats don't come off. When they talk, they don't look at you. They don't perspire.

COUNTESS Have they wives? Have they children?

THE RAGPICKER They buy the models out of shop windows, furs and all. They animate them by a secret process. Then they marry them. Naturally, they don't have children.

COUNTESS What work do they do?

THE RAGPICKER They don't do any work. Whenever they meet, they whisper, and then they pass each other thousand-franc notes. You see them standing on the corner by the Stock Exchange. You see them at auctions—in the back. They never raise a finger—they just stand there. In theater lobbies, by the box office—they never go inside. They don't do anything, but wherever you see them, things are not the same. I remember well the time when a cabbage could sell itself just by being a cabbage. Nowadays it's no good being a cabbage—unless you have an agent and pay him a commission. Nothing is free any more to sell itself or give itself away. These days, Countess, every cabbage has its pimp.

COUNTESS I can't believe that.

THE RAGPICKER Countess, little by little, the pimps have taken over the world. They don't do anything, they don't make anything—they just stand there and take their cut. It makes a difference. Look at the shopkeepers. Do you ever see one smiling at a customer any more? Certainly not. Their smiles are strictly for the pimps. The butcher has to smile at the meat-pimp, the florist at the rose-pimp, the grocer at the fresh-fruit-and-vegetable pimp. It's all organized down to the slightest detail. A pimp for bird-seed. A pimp for fishfood. That's why the cost of living keeps going up all the time. You buy a glass of beer—it costs twice as much as it used to. Why? 10 percent for the glass-pimp, 10 percent for the beer-pimp, 20 percent for the glass-of-beer-pimp—that's where our money goes. Personally, I prefer the old-fashioned type. Some of those men at least were loved by the women they sold. But what feelings can a pimp arouse in a leg of lamb? Pardon my language, Irma.

COUNTESS It's all right. She doesn't understand it.

THE RAGPICKER So now you know, Countess, why the world is no longer happy. We are the last of the free people of the earth. You saw them looking us over today. Tomorrow, the street-singer will start paying the song-pimp, and the garbage-pimp will be after me. I tell you, Countess, we're finished. It's the end of free enterprise in this world!

COUNTESS Is this true, Roderick?

PIERRE I'm afraid it's true.

COUNTESS Did you know about this, Irma?

IRMA All I know is the doorman says that faith is dead.

DOORMAN I've stopped taking bets over the phone.

JUGGLER The very air is different, Countess. You can't trust it any more. If I throw my torches up too high, they go out.

THE RAGPICKER The sky-pimp puts them out.

FLOWER GIRL My flowers don't last over night now. They wilt.

JUGGLER Have you noticed, the pigeons don't fly any more?

THE RAGPICKER They can't afford to. They walk.

COUNTESS They're a lot of fools and so are you! You should have told me at once! How can you bear to live in a world where there is unhappiness? Where a man is not his own master? Are you cowards? All we have to do is to get rid of these men.

PIERRE How can we get rid of them? They're too strong.

(*The* SERGEANT *walks up again*)

COUNTESS (*Smiling*) The Sergeant will help us.

SERGEANT Who? Me?

IRMA There are a great many of them, Countess. The Deaf-Mute knows them all. They employed him once, years ago, because he was deaf. (*The* DEAF-MUTE *wigwags a short speech*) They fired him because he wasn't blind. (*Another flash of sign language*) They're all connected like the parts of a machine.

COUNTESS So much the better. We shall drive the whole machine into a ditch.

SERGEANT It's not that easy, Countess. You never catch these birds napping. They change before your very eyes. I remember when I was in the detectives . . . You catch a president, pfft! He turns into a trustee. You catch him as trustee, and pfft! he's not a trustee—he's an honorary vice-chairman. You catch a Senator dead to rights: he becomes Minister of Justice. You get after the Minister of Justice—he is Chief of Police. And there you are—no longer in the detectives.

PIERRE He's right, Countess. They have all the power. And all the money. And they're greedy for more.

COUNTESS They're greedy? Ah, then, my friends, they're lost. If they're greedy, they're stupid. If they're greedy—don't worry, I know exactly what to do. Roderick, by tonight you will be an honest man. And, Juggler, your torches will stay lit. And your beer will flow freely again, Martial. And the world will be saved. Let's get to work.

THE RAGPICKER What are you going to do?

COUNTESS Have you any kerosene in the house, Irma?

IRMA Yes. Would you like some?

COUNTESS I want just a little. In a dirty bottle. With a little mud. And some mange-cure, if you have it. (*To the* DEAF-MUTE) Deaf-Mute! Take a letter. (IRMA *interprets in sign language. To the* SINGER) Singer, go and find Madame Constance.

(IRMA *and the* WAITER *go into the café*)

SINGER Yes, Countess.

COUNTESS Ask her to be at my house by two o'clock. I'll be waiting for her in the cellar. You may tell her we have to discuss the future of humanity. That's sure to bring her.

SINGER Yes, Countess.

COUNTESS And ask her to bring Mademoiselle Gabrielle and Madame Josephine with her. Do you know how to get in to speak to Madame Constance? You ring twice, and then meow three times like a cat. Do you know how to meow?

SINGER I'm better at barking.

COUNTESS Better practice meowing on the way. Incidentally, I think Madame Constance knows all the verses of your mazurka. Remind me to ask her.

SINGER Yes, Countess. (*Exit*)

(IRMA *comes in. She is shaking the oily concoction in a little perfume vial, which she now hands the* COUNTESS)

IRMA Here you are, Countess.

COUNTESS Thanks, Irma. (*She assumes a presidential manner*) Deaf-Mute! Ready?

(IRMA *interprets in sign language. The* WAITER *has brought out a portfolio of letter paper and placed it on a table. The* DEAF-MUTE *sits down before it, and prepares to write*)

IRMA (*Speaking for the* DEAF-MUTE) I'm ready.

COUNTESS My dear Mr.— What's his name?

(IRMA *wigwags the question to the* DEAF-MUTE, *who answers in the same manner. It is all done so deftly that it is as if the* DEAF-MUTE *were actually speaking*)

IRMA They are all called Mr. President.

COUNTESS My dear Mr. President: I have personally verified the existence of a spontaneous outcrop of oil in the cellar of Number 21 Rue de Chaillot, which is at present occupied by a dignified person of unstable mentality. (*The* COUNTESS *grins knowingly*) This explains why, fortunately for us, the discovery has so long been kept secret. If you should wish to verify the existence of this outcrop for yourself, you may call at the above address at three P.M. today. I am herewith enclosing a sample so that you may judge the quality and consistency of the crude. Yours very truly. Roderick, can you sign the prospector's name?

PIERRE You wish me to?

COUNTESS One forgery wipes out the other.

(PIERRE *signs the letter. The* DEAF-MUTE *types the address on an envelope*)

IRMA Who is to deliver this?

COUNTESS The Doorman, of course. On his bicycle. And as soon as you have delivered it, run over to the prospector's office. Leave word that the President expects to see him at my house at three.

DOORMAN Yes, Countess.

COUNTESS I shall leave you now. I have many pressing things to do. Among others, I must press my red gown.

RAGPICKER But this only takes care of two of them, Countess.

COUNTESS Didn't the Deaf-Mute say they are all connected like the works of a machine?

IRMA Yes.

COUNTESS Then, if one comes, the rest will follow. And we shall have them all. My boa, please.

DOORMAN The one that's stolen, Countess?

COUNTESS Naturally. The one the prospector stole.

DOORMAN It hasn't turned up yet, Countess. But someone has left an ermine collar.

COUNTESS Real ermine?

DOORMAN Looks like it.

COUNTESS Ermine and iris were made for each other. Let me see it.

DOORMAN Yes, Countess. (*Exit* DOORMAN)

COUNTESS Roderick, you shall escort me. You still look pale. I have some old Chartreuse at home. I always take a glass each year. Last year I forgot. You shall have it.

PIERRE If there is anything I can do, Countess . . . ?

COUNTESS There is a great deal you can do. There

are all the things that need to be done in a room that no man has been in for twenty years. You can untwist the cord on the blind and let in a little sunshine for a change. You can take the mirror off the wardrobe door, and deliver me once and for all from the old harpy that lives in the mirror. You can let the mouse out of the trap. I'm tired of feeding it. (*To her friends*) Each man to his post. See you later, my friends. (*The* DOORMAN *puts the ermine collar around her shoulders*) Thank you, my boy. It's rabbit. (*One o'clock strikes*) Your arm, Valentine.

PIERRE Valentine?

COUNTESS It's just struck one. At one, all men become Valentine.

PIERRE (*He offers his arm*) Permit me.

COUNTESS Or Valentino. It's obviously far from the same, isn't it, Irma? But they have that much choice. (*She sweeps out majestically with* PIERRE. *The others disperse. All but* IRMA)

IRMA (*Clearing off the table*) I hate ugliness. I love beauty. I hate meanness. I adore kindness. It may not seem so grand to some to be a waitress in Paris. I love it. A waitress meets all sorts of people. She observes life. I hate to be alone. I love people. But I have never said I love you to a man. Men try to make me say it. They put their arms around me—I pretend I don't see it. They pinch me—I pretend I don't feel it. They kiss me—I pretend I don't know it. They take me out in the evening and make me drink—but I'm careful, I never say it. If they don't like it, they can leave me alone. Because when I say I love you to Him, He will know just by looking in my eyes that many have held me and pinched me and kissed me, but I have never said I love you to anyone in the world before. Never. No. (*Looking off in the direction in which* PIERRE *has gone, she whispers softly:*) I love you.

VOICE (*From within the café*) Irma!

IRMA Coming. (*Exits*)

*Curtain*

# Act Two

SCENE *The cellar of the* COUNTESS' *house. An ancient vault set deep in the ground, with walls of solid masonry, part brick and part great ashlars, mossy and sweating. A staircase of medieval pattern is built into the thickness of the wall, and leads up to the street level from a landing halfway down. In the corners of the cellar are piled casks, packing cases, birdcages, and other odds and ends —the accumulation of centuries—the whole effect utterly fantastic.*

*In the center of the vast underground room, some furniture has been arranged to give an impression of a sitting-room of the 1890's. There is a venerable chaise-longue piled with cushions that once were gay, three armchairs, a table with an oil lamp and a bowl of flowers, a shaggy rug. It is two* P.M., *the same day.*

AT RISE *The* COUNTESS *is sitting over a bit of mending, in one of the armchairs.* IRMA *appears on the landing and calls down.*

IRMA Countess! The Sewer Man is here.

COUNTESS Thank goodness, Irma. Send him down. (*The* SEWER MAN *enters. He carries his hip-boots in his hand*) How do you do, Mr. Sewer Man? (*The* SEWER MAN *bows*) But why do you have your boots in your hand instead of on your feet?

SEWER MAN Etiquette, Countess. Etiquette.

COUNTESS How very American! I'm told that Americans nowadays apologize for their gloves if they happen to take one's hand. As if the skin of a human were nicer to touch than the skin of a sheep! And particularly if they have sweaty hands . . . !

SEWER MAN My feet never sweat, Countess.

COUNTESS How very nice! But please don't stand on ceremony here. Put your boots on. Put them on.

SEWER MAN (*Complying*) Thanks very much, Countess.

COUNTESS (*While he draws on his boots*) I'm sure you must have a very poor opinion of the upper world, from what you see of it. The way people throw their filth into your territory is absolutely scandalous! I burn all my refuse, and I scatter the ashes. All I ever throw in the drain is flowers. Did you happen to see a lily float by this morning? Mine. But perhaps you didn't notice?

SEWER MAN We notice a lot more down there, Countess, than you might think. You'd be surprised the things we notice. There's lots of things come along that were obviously intended for us—little gifts, you might call them—sometimes a brand-new shaving brush—sometimes, *The Brothers Karamazov* . . . Thanks for the lily, Countess. A very sweet thought.

COUNTESS Tomorrow you shall have this iris. But now, let's come to the point. I have two questions to ask you.

SEWER MAN Yes, Countess?

COUNTESS First—and this has nothing to do with our problem—it's just something that has been troubling me. . . . Tell me, is it true that the sewer men of Paris have a king?

SEWER MAN Oh, now, Countess, that's another of those fairy tales out of the Sunday supplements. It just seems those writers can't keep their minds off the sewers! It fascinates them. They keep thinking of us moving around in our underground canals like gondoliers in Venice, and it sends them into a fever of romance! The things they say about us! They say we have a race of girls down there who never see the light of day! It's completely fantastic! The girls naturally come out—every Christmas and Easter. And orgies by torchlight with gondolas and guitars! With troops of rats that dance as they follow the piper! What nonsense! The rats are not allowed to dance. No, no, no. Of course we have no king. Down in the sewers, you'll find nothing but good Republicans.

COUNTESS And no queen?

SEWER MAN No. We may run a beauty contest down there once in a while. Or crown a mermaid Queen of the May. But no queen what you'd call a queen. And, as for these swimming races they talk so much about . . . possibly once in a while—in the summer—in the dog days . . .

COUNTESS I believe you. I believe you. And now tell me. Do you remember that night I found you here in my cellar—looking very pale and strange—you were half-dead as a matter of fact—and I gave you some brandy . . .

SEWER MAN Yes, Countess.

COUNTESS That night you promised if ever I should need it—you would tell me the secret of this room.

SEWER MAN The secret of the moving stone?

COUNTESS I need it now.

SEWER MAN Only the King of the Sewer Men knows this secret.

COUNTESS I'm sure of it. I know most secrets, of course. As a matter of fact, I have three magic words that will open any door that words can open. I have tried them all—in various tones of voice. They don't seem to work. And this is a matter of life and death.

SEWER MAN Look, Countess. (*He locates a brick in the masonry, and pushes it. A huge block of stone slowly pivots and uncovers a trap from which a circular staircase winds into the bowels of the earth*)

COUNTESS Good heavens! Where do those stairs lead?

SEWER MAN Nowhere.

COUNTESS But they must go somewhere.

SEWER MAN They just go down.

COUNTESS Let's go and see.

SEWER MAN No, Countess. Never again. That time you found me, I had a pretty close shave. I kept going down and around, and down and around for an hour, a year—I don't know. There's no end to it, Countess. Once you start you can't stop. . . . Your head begins to turn—you're lost. No—once you start down, there's no coming up.

COUNTESS You came up.

SEWER MAN I—I am a special case. Besides, I had my tools, my ropes. And I stopped in time.

COUNTESS You could have screamed—shouted.

SEWER MAN You could fire off a cannon.

COUNTESS Who could have built a thing like this?

SEWER MAN Paris is old, you know. Paris is very old.

COUNTESS You don't suppose, by any chance, there is oil down there?

SEWER MAN There's only death down there.

COUNTESS I should have preferred a little oil too—or a vein of gold—or emeralds. You're quite sure there is nothing?

SEWER MAN Not even rats.

COUNTESS How does one lower this stone?

SEWER MAN Simple. To open, you press here. And to close it, you push there. (*He presses the brick. The stone descends*) Now there's two of us in the world that knows it.

COUNTESS I won't remember long. Is it all right if I repeat my magic words while I press it?

SEWER MAN It's bound to help. (IRMA *enters*)

IRMA Countess, Madame Constance and Mademoiselle Gabrielle are here.

COUNTESS Show them down, Irma. Thank you very much, Mr. Sewer Man.

SEWER MAN Like that story about the steam laundry that's supposed to be running day and night in my sewer . . . I can assure you . . .

COUNTESS (*Edging him toward the door*) Thank you very much.

SEWER MAN Pure imagination! They never work nights. (*He goes off, bowing graciously*)

(CONSTANCE, *the Madwoman of Passy, and* GABRIELLE, *the Madwoman of St. Sulpice,*[1] *come down daintily.* CONSTANCE *is all in white. She wears an enormous hat graced with ostrich plumes, and a lavender veil.* GABRIELLE *is costumed with the affected simplicity of the 1880's. She is atrociously made up in a remorseless parody of blushing innocence, and she minces down the stairs with macabre coyness*)

CONSTANCE Aurelia! Don't tell us they've found your feather boa?

GABRIELLE You don't mean Adolphe Bertaut has proposed at last! I knew he would.

COUNTESS How are you, Constance? (*She shouts*) How are you, Gabrielle?

GABRIELLE You needn't shout today, my dear. It's Wednesday. Wednesdays, I hear perfectly.

CONSTANCE It's Thursday.

GABRIELLE Oh, dear. Well, never mind. I'm going to make an exception just this once.

CONSTANCE (*To an imaginary dog who has stopped on the landing*) Come along, Dickie. Come along. And stop barking. What a racket you're making! Come on, darling—we've come to see the longest boa and the handsomest man in Paris. Come on.

COUNTESS Constance, it's not a question of my boa today. Nor of poor Adolphe. It's a question of the future of the human race.

CONSTANCE You think it has a future?

COUNTESS Please don't make silly jokes. Sit down and listen to me. Today we must make a decision which may alter the fate of the world.

CONSTANCE Couldn't we do it tomorrow? I want to wash my slippers. Now, Dickie—please!

COUNTESS We haven't a moment to waste. Where is Josephine? Well, we'd best have our tea, and the moment Josephine comes . . .

GABRIELLE Josephine is sitting on her bench in front of the palace waiting for President Wilson to come out. She says she's sorry, but she positively must see him today.

[1] Passy and St. Sulpice, like Chaillot, are fashionable sections of Paris.

CONSTANCE Dickie!

COUNTESS What a pity! (*She gets the tea things from the side table, pours tea and serves cake and honey*) I wish she were here to help us. She has a first-class brain.

CONSTANCE Go ahead, dear. We're listening. (*To* DICKIE) What is it, Dickie? You want to sit in Aunt Aurelia's lap. All right, darling. Go on. Jump, Dickie.

COUNTESS Constance, we love you, as you know. And we love Dickie. But this is a serious matter. So let's stop being childish for once.

CONSTANCE And what does that mean, if you please?

COUNTESS It means Dickie. You know perfectly well that we love him and fuss over him just as if he were still alive. He's a sacred memory and we wouldn't hurt his feelings for the world. But please don't plump him in my lap when I'm settling the future of mankind. His basket is in the corner—he knows where it is, and he can just go and sit in it.

CONSTANCE So you're against Dickie too! You too!

COUNTESS Constance! I'm not in the least against Dickie! I adore Dickie. But you know as well as I that Dickie is only a convention with us. It's a beautiful convention—but it doesn't have to bark all the time. Besides, it's you that spoil him. The time you went to visit your niece and left him with me, we got on marvelously together. He didn't bark, he didn't tear things, he didn't even eat. But when you're with him, one can pay attention to nothing else. I'm not going to take Dickie in my lap at a solemn moment like this, no, not for anything in the world. And that's that!

GABRIELLE (*Very sweetly*) Constance, dear, I don't mind taking him in my lap. He loves to sit in my lap, don't you, darling?

CONSTANCE Kindly stop putting on angelic airs, Gabrielle. I know you very well. You're much too sweet to be sincere. There's plenty of times that I make believe that Dickie is here, when really I've left him home, and you cuddle and pet him just the same.

GABRIELLE I adore animals.

CONSTANCE If you adore animals, you shouldn't pet them when they're not there. It's a form of hypocrisy.

COUNTESS Now, Constance, Gabrielle has as much right as you . . .

CONSTANCE Gabrielle has no right to do what she does. Do you know what she does? She invites *people* to come to tea with us. *People* whom we know nothing about. *People* who exist only in her imagination.

COUNTESS You think that's not an existence?

GABRIELLE I don't invite them at all. They come by themselves. What can I do?

CONSTANCE You might introduce us.

COUNTESS If you think they're only imaginary, there's no point in your meeting them, is there?

CONSTANCE Of course they're imaginary. But who likes to have imaginary people staring at one? Especially strangers.

GABRIELLE Oh, they're really very nice. . . .

CONSTANCE Tell me just one thing, Gabrielle—are they here now?

COUNTESS Am I to be allowed to speak? Or is this going to be the same as the argument about inoculating Josephine's cat, when we didn't get to the subject at all?

CONSTANCE Never! Never! Never! I'll never give my consent to that. (*To* DICKIE) I'd never do a thing like that to you, Dickie sweet. . . . Oh, no! Oh, no! (*She begins to weep softly*)

COUNTESS Good heavens! Now we have her in tears. What an impossible creature! With the fate of humanity hanging in the balance! All right, all right, stop crying. I'll take him in my lap. Come, Dickie, Dickie.

CONSTANCE No. He won't go now. Oh, how can you be so cruel? Don't you suppose I know about Dickie? Don't you think I'd rather have him here alive and woolly and frisking around the way he used to? You have your Adolphe. Gabrielle has her birds. But I have only Dickie. Do you think I'd be so silly about him if it wasn't that it's only by pretending that he's here all the time that I get him to come sometimes, really? Next time I won't bring him!

COUNTESS Now let's not get ourselves worked up over nothing. Come here, Dickie. . . . Irma is going to take you for a nice walk. (*She rings her bell*) Irma!

(IRMA *appears on the landing*)

CONSTANCE No. He doesn't want to go. Besides, I didn't bring him today. So there!

COUNTESS Very well, then. Irma, make sure the door is locked.

IRMA Yes, Countess. (IRMA *exits*)

CONSTANCE What do you mean? Why locked? Who's coming?

COUNTESS If you'd let me get a word in, you'd know by now. A terrible thing has happened. This morning, this very morning, exactly at noon . . .

CONSTANCE (*Thrilled*) Oh, how exciting!

COUNTESS Be quiet. This morning, exactly at noon, thanks to a young man who drowned himself in the Seine . . . Oh, yes, while I think of it—do you know a mazurka called *La Belle Polonaise?*

CONSTANCE Yes, Aurelia.

COUNTESS Could you sing it now? This very minute?

CONSTANCE Yes, Aurelia.

COUNTESS All of it?

CONSTANCE Yes, Aurelia. But who's interrupting now, Aurelia?

COUNTESS You're right. Well, this morning, exactly at noon, I discovered a horrible plot. There is a group of men who intend to tear down the whole city!

CONSTANCE Is that all?

GABRIELLE But I don't understand, Aurelia. Why should men want to tear down the city? It was they themselves who put it up.

COUNTESS You are so innocent, my poor Gabrielle. There are people in the world who want to destroy everything. They have the fever of destruction. Even when they pretend that they're building, it is only in order to destroy. When they put up a new building, they quietly knock down two old ones. They build cities so that they can destroy the countryside. They destroy space with telephones and time with airplanes. Humanity is now dedicated to the task of universal destruction. I am speaking, of course, primarily of the male sex.

GABRIELLE (*Shocked*) Oh . . . !

CONSTANCE Aurelia! Must you talk sex in front of Gabrielle?

COUNTESS There *are* two sexes.

CONSTANCE Gabrielle is a virgin, Aurelia!

COUNTESS Oh, she can't be as innocent as all that. She keeps canaries.

GABRIELLE I think you're being very cruel about men, Aurelia. Men are big and beautiful, and as loyal as dogs. I preferred not to marry, it's true. But I hear excellent reports from friends who have had an opportunity to observe them closely.

COUNTESS My poor darling! You are still living in a dream. But one day, you will wake up as I have, and then you will see what is happening in the world. The tide has turned, my dear. Men are changing back into beasts. They know it. They no longer try to hide it. There was once such a thing as manners. I remember a time when the hungriest was the one who took the longest to pick up his fork. The one with the broadest grin was the one who needed most to go to the . . . It was such fun to keep them grinning like that for hours. But now they no longer pretend. Just look at them—snuffling their soup like pigs, tearing their meat like tigers, crunching their lettuce like crocodiles! A man doesn't take your hand nowadays. He gives you his paw.

CONSTANCE Would that trouble you so much if they turned into animals? Personally, I think it's a good idea.

GABRIELLE Oh, I'd love to see them like that. They'd be sweet.

CONSTANCE It might be the salvation of the human race.

COUNTESS (*To* CONSTANCE) You'd make a fine rabbit, wouldn't you?

CONSTANCE I?

COUNTESS Naturally. You don't think it's only the men who are changing? You change along with them. Husbands and wives together. We're all one race, you know.

CONSTANCE You think so? And why would my poor husband have to be a rabbit if he were alive?

COUNTESS Remember his front teeth? When he nibbled his celery?

CONSTANCE I'm happy to say, I remember absolutely nothing about him. All I remember on that subject is the time that Father Lacordaire tried to kiss me in the park.

COUNTESS Yes, yes, of course.

CONSTANCE And what does that mean, if you please, "Yes, yes, of course"?

COUNTESS Constance, just this once, look us in the eye and tell us truly—did that really happen or did you read about it in a book?

CONSTANCE Now I'm being insulted!

COUNTESS We promise you faithfully that we'll believe it all over again afterwards, won't we, Gabrielle? But tell us the truth this once.

CONSTANCE How dare you question my memories? Suppose I said your pearls were false!

COUNTESS They were.

CONSTANCE I'm not asking what they were. I'm asking what they are. Are they false or are they real?

COUNTESS Everyone knows that little by little, as one wears pearls, they become real.

CONSTANCE And isn't it exactly the same with memories?

COUNTESS Now do not let us waste time. I must go on.

CONSTANCE I think Gabrielle is perfectly right about men. There are still plenty who haven't changed a bit. There's an old Senator who bows to Gabrielle every day when he passes her in front of the palace. And he takes off his hat each time.

GABRIELLE That's perfectly true, Aurelia. He's always pushing an empty baby carriage, and he always stops and bows.

COUNTESS Don't be taken in, Gabrielle. It's all make-believe. And all we can expect from these make-believe men is itself make-believe. They give us facepowder made of stones, sausages made of sawdust, shirts made of glass, stockings made of milk. It's all a vulgar pretence. And if that is the case, imagine what passes, these days, for virtue, sincerity, generosity, and love! I warn you, Gabrielle, don't let this Senator with the empty baby carriage pull the wool over your eyes.

GABRIELLE He's really the soul of courtesy. He seems very correct.

COUNTESS Those are the worst. Gabrielle, beware! He'll make you put on black riding boots, while he dances the can-can around you, singing God knows what filth at the top of his voice. The very thought makes one's blood run cold!

GABRIELLE You think that's what he has in mind?

COUNTESS Of course. Men have lost all sense of decency. They are all equally disgusting. Just look at them in the evening, sitting at their tables in the café, working away in unison with their toothpicks, hour after hour, digging up roast beef, veal, onion . . .

CONSTANCE They don't harm anyone that way.

COUNTESS Then why do you barricade your door, and make your friends meow before you let them come up? Incidentally, we must make an interesting sight, Gabrielle and I, yowling together on your doorstep like a couple of tomcats!

CONSTANCE There's no need at all for you to yowl together. One would be quite enough. And you know perfectly well why I have to do it. It's because there are murderers.

COUNTESS I don't quite see what prevents murderers from meowing like anybody else. But why are there murderers?

CONSTANCE Why? Because there are thieves.

COUNTESS And why are there thieves? Why is there almost nothing but thieves?

CONSTANCE Because they worship money. Because money is king.

COUNTESS Ah—now we've come to it. Because we live in the reign of the Golden Calf. Did you realize that, Gabrielle? Men now publicly worship the Golden Calf!

GABRIELLE How awful! Have the authorities been notified?

COUNTESS The authorities do it themselves, Gabrielle.

GABRIELLE Oh! Has anyone talked to the bishop?

COUNTESS Nowadays only money talks to the bishop. And so you see why I asked you to come here today. The world has gone out of its mind. Unless we do something, humanity is doomed! Constance, have you any suggestions?

CONSTANCE I know what I always do in a case like this. . . .

COUNTESS You write to the Prime Minister.

CONSTANCE He always does what I tell him.

COUNTESS Does he ever answer your letters?

CONSTANCE He knows I prefer him not to. It might excite gossip. Besides, I don't always write. Sometimes I wire. The time I told him about the Archbishop's frigidaire, it was by wire. And they sent a new one the very next day.

COUNTESS There was probably a commission in it for someone. And what do you suggest, Gabrielle?

CONSTANCE Now, how can she tell you until she's consulted her voices?

GABRIELLE I could go right home and consult them, and we could meet again after dinner.

COUNTESS There's no time for that. Besides, your voices are not real voices.

GABRIELLE (*Furious*) How dare you say a thing like that?

COUNTESS Where do your voices come from? Still from your sewing-machine?

GABRIELLE Not at all. They've passed into my hot-water bottle. And it's much nicer that way. They don't chatter any more. They gurgle. But they haven't been a bit nice to me lately. Last night they kept telling me to let my canaries out. "Let them out. Let them out. Let them out."

CONSTANCE Did you?

GABRIELLE I opened the cage. They wouldn't go.

COUNTESS I don't call that *voices*. Objects talk—everyone knows that. It's the principle of the phonograph. But to ask a hot-water bottle for advice is silly. What does a hot-water bottle know? No, all we have to consult here is our own judgment.

CONSTANCE Very well then, tell us what you have decided. Since you're asking our opinion, you've doubtless made up your mind.

COUNTESS Yes, I've thought the whole thing out. All I really needed to discover was the source of the infection. Today I found it.

CONSTANCE Where?

COUNTESS You'll see soon enough. I've baited a trap. In just a few minutes. the rats will be here.

GABRIELLE (*In alarm*) Rats!

COUNTESS Don't be alarmed. They're still in human form.

GABRIELLE Heavens! What are you going to do with them?

COUNTESS That's just the question. Suppose I get these wicked men all here at once—in my cellar—have I the right to exterminate them?

GABRIELLE To kill them? (COUNTESS *nods*)

CONSTANCE That's not a question for us. You'll have to ask Father Bridet.

COUNTESS I have asked him. Yes. One day, in confession, I told him frankly that I had a secret desire to destroy all wicked people. He said: "By all means, my child. And when you're ready to go into action, I'll lend you the jawbone of an ass."

CONSTANCE That's just talk. You get him to put that in writing.

GABRIELLE What's your scheme, Aurelia?

COUNTESS That's a secret.

CONSTANCE It's not so easy to kill them. Let's say you had a tank full of vitriol all ready for them. You could never get them to walk into it. There's nothing so stubborn as a man when you want him to do something.

COUNTESS Leave that to me.

CONSTANCE But if they're killed, they're bound to be missed, and then we'll be fined. They fine you for every little thing these days.

COUNTESS They won't be missed.

GABRIELLE I wish Josephine were here. Her sister's husband was a lawyer. She knows all about these things.

COUNTESS Do you miss a cold when it's gone? Or the germs that caused it? When the world feels well again, do you think it will regret its illness? No, it will stretch itself joyfully, and it will smile—that's all.

CONSTANCE Just a moment! Gabrielle, are they here now? Yes or no?

COUNTESS What's the matter with you now?

CONSTANCE I'm simply asking Gabrielle if her friends are in the room or not. I have a right to know.

GABRIELLE I'm not allowed to say.

CONSTANCE I know very well they are. I'm sure of it. Otherwise you wouldn't be making faces.

COUNTESS May I ask what difference it makes to you if her friends are in the room?

CONSTANCE Just this: If they're here, I'm not going to say another word! I'm certainly not going to commit myself in a matter involving the death sentence in the presence of third parties, whether they exist or not.

GABRIELLE That's not being very nice to my guests, is it?

COUNTESS Constance, you must be mad! Or are you so stupid as to think that just because we're alone, there's nobody with us? Do you consider us so boring or repulsive that of all the millions of beings, imaginary or otherwise, who are prowling about in space, there's not one who might possibly enjoy spending a little time with us? On the contrary, my dear—

my house is full of guests always. They know that here they have a place in the universe where they can come when they're lonely and be sure of a welcome. For my part, I'm delighted to have them.

GABRIELLE Thank you, Aurelia.

CONSTANCE You know perfectly well, Aurelia . . .

COUNTESS I know perfectly well that at this moment the whole universe is listening to us—and that every word we say echoes to the remotest star. To pretend otherwise is the sheerest hypocrisy.

CONSTANCE Then why do you insult me in front of everybody? I'm not mean. I'm shy. I feel timid about giving an opinion in front of such a crowd. Furthermore, if you think I'm so bad and so stupid, why did you invite me, in the first place?

COUNTESS I'll tell you. And I'll tell you why, disagreeable as you are, I always give you the biggest piece of cake and my best honey. It's because when you come there's always someone with you—and I don't mean Dickie—I mean someone who resembles you like a sister, only she's young and lovely, and she sits modestly to one side and smiles at me tenderly all the time you're bickering and quarreling, and never says a word. That's the Constance to whom I give the cake that you gobble, and it's because of her that you're here today, and it's her vote that I'm asking you to cast in this crucial moment. And not yours, which is of no importance whatever.

CONSTANCE I'm leaving.

COUNTESS Be so good as to sit down. I can't let her go yet.

CONSTANCE (*Crossing toward the stairs*) No. This is too much. I'm taking her with me.

(IRMA *enters*)

IRMA Madame Josephine.

COUNTESS Thank heaven!

GABRIELLE We're saved. (JOSEPHINE, *the Madwoman of La Concorde,*[2] *sweeps in majestically in a get-up somewhere between the regal and the priestly*)

JOSEPHINE My dear friends, today once again, I waited for President Wilson—but he didn't come out.

COUNTESS You'll have to wait quite a while longer before he does. He's been dead since 1924.

JOSEPHINE I have plenty of time.

COUNTESS In anyone else, Josephine, these extravagances might seem a little childish. But a person of your judgment doubtless has her reasons for wanting to talk to a man to whom no one would listen when he was alive. We have a legal problem for you. Suppose you had all the world's criminals here in this room. And suppose you had a way of getting rid of them forever. Would you have the right to do it?

JOSEPHINE Why not?

COUNTESS Exactly my point.

GABRIELLE But, Josephine, so many people!

JOSEPHINE *De minimis non curat lex.*[3] The more there are, the more legal it is. It's impersonal. It's even military. It's the cardinal principle of battle—you get all your enemies in one place, and you kill them all together at one time. Because if you had to track them down one by one in their houses and offices, you'd get tired, and sooner or later you'd stop. I believe your idea is very practical, Aurelia. I can't imagine why we never thought of it before.

GABRIELLE Well, if you think it's all right to do it. . . .

JOSEPHINE By all means. Your criminals have had a fair trial, I suppose?

COUNTESS Trial?

JOSEPHINE Certainly. You can't kill anybody without a trial. That's elementary. "No man shall be deprived of his life, liberty, and property without due process of law."

COUNTESS They deprive us of ours.

JOSEPHINE That's not the point. You're not accused of anything. Every accused—man, woman, or child—has the right to defend himself at the bar of justice. Even animals. Before the Deluge, you will recall, the Lord permitted Noah to speak in defense of his fellow mortals. He evidently stuttered. You know the result. On the other hand, Captain Dreyfus was not only innocent—he was defended by a marvelous orator. The result was precisely the same. So you see, in having a trial, you run no risk whatever.

COUNTESS But if I give them the slightest cause for suspicion—I'll lose them.

JOSEPHINE There's a simple procedure prescribed in such cases. You can summon the defendants by calling them three times—mentally, if you like. If they don't appear, the court may designate an attorney who will represent them. This attorney can then argue their case to the court, *in absentia,* and a judgment can then be rendered, *in contumacio.*[4]

COUNTESS But I don't know any attorneys. And we have only ten minutes.

GABRIELLE Hurry, Josephine, hurry!

JOSEPHINE In case of emergency, it is permissible for the court to order the first passer-by to act as attorney for the defense. A defense is like a baptism. Absolutely indispensable, but you don't have to know anything to do it. Ask Irma to get you somebody. Anybody.

COUNTESS The Deaf-Mute?

JOSEPHINE Well—that's getting it down a bit fine. That might be questionable on appeal.

COUNTESS (*Calls*) Irma! What about the Police Sergeant?

JOSEPHINE He won't do. He's under oath to the state.

(IRMA *appears*)

IRMA Yes, Countess?

COUNTESS Who's out there, Irma?

IRMA All our friends, Countess. There's the Ragpicker and . . .

COUNTESS Send down the Ragpicker.

CONSTANCE Do you think it's wise to have all those millionaires represented by a ragpicker?

JOSEPHINE It's a first-rate choice. Criminals are al-

[2] The central square of Paris.

[3] The law does not concern itself with trifles.

[4] In contempt of court.

ways represented by their opposites. Murderers, by someone who obviously wouldn't hurt a fly. Rapists, by a member of the League for Decency. Experience shows it's the only way to get an acquittal.

COUNTESS But we must not have an acquittal. That would mean the end of the world!

JOSEPHINE Justice is justice, my dear.

(*The* RAGPICKER *comes down, with a stately air. Behind him, on the landing, appear the other* VAGABONDS)

THE RAGPICKER Greetings, Countess. Greetings, ladies. My most sincere compliments.

COUNTESS Has Irma told you . . . ?

THE RAGPICKER She said something about a trial.

COUNTESS You have been appointed attorney for the defense.

THE RAGPICKER Terribly flattered, I'm sure.

COUNTESS You realize, don't you, how much depends on the outcome of this trial?

JOSEPHINE Do you know the defendants well enough to undertake the case?

THE RAGPICKER I know them to the bottom of their souls. I go through their garbage every day.

CONSTANCE And what do you find there?

THE RAGPICKER Mostly flowers.

GABRIELLE It's true, you know, the rich are always surrounded with flowers.

CONSTANCE How beautiful!

COUNTESS Are you trying to prejudice the court?

THE RAGPICKER Oh no, Countess, no.

COUNTESS We want a completely impartial defense.

THE RAGPICKER Of course, Countess, of course. Permit me to make a suggestion.

COUNTESS Will you preside, Josephine?

THE RAGPICKER Instead of speaking as attorney, suppose you let me speak directly as defendant. It will be more convincing, and I can get into it more.

JOSEPHINE Excellent idea. Motion granted.

COUNTESS We don't want you to be too convincing, remember.

THE RAGPICKER Impartial, Countess, impartial.

JOSEPHINE Well? Have you prepared your case?

THE RAGPICKER How rich am I?

JOSEPHINE Millions. Billions.

THE RAGPICKER How did I get them? Theft? Murder? Embezzlement?

COUNTESS Most likely.

THE RAGPICKER Do I have a wife? A mistress?

COUNTESS Everything.

THE RAGPICKER All right. I'm ready.

GABRIELLE Will you have some tea?

THE RAGPICKER Is that good?

CONSTANCE Very good for the voice. The Russians drink nothing but tea. And they talk like anything.

THE RAGPICKER All right. Tea.

JOSEPHINE (*To the* VAGABONDS) Come in. Come in. All of you. You may take places. The trial is public. (*The* VAGABONDS *dispose themselves on the steps and elsewhere*) Your bell, if you please, Aurelia.

COUNTESS But what if I should need to ring for Irma?

JOSEPHINE Irma will sit here, next to me. If you need her, she can ring for herself. (*To the* POLICE SERGEANT *and the* POLICEMAN) Conduct the accused to the bar. (*The officers conduct the* RAGPICKER *to a bar improvised with a rocking chair and a packing case marked FRAGILE. The* RAGPICKER *mounts the box. She rings the bell*) The court is now in session. (*All sit*) Counsel for the defense, you may take the oath.

THE RAGPICKER I swear to tell the truth, the whole truth, and nothing but the truth, so help me God.

JOSEPHINE Nonsense! You're not a witness. You're an attorney. It's your duty to lie, conceal, and distort everything, and slander everybody.

THE RAGPICKER All right. I swear to lie, conceal, and distort everything, and slander everybody.

(JOSEPHINE *rings stridently*)

JOSEPHINE Quiet! Begin.

THE RAGPICKER May it please the honorable, august and elegant Court . . .

JOSEPHINE Flattery will get you nowhere. That will do. The defense has been heard. Cross-examination.

COUNTESS Mr. President . . .

THE RAGPICKER (*Bowing with dignity*) Madame.

COUNTESS Do you know what you are charged with?

THE RAGPICKER I can't for the life of me imagine. My life is an open book. My ways are known to all. I am a pillar of the church and the sole support of the Opera. My hands are spotless.

COUNTESS What an atrocious lie! Just look at them!

CONSTANCE You don't have to insult the man. He's only lying to please you.

COUNTESS Be quiet, Constance! You don't get the idea at all. (*To the* RAGPICKER) You are charged with the crime of worshipping money.

THE RAGPICKER Worshipping money? Me?

JOSEPHINE Do you plead guilty or not guilty? Which is it?

THE RAGPICKER Why, Your Honor . . .

JOSEPHINE Yes or no?

THE RAGPICKER Yes or no? No! I don't worship money, Countess. Heavens, no! Money worships me. It adores me. It won't let me alone. It's damned embarrassing, I can tell you.

JOSEPHINE Kindly watch your language.

COUNTESS Defendant, tell the Court how you came by your money.

THE RAGPICKER The first time money came to me, I was a mere boy, a little golden-haired child in the bosom of my dear family. It came to me suddenly in the guise of a gold brick which, in my innocence, I picked out of a garbage can one day while playing. I was horrified, as you can imagine. I immediately tried to get rid of it by swapping it for a little rundown one-track railroad which, to my consternation, at once sold itself for a hundred times its value. In a desperate effort to get rid of this money, I began to buy things. I bought the Northern Refineries, the Galeries Lafayette,[5] and the Schneider-Creusot Munition Works. And now I'm stuck with them. It's a horrible fate—but I'm resigned to it. I don't ask for your

[5] One of the largest department stores in Paris.

sympathy, I don't ask for your pity—all I ask for is a little common human understanding . . . . (*He begins to cry*)

COUNTESS I object. This wretch is trying to play on the emotions of the Court.

JOSEPHINE The Court has no emotions.

THE RAGPICKER Everyone knows that the poor have no one but themselves to blame for their poverty. It's only just that they should suffer the consequences. But how is it the fault of the rich if they're rich?

COUNTESS Dry your tears. You're deceiving nobody. If, as you say, you're ashamed of your money, why is it you hold onto it with such a death-grip?

THE RAGPICKER Me?

STREET PEDDLER You never part with a franc!

JUGGLER You wouldn't even give the poor Deaf-Mute a sou!

THE RAGPICKER Me, hold onto money? What slander! What injustice! What a thing to say to me in the presence of this honorable, august, and elegant Court! I spend all my time trying to spend my money. If I have tan shoes, I buy black ones. If I have a bicycle, I buy a motor car. If I have a wife, I buy . . .

JOSEPHINE (*Rings*) Order!

THE RAGPICKER I dispatch a plane to Java for a bouquet of flowers. I send a steamer to Egypt for a basket of figs. I send a special representative to New York to fetch me an ice-cream cone. And if it's not just exactly right, back it goes. But no matter what I do, I can't get rid of my money! If I play a hundred to one shot, the horse comes in by twenty lengths. If I throw a diamond in the Seine, it turns up in the trout they serve me for lunch. Ten diamonds—ten trout. Well, now, do you suppose I can get rid of forty millions by giving a sou to a deaf-mute? Is it even worth the effort?

CONSTANCE He's right.

THE RAGPICKER Ah! You see, my dear? At last, there is somebody who understands me! Somebody who is not only beautiful, but extraordinarily sensitive and intelligent.

COUNTESS I object!

JOSEPHINE Overruled!

THE RAGPICKER I should be delighted to send you some flowers, Miss—directly I'm acquitted. What flowers do you prefer?

CONSTANCE Roses.

THE RAGPICKER You shall have a bale every morning for the next five years. Money means nothing to me.

CONSTANCE And amaryllis.

THE RAGPICKER I'll make a note of the name. (*In his best lyrical style*) The lady understands, ladies and gentlemen. The lady is no fool. She's been around and she knows what's what. If I gave the Deaf-Mute a franc, twenty francs, twenty million francs—I still wouldn't make a dent in the forty times a thousand million francs that I'm afflicted with! Right, little lady?

CONSTANCE Right.

JOSEPHINE Proceed.

THE RAGPICKER Like on the Stock Exchange. If *you* buy a stock, it sinks at once like a plummet. But if *I* buy a stock, it turns around and soars like an eagle. If I buy it at 33 . . .

PEDDLER It goes up to a thousand.

THE RAGPICKER It goes to twenty thousand! That's how I bought my twelve chateaux, my twenty villas, my 234 farms. That's how I endow the Opera and keep my twelve ballerinas.

FLOWER GIRL I hope every one of them deceives you every moment of the day!

THE RAGPICKER How can they deceive me? Suppose they try to deceive me with the male chorus, the general director, the assistant electrician, or the English horn—I own them all, body and soul. It would be like deceiving me with my big toe.

CONSTANCE Don't listen, Gabrielle.

GABRIELLE Listen to what?

THE RAGPICKER No. I am incapable of jealousy. I have all the women—or I can have them, which is the same thing. I get the thin ones with caviar—the fat ones with pearls . . . .

COUNTESS So you think there are no women with morals?

THE RAGPICKER I mix morals with mink—delicious combination. I drip pearls into protests. I adorn resistance with rubies. My touch is jeweled; my smile, a motor car. What woman can withstand me? I lift my little finger—and do they fall?— Like leaves in autumn—like tin cans from a second-story window.

CONSTANCE That's going a little too far!

COUNTESS You see where money leads.

THE RAGPICKER Of course. When you have no money, nobody trusts you, nobody believes you, nobody likes you. Because to have money is to be virtuous, honest, beautiful, and witty. And to be without is to be ugly and boring and stupid and useless.

COUNTESS One last question. Suppose you find this oil you're looking for. What do you propose to do with it?

THE RAGPICKER I propose to make war! I propose to conquer the world!

COUNTESS You have heard the defense, such as it is. I demand a verdict of guilty.

THE RAGPICKER What are you talking about? Guilty? I? I am never guilty!

JOSEPHINE I order you to keep quiet.

THE RAGPICKER I am never quiet!

JOSEPHINE Quiet, in the name of the law!

THE RAGPICKER I am the law. When I speak, that is the law. When I present my backside, it is etiquette to smile and to apply the lips respectfully. It is more than etiquette—it is a cherished national privilege, guaranteed by the Constitution.

JOSEPHINE That's contempt of court. The trial is over.

COUNTESS And the verdict?

ALL Guilty!

JOSEPHINE Guilty as charged.

COUNTESS Then I have full authority to carry out the sentence?

ALL Yes!

COUNTESS I can do what I like with them?

ALL Yes!

COUNTESS I have the right to exterminate them?

ALL Yes!

JOSEPHINE Court adjourned!

COUNTESS (*To the* RAGPICKER) Congratulations, Ragpicker. A marvelous defense. Absolutely impartial.

THE RAGPICKER Had I known a little before, I could have done better. I could have prepared a little speech, like the time I used to sell the Miracle Spot Remover. . . .

JOSEPHINE No need for that. You did very well, extempore. The likeness was striking and the style reminiscent of Clemenceau. I predict a brilliant future for you. Good-bye, Aurelia. I'll take our little Gabrielle home.

CONSTANCE I'm going to walk along the river. (*To* DICKIE) Oh! So here you are. And your ear all bloody! Dickie! Have you been fighting again? Oh, dear . . . !

COUNTESS (*To the* RAGPICKER) See that she gets home all right, won't you? She loses everything on the way. And in the queerest places. Her prayer book in the butcher shop. And her corset in church.

THE RAGPICKER (*Bowing and offering his arm*) Permit me, Madame.

STREET SINGER Oh, Countess—my mazurka. Remember?

COUNTESS Oh, yes. Constance, wait a moment. (*To the* SINGER) Well? Begin.

SINGER (*Sings*)

Do you hear, Mademoiselle,
Those musicians of hell?

CONSTANCE Why, of course, it's *La Belle Polonaise*. . . . (*She sings*)

From Poland to France
Comes this marvelous dance,
So gracious,
Audacious,
Will you foot it, perchance?

SINGER I'm saved!

JOSEPHINE (*Reappearing at the head of the stairs*)

Now my arm I entwine
Round these contours divine,
So pure, so impassioned,
Which Cupid has fashioned. . . .

GABRIELLE (*Reappearing also, she sings a quartet with the others*)

Come, let's dance the mazurka, that devilish measure,
'Tis a joy that's reserved to the gods for their pleasure—
Let's gallop, let's hop,
With never a stop,
My blond Polish miss,
Let our heads spin and turn
As the dance-floor we spurn—
There was never such pleasure as this!

(*They all exit, dancing*)

IRMA It's time for your afternoon nap.

COUNTESS But suppose they come, Irma!

IRMA I'll watch out for them.

COUNTESS Thank you, Irma. I *am* tired. (*She smiles*) Did you ever see a trial end more happily in your life?

IRMA Lie down and close your eyes a moment.

(*The* COUNTESS *stretches out on the chaise-longue and shuts her eyes.* IRMA *tiptoes out. In a moment,* PIERRE *comes down softly, the feather boa in his hands. He stands over the chaise-longue, looking tenderly down at the sleeping woman, then kneels beside her and takes her hand*)

COUNTESS (*Without opening her eyes*) Is it you, Adolphe Bertaut?

PIERRE It's only Pierre.

COUNTESS Don't lie to me, Adolphe Bertaut. These are your hands. Why do you complicate things always? Say that it's you.

PIERRE Yes. It is I.

COUNTESS Would it cost you so much to call me Aurelia?

PIERRE It's I, Aurelia.

COUNTESS Why did you leave me, Adolphe Bertaut? Was she so very lovely, this Georgette of yours?

PIERRE No. You are a thousand times lovelier.

COUNTESS But she was clever.

PIERRE She was stupid.

COUNTESS It was her soul, then, that drew you? When you looked into her eyes, you saw a vision of heaven, perhaps?

PIERRE I saw nothing.

COUNTESS That's how it is with men. They love you because you are beautiful and clever and soulful—and at the first opportunity they leave you for someone who is plain and dull and soulless. But why does it have to be like that, Adolphe Bertaut? Why?

PIERRE Why, Aurelia?

COUNTESS I know very well she wasn't rich. Because when I saw you that time at the grocer's, and you snatched the only good melon from right under my nose, your cuffs, my poor friend, were badly frayed. . . .

PIERRE Yes. She was poor.

COUNTESS "Was" poor? Is she dead then? If it's because she's dead that you've come back to me—then no. Go away. I will not take their leavings from the dead. I refuse to inherit you. . . .

PIERRE She's quite well.

COUNTESS Your hands are still the same, Adolphe Bertaut. Your touch is young and firm. Because it's the only part of you that has stayed with me. The rest of you is pretty far gone, I'm afraid. I can see why you'd rather not come near me when my eyes are open. It's thoughtful of you.

PIERRE Yes. I've aged.

COUNTESS Not I. I am young because I haven't had to live down my youth, like you. I have it with me still, as fresh and beautiful as ever. But when you walk now in the park at Colombes with Georgette, I'm sure . . .

PIERRE There is no longer a park at Colombes.

COUNTESS Is there a park still at St. Cloud? Is there a park at Versailles? I've never gone back to see. But I think, if they could move, those trees would have walked away in disgust the day you went there with Georgette. . . .

PIERRE They did. Not many are left.

COUNTESS You take her also, I suppose, to hear *Denise*?

PIERRE No one hears *Denise* any more.

COUNTESS It was on the way home from *Denise*, Adolphe Bertaut, that I first took your arm. Because it was windy and it was late. I have never set foot in that street again. I go the other way round. It's not easy, in the winter, when there's ice. One is quite apt to fall. I often do.

PIERRE Oh, my darling—forgive me.

COUNTESS No, never. I will never forgive you. It was very bad taste to take her to the very places where we'd been together.

PIERRE All the same, I swear, Aurelia . . .

COUNTESS Don't swear. I know what you did. You gave her the same flowers. You bought her the same chocolates. But has she any left? No. I have all your flowers still. I have twelve chocolates. No, I will never forgive you as long as I live.

PIERRE I always loved you, Aurelia.

COUNTESS You "loved" me? Then you too are dead, Adolphe Bertaut?

PIERRE No. I love you. I shall always love you, Aurelia.

COUNTESS Yes. I know. That much I've always known. I knew it the moment you went away, Adolphe, and I knew that nothing could ever change it. Georgette is in his arms now—yes. But he loves me. Tonight he's taken Georgette to hear *Denise*—yes. But he loves me. . . . I know it. You never loved her. Do you think I believed for one moment that absurd story about her running off with the osteopath? Of course not. Since you didn't love her, obviously she stayed with you. And, after that, when she came back, and I heard about her going off with the surveyor—I knew that couldn't be true, either. You'll never get rid of her, Adolphe Bertaut—never. Because you don't love her.

PIERRE I need your pity, Aurelia. I need your love. Don't forget me. . . .

COUNTESS Farewell, Adolphe Bertaut. Farewell. Let go my hand, and give it to little Pierre. (PIERRE *lets go her hand, and after a moment takes it again. The* COUNTESS *opens her eyes*) Pierre? Ah, it's you. Has he gone?

PIERRE Yes, Countess.

COUNTESS I didn't hear him go. Oh, he knows how to make a quick exit, that one. (*She sees the boa*) Good heavens! Wherever did you find it?

PIERRE In the wardrobe, Countess. When I took off the mirror.

COUNTESS Was there a purple felt shopping bag with it?

PIERRE Yes, Countess.

COUNTESS And a little child's sewing box?

PIERRE No, Countess.

COUNTESS Oh, they're frightened now. They're trembling for their lives. You see what they're up to? They're putting back all the things they have stolen. I never open that wardrobe, of course, on account of the old woman in the mirror. But I have sharp eyes. I don't need to open it to see what's in it. Up to this morning, that wardrobe was empty. And now—you see? But, dear me, how stupid they are! The one thing I really miss is my little sewing box. It's something they stole from me when I was a child. They haven't put it back? You're quite sure?

PIERRE What was it like?

COUNTESS Green cardboard with paper lace and gold stamping. I got it for Christmas when I was seven. They stole it the very next day. I cried my eyes out every time I thought of it—until I was eight.

PIERRE It's not there, Countess.

COUNTESS The thimble was gilt. I swore I'd never use any other. Look at my poor fingers. . . .

PIERRE They've kept the thimble too.

COUNTESS Splendid! Then I'm under no obligation to be merciful. Put the boa around my neck, Pierre. I want them to see me wearing it. They'll think it's a real boa.

(IRMA *runs in excitedly*)

IRMA Here they come, Countess! You were right—it's a procession. The street is full of limousines and taxis!

COUNTESS I will receive them. (*As* PIERRE *hesitates to leave her*) Don't worry. There's nothing to be frightened of. (PIERRE *goes out*) Irma, did you remember to stir the kerosene into the water?

IRMA Yes, Countess. Here it is.

COUNTESS (*Looking critically at the bottle*) You might as well pour in what's left of the tea. (IRMA *shakes up the liquid*) Don't forget, I'm supposed to be deaf. I want to hear what they're thinking.

IRMA Yes, Countess.

COUNTESS (*Putting the finishing touches to her make-up*) I don't have to be merciful—but, after all, I do want to be just. . . .

(IRMA *goes up to the landing and exits. As soon as she is alone, the* COUNTESS *presses the brick, and the trap door opens. There is a confused sound of auto horns in the street above, and the noise of an approaching crowd*)

IRMA (*Offstage*) Yes, Mr. President. Come in, Mr. President. You're expected, Mr. President. This way, Mr. President. (*The* PRESIDENTS *come down, led by the* PRESIDENT. *They all look alike, are dressed alike, and all have long cigars*) The Countess is quite deaf, gentlemen. You'll have to shout. (*She announces*) The presidents of the boards of directors!

THE PRESIDENT I had a premonition, Madame, when I saw you this morning, that we should meet again. (*The* COUNTESS *smiles vaguely. He continues, a tone louder*) I want to thank you for your trust. You may place yourself in our hands with complete confidence.

SECOND PRESIDENT Louder. The old trot can't hear you.

THE PRESIDENT I have a letter here, Madame, in which . . .

SECOND PRESIDENT Louder. Louder.

THIRD PRESIDENT (*Shouting*) Is it true that you've located . . . ? (*The* COUNTESS *stares at him blankly. He shouts at the top of his voice*) Oil? (*The* COUNTESS *nods with a smile, and points down. The* PRESIDENT *produces a legal paper and a fountain pen*) Sign here.

COUNTESS What is it? I haven't my glasses.

THE PRESIDENT Your contract. (*He offers the pen*)

COUNTESS Thank you.

SECOND PRESIDENT (*Normal voice*) What is it?

THIRD PRESIDENT Waiver of all rights. (*He takes it back signed*) Thank you. (*He hands it to the* SECOND PRESIDENT) Witness. (*The* SECOND PRESIDENT *witnesses it. The* PRESIDENT *passes it on to the* THIRD PRESIDENT) Notarize. (*The paper is notarized. The* PRESIDENT *turns to the* COUNTESS *and shouts*) My congratulations. And now, Madame— (*He produces a gold brick wrapped in tissue paper*) If you'll show us the well, this package is yours.

COUNTESS What is it?

THE PRESIDENT Pure gold. Twenty-four karat. For you.

COUNTESS Thank you very much. (*She takes it*) It's heavy.

SECOND PRESIDENT Are you going to give her that?

THE PRESIDENT Don't worry. We'll pick it up again on the way out. (*He shouts at the* COUNTESS, *pointing at the trap door*) Is this the way?

COUNTESS That's the way.

(*The* SECOND PRESIDENT *tries to slip in first. The* PRESIDENT *pulls him back*)

THE PRESIDENT Just a minute, Mr. President. After me, if you don't mind. And watch those cigars. It's oil, you know.

(*But as he is about to descend, the* COUNTESS *steps forward*)

COUNTESS Just one moment . . .

THE PRESIDENT Yes?

COUNTESS Did any of you happen to bring along a little sewing box?

THE PRESIDENT Sewing box? (*He pulls back another impatient* PRESIDENT) Take it easy.

COUNTESS Or a little gold thimble?

THE PRESIDENT Not me.

THE PRESIDENTS Not us.

COUNTESS What a pity!

THE PRESIDENT Can we go down now?

COUNTESS Yes. You may go down now. Watch your step!

(*They hurry down eagerly. When they have quite disappeared,* IRMA *appears on the landing and announces the next echelon*)

IRMA Countess, the Prospectors.

COUNTESS Heavens! Are there more than one?

IRMA There's a whole delegation.

COUNTESS Send them down.

(*The* PROSPECTOR *comes in, following his nose*)

IRMA Come in, please.

THE PROSPECTOR (*Sniffing the air like a bloodhound*) I smell something. . . . Who's that?

IRMA The Countess. She is very deaf.

THE PROSPECTOR Good.

(*The* PROSPECTORS *also look alike. Sharp clothes, Western hats, and long noses. They crowd down the stairs after the* PROSPECTOR, *sniffing in unison. The* PROSPECTOR *is especially talented. He casts about on the scent until it leads him to the decanter on the table. He pours himself a glass, drinks it off, and belches with much satisfaction. The others join him at once, and follow his example. They all belch in unison*)

THE PROSPECTORS Oil?

THE PROSPECTOR Oil!

COUNTESS Oil.

THE PROSPECTOR Traces? Puddles?

COUNTESS Pools. Gushers.

SECOND PROSPECTOR Characteristic odor? (*He sniffs*)

THE PROSPECTOR Chanel Number 5. Nectar! Undoubtedly—the finest—rarest! (*He drinks*) Sixty gravity crude: straight gasoline! (*To the* COUNTESS) How found? By blast? Drill?

COUNTESS By finger.

THE PROSPECTOR (*Whipping out a document*) Sign here, please.

COUNTESS What is it?

THE PROSPECTOR Agreement for dividing the profits . . . (*The* COUNTESS *signs*)

SECOND PROSPECTOR (*To* FIRST PROSPECTOR) What is it?

THE PROSPECTOR (*Pocketing the paper*) Application to enter a lunatic asylum. Down there?

COUNTESS Down there. (*The* PROSPECTORS *go down, sniffing*)

(IRMA *enters*)

IRMA The gentlemen of the press are here.

COUNTESS The rest of the machine! Show them in.

IRMA The Public Relations Counselors! (*They enter, all shapes and sizes, all in blue pin-striped suits and black homburg hats*) The Countess is very deaf, gentlemen. You'll have to shout!

FIRST PRESS AGENT You don't say— Delighted to make the acquaintance of so charming and beautiful a lady . . . .

SECOND PRESS AGENT Louder. She can't hear you.

FIRST PRESS AGENT What a face! (*Shouts*) Madame, we are the press. You know our power. We fix all values. We set all standards. Your entire future depends on us.

COUNTESS How do you do?

FIRST PRESS AGENT What will we charge the old trull? The usual thirty?

SECOND PRESS AGENT Forty.

THIRD PRESS AGENT Sixty.

FIRST PRESS AGENT All right—seventy-five. (*He fills in a form and offers it to the* COUNTESS) Sign here, Countess. This contract really gives you a break.

COUNTESS That is the entrance.

FIRST PRESS AGENT Entrance to what?

COUNTESS The oil well.

FIRST PRESS AGENT Oh, we don't need to see that, Madame.

COUNTESS Don't need to see it?

FIRST PRESS AGENT No, no—we don't have to see it to write about it. We can imagine it. An oil well is an oil well. "That's oil we know on earth, and oil we need to know." (*He bows*)

COUNTESS But if you don't see it, how can you be sure the oil is there?

FIRST PRESS AGENT If it's there, well and good. If it's not, by the time we get through, it will be. You underestimate the creative aspect of our profession, Madame. (*The* COUNTESS *shakes her head, handing back the papers*) I warn you, if you insist on rubbing our noses in this oil, it will cost you 10 percent extra.

COUNTESS It's worth it. (*She signs. They cross toward the trapdoor*)

SECOND PRESS AGENT (*Descending*) You see, Madame, we of the press can refuse a lady nothing.

THIRD PRESS AGENT Especially, such a lady. (THIRD PRESS AGENT *starts going down*)

SECOND PRESS AGENT (*Going down. Gallantly*) It's plain to see, Madame, that even fountains of oil have their nymphs. . . . I can use that somewhere. That's copy!

(*The* PRESS AGENTS *go down. As he disappears, the* FIRST PRESS AGENT *steals the gold brick and blows a kiss gallantly to the* COUNTESS, *who blows one back*)

(*There is a high-pitched chatter offstage, and* IRMA *comes in, trying hard to hold back* THREE WOMEN *who pay no attention to her whatever. These* WOMEN *are tall, slender, and as soulless as if they were molded of wax. They march down the steps, erect and abstracted like animated window models, but chattering incessantly*)

IRMA But, ladies, please—you have no business here—you are not expected. (*To the* COUNTESS) There are some strange ladies coming. . . .

COUNTESS Show them in, Irma. (*The* WOMEN *come down, without taking the slightest interest in their surroundings*) Who are you?

FIRST WOMAN Madame, we are the most powerful pressure group in the world.

SECOND WOMAN We are the ultimate dynamic.

THIRD WOMAN The mainspring of all combinations.

FIRST WOMAN Nothing succeeds without our assistance. Is that the well, Madame?

COUNTESS That is the well.

FIRST WOMAN Put out your cigarettes, girls. We don't want any explosions. Not with my brand-new eyelashes.

(*They go down, still chattering. The* COUNTESS *crosses to the wall to close the trap. As she does so, there is a commotion on the landing*)

IRMA Countess . . . (*A* MAN *rushes in breathlessly*)

MAN Just a minute! Just a minute! (*He rushes for the trap door*)

COUNTESS Wait! Who are you?

MAN I'm in a hurry. Excuse me. It's my only chance! (*He rushes down*)

COUNTESS But . . . (*But he is gone. She shrugs her shoulders, and presses the brick. The trap closes. She rings the bell for* IRMA) My gold brick! Why, they've stolen my gold brick! (*She moves toward the trap. It is now closed*) Well, let them take their god with them.

(IRMA *enters and sees with astonishment that the stage is empty of all but the* COUNTESS. *Little by little, the scene is suffused with light, faint at first, but increasing as if the very walls were glowing with the quiet radiance of universal joy. Only around the closed trap a shadow lingers*)

IRMA But what's happened? They've gone! They've vanished!

COUNTESS They've evaporated, Irma. They were wicked. Wickedness evaporates.

(PIERRE *enters. He is followed by the* VAGABONDS, *all of them. The new radiance of the world is now very perceptible. It glows from their faces*)

PIERRE Oh, Countess . . . !

WAITER Countess, everything's changed. Now you can breathe again. Now you can see.

PIERRE The air is pure! The sky is clear!

IRMA Life is beautiful again.

THE RAGPICKER (*Rushes in*) Countess—the pigeons! The pigeons are flying!

FLOWER GIRL They don't have to walk any more.

THE RAGPICKER They're flying. . . . The air is like crystal. And young grass is sprouting on the pavements.

COUNTESS Is it possible?

IRMA (*Interpreting for the* DEAF-MUTE) Now, Juggler, you can throw your fireballs up as high as you please—they won't go out.

SERGEANT On the street, utter strangers are shaking hands, they don't know why, and offering each other almond bars!

COUNTESS Oh, my friends . . .

WAITER Countess, we thank you. . . .

(*They go on talking with happy and animated gestures, but we no longer hear them, for their words blend into a strain of unearthly music which seems to thrill from the uttermost confines of the universe. And out of this music comes a voice*)

FIRST VOICE Countess . . . (*Only the* COUNTESS *hears it. She turns from the group of* VAGABONDS *in wonder*)

SECOND VOICE Countess . . .

THIRD VOICE Countess . . . (*As she looks up in rapture, the* FIRST VOICE *speaks again*)

FIRST VOICE Countess, we thank you. We are the friends of animals.

SECOND VOICE We are the friends of people.

THIRD VOICE We are the friends of friendship.

FIRST VOICE You have freed us!

SECOND VOICE From now on, there will be no hungry cats. . . .

THIRD VOICE And we shall tell the Duchess her dog's right name!

(*The* VOICES *fade off. And now another group of voices is heard*)

FIRST VOICE Countess, we thank you. We are the friends of flowers.

SECOND VOICE From now on, every plant in Paris will be watered. . . .

THIRD VOICE And the sewers will be fragrant with jasmine!

(*These voices, too, are silent. For an instant, the stage is vibrant with music. Then the* DEAF-MUTE *speaks, and his voice is the most beautiful of all*)

DEAF-MUTE Sadness flies on the wings of the morning, and out of the heart of darkness comes the light.

(*Suddenly a group of figures detaches itself from the shadows. These are exactly similar in face and figure and in dress. They are shabby in the fashion of 1900 and their cuffs are badly frayed. Each bears in his hand a ripe melon*)

FIRST ADOLPHE BERTAUT Countess, we thank you. We, too, are freed at last. We are the Adolphe Bertauts of the world.

SECOND ADOLPHE BERTAUT We are no longer timid.

THIRD ADOLPHE BERTAUT We are no longer weak.

FIRST ADOLPHE BERTAUT From this day on, we shall hold fast to what we love. For your sake, henceforth, we shall be handsome, and our cuffs forever immaculate and new. Countess, we bring you this melon and with it our hearts . . . ! (*They all kneel*) Will you do us the honor to be our wife?

COUNTESS (*Sadly*) Too late! Too late! (*She waves them aside. They take up their melons sadly and vanish. The voices of the* VAGABONDS *are heard again, and the music dies*) Too late! Too late!

PIERRE Too late, Countess?

IRMA Too late for what?

COUNTESS I say that it's too late for them. On the twenty-fourth of May, 1881, the most beautiful Easter in the memory of man, it was not too late. And on the fifth of September, 1887, the day they caught the trout and broiled it on the open fire by the brook at Villeneuve, it was not too late. And it was even not too late for them on the twenty-first of August, 1897, the day the Czar visited Paris with his guard. But they did nothing and they said nothing, and now—kiss each other, you two, this very instant!

IRMA You mean . . . ?

PIERRE You mean . . . ?

IRMA But, Countess . . .

COUNTESS It's three hours since you've met and known and loved each other. Kiss each other quickly. (PIERRE *hesitates*) Look at him. He hesitates. He trembles. Happiness frightens him. . . . How like a man! Oh, Irma, kiss him, kiss him! If two people who love each other let a single instant wedge itself between them, it grows—it becomes a month, a year, a century; it becomes too late. Kiss him, Irma, kiss him while there is time, or in a moment his hair will be white and there will be another madwoman in Paris! Oh, make her kiss him, all of you! (*They kiss*) Bravo! Oh, if only you'd had the courage to do that thirty years ago, how different I would be today! Dear Deaf-Mute, be still—your words dazzle our eyes! And Irma is too busy to translate for you. (*They kiss once more*) Well, there we are. The world is saved. And you see how simple it all was? Nothing is ever so wrong in this world that a sensible woman can't set it right in the course of an afternoon. Only, the next time, don't wait until things begin to look black. The minute you notice anything, tell me at once.

THE RAGPICKER We will, Countess. We will.

COUNTESS (*Puts on her hat. Her tone becomes business-like*) Irma. My bones. My gizzard.

IRMA I have them ready, Countess.

COUNTESS Good. (*She puts the bones into her basket and starts for the stairs*) Well, let's get on to more important things. Four o'clock. My poor cats must be starved. What a bore for them if humanity had to be saved every afternoon. They don't think much of it, as it is.

*Curtain*

# Jean Anouilh

# (1910- )

UNLIKE most leading French playwrights of the present day, Jean Anouilh has dedicated himself exclusively to the theatre. This concentration on a single art form is undoubtedly one of the main reasons for his unusual productivity: almost 30 plays by the age of 50. Since the late 1930's, he has written a play virtually every year. A new drama by Anouilh is almost sure to be the leading event of any Paris theatrical season, and performances in London, New York, and other theatrical capitals are likely to follow. This popularity is relatively recent. Prior to the end of the war, Anouilh was virtually unknown to the English-speaking public, and even afterwards, the reception of his plays on Broadway was at best lukewarm. The New York theatre public was disconcerted by his fantasy and distressed by his melancholy view of life; moreover, his plays are rooted deeply in French social relationships. The American success of Anouilh's recent historical plays marks a significant change in attitude and suggests that the time may now be ripe for a reappraisal of his earlier work.

His masters were Molière, Pirandello, Shaw and Giraudoux. His plays, like Molière's, are usually developed around a domestic crisis. The family is the center of dramatic action, and the main conflict often rises from the unwillingness or inability of one character to conform to the values of the others in his group. Pirandello, like Molière, inherited the tradition of *commedia dell' arte* with its free and easy improvisation of comic extravaganza, often turning on disguise and mistaken identity. The lesson of the Italian playwright's assault on the unity of the single personality in *Six Characters in Search of an Author* was not lost on the young French playwright at the beginning of his career. Shaw provided instruction in the art of satire as well as in the modernization of history. The process of unmasking so as to demonstrate the hypocrisy and corruption of the allegedly better classes of people is as essential to Anouilh as it is to Shaw. Giraudoux, through his reassertion of the magic of performance, also made a decisive impact on the young Anouilh, especially through *Siegfried* in 1928. In those days, Anouilh tells us, "I carried dog-eared copies of Shaw and Pirandello in my pockets; and yet, I was all alone." *Siegfried*, which he saw night after night and learned by heart, revealed to the young playwright a vision of what theatre might be.

Anouilh was born in Bordeaux. His father was a tailor, his mother a violinist in an orchestra at a casino where operettas were performed. The recurrent adventures in Anouilh's plays of actors and musicians, wholly bereft of glamour, may owe something to his childhood. At the age of ten he began writing one-act verse plays, imitations of Rostand; when he was 16, he completed his first full-length drama. Anouilh planned to be a lawyer, but lack of funds forced him to leave the university after a year and a half. He went to work for an advertising agency, writing copy in praise of underwear and cars. In 1930 he completed *Mandarine,* entitled after the gigolo hero willing to go to any lengths for the sake of money. The following year Louis Jouvet employed him as secretary to his company. Soon afterwards Anouilh married, and the penniless couple furnished their apartment with the sets from *Siegfried.* When the play was revived, the sets were taken away. Anouilh's early plays provide grim evidence of the poverty he suffered in the early years of his career. A lucky sale of film rights to a play that failed on the stage in 1935 marked the turning point in his fortune. Subsequently, plays that had been refused by all of the leading producers of Paris were presented with striking success.

In collecting his plays for publication, Anouilh has divided them under four headings: "Black," "Rose," "Brilliant," and "Grating." These adjectives are at best approximations of the prevailing mood; generally, a variety of tones and attitudes are set forth in a single play. The so-called "Black Plays" explore the failure of the individual to escape from his past. The first of these, *The Ermine* (*L'hermine,* 1931), demonstrates the corrupting effect of money on a poor young man in love with a rich heiress. His murder of her wealthy aunt, who opposes their marriage, is utterly futile, as is his obsession with money as a means of overcoming social distance. A similar situation is presented in his next play, *Jézabel* (1932), wherein a young man is hopelessly in love with a rich girl. In Anouilh's early plays squalor and poverty condemn their victims to a life of sordidness from which there is no escape. Perhaps the best, certainly the most complex, of the "Black Plays" is *La sauvage* (*Restless Heart,* 1934), again reflecting the young playwright's sharp sense of class lines. The world of the very rich is seen through the eyes of the very poor. The two lovers have no common ground; money is an impenetrable barrier. Thérèse, the poor girl who cannot adjust to the milieu of the rich, refuses the happiness that marriage with Florent seems to offer. Thérèse is unusual among Anouilh's heroines in her growth in self-understanding; her passion for integrity at the expense of a life of ease and comfort reveals an inner depth that raises her above the mere representatives of social classes. The last of the "Black Plays," *Le voyageur sans bagage* (*Traveller without Luggage,* 1936), was Anouilh's first considerable success. The hero, Gaston, has spent 18 years in an asylum as an amnesia victim; he discovers the viciousness of his earlier life and the depravity of his milieu. As a result, he rejects the rightful claims of his relatives and creates a new self which will presumably lead a new life. The emphasis, however, is on the darkness of the past, evaded by the hero only through disguise and fraud.

The role of masquerade as a higher form of reality, a means of overcoming the sordidness of the world, links the "Rose Plays" to the "Black." In 1936, Anouilh declared: "I discovered that a subject did not necessarily have to be treated in a rigid form, in the natural simplicity or even crudity it has at first. I realized that the dramatist could and should *play with* his characters, with their passions and their actions. . . . To 'play' with a subject is to create a new world of conventions and surround it with spells and a magic all your own. . . ." This theatricalism takes the form of a bold reliance on mask and costume as means of disguise, on speed, improvisation, and surprise. Anouilh's characters become conscious of the roles they are playing, and move freely in and out of their parts for purposes of ironic commentary or comic entertainment.

This interplay of the real and the make-believe is exploited for hilarious and farcical merriment in *Thieves' Carnival* (*Le Bal des Voleurs*). Written in 1932 but not produced until six years later, it marks the triumph in Anouilh's art of the utterly improbable. The comedy turns on an inversion of roles: the thieves become the dupes, easily and willingly taken in by Lady Hurf who sees the masquerade as a game which might relieve the boredom of her existence. The "Rose" and the "Black" draw close together in her sense of loneliness and melancholy; she knows that the game cannot last, but she is "as bored as a piece of old carpet" and the mad prank of entertaining and hoodwinking the rogues promises relief. For Lady Hurf, the thieves are marionettes, to perform for her amusement, but for Gustave and Juliette the fantasy becomes a serious involvement. Once again, Anouilh contrasts the poor boy and rich girl, deeply in love with one another but separated by money. Gustave is not duped by Edgard's desire to save the situation, but Juliette will find it easy to accept the lie in order to make their love realizable. Light and carefree, Anouilh's romantic fantasy is a tribute to his mastery of comic style.

The escape from emptiness and frustration through make-believe takes on a more serious tone in *Léocadia* (*Time Remembered,* 1939). The wealthy prince, Albert, cannot escape the image of the past, but this image is a gross distortion of his true relationship with the dead Léocadia. His aunt hires a milliner, Amanda, to play the role of the beloved, but she rebels against the falsity of her position and the stupidity of Albert's dream. None of Anouilh's plays more clearly points up his closeness to Pirandello in the interaction of pretense and reality and in the contrast between the actual and the imagined selves. The charm and innocence of Amanda represent happiness in the here and now; her victory is a deserved triumph over a vain mirage of an unreal, valueless past.

During the war Anouilh, like many of his contemporaries, wrote a number of plays recreating myths and legends of classical antiquity. His subsequent dramas, whether "Brilliant" or "Grating," reflect the playwright's harsher and more bitter attitude toward society. The process of unmasking is unrelieved by the tender warmth of the earlier plays. The bored dowagers, jealous husbands, naïve working girls, and depraved parents all mirror a sordid and unheroic society in which the individual's quest for integrity and meaning is defeated by the claims of painful reality. Over and over, Anouilh's heroines seem to tell us, "Love isn't what you think it is." Neither is money. In *L'Invitation au château* (*Ring Round the Moon,* 1947), Anouilh displays the fickleness of love and the meaninglessness of riches. The penniless dancer, Isabelle, and the millionaire, Messerschmann, tear up huge bundles of bank notes and fling the pieces in the faces of the audience. As he destroys the last bill, he turns to Isabelle and asks: "Are you happy now?" She replies, "No. Are you?" And he answers sadly, "Not at all." The happy ending cannot displace the dominant mood of futility and frustration.

The later plays are darker yet. *Ardèle* (1948), culminating in the double suicide of the hunchbacked lovers, strikes out savagely at the viciousness of "respectable" society. *Colombe* (1950) proves that no reconciliation is possible between a fanatically rigorous morality and one of easy accommodation. In *La valse des toréadors* (*The Waltz of the Toreadors,* 1951), marriage is reduced to mutual suffering and torture, relieved only by occasional and meaningless sexual adventures. *Ornifle* (1955) is a study in the extremes of meanness and corruption, while *Pauvre Bitos* (*Poor Bitos,* 1956) and *L'hurluberlu* (*The Fighting Cock,* 1958) unmask the merciless cruelty of absolute principle.

Only in his recent historical plays does Anouilh seem to move beyond this darkness. His drama of the life and death of Joan of Arc, *L'alouette* (*The Lark,* 1953), demonstrates the power of the individual to triumph over absolutism and compromise. In her rejection of a life of "happiness," Joan recalls Thérèse or Antigone, insisting on all or nothing. In *Becket* (1959), the same conflict of principle and expediency is resolved through the hero's death. After Becket's discovery of the honor of God, all other values become meaningless. He spurns the easy accommodation offered by King Henry and, like Antigone, pursues his destiny to its necessary end.

The inventiveness and charm of Anouilh's plays have assured their success in the theatre. Few writers have managed so well to please a variety of audiences and to reconcile the demands of art and commerce. Anouilh is a master of his craft. A poet of the theatre, he has invested the modern stage with fantasy, humor, and imaginative vitality. He has helped to shape and define contemporary drama through the originality of his art and, above all, through the magic of his style.

# THIEVES' CARNIVAL

## *A Play in Four Acts*

English version by Lucienne Hill

### CHARACTERS

PETERBONO, HECTOR, GUSTAVE — *Thieves*
LORD EDGARD
LADY HURF
EVA, JULIETTE — *Her nieces*
DUPONT-DUFORT SENIOR
DUPONT-DUFORT JUNIOR
TOWN CRIER
POLICEMEN
NURSEMAID
A CHILD
MUSICIAN

## Act One

*The public gardens of a watering-place which saw its heyday in the 1880's. In the middle, a bandstand. The orchestra is represented by a single musician, who at the rise of the curtain is executing a solo of superlative virtuosity on the clarinet. A woman deckchair attendant goes to and fro. The summer visitors stroll up and down to the rhythm of the music. In the foreground* EVA *and* HECTOR *are locked in a dramatic screen embrace. The music stops. So does the kiss, from which* HECTOR *emerges, reeling a little. Applause for the musician.*

HECTOR (*Covered in confusion*) I say, steady. They're applauding us!

EVA (*Bursts out laughing*) Of course not, it's the orchestra. I must say you appeal to me enormously.

HECTOR (*Instinctively fingering his hair and moustache*) What do you like about me, specially?

EVA Everything.

(*She blows him a kiss*)

We mustn't stay here, it's too risky. I'll see you tonight at eight in the Phoenix bar. And if you should meet me with my aunt, whatever you do, pretend you don't know me.

HECTOR (*Yearningly*) Your little hand, once more.

EVA Careful. My aunt's old friend Lord Edgard is over there by the bandstand reading his paper. He'll see us.

(*She holds out her hand, but turns away to watch* LORD EDGARD)

HECTOR (*Passionately*) I want to inhale the perfume of your hand!

(*He bends over her hand, and surreptitiously draws a jeweler's eyeglass from his pocket to take a closer look at* EVA'S *rings.* EVA *withdraws her hand, unaware of the manœuvre*)

EVA Till tonight.

(*She goes*)

HECTOR (*Weak at the knees*) My beloved . . .

(*He follows her out of sight, then comes downstage again, putting away his eyeglass, and mutters with icy self-possession*)

A good two hundred thousand. And not a flaw in the lot.

(*At this point the* TOWN CRIER *enters with his drum and the crowd gather round to listen*)

TOWN CRIER Townsmen of Vichy! The Municipality, anxious to preserve the well-being and security of the invalids and bathers, issues a warning for their information and protection! Numerous complaints from visitors have been lodged at the Town Hall and at the main police station, Market Street. A dangerous pack of picklepockets—

(*He has a little trouble with this word, at which the clarinet plays a little accompaniment. The* TOWN CRIER *swings round on him, furious*)

—a dangerous pack of pockpickets—

(*Again the clarinet renders the word in music*)

—is at this very hour within our gates. The local police is on the watch. Members of the Force, in plain clothes and in uniform, are ready to protect our visitors. . . .

(*Indeed, even as he speaks policemen are threading their several ways gracefully through the crowd*)

Visitors are nevertheless requested to exercise the greatest possible caution, particularly on the public highway, in public parks and in all other places of public resort. A reward in kind is offered by the Tourist Association to anyone supplying information leading to the apprehension of the felons! Tell your friends!

(*A roll of drums. During the proclamation* HECTOR *has relieved the* TOWN CRIER *of his enormous copper watch and bulging purse. The crowd scatters, and the drum and the harangue are heard again further off.* HECTOR *takes a seat, and the chair attendant approaches*)

CHAIR ATTENDANT Will you take a ticket, sir, please?

HECTOR (*Largely*) Since it's customary . . .

CHAIR ATTENDANT That'll be five francs, please.

(*While* HECTOR *feels for the money, the attendant steals his wallet, then the huge watch and the purse he has just taken from the* TOWN CRIER)

HECTOR (*Seizing the hand on its next trip into his pocket*) Hey! What do you think you're up to?

(*The attendant struggles to free herself, and loses her wig*)

Have you gone crazy?

(*He lifts his own wig and mustache a trifle*)

It's me!

(*The chair attendant readjusts her wig. It is* PETERBONO)

PETERBONO Sorry, old chap. It's me too. Had a good day?

HECTOR The purse and a watch, and a cigarette lighter.

PETERBONO (*Examining them*) I know that watch. It's the Town Crier's and it's made of copper. I put it back into his pocket, the poor devil, that and the purse, which you'll find if you check up contains just fifteen cents and the receipt for a registered parcel. As for the lighter, we've already got nine hundred and three, out of which only a couple work. I've known you do better, my lad!

HECTOR I've a date tonight with a girl who'll be mine before you can say mischief, and who wears over two hundred thousand francs' worth of diamonds on her middle finger.

PETERBONO We'll look into it. Have you noticed that little thing over there? The necklace?

HECTOR (*Examining the girl through the fieldglasses he wears round his neck*) Phew! The stones are enormous!

PETERBONO No wishful thinking. They're smaller to the naked eye. Still, off we go. Small change manœuvre. I get offensive and you interfere.

(*They cross to the girl with a terrible affectation of indifference*)

Ticket? Ticket?

(*The girl gives him a coin;* PETERBONO *begins to yell*)

I've got no change! I tell you I've got no change! No change, do you hear? No change at all, I keep on telling you!

HECTOR What's this? No change, eh? Excuse me, Mademoiselle, allow me to put this insolent baggage in her place!

(*There follows a tussle under cover of which* HECTOR *investigates the clasp of the girl's necklace*)

THE GIRL (*Violently freeing herself*) No, you don't!

HECTOR (*Taken aback*) What do you mean, no you don't!

PETERBONO No you don't what?

THE GIRL (*Lifting her wig. It is* GUSTAVE) It's me.

HECTOR (*Falling into a chair*) Charming!

PETERBONO (*Exploding*) That's what comes of not working to plan! I can't rely on anybody! Running errands, that's all you're fit for! Errand boys! If it weren't for your poor old mother who put you in my charge to learn the business, you'd be out on your ear, the pair of you. Do you hear me? Out on your ear! And without your week's pay in lieu of notice, make no mistake! And complain to the union if you dare! I'll tell them a thing or two, the dance you've led me, both of you!

(*To* GUSTAVE)

You! You haven't done a stroke today, naturally!

GUSTAVE Yes I have. I've done two. First, there's this magnificent wallet.

PETERBONO Let's have a look.

(*He examines it, then searches himself anxiously*)

Where did you get this? Who from?

GUSTAVE I got it in the Boulevard Ravachol off an old gentleman with a long white beard. . . .

PETERBONO (*Terrible in his anger*) —check trousers, olive-green jacket, and deer-stalker cap, am I right, pigeon-brain?

GUSTAVE (*Quaking*) Yes, sir. Did you see me?

PETERBONO (*Sinks into a chair, flattened by this latest blow*) That was me, idiot, that was me! At this rate we'll be lucky if we cover our expenses!

GUSTAVE But I've got something else, Mr. Peterbono, sir.

PETERBONO (*Profoundly discouraged*) If it's something else you stole from me you can imagine my curiosity.

GUSTAVE It isn't a thing, it's a girl. And she looks rich.

HECTOR (*Jumping up*) Good God! Don't say it's the same girl. A redhead? About twenty-five? Name of Eva?

GUSTAVE No. Dark hair, about twenty. Name of Juliette.

HECTOR Oh, that's all right.

PETERBONO What did you get?

GUSTAVE Nothing yet. But I helped her fish a kid out of the Thermes Fountain. We sat in the sun to dry and we got talking. She told me she liked me.

PETERBONO Any jewels?

GUSTAVE One very fine pearl.

PETERBONO Good. We must look into that. Hector, can you spare a moment this afternoon, other engagements permitting?

GUSTAVE No! I'd like to handle this myself.

PETERBONO What's this? What's this? Handle it yourself, would you? Well, whatever next?

GUSTAVE It was me she took a fancy to.

PETERBONO All the more reason. Hector will swallow her in one.

GUSTAVE No, I tell you! Not this one!

PETERBONO (*Severely*) Gustave, listen to me. Your mother put you in my care, and I took you into the firm as assistant decoy. You're young and you're ambitious. That's fine. I was ambitious myself when I was your age. But just a minute! In our profession, as in all professions, you have to work your way up from the bottom. Hector here is the finest professional seducer I know this side of Monte Carlo. There's a chap who hits the bull's eye three times out of four, and take it from me, that's a pretty handsome average. You don't mean to tell me that you, a mere apprentice, expect to turn out better work than that?

GUSTAVE To hell with it! I'll get her for myself.

PETERBONO (*Tight-lipped*) If you wish to do a job on the side in your spare time there's nothing to stop you. You'll owe me just the sixty-five per cent on what you make, that's all.

HECTOR (*Who has been watching a nursemaid during this altercation*) Peter?

PETERBONO Hector?

HECTOR That nursemaid over there. See the gold chain?

PETERBONO (*Contemptuously*) Pooh! It's probably gilded fuse wire.

HECTOR Listen, it's ten to seven. We've ten minutes in hand before supper.

PETERBONO Very well, if you're set on it. We'll give her the "Three Musketeers" Manœuvre.

HECTOR Three Musketeers Manœuvre?

PETERBONO It's the classic routine for nursemaids. Number one gets off with her, number two plays ten little pigs with the baby, and number three starts whistling bugle-calls without a break to make her senses reel.

(*They go. Enter* LADY HURF *and* JULIETTE)

JULIETTE The little boy was barely five years old. He was only in up to his waist, but he was frightened and he kept falling over. He would have drowned, I'm sure.

LADY HURF How dreadful! Have you noticed all these little chimney-pot hats everywhere? How absurd they look!

JULIETTE Fortunately this young man came to the rescue. He was wonderful, and very sweet.

LADY HURF All children are sweet at five. But at twelve they begin to get silly. That's why I never wanted any.

JULIETTE I was talking about the young man, Aunt.

LADY HURF Oh yes, of course. There's another of those grotesque little hats. The young man was very sweet —yes, go on.

JULIETTE That's all.

LADY HURF We must invite him to dinner.

JULIETTE He's gone. I'd never seen him before.

LADY HURF Good. One always knows far too many people. Besides, I can't stand stories about drowning. Your poor uncle swam like a lump of lead. He drowned himself seven times, I could have hit him. Ah, there's Edgard. Edgard, have you seen Eva?

LORD EDGARD (*Appearing from behind his paper*) How are you, my dear?

LADY HURF I asked if you'd seen Eva.

LORD EDGARD Eva? No, I haven't. That's very odd. Now what can I have done with her? Perhaps she's at the Baths.

LADY HURF At seven o'clock at night? Don't be silly.

JULIETTE Shall we try the Phoenix bar? She often goes there.

LADY HURF Edgard, don't stir from this spot for any reason whatsoever.

LORD EDGARD Very good, my dear.

LADY HURF (*Going*) But of course if you see her, run after her.

LORD EDGARD Very good, my dear.

LADY HURF Or better still, don't; you'd only lose her —just come and tell us which way she went.

LORD EDGARD Very good, my dear.

LADY HURF On second thoughts, no. You'd never manage to find us. Send one attendant after her, another attendant to let us know, and put a third in your place to tell us where you've gone so we can pick you up on the way home if we should happen to be passing.

LORD EDGARD Very good, my dear.

(*He retires stunned behind his paper. Exit* LADY HURF *with* JULIETTE. *Enter the* DUPONT-DUFORTS, *father and son, accompanied by the little jig on the clarinet, which is their signature tune*)

DUPONT-DUFORT SENIOR Let's follow. We'll meet them casually on the promenade, and try to tempt them to a cocktail. Didier, I don't know what's come over you. You, a hard-working, conscientious lad, brimful of initiative, and look at you. You're not paying an atom of attention to young Juliette.

DUPONT-DUFORT JUNIOR She snubs me.

DUPONT-DUFORT SENIOR What does that matter? To begin with, you aren't just anybody. You are Dupont-Dufort junior. Her aunt thinks a great deal of you. She's prepared to make any investment on your recommendation.

DUPONT-DUFORT JUNIOR That ought to be enough for us.

DUPONT-DUFORT SENIOR Son, in matters of money there's no such thing as enough. I'd far and away prefer you to pull off this marriage. Nothing short of that will put our bank fairly and squarely on its feet again. So let me see a bit of charm, a little fascination.

DUPONT-DUFORT JUNIOR Yes, Dad.

DUPONT-DUFORT SENIOR We couldn't wish for more propitious circumstances. They're bored to tears, and there's nobody here in the least presentable. So let's make ourselves agreeable, superlatively agreeable.

DUPONT-DUFORT JUNIOR Yes, Dad.

(*Exeunt the* DUPONT-DUFORTS. LORD EDGARD, *who has heard every word, looks over his* Times *to watch them go.* PETERBONO, HECTOR, *and* GUSTAVE *come in dressed as soldiers as the* MUSICIAN *begins his second number. The* POLICEMEN *enter at the same time from the other side. They all perform a flirtatious little ballet round the* NURSEMAID, *the manœuvres of the* POLICEMEN *seriously impeding those of the three thieves. The* NURSEMAID *finally goes; the* POLICEMEN, *twirling their white batons behind their backs, make gallant attempts to hinder her departure. During the ballet* LADY HURF *returns alone and goes to sit beside* LORD EDGARD. *The music stops at the exit of the* POLICEMEN *and the* NURSEMAID)

PETERBONO (*Thwarted*) Lads, that's the first time I've ever known the Three Musketeers Manœuvre to miscarry.

LADY HURF (*To* LORD EDGARD) Well, Edgard my dear, and what have you done with yourself today?

LORD EDGARD (*Surprised and embarrassed as always at* LADY HURF'S *customary abruptness*) I—er—I read *The Times*.

LADY HURF (*Sternly*) The same as yesterday?

LORD EDGARD (*Ingenuously*) Not the same copy as yesterday.

HECTOR (*Who has been watching the scene, gives a whistle of admiration*) See those pearls?

PETERBONO Four millions!

HECTOR How about it? What's it to be? Russian princes?

PETERBONO No. She knows her onions by the look of her. Ruined Spanish noblemen.

GUSTAVE That's bright of you. Whenever you masquerade as Spaniards you're rigged out like a couple of rats.

PETERBONO Quiet, shaver! You're speaking of a trade you know nothing about.

GUSTAVE Well, anyway, if you think I'm dressing up as your ecclesiastical secretary like the last time, it's no go. I'm not wearing a cassock in this heat.

PETERBONO Gustave, you're trying my patience! Come along, home! Hector and I will be Spanish Grandees, and you'll put on that cassock, heat or no heat.

(*The unwilling* GUSTAVE *is borne away, to the accompaniment of a little jig on the clarinet*)

LADY HURF (*Who has been deep in thought*) Edgard, the situation is grave. . . .

LORD EDGARD I know. According to *The Times*, the Empire . . .

LADY HURF No, no, here.

LORD EDGARD (*Looking round him anxiously*) Here?

LADY HURF Listen to me. We have two tender creatures in our care. Intrigues are fermenting—marriages are brewing. Personally I can't keep track of them—it gives me the vertigo. Who is to uncover them, Edgard, who is to supervise them?

LORD EDGARD Who?

LADY HURF Juliette is a scatterbrain. Eva is a scatterbrain. As for me, I haven't a notion what's going on and the mere idea of it bores me to extinction. Besides, I've no more common sense than those two senseless girls. That leaves you in the midst of these three scatterbrains.

LORD EDGARD That leaves me.

LADY HURF Which is another way of saying nobody. I am perplexed, excessively perplexed. Anything may happen in this watering-place. Intrigues spring up under one's very feet like so much jungle vegetation. Should we do better to leave Vichy, I wonder? Ought we perhaps to bury ourselves in some rustic backwater? Edgard, for heaven's sake say something! You are the guardian of these two young things, aren't you?

LORD EDGARD We might ask Dupont-Dufort his advice. He seems to be a man of character.

LADY HURF A deal too much character. What a ninny you are. He's the last man from whom we want advice. The Dupont-Duforts are after our money.

LORD EDGARD But they're rich.

LADY HURF Exactly. That's what worries me. They're after a lot of money. An investment or a marriage settlement. Our two little ones with their millions are exceptionally tempting morsels.

LORD EDGARD Could we not telegraph to England?

LADY HURF What for?

LORD EDGARD Scotland Yard might send us a detective.

LADY HURF That would be a great help, I must say! They're crooked as corkscrews, the lot of them!

LORD EDGARD The problem, then, is in effect insoluble.

LADY HURF Edgard, you simply must bestir yourself. Our fate, the girls' and mine, is in your hands.

LORD EDGARD (*Looks at his hands, very worried*) I don't know that I am very well equipped.

LADY HURF (*Sternly*) Edgard, do you call yourself a man? And a gentleman?

LORD EDGARD Yes.

LADY HURF Then make a decision!

LORD EDGARD (*Firmly*) Very well! I shall nevertheless summon a detective from Scotland Yard, with a special proviso that I want him honest.

LADY HURF Over my dead body! If he's honest, he'll philander with the kitchen-maids and he won't wash. It will be insufferable. And yet I don't know why I should be telling you all this. What do I want with absolute security? I'm as bored as a piece of old carpet!

LORD EDGARD Oh, my dear . . . !

LADY HURF That's all I am, a piece of old carpet.

LORD EDGARD You, who were once so beautiful.

LADY HURF Yes, in the nineteen-hundreds. Oh, I could scream with rage! I want to enjoy my last few years—I want to laugh a little. Sixty years I've spent deluded into thinking life a serious business. That's sixty years too long. I am in the mood, Edgard, for a gigantic piece of folly.

LORD EDGARD Nothing dangerous, I hope?

LADY HURF I don't know. I'll see what occurs to me.

(*She leans toward him*)

I think I should like to massacre the Dupont-Duforts.

(*In they come, accompanied by their particular little tune, with* EVA *and* JULIETTE)

DUPONT-DUFORT SENIOR How are you today, milady?

DUPONT-DUFORT JUNIOR Milady.

DUPONT-DUFORT SENIOR Ah, dear Lord Edgard.

LORD EDGARD (*Drawing him aside*) Take the greatest possible care.

DUPONT-DUFORT SENIOR But why, milord?

LORD EDGARD Hush! I can't tell you. But take care. Leave Vichy.

DUPONT-DUFORT JUNIOR We ran into these ladies on the promenade.

EVA Vichy's an impossible place. Nothing to do, nowhere to go, and all the men are hideous.

DUPONT-DUFORT JUNIOR Oh, how true! Quite, quite hideous, all of them!

DUPONT-DUFORT SENIOR All of them!

(*Aside to his son*)

Excellent thing for us.

EVA I have an engagement tonight, Aunt. I shall be late for dinner—if I'm back at all.

DUPONT-DUFORT SENIOR (*Aside to his son*) With you?

DUPONT-DUFORT JUNIOR No.

JULIETTE Eva, I haven't told you. I rescued a little boy who fell into the Thermes Fountain, and I met an enchanting young man, who helped me to save him.

LADY HURF Juliette talks of nothing else.

(*The* DUPONT-DUFORTS *look at each other anxiously*)

DUPONT-DUFORT SENIOR Wasn't that you?

DUPONT-DUFORT JUNIOR No.

JULIETTE We sat in the sun till we were dry, and chatted. You've no idea how pleasant he was! He's slight, with dark hair and—he's not the same as yours by any chance?

EVA No. Mine's tall, with red hair.

JULIETTE Thank goodness!

DUPONT-DUFORT SENIOR (*Whispers*) Sonny, you have absolutely *got* to sparkle.

(*Raising his voice*)

Didier, dear boy, have you been to the swimming-pool with these ladies yet? You must give them a demonstration of your impeccable crawl. You could have rescued the toddler with the greatest of ease.

JULIETTE Oh, the crawl would have been quite useless. The Thermes Fountain is only eighteen inches deep.

(*Toward the end of this scene,* PETERBONO, *as a very noble—all too noble—old Spanish gentleman,* HECTOR *as a Grandee, an equally spectacular achievement, and* GUSTAVE, *their ecclesiastical secretary, come in and slowly approach the others*)

PETERBONO Careful. This is big game. Stay close, and take no risks.

HECTOR Your monocle.

PETERBONO The big act, "Noblesse oblige." Wait for the word go. Gustave, two paces behind.

(*The clarinet strikes up a march, heroic and ultra-Spanish. Suddenly,* LADY HURF, *who has been watching this curious trio, runs to them and throws her arms round* PETERBONO'S *neck*)

LADY HURF Why, if it isn't that dear dear Duke of Miraflores!

(*Music stops*)

PETERBONO (*Surprised and uneasy*) Uh?

LADY HURF Don't say you've forgotten! Biarritz 1902. The luncheon parties at Pampeluna! The bull-fights! Lady Hurf.

PETERBONO Ah . . . ! Lady Hurf. Bull-fights. Lunch. Dear friend.

(*To the other two*)

I must have made up like one of her acquaintances.

LADY HURF I am so, so happy! I was disintegrating with boredom. But where is the Duchess?

PETERBONO Dead.

(*Tremolo from the orchestra*)

LADY HURF Oh, heavens! And your cousin the Count?

PETERBONO Dead.

(*Tremolo from the orchestra*)

LADY HURF Oh, heavens! And your friend, the Admiral?

PETERBONO Also dead.

(*The orchestra begins a funeral march.* PETERBONO *turns to his friends*)

Saved!

LADY HURF My poor friend. So many funerals.

PETERBONO Alas! However, may I present my son, Don Hector? And my ecclesiastical secretary, Dom Petrus?

LADY HURF Lord Edgard, whom you knew years ago. It was he whom you beat each morning at golf, and who was always losing his golf balls.

PETERBONO Ha, golf—yes. Dear friend.

LORD EDGARD (*Panic-stricken, to* LADY HURF) But, my dear—

LADY HURF (*Sternly*) What's the matter? Do you mean to say you don't remember the Duke?

LORD EDGARD This is insane. Come now, think back—

LADY HURF Your memory is abominable. Don't say another word or I shall lose my temper. My nieces, Eva and Juliette, who worry me so dreadfully because they're both very marriageable, and their dowries are exceptionally tempting to fortune-hunters.

(*The* DUPONT-DUFORTS *look at each other*)

DUPONT-DUFORT SENIOR Dignity, lad, dignity.

DUPONT-DUFORT JUNIOR She can't mean us.

(PETERBONO *and* HECTOR *indulge in violent nudging*)

LADY HURF I am so delighted to have met you again. Vichy is such a dull hole. Tell me, do you remember the Ridottos on the Riviera?

PETERBONO I should think I do!

DUPONT-DUFORT JUNIOR (*To his father*) We're forgotten.

DUPONT-DUFORT SENIOR Let's introduce ourselves. Dupont-Dufort, senior.

DUPONT-DUFORT JUNIOR Junior.

(*During the introductions,* EVA *stares hard at* HECTOR, *who simulates an enormous interest in the conversation.* GUSTAVE *has all but disappeared into his brief case, and rummages feverishly among his papers to avoid* JULIETTE'S *gaze, which is fixed on him in puzzled interest*)

LADY HURF You must be as bored as I am. It's an undreamed of stroke of fortune, our meeting, don't you think?

PETERBONO (*Nudging* HECTOR) Undreamed of.

HECTOR (*Nudging* PETERBONO) Yes. Undreamed of—absolutely undreamed of.

(*In their glee, they go much too far, but no one seems to notice*)

LADY HURF Your son is most charming. Don't you think so, Eva?

EVA Yes.

PETERBONO He was the most dashing officer in the entire Spanish army—before the revolution.

LADY HURF Alas! You suffered a great deal?

PETERBONO A great deal.

LADY HURF Where are you staying? Not at a hotel?

PETERBONO (*Vaguely*) Yes.

LADY HURF It's out of the question, Edgard! The Duke is staying at a hotel!

LORD EDGARD But, my dearest, I assure you—

LADY HURF Be quiet! Dear Duke, you cannot, you simply cannot stay at a hotel. Will you do us the honor of accepting our humble hospitality? Our villa is enormous, and we shall put the west wing entirely at your disposal.

PETERBONO Certainly, certainly, certainly, certainly—

(*Stupendous nudging between* PETERBONO *and* HECTOR. *The* DUPONT-DUFORTS *exchange crestfallen glances*)

LADY HURF You may, needless to say, bring your entourage.

(*She looks enquiringly at* GUSTAVE)

Is he looking for something?

PETERBONO A document, yes. Dom Petrus!

GUSTAVE (*Emerging from the brief case*) Your Grace?

(*He has put on some dark glasses*)

LADY HURF Has he got bad eyes?

PETERBONO Oh, very bad. His condition requires a certain amount of care. I couldn't burden you with his presence. Dom Petrus, we shall accept Lady Hurf's generous offer of hospitality. Call at the hotel, will you, and have our luggage sent on. And stay there until further notice. You will collect the mail and come to us each morning for instructions.

GUSTAVE (*Furious*) But, your Grace . . .

PETERBONO Enough!

GUSTAVE Your Grace—

PETERBONO Off with you!

(HECTOR *gives* GUSTAVE *a push, and he wanders reluctantly away*)

LADY HURF (*Moved*) Just as he used to be! That same commanding tone—the vocal magic of the Miraflores! Your cousin had it too.

PETERBONO Alas!

LADY HURF How did he die?

PETERBONO Er, how he died?

LADY HURF Yes—I was so fond of him.

PETERBONO You want me to relate the circumstances of his passing?

LADY HURF Yes.

PETERBONO (*Turns to* HECTOR *in his panic*) Well, he died . . .

(HECTOR *mimes a motor accident, but this* PETERBONO *cannot grasp*)

PETERBONO He died insane.

LADY HURF Ah, poor fellow! He always was eccentric. But your wife, the dear Duchess?

PETERBONO Dead.

LADY HURF Yes, I know. But how?

(HECTOR *touches his heart several times.* PETERBONO *is slow to take the suggestion, but as he has no imagination whatever himself, he gives way*)

PETERBONO Of love.

LADY HURF (*In confusion*) Oh, I beg your pardon! And your friend the Admiral?

PETERBONO Ah, now the Admiral . . .

(*He looks at* HECTOR, *who indicates that he has run out of ideas. He again misinterprets the pantomime*)

Drowned. But please excuse me, you are re-opening wounds which time has not yet healed.

LADY HURF Oh, forgive me, dear friend, forgive me!

(*To the others*)

What breeding! What grandeur in adversity! Don't you think so, Edgard?

LORD EDGARD My dear, I still insist that—

LADY HURF Do stop insisting. Can't you see the Duke is suffering?

DUPONT-DUFORT SENIOR (*To his son*) Let us join in the conversation.

DUPONT-DUFORT JUNIOR What an appalling avalanche of misfortunes!

DUPONT-DUFORT SENIOR Falling on such venerable heads!

(*No one listens*)

LADY HURF (*In a peal of laughter*) How beautiful Biarritz was in those days. Do you remember the balls?

PETERBONO Ah, the balls . . .

LADY HURF And Lina Veri?

PETERBONO Lina Veri. I can't quite recall . . .

LADY HURF Come, come. Why, you were intimate! (*To the others*) He's aged so much.

PETERBONO Oh, Lina Veri. Of course. The darling of Italian society.

LADY HURF No, no, no. She was a dancer.

PETERBONO Oh yes, but her mother was the darling of Italian society.

LADY HURF (*To the others*) He's wandering a little. He's very tired. My dear Duke, I would like to show you your apartments right away. The villa is close by, at the end of the avenue.

PETERBONO With pleasure.

(GUSTAVE *comes running in, this time as his own charming self, but magnificently dressed*)

GUSTAVE Good morning, Father!

PETERBONO (*Off his balance*) Little basket! Allow me to present my second son, Don Pedro, whom I'd forgotten to mention.

LADY HURF Gracious, you have another son? By whom?

PETERBONO (*Panicking again*) Ah, that's a long story—

(*He looks at* HECTOR, *who signs to him to go carefully*)

But that one also opens wounds as yet unhealed by time.

LADY HURF Come along, Edgard.

LORD EDGARD But, my dear—

LADY HURF And keep quiet!

(*They go,* HECTOR *paying elaborate attentions to* EVA, *who has continued to stare at him*)

JULIETTE (*To* GUSTAVE) Now will you kindly tell me what is going on?

GUSTAVE Ssh! I'll explain later.

(*They go too. The* DUPONT-DUFORTS *are left alone*)

DUPONT-DUFORT JUNIOR Father, they've forgotten us—!

DUPONT-DUFORT SENIOR All the same, we'll follow. And, Didier, twice the affability. Let's hope these young men are already attached or better still that they aren't interested in women!

(*They go*)

# Act Two

*A drawing-room in* LADY HURF'S *house. It is evening, after dinner, and* JULIETTE *and* GUSTAVE *are sitting side by side; a little romantic air is heard in the distance.*

JULIETTE It's nice here. No one is disturbing us tonight.

GUSTAVE Yes, it is nice.

JULIETTE For three days now you've been sad. Are you homesick for Spain?

GUSTAVE Oh no.

JULIETTE I'm sorry now I wouldn't work at my Spanish at school. We might have spoken it together. It would have been fun.

GUSTAVE I only speak a few words myself.

JULIETTE Do you? That's funny.

GUSTAVE Yes, it is rather.

(*A silence*)

JULIETTE It must be amusing to be a prince.

GUSTAVE Oh, one gets used to it, you know.

(*A silence*)

JULIETTE Don Pedro, what's the matter? We were much friendlier three days ago.

GUSTAVE Nothing's the matter.

(*A pause.* LORD EDGARD *crosses the room laden with papers*)

LORD EDGARD (*Muttering*) Though I should die in the endeavor, I'll set my mind at rest.

(*He drops his papers. They jump up to help him but he bars their path*)

Don't touch them! Don't touch them!

(*He picks up the papers himself and goes out muttering*)

This momentous discovery, if discovery there be, must be surrounded with the greatest possible precautions.

GUSTAVE What is he looking for? He's done nothing but ferret about among those old papers since we came here.

JULIETTE I don't know. He's a little mad. Only he's painstaking as well, you see, so sometimes the results are quite prodigious.

(*A little girl comes in*)

Oh, here's my little friend.

CHILD Mademoiselle Juliette, I've picked some daisies for you.

JULIETTE Thank you, darling.

CHILD They haven't very many petals. Daddy says they aren't the ones that lovers use.

JULIETTE Never mind.

CHILD Shall I get some others?

JULIETTE No. Yes. You're very sweet.

(*She kisses her*)

Run away now.

(*The* CHILD *goes.* JULIETTE *turns to* GUSTAVE, *shamefaced*)

JULIETTE Do you think it's silly of me?

GUSTAVE No.

JULIETTE You said you loved me, Don Pedro, yet for three days now you haven't even looked at me.

GUSTAVE I do love you, Juliette.

JULIETTE Then why—?

GUSTAVE I can't tell you.

JULIETTE My father wasn't titled, I know, but my aunt is a Lady, and my grandfather was an Honorable.

GUSTAVE How funny you are. It isn't that.

JULIETTE Do you think the Duke of Miraflores would consent to my marrying you?

GUSTAVE (*Smiling*) I'm sure he would.

JULIETTE Why do you look so sad then, if you love me and everyone approves?

GUSTAVE I can't tell you.

JULIETTE But you do feel, don't you, that our lives might meet and join one day?

GUSTAVE I would be lying if I told you I felt that.

JULIETTE (*Turning away*) That's unkind of you.

GUSTAVE Careful. Here's your cousin.

JULIETTE Come into the garden. It's getting dark. I want you to tell me everything.

(*The music fades as they go.* EVA *comes in, followed by* HECTOR, *in a totally different make-up from the one he wore in Act One*)

HECTOR There, you see, they've left us the place to ourselves.

EVA But I don't in the least need a place to myself—that's the pity of it—I could adapt myself quite easily to a great crowd around us.

HECTOR How cruel you are!

EVA I don't like you. I'm cruel to those I dislike. It's in my nature. But on the other hand, when someone appeals to me, there's hardly anything I wouldn't do for him.

HECTOR (*In despair*) Why, why can I not manage to appeal to you a second time?

EVA You know perfectly well why. You're not the same now.

HECTOR What abominable absent-mindedness! This disguise, I tell you, is the fancy of an aristocrat wearied to death of his own personality, a pastime which affords him an escape from his oppressive self. And for this accursed fancy, must I lose my love?

EVA I remember with delight a young man who spoke to me in the park. Find him for me. I might still think him lovable.

HECTOR This is ridiculous! Won't you even tell me if I'm getting warm? At least tell me, did I have a beard when I first appealed to you?

EVA But it wouldn't amuse me if I were to tell you.

HECTOR (*Who has turned away to change his make-up, turns back again wearing a completely new face*) It wasn't like this, I suppose?

EVA (*In a burst of laughter*) No, oh no!

HECTOR Yet you remember my voice, my eyes?

EVA Yes, but it isn't enough.

HECTOR I'm the same height as I was. I'm tall, well built—I assure you I am, very well built.

EVA I only judge by faces.

HECTOR This is horrible! Horrible! I'll never find the face that pleased you, ever! It wasn't as a woman, by any chance?

EVA What do you take me for?

HECTOR Or as a Chinaman?

EVA You're evidently out of your mind. I'll wait till you're in it again.

(*She goes to sit further off; he starts to follow her and she turns on him*)

No, no, no! For heaven's sake will you stop following me about and changing your beard every five minutes! You're making my head spin.

HECTOR (*Stricken*) And to think that idiot Peterbono keeps on swearing it was as a test-pilot!

(LORD EDGARD *crosses the room laden with papers*)

LORD EDGARD This is unthinkable! I must find this letter, from which the truth will spring in such a curious fashion.

(*He sees* HECTOR *in his latest make-up, drops his papers and leaps on him*)

At last! The detective from Scotland Yard.

HECTOR No sir.

(*He makes to go*)

LORD EDGARD Excellent! The perfect answer. I specially stipulated secrecy. But don't be afraid, I am Lord Edgard in person. You may disclose your identity.

HECTOR I tell you I'm not the man you're expecting.

(*He goes*)

LORD EDGARD (*Following him*) I see! I see! Perfect! You're keeping word for word to my instructions! I stressed the need for caution!

(LADY HURF *enters, holding a magazine*)

LADY HURF My little Eva is bored, isn't she?

(EVA *smiles and says nothing. Unseen by* LADY HURF, HECTOR *comes back in another make-up, which he silently shows* EVA. *She shakes her head and he retires, heavy-hearted.* LADY HURF *puts down her magazine with a sigh*)

My little Eva is as bored as she can be.

EVA (*With a smile*) Yes, Aunt.

LADY HURF So am I, darling, very bored.

EVA Only I'm twenty-five, so you see, it's rather sad.

LADY HURF You'll see how much sadder it can be when you are sixty. For you there's always love. As you may guess, it's several years now since I officially renounced it.

EVA Oh, love!

LADY HURF *What* a deep sigh! Since you've been a widow, surely you've had lovers?

EVA I never had a single one who loved me.

LADY HURF You want the moon. If your lovers bore you, marry one of them. That will give the others an added fascination.

EVA Marry? Whom?

LADY HURF Needless to say these Dupont-Duforts exasperate us both. What about the Spaniards?

EVA Prince Hector chases after me changing his mustache in the hope of rediscovering the one that first appealed to me.

LADY HURF Truly appealed to you?

EVA (*Smiling*) I don't remember.

LADY HURF They're curious individuals.

EVA Why?

LADY HURF Oh, I don't know. I tell you, I'm an old carcass who doesn't know what to do with herself. I've had everything a woman could reasonably, or even unreasonably, wish for. Money, power, lovers. Now that I'm old, I feel as alone inside my skin as I did as a little girl and they made me face the wall when I'd been naughty. And here's the rub; I know that between that little girl and this old woman, there has been, under the charivari and the noise, nothing but an even greater loneliness.

EVA I've always thought of you as happy.

LADY HURF You don't see much, do you? I am playing a part. Only, like everything else I do, I play it well, that's all. Yours now, you play badly, little girl.

(*She strokes her hair*)

Child, child, you will always find yourself pursued by desires with changing beards and never have the courage to tell one of them: stay as you are—I love you. Don't think yourself a martyr now. All women are the same. My little Juliette, though, will come through because she is romantic. Her simplicity will save her. It's a favor only granted to few.

EVA There are some who can love.

LADY HURF Yes. There are some who love a man. Who kill him with loving, who kill themselves for him, but they are seldom heiresses to millions.

(*She strokes her hair again, with a rueful smile*)

Ah, you'll finish up like me, an old woman covered in diamonds who plays at intrigues in an effort to forget that she has never lived. And yet, I'd like to laugh a little. Here am I, playing with fire, and the fire won't even burn my fingers.

EVA What do you mean, Aunt?

LADY HURF Shush—here come our marionettes.

(PETERBONO *and* HECTOR *appear in the doorway, preceded by the musician. and followed almost at once by the* DUPONT-DUFORTS. *They all rush toward the ladies, but it is the thieves who get there first to kiss their hands*)

(*Jumps to her feet and utters a sudden cry*)

Ah! I have an idea!

PETERBONO (*Frightened, to* HECTOR) She scares the life out of me. Every time she screams like that, I think my beard's loose.

LADY HURF Where is Juliette?

EVA In the garden, with Prince Pedro. They're inseparable.

PETERBONO Ah, the dear children!

LADY HURF (*Calling*) Juliette!

JULIETTE (*Coming in with* GUSTAVE) Did you want me, Aunt Emily?

LADY HURF (*Drawing her aside*) Your eyes are red, child. Now mind, you mustn't be unhappy, or I cut the strings and the puppets will fall down.

JULIETTE What do you mean, Aunt?

LADY HURF If I appear to be talking through my hat, it's precisely so you won't understand me. Come along, both of you.

(*She takes them by the waist and leads them into the garden*)

I have an idea to brighten up this evening; I want you to tell me what you think of it.

(*They go. The* DUPONT-DUFORTS *look at each other*)

DUPONT-DUFORT SENIOR After them, sonny. And a hundred times more charm. Remember, it's our future that's at stake.

DUPONT-DUFORT JUNIOR Yes, Pa.

(*Left alone, the three thieves can unbend*)

HECTOR (*Offering* PETERBONO *a box of cigars*) Would you care for a cigar?

PETERBONO (*Helping himself*) I'm savoring them. They're remarkably good.

HECTOR (*Pouring out*) A little brandy?

PETERBONO Thank you.

(*They drink*)

HECTOR Another cigar, perhaps?

PETERBONO (*Grabbing a fistful without more ado*) You're too kind. No, no really, you embarrass me.

(*He feels a slight remorse, and takes the box*)

But may I in return press you to a cigar?

HECTOR (*Pulling them out of his pockets in handfuls*) Thank you so much. I'm all right just now.

(*There is a moment of beatitude and exquisite refinement. They spread themselves blissfully on the sofa. Suddenly* HECTOR *indicates* GUSTAVE, *sitting sad and somber in his corner*)

PETERBONO (*Rises and goes to him*) What's wrong, laddie? Why so sad? Here you are with a wonderful room, lovely food, and a pretty little thing to flirt with, you're playing at princes, and for all that you can manage to be gloomy?

GUSTAVE I don't want to stay here.

(*The other two give a start*)

PETERBONO Uh? You want to leave?

GUSTAVE Yes.

PETERBONO Leave here?

GUSTAVE Yes—leave here.

PETERBONO Hector, the boy's lost his reason.

HECTOR What do you want to leave for?

GUSTAVE I'm in love with Juliette.

HECTOR Well then?

GUSTAVE Really in love.

HECTOR Well then?

PETERBONO Why not? You've never been better off. She takes you for a prince, and rich at that. Go in and win, lad, she's as good as yours.

GUSTAVE I don't want to take her, for a day, and then be forced to leave her.

PETERBONO You'll have to leave her one day.

GUSTAVE And—I'm ashamed of this game I have to play with her. I'd rather go away, now, and never see her again.

HECTOR He's out of his mind.

PETERBONO Completely.

GUSTAVE Look, what are we here for?

PETERBONO What are we here for? We're working, lad. It's the height of our season.

GUSTAVE We're here to do a job. Let's do it then and go.

PETERBONO And the preliminaries? Have you spared a single thought for the preliminaries?

GUSTAVE They've gone on long enough, your damn preliminaries.

PETERBONO I ask you, Hector, isn't it painful? Having to listen to an apprentice teaching us our trade!

HECTOR Of course we'll do a job; that's what we came for, but have you even the first idea what that job's going to be?

GUSTAVE Strip the drawing-room?

PETERBONO With carpet-bags, eh? Like raggle-taggle gypsies! The lowness, Hector, the abysmal lowness of this youngster's mind! Understand boy, that we haven't yet decided on the job we're going to do. And if our behavior strikes you, a novice, as peculiar, tell yourself it's because we're in the process of investigating the possibilities of this—establishment.

GUSTAVE You're lingering on here for the brandy and cigars, and because Hector still hopes he'll get Eva to remember him. But in actual fact you haven't the smallest inkling what you want to do. I may be an apprentice, but I'll tell you something—that's no way to work.

PETERBONO (*Running to* HECTOR) Hector, hold me back!

HECTOR (*Still blissfully smoking*) Gustave, don't be difficult. Try to understand.

PETERBONO Hector, hold me back!

HECTOR You see, we're wavering . . .

PETERBONO Hold me back, Hector! Hold me back!

HECTOR (*Takes his arm to please him*) All right, I've got you.

PETERBONO (*Deflated*) Just as well.

HECTOR (*To* GUSTAVE) We're wavering between several possible courses of action. . . .

GUSTAVE Which?

HECTOR Shall we confide in him, Pete? Is it safe to risk the indiscretion of a youth?

PETERBONO (*Shrugs*) Oh, confide in him, do. Since we're answerable to him now.

HECTOR Right. Tell him your idea first, Pete.

PETERBONO After you, Hector, after you.

HECTOR (*Embarrassed*) Aaaaaaah . . . well . . .

GUSTAVE You haven't thought of a thing!

HECTOR (*In righteous rage*) We haven't thought of a thing?!!! We're wavering between the trick of the dud check given in exchange for real jewels on a Saturday, which gives the weekend to make our getaway, or the trick of the good check received in exchange for dud jewels under the same conditions. We've also considered giving Lady Hurf some orchids sprayed with ether (taking good care not to smell them ourselves) so as to relieve her of the pearls as soon as she nods off.

PETERBONO (*Equally incensed*) Or we might provoke the Dupont-Duforts to a duel! We wound them and then in the commotion we make off with the silver!

GUSTAVE What if you're the ones to get wounded?

PETERBONO Impossible!

GUSTAVE Why?

PETERBONO (*Yelling*) I don't know. But it's impossible!

HECTOR Or again we could make out we'd been robbed and demand a colossal sum for hush-money!

PETERBONO Pretend we found a pearl in the oysters at dinner, for instance, and swap it for a pearl of Lady Hurf's, or something.

GUSTAVE There's no "r" in the month.

PETERBONO I said for instance!

GUSTAVE In other words you just don't know. Well, I'm going to do the job tonight, and then I'm off.

PETERBONO Tonight? And why not right away?

GUSTAVE Yes, why not right away? I want to go away. I want to leave here as soon as possible.

PETERBONO He'll be the ruin of us! Gustave, think of your poor old mother, who put you in my care!

GUSTAVE No!

PETERBONO I'll put my curse on you! Naturally you don't care a rap if I put my curse on you?

GUSTAVE No.

PETERBONO (*Bellowing*) Hector! Hold me back!

(*He seizes* GUSTAVE)

Just another fortnight. We'll do the job all right, but it's nice here, and it isn't so often we're in a nice place. . . .

GUSTAVE No. I'm too unhappy.

(*He goes*)

HECTOR (*Leaps after him*) After him! We've got to stop him before he starts a scandal.

PETERBONO (*Calling after him*) I've got an idea! Suppose we pretended not to know him?

(HECTOR *shrugs his shoulders and goes out, refusing even to consider such a solution*)

(*Enter* LORD EDGARD, *preceded by the musician playing a succession of tremolos as if he had intimations of a sudden blow of destiny. He is rummaging in his ever-present pile of papers. All of a sudden he utters a loud cry and falls in a dead faint among his scattered letters. The musician runs for help, emitting isolated notes from his instrument*)

JULIETTE (*Comes in*) Uncle, Uncle, what's the matter?

(*She props him up on a sofa and feels his hands*)

Ice-cold! What's this?

(*She picks up a letter, reads it, and hurriedly thrusts it into her pocket. Running out*)

Aunt Emily! Aunt Emily! Come quickly!

(*The clarinet in great confusion multiplies his tragic tremolos. Everyone comes rushing in shouting at once*)

Stroke!

At his age!

No, he's only fainted.

Stand back—give him air.

Get a doctor!

He's coming round.

He's all right now.

A sudden shock.

Perhaps he found what he was looking for.

(*The music stops. An enormous silence*)

PETERBONO (*Breathes to* HECTOR *in the silence*) The chance of a lifetime.

HECTOR Yes. But what do we do about it?

PETERBONO Well, nothing obviously, but it's still the chance of a lifetime.

LORD EDGARD (*Sitting up slowly, says in a toneless voice*) My friends, I have a ghastly piece of news for you. The Duke of Miraflores died in Biarritz in 1904.

(*Everyone looks at* PETERBONO, *who is very ill at ease. An impish little jig on the clarinet*)

PETERBONO Nonsense!

HECTOR (*Aside*) Talk about the chance of a lifetime!

PETERBONO This is a fine time to be funny! Ease over to the window.

LADY HURF Edgard, are you out of your mind?

LORD EDGARD No, I tell you. I've found the notification. I knew I'd find it eventually. Ever since the day—

(*He searches himself*)

Where is it? This is too much! Where is it? I had it a moment ago! Oh, my goodness! It's gone again.

DUPONT-DUFORT SENIOR Everything is coming to light!

DUPONT-DUFORT JUNIOR We are saved!

(*To* PETERBONO, *who is imperceptibly edging toward the window*)

Aren't you staying to make sure your host is all right?

PETERBONO Yes, oh yes!

LADY HURF Edgard, that's a ridiculous joke to play on the dear duke.

LORD EDGARD But, my dear, I guarantee—

LADY HURF Come along, dear Duke, and show him you aren't dead.

PETERBONO (*Uneasy*) No, no. I'm not dead.

LORD EDGARD Yet I found the notification. . . .

LADY HURF (*Pinching him*) Edgard, you're making a mistake, I'm sure. You must apologize.

LORD EDGARD (*Rubbing his arm*) Ouch! Why yes, now that you mention it, I think I must have been confusing him with the Duke of Orleans.

LADY HURF Of course. Shall we call the incident closed?

PETERBONO (*In great relief*) Completely closed.

LADY HURF Let's go outside, shall we? I've ordered coffee on the terrace. I want to tell you about my idea.

DUPONT-DUFORT SENIOR (*In step with her*) I think it's a wonderful idea.

LADY HURF (*Exasperated*) Wait a minute, my dear man, I haven't told you yet. Listen. They're holding a Thieves' Carnival tonight at the Casino. We're all going to dress up as thieves and go to it.

DUPONT-DUFORT SENIOR *and* JUNIOR (*Immediately burst out laughing*) He! He! He! How terribly, terribly amusing!

DUPONT-DUFORT SENIOR (*To his son as they go out*) Play up to her, son.

(*Exit*)

PETERBONO (*Furious, as he goes out with* HECTOR) I call that in very poor taste, don't you?

(JULIETTE *is alone. She stands motionless a moment. The music is heard some way away, playing a romantic theme.* JULIETTE *takes out the fatal letter and reads it*)

JULIETTE "We regret to announce the sad death of His Serene Highness the Duke of Miraflores y Grandes, Marquis of Priola, Count of Zeste and Galba. The funeral will take place . . ."

(*She stands in thought a moment*)

If his father isn't the Duke of Miraflores—then who can he be? Why has he taken the car out of the garage? Why is he hiding from me?

CHILD (*Entering*) Mademoiselle Juliette, I found some. Look, daisies with lots of petals.

JULIETTE Haven't you gone to bed yet?

CHILD I was picking daisies for you.

JULIETTE Thank you, you're an angel.

(*She kisses her*)

His father may be an adventurer, but you see, he loves me. He does love me, doesn't he?

CHILD Yes, of course he does.

JULIETTE We don't care, do we, if he's an adventurer, or worse? If you were me, you'd love him, wouldn't you, just the same? Only why does that hard look come into his eyes whenever I ask him about himself? If he has designs on me, and he'd be wise to have, because I'm very rich, he should be very pleasant to me all the time—whereas—do you think he prefers Eva? That would be terrible—

CHILD I don't know.

JULIETTE No, of course you don't. Come along, I'll take you home. Are you afraid of the dark?

CHILD No.

JULIETTE That's a good girl. Nor am I. There's nothing to be afraid of, you know. Thieves won't hurt you.

(*They go*)

# Act Three

*The same set. The room is dark; a figure is seen moving about with a torch. It is* GUSTAVE, *dressed in dark clothes and wearing a cap. He is silently examining the objects in the drawing-room. Suddenly he hears a noise and switches off the torch; a low whistle; two dark figures spring up, two torches flash, and focus on* GUSTAVE.

GUSTAVE Who's that?

FIGURE Tonight's the night.

GUSTAVE Peterbono?

FIGURE No. We're the new ones.

2ND FIGURE The new bandits.

GUSTAVE For God's sake, what's going on?

(*He draws a revolver*)

Hands up!

DUPONT-DUFORT SENIOR (*It is no other*) Ha ha ha! That's good! Where did you get the gun? It's magnificent!

GUSTAVE Stay where you are or I fire!

DUPONT-DUFORT SENIOR Come quietly! The game's up.

GUSTAVE Stay where you are, damn you!

(*He fires*)

DUPONT-DUFORT SENIOR (*Blissfully unaware of his danger*) Oh, well done! Bravo!

GUSTAVE What do you mean, Bravo?

(*He fires again*)

DUPONT-DUFORT JUNIOR It's a wonderful imitation! Where on earth did you buy those caps?

GUSTAVE For the last time, stay where you are!

(*He fires again and shatters a vase, which falls with a terrible clatter*)

DUPONT-DUFORT SENIOR Didier, why do you have to be so clumsy!

DUPONT-DUFORT JUNIOR (*Protesting in the dark*) But, Dad, I didn't do it!

DUPONT-DUFORT SENIOR Well, it can't have been I, can it? I'm in the middle of the room.

DUPONT-DUFORT JUNIOR But, Dad, so am I!

DUPONT-DUFORT SENIOR (*Suddenly anxious*) Well, then, who broke the vase?

LORD EDGARD (*Enters and switches on the light. He is dressed up as a policeman*) Now, now, what is all this noise? How do you like my helmet?

DUPONT-DUFORT SENIOR (*Who has got himself up, along with his son, in a terrifying apache disguise*) Superb, my lord, superb!

(*Exit* LORD EDGARD. DUPONT-DUFORT SENIOR *goes to* GUSTAVE)

My word, I don't think much of your costume. It doesn't come off—it's much too simple. It's the little touches that mean so much. For instance, look, this little scar here.

DUPONT-DUFORT JUNIOR And the black eye patch.

GUSTAVE What are you doing dressed up like that?

DUPONT-DUFORT SENIOR We're going to the Casino.

DUPONT-DUFORT JUNIOR To the Thieves' Carnival. And so are you.

GUSTAVE Oh? Oh yes, of course. So am I.

DUPONT-DUFORT SENIOR Only if I were you, I'd touch up your make-up, my boy. It's a shade too simple. You don't look a bit like a thief.

GUSTAVE You're quite right. I'll see to it at once.

(*He turns at the door*)

Tell me, is everybody going to the Thieves' Carnival?

DUPONT-DUFORT SENIOR Of course; everybody.

GUSTAVE That's fine. See you later.

(*He goes*)

DUPONT-DUFORT SENIOR Not an ounce of imagination in him, that boy.

DUPONT-DUFORT JUNIOR If the other two have rigged themselves up as absurdly as that, which they probably have, we're well on the way. The girls will have eyes for nobody but us!

DUPONT-DUFORT SENIOR Have you seen the latest batch of telegrams?

DUPONT-DUFORT JUNIOR Yes.

DUPONT-DUFORT SENIOR If we don't leave this house with a fat settlement, it's the colonies for us, I can tell you. Make yourself irresistible, there's a good boy.

DUPONT-DUFORT JUNIOR I'm doing my best, Dad.

DUPONT-DUFORT SENIOR I know you are. You're an honest, conscientious lad, but you mustn't slacken for one moment. The success of this evening's entertainment means a great deal to us. What's more, there's something shady about our rivals which is bound to give rise to a scandal one of these days. It was quite obviously Lady Hurf who made the old duffer keep quiet this afternoon, when he insisted the Duke of Miraflores died in 1904. Keep your eyes open, and be ready for any emergency.

DUPONT-DUFORT JUNIOR We have got to get rid of these gallivanters. It's a matter of life and death.

DUPONT-DUFORT SENIOR We'll let them dig their own graves, while we'll be more and more agreeable. Ssh! Here comes Lady Hurf.

(*Enter* LADY HURF *and* EVA, *as thieves in petticoats. The* DUPONT-DUFORTS *cough desperately to attract attention*)

LADY HURF (*Seeing them*) Oh, breathtaking! Aren't they, Eva? Breathtaking! Who would have thought they had it in them! What do you think of our guests, Eva?

EVA What a spectacular effect! How in the world did you manage it?

DUPONT-DUFORT SENIOR (*Simpering*) We're delighted.

DUPONT-DUFORT JUNIOR That we delight you.

LADY HURF They always look as though they're waiting for a tip.

EVA Which, in a way, they are.

LADY HURF The Duke and his sons are being very slow.

EVA I called out to them as I went by. They can't manage to dress up as thieves, they said.

LADY HURF (*As she goes*) Go up and fetch them, gentlemen, if you would be so good, and give them a few wrinkles.

DUPONT-DUFORT SENIOR Certainly! Certainly!

(*Aside to his son*)

Let us be pleasant.

DUPONT-DUFORT JUNIOR Very, very pleasant.

(*They bow themselves out*)

(*Exeunt*)

(JULIETTE *crosses furtively*)

EVA Why, you're not dressed!

JULIETTE I'm going up now.

EVA You'll make us late.

JULIETTE Go on ahead. I'll take the two-seater.

EVA (*Unexpectedly*) Are you in love with this boy?

JULIETTE Why do you ask me?

EVA Yes indeed, why does one ask people if they're in love, when one can tell at a glance, always.

JULIETTE Can you tell?

EVA Yes.

JULIETTE Well, you're wrong. I'm not in love with anyone.

(*She turns to go, when* EVA *calls her back*)

EVA Juliette! Why do you look upon me as your enemy?

JULIETTE You are my enemy.

EVA No, I love you very much. Sit down.

JULIETTE (*Turning on her*) You're in love with him too, that's it, isn't it? You're going to take him away from me, and you want to warn me first so that I won't be hurt too much? Why, you've even agreed on that between you, probably. You have, haven't you? Haven't you? For heaven's sake say something! Why do you smile like that?

EVA How lucky you are to be in love as much as that.

JULIETTE You're prettier than I am; you can get any man you want.

EVA Oh, if I could only bring myself to want one.

JULIETTE Don't you want him then?

EVA No, little silly.

JULIETTE Have you never spoken to him when I wasn't looking?

EVA Had I ever wanted to I should have found it very difficult. He only has to come near me by accident and you can't take your eyes off us.

JULIETTE I'm wary. I love him, you see.

EVA Little gambler!

JULIETTE You swear you've never set out to attract him?

EVA I swear.

JULIETTE Even the day you danced with him twice running?

EVA The orchestra had struck up a second tango.

JULIETTE Even the day you went out on the river while the Dupont-Duforts tried to teach me roulette?

EVA Even then. He looked so sad that I suggested he should row straight back, but we couldn't find you anywhere.

JULIETTE That day I'm not so sure. He had a strange look in his eyes that evening.

EVA Because he'd asked me if I thought you cared for him, and I said you were an unpredictable little girl and there was no knowing what went on inside your heart.

JULIETTE Was that truly why?

(*A little pause*)

All the same, I do think you might have told him something else.

EVA Are you satisfied now?

JULIETTE Did you never try to attract him, not even at the beginning, not even the very first day?

EVA Not even the first day.

JULIETTE Yes, then, I'm satisfied.

EVA Why will you never trust me? I feel like an old woman beside you sometimes.

JULIETTE You're so much better-looking than I am, so much more poised, more feminine.

EVA Do you think so?

JULIETTE It surprises me, you know, in spite of what you say. You must admit that he's a good deal more attractive than Hector, and you don't mind *his* attentions.

EVA Do you think I couldn't have denied myself a mere flirtation, when I could see you were so much in love?

JULIETTE That's grand of you.

EVA Oh no. I wish I could have wanted him so much that I'd have sacrificed you without giving you a moment's thought.

JULIETTE When you chew your pearls, I know there's something wrong.

EVA Yes, there's something wrong.

JULIETTE Yet you look so lovely tonight. You'll have all the men around you at the Ball.

EVA All of them.

JULIETTE I'm not joking.

EVA Nor am I. I'll have them all. And yet it's very sad.

JULIETTE Aren't you happy?

EVA No.

JULIETTE Yet it's so easy. You only need to let yourself go. Why, hardly a moment goes by that one isn't unhappy, yet I think that must be what it means, to be happy.

EVA You've always thought me cleverer, stronger, more beautiful, than you because the men flocked round me. And yet you see, there's only you who is alive, in this house—you're the only one perhaps in Vichy, perhaps in the whole world.

JULIETTE (*Smiling, lost in her dream*) Yes, I am alive.

EVA And untouched, and eager to believe. . . .

JULIETTE To believe everything.

EVA You've never had, as I have, a man without love in your bed. You haven't even a jewel at your throat, not a ring on your finger. You're wearing nothing but this simple linen dress, and you're twenty years old, and you are in love.

(JULIETTE *sits motionless, yielding to the unseen with a faint smile*)

(*Looking sharply at her*)

Juliette, why are you not in thieves' dress like the rest of us?

JULIETTE (*Bursting with sudden joy*) Oh, I'm too happy! I haven't the courage to stay beside you who are sad. When I'm a little less happy, I'll think of you, I swear I will!

(*She kisses her and runs off*)

Ssh!

EVA All this mystery! What are you trying to say?

(*Enter* LADY HURF *with the* DUPONT-DUFORTS)

LADY HURF We will make a truly magnificent entrance.

DUPONT-DUFORT SENIOR The Spanish gentlemen are ready

LADY HURF Do they look all right?

DUPONT-DUFORT SENIOR That's a matter of taste.

DUPONT-DUFORT JUNIOR Anyway, here they come.

(*Enter* PETERBONO *and* HECTOR. *They have contrived to disguise themselves as absolutely ludicrous comic opera bandits. They are greeted with shrieks of laughter*)

HECTOR What are they laughing at?

PETERBONO What do they *think* thieves look like? Don't they ever go to the theater?

LADY HURF But, my dear Duke, what are you supposed to be?

PETERBONO A thief.

HECTOR (*To* EVA) It wasn't like this, I suppose?

EVA Heavens, no!

PETERBONO (*To* LADY HURF) Don't you like us?

LADY HURF Enormously!

PETERBONO Admit there's something wrong.

LADY HURF My dear friend, one really can't expect a Spanish grandee to make much of a showing as a common thief.

PETERBONO Well said, eh, Hector?

(*Enormous nudgings*)

LADY HURF Come along, all of you. The car's waiting. Where is Lord Edgard? Still glued to the mirror I suppose. Edgard!

(*He appears, still in his own suit, and wearing his police helmet, but he has shaved off his moustache*)

LORD EDGARD Do you think I did well to shave off my moustache?

LADY HURF (*Without looking at him*) I don't know! Come along! To the Carnival!

(*The music immediately strikes up a lively quadrille, which the thieves dance with the ladies, without the* DUPONT-DUFORTS *getting a look in. Then follows a piece of extremely vulgar jive, and the* DUPONT-DUFORTS, *making the best of a bad job, finish up by dancing together with tremendous spirit. All the characters dance their way out*)

DUPONT-DUFORT SENIOR (*Bringing up the rear with his son*) Things are getting better and better and better.

DUPONT-DUFORT JUNIOR Let's be as witty as the very devil!

DUPONT-DUFORT SENIOR And, remember, Didier, twice as nice.

(*The room remains empty for an instant. A servant comes in to close the windows and turn out the lights. Another moment of silence, and* GUSTAVE *appears, and listens. The car is heard driving off. He goes right round the room, examining its contents one by one. All of a sudden he flattens himself against the wall*)

JULIETTE (*Enters, dressed for a journey*) Here I am.

GUSTAVE What are you doing here? Why didn't you go with the others?

JULIETTE I've come to find you.

GUSTAVE Get out of here, will you?

JULIETTE Why are you so harsh with me?

GUSTAVE Go on, get out!

JULIETTE I'll go, of course, if you don't want me, only I thought you would want me. What's the matter?

GUSTAVE I've got a headache. I want to stay here.

JULIETTE Why this yarn, to me?

GUSTAVE It isn't a yarn. Get out, will you? Go on, quick march!

JULIETTE But—you've never spoken to me like this!

GUSTAVE There's a first time for everything.

JULIETTE What have I done?

GUSTAVE Nothing in particular. It's too difficult to explain, and anyway you wouldn't understand.

JULIETTE But, Señor Pedro . . .

GUSTAVE There isn't any Señor Pedro, for a start. My name is Gustave. And secondly, will you please go away?

JULIETTE And there was I thinking that you loved me—

GUSTAVE We all make mistakes, don't we?

JULIETTE But you used to tell me so.

GUSTAVE I was lying.

JULIETTE Oh, no! I don't believe it!

GUSTAVE (*Going to her purposefully*) Listen, my little pet, I'm telling you to get out of here, double quick.

JULIETTE Why?

GUSTAVE You'll see why later on. In the meantime go up to your room and weep over your lost illusions.

(*He takes her arm to lead her to the door*)

What are you dressed up in this coat for? What kind of a costume is that meant to be?

JULIETTE Traveling costume.

GUSTAVE Traveling costume? You're mad.

JULIETTE Please don't be angry. I came to find you so we could go away. You told me once we'd go away together.

GUSTAVE I was joking. Anyway, how do you know I mean to go away?

JULIETTE I know.

GUSTAVE You look as though you know a lot of things. Come along with me.

JULIETTE We might meet one of the servants in the passage.

(*He looks at her*)

We'd better not move from here. We'll be quite safe in this room.

GUSTAVE The Dupont-Duforts must be waiting for you. Go and dress up as a pickpocket like the rest of them.

JULIETTE Don't pickpockets ever wear traveling clothes?

GUSTAVE You're not going to travel. You're going to a carnival.

JULIETTE Once they've stolen thieves go away as a rule. Why won't you let me come with you, since you're going away?

GUSTAVE (*Seizes her*) You know too much, my girl!

JULIETTE Oh, please, don't hurt me!

GUSTAVE Don't be afraid. Just a precaution.

(*He ties her to a chair, and searches in her handbag*)

JULIETTE Oh, don't rob my bag. There's nothing in it. Anyway, I give it to you.

GUSTAVE Thank you. All I want is a handkerchief.

JULIETTE What for?

GUSTAVE To gag you with.

(*He finds her handkerchief, which is microscopic*)

I ask you, what's the point of a handkerchief that size? Never mind, mine's clean.

JULIETTE I'm not going to scream—I swear I won't scream—Señor Pedro! Gustave—Gusta . . .

(*He gags her*)

GUSTAVE There. If you think this a Thieves' Carnival, my lass, you'll have to think again. I'm a real thief, I am. So is Hector, and so is the Duke of Miraflores. Except that those two, they're imbeciles as well. You've built yourself a castle in the air, that's all, and your aunt, who's got bats in her belfry, has built herself a dozen. But let me tell you *I* came to do a job, and I intend to do it.

(*She struggles*)

All right. All right. It's no good trying to soften me. I'm used to girls.

(*He begins to fill his sacks with the most unlikely objects in the room. After a while he looks at her with misgiving*)

It's not too tight, is it?

(*She shakes her head*)

That's a good girl. You see, old girl, I did a bit of billing and cooing, I know, but to be frank I didn't mean a word of it. I had to do it for the job.

(*She struggles again*)

Does that upset you? Yes, I know, it isn't very pretty. But then in every trade there's always a little bit like that which isn't very pretty. Apart from that, I'm an honest sort of chap in my own way. I follow my trade, simply, without frills and fancies. Not like Hector and Peterbono. Peterbono has to be the Duke of Miraflores. One must be honest in one's own particular line. Life's not worth living otherwise.

(*He takes a furtive look at her*)

You sure it's not too tight?

(*He gives her a smile*)

It worries me a bit, playing a trick like that on you, because you know, I lied just now. I am fond of you really.

(*He goes back to his work*)

After all, when God invented thieves He had to deprive them of a thing or two, so He took away from them the esteem of honest folk. When you come to think of it, it's not so terrible. It could have been much worse.

(*He shrugs, and laughs, without daring to meet her eyes*)

In a little while, you'll see, we'll have forgotten all about it.

(*He goes on collecting objects. She struggles again, and he looks at her*)

If there's anything you care for specially, you must tell me. I'll leave it for you, as a souvenir. I mean, I'd *like* to give you a little present.

(*She looks at him and he stops in embarrassment*)

Please, don't look at me like that! You're breaking my heart! Can't you see I've got to do this? So just let me get quietly on with my job.

(*She moves*)

Are you uncomfortable? You're not choking, are you?

Look, Juliette, if you swear not to call out, I'll take the gag off. Do you swear?

(*She nods*)

All right then, I trust you.

(*He removes the handkerchief*)

What are you going to say to me, now that you know I'm a real thief?

(*He sits down, resigned*)

JULIETTE (*The moment she is ungagged*) This is absurd! Absolutely absurd. Untie me at once!

GUSTAVE Oh, no! I'm a good sort, but business is business.

JULIETTE At least listen to me!

GUSTAVE What do you want to say?

JULIETTE You don't imagine I came to find you, wearing my traveling coat, merely in order to sit here like a nincompoop bound and gagged in a chair? Of course I know you're a thief. If you weren't a real thief, I wouldn't have thought you were planning to leave in the middle of the night, would I, seeing you're a guest of my aunt's?

GUSTAVE What are you talking about?

JULIETTE I've been telling you over and over again for the last hour. I love you. I saw you take a car out of the garage, I guessed you really were a thief, and that tonight was the night. As I supposed you'd go the moment the job was done, I dressed and got ready to go with you. You don't intend to stay, do you?

GUSTAVE That's no question to ask a thief.

JULIETTE Well then, take me with you.

GUSTAVE But I'm a thief.

JULIETTE (*Crying out in exasperation*) I tell you I know you're a thief! There's no need to go on and on about it. I wonder you don't draw attention to yourself. Come along, untie my hands.

GUSTAVE But, Juliette—

JULIETTE Untie my hands. They're terribly painful.

GUSTAVE Do you swear not to run away and raise the alarm?

JULIETTE Yes, yes, I swear. Oh, how stupid you are!

GUSTAVE I trust you of course, but I just don't understand.

(*He unties her. She immediately powders her face, and then gets up with determination*)

JULIETTE We've wasted at least a quarter of an hour. Make haste. It wouldn't do to get caught now. Have you enough with this lot?

(*She indicates the sacks with her foot*)

GUSTAVE What are you doing?

JULIETTE Really, I shall begin to wonder if you're all there soon. Yes, or no, do I appeal to you?

GUSTAVE Oh yes, but—

JULIETTE Good. That's the main thing. Now, listen to me. Gustave, if you like me, I love you and I want to be your wife—oh, don't worry, if you're afraid of awkward questions at the Registry Office, we won't get properly married. There. Now then—

(*She picks up one of the sacks*)

Is this all we're taking with us?

GUSTAVE (*Snatching the sack from her*) Juliette, no! You don't know what you're doing! You mustn't come with me. What would become of you?

JULIETTE I'd help you. I'd keep a look-out, and I'd whistle when I saw someone coming. I can whistle beautifully. Listen—

(*She gives an earsplitting whistle*)

GUSTAVE (*Terrified*) Ssssh! For heaven's sake!

(*They listen for a moment*)

JULIETTE (*Humbly*) I'm sorry. What a fool I am. Take me away. I'll whistle very quietly, I promise you, and then only when it's absolutely necessary.

GUSTAVE Juliette, this is only a whim. You're playing with me. It's unkind of you.

JULIETTE Oh no, you mustn't think that! Never think that! I love you.

GUSTAVE But do you know the dangers of this kind of life?

JULIETTE Yes. Kiss me.

GUSTAVE Juliette, it's good-bye to your tranquillity.

JULIETTE It was on the way to killing me, my tranquillity. Kiss me.

GUSTAVE But you're happy here, Juliette. You don't know what it means to be on the run, to be afraid. You're used to luxury.

JULIETTE Why, we're rich! Look at this! If it worries you, we won't steal so long as the police are out looking for me.

GUSTAVE Thieves aren't wealthy folk. You get precious little for what you sell.

JULIETTE Well, we'll be poor then. Kiss me.

(*They join in a long kiss*)

(*Radiantly*)

I am so happy. Now, hurry.

(*She stops*)

Why, you haven't taken the little Fragonards. You're mad, my darling, they're the most valuable things in the house.

(*She runs to take them down*)

And the little enamels.

(*She rummages in the sack*)

Leave the candlesticks. They're imitation bronze. You see how useful I am to you. I shall be such a help, you'll see. Kiss me.

GUSTAVE (*Taking her in his arms again*) My little robber girl.

(*They go*)

# Act Four

*In the conservatory, an hour later. The clarinet, which has begun by playing the Carnival theme, takes it up again in a nostalgic manner. The characters wander in in single file, heads hanging, and sit down, vexed and dejected.*

LADY HURF It's positively absurd.

HECTOR I do think they might have let us in.

LADY HURF Too absurd. Fancy writing the title of the Carnival in microscopic lettering. Economy is an absolute obsession with the French.

LORD EDGARD We were turned away in the most humiliating fashion.

EVA What do you expect, Uncle? I can quite see that our attire alarmed them.

LADY HURF A Carnival of Leaves! The idiocy of it!! A Carnival of Leaves!

DUPONT-DUFORT SENIOR What puzzles me is how you could confuse a Carnival of Leaves with a Carnival of Thieves.

LADY HURF You should have consulted the notices yourself then, my good friend, if your eyesight is so sharp.

DUPONT-DUFORT SENIOR But dammit . . .

DUPONT-DUFORT JUNIOR Don't be rash, Dad.

LADY HURF To begin with, it's thanks to your disguises that our party was shown the door.

PETERBONO I should definitely have got in, for one. It's a funny thing. They quite thought I was going as a palm tree.

LADY HURF Of course, but for them we should all have been admitted. What abominable taste! Look at them, will you? They might be a couple of pantomime buccaneers.

DUPONT-DUFORT SENIOR I should have thought for a Carnival of Thieves . . .

LADY HURF Leaves! Leaves! Leaves! Are you going to spend the rest of the evening calling it a Carnival of Thieves?

DUPONT-DUFORT JUNIOR Keep calm, Father.

(*To* LADY HURF)

We are dreadfully sorry.

DUPONT-DUFORT SENIOR (*Abjectly*) We'll never do it again.

LADY HURF A fine time to say so!

LORD EDGARD Could we not perhaps spend the evening as we are, among ourselves, so as not to waste our efforts altogether?

LADY HURF Edgard, what an insane idea. Let us go up and change. We'll play yet one more stupefying game of bridge.

(*She sighs and the guests sigh with her*)

LORD EDGARD If I'd known we were going to play bridge I would have preferred to keep my mustache.

LADY HURF (*Distractedly*) So would I!

(*To* PETERBONO, *on her way out*)

My dear Duke, can you forgive me for this wasted evening?

PETERBONO (*Nudging* HECTOR) No evening is ever really wasted.

LADY HURF Another time I'll be more careful when I read the posters, and more discriminating in my choice of company.

(*She goes with* EVA *and* LORD EDGARD)

PETERBONO Ring. Pearls.

HECTOR Pocket-book.

PETERBONO Perfect.

(*The* DUPONT-DUFORTS *find themselves alone*)

DUPONT-DUFORT SENIOR Things are going badly.

DUPONT-DUFORT JUNIOR Very badly.

DUPONT-DUFORT SENIOR These gay dogs are here on the same errand as we are, that's quite obvious, but everything is going their way and nothing is coming ours.

DUPONT-DUFORT JUNIOR (*Looking in a mirror*) Yet we achieved a really lovely make-up.

DUPONT-DUFORT SENIOR Not for a Carnival of Leaves.

DUPONT-DUFORT JUNIOR Fancy organizing a Carnival of Leaves!

DUPONT-DUFORT SENIOR Fancy, what's more, reading "Carnival of Thieves" when it's down in black and white on all the posters "Carnival of Leaves." The old goose!

DUPONT-DUFORT JUNIOR (*Catching sight of the drawing-room through the open window*) Daddy!

DUPONT-DUFORT SENIOR What is it?

DUPONT-DUFORT JUNIOR Look at the wall!

DUPONT-DUFORT SENIOR What about the wall?

DUPONT-DUFORT JUNIOR The Fragonards!

DUPONT-DUFORT SENIOR If you think at a time like this I feel like going into ecstasies over a lot of paintings!

DUPONT-DUFORT JUNIOR Daddy, the Fragonards aren't on the wall.

(*He rushes into the room*)

DUPONT-DUFORT SENIOR Well?

DUPONT-DUFORT JUNIOR (*From the room*) Nor are the enamels! The bronze candlesticks are missing! And the snuff-boxes! All the drawers are open!

(*Rushing out again*)

Daddy, there's been a burglary!

DUPONT-DUFORT SENIOR Let's go. They'll think we did it.

DUPONT-DUFORT JUNIOR Don't be ridiculous! We were at the Carnival with everybody else! Daddy! There's been a robbery here!

DUPONT-DUFORT SENIOR (*Who has been to make sure*) You're absolutely right. There's been a robbery. But what are you so pleased about? That won't set our affairs to rights.

DUPONT-DUFORT JUNIOR Don't you understand? There's been a robbery while we were at the Casino. Don't you see suspicion can only fall on the one person who made himself conspicuous by his absence? Now then, who, I ask you, made himself conspicuous by his absence?

DUPONT-DUFORT SENIOR Young Pedro?

DUPONT-DUFORT JUNIOR Of course! Young Pedro.

DUPONT-DUFORT SENIOR In that case, surely the others would be his accomplices.

DUPONT-DUFORT JUNIOR They are his accomplices. They came with us to allay suspicion, that's quite clear. But now you may be sure they're gone, or will have before very long.

DUPONT-DUFORT SENIOR Didier. you're magnificent! You do my old heart good. Kiss me, son! At last they are unmasked. They're done for, laddie, and our affairs have never looked so promising.

DUPONT-DUFORT JUNIOR We must clinch matters. There's to be no escape and no denial. We must telephone the police at once.

(*He picks up the receiver*)

Give me the police please. And hurry!

DUPONT-DUFORT SENIOR (*Trundling round the drawing-room and bellowing*) The Fragonards! The enamels! The candlesticks! The snuff-boxes! Two drawers burst open! Magnificent!

DUPONT-DUFORT JUNIOR Hallo? Is that the police station? This is the Villa des Boyards. A serious robbery has just taken place. Yes, the thieves are still on the premises. You'll catch them red-handed if you hurry. Hurry!

DUPONT-DUFORT SENIOR (*Coming back radiant*) Come to your father, laddie!

(*They embrace*)

DUPONT-DUFORT JUNIOR Let's call the company and confront the rascals! Hey there! Come quickly, everybody!

DUPONT-DUFORT SENIOR Hey there! Hey!

LORD EDGARD (*Entering. He, and likewise the others when they come down, have all changed back into their usual clothes*) What's the matter?

DUPONT-DUFORT JUNIOR There's been a burglary!

LORD EDGARD That's no surprise to anybody in these troubled times. Where?

DUPONT-DUFORT JUNIOR Here!

LORD EDGARD Here!

DUPONT-DUFORT SENIOR (*Breathless with excitement*) Here! Here in this very room!

LORD EDGARD In the drawing-room? What did they take?

DUPONT-DUFORT SENIOR (*Like a street hawker*) Fragonards! Enamels! Snuff-boxes! Candlesticks! Drawers! Come in and see! Come and see!

(LORD EDGARD *goes into the room, comes back and staggers into an armchair*)

LORD EDGARD Terrible! Terrible! I had an idea this would happen.

DUPONT-DUFORT SENIOR }<br>DUPONT-DUFORT JUNIOR } So had we!

LORD EDGARD Do you know who did it?

DUPONT-DUFORT SENIOR We have an idea!

LORD EDGARD So have I!

(*Enter* EVA)

My child, we've just been burgled!

EVA What?

DUPONT-DUFORT SENIOR (*Off again*) The Fragonards! The enamels! The candlesticks! The snuff-boxes!

EVA I'm glad about the candlesticks, they were appalling. But it's a shame about the Fragonards.

(*Hector enters triumphantly in a new make-up*)

HECTOR Eva, this time I've got it!

EVA No.

LORD EDGARD (*Leaping on him*) At last! The detective! My dear fellow, you're in the nick of time. A serious robbery has just been committed. We suspect some impostors whom we are entertaining at the moment, owing to a curious fancy of my cousin's. Kindly arrest them at once, my dear fellow.

EVA What's come over you, Uncle? That's Prince Hector. Hector, do take off that beard.

HECTOR (*Modestly, as he reveals himself*) Yes sir, it's me.

LORD EDGARD (*In a sudden rage*) How much longer do you intend to make a fool of me, young man?

HECTOR (*Backing imperceptibly toward the door*) But, your lordship, I'm not making a fool of you, really.

LORD EDGARD I can take a joke, in doubtful taste though it is with a man of my years, but don't repeat it a dozen times a day!

HECTOR (*Nearing the door*) But I'm not making a fool . . .

(*He bumps into the* DUPONT-DUFORTS, *who have cut off his retreat*)

DUPONT-DUFORT JUNIOR Oh no.

DUPONT-DUFORT SENIOR Of course you're not making a fool of him. Don't go. Everything will be all right.

HECTOR Look here, what's going on? Am I under suspicion?

EVA Gentlemen, will you please leave His Highness alone?

HECTOR I should think so. Why it's absurd, isn't it, Eva?

LADY HURF (*Entering with* PETERBONO) What is all this shouting? I've never heard such a commotion!

PETERBONO We simply can't hear ourselves speak!

LORD EDGARD It's terrible! There's been a dreadful robbery! I had my suspicions all along. I told you he died in 1904! I told you they were all impostors!

DUPONT-DUFORT SENIOR (*At the same time*) The Fragonards! The enamels! The snuff-boxes! The candlesticks! The drawers!

LADY HURF One at a time, please! I don't know what you're talking about. First of all I must sit down. I'm worn out.

(*During the ejaculations of the others, and the silence which follows,* HECTOR *is desperately indicating to* PETERBONO *that they must be off.* PETERBONO *thinks his cuff-links are undone, his tie crooked or that something is hanging down. He brushes himself, looks in the mirror, still fails to understand, and finally shrugs his shoulders and gives up*)

Now. Tell me all about it.

PETERBONO (*Engagingly*) Splendid idea. Tell us all about it.

LORD EDGARD (*Before they stop him*) Didn't I tell you he died in—

DUPONT-DUFORT SENIOR (*At the same time*) Everything! Everything! The Fragonards! The . . .

(*They look at each other and stop dead*)

EVA There's been a burglary.

LADY HURF A burglary?

EVA Yes. While we were out the enamels were stolen, and the Fragonards, and believe it or not, the candlesticks.

LADY HURF Oh good. They were imitation.

LORD EDGARD I told you so! I told you so!

LADY HURF One of the servants, I expect. Are they all here?

EVA I don't know.

DUPONT-DUFORT SENIOR We must inform the police.

LADY HURF No.

DUPONT-DUFORT SENIOR What do you mean, no?

LADY HURF No, I tell you. I will not have policemen in my house.

DUPONT-DUFORT JUNIOR But we've already telephoned, your ladyship.

LADY HURF My good sirs, have you completely forgotten your manners? I beg you to remember that this is my house. You appear to have abandoned every vestige of constraint these last few days.

DUPONT-DUFORT JUNIOR But we—

DUPONT-DUFORT SENIOR You see, we—

LADY HURF Eva, ring through at once and tell them not to come.

DUPONT-DUFORT SENIOR Too late. They're bound to be on the way.

(*All this time* PETERBONO *and* HECTOR *have been quietly edging toward the door. When* LADY HURF *tells* EVA *to call off the police, they stop, still hopeful. At these last words, they make a frenzied dash for it*)

Look! They're getting away!

DUPONT-DUFORT JUNIOR This is too much! We'll save you, whether you like it or not! Hands up!

DUPONT-DUFORT SENIOR Hands up!

(*They cover the thieves with their revolvers*)

LADY HURF Gentlemen, I am mistress in this house! I order you to put away those firearms!

DUPONT-DUFORT JUNIOR No!

DUPONT-DUFORT SENIOR No. You'll thank us for it later on.

LADY HURF Eva, I'm going to have hysterics! Call the servants! Emile! Here, quickly! Joseph! Help!

(*Enter* POLICE, *during her cries*)

POLICEMAN Here we are! Horace, you take the fat one!

(*They have seen these two horrible bandits pointing their guns at the gentry. Without a moment's indecision, they hurl themselves on the* DUPONT-DUFORTS)

Aha, me beauties! We've got you!

DUPONT-DUFORT SENIOR *and* JUNIOR (*Backing away*) But—but— We didn't do anything! No, no, not us! Not us! Quite the reverse! We're the ones who telephoned! This is preposterous! It's they!

(*They collide as they retreat, try to escape the other way and collide again, in the course of a droll little ballet which culminates in their capture*)

POLICEMEN (*Hoisting them on to their shoulders with the showmanship of circus acrobats*) Upsadaisy!

(*To* HECTOR)

If you'd like to give us a hand, sir, by taking the trouble to open the door, sir, it'd be much appreciated.

HECTOR No trouble. Absolutely no trouble at all.

(*The* POLICEMEN *carry off the* DUPONT-DUFORTS *despite their agonizing protestations*)

LORD EDGARD (*Wildly*) But, my dear . . .

LADY HURF (*Sternly*) Edgard! Be quiet.

DUPONT-DUFORT SENIOR (*Yelling in vain as he is borne away*) For God's sake say something! Tell them! Tell them!

DUPONT-DUFORT JUNIOR (*As he whirls past her*) Mademoiselle Eva!

(*They have gone, played out by their own little melody*)

LADY HURF (*Calmly*) There! That's a relief. Three whole weeks those folks have been here, and I hadn't a notion how to get rid of them.

LORD EDGARD (*Overcome by so many emotions, falls semiconscious into an armchair*) When I think I came here to cure my liver trouble!

LADY HURF Eva dear, run up and get your uncle his smelling-salts.

(EVA *goes.* LADY HURF *looks at* PETERBONO, *who ever since the arrest of the* DUPONT-DUFORTS *has been choking in the grip of irrepressible hysteria*)

My dear man, save your laughter. I know perfectly well you are the real thief.

(*He stops dead. She feels in his pocket*)

Give me back my pearls. You haven't been very clever.

PETERBONO What do you mean?

LADY HURF Have you a lot of luggage? How long will it take you to pack?

PETERBONO (*Piteously*) Not long.

LADY HURF Then I advise you to make the greatest possible haste upstairs.

PETERBONO Yes.

(*Enter* HECTOR)

HECTOR (*Superbly*) There. The rascals are in good hands, your Ladyship.

(PETERBONO *coughs*)

Father dear, are you not feeling well?

LADY HURF No, he's not feeling at all well. I think you had better both go up to your rooms.

HECTOR Really, Father? Where's the trouble exactly?

LORD EDGARD (*Himself once more*) I told you the Duke of Miraflores died in 1904!

LADY HURF I knew it long ago, my dear.

HECTOR (*Still not understanding* PETERBONO'*s desperate dumbshow, says waggishly*) Ha! Ha! Ha! Still the same old joke, eh?

LADY HURF The duke died in my arms, or near enough. So that I knew quite well whom we were dealing with. Only you see, my poor old Edgard, I was so very, very bored.

HECTOR (*Finally going to* PETERBONO) What's the matter, for heaven's sake?

PETERBONO Idiot! I've been trying to tell you for the last half-hour. The game's up, but she's letting us go free.

HECTOR Uh? Don't be silly, they've arrested the others.

LADY HURF (*Going to them with a smile*) You don't, I'm sure, want to await the visit of the inspector of police, gentlemen.

HECTOR This is unthinkable! What are we accused of? We were with you the whole evening!

PETERBONO Don't be canny. Come on.

HECTOR My dear father, I don't know what you're talking about. Madam, we are here as your guests, and this robbery is no reason to treat us, the Miraflores y Grandes, in this cavalier fashion.

PETERBONO (*Unable to suppress a giggle, despite the tragic situation*) Miraflores y Grandes! Oh, my Lord! You're off your head, old chap. Come on.

LADY HURF Go along, sir, do, as everyone advises you

HECTOR I will not tolerate this attitude.

(*To* PETERBONO)

Play up, will you?

EVA (*Coming back*) Here are the salts.

HECTOR I will not tolerate this attitude. Because if you consider our presence undesirable, I laugh to scorn—do you hear, to scorn, your utterly unfounded and insulting allegations. There's someone here, I know, who will think my presence far from undesirable. Eva, Eva my darling, I've found my face at last!

(*He turns away and rapidly re-creates the appearance he had in the first scene*)

PETERBONO Hector, stop playing about. The police are on their way.

HECTOR (*Making up*) Let me alone. We're saved, I tell you!

LADY HURF (*Sits down dispirited*) Edgard, if this headstrong child falls in love with him again, the situation is absolutely hopeless.

LORD EDGARD I have not the faintest idea of what is going on. What is he doing? Is this another piece of comicality? He goes very much too far, that boy.

HECTOR (*Turning round triumphantly*) Eva beloved! It *was* like this, wasn't it?

(*A silence.* EVA *looks at him. The others hold their breath*)

EVA (*Calmly breaking the tension*) Yes, that's how you were. Only I must have looked at you too hastily, I think, because now you don't appeal to me at all.

LADY HURF (*Leaping up*) Heaven be praised! Now, off with you! Quickly, off with you!

HECTOR But, Eva, listen! Eva, I can't believe . . .

PETERBONO (*In a whisper*) Hurry, idiot, hurry! She's taken back the necklace, but I've still got the ring.

(*They go with great dignity. A gay little tune signals their departure*)

LADY HURF (*Watching them go with a tender little smile*) Poor old fellow. I let him keep the ring. They stayed here a full fortnight after all, because of me. We haven't any right to make them waste their time. I imagine it's a trade which can't bring in all that much.

LORD EDGARD What I don't fathom is where the boy comes in.

(*The two women look at him in sudden anguish*)

The boy, the young one, who was so pleasant, you remember?

EVA Juliette! Where's Juliette?

LADY HURF Juliette! She didn't come to the Carnival. Isn't she upstairs? Perhaps in the morning-room? Or in the garden?

EVA I'll run and see. Oh, it's inconceivable.

LORD EDGARD What is inconceivable? I don't understand, quite.

(LADY HURF *drops on to the sofa, and plays nervously with her pearls*)

Why do you look so tragic? It's all over now, isn't it?

LADY HURF No, stupid, it is not all over. This boy has carried off Juliette along with the pictures in the drawing room. How many times did I tell you to bestir yourself and take precautions if we didn't want disaster?

EVA (*Coming back*) She's not upstairs. The servants are combing the grounds.

LADY HURF It's horrible!

LORD EDGARD Juliette, our little Juliette. Is it possible? Can she have been stolen?

EVA Yes.

LORD EDGARD But she's a big girl now. She could have defended herself. Or called for help. The house is overrun with staff.

LADY HURF Can't you understand? She's in his power! He's bewitched her. He'll make her steal for him, or walk the streets!

LORD EDGARD The streets.

(*It dawns on him*)

The Streets!

(*He staggers under the blow. The clarinet plays an air heavy with tragedy. The three of them lapse into pensive and painful silence. The clarinet resumes its tragic theme with an overtone of mockery, and then leads into the romance which is indeed altogether fitting at this moment, for* GUSTAVE *enters on tiptoe, laden with so many things that he cannot see where he is going. He is carrying* JULIETTE, *who is asleep, and his various sacks. He crosses the drawing room, unseen by anybody; suddenly he bumps into an armchair. He drops his sacks with a clatter, and startles the others, who see him and cry out*)

He's killed her!

(GUSTAVE, *terrified, makes to put* JULIETTE *down on the sofa, but at the cries she wakens and clings to him*)

JULIETTE No, no, no! Why did you bring me back? No, he's not to go! If he goes I'm going with him!

LADY HURF Juliette!

LORD EDGARD My child.

JULIETTE (*Screaming through a flood of tears*) Yes, you despise him, I know, but I love him. Don't try to tell me anything—I want to go with him because I love him. Don't say a word, I'd only hate you for it. Gustave, Gustave, why did you bring me back?

(*He struggles and tries to run away but she clutches him*)

No. Stay here, or let me come with you. Why did you bring me back? Was I too stupid for you? Too naïve? Is it because I fell asleep beside you in the car that you don't want me? It's true one doesn't as a rule doze off the night of one's elopement, but I was tired, my darling. I'm not used to staying up so late.

(*She hides her head in his arms*)

LORD EDGARD What is she saying?

LADY HURF (*Moved*) Do be quiet! It's very lovely what she is saying.

JULIETTE (*Turning to them like a little fury, without letting go of* GUSTAVE) No, no, I'm not ashamed! I'm not ashamed! You can say anything you like, I'll never be ashamed! I love him. I want him for my lover, since you will never let him be my husband. Look. I'm going to kiss him now in front of you.

(*She throws her arms round his neck. He holds back for a second, then as he sees her tousled hair and her radiant tear-stained face, he too forgets the others*)

GUSTAVE I love you, Juliette.

JULIETTE You see, we're kissing here, in front of them.

(*They kiss*)

LORD EDGARD (*Adjusting his pince-nez*) Why, they're kissing.

LADY HURF That's right. They're kissing. What about it? Did you never do as much?

(*She contemplates them, entranced*)

How enchanting they are!

LORD EDGARD Aren't they? Do you remember, Emily?

LADY HURF They make a delightful couple, don't they?

LORD EDGARD (*Lost in his memories*) Delightful. Do you remember? The Crystal Palace?

LADY HURF She's nearly as tall as he is. He is adorable. Look at the breeding in that profile. The exquisite shyness and yet the strength of it. He will make a fairy-tale husband for our terrible, gentle little Juliette.

(*She stops*)

Edgard, what are you talking me into? He's a thief!

LORD EDGARD (*Smiling*) Ah yes, a thief.

LADY HURF Well then, it's out of the question. He must go at once.

(*The clarinet stops from shock*)

LORD EDGARD (*Crestfallen*) But—but they love each other.

LADY HURF I know they love each other. But it's the only thing to do. Absolutely the only thing. She simply cannot marry a boy who has neither a father nor a mother.

LORD EDGARD Ah!

(*He thinks furiously for a moment, then cries suddenly*)

Wait a minute! Wait a minute!

(GUSTAVE *and* JULIETTE, *startled by his cry, come out of their embrace.* LORD EDGARD *runs out like one demented*)

LADY HURF Where do you suppose he's going?

JULIETTE I'll never leave him, never, never, never.

GUSTAVE (*Holding her to him, says by way of explanation*) We love each other.

(*The clarinet plays a little supplication*)

LADY HURF I gather so. But there it is. You're nothing but a nobody, if not worse. I'm afraid you'll have to go.

(*Another entreaty from the clarinet*)

JULIETTE If he goes I go with him.

LADY HURF This time we will be here to stop you.

(*The clarinet screams in heart-rending imploration.* LADY HURF *turns furiously on the musician*)

As for you, my good sir, you're beginning to get on my nerves! Go away!

(*The clarinet attempts a musical protest*)

Get out of here this instant!

(*She drives him out. Pathetically the musician goes, expressing his despair on his instrument.* LORD EDGARD *returns like a meteor, carrying ribbons, medals and a photograph. He marches threateningly over to* GUSTAVE)

LORD EDGARD You are twenty years old, are you not?

GUSTAVE Yes.

LORD EDGARD Right.

(*He looks at the photograph, looks at it a second time, backs, screwing up his eyes in the manner of a painter scrutinizing a picture*)

Hold your head up. Fine. Open your shirt. Fine. Now for the mark behind the ear.

(*He turns back his ear*)

Fine.

(*He shows him the medal*)

Do you recognize this medal?

GUSTAVE No.

LORD EDGARD (*Throwing it away*) Never mind. You are my son! My son who was stolen from me at a tender age.

(*He falls into his arms*)

LADY HURF Edgard, have you taken leave of your senses?

GUSTAVE (*Furiously*) Let me go, sir. I don't know what you're talking about.

(*To* JULIETTE)

What's the matter with him?

LORD EDGARD (*To* LADY HURF) Do you deny that a son was stolen from me at a tender age?

(*To* GUSTAVE)

Do you deny that you are uncertain of your paternal origins? Yes, yes, you are my son, my own son, my beloved son!

(*He falls on his neck again*)

JULIETTE Isn't that lucky! Gustave, isn't that lucky!

GUSTAVE (*Freeing himself roughly*) No, it won't work.

LORD EDGARD What won't work?

GUSTAVE I'm quite sure I'm not your son.

LORD EDGARD So I shall have waited twenty years for Heaven to give me back my child, and now when Heaven at last sees fit to give him back to me, it is this very child who refuses to acknowledge his own father!

GUSTAVE No. It's all a scheme because you can see your little girl is in love with me, but I'm sorry, I can't accept.

LADY HURF That's very honorable of him.

LORD EDGARD This is horrible! Horrible! My son denies me!

(*He prances with rage*)

GUSTAVE No, I can't accept. It's nice of you to do it, very nice of you. But I can't. I'm not one of your sort.

LADY HURF It is really unfortunate that this boy should be the only one amongst us to suffer from class-consciousness.

LORD EDGARD I am abominably humiliated. Such contempt from my own son! I shall crumple up with sorrow.

(*He does in fact crumple up with sorrow on the nearest sofa*)

Here I am, crumpled up. How much longer do I have to stay crumpled?

LADY HURF Couldn't you see your way to accepting? You're making your father very unhappy.

GUSTAVE How can I! I haven't any reason—

JULIETTE Oh, but you have! Come into the garden as you did before. I'm going to explain all your reasons to you. Do come, please. Come anyway. You haven't anything to lose after all, by coming into the garden. (*She drags him out*)

LADY HURF (*As soon as they're gone*) Edgard, it's not true! You never had a son stolen from you at a tender age!

LORD EDGARD No, it isn't true. It's a picture I cut out of a magazine.

LADY HURF So you've acted like an imbecile for over fifty years and yet you had it in you to think of that all by yourself.

EVA How happy they are going to be.

LADY HURF (*Dreamily*) Yes.

EVA And I shall continue to play the young and charming widow who is always such a great success.

LADY HURF My poor Eva, faith is a gift, alas, and there's no learning it. It's over, our fine escapade. Here we are alone again, like bobbing corks. It's only for those who have played it with all the zest of youth that the comedy is a success, and only then because they were playing their youth, a thing which succeeds always. They were not even conscious of the comedy. (*Enter a bearded gentleman*)

BEARDED GENTLEMAN I am from Scotland Yard.

LORD EDGARD (*Lets out a roar, leaps on to him and pulls his beard*) Oh no, it won't work this time!

DETECTIVE Stop it! You're hurting me!

LORD EDGARD (*Greatly astonished*) What! Do you mean it's your own?

DETECTIVE Of course it's my own!

LORD EDGARD Then you really are the detective I sent for?

DETECTIVE I've just said so, haven't I?

LORD EDGARD Well we don't need you any more. The entertainment is over.

DETECTIVE (*Blithely*) In that case . . .

(*He pulls his clarinet out of his pocket—for it is none other than the musician—and strikes up a quick-step which does duty as a finale. The characters come in through all the doors, dancing and exchanging beards*)

# ANTIGONE

The vogue of classical myth in modern drama testifies not only to the continuing vitality of the classical tradition, but to the preoccupation of recent playwrights with the relationship of man and the forces that shape or limit his destiny. Antique myth has facilitated the use of drama as a philosophical quest, opposing man and his gods, free will and determinism, a meaningful and meaningless view of the cosmos.

The question of the dignity of life and the meaning of heroic action became especially acute at a moment in history dominated by the police state and the concentration camp. The revival of classical mythology served not only to underscore the continuity of present and past, but to evade the capricious and stupid censorship of the Occupation authorities. Allegory, parable, and Aesopian style were but some of the tricks used to mask the drama of resistance and protest. Allusiveness and indirectness replaced bold literalness of statement. At one time during the Occupation, the *Antigone* dramas of Sophocles, Garnier, and Anouilh were all being performed at the same time. The interest of French playwrights in classical myth did not suddenly begin with World War II, but it acquired a new urgency; Frenchmen torn between collaboration and resistance saw in the ambiguities and tensions of the drama of ancient Greece a mirror of their own spiritual crisis.

The first of Anouilh's mythical plays, *Eurydice* (1941), is closely related in theme to the earlier "Black Plays." Orpheus, more lover than musician, is drawn instinctively to Eurydice but the sordidness of her past comes between them. After her death in an accident, the lovers are given a second chance, but Orpheus refuses happiness based on a lie. Their reunion comes only in death. Anouilh's modernization of the legend, in striking contrast to Cocteau's *Orphée,* emphasizes moral rather than mythical values. His subsequent classical recreations moved beyond the trials of personal experience to embrace political and philosophical conflicts of contemporary history. *Orestes,* begun in 1942 but unfinished, opposes the political expediency of Aegisthus to Electra's uncompromising demand for justice. The close relationship of Aegisthus to Creon in *Antigone* provides clear evidence of Anouilh's deep preoccupation with the claims of accommodation and resistance during the early days of the Occupation.

*Antigone* is modeled on the famous tragedy of Sophocles, but Anouilh's play is an interpretation, not merely a restatement. On the surface, the modern heroine rebels for the same reasons as her ancient forebear: out of a sense of injustice over the violation of a sacred law. As in the Greek drama, this conflict opposes the intransigent individual to the tyranny of the state. Yet, in the course of Anouilh's play, the grounds of tension shift from political to philosophical values; the central issue is the meaning of life itself and the impossibility of maintaining one's purity in a world that demands and imposes compromise. Antigone may not really know why she dies, for Creon convinces her of the futility and senselessness of her resistance, but he overstates his case and only proves that the life Antigone can have is not worth having. Creon is a far more sympathetic figure than we find in Sophocles, and it is understandable why some should see him as the hero of the play. The ambiguity is willful: Creon's practical wisdom points in the direction of Vichy collaboration, yet Antigone refuses the easy and safe way out: "what a person can do, a person ought to do." The appeal to heroism and self-sacrifice in the face of brutal oppression is also part of the play. Antigone's suicide marks her as one of the many Anouilh heroines who refuse happiness and, in their rigorous assertion of principle, challenge the easy ways of everyday existence. Both Antigone and Creon are right; their plea on behalf of contesting principles and values embraces but also goes far beyond the moral and political crisis of the early 1940's.

Anouilh's last play in the classical tradition, *Medea* (1946), is, like *Antigone,* an extended drama in one act. While the presentation of *Antigone* is openly theatrical, close in manner to a play within a play, *Medea* is simpler and more objective in technique. The rapier-like cut and thrust of argument in *Antigone* here gives way to passionate revelation of the inner self. *Medea* is essentially a study in psychopathology, an expression of the savage bestiality that defines for Medea the meaning of her existence.

The repudiation of romantic love and, indeed, of the romantic view of human relationships is as evident in Anouilh's mythical dramas as in his tragicomedies of modern life. A master showman as well as a poet, Anouilh has embodied serious philosophical convictions in plays that amuse and entertain even while they challenge our most cherished and most comfortable assumptions. Anouilh's theatre is indeed a world of pretense and make-believe, but it brings us face to face with our undisguised selves.

# ANTIGONE

## Translated by Lewis Galantière

### CHARACTERS

CHORUS
ANTIGONE
NURSE
ISMENE
HAEMON
CREON
FIRST GUARD, *Jonas*
SECOND GUARD, *a Corporal*
THIRD GUARD
MESSENGER
PAGE
EURYDICE

---

ANTIGONE, *her hands clasped round her knees, sits on the top step. The* THREE GUARDS *sit on the steps, in a small group, playing cards. The* CHORUS *stands on the top step.* EURYDICE *sits on the top step, just left of center, knitting. The* NURSE *sits on the second step, left of* EURYDICE. ISMENE *stands in front of arch, left, facing* HAEMON, *who stands left of her.* CREON *sits in the chair at right end of the table, his arm over the shoulder of his* PAGE, *who sits on the stool beside his chair. The* MESSENGER *is leaning against the downstage portal of the right arch. The curtain rises slowly; then the* CHORUS *turns and moves downstage.*

CHORUS Well, here we are.
These people are about to act out for you the story of Antigone.
That thin little creature sitting by herself, staring straight ahead, seeing nothing, is Antigone. She is thinking. She is thinking that the instant I finish telling you who's who and what's what in this play, she will burst forth as the tense, sallow, wilful girl whose family would never take her seriously and who is about to rise up alone against Creon, her uncle, the King.
Another thing that she is thinking is this: she is going to die. Antigone is young. She would much rather live than die. But there is no help for it. When your name is Antigone, there is only one part you can play; and she will have to play hers through to the end.
From the moment the curtain went up, she began to feel that inhuman forces were whirling her out of this world, snatching her away from her sister, Ismene, whom you see smiling and chatting with that young man; from all of us who sit or stand here, looking at her, not in the least upset ourselves—for we are not doomed to die tonight.
(CHORUS *turns and indicates* HAEMON)
The young man talking to Ismene—to the gay and beautiful Ismene—is Haemon. He is the King's son, Creon's son. Antigone and he are engaged to be married. You wouldn't have thought she was his type. He likes dancing, sports, competition; he likes women, too. Now look at Ismene again. She is certainly more beautiful than Antigone. She is the girl you'd think he'd go for. Well . . . There was a ball one night. Ismene wore a new evening frock. She was radiant. Haemon danced every dance with her. And yet, that same night, before the dance was over, suddenly he went in search of Antigone, found her sitting alone—like that, with her arms clasped round her knees—and asked her to marry him. We still don't know how it happened. It didn't seem to surprise Antigone in the least. She looked up at him out of those solemn eyes of hers, smiled sort of sadly and said "yes." That was all. The band struck up another dance. Ismene, surrounded by a group of young men, laughed out loud. And . . . well, here is Haemon expecting to marry Antigone. He won't, of course. He didn't know, when he asked her, that the earth wasn't meant to hold a husband of Antigone, and that this princely distinction was to earn him no more than the right to die sooner than he might otherwise have done.
(CHORUS *turns toward* CREON)
That gray-haired, powerfully built man sitting lost in thought, with his little page at his side, is Creon, the King. His face is lined. He is tired. He practices the difficult art of a leader of men. When he was younger, when Oedipus was King and Creon was no more than the King's brother-in-law, he was different. He loved music, bought rare manuscripts, was a kind of art patron. He would while away whole afternoons in the antique shops of this city of Thebes. But Oedipus died. Oedipus' sons died. Creon had to roll up his sleeves and take over the kingdom. Now and then, when he goes to bed weary with the day's work, he wonders whether this business of being a leader of men is worth the trouble. But when he wakes up, the prob-

lems are there to be solved; and like a conscientious workman, he does his job.

Creon has a wife, a Queen. Her name is Eurydice. There she sits, the old lady with the knitting, next to the Nurse who brought up the two girls. She will go on knitting all through the play, till the time comes for her to go to her room and die. She is a good woman, a worthy, loving soul. But she is no help to her husband. Creon has to face the music alone. Alone with his Page, who is too young to be of any help. The others? Well, let's see.

(*He points toward the* MESSENGER)

That pale young man leaning against the wall is the Messenger. Later on, he will come running in to announce that Haemon is dead. He has a premonition of catastrophe. That's what he is brooding over. That's why he won't mingle with the others.

As for those three red-faced card players—they are the guards. One smells of garlic, another of beer; but they're not a bad lot. They have wives they are afraid of, kids who are afraid of them; they're bothered by the little day-to-day worries that beset us all. At the same time—they are policemen: eternally innocent, no matter what crimes are committed; eternally indifferent, for nothing that happens can matter to them. They are quite prepared to arrest anybody at all, including Creon himself, should the order be given by a new leader.

That's the lot. Now for the play.

Oedipus, who was the father of the two girls, Antigone and Ismene, had also two sons, Eteocles and Polynices. After Oedipus died, it was agreed that the two sons should share his throne, each to reign over Thebes in alternate years.

(*Gradually, the lights on the stage have been dimmed*)

But when Eteocles, the elder son, had reigned a full year, and time had come for him to step down, he refused to yield up the throne to his younger brother. There was civil war. Polynices brought up allies—six foreign princes; and in the course of the war he and his foreigners were defeated, each in front of one of the seven gates of the city. The two brothers fought, and they killed one another in single combat just outside the city walls. Now Creon is King.

(CHORUS *is leaning, at this point, against the left proscenium arch. By now the stage is dark, with only the cyclorama bathed in dark blue. A single spot lights up the face of* CHORUS)

Creon has issued a solemn edict that Eteocles, with whom he had sided, is to be buried with pomp and honors, and that Polynices is to be left to rot. The vultures and the dogs are to bloat themselves on his carcass. Nobody is to go into mourning for him. No gravestone is to be set up in his memory. And above all, any person who attempts to give him religious burial will himself be put to death.

(*While* CHORUS *has been speaking the characters have gone out one by one.* CHORUS *disappears through the left arch.*

*It is dawn, gray and ashen, in a house asleep.* ANTIGONE *steals in from out-of-doors, through the arch, right. She is carrying her sandals in her hand. She pauses, looking off through the arch, taut, listening, then turns and moves across downstage. As she reaches the table, she sees the* NURSE *approaching through the arch, left. She runs quickly toward the exit. As she reaches the steps, the* NURSE *enters through arch and stands still when she sees* ANTIGONE)

NURSE Where have you been?

ANTIGONE Nowhere. It was beautiful. The whole world was gray when I went out. And now—you wouldn't recognize it. It's like a postcard: all pink, and green, and yellow. You'll have to get up earlier, Nurse, if you want to see a world without color.

NURSE It was still pitch black when I got up. I went to your room, for I thought you might have flung off your blanket in the night. You weren't there.

ANTIGONE (*Comes down the steps*) The garden was lovely. It was still asleep. Have you ever thought how lovely a garden is when it is not yet thinking of men?

NURSE You hadn't slept in your bed. I couldn't find you. I went to the back door. You'd left it open.

ANTIGONE The fields were wet. They were waiting for something to happen. The whole world was breathless, waiting. I can't tell you what a roaring noise I seemed to make alone on the road. It bothered me that whatever was waiting, wasn't waiting for me. I took off my sandals and slipped into a field. (*She moves down to the stool and sits*)

NURSE (*Kneels at* ANTIGONE'*s feet to chafe them and put on the sandals*) You'll do well to wash your feet before you go back to bed, Miss.

ANTIGONE I'm not going back to bed.

NURSE Don't be a fool! You get some sleep! And me, getting up to see if she hasn't flung off her blanket; and I find her bed cold and nobody in it!

ANTIGONE Do you think that if a person got up every morning like this, it would be just as thrilling every morning to be the first girl out of doors?

(NURSE *puts* ANTIGONE'*s left foot down, lifts her other foot and chafes it*)

NURSE Morning, my grandmother! It was night. It still is. And now, my girl, you'll stop trying to squirm out of this and tell me what you were up to. Where've you been?

ANTIGONE That's true. It was still night. There wasn't a soul out of doors but me who thought that it was morning. Don't you think it's marvelous—to be the first person who is aware that it is morning?

NURSE Oh, my little flibbertigibbet! Just can't imagine what I'm talking about, can she? Go on with you! I know that game. Where have you been, wicked girl?

ANTIGONE (*Soberly*) No. Not wicked.

NURSE You went out to meet someone, didn't you? Deny it if you can.

ANTIGONE Yes. I went out to meet someone.

NURSE A lover?

ANTIGONE Yes, Nurse. Yes, the poor dear. I have a lover.

NURSE (*Stands up; bursting out*) Ah, that's very nice now, isn't it? Such goings-on! You, the daughter of a king, running out to meet lovers. And we work our fingers to the bone for you, we slave to bring you up like young ladies! (*She sits on chair, right of table*) You're all alike, all of you. Even you—who never used to stop to primp in front of a looking-glass, or smear your mouth with rouge, or dindle and dandle to make the boys ogle you, and you ogle back. How many times I'd say to myself, "Now that one, now: I wish she was a little more of a coquette—always wearing the same dress, her hair tumbling round her face. One thing's sure," I'd say to myself, "none of the boys will look at her while Ismene's about, all curled and cute and tidy and trim. I'll have this one on my hands for the rest of my life." And now, you see? Just like your sister, after all. Only worse: a hypocrite. Who is the lad? Some little scamp, eh? Somebody you can't bring home and show to your family, and say, "Well, this is him, and I mean to marry him and no other." That's how it is, is it? Answer me!

ANTIGONE (*Smiling faintly*) That's how it is. Yes, Nurse.

NURSE Yes, says she! God save us! I took her when she wasn't that high. I promised her poor mother I'd make a lady of her. And look at her! But don't you go thinking this is the end of this, my young 'un. I'm only your nurse and you can play deaf and dumb with me; I don't count. But your Uncle Creon will hear of this! That, I promise you.

ANTIGONE (*A little weary*) Yes. Creon will hear of this.

NURSE And we'll hear what he has to say when he finds out that you go wandering alone o' nights. Not to mention Haemon. For the girl's engaged! Going to be married! Going to be married, and she hops out of bed at four in the morning to meet somebody else in a field. Do you know what I ought to do to you? Take you over my knee the way I used to do when you were little.

ANTIGONE Please, Nurse, I want to be alone.

NURSE And if you so much as speak of it, she says she wants to be alone!

ANTIGONE Nanny, you shouldn't scold, dear. This isn't a day when you should be losing your temper.

NURSE Not scold, indeed! Along with the rest of it, I'm to like it. Didn't I promise your mother? What would she say if she was here? "Old Stupid!" That's what she'd call me. "Old Stupid. Not to know how to keep my little girl pure! Spend your life making them behave, watching over them like a mother hen, running after them with mufflers and sweaters to keep them warm, and egg nogs to make them strong; and then at four o'clock in the morning, you who always complained you never could sleep a wink, snoring in your bed and letting them slip out into the bushes." That's what she'd say, your mother. And I'd stand there, dying of shame if I wasn't dead already. And all I could do would be not to dare look her in the face; and "That's true," I'd say. "That's all true what you say, Your Majesty."

ANTIGONE Nanny, dear. Dear Nanny. Don't cry. You'll be able to look Mamma in the face when it's your time to see her. And she'll say, "Good morning, Nanny. Thank you for my little Antigone. You did look after her so well." She knows why I went out this morning.

NURSE Not to meet a lover?

ANTIGONE No. Not to meet a lover.

NURSE Well, you've a queer way of teasing me, I must say! Not to know when she's teasing me! (*Rises to stand behind* ANTIGONE) I must be getting awfully old, that's what it is. But if you loved me, you'd tell me the truth. You'd tell me why your bed was empty when I went along to tuck you in. Wouldn't you?

ANTIGONE Please, Nanny, don't cry any more. (ANTIGONE *turns partly toward* NURSE, *puts an arm up to* NURSE'S *shoulder. With her other hand,* ANTIGONE *caresses* NURSE'S *face*). There now, my sweet red apple. Do you remember how I used to rub your cheeks to make them shine? My dear, wrinkled red apple! I didn't do anything tonight that was worth sending tears down the little gullies of your dear face. I am pure, and I swear that I have no other lover than Haemon. If you like, I'll swear that I shall never have any other lover than Haemon. Save your tears, Nanny, save them, Nanny dear; you may still need them. When you cry like that, I become a little girl again; and I mustn't be a little girl today. (ANTIGONE *rises and moves upstage*)

(ISMENE *enters through arch, left. She pauses in front of arch*)

ISMENE Antigone! What are you doing up at this hour? I've just been to your room.

NURSE The two of you, now! You're both going mad, to be up before the kitchen fire has been started. Do you like running about without a mouthful of breakfast? Do you think it's decent for the daughters of a king? (*She turns to* ISMENE) And look at you, with nothing on, and the sun not up! I'll have you both on my hands with colds before I know it.

ANTIGONE Nanny dear, go away now. It's not chilly, really. Summer's here. Go and make us some coffee. Please, Nanny, I'd love some coffee. It would do me so much good.

NURSE My poor baby! Her head's swimming, what with nothing on her stomach, and me standing here like an idiot when I could be getting her something hot to drink.

(NURSE *exits*)

(*A pause*)

ISMENE Aren't you well?

ANTIGONE Of course I am. Just a little tired. I got up too early. (ANTIGONE *sits on a chair, suddenly tired*)

ISMENE I couldn't sleep, either.

ANTIGONE Ismene, you ought not to go without your beauty sleep.

ISMENE Don't make fun of me.

ANTIGONE I'm not, Ismene, truly. This particular morning, seeing how beautiful you are makes everything easier for me. Wasn't I a miserable little beast when we were small? I used to fling mud at you, and put worms down your neck. I remember tying you to a tree and cutting off your hair. Your beautiful hair! How easy it must be never to be unreasonable with all that smooth silken hair so beautifully set round your head.

ISMENE (*Abruptly*) Why do you insist upon talking about other things?

ANTIGONE (*Gently*) I am not talking about other things.

ISMENE Antigone, I've thought about it a lot.

ANTIGONE Have you?

ISMENE I thought about it all night long. Antigone, you're mad.

ANTIGONE Am I?

ISMENE We cannot do it.

ANTIGONE Why not?

ISMENE Creon will have us put to death.

ANTIGONE Of course he will. That's what he's here for. He will do what he has to do, and we will do what we have to do. He is bound to put us to death. We are bound to go out and bury our brother. That's the way it is. What do you think we can do to change it?

ISMENE (*Releases* ANTIGONE'S *hand; draws back a step*) I don't want to die.

ANTIGONE I'd prefer not to die, myself.

ISMENE Listen to me, Antigone. I thought about it all night. I'm older than you are. I always think things over, and you don't. You are impulsive. You get a notion in your head and you jump up and do the thing straight off. And if it's silly, well, so much the worse for you. Whereas, *I* think things out.

ANTIGONE Sometimes it is better not to think too much.

ISMENE I don't agree with you! (ANTIGONE *looks at* ISMENE, *then turns and moves to chair behind table.* ISMENE *leans on end of table top, toward* ANTIGONE) Oh, I know it's horrible. And I pity Polynices just as much as you do. But all the same, I sort of see what Uncle Creon means.

ANTIGONE I don't want to "sort of see" anything.

ISMENE Uncle Creon is the king. He has to set an example!

ANTIGONE But I am not the king; and I don't have to set people examples. Little Antigone gets a notion in her head—the nasty brat, the wilful, wicked girl; and they put her in a corner all day, or they lock her up in the cellar. And she deserves it. She shouldn't have disobeyed!

ISMENE There you go, frowning, glowering, wanting your own stubborn way in everything. Listen to me. I'm right oftener than you are.

ANTIGONE I don't want to be right!

ISMENE At least you can try to understand.

ANTIGONE Understand! The first word I ever heard out of any of you was that word "understand." Why didn't I "understand" that I must not play with water—cold, black, beautiful flowing water—because I'd spill it on the palace tiles. Or with earth, because earth dirties a little girl's frock. Why didn't I "understand" that nice children don't eat out of every dish at once; or give everything in their pockets to beggars; or run in the wind so fast that they fall down; or ask for a drink when they're perspiring; or want to go swimming when it's either too early or too late, merely because they happen to feel like swimming. Understand! I don't want to understand. There'll be time enough to understand when I'm old. . . . If I ever *am* old. But not now.

ISMENE He is stronger than we are, Antigone. He is the king. And the whole city is with him. Thousands and thousands of them, swarming through all the streets of Thebes.

ANTIGONE I am not listening to you.

ISMENE His mob will come running, howling as it runs. A thousand arms will seize our arms. A thousand breaths will breathe into our faces. Like one single pair of eyes, a thousand eyes will stare at us. We'll be driven in a tumbrel through their hatred, through the smell of them and their cruel, roaring laughter. We'll be dragged to the scaffold for torture, surrounded by guards with their idiot faces all bloated, their animal hands clean-washed for the sacrifice, their beefy eyes squinting as they stare at us. And we'll know that no shrieking and no begging will make them understand that we want to live, for they are like slaves who do exactly as they've been told, without caring about right or wrong. And we shall suffer, we shall feel pain rising in us until it becomes so unbearable that we *know* it must stop. But it won't stop; it will go on rising and rising, like a screaming voice. Oh, I can't, I can't, Antigone!

(*A pause*)

ANTIGONE How well you have thought it all out.

ISMENE I thought of it all night long. Didn't you?

ANTIGONE Oh, yes.

ISMENE I'm an awful coward, Antigone.

ANTIGONE So am I. But what has that to do with it?

ISMENE But, Antigone! Don't you want to go on living?

ANTIGONE Go on living! Who was it that was always the first out of bed because she loved the touch of the cold morning air on her bare skin? Who was always the last to bed because nothing less than infinite weariness could wean her from the lingering night? Who wept when she was little because there were too many grasses in the meadow, too many creatures in the field, for her to know and touch them all?

ISMENE (*Clasps* ANTIGONE'S *hands, in a sudden rush of tenderness*) Darling little sister!

ANTIGONE (*Repulsing her*) No! For heaven's sake! Don't paw me! And don't let us start sniveling! You say you've thought it all out. The howling mob—the torture—the fear of death. . . . They've made up your mind for you. Is that it?

ISMENE Yes.

ANTIGONE All right. They're as good excuses as any.

ISMENE Antigone, be sensible. It's all very well for men to believe in ideas and die for them. But you are a girl!

ANTIGONE Don't I know I'm a girl? Haven't I spent my life cursing the fact that I was a girl?

ISMENE (*With spirit*) Antigone! You have everything in the world to make you happy. All you have to do is reach out for it. You are going to be married; you are young; you are beautiful—

ANTIGONE I am not beautiful.

ISMENE Yes, you are! Not the way other girls are. But it's always you that the little boys turn to look back at when they pass us in the street. And when you go by, the little girls stop talking. They stare and stare at you, until we've turned a corner.

ANTIGONE (*A faint smile*) "Little boys—little girls."

ISMENE (*Challengingly*) And what about Haemon? (*A pause*)

ANTIGONE I shall see Haemon this morning. I'll take care of Haemon. You always said I was mad; and it didn't matter how little I was or what I wanted to do. Go back to bed now, Ismene. The sun is coming up, and, as you see, there is nothing I can do today. Our brother Polynices is as well guarded as if he had won the war and were sitting on his throne. Go along. You are pale with weariness.

ISMENE What are you going to do?

NURSE (*Calls from off-stage*) Come along, my dove. Come to breakfast.

ANTIGONE I don't feel like going to bed. However, if you like, I'll promise not to leave the house till you wake up. Nurse is getting me breakfast. Go and sleep. The sun is just up. Look at you: you can't keep your eyes open. Go.

ISMENE And you will listen to reason, won't you? You'll let me talk to you about this again? Promise?

ANTIGONE I promise. I'll let you talk. I'll let all of you talk. Go to bed, now. (ISMENE *goes to arch and exits*) Poor Ismene!

NURSE (*Enters through arch, speaking as she enters*) Come along, my dove. I've made you some coffee and toast and jam. (*She turns toward arch as if to exit*)

ANTIGONE I'm not really hungry, Nurse.

(NURSE *stops, looks at* ANTIGONE, *then moves behind her*)

NURSE (*Very tenderly*) Where is your pain?

ANTIGONE Nowhere, Nanny dear. But you must keep me warm and safe, the way you used to do when I was little. Nanny! Stronger than all fever, stronger than any nightmare, stronger than the shadow of the cupboard that used to snarl at me and turn into a dragon on the bedroom wall. Stronger than the thousand insects gnawing and nibbling in the silence of the night. Stronger than the night itself, with the weird hooting of the nightbirds that frightened me even when I couldn't hear them. Nanny, stronger than death, give me your hand, Nanny, as if I were ill in bed, and you sitting beside me.

NURSE My sparrow, my lamb! What is it that's eating your heart out?

ANTIGONE Oh, it's just that I'm a little young still for what I have to go through. But nobody but you must know that.

NURSE (*Places her other arm round* ANTIGONE'S *shoulder*) A little young for what, my kitten?

ANTIGONE Nothing in particular, Nanny. Just—all this. Oh, it's so good that you are here. I can hold your callused hand, your hand that is so prompt to ward off evil. You are very powerful, Nanny.

NURSE What is it you want me to do for you, my baby?

ANTIGONE There isn't anything to do, except put your hand like this against my cheek. (*She places the* NURSE'S *hand against her cheek. A pause, then, as* ANTIGONE *leans back, her eyes shut*) There! I'm not afraid any more. Not afraid of the wicked ogre, nor of the sandman, nor of the dwarf who steals little children. (*A pause.* ANTIGONE *resumes on another note*) Nanny . . .

NURSE Yes?

ANTIGONE My dog, Puff . . .

NURSE (*Straightens up, draws her hand away*) Well?

ANTIGONE Promise me that you will never scold her again.

NURSE Dogs that dirty up a house with their filthy paws deserve to be scolded.

ANTIGONE I know. Just the same, promise me.

NURSE You mean you want me to let her make a mess all over the place and not say a thing?

ANTIGONE Yes, Nanny.

NURSE You're asking a lot. The next time she wets my living-room carpet, I'll—

ANTIGONE Please, Nanny, I beg of you!

NURSE It isn't fair to take me on my weak side, just because you look a little peaked today. . . . Well, have it your own way. We'll mop up and keep our mouth shut. You're making a fool of me, though.

ANTIGONE And promise me that you will talk to her. That you will talk to her often.

NURSE (*Turns and looks at* ANTIGONE) Me, talk to a dog!

ANTIGONE Yes. But mind you: you are not to talk to her the way people usually talk to dogs. You're to talk to her the way I talk to her.

NURSE I don't see why both of us have to make fools of ourselves. So long as you're here, one ought to be enough.

ANTIGONE But if there was a reason why I couldn't go on talking to her—

NURSE (*Interrupting*) Couldn't go on talking to her! And why couldn't you go on talking to her? What kind of poppycock—?

ANTIGONE And if she got too unhappy, if she moaned and moaned, waiting for me with her nose under the door as she does when I'm out all day, then the best thing, Nanny, might be to have her mercifully put to sleep.

NURSE Now what *has* got into you this morning? (HAEMON *enters through arch*) Running round in the darkness, won't sleep, won't eat—(ANTIGONE *sees* HAEMON)—and now it's her dog she wants killed. I never—

ANTIGONE (*Interrupting*) Nanny! Haemon is here. Go inside, please. And don't forget that you've promised me. (NURSE *goes to arch and exits.* ANTIGONE *rises*) Haemon, Haemon! Forgive me for quarreling with you last night. (*She crosses quickly to* HAEMON *and they embrace*) Forgive me for everything. It was all my fault. I beg you to forgive me.

HAEMON You know that I've forgiven you. You had hardly slammed the door, your perfume still hung in the room, when I had already forgiven you. (*He holds her in his arms and smiles at her. Then draws slightly back*) You stole that perfume. From whom?

ANTIGONE Ismene.

HAEMON And the rouge? and the face powder? and the frock? Whom did you steal them from?

ANTIGONE Ismene.

HAEMON And in whose honor did you get yourself up so elegantly?

ANTIGONE I'll tell you everything. (*She draws him closer*) Oh, darling, what a fool I was! To waste a whole evening! A whole, beautiful evening!

HAEMON We'll have other evenings, my sweet.

ANTIGONE Perhaps we won't.

HAEMON And other quarrels, too. A happy love is full of quarrels, you know.

ANTIGONE A happy love, yes. Haemon, listen to me.

HAEMON Yes?

ANTIGONE Don't laugh at me this morning. Be serious.

HAEMON I am serious.

ANTIGONE And hold me tight. Tighter than you have ever held me. I want all your strength to flow into me.

HAEMON There! With all my strength.

(*A pause*)

ANTIGONE (*Breathless*) That's good. (*They stand for a moment, silent and motionless*) Haemon! I wanted to tell you. You know—the little boy we were going to have when we were married?

HAEMON Yes?

ANTIGONE I'd have protected him against everything in the world.

HAEMON Yes, dearest.

ANTIGONE Oh, you don't know how I should have held him in my arms and given him my strength. He wouldn't have been afraid of anything, I swear he wouldn't. Not of the falling night, nor of the terrible noonday sun, nor of all the shadows or all the walls in the world. Our little boy, Haemon! His mother wouldn't have been very imposing: her hair wouldn't always have been brushed; but she would have been strong where he was concerned, so much stronger than all those real mothers with their real bosoms and their aprons round their middle. You believe that, don't you, Haemon?

HAEMON (*Soothingly*) Yes, yes, my darling.

ANTIGONE And you believe me when I say that you would have had a real wife?

HAEMON Darling, you are my real wife.

ANTIGONE (*Pressing against him and crying out*) Haemon, you loved me! You did love me that night, didn't you? You're sure of it!

HAEMON (*Rocking her gently*) What night, my sweet?

ANTIGONE And you are very sure, aren't you, that that night, at the dance, when you came to the corner where I was sitting, there was no mistake? It was me you were looking for? It wasn't another girl? And you're sure that never, not in your most secret heart of hearts, have you said to yourself that it was Ismene you ought to have asked to marry you?

HAEMON (*Reproachfully*) Antigone, you are idiotic. You might give me credit for knowing my own mind. It's you I love, and no one else.

ANTIGONE But you love me as a woman—as a woman wants to be loved, don't you? Your arms round me aren't lying, are they? Your hands, so warm against my back—they're not lying? This warmth that's in me; this confidence, this sense that I am safe, secure, that flows through me as I stand here with my cheek in the hollow of your shoulder: they are not lies, are they?

HAEMON Antigone, darling, I love you exactly as you love me. With all of myself.

(*They kiss*)

ANTIGONE I'm sallow, and I'm scrawny. Ismene is pink and golden. She's like a fruit.

HAEMON Look here, Antigone—

ANTIGONE Ah, dearest, I am ashamed of myself. But this morning, this special morning, I must know. Tell me the truth! I beg you to tell me the truth! When you think about me, when it strikes you suddenly that I am going to belong to you—do you have the feeling that—that a great empty space is being hollowed out inside you, that there is something inside you that is just—dying?

HAEMON Yes, I do, I do.

(*A pause*)

ANTIGONE That's the way I feel. And another thing. I wanted you to know that I should have been very proud to be your wife—the woman whose shoulder you would put your hand on as you sat down to table, absentmindedly, as upon a thing that belonged to you. (*After a moment, draws away from him. Her tone changes*) There! Now I have two things more to tell you. And when I have told them to you, you must go away instantly, without asking any questions. However strange they may seem to you. However much they may hurt you. Swear that you will!

HAEMON (*Beginning to be troubled*) What are these things that you are going to tell me?

ANTIGONE Swear, first, that you will go away without one word. Without so much as looking at me. (*She looks at him, wretchedness in her face*) You hear me, Haemon. Swear it, please. This is the last mad wish that you will ever have to grant me.

(*A pause*)

HAEMON I swear it, since you insist. But I must tell you that I don't like this at all.

ANTIGONE Please, Haemon. It's very serious. You must listen to me and do as I ask. First, about last night, when I came to your house. You asked me a moment ago why I wore Ismene's dress and rouge. It was because I was stupid. I wasn't very sure that you loved me as a woman; and I did it—because I wanted you to want me. I was trying to be more like other girls.

HAEMON Was *that* the reason? My poor—

ANTIGONE Yes. And you laughed at me. And we quarreled; and my awful temper got the better of me and I flung out of the house. . . . The real reason was that I wanted you to take me; I wanted to be your wife before—

HAEMON Oh, my darling—

ANTIGONE (*Shuts him off*) You swore you wouldn't ask any questions. You swore, Haemon. (*Turns her face away and goes on in a hard voice*) As a matter of fact, I'll tell you why. I wanted to be your wife last night because I love you that way very—very strongly. And also because— Oh, my darling, my darling, forgive me; I'm going to cause you quite a lot of pain. (*She draws away from him*) I wanted it also because I shall never, never be able to marry you, never! (HAEMON *is stupefied and mute; then he moves a step toward her*) Haemon! You took a solemn oath! You swore! Leave me quickly! Tomorrow the whole thing will be clear to you. Even before tomorrow: this afternoon. If you please, Haemon, go now. It is the only thing left that you can do for me if you still love me. (*A pause as* HAEMON *stares at her. Then he turns and goes out through the arch.* ANTIGONE *stands motionless, then moves to chair at end of table and lets herself gently down on it. In a mild voice, as of calm after storm*) Well, it's over for Haemon, Antigone.

(ISMENE *enters through arch, pauses for a moment in front of it when she sees* ANTIGONE, *then crosses behind table*)

ISMENE I can't sleep. I'm terrified. I'm so afraid that even though it is daylight, you'll still try to bury Polynices. Antigone, little sister, we all want to make you happy—Haemon, and Nurse, and I, and Puff whom you love. We love you, we are alive, we need you. And you remember what Polynices was like. He was our brother, of course. But he's dead; and he never loved you. He was a bad brother. He was like an enemy in the house. He never thought of you. Why should you think of him? What if his soul does have to wander through endless time without rest or peace? Don't try something that is beyond your strength. You are always defying the world, but you're only a girl, after all. Stay at home tonight. Don't try to do it, I beg you. It's Creon's doing, not ours.

ANTIGONE You are too late, Ismene. When you first saw me this morning, I had just come in from burying him.

(ANTIGONE *exits through arch*)

(*The lighting, which by this time has reached a point of early morning sun, is quickly dimmed out, leaving the stage bathed in a light blue color*)

(ISMENE *runs out after* ANTIGONE)

(*On* ISMENE'S *exit the lights are brought up suddenly to suggest a later period of the day*)

(CREON *and* PAGE *enter through curtain upstage.* CREON *stands on the top step; his* PAGE *stands at his right side*)

CREON A private of the guards, you say? One of those standing watch over the body? Show him in.

(*The* PAGE *crosses to arch and exits.* CREON *moves down to end of table.*

PAGE *re-enters, preceded by the* FIRST GUARD, *livid with fear.* PAGE *remains on upstage side of arch.* GUARD *salutes*)

GUARD Private Jonas, Second Battalion.

CREON What are you doing here?

GUARD It's like this, sir. Soon as it happened, we said: "Got to tell the chief about this before anybody else spills it. He'll want to know right away." So we tossed a coin to see which one would come up and tell you about it. You see, sir, we thought only one man had better come because, after all, you don't want to leave the body without a guard. Right? I mean, there's three of us on duty, guarding the body.

CREON What's wrong about the body?

GUARD Sir, I've been seventeen years in the service. Volunteer. Wounded three times. Two mentions. My record's clean. I know my busines and I know my place. I carry out orders. Sir, ask any officer in the battalion; they'll tell you. "Leave it to Jonas. Give him an order: he'll carry it out." That's what they'll tell you, sir. Jonas, that's me—that's my name.

CREON What's the matter with you, man? What are you shaking for?

GUARD By rights it's the corporal's job, sir. I've been recommended for a corporal but they haven't put it through yet. June, it was supposed to go through.

CREON (*Interrupts*) Stop chattering and tell me why you are here. If anything has gone wrong, I'll break all three of you.

GUARD Nobody can say we didn't keep our eye on that body. We had the two o'clock watch—the tough one. You know how it is, sir. It's nearly the end of the night. Your eyes are like lead. You've got a crick in the back of your neck. There's shadows, and the fog is beginning to roll in. A fine watch they give us! And me, seventeen years in the service. But we was doing our duty all right. On our feet, all of us. Anybody says we were sleeping is a liar. First place, it was too cold. Second place—(CREON *makes a gesture of impatience*) Yes, sir. Well, I turned round and looked at the body. We wasn't only ten feet away from it, but that's how I am. I was keeping my eye on it. (*Shouts*) Listen, sir, I was the first man to see it! Me! They'll tell you. I was the one let out that yell!

CREON What for? What was the matter?

GUARD Sir, the body! Somebody had been there and buried it. (CREON *comes down a step on the stair. The* GUARD *becomes more frightened*) It wasn't much, you understand. With us three there, it couldn't have been. Just covered over with a little dirt, that's all. But enough to hide it from the buzzards.

CREON By God, I'll—! (*He looks intently at the* GUARD)

You are sure that it couldn't have been a dog, scratching up the earth?

GUARD Not a chance, sir. That's kind of what we hoped it was. But the earth was scattered over the body just like the priests tell you you should do it. Whoever did that job knew what he was doing all right.

CREON Who could have dared? (*He turns and looks at the* GUARD) Was there anything to indicate who might have done it?

GUARD Not a thing, sir. Maybe we heard a footstep—I can't swear to it. Of course we started right in to search, and the corporal found a shovel, a kid's shovel no bigger than that, all rusty and everything. Corporal's got the shovel for you. We thought maybe a kid did it.

CREON (*To himself*) A kid! (*He looks away from the* GUARD) I broke the back of the rebellion; but like a snake, it is coming together again. Polynices' friends, with their gold, blocked by my orders in the banks of Thebes. The leaders of the mob, stinking of garlic and allied to envious princes. And the temple priests, always ready for a bit of fishing in troubled waters. A kid! I can imagine what he is like, their kid: a baby-faced killer, creeping in the night with a toy shovel under his jacket. (*He looks at his* PAGE) Though why shouldn't they have corrupted a real child? Very touching! Very useful to the party, an innocent child. A martyr. A real white-faced baby of fourteen who will spit with contempt at the guards who kill him. A free gift to their cause: the precious, innocent blood of a child on my hands. (*He turns to the* GUARD) They must have accomplices in the Guard itself. Look here, you. Who knows about this?

GUARD Only us three, sir. We flipped a coin, and I came right over.

CREON Right. Listen, now. You will continue on duty. When the relief squad comes up, you will tell them to return to barracks. You will uncover the body. If another attempt is made to bury it, I shall expect you to make an arrest and bring the person straight to me. And you will keep your mouths shut. Not one word of this to a human soul. You are all guilty of neglect of duty, and you will be punished; but if the rumor spreads through Thebes that the body received burial, you will be shot—all three of you.

GUARD (*excitedly*) Sir, we never told nobody, I swear we didn't! Anyhow, I've been up here. Suppose my pals spilled it to the relief; I couldn't have been with them and here too. That wouldn't be my fault if they talked. Sir, I've got two kids. You're my witness, sir, it couldn't have been me. I was here with you. I've got a witness! If anybody talked, it couldn't have been me! I was—

CREON (*Interrupting*) Clear out! If the story doesn't get round, you won't be shot. (*The* GUARD *salutes, turns and exits, at the double.* CREON *turns and paces upstage, then comes down to end of the table*) A child! (*He looks at* PAGE) Come along, my lad. Since we can't hope to keep this to ourselves, we shall have to be the first to give out the news. And after that, we shall have to clean up the mess. (PAGE *crosses to side of* CREON. CREON *puts his hand on* PAGE'S *shoulder*) Would you be willing to die for me? Would you defy the Guard with your little shovel? (PAGE *looks up at* CREON) Of course you would. You would do it, too. (*A pause.* CREON *looks away from* PAGE *and murmurs*) A child! (CREON *and* PAGE *go slowly upstage center to top step.* PAGE *draws aside the curtain, through which* CREON *exits with* PAGE *behind him*)

(*As soon as* CREON *and* PAGE *have disappeared,* CHORUS *enters and leans against the upstage portal of arch, left. The lighting is brought up to its brightest point to suggest midafternoon.* CHORUS *allows a pause to indicate that a crucial moment has been reached in the play, then moves slowly downstage, center. He stands for a moment silent, reflecting, and then smiles faintly*)

CHORUS The spring is wound up tight. It will uncoil of itself. That is what is so convenient in tragedy. The least little turn of the wrist will do the job. Anything will set it going: a glance at a girl who happens to be lifting her arms to her hair as you go by; a feeling when you wake up on a fine morning that you'd like a little respect paid to you today, as if it were as easy to order as a second cup of coffee; one question too many, idly thrown out over a friendly drink—and the tragedy is on.

The rest is automatic. You don't need to lift a finger. The machine is in perfect order; it has been oiled ever since time began, and it runs without friction. Death, treason, and sorrow are on the march; and they move in the wake of storm, of tears, of stillness. Every kind of stillness. The hush when the executioner's ax goes up at the end of the last act. The unbreathable silence when, at the beginning of the play, the two lovers, their hearts bared, their bodies naked, stand for the first time face to face in the darkened room, afraid to stir. The silence inside you when the roaring crowd acclaims the winner—so that you think of a film without a sound-track, mouths agape and no sound coming out of them, a clamor that is no more than a picture; and you, the victor, already vanquished, alone in the desert of your silence. That is tragedy.

Tragedy is clean, it is restful, it is flawless. It has nothing to do with melodrama—with wicked villains, persecuted maidens, avengers, sudden revelations, and eleventh-hour repentances. Death, in a melodrama, is really horrible because it is never inevitable. The dear old father might so easily have been saved; the honest young man might so easily have brought in the police five minutes earlier.

In a tragedy, nothing is in doubt and everyone's destiny is known. That makes for tranquillity. There is a sort of fellow-feeling among characters in a tragedy: he who kills is as innocent as he who gets killed: it's all a matter of what part you are playing. Tragedy is restful; and the reason is that hope, that foul, deceitful thing, has no part in it. There isn't any hope. You're trapped. The whole sky has fallen on you, and all you can do about it is to shout.

Don't mistake me: I said "shout": I did not say groan, whimper, complain. That, you cannot do. But you can shout aloud; you can get all those things said that you never thought you'd be able to say—or never even knew you had it in you to say. And you don't say these things because it will do any good to say them: you know better than that. You say them for their own sake; you say them because you learn a lot from them.

In melodrama, you argue and struggle in the hope of escape. That is vulgar; it's practical. But in tragedy, where there is no temptation to try to escape, argument is gratuitous: it's kingly.

(*Voices of the* GUARDS *and scuffling sounds heard through the archway.* CHORUS *looks in that direction, in a changed tone*)

The play is on. Antigone has been caught. For the first time in her life, little Antigone is going to be able to be herself.

(CHORUS *exits through arch*)

(*A pause, while the offstage voices rise in volume, then the* FIRST GUARD *enters, followed by* SECOND *and* THIRD GUARDS, *holding the arms of* ANTIGONE *and dragging her along. The* FIRST GUARD, *speaking as he enters, crosses swiftly to end of the table. The* TWO GUARDS *and* ANTIGONE *stop downstage*)

FIRST GUARD (*Recovered from his fright*) Come on, now, Miss, give it a rest. The chief will be here in a minute and you can tell him about it. All I know is my orders. I don't want to know what you were doing there. People always have excuses; but I can't afford to listen to them, see. Why, if we had to listen to all the people who want to tell us what's the matter with this country, we'd never get our work done. (*To the* GUARDS) You keep hold of her and I'll see that she keeps her face shut.

ANTIGONE They are hurting me. Tell them to take their dirty hands off me.

FIRST GUARD Dirty hands, eh? The least you can do is try to be polite, Miss. Look at me: I'm polite.

ANTIGONE Tell them to let me go. I shan't run away. My father was King Oedipus. I am Antigone.

FIRST GUARD King Oedipus' little girl! Well, well, well! Listen, Miss, the night watch never picks up a lady but they say, you better be careful: I'm sleeping with the police commissioner.

(*The* GUARDS *laugh*)

ANTIGONE I don't mind being killed, but I don't want them to touch me.

FIRST GUARD And what about stiffs, and dirt, and such like? You wasn't afraid to touch them, was you? "Their dirty hands!" Take a look at your own hands. (ANTIGONE, *handcuffed, smiles despite herself as she looks down at her hands. They are grubby*) You must have lost your shovel, didn't you? Had to go at it with your fingernails the second time, I'll bet. By God, I never saw such nerve! I turn my back for about five seconds; I ask a pal for a chew; I say "thanks"; I get the tobacco stowed away in my check—the whole thing don't take ten seconds; and there she is, clawing away like a hyena. Right out in broad daylight! And did she scratch and kick when I grabbed her! Straight for my eyes with them nails she went. And yelling something fierce about, "I haven't finished yet; let me finish!" She ain't got all her marbles!

SECOND GUARD I pinched a nut like that the other day. Right on the main square she was, hoisting up her skirts and showing her behind to anybody that wanted to take a look.

FIRST GUARD Listen, we're going to get a bonus out of this. What do you say we throw a party, the three of us?

SECOND GUARD At the old woman's? Behind Market Street?

THIRD GUARD Suits me. Sunday would be a good day. We're off duty Sunday. What do you say we bring our wives?

FIRST GUARD No. Let's have some fun this time. Bring your wife, there's always something goes wrong. First place, what do you do with the kids? Bring them, they always want to go to the can just when you're right in the middle of a game of cards or something. Listen, who would have thought an hour ago that us three would be talking about throwing a party now? The way I felt when the old man was interrogating me, we'd be lucky if we got off with being docked a month's pay. I want to tell you, I was scared.

SECOND GUARD You sure we're going to get a bonus?

FIRST GUARD Yes. Something tells me this is big stuff.

THIRD GUARD (*To* SECOND GUARD) What's-his-name, you know—in the Third Battalion? He got an extra month's pay for catching a fire-bug.

SECOND GUARD If we get an extra month's pay, I vote we throw the party at the Arabian's.

FIRST GUARD You're crazy! He charges twice as much for liquor as anybody else in town. Unless you want to go upstairs, of course. Can't do that at the old woman's.

THIRD GUARD Well, we can't keep this from our wives, no matter how you work it out. You get an extra month's pay, and what happens? Everybody in the battalion knows it, and your wife knows it too. They might even line up the battalion and give it to you in front of everybody, so how could you keep your wife from finding out?

FIRST GUARD Well, we'll see about that. If they do the job out in the barrack-yard—of course that means women, kids, everything.

ANTIGONE I should like to sit down, if you please.

(*A pause, as the* FIRST GUARD *thinks it over*)

FIRST GUARD Let her sit down. But keep hold of her. (*The two* GUARDS *start to lead her toward the chair at end of table. The curtain upstage opens, and* CREON *enters, followed by his* PAGE. FIRST GUARD *turns and moves upstage a few steps, sees* CREON) 'Tenshun! (*The three* GUARDS *salute.* CREON, *seeing* ANTIGONE *handcuffed to* THIRD GUARD, *stops on the top step, astonished*)

CREON Antigone! (*To the* FIRST GUARD) Take off those handcuffs! (FIRST GUARD *crosses above table to left of* ANTIGONE) What is this? (CREON *and his* PAGE *come down off the steps*)

(FIRST GUARD *takes key from his pocket and unlocks the cuff on* ANTIGONE'S *hand.* ANTIGONE *rubs her wrist as she crosses below table toward chair at end of table.* SECOND *and* THIRD GUARDS *step back to front of arch.* FIRST GUARD *turns upstage toward* CREON)

FIRST GUARD The watch, sir. We all came this time.

CREON Who is guarding the body?

FIRST GUARD We sent for the relief.

(CREON *comes down*)

CREON But I gave orders that the relief was to go back to barracks and stay there! (ANTIGONE *sits on chair at left of table*) I told you not to open your mouth about this!

FIRST GUARD Nobody's said anything, sir. We made this arrest, and brought the party in, the way you said we should.

CREON Fools! (*To* ANTIGONE) Where did these men find you?

FIRST GUARD Right by the body.

CREON What were you doing near your brother's body? You knew what my orders were.

FIRST GUARD What was she doing? Sir, that's why we brought her in. She was digging up the dirt with her nails. She was trying to cover up the body all over again.

CREON Do you realize what you are saying?

FIRST GUARD Sir, ask these men here. After I reported to you, I went back, and first thing we did, we uncovered the body. The sun was coming up and it was beginning to smell, so we moved it up on a little rise to get him in the wind. Of course, you wouldn't expect any trouble in broad daylight. But just the same, we decided one of us had better keep his eye peeled all the time. About noon, what with the sun and the smell, and as the wind dropped and I wasn't feeling none too good, I went over to my pal to get a chew. I just had time to say "thanks" and stick it in my mouth, when I turned round and there she was, clawing away at the dirt with both hands. Right out in broad daylight! Wouldn't you think when she saw me come running she'd stop and leg it out of there? Not her! She went right on digging as fast as she could, as if I wasn't there at all. And when I grabbed her, she scratched and bit and yelled to leave her alone, she hadn't finished yet, the body wasn't all covered yet, and the like of that.

CREON (*To* ANTIGONE) Is this true?

ANTIGONE Yes, it is true.

FIRST GUARD We scraped the dirt off as fast as we could, then we sent for the relief and we posted them. But we didn't tell them a thing, sir. And we brought in the party so's you could see her. And that's the truth, so help me God.

CREON (*To* ANTIGONE) And was it you who covered the body the first time? In the night?

ANTIGONE Yes, it was. With a toy shovel we used to take to the seashore when we were children. It was Polynices' own shovel; he had cut his name in the handle. That was why I left it with him. But these men took it away; so the next time, I had to do it with my hands.

FIRST GUARD Sir, she was clawing away like a wild animal. Matter of fact, first minute we saw her, what with the heat haze and everything, my pal says, "That must be a dog," he says. "Dog!" I says, "That's a girl, that is!" And it was.

CREON Very well (*Turns to the* PAGE) Show these men to the ante-room. (*The* PAGE *crosses to the arch, stands there, waiting.* CREON *moves behind the table. To the* FIRST GUARD) You three men will wait outside. I may want a report from you later.

FIRST GUARD Do I put the cuffs back on her, sir?

CREON No. (*The three* GUARDS *salute, do an about-turn and exit through arch, right.* PAGE *follows them out. A pause*) Had you told anybody what you meant to do?

ANTIGONE No.

CREON Did you meet anyone on your way—coming or going?

ANTIGONE No, nobody.

CREON Sure of that, are you?

ANTIGONE Perfectly sure.

CREON Very well. Now listen to me. You will go straight to your room. When you get there, you will go to bed. You will say that you are not well and that you have not been out since yesterday. Your nurse will tell the same story. (*He looks toward arch, through which the* GUARDS *have exited*) And I'll get rid of those three men.

ANTIGONE Uncle Creon, you are going to a lot of trouble for no good reason. You must know that I'll do it all over again tonight.

(*A pause. They look one another in the eye*)

CREON Why did you try to bury your brother?

ANTIGONE I owed it to him.

CREON I had forbidden it.

ANTIGONE I owed it to him. Those who are not buried wander eternally and find no rest. If my brother were alive, and he came home weary after a long day's hunting, I should kneel down and unlace his boots, I should fetch him food and drink, I should see that his bed was ready for him. Polynices is home from the hunt. I owe it to him to unlock the house of the dead in which my father and my mother are waiting to welcome him. Polynices has earned his rest.

CREON Polynices was a rebel and a traitor, and you know it.

ANTIGONE He was my brother.

CREON You heard my edict. It was proclaimed throughout Thebes. You read my edict. It was posted up on the city walls.

ANTIGONE Of course I did.

CREON You knew the punishment I decreed for any person who attempted to give him burial.

ANTIGONE Yes, I knew the punishment.

CREON Did you by any chance act on the assumption that a daughter of Oedipus, a daughter of Oedipus' stubborn pride, was above the law?

ANTIGONE No, I did not act on that assumption.

CREON Because if you had acted on that assumption,

Antigone, you would have been deeply wrong. Nobody has a more sacred obligation to obey the law than those who make the law. You are a daughter of law-makers, a daughter of kings, Antigone. You must observe the law.

ANTIGONE Had I been a scullery maid washing my dishes when that law was read aloud to me, I should have scrubbed the greasy water from my arms and gone out in my apron to bury my brother.

CREON What nonsense! If you had been a scullery maid, there would have been no doubt in your mind about the seriousness of that edict. You would have known that it meant death; and you would have been satisfied to weep for your brother in your kitchen. But you! You thought that because you come of the royal line, because you were my niece and were going to marry my son, I shouldn't dare have you killed.

ANTIGONE You are mistaken. Quite the contrary. I never doubted for an instant that you would have me put to death.

(*A pause, as* CREON *stares fixedly at her*)

CREON The pride of Oedipus! Oedipus and his headstrong pride all over again. I can see your father in you—and I believe you. Of course you thought that I should have you killed! Proud as you are, it seemed to you a natural climax in your existence. Your father was like that. For him as for you human happiness was meaningless; and mere human misery was not enough to satisfy his passion for torment. (*He sits on a stool behind the table*) You come of people for whom the human vestment is a kind of straitjacket: it cracks at the seams. You spend your lives wriggling to get out of it. Nothing less than a cosy tea party with death and destiny will quench your thirst. The happiest hour of your father's life came when he listened greedily to the story of how, unknown to himself, he had killed his own father and dishonored the bed of his own mother. Drop by drop, word by word, he drank in the dark story that the gods had destined him, first to live and then to hear. How avidly men and women drink the brew of such a tale when their names are Oedipus—and Antigone! And it is so simple, afterward, to do what your father did, to put out one's eyes and take one's daughter begging on the highways.

Let me tell you, Antigone: those days are over for Thebes. Thebes has a right to a king without a past. My name, thank God, is only Creon. I stand here with both feet firm on the ground; with both hands in my pockets; and I have decided that so long as I am king—being less ambitious than your father was—I shall merely devote myself to introducing a little order into this absurd kingdom; if that is possible.

Don't think that being a king seems to me romantic. It is my trade; a trade a man has to work at every day; and like every other trade, it isn't all beer and skittles. But since it is my trade, I take it seriously. And if, tomorrow, some wild and bearded messenger walks in from some wild and distant valley—which is what happened to your dad—and tells me that he's not quite sure who my parents were, but thinks that my wife Eurydice is actually my mother, I shall ask him to do me the kindness to go back where he came from; and I shan't let a little matter like that persuade me to order my wife to take a blood test and the police to let me know whether or not my birth certificate was forged. Kings, my girl, have other things to do than to surrender themselves to their private feelings. (*He looks at her and smiles*) Hand *you* over to be killed! (*He rises, moves to end of table and sits on the top of table*) I have other plans for you. You're going to marry Haemon; and I want you to fatten up a bit so that you can give him a sturdy boy. Let me assure you that Thebes needs that boy a good deal more than it needs your death. You will go to your room, now, and do as you have been told; and you won't say a word about this to anybody. Don't fret about the guards: I'll see that their mouths are shut. And don't annihilate me with those eyes. I know that you think I am a brute, and I'm sure you must consider me very prosaic. But the fact is, I have always been fond of you, stubborn though you always were. Don't forget that the first doll you ever had came from me. (*A pause.* ANTIGONE *says nothing, rises and crosses slowly below the table toward the arch.* CREON *turns and watches her; then*) Where are you going?

ANTIGONE (*Stops downstage. Without any show of rebellion*) You know very well where I am going.

CREON (*After a pause*) What sort of game are you playing?

ANTIGONE I am not playing games.

CREON Antigone, do you realize that if, apart from those three guards, a single soul finds out what you have tried to do, it will be impossible for me to avoid putting you to death? There is still a chance that I can save you; but only if you keep this to yourself and give up your crazy purpose. Five minutes more, and it will be too late. You understand that?

ANTIGONE I must go and bury my brother. Those men uncovered him.

CREON What good will it do? You know that there are other men standing guard over Polynices. And even if you did cover him over with earth again, the earth would again be removed.

ANTIGONE I know all that. I know it. But that much, at least, I can do. And what a person can do, a person ought to do.

(*Pause*)

CREON Tell me, Antigone, do you believe all that flummery about religious burial? Do you really believe that a so-called shade of your brother is condemned to wander for ever homeless if a little earth is not flung on his corpse to the accompaniment of some priestly abracadabra? Have you ever listened to the priests of Thebes when they were mumbling their formula? Have you ever watched those dreary bureaucrats while they were preparing the dead for burial—skipping half the gestures required by the ritual, swallowing half their words, hustling the dead into their graves out of fear that they might be late for lunch?

ANTIGONE Yes, I have seen all that.

CREON And did you never say to yourself as you

watched them, that if someone you really loved lay dead under the shuffling, mumbling ministrations of the priests, you would scream aloud and beg the priests to leave the dead in peace?

ANTIGONE Yes, I've thought all that.

CREON And you still insist upon being put to death—merely because I refuse to let your brother go out with that grotesque passport; because I refuse his body the wretched consolation of that mass-production jibber-jabber, which you would have been the first to be embarrassed by if I had allowed it. The whole thing is absurd!

ANTIGONE Yes, it's absurd.

CREON Then why, Antigone, why? For whose sake? For the sake of them that believe in it? To raise them against me?

ANTIGONE No.

CREON For whom then if not for them and not for Polynices either?

ANTIGONE For nobody. For myself.

(*A pause as they stand looking at one another*)

CREON You must want very much to die. You look like a trapped animal.

ANTIGONE Stop feeling sorry for me. Do as I do. Do your job. But if you are a human being, do it quickly. That is all I ask of you. I'm not going to be able to hold out for ever.

CREON (*Takes a step toward her*) I want to save you, Antigone.

ANTIGONE You are the king, and you are all-powerful. But that you cannot do.

CREON You think not?

ANTIGONE Neither save me nor stop me.

CREON Prideful Antigone! Little Oedipus!

ANTIGONE Only this can you do: have me put to death.

CREON Have you tortured, perhaps?

ANTIGONE Why would you do that? To see me cry? To hear me beg for mercy? Or swear whatever you wish, and then begin over again?

(*A pause*)

CREON You listen to me. You have cast me for the villain in this little play of yours, and yourself for the heroine. And you know it, you damned little mischief-maker! But don't you drive me too far! If I were one of your preposterous little tyrants that Greece is full of, you would be lying in a ditch this minute with your tongue pulled out and your body drawn and quartered. But you can see something in my face that makes me hesitate to send for the guards and turn you over to them. Instead, I let you go on arguing; and you taunt me, you take the offensive. (*He grasps her left wrist*) What are you driving at, you she-devil?

ANTIGONE Let me go. You are hurting my arm.

CREON (*Gripping her tighter*) I will not let you go.

ANTIGONE (*Moans*) Oh!

CREON I was a fool to waste words. I should have done this from the beginning. (*He looks at her*) I may be your uncle—but we are not a particularly affectionate family. Are we, eh? (*Through his teeth, as he twists*) Are we? (CREON *propels* ANTIGONE *round below him to his side*) What fun for you eh? To be able to spit in the face of a king who has all the power in the world; a man who has done his own killing in his day; who has killed people just as pitiable as you are—and who is still soft enough to go to all this trouble in order to keep you from being killed.

(*A pause*)

ANTIGONE Now you are squeezing my arm too tightly. It doesn't hurt any more.

(CREON *stares at her, then drops her arm*)

CREON I shall save you yet. (*He goes below the table to the chair at end of table, takes off his coat and places it on the chair*) God knows, I have things enough to do today without wasting my time on an insect like you. There's plenty to do, I assure you, when you've just put down a revolution. But urgent things can wait. I am not going to let politics be the cause of your death. For it is a fact that this whole business is nothing but politics: the mournful shade of Polynices, the decomposing corpse, the sentimental weeping and the hysteria that you mistake for heroism—nothing but politics.

Look here. I may not be soft, but I'm fastidious. I like things clean, ship-shape, well scrubbed. Don't think that I am not just as offended as you are by the thought of that meat rotting in the sun. In the evening, when the breeze comes in off the sea, you can smell it in the palace, and it nauseates me. But I refuse even to shut my window. It's vile; and I can tell you what I wouldn't tell anybody else: it's stupid, monstrously stupid. But the people of Thebes have got to have their noses rubbed into it a little longer. My God! If it was up to me, I should have had them bury your brother long ago as a mere matter of public hygiene. I admit that what I am doing is childish. But if the featherheaded rabble I govern are to understand what's what, that stench has got to fill the town for a month!

ANTIGONE (*Turns to him*) You are a loathsome man!

CREON I agree. My trade forces me to be. We could argue whether I ought or ought not to follow my trade; but once I take on the job, I must do it properly.

ANTIGONE Why do you do it at all?

CREON My dear, I woke up one morning and found myself King of Thebes. God knows, there were other things I loved in life more than power.

ANTIGONE Then you should have said no.

CREON Yes, I could have done that. Only, I felt that it would have been cowardly. I should have been like a workman who turns down a job that has to be done. So I said yes.

ANTIGONE So much the worse for you, then. I didn't say yes. I can say no to anything I think vile, and I don't have to count the cost. But because you said yes, all that you can do, for all your crown and your trappings, and your guards—all that you can do is to have me killed.

CREON Listen to me.

ANTIGONE If I want to. I don't have to listen to you if

I don't want to. You've said your *yes*. There is nothing more you can tell me that I don't know. You stand there, drinking in my words. (*She moves behind chair*) Why is it that you don't call your guards? I'll tell you why. You want to hear me out to the end; that's why.

CREON You amuse me.

ANTIGONE Oh, no, I don't. I frighten you. That is why you talk about saving me. Everything would be so much easier if you had a docile, tongue-tied little Antigone living in the palace. I'll tell you something, Uncle Creon: I'll give you back one of your own words. You are too fastidious to make a good tyrant. But you are going to have to put me to death today, and you know it. And that's what frightens you. God! Is there anything uglier than a frightened man!

CREON Very well. I am afraid, then. Does that satisfy you? I am afraid that if you insist upon it, I shall have to have you killed. And I don't want to.

ANTIGONE I don't have to do things that I think are wrong. If it comes to that, you didn't really want to leave my brother's body unburied, did you? Say it! Admit that you didn't.

CREON I have said it already.

ANTIGONE But you did it just the same. And now, though you don't want to do it, you are going to have me killed. And you call that being a king!

CREON Yes, I call that being a king.

ANTIGONE Poor Creon! My nails are broken, my fingers are bleeding, my arms are covered with the welts left by the paws of your guards—but I am a queen!

CREON Then why not have pity on me, and live? Isn't your brother's corpse, rotting there under my windows, payment enough for peace and order in Thebes? My son loves you. Don't make me add your life to the payment. I've paid enough.

ANTIGONE No, Creon! You said yes, and made yourself king. Now you will never stop paying.

CREON But God in Heaven! Won't you try to understand me! I'm trying hard enough to understand you! There had to be one man who said yes. Somebody had to agree to captain the ship. She had sprung a hundred leaks; she was loaded to the water-line with crime, ignorance, poverty. The wheel was swinging with the wind. The crew refused to work and were looting the cargo. The officers were building a raft, ready to slip overboard and desert the ship. The mast was splitting, the wind was howling, the sails were beginning to rip. Every man-jack on board was about to drown—and only because the only thing they thought of was their own skins and their cheap little day-to-day traffic. Was that a time, do you think, for playing with words like yes and no? Was that a time for a man to be weighing the pros and cons, wondering if he wasn't going to pay too dearly later on; if he wasn't going to lose his life, or his family, or his touch with other men? You grab the wheel, you right the ship in the face of a mountain of water. You shout an order, and if one man refuses to obey, you shoot straight into the mob. Into the mob, I say! The beast as nameless as the wave that crashes down upon your deck; as nameless as the whipping wind. The thing that drops when you shoot may be someone who poured you a drink the night before; but it has no name. And you, braced at the wheel, you have no name, either. Nothing has a name—except the ship, and the storm. (*A pause as he looks at her*) Now do you understand?

ANTIGONE I am not here to understand. That's all very well for you. I am here to say no to you, and die.

CREON It is easy to say no.

ANTIGONE Not always.

CREON It is easy to say no. To say yes, you have to sweat and roll up your sleeves and plunge both hands into life up to the elbows. It is easy to say no, even if saying no means death. All you have to do is to sit still and wait. Wait to go on living; wait to be killed. That is the coward's part. *No* is one of your man-made words. Can you imagine a world in which trees say *no* to the sap? In which beasts say *no* to hunger or to propagation? Animals are good, simple, tough. They move in droves, nudging one another onward, all traveling the same road. Some of them keel over; but the rest go on; and no matter how many may fall by the wayside, there are always those few left which go on bringing their young into the world, traveling the same road with the same obstinate will, unchanged from those who went before.

ANTIGONE Animals, eh, Creon! What a king you could be if only men were animals!

(*A pause.* CREON *turns and looks at her*)

CREON You despise me, don't you? (ANTIGONE *is silent.* CREON *goes on, as if to himself*) Strange. Again and again, I have imagined myself holding this conversation with a pale young man I have never seen in the flesh. He would have come to assassinate me, and would have failed. I would be trying to find out from him why he wanted to kill me. But with all my logic and all my powers of debate, the only thing I could get out of him would be that he despised me. Who would have thought that the white-faced boy would turn out to be you? And that the debate would arise out of something so meaningless as the burial of your brother?

ANTIGONE (*Repeats contemptuously*) Meaningless!

CREON (*Earnestly, almost desperately*) And yet, you must hear me out. My part is not an heroic one, but I shall play my part. I shall have you put to death. Only, before I do, I want to make one last appeal. I want to be sure that you know what you are doing as well as I know what I am doing. Antigone, do you know what you are dying for? Do you know the sordid story to which you are going to sign your name in blood, for all time to come?

ANTIGONE What story?

CREON The story of Eteocles and Polynices, the story of your brothers. You think you know it, but you don't. Nobody in Thebes knows that story but me. And it seems to me, this afternoon, that you have a right to know it too. (*A pause as* ANTIGONE *moves to chair and sits*) It's not a pretty story. (*He turns, gets stool from behind the table and places it between the the table and the chair*) You'll see. (*He looks at her for a moment*) Tell me, first. What do you remember about your brothers? They were older than you, so they must have looked down on you. And I imagine that they tormented you—pulled your pigtails, broke your dolls, whispered secrets to each other to put you in a rage.

ANTIGONE They were big and I was little.

CREON And later on, when they came home wearing evening clothes, smoking cigarettes, they would have nothing to do with you; and you thought they were wonderful.

ANTIGONE They were boys and I was a girl.

CREON You didn't know why, exactly, but you knew that they were making your mother unhappy. You saw her in tears over them; and your father would fly into a rage because of them. You heard them come in, slamming doors, laughing noisily in the corridors—insolent, spineless, unruly, smelling of drink.

ANTIGONE (*Staring outward*) Once, it was very early and we had just got up. I saw them coming home, and hid behind a door. Polynices was very pale and his eyes were shining. He was so handsome in his evening clothes. He saw me, and said: "Here, this is for you"; and he gave me a big paper flower that he had brought home from his night out.

CREON And of course you still have that flower. Last night, before you crept out, you opened a drawer and looked at it for a time, to give yourself courage.

ANTIGONE Who told you so?

CREON Poor Antigone! With her night-club flower. Do you know what your brother was?

ANTIGONE Whatever he was, I know that you will say vile things about him.

CREON A cheap, idiotic bounder, that is what he was. A cruel, vicious little voluptuary. A little beast with just wit enough to drive a car faster and throw more money away than any of his pals. I was with your father one day when Polynices, having lost a lot of money gambling, asked him to settle the debt; and when your father refused, the boy raised his hand against him and called him a vile name.

ANTIGONE That's a lie!

CREON He struck your father in the face with his fist. It was pitiful. Your father sat at his desk with his head in his hands. His nose was bleeding. He was weeping with anguish. And in a corner of your father's study, Polynices stood sneering and lighting a cigarette.

ANTIGONE That's a lie.

(*A pause*)

CREON When did you last see Polynices alive? When you were twelve years old. *That's* true, isn't it?

ANTIGONE Yes, that's true.

CREON Now you know why. Oedipus was too chicken-hearted to have the boy locked up. Polynices was allowed to go off and join the Argive army. And as soon as he reached Argos, the attempts upon your father's life began—upon the life of an old man who couldn't make up his mind to die, couldn't bear to be parted from his kingship. One after another, men slipped into Thebes from Argos for the purpose of assassinating him, and every killer we caught always ended by confessing who had put him up to it, who had paid him to try it. And it wasn't only Polynices. That is really what I am trying to tell you. I want you to know what went on in the back room, in the kitchen of politics; I want you to know what took place in the wings of this drama in which you are burning to play a part.

Yesterday, I gave Eteocles a State funeral, with pomp and honors. Today, Eteocles is a saint and a hero in the eyes of all Thebes. The whole city turned out to bury him. The schoolchildren emptied their savings-boxes to buy wreaths for him. Old men, orating in quavering, hypocritical voices, glorified the virtues of the great-hearted brother, the devoted son, the loyal prince. I made a speech myself; and every temple priest was present with an appropriate show of sorrow and solemnity in his stupid face. And military honors were accorded the dead hero.

Well, what else could I have done? People had taken sides in the civil war. Both sides couldn't be wrong; that would be too much. I couldn't have made them swallow the truth. Two gangsters was more of a luxury than I could afford. (*He pauses for a moment*) And this is the whole point of my story. Eteocles, that virtuous brother, was just as rotten as Polynices. That great-hearted son had done his best, too, to procure the assassination of his father. That loyal prince had also offered to sell out Thebes to the highest bidder. Funny, isn't it? Polynices lies rotting in the sun while Eteocles is given a hero's funeral and will be housed in a marble vault. Yet I have absolute proof that everything that Polynices did, Eteocles had plotted to do. They were a pair of blackguards—both engaged in selling out Thebes, and both engaged in selling out each other; and they died like the cheap gangsters they were, over a division of the spoils.

But, as I told you a moment ago, I had to make a martyr of one of them. I sent out to the holocaust for their bodies; they were found clasped in one another's arms—for the first time in their lives, I imagine. Each had been spitted on the other's sword, and the Argive cavalry had trampled them down. They were mashed to a pulp, Antigone. I had the prettier of the two carcases brought in, and gave it a State funeral; and I left the other to rot. I don't know which was which. And I assure you, I don't care. (*Long silence, neither looking at the other*)

ANTIGONE (*In a mild voice*) Why do you tell me all this?

CREON Would it have been better to let you die a victim to that obscene story?

ANTIGONE It might have been. I had my faith.

CREON What are you going to do now?

ANTIGONE (*Rises to her feet in a daze*) I shall go up to my room.

CREON Don't stay alone. Go and find Haemon. And get married quickly.

ANTIGONE (*In a whisper*) Yes.

CREON All this is really beside the point. You have your whole life ahead of you—and life is a treasure.

ANTIGONE Yes.

CREON And you were about to throw it away. Don't think me fatuous if I say that I understand you; and that at your age I should have done the same thing. A moment ago, when we were quarreling, you said I was drinking in your words. I was. But it wasn't you I was listening to; it was a lad named Creon who lived here in Thebes many years ago. He was thin and pale, as you are. His mind, too, was filled with thoughts of self-sacrifice. Go and find Haemon. And get married quickly, Antigone. Be happy. Life flows like water, and you young people let it run away through your fingers. Shut your hands; hold on to it, Antigone. Life is not what you think it is. Life is a child playing round your feet, a tool you hold firmly in your grip, a bench you sit down upon in the evening, in your garden. People will tell you that that's not life, that life is something else. They will tell you that because they need your strength and your fire, and they will want to make use of you. Don't listen to them. Believe me, the only poor consolation that we have in our old age is to discover that what I have just said to you is true. Life is nothing more than the happiness that you get out of it.

ANTIGONE (*Murmurs, lost in thought*) Happiness . . .

CREON (*Suddenly a little self-conscious*) Not much of a word, is it?

ANTIGONE (*Quietly*) What kind of happiness do you foresee for me? Paint me the picture of your happy Antigone. What are the unimportant little sins that I shall have to commit before I am allowed to sink my teeth into life and tear happiness from it? Tell me: to whom shall I have to lie? Upon whom shall I have to fawn? To whom must I sell myself? Whom do you want me to leave dying, while I turn away my eyes?

CREON Antigone, be quiet.

ANTIGONE Why do you tell me to be quiet when all I want to know is what I have to do to be happy? This minute; since it is this very minute that I must make my choice. You tell me that life is so wonderful. I want to know what I have to do in order to be able to say that myself.

CREON Do you love Haemon?

ANTIGONE Yes, I love Haemon. The Haemon I love is hard and young, faithful and difficult to satisfy, just as I am. But if what I love in Haemon is to be worn away like a stone step by the tread of the thing you call life, the thing you call happiness; if Haemon reaches the point where he stops growing pale with fear when I grow pale, stops thinking that I must have been killed in an accident when I am five minutes late, stops feeling that he is alone on earth when I laugh and he doesn't know why—if he too has to learn to say yes to everything—why, no, then, no! I do not love Haemon!

CREON You don't know what you are talking about!

ANTIGONE I do know what I am talking about! Now it is you who have stopped understanding. I am too far away from you now, talking to you from a kingdom you can't get into, with your quick tongue and your hollow heart. (*Laughs*) I laugh, Creon, because I see you suddenly as you must have been at fifteen: the same look of impotence in your face and the same inner conviction that there was nothing you couldn't do. What has life added to you, except those lines in your face, and that fat on your stomach?

CREON Be quiet, I tell you!

ANTIGONE Why do you want me to be quiet? Because you know that I am right? Do you think I can't see in your face that what I am saying is true? You can't admit it, of course; you have to go on growling and defending the bone you call happiness.

CREON It is your happiness, too, you little fool!

ANTIGONE I spit on your happiness! I spit on your idea of life—that life that must go on, come what may. You are all like dogs that lick everything they smell. You with your promise of a humdrum happiness—provided a person doesn't ask too much of life. I want everything of life, I do; and I want it now! I want it total, complete: otherwise I reject it! I will *not* be moderate. I will *not* be satisfied with the bit of cake you offer me if I promise to be a good little girl. I want to be sure of everything this very day; sure that everything will be as beautiful as when I was a little girl. If not, I want to die!

CREON Scream on, daughter of Oedipus! Scream on, in your father's own voice!

ANTIGONE In my father's own voice, yes! We are of the tribe that asks questions, and we ask them to the bitter end. Until no tiniest chance of hope remains to be strangled by our hands. We are of the tribe that hates your filthy hope, your docile, female hope; hope, your whore—

CREON (*Grasps her by her arms*) Shut up! If you could see how ugly you are, shrieking those words!

ANTIGONE Yes, I am ugly! Father was ugly, too. (CREON *releases her arms, turns and moves away. Stands with his back to* ANTIGONE) But Father became beautiful. And do you know when? (*She follows him to behind the table*) At the very end. When all his questions had been answered. When he could no longer doubt that he *had* killed his own father; that he *had* gone to bed with his own mother. When all hope was gone, stamped out like a beetle. When it was absolutely certain that nothing, nothing could save him. Then he was at peace; then he could smile, almost; then he became beautiful. . . . Whereas you! Ah, those faces of yours, you candidates for election to happiness! It's you who are the ugly ones, even the handsomest of you—with that ugly glint in the corner of your eyes, that ugly crease at the corner of your mouths. Creon, you spoke the word a moment ago: the kitchen of politics. You look it and you smell of it.

CREON (*Struggles to put his hand over her mouth*) I order you to shut up! Do you hear me!

ANTIGONE *You* order me? Cook! Do you really believe that you can give me orders?

CREON Antigone! The ante-room is full of people! Do you want them to hear you?

ANTIGONE Open the doors! Let us make sure that they can hear me!

CREON By God! You shut up, I tell you!

(ISMENE *enters through arch*)

ISMENE (*Distraught*) Antigone!

ANTIGONE (*Turns to* ISMENE) You, too? What do you want?

ISMENE Oh, forgive me, Antigone. I've come back. I'll be brave. I'll go with you now.

ANTIGONE Where will you go with me?

ISMENE (*To* CREON) Creon! If you kill her, you'll have to kill me too.

ANTIGONE Oh, no, Ismene. Not a bit of it. I die alone. You don't think I'm going to let you die with me after what I've been through? You don't deserve it.

ISMENE If you die, I don't want to live. I don't want to be left behind, alone.

ANTIGONE You chose life and I chose death. Now stop blubbering. You had your chance to come with me in the black night, creeping on your hands and knees. You had your chance to claw up the earth with your nails, as I did; to get yourself caught like a thief, as I did. And you refused it.

ISMENE Not any more. I'll do it alone tonight.

ANTIGONE (*Turns round toward* CREON) You hear that, Creon? The thing is catching! Who knows but that lots of people will catch the disease from me! What are you waiting for? Call in your guards! Come on, Creon! Show a little courage! It only hurts for a minute! Come on, cook!

CREON (*Turns toward arch and calls*) Guard!

(GUARDS *enter through arch*)

ANTIGONE (*In a great cry of relief*) At last, Creon!

(CHORUS *enters through left arch*)

CREON (*To the* GUARDS) Take her away! (CREON *goes up on top step*)

(GUARDS *grasp* ANTIGONE *by her arms, turn and hustle her toward the arch, right, and exit*)

(ISMENE *mimes horror, backs away toward the arch, left, then turns and runs out through the arch. A long pause, as* CREON *moves slowly downstage*)

CHORUS (*Behind* CREON. *Speaks in a deliberate voice*) You are out of your mind, Creon. What have you done?

CREON (*His back to* CHORUS) She had to die.

CHORUS You must not let Antigone die. We shall carry the scar of her death for centuries.

CREON No man on earth was strong enough to dissuade her. Death was her purpose, whether she knew it or not. Polynices was a mere pretext. When she had to give up that pretext, she found another one. She was bent upon only one thing: to reject life and to die.

CHORUS She is a mere child, Creon.

CREON What do you want me to do for her? Condemn her to live?

HAEMON (*Calls from offstage*) Father! (HAEMON *enters through arch, right.* CREON *turns toward him*)

CREON Haemon, forget Antigone. Forget her, my dearest boy.

HAEMON How can you talk like that?

CREON (*Grasps* HAEMON *by the hands*) I did everything I could to save her, Haemon. I used every argument. I swear I did. The girl doesn't love you. She could have gone on living for you; but she refused. She wanted it this way; she wanted to die.

HAEMON Father! The guards are dragging Antigone away! You've got to stop them! (*He breaks away from* CREON)

CREON (*Looks away from* HAEMON) I can't stop them. It's too late. Antigone has spoken. The story is all over Thebes. I cannot save her now.

CHORUS Creon, you must find a way. Lock her up. Say that she has gone out of her mind.

CREON Everybody will know it isn't so. The nation will say that I am making an exception of her because my son loves her. I cannot.

CHORUS You can still gain time, and get her out of Thebes.

CREON The mob already knows the truth. It is howling for her blood. I can do nothing.

HAEMON But, Father, you are master in Thebes!

CREON I am master under the law. Not above the law.

HAEMON You cannot let Antigone be taken from me. I am your son!

CREON I cannot do anything else, my poor boy. She must die and you must live.

HAEMON Live, you say! Live a life without Antigone? A life in which I am to go on admiring you as you busy yourself about your kingdom, make your persuasive speeches, strike your attitudes? Not without Antigone. I love Antigone. I will not live without Antigone!

CREON Haemon—you will have to resign yourself to life without Antigone. (*He moves to left of* HAEMON) Sooner or later there comes a day of sorrow in each man's life when he must cease to be a child and take up the burden of manhood. That day has come for you.

HAEMON (*Backs away a step*) That giant strength, that courage. That massive god who used to pick me up in his arms and shelter me from shadows and monsters—was that you, Father? Was it of you I stood in awe? Was that man you?

CREON For God's sake, Haemon, do not judge me! Not you, too!

HAEMON (*Pleading now*) This is all a bad dream, Father. You are not yourself. It isn't true that we have been backed up against a wall, forced to surrender. We don't have to say *yes* to this terrible thing. You are still king. You are still the father I revered. You have no right to desert me, to shrink into nothingness. The world will be too bare, I shall be too alone in the world, if you force me to disown you.

CREON The world *is* bare, Haemon, and you *are* alone. You must cease to think your father all-powerful. Look straight at me. See your father as he is. That is what it means to grow up and be a man.

HAEMON (*Stares at* CREON *for a moment*) I tell you that I will not live without Antigone. (*Turns and goes quickly out through arch*)

CHORUS Creon, the boy will go mad.

CREON Poor boy! He loves her.

CHORUS Creon, the boy is wounded to death.

CREON We are all wounded to death.

(FIRST GUARD *enters through arch, right, followed by* SECOND *and* THIRD GUARDS *pulling* ANTIGONE *along with them*)

FIRST GUARD Sir, the people are crowding into the palace!

ANTIGONE Creon, I don't want to see their faces. I don't want to hear them howl. You are going to kill me; let that be enough. I want to be alone until it is over.

CREON Empty the palace! Guards at the gates! (CREON *quickly crosses toward the arch and exits. Two* GUARDS *release* ANTIGONE *and exit behind* CREON. CHORUS *goes out through arch, left*)

(*The lighting dims so that only the area about the table is lighted. The cyclorama is covered with a dark blue color. The scene is intended to suggest a prison cell, filled with shadows and dimly lit.* ANTIGONE *moves to stool and sits. The* FIRST GUARD *stands upstage. He watches* ANTIGONE, *and as she sits, he begins pacing slowly downstage, then upstage*)

(*A pause*)

ANTIGONE (*Turns and looks at the* GUARD) It's you, is it?

GUARD What do you mean, me?

ANTIGONE The last human face that I shall see. (*A pause as they look at each other, then* GUARD *paces upstage; turns and crosses behind table*) Was it you that arrested me this morning?

GUARD Yes, that was me.

ANTIGONE You hurt me. There was no need for you to hurt me. Did I act as if I was trying to escape?

GUARD Come on now, Miss. It was my business to bring you in. I did it. (*A pause. He paces to and fro upstage. Only the sound of his boots is heard*)

ANTIGONE How old are you?

GUARD Thirty-nine.

ANTIGONE Have you any children?

GUARD Yes. Two.

ANTIGONE Do you love your children?

GUARD What's that got to do with you? (*A pause. He paces upstage and downstage*)

ANTIGONE How long have you been in the Guard?

GUARD Since the war. I was in the army. Sergeant. Then I joined the Guard.

ANTIGONE Does one have to have been an army sergeant to get into the Guard?

GUARD Supposed to be. Either that or on special detail. But when they make you a guard, you lose your stripes.

ANTIGONE (*Murmurs*) I see.

GUARD Yes. Of course, if you're a guard, everybody knows you're something special; they know you're an old N.C.O. Take pay, for instance. When you're a guard you get your pay, and on top of that you get six months' extra pay, to make sure you don't lose anything by not being a sergeant any more. And of course you do better than that. You get a house, coal, rations, extras for the wife and kids. If you've got two kids, like me, you draw better than a sergeant.

ANTIGONE (*Barely audible*) I see.

GUARD That's why sergeants, now, they don't like guards. Maybe you noticed they try to make out they're better than us? Promotion, that's what it is. In the army, anybody can get promoted. All you need is good conduct. Now in the Guard, it's slow, and you have to know your business—like how to make out a report and the like of that. But when you're an N.C.O. in the Guard, you've got something that even a sergeant-major ain't got. For instance—

ANTIGONE (*Breaking him off*) Listen.

GUARD Yes, Miss.

ANTIGONE I'm going to die soon.

(*The* GUARD *looks at her for a moment, then turns and moves away*)

GUARD For instance, people have a lot of respect for guards, they have. A guard may be a soldier, but he's kind of in the civil service, too.

ANTIGONE Do you think it hurts to die?

GUARD How would I know? Of course, if somebody sticks a saber in your guts and turns it round, it hurts.

ANTIGONE How are they going to put me to death?

GUARD Well, I'll tell you. I heard the proclamation all right. Wait a minute. How did it go now? (*He stares into space and recites from memory*) "In order that our fair city shall not be pol-luted with her sinful blood, she shall be im-mured—immured." That means, they shove you in a cave and wall up the cave.

ANTIGONE Alive?

GUARD Yes. . . . (*He moves away a few steps*)

ANTIGONE (*Murmurs*) O tomb! O bridal bed! Alone!

(ANTIGONE *sits there, a tiny figure in the middle of the stage. You would say she felt a little chilly. She wraps her arms round herself*)

GUARD Yes! Outside the south-east gate of the town. In the Cave of Hades. In broad daylight. Some detail, eh, for them that's on the job! First they thought maybe it was a job for the army. Now it looks like it's going to be the Guard. There's an outfit for you! Nothing the Guard can't do. No wonder the army's jealous.

ANTIGONE A pair of animals.

GUARD What do you mean, a pair of animals?

ANTIGONE When the winds blow cold, all they need do is to press close against one another. I am all alone.

GUARD Is there anything you want? I can send out for it, you know.

ANTIGONE You are very kind. (*A pause.* ANTIGONE

*looks up at the* GUARD) Yes, there is something I want. I want you to give someone a letter from me, when I am dead.

GUARD How's that again? A letter?

ANTIGONE Yes, I want to write a letter; and I want you to give it to someone for me.

GUARD (*Straightens up*) Now, wait a minute. Take it easy. It's as much as my job is worth to go handing out letters from prisoners.

ANTIGONE (*Removes a ring from her finger and holds it out toward him*) I'll give you this ring if you will do it.

GUARD Is it gold? (*He takes the ring from her*)

ANTIGONE Yes, it is gold.

GUARD (*Shakes his head*) Uh-uh. No can do. Suppose they go through my pockets. I might get six months for a thing like that. (*He stares at the ring, then glances off right to make sure that he is not being watched*) Listen, tell you what I'll do. You tell me what you want to say, and I'll write it down in my book. Then, afterward, I'll tear out the pages and give them to the party, see? If it's in my handwriting, it's all right.

ANTIGONE (*Winces*) In your handwriting? (*She shudders slightly*) No. That would be awful. The poor darling! In your handwriting.

GUARD (*Offers back the ring*) O.K. It's no skin off my nose.

ANTIGONE (*Quickly*) Of course, of course. No, keep the ring. But hurry. Time is getting short. Where is your notebook? (*The* GUARD *pockets the ring, takes his notebook and pencil from his pocket, puts his foot up on chair, and rests the notebook on his knee, licks his pencil*) Ready? (*He nods*) Write, now. "My darling . . ."

GUARD (*Writes as he mutters*) The boy friend, eh?

ANTIGONE "My darling. I wanted to die, and perhaps you will not love me any more . . ."

GUARD (*Mutters as he writes*) ". . . will not love me any more."

ANTIGONE "Creon was right, it's terrible; now, beside this man, I no longer know why I am dying. I am afraid . . ."

GUARD (*Repeats as he writes*) "Creon was right, it's terrible . . ."

ANTIGONE "Oh, Haemon, our little boy. Only now do I understand how easy it was to live."

GUARD (*Looks at her*) Wait a minute! How fast do you think I can write?

ANTIGONE (*Takes hold of herself*) Where are you?

GUARD (*Reads from his notebook*) "It's terrible now beside this man . . ."

ANTIGONE "I no longer know why I am dying."

GUARD (*Writing*) "I no longer know why I am dying." You never know why you're dying.

ANTIGONE (*Continuing*) "I'm afraid. . . ." No. Scratch that out. Nobody must know that. It's as if they saw me naked and touched me, after I was dead. Scratch it all out. Just write: "Forgive me."

GUARD (*Looks at* ANTIGONE) I cut out everything you said there at the end, and I put down, "Forgive me"?

ANTIGONE Yes. "Forgive me, my darling. You would all have been so happy except for Antigone. I love you."

GUARD (*Finishes the letter*) ". . . I love you." (*He looks at her*) Is that all?

ANTIGONE That's all.

GUARD (*Straightens up, looks at notebook*) Damn funny letter.

ANTIGONE I know.

GUARD (*Looks at her*) Who is it to? (*A sudden roll of drums begins and continues until after* ANTIGONE *exits. The* FIRST GUARD *pockets the notebook and shouts at* ANTIGONE) O.K. That's enough out of you! Come on!

(*At the sound of the drum roll,* SECOND *and* THIRD GUARDS *enter through the right arch.* ANTIGONE *rises.* GUARDS *seize her and exit with her*)

(*The lighting moves up to suggest late afternoon*)

(CHORUS *enters*)

CHORUS And now it is Creon's turn.

(MESSENGER *runs through the arch, right*)

MESSENGER The Queen . . . the Queen! Where is the Queen?

CHORUS What do you want with the Queen? What have you to tell the Queen?

MESSENGER News to break her heart. Antigone had just been thrust into the cave. They hadn't finished heaving the last blocks of stone into place when Creon and the rest heard a sudden moaning from the tomb. A hush fell over us all, for it was not the voice of Antigone. It was Haemon's voice that came forth from the tomb. Everybody looked at Creon; and he howled like a man demented: "Take away the stones! Take away the stones!" The slaves leaped at the wall of stones, and Creon worked with them, sweating and tearing at the blocks with his bleeding hands. Finally a narrow opening was forced, and into it slipped the smallest guard.

Antigone had hanged herself by the cord of her robe, by the red and golden twisted cord of her robe. The cord was round her neck like a child's collar. Haemon was on his knees, holding her in his arms and moaning, his face buried in her robe. More stones were removed, and Creon went into the tomb. He tried to raise Haemon to his feet. I could hear him begging Haemon to rise to his feet. Haemon was deaf to his father's voice, till suddenly he stood up of his own accord, his eyes dark and burning. Anguish was in his face, but it was the face of a little boy. He stared at his father. Then suddenly he struck him—hard; and he drew his sword. Creon leaped out of range. Haemon went on staring at him, his eyes full of contempt—a glance that was like a knife, and that Creon couldn't escape. The King stood trembling in the far corner of the tomb, and Haemon went on staring. Then, without a word, he stabbed himself and lay down beside Antigone, embracing her in a great pool of blood.

(*A pause as* CREON *and* PAGE *enter through arch on the* MESSENGER'S *last words.* CHORUS *and the*

MESSENGER *both turn to look at* CREON, *then the* MESSENGER *exits through curtain*)

CREON I have had them laid out side by side. They are together at last, and at peace. Two lovers on the morrow of their bridal. Their work is done.

CHORUS But not yours, Creon. You have still one thing to learn. Eurydice, the Queen, your wife—

CREON A good woman. Always busy with her garden, her preserves, her jerseys—those jerseys she never stopped knitting for the poor. Strange, how the poor never stop needing jerseys. One would almost think that was all they needed.

CHORUS The poor in Thebes are going to be cold this winter, Creon. When the Queen was told of her son's death, she waited carefully until she had finished her row, then put down her knitting calmly—as she did everything. She went up to her room, her lavender-scented room, with its embroidered doilies and its pictures framed in plush; and there, Creon, she cut her throat. She is laid out now in one of those two old-fashioned twin beds, exactly where you went to her one night when she was still a maiden. Her smile is still the same, scarcely a shade more melancholy. And if it were not for that great red blot on the bed linen by her neck, one might think she was asleep.

CREON (*In a dull voice*) She, too. They are all asleep. (*Pause*) It must be good to sleep.

CHORUS And now you are alone, Creon.

CREON Yes, all alone. (*To* PAGE) My lad.

PAGE Sir?

CREON Listen to me. They don't know it, but the truth is the work is there to be done, and a man can't fold his arms and refuse to do it. They say it's dirty work. But if we didn't do it, who would?

PAGE I don't know, sir.

CREON Of course you don't. You'll be lucky if you never find out. In a hurry to grow up, aren't you?

PAGE Oh yes, sir.

CREON I shouldn't be if I were you. Never grow up if you can help it. (*He is lost in thought as the hour chimes*) What time is it?

PAGE Five o'clock, sir.

CREON What have we on at five o'clock?

PAGE Cabinet meeting, sir.

CREON Cabinet meeting. Then we had better go along to it.

(CREON *and* PAGE *exit slowly through arch, left, and* CHORUS *moves downstage*)

CHORUS And there we are. It is quite true that if it had not been for Antigone they would all have been at peace. But that is over now. And they are all at peace. All those who were meant to die have died: those who believed one thing, those who believed the contrary thing, and even those who believed nothing at all, yet were caught up in the web without knowing why. All dead: stiff, useless, rotting. And those who have survived will now begin quietly to forget the dead: they won't remember who was who or which was which. It is all over. Antigone is calm tonight and we shall never know the name of the fever that consumed her. She has played her part.

(*Three* GUARDS *enter, resume their places on steps as at the rise of the curtain, and begin to play cards*)

A great melancholy wave of peace now settles down upon Thebes, upon the empty palace, upon Creon, who can now begin to wait for his own death.

Only the guards are left, and none of this matters to them. It's no skin off their noses. They go on playing cards.

(CHORUS *walks toward the arch, left, as the curtain falls*)

# Jean-Paul Sartre

## (1905-     )

JEAN-PAUL SARTRE is probably the most widely discussed and most controversial writer of our time. First and foremost a philosopher, he has wedded intelligence and imagination in a series of stories, novels, plays, critical essays, and treatises that are remarkable for their literary as well as their philosophical qualities. To date, Sartre has published nine plays. All of them are important contributions to the modern repertoire, but drama has had to take its turn along with Sartre's other activities. The immense prestige of Sartre the thinker has helped to call attention to his literary as well as his philosophical pursuits. The two go hand in hand in all of Sartre's writings. Nevertheless, the plays reveal such a gift for the theatre that one may be pardoned for wishing that Sartre had written many more, even at the expense of his more discursive preoccupations.

Sartre's notoriety is due mainly to his role as spokesman and popularizer of existentialism. Sartre did not invent either the term or the concepts associated with it, and he represents but one of several modes of existential thought; nonetheless, he is rightly considered the founder of a movement that has embraced every area of contemporary literature and life. Sartre's existentialism is above all a philosophy of responsible freedom: "To do and while doing to make oneself and to be nothing but the self which one has made." Everyone, according to Sartre, is responsible for everything. Freedom carries with it the anguish of this responsibility. Thought is never abstract; it affirms itself in action. Consciousness acquires meaning through choice; aims are judged not by intentions but by acts and accomplishments. Man's total responsibility imposes an analysis of the possibilities of choice and an acceptance of its consequences. Evasion of the claims of consciousness results in inauthentic action or "bad faith." Through his acts the individual shapes his own destiny and asserts the meaning of his existence, not only for himself, but as it will be judged by others. Each moment, every action, can mark a decisive choice in which the value of a whole life is summed up. This philosophy of crisis was particularly applicable to the daily conditions of life during the French Occupation and the Resistance. Although Sartre sees commitment or engagement as a universal condition, his particular expression of existentialism is closely tied to the bitter but also heroic events of the early 1940's.

Sartre began his career as a playwright in 1940 with a Christmas play based on a biblical theme and addressed to his fellow prisoners of war in a German internment camp. Before the war he was a professor of philosophy, but in the late 1930's he began to acquire a reputation in literary circles for his fiction and criticism. His first major play, *The Flies* (*Les Mouches,* 1943), was performed in Paris with the approval of the German censorship. Ostensibly a modernization of Aeschylus' *The Libation Bearers,* it is also an appeal to Frenchmen to rise up against tyranny and oppression. Orestes changes from a mild and compromising youth to a man of resolute action, not out of a desire to avenge the slain Agamemnon, but for the sake of the welfare of the community. The collective guilt of the citizens of Argos in permitting the murder and in suffering the tyranny of Aegisthus has led to their collective punishment in the form of the flies that Jupiter has sent to remind the men and women of Argos of their sinful condition. Aegisthus, much weaker than in other dramatizations of the legend, is simply a device by which the god imposes self-abasement and an appeal for divine grace on the whole community. Only Orestes and Electra resist Jupiter's authority in the name of personal and responsible freedom. Electra collapses under the threat of punishment; she refuses to share Orestes' resolve to move "toward ourselves" by rejecting a supernatural authority that would free man from the burden of responsibility. Orestes' decision is a liberating act, for he becomes the redeemer and savior of Argos, taking on the guilt of the community so that it may be free.

His second play, *No Exit* (*Huis Clos,* 1944), indicates a remarkable growth in construction and dialogue. In an influential essay entitled "Forgers of Myths," Sartre describes French drama of the Occupation and immediate postwar era as "violent and brief, centered around one single event," with small casts and with action concentrated within a short span of time. This austerity and intensity underlies a drama that is philosophical rather than psychological, presenting situations rather than characters, and freely combining fantasy and myth with literal representation. *No Exit* takes place in a hell markedly analogous to the real world. The history of the three damned souls is sordid and macabre, yet their past matters only insofar as it affects the choices made in the present. Garcin, Inez and Estelle each become aware of their need for the others; the gradual emergence of this interdependence leads to a circular pattern of relationships that defines the action of the play. All three are bound indissolubly together. Still, they are distinguished not only by class differences but by sharply varying degrees of insight into their own existence. Inez represents the fullest degree of inner clarity and authenticity, while Garcin is in the process of discovering the meaning of his life: his refusal to abandon Inez is an act of courage that will make it possible for him to pursue his relentless if painful self-examination. His climactic assertion, "Hell is—other people!" carries with it his recognition of the impossibility of moral judgment independent of the subjective evaluations of others. Neither in life nor in hell is evasion or indifference possible. *No Exit* is an intense and moving restatement of the primacy of personal authenticity and engagement. In its fitting together of imaginative and ideological values, it is probably Sartre's best play.

The experiences of the French Resistance, in which the playwright participated, provided the subject matter for his most brutal representation of physical suffering, *Morts sans sépulture* (literally translated as *Dead without Burial* but known in America as *The Victors*, 1946). Five *maquisards* captured by French collaborators are interrogated and tortured in the hope that they will reveal the hiding place of their leader. One commits suicide, one is killed by the others to prevent him from informing, and the remaining three are shot. Sartre's main concern is with how the condemned face death, but his gruesome portrayal of the realities of recent French history spares the audience nothing. Close to naturalism in its concentration on the excruciatingly painful, the play is at the same time a powerful and moving tribute to the heroism of ordinary men and women under unusual stress. In *The Respectful Prostitute* (*La Putain respectueuse*, 1946) Sartre employed the traditional devices of social realism to attack Negro persecution and the corruption of justice in the southern part of the United States. Combining melodrama with the "thesis play," it appealed to the fashionable anti-Americanism of the early days of the Liberation; the view of American society is cliché-ridden and distorted, but Sartre's exaggerations do not cancel out a degree of validity in his portrayal of moral and political degradation.

The tangled politics of Eastern Europe—possibly Hungary—in the closing days of World War II, when the Russians were advancing but the Germans were still on the scene and in control, provided the background of *Dirty Hands* (*Les Mains sales,* 1948), one of Sartre's most successful plays outside of France despite the cold reception of the New York production. Sartre's exposé of intellectual dishonesty, intrigue, and betrayal within the Communist party led left-wing critics to denounce the drama as anti-Communist, but Sartre insisted that this judgment in no way corresponded to his intention. The play deals not with politics but with the groundwork of ethical choice. Hugo is a weak and contemptible figure, a bourgeois intellectual seeking to play the part of a man of action. He kills Hoederer, the dissident Communist, out of a confusion of personal and ideological values, yet he gives this act a meaning by refusing to repudiate it even at the cost of his life. His liquidation coincides with his discovery of individual responsibility.

The quest for authenticity and the menace of betrayal, by one's self or by others, constitutes the dominant theme of Sartre's plays. *Le Diable et le Bon Dieu* (*The Devil and the Good Lord,* 1951) is probably Sartre's richest drama of ideas if not his most coherent. His hero, Goetz, does the devil's work and revels in it. Beginning as a prince of anarchy, he undergoes a conversion and, like Orestes, attempts to take on himself the sins of all mankind. Neither extreme of hatred or love is viable in the mixed and contradictory world of human experience. Goetz ends with the Nietzschean recognition that God is dead, Heaven is empty, and man must accept his burden of total responsibility. Goetz abandons his heroic but futile isolation and emerges as leader of the peasant rebellion. Sartre's historical play is crowded with turbulent mass scenes, yet the concentration on opposing principles of allegiance retards the action. The ideological antagonisms are seldom made sufficiently dramatic, yet Goetz himself is Sartre's most vivid and powerful character creation.

Sartre has attempted comedy only once, in *Nekrassov* (1955), a somewhat over-long satire of fashionable European anti-communism of allegedly American origin. More bitter and sardonic than humorous, it was not an immediate theatrical success. Sartre attributed this to the dominance of the theatre by the bourgeoisie, but workers also refused to buy tickets even at reduced rates. In his recent pronouncements Sartre has vigorously attacked the theatre as a bourgeois institution forcing on the playwright "an image of an unchanging man in an unchanging universe." He still insists on the role of commitment in moving the audience toward social change: "A play is something which hurls people into an understanding." It demands participation and personal response.

Sartre's latest play, *Les Séquestrés d'Altona* (*The Condemned of Altona,* 1959), is proof that despite the intermittent character of his compositions, his talent as a playwright is as vigorous as ever. Here he explores the problem of individual and collective war guilt within the family of a German industrialist, Von Gerlach. His son Frantz, a torturer and war criminal, lives in a secluded room, half-mad, evading his crime through the fiction that he is witness of his age, calling on posterity in the hope of exoneration. He refuses the life his ailing father offers him and they join in a symbolic double suicide out of their recognition of what they have done, leaving the other members of the household to take their places. Once again, violence, revolt, espionage, intrigue, personal and political betrayal, create a tense and moving drama wherein individual experiences are fused with social themes of intense relevance. Sartre wrote the play with reference to French conduct in Algeria, but the issues transcend any single topical application. Seriousness of purpose and complexity of thought are undiminished in his play, a continuing demonstration of the vital interplay of philosophy and drama on the contemporary stage.

# NO EXIT

## *A Play in One Act*

Translated by Stuart Gilbert

### CHARACTERS

VALET
GARCIN
ESTELLE
INEZ

*A drawing-room in Second Empire style.*[1] *A massive bronze ornament stands on the mantelpiece.*

GARCIN (*Enters, accompanied by the* ROOM-VALET, *and glances around him*) Hm! So here we are?

VALET Yes, Mr. Garcin.

GARCIN And this is what it looks like?

VALET Yes.

GARCIN Second Empire furniture, I observe. . . . Well, well, I dare say one gets used to it in time.

VALET Some do. Some don't.

GARCIN Are all the other rooms like this one?

VALET How could they be? We cater for all sorts: Chinamen and Indians, for instance. What use would they have for a Second Empire chair? [2]

GARCIN And what use do you suppose *I* have for one? Do you know who I was? . . . Oh, well, it's no great matter. And, to tell the truth, I had quite a habit of living among furniture that I didn't relish, and in false positions. I'd even come to like it. A false position in a Louis-Philippe dining-room—you know the style? [3]—well, that had its points, you know. Bogus in bogus, so to speak.

VALET And you'll find that living in a Second Empire drawing-room has its points.

GARCIN Really? . . . Yes, yes, I dare say. . . . (*He takes another look around*) Still, I certainly didn't expect—this! You know what they tell us down there?

VALET What about?

GARCIN About (*Makes a sweeping gesture*) this—er—residence.

VALET Really, sir, how could you believe such cock-and-bull stories? Told by people who'd never set foot here. For, of course, if they had—

GARCIN Quite so. (*Both laugh. Abruptly the laugh dies from* GARCIN's *face*) But, I say, where are the instruments of torture?

VALET The what?

GARCIN The racks and red-hot pincers and all the other paraphernalia?

VALET Ah, you must have your little joke, sir!

GARCIN My little joke? Oh, I see. No, I wasn't joking. (*A short silence. He strolls round the room*) No mirrors, I notice. No windows. Only to be expected. And nothing breakable. (*Bursts out angrily*) But, damn it all, they might have left me my toothbrush!

VALET That's good! So you haven't yet got over your —what-do-you-call-it?—sense of human dignity? Excuse me smiling.

GARCIN (*Thumping ragefully the arm of an armchair*) I'll ask you to be more polite. I quite realize the position I'm in, but I won't tolerate . . .

VALET Sorry, sir. No offense meant. But all our guests ask me the same questions. Silly questions, if you'll pardon me saying so. Where's the torture-chamber? That's the first thing they ask, all of them. They don't bother their heads about the bathroom requisites, that I can assure you. But after a bit, when they've got their nerve back, they start in about their toothbrushes and what-not. Good heavens, Mr. Garcin, can't you use your brains? What, I ask you, would be the point of brushing your teeth?

GARCIN (*More calmly*) Yes, of course you're right. (*He looks around again*) And why should one want to see oneself in a looking-glass? But that bronze contraption on the mantelpiece, that's another story. I suppose there will be times when I stare my eyes out at it. Stare my eyes out—see what I mean? . . . All right, let's put our cards on the table. I assure you I'm quite conscious of my position. Shall I tell you what it feels like? A man's drowning, choking, sinking by inches, till only his eyes are just above water. And what does he see? A bronze atrocity by—what's the

[1] Furniture of the Second Empire (1851-71) was an elaborately decorative pastiche of earlier styles.

[2] Second Empire chairs were sumptuously over-stuffed.

[3] The Louis-Philippe (1830-48) style was a rich and ornate imitation of eighteenth century modes.

fellow's name?—Barbedienne.[4] A collector's piece. As in a nightmare. That's their idea, isn't it? . . . No, I suppose you're under orders not to answer questions; and I won't insist. But don't forget, my man, I've a good notion of what's coming to me, so don't you boast you've caught me off my guard. I'm facing the situation, facing it. (*He starts pacing the room again*) So that's that; no toothbrush. And no bed, either. One never sleeps, I take it?

VALET That's so.

GARCIN Just as I expected. *Why* should one sleep? A sort of drowsiness steals on you, tickles you behind the ears, and you feel your eyes closing—but why sleep? You lie down on the sofa and—in a flash, sleep flies away. Miles and miles away. So you rub your eyes, get up, and it starts all over again.

VALET Romantic, that's what you are.

GARCIN Will you keep quiet, please! . . . I won't make a scene, I shan't be sorry for myself, I'll face the situation, as I said just now. Face it fairly and squarely. I won't have it springing at me from behind, before I've time to size it up. And you call that being "romantic"! . . . So it comes to this; one doesn't need rest. Why bother about sleep if one isn't sleepy? That stands to reason, doesn't it? Wait a minute, there's a snag somewhere; something disagreeable. Why, now, should it be disagreeable? . . . Ah, I see; it's life without a break.

VALET What do you mean by that?

GARCIN What do I mean? (*Eyes the* VALET *suspiciously*) I thought as much. That's why there's something so beastly, so damn bad-mannered, in the way you stare at me. They're paralyzed.

VALET What are you talking about?

GARCIN Your eyelids. We move ours up and down. Blinking, we call it. It's like a small black shutter that clicks down and makes a break. Everything goes black; one's eyes are moistened. You can't imagine how restful, refreshing, it is. Four thousand little rests per hour. Four thousand little respites—just think! . . . So that's the idea. I'm to live without eyelids. Don't act the fool, you know what I mean. No eyelids, no sleep; it follows, doesn't it? I shall never sleep again. But then—how shall I endure my own company? Try to understand. You see, I'm fond of teasing, it's a second nature with me—and I'm used to teasing myself. Plaguing myself, if you prefer; I don't tease nicely. But I can't go on doing that without a break. Down there I had my nights. I slept. I always had good nights. By way of compensation, I suppose. And happy little dreams. There was a green field. Just an ordinary field. I used to stroll in it. . . . Is it daytime now?

VALET Can't you see? The lights are on.

GARCIN Ah yes, I've got it. It's *your* daytime. And outside?

VALET Outside?

GARCIN Damn it, you know what I mean. Beyond that wall.

VALET There's a passage.

GARCIN And at the end of the passage?

VALET There's more rooms, more passages, and stairs.

GARCIN And what lies beyond them?

VALET That's all.

GARCIN But surely you have a day off sometimes. Where do you go?

VALET To my uncle's place. He's the head valet here. He has a room on the third floor.

GARCIN I should have guessed as much. Where's the light-switch?

VALET There isn't any.

GARCIN What? Can't one turn off the light?

VALET Oh, the management can cut off the current if they want to. But I can't remember their having done so on this floor. We have all the electricity we want.

GARCIN So one has to live with one's eyes open all the time?

VALET To *live,* did you say?

GARCIN Don't let's quibble over words. With one's eyes open. Forever. Always broad daylight in my eyes—and in my head. (*Short silence*) And suppose I took that contraption on the mantelpiece and dropped it on the lamp—wouldn't it go out?

VALET You can't move it. It's too heavy.

GARCIN (*Seizing the bronze ornament and trying to lift it*) You're right. It's too heavy.

(*A short silence follows*)

VALET Very well, sir, if you don't need me any more, I'll be off.

GARCIN What? You're going? (*The* VALET *goes up to the door*) Wait. (VALET *looks round*) That's a bell, isn't it? (VALET *nods*) And if I ring, you're bound to come?

VALET Well, yes, that's so—in a way. But you can never be sure about that bell. There's something wrong with the wiring, and it doesn't always work. (GARCIN *goes to the bell-push and presses the button. A bell purrs outside*)

GARCIN It's working all right.

VALET (*Looking surprised*) So it is. (*He, too, presses the button*) But I shouldn't count on it too much if I were you. It's—capricious. Well, I really must go now. (GARCIN *makes a gesture to detain him*) Yes, sir?

GARCIN No, never mind. (*He goes to the mantelpiece and picks up a paper-knife*) What's this?

VALET Can't you see? An ordinary paper-knife.

GARCIN Are there books here?

VALET No.

GARCIN Then what's the use of this? (VALET *shrugs his shoulders*) Very well. You can go. (VALET *goes out*)

(GARCIN *is by himself. He goes to the bronze ornament and strokes it reflectively. He sits down; then gets up, goes to the bell-push, and presses the button. The bell remains silent. He tries two or three times, without success. Then he tries to open the door, also without success. He calls the* VALET *several times, but gets no result. He beats the door with his fists, still calling. Suddenly he grows calm and sits down again. At the same moment the door opens and* INEZ *enters, followed by the* VALET)

[4] Ferdinand Barbedienne (1810-1892), noted for his bronze reproductions of famous statues.

VALET Did you call, sir?

GARCIN (*On the point of answering "Yes"—but then his eyes fall on* INEZ) No.

VALET (*Turning to* INEZ) This is your room, Madam. (INEZ *says nothing*) If there's any information you require—? (INEZ *still keeps silent, and the* VALET *looks slightly huffed*) Most of our guests have quite a lot to ask me. But I won't insist. Anyhow, as regards the toothbrush, and the electric bell, and that thing on the mantelshelf, this gentleman can tell you anything you want to know as well as I could. We've had a little chat, him and me. (VALET *goes out.* GARCIN *refrains from looking at* INEZ, *who is inspecting the room. Abruptly she turns to* GARCIN)

INEZ Where's Florence? (GARCIN *does not reply*) Didn't you hear? I asked you about Florence. Where is she?

GARCIN I haven't an idea.

INEZ Ah, that's the way it works, is it? Torture by separation. Well, as far as I'm concerned, you won't get anywhere. Florence was a tiresome little fool, and I shan't miss her in the least.

GARCIN I beg your pardon. Who do you suppose I am?

INEZ You? Why, the torturer, of course.

GARCIN (*Looks startled, then bursts out laughing*) Well, that's a good one! Too comic for words. I the torturer! So you came in, had a look at me, and thought I was—er—one of the staff. Of course, it's that silly fellow's fault; he should have introduced us. A torturer indeed! I'm Joseph Garcin, journalist and man of letters by profession. And as we're both in the same boat, so to speak, might I ask you, Mrs.—?

INEZ (*Testily*) Not "Mrs." I'm unmarried.

GARCIN Right. That's a start, anyway. Well, now that we've broken the ice, do you *really* think I look like a torturer? And, by the way, how does one recognize torturers when one sees them? Evidently you've ideas on the subject.

INEZ They look frightened.

GARCIN Frightened! But how ridiculous! Of whom should they be frightened? Of their victims?

INEZ Laugh away, but I know what I'm talking about. I've often watched my face in the glass.

GARCIN In the glass? (*He looks around him*) How beastly of them! They've removed everything in the least resembling a glass. (*Short silence*) Anyhow, I can assure you I'm not frightened. Not that I take my position lightly; I realize its gravity only too well. But I'm not afraid.

INEZ (*Shrugging her shoulders*) That's your affair. (*Silence*) Must you be here all the time, or do you take a stroll outside, now and then?

GARCIN The door's locked.

INEZ Oh! . . . That's too bad.

GARCIN I can quite understand that it bores you having me here. And I, too—well, quite frankly, I'd rather be alone. I want to think things out, you know; to set my life in order, and one does that better by oneself. But I'm sure we'll manage to pull along together somehow. I'm no talker, I don't move much; in fact I'm a peaceful sort of fellow. Only, if I may venture on a suggestion, we should make a point of being extremely courteous to each other. That will ease the situation for us both.

INEZ I'm not polite.

GARCIN Then I must be polite for two.

(*A longish silence.* GARCIN *is sitting on a sofa, while* INEZ *paces up and down the room*)

INEZ (*Fixing her eyes on him*) Your mouth!

GARCIN (*As if waking from a dream*) I beg your pardon.

INEZ Can't you keep your mouth still? You keep twisting it about all the time. It's grotesque.

GARCIN So sorry. I wasn't aware of it.

INEZ That's just what I reproach you with. (GARCIN'S *mouth twitches*) There you are! You talk about politeness, and you don't even try to control your face. Remember you're not alone; you've no right to inflict the sight of your fear on me.

GARCIN (*Getting up and going toward her*) How about you? Aren't you afraid?

INEZ What would be the use? There was some point in being afraid *before;* while one still had hope.

GARCIN (*In a low voice*) There's no more hope—but it's still "before." We haven't yet begun to suffer.

INEZ That's so. (*A short silence*) Well? What's going to happen?

GARCIN I don't know. I'm waiting.

(*Silence again.* GARCIN *sits down and* INEZ *resumes her pacing up and down the room.* GARCIN'S *mouth twitches; after a glance at* INEZ *he buries his face in his hands. Enter* ESTELLE *with the* VALET. ESTELLE *looks at* GARCIN, *whose face is still hidden by his hands.*)

ESTELLE (*to* GARCIN) No! Don't look up. I know what you're hiding with your hands. I know you've no face left. (GARCIN *removes his hands*) What! (*A short pause. Then, in a tone of surprise*) But I don't know you!

GARCIN I'm not the torturer, Madam.

ESTELLE I never thought you were. I—I thought someone was trying to play a rather nasty trick on me. (*To the* VALET) Is anyone else coming?

VALET No, Madam. No one else is coming.

ESTELLE Oh! Then we're to stay by ourselves, the three of us, this gentleman, this lady, and myself. (*She starts laughing*)

GARCIN (*Angrily*) There's nothing to laugh about.

ESTELLE (*Still laughing*) It's those sofas. They're so hideous. And just look how they've been arranged. It makes me think of New Year's Day—when I used to visit that boring old aunt of mine, Aunt Mary. Her house is full of horrors like that. . . . I suppose each of us has a sofa of his own. Is that one mine? (*To the* VALET) But you can't expect me to sit on that one. It would be too horrible for words. I'm in pale blue and it's vivid green.

INEZ Would you prefer mine?

ESTELLE That claret-colored one, you mean? That's very sweet of you, but really—no, I don't think it'd be so much better. What's the good of worrying, anyhow? We've got to take what comes to us, and I'll stick to the green one. (*Pauses*) The only one which might do, at a pinch, is that gentleman's. (*Another pause*)

INEZ Did you hear, Mr. Garcin?

GARCIN (*With a slight start*) Oh—the sofa, you mean. So sorry. (*He rises*) Please take it, Madam.

ESTELLE Thanks. (*She takes off her coat and drops it on the sofa. A short silence*) Well, as we're to live together, I suppose we'd better introduce ourselves. My name's Rigault. Estelle Rigault. (GARCIN *bows and is going to announce his name, but* INEZ *steps in front of him*)

INEZ And I'm Inez Serrano. Very pleased to meet you.

GARCIN (*Bowing again*) Joseph Garcin.

VALET Do you require me any longer?

ESTELLE No, you can go. I'll ring when I want you.

(*Exit* VALET, *with polite bows to everyone*)

INEZ You're very pretty. I wish we'd had some flowers to welcome you with.

ESTELLE Flowers? Yes, I loved flowers. Only they'd fade so quickly here, wouldn't they? It's so stuffy. Oh, well, the great thing is to keep as cheerful as we can, don't you agree? Of course, you, too, are—

INEZ Yes. Last week. What about you?

ESTELLE I'm—quite recent. Yesterday. As a matter of fact, the ceremony's not quite over. (*Her tone is natural enough, but she seems to be seeing what she describes*) The wind's blowing my sister's veil all over the place. She's trying her best to cry. Come, dear! Make another effort. That's better. Two tears, two little tears are twinkling under the black veil. Oh dear! What a sight Olga looks this morning! She's holding my sister's arm, helping her along. She's not crying, and I don't blame her; tears always mess one's face up, don't they? Olga was my bosom friend, you know.

INEZ Did you suffer much?

ESTELLE No. I was only half conscious, mostly.

INEZ What was it?

ESTELLE Pneumonia. (*In the same tone as before*) It's over now, they're leaving the cemetery. Good-by. Good-by. Quite a crowd they are. My husband's stayed at home. Prostrated with grief, poor man. (*To* INEZ) How about you?

INEZ The gas stove.

ESTELLE And you, Mr. Garcin?

GARCIN Twelve bullets through my chest. (ESTELLE *makes a horrified gesture*) Sorry! I fear I'm not good company among the dead.

ESTELLE Please, please don't use that word. It's so—so crude. In terribly bad taste, really. It doesn't mean much, anyhow. Somehow I feel we've never been so much alive as now. If we've absolutely got to mention this—this state of things, I suggest we call ourselves—wait!—absentees. Have you been—been absent for long?

GARCIN About a month.

ESTELLE Where do you come from?

GARCIN From Rio.

ESTELLE I'm from Paris. Have you anyone left down there?

GARCIN Yes, my wife. (*In the same tone as* ESTELLE *has been using*) She's waiting at the entrance of the barracks. She comes there every day. But they won't let her in. Now she's trying to peep between the bars. She doesn't yet know I'm—absent, but she suspects it. Now she's going away. She's wearing her black dress. So much the better, she won't need to change. She isn't crying, but she never did cry, anyhow. It's a bright sunny day and she's like a black shadow creeping down the empty street. Those big tragic eyes of hers—with that martyred look they always had. Oh, how she got on my nerves!

(*A short silence.* GARCIN *sits on the central sofa and buries his head in his hands*)

INEZ Estelle!

ESTELLE Please, Mr. Garcin!

GARCIN What is it?

ESTELLE You're sitting on my sofa.

GARCIN I beg your pardon. (*He gets up*)

ESTELLE You looked so—so far away. Sorry I disturbed you.

GARCIN I was setting my life in order. (INEZ *starts laughing*) You may laugh, but you'd do better to follow my example.

INEZ No need. My life's in perfect order. It tidied itself up nicely of its own accord. So I needn't bother about it now.

GARCIN Really? You imagine it's so simple as that. (*He runs his hand over his forehead*) Whew! How hot it is here! Do you mind if—? (*He begins taking off his coat*)

ESTELLE How dare you! (*More gently*) No, please don't. I loathe men in their shirt-sleeves.

GARCIN (*Putting on his coat again*) All right. (*A short pause*) Of course, I used to spend my nights in the newspaper office, and it was a regular Black Hole, so we never kept our coats on. Stiflingly hot it could be. (*Short pause. In the same tone as previously*) Stifling, that it *is*. It's night now.

ESTELLE That's so. Olga's undressing; it must be after midnight. How quickly the time passes, on earth!

INEZ Yes, after midnight. They've sealed up my room. It's dark, pitch-dark, and empty.

GARCIN They've slung their coats on the backs of the chairs and rolled up their shirt-sleeves above the elbow. The air stinks of men and cigar-smoke. (*A short silence*) I used to like living among men in their shirt-sleeves.

ESTELLE (*Aggressively*) Well, in that case our tastes differ. That's all it proves. (*Turning to* INEZ) What about you? Do you like men in their shirt-sleeves?

INEZ Oh, I don't care much for men any way.

ESTELLE (*Looking at the other two with a puzzled air*) Really I can't imagine why they put us three together. It doesn't make sense.

INEZ (*Stifling a laugh*) What's that you said?

ESTELLE I'm looking at you two and thinking that we're going to live together. . . . It's so absurd. I expected to meet old friends, or relatives.

INEZ Yes, a charming old friend—with a hole in the middle of his face.

ESTELLE Yes, him too. He danced the tango so divinely. Like a professional. . . . But why, why should we of all people be put together?

GARCIN A pure fluke, I should say. They lodge folks as they can, in the order of their coming. (*To* INEZ) Why are you laughing?

INEZ Because you amuse me, with your "flukes." As if they left anything to chance! But I suppose you've got to reassure yourself somehow.

ESTELLE (*Hesitantly*) I wonder, now. Don't you think we may have met each other at some time in our lives?

INEZ Never. I shouldn't have forgotten you.

ESTELLE Or perhaps we have friends in common. I wonder if you know the Dubois-Seymours?

INEZ Not likely.

ESTELLE But *everyone* went to their parties.

INEZ What's their job?

ESTELLE Oh, they don't do anything. But they have a lovely house in the country, and hosts of people visit them.

INEZ I didn't. I was a post-office clerk.

ESTELLE (*Recoiling a little*) Ah, yes. . . . Of course, in that case—(*A pause*) And you, Mr. Garcin?

GARCIN We've never met. I always lived in Rio.

ESTELLE Then you must be right. It's mere chance that has brought us together.

INEZ Mere chance? Then it's by chance this room is furnished as we see it. It's an accident that the sofa on the right is a livid green, and that one on the left's wine-red. Mere chance? Well, just try to shift the sofas and you'll see the difference quick enough. And that statue on the mantelpiece, do you think it's there by accident? And what about the heat here? How about that? (*A short silence*) I tell you they've thought it all out. Down to the last detail. Nothing was left to chance. This room was all set for us.

ESTELLE But really! Everything here's so hideous; all in angles, so uncomfortable. I always loathed angles.

INEZ (*Shrugging her shoulders*) And do you think *I* lived in a Second Empire drawing-room?

ESTELLE So it was all fixed up beforehand?

INEZ Yes. And they've put us together deliberately.

ESTELLE Then it's not mere chance that *you* precisely are sitting opposite *me?* But what can be the idea behind it?

INEZ Ask me another! I only know they're waiting.

ESTELLE I never could bear the idea of anyone's expecting something from me. It always made me want to do just the opposite.

INEZ Well, do it. Do it if you can. You don't even know what they expect.

ESTELLE (*Stamping her foot*) It's outrageous! So something's coming to me from you two? (*She eyes each in turn*) Something nasty, I suppose. There are some faces that tell me everything at once. Yours don't convey anything.

GARCIN (*Turning abruptly toward* INEZ) Look here! Why are we together? You've given us quite enough hints, you may as well come out with it.

INEZ (*In a surprised tone*) But I know nothing, absolutely nothing about it. I'm as much in the dark as you are.

GARCIN We've *got* to know. (*Ponders for a while*)

INEZ If only each of us had the guts to tell—

GARCIN Tell what?

INEZ Estelle!

ESTELLE Yes?

INEZ What have you done? I mean, why have they sent you here?

ESTELLE (*Quickly*) That's just it. I haven't a notion, not the foggiest. In fact, I'm wondering if there hasn't been some ghastly mistake. (*To* INEZ) Don't smile. Just think of the number of people who—who become absentees every day. There must be thousands and thousands, and probably they're sorted out by—by understrappers, you know what I mean. Stupid employees who don't know their job. So they're bound to make mistakes sometimes. . . . Do stop smiling. (*To* GARCIN) Why don't you speak? If they made a mistake in my case, they may have done the same about you. (*To* INEZ) And you, too. Anyhow, isn't it better to think we've got here by mistake?

INEZ Is that all you have to tell us?

ESTELLE What else should I tell? I've nothing to hide. I lost my parents when I was a kid, and I had my young brother to bring up. We were terribly poor and when an old friend of my people asked me to marry him I said yes. He was very well off, and quite nice. My brother was a very delicate child and needed all sorts of attention, so really that was the right thing for me to do, don't you agree? My husband was old enough to be my father, but for six years we had a happy married life. Then two years ago I met the man I was fated to love. We knew it the moment we set eyes on each other. He asked me to run away with him, and I refused. Then I got pneumonia and it finished me. That's the whole story. No doubt, by certain standards, I did wrong to sacrifice my youth to a man nearly three times my age. (*To* GARCIN) Do *you* think that could be called a sin?

GARCIN Certainly not. (*A short silence*) And now, tell me, do you think it's a crime to stand by one's principles?

ESTELLE Of course not. Surely no one could blame a man for that!

GARCIN Wait a bit! I ran a pacifist newspaper. Then war broke out. What was I to do? Everyone was watching me, wondering: "Will he dare?" Well, I dared. I folded my arms and they shot me. Had I done anything wrong?

ESTELLE (*Laying her hand on his arm*) Wrong? On the contrary. You were—

INEZ (*Breaks in ironically*) —a hero! And how about your wife, Mr. Garcin?

GARCIN That's simple. I'd rescued her from—from the gutter.

ESTELLE (*To* INEZ) You see! You see!

INEZ Yes, I see. (*A pause*) Look here! What's the

point of play-acting, trying to throw dust in each other's eyes? We're all tarred with the same brush.

ESTELLE (*Indignantly*) How dare you!

INEZ Yes, we are criminals—murderers—all three of us. We're in hell, my pets; they never make mistakes, and people aren't damned for nothing.

ESTELLE Stop! For heaven's sake—

INEZ In hell! Damned souls—that's us, all three!

ESTELLE Keep quiet! I forbid you to use such disgusting words.

INEZ A damned soul—that's you, my little plaster saint. And ditto our friend there, the noble pacifist. We've had our hour of pleasure, haven't we? There have been people who burned their lives out for our sakes—and we chuckled over it. So now we have to pay the reckoning.

GARCIN (*Raising his fist*) Will you keep your mouth shut, damn it!

INEZ (*Confronting him fearlessly, but with a look of vast surprise*) Well, well! (*A pause*) Ah, I understand now. I know why they've put us three together.

GARCIN I advise you to—to think twice before you say any more.

INEZ Wait! You'll see how simple it is. Childishly simple. Obviously there aren't any physical torments—you agree, don't you? And yet we're in hell. And no one else will come here. We'll stay in this room together, the three of us, for ever and ever. . . . In short, there's someone absent here, the official torturer.

GARCIN (*Sotto voce*) I'd noticed that.

INEZ It's obvious what they're after—an economy of man-power—or devil-power, if you prefer. The same idea as in the cafeteria, where customers serve themselves.

ESTELLE What ever do you mean?

INEZ I mean that each of us will act as torturer of the two others.

(*There is a short silence while they digest this information*)

GARCIN (*Gently*) No, I shall never be your torturer. I wish neither of you any harm, and I've no concern with you. None at all. So the solution's easy enough; each of us stays put in his or her corner and takes no notice of the others. You here, you here, and I there. Like soldiers at our posts. Also, we mustn't speak. Not one word. That won't be difficult; each of us has plenty of material for self-communings. I think I could stay ten thousand years with only my thoughts for company.

ESTELLE Have *I* got to keep silent, too?

GARCIN Yes. And that way we—we'll work out our salvation. Looking into ourselves, never raising our heads. Agreed?

INEZ Agreed.

ESTELLE (*After some hesitation*) I agree.

GARCIN Then—good-by.

(*He goes to his sofa and buries his head in his hands. There is a long silence; then* INEZ *begins singing to herself*)

INEZ (*Singing*)

What a crowd in Whitefriars Lane!
They've set trestles in a row,
With a scaffold and the knife,
And a pail of bran below.
Come, good folks, to Whitefriars Lane,
Come to see the merry show!

The headsman rose at crack of dawn,
He'd a long day's work in hand,
Chopping heads off generals,
Priests and peers and admirals,
All the highest in the land.
What a crowd in Whitefriars Lane!

See them standing in a line,
Ladies all dressed up so fine.
But their heads have got to go,
Heads and hats roll down below.
Come, good folks, to Whitefriars Lane,
Come to see the merry show!

(*Meanwhile* ESTELLE *has been plying her powder-puff and lipstick. She looks round for a mirror, fumbles in her bag, then turns toward* GARCIN)

ESTELLE Excuse me, have you a glass? (GARCIN *does not answer*) Any sort of glass, a pocket-mirror will do. (GARCIN *remains silent*) Even if you won't speak to me, you might lend me a glass.

(*His head still buried in his hands,* GARCIN *ignores her*)

INEZ (*Eagerly*) Don't worry. I've a glass in my bag. (*She opens her bag. Angrily*) It's gone! They must have taken it from me at the entrance.

ESTELLE How tiresome!

(*A short silence.* ESTELLE *shuts her eyes and sways, as if about to faint.* INEZ *runs forward and holds her up*)

INEZ What's the matter?

ESTELLE (*Opens her eyes and smiles*) I feel so queer. (*She pats herself*) Don't you ever get taken that way? When I can't see myself I begin to wonder if I really and truly exist. I pat myself just to make sure, but it doesn't help much.

INEZ You're lucky. I'm always conscious of myself—in my mind. Painfully conscious.

ESTELLE Ah yes, in your mind. But everything that goes on in one's head is so vague, isn't it? It makes one want to sleep. (*She is silent for a while*) I've six big mirrors in my bedroom. There they are. I can see them. But they don't see me. They're reflecting the carpet, the settee, the window—but how empty it is, a glass in which I'm absent! When I talked to people I always made sure there was one near by in which I could see myself. I watched myself talking. And somehow it kept me alert, seeing myself as the others saw me. . . . Oh dear! My lipstick! I'm sure I've put it on all crooked. No, I can't do without a looking-glass for ever and ever, I simply can't.

INEZ Suppose I try to be your glass? Come and pay me a visit, dear. Here's a place for you on my sofa.

ESTELLE But— (*Points to* GARCIN)

INEZ Oh, he doesn't count.

ESTELLE But we're going to—to hurt each other. You said it yourself.

INEZ Do I look as if I wanted to hurt you?

ESTELLE One never can tell.

INEZ Much more likely *you'll* hurt *me*. Still, what does it matter? If I've got to suffer, it may as well be at your hands, your pretty hands. Sit down. Come closer. Closer. Look into my eyes. What do you see?

ESTELLE Oh, I'm there! But so tiny I can't see myself properly.

INEZ But *I* can. Every inch of you. Now ask me questions. I'll be as candid as any looking-glass.

(ESTELLE *seems rather embarrassed and turns to* GARCIN, *as if appealing to him for help*)

ESTELLE Please, Mr. Garcin. Sure our chatter isn't bothering you?

(GARCIN *makes no reply*)

INEZ Don't worry about him. As I said, he doesn't count. We're by ourselves. . . . Ask away.

ESTELLE Are my lips all right?

INEZ Show! No, they're a bit smudgy.

ESTELLE I thought as much. Luckily (*Throws a quick glance at* GARCIN) no one's seen me. I'll try again.

INEZ That's better. No. Follow the line of your lips. Wait! I'll guide your hand. There. That's quite good.

ESTELLE As good as when I came in?

INEZ Far better. Crueler. Your mouth looks quite diabolical that way.

ESTELLE Good gracious! And you say you like it! How maddening, not being able to see for myself! You're quite sure, Miss Serrano, that it's all right now?

INEZ Won't you call me Inez?

ESTELLE Are you sure it looks all right?

INEZ You're lovely, Estelle.

ESTELLE But how can I rely upon your taste? Is it the same as *my* taste? Oh, how sickening it all is, enough to drive one crazy!

INEZ I *have* your taste, my dear, because I like you so much. Look at me. No, straight. Now smile. I'm not so ugly, either. Am I not nicer than your glass?

ESTELLE Oh, I don't know. You scare me rather. My reflection in the glass never did that; of course, I knew it so well. Like something I had tamed. . . . I'm going to smile, and my smile will sink down into your pupils, and heaven knows what it will become.

INEZ And why shouldn't you "tame" *me?* (*The women gaze at each other,* ESTELLE *with a sort of fearful fascination*) Listen! I want you to call me Inez. We must be great friends.

ESTELLE I don't make friends with women very easily.

INEZ Not with postal clerks, you mean? Hullo, what's that—that nasty red spot at the bottom of your cheek? A pimple?

ESTELLE A pimple? Oh, how simply foul! Where?

INEZ There. . . . You know the way they catch larks —with a mirror? I'm your lark-mirror, my dear, and you can't escape me. . . . There isn't any pimple, not a trace of one. So what about it? Suppose the mirror started telling lies? Or suppose I covered my eyes—as he is doing—and refused to look at you, all that loveliness of yours would be wasted on the desert air. No, don't be afraid, I can't help looking at you, I shan't turn my eyes away. And I'll be nice to you, ever so nice. Only you must be nice to me, too.

(*A short silence*)

ESTELLE Are you really—attracted by me?

INEZ Very much indeed.

(*Another short silence*)

ESTELLE (*Indicating* GARCIN *by a slight movement of her head*) But I wish he'd notice me, too.

INEZ Of course! Because he's a Man! (*To* GARCIN) You've won. (GARCIN *says nothing*) But look at her, damn it! (*Still no reply from* GARCIN) Don't pretend. You haven't missed a word of what we've said.

GARCIN Quite so; not a word. I stuck my fingers in my ears, but your voices thudded in my brain. Silly chatter. Now will you leave me in peace, you two? I'm not interested in you.

INEZ Not in me, perhaps—but how about this child? Aren't you interested in her? Oh, I saw through your game; you got on your high horse just to impress her.

GARCIN I asked you to leave me in peace. There's someone talking about me in the newspaper office and I want to listen. And, if it'll make you any happier, let me tell you that I've no use for the "child," as you call her.

ESTELLE Thanks.

GARCIN Oh, I didn't mean it rudely.

ESTELLE You cad!

(*They confront each other in silence for some moments*)

GARCIN So's that's that. (*Pause*) You know I begged you not to speak.

ESTELLE It's *her* fault; she started. I didn't ask anything of her and she came and offered me her—her glass.

INEZ So you say. But all the time you were making up to him, trying every trick to catch his attention.

ESTELLE Well, why shouldn't I?

GARCIN You're crazy, both of you. Don't you see where this is leading us? For pity's sake, keep your mouths shut. (*Pause*) Now let's all sit down again quite quietly; we'll look at the floor and each must try to forget the others are there.

(*A longish silence.* GARCIN *sits down. The women return hesitantly to their places. Suddenly* INEZ *swings round on him*)

INEZ To forget about the others? How utterly absurd! I *feel* you there, in every pore. Your silence clamors in my ears. You can nail up your mouth, cut your tongue out—but you can't prevent your *being there.* Can you stop your thoughts? I hear them ticking away like a clock tick-tock, tick-tock, and I'm certain you hear mine. It's all very well skulking on your sofa, but you're everywhere, and every sound comes to me soiled, because you've intercepted it on its way. Why, you've even stolen my face; you know it and I don't! And what about her, about Estelle? You've stolen her from me, too; if she and I were alone do you suppose she'd treat me as she does? No, take your hands from your face, I won't leave you in peace—that would suit your book too well. You'd go on sitting there, in a sort of trance, like a yogi, and even if I didn't see her

I'd feel it in my bones—that she was making every sound, even the rustle of her dress, for your benefit, throwing you smiles you didn't see. . . . Well, I won't stand for that, I prefer to choose my hell; I prefer to look you in the eyes and fight it out face to face.

GARCIN Have it your own way. I suppose we were bound to come to this; they knew what they were about, and we're easy game. If they'd put me in a room with men—men can keep their mouths shut. But it's no use wanting the impossible. (*He goes to* ESTELLE *and lightly fondles her neck*) So I attract you, little girl? It seems you were making eyes at me?

ESTELLE Don't touch me.

GARCIN Why not? We might, anyhow, be natural. . . . Do you know, I used to be mad about women? And some were fond of me. So we may as well stop posing, we've nothing to lose. Why trouble about politeness, and decorum, and the rest of it? We're between ourselves. And presently we shall be naked as—as newborn babes.

ESTELLE Oh, let me be!

GARCIN As new-born babes. Well, I'd warned you, anyhow. I asked so little of you, nothing but peace and a little silence. I'd put my fingers in my ears. Gomez was spouting away as usual, standing in the center of the room, with all the pressmen listening. In their shirtsleeves. I tried to hear, but it wasn't too easy. Things on earth move so quickly, you know. Couldn't you have held your tongues? Now it's over, he's stopped talking, and what he thinks of me has gone back into his head. Well, we've got to see it through somehow. . . . Naked as we were born. So much the better; I want to know whom I have to deal with.

INEZ You know already. There's nothing more to learn.

GARCIN You're wrong. So long as each of us hasn't made a clean breast of it—why they've damned him or her—we know nothing. Nothing that counts. You, young lady, you shall begin. Why? Tell us why. If you are frank, if we bring our specters into the open, it may save us from disaster. So—out with it! Why?

ESTELLE I tell you I haven't a notion. They wouldn't tell me why.

GARCIN That's so. They wouldn't tell me, either. But I've a pretty good idea. . . . Perhaps you're shy of speaking first? Right. I'll lead off. (*A short silence*) I'm not a very estimable person.

INEZ No need to tell us that. We know you were a deserter.

GARCIN Let that be. It's only a side-issue. I'm here because I treated my wife abominably. That's all. For five years. Naturally, she's suffering still. There she is: the moment I mention her, I see her. It's Gomez who interests me, and it's she I see. Where's Gomez got to? For five years. There! They've given her back my things; she's sitting by the window, with my coat on her knees. The coat with the twelve bullet-holes. The blood's like rust; a brown ring round each hole. It's quite a museum-piece, that coat; scarred with history. And I used to wear it, fancy! . . . Now, can't you shed a tear, my love? Surely you'll squeeze one out—at last? No? You can't manage it? . . . Night after night I came home blind drunk, stinking of wine and women. She'd sat up for me, of course. But she never cried, never uttered a word of reproach. Only her eyes spoke. Big, tragic eyes. I don't regret anything. I must pay the price, but I shan't whine. . . . It's snowing in the street. Won't you cry, confound you? That woman was a born martyr, you know; a victim by vocation.

INEZ (*Almost tenderly*) Why did you hurt her like that?

GARCIN It was so easy. A word was enough to make her flinch. Like a sensitive-plant. But never, never a reproach. I'm fond of teasing. I watched and waited. But no, not a tear, not a protest. I'd picked her up out of the gutter, you understand. . . . Now she's stroking the coat. Her eyes are shut and she's feeling with her fingers for the bullet-holes. What are you after? What do you expect? I tell you I regret nothing. The truth is, she admired me too much. Does that mean anything to you?

INEZ No. Nobody admired *me*.

GARCIN So much the better. So much the better for you. I suppose all this strikes you as very vague. Well, here's something you can get your teeth into. I brought a half-caste girl to stay in our house. My wife slept upstairs; she must have heard—everything. She was an early riser and, as I and the girl stayed in bed late, she served us our morning coffee.

INEZ You brute!

GARCIN Yes, a brute, if you like. But a well-beloved brute. (*A far-away look comes to his eyes*) No, it's nothing. Only Gomez, and he's not talking about *me*. . . . What were you saying? Yes, a brute. Certainly. Else why should I be here? (*To* INEZ) Your turn.

INEZ Well, I was what some people down there called "a damned bitch." Damned already. So it's no surprise, being here.

GARCIN Is that all you have to say?

INEZ No. There was that affair with Florence. A dead man's tale. With three corpses to it. He to start with; then she and I. So there's no one left, I've nothing to worry about; it was a clean sweep. Only that room. I see it now and then. Empty, with the doors locked. . . . No, they've just unlocked them. "To Let." It's to let; there's a notice on the door. That's—too ridiculous.

GARCIN Three. Three deaths, you said?

INEZ Three.

GARCIN One man and two women?

INEZ Yes.

GARCIN Well, well. (*A pause*) Did he kill himself?

INEZ He? No, he hadn't the guts for that. Still, he'd every reason; we led him a dog's life. As a matter of fact, he was run over by a street car. A silly sort of end. . . . I was living with them; he was my cousin.

GARCIN Was Florence fair?

INEZ Fair? (*Glances at* ESTELLE) You know, I don't regret a thing; still, I'm not so very keen on telling you the story.

GARCIN That's all right. . . . So you got sick of him?

INEZ Quite gradually. All sorts of little things got on my nerves. For instance, he made a noise when he was drinking—a sort of gurgle. Trifles like that. He was rather pathetic really. Vulnerable. Why are you smiling?

GARCIN Because I, anyhow, am *not* vulnerable.

INEZ Don't be too sure. . . . I crept inside her skin, she saw the world through my eyes. When she left him, I had her on my hands. We shared a bed-sitting-room at the other end of the town.

GARCIN And then?

INEZ Then that street car did its job. I used to remind her every day: "Yes, my pet, we killed him between us." (*A pause*) I'm rather cruel, really.

GARCIN So am I.

INEZ No, you're not cruel. It's something else.

GARCIN What?

INEZ I'll tell you later. When I say I'm cruel, I mean I can't get on without making people suffer. Like a live coal. A live coal in others' hearts. When I'm alone I flicker out. For six months I flamed away in her heart, till there was nothing but a cinder. One night she got up and turned on the gas while I was asleep. Then she crept back into bed. So now you know.

GARCIN Well! Well!

INEZ Yes? What's in your mind?

GARCIN Nothing. Only that it's not a pretty story.

INEZ Obviously. But what matter?

GARCIN As you say, what matter? (*To* ESTELLE) Your turn. What have you done?

ESTELLE As I told you, I haven't a notion. I rack my brain, but it's no use.

GARCIN Right. Then we'll give you a hand. That fellow with the smashed face, who was he?

ESTELLE Who—who do you mean?

INEZ You know quite well. The man you were so scared of seeing when you came in.

ESTELLE Oh, him! A friend of mine.

GARCIN Why were you afraid of him?

ESTELLE That's my business, Mr. Garcin.

INEZ Did he shoot himself on your account?

ESTELLE Of course not. How absurd you are!

GARCIN Then why should you have been so scared? He blew his brains out, didn't he? That's how his face got smashed.

ESTELLE Don't! Please don't go on.

GARCIN Because of you. Because of you.

INEZ He shot himself because of you.

ESTELLE Leave me alone! It's—it's not fair, bullying me like that. I want to go! I want to go!

(*She runs to the door and shakes it*)

GARCIN Go if you can. Personally, I ask for nothing better. Unfortunately, the door's locked.

(ESTELLE *presses the bell-push, but the bell does not ring.* INEZ *and* GARCIN *laugh.* ESTELLE *swings round on them, her back to the door*)

ESTELLE (*In a muffled voice*) You're hateful, both of you.

INEZ Hateful? Yes, that's the word. Now get on with it. That fellow who killed himself on your account—you were his mistress, eh?

GARCIN Of course she was. And he wanted to have her to himself alone. That's so, isn't it?

INEZ He danced the tango like a professional, but he was poor as a church mouse—that's right, isn't it?

(*A short silence*)

GARCIN Was he poor or not? Give a straight answer.

ESTELLE Yes, he was poor.

GARCIN And then you had your reputation to keep up. One day he came and implored you to run away with him, and you laughed in his face.

INEZ That's it. You laughed at him. And so he killed himself.

ESTELLE Did you use to look at Florence in that way?

INEZ Yes.

(*A short pause, then* ESTELLE *bursts out laughing*)

ESTELLE You've got it all wrong, you two. (*She stiffens her shoulders, still leaning against the door, and faces them. Her voice grows shrill, truculent*) He wanted me to have a baby. So there!

GARCIN And you didn't want one?

ESTELLE I certainly didn't. But the baby came, worse luck. I went to Switzerland for five months. No one knew anything. It was a girl. Roger was with me when she was born. It pleased him no end, having a daughter. It didn't please *me!*

GARCIN And then?

ESTELLE There was a balcony overlooking the lake. I brought a big stone. He could see what I was up to and he kept on shouting: "Estelle, for God's sake, don't!" I hated him then. He saw it all. He was leaning over the balcony and he saw the rings spreading on the water—

GARCIN Yes? And then?

ESTELLE That's all. I came back to Paris—and he did as he wished.

GARCIN You mean he blew his brains out?

ESTELLE It was absurd of him, really, my husband never suspected anything. (*A pause*) Oh, how I loathe you! (*She sobs tearlessly*)

GARCIN Nothing doing. Tears don't flow in this place.

ESTELLE I'm a coward. A coward! (*Pause*) If you knew how I hate you!

INEZ (*Taking her in her arms*) Poor child! (*To* GARCIN) So the hearing's over. But there's no need to look like a hanging judge.

GARCIN A hanging judge? (*He glances around him*) I'd give a lot to be able to see myself in a glass. (*Pause*) How hot it is! (*Unthinkingly he takes off his coat*) Oh, sorry! (*He starts putting it on again*)

ESTELLE Don't bother. You can stay in your shirt-sleeves. As things are—

GARCIN Just so. (*He drops his coat on the sofa*) You mustn't be angry with me, Estelle.

ESTELLE I'm not angry with you.

INEZ And what about me? Are you angry with me?

ESTELLE Yes.

(*A short silence*)

INEZ Well, Mr. Garcin, now you have us in the nude

all right. Do you understand things any better for that?

GARCIN I wonder. Yes, perhaps a trifle better. (*Timidly*) And now suppose we start trying to help each other.

INEZ I don't need help.

GARCIN Inez, they've laid their snare damned cunningly—like a cobweb. If you make any movement, if you raise your hand to fan yourself, Estelle and I feel a little tug. Alone, none of us can save himself or herself; we're linked together inextricably. So you can take your choice. (*A pause*) Hullo? What's happening?

INEZ They've let it. The windows are wide open, a man is sitting on my bed. *My* bed, if you please! They've let it, let it! Step in, step in, make yourself at home, you brute! Ah, there's a woman, too. She's going up to him, putting her hands on his shoulders. . . . Damn it, why don't they turn the lights on? It's getting dark. Now he's going to kiss her. But that's my room, *my* room! Pitch-dark now. I can't see anything, but I hear them whispering, whispering. Is he going to make love to her on *my* bed? What's that she said? That it's noon and the sun is shining? I must be going blind. (*A pause*) Blacked out. I can't see or hear a thing. So I'm done with the earth, it seems. No more alibis for me! (*She shudders*) I feel so empty, desiccated—really dead at last. All of me's here, in this room. (*A pause*) What were you saying? Something about helping me, wasn't it?

GARCIN Yes.

INEZ Helping me to do what?

GARCIN To defeat their devilish tricks.

INEZ And what do you expect me to do, in return?

GARCIN To help *me*. It only needs a little effort, Inez; just a spark of human feeling.

INEZ Human feeling. That's beyond my range. I'm rotten to the core.

GARCIN And how about me? (*A pause*) All the same, suppose we try?

INEZ It's no use. I'm all dried up. I can't give and I can't receive. How could *I* help you? A dead twig, ready for the burning. (*She falls silent, gazing at* ESTELLE, *who has buried her head in her hands*) Florence was fair, a natural blonde.

GARCIN Do you realize that this young woman's fated to be your torturer?

INEZ Perhaps I've guessed it.

GARCIN It's through her they'll get you. I, of course, I'm different—aloof. I take no notice of her. Suppose you had a try—

INEZ Yes?

GARCIN It's a trap. They're watching you, to see if you'll fall into it.

INEZ I know. And you're another trap. Do you think they haven't foreknown every word you say? And of course there's a whole nest of pitfalls that we can't see. Everything here's a booby-trap. But what do I care? I'm a pitfall, too. For her, obviously. And perhaps I'll catch her.

GARCIN You won't catch anything. We're chasing after each other, round and round in a vicious circle, like the horses on a merry-go-round. That's part of their plan, of course. . . . Drop it, Inez. Open your hands and let go of everything. Or else you'll bring disaster on all three of us.

INEZ Do I look the sort of person who lets go? I know what's coming to me. I'm going to burn, and it's to last forever. Yes, I *know* everything. But do you think I'll let go? I'll catch her, she'll see you through my eyes, as Florence saw that other man. What's the good of trying to enlist my sympathy? I assure you I know everything, and I can't feel sorry even for myself. A trap! Don't I know it, and that I'm in a trap myself, up to the neck, and there's nothing to be done about it? And if it suits their book, so much the better!

GARCIN (*Gripping her shoulders*) Well, *I*, anyhow, can feel sorry for you, too. Look at me, we're naked, naked right through, and I can see into your heart. That's one link between us. Do you think I'd want to hurt you? I don't regret anything, I'm dried up, too. But for you I can still feel pity.

INEZ (*Who has let him keep his hands on her shoulders until now, shakes herself loose*) Don't. I hate being pawed about. And keep your pity for yourself. Don't forget, Garcin, that there are traps for you, too, in this room. All nicely set for you. You'd do better to watch your own interests. (*A pause*) But, if you will leave us in peace, this child and me, I'll see I don't do you any harm.

GARCIN (*Gazes at her for a moment, then shrugs his shoulders*) Very well.

ESTELLE (*Raising her head*) Please, Garcin.

GARCIN What do you want of me?

ESTELLE (*Rises and goes up to him*) You can help *me*, anyhow.

GARCIN If you want help, apply to her.

(INEZ *has come up and is standing behind* ESTELLE, *but without touching her. During the dialogue that follows she speaks almost in her ear. But* ESTELLE *keeps her eyes on* GARCIN, *who observes her without speaking, and she addresses her answers to him, as if it were he who is questioning her*)

ESTELLE I implore you, Garcin—you gave me your promise, didn't you? Help me quick. I don't want to be left alone. Olga's taken him to a cabaret.

INEZ Taken whom?

ESTELLE Peter. . . . Oh, now they're dancing together.

INEZ Who's Peter?

ESTELLE Such a silly boy. He called me his glancing stream—just fancy! He was terribly in love with me . . . She's persuaded him to come out with her tonight.

INEZ Do you love him?

ESTELLE They're sitting down now. She's puffing like a grampus. What a fool the girl is to insist on dancing! But I dare say she does it to reduce. . . . No, of course I don't love him; he's only eighteen, and I'm not a baby-snatcher.

INEZ Then why bother about them? What difference can it make?

ESTELLE He belonged to me.

INEZ Nothing on earth belongs to you any more.

ESTELLE I tell you he was mine. All mine.

INEZ Yes, he *was* yours—once. But now— Try to make him hear, try to touch him. Olga can touch him, talk to him as much as she likes. That's so, isn't it? She can squeeze his hands, rub herself against him—

ESTELLE Yes, look! She's pressing her great fat chest against him, puffing and blowing in his face. But, my poor little lamb, can't you see how ridiculous she is? Why don't you laugh at her? Oh, once I'd have only had to glance at them and she'd have slunk away. Is there really nothing, nothing left of me?

INEZ Nothing whatever. Nothing of you's left on earth—not even a shadow. All you own is here. Would you like that paper-knife? Or that ornament on the mantelpiece? That blue sofa's yours. And I, my dear, am yours forever.

ESTELLE You mine! That's good! Well, which of you two would dare to call me his glancing stream, his crystal girl? You know too much about me, you know I'm rotten through and through. . . . Peter dear, think of me, fix your thoughts on me, and save me. All the time you're thinking "my glancing stream, my crystal girl," I'm only half here, I'm only half wicked, and half of me is down there with you, clean and bright and crystal-clear as running water. . . . Oh, just look at her face, all scarlet, like a tomato. No, it's absurd, we've laughed at her together, you and I, often and often. . . . What's that tune?—I always loved it. Yes, the *St. Louis Blues*. . . . All right, dance away, dance away. Garcin, I wish you could see her, you'd die of laughing. Only—she'll never know I *see* her. Yes, I see you, Olga, with your hair all anyhow, and you do look a dope, my dear. Oh, now you're treading on his toes. It's a scream! Hurry up! Quicker! Quicker! He's dragging her along, bundling her round and round—it's too ghastly! He always said I was so light, he loved to dance with me. (*She is dancing as she speaks*) I tell you, Olga, I can see you. No, she doesn't care, she's dancing through my gaze. What's that? What's that you said? "Our poor dear Estelle"? Oh, don't be such a humbug! You didn't even shed a tear at the funeral. . . . And she has the nerve to talk to him about her poor dear friend Estelle! How dare she discuss me with Peter? Now then, keep time. She never could dance and talk at once. Oh, what's that? No, no. Don't tell him. Please, please don't tell him. You can keep him, do what you like with him, but please don't tell him about —that! (*She has stopped dancing*) All right. You can have him now. Isn't it *foul,* Garcin? She's told him everything, about Roger, my trip to Switzerland, the baby. "Poor Estelle wasn't exactly—" No, I wasn't exactly— True enough. He's looking grave, shaking his head, but he doesn't seem so very much surprised, not what one would expect. Keep him, then—I won't haggle with you over his long eyelashes, his pretty girlish face. They're yours for the asking. His glancing stream, his crystal. Well, the crystal's shattered into bits. "Poor Estelle!" Dance, dance, dance. On with it. But do keep time. One, two. One, two. How I'd love to go down to earth for just a moment, and dance with him again. (*She dances again for some moments*) The music's growing fainter. They've turned down the lights, as they do for a tango. Why are they playing so softly? Louder, please. I can't hear. It's so far away, so far away. I—I can't hear a sound. (*She stops dancing*) All over. It's the end. The earth has left me. (*To* GARCIN) Don't turn from me—please. Take me in your arms. (*Behind* ESTELLE'S *back,* INEZ *signs to* GARCIN *to move away*)

INEZ (*Commandingly*) Now then, Garcin!

(GARCIN *moves back a step, and, glancing at* ESTELLE, *points to* INEZ)

GARCIN It's to her you should say that.

ESTELLE (*Clinging to him*) Don't turn away. You're a man, aren't you, and surely I'm not such a fright as all that! Everyone says I've lovely hair and, after all, a man killed himself on my account. You have to look at something, and there's nothing here to see except the sofas and that awful ornament and the table. Surely I'm better to look at than a lot of stupid furniture. Listen! I've dropped out of their hearts like a little sparrow fallen from its nest. So gather me up, dear, fold me to your heart—and you'll see how nice I can be.

GARCIN (*Freeing himself from her, after a short struggle*) I tell you it's to that lady you should speak.

ESTELLE To her? But she doesn't count, she's a woman.

INEZ Oh, I don't count? Is that what you think? But, my poor little fallen nestling, you've been sheltering in my heart for ages, though you didn't realize it. Don't be afraid; I'll keep looking at you for ever and ever, without a flutter of my eyelids, and you'll live in my gaze like a mote in a sunbeam.

ESTELLE A sunbeam indeed! Don't talk such rubbish! You've tried that trick already, and you should know it doesn't work.

INEZ Estelle! My glancing stream! My crystal!

ESTELLE *Your* crystal? It's grotesque. Do you think you can fool me with that sort of talk? Everyone knows by now what I did to my baby. The crystal's shattered, but I don't care. I'm just a hollow dummy, all that's left of me is the outside—but it's not for you.

INEZ Come to me, Estelle. You shall be whatever you like: a glancing stream, a muddy stream. And deep down in my eyes you'll see yourself just as you want to be.

ESTELLE Oh, leave me in peace. You haven't any eyes. Oh, damn it, isn't there anything I can do to get rid of you? I've an idea. (*She spits in* INEZ'S *face*) There!

INEZ Garcin, you shall pay for this.

(*A pause.* GARCIN *shrugs his shoulders and goes to* ESTELLE)

GARCIN So it's a man you need?

ESTELLE Not *any* man. You.

GARCIN No humbug now. Any man would do your

business. As I happen to be here, you want me. Right! (*He grips her shoulders*) Mind, I'm not your sort at all, really; I'm not a young nincompoop and I don't dance the tango.

ESTELLE I'll take you as you are. And perhaps I shall change you.

GARCIN I doubt it. I shan't pay much attention; I've other things to think about.

ESTELLE What things?

GARCIN They wouldn't interest you.

ESTELLE I'll sit on your sofa and wait for you to take some notice of me. I promise not to bother you at all.

INEZ (*With a shrill laugh*) That's right, fawn on him, like the silly bitch you are. Grovel and cringe! And he hasn't even good looks to commend him!

ESTELLE (*To* GARCIN) Don't listen to her. She has no eyes, no ears. She's—nothing.

GARCIN I'll give you what I can. It doesn't amount to much. I shan't love you; I know you too well.

ESTELLE Do you want me, anyhow?

GARCIN Yes.

ESTELLE I ask no more.

GARCIN In that case—(*He bends over her*)

INEZ Estelle! Garcin! You must be going crazy. You're not alone. I'm here too.

GARCIN Of course—but what does it matter?

INEZ Under my eyes? You couldn't—couldn't do it.

ESTELLE Why not? I often undressed with my maid looking on.

INEZ (*Gripping* GARCIN'*s arm*) Let her alone. Don't paw her with your dirty man's hands.

GARCIN (*Thrusting her away roughly*) Take care. I'm no gentleman, and I'd have no compunction about striking a woman.

INEZ But you promised me; you promised. I'm only asking you to keep your word.

GARCIN Why should I, considering you were the first to break our agreement?

(INEZ *turns her back on him and retreats to the far end of the room*)

INEZ Very well, have it your own way. I'm the weaker party, one against two. But don't forget I'm here, and watching. I shan't take my eyes off you. Garcin; when you're kissing her, you'll feel them boring into you. Yes, have it your own way, make love and get it over. We're in hell; my turn will come.

(*During the following scene she watches them without speaking*)

GARCIN (*Coming back to* ESTELLE *and grasping her shoulders*) Now then. Your lips. Give me your lips.

(*A pause. He bends to kiss her, then abruptly straightens up*)

ESTELLE (*Indignantly*) Really! (*A pause*) Didn't I tell you not to pay any attention to her?

GARCIN You've got it wrong. (*Short silence*) It's Gomez; he's back in the press-room. They've shut the windows; it must be winter down there. Six months since I— Well, I warned you I'd be absent-minded sometimes, didn't I? They're shivering, they've kept their coats on. Funny they should feel the cold like that, when I'm feeling so hot. Ah, this time he's talking about me.

ESTELLE Is it going to last long? (*Short silence*) You might at least tell me what he's saying.

GARCIN Nothing. Nothing worth repeating. He's a swine, that's all. (*He listens attentively*) A goddamned bloody swine. (*He turns to* ESTELLE) Let's come back to—to ourselves. Are you going to love me?

ESTELLE (*Smiling*) I wonder now!

GARCIN Will you trust me?

ESTELLE What a quaint thing to ask! Considering you'll be under my eyes all the time, and I don't think I've much to fear from Inez, so far as you're concerned.

GARCIN Obviously. (*A pause. He takes his hands off* ESTELLE'*s shoulders*) I was thinking of another kind of trust. (*Listens*) Talk away, talk away, you swine. I'm not there to defend myself. (*To* ESTELLE) Estelle, you *must* give me your trust.

ESTELLE Oh, what a nuisance you are! I'm giving you my mouth, my arms, my whole body—and everything could be so simple. . . . My trust! I haven't any to give, I'm afraid, and you're making me terribly embarrassed. You must have something pretty ghastly on your conscience to make such a fuss about my trusting you.

GARCIN They shot me.

ESTELLE I know. Because you refused to fight. Well, why shouldn't you?

GARCIN I—I didn't exactly refuse. (*In a far-away voice*) I must say he talks well, he makes out a good case against me, but he never says what I should have done instead. Should I have gone to the general and said: "General, I decline to fight"? A mug's game; they'd have promptly locked me up. But I wanted to show my colors, my true colors, do you understand? I wasn't going to be silenced. (*To* ESTELLE) So I—I took the train. . . . They caught me at the frontier.

ESTELLE Where were you trying to go?

GARCIN To Mexico. I meant to launch a pacifist newspaper down there. (*A short silence*) Well, why don't you speak?

ESTELLE What could I say? You acted quite rightly, as you didn't want to fight. (GARCIN *makes a fretful gesture*) But, darling, how on earth can I guess what you want me to answer?

INEZ Can't you guess? Well, *I* can. He wants you to tell him that he bolted like a lion. For "bolt" he did, and that's what's biting him.

GARCIN "Bolted," "went away"—we won't quarrel over words.

ESTELLE But you *had* to run away. If you'd stayed they'd have sent you to jail, wouldn't they?

GARCIN Of course. (*A pause*) Well, Estelle, am I a coward?

ESTELLE How can I say? Don't be so unreasonable, darling. I can't put myself in your skin. You must decide that for yourself.

GARCIN (*Wearily*) I can't decide.

ESTELLE Anyhow, you must remember. You must have had reasons for acting as you did.

GARCIN I had.

ESTELLE Well?

GARCIN But were they the real reasons?

ESTELLE You've a twisted mind, that's your trouble. Plaguing yourself over such trifles!

GARCIN I'd thought it all out, and I wanted to make a stand. But was that my real motive?

INEZ Exactly. That's the question. Was that your real motive? No doubt you argued it out with yourself, you weighed the pros and cons, you found good reasons for what you did. But fear and hatred and all the dirty little instincts one keeps dark—they're motives too. So carry on, Mr. Garcin, and try to be honest with yourself—for once.

GARCIN Do I need you to tell me that? Day and night I paced my cell, from the window to the door, from the door to the window. I pried into my heart, I sleuthed myself like a detective. By the end of it I felt as if I'd given my whole life to introspection. But always I harked back to the one thing certain—that I had acted as I did, I'd taken that train to the frontier. But why? Why? Finally I thought: My death will settle it. If I face death courageously, I'll prove I am no coward.

INEZ And how did you face death?

GARCIN Miserably. Rottenly. (INEZ *laughs*) Oh, it was only a physical lapse—that might happen to anyone; I'm not ashamed of it. Only everything's been left in suspense, forever. (*To* ESTELLE) Come here, Estelle. Look at me. I want to feel someone looking at me while they're talking about me on earth. . . . I like green eyes.

INEZ Green eyes! Just hark to him! And you, Estelle, do you like cowards?

ESTELLE If you knew how little I care! Coward or hero, it's all one—provided he kisses well.

GARCIN There they are, slumped in their chairs, sucking at their cigars. Bored they look. Half-asleep. They're thinking: "Garcin's a coward." But only vaguely, dreamily. One's got to think of something. "That chap Garcin was a coward." That's what they've decided, those dear friends of mine. In six months' time they'll be saying: "Cowardly as that skunk Garcin." You're lucky, you two; no one on earth is giving you another thought. But I—I'm long in dying.

INEZ What about your wife, Garcin?

GARCIN Oh, didn't I tell you? She's dead.

INEZ Dead?

GARCIN Yes, she died just now. About two months ago.

INEZ Of grief?

GARCIN What else should she die of? So all is for the best, you see; the war's over, my wife's dead, and I've carved out my place in history.

(*He gives a choking sob and passes his hand over his face.* ESTELLE *catches his arm*)

ESTELLE My poor darling! Look at me. Please look. Touch me. Touch me. (*She takes his hand and puts it on her neck*) There! Keep your hand there. (GARCIN *makes a fretful movement*) No, don't move. Why trouble what those men are thinking? They'll die off one by one. Forget them. There's only me, now.

GARCIN But *they* won't forget *me,* not they! They'll die, but others will come after them to carry on the legend. I've left my fate in their hands.

ESTELLE You think too much, that's your trouble.

GARCIN What else is there to do now? I was a man of action once. . . . Oh, if only I could be with them again, for just one day—I'd fling their lie in their teeth. But I'm locked out; they're passing judgment on my life without troubling about me, and they're right, because I'm dead. Dead and done with. (*Laughs*) A back number.

(*A short pause*)

ESTELLE (*Gently*) Garcin.

GARCIN Still there? Now listen! I want you to do me a service. No, don't shrink away. I know it must seem strange to you, having someone asking you for help; you're not used to that. But if you'll make the effort, if you'll only *will* it hard enough, I dare say we can really love each other. Look at it this way. A thousand of them are proclaiming I'm a coward; but what do numbers matter? If there's someone, just one person, to say quite positively I did not run away, that I'm not the sort who runs away, that I'm brave and decent and the rest of it—well, that one person's faith would save me. Will you have that faith in me? Then I shall love you and cherish you for ever. Estelle—will you?

ESTELLE (*Laughing*) Oh, you dear silly man, do you think I could love a coward?

GARCIN But just now you said—

ESTELLE I was only teasing you. I like men, my dear, who're real men, with tough skin and strong hands. You haven't a coward's chin, or a coward's mouth, or a coward's voice, or a coward's hair. And it's for your mouth, your hair, your voice, I love you.

GARCIN Do you mean this? *Really* mean it?

ESTELLE Shall I swear it?

GARCIN Then I snap my fingers at them all, those below and those in here. Estelle, we shall climb out of hell. (INEZ *gives a shrill laugh. He breaks off and stares at her*) What's that?

INEZ (*Still laughing*) But she doesn't mean a word of what she says. How can you be such a simpleton? "Estelle, am I a coward?" As if she cared a damn either way.

ESTELLE Inez, how dare you? (*To* GARCIN) Don't listen to her. If you want me to have faith in you, you must begin by trusting me.

INEZ That's right! That's right! Trust away! She wants a man—that far you can trust her—she wants a man's arm round her waist, a man's smell, a man's eyes glowing with desire. And that's all she wants. She'd assure you you were God Almighty if she thought it would give you pleasure.

GARCIN Estelle, is this true? Answer me. Is it true?

ESTELLE What do you expect me to say? Don't you realize how maddening it is to have to answer questions one can't make head or tail of? (*She stamps her foot*) You do make things difficult. . . . Anyhow, I'd love you just the same, even if you were a coward. Isn't that enough?

(*A short pause*)

GARCIN (*To the two women*) You disgust me, both of you.

(*He goes toward the door*)

ESTELLE What are you up to?

GARCIN I'm going.

INEZ (*Quickly*) You won't get far. The door is locked.

GARCIN I'll *make* them open it. (*He presses the bell-push. The bell does not ring*)

ESTELLE Please! Please!

INEZ (*To* ESTELLE) Don't worry, my pet. The bell doesn't work.

GARCIN I tell you they shall open. (*Drums on the door*) I can't endure it any longer, I'm through with you both. (ESTELLE *runs to him; he pushes her away*) Go away. You're even fouler than she. I won't let myself get bogged in your eyes. You're soft and slimy. Ugh! (*Bangs on the door again*) Like an octopus. Like a quagmire.

ESTELLE I beg you, oh, I beg you not to leave me. I'll promise not to speak again, I won't trouble you in any way—but don't go. I daren't be left alone with Inez, now she's shown her claws.

GARCIN Look after yourself. I never asked you to come here.

ESTELLE Oh, how mean you are! Yes, it's quite true you're a coward.

INEZ (*Going up to* ESTELLE) Well, my little sparrow fallen from the nest, I hope you're satisfied now. You spat in my face—playing up to him, of course—and we had a tiff on his account. But he's going, and a good riddance it will be. We two women will have the place to ourselves.

ESTELLE You won't gain anything. If that door opens, I'm going, too.

INEZ Where?

ESTELLE I don't care where. As far from you as I can.

(GARCIN *has been drumming on the door while they talk*)

GARCIN Open the door! Open, blast you! I'll endure anything, your red-hot tongs and molten lead, your racks and prongs and garrotes—all your fiendish gadgets, everything that burns and flays and tears—I'll put up with any torture you impose. Anything, anything would be better than this agony of mind, this creeping pain that gnaws and fumbles and caresses one and never hurts quite enough. (*He grips the door-knob and rattles it*) Now will you open? (*The door flies open with a jerk, and he just avoids falling*) Ah! (*A long silence*)

INEZ Well, Garcin? You're free to go.

GARCIN (*Meditatively*) Now I wonder why that door opened.

INEZ What are you waiting for? Hurry up and go.

GARCIN I shall not go.

INEZ And you, Estelle? (ESTELLE *does not move.* INEZ *bursts out laughing*) So what? Which shall it be? Which of the three of us will leave? The barrier's down, why are we waiting? . . . But what a situation! It's a scream! We're—inseparables!

(ESTELLE *springs at her from behind*)

ESTELLE Inseparables? Garcin, come and lend a hand. Quickly. We'll push her out and slam the door on her. That'll teach her a lesson.

INEZ (*Struggling with* ESTELLE) Estelle! I beg you, let me stay. I won't go, I won't go! Not into the passage.

GARCIN Let go of her.

ESTELLE You're crazy. She hates you.

GARCIN It's because of her I'm staying here.

(ESTELLE *releases* INEZ *and stares dumfoundedly at* GARCIN)

INEZ Because of me? (*Pause*) All right, shut the door. It's ten times hotter here since it opened. (GARCIN *goes to the door and shuts it*) Because of me, you said?

GARCIN Yes. *You,* anyhow, know what it means to be a coward.

INEZ Yes, I know.

GARCIN And you know what wickedness is, and shame, and fear. There were days when you peered into yourself, into the secret places of your heart, and what you saw there made you faint with horror. And then, next day, you didn't know what to make of it, you couldn't interpret the horror you had glimpsed the day before. Yes, you know what evil costs. And when you say I'm a coward, you know from experience what that means. Is that so?

INEZ Yes.

GARCIN So it's you whom I have to convince; you are of my kind. Did you suppose I meant to go? No, I couldn't leave you here, gloating over my defeat, with all those thoughts about me running in your head.

INEZ Do you really wish to convince me?

GARCIN That's the one and only thing I wish for now. I can't hear them any longer, you know. Probably that means they're through with me. For good and all. The curtain's down, nothing of me is left on earth—not even the name of coward. So, Inez, we're alone. Only you two remain to give a thought to me. She—she doesn't count. It's you who matter; you who hate me. If you'll have faith in me I'm saved.

INEZ It won't be easy. Have a look at me. I'm a hard-headed woman.

GARCIN I'll give you all the time that's needed.

INEZ Yes, we've lots of time in hand. *All* time.

GARCIN (*Putting his hands on her shoulders*) Listen! Each man has an aim in life, a leading motive; that's so, isn't it? Well, I didn't give a damn for wealth, or for love. I aimed at being a real man. A tough, as they say. I staked everything on the same horse. . . . Can one possibly be a coward when one's deliberately courted danger at every turn? And can one judge a life by a single action?

INEZ Why not? For thirty years you dreamt you were a hero, and condoned a thousand petty lapses—because a hero, of course, can do no wrong. An easy method, obviously. Then a day came when you were up against it, the red light of real danger—and you took the train to Mexico.

GARCIN I "dreamt," you say. It was no dream. When I chose the hardest path, I made my choice deliberately. A man is what he wills himself to be.

INEZ Prove it. Prove it was no dream. It's what one

does, and nothing else, that shows the stuff one's made of.

GARCIN I died too soon. I wasn't allowed time to—to do my deeds.

INEZ One always dies too soon—or too late. And yet one's whole life is complete at that moment, with a line drawn neatly under it, ready for the summing up. You are—your life, and nothing else.

GARCIN What a poisonous woman you are! With an answer for everything.

INEZ Now then! Don't lose heart. It shouldn't be so hard, convincing me. Pull yourself together, man, rake up some arguments. (GARCIN *shrugs his shoulders*) Ah, wasn't I right when I said you were vulnerable? Now you're going to pay the price, and what a price! You're a coward, Garcin, because I wish it. I wish it—do you hear?—I wish it. And yet, just look at me, see how weak I am, a mere breath on the air, a gaze observing you, a formless thought that thinks you. (*He walks toward her, opening his hands*) Ah, they're open now, those big hands, those coarse, man's hands! But what do you hope to do? You can't throttle thoughts with hands. So you've no choice, you must convince me, and you're at my mercy.

ESTELLE Garcin!

GARCIN What?

ESTELLE Revenge yourself.

GARCIN How?

ESTELLE Kiss me, darling—then you'll hear her squeal.

GARCIN That's true, Inez. I'm at your mercy, but you're at mine as well.

(*He bends over* ESTELLE. INEZ *gives a little cry*)

INEZ Oh, you coward, you weakling, running to women to console you!

ESTELLE That's right, Inez. Squeal away.

INEZ What a lovely pair you make! If you could see his big paw splayed out on your back, rucking up your skin and creasing the silk. Be careful, though! He's perspiring, his hand will leave a blue stain on your dress.

ESTELLE Squeal away, Inez, squeal away! . . . Hug me tight, darling; tighter still—that'll finish her off, and a good thing too!

INEZ Yes, Garcin, she's right. Carry on with it, press her to you till you feel your bodies melting into each other; a lump of warm, throbbing flesh. . . . Love's a grand solace, isn't it, my friend? Deep and dark as sleep. But I'll see you don't sleep.

(GARCIN *makes a slight movement*)

ESTELLE Don't listen to her. Press your lips to my mouth. Oh, I'm yours, yours, yours.

INEZ Well, what are you waiting for? Do as you're told. What a lovely scene: coward Garcin holding baby-killer Estelle in his manly arms! Make your stakes, everyone. Will coward Garcin kiss the lady, or won't he dare? What's the betting? I'm watching you, everybody's watching, I'm a crowd all by myself. Do you hear the crowd? Do you hear them muttering, Garcin? Mumbling and muttering. "Coward! Coward! Coward! Coward!"—that's what they're saying. . . . It's no use trying to escape, I'll never let you go. What do you hope to get from her silly lips? Forgetfulness? But I shan't forget you, not I! "It's I you must convince." So come to me. I'm waiting. Come along, now. . . . Look how obedient he is, like a well-trained dog who comes when his mistress calls. You can't hold him, and you never will.

GARCIN Will night never come?

INEZ Never.

GARCIN You will always see me?

INEZ Always.

(GARCIN *moves away from* ESTELLE *and takes some steps across the room. He goes to the bronze ornament*)

GARCIN This bronze. (*Strokes it thoughtfully*) Yes, now's the moment; I'm looking at this thing on the mantelpiece, and I understand that I'm in hell. I tell you, everything's been thought out beforehand. They knew I'd stand at the fireplace stroking this thing of bronze, with all those eyes intent on me. Devouring me. (*He swings round abruptly*) What? Only two of you? I thought there were more; many more. (*Laughs*) So this is hell. I'd never have believed it. You remember all we were told about the torture-chambers, the fire and brimstone, the "burning marl." Old wives' tales! There's no need for red-hot pokers. Hell is—other people!

ESTELLE My darling! Please—

GARCIN (*Thrusting her away*) No, let me be. She is between us. I cannot love you when she's watching.

ESTELLE Right! In that case, I'll stop her watching. (*She picks up the paper-knife from the table, rushes at* INEZ, *and stabs her several times*)

INEZ (*Struggling and laughing*) But, you crazy creature, what do you think you're doing? You know quite well I'm dead.

ESTELLE Dead?

(*She drops the knife. A pause.* INEZ *picks up the knife and jabs herself with it regretfully*)

INEZ Dead! Dead! Dead! Knives, poison, ropes—all useless. It has happened *already*, do you understand? Once and for all. So here we are, forever. (*Laughs*)

ESTELLE (*With a peal of laughter*) Forever. My God, how funny! Forever.

GARCIN (*Looks at the two women, and joins in the laughter*) For ever, and ever, and ever.

(*They slump onto their respective sofas. A long silence. Their laughter dies away and they gaze at each other*)

GARCIN Well, let's get on with it. . . .

*Curtain*

# Albert Camus

## (1913-1960)

THE INTELLECTUAL vigor and stylistic brilliance of Camus' novels, short stories, and essays almost obscure his equally genuine contribution to the modern theatre. Along with other French writers who responded to the challenge of existential thought, Camus viewed the writer's art as intimately bound up with a rigorous philosophical quest into the meaning of life. The interplay of poetry and dialectics shaped every line Camus wrote; yet his plays, like his other works, are not cold philosophical demonstrations, but lively and concrete expressions of thought converted into drama.

Camus' love of the theatre dates from the beginning of his literary career. At 21 he was an energetic participant in the intellectual and artistic life of Algiers. Moved by a passionate hatred of injustice, he joined the Communist party in 1934, only to leave it soon afterwards. With friends of similar revolutionary persuasion, he founded the Théâtre du Travail (Workers' Theatre), directed to a proletarian audience and to producing dramas of immediate social and political importance. In addition, the young Camus helped organize a touring company that played in the Algerian provinces. He acted in a number of plays, including his own adaptations of novels of Dostoevsky and Malraux; he was also scene designer, director, and manager of the company as well as playwright.

Camus' first play, *Revolt in the Asturias* (*Révolte dans les Asturies,* 1936) was actually a collaborative effort; five members of the Workers' Theatre contributed to the first draft, which was then edited and polished by Camus. The events of the drama were drawn from recent history: the rebellion of Spanish miners in 1934. After their initial success, the rebels set up a socialist state in Oviedo, only to be brutally crushed by government troops two weeks later. In its passionate probing into the meaning of death, this drama of abortive revolt prefigures everything Camus was to write. His love of theatrical experiment impelled him to place the set around the audience. The stage was arranged in two levels, with changes in scene design made only through the manipulation of lights. Camus felt that by placing the spectator in the center of the action, the performance would take on the immediacy of ritual participation: "The spectator must feel he is *in* Oviedo, not *in front* of it; everything goes on around him and he must be the center of the tragedy." The experiment took place in the hall of a café in a working-class district of Algiers. Camus felt it was a failure and subsequently refused to reprint the play; nevertheless, the opposition of mass forces, the rejection of traditional psychological and realistic drama, the imaginative use of décor, music, and choral fantasy, as in the voices of the dead miners lamenting their fate, all point to a vivid awareness of new possibilities of theatrical expression.

*Caligula,* by common consent Camus' best play, dates from 1938. The rather brief first version bore the subtitle: "The Meaning of Death." Closely related to the analysis of the absurdity of life later presented in the existential essay, *The Myth of Sisyphus, Caligula* is a drama rich in ideological texture. It makes considerable demands on both spectator and reader, yet from its premiere in 1945 with Gérard Philipe in the title role, it was clear that Camus had written, not a cold and abstract intellectual dialogue, but a taut and compelling play animated by a highly concrete and visual conception of drama. The 1938 text was expanded in 1945 and again in 1958, but the most recent changes are minor and incidental. Camus himself considered the version of 1945, here presented in translation, to be the best.

The playwright borrowed the starting point and many of the details of the action from Suetonius, with assistance from other ancient historians; yet Camus' hero belongs far more to the world of fantasy and make-believe than to historical reality. First and foremost, Caligula is not an emperor but an actor; life is a masquerade and cruelty is a mask for the actor's game of endless self-creation. The hero's attitude toward himself is insistently theatrical. His first and last action is to contemplate himself in a mirror, not merely out of narcissism, but to mark off the boundary between the real and fictitious selves. The whole of Caligula's existence is a performance wherein the hero is at once spectator and protagonist, delighting in the sheer pleasure of theatrical improvisation.

The key to Caligula's brutal mask is his obsession with the absurdity of existence: "Men die; and they are not happy." His tyranny is an effort to make the impossible possible. If life is meaningless, then power has no limits. Caligula plainly is not mad; he only appears so to those who fail to understand him. His monstrous depravity is an assertion of freedom as well as a surrender to an inner darkness. No name is ascribed to "the black ulcers that fester in his soul" and ultimately drive him to suicide. As Camus declared, by dint of his fidelity to himself Caligula is unfaithful to mankind: "If his truth is the denial of the gods, his error is the denial of men. He has not understood that you cannot destroy everything without destroying yourself." In his final soliloquy, Caligula questions the validity of his choice, but his last line reaffirms his challenge of the cosmos even while it points to the presence of his wild passion in all of us and to its continuation in history.

It is curious that some of Camus' interpreters have seen the play merely as a drama of ideas. There is little that is profound or complex about the ironic or perverse manifestations of Caligula's "madness"; the scenes of torture are painful and horrifying, but they lend immediacy and substance to the hero's inner struggle. His tricks, poses, and brutalities are as much a part of the play as his driving introspection. Camus, in his simple, direct and bare style, has created a figure endowed with a life of his own. No mere mouthpiece for the philosophy of the playwright, Caligula stands forth as a living tribute to the power of his creator to embody the intensity and passion of inner life.

*Caligula* undoubtedly constitutes Camus' greatest achievement in the theatre, but his other plays and adaptations are also remarkable dramatizations of the meaning of violence and death. *The Misunderstanding* (*Le Malentendu*, 1944) is a harsh and ironic portrayal of ruthlessness, in which the murderers unwittingly become their own victims. The returning son, Jan, delays revealing his identity, the better to learn how to make his mother and sister happy, and pays for it with his life. More significant, if even less successful at the box office, is *State of Siege* (*L'Etat de Siège*, 1948) often erroneously described as an adaptation of Camus' novel, *The Plague*. A free-flowing poetic fantasy, *State of Siege* combines lyricism, dance, music, song, and choral ode in a loose and turbulent spectacle suggestive of the "total theatre" of Paul Claudel. In his prefatory note, Camus insists that the work is to be viewed not as a traditional play but as a spectacle freely mixing all the forms of dramatic expression. It is a daring experiment, reminiscent at times of the frenzied passion and symbolic characterization of expressionism, but concerned essentially with political relationships rising out of the chaos of recent history. Concentration camps, mass executions, brain washing, thought control, the manipulation of history, the reduction of men to statistics, all prefigure the new Apocalypse, the dark vision of universal destruction with which the play closes. Rambling and at times incoherent, *State of Siege* led Camus into a blind alley; his subsequent plays, far more modest in scope, were marked by a more solid command of structure within a severely restricted conception of the limits of dramatic representation.

*The Just Assassins* (*Les Justes*, 1949) draws on the confessions of a political terrorist in the abortive Russian revolution of 1905 to explore once again the moral and philosophical consequences of violence. Camus' probing into the ideological basis of political assassination is given vividly concrete expression in the conflict within and among the revolutionaries. Kaliayev, who kills in order to make possible a just society, insists that there are boundaries beyond which the quest for justice cannot pass without corrupting itself. His acceptance of death is a conquest of the futility of life and a demonstration of the purity of his act of violence. "If I did not die," Kaliayev exclaims to his victim's widow, "it's then I'd be a murderer." The sharp opposition of ideas is at the same time the conflict of passionate human beings whose choice dooms them to excruciating inner suffering. Perhaps too much of the drama depends on narration rather than visual presentation, but the characters are vividly and convincingly drawn, and the patent application of the politics of violence to present-day Russia intensifies the urgency of Camus' plea for a just relationship of ends and means.

In the last decade of his life Camus continued his work in the theatre as an adapter, translator, and director. His grasp of the technical intricacies of production was extensive and sure. His translations of Lope de Vega and Calderón were a natural expression of his kinship with Spain—his mother was of Spanish origin—and of his admiration of the polished antithesis and symbolic spectacle of *siglo de oro* drama and its portrayal of the passion and mystery of human destiny. Even more striking and successful were his adaptations of Faulkner's *Requiem for a Nun* (1956) and Dostoevsky's *The Possessed* (1959). The former is a skillful arrangement of Faulkner's complex dramatic dialogue on moral anarchy and redemption through suffering. Camus is more concerned with clarity of motivation than with spiritual consequences, and the reduction of Faulkner's ambiguity and rhetoric, while essential to the demands of the stage, is not an unmixed gain. Camus was more self-effacing in his dramatization of *The Possessed*. The adaptation is crowded with incident, and, in its concentration on four central figures rather than one, betrays the same blurring of focus that we find in Dostoevsky's sprawling but absorbing political novel. As in *The Just Assassins*, the parallel between the Russia of today and that of a century ago transforms seemingly academic ideological debate into a sober and disturbing illumination of the meaning of political murder. Deservedly, the play was one of the triumphs of the French stage in 1959. Its powerful impact arose not only from the intrinsically dramatic substance of Dostoevsky's novel, but from the wonderful affinity of mind and spirit between the novelist and the playwright.

Camus is the author of but one great play, but his importance in the theatre of our time cannot be questioned. Had he not been cut off at the age of 46, he undoubtedly would have continued to write for the theatre. He was at work on a *Don Juan* drama at the time of his death. The play may well have provided yet one more dramatization of the greatness and misery of the absurd hero. In "The Myth of Sisyphus" the lover joins the conqueror, the actor and the writer in ceaselessly protesting against the dominion of death. Camus' drama was a vehicle for his philosophy but at its best it was something more as well: a vivid and impassioned expression of the agony and grandeur of living men.

# CALIGULA

## *A Play in Four Acts*

Translated by Stuart Gilbert

### CHARACTERS IN THE PLAY

CALIGULA
CÆSONIA
HELICON
SCIPIO
CHEREA
THE OLD PATRICIAN
METELLUS
LEPIDUS
INTENDANT
MEREIA
MUCIUS
MUCIUS' WIFE
PATRICIANS, KNIGHTS,
POETS, GUARDS, SERVANTS

## Act One

*A number of patricians, one a very old man, are gathered in a state room of the imperial palace. They are showing signs of nervousness.*

FIRST PATRICIAN Still no news.

THE OLD PATRICIAN None last night, none this morning.

SECOND PATRICIAN Three days without news. Strange indeed!

THE OLD PATRICIAN Our messengers go out, our messengers return. And always they shake their heads and say: "Nothing."

SECOND PATRICIAN They've combed the whole countryside. What more can be done?

FIRST PATRICIAN We can only wait. It's no use meeting trouble halfway. Perhaps he'll return as abruptly as he left us.

THE OLD PATRICIAN When I saw him leaving the palace, I noticed a queer look in his eyes.

FIRST PATRICIAN Yes, so did I. In fact I asked him what was amiss.

SECOND PATRICIAN Did he answer?

FIRST PATRICIAN One word: "Nothing."

(*A short silence.* HELICON *enters. He is munching onions*)

SECOND PATRICIAN (*In the same nervous tone*) It's all very perturbing.

FIRST PATRICIAN Oh, come now! All young fellows are like that.

THE OLD PATRICIAN You're right there. They take things hard. But time smooths everything out.

SECOND PATRICIAN Do you really think so?

THE OLD PATRICIAN Of course. For one girl dead, a dozen living ones.

HELICON Ah? So you think that there's a girl behind it?

FIRST PATRICIAN What else should there be? Anyhow—thank goodness!—grief never lasts forever. Is any one of us here capable of mourning a loss for more than a year on end?

SECOND PATRICIAN Not I, anyhow.

FIRST PATRICIAN No one can do that.

THE OLD PATRICIAN Life would be intolerable if one could.

FIRST PATRICIAN Quite so. Take my case. I lost my wife last year. I shed many tears, and then I forgot. Even now I feel a pang of grief at times. But, happily, it doesn't amount to much.

THE OLD PATRICIAN Yes, Nature's a great healer.

(CHEREA *enters*)

FIRST PATRICIAN Well . . ?

CHEREA Still nothing.

HELICON Come, gentlemen! There's no need for consternation.

FIRST PATRICIAN I agree.

HELICON Worrying won't mend matters—and it's lunchtime.

THE OLD PATRICIAN That's so. We mustn't drop the prey for the shadow.

CHEREA I don't like the look of things. But all was going too smoothly. As an emperor, he was perfection's self.

SECOND PATRICIAN Yes, exactly the emperor we wanted; conscientious and inexperienced.

FIRST PATRICIAN But what's come over you? There's no reason for all these lamentations. We've no ground for assuming he will change. Let's say he loved Drusilla. Only natural; she was his sister. Or say his love for her was something more than brotherly; shocking enough, I grant you. But it's really going too far, setting all Rome in a turmoil because the girl has died.

CHEREA Maybe. But, as I said, I don't like the look of things; this escapade alarms me.

THE OLD PATRICIAN Yes, there's never smoke without fire.

FIRST PATRICIAN In any case, the interests of the State should prevent his making a public tragedy of . . . of, let's say, a regrettable attachment. No doubt such things happen; but the less said the better.

HELICON How can you be sure Drusilla is the cause of all this trouble?

SECOND PATRICIAN Who else should it be?

HELICON Nobody at all, quite likely. When there's a host of explanations to choose from, why pick on the stupidest, most obvious one?

(*Young* SCIPIO *enters.* CHEREA *goes toward him*)

CHEREA Well?

SCIPIO Still nothing. Except that some peasants think they saw him last night not far from Rome, rushing through the storm.

(CHEREA *comes back to the patricians,* SCIPIO *following him*)

CHEREA That makes three days, Scipio, doesn't it?

SCIPIO Yes . . . I was there, following him as I usually do. He went up to Drusilla's body. He stroked it with two fingers, and seemed lost in thought for a long while. Then he swung round and walked out, calmly enough. . . . And ever since we've been hunting for him—in vain.

CHEREA (*Shaking his head*) That young man was too fond of literature.

SECOND PATRICIAN Oh, at his age, you know . . .

CHEREA At his age, perhaps; but not in his position. An artistic emperor is an anomaly. I grant you we've had one or two; misfits happen in the best of empires. But the others had the good taste to remember they were public servants.

FIRST PATRICIAN It made things run more smoothly.

THE OLD PATRICIAN One man, one job—that's how it should be.

SCIPIO What can we do, Cherea?

CHEREA Nothing.

SECOND PATRICIAN We can only wait. If he doesn't return, a successor will have to be found. Between ourselves—there's no shortage of candidates.

FIRST PATRICIAN No, but there's a shortage of the right sort.

CHEREA Suppose he comes back in an ugly mood?

FIRST PATRICIAN Oh, he's a mere boy; we'll make him see reason.

CHEREA And what if he declines to see it?

FIRST PATRICIAN (*Laughing*) In that case, my friend, don't forget I once wrote a manual of revolutions. You'll find all the rules there.

CHEREA I'll look it up—if things come to that. But I'd rather be left to my books.

SCIPIO If you'll excuse me. . . .

(*Goes out*)

CHEREA He's offended.

THE OLD PATRICIAN Scipio is young, and young people always hang together.

HELICON Scipio doesn't count, anyhow.

(*Enter a member of the imperial bodyguard*)

THE GUARDSMAN Caligula has been seen in the palace gardens.

(*All leave the room. The stage is empty for some moments. Then* CALIGULA *enters stealthily from the left. His legs are caked with mud, his garments dirty; his hair is wet, his look distraught. He brings his hand to his mouth several times. Then he approaches a mirror, stopping abruptly when he catches sight of his reflected self. After muttering some unintelligible words, he sits down on the right, letting his arms hang limp between his knees.* HELICON *enters, left. On seeing* CALIGULA, *he stops at the far end of the stage and contemplates him in silence.* CALIGULA *turns and sees him. A short silence*)

HELICON (*Across the stage*) Good morning, Caius.

CALIGULA (*In quite an ordinary tone*) Good morning, Helicon.

(*A short silence*)

HELICON You're looking tired.

CALIGULA I've walked a lot.

HELICON Yes, you've been away for quite a while.

(*Another short silence*)

CALIGULA It was hard to find.

HELICON What was hard to find?

CALIGULA What I was after.

HELICON Meaning?

CALIGULA (*In the same matter-of-fact tone*) The moon.

HELICON What?

CALIGULA Yes, I wanted the moon.

HELICON Ah. . . . (*Another silence.* HELICON *approaches* CALIGULA) And why did you want it?

CALIGULA Well . . . it's one of the things I haven't got.

HELICON I see. And now—have you fixed it up to your satisfaction?

CALIGULA No. I couldn't get it.

HELICON Too bad!

CALIGULA Yes, and that's why I'm tired. (*Pauses. Then*) Helicon!

HELICON Yes, Caius?

CALIGULA No doubt, you think I'm crazy.

HELICON As you know well, I never think.

CALIGULA Ah, yes. . . . Now, listen! I'm not mad; in fact I've never felt so lucid. What happened to me is quite simple; I suddenly felt a desire for the impossible. That's all. (*Pauses*) Things as they are, in my opinion, are far from satisfactory.

HELICON Many people share your opinion.

CALIGULA That is so. But in the past I didn't realize it. *Now* I know. (*Still in the same matter-of-fact tone*) Really, this world of ours, the scheme of things as they call it, is quite intolerable. That's why I want the moon, or happiness, or eternal life—something, in fact, that may sound crazy, but which isn't of this world.

HELICON That's sound enough in theory. Only, in practice one can't carry it through to its conclusion.

CALIGULA (*Rising to his feet, but still with perfect calmness*) You're wrong there. It's just because no one *dares* to follow up his ideas to the end that nothing is achieved. All that's needed, I should say, is to be logical right through, at all costs. (*He studies* HELICON'S *face*) I can see, too, what you're thinking. What a fuss over a woman's death! But that's not it. True enough, I seem to remember that a woman died some days ago; a woman whom I loved. But love, what is it? A side issue. And I swear to you her death is not the point; it's no more than the symbol of a truth that makes the moon essential to me. A childishly simple, obvious, almost silly truth, but one that's hard to come by and heavy to endure.

HELICON May I know what it is, this truth that you've discovered?

CALIGULA (*His eyes averted, in a toneless voice*) Men die; and they are not happy.

HELICON (*After a short pause*) Anyhow, Caligula, it's a truth with which one comes to terms, without much trouble. Only look at the people over there. This truth of yours doesn't prevent them from enjoying their meal.

CALIGULA (*With sudden violence*) All it proves is that I'm surrounded by lies and self-deception. But I've had enough of that; I wish men to live by the light of truth. And I've the power to make them do so. For I know what they need and haven't got. They're without understanding and they need a teacher; someone who knows what he's talking about.

HELICON Don't take offense, Caius, if I give you a word of advice. . . . But that can wait. First, you should have some rest.

CALIGULA (*Sitting down. His voice is gentle again*) That's not possible, Helicon. I shall never rest again.

HELICON But—why?

CALIGULA If I sleep, who'll give me the moon?

HELICON (*After a short silence*) That's true.

CALIGULA (*Rising to his feet again, with an effort*) Listen, Helicon . . . I hear footsteps, voices. Say nothing—and forget you've seen me.

HELICON I understand.

CALIGULA (*Looking back, as he moves toward the door*) And please help me, from now on.

HELICON I've no reason not to do so, Caius. But I know very few things, and few things interest me. In what way can I help you?

CALIGULA In the way of . . . the impossible.

HELICON I'll do my best.

(CALIGULA *goes out.* SCIPIO *and* CÆSONIA *enter hurriedly*)

SCIPIO No one! Haven't you seen him?

HELICON No.

CÆSONIA Tell me, Helicon. Are you quite sure he didn't say anything to you before he went away?

HELICON I'm not a sharer of his secrets, I'm his public. A mere onlooker. It's more prudent.

CÆSONIA Please don't talk like that.

HELICON My dear Cæsonia, Caius is an idealist as we all know. He follows his bent, and no one can foresee where it will take him. . . . But, if you'll excuse me, I'll go to lunch.

(*Exit* HELICON)

CÆSONIA (*Sinking wearily onto a divan*) One of the palace guards saw him go by. But all Rome sees Caligula everywhere. And Caligula, of course, sees nothing but his own idea.

SCIPIO What idea?

CÆSONIA How can I tell, Scipio?

SCIPIO Are you thinking of Drusilla?

CÆSONIA Perhaps. One thing is sure; he loved her. And it's a cruel thing to have someone die today whom only yesterday you were holding in your arms.

SCIPIO (*Timidly*) And you . . . ?

CÆSONIA Oh, I'm the old, trusted mistress. That's my role.

SCIPIO Cæsonia, we must save him.

CÆSONIA So you, too, love him?

SCIPIO Yes. He's been very good to me. He encouraged me; I shall never forget some of the things he said. He told me life isn't easy, but it has consolations: religion, art, and the love one inspires in others. He often told me that the only mistake one makes in life is to cause others suffering. He tried to be a just man.

CÆSONIA (*Rising*) He's only a child. (*She goes to the glass and scans herself*) The only god I've ever had is my body, and now I shall pray this god of mine to give Caius back to me.

(CALIGULA *enters. On seeing* CÆSONIA *and* SCIPIO *he hesitates, and takes a backward step. At the same moment several men enter from the opposite side of the room: patricians and the* INTENDANT *of the palace. They stop short when they see* CALIGULA. CÆSONIA *turns. She and* SCIPIO *hurry toward* CALIGULA, *who checks them with a gesture*)

INTENDANT (*In a rather quavering voice*) We . . . we've been looking for you, Cæsar, high and low.

CALIGULA (*In a changed, harsh tone*) So I see.

INTENDANT We . . . I mean . . .

CALIGULA (*Roughly*) What do you want?

INTENDANT We were feeling anxious, Cæsar.

CALIGULA (*Going toward him*) What business had you to feel anxious?

INTENDANT Well . . . er . . . (*He has an inspiration*) Well, as you know, there are points to be settled in connection with the Treasury.

CALIGULA (*Bursting into laughter*) Ah, yes. The Treasury! That's so. The Treasury's of prime importance.

INTENDANT Yes, indeed.

CALIGULA (*Still laughing, to* CÆSONIA) Don't you agree, my dear? The Treasury is all-important.

CÆSONIA No, Caligula. It's a secondary matter.

CALIGULA That only shows your ignorance. We are extremely interested in our Treasury. Everything's important: our fiscal system, public morals, foreign policy, army equipment, and agrarian laws. Everything's of cardinal importance, I assure you. And everything's on an equal footing: the grandeur of Rome and your attacks of arthritis. . . . Well, well, I'm going to apply my mind to all that. And, to begin with . . . Now listen well, Intendant.

INTENDANT We are listening, sir.

(*The patricians come forward*)

CALIGULA You're our loyal subjects, are you not?

INTENDANT (*In a reproachful tone*) Oh, Cæsar . . . !

CALIGULA Well, I've something to propose to you. We're going to make a complete change in our economic system. In two moves. Drastic and abrupt. I'll explain, Intendant . . . when the patricians have left. (*The patricians go out.* CALIGULA *seats himself beside* CÆSONIA, *with his arm around her waist*) Now mark my words. The first move's this. Every patrician, everyone in the Empire who has any capital —small or large, it's all the same thing—is ordered to disinherit his children and make a new will leaving his money to the State.

INTENDANT But Cæsar . . .

CALIGULA I've not yet given you leave to speak. As the need arises, we shall have these people die; a list will be drawn up by us fixing the order of their deaths. When the fancy takes us, we may modify that order. And, of course, we shall step into their money.

CÆSONIA (*Freeing herself*) But—what's come over you?

CALIGULA (*Imperturbably*) Obviously the order of their going has no importance. Or, rather, all these executions have an equal importance—from which it follows that none has any. Really all those fellows are on a par, one's as guilty as another. (*To the* INTENDANT, *peremptorily*) You are to promulgate this edict without a moment's delay and see it's carried out forthwith. The wills are to be signed by residents in Rome this evening; within a month at the latest by persons in the provinces. Send out your messengers.

INTENDANT Cæsar, I wonder if you realize . . .

CALIGULA Do I realize . . . ? Now, listen well, you fool! If the Treasury has paramount importance, human life has none. That should be obvious to you. People who think like you are bound to admit the logic of my edict, and since money is the only thing that counts, should set no value on their lives or anyone else's. I have resolved to be logical, and I have the power to enforce my will. Presently you'll see what logic's going to cost you! I shall eliminate contradictions and contradicters. If necessary, I'll begin with you.

INTENDANT Cæsar, my good will can be relied on, that I swear.

CALIGULA And mine, too; that I guarantee. Just see how ready I am to adopt your point of view, and give the Treasury the first place in my program. Really you should be grateful to me; I'm playing into your hand, and with your own cards. (*He pauses, before continuing in a flat, unemotional tone*) In any case there is a touch of genius in the simplicity of my plan—which clinches the matter. I give you three seconds in which to remove yourself. One . . .

(*The* INTENDANT *hurries out*)

CÆSONIA I can't believe it's you! But it was just a joke, wasn't it?—all you said to him.

CALIGULA Not quite that, Cæsonia. Let's say, a lesson in statesmanship.

SCIPIO But, Caius, it's . . . it's impossible!

CALIGULA That's the whole point.

SCIPIO I don't follow.

CALIGULA I repeat—that is my point. I'm exploiting the impossible. Or, more accurately, it's a question of making the impossible possible.

SCIPIO But that game may lead to—to anything! It's a lunatic's pastime.

CALIGULA No, Scipio. An emperor's vocation. (*He lets himself sink back wearily among the cushions*) Ah, my dears, at last I've come to see the uses of supremacy. It gives impossibilities a run. From this day on, so long as life is mine, my freedom has no frontier.

CÆSONIA (*Sadly*) I doubt if this discovery of yours will make us any happier.

CALIGULA So do I. But, I suppose, we'll have to live it through.

(CHEREA *enters*)

CHEREA I have just heard of your return. I trust your health is all it should be.

CALIGULA My health is duly grateful. (*A pause. Then, abruptly*) Leave us, Cherea. I don't want to see you.

CHEREA Really, Caius, I'm amazed . . .

CALIGULA There's nothing to be amazed at. I don't like literary men, and I can't bear lies.

CHEREA If we lie, it's often without knowing it. I plead Not Guilty.

CALIGULA Lies are never guiltless. And yours attribute importance to people and to things. That's what I cannot forgive you.

CHEREA And yet—since this world is the only one we have, why not plead its cause?

CALIGULA Your pleading comes too late, the verdict's given. . . . This world has no importance; once a man realizes that, he wins his freedom. (*He has risen to his feet*) And that is why I hate you, you and your kind; because you are not free. You see in me the one free man in the whole Roman Empire. You should be glad to have at last among you an emperor who points the way to freedom. Leave me, Cherea; and you, too, Scipio, go—for what is friendship? Go, both of you, and spread the news in Rome that freedom has been given her at last, and with the gift begins a great probation.

(*They go out.* CALIGULA *has turned away, hiding his eyes*)

CÆSONIA Crying?

CALIGULA Yes, Cæsonia.

CÆSONIA But, after all, what's changed in your life? You may have loved Drusilla, but you loved many others—myself included—at the same time. Surely that wasn't enough to set you roaming the countryside for three days and nights and bring you back with this . . . this cruel look on your face?

CALIGULA (*Swinging round on her*) What nonsense is this? Why drag in Drusilla? Do you imagine love's the only thing that can make a man shed tears?

CÆSONIA I'm sorry, Caius. Only I was trying to understand.

CALIGULA Men weep because . . . the world's all wrong. (*She comes toward him*) No, Cæsonia. (*She draws back*) But stay beside me.

CÆSONIA I'll do whatever you wish. (*Sits down*) At my age one knows that life's a sad business. But why deliberately set out to make it worse?

CALIGULA No, it's no good; you can't understand. But what matter? Perhaps I'll find a way out. Only, I feel a curious stirring within me, as if undreamed of things were forcing their way up into the light—and I'm helpless against them. (*He moves closer to her*) Oh, Cæsonia, I knew that men felt anguish, but I didn't know what that word anguish meant. Like everyone else I fancied it was a sickness of the mind—no more. But no, it's my body that's in pain. Pain everywhere, in my chest, in my legs and arms. Even my skin is raw, my head is buzzing, I feel like vomiting. But worst of all is this queer taste in my mouth. Not blood, or death, or fever, but a mixture of all three. I've only to stir my tongue, and the world goes black, and everyone looks . . . horrible. How hard, how cruel it is, this process of becoming a man!

CÆSONIA What you need, my dear, is a good, long sleep. Let yourself relax and, above all stop thinking. I'll stay by you while you sleep. And when you wake, you'll find the world's got back its savor. Then you must use your power to good effect—for loving better what you still find lovable. For the possible, too, deserves to be given a chance.

CALIGULA Ah but for that I'd need to sleep, to let myself go—and that's impossible.

CÆSONIA So one always thinks when one is overtired. A time comes when one's hand is firm again.

CALIGULA But one must know where to place it. And what's the use to me of a firm hand, what use is the amazing power that's mine, if I can't have the sun set in the east, if I can't reduce the sum of suffering and make an end of death? No, Cæsonia, it's all one whether I sleep or keep awake, if I've no power to tamper with the scheme of things.

CÆSONIA But that's madness, sheer madness. It's wanting to be a god on earth.

CALIGULA So you, too, think I'm mad. And yet—what is a god that I should wish to be his equal? No, it's something higher, far above the gods, that I'm aiming at, longing for with all my heart and soul. I am taking over a kingdom where the impossible is king.

CÆSONIA You can't prevent the sky from being the sky, or a fresh young face from aging, or a man's heart from growing cold.

CALIGULA (*With rising excitement*) I want . . . I want to drown the sky in the sea, to infuse ugliness with beauty, to wring a laugh from pain.

CÆSONIA (*Facing him with an imploring gesture*) There's good and bad, high and low, justice and injustice. And I swear to you these will never change.

CALIGULA (*In the same tone*) And I'm resolved to change them . . . I shall make this age of ours a kingly gift—the gift of equality. And when all is leveled out, when the impossible has come to earth and the moon is in my hands—then, perhaps, I shall be transfigured and the world renewed; then men will die no more and at last be happy.

CÆSONIA (*With a little cry*) And love? Surely you won't go back on love!

CALIGULA (*In a wild burst of anger*) Love, Cæsonia! (*He grips her shoulders and shakes her*) I've learned the truth about love; it's nothing, nothing! That fellow was quite right—you heard what he said, didn't you?—it's only the Treasury that counts. The fountainhead of all. Ah, now at last I'm going to live, really *live*. And living, my dear, is the opposite of loving. I know what I'm talking about—and I invite you to the most gorgeous of shows, a sight for gods to gloat on, a whole world called to judgment. But for that I must have a crowd—spectators, victims, criminals, hundreds and thousands of them. (*He rushes to the gong and begins hammering on it, faster and faster*) Let the accused come forward. I want my criminals, and they all are criminals. (*Still striking the gong*) Bring in the condemned men. I must have my public. Judges, witnesses, accused—all sentenced to death without a hearing. Yes, Cæsonia, I'll show them something they have never seen before, the one free man in the Roman Empire. (*To the clangor of the gong the palace has been gradually filling with noises; the clash of arms, voices, footsteps slow or hurried, coming nearer, growing louder. Some soldiers enter, and leave hastily*) And you, Cæsonia, shall obey me. You must stand by me to the end. It will be marvelous, you'll see. Swear to stand by me, Cæsonia.

CÆSONIA (*Wildly, between two gong strokes*) I needn't swear. You know I love you.

CALIGULA (*In the same tone*) You'll do all I tell you.

CÆSONIA All, all, Caligula—but do, please, stop. . . .

CALIGULA (*Still striking the gong*) You will be cruel.

CÆSONIA (*Sobbing*) Cruel.

CALIGULA (*Still beating the gong*) Cold and ruthless.

CÆSONIA Ruthless.

CALIGULA And you will suffer, too.

CÆSONIA Yes, yes—oh, no, please . . . I'm—I'm going mad, I think! (*Some patricians enter, followed by members of the palace staff. All look bewildered and perturbed.* CALIGULA *bangs the gong for the last time, raises his mallet, swings round and summons them in a shrill, half-crazy voice*)

CALIGULA Come here. All of you. Nearer. Nearer still. (*He is quivering with impatience*) Your Emperor commands you to come nearer. (*They come forward, pale with terror*) Quickly. And you, Cæsonia, come beside me. (*He takes her hand, leads her to the mirror, and with a wild sweep of his mallet effaces a reflection on its surface. Then gives a sudden laugh*)

All gone. You see, my dear? An end of memories; no more masks. Nothing, nobody left. Nobody? No, that's not true. Look, Cæsonia. Come here, all of you, and *look* . . .

(*He plants himself in front of the mirror in a grotesque attitude*)

CÆSONIA (*Staring, horrified, at the mirror*) Caligula!

(CALIGULA *lays a finger on the glass. His gaze steadies abruptly and when he speaks his voice has a new, proud ardor*)

CALIGULA Yes . . . Caligula.

*Curtain*

# Act Two

*Three years later.*

*A room in* CHEREA'S *house, where the patricians have met in secret.*

FIRST PATRICIAN It's outrageous, the way he's treating us.

THE OLD PATRICIAN He calls me "darling"! In public, mind you—just to make a laughingstock of me. Death's too good for him.

FIRST PATRICIAN And fancy making us run beside his litter when he goes into the country.

SECOND PATRICIAN He says the exercise will do us good.

THE OLD PATRICIAN Conduct like that is quite inexcusable.

THIRD PATRICIAN You're right. That's precisely the sort of thing one can't forgive.

FIRST PATRICIAN He confiscated your property, Patricius. He killed your father, Scipio. He's taken your wife from you, Octavius, and forced her to work in his public brothel. He has killed your son, Lepidus. I ask you, gentlemen, can you endure this? I, anyhow, have made up my mind. I know the risks, but I also know this life of abject fear is quite unbearable. Worse than death, in fact. Yes, as I said, my mind's made up.

SCIPIO He made my mind up for me when he had my father put to death.

FIRST PATRICIAN Well? Can you still hesitate?

A KNIGHT No. We're with you. He's transferred our stalls at the Circus to the public, and egged us on to fight with the rabble—just to have a pretext for punishing us, of course.

THE OLD PATRICIAN He's a coward.

SECOND PATRICIAN A bully.

THIRD PATRICIAN A buffoon.

THE OLD PATRICIAN He's impotent—that's his trouble, I should say.

(*A scene of wild confusion follows, weapons are brandished, a table is overturned, and there is a general rush toward the door. Just at this moment* CHEREA *strolls in, composed as usual, and checks their onrush*)

CHEREA What's all this about? Where are you going?

A PATRICIAN To the palace.

CHEREA Ah, yes. And I can guess why. But do you think you'll be allowed to enter?

THE PATRICIAN There's no question of asking leave.

CHEREA Lepidus, would you kindly shut that door? (*The door is shut.* CHEREA *goes to the overturned table and seats himself on a corner of it. The others turn toward him*) It's not so simple as you think, my friends. You're afraid, but fear can't take the place of courage and deliberation. In short, you're acting too hastily.

A KNIGHT If you're not with us, go. But keep your mouth shut.

CHEREA I suspect I'm with you. But make no mistake. Not for the same reasons.

A VOICE That's enough idle talk.

CHEREA (*Standing up*) I agree. Let's get down to facts. But, first, let me make myself clear. Though I am *with* you, I'm not *for* you. That, indeed, is why I think you're going about it the wrong way. You haven't taken your enemy's measure; that's obvious, since you attribute petty motives to him. But there's nothing petty about Caligula, and you're riding for a fall. You'd be better placed to fight him if you would try to see him as he really is.

A VOICE We see him as he is—a crazy tyrant.

CHEREA No. We've had experience of mad emperors. But this one isn't mad enough. And what I loathe in him is this: that he knows what he wants.

FIRST PATRICIAN And we, too, know it; he wants to murder us all.

CHEREA You're wrong. Our deaths are only a side issue. He's putting his power at the service of a loftier, deadlier passion; and it imperils everything we hold most sacred. True, it's not the first time Rome has seen a man wielding unlimited power; but it's the first time he sets no limit to his use of it, and counts mankind, and the world we know, for nothing. That's what appalls me in Caligula; that's what I want to fight. To lose one's life is no great matter; when the time comes I'll have the courage to lose mine. But what's intolerable is to see one's life being drained of meaning, to be told there's no reason for existing. A man can't live without some reason for living.

FIRST PATRICIAN Revenge is a good reason.

CHEREA Yes, and I propose to share it with you. But I'd have you know that it's not on your account, or to help you to avenge your petty humiliations. No, if I join forces with you, it's to combat a big idea—an ideal, if you like—whose triumph would mean the end of everything. I can endure your being made a mock of, but I cannot endure Caligula's carrying out his theories to the end. He is converting his philosophy into corpses and—unfortunately for us

—it's a philosophy that's logical from start to finish. And where one can't refute, one strikes.

A VOICE Yes. We must *act.*

CHEREA We must take action, I agree. But a frontal attack's quite useless when one is fighting an imperial madman in the full flush of his power. You can take arms against a vulgar tyrant, but cunning is needed to fight down disinterested malice. You can only urge it on to follow its bent, and bide your time until its logic founders in sheer lunacy. As you see, I prefer to be quite frank, and I warn you I'll be with you only for a time. Afterward, I shall do nothing to advance your interests; all I wish is to regain some peace of mind in a world that has regained a meaning. What spurs me on is not ambition but fear, my very reasonable fear of that inhuman vision in which my life means no more than a speck of dust.

FIRST PATRICIAN (*Approaching him*) I have an inkling of what you mean, Cherea. Anyhow, the great thing is that you, too, feel that the whole fabric of society is threatened. You, gentlemen, agree with me, I take it, that our ruling motive is of a moral order. Family life is breaking down, men are losing their respect for honest work, a wave of immorality is sweeping the country. Who of us can be deaf to the appeal of our ancestral piety in its hour of danger? Fellow conspirators, will you tolerate a state of things in which patricians are forced to run, like slaves, beside the Emperor's litter?

THE OLD PATRICIAN Will you allow them to be addressed as "darling"?

A VOICE And have their wives snatched from them?

ANOTHER VOICE And their money?

ALL TOGETHER No!

FIRST PATRICIAN Cherea, your advice is good, and you did well to calm our passion. The time is not yet ripe for action; the masses would still be against us. Will you join us in watching for the best moment to strike—and strike hard?

CHEREA Yes—and meanwhile let Caligula follow his dream. Or, rather, let's actively encourage him to carry out his wildest plans. Let's put method into his madness. And then, at last, a day will come when he's alone, a lonely man in an empire of the dead and kinsmen of the dead.

(*A general uproar. Trumpet calls outside. Then silence, but for whispers of a name:* "CALIGULA!" CALIGULA *enters with* CÆSONIA, *followed by* HELICON *and some soldiers. Pantomime.* CALIGULA *halts and gazes at the conspirators. Without a word he moves from one to the other, straightens a buckle on one man's shoulder, steps back to contemplate another, sweeps them with his gaze, then draws his hand over his eyes and walks out, still without a word*)

CÆSONIA (*Ironically, pointing to the disorder of the room*) Were you having a fight?

CHEREA Yes, we were fighting.

CÆSONIA (*In the same tone*) Really? Might I know what you were fighting about?

CHEREA About . . . nothing in particular.

CÆSONIA Ah? Then it isn't true.

CHEREA What isn't true?

CÆSONIA You were *not* fighting.

CHEREA Have it your own way. We weren't fighting.

CÆSONIA (*Smiling*) Perhaps you'd do better to tidy up the place. Caligula hates untidiness.

HELICON (*To the* OLD PATRICIAN) You'll end by making him do something out of character.

THE OLD PATRICIAN Pardon . . . I don't follow. What have we done to him?

HELICON Nothing. Just nothing. It's fantastic being futile to that point; enough to get on anybody's nerves. Try to put yourselves in Caligula's place. (*A short pause*) I see; doing a bit of plotting, weren't you now?

THE OLD PATRICIAN Really, that's too absurd. I hope Caligula doesn't imagine . . .

HELICON He doesn't imagine. He *knows.* But, I suppose, at bottom, he rather wants it. . . . Well, we'd better set to tidying up.

(*All get busy.* CALIGULA *enters and watches them*)

CALIGULA (*To the* OLD PATRICIAN) Good day, darling. (*To the others*) Gentlemen, I'm on my way to an execution. But I thought I'd drop in at your place, Cherea, for a light meal. I've given orders to have food brought here for all of us. But send for your wives first. (*A short silence*) Rufius should thank his stars that I've been seized with hunger. (*Confidentially*) Rufius, I may tell you, is the knight who's going to be executed. (*Another short silence*) What's this? None of you asks me why I've sentenced him to death? (*No one speaks. Meanwhile slaves lay the table and bring food*) Good for you! I see you're growing quite intelligent. (*He nibbles an olive*) It has dawned on you that a man needn't have done anything for him to die. (*He stops eating and gazes at his guests with a twinkle in his eye*) Soldiers, I am proud of you. (*Three or four women enter*) Good! Let's take our places. Anyhow. No order of precedence today. (*All are seated*) There's no denying it, that fellow Rufius is in luck. But I wonder if he appreciates this short reprieve. A few hours gained on death, why, they're worth their weight in gold! (*He begins eating; the others follow suit. It becomes clear that* CALIGULA'*s table manners are deplorable. There is no need for him to flick his olive stones onto his neighbors' plates, or to spit out bits of gristle over the dish, or to pick his teeth with his nails, or to scratch his head furiously. However, he indulges in these practices throughout the meal, without the least compunction. At one moment he stops eating, stares at* LEPIDUS, *one of the guests, and says roughly*) You're looking grumpy, Lepidus. I wonder, can it be because I had your son killed?

LEPIDUS (*Thickly*) Certainly not, Caius. Quite the contrary.

CALIGULA (*Beaming at him*) "Quite the contrary!" It's always nice to see a face that hides the secrets of the heart. Your face is sad. But what about your heart? Quite the contrary—isn't that so, Lepidus?

LEPIDUS (*Doggedly*) Quite the contrary, Cæsar.

CALIGULA (*More and more enjoying the situation*) Really, Lepidus, there's no one I like better than you. Now let's have a laugh together, my dear friend. Tell me a funny story.

LEPIDUS (*Who has overrated his endurance*) Please . . .

CALIGULA Good! Very good! Then it's I who'll tell the story. But you'll laugh, won't you, Lepidus? (*With a glint of malice*) If only for the sake of your other son. (*Smiling again*) In any case, as you've just told us, you're not in a bad humor. (*He takes a drink, then says in the tone of a teacher prompting a pupil*) Quite . . . quite the . . .

LEPIDUS (*Wearily*) Quite the contrary, Cæsar.

CALIGULA Splendid! (*Drinks again*) Now listen. (*In a gentle, faraway tone*) Once upon a time there was a poor young emperor whom nobody loved. He loved Lepidus, and to root out of his heart his love for Lepidus, he had his youngest son killed. (*In a brisker tone*) Needless to say, there's not a word of truth in it. Still it's a funny story, eh? But you're not laughing. Nobody's laughing. Now listen! (*In a burst of anger*) I insist on everybody's laughing. You, Lepidus, shall lead the chorus. Stand up, every one of you, and laugh. (*He thumps the table*) Do you hear what I say? I wish to see you laughing, all of you. (*All rise to their feet. During this scene all the players,* CALIGULA *and* CÆSONIA *excepted, behave like marionettes in a puppet play.* CALIGULA *sinks back on his couch, beaming with delight, and bursts into a fit of laughter*) Oh, Cæsonia! Just look at them! The game is up; honor, respectability, the wisdom of the nations, gone with the wind! The wind of fear has blown them all away. Fear, Cæsonia—don't you agree?—is a noble emotion, pure and simple, self-sufficient, like no other; it draws its patent of nobility straight from the guts. (*He strokes his forehead and drinks again. In a friendly tone*) Well, well, let's change the subject. What have you to say, Cherea? You've been very silent.

CHEREA I'm quite ready to speak, Caius. When you give me leave.

CALIGULA Excellent. Then—keep silent. I'd rather have a word from our friend Mucius.

MUCIUS (*Reluctantly*) As you will, Caius.

CALIGULA Then tell us something about your wife. And begin by sending her to this place, on my right. (MUCIUS' WIFE *seats herself beside* CALIGULA) Well, Mucius? We're waiting.

MUCIUS (*Hardly knowing what he says*) My wife . . . but . . . I'm very fond of her.

(*General laughter*)

CALIGULA Why, of course, my friend, of course. But how ordinary of you! So unoriginal! (*He is leaning toward her, tickling her shoulder playfully with his tongue*) By the way, when I came in just now, you were hatching a plot, weren't you? A nice bloody little plot?

OLD PATRICIAN Oh, Caius, how can you . . . ?

CALIGULA It doesn't matter in the least, my pet. Old age will be served. I won't take it seriously. Not one of you has the spunk for a heroic act. . . . Ah, it's just come to my mind, I have some affairs of state to settle. But, first, let the imperious desires that nature creates in us have their way.

(*He rises and leads* MUCIUS' WIFE *into an adjoining room.* MUCIUS *starts up from his seat*)

CÆSONIA (*Amiably*) Please, Mucius. Will you pour me out another glass of this excellent wine. (MUCIUS *complies; his movement of revolt is quelled. Everyone looks embarrassed. Chairs creak noisily. The ensuing conversation is in a strained tone.* CÆSONIA *turns to* CHEREA) Now, Cherea, suppose you tell me why you people were fighting just now?

CHEREA (*Coolly*) With pleasure, my dear Cæsonia. Our quarrel arose from a discussion whether poetry should be bloodthirsty or not.

CÆSONIA An interesting problem. Somewhat beyond my feminine comprehension, of course. Still it surprises me that your passion for art should make you come to blows.

CHEREA (*In the same rather stilted tone*) That I can well understand. But I remember Caligula's telling me the other day that all true passion has a spice of cruelty.

CÆSONIA (*Helping herself from the dish in front of her*) There's truth in that. Don't you agree, gentlemen?

THE OLD PATRICIAN Ah, yes. Caligula has a rare insight into the secret places of the heart.

FIRST PATRICIAN And how eloquently he spoke just now of courage!

SECOND PATRICIAN Really, he should put his ideas into writing. They would be most instructive.

CHEREA And, what's more, it would keep him busy. It's obvious he needs something to occupy his leisure.

CÆSONIA (*Still eating*) You'll be pleased to hear that Caligula shares your views; he's working on a book. Quite a big one, I believe.

(CALIGULA *enters, accompanied by* MUCIUS' WIFE)

CALIGULA Mucius, I return your wife, with many thanks. But excuse me, I've some orders to give.

(*He hurries out.* MUCIUS *has gone pale and risen to his feet*)

CÆSONIA (*To* MUCIUS, *who is standing*) This book of his will certainly rank among our Latin Classics. Are you listening, Mucius?

MUCIUS (*His eyes still fixed on the door by which* CALIGULA *went out*) Yes. And what's the book about, Cæsonia?

CÆSONIA (*Indifferently*) Oh, it's above my head, you know.

CHEREA May we assume it deals with the murderous power of poetry?

CÆSONIA Yes, something of that sort, I understand.

THE OLD PATRICIAN (*Cheerfully*) Well anyhow, as our friend Cherea said, it will keep him busy.

CÆSONIA Yes, my love. But I'm afraid there's one thing you won't like quite so much about this book, and that's its title.

CHEREA What is it?

CÆSONIA *Cold Steel.*

(CALIGULA *hurries in*)

CALIGULA Excuse me, but I've some urgent public work in hand. (*To the* INTENDANT) Intendant, you are to close the public granaries. I have signed a decree to that effect; you will find it in my study.

INTENDANT But, sire . . .

CALIGULA Famine begins tomorrow.

INTENDANT But . . . but heaven knows what may happen—perhaps a revolution.

CALIGULA (*Firmly and deliberately*) I repeat; famine begins tomorrow. We all know what famine means —a national catastrophe. Well, tomorrow there will be a catastrophe, and I shall end it when I choose. After all, I haven't so many ways of proving I am free. One is always free at someone else's expense. Absurd perhaps, but so it is. (*With a keen glance at* MUCIUS) Apply this principle to your jealousy—and you'll understand better. (*In a meditative tone*) Still, what an ugly thing is jealousy! A disease of vanity and the imagination. One pictures one's wife . . . (MUCIUS *clenches his fists and opens his mouth to speak. Before he can get a word out,* CALIGULA *cuts in*) Now, gentlemen, let's go on with our meal. . . . Do you know, we've been doing quite a lot of work, with Helicon's assistance? Putting the final touches to a little monograph on execution—about which you will have much to say.

HELICON Assuming we ask your opinion.

CALIGULA Why not be generous, Helicon, and let them into our little secrets? Come now, give them a sample. Section Three, first paragraph.

HELICON (*Standing, declaims in a droning voice*) "Execution relieves and liberates. It is universal, tonic, just in precept and in practice. A man dies because he is guilty. A man is guilty because he is one of Caligula's subjects. Now all men are Caligula's subjects. *Ergo,* all men are guilty and shall die. It is only a matter of time and patience."

CALIGULA (*Laughing*) There's logic for you, don't you agree? That bit about patience was rather neat, wasn't it? Allow me to tell you, that's the quality I most admire in you . . . your patience. Now, gentlemen, you can disperse. Cherea doesn't need your presence any longer. Cæsonia, I wish you to stay. You too, Lepidus. Also our old friend Mereia. I want to have a little talk with you about our National Brothel. It's not functioning too well; in fact, I'm quite concerned about it.

(*The others file out slowly.* CALIGULA *follows* MUCIUS *with his eyes*)

CHEREA At your orders, Caius. But what's the trouble? Is the staff unsatisfactory?

CALIGULA No, but the takings are falling off.

MEREIA Then you should raise the entrance fee.

CALIGULA There, Mereia, you missed a golden opportunity of keeping your mouth shut. You're too old to be interested in the subject, and I don't want your opinion.

MEREIA Then why ask me to stay?

CALIGULA Because, presently, I may require some cool, dispassionate advice.

(MEREIA *moves away*)

CHEREA If you wish to hear my views on the subject, Caius, I'd say, neither coolly nor dispassionately, that it would be a blunder to raise the scale of charges.

CALIGULA Obviously. What's needed is a bigger turnover. I've explained my plan of campaign to Cæsonia, and she will tell you all about it. As for me, I've had too much wine, I'm feeling sleepy.

(*He lies down and closes his eyes*)

CÆSONIA It's very simple. Caligula is creating a new order of merit.

CHEREA Sorry, I don't see the connection.

CÆSONIA No? But there is one. It will be called the Badge of Civic Merit and awarded to those who have patronized Caligula's National Brothel most assiduously.

CHEREA A brilliant idea!

CÆSONIA I agree. Oh, I forgot to mention that the badge will be conferred each month, after checking the admission tickets. Any citizen who has not obtained the badge within twelve months will be exiled, or executed.

CHEREA Why "or executed"?

CÆSONIA Because Caligula says it doesn't matter which —but it's important he should have the right of choosing.

CHEREA Bravo! The Public Treasury will wipe out its deficit in no time.

(CALIGULA *has half opened his eyes and is watching old* MEREIA *who, standing in a corner, has produced a small flask and is sipping its contents*)

CALIGULA (*Still lying on the couch*) What's that you're drinking, Mereia?

MEREIA It's for my asthma, Caius.

CALIGULA (*Rises, and thrusting the others aside, goes up to* MEREIA *and sniffs his mouth*) No, it's an antidote.

MEREIA What an idea, Caius! You must be joking. I have choking fits at night and I've been in the doctor's hands for months.

CALIGULA So you're afraid of being poisoned?

MEREIA My asthma . . .

CALIGULA No. Why beat about the bush? You're afraid I'll poison you. You suspect me. You're keeping an eye on me.

MEREIA Good heavens, no!

CALIGULA You suspect me. I'm not to be trusted, eh?

MEREIA Caius!

CALIGULA (*Roughly*) Answer! (*In a cool, judicial tone*) If you take an antidote, it follows that you credit me with the intention of poisoning you. Q.E.D.

MEREIA Yes . . . I mean . . . no!

CALIGULA And thinking I intend to poison you, you take steps to frustrate my plan. (*He falls silent. Meanwhile* CÆSONIA *and* CHEREA *have moved away, backstage.* LEPIDUS *is watching the speakers with an air of consternation*) That makes two crimes, Mereia, and a dilemma from which you can't escape. *Either* I have no wish to cause your death; in which case you are unjustly suspecting me, your emperor. *Or else* I desire your death; in which case, vermin that you are, you're trying to thwart my will. (*Another silence.* CALIGULA *contemplates the old man gloatingly*) Well, Mereia, what have you to say to my logic?

MEREIA It . . . it's sound enough, Caius. Only it doesn't apply to the case.

CALIGULA A third crime. You take me for a fool. Now sit down and listen carefully. (*To* LEPIDUS) Let everyone sit down. (*To* MEREIA) Of these three crimes only one does you honor; the second one—because by crediting me with a certain wish and presuming to oppose it you are deliberately defying me. You are a rebel, a leader of revolt. And that needs courage. (*Sadly*) I've a great liking for you, Mereia. And that is why you'll be condemned for crime number two, and not for either of the others. You shall die nobly, a rebel's death. (*While he talks* MEREIA *is shrinking together on his chair*) Don't thank me. It's quite natural. Here. (*Holds out a phial. His tone is amiable*) Drink this poison. (MEREIA *shakes his head. He is sobbing violently.* CALIGULA *shows signs of impatience*) Don't waste time. Take it. (MEREIA *makes a feeble attempt to escape. But* CALIGULA *with a wild leap is on him, catches him in the center of the stage and after a brief struggle pins him down on a low couch. He forces the phial between his lips and smashes it with a blow of his fist. After some convulsive movements* MEREIA *dies. His face is streaming with blood and tears.* CALIGULA *rises, wipes his hands absent-mindedly, then hands* MEREIA'S *flask to* CÆSONIA) What was it? An antidote?

CÆSONIA (*Calmly*) No, Caligula. A remedy for asthma.

(*A short silence*)

CALIGULA (*Gazing down at* MEREIA) No matter. It all comes to the same thing in the end. A little sooner, a little later. . . .

(*He goes out hurriedly, still wiping his hands*)

LEPIDUS (*In a horrified tone*) What . . . what shall we do?

CÆSONIA (*Coolly*) Remove that body to begin with, I should say. It's rather a beastly sight.

(CHEREA *and* LEPIDUS *drag the body into the wings*)

LEPIDUS (*To* CHEREA) We must act quickly.

CHEREA We'll need to be two hundred.

(*Young* SCIPIO *enters. Seeing* CÆSONIA, *he makes as if to leave*)

CÆSONIA Come.

SCIPIO What do you want?

CÆSONIA Come nearer. (*She pushes up his chin and looks him in the eyes. A short silence. Then, in a calm, unemotional voice*) He killed your father, didn't he?

SCIPIO Yes.

CÆSONIA Do you hate him?

SCIPIO Yes.

CÆSONIA And you'd like to kill him?

SCIPIO Yes.

CÆSONIA (*Withdrawing her hand*) But—why tell me this?

SCIPIO Because I fear nobody. Killing him or being killed—either way out will do. And anyhow you won't betray me.

CÆSONIA That's so. I won't betray you. But I want to tell you something—or, rather, I'd like to speak to what is best in you.

SCIPIO What's best in me is—my hatred.

CÆSONIA Please listen carefully to what I'm going to say. It may sound hard to grasp, but it's as clear as daylight, really. And it's something that would bring about the one real revolution in this world of ours, if people would only take it in.

SCIPIO Yes? What is it?

CÆSONIA Wait! Try to call up a picture of your father's death, of the agony on his face as they were tearing out his tongue. Think of the blood streaming from his mouth, and recall his screams, like a tortured animal's.

SCIPIO Yes.

CÆSONIA And now think of Caligula.

SCIPIO (*His voice rough with hatred*) Yes.

CÆSONIA Now listen. *Try to understand him.*

(*She goes out, leaving* SCIPIO *gaping after her in bewilderment.* HELICON *enters*)

HELICON Caligula will be here in a moment. Suppose you go for your meal, young poet?

SCIPIO Helicon, help me.

HELICON Too dangerous, my lamb. And poetry means nothing to me.

SCIPIO You can help me. You know . . . so many things.

HELICON I know that the days go by—and growing boys should have their meals on time . . . I know, too, that you could kill Caligula . . . and he wouldn't greatly mind it.

(HELICON *goes out.* CALIGULA *enters*)

CALIGULA Ah, it's you, Scipio. (*He pauses. One has the impression that he is somewhat embarrassed*) It's quite a long time since I saw you last. (*Slowly approaches* SCIPIO) What have you been up to? Writing more poems, I suppose. Might I see your latest composition?

SCIPIO (*Likewise ill at ease, torn between hatred and some less defined emotion*) Yes, Cæsar, I've written some more poems.

CALIGULA On what subject?

SCIPIO Oh, on nothing in particular. Well, on Nature in a way.

CALIGULA A fine theme. And a vast one. And what has Nature done for you?

SCIPIO (*Pulling himself together, in a somewhat truculent tone*) It consoles me for not being Cæsar.

CALIGULA Really? And do you think Nature could console me for being Cæsar?

SCIPIO (*In the same tone*) Why not? Nature has healed worse wounds than that.

CALIGULA (*In a curiously young, unaffected voice*) Wounds, you said? There was anger in your voice.

Because I put your father to death? . . . That word you used—if you only knew how apt it is! My wounds! (*In a different tone*) Well, well, there's nothing like hatred for developing the intelligence.

SCIPIO (*Stiffly*) I answered your question about Nature.

(CALIGULA *sits down, gazes at* SCIPIO, *then brusquely grips his wrists and forces him to stand up. He takes the young man's face between his hands*)

CALIGULA Recite your poem to me, please.

SCIPIO No, please, don't ask me that.

CALIGULA Why not?

SCIPIO I haven't got it on me.

CALIGULA Can't you remember it?

SCIPIO No.

CALIGULA Anyhow you can tell me what it's about.

SCIPIO (*Still hostile; reluctantly*) I spoke of a . . . a certain harmony . . .

CALIGULA (*Breaking in; in a pensive voice*) . . . between one's feet and the earth.

SCIPIO (*Looking surprised*) Yes, it's almost that . . . and it tells of the wavy outline of the Roman hills and the sudden thrill of peace that twilight brings to them . . .

CALIGULA And the cries of swifts winding through the green dusk.

SCIPIO (*Yielding more and more to his emotion*) Yes, yes! And that fantastic moment when the sky all flushed with red and gold swings round and shows its other side, spangled with stars.

CALIGULA And the faint smell of smoke and trees and streams that mingles with the rising mist.

SCIPIO (*In a sort of ecstasy*) Yes, and the chirr of crickets, the coolness veining the warm air, the rumble of carts and the farmers' shouts, dogs barking . . .

CALIGULA And the roads drowned in shadow winding through the olive groves . . .

SCIPIO Yes, yes. That's it, exactly. . . . But how did you know?

CALIGULA (*Drawing* SCIPIO *to his breast*) I wonder! Perhaps because the same eternal truths appeal to us both.

SCIPIO (*Quivering with excitement, burying his head on* CALIGULA'S *breast*) Anyhow, what does it matter! All I know is that everything I feel or think of turns to love.

CALIGULA (*Stroking his hair*) That, Scipio, is a privilege of noble hearts—and how I wish I could share your . . . your limpidity! But my appetite for life's too keen; Nature can never sate it. You belong to quite another world, and you can't understand. You are single-minded for good; and I am single-minded —for evil.

SCIPIO I *do* understand.

CALIGULA No. There's something deep down in me—an abyss of silence, a pool of stagnant water, rotting weeds. (*With an abrupt change of manner*) Your poem sounds very good indeed, but, if you really want my opinion. . . .

SCIPIO (*His head on* CALIGULA'S *breast, murmurs*) Yes?

CALIGULA All that's a bit . . . anemic.

SCIPIO (*Recoiling abruptly, as if stung by a serpent, and gazing, horrified, at* CALIGULA, *he cries hoarsely*) Oh, you brute! You loathsome brute! You've fooled me again. I know! You were playing a trick on me, weren't you? And now you're gloating over your success.

CALGULA (*With a hint of sadness*) There's truth in what you say. I *was* playing a part.

SCIPIO (*In the same indignant tone*) What a foul, black heart you have! And how all that wickedness and hatred must make you suffer!

CALIGULA (*Gently*) That's enough.

SCIPIO How I loathe you! And how I pity you!

CALIGULA (*Angrily*) Enough, I tell you.

SCIPIO And how horrible a loneliness like yours must be!

CALIGULA (*In a rush of anger, gripping the boy by the collar, and shaking him*) Loneliness! What do *you* know of it? Only the loneliness of poets and weaklings. You prate of loneliness, but you don't realize that one is *never* alone. Always we are attended by the same load of the future and the past. Those we have killed are always with us. But *they* are no great trouble. It's those we have loved, those who loved us and whom we did not love; regrets, desires, bitterness and sweetness, whores and gods, the celestial gang! Always, always with us! (*He releases* SCIPIO *and moves back to his former place*) Alone! Ah, if only in this loneliness, this ghoul-haunted wilderness of mine, I could know, but for a moment, real solitude, real silence, the throbbing stillness of a tree! (*Sitting down, in an access of fatigue*) Solitude? No, Scipio, mine is full of gnashings of teeth, hideous with jarring sounds and voices. And when I am with the women I make mine and darkness falls on us and I think, now my body's had its fill, that I can feel myself my own at last, poised between death and life—ah, then my solitude is fouled by the stale smell of pleasure from the woman sprawling at my side.

(*A long silence.* CALIGULA *seems weary and despondent.* SCIPIO *moves behind him and approaches hesitantly. He slowly stretches out a hand toward him, from behind, and lays it on his shoulder. Without looking round,* CALIGULA *places his hand on* SCIPIO'S)

SCIPIO All men have a secret solace. It helps them to endure, and they turn to it when life has wearied them beyond enduring.

CALIGULA Yes, Scipio.

SCIPIO Have you nothing of the kind in your life, no refuge, no mood that makes the tears well up, no consolation?

CALIGULA Yes, I have something of the kind.

SCIPIO What is it?

CALIGULA (*Very quietly*) Scorn.

*Curtain*

# Act Three

*A room in the imperial palace.*

*Before the curtain rises a rhythmic clash of cymbals and the thudding of a drum have been coming from the stage, and when it goes up we see a curtained-off booth, with a small proscenium in front, such as strolling players use at country fairs. On the little stage are* CÆSONIA *and* HELICON, *flanked by cymbal players. Seated on benches, with their backs to the audience, are some patricians and young* SCIPIO.

HELICON (*In the tone of a showman at a fair*) Walk up! Walk up! (*A clash of cymbals*) Once more the gods have come to earth. They have assumed the human form of our heaven-born emperor, known to men as Caligula. Draw near, mortals of common clay; a holy miracle is taking place before your eyes. By a divine dispensation peculiar to Caligula's hallowed reign, the secrets of the gods will be revealed to you. (*Cymbals*)

CÆSONIA Come, gentlemen. Come and adore him—and don't forget to give your alms. Today heaven and its mysteries are on show, at a price to suit every pocket.

HELICON For all to see, the secrets of Olympus, revelations in high places, featuring gods in undress, their little plots and pranks. Step this way! The whole truth about your gods! (*Cymbals*)

CÆSONIA Adore him, and give your alms. Come near, gentlemen. The show's beginning.

(*Cymbals. Slaves are placing various objects on the platform*)

HELICON An epoch-making reproduction of the life celestial, warranted authentic in every detail. For the first time the pomp and splendor of the gods are presented to the Roman public. You will relish our novel, breathtaking effects: flashes of lightning (*Slaves light Greek fires*), peals of thunder (*They roll a barrel filled with stones*), the divine event on its triumphal way. Now watch with all your eyes.

(*He draws aside the curtain. Grotesquely attired as Venus,* CALIGULA *beams down on them from a pedestal*)

CALIGULA (*Amiably*) I'm Venus today.

CÆSONIA Now for the adoration. Bow down. (*All but* SCIPIO *bend their heads*) And repeat after me the litany of Venus called Caligula.

"Our Lady of pangs and pleasures . . ."

THE PATRICIANS "Our Lady of pangs and pleasures . . ."

CÆSONIA "Born of the waves, bitter and bright with seafoam . . ."

THE PATRICIANS "Born of the waves, bitter and bright with seafoam . . ."

CÆSONIA "O Queen whose gifts are laughter and regrets . . ."

THE PATRICIANS "O Queen whose gifts are laughter and regrets . . ."

CÆSONIA "Rancors and raptures . . ."

THE PATRICIANS "Rancors and raptures . . ."

CÆSONIA "Teach us the indifference that kindles love anew . . ."

THE PATRICIANS "Teach us the indifference that kindles love anew . . ."

CÆSONIA "Make known to us the truth about this world—which is that it has none . . ."

THE PATRICIANS "Make known to us the truth about this world—which is that it has none . . ."

CÆSONIA "And grant us strength to live up to this verity of verities."

THE PATRICIANS "And grant us strength to live up to this verity of verities."

CÆSONIA Now, pause.

THE PATRICIANS Now, pause.

CÆSONIA (*After a short silence*) "Bestow your gifts on us, and shed on our faces the light of your impartial cruelty, your wanton hatred; unfold above our eyes your arms laden with flowers and murders . . ."

THE PATRICIANS ". . . your arms laden with flowers and murders."

CÆSONIA "Welcome your wandering children home, to the bleak sanctuary of your heartless, thankless love. Give us your passions without object, your griefs devoid of reason, your raptures that lead nowhere . . ."

THE PATRICIANS ". . . your raptures that lead nowhere . . ."

CÆSONIA (*Raising her voice*) "O Queen, so empty yet so ardent, inhuman yet so earthly, make us drunk with the wine of your equivalence, and surfeit us forever in the brackish darkness of your heart."

THE PATRICIANS "Make us drunk with the wine of your equivalence, and surfeit us forever in the brackish darkness of your heart." (*When the patricians have said the last response,* CALIGULA, *who until now has been quite motionless, snorts and rises*)

CALIGULA (*In a stentorian voice*) Granted, my children. Your prayer is heard. (*He squats cross-legged on the pedestal. One by one the patricians make obeisance, deposit their alms, and line up on the right. The last, in his flurry, forgets to make an offering.* CALIGULA *bounds to his feet*) Steady! Steady on! Come here, my lad. Worship's very well, but almsgiving is better. Thank you. We are appeased. Ah, if the gods had no wealth other than the love you mortals give them, they'd be as poor as poor Caligula. Now, gentlemen, you may go, and spread abroad the glad tidings of the miracle you've been allowed to witness. You have seen Venus, seen her godhead with your fleshly eyes, and Venus herself has spoken to you. Go, most favored gentlemen. (*The patricians begin to move away*) Just a moment. When you leave, mind you take the exit on your left. I have posted sentries in the others, with orders to kill you.

(*The patricians file out hastily, in some disorder. The slaves and musicians leave the stage*)

HELICON (*Pointing a threatening finger at* SCIPIO) Naughty boy, you've been playing the anarchist again.

SCIPIO (*To* CALIGULA) You spoke blasphemy, Caius.

CALIGULA Blasphemy? What's that?

SCIPIO You're befouling heaven, after bloodying the earth.

HELICON How this youngster loves big words! (*He stretches himself on a couch*)

CÆSONIA (*Composedly*) You should watch your tongue, my lad. At this moment men are dying in Rome for saying much less.

SCIPIO Maybe—but I've resolved to tell Caligula the truth.

CÆSONIA Listen to him, Caligula! That was the one thing missing in your Empire—a bold young moralist.

CALIGULA (*Giving* SCIPIO *a curious glance*) Do you really believe in the gods, Scipio?

SCIPIO No.

CALIGULA Then I fail to follow. If you don't believe, why be so keen to scent out blasphemy?

SCIPIO One may deny something without feeling called on to besmirch it, or deprive others of the right of believing in it.

CALIGULA But that's humility, the real thing, unless I'm much mistaken. Ah, my dear Scipio, how glad I am on your behalf—and a trifle envious, too. Humility's the one emotion I may never feel.

SCIPIO It's not I you're envious of; it's the gods.

CALIGULA If you don't mind, that will remain our secret—the great enigma of our reign. Really, you know, there's only one thing for which I might be blamed today—and that's this small advance I've made upon the path of freedom. For someone who loves power the rivalry of the gods is rather irksome. Well, I've proved to these imaginary gods that any man, without previous training, if he applies his mind to it, can play their absurd parts to perfection.

SCIPIO That, Caius, is what I meant by blasphemy.

CALIGULA No, Scipio, it's clear-sightedness. I've merely realized that there's only one way of getting even with the gods. All that's needed is to be as cruel as they.

SCIPIO All that's needed is to play the tyrant.

CALIGULA Tell me, my young friend. What exactly *is* a tyrant?

SCIPIO A blind soul.

CALIGULA That's a moot point. I should say the real tyrant is a man who sacrifices a whole nation to his ideal or his ambition. But I have no ideal, and there's nothing left for me to covet by way of power or glory. If I use this power of mine, it's to compensate.

SCIPIO For what?

CALIGULA For the hatred and stupidity of the gods.

SCIPIO Hatred does not compensate for hatred. Power is no solution. Personally I know only one way of countering the hostility of the world we live in.

CALIGULA Yes? And what is it?

SCIPIO Poverty.

CALIGULA (*Bending over his feet and scrutinizing his toes*) I must try that, too.

SCIPIO Meanwhile many men round you are dying.

CALIGULA Oh, come! Not so many as all that. Do you know how many wars I've refused to embark on?

SCIPIO No.

CALIGULA Three. And do you know why I refused?

SCIPIO Because the grandeur of Rome means nothing to you.

CALIGULA No. Because I respect human life.

SCIPIO You're joking, Caius.

CALIGULA Or, anyhow, I respect it more than I respect military triumphs. But it's a fact that I don't respect it more than I respect my own life. And if I find killing easy, it's because dying isn't hard for me. No, the more I think about it, the surer I feel that I'm no tyrant.

SCIPIO What does it matter, if it costs us quite as dear as if you were one?

CALIGULA (*With a hint of petulance*) If you had the least head for figures you'd know that the smallest war a tyrant—however levelheaded he might be—indulged in would cost you a thousand times more than all my vagaries (shall we call them?) put together.

SCIPIO Possibly. But at least there'd be *some* sense behind a war; it would be understandable—and to understand makes up for much.

CALIGULA There's no understanding fate; therefore I choose to play the part of fate. I wear the foolish, unintelligible face of a professional god. And that is what the men who were here with you have learned to adore.

SCIPIO That, too, Caius, is blasphemy.

CALIGULA No, Scipio, it's dramatic art. The great mistake you people make is not to take the drama seriously enough. If you did, you'd know that any man can play lead in the divine comedy and become a god. All he needs do is to harden his heart.

SCIPIO You may be right, Caius. But I rather think you've done everything that was needed to rouse up against you a legion of human gods, ruthless as yourself, who will drown in blood your godhead of a day.

CÆSONIA Really, Scipio!

CALIGULA (*Peremptorily*) No, don't stop him, Cæsonia. Yes, Scipio, you spoke truer than you knew; I've done everything needed to that end. I find it hard to picture the event you speak of—but I sometimes dream it. And in all those faces surging up out of the angry darkness, convulsed with fear and hatred, I see, and I rejoice to see, the only god I've worshipped on this earth; foul and craven as the human heart. (*Irritably*) Now go. I've had enough of you, more than enough. (*In a different tone*) I really must attend to my toenails; they're not nearly red enough, and I've no time to waste. (*All go, with the exception of* HELICON. *He hovers round* CALIGULA, *who is busy examining his toes*) Helicon!

HELICON Yes?

CALIGULA Getting on with your task?

HELICON What task?

CALIGULA You know . . . the moon.

HELICON Ah yes, the moon. . . . It's a matter of time and patience. But I'd like to have a word with you.

CALIGULA I might have patience; only I have not much time. So you must make haste.

HELICON I said I'd do my utmost. But, first, I have something to tell you. Very serious news.

CALIGULA (*As if he has not heard*) Mind you, I've had her already.

HELICON Whom?

CALIGULA The moon.

HELICON Yes, yes. . . . Now listen, please. Do you know there's a plot being hatched against your life?

CALIGULA What's more, I had her thoroughly. Only two or three times, to be sure. Still, I had her all right.

HELICON For the last hour I've been trying to tell you about it, only—

CALIGULA It was last summer. I'd been gazing at her so long, and stroking her so often on the marble pillars in the gardens that evidently she'd come to understand.

HELICON Please stop trifling, Caius. Even if you refuse to listen, it's my duty to tell you this. And if you shut your ears, it can't be helped.

CALIGULA (*Applying red polish to his toenails*) This varnish is no good at all. But, to come back to the moon—it was a cloudless August night. (HELICON *looks sulkily away, and keeps silence*) She was coy, to begin with. I'd gone to bed. First she was blood-red, low on the horizon. Then she began rising, quicker and quicker, growing brighter and brighter all the while. And the higher she climbed, the paler she grew, till she was like a milky pool in a dark wood rustling with stars. Slowly, shyly she approached, through the warm night air, soft, light as gossamer, naked in beauty. She crossed the threshold of my room, glided to my bed, poured herself into it, and flooded me with her smiles and sheen. . . . No, really this new varnish is a failure. . . . So you see, Helicon, I can say, without boasting, that I've had her.

HELICON Now will you listen, and learn the danger that's threatening you?

CALIGULA (*Ceasing to fiddle with his toes, and gazing at him fixedly*) All I want, Helicon, is—the moon. For the rest, I've always known what will kill me. I haven't yet exhausted all that is to keep me living. That's why I want the moon. And you must not return till you have secured her for me.

HELICON Very well. . . . Now I'll do my duty and tell you what I've learned. There's a plot against you. Cherea is the ringleader. I came across this tablet which tells you all you need to know. See, I put it here.

(*He places the tablet on one of the seats and moves away*)

CALIGULA Where are you off to, Helicon?

HELICON (*From the threshold*) To get the moon for you.

(*There is a mouselike scratching at the opposite door.* CALIGULA *swings round and sees the* OLD PATRICIAN)

THE OLD PATRICIAN (*Timidly*) May I, Caius . . .

CALIGULA (*Impatiently*) Come in! Come in! (*Gazes at him*) So, my pet, you've returned to have another look at Venus.

THE OLD PATRICIAN Well . . . no. It's not quite that. Ssh! Oh, sorry, Caius! I only wanted to say . . . You know I'm very, very devoted to you—and my one desire is to end my days in peace.

CALIGULA Be quick, man. Get it out!

THE OLD PATRICIAN Well, it's . . . it's like this. (*Hurriedly*) It's terribly serious, that's what I meant to say.

CALIGULA No, it isn't serious.

THE OLD PATRICIAN But—I don't follow. *What* isn't serious?

CALIGULA But what are we talking about, my love?

THE OLD PATRICIAN (*Glancing nervously round the room*) I mean to say . . . (*Wriggles, shuffles, then bursts out with it*) There's a plot afoot, against you.

CALIGULA There! You see. Just as I said; it isn't serious.

THE OLD PATRICIAN But, Caius, they mean to kill you.

CALIGULA (*Approaching him and grasping his shoulders*) Do you know why I can't believe you?

THE OLD PATRICIAN (*Raising an arm, as if to take an oath*) The gods bear witness, Caius, that . . .

CALIGULA (*Gently but firmly pressing him back toward the door*) Don't swear. I particularly ask you not to swear. Listen, instead. Suppose it were true, what you are telling me—I'd have to assume you were betraying your friends, isn't that so?

THE OLD PATRICIAN (*Flustered*) Well, Caius, considering the deep affection I have for you . . .

CALIGULA (*In the same tone as before*) And I cannot assume *that*. I've always loathed baseness of that sort so profoundly that I could never restrain myself from having a betrayer put to death. But I know the man you are, my worthy friend. And I'm convinced you neither wish to play the traitor nor to die.

THE OLD PATRICIAN Certainly not, Caius. Most certainly not.

CALIGULA So you see I was right in refusing to believe you. You wouldn't stoop to baseness, would you?

THE OLD PATRICIAN Oh, no, indeed!

CALIGULA Nor betray your friends?

THE OLD PATRICIAN I need hardly tell you that, Caius.

CALIGULA Therefore it follows that there isn't any plot. It was just a joke—between ourselves, rather a silly joke—what you've just been telling me, eh?

THE OLD PATRICIAN (*Feebly*) Yes, yes. A joke, merely a joke.

CALIGULA Good. So now we know where we are. Nobody wants to kill me.

THE OLD PATRICIAN Nobody. That's it. Nobody at all.

CALIGULA (*Drawing a deep breath; in measured tones*) Then—leave me, sweetheart. A man of honor is an animal so rare in the present-day world that I couldn't bear the sight of one too long. I must be left alone to relish this unique experience. (*For some moments he gazes, without moving, at the tablet. He picks it up and reads it. Then, again, draws a deep breath. Then summons a palace guard)*

CALIGULA Bring Cherea to me. (*The man starts to leave*) Wait! (*The man halts*) Treat him politely. (*The man goes out.* CALIGULA *falls to pacing the room. After a while he approaches the mirror*) You decided to be logical, didn't you, poor simpleton? Logic for ever! The question now is: Where will that take you? (*Ironically*) Suppose the moon were brought here, everything would be different. That was the idea, wasn't it? Then the impossible would become possible, in a flash the Great Change come, and all things be transfigured. After all, why shouldn't Helicon bring it off? One night, perhaps, he'll catch her sleeping in a lake, and carry her here, trapped in a glistening net, all slimy with weeds and water, like a pale bloated fish drawn from the depths. Why not, Caligula? Why not, indeed? (*He casts a glance round the room*) Fewer and fewer people round me; I wonder why. (*Addressing the mirror, in a muffled voice*) Too many dead, too many dead—that makes an emptiness. . . . No, even if the moon were mine, I could not retrace my way. Even were those dead men thrilling again under the sun's caress, the murders wouldn't go back underground for that. (*Angrily*) Logic, Caligula; follow where logic leads. Power to the uttermost; willfulness without end. Ah, I'm the only man on earth to know the secret—that power can never be complete without a total self-surrender to the dark impulse of one's destiny. No, there's no return. I must go on and on, until the consummation.

(CHEREA *enters.* CALIGULA *is slumped in his chair, the cloak drawn tightly round him*)

CHEREA You sent for me, Caius?

CALIGULA (*Languidly*) Yes, Cherea.

(*A short silence*)

CHEREA Have you anything particular to tell me?

CALIGULA No, Cherea.

(*Another silence*)

CHEREA (*With a hint of petulance*) Are you sure you really need my presence?

CALIGULA Absolutely sure, Cherea. (*Another silence. Then, as if suddenly recollecting himself*) I'm sorry for seeming so inhospitable. I was following up my thoughts, and— Now do sit down, we'll have a friendly little chat. I'm in a mood for some intelligent conversation. (CHEREA *sits down. For the first time since the play began,* CALIGULA *gives the impression of being his natural self*) Do you think, Cherea, that it's possible for two men of much the same temperament and equal pride to talk to each other with complete frankness—if only once in their lives? Can they strip themselves naked, so to speak, and shed their prejudices, their private interests, the lies by which they live?

CHEREA Yes, Caius, I think it possible. But I don't think you'd be capable of it.

CALIGULA You're right. I only wished to know if you agreed with me. So let's wear our masks, and muster up our lies. And we'll talk as fencers fight, padded on all the vital parts. Tell me, Cherea, why don't you like me?

CHEREA Because there's nothing likable about you, Caius. Because such feelings can't be had to order. And because I understand you far too well. One cannot like an aspect of oneself which one always tries to keep concealed.

CALIGULA But why is it you hate me?

CHEREA There, Caius, you're mistaken. I do not hate you. I regard you as noxious and cruel, vain and selfish. But I cannot hate you, because I don't think you are happy. And I cannot scorn you, because I know you are no coward.

CALIGULA Then why wish to kill me?

CHEREA I've told you why; because I regard you as noxious, a constant menace. I like, and need, to feel secure. So do most men. They resent living in a world where the most preposterous fancy may at any moment become a reality, and the absurd transfix their lives, like a dagger in the heart. I feel as they do; I refuse to live in a topsy-turvy world. I want to know where I stand, and to stand secure.

CALIGULA Security and logic don't go together.

CHEREA Quite true. My plan of life may not be logical, but at least it's sound.

CALIGULA Go on.

CHEREA There's no more to say. I'll be no party to your logic. I've a very different notion of my duties as a man. And I know that the majority of your subjects share my view. You outrage their deepest feelings. It's only natural that you should . . . disappear.

CALIGULA I see your point, and it's legitimate enough. For most men, I grant you, it's obvious. But *you*, I should have thought, would have known better. You're an intelligent man, and given intelligence, one has a choice: either to pay its price or to disown it. Why do you shirk the issue and neither disown it nor consent to pay its price?

CHEREA Because what I want is to live, and to be happy. Neither, to my mind, is possible if one pushes the absurd to its logical conclusions. As you see, I'm quite an ordinary sort of man. True, there are moments when, to feel free of them, I desire the death of those I love, or I hanker after women from whom the ties of family or friendship debar me. Were logic everything, I'd kill or fornicate on such occasions. But I consider that these passing fancies have no great importance. If everyone set to gratifying them, the world would be impossible to live in, and happiness, too, would go by the board. And these, I repeat, are the things that count, for me.

CALIGULA So, I take it, you believe in some higher principle?

CHEREA Certainly I believe that some actions are—shall I say?—more praiseworthy than others.

CALIGULA And *I* believe that all are on an equal footing.

CHEREA I know it, Caius, and that's why I don't hate you. I understand, and, to a point, agree with you. But you're pernicious, and you've got to go.

CALIGULA True enough. But why risk your life by telling me this?

CHEREA Because others will take my place, and because I don't like lying.

(*A short silence*)

CALIGULA Cherea!

CHEREA Yes, Caius?

CALIGULA Do you think that two men of similar temperament and equal pride can, if only once in their lives, open their hearts to each other?

CHEREA That, I believe, is what we've just been doing.

CALIGULA Yes, Cherea. But you thought I was incapable of it.

CHEREA I was wrong, Caius. I admit it, and I thank you. Now I await your sentence.

CALIGULA My sentence? Ah, I see. (*Producing the tablet from under his cloak*) You know what this is, Cherea?

CHEREA I knew you had it.

CALIGULA (*Passionately*) You knew I had it! So your frankness was all a piece of play acting. The two friends did *not* open their hearts to each other. Well, well! It's no great matter. Now we can stop playing at sincerity, and resume life on the old footing. But first I'll ask you to make just one more effort; to bear with my caprices and my tactlessness a little longer. Listen well, Cherea. This tablet is the one and only piece of evidence against you.

CHEREA Caius, I'd rather go. I'm sick and tired of all these antics. I know them only too well, and I've had enough. Let me go, please.

CALIGULA (*In the same tense, passionate voice*) No, stay. This tablet is the only evidence. Is that clear?

CHEREA Evidence? I never knew you needed evidence to send a man to his death.

CALIGULA That's true. Still, for once I wish to contradict myself. Nobody can object to that. It's so pleasant to contradict oneself occasionally; so restful. And I need rest, Cherea.

CHEREA I don't follow . . . and, frankly, I've no taste for these subtleties.

CALIGULA I know, Cherea, I know. You're not like me; you're an ordinary man, sound in mind and body. And naturally you've no desire for the extraordinary. (*With a burst of laughter*) You want to live and to be happy. That's all!

CHEREA I think, Caius, we'd better leave it at that. . . . Can I go?

CALIGULA Not yet. A little patience, if you don't mind —I shall not keep you long. You see this thing—this piece of evidence? I choose to assume that I can't sentence you to death without it. That's my idea . . . and my repose. Well! See what becomes of evidence in an emperor's hands. (*He holds the tablet to a torch.* CHEREA *approaches. The torch is between them. The tablet begins to melt*) You see, conspirator! The tablet's melting, and as it melts a look of innocence is dawning on your face. What a handsome forehead you have, Cherea! And how rare, how beautiful a sight is an innocent man! Admire my power. Even the gods cannot restore innocence without first punishing the culprit. But your emperor needs only a torch flame to absolve you and give you a new lease of hope. So carry on, Cherea; follow out the noble precepts we've been hearing, wherever they may take you. Meanwhile your emperor awaits his repose. It's his way of living and being happy.

(CHEREA *stares, dumfounded, at* CALIGULA. *He makes a vague gesture, seems to understand, opens his mouth to speak—and walks abruptly away. Smiling, holding the tablet to the flame,* CALIGULA *follows the receding figure with his gaze*)

*Curtain*

# Act Four

*A room in the imperial palace.*

*The stage is in semidarkness.* CHEREA *and* SCIPIO *enter.* CHEREA *crosses to the right, then comes back left to* SCIPIO.

SCIPIO (*Sulkily*) What do you want of me?

CHEREA There's no time to lose. And we must know our minds, we must be resolute.

SCIPIO Who says I'm not resolute?

CHEREA You didn't attend our meeting yesterday.

SCIPIO (*Looking away*) That's so, Cherea.

CHEREA Scipio, I am older than you, and I'm not in the habit of asking others' help. But, I won't deny it, I need you now. This murder needs honorable men to sponsor it. Among all these wounded vanities and sordid fears, our motives only, yours and mine, are disinterested. Of course I know that, if you leave us, we can count on your silence. But that is not the point. What I want is—for you to stay with us.

SCIPIO I understand. But I can't, oh, no, I *cannot* do as you wish.

CHEREA So you are with him?

SCIPIO No. But I cannot be against him. (*Pauses; then in a muffled voice*) Even if I killed him, my heart would still be with him.

CHEREA And yet—he killed your father!

SCIPIO Yes—and that's how it all began. But that, too, is how it ends.

CHEREA He denies what you believe in. He tramples on all that you hold sacred.

SCIPIO I know, Cherea. And yet something inside me is akin to him. The same fire burns in both our hearts.

CHEREA There are times when a man must make his choice. As for me, I have silenced in my heart all that might be akin to him.

SCIPIO But—*I*—I cannot make a choice. I have my

own sorrow, but I suffer with him, too; I share his pain. I understand all—that is my trouble.

CHEREA So that's it. You have chosen to take his side.

SCIPIO (*Passionately*) No, Cherea. I beg you, don't think that. I can never, never again take anybody's side.

CHEREA (*Affectionately; approaching* SCIPIO) Do you know, I hate him even more for having made of you —what he has made.

SCIPIO Yes, he has taught me to expect everything of life.

CHEREA No, he has taught you despair. And to have instilled despair into a young heart is fouler than the foulest of the crimes he has committed up to now. I assure you, *that* alone would justify me in killing him out of hand.

(*He goes toward the door.* HELICON *enters*)

HELICON I've been hunting for you high and low, Cherea. Caligula's giving a little party here, for his personal friends only. Naturally he expects you to attend it. (*To* SCIPIO) You, my boy, aren't wanted. Off you go!

SCIPIO (*Looking back at* CHEREA *as he goes out*) Cherea.

CHEREA (*Gently*) Yes, Scipio?

SCIPIO Try to understand.

CHEREA (*In the same gentle tone*) No, Scipio.

(SCIPIO *and* HELICON *go out. A clash of arms in the wings. Two soldiers enter at right, escorting the* OLD PATRICIAN *and the* FIRST PATRICIAN, *who show signs of alarm*)

FIRST PATRICIAN (*To one of the soldiers, in a tone which he vainly tries to steady*) But . . . but what *can* he want with us at this hour of the night?

SOLDIER Sit there. (*Points to the chairs on the right*)

FIRST PATRICIAN If it's only to have us killed—like so many others—why all these preliminaries?

SOLDIER Sit down, you old mule.

THE OLD PATRICIAN Better do as he says. It's clear he doesn't know anything.

SOLDIER Yes, darling, quite clear. (*Goes out*)

FIRST PATRICIAN We should have acted sooner; I always said so. Now we're in for the torture chamber.

(*The* SOLDIER *comes back with* CHEREA, *then goes out*)

CHEREA (*Seating himself. He shows no sign of apprehension*) Any idea what's happening?

FIRST PATRICIAN AND THE OLD PATRICIAN (*Speaking together*) He's found out about the conspiracy.

CHEREA Yes? And then?

THE OLD PATRICIAN (*Shuddering*) The torture chamber for us all.

CHEREA (*Still unperturbed*) I remember that Caligula once gave eighty-one thousand sesterces to a slave who, though he was tortured nearly to death, wouldn't confess to a theft he had committed.

FIRST PATRICIAN A lot of consolation that is—for us!

CHEREA Anyhow, it shows that he appreciates courage. You ought to keep that in mind. (*To the* OLD PATRICIAN) Would you very much mind not chattering with your teeth? It's a noise I particularly dislike.

THE OLD PATRICIAN I'm sorry, but—

FIRST PATRICIAN Enough trifling! Our lives are at stake.

CHEREA (*Coolly*) Do you know Caligula's favorite remark?

THE OLD PATRICIAN (*On the verge of tears*) Yes. He says to the executioner: "Kill him slowly, so that he feels what dying's like!"

CHEREA No, there's a better one. After an execution he yawns, and says quite seriously: "What I admire most is my imperturbability."

FIRST PATRICIAN Do you hear . . . ?

(*A clanking of weapons is heard off stage*)

CHEREA That remark betrays a weakness in his make-up.

THE OLD PATRICIAN Would you be kind enough to stop philosophizing? It's something I particularly dislike.

(*A slave enters and deposits a sheaf of knives on a seat*)

CHEREA (*Who has not noticed him*) Still, there's no denying it's remarkable, the effect this man has on all with whom he comes in contact. He forces one to think. There's nothing like insecurity for stimulating the brain. That, of course, is why he's so much hated.

THE OLD PATRICIAN (*Pointing a trembling finger*) Look!

CHEREA (*Noticing the knives, in a slightly altered tone*) Perhaps you were right.

FIRST PATRICIAN Yes, waiting was a mistake. We should have acted at once.

CHEREA I agree. Wisdom's come too late.

THE OLD PATRICIAN But it's . . . it's crazy. I don't want to die.

(*He rises and begins to edge away. Two soldiers appear, and, after slapping his face, force him back onto his seat. The* FIRST PATRICIAN *squirms in his chair.* CHEREA *utters some inaudible words. Suddenly a queer music begins behind the curtain at the back of the stage; a thrumming and tinkling of zithers and cymbals. The patricians gaze at each other in silence. Outlined on the illuminated curtain, in shadow play,* CALIGULA *appears, makes some grotesque dance movements, and retreats from view. He is wearing ballet dancer's skirts and his head is garlanded with flowers. A moment later a* SOLDIER *announces gravely:* "Gentlemen, the performance is over." *Meanwhile* CÆSONIA *has entered soundlessly behind the watching patricians. She speaks in an ordinary voice, but none the less they give a start on hearing it.*)

CÆSONIA Caligula has instructed me to tell you that, whereas in the past he always summoned you for affairs of state, today he invited you to share with him an artistic emotion. (*A short pause. Then she continues in the same tone*) He added, I may say, that anyone who has not shared in it will be beheaded. (*They keep silent*) I apologize for insisting, but I must ask you if you found that dance beautiful.

FIRST PATRICIAN (*After a brief hesitation*) Yes, Cæsonia. It was beautiful.

THE OLD PATRICIAN (*Effusively*) Lovely! Lovely!

CÆSONIA And you, Cherea?

CHEREA (*Icily*) It was . . . very high art.

CÆSONIA Good. Now I can describe your artistic emotions to Caligula.

(CÆSONIA *goes out*)

CHEREA And now we must act quickly. You two stay here. Before the night is out there'll be a hundred of us.

(*He goes out*)

THE OLD PATRICIAN No, no. *You* stay. Let me go, instead. (*Sniffs the air*) It smells of death here.

FIRST PATRICIAN And of lies. (*Sadly*) I said that dance was beautiful!

THE OLD PATRICIAN (*Conciliatingly*) And so it was, in a way. Most original.

(*Some patricians and knights enter hurriedly*)

SECOND PATRICIAN What's afoot? Do you know anything? The Emperor's summoned us here.

THE OLD PATRICIAN (*Absent-mindedly*) For the dance, maybe.

SECOND PATRICIAN What dance?

THE OLD PATRICIAN Well, I mean . . . er . . . the artistic emotion.

THIRD PATRICIAN I've been told Caligula's very ill.

FIRST PATRICIAN He's a sick man, yes . . .

THIRD PATRICIAN What's he suffering from? (*In a joyful tone*) By God, is he going to die?

FIRST PATRICIAN I doubt it. His disease is fatal—to others only.

THE OLD PATRICIAN That's one way of putting it.

SECOND PATRICIAN Quite so. But hasn't he some other disease less serious, and more to our advantage?

FIRST PATRICIAN No. That malady of his excludes all others.

(*He goes out.* CÆSONIA *enters. A short silence*)

CÆSONIA (*In a casual tone*) If you want to know, Caligula has stomach trouble. Just now he vomited blood.

(*The patricians crowd round her*)

SECOND PATRICIAN O mighty gods, I vow, if he recovers, to pay the Treasury two hundred thousand sesterces as a token of my joy.

THIRD PATRICIAN (*With exaggerated eagerness*) O Jupiter, take my life in place of his!

(CALIGULA *has entered, and is listening*)

CALIGULA (*Going up to the* SECOND PATRICIAN) I accept your offer, Lucius. And I thank you. My Treasurer will call on you tomorrow. (*Goes to the* THIRD PATRICIAN *and embraces him*) You can't imagine how touched I am. (*A short silence. Then, tenderly*) So you love me, Cassius, as much as that?

THIRD PATRICIAN (*Emotionally*) Oh, Cæsar, there's nothing, nothing I wouldn't sacrifice for your sake.

CALIGULA (*Embracing him again*) Ah, Cassius, this is really too much; I don't deserve all this love. (CASSIUS *makes a protesting gesture*) No, no, really I don't! I'm not worthy of it. (*He beckons to two soldiers*) Take him away. (*Gently, to* CASSIUS) Go, dear friend, and remember that Caligula has lost his heart to you.

THIRD PATRICIAN (*Vaguely uneasy*) But—where are they taking me?

CALIGULA Why, to your death, of course. Your generous offer was accepted, and I feel better already. Even that nasty taste of blood in my mouth has gone. You've cured me, Cassius. It's been miraculous, and how proud you must feel of having worked the miracle by laying your life down for your friend—especially when that friend's none other than Caligula! So now you see me quite myself again, and ready for a festive night.

THIRD PATRICIAN (*Shrieking, as he is dragged away*) No! No! I don't want to die. You can't be serious!

CALIGULA (*In a thoughtful voice, between the shrieks*) Soon the sea roads will be golden with mimosas. The women will wear their lightest dresses. And the sky! Ah, Cassius, what a blaze of clean, swift sunshine! The smiles of life. (CASSIUS *is near the door.* CALIGULA *gives him a gentle push. Suddenly his tone grows serious*) Life, my friend, is something to be cherished. Had you cherished it enough, you wouldn't have gambled it away so rashly. (CASSIUS *is led off.* CALIGULA *returns to the table*) The loser must pay. There's no alternative. (*A short silence*) Come, Cæsonia. (*He turns to the others*) By the way, an idea has just waylaid me, and it's such an apt one that I want to share it with you. Until now my reign has been too happy. There's been no world-wide plague, no religious persecution, not even a rebellion—nothing in fact to make us memorable. And that, I'd have you know, is why I try to remedy the stinginess of fate. I mean—I don't know if you've followed me—that, well (*He gives a little laugh*), it's I who replace the epidemics that we've missed. (*In a different tone*) That's enough. I see Cherea's coming. Your turn, Cæsonia. (CALIGULA *goes out.* CHEREA *and the* FIRST PATRICIAN *enter.* CÆSONIA *hurries toward* CHEREA)

CÆSONIA Caligula is dead.

(*She turns her head, as if to hide her tears; her eyes are fixed on the others, who keep silence. Everyone looks horrified, but for different reasons*)

FIRST PATRICIAN You . . . you're *sure* this dreadful thing has happened? It seems incredible. Only a short while ago he was dancing.

CÆSONIA Quite so—and the effort was too much for him. (CHEREA *moves hastily from one man to the other. No one speaks*) You've nothing to say, Cherea?

CHEREA (*In a low voice*) It's a great misfortune for us all, Cæsonia.

(CALIGULA *bursts in violently and goes up to* CHEREA)

CALIGULA Well played, Cherea. (*He spins round and stares at the others. Petulantly*) Too bad! It didn't come off. (*To* CÆSONIA) Don't forget what I told you.

(CALIGULA *goes out.* CÆSONIA *stares after him without speaking*)

THE OLD PATRICIAN (*Hoping against hope*) Is he ill, Cæsonia?

CÆSONIA (*With a hostile look*) No, my pet. But what

you don't know is that the man never has more than two hours' sleep and spends the best part of the night roaming about the corridors in his palace. Another thing you don't know—and you've never given a thought to—is what may pass in this man's mind in those deadly hours between midnight and sunrise. Is he ill? No, not ill—unless you invent a name and medicine for the black ulcers that fester in his soul.

CHEREA (*Seemingly affected by her words*) You're right, Cæsonia. We all know that Caius . . .

CÆSONIA (*Breaking in emotionally*) Yes, you know it—in your fashion. But, like all those who have none, you can't abide anyone who has too much soul. Healthy people loathe invalids. Happy people hate the sad. Too much soul! That's what bites you, isn't it? You prefer to label it a disease; that way all the dolts are justified and pleased. (*In a changed tone*) Tell me, Cherea. Has love ever meant anything to you?

CHEREA (*Himself again*) I'm afraid we're too old now, Cæsonia, to learn the art of love-making. And anyhow it's highly doubtful if Caligula will give us time to do so.

CÆSONIA (*Who has recovered her composure*) True enough. (*She sits down*) Oh, I was forgetting. . . . Caligula asked me to impart some news to you. You know, perhaps, that it's a red-letter day today, consecrated to art.

THE OLD PATRICIAN According to the calendar?

CÆSONIA No, according to Caligula. He's convoked some poets. He will ask them to improvise a poem on a set theme. And he particularly wants those of you who are poets to take part in the competition. He specially mentioned young Scipio and Metellus.

METELLUS But we're not ready.

CÆSONIA (*In a level tone, as if she has not heard him*) Needless to say there are prizes. There will be penalties, too. (*Looks of consternation*) Between ourselves, the penalties won't be so very terrible.

(CALIGULA *enters, looking gloomier than ever*)

CALIGULA All ready?

CÆSONIA Yes. (*To a soldier*) Bring in the poets.

(*Enter, two by two, a dozen poets, keeping step; they line up on the right of the stage*)

CALIGULA And the others?

CÆSONIA Metellus! Scipio!

(*They cross the stage and take their stand beside the poets.* CALIGULA *seats himself, backstage on the left, with* CÆSONIA *and the patricians. A short silence*)

CALIGULA Subject: death. Time limit: one minute.

(*The poets scribble feverishly on their tablets*)

THE OLD PATRICIAN Who will compose the jury?

CALIGULA I. Isn't that enough?

THE OLD PATRICIAN Oh, yes, indeed. Quite enough.

CHEREA Won't you take part in the competition, Caius?

CALIGULA Unnecessary. I made my poem on that theme long ago.

THE OLD PATRICIAN (*Eagerly*) Where can one get a copy of it?

CALIGULA No need to get a copy. I recite it every day, after my fashion. (CÆSONIA *eyes him nervously.* CALIGULA *rounds on her almost savagely*) Is there anything in my appearance that displeases you?

CÆSONIA (*Gently*) I'm sorry. . . .

CALIGULA No meekness, please. For heaven's sake, no meekness. You're exasperating enough as it is, but if you start being humble . . . (CÆSONIA *slowly moves away.* CALIGULA *turns to* CHEREA) I continue. It's the only poem I have made. And it's proof that I'm the only true artist Rome has known—the only one, believe me—to match his inspiration with his deeds.

CHEREA That's only a matter of having the power.

CALIGULA Quite true. Other artists create to compensate for their lack of power. I don't need to make a work of art; I *live* it. (*Roughly*) Well, poets, are you ready?

METELLUS I think so.

THE OTHERS Yes.

CALIGULA Good. Now listen carefully. You are to fall out of line and come forward one by one. I'll whistle. Number One will start reading his poem. When I whistle, he must stop, and the next begin. And so on. The winner, naturally, will be the one whose poem hasn't been cut short by the whistle. Get ready. (*Turning to* CHEREA, *he whispers*) You see, organization's needed for everything, even for art.

(*Blows his whistle*)

FIRST POET Death, when beyond thy darkling shore . . .

(*A blast of the whistle. The poet steps briskly to the left. The others will follow the same procedure. these movements should be made with mechanical precision*)

SECOND POET In their dim cave, the Fatal Sisters Three . . .

(*Whistle*)

THIRD POET Come to me death, beloved . . .

(*A shrill blast of the whistle. The* FOURTH POET *steps forward and strikes a dramatic posture. The whistle goes before he has opened his mouth*)

FIFTH POET When I was in my happy infancy . . .

CALIGULA (*Yelling*) Stop that! What earthly connection has a blockhead's happy infancy with the theme I set? The connection! Tell me the connection!

FIFTH POET But, Caius, I've only just begun, and . . .

(*Shrill blast*)

SIXTH POET (*In a high-pitched voice*) Ruthless, he goes his hidden ways . . .

(*Whistle*)

SEVENTH POET (*Mysteriously*) Oh, long, abstruse orison . . .

(*Whistle, broken off as* SCIPIO *comes forward without a tablet*)

CALIGULA You haven't a tablet?

SCIPIO I do not need one.

CALIGULA Well, let's hear you. (*He chews at his whistle*)

SCIPIO (*Standing very near* CALIGULA, *he recites listlessly, without looking at him*)

Pursuit of happiness that purifies the heart,
Skies rippling with light,
O wild, sweet, festal joys, frenzy without hope!

CALIGULA (*Gently*) Stop, please. The others needn't compete. (*To* SCIPIO) You're very young to understand so well the lessons we can learn from death.

SCIPIO (*Gazing straight at* CALIGULA) I was very young to lose my father.

CALIGULA (*Turning hastily*) Fall in, the rest of you. No, really a sham poet is too dreadful an infliction. Until now I'd thought of enrolling you as my allies; I sometimes pictured a gallant band of poets defending me in the last ditch. Another illusion gone! I shall have to relegate you to my enemies. So now the poets are against me—and that looks much like the end of all. March out in good order. As you go past you are to lick your tablets so as to efface the atrocities you scrawled on them. Attention! Forward! (*He blows his whistle in short rhythmic jerks. Keeping step, the poets file out by the right, tonguing their immortal tablets.* CALIGULA *adds in a lower tone*) Now leave me, everyone.

(*In the doorway, as they are going out,* CHEREA *touches the* FIRST PATRICIAN'S *shoulder, and speaks in his ear*)

CHEREA Now's our opportunity.

(SCIPIO, *who has overheard, halts on the threshold and walks back to* CALIGULA)

CALIGULA (*Acidly*) Can't you leave me in peace—as your father's doing?

SCIPIO No, Caius, all that serves no purpose now. For now I know, I *know* that you have made your choice.

CALIGULA Won't you leave me in peace!

SCIPIO Yes, you shall have your wish; I am going to leave you, for I think I've come to understand you. There's no way out left to us, neither to you nor to me—who am like you in so many ways. I shall go away, far away, and try to discover the meaning of it all. (*He gazes at* CALIGULA *for some moments. Then, with a rush of emotion*) Good-by, dear Caius. When all is ended, remember that I loved you. (*He goes out.* CALIGULA *makes a vague gesture. Then, almost savagely, he pulls himself together and takes some steps toward* CÆSONIA)

CÆSONIA What did he say?

CALIGULA Nothing you'd understand.

CÆSONIA What are you thinking about?

CALIGULA About him. And about you, too. But it amounts to the same thing.

CÆSONIA What is the matter?

CALIGULA (*Staring at her*) Scipio has gone. I am through with his friendship. But you, I wonder why you are still here. . . .

CÆSONIA Why, because you're fond of me.

CALIGULA No. But I think I'd understand—if I had you killed.

CÆSONIA Yes, that would be a solution. Do so, then. . . . But why, oh, why can't you relax, if only for a moment, and live freely, without constraint?

CALIGULA I have been doing that for several years; in fact I've made a practice of it.

CÆSONIA I don't mean that sort of freedom. I mean —Oh, don't you realize what it can be to live and love quite simply, naturally, in . . . in purity of heart?

CALIGULA This purity of heart you talk of—every man acquires it, in his own way. Mine has been to follow the essential to the end. . . . Still all that needn't prevent me from putting you to death. (*Laughs*) It would round off my career so well, the perfect climax. (*He rises and swings the mirror round toward himself. Then he walks in a circle, letting his arms hang limp, almost without gestures; there is something feral in his gait as he continues speaking*) How strange! When I don't kill, I feel alone. The living don't suffice to people my world and dispel my boredom. I have an impression of an enormous void when you and the others are here, and my eyes see nothing but empty air. No, I'm at ease only in the company of my dead. (*He takes his stand facing the audience, leaning a little forward. He has forgotten* CÆSONIA'S *presence*) Only the dead are real. They are of my kind. I see them waiting for me, straining toward me. And I have long talks with this man or that, who screamed to me for mercy and whose tongue I had cut out.

CÆSONIA Come. Lie down beside me. Put your head on my knees. (CALIGULA *does so*) That's better, isn't it? Now rest. How quiet it is here!

CALIGULA Quiet? You exaggerate, my dear. Listen! (*Distant metallic tinklings, as of swords or armor*) Do you hear those thousands of small sounds all around us, hatred stalking its prey? (*Murmuring voices, footsteps*)

CÆSONIA Nobody would dare. . . .

CALIGULA Yes, stupidity.

CÆSONIA Stupidity doesn't kill. It makes men slow to act.

CALIGULA It can be murderous, Cæsonia. A fool stops at nothing when he thinks his dignity offended. No, it's not the men whose sons or fathers I have killed who'll murder me. *They,* anyhow, have understood. They're with me, they have the same taste in their mouths. But the others—those I made a laughing-stock of—I've no defense against their wounded vanity.

CÆSONIA (*Passionately*) *We* will defend you. There are many of us left who love you.

CALIGULA Fewer every day. It's not surprising. I've done all that was needed to that end. And then— let's be fair—it's not only stupidity that's against me. There's the courage and the simple faith of men who ask to be happy.

CÆSONIA (*In the same tone*) No, *they* will not kill you. Or, if they tried, fire would come down from heaven and blast them, before they laid a hand on you.

CALIGULA From heaven! There is no heaven, my poor dear woman! (*He sits down*) But why this sudden access of devotion? It wasn't provided for in our agreement, if I remember rightly.

CÆSONIA (*Who has risen from the couch and is pacing the room*) Don't you understand? Hasn't it been enough to see you killing others, without my also knowing you'll be killed as well? Isn't it enough to feel you hard and cruel, seething with bitterness, when I hold you in my arms; to breathe a reek of murder when you lie on me? Day after day I see all that's human in you dying out, little by little. (*She turns toward him*) Oh, I know. I know I'm getting old, my beauty's on the wane. But it's you only I'm concerned for now; so much so that I've ceased troubling whether you love me. I only want you to get well, quite well again. You're still a boy, really; you've a whole life ahead of you. And, tell me, what greater thing can you want than a whole life?

CALIGULA (*Rising, looks at her fixedly*) You've been with me a long time now, a very long time.

CÆSONIA Yes. . . . But you'll keep me, won't you?

CALIGULA I don't know. I only know that, if you're with me still, it's because of all those nights we've had together, nights of fierce, joyless pleasure; it's because you alone know me as I am. (*He takes her in his arms, bending her head back a little with his right hand*) I'm twenty-nine. Not a great age really. But today when none the less my life seems so long, so crowded with scraps and shreds of my past selves, so complete in fact, you remain the last witness. And I can't avoid a sort of shameful tenderness for the old woman that you soon will be.

CÆSONIA Tell me that you mean to keep me with you.

CALIGULA I don't know. All I know—and it's the most terrible thing of all—is that this shameful tenderness is the one sincere emotion that my life has given up to now. (CÆSONIA *frees herself from his arms.* CALIGULA *follows her. She presses her back to his chest and he puts his arms round her*) Wouldn't it be better that the last witness should disappear?

CÆSONIA That has no importance. All I know is: I'm happy. What you've just said has made me very happy. But why can't I share my happiness with you?

CALIGULA Who says I'm unhappy?

CÆSONIA Happiness is kind. It doesn't thrive on bloodshed.

CALIGULA Then there must be two kinds of happiness, and I've chosen the murderous kind. For I *am* happy. There was a time when I thought I'd reached the extremity of pain. But, no, one can go farther yet. Beyond the frontier of pain lies a splendid, sterile happiness. Look at me. (*She turns toward him*) It makes me laugh, Cæsonia, when I think how for years and years all Rome carefully avoided uttering Drusilla's name. Well, all Rome was mistaken. Love isn't enough for me; I realized it then. And I realize it again today, when I look at you. To love someone means that one's willing to grow old beside that person. That sort of love is right outside my range. Drusilla old would have been far worse than Drusilla dead. Most people imagine that a man suffers because out of the blue death snatches away the woman he loves. But his real suffering is less futile; it comes from the discovery that grief, too, cannot last. Even grief is vanity.

You see, I had no excuses, not the shadow of a real love, neither bitterness nor profound regret. Nothing to plead in my defense! But today—you see me still freer than I have been for years; freed as I am from memories and illusion. (*He laughs bitterly*) I know now that nothing, *nothing* lasts. Think what that knowledge means! There have been just two or three of us in history who really achieved this freedom, this crazy happiness. Well, Cæsonia, you have seen out a most unusual drama. It's time the curtain fell, for you.

(*He stands behind her again, linking his forearm round* CÆSONIA'S *neck*)

CÆSONIA (*Terrified*) No, it's impossible! How can you call it happiness, this terrifying freedom?

CALIGULA (*Gradually tightening his grip on* CÆSONIA'S *throat*) Happiness it is, Cæsonia; I know what I'm saying. But for this freedom I'd have been a contented man. Thanks to it, I have won the godlike enlightenment of the solitary. (*His exaltation grows as little by little he strangles* CÆSONIA, *who puts up no resistance, but holds her hands half opened, like a suppliant's, before her. Bending his head, he goes on speaking, into her ear*) I live, I kill, I exercise the rapturous power of a destroyer, compared with which the power of a creator is merest child's play. And this, *this* is happiness; this and nothing else—this intolerable release, devastating scorn, blood, hatred all around me; the glorious isolation of a man who all his life long nurses and gloats over the ineffable joy of the unpunished murderer; the ruthless logic that crushes out human lives (*He laughs*), that's crushing yours out, Cæsonia, so as to perfect at last the utter loneliness that is my heart's desire.

CÆSONIA (*Struggling feebly*) Oh, Caius . . .

CALIGULA (*More and more excitedly*) No. No sentiment. I must have done with it, for the time is short. My time is very short, dear Cæsonia. (CÆSONIA *is gasping, dying.* CALIGULA *drags her to the bed and lets her fall on it. He stares wildly at her; his voice grows harsh and grating*) You, too, were guilty. But killing is not the solution. (*He spins round and gazes crazily at the mirror*) Caligula! You, too; you, too, are guilty. Then what of it—a little more, a little less? Yet who can condemn me in this world where there is no judge, where nobody is innocent? (*He brings his eyes close to his reflected face. He sounds genuinely distressed*) You see, my poor friend. Helicon has failed you. I won't have the moon. Never, never, never! But how bitter it is to know all, and to have to go through to the consummation! Listen! That was a sound of weapons. Innocence arming for the fray—and innocence will triumph. Why am I not in their place, among them? And I'm afraid. That's cruelest of all, after despising others, to find oneself as cowardly as they. Still, no matter. Fear, too, has an end. Soon I shall attain that emptiness beyond all understanding, in which the heart has rest. (*He steps back a few paces, then returns to the mirror. He seems calmer. When he speaks again his voice is steadier, less shrill*)

Yet, really, it's quite simple. If I'd had the moon, if love were enough, all might have been different. But where could I quench this thirst? What human heart, what god, would have for me the depth of a great lake? (*Kneeling, weeping*) There's nothing in this world, or in the other, made to my stature. And yet I know, and you, too, know (*Still weeping, he stretches out his arms toward the mirror*) that all I need is for the impossible to be. The impossible! I've searched for it at the confines of the world, in the secret places of my heart. I've stretched out my hands (*His voice rises to a scream*); see, I stretch out my hands, but it's always you I find, you only, confronting me, and I've come to hate you. I have chosen a wrong path, a path that leads to nothing. My freedom isn't the right one. . . . Nothing, nothing yet. Oh, how oppressive is this darkness! Helicon has not come; we shall be forever guilty. The air tonight is heavy as the sum of human sorrows. (*A clash of arms and whisperings are heard in the wings.* CALIGULA *rises, picks up a stool, and returns to the mirror, breathing heavily. He contemplates himself, makes a slight leap forward, and, watching the symmetrical movement of his reflected self, hurls the stool at it, screaming*) To history, Caligula! Go down to history! (*The mirror breaks and at the same moment armed conspirators rush in.* CALIGULA *swings round to face them with a mad laugh.* SCIPIO *and* CHEREA, *who are in front, fling themselves at him and stab his face with their daggers.* CALIGULA'*s laughter turns to gasps. All strike him, hurriedly, confusedly. In a last gasp, laughing and choking,* CALIGULA *shrieks*) I'm still alive!

*Curtain*

# Bertolt Brecht

## (1898-1956)

A REVOLUTIONARY playwright in both theme and technique, Bertolt Brecht was undoubtedly the most gifted writer of thoroughgoing Marxist persuasion in our time. His dedication to communism brought him notoriety and suspicion in the non-communist world, but his plays are the property of all who love the theatre. Brecht believed that his drama could only be rightly appreciated under world communism; yet his work has enjoyed enthusiastic applause in the West while it has been virtually ignored in Eastern Europe except in East Berlin. The posthumous publication of some of Brecht's manuscripts and uncompleted writings makes it plain that he was far more of a deviationist than even his sharpest critics among the orthodox Marxists supposed. Nonconformity, ambivalence, and paradox were as much a part of Brecht's character and personality as they were of his ideology and art.

Brecht was born in the Bavarian city of Augsburg, the son of a rather well-to-do manager of a paper factory. He aimed at a medical career and for a time attended the University of Munich, but his studies were interrupted by his conscription into military service in 1918. He served as a medical orderly in the closing months of the war, and the deep and uncompromising pacifism that runs through all his plays is thus rooted in concrete experience of the mutilation and carnage that war brings. In 1918 he wrote his first play, *Baal,* a turbulent account of the sordid adventures of an amoral and ruthless poet who murders his best friend in a fit of jealousy. Organized in 22 loosely connected scenes, the frenzied and explosive drama shows the playwright's indebtedness to Buechner's *Woyzeck* as well as his similarity to the expressionists. His second play, *Trommeln in der Nacht* (*Drums in the Night*), also dates from 1918. Bitterly nihilistic in implication, it portrays the home-coming of the veteran, Kragler, who learns that his fiancée, Anna, has been seduced by a war profiteer, and that the civilization which he risked his life to defend is not worth fighting for. Kragler turns his back on the Spartacist revolution to marry Anna, recognizing that his choice is further proof of the decay and degradation of the times. Brecht viewed his society in the 1920's with a jaundiced, cynical eye. The nihilism of the young playwright can be seen as essential preparation for the positive revolutionary commitment of the mature writer. Indeed, a demand for violent social change is already implicit in these early plays.

At the beginning of his career, Brecht sustained himself as a cabaret performer, singing witty ribald ballads to his own guitar accompaniment. His early theatrical successes, notably the award of the Kleist Prize in 1922 for *Drums in the Night,* opened other avenues and he served for a time as a play reader, first in Munich and then under Max Reinhardt in Berlin. He continued his theatrical experimentation in *In the Jungle of the Cities,* a study of violent homosexuality in a Chicago underworld setting, and in *A Man's a Man,* set in a make-believe India drawn from Kipling's *Barrack-Room Ballads,* in which brain washing and castration provide a violent counterpart to a comedy of transformation of personal identity.

By far the most successful of all of Brecht's works was the musical, *The Threepenny Opera,* written in 1928 in close collaboration with the composer, Kurt Weill. The popularity of the play is due in large measure to the music, but collaboration for Brecht was always an act of genuine participation in a group effort, and Brecht's own contribution to the music was by no means unimportant. The plot is a modernization of John Gay's hilarious comedy of 1728, *The Beggar's Opera,* with ballads taken from Villon and Kipling. Brecht followed the example of Shakespeare, Molière, and countless others in taking his plots from ready-made sources, but what he called his "basic laxity in matters of literary property" extended to the "borrowing" of sentences and whole passages of writings of others. The ballads of François Villon which he appropriated in this instance are perfectly in keeping with the mood and tone of the play. The robber Macheath heroically triumphs over the intrigues of the beggar-king, Peachum, and the cant hypocrisy of so-called respectable society. Duplicity and betrayal are the only means of self-preservation in a milieu where the sole premises of morality are money and power. Brecht, like Gay, rewards his victim of injustice by saving Macheath at the last moment through a fantastically contrived happy ending, crowned by rollicking merriment. The play is in fact an assault on the social values of the audience, and the commentary of the actors on the characters, along with the ironic or hortatory use of screens and captions, serves to provoke audience interpretation and judgment. *The Threepenny Opera* is a wonderful illustration of Brecht's fusion of instruction and entertainment.

It was in the middle years of the 1920's that Brecht

began the theoretical speculations that led him to the formulation of "epic theatre." Brecht's theory was not nearly as new as he believed nor as complex as some of his theorizing would suggest. For Brecht, epic style was episodic as well as spacious. In sharp contrast to the well-made play, with its tight construction and linear sequential action, he advocated a loose and flexible ordering of scenes, each episode constituting a complete narrative unit. In fact, the element of narrative is far more significant in Brecht's drama than in the older anecdotal plot. The stage itself is the narrator, commenting on the action through such devices as screens, captions, slides, film projections, the chorus, the off-stage narrator, or the actor stepping in and out of his role. The result is an anti-illusionist theatre wherein the onlooker is constantly reminded that he is the spectator of a play. All of these devices are for Brecht ways of preventing simple identification between audience and character. The theatre is a means of scientific and analytical demonstration: "Plays must be convincing like court pleas; the main thing is to teach the spectator to reach a verdict." This rational didacticism necessitates the process Brecht calls distancing or alienation, which is indispensable if the theatrical situation is to be understood and evaluated. The contrast between epic and dramatic theatre is based on the discussion in Aristotle's *Poetics* of the differences between epic and tragedy. Brecht opposed "epic theatre" to what he considered the "Aristotelian theatre." Nevertheless, at its best, "epic theatre" is marked by the same unity of action which is the cornerstone of Aristotelian drama.

Brecht's dramatic theory offers interesting and provocative insights into his conscious aims, but its importance as a description of his practice has undoubtedly been exaggerated. He may have succeeded in reducing the element of emotional involvement, but it is never wholly eliminated, and it is often a prominent and indeed decisive element in the reaction of his audience.

The increasingly Marxist and tendentious character of his plays made Brecht a logical target of the Nazis on their accession to power. He fled Germany in February of 1933, the day after the Reichstag fire. His books were subsequently burned, his plays were banned, and he was deprived of German citizenship. Brecht's exile spans the years from 1933 to 1948; he went first to Denmark, thence to Sweden and Finland, and finally to America via Vladivostok in 1941. During the war he lived in Santa Monica, California, continuing to write and making several unsuccessful efforts to gain professional production of his works in the United States. His theatre seemed strange to an American public fed on social realism; only in college and university circles did his plays gain a measure of acceptance in the United States.

Brecht's most important plays date from the late 1930's during his exile in Scandinavia. The inception and in some cases the completion of such masterpieces as *Mother Courage and Her Children, Galileo, The Good Woman of Setzuan,* and *Herr Puntila and His Servant Matti* belong to this unsettled period. All of these plays had their first performance in Zurich. Brecht's Galileo, who perseveres in his researches but does not publish them from fear of torture by the Inquisition, is at once both a hero and a criminal. A liberator in the quest for enlightenment, he has made himself subservient to ecclesiastical authority and has thereby abandoned his responsibility as a man of science. In an early version of the play, Galileo's capitulation was presented as an act of cunning, to gain time for his secret investigations. However, the final version, portraying Galileo as a social criminal, is undoubtedly in closer accord with orthodox Marxist dogma, even though the audience is likely to see Galileo in a more heroic cast. *Herr Puntila and His Servant Matti* is based in part on Finnish folk tales and is set in Finland. Puntila, a rich farmer, is harsh and selfish when sober, generous and kind when drunk. He insists that his daughter marry Matti, his chauffeur, but Puntila's conduct toward his servant varies so sharply according to his sobriety, that Matti refuses the marriage and leaves. Puntila is a wonderfully comic figure and his alternations of mood and character are far more striking than Brecht's statement of the relationship of capitalists and workers.

*Mother Courage and Her Children* offers yet another instance of the superiority of Brecht's art to his dialectics. The play is founded on a seventeenth-century picaresque novel by Grimmelshausen, but Brecht employed history only as a means of illuminating the present. His object, he explained, was to make the spectator see the blindness and stupidity of Mother Courage's dependence on war. Her life is plainly an open contradiction: no one can gain from a war, and the masses lose most. Once again, Brecht has penned a violent and passionate plea for pacifism. Mother Courage has only a momentary glance of insight into her condition, at the end of Scene Six; then she relapses, and we see her pulling her carriage alone at the end of the play, having learned nothing from experience. Plainly, Brecht did not envisage Mother Courage as a heroic character, yet most spectators are more affected by the mother than by the profiteer. Her plight arouses compassion, despite Brecht's insistence on distancing, and her vitality, wit, and spirited defense of her family arouse admiration. Much must depend on the interpretation provided by the actors. Brecht was a gifted director as well as a great playwright, and the production of *Mother Courage and Her Children* by his East Berlin company, the Berliner Ensemble, with his wife, Helene Weigel, in the leading role, is unquestionably one of the great theatrical events of the mid-century. In revisions made for the Berlin performance, Brecht hardened the character of Mother Courage, but the orthodox Marxists were still not satisfied: they felt she should end as a political activist. Brecht's theatricality moved him to the opposite pole from socialist realism; indeed, his ceaseless experimentation led to angry charges of formalism in Eastern Europe. In *Mother Courage and Her Children* his versatility and brilliance and his genuine compassion for the suffering of little people triumph over the rigidity of dialectics and dogma.

# MOTHER COURAGE AND HER CHILDREN

## *A Chronicle of the Thirty Years' War*

English Version by Eric Bentley[1]

CHARACTERS (*in order of appearance*)

There are 32 roles plus four "voices off" and three supers. But much doubling is possible; in fact, of all the actors, only the seven principals cannot double; these seven are Mother Courage, her three children, Cook, Chaplain, Yvette—even one of the children, Swiss Cheese, *could* double if absolutely necessary.

*Prologue*

MOTHER COURAGE SWISS CHEESE
EILIF CATHERINE

*Scene One*

RECRUITING OFFICER SERGEANT

*Scene Two*

COOK COMMANDER CHAPLAIN

*Scene Three*

ORDNANCE OFFICER SERGEANT
YVETTE POTTIER ONE EYE
SOLDIER COLONEL
(TWO SUPERS)

*Scene Four*

CLERK OLDER SOLDIER YOUNGER SOLDIER

*Scene Five*

FIRST SOLDIER PEASANT
SECOND SOLDIER PEASANT WOMAN

*Scene Six*

SOLDIER (*singing*)

*Scene Seven: no new characters*

*Scene Eight*

OLD WOMAN VOICES (*two*)
YOUNG MAN SOLDIER
(ONE SUPER)

*Scene Nine*

VOICE

*Scene Ten*

VOICE (*girl singing*)

*Scene Eleven*

LIEUTENANT OLD PEASANT
FIRST SOLDIER PEASANT WOMAN
SECOND SOLDIER YOUNG PEASANT

*Scene Twelve: no new characters*

THE TIME 1624-1636
THE PLACE *Sweden, Poland, Germany*

[1] The present text corresponds, in general, to the acting version used at the Munich Kammerspiele in 1950 when Brecht himself was the director and Eric Bentley an assistant. When the translation was produced by Unity Theater in London (1958), a few additional passages were taken over from the full-length German version of the play: these are printed here in English for the first time. In 1959 Eric Bentley revised his lyrics, and a new score was specially composed for them by Darius Milhaud.

## Prologue

*The wagon of a vivandière.* MOTHER COURAGE *sitting on it, singing. Her dumb daughter* CATHERINE *beside her playing the mouth organ. The wagon is drawn by her two sons,* EILIF *and* SWISS CHEESE, *who join in the refrain.*

Here's Mother Courage and her wagon!
  Hey, Captain, let them come and buy!
Beer by the keg! Wine by the flagon!
  Let your men drink before they die!
Sabres and swords are hard to swallow:
  First you must give them beer to drink.

Then they can face what is to follow—
    But let 'em swim before they sink!
        Christians, awake! The winter's gone!
        The snows depart. The dead sleep on.
        And though you may not long survive
        Get out of bed and look alive!

Your men will march till they are dead, sir,
    But cannot fight unless they eat.
The blood they spill for you is red, sir,
    What fires that blood is my red meat.
For meat and soup and jam and jelly
    In this old cart of mine are found:
So fill the hole up in your belly
    Before you fill one underground.
        Christians awake! The winter's gone!
        The snows depart. The dead sleep on.
        And though you may not long survive
        Get out of bed and look alive!

## Scene One

SPRING, 1624. IN DALARNA, SWEDEN, KING GUSTAVUS ADOLPHUS IS RECRUITING FOR THE CAMPAIGN IN POLAND. THE PROVISIONER ANNA FIERLING, KNOWN AS CANTEEN ANNA OR MOTHER COURAGE, LOSES A SON.[1]

*A highway in the neighborhood of a town. A top* SERGEANT *and a* RECRUITING OFFICER *stand shivering.*

OFFICER How the hell can you line up a squadron in *this* place? You know what I keep thinking about, Sergeant? Suicide. I'm supposed to slap four platoons together by the twelfth—four platoons the Chief's asking for! And they're so friendly around here I'm scared to sleep nights. Suppose I do get my hands on some character and squint at him so I don't notice he's chicken breasted and has varicose veins. I get him drunk and relaxed, he signs on the dotted line. I pay for the drinks, he steps outside for a minute. I get a hunch I should follow him to the door, and am I right! Off he's shot like a louse from a scratch. You can't take a man's word any more, Sergeant. There's no loyalty left in the world, no trust, no faith, no sense of honor. I'm losing my confidence in mankind, Sergeant.

SERGEANT What they could use round here is a good war. What else can you expect with peace running wild all over the place? You know what the trouble with peace is? No organization. When do you get organization? In a war. Peace is one big waste of equipment. Anything goes, no one gives a god damn. See the way they eat? Cheese on rye, bacon on the cheese? Disgusting! How many horses they got in this town? How many young men? Nobody knows! They haven't bothered to count 'em!! That's peace for you!!! I been in places where they haven't had a war in seventy years and you know what? The people can't remember their own names! They don't know who they are! It takes a war to fix all that. In a war everyone registers, everybody's name's on a list, their shoes are stacked, their corn's in the bag, you count it all up—cattle, men, et cetera—and take it away! Yeah, that's the story—no organization, no war!

OFFICER It's the God's truth.

SERGEANT Course, a war's like every real good deal, hard to get going. But when it's on the road, it's a pisser—everybody's scared off peace—like a crapshooter that keeps fading to cover his loss. Course, *until* it gets going, they're just as scared off war—afraid to try anything new.

OFFICER Look, a wagon! Two women and a couple of young punks. Stop the old lady, Sergeant. And if there's nothing doing this time, you won't catch *me* freezing my ass in the April wind!

MOTHER COURAGE (*Entering with her three children as in the prologue*) Good day to you, Sergeant!

SERGEANT (*Barring the way*) Good day! Who do you think *you* are?

MOTHER COURAGE Tradespeople!
(*She prepares to go*)

SERGEANT Halt! Where are you riffraff from?

EILIF The Second Protestant Regiment.

SERGEANT Where are your papers?

MOTHER COURAGE Papers?

SWISS CHEESE But this is Mother Courage!

SERGEANT Never heard of her. Where'd she get a name like that?

MOTHER COURAGE They call me Mother Courage because I was afraid I'd be ruined, so I drove through the bombardment of Riga like a madwoman, with fifty loaves of bread in my cart. They were getting moldy, I couldn't please myself.

SERGEANT No funny business! Where are your papers?

MOTHER COURAGE (*Rummaging among a mass of papers in a tin box, and clambering down from her cart*) Here, Sergeant! Here's a whole Bible I got in Altötting to wrap cucumbers in, and a map of Moravia, God knows if I'll ever get there, it's good enough for the cat if I don't. And here's a document to say my horse hasn't got hoof and mouth disease; too bad he died on us, he cost fifteen gilders, thank God I didn't pay it. Is that enough paper?

SERGEANT Are you making a pass at me? Well, you

[1] The scene headings in block capitals are projected on a front curtain. In the scene itself the location is indicated by large black letters hanging from the flies (e.g. SWEDEN in this first scene).

got another guess coming. You got to have a license and you know it.

MOTHER COURAGE Show a little respect for a lady and don't go telling these grown children of mine I'm making a pass at you, it's not proper, what would I want with *you?* My license in the Second Protestant Regiment is an honest face, even if *you* wouldn't know how to read it. I'll have no rubber stamp on it neither.

OFFICER There's insubordination for you, my dear Sergeant! (*To* MOTHER COURAGE) Do you know what we need in the army? (MOTHER COURAGE *starts to reply but he doesn't let her*) Discipline!

MOTHER COURAGE I'd have said frankfurters.

SERGEANT Name?

MOTHER COURAGE Anna Fierling.

SERGEANT So you're all Fierlings?

MOTHER COURAGE What do you mean? I was talking about me.

SERGEANT And I was talking about your children!

MOTHER COURAGE Must they all have the same name!

(*Indicating the elder son*)

This boy, for instance, his name is Eilif Noyocki—for the good reason that his father always said his name was Koyocki or Moyocki. The boy remembers him to this day, only it's another one he remembers to this day, a Frenchman with a pointed beard. Anyhow he certainly has his father's brains—that man would have the pants off a farmer's behind before he knew what had happened. So we all have our own names.

SERGEANT You're all called something different?

MOTHER COURAGE Are you pretending you don't get it?

SERGEANT (*Indicating Swiss Cheese*) He's Chinese, I suppose?

MOTHER COURAGE Wrong again. A Swiss.

SERGEANT After the Frenchman?

MOTHER COURAGE Frenchman? I don't know any Frenchman. Don't confuse the issue or we'll be here all day. He's a Swiss but he happens to be called Feyos, a name that has nothing to do with his father, who was called something else; he was a military engineer, if you please, and a drunkard.

(SWISS CHEESE *nods, beaming, and even* CATHERINE *is amused*)

SERGEANT Then how come his name's Feyos?

MOTHER COURAGE No harm meant, Sergeant, but you have no imagination. Of course he's called Feyos—when he came I was with a Hungarian, he didn't mind a bit, he had a floating kidney, though he never touched a drop, he was a very honest man. The boy takes after him.

SERGEANT But he wasn't his father!

MOTHER COURAGE I said he took after him. I call him Swiss Cheese because he's good at pulling the wagon.

(*Indicating her daughter*)

She's called Catherine Haupt. Half German.

SERGEANT A nice family I must say.

MOTHER COURAGE We've seen the whole world together, my wagon and me.

SERGEANT (*Writing*) We'll need all that in writing. You are from Bamberg in Bavaria. How do you come to be in this place?

MOTHER COURAGE I can't wait till the war decides to come to Bavaria.

OFFICER (*To* EILIF) And you two oxen pull the cart. Jacob Ox and Esau Ox! Do you ever get out of harness?

EILIF Can I smack him in the puss, Mother? I'd like to.

MOTHER COURAGE No, you can't, you stay where you are. And now, gentlemen, what about a fine pair of pistols? Or a belt—yours is practically worn through, Sergeant.

SERGEANT I'm after something else. I see these boys are straight as birch trees, broad in the chest, strong of limb—what are specimens like that doing out of the army I'd like to know?

MOTHER COURAGE (*Rapidly*) It's no use, Sergeant: the soldier's life is not for sons of mine!

OFFICER Why not? It means money. It means fame. Peddling boots is woman's work.

(*To* EILIF)

Just step up here and let me see if that's muscle or chicken fat.

MOTHER COURAGE Chicken fat. Give him a good hard look and he'll fall over.

OFFICER And kill a calf while he's falling if there's one in the way.

(*He tries to hustle* EILIF *off*)

MOTHER COURAGE Will you let him alone? He's not for you!

OFFICER He called my face a puss, that's an insult. The two of us will now go out in the field and settle this affair like men of honor.

EILIF Don't worry, I can handle him, Mother.

MOTHER COURAGE Stay here, you trouble maker! Never happy unless you're in a fight.

(*To the* OFFICER)

He has a knife in his boot and he knows how to use it.

OFFICER I'll draw it out of him like a milk tooth. Come on, young fellow!

MOTHER COURAGE Officer, I'll report you to the colonel, he'll throw you in jail. The lieutenant is courting my daughter!

SERGEANT Take it easy, brother.

(*To* MOTHER COURAGE)

What have you got against the service? Wasn't his father a soldier? Didn't he die a soldier's death? You said so yourself.

MOTHER COURAGE Yes, he's dead, but this one's just a baby, and you'll lead him to the slaughter for me, I know you. You'll get five gilders for him.

OFFICER First thing you know, you'll have a new cap and knee boots, how about it?

EILIF Not from you, thanks.

MOTHER COURAGE "Come on, let's go fishing," said the angler to the worm.

(*To* SWISS CHEESE)

Run and tell everybody they're trying to steal your brother!

(*She draws a knife*)

Now try and steal him! And I'll let you have it, I'll cut you down like dogs! Using *him* in your war! We sell linen, we sell ham, we're peaceful people!

SERGEANT You're peaceful all right, your knife proves it. Why, you should be ashamed of yourself. Give me that knife, you hag! You admit you live off the war, what else *would* you live off? Tell me: how can we have a war without soldiers?

MOTHER COURAGE Do they have to be mine?

SERGEANT So that's it. The war should swallow the pits and spit out the peach, huh? Your brood should get fat off the war, and the poor war shouldn't ask a thing in return; it can look after itself, huh? Call yourself Mother Courage and then get scared of the war—your breadwinner? Your sons aren't scared, I know that much.

EILIF No war can scare me.

SERGEANT Why should it? Look at me: the soldier's life hasn't done me any harm, has it? I enlisted at seventeen.

MOTHER COURAGE You haven't reached seventy.

SERGEANT I will, though.

MOTHER COURAGE Above ground?

SERGEANT Are you trying to rile me, telling me I'll die?

MOTHER COURAGE Suppose it's the truth? Suppose I can see it's your fate? Suppose I know you're just a corpse on furlough?

SWISS CHEESE She has second sight. Everyone says so. She can look into the future.

OFFICER Then go look into the sergeant's future, it might amuse him.

SERGEANT I don't believe in that stuff.

MOTHER COURAGE Your helmet!

(*He gives her his helmet*)

SERGEANT It means about as much as a crap in the grass. But anything for a laugh.

MOTHER COURAGE (*Takes a sheet of parchment and tears it in two pieces*) Eilif, Swiss Cheese, and Catherine, so should we all be torn asunder if we let ourselves be drawn too deep into the war!

(*To the* SERGEANT)

For you, I'll make an exception, and do it free. Death is black. I draw a black cross on this piece of paper

SWISS CHEESE And the other she leaves blank, see?

MOTHER COURAGE Then I fold them, put them in the helmet, and shuffle them up—mixed up like we all are from our mother's womb on. And now you draw and find out the answer.

(*The* SERGEANT *hesitates*)

OFFICER (*To* EILIF) I don't take just anybody, I'm particular, they all say so. And you're full of punch, I like that.

SERGEANT (*Fishing into the helmet*) It's a lot of bunk. Hogwash!

SWISS CHEESE He's drawn the black cross. His number's up!

OFFICER Don't let them frighten you, there aren't enough bullets to go round.

SERGEANT (*Hoarsely*) You swindled me.

MOTHER COURAGE You swindled yourself, the day you enlisted. And now we must drive on, there isn't a war every day in the week, we got to get to work.

SERGEANT Hell and damnation, you're not getting away with this. We're taking that bastard of yours with us, we'll make a soldier of him.

EILIF I'd like that, Mother.

MOTHER COURAGE Shut up, you Finnish devil!

EILIF And Swiss Cheese would like to be a soldier too.

MOTHER COURAGE That's news to me. I see I'll have to draw lots for all three of you.

(*She goes to the back to draw crosses on the slips*)

OFFICER (*To* EILIF) People've been saying the Swedish soldier is religious. That's malicious gossip, I can't tell you how much damage it's done us. We only sing on Sunday. One verse of a hymn. And then only if you have a voice.

MOTHER COURAGE (*Returns with the slips and throws them into the* SERGEANT'*s helmet*) Run away from their mother would they, the devils, and off to war like a cat to cream? Just let me consult these slips and they'll see the world's no promised land with its "Join up, son, you're officer material!"

(*She thrusts the helmet at* EILIF)

There, take yours, Eilif.

(*He does so. As he unfolds the paper she snatches it from him*)

There you are, a cross! If he's a soldier, his number's up, that's for sure.

OFFICER (*Still talking to Eilif*) If you're wetting your pants, I'll try your brother.

MOTHER COURAGE Now take yours, Swiss Cheese. You're a safer bet because you're my *good* boy.

(*He draws his lot*)

Why do you look so strangely at it? It *must* be blank.

(*She takes it from him*)

A cross? Oh, Swiss Cheese, there's no saving you either—unless you're a good boy through and through every minute of every day! Just look, Sergeant, a black cross, isn't it?

SERGEANT Another cross. But I don't see why *I* got one, I always stay well in the rear.

(*To the* OFFICER)

It can't be a trick, it gets her own children.

MOTHER COURAGE (*To* CATHERINE) And now all I have left is you, you're a cross in yourself, but you have a kind heart.

(*She holds the helmet up but takes the paper herself*)

Oh! I could give up in despair! I can't be right, I must have made a mistake. Don't be *too* kind, Catherine, don't be too kind, there's a cross in your path!

(*Breaking the mood*)

So now you all know: always be very careful! And now we'll get in and drive on.

(*She climbs on to the wagon*)

OFFICER (*To* SERGEANT) Do something.

SERGEANT I don't feel so well.

OFFICER Maybe you caught a cold when you took your helmet off. Try doing business with her.

(*Aloud*)

That belt, Sergeant, you could at least take a look at it, after all they live by trade, don't they, these good people? Hey, you! The sergeant will buy the belt!

MOTHER COURAGE Half a gilder. Worth four times the price.

SERGEANT It's not even a new one. But there's too much wind here, I'll go look at it behind your wagon.

MOTHER COURAGE It doesn't seem windy to me.

SERGEANT Hey, maybe it is worth half a gilder at that, there's silver on it.

MOTHER COURAGE (*Following him back of the wagon*) A solid six ounces worth.

OFFICER (*To* EILIF) I can let you have some cash in advance, come on!

(EILIF *is undecided*)

MOTHER COURAGE (*Behind the wagon with the* SERGEANT) Half a gilder then, quick.

SERGEANT I still don't see why I had to draw a cross. I told you I always stay in the rear, it's the only place that's safe. You send the others on ahead to win the laurels of victory or the glory of heroic defeat as the case may be. You've ruined my afternoon.

MOTHER COURAGE You mustn't take on so. Here, have a shot of brandy.

(*She gives him some*)

And go right on staying in the rear. Half a gilder.

OFFICER (*Has taken* EILIF *by the arm and is drawing him upstage*) Ten gilders in advance and you're a soldier of the king, my lad, a stout fellow! The women'll be mad about you. And you can smack me in the puss because I insulted you. (*Both leave*)

(CATHERINE *makes harsh noises*)

MOTHER COURAGE Coming, Catherine, coming! The sergeant's just paying his bill.

(*She bites the half gilder*)

To me, Sergeant, all money is suspect, but your half gilder's okay. Now we'll be off. Where's Eilif?

SWISS CHEESE Gone with the recruiting officer.

MOTHER COURAGE (*Stops in her tracks, a pause, then*) Oh, you simpleton!

(*To* CATHERINE)

And you could do nothing about it, you're dumb.

SERGEANT Take a shot yourself, Mother. That's how it goes. Your son's a soldier, he might do worse.

MOTHER COURAGE (*Motions* CATHERINE *down from the wagon*) You must help your brother now, Catherine.

(*Brother and sister get into harness together and pull the wagon,* MOTHER COURAGE *beside them*)

SERGEANT (*Looking after them*)

If from the war you'd like to borrow
Remember: the debt must be paid tomorrow!

# Scene Two

IN THE YEARS 1625 AND 1626 MOTHER COURAGE JOURNEYS THROUGH POLAND IN THE BAGGAGE TRAIN OF THE SWEDISH ARMY. SHE MEETS HER SON AGAIN BEFORE WALLHOF CASTLE. OF THE SUCCESSFUL SALE OF A CAPON AND GREAT DAYS FOR THE BRAVE SON.

*Tent of the Swedish Commander. Kitchen next to it. Sound of cannon. The* COOK *is quarreling with* MOTHER COURAGE *who is trying to sell him a capon.*

COOK (*Who has a Dutch accent*) Sixty hellers for that paltry poultry?

MOTHER COURAGE Paltry poultry? Why, he's the fattest fowl you ever saw! I see no reason why I shouldn't get sixty hellers for him—this Commander can eat till the cows come home.

COOK They're ten hellers a dozen on every street corner.

MOTHER COURAGE A capon like this on every street corner! With a siege going on and people all skin and bones? Maybe you can get a field rat! I said maybe. Because we're all out of *them* too. Didn't you see the soldiers running five deep after one hungry little field rat? All right then, in a siege, my price for a giant capon is fifty hellers.

COOK But we're not "in a siege," we're doing the besieging, it's the other side that's "in a siege" . . .

MOTHER COURAGE A fat lot of difference that makes, *we* don't have a thing to eat either. They took everything in the town with them before all this started, and now they've nothing to do but eat and drink. It's us I'm worried about. Look at the farmers round here, they haven't a thing.

COOK Sure they have. They hide it.

MOTHER COURAGE They have not! They're ruined. They're so hungry I've seen 'em digging up roots to eat. I could boil your leather belt and make their mouths water with it. That's how things are round here. And I'm supposed to let a capon go for forty hellers!

COOK Thirty. Not forty, I said thirty hellers.

MOTHER COURAGE I say this is no ordinary chicken. It was a talented animal, so I hear. It would only feed when they played it some music. In fact, it had its own way of marching. It was so intelligent it could count. Forty hellers is too much for all this? I know *your* problem: if you don't find something to eat and quick, the Chief will—cut—your—fat—head—off!

COOK All right, just watch.

(*He takes a piece of beef and lays his knife on it.*)

Here's a piece of beef, I'm going to roast it. I give you one more chance.

MOTHER COURAGE Roast it, go ahead, it's only one year old.

COOK One *day* old! Yesterday it was a cow. I saw it running around.

MOTHER COURAGE In that case it must have started stinking before it died.

COOK I don't care if I have to cook it five hours.

(*He cuts into it*)

MOTHER COURAGE Put plenty of pepper in.

(*The* SWEDISH COMMANDER, *a* CHAPLAIN *and* EILIF *enter the tent*)

COMMANDER (*Clapping* EILIF *on the shoulder*) In the Commander's tent with you, Eilif my son! Sit at my right hand, you happy warrior! You've played a hero's part, you've served the Lord in his own Holy War, *that's* the thing! And you'll get a gold bracelet out of it when we take the town if *I* have any say in the matter! We come to save their souls and what do they do, the filthy, irreligious sons of bitches? Drive their cattle away from *us,* while they stuff their priests with beef at both ends! But you showed 'em. So here's a can of red wine for you, we'll drink together!

(*They do so*)

The chaplain gets the dregs, he's religious. Now what would you like for dinner, my hearty?

EILIF How about a slice of meat?

COOK Nothing to eat, so he brings company to eat it!

(MOTHER COURAGE *makes him stop talking, she wants to listen*)

COMMANDER Cook, meat!

EILIF Tires you out, skinning peasants. Gives you an appetite.

MOTHER COURAGE Dear God, it's my Eilif!

COOK Who?

MOTHER COURAGE My eldest. It's two years since I saw him, he was stolen from me right off the street. He must be in high favor if the Commander's invited him to dinner. And what do you have to eat? Nothing. You hear what the Commander's guest wants? Meat! Better take my advice, buy the capon. The price is one gilder.

COMMANDER (*Who has sat down with* EILIF *and the* CHAPLAIN, *roaring*) Cook! Dinner, you pig, or I'll have your head!

COOK This is blackmail. Give me the damn thing!

MOTHER COURAGE Paltry poultry like this?

COOK You were right. Give it here. It's highway robbery, fifty hellers.

MOTHER COURAGE I said one gilder. Nothing's too high for my eldest, the Commander's guest of honor.

COOK Well, you might at least pluck the damn thing till I have a fire going.

MOTHER COURAGE (*Sitting down to pluck the capon*) I can't wait to see his face when he sees me. This is my brave son. I also have a stupid one but he's honest. The daughter is nothing. At least, she doesn't talk; we must be thankful for small mercies.

COMMANDER Have another glass, my son, it's my favorite Falernian. There's only one cask left—two at the most—but it's worth it to meet a soldier that still believes in God! Our chaplain here just looks on, he only preaches, he hasn't a clue how anything gets done. So now, Eilif my son, give us the details: tell us how you fixed the peasants and grabbed the twenty bullocks.

EILIF Well, it was like this. I found out that the peasants had hidden their oxen and—on the sly and chiefly at night—had driven them into a certain wood. The people from the town were to pick them up there. I let them get their oxen in peace—they ought to know better than me where they are, I said to myself. Meanwhile I made my men crazy for meat. Their rations were short and I made sure they got shorter. Their mouths'd water at the sound of any word beginning with M, like mother.

COMMANDER Smart kid.

EILIF Not bad. The rest was a snap. Only the peasants had clubs and outnumbered us three to one and made a murderous attack on us. Four of them drove me into a clump of trees, knocked my good sword from my hand, and yelled, "Surrender!" What now, I said to myself, they'll make mincemeat of me.

COMMANDER What did you do?

EILIF I laughed.

COMMANDER You what?

EILIF I laughed. And so we got to talking. I came right down to business and said: "Twenty gilders an ox is too much, I bid fifteen." Like I wanted to buy. That foxed 'em. So while they were scratching their heads, I reached for my good sword and cut 'em to pieces. Necessity knows no law, huh?

COMMANDER What do *you* say, keeper of souls?

CHAPLAIN Strictly speaking, that saying is not in the Bible. Our Lord made five hundred loaves out of five so that no such necessity would arise. When he told men to love their neighbors, their bellies were full. Nowadays things are different.

COMMANDER (*Laughing*) Quite different. A swallow of wine for those wise words, you pharisee!

(*To* EILIF)

You cut 'em to pieces in a good cause, our fellows were hungry and you gave 'em to eat. Doesn't it say in the Bible "Whatsoever thou doest to the least of these my children, thou doest unto me?" And what *did* you do to 'em? You got 'em the best steak dinner they ever tasted.

EILIF I reached for my good sword and cut 'em to pieces.

COMMANDER You have the makings of a Julius Caesar, why, you should be presented to the King!

EILIF I've seen him—from a distance of course. He seemed to shed a light all around. I must try to be like him!

COMMANDER I think you're succeeding, my boy! Oh, Eilif, you don't know how I value a brave soldier like you!

(*He takes him to the map*)

Take a look at our position, Eilif, it isn't all it might be, is it?

MOTHER COURAGE (*Who has been listening and is now plucking angrily at her capon*) He must be a very bad commander.

COOK Just a greedy one. Why bad?

MOTHER COURAGE Because he needs *brave* soldiers, that's why. If his plan of campaign was any good, why would he need *brave* soldiers, wouldn't plain, ordinary soldiers do? Whenever there are great virtues, it's a sure sign something's wrong.

COOK You mean, it's a sure sign something's right.

MOTHER COURAGE I mean what I say. Listen. When a king is a stupid king and leads his soldiers into a trap, they need this virtue of courage. When he's tight-fisted and hasn't enough soldiers, the few he does have need the heroism of Hercules—another virtue. And if he's a sloven and doesn't give a damn about anything, they have to fend for themselves and be wise as serpents or they're through. Loyalty's another virtue and you need plenty of it if the king's always asking too much of you. But in a good country the virtues wouldn't be necessary. Everybody could be quite ordinary, middling, and, for all of me, cowards.

COMMANDER I bet your father was a soldier.

EILIF I've heard he was a great soldier. My mother warned me. I know a song about that.

COMMANDER Sing it to us.

(*Roaring*)

Bring that meat!

EILIF It's called THE SONG OF THE FISHWIFE AND THE SOLDIER.

(*He sings and at the same time does a war dance with his saber*)

To a soldier lad comes an old fishwife
And this old fishwife, says she:
A gun will shoot, a knife will knife,
You will drown if you fall in the sea.
Keep away from the ice if you want my advice,
Says the old fishwife, says she.
The soldier laughs and loads his gun
Then grabs his knife and starts to run:
It's the life of a hero for me!
From the north to the south I shall march through the land
With a knife at my side and a gun in my hand!
Says the soldier lad, says he.

When the lad defies the fishwife's cries
The old fishwife, says she:
The young are young, the old are wise,
You will drown if you fall in the sea.
Don't ignore what I say or you'll rue it one day!
Says the old fishwife, says she.
But gun in hand and knife at side
The soldier steps into the tide:
It's the life of a hero for me!
When the new moon is shining on shingle roofs white
We are all coming back, go and pray for that night!
Says the soldier lad, says he.

And the fishwife old does what she's told:
Down upon her knees drops she.
When the smoke is gone, the air is cold,
Your heroic deeds won't warm me!
See the smoke, how it goes! May God scatter his foes!
Down upon her knees drops she.
But gun in hand and knife at side
The lad is swept out by the tide:
He floats with the ice to the sea.
And the new moon is shining on shingle roofs white
But the lad and his laughter are lost in the night:
He floats with the ice to the sea.

COMMANDER What a kitchen I've got! There's no end to the liberties they take!

EILIF (*Has entered the kitchen and embraced his mother*) To see you again! Where are the others?

MOTHER COURAGE (*In his arms*) Happy as ducks in a pond. Swiss Cheese is paymaster with the Second Protestant Regiment, so at least he isn't in the fighting, I couldn't keep him out altogether.

EILIF Are your feet holding up?

MOTHER COURAGE I've a bit of trouble getting my shoes on in the morning.

COMMANDER (*Who has come over*) So, you're his mother! I hope you have more sons for me like this fellow.

EILIF If I'm not the lucky one: you sit there in the kitchen and hear your son being feasted!

MOTHER COURAGE Yes. I heard all right.

(*Gives him a box on the ear*)

EILIF Because I took the oxen?

MOTHER COURAGE No. Because you didn't surrender when the four peasants let fly at you and tried to make mincemeat of you! Didn't I teach you to take care of yourself? Finnish devil!

(*The* COMMANDER *and the* CHAPLAIN *stand laughing in the doorway*)

# Scene Three

THREE YEARS PASS AND MOTHER COURAGE, WITH PARTS OF A FINNISH REGIMENT, IS TAKEN PRISONER. HER DAUGHTER IS SAVED, HER WAGON LIKEWISE, BUT HER HONEST SON DIES.

*A camp. The regimental flag is flying from a pole. Afternoon. All sorts of wares hanging on the wagon.* MOTHER COURAGE'S *clothes line is tied to the wagon at one end, to a cannon at the other. She and* CATHERINE *are folding the wash on the cannon. At the same time she is bargaining with an* ORDNANCE OFFICER *over a bag of bullets.* SWISS CHEESE, *in paymaster's uniform now, looks on.* YVETTE POTTIER, *a very good-looking young person, is sewing at a colored hat, a glass of brandy before her. She is in stocking feet. Her red boots are near by.*

OFFICER I'm letting you have the bullets for two gilders. Dirt cheap. 'Cause I need the money. The Colonel's been drinking with the officers for three days and we're out of liquor.

MOTHER COURAGE They're army property. If they find 'em on me, I'll be courtmartialed. You sell your bullets, you bastards, and send your men out to fight with nothing to shoot with.

OFFICER Aw, come on, one good turn deserves another.

MOTHER COURAGE I won't take army stuff. Not at *that* price.

OFFICER You can resell 'em for five gilders, maybe eight, to the Ordnance Officer of the Fourth Regiment. All you have to do is give him a receipt for twelve. He hasn't a bullet left.

MOTHER COURAGE Why don't you do it yourself?

OFFICER I don't trust him. We're friends.

MOTHER COURAGE (*Takes the bag*) Give it here.

(*To* CATHERINE)

Take it round the back and pay him a gilder and a half.

(*As the* OFFICER *protests*)

I said a gilder and a half!

(CATHERINE *drags the bag away. The* OFFICER *follows.* MOTHER COURAGE *speaks to* SWISS CHEESE)

Here's your underwear back, take care of it; it's October now, autumn may come at any time; I purposely don't say it must come, I've learnt from experience there's nothing that must come, not even the seasons. But your books *must* balance now you're the regimental paymaster. *Do* they balance?

SWISS CHEESE Yes, Mother.

MOTHER COURAGE Don't forget they made you paymaster because you're honest and so simple you'd never think of running off with the cash. Don't lose that underwear.

SWISS CHEESE No, Mother. I'll put it under the mattress.

(*He starts to go*)

OFFICER I'll go with you, paymaster.

MOTHER COURAGE Don't teach him how to finagle!

(*Without a good-by the* OFFICER *leaves with* SWISS CHEESE)

YVETTE (*Waving to him*) You might at least say good-by!

MOTHER COURAGE (*To* YVETTE) I don't like that. *He's* no sort of company for my Swiss Cheese. But the war's not making a bad start. Before all the different countries get into it, four of five years'll have gone by like nothing. If I look ahead and make no mistakes, business will be good. Don't you know you shouldn't drink in the morning with your illness?

YVETTE Who says I'm ill? That's libel!

MOTHER COURAGE They all say so.

YVETTE They're all liars. I'm desperate, Mother Courage. They all avoid me like a stinking fish. Because of those lies. So what am I fixing my hat for?

(*She throws it down*)

That's why I drink in the morning; I never used to, it gives you crow's feet, but now it's all one, every man in the regiment knows me. I should have stayed home when my first was unfaithful. But pride isn't for the likes of us, you eat dirt or down you go.

MOTHER COURAGE Now don't you start in again with your friend Peter and how it all happened—in front of my innocent daughter.

YVETTE She's the one that should hear it. So she'll get hardened against love.

MOTHER COURAGE That's something no one ever gets hardened against.

YVETTE He was an army cook, blond, a Dutchman, but thin. Catherine, beware of thin men! I didn't. I didn't even know he'd had another girl before me and she called him Peter Piper because he never took his pipe out of his mouth the whole time, it meant so little to him.

(*She sings* THE CAMP FOLLOWER'S SONG)

Scarce seventeen was I when
The foe came to our land
And laid aside his saber
And took me by the hand.
And we performed by day
The sacred rite of May
And we performed by night
Another sacred rite.
The regiment, well exercised,
Presented arms, then stood at ease,
Then took us off behind the trees
Where we fraternized.

Each of us had her foe and
A cook fell to my lot.
I hated him by daylight
But in the dark did not.
So we perform by day
The sacred rite of May
And we perform by night
That other sacred rite.
The regiment, well exercised,
Presents its arms, then stands at ease,
Then takes us off behind the trees
Where we fraternize.

Ecstasy filled my heart, O
My love seemed heaven-born!
But why were people saying
It was not love but scorn?
The springtime's soft amour
Through summer may endure
But swiftly comes the fall
And winter ends it all.
December came. All of the men
Filed past the trees where once we hid
Then quickly marched away and did
Not come back again.

I made the mistake of running after him, I never found him. It's ten years ago now.

(*With swaying gait she goes behind the wagon*)

MOTHER COURAGE You're leaving your hat.

YVETTE For the birds.

MOTHER COURAGE Let this be a lesson to you, Catherine, never start anything with a soldier. Love *is* like a heavenly dove, so watch out! He tells you he'd like to kiss the ground under your feet—did you wash 'em yesterday, while we're on the subject? And then if you don't look out, your number's up, you're his slave for life. Be glad you're dumb, Catherine: you'll never contradict yourself, you'll never want to bite your tongue off because you spoke out of turn. Dumbness is a gift from God. Here comes the Commander's Cook, what's biting *him?*

(*Enter the* COOK *and the* CHAPLAIN)

CHAPLAIN I bring a message from your son Eilif. The Cook came with me. You've made, ahem, an impression on him.

COOK I thought I'd get a little whiff of the balmy breeze.

MOTHER COURAGE Get it then, and welcome. But what does Eilif want? I've no money to spare.

CHAPLAIN Actually, I have something to tell his brother, the paymaster.

MOTHER COURAGE He isn't here. And he isn't anywhere else either. He's not his brother's paymaster, and I won't have him led into temptation.

(*She takes money from the purse at her belt*)

Give him this. It's a sin. He's speculating in mother love, he ought to be ashamed of himself.

COOK Not for long. He has to go with his regiment now—to his death maybe. Send some more money, or you'll be sorry. You women are hard—and sorry afterward. A glass of brandy wouldn't cost very much, but you don't give it, and six feet under goes your man and you can't dig him up again.

CHAPLAIN All very touching, my dear Cook, but to fall in this war is not a misfortune, it's a blessing. This is a holy war. Not just any old war but a religious one, and therefore pleasing unto God.

COOK Sure. In one sense it's a war because there's fleecing, bribing, plundering, not to mention a little raping, but it's different from all other wars because it's a holy war. That's clear. All the same, it makes you thirsty.

CHAPLAIN (*To* MOTHER COURAGE, *pointing at the* COOK) I tried to hold him off but he said you'd bewitched him. He dreams about you.

COOK (*Lighting a clay pipe*) Brandy from the fair hand of a lady, that's for me. And don't embarrass me any more: the stories the chaplain was telling on the way over still have me blushing.

MOTHER COURAGE A man of his cloth! I must get you both something to drink or you'll be making improper advances out of sheer boredom.

CHAPLAIN That is indeed a temptation, said the Court Chaplain, and gave way to it.

(*Turning toward* CATHERINE *as he strolls around*)

And who is this captivating young person?

MOTHER COURAGE She's not a captivating young person, she's a respectable young person.

(*The* CHAPLAIN *and the* COOK *go with* MOTHER COURAGE *behind the cart*)

MOTHER COURAGE The trouble here in Poland is that the Poles *would* keep meddling. It's true our Swedish King moved in on them with man, beast, and wagon, but instead of maintaining the peace the Poles were always meddling in their own affairs. They attacked the Swedish King when he was in the act of peacefully withdrawing. So they were guilty of a breach of the peace and their blood is on their own heads.

CHAPLAIN Anyway, our Gustavus Adolphus was thinking of nothing but their freedom. The German Kaiser enslaved them all, Poles and Germans alike, so our King *had* to liberate them.

COOK Just what *I* think. Your health! Your brandy is first rate, I'm never mistaken in a face.

(CATHERINE *looks after them, leaves the washing, and goes to the hat, picks it up, sits down, and takes up the red boots*)

And the war is a holy war.

(*Singing while* CATHERINE *puts the boots on*)

"A mighty fortress is our God . . ." (*He sings a verse or so of Luther's hymn*) And talking of King Gustavus, this freedom he tried to bring to Germany cost him a pretty penny. Back in Sweden he had to levy a salt tax, the poorer folks didn't like it a bit. Then, too, he had to lock up the Germans and even cut their heads off, they clung so to slavery and their Kaiser. Of course, if no one had *wanted* to be free, the King wouldn't have had any fun. First it was just Poland he tried to protect from bad men, specially the Kaiser, then his appetite grew with eating, and he ended protecting Germany too.

CHAPLAIN He had one thing in his favor anyway: the Word of God. Or they could have said he did it all for himself and for profits. He has a clear conscience, that man.

COOK (*With heavy irony*) Yes. He always put conscience first.

CHAPLAIN It's plain you're no Swede, or you'd speak differently of the Hero King!

MOTHER COURAGE What's more, you eat his bread.

COOK I don't eat his bread. I bake his bread.

MOTHER COURAGE He can never be conquered, and I'll tell you why: his men believe in him.

(*Earnestly*)

To hear the big fellows talk, they wage the war from fear of God and for all things bright and beautiful, but just look into it, and you'll see they're not so silly: they want a good profit out of it, or else the little fellows like you and me wouldn't back 'em up.

COOK Surely.

CHAPLAIN (*Indicating the Protestant flag*) And as a Dutchman you'd do well to see which flag's flying here before you express an opinion!

MOTHER COURAGE All good Protestants for ever!

COOK A health!

(CATHERINE *has begun to strut around with* YVETTE'*s hat on, copying* YVETTE'*s sexy walk.*

*Suddenly cannon and shots. Drums.* MOTHER COURAGE, *the* COOK, *and the* CHAPLAIN *rush round to the front of the cart, the two last with glasses in their hands. The* ORDNANCE OFFICER *and a* SOLDIER *come running to the cannon and try to push it along*)

MOTHER COURAGE What's the matter? Let me get my wash off that gun, you slobs!

(*She tries to do so*)

OFFICER The Catholics! Surprise attack! We don't know if we can get away!

(*To the* SOLDIER)

Get that gun!

(*Runs off*)

COOK For heaven's sake! I must go to the Commander. Mother Courage, I'll be back in a day or two—for a short conversation.

(*Rushes off*)

MOTHER COURAGE Hey, you're leaving your pipe!

COOK (*off*) Keep it for me, I'll need it!

MOTHER COURAGE This *would* happen when we were just making money.

CHAPLAIN Well, I must be going too. Yes, if the enemy's so close, it can be dangerous. "Blessed are the peacemakers," a good slogan in wartime! If only I had a cloak.

MOTHER COURAGE I'm lending no cloaks. Not even to save a life I'm not. I've had experience in that line.

CHAPLAIN But I'm in special danger. Because of my religion!

MOTHER COURAGE (*Brings him a cloak*) It's against my better judgment. Now run!

CHAPLAIN I thank you, you're very generous, but maybe I'd better stay and sit here. If I run, I might attract the enemy's attention. I might arouse suspicion.

MOTHER COURAGE (*To the* SOLDIER) Let it alone, you dope, who's going to pay you for this? It'll cost you your life, let me hold it for you.

SOLDIER (*Running away*) You're my witness: I tried!

MOTHER COURAGE I'll swear to it!

(*Seeing* CATHERINE *with the hat*)

What on earth are you up to—with a whore's hat! Take it off this minute! Are you crazy? With the enemy coming?

(*She tears the hat off her head*)

Do you want them to find you and make a whore of you? And she has the boots on too, straight from Babylon, I'll soon fix that.

(*She tries to get them off*)

Oh God, Chaplain, help me with these boots, I'll be right back!

(*She runs to the wagon*)

YVETTE (*Entering and powdering her face*) What's that you say; the Catholics are coming? Where's my hat? Who's been trampling on it!? I can't run around in that, what will they think of me? And I've no mirror either.

(*To the* CHAPLAIN, *coming very close*)

How do I look—too much powder?

CHAPLAIN Just, er, right.

YVETTE And where are my red boots?

(*She can't find them because* CATHERINE *is hiding her feet under her skirt*)

I left them here! Now I've got to go barefoot to my tent, it's a scandal!

(*Exit*)

(SWISS CHEESE *comes running in carrying a cash box*)

MOTHER COURAGE (*Enters with her hands covered with ashes*)

(*To* CATHERINE) Ashes!

(*To* SWISS CHEESE)

What you got there?

SWISS CHEESE The regimental cash box.

MOTHER COURAGE Throw it away! Your paymastering days are over!

SWISS CHEESE It's a trust!

(*He goes to the back*)

MOTHER COURAGE (*To the* CHAPLAIN) Off with your pastor's coat, Chaplain, or they'll recognize you, cloak or no cloak.

(*She is rubbing ashes into* CATHERINE's *face*)

Keep still. A little dirt, and you're safe. When a soldier sees a clean face, there's one more whore in the world. Specially a Catholic soldier. That should do, it looks like you've been rolling in muck. Don't tremble. Nothing can happen to you now.

(*To* SWISS CHEESE)

Where have you left that cash?

SWISS CHEESE I thought I'd just put it in the wagon.

MOTHER COURAGE (*Horrified*) What!? In my wagon? God punish you for a prize idiot! If I just look away for a moment! They'll hang all three of us!

SWISS CHEESE Then I'll put it somewhere else. Or escape with it.

MOTHER COURAGE You'll stay right here. It's too late.

CHAPLAIN (*Still changing his clothes*) For Heaven's sake: the Protestant flag!

MOTHER COURAGE (*Taking down the flag*) I don't notice it any more, I've had it twenty-five years.

(*The sound of cannon grows*)

(*Three days later. Morning. The cannon is gone.* MOTHER COURAGE, CATHERINE, *the* CHAPLAIN *and* SWISS CHEESE *sit anxiously eating*)

SWISS CHEESE This is the third day I've been sitting here doing nothing, and the Sergeant, who's always been patient with me, may be slowly beginning to ask, "Where on earth is Swiss Cheese with that cash box?"

MOTHER COURAGE Be glad they're not on the scent.

CHAPLAIN What about me? I can't hold service here or I'll be in hot water. It is written, "Out of the abundance of the heart, the tongue speaketh." But woe is me if *my* tongue speaketh!

MOTHER COURAGE That's how it is. Here you sit—one with his religion, the other with his cash box, I don't know which is more dangerous.

CHAPLAIN We're in God's hands now!

MOTHER COURAGE I hope we're not as desperate as *that,* but it *is* hard to sleep at night. 'Course it'd be easier if *you* weren't here, Swiss Cheese, all the same I've not done badly. When they questioned me, I always asked where I could buy holy candles a bit cheaper. I know these things because Swiss Cheese's father was a Catholic and made jokes about it. They didn't quite believe me but they needed a canteen, so they winked an eye. Maybe it's all for the best. We're prisoners. But so are lice in fur.

CHAPLAIN The milk is good. As far as quantity goes, we may have to reduce our Swedish appetites somewhat. We are defeated.

MOTHER COURAGE Who's defeated? The defeats and victories of the fellows at the top aren't always defeats and victories for the fellows at the bottom. Not at all. There've been cases where a defeat is a victory for the fellows at the bottom, it's only their honor that's lost, nothing serious. In Livonia once, our Chief took such a knock from the enemy, in the confusion I got a fine gray mare out of the baggage train, it pulled my wagon seven months—till we won and there was inventory. But in general both defeat and victory are a costly business for us that haven't got much. The best thing is for politics to kind of get stuck in the mud.

(*To* SWISS CHEESE)

Eat!

SWISS CHEESE I don't like it. How will the Sergeant pay his men?

MOTHER COURAGE Soldiers in flight don't get paid.

SWISS CHEESE Well, they could claim to be. No pay, no flight. They can refuse to budge.

MOTHER COURAGE Swiss Cheese, your sense of duty worries me. I've brought you up to be honest because you're not very bright. But don't go too far! And now I'm going with the Chaplain to buy a Catholic flag and some meat. A good thing they let me continue in business. In business you ask what price, not what religion. Protestant pants keep you just as warm.

(*She disappears into the wagon*)

CHAPLAIN She's worried about the cash box. Up to now they've ignored us—as if we were part of the wagon—but can it last?

SWISS CHEESE I can get rid of it.

CHAPLAIN That's almost *more* dangerous. Suppose you're seen. They have spies. Yesterday morning one jumped out of the very hole I was relieving myself in. I was so off guard I almost broke out in prayer—*that* would have given me away all right! I believe their favorite way of finding a Protestant is smelling his, um, excrement. The spy was a little brute with a bandage over one eye.

MOTHER COURAGE (*Clambering out of the wagon with a basket*) I've found you out, you shameless hussy!

(*She holds up* YVETTE'S *red boots in triumph*)

Yvette's red boots! She just snitched them—because you went and told her she was a captivating person.

(*She lays them in the basket*)

Stealing Yvette's boots! But *she* disgraces herself for money, *you* do it for nothing—for pleasure! Save your proud peacock ways for peacetime!

CHAPLAIN I don't find her proud.

MOTHER COURAGE I like her when people say "I never noticed the poor thing." I like her when she's a stone in Dalarna where there's nothing but stones.

(*To* SWISS CHEESE)

Leave the cash box where it is, do you hear? And pay attention to your sister, she needs it. Between the two of you, you'll be the death of me yet; I'd rather take care of a bag of fleas.

(*She leaves with the* CHAPLAIN. CATHERINE *clears the dishes away*)

SWISS CHEESE Not many days more when you can sit in the sun in your shirtsleeves.

(CATHERINE *points to a tree*)

Yes, the leaves are yellow already.

(*With gestures,* CATHERINE *asks if he wants a drink*)

I'm not drinking, I'm thinking.

(*Pause*)

She says she can't sleep. So I *should* take the cash box away. I've found a place for it. I'll keep it in the mole hole by the river till the time comes. I might get it tonight before sunrise and take it to the regiment. How far can they have fled in three days? The Sergeant's eyes'll pop out of his head. "You've disappointed me most pleasantly, Swiss Cheese," he'll say, "*I* trust you with the cash box and *you* bring it back!" Yes, Catherine, I *will* have a glass now!

(*When* CATHERINE *reappears behind the wagon two men confront her. One of them is a sergeant. The other doffs his hat and flourishes it in a showy greeting. He has a bandage over one eye*)

THE MAN WITH THE BANDAGE Good morning, young lady. Have you seen a staff officer from the Second Protestant Regiment?

(*Terrified,* CATHERINE *runs away, spilling her brandy. The two men look at each other and then withdraw after seeing* SWISS CHEESE)

SWISS CHEESE (*Starting up from his reflections*) You're spilling it! What's the matter with you, can't you see where you're going? I don't understand you. Anyway, I must be off, I've decided it's the thing to do.

(*He stands up. She does all she can to make him aware of the danger he is in. He only pushes her away*)

I'd like to know what you mean. I know you mean well, poor thing, you just can't get it out. And don't trouble yourself about the brandy; I'll live to drink so much of it, what's one glass?

(*He takes the cash box out of the wagon and puts it under his coat*)

I'll be right back. But don't hold me up or I'll have to scold you. Yes, I know you mean well. If you only could speak!

(*When she tries to hold him back he kisses her and pulls himself free. Exit. She is desperate and runs up and down, emitting little sounds.* MOTHER COURAGE *and the* CHAPLAIN *return.* CATHERINE *rushes at her mother*)

MOTHER COURAGE What *is* it, what *is* it, Catherine? Control yourself! Has someone done something to you? Where is Swiss Cheese?

(*To the* CHAPLAIN)

Don't stand around, get that Catholic flag up!

(*She takes a Catholic flag out of her basket and the* CHAPLAIN *runs it up the pole*)

CHAPLAIN (*Bitterly*) All good Catholics forever!

MOTHER COURAGE Now, Catherine, calm down and tell all about it, your mother understands. What, that little bastard of mine's taken the cash box away? I'll box his ears for him, the rascal! Now take your time and don't try to talk, use your hands. I don't like it when you howl like a dog, what'll the Chaplain think of you? See how shocked he looks. A man with one eye was here?

CHAPLAIN That fellow with one eye is an informer! Have they caught Swiss Cheese?

(CATHERINE *shakes her head, shrugs her shoulders*)

This is the end.

(*Voices off. The two men bring in* SWISS CHEESE)

SWISS CHEESE Let me go. I've nothing on me. You're breaking my shoulder! I am innocent.

SERGEANT This is where he comes from. These are his friends.

MOTHER COURAGE Us? Since when?

(*Putting things in her basket*)

SWISS CHEESE I don't even know 'em. I was just getting my lunch here. Ten hellers it cost me. Maybe you saw me sitting on that bench. It was too salty.

SERGEANT Who *are* you people, anyway?

MOTHER COURAGE Law abiding citizens! It's true what he says. He bought his lunch here. And it was too salty.

SERGEANT Are you pretending you don't know him?

MOTHER COURAGE I can't know all of them, can I? *I* don't ask, "What's your name and are you a heathen?" If they pay up, they're not heathens to me. Are you a heathen?

SWISS CHEESE Oh, no!

CHAPLAIN He sat there like a law-abiding chap and never once opened his mouth. Except to eat. Which is necessary.

SERGEANT Who do you think *you* are?

MOTHER COURAGE Oh, he's my barman. And you're thirsty, I'll bring you a glass of brandy; you must be footsore and weary!

SERGEANT No brandy on duty.

(*To* SWISS CHEESE)

You were carrying something. You must have hidden it by the river. We saw the bulge in your shirt.

MOTHER COURAGE Sure it was him?

SWISS CHEESE I think you mean another fellow. There *was* a fellow with something under his shirt, I saw him. I'm the wrong man.

MOTHER COURAGE I think so too. It's a misunderstanding. Could happen to anyone. Oh, I know what people are like, I'm Mother Courage, you've heard of me, everyone knows about me, and I can tell you this: he looks honest.

SERGEANT We're after the regimental cash box. And we know what the man looks like who's been keeping it. We've been looking for him two days. It's you.

SWISS CHEESE No, it's not!

SERGEANT And if you don't shell out, you're dead, see? Where is it?

MOTHER COURAGE (*Urgently*) 'Course he'd give it to you to save his life. He'd up and say, I do have it, here it is, you're stronger than me. He's not *that* stupid. Speak, little stupid, the Sergeant's giving you a chance!

SWISS CHEESE What if I don't have it?

SERGEANT Come with us. We'll get it out of you.

(*They take him off*)

MOTHER COURAGE (*Shouting after them*) He'd tell you! He's not *that* stupid! And leave his shoulder alone!!

(*She runs after them*)

(*The same evening. The* CHAPLAIN *and* CATHERINE *are rinsing glasses and polishing knives*)

CHAPLAIN Cases of people getting caught like this are by no means unknown in the history of religion. I am reminded of the Passion of Our Lord and Savior. There's an old song about it. (*He sings* THE SONG OF THE HOURS)

In the first hour of the day
Simple Jesus Christ was
Halèd as a murderer
Before the heathen Pilate.

Pilate found no fault in him
No cause to condemn him
So he sent the Lord away.
Let King Herod see him!

Hour the third: the Son of God
Was with scourges beaten
And they set a crown of thorns
On the head of Jesus.

And they dressed him as a king
Joked and jested at him
And the cross to die upon
He himself must carry.

Six: they stripped Lord Jesus bare.
To the cross they nailed him.
When the blood came gushing, he
Prayed and loud lamented.

From their neighbor crosses, thieves
Mocked him like the others.
And the bright sun crept away
Not to see such doings.

Nine: Lord Jesus cried aloud
That he was forsaken!
In a sponge upon a pole
Vinegar was fed him.

Then the Lord gave up the ghost
And the earth did tremble.
Temple curtain split in twain.
Cliffs fell in the ocean.

Evening: they broke the bones
Of the malefactors.
Then they took a spear and pierced
The side of gentle Jesus.

And the blood and water ran
And they laughed at Jesus.

Of this simple son of man
Such and more they tell us.

MOTHER COURAGE (*Entering, excited*) It's life and death. But the Sergeant will still listen to us. The only thing is, he mustn't know it's our Swiss Cheese, or they'll say we helped him. It's only a matter of money, but where can *we* get money? Wasn't Yvette here? I met her on the way over. She's picked up a Colonel! Maybe he'll buy her a canteen business!

CHAPLAIN You'd sell the wagon, everything?

MOTHER COURAGE Where else would I get the money for the Sergeant?

CHAPLAIN What are you to live off?

MOTHER COURAGE That's just it.

(*Enter* YVETTE POTTIER *with a hoary old* COLONEL)

YVETTE (*Embracing* MOTHER COURAGE) *Dear* Mistress Courage, we meet again!

(*Whispering*)

He didn't say no.

(*Aloud*)

This is my friend, my, um, business adviser. I happened to hear you might like to sell your wagon. Due to special circumstances. I'd like to think about it.

MOTHER COURAGE I want to pawn it, not sell it. And nothing hasty. In war time you don't find another wagon like that so easy.

YVETTE (*Disappointed*) Only pawn it? I thought you wanted to sell, I don't know if I'm interested.

(*To the* COLONEL)

What do *you* think, my dear?

COLONEL I quite agree with you, honey bun.

MOTHER COURAGE It's only for pawn.

YVETTE I thought you *had* to have the money.

MOTHER COURAGE (*Firmly*) I do have to have it. But I'd rather wear my feet off looking for an offer than just sell. We live off the wagon.

COLONEL Take it, take it!

YVETTE My friend thinks I should go ahead, but I'm not sure—if it's only for pawn. You think we should buy it outright, don't you?

COLONEL I do, bunny, I do!

MOTHER COURAGE Then you must find something that's for sale.

YVETTE Yes, we can go around looking for something, I *love* going around looking, I *love* going around with you, Poldy . . .

COLONEL Really? You do?

YVETTE Oh, it's *lovely!* I could take *weeks* of it!

COLONEL Really? You could?

YVETTE If you get the money, when are you thinking of paying it back?

MOTHER COURAGE In two weeks. Maybe in one.

YVETTE I can't make up my mind. Poldy, advise me, *chéri!*

(*She takes the* COLONEL *to one side*)

She'll *have* to sell, don't worry. That lieutenant—the blond one—you know the one I mean—he'll lend me the money. He's *mad* about me, he says I remind him of someone. What do you advise?

COLONEL Oh, I have to warn you against *him.* He's no good. He'll exploit the situation. I told you, bunny, I told you *I'd* buy you something, didn't I tell you that?

YVETTE I simply can't let you!

COLONEL Oh, please, please!

YVETTE Well, if you think the lieutenant might exploit the situation I *will* let you!

COLONEL I do think so.

YVETTE So you advise me to?

COLONEL I do, bunny, I do!

YVETTE (*Returning to* MOTHER COURAGE) My friend says all right. Write me out a receipt saying the wagon's mine when the two weeks are up—with everything in it. I'll just run through it all now, the two hundred gilders can wait.

(*To the* COLONEL)

You go on ahead to the camp, I'll follow, I must go over all this so nothing'll be missing later from *my* wagon!

COLONEL Wait, I'll help you up!

(*He does so*)

Come soon, honey-bunny!

(*Exit*)

MOTHER COURAGE Yvette, Yvette!

YVETTE There aren't many boots left!

MOTHER COURAGE Yvette, this is no time to go through the wagon, yours or not yours. You promised you'd talk to the Sergeant about Swiss Cheese. There isn't a minute to lose. He's up before the court martial one hour from now.

YVETTE I just want to check through these shirts.

MOTHER COURAGE (*Dragging her down the steps by the skirt*) You hyena, Swiss Cheese's life's at stake! And don't say who the money comes from. Pretend he's your sweetheart, for heaven's sake, or we'll all get it for helping him.

YVETTE I've arranged to meet One Eye in the bushes. He must be there by now.

CHAPLAIN And don't hand over all two hundred, a hundred and fifty's sure to be enough.

MOTHER COURAGE I'll thank you to keep your nose out of this, I'm not doing *you* out of your porridge. Now run, and no haggling, remember his life's at stake.

(*She pushes* YVETTE *off*)

CHAPLAIN I didn't want to talk you into anything, but what are we going to live on? You have an unmarriageable daughter round your neck.

MOTHER COURAGE I'm counting on that cash box, smart alec. They'll pay his expenses out of it.

CHAPLAIN You think she can work it?

MOTHER COURAGE It's to her interest: I pay out the two hundred and she gets the wagon. She knows what she's doing, she won't have her colonel on the string forever. Catherine, go and clean the knives, use pumice stone.

(*To the* CHAPLAIN)

And don't *you* stand around like Jesus in Gethsemane. Get a move on, wash those glasses. There'll be over fifty cavalrymen here tonight, can't you just hear them grumbling, "Isn't walking terrible, oh my poor feet!" I think they'll let us have him. Thanks be to

God they're corruptible. They're not wolves, they're human and after money. God is merciful, and men are bribable, that's how His will is done on earth as it is in Heaven. Corruption is our only hope. As long as there's corruption, there'll be merciful judges and even the innocent may get off!

YVETTE (*Comes panting in*) They'll do it for two hundred if you make it snappy, these things change from one minute to the next. I'd better take One Eye to my colonel right now. He confessed he had the cash box, they put the thumb screws on him. But he threw it in the river when he noticed them coming up behind him. So it's gone. Shall I run and get the money from my colonel?

MOTHER COURAGE The cash box gone? How'll I ever get my two hundred back?

YVETTE So you thought you could get it from the cash box? I *would* have been sunk. Not a hope, Mother Courage. If you want your Swiss Cheese, you'll have to pay. Or should I let the whole thing drop, so you can keep your wagon?

MOTHER COURAGE What can I do? I *can't* pay two hundred. You *should* have haggled with them. I must hold on to something, or any passer-by can kick me in the ditch. Go and say I'll pay a hundred and twenty or the deal's off. Even at that I lose the wagon.

YVETTE They won't do it. And anyway, One Eye's in a hurry. He looks over his shoulder the whole time, he's so worked up. Hadn't I better give them the whole two hundred?

MOTHER COURAGE (*Desperate*) I can't pay it! I've been working thirty years. She's twenty-five and still no husband, I have her to think of. So leave me alone, I know what I'm doing. A hundred and twenty or no deal.

YVETTE You know best.

(*Runs off*)

(MOTHER COURAGE *turns away and slowly walks a few paces to the rear. Then she turns round, looks neither at the* CHAPLAIN *nor her daughter, and sits down to help* CATHERINE *polish the knives*)

MOTHER COURAGE You'll have your brother back. I *will* pay two hundred—if I have to. With eighty gilders we could pack a hamper with goods and begin over. It wouldn't be the end of the world.

CHAPLAIN The Bible says, the Lord will provide.

MOTHER COURAGE (*To* CATHERINE) You must rub them dry.

YVETTE (*Comes running on*) They won't do it. I warned you. He said the drums would roll any second now and that's the sign a verdict has been pronounced. I offered a hundred and fifty, he didn't even shrug his shoulders. I could hardly get him to stay there while I came to you.

MOTHER COURAGE Tell him, I'll pay two hundred. Run!

(YVETTE *runs.* MOTHER COURAGE *sits, silent. The* CHAPLAIN *has stopped doing the glasses*)

I believe—I haggled too long.

(*In the distance, a roll of drums. The* CHAPLAIN *stands up and walks toward the rear.* MOTHER COURAGE *remains seated. It grows dark. It gets light again.* MOTHER COURAGE *has not moved*)

YVETTE (*Appears, pale*) Now you've done it—with your haggling. You can keep the wagon now. He got eleven bullets, that's all. I don't know why I still bother about you, you don't deserve it, but I just happened to learn they don't think the cash box is really in the river. They suspect it's here, they think you're connected with him. I think they mean to bring him here to see if you give yourself away when you see him. I warn you not to know him or we're in for it. And I better tell you straight, they're right behind me. Shall I keep Catherine away?

(MOTHER COURAGE *shakes her head*)

Does she know? Maybe she never heard the drums or didn't understand.

MOTHER COURAGE She knows. Bring her.

(YVETTE *brings* CATHERINE, *who walks over to her mother and stands by her.* MOTHER COURAGE *takes her hand. Two men come on with a stretcher; there is a sheet on it and something underneath. Beside them, the* SERGEANT. *They put the stretcher down*)

SERGEANT Here's a man we don't know the name of. But he has to be registered to keep the records straight. He bought a meal from you. Look at him, see if you know him.

(*He pulls back the sheet*)

Do you know him?

(MOTHER COURAGE *shakes her head*)

What? You never saw him before he took that meal?

(MOTHER COURAGE *shakes her head*)

Lift him up. Throw him on the junk heap. He has no one that knows him.

(*They carry him off*)

## Scene Four

MOTHER COURAGE SINGS *THE SONG OF THE GREAT CAPITULATION*

(*Outside an officer's tent,* MOTHER COURAGE *waits. A* CLERK *looks out of the tent*)

CLERK You want to speak to the captain? I know you. You had a Protestant paymaster with you, he was hiding out. Better make no complaint here.

MOTHER COURAGE I will too! I'm innocent and if I give up it'll look like I have a bad conscience. They cut everything in my wagon to ribbons with their sabers and then claimed a fine of five thalers for nothing and less than nothing.

CLERK For your own good, keep your trap shut. We haven't many canteens, so we let you stay in business, especially if you've a bad conscience and have to pay a fine now and then.

MOTHER COURAGE I'm going to lodge a complaint.

CLERK As you wish. Wait here till the captain has time.

(*Withdraws into the tent*)

YOUNG SOLDIER (*Comes storming in*) Screw the captain! Where *is* the son-of-a-bitch? Snitching my reward, spending it on brandy for his whores, I'll rip his belly open!

OLDER SOLDIER (*Coming after him*) Shut your hole, you'll wind up in the stocks.

YOUNG SOLDIER Come out, you thief, I'll make lamb chops out of you! I was the only one in the squad who swam the river and *he* grabs my money, I can't even buy a beer. Come on out! And let me slice you up!

OLD SOLDIER Holy Christ, he'll destroy himself!

YOUNG SOLDIER Let me go or I'll run *you* down too. This thing has got to be settled!

OLDER SOLDIER Saved the colonel's horse and didn't get the reward. He's young, he hasn't been at it long.

MOTHER COURAGE Let him go. He doesn't have to be chained, he's not a dog. Very reasonable to want a reward. Why else should he want to shine?

YOUNG SOLDIER He's in there pouring it down! You're all chickens. I done something special, I want the reward!

MOTHER COURAGE Young man, don't scream at *me*, I have my own troubles.

YOUNG SOLDIER He's whoring on my money and I'm hungry! I'll murder him!

MOTHER COURAGE I understand: you're hungry. You're angry: I understand that too.

YOUNG SOLDIER It's no use you talking, I won't stand for injustice!

MOTHER COURAGE You're quite right. But how long for? How long won't you stand injustice for? One hour? Or two? You haven't asked yourself that, have you? And yet it's the main thing. It's a misery to sit in the stocks. Especially if you leave it till then to decide you do stand for injustice.

YOUNG SOLDIER I don't know why I listen to you. Screw that captain! Where is he?

MOTHER COURAGE You listen because you know I'm right. Your rage has calmed down already. It was a short one and you'd need a long one. But where would you find it?

YOUNG SOLDIER Are you trying to say it's not right to ask for the money?

MOTHER COURAGE Just the opposite. I only say, your rage won't last. You'll get nowhere with it, it's a pity. If your rage was a long one, I'd urge you on. Slice him up, I'd advise you. But what's the use if you *don't* slice him up because you feel your tail between your legs? You stand there and the captain lets you have it.

OLDER SOLDIER You're quite right, he's nuts.

YOUNG SOLDIER All right, we'll see whether I slice him up or not.

(*Draws his sword*)

When he comes out, I slice him up!

CLERK (*Looking out*) The captain will be right out.

(*In the tone of military command*)

Be seated!

(*The* YOUNG SOLDIER *sits*)

MOTHER COURAGE What did I tell you? They know us inside out, they know their business. Be seated! And we sit. Oh, you needn't be embarrassed in front of me, I'm no better. We don't stick our necks out, do we? We're too well paid to keep 'em in. Let me tell you about the Great Capitulation.

(*She sings* THE SONG OF THE GREAT CAPITULATION)

Long, long ago, a green beginner
  I thought myself a special case.
(None of your ordinary, run of the mill girls, with my looks and my talent and my love of the higher things!)
I picked a hair out of my dinner
  And put the waiter in his place.
(All or nothing. Anyway, never the second best. I am the master of my fate. I'll take no orders from no one.)
Then a little bird whispers!
    The bird says: "Wait a year or so
    And marching with the band you'll go
    Keeping in step, now fast, now slow,
    And piping out your little spiel.
    Then one day the battalions wheel
    And you go down upon your knees
    To God Almighty if you please!"

My friend, before that year was over
  I'd learned to drink their cup of tea.
(Two children round your neck and the price of bread and what all!)
When they were through with me, moreover,
  They had me where they wanted me.
(You must get in with people. If you scratch my back, I'll scratch yours. Never stick your neck out!)
Then a little bird whispered!
    The bird says: "Scarce a year or so
    And marching with the band she'd go
    Keeping in step, now fast, now slow,
    And piping out her little spiel.
    Then one day the battalions wheel
    And she goes down upon her knees
    To God Almighty if you please!"

Our plans are big, our hopes colossal.
  We hitch our wagon to a star.
(Where there's a will, there's a way. You can't hold a good man down.)
"We can lift mountains," says the apostle.
  And yet: how heavy one cigar!
(You must cut your coat according to your cloth.)
That little bird whispers!
    The bird says: "Wait a year or so
    And marching with the band we go
    Keeping in step, now fast, now slow,
    And piping out our little spiel.
    Then one day the battalions wheel

And we go down upon our knees
To God Almighty if you please!"

MOTHER COURAGE And so I think you should stay here with your sword drawn if you're set on it and your anger is big enough. You have good cause, I admit. But if your anger is a short one, you'd better go.

YOUNG SOLDIER Aw, shove it!

(*He stumbles off, the other soldier following him*)

CLERK (*Sticks his head out*) The captain is here. You can lodge your complaint.

MOTHER COURAGE I've thought better of it. I'm not complaining.

(*Exit. The* CLERK *looks after her, shaking his head*)

## Scene Five

TWO YEARS HAVE PASSED. THE WAR COVERS WIDER AND WIDER TERRITORY. FOREVER ON THE MOVE THE LITTLE WAGON CROSSES POLAND, MORAVIA, BAVARIA, ITALY, AND AGAIN BAVARIA. 1631. TILLY'S VICTORY AT LEIPZIG COSTS MOTHER COURAGE FOUR SHIRTS.

*The wagon stands in a war-ruined village. Faint military music from the distance. Two soldiers are being served at a counter by* CATHERINE *and* MOTHER COURAGE. *One of them has a woman's fur coat about his shoulders.*

MOTHER COURAGE What, you can't pay? No money, no schnapps! They can play a victory march, they should pay their men.

FIRST SOLDIER I want my schnapps! I arrived too late for plunder. The Chief allowed one hour to plunder the town, it's a swindle. He's not inhuman, he says. So I guess they bought him off.

CHAPLAIN (*Staggering in*) There are more in the farmhouse. A whole family of peasants. Help me someone, I need linen!

(*The* SECOND SOLDIER *goes with him.* CATHERINE *is getting very excited. She tries to get her mother to bring linen out*)

MOTHER COURAGE I have none. I sold all my bandages to the regiment. I'm not tearing up my officer's shirts for these people.

CHAPLAIN (*Calling over his shoulder*) I said I need linen!

MOTHER COURAGE (*Stopping* CATHERINE *from entering the wagon*) Not a thing! They have nothing and they pay nothing!

CHAPLAIN (*To a woman he is carrying in*) Why did you stay out there in the line of fire?

WOMAN Our farm——

MOTHER COURAGE Think they'd ever let go of *anything*? And now I'm supposed to pay, Well, I won't!

FIRST SOLDIER They're Protestants, why should they be Protestants?

MOTHER COURAGE Protestant, Catholic, what do *they* care? Their farm's gone, that's what.

SECOND SOLDIER They're not Protestants anyway, they're Catholics.

FIRST SOLDIER In a bombardment we can't pick and choose.

PEASANT (*Brought on by* CHAPLAIN)
My arm's gone.

CHAPLAIN Where's that linen?

MOTHER COURAGE I can't give you any. With all I have to pay out—taxes, duties, bribes . . .

(CATHERINE *takes up a board and threatens her mother with it, emitting gurgling sounds*)

Are you out of your mind? Put that board down or I'll fetch you one, you lunatic! I'm giving nothing, I don't dare, I have myself to think of.

(*The* CHAPLAIN *lifts her bodily off the steps of the wagon and sets her down on the ground. He takes out shirts from the wagon and tears them in strips*)

My shirts, my officer's shirts!

(*From the house comes the cry of a child in pain*)

PEASANT The child's still in there!

(CATHERINE *runs in*)

MOTHER COURAGE Hold her back, the roof may fall in!

CHAPLAIN I'm not going back in there!

MOTHER COURAGE My officer's shirts, half a gilder apiece! I'm ruined.

(CATHERINE *brings a baby out of the ruins*)

MOTHER COURAGE Another baby to drag around, you must be pleased with yourself. Give it to its mother this minute!

(CATHERINE *is rocking the child and half humming a lullaby*)

CHAPLAIN (*Bandaging*) The blood's coming through.

MOTHER COURAGE There she sits, happy as a lark in all this!

(*Shouting toward the music*)

Stop that music, I can see your victory all right!

(*Seeing* FIRST SOLDIER *trying to make off with the bottle he's been drinking from*)

Stop, you pig, if you want *another* victory you must pay for it!

FIRST SOLDIER I'm broke.

MOTHER COURAGE (*Tearing the fur coat off him*) Then leave this, it's stolen goods anyhow.

(CATHERINE *rocks the child and raises it high above her head*)

## Scene Six

BEFORE THE CITY OF INGOLSTADT IN BAVARIA MOTHER COURAGE ATTENDS THE FUNERAL OF THE FALLEN COMMANDER, TILLY. CONVERSATIONS TAKE PLACE ABOUT WAR HEROES AND THE DURATION OF THE WAR. THE CHAPLAIN COMPLAINS THAT HIS TALENTS ARE LYING FALLOW AND CATHERINE GETS THE RED BOOTS. THE YEAR IS 1632.

*The inside of a canteen tent. The inner side of a counter at the rear. Rain. In the distance, drums and funeral music. The* CHAPLAIN *and the* REGIMENTAL CLERK *are playing checkers.* MOTHER COURAGE *and her* DAUGHTER *are taking inventory.*

CHAPLAIN The funeral procession is just starting out.

MOTHER COURAGE Pity about the Chief—twenty-two pairs, socks—getting killed that way. They say it was an accident. There was a fog over the fields that morning, and the fog was to blame. The Chief called up another regiment, told 'em to fight to the death, rode back again, missed his way in the fog, went forward instead of back, and ran straight into a bullet in the thick of the battle!

(*A whistle from the rear. She goes to the counter. To a soldier*)

It's a disgrace the way you're all skipping your Commander's funeral!

(*She pours a drink*)

CLERK They shouldn't have handed the money out before the funeral. Now the men are all getting drunk instead of going to it.

CHAPLAIN (*To the* CLERK) Don't you have to be there?

CLERK I stayed away because of the rain.

MOTHER COURAGE It's different for you, the rain might spoil your uniform.

VOICE FROM THE COUNTER Service! One brandy!

MOTHER COURAGE Your money first. No, you *can't* come inside the tent, not with those boots; you can drink outside, rain or no rain. I only let officers in here.

(*To the* CLERK)

The Chief had his troubles lately, I hear. There was unrest in the second regiment because he didn't pay 'em but said it was a holy war and they must fight it for free.

CHAPLAIN (*As music continues*) Now they're filing past the body.

MOTHER COURAGE I feel sorry for a commander or an emperor like that—when maybe he had something special in mind, something they'd talk about in times to come, something they'd raise a statue to him for. The conquest of the world now, *that's* a goal for a commander, he couldn't do better than *that,* could he? . . . Lord, worms have got into the biscuit. . . . In short he works his hands to the bone and then it's all spoiled by the common riffraff that only wants a jug of beer or a bit of company, not the higher things in life. The finest plans have always been spoiled by the littleness of them that should carry them out. Even emperors can't do it all by themselves. They count on support from their soldiers and the people round about. Am I right?

CHAPLAIN (*Laughing*) You're right, Mother Courage, till you come to the soldiers. They do what they can. Those fellows outside, for example, drinking their brandy in the rain, I'd trust 'em to fight a hundred years, one war after another, two at once if necessary. And I wasn't trained as a Commander.

MOTHER COURAGE . . . Seventeen leather belts . . . Then you don't think the war might end?

CHAPLAIN Because a Commander's dead? Don't be childish, they're a dime a dozen. There are always heroes.

MOTHER COURAGE Well, I wasn't asking just for the sake of argument. I was wondering if I should buy up a lot of supplies. They happen to be cheap right now. But if the war ended, I might just as well throw them away.

CHAPLAIN I realize you are serious, Mother Courage. Well, there have always been people going around saying someday the war will end. I say, you can't be sure the war will *ever* end. Of course it may have to pause occasionally—for breath, as it were—it can even meet with an accident—nothing on this earth is perfect—a war of which we could say it left nothing to be desired will probably never exist. A war can come to a sudden halt—from unforeseen causes—you can't think of everything—a little oversight, and the war's in the hole, and someone's got to pull it out again! The someone is the Emperor or the King or the Pope. They're such friends in need, the war has really nothing to worry about, it can look forward to a prosperous future.

A SOLDIER (*Sings at the counter*)

A schnapps, host, quick, make haste!
A soldier's no time to waste,
Must be for his Kaiser fighting!

Make it a double, this is a holiday.

MOTHER COURAGE If I was sure you're right . . .

CHAPLAIN Think it out for yourself, how *could* the war end?

SOLDIER

Your breast, girl, quick. make haste!
A soldier's no time to waste,
Must be to Moravia riding!

CLERK (*Of a sudden*) What about peace? Yes, peace. I'm from Bohemia, I'd like to get home once in a while.

CHAPLAIN You would, would you? Deaı old peace! What happens to the hole when the cheese is gone?

CLERK In the long run you can't live without peace!

CHAPLAIN Well, I'd say there's peace even in war, war has its . . . islands of peace. For war satisfies *all* needs, even those of peace, yes, they're provided for, or the war couldn't keep going. In war—as in the very thick of peace—you can take a crap, and between one battle and the next there's always a beer, and even on the march you can catch a nap—on your elbow maybe, in a gutter—something can always be managed. Of course you can't play cards during an attack, but neither can you while plowing the fields in peace-time; it's when the victory's won that there are possibilities. And can't you be fruitful and multiply in the very midst of slaughter—behind a barn or some place? Nothing can keep you from it very long in any event. And so the war has your offspring and can carry on. War is like love, it always finds a way. Why *should* it end?

(CATHERINE *has stopped working. She stares at the* CHAPLAIN)

MOTHER COURAGE Then I *will* buy those supplies, I'll rely on you.

(CATHERINE *suddenly bangs a basket of glasses down on the ground and runs out.* MOTHER COURAGE *laughs*)

Lord, Catherine's still going to wait for peace. I promised her she'll get a husband—when it's peace. (*Runs after her*)

CLERK (*Standing up*) I win. You were talking. You pay.

MOTHER COURAGE (*Returning with* CATHERINE) Be sensible, the war'll go on a bit longer, and we'll make a bit more money, then peace'll be all the nicer. Now you go into the town, it's not ten minutes walk, and bring the things from the Golden Lion, just the more expensive ones, we can get the rest later in the wagon. It's all arranged, the clerk will go with you, most of the soldiers are at the funeral, nothing can happen to you. Do a good job, don't lose anything, Catherine, think of your trousseau!

(CATHERINE *ties a cloth round her head and leaves with the* CLERK)

CHAPLAIN You don't mind her going with the clerk?

MOTHER COURAGE She's not so pretty anyone would want to ruin her.

CHAPLAIN The way you run your business and always come through is nothing short of commendable, Mother Courage—I see how you got your name.

MOTHER COURAGE Poorer people need courage. They're lost, that's why. That they even get up in the morning is something—in *their* plight. Or that they plow a field—in war time. Or that they have an Emperor and a Pope, what courage *that* takes, when you can lose your life by it! The poor! They hang each other one by one, they slaughter each other in the lump, so if they want to look each other in the face once in a while—well, it takes courage, that's all.

(*She sits, takes a small pipe from her pocket and smokes it*)

You might chop me a bit of firewood.

CHAPLAIN (*Reluctantly taking his coat off and preparing to chop wood*) Properly speaking, I'm a pastor of souls, not a woodcutter.

MOTHER COURAGE But I don't have a soul. And I do need wood.

CHAPLAIN What's that little pipe you've got there?

MOTHER COURAGE Just a pipe.

CHAPLAIN I think it's a very particular pipe.

MOTHER COURAGE Oh?

CHAPLAIN The cook's pipe in fact. Our Swedish Commander's cook.

MOTHER COURAGE If you know, why beat about the bush?

CHAPLAIN Because I don't know if you've been *aware* that's what you've been smoking. It was possible you just rummaged among your belongings and your fingers just lit on a pipe and you just took it. In pure absent-mindedness.

MOTHER COURAGE How do you know that's not it?

CHAPLAIN It isn't. You *are* aware of it.

(*He brings the ax down on the block with a crash*)

MOTHER COURAGE What if I was?

CHAPLAIN I must give you a warning, Mother Courage, it's my duty. You are unlikely ever again to see the gentleman but that's no pity, you're in luck. Mother Courage, he did not impress me as trustworthy. On the contrary.

MOTHER COURAGE Really? He was such a nice man.

CHAPLAIN Well! So that's what you call a nice man. I do not.

(*The ax falls again*)

Far be it from me to wish him ill, but I cannot—cannot—describe him as nice. No, no, he's a Don Juan, a cunning Don Juan. Just look at that pipe if you don't believe me. You must admit it tells everything about him.

MOTHER COURAGE I see nothing special in it. It's been, um, used.

CHAPLAIN It's bitten half-way through! He's a man of great violence! It is the pipe of a man of great violence, you can see *that* if you've any judgment left!

(*He deals the block a tremendous blow*)

MOTHER COURAGE Don't bite my chopping block half-way through!

CHAPLAIN I told you I had no training as a woodcutter. The care of souls was my field. Around here my gifts and capabilities are grossly misused. In physical labor my god-given talents find no—um—adequate expression—which is a sin. You haven't heard me preach. Why, I can put such spirit into a regiment with a single sermon that the enemy's a mere flock of sheep to them and their own lives no more than smelly old shoes to be thrown away at the thought of final victory! God has given me the gift of tongues. I can preach you out of your senses!

MOTHER COURAGE I need my senses, what would I do without them?

CHAPLAIN Mother Courage, I have often thought that —under a veil of plain speech—you conceal a heart. You are human, you need . . . warmth.

MOTHER COURAGE The best way of warming this tent is to chop plenty of firewood.

CHAPLAIN You're changing the subject. Seriously, my dear Courage, I sometimes ask myself how it would be if our relationship should be somewhat more firmly . . . cemented. I mean, now the wind of war has whirled us so strangely together.

MOTHER COURAGE The cement's pretty firm already. I cook your meals. And you lend a hand—at chopping firewood, for instance.

CHAPLAIN (*Going over to her, gesturing with the ax*) You know what I mean by a close relationship. It has nothing to do with eating and woodcutting and such base necessities. Let your heart speak!

MOTHER COURAGE Don't come at me like that with your ax, that'd be *too* close a relationship!

CHAPLAIN This is no laughing matter, I am in earnest. I've thought it all over.

MOTHER COURAGE Dear Chaplain, be a sensible fellow. I like you, and I don't want to heap coals of fire on your head. All I'm after is to bring me and my children through in that wagon. Now chop the firewood and we'll be warm of an evening, which is quite a lot these days. What's that?

(*She stands up.* CATHERINE *enters breathless with a nasty wound above her eye and brow. She is letting everything fall, parcels, leather goods, a drum, etc.*)

Catherine, what is it? Were you attacked? On the way back? It's not serious, only a flesh wound, I'll bandage it up for you, and you'll be better within the week. Didn't the clerk walk you back? That's because you're a good girl, he thought they'd leave you alone. The wound really isn't deep, it won't show, though I wouldn't mind if it did. The pretty girls have a bad time, they get dragged around till they're finished off, and the other ones get left alone. I've seen so many with pretty faces and they looked like something that would scare a wolf in no time. They can't go behind a tree without getting scared. They lead a horrible life. It's like with the trees: the straight and tall ones are cut down for roof timber while the crooked ones are left to enjoy life. That's it, now it's all bandaged. Now I've got something for you, I've been keeping it, just watch.

(*She digs* YVETTE POTTIER'S *red boots out of a bag*)

You see? You always wanted 'em and now you have 'em. Put them on before I think twice about it.

(*She helps her*)

It won't show at all! The boots have kept well, I cleaned them good before I put them away.

(CATHERINE *leaves the shoes and creeps into the wagon*)

CHAPLAIN (*When she's gone*) I hope she won't be disfigured?

MOTHER COURAGE There'll be a scar. She needn't wait for peace now.

CHAPLAIN She didn't let them get any of the stuff from her.

MOTHER COURAGE Maybe I shouldn't have been so strict with her. If only I ever knew what went on inside her head. One time she stayed out all night, once in all the years. I could never get out of her what happened, I racked my brains for quite a while.

(*She picks up the things* CATHERINE *spilled and sorts them angrily*)

This is war. A nice source of income to have!

(*Cannon shots*)

CHAPLAIN Now they're lowering the Commander in his grave! A historic moment.

MOTHER COURAGE It's a historic moment to me when they hit my daughter over the eye. She's all but finished now, she'll get no husband, and she's so crazy for children! Even her dumbness comes from the war. A soldier stuck something in her mouth when she was little. I'll not see Swiss Cheese again, and where my Eilif is the Good Lord knows. Curse the war!

## Scene Seven

*A highway. The* CHAPLAIN *and* CATHERINE *are pulling the wagon. It is dirty and neglected, though there are new goods hung round it.*

MOTHER COURAGE (*Walking beside the wagon and drinking heavily from a flask at her waist*) I won't have my war all spoiled for me! It destroys the weak, does it? Well, what does peace do for 'em? Huh?

(*She sings her song*)

So cheer up, boys, the rose is fading
When victory comes you may be dead
A war is just the same as trading
But not with cheese—with steel and lead!
Christians, awake! The winter's gone!
The snows depart, the dead sleep on.
And though you may not long survive
Get out of bed and look alive!

(*And the wagon moves on*)

## Scene Eight

1632. IN THIS SAME YEAR GUSTAVUS ADOLPHUS FELL IN THE BATTLE OF LÜTZEN. THE PEACE THREATENS MOTHER COURAGE WITH RUIN. HER BRAVE SON PERFORMS ONE HEROIC DEED TOO MANY AND COMES TO A SHAMEFUL END.

*A camp. A summer morning. In front of the wagon, an old woman and her son. The son is dragging a large bag of bedding.*

MOTHER COURAGE (*From inside the wagon*) Must you come at the crack of dawn?

YOUNG MAN We've been walking all night, twenty miles it was, we have to be back today.

MOTHER COURAGE (*Still inside*) What do I want with bed feathers? Take 'em to the town!

YOUNG MAN At least wait till you see 'em.

OLD WOMAN Nothing doing here either, let's go.

YOUNG MAN And let 'em sign away the roof over our heads for taxes? Maybe she'll pay three gilders if you throw in that bracelet.

(*Bells start ringing*)

You hear, Mother?

VOICES (*From the rear*) It's peace! The King of Sweden's killed!

MOTHER COURAGE (*Sticking her head out of the wagon. She hasn't done her hair yet*) Bells! What are the bells for, middle of the week?

CHAPLAIN (*Crawling out from under the wagon*) What's that they're shouting?

YOUNG MAN It's peace.

CHAPLAIN Peace!?

MOTHER COURAGE Don't tell me peace has broken out—when I've just gone and bought all these supplies!

CHAPLAIN (*Calling, toward the rear*) Is it peace?

VOICE (*From a distance*) Yes, the war stopped three weeks ago!

CHAPLAIN (*To* MOTHER COURAGE) Or why would they ring the bells?

VOICE A great crowd of Lutherans have just arrived with wagons—they brought the news.

YOUNG MAN It's peace, Mother.

(*The* OLD WOMAN *collapses*)

What's the matter?

MOTHER COURAGE (*Back in the wagon*) Catherine, it's peace! Put on your black dress, we're going to church, we owe it to Swiss Cheese!

YOUNG MAN The people here say so too, the war's over.

(*The* OLD WOMAN *stands up, dazed*)

I'll get the harness shop going again now, I promise you. Everything'll be all right, father will get his bed back. . . . Can you walk?

(*To the* CHAPLAIN)

She felt sick, it was the news. She didn't believe there'd ever be peace again. Father always said there would. We're going home.

(*They leave*)

MOTHER COURAGE (*Off*) Give her a schnapps!

CHAPLAIN They've left already.

MOTHER COURAGE (*Still off*) What's going on in the camp over there?

CHAPLAIN They're all getting together, I think I'll go over. Shall I put my pastor's clothes on again?

MOTHER COURAGE Better get the exact news first, and not risk being taken for the antichrist. I'm glad about the peace even though I'm ruined. At least I've got two of my children through the war. Now I'll see my Eilif again.

CHAPLAIN And who may this be coming down from the camp? Well, if it isn't our Swedish Commander's cook!

COOK (*Somewhat bedraggled, carrying a bundle*) Who's here? The Chaplain!

CHAPLAIN Mother Courage, a visitor!

(MOTHER COURAGE *clambers out*)

COOK Well, I promised I'd come over for a brief conversation as soon as I had time. I didn't forget your brandy, Mrs. Fierling.

MOTHER COURAGE Mr. Lamp, the Commander's cook! After all these years! Where is Eilif?

COOK Isn't he here yet? He went on ahead yesterday, he was on his way over.

CHAPLAIN I *will* put my pastor's clothes on.

(*He goes behind the wagon*)

MOTHER COURAGE He may be here any minute then.

(*Calls toward the wagon*)

Catherine, Eilif's coming! Bring a glass of brandy for the Cook, Catherine!

(CATHERINE *doesn't come*)

Pull your hair over it and have done, the Cook's no stranger. She won't come out. Peace is nothing to her, it was too long coming. Well, one more schnapps!

COOK Dear old peace!

(*He and* MOTHER COURAGE *sit*)

MOTHER COURAGE Cook, you come at a bad time: I'm ruined.

COOK What? That's terrible!

MOTHER COURAGE The peace has broken my neck. On the Chaplain's advice I've gone and bought a lot of supplies. Now everybody's leaving and I'm holding the bag.

COOK How ever could you listen to the Chaplain? If I'd had time—but the Catholics were too quick—I'd have warned you against him. He's a windbag. Well, so now he's the big wheel round here!

MOTHER COURAGE He's been doing the dishes for me and helping with the wagon.

COOK I'll bet he has. And I'll bet he's told you a few of his jokes. He has a most unhealthy attitude to women. I tried to influence him but it was no good. He isn't sound.

MOTHER COURAGE Are you sound?

COOK If I'm nothing else, I'm sound. Your health!

MOTHER COURAGE Sound! Only one person around here was ever sound, and I never had to slave as I did then. He sold the blankets off the children's beds in autumn. You aren't recommending yourself if you *admit* you're sound.

COOK You fight tooth and nail, don't you? I like that.

MOTHER COURAGE Don't tell me you dream of my teeth and nails.

COOK Well, here we sit, while the bells of peace do ring, and you pour your famous brandy as only you know how.

MOTHER COURAGE I don't think much of the bells of peace at the moment. I don't see how they can hand out all this pay that's in arrears. And then where shall I be with my famous brandy? Have you all been paid?

COOK (*Hesitating*) Not exactly. That's why we disbanded. In the circumstances, I thought, why stay? For the time being, I'll look up a couple of friends. So here I am.

MOTHER COURAGE In other words, you're broke.

COOK (*Annoyed by the bells*) It's about time they stopped that racket! I'd like to set myself up in some business. I'm fed up with being their cook. I'm supposed to make do with tree roots and shoe leather, and then they throw the soup in my face. Being a cook nowadays is a dog's life. I'd sooner do war service, but of course it's peace now. We'll discuss it later.

MOTHER COURAGE Oh, Cook, it's a dog's life.

COOK (*As the* CHAPLAIN *turns up, wearing his old costume*) We'll discuss it.

CHAPLAIN The coat's pretty good. Just a few moth holes.

COOK I don't know why you take the trouble. You won't find another job. Who could you incite now to earn an honorable wage or risk his life for a cause? Besides I have a bone to pick with you.

CHAPLAIN Have you?

COOK I have. You advised a lady to buy superfluous goods on the pretext that the war would never end.

CHAPLAIN (*Hotly*) I'd like to know what business it is of yours?

COOK It's unprincipled behavior! How can you give unwanted advice? And interfere with the conduct of other people's businesses?

CHAPLAIN Who's interfering now, I'd like to know?
(*Haughtily to* MOTHER COURAGE)
I had no idea you were such a close friend of this gentleman and had to account to *him* for everything.

MOTHER COURAGE Now don't get excited. The Cook's giving his personal opinion. You can't deny your war was a lemon.

CHAPLAIN You mustn't take the name of peace in vain. Remember, you're a hyena of the battlefield!

MOTHER COURAGE A what!?

COOK If you insult my girl friend, you'll have to reckon with me!

CHAPLAIN I am *not* speaking to you, your intentions are only too transparent!
(*To* MOTHER COURAGE)
But when I see *you* take peace between finger and thumb like a snotty old hanky, my humanity rebels! It shows that you want war, not peace, for what you get out of it. But don't forget the proverb: he who sups with the devil must use a long spoon!

MOTHER COURAGE Remember what one fox said to another that was caught in a trap? "If you stay there, you're just asking for trouble!" There isn't much love lost between me and the war. And when it comes to calling me a hyena, you and I part company.

CHAPLAIN Then why all this grumbling about the peace just as everyone's heaving a sigh of relief? Is it just for the junk in your wagon?

MOTHER COURAGE My goods are not junk. I live off them.

CHAPLAIN You live off war. Exactly.

COOK (*To the* CHAPLAIN) As a grown man, you should know better than to go around advising people.
(*To* MOTHER COURAGE)
Now, in your situation you'd be smart to get rid of certain goods at once—before the prices sink to zero. Get ready and get going, there isn't a moment to lose!

MOTHER COURAGE That's sensible advice, I think I'll take it.

CHAPLAIN Because the Cook says so.

MOTHER COURAGE Why didn't *you* say so? He's right, I must get to the market.
(*She climbs into the wagon*)

COOK One up for me, Chaplain. You have no presence of mind. You should have said, "*I* gave you advice? Why, I was just talking politics!" And you shouldn't take me on as a rival. Cockfights are not becoming to your cloth.

CHAPLAIN If you don't shut your trap, I'll murder you, whether it's becoming or not!

COOK (*Taking his boots off and unwinding the wrappings on his feet*) If you hadn't degenerated into a godless tramp, you could easily be quite a success these days. Cooks won't be needed, there's nothing to cook, but there's still plenty to believe, and people'll go right on believing it.

CHAPLAIN (*Changing his tone*) Cook, please don't drive me out! Since I became a tramp, I'm a somewhat better man. I couldn't preach to 'em any more. So where should I go?
(YVETTE POTTIER *enters, decked out in black, with a stick. She is much older, fatter, and heavily powdered. Behind her, a servant*)

YVETTE Hullo, everybody! Is this Mother Courage's establishment?

CHAPLAIN Quite right. And with whom have we the pleasure?

YVETTE I am Madame Colonel Starhemberg, good people. Where's Mother Courage?

CHAPLAIN (*Calling to the wagon*) Madame Colonel Starhemberg wants to speak with you!

MOTHER COURAGE (*From inside*) Coming!

YVETTE (*Calling*) It's Yvette!

MOTHER COURAGE (*Inside*) Yvette!

YVETTE Just to see how you're getting on!
(*As the* COOK *turns round in horror*)
Peter!

COOK Yvette!

YVETTE Of all things! How did *you* get here?

COOK On a cart.

CHAPLAIN Well! You know each other? Intimately?

YVETTE I'll say!
(*Scrutinizing the* COOK)
You're fat.

COOK For that matter, *you're* no beanpole.

YVETTE Anyway, nice meeting you, tramp. Now I can tell you what I think of you.

CHAPLAIN Do that, tell him all, but wait till Mother Courage comes out.

COOK Now don't make a scene . . .

MOTHER COURAGE (*Comes out, laden with goods*) Yvette!

(*They embrace*)

But why are you in mourning?

YVETTE Doesn't it suit me? My husband, the colonel, died several years ago.

MOTHER COURAGE The old fellow that nearly bought my wagon?

YVETTE Naw, not him—his older brother!

MOTHER COURAGE Good to see one person who got somewhere in the war.

YVETTE I've had my ups and downs.

MOTHER COURAGE Don't let's talk badly of Colonels. They make money like hay.

CHAPLAIN If I were you, I'd put my shoes on again. You promised to give us your opinion of this gentleman.

COOK Now, Yvette, don't make a stink!

MOTHER COURAGE He's a friend of mine, Yvette.

YVETTE He's—Peter Piper, that's what!

MOTHER COURAGE What!?

COOK Cut the nicknames. My name's Lamp.

MOTHER COURAGE (*Laughing*) Peter Piper? Who turned the women's heads? I'll have to sit down. And I've been keeping your pipe for you.

CHAPLAIN And smoking it.

YVETTE Lucky I can warn you against him. He's a bad lot. You won't find a worse on the whole coast of Flanders. He got more girls in trouble than . . .

COOK That's a long time ago, it isn't true any more.

YVETTE Stand up when you talk to a lady! Oh, how I loved that man! And all the time he was having a little bowlegged brunette. He got *her* in trouble too, of course.

COOK I seem to have brought *you* luck!

YVETTE Shut your trap, you hoary ruin! And you take care, Mother Courage, this type is still dangerous even in decay!

MOTHER COURAGE (*To* YVETTE) Come with me, I must get rid of this stuff before the prices fall.

YVETTE (*Concentrating on* COOK) Miserable cur!

MOTHER COURAGE Maybe you can help me at army headquarters, you have contacts.

YVETTE Damnable whore hunter!

MOTHER COURAGE (*Shouting into the wagon*) Catherine, church is all off, I'm going to market!

YVETTE Inveterate seducer!

MOTHER COURAGE (*Still to* CATHERINE) When Eilif comes, give him something to drink!

YVETTE I've put an end to your tricks, Peter Piper, and one day—in a better life than this—the Lord God will reward me!

(*She sniffs*)

Come, Mother Courage!

(*Leaves with* MOTHER COURAGE. *Pause*)

CHAPLAIN As our text this morning let us take the saying, the mills of God grind slowly. And you complain of my jokes!

COOK I have no luck. I'll be frank, I was hoping for a good hot dinner, I'm starving. And now they'll be talking about me, and she'll get a completely wrong picture. I think I should go before she comes back.

CHAPLAIN I think so too.

COOK Chaplain, the peace makes me sick. Mankind must perish by fire and sword, we're born and bred in sin! Oh, how I wish I was roasting a great fat capon for the Commander—God knows where *he's* got to—with mustard sauce and those little yellow carrots. . . .

CHAPLAIN Red cabbage—with capon, red cabbage.

COOK You're right. But he always wanted yellow carrots.

CHAPLAIN He never understood a thing.

COOK You always put plenty away.

CHAPLAIN Under protest.

COOK Anyway, you must admit, those were the days.

CHAPLAIN Yes, that I might admit.

COOK Now you've called her a hyena, there's not much future for you here either. What are you staring at?

CHAPLAIN It's Eilif!

(*Followed by two soldiers with halberds,* EILIF *enters. His hands are fettered. He is white as chalk*)

What's happened to you?

EILIF Where's Mother?

CHAPLAIN Gone to town.

EILIF They said she was here. I was allowed a last visit.

COOK (*To the soldiers*) Where are you taking him?

SOLDIER For a ride.

(*The other soldier makes the gesture of throat cutting*)

CHAPLAIN What has he done?

SOLDIER He broke in on a peasant. The wife is dead.

CHAPLAIN Eilif, how could you?

EILIF It's no different. It's what I did before.

COOK That was in wartime.

EILIF Shut your hole. Can I sit down till she comes?

SOLDIER No.

CHAPLAIN It's true. In wartime they honored him for it. He sat at the Commander's right hand. It was bravery. Couldn't we speak with the provost?

SOLDIER What's the use? Stealing cattle from a peasant, what's brave about that?

COOK It was just dumb.

EILIF If I'd been dumb, I'd have starved, smarty.

COOK So you were bright and paid for it.

CHAPLAIN At least we must bring Catherine out.

EILIF Let her alone. Just give me some brandy.

SOLDIER No.

CHAPLAIN What shall we tell your mother?

EILIF Tell her it was no different. Tell her it was the same. Aw, tell her nothing.

(*The soldiers take him away*)

CHAPLAIN I'll come with you, I'll . . .

EILIF I don't need a priest!

CHAPLAIN You don't know—yet.

(*Follows him*)

COOK (*Calling after him*) I'll have to tell her, she'll want to see him!

CHAPLAIN Better tell her nothing. Or maybe just that he was here, and he'll return, maybe tomorrow. Meantime I'll be back and can break the news.

(*Leaves quickly. The* COOK *looks after him, shakes his head, then walks uneasily around. Finally, he approaches the wagon*)

COOK Hi! Won't you come out? You want to run away from the peace, don't you? Well, so do I! I'm the Swedish Commander's cook, remember me? I was wondering if you got anything to eat in there—while we're waiting for your mother. I wouldn't mind a bit of bacon—or even bread—just to pass the time.

(*He looks in*)

She's got a blanket over her head.

(*The thunder of cannon*)

MOTHER COURAGE (*Running, out of breath, still carrying the goods*) Cook, the peace is over, the war's on again, has been for three days! I didn't get rid of this stuff after all, thank God! There's a shooting match in the town already—with the Lutherans. We must get away with the wagon. Pack, Catherine! What's on *your* mind? Something the matter?

COOK Nothing.

MOTHER COURAGE But there is, I see it in your face.

COOK Eilif was here. Only he had to go away again.

MOTHER COURAGE He was here? Then we'll see him on the march. I'll be with our side this time. How'd he look?

COOK The same.

MOTHER COURAGE He'll *never* change. And the war couldn't get *him,* he's bright. Help me with the packing.

(*She starts it*)

Did he tell you anything? Is he in good with the captain? Did he tell you about his heroic deeds?

COOK (*Darkly*) He's done one of them over again.

MOTHER COURAGE Tell me about it later.

(CATHERINE *appears*)

Catherine, the peace is all through, we're on the move again.

(*To the* COOK)

What *is* biting you?

COOK I'll enlist.

MOTHER COURAGE A good idea. Where's the Chaplain?

COOK In the town. With Eilif.

MOTHER COURAGE Stay with us a while, Mr. Lamp, I need a bit of help.

COOK This Yvette thing . . .

MOTHER COURAGE Hasn't done you any harm at all in my eyes. Just the opposite. Where there's smoke, there's fire, they say. You'll come?

COOK I won't say no.

MOTHER COURAGE The twelfth regiment's under way. Into harness with you! Maybe I'll see Eilif before the day is out, just think! Well, it wasn't such a long peace, we can't grumble. Let's go!

(*They move off.* MOTHER COURAGE *sings*)

Up hill, down dale, past dome and steeple,
  My wagon always moves ahead.
The war can care for all its people
  So long as there is steel and lead.
Though steel and lead are stout supporters
  A war needs human beings too.
Report today to your headquarters!
  If it's to last, this war needs you!
    Christians, awake! The winter's gone!
    The snows depart, the dead sleep on.
    And though you may not long survive
    Get out of bed and look alive!

## Scene Nine

THE HOLY WAR HAS LASTED SIXTEEN YEARS AND GERMANY HAS LOST HALF ITS INHABITANTS. THOSE WHO ARE SPARED IN BATTLE DIE BY PLAGUE. OVER ONCE BLOOMING COUNTRYSIDE HUNGER RAGES. TOWNS ARE BURNED DOWN. WOLVES PROWL THE EMPTY STREETS. IN THE AUTUMN OF 1634 WE FIND MOTHER COURAGE IN THE FICHTELGEBIRGE NOT FAR FROM THE ROAD THE SWEDISH ARMY IS TAKING. WINTER HAS COME EARLY AND IS HARD. BUSINESS IS BAD. ONLY BEGGING REMAINS. THE COOK RECEIVES A LETTER FROM UTRECHT AND IS SENT PACKING.

*In front of a half-ruined parsonage. Early winter. A gray morning. Gusts of wind.* MOTHER COURAGE *and the* COOK *at the wagon in shabby clothes.*

COOK There are no lights on, no one's up.

MOTHER COURAGE But it's a parsonage. The parson'll have to leave his feather bed and go ring the bells. Then he'll have himself a hot soup.

COOK Where'll he get it from? The whole village is starving.

MOTHER COURAGE The house is lived in. There was a dog barking.

COOK If the parson has anything, he'll stick to it.

MOTHER COURAGE Maybe if we sang him something . . .

COOK I've had enough. Anna, I didn't tell you, a letter came from Utrecht. My mother died of cholera, the inn is mine. There's the letter, if you don't believe me.

MOTHER COURAGE (*Reading*) Mr. Lamp, I'm tired of wandering, too. I feel like a butcher's dog taking meat to my customers and getting none myself. I've nothing more to sell and people have nothing to pay for it. In Saxony someone tried to saddle me with a chestful of books in return for two eggs. And in Württemberg they would have let me have their plough for a bag of salt. Nothing grows any more, only thorn bushes. I hear they've even caught nuns committing robbery.

COOK The world's dying out.

MOTHER COURAGE Sometimes I see myself driving through hell with this wagon and selling brimstone. And sometimes I'm driving through heaven handing out provisions to wandering souls! If only we could find a place where there's no shooting, me and my children—what's left of 'em—we might rest up a while.

COOK We could open this inn together. Think about it, Courage. *My* mind's made up. With or without you, I'm leaving for Utrecht. And today at that.

MOTHER COURAGE I must talk to Catherine, it's sudden.

(CATHERINE *emerges from the wagon*)

Catherine, I've something to tell you. The cook and I want to go to Utrecht, he's been left an inn. We'd be sure of our dinner: nice, hm? And you'd have a bed, what do you think of *that?* This is a dog's life, on the road, you might be killed any time, even now you're covered with lice. . . . I think we'll decide to go, Catherine.

COOK Anna, I must have a word with you alone.

MOTHER COURAGE Go back inside, Catherine.

(CATHERINE *does so*)

COOK I'm interrupting because there's a misunderstanding, Anna. I thought I wouldn't have to say it right out, but I see I must. If you're bringing *her,* it's all off.

(CATHERINE *has her head out of the back of the wagon and is listening*)

MOTHER COURAGE You mean I leave Catherine behind?

COOK What do you think? There's no room in the inn, it isn't one of those places with three counters. If the two of us stand on our hindlegs we can earn a living, but three's too many. Let Catherine keep your wagon.

MOTHER COURAGE I was thinking she might find a husband in Utrecht.

COOK Don't make me laugh. With that scar? And old as she is? And dumb?

MOTHER COURAGE Not so loud!

COOK Loud or soft, what is, is. That's another reason I can't have her in the inn, the customers wouldn't like it.

MOTHER COURAGE Not so loud, I said!

COOK There's a light in the parsonage, we can sing now!

(*They go over toward the wall*)

MOTHER COURAGE How could she pull the wagon by herself? The war frightens her. She has terrible dreams. I hear her groan at night, especially after battles. What she sees in her dreams I don't know. The other day I found a hedgehog with her that we'd run over.

COOK The inn's too small.

(*Calling*)

Worthy Sir, menials, and all within! We now present the song of Solomon, Julius Caesar, and other great souls who came to no good, so you can see we're law-abiding folk too, and have a hard time getting by, especially in winter.

(*He sings:* THE SONG OF THE GREAT SOULS OF THIS EARTH)

You've heard of wise old Solomon
    You know his history.
He thought so little of this earth
He cursed the hour of his birth
    Declaring: all is vanity.
How very wise was Solomon!
    But ere night came and day did go
This fact was clear to everyone:
    It was his wisdom that had brought him low.
*Better for you if you have none.*

For the virtues are dangerous in this world, as our fine song tells. You're better off without, you have a nice life, breakfast included—a good hot soup maybe. . . . I'm an example of a man who's not had any, and I'd like some, I'm a soldier, but what good did my bravery do me in all those battles? None at all. I might just as well have wet my pants like a coward and stayed home. For why?

And Julius Caesar, who was brave,
    You saw what came of him.
He sat like God on an altar-piece
    And yet they tore him limb from limb
While his prestige did still increase!
"Et tu, Brute, I am undone!"
    And ere night came and day did go
This fact was clear to everyone:
    It was his bravery that brought him low
*Better for you if you have none.*

(*Under his breath*)

They don't even look out.

(*Aloud*)

Worthy Sir, menials, and all within! You should say, no, courage isn't the thing to fill a man's belly, try honesty, that should be worth a dinner, at any rate it must have *some* effect. Let's see.

You all know honest Socrates
    Who always spoke the truth.
They owed him thanks for that, you'd think,
Yet they put hemlock in his drink
    And swore that he was bad for youth.
How honest was the people's son!
    But ere night came and day did go
This fact was clear to everyone:
    It was his honesty that brought him low.
*Better for you if you have none.*

Yes, we're told to be unselfish and share what we have but what if we have nothing? And those who do share it don't have an easy time either, for what's left when you're through sharing? Unselfishness is a very rare virtue—it doesn't pay.

Unselfish Martin could not bear
His fellow creature's woes.
He met a beggar in the snows
And gave him half his cloak to wear:
So both of them fell down and froze.
What an unselfish paragon!
But ere night came and day did go
This fact was clear to everyone:
It was unselfishness that brought him low.
*Better for you if you have none.*

That's how it is with us. We're law-abiding folk, we keep to ourselves, don't steal, don't kill, don't burn the place down. And in this way we sink lower and lower and the song proves true and there's no soup going. And if we were different, if we were thieves and killers, maybe we could eat our fill! For virtues bring no reward, only vices. Such is the world, need it be so?

God's Ten Commandments we have kept
And acted as we should.
It has not done us any good.
O you who sit beside a fire
Please help us now: our need is dire!
Strict godliness we've always shown
But ere night came and day did go
This fact was clear to every one:
It was our godliness that brought us low.
*Better for you if you have none.*

VOICE (*From above*) You there! Come up! There's some soup here for you!

MOTHER COURAGE Lamp, I couldn't swallow a thing. Was that your last word?

COOK Yes, Anna. Think it over.

MOTHER COURAGE There's nothing to think over.

COOK You're going to be silly, but what can I do? I'm not inhuman, it's just that the inn's a small one. And now we must go up, or it'll be no soap here too, and we've been singing in the cold for nothing.

MOTHER COURAGE I'll get Catherine.

COOK Better stick something in your pocket for her. If there are three of us, they won't like it.
(*Exeunt*)
(CATHERINE *clambers out of the wagon with a bundle. She makes sure they're both gone. Then, on a wagon wheel, she lays out a skirt of her mother's and a pair of the* COOK's *pants side by side and easy to see. She has just finished, and has picked her bundle up, when* MOTHER COURAGE *returns*)

MOTHER COURAGE (*With a plate of soup*) Catherine! Stay where you are, Catherine! Where do you think you're going with that bundle?
(*She examines the bundle*)
She's packed her things. Were you listening? I told him there was nothing doing, he can *have* Utrecht and his lousy inn, what would *we* want with a lousy inn?
(*She sees the skirt and pants*)
Oh, you're a stupid girl, Catherine, what if I'd seen that and you gone?
(*She takes hold of Catherine, who's trying to leave*)
And don't think I've sent him packing on your account. It was the wagon. You can't part us, I'm too used to it, *you* didn't come into it, it was the wagon. Now we're leaving, and we'll put the cook's things here where he'll find 'em, the stupid man.
(*She clambers up and throws a couple of things down to go with the pants*)
There! He's fired! The last man I'll take into *this* business! Now let's you and me be going. Get into harness. This winter'll pass—like all the others.
(*They harness themselves to the wagon, turn it around, and start out. A gust of wind. Enter the* COOK, *still chewing. He sees his things*)

## Scene Ten

*On the highway.* MOTHER COURAGE *and* CATHERINE *are pulling the wagon. They come to a prosperous farmhouse. Someone inside is singing* THE SONG OF SHELTER.

In March a tree we planted
To make the garden gay.
In June we were enchanted:
A lovely rose was blooming
The balmy air perfuming!
Blest of the gods are they
Who have a garden gay!
In June we were enchanted.

When snow falls helter-skelter
And loudly blows the storm
Our farmhouse gives us shelter.
The winter's in a hurry
But we've no cause to worry.
Cosy are we and warm
Though loudly blows the storm
Our farmhouse gives us shelter.

(MOTHER COURAGE *and* CATHERINE *have stopped to listen. Then they start out again*)

## Scene Eleven

JANUARY, 1636. CATHOLIC TROOPS THREATEN THE PROTESTANT TOWN OF HALLE. THE STONES BEGIN TO

TALK. MOTHER COURAGE LOSES HER DAUGHTER AND JOURNEYS ONWARD ALONE. THE WAR IS NOT YET NEAR ITS END.

*The wagon, very far gone now, stands near a farmhouse with a straw roof. It is night. Out of the wood come a* LIEUTENANT *and* THREE SOLDIERS *in full armor.*

LIEUTENANT And there mustn't be a sound. If anyone yells, cut him down.

FIRST SOLDIER But we'll have to knock—if we want a guide.

LIEUTENANT Knocking's a natural noise, it's all right, could be a cow hitting the wall of the cowshed.

(*The* SOLDIERS *knock at the farmhouse door. An old peasant woman opens. A hand is clapped over her mouth. Two soldiers enter*)

MAN'S VOICE What is it?

(*The* SOLDIERS *bring out an old peasant and his son*)

LIEUTENANT (*Pointing to the wagon on which* CATHERINE *has appeared*)

There's one.

(*A soldier pulls her out*)

Is this everybody that lives here?

PEASANTS (*Alternating*) That's our son. And that's a girl that can't talk. Her mother's in town buying up stocks because the shopkeepers are running away and selling cheap. They're canteen people.

LIEUTENANT I'm warning you. Keep quiet. One sound and you'll have a sword in your ribs. And I need someone to show us the path to the town.

(*Points to the* YOUNG PEASANT)

You! Come here!

YOUNG PEASANT I don't know any path!

SECOND SOLDIER (*Grinning*) He don't know any path!

YOUNG PEASANT I don't help Catholics.

LIEUTENANT (*To* SECOND SOLDIER) Show him your sword.

YOUNG PEASANT (*Forced to his knees, a sword at his throat*) I'd rather die!

SECOND SOLDIER (*Again mimicking*) He'd rather die!

FIRST SOLDIER I know how to change his mind.

(*Walks over to the cowshed*)

Two cows and a bull. Listen, you. If you aren't going to be reasonable, I'll saber your cattle.

YOUNG PEASANT Not the cattle!

PEASANT WOMAN (*Weeping*) Spare the cattle, Captain, or we'll starve!

LIEUTENANT If he must be pigheaded!

FIRST SOLDIER I think I'll start with the bull.

YOUNG PEASANT (*To the old one*) Do I have to?

(*The* OLDER ONE *nods*)

I'll do it.

PEASANT WOMAN Thank you, thank you, Captain, for sparing us, for ever and ever, Amen.

(*The old man stops her going on thanking him*)

FIRST SOLDIER I knew the bull came first all right!

(*Led by the* YOUNG PEASANT, *the* LIEUTENANT *and the* SOLDIERS *go on their way*)

OLD PEASANT I wish we knew what it was. Nothing good, I guess.

PEASANT WOMAN Maybe they're just scouts. What are you doing?

OLD PEASANT (*Setting a ladder against the roof and climbing up*) I'm seeing if they're alone.

(*On the roof*)

Things are moving—all over. I can see armor. And a cannon. There must be more than a regiment. God have mercy on the town and all within!

PEASANT WOMAN Are there lights in the town?

OLD PEASANT No, they're all asleep.

(*He climbs down*)

There'll be an attack, and they'll all be slaughtered in their beds.

PEASANT WOMAN The watchman'll give warning.

OLD PEASANT They must have killed the watchman in the tower on the hill or he'd have sounded his horn before this.

PEASANT WOMAN If there were more of us . . .

OLD PEASANT But being that we're alone with that cripple . . .

PEASANT WOMAN There's nothing we can do, is there?

OLD PEASANT Nothing.

PEASANT WOMAN We can't get down there. In the dark.

OLD PEASANT The whole hillside's swarming with 'em.

PEASANT WOMAN We could give a sign?

OLD PEASANT And be cut down for it?

PEASANT WOMAN No, there's nothing we can do.

(*To* CATHERINE)

Pray, poor thing, pray! There's nothing we can do to stop this bloodshed, so even if you can't talk, at least pray! He hears, if no one else does. I'll help you.

(ALL *kneel,* CATHERINE *behind*)

Our Father, which art in Heaven, hear our prayer, let not the town perish with all that lie therein asleep and fearing nothing. Wake them, that they rise and go to the walls and see the foe that comes with fire and sword in the night down the hill and across the fields. God protect our mother and make the watchman not sleep but wake ere it's too late. And save our son-in-law too, O God, he's there with his four children, let them not perish, they're innocent, they know nothing, one of them's not two years old, the eldest is seven.

(CATHERINE *rises, troubled*)

Heavenly Father, hear us, only Thou canst help us or we die, for we are weak and have no sword nor nothing; we cannot trust our own strength but only Thine, O Lord; we are in Thy hands, our cattle, our farm, and the town too, we're all in Thy hands, and the foe is nigh unto the walls with all his power.

(CATHERINE *unperceived, has crept off to the wagon, has taken something out of it, put it under her skirt, and has climbed up the ladder to the roof*)

Be mindful of the children in danger, especially the little ones, be mindful of the old folk who cannot move, and of all Christian souls, O Lord.

OLD PEASANT And forgive us our trespasses as we forgive them that trespass against us. Amen.

(*Sitting on the roof,* CATHERINE *takes a drum from under her skirt, and starts to beat it*)

PEASANT WOMAN Heavens, what's she doing?

OLD PEASANT She's out of her mind!

PEASANT WOMAN Bring her down, quick!

(*The* OLD PEASANT *runs to the ladder but* CATHERINE *pulls it up on the roof*)

She'll get us in trouble.

OLD PEASANT Stop it this minute, you silly cripple!

PEASANT WOMAN The soldiers'll come!

OLD PEASANT (*Looking for stones*) I'll stone you!

PEASANT WOMAN Have you no pity, don't you have a heart? We have relations there too, four grandchildren, but there's nothing we can do. If they find us now, it's the end, they'll stab us to death!

(CATHERINE *is staring into the far distance, toward the town. She goes on drumming*)

PEASANT WOMAN (*To the* PEASANT) I told you not to let that riffraff in your farm. What do *they* care if we lose our cattle?

LIEUTENANT (*Running back with* SOLDIERS *and* YOUNG PEASANT) I'll cut you all to bits!

PEASANT WOMAN We're innocent, sir, there's nothing we can do. She did it, a stranger!

LIEUTENANT Where's the ladder?

OLD PEASANT On the roof.

LIEUTENANT (*Calling*) Throw down the drum. I order you!

(*To* PEASANTS)

You're all in this, but you won't live to tell the tale.

OLD PEASANT They've been cutting down fir trees around here. If we bring a tall enough trunk we can knock her off the roof. . . .

FIRST SOLDIER (*To the* LIEUTENANT) I beg leave to make a suggestion.

(*He whispers something to the* LIEUTENANT, *who nods. To* CATHERINE)

Listen, you! We have an idea—for your own good. Come down and go with us to the town. Show us your mother and we'll spare her.

(CATHERINE *replies with more drumming*)

LIEUTENANT (*Pushing him away*) She doesn't trust you, no wonder with your face.

(*He calls up to* CATHERINE)

Hey, you! Suppose I give you my word? I'm an officer, my word's my bond!

(CATHERINE *again replies with drumming—harder this time*)

Nothing is sacred to her.

FIRST SOLDIER This can't go on, they'll sure as hell hear it in the town.

LIEUTENANT We must make another noise with something. Louder than that drum. What can we make a noise with?

FIRST SOLDIER But we mustn't make a noise!

LIEUTENANT A harmless noise, fool, a peacetime noise!

OLD PEASANT I could start chopping wood.

LIEUTENANT That's it!

(*The* PEASANT *brings his ax and chops away*)

Chop! Chop harder! Chop for your life! It's not enough.

(*To* FIRST SOLDIER)

You chop too!

OLD PEASANT I've only one ax.

LIEUTENANT We must set fire to the farm. Smoke her out.

OLD PEASANT That's no good, Captain, when they see fire from the town, they'll know everything.

(CATHERINE *is laughing now and drumming harder than ever*)

LIEUTENANT She's laughing at us, that's too much, I'll have her guts if it's the last thing I do. Bring a musket!

(*Two* SOLDIERS *off*)

PEASANT WOMAN I have it, Captain. That's their wagon over there, Captain. If we smash that, she'll stop. It's all they have, Captain.

LIEUTENANT (*To the* YOUNG PEASANT) Smash it!

(*Calling*)

If you don't stop that noise, we'll smash up your wagon!

(*The* YOUNG PEASANT *deals the wagon a couple of feeble blows with a board*)

PEASANT WOMAN (*To* CATHERINE) Stop, you little beast!

(CATHERINE *stares at the wagon and pauses. Noises of distress come out of her. She goes on drumming*)

LIEUTENANT Where are those sonsofbitches with that gun?

FIRST SOLDIER They can't have heard anything in the town or we'd hear their cannon.

LIEUTENANT (*Calling*) They don't hear you. And now we're going to shoot you. I'll give you one more chance: throw down that drum!

YOUNG PEASANT (*Dropping the board, screaming to* CATHERINE) Don't stop now! Go on, go on, go on . . .

(*The* SOLDIER *knocks him down and stabs him.* CATHERINE *starts crying but goes on drumming*)

PEASANT WOMAN Not in the back, you're killing him!

(*The* SOLDIERS *arrive with the musket*)

LIEUTENANT Set it up!

(*Calling while the musket is set up on forks*)

Once for all: stop that drumming!

(*Still crying,* CATHERINE *is drumming as hard as she can*)

Fire!

(*The* SOLDIERS *fire.* CATHERINE *is hit. She gives the drum another feeble beat or two, then collapses*)

LIEUTENANT That's an end to the noise.

(*But the last beats of the drum are lost in the din of cannon from the town. Mingled with the thunder of cannon, alarm-bells are heard in the distance*)

FIRST SOLDIER She made it.

## Scene Twelve

*Toward morning. The drums and pipes of troops on the march, receding. In front of the wagon* MOTHER COURAGE *sits by* CATHERINE'S *body. The peasants of the last scene are standing near.*

PEASANTS (*One sentence apiece*) You must leave. There's only one regiment to go. You can never get away by yourself.

MOTHER COURAGE Maybe she's asleep.

(*She sings*)

Lullay, lullay, what's that in the hay?
The neighbor's kids cry but mine are gay.
The neighbor's kids are dressed in dirt:
Your silks were cut from an angel's skirt.
They are all starving: you have a cake;
If it's too stale, you need but speak.
Lullay, lullay, what's rustling there?
One lad fell in Poland. The other is where?

You shouldn't have told her about the children.

PEASANTS If you hadn't gone off to the town to get your cut, maybe it wouldn't have happened.

MOTHER COURAGE I'm glad she can sleep.

PEASANTS (*One sentence apiece*) She's not asleep, it's time you realized. She's through. You must get away. There are wolves in these parts. And the bandits are worse.

MOTHER COURAGE (*Standing up*) That's right.

PEASANTS Have you no one now?

MOTHER COURAGE Yes. My son Eilif.

PEASANTS Find him then. Leave *her* to us. We'll give her a proper burial. You needn't worry.

MOTHER COURAGE Here's a little money for the expenses.

(*Harnessing herself to the wagon*)

I hope I can pull the wagon by myself. Yes, I'll manage, there's not much in it now.

(*Another regiment passes with pipe and drum*)

MOTHER COURAGE Hey! Take me with you!!

(*She starts pulling the wagon. Soldiers are heard singing*)

Dangers, surprises, devastations—
The war takes hold and will not quit.
But though it last three generations
We shall get nothing out of it.
Starvation, filth, and cold enslave us.
The army robs us of our pay.
Only a miracle can save us
And miracles have had their day.
Christians, awake! The winter's gone!
The snows depart. The dead sleep on.
And though you may not long survive
Get out of bed and look alive!

# THE GOOD WOMAN OF SETZUAN

BRECHT never succeeded in making himself a wholly acceptable adherent of the communist cause, but he made a conscientious and sustained effort to fuse Marxist ideology and theatrical art. In 1928 and 1929, he attended lectures on dialectical materialism at the Marxist Workers' Institute in Berlin, and gave expression to the problems of individual action and collective discipline in a number of short plays called *Lehrstücke* or teaching pieces, dramatizing representative situations as case studies for judgment by the author and actors, as well as by the audience. This highly abstract and formalized drama had its origins in the student opera, improvised in schools for the instruction of the performers, and in the Japanese Noh drama which Brecht read in the translations of Arthur Waley. The austerity and detachment of Oriental acting appealed to Brecht and supported his didacticism. He particularly admired the ability of Chinese actors to move outside of their parts and, at the same time, to reveal their awareness of the presence of the audience.

*Der gute Mensch von Sezuan* (*The Good Woman of Setzuan*) is literally translated as the good *person* of Setzuan, for the principal figure is both a man and a woman. In a prefatory note, Brecht states that the play was begun in Denmark in 1938 and completed in Sweden two years later. He calls it a parable piece, and adds that the province of Setzuan stands for any place where some men are exploited by others. The stage direction describing the capital of the province as "half Europeanized" reminds us of the broad application of the play to contemporary life. Brecht makes virtually no use of a specific scene or décor; the place could be anywhere in Europe.

Brecht's characters are flat; puppet-like, they serve as representatives of their class, yet they move with speed and spontaneity. The pattern of the drama is intricate. Scenes are blended with interludes in a structure of cumulative action, but each episode is a complete unit in itself. Brecht's morality play preaches indirectly, through question and illustration: Why don't the gods sustain good men? What happens to the virtuous in the world in which we live? The impotent and naïve gods are only a device; clearly, they inhabit another realm from that of Shen Te and her cousin. It is characteristic of Brecht's art that he does not spell out a solution; the open, unresolved conclusion is part of the deliberate appeal to the spectators: "find out the end yourselves!" Repeatedly, Brecht stated that his plays are based on the fundamental assumption that the world is changeable. The direction of change is indicated in the action, yet nowhere does the playwright mark out the precise course this change should follow or the specific consequences that should result. The critique of the existing order is negative. It is also hilarious. It is not likely that *The Good Woman of Setzuan* will make Marxists of the spectators, but its rapid antitheses, sardonic wit, and insight into human nature mark it as one of the great plays of our time.

Brecht returned to a Chinese model in his last major play, *The Caucasian Chalk Circle* (1945). A play within a play, it begins with a story-teller's description of the old legend of the circle used to determine the true parentage of a disputed child. The judge, Azdak, is a drunken and lecherous rogue who deserves hanging, but is chosen by victorious rebellious soldiers as the local magistrate: "The judge was always a rascal! Now the rascal shall be a judge." Azdak performs his office with uncommon sagacity; in a tenure rivaling the governorship of Sancho Panza, he sets forth principles for the just award of possession of disputed children or property, and saves his own skin into the bargain. A thoroughly likable scamp, Azdak is one of Brecht's most striking and most attractive comic characters. The lightness and simplicity of the action, the loose and seemingly random construction, the contrasting use of masks, the spirited interplay of song and choral narrative, all stamp the play as one of Brecht's finest accomplishments.

From 1949 to the end of his life Brecht lived in East Berlin but wrote no drama of intrinsic importance. He cleverly obtained Austrian citizenship, which enabled him to travel freely, and a West German publisher, which placed him somewhat beyond the reach of communist censorship. He conscientiously tried to serve his masters in his own way; when he received a Stalin Peace Prize in 1955, he promptly deposited the money in a Swiss bank. Had he maintained his health, he might have embarrassed his communist benefactors even more. Now that he is dead, Brecht receives vociferous acclaim from Marxist propagandists for reasons that have nothing to do with his art. We must make a sharp distinction between the use of Brecht as a communist weapon and the legacy of Brecht in the modern theatre. His dedication to his craft and his rare imaginative genius proclaim him unmistakably one of the great playwrights of our time.

# THE GOOD WOMAN OF SETZUAN

English Version by Eric Bentley*

Lyrics by Eric Bentley

## A Note on the Music for the Play

The Bentley lyrics were written for a score that had been composed to fit the German words. It is by Paul Dessau. Later Stefan Wolpe made another score specially for the Bentley words.

There are no "numbers" in the musical comedy sense, but the following songs are items in themselves and not just part of the dialogue:

1. The Song of the Smoke (Scene One).
2. The Song of the Water Seller in the Rain (Scene Three).
3. The Song of Defenselessness (Scene Four (a)).
4. The Song of St. Nevercome's Day (Scene Six).
5. The Song of the Eighth Elephant (Scene Eight).

Almost in the same category is the little song of the gods in Scene One (a), the musical theme of which, in the Dessau score, is repeated later. Most of Shen Te's bits of verse, in the score, are spoken (sometimes naturally, sometimes in *sprechstimme*) to musical accompaniment, but there are notes for In Our Country (Scene Three) and For No Reason a Plum (Scene Seven). The elaborate pantomime in which this last song occurs has instrumental music, not behind the lines, but between them: the monologue being, therefore, an alternation of music and words. The Dessau music is scored for six players: prepared piano, muted trumpet, clarinet, flute, percussion, guitar. The Stefan Wolpe music is for piano and voice only. E.B.

### CHARACTERS

WANG, *a water seller*
THREE GODS
SHEN TE, *a prostitute, later a shopkeeper*
MRS. SHIN, *former owner of Shen Te's shop*
A FAMILY OF EIGHT (HUSBAND, WIFE, BROTHER, SISTER-IN-LAW, GRANDFATHER, NEPHEW, NIECE, BOY)
AN UNEMPLOYED MAN
A CARPENTER
MRS. MI TZU, *Shen Te's landlady*
YANG SUN, *an unemployed pilot, later a factory manager*
AN OLD WHORE
A POLICEMAN
AN OLD MAN
AN OLD WOMAN, *his wife*
A PRIEST
MR. SHU FU, *a barber*
MRS. YANG, *mother of Yang Sun*
GENTLEMEN, VOICES, CHILDREN, *etc.*

* This translation was made in 1946-47 from a manuscript supplied by the author.

## Prologue

*A street. It is evening.* WANG, *the water seller, introduces himself to the audience.*

WANG I sell water here in the city of Setzuan.[1] It's a difficult business. When water is scarce, I have to go a long way to find any. And when it is plentiful, I am without income. But in our province there is nothing unusual about poverty. It is generally said that only the gods can still help us. From a cattle buyer who moves around a good deal, I learn to my unutterable joy that some of the highest gods are on their way to our province and may be expected here in Setzuan too. Heaven is said to be very disturbed by all the complaints that have been going up. For three days I have been waiting here at the entrance of the town, especially toward evening, so that I

[1] Later changed by Brecht to the Province of Szechwan. This, of course, makes it an actual place. (Tr. note)

may be the first to greet them. Later, I'd hardly have the opportunity to do so. The gods will be surrounded by important people. They'll be in constant demand. If only I recognize them! After all they needn't come together. Perhaps they'll come separately so as not to be so conspicuous. It can't be those people over there, they are coming from work. (*He looks at passing workers*) Their shoulders are crushed from all the carrying they do. That fellow there can't possibly be a god either, he has ink on his fingers. At best he's an office worker at a cement factory. Even those gentlemen there (*Two gentlemen pass*) don't seem like gods to me. They look like people who're always beating somebody, which gods don't need to do. But look at those three! They're quite a different matter. They're well fed, show no sign of having any occupation, and have dust on their shoes, which means they come from far away. They must be gods. Dispose of me, illustrious ones!

(*He throws himself down before them*)

THE FIRST GOD (*Pleased*) Have we been expected here?

WANG (*Giving them a drink*) For a long time. But I was the only one who *knew* you were coming.

THE FIRST GOD Well, we need somewhere to stay the night. Do you know a place?

WANG *A* place? Countless places! The whole town is at your service, illustrious ones! What sort of a place do you wish?

(*The* GODS *look meaningfully at each other*)

THE FIRST GOD Take the nearest house, my son! Try the very nearest house first.

WANG I'm a little afraid of making enemies of other mighty men if I favor one of them in particular. Few people can help us, you see, but almost everyone can hurt us.

THE FIRST GOD Well then, we order you: take the nearest house!

WANG That is Mr. Fo over there! Wait just one moment!

(*He runs to a house and knocks at the door. It is opened, but one can see that he is rejected. He returns, hesitantly*)

WANG That's annoying. Mr. Fo is not at home just now, and his servants don't dare do anything without orders from him, he's so very strict. He will certainly have a fit when he learns who they turned away, won't he?

THE GODS (*Smiling*) He certainly will.

WANG Well then, another moment! The house next door belongs to the widow Su. She'll be beside herself with joy.

(*He runs to the house but apparently is rejected there too*)

WANG I'll have to inquire over there. She says she has only one little tiny room and it isn't prepared. I can well understand she's ashamed because some corners of the house aren't so clean. That's what women are like, it's a disgrace. I'll go at once to Mr. Tscheng.

THE SECOND GOD The little room will be enough. Tell her we're coming.

WANG Even if it isn't clean? It may be swarming with spiders!

THE SECOND GOD That doesn't matter. Where there are spiders, there aren't so many flies.

THE THIRD GOD Never mind. (*Friendly, to* WANG) Go to Mr. Tscheng or some other place, my son. Spiders, after all, rather disgust me.

(WANG *knocks again somewhere and is admitted*)

VOICE FROM THE HOUSE Spare us your gods! We have other troubles!

WANG (*Back with the* GODS) Mr. Tscheng is quite upset. He has the whole house full of relations and doesn't dare show his face, illustrious ones! Between ourselves I believe there are bad people among them whom he doesn't want you to see. He is too afraid of your judgment, that's the thing.

THE THIRD GOD Are we so terrible, then?

WANG Only with bad people, isn't that so? It's well known, isn't it, that the province Kwan has been afflicted with floods for decades?

THE SECOND GOD Really? Why?

WANG Well, because there's no religion there!

THE SECOND GOD Nonsense. It's because they neglected the dam!

THE FIRST GOD Sst! (*To* WANG) Are you still hoping, my son?

WANG How can you ask such a thing? I only need to go one house farther along. From there on, there'll be plenty to choose from. Everyone's just itching to put you up. Accidental circumstances, you understand. I go!

(*He begins to leave and then, undecided, remains standing in the street*)

THE SECOND GOD What did I say?

THE THIRD GOD Of course it may really be "accidental circumstances."

THE SECOND GOD In Schun, in Kwan, and in Setzuan —"accidental circumstances" every time? There aren't any religious people left, that's the naked truth, and you don't want to face it. Our mission has failed, why not admit it?

THE FIRST GOD We might run across some good people at any moment. We mustn't expect things to be too cozy.

THE THIRD GOD The resolution said: "The world can remain as it is if enough people are found living lives worthy of human beings." Good people, in other words. The water seller himself is such a person unless I'm very much mistaken. (*He goes up to* WANG *who is still standing undecided*)

THE SECOND GOD He *is* very much mistaken. When this water man gave us a drink from his measuring cup, I noticed something. Here's the cup. (*He shows it to the* FIRST GOD)

THE FIRST GOD It has two bottoms.

THE SECOND GOD A swindler!

THE FIRST GOD All right, count *him* out. But what does it matter if *one* person is rotten? We'll find enough yet who'll meet our conditions. We have to find *one!* For two thousand years, they've been shouting: "The world can't go on as it is, no one on earth can *be* good and *stay* good." And now at last we've got to name the people who can keep our commandments.

THE THIRD GOD (*To* WANG) Is it so difficult to find a place?

WANG Not for you! What are you thinking of? It's all my fault a place wasn't found right away. I'm not going about it properly.

THE THIRD GOD Surely, that's not so.

(*He goes back*)

WANG They're noticing already. (*He accosts a gentleman*) Pardon me, worthy sir, for accosting you, but three of the highest gods, whose imminent arrival has been discussed for years by all Setzuan, have now actually appeared. They need a place to sleep. Do not pass by! See for yourself. One look will suffice. Don't wait, for heaven's sake. It's a chance in a lifetime! Be the first to ask the gods under your roof before they're snapped up by someone else. They will accept.

(*The gentleman has passed by*)

WANG (*Turning to another*) My dear sir, you've heard what's going on. Do you, perhaps, have spare rooms? They don't have to be palatial. It's the good intention that counts.

THE MAN How should I know what kind of gods you've got there? A fellow that lets people into his house likes to know what he's getting.

(*He goes into a tobacco store.* WANG *runs back to the* THREE GODS)

WANG I've found a gentleman who'll certainly take you.

(*He sees his cup on the ground, looks toward the* GODS *in confusion, takes it, and runs back again*)

THE FIRST GOD That doesn't sound encouraging.

WANG (*As the* MAN *is coming out of the store again*) Well, what about the rooms for the night?

THE MAN How do you know I don't live at an inn?

THE FIRST GOD He's getting nowhere. We can cross Setzuan off the list too.

WANG They're three of the very greatest gods! Really! Their statues in the temples are very well done. If you go quickly and invite them, they might accept!

THE MAN (*Laughing*) You must be trying to find a place for a nice bunch of crooks. (*Exit*)

WANG (*Abusing him*) You squinting scoundrel! Have you no religion? You'll all roast in boiling oil for your indifference! The gods spit on you! But you'll regret it! You'll have to pay. The whole pack of you, fourth cousins included. You've brought disgrace to all Setzuan. (*Pause*) And now only Shen Te the prostitute is left. She can't say no.

(*He calls "Shen Te!" Above,* SHEN TE *looks out of the window*)

WANG They're here. I can't find any place to put them. Can't you take them in for the night?

SHEN TE I don't think so, Wang. I'm expecting a gentleman. How is it you can't find any other place?

WANG I can't tell you now. Setzuan is one big dung heap.

SHEN TE When he comes I'd have to hide. Then maybe he'd go away again. He's expecting to take me out.

WANG In the meantime, couldn't we come up?

SHEN TE Well, you don't have to shout. Can we be open with them?

WANG No! They mustn't find out about your profession. We'd better wait downstairs. You won't go out with the gentleman then?

SHEN TE I'm not so well off. And if I don't pay my rent by tomorrow morning, I'll be thrown out.

WANG This is no time for calculations.

SHEN TE I'm not so sure. Stomachs rumble even on the emperor's birthday. But all right, I'll take them in. (*She can be seen putting out the light*)

THE FIRST GOD I think it's hopeless.

(*They step up to* WANG)

WANG (*Starting as he sees them standing behind him*) A place has been found. (*He wipes the sweat off*)

THE GODS It has? Let's see it then.

WANG There's no hurry. Take your time. The room still has to be fixed.

THE THIRD GOD Well then, we'll sit down here and wait.

WANG I'm afraid there's too much traffic right here. Perhaps we should go over there?

THE SECOND GOD We like to look at people. That's what we're here for.

WANG But . . . there's a draft.

THE SECOND GOD Oh, we're pretty tough.

WANG Perhaps you'd like me to show you Setzuan by night? We might take a little walk.

THE THIRD GOD We've done quite a bit of walking today already. (*Smiling*) But if you want to get us away from here, you need only say so.

(*They go back*)

THE THIRD GOD Is this all right with you?

(*They sit down on a doorstep.* WANG *sits down on the ground at a little distance*)

WANG (*Taking a deep breath*) You're staying with a single girl. She's the best woman—the best human being—in Setzuan.

THE THIRD GOD That's nice.

WANG (*To the audience*) When I picked up the cup a little while ago, they looked at me so strangely. Did they notice something? I don't dare look them in the eyes any more.

THE THIRD GOD You're quite exhausted.

WANG A little. From running.

THE FIRST GOD Do people have a hard time of it here?

WANG *Good* people do.

THE FIRST GOD (*Seriously*) And you?

WANG I know what you mean. I'm not good. But I don't have an easy time either.

(*In the meantime a gentleman has turned up in front of* SHEN TE'S *house. He has whistled several times. Each time* WANG *starts*)

THE THIRD GOD (*Softly, to* WANG) I think he's gone now.

WANG (*Confused*) Yes.

(*He gets up and runs to the square, leaving his carrying pole behind. But in the meantime the *waiting man has left, and* SHEN TE *has stepped through the door and, softly calling* "Wang!," *has gone down the street.* WANG, *now softly calling* "Shen Te!," *gets no reply*)

WANG She's left me in the lurch. She's gone off to get her rent together and now I've no place for the illustrious ones. They're tired and still waiting. I can't go back again and say nothing doing. My own little place, a sewer pipe, is out of the question. Moreover, the gods wouldn't want to stay with a fellow when they've seen through his dishonest dealings. I won't go back. Not for anything in the world. But my carrying pole is lying there. What'll I do? I don't dare to get it. Since I didn't succeed in doing anything for the gods, whom I revere, I'll leave Setzuan and hide from their sight.

(*He rushes off.* SHEN TE *returns. She is looking for* WANG *on the other side and sees the* GODS)

SHEN TE Are you the illustrious ones? My name is Shen Te. It would please me very much if you'd be content with my simple room.

THE THIRD GOD Where has the water seller gone to?

SHEN TE I must have missed him.

THE FIRST GOD He probably thought you weren't coming and didn't dare return to us.

THE THIRD GOD (*Picking up the carrying pole*) We'll leave this at your house. He'll be needing it.

(*Led by* SHEN TE, *they go into the house. It grows dark, then light again. It is dawn. Again led by* SHEN TE, *who lights their way with a lamp, the* GODS *pass through the door. They are taking leave*)

THE FIRST GOD My dear Shen Te, we must thank you for your hospitality. We shall not forget that it was you who took us in. Return the carrying pole to the water seller and tell him that we want to thank him too for showing us a good human being.

SHEN TE I'm not good. I have to confess something: when Wang asked me to put you up I hesitated.

THE FIRST GOD Hesitating doesn't matter if only you win out. You must know that you did more than give us a place to sleep. Many—even some of us gods—have been doubting whether good people still exist. To decide that question is the main object of our journey. Now that we've found a good human being, we shall joyously continue on our way. Goodbye!

SHEN TE Stop, illustrious ones! I'm not at all sure that I'm good. I'd like to be good of course, but how am I to pay my rent? Well, I'll confess it to you: I sell myself in order to live, and even so I can't get along. There are many others who have to do the same. I'm ready to do anything; but who isn't? I'd be happy to honor my father and my mother and speak the truth. It would be nice not to covet my neighbor's house. It would be pleasant to attach myself to one man and be faithful to him. I too should like not to exploit anyone, not to rob the helpless. But how? How? Even when I break only a *few* of the commandments, I can hardly survive.

THE FIRST GOD All these, Shen Te, are but the doubts of a good woman.

THE THIRD GOD Farewell, Shen Te! And give my best regards to the water seller. He was a good friend to us.

THE SECOND GOD I fear he's none the better for it.

THE THIRD GOD Best of luck to you!

THE FIRST GOD Above all, be good, Shen Te! Farewell!

(*They turn to go. They are already waving*)

SHEN TE (*Worried*) But I'm not sure of myself, illustrious ones! How can I be good when everything is so expensive?

THE SECOND GOD We can't do anything about that. We mustn't meddle with economics!

THE THIRD GOD Stop! Just one moment! Might she not fare better if she were a little richer?

THE SECOND GOD We can't give her anything. We couldn't account for it up above.

THE FIRST GOD Why not?

(*They put their heads together and talk excitedly*)

THE FIRST GOD (*Embarrassed, to* SHEN TE) You say you can't pay your rent. We're not paupers and of course we'll pay for the room. Here! (*He gives her money*) But don't tell anyone we paid. Such an action could be misinterpreted.

THE SECOND GOD It certainly could.

THE FIRST GOD But it's allowable. We *can* pay for the room without misgiving. There's nothing against it in the resolution. Well, goodbye!

(*The* GODS *quickly go*)

## Scene One

(*A small tobacco store. The store is not as yet completely furnished and has not opened*)

SHEN TE (*To the audience*) It's now three days since the gods went away. They said they wanted to pay me for the night's lodging. And when I looked to see what they'd given me, I saw that it was more than a thousand silver dollars. With the money I bought myself a tobacco store. Yesterday I moved in here and I hope now to be able to do a lot of good. There, for instance, is Mrs. Shin, the former owner of the store. Yesterday she came to ask for rice for her children. Today I see her again coming across the square with her pot.

(*Enter* MRS. SHIN. *The two women bow to each other*)

SHEN TE Good morning, Mrs. Shin.

MRS. SHIN Good morning, Miss Shen Te. How do you like it in your new home?

SHEN TE Very much. How did your children spend the night?

MRS. SHIN Oh dear, in a strange house, if you can call

that shack a house! The youngest is coughing already.

SHEN TE That's bad.

MRS. SHIN You don't know what's bad. You're well off. But you'll learn quite a lot in this dump. What a slum this neighborhood is!

SHEN TE Didn't you tell me the workers from the cement factory come here at noon?

MRS. SHIN Yes, but otherwise there isn't a soul that buys here, not even the neighbors.

SHEN TE You didn't tell me that when you sold me the store.

MRS. SHIN Don't start blaming me now! First you rob me and my children of our home and then you call it a dump! And a slum! That's the limit! (*She cries*)

SHEN TE (*Quickly*) I'll get your rice right away.

MRS. SHIN I also wanted to ask you to lend me some money.

SHEN TE (*Pouring rice into* MRS. SHIN's *pot*) I can't. You know I haven't sold anything.

MRS. SHIN But I need it. What am I to live off? You took everything away from me and now you cut my throat! I'll leave my children on your doorstep, you cutthroat! (*She tears the pot out of* SHEN TE's *hands*)

SHEN TE Don't be angry! You'll spill the rice!

(*Enter an elderly couple and a shabbily dressed young man*)

THE WIFE Ah, my dear Shen Te, we've heard you're so well off now. You've become a businesswoman! Imagine, we're without a roof over our heads. Our tobacco store has gone to pieces. We were wondering whether we couldn't spend the night with you. You know my nephew? He's come too. He never leaves us.

THE NEPHEW (*Looking around*) A nice store!

MRS. SHIN What sort of people are *they?*

SHEN TE They put me up when I first came in from the country. (*To the audience*) When the little money I had was gone, they threw me out on the street. Perhaps they're afraid now that I'll say no.

They are poor.
They have no shelter
They have no friends
They need somebody
How could one say no?

(*Friendly, to the newcomers*) Welcome! I'll gladly give you shelter. Though I only have one very small room behind the store.

THE HUSBAND That'll be enough. Don't worry.

THE WIFE (*While she brings tea to* SHEN TE) We better settle down back here, so we won't be in your way. I suppose you've chosen a tobacco store in memory of your first home. We'll be able to give you some hints. That's another reason why we came.

MRS. SHIN (*Sneering*) I hope customers will come too!

THE WIFE I guess that's meant for us.

THE HUSBAND Psst! Here comes a customer.

(*A ragged man comes in*)

THE RAGGED MAN Excuse me. I am unemployed.

(MRS. SHIN *laughs*)

SHEN TE Can I help you?

THE UNEMPLOYED I hear you're opening up tomorrow. Things sometimes get damaged when you're unpacking. Don't you have a spare cigarette?

THE WIFE What nerve, begging for tobacco! He might at least ask for bread!

THE UNEMPLOYED Bread is expensive. A few puffs at a cigarette and I'll be a new man. I'm all in.

SHEN TE (*Giving him cigarettes*) That's important, to be a new man. I'll open the store with you as my first customer. You'll bring me luck.

(*The* UNEMPLOYED *quickly lights a cigarette, inhales, and goes off, coughing*)

THE WIFE My dear Shen Te, was that right?

MRS. SHIN If you open up like this, in three days there'll be no store left.

THE HUSBAND I bet he still had money in his pocket.

SHEN TE But he said he hadn't.

THE NEPHEW How do you know he wasn't lying?

SHEN TE (*Angrily*) How do I know he *was* lying?

THE WIFE (*Shaking her head*) She can't say no! You're too good, Shen Te. If you want to keep your store, you must learn to say no, now and then.

THE HUSBAND Why don't you say it's not yours? Say it belongs to a relative who insists on an exact settlement of accounts. Can't you do that?

MRS. SHIN That could be done if one wasn't always pretending to be a benefactress.

SHEN TE (*Laughing*) Scold, scold, scold! If you're not careful I'll give you notice and pour the rice back.

THE WIFE (*Horrified*) The rice is yours, too?

SHEN TE (*To the audience*)

They are bad.
They are nobody's friend.
They begrudge everyone his rice.
They need everything themselves.
Who could scold them?

(*Enter a little man*)

MRS. SHIN (*Seeing him and hurriedly starting to go*) I'll see you tomorrow. (*Exit*)

THE LITTLE MAN (*Calling after her*) Stop, Mrs. Shin! It's you I'm looking for.

THE WIFE Does she come regularly? Does she have any claim on you?

SHEN TE She has no claim, but she's hungry: that's more than a claim.

THE LITTLE MAN *She* knows why she's running. You're the new owner? Oh, you're filling up the shelves already. But they don't belong to you, see! Unless you pay for them. The rascals who were here before didn't pay for them. (*To the others*) I'm the carpenter, you see.

SHEN TE But I thought they belonged to the furnishings, which I paid for.

THE CARPENTER Fraud! It's all a fraud! You're working together with that Shin woman of course. I demand my hundred silver dollars as sure as my name's Lin To.

SHEN TE How am I to pay it? I have no more money!

THE CARPENTER Then I'll have you arrested. You'll pay at once or I'll have you arrested.

THE HUSBAND (*Prompting* SHEN TE) Cousin!

SHEN TE Can't it wait till next month?

THE CARPENTER (*Shouting*) No!

SHEN TE Don't be hard, Mr. Lin To. I can't settle all claims at once. (*To the audience*)

A little indulgence and strength is redoubled.
Look, the cart horse stops and sniffs the grass:
Connive at this and the horse will pull better.
A little patience in June and the tree is heavy with peaches in August.
How should we live together without patience?
A short postponement, and the farthest goals are reached.

(*To the* CARPENTER) Be patient just for a little while, Mr. Lin To!

THE CARPENTER And who's patient with me and my family? (*He moves a shelf from the wall as if he wanted to take it with him*) Pay up, or I take the shelves away!

THE WIFE My dear Shen Te, why don't you let your cousin settle this affair? (*To the* CARPENTER) Write down your claim and Miss Shen Te's cousin will pay.

THE CARPENTER Cousin! I know these cousins!

THE NEPHEW Don't laugh like that! I know him personally.

THE HUSBAND What a man! Sharp as a knife!

THE CARPENTER All right, he'll get my bill! (*He puts down a shelf, sits on it, and writes out his bill*)

THE WIFE (*To* SHEN TE) If you don't stop him, he'll tear the shirt off your body to get his measly shelves. Never recognize a claim, justified or not, or in two minutes you'll be swamped with claims, justified or not. Throw a piece of meat into a garbage can, and all the mangy dogs of the district will be at each other's throats in your back yard. What are our law courts for?

SHEN TE If his work doesn't support him, the law courts won't. He's done some work and doesn't want to go empty-handed. And he's got a family. It's too bad I can't pay him. What will the gods say?

THE HUSBAND You did your share when you took *us* in. That's more than enough.

(*Enter a limping man and a pregnant woman*)

THE LIMPING MAN (*To the couple*) Oh, here you are! You're nice relatives! Leaving us standing on the street corner.

THE WIFE (*Embarrassed, to* SHEN TE) That's my brother Wung and my sister-in-law. (*To the two of them*) Stop grumbling. Go and sit quietly in the corner and don't disturb our old friend, Miss Shen Te. You can stay here, she's got nothing against it. (*To* SHEN TE) I think we've got to take these two in. My sister-in-law is in her fifth month. Or don't you agree?

SHEN TE Oh, yes. Welcome!

THE WIFE (*To the two*) Say thank you. The cups are back there. (*To* SHEN TE) They just wouldn't have known *where* to go. A good thing you got the store!

SHEN TE (*Laughing, and bringing tea, she says to the audience*) Yes, a good thing I did!

(*Enter the* LANDLADY, MRS. MI TZU, *a blank in her hand*)

THE LANDLADY Miss Shen Te, I am the landlady, Mrs. Mi Tzu. I hope we'll get on well together. Here is the lease. (*While* SHEN TE *is reading through the lease*) The opening of a little store is a beautiful moment, isn't it, ladies and gentlemen? (*She looks around*) There're still a few small gaps on the shelves, but it'll be all right. You'll be able to bring me some references, won't you?

SHEN TE Is that necessary?

THE LANDLADY I've no idea who you are.

THE HUSBAND Perhaps we can vouch for Miss Shen Te? We've known her since she came to town and will go through fire for her at any time.

THE LANDLADY And who are you?

THE HUSBAND I am the tobacco dealer Ma Fu.

THE LANDLADY Where's your store?

THE HUSBAND At the moment I don't have a store. I've just sold it.

THE LANDLADY I see. (*To* SHEN TE) And don't you know anyone else who could give me some information about you?

THE WIFE (*Prompting*) Cousin! Cousin!

THE LANDLADY You've got to have somebody to speak for you if you're coming into my house. This is a respectable house, my dear. Without some assurance I can't even sign the lease with you.

SHEN TE (*Slowly, with downcast eyes*) I have a cousin.

THE LANDLADY Oh, you have a cousin. On the square? Then we can go over there right away. What does he do?

SHEN TE He isn't living here. He's in another town.

THE WIFE Didn't you say he was in Shung?

SHEN TE Mr. . . . Shui Ta. In Shung.

THE HUSBAND But I know him! A tall thin fellow?

THE NEPHEW (*To the* CARPENTER) You were negotiating with Miss Shen Te's cousin too! About the shelves!

THE CARPENTER (*Surly*) I'm just writing out a bill for him. Here it is! (*He hands it over*) Tomorrow morning I'll be back. (*Exit*)

THE NEPHEW (*Calling after him and glancing at the* LANDLADY) Don't worry, the cousin will pay!

THE LANDLADY (*Examining* SHEN TE *closely*) Well, I'll be very pleased to meet him too. Good evening, Miss. (*Exit*)

THE WIFE (*After a pause*) Now the cat's out of the bag. You can be sure she'll know everything about you tomorrow morning.

THE SISTER-IN-LAW (*Softly to the* NEPHEW) This thing won't last long!

(*Enter a boy leading an old man*)

THE BOY (*Calling over his shoulder*) Here they are.

THE WIFE Good evening, Grandfather. (*To* SHEN TE) The good old man! He must have worried about us. And the boy, hasn't he grown? He eats like ten men.

Well, who else did you bring, for heaven's sake?

THE HUSBAND (*Looking outside*) Only our niece.

THE SISTER-IN-LAW (*Softly to the* NEPHEW *while a young girl comes in*) The rats climb onto the sinking ship!

THE WIFE (*To* SHEN TE) A young relative from the country. I hope we aren't too many for you. We weren't quite as many when you were living with us, were we? Yes, we got more and more. The less we had, the more there were of us. And the more there were of us, the less we had. But now we'll lock up, or there won't be a moment's peace. (*She locks the door and they all sit down*) We mustn't disturb you in your business, that's the main thing. Or how can the fire be kept burning? We thought we might arrange matters something like this: during the day the young ones will go off and only grandfather, the sister-in-law, and maybe I myself will stay. The others will look in at the most once or twice during the day, all right? Light the lamp over there and make yourself at home.

THE NEPHEW (*Humorously*) If only the cousin doesn't pop up tonight all of a sudden. The strict Mr. Shui Ta!

(*The* SISTER-IN-LAW *laughs*)

THE BROTHER (*Reaching for a cigarette*) One cigarette won't matter much.

THE HUSBAND I'm sure it won't.

(*They all help themselves to cigarettes. The* BROTHER *hands round a jug of wine*)

THE NEPHEW The cousin will pay for it.

THE GRANDFATHER (*Seriously to* SHEN TE) Good evening!

(SHEN TE *is confused by the belated greeting and bows. In one hand she holds the* CARPENTER'S *bill, in the other the lease*)

THE WIFE Couldn't you sing something to entertain our hostess a little?

THE NEPHEW Grandfather will start!

(*They sing*)

*SONG OF THE SMOKE*

I used to think (before old age beset me)
That brains could fill the pantry of the poor.
But where did all my cerebration get me?
I'm just as hungry as I was before.
So what's the use?
See the smoke float free
Into ever colder coldness!
It's the same with me.

The straight and narrow path leads to disaster
And so the crooked path I tried to tread.
That got me to disaster even faster.
(They say we shall be happy when we're dead.)
So what's the use?
See the smoke float free
Into ever colder coldness!
It's the same with me.

You older people, full of expectation,
At any moment now you'll walk the plank!
The future's for the younger generation!
Yes, even if that future is a blank.
So what's the use?
See the smoke float free
Into ever colder coldness!
It's the same with me.

THE NEPHEW Where did you get the wine?

THE SISTER-IN-LAW He pawned the bag of tobacco.

THE HUSBAND What? That tobacco was the only thing left to us! We didn't even touch it to pay for our lodgings! You swine!

THE BROTHER Do you call me a swine because my wife is cold? And you had a drink yourself? Give me the jug this minute!

(*They fight. The shelves fall over*)

SHEN TE (*Imploring them*) Oh, spare the store! Don't destroy everything! It's a gift of the gods! Take what there is, but don't destroy it all!

THE WIFE (*Skeptically*) The store is smaller than I thought. Perhaps we shouldn't have mentioned it to Auntie and the others. If they come too, it'll be very crowded.

THE SISTER-IN-LAW Our hostess is cooling off already.

(*There are voices outside and a knocking on the door*)

SHOUTS FROM OUTSIDE Open up! It's us!

THE WIFE Is that you, Auntie? What are we going to do?

SHEN TE O hope! My beautiful store! I bought it yesterday and today it's done for.

The little lifeboat
Is swiftly sent down.
Too many people greedily
Reach for it as they drown.

SHOUTS FROM OUTSIDE Open up!

# Scene One (a)

(*Below a bridge. The water seller crouches by the river*)

WANG (*Looking around*) Everything's quiet. It's four days now that I've been hiding out. They can't find me, because I'm keeping my eyes open. I fled along their road on purpose. On the second day, they passed the bridge, I heard their steps above me. Now they must be a long way off, and I'm safe.

(*He lies back and falls asleep. Music. The slope becomes transparent and the* GODS *appear*)

WANG (*Raising his arm to his face as if about to be struck*) Don't say anything! I know it all! I found no one who wants to take you, not in a single house! Now you know! Now you can go on!

THE FIRST GOD But you did find someone. When you

were away, she came. She took us in for the night, she watched over our sleep, and when we left her in the morning she showed us the way with a lamp. You mentioned her to us as a good woman and she was good.

WANG So it was Shen Te who took you in?

THE THIRD GOD Of course.

WANG And I had so little faith, I ran away! Only because I thought: "She can't come. Because she's not well off, she can't come."

THE GODS

O weak one!
O well-disposed but weak man!
Where there is need, he thinks, there is no goodness!
Where there is danger, he thinks, there is no courage!
O weakness always to believe the worst!
O hasty judgment! Frivolous despair!

WANG I'm very ashamed, illustrious ones!

THE FIRST GOD And now, water seller, do us a favor and go back quickly to the city of Setzuan. Look up the good Shen Te there and give us a report on her. She's well off now. She's supposed to have got some money for a little store so she can follow the inclinations of her heart. Show an interest in her goodness. No one can be good for long when goodness is not in demand. We will continue our journey. We will search and find other people who resemble our good woman from Setzuan: the talk about good people being no longer able to live on our earth will stop. (*They disappear*)

## Scene Two

(*The tobacco store. People sleeping everywhere. The lamp is still burning. A knocking*)

THE WIFE (*Getting up, sleepily*) Shen Te! Someone's knocking! Where is she, anyway?

THE NEPHEW I guess she's getting breakfast. The cousin will pay for it!

(*The* WIFE *laughs and shuffles to the door. Enter a young man, followed by the* CARPENTER)

THE YOUNG MAN I'm the cousin.

THE WIFE (*Falling from the clouds*) What?!

THE YOUNG MAN My name is Shui Ta.

THE GUESTS (*Shaking each other awake*) Her cousin! But that was a joke, she doesn't *have* a cousin! Someone's here saying he's her cousin! I don't believe it, so early in the morning!

THE NEPHEW If you're our hostess's cousin, go and get us some breakfast quickly!

SHUI TA (*Putting out the light*) The first customers will soon be here. Please get dressed so that I can open my store.

THE HUSBAND *Your* store? I thought the store belonged to our friend Shen Te. (SHUI TA *shakes his head*) What, it isn't her store at all?

THE SISTER-IN-LAW Then she's cheated us! Where is she, anyway?

SHUI TA She's been delayed. She wants me to tell you that, now *I'm* here, she can no longer do anything for you.

THE WIFE (*Deeply affected*) And we thought she was good!

THE NEPHEW Don't believe him! Look for her!

THE HUSBAND That's what we'll do. (*He organizes the search*) You and you and you and you, look for her everywhere. Grandfather and us, we'll stay here to hold the fort. In the meantime the boy can get us something to eat. (*To the* BOY) You see the bakery over there on the corner? Sneak over and stuff your shirt full.

THE SISTER-IN-LAW Take a few of the little light cakes too!

THE HUSBAND But be careful, don't let the baker catch you! And don't run into the policeman!

(*The* BOY *nods and goes off. The others finish dressing*)

SHUI TA This store has been your refuge. Won't you give it a bad reputation if you steal from the bakery?

THE NEPHEW Don't pay any attention to him. We'll find her soon enough. She'll give him a piece of her mind.

(*The* NEPHEW, *the* BROTHER, *the* SISTER-IN-LAW, *and the* NIECE *go out*)

THE SISTER-IN-LAW (*As she leaves*) Leave us some of the breakfast!

SHUI TA (*Calmly*) You won't find her. My cousin regrets of course that she can't abide by the law of hospitality for an unlimited period. But unfortunately there are too many of you. This is a tobacco store and Miss Shen Te has to live off it.

THE HUSBAND Our Shen Te just couldn't say a thing like that.

SHUI TA Perhaps you're right. (*To the* CARPENTER) The unfortunate thing is that the need in this city is too great for a single person to manage. In that regard, nothing has changed, unfortunately, since someone eleven hundred years ago composed these lines:

The governor, asked what was needed
To help the freezing people of the town, made answer:
"A blanket ten thousand feet long
Which would simply cover all the suburbs."

(*He starts to clean up the store*)

THE CARPENTER I see you're trying to put your cousin's affairs in order. There's a little debt, recognized by witnesses, and it needs settling. For the shelves. One hundred silver dollars.

SHUI TA (*Taking the bill out of his pocket, not un-*

*friendly*) Don't you think one hundred silver dollars a little much?

THE CARPENTER No. And I can't make any deductions. I have a wife and children to support.

SHUI TA (*Severely*) How many children?

THE CARPENTER Four.

SHUI TA Then I offer you twenty silver dollars.

(*The* HUSBAND *laughs*)

THE CARPENTER Are you crazy? The shelves are walnut!

SHUI TA Then take them away.

THE CARPENTER What d'you mean?

SHUI TA They cost too much. I beg you, take the walnut shelves away.

THE WIFE Well said! (*She laughs too*)

THE CARPENTER (*Uncertainly*) I demand that someone call Miss Shen Te. She seems to be a better person than you.

SHUI TA Certainly. She's ruined.

THE CARPENTER (*Resolutely taking some shelves and carrying them to the door*) You can pile up your tobacco goods on the floor! It suits me!

SHUI TA (*To the* HUSBAND) Help him!

THE HUSBAND (*He also grabs a shelf and, grinning, carries it to the door*) Out with the shelves!

THE CARPENTER You dog, do you want my family to starve?

SHUI TA Once more I offer you twenty silver dollars. I don't want to pile up my tobacco goods on the floor.

THE CARPENTER A hundred!

(SHUI TA *looks indifferently out of the window. The* HUSBAND *prepares to carry out more shelves*)

THE CARPENTER At least don't smash them against the door post, idiot! (*Desperately*) But they were made to measure! They fit this dump and nowhere else! The boards are spoiled, mister!

SHUI TA Exactly. That's why I'm offering you only twenty silver dollars. Because the boards are spoiled.

(*The* WIFE *squeals with pleasure*)

THE CARPENTER (*Suddenly tired*) I can't keep it up. Take the shelves and pay what you want.

SHUI TA Twenty silver dollars.

(*He places two large coins on the table. The* CARPENTER *takes them*)

THE HUSBAND (*Carrying back the shelves*) It's enough for a heap of spoiled boards!

THE CARPENTER Enough, maybe, to get drunk on! (*Exit*)

THE HUSBAND We got rid of *him!*

THE WIFE (*Weeping with merriment and drying her tears*) "They're walnut!" "Take them away!" "One hundred silver dollars! I have four children!" "Then I'll pay twenty!" "But they're spoiled." "Exactly! Twenty silver dollars!"—That's how one has to treat those scamps.

SHUI TA Yes. (*Earnestly*) Go away quickly!

THE HUSBAND Us?

SHUI TA Yes, you. You're thieves and parasites. If you go fast without wasting time talking back, you can still save yourselves.

THE HUSBAND It's best just not to answer him at all. Let's not shout on an empty stomach. I'd like to know where the boy is.

SHUI TA Yes, where's the boy? I told you before, I don't want him in my store with stolen cakes. (*Suddenly shouting*) Once more: Go!

(*They remain seated*)

SHUI TA (*Calmly again*) As you wish.

(*He goes to the door and bows low. A* POLICEMAN *appears in the doorway*)

SHUI TA I presume I am addressing the officer in charge of this neighborhood?

THE POLICEMAN Yes, Mr. . . .

SHUI TA Shui Ta. (*They smile at each other*) Nice weather today!

THE POLICEMAN A little warm, maybe?

SHUI TA A little warm, maybe.

THE HUSBAND (*Softly to the* WIFE) If he gabbles until the boy comes back, we're done for!

(*He tries secretly to make some signs at* SHUI TA)

SHUI TA (*Without paying attention to him*) It makes a difference whether one thinks of the weather from a cool store or from the dusty street.

THE POLICEMAN A big difference.

THE WIFE (*To the* HUSBAND) Don't worry! The boy won't come when he sees the policeman standing in the doorway.

SHUI TA Why don't you come in? It's really cooler in here. My cousin and I have opened a store. We attach the greatest importance, let me tell you, to being on good terms with the authorities.

THE POLICEMAN (*Entering*) You are very kind, Mr. Shui Ta. Yes, it's really cool in here.

THE HUSBAND (*Softly*) He's taking him in, specially so the boy won't see him.

SHUI TA Visitors. Distant acquaintances of my cousin, I hear. They are on a journey. (*They bow*) We were just about to take leave.

THE HUSBAND (*Hoarsely*) Well, we'll be going now.

SHUI TA I shall tell my cousin that you want to thank her for the rooms but that you had no time to await her return.

(*A noise from the street and shouts of:* "Stop thief!")

THE POLICEMAN What's that?

(*The* BOY *is in the doorway. Various kinds of cakes are falling out of his shirt. The* WIFE *waves him desperately back. He turns and starts to go*)

THE POLICEMAN Stop, you! (*He takes hold of the* BOY) Where did you get these cakes?

THE BOY Over there.

THE POLICEMAN Oh, theft, is it?

THE WIFE We didn't know anything about it. The boy did it on his own. (*To the* BOY) You good-for-nothing!

THE POLICEMAN Mr. Shui Ta, can you clarify the situation?

(SHUI TA *is silent*)

THE POLICEMAN Aha. You're all coming to the station with me.

SHUI TA I'm most distressed that such a thing could have happened in my establishment.

THE WOMAN He was watching when the boy went away!

SHUI TA I can assure you, officer, I should hardly have asked you in if I'd wanted to conceal a theft.

THE POLICEMAN That's right. And you will also understand, Mr. Shui Ta, that it's my duty to take those people away. (SHUI TA *bows*) Go on with you! (*He drives them out*)

THE GRANDFATHER (*Solemnly from the doorway*) Good day! (*Exeunt all except* SHUI TA, *who continues to tidy up. Enter the* LANDLADY)

THE LANDLADY So you're her cousin! What does it mean that the police are dragging people away from my house? What right has your Miss Shen Te to turn this store into a house of assignation? That's what happens if one takes in people who only yesterday lived in a two-bit hotel and went begging for bread to the corner bakery! You see, I know everything!

SHUI TA Yes, I see. You've been told bad things about my cousin. She is accused of having gone hungry! It's a notorious fact that she lived in poverty. She's got the worst possible reputation: that of being poor.

THE LANDLADY She was a common . . .

SHUI TA Pauper. Let's not mince words.

THE LANDLADY Oh, please, no sentimental rubbish. I'm speaking about her conduct, not her earnings. There must have been earnings, or this store wouldn't be here. Several elderly gentlemen must have taken care of that. How does one get a store at all? Sir, this is a respectable house! The people who pay rent here don't wish to live under the same roof with such a person. Yes, sir. (*Pause*) I'm not a monster but I've got to be careful.

SHUI TA (*Coldly*) Mrs. Mi Tzu, I'm busy. Just tell me how much it'll cost us to live in this respectable house.

THE LANDLADY You're a cool customer, I must say.

SHUI TA (*Taking the lease from the counter*) The rent is very high. I assume from the contract that it's payable by the month.

THE LANDLADY (*Quickly*) Not for people like your cousin!

SHUI TA What do you mean?

THE LANDLADY I mean that people like your cousin must pay the half-yearly rent of two hundred silver dollars in advance.

SHUI TA Two hundred silver dollars! Sheer usury! How am I to get it? I can't count on a large turnover here. My only hope lies in the sack makers at the cement factory. I've been told they smoke a lot because their work is exhausting. But then, *they* don't earn much either.

THE LANDLADY You should have thought of that earlier.

SHUI TA Mrs. Mi Tzu, have a heart! It's true, my cousin has made the unpardonable mistake of giving shelter to unfortunate persons. But she can improve. I'll see to it that she improves. And, tell me, how could you find a better tenant than one who knows the depths because she comes from them? She'll work her fingers to the bone to pay the rent on time. She'll do everything, sacrifice everything, sell everything, shun nothing, and all the time she'll be as humble as a little mouse and as quiet as a fly. She'll give way to you in anything before she'll go back where she came from. Such a tenant is worth her weight in gold.

THE LANDLADY Two hundred silver dollars payable in advance or she'll go back on the streets where she came from!

(*Enter the* POLICEMAN)

THE POLICEMAN Don't let me disturb you, Mr. Shui Ta!

THE LANDLADY The police certainly display a great interest in this store.

THE POLICEMAN Mrs. Mi Tzu, I hope you haven't got the wrong impression. Mr. Shui Ta has done us a service and I'm coming solely to thank him for it in the name of the police.

THE LANDLADY Well, that's nothing to me. I hope, Mr. Shui Ta, that my proposal will be agreeable to your cousin. I like to be on good terms with my tenants. Good day, gentlemen. (*Exit*)

SHUI TA Good day, Mrs. Mi Tzu.

THE POLICEMAN Are you having difficulties with Mrs. Mi Tzu.

SHUI TA She's demanding the rent in advance because my cousin doesn't seem to her respectable.

THE POLICEMAN And you don't have the money? (SHUI TA *is silent*) But surely a man like you, Mr. Shui Ta, can get credit?

SHUI TA Perhaps. But how can a woman like Shen Te get credit?

THE POLICEMAN Aren't you staying?

SHUI TA No. I can't come back either. I can lend her a helping hand only on my trip through town. I can only ward off the worst. Soon she'll have to rely on herself again. I'm wondering what will happen then? I'm worried.

THE POLICEMAN Mr. Shui Ta, I'm sorry you're in difficulties with the rent. I must admit that at first we looked at this store with mixed feelings. But your courageous behavior a little while ago showed us what you're made of. The authorities soon find out who they can trust.

SHUI TA (*Bitterly*) Officer, in order to save this little store, which my cousin regards as a gift of the gods, I'm ready to go to the very limit permitted by law. But hardness and cunning help only against inferiors. The lines are drawn cleverly. I feel like the man who dealt with the rats, only to find himself with rivers to cross. (*After a little pause*) Do you smoke?

THE POLICEMAN (*Putting two cigars into his pocket*) Us fellows at the station would hate to lose you, Mr. Shui Ta. But you've got to understand Mrs. Mi Tzu. Shen Te—let's not beat about the bush—lived by selling herself to men. You can object: what else could she have done? How, for instance, was she to pay her rent? But the fact remains: it isn't respectable. Why not? First: one doesn't sell love—beware of the love that's for sale! Second: it's respectable to go with someone you love but not with someone who's paying for it! Third: the proverb says, not for a handful of rice but for love! Well, you'll answer, what good is all this wisdom once the milk is spilt? What can she do? She's got to get hold of her half-year's rent or she'll be back on the streets. And how's she to get hold of the rent? Mr. Shui Ta, I have to tell you, I don't know. (*He's busy thinking*) Mr. Shui Ta, I've got it! Find her a husband!

(*Enter a little* OLD WOMAN)

THE OLD WOMAN A good cheap cigar for my husband. We'll have been married forty years tomorrow, you see, and we're having a little celebration.

SHUI TA (*Politely*) Forty years, and you still want to celebrate!

THE OLD WOMAN As far as our means allow! We own the carpet store across from here. I hope we'll be good neighbors. We should be. Times are bad.

SHUI TA (*Showing her various boxes*) A very old saying, I fear.

THE POLICEMAN Mr. Shui Ta, we need capital. Well, I propose a marriage.

SHUI TA (*Apologetically to the* OLD WOMAN) I've let myself be persuaded to bother this gentleman with my personal worries.

THE POLICEMAN We can't pay the half-year's rent. Very well. We marry a little money.

SHUI TA That won't be easy.

THE POLICEMAN Why not? She's a good match. She's got a small, growing store. (*To the* OLD WOMAN) What do *you* think about it?

THE OLD WOMAN (*Undecidedly*) Yes . . .

THE POLICEMAN An ad in the paper!

THE OLD WOMAN (*Reticently*) If the young lady agrees . . .

THE POLICEMAN What should she have against it? I'll make out the ad. One good turn deserves another. Don't think the authorities aren't concerned with the struggling small businessman! You lend us a helping hand and in turn we make up a matrimonial ad for you! Ha! ha! ha!

(*He eagerly takes out his notebook, wets the stump of a pencil, and writes away*)

SHUI TA (*Slowly*) It's not a bad idea.

THE POLICEMAN "What . . . decent . . . man with small capital . . . widower . . . not excluded . . . wishes . . . marriage . . . into flourishing tobacco store?" And then we'll add: "am . . . pretty . . . pleasant appearance." How's that?

SHUI TA If you don't think that's an exaggeration . . .

THE OLD WOMAN (*Kindly*) Not at all. I've seen her.

(*The* POLICEMAN *tears the page out of his notebook and hands it to* SHUI TA)

SHUI TA With horror I see how much luck one needs to keep above water. How many ideas! How many friends! (*To the* POLICEMAN) Despite my determination, I was at the end of my tether as far as the store rent was concerned. But then you came and helped me with good advice. Truly, now I see a way out!

# Scene Three

(*Evening in the city park. A young man*—YANG SUN—*in ragged clothes follows with his eyes an airplane which seems to be describing a curve high over the city park. He takes a rope out of his pocket and looks carefully around. As he is going toward a large willow, two prostitutes come along. The one is already old, the other is the niece from the family that has imposed itself on* SHEN TE)

THE YOUNG ONE Good evening, young gentleman. Coming with me, dearie?

SUN Perhaps, ladies. If you buy me something to eat.

THE OLD ONE You're nuts, aren't you? (*To the* YOUNG ONE) Let's go on. We're only wasting our time with him. He's the unemployed pilot.

THE YOUNG ONE But no one else will be left in the park, it'll rain in a minute.

THE OLD ONE You never know.

(*They go on.* SUN, *looking about, pulls out his rope and throws it round a willow branch. But again he is disturbed. The two prostitutes are coming quickly back. They don't see him*)

THE YOUNG ONE It's going to pour.

(SHEN TE *comes walking along*)

THE OLD ONE Look, here comes the monster! She brought disaster to you and your family!

THE YOUNG ONE It wasn't her. It was her cousin. She took us in and later offered to pay for the cakes. I have nothing against her.

THE OLD ONE But I have! (*Loudly*) Ah, here's our dear rich sister! She's got a store but she still wants to snatch our boy friends away.

SHEN TE Now don't bite my head off. I'm going to the tearoom by the pond.

THE YOUNG ONE Is it true you're going to marry a widower with three children?

SHEN TE Yes, I'm meeting him there.

SUN (*Impatiently*) Won't you get going, you whores! Can't a man be at peace even here?

THE OLD ONE Shut your trap!

(*Exeunt the two prostitutes*)

SUN (*Calling after them*) Vultures! (*To the audience*) Even at this remote spot they don't tire of fishing for victims! Even in the bushes, even when it's raining, they desperately search for customers!

SHEN TE (*Angrily*) Why do you swear at them? (*She notices the rope*) Oh!

SUN What are you gaping at?

SHEN TE What's the rope for?

SUN Go on, sister, go on! I've no money, nothing, not even a penny. And if I had a penny, I wouldn't buy you. First I'd buy a cup of water.

(*It starts raining*)

SHEN TE What's the rope for? You mustn't do that!

SUN What's that to you? Clear off!

SHEN TE It's raining.

SUN Don't you try to come under this tree.

SHEN TE (*Who stays standing in the rain without moving*) No.

SUN Sister, leave it, it won't help you. You can't do business with me. You're too ugly for me anyway. Crooked legs.

SHEN TE That isn't true.

SUN Don't show them! If it's raining, for heaven's sake come under the tree!

(*She goes slowly under the tree and sits down*)

SHEN TE Why did you want to do it?

SUN Do you want to know? Then I'll tell you: to get rid of you. (*Pause*) Do you know what it is to be a flier?

SHEN TE Yes, I've seen pilots in a tearoom.

SUN No, you haven't. Perhaps you've seen a couple of conceited idiots with leather helmets, fellows with no ear for a motor, no sense for a machine. They only get into a plane because they know how to bribe the manager at the airport. Tell one of them: "Take your plane two thousand feet up, let it fall down through the clouds, and then catch it with one flick of the wrist," and he'll say: "That's not in the contract." If you fly, and you don't land your plane as if you were landing on your own rear end, you are not a flier but a fool. I am a flier. And I'm also the biggest fool for reading all those books on flying in the school at Peking and missing out on one page of one book which says that there's no need for fliers any more. And so I'm a flier without a plane, a mail pilot without mail. *You* can't understand what that means.

SHEN TE I think I can.

SUN No, I'm telling you, you can't understand it. That means you can't understand it.

SHEN TE (*Half laughing, half crying*) When we were children we had a crane with a lame wing. He was friendly and didn't mind our jokes. He strutted along behind us, crying out to us not to run too fast. But in the fall and in the spring when large swarms of cranes were flying over the village, he became very restless. And I could understand why. (*She weeps*)

SUN Don't howl.

SHEN TE No.

SUN It hurts the complexion.

SHEN TE I'm stopping.

(*She dries her tears with her sleeve. Leaning against the tree, and without turning toward her, he reaches for her face*)

SUN You don't even know how to wipe your face properly.

(*He wipes it for her with a handkerchief. Pause*)

SUN If you *had* to stay here so I wouldn't hang myself, you might at least open your mouth.

SHEN TE I don't know anything.

SUN Why exactly do you want to cut me down from the tree, sister?

SHEN TE I'm frightened. I'm sure you only wanted to do it because the evening is so gloomy. (*To the audience*)

In our country
There should be no gloomy evenings.
High bridges over the river
The hour between night and morning
And the long winter: they too are dangerous.
For with all the misery
A little is enough
And men throw away
The unbearable life.

SUN Talk about yourself.

SHEN TE What about me? I have a little store.

SUN (*Mocking*) Oh, you don't walk the streets, you have a store!

SHEN TE (*Determinedly*) I have a store now, but, before, I was on the streets.

SUN And the store was a gift of the gods, I suppose?

SHEN TE Yes.

SUN One nice evening they were standing there and saying: Here's some money?

SHEN TE (*Laughing softly*) One morning.

SUN You're not exactly entertaining.

SHEN TE (*After a pause*) I can play the zither a little, and I can mimic people. (*In a low voice she imitates a man of dignity*) "Well, think of that, I must have left my money at home!" But then I got the store. And the first thing I did was to give away my zither. Now, I said to myself, I can be as dumb as a fish and it won't make any difference.

I'm rich now, I said.
I walk alone, I sleep alone.
For a whole year, I said,
I'll have nothing to do with a man.

SUN But now you're marrying one? The one in the tearoom by the pond?

(SHEN TE *is silent*)

SUN What exactly do you know of love?

SHEN TE Everything.

SUN Nothing, sister. (*Pause*) Or perhaps you liked it?

SHEN TE No.

SUN (*Without turning toward her, he strokes her face with his hand*) Is that pleasant?

SHEN TE Yes.

SUN You're easily satisfied, I must say. What a town!

SHEN TE Don't you have any friends?

SUN Lots, but none who want to hear I'm still without a job. They make a face as if someone was complaining that there's still water in the ocean. Do *you* have a friend maybe?

SHEN TE (*Hesitantly*) A cousin.

SUN Then beware of him.

SHEN TE He's only been here once. Now he's gone away and he'll never be back. But why are you talking so despairingly? To speak without hope, they say, is to speak without goodness.

SUN Just go on talking. A voice, after all, is a voice.

SHEN TE (*Eagerly*) Despite the great misery, there are still kind people. Once, when I was little, I fell down with a load of brushwood. An old man picked me up. He gave me some cheese too. I've often thought of that. Especially those who don't have much to eat like to give some away. People probably like to show what they can do, and how could they show it better than by being kind? Being wicked is just being clumsy. When someone sings a song or builds a machine or plants some rice, that's really a sort of kindness. And you're kind, too.

SUN It doesn't seem hard to be kind in your eyes.

SHEN TE No. Just now I felt a raindrop.

SUN Where?

SHEN TE Between the eyes.

SUN Nearer the right one or nearer the left?

SHEN TE Nearer the left.

SUN Good. (*After a while, sleepily*) And you're through with men?

SHEN TE (*Smiling*) But my legs aren't crooked.

SUN Perhaps not.

SHEN TE Definitely not.

SUN (*Tired, leaning against the tree*) I haven't eaten anything for two days or drunk anything for one. So I couldn't love you, sister, even if I wanted to.

SHEN TE It's lovely in the rain.

(WANG, *the water seller, appears. He sings*)

*THE SONG OF THE WATER SELLER IN THE RAIN*

"Buy my water," I am yelling
And my fury restraining
For no water I'm selling
'Cause it's raining, 'cause it's raining!
I keep yelling: "Buy my water!"
But no one's buying
Athirst and dying
And drinking and paying!
Buy water!
Buy water, you dogs!

Nice to dream of lovely weather!
Think of all the consternation
Were there no precipitation
Half a dozen years together!
Can't you hear them shrieking: "Water!"
Pretending they adore me?
They all would go down on their knees before me!
Down on your knees!
Go down on your knees, you dogs!

What are lawns and hedges thinking?
What are fields and forests saying?
"At the cloud's breast we are drinking!
And we've no idea who's paying!"
I keep yelling: "Buy my water!"
But no one's buying
Athirst and dying
And drinking and paying!
Buy water!
Buy water, you dogs!

(*The rain has stopped.* SHEN TE *sees* WANG *and runs toward him*)

SHEN TE Oh, Wang, are you back again? I've got your carrying pole at home.

WANG Thank you very much for keeping it! How are you, Shen Te?

SHEN TE I'm well. I've met a very clever and brave man. And I'd like to buy a cup of your water.

WANG Put your head back and open your mouth and you'll have as much water as you want. The willow over there is still dripping.

SHEN TE

But I want your water, Wang,
The water carried from far
The water that has made you tired
The water that will be hard to sell because it is raining.

And I need it for the gentleman over there.

He is a pilot.
A pilot is bolder than other men.
In the clouds' company!
Braving the great storms
He flies through the skies
And brings to friends in far-off lands
The friendly mail.

(*She pays and runs over to* SUN *with the cup*)

SHEN TE (*Calling back, laughing, to* WANG) He's fallen asleep. Despair and rain and I have made him tired.

# Scene Three (a)

(WANG'S *sleeping quarters in a sewer pipe. The water seller is asleep. Music. The sewer pipe becomes transparent and the* GODS *appear to the dreaming* WANG)

WANG (*Radiantly*) I've seen her, illustrious ones! She's still the same!

THE FIRST GOD We're glad to hear it.

WANG She loves! She's shown me her friend. She's really well off.

THE FIRST GOD That's good to hear. Let's hope it will give her strength in her striving toward the good.

WANG Absolutely! She does as many good deeds as she can.

THE FIRST GOD What sort of good deeds? Tell us about it, my dear Wang!

WANG She has a kind word for everyone.

THE FIRST GOD (*Eagerly*) Yes, and . . . ?

WANG It seldom happens that anyone leaves her little store without tobacco just because he has no money.

THE FIRST GOD That doesn't sound bad. Anything else?

WANG She gave lodging to a family of eight!

THE FIRST GOD (*Triumphantly to the* SECOND) Eight! (*To* WANG) And something else perhaps?

WANG She bought a cup of water from me, even though it was raining.

THE FIRST GOD Of course, all these smaller good deeds. That's understood.

WANG But they run into money. A little store doesn't make so much.

THE FIRST GOD Yes, surely. But a prudent gardener can produce miracles even on a tiny plot.

WANG She really does that! Every morning she hands out rice, and believe me, it takes more than half her earnings!

THE FIRST GOD (*A little disappointed*) I'm not saying anything. And for a beginning, I'm not dissatisfied.

WANG Just think, times aren't exactly good! Once, her store got into difficulties and she had to call a cousin to her aid.

As soon as there was a place that was shielded
 from the wind
The ruffled birds of the whole wintry sky
Came flying and fought for the place
And the hungry fox bit through the thin wall
And the one-legged wolf tipped the small dish over.

In short, she couldn't manage all the business herself any more. But they all agree that she's a good girl. Everywhere she's called the Angel of the Suburbs already. So much good comes from her store. Whatever the carpenter Lin To may say!

THE FIRST GOD What does that mean? Does the carpenter Lin To speak badly of her?

WANG Oh, he only says that the shelves in the store weren't paid for in full.

THE SECOND GOD What are you saying now? A carpenter wasn't paid? In Shen Te's store? How could she allow that?

WANG I guess she didn't have the money.

THE SECOND GOD All the same one pays what one owes. The mere appearance of injustice has to be avoided. First the letter of the commandment must be fulfilled. Then the spirit.

WANG But it was only her cousin, illustrious one, not she herself!

THE SECOND GOD Then that cousin must never cross her threshold again!

WANG (*Downcast*) I understand, illustrious one! In defense of Shen Te, let me at least say that her cousin is considered a highly respectable businessman. Even the police value him.

THE FIRST GOD Well, we don't want to damn this cousin without having heard him. I admit I don't understand anything about business. Perhaps one should make inquiries to find out what is customary. But anyway, business—is it so very necessary? They're always doing business nowadays! Did the Seven Good Kings do business? Did Kung the Just sell fish? What does business have to do with an honest and dignified life?

THE SECOND GOD (*With a bad cold*) In any case such a thing must not happen again. (*He turns to go. The two other* GODS *turn too*)

THE THIRD GOD (*The last to turn away, embarrassed*) You must forgive our harsh tone today. We're overtired and haven't slept enough. Lodgings for the night! The wealthy give us the very best of recommendations to the poor, but the poor don't have enough room.

THE GODS (*Moving away, grumbling*) Weak, the best of them! Nothing decisive! Little, little! Everything from the heart, of course, but it doesn't amount to much! At least, she should see that . . .

(*One no longer hears them*)

WANG (*Calling after them*) Oh, don't be angry, illustrious ones! Don't ask too much all at once!

## Scene Four

(*The square in front of* SHEN TE'S *tobacco store. A barber's shop, a carpet store, and* SHEN TE'S *tobacco store. It is morning. In front of* SHEN TE'S *store, two of the family of eight, the* GRANDFATHER *and the* SISTER-IN-LAW, *are waiting. Waiting also are the* UNEMPLOYED *and* MRS. SHIN)

THE SISTER-IN-LAW She didn't come home last night!

MRS. SHIN Unbelievable behavior! At last this crazy cousin has gone away and madam deigns, now and then at least, to give us a little bit of rice out of all her abundance. But already she's staying out all night, loitering around, God knows where!

(*Loud voices are heard from the barber's.* WANG *stumbles out, followed by the fat barber,* MR. SHU FU, *who is carrying a heavy curling iron*)

MR. SHU FU I'll teach you to bother my customers with your smelly water! Take your cup and get going!

(WANG *reaches for the cup held out by* MR. SHU FU, *who hits him on the hand with the curling iron.* WANG *cries out with pain*)

MR. SHU FU There you have it! Let it be a lesson to you! (*He goes puffing back into his store*)

THE UNEMPLOYED (*Picking up the cup and handing it to* WANG) You can report him to the police for hitting you like that.

WANG My hand's smashed.

THE UNEMPLOYED Is something broken?

WANG I can't move it.

THE UNEMPLOYED Sit down and pour a little water over it!

(WANG *sits down*)

MRS. SHIN You get the water cheap, anyway.

THE SISTER-IN-LAW You can't even get a little linen rag here at eight in the morning. She's got to go out! Adventures! What a scandal!

MRS. SHIN (*Gloomily*) She's forgotten us!

(SHEN TE *comes down the street carrying a dish of rice*)

SHEN TE (*To the audience*) I've never seen the town in the early morning before. At this hour I used to lie in bed with a dirty blanket over my head, afraid of waking up. Today I walked among the newspaper boys, among the men who rinse the pavement with water, and among the ox carts that bring fresh vegetables from the country. I've walked a long way from Sun's neighborhood over here, but I've been getting merrier at every step. I've always been told that if you're in love you walk on clouds, but the best thing is walking on the earth, on the pavement. I tell you, in the morning rows of houses look like rubbish heaps with lights on them. The sky is pink and transparent because there's no dust yet. I tell you, you miss much if you don't love, if you don't see your Setzuan at the hour when it rises from sleep like a sober old craftsman pumping his lungs full of fresh air and reaching for his tools, as the poets say. (*To the waiting people*) Good morning! Here's the rice! (*She distributes the rice, then notices* WANG) Good morning, Wang. I'm quite light-headed today. On the way home I looked at myself in every shop window, and now I feel like buying a shawl. (*After hesitating a little*) I'd so much like to be beautiful. (*She quickly goes into the carpet store*)

MR. SHU FU (*Who has stepped out again, to the audience*) I'm quite surprised to note how beautiful Miss Shen Te looks today. She's the owner of the tobacco store across the street and I've never really noticed her before. I've been looking at her for three minutes and I think I'm already in love with her. An incredibly attractive person! (*To* WANG) Clear off, you rascal! (*He goes back into his store.* SHEN TE, *the* OLD WOMAN, *and her husband the carpet dealer step out of the carpet store.* SHEN TE *is wearing a shawl, the carpet dealer is holding out a mirror*)

THE OLD WOMAN It's very pretty and not expensive because it has a little hole at the bottom.

SHEN TE (*Looking at the shawl on the* OLD WOMAN'S *arm*) The green one's nice too.

THE OLD WOMAN (*Smiling*) But unfortunately not the least bit damaged.

SHEN TE Yes, that's a shame. I can't spend too much, with my small store. I only take in a little and the expenses are great.

THE OLD WOMAN It's good deeds that cost you so much. Be careful. In the beginning, every dish of rice counts, doesn't it?

SHEN TE (*Trying on the shawl with the little hole in it*) Well, that's how things are. But at the moment I'm light-headed. I wonder if this color suits me?

THE OLD WOMAN That's a question to put to a *man.*

SHEN TE (*Turning to the* OLD MAN) Does it suit me?

THE OLD MAN Why don't you ask . . .

SHEN TE (*Very politely*) No, I'm asking you.

THE OLD MAN (*Also politely*) The shawl suits you. But wear it with the dull side turned out.

(SHEN TE *pays*)

THE OLD WOMAN If you don't like it, you can always exchange it. (*She pulls her aside*) Does he have any money?

SHEN TE (*Laughing*) Oh no!

THE OLD WOMAN Then how will you be able to pay the rent?

SHEN TE The rent? I'd completely forgotten it!

THE OLD WOMAN I thought as much. And next Monday is the first of the month. I'd like to talk something over with you. You know, my husband and I had a few doubts about the marriage ad after we got to know you. We decided to help you out if it comes to the worst. We've put aside a little money and can lend you two hundred silver dollars. If you wish you can pledge us your stock of tobacco. Of course we don't need a written agreement.

SHEN TE Do you really want to lend money to a light-headed person like me?

THE OLD WOMAN Well, to be honest, we might not lend it to your cousin—who's definitely not light-headed. But we don't worry about lending it to you.

THE OLD MAN (*Stepping up to them*) Settled?

SHEN TE I wish the gods could have heard your wife just now, Mr. Ma. They're looking for good people who're happy. And you must be happy helping me, for it was love that got me into trouble.

(*The old couple smile at each other*)

THE OLD MAN Here's the money.

(*He hands her an envelope.* SHEN TE *takes it and bows. The old couple bow too. They go back into their store*)

SHEN TE (*To* WANG, *holding up her envelope*) This is the rent for half a year! Isn't it just like a miracle? And how do you like my new shawl, Wang?

WANG Did you buy it for the fellow I saw in the city park?

(SHEN TE *nods*)

MRS. SHIN Maybe you better take a look at his smashed hand? Never mind telling him your doubtful adventures!

SHEN TE (*Taken aback*) What's the matter with your hand?

MRS. SHIN The barber smashed it with a curling iron in front of our eyes.

SHEN TE (*Horrified at her negligence*) And I didn't notice anything! You must go to the doctor this minute or your hand will get stiff and you'll never be able to work properly again. What a terrible misfortune! Quick, get up! Go, quickly!

THE UNEMPLOYED It's not the doctor he should go to but the judge! He can demand compensation from the barber, he's rich.

WANG You think there's a chance?

MRS. SHIN If it's really smashed. But is it?

WANG I think so. It's swollen up already. Maybe I could get a pension?

MRS. SHIN Of course you've got to have a witness.

WANG But you *all* saw it! You could *all* testify?

(*He looks round. The* UNEMPLOYED, *the* GRANDFATHER, *and the* SISTER-IN-LAW *sit by the wall of the house and eat. Nobody looks up*)

SHEN TE (*To* MRS. SHIN) But you saw it yourself!

MRS. SHIN I don't want anything to do with the police.

SHEN TE (*To the* SISTER-IN-LAW) What about you?

THE SISTER-IN-LAW Me? I wasn't looking!

MRS. SHIN Of course you were! I saw you! But you're afraid because the barber's a big shot.

SHEN TE (*To the* GRANDFATHER) I'm sure *you'll* testify!

THE SISTER-IN-LAW His testimony won't be accepted. He's gaga.

SHEN TE (*To the* UNEMPLOYED) It might be a matter of a pension for life.

THE UNEMPLOYED I've been picked up twice for begging. *My* testimony would only do him harm.

SHEN TE (*Not quite believing*) So none of you want to say what happened? His hand was smashed in broad daylight, all of you were watching, and nobody wants to speak! (*Angrily*)

Unhappy men!
Your brother is assaulted and you shut your eyes!
He is hit and cries aloud and you are silent?
The beast prowls, chooses his victim, and you say:
He's spared us because we do not show displeasure.
What sort of a city is this? What sort of people are you?
When injustice is done there should be revolt in the city.
And if there is no revolt, it were better that the city should perish in fire before night falls!

Wang, if no one present will be your witness, I will. I'll say *I* saw it.

MRS. SHIN That'll be perjury.

WANG I don't know if I can accept this. Though maybe I'll have to. (*Looking at his hand, worried*) Do you think it's swollen enough? I think maybe the swelling's gone down now?

THE UNEMPLOYED (*Reassuring him*) No, the swelling definitely hasn't gone down.

WANG Hasn't it? No, I guess it's *more* swollen, if anything. Maybe my wrist is broken after all! I'd better run to the judge this minute.

(*Carefully holding his hand and looking at it all the time, he runs off.* MRS. SHIN *runs into the barber's shop*)

THE UNEMPLOYED She wants to get on the right side of the barber.

THE SISTER-IN-LAW We can't change the world.

SHEN TE (*Discouraged*) I didn't want to scold you. I'm only afraid. No, I *did* want to scold. Get out of my sight!

(*The* UNEMPLOYED, *the* SISTER-IN-LAW, *and the* GRANDFATHER *go off, eating and sulking*)

SHEN TE (*To the audience*)

They no longer answer.
Where one puts them they stay
And if one sends them away
They quickly go.
Nothing moves their hearts.
Only the smell of food can make them look up.

(AN OLDISH WOMAN *comes running in*)

THE OLDISH WOMAN (*Out of breath*) Are you Miss Shen Te? My son. Has told me everything. I am. Sun's mother, Mrs. Yang. Just think, he has. chance now. To get a job as flier. This morning. Just now a letter. Came from Peking. From the manager of the airmail service.

SHEN TE He can fly again? Oh, Mrs. Yang!

MRS. YANG But the job. Costs a lot of money. Five hundred silver dollars.

SHEN TE That's a lot, but money mustn't stand in the way of a thing like that. After all, I've got the store!

MRS. YANG If you could only do something!

SHEN TE (*Embracing her*) If only I could!

MRS. YANG You would give a talented young man a chance?

SHEN TE How can they prevent a man from being useful? (*After a pause*) Only I won't get enough for the store, and these two hundred silver dollars cash are just borrowed. Take them with you at once. I'll pay them back by selling my tobacco stock. (*She gives her the old couple's money*)

MRS. YANG Oh, Miss Shen Te, that really is help at the right moment! And they were calling him the Dead Flier of Setzuan, they were all so convinced he'd never do any more flying!

SHEN TE But we need three hundred silver dollars more for the job. We've got to think, Mrs. Yang. (*Slowly*) I know someone who might be able to help me. Someone who helped me out once before. I didn't really want to call him again, he's so hard and cunning. It would certainly have to be the last time. But a flier's got to fly, that's clear.

(*Distant sound of engines*)

MRS. YANG If the man you're talking about could get the money! Look, that's the morning mail plane, going to Peking!

SHEN TE (*Decisively*) Wave, Mrs. Yang! I'm sure the pilot can see us! (*She waves with her shawl*) You wave too!

MRS. YANG (*Waving*) You know the pilot who's flying up there?

SHEN TE No. I know the pilot who *shall* be up there. He gave up hope but he *shall* fly, Mrs. Yang. One at least shall raise himself above this misery and above us all! (*To the audience*)

Yang Sun, my lover,
In the clouds' company!
Braving the great storms
Flying through the skies
And bringing to friends in distant lands
The friendly mail.

## Scene Four (a)

(*Before the curtain.* SHEN TE *appears with the suit and mask of* SHUI TA *in her hands. She sings*)

*THE SONG OF THE DEFENSELESSNESS OF THE GODS AND GOOD MEN*

In our country
A useful man needs luck
Only if he find strong backers
Can he show himself useful
The good can't defend themselves and
Even the gods are defenseless

Oh, why don't the gods have their own ammunition
And launch against badness their own expedition
Enthroning the good and preventing sedition
And bringing the world to a peaceful condition?

(*She puts on* SHUI TA's *suit and takes a few steps in his manner*)

Good men
Cannot long remain good in our country.
Where the plates are empty, the dinner guests fight.
Alas, the commandments of the gods
Are no use against want.
Oh, why don't the gods do the buying and selling
Injustice forbidding, starvation dispelling
Give bread to each city and joy to each dwelling?
Oh, why don't the gods do the buying and selling?

(*She puts on the mask of* SHUI TA *and now sings with his voice*)

You can only help one of your luckless brothers
By trampling down a dozen others
Why is it the gods do not feel indignation
And come down in fury to end exploitation
Defeat all defeat and forbid desperation
Refusing to tolerate such toleration?
Why is it?

## Scene Five

(*The tobacco store.* SHUI TA *sits behind the counter reading the paper. He doesn't pay the least attention to* MRS. SHIN, *who is cleaning up and talking at the same time*)

MRS. SHIN A little store like this soon comes to ruin when certain rumors start spreading in the neighborhood. Believe me. It's high time that a decent man like you started looking into this dubious affair between Miss Shen Te and that Yang Sun from Yellow Street. Don't forget Mr. Shu Fu, the barber next door, a man with twelve houses and only one wife, and she's old, only yesterday confessed a certain interest in Miss Shen Te. A very flattering interest, I thought. He even inquired about her means. And that, if I may say so, proves real affection.

(*Since she gets no answer, she finally goes out with the bucket*)

SUN'S VOICE (*From outside*) Is that Miss Shen Te's store?

MRS. SHIN'S VOICE Yes, this is it. But today her cousin's here.

(*With the light steps of* SHEN TE, SHUI TA *runs to a mirror. She is just about to start fixing her hair when she notices the mistake in the mirror. She turns away laughing softly. Enter* YANG SUN. *Behind him comes the inquisitive* MRS. SHIN. *She goes past him into the back room*)

SUN I'm Yang Sun. (SHUI TA *bows*) Is Shen Te here?

SHUI TA No, she's not.

SUN I guess you know what our relationship is? (*He begins to inspect the store*) A real live store! I always thought she was just talking big. (*He looks with satisfaction into the little boxes and china jars*) Man, I'm going to fly again! (*He takes a cigar and* SHUI TA *gives him a light*) D'you think we can squeeze another three hundred silver dollars out of the store?

SHUI TA May I ask if you intend to sell it right away?

SUN Well, do we have the three hundred in cash? (SHUI TA *shakes his head*) It was decent of her to come right out with the two hundred. But with three hundred still missing, they won't be much use.

SHUI TA Perhaps it was rather rash of her to promise you the money. It may cost her the store. Haste, they say, is the name of the wind that knocks down the scaffolding.

SUN I need the money quickly or not at all. And the girl isn't one to keep you waiting either. For one thing or another, you get me?

SHUI TA I get you.

SUN Uh-huh.

SHUI TA May I know what the five hundred silver dollars will be used for?

SUN Sure. I see I'm to be sounded out. The manager at the Peking airport is a friend of mine from flying school. He can get me the job if I cough up five hundred silver dollars.

SHUI TA Is not that sum unusually high?

SUN No. He'll have to fire one of his present pilots. For negligence. And the fellow he has in mind isn't negligent, because he's got a large family. You understand. All this, by the way, in confidence. Shen Te needn't know it.

SHUI TA Perhaps not. Just one thing—won't that manager sell *you* out next month?

SUN Not me. There won't be any negligence in my work. I was unemployed long enough.

SHUI TA (*Nodding*) The hungry dog pulls the cart home faster. (*He scrutinizes him*) The responsibility is very great. Mr. Yang Sun, you ask my cousin to give up her small possessions, to leave all her friends in this town, and to put her entire fate into your hands. I assume you intend to marry Shen Te?

SUN I'd be prepared to.

SHUI TA But isn't it a pity, then, to get rid of the store for a few silver dollars? We won't get much for it if we have to sell at once. The two hundred silver dollars you have in your hands would pay the rent for half a year. Wouldn't that tempt you to continue in the tobacco business?

SUN Would it tempt *me?* Is Yang Sun, the flier, to be seen standing behind the counter: "Do you wish a strong cigar or a mild one, worthy sir?" That's no business for the Yang Sun's, not in this century!

SHUI TA Allow me to ask, is flying very profitable?

SUN (*Pulling a letter out of his pocket*) Sir, I'd get two hundred and fifty silver dollars a month! Look at the letter yourself. Here's the stamp and the postmark. Peking.

SHUI TA Two hundred and fifty silver dollars? That's a lot.

SUN Do you think I fly for nothing?

SHUI TA The job seems to be good. Mr. Yang Sun, my cousin has commissioned me to help you to this post which means so much to you. From her own point of view, I cannot see any good reason why she shouldn't follow the inclinations of her heart. She has every right to experience the joys of love. I'm prepared to turn everything here to money. Here comes the landlady, Mrs. Mi Tzu, whom I'll ask to advise me about the sale.

THE LANDLADY (*Entering*) Good day, Mr. Shui Ta. I suppose it's about the rent which is due the day after tomorrow?

SHUI TA Mrs. Mi Tzu, circumstances have arisen which make it look doubtful whether my cousin will keep her store. She's planning to marry, and her future husband (*He introduces* YANG SUN), Mr. Yang Sun, will take her to Peking where they are to start a new life. If I can get enough for my tobacco, I shall sell out.

THE LANDLADY How much do you need?

SUN Three hundred down.

SHUI TA (*Quickly*) No, five hundred!

THE LANDLADY (*To* SUN) Perhaps I'll be able to help you. How much did your tobacco cost?

SHUI TA My cousin paid a thousand silver dollars for it and very little has been sold.

THE LANDLADY A thousand silver dollars! She was gypped of course. I'll tell you something: I'll pay you three hundred silver dollars for the whole store if you move out the day after tomorrow.

SUN We'll do that. It'll work, old man!

SHUI TA It's too little.

SUN It's enough!

SHUI TA I've got to have at least five hundred.

SUN What for?

SHUI TA (*To the* LANDLADY) Allow me to talk something over with my cousin's fiancé (*Aside to* SUN) All the tobacco here has been pledged to two old people for the two hundred silver dollars which were given to you yesterday.

SUN Is there a written agreement?

SHUI TA No.

SUN (*To the* LANDLADY) We can manage with three hundred.

THE LANDLADY But I've got to know whether the store is in debt.

SUN You answer!

SHUI TA The store is not in debt.

SUN When can the three hundred be had?

THE LANDLADY The day after tomorrow, and you can still think it over. You'll get more if you don't sell in such a rush. I'll pay three hundred, but only because I want to do my share in what seems to be a case of young love. (*Exit*)

SUN (*Calling after her*) We'll make the deal! Little boxes, jars and sacks, everything for three hundred and the pain's over. (*To* SHUI TA) Perhaps some other place we can get more by the day after tomorrow?

SHUI TA Not in such a short time. We won't have one silver dollar apart from the three hundred of Mrs. Mi Tzu. You have the money for the trip and the first few weeks?

SUN Sure.

SHUI TA How much is that?

SUN I'll dig it up, anyway, even if I have to steal it!

SHUI TA Oh, I see, this money too has to be dug up?

SUN Don't fall out of your shoes, old man, I'll get to Peking somehow.

SHUI TA It can't be so cheap for two people.

SUN *Two* people? I'm leaving the girl behind. At first, she'll only be a millstone round my neck.

SHUI TA I see.

SUN Why d'you look at me as if I was a leaking oil tank? You've got to manage the best you can.

SHUI TA And how is my cousin to live?

SUN Can't *you* do something for her?

SHUI TA I'll try. (*Pause*) I wish, Mr. Yang Sun, you'd hand over to me the two hundred silver dollars and would leave them here till you can show me two tickets to Peking.

SUN My dear man, I wish you'd mind your own business.

SHUI TA Miss Shen Te . . .

SUN Just leave the girl to me.

SHUI TA . . . might not want to sell her store when she learns that . . .

SUN She'll want to. Even then.

SHUI TA And you're not afraid of my interference?

SUN My dear sir!

SHUI TA You seem to forget she's a human being and has got some sense.

SUN (*Amused*) What certain people think about their female relatives and the effect of reasonable persuasion has always been a source of wonder to me. Have you ever heard of the power of love? The tickling of the flesh? You want to talk reason to her? She doesn't know what reason is! On the other hand, the poor creature's been abused all her life. I've only to put my hand on her shoulder and say "you're coming with me" and she hears bells and wouldn't know her own mother.

SHUI TA (*With difficulty*) Mr. Yang Sun!

SUN Mr. What's-your-name!

SHUI TA My cousin is devoted to you because . . .

SUN Shall we say because I've got my hand on her bosom? Put that in your pipe and smoke it! (*He takes another cigar, then puts a few in his pocket, and finally takes the whole box under his arm*) Don't you go to her with empty hands. We'll stick to the marriage. And she'll bring the three hundred or you'll bring them. Either she or you! (*Exit*)

MRS. SHIN (*Putting her head out of the back room*) Not exactly pleasant. And all of Yellow Street knows he's got the girl completely under his thumb.

SHUI TA (*Crying out*) The store's gone! He isn't in love! I'm lost! (*He begins to run round like an imprisoned animal, repeating,* "The store's gone!" *until he stops suddenly and begins to talk to* MRS. SHIN) Shin, you grew up in the gutter and so did I. Are we frivolous? No. Do we lack the necessary brutality? No. I'm ready to take you by the throat and shake you till you spit out the last penny you've stolen from me. You know that. The times are terrible, this town is hell, but gradually we manage to crawl up the smooth walls. Then bad luck overtakes one or another of us: he is in love. That's enough, he's lost. One weakness and you're finished. How are you to free yourself of *all* weaknesses, and especially of the deadliest of weaknesses, love? Love is absolutely impossible! It's much too expensive! But then, tell me yourself, can one live and be *always* on the watch? What sort of a world is this?

> Caresses turn to strangulation.
> The sigh of love turns to a cry of fear.
> Why are the vultures circling over there?
> A girl is going to meet her lover.

MRS. SHIN I think I better go and get the barber right away. You've got to talk with the barber. He's a man of honor. The barber, he's the right one for your cousin.

(*Receiving no answer, she runs off.* SHUI TA *runs around again until* MR. SHU FU *enters, followed by* MRS. SHIN, *who, however, on a sign from* MR. SHU FU, *is forced to withdraw*)

SHUI TA (*Hurrying toward him*) My dear sir, I know from hearsay that you have hinted at a certain interest in my cousin. Let me set aside all the laws of propriety and reserve: Miss Shen Te is at the moment in great danger.

MR. SHU FU Oh!

SHUI TA Only a few hours ago the possessor of her own store, my cousin is now little more than a beggar. Mr. Shu Fu, this store is ruined.

MR. SHU FU Mr. Shui Ta, the charm of Miss Shen Te lies not in the goodness of her store but in the goodness of her heart. The name which this neighborhood has given to the young lady tells all. They call her the Angel of the Suburbs!

SHUI TA My dear sir, this goodness has cost my cousin two hundred silver dollars on a single day. We have to put a stop to that.

MR. SHU FU Allow me to express a different opinion: we've got to open the gates wide to this goodness. It's in the nature of the young lady to do good. Every morning I affectionately watch her feeding four people. What does that signify? Why can't she feed four hundred? I hear, for instance, that she's racking her brains about how to shelter some homeless people. My cabins behind the cattle run are empty. They're at her disposal. And so on and so forth . . . Mr. Shui Ta, might I hope that Miss Shen Te would lend an ear to certain ideas which have come to me in the last few days? Ideas like these?

SHUI TA Mr. Shu Fu, she will listen to such high thoughts with admiration.

(*Enter* WANG *with the* POLICEMAN. MR. SHU FU *turns around and studies the shelves*)

WANG Is Miss Shen Te here?

SHUI TA No.

WANG I am Wang, the water seller. I guess you're Mr. Shui Ta?

SHUI TA Quite right. Good day, Wang.

WANG I'm a friend of Shen Te's.

SHUI TA You're one of her oldest friends, I know.

WANG (*To the* POLICEMAN) You see? (*To* SHUI TA) I'm coming because of my hand.

THE POLICEMAN It's smashed all right. There's no doubt about it.

SHUI TA (*Quickly*) I see you need a sling. (*He gets a shawl from the back room and throws it to* WANG)

WANG But that's her new shawl.

SHUI TA She no longer needs it.

WANG But she bought it to please a certain person.

SHUI TA As things have turned out, that is no longer necessary.

WANG (*Making himself a sling out of the shawl*) She's my only witness.

THE POLICEMAN Your cousin's supposed to've seen how the barber Shu Fu hit the water seller with the curling iron. D'you know anything about it?

SHUI TA I only know that my cousin wasn't present when the incident occurred.

WANG That's a misunderstanding! Just wait till Shen Te's here and everything will be cleared up. Shen Te'll bear witness to everything. Where is she?

SHUI TA (*Seriously*) Mr. Wang, you call yourself my cousin's friend. My cousin has a lot of worries right now. She's been terribly exploited from all sides. In the future, she won't be able to afford the smallest weakness. I'm convinced you won't ask her to lose all she has by making her say anything but the truth in this matter.

WANG (*Confused*) But *she* advised me to go to the judge.

SHUI TA Was the judge supposed to heal your hand? (MR. SHU FU *turns round*). Mr. Wang, it's one of my principles never to meddle in the quarrels of my friends. (SHUI TA *bows to* MR. SHU FU *who returns the bow*)

WANG (*Taking off the sling and putting it back, sadly*) I understand.

THE POLICEMAN And now I guess I can go again. You went to a decent man—the wrong fellow for your swindling. You better be a bit more careful next time, with your accusations. If Mr. Shu Fu didn't put mercy before justice, you could be jailed for libel. Off with you now.

(*Exeunt*)

SHUI TA I beg you to excuse this occurrence.

MR. SHU FU It's excused. (*Urgently*) And this affair with a "certain person" (*He points to the shawl*) is really over? Completely finished?

SHUI TA Completely. She's seen through him. Of course, it'll take time till she's got over everything.

MR. SHU FU We shall be careful. Delicate.

SHUI TA There are some fresh wounds.

MR. SHU FU She'll go to the country.

SHUI TA For some weeks. However, before that she'll be glad to talk everything over with someone she can trust.

MR. SHU FU At a small dinner in a small but good restaurant.

SHUI TA In a discreet way. I'll hurry to inform my cousin. She'll be reasonable. She's very worried about the store, which she regards as a gift of the gods. Be patient for a few minutes. (*Exit into the back room*)

MRS. SHIN (*Putting her head in*) May I congratulate you?

MR. SHU FU Mrs. Shin, you may let Miss Shen Te's protégés know today that I am giving them shelter in the cabins behind the cattle run.

(*She nods, grinning*)

MR. SHU FU (*Getting up, to the audience*) What do you think of me, ladies and gentlemen? Could anyone do more? Could anyone be less selfish? More far-sighted? A small dinner! What vulgar and clumsy thoughts this would bring into the minds of most people. But nothing like that will happen. Nothing. She won't be touched. Not even casually. Not even accidentally while passing the salt! Nothing but ideas will be exchanged. Two souls will find each other over the flowers on the table, white chrysanthemums by the way. (*He makes a note of that*) No, we won't exploit an unfortunate situation. We won't turn a disappointment to our advantage. Understanding and assistance will be offered. And almost without a sound. A single glance might perhaps acknowledge it. A glance which could also mean more.

MRS. SHIN So everything went as you wished, Mr. Shu Fu?

MR. SHU FU Oh, just as I wished! There'll presumably be a few changes in this district. A certain person has been shown the door and some of the plots against this shop will be spoiled. Certain people who still dare to harm the reputation of the chastest girl in this city will get into trouble with me in the future. What do you know about this Yang Sun?

MRS. SHIN He's the dirtiest, laziest . . .

MR. SHU FU He's nothing. He doesn't exist. He can't be found, Mrs. Shin.

(*Enter* SUN)

SUN What's going on here?

MRS. SHIN Mr. Shu Fu, d'you want me to call Mr. Shui Ta? He won't want strangers loitering around in the store.

MR. SHU FU Miss Shen Te is having an important talk with Mr. Shui Ta and mustn't be interrupted.

SUN What, she's here? I didn't see her go in! What sort of a talk is that? I've got to be in on it!

MR. SHU FU (*Preventing him from going into the back room*) You'll have to be patient, my dear sir. I think I know who you are. Please take note that Miss Shen Te and I are about to announce our engagement.

SUN What?

MRS. SHIN That surprises you, doesn't it?

(SUN *is fighting with the barber to get into the back room when* SHEN TE *steps out of it*)

MR. SHU FU Excuse me, dear Shen Te. Perhaps you could explain . . .

SUN What's the matter, Shen Te? Are you crazy?

SHEN TE (*Breathlessly*) Sun, my cousin and Mr. Shu Fu have come to an agreement: I'm to listen to Mr. Shu Fu's ideas about how to help the people of the neighborhood. (*Pause*) My cousin wants to part us.

SUN And you agree?

SHEN TE Yes.

(*Pause*)

SUN Did they tell you I'm a bad man?

(SHEN TE *is silent*)

SUN Maybe I *am* a bad man, Shen Te. And that's why I need you. I'm low. Without money, without manners. But I fight back. They're driving you into misfortune, Shen Te. (*He goes over to her and speaks in an undertone*) Just look at him! Do you have no eyes in your head? (*With his hand on her shoulder*) Poor creature, *now* what did they want you to do? Make a reasonable match! Without me they'd just have sacrificed you. Admit that, but for me, you would have gone away with him!

SHEN TE Yes.

SUN A man you don't love.

SHEN TE Yes.

SUN Have you forgotten everything? How it was raining?

SHEN TE No.

SUN How you cut me from the tree? How you bought me a cup of water? How you promised me the money so I could fly again?

SHEN TE (*Trembling*) What do you want?

SUN I want you to come with me.

SHEN TE Mr. Shu Fu, forgive me, I want to go away with Sun.

SUN We're lovers, you know. (*He leads her to the door*) Where is the key to the store? (*He takes it from her pocket and hands it to* MRS. SHIN) Leave it outside the door when you're through. Come on, Shen Te.

MR. SHU FU But this is rape! (*Shouting to the back*) Mr. Shui Ta!

SUN Tell him not to shout so much in here.

SHEN TE Please don't call my cousin, Mr. Shu Fu. He doesn't agree with me, I know. But he's not right, I can feel it. (*To the audience*)

I want to go with the one I love
I don't want to reckon what it will cost
I don't want to consider if it is wise
I want to go with the one I love.

SUN That's it.
(*Exeunt*)

## Scene Five (a)

(*Before the curtain.* SHEN TE, *in her wedding outfit and on the way to her wedding, turns to the audience*)

SHEN TE I've had a terrible experience. As I was stepping out of the house, gay and full of expectation, the carpet dealer's old wife was standing on the street. She was trembling all over, and she told me that her husband had fallen sick from excitement and worry about the money they'd lent me. She thought it best that I return the money to her now in any case. Of course I promised it to her. She was very relieved, wished me the best of luck with tears in her eyes and asked me to forgive her because she couldn't altogether trust my cousin, nor, unfortunately, Sun. I had to sit down when she'd gone, I was so alarmed by my own behavior. With my emotions in an uproar, I threw myself again into the arms of Yang Sun. I couldn't resist his voice and his caresses. The bad things he said to Shui Ta didn't teach Shen Te anything. Sinking into his arms, I thought: the gods wanted me to be good to myself too.

To let no one perish, not even one's self,
To fill everyone with happiness, even one's self,
That is good.

How could I simply forget those two good old people? Like a small hurricane, Sun just swept away my store and all my friends in the direction of Peking. But he's not bad and he loves me. As long as I'm with him, he won't do anything bad. What men say between themselves doesn't count. He just wants to seem big and powerful and above all hard-boiled. When I tell him that the old couple won't be able to pay their taxes, he'll understand everything. He'd rather go and work in the cement factory than owe his flying to a crime. Of course flying's a great passion with Sun. Shall I be strong enough to bring out the good in him? Now, on the way to my wedding, I waver between fear and joy. (*She goes quickly off*)

## Scene Six

(*A side room of a cheap restaurant in the suburbs. A waiter pours out wine for the wedding party. Near* SHEN TE *are the* GRANDFATHER, *the* SISTER-IN-LAW, *the* NIECE, MRS. SHIN, *and the* UNEMPLOYED. *In the corner, alone, stands a* PRIEST. *Down stage,* SUN *is talking with his mother,* MRS. YANG. *He is wearing a dinner jacket*)

SUN Something unpleasant, Mamma. She just told me in all innocence that she can't sell the store for me. Somebody or other is bringing a claim because they lent her the two hundred silver dollars which she gave to you. And her cousin said that there wasn't any written agreement.

MRS. YANG What did you say to her? Of course you can't marry her now.

SUN There's no sense in talking with her about these things. She's got a thick head. I've sent for her cousin.

MRS. YANG But he wants to marry her to the barber.

SUN I've put an end to that marriage. The barber's been insulted. Her cousin will soon understand that if I don't hand over the two hundred, the creditors will seize the store and the store will be gone, but if I don't get the three hundred, my job will be gone too.

MRS. YANG I'll look for him outside the restaurant. Go to your bride, now, Sun!

SHEN TE (*Pouring wine, to the audience*) I wasn't mistaken in him. I couldn't see a trace of disappointment in his face. He's perfectly cheerful though it must be a heavy blow for him to give up flying. I love him very much. (*She waves* SUN *over*) Sun, you haven't drunk a toast with the bride!

SUN What shall we drink to?

SHEN TE Let's drink to the future.
(*They drink*)

SUN When the bridegroom's tuxedo will no longer be borrowed!

SHEN TE But when the bride's dress will still get rained on now and then.

SUN To everything we wish for!

SHEN TE That it may quickly come true!

MRS. YANG (*On the way out, to* MRS. SHIN) I'm delighted with my son. I've always impressed it on him that he can get whoever he wants. Why, he's a trained mechanic and flier. And what does he tell me now? "I'm marrying for love, Mamma," he says, "money isn't everything." It's a love match! (*To the* SISTER-IN-LAW) It has to happen once, hasn't it? But it's hard for a mother, it's hard. (*Calling back to the* PRIEST) Don't cut it too short. If you take as much time for the ceremony as you took to haggle about the price, it'll be dignified all right. (*To* SHEN TE) We've got to postpone things a little still, my dear. One of our most beloved guests hasn't arrived yet. (*To all*) Excuse me, please. (*Exit*)

THE SISTER-IN-LAW We'll gladly be patient as long as there's wine.

(*They all sit down*)

THE UNEMPLOYED We're not missing anything.

SUN (*Loud and jokingly before the guests*) And before the marriage I've still got to give you a little quiz. A not unnecessary thing when a wedding is held at such short notice. (*To the guests*) I've no idea what sort of a wife I'm getting. That worries me. (*To* SHEN TE) For instance, can you make five cups of tea with three tea leaves?

SHEN TE No.

SUN I see I won't be getting any tea. Can you sleep on a sack of straw the size of the book the priest is reading?

SHEN TE With someone else?

SUN Alone.

SHEN TE In that case, no.

SUN I'm horrified at the wife I'm getting.

(*They all laugh. Behind* SHEN TE, MRS. YANG *steps into the doorway. With a shrug of her shoulders, she tells* SUN *that there's no sign of the expected guest*)

MRS. YANG (*To the* PRIEST, *who has shown her his watch*) Don't be in such a hurry. It can be a matter of minutes. I can see they're drinking and smoking and no one's in a hurry. (*She sits down by the guests*)

SHEN TE Don't we have to talk about how we're going to arrange everything?

MRS. YANG Oh, please, let's not talk shop. Shoptalk introduces a *common* note into the celebration, doesn't it?

(*The entrance bell rings. They all look to the door but nobody enters*)

SHEN TE Who's your mother waiting for, Sun?

SUN That's a surprise for you. By the way, how's your cousin Shui Ta? I got on with him. A very sensible man! What a brain! Why don't you say anything?

SHEN TE I don't know. I don't want to think of him.

SUN Why not?

SHEN TE Because you *shouldn't* get on well with him. If you love me, you can't love him.

SUN Then may the three devils fetch him: the Fog-devil, the Engine-trouble-devil, and the Empty-gas-tank devil! Drink, you stubborn girl! (*He makes her drink*)

THE SISTER-IN-LAW (*To* MRS. SHIN) Something's wrong here.

MRS. SHIN What else did you expect?

THE PRIEST (*Resolutely stepping up to* MRS. YANG, *a watch in his hand*) I've got to go, Mrs. Yang. I've got another wedding to attend to, and tomorrow morning a funeral.

MRS. YANG D'you think I like all this postponing? We were hoping to manage with one pitcher of wine. But look how it's coming to an end! (*Loudly to* SHEN TE) My dear Shen Te, I can't understand where your cousin can be all this time!

SHEN TE My cousin?

MRS. YANG But, my dear, it's him we're waiting for! I'm just old fashioned enough to think that such a close relative of the bride should be present at the wedding.

SHEN TE Oh Sun, is it because of the three hundred silver dollars?

SUN (*Without looking at her*) Can't you hear? She's old fashioned. Well, I'm considerate. We'll wait another fifteen minutes and if he hasn't come then because the three devils have got him, we'll start!

MRS. YANG I guess you all know already that my son is getting a job as a mail pilot. I'm very pleased about it. In these times, we have to make good money.

THE SISTER-IN-LAW It's to be in Peking, isn't it?

MRS. YANG Yes, in Peking.

SHEN TE You've got to tell your mother, Sun, that Peking is out of the question.

SUN Your cousin will tell her, if he agrees with you. Between us: I don't agree.

SHEN TE (*Appalled*) Sun!

SUN How I hate this Setzuan. What a town! Do you know what they all look like when I half close my eyes? Horses! They fret and screw their necks up: what's thundering there above them? How's that? They're no longer needed? What, their time's up already? Let them bite themselves to death in their horse town! O to get out of here!

SHEN TE But I've promised the money to the old couple.

SUN Yes, you told me. And since you do stupid things like that, it's lucky your cousin's coming. Drink, and leave business to us! We'll fix it up.

SHEN TE (*Horrified*) But my cousin can't come.

SUN What do you mean?

SHEN TE He can't come!

SUN And how do you figure our future? Tell me that.

SHEN TE I thought you still had the two hundred silver dollars. We could return them tomorrow and keep the tobacco, which is worth a lot more. Then we'll sell it together in front of the cement factory since we can't pay the half year's rent.

SUN Forget it! Forget it fast, sister! *I* am to stand on the street and sell tobacco to cement workers, I, Yang Sun, the flier! I'd rather run through all two hundred in one night! I'd rather throw it in the river! And your cousin knows me! I've arranged it with him. He's to bring the three hundred to the wedding.

SHEN TE My cousin can't come.

SUN And I thought he couldn't stay away.

SHEN TE He can't be where I am.

SUN How mysterious!

SHEN TE Sun, you've got to know it: he's not your friend. I'm the one that loves you. My cousin Shui Ta doesn't love anybody. He's my friend, but he's no friend to my friends. He was thinking of the job at Peking when he agreed to your getting the old couple's money. But he won't bring you the three hundred silver dollars to the wedding.

SUN And why not?

SHEN TE (*Looking into his eyes*) He says you only bought one ticket to Peking.

SUN Yes, that was so yesterday, but just look what I

can show him today! (*He pulls two pieces of paper halfway out of his breast pocket*) The old woman needn't see. Here's two tickets to Peking. One for me and one for you. Do you still think your cousin's against the marriage?

SHEN TE No. The job's good. And I don't have my store any more.

SUN Because of you I sold our furniture.

SHEN TE Don't go on! Don't show me the tickets! I'm too afraid I might simply go with you. But I can't give you the three hundred silver dollars, Sun. What's to become of the old couple?

SUN And what's to become of me? (*Pause*) Better drink some more! Or are you a cautious person? I don't want a cautious wife. If I drink, I'll fly again. And you, if you drink, you might possibly understand me.

SHEN TE Don't think I don't understand you. You want to fly and I can't help you.

SUN "Here's a plane, my darling, but it's only got one wing!"

SHEN TE Sun, we can't get the job at Peking honestly. That's why I need the two hundred silver dollars which you got from me. Give them to me now, Sun!

SUN "Give them to me now, Sun!" What exactly are you talking about? Are you my wife or aren't you? You're betraying me, you know that, don't you? Luckily for both of us, things don't depend on you. Everything's arranged.

MRS. YANG (*Icily*) Sun, are you sure the bride's cousin is coming? Since he's still not here it might almost seem that he has something against this marriage.

SUN What are you thinking of, Mamma? We're bosom friends! I'll open the door wide so he'll find us right away when he comes to be his friend Sun's best man. (*He goes to the door and kicks it open. Then he returns, staggering somewhat since he has already drunk too much, and sits down again beside* SHEN TE) We're waiting. Your cousin's got more sense than you. Love, he says wisely, goes with living! And, more important than that, he knows what it means to you: no more store and no marriage either!

(*Everyone is waiting*)

MRS. YANG Now!

(*Steps can be heard and everyone looks toward the door. But the steps pass*)

MRS. SHIN It's going to be a scandal. I can feel it. I can smell it. The bride is waiting for the wedding but the groom's waiting for her cousin.

SUN The cousin's taking his time.

SHEN TE (*Softly*) Oh, Sun!

SUN To sit here with the tickets in my pocket and next to me a fool who doesn't know arithmetic. I can foresee the day when you'll send the police to my house to get the two hundred silver dollars.

SHEN TE (*To the audience*) He is bad and he wants me to be bad too. Here I am, I love him, and he waits for the cousin. But around me are the frail: the old woman with her sick husband, the poor who in the morning wait for their rice at my door, and an unknown man from Peking who is worried about his job. And they all protect me by trusting me.

SUN (*Staring at the glass pitcher in which there is no wine left*) The glass pitcher of wine is our clock. We're poor people and when the guests have drunk the wine, the clock's run down forever.

(MRS. YANG *beckons him to be silent, for steps can again be heard*)

THE WAITER (*Entering*) Do you want another pitcher of wine, Mrs. Yang?

MRS. YANG No, I think we've got enough. Wine only makes you warm, doesn't it?

MRS. SHIN It's expensive too, I'd say.

MRS. YANG Drinking always makes me perspire.

THE WAITER Might I ask, then, for a settlement of the bill?

MRS. YANG (*Not hearing him*) Ladies and gentlemen, I ask you to be patient a little longer, the cousin *must* be on his way. (*To the* WAITER) Don't spoil the festivities!

THE WAITER I can't let you leave without settling the bill.

MRS. YANG But I'm known here!

THE WAITER Exactly.

MRS. YANG It's outrageous, the service today. What d'you say to that, Sun?

THE PRIEST I take my leave. (*He goes off, ponderously*)

MRS. YANG (*Desperately*) Just stay where you are! The priest's coming back in a few minutes.

SUN Never mind, Mamma. Ladies and gentlemen since the priest's gone away, we can't keep you.

THE SISTER-IN-LAW Come on, grandfather!

THE GRANDFATHER (*Earnestly emptying his glass*) To the bride!

THE NIECE (*To* SHEN TE) Don't hold it against him. He wants to be friendly. He likes you.

MRS. SHIN What a disgrace!

(*All the guests go off*)

SHEN TE Shall I go too, Sun?

SUN No, you'll wait. (*He drags her by her bridal ornaments, messing them up*) Isn't it your wedding? I'm still waiting and the old woman's waiting too. *She* wants to see her falcon (*He points at himself*) in the clouds! However, I almost believe now that it'll be Saint Nevercome's Day before she'll step to her door and see his plane thundering over her house. (*To the empty seats, as if the guests were still present*) Ladies and gentlemen, what's the matter with the conversation? Don't you like it here? The wedding, after all, is only postponed a bit because of the important guest who's expected and because the bride doesn't yet know the meaning of love. For your entertainment, I, the bridegroom, will sing you a song. (*He sings*)

*THE SONG OF ST. NEVERCOME'S DAY*

On a certain day, as is generally known,
One and all will be shouting: Hooray, hooray!
For the beggar maid's son has a solid-gold throne
And the day is St. Nevercome's Day

On St. Nevercome's, Nevercome's, Nevercome's
Day
He'll sit on his solid-gold throne

Oh, hooray, hooray! That day goodness will pay!
That day badness will cost you your head!
And merit and money will smile and be funny
While exchanging salt and bread
On St. Nevercome's Nevercome's, Nevercome's
Day
While exchanging salt and bread

And the grass, oh, the grass will look down at the
sky
And the pebbles will roll up the stream
And all men will be good without batting an eye
They will make of our earth a dream
On St. Nevercome's, Nevercome's, Nevercome's
Day
They will make of our earth a dream

And as for me, that's the day I shall be
A flyer and one of the best
Unemployed man, you will have work to do
Washerwoman, you'll get your rest
On St. Nevercome's, Nevercome's, Nevercome's
Day
Washerwoman, you'll get your rest

MRS. YANG He won't come now.

(*The three sit there, two of them looking toward the door*)

## Scene Six (a)

(WANG'S *sleeping quarters. Again the* GODS *appear to* WANG *in a dream. He has fallen asleep over a large book. Music*)

WANG I'm glad you've come, illustrious ones! Permit me a question which disturbs me deeply. In the ruined hut of a priest who has moved away to become a laborer in the cement factory, I found a book and in it a strange passage. I absolutely must read it to you. Here it is. (*With his left hand he turns the pages of an imaginary book above the real book which is lying in his lap. He lifts up the imaginary book to read from while the real book remains where it is*) "In Sung there is a place called Thorngrove. Catalpas, cypresses, and mulberry trees grow there. Now trees which are one or two spans in circumference are cut down by those who want sticks to make dog kennels with. Those of three or four feet in circumference are cut down by rich families in search of boards for coffins. Those of seven or eight feet in circumference are cut down by people seeking beams for their luxury villas. Thus none of the trees lives its allotted span, for all perish before their time is up by saw and ax. Such are the tribulations of usefulness."

THE THIRD GOD In that case the one men have least use for would be the best.

WANG No, only the happiest. It's the worst but also the happiest.

THE FIRST GOD The things people write!

THE SECOND GOD Why does this parable affect you so deeply, water seller?

WANG Because of Shen Te, illustrious one! She has come to grief in her love because she followed the commandment, love thy neighbor! Perhaps she is really *too* good for this world, illustrious ones!

THE FIRST GOD Nonsense, weak and wretched man! Lice and doubts, it seems, have almost eaten you up.

WANG Certainly, illustrious one, forgive me! I only thought you might be able to intervene.

THE FIRST GOD That's quite impossible. Our friend here (*He points to the* THIRD GOD *who has a black eye*) intervened in a quarrel only yesterday. You can see the consequences.

WANG But her cousin has to be called in again. He's an incredibly skillful man, as I found out for myself, but not even he could achieve anything. The store seems to be lost.

THE THIRD GOD (*A bit worried*) Perhaps we should help after all?

THE FIRST GOD I'm of the opinion that she should help herself.

THE SECOND GOD (*Sternly*) The worse the situation of a good man, the better he shows himself. Suffering ennobles!

THE FIRST GOD All our hopes rest on her.

THE THIRD GOD Things aren't what they might be with our search. Now and then we find some good beginnings, gratifying intentions, many high principles, but all that hardly constitutes a good human being. And when we do find halfway good people, they don't live in a dignified, human way. (*Confidentially*) Things are especially bad with our sleeping quarters. You can see where we spend the nights by the straw sticking to our clothes.

WANG Just one thing, couldn't you at least . . .

THE GODS No. We're onlookers. We firmly believe that our good woman will find her own way on this dark earth. The heavier the burden the greater will be her strength! Just wait, water seller, and, you'll see, everything will come to a good . . .

(*The figures of the* GODS *have grown paler, their voices softer, all the time. Now they disappear and their voices are no longer heard*)

## Scene Seven

*(The yard behind* SHEN TE's *tobacco store. On a cart there are a few house furnishings.* SHEN TE *and* MRS. SHIN *are taking down the washing from the line)*

MRS. SHIN I can't understand why you don't fight for your store tooth and nail.

SHEN TE What? I can't even pay the rent. The old couple's two hundred silver dollars have to be returned today but since I've given them to someone else, I'll have to sell my tobacco to Mrs. Mi Tzu.

MRS. SHIN Everything's gone then. No husband, no tobacco, no place to stay! That's what happens when somebody wants to be better than other people. What are you going to live off now?

SHEN TE I don't know. Perhaps I can earn a little by sorting tobacco.

MRS. SHIN What are Mr. Shui Ta's pants doing here? He must have gone away from here naked!

SHEN TE He's got another pair of trousers.

MRS. SHIN I thought you said he'd gone for good? Why did he leave his pants behind?

SHEN TE Perhaps he doesn't need them any more.

MRS. SHIN Shall I pack them away?

SHEN TE No.

(MR. SHU FU *comes running in)*

MR. SHU FU Don't say anything. I know all. You sacrificed your love and happiness so as not to ruin two old people who trusted you. It's not in vain that this neighborhood, this suspicious and malevolent neighborhood, calls you the Angel of the Suburbs. Your fiancé couldn't rise to your moral level, so you left him. And now you're closing your store, this little haven for so many! I can't let that pass. Morning after morning I watched from my doorstep the little crowd of wretched people in front of your store and you distributing rice with your own hands. Will that never happen again? Must the good woman of Setzuan perish? Oh, if only you'd permit me to assist you with your good works! No, don't say anything! I don't want any assurances. No avowals that you wish to accept my help! But here. *(He pulls out a checkbook and signs a check which he puts on her cart)* I'm making out a blank check to you. You can fill it out as you wish, for any sum. And now I go, quietly and modestly, making no claims, on tiptoe, full of veneration, selflessly. *(Exit)*

MRS. SHIN *(Examining the check)* You're saved! The likes of you are lucky: you always find some idiot. But now fall to! Fill it out for a thousand silver dollars and I'll take it to the bank before he comes to his senses.

SHEN TE Put the washing basket on the cart. I can pay the laundry bill without the check.

MRS. SHIN What? You don't want to take the check? It's a crime! Is it just because you think you'd have to marry him? Sheer madness! People like him *want* to be led by the nose! It's the greatest bliss they know. Or do you still want to hold on to your flier when Yellow Street and the whole neighborhood know how badly he treated you?

SHEN TE It all comes from poverty. *(To the audience)*

I saw him puff up his cheeks in his sleep. They
were bad cheeks.
But in the morning I held his coat against the light
and saw the walls through it.
When I heard his cunning laugh, I grew afraid.
But when I saw his shoes full of holes, I loved
him dearly.

MRS. SHIN So you're defending him after everything that's happened. I've never seen anyone quite as crazy. *(Angrily)* I shall breathe more easily when we're rid of you in this neighborhood.

SHEN TE *(Staggering while taking down the wash)* I'm a bit dizzy.

MRS. SHIN *(Taking the wash from her)* Do you often get dizzy when you stretch or bend? If only there isn't a little visitor on the way! *(She laughs)* What a pretty mess! If that's what's happened, it's all up with the big check! It wasn't meant for an occasion of that sort.

*(She goes to the back with a basket.* SHEN TE *looks after her without moving. Then she looks at her body, feels it, and a great joy comes over her face)*

SHEN TE *(Softly)* O joy! A human being is growing in my womb. Nothing can be seen yet. But he's there already. The world awaits him secretly. In the towns, people are saying: Someone's coming now who's got to be reckoned with. *(In pantomime she introduces her little son to the audience)* A flier!

Welcome a new conqueror of unknown mountains
and unreachable regions!
One who brings the mail from man to man over the
unpassable deserts!

*(She begins to walk up and down, leading her little son by the hand)* Come, son, look at the world! Here, that's a tree. Bow to it, greet it. *(She shows him how to bow)* That's it: now you know each other. Stop, here comes the water seller. A friend. Give him your hand. Don't be afraid. A glass of fresh water for my son, please. It's warm today. *(She gives him the glass)* O dear, the policeman! We'll make a big circle around him. Perhaps we'll get a few cherries over there in the rich Mr. Feh Pung's garden. But we mustn't be seen there. Come, fatherless boy! You too want cherries! Easy, easy, son! *(They walk carefully, looking around)* No, over here, the bushes will hide us. No, you can't go straight at them like that. *(He seems to pull her away. She resists)* We've got to be reasonable. *(Suddenly she gives in)* All right, if you really must go straight at them . . . *(She lifts him up)* Can you reach the cherries? Push them in your mouth, that's a safe place for them. *(She takes a cherry from him and puts it in her*

*mouth*) Tastes pretty good. O heavens, the policeman! Now we've got to run! (*They flee*) There's the street. Quiet now, we'll walk slowly so we won't be noticed. As if not the least thing had happened. (*She sings, walking along with the child*)

For no reason a plum
Attacked a bum.
But the man, very quick,
Bit the plum in the neck.

(WANG, *the water seller, has come in, leading a child by the hand. He watches* SHEN TE *with wonder.* WANG *coughs*)

SHEN TE Oh, Wang! Hello.

WANG Shen Te, I've heard you're not so well off. You even had to sell your store to pay your debts. But here's a child without a roof over his head. He was running about in the stockyards. He seems to be one of Lin To's children. You remember the carpenter? He lost his shop a few weeks ago and has been drinking ever since. His children go hungry and hang around the streets. What can be done for them?

SHEN TE (*Taking the child from him*) Come, little man! (*To the audience*)

You there! Someone is asking for shelter.
A bit of tomorrow is asking for a today!
His friend, the conqueror, whom you know,
Is his advocate.

(*To* WANG) He can easily live in Mr. Shu Fu's cabins where I also may be going. I'm to have a baby too. But don't tell anyone or Yang Sun will hear it, and we'd only be in his way. Look for Mr. Lin To downtown, and tell him to come here.

WANG Thanks a lot, Shen Te. I knew you'd find something. (*To the child*) You see, someone who's *good* always knows a way out. I'll run quickly and get your father. (*He starts to go*)

SHEN TE Oh Wang, now it comes back to me: how's your hand? I *wanted* to take the oath for you but my cousin . . .

WANG Don't worry about my hand. Look, I've already learned to get along without my right hand. I hardly need it any more. (*He shows her how he can handle his pole without using his right hand*) Watch how I do it!

SHEN TE But it mustn't grow stiff! There, take the cart, sell everything, and go to the doctor with the money. I'm ashamed to have let you down like this. And what will you think of my accepting the cabins from the barber?

WANG The homeless can live there now. And so can you. That's more important than my hand. Now I'm going to get the carpenter. (*Exit*)

SHEN TE Promise me you'll go to the doctor!

(MRS. SHIN *has returned and has been waving to her*)

MRS. SHIN Are you crazy? Giving away the cart with your very last possessions! What's his hand to you? If the barber hears of it, he'll chase you out of the only shelter you can get. You haven't paid me for the laundry!

SHEN TE Why are you so bad?

You tread on your fellow man.
Isn't it a strain?
Your veins swell with your efforts to be greedy.
Extended naturally, a hand gives and receives with equal ease.
Grabbing greedily, it has to strain. Alas!
What an enticement, to give! How pleasant, to be kind!
A good word slips out like a sigh of contentment.

(MRS. SHIN *goes angrily off*)

SHEN TE (*To the child*) Sit down here and wait till your father comes.

(*The child sits on the ground. Enter the* HUSBAND *and* WIFE *who came to live with* SHEN TE *on the day her store opened. They are dragging large sacks*)

THE WIFE Are you alone, Shen Te? (*Since* SHEN TE *nods, she calls in her* NEPHEW *who is also carrying a sack*) Where's your cousin?

SHEN TE He's gone away.

THE WIFE And is he coming back?

SHEN TE No. I'm giving up the store.

THE WIFE We know that. That's why we came. We've got a few sacks of raw tobacco here which someone owed us and we'd like to ask you to move them to your new home together with your belongings. We haven't got a place yet to take them to and we'd be so noticeable on the street. I don't see how you can deny us this small favor after all the trouble we got into in your store.

SHEN TE I'll gladly do you the favor.

THE HUSBAND And if someone should ask whose sacks these are, you can say they're yours.

SHEN TE Who should ask me?

THE WIFE (*Looking at her sharply*) The police, for instance. They are prejudiced against us and want to ruin us. Where should we put the sacks?

SHEN TE I don't know, just now I'd rather not do anything that might get me in jail.

THE WIFE That's just like you. We're to lose the few miserable sacks of tobacco too, the only things we saved!

(SHEN TE *maintains a stubborn silence*)

THE HUSBAND Just think, this tobacco could start us in the manufacturing business. We could go a long way!

SHEN TE All right, I'll keep the sacks for you. For the time being, we'll put them in the back room.

(*She goes in with them. The child looks after her. Then, shyly glancing about, he goes to the garbage can and fishes around in it. He starts to eat out of it.* SHEN TE *and the others come back*)

THE WIFE You understand, I guess, that we depend on you completely.

SHEN TE Yes. (*She sees the child and grows rigid*)

THE HUSBAND We'll look for you the day after tomorrow in Mr. Shu Fu's cabins.

SHEN TE Go now, quickly. I'm not well.

(*She pushes them off. Exeunt the three*)

SHEN TE He is hungry. He's fishing in the garbage can. (*She picks up the child and, in the following speech, expresses her horror at the fate of poor children. She shows the audience the little gray mouth. She asserts her determination under no circumstances to treat her own child with such cruelty. During her speech the musicians start playing "The Song of the Defenselessness of the Gods and Good Men"*)

O son! O flier! Into what a world will you come?
They want to let you fish in the garbage can, even
you!
Only look at the little gray mouth!
(*She shows the child to the audience*)
How do you treat your offspring?
Have you no mercy on the fruit of your womb?
No pity for yourselves, unhappy men?
I shall defend my own even if I have to be a tigress
to do it!
Having seen this, from now on, I divorce myself
from everybody!
I will not rest till I have saved my son, if only him!
What I have learned in my school, the gutter,
With fisticuffs and deceit,
Will now be of use to you, my son!
I will be good to you, and a tigress, a wild beast
To all others,
If I have to.
And I *shall* have to.

(*She goes off to change into the cousin's clothes*)

SHEN TE (*Going*) Once more it has to be. The last time, I hope.

(*She has taken with her* SHUI TA'*s trousers. The returning* MRS. SHIN *looks after her curiously. Enter the* SISTER-IN-LAW *and the* GRANDFATHER. *The music continues softly*)

THE SISTER-IN-LAW The store's closed. The furniture's in the yard. That's the end.

MRS. SHIN The results of frivolity, sensuality, and self-love. And where's the journey to? Down, down, down! Into Mr. Shu Fu's cabins. With you.

THE SISTER-IN-LAW She'll have a nice surprise! We've come to complain! Damp rat holes with rotten floors! The barber only offered them to us because his soap supplies got moldy there. "I have shelter for you, what do you say to that?" Shame! we say to that!

(*Enter the* UNEMPLOYED)

THE UNEMPLOYED Is it true, Shen Te's moving away?

THE SISTER-IN-LAW Yes, she wanted to sneak off. No one was supposed to find out.

MRS. SHIN She's ashamed because she's ruined.

THE UNEMPLOYED (*Excitedly*) She's got to call her cousin! Advise her to call her cousin! He's the only one who can still do something.

THE SISTER-IN-LAW That's true. He's stingy enough but at least he'll save her store and then she'll help us again.

THE UNEMPLOYED I wasn't thinking of us, I was thinking of her. But, you're right, she should call him for our sake too.

(*Enter* WANG *with the* CARPENTER. *He leads two children by the hand*)

THE CARPENTER I really can't thank you enough. (*To the others*) We're getting a place to live.

MRS. SHIN Where?

THE CARPENTER Mr. Shu Fu's cabins! And it was little Feng who brought the change about! (*He sees* FENG) Well, here you are! "Here is someone asking for shelter," Miss Shen Te is supposed to have said, and at once she got us a place to stay. (*To the two children*) Thank your brother, you two! (*The* CARPENTER *and his children gaily bow to the child*) Our thanks, little friend!

(SHUI TA *has entered*)

SHUI TA May I ask what you all want here?

THE UNEMPLOYED Mr. Shui Ta!

WANG Good day, Mr. Shui Ta. I didn't know you'd come back. You know the carpenter, Mr. Lin To. Miss Shen Te has promised him a place in Mr. Shu Fu's cabins.

SHUI TA Mr. Shu Fu's cabins are not available.

THE CARPENTER So we can't live there?

SHUI TA The space is reserved for something else.

THE SISTER-IN-LAW Does that mean *we* have to get out too?

SHUI TA I'm afraid so.

THE SISTER-IN-LAW But where are we all to go?

SHUI TA (*Shrugging his shoulders*) As I understand Miss Shen Te, who has gone on a journey, it is not her intention to withdraw her aid completely. However, in the future, things will be ordered a bit more reasonably. No more food without services rendered in return. Instead, everyone will be given the opportunity to work himself up in an honest way. Miss Shen Te has decided to give you all work. Those of you who want to follow me now into Shu Fu's cabins will not be led into nothingness.

THE SISTER-IN-LAW Does that mean we're all supposed to work for Shen Te now?

SHUI TA Yes. You'll be making tobacco. In the room inside are three bales of goods. Get them!

THE SISTER-IN-LAW Don't forget we owned a store once. We prefer to work for ourselves. We have our own tobacco.

SHUI TA (*To the* UNEMPLOYED *and the* CARPENTER) Perhaps *you* will want to work for Shen Te since you don't have your own tobacco.

(*The* CARPENTER *and the* UNEMPLOYED *go in dejectedly. The* LANDLADY *enters*)

THE LANDLADY Well, Mr. Shui Ta, how're things with the sale? Here I have three hundred silver dollars.

SHUI TA Mrs. Mi Tzu, I've decided not to sell, but to sign the lease.

THE LANDLADY What? All of a sudden you don't need the money for the flier?

SHUI TA No.

THE LANDLADY And do you have the rent?

SHUI TA (*Taking the barber's check from the cart and filling it out*) Here I have a check for ten thousand silver dollars, made out by Mr. Shu Fu, who's interested in my cousin. Mrs. Mi Tzu, look for yourself. The two hundred silver dollars for the next half year's rent will be in your hands before 6 P.M. And now, Mrs. Mi Tzu, allow me to continue my work. I'm very busy today and have to ask your pardon.

THE LANDLADY Oh I see, Mr. Shu Fu steps into the flier's shoes! Ten thousand silver dollars! Nevertheless, Mr. Shui Ta, the young girls of today surprise me. They are fickle. And superficial too.

(*She goes out. The* CARPENTER *and the* UNEMPLOYED *drag in the sacks*)

THE CARPENTER I don't know why I'm dragging your sacks.

SHUI TA It's enough that I know. Your son here has a healthy appetite. He wants to eat, Mr. Lin To.

THE SISTER-IN-LAW (*Seeing the sacks*) Has my brother-in-law been here?

MRS. SHIN Yes.

THE SISTER-IN-LAW I thought so. I know these sacks. That's our tobacco!

SHUI TA You better not say that so loud. This is my tobacco, as you can see from the fact that it was standing in my room. If you have any doubts, we can go to the police and remove them. Is that what you want?

THE SISTER-IN-LAW (*Angrily*) No.

SHUI TA It seems you don't have tobacco of your own after all. Under these circumstances you will perhaps grasp the saving hand which Miss Shen Te is holding out to you? Be so kind now as to show me the way to Mr. Shu Fu's cabins.

(*Taking the Carpenter's youngest child by the hand,* SHUI TA *goes off, followed by the* CARPENTER, *his other children, the* SISTER-IN-LAW, *the* GRANDFATHER, *and the* UNEMPLOYED. *The* SISTER-IN-LAW, *the* CARPENTER, *and the* UNEMPLOYED *drag the sacks*)

WANG He's a bad man. But Shen Te is good.

MRS. SHIN I don't know. A pair of pants is missing from the clothes line and her cousin's wearing them. That must mean something. I'd like to know what.

(*Enter the old couple*)

THE OLD WOMAN Isn't Miss Shen Te here?

MRS. SHIN (*Absent-mindedly*) Gone away.

THE OLD WOMAN That's strange. She was going to bring us something.

WANG (*Sadly looking at his hand*) She was going to help me too. My hand's getting all stiff. I'm sure she'll be back soon. The cousin has never stayed long.

MRS. SHIN He hasn't, has he?

# Scene Seven (a)

(WANG'S *sleeping quarters. Music. In his dream, the water seller tells the* GODS *his fears. The* GODS *are still on their long journey. They seem tired. Stopping for a moment, they look over their shoulders toward the water seller*)

WANG Before your sudden appearance woke me, illustrious ones, I was dreaming. I saw my dear sister Shen Te in great distress in the rushes by the river at the place where those who commit suicide are found. She was staggering strangely and held her head low as if she were dragging something soft but heavy which was pulling her down in the mud. When I called to her, she told me she had to take the package of rules to the other shore without getting it wet since that would wipe away the writing. Actually I couldn't see that she was carrying anything. But I remembered with fear that you, the gods, had spoken to her about the great virtues, in gratitude for her taking you in when you were hard put to it for sleeping quarters, O shame! I'm sure you'll understand my worries.

THE THIRD GOD What do you propose?

WANG Somewhat fewer rules, illustrious ones! A little relaxation of the book of rules, benevolent ones, in view of the bad times.

THE THIRD GOD As for instance, Wang, as for instance?

WANG As for instance that only good will be required, instead of love, or . . .

THE THIRD GOD But that would be even more difficult, unhappy one!

WANG Or fairness instead of justice.

THE THIRD GOD But that would mean more work!

WANG Then just propriety instead of honor.

THE THIRD GOD But, don't you see, that would mean *more* work, not less, you skeptic! (*Tired, they wander on*)

# Scene Eight

(SHUI TA'S *tobacco factory.* SHUI TA *has established a small tobacco factory in* MR. SHU FU'S *cabins. Behind bars, fearfully close together, are several families, especially women and children. Among them are the* SISTER-IN-LAW, *the* GRANDFATHER, *the* CARPENTER, *and his children. Enter* MRS. YANG *followed by* YANG SUN)

MRS. YANG (*To the audience*) I have to tell you how the wisdom and strength of the universally respected

Mr. Shui Ta has transformed my son Yang Sun from a depraved scamp into a useful person. As the whole neighborhood found out, Mr. Shui Ta opened a small but soon flourishing tobacco factory near the cattle runs. Three months ago I found it necessary to visit him there with my son. After a short time he received me.

(SHUI TA *comes out of the factory and goes to* MRS. YANG)

SHUI TA How can I help you, Mrs. Yang?

MRS. YANG Mr. Shui Ta, I'd like to put in a word for my son. This morning the police were at our house and we were told that you have brought an action in the name of Miss Shen Te for breach of promise of marriage. You also claim that Sun dishonestly got his hands on two hundred silver dollars.

SHUI TA Quite right, Mrs. Yang.

MRS. YANG Mr. Shui Ta, for the sake of the gods, couldn't you be merciful once more? The money's gone. He ran through it in two days when nothing came of the flying job. I know he's a good-for-nothing. He'd already sold my furniture and wanted to go to Peking without his old Mamma. (*She weeps*) Miss Shen Te thought very highly of him once.

SHUI TA What do you have to say, Mr. Yang Sun?

SUN (*Darkly*) The money's gone.

SHUI TA Mrs. Yang, because of my cousin's incomprehensible weakness for your depraved son, I'm prepared to give him another chance. She told me that she expected honest work to produce an improvement. He can have a job in my factory. We will deduct the two hundred silver dollars from his salary bit by bit.

SUN Then it's the factory or the jail?

SHUI TA Take your choice.

SUN And I guess I can't talk with Shen Te?

SHUI TA No.

SUN Where's my place?

MRS. YANG A thousand thanks, Mr. Shui Ta! You are infinitely kind. The gods will reward you. (*To* SUN) You've departed from the right path. Now try your hand at honest work till you can face your mother again!

(SUN *follows* SHUI TA *into the factory.* MRS. YANG *returns to the footlights*)

MRS. YANG The first weeks were hard for Sun. The work didn't agree with him. He had little opportunity to distinguish himself. But in the third week a small incident came to his aid.

(SUN *and the former* CARPENTER LIN TO *are each dragging two bales of tobacco*)

THE CARPENTER (*He stops, groaning, and sits down on a bale*) I can hardly go on. I'm not young enough for this work.

SUN (*Sitting down too*) Why don't you just throw the sacks in their faces?

THE CARPENTER And how're we to live? To get a bare living I've even got to use the children. If Miss Shen Te could see this! She was good.

SUN She was all right. If conditions hadn't been so lousy, we could have made out quite nicely together. I'd like to know where she is. We better go on. *He* usually comes about this time.

(*They get up.* SUN *sees* SHUI TA *approaching*)

SUN Give me one of your sacks, you cripple! (SUN *takes one of the bales from* LIN TO)

THE CARPENTER Thanks a lot! Now if *she* were here and saw how you help an old man you'd soon be in favor. Oh dear!

(*Enter* SHUI TA)

MRS. YANG And of course Mr. Shui Ta saw right away what it means to be a good worker not shrinking from any job. And he stepped in.

SHUI TA Stop, you! What's going on? Are you only carrying one sack?

THE CARPENTER I'm a bit tired today, Mr. Shui Ta, and Yang Sun was kind enough to . . .

SHUI TA You're going back to take three bales, my friend. What Yang Sun can do, you can do. Yang Sun has the right attitude and you have not.

MRS. YANG (*While the former* CARPENTER *gets two more bales*) Of course, not a word to Sun but Mr. Shui Ta was wise to the situation. And the following Saturday when the wages were being paid out . . .

(*A table is brought in and* SHUI TA *arrives with a bag of money. Standing next to the foreman—the former* UNEMPLOYED*—he pays the wages.* SUN *steps up to the table*)

THE UNEMPLOYED Yang Sun, six silver dollars.

SUN Excuse me, it can't be more than five. Only five silver dollars. (*He takes the list held by the foreman*) Please look, here are marked *six* working days. That's a mistake. I was absent one day because of some court business. (*Hypocritically*) I don't want anything I don't deserve, however lousy the pay is!

THE UNEMPLOYED Okay, five silver dollars! (*To* SHUI TA) A rare case, Mr. Shui Ta!

SHUI TA How can it say six days here if it was only five?

THE UNEMPLOYED I must have made a mistake, Mr. Shui Ta. (*To* SUN, *coldly*) It won't happen again.

SHUI TA (*Calling* SUN *aside*) I noticed the other day that you're a strong man and don't hold your strength back. You give it to the firm. Today I see you're even honest. Does it often happen that the foreman makes mistakes in favor of the employees?

SUN He's got friends among the workers and they look on him as one of themselves.

SHUI TA I see. Well, one good turn deserves another. Would you like some little recompense?

SUN No. But perhaps I may point to the fact that I'm also intelligent. I've had an education, you know. The foreman means well enough by the workers but he's uneducated and can't understand what the firm needs. Give me a trial period of one week, Mr. Shui Ta, and I think I'll be able to prove to you that my intelligence can be worth more to the firm than my physical strength.

MRS. YANG Those were daring words, but that evening I said to my son: You're a flier. Show that, even where you are now, you can rise! Fly, my falcon! And, really, education and intelligence can do great things! How can you belong to the better sort of people without them? My son worked true miracles in Mr. Shui Ta's factory!

(SUN *stands with his legs apart behind the workers. Above their heads is a basket of raw tobacco which they are handing along*)

SUN You there, I don't call that honest work! This basket has got to move faster! (*To a child*) Sit on the floor where you don't take up so much room! And you, yes, you over there, you can easily take on the pressing too! Lazy dogs, what're you getting paid for? Hurry up with the basket! The devil! Put grandfather on one side and let him pick with the children! No more laziness now! To my beat, the whole thing! (*He claps the rhythm with his hands and the basket moves faster*)

MRS. YANG And no enmity, no abuse from uneducated people—and there was plenty of it—could stop my son from doing his duty.

(*One of the workers starts the Song of the Eighth Elephant. The others join in the refrain*)

*SONG OF THE EIGHTH ELEPHANT*

Chang had seven elephants—all much the same—
But then there was Little Brother
The seven, they were wild, Little Brother, he was tame
And to guard them Chang chose Little Brother
Run faster!
Mr. Chang has a forest park
Which must be cleared before tonight
And already it's growing dark!

When the seven elephants cleared that forest park
Mr. Chang rode high on Little Brother
While the seven toiled and moiled till dark
On his big behind sat Little Brother
Dig faster!
Mr. Chang has a forest park
Which must be cleared before tonight
And already it's growing dark!

And the seven elephants worked many an hour
Till none of them could work another
Old Chang, he looked sour, on the seven, he did glower
But gave a pound of rice to Little Brother
What was that?
Mr. Chang has a forest park
Which must be cleared before tonight
And already it's growing dark!

And the seven elephants hadn't any tusks
The one that had the tusks was Little Brother!
Seven are no match for one, if the one has a gun!
How old Chang did laugh at Little Brother!
Keep on digging!
Mr. Chang has a forest park
Which must be cleared before tonight
And already it's growing dark!

(*Smoking a cigar,* SHUI TA *has come casually strolling forward.* YANG SUN, *laughing, has joined in the refrain of the third stanza and speeded up the tempo of the last by clapping his hands*)

MRS. YANG We really can't thank Mr. Shui Ta enough. Almost without lifting a finger, with wisdom and strength alone, he's brought out all the good that lay hidden in Sun. He didn't make his fantastic promises like his cousin whom they praise so highly. He just forced him into honest work. Today, Sun is quite a different person. You'll have to admit that! A noble man is like a bell. If you ring it, it rings, and if you don't, it don't, as the saying goes.

## Scene Nine

(SHEN TE'S *tobacco store. The store has become an office with club chairs and fine carpets. It is raining.* SHUI TA, *now fat, is sending away the* OLD MAN *and his wife.* MRS. SHIN, *amused, looks on. She is obviously in new clothes*)

SHUI TA I'm sorry I can't tell you when she'll be back.

THE OLD WOMAN We got a letter today with the two hundred silver dollars which we once lent her. It had no return address. But the letter must have come from Shen Te. We'd like to write to her. What's her address?

SHUI TA I'm sorry I don't know that either.

THE OLD MAN Let's go.

THE OLD WOMAN She's got to come back sometime.

(SHUI TA *bows. The two old people go off, uncertain and worried*)

MRS. SHIN They got their money too late. Now they've lost their store because they couldn't pay their taxes.

SHUI TA Why didn't they come to me?

MRS. SHIN People don't like to come to you. At first, I guess, they were waiting for Shen Te to come back, because they had nothing in writing. Then at the critical moment the old man got a fever and his wife stayed with him day and night.

SHUI TA (*He has to sit down; he is beginning to feel sick*) I'm dizzy again.

MRS. SHIN (*Attending to him*) You're in your seventh month! The excitement isn't good for you. You can be glad you've got me. No one can get along without help from others. Well, I'll be at your side when your hardest hour comes. (*She laughs*)

SHUI TA (*Weakly*) Can I count on it, Mrs. Shin?

MRS. SHIN I'll say. Of course it'll cost you a bit. Open your collar, you'll feel better.

SHUI TA (*Wretchedly*) It's all for the child's sake, Mrs. Shin.

MRS. SHIN All for the child.

SHUI TA I'm getting fat too fast. It must draw attention.

MRS. SHIN They put it down to your wealth.

SHUI TA And what'll happen to the little one?

MRS. SHIN You ask that three times a day. It'll be taken care of. It'll have the best that money can buy.

SHUI TA Yes. (*Anxiously*) And it must never see Shui Ta.

MRS. SHIN Never. Always Shen Te.

SHUI TA But the rumors in the neighborhood! The things the water seller says! The store is watched!

MRS. SHIN As long as the barber doesn't know anything, nothing's lost. Drink some of this water.

(*Enter* SUN *in a smart suit and with a businessman's brief case. He looks surprised at finding* SHUI TA *in* MRS. SHIN'S *arms*)

SUN I guess I'm intruding.

SHUI TA (*Getting up with difficulty and going to the door, staggering*) Until tomorrow, Mrs. Shin!

(MRS. SHIN, *putting on her gloves, smiles and goes off*)

SUN Gloves! Where from, what for, and how? Is she fleecing you maybe? (*Since* SHUI TA *does not answer*) Are even you susceptible to the tender emotions? Funny. (*He takes a sheet of paper out of his brief case*) Anyway, you haven't been at your best, lately, not as you used to be. Moods. Indecisions. Are you ill? The business suffers. Here's another letter from the police. They want to close the factory. They say that at the very most they can only permit twice the lawful number of workers. You've got to do something now, Mr. Shui Ta.

(SHUI TA *looks at him absent-mindedly for a moment. Then he goes into the back room and returns with a bag. He pulls out a new bowler hat and throws it on the desk*)

SHUI TA The firm wishes its representatives to be decently dressed.

SUN Did you buy that for me?

SHUI TA (*Indifferently*) Try it on and see if it fits.

(SUN *is surprised but puts it on.* SHUI TA *looks him over and puts the bowler in place*)

SUN Your servant! But don't evade me again! You've got to discuss the new project with the barber today.

SHUI TA The barber's demanding impossible conditions.

SUN Of what kind? If only you'd tell me.

SHUI TA (*Evasively*) The cabins are good enough.

SUN Yes, good enough for the rabble working there. But not good enough for the tobacco. It gets damp. Before the meeting I'll have a talk with Mrs. Mi Tzu about *her* buildings. If we have them, we can fire this bunch of beggars, abortions, and walking scarecrows. They're not good enough. We'll have a cup of tea, I'll stroke Mrs. Mi Tzu's fat knees, and we'll get her buildings half price.

SHUI TA (*Sharply*) No. In the interest of the firm's reputation, I want your behavior always to be personally reserved and coolly businesslike.

SUN Why are you so irritated? Are those unpleasant rumors bothering you?

SHUI TA I don't pay any attention to rumors.

SUN Then it must be the rain again. Rain always makes you irritable and melancholy. I'd like to know why.

(WANG *is heard singing "The Song of the Water Seller in the Rain"*)

SUN Here's that damned water seller. He'll be starting his heckling again.

WANG'S VOICE (*From outside*) Aren't there any good people left in the city of Setzuan? Not even here on the square where the good Shen Te used to live? Where is she who even when it was raining bought a little water from me in the gladness of her heart many months ago? Where is she now? Has no one seen her? Has no one heard from her? She went into this house one evening and never came out again.

SUN Shall I shut his trap for him? What's it to him where she is? By the way, I think you're only keeping it secret so that *I* won't find out.

WANG (*Entering*) Mr. Shui Ta, I'm asking you again when Shen Te will come back. It's six months now since she went away. (SHUI TA *is silent*) In the meantime much has happened which she would never have put up with. (SHUI TA *is still silent*) Mr. Shui Ta, there are rumors in the district that something must have happened to Shen Te. We, her friends, are very worried. Have the goodness to give us her address!

SHUI TA Unfortunately, I'm not free at the moment, Mr. Wang. Come back next week.

WANG (*Excitedly*) In the mornings there used to be rice at her door. For the needy. It has been there again lately!

SHUI TA And what do people conclude from this?

WANG That Shen Te hasn't gone away at all, but . . .

SHUI TA But what? (WANG *is silent*) Then I'll give you my answer. And it is final. If you're Shen Te's friend, Mr. Wang, ask about her as little as possible. That's my advice.

WANG Nice advice! Mr. Shui Ta, Shen Te told me before her disappearance that she was pregnant!

SUN What?

SHUI TA (*Quickly*) It's a lie!

WANG (*Very earnestly to* SHUI TA) Mr. Shui Ta, you mustn't believe that Shen Te's friends will stop asking about her. A good person isn't so easily forgotten. There aren't many. (*Exit*)

(*Motionless,* SHUI TA *looks after him, then goes quickly into the back room*)

SUN (*To the audience*) Shen Te pregnant! I'm beside myself! I've been swindled! She must have told her cousin right away and that scoundrel sent her away immediately! "Pack your suitcase and disappear before the child's father gets wind of it." It's absolutely unnatural. It's inhuman. I have a son, a Yang appears on the scene, and what happens? The girl disappears and I'm left here to slave! (*He gets angry*) I'm put off with a hat! (*He stamps on it*) Criminal! Thief! Kidnapper! And the girl's virtually without a protector! (*Sobbing can be heard from the back room. He stands still*) Did I hear sobbing? Who is it? It's stopped. What sobs are these? That cunning dog Shui Ta doesn't sob! Who sobs then? And what does it mean that the rice is said to be at the door in the mornings? Is the girl here after all? Is he just hiding her? Who else could be sobbing? That would be just the thing I want! If she's pregnant I've got to find her!

(SHUI TA *returns from the back room. He goes to the door and looks out into the rain*)

SUN Well, where is she?

SHUI TA (*Putting up his hand and listening*) Just a moment! It's nine o'clock. But one can't hear a thing today. The rain's too heavy.

SUN (*Ironically*) And what do you want to hear?

SHUI TA The mail plane.

SUN Stop fooling.

SHUI TA I was once told that you wanted to fly? Have you lost that desire?

SUN I'm not complaining about my present position, if that's what you mean. I don't care for night work, you know. Flying the mail is night work. The firm's become very dear to me, so to speak. It is after all the firm of my one-time future wife, even if she has gone away. And she has, hasn't she?

SHUI TA Why do you ask?

SUN Maybe because her affairs still don't leave me altogether unmoved.

SHUI TA That might interest my cousin.

SUN In any case, I'm still sufficiently concerned in her affairs not to close my eyes if, for instance, she were kept under lock and key.

SHUI TA By whom?

SUN By you!

(*Pause*)

SHUI TA What would you do?

SUN I might, to begin with, start arguing about my position in the firm.

SHUI TA Oh, I see. And if the firm, that is, if *I* should give you an adequate position, could I count on your giving up all further investigations concerning your one-time future wife?

SUN Perhaps.

SHUI TA And what sort of new position are you thinking of?

SUN The top one. I'd be thinking of throwing you out, for example.

SHUI TA And if, instead of me, the firm threw *you* out?

SUN I'd probably come back. And not alone.

SHUI TA But?

SUN With the police.

SHUI TA With the police. And suppose the police found no one here?

SUN Then I suppose they'd search this back room. Mr. Shui Ta, my longing for the lady of my heart is insatiable. I feel I must do something in order to fold her in my arms again. (*Calmly*) She's pregnant and needs someone around. I've got to talk it over with the water seller. (*He goes*)

(SHUI TA *looks after him without moving. Then he quickly returns to the back room. He brings out various belongings of* SHEN TE'S, *underwear, dresses, toilet articles. He looks a long time at the shawl which* SHEN TE *bought from the* OLD MAN *and his wife. He then makes all these things up into a bundle and. hearing a noise, hides it under the table. Enter the* LANDLADY *and* MR. SHU FU. *They greet* SHUI TA *and put away their umbrellas and rubbers*)

THE LANDLADY Fall's coming on, Mr. Shui Ta.

MR. SHU FU A sad season!

THE LANDLADY And where's your charming secretary? A terrible lady-killer! But I guess you don't know that side of him. All the same he knows how to combine charm with attention to business in a way which can only be to your advantage.

SHUI TA (*Bowing*) Won't you take a seat?

(*They sit down and start smoking*)

SHUI TA My friends, an unforeseen incident which might have certain consequences forces me to speed up the negotiations. Negotiations concerning the future of the project I've been working on. Mr. Shu Fu, my factory is in difficulties.

MR. SHU FU It always is.

SHUI TA But now the police are openly threatening to close it if I can't point to negotiations for a new project. Mr. Shu Fu, it's a question of my cousin's one piece of property. Now you've always displayed the liveliest interest in my cousin.

MR. SHU FU Mr. Shui Ta, I have a deep aversion to talking about your constantly expanding projects. I speak about a small dinner with your cousin; you hint at financial difficulties. I put cabins for the homeless at your cousin's disposal; you establish a factory there. I hand her a check; you present it. Your cousin disappears; you ask for ten thousand silver dollars, remarking that my cabins are too small. Sir, where *is* your cousin?

SHUI TA Mr. Shu Fu, don't worry. I can inform you today that she'll be back very soon.

MR. SHU FU Soon? When? You've been saying "soon" for weeks.

SHUI TA I'm not demanding new signatures from you. I've merely asked whether you'd show more interest in my project if my cousin returned.

MR. SHU FU I've told you a thousand times that I'm ready to discuss everything with your cousin and nothing with you. However, it seems that you want to put obstacles in the way of such a discussion.

SHUI TA Not any more.

MR. SHU FU When will it take place then?

SHUI TA (*Uncertainly*) In three months.

MR. SHU FU (*Annoyed*) Then I'll sign in three months.

SHUI TA But everything has to be prepared.

MR. SHU FU You can prepare everything, Shui Ta, if you're convinced that your cousin will really come at this time.

SHUI TA Mrs. Mi Tzu, are you, for your part, ready to confirm to the police that I may have your workrooms?

THE LANDLADY Certainly, if you'll let me have your secretary. You've known for weeks that's my condition. (*To* MR. SHU FU) The young man's so efficient in business and I need a manager.

SHUI TA You've got to understand that I can't do without Mr. Yang Sun just now, with all the difficulties I'm having. And my health has been failing me lately.

I was ready from the beginning to let you have him, but . . .

THE LANDLADY Yes, but?

(*Pause*)

SHUI TA All right, he'll call on you tomorrow, in your office.

MR. SHU FU I am very glad that you were able to reach this decision, Shui Ta. Should Miss Shen Te really come back, the young man's presence would be highly improper. As we know, he once exerted a most harmful influence over her.

SHUI TA (*Bowing*) Doubtless. Please excuse my long hesitation over the question of my cousin Shen Te and Mr. Yang Sun. It is not worthy of a businessman. But they were once very close to each other.

THE LANDLADY You're excused.

SHUI TA (*Looking toward the door*) My friends, let us now reach a settlement. In this once small and shabby store where the poor people of the neighborhood bought the good Shen Te's tobacco, we, her friends, are resolving to establish twelve beautiful new stores which in the future will sell Shen Te's good tobacco. I'm told people are calling me the Tobacco King of Setzuan. Actually I carried on this business solely in my cousin's interests. It will belong to her, her children, and her grandchildren.

(*The noise of a crowd can be heard from outside Enter* SUN, WANG, *and the* POLICEMAN)

THE POLICEMAN Mr. Shui Ta, I'm very sorry the excited state of this neighborhood forces me to follow up a report originating in your own firm. According to this report you are depriving your cousin Miss Shen Te of her freedom.

SHUI TA It's not true.

THE POLICEMAN Mr. Yang Sun here testifies that from the room behind your office he heard sobbing which could only come from a female.

THE LANDLADY That's ridiculous. I and Mr. Shu Fu, two respected citizens of this city whose evidence could hardly be doubted by the police, can testify that no one has been sobbing here. We are quietly smoking our cigars.

THE POLICEMAN Unfortunately I have orders to inspect the room in question.

(SHUI TA *opens the door. The* POLICEMAN *bows and steps into the doorway. He looks into the room, then turns round and smiles*)

THE POLICEMAN There's really nobody in there.

SUN (*Who has been following him*) But I heard sobbing! (*His eye lights on the table under which* SHUI TA *has pushed the bundle. He spots the bundle*) That wasn't here before! (*Opening it, he shows* SHEN TE'S *dresses and other things*)

WANG Those are Shen Te's things! (*He runs to the door and calls out*) Her clothes have been discovered here!

THE POLICEMAN (*Taking the things*) You declare that your cousin's gone away. A bundle with things of hers is found hidden under your table. Where can the girl be reached, Mr. Shui Ta?

SHUI TA I don't know her address.

THE POLICEMAN That is most regrettable.

SHOUTS FROM THE CROWD Shen Te's things have been found! The Tobacco King has murdered the girl and put her out of the way!

THE POLICEMAN Mr. Shui Ta, I shall have to ask you to follow me to the station.

SHUI TA (*Bowing to the* LANDLADY *and* MR. SHU FU) I have to apologize for this scandal, my friends. But there are still judges in Setzuan. I'm convinced that everything will shortly be cleared up. (*He goes out, the* POLICEMAN *at his back*)

WANG A terrible crime has been committed!

SUN (*Dismayed*) But I heard sobbing!

## Scene Nine (a)

(WANG'S *sleeping quarters. Music. For the last time the* GODS *appear to the water seller in his dream. They have changed considerably. There are unmistakable signs of a long journey, extreme exhaustion, and manifold unhappy experiences. One has had his hat struck off his head, one has lost a leg in a fox trap, and all three go barefoot*)

WANG At last you've come! Terrible things have been happening in Shen Te's tobacco store, illustrious ones. Shen Te went away again many months ago! Her cousin seized everything! Today he's been arrested. He's supposed to have murdered her to get her store. But I don't believe it. I had a dream in which she came and told me that her cousin's holding her prisoner. Oh, illustrious ones, you must come back at once and find her.

THE FIRST GOD This is terrible. Our whole search has come to grief. We didn't find many good people and those we found lived in a way quite unworthy of human beings. We'd already decided to confine ourselves to Shen Te.

THE SECOND GOD If she's still good!

WANG She certainly is, but she's disappeared!

THE FIRST GOD Then all is lost.

THE SECOND GOD Restrain yourself!

THE FIRST GOD What good would that do? If she can't be found, we've got to retire. What sort of world did we find? Misery, vulgarity, and waste everywhere! Even the countryside has fallen away from us. The lovely trees are decapitated by telephone wires and on the other side of the mountains we see heavy smoke clouds and hear the thunder of cannon. And nowhere a good man who can pull through!

THE THIRD GOD Alas, water seller, our commandments

seem to be deadly. I fear that all our moral rules have to be done away with. People keep busy just saving their skins. Good intentions bring them to the brink of the abyss, and good deeds throw them into it. (*To the other two* GODS) The world can't be lived in, you've got to admit!

THE SECOND GOD (*Vehemently*) No, it's people who are worthless!

THE THIRD GOD The world is too cold!

THE SECOND GOD People are too weak!

THE FIRST GOD Dignity, my friends, dignity! Brothers, we mustn't despair. We did find one human being who was good and stayed good. She's only disappeared. Let's hurry and find her! One is enough! Didn't we say that everything can still turn out well if there's one human being who can stand this world? Just one?

(*They quickly disappear*)

## Scene Ten

(*A courtroom. Groups:* MR. SHU FU *and the* LANDLADY. SUN *and his mother.* WANG, *the* CARPENTER, *the* GRANDFATHER, *the* YOUNG PROSTITUTE, *the* OLD MAN *and* WOMAN. MRS. SHIN, *the* POLICEMAN. *The* UNEMPLOYED, *the* SISTER-IN-LAW)

THE OLD MAN He's too powerful.

WANG He wants to open twelve new stores.

THE CARPENTER How can the judge give a fair sentence if the accused's friends—the barber Shu Fu and the landlady Mi Tzu—are also *his* friends?

THE SISTER-IN-LAW Mrs. Shin was seen last night carrying a fat goose into the judge's kitchen by order of Mr. Shui Ta. The fat was dripping through the basket.

THE OLD WOMAN (*To* WANG) Our poor Shen Te will never be found.

WANG No, only the gods can discover the truth.

THE POLICEMAN Order! The judges are coming!

(*Enter the three* GODS *in judges' robes. As they walk by the footlights on their way to their seats, one can hear them whispering*)

THE THIRD GOD We'll be found out. The certificates are very badly forged.

THE SECOND GOD And people will wonder about the judge's sudden indigestion.

THE FIRST GOD No, that's only natural. He ate half a goose.

MRS. SHIN These are *new* judges!

WANG And very good ones!

(*The third and last* GOD *hears this, turns round, and smiles at* WANG. *The* GODS *sit down. The* FIRST GOD *beats on the table with a hammer. The* POLICEMAN *brings in* SHUI TA *who is whistled at but walks with lordly steps*)

THE POLICEMAN Be prepared for a surprise. It isn't the just Fu Yi Tcheng. But the new judges look very mild too.

(SHUI TA *sees the* GODS *and faints*)

THE YOUNG PROSTITUTE What's the matter? The Tobacco King has fainted.

THE SISTER-IN-LAW Yes, at the sight of the new judges!

WANG He seems to know them! I don't understand that.

THE FIRST GOD Are you the tobacco merchant Shui Ta?

SHUI TA (*Weakly*) Yes.

THE FIRST GOD You have been accused of doing away with your own cousin Miss Shen Te, in order to take possession of her business. Do you plead guilty?

SHUI TA No.

THE FIRST GOD (*Turning the pages of documents*) We'll first hear the policeman of this neighborhood on the reputation of the accused and on the reputation of his cousin.

THE POLICEMAN (*Stepping forward*) Miss Shen Te was a girl who liked to please everyone, who lived and let live, as the saying goes. Mr. Shui Ta, on the other hand, is a man of principle. The generosity of Miss Shen Te forced him at times to strict measures. However, unlike the girl, he was always on the side of the law, your honor. Once, people to whom his cousin trustfully gave shelter were unmasked by him as a band of thieves. Another time he saved Miss Shen Te at the last moment from plain perjury. I know Mr. Shui Ta to be a respectable and law-abiding citizen.

THE FIRST GOD Are there others present who want to testify that the accused is incapable of his supposed crime?

(MR. SHU FU *and the* LANDLADY *step forward*)

THE POLICEMAN (*Whispering to the* GODS) Mr. Shu Fu, a very influential gentleman.

MR. SHU FU Mr. Shui Ta has the reputation of a highly respected businessman here in Setzuan. He is Vice-President of the Chamber of Commerce and is about to be made justice of the peace.

WANG (*Interrupting*) By you! You're doing business with him!

THE POLICEMAN (*Whispering*) A disagreeable character.

THE LANDLADY As President of the Community Chest I'd like to call the attention of the court to this fact: Mr. Shui Ta is not only about to give to his numerous employees the best possible rooms, well-lighted and healthy, but is also making regular contributions to our home for the disabled.

THE POLICEMAN (*Whispering*) Mrs. Mi Tzu, a close friend of the judge Fu Yi Tcheng!

THE FIRST GOD Yes, yes, but now we've got to hear whether anyone has *less* favorable evidence to bring forward.

(WANG, *the* CARPENTER, *the* OLD MAN *and* WOMAN,

*the* UNEMPLOYED, *the* SISTER-IN-LAW, *and the* YOUNG PROSTITUTE *step forward*)

THE POLICEMAN The scum of the neighborhood.

THE FIRST GOD Well, what do you know of the general behavior of Shui Ta?

SHOUTS (*Jumbled*) He's ruined us!
—He blackmailed me!
—He led us off on the wrong track!
—Exploited the helpless!
—Lied!
—Cheated!
—Murdered!

THE FIRST GOD Accused, what have you to say?

SHUI TA I have simply enabled my cousin to exist, your honor. I only came when she was in danger of losing her little store. I had to come three times. I never wanted to stay. But the last time circumstances forced me to remain. I never had anything but trouble. My cousin was popular; I did the dirty work. That's why I'm hated.

THE SISTER-IN-LAW You certainly are. Take our case, your honor! (*To* SHUI TA) I won't mention the sacks.

SHUI TA Why not? Why not?

THE SISTER-IN-LAW (*To the* GODS) Shen Te gave us shelter and *he* had us arrested.

SHUI TA You stole cakes!

THE SISTER-IN-LAW Now he pretends to be interested in the baker's cakes! He wanted the store for himself!

SHUI TA The store wasn't a public refuge, selfish creatures!

THE SISTER-IN-LAW But we had no place to stay!

SHUI TA There were too many of you!

WANG And they (*Pointing to the* OLD MAN *and* WOMAN) were selfish too?

THE OLD MAN We put our savings into Shen Te's store. Why did you make us lose *our* store?

SHUI TA Because my cousin was helping a flier to fly. I was to get the money!

WANG Maybe she wanted to help him to fly. What interested you was the well-paid job in Peking. The store wasn't good enough for you!

SHUI TA The rent was too high!

MRS. SHIN That's true enough.

SHUI TA And my cousin knew nothing about business!

MRS. SHIN That's true too! She was also in love with the flier.

SHUI TA Shouldn't she be allowed to love?

WANG Certainly! And why did you want to force her to marry a man she did not love, the barber over there?

SHUI TA The man she loved was a scoundrel.

WANG (*Pointing to* SUN) Him?

SUN (*Jumping up*) And because he was a scoundrel you took him into your office!

SHUI TA To improve you! To improve you!

THE SISTER-IN-LAW To make him into a slave-driver!

WANG And when he was improved, didn't you sell him to her? (*Pointing to the* LANDLADY) She shouted it around every place!

SHUI TA Because she wouldn't give me her buildings unless she had him to stroke her knees!

THE LANDLADY That's a lie! Don't talk of my buildings ever again. I'll have nothing more to do with you. Murderer! (*She rustles off, insulted*)

SUN (*Insisting on getting his word in*) Your honor, I must speak on his behalf!

THE SISTER-IN-LAW Naturally. You're in his employ.

THE UNEMPLOYED He's the worst slave-driver I've ever known. He's absolutely depraved.

SUN Your honor, the accused may have made whatever you say of me, but he's not a murderer. A few minutes before he was arrested I heard Shen Te's voice in his back room!

THE FIRST GOD (*Avidly*) So she's alive? Tell us exactly what you heard?

SUN (*Triumphantly*) Sobbing, your honor, sobbing!

THE THIRD GOD And you recognized her?

SUN Absolutely. How could I fail to recognize her voice?

MR. SHU FU Sure, *you* made her sob often enough!

SUN And yet I made her happy. But then he (*Pointing to* SHUI TA) wanted to sell her to you!

SHUI TA (*To* SUN) Because you didn't love her!

WANG No. For the money!

SHUI TA But what was the money needed for, your honor? (*To* SUN) You wanted her to sacrifice all her friends, but the barber offered his cabins and his money to help the poor. Moreover, I *had* to get her engaged to him so that she could still be good.

WANG Why didn't you let her be good when the big check was signed? Why did you send Shen Te's friends into the dirty sweatshops of your factory, Tobacco King?

SHUI TA For the child's sake!

THE CARPENTER And *my* children? What did you do with *my* children?

(SHUI TA *is silent*)

WANG Now you're silent! The gods gave the store to Shen Te as a little fountain of goodness. She always wanted to do good and you always came and spoiled it.

SHUI TA (*Beside himself*) Because otherwise the fountain would have dried up, fool!

MRS. SHIN That's true, your honor!

WANG What good is a fountain if you can't get at the water?

SHUI TA Good deeds mean ruin!

WANG (*Wildly*) But bad deeds mean a good life, don't they? What did you do with the good Shen Te, bad man? How many good people are there, illustrious ones? *She* was good! When that man over there smashed my hand, she wanted to testify for me. And now I testify for her. She was good, I swear! (*He raises his hand in an oath*)

THE THIRD GOD What's the matter with your hand, water seller? It's all stiff.

WANG (*Pointing to* SHUI TA) It's his fault, his alone! She wanted to give me money for the doctor but then *he* came along! You were her deadly enemy!

SHUI TA I was her only friend!

ALL Where is she?

SHUI TA Gone away!
WANG Where to?
SHUI TA I won't tell!
ALL And why did she have to go away?
SHUI TA (*Shouting*) Because you would have torn her to shreds! (*Sudden quiet. He sinks onto a chair*) I can't go on. I'll explain everything. If the hall is cleared and only the judges remain, I will make a confession.
ALL He's confessing! He's found out!
THE FIRST GOD (*Beating on the table with the hammer*) Let the hall be cleared!

(*The* POLICEMAN *clears the hall*)

MRS. SHIN (*Laughing as she goes*) There'll be a surprise!
SHUI TA Have they gone? All of them? I can no longer keep silence. I recognized you, illustrious ones!
THE SECOND GOD What did you do with our good woman of Setzuan?
SHUI TA Let me confess the terrible truth: I am she!
THE SECOND GOD Shen Te!
SHEN TE

Yes, it is I. Shui Ta and Shen Te. I am both.
Your former injunction to be good and yet to live
Tore me like lightning in halves.
I don't know how it happened.
To be good to others and to myself—
I couldn't do both at the same time.
To help others and to help myself was too hard.
Alas, your world is difficult! Too much misery, too much despair!
The hand that is extended to a beggar, the beggar at once tears off!
Whoever helps the lost is lost himself!
For who could long refuse to be bad when he who eats no meat must die?
All the things that were needed—where should I have taken them from?
From myself! But then I perished!
A load of good intentions weighed me down to the ground.
Yet when I was unjust I walked mightily about and ate good meat!
Something must be wrong with your world.
Why is malice well rewarded? Why do punishments await the good?
Oh, how I should have loved to pamper myself!
And there was also a secret knowledge in me.
My foster-mother washed me in water from the gutter:
That gave me a sharp eye.
Yet pity pained me so, I was an angry wolf at the sight of misery.
Then I felt how I was changing and kind words turned to ashes in my mouth.
And yet I wished to be an Angel to the Suburbs.
To give was a delight. A happy face, and I walked on clouds.
Condemn me: everything I did I did to help my neighbor,
To love my lover, and to save my little son from want.
For your great plans, O Gods! I was too poor and small.

THE FIRST GOD (*With all signs of horror*) Don't go on, unhappy woman! What should we think, we who are so happy to have found you again!
SHEN TE But I've got to tell you that I am the bad man whose crimes everyone was talking about!
THE FIRST GOD The good woman whose good deeds everyone was talking about!
SHEN TE The bad man too!
THE FIRST GOD A misunderstanding! Several unfortunate occurrences! Some heartless neighbors! An excess of zeal!
THE SECOND GOD But how is she to go on living?
THE FIRST GOD She can do it. She's strong, well built. She can stand a lot.
THE SECOND GOD But didn't you hear what she said?
THE FIRST GOD (*Vehemently*) It was confused, very confused! And incredible, highly incredible! Should we admit our commandments to be deadly? Should we renounce our commandments? (*Sullenly*) Never! Should the world be changed? How? By whom? No! Everything is in order! (*He suddenly beats on the table with the hammer*)

And now . . . (*He makes a sign and music is heard. Rosy light*) let us return.
This little world has much engaged us.
Its joy and its sorrow have refreshed and pained us.
Up there, however, beyond the stars,
We shall gladly think of you, Shen Te, the good woman
Who bears witness to our spirit down below,
Who, in cold darkness, carries a little lamp!
Goodbye! Do it well!

(*He makes a sign and the ceiling opens. A pink cloud comes down. On it the* THREE GODS *rise, very slowly*)

SHEN TE Oh, don't, illustrious ones! Don't go away! Don't leave me! How can I face the good old couple who've lost their store and the water seller with his stiff hand? And how can I defend myself from the barber whom I do not love and from Sun whom I do love? And I am with child. Soon there'll be a little son who'll want to eat. I can't stay here!

(*She turns with a hunted look toward the door which will let her tormentors in*)

THE FIRST GOD You can do it. Just be good and everything will turn out well!

(*Enter the witnesses. They look with surprise at the judges floating on their pink cloud*)

WANG Show respect! The gods have appeared among us! Three of the highest gods have come to Setzuan to find a good human being. They had found one already, but . . .
THE FIRST GOD No "but"! Here she is!
ALL Shen Te!
THE FIRST GOD She has not perished. She was only hidden. She will stay with you. A good human being!

SHEN TE But I need my cousin!

THE FIRST GOD Not too often!

SHEN TE At least once a week!

THE FIRST GOD Once a month. That's enough!

SHEN TE Oh, don't go away, illustrious ones! I haven't told you everything! I need you desperately!

(*The* GODS *sing*)

*THE TRIO OF THE VANISHING GODS ON THE CLOUD*

We, alas, may never stay
More than a fleeting year.
If you watch your treasure long
'Twill always disappear.
Down here the golden light of truth
With shadow is alloyed
That's why we take our leave
Returning to the void.

SHEN TE Help! (*Her cries continue through the song*)

THE GODS Our anxious search is over now
Let us to heaven ascend
The good, good woman of Setzuan
Praising, praising to the end.

(*As* SHEN TE *stretches out her arms to them in desperation, they disappear above, smiling and waving*)

# Epilogue[1]

(*One of the actors walks out in front of the curtain and apologetically addresses the audience*)

Ladies and gentlemen, don't be angry! Please!
We know the play is still in need of mending.
A golden legend floated on the breeze,
The breeze dropped, and we got a bitter ending.
Being dependent on your approbation
We wished, alas! our work might be commended.
*We're* disappointed too. With consternation
We see the curtain closed, the plot unended.
In your opinion, then, what's to be done?
Change human nature or—the world? Well: which?
Believe in bigger, better gods or—none?
How can we mortals be both good and rich?
The right way out of the calamity
You must find for yourselves. Ponder, my friends,
How man with man may live in amity
And good men—women also—reach good ends.
There must, there must, be *some* end that would fit.
Ladies and gentlemen, help us look for it!

[1] Added by Brecht after he read the notices of the Viennese production in 1947. (Tr. note)

# Carl Zuckmayer

# (1896- )

THE work of Carl Zuckmayer offers convincing proof of the continuity of German drama in our time, despite the suppression of creative activity by the Nazi dictatorship. Working within the solid and stable tradition of realistic and social drama, he has created a number of plays that are a living tribute to his artistry and his insight into the moral dilemmas of contemporary history.

From 1940 to 1946, the playwright lived and worked in the United States, yet largely because of the accidental character of dramatic production in America, his work is hardly known on this side of the Atlantic. In Germany, Austria, and German-speaking Switzerland, he has long been hailed as one of the most vigorous and most talented of playwrights on the contemporary scene.

Carl Zuckmayer was born in Nackenheim, a village in the Hessian Rhineland, in a rich vine-growing area along the river. He spent most of his early life in Mainz, and at the age of 17 volunteered as a soldier in the first World War. He participated in many bloody battles and distinguished himself by his bravery in combat, winning war decorations which were to serve him usefully in trying situations during the Nazi regime. Like many other German youths, Zuckmayer returned from the war with a deep sense of revulsion against militarism. This fervent pacifism is reflected in his early poetry and fiction. He studied at the Universities of Frankfurt and Heidelberg in 1918, and frequented bohemian literary circles. In 1920 he completed his first play, *Crossroads* (*Kreuzweg*), an expressionist fantasy marked by the abstraction and shrill exclamation of such contemporaries as Georg Kaiser and Ernst Toller. The critical reception was harsh; the play, produced by Leopold Jessner, had only three performances in Berlin—but it turned the young Zuckmayer decisively toward the drama. Thereafter, he remained for a time in Berlin, hoping to gain new access to the stage, but was soon reduced to a grinding poverty that forced him to the borderline of a criminal existence. In his autobiography, *Second Wind*, the playwright tells how he was unwittingly used as a dope peddler and was saved from imprisonment only through the kindness and cunning of a prostitute. The preoccupation in his later work with moral abdication and depravity may well have roots in his early Berlin experience.

His opportunity to enter directly into Berlin theatre life came in 1924, when Max Reinhardt engaged him as a play reader at the Deutsches Theater. Here he worked alongside of Bertolt Brecht, who was employed in the same capacity, and assisted in the production of such plays as Shaw's *Saint Joan* and Pirandello's *Six Characters in Search of an Author*. In December, 1925, Zuckmayer became famous overnight with the performance of his *The Happy Vineyard* (*Der Fröhliche Weinberg*). This play is a lusty Rabelaisian comedy set in the wine country of the Rhineland and animated by a healthy love of physical experience, the joy of good living, and by song, dance, and the discovery of love.

In the play, the owner of a prosperous vineyard, Gunderloch, is determined to spare his daughter Klärchen a childless marriage and will not consent to her betrothal until she is pregnant. Clever as well as pretty, Klärchen manages to hoodwink her arrogant and pedantic suitor, Knuzius, and to win the hand and love of the sailor, Jochen. The play is a rollicking comedy from start to finish, marked by an earthiness and humor that stand out in sharp contrast to the grim seriousness of puritanical morality. The exuberance and joy of nature testifies to the oneness of all living things permeated by the fecundity of the vines. Zuckmayer's play at once captured the public fancy and was played in one German city after another. The Nazis did not like it because of its assault on fashionable anti-Semitism and its exposé of the boorishness of would-be defenders of the purity of the fatherland: Knuzius, the arrogant suitor, ends drunk on a pile of manure. The Nazis and their adherents caused innumerable riots at performances of *The Happy Vineyard*, but these disturbances served largely to enhance its popularity.

Subsequently, Zuckmayer turned to historical drama in *Schinderhannes* (1927), the tragedy of a bandit leader during the Napoleonic era. The following year he completed *Katherina Knie*, the story of a troupe of traveling acrobats, and also adapted *What Price Glory?* by Maxwell Anderson and Lawrence Stallings for the German stage. His later adaptations include *A Farewell to Arms*, from Ernest Hemingway's novel, and the reworking of Gerhart Hauptmann's *Herbert Engelmann*, the story of a World War I veteran who loses his mental balance and gains relief only through suicide. In the late 1920's the playwright also began adapting stories for the films and created one of the great motion pictures of our time in *The Blue Angel* (*Der blaue Engel*) with Marlene Dietrich and Emil Jannings, based on a novel by Heinrich Mann. In 1936 Zuckmayer prepared the scenario for the film *Rembrandt* with Charles Laughton in the lead role.

Increasingly, Zuckmayer's plays came to bear more and more directly on the social scene. *The Captain of Köpenick* (*Der Hauptmann von Köpenick*) of 1931 is a trenchant satire on Prussian militarism in the early years of the century, based on an actual event of 1906. An ex-convict shoemaker, Wilhelm Voigt, is without identity papers after his release from jail and cannot obtain work. In jail, he and other convicts had learned military manners and tactics while endlessly rehearsing the battle of Sedan of the Franco-Prussian War at the behest of their warden. With the aid of a second-hand captain's uniform, Voigt assumes authority over a whole town. The comedy dissolves into hilarious laughter in the final scene when he views himself in a mirror, but the point of the play is its merciless exposure of the stultifying effect of rigorous discipline on the social and imaginative life of the German people. No one, unfortunately, is any wiser at the end of the play, but Voigt has been led to question the moral values of a community that places protocol and documents above men. Once again, Zuckmayer indirectly called attention to the lurking menace of authoritarianism.

In 1933, his open antagonism toward the Nazis forced him to emigrate to Austria, where his literary activity continued. The following year he completed *The Rogue of Bergen* (*Der Schelm von Bergen*), relating the trials of a wise and sympathetic public executioner and his son, destined by law as his successor and haunted by an unnatural love for his Empress. *Ulla Winblad,* a brutal account of the suffering and abortive love of the Swedish poet, Bellman, also dates from the 1930's. When the Nazis annexed Austria, Zuckmayer fled to Switzerland, closely pursued by the Gestapo. He then came, via Cuba, to the United States.

*The Devil's General,* his most famous play, was written in Vermont between 1942 and 1945. It was first produced in Zurich late in 1946, and became the most arresting and controversial play of the postwar German stage. It is without doubt the most powerful dramatization of the plight of the Germans under the Hitler regime—men torn between their sense of duty to Germany and their horror and disgust at the Nazi destruction of all human values. General Harras is a sympathetic figure, and his concern with the plight of Jewish and other victims of Nazi persecution is genuine and heroic. His opposition to the Nazis is instinctive and passionate, yet he has served their cause and is thereby condemned to death by himself as well as by others. He is incapable of the sabotage or resistance of Oderbruch, but he is also incapable of capitulating to the Nazi Party. Caught between the one and the other, he is crushed. His suicide is an act of expiation, the price to be paid for having served the devil.

Alongside of the personal tragedy of the hero, we experience the tragedy of the German people amid the spiritual anarchy and depravity of the Nazi period. *The Devil's General* reveals the wretchedness of Hitler's *Reich* in vivid documentary detail, a living reminder of the degradation of humanity. Lest we forget this chapter of recent history, the play recalls to us what it was like to be in Germany in 1941. It draws strongly on the personalities and events of the day, and provides a vivid description of the past along with an interpretation of its significance. Appropriately, the play is dedicated to three members of the German Resistance, who were hanged by the Nazis after the abortive attempt on Hitler's life of July 20, 1944.

General Harras is proof that not all Germans went mad in the 1930's and '40's, yet the German guilt is collective as well as individual. The play is a harsh and bitter critique of "a miserable nation" whose people have become "slaves of death." The paradox of the basically good man in the service of the devil is but an expression of the larger paradox of Germany itself, a mixture of the best and the worst in the history of Western civilization. For the Germany of 1941, retribution is inevitable; the final scene takes place the day before Pearl Harbor.

The technique of Zuckmayer's play is altogether traditional but its passion, verve, and vigor of language are Zuckmayer's own. It stands forth as the most powerful of all dramas on the recent war, a thought-provoking study of the plight of a single man whose insight into himself and his times moves him from helplessness to a kind of heroism.

In more recent plays, Zuckmayer has continued to explore the problem of individual freedom and responsibility in a confused and divided world. *The Song in the Fiery Furnace* (*Der Gesang im Feuerofen,* 1951) is based upon a newspaper account of conflict between members of the French Resistance and the German Occupation. Here again, the action turns on a moral dilemma, the conflicting claims of national loyalty and humanity. The Maquis leaders undergo a cruel death, but their death has meaning beyond the brutality of the present, and their forgiveness of the enemy points to a new code of human values. *The Cold Light* (*Das Kalte Licht,* 1954) draws upon the atomic espionage of Klaus Fuchs. Wolters, the hero, acts out of sincere but naïve convictions in betraying atomic secrets to the Russians. Inspired by the ideal of science as a common human enterprise, he believes he is aiding all mankind by his acts, but he is forced to recognize the false abstraction of his unpolitical guise and to accept full responsibility for his error. In the process of confession and expiation he, like General Harras, discovers and reasserts the meaning of humanity.

The central problem in Zuckmayer's recent plays is moral far more than political. The scene of the action is the individual conscience. In every case, self-destruction necessarily follows the moral awakening. The hero is driven to crime through his evasion of moral responsibility, yet finally emerges to reclaim his dignity and self-respect as well as his place in a community of free men. The values of love, justice and freedom, along with the sense of group identity and the ever-present awareness of joy in life, underlie the enduring vitality of Zuckmayer's theatre.

# THE DEVIL'S GENERAL

Translated by Ingrid G. Gilbert and William F. Gilbert

CHARACTERS

HARRAS, *General of the German Air Force, the Luftwaffe*
HANSEN, *his adjutant*
KORRIANKE, *his chauffeur*
FRIEDRICH EILERS, *Colonel and leader of a fighter squadron*
PFUNDTMAYER, *pilot—same age as* HARRAS
HARTMANN, *pilot—new generation*
WRITZKY, HASTENTEUFFEL } *two pilots*
VON MOHRUNGEN, *industrialist, president of the Air Force Procurement Office*
BARON PFLUNGK, *attaché of the Foreign Ministry*
DR. SCHMIDT-LAUSITZ, *Minister of Culture*
ODERBRUCH, *engineer in the Air Administration*
ANNE EILERS, *married to* FRIEDRICH *and daughter of* VON MOHRUNGEN
POOTSIE VON MOHRUNGEN, *her sister*
OLIVIA GEISS, *opera singer*
DIDDO GEISS, *her niece*
LYRA SCHOEPPKE, *another singer*
SCHLICK, *an artist*
OTTO, *restaurateur*
FRANÇOIS, DETLEV } *waiters*
BUDDY LAWRENCE, *an American journalist*
TWO WORKERS
A POLICE DETECTIVE

PLACE *Berlin.*

TIME *Late 1941, shortly before America's entry into the war.*

## Act One

### The Time Bomb

*A private dining room in* OTTO'S *restaurant. Conservative—"Old German"—furnishings. In the middle, a sumptuous buffet table for about fifteen people. In the background an "intimate corner" with easy chairs and a smoking table on which are cigars and liqueur, the "corner" half hidden by gathered drapes. When the curtain rises, the ceiling light is still burning, but* FRANÇOIS *and* HERR DETLEV *begin to light a great many candles in silver candelabra on the table and walls. Later they turn off the glaring overhead light. They are also putting the finishing touches to the table decorations. All windows are covered with thick black curtains. A fan hums softly.*

DETLEV What time is it?

FRANÇOIS Quarter to midnight.

DETLEV Gonna be a long night.

FRANÇOIS *C'est la vie.*

DETLEV When General Harras decides to live it up, you can count on a few being out of the running by sunrise.

FRANÇOIS What are you doing? No port! Harras starts off with an Armagnac! Double! Pass me the brandy glass.

DETLEV How do you know, sweetheart?

FRANÇOIS I know the General. He comes from the Reichschancery—a very official reception. *Donc*—he needs stronger stuff than the port. Logical, *n'est-ce pas?*

DETLEV It figures. When Harras has gazed his Fuehrer in the eye, he needs an internal wash.

FRANÇOIS (*Glancing over the platters of food*) Thank God for the occupied countries. What would the boss do without them? We serve nothing but the fruits . . . the fruits of victory. *Voilà:* the hors d'oeuvres—from Norway. The lobster—from Ostende. The goose liver—from Poland. The cheese—from Holland. The butter—from Denmark. And the fresh vegetables—from Italy. No caviar—from Moscow . . .

DETLEV But French champagne. (*He pops the cork on a bottle of champagne and tastes it*) *Prosit*—Oh, la-la!—Tastes better than Ribbentrop's domestic brew!

OTTO (*From outside*) François! The liver pâté for His Excellency! The tureen is not open!

FRANÇOIS (*To himself, bored*) You open it! I don't give a damn. (*He tastes the champagne*) Long live collaboration!

OTTO (*Appears at the door very excited*) Herr Detlev! François! Where in Heaven are you? There isn't a thing going on in here yet! How do you expect me to manage with those clumsy greenhorns out there? And especially today, a Reichstag[1] day. Every room crawling with big game: four Excellencies, two Ministers, a Field Marshal, bushels of Gauleiters,[2] and the very cream of the Opera.

DETLEV Begging your pardon, Herr Otto, we are on duty. General Harras requisitioned us expressly for his party. François and myself. On account of we're dependable, you know!

OTTO You've got time. He hasn't even driven up to the door yet, but where are Herr Jannings' pheasants? Herr Jannings is screaming for his pheasants!

DETLEV Let him scream! Herr Jannings can kiss my—

OTTO It's unbelievable! This is my reward—betrayed and sold out!—and I can't hire any replacements! After all I did for you! Who got you military exemptions, ration cards for heavy laborers! And so much more! If you two knife me in the back now . . .

FRANÇOIS Gently, Otto, gently! If you have done favors for us, after all, we have done some things for you, *n'est-ce pas?* The carloads from Brussels, that business in Paris, and—

OTTO Shut your mouth! For the last time, are you going to help over there—or not?

FRANÇOIS Remember your ulcer, Otto. Breathe deeply.

DETLEV Give Auntie a little kiss, François.

OTTO Herr Detlev—if times were different—I would throw you out on the spot. (*Screaming and red as a lobster*) On the spot!

DETLEV (*Amused*) On the spot. If times were different, of course. (FRANÇOIS *laughs*)

OTTO Quiet! Their Excellencies! (*Voices from outside*). (OTTO *at the door, speaking off*) Welcome to Otto's—General! President—Colonel—Baron—Doctor! My compliments ladies! Hat check! Be so kind, your wraps? Everything is ready, General. The lobster is blushing.

HARRAS (*From outside*) François! 'N Armagnac! Double!

[1] Elective legislative assembly of Germany.

[2] Gauleiters were district leaders of the Nazi party.

FRANÇOIS *Voilà!* (*He hurries off with the glass*)

DETLEV We'd better unscrew all the light bulbs.

OTTO Unscrew the bulbs? What for?

DETLEV Don't you know—when Harry gets loaded he shoots them down.

OTTO Leave two or three so he doesn't get mad; he might aim for the candles and hit my mirrors. (*Hurries out into the corridor*) A great honor, General, and a pleasure.

(DETLEV *is alone in the room for a moment. In a flash he opens an invisible door in the wall paneling, turns on a dial and closes the door.* HARRAS *enters, followed by* OTTO. *He is in full dress uniform, but his bearing and manner are casual, even somewhat sloppy. He still holds the empty glass in his hand and a cigarette dangles from the corner of his mouth. He can't be older than forty-five. His face is intelligent, youthful, even boyish, despite his thinning hair. By nature it is a gay face, carefree, pleasant, and a little mischievous. Now it seems to be suffused with a perceptible nervous tension. He looks around probingly*)

HARRAS Well, looks pretty decent. Almost like the good old times—in case you still remember, Otto.

OTTO Always good times with us, General. Old or not—we haven't changed. We do the best we can. Except for the mayonnaise—so many eggs, and that oil, you know—one can't do quite as one wishes. But I have prepared a tartar sauce for the General to go with the lobster. Your guests will scarcely taste the difference.

HARRAS Don't worry, Otto, anything will taste good to us. We have just come from a beer party with the Fuehrer. Besides, every man in the Luftwaffe has been issued synthetic taste buds.

OTTO Priceless, General! (*Laughs*) Your sense of humor's as sharp as ever.

HARRAS Ersatz humor, my friend, thistles, chicory and oak leaves. Well, now—is this still the real article? (*Holds out his glass.* FRANÇOIS *fills it*) Listen, there's something ticking in here.

OTTO Ticking? Where, General?

HARRAS Not in your head, Otto, I hope. Keep quiet . . . There.

OTTO I can't hear anything—but, then, maybe—a little hum—

DETLEV Must be the fan, General, or the heat.

OTTO Of course, the fan. We have to use it in the blackout. You can't open the windows, and the cigar smoke . . .

HARRAS Doesn't sound like a fan to me!

OTTO What amazing ears the General has!

HARRAS Some people go deaf flying. The opposite happened to me. I can identify twenty different types of planes just by the sound of the engines. Turn that thing off for a minute. (DETLEV *turns off the fan*) I still hear a tick.

DETLEV Then it's the heat. You save on coal: then your pipes drip.

OTTO Well now—there has never been any dripping in the pipes, if you please, Herr Detlev.

HARRAS (*Has stopped near the wall paneling*) Seems to come from somewhere in this wall. Could be the pipes after all. Unless, of course, it's a time bomb.

DETLEV That's it! A time bomb. (*Laughs and turns the fan on again*)

(*During the last few phrases several gentlemen have appeared at the door in the background. At first they're only half visible. Then there is great activity in the entrance; each wants to concede to the other. They are:* VON MOHRUNGEN, COLONEL EILERS, BARON PFLUNGK, DOCTOR SCHMIDT-LAUSITZ, HANSEN. *They press around the doorway murmuring courtesies such as:*

"After you, Mohrungen."

"But my dear Eilers, you, the guest of honor."

"Please, Doctor."

"Out of the question, the military first."

"Come, Baron."

"No, no, I'm at home here.")

HARRAS (*Has watched the scene with a big grin*) Who said there are no manners left in Germany. Hansen! Doff that helmet in reverence! There are lobsters present!

HANSEN (*A small, jovial, poodle-like rubber ball of a man in the uniform of a captain breaks through the group and storms the table*) Well then—to hell with formalities. To the attack! Le'me at them red devils! (*He begins to eat without further ado*)

(*The other gentlemen enter without further complications:* VON MOHRUNGEN *and* BARON PFLUNGK *in tails,* DOCTOR SCHMIDT-LAUSITZ *in party uniform,* COLONEL EILERS *in fancy dress uniform with many impressive medals.* MOHRUNGEN, *a good-looking man of about fifty with grey temples, representative of the old upper class of heavy industry. His junker-like conservative outlook is subdued by a southern German naturalness. . .* BARON PFLUNGK, *an elegant greyhound with smooth manners, completely without character . . .* DOCTOR SCHMIDT-LAUSITZ, *a narrow forehead with flashing eye glasses, behind them close-set eyes, barely visible, thin blond hair, in "regulation" outfit, tight-lipped, his posture and bearing stiff to the point of exaggeration. . .* COLONEL EILERS, *not older than thirty-five. Dark hair, tall, weather-tanned features, average except for an unusual seriousness which gives him sometimes an absent, almost sad expression*)

OTTO (*Somewhat uncertain*) Heil Hit—Good evening, von Mohrungen. Good eve—Heil Hitler, Doctor.

HARRAS Just say, "Good Adolf" or "Heil Evening." That will suit everybody. (*To the others*) I think we all know each other. This is our Minister of Culture, Doctor Schmidt-Lausitz, from the Propaganda Ministry. Culture and propaganda have been efficiently co-ordinated in the German Reich. Schmidt-Lausitz, as differentiated from Schmidt-Muddledorf, Schmidt-Fartheim, Schmidt-Burpbach, and other gentlemen without special distinguishing characteristics.

LAUSITZ I do not wish to intrude, General. I see—this is a private gathering. I only came along because I have to talk over a few details with Baron Pflungk and Colonel Eilers concerning the foreign press conference tomorrow and the shortwave broadcast to America.

HARRAS You will have ample opportunity to take care of that during the course of the evening. Stay, relax, Doctor. No one disturbs us. You've heard about my bad jokes already, I am sure. They are all entered in my personal file at Gestapo Headquarters.[3] Go ahead and read up on 'em.

LAUSITZ (*With a sour smile*) A joke's permissible, General, if it doesn't go too far.

HARRAS Let Himmler be our judge.[4] Fortify yourselves, gentlemen! You need it after you have nipped from the Holy Grail at the Reichschancery.

MOHRUNGEN My Lord, this almost looks like peacetime. Why it warms my heart.

HANSEN (*Eating*) And the pit of the stomach. Very much to your health, von Mohrungen.

HARRAS Well, it isn't every day we can have a feast. But when Friedrich Eilers has his big night then it must rain manna in the desert—excuse the non-Aryan comparison, Dr. Lausitz. Help yourself, Eilers. It's no steal from the national wealth, only a small compensation. If we leave any left-overs, the big shots across the hall will swill it down.

EILERS (*Smiling, a little embarrassed*) You do me too much honor, General. All this is really too much to ask for, here behind the lines. At the front we are very well taken care of, you know.

OTTO All ration-free goods, gentlemen, reserved for young heroes and old fighters. Except for the butter. For that, I regret—I will have to punch a little hole in your ration cards.

MOHRUNGEN Now I see how provincial I have become. Lobsters. Midnight supper. At home in Mannheim, everyone is in bed by eleven, not a place open. And whenever I've come to Berlin before, I've always taken the night plane back so I could be at the factory in the morning.

OTTO Officially we also close at eleven, Mr. von Mohrungen. We have to thank "Poppa" for all this. Since Poppa got a special permit for private parties Otto's has recovered some of the old "zing." Strength through Joy[5] is also the true motto of our business.

MOHRUNGEN I thought his father was no longer living.

HARRAS (*Laughing*) When you hear anyone in Berlin talking about "Poppa," my dear Mr. von Mohrungen, it always refers to "Fat Hermann" Goering,[6] our Reichsmarshal with the ersatz spare-tire 'round his middle.

PFLUNGK A nice sign of his popularity.

[3] "Gestapo" is a short form of *"Geheime Staatspolizei,"* the "Secret State Police" of Nazi Germany.

[4] Heinrich Himmler (1900-1945), chief of the Gestapo.

[5] Motto of the Hitler Youth.

[6] Hermann Goering (1893-1946), one of Hitler's earliest followers, was Commander-in-chief of the German Air Force and director of German industry and war production.

HARRAS (*Ironic*) Bravo, Baron. Fill 'em up, François. Here come the ladies.

(MRS. ANNE EILERS *and her sister,* MISS VON MOHRUNGEN, *called* "POOTSIE," *come freshly made-up from the powder room. Both are in evening gowns:* ANNE EILERS *elegant but simple.* "POOTSIE" *very elegant but somewhat shrill.* ANNE *is a beautiful tall woman in her middle twenties with a quiet, somewhat disinterested expression which only takes on life and warmth when it falls on her husband.* "POOTSIE," *a few years younger, has a provocatively good figure and an almost too pretty doll-like face with a touch of vulgarity and restless, insatiable eyes*)

HARRAS (*Introducing*) Minister of Culture, Dr. Schmidt-Lausitz—Mrs. Colonel Eilers—Miss von Mohrungen. Baron Pflungk, you know officially.

POOTSIE Miss von Mohrungen—that sounds so madly formal—downright reactionary. Why don't you call me Pootsie, like everyone else?

HARRAS I don't dare, Pootsie. Seems rather hasty to me. We just met a couple of hours ago.

POOTSIE I won't conceive if you do, I almost said. Bottoms up, Harry!

MOHRUNGEN But, Pootsie!

HARRAS Stop, young lady! Don't drink yet! Tear the goblet from her lips. François, a refill. (*Steps into the middle and a loose circle forms around him*) So—without further schmaltz, but from the heart, I drink to Friedrich Eilers, to his fiftieth air victory which we are celebrating today. To a hundred, and to his safe return home. Your health, Friedrich.

ALL To your health, Friedrich.

EILERS (*Gayly fending them off*) Thanks, thanks, I feel like a war memorial.

HARRAS Just what y'are. The name is Harry, Fred. (*They drink and shake hands*)

THE OTHERS (*Chiming in*) To General Harras! (*They drink*)

LAUSITZ (*Alone*) To the Fuehrer!

HARRAS Cheers, with an empty glass. The Fuehrer doesn't drink.

HANSEN (*Already a little drunk*) François! A glass of milk. A toast to the pious life.

HARRAS Shut your mouth, small fry. Just because I shoot my mouth off you don't have to follow suit—not by a long shot.

EILERS Bravo! To our best pilot-commander, General Harras.

HANSEN Excuse me, General.

MOHRUNGEN (*Has put his arm around* EILERS' *shoulder*) I can really be proud of my son-in-law.

ANNE We can all be proud, Poppa, the whole German nation.

HARRAS Best man in the Luftwaffe—or in the whole army.

EILERS Slightly exaggerated. I might say, everyone of our boys does his best. If there is anything to be proud of, then it's my squadron. Four of my officers were awarded the Iron Cross First Class today. And they all deserved it.

PFLUNGK (*Slightly personal, to* POOTSIE) Wasn't Lieutenant Hartmann among those decorated? Then we have double good reason for celebrating tonight.

POOTSIE (*Casually*) Do you know little Hartmann? Nice boy.

ANNE Why don't you admit you're engaged to him. Everyone knows it. You haven't made much of a secret of it up to now.

POOTSIE Engaged. Such a ghastly word. I don't like anything that sounds so middle-class. I mean—downright reactionary.

HARRAS Of course, in the Hitler Youth no one gets engaged any more. That holds you up too long; you might grow up in the meantime.

HANSEN You don't even bother getting married—just start right in and give a boost to the birth rate. Excuse me, General.

POOTSIE (*Also a little tipsy already, with a certain provocative manner which as yet does not differentiate between* HARRAS *and* BARON PFLUNGK) Always making fun of a poor li'l chick, huh? But today's girls aren't poor li'l chicks anymore by a long shot. We modern girls have nothing against marriage if it's the right man. But just stop and think for a minute all the rigmarole we have to go through; the proofs of Aryan blood, all the way down to your great-grandfather's big toe. Health certificate, proof of fertility, semen count, and so forth. Yes, it's all necessary on account of race—but who wants to wait around for all that? With your normal drives—you can grow old and rancid in the process.

MOHRUNGEN What a way to talk, Pootsie! Don't you think that goes too far!

POOTSIE Heavens no! We all talk like that in the Hitler Youth. That is the privilege of youth.

EILERS And what about the duties of youth. I hope you know what I mean.

POOTSIE My dear Mister Brother-in-law, above all, no gloom and doom this evening. Little Hartmann has already drearified me enough. Did he get all that from you?

EILERS (*More to* MOHRUNGEN *and* ANNE) Young Hartmann is really a very special case. Tireless in combat—downright daredevil. Almost too much for my blood. Trouble begins to cook up anywhere . . . Presto, he volunteers. Three times a day if the plane can stand it. Sometimes I almost think he—(*Doesn't finish the sentence*)

POOTSIE (*Chatting with* PFLUNGK) Hartmann's a good-looking pilot; you can't take that away from him. And anyway he's a sharp boy—three sports prizes, twelve planes shot down and tip-top ideology. But something's missing—I don't know what—real dash. He doesn't dance, imagine!

PFLUNGK That is a great mistake. You love to dance, I imagine, Miss von Mohrungen?

POOTSIE I'm mad about it as long as it isn't that national around-in-a-big-circle sort of thing. But it's Pootsie, please. When I was little I couldn't pronounce my real name so I named myself Pootsie and it stuck. (*She laughs, intoxicated with herself*)

PFLUNGK Very sweet. May I take you dancing sometime, Pootsie? To one of our diplomatic evenings while you're in Berlin? A private party, of course.

POOTSIE You bet you may. Did you know I am staying in Berlin? I've been accepted for training in the Party Women's Corps. Where do you have these dinner dances? At the "Eden" or at the "Old Queen"? (*They withdraw excitedly into one of the niches*)

MOHRUNGEN (*Has taken* HARRAS *aside for a moment*) Tell me, General, have you discovered anything new about the situation? It's going to come up in the meeting tomorrow. I'm afraid if we don't find an explanation quickly, there is going to be interference from certain parties—you know what I mean. I don't want to take a stand before I know your opinion.

HARRAS My opinion. Official—or personal?

MOHRUNGEN I think we can trust each other, General.

HARRAS To be frank—I haven't any opinion at all so far—only suspicions. It's a hell of a business. Fresh reports came in this afternoon. Between us, von Mohrungen—a failure of wing structure on a dozen brand new planes. I'm having the metal checked. But the whole thing's got me completely baffled—Careful—We will talk later.

LAUSITZ (*Has come close to them*) Am I intruding? Or don't you discuss professional secrets on a social occasion? Of course, I don't know anything about technical matters, but I find the whole aircraft industry very fascinating. . . .

HARRAS No professional secrets, Dr. Lausitz. Everything is as clear as daylight. Von Mohrungen controls procurements of raw materials, I control production. The Colonel and his fly-boys sit themselves down in the cockpit, swoop around up in the air until they've shot down fifty enemy kites. Then they pin 'em with a medal. Nothin' to it!

LAUSITZ Divided responsibility. Highly interesting. As I said, I don't understand anything about it. My province is Culture. Total mobilization of the German soul, you know. And enlightenment of the neutral foreign countries. That, too, is battle—even if not with weapons.

HARRAS I know. You use your mouth instead. That probably calls for a special kind of courage. I could never do it.

LAUSITZ You flatter me, General. (*Turns away*)

HANSEN (*Who had stepped up previously, softly*) Blockhead.

HARRAS (*Between his teeth*) Watch your step, small fry. Don't get plastered tonight.

HANSEN Don't worry. I only make as if. Am sharp as a tack. (HARRAS *nods to him and drinks hastily.* EILERS *and* ANNE *have stepped up to him*)

ANNE I just want to tell you, General Harras—I'll never forget this evening. What you said about Friedrich was more than an honor. There was so much warmth and friendship in it. I know how much it means to him. I'm sure he hasn't been this happy since he was a child.

EILERS Thank you, Anne. You put that just right. I wouldn't have been able to get it out like that.

HARRAS Yes, you're steeped in official stiffness, Freddie, but I know all about you anyway. I always felt closer to you than all the others even though you don't drink. Well, make an exception for once. (*He pours him a glass*)

EILERS (*Laughing*) Well, it can't do any harm—on furlough.

ANNE You should hear how Friedrich talks about you. It is enough to make a woman jealous. Harras comes first—after the Fuehrer, naturally, and then nobody else for a long time.

HARRAS And now you've met the old Harry in the flesh. Disappointing isn't he? Not a bit of that four-star dignity and not even a party member.

EILERS Well, yes—in that respect—maybe we think a little differently. But in the air it makes no difference. A man is a man up there.

ANNE Isn't it also a question of generation? We grew up with it. To us it is holy. The party gave us that little bit of meaning to life.

HARRAS The meaning of my life was always flying. I started out in 1914. And now I can't stop anymore. It's like liquor. (*He drinks*) Here's to you, children. You know, I'm so happy that we're together tonight. (*Slaps* EILERS *on the shoulder. To* ANNE) I've only laid eyes on the old man once since this Russia business started up and that was at an official staff meeting. Come on, sit down and open up your inner life. How are you, anyhow?—I mean—outside the service? At home! How are the children?

EILERS Haven't seen them yet—just got back from the front today. But you can imagine how I am looking forward to next week!

ANNE Oh, but the boys! They can't wait. The little one can say, "Daddy fly." And with it he goes, "Sssssss."

HARRAS Must be nice—to come home—to have children. . . .

EILERS (*Somewhat absently*) Yes—to come home—(*He becomes silent, stares at the glass that he holds in his hand*)

ANNE What's the matter with you, Friedrich?

EILERS (*As though waking up*) Oh—nothing. Excuse me, please. It was just funny—

HARRAS What was?

EILERS I saw myself suddenly—there, in the glass. A little distorted—but perfectly clear. My own face. Funny. You never really know what you look like. (*He stares almost frightened in front of himself*)

ANNE (*With a somewhat forced laugh*) You know—you're tipsy, Friedrich.

EILERS (*Agreeing, changed and unaffected*) It's true I really can't take a drop.

HARRAS Well, go and eat something. A lobster will do you more good than army pep-up pills.

EILERS (*Shaking his head, smiling*) Yes, I think I'll try that. (*He goes to the buffet*)

ANNE What happened to him? Was it really that little glass of wine?

HARRAS He should sleep it off for twenty-four hours.

And when he wakes up—then he should—the first thing—look into your eyes, Anne.

ANNE (*Presses his hand hastily*) Thanks, Harry. You are—you are wonderful. (*She goes quickly to* EILERS)

HARRAS (*To himself*) Damn it all. Damn it all. (*He drinks*)

OTTO (*Comes in beaming*) A real big night, General. Reichsmarshal Goering himself is coming. He will be right next door. We've had to clear away the lower ranks. Admission from now on only to Group Commanders and up! By the way, four junior officers are outside—from Colonel Eilers' squadron. They claim the General ordered them to report to him here. Should I let them in?

HARRAS (*Who at first barely listened, electrified*) Why sure! Hurry up! Before they're all scared stiff by the hullabaloo out there. Let 'em in!

OTTO As you order, General. Everything satisfactory? The champagne well chilled?

HARRAS Let's go, Otto! (OTTO *exits*) Pootsie! Hands off that diplomatic vest! Surprise coming up.

POOTSIE Another toast?

HARRAS Something like that. François, more glasses!

(*Enter* CAPTAIN PFUNDTMAYER, *1st Lt.* HASTENTEUFFEL, *2nd Lts.* WRITZKY *and* HARTMANN: PFUNDTMAYER *about as old as* HARRAS, *a Bavarian powerhouse;* HASTENTEUFFEL *more Westphalian, sharp-eyed with big hands and a heavy tongue;* WRITZKY *a "sharp boy" from Berlin, slightly effeminate but dashing and elegant;* HARTMANN *very young, slender, pale, with an attractive, smart, boyish face*)

PFUNDTMAYER (*Reporting in military fashion*) Captain Pfundtmayer and three officers from Colonel Eilers' Fighter Squadron reporting, sir!

HARRAS (*Official but barely able to hold back his laughter*) Thank you, Captain. Gentlemen, I have the honor to congratulate you on your decorations and bid you welcome to our little gathering.

PFUNDTMAYER (*Salutes*) The honor's all ours, General.

HARRAS (*Bursting out*) Pfundy! Y'old stud mule! You haven't grown any younger!

PFUNDTMAYER Harry, y'old struttin' rooster! Can a body still call you that, such a powerful big critter as you've turned out to be.

HARRAS (*To his other guests*) We were front line buddies—1914 to '18.

PFUNDTMAYER No, to '17—winter of '17, when they ketched me in the arse. My pig-luck!

MOHRUNGEN And the gentlemen have never met since?

HARRAS Just so happened we never did. But I've been prepared for a long time. Ten paces to the rear, Pfundy! D'ya still remember?

PFUNDTMAYER Me? I sure do!

HARRAS Ten paces to the rear, soldier!

(*He takes ten paces back,* HARRAS *the same; they face each other and march with a peculiar travesty of the parade step, each with a full glass in his hand so that it looks as though they would bump into each other and push the glasses into each other's faces. But at the last moment, belly to belly, they swerve the glasses sideways and put them to each other's mouth. Each empties the glass of the other with a gulp; then they about-face smartly so that for a moment they stand back to back. They march back in the same tempo to their starting point and fill the glasses anew. General bravos and clapping*)

HARRAS We used to greet each other like that every evening at the officers' mess—outside Verdun. Now there was a war!

PFUNDTMAYER We drunk a lot more, I'll admit that. The eats was worse though! (*Laughing to the point of tears*) What a rat-race! You still able t'shoot a glass off of my dome, Harry? Or don't ya dare n'more? (*He puts his glass on his broad skull*)

HARRAS Hansen, my Luger!

PFUNDTMAYER (*Takes the glass down quickly and drinks*) Naw, naw! I guess I can't afford to risk this set of brains. They're still prewar quality, you know. (*He shakes with laughter*)

HASTENTEUFFEL (*With a hoarse bass voice*) If the General would like to shoot—at your service, sir. (*He puts a small glass on his head and stands at attention*)

HARRAS Later, my friend, after the next bottle. Haven't got my famous steady hand yet.

WRITZKY May I present target with a cigarette? I have a long brand. (*He stands in profile with an extra long cigarette in his mouth*)

HARRAS You're all right, boys. Come, I'll introduce you around. You don't need any introduction, Lieutenant Hartmann. Go ahead, make yourself at home.

HARTMANN (*somewhat embarrassed*) Yes, indeed, General. Thank you, General. (*He stands in the foreground with* POOTSIE *while* HARRAS *leads the others around and loose groups are formed*)

POOTSIE (*Casual but friendly and not without pride*) Well, little man, how does it feel? All that laurel around so young a brow?

HARTMANN I don't know—I'm not all here, yet. Last night over Leningrad and now—it's all so fast.

POOTSIE Well, don't brood over it, young poet. Save the war experiences for your memoirs. Get hep, man. You're in Berlin, boy, at Otto's, the only place in the German Reich where there's still anything cooking. Do you know Baron Pflungk, Foreign Ministry? A charming man. He's going to take me to a diplomatic dinner dance. Next week he's flying to Vichy, Berne and so on and he has promised to bring me chocolate and some material for a dress. Isn't that madly sweet of him?

HARTMANN I'm very pleased.

PFLUNGK (*Introduces himself with a somewhat self-conscious false irony*) Pflungk, consoler of widows and orphans. But naturally, the question of "taking out" will only come up when your furlough is over, Lieutenant, and the young lady is bored. Or would you also do me the honor—perhaps next Saturday night—

POOTSIE Lord, no! I told you, he doesn't even dance. And anyway, what's the big idea? After all, we aren't married.

HARTMANN I—I really wanted to spend my furlough in the country. I thought—perhaps on the Rhine—near the Mohrungen estate—

POOTSIE Who's stopping you?

HARTMANN I didn't know you wanted to stay in Berlin. I thought—

POOTSIE Look, you won't catch me in the country. I never went much for that nature stuff. And in this day and age? Grim, I tell you. Everybody walks around with a face this long—like a state funeral. Naw, the only place you can live a little these days is Berlin.

PFLUNGK And that only on occasion.

POOTSIE Well, you've got to have connections, and you do, thank God. We'll have to get Harry to throw us a party in that apartment of his with the propeller bar. The goings-on there! Wow, the stories I've heard. (*She turns to* HARRAS *who is coming up with* PFUNDTMAYER *and another group*)

HARRAS That really fascinates you, doesn't it, little bride?

POOTSIE I'd like to be at an affair like that just once. Is it true that the serving girls only wear fig leaves at your festivities? I'll come as a servant girl, I warn you.

PFUNDTMAYER That would be a real thrill on a meatless day.

HASTENTEUFFEL (*His hoarse bass voice booming over from another corner where he stands with* MOHRUNGEN, EILERS, ANNE *and* DR. LAUSITZ) This Russian jumps me out of a cloud bank, low on the right, come up fast and lets me have it—a good burst—I throttle back, slide under him. I'm lucky—catch a cloud bank myself, spiral up fast, tear out in a Harras curve—you know, so far over you're almost head down—for which friend Russian is not prepared and nail him in the left wing. Three minutes after he jumps me I let him have it—down he goes, smoking like a stuck chimney. Don't kid yourself, those Russians make it plenty hot for us.

LAUSITZ In specific cases, that may be correct but the total picture proves them technologically and morally inferior.

EILERS Just as you say, Doctor. We're winning without a doubt. But I can tell you, the R.A.F. boys aren't joking any more either.

LAUSITZ Of course, a war for the life and death of the nation is no joke.

HARRAS Bravo, Dr. Lausitz. Go and breathe some real fighting spirit into these gentlemen.

LAUSITZ That is far from my intention.

HANSEN Is it absolutely necessary that we talk shop tonight?

PFUNDTMAYER I'd say you got yourself withdrawn at exactly the right time, Captain.

HANSEN Thanks, I did. (*With the left hand he lifts his right arm which is stiff*) With a small souvenir still in there from the London Blitz. It's just enough for me, especially in bad weather.

PFUNDTMAYER (*to* HARRAS) Here's to ya, old sojur! Important thing is we're still with it. I al'ays wish'd, m'self, it'uld start up ag'in. We had to bide our time long enough till it did. Now I just says to m'self, "If it only don't all fizzle out before I makes Lieutenant Colonel."

HARRAS Never mind, Pfundy, mebbe you'll still make "Ginrul"!

PFUNDTMAYER (*Slightly drunk*) Genurrull! Genurrull! You made it, Harry! But if ya really think about it—I was al'ays in the party—right from the Bloody March in '23—marched right behind the Fuehrer too—a little ta the left. And I lay in the puddles. But you, Harry—Well, I won't say nothing—

HARRAS Go ahead, say it, Pfundy! Get it off your chest!—Let's have it.

PFUNDTMAYER We old party men, we didn't have no time for careers. We was obliged first to "liquidate the enemy within." After that come business and family—there was a cross! I married inta the hops business, ya know. But it didn't pay off—Jews was in the competition and squeezed us out. Good buddy, that's when ya learn ta hate. When the party come to power I made out a little better. I did business with the Aryanization Program, cleaning out Jews. And now, in uniform, what am I now? A poor ole Captain—me, with my low party number and all. And you—you're the Genurrull! Ya call that justice?

HARRAS Well, now, listen here, ma friend. I have never been a Nazi. You're right. I'm a flier. I've risked my neck and earned my keep. I never married into nothing. I've never dipped into the party treasury, never stole anything from a Jew nor built myself villas from the proceeds. (*Stubborn—already slightly drunk*) General or clown. I'm a flier and that's all. And who ever don't like it, he can— (*An abashed silence*)

PFUNDTMAYER Well, what da ya know! (*With mouth open*)

LAUSITZ What the General means to say is the Fuehrer has given his life, which was passionately dedicated to aviation and to the Luftwaffe, a goal and an opportunity to serve the Fatherland from a leading position.

HARRAS Ya see—there you have, presto, the official translation. Thanks, Doctor—That's exactly what I meant.

LAUSITZ I don't doubt it.

HARRAS Why should you? You know my innermost thoughts.

LAUSITZ I believe I do, General.

HARRAS Well then—cheers! (*He empties a glass of Armagnac*)

(*During the last few sentences there has been noise and commotion in the background and now three ladies from the theatre sweep in, led by* OTTO. OLIVIA GEISS, *operetta diva, has the full bust of the professional singer but slim, almost delicate legs. She is almost forty, dressed too young for her age, very blonde, and still pretty. Her sympathetic face, already a little spongy, is slightly red from just having make-up removed. She's not very much made up now.* LYRA SCHOEPPKE *is red-haired and wears a monocle. She's powdered absolutely white so that it is hard to judge her age. She's wearing an excessively tight black silk dress which sharply accentuates her good figure.* DIDDO GEISS *is a very young blonde girl with an unusually fresh, natural face and large dark blue eyes. She seems more like a school-girl who is going to her first ball. She wears a bunch of fresh violets at her bosom*)

OLIVIA Harry! When I heard you were here—nobody could hold me back! We just rolled up—the opening night party of Reichsmarshal Goering. "Give old Harry a kiss for me," he said—but I don't really know whether that means anything to you.

HARRAS (*Holds out his cheek to her*) From you—always. From Poppa—only when I'm completely plastered. I haven't quite reached that point this evening.

OLIVIA Are you sober enough to meet my little niece? Because this child simply idolizes you! So don't disillusion her, if you'll be so kind. (*She falls into her native dialect*) Come here, little Diddo, now's your chance to meet a real hero—from the good old days when you really had to be somebody to get to the top. That was when the stars stood up front for the applause and the extras behind. Nowadays everybody's a hero—behind, up front, and in the middle.

HARRAS (*Strikes a pose in front of* DIDDO) Don't touch, please, the old gentleman is under national monument conservation. (DIDDO, *who has looked at him with barely concealed curiosity, laughs a little.* HARRAS *bends briefly over her hand. To* OLIVIA) And you've kept her hidden from me for nineteen years. I thought you were a friend of mine! (*He holds on to* DIDDO'*s hand while she blushes more and more under his interested, probing glance*)

PFLUNGK May I do the honors? (*He begins to introduce*) Mr. von Mohrungen, Colonel Eilers and Mrs. Eilers— (*He mumbles the other names while the gentlemen bow before* OLIVIA *and* LYRA, *then the ladies shake hands with them*)

POOTSIE Be daring, Hartmann! Step right up! Now's your chance to meet the famous Geiss who captivated our fathers and uncles when they were in puberty!

MOHRUNGEN (*Painfully embarrassed. Apologizing to* OLIVIA) Don't take her seriously, dear lady. My daughter has a peculiar sense of humor.

OLIVIA Know all about it. Today's youth. They'll play less hard-to-get when men get scarcer, like after the last war. Is the interesting lieutenant her fiancé?

MOHRUNGEN Yes, that is— (*Changing the subject*) What was the musical that opened this evening?

OLIVIA *The Merry Widow* for a change. That's the only thing the Fuehrer wants to hear besides Wagner. The whole thing was one of those gala occasions. Sort of an anniversary for me—twenty-five years ago I sang it for the first time—exactly to the day.

MOHRUNGEN (*Fascinated*) Wasn't that at Heidelberg? I saw you in that performance!

POOTSIE What did I tell you!

OLIVIA You remember it, Mr. von Mohrungen? Have I changed a little since then?

MOHRUNGEN If I may be privileged to witness one of your performances again, then I will permit myself an opinion. But for me you'll always be the best Merry Widow. Unsurpassed.

OLIVIA Oh, that old shoe—I can rattle it off like a worn-out record. If only once they would give me something new. But it'll never come to that anymore —not in my lifetime.

LYRA Don't make yourself out older than you are, Ollie.

OLIVIA Why? Youth must have a chance too. My niece had her first part tonight. The Lord Almighty himself was expected for the performance, but he didn't show up.

LYRA No dice. One of those rare times that I'm in a production, what happens?— Boom! Thunder in the East. My luck.

HARRAS (*to* DIDDO) If I had known—we all would have come to see you. Well, what were you like on stage?

DIDDO I haven't the faintest idea, General. I was— in a trance. When my cue came my heart went bump, bump, bump way up in my throat—well, it would have been easier to go to my own execution.

OLIVIA Such luck. Just think of it. She played like a young goddess. And in the intermission she was supposed to have been introduced. Of course, the Reichsmarshal was awfully sweet to her, but you know that isn't the same for these children. St. Peter instead of the Good Lord Himself, so to speak.

DIDDO I didn't know if he was really in his box or not. I just thought, "I wasn't this bad at rehearsal." And then after the curtain our director said to me, "No soap. Called away to the Eastern Front."

EILERS Called away to the front! The Fuehrer?

OLIVIA Well, instead you're meeting our Harry. He's a big wheel, too. (*She pats* HARRAS' *cheek*)

DIDDO I really almost wished for that more— (*Laughter*)— When I was little I used to look at your picture secretly—the one that sits on Aunt Ollie's bedside table.

LYRA Tut. Tut.

OLIVIA That's right. That's exactly where it stands. With flowers. It's a little yellow and faded.

HARRAS (*Passes his hand over his hair—to* DIDDO) You should have met me twenty years ago. I was young once too.

DIDDO Twenty years?—I wasn't in this world then!

OLIVIA But I was! Cheers, Harry! (*She drinks from his glass*)

PFLUNGK François! Detlev! Perhaps the ladies would like—

PFUNDTMAYER (*Who is devouring* LYRA *with his eyes*) Yes sir, let's all have a drink! Swill 'er down, everybody! This we gotta celebrate. What a sow!

LYRA To whom are you referring, Captain?

PFUNDTMAYER Beg pardon, Ma'am. What I mean— I'm just plain lucky. Ma first night in Berlin and lo and behold, ladies from the theatre. Ma sow-luck, I call it. (*They laugh*)

HARRAS (*Softly to* HANSEN) Call the ministry—see what's cooking.

HANSEN Orders! (*He goes out*)

LYRA Did you come here straight from the front, Captain?

PFUNDTMAYER You know it! Yesterday we still had dead Russians for evening chow. Ya know, I never really sniffed a lady from the theatre before up close over kümmel and corn, as they say.

POOTSIE Well go ahead and take a bite, Captain. You must have good teeth.

LYRA (*Ignoring* POOTSIE *pointedly*) You must tell me about your experiences, Captain. Madly exciting, I imagine—these duels in the air—man against man—like the tournaments of knights in days of old.

PFUNDTMAYER Exactly! Just exactly! Ya hear that, Hastenteiffie? We're knights in days of old, you and me! (*He laughs a booming laugh*)

LYRA (*Laughing with him*) I know I must sound terribly silly—

PFUNDTMAYER Not at all, Ma'am! Ma'am! (*He kisses her hand and pats it*)

OTTO (*Re-enters*) The Reichsmarshal[7] begs me to announce: Supper is served. I regret to have to recall you to the line of duty—but there is a small compensation for the gentlemen. The Reichsmarshal takes the liberty to invite the ladies and gentlemen of the Eilers Squadron to join him for a glass of champagne—He expects the gentlemen post-haste.

HARRAS Well, off you go, boys. Fat Hermann isn't on display every day. You can all cut yourselves a slice.

OTTO Not coming, General? The Reichsmarshal specifically requested—

HARRAS Little later. He will undoubtedly be able to tame his passion for me another fifteen minutes. Eilers, will you fly lead?

LAUSITZ (*To* EILERS) Might I speak with you beforehand—about our broadcast?—

EILERS Of course, Doctor (*To* PFUNDTMAYER) Pfundtmayer, please take my place? Introduce the men.

PFUNDTMAYER (*Beaming to* LYRA) Looka here—sowluck's what you gotta have.

POOTSIE The gentlemen *and* ladies, if you please. That means us. At times like this, little Pootsie can't be left out. Whatsa matter, beautiful dreamer? Still the melancholy Prince of Homburg? [8] (*She hooks arms with* HARTMANN *and* ANNE. *All exit except* HARRAS, EILERS, LAUSITZ, PFLUNGK, *and* MOHRUNGEN)

OLIVIA (*While going off—softly to* HARRAS) Harry. I have to speak to you alone for a moment.

HARRAS Not easy tonight. Urgent?

OLIVIA S.O.S.

HARRAS Well—maybe later. Otherwise—you have my private number.

OLIVIA I don't trust the phone. (*She goes off.* HANSEN *enters in the meantime, goes quickly to* HARRAS *and whispers something to him*)

MOHRUNGEN (*Watching* POOTSIE *go off, who is laughing and jabbering loudly*) These two girls of mine—what a difference!—It's hard to believe they're sisters. I have to admit, sometimes I'm just no match for Pootsie at all. I probably didn't pay enough attention to her upbringing. (*To* EILERS) Momma died too soon.

LAUSITZ I assume the Bund[9] relieved you of some of the worry of her upbringing.

MOHRUNGEN (*Somewhat bitter*) Yes, of that they relieved me.

HARRAS (*To* EILERS, *who looks worried*) Trouble spot around Moscow.

LAUSITZ It is a small matter of tactical regrouping. Principally due to weather. We were briefed on it at the Propaganda Ministry this evening already. The attack on Moscow and Petersburg will not be appreciably delayed. But this makes our shortwave broadcast all the more important—in order to prevent any kind of rumor mongering. If I could just have a moment with you . . . privately.

EILERS Crisis or not, Doctor, you'll have to tell me exactly what to do. I have a terrible case of stage fright already.

LAUSITZ (*Smiling*) There is no reason to be apprehensive, Colonel. All you have to do is to speak quite naturally—from your own true experiences. The script has been prepared. All you have to do is read it. Everything will be pre-recorded.

EILERS The most important thing to me is to catch the noon train. You understand, the children. I haven't been home for a year and naturally I don't want to lose a day.

LAUSITZ That can be easily arranged, Colonel. (*He takes the script from his briefcase*) Perhaps we could go into another room. You will excuse us, General?

HARRAS Please; gladly. (*After* LAUSITZ *and* EILERS *have gone out, speaking to* HANSEN, *who remains with* MOHRUNGEN *and* PFLUNGK) All right, let's have the latest. Tomorrow, these gentlemen will hear all about it anyhow.

HANSEN As far as they can tell at the Ministry, everything's freezing up in Russia. Way below zero. Von Bock got cold feet.[10] They say he hollered into the phone, "Retreat immediately, or I'll not be responsible." Whereupon the great Fuehrer swung himself into the saddle of his war-horse and headed East to see for himself. I'll call them again; they expect fresh reports any minute. (*He goes off*)

PFLUNGK That means we'll be having a new scapegoat soon. What is your opinion of the matter, General?

HARRAS Don't ask so sly, ole Saxon. Every messenger boy in the Reichschancery knows my opinion.

MOHRUNGEN Seriously, General—do you believe anything can go wrong—I mean, anything decisive?

HARRAS It's done gone already, von Mohrungen. You know it. Why ask me?

MOHRUNGEN You mean—the increased demand for raw material—

[7] Official title of Hermann Goering.

[8] An allusion to the hero of a play written in 1808 by Heinrich von Kleist.

[9] The reference is to the "Bund deutscher Mädel" or League of German Girls, organized by the Nazi party.

[10] Feodor von Bock (1880-1945), Field Marshal commanding the German Army attacking Moscow.

HARRAS I mean: Russia.

PFLUNGK Strategically speaking—if we had taken care of Russia—

HARRAS But we haven't—Not by a long shot. I don't know anything about strategy. I only know what it costs from the standpoint of the Luftwaffe. What it costs under the most favorable circumstances, and we're a long way from them.

MOHRUNGEN You don't think we'll be able to keep up with production?

HARRAS Figure it out for yourself. What will the western powers produce in two years?

PLFUNGK Aren't you overestimating the strength of the democracies?—You know they're undermined psychologically. And our U-boats—

HARRAS I seem to have heard that somewhere once before. Sounds sort of familiar. No—I remember 1916 too well—when a guy like myself in a pumped-up wreck of a crate tried to stink up a dozen or so of those psychologically undermined democrats. And more water in my bladder than gas in my tank. Hell. (*Drinks*)

MOHRUNGEN And how do you think the whole thing can be saved?—You don't mean to say, do you—that considering the other factors in our position, our reserves, and our synthetic materials—

HARRAS (*Shrugs his shoulders*) Ask the Foreign Ministry. (*Motions with his head toward* PFLUNGK. *Fills his glass*)

PFLUNGK In my opinion there is still a way out in case we can't attain a complete military victory. Keep America out of it. Cool down Japan. Negotiate peace in the Far East. Then, somehow, a separate peace with Russia even at the price of some zones of influence in the Balkans and the Near East; gentle pressure on London and a compromise between us and the British Empire. Then we'll see.

HARRAS (*Laughs*) Ribbentrop[11] Brand Champagne, 1914—late harvest. Before dinner the label on the bottle read differently. No children, the Champagne Fritz hasn't the faintest idea what to do and he ain't learnin' either. He thought he knew the British because a few snobbed-up Lords in London slapped him on the shoulder and a couple of crafty stockbrokers winked at him at dinner. But if he knows England, then I know the moon. If you mash a bulldog's rear against a wall he'll bite until either he's had it, or you've had it. There's only one way to play it, keep your own rear end free.

PFLUNGK General, I think you're mistaken about England. Henderson said in '39[12] . . .

HARRAS Doesn't interest me. I count the heads of my dear ones remaining and say, "Gone, for this!" Once upon a time there was a German Air Force, the most powerful in the world.

MOHRUNGEN Perhaps this jump to the East should have been prevented—

HARRAS By whom? Me or my grandmother? Go ahead and prevent, just once, in this country. I've put my foot in my mouth often enough. I ran to Hermann and stabbed him with the facts when I first glimpsed his secret orders at Luftwaffe Headquarters. Hermann wrinkled his nose and wiggled his jowls. Then he went and told it to Halder,[13] and he told it to Keitel,[14] and he told it to Brauchitsch,[15] and he dared to clear his throat quite audibly in the Eagle's Roost—but the Great Spirit was already chewing the carpet and spraying his famous intuition. Brrrr— (*He shakes himself with disgust*)

MOHRUNGEN (*Abashed*) Nevertheless—you have to admit that he has military instinct . . .

HARRAS I admit nothing. Absolutely nothing. Joan of Arc's voices with laryngitis. It makes me puke. Well, cheers. (*He drinks*)

(*From the other side of the restaurant where Goering's party is going on, the soft music of a record player has begun a waltz from* The Merry Widow. POOTSIE *appears at the door, excited*)

POOTSIE Baron Pflungk! They're dancing over there. He's madly nice—and not as fat as I thought, rather imposing, in fact. Only around his rear the seams almost burst when he stands up. Coming, Baron? A slow waltz with feeling. It will always be the most graceful dance.

PFLUNGK I love waltzes.

POOTSIE If the man can lead— (*While* PFLUNGK *dances out with her*) You can lead—I knew it immediately.

MOHRUNGEN (*Nervously fussing with his cigarette—to* HARRAS *with whom he is now alone*) Tell me, General, do you trust this Pflungk?

HARRAS Not as far as I can spit. Why should I? Whom can you trust anyhow?

MOHRUNGEN Aren't you a little careless?

HARRAS Sure. That's my method. (*He lights a cigarette*) They know what I think. So why not say it out loud. The minute I start being careful they'll think my pants are full and they can spit on my head.

MOHRUNGEN That's true. We're all suspect—everyone of us who doesn't belong to the party or to the inner circle. But you don't have to hand them the cue, so to speak.

HARRAS Opportunities they have a-plenty, if they want them. Their snuffle-hounds are leering around every hydrant. That lousy Schmidt—the gent with the German soul—who stands on Culture until it can't get up any more—I happen to know for a fact that he sends daily love letters to the Gestapo. These boys don't fool me. And if I can step on their toes, I do it with pleasure.

MOHRUNGEN You think they can't touch you—that you're indispensable . . .

HARRAS I don't *think* it. I know it up to a certain

[11] Joachim von Ribbentrop (1893-1946), German Minister of Foreign Affairs under Hitler.

[12] Neville Henderson (1882-1942), British ambassador to Germany identified with the policy of appeasement.

[13] Franz Halder (1884—) was Chief of the Army General Staff from 1938 to 1942.

[14] Wilhelm Keitel (1882-1946) was Hitler's Chief of Staff.

[15] Walther von Brauchitsch (1881-1948) was Commander in Chief of the Army until the end of 1941.

point. That gang wants to win the war—they can't turn back now. There's only a handful of people who can push the right button. Too bad I'm one of them. Anyway, I don't give one whoop in hell. (*He leans back in an easy chair and suddenly looks very tired*)

MOHRUNGEN (*Looks at him worriedly*) Are you really so pessimistic?

HARRAS I don't mean it that way. It's more personal. Of course, I know—they can liquidate me any day despite my indispensability. To the "Maiden" no one is indispensable—except Brueckner[16] who sits next to him with a loaded revolver when he goes for a drive. But what do I care? I've been risking my life for a quarter of a century about every second day and it was nice, everything considered. Enough girls—enough to drink—a lot of flying—and—a few good moments. What more can you want?

MOHRUNGEN You talk as though you were writing your own obituary!

HARRAS Better now than never. If I can't say what I think—have to watch the booze intake so the wrong joke don't slip out . . . If it comes to being careful, then the whole schmear don't pay any more at all.

MOHRUNGEN What does pay anyway?

HARRAS (*Leans forward, slaps him lightly on the knee*) Now don't you start, Mohrungen. You are a respectable member of society—not a quasi-adventurer, a cloud-hopper like me, but—a representative of sound, stable values. You have to keep your chin up.

MOHRUNGEN That's just it, General. One tries to maintain a decent standard—for Germany—or in my case for the economic health of our industry, and right before my eyes everything dissolves into mist and foul air.

HARRAS You shouldn't take what I said before so tragically. There's still a strong chance that we'll win the war. You can always count on a break from the fumbles of the other side. Otherwise, where would we be?

MOHRUNGEN Win—or lose, Harras, it isn't the same anymore. Sometimes I think—our Germany, the one we loved—is gone. Either way, beyond recall.

HARRAS What kind of Germany did we love? The old—with the stiff collar and the clamped monocle? Or the democratic, with the paunch and wobbly legs?

MOHRUNGEN Certainly not the one—for which we are both working now.

HARRAS Too bad you and your friends didn't think of that when you financed these bums.

MOHRUNGEN We saw it differently. We thought we were creating a weapon against Bolshevism, a weapon we could control.

HARRAS Yes, I know. Fritz Thyssen,[17] "The Sorcerer's Apprentice" or "The Strong Hand"—a very nice reading assignment for tomorrow's school children. You thought you would do the pushing, and you got pushed. I never kidded myself.

[16] Wilhelm Brueckner was Hitler's adjutant.

[17] A German industrialist who aided in Hitler's rise to power.

MOHRUNGEN Well then, what actually is your excuse? I beg your pardon, that goes too far.

HARRAS That doesn't go too far at all. The question is quite justified among friends.

MOHRUNGEN (*With warmth*) I thank you. (*Extends his hand to him*)

HARRAS (*Shaking his hand lightly*) Excuse? There is none. That is—if I had to write one for the principal upstairs— (*He points to heaven with his cigar*)—then it would be because of my mother. But otherwise—I'd have to admit I got on this bandwagon stone-cold sober—without any illusions. I knew the gang from the last time. When their turn came in '33—I knew for sure another little world war was being cooked up. Well, it just so happens I'm a fool about flying. Air combat without me—naw, I couldn't stand that. I said to myself, "—A man has got to stay in his corner of the ring." You can't very well change sides in the second round.

MOHRUNGEN Naturally not.

HARRAS Is it so natural? Perhaps—it is just habit. Comfort, the cradle of all vices, the law of inertia or the lack of inner ability to change. Just between us—wouldn't I have a better feeling in my stomach if I were bombing the Reichschancery instead of the Kremlin or Buckingham Palace!

MOHRUNGEN (*Has become pale*) For God's sake, dear General. For God's sake!

HARRAS Don't worry, von Mohrungen. I'm not doing it. I missed that train. I never had a real future with the others. Oh, I could have made a career out of being a stunt flier, daredevil, a sort of flying clown over there. I might have made the movies—but no more. Those boys have no imagination, and that was precisely the positive factor in this whole business here for me, at least. Nowhere else in the world but here would I have been given these possibilities, these unlimited means—this power. These five years, making the Luftwaffe airborne—I don't regret them. When an old wolf licks blood again, he runs with the pack even though all hell breaks loose. So you don't like the management! Spain, of course, was slightly sickening. But the first two years, when it really started up, we had something to offer, there was some style to it then. The best, most exact, most effective machinery that ever existed in the history of war.

MOHRUNGEN That is probably true of the whole army; our war machine is so carefully, so thoroughly integrated that it can stand any kind of strain.

HARRAS Maybe yes, maybe no. I know machines. I'm a technician. I know exactly how much depends on precise computations. But there is always the very last angle that is incomputable. It's called luck, touch, mercy, idea—character—or something else. It comes—from somewhere else and it's irrational.

MOHRUNGEN You were always a sort of artist. You've got it in you.

HARRAS Not quite that bad. A dash of it goes with the mechanics. At any rate, we're with this thing and we have no choice.

MOHRUNGEN (*Thoughtfully*) And aside from that, there are still—deeper ties. Or what did you mean before when you said, because of your mother?

HARRAS (*Laughs thoughtfully, speaks parenthetically, blowing smoke through his nose*) Oh, the old lady. She's childish, you know. She sits down there in Bavaria in her country house and is proud of me. I don't want to spoil her fun for these last few years. Medals and honors, epaulets, General's stripes, and so forth—you can have it, as far as I'm concerned. Even as a young man I didn't care about it. But Mother beams. Whenever I won anything my first thought was always: the telegram to Mother, honestly—I guess every man has some woman for whom he does what he does. Otherwise we wouldn't any of us work so hard, believe me. For me there was never a better woman.

MOHRUNGEN (*Somewhat absently, nodding to himself*) Yes—the mothers—

HARRAS (*Slightly embarrassed*) Emotional drivel! We'll never get the cart out of the mud with that! (*Stands up and begins to walk up and down*) We're in one hell of a mess, you know, you and I!

MOHRUNGEN (*Expectantly*) You mean—the matter of the faulty materials?

HARRAS (*Nods*) As far as we can tell, there is something wrong with the alloys that is throwing off the weight calculation. But where the actual source of the mistake is—there we are completely in the dark. I wouldn't have attached too much importance to the business—an error, carelessness can always occur once—but it repeated itself with a certain regularity. Three times, in three different deliveries of new fighter planes in one week. There is something fishy there.

MOHRUNGEN Do you think it's sabotage? Communists in the factories?

HARRAS Possible. But not very probable. The very regularity makes me think it's an organization led according to a plan. That doesn't check out with what we know about the underground.

MOHRUNGEN Who else could have such an organization? (*Perplexed, as* HARRAS *grins*) You mean—really? But—what possible motive could they have there—

HARRAS (*Shrugs his shoulders*) It's all guesswork. I have no proof. But it looks as though they were stoking a furnace in hell just for me. Me—personally. After all, I am directly responsible for all the aircraft materials that pass through my office and are approved by me.

MOHRUNGEN Then you must be able to exercise a certain control.

HARRAS (*Nervous*) My God, yes! A very definite control. But that has its limits! I can't very well tap every ingot of aluminum, and pull every foot of steel cable. I can make spot tests and check the work of the departments below me, but in the last analysis it is a question of personnel.

MOHRUNGEN That's probably somewhat complicated with such an enormous network of industries.

HARRAS It isn't too bad. All you need is a handful of men on whom you can rely absolutely.

MOHRUNGEN Do you have them?

HARRAS I have them. Oderbruch, for example.

MOHRUNGEN Oderbruch—that's your chief engineer.

HARRAS I created the position just for him. He is tireless, works night and day—and . . . he misses nothing. I'm blind by comparison.

MOHRUNGEN (*Smiling*) At last, a point where the great skeptic in you falls silent.

HARRAS You know, I don't trust anyone so easily. But the few people you've been together with once—in a real jam—in a plane dribbling off with the controls jammed—you know them. There are damned few. I can count them on the fingers of one hand. Hansen and Korrianke, my old chauffeur, and Oderbruch are the only ones I can rely on—but those, all the way.

MOHRUNGEN It can't possibly be the fault of the raw materials.

HARRAS That much is certain. You're not liable, Mohrungen.

MOHRUNGEN That's not necessarily true. Our light-metal factories, Waldhofen and Kaefertal, work mainly with alloys. The cartel system is powerful but today it depends 100 percent on co-operation with government agencies which dictate price and output to us.

HARRAS In other words, the procurement office is forced to take a stand 100 percent behind the viewpoint demanded of you from the powers above.

MOHRUNGEN I will never take a stand against my convictions . . . (HARRAS *is silent for a moment, looks at him*) I hope you assume nothing else about me.

HARRAS Then it would be best if tomorrow you enter into no discussion at all which—

MOHRUNGEN (*Interrupts, touches his arm*) Shhhh. I believe someone is listening!

HARRAS (*Indifferent*) Really? Who?

MOHRUNGEN I saw something in the hall.

HARRAS Heh! Is anybody there?

FRANÇOIS (*Appears at the door*) You called, General? More Armagnac?

HARRAS (*Laughs*) You're getting nervous, Mohrungen. Thank you, François—there's a full bottle here. But bring me the wine card later on—We'll need a change soon.

FRANÇOIS Of course, General. (*Goes off*)

MOHRUNGEN Don't you think that Frenchman is snooping around?

HARRAS Naw, naw—the boys here are OK. And what if he is? What can he hear? I don't know anything myself.

MOHRUNGEN A Gestapo plot—to sabotage its own armaments—I can hardly believe that, General.

HARRAS You mean, they could have my scalp cheaper? Possible. I don't know. It's only a suspicion. But you see, it is not just that the Heil-boys don't like my nose . . .

MOHRUNGEN I know, the Luftwaffe is at stake.

HARRAS Naturally. Whoever controls the air force has the balance of power in case of a fight between the army and the party—That is why the party, that is, the SS,[18] is trying so hard to get all the key positions in its claws. If they succeed, then they will have won the smoldering German civil war for the second time. And there are only a few heads that still stand in the way.

MOHRUNGEN The best, however.

HARRAS Or the thickest. However that may be, this business has to be stopped. Because it happens to be a real danger—I'm not talking about the politics now, but about our boys at the front. When they can't depend on their planes any more—

MOHRUNGEN What sort of man is this Oderbruch? Where does he come from?

HARRAS (*Laughs. Turns to* EILERS *who has just come in with* ANNE *on his arm*) Friedrich! What sort of a man is Oderbruch?

EILERS (*His face lights up*) Oderbruch? Well, how should I say it? You can trust him with your fortune without receipt. Even your wife and children.

HARRAS Bravo, Fred! A plus. You're getting to be a poet. (*To* MOHRUNGEN) He comes from a good home. Silesian Catholics, as far as I know. Old family of government officials, of course, without doremi. He began as a mechanic, and flew with me, then with Eilers. He has the kind of technical fingertip sensitivity and knowledge of the field that you only find once in a lifetime.

MOHRUNGEN Then you must be very happy to have him.

HARRAS You bet. (*To* EILERS) It got too wild for you two over there, eh?

EILERS (*Laughing*) Yes. A little wild. Pootsie is dancing polkas with the Reichsmarshal.

HARRAS Come, Mohrungen, let's have a look. (*While going off*) I put Oderbruch on the scent. I bet he'll find out where the dog is buried— (*He and* MOHRUNGEN *disappear*)

ANNE (*Puts her arm around* EILERS) Tired, darling?

EILERS (*Draws her close to him*) Not too bad. A little —worn out.

ANNE I think we could make our exit soon. Don't you?

EILERS Sure. It's only on account of Harras. He's really getting a kick out of this party. Let's stay another half hour.

ANNE But no longer. (*Tenderly*) You should be in bed.

EILERS When I'm with you—then I'm not tired any more. That's—better than sleep. (*He kisses her*) I missed you so.

ANNE (*Softly*) Don't you know—that I'm always with you? Day and night?

EILERS (*Nods*) I know. That's what keeps me going. Without that—it would be hard to take.

ANNE Is it that rough?

EILERS (*Sits down and leans back*) Yes. Being separated. Being away from home. As for the service routine—war, planes, combat—you get used to all that. And yet—it isn't right in the long run. I mean—killing people.

ANNE (*Strokes his hand*) It has to be. For the Fatherland. For the future. For a better world.

EILERS Yes, it's all necessary. (*Smiling—calmed*) Sometimes—there are moments—there is something strange about them, unreal, you know—almost like a fantasy. Moments when you forget everything. (*He speaks gropingly as if remembering a dream*) Last October we went up one night under a full moon—There was already a little snow on the ground—and everything looked like silver. I was alone in the lead plane watching the needle on the controls. But I was also somewhere else, at home, in the mountains. Suddenly, I heard myself reciting a poem about the moon that I had forgotten long ago—

> The moon in beds of sky
> Has looked down many a night
> Seen seas and fields go by
> Where boys, now men, have loved its light.

Isn't it beautiful?

ANNE Very beautiful.

EILERS By Matthias Claudius, I think. (*Shaking his head*) We are a funny people. Guernica, Coventry and Matthias Claudius.[19] How do they ever go together?

ANNE (*Intense, beseeching*) Don't question, darling. Believe. Believe. Remember what you wrote to me—when you left the first time? I know it by heart. I say it to myself over and over. "Let nothing confuse you—Let nothing make you waver. Believe with every fiber of your being in Germany—in yourself—in us —in our mission—Whoever believes will survive. Believe!"

EILERS I still do, my love. I will—to the end.

ANNE 'Til victory.

EILERS 'Til victory—and peace. Peace, Anne! That will come again too—someday. (*He laughs*) Think of it—the children—they won't even be able to imagine what's happening in the world today. Perhaps they will fly planes sometime with no gun turrets, with no bomb bays, planes with many windows and telescopes and instruments for measuring. Planes to see, study, explore—explore the whole world with open eyes, happy, unafraid—That's why I do all this. That's why.

ANNE (*Almost shy, whispering*) I love you. (*They sit silent for a moment, hand in hand*)

(*Music and the noise of voices have become louder in the background. Now* PFUNDTMAYER *and* LYRA SCHOEPPKE *appear in the corridor, sauntering arm in arm in the midst of conversation*)

[18] The SS or "Schutz-Staffeln" ("Protective Corps") was the military unit of the Nazi party.

[19] Matthias Claudius (1740-1815) was a famous lyric poet. The poem is "Ein Wiegenlied, bei Mondschein zu singen" —"A lullaby, to be sung in the moonlight." Guernica, a city in northern Spain, was destroyed by German planes in April, 1937. The English city of Coventry was bombed into ruins in raids of 1940 and 1941.

PFUNDTMAYER In Munich—on the Odeon Square, just to the left of the Fuehrer, smack in the puddles. I kin still see the brains of the guy next to me plastered all over the wall of the Preysing Palace.[20] Eferdinger, his name was, Larry.

LYRA (*Stuttering*) And nothing happened to you at all?

PFUNDTMAYER Nuttin' ever happens to me. Sow-luck, that's what ya gotta have. This—looka here, Ma'am, this is the blood medal. And you should only get a look at the scars I carry from the last World War—

LYRA Where were you wounded?

PFUNDTMAYER Down around my backsides, Ma'am. (*He laughs uproariously, as over a good joke.* LYRA *chimes in somewhat forcedly and they disappear.* HARRAS *enters arm in arm with* OLIVIA *and* DIDDO. *All three come into the room with a sort of dance-step softly humming the melody of a waltz.* HARRAS *is quite drunk but still in good form*)

HARRAS Look a' that, children. Look what's become of my party. Empty glasses, empty plates—and one lone pair of lovers. The sad remains. Whose party was this anyway? Reichsmarshal Fat Back's or mine?

EILERS (*Has gotten up smiling*) We'll round them up over there for the flight back, eh Anne?

HARRAS (*To* EILERS) Yes, do me a favor and call back your squadron. But don't you take off on me, Freddie. If you go, I go too.

ANNE He should really sleep soon—

HARRAS As you wish. As you wish. Let's all go sleep. Let's go sleep.

EILERS Oh no, Harras. We're staying. I can sleep on the train.

HARRAS You're a good guy, Freddie. You're a good guy. (*Slaps him on the shoulder*) A good guy, even if you don't drink and even if you are so solidly married.

ANNE (*Laughing*) I'm sorry, General.

HARRAS It's approved. It's approved. You're all right, Anne. You're all right. I think I'm already beginning to recover. Well, let's go, children. Bring the others back. It's high time we all had another drink.

EILERS Come, Anne. We'll be right back with the others. (*He and* ANNE *go off arm in arm*)

HARRAS (*Has mixed something in a glass and gives it to* DIDDO) Here, my child—try this. That's no cocktail. That is a Christian-Catholic Judo-Germanic Atheistic mixture. When you've downed that you'll believe in God again.

OLIVIA For Heaven's sake, Harry! Please don't get the child tipsy. Put it down, Diddo.

DIDDO Let me be. I know how much I can take. Your health, General.

HARRAS General. From your sweet lips. Can't stand to hear it. Makes me—downright melancholy, is what it makes me. Call me Harry. Would you like to?

DIDDO On one condition.

HARRAS Fulfilled, my child. What is it?

[20] Places in the center of Munich. The reference is to the attempted Nazi "Putsch" of 1923.

DIDDO That you don't call me "my child" anymore, because that makes me melancholy too.

HARRAS Agreed. Let's drink to it. You call me Harry and I call you Monkeywrench.

DIDDO Monkeywrench—O.K. by me. Not beautiful, but funny.

HARRAS There, you see. From now on the two of us will never be melancholy again.

DIDDO At least not when we're drinking something like this together.

HARRAS And when we are sober together—then especially not. The main thing—that we're together. And that we will be from now on—very often—won't we?

DIDDO (*Drinks and laughs*) I can say "yes" without hesitation. Tomorrow morning you will have forgotten it anyhow.

HARRAS My dear chi—pardon me. My dear Monkeywrench. You don't know me! You think I'm just a silly old booze-guzzler. Well, I am—But don't think that I will forget one word that either of us says tonight—or—or does not say— (*He stands very close to her and bends a little over her dress*) Fresh violets. Who gave you these?

DIDDO Aunt Ollie.

HARRAS Then it's all right.

DIDDO (*Somewhat bewildered*) I really think . . .

HARRAS What?

DIDDO You know, I almost think I would like some more of that Christian, Bolshevist mixture, or whatever it's called.

HARRAS Now I'll have to kiss you. (*He comes closer*)

DIDDO No—please—General!

HARRAS General—That'll cost you two kisses.

OLIVIA Say now, aren't you two even ashamed to carry on right here in the presence of an old lady? Kissing, Harry—with *your* breath! Don't light a match—There'll be an explosion!

HARRAS (*Pursuing* DIDDO) The explosion took place a while back—without a match!

OLIVIA Diddo . . . dear, could you leave us alone for a moment? You understand? I have something to tell him. Something serious. (*She takes his arm*)

DIDDO (*Saved*) Of course, Aunt Ollie. I'll go over there and hold off the others a little longer—OK?

OLIVIA Just five minutes.

HARRAS But—come back! Please!

DIDDO Maybe— (*She runs out*)

HARRAS (*Staring after her*) Absolutely—absolutely bewitching.

OLIVIA Listen, you—hands off, if you don't mind. That's too good for you.

HARRAS My dear good Mommy. You know me. Pure paternal feeling. Hand on my heart.

OLIVIA I know you, old Tom Cat. And I know girls. She's already lost her head over you. Though you'd think a young thing like that would dream of something prettier'n you! That's a girl for you. You're very impressive with your fame and your personality —and you use it shamelessly.

HARRAS (*Suddenly quite sober*) Yes, you're right, Ollie. It's unfair. Damned unfair. I'm going to be good;

you can depend on it. Well now, let's have it. Whatsa matter?

OLIVIA Is your head halfway clear now?

HARRAS Clear as pure alcohol. Hurry up, they're coming back in a minute.

OLIVIA (*Close to him, softly, desperate*) Bergmann got out of Buchenwald.[21] He was there for six months and they've messed him up so badly that he's in the hospital. Police hospital, naturally. But Jenny knows a doctor there who gives people death certificates. Then they can be smuggled out at night. Costs ten thousand. She's scrounged it up somehow and decided to escape with him. She says, if they ship him to Poland, he'll kill himself. Harry, you're the only one who can help . . .

HARRAS Just a minute. (*He takes a piece of ice out of the champagne cooler, pours a little cognac over it and begins to chew it*) He can't get out legally? Can't get a visa to someplace? Can't even buy one?

OLIVIA Not a chance. They're out to get him.

HARRAS Yes, I know. Those fellows will never be able to forgive him his Aryan wife. Not only did she marry a Jew, she's beautiful to boot and ran away from a Nazi on his account. No, he's not going to get an exit visa—unless it's to a camp.

OLIVIA I wouldn't come to you if there were any other way. But— (*Tears choke her voice*)

HARRAS (*His hand glides quickly over her hair*) Well now, just calm down for a minute. We'll figure out something. Is Jenny in good form? I mean, as a pilot? After all, she learned with me.

OLIVIA I don't know. But there is nothing she wouldn't do for him—nothing she couldn't do.

HARRAS Sure—a matter of life and death.

OLIVIA That's the way it stands either way. But for God's sake, Harry, I don't want you to get yourself—

HARRAS (*Cuts her off with a gesture, goes to the door, whistles a cavalry signal and calls*) Korrianke! (*Grinning to* OLIVIA) The likes of us have their bodyguard too, just like the other gangsters.

(KORRIANKE *enters at a trot. He is an older man, square built and slightly fat, with a red face and a double chin. Even though he wears the uniform of the Luftwaffe, the chauffeur in him is immediately apparent too. He has a thin, somewhat husky voice and lisps a little*)

KORRIANKE Ready for action, Herr General!

HARRAS Pay attention, Korriandoli. If someone comes in now, we are planning a trip to Kohlhasenbrück with Mrs. Geiss and her niece. Take out my calendar. You're the one who knows when I'm free. Get it?

KORRIANKE I'm with it, . . . Herr General. Kohlhasenbrück.

HARRAS (*In a lowered voice*) Do you remember Professor Bergmann? Samuel Bergmann, the surgeon?

KORRIANKE (*Lighting up*) The one who patched us up when we had that tough break with a curve at 120 m.p.h?

[21] A concentration camp near Weimar.

HARRAS Right. The magician who takes people's hearts out like a pocket watch, repairs them and puts them back again.

KORRIANKE Easy as pie.

HARRAS Cut it! They stuck him in a concentration camp for miscegenation and mauled him for six months.

KORRIANKE Sons of bitches, Herr General.

HARRAS Cut it! Remember his wife? I taught her to fly.

KORRIANKE A blonde! Hard to forget, Herr General. (*Smacks his lips*)

HARRAS Cut it!—Here's the pitch!—You will meet said doctor and the blonde in the apartment of Mrs. Geiss here— (*To* OLIVIA) When?

OLIVIA (*Pale, almost trembling*) Day after tomorrow, at night.

HARRAS Day after tomorrow, at night. The exact time I will tell you later. You will take along: for the professor, an old military coat and a cap of mine; for the lady—pilot's overalls, helmet and goggles. Do you think you can drive my car through to hangar 35 without being stopped for inspection?

KORRIANKE For certain, Herr General. Hangar 35. Easy as pie.

HARRAS All right Korrianke. (*Voices become audible outside. It is* PFUNDTMAYER *and* LYRA *who are fooling around in the hall. Speaking loudly*) Well then, Kohlhasenbrück—next Sunday.

KORRIANKE (*Loudly*) Kohlhasenbrück, Herr General. Just possible the ladies can go ice skating. There's a nip of frost in the air, Herr General.

HARRAS Yes, especially around Moscow.

KORRIANKE I'm with you completely, Herr General. (*Goes off*)

OLIVIA (*Quickly*) Harry—what is hangar 35?

HARRAS (*Softly*) There's a little sports plane there, always ready for flight with an exact map and directions for a fast, safe air route to Switzerland. For all emergencies.

OLIVIA And—Korrianke?

HARRAS Where do you think that guy left his front teeth? I fished him out of a concentration camp myself in '34.

OLIVIA Harry—you are— (*Reaches for his hand*)

HARRAS Pah. I've already forgotten the whole thing. (*He empties a big glass*) So, on Sunday, not too early though! Say around noon.

OLIVIA I'd love to.

HARRAS It's a deal . . . if "little violets" comes along.

OLIVIA You hen-happy old rooster! Just listen to you crow! (*Both laugh, from outside voices, calls, and laughing come closer.* PFUNDTMAYER *comes in,* LYRA, *then in short succession* WRITZKY, HASTENTEUFFEL, HARTMANN, EILERS, LAUSITZ.)

LYRA They're adjourning over there. Excuse us, Ollie, for breaking up your tête-à-tête, but you've flirted enough with your old flame. Are you coming up to my place now? Our director is there with half the company. We still have a little wine, too.

OLIVIA Heavens, yes, our colleagues. I don't know

—Actually, I'm a little tired. And that child has to go to bed.

LYRA (*Laughs*) "That child" has already said she'd come, Ollie. You can't send her home right after her first performance. She's beginning to grow out of diapers, you know.

PFUNDTMAYER Couldn't you manage to stay a little longer, Ma'am? Such a broken-off evening. Downright unhealthy, it is. I mean—we understand each other, Ma'am.

LYRA (*Formally*) Sorry, Captain. I am expecting guests at home. Why don't you come up to my place with your friends when you finish off here? You too, of course, Harry. We'd love to have you. We're sure to be up until the morning papers come out.

PFUNDTMAYER Accepted, Ma'am, accepted. Gonna come. Gonna bring a coupla bottles along. War's war!

LYRA That can never do any harm. God—if we only had some coffee. It isn't far, Motzstrasse 3, corner of Nollendorf. Just ring downstairs. Hurry up, Ollie, the Reichsmarshal is going to take us in his car—Well, then, let's say good night before it's morning.

OLIVIA Goodbye, Harry. (*She brushes his cheek with a kiss*)

HARRAS (*Has glanced nervously through the door*) See you soon. But where is Diddo?

LYRA If you mean the Junior Miss, she went on ahead with a couple of Lieutenants. (*She disappears with* OLIVIA)

WRITZKY (*Laughing as he enters*) Now, if that doesn't beat everything! The way he tells it himself, I think that's downright big of him. Have you heard the latest Goering joke, General?

HARRAS Which one?

WRITZKY The one where Goering gets to Heaven, meets Falstaff and they make a bet which one can wear the shortest sash around his middle, and the good Lord says . . .

HARRAS That one has a long grey beard.

WRITZKY Sorry, General. At the front we're always six months behind. Imagine though, he tells it himself and almost dies laughing! I think that's marvelous.

LAUSITZ The Reichsmarshal has a profound feeling for the German sense of humor.

HARRAS Yeah, and for his popularity. He's his own best press agent. The other day he released fifteen Goering jokes for night club repertoires. But woe to the poor comedian who tells it wrong and gets too much applause. Hup, two, three, four, and he's off on a long march to the Eastern Front, barefoot.

LAUSITZ Yes, the Reichsmarshal has an unusually highly developed sense of tact, a virtue some of us lack.

HARRAS Right. Why don't you install a tact-schooling department in the Propaganda Ministry. You could keep 'em real busy.

PFUNDTMAYER Do you know the latest Russian joke, Harry? It's a pisser—I heard it the other day at division club, and I writ it all down. (*Takes a small slip out of his pocket and checks up*) Jus' so I don't botch it all up. Two Russian officers bump into each other in the dark of night on the streets of Moscow, both of 'em plastered with vodka; one belches, the other belches; one draws his revolver and shoots; the other one shoots; they falls in a pool of blood; the ambulance comes and carts 'em off. It's good already, huh? 'N so, they're laying in the ambulance—one asks the other, "Say, Comrade, why did you shoot me?"—"Well, you know, when you belched, it smelled so good like pork sausage, I thought the Germans was here." Says the other one: "You was dreamin', brother of me heart. You've forgotten what pork sausage tastes like. That wasn't no pork sausage. That was a dead Commissar!"

HASTENTEUFFEL (*Without moving a muscle, in his deep bass*) Ha, ha, ha.

LAUSITZ Genuine front humor.

HARRAS Yes, humor is the gift of the Gods and badly rationed out on earth. What one has in excess, the other lacks.

PFUNDTMAYER (*Without feeling the irony*) We're funny birds! Harry, let's sing 'em a couple! (*Sings*)

Bonifacius Kiesewetter
Always was a bastard—

HARRAS (*Laughing*) I don't think the younger gentlemen know that one.

PFUNDTMAYER Don't matter. We'll teach 'em. While the ladies is in the toilet. That Lyra—she's really put together.

HARRAS The epitome of modern technology. You keep after her, old man!—We used to call her the service station.

PFUNDTMAYER The—what? Boy, that's a pisser. That hits it right in the bull's eye. (*Laughs, somewhat dumfounded*)

EILERS Harry, why don't you sing something? I've always heard about your improvisations but I was never around when you were in the mood.

HARRAS Am I in the mood now?

EILERS No? I thought you were.

HARRAS (*Pulls himself together*) Why sure, Freddie. When I look at you, the blues take off in squadron formation. But first, let's take in some high octane. Waiter! (DETLEV *enters*)

DETLEV The General wishes . . . ?

HARRAS Let's have the dream catalogue.

DETLEV The wine card, General? (*Hands it to him*)

HARRAS We'll need something special now. Not to guzzle—to drink—to enjoy—to celebrate—something noble, something festive, an augmentation of our existence. (*Leafs through the wine list*) You had a celestial bell in your prayer book—I haven't heard it ring for many years but I remember it exactly. There are eternal values involved here. Here it is!—I think this is your best and just right for tonight. Who knows for how much longer? Drivel! And this is it! (*He reads*) Lieserer Niederberg. Last dry grape harvest, special fermentation, from the vineyards of the Earl of Schorlemer-Lieser. How that rings! Like an October day.

DETLEV Beg pardon, General, but that one has a little cross.

HARRAS A little cross? What does that mean?

DETLEV Reserved. Not for sale. There may be only a few bottles left in the cellar.

HARRAS Those few bottles are just the ones that have been waiting for us. Reserved? For whom? Are you sure they weren't reserved for me?

DETLEV I'll check the reservation list. We have kept it for twenty years for our regular guests. 96. (*Taking the notebook from* FRANÇOIS *he leafs quickly through it*) 96. Here it is. Reserved for— (*He bites his lip*)

HARRAS Well, out with it.

DETLEV For Mr. Remarque,[22] General.

HARRAS For Mr. . . . ! (*He slaps his thighs and laughs uproariously*) That's the best one I've heard in a long time. Now there is true German loyalty. That's tradition. I suppose you are reserving it for a happy reunion. (*He laughs until he cries*)

DETLEV (*Embarrassed*) No one ever asked for the wine, General. Of course, the reservation is no longer valid, General. I'll bring it at once. (*He goes*)

LAUSITZ (*Has come closer*) For Erich Maria Remarque? The emigrant?

HARRAS (*Still more amused*) Imagine!—The poor man is stuck . . . in America with nothing to slurp but whiskey!

DETLEV Shall I put it on ice, General?

HARRAS Bring it on! Cellar temperature is just right for it. Let's drink to the old boy. I've worked myself through many a bout with him. He could gulp it down like a pelican. I drink like a chickadee by comparison.

LAUSITZ (*Livid with rage*) Fifty marks a bottle! You see how these Jewish swine carried on before we cleaned out the barn. While our kind had to slave away in some little hole of an editorial office.

HARRAS Perhaps you wrote too poorly for a better editorial office, Doctor. You may remember, in those days there was still a market for good German. And that Jewish business doesn't apply to this case. You know, I am sure, that Remarque is not a Jew.

LAUSITZ With riffraff like that there is no difference. (*Full of hate*) Remarque of Ullstein.[23] Whoever associates with Jews is himself a Jew.

HARRAS And whoever eats with pigs out of a trough is himself a pig.

LAUSITZ (*Cutting*) What do you mean by that, General?

HARRAS Just talking to myself.

PFUNDTMAYER (*Who hasn't understood anything*) You mean whoever picks other people's noses is himself a pig. That's a joke—ha, ha, ha! (*He laughs*)

WRITZKY Do you remember the joke from the Roehm period:[24] "Whoever puts his hand in other people's pants is one of the Storm Troopers." (*He sighs*) Those times are over. (*He and* PFUNDTMAYER *laugh alone*)

LAUSITZ (*After a sudden silence*) May I excuse myself? I am on duty early, General. (*He bows to* HARRAS) Gentlemen. (*He salutes*) Heil Hitler!

HARRAS Doctor. (*He bows slightly.* DOCTOR SCHMIDT-LAUSITZ *exits.* HARRAS *takes a very deep breath*) Thank God! Now—now I can sing, Freddie. But I just couldn't with that Super-Aryan Siegfried in the room. I'm no singer, you know, but now—I'd like to. (*Beaming with good humor*) Detlev! Where's that wine? (*He pours himself a drink—clears his throat*) Let's start off with a prehistoric pilot song. It comes down to us from the grasshopper period by old man Fokker himself.[25] The refrain is a canon. You'll all have to chime in, let's say—according to rank. Eilers first.

EILERS God forbid, I'm completely unmusical.

HARRAS Doesn't matter. It's not a question of music. (*He has taken a guitar hanging on the wall, strikes a few chords, and begins talking the song*)

To the tune of "Mademoiselle from Armentières."

We fly up in our aeroplanes
  Way up high.
We fly up in our aeroplanes
  Way up high.
We fly up in our aeroplanes
Looking down for Frenchy dames,
Walking on the earth below.
The dames we spied there from the air,
At closer look they had gray hair.
To hell with all the earth below.

We shoot our guns and drop our bombs
  Ack, ack, ack.
We shoot our guns and drop our bombs
  Ack, ack, ack.
We shoot our guns and drop our bombs
The S.O.B.'s are shooting back.
Mama, I am flying home!

(*All chime in with shouts and hand clapping, and the refrain is repeated at a faster tempo*)

EILERS (*Smiling*) That's good! We'll have to introduce that at the Officer's Club so a man can get his mind on something else for a change.

HARRAS Damn stupid, but beautiful—Children, all I say is, *prosit.* (DETLEV *has poured and passed the glasses*) You take a glass too, Hartmann. This isn't alcohol. This is liquid sunlight. Just smell it. (*All have lifted their glasses and are sniffing the wine*—HARRAS, *almost solemn*) It's better than ever. There is no time—there are no times for a thing like this. Do you know what you are drinking? Mosel wine! From the valley where the vine trees grip the slate slopes. Been growing for a thousand years—a thousand years of life and work and people—completely without propaganda.

[22] Erich Maria Remarque, an anti-militaristic novelist, lived in exile during the Hitler period.

[23] Ullstein was Remarque's publisher.

[24] The early days of the Nazi party (1923-34). Roehm was a notorious homosexual.

[25] Anthony Fokker (1890-1939) designed and built German pursuit planes during World War I.

EILERS (*Softly, raising his glass*) To Germany.

HARRAS (*His glass trembling*) To the Germany in which it grew. The true, the immortal Germany. (ANNE EILERS, POOTSIE, MOHRUNGEN, *and* BARON PFLUNGK *appear in the door*)

POOTSIE Well, what happened here—somebody die? Sounds like a funeral oration.

EILERS You missed something. Harry sang.

HARRAS Let's go, children—Let's boom once more for the ladies. Second verse:

We shoot some shells and drop some bombs
From our planes. (Repeat)
The shells we shoot, the bombs we drop;
This rotten war is getting hot.
On a furlough I shall go.

(*The others chime in,* HARRAS *with the guitar in his arms, more or less drunk, improvises a sort of mechanical dance, everybody laughs, claps, and sings*)

PFUNDTMAYER (*Calls out*) Harry, let's sing one from the last war! (*He starts it*)

I think—I think a pigeon flies
up there. . . . .

(HARRAS *plays and sings.* POOTSIE *and* PFLUNGK *dance.* PFUNDTMAYER *is waltzing with* HASTENTEUFFEL. WRITZKY *squeaks in a high voice in the manner of a female impersonator.* EILERS *has put his arm around* ANNE *and now they too begin to dance.* MOHRUNGEN *looks on smiling.* HARTMANN, *alone, suddenly empties the glass that he is still holding in his hand, fills it and empties it again.* HARRAS *is now starting in on popular songs of the last war which he combines and mixes up while the mood and the noise mount.*

HANSEN *has entered from the corridor. He has remained standing in the door. His face is serious. He signals to* HARRAS *with his eyes.* HARRAS, *the guitar on his arm and still playing, saunters over to him without attracting any attention while the others continue singing and dancing. Then the guitar playing breaks off*)

POOTSIE (*Singing the last phrase of a song alone*)

—"They don't take love so tragically."

(*It becomes still*)

HARRAS (*Slowly walks through the room, puts the guitar down between the empty plates and glasses on the table, turns around and looks at* EILERS. *It has become very quiet. Even* POOTSIE, *leaning against* PFLUNGK, *is silent. After a few seconds* HARRAS, *in a very calm and sober voice says:*) Gentlemen! The Eilers Squadron is ordered back to the front. All leaves are cancelled. You will report to the Air Ministry Transport Division at 8:30 a.m. and will take off in new planes for Army Headquarters at Smolensk. (*He is quiet for a moment and lights a cigarette*) Well, that's that! And not the first time either. I only wish I could come along. But I'm going to come and visit you soon, children, as soon as I can leave this store here alone for a few days.

EILERS (*Pale, resolute*) Gentlemen, I repeat: 8:30 a.m., Air Ministry, Transport Division. Heil Hitler! (*The officers stand at attention*)

HARTMANN (*His eyes flaming, lifts his hand*) Heil Hitler!

THE OTHERS (*Repeat formally*) Heil Hitler!

MOHRUNGEN (*Has taken* ANNE'S *hand and is stroking it*) That's war, my dear: when duty calls there is no private life. Don't let it upset you too much.

EILERS (*Smiling*) There might be a bright side to this thing! If they cash in on a week with us now, then they will have to give us Christmas leave this year. And what could be better than Christmas at home? Last year we spent the holiday on the North Sea patrol. (*His calm, measured thoughtfulness is genuine and begins to affect the others. The shock is wearing off. Everybody's talking*)

PFUNDTMAYER And I thought I had pig's luck. What a double cross jus' now when I've gone an' met the woman of ma life!

HASTENTEUFFEL With you it can only be a question of the pig 'a your life, you old pig-hunter.

PFUNDTMAYER (*Taking offense*) If ya don't mind, I'll have ta ask ya ta take that back. I don't take kindly to them jokes. They're just apt to make me real mad, I can tell you!

WRITZKY I suggest we let it out on the Russians. Let's steer clear of these misunderstandings among ourselves.

PFUNDTMAYER This shindig was just beginning to get off the ground. Aw, what the hell—there's still gonna be some roaring tonight.

EILERS I know you'll excuse us, Harry. I think it only sensible to get some sleep.

HARRAS Why sure. Go on home, children.

POOTSIE (*Has stepped up to* HARTMANN) You seem to be downright happy, little man. First time you've put on a human face all night! (HARTMANN *doesn't answer*)

PFUNDTMAYER Whoever goes home is a dog. 'Cept, of course, the married couples.

POOTSIE I like that. You're a real fighter,—a real hero. (*She puts her arm around* HARTMANN. *Without answering* HARTMANN *quietly but very definitely frees himself*) Well, pardon me, then don't. I won't throw myself at you.

HARRAS Ladies and gentlemen, you are at liberty. For the rest of the night, everyone can do as he pleases. I suppose you're still going up to Lyra's?

PFUNDTMAYER And how! We're going to hold out till eight, and then a cold rub-down. Brrrrr.

HARRAS Then step lively. Perhaps I'll follow you—after I settle up here. (*He says goodbye to* PFUNDTMAYER *and* HASTENTEUFFEL *with a handshake and the three exit*)

POOTSIE Ugh. Now it's getting dull. Shouldn't we go up for a little while too, Baron?

PFLUNGK To Lyra's? I don't think that would be altogether proper.

MOHRUNGEN Quite improper. You will now come up to the hotel, Pootsie.

POOTSIE My God—paternal authority, always at the wrong time. Isn't it lucky you have to go back to Mannheim.

MOHRUNGEN Pootsie—

POOTSIE All right, all right, little old man. I'm coming. (*She kisses him lightly on the forehead*)

MOHRUNGEN (*Beaming*) Well, you see, it's all for your own good.

PFLUNGK I can take all of you. My car is outside.

HARRAS (*With* ANNE *and* EILERS *at the door*) Good night, Anne. If you'll just leave your telephone number at the Air Ministry office I will have all radio reports that come in from the front called through to you so you will always have first-hand information when he can't write.

ANNE Many, many thanks. It was a beautiful evening. (*She presses his hand warmly*) Goodbye.

EILERS How about visiting us for Christmas, Harry, if I get leave?

HARRAS It's a promise.

(*During the last sentences* HARRAS *and* HANSEN *have accompanied the guests outside and now they disappear with them to the cloak room and from there we can still hear voices and goodbyes*)

POOTSIE (*Has remained standing with* HARTMANN *who hasn't gone out yet*) Aren't you coming along? The Baron would give you a lift.

HARTMANN I'm not tired.

POOTSIE You mad at me? (HARTMANN, *without looking at her, shakes his head*) We can still be good friends.

HARTMANN (*Stiff*) Of course.

POOTSIE Well then—goodbye. And lots of luck. (*With as much warmth as she can muster*) Keep well, dear. I'll think of you.

HARTMANN Thanks.

(*She brings her face close to his and offers him her lips, but he only bends briefly over her head; she shrugs her shoulders and exits. He straightens himself up, turns on his heels, goes slowly to the table, stands with his back to the audience and empties a glass*)

HARRAS (*Comes back with* HANSEN) Well, bud, now the two of us. . . . (*He notices* HARTMANN *and stops. Both look at him for a moment*)

HARTMANN (*Turns, hesitates, snaps to attention, then somewhat helpless*) May I take my leave, General?

HARRAS Why don't you help me finish this bottle, Lieutenant Hartmann?

HARTMANN (*Unsure*) I don't want to disturb you, General.

HARRAS But you aren't disturbing anyone, quite the contrary. I'd be glad to have you stay—You know what? You want to do me a little favor?

HARTMANN At your service, General.

HARRAS You go out there where my car is parked and have Korrianke give you my cigarette case. I've got some with tobacco. I can't stand the smell of that camel dung Rommel is sending home from the desert.

HARTMANN Gladly, General. (*He exits*)

HARRAS (*He looks after him, then to* HANSEN) What do you suppose is the matter with that boy? Sorrows of love? Or is there more behind it? Peculiar fellow. Hardly over twenty—didn't say a word all evening.

HANSEN Probably just one of them quiet ones, General. One of the silent types in this country, of which we've got a whole lot in the German Reich. Hi, how I like them, General. I could cheerfully jab them in the rear end with a darning needle for hours on end. They spread quiet all around them—so full of deep, significant thoughts because, as a matter of fact, they got nothin' at all to say. Nothin' at all even occurs to 'em and they're proud of it too. I know the kind. I'm from the North Sea coast myself. You can see one of them great big quiets standing around in every boathouse. They're locked-up natures, locked up like an empty chest. Them is deep people, deep like a pumped-out well. Not a drop in 'em. Nothin' but hollow bark, 'n the whole oak tree shakes if'n only a woodpecker taps on it with his beak. They're even quiet in bed, General. They just blow off quietly into eternity.

HARRAS (*Has listened thoughtfully, smiling*) It's all right, bud. You've got a good, clear head. (*Seeing* HARTMANN *come back*) Now leave us alone for a little while. But drink up first. Let's not waste anything.

HANSEN (*Empties his glass*) Has the General any other orders?

HARRAS Tell them outside to get my bill ready. We'll see each other later in the office.

HANSEN Anytime, General. (*He exits*)

HARRAS (*Fills his and* HARTMANN'S *glasses, takes a cigarette out of the case, and offers one to* HARTMANN *who declines.* HARRAS, *too, doesn't light his cigarette, just plays with it. Speaking almost to himself*) No—not with this wine, no smoking. A mortal sin, my father would have said, and he knew what he was talking about. *Prosit,* Hartmann.

HARTMANN Thanks, General. (*He doesn't drink, looks down on the floor*)

HARRAS (*Puts his glass down, pulls up a chair close to his and leans toward him*) Well, Hartmann, I want you to open up once. There's no sense your hanging around the bushes like a constipated bird-dog. Go ahead, burst, man! Explode! Curse yourself out! Say after me: "Damn it all to hell!" And when you say it, think about whomever or whatever you please. Come on, we'll do it together. One—two—three.

BOTH Damn it all to hell!

HARRAS Louder!

BOTH Damn it all to hell!!

HARRAS Still louder!

BOTH Damn it all to hell!!! (HARTMANN, *after the last time, empties his glass and throws it against the wall*)

HARRAS Bravo! You feel better now?

HARTMANN (*Breathing heavily and quite frightened by himself*) A little, General.

HARRAS Well, that's pretty good for a start. Sometimes

you just have to purify the atmosphere or you suffocate. Did you damn me along with the rest of 'em? We might have material for a conversation then.

HARTMANN I don't quite understand, General.

HARRAS Why be so cagey? You understand perfectly. I saw your face when I was badgering that culture-louse. You think my jokes outrageous, and my political position scandalous. Right?

HARTMANN I don't permit myself a judgment, General.

HARRAS But you have one just the same. No dodging, my boy! I know what you think. I don't hold it against you. Because those are not really your thoughts. It's only party education that was stuffed into you. It tells you: "That Harras—is a disgrace." But your better self has secret doubts like every better self. And now, Hartmann, let's forget the whole business for a while and make like we're human beings, right? Just forget I'm your general. Forget we don't think the same way. Just imagine we're old friends who've met at some stupid class reunion. Do you think you can manage that for five minutes?

HARTMANN No, General.

HARRAS (*Sighing*) A good beginning! Let's try another angle—If I start poking my nose into things you don't want to talk about, then you just say: "Cut it"—Will you do that?

HARTMANN (*Smiling slightly*) I hardly think so, General.

HARRAS You're a tough nut to crack. OK. I'll give it to you straight. What's the score with you and little Miss Pootsie? Is the bust-up really serious or is it only a temporary breakdown?

HARTMANN (*Unmoved, with an almost mask-like fixedness*) It's all over, General. Miss von Mohrungen has broken off the engagement. That is—we weren't officially engaged yet. But Mr. von Mohrungen had given his consent.

HARRAS So—hmmm. And why would that be?

HARTMANN (*Halting but always in the tone of a military report*) Because of the confusion in my family tree, General. You see, my family comes from the Rhineland. My father and grandfather were regular officers —There is no ground for suspicion of Jewish blood mixture. But—it appears that one of my great-grandmothers came from a foreign country. That happened frequently in old Rhineland families. She cannot be traced. The papers are simply not to be found.

HARRAS (*Has bitten his lip and is mumbling to himself*) So that's the problem! A poor boy running around with an undefinable great-grandmother. (*With rising rage*) To top it all off you don't know a thing about the extra-marital romances of your Mrs. Great-grandmother. You can never tell with these non-Germans, you know. She wouldn't have asked for Aryan papers. Or—are you possibly even a descendant of that Crusading Knight Hartmann who married into a wine firm in Jerusalem?

HARTMANN (*Matter of fact*) Racial investigation does not go back that far, General.

HARRAS But it must, it must! If it's worth doing at all —it's worth doing right! Just think of all the things that could have happened in the Rhineland, the great mill of nations, the wine-press of Europe! (*Calmer*) Just imagine the procession of your ancestors—since the birth of Christ. There was a Roman Captain, a dark fellow, brown as a ripe olive; he managed to teach Latin to his blonde girl on the banks of the Rhine; then a Jewish spice dealer came into the family, a serious man who converted to Christianity before the wedding and founded the Catholic tradition in the house. Then a Greek doctor, a Celtic Legionnaire, a Swedish Knight, one of Napoleon's soldiers, a deserting Cossack, a wandering miller's apprentice from Alsace, a fat boatsman from Holland, a Magyar, a dashing officer from Vienna, a French actor, a Bohemian musician; and all the whole mixed-up crowd that lived, brawled, drank, and sang and begot children along the River Rhine! That Goethe character, he came out of the same pot. Also a guy named Beethoven, and Gutenberg, and—ah, what the . . . look it up in the encyclopedia! They were the best, my friend! The best in the world! and why? Because the nations mixed like the waters from the springs and brooks and rivers that flow together in one great living stream. The Rhineland, that means: the West—That is natural nobility. Be proud of it, Hartmann—and hang the papers of your questionable grandmother in the toilet. *Prosit!*

HARTMANN (*Unchanged, only somewhat sadder*) Miss von Mohrungen has papers covering four generations. That is enough for a marriage contract with an SS man and for any party career. She will not settle for less than that. She is ambitious. She does not want to . . . take second best.

HARRAS (*Bursting out with a red face*) Then for Pete and Joe's sake be glad you're rid of the bitch! And don't hang your head—over a chippy like that! Damn it all! (*He pounds the table uncontrolled*) She's cheap like a half-eaten apple. She's not even worth a postage stamp. Fun for a week's leave at best. She's the type you whack on the naked rear so she'll have a souvenir. You'll forget her name before you're all the way down the stairs. (HARTMANN *has let his head sink on his chest.* HARRAS *falls silent—looks at* HARTMANN, *quite frightened, stands up—steps up to him, very tenderly*) My God, boy, did I hurt you? I didn't want that. It just sort of slipped out—in anger you understand. I know—you were serious about the girl. I respect that. I—didn't mean it like that.

HARTMANN (*Looks up, looks at* HARRAS) You meant it, General. (*Softly*) You were right.

HARRAS No. I was unjust. I went too far—and I'm sorry.

HARTMANN She told me I wasn't fit for modern life—because I couldn't take the affair lightly. Because I preferred not having any affair at all rather than debase my feeling for her. Perhaps it's true. Perhaps I'm not fit for our life, or not meant for it. But . . . I am good enough to die . . . General!

HARRAS Don't be a fool, boy. Life and death has nothing to do with it. You weren't meant for each other; that's all. Forget about her as fast as you can.

Grit your teeth and gulp it down. I know it tastes like snot and vomit at first. But believe me, a messed up affair of young love is no worse than the measles. It's just a childhood disease of the imagination, that's all. You get over it and when you do you're healthier than before. Don't even think about it anymore. There are better things in this world. Bigger ones.

HARTMANN Yes indeed, General. Death on the battlefield is big. And pure. And eternal.

HARRAS Come on, man! Don't feed me those old lines. It stinks—your "Death on the battlefield." I know you feel some sort of emotion when you say those things, but it's false, do you understand? Didn't you see the gory mess of bodies lying around? What's great about it? And eternal? It goes with war like digestion with eating. That's all. You're not supposed to be afraid of death; not if you're a man. You're not supposed to run away from it. But you *are* supposed to fight it, outwit it, hate it like the plague. If you glorify and go looking for it—you won't be a hero. You'll be an idiot.

HARTMANN I know. We may not risk our lives irresponsibly; they aren't ours to risk.

HARRAS Then whose are they, for God's sake?—Don't you dare say now: the Fuehrer's. Or else I'll see red.

HARTMANN (*Fixedly*) We must preserve the fighting strength of our squadron to the last drop of blood.

HARRAS (*Somewhat helpless*) Good God. If only once I didn't have to swallow that "last drop of blood" routine. Each dose makes me nauseous. You're supposed to keep your stupid drops of blood together, you understand! At least enough of them so you don't conk out. You're supposed to survive, do you hear? Come through, come down, come back! And bring your own hide with you, hale and hearty and as tough and soft and durable as well-tanned doeskin. Look, after all, I'm an old soldier myself. I know something about this business. And I tell you, anyone who's going to be worth anything in combat must have the hope and will to come out alive. If you wanna win, ya gotta survive first. Whoever fights without hope is half a casualty before he starts. And *hope* means you look forward to something, to living! With or without Pootsie. Cross her off. Don't you look forward to coming home when the war is over?

HARTMANN I don't know, General. (*Since* HARRAS *is looking at him questioningly—after a pause*) I don't have a real home that I can look forward to. My father fell in the last war. Three days before the end. I never knew him. My mother married again—a business man. He got rich while our nation grew poorer. I could never love or respect him. That alienated me from my mother. I kept thinking: "He takes and enjoys all that my father sacrificed for his country." I never had a home, General, until—

HARRAS Hmm?

HARTMANN —Until I joined the Hitler Youth. My home was the training camp. The Officers' School. And then—the Eilers Squadron. (*His face, which for a moment had grown softer, has locked itself again. He looks down*)

HARRAS (*Looks at him silently, filling the glasses. Then he begins to walk up and down, speaking slowly, softly, almost as if talking to himself*) Listen to me, Hartmann—or don't listen—whatever you want. I'll tell you what went through my head tonight looking at you. You're young but you don't know it. Life is in front of you—but you don't know what life is. You're stuck in an oyster's shell. You think your shell is the world, but you don't feel how all around you outside the enormous ocean roars. Take it from me, life is beautiful. The world is wonderful. We human beings try like hell to louse it up and even have a certain degree of success, but we are no match for it—for the original concept. I don't know who thought the whole thing up. I am no philosopher. I'm a technician, a soldier. But I know—the concept is good. The plan is right. The design is magnificent. And the meaning of it is—not: Power. Not: Luck. Not: Gratification. But—"Beauty." Or—"Joy." Or both. I don't care what you call it—maybe there's no word for it. It's something we feel and possess in our best moments. And that's the only reason we are alive. Are you listening, Hartmann, to what the old man is babbling?

HARTMANN (*Quiet, simply*) Yes.

HARRAS When you were a boy did you ever hunt butterflies in a meadow? You see!— You were after Beauty. The meadow with the dusty roadside bushes —that's our homeland. Also the clear brook into which we throw pebbles. Didn't you ever get frightened when the stone went kerplop into the water and disappeared? Our homeland, Hartmann, is the memory, the good and the bad. The meadows, the brooks are the puddles of memory—out of which we make pictures as large as Heaven and Hell. Do you have an idea what I'm talking about?

HARTMANN Yes.

HARRAS I'm talking about you, my boy, about you and about me. About us men, so to speak. Men are a funny species of animal. From time to time a great frenzy seizes them and they go berserk till they get it out of their systems. War is our oldest excuse for running riot. Of course men are never completely normal. There's always a screw loose somewhere—or something twisted in the inner mechanism. We stumble around here as though we were being paid for it. We build up a world and then we destroy it down to the foundation. Then there's a chance for a new plan to come up about which we don't have the foggiest notion. Maybe our enemy's design or the plan of the defeated, but the original design, the one that always continues to attract us—the fundamental basis of the whole show—that is beautiful even if we don't understand the formula. Why are rocks beautiful? And the Northern Lights? Or the grain in a piece of wood? And even some of our own creations motivated by viciousness—if they work, they're beautiful. A tank is beautiful. And a heavy bomber—a fighter plane—as beautiful as a horse taking a jump. And a curved steel bridge over a river. And an old worm-eaten hope-chest. A tree in autumn. A thunderstorm. A sunflower. And sometimes even a human face—Lord God Almighty, Hartmann! Don't you think it's worth it to live? To live a long, long time? To grow very old? (*He empties his glass.* HARTMANN *lifts his glass to his lips without drinking. He sits motionless and tears run down his face*)

DELTEV (*Looks in holding a plug-in telephone*) Sorry to disturb you, General. A call for you. (*He plugs in the telephone and at the same time puts the folded bill on the table and slowly goes back to the door*)

HARRAS (*He picks up the telephone*) Hello, Lyra! Of course, I'm in good shape. Come over? I don't know. Tell me, is the little one still there? Which little one—stupid question. Yes, please—like to talk to her. (*He waits for a minute with the telephone at his ear and with his free hand lights a cigarette and hums nervously to himself*) Good morning, Monkey-wrench. There's something I've got to tell you. I keep thinking about those violets you wore. Put them in water, will you? It would be too bad if they wilted. A little while ago they were so fresh . . . OK. That's a promise. What? Going to press them and keep them in my scrapbook like a little girl. Oh, yes, I'm serious. No—I'm coming over. You'll have to stay now. All right then. Sure I am, absolutely certain. In ten minutes. (*He hangs up—picks up the receiver again for a second, listens, and puts it back again. His glance glides over to* HARTMANN *whose head has sunk onto the back of the chair. He looks more dead than asleep.* HARRAS *goes quickly to the door, whistles and calls*) Korrianke!

(KORRIANKE *appears, behind him* DETLEV *and* FRANÇOIS. HARRAS *points with his head to the sleeping—or exhausted* HARTMANN)

KORRIANKE Champagne corpse, General?

HARRAS Naw—combat fatigue. Maybe the wine was too heavy. Take him home, Korrianke—put him to bed. See that he sleeps. When I get home we'll make him a good breakfast. He has to take off for the front at 8:30.

KORRIANKE The young man ought to report for sick call, General. He needs relaxation.

HARRAS He wouldn't do it. Well—let's move. Can you make it alone?

KORRIANKE Easy as pie. (*He lifts* HARTMANN *up with bear-like arms but with an almost maternal care and carries him out*)

HARRAS Take my car, it has better springs, and call me a taxi. (*He takes the check, looks it over hastily, takes a big bill out of his wallet and gives it to* DETLEV)

DETLEV I'll be right back with the change, sir.

HARRAS Nonsense. Split the difference between you.

DETLEV It's too much, General—

HARRAS You won't reform me any more, Detlev. He who is born a spendthrift, dies a—oh well, I'm too tired to be funny. Good night.

DETLEV *and* FRANÇOIS Good night, General. Many thanks. *Merci. Merci.*

HARRAS (*Picks up the telephone receiver once more and listens*) Funny noise in there. (*Puts the receiver back and listens toward the wall as he starts out*) Still ticking, too. So—tick! Who cares? (*He exits*)

(DETLEV *and* FRANÇOIS *remain alone.* FRANÇOIS *begins to put out the candles and is whistling softly to himself.* DETLEV *has watched* HARRAS *go out, waits until we hear the noise of the car starting—then he goes to the telephone—dials a number, waits.* FRANÇOIS *stops whistling—watches him, sipping from a glass of wine someone has left*)

DETLEV Hello? Detlev, here. Secret Office C, Captain Degenhardt—Yes, indeed, Captain. Everything went smoothly. But there was a slight ticking that almost gave it away. Beg your pardon? Only partly intelligible? That wasn't my fault, Captain. The noise here, you know—yes, indeed. At your service. Promptly, at your office. (*Hangs up*) Only worked part of the time. Something new . . . a radio dictaphone with telephonic recording device. There's a few wrinkles like that ticking they've still got to iron out.

FRANÇOIS (*Under his breath*) It's disgusting.

DETLEV (*Wheels around and stares at him*) You keep your trap shut and don't let out so much as a peep. If that Otto finds out, you'll see something. We have to keep him pure or he'll botch up the whole thing.

FRANÇOIS It's disgusting.

DETLEV (*Closer to him, menacingly*) I've got you in my hand—my barbed wire sweetheart. You want to land in a camp! Maybe ya like forced labor? (*Calmer*) Think I like to do it? Makes me puke. Show me a guy who isn't a son of a bitch around here. In this here country you're your own best friend. What are you supposed to do if one of them comes along and gives you a speech: "Well now, listen to me, Herr Detlev. You, as a waiter, have a special opportunity to serve the state." And all the time he gives you one of those ice cold stares—You don't say no, mister. Besides, I got a family.

FRANÇOIS *Merde.*

*Curtain*

# Act Two

## Stay of Execution or The Hand

GENERAL HARRAS' *apartment in a new western suburb of Berlin. A roomy studio apartment on the top floor of a modern building. It is furnished in modern style, solid and functional, but in a somewhat adventurous way. A few well made pieces of furniture: a long, narrow drawing table covered with all kinds of technical materials; a desk with pamphlets, documents and a telephone. An open red brick fireplace, a few comfortable chairs, and a few wooden ones, a lot of smoking equipment, a couch covered with a camel's hair cover, and a radio phonograph. The walls are painted in a light color and half covered with bookcases. Above these, a few old lutes, a collection of exotic butterflies, and a target with a lot of holes in it. A few woodcuts and pictures of animals by Franz Marc.*[1] *Here and there the wild grimace of an African dancing mask. In a corner a bow and arrow, an Arabian saddle and an African drum.*

*In a side room, a sort of dressing room which joins onto the studio. Half hidden by a bamboo screen, a bar has been built. Its frame is made of splintered propellors and all kinds of broken and shot-up parts of planes. Inside, the bar is full of fantastic stuff, trophies of war and travel, photographs of fliers, girls and wild animals.*

*At left and right doors lead to the kitchen and the hall. It is late afternoon but still light, shortly before dusk. Through the high studio window on the back wall one can see the wintry glaring-white sky over the city of Berlin. The blackout curtains are pulled back.*

KORRIANKE *stands motionless at the window and watches the street below with binoculars.* HANSEN, *smoking, walks back and forth with heavy, hasty steps, always coming back to the same spot.*

HANSEN (*After a while, remains standing, looks at his watch*) Damn it. It's more than a man can stand. (*He stamps his foot, goes to the telephone and dials a number*) Hello, Air Ministry? Captain Hansen speaking. Give me extension 1296—Oderbruch?—Anything new? No. Not here either—I told you already, at ten o'clock I got orders: "Be ready at his apartment." Now it's five. Yes, yes—rumors, . . . rumors. The whole history of the world is only a rumor. Trouble is, sometimes they are true. Naturally. As soon as I know anything. (*Hangs up*) Damn it all. (*Begins walking up and down again.* KORRIANKE *has put down the binoculars and listened to the conversation. Now he picks up the binoculars again and looks down in the street*) Stop that, man. It's completely pointless. You're driving me mad. This is not a regatta!

KORRIANKE (*Grimly*) Please, no nervous breakdown, Captain. You've been waiting seven hours—me, I bin waiting two weeks. So the word is: Calm down!

HANSEN He's driving me mad. Calm down! Do you know what my old commander used to say? Man, you should have been a bricklayer—nothing bothers you!

KORRIANKE (*Almost screaming*) For two weeks! An' it come like a bolt from the blue! We'd cooked up a little trip to Kohlhasen, car full of gas an' all—All of a sudden, he come up all alone 'n green around the gills an' says: "Korriandoli, step lively 'n get my small bag, toothbrush, 'n pajamas enough—I've got to go traveling f'r a few days!—Not another word and out he goes! I give a look down the stairs—what do I see? Mercedes-Benz, Model '41, black limousine, flag up front, party emblem and a big red G—Gestapo! So I says to myself. . . . Harras is in the soup, that's what I think.

HANSEN You have told me that story exactly eighteen times. Once more and I will have hysterics! (*Rummages around in his pockets and brings forth an empty cigarette box*) The devil. That was the last one. (*He throws the box away*)

KORRIANKE Captain, hand on your heart, do you believe the rumors?

HANSEN I believe nothing! What am I supposed to believe? Officially, the word is he's at the Eastern Front and there isn't nobody believes that! But that's still no grounds for you holding a wake.

KORRIANKE It's not like I was holding a wake, Captain. But it's supposed t'have come out in the foreign papers and on the British radio they said—

HANSEN That's hogwash! His friends at the press table in his favorite tavern launched that one because they like to think it helps him. Stupid idea! It can result in exactly the opposite.

KORRIANKE But I've been through it all myself. I've been behind the barbed wire. "You!—Say 'Heil Hitler,' " one of 'em says to me. I grit my teeth together, at that time I still had 'em—Crash!—I had a club in the snout—If Harras hadn't gotten me out—they would have finished me off piece by piece, easy as pie.

HANSEN That's not for generals. That only starts with captains and on down. I tell you, man, he'll fly himself out of it—he'll come back. And today. Why would they have ordered me to report here? To receive his ashes? They send those through the mail. (*Begins to pace back and forth*)

KORRIANKE The elevator! Pssst! The elevator is coming up! (*Through the open hall door we hear the whirring noise of an elevator. Both listen*)

HANSEN He's coming! (KORRIANKE *runs out. A man in civilian clothes comes in hastily. He has his hat pressed down over his face.* KORRIANKE *is close behind him*)

KORRIANKE Stop! Stop! Who are you anyway?

HANSEN (*Hand on his gun*) Halt! Stand still! What do you want here?

LAWRENCE (*Pushes back the brim of his hat*) Hello, Captain! How are you?

HANSEN Buddy, it's you!

LAWRENCE Yes, it's me—still in one piece, just a little out of breath. They had a guy shadowing me but I shook him.

(*He throws himself into a chair, exhausted and begins to smoke. He is in his middle twenties with intelligent, somewhat sad eyes. His face creates a clean-cut effect even though he is unshaved and dusty*)

HANSEN Unwind, Korrianke. You know Buddy Lawrence, don't you?—Our friend from the decadent American press.

LAWRENCE Was, Captain, was! My press card was

[1] Franz Marc (1880-1916) was a noted expressionist painter.

cancelled yesterday. Waiting for an exit permit. Hope I get it in time.

HANSEN Because you stuck your nose in this Harras affair?

LAWRENCE That was just foam on the beer. My stein was running over. (*He laughs*)

KORRIANKE You—Mister—did you report that General Harras is dead? Where did you hear that? What do you know about him? Where is General Harras?

LAWRENCE That's what I'm asking you. That's why I'm here. The afternoon editions say: "General Harras just returned from an inspection of the Eastern Front." Seen, he wasn't, by nobody. And the story that he'd been liquidated we got from the front.

HANSEN From the front? Everybody's superstitious at the front. They've got too much time. They eat too many beans and they squat around for hours in the latrine squeezing out rumors. But it isn't true. Can't be true. Or can it? Can it?

LAWRENCE (*Shrugs his shoulders*) I said to myself, if it isn't true then at least it makes a stink and people will ask about him. Sometimes that helps; sometimes it doesn't— (*He puts out a half-smoked cigarette*)

HANSEN How about a little business deal, sir? Two cigarettes for a cognac.

LAWRENCE Thanks. (*Drinks*) Just in time. On Kaiserstrasse I jumped off the bus and zigzagged for ten blocks. They're already in my apartment. But I was tipped off.

HANSEN Why don't you go to your Embassy?

LAWRENCE Stuffed shirts. Only in an emergency. I spent the night in the waiting rooms of assorted Berlin railroad stations. It was very educational. (*He yawns*)

KORRIANKE Pssst!! The elevator. (*They listen. Immediately after that, the doorbell rings*)

HANSEN Run, man.

KORRIANKE That isn't him. He's got a key.

HANSEN Ya damn fool. He could have lost it.

KORRIANKE Not him. Never. (*The doorbell rings again.* KORRIANKE *goes*)

HANSEN (*To* LAWRENCE) Wouldn't it be smarter if you made yourself scarce? (*Points to the kitchen door*) You never know.

LAWRENCE Not on a bet. Too nosey.

(*Both stare at the door. In walks* DR. SCHMIDT-LAUSITZ *in his black party uniform. He stands in the doorway for a moment and inspects the two without greeting,* KORRIANKE *right behind him*)

LAUSITZ (*Takes his hat off, suddenly turns around with a short jerk to* KORRIANKE, *hands him his hat*) Hang it up!

KORRIANKE (*Murmurs*) Delighted. Easy as pie.

LAUSITZ (*Steps forward, lifts his hand quickly*) Heil Hitler. (HANSEN *gives a military salute*)

LAWRENCE Howdy.

LAUSITZ I'm not at all surprised to find you here. We are oriented as to every one of your moves.

LAWRENCE Likewise the American Embassy, Mr. Cultural Propaganda.

LAUSITZ That is very wise. Should you meet with an accident—a traffic accident for example—you thus save the authorities the trouble of identifying the body.

LAWRENCE I wasn't thinking of a traffic accident.

LAUSITZ Then you should be more careful. About jumping off moving vehicles, I mean. Something could easily happen to you.

LAWRENCE Don't worry. I can take care of myself.

LAUSITZ Good for you. I trust that you have already applied for your exit visa? As a fellow human being, I'd advise you to hurry up about it.

LAWRENCE As a fellow human being, you are very cordial. As you see, I am already making my farewell calls. But I'm having trouble finding my friends at home. Alive, I mean.

LAUSITZ If you would like to say goodbye to General Harras why don't you try the Adlon Bar. He stopped off there to report to the foreign press on his inspection trip to the Eastern Front. The truly neutral foreign press, of course.

LAWRENCE I no longer have the honor to belong to that select group.

LAUSITZ I'm pleased to hear that you consider it an honor— In any case, the General will be telling about his experiences at the Eastern Front. That will nip all future rumor-mongering in the bud.

LAWRENCE A denial in advance? Just like a planned invasion.

LAUSITZ You can take it as you wish. Your point of view is no longer of interest here. (*He turns to* HANSEN) General Harras wishes to resume his official duties immediately. Before you report to him I would like to remind you of the great responsibility of his previous investigations. It rests not only with him, but also with his personal co-workers.

HANSEN I understand.

LAUSITZ Perhaps not completely. For example, should you have made observations about which you do not wish to enlighten the General immediately, then I will be at your disposal at any time for a confidential discussion. You might find that advantageous.

HANSEN I find it superfluous.

LAUSITZ As you wish. You will think it over. I myself have a number of more general points to clear up with General Harras as soon as he arrives here.

HANSEN Without witnesses, presumably.

LAUSITZ I assume the General would prefer a private conversation.

KORRIANKE (*Who, standing by the door, has made excited signs*) Elevator! Elevator! (*Short silence. Then the doorbell rings—*KORRIANKE *goes, disappointed. Immediately afterwards we hear him let out a sort of yodel that could also be a cry of pain or fright. Everybody is startled. Then we hear him yelling*) Captain, on the double. It's him!

HANSEN (*Wipes his brow*) Lord Almighty, ma legs won't work. (*He stumbles out*)

LAUSITZ (*With mocking glance to* LAWRENCE) The dead rise up. Are you about to see a spirit?

LAWRENCE Perhaps only a "corpse on furlough."

LAUSITZ That is what we all are. It is only a matter of

the time granted. Our Fuehrer issues both longer and shorter furlough permits.

LAWRENCE And God probably has no hand in this at all.

LAUSITZ He is allowed to sign them.

LAWRENCE Almost like old Hindenburg.[2]

LAUSITZ Something like that.

(LAUSITZ *gives a brief Hitler salute as* HARRAS *enters with the beaming* KORRIANKE *who carries coat, cap, and bag, and pours a large glass of Kirsch with his free hand.* HARRAS *is dressed in a grey field uniform, seems unchanged, only somewhat pale, with red-rimmed eyes*)

HARRAS (*While entering*) Naw, naw, children— I never lose keys or cigarette lighters or corkscrews. I only lose money. As for the key, it seems to have fascinated somebody else. (*Looks at* SCHMIDT-LAUSITZ) If, by any chance, you have any idea who might be bent on secret visits to my apartment, then tell them that the lock will be changed today.

KORRIANKE (*Puts his hand in his trouser pocket*) Small matter. Patent lock always on hand. Only have to switch 'em.

LAUSITZ I don't know what you're talking about.

HARRAS Not important, I got it from a detective story. Hey, Buddy! What are you doing here?

LAWRENCE Looking for trouble, I guess. Sorry to see you're still alive. I bet two years' poker winnings that the rumors were true.

HARRAS Double your bet and wait a few weeks. How about a drink, Buddy, you look worn out.

LAWRENCE What I need is a shave. May I use your shaving equipment?

HARRAS Of course. Courtesy of the Luftwaffe. (*To* KORRIANKE) Unpack my stuff and show him the bathroom.

KORRIANKE (*While going off with* LAWRENCE) Easy as pie. I'm going to whip up the lather myself. . . . Say, tell me, Yankee, do they really make good beer in Milwaukee . . . ? (*He disappears with* LAWRENCE)

HARRAS (*Changed, remains standing in front of* LAUSITZ, *stares at him, speaking softly with an effort at self-control*) I do not recall giving you permission to come here.

LAUSITZ I did not ask for permission, General. However, in your own interests—

HARRAS What do you care about my interests? The comedy is over. I can take off my make-up alone. What else do you want?

LAUSITZ I have an official message for you.

HARRAS An order?

LAUSITZ That is a matter of—interpretation.

HARRAS I can tell you right off, I don't take orders from you.

LAUSITZ Too bad. You don't seem to grasp the seriousness of your situation.

HARRAS You think I don't know the stakes in this game after two weeks in Hotel Gestapo. Your threats are nothing compared to the service I had there.

LAUSITZ Your bearing and physical condition prove that you cannot complain about your treatment.

HARRAS Maybe I'm supposed to thank you because they did not fracture my nose-bone? They'd have broken my eggs with rapture if I didn't have a few friends in the General Staff who could raise a rumpus. The spotlights over my bunk were sufficient for a little rehearsal. Only don't go thinking that you've cut me down to size. Not that way, my boy.

LAUSITZ Since you prefer to speak bluntly, I am at liberty to respond in kind. In your position I would not rely too heavily on the friends in the General Staff. And even less on the friends in foreign countries and public opinion. We take care of public opinion. You can leave that worry to us. You owe your temporary freedom to purely practical considerations. I have been delegated to clarify them for you.

HARRAS I have taken cognizance of the word "temporary." Even without it I would not confuse my present state with freedom. (*Sits down in a chair with his back to* LAUSITZ)

LAUSITZ You are being given an opportunity for complete rehabilitation, General. However, there is a time limit, non-extendable. As director of the department you are responsible for the recurrent sabotage in airplane production. This problem must be conclusively explained and removed within ten days.

HARRAS (*Without turning around*) Otherwise?

LAUSITZ There is no otherwise. The investigation, for which the secret police were forced to take you into custody, has, up to this point, not turned up any full proof against you. There is, however, ground for suspicion that you are covering up for anti-state elements or that you are preventing their prosecution by deliberate laxity. That would be abominable, morally even more abominable than the crime itself. You have ten days to disprove this suspicion by clearing up the problem completely. The whole case is now a matter of your personal survival. We expect a prompt settlement one way or the other.

HARRAS That means ten days "stay of execution."

LAUSITZ "Stay" is correct—As for "execution," you don't necessarily have to form an *idée fixe* on that detail.

HARRAS You mean there are more modern murder methods.

LAUSITZ That goes beyond the scope of my official information. I hope that now you know where you stand. (HARRAS *doesn't answer, just smokes*) Personally, I would like to add—

HARRAS Thanks. I know.

LAUSITZ You will hear it just the same. Personally, I wouldn't delay ten days—not even ten minutes, to render a person like you harmless.

HARRAS Likewise.

LAUSITZ I know. In me you see a mortal enemy. You are quite correct. There isn't room enough under the sun for us both.

[2] Paul von Hindenburg (1847-1934), Field Marshal in command of German armies during World War I and President of the Weimar Republic prior to Hitler's rise to power.

HARRAS Nor under my roof. Shall I leave?

LAUSITZ Your arrogance is out of place. Your mockery misses the mark. Your game is over. You will not rob us of the fruits of our battle. You thought you could skim off the cream here—lick yourself fat on it—and pour us into the pig's trough with the garbage. Your game is over. You miscalculated. It will turn out the other way.

HARRAS (*Indifferently*) Possible. It always turns out the other way. The wheel turns as long as it rolls.

LAUSITZ For you the wheel will not turn any more. Not to the top. You and your kind have looked down on us long enough. However, we don't look down long. We kick.

HARRAS Of course, and in the groin. And always against the defenseless ones. In packs and in tight formation with official sanction. (*He looks at* LAUSITZ *with an almost surprised, revolted look*) And dregs like you want to rule the world. You'll be amazed with your discoveries.

LAUSITZ For the time being the others are amazed. But you, General Harras, don't need to be conceited about your personal courage. Anyone can have that. And as far as honor is concerned, we define it. Despise us if you can afford it. We pay back. (HARRAS *takes a gun out of his pocket and unlocks the safety catch.* LAUSITZ *hastily goes to the door*) For God's sake, General Harras, you are taking the road to ruin.

HARRAS Don't worry. I'm just trying to steady my aim. (*He aims for the target on the wall and fires from a sitting position.* KORRIANKE *and* HANSEN *run in*) The gentleman wishes to leave. Elevator.

HANSEN (*Looking at the target*) 23. Not bad.

HARRAS Not good enough. (*Shoots again*)

HANSEN Bull's eye.

HARRAS All right. (LAUSITZ *goes off quickly without a goodbye.* KORRIANKE *follows. We hear the noise of the elevator.* HARRAS *puts the revolver away, takes the full glass. His hand trembles a little. He shakes his head, empties his glass and leans back.* HANSEN *and* KORRIANKE *return*) Open a window. Let some fresh air in here.

KORRIANKE Maybe I can still hit him! (*He runs to the window, opens it and spits down*) Tough luck, too much wind.

HARRAS (*Tired*) There, you see. Even the weather is against us. Who can win against such odds.

KORRIANKE (*Changed—white-faced—with clenched fists*) If something had happened to you, Herr General, I—I don't know what I—

HARRAS S'all right, Korriandoli. (*Goes to him and puts a cigarette in his mouth*) Go ahead and smoke one. Be calm and breathe deeply the doctor said as he turned on the gas. How do things stand here in the building? Are we safe from hidden ears in the walls?

KORRIANKE A coupla so-called telephone workers was here. Disorder men from the central exchange. Shoulda took a movie how cool I smile at 'em. No problem here I says. That l'tle mic'ophone certain parties built in here three weeks ago if that's why you come, we dug that out ourselves already. You don't need ta trouble yourselves there. We're trained technicians. 'N they retreated. "Have to make a report to the office," one of 'em mumbled.

HARRAS (*Laughs, slaps him on the shoulder*) Don't let 'em think we don't know the old tricks. Let 'em think up somethin' new so's we can have a l'tle change. (*Turns to* HANSEN) Good! We don't have to whisper. The shit is up to our chins and seems to be in the process of rising.

KORRIANKE Looks like we have to grow a little.

HARRAS I sort of have the feeling I'm growing shorter. What did the commentators say at the Ministry?

HANSEN Icy silence over a foggy ocean. Kesselring[8] palavered with the Chief and stalked through the corridors as though he had a time bomb up his rear. Nobody raised a visor. Everyone looked in the other direction except Oderbruch. He saw right through the pea soup. When we got the report, "General Harras whisked off to the front—alone—without staff, and so forth," he turned chalk white. We thought he'd pass out. After that he worked around the clock every night—I tried to keep up. When I gave out he still took material home with him.

HARRAS Yes, he's tops. Any result up to now?

HANSEN Nothing tangible—as far as the wing covering is concerned. The technical side I understand well enough.

HARRAS New accidents occurred?

KORRIANKE No more reports came in. Stopped suddenly about two weeks ago.

HARRAS Two weeks ago. That's weird. That smells like a sinister systematic plan. But where—where is the root?

HANSEN The important thing is—you'll fly lead again. Now we're certain to catch the fox.

HARRAS (*Softly to himself*) I think—there's no longer any point in it. I think—there's no point in it. No point at all.

(HANSEN *looks at* HARRAS *and bites his lip.* KORRIANKE *has brought in a loose, soft suede jacket which* HARRAS *changes for the coat of his uniform*)

KORRIANKE Mufti, mufti. Jus' like at Mother's.

HARRAS Thanks. How's our Yank?

KORRIANKE He's rolled himself up on the couch pounding his ear like a bear in winter. Didn't even hear the shooting.

HARRAS Let him sleep. Don't let him go out in the street alone anymore. We have to find a way to spirit him off to the Embassy. He knows too much. (*The telephone rings.* KORRIANKE *takes it off quickly before* HARRAS *can reach for it*)

KORRIANKE We're here, who's there? Sure, sure, but sure. Arrived promptly. What did the ole Easter Bunny tell you? Fresh as a daisy. Washed and shaved—What, sleep? Out of the question. Clear—understood, hup, hup—click, click. (*He hangs up*)

HARRAS Who was that?

[8] General Albert Kesselring (1885-1960) was in command of German aviation in the Russian sector in 1941-42. He was subsequently in charge of German forces in Italy.

KORRIANKE (*Beaming*) Wouldn't Herr General like to know!

HARRAS Well, what's going on?

KORRIANKE Regrettable lapse in your powers of observation, Herr General.

HARRAS What is this? Blindman's bluff?

KORRIANKE Excellent idea. Cold or hot. Eyes closed, if you please, and breathe through distended nostrils. Advance slowly. Sniff, sniff. Don'cha smell nothin'?

HARRAS Naw, what is it? Did you dig up a limburger?

KORRIANKE (*Disgusted*) I do believe you've lost your nose for fine detail. (*Puts a vase of flowers in front of* HARRAS' *face*)

HARRAS (*Opens his eyes*) Hmmmm. Violets. I really wouldn't have noticed it myself. Was she here?

KORRIANKE Every day, five o'clock on the dot after rehearsal. Have I heard anything? Is there any news? Do I know where you are and when are you coming back? I didn't. Sometimes I fibbed a little. So I told her stories about Herr General's childhood.

HARRAS Childhood! But I only met you in '17!

KORRIANKE 'S all the same. Every grown-up had a beautiful childhood. I know what a young lady like that wants to hear. (*Clicks his tongue*) Class, Herr General.

HARRAS Korrianke, you're turning into a matchmaker.

KORRIANKE There wasn't much matching to do, Herr General. An affair like that just matches itself. (*Bell rings*) But if you please, go easy at first. The little Miss was terrible upset. (*He runs out*)

HANSEN Discretion seems to be called for now. Under protest, I shall withdraw into my foreskin.

HARRAS Let's go, let's go! (*Quickly drinks a kirsch*)

HANSEN Mouthwash would be more advisable.

HARRAS Out!

(HANSEN *disappears through the other door while* KORRIANKE *lets* DIDDO *in from the hall and wants to leave again, but* DIDDO *hangs on to his hand, throws her arms around his neck and kisses him on the cheek*)

KORRIANKE (*Speaking over her head*) Blank cartridge, Herr General. Not meant for me personally. My dear little Miss, let's not have a nervous breakdown now. You know—when the steering wheel's gone and the brakes give out, then the thing to do is look Fate right in the eye without batting—

HARRAS Cut—

KORRIANKE —it. Easy as pie. (*Quickly goes off*)

DIDDO (*Half laughing, wipes her eyes*) But I'm not crying. I don't want to cry. Isn't it disgusting that you have to cry when you're happy.

HARRAS (*Comes up to her*) I don't call that crying, those few drops of holy water. That's family tradition like kissing harmless symbolic figures. I know all about that from Aunt Ollie. Is she all the time still smooching with the old prompter when she has someone else in mind?

DIDDO (*Laughs relieved*) Sometimes even me when there are no old ladies around. When I was a child it used to hurt my feelings. Now I can understand it. She wanted to come up. I was supposed to meet her at the Wittenberg subway station but I stood her up. I hope she waits a long time before she follows. Of course, I had to tell her everything—I heard from Korrianke. She—she was terribly worried.

HARRAS Nonsense. No reason to get upset just because I fly to the front. I've been flying around in the air for a quarter of a century and nothing's ever happened to me.

DIDDO (*Softly*) We were afraid it was true—what was being whispered.

HARRAS And if it had been true—would that have been so bad for you?

DIDDO (*Lowers her head*) Yes, or I wouldn't be here.

HARRAS (*Very serious*) Will you believe me if I tell you that nothing better ever happened to me? Please believe it.

DIDDO I believe it. I want to believe it. I can't really imagine what it would mean to you. But to me you are everything.

HARRAS And when you say that you don't even look at me.

DIDDO No—that is asking too much. But I would like to look at you. Quite thoroughly. After all, I hardly know you! Couldn't you look somewhere else for a minute? Maybe out the window?

HARRAS (*Turns his face to the window*) Sunset—made to order.

DIDDO Now I'm looking at you.

HARRAS Still?

DIDDO Still.

HARRAS Can I look at you now?

DIDDO Yes, you can turn around now.

HARRAS (*Looks into her face*) You—changed. You're older. More beautiful.

DIDDO Do you know why? (HARRAS *nods, takes a step toward her.* DIDDO *draws back somewhat*)

HARRAS Come. (*Almost without touching her, he leads her to an easy chair and sits down next to her on the arm*) I have to confess something to you. I didn't know this. I didn't expect it at all. I've had bad dreams recently—You didn't go with them. And ten minutes ago—or is it only five?—I had a moment there when everything was all the same to me—It may come back. Dying swan with heavenly harp. Worse than Ash Wednesday. But now—do you know how I feel now?

DIDDO (*Takes his hand*) Tell me.

HARRAS Playing hookey from school! Mardi Gras! Long vacations!

DIDDO (*Laughs*) You must have been quite a pest at home in school! Korrianke was telling me!

HARRAS Yes—he was always around!

DIDDO And at thirteen already after the girls!

HARRAS Told you that too?

DIDDO I think he left out the worst part!

HARRAS I'll have to button his lip.

DIDDO But he didn't say anything bad about you. Don't you know you're God Almighty to him? But you're a dangerous criminal as far as women are concerned—no one has to tell me that. I don't really care. I like it.

HARRAS (*Bends down to her*) Damn it—I should have guzzled mouthwash. Reeking of alcohol again.

DIDDO That goes with you. That's how I got to know you. Come— (*Takes his face in her hands and pulls it all the way over to her face. Kisses him on the lips and frees herself again immediately*) What does Korrianke say? Blank cartridge. Oh, I'm almost not scared of you anymore. But please, give me something to drink. Anything. I think I feel very weak.

HARRAS (*Pouring a drink*) And now just let someone come along and tell me that life isn't beautiful. A long time ago I tried to tell a young man that life was worth living if only you can look forward to something. I had almost forgotten it myself these last few days.

DIDDO (*Drinks with him*) Maybe you have to learn to be happy and rehearse until you can do it? But shouldn't that come from Heaven? We are always uneasy—burdened—I didn't really look forward to my first night at the theatre. There is too much fear in everything—And if you don't have any yourself then there are always others around frightening themselves. Surely it can't always have been like that? There must have been a time when you could simply be happy to be young? Weren't you?

HARRAS I don't remember now. I don't think it is easy to be young any time.

DIDDO No. I think it's a sort of a sickness. (*She shudders a little*) Sometimes I am only a feather in the wind that has no weight at all. Sometimes I'm as heavy as a stone at the bottom of a well. But—now I want to be happy! Quite madly happy. Surely it's no disgrace? Isn't it all right?

HARRAS It's more than all right. It comes—how did you say?—from Heaven. Your whole lifetime you're supposed to love and be happy. We need a whole world of joy—to outweigh all the misery—or else the world would get so heavy it wouldn't be able to turn anymore—Do you know we're both already a little drunk?

DIDDO Oh, it's wonderful. It's wonderful to be a little drunk—Aunt Ollie, you know, always takes everything so terribly tragically—it is really tragic too, of course. But after all, I can't help it that I'm not Jewish. I can't laugh anymore without her sighing. It's as though she held it against me, me personally. She worries about the poor Jews day and night—I believe the men she loved the most were all Jews—outside of—of course—

HARRAS (*Laughs*) You mean: present company excepted. You don't have to blush.

DIDDO I'm not blushing, you dangerous criminal. Look . . . I . . . often I don't know where I'm at anymore. I was only twelve in 1933. Aunt Ollie thinks everything is bad, and some of our colleagues think everything is good. They say the terrible stories are all enemy lies. And still others think some things are good and say "You can't tell, something better might follow"—Well, what am I supposed to think? If you come right down to it, you see only what crosses your path. I only know one thing. I would like to get out, out! Why, I couldn't even explain. But sometimes I think if I were my age and were Jewish and had to emigrate—maybe it wouldn't be so bad. Maybe it would even be better. To see the world—my God! New York! Just once, to be all the way to the top of a skyscraper and let your handkerchief fall down, and watch it get smaller like a snowflake over all the traffic! And the ocean—and the harbors—maybe China—or Rio de Janeiro. Me, I wouldn't care. I could do anything: wash dishes, wipe children, factory work—only to be free—outside! Sometimes I envy the Jews madly. I mean the ones outside.

HARRAS (*Takes her in his arms*) Maybe we'll be honorary Jews, us two. Maybe we'll wander through the world sometime. Maybe they'll throw us out at the right time because we're so illegally happy.

DIDDO I don't need the world when I'm with you. I want to stay with you today. Always. Come—take off my jacket for me now. (*Throws it behind her*) After all, I'm at home here. If Aunt Ollie says I look smooched up, it's completely all right with me.

HARRAS You are wonderful.

DIDDO You are wonderful.

HARRAS Gee, we are stupid.

DIDDO Gee, we are stupid.

HARRAS (*Bends her head back*) Come—kiss me—like that.

DIDDO Easy as pie—

HARRAS Cut—

DIDDO —it. (*Kisses him*)

HARRAS (*After a little while*) In a British play the maid would come in now to serve tea or the telephone would ring.

DIDDO Telephone!—God. it's getting dark already—Yes, I have to call somebody.

HARRAS No, I don't like that.

DIDDO But I promised—to make up my mind by tonight. I've been holding him off for two weeks—

HARRAS Him? Who?

DIDDO Roisterer—our new director—He made me a proposition—real wild—a lead! He likes to think I'm his discovery and he thinks he can put me over. He's worked on the play himself. They all say he is a genius.

HARRAS (*Grumbling*) Don't like it. Don't like it.

DIDDO I demanded a shameless salary and they said yes. That's the stupid part. But I would have to go to Vienna for six months, because it opens there first. Because, I think, he is from Vienna or from Linz. I don't know exactly. Anyway from Austria. I don't know my way around there.

HARRAS A Viennese from Linz like Hitler! That boy will go far. Oh, isn't this wonderful! Oh, isn't this marvelous! I'm already jealous!

DIDDO Of Roisterer? (*She laughs*) You should see him! He looks like a rabbit!

HARRAS For God's sake not that! Rabbits are terribly sexy. If the comparison occurs to you—

DIDDO Will you stop! Roisterer—it's just silly!

HARRAS They always say that.

DIDDO Well, if you're not . . .

HARRAS Please, don't wreck my beautiful jealousy! Nothing like this has happened to me for such a long time—to be so magnificently, so stupidly, in love.

DIDDO But I can't imagine me with Roisterer!

HARRAS You're not supposed to, you rascal!

DIDDO Besides, I'm turning it down. (*Runs to the telephone*) You don't really believe I'm going to leave now?

HARRAS (*Follows her quickly and puts his hand on the phone. Changed*) Wait a minute. Is there such a big hurry?

DIDDO I want to get it over with. It's only fair to let him know.

HARRAS You will have to think it over some more.

DIDDO There's nothing to think over.

HARRAS Maybe there is, from my point of view.

DIDDO (*Leans against him*) Please, please don't say I should think of my career. I don't give a hoot about it. I don't want to. What could come out of a career, if I thought about it now? It wouldn't be genuine. Let me stay here.

HARRAS (*Holds her close, breathes into her hair softly*) It isn't because of your career. Don't say anything now. I'll explain it to you later. Let me have a little time. When does he have to know?

DIDDO Before tonight's curtain—

HARRAS (*Looks at his watch*) We still have an hour. Will you give me an hour? No questions asked? And will you leave—the decision to me?—Just this once?

DIDDO (*Looks at him*) Yes.

HARRAS Thanks. (*Strokes her arm and her hand*)

DIDDO (*Touches his hand in which he is still holding the watch, touches his watch just as he is starting to put it away*) What a funny kind of watch you have—

HARRAS That's no watch. That's my time-grinder.

DIDDO I've never seen anything like it. It must be terribly old. Does it work?

HARRAS It runs so fast you have to chain it down. That is, if it doesn't stop. And then all ya have to do is this— (*He knocks the watch against the back of his head*)—Did you hear it ring? Genuine nickel plate. In an emergency you can use it as a weapon.

DIDDO Didn't anyone ever think of buying you a new watch?

HARRAS All the nicer girls. I could have had a collection, but I don't need it. But I guess I'll never part with this one.

DIDDO Where did you get it?

HARRAS Someone gave it to me. (*He puts the watch away*)

DIDDO You don't have to talk about it if you don't want to.

HARRAS He was the first pilot I shot down. He gave me a hard time. I was there when he died. He said: "Souvenir"—and gave me the watch. And grinned and smoked a cigarette. Suddenly I knew I would stay alive as long—as long as I had the watch. Of course, that's silly. Superstition. It's only true for you if it hits you. But when he grinned at me so calmly and a little sly, it suddenly struck me: "He knows." Dying people see more than the rest of us. Whoever has the watch stays alive so the other one isn't forgotten. You shouldn't really talk about things like that. I've never done it. Never before. . . .

DIDDO Don't you think you could talk about everything with me?

HARRAS (*Walks up and down, remains standing in front of her, speaks rapidly, softly*) You should know how things stand with me. I can't cheat on you. Right now my life is worth less than the old watch. They could both stop any minute. They're after me —and they've learned how to hunt. I'm trying to beat my way through—but I don't know if it will come off. The chances are slim. At any rate, I can still defend myself. And if I make it, it'll be because of you. I didn't want to tell you at first. Now the secrecy seems petty to me. It would have been nicer—a few more days or hours without any shadow. But what good would all this be between us if we didn't become confidants—bound together. For now and always.

DIDDO Now I know you love me. (*Embraces him*)

HARRAS (*Almost without tone*) For now and always.

(*Commotion outside—steps, lowered voices. The door is pushed open.* KORRIANKE *appears, behind him two men with Red Cross armbands carrying* OLIVIA *on a stretcher*)

KORRIANKE Right here on the couch. Look out—don't stumble over the carpet.

DIDDO (*Clinging to* HARRAS) Is she—is she—

KORRIANKE (*Quickly*) Don't worry. Problem with the tender sex. Fade out, technically speaking.

FIRST MAN Lucky she gave the address before she tipped over. Was right at the transfer station, Adolf Hitler Square—used to be Reichschancery Square.

SECOND MAN Me—she grabbed on ta ma sleeve and then she went, "Ugh," and then she was gone.

HARRAS I know all about it. I lived through it a hundred times about twenty years ago. She'll still be fainting when she's ninety.

(*The two men have put* OLIVIA *on the couch and have withdrawn into the corridor.* HARRAS *quickly hands them some bills while* KORRIANKE *is working over* OLIVIA, *puts a pillow under her head and is rubbing her joints*)

KORRIANKE Should I call a doctor?

HARRAS No, I think I can fix her myself. You take care of the two heroes—a beer and a cigar would go over, I bet. (*To* DIDDO) You'd better go out, too. She doesn't have to see you the minute she comes to. I'll call you.

KORRIANKE (*Going off*) A little cologne—or better yet, a few drops of Schnapps—

HARRAS I know something better. (*As soon as everybody is outside he winds his watch and holds it up to* OLIVIA'S *ear, lets the alarm ring and calls out in a changed voice*) Mrs. Geiss! Your cue! You're on!

(OLIVIA *opens her eyes, sits up and looks around*

*absently.* HARRAS *puts his watch back in his pocket and gets a bottle of red wine from the bar)*

OLIVIA I smell violets. Is my little girl here?

HARRAS (*Working on the bottle*) Came just a minute ago. You must have been at the wrong exit. She waited for you for an hour.

OLIVIA Tell me no stories. I'm very happy for her.

HARRAS Ping! (*He pulls the cork*)

OLIVIA That sounds good. I feel better already. I guess I made a fool of myself again—

HARRAS (*Gives her the cork*) First Aid. Ersatz smelling salts. (*Gets the glasses*)

OLIVIA The subway was jammed—I had to stand up the whole trip—And oh, the air!—Nobody has any soap these days.

HARRAS Yes. The heroic age stinks of dirty laundry. Have a drink. *Gesundheit.*

OLIVIA And then all the worry about you—the strain —You don't even know yet what happened!

HARRAS Bergmann? I haven't had time to ask Korrianke—

OLIVIA Go and make sure no one comes in—not the little one either. (*Starting*) My God—where's my pocketbook. Oh, here—thank the Lord. (*She rummages around in it*)

HARRAS (*At the door*) Everything's all fixed. Yes, she's chirping again. How about fixing up a little supper? Anything at all—a few hot sausages or something like that. I think we are going to have company. (*We hear* DIDDO *outside laughing with* KORRIANKE. HARRAS *closes the door.* OLIVIA *has taken an unopened letter out of her pocketbook, turns it nervously back and forth*) I couldn't get this Bergmann business out of my mind the whole time—Just didn't have a chance to do anything. Had to go away too suddenly. But now we'll certainly rock the baby. What's that?

OLIVIA Too late.

HARRAS (*Takes the letter, holds it unopened in his hand*) Did they escape?

OLIVIA Poison.

HARRAS And—Jenny?

OLIVIA Both of them—together. She didn't want to be without him. The doctor brought this to me. It's his goodbye to you.

HARRAS (*Sits down next to her on the couch*) Damn it all. Damn it all. Why couldn't they . . . a day later—I could have worked it—

OLIVIA It was too late anyway. He didn't care anymore.

HARRAS Damn it all. (*Turns on a reading lamp, opens the letter, reads it quickly, hands it to* OLIVIA)

OLIVIA (*With tears in her eyes*) I can't—I don't have my glasses—Do you mind?

HARRAS (*Without humor*) Cry-baby. (*Reads in a monotone voice*) "My Dear Friend—This is the only way to freedom possible for us. We are calm. I haven't the strength for what people call a 'new life' and I can't buy it with the sacrifices of my friends. I know what you were ready to do for us. You did it for others. Our blessings will forever—the thought that there are still human beings like you"—I can't go on. You know anyhow. Thanks, etc. (*He has become quite pale*)

OLIVIA (*Weeping*) You deserve it even if you didn't succeed this time. You can be proud of that letter.

HARRAS Proud? Of all things! (*Throws the letter on the desk*) Now let's look in the mirror and be moved by our reflection. What noble human beings we are! Everybody has his conscience-Jew or several of them so he can sleep nights. But you can't buy yourself free with that. That's self-deception. We're guilty for what's happening to thousands of people we don't know and can never help. Guilty and damned for all eternity. Permitting viciousness is worse than doing it.

OLIVIA But what in Heaven's name are we supposed to do? As it is you always have one foot in the clink. If you just carry a letter like this in your pocketbook! Are we supposed to take poison too?

HARRAS That isn't necessary. We'll all have our turn in due time. One after the other. It's already rising up out of their graves—high as the sky. Don't you see it? Didn't you ever see it?

OLIVIA What—who?

HARRAS (*Goes to the window*) Look out there. When I'm alone and it gets dark in the evening, it grows over there above the rooftops. Like this— (*He lifts his closed fist and slowly unfolds all his fingers upwards*) Only one hand. Five fingers. But—gigantic. Monstrous. Big enough to take hold of a city and lift it up and smash it to the ground. (*He lets his arm drop*) Then it shrivels up again. Then, it grows again. I know it's only the searchlights from the flak station radio tower, five searching pillars of light. That's all. But to me it's a hand. And I know whose hand it is. (*For a moment he stares into the twilight, then turns around*) And now you're going to say: "overstrained nerves " No. I don't have nerves! Never had any!

OLIVIA (*Sobbing*) My God, Harry! What did they do to you? If you give up, what's to become of us?

HARRAS (*Puts an arm around her shoulders*) But I'm not giving up. Quite the contrary. I'm just beginning all over again. I'm going to pop 'em one below the belt even if it's in the twelfth round. You just have to know whom you're dealing with.

OLIVIA Listen, Harry. You should take off. Anywhere, any country. It doesn't matter if they lock you up till the war is over. There's no point in staying here anymore.

HARRAS Yes, there is a point in it. I've got to find out the truth.

OLIVIA You know it anyway. No—you're careless. That's your old vice. It provokes you when things get dangerous. You're a man of thrills. You don't want to miss anything. And that's exactly why they're after you. As long as someone like you is around and able to give orders they feel hemmed in. That's why they want revenge.

HARRAS Maybe you're right. But I've still got things to do around here.

OLIVIA And besides, you had too much success with

women. That's the worst of it. With our Nazis everything is really jealousy, bed-jealousy above all. But on that point they're way below zero—almost the whole bunch of them. That's why they're always wanting to go to war and make out like great men—it's all a fake. Where a man has to show what he's really worth, a steeled body won't help, nor iron energy. Either you've got it or you haven't got it. But those boys—we know all about them. First great sounds—then it's all over before it really began and off they run, back to duty. *Nebbish!*

HARRAS For you the value of any man is completely fixed by a single definition. (*He smiles*)

OLIVIA But it is, isn't it? Except for geniuses, perhaps. Goethe is supposed to have been very superior in that department. About Napoleon you hear less that's good. But with your Adolf—there's nothing there at all—God, I hope the little one isn't listening.

HARRAS (*Quite gay, kisses her on the ear*) She can't learn anything wrong from you. You have a completely healthy personal viewpoint. Oh, Ollie, if there were no women and no music! Then the economic determinists would be right. Then the whole show would be nothing but a manufacturing process and our rain showers a sprinkler system. (*Turns on the radio*) Come, let's let it tinkle a bit so that Diddo knows it's all right to come in here again. (*On the radio, "Siegfried's death" from* Götterdämmerung)—Thank you, no. (*Turns it off*) Hitlerian destiny music. Or is it ours? Brmmm, brmmm, brmmm—Siegfried's death.

OLIVIA Maybe somebody's been killed—a general or something. They played that for Fritsch.[4]

HARRAS You have to dig that stuff out of your ears. Just wait—I've got something here. (*Puts a record on the phonograph which plays an old popular song hoarsely and dragging a bit*)

OLIVIA God, our old song!— (*She trills along a bit, puts her hand lightly on his shoulder. He holds her around her waist and rocks her a few steps in the rhythm of the melody*)

HARRAS Do you still remember? Russian Tea Room? Pigeon Casino? The Butterfly Room?

OLIVIA Sounds like Paradise Lost, and what shabby places. God, Harry, why were we so cynical? I mean, so frivolous?

HARRAS Were we?

OLIVIA We loved each other, and how! Why didn't we take it seriously? And build something together? Like a family. We'd be so much better off now.

HARRAS We weren't the right people for that, neither of us.

OLIVIA Why not? I think it was a sin—or cowardice. We should have been punished then. It was sin.

HARRAS But you were just going to play Joan of Arc.

OLIVIA Yes, that's the way it always was. I can't remember how many times it happened to me. I was as receptive as a field mouse. All a man had to do was to give me a friendly squeeze and I liked him until I remembered my other side. And always because of the same damned role. Finally I adopted Diddo, but it isn't any kind of life in the end. There's something false in it.

HARRAS (*Lets go of her. Plays the record again*) Listen, Ollie—maybe I'll try it yet. Or do you think it's too late? Am I too old for her?

OLIVIA There's no such thing. If it's really serious—

HARRAS I've never been more serious. Perhaps I'll pull my neck out of the noose yet. Many a condemned man has jumped off the scaffold. And if I get out of it, you'll get to be my mother-in-law.

OLIVIA Better'n nothing. Let's drink to it.

HARRAS (*Pouring*) Let's drink to it. (*Calls*) Hey, you in the kitchen, don't be so discreet!

HANSEN (*Pokes his head in*) Light music and heavy red wine! In matters of good taste we can always rely on the older generation.

HARRAS Don't brag, you bum. You're getting bald already.

HANSEN And you, General, haven't got any hair on your chest yet. (*Bows to* OLIVIA) Madam. . . .

OLIVIA Therein lies the secret of his charm. I never cared much for woolly bears. (*She puts the needle back and begins to dance with* HANSEN)

DIDDO (*Has come in*) Well, you seem to have recovered completely—Aunt Ollie. Who's taking who to the theatre tonight? (*Drinks from* HARRAS' *glass*)

KORRIANKE In an emergency that'll be accomplished with a wheelbarrow. (*Speaks from the door. The doorbell rings*) We seem to be getting an addition. (*Going off*) Supper's served, Herr General. The little Miss has a positive genius for making sandwiches. (*He goes off to the corridor*)

HARRAS You can found a household on that.

DIDDO Did she notice anything?

HARRAS Everything. Things like that always show up before they're even true—the science of wave transmission.

DIDDO So much the better. Then we don't have to watch out for our waves anymore.

HARRAS It's impossible anyway. They twitter like squirrels. (*He has put his arms around her without dancing*)

DIDDO (*Almost at his mouth completely entranced*) Since when do squirrels twitter— (*She breathes a kiss on his mouth*)

HARRAS (*Just like her*) Yes—since when do squirrels twitter—

DIDDO If you say they twitter, then they twitter.

HARRAS They twitter, you can depend on it. (*They disappear behind the bamboo screen. In the meantime* KORRIANKE *has appeared at the door and given signals to* HANSEN. HANSEN *excuses himself quietly from* OLIVIA*—goes to* KORRIANKE, *and leaves the room after a few whispered directions. The record is over. but still running.* OLIVIA *goes quickly to the player and turns it off*) What's the matter? Where's Hansen?

KORRIANKE Someone asked for him, Herr General.

(HARRAS *lets go of* DIDDO *and stands immobile for a moment. He is about to go to the door when*

[4] General Werner von Fritsch, former Chief of Staff, was killed before Warsaw in September, 1939.

HANSEN *comes back. He is slightly flushed and trying to appear unaffected*)

HANSEN Sorry to have to say goodbye, General. Two gentlemen with stiff hats and shiny boots. Rather plebeian company—but irresistible.

HARRAS Did they say what they wanted from you?

HANSEN Only answer a few questions—to relieve an urgent need. I've always wanted to see the Gestapo from the inside. It will be a completely one-sided pleasure. My name is Bunny and I don't know nuttin' about it. (*He laughs, embarrassed, falls silent and makes a signal to* HARRAS *which is proof of honor.* HARRAS *responds and returns it, then gives him his hand.* HANSEN *presses his hand silently, looks briefly into* HARRAS' *eyes and leaves. Silence.* HARRAS *goes to the telephone, hesitates. Mumbles*)

HARRAS There's no point in it. (KORRIANKE *brings in a full glass*) Thanks. (*Puts it untouched on the table*)

DIDDO Can they really—can they do anything to him?

HARRAS (*Shrugs his shoulders*) They know how to strike.

(*He stands with clenched fists.* OLIVIA *is holding* DIDDO'S *hand—Voices and laughter come from the hall outside. In walk* BARON PFLUNGK, VON MOHRUNGEN, *and* POOTSIE. POOTSIE *is wearing a party uniform, elegantly tailored, with a short skirt, long stockings and a tight blouse. In her garish manner she creates a rather exaggerated effect. The two gentlemen, on the other hand, are almost disturbed and breathless, not just from climbing the stairs*)

POOTSIE Please, let's close the elevator door for future generations. We thought the thing was out of commission. You must have shipped out a regiment up here! Just when we had climbed the last summit—zoom, it whizzed off. (*Looks around*) Well, so this is the ill-famed robber's cave. Not as barbaric as I thought.

MOHRUNGEN Pardon the invasion, General, but the hall door was open and naturally Pootsie was a full horse-length ahead of us. I'm a little too mature for nine floors.

PFLUNGK I trust we are not barging in at the wrong moment.

HARRAS You're just in time. At the stroke of twelve, spirits appear.

MOHRUNGEN (*Laughs, somewhat uncertain. Notices* OLIVIA) If I had known *you* were going to be here, Madam . . .

OLIVIA Then you would have shot up the stairs like a sky-rocket.

MOHRUNGEN Like cupid's arrow, Madam. Did you get my flowers?

OLIVIA The fastest method of travel. Cavalier, why didn't you come to the theatre?

MOHRUNGEN But I came! Didn't you get my flowers?

OLIVIA Why didn't you come back to my dressing room?

MOHRUNGEN Uninvited? Wouldn't that have been somewhat forward?

OLIVIA Well—aren't you the stormy one! Hold me back! Hold me back! So I've got a new admirer and already he doesn't dare.

MOHRUNGEN What is not may yet be. (*Kisses her hand. They withdraw to the bar*)

POOTSIE Poppa loves bacon. We're pretty well paired off here it seems; the old Geiss, the young Geiss, two harmless civilians and two able-bodied warriors. (*She goes up to* HARRAS) How do you like my new uniform? (*She salutes him*)

HARRAS Too brown.

POOTSIE You old tease. Maybe you prefer flesh color?

PFLUNGK Well, Pootsie, now that you've reached your desired goal, don't restrain your emotions. (*Turns to* DIDDO) I hope we're not intruding. Bachelor quarters always have a certain fascination for young ladies.

DIDDO (*Glancing at* POOTSIE) That depends on the young ladies.

POOTSIE (*To* HARRAS) Pflungk is absolutely harmless. He won't seduce your little Miss Innocent. Dry old herring-bones. You can take him on.

HARRAS Would you like something to drink?

POOTSIE Oh, how formal. Yes—a little fuel won't hurt. Who's that good-looking young man? (LAWRENCE *has come back in. He is washed and shaved and looks ten years younger*)

HARRAS That's my friend, Buddy Lawrence. Miss von Mohrungen.

POOTSIE American, I should have known. The Anglo-Saxon mixture type—broad shoulders, narrow hips, long skull, but nothing in it. No enlightenment, I mean. In your country they claim every "Man is born equal," even if he is a Jew.

LAWRENCE That's what we say. Were you ever there?

POOTSIE No, but we get all that in the course.

LAWRENCE What course?

POOTSIE NSRFF—Special School for Advanced Reichswomen Leadership Candidates.

LAWRENCE (*Pulls out his notebook*) You'll have to repeat that slowly.

POOTSIE In case I decide to grant you an interview, do you have a clean bill of health?

LAWRENCE You mean—am I kosher? Not in the full sense of the word.

POOTSIE It's not my worry. The censor will rap your knuckles. What do you want to know? Shoot.

LAWRENCE What do you learn in your course? What are you majoring in?

POOTSIE World outlook, of course, from the woman's point of view. We hear top authorities on the subject of race politics, breeding selection, sex hygiene, body culture. Right now the lecture series is based on Nietzsche's philosophy: The value of suffering in the Life of the Nation.

LAWRENCE (*Writing*) Is that of concern to women?

POOTSIE And how! The strength of the emotional life begins with the mother. Everything on a scientific basis, you understand? Biological, medical, philosophical. Question of suffering in Nietzsche, the ethical significance of pain, critique of the destructive effects of false pity. Of course, it's decadent. When I have a baby there won't be any anesthesia. It's going to be a matter of suffering wide awake and screaming till the seams burst.

HARRAS I'd like to midwife that. (*Downs a schnapps*)

POOTSIE I bet that would suit you. (*She talks more to him*) You should watch us do our exercises. Your tongue would hang out. Strapping girls, all of them, wearing nothing but panties.

HARRAS That would cure me.

POOTSIE We've gotten rid of all conventions; sex inhibitions, class consciousness, social differences; all that is abolished. Every German woman is—of nobility.

LAWRENCE How noble!

HARRAS What a shabby swindle! Your father, Pootsie, is making nice, round little millions in partnership with Hermann Goering and your noble German sisters spend their lives making munitions in his workshops so a salvo can be fired over the mass-grave of their bridegrooms.

POOTSIE You talk like a Jew.

HARRAS I am one—honorary degree.

POOTSIE Well, your big mouth impresses me. I suppose you're never afraid?

HARRAS Oh yes, Pootsie, I could be, of you.

POOTSIE Is that supposed to be a compliment?

HARRAS No—flattery.

POOTSIE Funny. All my affairs begin with a fight. (*Irritated, to* LAWRENCE) Now you can put a period. You won't get any more out of me. I have to undertake an inspection here. (*She turns away and walks around in the room*)

LAWRENCE (*To* HARRAS *who is handing him a glass*) Ghastly. I'm going to take her apart—if only she didn't have such a pretty rear. It's time I got out of here or I'm going to get vicious. I think I'll go now.

HARRAS (*Softly*) Impossible. The house is being watched—Are you all right?

LAWRENCE Perfect. As though I'd been on vacation.

HARRAS You look it. With you guys, a shave and a little sleep is enough.

LAWRENCE That comes from a clear conscience and a complete lack of mental burdens.

HARRAS (*Laughs*) I'm jealous. I'll straighten out your taste in women. I want you to meet a young lady who—to me—that is, I'm going to marry her.

LAWRENCE Congratulations. But isn't this quite sudden?

HARRAS Not at all. It was settled five minutes ago.

LAWRENCE Then what about my bet?

HARRAS Better write it off. I intend to live—now. I care.

LAWRENCE Do you think you can last? It's all got to blow up sometime.

HARRAS I'm going to try one way or another. (*Takes* LAWRENCE *to* DIDDO *who is standing at the window with* PFLUNGK)

POOTSIE (*Has looked around in the room*) The famous propeller bar? Sharp! (*Pointing to the junk*) He shot these down himself and reworked them. (*She scratches on a piece of metal*) Is that blood or rust?

MOHRUNGEN (*Who has come out of the bar with* OLIVIA, *somewhat embarrassed*) Really very interesting. All these trophies and souvenirs are a part of the history of modern war, so to speak.

HARRAS Most of them were peaceful crash landings. Africa, Greenland, and so forth. The seat is from my old Rumpler-pigeon, 1915.

PFLUNGK Original decor.

HARRAS Horrible, isn't it? Everybody is born with a certain amount of bad taste. You have to fight against it to raise your general level, a kind of aesthetic self-analysis.

MOHRUNGEN It's over my head.

HARRAS I have a hunch many a modern decorator would be happy if, at home, he could flop down on a plush sofa with embroidered pillows just like he did at Grandma's. It's about like that with my chamber of horrors.

POOTSIE Well, I like it. (*She rocks on the plane seat*)

HARRAS You would. I call it my reservoir of barbarism.

POOTSIE And who is the faded beau in the middle? (*She points to a wreathed photograph of a pilot*)

HARRAS (*Speaking more to* DIDDO) My best enemy from the last World War. His mother gave me the picture. I visited her afterward.

POOTSIE The famous chivalric gesture. Good for the historic reputation but antiquated. (DIDDO *turns sharply and goes out*) What's the matter with the little blonde—jealous already?

HARRAS Not at all. She's helping Korrianke so we can have a bite of something. Here comes Schlick. Now you will get to meet a celebrity. (KORRIANKE *has let in the painter* SCHLICK)

MOHRUNGEN Schlick—Schlick—what did I read about him . . . recently?

HARRAS That the exhibition of his paintings was banned. Doesn't please the first artist of our nation. Heil, great brush. You look parched. (*He fills a glass*)

(SCHLICK, *not at all Bohemian, but dressed in a somewhat negligent fashion with an unhealthy color to his face and a glassy look in his eyes, comes toward* HARRAS *swaying slightly. He creates the impression of a man who has been drinking since morning. In his hand he holds a portfolio of drawings which he throws on the table in front of* HARRAS *so that the individual pages fall out*)

SCHLICK Last series. Just finished it. (*He drinks hastily*)

HARRAS (*With a hasty glance at the pages, gathers them up hurriedly*) You're drunk. You stagger around in public with this stuff?

POOTSIE Something vulgar? Let's have a look.

HARRAS Not vulgar enough. More—abstract. It would bore you.

POOTSIE Well, I bet it's naked girls. You artists—we know all about you. (SCHLICK *stares at her quite fascinated. He doesn't speak.* POOTSIE *fixes her blouse so it's tighter*) You can show me everything. I'm an adult.

SCHLICK That one . . . that one! That's what I've been missing!—I need her. (*Takes a drawing pencil out of his pocket*) Nazi witchcraft. Imagination doesn't go that far.

HARRAS Shut up now. Drink something or sit down.

POOTSIE (*Half angry, half flattered*) I'll sit for you some other time. Right now, you're seeing double. What about me provokes you—face or figure?

SCHLICK (*Without interruption from* HARRAS) The evil. The embodiment of evil in the flesh, in the sex. Uniform over the body—naked lap in the face.

MOHRUNGEN Really, that is going a little too far. Don't forget, there are ladies present!

SCHLICK (*Turns to* MOHRUNGEN *and speaks clearly with the imperturbability of a man standing before his bathtub and preaching to the fishes*) It doesn't go too far at all. That's only the beginning. I'll have to explain it to you. It is of enormous significance. It concerns my series: "Blood and Soil."

POOTSIE Sounds quite according to regulations. Everybody paints that these days.

SCHLICK (*Laughs*) I discovered the formula, the original formula. I'm the only one who knows it. (*He speaks as if lecturing, without excitement*) Blood falls on the ground, drips, runs, spurts or streams. The earth swallows it like a lap swallows seed. That is the conception of evil, the birth of all misfortunes. Abel's blood flowed on the ground . . . with the first murder. That's when evil came into the world. Everybody knows that. But how come no one ever noticed that it came from a chemical combination? Blood and soil. The formula. The chemical combination. From this rise the diseases, the epidemics . . . because all their original germs go back to an original sourcegerm. Then the evil impulses: hate, revenge, jealousy, cruelty. The evil spirits: demons, devils, furies, the stranglers and the grabbers. Then the destructive wishes: the evil thoughts, every variety of lie, also the poisonous mushrooms, death in the womb, purple children. The inner decay, conceit, rottenness of soul, betrayal, fear, stinking self-deception—everything. That's how it began. That's how it goes on. There is no escape. Think of the stained earth of Russia, the dung of corpses, the fatal impregnation. It will all come back to us. I have drawn all that. (*He stares at* HARRAS *who is locking the portfolio in a drawer*) Maybe you're right. I don't suppose anybody can stand that. Perhaps I'd better jump out of a window.

HARRAS That's your first good idea tonight. There's a balcony next door. You can make a good, safe jump from there.

SCHLICK (*To the others*) Why don't you laugh? Go ahead. Laugh, please. I'm very funny. I'm also a bastard, just like you, ladies and gentlemen.

KORRIANKE (*On a sign from* HARRAS *has taken him by the arm*) Sour herring and a cheese sandwich. Then maybe a glass of beer. Guzzling with no blotter—Logical results. (*Wants to lead him to the kitchen*)

SCHLICK No, thanks. Don't need it. There are too many grabbers here for me. (*Frees himself, looks around in the air, to* HARRAS) Do you think they'll let you skip? Why you of all people? There are too many— (*Goes quickly, stumbling out the door,* KORRIANKE *follows. Oppressed silence, even* POOTSIE *seems somewhat subdued*)

POOTSIE Queer ole jug. Was he always like that?

HARRAS Not before 1933. He was still married then. His wife was Jewish. He agreed to a divorce—because he believed a German could only paint in Germany. His wife and the children are missing. And Schlick is still considered a degenerate artist. (HARRAS *with a nervous motion has almost automatically turned on the radio. A voice is snarling*)

VOICE . . . are standing their ground everywhere, despite premature snowstorms and unbearable cold, which is costing our troops the heaviest . . . (HARRAS *turns off the radio*)

OLIVIA Brrr. I thought I heard something about hot sausages before. That would be a positive salvation.

HARRAS Thanks, Ollie. Saved by the ground crew. Excuse me, please, I'm a bad host. May I trouble you to come to the kitchen? I have sort of a Tyrolean corner there instead of a dining room—No, Baron, no trouble at all—Just a bite so we can go on drinking. (*To* OLIVIA) Can I leave K.P. to you and Diddo? We will come along in a minute.

(*He remains behind with* MOHRUNGEN, *who has made a sign to him, while the others disappear into the kitchen from which we hear noises and voices*)

MOHRUNGEN Tell me— (*Lowers his voice*)—can one be overheard here?

HARRAS Only by your conscience, Mohrungen.

MOHRUNGEN I don't know what you mean, General. Please be serious. Everyone must clean his own house first.

HARRAS Good, let us sweep. You, as the elder and my guest, have precedence. Begin in front of your door. In front of mine the Gestapo has swept anyway, as you probably know. Of course, they sweep backwards—the dirt into the house.

MOHRUNGEN I cannot talk with you in that tone—

HARRAS Then let's go eat something.

MOHRUNGEN (*Holding him by his arm*) Why don't you listen to reason—your very life is at stake!

HARRAS That is my affair! Right now all I'm interested in is the position taken by your procurement office regarding the faulty materials.

MOHRUNGEN There was nothing else I could do, General. (*Stutters*) I acted—yes—according to my honest opinion. I couldn't take my personal feelings into account. The situation has gone so far that we cannot block it. Must not.

HARRAS In other words—you have taken a position against me. You have thrown the suspicion and responsibility completely onto my offices.

MOHRUNGEN (*Tortured*) I have only done my duty. As far as the manufacturing end is concerned, there is indisputable proof of my exoneration. All evidence points the other way.

HARRAS *My* way. There is no evidence this way or that.

MOHRUNGEN But what am I to do? You don't expect me to *ask* them to investigate me? Yes, I know you're suspicious. You may be right—I don't know—and—and I don't want to know! No, I don't want to know it! My position is difficult enough—I'm sorry to have to say it—through your failings! (*Whispering*) A part of our conversation at the restaurant was recorded—not very clearly, thank God. And there is nothing left for me to do except—please, won't you try to understand me?

HARRAS (*Cool, but not unfriendly*) I understand completely—Any human being wants to save himself.

MOHRUNGEN It is not a question of that.

HARRAS What else—?

MOHRUNGEN Listen to me for a minute—without prejudice. It is a matter of saving *you*. There is only one way for you and I want to help you. I don't mind telling you quite frankly, it is in my interest too.

HARRAS Yes?

MOHRUNGEN You know Funk?[5] At least he has a sense of humor and he likes to drink too—I know that he respects you. I could arrange a get-together —quite casually. Perhaps "a stein at dusk" in my hotel. He has enough influence to negotiate the necessary—

HARRAS What's my line in all this?

MOHRUNGEN You have got to join the Party, take a completely different position, make peace with Himmler—

HARRAS And deliver the Luftwaffe into the arms of the SS.

MOHRUNGEN But you can't prevent it anyway. It is the command of the hour. We are in a war and unity must come first, before personal doubts, scruples or feelings of the moment. You know, it's just as hard for me. But we must—we must save Germany from Bolshevism. Not only Germany. The world.

HARRAS Go ahead and save, Mohrungen. Save away. Save your executive board position and your dividends. But do me a favor, don't try and save me.

MOHRUNGEN Harras, you must realize you can't fly into the eye of the storm for long. Your ideals too are at stake. The whole of Christian civilization is at stake!

HARRAS Then save that too. After all, everybody is saving something these days. Religion, culture, democracy, the West—in every direction you blow your nose—a crusade for a big thing you can't even prove exists. I'd like to meet just one guy honest enough to admit that all he wants to save is his own skin. I sure would like to hang on to mine. But not by means of "a stein at dusk." My ideal is quite modest: Not to have to spit in my face. Not even in a cross-wind.

MOHRUNGEN (*His anger rising*) Do you mean to say— (*After a pause—softly*) That I have given up my honor?

HARRAS Yes.

MOHRUNGEN (*Turns away*) We don't live just to be happy, after all. After all, we do have to make sacrifices. I know—we're all going to the dogs. I don't have a will of my own anymore— (*He sobs*)

HARRAS I'm thirsty. There's beer in the kitchen.

[5] Walther Funk (1890-1960), president of the Reichsbank under Hitler.

MOHRUNGEN Can't you understand me at all?

HARRAS Oh, yes, Mohrungen, I understand completely. I didn't expect anything else. (*Goes to the kitchen door*)

POOTSIE (*Entering with a half-eaten frankfurter in her hand, followed by* PFLUNGK) Peace-time goods, completely free of horse-shoe nails. Go get yourself one. Momma Geiss is keeping it hot for you! You can discuss the military situation with your mouth full too, Poppa. (*To* HARRAS) May I use your telephone? Just once? Official business, of course.

HARRAS Certainly. Even if it's official love. Ouch! I don't usually think up anything that corny! You cramp my style, Pootsie.

POOTSIE Yes, war spoils everything, doesn't it?

HARRAS Come, Mohrungen. (HARRAS *goes with* MOHRUNGEN *off to the kitchen*)

PFLUNGK Now Pootsie, you don't want to telephone at all. Why did you step on my foot?

POOTSIE Never fear, noble one. Not on account of love making. It was just a trick. I discovered something here I want to study. Might interest you, too. Mad business, my friend. I just got a quick look at it before. (*She goes to the desk where* BERGMANN'S *letter was left and picks it up*) You just watch that nobody comes in. Somebody must have just brought it to him or he would have hidden it. Maybe that Geiss woman. I've been suspicious of her for a long time! (*She reads,* PFLUNGK *reading over her shoulder*)

PFLUNGK From one of his Jew-friends, naturally. He's supposed to have smuggled a couple of them over the border already.

POOTSIE But these are anti-state activities! This is high treason!

PFLUNGK Give me the letter.

POOTSIE Woudn't think of it.

PFLUNGK Give me the letter.

POOTSIE What do *you* want it for?

PFLUNGK You'll see. (*Tears the letter out of her hand and starts to throw it into the fireplace in which* KORRIANKE *has made a fire. However, he throws too short and* POOTSIE *catches it in mid-air before it can fall*)

POOTSIE Idiot. Can't even throw. Better take a course in light-athletics, you flap-tail. What's the big idea anyway?

PFLUNGK Because I don't want you to do anything foolish.

POOTSIE Foolish?

PFLUNGK With this letter you can destroy Harras—

POOTSIE So what.

PFLUNGK It would be foolish, even dangerous. Pootsie, you are too young to understand that. We are not unconquerable. In war there is fortune and misfortune, even for National Socialists. Things could be different sometime. Then you will need people like Harras. You might thank your lucky stars that you know such people. Know them well.

POOTSIE You are thinking a little too far, Baron.

PFLUNGK Better than too short. Have you considered, for example, that if he goes down the drain right now—then you've known him too well already. It would be the worst thing that could happen.

POOTSIE Aw, go take your shakes somewhere else! Boy, if you aren't a weak sister. You make me puke. Harras, at least, has some guts!

PFLUNGK What are you going to do with the letter?

POOTSIE That depends. That depends on him. Maybe —maybe I'll make him real big. Maybe I'll let him fall. (*Puts the letter inside her blouse*) Incidentally, if that Geiss girl gives me one more dirty look I'm going to paste her one. (*Voices grow louder, come nearer from the kitchen.* POOTSIE *quickly takes up the telephone receiver and pretends to talk*) Well then, shall we meet at the juice bar? On a bombless night, of course. (*Hangs up*)—Well, how was that for an act? Just let that Geiss girl put on an equal performance!

PFLUNGK (*Hastily*) I tell you you're playing with dynamite. You don't know what you are stirring up—

POOTSIE Tell it to your maiden aunt! (*She looks in the bar for cigarettes.* BARON PFLUNGK, *still whispering to her, follows her into the bar. The others have come back from the kitchen, some of them with glasses, some of them smoking.* MOHRUNGEN *and* OLIVIA *in a subdued conversation come up to the door and disappear again.* HARRAS *comes in with* DIDDO *and* LAWRENCE. *Turns to the window and starts to pull the drapes*)

HARRAS Time to put the blackout drapes between us and the enemy fliers.

DIDDO What a shame! The twilight is so lovely.

HARRAS *L'heure macabre.*[6] Deep sea station.

LAWRENCE Yes, there's something of the aquarium about it.

HARRAS When it gets dark the house sinks like a diving bell. The air is deep sea water, dusky dim. Fluorescent-eyed fish swim by slowly. The sluggish beat of their fins wipes across the window. Soft mouths swallow our eyes and blow them to the surface in a swirl of bubbles. Our faces grow blind. We see with our fingertips, hear with our tongues, smell with our spines and breathe with our brains. The secret sense awakens, the primitive sense, the one that embraces all senses and has no limits, no borders—very close to madness.

DIDDO (*Has put her arm in his*) I've always wanted to play a madwoman. I don't know why. Perhaps to get rid of something that's trapped inside me, that might not come out otherwise. But maybe that has no place on the stage. Do you know *Danton's Death* by Buechner? (HARRAS *nods*) Sometimes when I'm walking down the street, I'm Lucille—They've murdered my lover—The hangman of the revolution stalks through the night—And suddenly I must step out of the darkness and call: "Long Live the King!" That's how I would like to die. Is that mad? (HARRAS *draws her close to him but does not answer*)

LAWRENCE I envy you Germans your word "Wahnsinn"—the mad sense. It's a poet's word, almost a holy word. Also "Leidenschaft"—the pain of passion. Also "Ehrfurcht"—the spirit of honor. "Sehnsucht"—the sickness of longing. "Begeisterung"—fullness of spirit.

HARRAS You know our language.

LAWRENCE (*Sadly*) I love Germany.

HARRAS Is it still worth being loved? In spite of everything?

LAWRENCE Yeah, or I wouldn't have hung around this long with my head in the lion's mouth. Tomorrow I may be rotting in a camp. On account of just that German mad sense—your madness.

HARRAS I'm sick of it. It's laid too many rotten eggs for us—the house of mad Siegfried, the insane delusions of grandeur. Oh, Buddy, how I long sometimes for a simple nation—for football players, mechanics, gum chewers. How sick I am of Significance, the Intoxication of Death, the demonic Block Warden, the split inner life, the Faustian Mail Carrier. Our half-culture has filled our bellies with metaphysics and our heads with intestinal gas. "The indigestible pulls us on down." We have become a nation of constipated public school teachers who exchanged the rod for the riding whip in order to disfigure the human face. Cloudchasers and slaves of death. A miserable nation.

LAWRENCE I love the Germans.

HARRAS Me too. To the point of hate. Just like an actor who loves and hates the character he plays, the role to which he has been sentenced—love and hate.

LAWRENCE That goes for everyone.

HARRAS Yes, we all act. We are hidden in roles and don't know their end. We don't even know their character. How much evil is in yourself? Ask the author. Is he crazy? Or a swindler? Should he be worshiped —or nailed to the cross?

DIDDO And did he at least write good parts for us in a bad play? Or the other way around? What are we acting anyway? Grand opera—comedy—tragedy?

HARRAS (*Smiling*) Everything together, I think, and probably just the second act, because the third will be more cataclysmic.

LAWRENCE Perhaps it is only a prelude—a Tragic Festival Overture.

HARRAS "Germany, an endless prologue." (*He pulls the blackout curtains and turns on the lights*)

OLIVIA (*In the kitchen door*) Diddo, for Heaven's sake, I must get to the theatre. In one hour the curtain goes up.

HARRAS No hysteria. You can still make it in a taxi.

OLIVIA But you can't get one.

HARRAS Korrianke has a friend in the West End garage who always manages to roll. (*He calls*) Korrianke!—Korrianke, Mrs. Geiss needs the wheelbarrow and I need the evening paper. I'm dying to find out what experiences I had at the Eastern Front.

OLIVIA Korrianke is an archangel. Without him we'd be all loused up. Get ready, little one, so we don't get into a mess. I'm sorry, Mr. von Mohrungen—it's time for the show. (*Turns back into the next room*)

HARRAS (*To* LAWRENCE) Do me a favor and leave Diddo and me alone for a minute. Hold the others off. Thanks. (LAWRENCE *nods, turns to* POOTSIE *and*

[6] The dark hour.

PFLUNGK *who are coming out of the bar, arguing softly.* HARRAS *takes his watch out of his pocket*) Now pretend I'm showing you something. Don't answer. Pay attention; perhaps I'm going to fall out of character. Maybe I'll break contract. Maybe I'll pull a trick on the author. I'm thinking of clearing out—via air, with no ticket. (DIDDO *nods emphatically and pretends to be listening to the watch.* HARRAS *goes on*) When and how I don't know yet. If it works— (*He interrupts himself*) careful, they're coming back.

DIDDO (*Almost without tone, under her breath*) It must work. It must.

HARRAS You hear? It's ticking again. It isn't wrecked, not by a long shot. (*Puts the watch back*)

DIDDO It'll last a hundred years in your pocket.

HARRAS (*Laughing*) If the seam doesn't burst.

(KORRIANKE *has appeared in the hall door holding newspapers in his hand. At the same time* OLIVIA *rushes in, followed by* MOHRUNGEN)

OLIVIA Taxi? That's what I call blitz-service. Let's cut the long farewell scenes. Come, little Diddo, put on your jacket.

KORRIANKE General—

HARRAS (*Looks at him*) What's that look for? What's the matter?

KORRIANKE Something's happened.

MOHRUNGEN (*Has stepped up to* KORRIANKE) Special edition? Black border? Did somebody— (*Has taken one of the papers and turns pale*) Dear God— (*Drops the paper*)

HARRAS (*Without moving—almost with certainty*) Eilers?

POOTSIE (*Has run up to* MOHRUNGEN, *picks up the paper, reads*) "—fatal accident—crash over the field—unexplained mechanical defect—in the plane of Colonel Friedrich Eilers. . . . (MOHRUNGEN *takes her arm*) It isn't possible. . . . (*She is silent, looks at* HARRAS)

HARRAS (*Through his teeth*) From the paper—no telephone call—no telegram.

POOTSIE (*Softly, affected*) Anne—could she know?

MOHRUNGEN (*Completely broken*) We must try to call. I will go there on the next train—

PFLUNGK (*Reading*) "The Fuehrer has ordered a State funeral." That will console her a little.

MOHRUNGEN I hardly think so. (POOTSIE *strokes his hand. He nods wretchedly*)

OLIVIA And now you are supposed to sing. I don't want to go on at all any more. . . .

MOHRUNGEN I suddenly feel terribly old.

HARRAS (*Changed, with cold voice*) Korrianke, take the big car. Make it fast. Drive to Oderbruch—he's sure to be at home now. Bring him here. I don't want to use the phone. Tell him to bring all the records he has on hand. We must work. Take the apartment key. Send it up before you park the car. Don't lose a minute. (KORRIANKE *stands at attention, then goes*)

MOHRUNGEN (*To* PFLUNGK) Can you take us to the hotel, Baron? I must pack. Where's Pootsie?

PFLUNGK I don't know. She must have gone ahead.

MOHRUNGEN (*Calls*) Pootsie!—Why does she run away now?

PFLUNGK (*Shrugs his shoulders*) She has her moods. Don't worry, I will bring her. I—I don't need to say how deeply I sympathize with you.

MOHRUNGEN (*Nods absently*) Yes, thank you. (*His eyes meet* HARRAS, *grow hard*) This won't end here. This case is going to be cleared up conclusively. And without any personal considerations whatsoever. (HARRAS *returns his look—bows silently*)

PFLUNGK (*Embarrassed*) Goodbye, General—Thanks for the hospitality.

HARRAS Oh, please, would you drop Mr. Lawrence off—at the American Embassy. It's on your way.

PFLUNGK Gladly, with pleasure.

LAWRENCE You think of everything. Good luck, Harry. (*Puts out his hand*)

HARRAS Good luck to you. Your bet is getting hotter, contemporary. Put a month's salary on it. (*Briefly presses his hand.* MOHRUNGEN, PFLUNGK, *and* LAWRENCE *go off.* OLIVIA *hesitates at the door. We hear the elevator.* HARRAS *to* DIDDO—*calmly and firmly*) Go to Vienna. Everything's changed now.

DIDDO Not for me. I'm not weak. I won't leave you—not now.

HARRAS (*Takes her hands*) You are always with me.

DIDDO How can I be—when I'm far away?

HARRAS Much more so than here. What's coming now I have to do alone.

DIDDO How will I hear from you?

HARRAS I can reach you more easily there. You can count on hearing from me. Here you would be watched. Or—worse. Will you promise me that you will go?

DIDDO I'll go.

OLIVIA (*Softly*) Come now, Diddo.

(DIDDO *tears herself loose, goes quickly with* OLIVIA. HARRAS *alone in the brightly lit room grabs the back of a chair with an unconscious movement, grips it with his hands, closes his eyes. When he opens them* POOTSIE *is in the door. He stares at her, loosens the grip of his hands*)

HARRAS Where did you come from? Who let you in?

POOTSIE (*Without shyness, but not frivolous*) Nobody. I hid in the closet till they were gone. I must speak with you, Harras. Alone.

HARRAS You picked the wrong moment. I have work to do. I haven't time to chit-chat.

POOTSIE I am not that stupid, Harry. We all put on a little act. You do too. We have a habit of over-playing in public and forget ourselves that we are doing it. Harry, things can't go on like this with you.

HARRAS What do you mean by that?

POOTSIE You know, this business about Eilers hits close. It gave me quite a jolt. Not only because of Anne and her children—He was a fine man, a little soft maybe. You're better, as far as material goes. Of course, they say every flier gets it sometime. It's part of the business. But you, why do you insist on smashing yourself up? It doesn't add up!

HARRAS Maybe it does to me. And anyway, Pootsie, what business is it of yours?

POOTSIE I can't stand watching it. And I don't want

to. There aren't that many real men in the world. You are a man. It's a crying shame about you. Little Hartmann, for example—that wasn't easy for me at all. I like him a lot—He's a dear boy. But what am I supposed to do with him? A "dear boy" isn't enough for me, no matter how decent he is. I want a real man who can get to the top. You could make it, Harry. You've got to make it.

HARRAS Make what? The honorary chairmanship of "Strength Through Joy" or a gold wall-plaque in the Reichswoman's Corps? Are you giving me the propaganda treatment? Get yourself a pimp.

POOTSIE Don't get sarcastic. I know all about your line. You don't have to put on your act for me. You're just plain stupid and stubborn if you don't join the crowd. You're no Jew and no Communist. You know you can't fight it. Don't be a fool! You have blood, race, spirit. You were born to rule, to grasp, to possess. You didn't seem to mind becoming a Nazi General. The glamour, the power, that suited you, didn't it? So why quit now? Well why don't you aim a little higher? You've got the stuff for it.

HARRAS Thanks.

POOTSIE Nonsense. Don't give me that old drivel about freedom, humanity—Whoever rules is free. There are only two parties in the world: the one on top and the one on the bottom. The ones on the bottom are wrong and don't deserve any better. That's reality. You belong at the top, Harry, the very top!

HARRAS (*Between his teeth*) "At the top of the highest mountain," hmmmm?

POOTSIE Yes, damn it all. I'll show you the world—You can only see it from the top! Look down. You're used to heights. Go ahead, look down at the others. Yes-men, sponges, jellyfish. And our big shots—Some of them are able men, but none of them are really big men. Goering—a conceited dumpling. Milch[7] and Kesselring—they're half-dead like my father—a collection for the wax museum. Himmler is smart but no soldier. If you only wanted to, you could make them all dance to your tune. Are you afraid of blood? Are you a dishrag? Haven't you any "instinct" any more? In one year you could be the greatest of 'em all—the power behind the Fuehrer. And remove anybody who doesn't please you. Power is life. Power is pleasure. Harry, just say the word. I'll make you real big!

HARRAS You'll make me real big! And why, if I may ask? What's it to you? What do you get out of it?

POOTSIE I like you. That's why. You know it anyway, so why shouldn't I admit it? I liked you right off. And Pootsie gets what she wants. You need a woman who shakes you up, pulls on the reins and gives you the spurs so you shoot over the finish line. You need me, Harry.

HARRAS (*With a touch of sympathy*) I must disillusion you, Pootsie. You're making a mistake. I'm the wrong man. Look for another. There are so many. I don't need anyone. And if I need someone, I'll look for her myself.

POOTSIE You just don't dare. Scared you'll burn your tongue. Knock it off, will you. The Good Shepherd with the little lamb in his arms—it doesn't suit you. Go look in the mirror. You're a carnivorous animal. You've got eyes like a hawk and fangs like a wolf. What do you want with that green lamb's lettuce? She'll go flat on you before you've taken a bite. She'll lag behind.

HARRAS Run along now, Pootsie. I've warned you enough.

POOTSIE It would be smarter if you let yourself be warned, Harras. Don't push me too far. You don't smuggle old Jews over the border unpunished just to play the Good Samaritan. No one has the right to do that, not even you. Whatever has been condemned to come down must come down—It's hands off or you'll get slapped. What do you care about a handful of Jews? They've been trying to be the salt of the earth long enough. Now they can swallow salt until their gullets dry up. You want to gulp along with them?

HARRAS (*Has looked at the desk, stares at her*) What's this? Stealing, blackmail, extortion?

POOTSIE I'm through talking. He who doesn't hear, must feel.

HARRAS (*Jumping to the wall, tears a heavy African whip down and starts toward her*) Then you hear! If you don't get out on the spot I'm going to pull this thing across your face, straight across, so you'll be marked as long as you vegetate. (*Raises his arm*)

POOTSIE (*Raising her arms, backs quickly to the door and stands there*) So—that's the kind you are? You coward. I'll teach you. You dirty little dog. You traitor. (*She backs out and slams the door*)

(HARRAS *stands for a moment breathing heavily, then throws the whip away. Clutches his throat as though he couldn't breathe. Quickly goes through the room to a light switch and turns off all the lights until it's completely dark. Then to the window, pulls back the drapes, opens the window wide. Looks out, breathing deeply. The room is filled from outside with a weak shimmer of light that becomes stronger. In the middle of the black window five fanned beams grow slowly in height and stand in the frame of the window like the fingers of a giant outstretched hand.* HARRAS *stands for a minute motionless, then pulls the drapes violently and reels drunkenly back into the room. We can't see him. He seems to have sunk into a chair or to the floor. His voice comes out of the depths*)

HARRAS Lord in Heaven. I am afraid. I am afraid. I am afraid— (*Falls silent. A door opens.* HARRAS *in the darkness jumps up, screams*) Halt! Don't move! Who's there? (*The light goes on,* HARRAS *at the switch, a gun in his hand*)

(ODERBRUCH *stands in the door with a briefcase under his arm. He's a man in his forties, slim, ash blond, with simple, clear features and nothing par-*

[7] Erhard Milch was an air force commander and member of the German general staff.

*ticularly remarkable about him. He is wearing the unornamented uniform of the special technical troops, with no decorations. As he comes nearer we notice that he limps a little, almost imperceptibly. His speech is brief, measured, sometimes a little halting—controlled and thoughtful*)

ODERBRUCH Did I frighten you? Korrianke gave me the key. (*Goes to the desk and puts down the briefcase and the keys*)

HARRAS Oderbruch! Thank God you're here. I guess I was a little hysterical. (*He laughs briefly*) I had turned off the lights to let some air in. I must be a little hysterical. You never know what's sneaking around in the dark these days. I always thought I had no nerves.

ODERBRUCH You get to feel that way if you have to sit on them day and night. But you have to give them the reins, once in a while, or they get hardmouthed and don't function any more as a warning system.

HARRAS It's no wonder I'm jumpy. Things have been a bit thick lately—You know about Eilers? (ODERBRUCH *nods*) Since when?

ODERBRUCH Korrianke just told me. No one said anything at the office.

HARRAS Yes, they kept it "quiet." Why? Like so many other things . . . why? When I look at your old briefcase and your face, then I know we won't be stumped for too long. Lucky you were home. Did I disturb you?

ODERBRUCH (*Smiling*) It's my Thursday.

HARRAS Oh, that's right. I didn't have the faintest idea what day it is. I'm sorry.

ODERBRUCH It doesn't matter at such a time. Otherwise I cling to it like eternal bliss. You need a hobby like that to take you completely away from everything.

HARRAS I know, it's your one and only vice. What was it this evening?

ODERBRUCH Schubert—C Major Quintet, with two cellos. It wasn't easy to dig up the second cello. There aren't that many cellists.

HARRAS Probably not many who would dare play with you—Isn't it horrible about Eilers? Anyone else I could get over it more easily.

ODERBRUCH He was my friend too.

HARRAS If, at least, it had happened in combat. But this way it's murder. Treacherous murder. Do you have any explanation? A clue? Why Eilers of all people?

ODERBRUCH It could just as well have been anybody else. The Squadron had a delivery of new planes, all tested, all inspected.

HARRAS We'll have to order all of them back. Not one of them can be allowed off the ground.

ODERBRUCH I have already issued the order, on my own, from home.

HARRAS Good. We'll have to trace this thing right into the factories if need be. But I don't know if it's any use. There's something behind it all. Eilers was in nobody's way. He was the best squadron leader. He was a party member. You don't really believe it was an accident?

ODERBRUCH Accidents do happen.

HARRAS Yes—and a life is wrecked. Not only that, also a home, also a family. All those things are being destroyed, pulverized from within and without. There are hardly any real families left. If you had seen those two together! It was enough to make a strong man cry. I was planning to spend Christmas with them. If it had gotten somebody like us two lone wolves, it wouldn't have been half as bad. Do you want a drink? (*Fills two glasses*)

ODERBRUCH Thanks. After work.

HARRAS Didn't you ever think of getting married?

ODERBRUCH It's hard to say. At first it wasn't possible financially. Later no longer the right time.

HARRAS Those aren't real reasons. Not if you really wanted to.

ODERBRUCH You know, I was supposed to be a priest once. (*Smiling*) Maybe that stuck to me.

HARRAS With me it was just the opposite. I didn't want to miss anything—and now it seems to me I missed the best. You shouldn't leave love for nice weather. You should build it up like a house. You should make a bulwark of love out of your life!

ODERBRUCH That bulwark has to stand on sure ground —clean ground.

HARRAS That's your conservative upbringing, your uncle, the Archbishop. Or do you really think differently? (*Looks at him questioningly.* ODERBRUCH *doesn't answer*) For me a sport plane would be enough for a beginning, or a trailer. Gypsy wedding. Migratory bird menage. If only the world weren't blocked with barbed wire—

ODERBRUCH You can fly over it.

HARRAS Not if it's inside. The invisible barbed wire. (*Lowers his voice*) I must confess something to you, Oderbruch. I have thought of flight, for good reasons. Now Eilers holds me back. If I had skipped I wouldn't have told you. This way, I feel better that you know. You suspected it anyway.

ODERBRUCH I thank you.

HARRAS Do you know where I've been these last two weeks? Or can you imagine?

ODERBRUCH I can imagine.

HARRAS Then you know what the stakes are. Eilers is dead. They've come for Hansen. I have to get to the bottom of this. I have to end it at any cost. You are the only man who can help me. Tell me the truth. Do you think we can find it. The truth?

ODERBRUCH It will come to light one day.

HARRAS One day!—I have only ten left. (ODERBRUCH *takes the glass that* HARRAS *filled before and empties it.* HARRAS *is watching him.* HARRAS *goes up to him*) Oderbruch—do you know something you're keeping from me? Do you suspect someone? Are you hiding anything? Don't spare me, for Heaven's sake! for truth's sake! Don't spare anyone! Do you know something?

ODERBRUCH (*Puts down his glass*) Nothing but facts.

HARRAS Facts—What do they mean?—What's behind them?

ODERBRUCH It will come to light.

HARRAS And if it's too late? What if it's pitch black and the power lines are down?

ODERBRUCH It's never too late for the truth.

HARRAS Your calmness, man—I wish it would grow on me like a beard. Sometimes I wonder why you don't wear one.

ODERBRUCH (*Laughs a little*) That would be too much mask.

HARRAS Yes—it's better to hide yourself behind a naked face.

ODERBRUCH (*Starts to open his briefcase, letting the lock click*) Here are the results of our investigations to date. Of course, without the latest incident.

HARRAS (*Slaps him on the shoulder*) Let's get at it. (*He turns on the working light*) Is that the analysis of the tests on materials?

ODERBRUCH (*Nods*) Here are tests number one: Normal aluminum weights. Messerschmidt—alloy percentage. Tests number two: Variations . . . Slide rule calculations. Decreased angle of incline. Tests number three: . . .

(HARRAS *is bent over the table, mumbling. Sirens wail outside and get louder. Distant flak fire, coming nearer with the sound of bombers*)

HARRAS (*Lifts his head*) The gentlemen from the River Thames. Do you want to go to the cellar, Oderbruch?

ODERBRUCH Why? What for?

HARRAS You're right. The enemy is here. (*Both bend over their work*)

*Curtain*

# Act Three

## Damnation

### Act Three Takes Place on General Harras' Last Day of Grace

*Technical office at a military airfield outside Berlin. Cold, square construction of steel, cement, and glass. Worktable with metal edges and corners. Sketches of plane models and weather maps on the walls. No pictures or any kind of ornamentation. A small vase with a faded bunch of violets is standing on the ledge of an electrical switchboard. In the corner, a small sofa made up as a bed but not slept in. Next to it a small open suitcase. In the background, high windows with a view of hangars, sheds, runways and the starting apron. The reddish light of an early winter morning falls into the room. The lights are still burning.* HARRAS *at the worktable in an unbuttoned military jacket. Next to him is a breakfast tray with a thermos bottle. The worktable is covered with records, papers, test materials, and measuring instruments.* KORRIANKE, *at the sofa, is taking the bedding off and putting it in the suitcase.*

HARRAS (*Picking up a piece of paper and toying with the pen*) What's the date, Korrianke?

KORRIANKE Saturday, December 6, 1941.

HARRAS December 6—St. Nicholas Day. Apples and nuts for all the good children. Whips for the bad ones.

KORRIANKE Not even a calendar in this broken down shack. I'm going to requisition one.

HARRAS Doesn't pay any more. (*He yawns, puts down the pen and lights a cigarette*)

KORRIANKE You didn't sleep again, General.

HARRAS No time. I wasn't tired. Say, when did Eilers go down?

KORRIANKE Thursday of last week. Ten days ago.

HARRAS Hmmmm! Then today is the delivery date. What's the situation like out there?

KORRIANKE Two Panzers[1] 'n front the main portals. SS Guard, Shock Troops. Must've moved in cover of darkness. They didn't want ta let me in a'tall. Exit and entrance by special pass only.

HARRAS Then we're as good as prisoners.

KORRIANKE Not quite, General.

HARRAS No, not quite. (*Takes up the pen*) December 6. Apples and nuts. Stupid. I can't write letters. (*Gets up, stretches*)

KORRIANKE (*Goes to the table, takes the thermos bottle*) All gone?

HARRAS All gone—Listen, Korriandoli; quick, before somebody comes! In case anything goes wrong—stop shaking your head. Of course it can go wrong. You know that. So without your funny faces now . . . in case something happens to me, you take a vacation and leave immediately for Vienna. I'll leave you enough money. So—she doesn't do anything foolish! Think of something—something she can stand. You're such a good story teller. Damn it, you know what I mean.

KORRIANKE I know, General.

HARRAS A service for a friend. (*The telephone rings. He picks up the receiver*) Yes, indeed. In five minutes. (*Hangs up. Speaks hastily*) And something else. Have you thought of what you're going to do—I mean, in case I can't use you anymore. You're not too old for them to stick you right at the front. Maybe you can move to "Dodgeburg" with one of my friends in the occupied countries. You know your way around. But caution, old man—pay attention. Look sharp, keep your mouth shut, et cetera. They don't forget. Don't take chances!

KORRIANKE No, General. In case of an event, I'm going to report myself into the infantry, next load going east.

HARRAS To the East? You must have rocks in your head!

[1] Tanks.

KORRIANKE Wanna bet I don't, General? I ain't selling this little head, not even for a coffee bean. To the East—on to the East! I've a pow'ful drive for it. In the East standing guard in the dead of night—(*Raises his hand*) *Tovarischitschi! Tovarischitschi!* I know how ta do that, all right.

HARRAS I don't think I have to worry about you.

KORRIANKE No, General. (*The telephone rings again*)

HARRAS (*Presses a button on the phone*) As for the rest—everything like we planned it. Clear? You'll get set and wait in any event—till dark.

KORRIANKE Till judgment day, General.

HARRAS Not that long, I hope! That's just how long it may be before we see each other again. And what are we going to say then, Korrianke?

KORRIANKE *Prosit's* what we're going to say. Shed 35? And we're off to buy chocolate bars in Switzerland. Easy as pie! (*Stares at* HARRAS, *frightened. Repeats slowly*) Easy as pie, General.

HARRAS (*At the telephone*) Well, what is it?

KORRIANKE You forgot "Cut it!"

HARRAS Excuse me. I'm a little absent-minded. (*Roars*) Cut it!

KORRIANKE (*At attention—swallowing*) Thanks, General. (*Goes off quickly*)

HARRAS (*At his desk, crumples the paper he was going to write on, throws it in the wastebasket. Turns off the light. Takes up the telephone, pushes a button*) Chief Engineer, please. Oderbruch? Slept any?—Well, so, so. No, nothing important. Always the same picture. Yes, interrogation of the two workmen. Send the detective in here—or—no, you come with them and stay. (*He buttons his jacket, looks at the door. In walk* ODERBRUCH *and a man in civilian clothes*)

DETECTIVE Morning, General. I brought the two birds over as you ordered. But you won't get nothin' out of them. They're a couple of hard nuts. Cross-examination, spotlights, intimate approach—nothing works with them. Our old-fashioned methods don't work in this kind of a deal. And I don't work with the new methods in any kind of deal.

HARRAS It's possible they are innocent and really don't know anything.

DETECTIVE Then God have mercy on them. Have you read my report?

HARRAS Yes. (*To* ODERBRUCH) These men are on the suspected list, aren't they?

ODERBRUCH Yes, whatever that means. They worked on a shift that handled the faulty planes. That's all we know.

HARRAS And why were these two fished out?

DETECTIVE One is an old Social Democrat, unpopular in the Worker's Front, a grumbler. Has made remarks on several occasions, for example: Dr. Ley[2] could kiss his . . . and so forth. The other is suspected of sympathizing with a secret Communist Youth Organization.

HARRAS That isn't exactly proof that they're mixed up in this affair.

[2] Robert Ley (1890-1945) was head of the Nazi Labor Front.

DETECTIVE No—not exactly proof. They deny everything, of course. And when you get tough, they switch to complete blackout.

HARRAS Do me a favor, Detective. Let us talk to them alone. We might just possibly get more results that way.

DETECTIVE (*Shrugs his shoulders*) I doubt it. But—as you wish, General. (*Turns to the door and gives an order*)

(*A guard brings* THE TWO WORKMEN *in and goes off with* THE DETECTIVE. *The two men are not handcuffed and are wearing their work clothes.* THE OLDER ONE, *around fifty, has a bony weathered face and graying hair.* THE YOUNGER *is thin and very pale. Both seem calm and look at the floor*)

HARRAS (*Observes them for a moment*) Would you like to sit down?

THE OLDER (*Without looking up*) Thanks. We would rather stand.

HARRAS Yes, I imagine you're tired of sitting. Walk up and down if you like. I'm going to refrain from offering you a cigarette on purpose. That's an old bully's trick to get a man to talk. But it would be easier to get started if you looked at me.

THE OLDER (*With a suggestion of a smile*) That can be arranged.

HARRAS Well now! I don't want to do any squeezing. I'm not your enemy. I don't consider you guilty until you have been proven guilty. And I don't want to lead you on to squeal on your friends, and so forth. I'd just like to give you one piece of advice—while we are alone.

(THE WORKMEN *look at him unmoved*)

HARRAS To begin with I would like to say that personally I don't give a damn about your private political opinions. I'm here not as a policeman or a government representative. This investigation is not for my amusement nor your harassment. I carry the responsibility for our planes and the security of our pilots, that's all. Sabotage occurred and I want to see to it that it stops—nothing else. Sooner or later it will be uncovered anyway—and then, under more unpleasant circumstances for all concerned. If you had confidence in me we could all improve our position. I mean that the way I say it.

(THE WORKMEN *look at him, silent*)

HARRAS I'm sure you know you're up the proverbial creek. (THE WORKMEN *are silent*) Whether justly or unjustly is not the point here. But, of course, you know what the score is. If they want to suspect somebody, they can always find something suspicious. And the less they find the tougher they get. As long as you are being detained for interrogation purposes nothing much is going to happen to you. If you end up in jail or the workhouse you'll be in good shape. I don't want to talk you into making something up. But if you had anything at all to do with this business I'd like to point out to you that there is a type of confession which doesn't incriminate anyone else and which doesn't doom you completely. It would bring an impossible situation to a temporary standstill. It might be your salvation. (THE WORKMEN *look at him, silent*) To put it bluntly, this type of statement could keep you out of a concentration camp. You know what that means. I don't want to rush you. Take your time. Think it over.

THE OLDER There is nothing to think over. We have nothing to say.

HARRAS I'll give you a clue. Did you ever hear—from an unknown source—that certain parts were delivered without passing through military inspection? If that were true, you would only be guilty of negligence.

(*Silence*)

HARRAS Or did you ever get the impression that planes produced by your shift were subject to some kind of unfamiliar manipulation before they were shipped out? Or after they had passed the test stations? (*Somewhat more slowly, softly and intently*) Take the test stations. They're not the responsibility of your fellow workers. They're under the state police. Do you think the faulty material was slipped in there? Have you made any kind of—observations? (THE WORKERS *remain unchanged*)

HARRAS (*Even more slowly*) If you would like to tell me anything confidentially that you don't want repeated, I will give you my word that I will not betray it. That goes for my chief engineer, too. Isn't my word good enough?

(THE OLDER WORKMAN *shrugs his shoulders almost unnoticeably*)

HARRAS (*Close to them*) That is my last question and my last try to save you. It's up to you whether you decide to believe me or not. If you want to talk, whatever you say can be between us. We could decide together what we put down on the record. Fix it up for you the best we can. Do you have anything to say to me?

THE OLDER No.

HARRAS (*Looks at* THE YOUNGER ONE. THE YOUNGER ONE *bites his lips and shakes his head.* HARRAS *looks at* ODERBRUCH) Do you want to add anything? Any questions? (ODERBRUCH, *who has stood motionless in the background, motions him off*) Then I'm afraid we have to give up. (*Hesitates a moment*) I'm sorry. For you, too. (THE WORKMEN *remain unchanged.* HARRAS *goes to the table and pushes a buzzer. Takes out his cigarette case*) Now, at least, I can offer you a cigarette.

THE OLDER Thanks. I don't smoke.

(THE YOUNGER ONE *takes a cigarette without a word.* HARRAS *gives him a light. He smokes greedily. There is a knock.* HARRAS *opens the door.* THE DETECTIVE *comes in. Behind him* DR. SCHMIDT-LAUSITZ *and an* SS GUARD. THE GUARD *remains standing in the door*)

DETECTIVE What did I tell you, General? A waste of time. Or am I wrong?

LAUSITZ (*To* HARRAS) Any results? Did you take down a statement, General?

HARRAS No. Nothing was said to warrant a statement.

LAUSITZ And what is your personal impression of these suspects?

HARRAS I'd say these people have nothing to do with the matter.

LAUSITZ Possible. We shall see. (*To* THE DETECTIVE) You can issue the release papers.

DETECTIVE You mean I'm no longer responsible for these men?

LAUSITZ No. We have other plans for them. (*He looks at* THE WORKERS, *waits a while.* THE WORKERS *look down.* THE YOUNGER ONE *smokes.* LAUSITZ *signals to* THE SS GUARD) You will take charge of the prisoners. They will be in protective custody for an indefinite period with special directives. Prepare them for deportation! (THE SS GUARD *takes a step forward.* THE YOUNGER WORKER *lets his cigarette drop, steps on it. He sways a little. His head drops to his chest.* THE OLDER ONE *looks at him.* LAUSITZ *has watched them. He steps up to* THE YOUNGER ONE) Perhaps you wish to make a statement? (THE YOUNGER ONE *lifts up his head. He is very pale. He meets the glance of* THE OLDER ONE, *straightens up, stands motionless—Long silence*) Take them away! (THE SS GUARD *goes off with* THE TWO WORKERS. THE DETECTIVE *follows.* LAUSITZ *closes the door behind them.* HARRAS *has turned away, stepped up to the window and looks out.* ODERBRUCH *remains unchanged at the desk*) Well, that ends that—at least as far as you're concerned, General. Unless—you have some other solution to the problem—through your material tests?

HARRAS (*Over his shoulder*) I'm still working on them.

LAUSITZ Not indefinitely. I am commissioned to deliver this official order to you.

HARRAS (*Puts out his hand without leaving the window.* LAUSITZ *goes up to him slowly and hands him a paper.* HARRAS *looks at it briefly, turns to* ODERBRUCH) The investigation committee expects a final report—by seven o'clock tonight. (*He puts the paper in his pocket and looks out the window again*)

LAUSITZ I will appear at the appointed hour to receive it in order to forward it to a higher office. In the meantime, I do not wish to disturb you in your work—

HARRAS (*Looking out at the airfield with tension—without paying any attention to* LAUSITZ) There she is. M41-1304. (ODERBRUCH *steps up to him. Both look out*)

LAUSITZ (*Following their glance*) What sort of plane is that—that's being rolled down the runway?

ODERBRUCH A Messerschmidt—the sister-ship of the plane in which Eilers crashed. That was M41-1303. It went through the same manufacturing process and was shipped out with the same delivery but to a different front. We had quite a bit of trouble getting it back unflown. The control papers were in order.

LAUSITZ And is the plane—defective?

ODERBRUCH We don't know yet. We can't find anything wrong with it on the ground. We want to try it out in the air. Perhaps it is all right.

LAUSITZ Can that be tried out—without danger?

ODERBRUCH No, not quite, but with a parachute.

HARRAS (*To* LAUSITZ, *sarcastically*) Would you like to risk a little test flight with me?

LAUSITZ Thank you, no. For a trip like that I would prefer a less daredevil pilot.

HARRAS Afraid I might fly to hell with you?

LAUSITZ It might appeal to you to challenge the devil to a round of poker in hope of out-bluffing him.

HARRAS You still have too high an opinion of me.

LAUSITZ No higher than you deserve—What is it? (A GUARD *has come in, goes to* LAUSITZ *and whispers*) No objections. (*To* HARRAS) A Lieutenant Hartmann from the Eilers Squadron would like to see you. He's on sick leave—wounded. Would you care to see him?

HARRAS Hartmann—Oh, yes, Hartmann! Naturally—gladly. (*To* ODERBRUCH) We can't do very much right now anyway. I will call you up when I've drafted the report. (LAUSITZ *and* ODERBRUCH *go off. Almost at the same time* HARTMANN *comes in, remains standing at the door and salutes with his left hand. His right arm is in a black sling.* HARRAS *is changed, refreshed*) Hartmann, come on in. Let me inspect you! I'm really happy to see you—and on your feet already!—Hup 2, 3, 4! I hear they got you—Where, exactly?

HARTMANN Over the north sector, between Schluesselburg and the north coast. But I brought back the plane.

HARRAS Bravo. But I meant your wound.

HARTMANN That's not important, although I don't know if I'll be able to fly again. Mig fire—in the elbow joint.

HARRAS Something like Hansen, but with him there were bone splinters—that's why his arm is stiff.

HARTMANN And how is Captain Hansen?

HARRAS At the moment he's away on orders. Why don't you sit down! When did you get out of the repair shop?

HARTMANN Two days ago. I tried to call the General's private number. The Ministry said the General was here on a special job. I hope I'm not disturbing the General—

HARRAS For Pete's sake, drop that "General" stuff. You make me feel like a war memorial!

HARTMANN I thought I could ask the General—could ask you for—something to do, General. I feel strong enough for light duty. I'm left-handed, you know, General.

HARRAS (*Laughs*) Untamable. I'll bet you'd go on duty with your toes. (*Looks at* HARTMANN) You should give yourself a little time. A few weeks relaxation would be smarter. You don't look exactly blooming. Gotten a little transparent. Even thinner. Even more serious.

HARTMANN I don't know, General. I don't feel like relaxing. I think I would recover faster if I had something to do.

HARRAS Always gotta be on the go, eh?

HARTMANN (*Laughs*) Could you prescribe something else?

HARRAS Still the sorrows of love?

HARTMANN (*Smiles unmoved*) No, General—It's funny, I'd almost forgotten that.

HARRAS Now I could say, "What did I tell you"—but I won't.

HARTMANN (*Serious again*) At that time—I didn't know yet—(*Hesitates.* HARRAS *is silent—waits*) At that time, I was—I felt myself—very well armed—as if I had armor-plate. I didn't know how much you can learn in a few weeks—even in one hour.

HARRAS You don't mean—your wound.

HARTMANN No. That was almost a salvation—for the moment. May I ask you a question, General?

HARRAS Sure. Go ahead.

HARTMANN It's not simple. First, I must explain—Have you really time for me, General?

HARRAS At the moment I wouldn't know of anything better to do with my time. That's the truth.

HARTMANN Maybe—it's always been like this—and I just didn't see it. Didn't want to see it. Maybe it's just been like this since the war. (*He speaks rapidly, hastily, like someone who wants to get rid of something that he doesn't want to admit to himself*) The atrocity stories you hear about—they are all true. They aren't just rumors of horrors. I saw it with my own eyes. And they are the same—the same boys who lived with me in the Hitler Youth. We were all inspired. We'd stay up at night and sing and talk about ideals, sacrifice, contribution, and about duty, about cleanliness. I had a school friend—he wouldn't have hurt a fly—He was shy, sensitive. Did he only act like that? I met him again in Lodz—I didn't know he was with the Extermination Commandos. He took me along. "It's going to be quite a show," he said. He came from Bavaria. That's what they say there. They shot at defenseless people as a joke, they laughed when the victims whimpered with fear—they—I can't say it, General. That isn't part of war or goals or ideals. There is no justification for what they did. A thing like that is simply infamous. General, I am asking you, will we all get to be like that? Could I get to be like that? Is there no defense against it?

HARRAS Civilization has tried for thousands of years to build a protective wall against inhumanity. But it can be demolished in less than one man's lifetime—I know that's no answer. You haven't asked me yet what you really want to know.

HARTMANN In the Hitler Youth they told us we were the crusading knights of a new age. The old Christian time was supposed to have had its two thousand years. The new one was to be constructed from our plan, an empire of strength and magnificence in this world. I believed all that. It filled me with enthusiasm. But how can a new thing become strong and good if it begins by unleashing the lowest and meanest in human beings? How can anyone stand life in this new age if it begins with straight murder?

HARRAS There is no such thing as a "new age." Time—is always the same—great, untouchable, without beginning or end. And yet, whenever a human being makes a fresh start in life then the world is created anew.

HARTMANN That night at the restaurant, General, you

said so many things. They have all been going around in my head like a tune—all these weeks. But something was missing. Perhaps you'll laugh at me. Do you believe in God?

HARRAS (*After a long pause*) I don't know. I never met Him. But that was my fault—I didn't want to meet Him. He would have made me face decisions that I would rather avoid. I believed in the "thinkable" and the "knowable"—in what you can test, discover and find. But the greatest invention of all time, I did not recognize. Its name is God, in many forms —always God. It is an invention of the human soul or rather a discovery, a revealed knowledge. That's why it is true. Man doesn't dream anything that isn't true or that won't come true. If he dreams God, then God exists. I don't know Him but I have looked the devil in the eye. That's how I know that there must be a God. He hid his face from me. You will meet Him.

HARTMANN Did you ever pray?

HARRAS Yes, I think so. When I was very happy.

HARTMANN Then you must have met Him. Most people only pray when they're afraid.

HARRAS I don't know. I didn't take his hand. I chose the other one. But you—if you're asking me—you may have faith in Him.

HARTMANN It is very hard to have faith.

HARRAS It has always been hard—for everybody who questioned. For your generation it is probably the hardest. You were born the day justice fell apart. But believe me—there is a justice. No guilt will be erased. No debt will be cancelled. No eel will slip through the net. And the feasts and celebrations follow the big haul. Believe, Hartmann—go ahead and believe confidently in divine justice! It will not betray you.

HARTMANN I would like to work near you, General, even if you don't have any time for me. If only I could be allowed to be of some small help to you. Can't you find something for me to do in your office? I've had a little technical training.

HARRAS Near me—that—will not be so easy. But we'll see what we can do. (*Goes to the telephone, pushes a buzzer*) Chief Engineer!—Oderbruch? You've been looking for a reliable co-worker, right? There is a young officer who is no longer on flight duty. Yes, he has some technical background. Sound him out. I'll send him over. If he's worth anything he can stay on trial. (*Hangs up*) You can report to the Chief Engineer! Room 9.

HARTMANN I thank you, General. For everything.

HARRAS Thanks for stopping in, Hartmann. You told me more than I told you. Now I must work. We'll see each other later. (*Gives him his hand.* HARTMANN *exits*)

(HARRAS *steps up to the window and looks out. Mumbles "M 41 1304." In the corridor outside we hear loud voices, steps and calls.* HARRAS *turns around and looks at the door. The door opens. A woman stands in the doorway. She is dressed all in black and wears a black veil over her face. An officer is trying to stand in her way*)

OFFICER Halt! Stand back! I must insist on seeing your pass—(*The woman lifts her veil*)

ANNE I am Mrs. Eilers.

OFFICER Oh—I beg your pardon. (*He exits*)

HARRAS (*Goes toward her with his hands outstretched*) Anne. How good of you to come. Almost the hardest part of these last few days has been that I didn't have time to take your hand.

ANNE I don't want your hand. (*She stands motionless, with her head high and a fixed, almost blank face*)

HARRAS (*Looks at her. Lets his hands drop. After a pause*) Why did you come?

ANNE (*Hard, toneless*) I demand an accounting.

HARRAS From me?

ANNE Eilers did not die in combat. He was murdered. You are his murderer.

HARRAS (*With difficulty, searching for the words*) Anne—I know how hard this has hit you. It's a terrible misfortune; perhaps it could have been prevented but not by anything I might have done. Do you really believe that I failed him or worse? What have they been telling you? Yes, I carry the technical responsibility. How heavily I feel that responsibility I can't tell you. What happened to him also happened to me. But I don't know, even now, whether it was really a crime—or a vicious, murderous accident.

ANNE An accident does not murder. I don't know what you're talking about. I have talked with nobody since it happened. But I haven't closed my eyes. It opened my eyes. (*She looks at him with large burning eyes*)

HARRAS What do you accuse me of, Anne. What did I do?

ANNE Nothing, that's what you've done. You didn't believe in what Eilers believed. But you let him die for it, die senselessly. You stood by and never did a thing to save him. That sin can never be forgiven.

HARRAS Could I have saved him by believing in what was false? Could you save him? Did you try? Or even—think of it?

ANNE I didn't think—as long as Freddie was alive. I had to believe with him. I had to stand by him with my heart. Now I know that he died for nothing. But you, Harras, you always knew. You could have saved him, if not for a better life then for a better death. You knew that you were sending him to a senseless death. You are still doing it with thousands of others every day. Your war is murder. His was sacrifice.

HARRAS It was the same war. (*To himself*) It will be the same death.

ANNE You have nothing in common with him, in life or death. Friedrich Eilers would never have gone into a war he didn't believe was just. He would never have killed a man without believing that he was doing it for a just cause. You kill without justice or belief for a cause that you hate and despise. You are a murderer. Eilers was a hero.

HARRAS Then everyone is a hero who doesn't know what he is dying for. Then everyone is a murderer who can't change the world, every ordinary mortal on this earth.

ANNE Only he who knows and doesn't acknowledge it.

HARRAS What does a man know? What *can* a man know? (*He turns away*)

ANNE (*Steps up behind him. Speaks almost in his ear*) Do you believe this war is just? You know that it is unjust. Then why do you let it happen? Why don't you acknowledge it? Do you believe our leadership is good? You know it is ruinous. Why do you watch it? You put on a great show of courage with your sarcasm and lukewarm doubt. What good is that to anybody? You are a part of the rottenness. You are guilty of every murder committed in the name of Germany. You stink of death!

HARRAS (*Turns around to her*) Why did you come?

ANNE (*Almost whispering*) Because he loved you. His blood screams for yours.

HARRAS But that is madness, Anne. That is madness. Don't you see what is happening in the world? The nations are in turmoil. Do I know where they will end? Can I stop them? Change their direction? Can I stem the avalanche with my shoulders? Turn a flood with my hand? What can one helpless man do, Anne, in a world which sweeps him along its terrible course and pounds the thunder of its violence into his ear with every heartbeat? Who am I to change it? (ANNE *is silent.* HARRAS *almost crying out*) Who am I anyway? Am I more than a man? Can I know more—do more—suffer more—than a man? I'm no God. (*He stares up. It seems as though he would collapse*)

ANNE (*Unmoved*) A God became a man to be able to suffer like a man, to comfort and console all who mourn and suffer. But you, you are not fit to utter His name. You have forfeited that too. You don't believe in that either.

HARRAS (*Again controlled. Close to her*) And who are you, Anne? You come like the black angel from the kingdom of death and demand reckoning. You accuse and you judge. You have known grief that can't be relieved, felt a tragedy for which there is no consolation. But don't you know that everyone builds his own fate? Can you stand before the Divine Judge yourself—and say: "I believed in the good, I didn't know about the bad"? How could you ever have believed in a cause whose stinking rottenness burned your nose every day? How could you two pretend to talk about ideals when you looked into the faces of those who represent them? Everybody knows what's going on in this country! Those who don't know—don't want to know. And the ones who still "believe" in the sham—are kidding themselves.

ANNE (*Calmly, sadly*) We did believe. We had to or we couldn't have lived. We knew what was happening. But we had to take it in the bargain. Eilers struggled hard with it. We thought that everything new had to be born in pain and blood. We thought there was a hard shell to be broken through and cast off. We had examples—we looked for parallels in history. There were other times when men were sacrificed—heretics burned—innocent children killed—horrors committed in times of upheaval, great revolutions when new worlds opened. Those who believed in the future had to make peace with it and think their way through it. That's over. Now there is nothing left for me.

HARRAS All those you looked to as examples, Anne, believed in human beings and a way of life which could exist better than anything they destroyed. But the men who are blowing up our world despise human beings. That is their only philosophy. They can't imagine anything better. They are the evil means for an evil purpose. To them people are conniving, repulsive, stupid, cowardly, a mob. So they treat them accordingly. Beat them, burn them, and slaughter them! That's what they believe in. And they are right. We are hopeless, depraved, pitiful, wretched tramps.

ANNE Eilers wasn't wretched. Eilers is dead.

HARRAS What are you going to say about me when I'm dead?

ANNE Nothing. (*Pulls down her veil and exits*)

HARRAS Nothing. It checks. (*Slowly goes to the window and looks out*)

*Short Blackout*

*Distant drum music until the stage lights up for the last scene. The same room, reddish light from outside as at the beginning of the act, only deeper, warmer, as in the evening. The drums go on for a minute, then fanfares of a march for presenting arms.* HARRAS *is at the window as before.* ODERBRUCH *stands at the table reading a paper*

HARRAS Why the big blow?

ODERBRUCH Replacements moving out. Fresh young troops.

HARRAS At least this mess lets me out of having to give them a pep-talk. Did you read the report through? Correct?

ODERBRUCH It doesn't seem as though any of the known facts are missing.

HARRAS In other words: Everything is missing. Empty pages—You'll have to countersign.

ODERBRUCH You haven't signed yet yourself. (*Dips his pen*)

HARRAS Not yet—I can't tear myself away from this window. (*Opens one section of the window*) Not much of a view. Sand pines—flat earth and a thin sugar sprinkling of snow. Frost on the hangars. Clear sky. Above the haze, the sky is clear, and the air tastes like exhaust fumes, like grease, oil, and pine bark. A cold landscape. More like a work area—really just a lot. That's it! Let's go to the mountains for hunting—to the rolling hills for love—to the ocean for dreaming. For work, report here where plan and result cover each other. Landscape and construction; that's how I picture hell: steel, cement, aluminum, rubber, India rubber—durable materials, solid construction. Nothing artful, nothing artificial—but well made. Exact and generous, exciting and calming at the same time. Like the solution of a geometric problem. Damned solid and extremely fantastic. Buzzing, purring, shaking with imagination. Is the form of a fugue sober? Abstract? Cold, but certainly not lifeless. And when Bach composes it, then it grows heavenly wings. (*Closes the window*) Now it's getting cold. (ODERBRUCH *stands in the same spot and looks at* HARRAS. HARRAS *goes to the table*) Should I sign it now? I can sign it. I can also not sign it. It's all the same. It won't change a thing. The one thing that now seems fairly certain to me isn't in there.

ODERBRUCH (*With controlled suspense*) What "one thing"?

HARRAS (*Looks at him, hesitates a moment*) I'm almost certain that our friends, the Gestapo, don't know anything. On that point I was on the wrong track. They are hunting in the dark just like we are, hoping I'd turn up something. That's what they are waiting for up to this very moment. (*Hesitates again with a searching glance at* ODERBRUCH) Otherwise, why should they wait? The case against me is ready. Some dame who "loves me" has supplied them with plenty of material. But they're holding out this "last minute chance." They're holding out the grand opportunity of rehabilitation at the edge of the knife, hoping to learn something they don't know. Too bad I can't use it. No miracles will occur. Look in here. (*With a quick movement he opens a drawer and takes out a pistol. Grins*) Schmidt-Lausitz must have slipped it in here. It's my own. I had to hand it in. Tactful invitation to the dance. Gentleman's exit. How considerate! But I'm not going to do them that favor. The one good point in the situation is that now that dog doesn't dare come in here anymore. He has good reason too. It might not agree with him. And if he sends ten bullies ahead, five will have to bite the dust. This is no pigeon roost. (HARRAS *pockets the revolver.* ODERBRUCH *looks at him and moistens his lips*) I don't really care, but I'm not quite ready. It's a disgusting feeling to move out of a room without cleaning up. Oderbruch, I know I'm very close to the solution. Skin-close. Arm's length. I feel it—I sense it—with every nerve. It is only a thought—that stands in the way.

ODERBRUCH (*With emphasis*) Why don't you think it, General Harras?

HARRAS (*Looks at him a long time. Both are very pale. He speaks softly, deliberately*) Oderbruch. If I swear by a sacred oath, not by my honor, not as a general, officer, soldier, but as the man you know, the man with whom you flew for twelve years and as a man in his last hour, I swear to you that nothing you say will ever seep out of these four walls, nothing will ever cross this threshold that either of us may say now. Oderbruch, do you want to talk? (ODERBRUCH *is silent.* HARRAS *close to him*) The truth, Oderbruch! The truth! (*Stares into his eyes.* ODERBRUCH *returns his look and nods*) You, Oderbruch?

ODERBRUCH (*Almost toneless*) We.

(HARRAS *takes a deep breath and wipes the perspiration from his face. After a pause, speaks quietly*)

HARRAS Who is "We"? Who are the others?

ODERBRUCH We have no names.

HARRAS Don't you trust me now either? Who are you?

ODERBRUCH I said it. We fight, unknown, unnamed. We know about each other, but we hardly know each other. We have no names, only—a goal! And an enemy.

HARRAS Was Eilers the enemy? I thought—he was your friend?

ODERBRUCH I had none better. Outside of you, General.

HARRAS Why do you strike us out of the dark, out of ambush? Why do you hit us—instead of the enemy?

ODERBRUCH You are Hitler's weapon with which he can win. And if he wins, Harras—if Germany wins this war—then Germany is lost. Then the world is lost.

HARRAS Have you thought what defeat means? Foreign domination? New force? New subjugations?

ODERBRUCH There is no subjugation that would not be liberation—for our people.

HARRAS Is there really no other way to free Germany?

ODERBRUCH Do you know another way?

HARRAS If I knew it—then millions would know it.

ODERBRUCH There's your answer. There is no other way. We need the defeat—We must help it with our own hands. Only then can we rise up again, cleansed.

HARRAS Defeat—that is certain. Resurrection—is a dream.

ODERBRUCH No, it's a law of life, the one like the other. Both equally hard. Both written in blood.

HARRAS With the blood of friends?

ODERBRUCH Also with our own.

HARRAS Explain this thing to me, Oderbruch! Help me to understand it. How did you get to this point? You were non-political. You liked technology. You made music. What came over you?

ODERBRUCH What comes over anyone? Shame.

HARRAS Don't evade me, Oderbruch! Don't feed me with empty words. Tell me everything! How did you come to this point?

ODERBRUCH There isn't much to say. What came over me? You know my story. Family, tradition, career—it all collapsed when I was young. I became an apprentice, a mechanic. I went up. An accident threw me back. I went down. It was always very hard—until the evil came to power. Then, it went better. (*Smiling*) When our state went to the devil—I became a state employee. That's how it was for thousands in Hitler's empire. It is the career of one of his people.

HARRAS And—what happened?

ODERBRUCH Nothing that I can pin-point—No personal reason. No—human explanation. None of my brothers died in a concentration camp. I loved no Jewish girl. No friend of mine was hunted out of the country. I didn't know anyone who fell on June 30th.[3] But one day I was ashamed that I was German. Since then—I can't rest—till it's over.

HARRAS And the others?

[3] The ruthless and bloody purge of military and political leaders on June 30, 1934 was a turning point in Hitler's seizure of power.

ODERBRUCH Some came out of shame. Others were driven by anger or hate. Some because they loved their homeland—Many because they loved their work or the idea of freedom and the freedom of their brothers. But all—even those who hate irreconcilably—came because they loved something more than themselves. And there is no one among us who didn't come on his own.

HARRAS How many?

ODERBRUCH I don't know. We have no way to count. We are becoming fewer instead of more. Many disappear and never reappear. The two men today—I had never seen them before. They didn't know me. But I knew they belonged to us. (HARRAS *listens quietly, his face frozen*)

HARRAS What is your goal? What's the strategy? What is your immediate objective?

ODERBRUCH Destruction, a bitter solution, but the only one left us. We cannot stop for our friends. We can't stop to ask where a man's heart is, Harras, only where he stands. We don't stop for ourselves. We will all fall.

HARRAS That means—it is for nothing. Meaningless slaughter.

ODERBRUCH Not meaningless. Not for nothing. We know what for.

HARRAS What good is that—if you rot? What does that change if you get buried? Martyred, burned, and forgotten?

ODERBRUCH (*After a pause*) Gregory the Great said: "The martyr alone is nothing, but he who knows why he suffers, his testimony is stronger than death." We know why.

HARRAS (*Lurking, dangerous*) And you believe—I'm going to let myself be slaughtered with the others? Why me? I don't know why. I am alone. I didn't come by myself. Am I supposed to fold my hands and say, "Amen," when my life is at stake— (*Turns away and goes to the window*)

ODERBRUCH (*Softly*) Your soul is at stake.

HARRAS (*Wheels around*) And what if I don't have a soul? What if I wanted to sell it? A second time? Who told you that I won't betray you to save my own skin? Who told you that?

ODERBRUCH You swore by an oath, General Harras.

HARRAS (*Starts toward him*) This is the hour of the broken word, the day of perjury, the day of false oaths. It pays better than loyalty. Should I spare your life because you sacrifice mine? Perhaps I have a great need to go on living? Perhaps someone needs me? Perhaps someone waits for me? Who are you to think I will accept your verdict without defending myself? How dare you put your life in my hands? And the lives of all your friends too?!

ODERBRUCH Because in this hour you are one of us. You do not betray what you believe.

HARRAS (*After a pause—simply*) That was the signature. I accept. Too bad. My physical heart would have made it for a couple of decades more. (*He goes to the telephone and pushes a buzzer.* ODERBRUCH *leans against the table, pale, as if exhausted*) Commando guard! Dr. Schmidt-Lausitz! Harras speaking! Your case will be settled in ten minutes. Then you can come down for my reports. (*Puts the telephone down, takes it up again*) Chief Engineer's office. Ask Lieutenant Hartmann to come in please. (*Hangs up, turns to* ODERBRUCH, *speaks measuredly, almost dreamily*) Tell me one more thing, Oderbruch. What is it that you love more than yourselves? What do you believe in, what do you hope for so much that you defy Nero and his gladiators? Is it Heaven's mercy? Is it justice on earth?

ODERBRUCH Both in one. It is eternal justice.

HARRAS What is eternal justice?

ODERBRUCH Justice is the uncompromising ruling law to which spirit, nature and life are subservient. When it is fulfilled—it is called freedom.

HARRAS (*Looks at him, nods*) One more thing, Oderbruch. What kind of songs do you people sing? Are they the old songs that died long ago? Songs of unfulfilled hope, of despairing longing? After the day of fame? The last battle? The sun that never rises? What kind of songs do you sing?

ODERBRUCH One doesn't sing in the catacombs.

HARRAS There is no victory without a song.

ODERBRUCH We know we won't see the victory. But those who follow us, they will have their own songs.

HARRAS What kind of songs, Oderbruch?

ODERBRUCH New songs. Human songs, divine songs.

HARRAS Thank you. I know enough now. (*He takes the pen and signs the report. Hands it to* ODERBRUCH) Here. You'd better sign. I'd rather have everything in order. That's better for you, too. I must ask you to forgive me, Oderbruch. For one moment—one bad moment—I doubted you. Now I feel better. (*Briefly presses* ODERBRUCH's *hand, goes to the wall, takes down his flying jacket and his old helmet and puts them on*)

ODERBRUCH What do you plan to do?

HARRAS (*Grins*) Exit. My own way.

ODERBRUCH What are you going to do, General Harras? What's in your mind?

HARRAS Ever hear about a divine judgment?

ODERBRUCH What do you mean by that?

HARRAS An experiment. I have always liked to experiment.

ODERBRUCH All the exits are guarded.

HARRAS Except one. (*He points to the window*)

ODERBRUCH Yes, the direct one from this room to the airfield. But the guards are there.

HARRAS They don't scare me.

ODERBRUCH What are you going to do, Harras? (HARRAS *smiles, almost gaily, lights a cigarette.* ODERBRUCH *in a sudden wave of emotion*) General Harras—if you wait another ten minutes—until it's dark—We could get to hangar 35 without being seen. I'll help you start the engine. I'll get out of it somehow afterwards. If we make it quick we can get through.

HARRAS (*Casually, a little ironic*) I think the verdict is written in blood. (*Turns to a small door next to the window*)

ODERBRUCH (*Steps between him and the door*) I always hoped it would come to this talk. It's changed a lot of things. It isn't your death we need, Harras. You could do a lot of good abroad, in another country, General Harras. You could be of more use alive, General Harras, if you only wanted to. I have an address in Switzerland—

HARRAS (*Shakes his head, unperturbed*) Too late, my friend. I'm no good anymore for that type of thing. I've been the Devil's General on earth too long. I'm going to fly an advance mission for him in hell too—in preparation for his imminent arrival. Reconnaissance. Don't give up now, Oderbruch. You were right about everything. Keep your gun clean and hit the root first, then the crown. (*Bends over to him, softly, with almost a smile*) Besides, Korrianke is waiting in hangar 35, ready to go. I can still take that way out in case I think of it. But mercy? Naw, can't use it. (*There is a knock at the door*) Who's there?

HARTMANN You called for me, General?

HARRAS Yes, Hartmann, my boy. Lucky I've got another chance to see you. I have to rush off for an indefinite period. I want you to stay with Oderbruch. He will explain all the details to you. All of them, Oderbruch! (*Hesitates a moment, as if something occurred to him*) Tell me, Hartmann, do you have a watch?

HARTMANN Yes—a wrist watch with a luminous dial.

HARRAS Let's trade! Take mine for yours. (*Takes the wrist watch from* HARTMANN'S *left wrist and gives the old watch from his pocket to* HARTMANN) It isn't a very good deal for you, but it's durable. If it stops you hit it against the back of your head! See, like this. Then it'll run again. Don't lose it. (*Presses it into* HARTMANN'S *hand*) Souvenir. (*Turns, goes to the small side door, opens it a little and looks out*) Hmmmm! Light north wind. Smells of the sea. Good take off weather . . . for the R.A.F. Duck, children—and don't let them get you. (*He goes quickly,* ODERBRUCH *runs to the window, stares out*)

HARTMANN (*Follows to the window*) Is he flying to the front?

ODERBRUCH (*Pale, almost entreating*) Hangar 35—

HARTMANN Where is hangar 35?

ODERBRUCH (*Tears open the window, leans out*) He isn't going there—he—he's going the other way.

HARTMANN What kind of plane is that he's going to?

ODERBRUCH (*Almost mechanically*) M 41 1304. (*Shouts are heard outside. A few shots.* HARRAS' *voice is heard in a short, wild laugh. The roar of engines starting fills the room*) He's climbing . . . (*The engine noise gets louder and louder, drowning out the shouting and a few more shots*) They can't hit him—he's climbing—he'll get through. (*He and* HARTMANN, *close together by the window, stare upwards*)

HARTMANN There! (*He grabs* ODERBRUCH'S *arm. Then, he covers his face with his hands. The sound of the engine has suddenly ceased. Dead silence*)

ODERBRUCH (*Softly, after a pause*) Our Father, which art in Heaven . . . (HARTMANN'S *voice joins his, sobbing. The door opens.* SCHMIDT-LAUSITZ *runs in and rushes to the telephone*)

LAUSITZ Main Headquarters? The case is closed. Very smoothly. Perfect. General Harras was killed accidentally a few minutes ago, in the performance of his duties to the Fuehrer and the Third Reich. On a test flight. Yes, indeed. State funeral, with full military honors.

*Curtain*

# Thornton Wilder

## (1897-      )

In 1957 Wilder described himself as "not an innovator but a rediscoverer of forgotten goods and I hope a remover of obtrusive bric-a-brac." To playgoers who recall the delightful shock provided by their first experience of the Stage Manager setting the scenery-less *Our Town* or the flying flats and baby dinosaur of *The Skin of Our Teeth,* Wilder's distinction between "innovator" and "rediscoverer of forgotten goods" may be surprising. To many Americans he remains the innovator *par excellence* because of his removal of the "bric-a-brac" of realistic theatre as well as because of his success in locating the center of eternity in the daily events of human existence.

Out of the widest range of learning any American dramatist has brought to the composition of plays, Wilder has made viable a view of life and drama at once eclectic and individualistic. From the central documents of metaphysics and aesthetics, of ethics and history, of theology and psychology, he has fashioned a vision of man which, in both its coherence and its derivativeness, most nearly resembles that of a Renaissance Humanist. Indefatigable as a traveler, avid as a theatregoer, zestful as occasional actor (usually as the Stage Manager in *Our Town*), he has friends among the century's most creative figures in philosophy and the arts. He can speak of Sunday afternoons with Freud in Grinzing as easily as he can impart the wisdom of his close friend, Gertrude Stein. His plays, which—considering his fame—are remarkably few, have been produced throughout the world at moments in history when his humanism has had extraordinary impact: *The Skin of Our Teeth,* his sweet-and-sour tribute to mankind's powers of endurance, opened in 1942 as Americans (including Wilder) threw their energies into World War II, and it was playing in London and Germany at the war's end. In the postwar years, he has continued—in later plays such as his *Alcestiad* (or *A Life in the Sun*)—to probe man's relation to the universe, while his earlier plays continue to interpret America to the world. In the Age of Specialization and Iron Curtains, he is that rarity, the Universal Man.

Wilder was born April 17, 1897, in Madison, Wisconsin, to parents who placed a very high value on learning and religious training. His "very strict Calvinistic" father combined, as owner-editor of a newspaper, strong interests in economics, in which he had taken a doctorate at Yale, and politics, in which he took his views from Theodore Roosevelt. From 1905 to 1909, while his father was consul general in Shanghai and Hong Kong, Wilder attended a missionary school in China. He completed high school in California, then studied classics for two years at Oberlin College and later at Yale, from which—with time out for Coast Artillery service late in World War I—he graduated in 1920. After a year studying archaeology and art in Rome, he became a teacher, at first in New Jersey at the Lawrenceville School (1921-1928), later at the University of Chicago (1931-1936, and 1941). Although over-age when America entered World War II, Wilder sought a military assignment: from 1942 to 1945, he served in Air Force Intelligence in the United States, North Africa, and Italy. Since 1945, except for a brief return to the academic world to give the Charles Eliot Norton Lectures at Harvard in 1950-1951, Wilder has devoted himself to writing and traveling.

Before he entered Oberlin, Wilder was writing three-minute, usually three-character, plays, sixteen of which he chose to include in *The Angel That Troubled the Waters* (1928). In his Foreword, Wilder recalled his literary beginnings ("It is a discouraging business to be an author at sixteen . . . all aspiration and no fulfillment") and offered an apologia for didacticism. In one of these playlets, Mozart unsuccessfully begs Death (as Gray Steward) to let him finish his Requiem; in another, Shelley, expounding on Platonic essences in art, claims Ibsen's *Master Builder* as his own "Death of a Centaur," the poem he was planning on the day he drowned. Other characters include Our Lord, Christ, Satan, St. Francis, and Childe Roland, moving through "drifting violet mists" or viewing "the clockwork of the skies," only occasionally touching down in familiar reality. For the most part unactable, these parables foreshadow the abstract thematics and impeccable style of his later work.

Wilder's first full-length play, the four-act *The Trumpet Shall Sound,* appeared serially late in 1919 in the *Yale Literary Magazine.* It resembles an ultramundane combination of Shakespeare's *Measure for Measure* and Jonson's *The Alchemist*: a master (God) tests the mettle of his servants (Angels) by leaving his house (Heaven) briefly in their charge. It was given a laboratory production in 1926, the year Wilder's first novel, *The Cabala,* appeared. In 1928 Wilder won his first Pulitzer Prize for *The Bridge of San Luis Rey,* a complex study of destiny manifest in all its mysteries in eighteenth-century Peru. Publication in 1930 of his third novel, *The*

*Woman of Andros* (derived in part from Menander via Terence and even more remote in setting than its predecessors), moved the Marxist critic, Michael Gold, to attack Wilder for avoiding bitter realities of American life. Wilder was stoutly defended, but Gold's labels ("Prophet of the Genteel Christ" and "This Emily Post of culture") remained to tarnish Wilder's reputation in the 1930's when "social," rather than "cosmic," significance was the yardstick by which artistic stature was being measured.

Since 1930 Wilder has written two highly valued novels (*Heaven's My Destination,* 1935, and *The Ides of March,* 1948), but he has preferred to concentrate on theatre. Wearied by realism, Wilder determined to use the stage to capture "not verisimilitude but reality." From 1928 to 1930 he studied the experimentalist drama flourishing in European theatre and grounded his theoretical knowledge of world drama's full storehouse of theatrical conventions on a more practical base. He explored theatricalist dramaturgy by analyzing productions of Strindberg's anti-naturalism (long familiar to Wilder on the printed page), Pirandello, the Expressionists, and Obey and Cocteau who, with directors like Copeau and Pitoëff, were creating a "poetry of the theatre." To restore drama to its status as festival and communal ritual, he resolved to shake up a theatre he felt had become "evasive" and "soothing."

The first results of this determination appeared in *The Long Christmas Dinner and Other Plays* (1931). Three of the six one-acts in this collection show Wilder's mastery of the realistic mode he hoped to supplant. The others, finger-exercises for *Our Town* and *The Skin of Our Teeth,* were, as Wilder describes them, experiments in the manipulation of time and space: "In *The Happy Journey to Trenton and Camden,* four kitchen chairs represent an automobile and a family travels seventy miles in twenty minutes. Ninety years go by in *The Long Christmas Dinner*. In *Pullman Car Hiawatha,* some more plain chairs serve as berths and we hear the very vital statistics of the towns and fields that passengers are traversing; we hear their thoughts; we even hear the planets over their heads." In the last of these, he developed a device important to the success of *Our Town*: he restored to drama the narrator-chorus "with his point of view, his powers of analyzing the behavior of the characters, his ability to interfere and supply further facts about the past, about simultaneous actions not visible on the stage, and above *all* his function of pointing the moral and emphasizing the significance of the action." Taken together, these short plays are a storehouse of rediscovered goods from which he borrowed freely. They also show a "paleface" Wilder emerging as a "redskin" and discovering America in the twentieth century.

Wilder has adapted three widely varying plays for American production: Obey's theatricalist *Le viol de Lucrèce,* the realist *A Doll's House* (with Nora closing the door with far more finality than Ibsen indicated), and Sartre's *Morts sans sépulture* (retitled *The Victors*), a drama attractive to Wilder in its existentialism and portrayal of French Resistance fighters. In his own works, Wilder may be seen as a gifted adaptor-translator who has evoked commentary which, heavy with emphasis on sources, resembles the traditional scholarly introduction to a Shakespearean play. *The Bridge of San Luis Rey* is under debt to Mérimée and Conrad; Joyce's *Finnegans Wake,* as two Joycean scholars angrily demonstrated in 1942, is the primary source of *The Skin of Our Teeth*; Wilder's most recent play (*A Life in the Sun*) is based, like T. S. Eliot's *The Cocktail Party,* on Euripides' *Alcestis.* In its *direct* lineage *The Matchmaker* includes at least his own earlier *Merchant of Yonkers* (1938), in its turn freely adapted and gentled-down from *Einen Jux will er sich machen* (*Out for a Good Time*), a cynical comedy adapted (1842) by the Austrian, Johann Nestroy, from John Oxenham's *A Day Well Spent,* a London success of 1835. As with Shakespeare, comparison of Wilder's works with his sources leads to greater respect for the transforming artist. Dolly Levi, his wild-and-woolly matchmaker, is a hilarious original Wilder created in order to lighten his source's tone; however much else he borrowed from Joyce, Wilder did not find his brilliant mistress of ceremonies, Lilith-Lily Sabina-Miss Somerset, anywhere but in his own ruminations about the degree of audience involvement appropriate to *The Skin of Our Teeth.*

Neither so experimental nor so cosmic as *Our Town* and *The Skin of Our Teeth,* the better-known plays which in 1938 and 1943 brought Wilder his later Pulitzer awards, *The Matchmaker* was written just after *Our Town* made Grover's Corners, New Hampshire, the best-known village in the universe and the Mind of God. The philosophical affinity between the two plays is clear in the extent to which Wilder's description of *Our Town* fits both plays: "It is an attempt to find a value above all price for the smallest events in our daily life." *The Matchmaker*'s experimentalism is confined to testing the serviceability of the presentational aside and the adaptability of realistic settings to a farce filled with sudden disappearances, disguises, chases, mistaken identities—none of which would be possible on *Our Town's* bare stage.

The only serious charge brought against *The Skin of Our Teeth* and *Our Town* concerns the jarring juxtaposition of comedy and an essentially tragic view of man. Wilder himself has described how *Our Town*'s third act, centered on the eternity of death, evokes mixed reactions: "Many thank me for the 'comfort' they found in the last act of *Our Town*; others tell me that it is a desolating picture of our limitation to 'realize' life—almost too sad to endure." As a genre painting affectionately conceived and as a plea for "a fuller, freer participation in life," *The Matchmaker* is *Our Town* with its darker corners flooded with sunshine; the satire, even of Vandergelder's theory of profit, is too mild to be taken very seriously. In *Our Town* and *The Skin of Our Teeth,* Wilder paid tribute to the eternally recurrent powers of mankind to endure through the community and the family. In *The Matchmaker,* using every popular turn of classical comedy, Wilder paid tribute to mankind's powers to enjoy life through the exercise of the comic spirit.

# THE MATCHMAKER

## *A Farce in Four Acts*

### CHARACTERS

HORACE VANDERGELDER, *a merchant of Yonkers, New York*

CORNELIUS HACKL, BARNABY TUCKER, MALACHI STACK — *clerks in his store*

AMBROSE KEMPER, *an artist*

JOE SCANLON, *a barber*

RUDOLPH, AUGUST — *waiters*

A CABMAN

MRS. DOLLY LEVI, MISS FLORA VAN HUYSEN — *friends of Vandergelder's late wife*

MRS. IRENE MOLLOY, *a milliner*

MINNIE FAY, *her assistant*

ERMENGARDE, *Vandergelder's niece*

GERTRUDE, *Vandergelder's housekeeper*

MISS VAN HUYSEN'S COOK

ACT ONE *Vandergelder's house in Yonkers, New York.*

ACT TWO *Mrs. Molloy's hat shop, New York.*

ACT THREE *The Harmonia Gardens Restaurant on the Battery, New York.*

ACT FOUR *Miss Van Huysen's house, New York.*

TIME The early 80's.

This play is based upon a comedy by Johann Nestroy, *Einen Jux will er sich machen* (Vienna, 1842), which was in turn based upon an English original, *A Day Well Spent* (London, 1835) by John Oxenford.

## Act One

*Living room of Mr. Vandergelder's house, over his hay, feed, and provision store in Yonkers, fifteen miles north of New York City. Articles from the store have overflowed into this room; it has not been cleaned for a long time and is in some disorder, but it is not sordid or gloomy.*

*There are three entrances. One at the center back leads into the principal rooms of the house. One on the back right (all the directions are from the point of view of the actors) opens on steps which descend to the street door. One on the left leads to Ermengarde's room.*

*In the center of the room is a trap door; below it is a ladder descending to the store below.*

*Behind the trap door and to the left of it is a tall accountant's desk; to the left of it is an old-fashioned stove with a stovepipe going up into the ceiling. Before the desk is a tall stool. On the right of the stage is a table with some chairs about it.*

*Mr. Vandergelder's Gladstone bag, packed for a journey, is beside the desk.*

*It is early morning.*

VANDERGELDER, *sixty, choleric, vain and sly, wears a soiled dressing gown. He is seated with a towel about his neck, in a chair beside the desk, being shaved by* JOE SCANLON. VANDERGELDER *is smoking a cigar and holding a hand mirror.* AMBROSE KEMPER *is angrily striding about the room.*

VANDERGELDER (*Loudly*) I tell you for the hundredth time you will never marry my niece.

AMBROSE (*Thirty; dressed as an "artist"*) And I tell you for the thousandth time that I will marry your niece; and right soon, too.

VANDERGELDER Never!

AMBROSE Your niece is of age, Mr. Vandergelder. Your niece has consented to marry me. This is a free country, Mr. Vandergelder—not a private kingdom of your own.

VANDERGELDER There are no free countries for fools, Mr. Kemper. Thank you for the honor of your visit —good morning.

JOE (*Fifty; lanky, mass of gray hair falling into his eyes*) Mr. Vandergelder, will you please sit still one minute? If I cut your throat it'll be practically unintentional.

VANDERGELDER Ermengarde is not for you, nor for anybody else who can't support her.

AMBROSE I tell you I can support her. I make a very good living.

VANDERGELDER No, sir! A living is made, Mr. Kemper, by selling something that everybody needs at least once a year. Yes, sir! And a million is made by producing something that everybody needs every day. You artists produce something that nobody needs at any time. You may sell a picture once in a while, but you'll make no living. Joe, go over there and stamp three times. I want to talk to Cornelius. (JOE *crosses to trap door and stamps three times*)

AMBROSE Not only can I support her now, but I have considerable expectations.

VANDERGELDER *Expectations!* We merchants don't do business with them. I don't keep accounts with people who promise somehow to pay something someday, and I don't allow my niece to marry such people.

AMBROSE Very well, from now on you might as well know that I regard any way we can find to get married is right and fair. Ermengarde is of age, and there's no law . . . (VANDERGELDER *rises and crosses toward* AMBROSE. JOE SCANLON *follows him complainingly and tries to find a chance to cut his hair even while he is standing*)

VANDERGELDER Law? Let me tell you something, Mr. Kemper: most of the people in the world are fools. The law is there to prevent crime; we men of sense are there to prevent foolishness. It's I, and not the law, that will prevent Ermengarde from marrying you, and I've taken some steps already. I've sent her away to get this nonsense out of her head.

AMBROSE Ermengarde's . . . not here?

VANDERGELDER She's gone—east, west, north, south. I thank you for the honor of your visit. (*Enter* GERTRUDE—*eighty; deaf; half blind; and very pleased with herself*)

GERTRUDE Everything's ready, Mr. Vandergelder. Ermengarde and I have just finished packing the trunk.

VANDERGELDER Hold your tongue! (JOE *is shaving* VANDERGELDER'S *throat, so he can only wave his hands vainly*)

GERTRUDE Yes, Mr. Vandergelder, Ermengarde's ready to leave. Her trunk's all marked. Care Miss Van Huysen, 8 Jackson Street, New York.

VANDERGELDER (*Breaking away from* JOE) Hell and damnation! Didn't I tell you it was a secret?

AMBROSE (*Picks up hat and coat—kisses* GERTRUDE) Care Miss Van Huysen, 8 Jackson Street, New York. Thank you very much. Good morning, Mr. Vandergelder. (*Exit* AMBROSE, *to the street*)

VANDERGELDER It won't help you, Mr. Kemper— (*To* GERTRUDE) Deaf! And blind! At least you can do me the favor of being dumb!

GERTRUDE Chk—chk! Such a temper! Lord save us! (CORNELIUS *puts his head up through the trap door. He is thirty-three; mock-deferential—he wears a green apron and is in his shirt-sleeves*)

CORNELIUS Yes, Mr. Vandergelder?

VANDERGELDER Go in and get my niece's trunk and carry it over to the station. Wait! Gertrude, has Mrs. Levi arrived yet? (CORNELIUS *comes up the trap door, steps into the room and closes the trap door behind him*)

GERTRUDE Don't shout. I can hear perfectly well. Everything's clearly marked. (*Exit left*)

VANDERGELDER Have the buggy brought round to the front of the store in half an hour.

CORNELIUS Yes, Mr. Vandergelder.

VANDERGELDER This morning I'm joining my lodge parade and this afternoon I'm going to New York. Before I go, I have something important to say to you and Barnaby. Good news. Fact is—I'm going to promote you. How old are you?

CORNELIUS Thirty-three, Mr. Vandergelder.

VANDERGELDER What?

CORNELIUS Thirty-three.

VANDERGELDER That all? That's a foolish age to be at. I thought you were forty.

CORNELIUS Thirty-three.

VANDERGELDER A man's not worth a cent until he's forty. We just pay 'em wages to make mistakes—don't we, Joe?

JOE You almost lost an ear on it, Mr. Vandergelder.

VANDERGELDER I was thinking of promoting you to chief clerk.

CORNELIUS What am I now, Mr. Vandergelder?

VANDERGELDER You're an impertinent fool, that's what you are. Now, if you behave yourself, I'll promote you from impertinent fool to chief clerk, with a raise in your wages. And Barnaby may be promoted from idiot apprentice to incompetent clerk.

CORNELIUS Thank you, Mr. Vandergelder.

VANDERGELDER However, I want to see you again before I go. Go in and get my niece's trunk.

CORNELIUS Yes, Mr. Vandergelder. (*Exit* CORNELIUS, *left*)

VANDERGELDER Joe—the world's getting crazier every minute. Like my father used to say: the horses'll be taking over the world soon.

JOE (*Presenting mirror*) I did what I could, Mr. Vandergelder, what with you flying in and out of the chair. (*He wipes the last of the soap from Vandergelder's face*)

VANDERGELDER Fine, fine, Joe, you do a fine job, the same fine job you've done me for twenty years. Joe . . . I've got special reasons for looking my best today . . . isn't there something a little extry you could do, something a little special? I'll pay you right up to fifty cents—see what I mean? Do some of those things you do to the young fellas. Touch me up; smarten me up a bit.

JOE All I know is fifteen cents' worth, like usual, Mr. Vandergelder; and that includes everything that's decent to do to a man.

VANDERGELDER Now hold your horses, Joe—all I meant was . . .

JOE I've shaved you for twenty years and you never asked me no such question before.

VANDERGELDER Hold your horses, I say, Joe! I'm going to tell you a secret. But I don't want you telling it to that riffraff down to the barbershop what I'm going to tell you now. All I ask of you is a little extry because I'm thinking of getting married again; and this very afternoon I'm going to New York to call on my intended, a very refined lady.

JOE Your gettin' married is none of my business, Mr. Vandergelder. I done everything to you I know, and the charge is fifteen cents like it always was, and . . . (CORNELIUS *crosses, left to right, and exit, carrying a trunk on his shoulder.* ERMENGARDE *and* GERTRUDE *enter from left*) I don't dye no hair, not even for fifty cents I don't!

VANDERGELDER Joe Scanlon, get out!

JOE And lastly, it looks to me like you're pretty rash to judge which is fools and which isn't fools, Mr. Vandergelder. People that's et onions is bad judges of who's et onions and who ain't. Good morning, ladies; good morning, Mr. Vandergelder. (*Exit* JOE)

VANDERGELDER Well, what do you want?

ERMENGARDE (*Twenty-four; pretty, sentimental*) Uncle! You said you wanted to talk to us.

VANDERGELDER Oh yes. Gertrude, go and get my parade regalia—the uniform for my lodge parade.

GERTRUDE What? Oh yes. Lord have mercy! (*Exit* GERTRUDE, *back center*)

VANDERGELDER I had a talk with that artist of yours. He's a fool. (ERMENGARDE *starts to cry*) Weeping! Weeping! You can go down and weep for a while in New York where it won't be noticed. (*He sits on desk chair, puts tie round neck and calls her over to tie it for him*) Ermengarde! I told him that when you were old enough to marry you'd marry someone who could support you. I've done you a good turn. You'll come and thank me when you're fifty.

ERMENGARDE But Uncle, I love him!

VANDERGELDER I tell you you don't.

ERMENGARDE But I *do!*

VANDERGELDER And I tell you you don't. Leave those things to me.

ERMENGARDE If I don't marry Ambrose I know I'll die.

VANDERGELDER What of?

ERMENGARDE A broken heart.

VANDERGELDER Never heard of it. Mrs. Levi is coming in a moment to take you to New York. You are going to stay two or three weeks with Miss Van Huysen, an old friend of your mother's. (GERTRUDE *re-enters with coat, sash and sword. Enter from the street, right,* MALACHI STACK) You're not to receive any letters except from me. I'm coming to New York myself today and I'll call on you tomorrow. (*To* MALACHI) Who are you?

MALACHI (*Fifty. Sardonic. Apparently innocent smile; pretense of humility*) Malachi Stack, your honor. I heard you wanted an apprentice in the hay, feed, provision, and hardware business.

VANDERGELDER An apprentice at your age?

MALACHI Yes, your honor; I bring a lot of experience to it.

VANDERGELDER Have you any letters of recommendation?

MALACHI (*Extending a sheaf of soiled papers*) Yes, indeed, your honor! First-class recommendation.

VANDERGELDER Ermengarde! Are you ready to start?

ERMENGARDE Yes.

VANDERGELDER Well, go and get ready some more. Ermengarde! Let me know the minute Mrs. Levi gets here.

ERMENGARDE Yes, Uncle Horace. (ERMENGARDE *and* GERTRUDE *exit.* VANDERGELDER *examines the letters, putting them down one by one*)

VANDERGELDER I don't want an able seaman. Nor a typesetter. And I don't want a hospital cook.

MALACHI No, your honor, but it's all experience. Excuse me! (*Selects a letter*) This one is from your former partner, Joshua Van Tuyl, in Albany. (*He puts letters from table back into pocket*)

VANDERGELDER ". . . for the most part honest and reliable . . . occasionally willing and diligent." There seems to be a certain amount of hesitation about these recommendations.

MALACHI Businessmen aren't writers, your honor. There's only one businessman in a thousand that can write a good letter of recommendation, your honor. Mr. Van Tuyl sends his best wishes and wants to know if you can use me in the provision and hardware business.

VANDERGELDER Not so fast, not so fast! What's this "your honor" you use so much?

MALACHI Mr. Van Tuyl says you're President of the Hudson River Provision Dealers' Recreational, Musical, and Burial Society.

VANDERGELDER I am; but there's no "your honor" that goes with it. Why did you come to Yonkers?

MALACHI I heard that you'd had an apprentice that was a good-for-nothing, and that you were at your wit's end for another.

VANDERGELDER Wit's end, wit's end! There's no dearth of good-for-nothing apprentices.

MALACHI That's right, Mr. Vandergelder. It's employers

there's a dearth of. Seems like you hear of a new one dying every day.

VANDERGELDER What's that? Hold your tongue. I see you've been a barber, and a valet too. Why have you changed your place so often?

MALACHI Changed my place, Mr. Vandergelder? When a man's interested in experience . . .

VANDERGELDER Do you drink?

MALACHI No, thanks. I've just had breakfast.

VANDERGELDER I didn't ask you whether— Idiot! I asked you if you were a drunkard.

MALACHI No, sir! No! Why, looking at it from all sides I don't even like liquor.

VANDERGELDER Well, if you keep on looking at it from all sides, out you go. Remember that. Here. (*Gives him remaining letters*) With all your faults, I'm going to give you a try.

MALACHI You'll never regret it, Mr. Vandergelder. You'll never regret it.

VANDERGELDER Now today I want to use you in New York. I judge you know your way around New York?

MALACHI Do I know New York? Mr. Vandergelder, I know every hole and corner in New York.

VANDERGELDER Here's a dollar. A train leaves in a minute. Take that bag to the Central Hotel on Water Street, have them save me a room. Wait for me. I'll be there about four o'clock.

MALACHI Yes, Mr. Vandergelder. (*Picks up the bag, starts out, then comes back*) Oh, but first, I'd like to meet the other clerks I'm to work with.

VANDERGELDER You haven't time. Hurry now. The station's across the street.

MALACHI Yes, sir. (*Away—then back once more*) You'll see, sir, you'll never regret it. . . .

VANDERGELDER I regret it already. Go on. Off with you. (*Exit* MALACHI, *right. The following speech is addressed to the audience. During it* MR. VANDERGELDER *takes off his dressing gown, puts on his scarlet sash, his sword, and his bright-colored coat. He is already wearing light blue trousers with a red stripe down the sides*)

VANDERGELDER Ninety-nine per cent of the people in the world are fools and the rest of us are in great danger of contagion. But I wasn't always free of foolishness as I am now. I was once young, which was foolish; I fell in love, which was foolish; and I got married, which was foolish; and for a while I was poor, which was more foolish than all the other things put together. Then my wife died, which was foolish of her; I grew older, which was sensible of me; then I became a rich man, which is as sensible as it is rare. Since you see I'm a man of sense, I guess you were surprised to hear that I'm planning to get married again. Well, I've two reasons for it. In the first place, I like my house run with order, comfort, and economy. That's a woman's work; but even a woman can't do it well if she's merely being paid for it. In order to run a house well, a woman must have the feeling that she owns it. Marriage is a bribe to make a housekeeper think she's a householder. Did you ever watch an ant carry a burden twice its size? What excitement! What patience! What will! Well, that's what I think of when I see a woman running a house. What giant passions in those little bodies—what quarrels with the butcher for the best cut—what fury at discovering a moth in a cupboard! Believe me!—if women could harness their natures to something bigger than a house and a baby carriage—tck! tck!—they'd change the world. And the second reason, ladies and gentlemen? Well, I see by your faces you've guessed it already. There's nothing like mixing with women to bring out all the foolishness in a man of sense. And that's a risk I'm willing to take. I've just turned sixty, and I've just laid side by side the last dollar of my first half million. So if I should lose my head a little, I still have enough money to buy it back. After many years' caution and hard work, I have earned a right to a little risk and adventure, and I'm thinking of getting married. Yes, like all you other fools, I'm willing to risk a little security for a certain amount of adventure. Think it over. (*Exit back center.* AMBROSE *enters from the street, crosses left, and whistles softly.* ERMENGARDE *enters from left*)

ERMENGARDE Ambrose! If my uncle saw you!

AMBROSE Sh! Get your hat.

ERMENGARDE My hat!

AMBROSE Quick! Your trunk's at the station. Now quick! We're running away.

ERMENGARDE Running away!

AMBROSE Sh!

ERMENGARDE Where?

AMBROSE To New York. To get married.

ERMENGARDE Oh, Ambrose, I can't do that. Ambrose dear—it wouldn't be proper!

AMBROSE Listen. I'm taking you to my friend's house. His wife will take care of you.

ERMENGARDE But, Ambrose, a girl can't go on a train with a man. I can see you don't know anything about girls.

AMBROSE But I'm telling you we're going to get married!

ERMENGARDE Married! But what would *Uncle* say?

AMBROSE We don't care what Uncle'd say—we're eloping.

ERMENGARDE Ambrose Kemper! How can you use such an awful word!

AMBROSE Ermengarde, you have the soul of a field mouse.

ERMENGARDE (*Crying*) Ambrose, why do you say such cruel things to me? (*Enter* MRS. LEVI, *from the street, right. She stands listening*)

AMBROSE For the last time I beg you—get your hat and coat. The train leaves in a few minutes. Ermengarde, we'll get married tomorrow. . . .

ERMENGARDE Oh, Ambrose! I see you don't understand anything about weddings. Ambrose, don't you *respect* me? . . .

MRS. LEVI (*Uncertain age; mass of sandy hair; impoverished elegance; large, shrewd but generous nature, an assumption of worldly cynicism conceals a tireless amused enjoyment of life. She carries a hand-*

*bag and a small brown paper bag*) Good morning, darling girl—how are you? (*They kiss*)

ERMENGARDE Oh, good morning, Mrs. Levi.

MRS. LEVI And who is this gentleman who is so devoted to you?

ERMENGARDE This is Mr. Kemper, Mrs. Levi. Ambrose, this is . . . Mrs. Levi . . . she's an old friend. . . .

MRS. LEVI Mrs. Levi, born Gallagher. Very happy to meet you, Mr. Kemper.

AMBROSE Good morning, Mrs. Levi.

MRS. LEVI Mr. Kemper, *the artist!* Delighted! Mr. Kemper, may I say something very frankly?

AMBROSE Yes, Mrs. Levi.

MRS. LEVI This thing you were planning to do is a very great mistake.

ERMENGARDE Oh, Mrs. Levi, please explain to Ambrose—of *course!* I want to marry him, but to *elope!* . . . How . . .

MRS. LEVI Now, my dear girl, you go in and keep one eye on your uncle. I wish to talk to Mr. Kemper for a moment. You give us a warning when you hear your Uncle Horace coming. . . .

ERMENGARDE Ye-es, Mrs. Levi. (*Exit* ERMENGARDE, *back center*)

MRS. LEVI Mr. Kemper, I was this dear girl's mother's oldest friend. Believe me, I am on your side. I hope you two will be married very soon, and I think I can be of real service to you. Mr. Kemper, I always go right to the point.

AMBROSE What is the point, Mrs. Levi?

MRS. LEVI Mr. Vandergelder is a very rich man, Mr. Kemper, and Ermengarde is his only relative.

AMBROSE But I am not interested in Mr. Vandergelder's money. I have enough to support a wife and family.

MRS. LEVI Enough? How much is enough when one is thinking about children and the future? The future is the most expensive luxury in the world, Mr. Kemper.

AMBROSE Mrs. Levi, what is the point?

MRS. LEVI Believe me, Mr. Vandergelder wishes to get rid of Ermengarde, and if you follow my suggestions he will even permit her to marry you. You see, Mr. Vandergelder is planning to get married himself.

AMBROSE What? That monster!

MRS. LEVI Mr. Kemper!

AMBROSE Married! To you, Mrs. Levi?

MRS. LEVI (*Taken aback*) Oh, no, no . . . No! I am merely arranging it. I am helping him find a suitable bride.

AMBROSE For Mr. Vandergelder there are no suitable brides.

MRS. LEVI I think we can safely say that Mr. Vandergelder will be married to someone by the end of next week.

AMBROSE What are you suggesting, Mrs. Levi?

MRS. LEVI I am taking Ermengarde to New York on the next train. I shall not take her to Miss Van Huysen's, as is planned; I shall take her to my house. I wish you to call for her at my house at five-thirty. Here is my card.

AMBROSE "Mrs. Dolly Gallagher Levi. Varicose veins reduced."

MRS. LEVI (*Trying to take back card*) I beg your pardon . . .

AMBROSE (*Holding card*) I beg *your* pardon. "Consultations free."

MRS. LEVI I meant to give you my other card. Here.

AMBROSE "Mrs. Dolly Gallagher Levi. Aurora Hosiery. Instruction in the guitar and mandolin." You do all these things, Mrs. Levi?

MRS. LEVI Two and two make four, Mr. Kemper—always did. So you will come to my house at five-thirty. At about six I shall take you both with me to the Harmonia Gardens Restaurant on the Battery; Mr. Vandergelder will be there and everything will be arranged.

AMBROSE How?

MRS. LEVI Oh, I don't know. One thing will lead to another.

AMBROSE How do I know that I can trust you, Mrs. Levi? You could easily make our situation worse.

MRS. LEVI Mr. Kemper, your situation could not possibly be worse.

AMBROSE I wish I knew what you get out of this, Mrs. Levi.

MRS. LEVI That is a very proper question. I get two things: profit and pleasure.

AMBROSE How?

MRS. LEVI Mr. Kemper, I am a woman who arranges things. At present I am arranging Mr. Vandergelder's domestic affairs. Out of it I get—shall we call it: little pickings? I need little pickings, Mr. Kemper, and especially just now, when I haven't got my train fare back to New York. You see: I am frank with you.

AMBROSE That's your profit, Mrs. Levi; but where do you get your pleasure?

MRS. LEVI My pleasure? Mr. Kemper, when you artists paint a hillside or a river you change everything a little, you make thousands of little changes, don't you? Nature is never completely satisfactory and must be corrected. Well, I'm like you artists. Life as it is is never quite interesting enough for me—I'm bored, Mr. Kemper, with life as it is—and so I do things. I put my hand in here, and I put my hand in there, and I watch and I listen—and often I'm very much amused.

AMBROSE (*Rises*) Not in my affairs, Mrs. Levi.

MRS. LEVI Wait, I haven't finished. There's another thing. I'm very interested in this household here—in Mr. Vandergelder and all that idle, frozen money of his. I don't like the thought of it lying in great piles, useless, motionless, in the bank, Mr. Kemper. Money should circulate like rain water. It should be flowing down among the people, through dressmakers and restaurants and cabmen, setting up a little business here, and furnishing a good time there. Do you see what I mean?

AMBROSE Yes, I do.

MRS. LEVI New York should be a very happy city, Mr. Kemper, but it isn't. My late husband came from Vienna; now there's a city that understands this. I want New York to be more like Vienna and less like a collection of nervous and tired ants. And if you and Ermengarde get a good deal of Mr. Vandergelder's money, I want you to see that it starts flowing in and around a lot of people's lives. And for that reason I want you to come with me to the Harmonia Gardens Restaurant tonight. (*Enter* ERMENGARDE)

ERMENGARDE Mrs. Levi, Uncle Horace is coming.

MRS. LEVI Mr. Kemper, I think you'd better be going. . . . (AMBROSE *crosses to trap door and disappears down the ladder, closing trap as he goes*) Darling girl, Mr. Kemper and I have had a very good talk. You'll see: Mr. Vandergelder and I will be dancing at your wedding very soon— (*Enter* VANDERGELDER *at back. He has now added a splendid plumed hat to his costume and is carrying a standard or small flag bearing the initials of his lodge*) Oh, Mr. Vandergelder, how handsome you look! You take my breath away. Yes, my dear girl, I'll see you soon. (*Exit* ERMENGARDE *back center*) Oh, Mr. Vandergelder, I wish Irene Molloy could see you now. But then! I don't know what's come over you lately. You seem to be growing younger every day.

VANDERGELDER Allowing for exaggeration, Mrs. Levi. If a man eats careful there's no reason why he should look old.

MRS. LEVI You never said a truer word.

VANDERGELDER I'll never see fifty-five again.

MRS. LEVI Fifty-five! Why, I can see at a glance that you're the sort that will be stamping about at a hundred—and eating five meals a day, like my Uncle Harry. At fifty-five my Uncle Harry was a mere boy. I'm a judge of hands, Mr. Vandergelder—show me your hand. (*Looks at it*) Lord in heaven! What a life line!

VANDERGELDER Where?

MRS. LEVI From *here* to *here*. It runs right off your hand. I don't know where it goes. They'll have to hit you on the head with a mallet. They'll have to stifle you with a sofa pillow. You'll bury us all! However, to return to our business—Mr. Vandergelder, I suppose you've changed your mind again. I suppose you've given up all idea of getting married.

VANDERGELDER (*Complacently*) Not at all, Mrs. Levi. I have news for you.

MRS. LEVI News?

VANDERGELDER Mrs. Levi, I've practically decided to ask Mrs. Molloy to be my wife.

MRS. LEVI (*Taken aback*) You have?

VANDERGELDER Yes, I have.

MRS. LEVI Oh, you have! Well, I guess that's just about the best news I ever heard. So there's nothing more for me to do but wish you every happiness under the sun and say good-by. (*Crosses as if to leave*)

VANDERGELDER (*Stopping her*) Well—Mrs. Levi—Surely I thought—

MRS. LEVI Well, I did have a little suggestion to make —but I won't. You're going to marry Irene Molloy, and that closes the matter.

VANDERGELDER What suggestion was that, Mrs. Levi?

MRS. LEVI Well—I *had* found *another* girl for you.

VANDERGELDER Another?

MRS. LEVI The most wonderful girl, the ideal wife.

VANDERGELDER Another, eh? What's her name?

MRS. LEVI Her name?

VANDERGELDER Yes!

MRS. LEVI (*Groping for it*) Err . . . er . . . her *name?*—Ernestina—Simple. *Miss* Ernestina Simple. But now of course all that's too late. After all, you're engaged—you're practically engaged to marry Irene Molloy.

VANDERGELDER Oh, I ain't engaged to Mrs. Molloy!

MRS. LEVI Nonsense! You can't break poor Irene's heart now and change to another girl. . . . When a man at your time of life calls four times on an attractive widow like that—and sends her a pot of geraniums—that's practically an engagement!

VANDERGELDER That ain't an engagement!

MRS. LEVI And yet—! If only you were free! I've found this treasure of a girl. Every moment I felt like a traitor to Irene Molloy—but let me tell you: I couldn't help it. I told this girl all about you, just as though you were a free man. Isn't that dreadful? The fact is: she has fallen in love with you already.

VANDERGELDER Ernestina?

MRS. LEVI Ernestina Simple.

VANDERGELDER Ernestina Simple.

MRS. LEVI Of course she's a very different idea from Mrs. Molloy, Ernestina is. Like her name—simple, domestic, practical.

VANDERGELDER Can she cook?

MRS. LEVI Cook, Mr. Vandergelder? I've had two meals from her hands, and—as I live—I don't know what I've done that God should reward me with such meals. (*Pause*) Her duck! Her steak!

VANDERGELDER Eh! Eh! In this house we don't eat duck and steak every day, Mrs. Levi.

MRS. LEVI But didn't I tell you?—that's the wonderful part about it. Her duck—what was it? Pigeon! I'm alive to tell you. I don't know how she does it. It's a secret that's come down in her family. The greatest chefs would give their right hands to know it. And the steaks? Shoulder of beef—four cents a pound. Dogs wouldn't eat it. But when Ernestina passes her hands over it—! !

VANDERGELDER Allowing for exaggeration, Mrs. Levi.

MRS. LEVI No exaggeration. I'm the best cook in the world myself, and I *know* what's good.

VANDERGELDER Hm. How old is she, Mrs. Levi?

MRS. LEVI Nineteen, well—say twenty.

VANDERGELDER Twenty, Mrs. Levi? Girls of twenty are apt to favor young fellows of their own age.

MRS. LEVI But you don't listen to me. And you don't know the girl. Mr. Vandergelder, she has a positive horror of flighty, brainless young men. A fine head of gray hair, she says, is worth twenty shined up with goose grease. No, sir. "I like a man that's *settled*"—in so many words she said it.

VANDERGELDER That's . . . that's not usual, Mrs. Levi.

MRS. LEVI Usual? I'm not wearing myself to the bone

hunting up *usual* girls to interest you, Mr. Vandergelder. Usual, indeed. Listen to me. Do you know the sort of pictures she has on her wall? Is it any of these young Romeos and Lochinvars? No!—it's Moses on the Mountain—that's what she's got. If you want to make her happy, you give her a picture of Methuselah surrounded by his grandchildren. That's my advice to you.

VANDERGELDER I hope . . . hm . . . that she has some means, Mrs. Levi. I have a large household to run.

MRS. LEVI Ernestina? She'll bring you five thousand dollars a year.

VANDERGELDER Eh! Eh!

MRS. LEVI Listen to me, Mr. Vandergelder. You're a man of sense, I hope. A man that can reckon. In the first place, she's an orphan. She's been brought up with a great saving of food. What does she eat herself? Apples and lettuce. It's what she's been used to eat and what she likes best. She saves you two thousand a year right there. Secondly, she makes her own clothes—out of old tablecloths and window curtains. And she's the best-dressed woman in Brooklyn this minute. She saves you a thousand dollars right there. Thirdly, her health is of iron—

VANDERGELDER But, Mrs. Levi, that's not money in the pocket.

MRS. LEVI We're talking about marriage, aren't we, Mr. Vandergelder? The money she saves while she's in Brooklyn is none of your affair—but if she were your wife that would be *money*. Yes, sir, that's money.

VANDERGELDER What's her family?

MRS. LEVI Her father?—God be good to him! He was the best—what am I trying to say?—the best undertaker in Brooklyn, respected, esteemed. He knew all the best people—knew them well, even before they died. So—well, that's the way it is. (*Lowering her voice, intimately*) Now let me tell you a little more of her appearance. Can you hear me: as I say, a beautiful girl, beautiful, I've seen her go down the street—you know what I mean?—the young men get dizzy. They have to lean against lampposts. And she? Modest, eyes on the ground—I'm not going to tell you any more. . . . Couldn't you come to New York today?

VANDERGELDER I was thinking of coming to New York this afternoon. . . .

MRS. LEVI You were? Well now, I wonder if something could be arranged—oh, she's so eager to see you! Let me see . . .

VANDERGELDER Could I . . . Mrs. Levi, could I give you a little dinner, maybe?

MRS. LEVI Really, come to think of it, I don't see where I could get the time. I'm so busy over that wretched lawsuit of mine. Yes. If I win it, I don't mind telling you, I'll be what's called a very rich woman. I'll own half of Long Island, that's a fact. But just now I'm at my wit's end for a little help, just enough money to finish it off. My wit's end! (*She looks in her handbag. In order not to hear this,* VANDERGELDER *has a series of coughs, sneezes, and minor convulsions*) But perhaps I could arrange a little dinner; I'll see. Yes, for that lawsuit all I need is fifty dollars, and Staten Island's as good as mine. I've been trotting all over New York for you, trying to find you a suitable wife.

VANDERGELDER Fifty dollars! !

MRS. LEVI Two whole months I've been . . .

VANDERGELDER Fifty dollars, Mrs. Levi . . . is no joke. (*Producing purse*) I don't know where money's gone to these days. It's in hiding. . . . There's twenty . . . well, there's twenty-five. I can't spare no more, not now I can't.

MRS. LEVI Well, this will help—will help somewhat. Now let me tell you what we'll do. I'll bring Ernestina to that restaurant on the Battery. You know it: the Harmonia Gardens. It's good, but it's not flashy. Now, Mr. Vandergelder, I think it'd be nice if just this once you'd order a real nice dinner. I guess you can afford it.

VANDERGELDER Well, just this once.

MRS. LEVI A chicken wouldn't hurt.

VANDERGELDER Chicken! !—Well, just this once.

MRS. LEVI And a little wine.

VANDERGELDER Wine? Well, just this once.

MRS. LEVI Now about Mrs. Molloy—what do you think? Shall we call that subject closed?

VANDERGELDER No, not at all, Mrs. Levi, I want to have dinner with Miss . . . with Miss . . .

MRS. LEVI Simple.

VANDERGELDER With Miss Simple; but first I want to make another call on Mrs. Molloy.

MRS. LEVI Dear, dear, dear! And Miss Simple? What races you make me run! Very well; I'll meet you on one of those benches in front of Mrs. Molloy's hat store at four-thirty, as usual. (*Trap door rises, and* CORNELIUS' *head appears*)

CORNELIUS The buggy's here, ready for the parade, Mr. Vandergelder.

VANDERGELDER Call Barnaby. I want to talk to both of you.

CORNELIUS Yes, Mr. Vandergelder. (*Exit* CORNELIUS *down trap door. Leaves trap open*)

MRS. LEVI Now do put your thoughts in order, Mr. Vandergelder. I can't keep upsetting and disturbing the finest women in New York City unless you mean business.

VANDERGELDER Oh, I mean business all right!

MRS. LEVI I hope so. Because, you know, you're playing a very dangerous game.

VANDERGELDER Dangerous?—Dangerous, Mrs. Levi?

MRS. LEVI Of course, it's dangerous—and there's a name for it! You're tampering with these women's affections, aren't you? And the only way you can save yourself now is to be married to *someone* by the end of next week. So think that over! (*Exit center back. Enter* CORNELIUS *and* BARNABY, *by the trap door*)

VANDERGELDER This morning I'm joining my lodge

parade, and this afternoon I'm going to New York. When I come back, there are going to be some changes in the house here. I'll tell you what the change is, but I don't want you discussing it amongst yourselves: you're going to have a mistress.

BARNABY (*Seventeen; round-faced, wide-eyed innocence; wearing a green apron*) I'm too young, Mr. Vandergelder! !

VANDERGELDER Not yours! Death and damnation! Not yours, idiot—*mine!* (*Then, realizing*) Hey! Hold your tongue until you're spoken to! I'm thinking of getting married.

CORNELIUS (*Crosses, hand outstretched*) Many congratulations, Mr. Vandergelder, and my compliments to the lady.

VANDERGELDER That's none of your business. Now go back to the store. (*The* BOYS *start down the ladder,* BARNABY *first*) Have you got any questions you want to ask before I go?

CORNELIUS Mr. Vandergelder—er—Mr. Vandergelder, does the chief clerk get one evening off every week?

VANDERGELDER So that's the way you begin being chief clerk, is it? When I was your age I got up at five; I didn't close the shop until ten at night, and then I put in a good hour at the account books. The world's going to pieces. You elegant ladies lie in bed until six and at nine o'clock at night you rush to close the door so fast the line of customers bark their noses. No, sir—you'll attend to the store as usual, and on Friday and Saturday nights you'll remain open until ten—now hear what I say! This is the first time I've been away from the store overnight. When I come back I want to hear that you've run the place perfectly in my absence. If I hear of any foolishness, I'll discharge you. An evening free! Do you suppose that *I* had evenings free? (*At the top of his complacency*) If I'd had evenings free I wouldn't be what I am now! (*He marches out, right*)

BARNABY (*Watching him go*) The horses nearly ran away when they saw him. What's the matter, Cornelius?

CORNELIUS (*Sits in dejected thought*) Chief clerk! Promoted from chief clerk to chief clerk.

BARNABY Don't you like it?

CORNELIUS Chief clerk!—and if I'm good, in ten years I'll be promoted to chief clerk again. Thirty-three years old and I still don't get an evening free! When am I going to begin to live?

BARNABY Well—ah . . . you can begin to live on Sundays, Cornelius.

CORNELIUS That's not living. Twice to church, and old Wolf-trap's eyes on the back of my head the whole time. And as for holidays! What did we do last Christmas? All those canned tomatoes went bad and exploded. We had to clean up the mess all afternoon. Was that living?

BARNABY (*Holding his nose at the memory of the bad smell*) No! ! !

CORNELIUS (*Rising with sudden resolution*) Barnaby, how much money have you got—where you can get at it?

BARNABY Oh—three dollars. Why, Cornelius?

CORNELIUS You and I are going to New York.

BARNABY Cornelius! ! ! We can't! Close the store?

CORNELIUS Some more rotten-tomato cans are going to explode.

BARNABY Holy cabooses! How do you know?

CORNELIUS I know they're rotten. All you have to do is to light a match under them. They'll make such a smell that customers can't come into the place for twenty-four hours. That'll get us an evening free. We're going to New York too, Barnaby, we're going to live! I'm going to have enough adventures to last me until I'm *partner*. So go and get your Sunday clothes on.

BARNABY Wha-a-a-t?

CORNELIUS Yes, I mean it. We're going to have a good meal; and we're going to be in danger; and we're going to get almost arrested; and we're going to spend all our money.

BARNABY Holy cabooses! !

CORNELIUS And one more thing: we're not coming back to Yonkers until we've kissed a girl.

BARNABY Kissed a girl! Cornelius, you can't do that. You don't know any girls.

CORNELIUS I'm thirty-three. I've got to begin sometime.

BARNABY I'm only seventeen, Cornelius. It isn't so urgent for me.

CORNELIUS Don't start backing down now—if the worst comes to the worst and we get discharged from here we can always join the Army.

BARNABY Uh—did I hear you say that you'd be old Wolf-trap's partner?

CORNELIUS How can I help it? He's growing old. If you go to bed at nine and open the store at six, you get promoted upward whether you like it or not.

BARNABY My! Partner.

CORNELIUS Oh, there's no way of getting away from it. You and I will be Vandergelders.

BARNABY I? Oh, no—I may rise a little, but I'll never be a Vandergelder.

CORNELIUS Listen—everybody thinks when he gets rich he'll be a different kind of rich person from the rich people he sees around him; later on he finds out there's only one kind of rich person, and he's it.

BARNABY Oh, but I'll—

CORNELIUS No. The best of all would be a person who has all the good things a poor person has, and all the good meals a rich person has, but that's never been known. No, you and I are going to be Vandergelders; all the more reason, then, for us to try and get some living and some adventure into us now—will you come, Barnaby?

BARNABY (*In a struggle with his fears, a whirlwind of words*) But Wolf-trap—KRR-pt, Gertrude-KRR-pt— (*With a sudden cry of agreement*) Yes, Cornelius! (*Enter* MRS. LEVI, ERMENGARDE *and* GERTRUDE *from back center. The* BOYS *start down the ladder,* CORNELIUS *last*)

MRS. LEVI Mr. Hackl, is the trunk waiting at the station?

CORNELIUS Yes, Mrs. Levi. (*Closes the trap door*)

MRS. LEVI Take a last look, Ermengarde.

ERMENGARDE What?

MRS. LEVI Take a last look at your girlhood home, dear. I remember when I left my home. I gave a whinny like a young colt, and off I went. (ERMENGARDE *and* GERTRUDE *exit*)

ERMENGARDE (*As they go*) Oh, Gertrude, do you think I ought to get married this way? A young girl has to be so careful! (MRS. LEVI *is alone. She addresses the audience*)

MRS. LEVI You know, I think I'm going to have this room with *blue* wallpaper,—yes, in blue! (*Hurries out after the others.* BARNABY *comes up trap door, looks off right, then lies on floor, gazing down through the trap door*)

BARNABY All clear up here, Cornelius! Cornelius—hold the candle steady a minute—the bottom row's all right—but try the top now . . . they're swelled up like they are ready to bust! (*BANG*) Holy CABOOSES! (*BANG, BANG*) Cornelius! I can smell it up here! (*Rises and dances about, holding his nose*)

CORNELIUS (*Rushing up the trap door*) Get into your Sunday clothes, Barnaby. We're going to New York! (*As they run out . . . there is a big explosion. A shower of tomato cans comes up from below, as the curtain falls*)

*Curtain*

# Act Two

*Mrs. Molloy's hat shop, New York City.*

*There are two entrances. One door at the extreme right of the back wall, to Mrs. Molloy's workroom; one at the back left corner, to the street. The whole left wall is taken up with the show windows, filled with hats. It is separated from the shop by a low brass rail, hung with net; during the act both* MRS. MOLLOY *and* BARNABY *stoop under the rail and go into the shop window. By the street door stands a large cheval glass. In the middle of the back wall is a large wardrobe or clothes cupboard, filled with ladies' coats, large enough for* CORNELIUS *to hide in. At the left, beginning at the back wall, between the wardrobe and the workroom door, a long counter extends toward the audience, almost to the footlights. In the center of the room is a large round table with a low-hanging red cloth. There are a small gilt chair by the wardrobe and two chairs in front of the counter. Over the street door and the workroom door are bells which ring when the doors are opened.*

*As the curtain rises,* MRS. MOLLOY *is in the window, standing on a box, reaching up to put hats on the stand.* MINNIE FAY *is sewing by the counter.* MRS. MOLLOY *has on a pair of felt overshoes, to be removed later.*

MRS. MOLLOY Minnie, you're a fool. Of course I shall marry Horace Vandergelder.

MINNIE Oh, Mrs. Molloy! I didn't ask you. I wouldn't dream of asking you such a personal question.

MRS. MOLLOY Well, it's what you meant, isn't it? And there's your answer. I shall certainly marry Horace Vandergelder if he asks me. (*Crawls under window rail, into the room, singing loudly*)

MINNIE I know it's none of my business . . .

MRS. MOLLOY Speak up, Minnie, I can't hear you.

MINNIE . . . but do you . . . do you . . . ?

MRS. MOLLOY (*Having crossed the room, is busy at the counter*) Minnie, you're a fool. Say it: Do I love him? Of course, I don't love him. But I have two good reasons for marrying him just the same. Minnie, put something on that hat. It's not ugly enough. (*Throws hat over counter*)

MINNIE (*Catching and taking hat to table*) Not ugly enough!

MRS. MOLLOY I couldn't sell it. Put a . . . put a sponge on it.

MINNIE Why, Mrs. Molloy, you're in such a *mood* today.

MRS. MOLLOY In the first place I shall marry Mr. Vandergelder to get away from the millinery business. I've hated it from the first day I had anything to do with it. Minnie, I hate hats. (*Sings loudly again*)

MINNIE Why, what's the matter with the millinery business?

MRS. MOLLOY (*Crossing to window with two hats*) I can no longer stand being suspected of being a wicked woman, while I have nothing to show for it. I can't stand it. (*She crawls under rail into window*)

MINNIE Why, no one would dream of suspecting you—

MRS. MOLLOY (*On her knees, she looks over the rail*) Minnie, you're a fool. All millineresses are suspected of being wicked women. Why, half the time all those women come into the shop merely to look at me.

MINNIE Oh!

MRS. MOLLOY They enjoy the suspicion. But they aren't certain. If they were *certain* I was a wicked woman, they wouldn't put foot in this place again. Do I go to restaurants? No, it would be bad for business. Do I go to balls, or theatres, or operas? No, it would be bad for business. The only men I ever meet are feather merchants. (*Crawls out of window, but gazes intently into the street*) What are those two young men doing out there on that park bench? Take my word for it, Minnie, either I marry Horace Vandergelder, or I break out of this place like a fire engine. I'll go to every theatre and ball and opera in New York City. (*Returns to counter, singing again*)

MINNIE But Mr. Vandergelder's not . . .

MRS. MOLLOY Speak up, Minnie, I can't hear you.

MINNIE . . . I don't think he's attractive.

MRS. MOLLOY But what I think he is—and it's very important—I think he'd make a good fighter.

MINNIE Mrs. Molloy!

MRS. MOLLOY Take my word for it, Minnie: the best part of married life is the fights. The rest is merely so-so.

MINNIE (*Fingers in ears*) I won't listen.

MRS. MOLLOY Peter Molloy—God rest him!—was a fine arguing man. I pity the woman whose husband slams the door and walks out of the house at the beginning of an argument. Peter Molloy would stand up and fight for hours on end. He'd even throw things, Minnie, and there's no pleasure to equal that. When I felt tired I'd start a good bloodwarming fight and it'd take ten years off my age; now Horace Vandergelder would put up a good fight; I know it. I've a mind to marry him.

MINNIE I think they're just awful, the things you're saying today.

MRS. MOLLOY Well, I'm enjoying them myself, too.

MINNIE (*At the window*) Mrs. Molloy, those two men out in the street—

MRS. MOLLOY What?

MINNIE Those men. It looks as if they meant to come in here.

MRS. MOLLOY Well now, it's time some men came into this place. I give you the younger one, Minnie.

MINNIE Aren't you terrible! (MRS. MOLLOY *sits on center table, while* MINNIE *takes off her felt overshoes*)

MRS. MOLLOY Wait till I get my hands on that older one! Mark my words, Minnie, we'll get an adventure out of this yet. Adventure, adventure! Why does everybody have adventures except me, Minnie? Because I have no spirit, I have no gumption. Minnie, they're coming in here. Let's go into the workroom and make them wait for us for a minute.

MINNIE Oh, but Mrs. Molloy . . . my work! . . .

MRS. MOLLOY (*Running to workroom*) Hurry up, be quick now, Minnie! (*They go out to workroom.* BARNABY *and* CORNELIUS *run in from street, leaving front door open. They are dressed in the stiff discomfort of their Sunday clothes.* CORNELIUS *wears a bowler hat,* BARNABY *a straw hat too large for him*)

BARNABY No one's here.

CORNELIUS Some women were here a minute ago. I saw them. (*They jump back to the street door and peer down the street*) That's Wolf-trap all right! (*Coming back*) Well, we've got to hide here until he passes by.

BARNABY He's sitting down on that bench. It may be quite a while.

CORNELIUS When these women come in, we'll have to make conversation until he's gone away. We'll pretend we're buying a hat. How much money have you got now?

BARNABY (*Counting his money*) Forty cents for the train—seventy cents for dinner—twenty cents to see the whale—and a dollar I lost—I have seventy cents.

CORNELIUS And I have a dollar seventy-five. I wish I knew how much hats cost!

BARNABY Is this an adventure, Cornelius?

CORNELIUS No, but it may be.

BARNABY I think it is. There we wander around New York all day and nothing happens; and then we come to the quietest street in the whole city and suddenly Mr. Vandergelder turns the corner. (*Going to door*) I think that's an adventure. I think . . . Cornelius! That Mrs. Levi is there now. She's sitting down on the bench with him.

CORNELIUS What do you know about that! We know only one person in all New York City, and there she is!

BARNABY Even if our adventure came along now I'd be too tired to enjoy it. Cornelius, why isn't this an adventure?

CORNELIUS Don't be asking that. When you're in an adventure, you'll know it all right.

BARNABY Maybe I wouldn't. Cornelius, let's arrange a signal for you to give when an adventure's really going on. For instance, Cornelius, you say . . . uh . . . uh . . . *pudding;* you say *pudding* to me as if it's an adventure we're in.

CORNELIUS I wonder where the lady who runs this store is? What's her name again?

BARNABY Mrs. Molloy, hats for ladies.

CORNELIUS Oh, yes. I must think over what I'm going to say when she comes in. (*To counter*) "Good afternoon, Mrs. Molloy, wonderful weather we're having. We've been looking everywhere for some beautiful hats."

BARNABY That's fine, Cornelius!

CORNELIUS "Good afternoon, Mrs. Molloy; wonderful weather . . ." We'll make her think we're very rich. (*One hand in trouser pocket, the other on back of chair*) "Good afternoon, Mrs. Molloy . . ." You keep one eye on the door the whole time. "We've been looking everywhere for . . ." (*Enter* MRS. MOLLOY *from the workroom*)

MRS. MOLLOY (*Behind the counter*) Oh, I'm sorry. Have I kept you waiting? Good afternoon, gentlemen.

CORNELIUS (*Hat off*) Here, Cornelius Hackl.

BARNABY (*Hat off*) Here, Barnaby Tucker.

MRS. MOLLOY I'm very happy to meet you. Perhaps I can help you. Won't you sit down?

CORNELIUS Thank you, we will. (*The* BOYS *place their hats on the table, then sit down at the counter facing* MRS. MOLLOY) You see, Mrs. Molloy, we're looking for hats. We've looked everywhere. Do you know what we heard? Go to Mrs. Molloy's, they said. So we came here. Only place we *could* go . . .

MRS. MOLLOY Well, now, that's *very* complimentary.

CORNELIUS . . . and we were right. Everybody was right.

MRS. MOLLOY You wish to choose some hats for a friend?

CORNELIUS Yes, exactly. (*Kicks* BARNABY)

BARNABY Yes, exactly.

CORNELIUS We were thinking of five or six, weren't we, Barnaby?

BARNABY Er—five.

CORNELIUS You see, Mrs. Molloy, money's no object with us. None at all.

MRS. MOLLOY Why, Mr. Hackl . . .

CORNELIUS (*Rises and goes toward street door*) . . . I beg your pardon, what an interesting street! Something happening every minute. Passers-by, and . . . (BARNABY *runs to join him*)

MRS. MOLLOY You're from out of town, Mr. Hackl?

CORNELIUS (*Coming back*) Yes, ma'am—Barnaby, just keep your eye on the street, will you? You won't see that in Yonkers every day. (BARNABY *remains kneeling at street door*)

BARNABY Oh yes, I will.

CORNELIUS Not all of it.

MRS. MOLLOY Now this friend of yours—couldn't she come in with you someday and choose her hats herself?

CORNELIUS (*Sits at counter*) No. Oh, no. It's a surprise for her.

MRS. MOLLOY Indeed? That may be a little difficult, Mr. Hackl. It's not entirely customary— Your friend's very interested in the street, Mr. Hackl.

CORNELIUS Oh, yes. Yes. He has reason to be.

MRS. MOLLOY You said you were from out of town?

CORNELIUS Yes, we're from Yonkers.

MRS MOLLOY Yonkers?

CORNELIUS Yonkers . . . yes, Yonkers (*He gazes rapt into her eyes*) You should know Yonkers, Mrs. Molloy. Hudson River; Palisades; drives; some say it's the most beautiful town in the world; that's what they say.

MRS. MOLLOY Is that so!

CORNELIUS (*Rises*) Mrs. Molloy, if you ever had a Sunday free, I'd . . . we'd like to show you Yonkers. Y'know, it's very historic, too.

MRS. MOLLOY That's very kind of you. Well, perhaps . . . now about those hats. (*Takes two hats from under counter, and crosses to back center of the room*)

CORNELIUS (*Following*) Is there . . . Have you a . . . Maybe Mr. Molloy would like to see Yonkers too?

MRS. MOLLOY Oh, I'm a widow, Mr. Hackl.

CORNELIUS (*Joyfully*) You are! (*With sudden gravity*) Oh, that's too bad. Mr. Molloy would have enjoyed Yonkers.

MRS. MOLLOY Very likely. Now about these hats. Is your friend dark or light?

CORNELIUS Don't think about that for a minute. Any hat you'd like would be perfectly all right with her.

MRS. MOLLOY Really! (*She puts one on*) Do you like this one?

CORNELIUS (*In awe-struck admiration*) Barnaby! (*In sudden anger*) Barnaby! Look! (BARNABY *turns; unimpressed, he laughs vaguely, and turns to door again*) Mrs. Molloy, that's the most beautiful hat I ever saw. (BARNABY *now crawls under the rail into the window*)

MRS. MOLLOY Your friend is acting very strangely, Mr. Hackl.

CORNELIUS Barnaby, stop acting strangely. When the street's quiet and empty, come back and talk to us. What was I saying? Oh yes: Mrs. Molloy, you should know Yonkers.

MRS. MOLLOY (*Hat off*) The fact is, I have a friend in Yonkers. Perhaps you know him. It's always so foolish to ask in cases like that, isn't it? (*They both laugh over this with increasing congeniality.* MRS. MOLLOY *goes to counter with hats from table.* CORNELIUS *follows*) It's a Mr. Vandergelder.

CORNELIUS (*Stops abruptly*) What was that you said?

MRS. MOLLOY Then you do know him?

CORNELIUS Horace Vandergelder?

MRS. MOLLOY Yes, that's right.

CORNELIUS Know him! (*Look to* BARNABY) Why, no. No!

BARNABY No! No!

CORNELIUS (*Starting to glide about the room, in search of a hiding place*) I beg your pardon, Mrs. Molloy —what an attractive shop you have! (*Smiling fixedly at her he moves to the workshop door*) And where does this door lead to? (*Opens it, and is alarmed by the bell which rings above it*)

MRS. MOLLOY Why, Mr. Hackl, that's my workroom.

CORNELIUS Everything here is so interesting. (*Looks under counter*) Every corner. Every door, Mrs. Molloy. Barnaby, notice the interesting doors and cupboards. (*He opens the cupboard door*) Deeply interesting. Coats for ladies. (*Laughs*) Barnaby, make a note of the table. Precious piece of furniture, with a low-hanging cloth, I see. (*Stretches his leg under table*)

MRS. MOLLOY (*Taking a hat from box left of wardrobe*) Perhaps your friend might like some of this new Italian straw. Mr. Vandergelder's a substantial man and very well liked, they tell me.

CORNELIUS A lovely man, Mrs. Molloy.

MRS. MOLLOY Oh yes—charming, charming!

CORNELIUS (*Smiling sweetly*) Has only one fault, as far as I know; he's hard as nails; but apart from that, as you say, a charming nature, ma'am.

MRS. MOLLOY And a large circle of friends—?

CORNELIUS Yes, indeed, yes, indeed—five or six.

BARNABY Five!

CORNELIUS He comes and calls on you here from time to time, I suppose.

MRS. MOLLOY (*Turns from mirror where she has been putting a hat on*) This summer we'll be wearing ribbons down our back. Yes, as a matter of fact I am expecting a call from him this afternoon. (*Hat off*)

BARNABY I think . . . Cornelius! I think . . . !!

MRS. MOLLOY Now to show you some more hats—

BARNABY Look out! (*He takes a flying leap over the rail and flings himself under the table*)

CORNELIUS Begging your pardon, Mrs. Molloy. (*He jumps into the cupboard*)

MRS. MOLLOY Gentlemen! Mr. Hackl! Come right out of there this minute!

CORNELIUS (*Sticking his head out of the wardrobe door*) Help us just this once, Mrs. Molloy! We'll explain later!

MRS. MOLLOY Mr. Hackl!

BARNABY We're as innocent as can be, Mrs. Molloy.

MRS. MOLLOY But really! Gentlemen! I can't have this! *What are you doing?*

BARNABY Cornelius! Cornelius! Pudding?

CORNELIUS (*A shout*) Pudding! (*They disappear. Enter from the street* MRS. LEVI, *followed by* MR. VANDERGELDER. VANDERGELDER *is dressed in a too-bright checked suit, and wears a green derby—or bowler—hat. He is carrying a large ornate box of chocolates in one hand, and a cane in the other*)

MRS. LEVI Irene, my darling child, how *are* you? Heaven be good to us, how well you look! (*They kiss*)

MRS. MOLLOY But what a surprise! And Mr. Vandergelder in New York—what a pleasure!

VANDERGELDER (*Swaying back and forth on his heels complacently*) Good afternoon, Mrs. Molloy. (*They shake hands.* MRS. MOLLOY *brings chair from counter for him. He sits at left of table*)

MRS. LEVI Yes, Mr. Vandergelder's in New York. Yonkers lies up there—*decimated* today. Irene, we thought we'd pay you a very short call. Now you'll tell us if it's inconvenient, won't you?

MRS. MOLLOY (*Placing a chair for* MRS. LEVI *at right of table*) Inconvenient, Dolly! The idea! Why, it's sweet of you to come. (*She notices the boys' hats on the table—sticks a spray of flowers into crown of* CORNELIUS' *bowler and winds a piece of chiffon round* BARNABY'S *panama*)

VANDERGELDER We waited outside a moment.

MRS. LEVI Mr. Vandergelder thought he saw two customers coming in—two men.

MRS. MOLLOY Men! Men, Mr. Vandergelder? Why, what will you be saying next?

MRS. LEVI Then we'll sit down for a minute or two. . . .

MRS. MOLLOY (*Wishing to get them out of the shop into the workroom*) Before you sit down— (*She pushes them both*) Before you sit down, there's something I want to show you. I want to show Mr. Vandergelder my workroom, too.

MRS. LEVI I've seen the workroom a hundred times. I'll stay right here and try on some of these hats.

MRS. MOLLOY No, Dolly, you come too. I have something for you. Come along, everybody. (*Exit* MRS. LEVI *to workroom*) Mr. Vandergelder, I want your advice. You don't know how helpless a woman in business is. Oh, I feel I need advice every minute from a fine business head like yours. (*Exit* VANDERGELDER *to workroom.* MRS. MOLLOY *shouts this line and then slams the workroom door*) Now I shut the door!! (*Exit* MRS. MOLLOY. CORNELIUS *puts his head out of the wardrobe door and gradually comes out into the room, leaving door open*)

CORNELIUS Hsst!

BARNABY (*Pokes his head out from under the table*) Maybe she wants us to go, Cornelius?

CORNELIUS Certainly I won't go. Mrs. Molloy would think we were just thoughtless fellows. No, all I want is to stretch a minute.

BARNABY What are you going to do when he's gone, Cornelius? Are we just going to run away?

CORNELIUS Well . . . I don't know yet. I like Mrs. Molloy a lot. I wouldn't like her to think badly of me. I think I'll buy a hat. We can walk home to Yonkers, even if it takes us all night. I wonder how much hats cost. Barnaby, give me all the money you've got. (*As he leans over to take the money, he sneezes. Both return to their hiding places in alarm; then emerge again*) My, all those perfumes in that cupboard tickle my nose! But I like it in there . . . it's a woman's world, and very different.

BARNABY I like it where I am, too; only I'd like it better if I had a pillow.

CORNELIUS (*Taking coat from wardrobe*) Here, take one of these coats. I'll roll it up for you so it won't get mussed. Ladies don't like to have their coats mussed.

BARNABY That's fine. Now I can just lie here and hear Mr. Vandergelder talk. (CORNELIUS *goes slowly above table towards cheval mirror, repeating* MRS. MOLLOY'S *line dreamily*)

CORNELIUS This summer we'll be wearing ribbons down our back. . . .

BARNABY Can I take off my shoes, Cornelius? (CORNELIUS *does not reply. He comes to the footlights and addresses the audience, in completely simple naïve sincerity*)

CORNELIUS Isn't the world full of wonderful things? There we sit cooped up in Yonkers for years and years and all the time wonderful people like Mrs. Molloy are walking around in New York and we don't know them at all. I don't know whether—from where you're sitting—you can see—well, for instance, the way (*He points to the edge of his right eye*) her eye and forehead and cheek come together, up here. Can you? And the kind of fireworks that shoot out of her eyes all the time. I tell you right now: a fine woman is the greatest work of God. You can talk all you like about Niagara Falls and the Pyramids; they aren't in it at all. Of course, up there at Yonkers they came into the store all the time, and bought this and that, and I said, "Yes, ma'am," and "That'll be seventy-five cents, ma'am"; and I *watched* them. But today I've talked to one, equal to equal, equal to equal, and to the finest one that ever existed, in my opinion. They're so different from men! Everything that they say and do is so different that you feel like laughing all the time. (*He laughs*) Golly, they're different from men. And they're awfully mysterious, too. You never can be really sure what's going on in their heads. They have a kind of wall around them all the time—of pride and a sort of play-acting: I bet you could know a woman a hundred years without ever being really sure whether she liked you or not. This minute I'm in danger. I'm in danger of losing my job and my future and everything that people think is important; but I don't care. Even if I have to dig ditches for the rest of my life, I'll be a ditch digger who once had a wonderful day. Barnaby!

BARNABY Oh, you woke me up!

CORNELIUS (*Kneels*) Barnaby, we can't go back to Yonkers yet and you know why.

BARNABY Why not?

CORNELIUS We've had a good meal. We've had an adventure. We've been in danger of getting arrested. There's only one more thing we've got to do before we go back to be successes in Yonkers.

BARNABY Cornelius! You're never going to kiss Mrs. Molloy!

CORNELIUS Maybe.

BARNABY But she'll scream.

CORNELIUS Barnaby, you don't know anything at all. You might as well know right now that everybody except us goes through life kissing right and left all the time.

BARNABY (*Pauses for reflection: humbly*) Well, thanks for telling me, Cornelius. I often wondered. (*Enter* MRS. LEVI *from workroom*)

MRS. LEVI Just a minute, Irene. I must find my handkerchief. (CORNELIUS, *caught by the arrival of* MRS. LEVI, *drops to his hands and knees, and starts very slowly to crawl back to the wardrobe, as though the slowness rendered him invisible.* MRS. LEVI, *leaning over the counter, watches him. From the cupboard he puts his head out of it and looks pleadingly at her*) Why, Mr. Hackl, I thought you were up in Yonkers.

CORNELIUS I almost always am, Mrs. Levi. Oh, Mrs. Levi, don't tell Mr. Vandergelder! I'll explain everything later.

BARNABY (*Puts head out*) We're terribly innocent, Mrs. Levi.

MRS. LEVI Why, who's that?

BARNABY Barnaby Tucker—just paying a call.

MRS. LEVI (*Looking under counter and even shaking out her skirts*) Well, who else is here?

CORNELIUS Just the two of us, Mrs. Levi, that's all.

MRS. LEVI Old friends of Mrs. Molloy's, is that it?

CORNELIUS We never knew her before a few minutes ago, but we like her a lot—don't we, Barnaby? In fact, I think she's . . . I think she's the finest person in the world. I'm ready to tell that to anybody.

MRS. LEVI And does she think *you're* the finest person in the world?

CORNELIUS Oh, no. I don't suppose she even notices that I'm alive.

MRS. LEVI Well, I think she must notice that you're alive in that cupboard, Mr. Hackl. Well, if I were you, I'd get back into it right away. Somebody could be coming in any minute. (CORNELIUS *disappears. She sits unconcernedly in chair right. Enter* MRS. MOLLOY)

MRS. MOLLOY (*Leaving door open and looking about in concealed alarm*) Can I help you, Dolly?

MRS. LEVI No, no, no. I was just blowing my nose. (*Enter* VANDERGELDER *from workroom*)

VANDERGELDER Mrs. Molloy, I've got some advice to give you about your business. (MRS. MOLLOY *comes to the center of the room and puts* BARNABY'S *hat on floor in window, then* CORNELIUS' *hat on the counter*)

MRS. LEVI Oh, advice from Mr. Vandergelder! The whole city should hear this.

VANDERGELDER (*Standing in the workroom door, pompously*) In the first place, the aim of business is to make profit.

MRS. MOLLOY Is that so?

MRS. LEVI I never heard it put so clearly before. Did you hear it?

VANDERGELDER (*Crossing the room to the left*) You pay those girls of yours too much. You pay them as much as men. Girls like that enjoy their work. Wages, Mrs. Molloy, are paid to make people do work they don't want to do.

MRS. LEVI Mr. Vandergelder thinks so ably. And that's exactly the way his business is run up in Yonkers.

VANDERGELDER (*Patting her hand*) Mrs. Molloy, I'd like for you to come up to Yonkers.

MRS. MOLLOY That would be very nice. (*He hands her the box of chocolates*) Oh, thank you. As a matter of fact, I know someone from Yonkers, someone else.

VANDERGELDER (*Hangs hat on the cheval mirror*) Oh? Who's that? (MRS. MOLLOY *puts chocolates on table and brings gilt chair forward and sits center at table facing the audience*)

MRS. MOLLOY Someone quite well-to-do, I believe, though a little free and easy in his behavior. Mr. Vandergelder, do you know Mr. Cornelius Hackl in Yonkers?

VANDERGELDER I know him like I know my own boot. He's my head clerk.

MRS. MOLLOY Is that so?

VANDERGELDER He's been in my store for ten years.

MRS. MOLLOY Well, I never!

VANDERGELDER Where would you have known him? (MRS. MOLLOY *is in silent confusion. She looks for help to* MRS. LEVI, *seated at right end of table*)

MRS. LEVI (*Groping for means to help* MRS. MOLLOY) Err . . . blah . . . err . . . bl . . . er . . . Oh, just one of those chance meetings, I suppose.

MRS. MOLLOY Yes, oh yes! One of those chance meetings.

VANDERGELDER What? Chance meetings? Cornelius Hackl has no right to chance meetings. Where was it?

MRS. MOLLOY Really, Mr. Vandergelder, it's very unlike you to question me in such a way. I think Mr. Hackl is better known than you think he is.

VANDERGELDER Nonsense.

MRS. MOLLOY He's in New York often, and he's very well liked.

MRS. LEVI (*Having found her idea, with decision*) Well, the truth might as well come out now as later. Mr. Vandergelder, Irene is quite right. Your head clerk is often in New York. Goes everywhere; has an army of friends. Everybody knows Cornelius Hackl.

VANDERGELDER (*Laughs blandly and sits in chair at left of table*) He never comes to New York. He works all day in my store and at nine o'clock at night he goes to sleep in the bran room.

MRS. LEVI So you think. But it's not true.

VANDERGELDER Dolly Gallagher, you're crazy.

MRS. LEVI Listen to me. You keep your nose so deep in your account books you don't know what goes on. Yes, by day, Cornelius Hackl is your faithful trusted clerk—that's true; but by night! Well, he leads a double life, that's all! He's here at the opera; at the great restaurants; in all the fashionable homes . . . why, he's at the Harmonia Gardens Restaurant three nights a week. The fact is, he's the wittiest, gayest, naughtiest, most delightful man in New York. Well, he's just *the* famous Cornelius Hackl!

VANDERGELDER (*Sure of himself*) It ain't the same man. If I ever thought Cornelius Hackl came to New York, I'd discharge him.

MRS. LEVI Who took the horses out of Jenny Lind's carriage and pulled her through the streets?

MRS. MOLLOY Who?

MRS. LEVI Cornelius Hackl! Who dressed up as a waiter at the Fifth Avenue Hotel the other night and took an oyster and dropped it right down Mrs. . . . (*Rises*) No, it's too wicked to tell you!

MRS. MOLLOY Oh yes, Dolly, tell it! Go on!

MRS. LEVI No. But it *was* Cornelius Hackl.

VANDERGELDER (*Loud*) It ain't the same man. Where'd he get the money?

MRS. LEVI But he's very rich.

VANDERGELDER (*Rises*) Rich! I keep his money in my own safe. He has a hundred and forty-six dollars and thirty-five cents.

MRS. LEVI Oh, Mr. Vandergelder, you're killing me! Do come to your senses. He's one of *the* Hackls. (MRS. MOLLOY *sits at chair right of table where* MRS. LEVI *has been sitting*)

VANDERGELDER *The* Hackls?

MRS. LEVI They built the Raritan Canal.

VANDERGELDER Then why should he work in my store?

MRS. LEVI Well, I'll tell you. (*Sits at the center of the table, facing the audience*)

VANDERGELDER (*Striding about*) I don't want to hear! I've got a headache! I'm going home. *It ain't the same man!!* He sleeps in my bran room. You can't get away from facts. I just made him my chief clerk.

MRS. LEVI If you had any sense you'd make him partner. (*Rises, crosses to* MRS. MOLLOY) Now Irene, I can see you were as taken with him as everybody else is.

MRS. MOLLOY Why, I only met him once, very hastily.

MRS. LEVI Yes, but I can see that you were taken with him. Now don't you be thinking of marrying him!

MRS. MOLLOY (*Her hands on her cheeks*) Dolly! What are you saying! Oh!

MRS. LEVI Maybe it'd be fine. But think it over carefully. He breaks hearts like hickory nuts.

VANDERGELDER Who?

MRS. LEVI Cornelius Hackl!

VANDERGELDER Mrs. Molloy, how often has he called on you?

MRS. MOLLOY Oh, I'm telling the truth. I've only seen him once in my life. Dolly Levi's been exaggerating so. I don't know where to look! (*Enter* MINNIE *from workroom and crosses to window*)

MINNIE Excuse me, Mrs. Molloy. I must get together that order for Mrs. Parkinson.

MRS. MOLLOY Yes, we must get that off before closing.

MINNIE I want to send it off by the errand girl. (*Having taken a hat from the window*) Oh, I almost forgot the coat. (*She starts for the wardrobe*)

MRS. MOLLOY (*Running to the wardrobe to prevent her*) Oh, oh! I'll do that, Minnie! (*But she is too late.* MINNIE *opens the right-hand cupboard door and falls back in terror, and screams*)

MINNIE Oh, Mrs. Molloy! Help! There's a man! (MRS. MOLLOY *with the following speech pushes her back to the workroom door.* MINNIE *walks with one arm pointing at the cupboard. At the end of each of* MRS. MOLLOY'S *sentences she repeats—at the same pitch and degree—the words*) There's a man!

MRS. MOLLOY (*Slamming cupboard door*) Minnie, you imagined it. You're tired, dear. You go back in the workroom and lie down. Minnie, you're a fool; hold your tongue!

MINNIE There's a man! (*Exit* MINNIE *to workroom.* MRS. MOLLOY *returns to the front of the stage.* VANDERGELDER *raises his stick threateningly*)

VANDERGELDER If there's a man there, we'll get him out. Whoever you are, come out of there! (*Strikes table with his stick*)

MRS. LEVI (*Goes masterfully to the cupboard—sweeps her umbrella around among the coats and closes each door as she does so*) Nonsense! There's no man there. See! Miss Fay's nerves have been playing tricks on her. Come now, let's sit down again. What were you saying, Mr. Vandergelder? (*They sit,* MRS. MOLLOY *right,* MRS. LEVI *center,* VANDERGELDER *left. A sneeze is heard from the cupboard. They all rise, look towards cupboard, then sit again*) Well now . . . (*Another tremendous sneeze. With a gesture that says, "I can do no more"*) God bless you! (*They all rise.* MRS. MOLLOY *stands with her back to the cupboard*)

MRS. MOLLOY (*To* VANDERGELDER) Yes, there is a man in there. I'll explain it all to you another time. Thank you very much for coming to see me. Good afternoon, Dolly. Good afternoon, Mr. Vandergelder.

VANDERGELDER You're protecting a man in there!

MRS. MOLLOY (*With back to cupboard*) There's a very simple explanation, but for the present, good afternoon. (BARNABY *now sneezes twice, lifting the table each time.* VANDERGELDER, *right of table, jerks off the tablecloth.* BARNABY *pulls cloth under table and rolls himself up in it.* MRS. MOLLOY *picks up the box of chocolates, which has rolled on to the floor*)

MRS. LEVI Lord, the whole room's *crawling* with men! I'll never get over it.

VANDERGELDER The world is going to pieces! I can't believe my own eyes!

MRS. LEVI Come, Mr. Vandergelder. Ernestina Simple is waiting for us.

VANDERGELDER (*Finds his hat and puts it on*) Mrs. Molloy, I shan't trouble you again, and *vice versa.* (MRS. MOLLOY *is standing transfixed in front of cupboard, clasping the box of chocolates.* VANDERGELDER *snatches the box from her and goes out*)

MRS. LEVI (*Crosses to her*) Irene, when I think of all the interesting things you have in this room! (*Kisses her*) Make the most of it, dear. (*Raps cupboard*)

Good-by! (*Raps on table with umbrella*) Good-by! (*Exit* MRS. LEVI. MRS. MOLLOY *opens door of cupboard.* CORNELIUS *steps out*)

MRS. MOLLOY So that was one of your practical jokes, Mr. Hackl?

CORNELIUS No, no, Mrs. Molloy!

MRS. MOLLOY Come out from under that, Barnaby Tucker, you troublemaker! (*She snatches the cloth and spreads it back on table.* MINNIE *enters*) There's nothing to be afraid of, Minnie, I know all about these gentlemen.

CORNELIUS Mrs. Molloy, we realize that what happened here—

MRS. MOLLOY You think because you're rich you can make up for all the harm you do, is that it?

CORNELIUS No, no!

BARNABY (*On the floor putting shoes on*) No, no!

MRS. MOLLOY Minnie, this is the famous Cornelius Hackl who goes round New York tying people into knots; and that's Barnaby Tucker, another troublemaker.

BARNABY How d'you do?

MRS. MOLLOY Minnie, choose yourself any hat and coat in the store. We're going out to dinner. If this Mr. Hackl is so rich and gay and charming, he's going to be rich and gay and charming to us. He dines three nights a week at the Harmonia Gardens Restaurant, does he? Well, he's taking us there now.

MINNIE Mrs. Molloy, are you sure it's safe?

MRS. MOLLOY Minnie, hold your tongue. We're in a position to put these men into jail if they so much as squeak.

CORNELIUS Jail, Mrs. Molloy?

MRS. MOLLOY Jail, Mr. Hackl. Officer Cogarty does everything I tell him to do. Minnie, you and I have been respectable for years; now we're in disgrace, we might as well make the most of it. Come into the workroom with me; I know some ways we can perk up our appearances. Gentlemen, we'll be back in a minute.

CORNELIUS Uh—Mrs. Molloy, I hear there's an awfully good restaurant at the railway station.

MRS. MOLLOY (*High indignation*) Railway station? Railway station? Certainly not! No, sir! You're going to give us a good dinner in the heart of the fashionable world. Go on in, Minnie! Don't you boys forget that you've made us lose our reputations, and now the fashionable world's the only place we can eat. (MRS. MOLLOY *exits to workroom*)

BARNABY She's angry at us, Cornelius. Maybe we'd better run away now.

CORNELIUS No, I'm going to go through with this if it kills me. Barnaby, for a woman like that a man could consent to go back to Yonkers and be a success.

BARNABY All I know is no woman's going to make a success out of me.

CORNELIUS Jail or no jail, we're going to take those ladies out to dinner. So grit your teeth. (*Enter* MRS. MOLLOY *and* MINNIE *from workroom dressed for the street*)

MRS. MOLLOY Gentlemen, the cabs are at the corner, so forward march! (*She takes a hat—which will be* BARNABY'S *at the end of Act Three—and gives it to* MINNIE)

CORNELIUS Yes, ma'am. (BARNABY *stands shaking his empty pockets warningly*) Oh, Mrs. Molloy . . . is it far to the restaurant? Couldn't we walk?

MRS. MOLLOY (*Pauses a moment, then*) Minnie, take off your things. We're not going.

OTHERS Mrs. Molloy!

MRS. MOLLOY Mr. Hackl, I don't go anywhere I'm not wanted. Good night. I'm not very happy to have met you. (*She crosses the stage as though going to the workroom door*)

OTHERS Mrs. Molloy!

MRS. MOLLOY (*Going behind counter*) I suppose you think we're not fashionable enough for you? Well, I won't be a burden to you. Good night, Mr. Tucker. (*The others follow her behind counter:* CORNELIUS, BARNABY, *then* MINNIE)

CORNELIUS We want you to come with us more than anything in the world, Mrs. Molloy. (MRS. MOLLOY *turns and pushes the three back. They are now near the center of the stage, to the right of the table,* MRS. MOLLOY *facing the audience*)

MRS. MOLLOY No, you don't! Look at you! Look at the pair of them, Minnie! Scowling, both of them!

CORNELIUS Please, Mrs. Molloy!

MRS. MOLLOY Then smile. (*To* BARNABY) Go on, smile! No, that's not enough. Minnie, you come with me and we'll get our own supper.

CORNELIUS Smile, Barnaby, you lout!

BARNABY My face can't smile any stronger than that.

MRS. MOLLOY Then do something! Show some interest. Do something lively: sing!

CORNELIUS I can't sing, really I can't.

MRS. MOLLOY We're wasting our time, Minnie. They don't want us.

CORNELIUS Barnaby, what can you sing? Mrs. Molloy, all we know are sad songs.

MRS. MOLLOY That doesn't matter. If you want us to go out with you, you've got to sing something. (*All this has been very rapid; the boys turn up to counter, put their heads together, confer and abruptly turn, stand stiffly and sing "Tenting tonight; tenting tonight; tenting on the old camp ground." The four of them now repeat the refrain, softly harmonizing. At the end of the song, after a pause,* MRS. MOLLOY, *moved, says*)

MRS. MOLLOY We'll come! (*The boys shout joyfully*) You boys go ahead. (CORNELIUS *gets his hat from counter; as he puts it on he discovers the flowers on it.* BARNABY *gets his hat from window. They go out whistling.* MINNIE *turns and puts her hat on at the mirror*) Minnie, get the front door key—I'll lock the workroom. (MRS. MOLLOY *goes to workroom.* MINNIE *takes key from hook left of wardrobe and goes to* MRS. MOLLOY, *at the workroom door. She turns her around*)

MINNIE Why, Mrs. Molloy, you're crying! (MRS. MOLLOY *flings her arms around* MINNIE)

MRS. MOLLOY Oh, Minnie, the world is full of wonderful things. Watch me, dear, and tell me if my petticoat's showing. (*She crosses to door, followed by* MINNIE, *as the curtain falls*)

*Curtain*

# Act Three

*Veranda at the Harmonia Gardens Restaurant on the Battery, New York.*

*This room is informal and rustic. The main restaurant is indicated to be off stage back right.*

*There are three entrances: swinging double doors at the center of the back wall leading to the kitchen; one on the right wall (perhaps up a few steps and flanked by potted palms) to the street; one on the left wall to the staircase leading to the rooms above.*

*On the stage are two tables, left and right, each with four chairs. It is now afternoon and they are not yet set for dinner. Against the back wall is a large folding screen. Also against the back wall are hat and coat racks.*

*As the curtain rises,* VANDERGELDER *is standing, giving orders to* RUDOLPH, *a waiter.* MALACHI STACK *sits at table left.*

VANDERGELDER Now, hear what I say. I don't want you to make any mistakes. I want a table for three.

RUDOLPH (*Tall "snob" waiter, alternating between cold superiority and rage. German accent*) For three.

VANDERGELDER There'll be two ladies and myself.

MALACHI It's a bad combination, Mr. Vandergelder. You'll regret it.

VANDERGELDER And I want a chicken.

MALACHI A chicken! You'll regret it.

VANDERGELDER Hold your tongue. Write it down: chicken.

RUDOLPH Yes, sir. Chicken Esterhazy? Chicken cacciatore? Chicken à la crème—?

VANDERGELDER (*Exploding*) A chicken! A chicken like everybody else has. And with the chicken I want a bottle of wine.

RUDOLPH Moselle? Chablis? Vouvray?

MALACHI He doesn't understand you, Mr. Vandergelder. You'd better speak louder.

VANDERGELDER (*Spelling*) W-I-N-E.

RUDOLPH Wine.

VANDERGELDER Wine! And I want this table removed. We'll eat at that table alone. (*Exit* RUDOLPH *through service door at back*)

MALACHI There are some people coming in here now, Mr. Vandergelder. (VANDERGELDER *goes to back right to look at the newcomers*)

VANDERGELDER What! Thunder and damnation! It's my niece Ermengarde! What's she doing here?!— Wait till I get my hands on her.

MALACHI (*Running up to him*) Mr. Vandergelder! You must keep your temper!

VANDERGELDER And there's that rascal artist with her. Why, it's a plot. I'll throw them in jail.

MALACHI Mr. Vandergelder! They're old enough to come to New York. You can't throw people into jail for coming to New York.

VANDERGELDER And there's Mrs. Levi! What's she doing with them? It's a plot. It's a conspiracy! What's she saying to the cabman? Go up and hear what she's saying.

MALACHI (*Listening at entrance, right*) She's telling the cabman to wait, Mr. Vandergelder. She's telling the young people to come in and have a good dinner, Mr. Vandergelder.

VANDERGELDER I'll put an end to this.

MALACHI Now, Mr. Vandergelder, if you lose your temper, you'll make matters worse. Mr. Vandergelder, come here and take my advice.

VANDERGELDER Stop pulling my coat. What's your advice?

MALACHI Hide, Mr. Vandergelder. Hide behind this screen, and listen to what they're saying.

VANDERGELDER (*Being pulled behind the screen*) Stop pulling at me. (*They hide behind the screen as* MRS. LEVI, ERMENGARDE *and* AMBROSE *enter from the right.* AMBROSE *is carrying* ERMENGARDE'S *luggage*)

ERMENGARDE But I don't want to eat in a restaurant. It's not proper.

MRS. LEVI Now, Ermengarde, dear, there's nothing wicked about eating in a restaurant. There's nothing wicked, even, about being in New York. Clergymen just make those things up to fill out their sermons.

ERMENGARDE Oh, I wish I were in Yonkers, where *nothing* ever happens!

MRS. LEVI Ermengarde, you're hungry. That's what's troubling you.

ERMENGARDE Anyway, after dinner you must promise to take me to Aunt Flora's. She's been waiting for me all day and she must be half dead of fright.

MRS. LEVI All right, but, of course, you know at Miss Van Huysen's you'll be back in your uncle's hands.

AMBROSE (*Hands raised to heaven*) I can't stand it.

MRS. LEVI (*To* AMBROSE) Just keep telling yourself how pretty she is. Pretty girls have very little opportunity to improve their other advantages.

AMBROSE Listen, Ermengarde! You don't want to go back to your uncle. Stop and think! That old man with one foot in the grave!

MRS. LEVI And the other three in the cashbox.

AMBROSE Smelling of oats—

MRS. LEVI And axle grease.

MALACHI That's not true. It's only partly true.

VANDERGELDER (*Loudly*) Hold your tongue! I'm going to teach them a lesson.

MALACHI (*Whisper*) Keep your temper, Mr. Vandergelder. Listen to what they say.

MRS. LEVI (*Hears this; throws a quick glance toward the screen; her whole manner changes*) Oh dear, what was I saying? The Lord be praised, how glad I am that I found you two dreadful children just as you were about to break poor dear Mr. Vandergelder's heart.

AMBROSE He's got no heart to break!

MRS. LEVI (*Vainly signaling*) Mr. Vandergelder's a much kinder man than you think.

AMBROSE Kinder? He's a wolf.

MRS. LEVI Remember that he leads a very lonely life. Now you're going to have dinner upstairs. There are some private rooms up there—just meant for shy timid girls like Ermengarde. Come with me. (*She pushes the young people out left,* AMBROSE *carrying the luggage*)

VANDERGELDER (*Coming forward*) I'll show them! (*He sits at table right*)

MALACHI Everybody should eavesdrop once in a while, I always say. There's nothing like eavesdropping to show you that the world outside your head is different from the world inside your head.

VANDERGELDER (*Producing a pencil and paper*) I want to write a note. Go and call that cabman in here. I want to talk to him.

MALACHI No one asks advice of a cabman, Mr. Vandergelder. They see so much of life that they have no ideas left.

VANDERGELDER Do as I tell you.

MALACHI Yes, sir. Advice of a cabman! (*Exit right.* VANDERGELDER *writes his letter*)

VANDERGELDER "My dear Miss Van Huysen" (*To audience*) Everybody's dear in a letter. It's enough to make you give up writing 'em. "My dear Miss Van Huysen. This is Ermengarde and that rascal Ambrose Kemper. They are trying to run away. Keep them in your house until I come." (MALACHI *returns with an enormous* CABMAN *in a high hat and a long coat. He carries a whip*)

CABMAN (*Entering*) What's he want?

VANDERGELDER I want to talk to you.

CABMAN I'm engaged. I'm waiting for my parties.

VANDERGELDER (*Folding letter and writing address*) I know you are. Do you want to earn five dollars?

CABMAN Eh?

VANDERGELDER I asked you, do you want to earn five dollars?

CABMAN I don't know. I never tried.

VANDERGELDER When those parties of yours come downstairs, I want you to drive them to this address. Never mind what they say, drive them to this address. Ring the bell: give this letter to the lady of the house: see that they get in the door and keep them there.

CABMAN I can't make people go into a house if they don't want to.

VANDERGELDER (*Producing purse*) Can you for ten dollars?

CABMAN Even for ten dollars, I can't do it alone.

VANDERGELDER This fellow here will help you.

MALACHI (*Sitting at table left*) Now I'm pushing people into houses.

VANDERGELDER There's the address: Miss Flora Van Huysen, 8 Jackson Street.

CABMAN Even if I get them in the door I can't be sure they'll stay there.

VANDERGELDER For fifteen dollars you can.

MALACHI Murder begins at twenty-five.

VANDERGELDER Hold your tongue! (*To* CABMAN) The lady of the house will help you. All you have to do is to sit in the front hall and see that the man doesn't run off with the girl. I'll be at Miss Van Huysen's in an hour or two and I'll pay you then.

CABMAN If they call the police, I can't do anything.

VANDERGELDER It's perfectly honest business. Perfectly honest.

MALACHI Every man's the best judge of his own honesty.

VANDERGELDER The young lady is my niece. (*The* CABMAN *laughs, skeptically*) The young lady is my niece!! (*The* CABMAN *looks at Malachi and shrugs*) She's trying to run away with a good-for-nothing and we're preventing it.

CABMAN Oh, I know them, sir. They'll win in the end. Rivers don't run uphill.

MALACHI What did I tell you, Mr. Vandergelder? Advice of a cabman.

VANDERGELDER (*Hits table with his stick*) Stack! I'll be back in half an hour. See that the table's set for three. See that nobody else eats here. Then go and join the cabman on the box.

MALACHI Yes, sir. (*Exit* VANDERGELDER *right*)

CABMAN Who's your friend?

MALACHI Friend!! That's not a friend; that's an employer I'm trying out for a few days.

CABMAN You won't like him.

MALACHI I can see you're in business for yourself because you talk about liking employers. No one's ever liked an employer since business began.

CABMAN AW—!

MALACHI No, sir. I suppose you think *your horse* likes you?

CABMAN My old Clementine? She'd give her right feet for me.

MALACHI That's what all employers think. You imagine it. The streets of New York are full of cab horses winking at one another. Let's go in the kitchen and get some whisky. I can't push people into houses when I'm sober. No, I've had about fifty employers in my life, but this is the most employer of them all. He talks to everybody as though he were paying them.

CABMAN I had an employer once. He watched me from eight in the morning until six at night—just sat there and watched me. Oh, dear! Even my mother didn't think I was as interesting as that. (CABMAN *exits through service door*)

MALACHI (*Following him off*) Yes, being employed is like being loved: you know that somebody's thinking about you the whole time. (*Exits. Enter right,* MRS. MOLLOY, MINNIE, BARNABY *and* CORNELIUS)

MRS. MOLLOY See! Here's the place I meant! Isn't it fine? Minnie, take off your things; we'll be here for hours.

CORNELIUS (*Stopping at door*) Mrs. Molloy, are you sure you'll like it here? I think I feel a draught.

MRS. MOLLOY Indeed, I do like it. We're going to have a fine dinner right in this room; it's private, and it's elegant. Now we're all going to forget our troubles and call each other by our first names. Cornelius! Call the waiter.

CORNELIUS Wait—wait—I can't make a sound. I must have caught a cold on that ride. Wai— No! It won't come.

MRS. MOLLOY I don't believe you. Barnaby, you call him.

BARNABY (*Boldly*) Waiter! Waiter! (CORNELIUS *threatens him.* BARNABY *runs left*)

MINNIE I never thought I'd be in such a place in my whole life. Mrs. Molloy, is this what they call a "café"?

MRS. MOLLOY (*Sits at table left, facing audience*) Yes, this is a café. Sit down, Minnie. Cornelius, Mrs. Levi gave us to understand that every waiter in New York knew you.

CORNELIUS They will. (BARNABY *sits at chair left;* MINNIE *in chair back to audience. Enter* RUDOLPH *from service door*)

RUDOLPH Good evening, ladies and gentlemen.

CORNELIUS (*Shaking his hand*) How are you, Fritz? How are you, my friend?

RUDOLPH I am Rudolph.

CORNELIUS Of course. Rudolph, of course. Well, Rudolph, these ladies want a little something to eat—you know what I mean? Just if you can find the time —we know how busy you are.

MRS. MOLLOY Cornelius, there's no need to be so familiar with the waiter. (*Takes menu from* RUDOLPH)

CORNELIUS Oh, yes, there is.

MRS. MOLLOY (*Passing menu across*) Minnie, what do you want to eat?

MINNIE Just anything, Irene.

MRS. MOLLOY No, speak up, Minnie. What do you want?

MINNIE No, really, I have no appetite at all. (*Swings round in her chair and studies the menu, horrified at the prices*) Oh . . . Oh . . . I'd like some sardines on toast and a glass of milk.

CORNELIUS (*Takes menu from her*) Great grindstones! What a sensible girl. Barnaby, shake Minnie's hand. She's the most sensible girl in the world. Rudolph, bring us gentlemen two glasses of beer, a loaf of bread and some cheese.

MRS. MOLLOY (*Takes menu*) I never heard such nonsense. Cornelius, we've come here for a good dinner and a good time. Minnie, have you ever eaten pheasant?

MINNIE Pheasant? No-o-o-o!

MRS. MOLLOY Rudolph, have you any pheasant?

RUDOLPH Yes, ma'am. Just in from New Jersey today.

MRS. MOLLOY Even the pheasants are leaving New Jersey. (*She laughs loudly, pushing* CORNELIUS, *then* RUDOLPH; *not from menu*) Now, Rudolph, write this down: mock turtle soup; pheasant; mashed chestnuts; green salad; and some nice red wine. (RUDOLPH *repeats each item after her*)

CORNELIUS (*Losing all his fears, boldly*) All right, Barnaby, you watch me. (*He reads from the bill of fare*) Rudolph, write this down: Neapolitan ice cream; hothouse peaches; champagne . . .

ALL Champagne! (BARNABY *spins round in his chair*)

CORNELIUS (*Holds up a finger*) . . . and a German band. Have you got a German band?

MRS. MOLLOY No, Cornelius, I won't let you be extravagant. Champagne, but no band. Now, Rudolph, be quick about this. We're hungry. (*Exit* RUDOLPH *to kitchen.* MRS. MOLLOY *crosses to right*) Minnie, come upstairs. I have an idea about your hair. I think it'd be nice in two wee horns—

MINNIE (*Hurrying after her, turns and looks at the boys*) Oh! Horns! (*They go out right. There is a long pause.* CORNELIUS *sits staring after them*)

BARNABY Cornelius, in the Army, you have to peel potatoes all the time.

CORNELIUS (*Not turning*) Oh, that doesn't matter. By the time we get out of jail we can move right over to the Old Men's Home. (*Another waiter,* AUGUST, *enters from service door bearing a bottle of champagne in cooler, and five glasses.* MRS. MOLLOY *re-enters right, followed by* MINNIE, *and stops* AUGUST)

MRS. MOLLOY Waiter! What's that? What's that you have?

AUGUST (*Young waiter; baby face; is continually bursting into tears*) It's some champagne, ma'am.

MRS. MOLLOY Cornelius; it's our champagne. (ALL *gather round* AUGUST)

AUGUST No, no. It's for His Honor the Mayor of New York and he's very impatient.

MRS. MOLLOY Shame on him! The Mayor of New York has more important things to be impatient about. Cornelius, open it. (CORNELIUS *takes the bottle, opens it and fills the glasses*)

AUGUST Ma'am, he'll kill me.

MRS. MOLLOY Well, have a glass first and die happy.

AUGUST (*Sits at table right, weeping*) He'll kill me. (RUDOLPH *lays the cloth on the table, left*)

MRS. MOLLOY I go to a public restaurant for the first time in ten years and all the waiters burst into tears. There, take that and stop crying, love. (*She takes a glass to* AUGUST *and pats his head, then comes back*) Barnaby, make a toast!

BARNABY (*Center of the group, with naïve sincerity*) I? . . . uh . . . To all the ladies in the world . . . may I get to know more of them . . . and . . . may I get to know them better. (*There is a hushed pause*)

CORNELIUS (*Softly*) To the ladies!

MRS. MOLLOY That's *very* sweet and *very* refined. Minnie, for that I'm going to give Barnaby a kiss.

MINNIE Oh!

MRS. MOLLOY Hold your tongue, Minnie. I'm old enough to be his mother, and— (*Indicating a height three feet from the floor*) a dear wee mother I would have been too. Barnaby, this is for you from all the ladies in the world. (*She kisses him.* BARNABY *is at first silent and dazed, then*)

BARNABY Now I can go back to Yonkers, Cornelius. Pudding. Pudding. Pudding! (*He spins round and falls on his knees*)

MRS. MOLLOY Look at Barnaby. He's not strong enough for a kiss. His head can't stand it. (*Exit* AUGUST, *right service door, with tray and cooler. The sound of "Les Patineurs" waltz comes from off left.* CORNELIUS *sits in chair facing audience, top of table.* MINNIE *at left.* BARNABY *at right and* MRS. MOLLOY *back to audience*) Minnie, I'm enjoying myself. To think that this goes on in hundreds of places every night, while I sit at home darning my stockings. (MRS. MOLLOY *rises and dances, alone, slowly about the stage*) Cornelius, dance with me.

CORNELIUS (*Rises*) Irene, the Hackls don't dance. We're Presbyterian.

MRS. MOLLOY Minnie, you dance with me. (MINNIE *joins her.* CORNELIUS *sits again*)

MINNIE Lovely music.

MRS. MOLLOY Why, Minnie, you dance beautifully.

MINNIE We girls dance in the workroom when you're not looking, Irene.

MRS. MOLLOY You thought I'd be angry! Oh dear, no one in the world understands anyone else in the world. (*The girls separate.* MINNIE *dances off to her place at the table.* MRS. MOLLOY *sits thoughtfully at table right. The music fades away*) Cornelius! Jenny Lind and all those other ladies—do you see them all the time?

CORNELIUS (*Rises and joins her at table right*) Irene, I've put them right out of my head. I'm interested in . . . (RUDOLPH *has entered by the service door. He now flings a tablecloth between them on the table*)

MRS. MOLLOY Rudolph, what are you doing?

RUDOLPH A table's been reserved here. Special orders.

MRS. MOLLOY Stop right where you are. That party can eat inside. This veranda's ours.

RUDOLPH I'm very sorry. This veranda is open to anybody who wants it. Ah, there comes the man who brought the order. (*Enter* MALACHI *from the kitchen, drunk*)

MRS. MOLLOY (*To* MALACHI) Take your table away from here. We got here first, Cornelius, throw him out.

MALACHI Ma'am, my employer reserved this room at four o'clock this afternoon. You can go and eat in the restaurant. My employer said it was very important that he have a table alone.

MRS. MOLLOY No, sir. We got here first and we're going to stay here—alone, too. (MINNIE *and* BARNABY *come forward*)

RUDOLPH Ladies and gentlemen!

MRS. MOLLOY Shut up, you! (*To* MALACHI) You're an impertinent, idiotic kill-joy.

MALACHI (*Very pleased*) That's an insult!

MRS. MOLLOY All the facts about you are insults. (*To* CORNELIUS) Cornelius, do something. Knock it over! The table.

CORNELIUS Knock it over. (*After a shocked struggle with himself* CORNELIUS *calmly overturns the table.* AUGUST *rights the table and picks up cutlery, weeping copiously*)

RUDOLPH (*In cold fury*) I'm sorry, but this room can't be reserved for anyone. If you want to eat alone, you must go upstairs. I'm sorry, but that's the rule.

MRS. MOLLOY We're having a nice dinner alone and we're going to stay here. Cornelius, knock it over. (CORNELIUS *overturns the table again. The girls squeal with pleasure. The waiter* AUGUST *again scrambles for the silver*)

MALACHI Wait till you see my employer!

RUDOLPH (*Bringing screen down*) Ladies and gentlemen! I'll tell you what we'll do. There's a big screen here. We'll put the screen up between the tables. August, come and help me.

MRS. MOLLOY I won't eat behind a screen. I won't. Minnie, make a noise. We're not animals in a menagerie. Cornelius, no screen. Minnie, there's a fight. I feel ten years younger. No screen! No screen! (*During the struggle with the screen all talk at once*)

MALACHI (*Loud and clear and pointing to entrance at right*) Now you'll learn something. There comes my employer now, getting out of that cab.

CORNELIUS (*Coming to him, taking off his coat*) Where? I'll knock him down too. (BARNABY *has gone up to right entrance. He turns and shouts clearly*)

BARNABY Cornelius, it's Wolf-trap. Yes, it is!

CORNELIUS Wolf-trap! Listen, everybody. I think the screen's a good idea. Have you got any more screens, Rudolph? We could use three or four. (*He pulls the screen forward again*)

MRS. MOLLOY Quiet down, Cornelius, and stop changing your mind. Hurry up, Rudolph, we're ready for the soup. (*During the following scene* RUDOLPH *serves the meal at the table left, as unobtrusively as possible. The stage is now divided in half. The quartet's table is at the left. Enter* VANDERGELDER *from the right. He now wears overcoat and carries the box of chocolates*)

VANDERGELDER Stack! What's the meaning of this? I told you I wanted a table alone. What's that? (VANDERGELDER *hits the screen twice with his stick.* MRS. MOLLOY *hits back twice with a spoon. The four young people sit:* BARNABY *facing audience;* MRS. MOLLOY *right,* MINNIE *left, and* CORNELIUS *back to audience*)

MALACHI Mr. Vandergelder, I did what I could. Mr. Vandergelder, you wouldn't believe what wild savages the people of New York are. There's a woman over there, Mr. Vandergelder—civilization hasn't touched her.

VANDERGELDER Everything's wrong. You can't even manage a thing like that. Help me off with my coat. Don't kill me. Don't kill me. (*During the struggle with the overcoat* MR. VANDERGELDER'S *purse flies out of his pocket and falls by the screen.* VANDERGELDER *goes to the coat tree and hangs his coat up*)

MRS. MOLLOY Speak up! I can't hear you.

CORNELIUS My voice again. Barnaby, how's your throat? Can you speak?

BARNABY Can't make a sound.

MRS. MOLLOY Oh, all right. Bring your heads together, and we'll whisper.

VANDERGELDER Who are those people over there?

MALACHI Some city sparks and their girls, Mr. Vandergelder. What goes on in big cities, Mr. Vandergelder —best not think of it.

VANDERGELDER Has that couple come down from upstairs yet? I hope they haven't gone off without your seeing them.

MALACHI No, sir. Myself and the cabman have kept our eyes on everything.

VANDERGELDER (*Sits at right of table, profile to the audience*) I'll sit here and wait for my guests. You go out to the cab.

MALACHI Yes, sir. (VANDERGELDER *unfurls newspaper and starts to read.* MALACHI *sees the purse on the floor and picks it up*) Eh, What's that? A purse. Did you drop something, Mr. Vandergelder?

VANDERGELDER No. Don't bother me any more. Do as I tell you.

MALACHI (*Stooping over. Coming center*) A purse. That fellow over there must have let it fall during the misunderstanding about the screen. No, I won't look inside. Twenty-dollar bills, dozens of them. I'll go over and give it to him. (*Starts toward* CORNELIUS, *then turns and says to audience*) You're surprised? You're surprised to see me getting rid of this money so quickly, eh? I'll explain it to you. There was a time in my life when my chief interest was picking up money that didn't belong to me. The law is there to protect property, but—sure, the law doesn't care whether a property owner deserves his property or not, and the law has to be corrected. There are several thousands of people in this country engaged in correcting the law. For a while, I too was engaged in the redistribution of superfluities. A man works all his life and leaves a million to his widow. She sits in hotels and eats great meals and plays cards all afternoon and evening, with ten diamonds on her fingers. Call in the robbers! Call in the robbers! Or a man leaves it to his son who stands leaning against bars all night boring a bartender. Call in the robbers! Stealing's a weakness. There are some people who say you shouldn't have any weaknesses at all—no vices. But if a man has no vices, he's in great danger of making vices out of his virtues, and there's a spectacle. We've all seen them: men who were monsters of philanthropy and women who were dragons of purity. We've seen people who told the truth, though the Heavens fall—and the Heavens fell. No, no—nurse one vice in your bosom. Give it the attention it deserves and let your virtues spring up modestly around it. Then you'll have the miser who's no liar; and the drunkard who's the benefactor of a whole city. Well, after I'd had that weakness of stealing for a while, I found another: I took to whisky—whisky took to me. And then I discovered an important rule that I'm going to pass on to you: Never support two weaknesses at the same time. It's your combination sinners—your lecherous liars and your miserly drunkards—who dishonor the vices and bring them into bad repute. So now you see why I want to get rid of this money: I want to keep my mind free to do the credit to whisky that it deserves. And my last word to you, ladies and gentlemen, is this: one vice at a time. (*Goes over to* CORNELIUS) Can I speak to you for a minute?

CORNELIUS (*Rises*) You certainly can. We all want to apologize to you about that screen—that little misunderstanding. (*They all rise, with exclamations of apology*) What's your name, sir?

MALACHI Stack, sir. Malachi Stack. If the ladies will excuse you, I'd like to speak to you for a minute. (*Draws* CORNELIUS *down to front of stage*) Listen, boy, have you lost . . . ? Come here . . . (*Leads him further down, out of* VANDERGELDER'S *hearing*) Have you lost something?

CORNELIUS Mr. Stack, in this one day I've lost everything I own.

MALACHI There it is. (*Gives him purse*) Don't mention it.

CORNELIUS Why, Mr. Stack . . . you know what it is? It's a miracle. (*Looks toward the ceiling*)

MALACHI Don't mention it.

CORNELIUS Barnaby, come here a minute. I want you to shake hands with Mr. Stack. (BARNABY, *napkin tucked into his collar, joins them*) Mr. Stack's just found the purse I lost, Barnaby. You know—the purse full of money.

BARNABY (*Shaking his hand vigorously*) You're a wonderful man, Mr. Stack.

MALACHI Oh, it's nothing—nothing.

CORNELIUS I'm certainly glad I went to church all these years. You're a good person to know, Mr. Stack. In a way. Mr. Stack, where do you work?

MALACHI Well, I've just begun. I work for a Mr. Vandergelder in Yonkers. (CORNELIUS *is thunderstruck. He glances at* BARNABY *and turns to* MALACHI *with awe. All three are swaying slightly, back and forth*)

CORNELIUS You do? It's a miracle. (*He points to the ceiling*) Mr. Stack, I know you don't need it—but can I give you something for . . . for the good work?

MALACHI (*Putting out his hand*) Don't mention it. It's nothing. (*Starts to go left*)

CORNELIUS Take that. (*Hands him a note*)

MALACHI (*Taking note*) Don't mention it.

CORNELIUS And that. (*Another note*)

MALACHI (*Takes it and moves away*) I'd better be going.

CORNELIUS Oh, here. And that.

MALACHI (*Hands third note back*) No . . . I might get to like them. (*Exit left.* CORNELIUS *bounds exultantly back to table*)

CORNELIUS Irene, I feel a lot better about everything. Irene, I feel so well that I'm going to tell the truth.

MRS. MOLLOY I'd forgotten that, Minnie. Men get drunk so differently from women. All right, what is the truth?

CORNELIUS If I tell the truth, will you let me . . . will you let me put my arm around your waist? (MINNIE *screams and flings her napkin over her face*)

MRS. MOLLOY Hold your tongue, Minnie. All right, you can put your arm around my waist just to show it can be done in a gentlemanly way; but I might as well warn you: a corset is a corset.

CORNELIUS (*His arm around her; softly*) You're a wonderful person, Mrs. Molloy.

MRS. MOLLOY Thank you. (*She removes his hand from around her waist*) All right, now that's enough. What is the truth?

CORNELIUS Irene, I'm not as rich as Mrs. Levi said I was.

MRS. MOLLOY Not rich!

CORNELIUS I almost never came to New York. And I'm not like she said I was—bad. And I think you ought to know that at this very minute Mr. Vandergelder's sitting on the other side of that screen.

MRS. MOLLOY What! Well, he's not going to spoil any party of mine. So *that's* why we have been whispering? Let's forget all about Mr. Vandergelder and have some more wine. (*They start to sing softly: "The Sidewalks of New York." Enter* MRS. LEVI, *from the street, in an elaborate dress.* VANDERGELDER *rises*)

MRS. LEVI Good evening, Mr. Vandergelder.

VANDERGELDER Where's—where's Miss Simple?

MRS. LEVI Mr. Vandergelder, I'll never trust a woman again as long as I live.

VANDERGELDER Well? What is it?

MRS. LEVI She ran away this afternoon and got married!

VANDERGELDER She did?

MRS. LEVI Married, Mr. Vandergelder, to a young boy of fifty.

VANDERGELDER She did?

MRS. LEVI Oh, I'm as disappointed as you are. I-can't-eat-a-thing-what-have-you-ordered?

VANDERGELDER I ordered what you told me to, a chicken. (*Enter* AUGUST. *He goes to Vandergelder's table*)

MRS. LEVI I don't think I could face a chicken. Oh, waiter. How do you do? What's your name?

AUGUST August, ma'am.

MRS. LEVI August, this is Mr. Vandergelder of Yonkers—Yonkers' most influential citizen, in fact. I want you to see that he's served with the best you have and served promptly. And there'll only be the two of us. (MRS. LEVI *gives one set of cutlery to* AUGUST. VANDERGELDER *puts chocolate box under table*) Mr. Vandergelder's been through some trying experiences today—what with men hidden all over Mrs. Molloy's store—like Indians in ambush.

VANDERGELDER (*Between his teeth*) Mrs. Levi, you don't have to tell him everything about me. (*The quartet commences singing again very softly*)

MRS. LEVI Mr. Vandergelder, if you're thinking about getting married, you might as well learn right now you have to let women be women. Now, August, we want excellent service.

AUGUST Yes, ma'am. (*Exits to kitchen*)

VANDERGELDER You've managed things very badly. When I plan a thing it takes place. (MRS. LEVI *rises*) Where are you going?

MRS. LEVI Oh, I'd just like to see who's on the other side of that screen. (MRS. LEVI *crosses to the other side of the stage and sees the quartet. They are frightened and fall silent*)

CORNELIUS (*Rising*) Good evening, Mrs. Levi. (MRS. LEVI *takes no notice, but, taking up the refrain where they left off, returns to her place at the table right*)

VANDERGELDER Well, who was it?

MRS. LEVI Oh, just some city sparks entertaining their girls, I guess.

VANDERGELDER Always wanting to know everything; always curious about everything; always putting your nose into other people's affairs. Anybody who lived with you would get as nervous as a cat.

MRS. LEVI What? What's that you're saying?

VANDERGELDER I said anybody who lived with you would—

MRS. LEVI Horace Vandergelder, get that idea right out of your head this minute. I'm surprised that you even mentioned such a thing. Understand once and for all that I have no intention of marrying you.

VANDERGELDER I didn't mean that.

MRS. LEVI You've been hinting around at such a thing for some time, but from now on put such ideas right out of your head.

VANDERGELDER Stop talking that way. That's not what I meant at all.

MRS. LEVI I hope not. I should hope not. Horace Vandergelder, you go your way, (*Points a finger*) and I'll go mine. (*Points in same direction*) I'm not some Irene Molloy, whose head can be turned by a pot of geraniums. Why, the idea of you even suggesting such a thing.

VANDERGELDER Mrs. Levi, you misunderstood me.

MRS. LEVI I certainly hope I did. If I had any intention of marrying again it would be to a far more pleasure-loving man than you. Why I'd marry Cornelius Hackl before I'd marry you. (CORNELIUS *raises his head in alarm. The others stop eating and listen*) However, we won't discuss it any more. (*Enter* AUGUST *with a tray*) Here's August with our food. I'll serve it, August.

AUGUST Yes, ma'am. (*Exit* AUGUST)

MRS. LEVI Here's some white meat for you, and some giblets, very tender, and very good for you. No, as I said before, you go your way and I'll go mine—Start right in on the wine. I think you'll feel better at once. However, since you brought the matter up, there's one more thing I think I ought to say.

VANDERGELDER (*Rising in rage*) I didn't bring the matter up at all.

MRS. LEVI We'll have forgotten all about it in a moment, but—sit down, sit down, we'll close the matter forever in just a moment, but there's one more thing I ought to say. (VANDERGELDER *sits down*) It's true, I'm a woman who likes to know everything that's going on; who likes to manage things, you're perfectly right about that. But I wouldn't like to manage anything as disorderly as your household, as out of control, as untidy. You'll have to do that yourself, God helping you.

VANDERGELDER It's not out of control.

MRS. LEVI Very well, let's not say another word about it. Take some more of that squash, it's good. No, Horace, a complaining, quarrelsome, friendless soul like you is no sort of companion for me. You go your way, (*Peppers her own plate*) and I'll go mine. (*Peppers his plate*)

VANDERGELDER Stop saying that.

MRS. LEVI I won't say another word.

VANDERGELDER Besides . . . I'm not those things you said I am.

MRS. LEVI What?—Well, I guess you're friendless, aren't you? Ermengarde told me this morning you'd even quarreled with your barber—a man's who's held a razor to your throat for twenty years! Seems to me that that's sinking pretty low.

VANDERGELDER Well, . . . but . . . my clerks, they . . .

MRS. LEVI They like you? Cornelius Hackl and that Barnaby? Behind your back they call you Wolf-trap. (*Quietly the quartet at the other table have moved up to the screens—bringing chairs for* MRS. MOLLOY *and* MINNIE. *Wine glasses in hand, they overhear this conversation*)

VANDERGELDER (*Blanching*) They don't.

MRS. LEVI No, Horace. It looks to me as though I were the last person in the world that liked you, and even I'm just so-so. No, for the rest of my life I intend to have a good time. You'll be able to find some housekeeper who can prepare you three meals for a dollar a day—it can be done, you know, if you like cold baked beans. You'll spend your last days listening at keyholes, for fear someone's cheating you. Take some more of that.

VANDERGELDER Dolly, you're a damned exasperating woman.

MRS. LEVI There! You see? That's the difference between us. I'd be nagging you all day to get some spirit into you. You could be a perfectly charming, witty, amiable man, if you wanted to.

VANDERGELDER (*Rising, bellowing*) I don't want to be charming.

MRS. LEVI But you are. Look at you now. You can't hide it.

VANDERGELDER (*Sits*) Listen at keyholes! Dolly, you have no right to say such things to me.

MRS. LEVI At your age you ought to enjoy hearing the honest truth.

VANDERGELDER My age! My age! You're always talking about my age.

MRS. LEVI I don't know what your age is, but I do know that up at Yonkers with bad food and bad temper you'll double it in six months. Let's talk of something else; but before we leave the subject there's one more thing I *am* going to say.

VANDERGELDER Don't!

MRS. LEVI Sometimes, just sometimes, I think I'd be tempted to marry you out of sheer pity; and if the confusion in your house gets any worse I may *have* to.

VANDERGELDER I haven't asked you to marry me.

MRS. LEVI Well, *please don't*.

VANDERGELDER And my house is not in confusion.

MRS. LEVI What? With your niece upstairs in the restaurant right now?

VANDERGELDER I've fixed that better than you know.

MRS. LEVI And your clerks skipping around New York behind your back?

VANDERGELDER They're in Yonkers where they always are.

MRS. LEVI Nonsense!

VANDERGELDER What do you mean, nonsense?

MRS. LEVI Cornelius Hackl's the other side of that screen this very minute.

VANDERGELDER It ain't the same man!

MRS. LEVI All right. Go on. Push it, knock it down. Go and see.

VANDERGELDER (*Goes to screen, pauses in doubt, then returns to his chair again*) I don't believe it.

MRS. LEVI All right. All right. Eat your chicken. Of course, Horace, if your affairs went from bad to worse and you became actually miserable, I might feel that it was my duty to come up to Yonkers and be of some assistance to you. After all, I was your wife's oldest friend.

VANDERGELDER I don't know how you ever got any such notion. Now understand, once and for all, I have *no intention of marrying anybody*. Now, I'm tired and I don't want to talk. (CORNELIUS *crosses to extreme left,* MRS. MOLLOY *following him*)

MRS. LEVI I won't say another word, either.

CORNELIUS Irene, I think we'd better go. You take this money and pay the bill. Oh, don't worry, it's not mine.

MRS. MOLLOY No, no, I'll tell you what we'll do. You boys put on our coats and veils, and if he comes stamping over here, he'll think you're girls.

CORNELIUS What! Those things!

MRS. MOLLOY Yes. Come on. (*She and* MINNIE *take the clothes from the stand*)

VANDERGELDER (*Rises*) I've got a headache. I've had a bad day. I'm going to Flora Van Huysen's, and then I'm going back to my hotel. (*Reaches for his purse*) So, here's the money to pay for the dinner. (*Searching another pocket*) Here's the money to pay for the . . . (*Going through all his pockets*) Here's the money . . . I've lost my purse! !

MRS. LEVI Impossible! I can't imagine you without your purse.

VANDERGELDER It's been stolen. (*Searching overcoat*) Or I left it in the cab. What am I going to do? I'm new at the hotel; they don't know me. I've never been here before . . . Stop eating the chicken, I can't pay for it!

MRS. LEVI (*Laughing gaily*) Horace, I'll be able to find some money. Sit down and calm yourself.

VANDERGELDER Dolly Gallagher, I gave you twenty-five dollars this morning.

MRS. LEVI I haven't a cent. I gave it to my lawyer. We can borrow it from Ambrose Kemper, upstairs.

VANDERGELDER I wouldn't take it.

MRS. LEVI Cornelius Hackl will lend it to us.

VANDERGELDER He's in Yonkers—Waiter! (CORNELIUS *comes forward dressed in* MRS. MOLLOY's *coat, thrown over his shoulder like a cape.* MRS. LEVI *is enjoying herself immensely.* VANDERGELDER *again goes to back wall to examine the pockets of his overcoat*)

MRS. MOLLOY Cornelius, is that Mr. Vandergelder's purse?

CORNELIUS I didn't know it myself. I thought it was money just wandering around loose that didn't belong to anybody.

MRS. MOLLOY Goodness! That's what politicians think!

VANDERGELDER Waiter! (*A band off left starts playing a polka.* BARNABY *comes forward dressed in* MINNIE's *hat, coat, and veil*)

MINNIE Irene, doesn't Barnaby make a lovely girl? He just ought to stay that way. (MRS. LEVI *and* VANDERGELDER *move their table upstage while searching for the purse*)

MRS. MOLLOY Why should we have our evening spoiled? Cornelius, I can teach you to dance in a few minutes. Oh, he won't recognize you.

MINNIE Barnaby, it's the easiest thing in the world. (*They move their table up against the back wall*)

MRS. LEVI Horace, you danced with me at your wedding and you danced with me at mine. Do you remember?

VANDERGELDER No. Yes.

MRS. LEVI Horace, you were a good dancer then. Don't confess to me that you're too old to dance.

VANDERGELDER I'm not too old. I just don't want to dance.

MRS. LEVI Li ten to that music. Horace, do you remember the dances in the firehouse at Yonkers on Saturday nights? You gave me a fan. Come, come on! (VANDERGELDER *and* MRS. LEVI *start to dance.* CORNELIUS, *dancing with* MRS. MOLLOY, *bumps into* VANDERGELDER, *back to back.* VANDERGELDER, *turning, fails at first to recognize him, then does and roars*)

VANDERGELDER You're discharged! Not a word! You're fired! Where's that idiot, Barnaby Tucker? He's fired, too. (*The four young people, laughing, start rushing out the door to the street.* VANDERGELDER, *pointing at* MRS. MOLLOY, *shouts*) You're discharged!

MRS. MOLLOY (*Pointing at him*) *You're* discharged! (*Exit*)

VANDERGELDER You're discharged! (*Enter from left,* AMBROSE *and* ERMENGARDE. *To* ERMENGARDE) I'll lock you up for the rest of your life, young lady.

ERMENGARDE Uncle! (*She faints in* AMBROSE's *arms*)

VANDERGELDER (*To* AMBROSE) I'll have you arrested. Get out of my sight. I never want to see you again.

AMBROSE (*Carrying* ERMENGARDE *across to exit right*) You can't do anything to me, Mr. Vandergelder. (*Exit* AMBROSE *and* ERMENGARDE)

MRS. LEVI (*Who has been laughing heartily, follows the distraught* VANDERGELDER *about the stage as he continues to hunt for his purse*) Well, there's your life, Mr. Vandergelder! Without niece—without clerks—without bride—and without your purse. *Will you marry me now?*

VANDERGELDER No! (*To get away from her, he dashes into the kitchen*)

MRS. LEVI (*Still laughing, exclaims to the audience*) Damn!! (*And rushes off right*)

*Curtain*

# Act Four

*Miss Flora Van Huysen's house.*

*This is a prosperous spinster's living room and is filled with knickknacks, all in bright colors, and hung with family portraits, bird cages, shawls, etc. There is only one entrance—a large double door in the center of the back wall. Beyond it one sees the hall which leads left to the street door and right to the kitchen and the rest of the house. On the left are big windows hung with lace curtains on heavy draperies. Front left is Miss Van Huysen's sofa, covered with bright-colored cushions, and behind it a table. On the right is another smaller sofa.* MISS VAN HUYSEN *is lying on the sofa. The* COOK *is at the window, left.* MISS VAN HUYSEN, *fifty, florid, stout, and sentimental, is sniffing at smelling salts.* COOK (*enormous*) *holds a china mixing bowl.*

COOK No, ma'am. I could swear I heard a cab drawing up to the door.

MISS VAN HUYSEN You imagined it. Imagination. Everything in life . . . like that . . . disappointment . . . illusion. Our plans . . . our hopes . . . what becomes of them? Nothing. The story of my life. (*She sings for a moment*)

COOK Pray God nothing's happened to the dear girl. Is it a long journey from Yonkers?

MISS VAN HUYSEN No; but long enough for a thousand things to happen.

COOK Well, we've been waiting all day. Don't you think we ought to call the police about it?

MISS VAN HUYSEN The police! If it's God's will, the police can't prevent it. Oh, in three days, in a week, in a year, we'll know what's happened. . . . And if anything *has* happened to Ermengarde, it'll be a lesson to *him*—that's what it'll be.

COOK To who?

MISS VAN HUYSEN To that cruel uncle of hers, of course—to Horace Vandergelder, and to everyone else who tries to separate young lovers. Young lovers have enough to contend with as it is. Who should know that better than I? No one. The story of my life. (*Sings for a moment, then*) There! Now I hear a cab. Quick!

COOK No. No, ma'am. I don't see anything.

MISS VAN HUYSEN There! What did I tell you? Everything's imagination—illusion.

COOK But surely, if they'd changed their plans Mr. Vandergelder would have sent you a message.

MISS VAN HUYSEN Oh, I know what's the matter. That poor child probably thought she was coming to another prison—to another tyrant. If she'd known that I was her friend, and a friend of all young lovers, she'd be here by now. Oh, yes, she would. Her life shall not be crossed with obstacles and disappointments as . . . Cook, a minute ago my smelling salts were on this table. Now they've completely disappeared.

COOK Why, there they are, ma'am, right there in your hand.

MISS VAN HUYSEN Goodness! How did they get there? I won't inquire. Stranger things have happened!

COOK I suppose Mr. Vandergelder was sending her down with someone?

MISS VAN HUYSEN Two can go astray as easily as . . . (*She sneezes*)

COOK God bless you! (*Runs to window*) Now, here's a carriage stopping. (*The doorbell rings*)

MISS VAN HUYSEN Well, open the door, Cook. (COOK *exits*) It's probably some mistake. (*Sneezes again*) God bless you! (*Sounds of altercation off in hall*) It almost sounds as though I heard voices.

CORNELIUS (*Off*) I don't want to come in. This is a free country, I tell you.

CABMAN (*Off*) Forward march!

MALACHI (*Off*) In you go. We have orders.

CORNELIUS (*Off*) You can't make a person go where he doesn't want to go. (*Enter* MALACHI, *followed by* COOK. *The* CABMAN *bundles* BARNABY *and* CORNELIUS *into the room, but they fight their way back into the hall.* CORNELIUS *has lost* MRS. MOLLOY'S *coat, but* BARNABY *is wearing* MINNIE'S *clothes*)

MALACHI Begging your pardon, ma'am, are you Miss Van Huysen?

MISS VAN HUYSEN Yes, I am, unfortunately. What's all this noise about?

MALACHI There are two people here that Mr. Vandergelder said must be brought to this house and kept here until he comes. And here's his letter to you.

MISS VAN HUYSEN No one has any right to tell me whom I'm to keep in my house if they don't want to stay.

MALACHI You're right, ma'am. Everybody's always talking about people breaking into houses, ma'am; but there are more people in the world who want to break out of houses, that's what I always say— Bring them in, Joe. (*Enter* CORNELIUS *and* BARNABY *being pushed by the* CABMAN)

CORNELIUS This young lady and I have no business here. We jumped into a cab and asked to be driven to the station and these men brought us to the house and forced us to come inside. There's been a mistake.

CABMAN Is your name Miss Van Huysen?

MISS VAN HUYSEN Everybody's asking me if my name's Miss Van Huysen. I think that's a matter I can decide for myself. Now will you all be quiet while I read this letter? . . . "This is Ermengarde and that rascal Ambrose Kemper . . ." Now I know who you two are, anyway. "They are trying to run away . . ." Story of my life. "Keep them in your house until I come." Mr. Kemper, you have nothing to fear. (*To* CABMAN) Who are you?

CABMAN I'm Joe. I stay here until the old man comes. He owes me fifteen dollars.

MALACHI That's right, Miss Van Huysen, we must stay here to see they don't escape.

MISS VAN HUYSEN (*To* BARNABY) My dear child, take off your things. We'll all have some coffee. (*To* MALACHI *and* CABMAN) You two go out and wait in the hall. I'll send coffee out to you. Cook, take them. (COOK *pushes* MALACHI *and* CABMAN *into the hall*)

CORNELIUS Ma'am, we're not the people you're expecting, and there's no reason . . .

MISS VAN HUYSEN Mr. Kemper, I'm not the tyrant you think I am. . . . You don't have to be afraid of me. . . . I know you're trying to run away with this innocent girl. . . . All my life I have suffered from the interference of others. You shall not suffer as I did. So put yourself entirely in my hands. (*She lifts* BARNABY'S *veil*) Ermengarde! (*Kisses him on both cheeks*) Where's your luggage?

BARNABY It's—uh—uh—it's . . .

CORNELIUS Oh, I'll find it in the morning. It's been mislaid.

MISS VAN HUYSEN Mislaid! How like life! Well, Ermengarde; you shall put on some of my clothes.

BARNABY Oh, I know I wouldn't be happy, really.

MISS VAN HUYSEN She's a shy little thing, isn't she? Timid little darling! . . . Cook! Put some gingerbread in the oven and get the coffee ready . . .

COOK Yes, ma'am. (*Exits to kitchen*)

MISS VAN HUYSEN . . . while I go and draw a good hot bath for Ermengarde.

CORNELIUS Oh, oh—Miss Van Huysen . . .

MISS VAN HUYSEN Believe me, Ermengarde, your troubles are at an end. You two will be married tomorrow. (*To* BARNABY) My dear, you look just like I did at your age, and your sufferings have been as mine. While you're bathing, I'll come and tell you the story of my life.

BARNABY Oh, I don't want to take a bath. I always catch cold.

MISS VAN HUYSEN No, dear, you won't catch cold. I'll slap you all over. I'll be back in a minute. (*Exit*)

CORNELIUS (*Looking out of window*) Barnaby, do you think we could jump down from this window?

BARNABY Yes—we'd kill ourselves.

CORNELIUS We'll just have to stay here and watch for something to happen. Barnaby, the situation's desperate.

BARNABY It began getting desperate about half-past four and it's been getting worse ever since. Now I have to take a bath and get slapped all over. (*Enter* MISS VAN HUYSEN *from kitchen*)

MISS VAN HUYSEN Ermengarde, you've still got those wet things on. Your bath's nearly ready. Mr. Kemper, you come into the kitchen and put your feet in the oven. (*The doorbell rings. Enter* COOK) What's that? It's the doorbell. I expect it's your uncle.

COOK There's the doorbell. (*At window*) It's *another* man and a girl in a cab!

MISS VAN HUYSEN Well, go and let them in, Cook. Now, come with me, you two. Come, Ermengarde. (*Exit* COOK. MISS VAN HUYSEN *drags* CORNELIUS *and the protesting* BARNABY *off into the kitchen*)

COOK (*Off*) No, that's impossible. Come in, anyway. (*Enter* ERMENGARDE, *followed by* AMBROSE, *carrying the two pieces of luggage*) There's some mistake. I'll tell Miss Van Huysen, but there's some mistake.

ERMENGARDE But, I tell you, I *am* Mr. Vandergelder's niece; I'm Ermengarde.

COOK Beg your pardon, Miss, but you *can't* be Miss Ermengarde.

ERMENGARDE But—but—here I *am*. And that's my baggage.

COOK Well, I'll tell Miss Van Huysen who you *think* you are, but she won't like it. (*Exits*)

AMBROSE You'll be all right now, Ermengarde. I'd better go before she sees me.

ERMENGARDE Oh, no. You must stay. I feel so strange here.

AMBROSE I know, but Mr. Vandergelder will be here in a minute. . . .

ERMENGARDE Ambrose, you can't go. You can't leave me in this crazy house with those drunken men in the hall. Ambrose . . . Ambrose, let's say you're someone else that my uncle sent down to take care of me. Let's say you're—you're Cornelius Hackl!

AMBROSE Who's Cornelius Hackl?

ERMENGARDE You know. He's chief clerk in Uncle's store.

AMBROSE I don't want to be Cornelius Hackl. No, no, Ermengarde, come away with me now. I'll take you to my friend's house. Or I'll take you to Mrs. Levi's house.

ERMENGARDE Why, it was Mrs. Levi who threw us right at Uncle Horace's face. Oh, I wish I were back in Yonkers where nothing ever happens. (*Enter* MISS VAN HUYSEN)

MISS VAN HUYSEN What's all this I hear? Who do you say you are?

ERMENGARDE Aunt Flora . . . don't you remember me? I'm Ermengarde.

MISS VAN HUYSEN And you're Mr. Vandergelder's niece?

ERMENGARDE Yes, I am.

MISS VAN HUYSEN Well, that's very strange indeed, because he has just sent me another niece named Ermengarde. She came with a letter from him, explaining everything. Have you got a letter from him?

ERMENGARDE No . . .

MISS VAN HUYSEN Really!— And who is this?

ERMENGARDE This is Cornelius Hackl, Aunt Flora.

MISS VAN HUYSEN Never heard of him.

ERMENGARDE He's chief clerk in Uncle's store.

MISS VAN HUYSEN Never heard of him. The other Ermengarde came with the man she's in love with, and that *proves* it. She came with Mr. Ambrose Kemper.

AMBROSE (*Shouts*) Ambrose Kemper!

MISS VAN HUYSEN Yes, Mr. Hackl, and Mr. Ambrose Kemper is in the kitchen there now *with his feet in the oven.* (ERMENGARDE *starts to cry.* MISS VAN HUYSEN *takes her to the sofa. They both sit*) Dear child, what is your trouble?

ERMENGARDE Oh, dear. I don't know what to do.

MISS VAN HUYSEN (*In a low voice*) Are you in love with this man?

ERMENGARDE Yes, I am.

MISS VAN HUYSEN I could see it—and are people trying to separate you?

ERMENGARDE Yes, they are.

MISS VAN HUYSEN I could see it—who? Horace Vandergelder?

ERMENGARDE Yes.

MISS VAN HUYSEN That's enough for me. I'll put a stop to Horace Vandergelder's goings on. (MISS VAN HUYSEN *draws* AMBROSE *down to sit on her other side*) Mr. Hackl, think of me as your friend. Come in the kitchen and get warm. . . . (*She rises and starts to go out*) We can decide later who everybody is. My dear, would you like a good hot bath?

ERMENGARDE Yes, I would.

MISS VAN HUYSEN Well, when Ermengarde comes out you can go in. (*Enter* CORNELIUS *from the kitchen*)

CORNELIUS Oh, Miss Van Huysen . . .

ERMENGARDE Why, Mr. Hack—! !

CORNELIUS (*Sliding up to her, urgently*) Not yet! I'll explain. I'll explain everything.

MISS VAN HUYSEN Mr. Kemper!—Mr. Kemper! This is Mr. Cornelius Hackl. (*To* AMBROSE) Mr. Hackl, this is Mr. Ambrose Kemper. (*Pause, while the men glare at one another*) Perhaps you two know one another?

AMBROSE No!

CORNELIUS No, we don't.

AMBROSE (*Hotly*) Miss Van Huysen, I know that man is not Ambrose Kemper.

CORNELIUS (*Ditto*) And he's not Cornelius Hackl.

MISS VAN HUYSEN My dear young men, what does it matter what your names are? The important thing is that you are you. (*To* AMBROSE) You are alive and breathing, aren't you, Mr. Hackl? (*Pinches* AMBROSE'*s left arm*)

AMBROSE Ouch, Miss Van Huysen.

MISS VAN HUYSEN This dear child imagines she is Horace Vandergelder's niece Ermengarde.

ERMENGARDE But I am.

MISS VAN HUYSEN The important thing is that you're all in love. Everything else is illusion. (*She pinches* CORNELIUS' *arm*)

CORNELIUS Ouch! Miss Van Huysen!

MISS VAN HUYSEN (*Comes down and addresses the audience*) Everybody keeps asking me if I'm Miss Van Huys . . . (*She seems suddenly to be stricken with doubt as to who she is; her face shows bewildered alarm. She pinches herself on the upper arm and is abruptly and happily relieved*) Now, you two gentlemen sit down and have a nice chat while this dear child has a good hot bath. (*The doorbell rings.* ERMENGARDE *exit,* MISS VAN HUYSEN *about to follow her, but stops. Enter* COOK)

COOK There's the doorbell again.

MISS VAN HUYSEN Well, answer it. (*She and* ERMENGARDE *exit to kitchen*)

COOK (*At window, very happy about all these guests*) It's a cab and three ladies. I never saw such a night. (*Exit to front door*)

MISS VAN HUYSEN Gentlemen, you can rest easy. I'll see that Mr. Vandergelder lets his nieces marry you both. (*Enter* MRS. LEVI)

MRS. LEVI Flora, how are you?

MISS VAN HUYSEN Dolly Gallagher! What brings you here?

MRS. LEVI Great Heavens, Flora, what are those two drunken men doing in your hall?

MISS VAN HUYSEN I don't know. Horace Vandergelder sent them to me.

MRS. LEVI Well, I've brought you two girls in much the same condition. Otherwise they're the finest girls in the world. (*She goes up to the door and leads in* MRS. MOLLOY. MINNIE *follows*) I want you to meet Irene Molloy and Minnie Fay.

MISS VAN HUYSEN Delighted to know you.

MRS. LEVI Oh, I see you two gentlemen are here, too. Mr. Hackl, I was about to look for you (*Pointing about the room*) *somewhere* here.

CORNELIUS No, Mrs. Levi. I'm ready to face anything now.

MRS. LEVI Mr. Vandergelder will be here in a minute. He's downstairs trying to pay for a cab without any money.

MRS. MOLLOY (*Holding* VANDERGELDER'S *purse*) Oh, I'll help him.

MRS. LEVI Yes, will you, dear? You had to pay the restaurant bills. You must have hundreds of dollars there it seems.

MRS. MOLLOY This is his own purse he lost. I can't give it back to him without seeming . . .

MRS. LEVI I'll give it back to him— There, you help him with this now. (*She gives* MRS. MOLLOY *a bill and puts the purse airily under her arm*)

VANDERGELDER (*Off*) Will somebody please pay for this cab? (MRS. MOLLOY *exits to front door*)

MRS. MOLLOY (*Off stage*) I'll take care of that, Mr. Vandergelder. (*As* MR. VANDERGELDER *enters,* MALACHI *and the* CABMAN *follow him in.* VANDERGELDER *carries overcoat, stick, and box of chocolates*)

CABMAN Fifteen dollars, Mr. Vandergelder.

MALACHI Hello, Mr. Vandergelder.

VANDERGELDER (*To* MALACHI) You're discharged! (*To* CABMAN) You, too! (MALACHI *and* CABMAN *go out and wait in the hall*) So I've caught up with you at last! (*To* AMBROSE) I never want to see you again! (*To* CORNELIUS) You're discharged! Get out of this house, both of you. (*He strikes sofa with his stick; a second after,* MISS VAN HUYSEN *strikes him on the shoulder with a folded newspaper or magazine*)

MISS VAN HUYSEN (*Forcefully*) Now then you. Stop ordering people out of my house. You can shout and carry on in Yonkers, but when you're in my house you'll behave yourself.

VANDERGELDER They're both dishonest scoundrels.

MISS VAN HUYSEN Take your hat off. Gentlemen, you stay right where you are.

CORNELIUS Mr. Vandergelder, I can explain—

MISS VAN HUYSEN There aren't going to be any explanations. Horace, stop scowling at Mr. Kemper and forgive him.

VANDERGELDER That's not Kemper, that's a dishonest rogue named Cornelius Hackl.

MISS VAN HUYSEN You're crazy. (*Points to* AMBROSE) That's Cornelius Hackl.

VANDERGELDER I guess I know my own chief clerk.

MISS VAN HUYSEN I don't care what their names are. You shake hands with them both, or out you go.

VANDERGELDER Shake hands with those dogs and scoundrels!

MRS. LEVI Mr. Vandergelder, you've had a hard day. You don't want to go out in the rain now. Just for form's sake, you shake hands with them. You can start quarreling with them tomorrow.

VANDERGELDER (*Gives* CORNELIUS *one finger to shake*) There! Don't regard that as a handshake. (*He turns to* AMBROSE, *who mockingly offers him one finger*) Hey! I never want to see you again. (MRS. MOLLOY *enters from front door*)

MRS. MOLLOY Miss Van Huysen.

MISS VAN HUYSEN Yes, dear?

MRS. MOLLOY Do I smell coffee?

MISS VAN HUYSEN Yes, dear.

MRS. MOLLOY Can I have some, good and black?

MISS VAN HUYSEN Come along, everybody. We'll all go into the kitchen and have some coffee. (*As they all go*) Horace, you'll be interested to know there are two Ermengardes in there. . . .

VANDERGELDER Two! ! (*Last to go is* MINNIE, *who revolves about the room dreamily waltzing, a finger on her forehead.* MRS. LEVI *has been standing at one side. She now comes forward, in thoughtful mood.* MINNIE *continues her waltz round the left sofa and out to the kitchen.* MRS. LEVI, *left alone, comes to the front, addressing an imaginary Ephraim*)

MRS. LEVI Ephraim Levi, I'm going to get married again. Ephraim, I'm marrying Horace Vandergelder for his money. I'm going to send his money out doing all the things you taught me. Oh, it won't be a marriage in the sense that we had one—but I shall certainly make him happy, and Ephraim—I'm tired. I'm tired of living from hand to mouth, and I'm asking your permission, Ephraim—will you give me away? (*Now addressing the audience, she holds up the purse*) Money! Money!—it's like the sun we walk under; it can kill or cure— Mr. Vandergelder's money! Vandergelder's never tired of saying most of the people in the world are fools, and in a way he's right, isn't he? Himself, Irene, Cornelius, myself! But there comes a moment in everybody's life when he must decide whether he'll live among human beings or not—a fool among fools or a fool alone.

As for me, I've decided to live among them.

I wasn't always so. After my husband's death I retired into myself. Yes, in the evenings, I'd put out the cat, and I'd lock the door, and I'd make myself a little rum toddy; and before I went to bed I'd say a little prayer, thanking God that I was independent—that no one else's life was mixed up with mine. And when ten o'clock sounded from Trinity Church tower, I fell off to sleep and I was a perfectly contented woman. And one night, after two years of this, an oak leaf fell out of my Bible. I had placed it there on the day my husband asked me to marry him; a perfectly good oak leaf—but without color and without life. And suddenly I realized that for a long time I had not shed one tear; nor had I been filled with the wonderful hope that something or other would turn out well. I saw that I was like that oak leaf, and on that night I decided to rejoin the human race.

Yes, we're all fools and we're all in danger of destroying the world with our folly. But the surest way to keep us out of harm is to give us the four or five human pleasures that are our right in the world—and that takes a little *money!*

The difference between a little money and no money at all is enormous—and can shatter the world. And the difference between a little money and an enormous amount of money is very slight—and that, also, can shatter the world.

Money, I've always felt, money—pardon my expression—is like manure; it's not worth a thing unless it's spread about encouraging young things to grow.

Anyway—that's the opinion of the second Mrs. Vandergelder. (VANDERGELDER *enters with two cups of coffee. With his back, he closes both doors*)

VANDERGELDER Miss Van Huysen asked me to bring you this.

MRS. LEVI Thank you both. Sit down and rest yourself. What's been going on in the kitchen?

VANDERGELDER A lot of foolishness. Everybody falling in love with everybody. I forgave 'em; Ermengarde and that artist.

MRS. LEVI I knew you would.

VANDERGELDER I made Cornelius Hackl my partner.

MRS. LEVI You won't regret it.

VANDERGELDER Dolly, you said some mighty unpleasant things to me in the restaurant tonight . . . all that about my house . . . and everything.

MRS. LEVI Let's not say another word about it.

VANDERGELDER Dolly, you have a lot of faults—

MRS. LEVI Oh, I know what you mean.

VANDERGELDER You're bossy, scheming, inquisitive . . .

MRS. LEVI Go on.

VANDERGELDER But you're a wonderful woman. Dolly, marry me.

MRS. LEVI Horace! (*Rises*) Stop right there.

VANDERGELDER I know I've been a fool about Mrs. Molloy, and that other woman. But, Dolly, forgive me and marry me. (*He goes on his knees*)

MRS. LEVI Horace, I don't dare. No. I don't dare.

VANDERGELDER What do you mean?

MRS. LEVI You know as well as I do that you're the first citizen of Yonkers. Naturally, you'd expect your wife to keep open house, to have scores of friends in and out all the time. Any wife of yours should be used to that kind of thing.

VANDERGELDER (*After a brief struggle with himself*) Dolly, you can live any way you like.

MRS. LEVI Horace, you can't deny it, your wife would have to be a *somebody*. Answer me: am I a somebody?

VANDERGELDER You are . . . you are. Wonderful woman.

MRS. LEVI Oh, you're partial. (*She crosses, giving a big wink at the audience, and sits on sofa right.* VANDERGELDER *follows her on his knees*) Horace, it won't be enough for you to load your wife with money and jewels; to insist that she be a benefactress to half the town. (*He rises and, still struggling with himself, coughs so as not to hear this*) No, she must be a somebody. Do you really think I have it in me to be a credit to you?

VANDERGELDER Dolly, everybody knows that you could do anything you wanted to do.

MRS. LEVI I'll try. With your help, I'll try—and by the way, I found your purse. (*Holds it up*)

VANDERGELDER Where did you—! Wonderful woman!

MRS. LEVI It just walked into my hand. I don't know how I do it. Sometimes I frighten myself. Horace, take it. Money walks out of my hands, too.

VANDERGELDER Keep it. Keep it.

MRS. LEVI Horace! (*Half laughing, half weeping, and with an air of real affection for him*) I never thought . . . I'd ever . . . hear you say a thing like that! (BARNABY *dashes in from the kitchen in great excitement. He has discarded* MINNIE'S *clothes*)

BARNABY Oh! Excuse me. I didn't know anybody was here.

VANDERGELDER (*Bellowing*) Didn't know anybody was here. Idiot!

MRS. LEVI (*Putting her hand on* VANDERGELDER'S *arm; amiably*) Come in, Barnaby. Come in. (VANDERGELDER *looks at her a minute; then says, imitating her tone*)

VANDERGELDER Come in, Barnaby. Come in.

BARNABY Cornelius is going to marry Mrs. Molloy! !

MRS. LEVI Isn't that fine! Horace! . . . (MRS. LEVI *rises, and indicates that he has an announcement to make*)

VANDERGELDER Barnaby, go in and tell the rest of them that Mrs. Levi has consented—

MRS. LEVI *Finally* consented!

VANDERGELDER Finally consented to become my wife.

BARNABY Holy cabooses! (*Dashes back to the doorway*) Hey! Listen, everybody! Wolf-trap—I mean—Mr. Vandergelder is going to marry Mrs. Levi. (MISS VAN HUYSEN *enters followed by all the people in this act. She is now carrying the box of chocolates*)

MISS VAN HUYSEN Dolly, that's the best news I ever heard. (*She addresses the audience*) There isn't any more coffee; there isn't any more gingerbread; but there are three couples in my house and they're all going to get married. And do you know, one of those Ermengardes wasn't a dear little girl at all—she was a boy! Well, that's what life is: disappointment, illusion.

MRS. LEVI (*To audience*) There isn't any more coffee; there isn't any more gingerbread, and there isn't any more play—but there is one more thing we have to do. . . . Barnaby, come here. (*She whispers to him, pointing to the audience. Then she says to the audience*) I think the youngest person here ought to tell us what the moral of the play is. (BARNABY *is reluctantly pushed forward to the footlights*)

BARNABY Oh, I think it's about . . . I think it's about adventure. The test of an adventure is that when you're in the middle of it, you say to yourself, "Oh, now I've got myself into an awful mess; I wish I were sitting quietly at home." And the sign that something's wrong with you is when you sit quietly at home wishing you were out having lots of adventure. What we would like for you is that you have just the right amount of sitting quietly at home, and just the right amount of—adventure! So that now we all want to thank you for coming tonight, and we all hope that in your lives you have just the right amount of—adventure!

*Curtain*

# Tennessee Williams

## (1911-        )

In an early short story, "The Night of the Iguana," Tennessee Williams described a character's "sense of the enormous grotesquerie of the world," a phrase which can stand as the paradigm of his own world view. More recently he has described the human condition as one in which "we are all civilized, which means that we are all savages at heart but observing a few amenities of civilized behavior." Out of the compassion born of his own painful discovery of the ultimate loneliness and isolatedness of individual human experience, Williams has fashioned, in Arthur Miller's phrase, "a theatre with the blues" in which images of incredible brutality collide with those of fragile beauty. He has created a memorable gallery of phallic bulldozers and spinsterish, sex-starved field mice, libidinous avatars and compulsive sacrificial victims, all caught up in a social and moral condition where, in Williams' terms, "guilt is universal." In terms consonant with modern psychology's probings of civilization and its discontents, he has announced his point of view: "It is not the essential dignity but the essential ambiguity of man that I think needs to be stated."

Williams discovered man's ambiguity early in life. At 14 he found writing "an escape from the world of reality in which I felt acutely uncomfortable," and the world of his imagination has continued to command his greater loyalties, as evidenced by his continual reshaping of materials he has created. The evolution of *The Glass Menagerie* provides a typical instance of Williams' dedication to personal experiences he has objectified and made less painfully real in his imagination. The central incident of the abnormally shy Laura stirred out of her "glass menagerie" retreat by a dinner guest appears in an early short story, "Portrait of a Girl in Glass" (included in the collection, *One Arm*, 1948); Williams reportedly revised the story as a screen play, *The Gentleman Caller*; and when his scenario failed to interest his M-G-M employers, he fashioned a play, the loose episodic structure of which suggests its earlier cinematic form. Since the successful 1944 production, Williams has introduced countless other changes: many reflect lessons learned from Eddie Dowling's direction and Laurette Taylor's unforgettable interpretation of Amanda; other changes were introduced in the "acting version" published by Dramatists Play Service for amateur productions, and still others when he adapted it for the Warner Brothers film. Comparable is the history of *Battle of Angels,* disastrously produced by the Theatre Guild in 1940, rewritten as *Orpheus Descending* for a more successful 1957 production, and reworked again as the film, *The Fugitive Kind,* its title borrowed from one of Williams' earliest plays. His screen play, *Baby Doll,* was a brilliantly comic fusion of plots and characters drawn from several early one-acts. Unlike many other authors, Williams approaches revision with a zest and respectfulness engendered by a paternal sense of responsibility for his creations.

The geography of Williams' world is not so firmly localized as the neighboring Yoknapatawpha County of Faulkner's creation, but its central landmark, Moon Lake Casino, has the same vivid reality. With few exceptions (among which is *The Glass Menagerie*), Williams' plays are set in the Deep South, where he spent the first eight years of his life. Born March 26, 1911, in Columbus, Mississippi, Thomas Lanier Williams was the son of a robustious traveling salesman for a shoe company and an Episcopalian clergyman's daughter schooled in the genteel graces. The disparity in his parents' natures is reflected in Amanda Wingfield and the father whose glowing photograph gives him the reality of a fifth character in *The Glass Menagerie,* and again in Big Mama and Big Daddy in *Cat on a Hot Tin Roof.* In his maternal grandparents' rectory-home, Williams and his sister, Rose, were surrounded by doting adults who fostered a bookish, contemplative life repellent to Williams' extrovert father. The sheltered hothouse life Williams knew in Mississippi did not prepare him for a move in 1919 to the cheerless apartments and urban toughness of St. Louis, his home for almost twenty years. His sensitive nature resisted his father's persistent efforts to turn him into an All-American Boy who would not be "called a sissy by the neighborhood kids." His insecurity was exacerbated by the birth of a younger brother and by his mother's frequent illnesses. The adolescent Williams escaped a nightmarish reality only through steady moviegoing, his writing, and the sympathy of his sister, whose loneliness mirrored his own. Together they brightened their bleak living quarters to set off Rose's treasured glass animals which, in their transparent luminosity, became a symbol central in Williams' poetic art.

Williams' college education was marked by interruptions and transfers: after almost two years at the University of Missouri, he quit in 1933 and worked in a shoe warehouse; after two years of shoe-inventories, he suffered a nervous collapse, the victim of occupational boredom (clearly mirrored in Tom Wingfield) and of over-taxing himself in his compulsion to write his way out of St. Louis; in 1936 he enrolled at Washington University in St. Louis, then transferred to the University of Iowa where he studied theatre arts and playwriting. Soon after graduating in 1938, Williams took to the road, following the sun and savoring a life of independence in New Orleans, Mexico, Chicago, Florida, Los Angeles. He waited table, ushered in movie theatres, picked squabs at a pigeon ranch, ran elevators, worked in a bootery, angled unsuccessfully to join the WPA Writers Project—and constantly read, listened to music, and wrote poems, short stories, and plays. In 1939, he entered four early long plays (*Candles to the Sun, Fugitive Kind, Spring Storm,* and *Not About Nightingales*) and *American Blues,* a group of four one-acts, in the Group Theatre's playwriting contest. The one-acts brought him a special $100 award and, more important, the support of Audrey Wood, a New York agent who helped establish him as a promisingly serious young writer. Through her offices Williams received several foundation grants and, after the 1940 opening-and-closing in Boston of *Battle of Angels,* the distasteful but lucrative screen-writing contract which financed another period of productive vagabondage and writing.

Since December, 1944, when Chicago's drama critics drummed up enough support to keep *The Glass Menagerie* running for three months prior to its New York opening, Williams has become America's most honored dramatist. To his first Critics Circle award for *The Glass Menagerie* he has added double Pulitzer and Critics Circle awards for *A Streetcar Named Desire* (1947) and *Cat on a Hot Tin Roof* (1955). His best plays have been translated for productions throughout the world, and, with few exceptions, his works (including his novel, *The Roman Spring of Mrs. Stone*) have been effectively transferred to film. From the first, he has shown a mastery of all the extra-literary means by which poetic values can be evoked in the modern theatre. Although occasionally too ambitious and ripely over-ornate, his detailed specifications for musical themes, lighting and color effects, scenic and even dance elements are clearly indicative of a playwright who believes every theatrical effect must be carefully calculated in relation to the completed whole. Many of his plays invite heavy naturalistic staging, but Williams' usual approach to production remains the modified expressionism outlined in his Production Notes for *The Glass Menagerie.*

In his most searing representations of violence in his world of misfits, Williams' poetry of the theatre has softened without weakening action that might otherwise be unendurable. The violence which Williams admits has been the keynote of his full-length plays in the 1940-1960 period is usually also tempered by his richly inventive comic sense. Sometimes, as in *Baby Doll, The Rose Tattoo,* and *Period of Adjustment,* his humor erupts with a backwoods Rabelaisian lustiness in celebration *à la* D. H. Lawrence of the restorative powers of sexual fulfillment. More characteristically, however, his humor insinuates itself as a subtly modulated element in establishing the backgrounds against which violence explodes. Punctuated by the comically intrusive reality of "no-neck monster" grandchildren and a cancer-ridden Mississippi red neck's earthy vocabulary and exuberant vitality, Big Daddy and Brick's discussion of "mendacity," death, latent homosexuality, and life-denying self-disgust makes *Cat on a Hot Tin Roof*'s second act one of the most spellbinding in world drama. In the opening scenes of *A Streetcar Named Desire,* Williams' comic irony in pitting Stan Kowalski's exaggerated brutishness against Blanche DuBois' equally exaggerated daintiness is as central to our understanding as the controlling irony of the title for a tragedy in which Blanche's life-sustaining illusions are stripped away in a New Orleans slum called Elysian Fields.

Among the "*not* violent" plays, *The Glass Menagerie* is unquestionably his finest achievement. Williams has combined serious statement with comic insight in recreating the world in which he reached maturity. Violence, present both in the foreground—the explosive relationship between Amanda and Tom—and in the background, is subordinated to the reminiscent portrait of Laura, the peacemaker in a household ironically symbolic of the macrocosm. Tom has escaped from the tiny prison of the Wingfield apartment only to find himself in the larger prison of a world "lit by lightning" from which also there is no escape. Violence of the World War II "Now" is prefigured in the recollected "Then" through allusions to Guernica, labor troubles, Chamberlain's temporizing with the Master of Berchtesgaden, and especially by the World War I doughboy "smiling forever" in the blown-up photograph on the wall.

In the late 1940's Williams warned that, having put "all the nice things I have to say about people" in *The Glass Menagerie,* his future writing would be much harsher. In the early 1960's Williams is abandoning "the bestiality of life" and trying to "cast a kinder shadow, with more concentration on the quieter elements of existence." Possibly through psychoanalysis, but more probably through the extended self-analysis of a man who "can't expose a human weakness on the stage unless I know it through having it myself," Williams may succeed in leaving his "black" plays behind him. Musing on his "barrage of violence," Williams has tentatively justified his early preoccupation with man's destructive impulses: "If there is any truth in the Aristotelian idea that violence is purged by its poetic representation on a stage, then it may be that my cycle of violent plays have had a moral justification after all. I know that I have felt it. I have always felt a release from the sense of meaninglessness and death when a work of tragic intention has seemed to me to have achieved that intention, even if only approximately, nearly." Here Williams has described the effect—sometimes long-delayed or only faintly and reluctantly apprehended—his plays have had and will continue to have in the contemporary theatre.

## The Author's Production Notes

Being a "memory play," *The Glass Menagerie* can be presented with unusual freedom of convention. Because of its considerably delicate or tenuous material, atmospheric touches and subtleties of direction play a particularly important part. Expressionism and all other unconventional techniques in drama have only one valid aim, and that is a closer approach to truth. When a play employs unconventional techniques, it is not, or certainly shouldn't be, trying to escape its responsibility of dealing with reality, or interpreting experience, but is actually or should be attempting to find a closer approach, a more penetrating and vivid expression of things as they are. The straight realistic play with its genuine frigidaire and authentic ice-cubes, its characters that speak exactly as its audience speaks, corresponds to the academic landscape and has the same virtue of a photographic likeness. Everyone should know nowadays the unimportance of the photographic in art: that truth, life, or reality is an organic thing which the poetic imagination can represent or suggest, in essence, only through transformation, through changing into other forms than those which were merely present in appearance.

These remarks are not meant as a preface only to this particular play. They have to do with a conception of a new, plastic theatre which must take the place of the exhausted theatre of realistic conventions if the theatre is to resume vitality as a part of our culture.

### THE SCREEN DEVICE

There is *only one important difference between the original and acting version of the play* and that is the *omission* in the latter of the device which I tentatively included in my *original* script. This device was the use of a screen on which were projected magic-lantern slides bearing images or titles. I do not regret the omission of this device from the present Broadway production. The extraordinary power of Miss Taylor's performance made it suitable to have the utmost simplicity in the physical production. But I think it may be interesting to some readers to see how this device was conceived. So I am putting it into the published manuscript. These images and legends, projected from behind, were cast on a section of wall between the front-room and dining-room areas, which should be indistinguishable from the rest when not in use.

The purpose of this will probably be apparent. It is to give accent to certain values in each scene. Each scene contains a particular point (or several) which is structurally the most important. In an episodic play, such as this, the basic structure or narrative line may be obscured from the audience; the effect may seem fragmentary rather than architectural. This may not be the fault of the play so much as a lack of attention in the audience. The legend or image upon the screen will strengthen the effect of what is merely allusion in the writing and allow the primary point to be made more simply and lightly than if the entire responsibility were on the spoken lines. Aside from this structural value, I think the screen will have a definite emotional appeal, less definable but just as important. An imaginative producer or director may invent many other uses for this device than those indicated in the present script. In fact the possibilities of the device seem much larger to me than the instance of this play can possibly utilize.

### THE MUSIC

Another extra-literary accent in this play is provided by the use of music. A single recurring tune, "The Glass Menagerie," is used to give emotional emphasis to suitable passages. This tune is like circus music, not when you are on the grounds or in the immediate vicinity of the parade, but when you are at some distance and very likely thinking of something else. It seems under those circumstances to continue almost interminably and it weaves in and out of your preoccupied consciousness; then it is the lightest, most delicate music in the world and perhaps the saddest. It expresses the surface vivacity of life with the underlying strain of immutable and inexpressible sorrow. When you look at a piece of delicately spun glass you think of two things: how beautiful it is and how easily it can be broken. Both of those ideas should be woven into the recurring tune, which dips in and out of the play as if it were carried on a wind that changes. It serves as a thread of connection and allusion between the narrator with his separate point in time and space and the subject of his story. Between each episode it returns as reference to the emotion, nostalgia, which is the first condition of the play. It is primarily Laura's music and therefore comes out most clearly when the play focuses upon her and the lovely fragility of glass which is her image.

### THE LIGHTING

The lighting in the play is not realistic. In keeping with the atmosphere of memory, the stage is dim. Shafts of light are focused on selected areas or actors, sometimes in contradistinction to what is the apparent center. For instance, in the quarrel scene between Tom and Amanda, in which Laura has no active part, the clearest pool of light is on her figure. This is also true of the supper scene, when her silent figure on the sofa should remain the visual center. The light upon Laura should be distinct from the others, having a peculiar pristine clarity such as light used in early religious portraits of female saints or madonnas. A certain correspondence to light in religious paintings, such as El Greco's, where the figures are radiant in atmosphere that is relatively dusky, could be effectively used throughout the play. (It will also permit a more effective use of the screen.) A free, imaginative use of light can be of enormous value in giving a mobile, plastic quality to plays of a more or less static nature.

# THE GLASS MENAGERIE

## CHARACTERS

AMANDA WINGFIELD, *the mother*

A little woman of great but confused vitality clinging frantically to another time and place. Her characterization must be carefully created, not copied from type. She is not paranoiac, but her life is paranoia. There is much to admire in Amanda, and as much to love and pity as there is to laugh at. Certainly she has endurance and a kind of heroism, and though her foolishness makes her unwittingly cruel at times, there is tenderness in her slight person.

LAURA WINGFIELD, *her daughter*

Amanda, having failed to establish contact with reality, continues to live vitally in her illusions, but Laura's situation is even graver. A childhood illness has left her crippled, one leg slightly shorter than the other, and held in a brace. This defect need not be more than suggested on the stage. Stemming from this, Laura's separation increases till she is like a piece of her own glass collection, too exquisitely fragile to move from the shelf.

TOM WINGFIELD, *her son*

And the narrator of the play. A poet with a job in a warehouse. His nature is not remorseless, but to escape from a trap he has to act without pity.

JIM O'CONNOR, *the gentleman caller*

A nice, ordinary, young man.

SCENE *An Alley in St. Louis.*

PART I *Preparation for a Gentleman Caller*

PART II *The Gentleman Calls*

TIME *Now [c. 1944] and the Past.*

## Scene One

*The Wingfield apartment is in the rear of the building, one of those vast hive-like conglomerations of cellular living-units that flower as warty growths in overcrowded urban centers of lower middle-class population and are symptomatic of the impulse of this largest and fundamentally enslaved section of American society to avoid fluidity and differentiation and to exist and function as one interfused mass of automatism.*

*The apartment faces an alley and is entered by a fire escape, a structure whose name is a touch of accidental poetic truth, for all of these huge buildings are always burning with the slow and implacable fires of human desperation. The fire escape is included in the set—that is, the landing of it and steps descending from it.*

*The scene is memory and is therefore nonrealistic. Memory takes a lot of poetic license. It omits some details; others are exaggerated, according to the emotional value of the articles it touches, for memory is seated predominantly in the heart. The interior is therefore rather dim and poetic.*

*At the rise of the curtain, the audience is faced with the dark, grim rear wall of the Wingfield tenement. This building, which runs parallel to the footlights, is flanked on both sides by dark, narrow alleys which run into murky canyons of tangled clotheslines, garbage cans, and the sinister latticework of neighboring fire escapes. It is up and down these side alleys that exterior entrances and exits are made, during the play. At the end of* TOM's *opening commentary, the dark tenement wall slowly reveals (by means of a transparency) the interior of the ground floor Wingfield apartment.*

*Downstage is the living room, which also serves as a sleeping room for* LAURA, *the sofa unfolding to make her bed. Upstage, center, and divided by a wide arch or second proscenium with transparent faded portieres (or second curtain), is the dining room. In an old-fashioned what-not in the living room are seen scores of transparent glass animals. A blown-up photograph of the father hangs on the wall of the living room, facing the audience, to the left of the archway. It is the face of a very handsome young man in a doughboy's First World War cap. He is gallantly smiling, ineluctably smiling, as if to say, "I will be smiling forever."*

*The audience hears and sees the opening scene in the dining room through both the transparent fourth wall of the building and the transparent gauze portieres of the dining-room arch. It is during this revealing scene that the fourth wall slowly ascends, out of sight. This transparent exterior wall is not brought down again until the very end of the play, during* TOM's *final speech.*

*The narrator is an undisguised convention of the play. He takes whatever license with dramatic convention is convenient to his purposes.*

TOM *enters dressed as a merchant sailor from alley, stage left, and strolls across the front of the stage to the fire escape. There he stops and lights a cigarette. He addresses the audience.*

TOM Yes, I have tricks in my pocket, I have things up my sleeve. But I am the opposite of a stage magician. He gives you illusion that has the appearance of truth. I give you truth in the pleasant disguise of illusion.

To begin with, I turn back time. I reverse it to that quaint period, the thirties, when the huge middle class of America was matriculating in a school for the blind. Their eyes had failed them, or they had failed their eyes, and so they were having their fingers pressed forcibly down on the fiery Braille alphabet of a dissolving economy.

In Spain there was revolution. Here there was only shouting and confusion.

In Spain there was Guernica. Here there were disturbances of labor, sometimes pretty violent, in otherwise peaceful cities such as Chicago, Cleveland, Saint Louis . . .

This is the social background of the play.

(MUSIC)

The play is memory.

Being a memory play, it is dimly lighted, it is sentimental, it is not realistic.

In memory everything seems to happen to music. That explains the fiddle in the wings.

I am the narrator of the play, and also a character in it.

The other characters are my mother, Amanda, my sister, Laura, and a gentleman caller who appears in the final scenes.

He is the most realistic character in the play, being an emissary from a world of reality that we were somehow set apart from.

But since I have a poet's weakness for symbols, I am using this character also as a symbol; he is the long delayed but always expected something that we live for.

There is a fifth character in the play who doesn't appear except in this larger-than-life-size photograph over the mantel.

This is our father who left us a long time ago.

He was a telephone man who fell in love with long distances; he gave up his job with the telephone company and skipped the light fantastic out of town . . .

The last we heard of him was a picture post-card from Mazatlan, on the Pacific coast of Mexico, containing a message of two words—

"Hello— Good-bye!" and no address.

I think the rest of the play will explain itself. . . .

(AMANDA'S *voice becomes audible through the portieres*)

(LEGEND ON SCREEN: "OÙ SONT LES NEIGES" [1])

(*He divides the portieres and enters the upstage area*)

(AMANDA *and* LAURA *are seated at a drop-leaf table. Eating is indicated by gestures without food or utensils.* AMANDA *faces the audience,* TOM *and* LAURA *are seated in profile. The interior has lit up softly and through the scrim we see* AMANDA *and* LAURA *seated at the table in the upstage area*)

AMANDA (*Calling*) Tom?

TOM Yes, Mother.

AMANDA We can't say grace until you come to the table!

TOM Coming, Mother. (*He bows slightly and withdraws, reappearing a few moments later in his place at the table*)

AMANDA (*To her son*) Honey, don't *push* with your *fingers*. If you have to push with something, the thing to push with is a crust of bread. And chew—chew! Animals have sections in their stomachs which enable them to digest food without mastication, but human beings are supposed to chew their food before they swallow it down. Eat food leisurely, son, and really enjoy it. A well-cooked meal has lots of delicate flavors that have to be held in the mouth for appreciation. So chew your food and give your salivary glands a chance to function!

(TOM *deliberately lays his imaginary fork down and pushes his chair back from the table*)

[1] "Where are the snows [of yesteryear]?" part of the refrain of François Villon's "Ballade of Dead Ladies."

TOM I haven't enjoyed one bite of this dinner because of your constant directions on how to eat it. It's you that make me rush through meals with your hawk-like attention to every bite I take. Sickening—spoils my appetite—all this discussion of—animals' secretion—salivary glands—mastication!

AMANDA (*Lightly*) Temperament like a Metropolitan star! (*He rises and crosses downstage*) You're not excused from the table.

TOM I'm getting a cigarette.

AMANDA You smoke too much.

(LAURA *rises*)

LAURA I'll bring in the blanc mange.

(*He remains standing with his cigarette by the portieres during the following*)

AMANDA (*Rising*) No, sister, no, sister—you be the lady this time and I'll be the darky.

LAURA I'm already up.

AMANDA Resume your seat, little sister—I want you to stay fresh and pretty—for gentlemen callers!

LAURA I'm not expecting any gentlemen callers.

AMANDA (*Crossing out to kitchenette. Airily*) Sometimes they come when they are least expected! Why, I remember one Sunday afternoon in Blue Mountain—(*Enters kitchenette*)

TOM I know what's coming!

LAURA Yes. But let her tell it.

TOM Again?

LAURA She loves to tell it.

(AMANDA *returns with bowl of dessert*)

AMANDA One Sunday afternoon in Blue Mountain—your mother received—*seventeen!*—gentlemen callers! Why, sometimes there weren't chairs enough to accommodate them all. We had to send the nigger over to bring in folding chairs from the parish house.

TOM (*Remaining at portieres*) How did you entertain those gentlemen callers?

AMANDA I understood the art of conversation!

TOM I bet you could talk.

AMANDA Girls in those days *knew* how to talk, I can tell you.

TOM Yes?

(IMAGE: AMANDA AS A GIRL ON A PORCH, GREETING CALLERS)

AMANDA They knew how to entertain their gentlemen callers. It wasn't enough for a girl to be possessed of a pretty face and a graceful figure—although I wasn't slighted in either respect. She also needed to have a nimble wit and a tongue to meet all occasions.

TOM What did you talk about?

AMANDA Things of importance going on in the world! Never anything coarse or common or vulgar. (*She addresses* TOM *as though he were seated in the vacant chair at the table though he remains by portieres. He plays this scene as though he held the book*) My callers were gentlemen—all! Among my callers were some of the most prominent young planters of the Mississippi Delta—planters and sons of planters!

(TOM *motions for music and a spot of light on* AMANDA)

(*Her eyes lift, her face glows, her voice becomes rich and elegiac*)

(SCREEN LEGEND: "OÙ SONT LES NEIGES")

There was young Champ Laughlin who later became vice-president of the Delta Planters Bank.

Hadley Stevenson who was drowned in Moon Lake and left his widow one hundred and fifty thousand in Government bonds.

There were the Cutrere brothers, Wesley and Bates. Bates was one of my bright particular beaux! He got in a quarrel with that wild Wainwright boy. They shot it out on the floor of Moon Lake Casino. Bates was shot through the stomach. Died in the ambulance on his way to Memphis. His widow was also well-provided for, came into eight or ten thousand acres, that's all. She married him on the rebound—never loved her—carried my picture on him the night he died!

And there was that boy that every girl in the Delta had set her cap for! That beautiful, brilliant young Fitzhugh boy from Greene County!

TOM What did he leave his widow?

AMANDA He never married! Gracious, you talk as though all of my old admirers had turned up their toes to the daisies!

TOM Isn't this the first you've mentioned that still survives?

AMANDA That Fitzhugh boy went North and made a fortune—came to be known as the Wolf of Wall Street! He had the Midas touch, whatever he touched turned to gold!

And I could have been Mrs. Duncan J. Fitzhugh, mind you! But—I picked your *father!*

LAURA (*Rising*) Mother, let me clear the table.

AMANDA No, dear, you go in front and study your typewriter chart. Or practice your shorthand a little. Stay fresh and pretty!—It's almost time for our gentlemen callers to start arriving. (*She flounces girlishly toward the kitchenette*) How many do you suppose we're going to entertain this afternoon?

(TOM *throws down the paper and jumps up with a groan*)

LAURA (*Alone in the dining room*) I don't believe we're going to receive any, Mother.

AMANDA (*Reappearing, airily*) What? No one—not one? Your must be joking! (LAURA *nervously echoes her laugh. She slips in a fugitive manner through the half-open portieres and draws them gently behind her. A shaft of very clear light is thrown on her face against the faded tapestry of the curtains.* MUSIC: "THE GLASS MENAGERIE" UNDER FAINTLY. *Lightly*) Not one gentleman caller? It can't be true! There must be a flood, there must have been a tornado!

LAURA It isn't a flood, it's not a tornado, Mother. I'm just not popular like you were in Blue Mountain. . . . (TOM *utters another groan.* LAURA *glances at him with a faint, apologetic smile. Her voice catching a little*) Mother's afraid I'm going to be an old maid.

(*The Scene Dims Out with "Glass Menagerie" Music*)

## Scene Two

*"Laura, Haven't You Ever Liked Some Boy?"*

*On the dark stage the screen is lighted with the image of blue roses.*

*Gradually* LAURA'S *figure becomes apparent and the screen goes out.*

*The music subsides.*

LAURA *is seated in the delicate ivory chair at the small clawfoot table.*

*She wears a dress of soft violet material for a kimono—her hair tied back from her forehead with a ribbon.*

*She is washing and polishing her collection of glass.*

AMANDA *appears on the fire-escape steps. At the sound of her ascent,* LAURA *catches her breath, thrusts the bowl of ornaments away and seats herself stiffly before the diagram of the typewriter keyboard as though it held her spellbound.*

*Something has happened to* AMANDA. *It is written in her face as she climbs to the landing: a look that is grim and hopeless and a little absurd.*

*She has on one of those cheap or imitation velvety-looking cloth coats with imitation fur collar. Her hat is five or six years old, one of those dreadful cloche hats that were worn in the late twenties and she is clasping an enormous black patent-leather pocketbook with nickel clasps and initials. This is her full-dress outfit, the one she usually wears to the D.A.R.*

*Before entering she looks through the door.*

*She purses her lips, opens her eyes very wide, rolls them upward and shakes her head.*

*Then she slowly lets herself in the door. Seeing her mother's expression* LAURA *touches her lips with a nervous gesture.*

LAURA Hello, Mother, I was— (*She makes a nervous gesture toward the chart on the wall.* AMANDA *leans against the shut door and stares at* LAURA *with a martyred look*)

AMANDA Deception? Deception? (*She slowly removes her hat and gloves, continuing the sweet suffering stare. She lets the hat and gloves fall on the floor—a bit of acting*)

LAURA (*Shakily*) How was the D.A.R. meeting? (AMANDA *slowly opens her purse and removes a dainty white handkerchief which she shakes out delicately and delicately touches to her lips and nostrils*) Didn't you go to the D.A.R. meeting, Mother?

AMANDA (*Faintly, almost inaudibly*) —No—No. (*Then more forcibly*) I did not have the strength—to go to the D.A.R. In fact, I did not have the courage! I wanted to find a hole in the ground and hide myself in it forever! (*She crosses slowly to the wall and removes the diagram of the typewriter keyboard. She holds it in front of her for a second, staring at it sweetly and sorrowfully—then bites her lips and tears it in two pieces*)

LAURA (*Faintly*) Why did you do that, Mother? (AMANDA *repeats the same procedure with the chart of the Gregg Alphabet*) Why are you—

AMANDA Why? Why? How old are you, Laura?

LAURA Mother, you know my age.

AMANDA I thought that you were an adult; it seems that I was mistaken. (*She crosses slowly to the sofa and sinks down and stares at* LAURA)

LAURA Please don't stare at me, Mother. (AMANDA *closes her eyes and lowers her head. Count ten*)

AMANDA What are we going to do, what is going to become of us, what is the future? (*Count ten*)

LAURA Has something happened, Mother? (AMANDA *draws a long breath and takes out the handkerchief again. Dabbing process*) Mother, has—something happened?

AMANDA I'll be all right in a minute, I'm just bewildered —(*Count five*)—by life. . . .

LAURA Mother, I wish that you would tell me what's happened!

AMANDA As you know, I was supposed to be inducted into my office at the D.A.R. this afternoon. (IMAGE: A SWARM OF TYPEWRITERS) But I stopped off at Rubicam's Business College to speak to your teachers about your having a cold and ask them what progress they thought you were making down there.

LAURA Oh. . . .

AMANDA I went to the typing instructor and introduced myself as your mother. She didn't know who you were. Wingfield, she said. We don't have any such student enrolled at the school!

I assured her she did, that you had been going to classes since early in January.

"I wonder," she said, "if you could be talking about that terribly shy little girl who dropped out of school after only a few days' attendance?"

"No," I said, "Laura, my daughter, has been going to school every day for the past six weeks!"

"Excuse me," she said. She took the attendance book out and there was your name, unmistakably printed, and all the dates you were absent until they decided that you had dropped out of school.

I still said, "No, there must have been some mistake! There must have been some mix-up in the records!"

And she said, "No—I remember her perfectly now. Her hands shook so that she couldn't hit the right keys! The first time we gave a speed-test, she broke down completely—was sick at the stomach and almost had to be carried into the wash-room! After that morning she never showed up any more. We phoned the house but never got any answer"—while I was working at Famous and Barr, I suppose, demonstrating those— Oh!

I felt so weak I could barely keep on my feet!

I had to sit down while they got me a glass of water!

Fifty dollars' tuition, all of our plans—my hopes and ambitions for you—just gone up the spout, just gone up the spout like that.

(LAURA *draws a long breath and gets awkwardly to her feet. She crosses to the victrola and winds it up*)

What are you doing?

LAURA Oh! (*She releases the handle and returns to her seat*)

AMANDA Laura, where have you been going when you've gone out pretending that you were going to business college?

LAURA I've just been going out walking.

AMANDA That's not true.

LAURA It is. I just went walking.

AMANDA Walking? Walking? In winter? Deliberately courting pneumonia in that light coat? Where did you walk to, Laura?

LAURA All sorts of places—mostly in the park.

AMANDA Even after you'd started catching that cold?

LAURA It was the lesser of two evils, Mother. (IMAGE: WINTER SCENE IN PARK) I couldn't go back up. I—threw up—on the floor!

AMANDA From half past seven till after five every day you mean to tell me you walked around in the park, because you wanted to make me think that you were still going to Rubicam's Business College?

LAURA It wasn't as bad as it sounds. I went inside places to get warmed up.

AMANDA Inside where?

LAURA I went in the art museum and the bird-houses at the Zoo. I visited the penguins every day! Sometimes I did without lunch and went to the movies. Lately I've been spending most of my afternoons in the Jewel-box, that big glass house where they raise the tropical flowers.

AMANDA You did all this to deceive me, just for deception? (LAURA *looks down*) Why?

LAURA Mother, when you're disappointed, you get that awful suffering look on your face, like the picture of Jesus' mother in the museum!

AMANDA Hush!

LAURA I couldn't face it.

(*Pause. A whisper of strings*)

(LEGEND: "THE CRUST OF HUMILITY")

AMANDA (*Hopelessly fingering the huge pocketbook*) So what are we going to do the rest of our lives? Stay home and watch the parades go by? Amuse ourselves with the glass menagerie, darling? Eternally play those worn-out phonograph records your father left as a painful reminder of him?

We won't have a business career—we've given that up because it gave us nervous indigestion! (*Laughs wearily*) What is there left but dependency all our lives? I know so well what becomes of unmarried women who aren't prepared to occupy a position. I've seen such pitiful cases in the South—barely tolerated spinsters living upon the grudging patronage of sister's husband or brother's wife!—stuck away in some little mouse-trap of a room—encouraged by one in-law to visit another—little birdlike women without any nest—eating the crust of humility all their life!

Is that the future that we've mapped out for ourselves?

I swear it's the only alternative I can think of!

It isn't a very pleasant alternative, is it?

Of course—some girls *do marry.*

(LAURA *twists her hands nervously*)

Haven't you ever liked some boy?

LAURA Yes. I liked one once. (*Rises*) I came across his picture a while ago.

AMANDA (*With some interest*) He gave you his picture?

LAURA. No, it's in the year-book.

AMANDA (*Disappointed*) Oh—a high-school boy.

(SCREEN IMAGE: JIM AS HIGH-SCHOOL HERO BEARING A SILVER CUP)

LAURA Yes. His name was Jim. (LAURA *lifts the heavy annual from the claw-foot table*) Here he is in *The Pirates of Penzance.*

AMANDA (*Absently*) The what?

LAURA The operetta the senior class put on. He had a wonderful voice and we sat across the aisle from each other Mondays, Wednesdays, and Fridays in the Aud. Here he is with the silver cup for debating! See his grin?

AMANDA (*Absently*) He must have had a jolly disposition.

LAURA He used to call me—Blue Roses.

(IMAGE: BLUE ROSES)

AMANDA Why did he call you such a name as that?

LAURA When I had that attack of pleurosis—he asked me what was the matter when I came back. I said pleurosis—he thought that I said Blue Roses! So that's what he always called me after that. Whenever he saw me, he'd holler, "Hello, Blue Roses!" I didn't care for the girl that he went out with. Emily Meisenbach. Emily was the best-dressed girl at Soldan.[1] She never struck me, though, as being sincere. . . . It says in the Personal Section—they're engaged. That's—six years ago! They must be married by now.

AMANDA Girls that aren't cut out for business careers usually wind up married to some nice man. (*Gets up with a spark of revival*) Sister, that's what you'll do!

(LAURA *utters a startled, doubtful laugh. She reaches quickly for a piece of glass*)

LAURA But, Mother—

AMANDA Yes? (*Crossing to photograph*)

[1] A large, centrally-located St. Louis high school.

LAURA (*In a tone of frightened apology*) I'm—crippled!

(IMAGE: SCREEN)

AMANDA Nonsense! Laura, I've told you never, never to use that word. Why, you're not crippled, you just have a little defect—hardly noticeable, even! When people have some slight disadvantage like that, they cultivate other things to make up for it—develop charm—and vivacity—and—*charm!* That's all you have to do! (*She turns again to the photograph*) One thing your father had *plenty of*—was *charm!*

(TOM *motions to the fiddle in the wings*)

(*The Scene Fades Out with Music*)

# Scene Three

LEGEND ON SCREEN: "AFTER THE FIASCO—"
TOM *speaks from the fire-escape landing.*

TOM After the fiasco at Rubicam's Business College, the idea of getting a gentleman caller for Laura began to play a more and more important part in Mother's calculations.

It became an obsession. Like some archetype of the universal unconscious, the image of the gentleman caller haunted our small apartment. . . .

(IMAGE: YOUNG MAN AT DOOR WITH FLOWERS)

An evening at home rarely passed without some allusion to this image, this specter, this hope. . . .

Even when he wasn't mentioned, his presence hung in Mother's preoccupied look and in my sister's frightened, apologetic manner—hung like a sentence passed upon the Wingfields!

Mother was a woman of action as well as words. She began to take logical steps in the planned direction.

Late that winter and in the early spring—realizing that extra money would be needed to properly feather the nest and plume the bird—she conducted a vigorous campaign on the telephone, roping in subscribers to one of those magazines for matrons called *The Homemaker's Companion,* the type of journal that features the serialized sublimations of ladies of letters who think in terms of delicate cuplike breasts, slim, tapering waists, rich, creamy thighs, eyes like wood-smoke in autumn, fingers that soothe and caress like strains of music, bodies as powerful as Etruscan sculpture.

(SCREEN IMAGE: GLAMOR MAGAZINE COVER)

(AMANDA *enters with phone on long extension cord. She is spotted in the dim stage*)

AMANDA Ida Scott? This is Amanda Wingfield!

We *missed* you at the D.A.R. last Monday!

I said to myself: She's probably suffering with that sinus condition! How is that sinus condition?

Horrors! Heaven have mercy!—You're a Christian martyr, yes, that's what you are, a Christian martyr!

Well, I just now happened to notice that your subscription to the *Companion*'s about to expire! Yes, it expires with the next issue, honey!—just when that wonderful new serial by Bessie Mae Hopper is getting off to such an exciting start. Oh, honey, it's something that you can't miss! You remember how *Gone With the Wind* took everybody by storm? You simply couldn't go out if you hadn't read it. All everybody *talked* was Scarlett O'Hara. Well, this is a book that critics already compare to *Gone With the Wind.* It's the *Gone With the Wind* of the post-World War generation!—What?—Burning?—Oh, honey, don't let them burn, go take a look in the oven and I'll hold the wire! Heavens—I think she's hung up!

*DIM OUT*

(LEGEND ON SCREEN: "YOU THINK I'M IN LOVE WITH CONTINENTAL SHOEMAKERS?")

(*Before the stage is lighted, the violent voices of* TOM *and* AMANDA *are heard*)

(*They are quarreling behind the portieres. In front of them stands* LAURA *with clenched hands and panicky expression*)

(*A clear pool of light on her figure throughout this scene*)

TOM What in Christ's name am I—

AMANDA (*Shrilly*) Don't you use that—

TOM Supposed to do!

AMANDA Expression! Not in my—

TOM Ohhh!

AMANDA Presence! Have you gone out of your senses?

TOM I have, that's true, *driven* out!

AMANDA What is the matter with you, you—big—big—*idiot!*

TOM Look!—I've got *no thing,* no single thing—

AMANDA Lower your voice!

TOM In my life here that I can call my *own!* Everything is—

AMANDA Stop that shouting!

TOM Yesterday you confiscated my books! You had the nerve to—

AMANDA I took that horrible novel back to the library—yes! That hideous book by that insane Mr. Lawrence. (TOM *laughs wildly*) I cannot control the output of diseased minds or people who cater to them— (TOM *laughs still more wildly*) BUT I WON'T ALLOW SUCH FILTH BROUGHT INTO MY HOUSE! No, no, no, no, no!

TOM House, house! Who pays rent on it, who makes a slave of himself to—

AMANDA (*Fairly screeching*) Don't you DARE to—

TOM No, no, *I* mustn't say things! *I've* got to just—

AMANDA Let me tell you—

TOM I don't want to hear any more! (*He tears the portieres open. The upstage area is lit with a turgid smoky red glow*)

(AMANDA'S *hair is in metal curlers and she wears a very old bathrobe, much too large for her slight figure, a relic of the faithless Mr. Wingfield*)

(*An upright typewriter and a wild disarray of manuscripts is on the drop-leaf table. The quarrel was probably precipitated by* AMANDA'S *interruption of his creative labor. A chair lying overthrown on the floor*)

(*Their gesticulating shadows are cast on the ceiling by the fiery glow*)

AMANDA You *will* hear more, you—

TOM No, I won't hear more, I'm going out!

AMANDA You come right back in—

TOM Out, out, out! Because I'm—

AMANDA Come back here, Tom Wingfield! I'm not through talking to you!

TOM Oh, go—

LAURA (*Desperately*) —Tom!

AMANDA You're going to listen, and no more insolence from you! I'm at the end of my patience!

(*He comes back toward her*)

TOM What do you think I'm at? Aren't I supposed to have any patience to reach the end of, Mother? I know, I know. It seems unimportant to you, what I'm *doing*—what I *want* to do—having a little *difference* between them! You don't think that—

AMANDA I think you've been doing things that you're ashamed of. That's why you act like this. I don't believe that you go every night to the movies. Nobody goes to the movies night after night. Nobody in their right minds goes to the movies as often as you pretend to. People don't go to the movies at nearly midnight, and movies don't let out at two A.M. Come in stumbling. Muttering to yourself like a maniac! You get three hours' sleep and then go to work. Oh, I can picture the way you're doing down there. Moping, doping, because you're in no condition.

TOM (*Wildly*) No, I'm in no condition!

AMANDA What right have you got to jeopardize your job? Jeopardize the security of us all? How do you think we'd manage if you were—

TOM Listen! You think I'm crazy *about the warehouse?* (*He bends fiercely toward her slight figure*) You think I'm in love with the Continental Shoemakers? You think I want to spend fifty-five *years* down there in that—*celotex interior!* with—*fluorescent—tubes!* Look! I'd rather somebody picked up a crowbar and battered out my brains—than go back mornings! I *go!* Every time you come in yelling that God damn *"Rise and Shine!" "Rise and Shine!"* I say to myself, "How *lucky dead* people are!" But I get up. I *go!* For sixty-five dollars a month I give up all that I dream of doing and being *ever!* And you say self—*self's* all I ever think of. Why, listen, if self is what I thought of, Mother, I'd be where he is—GONE! (*Pointing to father's picture*) As far as the system of transportation reaches! (*He starts past her. She grabs his arm*) Don't grab at me, Mother!

AMANDA Where are you going?

TOM I'm going to the *movies!*

AMANDA I don't believe that lie!

TOM (*Crouching toward her, overtowering her tiny figure. She backs away, gasping*) I'm going to opium dens! Yes, opium dens, dens of vice and criminals' hang-outs, Mother. I've joined the Hogan gang, I'm a hired assassin, I carry a tommy-gun in a violin case! I run a string of cat-houses in the Valley! They call me Killer, Killer Wingfield, I'm leading a double-life, a simple, honest warehouse worker by day, by night a dynamic *czar* of the *underworld, Mother.* I go to gambling casinos, I spin away fortunes on the roulette table! I wear a patch over one eye and a false mustache, sometimes I put on green whiskers. On those occasions they call me—*El Diablo!* Oh, I could tell you things to make you sleepless! My enemies plan to dynamite this place. They're going to blow us all sky-high some night! I'll be glad, very happy, and so will you! You'll go up, up on a broomstick, over Blue Mountain with seventeen gentlemen callers! You ugly —babbling old—*witch. . . .* (*He goes through a series of violent, clumsy movements, seizing his overcoat, lunging to the door, pulling it fiercely open. The women watch him, aghast. His arm catches in the sleeve of the coat as he struggles to pull it on. For a moment he is pinioned by the bulky garment. With an outraged groan he tears the coat off again, splitting the shoulder of it, and hurls it across the room. It strikes against the shelf of* LAURA'S *glass collection, there is a tinkle of shattering glass.* LAURA *cries out as if wounded*)

(MUSIC. LEGEND: "THE GLASS MENAGERIE")

LAURA (*Shrilly*) *My glass!*—menagerie. . . . (*She covers her face and turns away*)

(*But* AMANDA *is still stunned and stupefied by the "ugly witch" so that she barely notices this occurrence. Now she recovers her speech*)

AMANDA (*In an awful voice*) I won't speak to you—until you apologize! (*She crosses through portieres and draws them together behind her.* TOM *is left with* LAURA. LAURA *clings weakly to the mantel with her face averted.* TOM *stares at her stupidly for a moment. Then he crosses to shelf. Drops awkwardly on his knees to collect the fallen glass, glancing at* LAURA *as if he would speak but couldn't*)

(*"The Glass Menagerie" steals in as the Scene Dims Out*)

## Scene Four

*The interior is dark. Faint light in the alley.*

*A deep-voiced bell in a church is tolling the hour of five as the scene commences.*

TOM *appears at the top of the alley. After each solemn boom of the bell in the tower, he shakes a little noise-maker or rattle as if to express the tiny spasm of man in contrast to the sustained power and dignity of the Almighty. This and the unsteadiness of his advance make it evident that he has been drinking.*

*As he climbs the few steps to the fire-escape landing light steals up inside.* LAURA *appears in night-dress, observing* TOM'S *empty bed in the front room.*

TOM *fishes in his pockets for door key, removing a motley assortment of articles in the search, including a perfect shower of movie-ticket stubs and an empty bottle. At last he finds the key, but just as he is about to insert it, it slips from his fingers. He strikes a match and crouches below the door.*

TOM (*Bitterly*) One crack—and it falls through!
(LAURA *opens the door*)

LAURA Tom, Tom, what are you doing?

TOM Looking for a door key.

LAURA Where have you been all this time?

TOM I have been to the movies.

LAURA All this time at the movies?

TOM There was a very long program. There was a Garbo picture and a Mickey Mouse and a travelogue and a newsreel and a preview of coming attractions. And there was an organ solo and a collection for the milk-fund—simultaneously—which ended up in a terrible fight between a fat lady and an usher!

LAURA (*Innocently*) Did you have to stay through everything?

TOM Of course! And, oh, I forgot! There was a big stage show! The headliner on this stage show was Malvolio the Magician. He performed wonderful tricks, many of them, such as pouring water back and forth between pitchers. First it turned to wine and then it turned to beer and then it turned to whiskey. I know it was whiskey it finally turned into because he needed somebody to come up out of the audience to help him, and I came up—both shows! It was Kentucky Straight Bourbon. A very generous fellow, he gave souvenirs. (*He pulls from his back pocket a shimmering rainbow-colored scarf*) He gave me this. This is his magic scarf. You can have it, Laura. You wave it over a canary cage and you get a bowl of gold-fish. You wave it over the gold-fish bowl and they fly away canaries. . . . But the wonderfullest trick of all was the coffin trick. We nailed him into a coffin and he got out of the coffin without removing one nail. (*He has come inside*) There is a trick that would come in handy for me—get me out of this 2 by 4 situation! (*Flops onto bed and starts removing shoes*)

LAURA Tom—Shhh!

TOM What're you shushing me for?

LAURA You'll wake up Mother.

TOM Goody, goody! Pay 'er back for all those "Rise an' Shines." (*Lies down, groaning*) You know it don't take much intelligence to get yourself into a nailed-up coffin, Laura. But who in hell ever got himself out of one without removing one nail?
(*As if in answer, the father's grinning photograph lights up*)

*SCENE DIMS OUT*

(*Immediately following: The church bell is heard striking six. At the sixth stroke the alarm clock goes off in* AMANDA'S *room, and after a few moments we hear her calling: "Rise and Shine! Rise and Shine! Laura, go tell your brother to rise and shine!"*)

TOM (*Sitting up slowly*) I'll rise—but I won't shine.
(*The light increases*)

AMANDA Laura, tell your brother his coffee is ready.
(LAURA *slips into front room*)

LAURA Tom!—It's nearly seven. Don't make Mother nervous. (*He stares at her stupidly. Beseechingly*) Tom, speak to Mother this morning. Make up with her, apologize, speak to her!

TOM She won't to me. It's her that started not speaking.

LAURA If you just say you're sorry she'll start speaking.

TOM Her not speaking—is that such a tragedy?

LAURA Please—please!

AMANDA (*Calling from kitchenette*) Laura, are you going to do what I asked you to do, or do I have to get dressed and go out myself?

LAURA Going, going—soon as I get on my coat! (*She pulls on a shapeless felt hat with nervous, jerky movement, pleadingly glancing at* TOM. *Rushes awkwardly for coat. The coat is one of* AMANDA'S, *inaccurately made-over, the sleeves too short for* LAURA) Butter and what else?

AMANDA (*Entering upstage*) Just butter. Tell them to charge it.

LAURA Mother, they make such faces when I do that.

AMANDA Sticks and stones can break our bones, but the expression on Mr. Garfinkel's face won't harm us! Tell your brother his coffee is getting cold.

LAURA (*At door*) Do what I asked you, will you, will you, Tom?
(*He looks sullenly away*)

AMANDA Laura, go now or just don't go at all!

LAURA (*Rushing out*) Going—going! (*A second later she cries out.* TOM *springs up and crosses to door.* AMANDA *rushes anxiously in.* TOM *opens the door*)

TOM Laura?

LAURA I'm all right. I slipped, but I'm all right.

AMANDA (*Peering anxiously after her*) If anyone breaks a leg on those fire-escape steps, the landlord ought to be sued for every cent he possesses! (*She shuts door. Remembers she isn't speaking and returns to other room*)

(*As* TOM *enters listlessly for his coffee, she turns her back to him and stands rigidly facing the window on the gloomy gray vault of the areaway. Its light on her face with its aged but childish features is cruelly sharp, satirical as a Daumier print*)

(MUSIC UNDER: "AVE MARIA")

(TOM *glances sheepishly but sullenly at her averted figure and slumps at the table. The coffee is scalding hot; he sips it and gasps and spits it back in the cup. At his gasp,* AMANDA *catches her breath and half turns. Then catches herself and turns back to window*)

(TOM *blows on his coffee, glancing sidewise at his mother. She clears her throat.* TOM *clears his. He starts to rise. Sinks back down again, scratches his head, clears his throat again.* AMANDA *coughs.* TOM *raises his cup in both hands to blow on it, his eyes staring over the rim of it at his mother for several moments. Then he slowly sets the cup down and awkwardly and hesitantly rises from the chair*)

TOM (*Hoarsely*) Mother. I—I apologize, Mother. (AMANDA *draws a quick, shuddering breath. Her face works grotesquely. She breaks into childlike tears*) I'm sorry for what I said, for everything that I said, I didn't mean it.

AMANDA (*Sobbingly*) My devotion has made me a witch and so I make myself hateful to my children!

TOM *No,* you *don't.*

AMANDA I worry so much, don't sleep, it makes me nervous!

TOM (*Gently*) I understand that.

AMANDA I've had to put up a solitary battle all these years. But you're my right-hand bower! Don't fall down, don't fail!

TOM (*Gently*) I try, Mother.

AMANDA (*With great enthusiasm*) Try and you will SUCCEED! (*The notion makes her breathless*) Why, you—you're just *full* of natural endowments! Both my children—they're *unusual* children! Don't you think I know it? I'm so—*proud!* Happy and—feel I've—so much to be thankful for but— Promise me one thing, Son!

TOM What, Mother?

AMANDA Promise, Son, you'll—never be a drunkard!

TOM (*Turns to her grinning*) I will never be a drunkard, Mother.

AMANDA That's what frightened me so, that you'd be drinking! Eat a bowl of Purina!

TOM Just coffee, Mother.

AMANDA Shredded wheat biscuit?

TOM No. No, Mother, just coffee.

AMANDA You can't put in a day's work on an empty stomach. You've got ten minutes—don't gulp! Drinking too-hot liquids makes cancer of the stomach. . . . Put cream in.

TOM No, thank you.

AMANDA To cool it.

TOM No! No, thank you, I want it black.

AMANDA I know, but it's not good for you. We have to do all that we can to build ourselves up. In these trying times we live in, all that we have to cling to is—each other. . . . That's why it's so important to — Tom, I—I sent out your sister so I could discuss something with you. If you hadn't spoken I would have spoken to you. (*Sits down*)

TOM (*Gently*) What is it, Mother, that you want to discuss?

AMANDA *Laura!*

(TOM *puts his cup down slowly*)

(LEGEND ON SCREEN: "LAURA")

(MUSIC: "THE GLASS MENAGERIE")

TOM —Oh—Laura . . .

AMANDA (*Touching his sleeve*) You know how Laura is. So quiet but—still water runs deep! She notices things and I think she—broods about them. (TOM *looks up*) A few days ago I came in and she was crying.

TOM What about?

AMANDA You.

TOM Me?

AMANDA She has an idea that you're not happy here.

TOM What gave her that idea?

AMANDA What gives her any idea? However, you do act strangely. I—I'm not criticizing, understand *that!* I know your ambitions do not lie in the warehouse, that like everybody in the whole wide world—you've had to—make sacrifices, but—Tom—Tom—life's not easy, it calls for—Spartan endurance! There's so many things in my heart that I cannot describe to you! I've never told you but I—*loved* your father. . . .

TOM (*Gently*) I know that, Mother.

AMANDA And you—when I see you taking after his ways! Staying out late—and—well, you *had* been drinking the night you were in that—terrifying condition! Laura says that you hate the apartment and that you go out nights to get away from it! Is that true, Tom?

TOM No. You say there's so much in your heart that you can't describe to me. That's true of me, too. There's so much in my heart that I can't describe to *you!* So let's respect each other's—

AMANDA But, why—*why,* Tom—are you always so *restless?* Where do you *go* to, nights?

TOM I—go to the movies.

AMANDA Why do you go to the movies so much, Tom?

TOM I go to the movies because—I like adventure. Adventure is something I don't have much of at work, so I go to the movies.

AMANDA But, Tom, you go to the movies *entirely* too *much!*

TOM I like a lot of adventure.

(AMANDA *looks baffled, then hurt. As the familiar inquisition resumes he becomes hard and impatient again.* AMANDA *slips back into her querulous attitude toward him*)

(IMAGE ON SCREEN: SAILING VESSEL WITH JOLLY ROGER)

AMANDA Most young men find adventure in their careers.

TOM Then most young men are not employed in a warehouse.

AMANDA The world is full of young men employed in warehouses and offices and factories.

TOM Do all of them find adventure in their careers?

AMANDA They do or they do without it! Not everybody has a craze for adventure.

TOM Man is by instinct a lover, a hunter, a fighter, and none of those instincts are given much play at the warehouse!

AMANDA Man is by instinct! Don't quote instinct to me! Instinct is something that people have got away from! It belongs to animals! Christian adults don't want it!

TOM What do Christian adults want, then, Mother?

AMANDA Superior things! Things of the mind and the spirit! Only animals have to satisfy instincts! Surely your aims are somewhat higher than theirs! Than monkeys—pigs—

TOM I reckon they're not.

AMANDA You're joking! However, that isn't what I wanted to discuss.

TOM (*Rising*) I haven't much time.

AMANDA (*Pushing his shoulders*) Sit down.

TOM You want me to punch in red at the warehouse, Mother?

AMANDA You have five minutes. I want to talk about Laura.

(LEGEND: "PLANS AND PROVISIONS")

TOM All right! What about Laura?

AMANDA We have to be making some plans and provisions for her. She's older than you, two years, and nothing has happened. She just drifts along doing nothing. It frightens me terribly how she just drifts along.

TOM I guess she's the type that people call home girls.

AMANDA There's no such type, and if there is, it's a pity! That is, unless the home is hers, with a husband!

TOM What?

AMANDA Oh, I can see the handwriting on the wall as plain as I see the nose in front of my face! It's terrifying!

More and more you remind me of your father! He was out all hours without explanation!—Then *left! Good-bye!*

And me with the bag to hold. I saw that letter you got from the Merchant Marine. I know what you're dreaming of. I'm not standing here blindfolded.

Very well, then. Then *do* it!

But not till there's somebody to take your place.

TOM What do you mean?

AMANDA I mean that as soon as Laura has got somebody to take care of her, married, a home of her own, independent—why, then you'll be free to go wherever you please, on land, on sea, whichever way the wind blows you!

But until that time you've got to look out for your sister. I don't say me because I'm old and don't matter! I say for your sister because she's young and dependent.

I put her in business college—a dismal failure! Frightened her so it made her sick at the stomach.

I took her over to the Young People's League at the church. Another fiasco. She spoke to nobody, nobody spoke to her. Now all she does is fool with those pieces of glass and play those worn-out records. What kind of a life is that for a girl to lead?

TOM What can I do about it?

AMANDA Overcome selfishness!

Self, self, self is all that you ever think of!

(TOM *springs up and crosses to get his coat. It is ugly and bulky. He pulls on a cap with earmuffs*)

Where is your muffler? Put your wool muffler on!

(*He snatches it angrily from the closet and tosses it around his neck and pulls both ends tight*)

Tom! I haven't said what I had in mind to ask you.

TOM I'm too late to—

AMANDA (*Catching his arm—very importunately. Then shyly*) Down at the warehouse, aren't there some—nice young men?

TOM No!

AMANDA There *must* be—*some* . . .

TOM Mother—(*Gesture*)

AMANDA Find out one that's clean-living—doesn't drink and—ask him out for sister!

TOM What?

AMANDA For *sister!* To *meet!* Get *acquainted!*

TOM (*Stamping to door*) Oh, my *go-osh!*

AMANDA Will you? (*He opens door. Imploringly*) Will you? (*He starts down*) Will you? *Will* you, dear?

TOM (*Calling back*) YES!

(AMANDA *closes the door hesitantly and with a troubled but faintly hopeful expression*)

(SCREEN IMAGE: GLAMOR MAGAZINE COVER)

(*Spot* AMANDA *at phone*)

AMANDA Ella Cartwright? This is Amanda Wingfield!

How are you, honey?

How is that kidney condition? (*Pause*)

*Horrors!* (*Pause*)

You're a Christian martyr, yes, honey, that's what you are, a Christian martyr!

Well, I just now happened to notice in my little red book that your subscription to the *Companion* has just run out! I knew that you wouldn't want to miss out on the wonderful serial starting in this new issue. It's by Bessie Mae Hopper, the first thing she's written since *Honeymoon for Three*.

Wasn't that a strange and interesting story? Well, this one is even lovelier, I believe. It has a sophisticated, society background. It's all about the horsey set on Long Island!

(*Fade Out*)

## Scene Five

LEGEND ON SCREEN: "ANNUNCIATION." *Fade with music.*

*It is early dusk of a spring evening. Supper has just been finished in the Wingfield apartment.* AMANDA *and* LAURA *in light-colored dresses are removing dishes from the table, in the upstage area, which is shadowy, their movements formalized almost as a dance or ritual, their moving forms as pale and silent as moths.*

TOM, *in white shirt and trousers, rises from the table and crosses toward the fire-escape.*

AMANDA (*As he passes her*) Son, will you do me a favor?

TOM What?

AMANDA Comb your hair! You look so pretty when your hair is combed! (TOM *slouches on sofa with evening paper. Enormous caption "Franco Triumphs"*) There is only one respect in which I would like you to emulate your father.

TOM What respect is that?

AMANDA The care he always took of his appearance. He never allowed himself to look untidy. (*He throws down the paper and crosses to fire-escape*) Where are you going?

TOM I'm going out to smoke.

AMANDA You smoke too much. A pack a day at fifteen cents a pack. How much would that amount to in a month? Thirty times fifteen is how much, Tom? Figure it out and you will be astounded at what you could save. Enough to give you a night-school course in accounting at Washington U! Just think what a wonderful thing that would be for you, Son!

(TOM *is unmoved by the thought*)

TOM I'd rather smoke. (*He steps out on landing, letting the screen door slam*)

AMANDA (*Sharply*) I know! That's the tragedy of it. . . . (*Alone, she turns to look at her husband's picture*)

(DANCE MUSIC: "ALL THE WORLD IS WAITING FOR THE SUNRISE!")

TOM (*To the audience*) Across the alley from us was the Paradise Dance Hall. On evenings in spring the windows and doors were open and the music came outdoors. Sometimes the lights were turned out except for a large glass sphere that hung from the ceiling. It would turn slowly about and filter the dusk with delicate rainbow colors. Then the orchestra played a waltz or a tango, something that had a slow and sensuous rhythm. Couples would come outside, to the relative privacy of the alley. You could see them kissing behind ash-pits and telephone poles.

This was the compensation for lives that passed like mine, without any change or adventure.

Adventure and change were imminent in this year. They were waiting around the corner for all these kids.

Suspended in the mist over Berchtesgaden, caught in the folds of Chamberlain's umbrella—

In Spain there was Guernica!

But here there was only hot swing music and liquor, dance halls, bars, and movies, and sex that hung in the gloom like a chandelier and flooded the world with brief, deceptive rainbows. . . .

All the world was waiting for bombardments!

(AMANDA *turns from the picture and comes outside*)

AMANDA (*Sighing*) A fire-escape landing's a poor excuse for a porch. (*She spreads a newspaper on a step and sits down, gracefully and demurely as if she were settling into a swing on a Mississippi veranda*) What are you looking at?

TOM The moon.

AMANDA Is there a moon this evening?

TOM It's rising over Garfinkel's Delicatessen.

AMANDA So it is! A little silver slipper of a moon. Have you made a wish on it yet?

TOM Um-hum.

AMANDA What did you wish for?

TOM That's a secret.

AMANDA A secret, huh? Well, I won't tell mine either. I will be just as mysterious as you.

TOM I bet I can guess what yours is.

AMANDA Is my head so transparent?

TOM You're not a sphinx.

AMANDA No, I don't have secrets. I'll tell you what I wished for on the moon. Success and happiness for my precious children! I wish for that whenever there's a moon, and when there isn't a moon, I wish for it, too.

TOM I thought perhaps you wished for a gentleman caller.

AMANDA Why do you say that?

TOM Don't you remember asking me to fetch one?

AMANDA I remember suggesting that it would be nice for your sister if you brought home some nice young man from the warehouse. I think that I've made that suggestion more than once.

TOM Yes, you have made it repeatedly.

AMANDA Well?

TOM We are going to have one.

AMANDA *What?*

TOM A gentleman caller!

(THE ANNUNCIATION IS CELEBRATED WITH MUSIC)

(AMANDA *rises*)

(IMAGE ON SCREEN: CALLER WITH BOUQUET)

AMANDA You mean you have asked some nice young man to come over?

TOM Yep. I've asked him to dinner.

AMANDA You really did?

TOM I did!

AMANDA You did, and did he—*accept?*

TOM He did!

AMANDA Well, well—well, well! That's—lovely!

TOM I thought that you would be pleased.

AMANDA It's definite, then?

TOM Very definite.

AMANDA Soon?

TOM Very soon.

AMANDA For heaven's sake, stop putting on and tell me some things, will you?

TOM What things do you want me to tell you?

AMANDA *Naturally* I would like to know when he's *coming!*

TOM He's coming tomorrow.

AMANDA *Tomorrow?*

TOM Yep. Tomorrow.

AMANDA But, Tom!

TOM Yes, Mother?

AMANDA Tomorrow gives me no time!

TOM Time for what?

AMANDA Preparations! Why didn't you phone me at once, as soon as you asked him, the minute that he accepted? Then, don't you see, I could have been getting ready!

TOM You don't have to make any fuss.

AMANDA Oh, Tom, Tom, Tom, of course I have to make a fuss! I want things nice, not sloppy! Not thrown together. I'll certainly have to do some fast thinking, won't I?

TOM I don't see why you have to think at all.

AMANDA You just don't know. We can't have a gentleman caller in a pig-sty! All my wedding silver has to be polished, the monogrammed table linen ought to be laundered! The windows have to be washed and fresh curtains put up. And how about clothes? We have to *wear* something, don't we?

TOM Mother, this boy is no one to make a fuss over!

AMANDA Do you realize he's the first young man we've introduced to your sister?

It's terrible, dreadful, disgraceful that poor little sister has never received a single gentleman caller! Tom, come inside! (*She opens the screen door*)

TOM What for?

AMANDA I want to ask you some things.

TOM If you're going to make such a fuss, I'll call it off, I'll tell him not to come!

AMANDA You certainly won't do anything of the kind. Nothing offends people worse than broken engagements. It simply means I'll have to work like a Turk! We won't be brilliant, but we will pass inspection. Come on inside. (TOM *follows, groaning*) Sit down.

TOM Any particular place you would like me to sit?

AMANDA Thank heavens I've got that new sofa! I'm also making payments on a floor lamp I'll have sent out! And put the chintz covers on, they'll brighten things up! Of course I'd hoped to have these walls repapered. . . . What is the young man's name?

TOM His name is O'Connor.

AMANDA That, of course, means fish—tomorrow is Friday! I'll have that salmon loaf—with Durkee's dressing! What does he do? He works at the warehouse?

TOM Of course! How else would I—

AMANDA Tom, he—doesn't drink?

TOM Why do you ask me that?

AMANDA Your father *did!*

TOM Don't get started on that!

AMANDA He *does* drink, then?

TOM Not that I know of!

AMANDA Make sure, be certain! The last thing I want for my daughter's a boy who drinks!

TOM Aren't you being a little bit premature? Mr. O'Connor has not yet appeared on the scene!

AMANDA But will tomorrow. To meet your sister, and what do I know about his character? Nothing! Old maids are better off than wives of drunkards!

TOM Oh, my God!

AMANDA Be still!

TOM (*Leaning forward to whisper*) Lots of fellows meet girls whom they don't marry!

AMANDA Oh, talk sensibly, Tom—and don't be sarcastic! (*She has gotten a hairbrush*)

TOM What are you doing?

AMANDA I'm brushing that cow-lick down!

What is this young man's position at the warehouse?

TOM (*Submitting grimly to the brush and the interrogation*) This young man's position is that of a shipping clerk, Mother.

AMANDA Sounds to me like a fairly responsible job, the sort of a job *you* would be in if you just had more *get-up*.

What is his salary? Have you any idea?

TOM I would judge it to be approximately eighty-five dollars a month.

AMANDA Well—not princely, but—

TOM Twenty more than I make.

AMANDA Yes, how well I know! But for a family man, eighty-five dollars a month is not much more than you can just get by on. . . .

TOM Yes, but Mr. O'Connor is not a family man.

AMANDA He might be, mightn't he? Some time in the future?

TOM I see. Plans and provisions.

AMANDA You are the only young man that I know of who ignores the fact that the future becomes the present, the present the past, and the past turns into everlasting regret if you don't plan for it!

TOM I will think that over and see what I can make of it.

AMANDA Don't be supercilious with your mother! Tell me some more about this—what do you call him?

TOM James D. O'Connor. The D. is for Delaney.

AMANDA Irish on *both* sides! *Gracious!* And doesn't drink?

TOM Shall I call him up and ask him right this minute?

AMANDA The only way to find out about those things is to make discreet inquiries at the proper moment. When I was a girl in Blue Mountain and it was suspected that a young man drank, the girl whose attentions he had been receiving, if any girl *was,* would sometimes speak to the minister of his church, or rather her father would if her father was living, and sort of feel him out on the young man's character. That is the way such things are discreetly handled to keep a young woman from making a tragic mistake!

TOM Then how did you happen to make a tragic mistake?

AMANDA That innocent look of your father's had everyone fooled!

He *smiled*—the world was *enchanted!*

No girl can do worse than put herself at the mercy of a handsome appearance!

I hope that Mr. O'Connor is not too good-looking.

TOM No, he's not too good-looking. He's covered with freckles and hasn't too much of a nose.

AMANDA He's not right-down homely, though?

TOM Not right-down homely. Just medium homely, I'd say.

AMANDA Character's what to look for in a man.

TOM That's what I've always said, Mother.

AMANDA You've never said anything of the kind and I suspect you would never give it a thought.

TOM Don't be so suspicious of me.

AMANDA At least I hope he's the type that's up and coming.

TOM I think he really goes in for self-improvement.

AMANDA What reason have you to think so?

TOM He goes to night school.

AMANDA (*Beaming*) Splendid! What does he do, I I mean study?

TOM Radio engineering and public speaking!

AMANDA Then he has visions of being advanced in the world!

Any young man who studies public speaking is aiming to have an executive job some day!

And radio engineering? A thing for the future!

Both of these facts are very illuminating. Those are the sort of things that a mother should know concerning any young man who comes to call on her daughter. Seriously or—not.

TOM One little warning. He doesn't know about Laura. I didn't let on that we had dark ulterior motives. I just said, why don't you come and have dinner with us? He said okay and that was the whole conversation.

AMANDA I bet it was! You're eloquent as an oyster.

However, he'll know about Laura when he gets here. When he sees how lovely and sweet and pretty she is, he'll thank his lucky stars he was asked to dinner.

TOM Mother, you mustn't expect too much of Laura.

AMANDA What do you mean?

TOM Laura seems all those things to you and me because she's ours and we love her. We don't even notice she's crippled any more.

AMANDA Don't say crippled! You know that I never allow that word to be used!

TOM But face facts, Mother. She is and—that's not all—

AMANDA What do you mean "not all"?

TOM Laura is very different from other girls.

AMANDA I think the difference is all to her advantage.

TOM Not quite all—in the eyes of others—strangers—she's terribly shy and lives in a world of her own and those things make her seem a little peculiar to people outside the house.

AMANDA Don't say peculiar.

TOM Face the facts. She is.

(THE DANCE-HALL MUSIC CHANGES TO A TANGO THAT HAS A MINOR AND SOMEWHAT OMINOUS TONE)

AMANDA In what way is she peculiar—may I ask?

TOM (*Gently*) She lives in a world of her own—a world of—little glass ornaments, Mother. . . . (*Gets up.* AMANDA *remains holding brush, looking at him, troubled*) She plays old phonograph records and—that's about all— (*He glances at himself in the mirror and crosses to door*)

AMANDA (*Sharply*) Where are you going?

TOM I'm going to the movies. (*Out screen door*)

AMANDA Not to the movies, every night to the movies! (*Follows quickly to screen door*) I don't believe you always go to the movies! (*He is gone.* AMANDA *looks worriedly after him for a moment. Then vitality and optimism return and she turns from the door. Crossing to portieres*) Laura! Laura! (LAURA *answers from kitchenette*)

LAURA Yes, Mother.

AMANDA Let those dishes go and come in front! (LAURA *appears with dish towel. Gaily*) Laura, come here and make a wish on the moon!

(SCREEN IMAGE: MOON)

LAURA (*Entering*) Moon—moon?

AMANDA A little silver slipper of a moon.

Look over your left shoulder, Laura, and make a wish!

(LAURA *looks faintly puzzled as if called out of sleep.* AMANDA *seizes her shoulders and turns her at an angle by the door*)

Now!

Now, darling, *wish!*

LAURA What shall I wish for, Mother?

AMANDA (*Her voice trembling and her eyes suddenly filling with tears*) Happiness! Good fortune!

(*The violin rises and the stage dims out*)

(*The Curtain Falls*)

## Scene Six

(IMAGE: HIGH SCHOOL HERO)

TOM And so the following evening I brought Jim home to dinner. I had known Jim slightly in high school. In high school Jim was a hero. He had tremendous Irish good nature and vitality with the scrubbed and polished look of white chinaware. He seemed to move in a continual spotlight. He was a star in basketball, captain of the debating club, president of the senior class and the glee club, and he sang the male lead in the annual light operas. He was always running or bounding, never just walking. He seemed always at the point of defeating the law of gravity. He was shooting with such velocity through his adolescence that you would logically expect him to arrive at nothing short of the White House by the time he was thirty. But Jim apparently ran into more interference after his graduation from Soldan. His speed had definitely slowed. Six years after he left high school he was holding a job that wasn't much better than mine.

(IMAGE: CLERK)

He was the only one at the warehouse with whom I was on friendly terms. I was valuable to him as someone who could remember his former glory, who had seen him win basketball games and the silver cup in debating. He knew of my secret practice of retiring to a cabinet of the wash-room to work on poems when business was slack in the warehouse. He called me Shakespeare. And while the other boys in the warehouse regarded me with suspicious hostility, Jim took a humorous attitude toward me. Gradually his attitude affected the others, their hostility wore off and they also began to smile at me as people smile at an oddly fashioned dog who trots across their path at some distance.

I knew that Jim and Laura had known each other at Soldan, and I had heard Laura speak admiringly of his voice. I didn't know if Jim remembered her or not. In high school Laura had been as unobtrusive as Jim had been astonishing. If he did remember Laura, it was not as my sister, for when I asked him to dinner, he grinned and said, "You know, Shakespeare, I never thought of you as having folks!"

He was about to discover that I did. . . .

(LIGHT UP STAGE)

(LEGEND ON SCREEN: "THE ACCENT OF A COMING FOOT")

(*Friday evening. It is about five o'clock of a late spring evening which comes "scattering poems in the sky"*)

(*A delicate lemony light is in the Wingfield apartment*)

(AMANDA *has worked like a Turk in preparation for the gentleman caller. The results are astonishing. The new floor lamp with its rose-silk shade is in place, a colored paper lantern conceals the broken light fixture in the ceiling, new billowing white curtains are at the windows, chintz covers are on chairs and sofa, a pair of new sofa pillows make their initial appearance*)

(*Open boxes and tissue paper are scattered on the floor*)

(LAURA *stands in the middle with lifted arms while* AMANDA *crouches before her, adjusting the hem of the new dress, devout and ritualistic. The dress is colored and designed by memory. The arrangement of* LAURA'S *hair is changed; it is softer and more becoming. A fragile, unearthly prettiness has come out in* LAURA: *she is like a piece of translucent glass touched by light, given a momentary radiance, not actual, not lasting*)

AMANDA (*Impatiently*) Why are you trembling?

LAURA Mother, you've made me so nervous!

AMANDA How have I made you nervous?

LAURA By all this fuss! You make it seem so important!

AMANDA I don't understand you, Laura. You couldn't be satisfied with just sitting home, and yet whenever I try to arrange something for you, you seem to resist it.

(*She gets up*)

Now take a look at yourself.

No, wait! Wait just a moment—I have an idea!

LAURA What is it now?

(AMANDA *produces two powder puffs which she wraps in handkerchiefs and stuffs in* LAURA'S *bosom*)

LAURA Mother, what are you doing?

AMANDA They call them "Gay Deceivers"!

LAURA I won't wear them!

AMANDA You will!

LAURA Why should I?

AMANDA Because, to be painfully honest, your chest is flat.

LAURA You made it seem like we were setting a trap.

AMANDA All pretty girls are a trap, a pretty trap, and men expect them to be.

(LEGEND: "A PRETTY TRAP")

Now look at yourself, young lady. This is the prettiest you will ever be!

I've got to fix myself now! You're going to be surprised by your mother's appearance! (*She crosses through portieres, humming gaily*)

(LAURA *moves slowly to the long mirror and stares solemnly at herself*)

(*A wind blows the white curtains inward in a slow, graceful motion and with a faint, sorrowful sighing*)

AMANDA (*Off stage*) It isn't dark enough yet. (*She turns slowly before the mirror with a troubled look*)

(LEGEND ON SCREEN: "THIS IS MY SISTER: CELEBRATE HER WITH STRINGS!" MUSIC)

AMANDA (*Laughing, off*) I'm going to show you something. I'm going to make a spectacular appearance!

LAURA What is it, Mother?

AMANDA Possess your soul in patience—you will see! Something I've resurrected from that old trunk! Styles haven't changed so terribly much after all. . . .

(*She parts the portieres*)

Now just look at your mother!

(*She wears a girlish frock of yellowed voile with a blue silk sash. She carries a bunch of jonquils—the legend of her youth is nearly revived. Feverishly*)

This is the dress in which I led the cotillion. Won the cakewalk twice at Sunset Hill, wore one spring to the Governor's ball in Jackson!

See how I sashayed around the ballroom, Laura?

(*She raises her skirt and does a mincing step around the room*)

I wore it on Sundays for my gentlemen callers! I had it on the day I met your father—

I had malaria fever all that spring. The change of climate from East Tennessee to the Delta—weakened resistance—I had a little temperature all the time—not enough to be serious—just enough to make me restless and giddy!—Invitations poured in—parties all over the Delta!—"Stay in bed," said Mother, "you have fever!"—but I just wouldn't—I took quinine but kept on going, going!—Evenings, dances!—Afternoons, long, long rides! Picnics—lovely!—So lovely, that country in May—All lacy with dogwood, literally flooded with jonquils!—That was the spring I had the craze for jonquils. Jonquils became an absolute obsession. Mother said, "Honey, there's no more room for jonquils." And still I kept on bringing in more jonquils. Whenever, wherever I saw them, I'd say, "Stop! Stop! I see jonquils!" I made the young men help me gather the jonquils! It was a joke, Amanda and her jonquils! Finally there were no more vases to hold them, every available space was filled with jonquils. No vases to hold them? All right, I'll hold them myself! And then I—(*She stops in front of the picture.* MUSIC) met your father!

Malaria fever and jonquils and then—this—boy. . . .

(*She switches on the rose-colored lamp*)

I hope they get here before it starts to rain.

(*She crosses upstage and places the jonquils in bowl on table*)

I gave your brother a little extra change so he and Mr. O'Connor could take the service car home.

LAURA (*With altered look*) What did you say his name was?

AMANDA O'Connor.

LAURA What is his first name?

AMANDA I don't remember. Oh, yes, I do. It was—Jim!

(LAURA *sways slightly and catches hold of a chair*)

(LEGEND ON SCREEN: "NOT JIM!")

LAURA (*Faintly*) Not—Jim.

AMANDA Yes, that was it, it was Jim! I've never known a Jim that wasn't nice!

(MUSIC: OMINOUS)

LAURA Are you sure his name is Jim O'Connor?

AMANDA Yes. Why?

LAURA Is he the one that Tom used to know in high school?

AMANDA He didn't say so. I think he just got to know him at the warehouse.

LAURA There was a Jim O'Connor we both knew in high school—(*Then, with effort*) If that is the one that Tom is bringing to dinner—you'll have to excuse me, I won't come to the table.

AMANDA What sort of nonsense is this?

LAURA You asked me once if I'd ever liked a boy. Don't you remember I showed you this boy's picture?

AMANDA You mean the boy you showed me in the year book?

LAURA Yes, that boy.

AMANDA Laura, Laura, were you in love with that boy?

LAURA I don't know, Mother. All I know is I couldn't sit at the table if it was him!

AMANDA It won't be him! It isn't the least bit likely. But whether it is or not, you will come to the table. You will not be excused.

LAURA I'll have to be, Mother.

AMANDA I don't intend to humor your silliness, Laura. I've had too much from you and your brother, both!

So just sit down and compose yourself till they come. Tom has forgotten his key so you'll have to let them in, when they arrive.

LAURA (*Panicky*) Oh, Mother—*you* answer the door!

AMANDA (*Lightly*) I'll be in the kitchen—busy!

LAURA Oh, Mother, please answer the door, don't make me do it!

AMANDA (*Crossing into kitchenette*) I've got to fix the dressing for the salmon. Fuss, fuss—silliness!—over a gentleman caller!

(*Door swings shut.* LAURA *is left alone*)

(LEGEND: "TERROR!")

(*She utters a low moan and turns off the lamp—sits stiffly on the edge of the sofa, knotting her fingers together*)

(LEGEND ON SCREEN: "THE OPENING OF A DOOR!")

(TOM *and* JIM *appear on the fire-escape steps and climb to landing. Hearing their approach,* LAURA *rises with a panicky gesture. She retreats to the portieres*)

(*The doorbell.* LAURA *catches her breath and touches her throat. Low drums*)

AMANDA (*Calling*) Laura, sweetheart! The door!

(LAURA *stares at it without moving*)

JIM I think we just beat the rain.

TOM Uh-huh. (*He rings again, nervously.* JIM *whistles and fishes for a cigarette*)

AMANDA (*Very, very gaily*) Laura, that is your brother and Mr. O'Connor! Will you let them in, darling?

(LAURA *crosses toward kitchenette door*)

LAURA (*Breathlessly*) Mother—you go to the door!

(AMANDA *steps out of kitchenette and stares furiously at* LAURA. *She points imperiously at the door*)

LAURA Please, please!

AMANDA (*In a fierce whisper*) What is the matter with you, you silly thing?

LAURA (*Desperately*) Please, you answer it, *please!*

AMANDA I told you I wasn't going to humor you, Laura. Why have you chosen this moment to lose your mind?

LAURA Please, please, please, you go!

AMANDA You'll have to go to the door because I can't!

LAURA (*Despairingly*) I can't either!

AMANDA *Why?*

LAURA I'm *sick!*

AMANDA I'm sick, too—of your nonsense! Why can't you and your brother be normal people? Fantastic whims and behavior!

(TOM *gives a long ring*)

Preposterous goings on! Can you give me one reason—(*Calls out lyrically*) COMING! JUST ONE SECOND! —why you should be afraid to open a door? Now you answer it, Laura!

LAURA Oh, oh, oh . . . (*She returns through the portieres. Darts to the victrola and winds it frantically and turns it on*)

AMANDA Laura Wingfield, you march right to that door!

LAURA Yes—yes, Mother!

(*A faraway, scratchy rendition of "Dardanella" softens the air and gives her strength to move through it. She slips to the door and draws it cautiously open*)

(TOM *enters with the caller,* JIM O'CONNOR)

TOM Laura, this is Jim. Jim, this is my sister, Laura.

JIM (*Stepping inside*) I didn't know that Shakespeare had a sister!

LAURA (*Retreating stiff and trembling from the door*) How—how do you do?

JIM (*Heartily extending his hand*) Okay!

(LAURA *touches it hesitantly with hers*)

JIM Your hand's *cold,* Laura!

LAURA Yes, well—I've been playing the victrola. . . .

JIM Must have been playing classical music on it! You ought to play a little hot swing music to warm you up!

LAURA Excuse me—I haven't finished playing the victrola. . . .

(*She turns awkwardly and hurries into the front room. She pauses a second by the victrola. Then catches her breath and darts through the portieres like a frightened deer*)

JIM (*Grinning*) What was the matter?

TOM Oh—with Laura? Laura is—terribly shy.

JIM Shy, huh? It's unusual to meet a shy girl nowadays. I don't believe you ever mentioned you had a sister.

TOM Well, now you know. I have one. Here is the *Post Dispatch.* You want a piece of it?

JIM Uh-huh.

TOM What piece? The comics?

JIM Sports! (*Glances at it*) Ole Dizzy Dean is on his bad behavior.

TOM (*Disinterest*) Yeah? (*Lights cigarette and crosses back to fire-escape door*)

JIM Where are *you* going?

TOM I'm going out on the terrace.

JIM (*Goes after him*) You know, Shakespeare—I'm going to sell you a bill of goods!

TOM What goods?

JIM A course I'm taking.

TOM Huh?

JIM In public speaking! You and me, we're not the warehouse type.

TOM Thanks—that's good news.

But what has public speaking got to do with it?

JIM It fits you for—executive positions!

TOM Awww.

JIM I tell you it's done a helluva lot for me.

(IMAGE: EXECUTIVE AT DESK)

TOM In what respect?

JIM In every! Ask yourself what is the difference between you an' me and men in the office down front? Brains?—No!—Ability?—No! Then what? Just one little thing—

TOM What is that one little thing?

JIM Primarily it amounts to—social poise! Being able to square up to people and hold your own on any social level!

AMANDA (*Off stage*) Tom?

TOM Yes, Mother?

AMANDA Is that you and Mr. O'Connor?

TOM Yes, Mother.

AMANDA Well, you just make yourselves comfortable in there.

TOM Yes, Mother.

AMANDA Ask Mr. O'Connor if he would like to wash his hands.

JIM Aw, no—no—thank you—I took care of that at the warehouse. Tom—

TOM Yes?

JIM Mr. Mendoza was speaking to me about you.

TOM Favorably?

JIM What do you think?

TOM Well—

JIM You're going to be out of a job if you don't wake up.

TOM I am waking up—

JIM You show no signs.

TOM The signs are interior.

(IMAGE ON SCREEN: THE SAILING VESSEL WITH JOLLY ROGER AGAIN)

TOM I'm planning to change. (*He leans over the rail speaking with quiet exhilaration. The incandescent marquees and signs of the first-run movie houses light his face from across the alley. He looks like a voyager*) I'm right at the point of committing myself to a future that doesn't include the warehouse and Mr. Mendoza or even a night-school course in public speaking.

JIM What are you gassing about?

TOM I'm tired of the movies.

JIM Movies!

TOM Yes, movies! Look at them— (*A wave toward the marvels of Grand Avenue*) All of those glamorous people—having adventures—hogging it all, gobbling the whole thing up! You know what happens? People go to the *movies* instead of *moving!* Hollywood characters are supposed to have all the adventures for everybody in America, while everybody in America sits in a dark room and watches them have them! Yes, until there's a war. That's when adventure becomes available to the masses! *Everyone's* dish, not only Gable's! Then the people in the dark room come out of the dark room to have some adventures themselves—Goody, goody!—It's our turn now, to go to the South Sea Island—to make a safari—to be exotic, far-off!—But I'm not patient. I don't want to wait till then. I'm tired of the *movies* and I am *about* to *move!*

JIM (*Incredulously*) Move?

TOM Yes.

JIM When?

TOM Soon!

JIM Where? Where?

(THEME THREE MUSIC SEEMS TO ANSWER THE QUESTION, WHILE TOM THINKS IT OVER. HE SEARCHES AMONG HIS POCKETS)

TOM I'm starting to boil inside. I know I seem dreamy, but inside—well, I'm boiling!—Whenever I pick up a shoe, I shudder a little thinking how short life is and what I am doing!—Whatever that means, I know it doesn't mean shoes—except as something to wear on a traveler's feet! (*Finds paper*) Look—

JIM What?

TOM I'm a member.

JIM (*Reading*) The Union of Merchant Seamen.

TOM I paid my dues this month, instead of the light bill.

JIM You will regret it when they turn the lights off.

TOM I won't be here.

JIM How about your mother?

TOM I'm like my father. The bastard son of a bastard! See how he grins? And he's been absent going on sixteen years!

JIM You're just talking, you drip. How does your mother feel about it?

TOM Shhh!—Here comes Mother! Mother is not acquainted with my plans!

AMANDA (*Enters portieres*) Where are you all?

TOM On the terrace, Mother.

(*They start inside. She advances to them.* TOM *is distinctly shocked at her appearance. Even* JIM *blinks a little. He is making his first contact with girlish Southern vivacity and in spite of the night-school course in public speaking is somewhat thrown off the beam by the unexpected outlay of social charm*)

(*Certain responses are attempted by* JIM *but are swept aside by* AMANDA*'s gay laughter and chatter.* TOM *is embarrassed but after the first shock* JIM *reacts very warmly, grins and chuckles, is altogether won over*)

(IMAGE: AMANDA AS A GIRL)

AMANDA (*Coyly smiling, shaking her girlish ringlets*) Well, well, well, so this is Mr. O'Connor. Introductions entirely unnecessary. I've heard so much about you from my boy. I finally said to him, Tom—good gracious!—why don't you bring this paragon to supper? I'd like to meet this nice young man at the warehouse!—Instead of just hearing him sing your praises so much!

I don't know why my son is so stand-offish—that's not Southern behavior!

Let's sit down and—I think we could stand a little more air in here! Tom, leave the door open. I felt a nice fresh breeze a moment ago. Where has it gone to?

Mmm, so warm already! And not quite summer, even. We're going to burn up when summer really gets started.

However, we're having—we're having a very light supper. I think light things are better fo' this time of year. The same as light clothes are. Light clothes an' light food are what warm weather calls fo'. You know our blood gets so thick during th' winter—it takes a while fo' us to *adjust* ou'selves!—when the season changes . . .

It's come so quick this year. I wasn't prepared. All of a sudden—heavens! Already summer!—I ran to the trunk an' pulled out this light dress— Terribly old! Historical almost! But feels so good—so good an' co-ol, y' know. . . .

TOM Mother—

AMANDA Yes, honey?

TOM How about—supper?

AMANDA Honey, you go ask Sister if supper is ready! You know that Sister is in full charge of supper!

Tell her you hungry boys are waiting for it.

(*To* JIM)

Have you met Laura?

JIM She—

AMANDA Let you in? Oh, good, you've met already! It's rare for a girl as sweet an' pretty as Laura to be domestic! But Laura is, thank heavens, not only pretty but also very domestic. I'm not at all. I never was a bit. I never could make a thing but angel-food cake. Well, in the South we had so many servants. Gone, gone, gone. All vestige of gracious living! Gone completely! I wasn't prepared for what the future brought me. All of my gentlemen callers were sons of planters and so of course I assumed that I would be married to one and raise my family on a large piece of land with plenty of servants. But man proposes—and woman accepts the proposal!—To vary that old, old saying a little bit—I married no planter! I married a man who worked for the telephone company!—That gallantly smiling gentleman over there! (*Points to the picture*) A telephone man who—fell in love with long-distance!—Now he travels and I don't even know where!—But what am I going on for about my —tribulations?

Tell me yours—I hope you don't have any!

Tom?

TOM (*Returning*) Yes, Mother?

AMANDA Is supper nearly ready?

TOM It looks to me like supper is on the table.

AMANDA Let me look— (*She rises prettily and looks through portieres*) Oh, lovely!—But where is Sister?

TOM Laura is not feeling well and she says that she thinks she'd better not come to the table.

AMANDA What?—Nonsense!—Laura? Oh, Laura!

LAURA (*Off stage, faintly*) Yes, Mother.

AMANDA You really must come to the table. We won't be seated until you come to the table!

Come in, Mr. O'Connor. You sit over there, and I'll—

Laura? Laura Wingfield!

You're keeping us waiting, honey! We can't say grace until you come to the table!

(*The back door is pushed weakly open and* LAURA *comes in. She is obviously quite faint, her lips trembling, her eyes wide and staring. She moves unsteadily toward the table*)

(LEGEND: "TERROR!")

(*Outside a summer storm is coming abruptly. The white curtains billow inward at the windows and there is a sorrowful murmur and deep blue dusk*)

(LAURA *suddenly stumbles—she catches at a chair with a faint moan*)

TOM Laura!

AMANDA Laura!

(*There is a clap of thunder*)

(LEGEND: "AH!")

(*Despairingly*)

Why, Laura, you *are* sick, darling! Tom, help your sister into the living room, dear!

Sit in the living room, Laura—rest on the sofa.

Well!

(*To the gentleman caller*)

Standing over the hot stove made her ill!—I told her that it was just too warm this evening, but—

(TOM *comes back in.* LAURA *is on the sofa*)

Is Laura all right now?

TOM Yes.

AMANDA What *is* that? Rain? A nice cool rain has come up!

(*She gives the gentleman caller a frightened look*)

I think we may—have grace—now. . . .

(TOM *looks at her stupidly*)

Tom, honey—you say grace!

TOM Oh . . .

"For these and all thy mercies—"

(*They bow their heads,* AMANDA *stealing a nervous glance at* JIM. *In the living room* LAURA, *stretched on the sofa, clenches her hand to her lips, to hold back a shuddering sob*)

God's Holy Name be praised—

(*The Scene Dims Out*)

## Scene Seven

*A Souvenir.*

*Half an hour later. Dinner is just being finished in the upstage area which is concealed by the drawn portieres.*

*As the curtain rises* LAURA *is still huddled upon the sofa, her feet drawn under her, her head resting on a pale blue pillow, her eyes wide and mysteriously watchful. The new floor lamp with its shade of rose-colored silk gives a soft, becoming light to her face, bringing out the fragile, unearthly prettiness which usually escapes attention. There is a steady murmur of rain, but it is slackening and stops soon after the scene begins; the air outside becomes pale and luminous as the moon breaks out.*

*A moment after the curtain rises, the lights in both rooms flicker and go out.*

JIM Hey, there, Mr. Light Bulb!

(AMANDA *laughs nervously*)

(LEGEND: "SUSPENSION OF A PUBLIC SERVICE")

AMANDA Where was Moses when the lights went out? Ha-ha. Do you know the answer to that one, Mr. O'Connor?

JIM No, Ma'am, what's the answer?

AMANDA In the dark!

(JIM *laughs appreciatively*)

Everbody sit still. I'll light the candles. Isn't it lucky we have them on the table? Where's a match? Which of you gentlemen can provide a match?

JIM Here.

AMANDA Thank you, sir.

JIM Not at all, Ma'am!

AMANDA I guess the fuse has burnt out. Mr. O'Connor, can you tell a burnt-out fuse? I know I can't and Tom is a total loss when it comes to mechanics.

(SOUND: GETTING UP: VOICES RECEDE A LITTLE TO KITCHENETTE)

Oh, be careful you don't bump into something. We don't want our gentleman caller to break his neck. Now wouldn't that be a fine howdy-do?

JIM Ha-ha!

Where is the fuse-box?

AMANDA Right here next to the stove. Can you see anything?

JIM Just a minute.

AMANDA Isn't electricity a mysterious thing?

Wasn't it Benjamin Franklin who tied a key to a kite?

We live in such a mysterious universe, don't we? Some people say that science clears up all the mysteries for us. In my opinion it only creates more!

Have you found it yet?

JIM No, Ma'am. All these fuses look okay to me.

AMANDA Tom!

TOM Yes, Mother?

AMANDA That light bill I gave you several days ago. The one I told you we got the notices about?

(LEGEND: "HA!")

TOM Oh—Yeah.

AMANDA You didn't neglect to pay it by any chance?

TOM Why, I—

AMANDA Didn't! I might have known it!

JIM Shakespeare probably wrote a poem on that light bill, Mrs. Wingfield.

AMANDA I might have known better than to trust him with it! There's such a high price for negligence in this world!

JIM Maybe the poem will win a ten-dollar prize.

AMANDA We'll just have to spend the remainder of the evening in the nineteenth century, before Mr. Edison made the Mazda lamp!

JIM Candelight is my favorite kind of light.

AMANDA That shows you're romantic! But that's no excuse for Tom.

Well, we got through dinner. Very considerate of them to let us get through dinner before they plunged us into everlasting darkness, wasn't it, Mr. O'Connor?

JIM Ha-ha!

AMANDA Tom, as a penalty for your carelessness you can help me with the dishes.

JIM Let me give you a hand.

AMANDA Indeed you will not!

JIM I ought to be good for something.

AMANDA Good for something? (*Her tone is rhapsodic*) *You?* Why, Mr. O'Connor, nobody, *nobody's* given me this much entertainment in years—as you have!

JIM Aw, now, Mrs. Wingfield!

AMANDA I'm not exaggerating, not one bit! But Sister is all by her lonesome. You go keep her company in the parlor!

I'll give you this lovely old candelabrum that used to be on the altar at the Church of the Heavenly Rest. It was melted a little out of shape when the church burnt down. Lightning struck it one spring. Gypsy Jones was holding a revival at the time and he intimated that the church was destroyed because the Episcopalians gave card parties.

JIM Ha-ha!

AMANDA And how about you coaxing Sister to drink a little wine? I think it would be good for her! Can you carry both at once?

JIM Sure. I'm Superman!

AMANDA Now, Thomas, get into this apron!

(*The door of kitchenette swings closed on* AMANDA'S *gay laughter; the flickering light approaches the portieres*)

(LAURA *sits up nervously as he enters. Her speech at first is low and breathless from the almost intolerable strain of being alone with a stranger*)

(THE LEGEND: "I DON'T SUPPOSE YOU REMEMBER ME AT ALL!")

(*In her first speeches in this scene, before* JIM'S *warmth overcomes her paralyzing shyness,* LAURA'S *voice is thin and breathless as though she has just run up a steep flight of stairs*)

(JIM'S *attitude is gently humorous. In playing this scene it should be stressed that while the incident is apparently unimportant, it is to* LAURA *the climax of her secret life*)

JIM Hello, there, Laura.

LAURA (*Faintly*) Hello. (*She clears her throat*)

JIM How are you feeling now? Better?

LAURA Yes. Yes, thank you.

JIM This is for you. A little dandelion wine. (*He extends it toward her with extravagant gallantry*)

LAURA Thank you.

JIM Drink it—but don't get drunk!

(*He laughs heartily.* LAURA *takes the glass uncertainly; laughs shyly*)

Where shall I set the candles?

LAURA Oh—oh, anywhere . . .

JIM How about here on the floor? Any objections?

LAURA No.

JIM I'll spread a newspaper under to catch the drippings. I like to sit on the floor. Mind if I do?

LAURA Oh, no.

JIM Give me a pillow?

LAURA What?

JIM A pillow!

LAURA Oh . . . (*Hands him one quickly*)

JIM How about you? Don't you like to sit on the floor?

LAURA Oh—yes.

JIM Why don't you, then?

LAURA I—will.

JIM Take a pillow! (LAURA *does. Sits on the other side of the candelabrum.* JIM *crosses his legs and smiles engagingly at her*) I can't hardly see you sitting way over there.

LAURA I can—see you.

JIM I know, but that's not fair, I'm in the limelight. (LAURA *moves her pillow closer*) Good! Now I can see you! Comfortable?

LAURA Yes.

JIM So am I. Comfortable as a cow! Will you have some gum?

LAURA No, thank you.

JIM I think that I will indulge, with your permission. (*Musingly unwraps it and holds it up*) Think of the fortune made by the guy that invented the first piece of chewing gum. Amazing, huh? The Wrigley Building is one of the sights of Chicago—I saw it summer before last when I went up to the Century of Progress. Did you take in the Century of Progress?

LAURA No, I didn't.

JIM Well, it was quite a wonderful exposition. What impressed me most was the Hall of Science. Gives you an idea of what the future will be in America, even more wonderful than the present time is! (*Pause. Smiling at her*) Your brother tells me you're shy. Is that right, Laura?

LAURA I—don't know.

JIM I judge you to be an old-fashioned type of girl. Well, I think that's a pretty good type to be. Hope you don't think I'm being too personal—do you?

LAURA (*Hastily, out of embarrassment*) I believe I *will* take a piece of gum, if you—don't mind. (*Clearing her throat*) Mr. O'Connor, have you—kept up with your singing?

JIM Singing? Me?

LAURA Yes. I remember what a beautiful voice you had.

JIM When did you hear me sing?

(VOICE OFF STAGE IN THE PAUSE)

VOICE (*Off stage*)

O blow, ye winds, heigh-ho,
A-roving I will go!
I'm off to my love
With a boxing glove—
Ten thousand miles away!

JIM You say you've heard me sing?

LAURA Oh, yes! Yes, very often. . . . I—don't suppose—you remember me—at all?

JIM (*Smiling doubtfully*) You know I have an idea I've seen you before. I had that idea soon as you opened the door. It seemed almost like I was about to remember your name. But the name that I started to call you—wasn't a name! And so I stopped myself before I said it.

LAURA Wasn't it—Blue Roses?

JIM (*Springs up. Grinning*) Blue Roses!—My gosh, yes—Blue Roses!

That's what I had on my tongue when you opened the door!

Isn't it funny what tricks your memory plays? I didn't connect you with high school somehow or other.

But that's where it was; it was high school. I didn't even know you were Shakespeare's sister!

Gosh, I'm sorry.

LAURA I didn't expect you to. You—barely knew me!

JIM But we did have a speaking acquaintance, huh?

LAURA Yes, we—spoke to each other.

JIM When did you recognize me?

LAURA Oh, right away!

JIM Soon as I came in the door?

LAURA When I heard your name I thought it was probably you. I knew that Tom used to know you a little in high school. So when you came in the door—Well, then I was—sure.

JIM Why didn't you *say* something, then?

LAURA (*Breathlessly*) I didn't know what to say, I was—too surprised!

JIM For goodness' sakes! You know, this sure is funny!

LAURA Yes! Yes, isn't it, though . . .

JIM Didn't we have a class in something together?

LAURA Yes, we did.

JIM What class was that?

LAURA It was—singing—Chorus!

JIM Aw!

LAURA I sat across the aisle from you in the Aud.

JIM Aw.

LAURA Mondays, Wednesdays, and Fridays.

JIM Now I remember—you always came in late.

LAURA Yes, it was so hard for me, getting upstairs. I had that brace on my leg—it clumped so loud!

JIM I never heard any clumping.

LAURA (*Wincing at the recollection*) To me it sounded like—thunder!

JIM Well, well, well, I never even noticed.

LAURA And everybody was seated before I came in. I had to walk in front of all those people. My seat was in the back row. I had to go clumping all the way up the aisle with everyone watching!

JIM You shouldn't have been self-conscious.

LAURA I know, but I was. It was always such a relief when the singing started.

JIM Aw, yes, I've placed you now! I used to call you Blue Roses. How was it that I got started calling you that?

LAURA I was out of school a little while with pleurosis. When I came back you asked me what was the matter. I said I had pleurosis—you thought I said Blue Roses. That's what you always called me after that!

JIM I hope you didn't mind.

LAURA Oh, no—I liked it. You see, I wasn't acquainted with many—people. . . .

JIM As I remember you sort of stuck by yourself.

LAURA I—I—never have had much luck at—making friends.

JIM I don't see why you wouldn't.

LAURA Well, I—started out badly.

JIM You mean being—

LAURA Yes, it sort of—stood between me—

JIM You shouldn't have let it!

LAURA I know, but it did, and—

JIM You were shy with people!

LAURA I tried not to be but never could—

JIM Overcome it?

LAURA No, I—I never could!

JIM I guess being shy is something you have to work out of kind of gradually.

LAURA (*Sorrowfully*) Yes—I guess it—

JIM Takes time!

LAURA Yes.

JIM People are not so dreadful when you know them. That's what you have to remember! And everybody has problems, not just you, but practically everybody has got some problems.

You think of yourself as having the only problems, as being the only one who is disappointed. But just look around you and you will see lots of people as disappointed as you are. For instance, I hoped when I was going to high school that I would be further along at this time, six years later, than I am now—You remember that wonderful write-up I had in *The Torch?*

LAURA Yes! (*She rises and crosses to table*)

JIM It said I was bound to succeed in anything I went into! (*Laura returns with the annual*) Holy Jeez! *The Torch!* (*He accepts it reverently. They smile across it with mutual wonder.* LAURA *crouches beside him and they begin to turn through it.* LAURA'S *shyness is dissolving in his warmth*)

LAURA Here you are in *The Pirates of Penzance!*

JIM (*Wistfully*) I sang the baritone lead in that operetta.

LAURA (*Raptly*) So—*beautifully!*

JIM (*Protesting*) Aw—

LAURA Yes, yes—beautifully—beautifully!

JIM You heard me?

LAURA All three times!

JIM No!

LAURA Yes!

JIM All three performances?

LAURA (*Looking down*) Yes.

JIM Why?

LAURA I—wanted to ask you to—autograph my program.

JIM Why didn't you ask me to?

LAURA You were always surrounded by your own friends so much that I never had a chance to.

JIM You should have just—

LAURA Well, I—thought you might think I was—

JIM Thought I might think you was—what?

LAURA Oh—

JIM (*With reflective relish*) I was beleaguered by females in those days.

LAURA You were terribly popular!

JIM Yeah—

LAURA You had such a—friendly way—

JIM I was spoiled in high school.

LAURA Everybody—liked you!

JIM Including you?

LAURA I—yes, I—I did, too— (*She gently closes the book in her lap*)

JIM Well, well, well!—Give me that program, Laura. (*She hands it to him. He signs it with a flourish*) There you are—better late than never!

LAURA Oh, I—what a—surprise!

JIM My signature isn't worth very much right now.
But some day—maybe—it will increase in value!
Being disappointed is one thing and being discouraged is something else. I am disappointed but I am not discouraged.
I'm twenty-three years old.
How old are you?

LAURA I'll be twenty-four in June.

JIM That's not old age!

LAURA No, but—

JIM You finished high school?

LAURA (*With difficulty*) I didn't go back.

JIM You mean you dropped out?

LAURA I made bad grades in my final examinations. (*She rises and replaces the book and the program. Her voice strained*) How is—Emily Meisenbach getting along?

JIM Oh, that kraut-head!

LAURA Why do you call her that?

JIM That's what she was.

LAURA You're not still—going with her?

JIM I never see her.

LAURA It said in the Personal Section that you were—engaged!

JIM I know, but I wasn't impressed by that—propaganda!

LAURA It wasn't—the truth?

JIM Only in Emily's optimistic opinion!

LAURA Oh—

(LEGEND: "WHAT HAVE YOU DONE SINCE HIGH SCHOOL?")

(JIM *lights a cigarette and leans indolently back on his elbows, smiling at* LAURA *with a warmth and charm which lights her inwardly with altar candles. She remains by the table and turns in her hands a piece of glass to cover her tumult*)

JIM (*After several reflective puffs on a cigarette*) What have you done since high school? (*She seems not to hear him*) Huh? (LAURA *looks up*) I said what have you done since high school, Laura?

LAURA Nothing much.

JIM You must have been doing something these six long years.

LAURA Yes.

JIM Well, then, such as what?

LAURA I took a business course at business college—

JIM How did that work out?

LAURA Well, not very—well—I had to drop out, it gave me—indigestion—

(JIM *laughs gently*)

JIM What are you doing now?

LAURA I don't do anything—much. Oh, please don't think I sit around doing nothing! My glass collection takes up a good deal of time. Glass is something you have to take good care of.

JIM What did you say—about glass?

LAURA Collection I said—I have one—(*She clears her throat and turns away again, acutely shy*)

JIM (*Abruptly*) You know what I judge to be the trouble with you?

Inferiority complex! Know what that is? That's what they call it when someone low-rates himself!

I understand it because I had it, too. Although my case was not so aggravated as yours seems to be. I had it until I took up public speaking, developed my voice, and learned that I had an aptitude for science. Before that time I never thought of myself as being outstanding in any way whatsoever!

Now I've never made a regular study of it, but I have a friend who says I can analyze people better than doctors that make a profession of it. I don't claim that to be necessarily true, but I can sure guess a person's psychology. Laura! (*Takes out his gum*) Excuse me, Laura. I always take it out when the flavor is gone. I'll use this scrap of paper to wrap it in. I know how it is to get it stuck on a shoe.

Yep—that's what I judge to be your principal trouble. A lack of confidence in yourself as a person. You don't have the proper amount of faith in yourself. I'm basing that fact on a number of your remarks and also on certain observations I've made. For instance that clumping you thought was so awful in high school. You say that you even dreaded to walk into class. You see what you did? You dropped out of school, you gave up an education because of a clump, which as far as I know was practically nonexistent! A little physical defect is what you have. Hardly noticeable even! Magnified thousands of times by imagination!

You know what my strong advice to you is? Think of yourself as *superior* in some way!

LAURA In what way would I think?

JIM Why, man alive, Laura! Just look about you a little. What do you see? A world full of common people! All of 'em born and all of 'em going to die!

Which of them has one-tenth of your good points! Or mine! Or anyone else's, as far as that goes—Gosh!

Everybody excels in some one thing. Some in many!

(*Unconsciously glances at himself in the mirror*)

All you've got to do is discover in *what!*

Take me, for instance.

(*He adjusts his tie at the mirror*)

My interest happens to lie in electro-dynamics. I'm taking a course in radio engineering at night school, Laura, on top of a fairly responsible job at the warehouse. I'm taking that course and studying public speaking.

LAURA Ohhhh.

JIM Because I believe in the future of television!

(*Turning back to her*)

I wish to be ready to go up right along with it. Therefore I'm planning to get in on the ground floor. In fact I've already made the right connections and all that remains is for the industry itself to get under way! Full steam—

(*His eyes are starry*)

*Knowledge*—Zzzzzp! *Money*—Zzzzzzp!—*Power!*

That's the cycle democracy is built on!

(*His attitude is convincingly dynamic.* LAURA *stares at him, even her shyness eclipsed in her absolute wonder. He suddenly grins*)

I guess you think I think a lot of myself!

LAURA No—o-o-o, I—

JIM Now how about you? Isn't there something you take more interest in than anything else?

LAURA Well, I do—as I said—have my—glass collection—

(*A peal of girlish laughter from the kitchen*)

JIM I'm not right sure I know what you're talking about.

What kind of glass is it?

LAURA Little articles of it, they're ornaments mostly!

Most of them are little animals made out of glass, the tiniest little animals in the world. Mother calls them a glass menagerie!

Here's an example of one, if you'd like to see it!

This one is one of the oldest. It's nearly thirteen.

(MUSIC: "THE GLASS MENAGERIE")

(*He stretches out his hand*)

Oh, be careful—if you breathe, it breaks!

JIM I'd better not take it. I'm pretty clumsy with things.

LAURA Go on, I trust you with him!

(*Places it is his palm*)

There now—you're holding him gently!

Hold him over the light, he loves the light! You see how the light shines through him?

JIM It sure does shine!

LAURA I shouldn't be partial, but he is my favorite one.

JIM What kind of a thing is this one supposed to be?

LAURA Haven't you noticed the single horn on his forehead?

JIM A unicorn, huh?

LAURA Mmm-hmmm!

JIM Unicorns, aren't they extinct in the modern world?

LAURA I know!

JIM Poor little fellow, he must feel sort of lonesome.

LAURA (*Smiling*) Well, if he does he doesn't complain about it. He stays on a shelf with some horses that don't have horns and all of them seem to get along nicely together.

JIM How do you know?

LAURA (*Lightly*) I haven't heard any arguments among them!

JIM (*Grinning*) No arguments, huh? Well, that's a pretty good sign! Where shall I set him?

LAURA Put him on the table. They all like a change of scenery once in a while!

JIM (*Stretching*) Well, well, well, well—

Look how big my shadow is when I stretch!

LAURA Oh, oh, yes—it stretches across the ceiling!

JIM (*Crossing to door*) I think it's stopped raining. (*Opens fire-escape door*) Where does the music come from?

LAURA From the Paradise Dance Hall across the alley.

JIM How about cutting the rug a little, Miss Wingfield?

LAURA Oh, I—

JIM Or is your program filled up? Let me have a look at it. (*Grasps imaginary card*) Why, every dance is taken! I'll just have to scratch some out. (WALTZ MUSIC: "LA GOLONDRINA") Ahhh, a waltz! (*He executes some sweeping turns by himself then holds his arms toward* LAURA)

LAURA (*Breathlessly*) I—can't dance!

JIM There you go, that inferiority stuff!

LAURA I've never danced in my life!

JIM Come on, try!

LAURA Oh, but I'd step on you!

JIM I'm not made out of glass.

LAURA How—how—how do we start?

JIM Just leave it to me. You hold your arms out a little.

LAURA Like this?

JIM A little bit higher. Right. Now don't tighten up, that's the main thing about it—relax.

LAURA (*Laughing breathlessly*) It's hard not to.

JIM Okay.

LAURA I'm afraid you can't budge me.

JIM What do you bet I can't (*He swings her into motion*)

LAURA Goodness, yes, you can!

JIM Let yourself go, now, Laura, just let yourself go.

LAURA I'm—

JIM Come on!

LAURA Trying!

JIM Not so stiff— Easy does it!

LAURA I know but I'm—

JIM Loosen th' backbone! There now, that's a lot better.

LAURA Am I?

JIM Lots, lots better! (*He moves her about the room in a clumsy waltz*)

LAURA Oh, my!

JIM Ha-ha!

LAURA Oh, my goodness!

JIM Ha-ha-ha! (*They suddenly bump into the table.* JIM *stops*) What did we hit on?

LAURA Table.

JIM Did something fall off it? I think—

LAURA Yes.

JIM I hope it wasn't the little glass horse with the horn!

LAURA Yes.

JIM Aw, aw, aw. Is it broken?

LAURA Now it is just like all the other horses.

JIM It's lost its—

LAURA Horn!

It doesn't matter. Maybe it's a blessing in disguise.

JIM You'll never forgive me. I bet that that was your favorite piece of glass.

LAURA I don't have favorites much. It's no tragedy, Freckles. Glass breaks so easily. No matter how careful you are. The traffic jars the shelves and things fall off them.

JIM Still I'm awfully sorry that I was the cause.

LAURA (*Smiling*) I'll just imagine he had an operation. The horn was removed to make him feel less—freakish!

(*They both laugh*)

Now he will feel more at home with the other horses, the ones that don't have horns. . . .

JIM Ha-ha, that's very funny!

(*Suddenly serious*)

I'm glad to see that you have a sense of humor.

You know—you're—well—very different!

Surprisingly different from anyone else I know!

(*His voice becomes soft and hesitant with a genuine feeling*)

Do you mind me telling you that?

(LAURA *is abashed beyond speech*)

I mean it in a nice way. . . .

(LAURA *nods shyly, looking away*)

You make me feel sort of—I don't know how to put it!

I'm usually pretty good at expressing things, but—

This is something that I don't know how to say!

(LAURA *touches her throat and clears it—turns the broken unicorn in her hands*)

(*Even softer*)

Has anyone ever told you that you were pretty?

(PAUSE: MUSIC)

(LAURA *looks up slowly, with wonder, and shakes her head*)

Well, you are! In a very different way from anyone else.

And all the nicer because of the difference, too.

(*His voice becomes low and husky.* LAURA *turns away, nearly faint with the novelty of her emotions*)

I wish that you were my sister. I'd teach you to have some confidence in yourself. The different people are not like other people, but being different is nothing to be ashamed of. Because other people are not such wonderful people. They're one hundred times one thousand. You're one times one! They walk all over the earth. You just stay here. They're common as—weeds, but—you—well, you're—*Blue Roses!*

(IMAGE ON SCREEN: BLUE ROSES)

(MUSIC CHANGES)

LAURA But blue is wrong for—roses. . . .

JIM It's right for you!—You're—pretty!

LAURA In what respect am I pretty?

JIM In all respects—believe me! Your eyes—your hair—are pretty! Your hands are pretty!

(*He catches hold of her hand*)

You think I'm making this up because I'm invited to dinner and have to be nice. Oh, I could do that! I could put on an act for you, Laura, and say lots of things without being very sincere. But this time I am. I'm talking to you sincerely. I happened to notice you had this inferiority complex that keeps you from feeling comfortable with people. Somebody needs to build your confidence up and make you proud instead of shy and turning away and—blushing—

Somebody—ought to—

Ought to—*kiss* you, Laura!

(*His hand slips slowly up her arm to her shoulder*)

(MUSIC SWELLS TUMULTUOUSLY)

(*He suddenly turns her about and kisses her on the lips*)

(*When he releases her,* LAURA *sinks on the sofa with a bright, dazed look*)

(JIM *backs away and fishes in his pocket for a cigarette*)

(LEGEND ON SCREEN: "SOUVENIR")

Stumble-john!

(*He lights the cigarette, avoiding her look*)

(*There is a peal of girlish laughter from* AMANDA *in the kitchen*)

(LAURA *slowly raises and opens her hand. It still contains the little broken glass animal. She looks at it with a tender, bewildered expression*)

Stumble-john!

I shouldn't have done that— That was way off the beam. You don't smoke, do you?

(*She looks up, smiling, not hearing the question*)

(*He sits beside her a little gingerly. She looks at him speechlessly—waiting*)

(*He coughs decorously and moves a little farther aside as he considers the situation and senses her feelings, dimly, with perturbation*)

(*Gently*)

Would you—care for a—mint?

(*She doesn't seem to hear him but her look grows brighter even*)

Peppermint—Life-Saver?

My pocket's a regular drug store—wherever I go . . .

(*He pops a mint in his mouth. Then gulps and decides to make a clean breast of it. He speaks slowly and gingerly*)

Laura, you know, if I had a sister like you, I'd do the same thing as Tom. I'd bring out fellows and—introduce her to them. The right type of boys of a type to—appreciate her.

Only—well—he made a mistake about me.

Maybe I've got no call to be saying this. That may not have been the idea in having me over. But what if it was?

There's nothing wrong about that. The only trouble is that in my case—I'm not in a situation to—do the right thing.

I can't take down your number and say I'll phone.

I can't call up next week and—ask for a date.

I thought I had better explain the situation in case you—misunderstood it and—hurt your feelings. . . .

(*Pause*)

(*Slowly, very slowly,* LAURA'S *look changes, her eyes returning slowly from his to the ornament in her palm*)

(AMANDA *utters another gay laugh in the kitchen*)

LAURA (*Faintly*) You—won't—call again?

JIM No, Laura, I can't.

(*He rises from the sofa*)

As I was just explaining, I've—got strings on me.

Laura, I've—been going steady!

I go out all of the time with a girl named Betty. She's a home-girl like you, and Catholic, and Irish, and in a great many ways we—get along fine.

I met her last summer on a moonlight boat trip up the river to Alton, on the *Majestic*.

Well—right away from the start it was—love!

(LEGEND: LOVE!)

(LAURA *sways slightly forward and grips the arm of the sofa. He fails to notice, now enrapt in his own comfortable being*)

Being in love has made a new man of me!

(*Leaning stiffly forward, clutching the arm of the sofa,* LAURA *struggles visibly with her storm. But* JIM *is oblivious, she is a long way off*)

The power of love is really pretty tremendous!

Love is something that—changes the whole world, Laura!

(*The storm abates a little and* LAURA *leans back. He notices her again*)

It happened that Betty's aunt took sick, she got a wire and had to go to Centralia. So Tom—when he asked me to dinner—I naturally just accepted the invitation, not knowing that you—that he—that I—

(*He stops awkwardly*)

Huh—I'm a stumble-john!

(*He flops back on the sofa*)

(*The holy candles in the altar of* LAURA'S *face have been snuffed out. There is a look of almost infinite desolation*)

(JIM *glances at her uneasily*)

I wish that you would—say something. (*She bites her lip which was trembling and then bravely smiles. She opens her hand again on the broken glass ornament. Then she gently takes his hand and raises it level with her own. She carefully places the unicorn in the palm of his hand, then pushes his fingers closed upon it*) What are you—doing that for? You want me to have him?—Laura? (*She nods*) What for?

LAURA A—souvenir . . .

(*She rises unsteadily and crouches beside the victrola to wind it up*)

(LEGEND ON SCREEN: "THINGS HAVE A WAY OF TURNING OUT SO BADLY!")

(OR IMAGE: "GENTLEMAN CALLER WAVING GOOD-BYE!—GAILY")

(*At this moment* AMANDA *rushes brightly back in the front room. She bears a pitcher of fruit punch in an old-fashioned cut-glass pitcher and a plate of macaroons. The plate has a gold border and poppies painted on it*)

AMANDA Well, well, well! Isn't the air delightful after the shower? I've made you children a little liquid refreshment.

(*Turns gaily to the gentleman caller*)

Jim, do you know that song about lemonade?

"Lemonade, lemonade
Made in the shade and stirred with a spade—
Good enough for any old maid!"

JIM (*Uneasily*) Ha-ha! No—I never heard it.

AMANDA Why, Laura! You look so serious!

JIM We were having a serious conversation.

AMANDA Good! Now you're better acquainted!

JIM (*Uncertainly*) Ha-ha! Yes.

AMANDA You modern young people are much more serious-minded than my generation. I was so gay as a girl!

JIM You haven't changed, Mrs. Wingfield.

AMANDA Tonight I'm rejuvenated! The gaiety of the occasion, Mr. O'Connor!

(*She tosses her head with a peal of laughter. Spills lemonade*)

Oooo! I'm baptizing myself!

JIM Here—let me—

AMANDA (*Setting the pitcher down*) There now. I discovered we had some maraschino cherries. I dumped them in, juice and all!

JIM You shouldn't have gone to that trouble, Mrs. Wingfield.

AMANDA Trouble, trouble? Why, it was loads of fun!

Didn't you hear me cutting up in the kitchen? I bet your ears were burning! I told Tom how outdone with him I was for keeping you to himself so long a time! He should have brought you over much, much sooner! Well, now that you've found your way, I want you to be a very frequent caller! Not just occasional but all the time.

Oh, we're going to have a lot of gay times together! I see them coming!

Mmm, just breathe that air! So fresh, and the moon's so pretty!

I'll skip back out—I know where my place is when young folks are having a—serious conversation!

JIM Oh, don't go out, Mrs. Wingfield. The fact of the matter is I've got to be going.

AMANDA Going, now? You're joking! Why, it's only the shank of the evening, Mr. O'Connor!

JIM Well, you know how it is.

AMANDA You mean you're a young workingman and have to keep workingmen's hours. We'll let you off early tonight. But only on the condition that next time you stay later.

What's the best night for you? Isn't Saturday night the best night for you workingmen?

JIM I have a couple of time-clocks to punch, Mrs. Wingfield. One at morning, another one at night!

AMANDA My, but you *are* ambitious! You work at night, too?

JIM No, Ma'am, not work but—Betty! (*He crosses deliberately to pick up his hat. The band at the Paradise Dance Hall goes into a tender waltz*)

AMANDA Betty? Betty? Who's—Betty!

(*There is an ominous cracking sound in the sky*)

JIM Oh, just a girl. The girl I go steady with! (*He smiles charmingly. The sky falls*)

(LEGEND: "THE SKY FALLS")

AMANDA (*A long-drawn exhalation*) Ohhhh . . . Is it a serious romance, Mr. O'Connor?

JIM We're going to be married the second Sunday in June.

AMANDA Ohhhh—how nice!

Tom didn't mention that you were engaged to be married.

JIM The cat's not out of the bag at the warehouse yet.

You know how they are. They call you Romeo and stuff like that.

(*He stops at the oval mirror to put on his hat. He carefully shapes the brim and the crown to give a discreetly dashing effect*)

It's been a wonderful evening, Mrs. Wingfield. I guess this is what they mean by Southern hospitality.

AMANDA It really wasn't anything at all.

JIM I hope it don't seem like I'm rushing off. But I promised Betty I'd pick her up at the Wabash depot, an' by the time I get my jalopy down there her train'll be in. Some women are pretty upset if you keep 'em waiting.

AMANDA Yes, I know— The tyranny of women!

(*Extends her hand*)

Good-bye, Mr. O'Connor.

I wish you luck—and happiness—and success! All three of them, and so does Laura!—Don't you, Laura?

LAURA Yes!

JIM (*Taking her hand*) Good-bye, Laura. I'm certainly going to treasure that souvenir. And don't you forget the good advice I gave you.

(*Raises his voice to a cheery shout*)

So long, Shakespeare!

Thanks again, ladies— Good night!

(*He grins and ducks jauntily out*)

(*Still bravely grimacing,* AMANDA *closes the door on the gentleman caller. Then she turns back to the room with a puzzled expression. She and* LAURA *don't dare to face each other.* LAURA *crouches beside the victrola to wind it*)

AMANDA (*Faintly*) Things have a way of turning out so badly.

I don't believe that I would play the victrola.

Well, well—well—

Our gentleman caller was engaged to be married!

Tom!

TOM (*From back*) Yes, Mother?

AMANDA Come in here a minute. I want to tell you something awfully funny.

TOM (*Enters with macaroon and a glass of the lemonade*) Has the gentleman caller gotten away already?

AMANDA The gentleman caller has made an early departure.

What a wonderful joke you played on us!

TOM How do you mean?

AMANDA You didn't mention that he was engaged to be married.

TOM Jim? Engaged?

AMANDA That's what he just informed us.

TOM I'll be jiggered! I didn't know about that.

AMANDA That seems very peculiar.

TOM What's peculiar about it?

AMANDA Didn't you call him your best friend down at the warehouse?

TOM He is, but how did I know?

AMANDA It seems extremely peculiar that you wouldn't know your best friend was going to be married!

TOM The warehouse is where I work, not where I know things about people!

AMANDA You don't know things anywhere! You live in a dream; you manufacture illusions!

(*He crosses to door*)

Where are you going?

TOM I'm going to the movies.

AMANDA That's right, now that you've had us make such fools of ourselves. The effort, the preparations, all the expense! The new floor lamp, the rug, the clothes for Laura! All for what? To entertain some other girl's fiancé!

Go to the movies, go! Don't think about us, a mother deserted, an unmarried sister who's crippled and has no job! Don't let anything interfere with your selfish pleasure!

Just go, go, go—to the movies!

TOM All right, I will! The more you shout about my selfishness to me the quicker I'll go, and I won't go to the movies!

AMANDA Go, then! Then go to the moon—you selfish dreamer!

(TOM *smashes his glass on the floor. He plunges out on the fire escape, slamming the door.* LAURA *screams—cut by door*)

(*Dance-hall music up.* TOM *goes to the rail and grips it desperately, lifting his face in the chill white moonlight penetrating the narrow abyss of the alley*)

(LEGEND ON SCREEN: "AND SO GOOD-BYE . . .")

(TOM'S *closing speech is timed with the interior pantomime. The interior scene is played as though viewed through soundproof glass.* AMANDA *appears to be making a comforting speech to* LAURA *who is huddled upon the sofa. Now that we cannot hear the mother's speech, her silliness is gone and she has dignity and tragic beauty.* LAURA'S *dark hair hides her face until at the end of the speech she lifts it to smile at her mother.* AMANDA'S *gestures are slow and graceful, almost dancelike, as she comforts the daughter. At the end of her speech she glances a moment at the father's picture—then withdraws through the portieres. At close of* TOM'S *speech,* LAURA *blows out the candles, ending the play*)

TOM I didn't go to the moon, I went much further—for time is the longest distance between two places—

Not long after that I was fired for writing a poem on the lid of a shoe-box.

I left Saint Louis. I descended the steps of this fire escape for a last time and followed, from then on, in my father's footsteps, attempting to find in motion what was lost in space—

I traveled around a great deal. The cities swept about me like dead leaves, leaves that were brightly colored but torn away from the branches.

I would have stopped, but I was pursued by something.

It always came upon me unawares, taking me altogether by surprise. Perhaps it was a familiar bit of music. Perhaps it was only a piece of transparent glass—

Perhaps I am walking along a street at night, in some strange city, before I have found companions. I pass the lighted window of a shop where perfume is sold. The window is filled with pieces of colored glass, tiny transparent bottles in delicate colors, like bits of a shattered rainbow.

Then all at once my sister touches my shoulder. I turn around and look into her eyes . . .

Oh, Laura, Laura, I tried to leave you behind me, but I am more faithful than I intended to be!

I reach for a cigarette, I cross the street, I run into the movies or a bar, I buy a drink, I speak to the nearest stranger—anything that can blow your candles out!

(LAURA *bends over the candles*)

—for nowadays the world is lit by lightning! Blow out your candles, Laura—and so good-bye. . . .

(*She blows the candles out*)

(*The Scene Dissolves*)

# Arthur Miller

## (1915- )

Of the younger American dramatists emergent since 1940, only Arthur Miller and Tennessee Williams have been accorded respectful attention throughout the world. In a theatre dominated by teams of skillful journeymen adapting the works of others, each has kept an owner's strong pride in his works. Critics early linked Williams with the Chekhovian "mood play" and Miller with the Ibsenite "problem play," but each has subsequently achieved a versatility which calls into question all generalizations concerning the traditions in which he writes. Steeped in the masterworks of world drama and working in a theatre that accommodates both realism and theatricalism, each knows he must find for himself the organic fusion of form and content most effective for communicating his own responses to contemporary America. Their individual voices can be heard in everything they have written, and through their compelling subjectivism they have advanced American drama toward the maturity O'Neill envisioned.

Miller mirrored his own youth when, in *Death of a Salesman,* he portrayed the adolescence of Biff and Happy Loman. Born October 17, 1915, Miller spent twenty years in the New York and Brooklyn neighborhoods in which Willy Loman's house stands. Brought as a child from Austria, Miller's father worked hard in America and, like Charley in *Death of a Salesman,* succeeded with his own small manufacturing concern; Miller's mother, a native New Yorker, was a manufacturer's daughter. Miller was an indifferent student, preferring athletics to ideas. After graduating from high school, he worked as a stock clerk in an auto parts warehouse, a scene he later recreated in the touching one-act play, *A Memory of Two Mondays* (1955). Suddenly inspired by reading *The Brothers Karamazov,* Miller resolved to become a writer. Despite his mediocre academic record, he was accepted, at 20, as a journalism student at the University of Michigan. There he first experienced the midwestern small-town life which he used as the background of his first produced plays. In Ann Arbor, he studied playwriting with Kenneth Thorpe Rowe and, in two successive years, won Jule and Avery Hopwood Awards for plays which later brought him the Theatre Guild National Award. After graduation in 1938, Miller returned to New York and a succession of writing jobs, briefly with the Federal Theatre Project, then with CBS and NBC radio workshops.

Disqualified for military service by an old football injury, Miller knew the not-uncomplicated life of a male civilian during wartime. He married a Michigan classmate in 1940, and after the arrival of a daughter and a son, he supplemented his irregular writer's income by doing manual labor. Out of his experiences visiting Army camps to collect background material for the film, *The Story of G. I. Joe,* he fashioned a forthright diary-form report, *Situation Normal,* published in 1944; later he converted a play-outline into *Focus* (1945), a novel about anti-Semitism in a small town. *Focus* brought him critical praise which did not alter his resolve to bring to the theatre "the thickness, awareness, and complexity" he admired in Dostoevsky.

Its disastrous four-performance run mocked his title, but *The Man Who Had All the Luck* (1944), Miller's first Broadway production, prefigured his later work. Here he framed the question he later made crucial in Willy Loman's agony: Is success a matter of sheer luck or honest effort? In eight scenes, enlivened by a robust folk comedy he has rarely employed since, Miller explored American success-myths at the grassroots level. Miller's hero, David Beeves, is fearful because he has all he ever wanted. The play charts David's fumblings with determinism and free will: Is he a jellyfish floating with the tide, or is he, in some imperceptible way, the master of his fate? Certain that his good luck will be balanced out by misfortune, David woos the compensatory retribution he expects, only to discover in his common sense the missing key to his success in life. Critics called this play "Saroyanesque," perhaps because of its episodic movement through time and because of its wistful optimism. Although presented within a framework of ironic parable, Miller's portrayal of a common man confronting his inner anxieties pointed the way to deeper and more serious self-confrontations in his later plays.

Miller's next play, *All My Sons,* grew out of a friend's account of a woman whose moral values led her to report her own father for selling defective machinery to the Army. Miller's version concerns a popular and successful industrialist, Joe Keller, and his combat-veteran son, Chris, who returns to partnership in the business the father has proudly built up for his sons. An older son, a pilot killed in action, is a living presence among the Kellers, chiefly because his mother refuses to believe he is dead. *All My Sons* reflects Miller's admiration for Ibsen, not only in its heavy reliance on delayed exposition and painstakingly controlled patterns of causality, but also in its parallels with *Pillars of Society,* in which Ibsen had shown a highly respected shipowner unwittingly sealing his son's doom by approving another voyage for the unseaworthy ship on which his son has stowed away. Miller, however, concentrates on Chris's moral indignation when he uncovers his father's crimes: not only was Joe Keller personally responsible for selling cracked engine-heads which caused 21 fatal airplane crashes, but he let his foreman go to prison for the crime. Finally awakened out of his "unrelatedness" to a sense of his responsibility for all men's sons, Joe Keller commits suicide. In 1947, America was still sorting itself out after the war, and Miller's study of veterans returning to confront civilian complacency and evidence of war-profiteering had an urgency which has only slightly diminished since then. In a year when no play was given a Pulitzer Prize, *All My Sons* won the Critics Circle Award over O'Neill's *The Iceman Cometh.* Besides giving Miller a foothold in the theatre, *All My Sons* marked the end of his Ibsenism: except for adapting *An Enemy of the People* in 1950 and issuing a few informed defenses of the Norwegian's dramaturgy, Miller has, since 1947, given critics little reason to align him with Ibsen.

His next play challenged the critics' descriptive powers. Directed by Elia Kazan, staged with remarkable "expressionistic" fluidity in a skeletal setting by Jo Mielziner, and with Lee J. Cobb creating the definitive Willy Loman, *Death of a Salesman* opened on February 10, 1949. It immediately became perhaps the most admired and most controversial play in the American theatre. In answer to those critics who applied neo-Aristotelian canons of tragedy to his play, Miller said: "I believe that the common man is as apt a subject for tragedy in its highest sense as kings were." Other controversy centers on Miller's politics. In his important Preface to his *Collected Plays* (1957), Miller describes attacks on *All My Sons* and *Death of a Salesman* from right- and left-wing critics, in America and abroad. Labeled Marxist for their allegedly unflattering pictures of Americans, the plays were also rejected, especially in Russia, as not Marxist enough. Miller has argued eloquently for the autonomy of art, but "muffled debate" about the propaganda content of his plays continues, as evidenced in 1961 by the unauthorized Russian filming of *Death of a Salesman* (called *You Can't Cross the Bridge*), presumably sponsored to illustrate American decadence.

To most audiences, however, *Death of a Salesman* is a deeply private experience. Miller assumed that "everyone knew Willy Loman" and the values by which he lived and was destroyed. Miller recalls that at Michigan he had started a play about the salesman acquaintance who finally emerged as Willy. The less remote origin, however, was the image of "an enormous face the height of the proscenium arch which would appear and then open up, and we would see the inside of a man's head." With a first title, *The Inside of His Head,* Miller set out to show the "mass of contradictions" and the cataclysmic interplay of Willy's past and present. He began writing, knowing only that Willy would destroy himself: "I was convinced only that if I could make him remember enough he would kill himself, and the structure of the play was determined by what was needed to draw up his memories like a mass of tangled roots without end or beginning." Miller was shocked when he saw how *Death of a Salesman* moved audiences to tears, for he had never thought the play "a document of pessimism."

In 1953, soon after he won Pulitzer and Critics Circle awards for *Death of a Salesman,* Miller found himself deeply disturbed by the insidious effects of McCarthyism in American life. Reminded of the Salem witch trials and, especially, of the accusations filed against John and Elizabeth Proctor by a sex-obsessed servant girl, Miller wrote *The Crucible.* In its searching depiction of the Proctors' ennobling struggle to retain their moral identity in the face of death, Miller's "existentialist" tragedy invites comparison with Shaw's *Saint Joan* and Eliot's *Murder in the Cathedral.* Only moderately successful on Broadway, *The Crucible* has fared better in revivals, especially in Europe, and in Sartre's stage and film adaptations. Miller's compelling study of a Puritan community caught up in mass hysteria now seems certain to outlive memories of Senator McCarthy, if not of the witch-hunts associated with his name.

In 1955, Miller's one-act plays, *A Memory of Two Mondays* and *A View from the Bridge,* were produced. In the latter play (expanded to two acts before its 1956 London production), Miller sought to achieve the rapid flow and tragic inevitability he admires in Greek drama. Using a narrator-chorus, he traces the descent of a Brooklyn longshoreman, Eddie Carbone, into a labyrinth of libidinous forces beyond his grasp: in the background is a clash between Italian and American codes of family loyalty which ultimately results in Eddie's death; in the foregound is a maze of incest, homosexuality, domestic discord, jealousy, and fear in which the uncomprehending Eddie is the agent of his own destruction. In no play has Miller better realized his conception of the "social play" and its goal of showing "we are made and yet are more than what made us."

During the late 1950's, Miller has written less as a playwright than as a theorist of tragedy in a democratic and industrialized society. He has been interested in motion pictures, not only because of his five-year marriage to Marilyn Monroe, but also because his major plays have been adapted as films. *The Misfits* (1961), his first screenplay, proved an imperfect fusion of theatrical and cinematic elements, but it revealed Miller's continuing interest in the tension between individualism and "wanting to belong" in which Willy Loman's tragedy is rooted. Miller's next plays are eagerly awaited. Dedicated to creating a theatre in which "an adult who wants to live can find plays that will heighten his awareness of what living in our time involves," Miller has already established—with *Death of a Salesman, The Crucible,* and *A View from the Bridge*—his preëminence in such a theatre.

# DEATH OF A SALESMAN

## *Certain Private Conversations in Two Acts and a Requiem*

CAST (IN ORDER OF APPEARANCE)

WILLY LOMAN
LINDA
BIFF
HAPPY
BERNARD
THE WOMAN (MISS FRANCIS)
CHARLEY
UNCLE BEN
HOWARD WAGNER
JENNY
STANLEY
MISS FORSYTHE
LETTA

*The action takes place in Willy Loman's house and yard and in various places he visits in the New York and Boston of today.*

*Throughout the play, in the stage directions, left and right mean stage left and stage right.*

## Act One

*A melody is heard, played upon a flute. It is small and fine, telling of grass and trees and the horizon. The curtain rises.*

*Before us is the Salesman's house. We are aware of towering, angular shapes behind it, surrounding it on all sides. Only the blue light of the sky falls upon the house and forestage; the surrounding area shows an angry glow of orange. As more light appears, we see a solid vault of apartment houses around the small, fragile-seeming home. An air of the dream clings to the place, a dream rising out of reality. The kitchen at center seems actual enough, for there is a kitchen table with three chairs, and a refrigerator. But no other fixtures are seen. At the back of the kitchen there is a draped entrance, which leads to the living-room. To the right of the kitchen, on a level raised two feet, is a bedroom furnished only with a brass bedstead and a straight chair. On a shelf over the bed a silver athletic trophy stands. A window opens onto the apartment house at the side.*

*Behind the kitchen, on a level raised six and a half feet, is the boys' bedroom, at present barely visible. Two beds are dimly seen, and at the back of the room a dormer window. (This bedroom is above the unseen living-room.) At the left a stairway curves up to it from the kitchen.*

*The entire setting is wholly or, in some places, partially transparent. The roof-line of the house is one-dimensional; under and over it we see the apartment buildings. Before the house lies an apron, curving beyond the forestage into the orchestra. This forward area serves as the back yard as well as the locale of all* WILLY'S *imaginings and of his city scenes. Whenever the action is in the present the actors observe the imaginary wall-lines, entering the house only through its door at the left. But in the scenes of the past these boundaries are broken, and characters enter or leave a room by stepping "through" a wall onto the forestage.*

*From the right,* WILLY LOMAN, *the Salesman, enters, carrying two large sample cases. The flute plays on. He hears but is not aware of it. He is past sixty years of age, dressed quietly. Even as he crosses the stage to the doorway of the house, his exhaustion is apparent. He unlocks the door, comes into the kitchen, and thankfully lets his burden down, feeling the soreness of his palms. A word-sigh escapes his lips—it might be "Oh, boy, oh, boy." He closes the door, then carries his cases out into the living-room, through the draped kitchen doorway.*

LINDA, *his wife, has stirred in her bed at the right. She gets out and puts on a robe, listening.*

*Most often jovial, she has developed an iron repression of her exceptions to* WILLY'S *behavior—she more than loves him, she admires him, as though his mercurial nature, his temper, his massive dreams and little cruelties, served her only as sharp reminders of the turbulent longings within him, longings which she shares but lacks the temperament to utter and follow to their end.*

LINDA (*Hearing* WILLY *outside the bedroom, calls with some trepidation*) Willy!

WILLY It's all right. I came back.

LINDA Why? What happened? (*Slight pause*) Did something happen, Willy?

WILLY No, nothing happened.

LINDA You didn't smash the car, did you?

WILLY (*With casual irritation*) I said nothing happened. Didn't you hear me?

LINDA Don't you feel well?

WILLY I'm tired to the death. (*The flute has faded away. He sits on the bed beside her, a little numb*) I couldn't make it. I just couldn't make it, Linda.

LINDA (*Very carefully, delicately*) Where were you all day? You look terrible.

WILLY I got as far as a little above Yonkers. I stopped for a cup of coffee. Maybe it was the coffee.

LINDA What?

WILLY (*After a pause*) I suddenly couldn't drive any more. The car kept going off onto the shoulder, y'know?

LINDA (*Helpfully*) Oh. Maybe it was the steering again. I don't think Angelo knows the Studebaker.

WILLY No, it's me, it's me. Suddenly I realize I'm goin' sixty miles an hour and I don't remember the last five minutes. I'm—I can't seem to—keep my mind to it.

LINDA Maybe it's your glasses. You never went for your new glasses.

WILLY No, I see everything. I came back ten miles an hour. It took me nearly four hours from Yonkers.

LINDA (*Resigned*) Well, you'll just have to take a rest, Willy, you can't continue this way.

WILLY I just got back from Florida.

LINDA But you didn't rest your mind. Your mind is over-active, and the mind is what counts, dear.

WILLY I'll start out in the morning. Maybe I'll feel better in the morning. (*She is taking off his shoes*) These goddam arch supports are killing me.

LINDA Take an aspirin. Should I get you an aspirin? It'll soothe you.

WILLY (*With wonder*) I was driving along, you understand? And I was fine. I was even observing the scenery. You can imagine, me looking at scenery, on the road every week of my life. But it's so beautiful up there, Linda, the trees are so thick, and the sun is warm. I opened the windshield and just let the warm air bathe over me. And then all of a sudden I'm goin' off the road! I'm tellin' ya, I absolutely forgot I was driving. If I'd've gone the other way over the white line I might've killed somebody. So I went on again—and five minutes later I'm dreamin' again, and I nearly—(*He presses two fingers against his eyes*) I have such thoughts, I have such strange thoughts.

LINDA Willy, dear. Talk to them again. There's no reason why you can't work in New York.

WILLY They don't need me in New York. I'm the New England man. I'm vital in New England.

LINDA But you're sixty years old. They can't expect you to keep traveling every week.

WILLY I'll have to send a wire to Portland. I'm supposed to see Brown and Morrison tomorrow morning at ten o'clock to show the line. Goddammit, I could sell them! (*He starts putting on his jacket*)

LINDA (*Taking the jacket from him*) Why don't you go down to the place tomorrow and tell Howard you've simply got to work in New York? You're too accommodating, dear.

WILLY If old man Wagner was alive I'd a been in charge of New York now! That man was a prince, he was a masterful man. But that boy of his, that Howard, he don't appreciate. When I went north the first time, the Wagner Company didn't know where New England was!

LINDA Why don't you tell those things to Howard, dear?

WILLY (*Encouraged*) I will, I definitely will. Is there any cheese?

LINDA I'll make you a sandwich.

WILLY No, go to sleep. I'll take some milk. I'll be up right away. The boys in?

LINDA They're sleeping. Happy took Biff on a date tonight.

WILLY (*Interested*) That so?

LINDA It was so nice to see them shaving together, one behind the other, in the bathroom. And going out together. You notice? The whole house smells of shaving lotion.

WILLY Figure it out. Work a lifetime to pay off a house. You finally own it, and there's nobody to live in it.

LINDA Well, dear, life is a casting off. It's always that way.

WILLY No, no, some people—some people accomplish something. Did Biff say anything after I went this morning?

LINDA You shouldn't have criticized him, Willy, especially after he just got off the train. You mustn't lose your temper with him.

WILLY When the hell did I lose my temper? I simply asked him if he was making any money. Is that a criticism?

LINDA But, dear, how could he make any money?

WILLY (*Worried and angered*) There's such an undercurrent in him. He became a moody man. Did he apologize when I left this morning?

LINDA He was crestfallen, Willy. You know how he admires you. I think if he finds himself, then you'll both be happier and not fight any more.

WILLY How can he find himself on a farm? Is that a life? A farmhand? In the beginning, when he was young, I thought, well, a young man, it's good for him to tramp around, take a lot of different jobs. But it's more than ten years now and he has yet to make thirty-five dollars a week!

LINDA He's finding himself, Willy.

WILLY Not finding yourself at the age of thirty-four is a disgrace!

LINDA Shh!

WILLY The trouble is he's lazy, goddammit!

LINDA Willy, please!

WILLY Biff is a lazy bum!

LINDA They're sleeping. Get something to eat. Go on down.

WILLY Why did he come home? I would like to know what brought him home.

LINDA I don't know. I think he's still lost, Willy. I think he's very lost.

WILLY Biff Loman is lost. In the greatest country in the world a young man with such—personal attractiveness, gets lost. And such a hard worker. There's one thing about Biff—he's not lazy.

LINDA Never.

WILLY (*With pity and resolve*) I'll see him in the morning; I'll have a nice talk with him. I'll get him a job selling. He could be big in no time. My God! Remember how they used to follow him around in high school? When he smiled at one of them their faces lit up. When he walked down the street . . . (*He loses himself in reminiscences*)

LINDA (*Trying to bring him out of it*) Willy, dear, I got a new kind of American-type cheese today. It's whipped.

WILLY Why do you get American when I like Swiss?

LINDA I just thought you'd like a change—

WILLY I don't want a change! I want Swiss cheese. Why am I always being contradicted?

LINDA (*With a covering laugh*) I thought it would be a surprise.

WILLY Why don't you open a window in here, for God's sake?

LINDA (*With infinite patience*) They're all open, dear.

WILLY The way they boxed us in here. Bricks and windows, windows and bricks.

LINDA We should've bought the land next door.

WILLY The street is lined with cars. There's not a breath of fresh air in the neighborhood. The grass don't grow any more, you can't raise a carrot in the back yard. They should've had a law against apartment houses. Remember those two beautiful elm trees out there? When I and Biff hung the swing between them?

LINDA Yeah, like being a million miles from the city.

WILLY They should've arrested the builder for cutting those down. They massacred the neighborhood. (*Lost*) More and more I think of those days, Linda. This time of year it was lilac and wisteria. And then the peonies would come out, and the daffodils. What fragrance in this room!

LINDA Well, after all, people had to move somewhere.

WILLY No, there's more people now.

LINDA I don't think there's more people. I think—

WILLY There's more people! That's what's ruining this country! Population is getting out of control. The competition is maddening! Smell the stink from that apartment house! And another one on the other side . . . How can they whip cheese?

(*On* WILLY's *last line,* BIFF *and* HAPPY *raise themselves up in their beds, listening*)

LINDA Go down, try it. And be quiet.

WILLY (*Turning to* LINDA, *guiltily*) You're not worried about me, are you, sweetheart?

BIFF What's the matter?

HAPPY Listen!

LINDA You've got too much on the ball to worry about.

WILLY You're my foundation and my support, Linda.

LINDA Just try to relax, dear. You make mountains out of molehills.

WILLY I won't fight with him any more. If he wants to go back to Texas, let him go.

LINDA He'll find his way.

WILLY Sure. Certain men just don't get started till later in life. Like Thomas Edison, I think. Or B. F. Goodrich. One of them was deaf. (*He starts for the bedroom doorway*) I'll put my money on Biff.

LINDA And Willy—if it's warm Sunday, we'll drive in the country. And we'll open the windshield, and take lunch.

WILLY No, the windshields don't open on the new cars.

LINDA But you opened it today.

WILLY Me? I didn't. (*He stops*) Now isn't that peculiar! Isn't that a remarkable— (*He breaks off in amazement and fright as the flute is heard distantly*)

LINDA What, darling?

WILLY That is the most remarkable thing.

LINDA What, dear?

WILLY I was thinking of the Chevvy. (*Slight pause*) Nineteen twenty-eight . . . when I had that red Chevvy— (*Breaks off*) That funny? I coulda sworn I was driving that Chevvy today.

LINDA Well, that's nothing. Something must've reminded you.

WILLY Remarkable. Ts. Remember those days? The way Biff used to simonize that car? The dealer refused to believe there was eighty thousand miles on it. (*He shakes his head*) Heh! (*To* LINDA) Close your eyes, I'll be right up. (*He walks out of the bedroom*)

HAPPY (*To* BIFF) Jesus, maybe he smashed up the car again!

LINDA (*Calling after* WILLY) Be careful on the stairs, dear! The cheese is on the middle shelf! (*She turns, goes over to the bed, takes his jacket, and goes out of the bedroom*)

(*Light has risen on the boys' room. Unseen,* WILLY *is heard talking to himself, "Eighty thousand miles," and a little laugh.* BIFF *gets out of bed, comes downstage a bit, and stands attentively.* BIFF *is two years older than his brother* HAPPY, *well built, but in these days bears a worn air and seems less self-assured. He has succeeded less, and his dreams are stronger and less acceptable than* HAPPY's. HAPPY *is tall, powerfully made. Sexuality is like a visible color on him, or a scent that many women have discovered. He, like his brother, is lost, but in a different way, for he has never allowed himself to turn his face toward defeat and is thus more confused and hard-skinned, although seemingly more content)*

HAPPY (*Getting out of bed*) He's going to get his license taken away if he keeps that up. I'm getting nervous about him, y'know, Biff?

BIFF His eyes are going.

HAPPY No, I've driven with him. He sees all right. He just doesn't keep his mind on it. I drove into the city with him last week. He stops at a green light and then it turns red and he goes. (*He laughs*)

BIFF Maybe he's color-blind.

HAPPY Pop? Why he's got the finest eye for color in the business. You know that.

BIFF (*Sitting down on his bed*) I'm going to sleep.

HAPPY You're not still sour on Dad, are you, Biff?

BIFF He's all right, I guess.

WILLY (*Underneath them, in the living-room*) Yes, sir, eighty thousand miles—eighty-two thousand!

BIFF You smoking?

HAPPY (*Holding out a pack of cigarettes*) Want one?

BIFF (*Taking a cigarette*) I can never sleep when I smell it.

WILLY What a simonizing job, heh!

HAPPY (*With deep sentiment*) Funny, Biff, y'know? Us sleeping in here again? The old beds. (*He pats his bed affectionately*) All the talk that went across those two beds, huh? Our whole lives.

BIFF Yeah. Lotta dreams and plans.

HAPPY (*With a deep and masculine laugh*) About five hundred women would like to know what was said in this room.

(*They share a soft laugh*)

BIFF Remember that big Betsy something—what the hell was her name—over on Bushwick Avenue?

HAPPY (*Combing his hair*) With the collie dog!

BIFF That's the one. I got you in there, remember?

HAPPY Yeah, that was my first time—I think. Boy, there was a pig! (*They laugh, almost crudely*) You taught me everything I know about women. Don't forget that.

BIFF I bet you forgot how bashful you used to be. Especially with girls.

HAPPY Oh, I still am, Biff.

BIFF Oh, go on.

HAPPY I just control it, that's all. I think I got less bashful and you got more so. What happened, Biff? Where's the old humor, the old confidence? (*He shakes* BIFF'*s knee.* BIFF *gets up and moves restlessly about the room*) What's the matter?

BIFF Why does Dad mock me all the time?

HAPPY He's not mocking you, he—

BIFF Everything I say there's a twist of mockery on his face. I can't get near him.

HAPPY He just wants you to make good, that's all. I wanted to talk to you about Dad for a long time, Biff. Something's—happening to him. He—talks to himself.

BIFF I noticed that this morning. But he always mumbled.

HAPPY But not so noticeable. It got so embarrassing I sent him to Florida. And you know something? Most of the time he's talking to you.

BIFF What's he say about me?

HAPPY I can't make it out.

BIFF What's he say about me?

HAPPY I think the fact that you're not settled, that you're still kind of up in the air . . .

BIFF There's one or two other things depressing him, Happy.

HAPPY What do you mean?

BIFF Never mind. Just don't lay it all to me.

HAPPY But I think if you just got started—I mean—is there any future for you out there?

BIFF I tell ya, Hap, I don't know what the future is. I don't know—what I'm supposed to want.

HAPPY What do you mean?

BIFF Well, I spent six or seven years after high school trying to work myself up. Shipping clerk, salesman, business of one kind or another. And it's a measly manner of existence. To get on that subway on the hot mornings in summer. To devote your whole life to keeping stock, or making phone calls, or selling or buying. To suffer fifty weeks of the year for the sake of a two-week vacation, when all you really desire is to be outdoors, with your shirt off. And always to have to get ahead of the next fella. And still—that's how you build a future.

HAPPY Well, you really enjoy it on a farm? Are you content out there?

BIFF (*With rising agitation*) Hap, I've had twenty or thirty different kinds of jobs since I left home before the war, and it always turns out the same. I just realized it lately. In Nebraska when I herded cattle, and the Dakotas, and Arizona, and now in Texas. It's why I came home now, I guess, because I realized it. This farm I work on, it's spring there now, see? And they've got about fifteen new colts. There's nothing more inspiring or—beautiful than the sight of a mare and a new colt. And it's cool there now, see? Texas is cool now, and it's spring. And whenever spring comes to where I am, I suddenly get the feeling, my God, I'm not gettin' anywhere! What the hell am I doing, playing around with horses, twenty-eight dollars a week! I'm thirty-four years old, I oughta be makin' my future. That's when I come running home. And now, I get here, and I don't know what to do with myself. (*After a pause*) I've always made a point of not wasting my life, and every time I come back here I know that all I've done is to waste my life.

HAPPY You're a poet, you know that, Biff? You're a—you're an idealist!

BIFF No, I'm mixed up very bad. Maybe I oughta get married. Maybe I oughta get stuck into something. Maybe that's my trouble. I'm like a boy. I'm not married, I'm not in business, I just—I'm like a boy. Are you content, Hap? You're a success, aren't you? Are you content?

HAPPY Hell, no!

BIFF Why? You're making money, aren't you?

HAPPY (*Moving about with energy, expressiveness*) All I can do now is wait for the merchandise manager to die. And suppose I get to be merchandise manager? He's a good friend of mine, and he just built a terrific estate on Long Island. And he lived there about two months and sold it, and now he's building another one. He can't enjoy it once it's finished. And I know that's just what I would do. I don't know what the hell I'm workin' for. Sometimes I sit in my apartment—all alone. And I think of the rent I'm paying. And it's crazy. But then, it's what I always wanted. My own apartment, a car, and plenty of women. And still, goddammit, I'm lonely.

BIFF (*With enthusiasm*) Listen, why don't you come out West with me?

HAPPY You and I, heh?

BIFF Sure, maybe we could buy a ranch. Raise cattle, use our muscles. Men built like we are should be working out in the open.

HAPPY (*Avidly*) The Loman Brothers, heh?

BIFF (*With vast affection*) Sure, we'd be known all over the counties!

HAPPY (*Enthralled*) That's what I dream about, Biff. Sometimes I want to just rip my clothes off in the middle of the store and outbox that goddam merchandise manager. I mean I can outbox, outrun, and outlift anybody in that store, and I have to take orders from those common, petty sons-of-bitches till I can't stand it any more.

BIFF I'm tellin' you, kid, if you were with me I'd be happy out there.

HAPPY (*Enthused*) See, Biff, everybody around me is so false that I'm constantly lowering my ideals . . .

BIFF Baby, together we'd stand up for one another, we'd have someone to trust.

HAPPY If I were around you—

BIFF Hap, the trouble is we weren't brought up to grub for money. I don't know how to do it.

HAPPY Neither can I!

BIFF Then let's go!

HAPPY The only thing is—what can you make out there?

BIFF But look at your friend. Builds an estate and then hasn't the peace of mind to live in it.

HAPPY Yeah, but when he walks into the store the waves part in front of him. That's fifty-two thousand dollars a year coming through the revolving door, and I got more in my pinky finger than he's got in his head.

BIFF Yeah, but you just said—

HAPPY I gotta show some of those pompous, self-important executives over there that Hap Loman can make the grade. I want to walk into the store the way he walks in. Then I'll go with you, Biff. We'll be together yet, I swear. But take those two we had tonight. Now weren't they gorgeous creatures?

BIFF Yeah, yeah, most gorgeous I've had in years.

HAPPY I get that any time I want, Biff. Whenever I feel disgusted. The only trouble is, it gets like bowling or something. I just keep knockin' them over and it doesn't mean anything. You still run around a lot?

BIFF Naa. I'd like to find a girl—steady, somebody with substance.

HAPPY That's what I long for.

BIFF Go on! You'd never come home.

HAPPY I would! Somebody with character, with resistance! Like Mom, y'know? You're gonna call me a bastard when I tell you this. That girl Charlotte I was with tonight is engaged to be married in five weeks. (*He tries on his new hat*)

BIFF No kiddin'!

HAPPY Sure, the guy's in line for the vice-presidency of the store. I don't know what gets into me, maybe I just have an overdeveloped sense of competition or something, but I went and ruined her, and furthermore I can't get rid of her. And he's the third executive I've done that to. Isn't that a crummy characteristic? And to top it all, I go to their weddings! (*Indignantly, but laughing*) Like I'm not supposed to take bribes. Manufacturers offer me a hundred-dollar bill now and then to throw an order their way. You know how honest I am, but it's like this girl, see. I hate myself for it. Because I don't want the girl, and, still, I take it and—I love it!

BIFF Let's go to sleep.

HAPPY I guess we didn't settle anything, heh?

BIFF I just got one idea that I think I'm going to try.

HAPPY What's that?

BIFF Remember Bill Oliver?

HAPPY Sure, Oliver is very big now. You want to work for him again?

BIFF No, but when I quit he said something to me. He put his arm on my shoulder, and he said, "Biff, if you ever need anything, come to me."

HAPPY I remember that. That sounds good.

BIFF I think I'll go to see him. If I could get ten thousand or even seven or eight thousand dollars I could buy a beautiful ranch.

HAPPY I bet he'd back you. 'Cause he thought highly of you, Biff. I mean, they all do. You're well liked, Biff. That's why I say to come back here, and we both have the apartment. And I'm tellin' you, Biff, any babe you want . . .

BIFF No, with a ranch I could do the work I like and still be something. I just wonder, though. I wonder if Oliver still thinks I stole that carton of basketballs.

HAPPY Oh, he probably forgot that long ago. It's almost ten years. You're too sensitive. Anyway, he didn't really fire you.

BIFF Well, I think he was going to. I think that's why I quit. I was never sure whether he knew or not. I know he thought the world of me, though. I was the only one he'd let lock up the place.

WILLY (*Below*) You gonna wash the engine, Biff?

HAPPY Shh!

(BIFF *looks at* HAPPY, *who is gazing down, listening.* WILLY *is mumbling in the parlor*)

HAPPY You hear that?

(*They listen.* WILLY *laughs warmly*)

BIFF (*Growing angry*) Doesn't he know Mom can hear that?

WILLY Don't get your sweater dirty, Biff!

(*A look of pain crosses* BIFF's *face*)

HAPPY Isn't that terrible? Don't leave again, will you? You'll find a job here. You gotta stick around. I don't know what to do about him, it's getting embarrassing.

WILLY What a simonizing job!

BIFF Mom's hearing that!

WILLY No kiddin', Biff, you got a date? Wonderful!

HAPPY Go on to sleep. But talk to him in the morning, will you?

BIFF (*Reluctantly getting into bed*) With her in the house. Brother!

HAPPY (*Getting into bed*) I wish you'd have a good talk with him.

(*The light on their room begins to fade*)

BIFF (*To himself in bed*) That selfish, stupid . . .

HAPPY Sh . . . Sleep, Biff.

(*Their light is out. Well before they have finished speaking,* WILLY's *form is dimly seen below in the darkened kitchen. He opens the refrigerator, searches in there, and takes out a bottle of milk. The apartment houses are fading out, and the entire house and surroundings become covered with leaves. Music insinuates itself as the leaves appear*)

WILLY Just wanna be careful with those girls, Biff, that's all. Don't make any promises. No promises of any kind. Because a girl, y'know, they always believe what you tell 'em, and you're very young, Biff, you're too young to be talking seriously to girls.

(*Light rises on the kitchen.* WILLY, *talking, shuts the refrigerator door and comes downstage to the kitchen table. He pours milk into a glass. He is totally immersed in himself, smiling faintly*)

WILLY Too young entirely, Biff. You want to watch your schooling first. Then when you're all set, there'll be plenty of girls for a boy like you. (*He smiles broadly at a kitchen chair*) That so? The girls pay for you? (*He laughs*) Boy, you must really be makin' a hit.

(WILLY *is gradually addressing—physically—a point offstage, speaking through the wall of the kitchen, and his voice has been rising in volume to that of a normal conversation*)

WILLY I been wondering why you polish the car so careful. Ha! Don't leave the hubcaps, boys. Get the chamois to the hubcaps. Happy, use newspaper on the windows, it's the easiest thing. Show him how to do it, Biff! You see, Happy? Pad it up, use it like a pad. That's it, that's it, good work. You're doin' all right, Hap. (*He pauses, then nods in approbation for a few seconds, then looks upward*) Biff, first thing we gotta do when we get time is clip that big branch over the house. Afraid it's gonna fall in a storm and hit the roof. Tell you what. We get a rope and sling her around, and then we climb up there with a couple of saws and take her down. Soon as you finish the car, boys, I wanna see ya. I got a surprise for you, boys.

BIFF (*Offstage*) Whatta ya got, Dad?

WILLY No, you finish first. Never leave a job till you're finished—remember that. (*Looking toward the "big trees"*) Biff, up in Albany I saw a beautiful hammock. I think I'll buy it next trip, and we'll hang it right between those two elms. Wouldn't that be something? Just swingin' there under those branches. Boy, that would be . . .

(YOUNG BIFF *and* YOUNG HAPPY *appear from the direction* WILLY *was addressing.* HAPPY *carries rags and a pail of water.* BIFF, *wearing a sweater with a block "S," carries a football.*)

BIFF (*Pointing in the direction of the car offstage*) How's that, Pop, professional?

WILLY Terrific. Terrific job, boys. Good work, Biff.

HAPPY Where's the surprise, Pop?

WILLY In the back seat of the car.

HAPPY Boy! (*He runs off*)

BIFF What is it, Dad? Tell me, what'd you buy?

WILLY (*Laughing, cuffs him*) Never mind, something I want you to have.

BIFF (*Turns and starts off*) What is it, Hap?

HAPPY (*Offstage*) It's a punching bag!

BIFF Oh, Pop!

WILLY It's got Gene Tunney's signature on it!

(HAPPY *runs onstage with a punching bag*)

BIFF Gee, how'd you know we wanted a punching bag?

WILLY Well, it's the finest thing for the timing.

HAPPY (*Lies down on his back and pedals with his feet*) I'm losing weight, you notice, Pop?

WILLY (*To* HAPPY) Jumping rope is good too.

BIFF Did you see the new football I got?

WILLY (*Examining the ball*) Where'd you get a new ball?

BIFF The coach told me to practice my passing.

WILLY That so? And he gave you the ball, heh?

BIFF Well, I borrowed it from the locker room. (*He laughs confidentially*)

WILLY (*Laughing with him at the theft*) I want you to return that.

HAPPY I told you he wouldn't like it!

BIFF (*Angrily*) Well, I'm bringing it back!

WILLY (*Stopping the incipient argument, to* HAPPY) Sure, he's gotta practice with a regulation ball, doesn't he? (*To* BIFF) Coach'll probably congratulate you on your initiative!

BIFF Oh, he keeps congratulating my initiative all the time, Pop.

WILLY That's because he likes you. If somebody else took that ball there'd be an uproar. So what's the report, boys, what's the report?

BIFF Where'd you go this time, Dad? Gee we were lonesome for you.

WILLY (*Pleased, puts an arm around each boy and they come down to the apron*) Lonesome, heh?

BIFF Missed you every minute.

WILLY Don't say? Tell you a secret, boys. Don't breathe it to a soul. Someday I'll have my own business, and I'll never have to leave home any more.

HAPPY Like Uncle Charley, heh?

WILLY Bigger than Uncle Charley! Because Charley is not—liked. He's liked, but he's not—well liked.

BIFF Where'd you go this time, Dad?

WILLY Well, I got on the road, and I went north to Providence. Met the Mayor.

BIFF The Mayor of Providence!

WILLY He was sitting in the hotel lobby.

BIFF What'd he say?

WILLY He said, "Morning!" And I said, "You got a fine city here, Mayor." And then he had coffee with me. And then I went to Waterbury. Waterbury is a fine city. Big clock city, the famous Waterbury clock. Sold a nice bill there. And then Boston—Boston is the cradle of the Revolution. A fine city. And a couple of other towns in Mass., and on to Portland and Bangor and straight home!

BIFF Gee, I'd love to go with you sometime, Dad.

WILLY Soon as summer comes.

HAPPY Promise?

WILLY You and Hap and I, and I'll show you all the towns. America is full of beautiful towns and fine, upstanding people. And they know me, boys, they know me up and down New England. The finest people. And when I bring you fellas up, there'll be open sesame for all of us, 'cause one thing, boys: I have friends. I can park my car in any street in New England, and the cops protect it like their own. This summer, heh?

BIFF *and* HAPPY, *together:* Yeah! You bet!

WILLY We'll take our bathing suits.

HAPPY We'll carry your bags, Pop!

WILLY Oh, won't that be something! Me comin' into the Boston stores with you boys carryin' my bags. What a sensation!

(BIFF *is prancing around, practicing passing the ball*)

WILLY You nervous, Biff, about the game?

BIFF Not if you're gonna be there.

WILLY What do they say about you in school, now that they made you captain?

HAPPY There's a crowd of girls behind him every time the classes change.

BIFF (*Taking* WILLY'S *hand*) This Saturday, Pop, this Saturday—just for you, I'm going to break through for a touchdown.

HAPPY You're supposed to pass.

BIFF I'm takin' one play for Pop. You watch me, Pop, and when I take off my helmet, that means I'm breakin' out. Then you watch me crash through that line!

WILLY (*Kisses* BIFF) Oh, wait'll I tell this in Boston!

(BERNARD *enters in knickers. He is younger than* BIFF, *earnest and loyal, a worried boy*)

BERNARD Biff, where are you? You're supposed to study with me today.

WILLY Hey, looka Bernard. What're you lookin' so anemic about, Bernard?

BERNARD He's gotta study, Uncle Willy. He's got Regents next week.

HAPPY (*Tauntingly, spinning* BERNARD *around*) Let's box, Bernard!

BERNARD Biff! (*He gets away from* HAPPY) Listen, Biff, I heard Mr. Birnbaum say that if you don't start studyin' math he's gonna flunk you, and you won't graduate. I heard him!

WILLY You better study with him, Biff. Go ahead now.

BERNARD I heard him!

BIFF Oh, Pop, you didn't see my sneakers! (*He holds up a foot for* WILLY *to look at*)

WILLY Hey, that's a beautiful job of printing!

BERNARD (*Wiping his glasses*) Just because he printed University of Virginia on his sneakers doesn't mean they've got to graduate him, Uncle Willy!

WILLY (*Angrily*) What're you talking about? With scholarships to three universities they're gonna flunk him?

BERNARD But I heard Mr. Birnbaum say—

WILLY Don't be a pest, Bernard! (*To his boys*) What an anemic!

BERNARD Okay, I'm waiting for you in my house, Biff.

(BERNARD *goes off. The Lomans laugh*)

WILLY Bernard is not well liked, is he?

BIFF He's liked, but he's not well liked.

HAPPY That's right, Pop.

WILLY That's just what I mean. Bernard can get the best marks in school, y'understand, but when he gets out in the business world, y'understand, you are going to be five times ahead of him. That's why I thank Almighty God you're both built like Adonises. Because the man who makes an appearance in the business world, the man who creates personal interest, is the man who gets ahead. Be liked and you will never want. You take me, for instance. I never have to wait in line to see a buyer. "Willy Loman is here!" That's all they have to know, and I go right through.

BIFF Did you knock them dead, Pop?

WILLY Knocked 'em cold in Providence, slaughtered 'em in Boston.

HAPPY (*On his back, pedaling again*) I'm losing weight, you notice, Pop?

(LINDA *enters, as of old, a ribbon in her hair, carrying a basket of washing*)

LINDA (*With youthful energy*) Hello, dear!

WILLY Sweetheart!

LINDA How'd the Chevvy run?

WILLY Chevrolet, Linda, is greatest car ever built. (*To the boys*) Since when do you let your mother carry wash up the stairs?

BIFF Grab hold there, boy!

HAPPY Where to, Mom?

LINDA Hang them up on the line. And you better go down to your friends, Biff. The cellar is full of boys. They don't know what to do with themselves.

BIFF Ah, when Pop comes home they can wait!

WILLY (*Laughs appreciatively*) You better go down and tell them what to do, Biff.

BIFF I think I'll have them sweep out the furnace room.

WILLY Good work, Biff.

BIFF (*Goes through wall-line of kitchen to doorway at back and calls down*) Fellas! Everybody sweep out the furnace room! I'll be right down!

VOICES All right! Okay, Biff.

BIFF George and Sam and Frank, come out back! We're hangin' up the wash! Come on, Hap, on the double! (*He and* HAPPY *carry out the basket*)

LINDA The way they obey him!

WILLY Well, that's training, the training. I'm tellin' you, I was sellin' thousands and thousands, but I had to come home.

LINDA Oh, the whole block'll be at that game. Did you sell anything?

WILLY I did five hundred gross in Providence and seven hundred gross in Boston.

LINDA No! Wait a minute, I've got a pencil. (*She pulls pencil and paper out of her apron pocket*) That makes your commission . . . two hundred—my God! Two hundred and twelve dollars!

WILLY Well, I didn't figure it yet, but . . .

LINDA How much did you do?

WILLY Well, I—I did—about a hundred and eighty gross in Providence. Well, no—it came to—roughly two hundred gross on the whole trip.

LINDA (*Without hesitation*) Two hundred gross. That's . . . (*She figures*)

WILLY The trouble was that three of the stores were half closed for inventory in Boston. Otherwise I woulda broke records.

LINDA Well, it makes seventy dollars and some pennies. That's very good.

WILLY What do we owe?

LINDA Well, on the first there's sixteen dollars on the refrigerator—

WILLY Why sixteen?

LINDA Well, the fan belt broke, so it was a dollar eighty.

WILLY But it's brand new.

LINDA Well, the man said that's the way it is. Till they work themselves in, y'know.

(*They move through the wall-line into the kitchen*)

WILLY I hope we didn't get stuck on that machine.

LINDA They got the biggest ads of any of them!

WILLY I know, it's a fine machine. What else?

LINDA Well, there's nine-sixty for the washing machine. And for the vacuum cleaner there's three and a half due on the fifteenth. Then the roof, you got twenty-one dollars remaining.

WILLY It don't leak, does it?

LINDA No, they did a wonderful job. Then you owe Frank for the carburetor.

WILLY I'm not going to pay that man! That goddam Chevrolet, they ought to prohibit the manufacture of that car!

LINDA Well, you owe him three and a half. And odds and ends, comes to around a hundred and twenty dollars by the fifteenth.

WILLY A hundred and twenty dollars! My God, if business don't pick up I don't know what I'm gonna do!

LINDA Well, next week you'll do better.

WILLY Oh, I'll knock 'em dead next week. I'll go to Hartford. I'm very well liked in Hartford. (*Pause*) You know, the trouble is, Linda, people don't seem to take to me.

(*They move onto the forestage*)

LINDA Oh, don't be foolish.

WILLY I know it when I walk in. They seem to laugh at me.

LINDA Why? Why would they laugh at you? Don't talk that way, Willy.

(WILLY *moves to the edge of the stage.* LINDA *goes into the kitchen and starts to darn stockings*)

WILLY I don't know the reason for it, but they just pass me by. I'm not noticed.

LINDA But you're doing wonderful, dear. You're making seventy to a hundred dollars a week.

WILLY But I gotta be at it ten, twelve hours a day. Other men—I don't know—they do it easier. I don't know why—I can't stop myself—I talk too much. A man oughta come in with a few words. One thing about Charley. He's a man of few words, and they respect him.

LINDA You don't talk too much, you're just lively.

WILLY (*Smiling*) Well, I figure, what the hell, life is short, a couple of jokes. (*To himself*) I joke too much! (*The smile goes*)

LINDA Why? You're—

WILLY I'm fat. I'm very—foolish to look at, Linda. I didn't tell you, but Christmas time I happened to be calling on F. H. Stewarts, and a salesman I know, as I was going in to see the buyer, I heard him say something about—walrus. And I—I cracked him right across the face. I won't take that. I simply will not take that. But they do laugh at me. I know that.

LINDA Darling . . .

WILLY I gotta overcome it. I know I gotta overcome it. I'm not dressing to advantage, maybe.

LINDA Willy, darling, you're the handsomest man in the world—

WILLY Oh, no, Linda.

LINDA To me you are. (*Slight pause*) The handsomest.

(*From the darkness is heard the laughter of a woman.* WILLY *doesn't turn to it, but it continues through* LINDA*'s lines*)

LINDA And the boys, Willy. Few men are idolized by their children the way you are.

(*Music is heard as behind a scrim, to the left of the house,* THE WOMAN, *dimly seen, is dressing*)

WILLY (*With great feeling*) You're the best there is, Linda, you're a pal, you know that? On the road—on the road I want to grab you sometimes and just kiss the life outa you.

(*The laughter is loud now, and he moves into a brightening area at the left, where* THE WOMAN *has come from behind the scrim and is standing, putting on her hat, looking into a "mirror" and laughing*)

WILLY 'Cause I get so lonely—especially when business is bad and there's nobody to talk to. I get the feeling that I'll never sell anything again, that I won't make a living for you, or a business, a business for the boys. (*He talks through* THE WOMAN's *subsiding laughter;* THE WOMAN *primps at the "mirror"*) There's so much I want to make for—

THE WOMAN Me? You didn't make me, Willy. I picked you.

WILLY (*Pleased*) You picked me?

THE WOMAN (*Who is quite proper-looking,* WILLY's *age*) I did. I've been sitting at that desk watching all the salesmen go by, day in, day out. But you've got such a sense of humor, and we do have such a good time together, don't we?

WILLY Sure, sure. (*He takes her in his arms*) Why do you have to go now?

THE WOMAN It's two o'clock . . .

WILLY No, come on in! (*He pulls her*)

THE WOMAN . . . my sisters'll be scandalized. When'll you be back?

WILLY Oh, two weeks about. Will you come up again?

THE WOMAN Sure thing. You do make me laugh. It's good for me. (*She squeezes his arm, kisses him*) And I think you're a wonderful man.

WILLY You picked me, heh?

THE WOMAN Sure. Because you're so sweet. And such a kidder.

WILLY Well, I'll see you next time I'm in Boston.

THE WOMAN I'll put you right through to the buyers.

WILLY (*Slapping her bottom*) Right. Well, bottoms up!

THE WOMAN (*Slaps him gently and laughs*) You just kill me, Willy. (*He suddenly grabs her and kisses her roughly*) You kill me. And thanks for the stockings. I love a lot of stockings. Well, good night.

WILLY Good night. And keep your pores open!

THE WOMAN Oh, Willy!

(THE WOMAN *bursts out laughing, and* LINDA's *laughter blends in.* THE WOMAN *disappears into the dark. Now the area at the kitchen table brightens.* LINDA *is sitting where she was at the kitchen table, but now is mending a pair of her silk stockings*)

LINDA You are, Willy. The handsomest man. You've got no reason to feel that—

WILLY (*Coming out of* THE WOMAN's *dimming area and going over to* LINDA) I'll make it all up to you, Linda, I'll—

LINDA There's nothing to make up, dear. You're doing fine, better than—

WILLY (*Noticing her mending*) What's that?

LINDA Just mending my stockings. They're so expensive—

WILLY (*Angrily, taking them from her*) I won't have you mending stockings in this house! Now throw them out!

(LINDA *puts the stockings in her pocket*)

BERNARD (*Entering on the run*) Where is he? If he doesn't study!

WILLY (*Moving to the forestage, with great agitation*) You'll give him the answers!

BERNARD I do, but I can't on a Regents! That's a state exam! They're liable to arrest me!

WILLY Where is he? I'll whip him, I'll whip him!

LINDA And he'd better give back that football, Willy, it's not nice.

WILLY Biff! Where is he? Why is he taking everything?

LINDA He's too rough with the girls, Willy. All the mothers are afraid of him!

WILLY I'll whip him!

BERNARD He's driving the car without a license!

(THE WOMAN's *laugh is heard*)

WILLY Shut up!

LINDA All the mothers—

WILLY Shut up!

BERNARD (*Backing quietly away and out*) Mr. Birnbaum says he's stuck up.

WILLY Get outa here!

BERNARD If he doesn't buckle down he'll flunk math! (*He goes off*)

LINDA He's right, Willy, you've gotta—

WILLY (*Exploding at her*) There's nothing the matter with him! You want him to be a worm like Bernard? He's got spirit, personality . . .

(*As he speaks,* LINDA, *almost in tears, exits into the living-room.* WILLY *is alone in the kitchen, wilting and staring. The leaves are gone. It is night again, and the apartment houses look down from behind*)

WILLY Loaded with it. Loaded! What is he stealing? He's giving it back, isn't he? Why is he stealing? What did I tell him? I never in my life told him anything but decent things.

(HAPPY *in pajamas has come down the stairs;* WILLY *suddenly becomes aware of* HAPPY's *presence*)

HAPPY Let's go now, come on.

WILLY (*Sitting down at the kitchen table*) Huh! Why did she have to wax the floors herself? Every time she waxes the floors she keels over. She knows that!

HAPPY Shh! Take it easy. What brought you back tonight?

WILLY I got an awful scare. Nearly hit a kid in Yonkers. God! Why didn't I go to Alaska with my brother Ben that time! Ben! That man was a genius, that man was success incarnate! What a mistake! He begged me to go.

HAPPY Well, there's no use in—

WILLY You guys! There was a man started with the clothes on his back and ended up with diamond mines!

HAPPY Boy, someday I'd like to know how he did it.

WILLY What's the mystery? The man knew what he wanted and went out and got it! Walked into a jungle, and comes out, the age of twenty-one, and he's rich! The world is an oyster, but you don't crack it open on a mattress!

HAPPY Pop, I told you I'm gonna retire you for life.

WILLY You'll retire me for life on seventy goddam dollars a week? And your women and your car and your apartment, and you'll retire me for life! Christ's sake, I couldn't get past Yonkers today! Where are you guys, where are you? The woods are burning! I can't drive a car!

(CHARLEY *has appeared in the doorway. He is a large man, slow of speech, laconic, immovable. In all he says, despite what he says, there is pity, and, now, trepidation. He has a robe over pajamas, slippers on his feet. He enters the kitchen*)

CHARLEY Everything all right?

HAPPY Yeah, Charley, everything's . . .

WILLY What's the matter?

CHARLEY I heard some noise. I thought something happened. Can't we do something about the walls? You sneeze in here, and in my house hats blow off.

HAPPY Let's go to bed, Dad. Come on.

(CHARLEY *signals to* HAPPY *to go*)

WILLY You go ahead, I'm not tired at the moment.

HAPPY (*To* WILLY) Take it easy, huh? (*He exits*)

WILLY What're you doin' up?

CHARLEY (*Sitting down at the kitchen table opposite* WILLY) Couldn't sleep good. I had a heartburn.

WILLY Well, you don't know how to eat.

CHARLEY I eat with my mouth.

WILLY No, you're ignorant. You gotta know about vitamins and things like that.

CHARLEY Come on, let's shoot. Tire you out a little.

WILLY (*Hesitantly*) All right. You got cards?

CHARLEY (*Taking a deck from his pocket*) Yeah, I got them. Someplace. What is it with those vitamins?

WILLY (*Dealing*) They build up your bones. Chemistry.

CHARLEY Yeah, but there's no bones in a heartburn.

WILLY What are you talkin' about? Do you know the first thing about it?

CHARLEY Don't get insulted.

WILLY Don't talk about something you don't know anything about.

(*They are playing. Pause*)

CHARLEY What're you doin' home?

WILLY A little trouble with the car.

CHARLEY Oh. (*Pause*) I'd like to take a trip to California.

WILLY Don't say.

CHARLEY You want a job?

WILLY I got a job, I told you that. (*After a slight pause*) What the hell are you offering me a job for?

CHARLEY Don't get insulted.

WILLY Don't insult me.

CHARLEY I don't see no sense in it. You don't have to go on this way.

WILLY I got a good job. (*Slight pause*) What do you keep comin' in here for?

CHARLEY You want me to go?

WILLY (*After a pause, withering*) I can't understand it. He's going back to Texas again. What the hell is that?

CHARLEY Let him go.

WILLY I got nothin' to give him, Charley, I'm clean, I'm clean.

CHARLEY He won't starve. None a them starve. Forget about him.

WILLY Then what have I got to remember?

CHARLEY You take it too hard. To hell with it. When a deposit bottle is broken you don't get your nickel back.

WILLY That's easy enough for you to say.

CHARLEY That ain't easy for me to say.

WILLY Did you see the ceiling I put up in the living-room?

CHARLEY Yeah, that's a piece of work. To put up a ceiling is a mystery to me. How do you do it?

WILLY What's the difference?

CHARLEY Well, talk about it.

WILLY You gonna put up a ceiling?

CHARLEY How could I put up a ceiling?

WILLY Then what the hell are you bothering me for?

CHARLEY You're insulted again.

WILLY A man who can't handle tools is not a man. You're disgusting.

CHARLEY Don't call me disgusting, Willy.

(UNCLE BEN, *carrying a valise and an umbrella, enters the forestage from around the right corner of the house. He is a stolid man, in his sixties, with a mustache and an authoritative air. He is utterly certain of his destiny, and there is an aura of far places about him. He enters exactly as* WILLY *speaks*)

WILLY I'm getting awfully tired, Ben.

(BEN'*s music is heard.* BEN *looks around at everything*)

CHARLEY Good, keep playing; you'll sleep better. Did you call me Ben?

(BEN *looks at his watch*)

WILLY That's funny. For a second there you reminded me of my brother Ben.

BEN I only have a few minutes. (*He strolls, inspecting the place.* WILLY *and* CHARLEY *continue playing*)

CHARLEY You never heard from him again, heh? Since that time?

WILLY Didn't Linda tell you? Couple of weeks ago we got a letter from his wife in Africa. He died.

CHARLEY That so.

BEN (*Chuckling*) So this is Brooklyn, eh?

CHARLEY Maybe you're in for some of his money.

WILLY Naa, he had seven sons. There's just one opportunity I had with that man . . .

BEN I must make a train, William. There are several properties I'm looking at in Alaska.

WILLY Sure, sure! If I'd gone with him to Alaska that time, everything would've been totally different.

CHARLEY Go on, you'd froze to death up there.

WILLY What're you talking about?

BEN Opportunity is tremendous in Alaska, William. Surprised you're not up there.

WILLY Sure, tremendous.

CHARLEY Heh?

WILLY There was the only man I ever met who knew the answers.

CHARLEY Who?

BEN How are you all?

WILLY (*Taking a pot, smiling*) Fine, fine.

CHARLEY Pretty sharp tonight.

BEN Is Mother living with you?

WILLY No, she died a long time ago.
CHARLEY Who?
BEN That's too bad. Fine specimen of a lady, Mother.
WILLY (*To* CHARLEY) Heh?
BEN I'd hoped to see the old girl.
CHARLEY Who died?
BEN Heard anything from Father, have you?
WILLY (*Unnerved*) What do you mean, who died?
CHARLEY (*Taking a pot*) What're you talkin' about?
BEN (*Looking at his watch*) William, it's half-past eight!
WILLY (*As though to dispel his confusion he angrily stops* CHARLEY'*s hand*) That's my build!
CHARLEY I put the ace—
WILLY If you don't know how to play the game I'm not gonna throw my money away on you!
CHARLEY (*Rising*) It was my ace, for God's sake!
WILLY I'm through, I'm through!
BEN When did Mother die?
WILLY Long ago. Since the beginning you never knew how to play cards.
CHARLEY (*Picks up the cards and goes to the door*) All right! Next time I'll bring a deck with five aces.
WILLY I don't play that kind of game!
CHARLEY (*Turning to him*) You ought to be ashamed of yourself!
WILLY Yeah?
CHARLEY Yeah! (*He goes out*)
WILLY (*Slamming the door after him*) Ignoramus!
BEN (*As* WILLY *comes toward him through the wall-line of the kitchen*) So you're William.
WILLY (*Shaking* BEN'*s hand*) Ben! I've been waiting for you so long! What's the answer? How did you do it?
BEN Oh, there's a story in that.

(LINDA *enters the forestage, as of old, carrying the wash basket*)

LINDA Is this Ben?
BEN (*Gallantly*) How do you do, my dear.
LINDA Where've you been all these years? Willy's always wondered why you—
WILLY (*Pulling* BEN *away from her impatiently*) Where is Dad? Didn't you follow him? How did you get started?
BEN Well, I don't know how much you remember.
WILLY Well, I was just a baby, of course, only three or four years old—
BEN Three years and eleven months.
WILLY What a memory, Ben!
BEN I have many enterprises, William, and I have never kept books.
WILLY I remember I was sitting under the wagon in—was it Nebraska?
BEN It was South Dakota, and I gave you a bunch of wild flowers.
WILLY I remember you walking away down some open road.
BEN (*Laughing*) I was going to find Father in Alaska.
WILLY Where is he?
BEN At that age I had a very faulty view of geography, William. I discovered after a few days that I was heading due south, so instead of Alaska, I ended up in Africa.
LINDA Africa!
WILLY The Gold Coast!
BEN Principally diamond mines.
LINDA Diamond mines!
BEN Yes, my dear. But I've only a few minutes—
WILLY No! Boys! Boys! (YOUNG BIFF *and* HAPPY *appear*) Listen to this. This is your Uncle Ben, a great man! Tell my boys, Ben!
BEN Why, boys, when I was seventeen I walked into the jungle, and when I was twenty-one I walked out. (*He laughs*) And by God I was rich.
WILLY (*To the boys*) You see what I been talking about? The greatest things can happen!
BEN (*Glancing at his watch*) I have an appointment in Ketchikan Tuesday week.
WILLY No, Ben! Please tell about Dad. I want my boys to hear. I want them to know the kind of stock they spring from. All I remember is a man with a big beard, and I was in Mamma's lap, sitting around a fire, and some kind of high music.
BEN His flute. He played the flute.
WILLY Sure, the flute, that's right!

(*New music is heard, a high, rollicking tune*)

BEN Father was a very great and a very wild-hearted man. We would start in Boston, and he'd toss the whole family into the wagon, and then he'd drive the team right across the country; through Ohio, and Indiana, Michigan, Illinois, and all the Western states. And we'd stop in the towns and sell the flutes that he'd made on the way. Great inventor, Father. With one gadget he made more in a week than a man like you could make in a lifetime.
WILLY That's just the way I'm bringing them up, Ben—rugged, well liked, all-around.
BEN Yeah? (*To* BIFF) Hit that, boy—hard as you can. (*He pounds his stomach*)
BIFF Oh, no, sir!
BEN (*Taking boxing stance*) Come on, get to me! (*He laughs*)
WILLY Go to it, Biff! Go ahead, show him!
BIFF Okay! (*He cocks his fists and starts in*)
LINDA (*To* WILLY) Why must he fight, dear?
BEN (*Sparring with* BIFF) Good boy! Good boy!
WILLY How's that, Ben, heh?
HAPPY Give him the left, Biff!
LINDA Why are you fighting?
BEN Good boy! (*Suddenly comes in, trips* BIFF, *and stands over him, the point of his umbrella poised over* BIFF'*s eye*)
LINDA Look out, Biff!
BIFF Gee!
BEN (*Patting* BIFF'*s knee*) Never fight fair with a stranger, boy. You'll never get out of the jungle that way. (*Taking* LINDA'*s hand and bowing*) It was an honor and a pleasure to meet you, Linda.
LINDA (*Withdrawing her hand coldly, frightened*) Have a nice—trip.
BEN (*To* WILLY) And good luck with your—what do you do?

WILLY Selling.

BEN Yes. Well . . . (*He raises his hand in farewell to all*)

WILLY No, Ben, I don't want you to think . . . (*He takes* BEN'S *arm to show him*) It's Brooklyn, I know, but we hunt too.

BEN Really, now.

WILLY Oh, sure, there's snakes and rabbits and— that's why I moved out here. Why, Biff can fell any one of these trees in no time! Boys! Go right over to where they're building the apartment house and get some sand. We're gonna rebuild the entire front stoop right now! Watch this, Ben!

BIFF Yes, sir! On the double, Hap!

HAPPY (*As he and* BIFF *run off*) I lost weight, Pop, you notice?

(CHARLEY *enters in knickers, even before the boys are gone*)

CHARLEY Listen, if they steal any more from that building the watchman'll put the cops on them!

LINDA (*To* WILLY) Don't let Biff . . .

(BEN *laughs lustily*)

WILLY You shoulda seen the lumber they brought home last week. At least a dozen six-by-tens worth all kinds a money.

CHARLEY Listen, if that watchman—

WILLY I gave them hell, understand. But I got a couple of fearless characters there.

CHARLEY Willy, the jails are full of fearless characters.

BEN (*Clapping* WILLY *on the back, with a laugh at* CHARLEY) And the stock exchange, friend!

WILLY (*Joining in* BEN'S *laughter*) Where are the rest of your pants?

CHARLEY My wife bought them.

WILLY Now all you need is a golf club and you can go upstairs and go to sleep. (*To* BEN) Great athlete! Between him and his son Bernard they can't hammer a nail!

BERNARD (*Rushing in*) The watchman's chasing Biff!

WILLY (*Angrily*) Shut up! He's not stealing anything!

LINDA (*Alarmed, hurrying off left*) Where is he? Biff, dear! (*She exits*)

WILLY (*Moving toward the left, away from* BEN) There's nothing wrong. What's the matter with you?

BEN Nervy boy. Good!

WILLY (*Laughing*) Oh, nerves of iron, that Biff!

CHARLEY Don't know what it is. My New England man comes back and he's bleedin', they murdered him up there.

WILLY It's contacts, Charley, I got important contacts!

CHARLEY (*Sarcastically*) Glad to hear it, Willy. Come in later, we'll shoot a little casino. I'll take some of your Portland money. (*He laughs at* WILLY *and exits*)

WILLY (*Turning to* BEN) Business is bad, it's murderous. But not for me, of course.

BEN I'll stop by on my way back to Africa.

WILLY (*Longingly*) Can't you stay a few days? You're just what I need, Ben, because I—I have a fine position here, but I—well, Dad left when I was such a baby and I never had a chance to talk to him and I still feel—kind of temporary about myself.

BEN I'll be late for my train.

(*They are at opposite ends of the stage*)

WILLY Ben, my boys—can't we talk? They'd go into the jaws of hell for me, see, but I—

BEN William, you're being first-rate with your boys. Outstanding, manly chaps!

WILLY (*Hanging on to his words*) Oh, Ben, that's good to hear! Because sometimes I'm afraid that I'm not teaching them the right kind of— Ben, how should I teach them?

BEN (*Giving great weight to each word, and with a certain vicious audacity*) William, when I walked into the jungle, I was seventeen. When I walked out I was twenty-one. And, by God, I was rich! (*He goes off into darkness around the right corner of the house*)

WILLY . . . was rich! That's just the spirit I want to imbue them with! To walk into a jungle! I was right! I was right! I was right!

(BEN *is gone, but* WILLY *is still speaking to him as* LINDA, *in nightgown and robe, enters the kitchen, glances around for* WILLY, *then goes to the door of the house, looks out and sees him. Comes down to his left. He looks at her*)

LINDA Willy, dear? Willy?

WILLY I was right!

LINDA Did you have some cheese? (*He can't answer*) It's very late, darling. Come to bed, heh?

WILLY (*Looking straight up*) Gotta break your neck to see a star in this yard.

LINDA You coming in?

WILLY Whatever happened to that diamond watch fob? Remember? When Ben came from Africa that time? Didn't he give me a watch fob with a diamond in it?

LINDA You pawned it, dear. Twelve, thirteen years ago. For Biff's radio correspondence course.

WILLY Gee, that was a beautiful thing. I'll take a walk.

LINDA But you're in your slippers.

WILLY (*Starting to go around the house at the left*) I was right! I was! (*Half to* LINDA, *as he goes, shaking his head*) What a man! There was a man worth talking to. I was right!

LINDA (*Calling after* WILLY) But in your slippers, Willy!

(WILLY *is almost gone when* BIFF, *in his pajamas, comes down the stairs and enters the kitchen*)

BIFF What is he doing out there?

LINDA Sh!

BIFF God Almighty, Mom, how long has he been doing this?

LINDA Don't, he'll hear you.

BIFF What the hell is the matter with him?

LINDA It'll pass by morning.

BIFF Shouldn't we do anything?

LINDA Oh, my dear, you should do a lot of things, but there's nothing to do, so go to sleep.

(HAPPY *comes down the stair and sits on the steps*)

HAPPY I never heard him so loud, Mom.

LINDA Well, come around more often; you'll hear him.

(*She sits down at the table and mends the lining of* WILLY'S *jacket*)

BIFF Why didn't you ever write me about this, Mom?

LINDA How would I write to you? For over three months you had no address.

BIFF I was on the move. But you know I thought of you all the time. You know that, don't you, pal?

LINDA I know, dear, I know. But he likes to have a letter. Just to know that there's still a possibility for better things.

BIFF He's not like this all the time, is he?

LINDA It's when you come home he's always the worst.

BIFF When I come home?

LINDA When you write you're coming, he's all smiles, and talks about the future, and—he's just wonderful. And then the closer you seem to come, the more shaky he gets, and then, by the time you get here, he's arguing, and he seems angry at you. I think it's just that maybe he can't bring himself to—to open up to you. Why are you so hateful to each other? Why is that?

BIFF (*Evasively*) I'm not hateful, Mom.

LINDA But you no sooner come in the door than you're fighting!

BIFF I don't know why. I mean to change. I'm tryin', Mom, you understand?

LINDA Are you home to stay now?

BIFF I don't know. I want to look around, see what's doin'.

LINDA Biff, you can't look around all your life, can you?

BIFF I just can't take hold, Mom. I can't take hold of some kind of a life.

LINDA Biff, a man is not a bird, to come and go with the springtime.

BIFF Your hair . . . (*He touches her hair*) Your hair got so gray.

LINDA Oh, it's been gray since you were in high school. I just stopped dyeing it, that's all.

BIFF Dye it again, will ya? I don't want my pal looking old. (*He smiles*)

LINDA You're such a boy! You think you can go away for a year and . . . You've got to get it into your head now that one day you'll knock on this door and there'll be strange people here—

BIFF What are you talking about? You're not even sixty, Mom.

LINDA But what about your father?

BIFF (*Lamely*) Well, I meant him too.

HAPPY He admires Pop.

LINDA Biff, dear, if you don't have any feeling for him, then you can't have any feeling for me.

BIFF Sure I can, Mom.

LINDA No. You can't just come to see me, because I love him. (*With a threat, but only a threat, of tears*) He's the dearest man in the world to me, and I won't have anyone making him feel unwanted and low and blue. You've got to make up your mind now, darling, there's no leeway any more. Either he's your father and you pay him that respect, or else you're not to come here. I know he's not easy to get along with—nobody knows that better than me—but . . .

WILLY (*From the left, with a laugh*) Hey, hey, Biffo!

BIFF (*Starting to go out after* WILLY) What the hell is the matter with him? (HAPPY *stops him*)

LINDA Don't—don't go near him!

BIFF Stop making excuses for him! He always, always wiped the floor with you. Never had an ounce of respect for you.

HAPPY He's always had respect for—

BIFF What the hell do you know about it?

HAPPY (*Surlily*) Just don't call him crazy!

BIFF He's got no character— Charley wouldn't do this. Not in his own house—spewing out that vomit from his mind.

HAPPY Charley never had to cope with what he's got to.

BIFF People are worse off than Willy Loman. Believe me, I've seen them!

LINDA Then make Charley your father, Biff. You can't do that, can you? I don't say he's a great man. Willy Loman never made a lot of money. His name was never in the paper. He's not the finest character that ever lived. But he's a human being, and a terrible thing is happening to him. So attention must be paid. He's not to be allowed to fall into his grave like an old dog. Attention, attention must be finally paid to such a person. You called him crazy—

BIFF I didn't mean—

LINDA No, a lot of people think he's lost his—balance. But you don't have to be very smart to know what his trouble is. The man is exhausted.

HAPPY Sure!

LINDA A small man can be just as exhausted as a great man. He works for a company thirty-six years this March, opens up unheard-of territories to their trademark, and now in his old age they take his salary away.

HAPPY (*Indignantly*) I didn't know that, Mom.

LINDA You never asked, my dear! Now that you get your spending money someplace else you don't trouble your mind with him.

HAPPY But I gave you money last—

LINDA Christmas time, fifty dollars! To fix the hot water it cost ninety-seven fifty! For five weeks he's been on straight commission, like a beginner, an unknown!

BIFF Those ungrateful bastards!

LINDA Are they any worse than his sons? When he brought them business, when he was young, they were glad to see him. But now his old friends, the old buyers that loved him so and always found some order to hand him in a pinch—they're all dead, retired. He used to be able to make six, seven calls a day in Boston. Now he takes his valises out of the car and puts them back and takes them out again and he's exhausted. Instead of walking he talks now. He drives seven hundred miles, and when he gets there no one knows him any more, no one welcomes him. And what goes through a man's mind, driving seven hundred miles home without having earned a cent?

Why shouldn't he talk to himself? Why? When he has to go to Charley and borrow fifty dollars a week and pretend to me that it's his pay? How long can that go on? How long? You see what I'm sitting here and waiting for? And you tell me he has no character? The man who never worked a day but for your benefit? When does he get the medal for that? Is this his reward—to turn around at the age of sixty-three and find his sons, who he loved better than his life, one a philandering bum—

HAPPY Mom!

LINDA That's all you are, my baby! (*To* BIFF) And you! What happened to the love you had for him? You were such pals! How you used to talk to him on the phone every night! How lonely he was till he could come home to you!

BIFF All right, Mom. I'll live here in my room, and I'll get a job. I'll keep away from him, that's all.

LINDA No, Biff. You can't stay here and fight all the time.

BIFF He threw me out of this house, remember that.

LINDA Why did he do that? I never knew why.

BIFF Because I know he's a fake and he doesn't like anybody around who knows!

LINDA Why a fake? In what way? What do you mean?

BIFF Just don't lay it all at my feet. It's between me and him—that's all I have to say. I'll chip in from now on. He'll settle for half my pay check. He'll be all right. I'm going to bed. (*He starts for the stairs*)

LINDA He won't be all right.

BIFF (*Turning on the stairs, furiously*) I hate this city and I'll stay here. Now what do you want?

LINDA He's dying, Biff.

(HAPPY *turns quickly to her, shocked*)

BIFF (*After a pause*) Why is he dying?

LINDA He's been trying to kill himself.

BIFF (*With great horror*) How?

LINDA I live from day to day.

BIFF What're you talking about?

LINDA Remember I wrote you that he smashed up the car again? In February?

BIFF Well?

LINDA The insurance inspector came. He said that they have evidence. That all these accidents in the last year—weren't—weren't—accidents.

HAPPY How can they tell that? That's a lie.

LINDA It seems there's a woman . . . (*She takes a breath as*

BIFF (*Sharply but contained*) What woman?
LINDA (*Simultaneously*) . . . and this woman . . .

LINDA What?

BIFF Nothing. Go ahead.

LINDA What did you say?

BIFF Nothing. I just said what woman?

HAPPY What about her?

LINDA Well, it seems she was walking down the road and saw his car. She says that he wasn't driving fast at all, and that he didn't skid. She says he came to that little bridge, and then deliberately smashed into the railing, and it was only the shallowness of the water that saved him.

BIFF Oh, no, he probably just fell asleep again.

LINDA I don't think he fell asleep.

BIFF Why not?

LINDA Last month . . . (*With great difficulty*) Oh, boys, it's so hard to say a thing like this! He's just a big stupid man to you, but I tell you there's more good in him than in many other people. (*She chokes, wipes her eyes*) I was looking for a fuse. The lights blew out, and I went down the cellar. And behind the fuse box—it happened to fall out—was a length of rubber pipe—just short.

HAPPY No kidding?

LINDA There's a little attachment on the end of it. I knew right away. And sure enough, on the bottom of the water heater there's a new little nipple on the gas pipe.

HAPPY (*Angrily*) That—jerk.

BIFF Did you have it taken off?

LINDA I'm—I'm ashamed to. How can I mention it to him? Every day I go down and take away that little rubber pipe. But, when he comes home, I put it back where it was. How can I insult him that way? I don't know what to do. I live from day to day, boys. I tell you, I know every thought in his mind. It sounds so old-fashioned and silly, but I tell you he put his whole life into you and you've turned your backs on him. (*She is bent over in the chair, weeping, her face in her hands*) Biff, I swear to God! Biff, his life is in your hands!

HAPPY (*To* BIFF) How do you like that damned fool!

BIFF (*Kissing her*) All right, pal, all right. It's all settled now. I've been remiss. I know that, Mom. But now I'll stay, and I swear to you, I'll apply myself. (*Kneeling in front of her, in a fever of self-reproach*) It's just—you see, Mom, I don't fit in business. Not that I won't try. I'll try, and I'll make good.

HAPPY Sure you will. The trouble with you in business was you never tried to please people.

BIFF I know, I—

HAPPY Like when you worked for Harrison's. Bob Harrison said you were tops, and then you go and do some damn fool thing like whistling whole songs in the elevator like a comedian.

BIFF (*Against* HAPPY) So what? I like to whistle sometimes.

HAPPY You don't raise a guy to a responsible job who whistles in the elevator!

LINDA Well, don't argue about it now.

HAPPY Like when you'd go off and swim in the middle of the day instead of taking the line around.

BIFF (*His resentment rising*) Well, don't you run off? You take off sometimes, don't you? On a nice summer day?

HAPPY Yeah, but I cover myself!

LINDA Boys!

HAPPY If I'm going to take a fade the boss can call any number where I'm supposed to be and they'll swear to him that I just left. I'll tell you something that I hate to say, Biff, but in the business world some of them think you're crazy.

BIFF (*Angered*) Screw the business world!
HAPPY All right, screw it! Great, but cover yourself!
LINDA Hap, Hap!
BIFF I don't care what they think! They've laughed at Dad for years, and you know why? Because we don't belong in this nuthouse of a city! We should be mixing cement on some open plain, or—or carpenters. A carpenter is allowed to whistle!

(WILLY *walks in from the entrance of the house, at left*)

WILLY Even your grandfather was better than a carpenter. (*Pause. They watch him*) You never grew up. Bernard does not whistle in the elevator, I assure you.
BIFF (*As though to laugh* WILLY *out of it*) Yeah, but you do, Pop.
WILLY I never in my life whistled in an elevator! And who in the business world thinks I'm crazy?
BIFF I didn't mean it like that, Pop. Now don't make a whole thing out of it, will ya?
WILLY Go back to the West! Be a carpenter, a cowboy, enjoy yourself!
LINDA Willy, he was just saying—
WILLY I heard what he said!
HAPPY (*Trying to quiet* WILLY) Hey, Pop, come on now . . .
WILLY (*Continuing over* HAPPY'*s line*) They laugh at me, heh? Go to Filene's, go to the Hub, go to Slattery's, Boston. Call out the name Willy Loman and see what happens! Big shot!
BIFF All right, Pop.
WILLY Big!
BIFF All right!
WILLY Why do you always insult me?
BIFF I didn't say a word. (*To* LINDA) Did I say a word?
LINDA He didn't say anything, Willy.
WILLY (*Going to the doorway of the living-room*) All right, good night, good night.
LINDA Willy, dear, he just decided . . .
WILLY (*To* BIFF) If you get tired hanging around tomorrow, paint the ceiling I put up in the living-room.
BIFF I'm leaving early tomorrow.
HAPPY He's going to see Bill Oliver, Pop.
WILLY (*Interestedly*) Oliver? For what?
BIFF (*With reserve, but trying, trying*) He always said he'd stake me. I'd like to go into business, so maybe I can take him up on it.
LINDA Isn't that wonderful?
WILLY Don't interrupt. What's wonderful about it? There's fifty men in the City of New York who'd stake him. (*To* BIFF) Sporting goods?
BIFF I guess so. I know something about it and—
WILLY He knows something about it! You know sporting goods better than Spalding, for God's sake! How much is he giving you?
BIFF I don't know, I didn't even see him yet, but—
WILLY Then what're you talkin' about?
BIFF (*Getting angry*) Well, all I said was I'm gonna see him, that's all!
WILLY (*Turning away*) Ah, you're counting your chickens again.
BIFF (*Starting left for the stairs*) Oh, Jesus, I'm going to sleep!
WILLY (*Calling after him*) Don't curse in this house!
BIFF (*Turning*) Since when did you get so clean?
HAPPY (*Trying to stop them*) Wait a . . .
WILLY Don't use that language to me! I won't have it!
HAPPY (*Grabbing* BIFF, *shouts*) Wait a minute! I got an idea. I got a feasible idea. Come here, Biff, let's talk this over now, let's talk some sense here. When I was down in Florida last time, I thought of a great idea to sell sporting goods. It just came back to me. You and I, Biff—we have a line, the Loman Line. We train a couple of weeks, and put on a couple of exhibitions, see?
WILLY That's an idea!
HAPPY Wait! We form two basketball teams, see? Two waterpolo teams. We play each other. It's a million dollars' worth of publicity. Two brothers, see? The Loman Brothers. Displays in the Royal Palms—all the hotels. And banners over the ring and the basketball court: "Loman Brothers." Baby, we could sell sporting goods!
WILLY That is a one-million-dollar idea!
LINDA Marvelous!
BIFF I'm in great shape as far as that's concerned.
HAPPY And the beauty of it is, Biff, it wouldn't be like a business. We'd be out playin' ball again . . .
BIFF (*Enthused*) Yeah, that's . . .
WILLY Million-dollar . . .
HAPPY And you wouldn't get fed up with it, Biff. It'd be the family again. There'd be the old honor, and comradeship, and if you wanted to go off for a swim or somethin'—well, you'd do it! Without some smart cooky gettin' up ahead of you!
WILLY Lick the world! You guys together could absolutely lick the civilized world.
BIFF I'll see Oliver tomorrow. Hap, if we could work that out . . .
LINDA Maybe things are beginning to—
WILLY (*Wildly enthused, to* LINDA) Stop interrupting! (*To* BIFF) But don't wear sport jacket and slacks when you see Oliver.
BIFF No, I'll—
WILLY A business suit, and talk as little as possible, and don't crack any jokes.
BIFF He did like me. Always liked me.
LINDA He loved you!
WILLY (*To* LINDA) Will you stop! (*To* BIFF) Walk in very serious. You are not applying for a boy's job. Money is to pass. Be quiet, fine, and serious. Everybody likes a kidder, but nobody lends him money.
HAPPY I'll try to get some myself, Biff. I'm sure I can.
WILLY I see great things for you kids, I think your troubles are over. But remember, start big and you'll end big. Ask for fifteen. How much you gonna ask for?
BIFF Gee, I don't know—
WILLY And don't say "Gee." "Gee" is a boy's word. A man walking in for fifteen thousand dollars does not say "Gee!"

BIFF Ten, I think, would be top though.

WILLY Don't be so modest. You always started too low. Walk in with a big laugh. Don't look worried. Start off with a couple of your good stories to lighten things up. It's not what you say, it's how you say it—because personality always wins the day.

LINDA Oliver always thought the highest of him—

WILLY Will you let me talk?

BIFF Don't yell at her, Pop, will ya?

WILLY (*Angrily*) I was talking, wasn't I?

BIFF I don't like you yelling at her all the time, and I'm tellin' you, that's all.

WILLY What're you, takin' over this house?

LINDA Willy—

WILLY (*Turning on her*) Don't take his side all the time, goddammit!

BIFF (*Furiously*) Stop yelling at her!

WILLY (*Suddenly pulling on his cheek, beaten down, guilt ridden*) Give my best to Bill Oliver—he may remember me. (*He exits through the living-room doorway*)

LINDA (*Her voice subdued*) What'd you have to start that for? (BIFF *turns away*) You see how sweet he was as soon as you talked hopefully? (*She goes over to* BIFF) Come up and say good night to him. Don't let him go to bed that way.

HAPPY Come on, Biff, let's buck him up.

LINDA Please, dear. Just say good night. It takes so little to make him happy. Come. (*She goes through the living-room doorway, calling upstairs from within the living-room*) Your pajamas are hanging in the bathroom, Willy!

HAPPY (*Looking toward where* LINDA *went out*) What a woman! They broke the mold when they made her. You know that, Biff?

BIFF He's off salary. My God, working on commission!

HAPPY Well, let's face it: he's no hot-shot selling man. Except that sometimes, you have to admit, he's a sweet personality.

BIFF (*Deciding*) Lend me ten bucks, will ya? I want to buy some new ties.

HAPPY I'll take you to a place I know. Beautiful stuff. Wear one of my striped shirts tomorrow.

BIFF She got gray. Mom got awful old. Gee, I'm gonna go in to Oliver tomorrow and knock him for a—

HAPPY Come on up. Tell that to Dad. Let's give him a whirl. Come on.

BIFF (*Steamed up*) You know, with ten thousand bucks, boy!

HAPPY (*As they go into the living-room*) That's the talk, Biff, that's the first time I've heard the old confidence out of you! (*From within the living-room, fading off*) You're gonna live with me, kid, and any babe you want just say the word . . . (*The last lines are hardly heard. They are mounting the stairs to their parents' bedroom*)

LINDA (*Entering her bedroom and addressing* WILLY, *who is in the bathroom. She is straightening the bed for him*) Can you do anything about the shower? It drips.

WILLY (*From the bathroom*) All of a sudden everything falls to pieces! Goddam plumbing, oughta be sued, those people. I hardly finished putting it in and the thing . . . (*His words rumble off*)

LINDA I'm just wondering if Oliver will remember him. You think he might?

WILLY (*Coming out of the bathroom in his pajamas*) Remember him? What's the matter with you, you crazy? If he'd've stayed with Oliver he'd be on top by now! Wait'll Oliver gets a look at him. You don't know the average caliber any more. The average young man today— (*He is getting into bed*)—is got a caliber of zero. Greatest thing in the world for him was to bum around.

(BIFF *and* HAPPY *enter the bedroom. Slight pause*)

WILLY (*Stops short, looking at* BIFF) Glad to hear it, boy.

HAPPY He wanted to say good night to you, sport.

WILLY (*To* BIFF) Yeah. Knock him dead, boy. What'd you want to tell me?

BIFF Just take it easy, Pop. Good night. (*He turns to go*)

WILLY (*Unable to resist*) And if anything falls off the desk while you're talking to him—like a package or something—don't you pick it up. They have office boys for that.

LINDA I'll make a big breakfast—

WILLY Will you let me finish? (*To* BIFF) Tell him you were in the business in the West. Not farm work.

BIFF All right, Dad.

LINDA I think everything—

WILLY (*Going right through her speech*) And don't undersell yourself. No less than fifteen thousand dollars.

BIFF (*Unable to bear him*) Okay. Good night, Mom. (*He starts moving*)

WILLY Because you got a greatness in you, Biff, remember that. You got all kinds a greatness . . . (*He lies back, exhausted.* BIFF *walks out*)

LINDA (*Calling after* BIFF) Sleep well, darling!

HAPPY I'm gonna get married, Mom. I wanted to tell you.

LINDA Go to sleep, dear.

HAPPY (*Going*) I just wanted to tell you.

WILLY Keep up the good work. (HAPPY *exits*) God . . . remember that Ebbets Field game? The championship of the city?

LINDA Just rest. Should I sing to you?

WILLY Yeah. Sing to me. (LINDA *hums a soft lullaby*) When that team came out—he was the tallest, remember?

LINDA Oh, yes. And in gold.

(BIFF *enters the darkened kitchen, takes a cigarette, and leaves the house. He comes downstage into a golden pool of light. He smokes, staring at the night*)

WILLY Like a young god. Hercules—something like that. And the sun, the sun all around him. Remember how he waved to me? Right up from the field, with the representatives of three colleges standing by? And the buyers I brought, and the cheers when he came out—Loman, Loman, Loman! God Almighty, he'll be great yet. A star like that, magnificent, can never really fade away!

(*The light on* WILLY *is fading. The gas heater begins to glow through the kitchen wall, near the stairs, a blue flame beneath red coils*)

LINDA (*Timidly*) Willy dear, what has he got against you?

WILLY I'm so tired. Don't talk any more.

(BIFF *slowly returns to the kitchen. He stops, stares toward the heater*)

LINDA Will you ask Howard to let you work in New York?

WILLY First thing in the morning. Everything'll be all right.

(BIFF *reaches behind the heater and draws out a length of rubber tubing. He is horrified and turns his head toward* WILLY'S *room, still dimly lit, from which the strains of* LINDA'S *desperate but monotonous humming rise*)

WILLY (*Staring through the window into the moonlight*) Gee, look at the moon moving between the buildings!

(BIFF *wraps the tubing around his hand and quickly goes up the stairs*)

*Curtain*

# Act Two

*Music is heard, gay and bright. The curtain rises as the music fades away.* WILLY, *in shirt sleeves, is sitting at the kitchen table, sipping coffee, his hat in his lap.* LINDA *is filling his cup when she can.*

WILLY Wonderful coffee. Meal in itself.

LINDA Can I make you some eggs?

WILLY No. Take a breath.

LINDA You look so rested, dear.

WILLY I slept like a dead one. First time in months. Imagine, sleeping till ten on a Tuesday morning. Boys left nice and early, heh?

LINDA They were out of here by eight o'clock.

WILLY Good work!

LINDA It was so thrilling to see them leaving together. I can't get over the shaving lotion in this house!

WILLY (*Smiling*) Mmm—

LINDA Biff was very changed this morning. His whole attitude seemed to be hopeful. He couldn't wait to get downtown to see Oliver.

WILLY He's heading for a change. There's no question, there simply are certain men that take longer to get—solidified. How did he dress?

LINDA His blue suit. He's so handsome in that suit. He could be a—anything in that suit!

(WILLY *gets up from the table.* LINDA *holds his jacket for him*)

WILLY There's no question, no question at all. Gee, on the way home tonight I'd like to buy some seeds.

LINDA (*Laughing*) That'd be wonderful. But not enough sun gets back there. Nothing'll grow any more.

WILLY You wait, kid, before it's all over we're gonna get a little place out in the country, and I'll raise some vegetables, a couple of chickens . . .

LINDA You'll do it yet, dear.

(WILLY *walks out of his jacket.* LINDA *follows him*)

WILLY And they'll get married, and come for a weekend. I'd build a little guest house. 'Cause I got so many fine tools, all I'd need would be a little lumber and some peace of mind.

LINDA (*Joyfully*) I sewed the lining . . .

WILLY I could build two guest houses, so they'd both come. Did he decide how much he's going to ask Oliver for?

LINDA (*Getting him into the jacket*) He didn't mention it, but I imagine ten or fifteen thousand. You going to talk to Howard today?

WILLY Yeah. I'll put it to him straight and simple. He'll just have to take me off the road.

LINDA And Willy, don't forget to ask for a little advance, because we've got the insurance premium. It's the grace period now.

WILLY That's a hundred . . . ?

LINDA A hundred and eight, sixty-eight. Because we're a little short again.

WILLY Why are we short?

LINDA Well, you had the motor job on the car . . .

WILLY That goddam Studebaker!

LINDA And you got one more payment on the refrigerator . . .

WILLY But it just broke again!

LINDA Well, it's old, dear.

WILLY I told you we should've bought a well-advertised machine. Charley bought a General Electric and it's twenty years old and it's still good, that son-of-a-bitch.

LINDA But, Willy—

WILLY Whoever heard of a Hastings refrigerator? Once in my life I would like to own something outright before it's broken! I'm always in a race with the junkyard! I just finished paying for the car and it's on its last legs. The refrigerator consumes belts like a goddam maniac. They time those things. They time them so when you finally paid for them, they're used up.

LINDA (*Buttoning up his jacket as he unbuttons it*) All told, about two hundred dollars would carry us, dear. But that includes the last payment on the mortgage. After this payment, Willy, the house belongs to us.

WILLY It's twenty-five years!

LINDA Biff was nine years old when we bought it.

WILLY Well, that's a great thing. To weather a twenty-five year mortgage is—

LINDA It's an accomplishment.

WILLY All the cement, the lumber, the reconstruction I put in this house! There ain't a crack to be found in it any more.

LINDA Well, it served its purpose.

WILLY What purpose? Some stranger'll come along, move in, and that's that. If only Biff would take this house, and raise a family . . . (*He starts to go*) Good-by, I'm late.

LINDA (*Suddenly remembering*) Oh, I forgot! You're supposed to meet them for dinner.

WILLY Me?

LINDA At Frank's Chop House on Forty-eighth near Sixth Avenue.

WILLY Is that so! How about you?

LINDA No, just the three of you. They're gonna blow you to a big meal!

WILLY Don't say! Who thought of that?

LINDA Biff came to me this morning, Willy, and he said, "Tell Dad, we want to blow him to a big meal." Be there six o'clock. You and your two boys are going to have dinner.

WILLY Gee whiz! That's really somethin'. I'm gonna knock Howard for a loop, kid. I'll get an advance, and I'll come home with a New York job. Goddammit, now I'm gonna do it!

LINDA Oh, that's the spirit, Willy!

WILLY I will never get behind a wheel the rest of my life!

LINDA It's changing, Willy, I can feel it changing!

WILLY Beyond a question. G'by, I'm late. (*He starts to go again*)

LINDA (*Calling after him as she runs to the kitchen table for a handkerchief*) You got your glasses?

WILLY (*Feels for them, then comes back in*) Yeah, yeah, got my glasses.

LINDA (*Giving him the handkerchief*) And a handkerchief.

WILLY Yeah, handkerchief.

LINDA And your saccharine?

WILLY Yeah, my saccharine.

LINDA Be careful on the subway stairs.

(*She kisses him, and a silk stocking is seen hanging from her hand.* WILLY *notices it*)

WILLY Will you stop mending stockings? At least while I'm in the house. It gets me nervous. I can't tell you. Please.

(LINDA *hides the stocking in her hand as she follows* WILLY *across the forestage in front of the house*)

LINDA Remember, Frank's Chop House.

WILLY (*Passing the apron*) Maybe beets would grow out there.

LINDA (*Laughing*) But you tried so many times.

WILLY Yeah. Well, don't work hard today. (*He disappears around the right corner of the house*)

LINDA Be careful!

(*As* WILLY *vanishes,* LINDA *waves to him. Suddenly the phone rings. She runs across the stage and into the kitchen and lifts it*)

LINDA Hello? Oh, Biff! I'm so glad you called, I just . . . Yes, sure, I told him. Yes, he'll be there for dinner at six o'clock, I didn't forget. Listen, I was just dying to tell you. You know that little rubber pipe I told you about? That he connected to the gas heater? I finally decided to go down the cellar this morning and take it away and destroy it. But it's gone! Imagine? He took it away himself, it isn't there! (*She listens*) When? Oh, then you took it. Oh—nothing, it's just that I'd hoped he'd taken it away himself. Oh, I'm not worried, darling, because this morning he left in such high spirits, it was like the old days! I'm not afraid any more. Did Mr. Oliver see you? . . . Well, you wait there then. And make a nice impression on him, darling. Just don't perspire too much before you see him. And have a nice time with Dad. He may have big news too! . . . That's right, a New York job. And be sweet to him tonight, dear. Be loving to him. Because he's only a little boat looking for a harbor. (*She is trembling with sorrow and joy*) Oh, that's wonderful, Biff, you'll save his life. Thanks, darling. Just put your arm around him when he comes into the restaurant. Give him a smile. That's the boy . . . Good-by, dear. . . . You got your comb? . . . That's fine. Good-by, Biff dear.

(*In the middle of her speech, Howard Wagner, thirty-six, wheels on a small typewriter table on which is a wire-recording machine and proceeds to plug it in. This is on the left forestage. Light slowly fades on Linda as it rises on Howard. Howard is intent on threading the machine and only glances over his shoulder as Willy appears*)

WILLY Pst! Pst!

HOWARD Hello, Willy, come in.

WILLY Like to have a little talk with you, Howard.

HOWARD Sorry to keep you waiting. I'll be with you in a minute.

WILLY What's that, Howard?

HOWARD Didn't you ever see one of these? Wire recorder.

WILLY Oh. Can we talk a minute?

HOWARD Records things. Just got delivery yesterday. Been driving me crazy, the most terrific machine I ever saw in my life. I was up all night with it.

WILLY What do you do with it?

HOWARD I bought it for dictation, but you can do anything with it. Listen to this. I had it home last night. Listen to what I picked up. The first one is my daughter. Get this. (*He flicks the switch and "Roll out the Barrel" is heard being whistled*) Listen to that kid whistle.

WILLY That is lifelike, isn't it?

HOWARD Seven years old. Get that tone.

WILLY Ts, ts. Like to ask a little favor of you . . .

(*The whistling breaks off, and the voice of* HOWARD'S *daughter is heard*)

HIS DAUGHTER "Now you, Daddy."

HOWARD She's crazy for me! (*Again the same song is whistled*) That's me! Ha! (*He winks*)

WILLY You're very good!

(*The whistling breaks off again. The machine runs silent for a moment*)

HOWARD Sh! Get this now, this is my son.

HIS SON "The capital of Alabama is Montgomery; the capital of Arizona is Phoenix; the capital of Arkansas is Little Rock; the capital of California is Sacramento . . ." (*And on, and on*)

HOWARD (*Holding up five fingers*) Five years old, Willy!

WILLY He'll make an announcer some day!

HIS SON (*Continuing*) "The capital . . ."

HOWARD Get that—alphabetical order! (*The machine breaks off suddenly*) Wait a minute. The maid kicked the plug out.

WILLY It certainly is a—

HOWARD Sh, for God's sake!

HIS SON "It's nine o'clock, Bulova watch time. So I have to go to sleep."

WILLY That really is—

HOWARD Wait a minute! The next is my wife.

(*They wait*)

HOWARD'S VOICE "Go on, say something." (*Pause*) "Well, you gonna talk?"

HIS WIFE "I can't think of anything."

HOWARD'S VOICE "Well, talk—it's turning."

HIS WIFE (*Shyly, beaten*) "Hello." (*Silence*) "Oh, Howard, I can't talk into this . . ."

HOWARD (*Snapping the machine off*) That was my wife.

WILLY That is a wonderful machine. Can we—

HOWARD I tell you, Willy, I'm gonna take my camera, and my bandsaw, and all my hobbies, and out they go. This is the most fascinating relaxation I ever found.

WILLY I think I'll get one myself.

HOWARD Sure, they're only a hundred and a half. You can't do without it. Supposing you wanna hear Jack Benny, see? But you can't be at home at that hour. So you tell the maid to turn the radio on when Jack Benny comes on, and this automatically goes on with the radio . . .

WILLY And when you come home you . . .

HOWARD You can come home twelve o'clock, one o'clock, any time you like, and you get yourself a Coke and sit yourself down, throw the switch, and there's Jack Benny's program in the middle of the night!

WILLY I'm definitely going to get one. Because lots of time I'm on the road, and I think to myself, what I must be missing on the radio!

HOWARD Don't you have a radio in the car?

WILLY Well, yeah, but whoever thinks of turning it on?

HOWARD Say, aren't you supposed to be in Boston?

WILLY That's what I want to talk to you about, Howard. You got a minute? (*He draws a chair in from the wing*)

HOWARD What happened? What're you doing here?

WILLY Well . . .

HOWARD You didn't crack up again, did you?

WILLY Oh, no. No . . .

HOWARD Geez, you had me worried there for a minute. What's the trouble?

WILLY Well, tell you the truth, Howard. I've come to the decision that I'd rather not travel any more.

HOWARD Not travel! Well, what'll you do?

WILLY Remember, Christmas time, when you had the party here? You said you'd try to think of some spot for me here in town.

HOWARD With us?

WILLY Well, sure.

HOWARD Oh, yeah, yeah. I remember. Well, I couldn't think of anything for you, Willy.

WILLY I tell ya, Howard. The kids are all grown up, y'know. I don't need much any more. If I could take home—well, sixty-five dollars a week, I could swing it.

HOWARD Yeah, but Willy, see I—

WILLY I tell ya why, Howard. Speaking frankly and between the two of us, y'know—I'm just a little tired.

HOWARD Oh, I could understand that, Willy. But you're a road man, Willy, and we do a road business. We've only got a half-dozen salesmen on the floor here.

WILLY God knows, Howard, I never asked a favor of any man. But I was with the firm when your father used to carry you in here in his arms.

HOWARD I know that, Willy, but—

WILLY Your father came to me the day you were born and asked me what I thought of the name of Howard, may he rest in peace.

HOWARD I appreciate that, Willy, but there just is no spot here for you. If I had a spot I'd slam you right in, but I just don't have a single solitary spot.

(*He looks for his lighter.* WILLY *has picked it up and gives it to him. Pause*)

WILLY (*With increasing anger*) Howard, all I need to set my table is fifty dollars a week.

HOWARD But where am I going to put you, kid?

WILLY Look, it isn't a question of whether I can sell merchandise, is it?

HOWARD No, but it's business, kid, and everybody's gotta pull his own weight.

WILLY (*Desperately*) Just let me tell you a story, Howard—

HOWARD 'Cause you gotta admit, business is business.

WILLY (*Angrily*) Business is definitely business, but just listen for a minute. You don't understand this. When I was a boy—eighteen, nineteen—I was already on the road. And there was a question in my mind as to whether selling had a future for me. Because in those days I had a yearning to go to Alaska. See, there were three gold strikes in one month in Alaska, and I felt like going out. Just for the ride, you might say.

HOWARD (*Barely interested*) Don't say.

WILLY Oh, yeah, my father lived many years in Alaska. He was an adventurous man. We've got quite a little streak of self-reliance in our family. I thought I'd go out with my older brother and try to locate him, and maybe settle in the North with the old man. And I was almost decided to go, when I met a salesman in the Parker House. His name was Dave Singleman. And he was eighty-four years old, and he'd drummed merchandise in thirty-one states. And old Dave, he'd go up to his room, y'understand, put on his green velvet slippers—I'll never forget—and pick up his phone and call the buyers, and without ever leaving his room, at the age of eighty-four, he made his living. And when I saw that, I realized that selling was the greatest career a man could want. 'Cause what could be more satisfying than to be able to go, at the age of eighty-four, into twenty or thirty different cities, and pick up a phone, and be remembered and loved and helped by so many different people? Do you know? when he died—and by the way he died the death of a salesman, in his green velvet slippers in the smoker of the New York, New Haven and Hartford, going into Boston—when he died, hundreds of salesmen and buyers were at his funeral. Things were sad on a lotta trains for months after that. (*He stands up.* HOWARD *has not looked at him*) In those days there was personality in it, Howard. There was respect, and comradeship, and gratitude in it. Today, it's all cut and dried, and there's no chance for bringing friendship to bear—or personality. You see what I mean? They don't know me any more.

HOWARD (*Moving away, to the right*) That's just the thing, Willy.

WILLY If I had forty dollars a week—that's all I'd need. Forty dollars, Howard.

HOWARD Kid, I can't take blood from a stone, I—

WILLY (*Desperation is on him now*) Howard, the year Al Smith was nominated, your father came to me and—

HOWARD (*Starting to go off*) I've got to see some people, kid.

WILLY (*Stopping him*) I'm talking about your father! There were promises made across this desk! You mustn't tell me you've got people to see—I put thirty-four years into this firm, Howard, and now I can't pay my insurance! You can't eat the orange and throw the peel away—a man is not a piece of fruit! (*After a pause*) Now pay attention. Your father—in 1928 I had a big year. I averaged a hundred and seventy dollars a week in commissions.

HOWARD (*Impatiently*) Now, Willy, you never averaged—

WILLY (*Banging his hand on the desk*) I averaged a hundred and seventy dollars a week in the year of 1928! And your father came to me—or rather, I was in the office here—it was right over this desk—and he put his hand on my shoulder—

HOWARD (*Getting up*) You'll have to excuse me, Willy, I gotta see some people. Pull yourself together. (*Going out*) I'll be back in a little while.

(*On* HOWARD*'s exit, the light on his chair grows very bright and strange*)

WILLY Pull myself together! What the hell did I say to him? My God, I was yelling at him! How could I! (WILLY *breaks off, staring at the light, which occupies the chair, animating it. He approaches this chair, standing across the desk from it*) Frank, Frank, don't you remember what you told me that time? How you put your hand on my shoulder, and Frank . . . (*He leans on the desk and as he speaks the dead man's name he accidentally switches on the recorder, and instantly*)

HOWARD'S SON ". . . of New York is Albany. The capital of Ohio is Cincinnati, the capital of Rhode Island is . . ." (*The recitation continues*)

WILLY (*Leaping away with fright, shouting*) Ha! Howard! Howard! Howard!

HOWARD (*Rushing in*) What happened?

WILLY (*Pointing at the machine, which continues nasally, childishly, with the capital cities*) Shut it off! Shut it off!

HOWARD (*Pulling the plug out*) Look, Willy . . .

WILLY (*Pressing his hands to his eyes*) I gotta get myself some coffee. I'll get some coffee . . .

(WILLY *starts to walk out.* HOWARD *stops him*)

HOWARD (*Rolling up the cord*) Willy, look . . .

WILLY I'll go to Boston.

HOWARD Willy, you can't go to Boston for us.

WILLY Why can't I go?

HOWARD I don't want you to represent us. I've been meaning to tell you for a long time now.

WILLY Howard, are you firing me?

HOWARD I think you need a good long rest, Willy.

WILLY Howard—

HOWARD And when you feel better, come back, and we'll see if we can work something out.

WILLY But I gotta earn money, Howard. I'm in no position to—

HOWARD Where are your sons? Why don't your sons give you a hand?

WILLY They're working on a very big deal.

HOWARD This is no time for false pride, Willy. You go to your sons and you tell them that you're tired. You've got two great boys, haven't you?

WILLY Oh, no question, no question, but in the meantime . . .

HOWARD Then that's that, heh?

WILLY All right, I'll go to Boston tomorrow.

HOWARD No, no.

WILLY I can't throw myself on my sons. I'm not a cripple!

HOWARD Look, kid, I'm busy this morning.

WILLY (*Grasping* HOWARD*'s arm*) Howard, you've got to let me go to Boston!

HOWARD (*Hard, keeping himself under control*) I've got a line of people to see this morning. Sit down, take five minutes, and pull yourself together, and then go home, will ya? I need the office, Willy. (*He starts to go, turns, remembering the recorder, starts to push off the table holding the recorder*) Oh, yeah. Whenever you can this week, stop by and drop off the samples. You'll feel better, Willy, and then come back and we'll talk. Pull yourself together, kid, there's people outside.

(HOWARD *exits, pushing the table off left.* WILLY *stares into space, exhausted. Now the music is heard—*BEN*'s music—first distantly, then closer,*

*closer. As* WILLY *speaks,* BEN *enters from the right. He carries valise and umbrella*)

WILLY Oh, Ben, how did you do it? What is the answer? Did you wind up the Alaska deal already?

BEN Doesn't take much time if you know what you're doing. Just a short business trip. Boarding ship in an hour. Wanted to say good-by.

WILLY Ben, I've got to talk to you.

BEN (*Glancing at his watch*) Haven't the time, William.

WILLY (*Crossing the apron to* BEN) Ben, nothing's working out. I don't know what to do.

BEN Now, look here, William. I've bought timberland in Alaska and I need a man to look after things for me.

WILLY God, timberland! Me and my boys in those grand outdoors!

BEN You've a new continent at your doorstep, William. Get out of these cities, they're full of talk and time payments and courts of law. Screw on your fists and you can fight for a fortune up there.

WILLY Yes, yes! Linda, Linda!

(LINDA *enters as of old, with the wash*)

LINDA Oh, you're back?

BEN I haven't much time.

WILLY No, wait! Linda, he's got a proposition for me in Alaska.

LINDA But you've got— (*To* BEN) He's got a beautiful job here.

WILLY But in Alaska, kid, I could—

LINDA You're doing well enough, Willy!

BEN (*To* LINDA) Enough for what, my dear?

LINDA (*Frightened of* BEN *and angry at him*) Don't say those things to him! Enough to be happy right here, right now. (*To* WILLY, *while* BEN *laughs*) Why must everybody conquer the world? You're well liked, and the boys love you, and someday— (*To* BEN)—why, old man Wagner told him just the other day that if he keeps it up he'll be a member of the firm, didn't he, Willy?

WILLY Sure, sure. I am building something with this firm, Ben, and if a man is building something he must be on the right track, mustn't he?

BEN What are you building? Lay your hand on it. Where is it?

WILLY (*Hesitantly*) That's true, Linda, there's nothing.

LINDA Why? (*To* BEN) There's a man eighty-four years old—

WILLY That's right, Ben, that's right. When I look at that man I say, what is there to worry about?

BEN Bah!

WILLY It's true, Ben. All he has to do is go into any city, pick up the phone, and he's making his living and you know why?

BEN (*Picking up his valise*) I've got to go.

WILLY (*Holding* BEN *back*) Look at this boy!

(BIFF, *in his high school sweater, enters carrying suitcase.* HAPPY *carries* BIFF'*s shoulder guards, gold helmet, and football pants*)

WILLY Without a penny to his name, three great universities are begging for him, and from there the sky's the limit, because it's not what you do, Ben. It's who you know and the smile on your face! It's contacts, Ben, contacts! The whole wealth of Alaska passes over the lunch table at the Commodore Hotel, and that's the wonder, the wonder of this country, that a man can end with diamonds here on the basis of being liked! (*He turns to* BIFF) And that's why when you get out on that field today it's important. Because thousands of people will be rooting for you and loving you. (*To* BEN, *who has again begun to leave*) And Ben! when he walks into a business office his name will sound out like a bell and all the doors will open to him! I've seen it, Ben, I've seen it a thousand times! You can't feel it with your hand like timber, but it's there!

BEN Good-by, William.

WILLY Ben, am I right? Don't you think I'm right? I value your advice.

BEN There's a new continent at your doorstep, William. You could walk out rich. Rich! (*He is gone*)

WILLY We'll do it here, Ben! You hear me? We're gonna do it here!

(*Young* BERNARD *rushes in. The gay music of the* BOYS *is heard*)

BERNARD Oh, gee, I was afraid you left already!

WILLY Why? What time is it?

BERNARD It's half-past one!

WILLY Well, come on, everybody! Ebbets Field next stop! Where's the pennants? (*He rushes through the wall-line of the kitchen and out into the living-room*)

LINDA (*To* BIFF) Did you pack fresh underwear?

BIFF (*Who has been limbering up*) I want to go!

BERNARD Biff, I'm carrying your helmet, ain't I?

HAPPY No, I'm carrying the helmet.

BERNARD Oh, Biff, you promised me.

HAPPY I'm carrying the helmet.

BERNARD How am I going to get in the locker room?

LINDA Let him carry the shoulder guards. (*She puts her coat and hat on in the kitchen*)

BERNARD Can I, Biff? 'Cause I told everybody I'm going to be in the locker room.

HAPPY In Ebbets Field it's the clubhouse.

BERNARD I meant the clubhouse. Biff!

HAPPY Biff!

BIFF (*Grandly, after a slight pause*) Let him carry the shoulder guards.

HAPPY (*As he gives* BERNARD *the shoulder guards*) Stay close to us now.

(WILLY *rushes in with the pennants*)

WILLY (*Handing them out*) Everybody wave when Biff comes out on the field. (HAPPY *and* BERNARD *run off*) You set now, boy?

(*The music has died away*)

BIFF Ready to go, Pop. Every muscle is ready.

WILLY (*At the edge of the apron*) You realize what this means?

BIFF That's right, Pop.

WILLY (*Feeling* BIFF'*s muscles*) You're comin' home this afternoon captain of the All-Scholastic Championship Team of the City of New York.

BIFF I got it, Pop. And remember, pal, when I take off my helmet, that touchdown is for you.

WILLY Let's go! (*He is starting out, with his arm around* BIFF, *when* CHARLEY *enters, as of old, in knickers*) I got no room for you, Charley.

CHARLEY Room? For what?

WILLY In the car.

CHARLEY You goin' for a ride? I wanted to shoot some casino.

WILLY (*Furiously*) Casino! (*Incredulously*) Don't you realize what today is?

LINDA Oh, he knows, Willy. He's just kidding you.

WILLY That's nothing to kid about!

CHARLEY No, Linda, what's goin' on?

LINDA He's playing in Ebbets Field.

CHARLEY Baseball in this weather?

WILLY Don't talk to him. Come on, come on! (*He is pushing them out*)

CHARLEY Wait a minute, didn't you hear the news?

WILLY What?

CHARLEY Don't you listen to the radio? Ebbets Field just blew up.

WILLY You go to hell! (CHARLEY *laughs. Pushing them out*) Come on, come on! We're late.

CHARLEY (*As they go*) Knock a homer, Biff, knock a homer!

WILLY (*The last to leave, turning to* CHARLEY) I don't think that was funny, Charley. This is the greatest day of his life.

CHARLEY Willy, when are you going to grow up?

WILLY Yeah, heh? When this game is over, Charley, you'll be laughing out of the other side of your face. They'll be calling him another Red Grange. Twenty-five thousand a year.

CHARLEY (*Kidding*) Is that so?

WILLY Yeah, that's so.

CHARLEY Well, then, I'm sorry, Willy. But tell me something.

WILLY What?

CHARLEY Who is Red Grange?

WILLY Put up your hands. Goddam you, put up your hands!

(CHARLEY, *chuckling, shakes his head and walks away, around the left corner of the stage.* WILLY *follows him. The music rises to a mocking frenzy*)

WILLY Who the hell do you think you are, better than everybody else? You don't know everything, you big, ignorant, stupid . . . Put up your hands!

(*Light rises, on the right side of the forestage, on a small table in the reception room of* CHARLEY'S *office. Traffic sounds are heard.* BERNARD, *now mature, sits whistling to himself. A pair of tennis rackets and an overnight bag are on the floor beside him*)

WILLY (*Offstage*) What are you walking away for? Don't walk away! If you're going to say something say it to my face! I know you laugh at me behind my back. You'll laugh out of the other side of your goddam face after this game. Touchdown! Touchdown! Eighty thousand people! Touchdown! Right between the goal posts.

(BERNARD *is a quiet, earnest, but self-assured young man.* WILLY'S *voice is coming from right upstage now.* BERNARD *lowers his feet off the table and listens.* JENNY, *his father's secretary, enters*)

JENNY (*Distressed*) Say, Bernard, will you go out in the hall?

BERNARD What is that noise? Who is it?

JENNY Mr. Loman. He just got off the elevator.

BERNARD (*Getting up*) Who's he arguing with?

JENNY Nobody. There's nobody with him. I can't deal with him any more, and your father gets all upset every time he comes. I've got a lot of typing to do, and your father's waiting to sign it. Will you see him?

WILLY (*Entering*) Touchdown! Touch— (*He sees* JENNY) Jenny, Jenny, good to see you. How're ya? Workin'? Or still honest?

JENNY Fine. How've you been feeling?

WILLY Not much any more, Jenny. Ha, Ha! (*He is surprised to see the rackets*)

BERNARD Hello, Uncle Willy.

WILLY (*Almost shocked*) Bernard! Well, look who's here! (*He comes quickly, guiltily, to* BERNARD *and warmly shakes his hand*)

BERNARD How are you? Good to see you.

WILLY What are you doing here?

BERNARD Oh, just stopped by to see Pop. Get off my feet till my train leaves. I'm going to Washington in a few minutes.

WILLY Is he in?

BERNARD Yes, he's in his office with the accountant. Sit down.

WILLY (*Sitting down*) What're you going to do in Washington?

BERNARD Oh, just a case I've got there, Willy.

WILLY That so? (*Indicating the rackets*) You going to play tennis there?

BERNARD I'm staying with a friend who's got a court.

WILLY Don't say. His own tennis court. Must be fine people, I bet.

BERNARD They are, very nice. Dad tells me Biff's in town.

WILLY (*With a big smile*) Yeah, Biff's in. Working on a very big deal, Bernard.

BERNARD What's Biff doing?

WILLY Well, he's been doing very big things in the West. But he decided to establish himself here. Very big. We're having dinner. Did I hear your wife had a boy?

BERNARD That's right. Our second.

WILLY Two boys! What do you know!

BERNARD What kind of a deal has Biff got?

WILLY Well, Bill Oliver—very big sporting-goods man—he wants Biff very badly. Called him in from the West. Long distance, carte blanche, special deliveries. Your friends have their own private tennis court?

BERNARD You still with the old firm, Willy?

WILLY (*After a pause*) I'm—I'm overjoyed to see how you made the grade, Bernard, overjoyed. It's an encouraging thing to see a young man really—really— Looks very good for Biff—very— (*He breaks *off, then)* Bernard— *(He is so full of emotion, he breaks off again)*

BERNARD What is it, Willy?

WILLY *(Small and alone)* What—what's the secret?

BERNARD What secret?

WILLY How—how did you? Why didn't he ever catch on?

BERNARD I wouldn't know that, Willy.

WILLY *(Confidentially, desperately)* You were his friend, his boyhood friend. There's something I don't understand about it. His life ended after that Ebbets Field game. From the age of seventeen nothing good ever happened to him.

BERNARD He never trained himself for anything.

WILLY But he did, he did. After high school he took so many correspondence courses. Radio mechanics; television; God knows what, and never made the slightest mark.

BERNARD *(Taking off his glasses)* Willy, do you want to talk candidly?

WILLY *(Rising, faces* BERNARD*)* I regard you as a very brilliant man, Bernard. I value your advice.

BERNARD Oh, the hell with the advice, Willy. I couldn't advise you. There's just one thing I've always wanted to ask you. When he was supposed to graduate, and the math teacher flunked him—

WILLY Oh, that son-of-a-bitch ruined his life.

BERNARD Yeah, but, Willy, all he had to do was go to summer school and make up that subject.

WILLY That's right, that's right.

BERNARD Did you tell him not to go to summer school?

WILLY Me? I begged him to go. I ordered him to go!

BERNARD Then why wouldn't he go?

WILLY Why? Why! Bernard, that question has been trailing me like a ghost for the last fifteen years. He flunked the subject, and laid down and died like a hammer hit him!

BERNARD Take it easy, kid.

WILLY Let me talk to you—I got nobody to talk to. Bernard, Bernard, was it my fault? Y'see? It keeps going around in my mind, maybe I did something to him. I got nothing to give him.

BERNARD Don't take it so hard.

WILLY Why did he lay down? What is the story there? You were his friend!

BERNARD Willy, I remember, it was June, and our grades came out. And he'd flunked math.

WILLY That son-of-a-bitch!

BERNARD No, it wasn't right then. Biff just got very angry, I remember, and he was ready to enroll in summer school.

WILLY *(Surprised)* He was?

BERNARD He wasn't beaten by it at all. But then, Willy, he disappeared from the block for almost a month. And I got the idea that he'd gone up to New England to see you. Did he have a talk with you then?

(WILLY *stares in silence)*

BERNARD Willy?

WILLY *(With a strong edge of resentment in his voice)* Yeah, he came to Boston. What about it?

BERNARD Well, just that when he came back—I'll never forget this, it always mystifies me. Because I'd thought so well of Biff, even though he'd always taken advantage of me. I loved him, Willy, y'know? And he came back after that month and took his sneakers—remember those sneakers with "University of Virginia" printed on them? He was so proud of those, wore them every day. And he took them down in the cellar, and burned them up in the furnace. We had a fist fight. It lasted at least half an hour. Just the two of us, punching each other down the cellar, and crying right through it. I've often thought of how strange it was that I knew he'd given up his life. What happened in Boston, Willy?

(WILLY *looks at him as at an intruder)*

BERNARD I just bring it up because you asked me.

WILLY *(Angrily)* Nothing. What do you mean, "What happened?" What's that got to do with anything?

BERNARD Well, don't get sore.

WILLY What are you trying to do, blame it on me? If a boy lays down is that my fault?

BERNARD Now, Willy, don't get—

WILLY Well, don't—don't talk to me that way! What does that mean, "What happened?"

(CHARLEY *enters. He is in his vest, and he carries a bottle of bourbon)*

CHARLEY Hey, you're going to miss that train. *(He waves the bottle)*

BERNARD Yeah, I'm going. *(He takes the bottle)* Thanks, Pop. *(He picks up his rackets and bag)* Good-by, Willy, and don't worry about it. You know, "If at first you don't succeed . . ."

WILLY Yes, I believe in that.

BERNARD But sometimes, Willy, it's better for a man just to walk away.

WILLY Walk away?

BERNARD That's right.

WILLY But if you can't walk away?

BERNARD *(After a slight pause)* I guess that's when it's tough. *(Extending his hand)* Good-by, Willy.

WILLY *(Shaking* BERNARD'S *hand)* Good-by, boy.

CHARLEY *(An arm on* BERNARD'S *shoulder)* How do you like this kid? Gonna argue a case in front of the Supreme Court.

BERNARD *(Protesting)* Pop!

WILLY *(Genuinely shocked, pained, and happy)* No! The Supreme Court!

BERNARD I gotta run. 'By, Dad!

CHARLEY Knock 'em dead, Bernard!

(BERNARD *goes off)*

WILLY *(As* CHARLEY *takes out his wallet)* The Supreme Court! And he didn't even mention it!

CHARLEY *(Counting out money on the desk)* He don't have to—he's gonna do it.

WILLY And you never told him what to do, did you? You never took any interest in him.

CHARLEY My salvation is that I never took any interest in anything. There's some money—fifty dollars. I got an accountant inside.

WILLY Charley, look . . . *(With difficulty)* I got my insurance to pay. If you can manage it—I need a hundred and ten dollars.

(CHARLEY *doesn't reply for a moment; merely stops moving*)

WILLY I'd draw it from my bank but Linda would know, and I . . .

CHARLEY Sit down, Willy.

WILLY (*Moving toward the chair*) I'm keeping an account of everything, remember. I'll pay every penny back. (*He sits*)

CHARLEY Now listen to me, Willy.

WILLY I want you to know I appreciate . . .

CHARLEY (*Sitting down on the table*) Willy, what're you doin'? What the hell is goin' on in your head?

WILLY Why? I'm simply . . .

CHARLEY I offered you a job. You can make fifty dollars a week. And I won't send you on the road.

WILLY I've got a job.

CHARLEY Without pay? What kind of a job is a job without pay? (*He rises*) Now, look, kid, enough is enough. I'm no genius but I know when I'm being insulted.

WILLY Insulted!

CHARLEY Why don't you want to work for me?

WILLY What's the matter with you? I've got a job.

CHARLEY Then what're you walkin' in here every week for?

WILLY (*Getting up*) Well, if you don't want me to walk in here—

CHARLEY I am offering you a job.

WILLY I don't want your goddam job!

CHARLEY When the hell are you going to grow up?

WILLY (*Furiously*) You big ignoramus, if you say that to me again I'll rap you one! I don't care how big you are! (*He's ready to fight*)

(*Pause*)

CHARLEY (*Kindly, going to him*) How much do you need, Willy?

WILLY Charley, I'm strapped, I'm strapped. I don't know what to do. I was just fired.

CHARLEY Howard fired you?

WILLY That snotnose. Imagine that? I named him. I named him Howard.

CHARLEY Willy, when're you gonna realize that them things don't mean anything? You named him Howard, but you can't sell that. The only thing you got in this world is what you can sell. And the funny thing is that you're a salesman, and you don't know that.

WILLY I've always tried to think otherwise, I guess. I always felt that if a man was impressive, and well liked, that nothing—

CHARLEY Why must everybody like you? Who liked J. P. Morgan? Was he impressive? In a Turkish bath he'd look like a butcher. But with his pockets on he was very well liked. Now listen, Willy, I know you don't like me, and nobody can say I'm in love with you, but I'll give you a job because—just for the hell of it, put it that way. Now what do you say?

WILLY I—I just can't work for you, Charley.

CHARLEY What're you, jealous of me?

WILLY I can't work for you, that's all, don't ask me why.

CHARLEY (*Angered, takes out more bills*) You been jealous of me all your life, you damned fool! Here, pay your insurance. (*He puts the money in* WILLY'S *hand*)

WILLY I'm keeping strict accounts.

CHARLEY I've got some work to do. Take care of yourself. And pay your insurance.

WILLY (*Moving to the right*) Funny, y'know? After all the highways, and the trains, and the appointments, and the years, you end up worth more dead than alive.

CHARLEY Willy, nobody's worth nothin' dead. (*After a slight pause*) Did you hear what I said?

(WILLY *stands still, dreaming*)

CHARLEY Willy!

WILLY Apologize to Bernard for me when you see him. I didn't mean to argue with him. He's a fine boy. They're all fine boys, and they'll end up big—all of them. Someday they'll all play tennis together. Wish me luck, Charley. He saw Bill Oliver today.

CHARLEY Good luck.

WILLY (*On the verge of tears*) Charley, you're the only friend I got. Isn't that a remarkable thing? (*He goes out*)

CHARLEY Jesus!

(CHARLEY *stares after him a moment and follows. All light blacks out. Suddenly raucous music is heard, and a red glow rises behind the screen at right.* STANLEY, *a young waiter, appears, carrying a table, followed by* HAPPY, *who is carrying two chairs*)

STANLEY (*Putting the table down*) That's all right, Mr. Loman, I can handle it myself. (*He turns and takes the chairs from* HAPPY *and places them at the table*)

HAPPY (*Glancing around*) Oh, this is better.

STANLEY Sure, in the front there you're in the middle of all kinds a noise. Whenever you got a party, Mr. Loman, you just tell me and I'll put you back here. Y'know, there's a lotta people they don't like it private, because when they go out they like to see a lotta action around them because they're sick and tired to stay in the house by theirself. But I know you, you ain't from Hackensack. You know what I mean?

HAPPY (*Sitting down*) So how's it coming, Stanley?

STANLEY Ah, it's a dog's life. I only wish during the war they'd a took me in the Army. I coulda been dead by now.

HAPPY My brother's back, Stanley.

STANLEY Oh, he come back, heh? From the Far West.

HAPPY Yeah, big cattle man, my brother, so treat him right. And my father's coming too.

STANLEY Oh, your father too!

HAPPY You got a couple of nice lobsters?

STANLEY Hundred per cent, big.

HAPPY I want them with the claws.

STANLEY Don't worry, I don't give you no mice. (HAPPY *laughs*) How about some wine? It'll put a head on the meal.

HAPPY No. You remember, Stanley, that recipe I brought you from overseas? With the champagne in it?

STANLEY Oh, yeah, sure. I still got it tacked up yet in the kitchen. But that'll have to cost a buck apiece anyways.

HAPPY That's all right.

STANLEY What'd you, hit a number or somethin'?

HAPPY No, it's a little celebration. My brother is—I think he pulled off a big deal today. I think we're going into business together.

STANLEY Great! That's the best for you. Because a family business, you know what I mean?—that's the best.

HAPPY That's what I think.

STANLEY 'Cause what's the difference? Somebody steals? It's in the family. Know what I mean? (*Sotto voce*) Like this bartender here. The boss is goin' crazy what kinda leak he's got in the cash register. You put it in but it don't come out.

HAPPY (*Raising his head*) Sh!

STANLEY What?

HAPPY You notice I wasn't lookin' right or left, was I?

STANLEY No.

HAPPY And my eyes are closed.

STANLEY So what's the—?

HAPPY Strudel's comin'.

STANLEY (*Catching on, looks around*) Ah, no, there's no—

(*He breaks off as a furred, lavishly dressed girl enters and sits at the next table. Both follow her with their eyes*)

STANLEY Geez, how'd ya know?

HAPPY I got radar or something. (*Staring directly at her profile*) Oooooooo . . . Stanley.

STANLEY I think that's for you, Mr. Loman.

HAPPY Look at that mouth. Oh, God. And the binoculars.

STANLEY Geez, you got a life, Mr. Loman.

HAPPY Wait on her.

STANLEY (*Going to the* GIRL'*s table*) Would you like a menu, ma'am?

GIRL I'm expecting someone, but I'd like a—

HAPPY Why don't you bring her—excuse me, miss, do you mind? I sell champagne, and I'd like you to try my brand. Bring her a champagne, Stanley.

GIRL That's awfully nice of you.

HAPPY Don't mention it. It's all company money. (*He laughs*)

GIRL That's a charming product to be selling, isn't it?

HAPPY Oh, gets to be like everything else. Selling is selling, y'know.

GIRL I suppose.

HAPPY You don't happen to sell, do you?

GIRL No, I don't sell.

HAPPY Would you object to a compliment from a stranger? You ought to be on a magazine cover.

GIRL (*Looking at him a little archly*) I have been.

(STANLEY *comes in with a glass of champagne*)

HAPPY What'd I say before, Stanley? You see? She's a cover girl.

STANLEY Oh, I could see. I could see.

HAPPY (*To the* GIRL) What magazine?

GIRL Oh, a lot of them. (*She takes the drink*) Thank you.

HAPPY You know what they say in France, don't you? "Champagne is the drink of the complexion"—Hya, Biff!

(BIFF *has entered and sits with* HAPPY)

BIFF Hello, kid. Sorry I'm late.

HAPPY I just got here. Uh, Miss—?

GIRL Forsythe.

HAPPY Miss Forsythe, this is my brother.

BIFF Is Dad here?

HAPPY His name is Biff. You might've heard of him. Great football player.

GIRL Really? What team?

HAPPY Are you familiar with football?

GIRL No, I'm afraid I'm not.

HAPPY Biff is quarterback with the New York Giants.

GIRL Well, that is nice, isn't it? (*She drinks*)

HAPPY Good health.

GIRL I'm happy to meet you.

HAPPY That's my name. Hap. It's really Harold, but at West Point they called me Happy.

GIRL (*Now really impressed*) Oh, I see. How do you do? (*She turns her profile*)

BIFF Isn't Dad coming?

HAPPY You want her?

BIFF Oh, I could never make that.

HAPPY I remember the time that idea would never come into your head. Where's the old confidence, Biff?

BIFF I just saw Oliver—

HAPPY Wait a minute. I've got to see that old confidence again. Do you want her? She's on call.

BIFF Oh, no. (*He turns to look at the* GIRL)

HAPPY I'm telling you. Watch this. (*Turning to the* GIRL) Honey? (*She turns to him*) Are you busy?

GIRL Well, I am . . . but I could make a phone call.

HAPPY Do that, will you, honey? And see if you can get a friend. We'll be here for a while. Biff is one of the greatest football players in the country.

GIRL (*Standing up*) Well, I'm certainly happy to meet you.

HAPPY Come back soon.

GIRL I'll try.

HAPPY Don't try, honey, try hard.

(*The* GIRL *exits.* STANLEY *follows, shaking his head in bewildered admiration*)

HAPPY Isn't that a shame now? A beautiful girl like that? That's why I can't get married. There's not a good woman in a thousand. New York is loaded with them, kid!

BIFF Hap, look—

HAPPY I told you she was on call!

BIFF (*Strangely unnerved*) Cut it out, will ya? I want to say something to you.

HAPPY Did you see Oliver?

BIFF I saw him all right. Now look, I want to tell Dad a couple of things and I want you to help me.

HAPPY What? Is he going to back you?

BIFF Are you crazy? You're out of your goddam head, you know that?

HAPPY Why? What happened?

BIFF (*Breathlessly*) I did a terrible thing today, Hap. It's been the strangest day I ever went through. I'm all numb, I swear.

HAPPY You mean he wouldn't see you?

BIFF Well, I waited six hours for him, see? All day. Kept sending my name in. Even tried to date his secretary so she'd get me to him, but no soap.

HAPPY Because you're not showin' the old confidence, Biff. He remembered you, didn't he?

BIFF (*Stopping* HAPPY *with a gesture*) Finally, about five o'clock, he comes out. Didn't remember who I was or anything. I felt like such an idiot, Hap.

HAPPY Did you tell him my Florida idea?

BIFF He walked away. I saw him for one minute. I got so mad I could've torn the walls down! How the hell did I ever get the idea I was a salesman there? I even believed myself that I'd been a salesman for him! And then he gave me one look and—I realized what a ridiculous lie my whole life has been! We've been talking in a dream for fifteen years. I was a shipping clerk.

HAPPY What'd you do?

BIFF (*With great tension and wonder*) Well, he left, see. And the secretary went out. I was all alone in the waiting-room. I don't know what came over me, Hap. The next thing I know I'm in his office—paneled walls, everything. I can't explain it. I—Hap, I took his fountain pen.

HAPPY Geez, did he catch you?

BIFF I ran out. I ran down all eleven flights. I ran and ran and ran.

HAPPY That was an awful dumb—what'd you do that for?

BIFF (*Agonized*) I don't know, I just—wanted to take something, I don't know. You gotta help me, Hap, I'm gonna tell Pop.

HAPPY You crazy? What for?

BIFF Hap, he's got to understand that I'm not the man somebody lends that kind of money to. He thinks I've been spiting him all these years and it's eating him up.

HAPPY That's just it. You tell him something nice.

BIFF I can't.

HAPPY Say you got a lunch date with Oliver tomorrow.

BIFF So what do I do tomorrow?

HAPPY You leave the house tomorrow and come back at night and say Oliver is thinking it over. And he thinks it over for a couple of weeks, and gradually it fades away and nobody's the worse.

BIFF But it'll go on forever!

HAPPY Dad is never so happy as when he's looking forward to something!

(WILLY *enters*)

HAPPY Hello, scout!

WILLY Gee, I haven't been here in years!

(STANLEY *has followed* WILLY *in and sets a chair for him.* STANLEY *starts off but* HAPPY *stops him*)

HAPPY Stanley!

(STANLEY *stands by, waiting for an order*)

BIFF (*Going to* WILLY *with guilt, as to an invalid*) Sit down, Pop. You want a drink?

WILLY Sure, I don't mind.

BIFF Let's get a load on.

WILLY You look worried.

BIFF N-no. (*To* STANLEY) Scotch all around. Make it doubles.

STANLEY Doubles, right. (*He goes*)

WILLY You had a couple already, didn't you?

BIFF Just a couple, yeah.

WILLY Well, what happened, boy? (*Nodding affirmatively, with a smile*) Everything go all right?

BIFF (*Takes a breath, then reaches out and grasps* WILLY's *hand*) Pal . . . (*He is smiling bravely, and* WILLY *is smiling too*) I had an experience today.

HAPPY Terrific, Pop.

WILLY That so? What happened?

BIFF (*High, slightly alcoholic, above the earth*) I'm going to tell you everything from first to last. It's been a strange day. (*Silence. He looks around, composes himself as best he can, but his breath keeps breaking the rhythm of his voice*) I had to wait quite a while for him, and—

WILLY Oliver?

BIFF Yeah, Oliver. All day, as a matter of cold fact. And a lot of—instances—facts, Pop, facts about my life came back to me. Who was it, Pop? Who ever said I was a salesman with Oliver?

WILLY Well, you were.

BIFF No, Dad, I was a shipping clerk.

WILLY But you were practically—

BIFF (*With determination*) Dad, I don't know who said it first, but I was never a salesman for Bill Oliver.

WILLY What're you talking about?

BIFF Let's hold on to the facts tonight, Pop. We're not going to get anywhere bullin' around. I was a shipping clerk.

WILLY (*Angrily*) All right, now listen to me—

BIFF Why don't you let me finish?

WILLY I'm not interested in stories about the past or any crap of that kind because the woods are burning, boys, you understand? There's a big blaze going on all around. I was fired today.

BIFF (*Shocked*) How could you be?

WILLY I was fired, and I'm looking for a little good news to tell your mother, because the woman has waited and the woman has suffered. The gist of it is that I haven't got a story left in my head, Biff. So don't give me a lecture about facts and aspects. I am not interested. Now what've you got to say to me?

(STANLEY *enters with three drinks. They wait until he leaves*)

WILLY Did you see Oliver?

BIFF Jesus, Dad!

WILLY You mean you didn't go up there?

HAPPY Sure he went up there.

BIFF I did. I—saw him. How could they fire you?

WILLY (*On the edge of his chair*) What kind of a welcome did he give you?

BIFF He won't even let you work on commission?

WILLY I'm out! (*Driving*) So tell me, he gave you a warm welcome?

HAPPY Sure, Pop, sure!

BIFF (*Driven*) Well, it was kind of—

WILLY I was wondering if he'd remember you. (*To* HAPPY) Imagine, man doesn't see him for ten, twelve years and gives him that kind of a welcome!

HAPPY Damn right!

BIFF (*Trying to return to the offensive*) Pop, look—

WILLY You know why he remembered you, don't you? Because you impressed him in those days.

BIFF Let's talk quietly and get this down to the facts, huh?

WILLY (*As though* BIFF *had been interrupting*) Well, what happened? It's great news, Biff. Did he take you into his office or'd you talk in the waiting-room?

BIFF Well, he came in, see, and—

WILLY (*With a big smile*) What'd he say? Betcha he threw his arm around you.

BIFF Well, he kinda—

WILLY He's a fine man. (*To* HAPPY) Very hard man to see, y'know.

HAPPY (*Agreeing*) Oh, I know.

WILLY (*To* BIFF) Is that where you had the drinks?

BIFF Yeah, he gave me a couple of—no, no!

HAPPY (*Cutting in*) He told him my Florida idea.

WILLY Don't interrupt. (*To* BIFF) How'd he react to the Florida idea?

BIFF Dad, will you give me a minute to explain?

WILLY I've been waiting for you to explain since I sat down here! What happened? He took you into his office and what?

BIFF Well—I talked. And—and he listened, see.

WILLY Famous for the way he listens, y'know. What was his answer?

BIFF His answer was— (*He breaks off, suddenly angry*) Dad, you're not letting me tell you what I want to tell you!

WILLY (*Accusing, angered*) You didn't see him, did you?

BIFF I did see him!

WILLY What'd you insult him or something? You insulted him, didn't you?

BIFF Listen, will you let me out of it, will you just let me out of it!

HAPPY What the hell!

WILLY Tell me what happened!

BIFF (*To* HAPPY) I can't talk to him!

(*A single trumpet note jars the ear. The light of green leaves stains the house, which holds the air of night and a dream.* YOUNG BERNARD *enters and knocks on the door of the house*)

YOUNG BERNARD (*Frantically*) Mrs. Loman, Mrs. Loman!

HAPPY Tell him what happened!

BIFF (*To* HAPPY) Shut up and leave me alone!

WILLY No, no! You had to go and flunk math!

BIFF What math? What're you talking about?

YOUNG BERNARD Mrs. Loman, Mrs. Loman!

(LINDA *appears in the house, as of old*)

WILLY (*Wildly*) Math, math, math!

BIFF Take it easy, Pop!

YOUNG BERNARD Mrs. Loman!

WILLY (*Furiously*) If you hadn't flunked you'd've been set by now!

BIFF Now, look, I'm gonna tell you what happened, and you're going to listen to me.

YOUNG BERNARD Mrs. Loman!

BIFF I waited six hours—

HAPPY What the hell are you saying?

BIFF I kept sending in my name but he wouldn't see me. So finally he . . . (*He continues unheard as light fades low on the restaurant*)

YOUNG BERNARD Biff flunked math!

LINDA No!

YOUNG BERNARD Birnbaum flunked him! They won't graduate him!

LINDA But they have to. He's gotta go to the university. Where is he? Biff! Biff!

YOUNG BERNARD No, he left. He went to Grand Central.

LINDA Grand— You mean he went to Boston!

YOUNG BERNARD Is Uncle Willy in Boston?

LINDA Oh, maybe Willy can talk to the teacher. Oh, the poor, poor boy!

(*Light on house area snaps out*)

BIFF (*At the table, now audible, holding up a gold fountain pen*) . . . so I'm washed up with Oliver, you understand? Are you listening to me?

WILLY (*At a loss*) Yeah, sure. If you hadn't flunked—

BIFF Flunked what? What're you talking about?

WILLY Don't blame everything on me! I didn't flunk math—you did! What pen?

HAPPY That was awful dumb, Biff, a pen like that is worth—

WILLY (*Seeing the pen for the first time*) You took Oliver's pen?

BIFF (*Weakening*) Dad, I just explained it to you.

WILLY You stole Bill Oliver's fountain pen!

BIFF I didn't exactly steal it! That's just what I've been explaining to you!

HAPPY He had it in his hand and just then Oliver walked in, so he got nervous and stuck it in his pocket!

WILLY My God, Biff!

BIFF I never intended to do it, Dad!

OPERATOR'S VOICE Standish Arms, good evening!

WILLY (*Shouting*) I'm not in my room!

BIFF (*Frightened*) Dad, what's the matter? (*He and* HAPPY *stand up*)

OPERATOR Ringing Mr. Loman for you!

WILLY I'm not there, stop it!

BIFF (*Horrified, gets down on one knee before* WILLY) Dad, I'll make good, I'll make good. (WILLY *tries to get to his feet.* BIFF *holds him down*) Sit down now.

WILLY No, you're no good, you're no good for anything.

BIFF I am, Dad, I'll find something else, you understand? Now don't worry about anything. (*He holds up* WILLY'*s face*) Talk to me, Dad.

OPERATOR Mr. Loman does not answer. Shall I page him?

WILLY (*Attempting to stand, as though to rush and silence the* OPERATOR) No, no, no!

HAPPY He'll strike something, Pop.

WILLY No, no . . .

BIFF (*Desperately, standing over* WILLY) Pop, listen! Listen to me! I'm telling you something good. Oliver talked to his partner about the Florida idea. You listening? He—he talked to his partner, and he came to me . . . I'm going to be all right, you hear? Dad. listen to me, he said it was just a question of the amount!

WILLY Then you . . . got it?

HAPPY He's gonna be terrific, Pop!

WILLY (*Trying to stand*) Then you got it, haven't you? You got it! You got it!

BIFF (*Agonized, holds* WILLY *down*) No, no. Look, Pop. I'm supposed to have lunch with them tomorrow. I'm just telling you this so you'll know that I can still make an impression, Pop. And I'll make good somewhere, but I can't go tomorrow, see?

WILLY Why not? You simply—

BIFF But the pen, Pop!

WILLY You give it to him and tell him it was an oversight!

HAPPY Sure, have lunch tomorrow!

BIFF I can't say that—

WILLY You were doing a crossword puzzle and accidentally used his pen!

BIFF Listen, kid, I took those balls years ago, now I walk in with his fountain pen? That clinches it, don't you see? I can't face him like that! I'll try elsewhere.

PAGE'S VOICE Paging Mr. Loman!

WILLY Don't you want to be anything?

BIFF Pop, how can I go back?

WILLY You don't want to be anything, is that what's behind it?

BIFF (*Now angry at* WILLY *for not crediting his sympathy*) Don't take it that way! You think it was easy walking into that office after what I'd done to him? A team of horses couldn't have dragged me back to Bill Oliver!

WILLY Then why'd you go?

BIFF Why did I go? Why did I go! Look at you! Look at what's become of you!

(*Off left,* THE WOMAN *laughs*)

WILLY Biff, you're going to go to that lunch tomorrow, or—

BIFF I can't go. I've got no appointment!

HAPPY Biff, for . . . !

WILLY Are you spiting me?

BIFF Don't take it that way! Goddammit!

WILLY (*Strikes* BIFF *and falters away from the table*) You rotten little louse! Are you spiting me?

THE WOMAN Someone's at the door, Willy!

BIFF I'm no good, can't you see what I am?

HAPPY (*Separating them*) Hey, you're in a restaurant! Now cut it out, both of you! (*The girls enter*) Hello, girls, sit down.

(THE WOMAN *laughs, off left*)

MISS FORSYTHE I guess we might as well. This is Letta.

THE WOMAN Willy, are you going to wake up?

BIFF (*Ignoring* WILLY) How're ya, miss, sit down. What do you drink?

MISS FORSYTHE Letta might not be able to stay long.

LETTA I gotta get up very early tomorrow. I got jury duty. I'm so excited! Were you fellows ever on a jury?

BIFF No, but I been in front of them! (*The girls laugh*) This is my father.

LETTA Isn't he cute? Sit down with us, Pop.

HAPPY Sit him down, Biff!

BIFF (*Going to him*) Come on, slugger, drink us under the table. To hell with it! Come on, sit down, pal.

(*On* BIFF'*s last insistence,* WILLY *is about to sit*)

THE WOMAN (*Now urgently*) Willy, are you going to answer the door!

(THE WOMAN'*s call pulls* WILLY *back. He starts right, befuddled*)

BIFF Hey, where are you going?

WILLY Open the door.

BIFF The door?

WILLY The washroom . . . the door . . . where's the door?

BIFF (*Leading* WILLY *to the left*) Just go straight down.

(WILLY *moves left*)

THE WOMAN Willy, Willy, are you going to get up, get up, get up, get up?

(WILLY *exits left*)

LETTA I think it's sweet you bring your daddy along.

MISS FORSYTHE Oh, he isn't really your father!

BIFF (*At left, turning to her resentfully*) Miss Forsythe, you've just seen a prince walk by. A fine, troubled prince. A hard-working, unappreciated prince. A pal, you understand? A good companion. Always for his boys.

LETTA That's so sweet.

HAPPY Well, girls, what's the program? We're wasting time. Come on, Biff. Gather round. Where would you like to go?

BIFF Why don't you do something for him?

HAPPY Me!

BIFF Don't you give a damn for him, Hap?

HAPPY What're you talking about? I'm the one who—

BIFF I sense it, you don't give a good goddam about him. (*He takes the rolled-up hose from his pocket and puts it on the table in front of* HAPPY) Look what I found in the cellar, for Christ's sake. How can you bear to let it go on?

HAPPY Me? Who goes away? Who runs off and—

BIFF Yeah, but he doesn't mean anything to you. You could help him—I can't! Don't you understand what I'm talking about? He's going to kill himself, don't you know that?

HAPPY Don't I know it! Me!

BIFF Hap, help him! Jesus . . . help him . . . Help me, help me, I can't bear to look at his face! (*Ready to weep, he hurries out, up right*)

HAPPY (*Starting after him*) Where are you going?

MISS FORSYTHE What's he so mad about?

HAPPY Come on, girls, we'll catch up with him.

MISS FORSYTHE (*As* HAPPY *pushes her out*) Say, I don't like that temper of his!

HAPPY He's just a little overstrung, he'll be all right!

WILLY (*Off left, as* THE WOMAN *laughs*) Don't answer! Don't answer!

LETTA Don't you want to tell your father—

HAPPY No, that's not my father. He's just a guy. Come on, we'll catch Biff, and, honey, we're going to paint this town! Stanley, where's the check! Hey, Stanley!

(*They exit.* STANLEY *looks toward left*)

STANLEY (*Calling to* HAPPY *indignantly*) Mr. Loman! Mr. Loman!

(STANLEY *picks up a chair and follows them off. Knocking is heard off left.* THE WOMAN *enters, laughing.* WILLY *follows her. She is in a black slip; he is buttoning his shirt. Raw, sensuous music accompanies their speech*)

WILLY Will you stop laughing? Will you stop?

THE WOMAN Aren't you going to answer the door? He'll wake the whole hotel.

WILLY I'm not expecting anybody.

THE WOMAN Whyn't you have another drink, honey, and stop being so damn self-centered?

WILLY I'm so lonely.

THE WOMAN You know you ruined me, Willy? From now on, whenever you come to the office, I'll see that you go right through to the buyers. No waiting at my desk any more, Willy. You ruined me.

WILLY That's nice of you to say that.

THE WOMAN Gee, you are self-centered! Why so sad? You are the saddest, self-centeredest soul I ever did see-saw. (*She laughs. He kisses her*) Come on inside, drummer boy. It's silly to be dressing in the middle of the night. (*As knocking is heard*) Aren't you going to answer the door?

WILLY They're knocking on the wrong door.

THE WOMAN But I felt the knocking. And he heard us talking in here. Maybe the hotel's on fire!

WILLY (*His terror rising*) It's a mistake.

THE WOMAN Then tell him to go away!

WILLY There's nobody there.

THE WOMAN It's getting on my nerves, Willy. There's somebody standing out there and it's getting on my nerves!

WILLY (*Pushing her away from him*) All right, stay in the bathroom here, and don't come out. I think there's a law in Massachusetts about it, so don't come out. It may be that new room clerk. He looked very mean. So don't come out. It's a mistake, there's no fire.

(*The knocking is heard again. He takes a few steps away from her, and she vanishes into the wing. The light follows him, and now he is facing* YOUNG BIFF, *who carries a suitcase.* BIFF *steps toward him. The music is gone*)

BIFF Why didn't you answer?

WILLY Biff! What are you doing in Boston?

BIFF Why didn't you answer? I've been knocking for five minutes, I called you on the phone—

WILLY I just heard you. I was in the bathroom and had the door shut. Did anything happen home?

BIFF Dad—I let you down.

WILLY What do you mean?

BIFF Dad . . .

WILLY Biffo, what's this about? (*Putting his arm around* BIFF) Come on, let's go downstairs and get you a malted.

BIFF Dad, I flunked math.

WILLY Not for the term?

BIFF The term. I haven't got enough credits to graduate.

WILLY You mean to say Bernard wouldn't give you the answers?

BIFF He did, he tried, but I only got a sixty-one.

WILLY And they wouldn't give you four points?

BIFF Birnbaum refused absolutely. I begged him, Pop, but he won't give me those points. You gotta talk to him before they close the school. Because if he saw the kind of man you are, and you just talked to him in your way, I'm sure he'd come through for me. The class came right before practice, see, and I didn't go enough. Would you talk to him? He'd like you, Pop. You know the way you could talk.

WILLY You're on. We'll drive right back.

BIFF Oh, Dad, good work! I'm sure he'll change it for you!

WILLY Go downstairs and tell the clerk I'm checkin' out. Go right down.

BIFF Yes, sir! See, the reason he hates me, Pop—one day he was late for class so I got up at the blackboard and imitated him. I crossed my eyes and talked with a lithp.

WILLY (*Laughing*) You did? The kids like it?

BIFF They nearly died laughing!

WILLY Yeah! What'd you do?

BIFF The thquare root of thixthy twee is . . . (WILLY *bursts out laughing;* BIFF *joins him*) And in the middle of it he walked in!

(WILLY *laughs and* THE WOMAN *joins in offstage*)

WILLY (*Without hesitation*) Hurry downstairs and—

BIFF Somebody in there?

WILLY No, that was next door.

(THE WOMAN *laughs offstage*)

BIFF Somebody got in your bathroom!

WILLY No, it's the next room, there's a party—

THE WOMAN (*Enters, laughing. She lisps this*) Can I come in? There's something in the bathtub, Willy, and it's moving!

(WILLY *looks at* BIFF, *who is staring open-mouthed and horrified at* THE WOMAN)

WILLY Ah—you better go back to your room. They must be finished painting by now. They're painting her room so I let her take a shower here. Go back, go back . . . (*He pushes her*)

THE WOMAN (*Resisting*) But I've got to get dressed, Willy, I can't—

WILLY Get out of here! Go back, go back . . . (*Suddenly striving for the ordinary*) This is Miss Francis, Biff, she's a buyer. They're painting her room. Go back, Miss Francis, go back . . .

THE WOMAN But my clothes, I can't go out naked in the hall!

WILLY (*Pushing her offstage*) Get outa here! Go back, go back!

(BIFF *slowly sits down on his suitcase as the argument continues offstage*)

THE WOMAN Where's my stockings? You promised me stockings, Willy!

WILLY I have no stockings here!

THE WOMAN You had two boxes of size nine sheers for me, and I want them!

WILLY Here, for God's sake, will you get outa here!

THE WOMAN (*Enters holding a box of stockings*) I just hope there's nobody in the hall. That's all I hope. (*To* BIFF) Are you football or baseball?

BIFF Football.

THE WOMAN (*Angry, humiliated*) That's me too. G'night. (*She snatches her clothes from* WILLY, *and walks out*)

WILLY (*After a pause*) Well, better get going. I want to get to the school first thing in the morning. Get my suits out of the closet. I'll get my valise. (BIFF *doesn't move*) What's the matter? (BIFF *remains motionless, tears falling*) She's a buyer. Buys for J. H. Simmons. She lives down the hall—they're painting. You don't imagine— (*He breaks off. After a pause*) Now listen, pal, she's just a buyer. She sees merchandise in her room and they have to keep it looking just so . . . (*Pause. Assuming command*) All right, get my suits. (BIFF *doesn't move*) Now stop crying and do as I say. I gave you an order. Biff, I gave you an order! Is that what you do when I give you an order? How dare you cry! (*Putting his arm around* BIFF) Now look, Biff, when you grow up you'll understand about these things. You mustn't—you mustn't overemphasize a thing like this. I'll see Birnbaum first thing in the morning.

BIFF Never mind.

WILLY (*Getting down beside* BIFF) Never mind! He's going to give you those points. I'll see to it.

BIFF He wouldn't listen to you.

WILLY He certainly will listen to me. You need those points for the U. of Virginia.

BIFF I'm not going there.

WILLY Heh? If I can't get him to change that mark you'll make it up in summer school. You've got all summer to—

BIFF (*His weeping breaking from him*) Dad . . .

WILLY (*Infected by it*) Oh, my boy . . .

BIFF Dad . . .

WILLY She's nothing to me, Biff. I was lonely, I was terribly lonely.

BIFF You—you gave her Mama's stockings! (*His tears break through and he rises to go*)

WILLY (*Grabbing for* BIFF) I gave you an order!

BIFF Don't touch me, you—liar!

WILLY Apologize for that!

BIFF You fake! You phony little fake! You fake! (*Overcome, he turns quickly and weeping fully goes out with his suitcase.* WILLY *is left on the floor on his knees*)

WILLY I gave you an order! Biff, come back here or I'll beat you! Come back here! I'll whip you!

(STANLEY *comes quickly in from the right and stands in front of* WILLY)

WILLY (*Shouts at* STANLEY) I gave you an order . . .

STANLEY Hey, let's pick it up, pick it up, Mr. Loman. (*He helps* WILLY *to his feet*) Your boys left with the chippies. They said they'll see you home.

(*A second waiter watches some distance away*)

WILLY But we were supposed to have dinner together.

(*Music is heard,* WILLY'S *theme*)

STANLEY Can you make it?

WILLY I'll—sure, I can make it. (*Suddenly concerned about his clothes*) Do I—I look all right?

STANLEY Sure, you look all right. (*He flicks a speck off* WILLY'S *lapel*)

WILLY Here—here's a dollar.

STANLEY Oh, your son paid me. It's all right.

WILLY (*Putting it in* STANLEY'S *hand*) No, take it. You're a good boy.

STANLEY Oh, no, you don't have to . . .

WILLY Here—here's some more, I don't need it any more. (*After a slight pause*) Tell me—is there a seed store in the neighborhood?

STANLEY Seeds? You mean like to plant?

(*As* WILLY *turns,* STANLEY *slips the money back into his jacket pocket*)

WILLY Yes. Carrots, peas . . .

STANLEY Well, there's hardware stores on Sixth Avenue, but it may be too late now.

WILLY (*Anxiously*) Oh, I'd better hurry. I've got to get some seeds. (*He starts off to the right*) I've got to get some seeds, right away. Nothing's planted. I don't have a thing in the ground.

(WILLY *hurries out as the light goes down.* STANLEY *moves over to the right after him, watches him off. The other waiter has been staring at* WILLY)

STANLEY (*To the waiter*) Well, whatta you looking at?

(*The waiter picks up the chairs and moves off right.* STANLEY *takes the table and follows him. The light fades on this area. There is a long pause, the sound of the flute coming over. The light gradually rises on the kitchen, which is empty.* HAPPY *appears at the door of the house, followed by* BIFF. HAPPY *is carrying a large bunch of long-stemmed roses. He enters the kitchen, looks around for* LINDA. *Not seeing her, he turns to* BIFF, *who is just outside the house door, and makes a gesture with his hands, indicating "Not here, I guess." He looks into the living-room and freezes. Inside,* LINDA, *unseen, is seated,* WILLY'S *coat on her lap. She rises ominously and quietly and moves toward* HAPPY, *who backs up into the kitchen, afraid*)

HAPPY Hey, what're you doing up? (LINDA *says nothing but moves toward him implacably*) Where's Pop? (*He keeps backing to the right, and now* LINDA *is in full view in the doorway to the living-room*) Is he sleeping?

LINDA Where were you?

HAPPY (*Trying to laugh it off*) We met two girls, Mom, very fine types. Here, we brought you some flowers. (*Offering them to her*) Put them in your room, Ma.

(*She knocks them to the floor at* BIFF*'s feet. He has now come inside and closed the door behind him. She stares at* BIFF, *silent*)

HAPPY Now what'd you do that for? Mom, I want you to have some flowers—

LINDA (*Cutting* HAPPY *off, violently to* BIFF) Don't you care whether he lives or dies?

HAPPY (*Going to the stairs*) Come upstairs, Biff.

BIFF (*With a flare of disgust, to* HAPPY) Go away from me! (*To* LINDA) What do you mean, lives or dies? Nobody's dying around here, pal.

LINDA Get out of my sight! Get out of here!

BIFF I wanna see the boss.

LINDA You're not going near him!

BIFF Where is he? (*He moves into the living-room and* LINDA *follows*)

LINDA (*Shouting after* BIFF) You invite him for dinner. He looks forward to it all day— (BIFF *appears in his parents' bedroom, looks around, and exits*)—and then you desert him there. There's no stranger you'd do that to!

HAPPY Why? He had a swell time with us. Listen, when I— (LINDA *comes back into the kitchen*)—desert him I hope I don't outlive the day!

LINDA Get out of here!

HAPPY Now look, Mom . . .

LINDA Did you have to go to women tonight? You and your lousy rotten whores!

(BIFF *re-enters the kitchen*)

HAPPY Mom, all we did was follow Biff around trying to cheer him up! (*To* BIFF) Boy, what a night you gave me!

LINDA Get out of here, both of you, and don't come back! I don't want you tormenting him any more. Go on now, get your things together! (*To* BIFF) You can sleep in his apartment. (*She starts to pick up the flowers and stops herself*) Pick up this stuff, I'm not your maid any more. Pick it up, you bum, you!

(HAPPY *turns his back to her in refusal.* BIFF *slowly moves over and gets down on his knees, picking up the flowers*)

LINDA You're a pair of animals! Not one, not another living soul would have had the cruelty to walk out on that man in a restaurant!

BIFF (*Not looking at her*) Is that what he said?

LINDA He didn't have to say anything. He was so humiliated he nearly limped when he came in.

HAPPY But, Mom, he had a great time with us—

BIFF (*Cutting him off violently*) Shut up!

(*Without another word,* HAPPY *goes upstairs*)

LINDA You! You didn't even go in to see if he was all right!

BIFF (*Still on the floor in front of* LINDA, *the flowers in his hand; with self-loathing*) No. Didn't. Didn't do a damned thing. How do you like that, heh? Left him babbling in a toilet.

LINDA You louse. You . . .

BIFF Now you hit it on the nose! (*He gets up, throws the flowers in the wastebasket*) The scum of the earth, and you're looking at him!

LINDA Get out of here!

BIFF I gotta talk to the boss, Mom. Where is he?

LINDA You're not going near him. Get out of this house!

BIFF (*With absolute assurance, determination*) No. We're gonna have an abrupt conversation, him and me.

LINDA You're not talking to him!

(*Hammering is heard from outside the house, off right.* BIFF *turns toward the noise*)

LINDA (*Suddenly pleading*) Will you please leave him alone?

BIFF What's he doing out there?

LINDA He's planting the garden!

BIFF (*Quietly*) Now? Oh, my God!

(BIFF *moves outside,* LINDA *following. The light dies down on them and comes up on the center of the apron as* WILLY *walks into it. He is carrying a flashlight, a hoe, and a handful of seed packets. He raps the top of the hoe sharply to fix it firmly, and then moves to the left, measuring off the distance with his foot. He holds the flashlight to look at the seed packets, reading off the instructions. He is in the blue of night*)

WILLY Carrots . . . quarter-inch apart. Rows . . . one-foot rows. (*He measures it off*) One foot. (*He puts down a package and measures off*) Beets. (*He puts down another package and measures again*) Lettuce. (*He reads the package, puts it down*) One foot— (*He breaks off as* BEN *appears at the right and moves slowly down to him*) What a proposition, ts, ts. Terrific, terrific. 'Cause she's suffered, Ben, the woman has suffered. You understand me? A man can't go out the way he came in, Ben, a man has got to add up to something. You can't, you can't (BEN *moves toward him as though to interrupt*) You gotta consider, now. Don't answer so quick. Remember, it's a guaranteed twenty-thousand-dollar proposition. Now look, Ben, I want you to go through the ins and outs of this thing with me. I've got nobody to talk to, Ben, and the woman has suffered, you hear me?

BEN (*Standing still, considering*) What's the proposition?

WILLY It's twenty thousand dollars on the barrelhead. Guaranteed, gilt-edged, you understand?

BEN You don't want to make a fool of yourself. They might not honor the policy.

WILLY How can they dare refuse? Didn't I work like a coolie to meet every premium on the nose? And now they don't pay off? Impossible!

BEN It's called a cowardly thing, William.

WILLY Why? Does it take more guts to stand here the rest of my life ringing up a zero?

BEN (*Yielding*) That's a point, William. (*He moves, thinking, turns*) And twenty thousand—that *is* something one can feel with the hand, it is there.

WILLY (*Now assured, with rising power*) Oh, Ben, that's the whole beauty of it! I see it like a diamond, shining in the dark, hard and rough, that I can pick up and touch in my hand. Not like—like an appointment! This would not be another damned-fool appointment, Ben, and it changes all the aspects. Because he thinks I'm nothing, see, and so he spites me. But the funeral— (*Straightening up*) Ben, that funeral will be massive! They'll come from Maine, Massachusetts, Vermont, New Hampshire! All the old-timers with the strange license plates—that boy will be thunder-struck, Ben, because he never realized—I am known! Rhode Island, New York, New Jersey —I am known, Ben, and he'll see it with his eyes once and for all. He'll see what I am, Ben! He's in for a shock, that boy!

BEN (*Coming down to the edge of the garden*) He'll call you a coward.

WILLY (*Suddenly fearful*) No, that would be terrible.

BEN Yes. And a damned fool.

WILLY No, no, he mustn't, I won't have that! (*He is broken and desperate*)

BEN He'll hate you, William.

(*The gay music of the* BOYS *is heard*)

WILLY Oh, Ben, how do we get back to all the great times? Used to be so full of light, and comradeship, the sleigh-riding in winter, and the ruddiness on his cheeks. And always some kind of good news coming up, always something nice coming up ahead. And never even let me carry the valises in the house, and simonizing, simonizing that little red car! Why, why can't I give him something and not have him hate me?

BEN Let me think about it. (*He glances at his watch*) I still have a little time. Remarkable proposition, but you've got to be sure you're not making a fool of yourself.

(BEN *drifts off upstage and goes out of sight.* BIFF *comes down from the left*)

WILLY (*Suddenly conscious of* BIFF, *turns and looks up at him, then begins picking up the packages of seeds in confusion*) Where the hell is that seed? (*Indignantly*) You can't see nothing out here! They boxed in the whole goddam neighborhood!

BIFF There are people all around here. Don't you realize that?

WILLY I'm busy. Don't bother me.

BIFF (*Taking the hoe from* WILLY) I'm saying good-by to you, Pop. (WILLY *looks at him, silent, unable to move*) I'm not coming back any more.

WILLY You're not going to see Oliver tomorrow?

BIFF I've got no appointment, Dad.

WILLY He put his arm around you, and you've got no appointment?

BIFF Pop, get this now, will you? Everytime I've left it's been a fight that sent me out of here. Today I realized something about myself and I tried to explain it to you and I—I think I'm just not smart enough to make any sense out of it for you. To hell with whose fault it is or anything like that. (*He takes* WILLY'*s arm*) Let's just wrap it up, heh? Come on in, we'll tell Mom. (*He gently tries to pull* WILLY *to left*)

WILLY (*Frozen, immobile, with guilt in his voice*) No, I don't want to see her.

BIFF Come on! (*He pulls again, and* WILLY *tries to pull away*)

WILLY (*Highly nervous*) No, no, I don't want to see her.

BIFF (*Tries to look into* WILLY'*s face, as if to find the answer there*) Why don't you want to see her?

WILLY (*More harshly now*) Don't bother me, will you?

BIFF What do you mean, you don't want to see her? You don't want them calling you yellow, do you? This isn't your fault; it's me, I'm a bum. Now come inside! (WILLY *strains to get away*) Did you hear what I said to you?

(WILLY *pulls away and quickly goes by himself into the house.* BIFF *follows*)

LINDA (*To* WILLY) Did you plant, dear?

BIFF (*At the door, to* LINDA) All right, we had it out. I'm going and I'm not writing any more.

LINDA (*Going to* WILLY *in the kitchen*) I think that's the best way, dear. 'Cause there's no use drawing it out, you'll just never get along.

(WILLY *doesn't respond*)

BIFF People ask where I am and what I'm doing, you don't know, and you don't care. That way it'll be off your mind and you can start brightening up again. All right? That clears it, doesn't it? (WILLY *is silent, and* BIFF *goes to him*) You gonna wish me luck, scout? (*He extends his hand*) What do you say?

LINDA Shake his hand, Willy.

WILLY (*Turning to her, seething with hurt*) There's no necessity to mention the pen at all, y'know.

BIFF (*Gently*) I've got no appointment, Dad.

WILLY (*Erupting fiercely*) He put his arm around . . . ?

BIFF Dad, you're never going to see what I am, so what's the use of arguing? If I strike oil I'll send you a check. Meantime forget I'm alive.

WILLY (*To* LINDA) Spite, see?

BIFF Shake hands, Dad.

WILLY Not my hand.

BIFF I was hoping not to go this way.

WILLY Well, this is the way you're going. Good-by.

(BIFF *looks at him a moment, then turns sharply and goes to the stairs*)

WILLY (*Stops him with*) May you rot in hell if you leave this house!

BIFF (*Turning*) Exactly what is it that you want from me?

WILLY I want you to know, on the train, in the mountains, in the valleys, wherever you go, that you cut down your life for spite!

BIFF No, no.

WILLY Spite, spite, is the word of your undoing! And when you're down and out, remember what did it. When you're rotting somewhere beside the railroad tracks, remember, and don't you dare blame it on me!

BIFF I'm not blaming it on you!

WILLY I won't take the rap for this, you hear?

(HAPPY *comes down the stairs and stands on the bottom step, watching*)

BIFF That's just what I'm telling you!

WILLY (*Sinking into a chair at the table, with full accu-*

*sation*) You're trying to put a knife in me—don't think I don't know what you're doing!

BIFF All right, phony! Then let's lay it on the line. (*He whips the rubber tube out of his pocket and puts it on the table*)

HAPPY You crazy—

LINDA Biff! (*She moves to grab the hose, but* BIFF *holds it down with his hand*)

BIFF Leave it there! Don't move it!

WILLY (*Not looking at it*) What is that?

BIFF You know goddam well what that is.

WILLY (*Caged, wanting to escape*) I never saw that.

BIFF You saw it. The mice didn't bring it into the cellar! What is this supposed to do, make a hero out of you? This supposed to make me sorry for you?

WILLY Never heard of it.

BIFF There'll be no pity for you, you hear it? No pity!

WILLY (*To* LINDA) You hear the spite!

BIFF No, you're going to hear the truth—what you are and what I am!

LINDA Stop it!

WILLY Spite!

HAPPY (*Coming down toward* BIFF) You cut it now!

BIFF (*To* HAPPY) The man don't know who we are! The man is gonna know! (*To* WILLY) We never told the truth for ten minutes in this house!

HAPPY We always told the truth!

BIFF (*Turning on him*) You big blow, are you the assistant buyer? You're one of the two assistants to the assistant, aren't you?

HAPPY Well, I'm practically—

BIFF You're practically full of it! We all are! And I'm through with it. (*To* WILLY) Now hear this, Willy, this is me.

WILLY I know you!

BIFF You know why I had no address for three months? I stole a suit in Kansas City and I was in jail. (*To* LINDA, *who is sobbing*) Stop crying. I'm through with it.

(LINDA *turns away from them, her hands covering her face*)

WILLY I suppose that's my fault!

BIFF I stole myself out of every good job since high school!

WILLY And whose fault is that?

BIFF And I never got anywhere because you blew me so full of hot air I could never stand taking orders from anybody! That's whose fault it is!

WILLY I hear that!

LINDA Don't, Biff!

BIFF It's goddam time you heard that! I had to be boss big shot in two weeks, and I'm through with it!

WILLY Then hang yourself! For spite, hang yourself!

BIFF No! Nobody's hanging himself, Willy! I ran down eleven flights with a pen in my hand today. And suddenly I stopped, you hear me? And in the middle of that office building, do you hear this? I stopped in the middle of that building and I saw—the sky. I saw the things that I love in this world. The work and the food and time to sit and smoke. And I looked at the pen and said to myself, what the hell am I grabbing this for? Why am I trying to become what I don't want to be? What am I doing in an office, making a contemptuous, begging fool of myself, when all I want is out there, waiting for me the minute I say I know who I am! Why can't I say that, Willy? (*He tries to make* WILLY *face him, but* WILLY *pulls away and moves to the left*)

WILLY (*With hatred, threateningly*) The door of your life is wide open!

BIFF Pop! I'm a dime a dozen, and so are you!

WILLY (*Turning on him now in an uncontrolled outburst*) I am not a dime a dozen! I am Willy Loman, and you are Biff Loman!

(BIFF *starts for* WILLY, *but is blocked by* HAPPY. *In his fury,* BIFF *seems on the verge of attacking his father*)

BIFF I am not a leader of men, Willy, and neither are you. You were never anything but a hard-working drummer who landed in the ash can like all the rest of them! I'm one dollar an hour, Willy! I tried seven states and couldn't raise it. A buck an hour! Do you gather my meaning? I'm not bringing home any prizes any more, and you're going to stop waiting for me to bring them home!

WILLY (*Directly to* BIFF) You vengeful, spiteful mutt!

(BIFF *breaks from* HAPPY. WILLY, *in fright, starts up the stairs.* BIFF *grabs him*)

BIFF (*At the peak of his fury*) Pop, I'm nothing! I'm nothing, Pop. Can't you understand that? There's no spite in it any more. I'm just what I am, that's all.

(BIFF'S *fury has spent itself, and he breaks down, sobbing, holding on to* WILLY, *who dumbly fumbles for* BIFF'S *face*)

WILLY (*Astonished*) What're you doing? What're you doing? (*To* LINDA) Why is he crying?

BIFF (*Crying, broken*) Will you let me go, for Christ's sake? Will you take that phony dream and burn it before something happens? (*Struggling to contain himself, he pulls away and moves to the stairs*) I'll go in the morning. Put him—put him to bed. (*Exhausted,* BIFF *moves up the stairs to his room*)

WILLY (*After a long pause, astonished, elevated*) Isn't that—isn't that remarkable? Biff—he likes me!

LINDA He loves you, Willy!

HAPPY (*Deeply moved*) Always did, Pop.

WILLY Oh, Biff! (*Staring wildly*) He cried! Cried to me. (*He is choking with his love, and now cries out his promise*) That boy—that boy is going to be magnificent!

(BEN *appears in the light just outside the kitchen*)

BEN Yes, outstanding, with twenty thousand behind him.

LINDA (*Sensing the racing of his mind, fearfully, carefully*) Now come to bed, Willy. It's all settled now.

WILLY (*Finding it difficult not to rush out of the house*) Yes, we'll sleep. Come on. Go to sleep, Hap.

BEN And it does take a great kind of a man to crack the jungle.

(*In accents of dread,* BEN'S *idyllic music starts up*)

HAPPY (*His arm around* LINDA) I'm getting married, Pop, don't forget it. I'm changing everything. I'm gonna run that department before the year is up. You'll see, Mom. (*He kisses her*)

BEN The jungle is dark but full of diamonds, Willy.

(WILLY *turns, moves, listening to* BEN)

LINDA Be good. You're both good boys, just act that way, that's all.

HAPPY 'Night, Pop. (*He goes upstairs*)

LINDA (*To* WILLY) Come, dear.

BEN (*With greater force*) One must go in to fetch a diamond out.

WILLY (*To* LINDA, *as he moves slowly along the edge of the kitchen, toward the door*) I just want to get settled down, Linda. Let me sit alone for a little.

LINDA (*Almost uttering her fear*) I want you upstairs.

WILLY (*Taking her in his arms*) In a few minutes, Linda. I couldn't sleep right now. Go on, you look awful tired. (*He kisses her*)

BEN Not like an appointment at all. A diamond is rough and hard to the touch.

WILLY Go on now. I'll be right up.

LINDA I think this is the only way, Willy.

WILLY Sure, it's the best thing.

BEN Best thing!

WILLY The only way. Everything is gonna be—go on, kid, get to bed. You look so tired.

LINDA Come right up.

WILLY Two minutes.

(LINDA *goes into the living-room, then reappears in her bedroom.* WILLY *moves just outside the kitchen door*)

WILLY Loves me. (*Wonderingly*) Always loved me. Isn't that a remarkable thing? Ben, he'll worship me for it!

BEN (*With promise*) It's dark there, but full of diamonds.

WILLY Can you imagine that magnificence with twenty thousand dollars in his pocket?

LINDA (*Calling from her room*) Willy! Come up!

WILLY (*Calling into the kitchen*) Yes! Yes. Coming! It's very smart, you realize that, don't you, sweetheart? Even Ben sees it. I gotta go, baby. 'By! 'By! (*Going over to* BEN, *almost dancing*) Imagine? When the mail comes he'll be ahead of Bernard again!

BEN A perfect proposition all around.

WILLY Did you see how he cried to me? Oh, if I could kiss him, Ben!

BEN Time, William, time!

WILLY Oh, Ben, I always knew one way or another we were gonna make it, Biff and I!

BEN (*Looking at his watch*) The boat. We'll be late. (*He moves slowly off into the darkness*)

WILLY (*Elegiacally, turning to the house*) Now when you kick off, boy, I want a seventy-yard boot, and get right down the field under the ball, and when you hit, hit low and hit hard, because it's important, boy. (*He swings around and faces the audience*) There's all kinds of important people in the stands, and the first thing you know . . . (*Suddenly realizing he is alone*) Ben! Ben, where do I . . . ? (*He makes a sudden movement of search*) Ben, how do I . . . ?

LINDA (*Calling*) Willy, you coming up?

WILLY (*Uttering a gasp of fear, whirling about as if to quiet her*) Sh! (*He turns around as if to find his way; sounds, faces, voices, seem to be swarming in upon him and he flicks at them, crying*) Sh! Sh! (*Suddenly music, faint and high, stops him. It rises in intensity, almost to an unbearable scream. He goes up and down on his toes, and rushes off around the house*) Shhh!

LINDA Willy?

(*There is no answer.* LINDA *waits.* BIFF *gets up off his bed. He is still in his clothes.* HAPPY *sits up.* BIFF *stands listening*)

LINDA (*With real fear*) Willy, answer me! Willy!

(*There is the sound of a car starting and moving away at full speed*)

LINDA No!

BIFF (*Rushing down the stairs*) Pop!

(*As the car speeds off, the music crashes down in a frenzy of sound, which becomes the soft pulsation of a single cello string.* BIFF *slowly returns to his bedroom. He and* HAPPY *gravely don their jackets.* LINDA *slowly walks out of her room. The music has developed into a dead march. The leaves of day are appearing over everything.* CHARLEY *and* BERNARD, *somberly dressed, appear and knock on the kitchen door.* BIFF *and* HAPPY *slowly descend the stairs to the kitchen as* CHARLEY *and* BERNARD *enter. All stop a moment when* LINDA, *in clothes of mourning, bearing a little bunch of roses, comes through the draped doorway into the kitchen. She goes to* CHARLEY *and takes his arm. Now all move toward the audience, through the wall-line of the kitchen. At the limit of the apron,* LINDA *lays down the flowers, kneels, and sits back on her heels. All stare down at the grave*)

# Requiem

CHARLEY It's getting dark, Linda.

(LINDA *doesn't react. She stares at the grave*)

BIFF How about it, Mom? Better get some rest, heh? They'll be closing the gate soon.

(LINDA *makes no move. Pause*)

HAPPY (*Deeply angered*) He had no right to do that. There was no necessity for it. We would've helped him.

CHARLEY (*Grunting*) Hmmm.

BIFF Come along, Mom.

LINDA Why didn't anybody come?

CHARLEY It was a very nice funeral.

LINDA But where are all the people he knew? Maybe they blame him.

CHARLEY Naa. It's a rough world, Linda. They wouldn't blame him.

LINDA I can't understand it. At this time especially. First time in thirty-five years we were just about free and clear. He only needed a little salary. He was even finished with the dentist.

CHARLEY No man only needs a little salary.

LINDA I can't understand it.

BIFF There were a lot of nice days. When he'd come home from a trip; or on Sundays, making the stoop; finishing the cellar; putting on the new porch; when he built the extra bathroom; and put up the garage. You know something, Charley, there's more of him in that front stoop than in all the sales he ever made.

CHARLEY Yeah. He was a happy man with a batch of cement.

LINDA He was so wonderful with his hands.

BIFF He had the wrong dreams. All, all, wrong.

HAPPY (*Almost ready to fight* BIFF) Don't say that!

BIFF He never knew who he was.

CHARLEY (*Stopping* HAPPY'S *movement and reply. To* BIFF) Nobody dast blame this man. You don't understand: Willy was a salesman. And for a salesman, there is no rock bottom to the life. He don't put a bolt to a nut, he don't tell you the law or give you medicine. He's a man way out there in the blue, riding on a smile and a shoeshine. And when they start not smiling back—that's an earthquake. And then you get yourself a couple of spots on your hat, and you're finished. Nobody dast blame this man. A salesman is got to dream, boy. It comes with the territory.

BIFF Charley, the man didn't know who he was.

HAPPY (*Infuriated*) Don't say that!

BIFF Why don't you come with me, Happy?

HAPPY I'm not licked that easily. I'm staying right in this city, and I'm gonna beat this racket! (*He looks at* BIFF, *his chin set*) The Loman Brothers!

BIFF I know who I am, kid.

HAPPY All right, boy. I'm gonna show you and everybody else that Willy Loman did not die in vain. He had a good dream. It's the only dream you can have —to come out number-one man. He fought it out here, and this is where I'm gonna win it for him.

BIFF (*With a hopeless glance at* HAPPY, *bends toward his mother*) Let's go, Mom.

LINDA I'll be with you in a minute. Go on, Charley. (*He hesitates*) I want to, just for a minute. I never had a chance to say good-by.

(CHARLEY *moves away, followed by* HAPPY. BIFF *remains a slight distance up and left of* LINDA. *She sits there, summoning herself. The flute begins, not far away, playing behind her speech*)

LINDA Forgive me, dear. I can't cry. I don't know what it is, but I can't cry. I don't understand it. Why did you ever do that? Help me, Willy, I can't cry. It seems to me that you're just on another trip. I keep expecting you. Willy, dear, I can't cry. Why did you do it? I search and search and I search, and I can't understand it, Willy. I made the last payment on the house today. Today, dear. And there'll be nobody home. (*A sob rises in her throat*) We're free and clear. (*Sobbing more fully, released*) We're free. (BIFF *comes slowly toward her*) We're free . . . We're free . . .

(BIFF *lifts her to her feet and moves out up right with her in his arms.* LINDA *sobs quietly.* BERNARD *and* CHARLEY *come together and follow them, followed by* HAPPY. *Only the music of the flute is left on the darkening stage as over the house the hard towers of the apartment buildings rise into sharp focus, and*

*The Curtain Falls*)

# Paddy Chayefsky

## (1923- )

IN THE closing sentences of "1900-1950," the final essay in his *In Search of Theater,* Eric Bentley wrote what must qualify as the faintest praise the mass media have ever received. In his retrospect of the first half of this century, a period marked by extraordinary, if diminishingly remarkable, advances in drama and theatre arts, Bentley concluded: "If (as nothing is eternal) the elimination of theater by its rivals becomes inevitable, we must start thinking wishfully about the future of film and television. As media there is nothing wrong with them." The essay was dated 1949, when television was still innocent in its groping experimentalism. Included in a collection published in 1953, its appearance coincided with awakening hopes that television might, indeed, prove hospitable to drama of high quality. From 1952 until 1957, the networks offered many teleplays stamped with promise, skillfulness, and power, qualities largely absent from Broadway during the same period. Among such young television playwrights as Reginald Rose, Horton Foote, Robert Alan Aurthur, Tad Mosel, Rod Serling, and Paddy Chayefsky could be heard individual voices emergent from an impressively wide background of experience.

Along with Serling, Paddy Chayefsky was the best known of these writers. Without Serling's restlessness and exploratory bent, Chayefsky concentrated on the environment he knew best: he populated his plays with New York garment workers, print shop compositors and linotypists, bookkeepers, butchers, callous weekend wolves prowling the Waverly Ballrooms, and young married couples resisting boredom, babies, and built-in-babysitter grandmothers. To an older generation, Chayefsky's "world of the mundane, the ordinary, and the untheatrical" was reminiscent of the world Odets had chronicled in the middle 1930's. Indeed, Chayefsky has ranked Odets—along with Lillian Hellman (whose *The Children's Hour* he once copied out word-by-word in order to master play structure)—as a major influence on his work: "It would be difficult to find a writer of my generation, especially a New York writer, who doesn't owe his very breath—his entire attitude toward the theater—to Odets." To a younger generation, Chayefsky's characters were as familiar as life itself: stripped of their "New Yorkese," that indistinct but recognizable dialect compounded of Jewish, Irish, Italian, and Radio Announcer idiom and rhythms, his characters and their problems had counterparts in every American metropolitan center.

Commenting on *Marty* as representing "the sort of material that does best on television," Chayefsky wrote: "The main characters are typical, rather than exceptional; the situations are easily identifiable by the audience; and the relationships are as common as people. . . . I tried to write the dialogue as if it had been wire-tapped. I tried to envision the scenes as if a camera had been focused upon the unsuspecting characters and had caught them in an untouched moment of life." His words recall Synge demonstrating how "all art is a collaboration" by reference to the "chink in the floor," the listening-post which opened his mind to the rich living language of servant girls. Like Synge, Chayefsky has been both admired and derided for his eavesdropping as the "master of the tape-recording school of dramatic writing."

Despite the Irish flavor of "Paddy" (a wartime nickname Chayefsky kept for professional identification), Sidney Chayefsky was born in 1923 into what he has called "a standard Jewish family with standard Jewish values." In 1934, when his father faced bankruptcy, the meaning of the Depression was brought home to a boy whose education had been focused on the arts—piano, literature, and, especially through his father's enthusiasm, the popular Yiddish theatre. From the Bronx's DeWitt Clinton High School, where he edited the magazine and newspaper, Chayefsky went to City College. During the second World War, he was a machine gunner. Convalescent in an Army hospital after he had been wounded by an exploding land mine, Chayefsky wrote *No T/O for Love,* a musical comedy produced in London and various Army camps. After the war, when he was working in a print shop, Garson Kanin, a wartime acquaintance, gave him $500 as palpable encouragement to write plays. Before he found his way into television, he was a student at the Hollywood Actors' Lab, a gag writer and occasional nightclub performer, and a writer for motion pictures and radio. Before September, 1952, when *Holiday Song,* adapted from a *Reader's Digest* story, brought him his first television success, Chayefsky wrote for such weekly half-hour programs as "Danger" and "Manhunt."

Working with such energetic young producers and directors as Fred Coe and Delbert Mann on the Sunday evening hour-long dramatic series, the Philco-Goodyear Playhouse, Chayefsky discovered the differences between writing as a journeyman and writing as an artist.

In 1953, his drama, *Marty,* won awards for Chayefsky and for Rod Steiger, the first actor to portray Marty; in early 1956, the filmed *Marty* (expanded, but little altered) received many prizes, not the least of which were Oscars for Ernest Borgnine as Best Actor, and for its producers for the Best Film of 1955.

Until 1957, strong emphasis was placed on original plays which, in network jargon, "emanated live" from New York studios. During this early period, production was in the hands of young men who were encouraged to experiment boldly in order to explore the new medium. After 1957, the center of television operations shifted to California, more emphasis was placed on filmed series with limitless rerun (and resale) possibilities in foreign as well as domestic markets, and the opportunities for television dramatists changed radically. By 1961, it was rare to find teleplays of the stature achieved by Serling's *Requiem for a Heavyweight* or Chayefsky's *Marty*. The showcases for such drama had all but disappeared.

Chayefsky's career after 1957 mirrors these changes clearly. He adapted his own most effective teleplays for films and in the filmed *Bachelor Party,* at least, as the camera followed his roving band of office workers out to recapture a fading footloose youth, Chayefsky approximated the achievement of *Marty*. *Middle of the Night,* Chayefsky's study of a May-October romance, began as a teleplay in 1954; it was adapted first for Broadway production; when Edward G. Robinson completed a long and successful run in the play, Chayefsky rewrote it for the films. With *The Goddess,* Chayefsky wrote directly for motion pictures. In detailing Emily Ann Faulkner's progress from an unhappy childhood in a fundamentalist Maryland town to precarious fame in Hollywood as the "Goddess" Rita Shawn, Chayefsky abandoned his familiar New York locales but not the themes of loneliness and quiet heroism which appear in all of his plays. In moving with such ease from television to Broadway and Hollywood, he invited the charge that he was a mere pieman responding to "show business" pressures to peddle his wares while they were still hot in every available market. In fact, however, Chayefsky was learning the facts of life about drama in the Age of Mass Communications. Not only was he becoming expert in the limitations and the challenges of each medium, but he was learning that a good play, honestly conceived and well written, will always find production and will always draw audiences. He was also learning that, if he had any hope of preserving the integrity of his works, he must exercise his auctorial rights by preparing them himself for their transfers from one medium to another.

In November, 1959, when *The Tenth Man* opened for a long and successful run, Chayefsky came full circle: once again he was writing directly for the theatre. For his tragicomic study of bedeviled moderns, he created a run-down synagogue in which a *dybbuk* (evil spirit) is exorcised and unbelievers, old and young alike, glimpse a lost faith. Reflecting a widespread mid-century concern, Chayefsky described his intentions: "All I meant to say was that it is better to have faith in something—some form of dedication—than to believe in nothing, for belief in nothing is utter futility and endless despair." In what may indicate a deepening of his interests, Chayefsky prepared to write *The Tenth Man* by doing months of "the most enjoyable research" on Jewish mysticism, and by reading European folk comedies, older Yiddish drama, and the works of Zuckmayer and Molnár. In his concern to leave "literal reality" behind him, Chayefsky was rediscovering a rich source of dramatic materials in Jewish drama. When Louis Kronenberger described *The Tenth Man* as a combination of "surrealism and photography, insanity and farce, demonology and Freud," he might also have been describing the dramatic tradition in which Ansky's *The Dybbuk* had been conceived. After *The Tenth Man,* Chayefsky took his wife and children on a trip to Israel and, for his next play, turned his attention to the Biblical figure of Gideon and the visitations of the Angel of God who stirs him to greatness.

In all his plays, Chayefsky has focused attention on the Affirming Man, a theme sometimes traced back to the television writer's responsiveness to sponsors' demands for cheer and moral uplift in television drama. As his work has developed, however, it has become clear that Chayefsky is responsive, not to sponsors, but to the little victories through which moderns assert their humanity. In *Middle of the Night,* the protagonist reaches dignity by taking the calculated risk of marrying a lonely young woman who will always be mistaken for his daughter; in *The Mother,* an elderly woman insists that her married children allow her to work and take care of herself. Although *The Tenth Man* disappointed some critics because of its ending, Chayefsky showed how, when "a skeptical young man who is a suicidal maniac and a devout Jewish girl, a catatonic schizophrenic who seems possessed by evil spirits, go and get married," they defy the odds which may still doom them to lives of "utter futility and endless despair." The unbeliever, recruited to complete the quorum for morning prayers in a Mineola synagogue, surmounts his boredom in a world from which he has never quite managed to dispatch himself ("I have tried to commit suicide so many times now it has become something of a family joke"). Marty Pilletti is also bored—with the endless questions about his marital prospects, with the regular week-end debates with Angie ("Well, what do you feel like doing tonight?"), with his self-disgust over being "a fat, ugly little man," worrying from year to year whether he can find a date for New Year's Eve. With all the dignity and innocence of a Chaplin tramp, Marty makes *his* affirming gesture: lifting "a determined finger," he dials "a dog." It is a small gesture, but it signifies Chayefsky's understanding of dramatic art.

# MARTY

## CAST

MARTY PILLETTI
CLARA DAVIS
ANGIE
MOTHER
AUNT CATHERINE
VIRGINIA
THOMAS
YOUNG MAN
CRITIC
BARTENDER
TWENTY-YEAR-OLD
ITALIAN WOMAN
SHORT GIRL
GIRL
YOUNG MOTHER
STAG
FORTY-YEAR-OLD

## Act One

FADE IN: *A butcher shop in the Italian district of New York City. Actually, we fade in on a close-up of a butcher's saw being carefully worked through a side of beef, and we dolly back to show the butcher at work, and then the whole shop. The butcher is a mild-mannered, stout, short, balding young man of thirty-six. His charm lies in an almost indestructible good-natured amiability.*

*The shop contains three women customers. One is a* YOUNG MOTHER *with a baby carriage. She is chatting with a second woman of about forty at the door. The customer being waited on at the moment is a stout, elderly* ITALIAN WOMAN *who is standing on tiptoe, peering over the white display counter, checking the butcher as he saws away.*

ITALIAN WOMAN Your kid brother got married last Sunday, eh, Marty?

MARTY (*Absorbed in his work*) That's right, Missus Fusari. It was a very nice affair.

ITALIAN WOMAN That's the big tall one, the fellow with the mustache.

MARTY (*Sawing away*) No, that's my other brother Freddie. My other brother Freddie, he's been married four years already. He lives down on Quincy Street. The one who got married Sunday, that was my little brother Nickie.

ITALIAN WOMAN I thought he was a big, tall, fat fellow. Didn't I meet him here one time? Big, tall, fat fellow, he tried to sell me life insurance?

MARTY (*Sets the cut of meat on the scale, watches its weight register*) No, that's my sister Margaret's husband Frank. My sister Margaret, she's married to the insurance salesman. My sister Rose, she married a contractor. They moved to Detroit last year. And my other sister, Frances, she got married about two and a half years ago in Saint John's Church on Adams Boulevard. Oh, that was a big affair. Well, Missus Fusari, that'll be three dollars, ninety-four cents. How's that with you?

(*The* ITALIAN WOMAN *produces an old leather change purse from her pocketbook and painfully extracts three single dollar bills and ninety-four cents to the penny and lays the money piece by piece on the counter*)

YOUNG MOTHER (*Calling from the door*) Hey, Marty, I'm inna hurry.

MARTY (*Wrapping the meat, calls amiably back*) You're next right now, Missus Canduso.

(*The old* ITALIAN WOMAN *has been regarding* MARTY *with a baleful scowl*)

ITALIAN WOMAN Well, Marty, when you gonna get married? You should be ashamed. All your brothers and sisters, they all younger than you, and they married, and they got children. I just saw your mother inna fruit shop, and she says to me: "Hey, you know a nice girl for my boy Marty?" Watsa matter with you? That's no way. Watsa matter with you? Now, you get married, you hear me what I say?

MARTY (*Amiably*) I hear you, Missus Fusari.

(*The old lady takes her parcel of meat, but apparently feels she still hasn't quite made her point*)

ITALIAN WOMAN My son Frank, he was married when he was nineteen years old. Watsa matter with you?

MARTY Missus Fusari, Missus Canduso over there, she's inna big hurry, and . . .

ITALIAN WOMAN You be ashamed of yourself.

(*She takes her package of meat, turns, and shuffles to the door and exits.* MARTY *gathers up the money on the counter, turns to the cash register behind him to ring up the sale*)

YOUNG MOTHER Marty, I want a nice big fat pullet, about four pounds. I hear your kid brother got married last Sunday.

MARTY Yeah, it was a very nice affair, Missus Canduso.

YOUNG MOTHER Marty, you oughtta be ashamed. All your kid brothers and sisters, married and have children. When you gonna get married?

(CLOSE-UP: MARTY. *He sends a glance of weary exasperation up to the ceiling. With a gesture of mild irritation, he pushes the plunger of the cash register. It makes a sharp ping.*

DISSOLVE TO: *Close-up of television set. A baseball game is in progress. Camera pulls back to show we are in a typical neighborhood bar—red leatherette booths—a jukebox, some phone booths. About half the bar stools are occupied by neighborhood folk.* MARTY *enters, pads amiably to one of the booths where a young man of about thirty-odd already sits. This is* ANGIE. MARTY *slides into the booth across from* ANGIE. ANGIE *is a little wasp of a fellow. He has a newspaper spread out before him to the sports pages.* MARTY *reaches over and pulls one of the pages over for himself to read. For a moment the two friends sit across from each other, reading the sports pages. Then* ANGIE, *without looking up, speaks*)

ANGIE Well, what do you feel like doing tonight?

MARTY I don't know, Angie. What do you feel like doing?

ANGIE Well, we oughtta do something. It's Saturday night. I don't wanna go bowling like last Saturday. How about calling up that big girl we picked up inna movies about a month ago in the RKO Chester?

MARTY (*Not very interested*) Which one was that?

ANGIE That big girl that was sitting in front of us with the skinny friend.

MARTY Oh, yeah.

ANGIE We took them home alla way out in Brooklyn. Her name was Mary Feeney. What do you say? You think I oughtta give her a ring? I'll take the skinny one.

MARTY It's five o'clock already, Angie. She's probably got a date by now.

ANGIE Well, let's call her up. What can we lose?

MARTY I didn't like her, Angie. I don't feel like calling her up.

ANGIE Well, what do you feel like doing tonight?

MARTY I don't know. What do you feel like doing?

ANGIE Well, we're back to that, huh? I say to you: "What do you feel like doing tonight?" And you say to me: "I don't know, what do you feel like doing?" And then we wind up sitting around your house with a couple of cans of beer, watching Sid Caesar on television. Well, I tell you what I feel like doing. I feel like calling up this Mary Feeney. She likes you.

(MARTY *looks up quickly at this*)

MARTY What makes you say that?

ANGIE I could see she likes you.

MARTY Yeah, sure.

ANGIE (*Half rising in his seat*) I'll call her up.

MARTY You call her up for yourself, Angie. I don't feel like calling her up.

(ANGIE *sits down again. They both return to reading the paper for a moment. Then* ANGIE *looks up again*)

ANGIE Boy, you're getting to be a real drag, you know that?

MARTY Angie, I'm thirty-six years old. I been looking for a girl every Saturday night of my life. I'm a little, short, fat fellow, and girls don't go for me, that's all. I'm not like you. I mean, you joke around, and they laugh at you, and you get along fine. I just stand around like a bug. What's the sense of kidding myself? Everybody's always telling me to get married. Get married. Get married. Don't you think I wanna get married? I wanna get married. They drive me crazy. Now, I don't wanna wreck your Saturday night for you, Angie. You wanna go somewhere, you go ahead. I don't wanna go.

ANGIE Boy, they drive me crazy too. My old lady, every word outta her mouth, when you gonna get married?

MARTY My mother, boy, she drives me crazy.

(ANGIE *leans back in his seat, scowls at the paper-napkin container.* MARTY *returns to the sports page. For a moment a silence hangs between them. Then . . .*)

ANGIE So what do you feel like doing tonight?

MARTY (*Without looking up*) I don't know. What do you feel like doing?

(*They both just sit,* ANGIE *frowning at the napkin container,* MARTY *at the sports page.*

*The camera slowly moves away from the booth, looks down the length of the bar, up the wall, past the clock—which reads ten to five—and over to the television screen, where the baseball game is still going on.*

DISSOLVE SLOWLY TO: *The television screen, now blank. The clock now reads a quarter to six.*

*Back in the booth,* MARTY *now sits alone. In front of him are three empty beer bottles and a beer glass, half filled. He is sitting there, his face expressionless, but his eyes troubled. Then he pushes himself slowly out of the booth and shuffles to the phone booth; he goes inside, closing the booth door carefully after him. For a moment* MARTY *just sits squatly. Then with some exertion—due to the cramped quarters—he contrives to get a small address book out of his rear pants pocket. He slowly flips through it, finds the page he wants, and studies it, scowling; then he takes a dime from the change he has just received, plunks it into the proper slot, waits for a dial tone . . . then carefully dials a number. . . . He waits. He is beginning to sweat a bit in the hot little booth, and his chest begins to rise and fall deeply)*

MARTY (*With a vague pretense at good diction*) Hello, is this Mary Feeney? . . . Could I please speak to Miss Mary Feeney? . . . Just tell her an old friend . . .

(*He waits again. With his free hand he wipes the gathering sweat from his brow*)

. . . Oh, hello there, is this Mary Feeney? Hello there, this is Marty Pilletti. I wonder if you recall me . . . Well, I'm kind of a stocky guy. The last time we met was inna movies, the RKO Chester. You was with another girl, and I was with a friend of mine name Angie. This was about a month ago . . .

(*The girl apparently doesn't remember him. A sort of panic begins to seize* MARTY. *His voice rises a little*)

The RKO Chester on Payne Boulevard. You was sitting in front of us, and we was annoying you, and you got mad, and . . . I'm the fellow who works inna butcher shop . . . come on, you know who I am! . . . That's right, we went to Howard Johnson's and we had hamburgers. You hadda milk shake . . . Yeah, that's right. I'm the stocky one, the heavy-set fellow. . . . Well, I'm glad you recall me, because I hadda swell time that night, and I was just wondering how everything was with you. How's everything? . . . That's swell . . . Yeah, well, I'll tell you why I called . . . I was figuring on taking in a movie tonight, and I was wondering if you and your friend would care to see a movie tonight with me and my friend . . . (*His eyes are closed now.*) Yeah, tonight. I know it's pretty late to call for a date, but I didn't know myself till . . . Yeah, I know, well how about . . . Yeah, I know, well maybe next Saturday night. You free next Saturday night? . . . Well, how about the Saturday after that? . . . Yeah, I know . . . Yeah . . . Yeah . . . Oh, I understand, I mean . . .

(*He just sits now, his eyes closed, not really listening. After a moment he returns the receiver to its cradle and sits, his shoulders slack, his hands resting listlessly in the lap of his spotted white apron. . . . Then he opens his eyes, straightens himself, pushes the booth door open, and advances out into the bar. He perches on a stool across the bar from the* BARTENDER, *who looks up from his magazine*)

BARTENDER I hear your kid brother got married last week, Marty.

MARTY (*Looking down at his hands on the bar*) Yeah, it was a very nice affair.

BARTENDER Well, Marty, when you gonna get married?

(MARTY *tenders the bartender a quick scowl, gets off his perch, and starts for the door—untying his apron as he goes*)

MARTY If my mother calls up, Lou, tell her I'm on my way home.

(DISSOLVE TO: *Marty's* MOTHER *and a young couple sitting around the table in the dinning room of Marty's home. The young couple—we will soon find out—are* THOMAS, *Marty's cousin, and his wife,* VIRGINIA. *They have apparently just been telling the mother some sad news, and the three are sitting around frowning.*

*The dining room is a crowded room filled with chairs and lamps, pictures and little statues, perhaps even a small grotto of little vigil lamps. To the right of the dining room is the kitchen, old-fashioned, Italian, steaming, and overcrowded. To the left of the dining room is the living room, furnished in same fashion as the dining room. Just off the living room is a small bedroom, which is Marty's. This bedroom and the living room have windows looking out on front. The dining room has windows looking out to side alleyway. A stairway in the dining room leads to the second floor.*

*The* MOTHER *is a round, dark, effusive little woman*)

MOTHER (*After a pause*) Well, Thomas, I knew sooner or later this was gonna happen. I told Marty, I said: "Marty, you watch. There's gonna be real trouble over there in your cousin Thomas' house." Because your mother was here, Thomas, you know?

THOMAS When was this, Aunt Theresa?

MOTHER This was one, two, three days ago. Wednesday. Because I went to the fruit shop on Wednesday, and I came home. And I come arounna back, and there's your mother sitting onna steps onna porch. And I said: "Catherine, my sister, wadda you doing here?" And she look uppa me, and she beganna cry.

THOMAS (*To his wife*) Wednesday. That was the day you threw the milk bottle.

MOTHER That's right. Because I said to her: "Catherine, watsa matter?" And she said to me: "Theresa, my daughter-in-law, Virginia, she just threw the milk bottle at me."

VIRGINIA Well, you see what happen, Aunt Theresa . . .

MOTHER I know, I know . . .

VIRGINIA She comes inna kitchen, and she begins poking her head over my shoulder here and poking her head over my shoulder there . . .

MOTHER I know, I know . . .

VIRGINIA And she begins complaining about this, and she begins complaining about that. And she got me so nervous, I spilled some milk I was making for the baby. You see, I was making some food for the baby, and . . .

MOTHER So I said to her, "Catherine . . ."

VIRGINIA So, she got me so nervous I spilled some milk. So she said: "You're spilling the milk." She says: "Milk costs twenty-four cents a bottle. Wadda you, a banker?" So I said: "Mama, leave me alone, please. You're making me nervous. Go on in the other room and turn on the television set." So then she began telling me how I waste money, and how I can't cook, and how I'm raising my baby all wrong, and she kept talking about these couple of drops of milk I spilt, and I got so mad, I said: "Mama, you wanna see me really spill some milk?" So I took the bottle and threw it against the door. I didn't throw it at her. That's just something she made up. I didn't throw it anywheres near her. Well, of course, alla milk went all over the floor. The whole twenty-four cents. Well, I was sorry right away, you know, but she ran outta the house.

(*Pause*)

MOTHER Well, I don't know what you want me to do, Virginia. If you want me, I'll go talk to her tonight.

(THOMAS *and* VIRGINIA *suddenly frown and look down at their hands as if of one mind*)

THOMAS Well, I'll tell you, Aunt Theresa . . .

VIRGINIA Lemme tell it, Tommy.

THOMAS Okay.

VIRGINIA (*Leaning forward to the* MOTHER) We want you to do a very big favor for us, Aunt Theresa.

MOTHER Sure.

VIRGINIA Aunt Theresa, you got this big house here. You got four bedrooms upstairs. I mean, you got this big house just for you and Marty. All your other kids are married and got their own homes. And I thought maybe Tommy's mother could come here and live with you and Marty.

MOTHER Well . . .

VIRGINIA She's miserable living with Tommy and me, and you're the only one that gets along with her. Because I called up Tommy's brother, Joe, and I said: "Joe, she's driving me crazy. Why don't you take her for a couple of years?" And he said: "Oh, no!" I know I sound like a terrible woman . . .

MOTHER No, Virginia, I know how you feel. My husband, may God bless his memory, his mother, she lived with us for a long time, and I know how you feel.

VIRGINIA (*Practically on the verge of tears*) I just can't stand it no more! Every minute of the day! Do this! Do that! I don't have ten minutes alone with my husband! We can't even have a fight! We don't have no privacy! Everybody's miserable in our house!

THOMAS All right, Ginnie, don't get so excited.

MOTHER She's right. She's right. Young husband and wife, they should have their own home. And my sister, Catherine, she's my sister, but I gotta admit, she's an old goat. And plenny-a times in my life I feel like throwing the milk bottle at her myself. And I tell you now, as far as I'm concerned, if Catherine wantsa come live here with me and Marty, it's all right with me.

(VIRGINIA *promptly bursts into tears*)

THOMAS (*Not far from tears himself, lowers his face*) That's very nice-a you, Aunt Theresa.

MOTHER We gotta ask Marty, of course, because this is his house too. But he's gonna come home any minute now.

VIRGINIA (*Having mastered her tears*) That's very nice-a you, Aunt Theresa.

MOTHER (*Rising*) Now, you just sit here. I'm just gonna turn onna small fire under the food.

(*She exits into the kitchen*)

VIRGINIA (*Calling after her*) We gotta go right away because I promised the baby sitter we'd be home by six, and it's after six now . . .

(*She kind of fades out. A moment of silence.* THOMAS *takes out a cigarette and lights it*)

THOMAS (*Calling to his aunt in the kitchen*) How's Marty been lately, Aunt Theresa?

MOTHER (*Off in kitchen*) Oh, he's fine. You know a nice girl he can marry?

(*She comes back into the dining room, wiping her hands on a kitchen towel*)

I'm worried about him, you know? He's thirty-six years old, gonna be thirty-seven in January.

THOMAS Oh, he'll get married, don't worry, Aunt Theresa.

MOTHER (*Sitting down again*) Well, I don't know. You know a place where he can go where he can find a bride?

THOMAS The Waverly Ballroom. That's a good place to meet girls, Aunt Theresa. That's a kind of big dance hall, Aunt Theresa. Every Saturday night, it's just loaded with girls. It's a nice place to go. You pay seventy-seven cents. It used to be seventy-seven cents. It must be about a buck and a half now. And you go in and you ask some girl to dance. That's how I met Virginia. Nice, respectable place to meet girls. You tell Marty, Aunt Theresa, you tell him: "Go to the Waverly Ballroom. It's loaded with tomatoes."

MOTHER (*Committing the line to memory*) The Waverly Ballroom. It's loaded with tomatoes.

THOMAS Right.

VIRGINIA You tell him, go to the Waverly Ballroom.

(*There is the sound of a door being unlatched off through the kitchen. The* MOTHER *promptly rises*)

MOTHER He's here.

(*She hurries into the kitchen. At the porch entrance to the kitchen,* MARTY *has just come in. He is closing the door behind him. He carries his butcher's apron in a bundle under his arm*)

MARTY Hello, Ma.

(*She comes up to him, lowers her voice to a whisper*)

MOTHER (*Whispers*) Marty, Thomas and Virginia are here. They had another big fight with your Aunt Catherine. So they ask me, would it be all right if Catherine come to live with us. So I said, all right with me, but we have to ask you. Marty, she's a lonely old lady. Nobody wants her. Everybody's throwing her outta their house. . . .

MARTY Sure, Ma, it's okay with me.

(*The* MOTHER*'s face breaks into a fond smile. She reaches up and pats his cheek with genuine affection*)

MOTHER You gotta good heart. (*Turning and leading the way back to the dining room.* THOMAS *has risen*) He says okay, it's all right Catherine comes here.

THOMAS Oh, Marty, thanks a lot. That really takes a load offa my mind.

MARTY Oh, we got plenny-a room here.

MOTHER Sure! Sure! It's gonna be nice! It's gonna be nice! I'll come over tonight to your house, and I talk to Catherine, and you see, everything is gonna work out all right.

THOMAS I just wanna thank you people again because the situation was just becoming impossible.

MOTHER Siddown, Thomas, siddown. All right, Marty, siddown. . . .

(*She exits into the kitchen.*

MARTY *has taken his seat at the head of the table and is waiting to be served.* THOMAS *takes a seat around the corner of the table from him and leans across to him*)

THOMAS You see, Marty, the kinda thing that's been happening in our house is Virginia was inna kitchen making some food for the baby. Well, my mother comes in, and she gets Virginia so nervous, she spills a couple-a drops . . .

VIRGINIA (*Tugging at her husband*) Tommy, we gotta go. I promise the baby sitter six o'clock.

THOMAS (*Rising without interrupting his narrative*) So she starts yelling at Virginia, waddaya spilling the milk for. So Virginia gets mad . . .

(*His wife is slowly pulling him to the kitchen door*) She says, "You wanna really see me spill milk?" So Virginia takes the bottle and she throws it against the wall. She's got a real Italian temper, my wife, you know that . . .

(*He has been tugged to the kitchen door by now*)

VIRGINIA Marty, I don't have to tell you how much we appreciate what your mother and you are doing for us.

THOMAS All right, Marty, I'll see you some other time . . . I'll tell you all about it.

MARTY I'll see you, Tommy.

(THOMAS *disappears into the kitchen after his wife*)

VIRGINIA (*Off, calling*) Good-by, Marty!

(*Close in on* MARTY, *sitting at table*)

MARTY Good-by, Virginia! See you soon!

(*He folds his hands on the table before him and waits to be served.*

*The* MOTHER *enters from the kitchen. She sets the meat plate down in front of him and herself takes a chair around the corner of the table from him.* MARTY *without a word takes up his knife and fork and attacks the mountain of food in front of him. His mother sits quietly, her hands a little nervous on the table before her, watching him eat. Then . . .*)

MOTHER So what are you gonna do tonight, Marty?

MARTY I don't know, Ma. I'm all knocked out. I may just hang arounna house.

(*The* MOTHER *nods a couple of times. There is a moment of silence. Then . . .*)

MOTHER Why don't you go to the Waverly Ballroom?

(*This gives* MARTY *pause. He looks up*)

MARTY What?

MOTHER I say, why don't you go to the Waverly Ballroom? It's loaded with tomatoes.

(MARTY *regards his mother for a moment*)

MARTY It's loaded with what?

MOTHER Tomatoes.

MARTY (*Snorts*) Ha! Who told you about the Waverly Ballroom?

MOTHER Thomas, he told me it was a very nice place.

MARTY Oh, Thomas. Ma, it's just a big dance hall, and that's all it is. I been there a hundred times. Loaded with tomatoes. Boy, you're funny, Ma.

MOTHER Marty, I don't want you hang arounna house tonight. I want you to go take a shave and go out and dance.

MARTY Ma, when are you gonna give up? You gotta bachelor on your hands. I ain't never gonna get married.

MOTHER You gonna get married.

MARTY Sooner or later, there comes a point in a man's life when he gotta face some facts, and one fact I gotta face is that whatever it is that women like, I ain't got it. I chased enough girls in my life. I went to enough dances. I got hurt enough. I don't wanna get hurt no more. I just called a girl this afternoon, and I got a real brush-off, boy. I figured I was past the point of being hurt, but that hurt. Some stupid woman who I didn't even wanna call up. She gave me the brush. That's the history of my life. I don't wanna go to the Waverly Ballroom because all that ever happened to me there was girls made me feel like I was a bug. I got feelings, you know. I had enough pain. No, thank you.

MOTHER Marty . . .

MARTY Ma, I'm gonna stay home and watch Sid Caesar.

MOTHER You gonna die without a son.

MARTY So I'll die without a son.

MOTHER Put on your blue suit . . .

MARTY Blue suit, gray suit, I'm still a fat little man. A fat little ugly man.

MOTHER You not ugly.

MARTY (*His voice rising*) I'm ugly . . . I'm ugly! . . . I'm UGLY!

MOTHER Marty . . .

MARTY (*Crying aloud, more in anguish than in anger*) Ma! Leave me alone! . . .

(*He stands abruptly, his face pained and drawn. He makes half-formed gestures to his mother, but he can't find words at the moment. He turns and marches a few paces away, turns to his mother again*)

MARTY Ma, waddaya want from me?! Waddaya want from me?! I'm miserable enough as it is! Leave me alone! I'll go to the Waverly Ballroom! I'll put onna blue suit and I'll go! And you know what I'm gonna get for my trouble? Heartache! A big night of heartache!

(*He sullenly marches back to his seat, sits down, picks up his fork, plunges it into the lasagna, and stuffs a mouthful into his mouth; he chews vigorously for a moment. It is impossible to remain angry for long. After a while he is shaking his head and muttering*)

MARTY Loaded with tomatoes . . . boy, that's rich . . .

*(He plunges his fork in again. Camera pulls slowly away from him and his mother, who is seated—watching him)*

*Fade Out*

# Act Two

FADE IN: *Exterior, three-story building. Pan up to second floor . . . bright neon lights reading "Waverly Ballroom" . . . The large, dirty windows are open; and the sound of a fair-to-middling swing band whooping it up comes out.*

DISSOLVE TO: *Interior, Waverly Ballroom—large dance floor crowded with jitterbugging couples, eight-piece combination hitting a loud kick. Ballroom is vaguely dark, made so by papier-mâché over the chandeliers to create alleged romantic effect. The walls are lined with stags and waiting girls, singly and in small murmuring groups. Noise and mumble and drone.*

DISSOLVE TO: *Live shot—a row of stags along a wall. Camera is looking lengthwise down the row. Camera dollies slowly past each face, each staring out at the dance floor, watching in his own manner of hungry eagerness. Short, fat, tall, thin stags. Some pretend diffidence. Some exhibit patent hunger.*

*Near the end of the line, we find* MARTY *and* ANGIE, *freshly shaved and groomed. They are leaning against the wall, smoking, watching their more fortunate brethren out on the floor.*

ANGIE Not a bad crowd tonight, you know?

MARTY There was one nice-looking one there in a black dress and beads, but she was a little tall for me.

ANGIE *(Looking down past* MARTY *along the wall right into the camera)* There's a nice-looking little short one for you right now.

MARTY *(Following his gaze)* Where?

ANGIE Down there. That little one there.

*(The camera cuts about eight faces down, to where the girls are now standing. Two are against the wall. One is facing them, with her back to the dance floor. This last is the one* ANGIE *has in mind. She is a cute little kid, about twenty, and she has a bright smile on—as if the other two girls are just amusing her to death)*

MARTY Yeah, she looks all right from here.

ANGIE Well, go on over and ask her. You don't hurry up, somebody else'll grab her.

*(*MARTY *scowls, shrugs)*

MARTY Okay, let's go.

*(They slouch along past the eight stags, a picture of nonchalant unconcern. The three girls, aware of their approach, stiffen, and their chatter comes to a halt.* ANGIE *advances to one of the girls along the wall)*

ANGIE Waddaya say, you wanna dance?

*(The girl looks surprised—as if this were an extraordinary invitation to receive in this place—looks confounded at her two friends, shrugs, detaches herself from the group, moves to the outer fringe of the pack of dancers, raises her hand languidly to dancing position, and awaits* ANGIE *with ineffable boredom.* MARTY, *smiling shyly, addresses the short girl)*

MARTY Excuse me, would you care for this dance?

*(The short girl gives* MARTY *a quick glance of appraisal, then looks quickly at her remaining friend)*

SHORT GIRL *(Not unpleasantly)* Sorry. I just don't feel like dancing just yet.

MARTY Sure.

*(He turns and moves back past the eight stags, all of whom have covertly watched his attempt. He finds his old niche by the wall, leans there. A moment later he looks guardedly down to where the short girl and her friend are. A young, dapper boy is approaching the short girl. He asks her to dance. The short girl smiles, excuses herself to her friend, and follows the boy out onto the floor.* MARTY *turns back to watching the dancers bleakly. A moment later he is aware that someone on his right is talking to him. . . . He turns his head. It is a young man of about twenty-eight)*

MARTY You say something to me?

YOUNG MAN Yeah. I was just asking you if you was here stag or with a girl.

MARTY I'm stag.

YOUNG MAN Well, I'll tell you. I got stuck onna blind date with a dog, and I just picked up a nice chick, and I was wondering how I'm gonna get ridda the dog. Somebody to take her home, you know what I mean? I be glad to pay you five bucks if you take the dog home for me.

MARTY *(A little confused)* What?

YOUNG MAN I'll take you over, and I'll introduce you as an old army buddy of mine, and then I'll cut out. Because I got this chick waiting for me out by the hatcheck, and I'll pay you five bucks.

MARTY *(Stares at the* YOUNG MAN*)* Are you kidding?

YOUNG MAN No, I'm not kidding.

MARTY You can't just walk off onna girl like that.

*(The* YOUNG MAN *grimaces impatiently and moves down the line of stags. . . .* MARTY *watches him, still a little shocked at the proposition. About two stags down, the* YOUNG MAN *broaches his plan to another* STAG. *This* STAG, *frowning and pursing his lips, seems more receptive to the idea. . . . The* YOUNG MAN *takes out a wallet and gives the* STAG *a five-dollar bill. The* STAG *detaches himself from the wall and, a little ill at ease, follows the* YOUNG MAN *back past* MARTY *and into the lounge.* MARTY

*pauses a moment and then, concerned, walks to the archway that separates the lounge from the ballroom and looks in.*

*The lounge is a narrow room with a bar and booths. In contrast to the ballroom, it is brightly lighted—causing* MARTY *to squint.*

*In the second booth from the archway sits a* GIRL, *about twenty-eight. Despite the careful grooming that she has put into her cosmetics, she is blatantly plain. The* YOUNG MAN *and the* STAG *are standing, talking to her. She is looking up at the* YOUNG MAN, *her hands nervously gripping her Coca-Cola glass. We cannot hear what the* YOUNG MAN *is saying, but it is apparent that he is introducing his new-found army buddy and is going through some cock-and-bull story about being called away on an emergency. The* STAG *is presented as her escort-to-be, who will see to it that she gets home safely. The* GIRL *apparently is not taken in at all by this, though she is trying hard not to seem affected.*

*She politely rejects the* STAG'*s company and will get home by herself, thanks for asking anyway. The* YOUNG MAN *makes a few mild protestations, and then he and the* STAG *leave the booth and come back to the archway from where* MARTY *has been watching the scene. As they pass* MARTY, *we overhear a snatch of dialogue)*

YOUNG MAN . . . In that case, as long as she's going home alone, give me the five bucks back. . . .

STAG . . . Look, Mac, you paid me five bucks. I was willing. It's my five bucks. . . .

(*They pass on.* MARTY *returns his attention to the* GIRL. *She is still sitting as she was, gripping and ungripping the glass of Coca-Cola in front of her. Her eyes are closed. Then, with a little nervous shake of her head, she gets out of the booth and stands—momentarily at a loss for what to do next. The open fire doors leading out onto the large fire escape catch her eye. She crosses to the fire escape, nervous, frowning, and disappears outside.*

MARTY *stares after her, then slowly shuffles to the open fire-escape doorway. It is a large fire escape, almost the size of a small balcony. The* GIRL *is standing by the railing, her back to the doorway, her head slunk on her bosom. For a moment* MARTY *is unaware that she is crying. Then he notices the shivering tremors running through her body and the quivering shoulders. He moves a step onto the fire escape. He tries to think of something to say)*

MARTY Excuse me, Miss. Would you care to dance?

(*The* GIRL *slowly turns to him, her face streaked with tears, her lip trembling. Then, in one of those peculiar moments of simultaneous impulse, she lurches to* MARTY *with a sob, and* MARTY *takes her to him. For a moment they stand in an awkward embrace,* MARTY *a little embarrassed, looking out through the doors to the lounge, wondering if anybody is seeing them. Reaching back with one hand, he closes the fire doors, and then, replacing the hand around her shoulder, he stands stiffly, allowing her to cry on his chest.*

DISSOLVE TO: *Exterior, apartment door. The* MOTHER *is standing, in a black coat and a hat with a little feather, waiting for her ring to be answered. The door opens.* VIRGINIA *stands framed in the doorway)*

VIRGINIA Hello, Aunt Theresa, come in.

(*The* MOTHER *goes into the small foyer.* VIRGINIA *closes the door)*

MOTHER (*In a low voice, as she pulls her coat off*) Is Catherine here?

VIRGINIA (*Helps her off with coat, nods—also in a low voice*) We didn't tell her nothing yet. We thought we'd leave it to you. We thought you'd put it like how you were lonely, and why don't she come to live with you. Because that way it looks like she's doing you a favor, insteada we're throwing her out, and it won't be so cruel on her. Thomas is downstairs with the neighbors . . . I'll go call him.

MOTHER You go downstairs to the neighbors and stay there with Thomas.

VIRGINIA Wouldn't it be better if we were here?

MOTHER You go downstairs. I talk to Catherine alone. Otherwise, she's gonna start a fight with you.

(*A shrill, imperious woman's voice from an offstage room suddenly breaks into the muttered conference in the foyer)*

AUNT (*Off*) Who's there?! Who's there?!

(*The* MOTHER *heads up the foyer to the living room, followed by* VIRGINIA, *holding the* MOTHER'*s coat)*

MOTHER (*Calls back*) It's me, Catherine! How you feel?

(*At the end of the foyer, the two sisters meet. The* AUNT *is a spare, gaunt woman with a face carved out of granite. Tough, embittered, deeply hurt type of face)*

AUNT Hey! What are you doing here?

MOTHER I came to see you. (*The two sisters quickly embrace and release each other*) How you feel?

AUNT I gotta pain in my left side and my leg throbs like a drum.

MOTHER I been getting pains in my shoulder.

AUNT I got pains in my shoulder, too. I have a pain in my hip, and my right arm aches so much I can't sleep. It's a curse to be old. How you feel?

MOTHER I feel fine.

AUNT That's nice.

(*Now that the standard greetings are over,* AUNT CATHERINE *abruptly turns and goes back to her chair. It is obviously her chair. It is an old, heavy oaken chair with thick armrests. The rest of the apartment is furnished in what is known as "modern"—a piece from* House Beautiful *here, a piece from* Better Homes and Gardens *there.* AUNT CATHERINE *sits, erect and forbidding, in her chair. The* MOTHER *seats herself with a sigh in a neighboring chair.* VIRGINIA, *having hung the* MOTHER'*s coat, now turns to the two older women. A pause)*

VIRGINIA I'm going downstairs to the Cappacini's. I'll be up inna little while.

(AUNT CATHERINE *nods expressionlessly.* VIRGINIA

*looks at her for a moment, then impulsively crosses to her mother-in-law)*

VIRGINIA You feel all right?

*(The old lady looks up warily, suspicious of this sudden solicitude)*

AUNT I'm all right.

*(*VIRGINIA *nods and goes off to the foyer. The two old sisters sit, unmoving, waiting for the door to close behind* VIRGINIA. *Then the* MOTHER *addresses herself to* AUNT CATHERINE*)*

MOTHER We gotta post card from my son, Nickie, and his bride this morning. They're in Florida inna big hotel. Everything is very nice.

AUNT That's nice.

MOTHER Catherine, I want you come live with me in my house with Marty and me. In my house, you have your own room. You don't have to sleep onna couch inna living room like here.

*(The* AUNT *looks slowly and directly at the* MOTHER*)*

Catherine, your son is married. He got his own home. Leave him in peace. He wants to be alone with his wife. They don't want no old lady sitting inna balcony. Come and live with me. We will cook in the kitchen and talk like when we were girls. You are dear to me, and you are dear to Marty. We are pleased for you to come.

AUNT Did they come to see you?

MOTHER Yes.

AUNT Did my son Thomas come with her?

MOTHER Your son Thomas was there.

AUNT Did he also say he wishes to cast his mother from his house?

MOTHER Catherine, don't make an opera outta this. The three-a you anna baby live in three skinny rooms. You are an old goat, and she has an Italian temper. She is a good girl, but you drive her crazy. Leave them alone. They have their own life.

*(The old* AUNT *turns her head slowly and looks her sister square in the face. Then she rises slowly from her chair)*

AUNT *(Coldly)* Get outta here. This is my son's house. This is where I live. I am not to be cast out inna street like a newspaper.

*(The* MOTHER *likewise rises. The two old women face each other directly)*

MOTHER Catherine, you are very dear to me. We have cried many times together. When my husband died, I would have gone insane if it were not for you. I ask you to come to my house because I can make you happy. Please come to my house.

*(The two sisters regard each other. Then* AUNT CATHERINE *sits again in her oaken chair, and the* MOTHER *returns to her seat. The hardened muscles in the old* AUNT*'s face suddenly slacken, and she turns to her sister)*

AUNT Theresa, what shall become of me?

MOTHER Catherine . . .

AUNT It's gonna happen to you. Mark it well. These terrible years. I'm afraida look inna mirror. I'm afraid I'm gonna see an old lady with white hair, like the old ladies inna park, little bundles inna black shawl, waiting for the coffin. I'm fifty-six years old. What am I to do with myself? I have strength in my hands. I wanna cook. I wanna clean. I wanna make dinner for my children. I wanna be of use to somebody. Am I an old dog to lie in fronta the fire till my eyes close? These are terrible years, Theresa! Terrible years!

MOTHER Catherine, my sister . . .

*(The old* AUNT *stares, distraught, at the* MOTHER*)*

AUNT It's gonna happen to you! It's gonna happen to you! What will you do if Marty gets married?! What will you cook?! What happen to alla children tumbling in alla rooms?! Where is the noise?! It is a curse to be a widow! A curse! What will you do if Marty gets married?! What will you do?!

*(She stares at the* MOTHER*—her deep, gaunt eyes haggard and pained. The* MOTHER *stares back for a moment, then her own eyes close. The* AUNT *has hit home. The* AUNT *sinks back onto her chair, sitting stiffly, her arms on the thick armrests. The* MOTHER *sits hunched a little forward, her hands nervously folded in her lap)*

AUNT *(Quietly)* I will put my clothes inna bag and I will come to you tomorrow.

*(The camera slowly dollies back from the two somber sisters.*

SLOW FADE-OUT.

CUT TO *Close-up, intimate,* MARTY *and the* GIRL *dancing cheek to cheek. Occasionally the heads of other couples slowly waft across the camera view, temporarily blocking out view of* MARTY *and the* GIRL. *Camera stays with them as the slow dance carries them around the floor. Tender scene)*

GIRL . . . The last time I was here the same sort of thing happened.

MARTY Yeah?

GIRL Well, not exactly the same thing. The last time I was up here about four months ago. Do you see that girl in the gray dress sitting over there?

MARTY Yeah.

GIRL That's where I sat. I sat there for an hour and a half without moving a muscle. Now and then, some fellow would sort of walk up to me and then change his mind. I just sat there, my hands in my lap. Well, about ten o'clock, a bunch of kids came in swaggering. They weren't more than seventeen, eighteen years old. Well, they swaggered down along the wall, leering at all the girls. I thought they were kind of cute . . . and as they passed me, I smiled at them. One of the kids looked at me and said: "Forget it, ugly, you ain't gotta chance." I burst out crying. I'm a big crier, you know.

MARTY So am I.

GIRL And another time when I was in college . . .

MARTY I cry alla time. Any little thing. I can recognize pain a mile away. My brothers, my brother-in-laws, they're always telling me what a goodhearted guy I am. Well, you don't get goodhearted by accident. You get kicked around long enough you get to be a real professor of pain. I know exactly how you feel. And I also want you to know I'm having a very good time with you now and really enjoying myself. So you see, you're not such a dog as you think you are.

GIRL I'm having a very good time too.

MARTY So there you are. So I guess I'm not such a dog as I think I am.

GIRL You're a very nice guy, and I don't know why some girl hasn't grabbed you off long ago.

MARTY I don't know either. I think I'm a very nice guy. I also think I'm a pretty smart guy in my own way.

GIRL I think you are.

MARTY I'll tell you some of my wisdom which I thunk up on those nights when I got stood up, and nights like that, and you walk home thinking: "Watsa matter with me? I can't be that ugly." Well, I figure, two people get married, and they gonna live together forty, fifty years. So it's just gotta be more than whether they're good-looking or not. My father was a real ugly man, but my mother adored him. She told me that she used to get so miserable sometimes, like everybody, you know? And she says my father always tried to understand. I used to see them sometimes when I was a kid, sitting in the living room, talking and talking, and I used to adore my old man because he was so kind. That's one of the most beautiful things I have in my life, the way my father and my mother were. And my father was a real ugly man. So it don't matter if you look like a gorilla. So you see, dogs like us, we ain't such dogs as we think we are.

(*They dance silently for a moment, cheeks pressed against each other. Close-ups of each face*)

GIRL I'm twenty-nine years old. How old are you?

MARTY Thirty-six.

(*They dance silently, closely. Occasionally the heads of other couples sway in front of the camera, blocking our view of* MARTY *and the* GIRL. *Slow, sweet dissolve.*

DISSOLVE TO: *Interior, kitchen,* MARTY'*s home. Later that night. It is dark. Nobody is home. The rear porch door now opens, and the silhouettes of* MARTY *and the* GIRL *appear—blocking up the doorway*)

MARTY Wait a minute. Lemme find the light.

(*He finds the light. The kitchen is suddenly brightly lit. The two of them stand squinting to adjust to the sudden glare*)

MARTY I guess my mother ain't home yet. I figure my cousin Thomas and Virginia musta gone to the movies, so they won't get back till one o'clock, at least.

(*The* GIRL *has advanced into the kitchen, a little ill at ease, and is looking around.* MARTY *closes the porch door*)

MARTY This is the kitchen.

GIRL Yes, I know.

(MARTY *leads the way into the dining room*)

MARTY Come on inna dining room. (*He turns on the light in there as he goes. The* GIRL *follows him in*) Siddown, take off your coat. You want something to eat? We gotta whole halfa chicken left over from yesterday.

GIRL (*Perching tentatively on the edge of a chair*) No, thank you. I don't think I should stay very long.

MARTY Sure. Just take off your coat a minute.

(*He helps her off with her coat and stands for a moment behind her, looking down at her. Conscious of his scrutiny, she sits uncomfortably, her breasts rising and falling unevenly.* MARTY *takes her coat into the dark living room. The* GIRL *sits patiently, nervously.* MARTY *comes back, sits down on another chair. Awkward silence*)

MARTY So I was telling you, my kid brother Nickie got married last Sunday . . . That was a very nice affair. And they had this statue of some woman, and they had whisky spouting outta her mouth. I never saw anything so grand in my life. (*The silence falls between them again.*) And watta meal. I'm a butcher, so I know a good hunka steak when I see one. That was choice filet, right off the toppa the chuck. A buck-eighty a pound. Of course, if you wanna cheaper cut, get rib steak. That gotta lotta waste on it, but it comes to about a buck and a quarter a pound, if it's trimmed. Listen, Clara, make yourself comfortable. You're all tense.

GIRL Oh, I'm fine.

MARTY You want me to take you home, I'll take you home.

GIRL Maybe that would be a good idea.

(*She stands. He stands, frowning, a little angry—turns sullenly and goes back into the living room for her coat. She stands unhappily. He comes back and wordlessly starts to help her into her coat. He stands behind her, his hands on her shoulders. He suddenly seizes her, begins kissing her on the neck. Camera comes up quickly to intensely intimate close-up, nothing but the heads. The dialogue drops to quick, hushed whispers*)

GIRL No, Marty, please . . .

MARTY I like you, I like you, I been telling you all night I like you . . .

GIRL Marty . . .

MARTY I just wanna kiss, that's all . . .

(*He tries to turn her face to him. She resists*)

GIRL No . . .

MARTY Please . . .

GIRL No . . .

MARTY Please . . .

GIRL Marty . . .

(*He suddenly releases her, turns away violently*)

MARTY (*Crying out*) All right! I'll take you home! All right! (*He marches a few angry paces away, deeply disturbed. Turns to her*) All I wanted was a lousy kiss! What am I, a leper or something?!

(*He turns and goes off into the living room to hide the flush of hot tears threatening to fill his eyes. The* GIRL *stands, herself on the verge of tears*)

GIRL (*Mutters, more to herself than to him*) I just didn't feel like it, that's all.

(*She moves slowly to the archway leading to the

*living room.* MARTY *is sitting on the couch, hands in his lap, looking straight ahead. The room is dark except for the overcast of the dining-room light reaching in. The* GIRL *goes to the couch, perches on the edge beside him. He doesn't look at her*)

MARTY Well, that's the history of my life. I'm a little, short, fat, ugly guy. Comes New Year's Eve, everybody starts arranging parties, I'm the guy they gotta dig up a date for. I'm old enough to know better. Let me get a packa cigarettes, and I'll take you home.

(*He starts to rise, but doesn't . . . sinks back onto the couch, looking straight ahead. The* GIRL *looks at him, her face peculiarly soft and compassionate*)

GIRL I'd like to see you again, very much. The reason I didn't let you kiss me was because I just didn't know how to handle the situation. You're the kindest man I ever met. The reason I tell you this is because I want to see you again very much. Maybe, I'm just so desperate to fall in love that I'm trying too hard. But I know that when you take me home, I'm going to just lie on my bed and think about you. I want very much to see you again.

(MARTY *stares down at his hands in his lap*)

MARTY (*Without looking at her*) Waddaya doing tomorrow night?

GIRL Nothing.

MARTY I'll call you up tomorrow morning. Maybe we'll go see a movie.

GIRL I'd like that very much.

MARTY The reason I can't be definite about it now is my Aunt Catherine is probably coming over tomorrow, and I may have to help out.

GIRL I'll wait for your call.

MARTY We better get started to your house because the buses only run about one an hour now.

GIRL All right.

(*She stands*)

MARTY I'll just get a packa cigarettes.

(*He goes into his bedroom. We can see him through the doorway, opening his bureau drawer and extracting a pack of cigarettes. He comes out again and looks at the girl for the first time. They start to walk to the dining room. In the archway,* MARTY *pauses, turns to the* GIRL)

MARTY Waddaya doing New Year's Eve?

GIRL Nothing.

(*They quietly slip into each other's arms and kiss. Slowly their faces part, and* MARTY*'s head sinks down upon her shoulder. He is crying. His shoulders shake slightly. The* GIRL *presses her cheek against the back of his head. They stand . . . there is the sound of the rear porch door being unlatched. They both start from their embrace. A moment later the* MOTHER*'s voice is heard off in the kitchen*)

MOTHER Hallo! Hallo, Marty? (*She comes into the dining room, stops at the sight of the* GIRL) Hallo, Marty, when you come home?

MARTY We just got here about fifteen minutes ago, Ma. Ma, I want you to meet Miss Clara Davis. She's a graduate of New York University. She teaches history in Benjamin Franklin High School.

(*This seems to impress the* MOTHER)

MOTHER Siddown, siddown. You want some chicken? We got some chicken in the icebox.

GIRL No, Mrs. Pilletti, we were just going home. Thank you very much anyway.

MOTHER Well, siddown a minute. I just come inna house. I'll take off my coat. Siddown a minute.

(*She pulls her coat off*)

MARTY How'd you come home, Ma? Thomas give you a ride?

(*The* MOTHER *nods*)

MOTHER Oh, it's a sad business, a sad business.

(*She sits down on a dining-room chair, holding her coat in her lap. She turns to the* GIRL, *who likewise sits*)

MOTHER My sister Catherine, she don't get along with her daughter-in-law, so she's gonna come live with us.

MARTY Oh, she's coming, eh, Ma?

MOTHER Oh, sure. (*To the* GIRL) It's a very sad thing. A woman, fifty-six years old, all her life, she had her own home. Now, she's just an old lady, sleeping on her daughter-in-law's couch. It's a curse to be a mother, I tell you. Your children grow up and then what is left for you to do? What is a mother's life but her children? It is a very cruel thing when your son has no place for you in his home.

GIRL Couldn't she find some sort of hobby to fill out her time?

MOTHER Hobby! What can she do? She cooks and she cleans. You gotta have a house to clean. You gotta have children to cook for. These are the terrible years for a woman, the terrible years.

GIRL You mustn't feel too harshly against her daughter-in-law. She also wants to have a house to clean and a family to cook for.

(*The* MOTHER *darts a quick, sharp look at the* GIRL*—then looks back to her hands, which are beginning to twist nervously*)

MOTHER You don't think my sister Catherine should live in her daughter-in-law's house?

GIRL Well, I don't know the people, of course, but, as a rule, I don't think a mother-in-law should live with a young couple.

MOTHER Where do you think a mother-in-law should go?

GIRL I don't think a mother should depend so much upon her children for her rewards in life.

MOTHER That's what it says in the book in New York University. You wait till you are a mother. It don't work out that way.

GIRL Well, it's silly for me to argue about it. I don't know the people involved.

MARTY Ma, I'm gonna take her home now. It's getting late, and the buses only run about one an hour.

MOTHER (*Standing*) Sure.

(*The* GIRL *stands*)

GIRL It was very nice meeting you, Mrs. Pilletti. I hope I'll see you again.

MOTHER Sure.

(MARTY *and the girl move to the kitchen*)

MARTY All right, Ma. I'll be back in about an hour.

MOTHER Sure.

GIRL Good night, Mrs. Pilletti.

MOTHER Good night.

(MARTY *and the* GIRL *exit into the kitchen. The* MOTHER *stands, expressionless, by her chair watching them go. She remains standing rigidly even after the porch door can be heard being opened and shut. The camera moves up to a close-up of the* MOTHER. *Her eyes are wide. She is staring straight ahead. There is fear in her eyes*)

*Fade Out*

# Act Three

FADE IN *Film—close-up of church bells clanging away. Pan down church to see typical Sunday morning, people going up the steps of a church and entering. It is a beautiful June morning.*

DISSOLVE TO *Interior, Marty's bedroom—sun fairly streaming through the curtains.* MARTY *is standing in front of his bureau, slipping his arms into a clean white shirt. He is freshly shaved and groomed. Through the doorway of his bedroom we can see the* MOTHER *in the dining room, in coat and hat, all set to go to Mass, taking the last breakfast plates away and carrying them into the kitchen. The camera moves across the living room into the dining room. The* MOTHER *comes out of the kitchen with a paper napkin and begins crumbing the table.*

*There is a knock on the rear porch door. The* MOTHER *leaves her crumbing and goes into the kitchen. Camera goes with her. She opens the rear door to admit* AUNT CATHERINE, *holding a worn old European carpetbag. The* AUNT *starts to go deeper into the kitchen, but the* MOTHER *stays her with her hand.*

MOTHER (*In low, conspiratorial voice*) Hey, I come home from your house last night, Marty was here with a girl.

AUNT Who?

MOTHER Marty.

AUNT Your son Marty?

MOTHER Well, what Marty you think is gonna be here in this house with a girl?

AUNT Were the lights on?

MOTHER Oh, sure. (*Frowns suddenly at her sister*) The girl is a college graduate.

AUNT They're the worst. College girls are one step from the streets. They smoke like men inna saloon.

(*The* AUNT *puts her carpetbag down and sits on one of the wooden kitchen chairs. The* MOTHER *sits on another*)

MOTHER That's the first time Marty ever brought a girl to this house. She seems like a nice girl. I think he has a feeling for this girl.

(*At this moment a burst of spirited whistling emanates from* MARTY'*s bedroom.*

CUT TO MARTY'*s bedroom—*MARTY *standing in front of his mirror, buttoning his shirt or adjusting his tie, whistling a gay tune.*

CUT BACK TO *The two sisters, both their faces turned in the direction of the whistling. The whistling abruptly stops. The two sisters look at each other. The* AUNT *shrugs*)

MOTHER He been whistling like that all morning.

(*The* AUNT *nods bleakly*)

AUNT He is bewitched. You will see. Today, tomorrow, inna week, he's gonna say to you: "Hey, Ma, it's no good being a single man. I'm tired running around." Then he's gonna say: "Hey, Ma, wadda we need this old house? Why don't we sell this old house, move into a nicer parta town? A nice little apartment?"

MOTHER I don't sell this house, I tell you that. This is my husband's house, and I had six children in this house.

AUNT You will see. A couple-a months, you gonna be an old lady, sleeping onna couch in your daughter-in-law's house.

MOTHER Catherine, you are a blanket of gloom. Wherever you go, the rain follows. Some day, you gonna smile, and we gonna declare a holiday.

(*Another burst of spirited whistling comes from* MARTY, *off. It comes closer, and* MARTY *now enters in splendid spirits, whistling away. He is slipping into his jacket*)

MARTY (*Ebulliently*) Hello, Aunt Catherine! How are you? You going to Mass with us?

AUNT I was at Mass two hours ago.

MARTY Well, make yourself at home. The refrigerator is loaded with food. Go upstairs, take any room you want. It's beautiful outside, ain't it?

AUNT There's a chill. Watch out, you catch a good cold and pneumonia.

MOTHER My sister Catherine, she can't even admit it's a beautiful day.

(MARTY*—now at the sink, getting himself a glass of water—is examining a piece of plaster that has fallen from the ceiling*)

MARTY (*Examining the chunk of plaster in his palm*) Boy, this place is really coming to pieces. (*Turns to* MOTHER) You know, Ma, I think, sometime we oughtta sell this place. The plumbing is rusty—everything. I'm gonna have to replaster that whole ceiling now. I think we oughtta get a little apartment somewheres in a nicer parta town. . . . You all set, Ma?

MOTHER I'm all set.

(*She starts for the porch door. She slowly turns*

*and looks at* MARTY, *and then at* AUNT CATHERINE *—who returns her look.* MOTHER *and* MARTY *exit.*

DISSOLVE TO *Church. The* MOTHER *comes out of the doors and down a few steps to where* MARTY *is standing, enjoying the clearness of the June morning)*

MOTHER In a couple-a minutes nine o'clock Mass is gonna start—in a couple-a minutes . . . (*To passers-by off*) hallo, hallo . . . (*To* MARTY) Well, that was a nice girl last night, Marty. That was a nice girl.

MARTY Yeah.

MOTHER She wasn't a very good-looking girl, but she look like a nice girl. I said, she wasn't a very good-looking girl, not very pretty.

MARTY I heard you, Ma.

MOTHER She look a little old for you, about thirty-five, forty years old?

MARTY She's twenny-nine, Ma.

MOTHER She's more than twenny-nine years old, Marty. That's what she tells you. She looks thirty-five, forty. She didn't look Italian to me. I said, is she an Italian girl?

MARTY I don't know. I don't think so.

MOTHER She don't look like Italian to me. What kinda family she come from? There was something about her I don't like. It seems funny, the first time you meet her she comes to your empty house alone. These college girls, they all one step from the streets.

(MARTY *turns, frowning, to his* MOTHER)

MARTY What are you talkin' about? She's a nice girl.

MOTHER I don't like her.

MARTY You don't like her? You only met her for two minutes.

MOTHER Don't bring her to the house no more.

MARTY What didn't you like about her?

MOTHER I don't know! She don't look like Italian to me, plenty nice Italian girls around.

MARTY Well, let's not get into a fight about it, Ma. I just met the girl. I probably won't see her again.

(MARTY *leaves frame*)

MOTHER Eh, I'm no better than my sister Catherine.

(DISSOLVE TO *Interior, the bar . . . about an hour later. The after-Mass crowd is there, about six men ranging from twenty to forty. A couple of women in the booths. One woman is holding a glass of beer in one hand and is gently rocking a baby carriage with the other.*

*Sitting in the booth of Act I are Angie and three other fellows, ages twenty, thirty-two, and forty. One of the fellows, aged thirty-two, is giving a critical resumé of a recent work of literature by Mickey Spillane*)

CRITIC . . . So the whole book winds up, Mike Hammer, he's inna room there with this doll. So he says: "You rat, you are the murderer." So she begins to con him, you know? She tells him how she loves him. And then Bam! He shoots her in the stomach. So she's laying there, gasping for breath, and she says: "How could you do that?" And he says: "It was easy."

TWENTY-YEAR-OLD Boy, that Mickey Spillane. Boy, he can write.

ANGIE (*Leaning out of the booth and looking down the length of the bar, says with some irritation*) What's keeping Marty?

CRITIC What I like about Mickey Spillane is he knows how to handle women. In one book, he picks up a tomato who gets hit with a car, and she throws a pass at him. And then he meets two beautiful twins, and they throw passes at him. And then he meets some beautiful society leader, and she throws a pass at him, and . . .

TWENTY-YEAR-OLD Boy, that Mickey Spillane, he sure can write . . .

ANGIE (*Looking out, down the bar again*) I don't know watsa matter with Marty.

FORTY-YEAR-OLD Boy, Angie, what would you do if Marty ever died? You'd die right with him. A couple-a old bachelors hanging to each other like barnacles. There's Marty now.

(ANGIE *leans out of the booth*)

ANGIE (*Calling out*) Hello, Marty, where you been?

(CUT TO *front end of the bar.* MARTY *has just come in. He waves back to* ANGIE, *acknowledges another hello from a man by the bar, goes over to the bar, and gets the bartender's attention*)

MARTY Hello, Lou, gimme change of a half and put a dime in it for a telephone call.

(*The* BARTENDER *takes the half dollar, reaches into his apron pocket for the change*)

BARTENDER I hear you was at the Waverly Ballroom last night.

MARTY Yeah. Angie tell you?

BARTENDER (*Picking out change from palm full of silver*) Yeah, I hear you really got stuck with a dog.

(MARTY *looks at him*)

MARTY She wasn't so bad.

BARTENDER (*Extending the change*) Angie says she was a real scrawny-looking thing. Well, you can't have good luck alla time.

(MARTY *takes the change slowly and frowns down at it. He moves down the bar and would make for the telephone booth, but* ANGIE *hails him from the booth*)

ANGIE Who you gonna call, Marty?

MARTY I was gonna call that girl from last night, take her to a movie tonight.

ANGIE Are you kidding?

MARTY She was a nice girl. I kinda liked her.

ANGIE (*Indicating the spot in the booth vacated by the* FORTY-YEAR-OLD) Siddown. You can call her later.

(MARTY *pauses, frowning, and then shuffles to the booth where* ANGIE *and the other two sit. The* CRITIC *moves over for* MARTY. *There is an exchange of hellos*)

TWENTY-YEAR-OLD I gotta girl, she's always asking me to marry her. So I look at that face, and I say to myself: "Could I stand looking at that face for the resta my life?"

CRITIC Hey, Marty, you ever read a book called *I, the Jury*, by Mickey Spillane?

MARTY No.

ANGIE Listen, Marty, I gotta good place for us to go

tonight. The kid here, he says, he was downna bazaar at Our Lady of Angels last night and . . .

MARTY I don't feel like going to the bazaar, Angie. I thought I'd take this girl to a movie.

ANGIE Boy, you really musta made out good last night.

MARTY We just talked.

ANGIE Boy, she must be some talker. She musta been about fifty years old.

CRITIC I always figger a guy oughtta marry a girl who's twenny years younger than he is, so that when he's forty, his wife is a real nice-looking doll.

TWENTY-YEAR-OLD That means he'd have to marry the girl when she was one year old.

CRITIC I never thoughta that.

MARTY I didn't think she was so bad-looking.

ANGIE She musta kept you inna shadows all night.

CRITIC Marty, you don't wanna hang around with dogs. It gives you a bad reputation.

ANGIE Marty, let's go downna bazaar.

MARTY I told this dog I was gonna call her today.

ANGIE Brush her.

(MARTY *looks questioningly at* ANGIE)

MARTY You didn't like her at all?

ANGIE A nothing. A real nothing.

(MARTY *looks down at the dime he has been nervously turning between two fingers and then, frowning, he slips it into his jacket pocket. He lowers his face and looks down, scowling at his thoughts. Around him, the voices clip along*)

CRITIC What's playing on Fordham Road? I think there's a good picture in the Loew's Paradise.

ANGIE Let's go down to Forty-second Street and walk around. We're sure to wind up with something.

(*Slowly* MARTY *begins to look up again. He looks from face to face as each speaks*)

CRITIC I'll never forgive La Guardia for cutting burlesque outta New York City.

TWENTY-YEAR-OLD There's burlesque over in Union City. Let's go to Union City. . . .

ANGIE Ah, they're always crowded on Sunday night.

CRITIC So wadda you figure on doing tonight, Angie?

ANGIE I don't know. Wadda you figure on doing?

CRITIC I don't know. (*Turns to the* TWENTY-YEAR-OLD) Wadda you figure on doing?

(*The* TWENTY-YEAR-OLD *shrugs.*

*Suddenly* MARTY *brings his fist down on the booth table with a crash. The others turn, startled, toward him.* MARTY *rises in his seat*)

MARTY "What are you doing tonight?" "I don't know, what are you doing?" Burlesque! Loew's Paradise! Miserable and lonely! Miserable and lonely and stupid! What am I, crazy or something?! I got something good! What am I hanging around with you guys for?!

(*He has said this in tones so loud that it attracts the attention of everyone in the bar. A little embarrassed,* MARTY *turns and moves quickly to the phone booth, pausing outside the door to find his dime again.* ANGIE *is out of his seat immediately and hurries after him*)

ANGIE (*A little shocked at* MARTY'*s outburst*) Watsa matter with you?

MARTY (*In a low, intense voice*) You don't like her. My mother don't like her. She's a dog, and I'm a fat, ugly little man. All I know is I had a good time last night. I'm gonna have a good time tonight. If we have enough good times together, I'm going down on my knees and beg that girl to marry me. If we make a party again this New Year's, I gotta date for the party. You don't like her, that's too bad. (*He moves into the booth, sits, turns again to* ANGIE, *smiles*) When you gonna get married, Angie? You're thirty-four years old. All your kid brothers are married. You oughtta be ashamed of yourself.

(*Still smiling at his private joke, he puts the dime into the slot and then—with a determined finger—he begins to dial*)

*Fade Out*

# John Osborne

## (1929- )

British theatre was caught in post-Shavian doldrums of the cup-and-saucer, cocktails-and-adultery banality parodied by Ionesco when, in May, 1956, John Osborne's *Look Back in Anger* opened and, in Louis Kronenberger's Orwellian phrase, "jabbed some good spiny cactus into England's aspidistra drama." Controversy, such as no British playwright had stirred for longer than London critics could remember, fostered an image of Osborne as leader of the "Angry Young Men," the Roaring Literary Lions of the Welfare State. Was his trumpeting protagonist, Jimmy Porter, merely a rejuvenated Jack Tanner, a mouthpiece for Osborne's own blistering attack on the Establishment? Or had Osborne conceived his ejaculatory misanthrope as an object of satire, a scapegoat whose unhappy lot it is to be both "a magical protector against evil forces" and "rejected as a loathsome sacrifice"? In *The Power of Satire,* Robert C. Elliott suggests that Jimmy Porter evokes ambivalent responses—in audiences as well as in Osborne's other characters—because, like other great misanthropes in literature, he *demands* to be at once embraced and rejected, at once petted and punished. Like Thersites, Timon of Athens, Alceste, and Lemuel Gulliver before him, Jimmy Porter has enabled Osborne's audiences to rediscover that "reluctant delight" man has but rarely in modern times been able to derive from satire.

Before the excitement over his initial success had died down, Osborne was represented again with *The Entertainer* and *Epitaph for George Dillon,* an earlier play on which he had collaborated with Anthony Creighton when both were unemployed actor-playwrights. Fears that Osborne's plays would mean little outside Great Britain were dispelled when *Look Back in Anger* won the New York Drama Critics Circle Award as the best "foreign" play of the 1957-1958 season. That it won against such competition as *The Entertainer,* Maurice Valency's adaptation of Duerrenmatt's *The Visit,* and *Summer of the 17th Doll* by the Australian, Ray Lawler, lent this award a distinction it does not always carry.

Osborne's overnight rise to fame reminded American critics of Odets' sudden emergence in 1935 as spokesman for another generation. In *Awake and Sing!* Odets had shown Ralph, seeking escape from the Bronx, and his elders, grasping their moments of escape in Caruso records, in the Katzenjammer Kids and Mickey Mouse, or in Belle Baker singing "Eli, Eli" on a vaudeville bill. Osborne juxtaposes Colonel Redfern, cherishing his memories of the "Maharajah's army" he once commanded, and Jimmy Porter, swinging crazily between enervating attacks on the Establishment, rehearsals of esoteric new music-hall turns, and preludes to fun and erotic games in a Winnie-the-Pooh world of "rather mad, slightly satanic, and very timid little animals" trying to avoid the "cruel steel traps" the world has set for them. Osborne sounded a note strongly reminiscent of Ibsen and Shaw—and Odets—in writing that the theatre is "what I always dreamed it might be: a weapon . . . one of the decisive weapons of our time." When he described the kind of theatre "that matters the most" as "one that offers a vital, emotional dynamic to ordinary people, that breaks down class barriers, and all the many obstacles set in the way of feeling," *Look Back in Anger* and *The Entertainer* had already proved Osborne's capabilities for serving such a theatre.

Born in London on December 12, 1929, Osborne grew up in the world of working parents he has described in "They Call It Cricket," the credo he wrote for *Declaration* (edited by Tom Maschler; first published, 1957). His maternal grandparents "managed a succession of pubs in London" until, as he reports, his grandfather "lost it all." His mother "has worked behind the bar most of her life" and "still does because she likes to 'be with other people.' " His father, a commercial artist and occasional publican, came from a South Wales family which, in its gentleness, was a marked contrast to Osborne's boisterous relatives on his mother's side: "Not only were their voices soft, but they actually *listened* to what you were saying." In the differences between the two families, Osborne studied the psychological mechanisms of extravagant self-advertising and repressed affection apparent in all his most compelling characters. In a judgment which exemplifies his brand of existentialist belief that "to become angry is to care," Osborne wrote of his mother's family: "I've no doubt that they were often boring, but life still had meaning for them. Even if they did get drunk and fight, they were responding; they were not defeated."

Osborne's formal education ended when he received a general certificate of education from Belmont College. After a dreary stint of writing for trade journals, he found his way into the threatre, first as tutor to child actors in a touring company, and later—beginning in 1948—in provincial repertory as an actor specializing, according to his report, in old men. He had started writing plays while he was still in his teens. After an early work, *The Devil Inside,* was produced in the provinces, Osborne wrote several plays, including *Look Back in Anger,* which were rejected by many managers before they finally found their way into production.

As has been the case frequently in modern drama, Osborne's early successes are linked with the fortunes of a single theatre. In 1956, guided by the actor-director, George Devine, the English Stage Company began its operations, dedicated to the encouragement of new playwrights. The company moved into the reconstructed Royal Court Theatre, where Devine hoped to revitalize a tradition which had made the old Court one of London's most famous theatres. Especially under the management of Granville-Barker and Vedrenne (1904-1907), the Court had offered repertories which educated Edwardian London in the masterworks of modern drama. It was there Shaw had supervised productions of his own plays and Granville-Barker had perfected his uncluttered "Elizabethan" staging of Shakespeare. Devine set out to re-establish the Royal Court as a theatre where "the play is more important than the actors, the director, the designer." The third play put into the English Stage Company's first repertory, *Look Back in Anger,* at once brought Osborne to prominence, and made May 8, 1956 at the Royal Court what has been called "a decisive date which marks a turning point in recent theatrical history."

Devine has recorded how, after reading (and presumably rejecting) several hundred new plays, he came upon *Look Back in Anger*: "When I opened the script of this one, the text leapt to life off the page. It is an experience that occurs very rarely: but as it came to me out of the post from an entirely unknown and penniless writer I always live in hopes that it will happen again. We put this play on because we thought it *had* to be put on." Most critics received the play coolly, but Kenneth Tynan, reviewing for the influential *Observer,* championed it vigorously. Although there was nothing strikingly original in its form, *Look Back in Anger*—in its characters—seemed to signal a reawakening of British drama. It led Ivor Brown to complain of "misanthropy among the garbage cans," of Jimmy Porter as a "cavilling chatterbox," and of Osborne as giving "the appearance of cultivating squalor for squalor's sake," but to Henry Hewes, reviewing the American production for *Saturday Review,* it was "the loudest and most beautiful yelp to be raised in the English theatre in this century." In 1960, revising his *Trends in 20th Century Drama* (first published in 1956), Frederick Lumley added a chapter on Osborne who had, in less than four years, established himself completely. Lumley wrote: "Even if *Look Back in Anger* was not the best play of the decade, it can be called the most important, for whatever may be the shortcomings of Osborne, a play which establishes a new intellectual climate, a return to a directness of language long absent, can have an important influence on the future."

An immediate "influence" of Osborne's first success was the Royal Court production of *The Entertainer* on April 10, 1957. Sir Laurence Olivier abandoned Shakespeare in order to portray the second-rate comic, Archie Rice, whose life and loyalties have been constricted by music-hall audiences "dead behind the eyes." Using fifteen "numbers" of varying duration in place of conventional acts and scenes, Osborne succeeded in mirroring a "dying" world: "I have . . . used some of the techniques of the music hall . . . because I believe that these can solve some of the eternal problems of time and space that face the dramatist, and also, it has been relevant to the story and setting. Not only has this technique its own traditions, its own convention and symbol, its own mystique, it cuts right across the restrictions of the so-called naturalistic stage. Its contact is immediate, vital, and direct."

After *The Entertainer,* the Osborne-Creighton *Epitaph for George Dillon* met the unenviable challenge of following the music-hall headliner. It opened at the Royal Court on February 11, 1958. A possibly talented actor-playwright forced to compromise with a world drenched in the light from television sets, George Dillon succeeds by failing. He allows his play to be retitled "Telephone Tart" and tailored for mass consumption and himself to be led into suburban London domesticity. In his sardonic epitaph ("probably a pastiche of someone or other"), George Dillon includes, along with many other signs of defeat, "He achieved nothing he set out to do." The play's action follows the seasons, from Spring (Act I) to Autumn and Winter (Act III), in ironic counterpoint to George's courtship of success.

In May, 1959, Osborne directed his musical comedy, *The World of Paul Slickey,* into London's Palace. Jack Oakham, *alias* Paul Slickey, columnist for "The Daily Racket," attacks everything from the Establishment to Rock 'n' Roll, and changes his sex in the process. Although it was a logical extension of Osborne's satire, the work failed. At best, it led some critics to hope Osborne might salvage some of his materials for a shorter, more severely disciplined satirical revue.

Martin Luther, the Great Protestant, perhaps the first Angry Young Man in modern times, next occupied Osborne's mind. His *Luther,* originally scheduled to open at Spoleto's Festival of Two Worlds but cancelled after Italian censors banned it, opened in Paris in July, 1961. John Osborne, who could—in his own person—pepper "They Call It Cricket" with such Jimmy Porterisms as "My objection to the Royalty symbol is that it is dead; it is the gold filling in a mouthful of decay," was entering the 1960's in a blaze of notoriety. Wanting "to make people feel, to give them lessons in feeling," Osborne might or might not inherit Shaw's mantle, but he had already assured his position as a major playwright. In creating Jimmy Porter, Archie Rice, and George Dillon, Osborne had helped to open the way for the extraordinary talents of many new playwrights. Such dramatists as Harold Pinter, Arnold Wesker, Shelagh Delaney, John Mortimer, Robert Bolt, John Whiting, Brendan Behan, Beverley Cross, Peter Shaffer, N. F. Simpson, and John Arden promised that the British drama of the 1960's would be vital, richly experimental, once again responsive to the twentieth century.

# LOOK BACK IN ANGER

## *A Play in Three Acts*

### CAST

In Order of Appearance

JIMMY PORTER
CLIFF LEWIS
ALISON PORTER
HELENA CHARLES
COLONEL REDFERN

*The action throughout takes place in the Porters' one-room flat in the Midlands.*

TIME *The present* [i.e., the early 1950's]

ACT I *Early evening, April*

ACT II

Scene 1 *Two weeks later*
Scene 2 *The following evening*

ACT III

Scene 1 *Several months later*
Scene 2 *A few minutes later*

## Act One

*The Porters' one-room flat in a large Midland town. Early evening. April.*

*The scene is a fairly large attic room, at the top of a large Victorian house. The ceiling slopes down quite sharply from L. to R. Down R. are two small low windows. In front of these is a dark oak dressing table. Most of the furniture is simple, and rather old. Up R. is a double bed, running the length of most of the back wall, the rest of which is taken up with a shelf of books. Down R. below the bed is a heavy chest of drawers, covered with books, neckties, and odds and ends, including a large, tattered toy teddy bear and soft, woolly squirrel. Up L. is a door. Below this a small wardrobe. Most of the wall L. is taken up with a high, oblong window. This looks out on to the landing, but light comes through it from a skylight beyond. Below the wardrobe is a gas stove, and, beside this, a wooden food cupboard, on which is a small, portable radio. Down C. is a sturdy dining table and three chairs, and, below this, L. and R., two deep, shabby leather armchairs.*

*At rise of curtain,* JIMMY *and* CLIFF *are seated in the two armchairs R. and L., respectively. All that we can see of either of them is two pairs of legs, sprawled way out beyond the newspapers which hide the rest of them from sight. They are both reading. Beside them, and between them, is a jungle of newspapers and weeklies. When we do eventually see them, we find that* JIMMY *is a tall, thin young man about twenty-five, wearing a very worn tweed jacket and flannels. Clouds of smoke fill the room from the pipe he is smoking. He is a disconcerting mixture of sincerity and cheerful malice, of tenderness and freebooting cruelty; restless, importunate, full of pride, a combination which alienates the sensitive and insensitive alike. Blistering honesty, or apparent honesty, like his, makes few friends. To many he may seem sensitive to the point of vulgarity. To others, he is simply a loudmouth. To be as vehement as he is is to be almost noncommittal.* CLIFF *is the same age, short, dark, big-boned, wearing a pullover and grey, new, but very creased trousers. He is easy and relaxed, almost to lethargy, with the rather sad, natural intelligence of the self-taught. If* JIMMY *alienates love,* CLIFF *seems to exact it—demonstrations of it, at least, even from the cautious. He is a soothing, natural counterpoint to* JIMMY.

*Standing L., below the food cupboard, is* ALISON. *She is leaning over an ironing board. Beside her is a pile of clothes. Hers is the most elusive person-*

*ality to catch in the uneasy polyphony of these three people. She is tuned in a different key, a key of well-bred malaise that is often drowned in the robust orchestration of the other two. Hanging over the grubby, but expensive, skirt she is wearing is a cherry red shirt of* JIMMY'S, *but she manages somehow to look quite elegant in it. She is roughly the same age as the men. Somehow, their combined physical oddity makes her beauty more striking than it really is. She is tall, slim, dark. The bones of her face are long and delicate. There is a surprising reservation about her eyes, which are so large and deep they should make equivocation impossible. The room is still, smoke-filled. The only sound is the occasional thud of* ALISON'S *iron on the board. It is one of those chilly Spring evenings, all cloud and shadows. Presently,* JIMMY *throws his paper down.*

JIMMY Why do I do this every Sunday? Even the book reviews seem to be the same as last week's. Different books—same reviews. Have you finished that one yet?

CLIFF Not yet.

JIMMY I've just read three whole columns on the English Novel. Half of it's in French. Do the Sunday papers make *you* feel ignorant?

CLIFF Not 'arf.

JIMMY Well, you *are* ignorant. You're just a peasant. (*To* ALISON) What about you? You're not a peasant are you?

ALISON (*Absently*) What's that?

JIMMY I said do the papers make you feel you're not so brilliant after all?

ALISON Oh—I haven't read them yet.

JIMMY I didn't ask you that. I said——

CLIFF Leave the poor girlie alone. She's busy.

JIMMY Well, she can talk, can't she? You can talk, can't you? You can express an opinion. Or does the White Woman's Burden make it impossible to think?

ALISON I'm sorry. I wasn't listening properly.

JIMMY You bet you weren't listening. Old Porter talks, and everyone turns over and goes to sleep. And Mrs. Porter gets 'em all going with the first yawn.

CLIFF Leave her alone, I said.

JIMMY (*Shouting*) All right, dear. Go back to sleep. It was only me talking. You know? Talking? Remember? I'm sorry.

CLIFF Stop yelling. I'm trying to read.

JIMMY Why do you bother? You can't understand a word of it.

CLIFF Uh huh.

JIMMY You're too ignorant.

CLIFF Yes, and uneducated. Now shut up, will you?

JIMMY Why don't you get my wife to explain it to you? She's educated. (*To her*) That's right, isn't it?

CLIFF (*Kicking out at him from behind his paper*) Leave her alone, I said.

JIMMY Do that again, you Welsh ruffian, and I'll pull your ears off.

(*He bangs* CLIFF'S *paper out of his hands*)

CLIFF (*Leaning forward*) Listen—I'm trying to better myself. Let me get on with it, you big, horrible man. Give it me. (*Puts his hand out for paper*)

ALISON Oh, give it to him, Jimmy, for heaven's sake! I can't think!

CLIFF Yes, come on, give me the paper. She can't think.

JIMMY Can't think! (*Throws the paper back at him*) She hasn't had a thought for years! Have you?

ALISON No.

JIMMY (*Picks up a weekly*) I'm getting hungry.

ALISON Oh, no, not already!

CLIFF He's a bloody pig.

JIMMY I'm not a pig. I just like food—that's all.

CLIFF Like it! You're like a sexual maniac—only with you it's food. You'll end up in the *News of the World*,[1] boyo, you wait. James Porter, aged twenty-five, was bound over last week after pleading guilty to interfering with a small cabbage and two tins of beans on his way home from "The Builder's Arms." The accused said he hadn't been feeling well for some time, and had been having black-outs. He asked for his good record as an air-raid warden, second class, to be taken into account.

JIMMY (*Grins*) Oh, yes, yes, yes. I like to eat. I'd like to live too. Do you mind?

CLIFF Don't see any use in your eating at all. You never get any fatter.

JIMMY People like me don't get fat. I've tried to tell you before. We just burn everything up. Now shut up while I read. You can make me some more tea.

CLIFF Good God, you've just had a great potful! I only had one cup.

JIMMY Like hell! Make some more.

CLIFF (*To* ALISON) Isn't that right? Didn't I only have one cup?

ALISON (*Without looking up*) That's right.

CLIFF There you are. And she only had one cup too. I saw her. You guzzled the lot.

JIMMY (*Reading his weekly*) Put the kettle on.

CLIFF Put it on yourself. You've creased up my paper.

JIMMY I'm the only one who knows how to treat a paper, or anything else, in this house. (*Picks up another paper*) Girl here wants to know whether her boy friend will lose all respect for her if she gives him what he asks for. Stupid bitch.

CLIFF Just let me get at her, that's all.

JIMMY Who buys this damned thing? (*Throws it down*) Haven't you read the other posh[2] paper yet?

CLIFF Which?

JIMMY Well, there are only two posh papers on a Sunday[3]—the one you're reading, and this one. Come on, let me have that one, and you take this.

CLIFF Oh, all right (*They exchange*) I was only read-

[1] A popular scandal-sheet.

[2] To the British, *posh* immediately signifies the speaker's lower-middle-class status; an upper-class Englishman would not use the word, which means "swell" or "high class."

[3] The two "posh" Sunday newspapers are the London *Times* and *The Observer*.

ing the Bishop of Bromley. (*Puts out his hand to* ALISON) How are you, dullin'?

ALISON All right, thank you, dear.

CLIFF (*Grasping her hand*) Why don't you leave all that, and sit down for a bit? You look tired.

ALISON (*Smiling*) I haven't much more to do.

CLIFF (*Kisses her hand, and puts her fingers in his mouth*) She's a beautiful girl, isn't she?

JIMMY That's what they all tell me.

(*His eyes meet hers*)

CLIFF It's a lovely, delicious paw you've got. Ummmmm. I'm going to bite it off.

ALISON Don't! I'll burn his shirt.

JIMMY Give her her finger back, and don't be so sickening. What's the Bishop of Bromley say?

CLIFF (*Letting go of* ALISON) Oh, it says here that he makes a very moving appeal to all Christians to do all they can to assist in the manufacture of the H-Bomb.

JIMMY Yes, well, that's quite moving, I suppose. (*To* ALISON) Are you moved, my darling?

ALISON Well, naturally.

JIMMY There you are: even my wife is moved. I ought to send the Bishop a subscription. Let's see. What else does he say. Dumdidumdidumdidum. Ah, yes. He's upset because someone has suggested that he supports the rich against the poor. He says he denies the difference of class distinctions. "This idea has been persistently and wickedly fostered by—the working classes!" Well!

(*He looks up at both of them for reaction, but* CLIFF *is reading, and* ALISON *is intent on her ironing*)

JIMMY (*To* CLIFF) Did you read that bit?

CLIFF Um?

(*He has lost them, and he knows it, but he won't leave it*)

JIMMY (*To* ALISON) You don't suppose your father could have written it, do you?

ALISON Written what?

JIMMY What I just read out, of course.

ALISON Why should my father have written it?

JIMMY Sounds rather like Daddy, don't you think?

ALISON Does it?

JIMMY Is the Bishop of Bromley his nom de plume, do you think?

CLIFF Don't take any notice of him. He's being offensive. And it's so easy for him.

JIMMY (*Quickly*) Did you read about the woman who went to the mass meeting of a certain American evangelist at Earls Court? She went forward, to declare herself for love or whatever it is, and, in the rush of converts to get to the front, she broke four ribs and got kicked in the head. She was yelling her head off in agony, but with 50,000 people putting all they'd got into "Onward Christian Soldiers," nobody even knew she was there. (*He looks up sharply for a response, but there isn't any*) Sometimes, I wonder if there isn't something wrong with me. What about that tea?

CLIFF (*Still behind paper*) What tea?

JIMMY Put the kettle on.

(ALISON *looks up at him*)

ALISON Do you want some more tea?

JIMMY I don't know. No, I don't think so.

ALISON Do you want some, Cliff?

JIMMY No, he doesn't. How much longer will you be doing that?

ALISON Won't be long.

JIMMY God, how I hate Sundays! It's always so depressing, always the same. We never seem to get any further, do we? Always the same ritual. Reading the papers, drinking tea, ironing. A few more hours, and another week gone. Our youth is slipping away. Do you know that?

CLIFF (*Throws down paper*) What's that?

JIMMY (*Casually*) Oh, nothing, nothing. Damn you, damn both of you, damn them all.

CLIFF Let's go to the pictures. (*To* ALISON) What do you say, lovely?

ALISON I don't think I'll be able to. Perhaps Jimmy would like to go. (*To* JIMMY) Would you like to?

JIMMY And have my enjoyment ruined by the Sunday night yobs[4] in the front row? No, thank you. (*Pause*) Did you read Priestley's piece this week? Why on earth I ask, I don't know. I know damned well you haven't. Why do I spend ninepence on that damned paper every week? Nobody reads it except me. Nobody can be bothered. No one can raise themselves out of their delicious sloth. You two will drive me round the bend soon—I know it, as sure as I'm sitting here. I know you're going to drive me mad. Oh, heavens, how I long for a little ordinary human enthusiasm. Just enthusiasm—that's all. I want to hear a warm, thrilling voice cry out Hallelujah! (*He bangs his breast theatrically*) Hallelujah! I'm alive! I've an idea. Why don't we have a little game? Let's pretend that we're human beings, and that we're actually alive. Just for a while. What do you say? Let's pretend we're human. (*He looks from one to the other*) Oh, brother, it's such a long time since I was with anyone who got enthusiastic about anything.

CLIFF What did he say?

JIMMY (*Resentful of being dragged away from his pursuit of* ALISON) What did who say?

CLIFF Mr. Priestley.

JIMMY What he always says, I suppose. He's like Daddy—still casting well-fed glances back to the Edwardian twilight from his comfortable, disenfranchised wilderness. What the devil have you done to those trousers?

CLIFF Done?

JIMMY Are they the ones you bought last week-end? Look at them. Do you see what he's done to those new trousers?

ALISON You are naughty, Cliff. They look dreadful.

JIMMY You spend good money on a new pair of

[4] In American English, we might use "slobs."

trousers, and then sprawl about in them like a savage. What do you think you're going to do when I'm not around to look after you? Well, what are you going to do? Tell me?

CLIFF (*Grinning*) I don't know. (*To* ALISON) What am I going to do, lovely?

ALISON You'd better take them off.

JIMMY Yes, go on. Take 'em off. And I'll kick your behind for you.

ALISON I'll give them a press while I've got the iron on.

CLIFF O.K. (*Starts taking them off*) I'll just empty the pockets. (*Takes out keys, matches, handkerchief*)

JIMMY Give me those matches, will you?

CLIFF Oh, you're not going to start up that old pipe again, are you? It stinks the place out. (*To* ALISON) Doesn't it smell awful?

(JIMMY *grabs the matches, and lights up*)

ALISON I don't mind it. I've got used to it.

JIMMY She's a great one for getting used to things. If she were to die, and wake up in paradise—after the first five minutes, she'd have got used to it.

CLIFF (*Hands her the trousers*) Thank you, lovely. Give me a cigarette, will you?

JIMMY Don't give him one.

CLIFF I can't stand the stink of that old pipe any longer. I must have a cigarette.

JIMMY I thought the doctor said no cigarettes?

CLIFF Oh, why doesn't he shut up?

JIMMY All right. They're your ulcers. Go ahead, and have a bellyache, if that's what you want. I give up. I give up. I'm sick of doing things for people. And all for what?

(ALISON *gives* CLIFF *a cigarette. They both light up, and she goes on with her ironing*)

Nobody thinks, nobody cares. No beliefs, no convictions and no enthusiasm. Just another Sunday evening.

(CLIFF *sits down again, in his pullover and shorts*)

Perhaps there's a concert on. (*Picks up* Radio Times) Ah. (*Nudges* CLIFF *with his foot*) Make some more tea.

(CLIFF *grunts. He is reading again*)

Oh, yes. There's a Vaughan Williams. Well, that's something, anyway. Something strong, something simple, something English. I suppose people like me aren't supposed to be very patriotic. Somebody said—what was it—we get our cooking from Paris (that's a laugh), our politics from Moscow, and our morals from Port Said. Something like that, anyway. Who was it? (*Pause*) Well, you wouldn't know anyway. I hate to admit it, but I think I can understand how her Daddy must have felt when he came back from India, after all those years away. The old Edwardian brigade do make their brief little world look pretty tempting. All homemade cakes and croquet, bright ideas, bright uniforms. Always the same picture: high summer, the long days in the sun, slim volumes of verse, crisp linen, the smell of starch. What a romantic picture. Phony, too, of course. It must have rained sometimes. Still, even I regret it somehow, phony or not. If you've no world of your own, it's rather pleasant to regret the passing of someone else's. I must be getting sentimental. But I must say it's pretty dreary living in the American Age—unless you're an American, of course. Perhaps all our children will be Americans. That's a thought, isn't it?

(*He gives* CLIFF *a kick, and shouts at him*)

I said that's a thought!

CLIFF You did?

JIMMY You sit there like a lump of dough. I thought you were going to make me some tea.

(CLIFF *groans.* JIMMY *turns to* ALISON)

Is your friend Webster coming tonight?

ALISON He might drop in. You know what he is.

JIMMY Well, I hope he doesn't. I don't think I could take Webster tonight.

ALISON I thought you said he was the only person who spoke your language.

JIMMY So he is. Different dialect but same language. I like him. He's got bite, edge, drive——

ALISON Enthusiasm.

JIMMY You've got it. When he comes here, I begin to feel exhilarated. He doesn't like me, but he gives me something, which is more than I get from most people. Not since——

ALISON Yes, we know. Not since you were living with Madeline.

(*She folds some of the clothes she has already ironed, and crosses to the bed with them*)

CLIFF (*Behind paper again*) Who's Madeline?

ALISON Oh, wake up, dear. You've heard about Madeline enough times. She was his mistress. Remember? When he was fourteen. Or was it thirteen?

JIMMY Eighteen.

ALISON He owes just about everything to Madeline.

CLIFF I get mixed up with all your women. Was she the one all those years older than you?

JIMMY Ten years.

CLIFF Proper little Marchbanks,[5] you are!

JIMMY What time's that concert on? (*Checks paper*)

CLIFF (*Yawns*) Oh, I feel so sleepy. Don't feel like standing behind that blinking sweet-stall again tomorrow. Why don't you do it on your own, and let me sleep in?

JIMMY I've got to be at the factory first thing, to get some more stock, so you'll have to put it up on your own. Another five minutes.

(ALISON *has returned to her ironing board. She stands with her arms folded, smoking, staring thoughtfully*)

She had more animation in her little finger than you two put together.

CLIFF Who did?

ALISON Madeline.

JIMMY Her curiosity about things, and about people was staggering. It wasn't just a naïve nosiness. With her, it was simply the delight of being awake, and watching.

(ALISON *starts to press* CLIFF'S *trousers*)

[5] The young poet in Shaw's *Candida.*

CLIFF (*Behind paper*) Perhaps I will make some tea, after all.

JIMMY (*Quietly*) Just to be with her was an adventure. Even to sit on the top of a bus with her was like setting out with Ulysses.

CLIFF Wouldn't have said Webster was much like Ulysses. He's an ugly little devil.

JIMMY I'm not talking about Webster, stupid. He's all right though, in his way. A sort of female Emily Brontë. He's the only one of your friends (*To* ALISON) who's worth tuppence, anyway. I'm surprised you get on with him.

ALISON So is he, I think.

JIMMY (*Rising to window R., and looking out*) He's not only got guts, but sensitivity as well. That's about the rarest combination I can think of. None of your other friends have got either.

ALISON (*Very quietly and earnestly*) Jimmy, please—don't go on.

(*He turns and looks at her. The tired appeal in her voice has pulled him up suddenly. But he soon gathers himself for a new assault. He walks C., behind* CLIFF, *and stands, looking down at his head*)

JIMMY Your friends—there's a shower for you.

CLIFF (*Mumbling*) Dry up. Let her get on with my trousers.

JIMMY (*Musingly*) Don't think I could provoke her. Nothing I could do would provoke her. Not even if I were to drop dead.

CLIFF Then drop dead.

JIMMY They're either militant like her Mummy and Daddy. Militant, arrogant, and full of malice. Or vague. She's somewhere between the two.

CLIFF Why don't you listen to that concert of yours? And don't stand behind me. That blooming droning on behind me gives me a funny feeling down the spine.

(JIMMY *gives his ears a twist and* CLIFF *roars with pain.* JIMMY *grins back at him*)

That hurt, you rotten sadist! (*To* ALISON) I wish you'd kick his head in for him.

JIMMY (*Moving in between them*) Have you ever seen her brother? Brother Nigel? The straight-backed, chinless wonder from Sandhurst? I only met him once myself. He asked me to step outside when I told his mother she was evil minded.

CLIFF And did you?

JIMMY Certainly not. He's a big chap. Well, you've never heard so many well-bred commonplaces come from beneath the same bowler hat. The Platitude from Outer Space—that's brother Nigel. He'll end up in the Cabinet one day, make no mistake. But somewhere at the back of that mind is the vague knowledge that he and his pals have been plundering and fooling everybody for generations. (*Going upstage, and turning*) Now Nigel is just about as vague as you can get without being actually invisible. And invisible politicians aren't much use to anyone—not even to *his* supporters! And nothing is more vague about Nigel than his knowledge. His knowledge of life and ordinary human beings is so hazy, he really deserves some sort of decoration for it—a medal inscribed "For Vaguery in the Field." But it wouldn't do for him to be troubled by any stabs of conscience, however vague. (*Moving down again*) Besides, he's a patriot and an Englishman, and he doesn't like the idea that he may have been selling out his countrymen all these years, so what does he do? The only thing he *can* do—seek sanctuary in his own stupidity. The only way to keep things as much like they always have been as possible, is to make any alternative too much for your poor, tiny brain to grasp. It takes some doing nowadays. It really does. But they knew all about character building at Nigel's school, and he'll make it all right. Don't you worry, he'll make it. And, what's more, he'll do it better than anybody else!

(*There is no sound, only the plod of* ALISON'S *iron. Her eyes are fixed on what she is doing.* CLIFF *stares at the floor. His cheerfulness has deserted him for the moment.* JIMMY *is rather shakily triumphant. He cannot allow himself to look at either of them to catch their response to his rhetoric, so he moves across to the window, to recover himself, and look out*)

It's started to rain. That's all it needs. This room and the rain.

(*He's been cheated out of his response, but he's got to draw blood somehow*)

(*Conversationally*) Yes, that's the little woman's family. You know Mummy and Daddy, of course. And don't let the Marquess of Queensberry manner fool you. They'll kick you in the groin while you're handing your hat to the maid. As for Nigel and Alison——(*In a reverent, Stuart Hibberd*[6] *voice*) Nigel and Alison. They're what they sound like: sycophantic, phlegmatic, and pusillanimous.

CLIFF I'll bet that concert's started by now. Shall I put it on?

JIMMY I looked up that word the other day. It's one of those words I've never been quite sure of, but always thought I knew.

CLIFF What was that?

JIMMY I told you—pusillanimous. Do you know what it means?

(CLIFF *shakes his head*)

Neither did I really. All this time, I have been married to this woman, this monument to non-attachment, and suddenly I discover that there is actually a word that sums her up. Not just an adjective in the English language to describe her with—it's her name! Pusillanimous! It sounds like some fleshy Roman matron, doesn't it? The Lady Pusillanimous seen here with her husband Sextus, on their way to the Games.

(CLIFF *looks troubled, and glances uneasily at* ALISON)

Poor old Sextus! If he were put into a Hollywood film, he's so unimpressive, they'd make some poor British actor play the part. He doesn't know it, but those

[6] A B.B.C. news commentator.

beefcake Christians will make off with his wife in the wonder of stereophonic sound before the picture's over.

(ALISON *leans against the board, and closes her eyes*)

The Lady Pusillanimous has been promised a brighter easier world than old Sextus can ever offer her. Hi, Pusey! What say we get the hell down to the Arena, and maybe feed ourselves to a couple of lions, huh?

ALISON God help me, if he doesn't stop, I'll go out of my mind in a minute.

JIMMY Why don't you? That would be something, anyway. (*Crosses to chest of drawers R.*) But I haven't told you what it means yet, have I? (*Picks up dictionary*) I don't have to tell her—she knows. In fact, if my pronunciation is at fault, she'll probably wait for a suitably public moment to correct it. Here it is. I quote: Pusillanimous. Adjective. Wanting of firmness of mind, of small courage, having a little mind, mean-spirited, cowardly, timid of mind. From the Latin *pusillus,* very little, and *animus,* the mind. (*Slams the book shut*) That's my wife! That's *her,* isn't it? Behold the Lady Pusillanimous. (*Shouting hoarsely*) Hi, Pusey! When's your next picture?

(JIMMY *watches her, waiting for her to break. For no more than a flash,* ALISON'S *face seems to contort, and it looks as though she might throw her head back, and scream. But it passes in a moment. She is used to these carefully rehearsed attacks, and it doesn't look as though he will get his triumph tonight. She carries on with her ironing.* JIMMY *crosses, and switches on the radio. The Vaughan Williams concert has started. He goes back to his chair, leans back in it, and closes his eyes*)

ALISON (*Handing* CLIFF *his trousers*) There you are, dear. They're not very good, but they'll do for now.

(CLIFF *gets up and puts them on*)

CLIFF Oh, that's lovely.

ALISON Now try and look after them. I'll give them a real press later on.

CLIFF Thank you, you beautiful, darling girl.

(*He puts his arms round her waist, and kisses her. She smiles, and gives his nose a tug.* JIMMY *watches from his chair*)

ALISON (*To* CLIFF) Let's have a cigarette, shall we?

CLIFF That's a good idea. Where are they?

ALISON On the stove. Do you want one, Jimmy?

JIMMY No, thank you, I'm trying to listen. Do you mind?

CLIFF Sorry, your lordship.

(*He puts a cigarette in* ALISON'S *mouth, and one in his own, and lights up.* CLIFF *sits down, and picks up his paper.* ALISON *goes back to her board.* CLIFF *throws down paper, picks up another, and thumbs through that*)

JIMMY Do you have to make all that racket?

CLIFF Oh, sorry.

JIMMY It's quite a simple thing, you know—turning over a page. Anyway, that's my paper. (*Snatches it away*)

CLIFF Oh, don't be so mean!

JIMMY Price ninepence, obtainable from any newsagent's. Now let me hear the music, for God's sake.

(*Pause*)

(*To* ALISON) Are you going to be much longer doing that?

ALISON Why?

JIMMY Perhaps you haven't noticed it, but it's interfering with the radio.

ALISON I'm sorry. I shan't be much longer.

(*A pause. The iron mingles with the music.* CLIFF *shifts restlessly in his chair,* JIMMY *watches* ALISON, *his foot beginning to twitch dangerously. Presently, he gets up quickly, crossing below* ALISON *to the radio, and turns it off*)

What did you do that for?

JIMMY I wanted to listen to the concert, that's all.

ALISON Well, what's stopping you?

JIMMY Everyone's making such a din—that's what's stopping me.

ALISON Well, I'm very sorry, but I can't just stop everything because you want to listen to music.

JIMMY Why not?

ALISON Really, Jimmy, you're like a child.

JIMMY Don't try and patronize me. (*Turning to* CLIFF) She's so clumsy. I watch for her to do the same things every night. The way she jumps on the bed, as if she were stamping on someone's face, and draws the curtains back with a great clatter, in that casually destructive way of hers. It's like someone launching a battleship. Have you ever noticed how noisy women are? (*Crosses below chairs to L.C.*) Have you? The way they kick the floor about, simply walking over it? Or have you watched them sitting at their dressing tables, dropping their weapons and banging down their bits of boxes and brushes and lipsticks?

(*He faces her dressing table*)

I've watched her doing it night after night. When you see a woman in front of her bedroom mirror, you realise what a refined sort of a butcher she is. (*Turns in*) Did you ever see some dirty old Arab, sticking his fingers into some mess of lamb fat and gristle? Well, she's just like that. Thank God they don't have many women surgeons! Those primitive hands would have your guts out in no time. Flip! Out it comes, like the powder out of its box. Flop! Back it goes, like the powder puff on the table.

CLIFF (*Grimacing cheerfully*) Ugh! Stop it!

JIMMY (*Moving upstage*) She'd drop your guts like hair clips and fluff all over the floor. You've got to be fundamentally insensitive to be as noisy and as clumsy as that.

(*He moves C., and leans against the table*)

I had a flat underneath a couple of girls once. You heard every damned thing those bastards did, all day and night. The most simple, everyday actions were a sort of assault course on your sensibilities. I used to plead with them. I even got to screaming the most ingenious obscenities I could think of, up the stairs at them. But nothing, nothing, would move them. With those two, even a simple visit to the lavatory sounded like a medieval siege. Oh, they beat me in the end—I had to go. I expect they're still at it. Or they're probably married by now, and driving some other poor devils out of their minds. Slamming their doors, stamping their high heels, banging their irons and saucepans—the eternal flaming racket of the female.

(*Church bells start ringing outside*)

JIMMY Oh, hell! Now the bloody bells have started!

(*He rushes to the window*)

Wrap it up, will you? Stop ringing those bells! There's somebody going crazy in here! I don't want to hear them!

ALISON Stop shouting! (*Recovering immediately*) You'll have Miss Drury up here.

JIMMY I don't give a damn about Miss Drury—that mild old gentlewoman doesn't fool me, even if she takes in you two. She's an old robber. She gets more than enough out of us for this place every week. Anyway, she's probably in church, (*Points to the window*) swinging on those bloody bells!

(CLIFF *goes to the window, and closes it*)

CLIFF Come on, now, be a good boy. I'll take us all out, and we'll have a drink.

JIMMY They're not open yet. It's Sunday. Remember? Anyway, it's raining.

CLIFF Well, shall we dance?

(*He pushes* JIMMY *round the floor, who is past the mood for this kind of fooling*)

Do you come here often?

JIMMY Only in the mating season. All right, all right, very funny.

(*He tries to escape, but* CLIFF *holds him like a vise*)

Let me go.

CLIFF Not until you've apologized for being nasty to everyone. Do you think bosoms will be in or out, this year?

JIMMY Your teeth will be out in a minute, if you don't let go!

(*He makes a great effort to wrench himself free, but* CLIFF *hangs on. They collapse to the floor C., below the table, struggling.* ALISON *carries on with her ironing. This is routine, but she is getting close to breaking point, all the same.* CLIFF *manages to break away, and finds himself in front of the ironing board.* JIMMY *springs up. They grapple*)

ALISON Look out, for heaven's sake! Oh, it's more like a zoo every day!

(JIMMY *makes a frantic, deliberate effort, and manages to push* CLIFF *on to the ironing board, and into* ALISON. *The board collapses.* CLIFF *falls against her, and they end up in a heap on the floor.* ALISON *cries out in pain.* JIMMY *looks down at them, dazed and breathless*)

CLIFF (*Picking himself up*) She's hurt. Are you all right?

ALISON Well, does it look like it!

CLIFF She's burnt her arm on the iron.

JIMMY Darling, I'm sorry.

ALISON Get out!

JIMMY I'm sorry, believe me. You think I did it on pur——

ALISON (*Her head shaking helplessly*) Clear out of my *sight!*

(*He stares at her uncertainly.* CLIFF *nods to him, and he turns and goes out of the door*)

CLIFF Come and sit down.

(*He leads her to the armchair R.*)

You look a bit white. Are you all right?

ALISON Yes. I'm all right now.

CLIFF Let's have a look at your arm. (*Examines it*) Yes, it's quite red. That's going to be painful. What should I do with it?

ALISON Oh, it's nothing much. A bit of soap on it will do. I never can remember what you do with burns.

CLIFF I'll just pop down to the bathroom and get some. Are you sure you're all right?

ALISON Yes.

CLIFF (*Crossing to door*) Won't be a minute. (*Exit*)

(*She leans back in the chair, and looks up at the ceiling. She breathes in deeply, and brings her hands up to her face. She winces as she feels the pain in her arm, and she lets it fall. She runs her hand through her hair*)

ALISON (*In a clenched whisper*) Oh, God!

(CLIFF *re-enters with a bar of soap*)

CLIFF It's this scented muck. Do you think it'll be all right?

ALISON That'll do.

CLIFF Here we are then. Let's have your arm.

(*He kneels down beside her, and she holds out her arm*)

I've put it under the tap. It's quite soft. I'll do it ever so gently.

(*Very carefully, he rubs the soap over the burn*)

All right? (*She nods*) You're a brave girl.

ALISON I don't feel very brave. (*Tears harshening her voice*) I really don't, Cliff. I don't think I can take much more. (*Turns her head away*) I think I feel rather sick.

CLIFF All over now. (*Puts the soap down*) Would you like me to get you something?

(*She shakes her head. He sits on the arm of the chair, and puts his arm round her. She leans her head back on to him*)

Don't upset yourself, lovely.

(*He massages the back of her neck, and she lets her head fall forward*)

ALISON Where is he?

CLIFF In my room.

ALISON What's he doing?

CLIFF Lying on the bed. Reading, I think. (*Stroking her neck*) That better?

(*She leans back, and closes her eyes again*)

ALISON Bless you.

(*He kisses the top of her head*)

CLIFF I don't think I'd have the courage to live on my own again—in spite of everything. I'm pretty rough, and pretty ordinary really, and I'd seem worse on my own. And you get fond of people too, worse luck.

ALISON I don't think I want anything more to do with love. Any more. I can't take it on.

CLIFF You're too young to start giving up. Too young,

and too lovely. Perhaps I'd better put a bandage on that—do you think so?

ALISON There's some on my dressing table.

(CLIFF *crosses to the dressing table R.*)

I keep looking back, as far as I remember, and I can't think what it was to feel young, really young. Jimmy said the same thing to me the other day. I pretended not to be listening—because I knew that would hurt him, I suppose. And—of course—he got savage, like tonight. But I knew just what he meant. I suppose it would have been so easy to say, "Yes, darling, I know just what you mean. I know what you're feeling." (*Shrugs*) It's those easy things that seem to be so impossible with us.

(CLIFF *stands down R., holding the bandage, his back to her*)

CLIFF I'm wondering how much longer I can go on watching you two tearing the insides out of each other. It looks pretty ugly sometimes.

ALISON You wouldn't seriously think of leaving us, would you?

CLIFF I suppose not. (*Crosses to her*)

ALISON I think I'm frightened. If only I knew what was going to happen.

CLIFF (*Kneeling on the arm of her chair*) Give it here. (*She holds out her arm*) Yell out if I hurt you. (*He bandages it for her*)

ALISON (*Staring at her outstretched arm*) Cliff——

CLIFF Um? (*Slight pause*) What is it, lovely?

ALISON Nothing.

CLIFF I said: what is it?

ALISON You see——(*Hesitates*) I'm pregnant.

CLIFF (*After a few moments*) I'll need some scissors.

ALISON They're over there.

CLIFF (*Crossing to the dressing table*) That is something, isn't it? When did you find this out?

ALISON Few days ago. It was a bit of a shock.

CLIFF Yes, I dare say.

ALISON After three years of married life, I have to get caught out now.

CLIFF None of us infallible, I suppose. (*Crosses to her*) Must say I'm surprised, though.

ALISON It's always been out of the question. What with—this place, and no money, and oh—everything. He's resented it, I know. What can you do?

CLIFF You haven't told him yet.

ALISON Not yet.

CLIFF What are you going to do?

ALISON I've no idea.

CLIFF (*Having cut her bandage, he starts tying it*) That too tight?

ALISON Fine, thank you.

(*She rises, goes to the ironing board, folds it up, and leans it against the food cupboard R.*)

CLIFF Is it . . . Is it . . . ?

ALISON Too late to avert the situation? (*Places the iron on the rack of the stove*) I'm not certain yet. Maybe not. If not, there won't be any problem, will there?

CLIFF And if it is too late?

(*Her face is turned away from him. She simply shakes her head*)

Why don't you tell him now?

(*She kneels down to pick up the clothes on the floor, and folds them up*)

After all, he does love you. You don't need me to tell you that.

ALISON Can't you see? He'll suspect my motives at once. He never stops telling himself that I know how vulnerable he is. Tonight it might be all right—we'd make love. But later, we'd both lie awake, watching for the light to come through that little window, and dreading it. In the morning, he'd feel hoaxed, as if I were trying to kill him in the worst way of all. He'd watch me growing bigger every day, and I wouldn't dare to look at him.

CLIFF You may have to face it, lovely.

ALISON Jimmy's got his own private morality, as you know. What my mother calls "loose." It is pretty free, of course, but it's very harsh too. You know, it's funny, but we never slept together before we were married.

CLIFF It certainly is—knowing him!

ALISON We knew each other such a short time, everything moved at such a pace, we didn't have much opportunity. And, afterwards, he actually taunted me with my virginity. He was quite angry about it, as if I had deceived him in some strange way. He seemed to think an untouched woman would defile him.

CLIFF I've never heard you talking like this about him. He'd be quite pleased.

ALISON Yes, he would.

(*She gets up, the clothes folded over her arm*)

Do you think he's right?

CLIFF What about?

ALISON Oh—everything.

CLIFF Well, I suppose he and I think the same about a lot of things, because we're alike in some ways. We both come from working people, if you like. Oh, I know some of his mother's relatives are pretty posh, but he hates them as much as he hates yours. Don't quite know why. Anyway, he gets on with me because I'm common. (*Grins*) Common as dirt, that's me.

(*She puts her hand on his head, and strokes it thoughtfully*)

ALISON You think I should tell him about the baby?

(*He gets up, and puts his arm round her*)

CLIFF It'll be all right—you see. Tell him.

(*He kisses her. Enter* JIMMY. *He looks at them curiously, but without surprise. They are both aware of him, but make no sign of it. He crosses to the armchair L., and sits down next to them. He picks up a paper, and starts looking at it.* CLIFF *glances at him,* ALISON'*s head against his cheek*)

There you are, you old devil, you! Where have you been?

JIMMY You know damn well where I've been. (*Without looking at her*) How's your arm?

ALISON Oh, it's all right. It wasn't much.

CLIFF She's beautiful, isn't she?

JIMMY You seem to think so.

(CLIFF *and* ALISON *still have their arms round one another*)

CLIFF Why the hell she married you, I'll never know.

JIMMY You think she'd have been better off with you?

CLIFF I'm not her type. Am I, dullin'?

ALISON I'm not sure what my type is.

JIMMY Why don't you both get into bed, and have done with it.

ALISON You know, I think he really means that.

JIMMY I do. I can't concentrate with you two standing there like that.

CLIFF He's just an old Puritan at heart.

JIMMY Perhaps I am, at that. Anyway, you both look pretty silly slobbering over each other.

CLIFF I think she's beautiful. And so do you, only you're too much of a pig to say so.

JIMMY You're just a sexy little Welshman, and you know it! Mummy and Daddy turn pale, and face the east every time they remember she's married to me. But if they saw all this going on, they'd collapse. Wonder what they *would* do, incidentally. Send for the police I expect. (*Genuinely friendly*) Have you got a cigarette?

ALISON (*Disengaging*) I'll have a look.

(*She goes to her handbag on the table C.*)

JIMMY (*Pointing at* CLIFF) He gets more like a little mouse every day, doesn't he?

(*He is trying to re-establish himself*)

He really does look like one. Look at those ears, and that face, and the little short legs.

ALISON (*Looking through her bag*) That's because he *is* a mouse.

CLIFF Eek! Eek! I'm a mouse.

JIMMY A randy little mouse.

CLIFF (*Dancing round the table, and squeaking*) I'm a mouse, I'm a mouse, I'm a randy little mouse. That's a mourris dance.

JIMMY A what?

CLIFF A *Mourris Dance*. That's a Morris Dance strictly for mice.

JIMMY You stink. You really do. Do you know that?

CLIFF Not as bad as you, you horrible old bear. (*Goes over to him, and grabs his foot*) You're a stinking old bear, you hear me?

JIMMY Let go of my foot, you whimsy little half-wit. You're making my stomach heave. I'm resting! If you don't let go, I'll cut off your nasty, great, slimy tail!

(CLIFF *gives him a tug, and* JIMMY *falls to the floor.* ALISON *watches them, relieved and suddenly full of affection*)

ALISON I've run out of cigarettes.

(CLIFF *is dragging* JIMMY *along the floor by his feet*)

JIMMY (*Yelling*) Go out and get me some cigarettes, and stop playing the fool!

CLIFF O.K.

(*He lets go of* JIMMY*'s legs suddenly, who yells again as his head bangs on the floor*)

ALISON Here's half a crown. (*Giving it him*) The shop on the corner will be open.

CLIFF Right you are. (*Kisses her on the forehead quickly*) Don't forget. (*Crosses upstage to door*)

JIMMY Now get to hell out of here!

CLIFF (*At door*) Hey, shorty!

JIMMY What do you want?

CLIFF Make a nice pot of tea.

JIMMY (*Getting up*) I'll kill you first.

CLIFF (*Grinning*) That's my boy! (*Exit*)

(JIMMY *is now beside* ALISON, *who is still looking through her handbag. She becomes aware of his nearness, and, after a few moments, closes it. He takes hold of her bandaged arm*)

JIMMY How's it feeling?

ALISON Fine. It wasn't anything.

JIMMY All this fooling about can get a bit dangerous.

(*He sits on the edge of the table, holding her hand*)

I'm sorry.

ALISON I know.

JIMMY I mean it.

ALISON There's no need.

JIMMY I did it on purpose.

ALISON Yes.

JIMMY There's hardly a moment when I'm not—watching and wanting you. I've got to hit out somehow. Nearly four years of being in the same room with you, night and day, and I still can't stop my sweat breaking out when I see you doing—something as ordinary as leaning over an ironing board.

(*She strokes his head, not sure of herself yet*)

(*Sighing*) Trouble is— Trouble is you get used to people. Even their trivialities become indispensable to you. Indispensable, and a little mysterious.

(*He slides his head forward, against her, trying to catch his thoughts*)

I think . . . I must have a lot of—old stock. . . . Nobody wants it. . . .

(*He puts his face against her belly She goes on stroking his head, still on guard a little. Then he lifts his head, and they kiss passionately*)

What are we going to do tonight?

ALISON What would you like to do? Drink?

JIMMY I know what I want now.

(*She takes his head in her hands and kisses him*)

ALISON Well, you'll have to wait till the proper time.

JIMMY There's no such thing.

ALISON Cliff will be back in a minute.

JIMMY What did he mean by "don't forget"?

ALISON Something I've been meaning to tell you.

JIMMY (*Kissing her again*) You're fond of him, aren't you?

ALISON Yes, I am.

JIMMY He's the only friend I seem to have left now. People go away. You never see them again. I can remember lots of names—men and women. When I was at school—Watson, Roberts, Davies. Jenny, Madeline, Hugh . . . (*Pause*) And there's Hugh's mum, of course. I'd almost forgotten her. She's been a good friend to us, if you like. She's even letting me buy the sweet-stall off her in my own time. She only bought it for us, anyway. She's so fond of you. I can never understand why you're so—distant with her.

ALISON (*Alarmed at this threat of a different mood*) Jimmy—please no!

JIMMY (*Staring at her anxious face*) You're very beautiful. A beautiful, great-eyed squirrel.

(*She nods brightly, relieved*)

Hoarding, nut-munching squirrel. (*She mimes this delightedly*) With highly polished, gleaming fur, and an ostrich feather of a tail.

ALISON Wheeeeeeeee!

JIMMY How I envy you.

(*He stands, her arms around his neck*)

ALISON Well, you're a jolly super bear, too. A really soooooooooooooooper, marvelous bear.

JIMMY Bears and squirrels *are* marvelous.

ALISON Marvelous *and* beautiful.

(*She jumps up and down excitedly, making little "paw gestures"*)

Oooooooh! Oooooooh!

JIMMY What the hell's that?

ALISON That's a dance squirrels do when they're happy.

(*They embrace again*)

JIMMY What makes you think you're happy?

ALISON Everything just seems all right suddenly. That's all. Jimmy——

JIMMY Yes?

ALISON You know I told you I'd something to tell you?

JIMMY Well?

(CLIFF *appears in the doorway*)

CLIFF Didn't get any further than the front door. Miss Drury hadn't gone to church after all. I couldn't get away from her. (*To* ALISON) Someone on the phone for you.

ALISON On the phone? Who on earth is it?

CLIFF Helena something.

(JIMMY *and* ALISON *look at each other quickly*)

JIMMY (*To* CLIFF) Helena Charles?

CLIFF That's it.

ALISON Thank you, Cliff. (*Moves upstage*) I won't be a minute.

CLIFF You will. Old Miss Drury will keep you down there forever. She doesn't think we keep this place clean enough. (*Comes and sits in the armchair down R.*) Thought you were going to make me some tea, you rotter.

(JIMMY *makes no reply*)

What's the matter, boyo?

JIMMY (*Slowly*) That bitch.

CLIFF Who?

JIMMY (*To himself*) Helena Charles.

CLIFF Who is this Helena?

JIMMY One of her old friends. And one of my natural enemies. You're sitting on my chair.

CLIFF Where are we going for a drink?

JIMMY I don't know.

CLIFF Well, you were all for it earlier on.

JIMMY What does she want? What would make her ring up? It can't be for anything pleasant. Oh, well, we shall soon know. (*He settles on the table*) Few minutes ago things didn't seem so bad either. I've just about had enough of this "expense of spirit"[7] lark, as far as women are concerned. Honestly, it's enough to make you become a scoutmaster or something, isn't it? Sometimes I almost envy old Gide and the Greek Chorus boys. Oh, I'm not saying that it mustn't be hell for them a lot of the time. But, at least, they do seem to have a cause—not a particularly good one, it's true. But plenty of them do seem to have a revolutionary fire about them, which is more than you can say for the rest of us. Like Webster, for instance. He doesn't like me—they hardly ever do.

(*He is talking for the sake of it, only half listening to what he is saying*)

I dare say he suspects me because I refuse to treat him either as a clown or as a tragic hero. He's like a man with a strawberry mark—he keeps thrusting it in your face because he can't believe it doesn't interest or horrify you particularly. (*Picks up* ALISON's *handbag thoughtfully, and starts looking through it*) As if I give a damn which way he likes his meat served up. I've got my own strawberry mark—only it's in a different place. No, as far as the Michaelangelo Brigade's concerned, I must be a sort of right-wing deviationist. If the Revolution ever comes, I'll be the first to be put up against the wall, with all the other poor old liberals.

CLIFF (*Indicating* ALISON's *handbag*) Wouldn't you say that that was her private property?

JIMMY You're quite right. But do you know something? Living night and day with another human being has made me predatory and suspicious. I know that the only way of finding out exactly what's going on is to catch them when they don't know you're looking. When she goes out, I go through everything —trunks, cases, drawers, bookcase, everything. Why? To see if there is something of me somewhere, a reference to me. I want to know if I'm being betrayed.

CLIFF You look for trouble, don't you?

JIMMY Only because I'm pretty certain of finding it. (*Brings out a letter from the handbag*) Look at that! Oh, I'm such a fool. This is happening every five minutes of the day. She gets letters. (*He holds it up*) Letters from her mother, letters in which I'm not mentioned at all because my name is a dirty word. And what does she do?

(*Enter* ALISON. *He turns to look at her*)

She writes long letters back to Mummy, and never mentions me at all, because I'm just a dirty word to her too.

(*He throws the letter down at her feet*)

Well, what did your friend want?

ALISON She's at the station. She's—coming over.

JIMMY I see. She said, "Can I come over?" And you said, "My husband, Jimmy—if you'll forgive me using such a dirty word, will be delighted to see you. He'll kick your face in!"

(*He stands up, unable to sustain his anger, poised on the table*)

[7] See Shakespeare's Sonnet 129, a strong rejection of physical love, "lust in action."

ALISON (*Quietly*) She's playing with the company at the Hippodrome this week, and she's got no digs. She can't find anywhere to stay——

JIMMY That I don't believe!

ALISON So I said she could come here until she fixes something else. Miss Drury's got a spare room downstairs.

JIMMY Why not have her in here? Did you tell her to bring her armor? Because she's going to need it!

ALISON (*Vehemently*) Oh, why don't you shut up, please!

JIMMY Oh, my dear wife, you've got so much to learn. I only hope you learn it one day. If only something—something would happen to you, and wake you out of your beauty sleep! (*Coming in close to her*) If you could have a child, and it would die. Let it grow, let a recognizable human face emerge from that little mass of indiarubber and wrinkles. (*She retreats away from him*) Please—if only I could watch you face that. I wonder if you might even become a recognizable human being yourself. But I doubt it.

(*She moves away, stunned, and leans on the gas stove down L. He stands rather helplessly on his own*)

Do you know I have never known the great pleasure of lovemaking when I didn't desire it myself? Oh, it's not that she hasn't her own kind of passion. She has the passion of a python. She just devours me whole every time, as if I were some over-large rabbit. That's me. That bulge around her navel—if you're wondering what it is—it's me. Me, buried alive down there, and going mad, smothered in that peaceful looking coil. Not a sound, not a flicker from her—she doesn't even rumble a little. You'd think that this indigestible mess would stir up some kind of tremor in those distended, overfed tripes—but not her!

(*Crosses up to the door*)

She'll go on sleeping and devouring until there's nothing left of me. (*Exit*)

(ALISON'S *head goes back as if she were about to make some sound. But her mouth remains open and trembling, as* CLIFF *looks on*)

*Curtain*

# Act Two, Scene One

*Two weeks later. Evening.*

ALISON *is standing over the gas stove, pouring water from the kettle into a large teapot. She is only wearing a slip, and her feet are bare. In the room across the hall,* JIMMY *is playing on his jazz trumpet, in intermittent bursts.* ALISON *takes the pot to the table C., which is laid for four people. The Sunday paper jungle around the two armchairs is as luxuriant as ever. It is late afternoon, the end of a hot day. She wipes her forehead. She crosses to the dressing table R., takes out a pair of stockings from one of the drawers, and sits down on the small chair beside it to put them on. While she is doing this, the door opens and* HELENA *enters. She is the same age as* ALISON, *medium height, carefully and expensively dressed. Now and again, when she allows her rather judicial expression of alertness to soften, she is very attractive. Her sense of matriarchal authority makes most men who meet her anxious, not only to please but impress, as if she were the gracious representative of visiting royalty. In this case, the royalty of that middle-class womanhood, which is so eminently secure in its divine rights, that it can afford to tolerate the parliament, and reasonably free assembly of its menfolk. Even from other young women, like* ALISON, *she receives her due of respect and admiration. In* JIMMY, *as one would expect, she arouses all the rabble-rousing instincts of his spirit. And she is not accustomed to having to defend herself against catcalls. However, her sense of modestly exalted responsibility enables her to behave with an impressive show of strength and dignity, although the strain of this is beginning to tell on her a little. She is carrying a large salad colander.*

ALISON Did you manage all right?

HELENA Of course. I've prepared most of the meals in the last week, you know.

ALISON Yes, you have. It's been wonderful having someone to help. Another woman, I mean.

HELENA (*Crossing down L.*) I'm enjoying it. Although I don't think I shall ever get used to having to go down to the bathroom every time I want some water for something.

ALISON It is primitive, isn't it?

HELENA Yes. It is rather.

(*She starts tearing up green salad on to four plates, which she takes from the food cupboard*)

Looking after one man is really enough, but two is rather an undertaking.

ALISON Oh, Cliff looks after himself, more or less. In fact, he helps me quite a lot.

HELENA Can't say I'd noticed it.

ALISON You've been doing it instead, I suppose.

HELENA I see.

ALISON You've settled in so easily somehow.

HELENA Why shouldn't I?

ALISON It's not exactly what you're used to, is it?

HELENA And are you used to it?

ALISON Everything seems very different here now—with you here.

HELENA Does it?

ALISON Yes. I was on my own before——

HELENA Now you've got me. So you're not sorry you asked me to stay?

ALISON Of course not. Did you tell him his tea was ready?

HELENA I banged on the door of Cliff's room, and yelled. He didn't answer, but he must have heard. I don't know where Cliff is.

ALISON (*Leaning back in her chair*) I thought I'd feel cooler after a bath, but I feel hot again already. God, I wish he'd lose that damned trumpet.

HELENA I imagine that's for my benefit.

ALISON Miss Drury will ask us to go soon, I know it. Thank goodness, she isn't in. Listen to him.

HELENA Does he drink?

ALISON Drink? (*Rather startled*) He's not an alcoholic, if that's what you mean.

(*They both pause, listening to the trumpet*)

He'll have the rest of the street banging on the door next.

HELENA (*Pondering*) It's almost as if he wanted to kill someone with it. And me in particular. I've never seen such hatred in someone's eyes before. It's slightly horrifying. Horrifying (*Crossing to food cupboard for tomatoes, beetroot, and cucumber*) and oddly exciting.

(ALISON *faces her dressing mirror, and brushes her hair*)

ALISON He had his own jazz band once. That was when he was still a student, before I knew him. I rather think he'd like to start another, and give up the stall altogether.

HELENA Is Cliff in love with you?

ALISON (*Stops brushing for a moment*) No . . . I don't think so.

HELENA And what about you? You look as though I've asked you a rather peculiar question. The way things are, you might as well be frank with me. I only want to help. After all, your behaviour together is a little strange—by most people's standards, to say the least.

ALISON You mean you've seen us embracing each other?

HELENA Well, it doesn't seem to go on as much as it did, I admit. Perhaps he finds my presence inhibiting—even if Jimmy's isn't.

ALISON We're simply fond of each other—there's no more to it than that.

HELENA Darling, really! It can't be as simple as that.

ALISON You mean there must be something physical too? I suppose there is, but it's not exactly a consuming passion with either of us. It's just a relaxed, cheerful sort of thing, like being warm in bed. You're too comfortable to bother about moving for the sake of some other pleasure.

HELENA I find it difficult to believe anyone's that lazy!

ALISON I think *we* are.

HELENA And what about Jimmy? After all, he is your husband. Do you mean to say he actually approves of it?

ALISON It isn't easy to explain. It's what he would call a question of allegiances, and he expects you to be pretty literal about them. Not only about himself and all the things he believes in, his present and his future, but his past as well. All the people he admires and loves, and has loved. The friends he used to know, people I've never even known—and probably wouldn't have liked. His father, who died years ago. Even the other women he's loved. Do you understand?

HELENA Do you?

ALISON I've tried to. But I still can't bring myself to feel the way he does about things. I can't believe that he's right somehow.

HELENA Well, that's something, anyway.

ALISON If things have worked out with Cliff, it's because he's kind and lovable, and I've grown genuinely fond of him. But it's been a fluke. It's worked because Cliff is such a nice person anyway. With Hugh, it was quite different.

HELENA Hugh?

ALISON Hugh Tanner. He and Jimmy were friends almost from childhood. Mrs. Tanner is his mother——

HELENA Oh yes—the one who started him off in the sweet business.

ALISON That's right. Well, after Jimmy and I were married, we'd no money—about eight pounds ten in actual fact—and no home. He didn't even have a job. He'd only left the university about a year. (*Smiles*) No—left. I don't think one "comes down" [1] from Jimmy's university. According to him, it's not even red brick, but white tile. Anyway, we went off to live in Hugh's flat. It was over a warehouse in Poplar.

HELENA Yes. I remember seeing the postmark on your letters.

ALISON Well, that was where I found myself on my wedding night. Hugh and I disliked each other on sight, and Jimmy knew it. He was so proud of us both, so pathetically anxious that we should take to each other. Like a child showing off his toys. We had a little wedding celebration, and the three of us tried to get tight on some cheap port they'd brought in. Hugh got more and more subtly insulting—he'd a rare talent for that. Jimmy got steadily depressed, and I just sat there, listening to their talk, looking and feeling very stupid. For the first time in my life, I was cut off from the kind of people I'd always known, my family, my friends, everybody. And I'd burnt my boats. After all those weeks of brawling with Mummy and Daddy about Jimmy, I knew I couldn't appeal to them without looking foolish and cheap. It was just before the General Election, I remember, and Nigel was busy getting himself into Parliament. He didn't have time for anyone but his constituents. Oh, he'd have been sweet and kind, I know.

HELENA (*Moving in C.*) Darling, why didn't you come to me?

ALISON You were away on tour in some play, I think.

HELENA So I was.

ALISON Those next few months at the flat in Poplar were a nightmare. I suppose I must be soft and

[1] Alison means that Jimmy's "white tile" university was not respected enough to use "come down," the Oxford and Cambridge term for "graduate."

squeamish, and snobbish, but I felt as though I'd been dropped in a jungle. I couldn't believe that two people, two educated people could be so savage, and so—so uncompromising. Mummy has always said that Jimmy is utterly ruthless, but she hasn't met Hugh. He takes the first prize for ruthlessness—from all comers. Together, they were frightening. They both came to regard me as a sort of hostage from those sections of society they had declared war on.

HELENA How were you living all this time?

ALISON I had a tiny bit coming in from a few shares I had left, but it hardly kept us. Mummy had made me sign everything else over to her, in trust, when she knew I was really going to marry Jimmy.

HELENA Just as well, I imagine.

ALISON They soon thought of a way out of that. A brilliant campaign. They started inviting themselves—through me—to people's houses, friends of Nigel's and mine, friends of Daddy's, oh everyone: the Arksdens, the Tarnatts, the Wains——

HELENA Not the Wains?

ALISON Just about everyone I'd ever known. Your people must have been among the few we missed out. It was just enemy territory to them, and, as I say, they used me as a hostage. We'd set out from headquarters in Poplar, and carry out our raids on the enemy in W.1, S.W.1, S.W.3, and W.8.[2] In my name, we'd gatecrash everywhere—cocktails, week-ends, even a couple of houseparties. I used to hope that one day, somebody would have the guts to slam the door in our faces, but they didn't. They were too well-bred, and probably sorry for me as well. Hugh and Jimmy despised them for it. So we went on plundering them, wolfing their food and drinks, and smoking their cigars like ruffians. Oh, they enjoyed themselves.

HELENA Apparently.

ALISON Hugh fairly revelled in the role of the barbarian invader. Sometimes I thought he might even dress the part—you know, furs, spiked helmet, sword. He even got a fiver out of Old Man Wain once. Blackmail, of course. People would have signed almost anything to get rid of us. He told him that we were about to be turned out of our flat for not paying the rent. At least it was true.

HELENA I don't understand you. You must have been crazy.

ALISON Afraid more than anything.

HELENA But letting them do it! Letting them get away with it! You managed to stop them stealing the silver, I suppose?

ALISON Oh, they knew their guerrilla warfare better than that. Hugh tried to seduce some fresh-faced young girl at the Arksdens' once, but that was the only time we were more or less turned out.

HELENA It's almost unbelievable. I don't understand your part in it all. Why? That's what I don't see. Why did you——

ALISON Marry him? There must be about six different answers. When the family came back from India, everything seemed, I don't know—unsettled? Anyway, Daddy seemed remote and rather irritable. And Mummy—well, you know Mummy. I didn't have much to worry about. I didn't know I was born as Jimmy says. I met him at a party. I remember it so clearly. I was almost twenty-one. The men there all looked as though they distrusted him, and as for the women, they were all intent on showing their contempt for this rather odd creature, but no one seemed quite sure how to do it. He'd come to the party on a bicycle, he told me, and there was oil all over his dinner jacket. It had been such a lovely day, and he'd been in the sun. Everything about him seemed to burn, his face, the edges of his hair glistened and seemed to spring off his head, and his eyes were so blue and full of the sun. He looked so young and frail, in spite of the tired line of his mouth. I knew I was taking on more than I was ever likely to be capable of bearing, but there never seemed to be any choice. Well, the howl of outrage and astonishment went up from the family, and that did it. Whether or no he was in love with me, that did it. He made up his mind to marry me. They did just about everything they could think of to stop us.

HELENA Yes, it wasn't a very pleasant business. But you can see their point.

ALISON Jimmy went into battle with his axe swinging round his head—frail, and so full of fire. I had never seen anything like it. The old story of the knight in shining armor—except that his armor didn't really shine very much.

HELENA And what about Hugh?

ALISON Things got steadily worse between us. He and Jimmy even went to some of Nigel's political meetings. They took bunches of their Poplar cronies with them, and broke them up for him.

HELENA He's really a savage, isn't he?

ALISON Well, Hugh was writing some novel or other, and he made up his mind he must go abroad—to China, or some God-forsaken place. He said that England was finished for us, anyway. All the old gang was back—Dame Alison's Mob, as he used to call it. The only real hope was to get out, and try somewhere else. He wanted us to go with him, but Jimmy refused to go. There was a terrible, bitter row over it. Jimmy accused Hugh of giving up, and he thought it was wrong of him to go off forever, and leave his mother all on her own. He was upset by the whole idea. They quarrelled for days over it. I almost wished they'd both go, and leave me behind. Anyway, they broke up. A few months later we came up here, and Hugh went off to find the New Millennium on his own. Sometimes, I think Hugh's mother blames me for it all. Jimmy, too, in a way, although he's never said so. He never mentions it. But whenever that woman looks at me, I can feel her thinking, "If it hadn't been for you, everything would have been all right. We'd have all been happy." Not that I dislike her—I don't. She's very sweet, in fact. Jimmy seems to adore her principally because she's been poor almost all her life, and she's frankly

[2] Postal-zone designations (West 1, Southwest 1, *etc.*) for the upper-class, fashionable sections of London.

ignorant. I'm quite aware how snobbish that sounds, but it happens to be the truth.

HELENA Alison, listen to me. You've got to make up your mind what you're going to do. You're going to have a baby, and you have a new responsibility. Before, it was different—there was only yourself at stake. But you can't go on living in this way any longer. (*To her*)

ALISON I'm so tired. I dread him coming into the room.

HELENA Why haven't you told him you're going to have a child?

ALISON I don't know. (*Suddenly anticipating* HELENA'S *train of thought*) Oh, it's his, all right. There couldn't be any doubt of that. You see——(*She smiles*) I've never really wanted anyone else.

HELENA Listen, darling—you've got to tell him. Either he learns to behave like anyone else, and looks after you——

ALISON Or?

HELENA Or you must get out of this mad-house. (*Trumpet crescendo*) This menagerie. He doesn't seem to know what love or anything else means.

ALISON (*Pointing to chest of drawers up R.*) You see that bear, and that squirrel? Well, that's him, and that's me.

HELENA Meaning?

ALISON The game we play: bears and squirrels, squirrels and bears.

(HELENA *looks rather blank*)

Yes, it's quite mad, I know. Quite mad. (*Picks up the two animals*) That's him. . . . And that's me. . . .

HELENA I didn't realise he was a bit fey, as well as everything else!

ALISON Oh, there's nothing fey about Jimmy. It's just all we seem to have left. Or had left. Even bears and squirrels seem to have gone their own ways now.

HELENA Since I arrived?

ALISON It started during those first months we had alone together—after Hugh went abroad. It was the one way of escaping from everything—a sort of unholy priest-hole of being animals to one another. We could become little furry creatures with little furry brains. Full of dumb, uncomplicated affection for each other. Playful, careless creatures in their own cosy zoo for two. A silly symphony for people who couldn't bear the pain of being human beings any longer. And now, even they are dead, poor little silly animals. They were all love, and no brains. (*Puts them back*)

HELENA (*Gripping her arm*) Listen to me. You've got to fight him. Fight, or get out. Otherwise, he *will* kill you.

(*Enter* CLIFF)

CLIFF There you are, dullin'. Hullo, Helena. Tea ready?

ALISON Yes, dear, it's all ready. Give Jimmy a call, will you?

CLIFF Right. (*Yelling back through door*) Hey, you horrible man! Stop that bloody noise, and come and get your tea! (*Coming in C.*) Going out?

HELENA (*Crossing to L.*) Yes.

CLIFF Pictures?

HELENA No. (*Pause*) Church.

CLIFF (*Really surprised*) Oh! I see. Both of you?

HELENA Yes. Are you coming?

CLIFF Well. . . . I—I haven't read the papers properly yet. Tea, tea, tea! Let's have some tea, shall we?

(*He sits at the upstage end of the table.* HELENA *puts the four plates of salad on it, sits down L., and they begin the meal.* ALISON *is making up her face at her dressing table. Presently,* JIMMY *enters. He places his trumpet on the bookcase, and comes above the table*)

Hullo, boyo. Come and have your tea. That blinkin' trumpet—why don't you stuff it away somewhere?

JIMMY You like it all right. Anyone who doesn't like real jazz, hasn't any feeling either for music or people. (*He sits R. end of table*)

HELENA Rubbish.

JIMMY (*To* CLIFF) That seems to prove my point for you. Did you know that Webster played the banjo?

CLIFF No, does he really?

HELENA He said he'd bring it along next time he came.

ALISON (*Muttering*) Oh, no!

JIMMY Why is it that nobody knows how to treat the papers in this place? Look at them. I haven't even glanced at them yet—not the posh ones, anyway.

CLIFF By the way, can I look at your *New*——

JIMMY No, you can't! (*Loudly*) You want anything, you pay for it. Like I have to. Price——

CLIFF Price ninepence, obtainable from any bookstall! You're a mean old man, that's what you are.

JIMMY What do you want to read it for, anyway? You've no intellect, no curiosity. It all just washes over you. Am I right?

CLIFF Right.

JIMMY What are you, you Welsh trash?

CLIFF Nothing, that's what I am.

JIMMY Nothing, are you? Blimey, you ought to be Prime Minister. You must have been talking to some of my wife's friends. They're a very intellectual set, aren't they? I've seen 'em.

(CLIFF *and* HELENA *carry on with their meal*)

They all sit around feeling very spiritual, with their mental hands on each other's knees, discussing sex as if it were the Art of Fugue. If you don't want to be an emotional old spinster, just you listen to your dad!

(*He starts eating. The silent hostility of the two women has set him off on the scent, and he looks quite cheerful, although the occasional, thick edge of his voice belies it*)

You know your trouble, son? Too anxious to please.

HELENA Thank heavens somebody is!

JIMMY You'll end up like one of those chocolate meringues my wife is so fond of. My wife—that's the one on the tom-toms behind me. Sweet and sticky on the outside, and sink your teeth in it, (*Savoring every word*) inside, all white, messy, and disgusting. (*Offering teapot sweetly to* HELENA) Tea?

HELENA Thank you.

*(He smiles, and pours out a cup for her)*

JIMMY That's how you'll end up, my boy—black hearted, evil minded, and vicious.

HELENA *(Taking cup)* Thank you.

JIMMY And those old favorites, your friends and mine: sycophantic, phlegmatic, and, of course, top of the bill—pusillanimous.

HELENA *(To* ALISON*)* Aren't you going to have your tea?

ALISON Won't be long.

JIMMY Thought of the title for a new song today. It's called "You can quit hanging round my counter, Mildred, 'cos you'll find my position is closed." *(Turning to* ALISON *suddenly)* Good?

ALISON Oh, very good.

JIMMY Thought you'd like it. If I can slip in a religious angle, it should be a big hit. *(To* HELENA*)* Don't you think so? I was thinking you might help me there. *(She doesn't reply)* It might help you if I recite the lyrics. Let's see now, it's something like this:

I'm so tired of necking,
Of pecking, home wrecking,
Of empty bed blues—
Just pass me the booze.
I'm tired of being hetero,
Rather ride on the metero,
Just pass me the booze.
This perpetual whoring
Gets quite dull and boring,
So avoid that old python coil,
And pass me the celibate oil.
You can quit, etc.

No?

CLIFF Very good, boyo.

JIMMY Oh, yes, and I know what I meant to tell you —I wrote a poem while I was at the market yesterday. If you're interested, which you obviously are. *(To* HELENA*)* It should appeal to you, in particular. It's soaked in the theology of Dante, with a good slosh of Eliot as well. It starts off "There are no dry cleaners in Cambodia!"

CLIFF What do you call it?

JIMMY "The Cess Pool." Myself being a stone dropped in it, you see——

CLIFF You should be dropped in it, all right.

HELENA *(To* JIMMY*)* Why do you try so hard to be unpleasant?

*(He turns very deliberately, delighted that she should rise to the bait so soon—he's scarcely in his stride yet)*

JIMMY What's that?

HELENA Do you have to be so offensive?

JIMMY You mean now? You think I'm being offensive? You under-estimate me. *(Turning to* ALISON*)* Doesn't she?

HELENA I think you're a very tiresome young man.

*(A slight pause as his delight catches up with him. He roars with laughter)*

JIMMY Oh dear, oh dear! My wife's friends! Pass Lady Bracknell the cucumber sandwiches,[3] will you?

*(He returns to his meal, but his curiosity about* ALISON'S *preparations at the mirror won't be denied any longer. He turns round casually, and speaks to her)*

Going out?

ALISON That's right.

JIMMY On a Sunday evening in this town? Where on earth are you going?

ALISON *(Rising)* I'm going out with Helena.

JIMMY That's not a direction—that's an affliction.

*(She crosses to the table, and sits down C. He leans forward, and addresses her again)*

I didn't ask you what was the matter with you. I asked you where you were going.

HELENA *(Steadily)* She's going to church.

*(He has been prepared for some plot, but he is as genuinely surprised by this as* CLIFF *was a few minutes earlier)*

JIMMY You're doing what?

*(Silence)*

Have you gone out of your mind or something? *(To* HELENA*)* You're determined to win her, aren't you? So it's come to this now! How feeble can you get? *(His rage mounting within)* When I think of what I did, what I endured, to get you out——

ALISON *(Recognizing an onslaught on the way, starts to panic)* Oh yes, we all know what you did for me! You rescued me from the wicked clutches of my family, and all my friends! I'd still be rotting away at home, if you hadn't ridden up on your charger, and carried me off!

*(The wild note in her voice has reassured him. His anger cools and hardens. His voice is quite calm when he speaks)*

JIMMY The funny thing is, you know, I really did have to ride up on a white charger—off-white, really. Mummy locked her up in their eight-bedroomed castle, didn't she? There is no limit to what the middle-aged mummy will do in the holy crusade against ruffians like me. Mummy and I took one quick look at each other, and, from then on, the age of chivalry was dead. I knew that, to protect her innocent young, she wouldn't hesitate to cheat, lie, bully, and blackmail. Threatened with me, a young man without money, background, or even looks, she'd bellow like a rhinoceros in labor—enough to make every male rhino for miles turn white, and pledge himself to celibacy. But even I under-estimated her strength. Mummy may look over-fed and a bit flabby on the outside, but don't let that well-bred guzzler fool you. Underneath all that, she's armor-plated——

*(He clutches wildly for something to shock* HELENA *with)*

She's as rough as a night in a Bombay brothel, and as tough as a matelot's arm. She's probably in that bloody cistern, taking down every word we say.

[3] The managing-guardian in Oscar Wilde's *The Importance of Being Earnest* (1895). Wilde used cucumber sandwiches in the "tea scene" in Act I.

(*Kicks cistern*) Can you 'ear me, mother. (*Sits on it, beats like bongo drums*) Just about get her in there. Let me give you an example of this lady's tactics. You may have noticed that I happen to wear my hair rather long. Now, if my wife is honest, or concerned enough to explain, she could tell you that this is not due to any dark, unnatural instincts I possess, but because (a) I can usually think of better things than a haircut to spend two bob on, and (b) I prefer long hair. But that obvious, innocent explanation didn't appeal to Mummy at all. So she hires detectives to watch me, to see if she can't somehow get me into the *News of the World*. All so that I shan't carry off her daughter on that poor old charger of mine, all tricked out and caparisoned in discredited passions and ideals! The old grey mare that actually once led the charge against the old order—well, she certainly ain't what she used to be. It was all she could do to carry me, but your weight (*To* ALISON) was too much for her. She just dropped dead on the way.

CLIFF (*Quietly*) Don't let's brawl, boyo. It won't do any good.

JIMMY Why *don't* we brawl? It's the only thing left I'm any good at.

CLIFF Jimmy, boy——

JIMMY (*To* ALISON) You've let this genuflecting sin-jobber win you over, haven't you? She's got you back, hasn't she?

HELENA Oh, for heaven's sake, don't be such a bully! You've no right to talk about her mother like that!

JIMMY (*Capable of anything now*) I've got every right. That old bitch should be dead! (*To* ALISON) Well? Aren't I right?

(CLIFF *and* HELENA *look at* ALISON *tensely, but she just gazes at her plate*)

I said she's an old bitch, and should be dead! What's the matter with you? Why don't you leap to her defence!

(CLIFF *gets up quickly, and takes his arm*)

CLIFF Jimmy, don't!

(JIMMY *pushes him back savagely, and he sits down helplessly, turning his head away on to his hand*)

JIMMY If someone said something like that about me, she'd react soon enough—she'd spring into her well-known lethargy, and say nothing! I say she ought to be dead. (*He brakes for a fresh spurt later. He's saving his strength for the knock-out*) My God, those worms will need a good dose of salts the day they get through her! Oh what a bellyache you've got coming to you, my little wormy ones! Alison's mother is on the way! (*In what he intends to be a comic declamatory voice*) She will pass away, my friends, leaving a trail of worms gasping for laxatives behind her—from purgatives to purgatory.

(*He smiles down at* ALISON, *but still she hasn't broken.* CLIFF *won't look at them. Only* HELENA *looks at him. Denied the other two, he addresses her*)

Is anything the matter?

HELENA I feel rather sick, that's all. Sick with contempt and loathing.

(*He can feel her struggling on the end of his line, and he looks at her rather absently*)

JIMMY One day, when I'm no longer spending my days running a sweet-stall, I may write a book about us all. It's all here. (*Slapping his forehead*) Written in flames a mile high. And it won't be recollected in tranquillity either, picking daffodils with Auntie Wordsworth. It'll be recollected in fire, and blood. My blood.

HELENA (*Thinking patient reasonableness may be worth a try*) She simply said that she's going to church with me. I don't see why that calls for this incredible outburst.

JIMMY Don't you? Perhaps you're not as clever as I thought.

HELENA You think the world's treated you pretty badly, don't you?

ALISON (*Turning her face away L.*) Oh, don't try and take his suffering away from him—he'd be lost without it.

(*He looks at her in surprise, but he turns back to* HELENA. ALISON *can have her turn again later*)

JIMMY I thought this play you're touring in finished up on Saturday week?

HELENA That's right.

JIMMY Eight days ago, in fact.

HELENA Alison wanted me to stay.

JIMMY What are you plotting?

HELENA Don't you think we've had enough of the heavy villain?

JIMMY (*To* ALISON) You don't believe in all that stuff. Why you don't believe in anything. You're just doing it to be vindictive, aren't you? Why—why are you letting her influence you like this?

ALISON (*Starting to break*) Why, why, why, why! (*Putting her hands over her ears*) That word's pulling my head off!

JIMMY And as long as you're around, I'll go on using it.

(*He crosses down to the armchair, and seats himself on the back of it. He addresses* HELENA'*s back*)

JIMMY The last time she was in a church was when she was married to me. I expect that surprises you, doesn't it? It was expediency, pure and simple. We were in a hurry, you see. (*The comedy of this strikes him at once, and he laughs*) Yes, we were actually in a hurry! Lusting for the slaughter! Well, the local registrar was a particular pal of Daddy's, and we knew he'd spill the beans to the Colonel like a shot. So we had to seek out some local vicar who didn't know him quite so well. But it was no use. When my best man—a chap I'd met in the pub that morning—and I turned up, Mummy and Daddy were in the church already. They'd found out at the last moment, and had come to watch the execution carried out. How I remember looking down at them, full of beer for breakfast, and feeling a bit buzzed. Mummy was slumped over her pew in a heap—the noble, female rhino, pole-axed at last! And Daddy sat beside her, upright and unafraid, dreaming of his days among the Indian Princes, and unable to believe he'd left his horsewhip at home. Just the two of them in that empty church—them and me. (*Coming out of his remembrance suddenly*) I'm not sure what happened after that. We must have been married, I suppose. I think I remember being sick in the vestry. (*To* ALISON) Was I?

HELENA Haven't you finished?

(*He can smell blood again, and he goes on calmly, cheerfully*)

JIMMY (*To* ALISON) Are you going to let yourself be taken in by this saint in Dior's clothing? I will tell you the simple truth about her. (*Articulating with care*) She is a cow. I wouldn't mind that so much, but she seems to have become a sacred cow as well!

CLIFF You've gone too far, Jimmy. Now dry up!

HELENA Oh, let him go on.

JIMMY (*To* CLIFF) I suppose you're going over to that side as well. Well, why don't you? Helena will help to make it pay off for you. She's an expert in the New Economics—the Economics of the Supernatural. It's all a simple matter of payments and penalties. (*Rises*) She's one of those apocalyptic share pushers who are spreading all those rumours about a transfer of power.

(*His imagination is racing, and the words pour out*)

Reason and Progress, the old firm, is selling out! Everyone get out while the going's good. Those forgotten shares you had in the old traditions, the old beliefs are going up—up and up and up. (*Moves up L.*) There's going to be a change over. A new Board of Directors, who are going to see that the dividends are always attractive, and that they go to the right people. (*Facing them*) Sell out everything you've got: all those stocks in the old, free inquiry. (*Crosses to above table*) The Big Crash is coming, you can't escape it, so get in on the ground floor with Helena and her friends while there's still time. And there isn't much of it left. Tell me, what could be more gilt-edged than the next world! It's a capital gain, and it's all yours.

(*He moves round the table, back to his chair R.*)

You see, I know Helena and her kind so very well. In fact, her kind are everywhere, you can't move for them. They're a romantic lot. They spend their time mostly looking forward to the past. The only place they can see the light is the Dark Ages. She's moved long ago into a lovely little cottage of the soul, cut right off from the ugly problems of the twentieth century altogether. She prefers to be cut off from all the conveniences we've fought to get for centuries. She'd rather go down to the ecstatic little shed at the bottom of the garden to relieve her sense of guilt. Our Helena is full of ecstatic wind—(*He* leans across *the table at her*) aren't you?

(*He waits for her to reply*)

HELENA (*Quite calmly*) It's a pity you've been so far away all this time. I would probably have slapped your face.

(*They look into each other's eyes across the table. He moves slowly up, above* CLIFF, *until he is beside her*)

You've behaved like this ever since I first came.

JIMMY Helena, have you ever watched somebody die?

(*She makes a move to rise*)

No, don't move away.

(*She remains seated, and looks up at him*)

It doesn't look dignified enough for you.

HELENA (*Like ice*) If you come any nearer, I will slap your face.

(*He looks down at her, a grin smouldering round his mouth*)

JIMMY I hope you won't make the mistake of thinking for one moment that I am a gentleman.

HELENA I'm not very likely to do that.

JIMMY (*Bringing his face close to hers*) I've no public school scruples about hitting girls. (*Gently*) If you slap my face—by God, I'll lay you out!

HELENA You probably would. You're the type.

JIMMY You bet I'm the type. I'm the type that detests physical violence. Which is why, if I find some woman trying to cash in on what she thinks is my defenseless chivalry by lashing out with her frail little fists, I lash back at her.

HELENA Is that meant to be subtle, or just plain Irish?

(*His grin widens*)

JIMMY I think you and I understand one another all right. But you haven't answered my question. I said: have you watched somebody die?

HELENA No, I haven't.

JIMMY Anyone who's never watched somebody die is suffering from a pretty bad case of virginity.

(*His good humor of a moment ago deserts him, as he begins to remember*)

For twelve months, I watched my father dying—when I was ten years old. He'd come back from the war in Spain, you see. And certain god-fearing gentlemen there had made such a mess of him, he didn't have long left to live. Everyone knew it—even I knew it.

(*He moves R.*)

But, you see, I was the only one who cared. (*Turns to the window*) His family were embarrassed by the whole business. Embarrassed and irritated. (*Looking out*) As for my mother, all she could think about was the fact that she had allied herself to a man who seemed to be on the wrong side in all things. My mother was all for being associated with minorities, provided they were the smart, fashionable ones.

(*He moves up C. again*)

We all of us waited for him to die. The family sent him a cheque every month, and hoped he'd get on with it quietly, without too much vulgar fuss. My mother looked after him without complaining, and that was about all. Perhaps she pitied him. I suppose she was capable of that. (*With a kind of appeal in his voice*) But I was the only one who cared!

(*He moves L., behind the armchair*)

Every time I sat on the edge of his bed, to listen to him talking or reading to me, I had to fight back my tears. At the end of twelve months, I was a veteran.

(*He leans forward on the back of the armchair*)

All that that feverish failure of a man had to listen to him was a small, frightened boy. I spent hour upon hour in that tiny bedroom. He would talk to me for hours, pouring out all that was left of his life to one, lonely, bewildered little boy, who could barely understand half of what he said. All he could feel was the despair and the bitterness, the sweet, sickly smell of a dying man.

(*He moves around the chair*)

You see, I learnt at an early age what it was to be angry—angry and helpless. And I can never forget it. (*Sits*) I knew more about—love . . . betrayal . . . and death, when I was ten years old than you will probably ever know all your life.

(*They all sit silently. Presently,* HELENA *rises*)

HELENA Time we went.

(ALISON *nods*)

I'll just get my things together. (*Crosses to door*) I'll see you downstairs. (*Exit*)

(*A slight pause*)

JIMMY (*Not looking at her, almost whispering*) Doesn't it matter to you—what people do to me? What are you trying to do to me? I've given you just everything. Doesn't it mean *anything* to you?

(*Her back stiffens. His axe-swinging bravado has vanished, and his voice crumples in disabled rage*)

JIMMY You Judas! You phlegm! She's taking you with her, and you're so bloody feeble, you'll let her do it!

(ALISON *suddenly takes hold of her cup, and hurls it on the floor. He's drawn blood at last. She looks down at the pieces on the floor, and then at him. Then she crosses R., takes out a dress on a hanger, and slips it on. As she is zipping up the side, she feels giddy, and she has to lean against the wardrobe for support. She closes her eyes*)

ALISON (*Softly*) All I want is a little peace.

JIMMY Peace! God! She wants peace! (*Hardly able to get his words out*) My heart is so full, I feel ill—and she wants peace!

(*She crosses to the bed to put on her shoes.* CLIFF *gets up from the table, and sits in the armchair R. He picks up a paper, and looks at that.* JIMMY *has recovered slightly, and manages to sound almost detached*)

I rage, and shout my head off, and everyone thinks "poor chap!" or "what an objectionable young man!" But that girl there can twist your arm off with her silence. I've sat in this chair in the dark for hours. And, although she knows I'm feeling as I feel now, she's turned over, and gone to sleep. (*He gets up and faces* CLIFF, *who doesn't look up from his paper*) One of us is crazy. One of us is mean and stupid and crazy. Which is it? Is it me? Is it me, standing here like an hysterical girl, hardly able to get my words out? Or is it her? Sitting there, putting on her shoes to go out with that—— (*But inspiration has deserted him by now*) Which is it?

(CLIFF *is still looking down at his paper*)

I wish to heaven you'd try loving her, that's all.

(*He moves up C., watching her look for her gloves*)

Perhaps, one day, you may want to come back. I shall wait for that day. I want to stand up in your tears, and splash about in them, and sing. I want to be there when you grovel. I want to be there, I want to watch it, I want the front seat.

(HELENA *enters, carrying two prayer books*)

I want to see your face rubbed in the mud—that's all I can hope for. There's nothing else I want any longer.

HELENA (*After a moment*) There's a phone call for you.

JIMMY (*Turning*) Well, it can't be anything good, can it? (*Exit*)

HELENA All ready?

ALISON Yes—I think so.

HELENA You feel all right, don't you? (*She nods*) What's he been raving about now? Oh, what does it matter? He makes me want to claw his hair out by the roots. When I think of what you will be going through in a few months' time—and all for him! It's as if you'd done *him* wrong! These *men!* (*Turning on* CLIFF) And all the time you just sit there, and do nothing!

CLIFF (*Looking up slowly*) That's right—I just sit here.

HELENA What's the matter with you? What sort of a man are you?

CLIFF I'm not the District Commissioner, you know. Listen, Helena—I don't feel like Jimmy does about you, but I'm not exactly on your side, either. And since you've been here, everything's certainly been worse than it's ever been. This has always been a battlefield, but I'm pretty certain that if I hadn't been here, everything would have been over between these two long ago. I've been a—a no-man's land between them. Sometimes, it's been still and peaceful, no incidents, and we've all been reasonably happy. But most of the time, it's simply a very narrow strip of plain hell. But where I come from, we're used to brawling and excitement. Perhaps I even enjoy being in the thick of it. I love these two people very much. (*He looks at her steadily, and adds simply*) And I pity all of us.

HELENA Are you including me in that? (*But she goes on quickly to avoid his reply*) I don't understand him, you, or any of it. All I know is that none of you seems to know how to behave in a decent, civilized way. (*In command now*) Listen, Alison—I've sent your father a wire.

ALISON (*Numbed and vague by now*) Oh?

(HELENA *looks at her, and realizes quickly that everything now will have to depend on her own authority. She tries to explain patiently*)

HELENA Look, dear—he'll get it first thing in the morning. I thought it would be better than trying to explain the situation over the phone. I asked him to come up, and fetch you home tomorrow.

ALISON What did you say?

HELENA Simply that you wanted to come home, and would he come up for you.

ALISON I see.

HELENA I knew that would be quite enough. I told him there was nothing to worry about, so they won't worry and think there's been an accident or anything. I had to do something, dear. (*Very gently*) You didn't mind, did you?

ALISON No, I don't mind. Thank you.

HELENA And you will go when he comes for you?

ALISON (*Pause*) Yes. I'll go.

HELENA (*Relieved*) I expect he'll drive up. He should be here about tea-time. It'll give you plenty of time to get your things together. And, perhaps, after you've gone—Jimmy (*Saying the word almost with difficulty*) will come to his senses, and face up to things.

ALISON Who was on the phone?

HELENA I didn't catch it properly. It rang after I'd sent the wire off—just as soon as I put the receiver down almost. I had to go back down the stairs again. Sister somebody, I think.

ALISON Must have been a hospital or something. Unless he knows someone in a convent—*that* doesn't seem very likely, does it? Well, we'll be late, if we don't hurry.

(*She puts down one of the prayer books on the table. Enter* JIMMY. *He comes down C., between the two women*)

CLIFF All right, boyo?

JIMMY (*To* ALISON) It's Hugh's mum. She's—had a stroke.

(*Slight pause*)

ALISON I'm sorry.

(JIMMY *sits on the bed*)

CLIFF How bad is it?

JIMMY They didn't say much. But I think she's dying.

CLIFF Oh dear. . . .

JIMMY (*Rubbing his fist over his face*) It doesn't make any sense at all. Do you think it does?

ALISON I'm sorry—I really am.

CLIFF Anything I can do?

JIMMY The London train goes in half an hour. You'd better order me a taxi.

CLIFF Right. (*He crosses to the door, and stops*) Do you want me to come with you, boy?

JIMMY No thanks. After all, you hardly knew her. It's not for you to go.

(HELENA *looks quickly at* ALISON)

She may not even remember me, for all I know.

CLIFF O.K. (*Exit*)

JIMMY I remember the first time I showed her your photograph—just after we were married. She looked at it, and the tears just welled up in her eyes, and she said: "But she's so beautiful! She's so beautiful!" She kept repeating it as if she couldn't believe it. Sounds a bit simple and sentimental when you repeat it. But it was pure gold the way she said it.

(*He looks at her. She is standing by the dressing table, her back to him*)

She got a kick out of you, like she did out of everything else. Hand me my shoes, will you?

(*She kneels down, and hands them to him*)

(*Looking down at his feet*) You're coming with me, aren't you? She (*He shrugs*) hasn't got anyone else now. I . . . need you . . . to come with me.

(*He looks into her eyes, but she turns away, and stands up. Outside, the church bells start ringing.* HELENA *moves up to the door and waits, watching them closely.* ALISON *stands quite still,* JIMMY'S *eyes burning into her. Then, she crosses in front of him to the table where she picks up the prayer book, her back to him. She wavers, and seems about to say something, but turns upstage instead, and walks quickly to the door*)

ALISON (*Hardly audible*) Let's go.

(*She goes out,* HELENA *following.* JIMMY *gets up, looks about him unbelievingly, and leans against the chest of drawers. The teddy bear is close to his face, and he picks it up gently, looks at it quickly, and throws it downstage. It hits the floor with a thud, and it makes a rattling, groaning sound—as guaranteed in the advertisement.* JIMMY *falls forward on to the bed, his face buried in the covers*)

*Quick Curtain*

## Act Two, Scene Two

*The following evening. When the curtain rises,* ALISON *is discovered R., going from her dressing table to the bed, and packing her things into a suitcase. Sitting down L. is her father,* COLONEL REDFERN, *a large handsome man, about sixty. Forty years of being a soldier sometimes conceals the essentially gentle, kindly man underneath. Brought up to command respect, he is often slightly withdrawn and uneasy now that he finds himself in a world where his authority has lately become less and less unquestionable. His wife would relish the present situation, but he is only disturbed and bewildered by it. He looks around him, discreetly scrutinizing everything.*

COLONEL (*Partly to himself*) I'm afraid it's all beyond me. I suppose it always will be. As for Jimmy—he just speaks a different language from any of us. Where did you say he'd gone?

ALISON He's gone to see Mrs. Tanner.

COLONEL Who?

ALISON Hugh Tanner's mother.

COLONEL Oh, I see.

ALISON She's been taken ill—a stroke. Hugh's abroad, as you know, so Jimmy's gone to London to see her.

(*He nods*)

He wanted me to go with him.

COLONEL Didn't she start him off in this sweet-stall business?

ALISON Yes.

COLONEL What is she like? Nothing like her son, I trust?

ALISON Not remotely. Oh—how can you describe her? Rather—ordinary. What Jimmy insists on calling "working class." A charwoman who married an actor, worked hard all her life, and spent most of it struggling to support her husband and her son. Jimmy and she are very fond of each other.

COLONEL So you didn't go with him?

ALISON No.

COLONEL Who's looking after the sweet-stall?

ALISON Cliff. He should be in soon.

COLONEL Oh, yes, of course—Cliff. Does he live here, too?

ALISON Yes. His room is just across the landing.

COLONEL Sweet-stall. It does seem an extraordinary thing for an educated young man to be occupying himself with. Why should he want to do that, of all things? I've always thought he must be quite clever in his way.

ALISON (*No longer interested in this problem*) Oh, he tried so many things—journalism, advertising, even vacuum cleaners for a few weeks. He seems to have been as happy doing this as anything else.

COLONEL I've often wondered what it was like—where you were living, I mean. You didn't tell us very much in your letters.

ALISON There wasn't a great deal to tell you. There's not much social life here.

COLONEL Oh, I know what you mean. You were afraid of being disloyal to your husband.

ALISON Disloyal! (*She laughs*) He thought it was high treason of me to write to you at all! I used to have to dodge downstairs for the post, so that he wouldn't see I was getting letters from home. Even then I had to hide them.

COLONEL He really does hate us, doesn't he?

ALISON Oh, yes—don't have any doubts about that. He hates all of us.

COLONEL (*Sighs*) It seems a great pity. It was all so unfortunate—unfortunate and unnecessary. I'm afraid I can't help feeling that he must have had a certain amount of right on his side.

ALISON (*Puzzled by this admission*) Right on his side?

COLONEL It's a little late to admit it, I know, but your mother and I weren't entirely free from blame. I have never said anything—there was no point afterwards—but I have always believed that she went too far over Jimmy. Of course, she was extremely upset at the time—we both were—and that explains a good deal of what happened. I did my best to stop her, but she was in such a state of mind, there was simply nothing I could do. She seemed to have made up her mind that if he was going to marry you, he must be a criminal, at the very least. All those inquiries, the private detectives—the accusations. I hated every moment of it.

ALISON I suppose she was trying to protect me—in a rather heavy-handed way, admittedly.

COLONEL I must confess I find that kind of thing rather horrifying. Anyway, I try to think now that it never happened. I didn't approve of Jimmy at all, and I don't suppose I ever should, but, looking back on it, I think it would have been better, for all concerned, if we had never attempted to interfere. At least, it would have been a little more dignified.

ALISON It wasn't your fault.

COLONEL I don't know. We were all to blame, in our different ways. No doubt Jimmy acted in good faith. He's honest enough, whatever else he may be. And your mother—in her heavy-handed way, as you put it—acted in good faith as well. Perhaps you and I were the ones most to blame.

ALISON You and I!

COLONEL I think you may take after me a little, my dear. You like to sit on the fence because it's comfortable and more peaceful.

ALISON Sitting on the fence! I married him, didn't I?

COLONEL Oh, yes, you did.

ALISON In spite of all the humiliating scenes and the threats! What did you say to me at the time? Wasn't I letting you down, turning against you, how could I do this to you, etcetera?

COLONEL Perhaps it might have been better if you hadn't written letters to us—knowing how we felt about your husband, and after everything that had happened. (*He looks at her uncomfortably*) Forgive me, I'm a little confused, what with everything—the telegram, driving up here suddenly. . . .

(*He trails off rather helplessly. He looks tired. He glances at her nervously, a hint of accusation in his eyes, as if he expected her to defend herself further. She senses this, and is more confused than ever*)

ALISON Do you know what he said about Mummy? He said she was an overfed, overprivileged old bitch. "A good blow-out for the worms" was his expression, I think.

COLONEL I see. And what does he say about me?

ALISON Oh, he doesn't seem to mind you so much. In fact, I think he rather likes you. He likes you because he can feel sorry for you. (*Conscious that what she says is going to hurt him*) "Poor old Daddy—just one of those sturdy old plants left over from the Edwardian Wilderness that can't understand why the sun isn't shining any more." (*Rather lamely*) Something like that, anyway.

COLONEL He has quite a turn of phrase, hasn't he? (*Simply, and without malice*) Why did you ever have to meet this young man?

ALISON Oh, Daddy, please don't put me on trial now. I've been on trial every day and night of my life for nearly four years.

COLONEL But why should he have married you, feeling as he did about everything?

ALISON That is the famous American question—you know, the sixty-four dollar one! Perhaps it was revenge.

(*He looks up uncomprehendingly*)
Oh yes. Some people do actually marry for revenge. People like Jimmy, anyway. Or perhaps he should have been another Shelley, and can't understand now why I'm not another Mary, and you're not William Godwin. He thinks he's got a sort of genius for love and friendship—on his own terms. Well, for twenty years, I'd lived a happy, uncomplicated life, and suddenly, this—this spiritual barbarian—throws down the gauntlet at me. Perhaps only another woman could understand what a challenge like that means—although I think Helena was as mystified as you are.

COLONEL I am mystified. (*He rises, and crosses to the window R.*) Your husband has obviously taught you a great deal, whether you realize it or not. What any of it means, I don't know. I always believed that people married each other because they were in love. That always seemed a good enough reason to me. But apparently, that's too simple for young people nowadays. They have to talk about challenges and revenge. I just can't believe that love between men and women is really like that.

ALISON Only some men and women.

COLONEL But why you? My daughter. . . . No. Perhaps Jimmy is right. Perhaps I am a—what was it? an old plant left over from the Edwardian Wilderness. And I can't understand why the sun isn't shining any more. You can see what he means, can't you? It was March, 1914, when I left England, and, apart from leaves every ten years or so, I didn't see much of my own country until we all came back in '47. Oh, I knew things had changed, of course. People told you all the time the way it was going—going to the dogs, as the Blimps[1] are supposed to say. But it seemed very unreal to me, out there. The England I remembered was the one I left in 1914, and I was happy to go on remembering it that way. Beside, I had the Maharajah's army to command—that was my world, and I loved it, all of it. At the time, it looked like going on forever. When I think of it now, it seems like a dream. If only it could have gone on forever. Those long, cool evenings up in the hills, everything purple and golden. Your mother and I were so happy then. It seemed as though we had everything we could ever want. I think the last day the sun shone was when that dirty little train steamed out of that crowded, suffocating Indian station, and the battalion band playing for all it was worth. I knew in my heart it was all over then. Everything.

ALISON You're hurt because everything is changed. Jimmy is hurt because everything is the same. And neither of you can face it. Something's gone wrong somewhere, hasn't it?

COLONEL It looks like it, my dear.

(*She picks up the squirrel from the chest of drawers, is about to put it in her suitcase, hesitates, and then puts it back. The* COLONEL *turns and looks at her. She moves down toward him, her head turned away. For a few moments, she seems to be standing on the edge of choice. The choice made, her body wheels round suddenly, and she is leaning against him, weeping softly*)

(*After a pause*) This is a big step you're taking. You've made up your mind to come back with me? Is that really what you want?

(*Enter* HELENA)

HELENA I'm sorry. I came in to see if I could help you pack, Alison. Oh, you look as though you've finished.

(ALISON *leaves her father, and moves to the bed, pushing down the lid of her suitcase*)

ALISON All ready.

HELENA Have you got everything?

ALISON Well, no. But Cliff can send the rest on sometime, I expect. He should have been back by now. Oh, of course, he's had to put the stall away on his own today.

COLONEL (*Crossing and picking up the suitcase*) Well, I'd better put this in the car then. We may as well get along. Your mother will be worried, I know. I promised her I'd ring her when I got here. She's not very well.

HELENA I hope my telegram didn't upset her too much. Perhaps I shouldn't have——

COLONEL Not at all. We were very grateful that you did. It was very kind of you, indeed. She tried to insist on coming with me, but I finally managed to talk her out of it. I thought it would be best for everyone. What about your case, Helena? If you care to tell me where it is, I'll take it down with this one.

HELENA I'm afraid I shan't be coming tonight.

ALISON (*Very surprised*) Aren't you coming with us?

(*Enter* CLIFF)

HELENA I'd like to, but the fact is I've an appointment tomorrow in Birmingham—about a job. They've just sent me a script. It's rather important, and I don't want to miss it. So it looks as though I shall have to stay here tonight.

ALISON Oh, I see. Hullo, Cliff.

CLIFF Hullo, there.

ALISON Daddy—this is Cliff.

COLONEL How do you do, Cliff.

CLIFF How do you do, sir.

(*Slight pause*)

COLONEL Well, I'd better put this in the car, hadn't I? Don't be long, Alison. Good-bye, Helena. I expect we shall be seeing you again soon, if you're not busy.

HELENA Oh, yes, I shall be back in a day or two.

(CLIFF *takes off his jacket*)

COLONEL Well, then—good-bye, Cliff.

CLIFF Good-bye, sir.

(*The* COLONEL *goes out.* CLIFF *comes down L.* HELENA *moves C.*)

You're really going then?

ALISON Really going.

CLIFF I should think Jimmy would be back pretty soon. You won't wait?

ALISON No, Cliff.

[1] Especially during World War II and as popularized in the political cartoons of David Low, Colonel Blimp symbolized the arch-conservative, traditionalist, stiff-upper-lip Englishman whose values and whose world were crumbling away.

CLIFF Who's going to tell him?

HELENA I can tell him. That is, if I'm here when he comes back.

CLIFF (*Quietly*) You'll be here. (*To* ALISON) Don't you think you ought to tell him yourself?

(*She hands him an envelope from her handbag. He takes it*)

Bit conventional, isn't it?

ALISON I'm a conventional girl.

(*He crosses to her, and puts his arms round her*)

CLIFF (*Back over his shoulder, to* HELENA) I hope you're right, that's all.

HELENA What do you mean? You hope *I'm* right?

CLIFF (*To* ALISON) The place is going to be really cock-eyed now. You know that, don't you?

ALISON Please, Cliff——

(*He nods. She kisses him*)

I'll write to you later.

CLIFF Good-bye, lovely.

ALISON Look after him.

CLIFF We'll keep the old nut-house going somehow.

(*She crosses C., in between the two of them, glances quickly at the two armchairs, the papers still left around them from yesterday.* HELENA *kisses her on the cheek, and squeezes her hand*)

HELENA See you soon.

(ALISON *nods, and goes out quickly.* CLIFF *and* HELENA *are left looking at each other*)

Would you like me to make you some tea?

CLIFF No, thanks.

HELENA Think I might have some myself, if you don't mind.

CLIFF So you're staying?

HELENA Just for tonight. Do you object?

CLIFF Nothing to do with me. (*Against the table C.*) Of course, he may not be back until later on.

(*She crosses L., to the window, and lights a cigarette*)

HELENA What do you think he'll do? Perhaps he'll look out one of his old girl friends. What about this Madeline?

CLIFF What about her?

HELENA Isn't she supposed to have done a lot for him? Couldn't he go back to her?

CLIFF I shouldn't think so.

HELENA What happened?

CLIFF She was nearly old enough to be his mother. I expect that's something to do with it! Why the hell should I know!

(*For the first time in the play, his good humor has completely deserted him. She looks surprised*)

HELENA You're his friend, aren't you? Anyway, he's not what you'd call reticent about himself, is he? I've never seen so many souls stripped to the waist since I've been here.

(*He turns to go*)

HELENA Aren't you staying?

CLIFF No, I'm not. There was a train in from London about five minutes ago. And, just in case he may have been on it, I'm going out.

HELENA Don't you think you ought to be here when he comes?

CLIFF I've had a hard day, and I don't think I want to see anyone hurt until I've had something to eat first, and perhaps a few drinks as well. I think I might pick up some nice, pleasant little tart in a milk bar, and sneak her in past old mother Drury. Here! (*Tossing the letter at her*) You give it to him! (*Crossing to door*) He's all yours. (*At door*) And I hope he rams it up your nostrils! (*Exit*)

(*She crosses to the table, and stubs out her cigarette. The front door downstairs is heard to slam. She moves to the wardrobe, opens it idly. It is empty, except for one dress, swinging on a hanger. She goes over to the dressing table, now cleared but for a framed photograph of* JIMMY. *Idly, she slams the empty drawers open and shut. She turns upstage to the chest of drawers, picks up the toy bear, and sits on the bed, looking at it. She lays her head back on the pillow, still holding the bear. She looks up quickly as the door crashes open, and* JIMMY *enters. He stands looking at her, then moves down C., taking off his raincoat, and throwing it over the table. He is almost giddy with anger, and has to steady himself on the chair. He looks up*)

JIMMY That old bastard nearly ran me down in his car! Now, if he'd killed me, that really would have been ironical. And how right and fitting that my wife should have been a passenger. A passenger! What's the matter with everybody? (*Crossing up to her*) Cliff practically walked into me, coming out of the house. He belted up the other way, and pretended not to see me. Are you the only one who's not afraid to stay?

(*She hands him* ALISON*'s note. He takes it*)

Oh, it's one of these, is it? (*He rips it open*)

(*He reads a few lines, and almost snorts with disbelief*)

Did you write this for her! Well, listen to this then! (*Reading*) "My dear—I must get away. I don't suppose you will understand, but please try. I need peace so desperately, and, at the moment, I am willing to sacrifice everything just for that. I don't know what's going to happen to us. I know you will be feeling wretched and bitter, but try to be a little patient with me. I shall always have a deep, loving need of you—Alison." Oh, how could she be so bloody wet! "Deep loving need!" That makes me puke! (*Crossing to R.*) She couldn't say, "You rotten bastard! I hate your guts, I'm clearing out, and I hope you rot!" No, she has to make a polite, emotional mess out of it! (*Seeing the dress in the wardrobe, he rips it out, and throws it in the corner up L.*) "Deep, loving need!" I never thought she was capable of being as phony as that! What is that —a line from one of those plays you've been in? What are you doing here anyway? You'd better keep out of my way, if you don't want your head kicked in.

HELENA (*Calmly*) If you'll stop thinking about yourself for one moment, I'll tell you something I think you ought to know. Your wife is going to have a baby.

(*He just looks at her*)

Well? Doesn't that mean anything? Even to you?

(*He is taken aback, but not so much by the news, as by her*)

JIMMY All right—yes. I am surprised. I give you that. But, tell me. Did you honestly expect me to go soggy at the knees, and collapse with remorse! (*Leaning nearer*) Listen, if you'll stop breathing your female wisdom all over me, I'll tell you something: I don't care. (*Beginning quietly*) I don't care if she's going to have a baby. I don't care if it has two heads! (*He knows her fingers are itching*) Do I disgust you? Well, go on—slap my face. But remember what I told you before, will you? For eleven hours, I have been watching someone I love very much going through the sordid process of dying. She was alone, and I was the only one with her. And when I have to walk behind that coffin on Thursday, I'll be on my own again. Because that bitch won't even send her a bunch of flowers—I know! She made the great mistake of all her kind. She thought that because Hugh's mother was a deprived and ignorant old woman, who said all the wrong things in all the wrong places, she couldn't be taken seriously. And you think I should be overcome with awe because that cruel, stupid girl is going to have a baby! (*Anguish in his voice*) I can't believe it! I can't. (*Grabbing her shoulder*) Well, the performance is over. Now leave me alone, and *get out*, you evil-minded little virgin.

(*She slaps his face savagely. An expression of horror and disbelief floods his face. But it drains away, and all that is left is pain. His hand goes up to his head, and a muffled cry of despair escapes him.* HELENA *tears his hand away, and kisses him passionately, drawing him down beside her*)

*Curtain*

# Act Three, Scene One

*Several months later. A Sunday evening.* ALISON'S *personal belongings, such as her make-up things on the dressing table, for example, have been replaced by* HELENA'S.

*At rise of curtain, we find* JIMMY *and* CLIFF *sprawled in their respective armchairs, immersed in the Sunday newspapers.* HELENA *is standing down L. leaning over the ironing board, a small pile of clothes beside her. She looks more attractive than before, for the setting of her face is more relaxed. She still looks quite smart, but in an unpremeditated, careless way; she wears an old shirt of* JIMMY'S.

CLIFF That stinking old pipe!

(*Pause*)

JIMMY Shut up.

CLIFF Why don't you do something with it?

JIMMY Why do I spend half of Sunday reading the papers?

CLIFF (*Kicks him without lowering his paper*) It stinks!

JIMMY So do you, but I'm not singing an aria about it. (*Turns to the next page*) The dirty ones get more and more wet round the mouth, and the posh ones are more pompous than ever. (*Lowering paper, and waving pipe at* HELENA) Does this bother you?

HELENA No. I quite like it.

JIMMY (*To* CLIFF) There you are—she likes it!

(*He returns to his paper.* CLIFF *grunts*)

Have you read about the grotesque and evil practices going on in the Midlands?

CLIFF Read about the what?

JIMMY Grotesque and evil practices going on in the Midlands.

CLIFF No, what about 'em?

JIMMY Seems we don't know the old place. It's all in here. Startling Revelations this week! Pictures too. Reconstructions of midnight invocations to the Coptic Goddess of fertility.

HELENA Sounds madly depraved.

JIMMY Yes, it's rather us, isn't it? My gosh, look at 'em! Snarling themselves silly. Next week a well-known debutante relates how, during an evil orgy in Market Harborough, she killed and drank the blood of a white cockerel. Well—I'll bet Fortnums[1] must be doing a roaring line in sacrificial cocks! (*Thoughtful*) Perhaps that's what Miss Drury does on Sunday evenings. She puts in a stint as evil high priestess down at the Y.W.—probably having a workout at this very moment. (*To* HELENA) You never dabbled in this kind of thing, did you?

HELENA (*Laughs*) Not lately!

JIMMY Sounds rather your cup of tea—cup of blood, I should say. (*In an imitation of a Midlands accent*) Well, I mean, it gives you something to do, doesn't it? After all, it wouldn't do if we was all alike, would it? It'd be a funny world if we was all the same, that's what *I* always say! (*Resuming in his normal voice*) All I know is that somebody's been sticking pins into *my* wax image for years. (*Suddenly*) Of course: Alison's mother! Every Friday, the wax arrives from Harrods,[1] and all through the week-end, she's stabbing away at it with a hatpin! Ruined her bridge game, I dare say.

HELENA Why don't *you* try it?

JIMMY Yes, it's an idea. (*Pointing to* CLIFF) Just for a start, we could roast him over the gas stove. Have we got enough shillings for the meter? It seems to be

[1] Fortnums and Harrods are high-class London department stores, patronized normally by what Jimmy would call the "posh crowd."

just the thing for these autumn evenings. After all, the whole point of a sacrifice is that you give up something you never really wanted in the first place. You know what I mean? People are doing it around you all the time. They give up their careers, say—or their beliefs—or sex. And everyone thinks to themselves: how wonderful to be able to do that. If only I were capable of doing that! But the truth of it is that they've been kidding themselves, and they've been kidding you. It's not awfully difficult—giving up something you were incapable of ever really wanting. We shouldn't be admiring them. We should feel rather sorry for them. (*Coming back from this sudden, brooding excursion, and turning to* CLIFF) You'll make an admirable sacrifice.

CLIFF (*Mumbling*) Dry up! I'm trying to read.

JIMMY Afterwards, we can make a loving cup from his blood. Can't say I fancy that so much. I've seen it—it looks like cochineal, ever so common. (*To* HELENA) Yours would be much better—pale Cambridge blue, I imagine. No? And afterwards, we could make invocations to the Coptic Goddess of fertility. Got any idea how you do that? (*To* CLIFF) Do you know?

CLIFF Shouldn't have thought *you* needed to make invocations to the Coptic whatever-she-is!

JIMMY Yes, I see what you mean. (*To* HELENA) Well, we don't want to *ask* for trouble, do we? Perhaps it might appeal to the lady here—she's written a long letter all about artificial insemination. It's headed: Haven't we tried God's patience enough! (*Throws the paper down*) Let's see the other posh one.

CLIFF Haven't finished yet.

JIMMY Well, hurry up. I'll have to write and ask them to put hyphens in between the syllables for you. There's a particularly savage correspondence going on in there about whether Milton wore braces or not. I just want to see who gets shot down this week.

CLIFF Just read that. Don't know what it was about, but a Fellow of All Souls seems to have bitten the dust, and the Athenaeum's going up in flames, so the Editor declares that this correspondence is now closed.

JIMMY I think you're actually acquiring yourself a curiosity, my boy. Oh, yes, and then there's an American professor from Yale or somewhere, who believes that when Shakespeare was writing *The Tempest,* he changed his sex. Yes, he was obliged to go back to Stratford because the other actors couldn't take him seriously any longer. This professor chap is coming over here to search for certain documents which will prove that poor old W.S. ended up in someone else's second best bed—a certain Warwickshire farmer's, whom he married after having three children by him.

(HELENA *laughs.* JIMMY *looks up quizzically*)

Is anything the matter?

HELENA No, nothing. I'm only beginning to get used to him. I never (*This is to* CLIFF) used to be sure when he was being serious, or when he wasn't.

CLIFF Don't think he knows himself half the time. When in doubt, just mark it down as an insult

JIMMY Hurry up with that paper, and shut up! What are we going to do tonight? There isn't even a decent concert on. (*To* HELENA) Are you going to Church?

HELENA (*Rather taken aback*) No. I don't think so. Unless you want to.

JIMMY Do I detect a growing, satanic glint in her eyes lately? Do you think it's living in sin with me that does it? (*To* HELENA) Do you feel very sinful, my dear? Well? Do you?

(*She can hardly believe that this is an attack, and she can only look at him, uncertain of herself*)

Do you feel sin crawling out of your ears, like stored up wax or something? Are you wondering whether I'm joking or not? Perhaps I ought to wear a red nose and funny hat. I'm just curious, that's all.

(*She is shaken by the sudden coldness in his eyes, but before she has time to fully realize how hurt she is, he is smiling at her, and shouting cheerfully at Cliff*)

Let's have that paper, stupid!

CLIFF Why don't you drop dead!

JIMMY (*To* HELENA) Will you be much longer doing that?

HELENA Nearly finished.

JIMMY Talking of sin, wasn't that Miss Drury's Reverend friend I saw you chatting with yesterday? Helena darling, I said wasn't that. . . .

HELENA Yes, it was.

JIMMY My dear, you don't have to be on the defensive you know.

HELENA I'm not on the defensive.

JIMMY After all, there's no reason why we shouldn't have the parson to tea up here. Why don't we? Did you find that you had much in common?

HELENA No, I don't think so.

JIMMY Do you think that some of this spiritual beefcake would make a man of me? Should I go in for this moral weight lifting and get myself some overdeveloped muscle? I was a liberal skinny weakling. I too was afraid to strip down to my soul, but now everyone looks at my superb physique in envy. I can perform any kind of press there is without betraying the least sign of passion or kindliness.

HELENA All right, Jimmy.

JIMMY Two years ago I couldn't even lift up my head—now I have more uplift than a film starlet.

HELENA Jimmy, can we have one day, just one day, without tumbling over religion or politics?

CLIFF Yes, change the record, old boy, or pipe down.

JIMMY (*Rising*) Thought of the title for a new song today. It's called "My mother's in the madhouse—that's why I'm in love with you." The lyrics are catchy, too. I was thinking we might work it into the act.

HELENA Good idea.

JIMMY I was thinking we'd scrub Jock and Day, and call ourselves something else. "And jocund day stands tiptoed on the misty mountain tops." [2] It's too intellectual! Anyway, I shouldn't think people will want

[2] Jimmy derives his pun from *Romeo and Juliet,* Act III, Scene 5, lines 9-10.

to be reminded of that peculiar man's plays after Harvard and Yale have finished with him. How about something bright and snappy? I know—— What about—T. S. Eliot and Pam!

CLIFF (*Casually falling in with this familiar routine*) Mirth, mellerdy, and madness!

JIMMY (*Sitting at the table R. and "strumming" it*) Bringing quips and strips for you!

(*They sing together*)

"For we may be guilty, darling. . . .
But we're both insane as well!"

(JIMMY *stands up, and rattles his lines off at almost unintelligible speed*)

Ladies and gentlemen, as I was coming to the theater tonight, I was passing through the stage door, and a man comes up to me, and 'e says:

CLIFF 'Ere! Have you seen nobody?

JIMMY Have I seen who?

CLIFF Have you seen nobody?

JIMMY Of course, I haven't seen nobody! Kindly don't waste my time! Ladies and gentlemen, a little recitation entitled "She said she was called a little Gidding,[3] but she was more like a gelding iron!" Thank you. "She said she was called little Gidding——"

CLIFF Are you quite sure you haven't seen nobody?

JIMMY Are you still here?

CLIFF I'm looking for nobody!

JIMMY *Will* you kindly go away! "She said she was called little Gidding——"

CLIFF Well, I can't find nobody anywhere, and I'm supposed to give him this case!

JIMMY Will you kindly stop interrupting per*lease!* Can't you see I'm trying to entertain these ladies and gentlemen? Who is this nobody you're talking about?

CLIFF I was told to come here and give this case to nobody.

JIMMY You were told to come here and give this case to nobody.

CLIFF That's right. And when I gave it to him, nobody would give me a shilling.

JIMMY And when you gave it to him, nobody would give you a shilling.

CLIFF That's right.

JIMMY Well, what about it?

CLIFF Nobody's not here!

JIMMY Now, let me get this straight: when you say nobody's here, you don't mean nobody's here?

CLIFF No.

JIMMY No.

JIMMY You mean—nobody's here.

CLIFF That's right.

JIMMY Well, why didn't you say so before?

HELENA (*Not quite sure if this is really her cue*) Hey! You down there!

JIMMY Oh, it goes on for hours yet, but never mind. What is it, sir?

HELENA (*Shouting*) I think your sketch stinks! I say—I think your sketch stinks!

JIMMY He thinks it stinks. And, who, pray, might you be?

HELENA Me? Oh—(*With mock modesty*) I'm nobody.

JIMMY Then here's your bloody case!

(*He hurls a cushion at her, which hits the ironing board.*

HELENA My ironing board!

(*The two men do a Flanagan and Allen,*[4] *moving slowly in step, as they sing*)

Now there's a certain little lady, and you all know who I mean,
She may have been to Roedean,[5] but to me she's still a queen.
Someday I'm goin' to marry her,
When times are not so bad,
Her mother doesn't care for me
So I'll 'ave to ask 'er dad.
We'll build a little home for two,
And have some quiet menage,
We'll send our kids to public school
And live on bread and marge.
Don't be afraid to sleep with your sweetheart,
Just because she's better than you.
Those forgotten middle-classes may have fallen on their noses,
But a girl who's true blue,
Will still have something left for you,
The angels up above, will know that you're in love
So don't be afraid to sleep with your sweetheart,
Just because she's better than you. . . .
They call me Sydney,
Just because she's better than you.

(*But* JIMMY *has had enough of this gag by now, and he pushes* CLIFF *away*)

JIMMY Your damned great feet! That's the second time you've kicked my ankle! It's no good—Helena will have to do it. Go on, go and make some tea, and we'll decide what we're going to do.

CLIFF Make some yourself!

(*He pushes him back violently,* JIMMY *loses his balance, and falls over*)

JIMMY You rough bastard!

(*He leaps up, and they grapple, falling on to the floor with a crash. They roll about, grunting and gasping.* CLIFF *manages to kneel on* JIMMY'S *chest*)

CLIFF (*Breathing heavily*) I want to read the papers!

JIMMY You're a savage, a hooligan! You really are! Do you know that! You don't deserve to live in the same house with decent, sensitive people!

CLIFF Are you going to dry up, or do I read the papers down here?

(JIMMY *makes a supreme effort, and* CLIFF *topples to the floor*)

JIMMY You've made me wrench my guts!

(*He pushes the struggling* CLIFF *down*)

[3] "Little Gidding" is the last of T. S. Eliot's *Four Quartets* (published 1943); the chain of punning here begins with Jimmy's retitling of the act.

[4] Popular music hall song-and-dance team.

[5] A fashionable girls' school near Brighton; a "Roedean girl" is caricatured as a hearty, tweedy, "field-hockey" Amazon.

CLIFF Look what you're doing! You're ripping my shirt. Get *off!*

JIMMY Well, what do you want to wear a shirt for? (*Rising*) A tough character like you! Now go and make me some tea.

CLIFF It's the only clean one I've got. Oh, you big oaf!

(*Getting up from the floor, and appealing to* HELENA)

Look! It's filthy!

HELENA Yes, it is. He's stronger than he looks. If you like to take it off now, I'll wash it through for you. It'll be dry by the time we want to go out.

(CLIFF *hesitates*)

What's the matter, Cliff?

CLIFF Oh, it'll be all right.

JIMMY Give it to her, and quit moaning!

CLIFF Oh, all right.

(*He takes it off, and gives it to her*)

Thanks, Helena.

HELENA (*Taking it*) Right. I won't be a minute with it.

(*She goes out.* JIMMY *flops into his armchair R.*)

JIMMY (*Amused*) You look like Marlon Brando or something. (*Slight pause*) You don't care for Helena, do you?

CLIFF You didn't seem very keen yourself once. (*Hesitating, then quickly*) It's not the same, is it?

JIMMY (*Irritably*) No, of course it's not the same, you idiot! It never is! Today's meal is always different from yesterday's and the last woman isn't the same as the one before. If you can't accept that, you're going to be pretty unhappy, my boy.

CLIFF (*Sits on the arm of his chair, and rubs his feet*) Jimmy—I don't think I shall stay here much longer.

JIMMY (*Rather casually*) Oh, why not?

CLIFF (*Picking up his tone*) Oh, I don't know. I've just thought of trying somewhere different. The sweet-stall's all right, but I think I'd like to try something else. You're highly educated, and it suits you, but I need something a bit better.

JIMMY Just as you like, my dear boy. It's your business, not mine.

CLIFF And another thing—I think Helena finds it rather a lot of work to do with two chaps about the place. It won't be so much for her if there's just the two of you. Anyway, I think I ought to find some girl who'll just look after me.

JIMMY Sounds like a good idea. Can't think who'd be stupid enough to team themselves up with you though. Perhaps Helena can think of somebody for you—one of her posh girl friends with lots of money, and no brains. That's what you want.

CLIFF Something like that.

JIMMY Any idea what you're going to do?

CLIFF Not much.

JIMMY That sounds like you, all right! Shouldn't think you'll last five minutes without me to explain the score to you.

CLIFF (*Grinning*) Don't suppose so.

JIMMY You're such a scruffy little beast—I'll bet some respectable little madam from Pinner or Guildford [6] gobbles you up in six months. She'll marry you, send you out to work, and you'll end up as clean as a new pin.

CLIFF (*Chuckling*) Yes, I'm stupid enough for that, too!

JIMMY (*To himself*) I seem to spend my life saying good-bye.

(*Slight pause*)

CLIFF My feet hurt.

JIMMY Try washing your socks. (*Slowly*) It's a funny thing. You've been loyal, generous, and a good friend. But I'm quite prepared to see you wander off, find a new home, and make out on your own. And all because of something I want from that girl downstairs, something I know in my heart she's incapable of giving. You're worth a half a dozen Helenas to me or to anyone. And, if you were in my place, you'd do the same thing. Right?

CLIFF Right.

JIMMY Why, why, why, why do we let these women bleed us to death? Have you ever had a letter, and on it is franked "Please Give Your Blood Generously"? Well, the Postmaster-General does that, on behalf of all the women of the world. I suppose people of our generation aren't able to die for good causes any longer. We had all that done for us, in the thirties and the forties, when we were still kids. (*In his familiar, semi-serious mood*) There aren't any good, brave causes left. If the big bang does come, and we all get killed off, it won't be in aid of the old-fashioned, grand design. It'll just be for the Brave New-nothing-very-much-thank-you. About as pointless and inglorious as stepping in front of a bus. No, there's nothing left for it, me boy, but to let yourself be butchered by the women.

(*Enter* HELENA)

HELENA Here you are, Cliff. (*Handing him the shirt*)

CLIFF Oh, thanks, Helena, very much. That's decent of you.

HELENA Not at all. I should dry it over the gas—the fire in your room would be better. There won't be much room for it over that stove.

CLIFF Right, I will. (*Crosses to door*)

JIMMY And hurry up about it, stupid. We'll all go out, and have a drink soon. (*To* HELENA) O.K.?

HELENA O.K.

JIMMY (*Shouting to* CLIFF *on his way out*) But make me some tea first, you madcap little Charlie.

(*She crosses down L.*) Darling, I'm sick of seeing you behind that damned ironing board!

HELENA (*Wryly*) Sorry.

JIMMY Get yourself glammed up, and we'll hit the town. See you've put a shroud over Mummy, I think you should have laid a Union Jack over it.

HELENA Is anything wrong?

JIMMY Oh, don't frown like that—you look like the presiding magistrate!

[6] Towns in the Midlands, synonymous with middle-class respectability; *cf.* America's Scarsdale, N. Y., or Columbus. Ohio.

HELENA How should I look?

JIMMY As if your heart stirred a little when you looked at me.

HELENA Oh, it does that, all right.

JIMMY Cliff tells me he's leaving us.

HELENA I know. He told me last night.

JIMMY Did he? I always seem to be at the end of the queue when they're passing information out.

HELENA I'm sorry he's going.

JIMMY Yes, so am I. He's a sloppy, irritating bastard, but he's got a big heart. You can forgive somebody almost anything for that. He's had to learn how to take it, and he knows how to hand it out. Come here.

(*He is sitting on the arm of his chair. She crosses to him, and they look at each other. Then she puts out her hand, and runs it over his head, fondling his ear and neck*)

Right from that first night, you have always put out your hand to me first. As if you expected nothing, or worse than nothing, and didn't care. You made a good enemy, didn't you? What they call a worthy opponent. But then, when people put down their weapons, it doesn't mean they've necessarily stopped fighting.

HELENA (*Steadily*) I love you.

JIMMY I think perhaps you do. Yes, I think perhaps you do. Perhaps it means something to lie with your victorious general in your arms. Especially, when he's heartily sick of the whole campaign, tired out, hungry, and dry.

(*His lips find her fingers, and he kisses them. She presses his head against her*)

You stood up, and came out to meet me. Oh, Helena—

(*His face comes up to her, and they embrace fiercely*)

Don't let anything go wrong!

HELENA (*Softly*) Oh, my darling——

JIMMY Either you're with me or against me.

HELENA I've always wanted you—always!

(*They kiss again*)

JIMMY T. S. Eliot and Pam, we'll make a good double. If you'll help me. I'll close that damned sweet-stall, and we'll start everything from scratch. What do you say? We'll get away from this place.

HELENA (*Nodding happily*) I say that's wonderful.

JIMMY (*Kissing her quickly*) Put all that junk away, and we'll get out. We'll get pleasantly, joyfully tiddly, we'll gaze at each other tenderly and lecherously in "The Builder's Arms," and then we'll come back here, and I'll make such love to you, you'll not care about anything else at all.

(*She moves away L., after kissing his hand*)

HELENA I'll just change out of your old shirt. (*Folding ironing board*)

JIMMY (*Moving to door*) Right. I'll hurry up the little man.

(*But before he reaches the door, it opens and* ALISON *enters. She wears a raincoat, her hair is untidy, and she looks rather ill. There is a stunned pause*)

ALISON (*Quietly*) Hullo.

JIMMY (*To* HELENA, *after a moment*) Friend of yours to see you.

(*He goes out quickly, and the two women are left looking at each other*)

*Quick Curtain*

# Act Three, Scene Two

*It is a few minutes later. From* CLIFF'S *room, across the landing, comes the sound of* JIMMY'S *jazz trumpet.*

*At rise of the Curtain,* HELENA *is standing L. of the table, pouring out a cup of tea.* ALISON *is sitting on the armchair R. She bends down and picks up* JIMMY'S *pipe. Then she scoops up a little pile of ash from the floor, and drops it in the ashtray on the arm of the chair.*

ALISON He still smokes this foul old stuff. I used to hate it at first, but you get used to it.

HELENA Yes.

ALISON I went to the pictures last week, and some old man was smoking it in front, a few rows away. I actually got up, and sat right behind him.

HELENA (*Coming down with cup of tea*) Here, have this. It usually seems to help.

ALISON (*Taking it*) Thanks.

HELENA Are you sure you feel all right now?

ALISON (*Nods*) It was just—oh, everything. It's my own fault—entirely. I must be mad, coming here like this. I'm sorry, Helena.

HELENA Why should you be sorry—you of all people?

ALISON Because it was unfair and cruel of me to come back. I'm afraid a sense of timing is one of the things I seem to have learnt from Jimmy. But it's something that can be in very bad taste. (*Sips her tea*) So many times, I've just managed to stop myself coming here—right at the last moment. Even today, when I went to the booking office at St. Pancras, it was like a charade, and I never believed that I'd let myself walk on to that train. And when I was on it, I got into a panic. I felt like a criminal. I told myself I'd turn round at the other end, and come straight back. I couldn't even believe that this place existed any more. But once I got here, there was nothing I could do. I had to convince myself that everything I remembered about this place had really happened to me once.

(*She lowers her cup, and her foot plays with the newspapers on the floor*)

How many times in these past few months I've thought of the evenings we used to spend here in this room. Suspended and rather remote. You make a good cup of tea.

HELENA (*Sitting L. of table*) Something Jimmy taught *me.*

ALISON (*Covering her face*) Oh, why am I here! You must all wish me a thousand miles away!

HELENA I don't wish anything of the kind. You've more right to be here than I.

ALISON Oh, Helena, don't bring out the book of rules——

HELENA You are his wife, aren't you? Whatever I have done, I've never been able to forget that fact. You have all the rights——

ALISON Helena—even I gave up believing in the divine rights of marriage long ago. Even before I met Jimmy. They've got something different now—constitutional monarchy. You are where you are by consent. And if you start trying any strong arm stuff, you're out. And I'm out.

HELENA Is that something you learnt from him?

ALISON Don't make me feel like a blackmailer or something, please! I've done something foolish, and rather vulgar in coming here tonight. I regret it, and I detest myself for doing it. But I did not come here in order to gain anything. Whatever it was—hysteria or just macabre curiosity, I'd certainly no intention of making any kind of breach between you and Jimmy. You must believe that.

HELENA Oh, I believe it all right. That's why everything seems more wrong and terrible than ever. You didn't even reproach me. You should have been outraged, but you weren't. (*She leans back, as if she wanted to draw back from herself*) I feel so—*ashamed.*

ALISON You talk as though he were something you'd swindled me out of——

HELENA (*Fiercely*) And you talk as if he were a book or something you pass around to anyone who happens to want it for five minutes. What's the matter with you? You sound as though you were quoting *him* all the time. I thought you told me once you couldn't bring yourself to believe in him.

ALISON I don't think I ever believed in your way either.

HELENA At least, I still believe in right and wrong! Not even the months in this madhouse have stopped me doing that. Even though everything I have done is wrong, at least I have known it was wrong.

ALISON You loved him, didn't you? That's what you wrote, and told me.

HELENA And it was true.

ALISON It was pretty difficult to believe at the time. I couldn't understand it.

HELENA I could hardly believe it myself.

ALISON Afterwards, it wasn't quite so difficult. You used to say some pretty harsh things about him. Not that I was sorry to hear them—they were rather comforting then. But you even shocked me sometimes.

HELENA I suppose I was a little over-emphatic. There doesn't seem much point in trying to explain everything, does there?

ALISON Not really.

HELENA Do you know—I have discovered what is wrong with Jimmy? It's very simple really. He was born out of his time.

ALISON Yes. I know.

HELENA There's no place for people like that any longer—in sex, or politics, or anything. That's why he's so futile. Sometimes, when I listen to him, I feel he thinks he's still in the middle of the French Revolution. And that's where he ought to be, of course. He doesn't know where he is, or where he's going. He'll never do anything, and he'll never amount to anything.

ALISON I suppose he's what you'd call an Eminent Victorian.[1] Slightly comic—in a way. . . . We seem to have had this conversation before.

HELENA Yes, I remember everything you said about him. It horrified me. I couldn't believe that you could have married someone like that. Alison—it's all over between Jimmy and me. I can see it now. I've got to get out. No—listen to me. When I saw you standing there tonight, I knew that it was all utterly wrong. That I didn't believe in any of this, and not Jimmy or anyone could make me believe otherwise. (*Rising*) How could I have ever thought I could get away with it! He wants one world and I want another, and lying in that bed won't ever change it! I believe in good and evil, and I don't have to apologize for that. It's quite a modern, scientific belief now, so they tell me. And, by everything I have ever believed in, or wanted, what I have been doing is wrong and evil.

ALISON Helena—you're not going to leave him?

HELENA Yes, I am. (*Before* ALISON *can interrupt, she goes on*) Oh, I'm not stepping aside to let you come back. You can do what you like. Frankly, I think you'd be a fool—but that's your own business. I think I've given you enough advice.

ALISON But he—he'll have no one.

HELENA Oh, my dear, he'll find somebody. He'll probably hold court here like one of the Renaissance popes. Oh, I know I'm throwing the book of rules at you, as you call it, but, believe me, you're never going to be happy without it. I tried throwing it away all these months, but I know now it just doesn't work. When you came in at that door, ill and tired and hurt, it was all over for me. You see—I didn't know about the baby. It was such a shock. It's like a judgment on us.

ALISON You saw me, and I had to tell you what had happened. I lost the child. It's a simple fact. There is no judgment, there's no blame——

HELENA Maybe not. But I feel it just the same.

ALISON But don't you see? It isn't logical!

HELENA No, it isn't. (*Calmly*) But I know it's right.

(*The trumpet gets louder*)

ALISON Helena (*Going to her*), you mustn't leave him. He needs you, I know he needs you——

HELENA Do you think so?

[1] Alison's allusion is to Lytton Strachey's poisonously understated volume of biographical studies, *Eminent Victorians* (1918).

ALISON Maybe you're not the right one for him—we're neither of us right——

HELENA (*Moving upstage*) Oh, why doesn't he stop that damned noise!

ALISON He wants something quite different from us. What it is exactly I don't know—a kind of cross between a mother and a Greek courtesan, a henchwoman, a mixture of Cleopatra and Boswell. But give him a little longer——

HELENA (*Wrenching the door open*) Please! Will you stop that! I can't think!

(*There is a slight pause, and the trumpet goes on. She puts her hands to her head*)

Jimmy, for God's sake!

(*It stops*)

Jimmy, I want to speak to you.

JIMMY (*Off*) Is your friend still with you?

HELENA Oh, don't be an idiot, and come in here!

(*She moves down L.*)

ALISON (*Rising*) He doesn't want to see me.

HELENA Stay where you are, and don't be silly. I'm sorry. It won't be very pleasant, but I've made up my mind to go, and I've got to tell him now.

(*Enter* JIMMY)

JIMMY Is this another of your dark plots? (*He looks at* ALISON) Hadn't she better sit down? She looks a bit ghastly.

HELENA I'm so sorry, dear. Would you like some more tea, or an aspirin or something?

(ALISON *shakes her head, and sits. She can't look at either of them*)

(*To* JIMMY, *the old authority returning*) It's not very surprising, is it? She's been very ill, she's——

JIMMY (*Quietly*) You don't have to draw a diagram for me—I can see what's happened to her.

HELENA And doesn't it mean anything to you?

JIMMY I don't exactly relish the idea of anyone being ill, or in pain. It was my child, too, you know. But (*He shrugs*) it isn't my first loss.

ALISON (*On her breath*) It was mine.

(*He glances at her, but turns back to* HELENA *quickly*)

JIMMY What are you looking so solemn about? What's she doing here?

ALISON I'm sorry, I'm—— (*Presses her hand over her mouth*)

(HELENA *crosses to* JIMMY *C., and grasps his hand*)

HELENA Don't, please. Can't you see the condition she's in? She's done nothing, she's said nothing, none of it's her fault.

(*He takes his hand away, and moves away a little downstage*)

JIMMY What isn't her fault?

HELENA Jimmy—I don't want a brawl, so please——

JIMMY Let's hear it, shall we?

HELENA Very well. I'm going downstairs to pack my things. If I hurry, I shall just catch the 7:15 to London.

(*They both look at him, but he simply leans forward against the table, not looking at either of them*)

This is not Alison's doing—you must understand that. It's my own decision entirely. In fact, she's just been trying to talk me out of it. It's just that suddenly, tonight, I see what I have really known all along. That you can't be happy when what you're doing is wrong, or is hurting someone else. I suppose it could never have worked, anyway, but I do love you, Jimmy. I shall never love anyone as I have loved you. (*Turns away L.*) But I can't go on. (*Passionately and sincerely*) I can't take part—in all this suffering. I can't!

(*She appeals to him for some reaction, but he only looks down at the table, and nods.* HELENA *recovers, and makes an effort to regain authority*)

(*To* ALISON) You probably won't feel up to making that journey again tonight, but we can fix you up at an hotel before I go. There's about half an hour. I'll just make it.

(*She turns up to the door, but* JIMMY'S *voice stops her*)

JIMMY (*In a low, resigned voice*) They all want to escape from the pain of being alive. And, most of all, from love. (*Crosses to the dressing table*) I always knew something like this would turn up—some problem, like an ill wife—and it would be too much for those delicate, hot-house feelings of yours.

(*He sweeps up* HELENA'S *things from the dressing table, and crosses over to the wardrobe. Outside, the church bells start ringing*)

It's no good trying to fool yourself about love. You can't fall into it like a soft job, without dirtying up your hands. (*Hands her the make-up things, which she takes. He opens the wardrobe*) It takes muscle and guts. And if you can't bear the thought (*Takes out a dress on a hanger*) of messing up your nice, clean soul, (*Crossing back to her*) you'd better give up the whole idea of life, and become a saint. (*Puts the dress in her arms*) Because you'll never make it as a human being. It's either this world or the next.

(*She looks at him for a moment, and then goes out quickly. He is shaken, and he avoids* ALISON'S *eyes, crossing to the window. He rests against it, then bangs his fist against the frame*)

Oh, those bells!

(*The shadows are growing around them.* JIMMY *stands, his head against the window pane.* ALISON *is huddled forward in the armchair R. Presently, she breaks the stillness, and rises to above the table*)

ALISON I'm . . . sorry. I'll go now.

(*She starts to move upstage. But his voice pulls her up*)

JIMMY You never even sent any flowers to the funeral. Not—a little bunch of flowers. You had to deny me that, too, didn't you?

(*She starts to move, but again he speaks*)

The injustice of it is almost perfect! The wrong people going hungry, the wrong people being loved, the wrong people dying!

(*She moves to the gas stove. He turns to face her*)
Was I really wrong to believe that there's a—a kind of—burning virility of mind and spirit that looks for something as powerful as itself? The heaviest, strongest creatures in this world seem to be the loneliest. Like the old bear, following his own breath in the dark forest. There's no warm pack, no herd to comfort him. That voice that cries out doesn't *have* to be a weakling's, does it?

(*He moves in a little*)

Do you remember that first night I saw you at that grisly party? You didn't really notice me, but I was watching you all the evening. You seemed to have a wonderful relaxation of spirit. I knew that was what I wanted. You've got to be really brawny to have that kind of strength—the strength to relax. It was only after we were married that I discovered that it wasn't relaxation at all. In order to relax, you've first got to sweat your guts out. And, as far as you were concerned, you'd never had a hair out of place, or a bead of sweat anywhere.

(*A cry escapes from her, and her fist flies to her mouth. She moves down to below the table, leaning on it*)

I may be a lost cause, but I thought if you loved me, it needn't matter.

(*She is crying silently. He moves down to face her*)

ALISON It doesn't matter! I was wrong, I was wrong! I don't want to be neutral, I don't want to be a saint. I want to be a lost cause. I want to be corrupt and futile!

(*All he can do is watch her helplessly. Her voice takes on a little strength, and rises*)

Don't you understand? It's gone! It's gone! That—that helpless human being inside my body. I thought it was so safe, and secure in there. Nothing could take it from me. It was mine, my responsibility. But it's lost.

(*She slides down against the leg of the table to the floor*)

All I wanted was to die. I never knew what it was like. I didn't know it could be like that! I was in pain, and all I could think of was you, and what I'd lost. (*Scarcely able to speak*) I thought: if only—if only he could see me now, so stupid, and ugly, and ridiculous. This is what he's been longing for me to feel. This is what he wants to splash about in! I'm in the fire, and I'm burning, and all I want is to die! It's cost him his child, and any others I might have had! But what does it matter—this is what he wanted from me!

(*She raises her face to him*)

Don't you see! I'm in the mud at last! I'm groveling! I'm crawling! Oh, God——

(*She collapses at his feet. He stands, frozen for a moment, then he bends down and takes her shaking body in his arms. He shakes his head, and whispers*)

JIMMY Don't. Please, don't. . . . I can't——

(*She gasps for her breath against him*)

You're all right. You're all right now. Please, I—I. . . . Not any more. . . .

(*She relaxes suddenly. He looks down at her, full of fatigue, and says with a kind of mocking, tender irony*)

We'll be together in our bear's cave, and our squirrel's drey, and we'll live on honey, and nuts—lots and lots of nuts. And we'll sing songs about ourselves—about warm trees and snug caves, and lying in the sun. And you'll keep those big eyes on my fur, and help me keep my claws in order, because I'm a bit of a soppy, scruffy sort of a bear. And I'll see that you keep that sleek, bushy tail glistening as it should, because you're a very beautiful squirrel, but you're none too bright either, so we've got to be careful. There are cruel steel traps lying about everywhere, just waiting for rather mad, slightly satanic, and very timid little animals. Right?

(ALISON *nods*)

(*Pathetically*) Poor squirrels!

ALISON (*With the same comic emphasis*) Poor bears! (*She laughs a little. Then looks at him very tenderly, and adds very, very softly*) Oh, poor, poor bears!

(*Slides her arms around him*)

*Curtain*

# Samuel Beckett

## (1906- )

WITH the opening of *En Attendant Godot* early in January, 1953, at the Théâtre de Babylone in Paris, one more Irish expatriate, Samuel Beckett, made a major contribution to twentieth-century drama. Beckett acted as his own translator in preparing the subsequent English version, *Waiting for Godot;* others have been responsible for translations into the more than twenty languages in which it has now been performed throughout the world. Despite his disavowals of any deep interest in the theatre, Beckett has continued to write plays, all of which have been immediately recognized as works central to the "Theatre of the Absurd."

Beckett has described his characters as "people [who] seem to be falling to bits," as individuals who "have nothing." His characters usually have names, but these names may shift, merge with other names, or just vanish into thin air. His characters inhabit locales which partake of familiar geography. However, despite his characters' occasional references to Lake Como, Sedan, and the Ardennes (as in *Endgame*) or to the Eiffel Tower, the Dead Sea, Connemara, and the Pyrenees (as in *Waiting for Godot*), ultimately topographical substance evaporates as surely as human nomenclature in Beckett's symbolist drama. Most important, however, is the evanescence of his characters' touching efforts to communicate—with others or sometimes, as in *Krapp's Last Tape,* with themselves in earlier periods of life. Discourse is broken, fragmentary, incomplete, automatic, filled as much with pauses as with phrases, all somehow conveying his characters' amazed wonderment that a sound has been uttered or an idea suggested. Beckett has mastered the language of Inarticulate Man inhabiting a limbo of futility, tedium, physical discomfort, and "waiting it out." Words and pauses, significant only as the marks of interior communication or a breakdown in human intercourse, are for Beckett millstones which weigh man down even as they signify his humanity. Beckett, like Ionesco, is a prose-poet of the ultimate unintelligibility of the seemingly intelligible. Their universe, conceived as constantly flying away from any center—and thus *ab surd,* is a wasteland of words.

The end towards which Beckett seems constantly to be moving may be the wordless pantomimic drama exemplified in his own *Acte sans paroles* (*Act without Words*), the "mime" originally performed on the same bill with *Endgame* (1957). In this tiny scenario of stage-directions, Beckett distilled the essence of his tragicomic view of life: in the dazzling light of a desert which is just a stage, a man is forever trapped. A "being" offstage is implied by a whistle and by stage properties tantalizingly dropped on strings from the flies. The nameless hero attempts to escape from the desert-stage, only to be thrown back by the offstage presence. He grasps at a carafe of water dangled always just out of his reach. At the end of the play, he lies in the foetal position, staring out at the audience; the carafe is dangled close to his face, but immobilized by his frustration he merely ignores it. There is no exit. The protagonist begins and ends alone—on a bare stage.

The bases of Beckett's philosophy still await discovery by one of the numerous critics now zealously probing his works with the same respectful diligence once reserved for Dostoevsky, Kafka, and Joyce, three authors with whom he is frequently compared. Beckett maintains a guarded silence on the "meaning" of his works, and he is undoubtedly vastly amused by some of the delicately spun theories his works have inspired. When one British critic asked him pointblank about *Waiting for Godot*'s meaning, Beckett quickly closed the conversation: "I take no sides about that." On the rare occasions when he has spoken of himself, he has volunteered little more than the vital statistics he might provide to renew his Irish passport. He was born in Dublin in 1906, and like Synge and O'Casey, grew up as a Protestant—"almost a Quaker," he told one interviewer. His comfortably situated middle-class parents gave their second son a good education, first at Portora Royal School (where Oscar Wilde had been educated), then at Dublin's Trinity College. In 1927, very much on schedule, Beckett at 21 received his baccalaureate in French and Italian, and an exchange lectureship at the École Normale Supérieure in Paris. During his first long stay in Paris, he published a long poem, *Whoroscope.* In 1931, he returned to Trinity as a lecturer in French and candidate for the Master's degree. Although he completed work on the advanced degree, Beckett found teaching uncongenial; since 1932, except for occasional short visits to his family, Beckett has lived in France. Asked why Ireland seemed so intolerable, Beckett has given the same explanation offered by O'Casey, who began his self-exile about the same time: the strict censorship of books and ideas and the clergy's power in Irish politics created an oppressive anti-intellectualism. In recent years, efforts have been made to honor O'Casey, Joyce, and Beckett in Ireland, but it appears that the exiles' complaints may still be justified. In 1958, for example, when O'Casey's new play, *The Drums of Father Ned,* was banned from Dublin's International Theatre Festival, Beckett supported O'Casey by banning performances of his own plays in Ireland. His works (three mime plays and the radio drama, *All That Fall*) scheduled for the 1958 Festival program have not been seen in Ireland.

From 1927 until the late 1940's, Beckett wrote in English. His earlier publications included a critical study of Proust, a collection of short stories (*More Pricks than Kicks*), a volume of poems (*Echo's Bones*), two novels (*Murphy* and *Watt*), and an essay on James Joyce. During the 1930's in Paris, Beckett, like Joyce's other friends, helped in various ways—reading, doing odd jobs—to make Joyce's difficult final years productive. Since 1937 Beckett's residence has been a Paris apartment. Especially since 1946 when he began to write almost exclusively in French, it has not been clear whether he should be classified as Irish or French. Most of his fictional characters and settings have remained Irish in flavor, if not always in any palpable reality. Visiting in Ireland when World War II began, Beckett immediately returned to Paris: "I preferred France in war to Ireland in peace." During the Nazi Occupation, he took refuge in the Unoccupied Zone of Vaucluse in southeastern France. In 1945, he returned briefly to Ireland, joined the Irish Red Cross, and soon was back in France as interpreter and storekeeper. In 1947, installed again in his Paris flat, he began writing in French his trilogy of novels: *Molloy* (1951), *Malone Meurt* (*Malone Dies,* 1952), and *l'Innommable* (*The Unnameable,* 1953). Like his plays, these novels are concerned with deterioration. In a more recent work, *Textes pour Rien* (*Texts for Nothing*), he tried unsuccessfully to "get out of the attitude of disintegration." Although he may keep trying to extricate himself from his cosmic melancholy, he will undoubtedly continue to concentrate on impotence and ignorance as themes eminently suited to his tastes: "I think anyone nowadays who pays the slightest attention to his own experience finds it the experience of a non-knower, a non-can-er [somebody who cannot]." Certainly his characters probe their experience even though, as non-knowers, they can arrive at no final comprehension beyond incomprehension. "I'm not interested in any system," Beckett has said, "I can't see any trace of any system anywhere."

Although he finds no evidence of systems operating in the universe, all his plays are constructed according to a system of antitheses in which either/or dichotomies are transformed into both/and unities. In *Waiting for Godot,* for example, audiences are struck first by simplistic polarities: wait or not wait; Godot will come or Godot will not come (he doesn't come but he may still come); of the two thieves on the cross, one was blessed but the other was damned; of the two tramp-protagonists, Vladimir (Didi) is Intellect but Estragon (Gogo) is Body; one of Gogo's boots goes on easily but the other will scarcely go on at all; of the two strange travelers linked by an umbilical cord of rope, Pozzo seems the Master-Mother while Lucky seems the Servant-Child—until Act II, when the relationship is inverted. At the end of this "tragicomedy," Didi and Gogo announce they will go, but they do not move. Finally, audiences recognize that Beckett does not emphasize the separateness of Mind and Matter, Blessedness and Damnation, Going or Staying. Instead, he defies obvious allegorical transliteration by, if not reconciling, at least resolving his contradictory principles into a single idea. Didi and Gogo may talk of separating and going their own ways, but they remain together to insure the survival of both—or of neither. In this paradox is found the comic/tragic antithesis around which controversy over the play's "meaning" revolves. To audiences who find Didi and Gogo's ribaldry and mutual reliance touchingly comic, Beckett is less than the complete pessimist he seems to those who see only two Everyman Tramps fading away as they wait without waiting for a mysterious Mr. Godot whose existence is verified only by a Shepherd Boy uncertain whether Godot's beard is white or black.

*Waiting for Godot* was succeeded by *All That Fall,* a radio play Beckett wrote on commission for the BBC "Third Programme." Remindful of Synge's *The Well of the Saints,* this sound-effects engineer's delight traces the difficult journey of a grotesquely fat old woman, Maddy Rooney, to the railroad station to meet her blind husband, Dan. *Embers* is another radio play in which voices merge with sounds of the elements and of machines. Beckett's typical plays are short and require a small cast: in *Krapp's Last Tape,* an old man connects with his youth through electronics; the recent *Happy Days* shows an elderly pair in a setting of scorched grass against a backdrop where sky and plain meet in stage-infinity.

Beckett has described *Endgame* (in the French original, *Fin de Partie*) as "rather difficult and elliptic" and "more inhuman than *Godot.*" To anyone familiar with such works as Strindberg's *Ghost Sonata,* however, *Endgame* poses no difficulties. Critics have pointed out Beckett's striking Biblical parallels and echoes, Shakespearean allusions, multilingual puns *à la Finnegans Wake,* and analogies with chess strategy and play-acting as a game. *Endgame* is a work of extraordinary verbal richness achieved with astonishing economy. As even a partial list shows, Beckett's characteristic polarities are abundantly present: death/life; here inside/there outside; left/right; blindness/sight; sitting down/standing up; impotence/procreation; decaying flesh (Hamm)/preservative spice (Clov[e]); Hamm[er]/Nail (in French, *clou;* in German, *Naegel,* the sources of Clov and the pun-names, Nagg and Nell). The action may be understood as occurring in outer space or within a human skull with its two window-eyes looking out on sea and land—and the small child Clov thinks he sees outside the bare interior. One of Beckett's most perceptive critics, Ruby Cohn, has described *Endgame* as presenting "the death of the stock props of Western civilization —family cohesion, filial, parental, and connubial love, faith in God, artistic appreciation and creation." These are only a handful of Beckett's themes in his probing of the existential mysteries.

# ENDGAME

## *A Play in One Act*

Translated from the French by the Author

CHARACTERS

NAGG
NELL
HAMM
CLOV

*Bare interior. Gray light. Left and right back, high up, two small windows, curtains drawn. Front right, a door. Hanging near door, its face to wall, a picture. Front left, touching each other, covered with an old sheet, two ashbins. Center, in an armchair on castors, covered with an old sheet,* HAMM. *Motionless by the door, his eyes fixed on* HAMM, CLOV. *Very red face. Brief tableau.*

CLOV *goes and stands under window left. Stiff, staggering walk. He looks up at window left. He turns and looks at window right. He goes and stands under window right. He looks up at window right. He turns and looks at window left. He goes out, comes back immediately with a small step-ladder, carries it over and sets it down under window left, gets up on it, draws back curtain. He gets down, takes six steps (for example) towards window right, goes back for ladder, carries it over and sets it down under window right, gets up on it, draws back curtain. He gets down, takes three steps towards window left, goes back for ladder, carries it over and sets it down under window left, gets up on it, looks out of window. Brief laugh. He gets down, takes one step towards window right, goes back for ladder, carries it over and sets it down under window right, gets up on it, looks out of window. Brief laugh. He gets down, goes with ladder towards ashbins, halts, turns, carries back ladder and sets it down under window right, goes to ashbins, removes sheet covering them, folds it over his arm. He raises one lid, stoops and looks into bin. Brief laugh. He closes lid. Same with other bin. He goes to* HAMM, *removes sheet covering him, folds it over his arm. In a dressing-gown, a stiff toque on his head, a large blood-stained handkerchief over his face, a whistle hanging from his neck, a rug over his knees, thick socks on his feet,* HAMM *seems to be asleep.* CLOV *looks him over. Brief laugh. He goes to door, halts, turns towards auditorium.*

CLOV (*Fixed gaze, tonelessly*) Finished, it's finished, nearly finished, it must be nearly finished. (*Pause*) Grain upon grain, one by one, and one day, suddenly, there's a heap, a little heap, the impossible heap. (*Pause*) I can't be punished any more. (*Pause*) I'll go now to my kitchen, ten feet by ten feet by ten feet, and wait for him to whistle me. (*Pause*) Nice dimensions, nice proportions, I'll lean on the table, and look at the wall, and wait for him to whistle me. (*He remains a moment motionless, then goes out. He comes back immediately, goes to window right, takes up the ladder and carries it out. Pause.* HAMM *stirs. He yawns under the handkerchief. He removes the handkerchief from his face. Very red face. Black glasses*)

HAMM Me— (*He yawns*) —to play. (*He holds the handkerchief spread out before him*) Old stancher! (*He takes off his glasses, wipes his eyes, his face, the glasses, puts them on again, folds the handkerchief and puts it back neatly in the breast-pocket of his dressing-gown. He clears his throat, joins the tips of his fingers*) Can there be misery— (*He yawns*) —loftier than mine? No doubt. Formerly. But now? (*Pause*) My father? (*Pause*) My mother? (*Pause*) My . . . dog? (*Pause*) Oh I am willing to believe they suffer as much as such creatures can suffer. But does that mean their sufferings equal mine? No doubt. (*Pause*) No, all is a— (*He yawns*) —bsolute, (*Proudly*) the bigger a man is the fuller he is. (*Pause. Gloomily*) And the emptier. (*He sniffs*) Clov! (*Pause*) No, alone. (*Pause*) What dreams! Those forests! (*Pause*) Enough, it's time it ended, in the shelter too. (*Pause*) And yet I hesitate, I hesitate to . . . to end. Yes, there it is, it's time it ended and yet I hesitate to— (*He yawns*) —to end. (*Yawns*) God, I'm tired, I'd be better off in bed. (*He whistles. Enter* CLOV *immediately. He halts beside the chair*) You pollute the air! (*Pause*) Get me ready, I'm going to bed.

CLOV I've just got you up.

HAMM And what of it?

CLOV I can't be getting you up and putting you to bed every five minutes, I have things to do. (*Pause*)

HAMM Did you ever see my eyes?

CLOV No.

HAMM Did you never have the curiosity, while I was sleeping, to take off my glasses and look at my eyes?

CLOV Pulling back the lids? (*Pause*) No.

HAMM One of these days I'll show them to you. (*Pause*) It seems they've gone all white. (*Pause*) What time is it?

CLOV The same as usual.

HAMM (*Gesture towards window right*) Have you looked?

CLOV Yes.

HAMM Well?

CLOV Zero.

HAMM It'd need to rain.

CLOV It won't rain. (*Pause*)

HAMM Apart from that, how do you feel?

CLOV I don't complain.

HAMM You feel normal?

CLOV (*Irritably*) I tell you I don't complain.

HAMM I feel a little queer. (*Pause*) Clov!

CLOV Yes.

HAMM Have you not had enough?

CLOV Yes! (*Pause*) Of what?

HAMM Of this . . . this . . . thing.

CLOV I always had. (*Pause*) Not you?

HAMM (*Gloomily*) Then there's no reason for it to change.

CLOV It may end. (*Pause*) All life long the same questions, the same answers.

HAMM Get me ready. (CLOV *does not move*) Go and get the sheet. (CLOV *does not move*) Clov!

CLOV Yes.

HAMM I'll give you nothing more to eat.

CLOV Then we'll die.

HAMM I'll give you just enough to keep you from dying. You'll be hungry all the time.

CLOV Then we won't die. (*Pause*) I'll go and get the sheet. (*He goes towards the door*)

HAMM No! (CLOV *halts*) I'll give you one biscuit per day. (*Pause*) One and a half. (*Pause*) Why do you stay with me?

CLOV Why do you keep me?

HAMM There's no one else.

CLOV There's nowhere else. (*Pause*)

HAMM You're leaving me all the same.

CLOV I'm trying.

HAMM You don't love me.

CLOV No.

HAMM You loved me once.

CLOV Once!

HAMM I've made you suffer too much. (*Pause*) Haven't I?

CLOV It's not that.

HAMM (*Shocked*) I haven't made you suffer too much?

CLOV Yes!

HAMM (*Relieved*) Ah you gave me a fright! (*Pause. Coldly*) Forgive me. (*Pause. Louder*) I said, Forgive me.

CLOV I heard you. (*Pause*) Have you bled?

HAMM Less. (*Pause*) Is it not time for my pain-killer?

CLOV No. (*Pause*)

HAMM How are your eyes?

CLOV Bad.

HAMM How are your legs?

CLOV Bad.

HAMM But you can move.

CLOV Yes.

HAMM (*Violently*) Then move! (CLOV *goes to back wall, leans against it with his forehead and hands*) Where are you?

CLOV Here.

HAMM Come back! (CLOV *returns to his place beside the chair*) Where are you?

CLOV Here.

HAMM Why don't you kill me?

CLOV I don't know the combination of the cupboard. (*Pause*)

HAMM Go and get two bicycle-wheels.

CLOV There are no more bicycle-wheels.

HAMM What have you done with your bicycle?

CLOV I never had a bicycle.

HAMM The thing is impossible.

CLOV When there were still bicycles I wept to have one. I crawled at your feet. You told me to go to hell. Now there are none.

HAMM And your rounds? When you inspected my paupers. Always on foot?

CLOV Sometimes on horse. (*The lid of one of the bins lifts and the hands of* NAGG *appear, gripping the rim. Then his head emerges. Nightcap. Very white face.* NAGG *yawns, then listens*) I'll leave you, I have things to do.

HAMM In your kitchen?

CLOV Yes.

HAMM Outside of here it's death. (*Pause*) All right, be off. (*Exit* CLOV. *Pause*) We're getting on.

NAGG Me pap!

HAMM Accursed progenitor!

NAGG Me pap!

HAMM The old folks at home! No decency left! Guzzle, guzzle, that's all they think of. (*He whistles. Enter* CLOV. *He halts beside the chair*) Well! I thought you were leaving me.

CLOV Oh not just yet, not just yet.

NAGG Me pap!

HAMM Give him his pap.

CLOV There's no more pap.

HAMM (*To* NAGG) Do you hear that? There's no more pap. You'll never get any more pap.

NAGG I want me pap!

HAMM Give him a biscuit. (*Exit* CLOV) Accursed fornicator! How are your stumps?

NAGG Never mind me stumps. (*Enter* CLOV *with biscuit*)

CLOV I'm back again, with the biscuit. (*He gives biscuit to* NAGG *who fingers it, sniffs it*)

NAGG (*Plaintively*) What is it?

CLOV Spratt's medium.

NAGG (*As before*) It's hard! I can't!

HAMM Bottle him! (CLOV *pushes* NAGG *back into the bin, closes the lid*)

CLOV (*Returning to his place beside the chair*) If age but knew!

HAMM Sit on him!

CLOV I can't sit.

HAMM True. And I can't stand.

CLOV So it is.

HAMM Every man his speciality. (*Pause*) No phone calls? (*Pause*) Don't we laugh?

CLOV (*After reflection*) I don't feel like it.

HAMM (*After reflection*) Nor I. (*Pause*) Clov!

CLOV Yes.

HAMM Nature has forgotten us.

CLOV There's no more nature.

HAMM No more nature! You exaggerate.

CLOV In the vicinity.

HAMM But we breathe, we change! We lose our hair, our teeth! Our bloom! Our ideals!

CLOV Then she hasn't forgotten us.

HAMM But you say there is none.

CLOV (*Sadly*) No one that ever lived ever thought so crooked as we.

HAMM We do what we can.

CLOV We shouldn't. (*Pause*)

HAMM You're a bit of all right, aren't you?

CLOV A smithereen. (*Pause*)

HAMM This is slow work. (*Pause*) Is it not time for my pain-killer?

CLOV No. (*Pause*) I'll leave you, I have things to do.

HAMM In your kitchen?

CLOV Yes.

HAMM What, I'd like to know.

CLOV I look at the wall.

HAMM The wall! And what do you see on your wall? Mene, mene? [1] Naked bodies?

CLOV I see my light dying.

HAMM Your light dying! Listen to that! Well, it can die just as well here, *your* light. Take a look at me and then come back and tell me what you think of *your* light. (*Pause*)

CLOV You shouldn't speak to me like that. (*Pause*)

HAMM (*Coldly*) Forgive me. (*Pause. Louder*) I said, Forgive me.

CLOV I heard you. (*The lid of* NAGG*'s bin lifts. His hands appear, gripping the rim. Then his head emerges. In his mouth the biscuit. He listens*)

HAMM Did your seeds come up?

CLOV No.

HAMM Did you scratch round them to see if they had sprouted?

CLOV They haven't sprouted.

HAMM Perhaps it's still too early.

CLOV If they were going to sprout they would have sprouted. (*Violently*) They'll never sprout! (*Pause.* NAGG *takes biscuit in his hand*)

HAMM This is not much fun. (*Pause*) But that's always the way at the end of the day, isn't it, Clov?

CLOV Always.

HAMM It's the end of the day like any other day, isn't it, Clov?

CLOV Looks like it. (*Pause*)

HAMM (*Anguished*) What's happening, what's happening?

CLOV Something is taking its course. (*Pause*)

HAMM All right, be off. (*He leans back in his chair, remains motionless.* CLOV *does not move, heaves a great groaning sigh.* HAMM *sits up*) I thought I told you to be off.

CLOV I'm trying. (*He goes to door, halts*) Ever since I was whelped. (*Exit* CLOV)

HAMM We're getting on. (*He leans back in his chair, remains motionless.* NAGG *knocks on the lid of the other bin. Pause. He knocks harder. The lid lifts and the hands of* NELL *appear, gripping the rim. Then her head emerges. Lace cap. Very white face*)

NELL What is it, my pet? (*Pause*) Time for love?

NAGG Were you asleep?

NELL Oh no!

NAGG Kiss me.

NELL I can't.

NAGG Try. (*Their heads strain towards each other, fail to meet, fall apart again*)

NELL Why this farce, day after day? (*Pause*)

NAGG I've lost me tooth.

NELL When?

NAGG I had it yesterday.

NELL (*Elegiac*) Ah yesterday! (*They turn painfully towards each other*)

NAGG Can you see me?

NELL Hardly. And you?

NAGG What?

NELL Can you see me?

NAGG Hardly.

NELL So much the better, so much the better.

NAGG Don't say that. (*Pause*) Our sight has failed.

NELL Yes. (*Pause. They turn away from each other*)

NAGG Can you hear me?

NELL Yes. And you?

NAGG Yes. (*Pause*) Our hearing hasn't failed.

NELL Our what?

NAGG Our hearing.

NELL No. (*Pause*) Have you anything else to say to me?

NAGG Do you remember—

NELL No.

NAGG When we crashed on our tandem and lost our shanks. (*They laugh heartily*)

NELL It was in the Ardennes. (*They laugh less heartily*)

[1] See *The Book af Daniel,* 5:26: "God hath numbered thy kingdom, and brought it to an end."

NAGG On the road to Sedan.[2] (*They laugh still less heartily*) Are you cold?

NELL Yes, perished. And you?

NAGG (*Pause*) I'm freezing. (*Pause*) Do you want to go in?

NELL Yes.

NAGG Then go in. (NELL *does not move*) Why don't you go in?

NELL I don't know. (*Pause*)

NAGG Has he changed your sawdust?

NELL It isn't sawdust. (*Pause. Wearily*) Can you not be a little accurate, Nagg?

NAGG Your sand then. It's not important.

NELL It is important. (*Pause*)

NAGG It was sawdust once.

NELL Once!

NAGG And now it's sand. (*Pause*) From the shore. (*Pause. Impatiently*) Now it's sand he fetches from the shore.

NELL Now it's sand.

NAGG Has he changed yours?

NELL No.

NAGG Nor mine. (*Pause*) I won't have it! (*Pause. Holding up the biscuit*) Do you want a bit?

NELL No. (*Pause*) Of what?

NAGG Biscuit. I've kept you half. (*He looks at the biscuit. Proudly*) Three quarters. For you. Here. (*He proffers the biscuit*) No? (*Pause*) Do you not feel well?

HAMM (*Wearily*) Quiet, quiet, you're keeping me awake. (*Pause*) Talk softer. (*Pause*) If I could sleep I might make love. I'd go into the woods. My eyes would see . . . the sky, the earth. I'd run, run, they wouldn't catch me. (*Pause*) Nature! (*Pause*) There's something dripping in my head. (*Pause*) A heart, a heart in my head. (*Pause*)

NAGG (*Soft*) Do you hear him? A heart in his head! (*He chuckles cautiously*)

NELL One mustn't laugh at those things, Nagg. Why must you always laugh at them?

NAGG Not so loud!

NELL (*Without lowering her voice*) Nothing is funnier than unhappiness, I grant you that. But—

NAGG (*Shocked*) Oh!

NELL Yes, yes, it's the most comical thing in the world. And we laugh, we laugh, with a will, in the beginning. But it's always the same thing. Yes, it's like the funny story we have heard too often, we still find it funny, but we don't laugh any more. (*Pause*) Have you anything else to say to me?

NAGG No.

NELL Are you quite sure? (*Pause*) Then I'll leave you.

NAGG Do you not want your biscuit? (*Pause*) I'll keep it for you. (*Pause*) I thought you were going to leave me.

NELL I am going to leave you.

NAGG Could you give me a scratch before you go?

NELL No. (*Pause*) Where?

NAGG In the back.

[2] A town in northeast France.

NELL No. (*Pause*) Rub yourself against the rim.

NAGG It's lower down. In the hollow.

NELL What hollow?

NAGG The hollow! (*Pause*) Could you not? (*Pause*) Yesterday you scratched me there.

NELL (*Elegiac*) Ah yesterday!

NAGG Could you not? (*Pause*) Would you like me to scratch you? (*Pause*) Are you crying again?

NELL I was trying. (*Pause*)

HAMM Perhaps it's a little vein. (*Pause*)

NAGG What was that he said?

NELL Perhaps it's a little vein.

NAGG What does that mean? (*Pause*) That means nothing. (*Pause*) Will I tell you the story of the tailor?

NELL No. (*Pause*) What for?

NAGG To cheer you up.

NELL It's not funny.

NAGG It always made you laugh. (*Pause*) The first time I thought you'd die.

NELL It was on Lake Como.[3] (*Pause*) One April afternoon. (*Pause*) Can you believe it?

NAGG What?

NELL That we once went out rowing on Lake Como. (*Pause*) One April afternoon.

NAGG We had got engaged the day before.

NELL Engaged!

NAGG You were in such fits that we capsized. By rights we should have been drowned.

NELL It was because I felt happy.

NAGG (*Indignant*) It was not, it was not, it was my story and nothing else. Happy! Don't you laugh at it still? Every time I tell it. Happy!

NELL It was deep, deep. And you could see down to the bottom. So white. So clean.

NAGG Let me tell it again. (*Raconteur's voice*) An Englishman, needing a pair of striped trousers in a hurry for the New Year festivities, goes to his tailor who takes his measurements. (*Tailor's voice*) "That's the lot, come back in four days, I'll have it ready." Good. Four days later. (*Tailor's voice*) "So sorry, come back in a week, I've made a mess of the seat." Good, that's all right, a neat seat can be very ticklish. A week later. (*Tailor's voice*) "Frightfully sorry, come back in ten days, I've made a hash of the crotch." Good, can't be helped, a snug crotch is always a teaser. Ten days later. (*Tailor's voice*) "Dreadfully sorry, come back in a fortnight, I've made a balls of the fly." Good, at a pinch, a smart fly is a stiff proposition. (*Pause. Normal voice*) I never told it worse. (*Pause. Gloomy*) I tell this story worse and worse. (*Pause. Raconteur's voice*) Well, to make it short, the bluebells are blowing and he ballockses the buttonholes. (*Customer's voice*) "God damn you to hell, Sir, no, it's indecent, there are limits! In six days, do you hear me, six days, God made the world. Yes Sir, no less Sir, the WORLD! And you are not bloody well capable of making me a pair of trousers in three months!"

[3] A resort in northwest Italy, near Switzerland.

(*Tailor's voice, scandalized*) "But my dear Sir, my dear Sir, look— (*Disdainful gesture, disgustedly*) —at the world— (*Pause*) and look— (*Loving gesture, proudly*) —at my TROUSERS!" (*Pause. He looks at* NELL *who has remained impassive, her eyes unseeing, breaks into a high forced laugh, cuts it short, pokes his head towards* NELL, *launches his laugh again*)

HAMM Silence! (NAGG *starts, cuts short his laugh*)

NELL You could see down to the bottom.

HAMM (*Exasperated*) Have you not finished? Will you never finish? (*With sudden fury*) Will this never finish? (NAGG *disappears into his bin, closes the lid behind him.* NELL *does not move. Frenziedly*) My kingdom for a nightman! (*He whistles. Enter* CLOV) Clear away this muck! Chuck it in the sea! (CLOV *goes to bins, halts*)

NELL So white.

HAMM What? What's she blathering about? (CLOV *stoops, takes* NELL'S *hand, feels her pulse*)

NELL (*To* CLOV) Desert! (CLOV *lets go her hand, pushes her back in the bin, closes the lid*)

CLOV (*Returning to his place beside the chair*) She has no pulse.

HAMM What was she drivelling about?

CLOV She told me to go away, into the desert.

HAMM Damn busybody! Is that all?

CLOV No.

HAMM What else?

CLOV I didn't understand.

HAMM Have you bottled her?

CLOV Yes.

HAMM Are they both bottled?

CLOV Yes.

HAMM Screw down the lids. (CLOV *goes towards door*) Time enough. (CLOV *halts*) My anger subsides, I'd like to pee.

CLOV (*With alacrity*) I'll go and get the catheter. (*He goes towards door*)

HAMM Time enough. (CLOV *halts*) Give me my pain-killer.

CLOV It's too soon. (*Pause*) It's too soon on top of your tonic, it wouldn't act.

HAMM In the morning they brace you up and in the evening they calm you down. Unless it's the other way round. (*Pause*) That old doctor, he's dead naturally?

CLOV He wasn't old.

HAMM But he's dead?

CLOV Naturally. (*Pause*) *You* ask *me* that? (*Pause*)

HAMM Take me for a little turn. (CLOV *goes behind the chair and pushes it forward*) Not too fast! (CLOV *pushes chair*) Right round the world! (CLOV *pushes chair*) Hug the walls, then back to the center again. (CLOV *pushes chair*) I was right in the center, wasn't I?

CLOV (*Pushing*) Yes.

HAMM We'd need a proper wheel-chair. With big wheels. Bicycle wheels! (*Pause*) Are you hugging?

CLOV (*Pushing*) Yes.

HAMM (*Groping for wall*) It's a lie! Why do you lie to me?

CLOV (*Bearing closer to wall*) There! There!

HAMM Stop! (CLOV *stops chair close to back wall.* HAMM *lays his hand against wall*) Old wall! (*Pause*) Beyond is the . . . other hell. (*Pause. Violently*) Closer! Closer! Up against!

CLOV Take away your hand. (HAMM *withdraws his hand.* CLOV *rams chair against wall*) There! (HAMM *leans towards wall, applies his ear to it*)

HAMM Do you hear? (*He strikes the wall with his knuckles*) Do you hear? Hollow bricks! (*He strikes again*) All that's hollow! (*Pause. He straightens up. Violently*) That's enough. Back!

CLOV We haven't done the round.

HAMM Back to my place! (CLOV *pushes chair back to center*) Is that my place?

CLOV Yes, that's your place.

HAMM Am I right in the center?

CLOV I'll measure it.

HAMM More or less! More or less!

CLOV (*Moving chair slightly*) There!

HAMM I'm more or less in the center?

CLOV I'd say so.

HAMM You'd say so! Put me right in the center!

CLOV I'll go and get the tape.

HAMM Roughly! Roughly! (CLOV *moves chair slightly*) Bang in the center!

CLOV There! (*Pause*)

HAMM I feel a little too far to the left. (CLOV *moves chair slightly*) Now I feel a little too far to the right. (CLOV *moves chair slightly*) I feel a little too far forward. (CLOV *moves chair slightly*) Now I feel a little too far back. (CLOV *moves chair slightly*) Don't stay there (*i.e. behind the chair*), you give me the shivers. (CLOV *returns to his place beside the chair*)

CLOV If I could kill him I'd die happy. (*Pause*)

HAMM What's the weather like?

CLOV As usual.

HAMM Look at the earth.

CLOV I've looked.

HAMM With the glass?

CLOV No need of the glass.

HAMM Look at it with the glass.

CLOV I'll go and get the glass. (*Exit* CLOV)

HAMM No need of the glass! (*Enter* CLOV *with telescope*)

CLOV I'm back again, with the glass. (*He goes to window right, looks up at it*) I need the steps.

HAMM Why? Have you shrunk? (*Exit* CLOV *with telescope*) I don't like that, I don't like that. (*Enter* CLOV *with ladder, but without telescope*)

CLOV I'm back again, with the steps. (*He sets down ladder under window right, gets up on it, realizes he has not the telescope, gets down*) I need the glass. (*He goes towards door*)

HAMM (*Violently*) But you have the glass!

CLOV (*Halting, violently*) No, I haven't the glass! (*Exit* CLOV)

HAMM This is deadly. (*Enter* CLOV *with telescope. He goes towards ladder*)

CLOV Things are livening up. (*He gets up on ladder, raises the telescope, lets it fall*) I did it on purpose. (*He gets down, picks up the telescope, turns it on auditorium*) I see . . . a multitude . . . in transports . . . of joy. (*Pause*) That's what I call a magnifier. (*He lowers the telescope, turns towards* HAMM) Well? Don't we laugh?

HAMM (*After reflection*) I don't.

CLOV (*After reflection*) Nor I. (*He gets up on ladder, turns the telescope on the without*) Let's see. (*He looks, moving the telescope*) Zero . . . (*He looks*) . . . zero . . . (*He looks*) . . . and zero.

HAMM Nothing stirs. All is—

CLOV Zer—

HAMM (*Violently*) Wait till you're spoken to! (*Normal voice*) All is . . . all is . . . all is what? (*Violently*) All is what?

CLOV What all is? In a word? Is that what you want to know? Just a moment. (*He turns the telescope on the without, looks, lowers the telescope, turns towards* HAMM) Corpsed. (*Pause*) Well? Content?

HAMM Look at the sea.

CLOV It's the same.

HAMM Look at the ocean! (CLOV *gets down, takes a few steps towards window left, goes back for ladder, carries it over and sets it down under window left, gets up on it, turns the telescope on the without, looks at length. He starts, lowers the telescope, examines it, turns it again on the without*)

CLOV Never seen anything like that!

HAMM (*Anxious*) What? A sail? A fin? Smoke?

CLOV (*Looking*) The light is sunk.

HAMM (*Relieved*) Pah! We all knew that.

CLOV (*Looking*) There was a bit left.

HAMM The base.

CLOV (*Looking*) Yes.

HAMM And now?

CLOV (*Looking*) All gone.

HAMM No gulls?

CLOV (*Looking*) Gulls!

HAMM And the horizon? Nothing on the horizon?

CLOV (*Lowering the telescope, turning towards* HAMM, *exasperated*) What in God's name could there be on the horizon? (*Pause*)

HAMM The waves, how are the waves?

CLOV The waves? (*He turns the telescope on the waves*) Lead.

HAMM And the sun?

CLOV (*Looking*) Zero.

HAMM But it should be sinking. Look again.

CLOV (*Looking*) Damn the sun.

HAMM Is it night already then?

CLOV (*Looking*) No.

HAMM Then what is it?

CLOV (*Looking*) Gray. (*Lowering the telescope, turning towards* HAMM, *louder*) Gray! (*Pause. Still louder*) GRRAY! (*Pause. He gets down, approaches* HAMM *from behind, whispers in his ear*)

HAMM (*Starting*) Gray! Did I hear you say gray?

CLOV Light black. From pole to pole.

HAMM You exaggerate. (*Pause*) Don't stay there, you give me the shivers. (CLOV *returns to his place beside the chair*)

CLOV Why this farce, day after day?

HAMM Routine. One never knows. (*Pause*) Last night I saw inside my breast. There was a big sore.

CLOV Pah! You saw your heart.

HAMM No, it was living. (*Pause. Anguished*) Clov!

CLOV Yes.

HAMM What's happening?

CLOV Something is taking its course. (*Pause*)

HAMM Clov!

CLOV (*Impatiently*) What is it?

HAMM We're not beginning to . . . to . . . mean something?

CLOV Mean something! You and I, mean something! (*Brief laugh*) Ah that's a good one!

HAMM I wonder. (*Pause*) Imagine if a rational being came back to earth, wouldn't he be liable to get ideas into his head if he observed us long enough. (*Voice of rational being*) Ah, good, now I see what it is, yes, now I understand what they're at! (CLOV *starts, drops the telescope and begins to scratch his belly with both hands. Normal voice*) And without going so far as that, we ourselves . . . (*With emotion*) . . . we ourselves . . . at certain moments . . . (*Vehemently*) To think perhaps it won't all have been for nothing!

CLOV (*Anguished, scratching himself*) I have a flea!

HAMM A flea! Are there still fleas?

CLOV On me there's one. (*Scratching*) Unless it's a crablouse.

HAMM (*Very perturbed*) But humanity might start from there all over again! Catch him, for the love of God!

CLOV I'll go and get the powder. (*Exit* CLOV)

HAMM A flea! This is awful! What a day! (*Enter* CLOV *with a sprinkling-tin*)

CLOV I'm back again, with the insecticide.

HAMM Let him have it! (CLOV *loosens the top of his trousers, pulls it forward and shakes powder into the aperture. He stoops, looks, waits, starts, frenziedly shakes more powder, stoops, looks, waits*)

CLOV The bastard!

HAMM Did you get him?

CLOV Looks like it. (*He drops the tin and adjusts his trousers*) Unless he's laying doggo.

HAMM Laying! Lying you mean. Unless he's *lying* doggo.

CLOV Ah? One says lying? One doesn't say laying?

HAMM Use your head, can't you. If he was laying we'd be bitched.

CLOV Ah. (*Pause*) What about that pee?

HAMM I'm having it.

CLOV Ah that's the spirit, that's the spirit! (*Pause*)

HAMM (*With ardor*) Let's go from here, the two of us! South! You can make a raft and the currents will carry us away, far away, to other . . . mammals!

CLOV God forbid!

HAMM Alone, I'll embark alone! Get working on that raft immediately. Tomorrow I'll be gone for ever.

CLOV (*Hastening towards door*) I'll start straight away.

HAMM Wait! (CLOV *halts*) Will there be sharks, do you think?

CLOV Sharks? I don't know. If there are there will be. (*He goes towards door*)

HAMM Wait! (CLOV *halts*) Is it not yet time for my pain-killer?

CLOV (*Violently*) No! (*He goes towards door*)

HAMM Wait! (CLOV *halts*) How are your eyes?

CLOV Bad.

HAMM But you can see.

CLOV All I want.

HAMM How are your legs?

CLOV Bad.

HAMM But you can walk.

CLOV I come . . . and go.

HAMM In my house. (*Pause. With prophetic relish*) One day you'll be blind, like me. You'll be sitting there, a speck in the void, in the dark, for ever, like me. (*Pause*) One day you'll say to yourself, I'm tired, I'll sit down, and you'll go and sit down. Then you'll say, I'm hungry, I'll get up and get something to eat. But you won't get up. You'll say, I shouldn't have sat down, but since I have I'll sit on a little longer, then I'll get up and get something to eat. But you won't get up and you won't get anything to eat. (*Pause*) You'll look at the wall a while, then you'll say, I'll close my eyes, perhaps have a little sleep, after that I'll feel better, and you'll close them. And when you open them again there'll be no wall any more. (*Pause*) Infinite emptiness will be all around you, all the resurrected dead of all the ages wouldn't fill it, and there you'll be like a little bit of grit in the middle of the steppe. (*Pause*) Yes, one day you'll know what it is, you'll be like me, except that you won't have anyone with you, because you won't have had pity on anyone and because there won't be anyone left to have pity on. (*Pause*)

CLOV It's not certain. (*Pause*) And there's one thing you forget.

HAMM Ah?

CLOV I can't sit down.

HAMM (*Impatiently*) Well you'll lie down then, what the hell! Or you'll come to a standstill, simply stop and stand still, the way you are now. One day you'll say, I'm tired, I'll stop. What does the attitude matter? (*Pause*)

CLOV So you all want me to leave you.

HAMM Naturally.

CLOV Then I'll leave you.

HAMM You can't leave us.

CLOV Then I won't leave you. (*Pause*)

HAMM Why don't you finish us? (*Pause*) I'll tell you the combination of the cupboard if you promise to finish me.

CLOV I couldn't finish you.

HAMM Then you won't finish me. (*Pause*)

CLOV I'll leave you, I have things to do.

HAMM Do you remember when you came here?

CLOV No. Too small, you told me.

HAMM Do you remember your father.

CLOV (*Wearily*) Same answer. (*Pause*) You've asked me these questions millions of times.

HAMM I love the old questions. (*With fervor*) Ah the old questions, the old answers, there's nothing like them! (*Pause*) It was I was a father to you.

CLOV Yes. (*He looks at* HAMM *fixedly*) You were that to me.

HAMM My house a home for you.

CLOV Yes. (*He looks about him*) This was that for me.

HAMM (*Proudly*) But for me, (*Gesture towards himself*) no father. But for Hamm, (*Gesture towards surroundings*) no home. (*Pause*)

CLOV I'll leave you.

HAMM Did you ever think of one thing?

CLOV Never.

HAMM That here we're down in a hole. (*Pause*) But beyond the hills? Eh? Perhaps it's still green. Eh? (*Pause*) Flora! Pomona! (*Ecstatically*) Ceres![4] (*Pause*) Perhaps you won't need to go very far.

CLOV I can't go very far. (*Pause*) I'll leave you.

HAMM Is my dog ready?

CLOV He lacks a leg.

HAMM Is he silky?

CLOV He's a kind of Pomeranian.

HAMM Go and get him.

CLOV He lacks a leg.

HAMM Go and get him! (*Exit* CLOV) We're getting on. (*Enter* CLOV *holding by one of its three legs a black toy dog*)

CLOV Your dogs are here. (*He hands the dog to* HAMM *who feels it, fondles it*)

HAMM He's white, isn't he?

CLOV Nearly.

HAMM What do you mean, nearly? Is he white or isn't he?

CLOV He isn't. (*Pause*)

HAMM You've forgotten the sex.

CLOV (*Vexed*) But he isn't finished. The sex goes on at the end. (*Pause*)

HAMM You haven't put on his ribbon.

CLOV (*Angrily*) But he isn't finished, I tell you! First you finish your dog and then you put on his ribbon! (*Pause*)

HAMM Can he stand?

CLOV I don't know.

HAMM Try. (*He hands the dog to* CLOV *who places it on the ground*) Well?

CLOV Wait! (*He squats down and tries to get the dog to stand on its three legs, fails, lets it go. The dog falls on its side*)

HAMM (*Impatiently*) Well?

CLOV He's standing.

HAMM (*Groping for the dog*) Where? Where is he? (CLOV *holds up the dog in a standing position*)

CLOV There. (*He takes* HAMM's *hand and guides it towards the dog's head*)

[4] Goddess of fertility and flowers. Goddess of fruit. Goddess of the earth.

HAMM (*His hand on the dog's head*) Is he gazing at me?

CLOV Yes.

HAMM (*Proudly*) As if he were asking me to take him for a walk?

CLOV If you like.

HAMM (*As before*) Or as if he were begging me for a bone. (*He withdraws his hand*) Leave him like that, standing there imploring me. (CLOV *straightens up. The dog falls on its side*)

CLOV I'll leave you.

HAMM Have you had your visions?

CLOV Less.

HAMM Is Mother Pegg's light on?

CLOV Light! How could anyone's light be on?

HAMM Extinguished!

CLOV Naturally it's extinguished. If it's not on it's extinguished.

HAMM No, I mean Mother Pegg.

CLOV But naturally she's extinguished! (*Pause*) What's the matter with you today?

HAMM I'm taking my course. (*Pause*) Is she buried?

CLOV Buried! Who would have buried her?

HAMM You.

CLOV Me! Haven't I enough to do without burying people?

HAMM But you'll bury me.

CLOV No I won't bury you. (*Pause*)

HAMM She was bonny once, like a flower of the field. (*With reminiscent leer*) And a great one for the men!

CLOV We too were bonny—once. It's a rare thing not to have been bonny—once. (*Pause*)

HAMM Go and get the gaff. (CLOV *goes to door, halts*)

CLOV Do this, do that, and I do it. I never refuse. Why?

HAMM You're not able to.

CLOV Soon I won't do it any more.

HAMM You won't be able to any more. (*Exit* CLOV) Ah the creatures, the creatures, everything has to be explained to them. (*Enter* CLOV *with gaff*)

CLOV Here's your gaff. Stick it up. (*He gives the gaff to* HAMM *who, wielding it like a puntpole, tries to move his chair*)

HAMM Did I move?

CLOV No. (HAMM *throws down the gaff*)

HAMM Go and get the oilcan.

CLOV What for?

HAMM To oil the castors.

CLOV I oiled them yesterday.

HAMM Yesterday! What does that mean? Yesterday!

CLOV (*Violently*) That means that bloody awful day, long ago, before this bloody awful day. I use the words you taught me. If they don't mean anything any more, teach me others. Or let me be silent. (*Pause*)

HAMM I once knew a madman who thought the end of the world had come. He was a painter—and engraver. I had a great fondness for him. I used to go and see him, in the asylum. I'd take him by the hand and drag him to the window. Look! There! All that rising corn! And there! Look! The sails of the herring fleet! All that loveliness! (*Pause*) He'd snatch away his hand and go back into his corner. Appalled. All he had seen was ashes. (*Pause*) He alone had been spared. (*Pause*) Forgotten. (*Pause*) It appears the case is . . . was not so . . . so unusual.

CLOV A madman? When was that?

HAMM Oh way back, way back, you weren't in the land of the living.

CLOV God be with the days! (*Pause.* HAMM *raises his toque*)

HAMM I had a great fondness for him. (*Pause. He puts on his toque again*) He was a painter—and engraver.

CLOV There are so many terrible things.

HAMM No, no, there are not so many now. (*Pause*) Clov!

CLOV Yes.

HAMM Do you not think this has gone on long enough?

CLOV Yes! (*Pause*) What?

HAMM This . . . this . . . thing.

CLOV I've always thought so. (*Pause*) You not?

HAMM (*Gloomily*) Then it's a day like any other day.

CLOV As long as it lasts. (*Pause*) All life long the same inanities.

HAMM I can't leave you.

CLOV I know. And you can't follow me. (*Pause*)

HAMM If you leave me how shall I know?

CLOV (*Briskly*) Well you simply whistle me and if I don't come running it means I've left you. (*Pause*)

HAMM You won't come and kiss me goodbye?

CLOV Oh I shouldn't think so. (*Pause*)

HAMM But you might be merely dead in your kitchen.

CLOV The result would be the same.

HAMM Yes, but how would I know, if you were merely dead in your kitchen?

CLOV Well . . . sooner or later I'd start to stink.

HAMM You stink already. The whole place stinks of corpses.

CLOV The whole universe.

HAMM (*Angrily*) To hell with the universe. (*Pause*) Think of something.

CLOV What?

HAMM An idea, have an idea. (*Angrily*) A bright idea!

CLOV Ah good. (*He starts pacing to and fro, his eyes fixed on the ground, his hands behind his back. He halts*) The pains in my legs! Its unbelievable! Soon I won't be able to think any more.

HAMM You won't be able to leave me. (CLOV *resumes his pacing*) What are you doing?

CLOV Having an idea. (*He paces*) Ah! (*He halts*)

HAMM What a brain! (*Pause*) Well?

CLOV Wait! (*He meditates. Not very convinced*) Yes . . . (*Pause. More convinced*) Yes! (*He raises his head*) I have it! I set the alarm. (*Pause*)

HAMM This is perhaps not one of my bright days, but frankly—

CLOV You whistle me. I don't come. The alarm rings. I'm gone. It doesn't ring. I'm dead. (*Pause*)

HAMM Is it working? (*Pause. Impatiently*) The alarm, is it working?

CLOV Why wouldn't it be working?

HAMM Because it's worked too much.

CLOV But it's hardly worked at all.

HAMM (*Angrily*) Then because it's worked too little!

CLOV I'll go and see. (*Exit* CLOV. *Brief ring of alarm off. Enter* CLOV *with alarm-clock. He holds it against* HAMM'S *ear and releases alarm. They listen to it ringing to the end. Pause*) Fit to wake the dead! Did you hear it?

HAMM Vaguely.

CLOV The end is terrific!

HAMM I prefer the middle. (*Pause*) Is it not time for my pain-killer?

CLOV No! (*He goes to door, turns*) I'll leave you.

HAMM It's time for my story. Do you want to listen to my story?

CLOV No.

HAMM Ask my father if he wants to listen to my story. (CLOV *goes to bins, raises the lid of* NAGG'S, *stoops, looks into it. Pause. He straightens up*)

CLOV He's asleep.

HAMM Wake him. (CLOV *stoops, wakes* NAGG *with the alarm. Unintelligible words.* CLOV *straightens up*)

CLOV He doesn't want to listen to your story.

HAMM I'll give him a bon-bon. (CLOV *stoops. As before*)

CLOV He wants a sugar-plum.

HAMM He'll get a sugar-plum. (CLOV *stoops. As before*)

CLOV It's a deal. (*He goes towards door.* NAGG'S *hands appear, gripping the rim. Then the head emerges.* CLOV *reaches door, turns*) Do you believe in the life to come?

HAMM Mine was always that. (*Exit* CLOV) Got him that time!

NAGG I'm listening.

HAMM Scoundrel! Why did you engender me?

NAGG I didn't know.

HAMM What? What didn't you know?

NAGG That it'd be you. (*Pause*) You'll give me a sugar-plum?

HAMM After the audition.

NAGG You swear?

HAMM Yes.

NAGG On what?

HAMM My honor. (*Pause. They laugh heartily*)

NAGG Two.

HAMM One.

NAGG One for me and one for—

HAMM One! Silence! (*Pause*) Where was I? (*Pause. Gloomily*) It's finished, we're finished. (*Pause*) Nearly finished. (*Pause*) There'll be no more speech. (*Pause*) Something dripping in my head, ever since the fontanelles. (*Stifled hilarity of* NAGG) Splash, splash, always on the same spot. (*Pause*) Perhaps it's a little vein. (*Pause*) A little artery. (*Pause. More animated*) Enough of that, it's story time, where was I? (*Pause. Narrative tone*) The man came crawling towards me, on his belly. Pale, wonderfully pale and thin, he seemed on the point of— (*Pause. Normal tone*) No. I've done that bit. (*Pause. Narrative tone*) I calmly filled my pipe—the meerschaum, lit it with . . . let us say a vesta, drew a few puffs. Aah! (*Pause*) Well, what is it *you* want? (*Pause*) It was an extraordinarily bitter day, I remember, zero by the thermometer. But considering it was Christmas Eve there was nothing . . . extraordinary about that. Seasonable weather, for once in a way. (*Pause*) Well, what ill wind blows you my way? He raised his face to me, black with mingled dirt and tears. (*Pause. Normal tone*) That should do it. (*Narrative tone*) No no, don't look at me, don't look at me. He dropped his eyes and mumbled something, apologies I presume. (*Pause*) I'm a busy man, you know, the final touches, before the festivities, you know what it is. (*Pause. Forcibly*) Come on now, what is the object of this invasion? (*Pause*) It was a glorious bright day, I remember, fifty by the heliometer, but already the sun was sinking down into the . . . down among the dead. (*Normal tone*) Nicely put, that. (*Narrative tone*) Come on now, come on, present your petition and let me resume my labors. (*Pause. Normal tone*) There's English for you. Ah well . . . (*Narrative tone*) It was then he took the plunge. It's my little one, he said. Tsstss, a little one, that's bad. My little boy, he said, as if the sex mattered. Where did he come from? He named the hole. A good half-day, on horse. What are you insinuating? That the place is still inhabited? No no, not a soul, except himself and the child—assuming he existed. Good. I inquired about the situation at Kov, beyond the gulf. Not a sinner. Good. And you expect me to believe you have left your little one back there, all alone, and alive into the bargain? Come now! (*Pause*) It was a howling wild day, I remember, a hundred by the anemometer. The wind was tearing up the dead pines and sweeping them . . . away. (*Pause. Normal tone*) A bit feeble, that. (*Narrative tone*) Come on, man, speak up, what is it you want from me, I have to put up my holly. (*Pause*) Well to make it short it finally transpired that what he wanted from me was . . . bread for his brat? Bread? But I have no bread, it doesn't agree with me. Good. Then perhaps a little corn? (*Pause. Normal tone*) That should do it. (*Narrative tone*) Corn, yes, I have corn, it's true, in my granaries. But use your head. I give you some corn, a pound, a pound and a half, you bring it back to your child and you make him—if he's still alive—a nice pot of porridge, (NAGG *reacts*) a nice pot and a half of porridge, full of nourishment. Good. The colors come back into his little cheeks—perhaps. And then? (*Pause*) I lost patience. (*Violently*) Use your head, can't you, use your head, you're on earth, there's no cure for that! (*Pause*) It was an exceedingly dry day, I remember, zero by the hygrometer. Ideal weather, for my lumbago. (*Pause. Violently*) But what in God's name do you imagine? That the earth will awake in spring? That the rivers and seas will run with fish again? That there's manna in heaven still for imbeciles like you? (*Pause*) Gradually I cooled down, sufficiently at least to ask him how long he had taken on the way. Three whole days. Good. In what condition he had left the child. Deep in sleep. (*Forcibly*) But deep in what sleep, deep in what sleep already? (*Pause*) Well to make it short I finally offered to take him into my service. He had touched a chord. And then I imagined already that I wasn't much longer for this world. (*He laughs. Pause*) Well? (*Pause*) Well? Here if you were careful you might die a nice natural death, in peace and comfort. (*Pause*) Well? (*Pause*) In the end he asked me would I consent to take in the child as well—if he were still alive. (*Pause*) It was the moment I was waiting for. (*Pause*) Would I consent to take in the child . . . (*Pause*) I can see him still, down on his knees, his hands flat on the ground, glaring at me with his mad eyes, in defiance of my wishes. (*Pause. Normal tone*) I'll soon have finished with this story. (*Pause*) Unless I bring in other characters. (*Pause*) But where would I find them? (*Pause*) Where would I look for them? (*Pause. He whistles. Enter* CLOV) Let us pray to God.

NAGG Me sugar-plum!

CLOV There's a rat in the kitchen!

HAMM A rat! Are there still rats?

CLOV In the kitchen there's one.

HAMM And you haven't exterminated him?

CLOV Half. You disturbed us.

HAMM He can't get away?

CLOV No.

HAMM You'll finish him later. Let us pray to God.

CLOV Again!

NAGG Me sugar-plum!

HAMM God first! (*Pause*) Are you right?

CLOV (*Resigned*) Off we go.

HAMM (*To* NAGG) And you?

NAGG (*Clasping his hands, closing his eyes, in a gabble*) Our Father which art—

HAMM Silence! In silence! Where are your manners? (*Pause*) Off we go. (*Attitudes of prayer. Silence. Abandoning his attitude, discouraged*) Well?

CLOV (*Abandoning his attitude*) What a hope! And you?

HAMM Sweet damn all! (*To* NAGG) And you?

NAGG Wait! (*Pause. Abandoning his attitude*) Nothing doing!

HAMM The bastard! He doesn't exist!

CLOV Not yet.

NAGG Me sugar-plum!

HAMM There are no more sugar-plums! (*Pause*)

NAGG It's natural. After all I'm your father. It's true if it hadn't been me it would have been someone else. But that's no excuse. (*Pause*) Turkish Delight, for example, which no longer exists, we all know that, there is nothing in the world I love more. And one day I'll ask you for some, in return for a kindness, and you'll promise it to me. One must live with the times. (*Pause*) Whom did you call when you were a tiny boy, and were frightened, in the dark? Your mother? No. Me. We let you cry. Then we moved you out of earshot, so that we might sleep in peace. (*Pause*) I was asleep, as happy as a king, and you woke me up to have me listen to you. It wasn't indispensable, you didn't really need to have me listen to you. (*Pause*) I hope the day will come when you'll really need to have me listen to you, and need to hear my voice, any voice. (*Pause*) Yes, I hope I'll live till then, to hear you calling me like when you were a tiny boy, and were frightened, in the dark, and I was your only hope. (*Pause.* NAGG *knocks on lid of* NELL'S *bin. Pause*) Nell! (*Pause. He knocks louder. Pause. Louder*) Nell! (*Pause.* NAGG *sinks back into his bin, closes the lid behind him. Pause*)

HAMM Our revels now are ended. (*He gropes for the dog*) The dog's gone.

CLOV He's not a real dog, he can't go.

HAMM (*Groping*) He's not there.

CLOV He's lain down.

HAMM Give him up to me. (CLOV *picks up the dog and gives it to* HAMM. HAMM *holds it in his arms. Pause.* HAMM *throws away the dog*) Dirty brute! (CLOV *begins to pick up the objects lying on the ground*) What are you doing?

CLOV Putting things in order. (*He straightens up. Fervently*) I'm going to clear everything away! (*He starts picking up again*)

HAMM Order!

CLOV (*Straightening up*) I love order. It's my dream. A world where all would be silent and still and each thing in its last place, under the last dust. (*He starts picking up again*)

HAMM (*Exasperated*) What in God's name do you think you are doing?

CLOV (*Straightening up*) I'm doing my best to create a little order.

HAMM Drop it! (CLOV *drops the objects he has picked up*)

CLOV After all, there or elsewhere. (*He goes towards door*)

HAMM (*Irritably*) What's wrong with your feet?

CLOV My feet?

HAMM Tramp! Tramp!

CLOV I must have put on my boots.

HAMM Your slippers were hurting you? (*Pause*)

CLOV I'll leave you.

HAMM No!

CLOV What is there to keep me here?

HAMM The dialogue. (*Pause*) I've got on with my story. (*Pause*) I've got on with it well. (*Pause. Irritably*) Ask me where I've got to.

CLOV Oh, by the way, your story?

HAMM (*Surprised*) What story?

CLOV The one you've been telling yourself all your days.

HAMM Ah you mean my chronicle?

CLOV That's the one. (*Pause*)

HAMM (*Angrily*) Keep going, can't you, keep going!

CLOV You've got on with it, I hope.

HAMM (*Modestly*) Oh not very far, not very far. (*He sighs*) There are days like that, one isn't inspired. (*Pause*) Nothing you can do about it, just wait for it to come. (*Pause*) No forcing, no forcing, it's fatal. (*Pause*) I've got on with it a little all the same. (*Pause*) Technique, you know. (*Pause. Irritably*) I say I've got on with it a little all the same.

CLOV (*Admiringly*) Well I never! In spite of everything you were able to get on with it!

HAMM (*Modestly*) Oh not very far, you know, not very far, but nevertheless, better than nothing.

CLOV Better than nothing! Is it possible?

HAMM I'll tell you how it goes. He comes crawling on his belly—

CLOV Who?

HAMM What?

CLOV Who do you mean, he?

HAMM Who do I mean! Yet another.

CLOV Ah him! I wasn't sure.

HAMM Crawling on his belly, whining for bread for his brat. He's offered a job as gardener. Before— (CLOV *bursts out laughing*) What is there so funny about that?

CLOV A job as gardener!

HAMM Is that what tickles you?

CLOV It must be that.

HAMM It wouldn't be the bread?

CLOV Or the brat. (*Pause*)

HAMM The whole thing is comical, I grant you that. What about having a good guffaw the two of us together?

CLOV (*After reflection*) I couldn't guffaw again today.

HAMM (*After reflection*) Nor I. (*Pause*) I continue then. Before accepting with gratitude he asks if he may have his little boy with him.

CLOV What age?

HAMM Oh tiny.

CLOV He would have climbed the trees.

HAMM All the little odd jobs.

CLOV And then he would have grown up.

HAMM Very likely. (*Pause*)

CLOV Keep going, can't you, keep going!

HAMM That's all. I stopped there. (*Pause*)

CLOV Do you see how it goes on.

HAMM More or less.

CLOV Will it not soon be the end?

HAMM I'm afraid it will.

CLOV Pah! You'll make up another.

HAMM I don't know. (*Pause*) I feel rather drained. (*Pause*) The prolonged creative effort. (*Pause*) If I could drag myself down to the sea! I'd make a pillow of sand for my head and the tide would come.

CLOV There's no more tide. (*Pause*)

HAMM Go and see is she dead. (CLOV *goes to bins, raises the lid of* NELL'S, *stoops, looks into it. Pause*)

CLOV Looks like it. (*He closes the lid, straightens up.* HAMM *raises his toque. Pause. He puts it on again*)

HAMM (*With his hand to his toque*) And Nagg? (CLOV *raises lid of* NAGG'S *bin, stoops, looks into it. Pause*)

CLOV Doesn't look like it. (*He closes the lid, straightens up*)

HAMM (*Letting go his toque*) What's he doing? (CLOV *raises lid of* NAGG'S *bin, stoops, looks into it. Pause*)

CLOV He's crying. (*He closes lid, straightens up*)

HAMM Then he's living. (*Pause*) Did you ever have an instant of happiness?

CLOV Not to my knowledge. (*Pause*)

HAMM Bring me under the window. (CLOV *goes towards chair*) I want to feel the light on my face. (CLOV *pushes chair*) Do you remember, in the beginning, when you took me for a turn? You used to hold the chair too high. At every step you nearly tipped me out. (*With senile quaver*) Ah great fun, we had, the two of us, great fun. (*Gloomily*) And then we got into the way of it. (CLOV *stops the chair under window right*) There already? (*Pause. He tilts back his head*) Is it light?

CLOV It isn't dark.

HAMM (*Angrily*) I'm asking you is it light.

CLOV Yes. (*Pause*)

HAMM The curtain isn't closed?

CLOV No.

HAMM What window is it?

CLOV The earth.

HAMM I knew it! (*Angrily*) But there's no light there! The other! (CLOV *pushes chair towards window left*) The earth! (CLOV *stops the chair under window left* HAMM *tilts back his head*) That's what I call light! (*Pause*) Feels like a ray of sunshine. (*Pause*) No?

CLOV No.

HAMM It isn't a ray of sunshine I feel on my face?

CLOV No. (*Pause*)

HAMM Am I very white? (*Pause. Angrily*) I'm asking you am I very white!

CLOV Not more so than usual. (*Pause*)

HAMM Open the window.

CLOV What for?

HAMM I want to hear the sea.

CLOV You wouldn't hear it.

HAMM Even if you opened the window?

CLOV No.

HAMM Then it's not worth while opening it?

CLOV No.

HAMM (*Violently*) Then open it! (CLOV *gets up on the ladder, opens the window. Pause*) Have you opened it?

CLOV Yes. (*Pause*)

HAMM You swear you've opened it?

CLOV Yes. (*Pause*)

HAMM Well . . . ! (*Pause*) It must be very calm. (*Pause. Violently*) I'm asking you is it very calm!

CLOV Yes.

HAMM It's because there are no more navigators. (*Pause*) You haven't much conversation all of a sudden. Do you not feel well?

CLOV I'm cold.

HAMM What month are we? (*Pause*) Close the window, we're going back. (CLOV *closes the window, gets down, pushes the chair back to its place, remains standing behind it, head bowed*) Don't stay there, you give me the shivers! (CLOV *returns to his place beside the chair*) Father! (*Pause. Louder*) Father! (*Pause*) Go and see did he hear me. (CLOV *goes to* NAGG'S *bin, raises the lid, stoops. Unintelligible words.* CLOV *straightens up*)

CLOV Yes.

HAMM Both times? (CLOV *stoops. As before*)

CLOV Once only.

HAMM The first time or the second? (CLOV *stoops. As before*)

CLOV He doesn't know.

HAMM It must have been the second.
CLOV We'll never know. (*He closes lid*)
HAMM Is he still crying?
CLOV No.
HAMM The dead go fast. (*Pause*) What's he doing?
CLOV Sucking his biscuit.
HAMM Life goes on. (CLOV *returns to his place beside the chair*) Give me a rug, I'm freezing.
CLOV There are no more rugs. (*Pause*)
HAMM Kiss me. (*Pause*) Will you not kiss me?
CLOV No.
HAMM On the forehead.
CLOV I won't kiss you anywhere. (*Pause*)
HAMM (*Holding out his hand*) Give me your hand at least. (*Pause*) Will you not give me your hand?
CLOV I won't touch you. (*Pause*)
HAMM Give me the dog. (CLOV *looks round for the dog*) No!
CLOV Do you not want your dog?
HAMM No.
CLOV Then I'll leave you.
HAMM (*Head bowed, absently*) That's right. (CLOV *goes to door, turns*)
CLOV If I don't kill that rat he'll die.
HAMM (*As before*) That's right. (*Exit* CLOV. *Pause*) Me to play. (*He takes out his handkerchief, unfolds it, holds it spread out before him*) We're getting on. (*Pause*) You weep, and weep, for nothing, so as not to laugh, and little by little . . . you begin to grieve. (*He folds the handkerchief, puts it back in his pocket, raises his head*) All those I might have helped. (*Pause*) Helped! (*Pause*) Saved. (*Pause*) Saved! (*Pause*) The place was crawling with them! (*Pause. Violently*) Use your head, can't you, use your head, you're on earth, there's no cure for that! (*Pause*) Get out of here and love one another! Lick your neighbor as yourself! (*Pause. Calmer*) When it wasn't bread they wanted it was crumpets. (*Pause. Violently*) Out of my sight and back to your petting parties! (*Pause*) All that, all that! (*Pause*) Not even a real dog! (*Calmer*) The end is in the beginning and yet you go on. (*Pause*) Perhaps I could go on with my story, end it and begin another. (*Pause*) Perhaps I could throw myself out on the floor. (*He pushes himself painfully off his seat, falls back again*) Dig my nails into the cracks and drag myself forward with my fingers. (*Pause*) It will be the end and there I'll be, wondering what can have brought it on and wondering what can have . . . (*He hesitates*) . . . why it was so long coming. (*Pause*) There I'll be, in the old shelter, along against the silence and . . . (*He hesitates*) the stillness. If I can hold my peace, and sit quiet, it will be all over with sound, and motion, all over and done with. (*Pause*) I'll have called my father and I'll have called my . . . (*He hesitates*) my son. And even twice, or three times, in case they shouldn't have heard me, the first time, or the second. (*Pause*) I'll say to myself, He'll come back. (*Pause*) And then? (*Pause*) And then? (*Pause*) He couldn't, he has gone too far. (*Pause*) And then? (*Pause. Very agitated*) All kinds of fantasies! That I'm being watched! A rat! Steps! Breath held and then . . . (*He breathes out*) Then babble, babble, words, like the solitary child who turns himself into children, two, three, so as to be together, and whisper together, in the dark. (*Pause*) Moment upon moment, pattering down, like the millet grains of . . . (*He hesitates*) . . . that old Greek, and all life long you wait for that to mount up to a life. (*Pause. He opens his mouth to continue, renounces*) Ah let's get it over! (*He whistles. Enter* CLOV *with alarm-clock. He halts beside the chair*) What? Neither gone nor dead?
CLOV In spirit only.
HAMM Which?
CLOV Both.
HAMM Gone from me you'd be dead.
CLOV And vice versa.
HAMM Outside of here it's death! (*Pause*) And the rat?
CLOV He's got away.
HAMM He can't go far. (*Pause. Anxious*) Eh?
CLOV He doesn't need to go far. (*Pause*)
HAMM Is it not time for my pain-killer?
CLOV Yes.
HAMM Ah! At last! Give it to me! Quick! (*Pause*)
CLOV There's no more pain-killer. (*Pause*)
HAMM (*Appalled*) Good . . . ! (*Pause*) No more pain-killer!
CLOV No more pain-killer. You'll never get any more pain-killer. (*Pause*)
HAMM But the little round box. It was full!
CLOV Yes. But now it's empty. (*Pause.* CLOV *starts to move about the room. He is looking for a place to put down the alarm-clock*)
HAMM (*Soft*) What'll I do? (*Pause. In a scream*) What'll I do? (CLOV *sees the picture, takes it down, stands it on the floor with its face to the wall, hangs up the alarm-clock in its place*) What are you doing?
CLOV Winding up.
HAMM Look at the earth.
CLOV Again!
HAMM Since it's calling to you.
CLOV Is your throat sore? (*Pause*) Would you like a lozenge? (*Pause*) No. (*Pause*) Pity. (CLOV *goes, humming, towards window right, halts before it, looks up at it*)
HAMM Don't sing.
CLOV (*Turning towards* HAMM) One hasn't the right to sing any more?
HAMM No.
CLOV Then how can it end?
HAMM You want it to end?
CLOV I want to sing.
HAMM I can't prevent you. (*Pause.* CLOV *turns towards window right*)
CLOV What did I do with that steps? (*He looks around for ladder*) You didn't see that steps? (*He sees it*) Ah, about time. (*He goes towards window left*) Sometimes I wonder if I'm in my right mind. Then it passes over and I'm as lucid as before. (*He*

*gets up on ladder, looks out of window*) Christ, she's under water! (*He looks*) How can that be? (*He pokes forward his head, his hand above his eyes*) It hasn't rained. (*He wipes the pane, looks. Pause*) Ah what a fool I am! I'm on the wrong side! (*He gets down, takes a few steps towards window right*) Under water! (*He goes back for ladder*) What a fool I am! (*He carries ladder towards window right*) Sometimes I wonder if I'm in my right senses. Then it passes off and I'm as intelligent as ever. (*He sets down ladder under window right, gets up on it, looks out of window. He turns towards* HAMM) Any particular sector you fancy? Or merely the whole thing?

HAMM Whole thing.

CLOV The general effect? Just a moment. (*He looks out of window. Pause*)

HAMM Clov.

CLOV (*Absorbed*) Mmm.

HAMM Do you know what it is?

CLOV (*As before*) Mmm.

HAMM I was never there. (*Pause*) Clov!

CLOV (*Turning towards* HAMM, *exasperated*) What is it?

HAMM I was never there.

CLOV Lucky for you. (*He looks out of window*)

HAMM Absent, always. It all happened without me. I don't know what's happened. (*Pause*) Do you know what's happened? (*Pause*) Clov!

CLOV (*Turning towards* HAMM, *exasperated*) Do you want me to look at this muckheap, yes or no?

HAMM Answer me first.

CLOV What?

HAMM Do you know what's happened?

CLOV When? Where?

HAMM (*Violently*) When! What's happened? Use your head, can't you! What has happened?

CLOV What for Christ's sake does it matter? (*He looks out of window*)

HAMM I don't know. (*Pause.* CLOV *turns towards* HAMM)

CLOV (*Harshly*) When old Mother Pegg asked you for oil for her lamp and you told her to get out to hell, you knew what was happening then, no? (*Pause*) You know what she died of, Mother Pegg? Of darkness.

HAMM (*Feebly*) I hadn't any.

CLOV (*As before*) Yes, you had. (*Pause*)

HAMM Have you the glass?

CLOV No, it's clear enough as it is.

HAMM Go and get it. (*Pause.* CLOV *casts up his eyes, brandishes his fists. He loses balance, clutches on to the ladder. He starts to get down, halts*)

CLOV There's one thing I'll never understand. (*He gets down*) Why I always obey you. Can you explain that to me?

HAMM No. . . . Perhaps it's compassion. (*Pause*) A kind of great compassion. (*Pause*) Oh you won't find it easy, you won't find it easy. (*Pause.* CLOV *begins to move about the room in search of the telescope*)

CLOV I'm tired of our goings on, very tired. (*He searches*) You're not sitting on it? (*He moves the chair, looks at the place where it stood, resumes his search*)

HAMM (*Anguished*) Don't leave me there! (*Angrily* CLOV *restores the chair to its place*) Am I right in the center?

CLOV You'd need a microscope to find this—(*He sees the telescope*) Ah, about time. (*He picks up the telescope, gets up on the ladder, turns the telescope on the without*)

HAMM Give me the dog.

CLOV (*Looking*) Quiet!

HAMM (*Angrily*) Give me the dog! (CLOV *drops the telescope, clasps his hands to his head. Pause. He gets down precipitately, looks for the dog, sees it, picks it up, hastens towards* HAMM *and strikes him violently on the head with the dog*)

CLOV There's your dog for you! (*The dog falls to the ground. Pause*)

HAMM He hit me!

CLOV You drive me mad, I'm mad!

HAMM If you must hit me, hit me with the ax. (*Pause*) Or with the gaff, hit me with the gaff. Not with the dog. With the gaff. Or with the ax. (CLOV *picks up the dog and gives it to* HAMM *who takes it in his arms*)

CLOV (*Imploringly*) Let's stop playing!

HAMM Never! (*Pause*) Put me in my coffin.

CLOV There are no more coffins.

HAMM Then let it end! (CLOV *goes towards ladder*) With a bang! (CLOV *gets up on ladder, gets down again, looks for telescope, sees it, picks it up, gets up ladder, raises telescope*) Of darkness! And me? Did anyone ever have pity on me?

CLOV (*Lowering the telescope, turning towards* HAMM) What? (*Pause*) Is it me you're referring to?

HAMM (*Angrily*) An aside, ape! Did you never hear an aside before? (*Pause*) I'm warming up for my last soliloquy.

CLOV I warn you. I'm going to look at this filth since it's an order. But it's the last time. (*He turns the telescope on the without*) Let's see. (*He moves the telescope*) Nothing . . . nothing . . . good . . . good . . . nothing . . . goo—(*He starts, lowers the telescope, examines it, turns it again on the without. Pause*) Bad luck to it!

HAMM More complications! (CLOV *gets down*) Not an underplot, I trust. (CLOV *moves ladder nearer window, gets up on it, turns telescope on the without*)

CLOV (*Dismayed*) Looks like a small boy!

HAMM (*Sarcastic*) A small . . . boy!

CLOV I'll go and see. (*He gets down, drops the telescope, goes towards door, turns*) I'll take the gaff. (*He looks for the gaff, sees it, picks it up, hastens towards door*)

HAMM No! (CLOV *halts*)

CLOV No? A potential procreator?

HAMM If he exists he'll die there or he'll come here. And if he doesn't . . . (*Pause*)

CLOV You don't believe me? You think I'm inventing? (*Pause*)

HAMM It's the end, Clov, we've come to the end. I don't need you any more. (*Pause*)

CLOV Lucky for you. (*He goes towards door*)

HAMM Leave me the gaff. (CLOV *gives him the gaff, goes towards door, halts, looks at alarm-clock, takes it down, looks round for a better place to put it, goes to bins, puts it on lid of* NAGG's *bin. Pause*)

CLOV I'll leave you. (*He goes towards door*)

HAMM Before you go . . . (CLOV *halts near door*) . . . say something.

CLOV There is nothing to say.

HAMM A few words . . . to ponder . . . in my heart.

CLOV Your heart!

HAMM Yes. (*Pause. Forcibly*) Yes! (*Pause*) With the rest, in the end, the shadows, the murmurs, all the trouble, to end up with. (*Pause*) Clov. . . . He never spoke to me. Then, in the end, before he went, without my having asked him, he spoke to me. He said . . .

CLOV (*Despairingly*) Ah . . . !

HAMM Something . . . from your heart.

CLOV My heart!

HAMM A few words . . . from your heart. (*Pause*)

CLOV (*Fixed gaze, tonelessly, towards auditorium*) They said to me, That's love, yes, yes, not a doubt, now you see how—

HAMM Articulate!

CLOV (*As before*) How easy it is. They said to me, That's friendship, yes, yes, no question, you've found it. They said to me, Here's the place, stop, raise your head and look at all that beauty. That order! They said to me, Come now, you're not a brute beast, think upon these things and you'll see how all becomes clear. And simple! They said to me, What skilled attention they get, all these dying of their wounds.

HAMM Enough!

CLOV (*As before*) I say to myself—sometimes, Clov, you must learn to suffer better than that if you want them to weary of punishing you—one day. I say to myself—sometimes, Clov, you must be there better than that if you want them to let you go—one day. But I feel too old, and too far, to form new habits. Good, it'll never end, I'll never go. (*Pause*) Then one day, suddenly, it ends, it changes, I don't understand, it dies, or it's me, I don't understand, that either. I ask the words that remain—sleeping, waking, morning, evening. They have nothing to say. (*Pause*) I open the door of the cell and go. I am so bowed I only see my feet, if I open my eyes, and between my legs a little trail of black dust. I say to myself that the earth is extinguished, though I never saw it lit. (*Pause*) It's easy going. (*Pause*) When I fall I'll weep for happiness. (*Pause. He goes towards door*)

HAMM Clov! (CLOV *halts, without turning*) Nothing. (CLOV *moves on*) Clov! (CLOV *halts, without turning*)

CLOV This is what we call making an exit.

HAMM I'm obliged to you, Clov. For your services.

CLOV (*Turning, sharply*) Ah pardon, it's I am obliged to you.

HAMM It's we are obliged to each other. (*Pause.* CLOV *goes toward door*) One thing more. (CLOV *halts*) A last favor. (*Exit* CLOV) Cover me with the sheet. (*Long pause*) No? Good. (*Pause*) Me to play. (*Pause. Wearily*) Old endgame lost of old, play and lose and have done with losing. (*Pause. More animated*) Let me see. (*Pause*) Ah yes! (*He tries to move the chair, using the gaff as before. Enter* CLOV, *dressed for the road. Panama hat, tweed coat, raincoat over his arm, umbrella, bag. He halts by the door and stands there, impassive and motionless, his eyes fixed on* HAMM, *till the end.* HAMM *gives up*) Good. (*Pause*) Discard. (*He throws away the gaff, makes to throw away the dog, thinks better of it*) Take it easy. (*Pause*) And now? (*Pause*) Raise hat. (*He raises his toque*) Peace to our . . . arses. (*Pause*) And put on again. (*He puts on his toque*) Deuce. (*Pause. He takes off his glasses*) Wipe. (*He takes out his handkerchief and, without unfolding it, wipes his glasses*) And put on again. (*He puts on his glasses, puts back the handkerchief in his pocket*) We're coming. A few more squirms like that and I'll call. (*Pause*) A little poetry. (*Pause*) You prayed—(*Pause. He corrects himself*) You CRIED for night; it comes—(*Pause. He corrects himself*) It FALLS: now cry in darkness. (*He repeats, chanting*) You cried for night; it falls: now cry in darkness. (*Pause*) Nicely put, that. (*Pause*) And now? (*Pause*) Moments for nothing, now as always, time was never and time is over, reckoning closed and story ended. (*Pause. Narrative tone*) If he could have his child with him. . . . (*Pause*) It was the moment I was waiting for. (*Pause*) You don't want to abandon him? You want him to bloom while you are withering? Be there to solace your last million last moments? (*Pause*) He doesn't realize, all he knows is hunger, and cold, and death to crown it all. But you! You ought to know what the earth is like, nowadays. Oh I put him before his responsibilities! (*Pause. Normal tone*) Well, there we are, there I am, that's enough. (*He raises the whistle to his lips, hesitates, drops it. Pause*) Yes, truly! (*He whistles. Pause. Louder. Pause*) Good. (*Pause*) Father! (*Pause. Louder*) Father! (*Pause*) Good. (*Pause*) We're coming. (*Pause*) And to end up with? (*Pause*) Discard. (*He throws away the dog. He tears the whistle from his neck*) With my compliments. (*He throws whistle towards auditorium. Pause. He sniffs. Soft*) Clov! (*Long pause*) No? Good. (*He takes out the handkerchief*) Since that's the way we're playing it . . . (*He unfolds handkerchief*) . . . let's play it that way . . . (*He unfolds*) . . . and speak no more about it . . . (*He finishes unfolding*) . . . speak no more. (*He holds handkerchief spread out before him*) Old stancher! (*Pause*) You . . . remain. (*Pause. He covers his face with handkerchief, lowers his arms to armrests, remains motionless. Brief tableau*)

*Curtain*

# Eugène Ionesco

## (1912- )

SINCE his explosion onto the contemporary theatrical scene in 1950, Ionesco has become one of the most prolific and controversial of present-day playwrights. Along with Beckett and other writers of the Paris avant-garde, he has created a revolution in dramatic form. Starting from the existential premise of the absurdity of the universe, Ionesco has turned the impossible and fantastic into a real and wholly probable representation of experience. Enlivened by his delight in outrageous mystification, Ionesco's compositions bring together the humorous and the pathetic, the farcical and the grotesque. Devotees of clarity and easy intelligibility in the theatre have found his plays irritating, and some have called them an extravagant hoax, "hollow and pretentious fakery," or worse. Ionesco makes severe demands on his public; he may not yield to ready explanation at a single reading or performance, but he is neither a lunatic nor a charlatan. His frequent and careful attempts to explain his approach to the theatre, along with his rapid conquest of the stage all over the world, suggest that he is a serious artist whose work invites our attention.

French on his mother's side, Ionesco spent his early years moving between Paris and his native Rumania. He taught school in Rumania in the early 1930's; in 1938, out of a deep feeling of revulsion for the native fascism of the Iron Guard and the widespread acceptance of Nazi ideology, he became a French citizen. He literally stumbled into the drama in 1948 when he wrote his first play, *The Bald Soprano* (*La Cantatrice Chauve*), as a parody of a primer he had bought to learn conversational English. Copying out sentences and committing them to memory, Ionesco was struck by the universality of the banalities of dialogue between the Smiths and the Martins. "A good part of the play," he declared, "is composed of sentence fragments drawn from my English primer and set end to end."

*The Bald Soprano* is a parody, not only of the theatre as the subtitle "anti-play" indicates, but of human utterance and experience. The dullness of everyday routine is carried to its farthest limits. The Smiths and the Martins are bored almost beyond belief; blissfully happy, they live, the playwright has declared, in a perfect society—perhaps the world of tomorrow—where all social problems have been resolved and men and women live in perfect harmony and contentment. Ionesco's farce demonstrates the emptiness of life in a world without problems. The play is literally about nothing; the stupid and banal talk flows naturally from the emptiness of daily life. *The Bald Soprano* was not meant to be funny and Ionesco insists that the laughter of the audiences came as a complete shock. In composing the play, he saw it as an expression of the tragedy of language; the characters mouth slogans and clichés of mass conformity, but they can no longer talk because they cannot think or feel. They have no personal identity: "you can put Martin in place of Smith and vice versa, no one will notice." At the climax, the rhythm and intensity of utterance mounts to a paroxysm wherein speech itself breaks down into vocables. Language is pulverized into meaningless sounds, a verbal irrationality that underscores the chaotic void of the world of experience.

Ionesco's dramatic devices are part of a dense and intricate artistic pattern. Dialogue is a series of *non sequiturs,* incongruous analogies, arbitrary associations, forced and ridiculous inferences, and gross distortions of the familiar and commonplace. Contradiction and antagonism are at the foundation of the playwright's vision of reality. It would be revealing to examine his indebtedness to the treatise of his countryman, Stéphane Lupasco, on logic and contradiction (*Logique et contradiction*, 1947), an effort to establish a new rationale for simultaneous contradictory truths. Identity, according to Lupasco, is never static; concepts, like objects, derive their movement and value out of unresolved antagonisms in dynamic opposition. The absurd has a lucidity of its own.

In the theatre Ionesco's love of paradox and ambiguity often takes a farcical and grotesque form. Distortions of size and shape go hand in hand with distortions of speech, in a language reminiscent of Rabelais in its exuberant neologisms. The volatile fantasy of dreams and hallucinations, the black humor and love of shock and surprise, all point to a close affinity between Ionesco and surrealist dramatists like Apollinaire, García Lorca, or Gertrude Stein. Ionesco has recognized the similarity ("the 'surreal' is there, within our reach, in our daily conversation") but insists that he is more lucid in his organization of dreams and other modes of subconscious experience. This is certainly true in his most recent work. Like the surrealists, he views art as "the exteriorization of a psychic dynamism." Truth, he insists, is not in the realm of literal reality; it lies "in our dreams, in the imagination." In his theatre, the subterranean, inner world takes on new shape and immediacy. Ionesco's theatrical genius is perhaps most strikingly revealed in his uncanny ability to find dramatic equivalents or metaphors for the ordinary experiences of modern life. His fables are ingenious abstractions of the absurdity of lived reality.

In his second play, *The Lesson* (1951), Ionesco merged the relationship of teacher and pupil with that of murderer and victim. The academic satire in the plight of the stupid pupil aiming at "the total doctorate" gives way to a brutal climax, suggestive of the monstrous depravity and horror of mass extermination and the concentration camp. *The Chairs* (1952), subtitled "a tragic farce," expresses the emptiness and frustration of rootless and alienated lives. The incessant filling of the stage with dozens of chairs represents the invasion of the world of man by things, objects, which clutter his surroundings and impede his movement. The burlesque of public meetings is also a harsh attack on clichés of social improvement and progress. Ionesco believes that the theatre of politics and propaganda, ideologies and theses, has flattened man out; hence, his rejection of Brecht's "Epic Theatre" along with middle-class social drama.

Although Ionesco has declared that engaged theatre leads to the concentration camp, he too is a deeply committed playwright, committed to the absolute freedom of the individual even to the point of utter irresponsibility. Yet this anarchy is not nihilistic; it represents a genuine assertion of personal value in a world dominated by nationalism, bureaucracy, conformity, and "group-think." In *Victims of Duty* (1953) a chance visit turns into a police interrogation and torture of the good citizen, Choubert, with the cries of the victim punctuated by a mock-serious discourse on the limits of the modern theatre, "still a prisoner of outmoded forms." *Jack or the Submission* (1955) depicts the coercion of the intransigent individual by the family. The hero's attitude toward potatoes with bacon offers a fine example of Ionesco's magnification of the trivial. Jack's fiancée with two noses suddenly turns into her double with three! The parody of romantic love and marriage is sustained in a sequel, *The Future Is in Eggs* (1959), wherein parental demands for offspring result in an inundation of eggs covering Jack from head to foot. As the eggs are piled higher and higher on top of him, he utters a feeble plea on behalf of pessimists, anarchists and nihilists amid the humanistic orgy in praise of procreation.

The breakdown of language and the oppression of the individual by the world of objects are dramatized again in *Amédée or How to Get Rid of It* (1954) by the sprouting of mushrooms in the dining room of the apartment and the gigantic growth of the corpse in the next room, smashing through the walls. Clutter is the principal subject of *The New Tenant* (1956), wherein the passive victim is completely walled in by his furniture. As in Sartre's *Nausea,* the sense of the absurd rises out of man's consciousness of his superfluity amid the alien and unremitting pressure of things. Through repetition, multiplication, and acceleration of movement toward a climax, Ionesco turns the suffering of his entrapped puppets into entertaining farce; but their essential condition is nonetheless grim and painful. In his *Impromptu de l'Alma* (*Improvisation,* 1956), a satire of drama critics patterned after Molière, Ionesco as a character in the action describes a play he is writing about Ionesco. In the course of this theatrical interlude, the playwright sets forth a serious defense of his own work: "I have tried to exteriorize the anguish of my characters through objects, to endow the scenery with speech, to give a visual quality to the dramatic action, to render concrete images of terror or regret, of remorse or alienation. . . ." Given the human condition, theatre for Ionesco cannot be optimistic.

His most recent plays point to an evolution away from the compressed one-act structure and the grotesque comedy of verbal wit to a more complex delineation of human relationships and the mysteries of dreams and the unconscious. Whereas his "pure theatre" comprised what he called "a progression through an increasingly intense and revealing series of emotional states," plot now acquires a degree of solidity and clarity, as well as intrinsic interest. *The Killer* (1959) is again an assault on ideological platitudes; out of a sense of "human brotherhood," Bérenger, the "dismally neutral" citizen, seeks out and finds reasons to justify his own murder even while the killer is advancing on him with drawn knife. Bérenger is also the hero of Ionesco's most successful play, *Rhinoceros* (1960), but here he is an individual in a world of conformists. Ionesco is not concerned with the dangers of vague imitation or conformity but with the brutalization of men, changed by dogma, inertia or stupidity, into horrible beasts. *Rhinoceros,* first composed as a short story, is plainly a political play, inspired perhaps by the playwright's memories of the rush of Rumanians to join the ranks of the fascist Iron Guard in the 1930's or the rise of Nazism in Germany and its spread to Bucharest, Paris, and other capitals of Europe. The rhinoceros, with its thick hide, clumsy gait, and small brain is a perfect analogue of dull-witted bestiality. Bérenger's anarchism takes the form of physical as well as moral resistance as he seizes his rifle and aims it at the beasts; the little man emerges as a lonely but authentic hero.

In Ionesco's theatre, everyone is a Displaced Person. Alienation, the failure of communication, the paralysis of conformity, along with empty eroticism, corruption and betrayal in human relations, and a vision of a future "utopia" darker than any yet imagined, make up the world of his plays. It is a terrifying and painful vision, but one that, by its very existence, points to the urgency of alternatives. Ionesco is not a reformer; his plays, he declares, reflect "a mood and not an ideology, an impulse and not a program." All the same, the subversion of false and meaningless ideologies and attitudes is a necessary first step toward a reformulation of values. Where language can no longer carry significant meaning, gestures must take the place of words. Through mime and vaudeville, fable and farce, Ionesco has revealed the humor present in human freedom as well as the anguish present in our awareness of cosmic absurdity.

# THE BALD SOPRANO

## *Anti-play*

Translated by Donald M. Allen

### THE CHARACTERS

MR. SMITH
MRS. SMITH
MR. MARTIN
MRS. MARTIN
MARY, *the maid*
THE FIRE CHIEF

SCENE *A middle-class English interior, with English armchairs. An English evening. Mr. Smith, an Englishman, seated in his English armchair and wearing English slippers, is smoking his English pipe and reading an English newspaper, near an English fire. He is wearing English spectacles and a small gray English mustache. Beside him, in another English armchair, Mrs. Smith, an Englishwoman, is darning some English socks. A long moment of English silence. The English clock strikes 17 English strokes.*

MRS. SMITH There, it's nine o'clock. We've drunk the soup, and eaten the fish and chips, and the English salad. The children have drunk English water. We've eaten well this evening. That's because we live in the suburbs of London and because our name is Smith.

MR. SMITH (*Continues to read, clicks his tongue*)

MRS. SMITH Potatoes are very good fried in fat; the salad oil was not rancid. The oil from the grocer at the corner is better quality than the oil from the grocer across the street. It is even better than the oil from the grocer at the bottom of the street. However, I prefer not to tell them that their oil is bad.

MR. SMITH (*Continues to read, clicks his tongue*)

MRS. SMITH However, the oil from the grocer at the corner is still the best.

MR. SMITH (*Continues to read, clicks his tongue*)

MRS. SMITH Mary did the potatoes very well, this evening. The last time she did not do them well. I do not like them when they are well done.

MR. SMITH (*Continues to read, clicks his tongue*)

MRS. SMITH The fish was fresh. It made my mouth water. I had two helpings. No, three helpings. That made me go to the toilet. You also had three helpings. However, the third time you took less than the first two times, while as for me, I took a great deal more. I eat better than you this evening. Why is that? Usually, it is you who eats more. It is not appetite you lack.

MR. SMITH (*Clicks his tongue*)

MRS. SMITH But still, the soup was perhaps a little too salt. It was saltier than you. Ha, ha, ha. It also had too many leeks and not enough onions. I regret I didn't advise Mary to add some aniseed stars. The next time I'll know better.

MR. SMITH (*Continues to read, clicks his tongue*)

MRS. SMITH Our little boy wanted to drink some beer; he's going to love getting tiddly. He's like you. At table did you notice how he stared at the bottle? But I poured some water from the jug into his glass. He was thirsty and he drank it. Helen is like me: she's a good manager, thrifty, plays the piano. She never asks to drink English beer. She's like our little daughter who drinks only milk and eats only porridge. It's obvious that she's only two. She's named Peggy. The quince and bean pie was marvelous. It would have been nice, perhaps, to have had a small glass of Australian Burgundy with the sweet, but I did not bring the bottle to the table because I did not wish to set the children a bad example of gluttony. They must learn to be sober and temperate.

MR. SMITH (*Continues to read, clicks his tongue*)

MRS. SMITH Mrs. Parker knows a Rumanian grocer by the name of Popesco Rosenfeld, who has just come from Constantinople. He is a great specialist in yogurt. He has a diploma from the school of yogurt-making in Adrianople. Tomorrow I shall buy a large pot of native Rumanian yogurt from him. One doesn't often find such things here in the suburbs of London.

MR. SMITH (*Continues to read, clicks his tongue*)

MRS. SMITH Yogurt is excellent for the stomach, the kidneys, the appendicitis, and apotheosis. It was Doctor Mackenzie-King who told me that, he's the one who takes care of the children of our neighbors, the Johns. He's a good doctor. One can trust him. He never prescribes any medicine that he's not tried out on himself first. Before operating on Parker, he had his own liver operated on first, although he was not the least bit ill.

MR. SMITH But how does it happen that the doctor pulled through while Parker died?

MRS. SMITH Because the operation was successful in the doctor's case and it was not in Parker's.

MR. SMITH Then Mackenzie is not a good doctor. The operation should have succeeded with both of them or else both should have died.

MRS. SMITH Why?

MR. SMITH A conscientious doctor must die with his patient if they can't get well together. The captain of a ship goes down with his ship into the briny deep, he does not survive alone.

MRS. SMITH One cannot compare a patient with a ship.

MR. SMITH Why not? A ship has its diseases too; moreover, your doctor is as hale as a ship; that's why he should have perished at the same time as his patient, like the captain and his ship.

MRS. SMITH Ah! I hadn't thought of that . . . Perhaps it is true. . . . And then, what conclusion do you draw from this?

MR. SMITH All doctors are quacks. And all patients too. Only the Royal Navy is honest in England.

MRS. SMITH But not sailors.

MR. SMITH Naturally (*A pause. Still reading his paper*) Here's a thing I don't understand. In the newspaper they always give the age of deceased persons but never the age of the newly born. That doesn't make sense.

MRS. SMITH I never thought of that!

(*Another moment of silence. The clock strikes seven times. Silence. The clock strikes three times. Silence. The clock doesn't strike*)

MR. SMITH (*Still reading his paper*) Tsk, it says here that Bobby Watson died.

MRS. SMITH My God, the poor man! When did he die?

MR. SMITH Why do you pretend to be astonished? You know very well that he's been dead these past two years. Surely you remember that we attended his funeral a year and a half ago.

MRS. SMITH Oh yes, of course I do remember. I remembered it right away, but I don't understand why you yourself were so surprised to see it in the paper.

MR. SMITH It wasn't in the paper. It's been three years since his death was announced. I remembered it through an association of ideas.

MRS. SMITH What a pity! He was so well preserved.

MR. SMITH He was the handsomest corpse in Great Britain. He didn't look his age. Poor Bobby, he'd been dead for four years and he was still warm. A veritable living corpse. And how cheerful he was!

MRS. SMITH Poor Bobby.

MR. SMITH Which poor Bobby do you mean?

MRS. SMITH It is his wife that I mean. She is called Bobby too, Bobby Watson. Since they both had the same name, you could never tell one from the other when you saw them together. It was only after his death that you could really tell which was which. And there are still people today who confuse her with the deceased and offer their condolences to him. Do you know her?

MR. SMITH I only met her once, by chance, at Bobby's burial.

MRS. SMITH I've never seen her. Is she pretty?

MR. SMITH She has regular features and yet one cannot say that she is pretty. She is too big and stout. Her features are not regular but still one can say that she is very pretty. She is a little too small and too thin. She's a voice teacher.

(*The clock strikes five times. A long silence*)

MRS. SMITH And when do they plan to be married, those two?

MR. SMITH Next spring, at the latest.

MRS. SMITH We shall have to go to their wedding, I suppose.

MR. SMITH We shall have to give them a wedding present. I wonder what?

MRS. SMITH Why don't we give them one of the seven silver salvers that were given us for our wedding and which have never been of any use to us? (*Silence*)

MRS. SMITH How sad for her to be left a widow so young.

MR. SMITH Fortunately, they had no children.

MRS. SMITH That was all they needed! Children! Poor woman, how could she have managed!

MR. SMITH She's still young. She might very well remarry. She looks so well in mourning.

MRS. SMITH But who would take care of the children? You know very well that they have a boy and a girl. What are their names?

MR. SMITH Bobby and Bobby like their parents. Bobby Watson's uncle, old Bobby Watson, is a rich man and very fond of the boy. He might very well pay for Bobby's education.

MRS. SMITH That would be proper. And Bobby Watson's aunt, old Bobby Watson, might very well, in her turn, pay for the education of Bobby Watson, Bobby Watson's daughter. That way Bobby, Bobby Watson's mother, could remarry. Has she anyone in mind?

MR. SMITH Yes, a cousin of Bobby Watson's.

MRS. SMITH Who? Bobby Watson?

MR. SMITH Which Bobby Watson do you mean?

MRS. SMITH Why, Bobby Watson, the son of old Bobby Watson, the late Bobby Watson's other uncle.

MR. SMITH No, it's not that one, it's someone else. It's Bobby Watson, the son of old Bobby Watson, the late Bobby Watson's aunt.

MRS. SMITH Are you referring to Bobby Watson the commercial traveler?

MR. SMITH All the Bobby Watsons are commercial travelers.

MRS. SMITH What a difficult trade! However, they do well at it.

MR. SMITH Yes, when there's no competition.

MRS. SMITH And when is there no competition?

MR. SMITH On Tuesdays, Thursdays, and Tuesdays.

MRS. SMITH Ah! Three days a week? And what does Bobby Watson do on those days?

MR. SMITH He rests, he sleeps.

MRS. SMITH But why doesn't he work those three days if there's no competition?

MR. SMITH I don't know everything. I can't answer all your idiotic questions!

MRS. SMITH (*Offended*) Oh! Are you trying to humiliate me?

MR. SMITH (*All smiles*) You know very well that I'm not.

MRS. SMITH Men are all alike! You sit there all day long, a cigarette in your mouth, or you powder your nose and rouge your lips, fifty times a day, or else you drink like a fish.

MR. SMITH But what would you say if you saw men acting like women do, smoking all day long, powdering, rouging their lips, drinking whisky?

MRS. SMITH It's nothing to me! But if you're only saying that to annoy me . . . I don't care for that kind of joking, you know that very well!

(*She hurls the socks across the stage and shows her teeth. She gets up*)

MR. SMITH (*Also getting up and going toward his wife, tenderly*) Oh, my little ducky daddles, what a little spitfire you are! You know that I only said it as a joke! (*He takes her by the waist and kisses her*) What a ridiculous pair of old lovers we are! Come, let's put out the lights and go bye-byes.

MARY (*Entering*) I'm the maid. I have spent a very pleasant afternoon. I've been to the cinema with a man and I've seen a film with some women. After the cinema, we went to drink some brandy and milk and then read the newspaper.

MRS. SMITH I hope that you've spent a pleasant afternoon, that you went to the cinema with a man and that you drank some brandy and milk.

MR. SMITH And the newspaper.

MARY Mr. and Mrs. Martin, your guests, are at the door. They were waiting for me. They didn't dare come in by themselves. They were supposed to have dinner with you this evening.

MRS. SMITH Oh, yes. We were expecting them. And we were hungry. Since they didn't put in an appearance, we were going to start dinner without them. We've had nothing to eat all day. You should not have gone out!

MARY But it was you who gave me permission.

MR. SMITH We didn't do it on purpose.

MARY (*Bursts into laughter, then she bursts into tears. Then she smiles*) I bought me a chamber pot.

MRS. SMITH My dear Mary, please open the door and ask Mr. and Mrs. Martin to step in. We will change quickly.

(MR. *and* MRS. SMITH *exit right.* MARY *opens the door at the left by which* MR. *and* MRS. MARTIN *enter*)

MARY Why have you come so late! You are not very polite. People should be punctual. Do you understand? But sit down there, anyway, and wait now that you're here.

(*She exits.* MR. *and* MRS. MARTIN *sit facing each other, without speaking. They smile timidly at each other. The dialogue which follows must be spoken in voices that are drawling, monotonous, a little singsong, without nuances*)

MR. MARTIN Excuse me, madam, but it seems to me, unless I'm mistaken, that I've met you somewhere before.

MRS. MARTIN I, too, sir. It seems to me that I've met you somewhere before.

MR. MARTIN Was it, by any chance, at Manchester that I caught a glimpse of you, madam?

MRS. MARTIN That is very possible. I am originally from the city of Manchester. But I do not have a good memory, sir. I cannot say whether it was there that I caught a glimpse of you or not!

MR. MARTIN Good God, that's curious! I, too, am originally from the city of Manchester, madam!

MRS. MARTIN That is curious!

MR. MARTIN Isn't that curious! Only, I, madam, I left the city of Manchester about five weeks ago.

MRS. MARTIN That is curious! What a bizarre coincidence! I, too, sir, I left the city of Manchester about five weeks ago.

MR. MARTIN Madam, I took the 8:30 morning train which arrives in London at 4:45.

MRS. MARTIN That is curious! How very bizarre! And what a coincidence! I took the same train, sir, I too.

MR. MARTIN Good Lord, how curious! Perhaps then, madam, it was on the train that I saw you?

MRS. MARTIN It is indeed possible; that is, not unlikely. It is plausible and, after all, why not!—But I don't recall it, sir!

MR. MARTIN I traveled second class, madam. There is no second class in England, but I always travel second class.

MRS. MARTIN That is curious! How very bizarre! And what a coincidence! I, too, sir, I traveled second class.

MR. MARTIN How curious that is! Perhaps we did meet in second class, my dear lady!

MRS. MARTIN That is certainly possible, and it is not at all unlikely. But I do not remember very well, my dear sir!

MR. MARTIN My seat was in coach No. 8, compartment 6, my dear lady.

MRS. MARTIN How curious that is! My seat was also in coach No. 8, compartment 6, my dear sir!

MR. MARTIN How curious that is and what a bizarre coincidence! Perhaps we met in compartment 6, my dear lady?

MRS. MARTIN It is indeed possible, after all! But I do not recall it, my dear sir!

MR. MARTIN To tell the truth, my dear lady, I do not remember it either, but it is possible that we caught a glimpse of each other there, and as I think of it, it seems to me even very likely.

MRS. MARTIN Oh! truly, of course, truly, sir!

MR. MARTIN How curious it is! I had seat No. 3, next to the window, my dear lady.

MRS. MARTIN Oh, good Lord, how curious and bizarre! I had seat No. 6, next to the window, across from you, my dear sir.

MR. MARTIN Good God, how curious that is and what a coincidence! We were then seated facing each other, my dear lady! It is there that we must have seen each other!

MRS. MARTIN How curious it is! It is possible, but I do not recall it, sir!

MR. MARTIN To tell the truth, my dear lady, I do not remember it either. However, it is very possible that we saw each other on that occasion.

MRS. MARTIN It is true, but I am not at all sure of it, sir.

MR. MARTIN Dear madam, were you not the lady who asked me to place her suitcase in the luggage rack and who thanked me and gave me permission to smoke?

MRS. MARTIN But of course, that must have been I, sir. How curious it is, how curious it is, and what a coincidence!

MR. MARTIN How curious it is, how bizarre, what a coincidence! And well, well, it was perhaps at that moment that we came to know each other, madam?

MRS. MARTIN How curious it is and what a coincidence! It is indeed possible, my dear sir! However, I do not believe that I recall it.

MR. MARTIN Nor do I, madam. (*A moment of silence. The clock strikes twice, then once*) Since coming to London, I have resided in Bromfield Street, my dear lady.

MRS. MARTIN How curious that is, how bizarre! I, too, since coming to London, I have resided in Bromfield Street, my dear sir.

MR. MARTIN How curious that is, well then, well then, perhaps we have seen each other in Bromfield Street, my dear lady.

MRS. MARTIN How curious that is, how bizarre! It is indeed possible, after all! But I do not recall it, my dear sir.

MR. MARTIN I reside at No. 19, my dear lady.

MRS. MARTIN How curious that is. I also reside at No. 19, my dear sir.

MR. MARTIN Well then, well then, well then, well then, perhaps we have seen each other in that house, dear lady?

MRS. MARTIN It is indeed possible but I do not recall it, dear sir.

MR. MARTIN My flat is on the fifth floor, No. 8, my dear lady.

MRS. MARTIN How curious it is, good Lord, how bizarre! And what a coincidence! I too reside on the fifth floor, in flat No. 8, dear sir!

MR. MARTIN (*Musing*) How curious it is, how curious it is, how curious it is, and what a coincidence! You know, in my bedroom there is a bed, and it is covered with a green eiderdown. This room, with the bed and the green eiderdown, is at the end of the corridor between the toilet and the bookcase, dear lady!

MRS. MARTIN What a coincidence, good Lord, what a coincidence! My bedroom, too, has a bed with a green eiderdown and is at the end of the corridor, between the toilet, dear sir, and the bookcase!

MR. MARTIN How bizarre, curious, strange! Then, madam, we live in the same room and we sleep in the same bed, dear lady. It is perhaps there that we have met!

MRS. MARTIN How curious it is and what a coincidence! It is indeed possible that we have met there, and perhaps even last night. But I do not recall it, dear sir!

MR. MARTIN I have a little girl, my little daughter, she lives with me, dear lady. She is two years old, she's blonde, she has a white eye and a red eye, she is very pretty, her name is Alice, dear lady.

MRS. MARTIN What a bizarre coincidence! I, too, have a little girl. She is two years old, has a white eye and a red eye, she is very pretty, and her name is Alice, too, dear sir!

MR. MARTIN (*In the same drawling, monotonous voice*) How curious it is and what a coincidence! And bizarre! Perhaps they are the same, dear lady!

MRS. MARTIN How curious it is! It is indeed possible, dear sir. (*A rather long moment of silence. The clock strikes 29 times*)

MR. MARTIN (*After having reflected at length, gets up slowly and, unhurriedly, moves toward* MRS. MARTIN, *who, surprised by his solemn air, has also gotten up very quietly.* MR. MARTIN, *in the same flat, monotonous voice, slightly singsong*) Then, dear lady, I believe that there can be no doubt about it, we have seen each other before and you are my own wife . . . Elizabeth, I have found you again!

(MRS. MARTIN *approaches* MR. MARTIN *without haste. They embrace without expression. The clock strikes once, very loud. This striking of the clock must be so loud that it makes the audience jump. The Martins do not hear it*)

MRS. MARTIN Donald, it's you, darling!

(*They sit together in the same armchair, their arms around each other, and fall asleep. The clock strikes several more times.* MARY, *on tiptoe, a finger to her lips, enters quietly and addresses the audience*)

MARY Elizabeth and Donald are now too happy to be able to hear me. I can therefore let you in on a secret. Elizabeth is not Elizabeth, Donald is not Donald. And here is the proof: the child that Donald spoke of is not Elizabeth's daughter, they are not the same person. Donald's daughter has one white eye and one red eye like Elizabeth's daughter. Whereas Donald's child has a white right eye and a red left eye, Elizabeth's child has a red right eye and a white left eye! Thus all of Donald's system of deduction collapses when it comes up against this last obstacle which destroys his whole theory. In spite of the extraordinary coincidences which seem to be definitive proofs, Donald and Elizabeth, not being the parents of the same child, are not Donald and Elizabeth. It is in vain that he thinks he is Donald, it is in vain that she thinks she is Elizabeth. He believes in vain that she is Elizabeth. She believes in vain that he is Donald—they are sadly deceived. But who is the true Donald? Who is the true Elizabeth? Who has any interest in prolonging this confusion? I don't know. Let's not try to know. Let's leave things as they are. (*She takes several steps toward the door, then returns and says to the audience*) My real name is Sherlock Holmes. (*She exits*)

(*The clock strikes as much as it likes. After several seconds,* MR. *and* MRS. MARTIN *separate and take the chairs they had at the beginning*)

MR. MARTIN Darling, let's forget all that has not passed between us, and, now that we have found each other again, let's try not to lose each other any more, and live as before.

MRS. MARTIN Yes, darling.

(MR. *and* MRS. SMITH *enter from the right, wearing the same clothes*)

MRS. SMITH Good evening, dear friends! Please forgive us for having made you wait so long. We thought that we should extend you the courtesy to which you are entitled and as soon as we learned that you had been kind enough to give us the pleasure of coming to see us without prior notice we hurried to dress for the occasion.

MR. SMITH (*Furious*) We've had nothing to eat all day. And we've been waiting four whole hours for you. Why have you come so late?

(MR. *and* MRS. SMITH *sit facing their guests. The striking of the clock underlines the speeches, more or less strongly, according to the case. The* MARTINS, *particularly* MRS. MARTIN, *seem embarrassed and timid. For this reason the conversation begins with difficulty and the words are uttered, at the beginning, awkwardly. A long embarrassed silence at first, then other silences and hesitations follow*)

MR. SMITH Hm. (*Silence*)

MRS. SMITH Hm, hm. (*Silence*)

MRS. MARTIN Hm, hm, hm. (*Silence*)

MR. MARTIN Hm, hm, hm, hm. (*Silence*)

MRS. MARTIN Oh, but definitely. (*Silence*)

MR. MARTIN We all have colds. (*Silence*)

MR. SMITH Nevertheless, it's not chilly. (*Silence*)

MRS. SMITH There's no draft. (*Silence*)

MR. MARTIN Oh no, fortunately. (*Silence*)

MR. SMITH Oh dear, oh dear, oh dear. (*Silence*)

MR. MARTIN Don't you feel well? (*Silence*)

MRS. SMITH No, he's wet his pants. (*Silence*)

MRS. MARTIN Oh, sir, at your age, you shouldn't. (*Silence*)

MR. SMITH The heart is ageless. (*Silence*)

MR. MARTIN That's true. (*Silence*)

MRS. SMITH So they say. (*Silence*)

MRS. MARTIN They also say the opposite. (*Silence*)

MR. SMITH The truth lies somewhere between the two. (*Silence*)

MR. MARTIN That's true. (*Silence*)

MRS. SMITH (*To the* MARTINS) Since you travel so much, you must have many interesting things to tell us.

MR. MARTIN (*To his wife*) My dear, tell us what you've seen today.

MRS. MARTIN It's scarcely worth the trouble, for no one would believe me.

MR. SMITH We're not going to question your sincerity!

MRS. SMITH You will offend us if you think that.

MR. MARTIN (*To his wife*) You will offend them, my dear, if you think that . . .

MRS. MARTIN (*Graciously*) Oh well, today I witnessed something extraordinary. Something really incredible.

MR. MARTIN Tell us quickly, my dear.

MR. SMITH Oh, this is going to be amusing.

MRS. SMITH At last.

MRS. MARTIN Well, today, when I went shopping to buy some vegetables, which are getting to be dearer and dearer . . .

MRS. SMITH Where is it all going to end!

MR. SMITH You shouldn't interrupt, my dear, it's very rude.

MRS. MARTIN In the street, near a café, I saw a man, properly dressed, about fifty years old, or not even that, who . . .

MR. SMITH Who, what?

MRS. SMITH Who, what?

MR. SMITH (*To his wife*) Don't interrupt, my dear, you're disgusting.

MRS. SMITH My dear, it is you who interrupted first, you boor.

MR. SMITH (*To his wife*) Hush. (*To* MRS. MARTIN) What was this man doing?

MRS. MARTIN Well, I'm sure you'll say that I'm making it up—he was down on one knee and he was bent over.

MR. MARTIN, MR. SMITH, MRS. SMITH Oh!

MRS. MARTIN Yes, bent over.

MR. SMITH Not possible.

MRS. MARTIN Yes, bent over. I went near him to see what he was doing . . .

MR. SMITH And?

MRS. MARTIN He was tying his shoe lace which had come undone.

MR. MARTIN, MR. SMITH, MRS. SMITH Fantastic!

MR. SMITH If someone else had told me this, I'd not believe it.

MR. MARTIN Why not? One sees things even more extraordinary every day, when one walks around. For instance, today in the Underground I myself saw a man, quietly sitting on a seat, reading his newspaper.

MRS. SMITH What a character!

MR. SMITH Perhaps it was the same man!

(*The doorbell rings*)

MR. SMITH Goodness, someone is ringing.

MRS. SMITH There must be somebody there. I'll go and see. (*She goes to see, she opens the door and closes it, and comes back*) Nobody. (*She sits down again*)

MR. MARTIN I'm going to give you another example . . .

(*Doorbell rings again*)

MR. SMITH Goodness, someone is ringing.

MRS. SMITH There must be somebody there. I'll go and see. (*She goes to see, opens the door, and comes back*) No one. (*She sits down again*)

MR. MARTIN (*Who has forgotten where he was*) Uh . . .

MRS. MARTIN You were saying that you were going to give us another example.

MR. MARTIN Oh, yes . . .

(*Doorbell rings again*)

MR. SMITH Goodness, someone is ringing.

MRS. SMITH I'm not going to open the door again.

MR. SMITH Yes, but there must be someone there!

MRS. SMITH The first time there was no one. The second time, no one. Why do you think that there is someone there now?

MR. SMITH Because someone has rung!

MRS. MARTIN That's no reason.

MR. MARTIN What? When one hears the doorbell ring, that means someone is at the door ringing to have the door opened.

MRS. MARTIN Not always. You've just seen otherwise!

MR. MARTIN In most cases, yes.

MR. SMITH As for me, when I go to visit someone, I ring in order to be admitted. I think that everyone does the same thing and that each time there is a ring there must be someone there.

MRS. SMITH That is true in theory. But in reality things happen differently. You have just seen otherwise.

MRS. MARTIN Your wife is right.

MR. MARTIN Oh! You women! You always stand up for each other.

MRS. SMITH Well, I'll go and see. You can't say that I am obstinate, but you will see that there's no one there! (*She goes to look, opens the door and closes it*) You see, there's no one there. (*She returns to her seat*)

MRS. SMITH Oh, these men who always think they're right and who're always wrong!

(*The doorbell rings again*)

MR. SMITH Goodness, someone is ringing. There must be someone there.

MRS. SMITH (*In a fit of anger*) Don't send me to open the door again. You've seen that it was useless. Experience teaches us that when one hears the doorbell ring it is because there is never anyone there.

MRS. MARTIN Never.

MR. MARTIN That's not entirely accurate.

MR. SMITH In fact it's false. When one hears the doorbell ring it is because there is someone there.

MRS. SMITH He won't admit he's wrong.

MRS. MARTIN My husband is very obstinate, too.

MR. SMITH There's someone there.

MR. MARTIN That's not impossible.

MRS. SMITH (*To her husband*) No.

MR. SMITH Yes.

MRS. SMITH I tell you *no*. In any case you are not going to disturb me again for nothing. If you wish to know, go and look yourself!

MR. SMITH I'll go.

(MRS. SMITH *shrugs her shoulders.* MRS. MARTIN *tosses her head*)

MR. SMITH (*Opening the door*) Oh! how do you do. (*He glances at* MRS. SMITH *and the* MARTINS, *who are all surprise*) It's the Fire Chief!

FIRE CHIEF (*He is of course in uniform and is wearing an enormous shining helmet*) Good evening, ladies and gentlemen. (*The* SMITHS *and the* MARTINS *are still slightly astonished.* MRS. SMITH *turns her head away, in a temper, and does not reply to his greeting*) Good evening, Mrs. Smith. You appear to be angry.

MRS. SMITH Oh!

MR. SMITH You see it's because my wife is a little chagrined at having been proved wrong.

MR. MARTIN There's been an argument between Mr. and Mrs. Smith, Mr. Fire Chief.

MRS. SMITH (*To* MR. MARTIN) This is no business of yours! (*To* MR. SMITH) I beg you not to involve outsiders in our family arguments.

MR. SMITH Oh, my dear, this is not so serious. The Fire Chief is an old friend of the family. His mother courted me, and I knew his father. He asked me to give him my daughter in marriage if ever I had one. And he died waiting.

MR. MARTIN That's neither his fault, nor yours.

FIRE CHIEF Well, what is it all about?

MRS. SMITH My husband was claiming . . .

MR. SMITH No, it was you who was claiming.

MR. MARTIN Yes, it was she.

MRS. MARTIN No, it was he.

FIRE CHIEF Don't get excited. You tell me, Mrs. Smith.

MRS. SMITH Well, this is how it was. It is difficult for me to speak openly to you, but a fireman is also a confessor.

FIRE CHIEF Well then?

MRS. SMITH We were arguing because my husband said that each time the doorbell rings there is always someone there.

MR. MARTIN It is plausible.

MRS. SMITH And I was saying that each time the doorbell rings there is never anyone there.

MRS. MARTIN It might seem strange.

MRS. SMITH But it has been proved, not by theoretical demonstrations, but by facts.

MR. SMITH That's false, since the Fire Chief is here. He rang the bell, I opened the door, and there he was.

MRS. MARTIN When?

MR. MARTIN But just now.

MRS. SMITH Yes, but it was only when you heard the doorbell ring the fourth time that there was someone there. And the fourth time does not count.

MRS. MARTIN Never. It is only the first three times that count.

MR. SMITH Mr. Fire Chief, permit me in my turn to ask you several questions.

FIRE CHIEF Go right ahead.

MR. SMITH When I opened the door and saw you, it was really you who had rung the bell?

FIRE CHIEF Yes, it was I.

MR. MARTIN You were at the door? And you rang in order to be admitted?

FIRE CHIEF I do not deny it.

MR. SMITH (*To his wife, triumphantly*) You see? I was right. When you hear the doorbell ring, that means someone rang it. You certainly cannot say that the Fire Chief is not someone.

MRS. SMITH Certainly not. I repeat to you that I was speaking of only the first three times, since the fourth time does not count.

MRS. MARTIN And when the doorbell rang the first time, was it you?

FIRE CHIEF No, it was not I.

MRS. MARTIN You see? The doorbell rang and there was no one there.

MR. MARTIN Perhaps it was someone else?

MR. SMITH Were you standing at the door for a long time?

FIRE CHIEF Three-quarters of an hour.

MR. SMITH And you saw no one?

FIRE CHIEF No one. I am sure of that.

MRS. MARTIN And did you hear the bell when it rang the second time?

FIRE CHIEF Yes, and that wasn't I either. And there was still no one there.

MRS. SMITH Victory! I was right.

MR. SMITH (*To his wife*) Not so fast. (*To the* FIRE CHIEF) And what were you doing at the door?

FIRE CHIEF Nothing. I was just standing there. I was thinking of many things.

MR. MARTIN (*To the Fire Chief*) But the third time—it was not you who rang?

FIRE CHIEF Yes, it was I.

MR. SMITH But when the door was opened nobody was in sight.

FIRE CHIEF That was because I had hidden myself—as a joke.

MRS. SMITH Don't make jokes, Mr. Fire Chief. This business is too sad.

MR. MARTIN In short, we still do not know whether, when the doorbell rings, there is someone there or not!

MRS. SMITH Never anyone.

MR. SMITH Always someone.

FIRE CHIEF I am going to reconcile you. You both are partly right. When the doorbell rings, sometimes there is someone, other times there is no one.

MR. MARTIN This seems logical to me.

MRS. MARTIN I think so too.

FIRE CHIEF Life is very simple, really. (*To the* SMITHS) Go on and kiss each other.

MRS. SMITH We just kissed each other a little while ago.

MR. MARTIN They'll kiss each other tomorrow. They have plenty of time.

MRS. SMITH Mr. Fire Chief, since you have helped us settle this, please make yourself comfortable, take off your helmet and sit down for a moment.

FIRE CHIEF Excuse me, but I can't stay long. I should like to remove my helmet, but I haven't time to sit down. (*He sits down, without removing his helmet*) I must admit that I have come to see you for another reason. I am on official business.

MRS. SMITH And what can we do for you, Mr. Fire Chief?

FIRE CHIEF I must beg you to excuse my indiscretion (*Terribly embarrassed*) . . . uhm (*He points a finger at the* MARTINS) . . . you don't mind . . . in front of them . . .

MRS. MARTIN Say whatever you like.

MR. MARTIN We're old friends. They tell us everything.

MR. SMITH Speak.

FIRE CHIEF Eh, well—is there a fire here?

MRS. SMITH Why do you ask us that?

FIRE CHIEF It's because—pardon me—I have orders to extinguish all the fires in the city.

MRS. MARTIN All?

FIRE CHIEF Yes, all.

MRS. SMITH (*Confused*) I don't know . . . I don't think so. Do you want me to go and look?

MR. SMITH (*Sniffing*) There can't be one here. There's no smell of anything burning.

FIRE CHIEF (*Aggrieved*) None at all? You don't have a little fire in the chimney, something burning in the attic or in the cellar? A little fire just starting, at least?

MRS. SMITH I am sorry to disappoint you but I do not believe there's anything here at the moment. I promise that I will notify you when we do have something.

FIRE CHIEF Please don't forget, it would be a great help.

MRS. SMITH That's a promise.

FIRE CHIEF (*To the* MARTINS) And there's nothing burning at your house either?

MRS. MARTIN No, unfortunately.

MR. MARTIN (*To the* FIRE CHIEF) Things aren't going so well just now.

FIRE CHIEF Very poorly. There's been almost nothing, a few trifles—a chimney, a barn. Nothing important. It doesn't bring in much. And since there are no returns, the profits on output are very meager.

MR. SMITH Times are bad. That's true all over. It's the same this year with business and agriculture as it is with fires, nothing is prospering.

MR. MARTIN No wheat, no fires.

FIRE CHIEF No floods either.

MRS. SMITH But there is some sugar.

MR. SMITH That's because it is imported.

MRS. MARTIN It's harder in the case of fires. The tariffs are too high!

FIRE CHIEF All the same, there's an occasional asphyxiation by gas, but that's unusual too. For instance, a young woman asphyxiated herself last week—she had left the gas on.

MRS. MARTIN Had she forgotten it?

FIRE CHIEF No, but she thought it was her comb.

MR. SMITH These confusions are always dangerous!

MRS. SMITH Did you go to see the match dealer?

FIRE CHIEF There's nothing doing there. He is insured against fires.

MR. MARTIN Why don't you go see the Vicar of Wakefield, and use my name?

FIRE CHIEF I don't have the right to extinguish clergymen's fires. The Bishop would get angry. Besides they extinguish their fires themselves, or else they have them put out by vestal virgins.

MR. SMITH Go see the Durands.

FIRE CHIEF I can't do that either. He's not English. He's only been naturalized. And naturalized citizens have the right to have houses, but not the right to have them put out if they're burning.

MRS. SMITH Nevertheless, when they set fire to it last year, it was put out just the same.

FIRE CHIEF He did that all by himself. Clandestinely. But it's not I who would report him.

MR. SMITH Neither would I.

MRS. SMITH Mr. Fire Chief, since you are not too pressed, stay a little while longer. You would be doing us a favor.

FIRE CHIEF Shall I tell you some stories?

MRS. SMITH Oh, by all means, how charming of you. (*She kisses him*)

MR. SMITH, MRS. MARTIN, MR. MARTIN Yes, yes, some stories, hurrah!

(*They applaud*)

MR. SMITH And what is even more interesting is the fact that firemen's stories are all true, and they're based on experience.

FIRE CHIEF I speak from my own experience. Truth, nothing but the truth. No fiction.

MR. MARTIN That's right. Truth is never found in books, only in life.

MRS. SMITH Begin!

MR. MARTIN Begin!

MRS. MARTIN Be quiet, he is beginning.

FIRE CHIEF (*Coughs slightly several times*) Excuse me, don't look at me that way. You embarrass me. You know that I am shy.

MRS. SMITH Isn't he charming! (*She kisses him*)

FIRE CHIEF I'm going to try to begin anyhow. But promise me that you won't listen.

MRS. MARTIN But if we don't listen to you we won't hear you.

FIRE CHIEF I didn't think of that!

MRS. SMITH I told you, he's just a boy.

MR. MARTIN, MR. SMITH Oh, the sweet child! (*They kiss him*)

MRS. MARTIN Chin up!

FIRE CHIEF Well, then! (*He coughs again in a voice shaken by emotion*) "The Dog and the Cow," an experimental fable. Once upon a time another cow asked another dog: "Why have you not swallowed your trunk?" "Pardon me," replied the dog, "it is because I thought that I was an elephant."

MRS. MARTIN What is the moral?

FIRE CHIEF That's for you to find out.

MR. SMITH He's right.

MRS. SMITH (*Furious*) Tell us another.

FIRE CHIEF A young calf had eaten too much ground glass. As a result, it was obliged to give birth. It brought forth a cow into the world. However, since the calf was male, the cow could not call him Mamma. Nor could she call him Papa, because the calf was too little. The calf was then obliged to get married and the registry office carried out all the details completely à la mode.

MR. SMITH À la mode de Caen.

MR. MARTIN Like tripe with onions.

FIRE CHIEF You've heard that one?

MRS. SMITH It was in all the papers.

MRS. MARTIN It happened not far from our house.

FIRE CHIEF I'll tell you another: "The Cock." Once upon a time, a cock wished to play the dog. But he had no luck because everyone recognized him right away.

MRS. SMITH On the other hand, the dog that wished to play the cock was never recognized.

MR. SMITH I'll tell you one: "The Snake and the Fox." Once upon a time, a snake came up to a fox and said: "It seems to me that I know you!" The fox replied to him: "Me too." "Then," said the snake, "give me some money." "A fox doesn't give money," replied the tricky animal, who, in order to escape, jumped down into a deep ravine full of strawberries and chicken honey. But the snake was there waiting for him with a Mephistophelean laugh. The fox pulled out his knife, shouting: "I'm going to teach you how to live!" Then he took to flight, turning his back. But he had no luck. The snake was quicker. With a well-chosen blow of his fist, he struck the fox in the middle of his forehead, which broke into a thousand pieces, while he cried: "No! No! Four times no! I'm not your daughter."

MRS. MARTIN It's interesting.

MRS. SMITH It's not bad.

MR. MARTIN (*Shaking* MR. SMITH's *hand*) My congratulations.

FIRE CHIEF (*Jealous*) Not so good. And anyway, I've heard it before.

MR. SMITH It's terrible.

MRS. SMITH But it wasn't even true.

MRS. MARTIN Yes, unfortunately.

MR. MARTIN (*To* MRS. SMITH) It's your turn, dear lady.

MRS. SMITH I only know one. I'm going to tell it to you. It's called "The Bouquet."

MR. SMITH My wife has always been romantic.

MR. MARTIN She's a true Englishwoman.

MRS. SMITH Here it is: Once upon a time, a fiancé gave a bouquet of flowers to his fiancée, who said, "Thanks"; but before she had said, "Thanks," he, without saying a single word, took back the flowers he had given her in order to teach her a good lesson, and he said, "I take them back." He said, "Goodbye," and took them back and went off in all directions.

MR. MARTIN Oh, charming! (*He either kisses or does not kiss* MRS. SMITH)

MRS. MARTIN You have a wife, Mr. Smith, of whom all the world is jealous.

MR. SMITH It's true. My wife is intelligence personified. She's even more intelligent than I. In any case, she is much more feminine, everyone says so.

MRS. SMITH (*To the* FIRE CHIEF) Let's have another, Mr. Fire Chief.

FIRE CHIEF Oh, no, it's too late.

MR. MARTIN Tell us one, anyway

FIRE CHIEF I'm too tired.

MR. SMITH Please do us a favor.

MR. MARTIN I beg you.

FIRE CHIEF No.

MRS. MARTIN You have a heart of ice. We're sitting on hot coals.

MRS. SMITH (*Falls on her knees sobbing, or else she does not do this*) I implore you!

FIRE CHIEF Righto.

MR. SMITH (*In* MRS. MARTIN'S *ear*) He agrees! He's going to bore us again.

MRS. MARTIN Shh.

MRS. SMITH No luck. I was too polite.

FIRE CHIEF "The Headcold." My brother-in-law had, on the paternal side, a first cousin whose maternal uncle had a father-in-law whose paternal grandfather had married as his second wife a young native whose brother he had met on one of his travels, a girl of whom he was enamored and by whom he had a son who married an intrepid lady pharmacist who was none other than the niece of an unknown fourth-class petty officer of the Royal Navy and whose adopted father had an aunt who spoke Spanish fluently and who was, perhaps, one of the granddaughters of an engineer who died young, himself the grandson of the owner of a vineyard which produced mediocre wine, but who had a second cousin, a stay-at-home, a sergeant-major, whose son had married a very pretty young woman, a divorcée, whose first husband was the son of a loyal patriot who, in the hope of making his fortune, had managed to bring up one of his daughters so that she could marry a footman who had known Rothschild, and whose brother, after having changed his trade several times, married and had a daughter whose stunted great-grandfather wore spectacles which had been given him by a cousin of his, the brother-in-law of a man from Portugal, natural son of a miller, not too badly off, whose foster-brother had married the daughter of a former country doctor, who was himself a foster-brother of the son of a forester, himself the natural son of another country doctor, married three times in a row, whose third wife . . .

MR. MARTIN I knew that third wife, if I'm not mistaken. She ate chicken sitting on a hornet's nest.

FIRE CHIEF It's not the same one.

MRS. SMITH Shh!

FIRE CHIEF As I was saying . . . whose third wife was the daughter of the best midwife in the region and who, early left a widow . . .

MR. SMITH Like my wife.

FIRE CHIEF . . . Had married a glazier who was full of life and who had had, by the daughter of a station master, a child who had burned his bridges . . .

MRS. SMITH His britches?

MR. MARTIN No his bridge game.

FIRE CHIEF And had married an oyster woman, whose father had a brother, mayor of a small town, who had taken as his wife a blonde schoolteacher, whose cousin, a fly fisherman . . .

MR. MARTIN A fly by night?

FIRE CHIEF . . . Had married another blonde schoolteacher, named Marie, too, whose brother was married to another Marie, also a blonde schoolteacher . . .

MR. SMITH Since she's blonde, she must be Marie.

FIRE CHIEF . . . And whose father had been reared in Canada by an old woman who was the niece of a priest whose grandmother, occasionally in the winter, like everyone else, caught a cold.

MRS. SMITH A curious story. Almost unbelievable.

MR. MARTIN If you catch a cold, you should get yourself a colt.

MR. SMITH It's a useless precaution, but absolutely necessary.

MRS. MARTIN Excuse me, Mr. Fire Chief, but I did not follow your story very well. At the end, when we got to the grandmother of the priest, I got mixed up.

MR. SMITH One always gets mixed up in the hands of a priest.

MRS. SMITH Oh yes, Mr. Fire Chief, begin again. Everyone wants to hear.

FIRE CHIEF Ah, I don't know whether I'll be able to. I'm on official business. It depends on what time it is.

MRS. SMITH We don't have the time, here.

FIRE CHIEF But the clock?

MR. SMITH It runs badly. It is contradictory, and always indicates the opposite of what the hour really is.

(*Enter* MARY)

MARY Madam . . . sir . . .

MRS. SMITH What do you want?

MR. SMITH What have you come in here for?

MARY I hope, madam and sir will excuse me . . . and these ladies and gentlemen too . . . I would like . . . I would like . . . to tell you a story, myself.

MRS. MARTIN What is she saying?

MR. MARTIN I believe that our friends' maid is going crazy . . . she wants to tell us a story, too.

FIRE CHIEF Who does she think she is? (*He looks at her*) Oh!

MRS. SMITH Why are you butting in?

MR. SMITH This is really uncalled for, Mary . . .

FIRE CHIEF Oh! But it is she! Incredible!

MR. SMITH And you?

MARY Incredible! Here!

MRS. SMITH What does all this mean?

MR. SMITH You know each other?

FIRE CHIEF And how!

(MARY *throws herself on the neck of the* FIRE CHIEF)

MARY I'm so glad to see you again . . . at last!

MR. AND MRS. SMITH Oh!

MR. SMITH This is too much, here, in our home, in the suburbs of London.

MRS. SMITH It's not proper! . . .

FIRE CHIEF It was she who extinguished my first fires.

MARY I'm your little firehose.

MR. MARTIN If that is the case . . . dear friends . . . these emotions are understandable, human, honorable . . .

MRS. MARTIN All that is human is honorable.

MRS. SMITH Even so, I don't like to see it . . . here among us . . .

MR. SMITH She's not been properly brought up . . .

FIRE CHIEF Oh, you have too many prejudices.

MRS. MARTIN What I think is that a maid, after all—even though it's none of my business—is never anything but a maid . . .

MR. MARTIN Even if she can sometimes be a rather good detective.

FIRE CHIEF Let me go.

MARY Don't be upset! . . . They're not so bad really.

MR. SMITH Hm . . . hm . . . you two are very touching, but at the same time, a little . . . a little . . .

MR. MARTIN Yes, that's exactly the word.

MR. SMITH . . . A little too exhibitionistic . . .

MR. MARTIN There is a native British modesty—forgive me for attempting, yet again, to define my thought—not understood by foreigners, even by specialists, thanks to which, if I may thus express myself . . . of course, I don't mean to refer to you . . .

MARY I was going to tell you . . .

MR. SMITH Don't tell us anything . . .

MARY Oh yes!

MRS. SMITH Go, my little Mary, go quietly to the kitchen and read your poems before the mirror . . .

MR. MARTIN You know, even though I'm not a maid, I also read poems before the mirror.

MRS. MARTIN This morning when you looked at yourself in the mirror you didn't see yourself.

MR. MARTIN That's because I wasn't there yet . . .

MARY All the same, I could, perhaps, recite a little poem for you.

MRS. SMITH My little Mary, you are frightfully obstinate.

MARY I'm going to recite a poem, then, is that agreed? It is a poem entitled "The Fire" in honor of the Fire Chief:

The Fire

The polyploids were burning in the wood
A stone caught fire
The castle caught fire
The forest caught fire
The men caught fire
The women caught fire
The birds caught fire
The fish caught fire
The water caught fire
The sky caught fire
The ashes caught fire
The smoke caught fire
The fire caught fire
Everything caught fire
Caught fire, caught fire.

(*She recites the poem while the* SMITHS *are pushing her offstage*)

MRS. MARTIN That sent chills up my spine . . .

MR. MARTIN And yet there's a certain warmth in those lines . . .

FIRE CHIEF I thought it was marvelous.

MRS. SMITH All the same . . .

MR. SMITH You're exaggerating . . .

FIRE CHIEF Just a minute . . . I admit . . . all this is very subjective . . . but this is my conception of the world. My world. My dream. My ideal . . . And now this reminds me that I must leave. Since you don't have the time here, I must tell you that in exactly three-quarters of an hour and sixteen minutes, I'm having a fire at the other end of the city. Consequently, I must hurry. Even though it will be quite unimportant.

MRS. SMITH What will it be? A little chimney fire?

FIRE CHIEF Oh, not even that. A straw fire and a little heartburn.

MR. SMITH Well, we're sorry to see you go.

MRS. SMITH You have been very entertaining.

MRS. MARTIN Thanks to you, we have passed a truly Cartesian quarter of an hour.

FIRE CHIEF (*Moving toward the door, then stopping*) Speaking of that—the bald soprano? (*General silence, embarrassment*)

MRS. SMITH She always wears her hair in the same style.

FIRE CHIEF Ah! Then goodbye, ladies and gentlemen.

MR. MARTIN Good luck, and a good fire!

FIRE CHIEF Let's hope so. For everybody.

(FIRE CHIEF *exits. All accompany him to the door and then return to their seats*)

MRS. MARTIN I can buy a pocketknife for my brother, but you can't buy Ireland for your grandfather.

MR. SMITH One walks on his feet, but one heats with electricity or coal.

MR. MARTIN He who sells an ox today, will have an egg tomorrow.

MRS. SMITH In real life, one must look out of the window.

MRS. MARTIN One can sit down on a chair, when the chair doesn't have any.

MR. SMITH One must always think of everything.

MRS. MARTIN The ceiling is above, the floor is below.

MRS. SMITH When I say yes, it's only a manner of speaking.

MRS. MARTIN To each his own.

MR. SMITH Take a circle, caress it, and it will turn vicious.

MRS. SMITH A schoolmaster teaches his pupils to read, but the cat suckles her young when they are small.

MRS. MARTIN Nevertheless, it was the cow that gave us tails.

MR. SMITH When I'm in the country, I love the solitude and the quiet.

MR. MARTIN You are not old enough yet for that.

MRS. SMITH Benjamin Franklin was right; you are more nervous than he.

MRS. MARTIN What are the seven days of the week?

MR. SMITH Monday, Tuesday, Wednesday, Thursday, Friday, Saturday, Sunday.[1]

[1] In English in the original.—Translator's note.

MR. MARTIN Edward is a clerk; his sister Nancy is a typist, and his brother William a shop-assistant.[2]

MRS. SMITH An odd family!

MRS. MARTIN I prefer a bird in the bush to a sparrow in a barrow.

MR. SMITH Rather a steak in a chalet than gristle in a castle.

MR. MARTIN An Englishman's home is truly his castle.

MRS. SMITH I don't know enough Spanish to make myself understood.

MRS. MARTIN I'll give you my mother-in-law's slippers if you'll give me your husband's coffin.

MR. SMITH I'm looking for a monophysite priest to marry to our maid.

MR. MARTIN Bread is a staff, whereas bread is also a staff, and an oak springs from an oak every morning at dawn.

MRS. SMITH My uncle lives in the country, but that's none of the midwife's business.

MR. MARTIN Paper is for writing, the cat's for the rat. Cheese is for scratching.

MRS. SMITH The car goes very fast, but the cook beats batter better.

MR. SMITH Don't be turkeys; rather kiss the conspirator.

MR. MARTIN Charity begins at home.[2]

MRS. SMITH I'm waiting for the aqueduct to come and see me at my windmill.

MR. MARTIN One can prove that social progress is definitely better with sugar.

MR. SMITH To hell with polishing!

(*Following this last speech of* MR. SMITH, *the others are silent for a moment, stupefied. We sense that there is a certain nervous irritation. The strokes of the clock are more nervous too. The speeches which follow must be said, at first, in a glacial, hostile tone. The hostility and the nervousness increase. At the end of this scene, the four characters must be standing very close to each other, screaming their speeches, raising their fists, ready to throw themselves upon each other.*)

MR. MARTIN One doesn't polish spectacles with black wax.

MRS. SMITH Yes, but with money one can buy anything.

MR. MARTIN I'd rather kill a rabbit than sing in the garden.

MR. SMITH Cockatoos, cockatoos, cockatoos, cockatoos, cockatoos, cockatoos, cockatoos, cockatoos, cockatoos, cockatoos.

MRS. SMITH Such caca, such caca, such caca, such caca, such caca, such caca, such caca, such caca, such caca.

MR. MARTIN Such cascades of cacas, such cascades of cacas, such cascades of cacas, such cascades of cacas, such cascades of cacas, such cascades of cacas, such cascades of cacas, such cascades of cacas.

MR. SMITH Dogs have fleas, dogs have fleas.

[2] In English in the original.—Translator's note.

MRS. MARTIN Cactus, coccyx! crocus! cockaded! cockroach!

MRS. SMITH Incasker, you incask us.

MR. MARTIN I'd rather lay an egg in a box than go and steal an ox.

MRS. MARTIN (*Opening her mouth very wide*) Ah! oh! ah! oh! Let me gnash my teeth.

MR. SMITH Crocodile!

MR. MARTIN Let's go and slap Ulysses.

MR. SMITH I'm going to live in my cabana among my cacao trees.

MRS. MARTIN Cacao trees on cacao farms don't bear coconuts, they yield cocoa! Cacao trees on cacao farms don't bear coconuts, they yield cocoa! Cacao trees on cacao farms don't bear coconuts, they yield cocoa.

MRS. SMITH Mice have lice, lice haven't mice.

MRS. MARTIN Don't ruche my brooch!

MR. MARTIN Don't smooch the brooch!

MR. SMITH Groom the goose, don't goose the groom.

MRS. MARTIN The goose grooms.

MRS. SMITH Groom your tooth.

MR. MARTIN Groom the bridegroom, groom the bridegroom.

MR. SMITH Seducer seduced!

MRS. MARTIN Scaramouche!

MRS. SMITH Sainte-Nitouche!

MR. MARTIN Go take a douche.

MR. SMITH I've been goosed.

MRS. MARTIN Sainte-Nitouche stoops to my cartouche.

MRS. SMITH "Who'd stoop to blame? . . . and I never choose to stoop."

MR. MARTIN Robert!

MR. SMITH Browning!

MRS. MARTIN, MR. SMITH Rudyard.

MRS. SMITH, MR. MARTIN Kipling.

MRS. MARTIN, MR. SMITH Robert Kipling!

MRS. SMITH, MR. MARTIN Rudyard Browning.

MRS. MARTIN Silly gobblegobblers, silly gobblegobblers.

MR. MARTIN Marietta, spot the pot!

MRS. SMITH Krishnamurti, Krishnamurti, Krishnamurti!

MR. SMITH The pope elopes! The pope's got no horoscope. The horoscope's bespoke.

MRS. MARTIN Bazaar, Balzac, bazooka!

MR. MARTIN Bizarre, beaux-arts, brassieres!

MR. SMITH A, e, i, o, u, a, e, i, o, u, a, e, i, o, u, i!

MRS. MARTIN B, c, d, f, g, l, m, n, p, r, s, t, v, w, x, z!

MR. MARTIN From sage to stooge, from stage to serge!

MRS. SMITH (*Imitating a train*) Choo, choo, choo, choo, choo, choo, choo, choo, choo, choo, choo!

MR. SMITH It's!

MRS. MARTIN Not!

MR. MARTIN That!

MRS. SMITH Way!

MR. SMITH It's!

MRS. MARTIN O!

MR. MARTIN Ver!

MRS. SMITH Here!

(*All together, completely infuriated, screaming in each others' ears. The light is extinguished. In the darkness we hear, in an increasingly rapid rhythm*)

ALL TOGETHER It's not that way, it's over here, it's not that way, it's over here, it's not that way, it's over here, it's not that way, it's over here!

(*The words cease abruptly. Again, the lights come on.* MR. *and* MRS. MARTIN *are seated like the* SMITHS *at the beginning of the play. The play begins again with the* MARTINS, *who say exactly the same lines as the* SMITHS *in the first scene, while the curtain softly falls*)

# Friedrich Duerrenmatt

## (1921- )

THE SATIRIC, unheroic, and grotesque drama that emerged from the pens of new European writers after World War II constituted an effort to make the theatre respond to the moral and intellectual chaos of our time. The most daring innovators of the early years of the century—Strindberg, Wedekind, and the expressionists—had conclusively demonstrated the power of the theatre to capture the fluidity and tension of unconscious experience and to transcend the limitations of space, time, and linear causality. The violence and frenzy of inner life explored by the expressionists represented far more accurately the terrifying anarchy of twentieth-century history than did the simpler drama of representational realism. In drama as in other literary forms, allegory, fable, parable, and other symbolic devices came to replace the older concern with literal anecdote. In his assimilation and use of theatricalist experimentation, Duerrenmatt is a wholly representative and traditional mid-century playwright.

Duerrenmatt was born in the Swiss village of Konolfingen, where his father was a pastor. His grandfather, Ulrich, had been active in nineteenth-century Swiss politics and was well known as a satiric poet and political eccentric (he once spent ten days in jail because of a poem). This combination of rural villager and dissident intellectual is also present in his grandson. Friedrich Duerrenmatt was educated first in Bern and then in Zurich where he attended the university. His first ambition was to become a painter and his early plays were published accompanied by his own illustrations. His style in painting, drawing upon Bosch, Barlach, Rouault, and the German expressionists, bears significant analogies to his drama. In the early 1940's he began his literary career with fictional sketches and prose fragments somewhat suggestive of the manner of Ernst Jünger in their shrill, "high frequency" style. His first play, *Es steht geschrieben* (*Thus Is It Written*), was composed in 1945-46 and first performed in Zurich in 1947. On the surface a historical drama dealing with the defeat of a fanatical group of Anabaptists in Münster during the Thirty Years' War, it is in fact a parody of history. From the beginning of his career, Duerrenmatt has been deeply concerned with moral and religious values. His strict Protestant training and his early interest in Kierkegaard and Kafka may help to explain his preoccupation with sin, suffering, and the quest for redemption in a seemingly alien or indifferent universe. He writes, he has stated, out of an awareness of the absurdity of the world, but also out of an awareness of the possibility of noble and responsible choice. His second play, *Der Blinde* (*The Blind Man*, 1948), has as its central character the blind Duke Knechtling, living in a world of ruins which he believes to be intact. He loses his son and daughter, his city is destroyed, and in the final panorama of desolation and waste, he stands forth naked before God and exclaims, "Become blind and ye shall see." The play is permeated with biblical rhythms and overtones in a language that moves freely between poetic and conversational styles. It is a striking illustration of Duerrenmatt's conception of theatre as a moral revelation and cosmic quest.

*Romulus the Great* (1949), subtitled "an unhistorical historical comedy," is a spirited modernization of a crucial event of the past, somewhat in the manner of Shaw's *Caesar and Cleopatra.* The action takes place on the Ides of March, 476 A.D., when the dying Roman Empire is conquered by the invading barbarian forces. Romulus, the last emperor, willfully conspires to bring about Rome's destruction. He acts not as a traitor but as a judge, mindful of the black villainy that stains the pages of Roman history. Rome has chosen power and tyranny over truth and humanity, and must be destroyed. Paradoxically, the leader of the Germans, Odoaker, is forced against his will to be a conqueror. Both figures are essentially unheroic. Romulus, who violates all the traditions of Roman emperors, is the personification of deliberate irresponsibility; he "contracts out" of the obligation his society would force upon him, and accepts a pension from the Germans which will enable him to live in comfortable retirement. The comedy ends with reflections on the possible course of history under the control of the Germans and the hope that mankind can enjoy a few peaceful and unheroic years.

The interplay of capricious fantasy and broad, irreverent comedy underlies Duerrenmatt's wholesome eclecticism. Aristophanes, Nestroy, Wedekind, Brecht, Wilder, and many more great comic and satiric playwrights have contributed to the variety of styles present in his works. Not only is each play utterly unlike its predecessor, but there is a wonderful mixture of styles within the plays. *Die Ehe des Herrn Mississippi* (*The Marriage of Mr. Mississippi*) was first produced in Munich in 1952. Written in a modified expressionist style, the play is a fluid and sprawling panorama of violence and intrigue. The hero, Florestan Mississippi, incarnates the passion for absolute justice and attempts to revive the Mosaic law. The futility of his quest ends in his ruin and the destruction of all who are associated with him. The other figures in the play are equally fantastic: Anastasia, a younger sister to Wedekind's Lulu, who poisons Florestan; St. Claude, the renegade Communist whose execution provides a frame for the dramatic action; and Übelohe, who takes up a life of wretchedness and poverty after his rejection by Anastasia. His final chorus is a hymn to man's reckless courage and God's glory.

Duerrenmatt turned away from almost bewildering incoherence to satirize the cult of power and institutional bureaucracy in the lively comedy, *An Angel Comes to Babylon* (1953). The angel arrives with the astonishingly beautiful girl, Kurubi, to be given to the most unfortunate man on earth. The choice falls on Akki, the sole beggar remaining alive; but King Nebukadnezar, out to convert all beggars to public servants, disguises himself as a beggar and proves himself even more insignificant than Akki. Nevertheless, he spurns the prize to return to his empire. The mere presence of Kurubi demoralizes the populace and she must be removed from the scene; the king gives her to his hangman, Akki in disguise, and they flee together. The mood of Duerrenmatt's comedy is suggestive of the innocent gaiety of Giraudoux or the early Anouilh as well as of the cynical satire of Brecht. Akki begs not for gain but out of principle: a demonstration of his intrinsic superiority. He is in fact an artist, indifferent to riches or power, dedicated to the pursuit of his art as a perpetual confirmation of his genius. His pungent analysis of society exposes the naked power relationship of the governor and the governed. The final triumph of the beggar is the victory of innocence and ingenuity over corruption and strength: the meek and lowly do indeed inherit the earth. The king will content himself with building the tower of Babel: a contest with God wherein the results may safely be predicted by the audience. *An Angel Comes to Babylon* deserves to be widely read and performed, if only for the wit and wisdom of Duerrenmatt's incredible beggar, Akki, one of the most engaging character creations of contemporary drama.

By far Duerrenmatt's most successful play has been the tragicomedy, *The Visit,* first performed in 1956. Here again, the playwright combines expressionistic devices with a lively and imaginative sense of the shocking and the macabre. In his essay, "Problems of the Theatre," he dwells at some length on the necessity for tragicomedy and the grotesque in modern drama: "Tragedy presupposes guilt, despair, moderation, lucidity, vision, a sense of responsibility. In the Punch-and-Judy show of our century, in this back-sliding of the white race, there are no more guilty and also, no responsible men. It is always, 'We couldn't help it' and 'We didn't really want that to happen.' . . . We are all collectively guilty, collectively bogged down in the sins of our fathers and of our forefathers. . . . Comedy alone is suitable for us. Our world has led to the grotesque as well as to the atom bomb. . . . But the tragic is still possible even if pure tragedy is not." Güllen is at once no place and every place. A purely imaginary locale somewhere in central Europe, the town is a microcosm of the modern metropolis. The dominant preoccupations and values are the same. The play presents a mirror of a community; despite the vivid concreteness of the central characters, the town of Güllen is itself the protagonist of the drama.

In an interview in 1958, Duerrenmatt declared: "When you write a play you don't do it to teach a lesson or prove a point or build a philosophy because you can never force art to prove anything." The thesis or ideology present in the drama emerges from it; the play itself, he insists, is the response to a specifically dramatic situation: "I describe human beings, not marionettes, an action, not an allegory; I set forth a world, not a moral." This world is itself the invention of the playwright. His drama is far removed from the literal reproduction of everyday life. The underlying conception of the play is poetic, not didactic.

It would be incorrect to reduce the complexity of the drama to strict allegory. In a note to the play, Duerrenmatt remarks: "Claire Zachanassian represents neither justice nor the Marshall Plan nor even the Apocalypse; let her be only what she is: the richest woman in the world, whose fortune has put her in a position to act like the heroine of a Greek tragedy: absolute, cruel, something like Medea." She may seem to present a rather complex study in psychopathology, but her manner is graceful and even refined. She is no mere abstract representation of cosmic evil or of outraged justice. The full title of the play, *Der Besuch der alten Dame* (*The Visit of the Old Lady*) emphasizes the impact of her personality on the community at large. The role of Claire has been somewhat softened and subdued in the version of the play prepared for the New York production. The playwright participated in the reworking, in accord with his view that plays must be adapted to the local conditions under which they are produced. Alfred Ill was renamed Anton Schill and many other details were altered, without affecting the principal line of dramatic action. Schill is akin to the ancient scapegoat whose ritual murder purges the community of its uncleanliness. The purgation is ironic, for the community itself becomes polluted through the surrender of its integrity and humanity. Claire justifies herself by exclaiming: "The world made me into a whore; now I make the world into a brothel." In an epilogue written for the original production, Duerrenmatt presents the effects of Claire's philanthropy. Güllen becomes a mechanized "utopia" similar to the grim vision of future technological civilization in Aldous Huxley's *Brave New World.* The final chorus of the townspeople, a parody of Greek drama, is an appeal for divine protection of their newly gained happiness. Schill's death brings with it the spiritual death of the community. It is possible to understand the capitulation of the town: "The temptation is too great, the poverty too bitter." Schill, in his death, towers magnificently above his assailants, a tribute to the grandeur of an ordinary man whose dignity and courage throw into sharp relief the material and spiritual corruption of his society.

# THE VISIT

Adapted by Maurice Valency

### CHARACTERS

*(In order of appearance)*

HOFBAUER (FIRST MAN)
HELMESBERGER (SECOND MAN)
WECHSLER (THIRD MAN)
VOGEL (FOURTH MAN)
PAINTER
STATION MASTER
BURGOMASTER
TEACHER
PASTOR
ANTON SCHILL
CLAIRE ZACHANASSIAN
CONDUCTOR
PEDRO CABRAL
BOBBY
POLICEMAN
FIRST GRANDCHILD
SECOND GRANDCHILD
MIKE
MAX
FIRST BLIND MAN
SECOND BLIND MAN
ATHLETE
FRAU BURGOMASTER
FRAU SCHILL
DAUGHTER
SON
DOCTOR NÜSSLIN
FRAU BLOCK (FIRST WOMAN)
TRUCK DRIVER
REPORTER
TOWNSMAN

*The action of the play takes place in and around the little town of Güllen, somewhere in Europe.*

*There are three acts.*

## Act One

*A railway-crossing bell starts ringing. Then is heard the distant sound of a locomotive whistle. The curtain rises.*

*The scene represents, in the simplest possible manner, a little town somewhere in Central Europe. The time is the present. The town is shabby and ruined, as if the plague had passed there. Its name, Güllen, is inscribed on the shabby signboard which adorns the façade of the railway station. This edifice is summarily indicated by a length of rusty iron paling, a platform parallel to the proscenium, beyond which one imagines the rails to be, and a baggage truck standing by a wall on which a torn timetable, marked* "Fahrplan," *is affixed by three nails. In the station wall is a door with a sign:* "Eintritt Verboten."[1] *This leads to the* STATION MASTER'S *office.*

*Left of the station is a little house of gray stucco, formerly whitewashed. It has a tile roof, badly in need of repair. Some shreds of travel posters still adhere to the windowless walls. A shingle hanging over the entrance, left, reads:* "Männer."[2] *On the other side of the shingle reads:* "Damen."[3] *Along the wall of the little house there is a wooden bench, backless, on which four men are lounging cheerlessly, shabbily dressed, with cracked shoes. A fifth man is busied with paintpot and brush. He is kneeling on the ground, painting a strip of canvas with the words:* "Welcome, Clara."

[1] No Entrance.
[2] Men.
[3] Ladies.

*The warning signal rings uninterruptedly. The sound of the approaching train comes closer and closer. The* STATION MASTER *issues from his office, advances to the center of the platform and salutes.*

*The train is heard thundering past in a direction parallel to the footlights, and is lost in the distance. The men on the bench follow its passing with a slow movement of their heads, from left to right.*

FIRST MAN The "Emperor." Hamburg-Naples.

SECOND MAN Then comes the "Diplomat."

THIRD MAN Then the "Banker."

FOURTH MAN And at eleven twenty-seven the "Flying Dutchman." Venice-Stockholm.

FIRST MAN Our only pleasure—watching trains.

(*The station bell rings again. The* STATION MASTER *comes out of his office and salutes another train. The men follow its course, right to left*)

FOURTH MAN Once upon a time the "Emperor" and the "Flying Dutchman" used to stop here in Güllen. So did the "Diplomat," the "Banker," and the "Silver Comet."

SECOND MAN Now it's only the local from Kaffigen and the twelve-forty from Kalberstadt.

THIRD MAN The fact is, we're ruined.

FIRST MAN What with the Wagonworks shut down . . .

SECOND MAN The Foundry finished . . .

FOURTH MAN The Golden Eagle Pencil Factory all washed up . . .

FIRST MAN It's life on the dole.

SECOND MAN Did you say life?

THIRD MAN We're rotting.

FIRST MAN Starving.

SECOND MAN Crumbling.

FOURTH MAN The whole damn town.

(*The station bell rings*)

THIRD MAN Once we were a center of industry.

PAINTER A cradle of culture.

FOURTH MAN One of the best little towns in the country.

FIRST MAN In the world.

SECOND MAN Here Goethe slept.

FOURTH MAN Brahms composed a quartet.

THIRD MAN Here Berthold Schwarz invented gunpowder.[4]

PAINTER And I once got first prize at the Dresden Exhibition of Contemporary Art. What am I doing now? Painting signs.

(*The station bell rings. The* STATION MASTER *comes out. He throws away a cigarette butt. The men scramble for it*)

FIRST MAN Well, anyway, Madame Zachanassian will help us.

FOURTH MAN If she comes . . .

THIRD MAN If she comes.

SECOND MAN Last week she was in France. She gave them a hospital.

FIRST MAN In Rome she founded a free public nursery.

THIRD MAN In Leuthenau, a bird sanctuary.

PAINTER They say she got Picasso to design her car.

FIRST MAN Where does she get all that money?

SECOND MAN An oil company, a shipping line, three banks and five railways—

FOURTH MAN And the biggest string of geisha houses in Japan.

(*From the direction of the town come the* BURGOMASTER, *the* PASTOR, *the* TEACHER *and* ANTON SCHILL. *The* BURGOMASTER, *the* TEACHER *and* SCHILL *are men in their fifties. The* PASTOR *is ten years younger. All four are dressed shabbily and are sad-looking. The* BURGOMASTER *looks official.* SCHILL *is tall and handsome, but graying and worn; nevertheless a man of considerable charm and presence. He walks directly to the little house and disappears into it*)

PAINTER Any news, Burgomaster? Is she coming?

ALL Yes, is she coming?

BURGOMASTER She's coming. The telegram has been confirmed. Our distinguished guest will arrive on the twelve-forty from Kalberstadt. Everyone must be ready.

TEACHER The mixed choir is ready. So is the children's chorus.

BURGOMASTER And the church bell, Pastor?

PASTOR The church bell will ring. As soon as the new bell ropes are fitted. The man is working on them now.

BURGOMASTER The town band will be drawn up in the market place and the Athletic Association will form a human pyramid in her honor—the top man will hold the wreath with her initials. Then lunch at the Golden Apostle. I shall say a few words.

TEACHER Of course.

BURGOMASTER I had thought of illuminating the town hall and the cathedral, but we can't afford the lamps.

PAINTER Burgomaster—what do you think of this?

(*He shows the banner*)

BURGOMASTER (*Calls*) Schill! Schill!

TEACHER Schill!

(SCHILL *comes out of the little house*)

SCHILL Yes, right away. Right away.

BURGOMASTER This is more in your line. What do you think of this?

SCHILL (*Looks at the sign*) No, no, no. That certainly won't do, Burgomaster. It's much too intimate. It shouldn't read: "Welcome, Clara." It should read: "Welcome, Madame . . ."

TEACHER Zachanassian.

BURGOMASTER Zachanassian.

SCHILL Zachanassian.

PAINTER But she's Clara to us.

FIRST MAN Clara Wäscher.

SECOND MAN Born here.

THIRD MAN Her father was a carpenter. He built this.

(*All turn and stare at the little house*)

SCHILL All the same . . .

PAINTER If I . . .

[4] Berthold Schwarz was a German monk who lived in the fourteenth century. The invention of gunpowder has been attributed to him and to many others.

BURGOMASTER No, no, no. He's right. You'll have to change it.

PAINTER Oh, well, I'll tell you what I'll do. I'll leave this and I'll put "Welcome, Madame Zachanassian" on the other side. Then if things go well, we can always turn it around.

BURGOMASTER Good idea. (*To* SCHILL) Yes?

SCHILL Well, anyway, it's safer. Everything depends on the first impression.

(*The train bell is heard. Two clangs. The* PAINTER *turns the banner over and goes to work*)

FIRST MAN Hear that? The "Flying Dutchman" has just passed through Leuthenau.

FOURTH MAN Eleven twenty.

BURGOMASTER Gentlemen, you know that the millionairess is our only hope.

PASTOR Under God.

BURGOMASTER Under God. Naturally. Schill, we depend entirely on you.

SCHILL Yes, I know. You keep telling me.

BURGOMASTER After all, you're the only one who really knew her.

SCHILL Yes, I knew her.

PASTOR You were really quite close to one another, I hear, in those days.

SCHILL Close? Yes, we were close, there's no denying it. We were in love. I was young—good-looking, so they said—and Clara—you know, I can still see her in the great barn coming toward me—like a light out of the darkness. And in the Konradsweil Forest she'd come running to meet me—barefooted—her beautiful red hair streaming behind her. Like a witch. I was in love with her, all right. But you know how it is when you're twenty.

PASTOR What happened?

SCHILL (*Shrugs*) Life came between us.

BURGOMASTER You must give me some points about her for my speech.

(*He takes out his notebook*)

SCHILL I think I can help you there.

TEACHER Well, I've gone through the school records. And the young lady's marks were, I'm afraid to say, absolutely dreadful. Even in deportment. The only subject in which she was even remotely passable was natural history.

BURGOMASTER Good in natural history. That's fine. Give me a pencil.

(*He makes a note*)

SCHILL She was an outdoor girl. Wild. Once, I remember, they arrested a tramp, and she threw stones at the policeman. She hated injustice passionately.

BURGOMASTER Strong sense of justice. Excellent.

SCHILL And generous . . .

ALL Generous?

SCHILL Generous to a fault. Whatever little she had, she shared—so good-hearted. I remember once she stole a bag of potatoes to give to a poor widow.

BURGOMASTER (*Writing in notebook*) Wonderful generosity—

TEACHER Generosity.

BURGOMASTER That, gentlemen, is something I must not fail to make a point of.

SCHILL And such a sense of humor. I remember once when the oldest man in town fell and broke his leg, she said, "Oh, dear, now they'll have to shoot him."

BURGOMASTER Well, I've got enough. The rest, my friend, is up to you.

(*He puts the notebook away*)

SCHILL Yes, I know, but it's not so easy. After all, to part a woman like that from her millions—

BURGOMASTER Exactly. Millions. We have to think in big terms here.

TEACHER If she's thinking of buying us off with a nursery school—

ALL Nursery school!

PASTOR Don't accept.

TEACHER Hold out.

SCHILL I'm not so sure that I can do it. You know, she may have forgotten me completely.

BURGOMASTER (*He exchanges a look with the* TEACHER *and the* PASTOR) Schill, for many years you have been our most popular citizen. The most respected and the best loved.

SCHILL Why, thank you . . .

BURGOMASTER And therefore I must tell you—last week I sounded out the political opposition, and they agreed. In the spring you will be elected to succeed me as Burgomaster. By unanimous vote.

(*The others clap their hands in approval*)

SCHILL But, my dear Burgomaster—!

BURGOMASTER It's true.

TEACHER I'm a witness. I was at the meeting.

SCHILL This is—naturally, I'm terribly flattered— It's a completely unexpected honor.

BURGOMASTER You deserve it.

SCHILL Burgomaster! Well, well—! (*Briskly*) Gentlemen, to business. The first chance I get, of course, I shall discuss our miserable position with Clara.

TEACHER But tactfully, tactfully—

SCHILL What do you take me for? We must feel our way. Everything must be correct. Psychologically correct. For example, here at the railway station, a single blunder, one false note, could be disastrous.

BURGOMASTER He's absolutely right. The first impression colors all the rest. Madame Zachanassian sets foot on her native soil for the first time in many years. She sees our love and she sees our misery. She remembers her youth, her friends. The tears well up into her eyes. Her childhood companions throng about her. I will naturally not present myself like this, but in my black coat with my top hat. Next to me, my wife. Before me, my two grandchildren all in white, with roses. My God, if it only comes off as I see it! If only it comes off. (*The station bell begins ringing*) Oh, my God! Quick! We must get dressed.

FIRST MAN It's not her train. It's only the "Flying Dutchman."

PASTOR (*Calmly*) We have still two hours before she arrives.

SCHILL For God's sake, don't let's lose our heads. We still have a full two hours.

BURGOMASTER Who's losing their heads? (*To* FIRST *and* SECOND MAN) When her train comes, you two, Helmesberger and Vogel, will hold up the banner with "Welcome Madame Zachanassian." The rest will applaud.

THIRD MAN Bravo!

(*He applauds*)

BURGOMASTER But, please, one thing—no wild cheering like last year with the government relief committee. It made no impression at all and we still haven't received any loan. What we need is a feeling of genuine sincerity. That's how we greet with full hearts our beloved sister who has been away from us so long. Be sincerely moved, my friends, that's the secret; be sincere. Remember you're not dealing with a child. Next a few brief words from me. Then the church bell will start pealing—

PASTOR If he can fix the ropes in time.

(*The station bell rings*)

BURGOMASTER —Then the mixed choir moves in. And then—

TEACHER We'll form a line down here.

BURGOMASTER Then the rest of us will form in two lines leading from the station—

(*He is interrupted by the thunder of the approaching train. The men crane their heads to see it pass. The* STATION MASTER *advances to the platform and salutes. There is a sudden shriek of air brakes. The train screams to a stop. The four men jump up in consternation*)

PAINTER But the "Flying Dutchman" never stops!

FIRST MAN It's stopping.

SECOND MAN In Güllen!

THIRD MAN In the poorest—

FIRST MAN The dreariest—

SECOND MAN The lousiest—

FOURTH MAN The most God-forsaken hole between Venice and Stockholm.

STATION MASTER It cannot stop!

(*The train noises stop. There is only the panting of the engine*)

PAINTER It's stopped!

(*The* STATION MASTER *runs out*)

OFFSTAGE VOICES What's happened? Is there an accident?

(*A hubbub of offstage voices, as if the passengers on the invisible train were alighting*)

CLAIRE (*Offstage*) Is this Güllen?

CONDUCTOR (*Offstage*) Here, here, what's going on?

CLAIRE (*Offstage*) Who the hell are you?

CONDUCTOR (*Offstage*) But you pulled the emergency cord, madame!

CLAIRE (*Offstage*) I always pull the emergency cord.

STATION MASTER (*Offstage*) I must ask you what's going on here.

CLAIRE (*Offstage*) And who the hell are you?

STATION MASTER (*Offstage*) I'm the Station Master, madame, and I must ask you—

CLAIRE (*Enters*) No!

(*From the right* CLAIRE ZACHANASSSIAN *appears. She is an extraordinary woman. She is in her fifties, red-haired, remarkably dressed, with a face as impassive as that of an ancient idol, beautiful still, and with a singular grace of movement and manner. She is simple and unaffected, yet she has the haughtiness of a world power. The entire effect is striking to the point of the unbelievable. Behind her comes her fiancé,* PEDRO CABRAL, *tall, young, very handsome, and completely equipped for fishing, with creel and net, and with a rod case in his hand. An excited* CONDUCTOR *follows*)

CONDUCTOR But, madame, I must insist! You have stopped "The Flying Dutchman." I must have an explanation.

CLAIRE Nonsense. Pedro.

PEDRO Yes, my love?

CLAIRE This is Güllen. Nothing has changed. I recognize it all. There's the forest of Konradsweil. There's a brook in it full of trout, where you can fish. And there's the roof of the great barn. Ha! God! What a miserable blot on the map.

(*She crosses the stage and goes off with* PEDRO)

SCHILL My God! Clara!

TEACHER Claire Zachanassian!

ALL Claire Zachanassian!

BURGOMASTER And the town band? The town band! Where is it?

TEACHER The mixed choir! The mixed choir!

PASTOR The church bell! The church bell!

BURGOMASTER (*To the* FIRST MAN) Quick! My dress coat. My top hat. My grandchildren. Run! Run! (FIRST MAN *runs off. The* BURGOMASTER *shouts after him*) And don't forget my wife!

(*General panic. The* THIRD MAN *and* FOURTH MAN *hold up the banner, on which only part of the name has been painted: "Welcome Mad—"* CLAIRE *and* PEDRO *re-enter, right*)

CONDUCTOR (*Mastering himself with an effort*) Madame. The train is waiting. The entire international railway schedule has been disrupted. I await your explanation.

CLAIRE You're a very foolish man. I wish to visit this town. Did you expect me to jump off a moving train?

CONDUCTOR (*Stupefied*) You stopped the "Flying Dutchman" because you wished to visit the town?

CLAIRE Naturally.

CONDUCTOR (*Inarticulate*) Madame!

STATION MASTER Madame, if you wished to visit the town, the twelve forty from Kalberstadt was entirely at your service. Arrival in Güllen, one seventeen.

CLAIRE The local that stops at Loken, Beisenbach, and Leuthenau? Do you expect me to waste three-quarters of an hour chugging dismally through this wilderness?

CONDUCTOR Madame, you shall pay for this!

CLAIRE Bobby, give him a thousand marks.

(BOBBY, *her butler, a man in his seventies, wearing dark glasses, opens his wallet. The townspeople gasp*)

CONDUCTOR (*Taking the money in amazement*) But, madame!

CLAIRE And three thousand for the Railway Widows' Relief Fund.

CONDUCTOR (*With the money in his hands*) But we have no such fund, madame.

CLAIRE Now you have.

(*The* BURGOMASTER *pushes his way forward*)

BURGOMASTER (*He whispers to the* CONDUCTOR *and* TEACHER) The lady is Madame Claire Zachanassian!

CONDUCTOR Claire Zachanassian? Oh, my God! But that's naturally quite different. Needless to say, we would have stopped the train if we'd had the slightest idea. (*He hands the money back to* BOBBY) Here, please. I couldn't dream of it. Four thousand. My God!

CLAIRE Keep it. Don't fuss.

CONDUCTOR Would you like the train to wait, madame, while you visit the town? The administration will be delighted. The cathedral porch. The town hall—

CLAIRE You may take the train away. I don't need it any more.

STATION MASTER All aboard!

(*He puts his whistle to his lips.* PEDRO *stops him*)

PEDRO But the press, my angel. They don't know anything about this. They're still in the dining car.

CLAIRE Let them stay there. I don't want the press in Güllen at the moment. Later they will come by themselves. (To STATION MASTER) And now what are you waiting for?

STATION MASTER All aboard!

(*The* STATION MASTER *blows a long blast on his whistle. The train leaves. Meanwhile, the* FIRST MAN *has brought the* BURGOMASTER'*s dress coat and top hat. The* BURGOMASTER *puts on the coat, then advances slowly and solemnly*)

CONDUCTOR I trust madame will not speak of this to the administration. It was a pure misunderstanding. (*He salutes and runs for the train as it starts moving*)

BURGOMASTER (*Bows*) Gracious lady, as Burgomaster of the town of Güllen, I have the honor—

(*The rest of the speech is lost in the roar of the departing train. He continues speaking and gesturing, and at last bows amid applause as the train noises end*)

CLAIRE Thank you, Mr. Burgomaster.

(*She glances at the beaming faces, and lastly at* SCHILL, *whom she does not recognize. She turns upstage*)

SCHILL Clara!

CLAIRE (*Turns and stares*) Anton?

SCHILL Yes. It's good that you've come back.

CLAIRE Yes. I've waited for this moment. All my life. Ever since I left Güllen.

SCHILL (*A little embarrassed*) That is very kind of you to say, Clara.

CLAIRE And have you thought about me?

SCHILL Naturally. Always. You know that.

CLAIRE Those were happy times we spent together.

SCHILL Unforgettable.

(*He smiles reassuringly at the* BURGOMASTER)

CLAIRE Call me by the name you used to call me.

SCHILL (*Whispers*) My kitten.

CLAIRE What?

SCHILL (*Louder*) My kitten.

CLAIRE And what else?

SCHILL Little witch.

CLAIRE I used to call you my black panther. You're gray now, and soft.

SCHILL But you are still the same, little witch.

CLAIRE I am the same? (*She laughs*) Oh, no, my black panther, I am not at all the same.

SCHILL (*Gallantly*) In my eyes you are. I see no difference.

CLAIRE Would you like to meet my fiancé? Pedro Cabral. He owns an enormous plantation in Brazil.

SCHILL A pleasure.

CLAIRE We're to be married soon.

SCHILL Congratulations.

CLAIRE He will be my eighth husband. (PEDRO *stands by himself downstage, right*) Pedro, come here and show your face. Come along, darling—come here! Don't sulk. Say hello.

PEDRO Hello.

CLAIRE A man of few words! Isn't he charming? A diplomat. He's interested only in fishing. Isn't he handsome, in his Latin way? You'd swear he was a Brazilian. But he's not—he's a Greek. His father was a White Russian. We were betrothed by a Bulgarian priest. We plan to be married in a few days here in the cathedral.

BURGOMASTER Here in the cathedral? What an honor for us!

CLAIRE No. It was my dream, when I was seventeen, to be married in Güllen cathedral. The dreams of youth are sacred, don't you think so, Anton?

SCHILL Yes, of course.

CLAIRE Yes, of course. I think so, too. Now I would like to look at the town. (*The mixed choir arrives, breathless, wearing ordinary clothes with green sashes*) What's all this? Go away. (*She laughs*) Ha! Ha! Ha!

TEACHER Dear lady—(*He steps forward, having put on a sash also*) Dear lady, as Rector of the high school and a devotee of that noble muse, Music, I take pleasure in presenting the Güllen mixed choir.

CLAIRE How do you do?

TEACHER Who will sing for you an ancient folk song of the region, with specially amended words—if you will deign to listen.

CLAIRE Very well. Fire away.

(*The* TEACHER *blows a pitch pipe. The mixed choir begins to sing the ancient folk song with the amended words. Just then the station bell starts ringing. The song is drowned in the roar of the passing express. The* STATION MASTER *salutes. When the train has passed, there is applause*)

BURGOMASTER The church bell! The church bell! Where's the church bell?

(*The* PASTOR *shrugs helplessly*)

CLAIRE Thank you, Professor. They sang beautifully. The big little blond bass—no, not that one—the one with the big Adam's apple—was most impressive. (*The* TEACHER *bows. The* POLICEMAN *pushes his way professionally through the mixed choir and comes to attention in front of* CLAIRE ZACHANASSIAN) Now, who are you?

POLICEMAN (*Clicks heels*) Police Chief Schultz. At your service.

CLAIRE (*She looks him up and down*) I have no need of you at the moment. But I think there will be work for you by and by. Tell me, do you know how to close an eye from time to time?

POLICEMAN How else could I get along in my profession?

CLAIRE You might practice closing both.

SCHILL (*Laughs*) What a sense of humor, eh?

BURGOMASTER (*Puts on the top hat*) Permit me to present my grandchildren, gracious lady. Hermine and Adolphine. There's only my wife still to come.

(*He wipes the perspiration from his brow, and replaces the hat. The little girls present the roses with elaborate curtsies*)

CLAIRE Thank you, my dears. Congratulations, Burgomaster. Extraordinary children.

(*She plants the roses in* PEDRO'S *arms. The* BURGOMASTER *secretly passes his top hat to the* PASTOR, *who puts it on*)

BURGOMASTER Our pastor, madame.

(*The* PASTOR *takes off the hat and bows*)

CLAIRE Ah. The pastor. How do you do? Do you give consolation to the dying?

PASTOR (*A bit puzzled*) That is part of my ministry, yes.

CLAIRE And to those who are condemned to death?

PASTOR Capital punishment has been abolished in this country, madame.

CLAIRE I see. Well, it could be restored, I suppose.

(*The* PASTOR *hands back the hat. He shrugs his shoulders in confusion*)

SCHILL (*Laughs*) What an original sense of humor!

(*All laugh, a little blankly*)

CLAIRE Well, I can't sit here all day—I should like to see the town.

(*The* BURGOMASTER *offers his arm*)

BURGOMASTER May I have the honor, gracious lady?

CLAIRE Thank you, but these legs are not what they were. This one was broken in five places.

SCHILL (*Full of concern*) My kitten!

CLAIRE When my airplane bumped into a mountain in Afghanistan. All the others were killed. Even the pilot. But as you see, I survived. I don't fly any more.

SCHILL But you're as strong as ever now.

CLAIRE Stronger.

BURGOMASTER Never fear, gracious lady. The town doctor has a car.

CLAIRE I never ride in motors.

BURGOMASTER You never ride in motors?

CLAIRE Not since my Ferrari crashed in Hong Kong.

SCHILL But how do you travel, then, little witch? On a broom?

CLAIRE Mike—Max! (*She claps her hands. Two huge bodyguards come in, left, carrying a sedan chair. She sits in it*) I travel this way—a bit antiquated, of course. But perfectly safe. Ha! Ha! Aren't they magnificent? Mike and Max. I bought them in America. They were in jail, condemned to the chair. I had them pardoned. Now they're condemned to my chair. I paid fifty thousand dollars apiece for them. You couldn't get them now for twice the sum. The sedan chair comes from the Louvre. I fancied it so much that the President of France gave it to me. The French are so impulsive, don't you think so, Anton? Go!

(MIKE *and* MAX *start to carry her off*)

BURGOMASTER You wish to visit the cathedral? And the old town hall?

CLAIRE No. The great barn. And the forest of Konradsweil. I wish to go with Anton and visit our old haunts once again.

THE PASTOR Very touching.

CLAIRE (*To the butler*) Will you send my luggage and the coffin to the Golden Apostle?

BURGOMASTER The coffin?

CLAIRE Yes. I brought one with me. Go!

TEACHER Hip-hip—

ALL Hurrah! Hip-hip, hurrah! Hurrah!

(*They bear off in the direction of the town. The* TOWNSPEOPLE *burst into cheers. The church bell rings*)

BURGOMASTER Ah, thank God—the bell at last.

(*The* POLICEMAN *is about to follow the others, when the two* BLIND MEN *appear. They are not young, yet they seem childish—a strange effect. Though they are of different height and features, they are dressed exactly alike, and so create the effect of being twins. They walk slowly, feeling their way. Their voices, when they speak, are curiously high and flutelike, and they have a curious trick of repetition of phrases*)

FIRST BLIND MAN We're in—

BOTH BLIND MEN Güllen.

FIRST BLIND MAN We breathe—

SECOND BLIND MAN We breathe—

BOTH BLIND MEN We breathe the air, the air of Güllen.

POLICEMAN (*Startled*) Who are you?

FIRST BLIND MAN We belong to the lady.

SECOND BLIND MAN We belong to the lady. She calls us—

FIRST BLIND MAN Kobby.

SECOND BLIND MAN And Lobby.

POLICEMAN Madame Zachanassian is staying at the Golden Apostle.

FIRST BLIND MAN We're blind.

SECOND BLIND MAN We're blind.

POLICEMAN Blind? Come along with me, then. I'll take you there.

FIRST BLIND MAN Thank you, Mr. Policeman.

SECOND BLIND MAN Thanks very much.

POLICEMAN Hey! How do you know I'm a policeman, if you're blind?

BOTH BLIND MEN By your voice. By your voice.

FIRST BLIND MAN All policemen sound the same.

POLICEMAN You've had a lot to do with the police, have you, little men?

FIRST BLIND MAN Men he calls us!

BOTH BLIND MEN Men!

POLICEMAN What are you then?
BOTH BLIND MEN You'll see. You'll see.
(*The* POLICEMAN *claps his hands suddenly. The* BLIND MEN *turn sharply toward the sound. The* POLICEMAN *is convinced they are blind*)
POLICEMAN What's your trade?
BOTH BLIND MEN We have no trade.
SECOND BLIND MAN We play music.
FIRST BLIND MAN We sing.
SECOND BLIND MAN We amuse the lady.
FIRST BLIND MAN We look after the beast.
SECOND BLIND MAN We feed it.
FIRST BLIND MAN We stroke it.
SECOND BLIND MAN We take it for walks.
POLICEMAN What beast?
BOTH BLIND MEN You'll see—you'll see.
SECOND BLIND MAN We give it raw meat.
FIRST BLIND MAN And she gives us chicken and wine.
SECOND BLIND MAN Every day—
BOTH BLIND MEN Every day.
POLICEMAN Rich people have strange tastes.
BOTH BLIND MEN Strange tastes—strange tastes.
(*The* POLICEMAN *puts on his helmet*)
POLICEMAN Come along, I'll take you to the lady.
(*The two* BLIND MEN *turn and walk off*)
BOTH BLIND MEN We know the way—we know the way.
(*The station and the little house vanish. A sign representing the Golden Apostle descends. The scene dissolves into the interior of the inn. The Golden Apostle is seen to be in the last stages of decay. The walls are cracked and moldering, and the plaster is falling from the ancient lath. A table represents the café of the inn. The* BURGOMASTER *and the* TEACHER *sit at this table, drinking a glass together. A procession of* TOWNSPEOPLE, *carrying many pieces of luggage, passes. Then comes a coffin, and, last, a large box covered with a canvas. They cross the stage from right to left*)
BURGOMASTER Trunks. Suitcases. Boxes. (*He looks up apprehensively at the ceiling*) The floor will never bear the weight. (*As the large covered box is carried in, he peers under the canvas, then draws back*) Good God!
TEACHER Why, what's in it?
BURGOMASTER A live panther. (*They laugh. The* BURGOMASTER *lifts his glass solemnly*) Your health, Professor. Let's hope she puts the Foundry back on its feet.
TEACHER (*Lifts his glass*) And the Wagonworks.
BURGOMASTER And the Golden Eagle Pencil Factory. Once that starts moving, everything else will go. *Prosit.*[5]
(*They touch glasses and drink*)
TEACHER What does she need a panther for?
BURGOMASTER Don't ask me. The whole thing is too much for me. The Pastor had to go home and lie down.
TEACHER (*Sets down his glass*) If you want to know the truth, she frightens me.

[5] Your health.

BURGOMASTER (*Nods gravely*) She's a strange one.
TEACHER You understand, Burgomaster, a man who for twenty-two years has been correcting the Latin compositions of the students of Güllen is not unaccustomed to surprises. I have seen things to make one's hair stand on end. But when this woman suddenly appeared on the platform, a shudder tore through me. It was as though out of the clear sky all at once a fury descended upon us, beating its black wings—
(*The* POLICEMAN *comes in. He mops his face*)
POLICEMAN Ah! Now the old place is livening up a bit!
BURGOMASTER Ah, Schultz, come and join us.
POLICEMAN Thank you. (*He calls*) Beer!
BURGOMASTER Well, what's the news from the front?
POLICEMAN I'm just back from Schiller's barn. My God! What a scene! She had us all tiptoeing around in the straw as if we were in church. Nobody dared to speak above a whisper. And the way she carried on! I was so embarrassed I let them go to the forest by themselves.
BURGOMASTER Does the fiancé go with them?
POLICEMAN With his fishing rod and his landing net. In full marching order. (*He calls again*) Beer!
BURGOMASTER That will be her seventh husband.
TEACHER Her eighth.
BURGOMASTER But what does she expect to find in the Konradsweil forest?
POLICEMAN The same thing she expected to find in the old barn, I suppose. The—the—
TEACHER The ashes of her youthful love.
POLICEMAN Exactly.
TEACHER It's poetry.
POLICEMAN Poetry.
TEACHER Sheer poetry! It makes one think of Shakespeare, of Wagner. Of Romeo and Juliet.
(*The* SECOND MAN *comes in as a waiter. The* POLICEMAN *is served his beer*)
BURGOMASTER Yes, you're right. (*Solemnly*) Gentlemen, I would like to propose a toast. To our great and good friend, Anton Schill, who is even now working on our behalf.
POLICEMAN Yes! He's really working.
BURGOMASTER Gentlemen, to the best-loved citizen of this town. My successor, Anton Schill!
(*They raise their glasses. At this point an unearthly scream is heard. It is the black panther howling offstage. The sign of the Golden Apostle rises out of sight. The lights go down. The inn vanishes. Only the wooden bench, on which the four men were lounging in the opening scene, is left on the stage, downstage right. The procession comes on upstage. The two bodyguards carry in* CLAIRE's *sedan chair. Next to it walks* SCHILL. PEDRO *walks behind, with his fishing rod. Last come the two* BLIND MEN *and the butler.* CLAIRE *alights*)
CLAIRE Stop! Take my chair off somewhere else. I'm tired of looking at you. (*The bodyguards and the sedan chair go off*) Pedro darling, your brook is just

a little further along down that path. Listen. You can hear it from here. Bobby, take him and show him where it is.

BOTH BLIND MEN We'll show him the way—we'll show him the way.

(*They go off, left.* PEDRO *follows.* BOBBY *walks off, right*)

CLAIRE Look, Anton. Our tree. There's the heart you carved in the bark long ago.

SCHILL Yes. It's still there.

CLAIRE How it has grown! The trunk is black and wrinkled. Why, its limbs are twice what they were. Some of them have died.

SCHILL It's aged. But it's there.

CLAIRE Like everything else. (*She crosses, examining other trees*) Oh, how tall they are. How long it is since I walked here, barefoot over the pine needles and the damp leaves! Look, Anton. A fawn.

SCHILL Yes, a fawn. It's the season.

CLAIRE I thought everything would be changed. But it's all just as we left it. This is the seat we sat on years ago. Under these branches you kissed me. And over there under the hawthorn, where the moss is soft and green, we would lie in each other's arms. It is all as it used to be. Only we have changed.

SCHILL Not so much, little witch. I remember the first night we spent together, you ran away and I chased you till I was quite breathless—

CLAIRE Yes.

SCHILL Then I was angry and I was going home, when suddenly I heard you call and I looked up, and there you were sitting in a tree, laughing down at me.

CLAIRE No. It was in the great barn. I was in the hayloft.

SCHILL Were you?

CLAIRE Yes. What else do you remember?

SCHILL I remember the morning we went swimming by the waterfall, and afterwards we were lying together on the big rock in the sun, when suddenly we heard footsteps and we just had time to snatch up our clothes and run behind the bushes when the old pastor appeared and scolded you for not being in school.

CLAIRE No. It was the schoolmaster who found us. It was Sunday and I was supposed to be in church.

SCHILL Really?

CLAIRE Yes. Tell me more.

SCHILL I remember the time your father beat you, and you showed me the cuts on your back, and I swore I'd kill him. And the next day I dropped a tile from a roof top and split his head open.

CLAIRE You missed him.

SCHILL No!

CLAIRE You hit old Mr. Reiner.

SCHILL Did I?

CLAIRE Yes. I was seventeen. And you were not yet twenty. You were so handsome. You were the best-looking boy in town.

(*The two* BLIND MEN *begin playing mandolin music offstage, very softly*)

SCHILL And you were the prettiest girl.

CLAIRE We were made for each other.

SCHILL So we were.

CLAIRE But you married Mathilde Blumhard and her store, and I married old Zachanassian and his oil wells. He found me in a whorehouse in Hamburg. It was my hair that entangled him, the old golden beetle.

SCHILL Clara!

CLAIRE (*She claps her hands*) Bobby! A cigar.

(BOBBY *appears with a leather case. He selects a cigar, puts it in a holder, lights it, and presents it to* CLAIRE)

SCHILL My kitten smokes cigars!

CLAIRE Yes. I adore them. Would you care for one?

SCHILL Yes, please. I've never smoked one of those.

CLAIRE It's a taste I acquired from old Zachanassian. Among other things. He was a real connoisseur.

SCHILL We used to sit on this bench once, you and I, and smoke cigarettes. Do you remember?

CLAIRE Yes. I remember.

SCHILL The cigarettes I bought from Mathilde.

CLAIRE No. She gave them to you for nothing.

SCHILL Clara—don't be angry with me for marrying Mathilde.

CLAIRE She had money.

SCHILL But what a lucky thing for you that I did!

CLAIRE Oh?

SCHILL You were so young, so beautiful. You deserved a far better fate than to settle in this wretched town without any future.

CLAIRE Yes?

SCHILL If you had stayed in Güllen and married me, your life would have been wasted, like mine.

CLAIRE Oh?

SCHILL Look at me. A wretched shopkeeper in a bankrupt town!

CLAIRE But you have your family.

SCHILL My family! Never for a moment do they let me forget my failure, my poverty.

CLAIRE Mathilde has not made you happy?

SCHILL (*Shrugs*) What does it matter?

CLAIRE And the children?

SCHILL (*Shakes his head*) They're so completely materialistic. You know, they have no interest whatever in higher things.

CLAIRE How sad for you.

(*A moment's pause, during which only the faint tinkling of the music is heard*)

SCHILL Yes. You know, since you went away my life has passed by like a stupid dream. I've hardly once been out of this town. A trip to a lake years ago. It rained all the time. And once five days in Berlin. That's all.

CLAIRE The world is much the same everywhere.

SCHILL At least you've seen it.

CLAIRE Yes. I've seen it.

SCHILL You've lived in it.

CLAIRE I've lived in it. The world and I have been on very intimate terms.

SCHILL Now that you've come back, perhaps things will change.

CLAIRE Naturally. I certainly won't leave my native town in this condition.

SCHILL It will take millions to put us on our feet again.

CLAIRE I have millions.

SCHILL One, two, three.

CLAIRE Why not?

SCHILL You mean—you will help us?

CLAIRE Yes.

(*A woodpecker is heard in the distance*)

SCHILL I knew it—I knew it. I told them you were generous. I told them you were good. Oh, my kitten, my kitten.

(*He takes her hand. She turns her head away and listens*)

CLAIRE Listen! A woodpecker.

SCHILL It's all just the way it was in the days when we were young and full of courage. The sun high above the pines. White clouds, piling up on one another. And the cry of the cuckoo in the distance. And the wind rustling the leaves, like the sound of surf on a beach. Just as it was years ago. If only we could roll back time and be together always.

CLAIRE Is that your wish?

SCHILL Yes. You left me, but you never left my heart. (*He raises her hand to his lips*) The same soft little hand.

CLAIRE No, not quite the same. It was crushed in the plane accident. But they mended it. They mend everything nowadays.

SCHILL Crushed? You wouldn't know it. See, another fawn.

CLAIRE The old wood is alive with memories.

(PEDRO *appears, right, with a fish in his hand*)

PEDRO See what I've caught, darling. See? A pike. Over two kilos.

(*The* BLIND MEN *appear onstage*)

BOTH BLIND MEN (*Clapping their hands*) A pike! A pike! Hurrah! Hurrah!

(*As the* BLIND MEN *clap their hands,* CLAIRE *and* SCHILL *exit, and the scene dissolves. The clapping of hands is taken up on all sides. The townspeople wheel in the walls of the café. A brass band strikes up a march tune. The door of the Golden Apostle descends. The townspeople bring in tables and set them with ragged tablecloths, cracked china, and glassware. There is a table in the center, upstage, flanked by two tables perpendicular to it, right and left. The* PASTOR *and the* BURGOMASTER *come in.* SCHILL *enters. Other townspeople filter in, left and right. One, the* ATHLETE, *is in gymnastic costume. The applause continues*)

BURGOMASTER She's coming! (CLAIRE *enters upstage, center, followed by* BOBBY) The applause is meant for you, gracious lady.

CLAIRE The band deserves it more than I. They blow from the heart. And the human pyramid was beautiful. You, show me your muscles. (*The* ATHLETE *kneels before her*) Superb. Wonderful arms, powerful hands. Have you ever strangled a man with them?

ATHLETE Strangled?

CLAIRE Yes. It's perfectly simple. A little pressure in the proper place, and the rest goes by itself. As in politics.

(*The* BURGOMASTER'S *wife comes up, simpering*)

BURGOMASTER (*Presents her*) Permit me to present my wife, Madame Zachanassian.

CLAIRE Annette Dummermuth. The head of our class.

BURGOMASTER (*He presents another sour-looking woman*) Frau Schill.

CLAIRE Mathilde Blumhard. I remember the way you used to follow Anton with your eyes, from behind the shop door. You've grown a little thin and dry, my poor Mathilde.

SCHILL My daughter, Ottilie.

CLAIRE Your daughter . . .

SCHILL My son, Karl.

CLAIRE Your son. Two of them!

(*The town* DOCTOR *comes in, right. He is a man of fifty, strong and stocky, with bristly black hair, a mustache, and a saber cut on his cheek. He is wearing an old cutaway*)

DOCTOR Well, well, my old Mercedes got me here in time after all!

BURGOMASTER Dr. Nüsslin, the town physician. Madame Zachanassian.

DOCTOR Deeply honored, madame.

(*He kisses her hand.* CLAIRE *studies him*)

CLAIRE It is you who signs the death certificates?

DOCTOR Death certificates?

CLAIRE When someone dies.

DOCTOR Why certainly. That is one of my duties.

CLAIRE And when the heart dies, what do you put down? Heart failure?

SCHILL (*Laughing*) What a golden sense of humor!

DOCTOR Bit grim, wouldn't you say?

SCHILL (*Whispers*) Not at all, not at all. She's promised us a million.

BURGOMASTER (*Turns his head*) What?

SCHILL A million!

ALL (*Whisper*) A million!

(CLAIRE *turns toward them*)

CLAIRE Burgomaster.

BURGOMASTER Yes?

CLAIRE I'm hungry. (*The girls and the waiter fill glasses and bring food. There is a general stir. All take their places at the tables*) Are you going to make a speech?

(*The* BURGOMASTER *bows.* CLAIRE *sits next to the* BURGOMASTER. *The* BURGOMASTER *rises, tapping his knife on his glass. He is radiant with good will. All applaud*)

BURGOMASTER Gracious lady and friends. Gracious lady, it is now many years since you first left your native town of Güllen, which was founded by the Elector Hasso and which nestles in the green slope between the forest of Konradsweil and the beautiful valley of Pückenried. Much has taken place in this time, much that is evil.

TEACHER That's true.

BURGOMASTER The world is not what it was; it has become harsh and bitter, and we too have had our share of harshness and bitterness. But in all this time, dear lady, we have never forgotten our little Clara. (*Applause*) Many years ago you brightened the town with your pretty face as a child, and now once again you brighten it with your presence. (*Polite applause*) We haven't forgotten you, and we haven't forgotten your family. Your mother, beautiful and robust even in her old age—(*He looks for his notes on the table*) —although unfortunately taken from us in the bloom of her youth by an infirmity of the lungs. Your respected father, Siegfried Wäscher, the builder, an example of whose work next to our railway station is often visited—(SCHILL *covers his face*)—that is to say, admired—a lasting monument of local design and local workmanship. And you, gracious lady, whom we remember as a golden-haired—(*He looks at her*) —little red-headed sprite romping about our peaceful streets—on your way to school—which of us does not treasure your memory? (*He pokes nervously at his notebook*) We well remember your scholarly attainments—

TEACHER Yes.

BURGOMASTER Natural history . . . Extraordinary sense of justice . . . And, above all, your supreme generosity. (*Great applause*) We shall never forget how you once spent the whole of your little savings to buy a sack of potatoes for a poor starving widow who was in need of food. Gracious lady, ladies and gentlemen, today our little Clara has become the world-famous Claire Zachanassian who has founded hospitals, soup kitchens, charitable institutes, art projects, libraries, nurseries, and schools, and now that she has at last once more returned to the town of her birth, sadly fallen as it is, I say in the name of all her loving friends who have sorely missed her: Long live our Clara!

ALL Long live our Clara!

(*Cheers. Music. Fanfare. Applause.* CLAIRE *rises*)

CLAIRE Mr. Burgomaster. Fellow townsmen. I am greatly moved by the nature of your welcome and the disinterested joy which you have manifested on the occasion of my visit to my native town. I was not quite the child the Burgomaster described in his gracious address . . .

BURGOMASTER Too modest, madame.

CLAIRE In school I was beaten—

TEACHER Not by me.

CLAIRE And the sack of potatoes which I presented to Widow Boll, I stole with the help of Anton Schill, not to save the old trull from starvation, but so that for once I might sleep with Anton in a real bed instead of under the trees of the forest. (*The townspeople look grave, embarrassed*) Nevertheless, I shall try to deserve your good opinion. In memory of the seventeen years I spent among you, I am prepared to hand over as a gift to the town of Güllen the sum of one billion marks. Five hundred million to the town, and five hundred million to be divided per capita among the citizens.

(*There is a moment of dead silence*)

BURGOMASTER A billion marks?

CLAIRE On one condition.

(*Suddenly a movement of uncontrollable joy breaks out. People jump on chairs, dance about, yell excitedly. The* ATHLETE *turns handsprings in front of the speaker's table*)

SCHILL Oh, Clara, you astonishing, incredible, magnificent woman! What a heart! What a gesture! Oh —my little witch!

(*He kisses her hand*)

BURGOMASTER (*Holds up his arms for order*) Quiet! Quiet, please! On one condition, the gracious lady said. Now, madame, may we know what that condition is?

CLAIRE I will tell you. In exchange for my billion marks, I want justice.

(*Silence*)

BURGOMASTER Justice, madame?

CLAIRE I wish to buy justice.

BURGOMASTER But justice cannot be bought, madame

CLAIRE Everything can be bought.

BURGOMASTER I don't understand at all.

CLAIRE Bobby, step forward.

(*The butler goes to the center of the stage. He takes off his dark glasses and turns his face with a solemn air*)

BOBBY Does anyone here present recognize me?

FRAU SCHILL Hofer! Hofer!

ALL Who? What's that?

TEACHER Not Chief Magistrate Hofer?

BOBBY Exactly. Chief Magistrate Hofer. When Madame Zachanassian was a girl, I was presiding judge at the criminal court of Güllen. I served there until twenty-five years ago, when Madame Zachanassian offered me the opportunity of entering her service as butler. I accepted. You may consider it a strange employment for a member of the magistracy, but the salary—

(CLAIRE *bangs the mallet on the table*)

CLAIRE Come to the point.

BOBBY You have heard Madame Zachanassian's offer. She will give you a billion marks—when you have undone the injustice that she suffered at your hands here in Güllen as a girl.

(*All murmur*)

BURGOMASTER Injustice at our hands? Impossible!

BOBBY Anton Schill . . .

SCHILL Yes?

BOBBY Kindly stand.

(SCHILL *rises. He smiles, as if puzzled. He shrugs*)

SCHILL Yes?

BOBBY In those days, a bastardy case was tried before me. Madame Claire Zachanassian, at that time called Clara Wäscher, charged you with being the father of her illegitimate child. (*Silence*) You denied the charge. And produced two witnesses in your support.

SCHILL That's ancient history. An absurd business. We were children. Who remembers?

CLAIRE Where are the blind men?

BOTH BLIND MEN Here we are. Here we are.

(MIKE *and* MAX *push them forward*)

BOBBY You recognize these men, Anton Schill?

SCHILL I never saw them before in my life. What are they?

BOTH BLIND MEN We've changed. We've changed.

BOBBY What were your names in your former life?

FIRST BLIND MAN I was Jacob Hueblein. Jacob Hueblein.

SECOND BLIND MAN I was Ludwig Sparr. Ludwig Sparr.

BOBBY (*To* SCHILL) Well?

SCHILL These names mean nothing to me.

BOBBY Jacob Hueblein and Ludwig Sparr, do you recognize the defendant?

FIRST BLIND MAN We're blind.

SECOND BLIND MAN We're blind.

SCHILL Ha-ha-ha!

BOBBY By his voice?

BOTH BLIND MEN By his voice. By his voice.

BOBBY At that trial, I was the judge. And you?

BOTH BLIND MEN We were the witnesses.

BOBBY And what did you testify on that occasion?

FIRST BLIND MAN That we had slept with Clara Wäscher.

SECOND BLIND MAN Both of us. Many times.

BOBBY And was it true?

FIRST BLIND MAN No.

SECOND BLIND MAN We swore falsely.

BOBBY And why did you swear falsely?

FIRST BLIND MAN Anton Schill bribed us.

SECOND BLIND MAN He bribed us.

BOBBY With what?

BOTH BLIND MEN With a bottle of schnapps.

BOBBY And now tell the people what happened to you. (*They hesitate and whimper*) Speak!

FIRST BLIND MAN (*In a low voice*) She tracked us down.

BOBBY Madame Zachanassian tracked them down. Jacob Hueblein was found in Canada. Ludwig Sparr in Australia. And when she found you, what did she do to you?

SECOND BLIND MAN She handed us over to Mike and Max.

BOBBY And what did Mike and Max do to you?

FIRST BLIND MAN They made us what you see.

(*The* BLIND MEN *cover their faces.* MIKE *and* MAX *push them off*)

BOBBY And there you have it. We are all present in Güllen once again. The plaintiff. The defendant. The two false witnesses. The judge. Many years have passed. Does the plaintiff have anything further to add?

CLAIRE There is nothing to add.

BOBBY And the defendant?

SCHILL Why are you doing this? It was all dead and buried.

BOBBY What happened to the child that was born?

CLAIRE (*In a low voice*) It lived a year.

BOBBY And what happened to you?

CLAIRE I became a whore.

BOBBY Why?

CLAIRE The judgment of the court left me no alternative. No one would trust me. No one would give me work.

BOBBY So. And now, what is the nature of the reparation you demand?

CLAIRE I want the life of Anton Schill.

(FRAU SCHILL *springs to Anton's side. She puts her arms around him. The children rush to him. He breaks away*)

FRAU SCHILL Anton! No! No!

SCHILL No— No— She's joking. That happened long ago. That's all forgotten.

CLAIRE Nothing is forgotten. Neither the mornings in the forest, nor the nights in the great barn, nor the bedroom in the cottage, nor your treachery at the end. You said this morning that you wished that time might be rolled back. Very well—I have rolled it back. And now it is I who will buy justice. You bought it with a bottle of schnapps. I am willing to pay one billion marks.

(*The* BURGOMASTER *stands up, very pale and dignified*)

BURGOMASTER Madame Zachanassian, we are not in the jungle. We are in Europe. We may be poor, but we are not heathens. In the name of the town of Güllen, I decline your offer. In the name of humanity. We shall never accept.

(*All applaud wildly. The applause turns into a sinister rhythmic beat. As* CLAIRE *rises, it dies away. She looks at the crowd, then at the* BURGOMASTER)

CLAIRE Thank you, Burgomaster. (*She stares at him a long moment*) I can wait.

(*She turns and walks off*)

*Curtain*

# Act Two

*The façade of the Golden Apostle, with a balcony on which chairs and a table are set out. To the right of the inn is a sign which reads:* "ANTON SCHILL, HANDLUNG." [1] *Under the sign the shop is represented by a broken counter. Behind the counter are some shelves with tobacco, cigarettes, and liquor bottles. There are two milk cans. The shop door is imaginary, but each entrance is indicated by a doorbell with a tinny sound.*

*It is early morning.*

SCHILL *is sweeping the shop. The* SON *has a pan and brush and also sweeps. The* DAUGHTER *is dusting. They are singing "The Happy Wanderer."*

[1] "Anton Schill, Merchandise."

SCHILL Karl—

(KARL *crosses with a dustpan.* SCHILL *sweeps dust into the pan. The doorbell rings. The* THIRD MAN *appears, carrying a crate of eggs*)

THIRD MAN 'Morning.

SCHILL Ah, good morning, Wechsler.

THIRD MAN Twelve dozen eggs, medium brown. Right?

SCHILL Take them, Karl. (*The* SON *puts the crate in a corner*) Did they deliver the milk yet?

SON Before you came down.

THIRD MAN Eggs are going up again, Herr Schill. First of the month.

(*He gives* SCHILL *a slip to sign*)

SCHILL What? Again? And who's going to buy them?

THIRD MAN Fifty pfennig a dozen.

SCHILL I'll have to cancel my order, that's all.

THIRD MAN That's up to you, Herr Schill.

(SCHILL *signs the slip*)

SCHILL There's nothing else to do. (*He hands back the slip*) And how's the family?

THIRD MAN Oh, scraping along. Maybe now things will get better.

SCHILL Maybe.

THIRD MAN (*Going*) 'Morning.

SCHILL Close the door. Don't let the flies in. (*The children resume their singing*) Now, listen to me, children. I have a little piece of good news for you. I didn't mean to speak of it yet awhile, but well, why not? Who do you suppose is going to be the next Burgomaster? Eh? (*They look up at him*) Yes, in spite of everything. It's settled. It's official. What an honor for the family, eh? Especially at a time like this. To say nothing of the salary and the rest of it.

SON Burgomaster!

SCHILL Burgomaster. (*The* SON *shakes him warmly by the hand. The* DAUGHTER *kisses him*) You see, you don't have to be entirely ashamed of your father. (*Silence*) Is your mother coming down to breakfast soon?

DAUGHTER Mother's tired. She's going to stay upstairs.

SCHILL You have a good mother, at least. There you are lucky. Oh, well, if she wants to rest, let her rest. We'll have breakfast together, the three of us. I'll fry some eggs and open a tin of the American ham. This morning we're going to breakfast like kings.

SON I'd like to, only—I can't.

SCHILL You've got to eat, you know.

SON I've got to run down to the station. One of the laborers is sick. They said they could use me.

SCHILL You want to work on the rails in all this heat? That's no work for a son of mine.

SON Look, Father, we can use the money.

SCHILL Well, if you feel you have to.

(*The son goes to the door. The* DAUGHTER *moves toward* SCHILL)

DAUGHTER I'm sorry, Father. I have to go too.

SCHILL You too? And where is the young lady going, if I may be so bold?

DAUGHTER There may be something for me at the employment agency.

SCHILL Employment agency?

DAUGHTER It's important to get there early.

SCHILL All right. I'll have something nice for you when you get home.

SON *and* DAUGHTER (*Salute*) Good day, Burgomaster.

(*The* SON *and* DAUGHTER *go out. The* FIRST MAN *comes into* SCHILL'S *shop. Mandolin and guitar music are heard offstage*)

SCHILL Good morning, Hofbauer.

FIRST MAN Cigarettes. (SCHILL *takes a pack from the shelf*) Not those. I'll have the green today.

SCHILL They cost more.

FIRST MAN Put it in the book.

SCHILL What?

FIRST MAN Charge it.

SCHILL Well, all right, I'll make an exception this time—seeing it's you, Hofbauer.

(SCHILL *writes in his cash book*)

FIRST MAN (*Opening the pack of cigarettes*) Who's that playing out there?

SCHILL The two blind men.

FIRST MAN They play well.

SCHILL To hell with them.

FIRST MAN They make you nervous? (SCHILL *shrugs. The* FIRST MAN *lights a cigarette*) She's getting ready for the wedding, I hear.

SCHILL Yes. So they say.

(*Enter the* FIRST *and* SECOND WOMAN. *They cross to the counter*)

FIRST WOMAN Good morning, good morning.

SECOND WOMAN Good morning.

FIRST MAN Good morning.

SCHILL Good morning, ladies.

FIRST WOMAN Good morning, Herr Schill.

SECOND WOMAN Good morning.

FIRST WOMAN Milk please, Herr Schill.

SCHILL Milk.

SECOND WOMAN And milk for me too.

SCHILL A liter of milk each. Right away.

FIRST WOMAN Whole milk, please, Herr Schill.

SCHILL Whole milk?

SECOND WOMAN Yes. Whole milk, please.

SCHILL Whole milk, I can only give you half a liter each of whole milk.

FIRST WOMAN All right.

SCHILL Half a liter of whole milk here, and half a liter of whole milk here. There you are.

FIRST WOMAN And butter please, a quarter kilo.

SCHILL Butter, I haven't any butter. I can give you some very nice lard?

FIRST WOMAN No. Butter.

SCHILL Goose fat? (*The* FIRST WOMAN *shakes her head*) Chicken fat?

FIRST WOMAN Butter.

SCHILL Butter. Now, wait a minute, though. I have a tin of imported butter here somewhere. Ah. There you are. No, sorry, she asked first, but I can order some for you from Kalberstadt tomorrow.

SECOND WOMAN And white bread.

SCHILL White bread.

(*He takes a loaf and a knife*)

SECOND WOMAN The whole loaf.

SCHILL But a whole loaf would cost . . .

SECOND WOMAN Charge it.

SCHILL Charge it?

FIRST WOMAN And a package of milk chocolate.

SCHILL Package of milk chocolate—right away.

SECOND WOMAN One for me, too, Herr Schill.

SCHILL And a package of milk chocolate for you, too.

FIRST WOMAN We'll eat it here, if you don't mind.

SCHILL Yes, please do.

SECOND WOMAN It's so cool at the back of the shop.

SCHILL Charge it?

WOMEN Of course.

SCHILL All for one, one for all.

(*The* SECOND MAN *enters*)

SECOND MAN Good morning.

THE TWO WOMEN Good morning.

SCHILL Good morning, Helmesberger.

SECOND MAN It's going to be a hot day.

SCHILL Phew!

SECOND MAN How's business?

SCHILL Fabulous. For a while no one came, and now all of a sudden I'm running a luxury trade.

SECOND MAN Good!

SCHILL Oh, I'll never forget the way you all stood by me at the Golden Apostle in spite of your need, in spite of everything. That was the finest hour of my life.

FIRST MAN We're not heathens, you know.

SECOND MAN We're behind you, my boy; the whole town's behind you.

FIRST MAN As firm as a rock.

FIRST WOMAN (*Munching her chocolate*) As firm as a rock, Herr Schill.

BOTH WOMEN As firm as a rock.

SECOND MAN There's no denying it—you're the most popular man in town.

FIRST MAN The most important.

SECOND MAN And in the spring, God willing, you will be our Burgomaster.

FIRST MAN Sure as a gun.

ALL Sure as a gun.

(*Enter* PEDRO *with fishing equipment and a fish in his landing net*)

PEDRO Would you please weigh my fish for me?

SCHILL (*Weighs it*) Two kilos.

PEDRO Is that all?

SCHILL Two kilos exactly.

PEDRO Two kilos!

(*He gives* SCHILL *a tip and exits*)

SECOND WOMAN The fiancé.

FIRST WOMAN They're to be married this week. It will be a tremendous wedding.

SECOND WOMAN I saw his picture in the paper.

FIRST WOMAN (*Sighs*) Ah, what a man!

SECOND MAN Give me a bottle of schnapps.

SCHILL The usual?

SECOND MAN No, cognac.

SCHILL Cognac? But cognac costs twenty-two marks fifty.

SECOND MAN We all have to splurge a little now and again—

SCHILL Here you are. Three Star.

SECOND MAN And a package of pipe tobacco.

SCHILL Black or blond?

SECOND MAN English.

SCHILL English! But that makes twenty-three marks eighty.

SECOND MAN Chalk it up.

SCHILL Now, look. I'll make an exception this week. Only, you will have to pay me the moment your unemployment check comes in. I don't want to be kept waiting. (*Suddenly*) Helmesberger, are those new shoes you're wearing?

SECOND MAN Yes, what about it?

SCHILL You too, Hofbauer. Yellow shoes! Brand new!

FIRST MAN So?

SCHILL (*To the women*) And you. You all have new shoes! New shoes!

FIRST WOMAN A person can't walk around forever in the same old shoes.

SECOND WOMAN Shoes wear out.

SCHILL And the money. Where does the money come from?

FIRST WOMAN We got them on credit, Herr Schill.

SECOND WOMAN On credit.

SCHILL On credit? And where all of a sudden do you get credit?

SECOND MAN Everybody gives credit now.

FIRST WOMAN You gave us credit yourself.

SCHILL And what are you going to pay with? Eh? (*They are all silent.* SCHILL *advances upon them threateningly*) With what? Eh? With what? With what?

(*Suddenly he understands. He takes his apron off quickly, flings it on the counter, gets his jacket, and walks off with an air of determination. Now the shop sign vanishes. The shelves are pushed off. The lights go up on the balcony of the Golden Apostle, and the balcony unit itself moves forward into the optical center.* CLAIRE *and* BOBBY *step out on the balcony.* CLAIRE *sits down.* BOBBY *serves coffee*)

CLAIRE A lovely autumn morning. A silver haze on the streets and a violet sky above. Count Holk would have liked this. Remember him, Bobby? My third husband?

BOBBY Yes, madame.

CLAIRE Horrible man!

BOBBY Yes, madame.

CLAIRE Where is Monsieur Pedro? Is he up yet?

BOBBY Yes, madame. He's fishing.

CLAIRE Already? What a singular passion!

(PEDRO *comes in with the fish*)

PEDRO Good morning, my love.

CLAIRE Pedro! There you are.

PEDRO Look, my darling. Four kilos!

CLAIRE A jewel! I'll have it grilled for your lunch. Give it to Bobby.

PEDRO Ah—it is so wonderful here! I like your little town.

CLAIRE Oh, do you?

PEDRO Yes. These people, they are all so—what is the word?

CLAIRE Simple, honest, hard-working, decent.

PEDRO But, my angel, you are a mind reader. That's just what I was going to say—however did you guess?

CLAIRE I know them.

PEDRO Yet when we arrived it was all so dirty, so —what is the word?

CLAIRE Shabby.

PEDRO Exactly. But now everywhere you go, you see them busy as bees, cleaning their streets—

CLAIRE Repairing their houses, sweeping—dusting—hanging new curtains in the windows—singing as they work.

PEDRO But you astonishing, wonderful woman! You can't see all that from here.

CLAIRE I know them. And in their gardens—I am sure that in their gardens they are manuring the soil for the spring.

PEDRO My angel, you know everything. This morning on my way fishing I said to myself, look at them all manuring their gardens. It is extraordinary—and it's all because of you. Your return has given them a new—what is the word?

CLAIRE Lease on life?

PEDRO Precisely.

CLAIRE The town was dying, it's true. But a town doesn't have to die. I think they realize that now. People die, not towns. Bobby! (BOBBY *appears*) A cigar.

(*The lights fade on the balcony, which moves back upstage. Somewhat to the right, a sign descends. It reads:* "Polizei." *The* POLICEMAN *pushes a desk under it. This, with the bench, becomes the police station. He places a bottle of beer and a glass on the desk, and goes to hang up his coat offstage. The telephone rings*)

POLICEMAN Schultz speaking. Yes, we have a couple of rooms for the night. No, not for rent. This is not the hotel. This is the Güllen police station.

(*He laughs and hangs up.* SCHILL *comes in. He is evidently nervous*)

SCHILL Schultz.

POLICEMAN Hello, Schill. Come in. Sit down. Beer?

SCHILL Please.

(*He drinks thirstily*)

POLICEMAN What can I do for you?

SCHILL I want you to arrest Madame Zachanassian.

POLICEMAN Eh?

SCHILL I said I want you to arrest Madame Zachanassian.

POLICEMAN What the hell are you talking about?

SCHILL I ask you to arrest this woman at once.

POLICEMAN What offense has the lady committed?

SCHILL You know perfectly well. She offered a billion marks—

POLICEMAN And you want her arrested for that?

(*He pours beer into his glass*)

SCHILL Schultz! It's your duty.

SCHULTZ Extraordinary! Extraordinary idea!

(*He drinks his beer*)

SCHILL I'm speaking to you as your next Burgomaster.

POLICEMAN Schill, that's true. The lady offered us a billion marks. But that doesn't entitle us to take police action against her.

SCHILL Why not?

POLICEMAN In order to be arrested, a person must first commit a crime.

SCHILL Incitement to murder.

POLICEMAN Incitement to murder is a crime. I agree.

SCHILL Well?

POLICEMAN And such a proposal—if serious—constitutes an assault.

SCHILL That's what I mean.

POLICEMAN But her offer can't be serious.

SCHILL Why?

POLICEMAN The price is too high. In a case like yours, one pays a thousand marks, at the most two thousand. But not a billion! That's ridiculous. And even if she meant it, that would only prove she was out of her mind. And that's not a matter for the police.

SCHILL Whether she's out of her mind or not, the danger to me is the same. That's obvious.

POLICEMAN Look, Schill, you show us where anyone threatens your life in any way—say, for instance, a man points a gun at you—and we'll be there in a flash.

SCHILL (*Gets up*) So I'm to wait till someone points a gun at me?

POLICEMAN Pull yourself together, Schill. We're all for you in this town.

SCHILL I wish I could believe it.

POLICEMAN You don't believe it?

SCHILL No. No, I don't. All of a sudden my customers are buying white bread, whole milk, butter, imported tobacco. What does it mean?

POLICEMAN It means business is picking up.

SCHILL Helmesberger lives on the dole; he hasn't earned anything in five years. Today he bought French cognac.

POLICEMAN I'll have to try your cognac one of these days.

SCHILL And shoes. They all have new shoes.

POLICEMAN And what have you got against new shoes? I'm wearing a new pair myself.

(*He holds out his foot*)

SCHILL You too?

POLICEMAN Why not?

(*He pours out the rest of his beer*)

SCHILL Is that Pilsen you're drinking now?

POLICEMAN It's the only thing.

SCHILL You used to drink the local beer.

POLICEMAN Hogwash.

(*Radio music is heard offstage*)

SCHILL Listen. You hear?

POLICEMAN "The Merry Widow." Yes.

SCHILL No. It's a radio.

POLICEMAN That's Bergholzer's radio.

SCHILL Bergholzer!

POLICEMAN You're right. He should close his window when he plays it. I'll make a note to speak to him.

(*He makes a note in his notebook*)

SCHILL And how can Bergholzer pay for a radio?

POLICEMAN That's his business.

SCHILL And you, Schultz, with your new shoes and your imported beer—how are you going to pay for them?

POLICEMAN That's my business. (*His telephone rings. He picks it up*) Police Station, Güllen. What? What? Where? Where? How? Right, we'll deal with it.

(*He hangs up*)

SCHILL (*He speaks during the* POLICEMAN's *telephone conversation*) Schultz, listen. No. Schultz, please —listen to me. Don't you see they're all . . . Listen, please. Look, Schultz. They're all running up debts. And out of these debts comes this sudden prosperity. And out of this prosperity comes the absolute need to kill me.

POLICEMAN (*Putting on his jacket*) You're imagining things.

SCHILL All she has to do is to sit on her balcony and wait.

POLICEMAN Don't be a child.

SCHILL You're all waiting.

POLICEMAN (*Snaps a loaded clip into the magazine of a rifle*) Look, Schill, you can relax. The police are here for your protection. They know their job. Let anyone, any time, make the slightest threat to your life, and all you have to do is let us know. We'll do the rest . . . Now, don't worry.

SCHILL No, I won't.

POLICEMAN And don't upset yourself. All right?

SCHILL Yes. I won't. (*Then suddenly, in a low tone*) You have a new gold tooth in your mouth!

POLICEMAN What are you talking about?

SCHILL (*Taking the* POLICEMAN's *head in his hands, and forcing his lips open*) A brand new, shining gold tooth.

POLICEMAN (*Breaks away and involuntarily levels the gun at* SCHILL) Are you crazy? Look, I've no time to waste. Madame Zachanassian's panther's broken loose.

SCHILL Panther?

POLICEMAN Yes, it's at large. I've got to hunt it down.

SCHILL You're not hunting a panther and you know it. It's me you're hunting!

(*The* POLICEMAN *clicks on the safety and lowers the gun*)

POLICEMAN Schill! Take my advice. Go home. Lock the door. Keep out of everyone's way. That way you'll be safe. Cheer up! Good times are just around the corner!

(*The lights dim in this area and light up on the balcony.* PEDRO *is lounging in a chair.* CLAIRE *is smoking*)

PEDRO Oh, this little town oppresses me.

CLAIRE Oh, does it? So you've changed your mind?

PEDRO It is true, I find it charming, delightful—

CLAIRE Picturesque.

PEDRO Yes. After all, it's the place where you were born. But it is too quiet for me. Too provincial. Too much like all small towns everywhere. These people —look at them. They fear nothing, they desire nothing, they strive for nothing. They have everything they want. They are asleep.

CLAIRE Perhaps one day they will come to life again.

PEDRO My God—do I have to wait for that?

CLAIRE Yes, you do. Why don't you go back to your fishing?

PEDRO I think I will.

(PEDRO *turns to go*)

CLAIRE Pedro.

PEDRO Yes, my love?

CLAIRE Telephone the president of Hambro's Bank.[2] Ask him to transfer a billion marks to my current account.

PEDRO A billion? Yes, my love.

(*He goes. The lights fade on the balcony. A sign is flown in. It reads:* "Rathaus."[3] *The* THIRD MAN *crosses the stage, right to left, wheeling a new television set on a hand truck. The counter of* SCHILL's *shop is transformed into the* BURGOMASTER's *office. The* BURGOMASTER *comes in. He takes a revolver from his pocket, examines it and sets it down on the desk. He sits down and starts writing.* SCHILL *knocks*)

BURGOMASTER Come in.

SCHILL I must have a word with you, Burgomaster.

BURGOMASTER Ah, Schill. Sit down, my friend.

SCHILL Man to man. As your successor.

BURGOMASTER But of course. Naturally.

(SCHILL *remains standing. He looks at the revolver*)

SCHILL Is that a gun?

BURGOMASTER Madame Zachanassian's black panther's broken loose. It's been seen near the cathedral. It's as well to be prepared.

SCHILL Oh, yes. Of course.

BURGOMASTER I've sent out a call for all able-bodied men with firearms. The streets have been cleared. The children have been kept in school. We don't want any accidents.

SCHILL (*Suspiciously*) You're making quite a thing of it.

BURGOMASTER (*Shrugs*) Naturally. A panther is a dangerous beast. Well? What's on your mind? Speak out. We're old friends.

SCHILL That's a good cigar you're smoking, Burgomaster.

BURGOMASTER Yes. Havana.

SCHILL You used to smoke something else.

BURGOMASTER Fortuna.

SCHILL Cheaper.

BURGOMASTER Too strong.

SCHILL A new tie? Silk?

BURGOMASTER Yes. Do you like it?

SCHILL And have you also bought new shoes?

BURGOMASTER (*Brings his feet out from under the desk*) Why, yes. I ordered a new pair from Kalberstadt. Extraordinary! However did you guess?

SCHILL That's why I'm here.

(*The* THIRD MAN *knocks*)

[2] One of the principal banks of England.

[3] "City Hall."

BURGOMASTER Come in.

THIRD MAN The new typewriter, sir.

BURGOMASTER Put it on the table. (*The* THIRD MAN *sets it down and goes*) What's the matter with you? My dear fellow, aren't you well?

SCHILL It's you who don't seem well, Burgomaster.

BURGOMASTER What do you mean?

SCHILL You look pale.

BURGOMASTER I?

SCHILL Your hands are trembling. (*The* BURGOMASTER *involuntarily hides his hands*) Are you frightened?

BURGOMASTER What have I to be afraid of?

SCHILL Perhaps this sudden prosperity alarms you.

BURGOMASTER Is prosperity a crime?

SCHILL That depends on how you pay for it.

BURGOMASTER You'll have to forgive me, Schill, but I really haven't the slightest idea what you're talking about. Am I supposed to feel like a criminal every time I order a new typewriter?

SCHILL Do you?

BURGOMASTER Well, I hope you haven't come here to talk about a new typewriter. Now, what was it you wanted?

SCHILL I have come to claim the protection of the authorities.

BURGOMASTER Ei! Against whom?

SCHILL You know against whom.

BURGOMASTER You don't trust us?

SCHILL That woman has put a price on my head.

BURGOMASTER If you don't feel safe, why don't you go to the police?

SCHILL I have just come from the police.

BURGOMASTER And?

SCHILL The chief has a new gold tooth in his mouth.

BURGOMASTER A new—? Oh, Schill, really! You're forgetting. This is Güllen, the town of humane traditions. Goethe slept here. Brahms composed a quartet. You must have faith in us. This is a law-abiding community.

SCHILL Then arrest this woman who wants to have me killed.

BURGOMASTER Look here, Schill. God knows the lady has every right to be angry with you. What you did there wasn't very pretty. You forced two decent lads to perjure themselves and had a young girl thrown out on the streets.

SCHILL That young girl owns half the world.

(*A moment's silence*)

BURGOMASTER Very well, then, we'll speak frankly.

SCHILL That's why I'm here.

BURGOMASTER Man to man, just as you said. (*He clears his throat*) Now—after what you did, you have no moral right to say a word against this lady. And I advise you not to try. Also—I regret to have to tell you this—there is no longer any question of your being elected Burgomaster.

SCHILL Is that official?

BURGOMASTER Official.

SCHILL I see.

BURGOMASTER The man who is chosen to exercise the high post of Burgomaster must have, obviously, certain moral qualifications. Qualifications which, unhappily, you no longer possess. Naturally, you may count on the esteem and friendship of the town, just as before. That goes without saying. The best thing will be to spread the mantle of silence over the whole miserable business.

SCHILL So I'm to remain silent while they arrange my murder?

(*The* BURGOMASTER *gets up*)

BURGOMASTER (*Suddenly noble*) Now, who is arranging your murder? Give me the names and I will investigate the case at once. Unrelentingly. Well? The names?

SCHILL You.

BURGOMASTER I resent this. Do you think we want to kill you for money?

SCHILL No. You don't want to kill me. But you want to have me killed.

(*The lights go down. The stage is filled with men prowling about with rifles, as if they were stalking a quarry. In the interval the* POLICEMAN'*s bench and the* BURGOMASTER'*s desk are shifted somewhat, so that they will compose the setting for the sacristy. The stage empties. The lights come up on the balcony.* CLAIRE *appears*)

CLAIRE Bobby, what's going on here? What are all these men doing with guns? Whom are they hunting?

BOBBY The black panther has escaped, madame.

CLAIRE Who let him out?

BOBBY Kobby and Lobby, madame.

CLAIRE How excited they are! There may be shooting?

BOBBY It is possible, madame.

(*The lights fade on the balcony. The sacristan comes in. He arranges the set, and puts the altar cloth on the altar. Then* SCHILL *comes on. He is looking for the* PASTOR. *The* PASTOR *enters, left. He is wearing his gown and carrying a rifle*)

SCHILL Sorry to disturb you, Pastor.

PASTOR God's house is open to all. (*He sees that* SCHILL *is staring at the gun*) Oh, the gun? That's because of the panther. It's best to be prepared.

SCHILL Pastor, help me.

PASTOR Of course. Sit down. (*He puts the rifle on the bench*) What's the trouble?

SCHILL (*Sits on the bench*) I'm frightened.

PASTOR Frightened? Of what?

SCHILL Of everyone. They're hunting me down like a beast.

PASTOR Have no fear of man, Schill. Fear God. Fear not the death of the body. Fear the death of the soul. Zip up my gown behind, Sacristan.

SCHILL I'm afraid, Pastor.

PASTOR Put your trust in heaven, my friend.

SCHILL You see, I'm not well. I shake. I have such pains around the heart. I sweat.

PASTOR I know. You're passing through a profound psychic experience.

SCHILL I'm going through hell.

PASTOR The hell you are going through exists only within yourself. Many years ago you betrayed a girl shamefully, for money. Now you think that we shall sell you just as you sold her. No, my friend, you are projecting your guilt upon others. It's quite natural. But remember, the root of our torment lies always within ourselves, in our hearts, in our sins. When you have understood this, you can conquer the fears that oppress you; you have weapons with which to destroy them.

SCHILL Siemethofer has bought a new washing machine.

PASTOR Don't worry about the washing machine. Worry about your immortal soul.

SCHILL Stockers has a television set.

PASTOR There is also great comfort in prayer. Sacristan, the bands. (SCHILL *crosses to the altar and kneels. The sacristan ties on the* PASTOR'S *bands*) Examine your conscience, Schill. Repent. Otherwise your fears will consume you. Believe me, this is the only way. We have no other. (*The church bell begins to peal.* SCHILL *seems relieved*) Now I must leave you. I have a baptism. You may stay as long as you like. Sacristan, the Bible, Liturgy, and Psalter. The child is beginning to cry. I can hear it from here. It is frightened. Let us make haste to give it the only security which this world affords.

SCHILL A new bell?

PASTOR Yes. Its tone is marvelous, don't you think? Full. Sonorous.

SCHILL (*Steps back in horror*) A new bell! You too, Pastor? You too?

(*The* PASTOR *clasps his hands in horror. Then he takes* SCHILL *into his arms*)

PASTOR Oh, God, God forgive me. We are poor, weak things, all of us. Do not tempt us further into the hell in which you are burning. Go, Schill, my friend, go my brother, go while there is time.

(*The* PASTOR *goes.* SCHILL *picks up the rifle with a gesture of desperation. He goes out with it. As the lights fade, men appear with guns. Two shots are fired in the darkness. The lights come up on the balcony, which moves forward*)

CLAIRE Bobby! What was that shooting? Have they caught the panther?

BOBBY He is dead, madame.

CLAIRE There were two shots.

BOBBY The panther is dead, madame.

CLAIRE I loved him. (*Waves* BOBBY *away*) I shall miss him.

(*The* TEACHER *comes in with two little girls, singing. They stop under the balcony*)

TEACHER Gracious lady, be so good as to accept our heartfelt condolences. Your beautiful panther is no more. Believe me, we are deeply pained that so tragic an event should mar your visit here. But what could we do? The panther was savage, a beast. To him our human laws could not apply. There was no other way—(SCHILL *appears with the gun. He looks dangerous. The girls run off, frightened. The* TEACHER *follows the girls*) Children—children—children!

CLAIRE Anton, why are you frightening the children?

(*He works the bolt, loading the chamber, and raises the gun slowly*)

SCHILL Go away, Claire—I warn you. Go away.

CLAIRE How strange it is, Anton! How clearly it comes back to me! The day we saw one another for the first time, do you remember? I was on a balcony then. It was a day like today, a day in autumn without a breath of wind, warm as it is now—only lately I am always cold. You stood down there and stared at me without moving. I was embarrassed. I didn't know what to do. I wanted to go back into the darkness of the room, where it was safe, but I couldn't. You stared up at me darkly, almost angrily, as if you wished to hurt me, but your eyes were full of passion. (SCHILL *begins to lower the rifle involuntarily*) Then, I don't know why, I left the balcony and I came down and stood in the street beside you. You didn't greet me, you didn't say a word, but you took my hand and we walked together out of the town into the fields, and behind us came Kobby and Lobby, like two dogs, sniveling and giggling and snarling. Suddenly you picked up a stone and hurled it at them, and they ran yelping back into the town, and we were alone. (SCHILL *has lowered the rifle completely. He moves forward toward her, as close as he can come*) That was the beginning, and everything else had to follow. There is no escape.

(*She goes in and closes the shutters.* SCHILL *stands immobile. The* TEACHER *tiptoes in. He stares at* SCHILL, *who doesn't see him. Then he beckons to the children*)

TEACHER Come, children, sing. Sing.

(*They begin singing. He creeps behind* SCHILL *and snatches away the rifle.* SCHILL *turns sharply. The* PASTOR *comes in*)

PASTOR Go, Schill—go!

(SCHILL *goes out. The children continue singing, moving across the stage and off. The Golden Apostle vanishes. The crossing bell is heard. The scene dissolves into the railway-station setting, as in Act One. But there are certain changes. The timetable marked* "Fahrplan" *is now new, the frame freshly painted. There is a new travel poster on the station wall. It has a yellow sun and the words:* "Reist in den Süden." [4] *On the other side of the Fahrplan is another poster with the words:* "Die Passionsspiele Oberammergau." [5] *The sound of passing trains covers the scene change.* SCHILL *appears with an old valise in his hand, dressed in a shabby trench coat, his hat on his head. He looks about with a furtive air, walking slowly to the platform. Slowly, as if by chance, the townspeople enter, from all sides.* SCHILL *hesitates, stops*)

BURGOMASTER (*From upstage, center*) Good evening, Schill.

SCHILL Good evening.

POLICEMAN Good evening.

SCHILL Good evening.

PAINTER (*Enters*) Good evening.

[4] "Travel in the South."

[5] "The Oberammergau Passion Play," portraying the suffering and death of Jesus, is performed in the south German village every ten years.

SCHILL Good evening.
DOCTOR Good evening.
SCHILL Good evening.
BURGOMASTER So you're taking a little trip?
SCHILL Yes. A little trip.
POLICEMAN May one ask where to?
SCHILL I don't know.
PAINTER Don't know?
SCHILL To Kalberstadt.
BURGOMASTER (*With disbelief, pointing to the valise*) Kalberstadt?
SCHILL After that—somewhere else.
PAINTER Ah. After that somewhere else.
(*The* FOURTH MAN *walks in*)
SCHILL I thought maybe Australia.
BURGOMASTER Australia!
ALL Australia!
SCHILL I'll raise the money somehow.
BURGOMASTER But why Australia?
POLICEMAN What would you be doing in Australia?
SCHILL One can't always live in the same town, year in, year out.
PAINTER But Australia—
DOCTOR It's a risky trip for a man of your age.
BURGOMASTER One of the lady's little men ran off to Australia . . .
ALL Yes.
POLICEMAN You'll be much safer here.
PAINTER Much!
(SCHILL *looks about him in anguish, like a beast at bay*)
SCHILL (*Low voice*) I wrote a letter to the administration at Kaffigen.
BURGOMASTER Yes? And?
(*They are all intent on the answer*)
SCHILL They didn't answer.
(*All laugh*)
DOCTOR Do you mean to say you don't trust old friends? That's not very flattering, you know.
BURGOMASTER No one's going to do you any harm here.
DOCTOR No harm here.
SCHILL They didn't answer because our postmaster held up my letter.
PAINTER Our postmaster? What an idea.
BURGOMASTER The postmaster is a member of the town council.
POLICEMAN A man of the utmost integrity.
DOCTOR He doesn't hold up letters. What an idea!
(*The crossing bell starts ringing*)
STATION MASTER (*Announces*) Local to Kalberstadt!
(*The townspeople all cross down to see the train arrive. Then they turn, with their backs to the audience, in a line across the stage.* SCHILL *cannot get through to reach the train*)
SCHILL (*In a low voice*) What are you all doing here? What do you want of me?
BURGOMASTER We don't like to see you go.
DOCTOR We've come to see you off.
(*The sound of the approaching train grows louder*)
SCHILL I didn't ask you to come.
POLICEMAN But we have come.
DOCTOR As old friends.
ALL As old friends.
(*The* STATION MASTER *holds up his paddle. The train stops with a screech of brakes. We hear the engine panting offstage*)
VOICE (*Offstage*) Güllen!
BURGOMASTER A pleasant journey.
DOCTOR And long life!
PAINTER And good luck in Australia!
ALL Yes, good luck in Australia.
(*They press around him jovially. He stands motionless and pale*)
SCHILL Why are you crowding me?
POLICEMAN What's the matter now?
(*The* STATION MASTER *blows a long blast on his whistle*)
SCHILL Give me room.
DOCTOR But you have plenty of room.
(*They all move away from him*)
POLICEMAN Better get aboard, Schill.
SCHILL I see. I see. One of you is going to push me under the wheels.
POLICEMAN Oh, nonsense. Go on, get aboard.
SCHILL Get away from me, all of you.
BURGOMASTER I don't know what you want. Just get on the train.
SCHILL No. One of you will push me under.
DOCTOR You're being ridiculous. Now, go on, get on the train.
SCHILL Why are you all so near me?
DOCTOR The man's gone mad.
STATION MASTER 'Board!
(*He blows his whistle. The engine bell clangs. The train starts*)
BURGOMASTER Get aboard man. Quick.
(*The following speeches are spoken all together until the train noises fade away*)
DOCTOR The train's starting.
ALL Get aboard, man. Get aboard. The train's starting.
SCHILL If I try to get aboard, one of you will hold me back.
ALL No, no.
BURGOMASTER Get on the train.
SCHILL (*In terror, crouches against the wall of the* STATION MASTER'S *office*) No—no—no. No. (*He falls on his knees. The others crowd around him. He cowers on the ground, abjectly. The train sounds fade away*) Oh, no—no—don't push me, don't push me!
POLICEMAN There. It's gone off without you.
(*Slowly they leave him. He raises himself up to a sitting position, still trembling. A* TRUCK DRIVER *enters with an empty can*)
TRUCK DRIVER Do you know where I can get some water? My truck's boiling over. (SCHILL *points to the station office*) Thanks. (*He enters the office, gets the water and comes out. By this time,* SCHILL *is erect*) Missed your train?

SCHILL Yes.

TRUCK DRIVER To Kalberstadt?

SCHILL Yes.

TRUCK DRIVER Well, come with me. I'm going that way.

SCHILL This is my town. This is my home. (*With strange new dignity*) No, thank you. I've changed my mind. I'm staying.

TRUCK DRIVER (*Shrugs*) All right.

(*He goes out.* SCHILL *picks up his bag, looks right and left, and slowly walks off*)

*Curtain*

# Act Three

*Music is heard. Then the curtain rises on the interior of the old barn, a dim, cavernous structure. Bars of light fall across the shadowy forms, shafts of sunlight from the holes and cracks in the walls and roof. Overhead hang old rags, decaying sacks, great cobwebs. Extreme left is a ladder leading to the loft. Near it, an old haycart. Left,* CLAIRE ZACHANASSIAN *is sitting in her gilded sedan chair, motionless, in her magnificent bridal gown and veil. Near the chair stands an old keg.*

BOBBY (*Comes in, treading carefully*) The doctor and the teacher from the high school to see you, madame.

CLAIRE (*Impassive*) Show them in.

(BOBBY *ushers them in as if they were entering a hall of state. The two grope their way through the litter. At last they find the lady, and bow. They are both well dressed in new clothes, but are very dusty*)

BOBBY Dr. Nüsslin and Professor Müller.

DOCTOR Madame.

CLAIRE You look dusty, gentlemen.

DOCTOR (*Dusts himself off vigorously*) Oh, forgive us. We had to climb over an old carriage.

TEACHER Our respects.

DOCTOR A fabulous wedding.

TEACHER Beautiful occasion.

CLAIRE It's stifling here. But I love this old barn. The smell of hay and old straw and axle grease—it is the scent of my youth. Sit down. All this rubbish—the haycart, the old carriage, the cask, even the pitchfork—it was all here when I was a girl.

TEACHER Remarkable place.

(*He mops his brow*)

CLAIRE I thought the pastor's text was very appropriate. The lesson a trifle long.

TEACHER I Corinthians 13.[1]

[1] See I Corinthians 13:13: "But now abideth faith, hope, love, these three; and the greatest of these is love."

CLAIRE Your choristers sang beautifully, Professor.

TEACHER Bach. From the *St. Matthew Passion.*

DOCTOR Güllen has never seen such magnificence! The flowers! The jewels! And the people.

TEACHER The theatrical world, the world of finance, the world of art, the world of science . . .

CLAIRE All these worlds are now back in their Cadillacs, speeding toward the capital for the wedding reception. But I'm sure you didn't come here to talk about them.

DOCTOR Dear lady, we should not intrude on your valuable time. Your husband must be waiting impatiently.

CLAIRE No, no, I've packed him off to Brazil.

DOCTOR To Brazil, madame?

CLAIRE Yes. For his honeymoon.

TEACHER *and* DOCTOR Oh! But your wedding guests?

CLAIRE I've planned a delightful dinner for them. They'll never miss me. Now what was it you wished to talk about?

TEACHER About Anton Schill, madame.

CLAIRE Is he dead?

TEACHER Madame, we may be poor. But we have our principles.

CLAIRE I see. Then what do you want?

TEACHER (*He mops his brow again*) The fact is, madame, in anticipation of your well-known munificence, that is, feeling that you would give the town some sort of gift, we have all been buying things. Necessities . . .

DOCTOR With money we don't have.

(*The* TEACHER *blows his nose*)

CLAIRE You've run into debt?

DOCTOR Up to here.

CLAIRE In spite of your principles?

TEACHER We're human, madame.

CLAIRE I see.

TEACHER We have been poor for a long time. A long, long time.

DOCTOR (*He rises*) The question is, how are we going to pay?

CLAIRE You already know.

TEACHER (*Courageously*) I beg you, Madame Zachanassian, put yourself in our position for a moment. For twenty-two years I've been cudgeling my brains to plant a few seeds of knowledge in this wilderness. And all this time, my gallant colleague, Dr. Nüsslin, has been rattling around in his ancient Mercedes, from patient to patient, trying to keep these wretches alive. Why? Why have we spent our lives in this miserable hole? For money? Hardly. The pay is ridiculous.

DOCTOR And yet, the professor here has declined an offer to head the high school in Kalberstadt.

TEACHER And Dr. Nüsslin has refused an important post at the University of Erlangen. Madame, the simple fact is, we love our town. We were born here. It is our life.

DOCTOR That's true.

TEACHER What has kept us going all these years is the

hope that one day the community will prosper again as it did in the days when we were young.

CLAIRE Good.

TEACHER Madame, there is no reason for our poverty. We suffer here from a mysterious blight. We have factories. They stand idle. There is oil in the valley of Pückenried.

DOCTOR There is copper under the Konradsweil Forest. There is power in our streams, in our waterfalls.

TEACHER We are not poor, madame. If we had credit, if we had confidence, the factories would open, orders and commissions would pour in. And our economy would bloom together with our cultural life. We would become once again like the towns around us, healthy and prosperous.

DOCTOR If the Wagonworks were put on its feet again—

TEACHER The Foundry.

DOCTOR The Golden Eagle Pencil Factory.

TEACHER Buy these plants, madame. Put them in operation once more, and I swear to you, Güllen will flourish and it will bless you. We don't need a billion marks. Ten million, properly invested, would give us back our life, and incidentally return to the investor an excellent dividend. Save us, madame. Save us, and we will not only bless you, we will make money for you.

CLAIRE I don't need money.

DOCTOR Madame, we are not asking for charity. This is business.

CLAIRE It's a good idea . . .

DOCTOR Dear lady! I knew you wouldn't let us down.

CLAIRE But it's out of the question. I cannot buy the Wagonworks. I already own them.

DOCTOR The Wagonworks?

TEACHER And the Foundry?

CLAIRE And the Foundry.

DOCTOR And the Golden Eagle Pencil Factory?

CLAIRE Everything. The valley of Pückenried with its oil, the forest of Konradsweil with its ore, the barn, the town, the streets, the houses, the shops, everything. I had my agents buy up this rubbish over the years, bit by bit, piece by piece, until I had it all. Your hopes were an illusion, your vision empty, your self-sacrifice a stupidity, your whole life completely senseless.

TEACHER Then the mysterious blight—

CLAIRE The mysterious blight was I.

DOCTOR But this is monstrous!

CLAIRE Monstrous. I was seventeen when I left this town. It was winter. I was dressed in a sailor suit and my red braids hung down my back. I was in my seventh month. As I walked down the street to the station, the boys whistled after me, and someone threw something. I sat freezing in my seat in the Hamburg Express. But before the roof of the great barn was lost behind the trees, I had made up my mind that one day I would come back . . .

TEACHER But, madame—

CLAIRE (*She smiles*) And now I have. (*She claps her hands*) Mike. Max. Take me back to the Golden Apostle. I've been here long enough.

(MIKE *and* MAX *start to pick up the sedan chair. The* TEACHER *pushes* MIKE *away*)

TEACHER Madame. One moment. Please. I see it all now. I had thought of you as an avenging fury, a Medea, a Clytemnestra—but I was wrong. You are a warm-hearted woman who has suffered a terrible injustice, and now you have returned and taught us an unforgettable lesson. You have stripped us bare. But now that we stand before you naked, I know you will set aside these thoughts of vengeance. If we made you suffer, you too have put us through the fire. Have mercy, madame.

CLAIRE When I have had justice. Mike!

(*She signals to* MIKE *and* MAX *to pick up the sedan chair. They cross the stage. The* TEACHER *bars the way*)

TEACHER But, madame, one injustice cannot cure another. What good will it do to force us into crime? Horror succeeds horror, shame is piled on shame. It settles nothing.

CLAIRE It settles everything.

(*They move upstage toward the exit. The* TEACHER *follows*)

TEACHER Madame, this lesson you have taught us will never be forgotten. We will hand it down from father to son. It will be a monument more lasting than any vengeance. Whatever we have been, in the future we shall be better because of you. You have pushed us to the extreme. Now forgive us. Show us the way to a better life. Have pity, madame—pity. That is the highest justice.

(*The sedan chair stops*)

CLAIRE The highest justice has no pity. It is bright and pure and clear. The world made me into a whore; now I make the world into a brothel. Those who wish to go down, may go down. Those who wish to dance with me, may dance with me. (*To her porters*) Go.

(*She is carried off. The lights black out. Downstage, right, appears* SCHILL'S *shop. It has a new sign, a new counter. The doorbell, when it rings, has an impressive sound.* FRAU SCHILL *stands behind the counter in a new dress. The* FIRST MAN *enters, left. He is dressed as a prosperous butcher, a few bloodstains on his snowy apron, a gold watch chain across his open vest*)

FIRST MAN What a wedding! I'll swear the whole town was there. Cigarettes.

FRAU SCHILL Clara is entitled to a little happiness after all. I'm happy for her. Green or white?

FIRST MAN Turkish. The bridesmaids! Dancers and opera singers. And the dresses! Down to here.

FRAU SCHILL It's the fashion nowadays.

FIRST MAN Reporters! Photographers! From all over the world! (*In a low voice*) They will be here any minute.

FRAU SCHILL What have reporters to do with us? We are simple people, Herr Hofbauer. There is nothing for them here.

FIRST MAN They're questioning everybody. They're

asking everything. (*The* FIRST MAN *lights a cigarette. He looks up at the ceiling*) Footsteps.

FRAU SCHILL He's pacing the room. Up and down. Day and night.

FIRST MAN Haven't seen him all week.

FRAU SCHILL He never goes out.

FIRST MAN It's his conscience. That was pretty mean, the way he treated poor Madame Zachanassian.

FRAU SCHILL That's true. I feel very badly about it myself.

FIRST MAN To ruin a young girl like that— God doesn't forgive it. (FRAU SCHILL *nods solemnly with pursed lips. The butcher gives her a level glance*) Look, I hope he'll have sense enough to keep his mouth shut in front of the reporters.

FRAU SCHILL I certainly hope so.

FIRST MAN You know his character.

FRAU SCHILL Only too well, Herr Hofbauer.

FIRST MAN If he tries to throw dirt at our Clara and tell a lot of lies, how she tried to get us to kill him, which anyway she never meant—

FRAU SCHILL Of course not.

FIRST MAN —Then we'll really have to do something! And not because of the money— (*He spits*) But out of ordinary human decency. God knows Madame Zachanassian has suffered enough through him already.

FRAU SCHILL She has indeed.

(*The* TEACHER *comes in. He is not quite sober*)

TEACHER (*Looks about the shop*) Has the press been here yet?

FIRST MAN No.

TEACHER It's not my custom, as you know, Frau Schill —but I wonder if I could have a strong alcoholic drink?

FRAU SCHILL It's an honor to serve you, Herr Professor. I have a good Steinhäger.[2] Would you like to try a glass?

TEACHER A very small glass.

(FRAU SCHILL *serves bottle and glass. The* TEACHER *tosses off a glass*)

FRAU SCHILL Your hand is shaking, Herr Professor.

TEACHER To tell the truth, I have been drinking a little already.

FRAU SCHILL Have another glass. It will do you good. (*He accepts another glass*)

TEACHER Is that he up there, walking?

FRAU SCHILL Up and down. Up and down.

FIRST MAN It's God punishing him.

(*The* PAINTER *comes in with the* SON *and the* DAUGHTER)

PAINTER Careful! A reporter just asked us the way to this shop.

FIRST MAN I hope you didn't tell him.

PAINTER I told him we were strangers here.

(*They all laugh. The door opens. The* SECOND MAN *darts into the shop*)

SECOND MAN Look out, everybody! The press! They are across the street in your shop, Hofbauer.

FIRST MAN My boy will know how to deal with them.

SECOND MAN Make sure Schill doesn't come down, Hofbauer.

FIRST MAN Leave that to me.

(*They group themselves about the shop*)

TEACHER Listen to me, all of you. When the reporters come I'm going to speak to them. I'm going to make a statement. A statement to the world on behalf of myself as Rector of Güllen High School and on behalf of you all, for all your sakes.

PAINTER What are you going to say?

TEACHER I shall tell the truth about Claire Zachanassian.

FRAU SCHILL You're drunk, Herr Professor; you should be ashamed of yourself.

TEACHER I should be ashamed? You should all be ashamed!

SON Shut your trap. You're drunk.

DAUGHTER Please, Professor—

TEACHER Girl, you disappoint me. It is your place to speak. But you are silent and you force your old teacher to raise his voice. I am going to speak the truth. It is my duty and I am not afraid. The world may not wish to listen, but no one can silence me. I'm not going to wait—I'm going over to Hofbauer's shop now.

ALL No, you're not. Stop him. Stop him.

(*They all spring at the* TEACHER. *He defends himself. At this moment,* SCHILL *appears through the door upstage. In contrast to the others, he is dressed shabbily in an old black jacket, his best*)

SCHILL What's going on in my shop? (*The townsmen let go of the* TEACHER *and turn to stare at* SCHILL) What's the trouble, Professor?

TEACHER Schill, I am speaking out at last! I am going to tell the press everything.

SCHILL Be quiet, Professor.

TEACHER What did you say?

SCHILL Be quiet.

TEACHER You want me to be quiet?

SCHILL Please.

TEACHER But, Schill, if I keep quiet, if you miss this opportunity—they're over in Hofbauer's shop now . . .

SCHILL Please.

TEACHER As you wish. If you too are on their side, I have no more to say.

(*The doorbell jingles. A* REPORTER *comes in*)

REPORTER Is Anton Schill here? (*Moves to* SCHILL) Are you Herr Schill?

SCHILL What?

REPORTER Herr Schill.

SCHILL Er—no. Herr Schill's gone to Kalberstadt for the day.

REPORTER Oh, thank you. Good day.

(*He goes out*)

PAINTER (*Mops his brow*) Whew! Close shave.

(*He follows the* REPORTER *out*)

SECOND MAN (*Walking up to* SCHILL) That was pretty smart of you to keep your mouth shut. You know what to expect if you don't.

(*He goes*)

[2] A kind of gin.

FIRST MAN Give me a Havana. (SCHILL *serves him*) Charge it. You bastard!

(*He goes.* SCHILL *opens his account book*)

FRAU SCHILL Come along, children—

(FRAU SCHILL, *the* SON *and the* DAUGHTER *go off, upstage*)

TEACHER They're going to kill you. I've known it all along, and you too, you must have known it. The need is too strong, the temptation too great. And now perhaps I too will join against you. I belong to them and, like them, I can feel myself hardening into something that is not human—not beautiful.

SCHILL It can't be helped.

TEACHER Pull yourself together, man. Speak to the reporters; you've no time to lose.

(SCHILL *looks up from his account book*)

SCHILL No. I'm not going to fight any more.

TEACHER Are you so frightened that you don't dare open your mouth?

SCHILL I made Claire what she is, I made myself what I am. What should I do? Should I pretend that I'm innocent?

TEACHER No, you can't. You are as guilty as hell.

SCHILL Yes.

TEACHER You are a bastard.

SCHILL Yes.

TEACHER But that does not justify your murder. (SCHILL *looks at him*) I wish I could believe that for what they're doing—for what they're going to do—they will suffer for the rest of their lives. But it's not true. In a little while they will have justified everything and forgotten everything.

SCHILL Of course.

TEACHER Your name will never again be mentioned in this town. That's how it will be.

SCHILL I don't hold it against you.

TEACHER But I do. I will hold it against myself all my life. That's why—

(*The doorbell jingles. The* BURGOMASTER *comes in. The* TEACHER *stares at him, then goes out without another word*)

BURGOMASTER Good afternoon, Schill. Don't let me disturb you. I've just dropped in for a moment.

SCHILL I'm just finishing my accounts for the week. (*A moment's pause*)

BURGOMASTER The town council meets tonight. At the Golden Apostle. In the auditorium.

SCHILL I'll be there.

BURGOMASTER The whole town will be there. Your case will be discussed and final action taken. You've put us in a pretty tight spot, you know.

SCHILL Yes. I'm sorry.

BURGOMASTER The lady's offer will be rejected.

SCHILL Possibly.

BURGOMASTER Of course, I may be wrong.

SCHILL Of course.

BURGOMASTER In that case—are you prepared to accept the judgment of the town? The meeting will be covered by the press, you know.

SCHILL By the press?

BURGOMASTER Yes, and the radio and the newsreel. It's a very ticklish situation. Not only for you—believe me, it's even worse for us. What with the wedding, and all the publicity, we've become famous. All of a sudden our ancient democratic institutions have become of interest to the world.

SCHILL Are you going to make the lady's condition public?

BURGOMASTER No, no, of course not. Not directly. We will have to put the matter to a vote—that is unavoidable. But only those involved will understand.

SCHILL I see.

BURGOMASTER As far as the press is concerned, you are simply the intermediary between us and Madame Zachanassian. I have whitewashed you completely.

SCHILL That is very generous of you.

BURGOMASTER Frankly, it's not for your sake, but for the sake of your family. They are honest and decent people.

SCHILL Oh—

BURGOMASTER So far we've all played fair. You've kept your mouth shut and so have we. Now can we continue to depend on you? Because if you have any idea of opening your mouth at tonight's meeting, there won't be any meeting.

SCHILL I'm glad to hear an open threat at last.

BURGOMASTER We are not threatening you. You are threatening us. If you speak, you force us to act—in advance.

SCHILL That won't be necessary.

BURGOMASTER So if the town decides against you?

SCHILL I will accept their decision.

BURGOMASTER Good. (*A moment's pause*) I'm delighted to see there is still a spark of decency left in you. But—wouldn't it be better if we didn't have to call a meeting at all? (*He pauses. He takes a gun from his pocket and puts it on the counter*) I've brought you this.

SCHILL Thank you.

BURGOMASTER It's loaded.

SCHILL I don't need a gun.

BURGOMASTER (*He clears his throat*) You see? We could tell the lady that we had condemned you in secret session and you had anticipated our decision. I've lost a lot of sleep getting to this point, believe me.

SCHILL I believe you.

BURGOMASTER Frankly, in your place, I myself would prefer to take the path of honor. Get it over with, once and for all. Don't you agree? For the sake of your friends! For the sake of our children, your own children—you have a daughter, a son—Schill, you know our need, our misery.

SCHILL You've put me through hell, you and your town. You were my friends, you smiled and reassured me. But day by day I saw you change—your shoes, your ties, your suits—your hearts. If you had been honest with me then, perhaps I would feel differently toward you now. I might even use that gun you brought me. For the sake of my friends. But now I have conquered my fear. Alone. It was hard, but it's done. And now you will have to judge me. And I will accept your judgment. For me that will be justice. How it will be for you, I don't know. (*He turns away*) You may kill me if you like. I won't complain, I won't protest, I won't defend myself. But I won't do your job for you either.

BURGOMASTER (*Takes up his gun*) There it is. You've had your chance and you won't take it. Too bad. (*He takes out a cigarette*) I suppose it's more than we can expect of a man like you. (SCHILL *lights the* BURGOMASTER's *cigarette*) Good day.

SCHILL Good day. (*The* BURGOMASTER *goes.* FRAU SCHILL *comes in, dressed in a fur coat. The* DAUGHTER *is in a new red dress. The* SON *has a new sports jacket*) What a beautiful coat, Mathilde!

FRAU SCHILL Real fur. You like it?

SCHILL Should I? What a lovely dress, Ottilie!

DAUGHTER *C'est très chic, n'est-ce pas?* [3]

SCHILL What?

FRAU SCHILL Ottilie is taking a course in French.

SCHILL Very useful. Karl—whose automobile is that out there at the curb?

SON Oh, it's only an Opel. They're not expensive.

SCHILL You bought yourself a car?

SON On credit. Easiest thing in the world.

FRAU SCHILL Everyone's buying on credit now, Anton. These fears of yours are ridiculous. You'll see. Clara has a good heart. She only means to teach you a lesson.

DAUGHTER She means to teach you a lesson, that's all.

SON It's high time you got the point, Father.

SCHILL I get the point. (*The church bells start ringing*) Listen. The bells of Güllen. Do you hear?

SON Yes, we have four bells now. It sounds quite good.

DAUGHTER Just like Gray's Elegy.

SCHILL What?

FRAU SCHILL Ottilie is taking a course in English literature.

SCHILL Congratulations! It's Sunday. I should very much like to take a ride in your car. Our car.

SON You want to ride in the car?

SCHILL Why not? I want to ride through the Konradsweil Forest. I want to see the town where I've lived all my life.

FRAU SCHILL I don't think that will look very nice for any of us.

SCHILL No—perhaps not. Well, I'll go for a walk by myself.

FRAU SCHILL Then take us to Kalberstadt, Karl, and we'll go to a cinema.

SCHILL A cinema? It's a good idea.

FRAU SCHILL See you soon, Anton.

SCHILL Good-bye, Ottilie. Good-bye, Karl. Good-bye, Mathilde.

FAMILY Good-bye.

(*They go out*)

SCHILL Good-bye. (*The shop sign flies off. The lights black out. They come up at once on the forest scene*) Autumn. Even the forest has turned to gold.

[3] It's very smart, isn't it?

(SCHILL *wanders down to the bench in the forest. He sits.* CLAIRE's *voice is heard*)

CLAIRE (*Offstage*) Stop. Wait here. (CLAIRE *comes in. She gazes slowly up at the trees, kicks at some leaves. Then she walks slowly down center. She stops before a tree, glances up the trunk*) Bark-borers. The old tree is dying.

(*She catches sight of* SCHILL)

SCHILL Clara.

CLAIRE How pleasant to see you here. I was visiting my forest. May I sit by you?

SCHILL Oh, yes. Please do. (*She sits next to him*) I've just been saying good-bye to my family. They've gone to the cinema. Karl has bought himself a car.

CLAIRE How nice.

SCHILL Ottilie is taking French lessons. And a course in English literature.

CLAIRE You see? They're beginning to take an interest in higher things.

SCHILL Listen. A finch. You hear?

CLAIRE Yes. It's a finch. And a cuckoo in the distance. Would you like some music?

SCHILL Oh, yes. That would be very nice.

CLAIRE Anything special?

SCHILL "Deep in the Forest."

CLAIRE Your favorite song. They know it.

(*She raises her hand. Offstage, the mandolin and guitar play the tune softly*)

SCHILL We had a child?

CLAIRE Yes.

SCHILL Boy or girl?

CLAIRE Girl.

SCHILL What name did you give her?

CLAIRE I called her Genevieve.

SCHILL That's a very pretty name.

CLAIRE Yes.

SCHILL What was she like?

CLAIRE I saw her only once. When she was born. Then they took her away from me.

SCHILL Her eyes?

CLAIRE They weren't open yet.

SCHILL And her hair?

CLAIRE Black, I think. It's usually black at first.

SCHILL Yes, of course. Where did she die, Clara?

CLAIRE In some family. I've forgotten their name. Meningitis, they said. The officials wrote me a letter.

SCHILL Oh, I'm so very sorry, Clara.

CLAIRE I've told you about our child. Now tell me about myself.

SCHILL About yourself?

CLAIRE Yes. How I was when I was seventeen in the days when you loved me.

SCHILL I remember one day you waited for me in the great barn. I had to look all over the place for you. At last I found you lying in the haycart with nothing on and a long straw between your lips . . .

CLAIRE Yes. I was pretty in those days.

SCHILL You were beautiful, Clara.

CLAIRE You were strong. The time you fought with those two railway men who were following me, I wiped the blood from your face with my red petticoat. (*The music ends*) They've stopped.

SCHILL Tell them to play "Thoughts of Home."

CLAIRE They know that too.

(*The music plays*)

SCHILL Here we are, Clara, sitting together in our forest for the last time. The town council meets tonight. They will condemn me to death, and one of them will kill me. I don't know who and I don't know where. Clara, I only know that in a little while a useless life will come to an end.

(*He bows his head on her bosom. She takes him in her arms*)

CLAIRE (*Tenderly*) I shall take you in your coffin to Capri. You will have your tomb in the park of my villa, where I can see you from my bedroom window. White marble and onyx in a grove of green cypress. With a beautiful view of the Mediterranean.

SCHILL I've always wanted to see it.

CLAIRE Your love for me died years ago, Anton. But my love for you would not die. It turned into something strong, like the hidden roots of the forest; something evil, like white mushrooms that grow unseen in the darkness. And slowly it reached out for your life. Now I have you. You are mine. Alone. At last, and forever, a peaceful ghost in a silent house.

(*The music ends*)

SCHILL The song is over.

CLAIRE Adieu, Anton.

(CLAIRE *kisses* ANTON, *a long kiss. Then she rises*)

SCHILL Adieu.

(*She goes.* SCHILL *remains sitting on the bench. A row of lamps descends from the flies. The townsmen come in from both sides, each bearing his chair. A table and chairs are set upstage, center. On both sides sit the townspeople. The* POLICEMAN, *in a new uniform, sits on the bench behind* SCHILL. *All the townsmen are in new Sunday clothes. Around them are technicians of all sorts, with lights, cameras, and other equipment. The townswomen are absent. They do not vote. The* BURGOMASTER *takes his place at the table, center. The* DOCTOR *and the* PASTOR *sit at the same table, at his right, and the* TEACHER *in his academic gown, at his left*)

BURGOMASTER (*At a sign from the radio technician, he pounds the floor with his wand of office*) Fellow citizens of Güllen, I call this meeting to order. The agenda: there is only one matter before us. I have the honor to announce officially that Madame Claire Zachanassian, daughter of our beloved citizen, the famous architect Siegfried Wäscher, has decided to make a gift to the town of one billion marks. Five hundred million to the town, five hundred million to be divided per capita among the citizens. After certain necessary preliminaries, a vote will be taken, and you, as citizens of Güllen, will signify your will by a show of hands. Has anyone any objection to this mode of procedure? The pastor? (*Silence*) The police? (*Silence*) The town health official? (*Silence*) The Rector of Güllen High School? (*Silence*) The political opposition? (*Silence*) I shall then proceed to the vote—(*The* TEACHER *rises. The* BURGOMASTER *turns in surprise and irritation*) You wish to speak?

TEACHER Yes.

BURGOMASTER Very well.

(*He takes his seat. The* TEACHER *advances. The movie camera starts running*)

TEACHER Fellow townsmen. (*The photographer flashes a bulb in his face*) Fellow townsmen. We all know that by means of this gift, Madame Claire Zachanassian intends to attain a certain object. What is this object? To enrich the town of her youth, yes. But more than that, she desires by means of this gift to re-establish justice among us. This desire expressed by our benefactress raises an all-important question. Is it true that our community harbors in its soul such a burden of guilt?

BURGOMASTER Yes! True!

SECOND MAN Crimes are concealed among us.

THIRD MAN (*He jumps up*) Sins!

FOURTH MAN (*He jumps up also*) Perjuries.

PAINTER Justice!

TOWNSMEN Justice! Justice!

TEACHER Citizens of Güllen, this, then, is the simple fact of the case. We have participated in an injustice. I thoroughly recognize the material advantages which this gift opens to us—I do not overlook the fact that it is poverty which is the root of all this bitterness and evil. Nevertheless, there is no question here of money.

TOWNSMEN No! No!

TEACHER Here there is no question of our prosperity as a community, or our well-being as individuals—The question is—must be—whether or not we wish to live according to the principles of justice, those principles for which our forefathers lived and fought and for which they died, those principles which form the soul of our Western culture.

TOWNSMEN Hear! Hear!

(*Applause*)

TEACHER (*Desperately, realizing that he is fighting a losing battle, and on the verge of hysteria*) Wealth has meaning only when benevolence comes of it, but only he who hungers for grace will receive grace. Do you feel this hunger, my fellow citizens, this hunger of the spirit, or do you feel only that other profane hunger, the hunger of the body? That is the question which I, as Rector of your high school, now propound to you. Only if you can no longer tolerate the presence of evil among you, only if you can in no circumstances endure a world in which injustice exists, are you worthy to receive Madame Zachanassian's billion and fulfill the condition bound up with this gift. If not—(*Wild applause. He gestures desperately for silence*) If not, then God have mercy on us!

(*The townsmen crowd around him, ambiguously, in a mood somewhat between threat and congratulation. He takes his seat, utterly crushed, exhausted by his effort. The* BURGOMASTER *advances and takes charge once again. Order is restored*)

BURGOMASTER Anton Schill—(*The* POLICEMAN *gives* SCHILL *a shove.* SCHILL *gets up*) Anton Schill, it is through you that this gift is offered to the town. Are you willing that this offer should be accepted?

(SCHILL *mumbles something*)

RADIO REPORTER (*Steps to his side*) You'll have to speak up a little, Herr Schill.

SCHILL Yes.

BURGOMASTER Will you respect our decision in the matter before us?

SCHILL I will respect your decision.

BURGOMASTER Then I proceed to the vote. All those who are in accord with the terms on which this gift is offered will signify the same by raising their right hands. (*After a moment, the* POLICEMAN *raises his hand. Then one by one the others. Last of all, very slowly, the* TEACHER) All against? The offer is accepted. I now solemnly call upon you, fellow townsmen, to declare in the face of all the world that you take this action, not out of love for worldly gain . . .

TOWNSMEN (*In chorus*) Not out of love for worldly gain . . .

BURGOMASTER But out of love for the right.

TOWNSMEN But out of love for the right.

BURGOMASTER (*Holds up his hand, as if taking an oath*) We join together, now, as brothers . . .

TOWNSMEN (*Hold up their hands*) We join together, now, as brothers . . .

BURGOMASTER To purify our town of guilt . . .

TOWNSMEN To purify our town of guilt . . .

BURGOMASTER And to reaffirm our faith . . .

TOWNSMEN And to reaffirm our faith . . .

BURGOMASTER In the eternal power of justice.

TOWNSMEN In the eternal power of justice.

(*The lights go off suddenly*)

SCHILL (*A scream*) Oh, God!

VOICE I'm sorry, Herr Burgomaster. We seem to have blown a fuse. (*The lights go on*) Ah—there we are. Would you mind doing that last bit again?

BURGOMASTER Again?

THE CAMERAMAN (*Walks forward*) Yes, for the newsreel.

BURGOMASTER Oh, the newsreel. Certainly.

THE CAMERAMAN Ready now? Right.

BURGOMASTER And to reaffirm our faith . . .

TOWNSMEN And to reaffirm our faith . . .

BURGOMASTER In the eternal power of justice.

TOWNSMEN In the eternal power of justice.

THE CAMERAMAN (*To his assistant*) It was better before, when he screamed "Oh, God."

(*The assistant shrugs*)

BURGOMASTER Fellow citizens of Güllen, I declare this meeting adjourned. The ladies and gentlemen of the press will find refreshments served downstairs, with the compliments of the town council. The exits lead directly to the restaurant.

THE CAMERAMAN Thank you.

(*The newsmen go off with alacrity. The townsmen remain on the stage.* SCHILL *gets up*)

POLICEMAN (*Pushes* SCHILL *down*) Sit down.

SCHILL Is it to be now?

POLICEMAN Naturally, now.

SCHILL I thought it might be best to have it at my house.

POLICEMAN It will be here.

BURGOMASTER Lower the lights. (*The lights dim*) Are they all gone?

VOICE All gone.

BURGOMASTER The gallery?

SECOND VOICE Empty.

BURGOMASTER Lock the doors.

THE VOICE Locked here.

SECOND VOICE Locked here.

BURGOMASTER Form a lane. (*The men form a lane. At the end stands the* ATHLETE *in elegant white slacks, a red scarf around his singlet*) Pastor. Will you be so good?

(*The* PASTOR *walks slowly to* SCHILL)

PASTOR Anton Schill, your heavy hour has come.

SCHILL May I have a cigarette?

PASTOR Cigarette, Burgomaster.

BURGOMASTER Of course. With pleasure. And a good one.

(*He gives his case to the* PASTOR, *who offers it to* SCHILL. *The* POLICEMAN *lights the cigarette. The* PASTOR *returns the case*)

PASTOR In the words of the prophet Amos—

SCHILL Please—

(*He shakes his head*)

PASTOR You're no longer afraid?

SCHILL No. I'm not afraid.

PASTOR I will pray for you.

SCHILL Pray for us all.

(*The* PASTOR *bows his head*)

BURGOMASTER Anton Schill, stand up!

(SCHILL *hesitates*)

POLICEMAN Stand up, you swine!

BURGOMASTER Schultz, please.

POLICEMAN I'm sorry. I was carried away. (SCHILL *gives the cigarette to the* POLICEMAN. *Then he walks slowly to the center of the stage and turns his back on the audience*) Enter the lane.

(SCHILL *hesitates a moment. He goes slowly into the lane of silent men. The* ATHLETE *stares at him from the opposite end.* SCHILL *looks in turn at the hard faces of those who surround him, and sinks slowly to his knees. The lane contracts silently into a knot as the men close in and crouch over. Complete silence. The knot of men pulls back slowly, coming downstage. Then it opens. Only the* DOCTOR *is left in the center of the stage, kneeling by the corpse, over which the* TEACHER'S *gown has been spread. The* DOCTOR *rises and takes off his stethoscope*)

PASTOR Is it all over?

DOCTOR Heart failure.

BURGOMASTER Died of joy.

ALL Died of joy.

(*The townsmen turn their backs on the corpse and at once light cigarettes. A cloud of smoke rises over them. From the left comes* CLAIRE ZACHANASSIAN, *dressed in black, followed by* BOBBY.

*She sees the corpse. Then she walks slowly to center stage and looks down at the body of* SCHILL)

CLAIRE Uncover him. (BOBBY *uncovers* SCHILL's *face. She stares at it a long moment. She sighs*) Cover his face.

(BOBBY *covers it.* CLAIRE *goes out, up center.* BOBBY *takes the check from his wallet, holds it out peremptorily to the* BURGOMASTER, *who walks over from the knot of silent men. He holds out his hand for the check. The lights fade. At once the warning bell is heard, and the scene dissolves into the setting of the railway station. The gradual transformation of the shabby town into a thing of elegance and beauty is now accomplished. The railway station glitters with neon lights and is surrounded with garlands, bright posters, and flags. The townsfolk, men and women, now in brand new clothes, form themselves into a group in front of the station. The sound of the approaching train grows louder. The train stops*)

STATION MASTER Güllen-Rome Express. All aboard, please. (*The church bells start pealing. Men appear with trunks and boxes, a procession which duplicates that of the lady's arrival, but in inverse order. Then come the* TWO BLIND MEN, *then* BOBBY, *and* MIKE *and* MAX *carrying the coffin. Lastly* CLAIRE. *She is dressed in modish black. Her head is high, her face as impassive as that of an ancient idol. The procession crosses the stage and goes off. The people bow in silence as the coffin passes. When* CLAIRE *and her retinue have boarded the train, the* STATION MASTER *blows a long blast*) 'Bo—ard!

(*He holds up his paddle. The train starts and moves off slowly, picking up speed. The crowd turns slowly, gazing after the departing train in complete silence. The train sounds fade*)

*The curtain falls slowly*

# Max Frisch

## (1911- )

THE isolation of Switzerland during the last war, a little country surrounded by gigantic military powers, brought with it a quickening of vitality in all areas of artistic and cultural expression. The presence in Zurich of a cosmopolitan and cultivated public, including large numbers of German emigrés, as well as a long tradition of flourishing theatrical activity, helped to sustain theatre in the German language during the war when elsewhere it had all but vanished as a creative force in modern life. The provincialism and strong sense of local cultural affiliation of the Swiss served as a positive advantage, as a source of objectivity and independence in judging the terrible events of contemporary European life. The Swiss playwrights who emerged during the second World War were not great technical innovators, but they were keenly alive to the rich variety of techniques made available by the experimentation of other playwrights. The example of Brecht was of capital importance. Brecht was in close contact with Zurich theatrical circles all during the war, and several of his best plays, including *Mother Courage* and *The Good Woman of Setzuan,* received their première at the Zurich Schauspielhaus. Along with the anti-illusionist and anti-bourgeois qualities of Brecht's art, Swiss playwrights drew directly on his irony, cynicism, pacifism, and exhilarating sense of comedy. As in Brecht's own development, the cabaret made an important contribution to the art of the drama. Zurich enjoyed a long tradition of cabaret theatre, with its pungent social satire and political criticism. In cafés like the "Cornichon" ("Dill Pickle"), young playwrights such as Max Frisch and Friedrich Duerrenmatt could experience the dramatic effectiveness of skits, songs, fragmentary narrative, burlesque, parody, grotesque comedy and cynical wit. The vogue of caricature and farce, of spontaneity and improvisation, of the coarse and comic reduction of the lofty and serious, stems directly from cabaret performance with its conscious theatricality and trenchant commentary on manners and men.

Max Frisch was born in Zurich in 1911, the son of an architect. After two years of study at the University of Zurich, he became a journalist, writing articles on sports and travel for various German newspapers. This activity led him to visit many parts of Eastern and Central Europe in the 1930's. His first serious literary effort was a play, *Steel,* written at the age of 16 and sent to Max Reinhardt in Berlin. It was not performed. Other early plays, inspired in part by the study of Ibsen, included a marriage comedy and a farce dealing with the conquest of the moon. At the age of 26 Frisch destroyed all of his early unpublished writings. He returned to school to study architecture and received his diploma in 1940. As a practicing architect, he came into close contact with the bureaucratic institutions of modern city life and with the conflict of art and expediency in modern architecture. The dissatisfaction of the architect with Swiss sanity, sobriety, eagerness for compromise, and lack of imaginative boldness, is reflected in his plays. After the early 1940's, Frisch's literary preoccupations left little time for the practice of his profession, but his training and attitudes are an important part of his artistic personality. It was as both an architect and a playwright that he visited the United States in 1951-52, through a grant from the Rockefeller Foundation. He has also made two visits to Mexico, and has traveled throughout Eastern as well as Western Europe. This cosmopolitanism has placed Frisch in a somewhat paradoxical situation in his provincial Swiss environment, in which the internationalist playwright is at once a citizen and an outsider.

Well before achieving recognition as a playwright, Frisch was considered a promising writer of fiction and literary prose. In the 1930's he published two novels dealing with adolescent and Alpine life, followed by a collection of notebook jottings written while on border patrol duty in 1939. The diary in fragmentary form is clearly among his literary preferences. Frisch's later novels explore the problems of paternity and marriage, and the clash between our conscious and unconscious selves, themes that were readily transferred to the drama. His best known novel, *Stiller* (1954), is a probing study of a sculptor who takes on a double personality in order to escape the image others form of him. The ambivalent attitude of Stiller to his society and its clichés of freedom is a restatement of the problem of the Swiss intellectual as mirrored in Frisch's essays and plays.

Frisch's first successful dramas are close to the surface of contemporary experience even while exploring new and experimental techniques. *Now They Are Singing Again* (*Nun singen sie wieder*), produced in 1945, is a requiem for the victims of Nazi barbarism wherein the living and the dead move side by side in a free fantasy, reminiscent of Wilder's *Our Town.* Despite the playwright's genuine pity for the victims, he seems to suggest that the dead have died in vain and the living have learned nothing from the catastrophe. *Santa Cruz,* first performed in 1946, is in the tradition of Strindberg's dream play, with time and space freely transposed in a blending of escapism and suffering. *The Chinese Wall* (*Die chinesische Mauer*), written about the same time, is even more experimental in its use of masks, artifice, and dance. The historical fantasy re-creates great figures of the European past at the Chinese Emperor's court. Columbus, Cleopatra, Don Juan and Napoleon are among his guests. The Emperor's boasting tirade about the invincibility of his army is painfully suggestive of the mad speeches of Hitler. Frisch approached the German problem directly in a play of 1949, *As the War Finished* (*Als der Krieg zu Ende war*), written in epic style and set in the living room and basement of a half-destroyed house in Berlin occupied by Russian officers and soldiers. The German Captain Anders, an executioner of Warsaw, is hidden by his wife Agnes, who agrees to make love with the Russian Colonel on condition that the basement is not to be entered. Agnes falls genuinely in love with the Russian, who spurns her after her husband's accidental capture. The play ends in misunderstanding, despair, and suicide. Agnes, heroine and victim, is at the same time interpreter and chorus of the play, speaking directly to the audience and attempting to explain the meaning of both the past and future events surrounding the action.

In *Count Öderland* (*Graf Öderland*), written in 1951 and revised five years later, a provincial lawyer, disgusted with the emptiness and corruption of a mechanized routine existence, seizes an axe and runs berserk as a criminal and revolutionary. Confronted with the necessity of ruling as leader of a successful uprising, he kills himself. The problem of social imprisonment is unresolved by the devotion to crime as a way of life. *Count Öderland* is Frisch's closest approximation to an existential drama, wherein crime follows upon an intellectual choice and collides with the absurdity of existence. The hero's violence is pointless and ends only in self-destruction. The plight of the intellectual amid the banalities of common life is again explored in *Don Juan or the Love of Geometry,* written in 1952 and performed the following year. Frisch's Don Juan is no seeker of coarse pleasures or sensual ecstasies. He passes his time in the study of Arabic mathematical treatises, and his love for geometry prevents him from accepting human love with its contradictory, anti-geometrical character. Closer to Faust than to Casanova, he ends seduced rather than seducing, driven to marriage through an adventure without love. Frisch's open irony and love of parody of traditional themes and values is nowhere more in evidence.

*Biedermann and the Firebugs* (*Biedermann und die Brandstifter*) was first written as a radio play in 1953. Its première took place in Zurich in March, 1958, and since then it has made its way rapidly to the forefront of the repertory of contemporary European drama. The plot may have its origins in observations in Frisch's diary in 1948, inspired by events in Czechoslovakia and the relation of Beneš and the democratic government to Gottwald and the Communists. In a larger sense, the stupidity and fear of Gottlieb Biedermann points to that of the Western nations during the rise of Hitler, or to the presence of cowardice and moral flabbiness in all of us. Biedermann, we are reminded a moment before the catastrophe, is also *"Jedermann"* or "Everyman." The parody of the morality play points at the same time to the collective involvement of the audience. The cosmic plane of action and disjunct, fragmentary movement, along with such episodes as the open theatricality of Scene Seven, point clearly to Wilder's *The Skin of Our Teeth* along with Brecht's *Lehrstücke* and parables, as Frisch's models. Biedermann is a representative of the civilized middle classes, devoted to his business enterprises but incapable of decisive action in a moment of crisis. His courteous treatment of the firebugs as honored guests hastens rather than prevents the disaster. Their elaborate and meticulous preparations, along with the warnings of the Chorus of Firemen, inject a sense of foreboding and of dark humor into the play. From the very beginning, the fate of the victims is unavoidable. The Epilogue, added for the Frankfurt performance in 1959, is sheer theatrical extravaganza: the victims demand not mercy but reparations, and hell goes on strike for want of sinners! Frisch has skillfully exploited the techniques of burlesque, parody, and grotesque comedy that have become an essential part of the resources of the modern playwright. His more recent efforts, *The Great Fury of Philipp Hotz* and *Andorra,* provide further evidence of his keen if angular involvement in the problems of our time and his unmistakable claim to eminence among the leading playwrights of the middle years of our century. The performance of his major plays throughout Europe and America is sure to be among the most significant events of the contemporary theatre in the years ahead.

# BIEDERMANN AND THE FIREBUGS

## *A learning-play without a lesson*

Adapted by Mordecai Gorelik

### CHARACTERS

GOTTLIEB BIEDERMANN
BABETTE, *his wife*
ANNA, *a maidservant*
SEPP SCHMITZ, *a wrestler*
WILLI EISENRING, *a waiter*
A POLICEMAN
A PH.D.
MRS. KNECHTLING
THE CHORUS OF FIREMEN

SCENE *A simultaneous setting, showing the living room and the attic of* BIEDERMANN'S *house.*

TIME *Now.*

## Scene One

*The stage is dark; then a match flares, illuminating the face of* HERR BIEDERMANN. *He is lighting a cigar, and as the stage grows more visible he looks about him. He is surrounded by* FIREMEN *wearing their helmets.*

BIEDERMANN You can't even light a cigar any more without thinking of houses on fire . . . It's disgusting! (*He hides the burning cigar and exits. The* FIREMEN *come forward in the manner of an antique* CHORUS. *The town clock booms the quarter-hour*)

CHORUS Fellow-citizens, we,
Guardians of the city.
Watchers, listeners,
Friends of the friendly town.

LEADER Which pays our salaries.

CHORUS Uniformed, equipped,
We guard your homes,
Patrol your streets,
Vigilant, tranquil.

LEADER Resting from time to time,
But alert, unsleeping.

CHORUS Watching, listening,
Lest hidden danger
Come to light
Too late.
(*The clock strikes half-hour*)

LEADER Much goes up in flames,
But not always
Because of fate.

CHORUS Call it fate, they tell you,
And ask no questions.
But mischief alone
Can destroy whole cities.

LEADER Stupidity alone—

CHORUS Stupidity, all-too-human—

LEADER Can undo our citizens,
Our all-too-mortal citizens.
(*The clock strikes three-quarters*)

CHORUS Use your head;
A stitch in time saves nine.

LEADER Exactly.

CHORUS Just because it happened,
Don't put the blame on God,
Nor on our human nature,
Nor on our fruitful earth,
Nor on our radiant sun . . .
Just because it happened,
Must you call the damned thing Fate?
(*The clock strikes four-quarters*)

LEADER Our watch begins.
(*The* CHORUS *sits. The clock strikes nine o'clock*)

## Scene Two

## The Living Room

GOTTLIEB BIEDERMANN *is reading the paper and smoking a cigar.* ANNA, *the maid-servant, in a white apron, brings him a bottle of wine.*

ANNA Herr Biedermann? (*No answer*) Herr Biedermann— (*He puts down his paper*)

BIEDERMANN They ought to hang them! I've said so all along! Another fire! And always the same story: another peddler shoe-horning his way into somebody's attic—another "harmless" peddler— (*He picks up the bottle*) They ought to hang every one of them! (*He picks up the corkscrew*)

ANNA He's still here, Herr Biedermann. The peddler. He wants to talk to you.

BIEDERMANN I'm not in!

ANNA Yes, sir, I told him—an hour ago. He says he knows you. I can't throw him out, Herr Biedermann.

BIEDERMANN Why not?

ANNA He's too strong.

BIEDERMANN Let him come to the office tomorrow.

ANNA Yes sir. I told him three times. He says he's not interested. He doesn't want any hair tonic.

BIEDERMANN What *does* he want?

ANNA Kindness, he says. Humanity.

BIEDERMANN (*Sniffs at the cork*) Tell him I'll throw him out myself if he doesn't get going at once. (*He fills his glass carefully*) Humanity! (*He tastes the wine*) Let him wait in the hall for me. If he's selling suspenders or razors . . . I'm not inhuman, you know, Anna. But they mustn't come into the house—I've told you that a hundred times! Even if we have three vacant beds, it's out of the question! Where a thing like that can lead to, these days— (ANNA *is about to go when* SCHMITZ *enters. He is athletic, in a costume reminiscent partly of the prison, partly of the circus; his arms are tattooed and there are leather straps on his wrists.* ANNA *edges out.* BIEDERMANN *sips his wine, unaware of* SCHMITZ, *who waits until he turns around*)

SCHMITZ Good evening. (BIEDERMANN *drops his cigar in surprise*) Your cigar, Herr Biedermann. (*He picks up the cigar and hands it to* BIEDERMANN)

BIEDERMANN Look here—

SCHMITZ Good evening.

BIEDERMANN What is this? I told the girl distinctly to have you wait in the hall.

SCHMITZ My name is Schmitz.

BIEDERMANN Without even knocking!

SCHMITZ Sepp Schmitz. (*Silence*) Good evening.

BIEDERMANN What do you want?

SCHMITZ You needn't worry, Herr Biedermann. I'm not a peddler.

BIEDERMANN No?

SCHMITZ A heavyweight wrestler. I mean I *used* to be.

BIEDERMANN And now?

SCHMITZ Unemployed. (*Pause*) Don't worry, sir, I'm not looking for a job—I'm fed up with wrestling. I came in here because it's raining hard outside. (*Pause*) It's warm in here. (*Pause*) I hope I'm not intruding . . . (*Pause*)

BIEDERMANN Cigar? (*He offers one*)

SCHMITZ You know, it's awful, Herr Biedermann—with a build like mine, everybody gets scared—Thank you. (BIEDERMANN *gives him a light*) Thank you. (*They stand there, smoking*)

BIEDERMANN Get to the point.

SCHMITZ My name is Schmitz.

BIEDERMANN You've said that . . . Delighted.

SCHMITZ I have no place to sleep. (*He holds the cigar to his nose, enjoying the aroma*) No place to sleep.

BIEDERMANN Would you like—some bread?

SCHMITZ If that's all there is.

BIEDERMANN A glass of wine?

SCHMITZ Bread and wine . . . If it's no trouble, sir; if it's no trouble. (BIEDERMANN *goes to the door*)

BIEDERMANN Anna! (*He comes back*)

SCHMITZ The girl said you were going to throw me out personally, Herr Biedermann, but I knew you didn't mean it. (ANNA *has entered*)

BIEDERMANN Anna, bring another glass.

ANNA Yes sir.

BIEDERMANN And some bread.

SCHMITZ And if you don't mind, Fräulein, a little butter. Some cheese or cold cuts. Only don't go to any trouble. Some pickles, a tomato or something, some mustard—whatever you have, Fräulein.

ANNA Yes sir.

SCHMITZ If it's no trouble. (ANNA *exits*)

BIEDERMANN You told the girl you knew me.

SCHMITZ That's right, sir.

BIEDERMANN How do you know me?

SCHMITZ I know you at your best, sir. Last night at the pub—you didn't see me; I was sitting in the corner. The whole place liked the way you kept banging at the table.

BIEDERMANN What did I say?

SCHMITZ Exactly the right thing, Herr Biedermann! (*He takes a puff at his cigar*) "They ought to hang them all! The sooner the better—the whole bunch! All those firebugs!" (BIEDERMANN *offers him a chair*)

BIEDERMANN Sit down. (SCHMITZ *sits*)

SCHMITZ This country needs men like you, sir.

BIEDERMANN I know, but—

SCHMITZ No buts, Herr Biedermann, no buts. You're the old-time type of solid citizen. That's why your slant on things—

BIEDERMANN Certainly, but—

SCHMITZ That's why.

BIEDERMANN Why what?

SCHMITZ You have a conscience. Everybody in the pub could see that. A solid conscience.

BIEDERMANN Naturally, but—

SCHMITZ Herr Biedermann, it's not natural at all. Not these days. In the circus, where I did my wrestling, for instance—before it burned down, the whole damned circus—our manager, for instance; you know what he told me? "Sepp," he says (They call me Sepp), "You know me. Will you tell me what I need a conscience for?" Just like that! "What my animals need is a whip," he says. That's the sort of character he is! "A conscience!" He'd laugh out loud. "If anybody has a conscience, you can make a bet it's a bad one." (*Enjoying his cigar*) God rest him!

BIEDERMANN Is he dead?

SCHMITZ Burned to a frazzle, with everything he owned. (*A pendulum clock strikes nine*)

BIEDERMANN I don't know what's keeping that girl so long.

SCHMITZ I've got time. (*Their eyes meet*) You haven't an empty bed in the house, Herr Biedermann. The girl told me.

BIEDERMANN Why do you laugh?

SCHMITZ "Sorry, no empty bed." That's what they all say . . . What's the result? Somebody like me, with no place to sleep— Anyway I don't want a bed.

BIEDERMANN No?

SCHMITZ Oh, I'm used to sleeping on the floor. My father was a miner. I'm used to it. (*He puffs at his cigar*) No apologies necessary, sir. You're not one of those birds who crap off in public—when *you* say something I believe it. What are things coming to if people can't believe each other any more? Nothing but suspicion all over! Am I right? But *you* still believe in yourself and others. Right? You're about the only man left in this town who doesn't say right off that people like us are firebugs.

BIEDERMANN Here's an ash-tray.

SCHMITZ Or am I wrong? (*He taps the ash off his cigar carefully*) People don't believe in God any more —they believe in the Fire Department.

BIEDERMANN What do you mean by that?

SCHMITZ Nothing but the truth. (ANNA *comes in with a tray*)

ANNA We have no cold cuts.

SCHMITZ This will do fine, Fräulein, this will do. Only you forgot the mustard.

ANNA Excuse me. (*Exits*)

BIEDERMANN Eat. (*He fills the glasses*)

SCHMITZ You don't get a reception like this every place you go, Herr Biedermann, let me tell you that! I've had some experiences! Somebody like me comes to the door—no necktie, no place to stay, hungry; "Sit down," they say, "Have a seat"—and meanwhile they call the police. How do you like that? All I ask for is a place to sleep, that's all. A good wrestler who's wrestled all his life—and some bird who never wrestled at all grabs me by the collar! "What's this?" I ask myself. I turn around just to look, and first thing you know he's broken his shoulder! (*Picks up his glass*) *Prosit!* (*They drink, and* SCHMITZ *starts eating*)

BIEDERMANN That's how it goes, these days. You can't open a newspaper without reading about another arson case. The same old story: another peddler asking for a place to sleep, and next morning the house is in flames. I mean to say . . . well, frankly, I can understand a certain amount of distrust . . . (*Reaches for his newspaper*) Look at this! (*He lays the paper next to* SCHMITZ*'s plate*)

SCHMITZ I saw it.

BIEDERMANN A whole district in flames. (*He gets up to show it to* SCHMITZ) Just read that! (SCHMITZ *eats, reads and drinks*)

SCHMITZ Is this wine Beaujolais?

BIEDERMANN Yes.

SCHMITZ Could be a little warmer. (*He reads, over his plate*) "Apparently the fire was planned and executed in the same way as the previous one." (*They exchange a glance*)

BIEDERMANN Isn't that the limit?

SCHMITZ That's why I don't care to read newspapers. Always the same thing.

BIEDERMANN Yes, yes, naturally . . . But that's no answer to the problem, to stop reading the papers. After all you have to know what you're up against.

SCHMITZ What for?

BIEDERMANN Why, because.

SCHMITZ It'll happen anyway, Herr Biedermann, it'll happen anyway. (*He sniffs the sausage*) God's will. (*He slices the sausage*)

BIEDERMANN You think so? (ANNA *brings the mustard*)

SCHMITZ Thank you, Fräulein, thank you.

ANNA Anything else you'd like?

SCHMITZ Not today. (ANNA *stops at the door*) Mustard is my favorite dish. (*He squeezes mustard out of the tube*)

BIEDERMANN How do you mean, God's will?

SCHMITZ God knows . . . (*He continues to eat with his eye on the paper*) "Expert opinion is that apparently the fire was planned and executed in the same way as the previous one." (*He laughs shortly, and fills his glass*)

ANNA Herr Biedermann?

BIEDERMANN What is it now?

ANNA Herr Knechtling would like to speak to you.

BIEDERMANN Knechtling? Now? Knechtling?

ANNA He says—

BIEDERMANN Out of the question.

ANNA He says he simply can't understand you.

BIEDERMANN Why must he understand me?

ANNA He has a sick wife and three children, he says—

BIEDERMANN Out of the question! (*He gets up impatiently*) Herr Knechtling! Herr Knechtling! Let Herr Knechtling leave me alone, dammit! Or let him get a lawyer! Please—let him! I'm through for the day . . . Herr Knechtling! All this to-do because I gave him his notice! Let him get a lawyer, by all means! I'll get one, too . . . Royalties on his invention! Let him put his head over the gas jet or get a lawyer! If Herr Knechtling can afford indulging in lawyers! Please—let him! (*Controlling himself, with a glance at* SCHMITZ) Tell Herr Knechtling I have a visitor. (ANNA *exits*) Excuse me.

SCHMITZ This is your house, Herr Biedermann.

BIEDERMANN How is the food? (*He sits, observing* SCHMITZ*, who attacks his food with enthusiasm*)

SCHMITZ Who'd have thought you could still find it, these days?

BIEDERMANN Mustard?

SCHMITZ Humanity! (*He screws the top of the mustard tube back on*) Here's what I mean: you don't grab me by the collar and throw me out in the rain, Herr Biedermann—*That's* what we need, Herr Biedermann! Humanity! (*He pours himself a drink*) God will reward you! (*He drinks with gusto*)

BIEDERMANN You mustn't think I'm inhuman, Herr Schmitz.

SCHMITZ Herr Biedermann!

BIEDERMANN That's what Frau Knechtling thinks.

SCHMITZ Would you be giving me a place to sleep tonight if you were inhuman?—Ridiculous!

BIEDERMANN Of course!

SCHMITZ Even if it's a bed in the attic. (*He puts down his glass*) Now our wine's the right temperature. (*The doorbell rings*) Police?

BIEDERMANN My wife. (*The doorbell rings again*) Come along, Herr Schmitz . . . But mind you, no noise! My wife has a heart condition— (WOMEN'*s voices are heard offstage.* BIEDERMANN *motions to* SCHMITZ *to hurry. They pick up the tray, bottles and glasses and tiptoe toward stage right, where the* CHORUS *is sitting*)

BIEDERMANN Excuse me! (*He steps over the bench*)

SCHMITZ Excuse me! (*He steps over the bench. He and* BIEDERMANN *disappear.* FRAU BIEDERMANN *enters, left, accompanied by* ANNA, *who takes her wraps*)

BABETTE Where's my husband?—You know, Anna, we're not narrow-minded, and I don't mind your having a boy friend. But if you're going to park him in the house—

ANNA But I don't have a boy friend, Frau Biedermann.

BABETTE Then whose rusty bicycle is that, outside the front door? It scared me to death!

## The Attic

(BIEDERMANN *switches on the light and gestures for* SCHMITZ *to come in. They speak in whispers*)

BIEDERMANN Here's the light-switch. If you get cold there's an old sheepskin around here somewhere. Only for Heaven's sake be quiet! Take off your shoes! (SCHMITZ *puts down the tray, takes off one shoe*) Herr Schmitz?

SCHMITZ Herr Biedermann?

BIEDERMANN You promise me, though, you're not a firebug? (SCHMITZ *starts to laugh*) Sh!! (*He nods goodnight and exits, closing the door.* SCHMITZ *takes off his other shoe*)

## The Living Room

(BABETTE *has heard something; she listens, frightened. Then, relieved, she turns to the audience*)

BABETTE Gottlieb, my husband, promised to go up to the attic every evening, personally, to see if there is any firebug up there. I'm so thankful! Otherwise I'd lie awake half the night.

## The Attic

(SCHMITZ, *now in his socks, goes to the light-switch and snaps out the light*)

CHORUS Fellow-citizens, we,
Shield of the innocent.
Guardians ever-tranquil,
Shield of the sleeping city.
Standing or
Sitting,
Ever on guard.

LEADER Taking a quiet smoke, now and again, to pass the time.

CHORUS Watching,
Listening,
Lest malignant fire leap out
Above these cozy rooftops
To undo our city.
(*The town clock strikes three*)

LEADER Everyone knows we're here,
Ready on call.
(*He fills his pipe*)

CHORUS Who turns the light on at this wee, small hour?
Woe!
Nerve-shattered,
Uncomforted by sleep,
The wife appears.
(BABETTE *enters in a bathrobe*)

BABETTE Somebody coughed! (*A snore*) Gottlieb, did you hear that? (*A cough*) Somebody's there! (*A snore*) That's men for you! A sleeping pill is all they need!

(*The town clock strikes four*)

LEADER Four o'clock.
(BABETTE *turns off the light again*)
We were not called.
(*He puts away his pipe. The stage lightens*)

CHORUS O radiant sun!
O godlike eye!
Light up the day above our cozy roofs!
Thanks be!
No harm has come to our sleeping town.
Not yet.
Thanks be!
(*The* CHORUS *sits*)

# Scene Three

## The Living Room

BIEDERMANN, *his hat and coat on, his briefcase under his arm, is drinking a cup of coffee standing up, and is speaking to* BABETTE, *who is offstage.*

BIEDERMANN For the last time—he's not a firebug!

BABETTE'S VOICE How do you know?

BIEDERMANN I asked him myself, point blank— Can't you think of anything else in this world? You and your firebugs—you're enough to drive a man insane! (BABETTE *enters with the cream pitcher*)

BABETTE Don't yell at me.

BIEDERMANN I'm not yelling at you, Babette, I'm merely yelling. (*She pours cream into his cup*) I have to go. (*He drinks his coffee. It's too hot*) If everybody goes around thinking everybody else is an arsonist— You've got to have a little trust in people, Babette, just a little! (*He looks at his watch*)

BABETTE I don't agree. You're too good-hearted, Gottlieb. You listen to the promptings of your heart, but I'm the one who can't sleep all night . . . I'll give him some breakfast and then I'll send him on his way, Gottlieb.

BIEDERMANN Do that.

BABETTE In a nice way, of course, without offending him.

BIEDERMANN Do that. (*He puts his cup down*) I have to see my lawyer. (*He gives* BABETTE *a perfunctory kiss. They do not notice* SCHMITZ, *who enters, the sheepskin around his shoulders*)

BABETTE Why did you give Knechtling his notice?

BIEDERMANN I don't need him any more.

BABETTE But you were always so pleased with him!

BIEDERMANN That's just what he's presuming on, now! Royalties on his invention—that's what he wants! Invention! Our hair tonic is merchandise, that's all—it's no invention! All those good folk who pour our tonic on their domes could use their own piss for all the good it does them!

BABETTE Gottlieb!

BIEDERMANN It's true, though. (*He checks to see if he has everything in his briefcase*) I'm too goodhearted—you're right. But I'll take care of this Knechtling! (*He is about to go when he sees* SCHMITZ)

SCHMITZ Good morning, everybody.

BIEDERMANN Herr Schmitz— (SCHMITZ *offers his hand*)

SCHMITZ Call me Sepp.

BIEDERMANN (*Ignores his hand*) My wife will speak with you, Herr Schmitz. I have to go, I'm sorry. Good luck . . . (*Changes his mind and shakes hands*) Good luck, Sepp. (BIEDERMANN *exits*)

SCHMITZ Good luck, Gottlieb. (BABETTE *looks at him*) That's your husband's name, isn't it—Gottlieb?

BABETTE How did you sleep?

SCHMITZ Thank you, madam—kind of freezing. But I made use of this sheepskin. Reminded me of old days in the mines. I'm used to the cold.

BABETTE Your breakfast is ready.

SCHMITZ Really, madam! (*She motions for him to sit*) No, really, I— (*She fills his cup*)

BABETTE You must pitch in, Sepp. You have a long way to go, I'm sure.

SEPP How do you mean? (*She points to the chair again*)

BABETTE Would you care for a soft-boiled egg?

SCHMITZ Two.

BABETTE Anna!

SCHMITZ I feel right at home, madam. (*He sits.* ANNA *enters*)

BABETTE Two soft-boiled eggs.

ANNA Yes ma'am.

SCHMITZ Three and a half minutes.

ANNA Very well. (ANNA *starts to leave*)

SCHMITZ Fräulein— (ANNA *stops at the door*) Good morning.

ANNA Morning. (*She exits*)

SCHMITZ The look she gave me! If it was up to her I'd still be out there in the pouring rain. (BABETTE *fills his cup*)

BABETTE Herr Schmitz—

SCHMITZ Yeah?

BABETTE If I may speak frankly—

SCHMITZ Aren't you kind of shaky, madam?

BABETTE Herr Schmitz—

SCHMITZ What's troubling you?

BABETTE Here's some cheese.

SCHMITZ Thank you.

BABETTE Marmalade.

SCHMITZ Thank you.

BABETTE Honey.

SCHMITZ One at a time, madam, one at a time. (*He leans back, eating his bread and butter; attentively*) Well?

BABETTE Frankly, Herr Schmitz—

SCHMITZ Just call me Sepp.

BABETTE Frankly—

SCHMITZ You'd like to get rid of me.

BABETTE No, Herr Schmitz, no! I wouldn't put it that way—

SCHMITZ How would you put it? (*He takes some cheese*) Tilsit cheese is my dish. (*He leans back, eating; attentively*) Madam thinks I'm a firebug.

BABETTE Please don't misunderstand me. What did I say? The last thing I want to do is hurt your feelings, Herr Schmitz . . . You've got me all confused now. Who ever mentioned firebugs? Even your manners, Herr Schmitz; I'm not complaining.

SCHMITZ I know. I have no manners.

BABETTE That's not it, Herr Schmitz—

SCHMITZ I smack my lips when I eat.

BABETTE Nonsense.

SCHMITZ That's what they used to tell me at the orphanage: "Schmitz, don't smack your lips when you eat!" (BABETTE *is about to pour more coffee*)

BABETTE You don't understand me. Really, you don't in the least! (SCHMITZ *places his hand over his cup*)

SCHMITZ I'm going.

BABETTE Herr Schmitz—

SCHMITZ I'm going.

BABETTE Another cup of coffee? (*He shakes his head*) Half a cup? (*He shakes his head*) You mustn't take it like that, Herr Schmitz. I didn't mean to hurt your feelings. I didn't say a single word about you making noises while you eat. (*He gets up*) Have I hurt your feelings? (*He folds his napkin*)

SCHMITZ It's not your lookout, madam, if I have no

manners. My father was a coal-miner. Where would people like us get any manners? Starving and freezing, madam—that's something I don't mind; but no education, madam, no manners, madam, no refinement—

BABETTE I understand.

SCHMITZ I'm going.

BABETTE Where?

SCHMITZ Out in the rain.

BABETTE Oh, no!

SCHMITZ I'm used to it.

BABETTE Herr Schmitz . . . don't look at me like that. Your father was a miner—I can understand it. You had an unfortunate childhood—

SCHMITZ No childhood at all, madam. (*He looks down at his fingers*) None at all. My mother died when I was seven . . . (*He turns away to wipe his eyes*)

BABETTE Sepp!— But Sepp—

(ANNA *brings the soft-boiled eggs*)

ANNA Anything else you'd like? (*She gets no answer; exits*)

BABETTE I haven't ordered you to leave, Herr Schmitz. I never said that. After all, what did I say? You misunderstand me, Herr Schmitz. Really, I mean it —won't you believe me? (*She takes his sleeve—with some hesitation*) Come, Sepp—finish eating! (SCHMITZ *sits down again*) What do you take us for? I haven't even noticed that you smack your lips. Honestly! Even if I did—we don't care a bit about external things. We're not like that at all, Herr Schmitz . . . (*He cracks his egg*)

SCHMITZ God will reward you!

BABETTE Here's the salt. (*He eats the egg with a spoon*)

SCHMITZ It's true, madam, you didn't order me away. You didn't say a word about it. That's true. Pardon me, madam, for not understanding.

BABETTE Is the egg all right?

SCHMITZ A little soft . . . Do pardon me, won't you? (*He has finished the egg*) What were you going to say, madam, when you started to say, very frankly—

BABETTE Well, I was going to say . . . (*He cracks the second egg*)

SCHMITZ God will reward you. (*He starts on the second egg*) My friend Willi says you can't find it any more, he says. Private charity. No fine people left; everything State-controlled. No real people left, these days . . . He says. The world is going to the dogs—that's why! (*He salts his egg*) Wouldn't he be surprised to get a breakfast like this! Wouldn't he open his eyes, my friend, Willi! (*The doorbell rings*) That could be him. (*It rings again*)

BABETTE Who is Willi?

SCHMITZ You'll see, madam. Willi's refined. Used to be a waiter at the Metropol. Before it burned down . . .

BABETTE Burned down?

SCHMITZ Head waiter. (ANNA *enters*)

BABETTE Who is it?

ANNA A gentleman.

BABETTE What does he want?

ANNA From the fire insurance, he says. To look over the house. (BABETTE *gets up*) He's wearing a frock coat—

SCHMITZ My friend Willi!

CHORUS Now two of them dismay us—
Two bicycles, both rusty.
To whom do they belong?

LEADER One yesterday's arrival.
One today's.

CHORUS Woe!

LEADER Night once again, and our watch.

(*The town clock strikes*)

CHORUS How much the coward fears where nothing threatens!
Dreading his own shadow,
Whirling at each sound,
Until his fears overtake him
At his own bedside!

(*The town clock strikes*)

LEADER They never leave their room, these two.
What is the reason?

(*The town clock strikes*)

CHORUS Blind, ah, blind is the weakling!
Trembling, expectant of evil,
Yet hoping somehow to avoid it!
Defenseless!
Ah, weary of menacing evil,
With open arms he receives it!

(*The town clock strikes*)

Woe!

(*The* CHORUS *sits*)

# Scene Four

## The Attic

*SCHMITZ is dressed as before. EISENRING has removed the jacket of his frock coat and is in a white vest and shirtsleeves. He and SCHMITZ are rolling tin barrels into a corner of the attic. The barrels are the type used for storing gasoline. Both vagabonds are in their socks and are working as quietly as they can.*

EISENRING Quiet! Quiet!

SCHMITZ Suppose he calls the police?

EISENRING Keep going.

SCHMITZ What then?

EISENRING Easy! Easy! (*They roll the barrels up to those already stacked in the shadows.* EISENRING *wipes his fingers with some cotton waste*)

EISENRING Why would he call the police?

SCHMITZ Why not?

EISENRING Because he's guilty himself—that's why. (*Doves are heard cooing*) It's morning. Bed-time! (*He throws away the rag*) Above a certain income every citizen is guilty one way or another. Have no fear. (*There is a sudden knocking on the locked door*)

BIEDERMANN'S VOICE Open up! Open up, there! (*He pounds on the door and shakes it*)

EISENRING That's no call for breakfast.

BIEDERMANN Open, I say! Immediately!

SCHMITZ He was never like that before. (*The banging on the door gets louder. Without haste, but briskly,* EISENRING *puts on his jacket, straightens his tie and flicks the dust from his trousers. Then he opens the door.* BIEDERMANN *enters. He is in his bathrobe. He does not see* EISENRING, *who is now behind the open door*)

BIEDERMANN Herr Schmitz!

SCHMITZ Good morning, sir. I hope this noise didn't wake you.

BIEDERMANN Herr Schmitz—

SCHMITZ It won't happen again, I assure you.

BIEDERMANN Leave this house! (*Pause*) I say leave this house!

SCHMITZ When?

BIEDERMANN At once!

SCHMITZ But—

BIEDERMANN Or my wife will call the police. And I can't and won't stop her.

SCHMITZ Hm . . .

BIEDERMANN I said right away, and I mean it. What are you waiting for? (SCHMITZ *picks up his shoes*) I'll have no discussion about it!

SCHMITZ Did I say anything?

BIEDERMANN If you think you can do as you like here because you're a wrestler— A racket like that, all night— (*Points to the door*) Out, I say! Get out! SCHMITZ *turns to* EISENRING)

SCHMITZ He was never like that before . . . (BIEDERMANN *sees* EISENRING *and is speechless*)

EISENRING My name is Eisenring.

BIEDERMANN What's the meaning of this?

EISENRING Willi Maria Eisenring.

BIEDERMANN Why are there two of you suddenly? (SCHMITZ *and* EISENRING *look at each other*) Without even asking!

EISENRING There, you see!

BIEDERMANN What's going on here?

EISENRING (*To* SCHMITZ) Didn't I tell you? Didn't I say it's no way to act, Sepp? Where are your manners? Without even asking! Suddenly two of us!

BIEDERMANN I'm beside myself!

EISENRING There, you see! (*He turns to* BIEDERMANN) That's what I told him! (*Back to* SCHMITZ) Didn't I? (SCHMITZ *hangs his head*)

BIEDERMANN Where do you think you are? Let's get one thing clear, gentlemen—I'm the owner of this house! I ask you—where do you think you are? (*Pause*)

EISENRING Answer when the gentleman asks you something! (*Pause*)

SCHMITZ Willi is a friend of mine . . .

BIEDERMANN And so?

SCHMITZ We were schoolmates together.

BIEDERMANN And so?

SCHMITZ And so I thought . . .

BIEDERMANN What?

SCHMITZ I thought . . . (*Pause*)

EISENRING You didn't think! (*He turns to* BIEDERMANN) I understand fully, Herr Biedermann. All you want to do is what's right—let's get that clear! (*He shouts at* SCHMITZ) You think the owner of this house is going to be pushed around? (*He turns to* BIEDERMANN *again*) Sepp didn't consult you at all?

BIEDERMANN Not one word!

EISENRING Sepp—

BIEDERMANN Not a word!

EISENRING (*To* SEPP) And then you're surprised when people throw you out in the street! (*He laughs contemptuously*)

BIEDERMANN There's nothing to laugh at, gentlemen! I'm serious! My wife has a heart condition—

EISENRING There, you see!

BIEDERMANN She didn't sleep half the night because of your noise. And anyway, what are you doing here? (*He looks around*) What the devil are these barrels doing here? (SCHMITZ *and* EISENRING *look hard where there are no barrels*) If you don't mind —what are these? (*He raps on a barrel*)

SCHMITZ Barrels . . .

BIEDERMANN Where did *they* come from?

SCHMITZ Do you know, Willi? Where they came from?

EISENRING It says "Imported" on the label.

BIEDERMANN Gentlemen—

EISENRING It says so on them somewhere! (EISENRING *and* SCHMITZ *look for a label*)

BIEDERMANN I'm speechless! What do you think you're doing? My whole attic is full of barrels—floor to ceiling! All the way from floor to ceiling!

EISENRING I knew it! (EISENRING *swings around*) Sepp had it figured out all wrong. (*To* SCHMITZ) Twelve by fifteen meters, you said. There's not a hundred square meters in this attic!—I couldn't leave my barrels in the street, Herr Biedermann; you can understand that—

BIEDERMANN I don't understand a thing! (SCHMITZ *shows him a label*)

SCHMITZ Here, Herr Biedermann—here's the label.

BIEDERMANN I'm speechless! (*He inspects the label*)

## Downstairs

(ANNA *leads a* POLICEMAN *into the living room*)

ANNA I'll call him. (*She exits. The* POLICEMAN *waits*)

## Upstairs

BIEDERMANN Gasoline?

## Downstairs

(ANNA *returns*)

ANNA What's it about, officer?

POLICEMAN Official business. (ANNA *goes out again. The* POLICEMAN *waits*)

## Upstairs

BIEDERMANN Is it true, sirs? Is it true?

EISENRING Is what true?

BIEDERMANN What's printed on this label? (*He shows them the label*) What do you take me for? I've never in my life been through anything like this! Do you think I can't read? (*They look at the label*) If you don't mind! (*He laughs sourly*) Gasoline! (*In the voice of a district attorney*) What is in those barrels?

EISENRING Gasoline!

BIEDERMANN Never mind your jokes! I'm asking you for the last time—what's in those barrels? You know as well as I do—this attic is no place for gasoline! (*He runs his finger over one of the barrels*) If you don't mind—just smell that for yourselves! (*He waves his finger under their noses*) Is that gasoline or isn't it? (*They sniff and exchange glances*)

EISENRING It is.

SCHMITZ It is.

BOTH No doubt whatever.

BIEDERMANN Are you insane? My whole attic full of gasoline—

SCHMITZ That's just why we don't smoke up here, Herr Biedermann.

BIEDERMANN What do you think you're doing? A thing like that—when every single newspaper is warning people to watch out for fires! My wife will have a heart attack!

EISENRING There, you see!

BIEDERMANN Don't keep saying, "There, you see!"

EISENRING You can't do that to a lady, Sepp. Not to a housewife. I know housewives. (ANNA *calls up the stairs*)

ANNA Herr Biedermann! Herr Biedermann! (BIEDERMANN *shuts the door*)

BIEDERMANN Herr Schmitz! Herr—

EISENRING Eisenring.

BIEDERMANN If you don't get these barrels out of the house this instant—and I mean this instant—

EISENRING You'll call the police.

BIEDERMANN Yes!

SCHMITZ There, you see! (ANNA *calls up the stairs*)

ANNA Herr Biedermann!

BIEDERMANN (*Lowers his voice*) That's my last word.

EISENRING What word?

BIEDERMANN I won't stand for it! I won't stand for gasoline in my attic! Once for all! (*There is a knock at the door*) I'm coming down! (*He opens the door. The* POLICEMAN *enters*)

POLICEMAN Ah, there you are, Herr Biedermann! You don't have to come down; I won't take much of your time.

BIEDERMANN Good morning!

POLICEMAN Good morning!

EISENRING Morning!

SCHMITZ Morning! (SCHMITZ *and* EISENRING *nod courteously*)

POLICEMAN There's been an accident.

BIEDERMANN Good Heavens!

POLICEMAN An elderly man. His wife says he used to work for you . . . An inventor. Put his head over the gas jet of his kitchen stove last night. (*He consults his notebook*) Knechtling, Johann. Number 11 Rossgasse. (*He puts his notebook away*) Did you know anybody by that name?

BIEDERMANN I—

POLICEMAN Maybe you'd rather we talked about this privately, Herr Biedermann?

BIEDERMANN Yes.

POLICEMAN It doesn't concern these employees of yours.

BIEDERMANN No . . . (*He stops at the door*) If anyone wants me, gentlemen, I'll be at the police station. I'll be right back. (SCHMITZ *and* EISENRING *nod*)

POLICEMAN Herr Biedermann—

BIEDERMANN I'm ready.

POLICEMAN What have you got in those barrels?

BIEDERMAN These?

POLICEMAN If I may ask?

BIEDERMAN . . . Hair tonic . . . (*He looks at* SCHMITZ *and* EISENRING)

EISENRING Hormotone.

SCHMITZ Science's gift to the well-groomed.

EISENRING Hormotone.

SCHMITZ Try a bottle today.

EISENRING You won't regret it.

BOTH Hormotone. Hormotone. Hormotone. (*The* POLICEMAN *laughs*)

BIEDERMANN Is he dead? (BIEDERMANN *and the* POLICEMAN *exit*)

EISENRING A real sweetheart!

SCHMITZ Didn't I tell you?

EISENRING But he didn't mention breakfast.

SCHMITZ He was never like that before. (EISENRING *reaches in his pants pocket*)

EISENRING Have you the detonator cap? (SCHMITZ *reaches in his pants pocket*)

SCHMITZ He was never that way before.

CHORUS O radiant sun!
O godlike eye!
Light up the day again above our cozy roofs!

LEADER Today same as yesterday.

CHORUS Hail!

LEADER No harm has come to our sleeping city.

CHORUS Hail!

LEADER Not yet . . .

CHORUS Hail!

(*Traffic noises offstage; honking, streetcars*)

LEADER Wise is man,
And able to ward off most perils,
If, sharp of mind and alert,

He heeds signs of coming disaster
In time.

CHORUS And if he does not?

LEADER He, who
Attentive to possible dangers,
Studies his newspaper daily—
Is daily, at breakfast, dismayed
By distant tidings, whose meaning
Is daily digested to spare him
Fatigue of his own stressful brain work—
Learning daily what's happened afar—
Can he so quickly discern
What is happening under his roof-tree?
Things that are—

CHORUS Unpublished!

LEADER Disgraceful!

CHORUS Inglorious!

LEADER Real!

CHORUS Things not easy to face! For, if he—
(*The* LEADER *interrupts with a gesture*)

LEADER He's coming.
(*The* CHORUS *breaks formation*)

CHORUS No harm has come to the sleeping city.
No harm yesterday or today.
Ignoring all omens,
The freshly-shaved citizen
Speeds to his office . . .
(*Enter* BIEDERMANN *in hat and coat, his briefcase under his arm*)

BIEDERMANN Taxi! . . . Taxi! . . . Taxi! (*The* CHORUS *is in his way*) What's the trouble?

CHORUS Woe!

BIEDERMANN What's up?

CHORUS Woe!

BIEDERMANN You've said that!

CHORUS Three times woe!

BIEDERMANN But why?

LEADER All-too-strangely a fiery prospect
Unfolds to our eyes.
And to yours.
Shall I be plainer?
Gasoline in the attic—

BIEDERMANN (*Shouts*) Is that *your* business? (*Silence*) Let me through— I have to see my lawyer— What do you want of me? I'm not guilty . . . (*Unnerved*) What's this—an inquest? (*Masterfully*) Let me through, please! (*The* CHORUS *remains motionless*)

CHORUS Far be it from us, the Chorus,
To judge a hero of drama—

LEADER But we *do* see the oncoming peril,
See clearly the menacing danger!

CHORUS Making a simple inquiry
About an impending disaster—
Uttering, merely, a warning—
Civic-minded, the Chorus comes forward,
Bathed, alas, in cold sweat,
In half-fainting fear of that moment
That calls for the hoses of firemen!
(BIEDERMANN *looks at his wrist watch*)

BIEDERMANN I'm in a hurry.

CHORUS Woe!

LEADER All that gasoline, Gottlieb
Biedermann!
How could you take it?

BIEDERMANN Take it?

LEADER You know very well,
The world is a brand for the burning!
Yet, knowing it, what did you think?

BIEDERMAN Think? (*He appraises the* CHORUS) My dear sirs, I am a free and independent citizen. I can think anything I like. What are all these questions? I have the right, my dear sirs, not to think at all if I feel like it! Aside from the fact that whatever goes on under my own roof— Let's get one thing clear, gentlemen: I am the owner of the house!

CHORUS Sacred, sacred to us
Is property,
Whatever befall!
Though we be scorched,
Though we be cindered—
Sacred, sacred to us!

BIEDERMANN Well, then— (*Silence*) Why can't I go through? (*Silence*) Why must you always imagine the worst? Where will that get you? All I want is some peace and quiet, not a thing more . . . As for those two gentlemen—aside from the fact that I have other troubles right now . . . (BABETTE *enters in street clothes*) What do *you* want here?

BABETTE Am I interrupting?

BIEDERMANN Can't you see I'm in conference? (BABETTE *nods to the* CHORUS, *then whispers in* BIEDERMANN'*s ear*) With ribbons, of course. Never mind the cost. As long as it's a wreath. (BABETTE *nods to the* CHORUS)

BABETTE Excuse me, sirs. (*She exits*)

BIEDERMANN To cut it short, gentlemen, I'm fed up! You and your firebugs! I don't even go to the pub any more—that's how fed up I am! Is there nothing else to talk about these days? Let's get one thing straight—if you go around thinking everybody except yourself is an arsonist, how are things ever going to improve? A little trust in people, for Heaven's sake! A little good will! Why keep looking at the bad side? Why go on the assumption that everybody else is a firebug? A little confidence, a little— (*Pause*) You can't go on living in fear! (*Pause*) You think I closed my eyes last night for one instant? I'm not an imbecile, you know! Gasoline is gasoline! I had the worst kind of thoughts running through my head last night . . . I climbed up on the table to listen—even got up on the bureau and put my ear to the ceiling! They were snoring, mind you—snoring! At least four times I climbed up on that bureau. Peacefully snoring! Just the same I got as far as the stairs, once—believe it or not—in my pajamas—and frantic, I tell you—frantic! I was all ready to wake up those two scoundrels and throw them out in the street, along with their barrels. Single-handedly, without compunction, in the middle of the night!

CHORUS Single-handedly?

BIEDERMANN Yes.

CHORUS Without compunction?

BIEDERMANN Yes.

CHORUS In the middle of the night?

BIEDERMANN Just about to! If my wife hadn't come after me, afraid I'd catch cold— (*Embarrassed, he reaches for a cigar*)

LEADER How shall I put it?
Sleepless he passed the night.
That they'd take advantage of a man's good nature—
Was that conceivable?
Suspicion came over him. Why?
(BIEDERMANN *lights his cigar*)

CHORUS No it's not easy for the citizen,
Tough in business
But really soft of heart,
Always ready,
Ready always to do good.

LEADER If that's how he happens to feel.

CHORUS Hoping that goodness
Will come of goodness.
How mistaken can you be?

BIEDERMANN What are you getting at?

CHORUS It seems to us there's a stink of gasoline.
(BIEDERMANN *sniffs*)

BIEDERMANN I don't smell anything.

CHORUS Woe to us!

BIEDERMANN Not a thing.

CHORUS Woe to us!

LEADER How soon he's got accustomed to bad smells!

CHORUS Woe to us!

BIEDERMANN And don't keep giving us that defeatism, gentlemen. Don't keep saying all the time, "Woe to us!" (*A car honks offstage*) Taxi!—Taxi! (*A car stops offstage*) If you'll excuse me— (*He hurries off*)

CHORUS Citizen—where to?
(*The car drives off*)

LEADER What is his recourse, poor wretch?
Forceful, yet fearful,
Milk-white of face,
Fearful yet firm—
Against what?
(*The car is heard honking*)

CHORUS So soon accustomed to bad smells!
(*The car is heard distantly honking*)
Woe to us!

LEADER Woe to you!
(*The* CHORUS *retires. All but the* LEADER, *who takes out his pipe*)
He who dreads change
More than disaster,
How can he fight
When disaster impends?
(*He follows the* CHORUS *out*)

# Scene Five

## The Attic

EISENRING *is alone, unwinding cord from a reel and singing "Lily Marlene" while he works. He stops whistling, wets his forefinger and holds it up to the dormer window to test the wind.*

## The Living Room

(BIEDERMANN *enters, cigar in mouth, followed by* BABETTE. *He takes off his coat and throws down his briefcase*)

BIEDERMANN Do as I say.

BABETTE A goose?

BIEDERMANN A goose! (*He takes off his tie without removing his cigar*)

BABETTE Why are you taking off your necktie, Gottlieb?

BIEDERMANN If I report those two boys to the police I'll make them my enemies. What good will that do me? Just one match and the whole house is up in flames! What good will that do us? On the other hand, if I go up there and invite them to dinner, why—

BABETTE Why, what?

BIEDERMANN Why, then we'll be friends. (*He takes off his jacket, hands it to* BABETTE *and exits*)

BABETTE (*Speaking to* ANNA, *offstage*) Just so you'll know, Anna: you can't get off this evening—we're having company. Set places for four.

## The Attic

(EISENRING *singing "Lily Marlene." There is a knock at the door*)

EISENRING Come in! (*He goes on singing. No one enters*) Come in! (BIEDERMANN *enters in shirtsleeves, holding his cigar*) Good day, Herr Biedermann!

BIEDERMANN (*Tactfully*) May I come in?

EISENRING I hope you slept well last night?

BIEDERMANN Thank you—miserably.

EISENRING So did I. It's this wind. (*He goes on working with the reel*)

BIEDERMANN If I'm not disturbing you—

EISENRING This is your house, Herr Biedermann.

BIEDERMANN If I'm not in the way— (*The cooing of doves is heard*) Where is our friend?

EISENRING Sepp? He went to work this morning, the lazy dog—he didn't want to go without breakfast! I sent him out for some sawdust.

BIEDERMANN Sawdust?

EISENRING It helps spread the sparks. (BIEDERMANN *laughs politely at what sounds like a poor joke*)

BIEDERMANN I was going to say, Herr Eisenring—

EISENRING That you still want to kick us out?

BIEDERMANN In the middle of the night—I'm out of sleeping pills—it suddenly struck me: you folks have no toilet facilities up here.

EISENRING We have the roof gutter.

BIEDERMANN Well, just as you like, of course. It merely struck me you might like to wash or take a shower— I kept thinking of that all night . . . You're very welcome to use my bathroom. I told Anna to hang up some towels for you there. (EISENRING *shakes his head*) Why do you shake your head?

EISENRING Where on earth did he put it?

BIEDERMANN What?

EISENRING You haven't seen a detonator cap? (*He searches around*) Don't trouble yourself, Herr Biedermann. In jail, you know, we had no bathrooms either.

BIEDERMANN In jail?

EISENRING Didn't Sepp tell you I just came out of prison?

BIEDERMANN No.

EISENRING Not a word about it?

BIEDERMANN No.

EISENRING All he likes to talk about is himself. There *are* such people!— Is it our fault, after all, if his youth was tragic? Did *you* have a tragic youth, Herr Biedermann? *I* didn't. I could have gone to college; my father wanted me to be a lawyer . . . (*He stands at the attic window murmuring to the doves*) Grrr! Grrr! Grrr! (BIEDERMANN *re-lights his cigar*)

BIEDERMANN Frankly, Herr Eisenring, I couldn't sleep all night. Is there really gasoline in those barrels?

EISENRING You don't trust us.

BIEDERMANN I'm merely asking.

EISENRING Herr Biedermann, what do you take us for? Frankly, what sort of people—

BIEDERMANN Herr Eisenring, you mustn't think I have no sense of humor. Only your idea of a joke—well—

EISENRING That's something we've learned.

BIEDERMANN What is?

EISENRING That a joke is first-class camouflage. Next comes sentiment: like when Sepp talks about a childhood in the coal mines, orphanages, circuses and so forth. But the best camouflage of all—in my opinion—is the plain and simple truth. Because nobody ever believes it.

## The Living Room

(ANNA *shows in the* WIDOW KNECHTLING, *dressed in black*)

ANNA Take a seat, please. (*The* WIDOW *sits*) But if you are Frau Knechtling, it's no use. Herr Biedermann wants nothing to do with you, he said. (*The* WIDOW *gets up*) Take a seat, please! (*The* WIDOW *sits down again*) But don't get up any hopes. (ANNA *exits*)

## The Attic

(EISENRING *is busy with one thing or another.* BIEDERMANN *is smoking*)

EISENRING I wonder what's keeping Sepp. Sawdust can't be so hard to find. I hope they haven't nabbed him.

BIEDERMANN Nabbed?

EISENRING Why do you smile?

BIEDERMANN When you use words like that, Herr Eisenring, it's as though you came from another world. Nab him! Like another world! *Our* kind of people seldom get nabbed!

EISENRING Because your kind of people seldom steal sawdust. That's obvious, Herr Biedermann. That's the class difference.

BIEDERMANN Absurd!

EISENRING You don't mean to say, Herr Biedermann—

BIEDERMANN I don't hold with class differences—you must have realized that by now, Herr Eisenring. I'm not old-fashioned—just the opposite, in fact. And I regret that the lower classes still talk about class differences. Aren't we all of us—rich or poor—the creation of one Creator? The middle class, too. Are we not—you and I—human beings, made of flesh and blood? . . . I don't know, sir, whether you smoke cigars— (*He offers one, but* EISENRING *shakes his head*) I don't mean reducing people to a common level, you understand. There will always be rich and poor, Heaven knows—but why can't we just shake hands? A little good will, for Heaven's sake, a little idealism, a little—and we'd all have peace and quiet, both the poor and the rich. Don't you agree?

EISENRING If I may speak frankly, Herr Biedermann—

BIEDERMANN Please do.

EISENRING You won't take it amiss?

BIEDERMANN The more frankly the better.

EISENRING Frankly speaking, you oughtn't to smoke here. (BIEDERMANN, *startled, puts out his cigar*) I can't make rules for you here, Herr Biedermann. After all, it's your house. Still and all—

BIEDERMANN Naturally.

EISENRING (*Looking down*) There it is! (*He takes something off the floor and blows it clean before attaching it to the wire. He starts whistling "Lily Marlene"*)

BIEDERMANN Tell me, Herr Eisenring, what is that you're doing? If I may ask? What is that thing?

EISENRING A detonator.

BIEDERMANN A——?

EISENRING And this is a fuse.

BIEDERMANN A——?

EISENRING Sepp says they've developed better ones lately. But they don't have them yet, in the stores. Buying them's out of the question for us, of course. Anything that has to do with war is frightfully expensive. Always the best quality . . .

BIEDERMANN A fuse, you say?

EISENRING A time-fuse. (*He hands* BIEDERMANN *one end of the cord*) If you'd be kind enough, Herr Biedermann, to hold this end— (BIEDERMANN *holds it for him*)

BIEDERMANN All joking aside, my friend—

EISENRING One second— (*He whistles "Lily Marlene,"*

*measuring the fuse*) Thank you, Herr Biedermann. (BIEDERMANN *suddenly laughs*)

BIEDERMANN Ha, ha! You can't put a scare into me, Willi! Though I must say, you count on people's sense of humor! The way you talk, I can understand your getting arrested now and then. You know, not everybody has my sense of humor!

EISENRING You have to find the right man.

BIEDERMANN At the pub, for instance—just say you believe in the natural goodness of man, and they have you marked down.

EISENRING Ha!

BIEDERMANN And still I won't mention how much I donated to our Fire Department!

EISENRING Ha! (*He puts down the fuse*) Those who have no sense of humor get what's coming to them just the same when the time comes—so don't let *that* worry you. (BIEDERMANN *sits down on a barrel. He has broken into a sweat*) What's the trouble, Herr Biedermann? You've gone quite pale. (*He claps him on the shoulder*) It's the smell. I know, if you're not used to it . . . I'll open the window for you, too. (*He opens the door*)

BIEDERMANN Thanks . . . (ANNA *calls up the stairs*)

ANNA Herr Biedermann! Herr Biedermann!

EISENRING The police again?

ANNA Herr Biedermann!

EISENRING It's a Police State!

ANNA Herr Biedermann—

BIEDERMANN I'm coming! (*They both whisper from here on*) Herr Eisenring, do you like goose?

EISENRING Goose?

BIEDERMANN Roast goose.

EISENRING Why?

BIEDERMANN Stuffed with chestnuts?

EISENRING And red cabbage?

BIEDERMANN Yes . . . I was going to say: my wife and I—I, especially—if we may have the pleasure . . . I don't mean to obtrude, Herr Eisenring, but if you'd care to join us at a little supper, you and Sepp—

EISENRING Today?

BIEDERMANN Or tomorrow, if you prefer—

EISENRING We probably won't stay until tomorrow. But today—of course, Herr Biedermann, with pleasure.

BIEDERMANN Shall we say seven o'clock? (ANNA *calls up the stairs*)

ANNA Herr Biedermann! (*They shake hands*)

BIEDERMANN (*At the door with a twinkle*) All set?

EISENRING All set! (BIEDERMANN *nods genially; then looks once more at the barrels and the fuse*)

EISENRING All set. (BIEDERMANN *exits.* EISENRING *goes to work again, whistling. The* CHORUS *enters as for the end of the scene. They are interrupted by the sound of a crash, as of something falling in the attic*)

## The Attic

EISENRING You can come out, Professor. (*A* PH.D., *wearing horn-rimmed glasses, crawls out of the pile of barrels*) You heard: we're invited to dinner, Sepp and me. You'll keep an eye on things. Nobody's to come in here and smoke, understand? Not before we're ready. (*The* PH.D. *polishes his glasses*) I often ask myself, Professor, why in hell you hang around with us. You don't enjoy a good, crackling fire, or flames, or sparks. Or sirens that go off too late—or dogs barking—or people shrieking—or smoke. Or ashes . . . (*The* PH.D. *solemnly adjusts his glasses.* EISENRING *laughs*) Do-gooder! (*He whistles gently to himself, surveying the* PROFESSOR) I don't like you eggheads— I've told you that before, Professor. You get no real fun out of anything. You're all so idealistic, so solemn . . . You can't be trusted. That's no fun, Professor. (*He goes back to his work, whistling*)

CHORUS Ready for action,
Axes and fire-hose;
Polished and oiled,
Every brass fitting.
Every man of us tested and ready.

LEADER We'll be facing a high wind.

CHORUS Every man of us tested and ready.
Our brass fire-pump
Polished and oiled,
Tested for pressure.

LEADER And the fire-hydrants?

CHORUS Everything ready.

LEADER Tested and ready for action.

(*Enter* BABETTE *with a goose, and the* PH.D.)

BABETTE Yes, Professor, I know, but my husband . . . Yes, I understand it's urgent, Professor. I'll tell him— (*She leaves the* PROFESSOR *and comes to the footlights*) My husband ordered a goose. See, this is it. And I have to roast it, so we can be friends with those people upstairs. (*Church bells ring*) It's Saturday night—you can hear the bells ringing. I have an odd feeling, somehow, that it may be the last time we'll hear them. (BIEDERMANN *calls, "Babette!"*) I don't know ladies, if Gottlieb is always right . . . You know what he says? "Certainly they're scoundrels, Babette, but if I make enemies of them, it's goodbye to our hair tonic!" (BIEDERMANN *calls. "Babette!"*) Gottlieb's like that. Good-hearted. Always too good-hearted! (*She exits with the goose*)

CHORUS This son of good family,
A wearer of glasses,
Pale, studious, trusting,
But trusting no longer
In power of goodness,
Will do anything now, for
Ends justify means.
(So he hopes.)
Ah, honest-dishonest!
Now wiping his glasses
To see things more clearly,

*He* sees no barrels—
No gasoline barrels!
It's an idea he sees—
An abstract conception—
Until it explodes!

PH.D. Good evening . . .

LEADER To the pumps!
The ladders!
The engines!
(*The* FIREMEN *rush to their posts*)

LEADER Good evening.
(*To the audience, as shouts of "Ready!" echo through the theatre*)
We're ready.

## Scene Six

### The Living Room

*The* WIDOW KNECHTLING *is still there, standing and waiting. Outside, the bells are ringing loudly.* ANNA *is setting the table.* BIEDERMANN *brings in two chairs.*

BIEDERMANN You can see, can't you, Frau Knechtling? I haven't time now—no time to think about the dead . . . I told you, go see my lawyer. (*The* WIDOW KNECHTLING *leaves*) You can't hear yourself think, with that noise. Close the window. (ANNA *shuts the window. The sound of the bells is fainter*) I said a simple, informal dinner. What are those idiotic candelabra for?

ANNA But, Herr Biedermann, we always have those!

BIEDERMANN I said simple, informal—not show-off! Fingerbowls! Knife-rests! Nothing but crystal and silver! What does that look like? (*He picks up the knife-rests and shoves them into his pants pocket*) Can't you see I'm wearing my oldest jacket? And you . . . Leave the carving knife, Anna—we'll need it; but away with the rest of this silver! Those two gentlemen must feel at home!—Where's the cork-screw?

ANNA Here.

BIEDERMANN Don't we have anything simpler?

ANNA In the kitchen. But that one is rusty.

BIEDERMANN Bring it here. (*He takes a silver ice-bucket off the table*) What's this for?

ANNA For the wine.

BIEDERMANN Silver! (*He glares at the bucket, then at* ANNA) Do we always use that, too?

ANNA We're going to need it, Herr Biedermann.

BIEDERMANN Humanity, brotherhood—that's what we need here! Away with that thing! And what are those, will you tell me?

ANNA Napkins.

BIEDERMANN Damask napkins!

ANNA We don't have any others. (BIEDERMANN *shoves the napkins into the silver bucket*)

BIEDERMANN There are whole nations, Anna, that live without napkins! (BABETTE *enters with a large wreath.* BIEDERMANN, *standing in front of the table, does not see her come in*) And why a cloth on the table?

BABETTE Gottlieb?

BIEDERMANN Let's have no class distinctions! (*He sees* BABETTE) What is that wreath?

BABETTE It's what we ordered—Gottlieb, what do you think?! They sent the wreath here by mistake! And I gave them the address myself—Knechtling's address—I wrote it down, even! And the ribbon and everything—they've got it all backward!

BIEDERMANN What's wrong with the ribbon?

BABETTE And the clerk says they sent the bill to Frau Knechtling! (*She shows him the ribbon:* "TO OUR DEAR, DEPARTED GOTTLIEB BIEDERMANN." *He considers the ribbon*)

BIEDERMANN We won't accept it, that's all! I should say not! They've got to exchange it! (*He goes back to the table*) Don't upset me, will you, Babette? I can't think of everything— (BABETTE *exits*) Take that tablecloth away. Help me, Anna. And remember —no serving! You come in and put the pan on the table.

ANNA The roast-pan?! (*He takes away the tablecloth*)

BIEDERMANN That's better! A wooden table, that's all. Just a table for supper. (*He hands* ANNA *the tablecloth*)

ANNA You mean that, Herr Biedermann—just bring in the goose in the pan? (*She folds up the tablecloth*) What wine shall I bring?

BIEDERMANN I'll get it myself.

ANNA Herr Biedermann!

BIEDERMANN What now?

ANNA I don't have any sweater, sir—any old sweater, as if I belonged to the family.

BIEDERMANN Borrow one of my wife's.

ANNA The yellow or the red one?

BIEDERMANN Don't be so fussy! No apron or cap, understand? And get rid of these candelabra. And make sure especially, Anna, that everything's not so neat!—I'll be in the cellar. (BIEDERMANN *exits*)

ANNA "Make sure especially, Anna, that everything's not so neat!" (*She throws the tablecloth down on the floor and stomps on it with both feet*) How's that? (SCHMITZ *and* EISENRING *enter, each holding a rose*)

BOTH Good evening, Fräulein. (ANNA *exits without looking at them*)

EISENRING Why no sawdust?

SCHMITZ Confiscated. Police measure. Precaution. They're picking up anybody who sells or owns sawdust without written permission. Precautions all over the place. (*He combs his hair*)

EISENRING Have you got matches?

SCHMITZ No.

EISENRING Neither have I. (SCHMITZ *blows his comb clean*)

SCHMITZ We'll have to ask him for them.

EISENRING Biedermann?

SCHMITZ Don't forget. (*He puts away his comb and sniffs*) Mmm! That smells good!

## Scene Seven

BIEDERMANN *comes to the footlights with a bottle.*

BIEDERMANN You can think what you like about me, gentlemen. But just answer one question— (*Laughter and loud voices offstage*) I say to myself: as long as they're laughing and drinking, we're safe. The best bottles out of my cellar! I tell you, if anybody had told me a week ago . . . When did *you* guess they were arsonists, gentlemen? This sort of thing doesn't happen the way you think. It comes on you slowly—slowly, at first—then sudden suspicion! Though I was suspicious at once—one's always suspicious! But tell me the truth, sirs—what would *you* have done? If you were in my place, for God's sake? And when? *When* would you have done it? At what point? (*He waits for an answer. Silence*) I've got to go. (*He leaves the stage quickly*)

## Scene Eight

### The Living Room

*The dinner is in full swing. Laughter.* BIEDERMANN, *especially, cannot contain himself at the joke he's just heard. Only* BABETTE *is not laughing.*

BIEDERMANN Oil waste! Did you hear that, Babette? Oil waste, he says! Oil waste burns better!

BABETTE I don't see what's funny.

BIEDERMANN Oil waste! You know what that is?

BABETTE Yes.

BIEDERMANN You have no sense of humor, Babette. (*He puts the bottle on the table*)

BABETTE All right, then, explain it.

BIEDERMANN Okay!—This morning Willi told Sepp to go out and steal some sawdust. Sawdust—get it? And just now, when I asked Sepp if he got any, he said he couldn't find any sawdust—he found some oil waste instead. Get it? And Willi says, "Oil waste burns better!"

BABETTE I understood all that.

BIEDERMANN You did?

BABETTE What's funny about it? (BIEDERMANN *gives up*)

BIEDERMANN Let's drink, men! (BIEDERMANN *removes the cork from the bottle*)

BABETTE Is that the truth, Herr Schmitz? Did you bring oil waste up to our attic?

BIEDERMANN This will kill you, Babette! This morning we even measured the fuse together, Willi and I!

BABETTE The fuse?

BIEDERMANN The time-fuse. (*He fills the glasses*)

BABETTE Seriously—what does that mean? (BIEDERMANN *laughs*)

BIEDERMANN Seriously! You hear that? Seriously! . . . Don't let them kid you, Babette. I told you—our friends have their own way of kidding! Different company, different jokes—that's what I always say . . . All we need now is to have them ask me for matches! (SCHMITZ *and* EISENRING *exchange glances*) These gentlemen took me for some Milquetoast, for some dope without humor— (*He lifts his glass*) Prosit!

EISENRING Prosit!

SCHMITZ Prosit!

BIEDERMANN To our friendship! (*They drink the toast standing up, then sit down again*) We're not doing serving. Just help yourselves, gentlemen.

SCHMITZ I can't eat any more.

EISENRING Don't restrain yourself, Sepp, you're not at the orphanage. (*He helps himself to more goose*) Your goose is wonderful, madam.

BABETTE I'm glad to hear it.

EISENRING Roast goose and stuffing! Now all we need is a tablecloth.

BABETTE You hear that, Gottlieb?

EISENRING We don't have to have one. Not one of those tablecloths, white damask, with silverware on it—

BIEDERMANN (*Loudly*) Anna!

EISENRING Damask, with flowers all over it—a white flower pattern—we don't have to have one. We didn't have any in prison.

BABETTE In prison?

BIEDERMANN Where is that girl?

BABETTE Have you been in prison? (ANNA *enters. She is wearing a bright red sweater*)

BIEDERMANN A tablecloth here—immediately!

ANNA Yes sir.

BIEDERMANN And if you have some fingerbowls or something—

ANNA Yes sir.

EISENRING Madam, you may think it's childish, but that's how the little man is. Take Sepp, for instance—he grew up in the coal mines, but it's the dream of his miserable life, a table like this, with crystal and silver! Would you believe it? He never heard of a knife-rest!

BABETTE But, Gottlieb, we have all those things!

EISENRING Of course we don't *have* to have them here—

ANNA Very well.

EISENRING If you have any napkins, Fräulein, out with them!

ANNA But Herr Biedermann said—

BIEDERMANN Out with them!

ANNA Yes sir. (*She starts to bring back the table service*)

EISENRING I hope you won't take it amiss, madam, but when you're just out of prison—months at a time with no refinement whatever— (*He shows the tablecloth to* SCHMITZ) You know what this is? (*To* BABETTE) He never saw one before! (*He turns back to* SCHMITZ) This is damask!

SCHMITZ What do you want me to do with it? (EISENRING *ties the tablecloth around his neck*)

EISENRING There— (BIEDERMANN *tries to find this amusing. He laughs*)

BABETTE Where are the knife-rests, Anna?

ANNA Herr Biedermann—

BIEDERMANN Out with them!

ANNA But you said "Take them away!" before!

BIEDERMANN Bring them here, I tell you! Where are they, goddamit?

ANNA In your pants pocket. (BIEDERMANN *reaches in his pants pocket and finds them*)

EISENRING Don't get excited.

ANNA I can't help it!

EISENRING No excitement, now, Fräulein— (ANNA *bursts into sobs and runs out*)

EISENRING It's this wind. (*Pause*)

BIEDERMANN Drink up, friends! (*They drink. A silence*)

EISENRING I ate roast goose every day when I was a waiter. I used to flit down those corridors holding a platter like this . . . How do you suppose, madam, waiters clean off their hands? In their hair, that's how —while there's others who use crystal fingerbowls. That's something I'll never forget. (*He dips his fingers in the fingerbowl*) Have you ever heard of a trauma?

BIEDERMANN No.

EISENRING I learned all about it in jail. (*He wipes his fingers dry*)

BABETTE And how did you happen to be there, Herr Eisenring?

BIEDERMANN Babette!

EISENRING How did I get into jail?

BIEDERMANN One doesn't ask questions like that!

EISENRING I wonder at that myself . . . I was a waiter —a little head waiter. Suddenly they made me out a great arsonist.

BIEDERMANN Hm.

EISENRING They called for me at my own home.

BIEDERMANN Hm.

EISENRING I was so amazed, I gave in.

BIEDERMANN Hm.

EISENRING I had luck, madam—seven really charming policemen. I said, "I have no time—I have to go to work." They answered, "Your restaurant's burned to the ground."

BIEDERMANN Burned to the ground?

EISENRING Overnight, apparently.

BABETTE Burned to the ground?

EISENRING "Fine," I said, "Then I *have* time . . ." Just a black, smoking hulk—that's all that was left of that place. I saw it as we drove by. Through those windows, you know, the little barred windows they have in those prison vans— (*He sips his wine delicately*)

BIEDERMANN And then? (EISENRING *studies the wine-label*)

EISENRING We used to keep this, too: '49, Cave de l'Echannon . . . And then? Let Sepp tell you the rest—As I was sitting in that police station, playing with my handcuffs, who do you think they brought in? —That one, there! (SCHMITZ *beams*) Prosit, Sepp!

SCHMITZ Prosit, Willi! (*They drink*)

BIEDERMANN And then?

SCHMITZ "Are you the firebug?" they asked him, and offered him cigarettes. He said, "Excuse me, I have no matches, Herr Commissioner, although you think I'm a firebug—" (*They laugh uproariously and slap each other's thighs*)

BIEDERMANN Hm. (ANNA *enters, in cap and apron again. She hands* BIEDERMANN *a visiting card*)

ANNA It's urgent, he says.

BIEDERMANN When I have visitors— (SCHMITZ *and* EISENRING *clink glasses again*)

SCHMITZ Prosit, Willi!

EISENRING Prosit, Sepp! (*They drink.* BIEDERMANN *studies the visiting card*)

BABETTE Who is it, Gottlieb?

BIEDERMANN It's a professor . . . (ANNA *is busy at the sideboard*)

EISENRING And what are those other things, Fräulein —those silver things?

ANNA The candlesticks?

EISENRING Why do you hide them?

BIEDERMANN Bring them here!

ANNA But you said, yourself, Herr Biedermann—

BIEDERMANN I say bring them here! (ANNA *places the candelabra on the table*)

EISENRING What do you say to that, Sepp? They have candlesticks and they hide them! Real silver candlesticks—what more do you want?—Have you a match? (*He reaches into his pants pocket*)

SCHMITZ Me? No. (*He reaches into his pants pocket*)

EISENRING Sorry, no matches, Herr Biedermann.

BIEDERMANN I have some.

EISENRING Let's have them.

BIEDERMANN I'll light the candles. Let me—I'll do it. (*He begins lighting the candles*)

BABETTE (*To* ANNA) What does the visitor want?

ANNA I don't know, ma'am. He says he can no longer be silent. And he's waiting on the stoop.

BABETTE It's private, he says?

ANNA Yes, ma'am. He says he has a revelation to make.

BABETTE A revelation?

ANNA That's how he talks. I can't follow it, even when he repeats it. He wants to remove himself, so he says . . . (BIEDERMANN *is still lighting candles*)

EISENRING It creates an atmosphere, doesn't it, madam? Candlelight, I mean.

BABETTE Yes, it does.

EISENRING I'm all for atmosphere. Refined, candlelight atmosphere—

BIEDERMANN I'm happy to know that. (*All the candles are lit*)

EISENRING Schmitz, don't smack your lips when you eat! (BABETTE *takes* EISENRING *aside*)

BABETTE Let him alone!

EISENRING He has no manners, madam. Excuse me—it's awful. But where could he have picked up any manners? From the coal mines to the orphanage—

BABETTE I know.

EISENRING From the orphanage to the circus.

BABETTE I know.

EISENRING From the circus to the theatre—

BABETTE I didn't know.

EISENRING A football of fate, madam. (BABETTE *turns to* SCHMITZ)

BABETTE In the theatre! Were you, really? (SCHMITZ *gnaws on a drumstick and nods*) Where?

SCHMITZ Upstage.

EISENRING Really talented, too! Sepp as a ghost! Can you imagine it?

SCHMITZ Not any more, though.

EISENRING Why not?

SCHMITZ I was in the theatre only a week, madam, before it burned to the ground.

BABETTE Burned to the ground?

EISENRING (*To* SCHMITZ) Don't be so diffident!

BIEDERMANN Burned to the ground?

EISENRING Don't be so diffident! (*He unties the tablecloth* SCHMITZ *has been wearing and throws it over* SCHMITZ*'s head*) Come on! (SCHMITZ *gets up with the tablecloth over him*) Doesn't he look like a ghost?

ANNA I'm frightened!

EISENRING Come here, little girl! (*He pulls* ANNA *onto his lap. She hides her face in her hands*)

SCHMITZ "Who calleth?"

EISENRING That's theatre language, madam. They call that a cue. He learned it in less than a week, before the theatre burned down.

BABETTE Please don't keep talking of fires!

SCHMITZ "Who calleth?"

EISENRING Ready— (*Everybody waits expectantly.* EISENRING *has a tight grip on* ANNA)

SCHMITZ "EVERYMAN! EVERYMAN!"

BABETTE Gottlieb?

BIEDERMANN Quiet!

BABETTE We saw that in Salzburg!

SCHMITZ "BIEDERMANN! BIEDERMANN!"

EISENRING He's terrific!

SCHMITZ "BIEDERMANN! BIEDERMANN!"

EISENRING You must say, "Who are you?"

BIEDERMANN Me?

EISENRING Or he can't say his lines.

SCHMITZ "EVERYMAN! BIEDERMANN!"

BIEDERMANN All right, then—who am I?

BABETTE No! You must ask him who *he* is.

BIEDERMANN I see.

SCHMITZ "DOST THOU HEAR ME?"

EISENRING No, no, Sepp—start it again. (*They change their positions*)

SCHMITZ "EVERYMAN! BIEDERMANN!"

BABETTE Are you the Angel of Death, maybe?

BIEDERMANN Nonsense!

BABETTE What else *could* he be?

BIEDERMANN Ask him. He might be the ghost in "Hamlet." Or that other one—what's-his-name—in "Macbeth."

SCHMITZ "WHO CALLS ME?"

EISENRING Go on.

SCHMITZ "GOTTLIEB BIEDERMANN!"

BABETTE Go ahead, ask him. He's talking to you.

SCHMITZ "DOST THOU HEAR ME?"

BIEDERMANN Who are you?

SCHMITZ "I AM THE GHOST OF—KNECHTLING." (BABETTE *springs up with a scream*)

EISENRING Stop! (*He pulls the tablecloth off* SCHMITZ) Idiot! How could you do such a thing? Knechtling was buried today!

SCHMITZ That's why I thought of him. (BABETTE *hides her face in her hands*)

EISENRING He's not Knechtling, madam. (*He shakes his head over* SCHMITZ) What crudeness!

SCHMITZ He was on my mind . . .

EISENRING Of all things—Knechtling! Herr Biedermann's best old employee! Imagine it: buried today—cold and stiff—not yet mouldy—pale as this tablecloth—white and shiny as damask— To go and act Knechtling— (*He takes* BABETTE *by the shoulder*) Honest to God, madam, it's Sepp—it's not Knechtling at all. (SCHMITZ *wipes off his sweat*)

SCHMITZ I'm sorry . . .

BIEDERMANN Let's sit down again.

ANNA Is it over?

BIEDERMANN Would you care for cigars, sirs? (*He offers a box of cigars*)

EISENRING (*To* SCHMITZ) Idiot! You see how Herr Biedermann is shaking! . . . Thank you, Herr Biedermann!—You think that's funny, Sepp? When you know very well that Knechtling laid his head over a gas jet? After everything Gottlieb did for him? He gave this Knechtling fourteen years' work—and this is his thanks!

BIEDERMANN Let's not talk about it.

EISENRING (*To* SCHMITZ) And that's your thanks for the goose! (*They attend to their cigars*)

SCHMITZ Would you like me to sing something?

EISENRING What?

SCHMITZ "Fox, you stole that lovely goosie . . ." (*He sings loudly*)

"Fox, you stole that lovely goosie,
Give it back again!"

EISENRING That's enough.

SCHMITZ "Give it back again!
Or they'll get you in the shnoosie—"

EISENRING He's drunk.

SCHMITZ "With their shooting-gun!"

EISENRING Pay no attention to him.

SCHMITZ "Give it back again!
Or they'll get you in the shnoosie
With their shooting-gun!"

BIEDERMANN "Shooting-gun!" That's good! (*The men all join in the song*)
"Fox, you stole that lovely goosie . . ."
(*They harmonize, now loudly, now softly. Laughter and loud cheer. There is a pause, and* BIEDERMANN *picks up again, leading the hilarity until they've all had it*)

BIEDERMANN So— Prosit! (*They raise their glasses. Fire sirens are heard near by*) What was that?

EISENRING Sirens.

BIEDERMANN Joking aside—

BABETTE Firebugs! Firebugs!

BIEDERMANN Don't yell like that! (BABETTE *runs to the window and throws it open. The sound of the sirens comes nearer, with a howl that goes to the marrow. The fire engines roar past*)

BIEDERMANN At least it's not here.

BABETTE I wonder where?

EISENRING From where the wind is blowing.

BIEDERMANN Not here, anyway.

EISENRING That's how we generally work it. Coax the Fire Department out to some cheap suburb or other, and then, when things really let loose, they find their way blocked.

BIEDERMANN No, gentlemen—all joking aside—

SCHMITZ That's how we do it—joking aside—

BIEDERMANN Please—enough of this nonsense! Don't overdo it! Look at my wife—white as chalk!

BABETTE And you too!

BIEDERMANN Besides, a fire alarm is nothing to laugh at, gentlemen. Somewhere some place is burning, or the Fire Department wouldn't be rushing there. (EISENRING *looks at his watch*)

EISENRING We've got to go, now.

BIEDERMANN Now?

EISENRING Sorry.

SCHMITZ "Or they'll get you in the shnoosie . . ." (*The sirens are heard again*)

BIEDERMANN Bring us some coffee, Babette! (BABETTE *goes out*) And you, Anna—do you have to stand there and gape? (ANNA *goes out*) Just between us, gentlemen: enough is enough. My wife has a heart condition. Let's have no more joking about fires.

SCHMITZ We're not joking, Herr Biedermann.

EISENRING We're firebugs.

BIEDERMANN No, gentlemen, quite seriously—

EISENRING Quite seriously.

SCHMITZ Yeah, quite seriously. Why don't you believe us?

EISENRING Your house is very favorably situated, Herr Biedermann, you must admit that. Five villas like yours around the gas works . . . It's true they keep a close watch on the gas works. Still, there's a good stiff wind blowing—

BIEDERMANN It can't be—

SCHMITZ Let's have plain talk! You think we're firebugs—

BIEDERMANN (*Like a whipped dog*) No, no, I don't think you are! You do me an injustice, gentlemen—I don't think you're firebugs . . .

EISENRING You swear you don't?

BIEDERMANN No! No! No! I don't believe it!

SCHMITZ What *do* you think we are?

BIEDERMANN You're my friends . . . (*They clap him on the shoulder and start to leave*)

EISENRING It's time to leave.

BIEDERMANN Gentlemen, I swear to you by all that's holy—

EISENRING By all that's holy?

BIEDERMANN Yes. (*He raises his hand as though to take an oath*)

SCHMITZ Willi doesn't believe in anything holy, Herr Biedermann. Any more than you do. You'll waste your time swearing. (*They go to the door*)

BIEDERMANN What can I do to make you believe me? (*He blocks the doorway*)

EISENRING Give us some matches.

BIEDERMANN Some—

EISENRING We have no more matches.

BIEDERMANN You want me to—

EISENRING If you don't think we're firebugs.

BIEDERMANN Matches—

SCHMITZ To show your belief in us, he means. (BIEDERMANN *reaches in his pocket*)

EISENBERG See how he hesitates?

BIEDERMANN Sh! Not in front of my wife . . . (BABETTE *returns*)

BABETTE Your coffee will be ready in a minute. (*Pause*) Must you go?

BIEDERMANN (*Formally*) At least you've felt, while here, my friends . . . I don't want to make a speech on this occasion, but may we not drink, before you go, to our eternal friendship? (*He picks up a bottle and the corkscrew*)

EISENRING Tell your very charming husband, madam, that he needn't open any more bottles on our account. It isn't worth the trouble any more.

BIEDERMANN It's no trouble, my friends, no trouble at all. If there's anything else you'd like—anything at all— (*He fills the glasses once more and hands them out*) My friends! (*They clink glasses*) Sepp—Willi— (*He kisses them each on the cheek. All drink*)

EISENRING Just the same, we must go now.

SCHMITZ Unfortunately.

EISENRING Madam— (*Sirens*)

BABETTE It's been such a nice evening. (*Alarm bells*)

EISENRING Just one thing, now, Gottlieb—

BIEDERMANN What is it?

EISENRING I've mentioned it to you before.

BIEDERMANN Anything you like. Just name it.

EISENRING The matches. (ANNA *has entered with coffee*)

BABETTE Why, what is it, Anna?

ANNA The coffee.

BABETTE You're all upset, Anna!

ANNA Back there—Frau Biedermann—the sky! You can see it from the kitchen—the whole sky is burning, Frau Biedermann! (*The scene is turning red as*

SCHMITZ *and* EISENRING *make their bows and exit.* BIEDERMANN *is left pale and shaken*)

BIEDERMANN Not our house, fortunately . . . Not our house . . . Not our . . . (*The* PH.D. *enters*) Who are you, and what do you want?

PH.D. I can no longer be silent. (*He takes out a paper and reads*) "Cognizant of the events now transpiring, whose iniquitous nature must be readily apparent, the undersigned submits to the authorities the subsequent statement . . ." (*Amid the shrieking of sirens he reads an involved statement, of which no one understands a word. Dogs howl, bells ring, there is the scream of departing sirens and the crackling of flames. The* PH.D. *hands* BIEDERMANN *the paper*) I remove myself . . .

BIEDERMANN But—

PH.D. I have said my say. (*He takes off and folds up his glasses*) Sir, as a serious-minded uplifter, I knew what they were doing in your attic. I did *not* know, however, that they were doing it just for fun!

BIEDERMANN Professor— (*The* PH.D. *removes himself*) What will I do with this, Professor? (*The* PH.D. *climbs over the footlights and takes a seat in the audience*)

BABETTE Gottlieb—

BIEDERMANN He's gone.

BABETTE What did you give them? Matches? Not matches?

BIEDERMANN Why not?

BABETTE Not matches?

BIEDERMANN If they really were firebugs, do you think they wouldn't have matches? Don't be foolish, Babette! (*The clock strikes. Silence. The red light onstage begins deepening into blackness. Sirens. Bells ring. Dogs howl. Cars honk . . . A crash of collapsing buildings. A crackling of flames. Screams and outcries . . . fading. The* CHORUS *comes on again*)

CHORUS Useless, quite useless.
And nothing more useless
Than this useless story.
For arson, once kindled,
Kills many,
Leaves few,
And accomplishes nothing.
(*First detonation*)

LEADER That was the gas works.
(*Second detonation*)

CHORUS Long foreseen, disaster
Has reached us at last.
Horrendous arson!
Unquenchable fire!
Fate—so they call it!
(*Third detonation*)

LEADER More gas tanks.
(*There is a series of frightful explosions*)

CHORUS Woe to us! Woe to us! Woe!
(*The house lights go up*)

# Scene Nine

## Epilog

### CHARACTERS OF THE EPILOG

HERR BIEDERMANN
BABETTE
ANNA
BEELZEBUB
A PERSONAGE
A POLICEMAN
A RING-TAILED MONKEY
THE WIDOW KNECHTLING
THE CHORUS

BABETTE *and* BIEDERMANN *are revealed, standing in the same positions as at the end of the previous scene.*

BABETTE Gottlieb?

BIEDERMANN Sh!

BABETTE Are we dead? (*A parrot screeches*)

BIEDERMANN Why didn't you come down before the stairs caught fire? Why did you run to our bedroom again?

BABETTE I went back for my jewelry.

BIEDERMANN Of course we're dead. (*The parrot squawks*)

BABETTE Gottlieb?

BIEDERMANN Quiet, now.

BABETTE Where are we?

BIEDERMANN In heaven, of course. Where else? (*A baby cries*)

BABETTE I never imagined heaven was like this. (*The baby cries again*)

BIEDERMANN Don't lose your faith at a time like this!

BABETTE Did *you* imagine it this way? (*The parrot screeches*) Gottlieb?

BIEDERMANN Don't lose your faith at a time like this.

BABETTE We've been waiting half an eternity. (*The baby cries*) And now that baby again! (*The parrot screeches*) Gottlieb?

BIEDERMANN What now?

BABETTE How did that parrot get into heaven? (*A doorbell rings*)

BIEDERMANN Don't upset me, Babette. Why can't a parrot go to heaven? If he's led a good life? (*The doorbell rings again*) What was that?

BABETTE Our doorbell.

BIEDERMANN Who can *that* be? (*The baby, the bell and the parrot all sound off together*)

BABETTE Who needs that parrot? And that baby, too! I won't be able to take it, Gottlieb—a racket like that, forever! Why, it's just like the slums!

BIEDERMANN Sh!

BABETTE They can't expect us to—

BIEDERMANN Calm down.

BABETTE People like us are not used to it.

BIEDERMANN (*Considering it*) Why wouldn't we be in heaven? Everybody we know is there—even my lawyer. This *must* be heaven! We've done nothing wrong— (*The doorbell rings*)

BABETTE Shouldn't we answer the doorbell? (*It rings again*) How did they get hold of our bell? (*It rings again*) Maybe an angel calling . . .

BIEDERMANN I'm perfectly innocent. I honored my father and mother—you know that, Babette. Especially Mother—you were sore about that often enough. I never made a graven image of God—never thought of it, even. I never stole; we always had what we needed. I never killed anybody. I never worked Sundays. I never coveted my neighbor's house. Or if I did, I paid cash for it. Buying's permitted, I'm sure. And I never caught myself lying. I never committed adultery, Babette—I mean it; compared with others, at least . . . You are my witness, Babette, before the angels. I had only one earthly fault: I was too good-hearted. (*The parrot screeches*)

BABETTE Can you understand what it's saying?

BIEDERMANN Did *you* kill anybody, Babette? I'm only asking, that's all. Or worship other gods? Outside of a little Yoga? Did you ever commit adultery?

BABETTE With whom?

BIEDERMANN Well, then— (*The doorbell rings*) We *must* be in heaven. (ANNA *enters in cap and apron*)

BABETTE How did Anna get into heaven? (ANNA *walks past. She has long, green hair*) I hope she didn't notice that you gave them the matches. She might report it.

BIEDERMANN The matches!

BABETTE I warned you they were firebugs, Gottlieb. I warned you from the beginning. (ANNA *comes back with a* POLICEMAN. *The* POLICEMAN *has little white wings*)

ANNA I'll call him. (*She exits. The* POLICEMAN *waits*)

BIEDERMANN You see? An angel. (*The* POLICEMAN *salutes*)

BABETTE I thought angels looked different.

BIEDERMANN This isn't the Middle Ages.

BABETTE Didn't *you* think they looked different? (*The* POLICEMAN *turns around. Continues to wait*) Should we kneel, do you think?

BIEDERMANN Ask him if this is heaven. (*Encouraging her with a nod*) We've been waiting half an eternity, tell him.

BABETTE My husband and I—

BIEDERMANN Tell him we're victims.

BABETTE My husband and I are victims.

BIEDERMANN Our house is ruined.

BABETTE My husband and I—

BIEDERMANN Tell him!

BABETTE Ruined.

BIEDERMAN He simply can't imagine what we've gone through. Tell him! We've lost everything, tell him. And it's in no way our fault.

BABETTE You can't imagine—

BIEDERMANN What we've gone through.

BABETTE All my jewelry melted.

BIEDERMANN Tell him we're innocent.

BABETTE Besides, we're innocent.

BIEDERMANN Compared with others.

BABETTE Compared with others. (*The* ANGEL-POLICEMAN *takes out a cigar*)

POLICEMAN Have you a match? (BIEDERMANN *turns pale*)

BIEDERMANN I? A match? (*A tongue of flame shoots up from the ground*)

POLICEMAN I've got a light, thanks. Never mind. (BABETTE *and* BIEDERMANN *stare at the flame, astonished*)

BABETTE Gottlieb—

BIEDERMANN Quiet!

BABETTE What does all this mean? (*Enter a* RING-TAILED MONKEY)

MONKEY Who are these people?

POLICEMAN A couple of the damned. (*He hands over a report. The* MONKEY *puts on his glasses*)

BABETTE Gottlieb, we know him!

BIEDERMANN Where from?

BABETTE The professor. Don't you remember? (*The* MONKEY *leafs through the report*)

MONKEY How are things upstairs?

POLICEMAN No use complaining. Nobody knows where God lives, but otherwise everything's fine. No use complaining, thank you.

MONKEY (*Indicating the report*) Why was this bunch sent here? (*The* POLICEMAN *glances at the report*)

POLICEMAN Freethinkers. (*The* MONKEY *has ten rubber stamps. He chooses from them, stamping each document*)

MONKEY "THOU SHALT HAVE NO OTHER GODS BEFORE ME."

POLICEMAN A doctor who gave wrong injections.

MONKEY "THOU SHALT NOT KILL."

POLICEMAN A board chairman with seven secretaries —all blonde.

MONKEY "THOU SHALT NOT COMMIT ADULTERY."

POLICEMAN An abortionist.

MONKEY "THOU SHALT NOT KILL."

POLICEMAN A drunk driver.

MONKEY "THOU SHALT NOT KILL."

POLICEMAN Refugees.

MONKEY What's their sin?

POLICEMAN Fifty-two potatoes, one umbrella, two wool blankets.

MONKEY "THOU SHALT NOT STEAL."

POLICEMAN A tax consultant.

MONKEY "THOU SHALT NOT BEAR FALSE WITNESS."

POLICEMAN Another drunk driver. (*The* MONKEY *stamps the paper silently*) Another freethinker. (*Ditto*) Seven underground fighters. Sent to heaven by mistake. They were caught and shot by a firing squad; but it seems they did some so-called liberating before then.

MONKEY Hm.

POLICEMAN Liberating while out of uniform.

MONKEY "THOU SHALT NOT STEAL."

POLICEMAN Another abortionist.

MONKEY "THOU SHALT NOT KILL."

POLICEMAN And here's the rest.

MONKEY "THOU SHALT NOT COMMIT ADULTERY." (*He stamps at least thirteen more reports*) Nothing but middle-class! Old Nick will be furious! And all these juvenile delinquents! I'm almost afraid of turning in this report! No general, no cabinet minister—not one celebrity in the lot!

POLICEMAN Ts. Ts.

MONKEY Take them down below. Beelzebub's already got the heat turned on, I think, or is about to. (THE POLICEMAN *salutes and exits*)

BABETTE Gottlieb, we are in hell!

BIEDERMANN Don't scream like that.

BABETTE Gottlieb— (*She breaks into sobs*)

BIEDERMANN There's something wrong here, Professor—it's got to be changed. How is it we're in hell, my wife and I? (*To* BABETTE) Keep calm, Babette, this *must* be a mistake. (*To the* MONKEY) Let me speak with the Devil.

BABETTE Gottlieb—

BIEDERMANN May I speak with the Devil, please?

MONKEY (*With a gesture*) Sit down, please. (BIEDERMANN *and* BABETTE *see no seats to sit down on*) What do you want to see him about? (BIEDERMANN *hands him a card*) What is that?

BIEDERMANN Driver's license—identification.

MONKEY Not required. (*He returns it without looking at it*) You're Gottlieb Biedermann? Manufacturer? Big bank account?

BIEDERMANN How did you know?

MONKEY Number 33 Rosenweg? The Devil knows you well. (BABETTE *and* BIEDERMANN *look at each other*) Take seats, please. (*Two burned chairs appear onstage*)

BABETTE Gottlieb—our chairs!

MONKEY Sit down, please. (*They sit*) Do you smoke?

BIEDERMANN Not any more.

MONKEY Your own cigars, you know. (*He helps himself to a cigar*) They were burned, too. I'm sure that doesn't surprise you. (*Flames shoot up from the floor*) I have a light, thank you. (*He lights his cigar and takes a puff*) Now come to the point—what is it you want? Some bread? Some wine, maybe?

BIEDERMANN We have no place to sleep! (*The* MONKEY *calls*)

MONKEY Anna!

BABETTE We're not beggars, we're victims.

BIEDERMANN We don't want charity. We're not used to it.

BABETTE And we don't need it. (ANNA *appears*)

ANNA Yes?

MONKEY They don't want charity.

ANNA That's all right, then. (*She exits*)

BABETTE We had our own home.

BIEDERMANN We demand compensation! (*The* MONKEY *withdraws without answering, as is the way of bureaucrats*)

BABETTE What does he mean, "The Devil knows you"?

BIEDERMANN How should *I* know? (*A pendulum clock strikes*)

BABETTE Our grandfather clock! (*It strikes nine*)

BIEDERMANN I shall insist that everything be put back where it was! We were insured! (*The* MONKEY *returns from stage left*)

MONKEY One moment, please. (*Exits stage right*)

BIEDERMANN These devils put on an act!

BABETTE Sh!

BIEDERMANN Next thing you know they'll ask for our fingerprints, like the police. To try and give us a bad conscience. (BABETTE *puts her hand on his arm comfortingly*) My conscience is clear. So is yours—

BABETTE What if they ask about the matches?

BIEDERMANN I gave those boys matches, that's true. But what of it? So did everybody else. Or the whole city wouldn't have burned down the way it did. I saw the flames spring out over every roof . . . And don't forget I acted in good faith!

BABETTE You're too excited.

BIEDERMANN And even if everybody did it, you can't throw everybody into hell! What about forgiveness? (*The* MONKEY *returns*)

MONKEY The Lord of the Underworld isn't back yet. Would you care to speak with Beelzebub instead?

BABETTE Beelzebub?

MONKEY He's around. But I warn you he smells something awful. He's the one with the horns, the hoofs and the tail . . . But don't expect much from *him*, madam—a poor devil like Sepp!

BIEDERMANN Sepp? (BABETTE *jumps up in alarm*)

BABETTE Gottlieb, what did I tell you?

BIEDERMANN Babette! (*He gives her a look that sits her down again*) My wife couldn't sleep nights. That's when you toss and worry. But by day, Professor, we had no ground for suspicion—none whatever. (BABETTE *gives him a look*) At least *I* didn't.

BABETTE Then why were you going to throw them out of the house?

BIEDERMANN I didn't throw them out.

BABETTE That's just it.

BIEDERMANN Why didn't *you* throw them out? Instead of feeding them toast and marmalade and soft-boiled eggs? (*The* MONKEY *puffs at his cigar*) To be brief, Professor, we had no idea what was going on at home. No idea. (*Trumpets sound*)

MONKEY That's him—the Lord of the Underworld. (*Trumpets*) In a terrible temper, no doubt. He's been up to heaven; probably had another tough session.

BIEDERMANN On my account?

MONKEY On account of this last amnesty . . . (*He whispers in* BIEDERMANN*'s ear*)

BIEDERMANN I've heard about that.

MONKEY And what do you say to this? (*He whispers again*)

BIEDERMANN You think so?

MONKEY If heaven thinks we're going to stand for anything and everything— (*He whispers again*)

BIEDERMANN You mean it? (*Trumpets*)

MONKEY He's coming! (*The* MONKEY *exits*)

BABETTE What did he say?

BIEDERMANN They may close the doors of hell; no more people admitted. Because hell is going on strike.

(*Doorbell rings*) He says they're furious down here. They've been expecting a whole army of big shots, and it seems heaven has pardoned them all. He says it's a hell of a crisis. (ANNA *crosses from left to right*) What's Anna doing here?

BABETTE I didn't tell you: she stole a pair of my new nylons. (ANNA *comes in with the* WIDOW KNECHTLING)

ANNA Sit down, please. But don't get up any hopes: your husband committed suicide, you know. (ANNA *exits. The* WIDOW *remains standing, there being no more seats*)

BABETTE It's Frau Knechtling! What does she want here? (*She gives the* WIDOW *a smile*) She's going to testify against us, Gottlieb.

BIEDERMANN Let her! (*The trumpets sound closer*) Why couldn't Knechtling have waited a week or two? He could have taken me aside at a favorable moment and talked it over, couldn't he? How could I know he was going to commit suicide just because I gave him his notice? (*The trumpets sound closer*) I'm not worried. (*The trumpets sound closer*) Those matches!

BABETTE Maybe nobody saw you.

BIEDERMANN There've always been disasters! Always were and always will be! . . . Besides, look at our city now—everything glass and aluminum! In fact it's a blessing, really, that the town burned down. From the standpoint of city planning . . . (*Trumpets, then organ music. Enter a* PERSONAGE, *pompous and resplendent, in a costume slightly reminiscent of a bishop.* BIEDERMANN *and* BABETTE *kneel at the footlights. The* PERSONAGE *takes center stage*)

PERSONAGE (*Calls*) Anna! (*He starts to take off his violet gloves*) I'm back from heaven.

BIEDERMANN (*To* BABETTE) You hear that?

PERSONAGE It's hopeless. (*He calls*) Anna! (*He goes on taking off his gloves*) I wonder if it really was heaven I saw—even though they told me it was. They had incense coming out of loudspeakers. And the medals on everybody! My old friends, the mass-murderers, with chests full of medals! And the angels hovering over them, full of smiles! Everybody chatting, strolling, drinking toasts! The saints had nothing to say; they're made of wood, on permanent loan from somewhere. As for the princes of the church—I tried to ask them where God lives, but they shut up, too, even though they're *not* made of wood . . . (*He calls*) Anna! (*He removes his hood. It is* EISENRING) I was disguised, of course. And the folks who are running things up there—and are busy blessing themselves—didn't recognize me. I added my blessing . . . (ANNA *and the* MONKEY *enter and bow*) Remove this clothing. (*The* PERSONAGE *holds out his arms to permit his four silken garments, one over the other, to be unbuttoned. These are, in order, silver, gold, violet and blood-red. The organ music ends.* BIEDERMANN *and* BABETTE *continue to kneel*) Bring my tail-coat.

ANNA Yes sir.

PERSONAGE And my head-waiter's wig. (ANNA *and the* MONKEY *remove his first garment*) I have some doubts whether it was God Himself who received me. He knew everything, and when He spoke He said exactly what the newspapers say, word for word. (*The parrot shrieks*) Where is Beelzebub?

MONKEY At the furnaces.

PERSONAGE Let him appear. (*The stage suddenly turns red*) What is this glare?

MONKEY He's heating the furnaces. A new batch of sinners; the usual kind. (*They remove the second garment*)

PERSONAGE Let him put out the furnaces.

MONKEY Put them out?

PERSONAGE Put them out! (*The parrot shrieks*) How is my parrot? (*He notices* BABETTE *and* BIEDERMANN) Ask those people why they're praying.

MONKEY They're not praying.

PERSONAGE They're kneeling.

MONKEY They want their home back. Compensation. (*The parrot screeches*)

PERSONAGE My lovely parrot! I found him in a burning house. The only creature who doesn't change his tune! He's going to ride on my shoulder when I go up to earth again. (ANNA *and the* MONKEY *remove his third garment*) Bring the bicycles, Professor. (*The* MONKEY *bows and exits*)

BIEDERMANN Willi, don't you know me? I'm your friend Gottlieb!

BABETTE We're innocent, Herr Eisenring! (ANNA *removes the* PERSONAGE'S *fourth garment*) Why does he pretend not to know us?

PERSONAGE Bring two velvet cushions, Anna, foı these people who are kneeling.

ANNA Yes sir. (*She exits*)

PERSONAGE I remember everything, Gottlieb. You went so far as to kiss the Devil. (*The parrot calls*)

BABETTE But, Willi, if we had known you were the Devil—if we had had the slightest inkling— (ANNA *brings the frock-coat and the cushions*)

PERSONAGE Thank you, Anna. They won't need those cushions now—Where's Beelzebub?

BEELZEBUB (*Appears*) Here. (*It is* SEPP, *wearing horns, hoofs and goat tail, and carrying a huge shovel*)

PERSONAGE Don't roar like that!—We're going back to earth, Sepp. (ANNA *is helping him dress*) Have you put out the ovens?

BEELZEBUB No. I've just shoveled more coal on. (*A reflection of flames flickers over the stage*)

PERSONAGE Do as I tell you. (*He calls*) Professor! (*To* SEPP) I got nowhere with heaven. They won't give up a single one of their sinners.

BEELZEBUB Not even one? (*The* MONKEY *enters*)

PERSONAGE Call the Fire Department! (*The* MONKEY *bows and exits*) Not one! They're all saved! Anybody who kills while in uniform. Or who promises to wear a uniform while killing. Or who orders killing by others in uniform—all are saved!

BEELZEBUB Saved?!

PERSONAGE Don't roar like that! (*An echo is heard from above*)

ECHO Saved! Saved! Saved! (BEELZEBUB *glares up at the sound*)

PERSONAGE Get your earthly clothes on, Sepp; we're going back to work. (*The* CHORUS *enters*)

CHORUS Woe!

BABETTE Gottlieb, what are *they* doing here?

CHORUS Fellow-citizens, see
Our pitiful helplessness!
Tested and ready were we,
Equipped with engines and hose;
Now we're forever condemned
To view the fires of hell
As they roast our citizens well.

PERSONAGE Gentlemen, put out the fires of hell! (*The* CHORUS *is startled*) I don't intend to run hell for the sake of middle-of-the-roaders, lowbrows, highbrows, liberals, pickpockets, adulterers, slackers and servant girls who steal nylon stockings! (*The* CHORUS *is motionless*) What are you waiting for?

CHORUS Ready for action
Axes and fire-hose;
Polished and oiled,
Every brass fitting;
Every man of us tested and ready.
Our brass fire-pump
Polished and oiled,
Tested for pressure.

LEADER And the fire-hydrants?

CHORUS Tested and ready for action.

PERSONAGE Then get going! (*The flickering red light, which had begun to die down, blazes up again*)

LEADER To the hoses!
The pumps!
The ladders!
(*The* FIREMEN *quickly take places*)

PERSONAGE Ready! (*The hiss of water is heard. The flames start to go out*) And now, my wig, my bicycle and my parrot!

BEELZEBUB What have they done to my childhood belief? "Thou shalt not kill," they said, And I believed them! (*The* PERSONAGE *polishes his fingernails*) I, Sepp Schmitz, son of a miner and a gipsy—I belong to the Devil. "Go to the devil, Sepp," they said, and I went. I told lies, because lies make things easier. I stole where I listed and whored where I lusted. The villages feared me, for I was strong with the strength of the Devil. I tripped up the villagers on their way to church. I burned down their barns on Sundays while they prayed. I laughed at their loving God, who had no love for me . . . Who closed the mine-shaft that buried my father? My mother, praying for me, died of grief at my capers . . . I burned down the orphans' home—for fun! I burned down the circus—for fun! I set fire to town after town—all for fun, for fun! (*The* PERSONAGE *laughs*) There's nothing to laugh at, Willi! (ANNA *brings the wig. The* MONKEY *brings two rusty bicycles*) There's nothing to laugh at. What have they done with my childhood belief? It's enough to make one throw up! (*The* PERSONAGE *has put on his wig*)

PERSONAGE Make ready! (*He takes one of the rusty bicycles*) How I burn to see them again—the big boys who never get sent here . . . And a good, crackling fire—alarms that are always too late—smoke—the howling of dogs and of people—and ashes! (BEELZEBUB *takes off his hoofs and his tail*) Are we ready? (*He jumps on his bicycle and rings the bell*)

BEELZEBUB One moment—

LEADER Stop pumping!
Down hoses!
Turn off the water!
(*The red shimmer dies out completely*)

PERSONAGE Your horns, Sepp! (BEELZEBUB *removes his horns, jumps on the other bicycle and rings the bell*)

PERSONAGE (*To* ANNA) Thank you, my girl . . . But you're always so gloomy! I heard you laugh only once—when we were singing that song. (ANNA *laughs*) Some day we'll sing it again.

ANNA Oh, please do! (*The* CHORUS *comes forward*)

CHORUS Fellow-citizens, we—

PERSONAGE Make it short, please!

CHORUS Hell's fires are out.

PERSONAGE Thank you. (*He reaches in his pants pocket*) Got any matches?

BEELZEBUB No. Have you?

PERSONAGE Never mind. Somebody'll give us some. (*The* MONKEY *enters with the parrot*) My parrot! (*He perches the parrot on his right shoulder*) Before I forget, Professor: we're taking in no more souls. Tell heaven hell is on strike. And if any angel comes looking for us, tell him we're back on earth. (BEELZEBUB *rings his bicycle bell*) Let's go. (SCHMITZ *and* EISENRING *ride away, waving*)

BOTH Good luck, Gottlieb, good luck! (*The* CHORUS *comes forward*)

CHORUS O radiant sun!
O godlike eye!
Light up the day—

LEADER Above our rebuilt city.

CHORUS Hallelujah!
(*The parrot squawks far off*)

BABETTE Gottlieb?

BIEDERMANN Sh!

BABETTE Are we saved?

BIEDERMANN Don't lose your faith at a time like this. (*The* WIDOW KNECHTLING *exits*)

CHORUS Hallelujah!

BABETTE Frau Knechtling is gone—

CHORUS Lovelier than before,
Risen from its ruins and its ashes
Is our city.
Removed and forgotten is the rubbish;
Forgotten, too, the men and women
Whose cries rose from the flames.

BIEDERMANN Life goes on.

CHORUS Historic are they now,
Those people.
And silent.

LEADER Hallelujah!

CHORUS Lovelier than before,
And richer,
Skyscraper-modern,
All chrome and glass,

Yet ever the same
At heart.
Hallelujah!
Reborn is our city!
(*Organ music*)

BABETTE Gottlieb?

BIEDERMANN What is it?

BABETTE Do you think we're saved?

BIEDERMANN Yes, I think so . . .

(*The organ music swells.* BABETTE *and* BIEDERMANN *are on their knees*)

# A Selective Bibliography of Works in English on Modern Drama and Theatre

CONTENTS

## I. STANDARD REFERENCE WORKS ON DRAMA AND THEATRE

Baker, Blanch M. (compiler), *Theatre and Allied Arts: A Guide to Books Dealing with the History, Criticism, and Technic of the Drama and Theatre and Related Arts and Crafts,* revised and enlarged edition of *Dramatic Bibliography* (published in 1933), New York, 1952

Clark, Barrett H., *European Theories of the Drama* (revised edition with a Supplement on the American Drama), New York, 1947

Hartnoll, Phyllis (editor), *The Oxford Companion to the Theatre,* revised edition, London, 1957

Melnitz, William W. (editor), *Theatre Arts Publications in the United States (1947-1952)*, AETA Monograph No. 1, Dubuque, Iowa, 1959

Ottemiller, John H., *Index to Plays in Collections,* revised edition, Washington, 1957

Shipley, Joseph T., *Guide to Great Plays,* Washington, 1956

Sobel, Bernard (editor), *Theatre Handbook and Digest of Plays,* revised edition, New York, 1959

Stallings, Roy, and Paul Myers (compilers), *A Guide to Theatre Reading,* New York, 1949

Vowles, Richard B. (compiler), *Dramatic Theory: A Bibliography,* New York, 1956

## II. SOME PERIODICALS DEVOTED PRIMARILY TO MODERN DRAMA

*Drama Survey*

*Educational Theatre Journal*

*Modern Drama*

*Shaw Review*

*Theatre Arts*

*Tulane Drama Review*

*World Theatre*

## III. SOME USEFUL PICTORIAL COLLECTIONS

Altman, George, Ralph Freud, Kenneth Macgowan, and William Melnitz, *Theatre Pictorial,* Berkeley, 1953

Anderson, John (and René Fülöp-Miller), *The American Theatre, and The Motion Picture in America,* New York, 1938

Blum, Daniel C. (editor), *Theatre World* (annual since 1944-45), New York

———, *Great Stars of the American Stage,* New York, 1952

———, *A Pictorial History of the American Theatre: 100 Years, 1860-1960,* Philadelphia, 1960

Carter, Huntly, *The New Spirit in the European Theatre: 1914-1924,* London, 1925

Cheney, Sheldon, *Stage Decoration,* New York, 1928

Fuerst, W. R., and Samuel J. Hume, *Twentieth Century Stage Decoration,* two volumes, New York, 1929

Hainaux, René (editor), *Stage Design Throughout the World Since 1935,* New York, 1956

Hobson, Harold (editor), *International Theatre Annual* (annual since 1956), New York

Isaacs, Edith J. R., *Architecture for the New Theatre,* New York, 1935

Jones, Robert Edmond, *Drawings for the Theatre,* New York, 1925

Komisarjevsky, Theodore, and Lee Simonson, *Settings and Costumes of the Modern Stage,* New York, 1933

Macgowan, Kenneth, *The Theatre of Tomorrow,* New York, 1921

———, and Robert Edmond Jones, *Continental Stagecraft,* New York, 1922

———, and William Melnitz, *The Living Stage,* New York, 1955

Nicoll, Allardyce, *The Development of the Theatre,* revised edition, New York, 1958

Oenslager, Donald, *Scenery Then and Now,* New York, 1936

Prideaux, Tom, *World Theatre in Pictures,* New York, 1953

Simonson, Lee, *The Art of Scenic Design,* New York, 1950

———, *The Stage is Set,* New York, 1932

Stephens, Frances (editor), *Theatre World Annual* (annual since 1949-1950), London

## IV. GENERAL AND SPECIAL STUDIES

### A. GENERAL STUDIES OF THE DRAMA

Archer, William, *Play-Making,* New York, 1938

Baker, George Pierce, *Dramatic Technique,* Boston, 1919

Barrault, Jean-Louis, *Reflections on the Theatre* (translated by Barbara Wall), London, 1951

———, *The Theatre of Jean-Louis Barrault* (translated and edited by Joseph Chiari), New York, 1961

Cole, Toby (editor), *Playwrights on Playwriting. The Meaning and Making of Modern Drama from Ibsen to Ionesco,* New York, 1960

Craig, Edward Gordon, *The Theatre—Advancing,* Boston, 1919

Craig, Edward Gordon, *On the Art of the Theatre,* New York, 1925; 1957

Disher, Maurice W., *Melodrama,* London, 1954

Drew, Elizabeth, *Discovering Drama,* New York, 1937

Eliot, T. S., *Poetry and Drama,* Cambridge, Massachusetts, 1951

Feibleman, James K., *In Praise of Comedy,* New York, 1939

Fergusson, Francis, *The Idea of the Theatre,* Princeton, 1949

Ghéon, Henri, *The Art of the Theatre,* New York, 1960

Hamilton, Clayton M., *The Theory of the Theatre,* New York, 1939

Harris, Mark, *The Case for Tragedy,* New York, 1932

Henn, T. R., *The Harvest of Tragedy,* London, 1956

James, Henry, *The Scenic Art* (edited by Allan Wade), New Brunswick, 1948

Kerr, Walter, *How Not to Write a Play,* New York, 1955

Kozlenko, William (editor), *The One-Act Play Today,* New York, 1938

Kronenberger, Louis, *The Thread of Laughter,* New York, 1952

Lawson, John Howard, *Theory and Technique of Playwriting and Screen-Writing,* New York, 1936; revised, 1960

MacCarthy, Desmond, *Drama,* New York, 1940

McCollum, William G., *Tragedy,* New York, 1957

Mandel, Oscar, *A Definition of Tragedy,* New York, 1961

Matthews, Brander (editor), *Papers on Playmaking,* New York, 1957 (reissued)

———, *A Study of the Drama,* New York, 1910

Monro, D. H., *Argument of Laughter,* London, 1951

Montague, C. E., *Dramatic Values,* New York, 1925

Muller, Herbert J., *The Spirit of Tragedy,* New York, 1956

Nicoll, Allardyce, *The Theory of Drama,* London, 1931

Olson, Elder, *Tragedy and the Theory of Drama,* Detroit, 1961

Peacock, Ronald, *The Art of Drama,* London, 1956

Potts, L. J., *Comedy,* London, 1949

Raphaelson, Samson, *The Human Nature of Playwriting,* New York, 1949

Rowe, Kenneth Thorpe, *A Theatre in Your Head,* New York, 1960

———, *Write That Play,* New York, 1939

Sewall, Richard B., *The Vision of Tragedy,* New Haven, 1959

Sharpe, Robert Boies, *Irony in the Drama: An Essay on Impersonation, Shock, and Catharsis,* Chapel Hill, 1959

Smith, Willard, *The Nature of Comedy,* Boston, 1930

Steiner, George, *The Death of Tragedy,* New York, 1961

Stuart, Donald Clive, *The Development of Dramatic Art,* New York, 1928

Styan, J. L., *The Elements of Drama,* Cambridge, 1960

Thompson, Alan Reynolds, *The Anatomy of Drama,* Berkeley, 1942; 1946

———, *The Dry Mock, A Study of Irony in Drama,* Berkeley, 1948

van Druten, John, *Playwright at Work,* New York, 1953

Young, Stark, *The Theatre,* New York, 1927; 1954


### B. HISTORIES OF MODERN DRAMA

#### 1. *Comparative and General*


Archer, William, *The Old Drama and the New,* New York, 1923

Balmforth, Ramsden, *The Problem Play, and Its Influence on Modern Thought and Life,* New York, 1928

Bentley, Eric, *The Playwright as Thinker,* New York, 1946; revised, 1955

Block, Anita, *The Changing World in Plays and Theatre,* Boston, 1939

Chandler, Frank W., *Modern Continental Playwrights,* New York, 1931

Charques, Richard D. (editor), *Footnotes to the Theatre,* London, 1938

Cheney, Sheldon, *The Art Theatre,* New York, 1925

———, *The Theatre: Three Thousand Years of Drama, Acting, and Stagecraft,* New York, 1929; revised, 1947

Clark, Barrett H., *A Study of the Modern Drama,* New York, 1938

———, and George Freedley (editors), *A History of Modern Drama,* New York, 1947

Dickinson, Thomas H. (editor), *The Theatre in a Changing Europe,* New York, 1937

Dukes, Ashley, *The Youngest Drama: Studies of Fifty Dramatists,* Chicago, 1924

Esslin, Martin, *The Theatre of the Absurd,* Garden City, 1961

Flanagan, Hallie, *Shifting Scenes of the Modern European Theatre,* New York, 1928

Freedley, George, and John A. Reeves, *A History of the Theatre,* New York, 1941; revised, 1955

Gassner, John, *Form and Idea in Modern Theatre,* New York, 1956

———, *Masters of the Drama,* revised edition, New York, 1954

Goldberg, Isaac, *The Drama of Transition,* Cincinnati, 1922

Gorelik, Mordecai, *New Theatres for Old,* New York, 1940

Henderson, Archibald, *European Dramatists,* New York, 1926

Hudson, Lynton, *The Twentieth Century Drama,* London, 1946

Huneker, James, *Egoists: A Book of Supermen,* London, 1909

———, *Iconoclasts: A Book of Dramatists,* London, 1905

Kerman, Joseph, *Opera as Drama,* New York, 1956

Krutch, Joseph Wood, *"Modernism" in Modern Drama,* Ithaca, 1953

———, *The Modern Temper,* New York, 1929

Lamm, Martin, *Modern Drama* (translated by K. Elliott), Oxford, 1952

Lewisohn, Ludwig, *The Drama and the Stage,* New York, 1922

———, *The Modern Drama,* New York, 1915

Lumley, Frederick, *Trends in 20th Century Drama,* Fairlawn, 1956; revised, 1960

Miller, Anna Irene, *The Independent Theatre in Europe, 1887 to the Present,* New York, 1931

Moderwell, Hiram Kelly, *The Theatre of Today,* New York, 1927

Nelson, Robert J., *Play Within A Play. The Dramatist's Conception of His Art: Shakespeare to Anouilh,* New Haven, 1958

Nicoll, Allardyce, *World Drama from Aeschylus to Anouilh,* New York, 1959

Palmer, John, *Studies in the Contemporary Theatre,* Boston, 1927

Peacock, Ronald, *The Poet in the Theatre,* New York, 1946; 1960 (enlarged)

Perry, Henry Ten Eyck, *Masters of Dramatic Comedy and Their Social Themes,* Cambridge, Massachusetts, 1939

Sayler, Oliver M., *Revolt in the Arts,* New York, 1930

Short, Ernest H., *Theatrical Cavalcade,* London, 1942

Southern, Richard, *The Seven Ages of the Theatre,* New York, 1961

Speaight, Robert, *Christian Theatre,* New York, 1960

———, *Drama Since 1939,* London, 1947

Stein, Jack, *Richard Wagner and the Synthesis of the Arts,* Detroit, 1960

Stevens, Thomas Wood, *The Theatre from Athens to Broadway,* New York, 1932

Weinstein, Leo, *The Metamorphoses of Don Juan,* Stanford, 1959

Williams, Raymond, *Drama from Ibsen to Eliot,* London, 1952

2. *American*

Chapman, John (editor), *The Burns Mantle Best Plays of 1947-1948* (through 1951-1952), New York

———, *Theatre '53—Theatre '56* (subsequently titled *Broadway's Best, 1957* to date), New York

———, and Garrison P. Sherwood (editors), *Best Plays of 1894-1899,* New York, 1955

Clurman, Harold, *The Fervent Years: The Story of the Group Theatre and the Thirties,* New York, 1945; revised, 1957

Deutsch, Helen, and Stella Hanau, *The Provincetown,* New York, 1931

Dickinson, Thomas H., *Playwrights of the New American Theater,* New York, 1925

Downer, Alan S., *Fifty Years of American Drama, 1900-1950,* Chicago, 1951

———, *Recent American Drama,* Minneapolis, 1961

Eaton, Walter Pritchard (editor), *The Theatre Guild: The First Ten Years,* New York, 1929

Flanagan, Hallie, *Arena: The Story of the Federal Theatre,* New York, 1940

Flexner, Eleanor, *American Playwrights, 1918-1938: The Theatre Retreats from Reality,* New York, 1938

Gagey, Edmond M., *Revolution in the American Drama,* New York, 1947

Gibson, William, *The Seesaw Log,* New York, 1959

Helburn, Theresa, *A Wayward Quest,* Boston, 1960

Hewitt, Barnard, *Theatre U.S.A., 1668-1957,* New York, 1959

Houghton, Norris, *Advance from Broadway,* New York, 1941

Hughes, Glenn, *A History of the American Theatre, 1700-1950,* New York, 1951

Isaacs, Edith J. R., *The Negro in the American Theatre,* New York, 1935; 1947

Kinne, Wisner Payne, *George Pierce Baker and the American Theatre,* Cambridge, Massachusetts, 1954

Kronenberger, Louis (editor), *The Best Plays of 1952-1953* (and subsequent), New York

Krutch, Joseph Wood, *The American Drama Since 1918,* New York, 1939; revised, 1957

Langner, Lawrence, *The Magic Curtain,* New York, 1951

Macgowan, Kenneth, *Footlights Across America. Towards A National Theatre,* New York, 1929

Mantle, Burns, *American Playwrights of Today,* New York, 1929

———, *Contemporary American Playwrights,* New York, 1938

——— (editor), *Best Plays of 1919-1920* (through 1946-1947), New York

———, and Garrison P. Sherwood (editors), *Best Plays of 1899-1909,* New York, 1944

———, *Best Plays of 1909-1919,* New York, 1943

Martin, Boyd, *Modern American Drama and Stage,* London, 1943

Mersand, Joseph, *American Drama Since 1930,* New York, 1949

Miller, Jordan Y. (editor), *American Dramatic Literature,* New York, 1961

Morris, Lloyd, *Curtain Time: The Story of the American Theater,* New York, 1953

Moses, Montrose J., *The American Dramatist,* Boston, 1925

———, and John Mason Brown, *The American Theatre As Seen By Its Critics, 1752-1934,* New York, 1934

Nannes, Casper H., *Politics in the American Drama,* Washington, 1960

O'Hara, Frank H., *Today in American Drama,* Chicago, 1939

Quinn, Arthur Hobson, *A History of American Drama from the Civil War to the Present Day,* New York, 1937 (revised)

Rice, Elmer, *The Living Theatre,* New York, 1959

Sayler, Oliver M., *Our American Theatre, 1908-1923,* New York, 1923

Seldes, Gilbert, *The Seven Lively Arts,* New York, 1924

Sievers, W. David, *Freud on Broadway. A History of Psychoanalysis and the American Drama,* New York, 1955

Weales, Gerald, *American Drama Since World War II,* New York, 1962

Whitman, Willson, *Bread and Circuses, A Study of the Federal Theatre,* New York, 1937

3. *English and Irish*

Agate, James, *A Short View of the English Stage: 1920-1926,* London, 1926

Boyd, Ernest A., *The Contemporary Drama of Ireland,* Boston, 1917; 1924

Byrne, Dawson, *The Story of Ireland's National Theatre,* Dublin, 1929

Cunliffe, John W., *Modern English Playwrights,* New York, 1927

Dickinson, Thomas H., *The Contemporary Drama of England,* Boston, 1931

Donoghue, Denis, *The Third Voice. Modern British and American Verse Drama,* Princeton, 1959

Downer, Alan S., *The British Drama,* New York, 1950

Ellis-Fermor, Una M., *The Irish Dramatic Movement,* London, 1939; 1954

Fay, Gerard, *The Abbey Theatre,* New York, 1958

Fay, William G., and Catherine Carswell, *The Fays of the Abbey Theatre,* New York, 1935

Guthrie, Tyrone, *A Life in the Theatre,* New York, 1959

Howarth, Herbert, *The Irish Writers, 1880-1940,* New York, 1959

Hudson, Lynton, *The English Stage, 1850-1950,* London, 1951

Kavanagh, Peter, *The Story of the Abbey Theatre,* New York, 1950

Knight, G. Wilson, *The Golden Labyrinth: A Study of the English Drama,* London, 1961

MacCarthy, Desmond, *The Court Theatre, 1904-1907,* London, 1907

Malone, Andrew E., *The Irish Drama, 1896-1928,* New York, 1929

Morgan, A. E., *Tendencies of Modern English Drama,* New York, 1924

Nicoll, Allardyce, *A History of the English Drama, 1660-1900, Volume 5* (*Late 19th Century Drama, 1850-1900*), Cambridge, 1959

———, *British Drama,* London, 1947 (revised)

Orme, Michael, *J. T. Grein: The Story of a Pioneer, 1862-1935,* London, 1936

Reynolds, Ernest R., *Modern English Drama: A Survey of the Theatre from 1900,* London, 1949

Robinson, Lennox, *Ireland's Abbey Theatre, 1899-1951,* London, 1951

——— (editor), *The Irish Theatre: Lectures Delivered During the Abbey Theatre Festival Held in Dublin in August, 1938,* London, 1939

Rowell, George, *The Victorian Theatre: A Survey,* London, 1956

Shaw, George Bernard, *Our Theatres in the Nineties,* London, 1931

Short, Ernest H., *Sixty Years of Theatre,* London, 1951

Thouless, Priscilla, *Modern Poetic Drama,* Oxford, 1934

Trewin, J. C., *Dramatists of Today,* London, 1953

———, *The English Theatre,* London, 1948

———, *The Theatre Since 1900,* London, 1951

Ussher, Arland, *Three Great Irishmen: Shaw, Yeats, Joyce,* New York, 1953

Weales, Gerald, *Religion in Modern English Drama,* Philadelphia, 1961

Wilson, A. E., *Post-War Theatre,* London, 1949

———, *The Edwardian Theatre,* London, 1951

Wimsatt, William K., Jr. (editor), *English Stage Comedy,* New York, 1955

4. *French*

Artaud, Antonin, *The Theatre and Its Double* (translated by Mary Caroline Richards), New York, 1958

Chandler, Frank W., *The Contemporary Drama of France,* Boston, 1920

Chiari, Joseph, *The Contemporary French Theatre: The Flight from Naturalism,* New York, 1959

Fowlie, Wallace, *Age of Surrealism,* New York, 1950

———, *Dionysus in Paris. A Guide to Contemporary French Theatre,* New York, 1960

Grossvogel, David I., *The Self-Conscious Stage in Modern French Drama,* New York, 1958 (re-issued as *Modern French Drama,* 1961)

Guicharnaud, Jacques, with June Beckelman, *Modern French Theatre from Giraudoux to Beckett,* New Haven, 1961

Hobson, Harold, *The French Theatre of Today,* London, 1953

Knapp, Bettina, *Louis Jouvet, Man of the Theatre,* New York, 1957

Lilar, Suzanne, *The Belgian Theater Since 1890,* New York, 1950

Pucciani, Oreste (editor), *The French Theatre Since 1930,* Boston, 1954

Smith, Hugh Allison, *Main Currents of Modern French Drama,* New York, 1925

Stanton, Stephen (editor), *Camille and Other Plays,* New York, 1957

Waxman, Samuel M., *Antoine and the Théâtre Libre,* Cambridge, Massachusetts, 1926

5. *German*

Bahr, Hermann, *Expressionism* (translated by R. F. Gribble), London, 1925

Feise, Ernst, *Fifty Years of German Drama (1880-1930): A Bibliography,* Baltimore, 1941

Garten, H. F., *Modern German Drama,* Fairlawn, 1959

Hill, Claude, and Ralph Ley, *The Drama of German Expressionism: A German-English Bibliography,* Chapel Hill, 1960

Samuel, Richard, and R. Hinton Thomas, *Expressionism in German Life, Literature and the Theatre (1910-1924),* Cambridge, 1939

Sokel, Walter H., *The Writer in Extremis. Expressionism in Twentieth-Century German Literature,* Stanford, 1959

6. *Russian*

Bakshy, Alexander, *The Path of the Modern Russian Stage,* Boston, 1918

Bowers, Faubion, *Broadway, U.S.S.R.: Theatre, Ballet, and Entertainment in Russia Today,* New York, 1959

Carter, Huntly, *The New Spirit in the Russian Theatre, 1917-1928,* London, 1929

Dana, H. W. L., *A Handbook on Soviet Drama,* New York, 1938

———, *Drama in Wartime Russia,* New York, 1943

Fülöp-Miller, René, and Joseph Gregor, *The Russian Theatre* (translated by Paul England), Philadelphia, 1930

Gorchakov, Nikolai A., *The Theatre in Soviet Russia,* New York, 1957

Houghton, Norris, *Moscow Rehearsals,* New York, 1936

———, *Return Engagement,* New York, 1962

Macleod, Joseph, *Actors Cross the Volga,* London, 1946

———, *The New Soviet Theatre,* London, 1943

Nemirovitch-Danchenko, Vladimir, *My Life in the Russian Theatre* (translated by John Cournos), London, 1937

Sayler, Oliver M., *Inside the Moscow Art Theatre,* New York, 1925

———, *The Russian Theatre,* New York, 1923 (enlarged)

Slonim, Marc, *Russian Theatre: From the Empire to the Soviets,* New York, 1961

Stanislavsky, Konstantin, *My Life in Art* (translated by G. Ivanov-Mumjiev), Moscow, c. 1958 (the authorized version of Stanislavsky's commentary)

Van Gyseghem, Andre, *Theatre in Soviet Russia,* London, 1943

Varneke, B. V., *A History of the Russian Theatre,* New York, 1951

Wiener, Leo, *The Contemporary Drama of Russia,* Boston, 1924

C. COLLECTIONS OF ESSAYS AND REVIEWS

Agate, James, *Red Letter Nights,* London, 1944

———, *The Contemporary Theatre,* London, 1924 (and subsequent years)

Anderson, Maxwell, *Off Broadway: Essays About the Theatre,* New York, 1947

Atkinson, Brooks, *Broadway Scrapbook,* New York, 1947

Beerbohm, Max, *Around Theatres,* New York, 1954

Bentley, Eric, *In Search of Theater,* New York, 1953

———, *The Dramatic Event: An American Chronicle,* New York, 1954

———, *What Is Theatre?,* Boston, 1956

Block, Haskell M., and Herman Salinger (editors), *The Creative Vision, Modern European Writers on Their Art,* New York, 1960

Brown, Ivor, *Theatre, 1954-1955,* London, 1955

———, *Theatre, 1955-1956,* London, 1956

Brown, John Mason, *As They Appear,* New York, 1952

———, *Broadway in Review,* New York, 1940

———, *Seeing Things,* New York, 1946

———, *Seeing More Things,* New York, 1948

———, *Still Seeing Things,* New York, 1950

———, *The Modern Theatre in Revolt,* New York, 1929

———, *Two On the Aisle: Ten Years of the American Theatre in Perspective,* New York, 1938

Clurman, Harold, *Lies Like Truth,* New York, 1958

Darlington, W. A., *Six Thousand and One Nights: 40 Years A Dramatic Critic,* London, 1960

Fergusson, Francis, *The Human Image in Dramatic Literature,* Garden City, 1957

Gassner, John, *Theatre at the Crossroads: Plays and Playwrights of the Mid-Century American Stage,* New York, 1960

———, *The Theatre in Our Times: A Survey of the Men, Materials and Movements in the Modern Theatre,* New York, 1954

Gilder, Rosamond, Hermine Rich Isaacs, Robert M. MacGregor, and Edward Reed (editors), *Theatre Arts Anthology: A Record and A Prophecy,* New York, 1950

Hobson, Harold, *The Theatre Now,* London, 1953

———, *Verdict at Midnight. Sixty Years of Dramatic Criticism,* London, 1952

Kerr, Walter, *Pieces at Eight,* New York, 1957

McCarthy, Mary, *On the Contrary. Articles of Belief, 1946-1961,* New York, 1961

———, *Sights and Spectacles, Theatre Chronicles 1937-1956,* New York, 1957

Morehouse, Ward, *Matinee Tomorrow: Fifty Years of Our Theatre,* New York, 1949

Nathan, George Jean, *The Theatre in the Fifties,* New York, 1953

———, *The World of George Jean Nathan* (edited by Charles Angoff), New York, 1952

———, *The Theatre Book of the Year, 1942-1943* (and subsequent to 1950-1951), New York

*New York Theatre Critics' Reviews,* New York, 1940 to date

Trewin, J. C., *A Play Tonight (English Theatre Between 1949 and 1952),* London, 1952

Tynan, Kenneth, *Curtains,* New York, 1961

van Thal, Herbert (editor), *James Agate, An Anthology,* New York, 1961

Williamson, Audrey, *Contemporary Theatre, 1953-1956,* London, 1956

———, *Theatre of Two Decades,* London, 1951

Worsley, T. C., *The Fugitive Art,* London, 1952

Young, Stark, *Immortal Shadows,* New York, 1948

———, *The Flower in Drama,* New York, 1955 (reissue)

### D. STAGING AND PRODUCTION

Appia, Adolphe, *The Work of Living Art,* Miami, 1961

Carter, Huntly, *The Theatre of Max Reinhardt,* London, 1914

Cole, Toby, and Helen Krich Chinoy (editors), *Actors on Acting,* New York, 1949

———, *Directing the Play,* Indianapolis and New York, 1953

Fuchs, George, *Revolution in the Theatre: Conclusions Concerning the Munich Artists' Theatre* (translated by C. C. Kuhn), Ithaca, 1959

Funke, Lewis, and John E. Booth (editors), *Actors Talk About Acting,* New York, 1961

Goodman, Randolph, *Drama On Stage,* New York, 1961

Gorchakov, Nikolai, *The Vakhtangov School of Stage Art,* Moscow, c. 1959

Gropius, Walter (editor), *The Theatre of Bauhaus,* Middletown, 1961

Jones, Margo, *Theatre in the Round,* New York, 1951

Jones, Robert Edmond, *The Dramatic Imagination,* New York, 1941

Komisarjevsky, Theodore, *Myself and the Theatre,* London, 1929

Nagler, Alois M., *Sources of Theatrical History,* New York, 1955

Nicoll, Allardyce, *Film and Theatre,* New York, 1936

Saint-Denis, Michel, *Theatre: The Rediscovery of Style,* New York, 1960

Sayler, Oliver M. (editor), *Max Reinhardt and His Theatre,* New York, 1924

Simonson, Lee, *Part of a Lifetime,* New York, 1943

Stanislavsky, Constantin, *An Actor Prepares* (translated by E. R. Hapgood), New York, 1936

———, *Stanislavsky On the Art of the Stage* (translated by David Magarshack), London, 1950

Vardac, A. Nicholas, *Stage to Screen, Theatrical Method from Garrick to Griffith,* Cambridge, Massachusetts, 1949

## V. INDIVIDUAL AUTHORS

(Cross-references at the ends of entries for individual authors refer to books in sections I-IV. Asterisks denote titles containing bibliographies.)


### JEAN ANOUILH

Champigny, Robert, "Theatre in a Mirror: Anouilh," *Yale French Studies,* 14 (Winter, 1954-1955)

Marsh, Edward Owen, *Jean Anouilh, Poet of Pierrot and Pantaloon,* London, 1953

Pronko, Leonard Cabell, *The World of Jean Anouilh,* Berkeley, 1961

See also: IV,B,1: Lumley
IV,B,4: Chiari; Fowlie, *Dionysus;* Grossvogel; Guicharnaud; Hobson; Pucciani
IV,C: Gassner, *Crossroads;* Tynan

### SAMUEL BECKETT

See Samuel Beckett Issue of *Perspective, XI* (Autumn, 1959)

Cohn, Ruby, "A Checklist of Beckett Criticism," *Perspective* (Autumn, 1959)

———, "*Endgame:* The Gospel According to Sad Sam Beckett," *Accent, XX* (Autumn, 1960)

Eastman, Richard, "The Strategy of Samuel Beckett's *Endgame,*" *Modern Drama, II* (May, 1959)

Kenner, Hugh, *Samuel Beckett,* New York, 1962

Mayoux, Jean-Jacques, "The Theatre of Samuel Beckett," *Perspective* (Autumn, 1959)

See also: IV,B,1: Esslin; Lumley
IV,B,4: Chiari; Fowlie, *Dionysus;* Grossvogel; Guicharnaud
IV,C: Gassner, *Crossroads;* Tynan

### BERTOLT BRECHT

See the Brecht Issue of *Tulane Drama Review,* 6 (September, 1961)

* Esslin, Martin, *Brecht, A Choice of Evils,* London, 1959; reprinted with changes as *Brecht: The Man and His Work,* Garden City, 1960

Gray, Ronald, *Bertolt Brecht,* New York, 1961

Hecht, Werner, "The Development of Brecht's Theory of Epic Theatre, 1918-1933" (translated by B. Q. Morgan), *Tulane Drama Review,* 6 (September, 1961)

Willett, John, *The Theatre of Bertolt Brecht. A Study from Eight Aspects,* London, 1959

See also: IV,A: Fergusson, *Image*
IV,B,1: Bentley, *Thinker;* Lumley
IV,B,5: Garten
IV,C: Bentley, *Search;* Block and Salinger; Gassner, *Our Times;* Cole; Tynan

### ALBERT CAMUS

Brée, Germaine, *Camus,* New Brunswick, 1959

Camus, Albert, "Why I Work in the Theatre," *Theatre Arts* (December, 1960)

Cruikshank, John, *Albert Camus and the Literature of Revolt,* Oxford, 1960

Hanna, Thomas, *The Thought and Art of Albert Camus,* Chicago, 1958

Maquet, Albert, *Albert Camus, or the Invincible Summer,* London, 1958

Reck, Rima Drell, "The Theater of Albert Camus," *Modern Drama, IV* (May, 1961)

Sonnenfeld, Albert, "Albert Camus as Dramatist: The Sources of His Failure," *Tulane Drama Review,* 5 (June, 1961)

Thody, Philip, *Albert Camus: A Study of His Work,* New York, 1959, revised 1961

See also: IV,B,4: Fowlie, *Dionysus;* Guicharnaud; Pucciani
IV, C: Tynan

### PADDY CHAYEFSKY

Chayefsky, Paddy, Essays in *Television Plays,* New York, 1955

Sayre, Nora, and Robert B. Silvers, "An Interview with Paddy Chayefsky," *Horizon, III* (September, 1960)

Wadsworth, Frank, "The TV Plays of Paddy Chayefsky," *Quarterly of Film, Radio, and Television, X* (Winter, 1955)

Weales, Gerald, "Marty and His Friends and Neighbors," *Commentary, XX* (September, 1955)

See also: IV,B,2: Downer, *Recent*
IV,C: Gassner, *Crossroads;* Tynan

### ANTON CHEKHOV

See the Chekhov Centenary Issue of *World Theatre, IX* (1960)

Bruford, W. H., *Chekhov and His Russia,* New Haven, 1947

Gerhardi, William, *Anton Chekhov, A Critical Study,* New York, 1923

Gorki, Maxim, *Reminiscences of Tolstoy, Chekhov, and Andreyev,* New York, 1921

Hingley, Ronald, *Chekhov,* London, 1950

Koteliansky, S. S., *Anton Tchekhov: Literary and Theatrical Reminiscences,* London, 1927

———, and P. Tomlinson, *Life and Letters of Anton Tchekhov,* New York, 1925

Magarshack, David, *Chekhov: A Life,* New York, 1953

———, *Chekhov the Dramatist,* London, 1952

Yachnin, Rissa, *Chekhov in English: A Selective List of Works By and About Him, 1949-1960,* New York Public Library, 1960

See also: IV,A: Cole; Fergusson, *Idea*
IV,B,6: Nemirov-Danchenko; Slonim; Stanislavsky
IV,C: Bentley, *Search* and *What is Theatre?;* Cole; Young, *Shadows*

JEAN COCTEAU

Cocteau, Jean, *Journals of Jean Cocteau* (edited by Wallace Fowlie), New York, 1956

Crosland, Margaret, *Jean Cocteau,* London, 1955

* Oxenhandler, Neal, *Scandal and Parade: The Theatre of Jean Cocteau,* New Brunswick, 1957

See also: IV,A: Cole; Fergusson, *Idea*
IV,B,1: Bentley, *Thinker*
IV,B,4: Chiari; Fowlie, *Dionysus;* Grossvogel, Guicharnaud; Pucciani
IV,C: Bentley, *Search;* Block and Salinger; Cole

FRIEDRICH DUERRENMATT

Askew, Melvin W., "Duerrenmatt's *The Visit of the Old Lady,*" *Tulane Drama Review,* 5 (June, 1961)

Duerrenmatt, Friedrich, "Problems of the Theatre," *Tulane Drama Review,* 3 (October, 1958)

Klarmann, Adolf, "Friedrich Duerrenmatt and the Tragic Sense of Comedy," *Tulane Drama Review,* 4 (May, 1960)

Rogoff, Gordon, "Mr. Duerrenmatt Buys New Shoes," *Tulane Drama Review,* 3 (October, 1958)

See also: IV,A: Cole
IV,B,5: Garten
IV,D: Goodman

MAX FRISCH

Frisch, Max, "Recollections of Brecht," *Tulane Drama Review,* 6 (September, 1961)

———, "On the Nature of the Theatre" (translated by Carl Richard Mueller), *Tulane Drama Review,* 6 (March, 1962)

Wellwarth, George, "Friedrich Duerrenmatt and Max Frisch: Two Views of the Drama," *Tulane Drama Review,* 6 (March, 1962)

See also: IV,B,1: Esslin
IV,B,5: Garten

FEDERICO GARCÍA LORCA

Barea, Arturo, *Lorca, The Poet and His People,* New York, 1949; 1958

Barnes, Robert, "The Fusion of Poetry and Drama in *Blood Wedding,*" *Modern Drama,* 2 (February, 1960)

Campbell, Roy, *Lorca,* New Haven, 1952

Honig, Edwin, *Garcia Lorca,* New York, 1944; 1948

Trend, J. B., *Lorca and the Spanish Poetic Tradition,* Oxford, 1956

See also: IV,A: Cole; Fergusson, *Image*
IV,B,1: Lumley
IV,C: Bentley, *Search;* Block and Salinger; Cole; Gassner, *Our Times;* Young, *Shadows*

JEAN GIRAUDOUX

See Giraudoux Issue of *Tulane Drama Review,* 3 (May, 1959)

Inskip, Donald, *Jean Giraudoux, The Making of a Dramatist,* Oxford, 1958

Lesage, Laurent, "Jean Giraudoux, Surrealism, and the German Romantic Ideal," *Illinois Studies in Language and Literature, XXXVI,* No. 3, 1952

———, *Jean Giraudoux, His Life and Works,* University Park, 1959

May, Georges, "Jean Giraudoux: Diplomacy and Dramaturgy," *Yale French Studies,* 5 (Spring, 1950)

See also: IV,A: Cole
IV,B,4: Chiari; Fowlie, *Dionysus;* Grossvogel; Guicharnaud; Pucciani
IV,C: Gassner, *Our Times* and *Crossroads;* Tynan

MAXIM GORKI

Bakshy, Alexander, *The Path of the Modern Russian Stage and Other Essays,* London, 1916

Gorki, Maxim, *Reminiscences of Tolstoy, Chekhov, and Andreyev,* New York, 1921

Kaun, Alexander, *Maxim Gorki and His Russia,* New York, 1931

See also: IV,B,6: Nemirovich-Danchenko; Slonim; Stanislavsky

GERHART HAUPTMANN

Garten, H. F., *Gerhart Hauptmann,* New Haven, 1954

Reichart, Walter A., "Fifty Years of Hauptmann Study in America (1894-1944): A Bibliography," *Monatshefte für Dt. Unterricht, 38* (1945).

Sinden, Margaret, *Gerhart Hauptmann: The Prose Plays,* Toronto, 1957

See also: IV,B,5: Garten

HUGO VON HOFMANNSTHAL

Hammelmann, H. A., *Hugo von Hofmannsthal,* New Haven, 1957

Schwarz, Alfred, "The Allegorical Theatre of Hugo von Hofmannsthal," *Tulane Drama Review,* 4 (March, 1960)

See also: IV,B,5: Garten

HENRIK IBSEN

See "Contemporary Classics" Issue of *World Theatre, VI* (Spring, 1957)

Arestad, Sverre, "*Peer Gynt* and the Idea of Self," *Modern Drama,* 3 (September, 1960)

Bradbrook, Muriel C., *Ibsen, The Norwegian,* London, 1946

Downs, Brian W., *A Study of Six Plays by Ibsen,* Cambridge, 1950

———, *Ibsen: The Intellectual Background,* Cambridge, 1946

Koht, Halvdan, *The Life of Ibsen,* New York, 1931

McFarlane, James W., *Ibsen and the Temper of Norwegian Literature,* London, 1960

Northam, John, *Ibsen's Dramatic Method,* London, 1953

Shaw, George Bernard, *The Quintessence of Ibsenism,* London, 1891; 1913

Tennant, P. F. D., *Ibsen's Dramatic Technique,* Cambridge, 1948

Weigand, Hermann J., *The Modern Ibsen: A Reconsideration,* New York, 1925

Zucker, Adolph E., *Ibsen, The Master Builder,* London, 1929

See also: IV,A: Cole; Fergusson, *Idea;* James; Thompson, *Mock*
IV,B,1: Bentley, *Thinker;* Huneker, *Iconoclasts* and *Egoists;* Lamm; Peacock, *Poet;* Williams
IV,C: Beerbohm; Cole

EUGÈNE IONESCO

Coe, Richard N., *Eugene Ionesco,* New York, 1961

Ionesco, Eugene, "Discovering the Theatre" (translated by Leonard Pronko), *Tulane Drama Review,* 4 (September, 1959)

———, "Eugene Ionesco Opens Fire," *World Theatre, VII,* No. 3 (1959); reprinted as "The Avant-Garde Theatre," *Tulane Drama Review,* 5 (December, 1960)

———, "Theatre and Anti-Theatre," *Theatre Arts* (July, 1958)

———, "The Tragedy of Language: How an English Primer Became My First Play" (translated by Jack Undank), *Tulane Drama Review,* 4 (March, 1960)

Lamont, Rosette C., "The Outrageous Ionesco" (an interview), *Horizon, III* (May, 1961)

Pronko, Leonard C., "The Anti-Spiritual Victory in the Theatre of Ionesco," *Modern Drama,* 2 (May, 1959)

Watson, Donald, "The Plays of Ionesco," *Tulane Drama Review,* 3 (October, 1958)

See also: IV,A: Cole
IV,B,1: Esslin; Lumley
IV,B,4: Fowlie, *Dionysus;* Grossvogel; Guicharnaud
IV,C: Tynan

GEORG KAISER

Kenworthy, B. J., *Georg Kaiser,* Oxford, 1957

See also: IV,B,5: Garten; Samuel and Thomas; Sokel

MAURICE MAETERLINCK

Bithell, Jethro, *Life and Writings of Maurice Maeterlinck,* London, 1930

Daniels, May, *The French Drama of the Unspoken,* Edinburgh, 1953

Halls, W. D., *Maurice Maeterlinck, A Study of His Life and Thoughts,* Oxford, 1960

See also: I: Clark, *Theories*
IV,B,1: Bentley, *Thinker;* Huneker, *Iconoclasts*

ARTHUR MILLER

Brandon, Henry, "The State of the Theatre: A Conversation with Arthur Miller," *Harper's,* CCXXI (November, 1960)

Hurrell, John D., *Two Modern American Tragedies: Reviews and Criticism of "Death of a Salesman" and "A Streetcar Named Desire,"* New York, 1961

Miller, Arthur, Preface to *Death of a Salesman,* New York, 1949

———, Introductions to *A View from the Bridge,* New York, 1955; 1960

———, Introduction to *Collected Plays,* New York, 1957

———, "The Family in Modern Drama," *Atlantic Monthly,* CXCVII (April, 1956)

———, "The Shadows of the Gods," *Harper's,* CCXVII (August, 1958)

———, "Tragedy and the Common Man," *Theatre Arts* (March, 1951)

———, and others, "A Matter of Hopelessness in *Death of a Salesman:* A Symposium," *Tulane Drama Review,* 2 (May, 1958)

Welland, Dennis, *Arthur Miller,* London, 1961

Williams, Raymond, "The Realism of Arthur Miller," *Critical Quarterly,* I (Summer, 1959)

See also: IV,A: Cole
IV,B,1: Bentley, *Thinker;* Krutch, *Modernism;* Lumley
IV,B,2: Downer, *Fifty* and *Recent;* Krutch, *Since 1918;* Sievers
IV,C: Bentley, *Search;* Gassner, *Our Times* and *Crossroads;* Tynan

### SEAN O'CASEY

See O'Casey and Synge Issue of *Modern Drama,* 4 (December, 1961)

Hogan, Robert, *The Experiments of Sean O'Casey,* New York, 1960

Koslow, Jules, *The Green and the Red: Sean O'Casey, The Man and His Plays,* New York, 1950

Krause, David, *Sean O'Casey, The Man and His Work,* New York, 1960

See also: IV,A: Cole
IV,B,1: Williams
IV,B,3: Byrne; Kavanagh; Robinson
IV,C: Atkinson; Gassner, *Our Times*

### CLIFFORD ODETS

Fergusson, Francis, "Beyond the Close Embrace," *Anchor Review* (1955)

Warshow, Robert, "Poet of the Jewish Middle Class," *Commentary* (May, 1946)

See also: IV,B,1: Block; Lumley
IV,B,2: Clurman, *Fervent;* Downer, *Fifty;* Flexner; Gagey; Krutch, *Since 1918;* Sievers
IV,C: Bentley, *What is Theatre?;* Clurman, *Lies;* McCarthy

### EUGENE O'NEILL

See O'Neill Issue of *Modern Drama,* 3 (December, 1960)

Alexander, Doris, *The Tempering of Eugene O'Neill,* New York, 1962

Bowen, Croswell, with Shane O'Neill, *The Curse of the Misbegotten: A Tale of the House of O'Neill,* New York, 1959

Bryer, Jackson R., "Forty Years of O'Neill Criticism: A Selected Bibliography," *Modern Drama,* 4 (September, 1961)

Cargill, Oscar, N. B. Fagin, and William J. Fisher (editors), *O'Neill and His Plays,* New York, 1961

Clark, Barrett H., *Eugene O'Neill, The Man and His Plays,* New York, 1947

Engel, Edwin, *The Haunted Heroes of Eugene O'Neill,* Cambridge, Massachusetts, 1953

Falk, Doris V., *Eugene O'Neill and the Tragic Tension: An Interpretive Study of the Plays,* New Brunswick, 1958

Gassner, John, *Eugene O'Neill,* Minneapolis, 1960

Gelb, Barbara and Arthur, *O'Neill,* New York, 1962

Skinner, Richard Dana, *Eugene O'Neill: A Poet's Quest,* New York, 1935

Winther, Sophus K., *Eugene O'Neill: A Critical Study,* New York, revised 1961

See also: IV,A: Cole
IV,B,1: Bentley, *Thinker;* Block; Krutch, *Modernism*
IV,B,2: Deutsch and Hanau; Downer, *Fifty;* Flexner; Gagey; Krutch, *Since 1918;* Sievers
IV,C: Bentley, *Search;* Gassner, *Our Times* and *Crossroads;* McCarthy; Nathan, various collections; Young, *Shadows*
IV,D: Langner

### JOHN OSBORNE

Allsop, Kenneth, *The Angry Decade: A Survey of the Cultural Revolt of the Nineteen-Fifties,* London, 1958

Deming, Barbara, "John Osborne's War Against the Philistines," *Hudson Review,* XI (Fall, 1958)

Dyson, A. E., *"Look Back in Anger," Critical Quarterly* 1 (Winter, 1959)

Kitchin, L., *Mid-Century Drama,* London, 1960

Osborne, John, "Introduction," *International Theatre Annual* No. 2 (1957)

———, "They Call It Cricket," *Declaration* (edited by Tom Maschler), New York, 1958

See also: IV,A: Cole
IV,B,1: Lumley
IV,C: Clurman, *Lies;* Gassner, *Crossroads;* Tynan

### LUIGI PIRANDELLO

Bishop, Thomas, *Pirandello and the French Theatre,* New York, 1960

MacClintock, Lander, *The Age of Pirandello,* Bloomington, 1951

Pirandello, Luigi, *Naked Masks* (edited by Eric Bentley), New York, 1952

Starkie, Walter, *Luigi Pirandello: 1867-1936,* New York, 1937

Vittorini, Domenico, *The Drama of Luigi Pirandello,* Philadelphia, 1935; 1958

See also: IV,A: Cole; Fergusson, *Idea*

(continued)

IV,B,1: Bentley, *Thinker;* Krutch, *Modernism;* Lumley; Williams
IV,C: Bentley, *Search;* Block and Salinger; Gassner, *Our Times;* Young, *Shadows*

WILLIAM SAROYAN

Clurman, Harold, "The Theatre of the Thirties," *Tulane Drama Review,* 4 (December, 1959)

Saroyan, William, Prefaces and essays in *The Time of Your Life,* New York, 1939; *Three Plays,* New York, 1939; *Razzle Dazzle,* New York, 1942; *Don't Go Away Mad,* New York, 1951

———, "Coming Reality: Preface to *The Time of Your Life,*" *Theatre Arts* (December, 1939)

See also: IV,B,1: Gassner, *Form*
IV,B,2: Gagey; Sievers
IV,C: Atkinson; Brown, John Mason, *Broadway;* Clurman, *Lies;* Gassner, *Our Times* and *Crossroads;* McCarthy, *Sights;* Nathan, various collections; Young, *Shadows*
IV,D: Langner

JEAN-PAUL SARTRE

See Sartre Issues of *Yale French Studies,* 1 (Spring/Summer, 1948), and *Tulane Drama Review,* 5 (March, 1961)

Greene, Norman N., *Jean-Paul Sartre: The Existentialist Ethic,* Ann Arbor, 1960

Grene, Marjorie, *Dreadful Freedom: A Critique of Existentialism,* Chicago, 1948; reissued as *Introduction to Existentialism,* Chicago, 1959

Murdoch, Iris, *Sartre, Romantic Rationalist,* New Haven, 1953

Sartre, Jean-Paul, "Forgers of Myths—The Young Playwrights of France" (translated by Rosamond Gilder), *Theatre Arts Anthology,* New York, 1951

———, "The Theatre: An Interview" (translated by Richard Seaver), *Evergreen Review,* Vol. 4, No. 11 (January/February, 1960)

Thody, Philip, *Jean-Paul Sartre: A Literary and Political Study,* New York, 1960

See also: IV,B,1: Bentley, *Thinker;* Lumley
IV,B,4: Chiari; Fowlie, *Dionysus;* Grossvogel; Guicharnaud; Hobson; Pucciani
IV,C: Block and Salinger; Cole; Gassner, *Our Times*

ARTHUR SCHNITZLER

Hill, Claude, "The Stature of Arthur Schnitzler," *Modern Drama,* 4 (May, 1961)

Liptzin, Sol, *Arthur Schnitzler,* New York, 1932

See also: IV,B,1: Bentley, *Thinker*
IV,B,5: Garten

GEORGE BERNARD SHAW

See Shaw Issue of *Modern Drama,* 2 (September, 1959), the "Contemporary Classics" Issue of *World Theatre,* VI (Spring, 1957), and, for current bibliography, *The Shaw Review* (until 1960, *The Shaw Bulletin*)

* Bentley, Eric, *Bernard Shaw,* New York, 1947; amended as *Bernard Shaw, 1856-1950,* 1957

Chesterton, G. K., *George Bernard Shaw,* London, 1909

Ervine, St. John, *Bernard Shaw, His Life, Works, and Friends,* New York, 1956

* Henderson, Archibald, *Bernard Shaw: Playboy and Prophet,* New York, 1932

* ———, *George Bernard Shaw: Man of the Century,* New York, 1956

* Irvine, William, *The Universe of G.B.S.,* New York, 1949

Kozelka, Paul, *A Glossary to the Plays of Bernard Shaw,* New York, 1959

Kronenberger, Louis (editor), *George Bernard Shaw. A Critical Survey,* Cleveland and New York, 1953

MacCarthy, Desmond, *Shaw's Plays in Review,* New York, 1951

Mander, Raymond, and Joe Mitcheson, *The Theatrical Companion to Shaw: A Pictorial Record of the First Performances of the Plays of G.B.S. with Synopses, Casts and Detailed Notes,* New York, 1955

Nethercot, Arthur H., *Men and Supermen: The Shavian Portrait Gallery,* Cambridge, Massachusetts, 1954

Pearson, Hesketh, *G.B.S. A Full-Length Portrait,* New York, 1942

———, *G.B.S. A Postscript,* New York, 1950

Strauss, Ernest, *Bernard Shaw, Art, and Socialism,* London, 1942

West, Alick, *George Bernard Shaw: A Good Man Fallen Among Fabians,* New York, 1950

Winsten, Stephen (editor), *G.B.S. 90,* New York, 1946

Collections of Shaw's writings (on music, drama, Shakespeare, politics, etc.) continue to appear, outnumbered only by articles on Shaw's works and life. Useful selective bibliographies—in addition to Charles A. Carpenter's "Continuing Checklist of Shaviana" in *The Shaw Review*—are the following:

Farley, Earl, and Marvin Carlson, "A Selected Bibliography (1945-1955)," Parts I and II, *Modern Drama,* 2 (September and December, 1959)

Keough, Lawrence C., "George Bernard Shaw, 1946-1955: A Selected Bibliography," *Bulletin of Bibliography,* XXII (1959) and XXIII (1960)

AUGUST STRINDBERG

See Strindberg Issue of *Modern Drama,* 5 (December, 1962) and "Modern Theatre in Sweden" Issue of *Tulane Drama Review,* 6 (December, 1961)

Bergholz, Harry, "Toward an Authentic Text of Strindberg's *Fröken Julie," Orbis Litterarum,* IX (1954)

Campbell, George A., *Strindberg,* New York, 1933

Dahlström, Carl E. W. L., *Strindberg's Dramatic Expressionism,* Ann Arbor, 1930

* Gustafson, Alrik, *A History of Swedish Literature,* Minneapolis, 1961, see especially, Chapter 8 and its bibliography

Johnson, Walter, "Strindberg and the Danse Macabre," *Modern Drama,* 3 (May, 1960)

McGill, V. J., *August Strindberg: The Bedevilled Viking,* London, 1930

Milton, J. R., "The Esthetic Fault of Strindberg's Dream Plays," *Tulane Drama Review,* 4 (March, 1960)

Mortensen, Brita M. E. and Brian W. Downs, *Strindberg: An Introduction to His Life and Works,* Cambridge, 1949

Sprigge, Elizabeth, *The Strange Life of August Strindberg,* New York, 1949

Strindberg, August, *Letters of Strindberg to Harriet Bosse* (edited and translated by Arvid Paulson), New York, 1959

Young, Vernon, "The History of *Miss Julia," Hudson Review,* VIII (1955)

See also: IV,B,1: Bentley, *Thinker and Search;* Gassner, *Our Times;* Henderson; Huneker, *Iconoclasts;* Krutch, *Modernism;* Lamm; Lewisohn; Williams
IV,C: Cole

JOHN MILLINGTON SYNGE

See Synge and O'Casey Issue of *Modern Drama,* 4 (December, 1961)

Bickley, Francis L., *J. M. Synge and the Irish Dramatic Movement,* Boston, 1912

Bourgeois, Maurice, *John Millington Synge and the Irish Theatre,* London, 1913

Corkery, Daniel, *Synge and Anglo-Irish Literature,* Oxford, 1947

Greene, David H. and Edward M. Stephens, *J. M. Synge, 1871-1909,* New York, 1959

Gregory, Lady Augusta, *Our Irish Theatre: A Chapter of Autobiography,* New York, 1913

Price, Alan, *Synge and Anglo-Irish Drama,* London, 1961

Setterquist, J., *Ibsen and the Beginnings of Anglo-Irish Drama,* Upsala, 1951

Yeats, William Butler, *Autobiography,* New York, 1938

———, *Essays,* New York, 1924

See also: IV,A: Peacock; Styan
IV,B,1: Bentley, *Search;* Gassner, *Our Times;* Williams
IV,B,3: Boyd; Byrne; Ellis-Fermor; Fay; Howarth; Kavanagh; Malone; Robinson

FRANK WEDEKIND

Feuchtwanger, Lion, "Introduction," *Five Tragedies of Sex* (translated by Frances Fawcett and Stephen Spender), New York, 1952

Hill, Claude, "Wedekind in Retrospect," *Modern Drama,* 3 (May, 1960)

See also: IV,B,1: Bentley, *Thinker*
IV,B,5: Garten; Samuel and Thomas; Sokel

THORNTON WILDER

* Burbank, Rex, *Thornton Wilder,* New York, 1961

* Edelstein, J. M., *A Bibliographical Checklist of the Writings of Thornton Wilder,* New Haven, 1959

Firebaugh, Joseph, "The Humanism of Thornton Wilder," *The Pacific Spectator,* IV (Autumn, 1950)

Fulton, A. R., "Expressionism—Twenty Years After," *Sewanee Review,* LII (Summer, 1944)

Hewitt, Barnard, "Thornton Wilder Says 'Yes'," *Tulane Drama Review,* 4 (December, 1959)

Kohler, Dayton, "Thornton Wilder," *English Journal,* XXVIII (January, 1939)

Wilder, Thornton, "Interview," *The "Paris Review" Interviews: Writers at Work* (edited by Malcolm Cowley), New York, 1958

———, "Preface," *Three Plays,* New York, 1957

———, "Some Thoughts on Playwriting," *The Intent of the Artist* (edited by Augusto Centeno), Princeton, 1941

See also: IV,A: Fergusson, *Image*
IV,B,1: Gassner, *Our Times* and *Form*
IV,B,2: Gagey; Sievers
IV,C: Atkinson; Clurman, *Lies;* Cole; McCarthy

TENNESSEE WILLIAMS

Carpenter, Charles A., Jr., and Elizabeth Cook, "Addenda to 'Tennessee Williams: A Selected Bibliography,'" *Modern Drama,* 2 (December, 1959)

Dony, Nadine, "Tennessee Williams: A Selected Bibliography," *Modern Drama,* 1 (December, 1958)

Dusenbury, Winifred L., *The Theme of Loneliness in American Drama,* Gainesville, 1960

Falk, Signi, *Tennessee Williams,* New York, 1961

Funke, Lewis, and John E. Booth, "Williams on Williams," *Theatre Arts* (January, 1962)

Hurrell, John D., *Two Modern American Tragedies: Reviews and Criticism of "Death of a Salesman" and "A Streetcar Named Desire,"* New York, 1961

Nelson, Benjamin, *Tennessee Williams: The Man and His Work,* New York, 1961

Popkin, Henry, "The Plays of Tennessee Williams," *Tulane Drama Review,* 4 (March, 1960)

Tischler, Nancy M., *Tennessee Williams: Rebellious Puritan,* New York, 1961

Vowles, Richard B., "Tennessee Williams and Strindberg," *Modern Drama,* 1 (December, 1958)

———, "Tennessee Williams: The World of His Imagery," *Tulane Drama Review,* 3 (December, 1958)

Williams, Tennessee, "Foreword," *Sweet Bird of Youth,* New York, 1959

———, "Foreword" and "Afterword," *Camino Real,* Norfolk, 1953

———, "Person-to-Person," *Cat on a Hot Tin Roof,* New York, 1955

———, "Something wild . . . ," *27 Wagons Full of Cotton,* second edition, Norfolk, 1953

———, "The Catastrophe of Success," *The Glass Menagerie* (New Classics edition), New York, 1949

———, "The Past, the Present and the Perhaps," *Orpheus Descending, with Battle of Angels,* New York, 1958

———, "The Timeless World of a Play," *The Rose Tattoo,* New York, 1951

———, "The World I Live In—Tennessee Williams Interviews Himself," *Observer* (April 7, 1957); reprinted in *Mayfair* (June, 1957)

See also: IV,B,1: Bentley, *Search;* Gassner, *Our Times* and *Crossroads;* Krutch, *Modernism*
IV,B,2: Downer, *Fifty* and *Recent;* Krutch, *Since 1918;* Sievers
IV,C: Bentley, *What is Theatre?* and *Event;* Cole; McCarthy; Tynan; Young, *Shadows*
IV,D: Goodman

#### WILLIAM BUTLER YEATS

Bjersby, Birgit M. H., *The Interpretation of the Cuchulain Legend in the Works of William Butler Yeats,* Upsala, 1950

Ellmann, Richard, *The Identity of Yeats,* New York, 1954

———, *Yeats: The Man and the Masks,* New York, 1948

* Hall, James, and Martin Steinmann (editors), *The Permanence of Yeats: Selected Criticism,* New York, 1950

Henn, T. R., *The Lonely Tower,* London, 1950

Hone, Joseph M., *William Butler Yeats, 1865-1939,* New York, 1943

Jeffares, Alexander N., *William Butler Yeats, Man and Poet,* London, 1949

Kermode, Frank, *Romantic Image,* New York, 1957

Popkin, Henry, "Yeats as Dramatist," *Tulane Drama Review,* 3 (March, 1959)

Saul, George Brandon, *Prolegomena to the Study of Yeats's Plays,* Philadelphia, 1958

Ure, Peter, *Towards A Mythology: Studies in the Poetry of William Butler Yeats,* London, 1946

Wilson, Francis A. C., *William Butler Yeats and Tradition,* New York, 1958

———, *Yeats's Iconography,* London, 1960

Yeats, William Butler, *Autobiographies,* London, 1955

———, *Essays,* London, 1924

———, *Essays 1931 to 1936,* Dublin, 1937

———, *Four Plays for Dancers,* London, 1921

———, *Plays and Controversies,* London, 1923

See also: IV,A: Peacock
IV,B,1: Bentley, *Thinker* and *Search;* Gassner, *Our Times;* Williams
IV,B,3: Boyd; Byrne; Donoghue; Ellis-Fermor; Fay; Howarth; Robinson; Ussher

#### CARL ZUCKMAYER

Zuckmayer, Carl, *Second Wind. Parts of an Autobiography,* London, 1941

See also: IV,B,1: Bentley, *Search;* Gassner, *Our Times*
IV,B,5: Garten

HASKELL M. BLOCK is Professor of Comparative Literature at Brooklyn College of the City University of New York. He received his A.B. from the University of Chicago, where he was elected to Phi Beta Kappa, his A.M. from Harvard University, and his doctorate from the University of Paris. He has taught at Harvard University, Queens College, and the University of Wisconsin. In 1956-1957 he was a Fulbright Research scholar at the University of Cologne. He is the author of essays on European dramatic naturalism, symbolist drama, expressionism in the modern American theatre, and individual studies of Hofmannsthal, Yeats, Camus, and other playwrights. He has edited and translated Molière's *Tartuffe* and the Modern Library edition of Voltaire, and is co-editor of *The Creative Vision: Modern European Writers on Their Art*. He has also edited a volume on *The Teaching of World Literature* and recently completed a critical study on *Mallarmé and the Symbolist Drama.*

ROBERT G. SHEDD is Professor of English and the Humanities at the University of Maryland, Baltimore County. He previously taught at Ohio State University. He received his A.B., A.M., and Ph.D. degrees from the University of Michigan, where he was elected to Phi Beta Kappa. He won the Avery Hopwood Award there in 1948 for two plays, the realistic *Summer Solstice* and an experiment in expressionism, *The Conventions at LaVivrus*. His dissertation was a study of Shakespeare's *Measure for Measure.* His adaptation of Molière's *Tartuffe* has been produced in many college theatres. He has written widely in the areas of Shakespearean and modern drama, and has directed the recent conferences on modern drama held in conjunction with the annual meetings of the Modern Language Association. An Associate Editor of the quarterly journal, *Modern Drama,* he is also editor of its annual selective bibliography of materials on the modern drama.